D0606372

ATLAS OF THE WORLD

MetroBooks

Table of Contents

iv - v .... How to Use the Atlas

The Real World
vi - vii .... Introduction
viii - ix .... Climate
x - xi .... Population
xii - xv .... Peoples and Countries
xvi .... World Time Zones

Maps and Index of the United States
S•1 .... Introduction
S•2 - S•3 .... United States
S•4 .... Alabama
S•5 .... Alaska
S•6 .... Arizona
S•7 .... Arkansas
S•8 .... California
S•9 .... Colorado
S•10 .... Connecticut
S•11 .... Delaware
S•12 .... Florida
S•13 .... Georgia
S•14 .... Hawaii
S•15 .... Idaho
S•16 .... Illinois
S•17 .... Indiana
S•18 .... Iowa
S•19 .... Kansas
S•20 .... Kentucky
S•21 .... Louisiana
S•22 .... Maine
S•23 .... Maryland
S•24 .... Massachusetts
S•25 .... Michigan
S•26 .... Minnesota
S•27 .... Mississippi
S•28 .... Missouri
S•29 .... Montana
S•30 .... Nebraska
S•31 .... Nevada
S•32 .... New Hampshire
S•33 .... New Jersey
S•34 .... New Mexico
S•35 .... New York
S•36 .... North Carolina
S•37 .... North Dakota
S•38 .... Ohio
S•39 .... Oklahoma
S•40 .... Oregon
S•41 .... Pennsylvania
S•42 .... Rhode Island
S•43 .... South Carolina
S•44 .... South Dakota
S•45 .... Tennessee
S•46 .... Texas
S•47 .... Utah
S•48 .... Vermont
S•49 .... Virginia
S•50 .... Washington
S•51 .... West Virginia
S•52 .... Wisconsin
S•53 .... Wyoming
S•54 - S•64 .... Index

Maps and Index of the World
1 .... Introduction
2-3 .... World, Political
4-5 .... World, Physical

Chairman, President, & CEO, Rand McNally & Company
Henry J. Feinberg

Senior Vice President, Marketing
Margaret A. Stender

Director, Reference Publishing
Kendra L. Ensor

Editors
Kathryn Martin O'Neil
Brett R. Gover
Ann T. Natunewicz

Art Direction and Design
John C. Nelson
Peggy R. Hogan

Marketing
Amy C. Krouse
JoEllen A. Klein

Photo Research
Feldman and Associates, Inc.

Manufacturing
Terry D. Rieger

Cartography Directors
V. Patrick Healy
Jon M. Leverenz

Cartography (U.S.)
Robert K. Argersinger
Barbara Benstead-Strassheim
David M. Bukala
Kerry B. Chambers
Marzee L. Eckhoff
Julie A. Geyer
Winifred V. Farbman
Susan K. Hudson
Elizabeth A. Hunt
Gwynn A. Hurshman
William R. Karbler
Brian M. Lash
Nina Lusterman
Erik A. Pedersen
Thomas F. Vitacco
David R. Walters
Richard A. Wanzo
James Wooden
David C. Zapenski

Cartography (U.K.)
Craig Asquith

Cartography (Italy)
Giovanni Baselli
Ubaldo Uberti

Credits

Jacket
© Earth Image/Tony Stone Images (globe), © PhotoDisc (coastline)

The Real World
Developed by Rand McNally with Dr. Marvin W. Mikesell, University of Chicago.

Satellite image on pages vi-vii: Mendoza, Argentina. Processed by Earth Information Systems Corporation, Austin, TX.; Laser film by Cirrus Technologies, Inc., Nashau, NH.

An Imprint of the Michael Friedman Publishing Group, Inc.

Library of Congress Cataloging-in-Publication Data available upon request.
ISBN 1-58663-242-6

Printed in Singapore by Tien Wah Press (Pte) Ltd

3 5 7 9 10 8 6 4 2

For bulk purchases and special sales, please contact:
Michael Freidman Publishing Group, Inc.
Attention: Sales Department
230 Fifth Avenue
New York, NY 10001
212/685-6610 FAX 212/685-3916

Visit our website:
www.metrobooks.com

Europe

6-7 .... Europe, Political
8-9 .... Northern Europe and Scandinavia
10-11 .... Baltic Regions and Moscow
12-13 .... British Isles
14-15 .... Northern France, Belgium, and the Netherlands
16-17 .... Germany, Czech Republic, Slovakia, and Poland
18-19 .... Southern France and Switzerland
20-21 .... Spain and Portugal
22-23 .... Northern Italy, Austria, and the Balkans
24-25 .... Southern Italy
26-27 .... Hungary, Yugoslavia, Romania, and Bulgaria
28-29 .... Greece and Western Turkey

Asia

30-31 .... Asia, Political
32-33 .... Northwestern Asia
34-35 .... Northeastern Asia
36-37 .... China, Korea, and Japan
38-39 .... Japan, Korea, and Northeastern China
40-41 .... Central and Southern Japan
42-43 .... Eastern China
44-45 .... Southeast Asia
46-47 .... Southern Asia
48-49 .... Myanmar, Thailand, and Singapore
50-51 .... Borneo, Java, and Sumatra
52 .... Philippines
53 .... Southern India
54-55 .... Northern India
56-57 .... Southwestern Asia
58-59 .... Israel, Lebanon, and Jordan

Africa

60-61 .... Africa, Political
62-63 .... Northeastern Africa
64-65 .... Northwestern Africa
66-67 .... Central Africa
68-69 .... Southern Africa
70-71 .... South Africa

Australia and Oceania

72-73 .... Australia and Oceania, Political
74-75 .... Australia
76-77 .... Southeastern Australia
78-79 .... Islands of the Pacific
80 .... New Zealand
81 .... Antarctica

South America

82-83 .... South America, Political
84-85 .... Northern South America
86-87 .... Venezuela and Colombia
88-89 .... Eastern Brazil
90-91 .... Southern South America
92-93 .... Central Argentina and Chile

North America

94-95 .... North America, Political
96-97 .... Mexico, Central America, and the Caribbean
98-99 .... Northwestern Mexico and Southwestern United States
100-101 .... Central Mexico
102-103 .... Central America
104-105 .... Islands of the Caribbean
106-107 .... Canada
108-109 .... United States
110-111 .... Northeastern United States and Southeastern
112-113 .... Great Lakes
114-115 .... Central Atlantic States
116-117 .... Southeastern United States
118-119 .... Northern Midwest
120-121 .... Midwest
122-123 .... Mississippi Delta
124-125 .... Northern Great Plains
126-127 .... Central Great Plains
128-129 .... Southern Great Plains
130-131 .... Southern Texas
132-133 .... Arizona and Utah
134-135 .... California, Nevada, and Hawaii
136-137 .... Northwestern United States
138-139 .... Southwestern Canada
140 .... Alaska and the Aleutians
141 .... Greenland

142-143 .... Pacific and Indian Oceans
144 .... Atlantic Ocean

I•1 to I•64 ...... Index

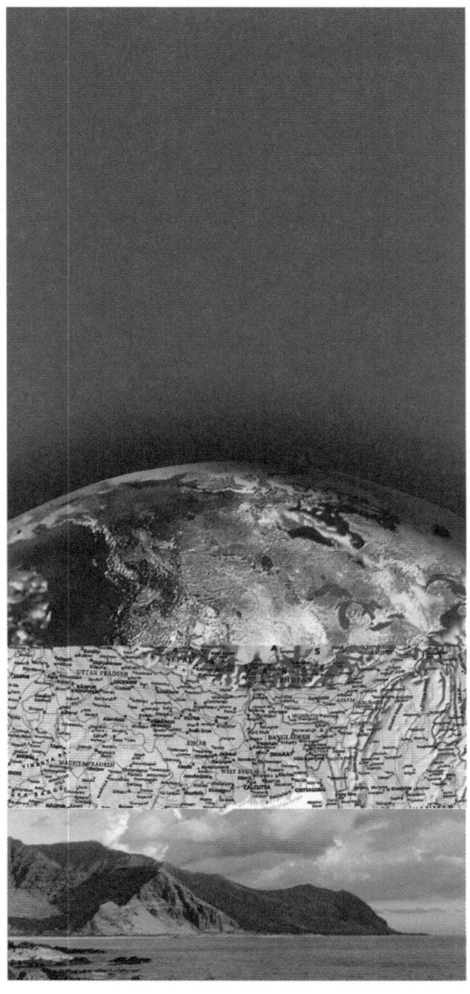

How to use the Atlas

What is an Atlas?

A set of maps bound together is called an atlas. Abraham Ortelius' *Theatrum orbis terrarum*, published in 1570, is considered to be the first modern "atlas," although it was not referred to as such for almost 20 years. In 1589, Gerardus Mercator *(figure 1)* coined the term when he named his collection of maps after Atlas, the mythological Titan who carried Earth on his shoulders as punishment for warring against Zeus. Since then, the definition of "atlas" has been expanded, and atlases often include additional geographic information in diagrams, tables, and text.

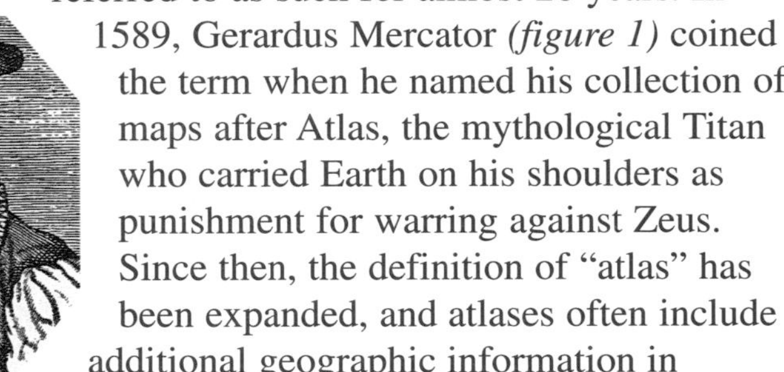

figure 1

Latitude and Longitude

The terms "latitude" and "longitude" refer to the grid of horizontal and vertical lines found on most maps and globes. Any point on Earth can be located by its precise latitude and longitude coordinates.

figure 2

The imaginary horizontal line that circles Earth halfway between the North and South poles is called the equator; it represents 0° latitude and lies 90° from either pole. The other lines of latitude, or parallels, measure distances north or south from the equator *(figure 2)*. The imaginary vertical line that measures 0° longitude runs through the Greenwich Observatory in the United Kingdom, and is called the Prime Meridian. The other lines of longitude, or meridians, measure distances east or west from the prime meridian *(figure 3)*, up to a maximum of 180°. Lines of latitude and longitude cross each other, forming a grid *(figure 4)*.

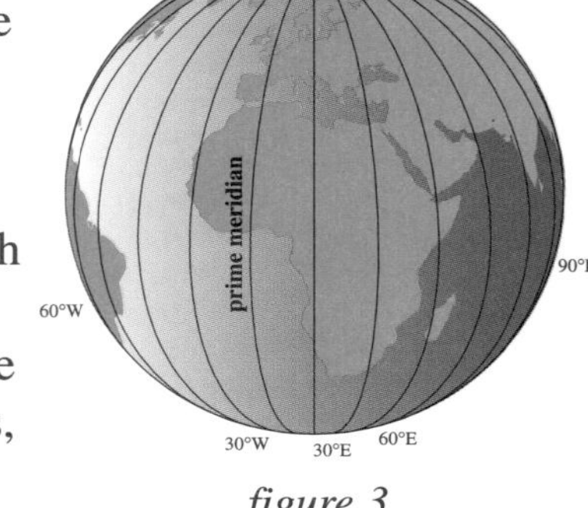

figure 3

Map Projections

Every cartographer is faced with the problem of transforming the curved surface of Earth onto a flat plane with a minimum of distortion. The systematic transformation of locations on Earth (a spherical surface) to locations on a map (a flat surface) is called projection.

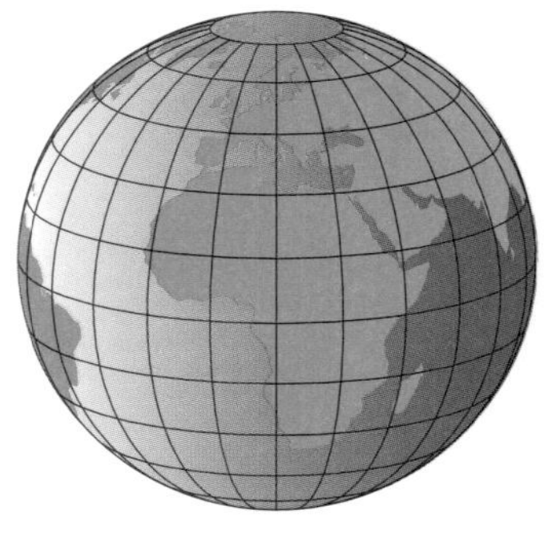

figure 4

It is not possible to represent on a flat map the spatial relationships of angle, distance, direction, and area that only a globe can show faithfully. As a result, projections inevitably involve some distortion. On large-scale maps representing a few square miles, the distortion is generally negligible. But on maps depicting large countries, continents, or the entire world, the amount of distortion can be significant. On maps which use the Mercator Projection (*figure 5*), for example, distortion increases with distance from the equator. Thus the island of Greenland appears larger than the entire continent of South America, although South America is in fact nine time larger. In contrast, the Robinson Projection (*figure 6*) renders the world's major land areas in generally correct proportion to one another, although distortion is still apparent in areas such as Antarctica, which is actually smaller than all of the continents except Europe and Australia.

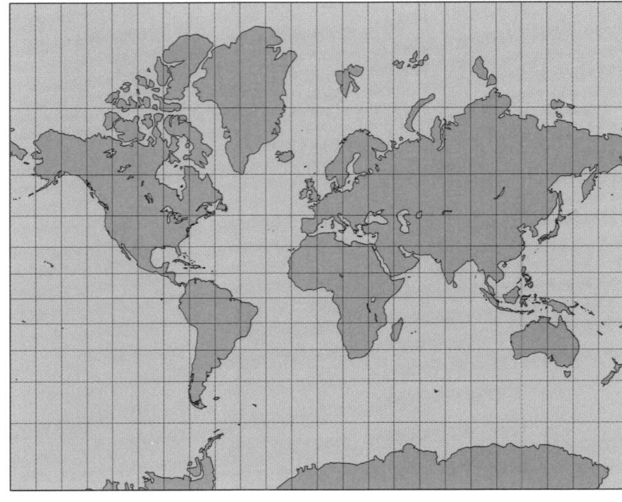

figure 5

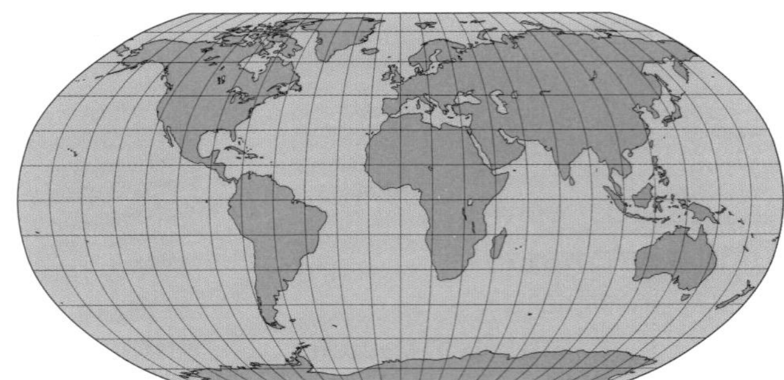

figure 6

There are an infinite number of possible map projections, all of which distort one or more of the characteristics of the globe in varying degrees. The projection that a cartographer chooses depends on the size and location of the area being projected and the purpose of the map. In this atlas, most of the maps are drawn on projections that give a consistent or only slightly distorted area scale, good land and ocean shape, parallels that are parallel, and as consistent a linear scale as possible throughout the projection.

Map Scale

The scale of a map is the relationship between distances or areas shown on the map and the corresponding distances or areas on Earth's surface. Large-scale maps show relatively small areas in greater detail than do small-scale maps, such as those of individual continents or of the world.

There are three different ways to express scale. Most often scale is given as a fraction, such as 1:10,000,000, which means that the ratio of distances on the map to actual distances on Earth is 1 to 10,000,000. Scale can also be expressed as a phrase, such as "One inch represents approximately ten million miles." Finally, scale can be illustrated via a bar scale on which various distances are labeled *(figure 7)*. Any of these three scale expressions can be used to calculate distances on a map.

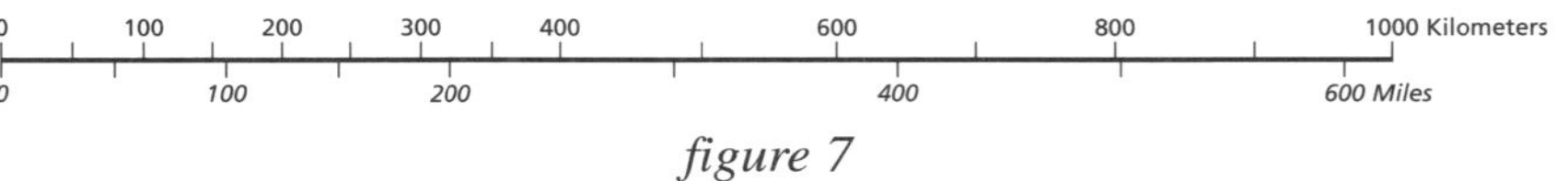

figure 7

Measuring Distances

Using a bar scale, it is possible to calculate the distance between any two points on a map. To find the approximate distance between São Paulo and Rio de Janeiro, Brazil, for example, follow these steps:

1) Lay a piece of paper on the right-hand page of the "Eastern Brazil" map found on pages 88-89, lining up its edge with the city dots for São Paulo and Rio de Janeiro. Make a mark on the paper next to each dot *(figure 8)*.

2) Place the paper along the scale bar found below the map, and position the first mark at 0. The second mark falls about a quarter of the way between the 200-mile tick and the 300-mile tick, indicating that the distance separating the two cities is approximately 225 miles *(figure 9)*.

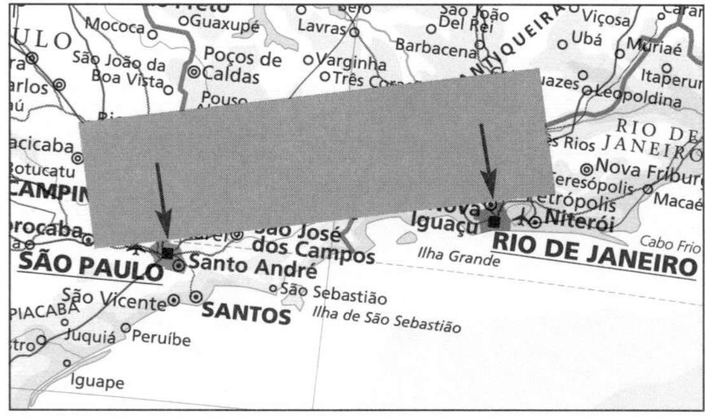

figure 8

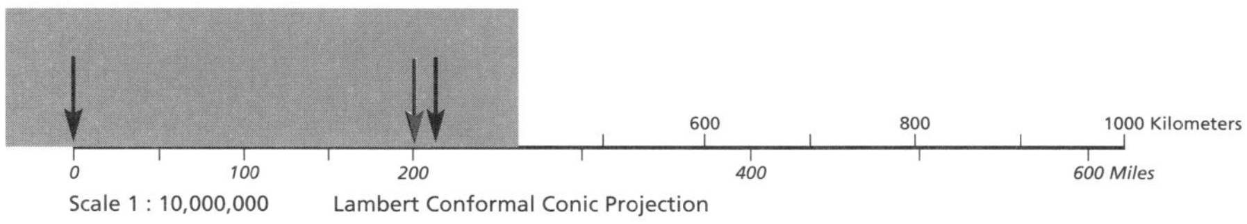

600 800 1000 Kilometers

0 100 200 400 600 Miles

Scale 1 : 10,000,000 Lambert Conformal Conic Projection

figure 9

3) To confirm this measurement, make a third pencil mark (shown in red in *figure 9*) at the 200-mile tick. Slide the paper to the left so that this mark lines up with 0. The Rio de Janeiro mark now falls very close to the 25-mile tick, which is unlabelled. Thus, São Paulo and Rio de Janeiro are indeed approximately 225 (200 + 25) miles apart.

Using the Index to Find Places

One of the most important purposes of an atlas is to help the reader locate cities, towns, and geographic features such as rivers, lakes, and mountains. This atlas uses a "bingo key" indexing system. In the index, found on pages **I•1** through **I•64**, every entry is assigned an alpha-numeric code that consists of a letter and a number. This code relates to the red letters and numbers that run along the perimeter of each map. To locate places or features, follow the steps outlined in this example for the city of Bratsk, Russia.

1) Look up Bratsk in the index. The entry *(figure 10)* contains the following information: the place name (Bratsk), the name of the country (Russia) in which Bratsk is located, the map reference key (C18) that corresponds to Bratsk's location on the map, and the page number (32) of the map on which Bratsk can be found.

Entry	Key	Page
Brassey, Banjaran, mts., Malay	A10	50
Brass Islands, is., V.I.U.S.	o7	104 b
Brasstown Bald, mtn., Ga., U.S.	B2	116
Bratca, Rom.	C9	26
Bratislava, Slov.	H13	16
Bratislava, state, Slov.	H13	16
Bratsk, Russia	C18	32
Bratskoe vodohranilisce, res., Russia	C18	32

figure 10

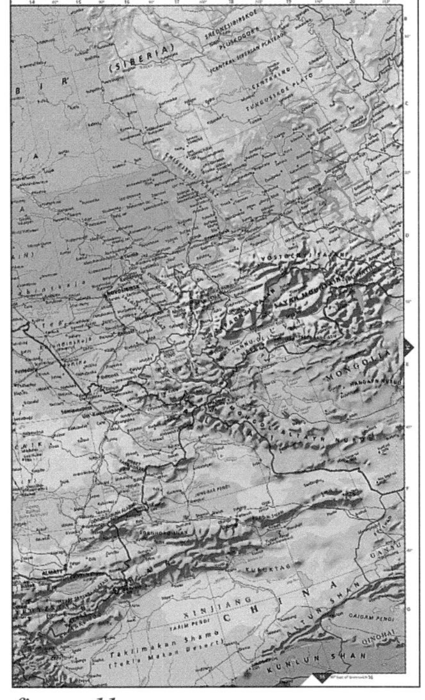

figure 11

2) Turn to the Northwestern Asia map on pages 32-33. Look along either the left or right-hand margin for the red letter "C"—the letter code given for Bratsk. The "C" denotes a band that arcs horizontally across the map, between the grid lines representing 55° and 60° North latitude. Then, look along either the top or bottom margin for the red number "18"—the numerical part of the code given for Bratsk. The "18" denotes a widening vertical band, between the grid lines representing 100° and 105° East longitude, which angles from the top center of the map to right-hand edge.

3) Using your finger, follow the horizontal "C" band and the vertical "18" band to the area where they overlap *(figure 11)*. Bratsk lies within this overlap area.

Physical Maps and Political Maps

Most of the maps in the *Atlas of the World* are physical maps, like the one shown in *figure 12*, emphasizing terrain, landforms, and elevation. Political maps, as in *figure 13*, emphasize countries and other political units over topography. The atlas includes political maps of the world and each of the continents except Antarctica.

figure 12

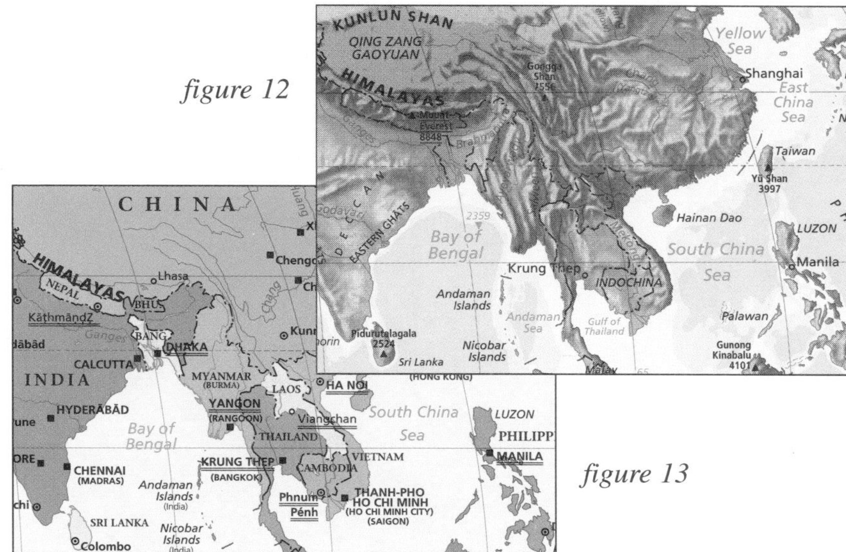

figure 13

How Maps Show Topography

The physical maps in this atlas use two techniques to depict Earth's topography. Variations in elevation are shown through a series of colors called hypsometric tints. Areas below sea level appear as a dark green; as the elevation rises, the tints move successively through lighter green, yellow, and orange. Similarly, variations in ocean depth are represented by bathymetric tints. The shallowest areas appear as light blue; darker tints of blue indicate greater depths. The hypsometric/ bathymetric scale that accompanies each map identifies, in feet and meters, all of the elevation and depth categories that appear on the map.

Principal landforms, such as mountain ranges and valleys, are rendered in shades of gray, a technique known as shaded relief. The combination of hypsometric tints and shaded relief provides the map reader with a three-dimensional picture of Earth's surface *(figure 14)*.

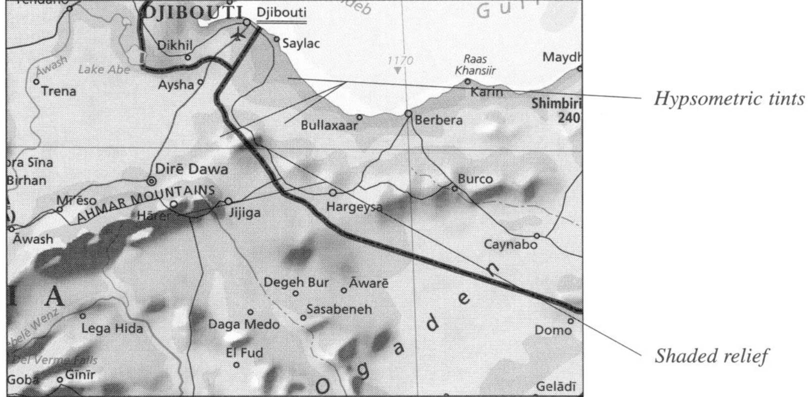

figure 14

The Real World

Marvin W. Mikesell
Professor of Geography, University of Chicago

VIEWED FROM SPACE, THE EARTH APPEARS AS A MAJESTIC SPHERE, BLUE-GRAY AND WHITE, OUTLINED AGAINST THE STARRY BLACKNESS OF THE UNIVERSE. SWIRLING CLOUD FORMATIONS STREAK THE ATMOSPHERE, GIVING THE SPHERE'S SURFACE THE LOOK OF POLISHED MARBLE.

As we draw closer to the planet, the solid blue-gray separates into the great oceans and land masses of this world. Reaching the outer atmosphere, we can begin to make out the complex shades of blue, green, and brown that speak of the Earth's astonishing diversity of terrain, vegetation and climatic zones.

At this distance, mountain ranges appear as little more than wrinkles in the planet's surface, rivers as fine, branching lines tracing across the continents, and lakes as still, blue puddles. Moving closer toward the surface, we discern the shapes of ancient craters, volcanoes, fissures and canyons, great stretches of desert, and long, fertile valleys surrounded by arid lands.

But only when we descend to the lower atmosphere do the telltale signs of human existence become visible. Cities line the coastal fringes of the continents and dot the inner regions, glowing at night like constellations. Highways and railroads criss-cross the settled areas of the Earth, often paralleling coastlines or river courses. Patchworks of farmlands, quarries, mines, and logging operations mark our economic activities around the globe.

Scholars generally believe that there is a fundamental order and logic in the distribution of humanity and our activities over the Earth—a kind of "human geography" ruled by natural and cultural forces. The following sequence of special maps explores this order and logic, portraying the major geographic distributions affecting human existence. By understanding more about human geography, we may learn how to deal with the problems we face and to preserve the diversity and beauty of the planet we have affected so profoundly.

WHILE CALM, CLEAR SKIES PREVAIL OVER NORTH AMERICA'S GREAT PLAINS, A VIOLENT HURRICANE BATTERS A CHAIN OF CARIBBEAN ISLANDS. IN EASTERN AFRICA, RAINSTORMS break a two-year drought, but northern European farmers watch their crops dry up in a heat wave. Mild spring winds arrive over Argentina, and in southeast Asia monsoon winds bring lightning and torrential rains.

The infinite variety of our planet's weather is created by the complex relationship of air, water, and land. Air masses ebb and flow around the globe, as moist tropical air moves toward the poles and drier polar air descends toward the equator. The spinning of the Earth helps to direct the air masses. Ocean currents circulate "rivers" of warmer and cooler waters around the globe. Great mountain ranges trap air masses and disrupt the worldwide flow. The 23½° inclination of our planet as it revolves around the sun creates the yearly cycle of seasons.

Over time, this constant interaction of natural forces establishes consistent weather patterns which, in turn, define the major climatic regions of the world, which are depicted on the adjacent map. Within each region, characteristic soils and related plant and animal life evolve.

Generally predictable patterns of weather within these regions have permitted humanity to develop an array of economic and cultural systems, each closely related to the area's normal climatic conditions.

It is the abnormal climatic occurrence—sometimes called a "climatic anomaly"—that causes the most human turmoil, as well as shock to the natural order. For example, a combination of cold Pacific currents and dry air masses makes the northern coast of Chile one of the driest places on Earth. The lifestyle of the region is based upon this prevailing climate. When the phenomenon known as *El Niño* occurs, the usual northerly flow of cold air and water reverses itself, and warm equatorial air and water flow south onto the coast of Chile. These unexpected conditions dramatically increase rainfall, leading to disastrous flooding, and completely disrupting the cultural and natural order.

Today there is growing awareness and concern about humanity's increasing impact on climate. In many large urban areas, the heat-absorbing artificial terrain, combined with air pollution from automobiles and industry, has created "micro-climates" characterized by higher temperatures and excessive smog. A far greater potential problem is global warming resulting from the so-called "greenhouse effect." The burning of fossil fuels adds carbon dioxide to the atmosphere, which causes the atmosphere to trap heat that would normally radiate out into space. If global temperatures rise even a few degrees, the consequences could be disastrous.

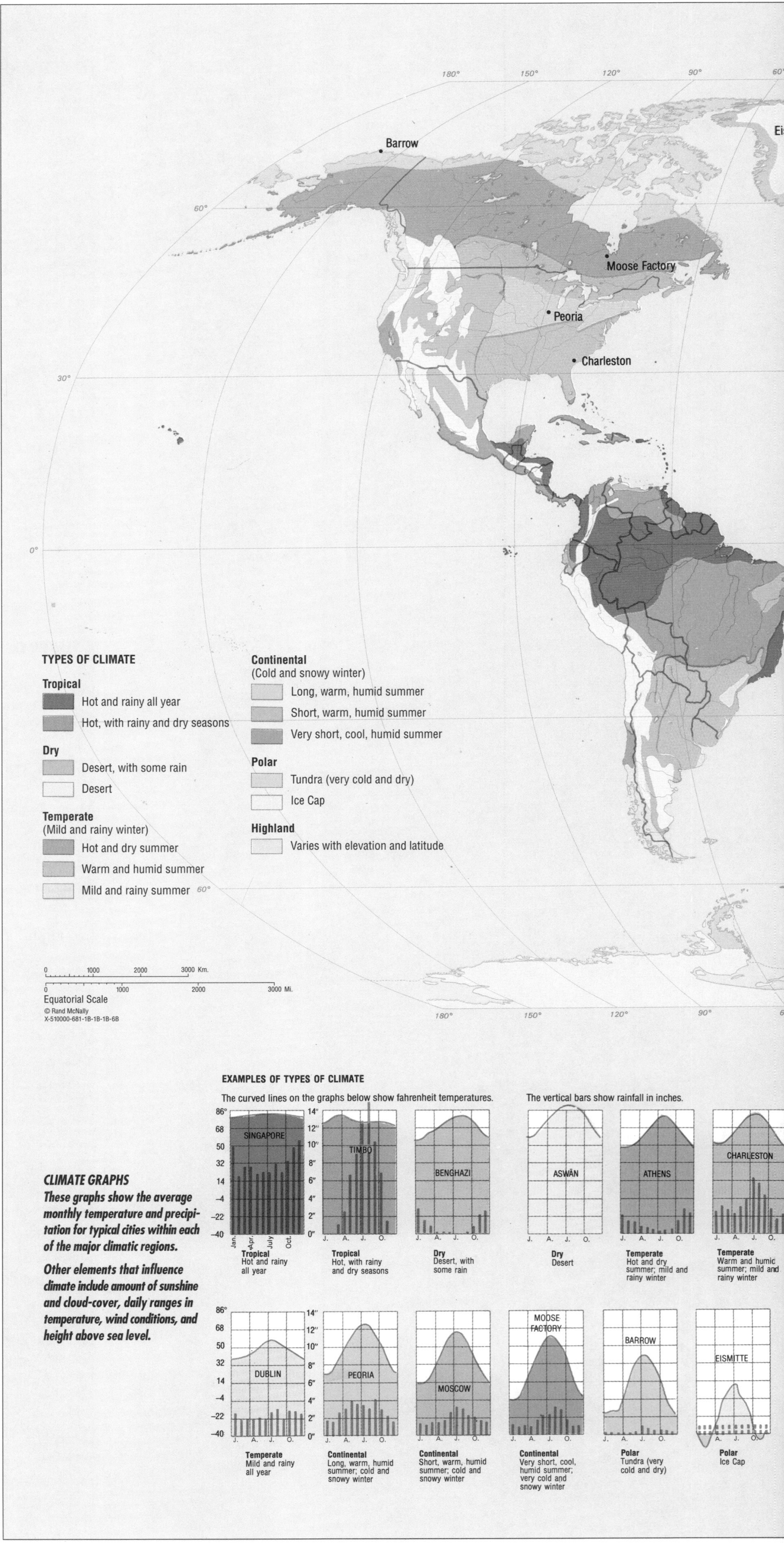

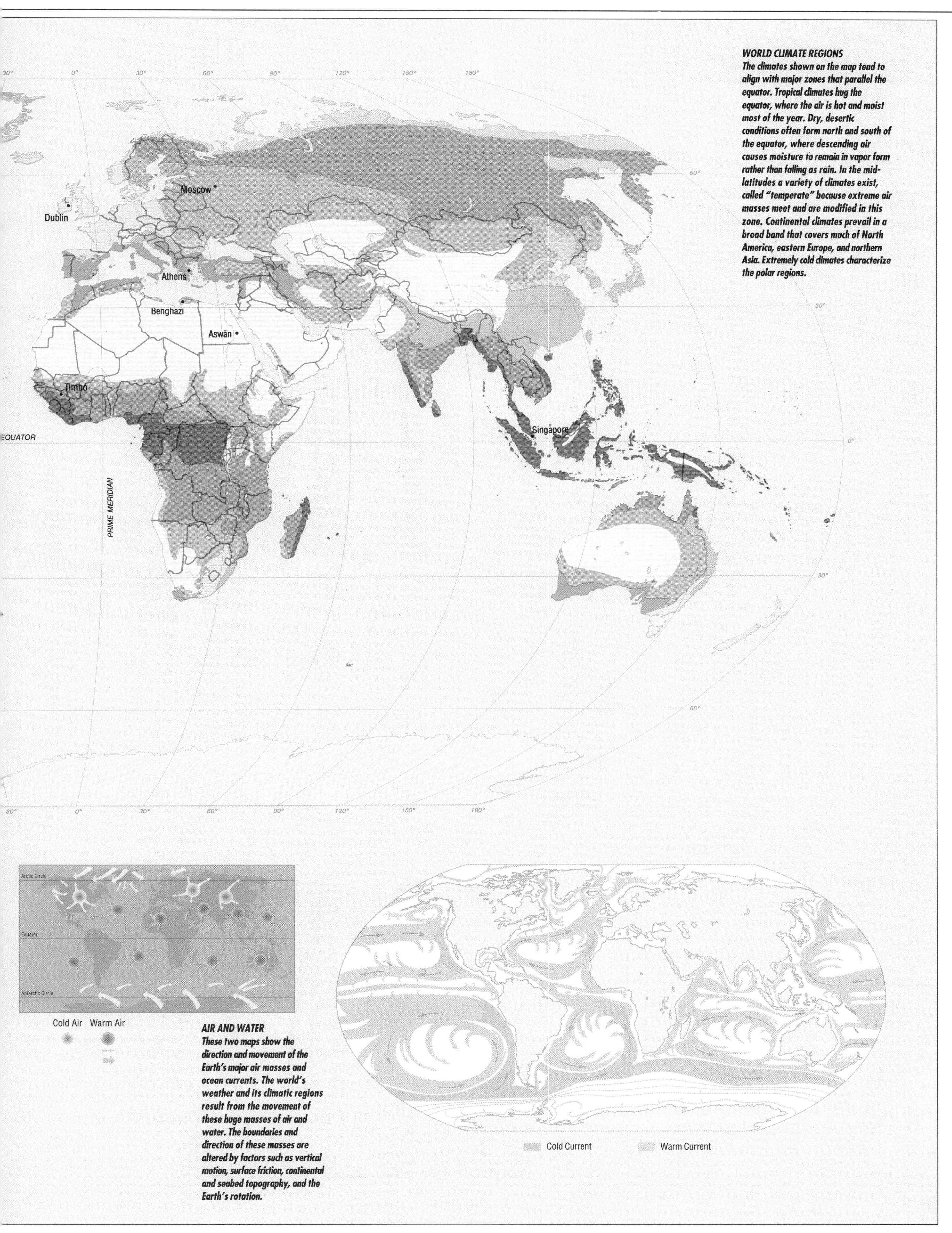

WORLD CLIMATE REGIONS
The climates shown on the map tend to align with major zones that parallel the equator. Tropical climates hug the equator, where the air is hot and moist most of the year. Dry, desertic conditions often form north and south of the equator, where descending air causes moisture to remain in vapor form rather than falling as rain. In the mid-latitudes a variety of climates exist, called "temperate" because extreme air masses meet and are modified in this zone. Continental climates prevail in a broad band that covers much of North America, eastern Europe, and northern Asia. Extremely cold climates characterize the polar regions.

AIR AND WATER
These two maps show the direction and movement of the Earth's major air masses and ocean currents. The world's weather and its climatic regions result from the movement of these huge masses of air and water. The boundaries and direction of these masses are altered by factors such as vertical motion, surface friction, continental and seabed topography, and the Earth's rotation.

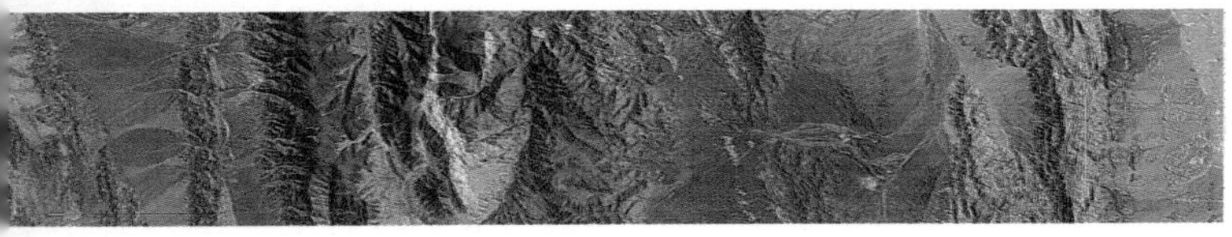

NEARLY 1.6 MILLION YEARS AGO, OUR HUMAN ANCESTORS STRUGGLED TO SURVIVE IN THE FORESTS AND FERTILE PLAINS OF EASTERN AFRICA. TODAY, HUMANITY inhabits every continent on earth. World population is approaching 6 billion, with 80 million new lives added every year. More people are alive now than have existed since the dawn of human history.

This explosive growth is fueled not only by a rising birth rate but by longer average life spans and by a sharp reduction in the number of children who die young. With births far outstripping deaths, predictions are that world population will not stablize until the year 2010, when over 10 billion people will share the planet.

The most densely settled parts of the Earth appear in the industrial areas of Europe, North America, and Japan, and the predominantly rural areas of India, China, and Southeast Asia. In developed areas, modern technology has encouraged the growth of large urban districts. The heavily populated rural areas of Asian countries reflect nearly 4,000 years of agricultural civilization.

Even with the surge in population, however, substantial areas of the Earth remain underpopulated or virtually empty. Some regions offer striking contrasts between crowded and open spaces. In Russia, a narrow band of population stretches along the Trans-Siberian Railway. The eastern shore of the Mediterranean Sea, with its crowded coastal fringe of Israel, Lebanon, and Syria, stands out sharply against the barren, uninhabited land beyond.

Several natural and cultural factors help explain the uneven distribution of humanity. Nature imposes limits on agricultural development: many areas are too dry or mountainous or have growing seasons too short to support a large population. The harsher climate and terrain of the polar regions and great deserts of the world show only widely scattered human settlements.

Cultural factors also influence where populations are likely to concentrate. Nearly 2.5 billion people now live in urban centers, half of them in cities that number 500,000 or more. By the year 2000, the urban population in less-developed countries will double, as the rural poor seek greater opportunities in the already-crowded cities. Religion and cultural values also influence a nation's ability to control its birth rate. Until curbing population becomes a worldwide goal, our growing numbers will continue to exert increasing pressure on the Earth's resources.

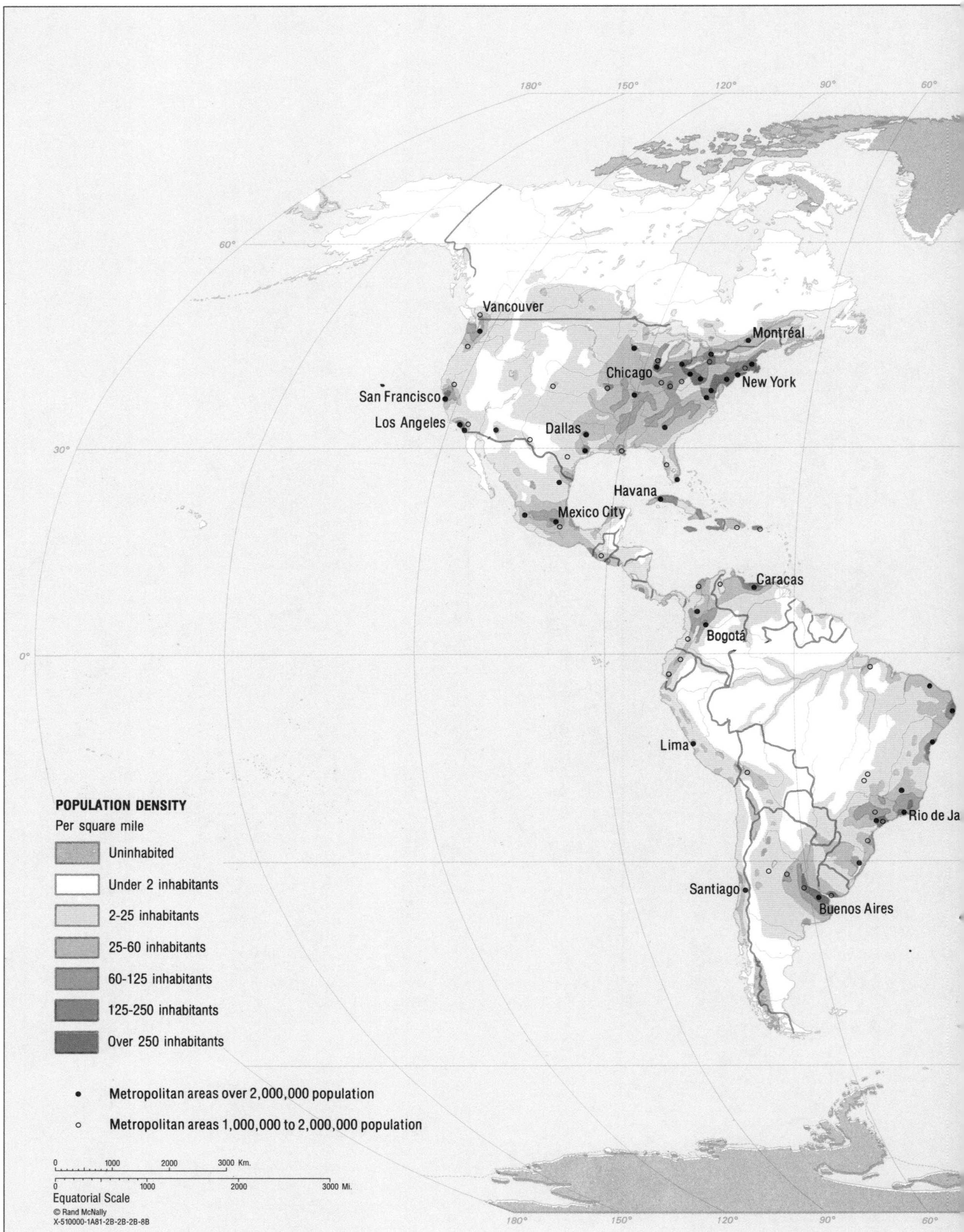

Vancouver
Montréal
Chicago
New York
San Francisco
Los Angeles
Dallas
Havana
Mexico City
Caracas
Bogotá
Lima
Rio de Ja
Santiago
Buenos Aires

POPULATION DENSITY
Per square mile
- Uninhabited
- Under 2 inhabitants
- 2-25 inhabitants
- 25-60 inhabitants
- 60-125 inhabitants
- 125-250 inhabitants
- Over 250 inhabitants

- • Metropolitan areas over 2,000,000 population
- ○ Metropolitan areas 1,000,000 to 2,000,000 population

0 1000 2000 3000 Km.
0 1000 2000 3000 Mi.
Equatorial Scale
© Rand McNally
X-510000-1A81-28-28-28-88

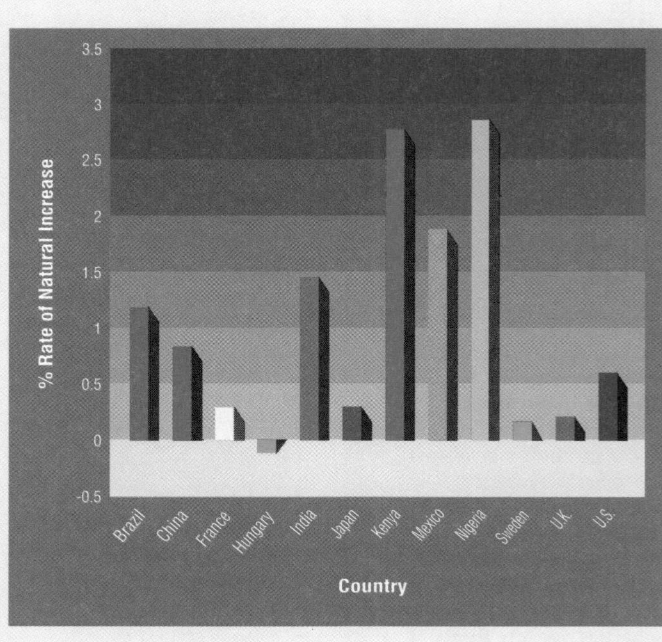

POPULATION GROWTH
In densely populated countries, extremely high growth rates can cripple efforts to develop viable economies. Through state-encouraged family planning, China has managed to decrease its growth rate and thus improve the economic well-being of its people. Low rates of growth in industrialized countries have resulted in economies which are able to support relatively high standards of living.

(Rate of natural growth per year = birth rate minus death rate. Immigration and emigration are not included in this formulation.)

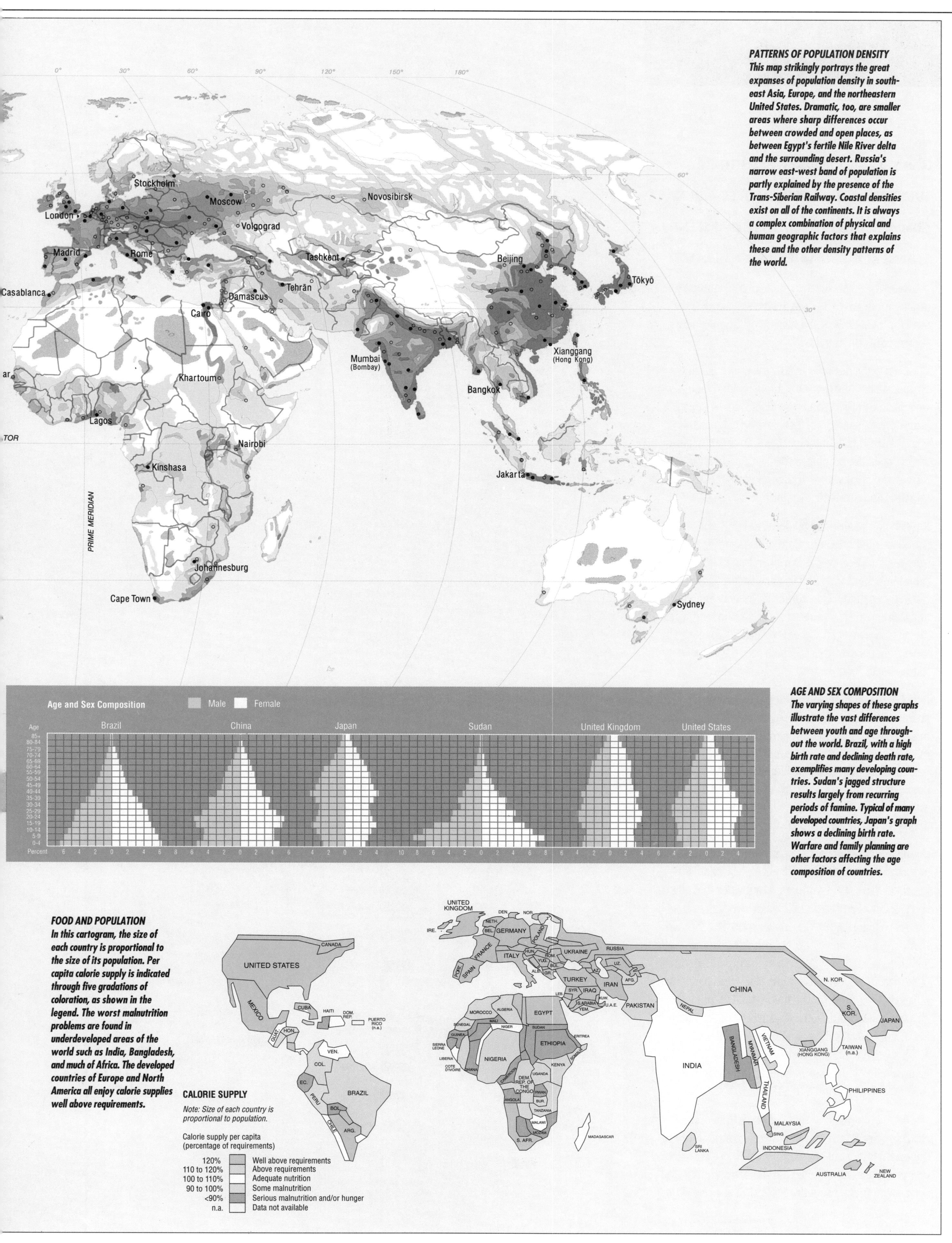

PATTERNS OF POPULATION DENSITY

This map strikingly portrays the great expanses of population density in southeast Asia, Europe, and the northeastern United States. Dramatic, too, are smaller areas where sharp differences occur between crowded and open places, as between Egypt's fertile Nile River delta and the surrounding desert. Russia's narrow east-west band of population is partly explained by the presence of the Trans-Siberian Railway. Coastal densities exist on all of the continents. It is always a complex combination of physical and human geographic factors that explains these and the other density patterns of the world.

AGE AND SEX COMPOSITION

The varying shapes of these graphs illustrate the vast differences between youth and age throughout the world. Brazil, with a high birth rate and declining death rate, exemplifies many developing countries. Sudan's jagged structure results largely from recurring periods of famine. Typical of many developed countries, Japan's graph shows a declining birth rate. Warfare and family planning are other factors affecting the age composition of countries.

FOOD AND POPULATION

In this cartogram, the size of each country is proportional to the size of its population. Per capita calorie supply is indicated through five gradations of coloration, as shown in the legend. The worst malnutrition problems are found in underdeveloped areas of the world such as India, Bangladesh, and much of Africa. The developed countries of Europe and North America all enjoy calorie supplies well above requirements.

LANGUAGE, RELIGION, AND ETHNIC IDENTITY—THESE HELP TO DEFINE HUMAN COMMUNITIES IN A WAY THAT TRANSCENDS POLITICAL BOUNDARIES. LANGUAGE, OF course, is the most effective means of communication among members of a group. It serves as a cohesive force for the members and helps to distinguish one community from another.

The map to the right shows only the major language groups, such as the Germanic branch of the Indo-European family. A map that displayed all known languages would require thousands of colors and labels. The Chinese branch of the Sino-Tibetan family ranks first in the number of speakers. English ranks second, but is the world's most important medium for scientific and commercial communication.

English enjoys absolute predominance in only four countries: the United Kingdom, the U.S., Australia, and New Zealand. However, it is spoken by a majority of people in Ireland and Canada and is the preferred second language in many other countries. French, Spanish, and Russian are also widely used as second languages. The importance of two other languages is suggested by the number of countries in which they have official status: Arabic (18 countries) and Spanish (20 countries).

Religion, like language, is a means of communication and a mechanism that promotes social cohesion. The map here shows the most important universalizing religions (Christianity, Islam, and Buddhism) that are held to be appropriate for all of humankind and so are propagated by missionary activities. Religions associated with particular peoples, such as Judaism and Hinduism, seldom entail missionary activity.

Countries cannot always be neatly divided into religious groups, however. In China, for example, Buddhism, Confucianism, and Taoism are so entwined that one has to speak of a Chinese religious system rather than a Chinese religion. Elsewhere in the world, and especially in Africa, a wide array of tribal religions can be identified, and many of these have incorporated some of the practices and beliefs of one of the universalizing religions. Over time, most religions tend to split into factions or denominations. The division of Christianity into Catholic, Orthodox, and Protestant branches is striking evidence of this tendency, as is the split of the Islamic religion into Sunni and Shi'ite factions after the death of Muhammad in A.D. 632.

The country boundaries that appear as lines under the patterns of religions and languages remind us of an important fact about our world: very few of the 184 member states of the United Nations are nations in the strict or singular sense of the word. Most are a collection

Continued on page xiv

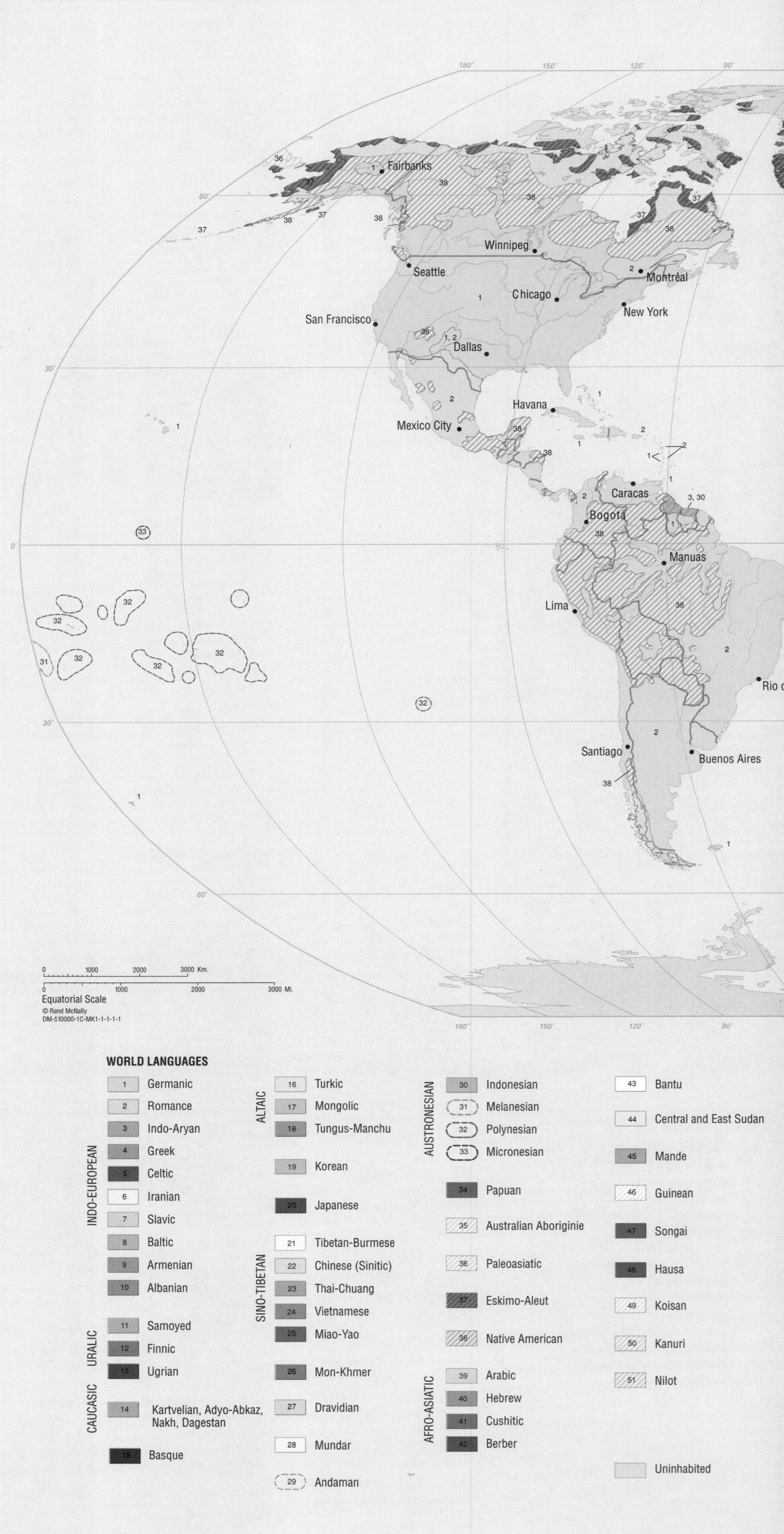

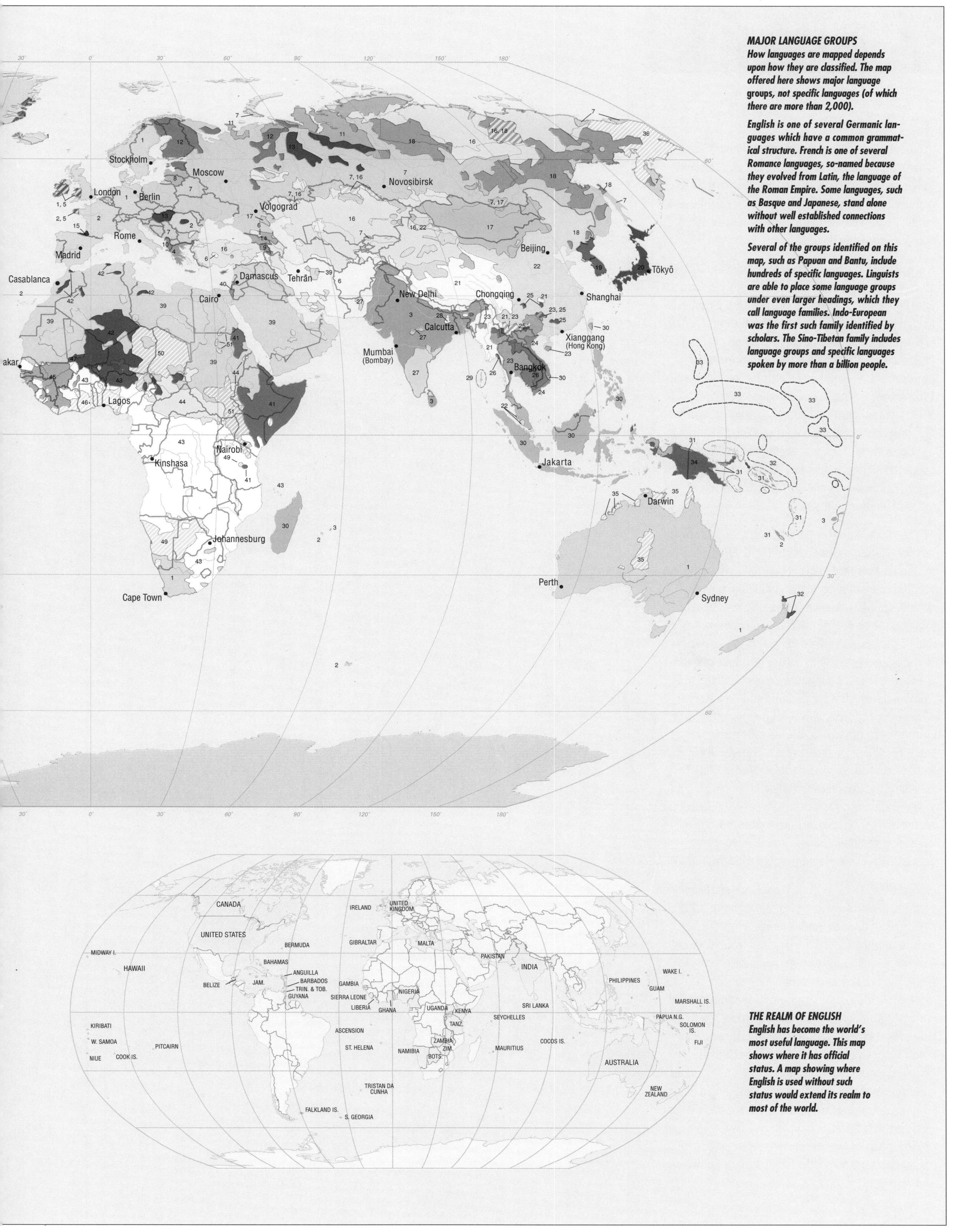

MAJOR LANGUAGE GROUPS

How languages are mapped depends upon how they are classified. The map offered here shows major language groups, not specific languages (of which there are more than 2,000).

English is one of several Germanic languages which have a common grammatical structure. French is one of several Romance languages, so-named because they evolved from Latin, the language of the Roman Empire. Some languages, such as Basque and Japanese, stand alone without well established connections with other languages.

Several of the groups identified on this map, such as Papuan and Bantu, include hundreds of specific languages. Linguists are able to place some language groups under even larger headings, which they call language families. Indo-European was the first such family identified by scholars. The Sino-Tibetan family includes language groups and specific languages spoken by more than a billion people.

THE REALM OF ENGLISH

English has become the world's most useful language. This map shows where it has official status. A map showing where English is used without such status would extend its realm to most of the world.

Continued from page xii

of different groups speaking a variety of languages and maintaining diverse religious and cultural beliefs. In Western Europe, only Denmark and Portugal are homogeneous countries where everyone speaks the same language and belongs to the same church. In Africa, only Tunisia shares this distinction.

It is hard to find a comparable example in the Middle East, even among countries predominantly Islamic in faith and Arabic in speech. Saudi Arabia, if its large foreign labor population is ignored, is the only example of a true nation state in this region. Elsewhere in Asia, Japan and the two Korean states are rare exceptions to the more common pattern of cultural complexity. In Latin America, Spanish or Portuguese speech and Roman Catholicism are cultural common denominators, but Native American languages are still spoken in most countries. In contrast, Argentina and Brazil are cultural melting pots like the United States. Costa Rica and Uruguay may be the only New World states without significant minorities.

The fact that cultural uniformity is so rare, and only one perfect example can be cited (Iceland), means that the familiar political map not only differs from the less familiar maps of language and religion, but may actually conflict with them. Some countries have laws and institutions that permit citizens of different faiths and languages to live in peace and prosperity. For example, the Swiss live in harmony in spite of speaking four languages (German, French, Italian, and Romansch) and having Catholic and Protestant affiliations. Unfortunately, such happy examples of cultural accommodation are offset by numerous instances of tension and conflict. The ethnic warfare within recent decades in Sri Lanka, Bosnia, Sudan, Lebanon, and Rwanda are conspicuous examples of the potential for violence that often exists in states that are not true nation states or have borders that do not coincide with ethnic realities. The collapse of the Soviet Union exposed many problems of this nature.

Since the world is never likely to have only one language or one religion, comparison of maps showing cultural patterns with those indicating political jurisdiction reveals an important truth about our troubled world. In order to understand why ethnic conflict occurs so frequently we need an appropriate vocabulary. We need to be able to distinguish among the following cultural-political categories: *nation states* (homogeneous countries, such as Iceland and Denmark); *multinational states* (countries made up of diverse ethnic and linguistic groups, such as India); *multi-state nations* (multiple countries that share language and religion, such as the Arabic-Islamic realm); *non-nation states* (Vatican City is the only example); and, finally, *non-state nations* (regions where people share language and religion but have no political state, such as Kurdistan and Palestine).

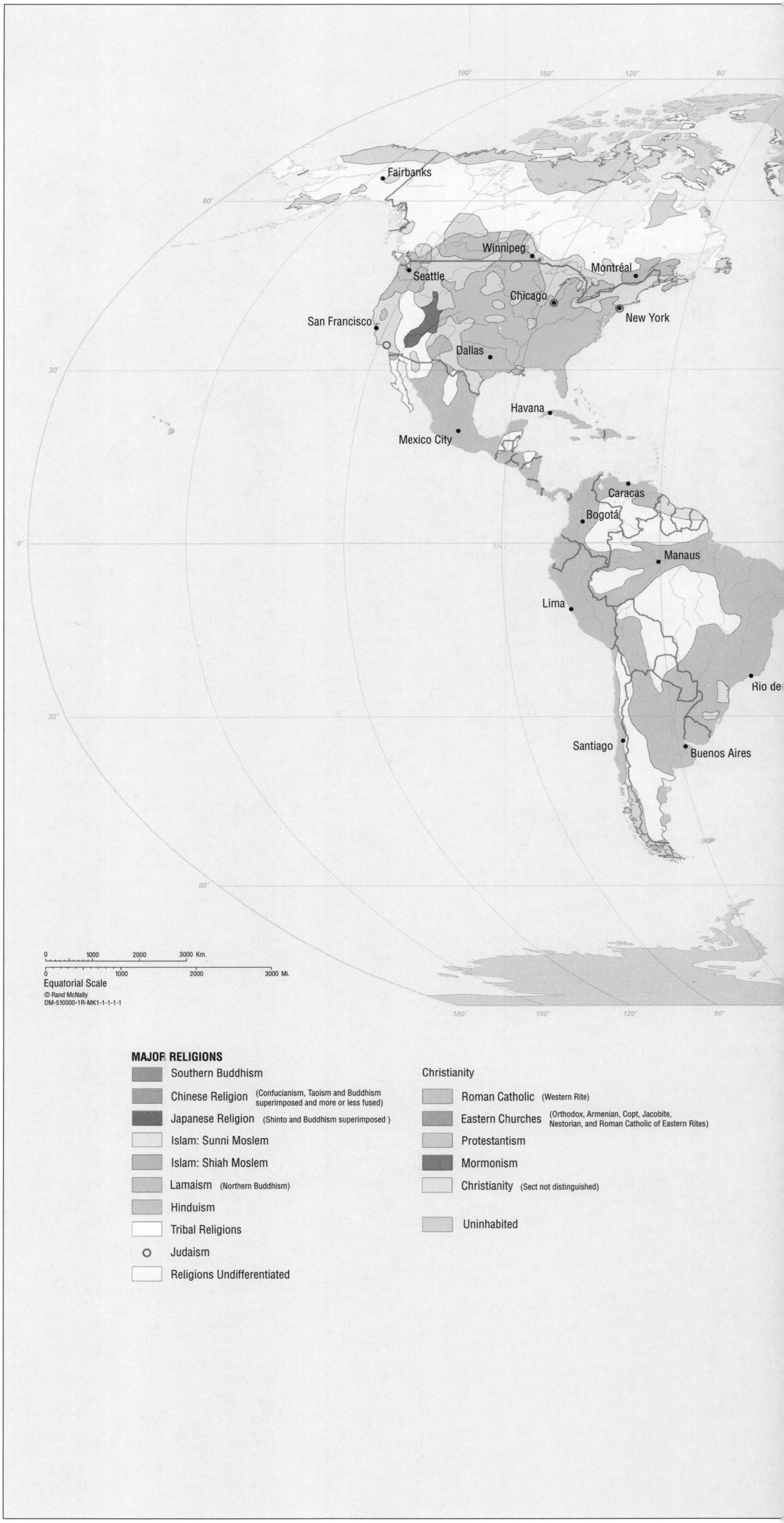

Fairbanks
Winnipeg
Montréal
Seattle
Chicago
New York
San Francisco
Dallas
Havana
Mexico City
Caracas
Bogotá
Manaus
Lima
Rio de
Santiago
Buenos Aires

0 1000 2000 3000 Km.
0 1000 2000 3000 Mi.
Equatorial Scale
© Rand McNally
DM-510000-1R-MK1-1-1-1-1

MAJOR RELIGIONS

- Southern Buddhism
- Chinese Religion (Confucianism, Taoism and Buddhism superimposed and more or less fused)
- Japanese Religion (Shinto and Buddhism superimposed)
- Islam: Sunni Moslem
- Islam: Shiah Moslem
- Lamaism (Northern Buddhism)
- Hinduism
- Tribal Religions
- Judaism
- Religions Undifferentiated

Christianity

- Roman Catholic (Western Rite)
- Eastern Churches (Orthodox, Armenian, Copt, Jacobite, Nestorian, and Roman Catholic of Eastern Rites)
- Protestantism
- Mormonism
- Christianity (Sect not distinguished)
- Uninhabited

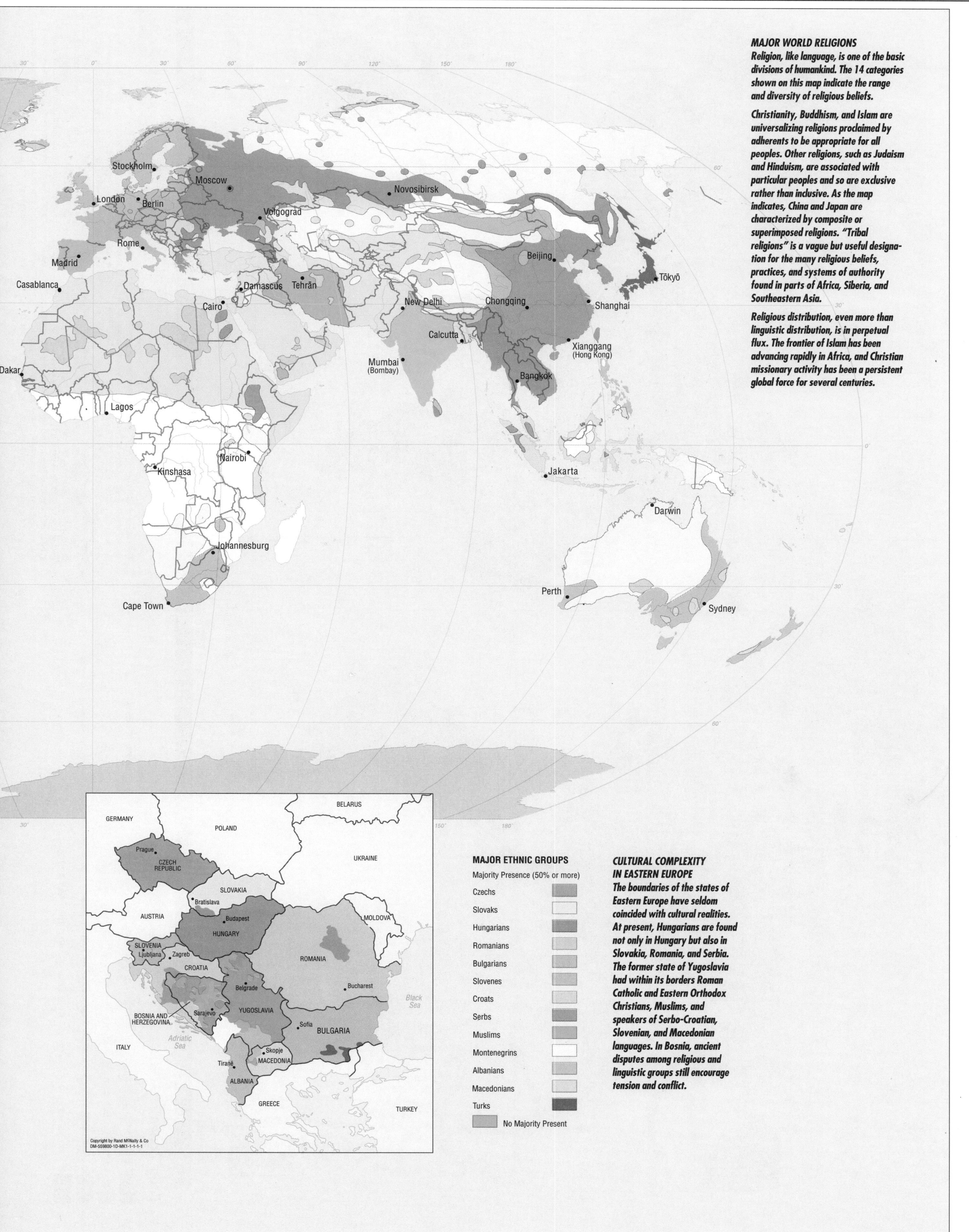

MAJOR WORLD RELIGIONS
Religion, like language, is one of the basic divisions of humankind. The 14 categories shown on this map indicate the range and diversity of religious beliefs.

Christianity, Buddhism, and Islam are universalizing religions proclaimed by adherents to be appropriate for all peoples. Other religions, such as Judaism and Hinduism, are associated with particular peoples and so are exclusive rather than inclusive. As the map indicates, China and Japan are characterized by composite or superimposed religions. "Tribal religions" is a vague but useful designation for the many religious beliefs, practices, and systems of authority found in parts of Africa, Siberia, and Southeastern Asia.

Religious distribution, even more than linguistic distribution, is in perpetual flux. The frontier of Islam has been advancing rapidly in Africa, and Christian missionary activity has been a persistent global force for several centuries.

MAJOR ETHNIC GROUPS

Majority Presence (50% or more)

- Czechs
- Slovaks
- Hungarians
- Romanians
- Bulgarians
- Slovenes
- Croats
- Serbs
- Muslims
- Montenegrins
- Albanians
- Macedonians
- Turks

No Majority Present

CULTURAL COMPLEXITY IN EASTERN EUROPE
The boundaries of the states of Eastern Europe have seldom coincided with cultural realities. At present, Hungarians are found not only in Hungary but also in Slovakia, Romania, and Serbia. The former state of Yugoslavia had within its borders Roman Catholic and Eastern Orthodox Christians, Muslims, and speakers of Serbo-Croatian, Slovenian, and Macedonian languages. In Bosnia, ancient disputes among religious and linguistic groups still encourage tension and conflict.

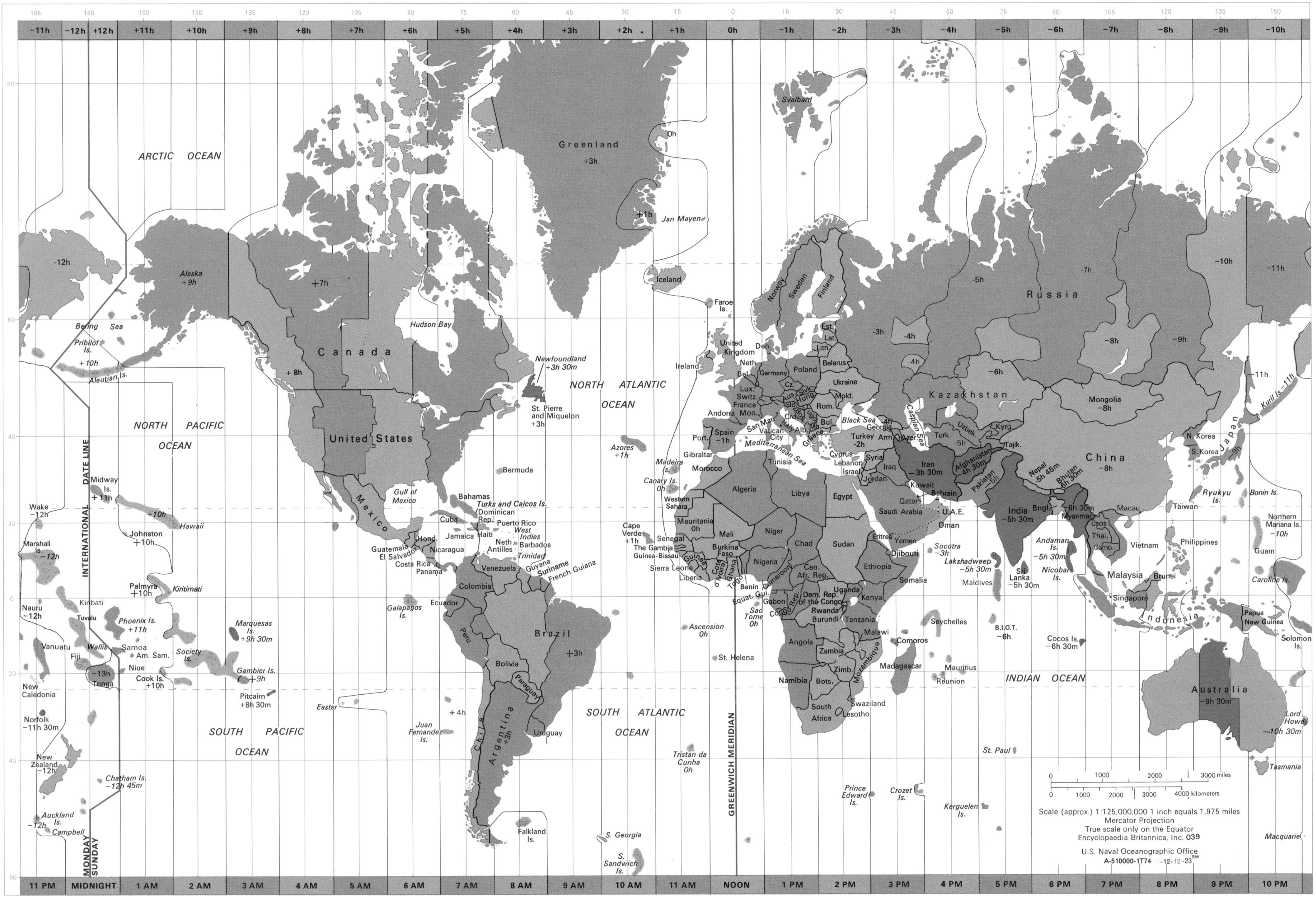

Time Zones

- Standard time zone of even-numbered hours from Greenwich time
- Standard time zone of odd-numbered hours from Greenwich time
- Time varies from the standard time zone by half an hour
- Time varies from the standard time zone by other than half an hour

h m — hours, minutes

Scale (approx.) 1:125,000,000 1 inch equals 1,975 miles
Mercator Projection
True scale only on the Equator
Encyclopaedia Britannica, Inc. 039

U.S. Naval Oceanographic Office
A-510000-1T74 -12-12-23[RW]

The standard time zone system, fixed by international agreement and by law in each country, is based on a theoretical division of the globe into 24 zones of 15° longitude each. The mid-meridian of each zone fixes the hour for the entire zone. The zero time zone extends 7½° east and 7½° west of the Greenwich meridian, 0° longitude. Since the earth rotates toward the east, time zones to the west of Greenwich are earlier, to the east, later.
Plus and minus hours at the top of the map are added to or subtracted from local time to find Greenwich time. Local standard time can be determined for any area in the world by adding one hour for each time zone counted in an easterly direction from one's own, or by subtracting one hour for each zone counted in a westerly direction. To separate one day from the next, the 180th meridian has been designated as the international date line.
On both sides of the line the time of day is the same, but west of the line it is one day later than it is to the east.
Countries that adhere to the international zone system adopt the zone applicable to their location. Some countries, however, establish time zones based on political boundaries, or adopt the time zone of a neighboring unit. For all or part of the year some countries also advance their time by one hour, thereby utilizing more daylight hours each day.

Maps and Index of the United States

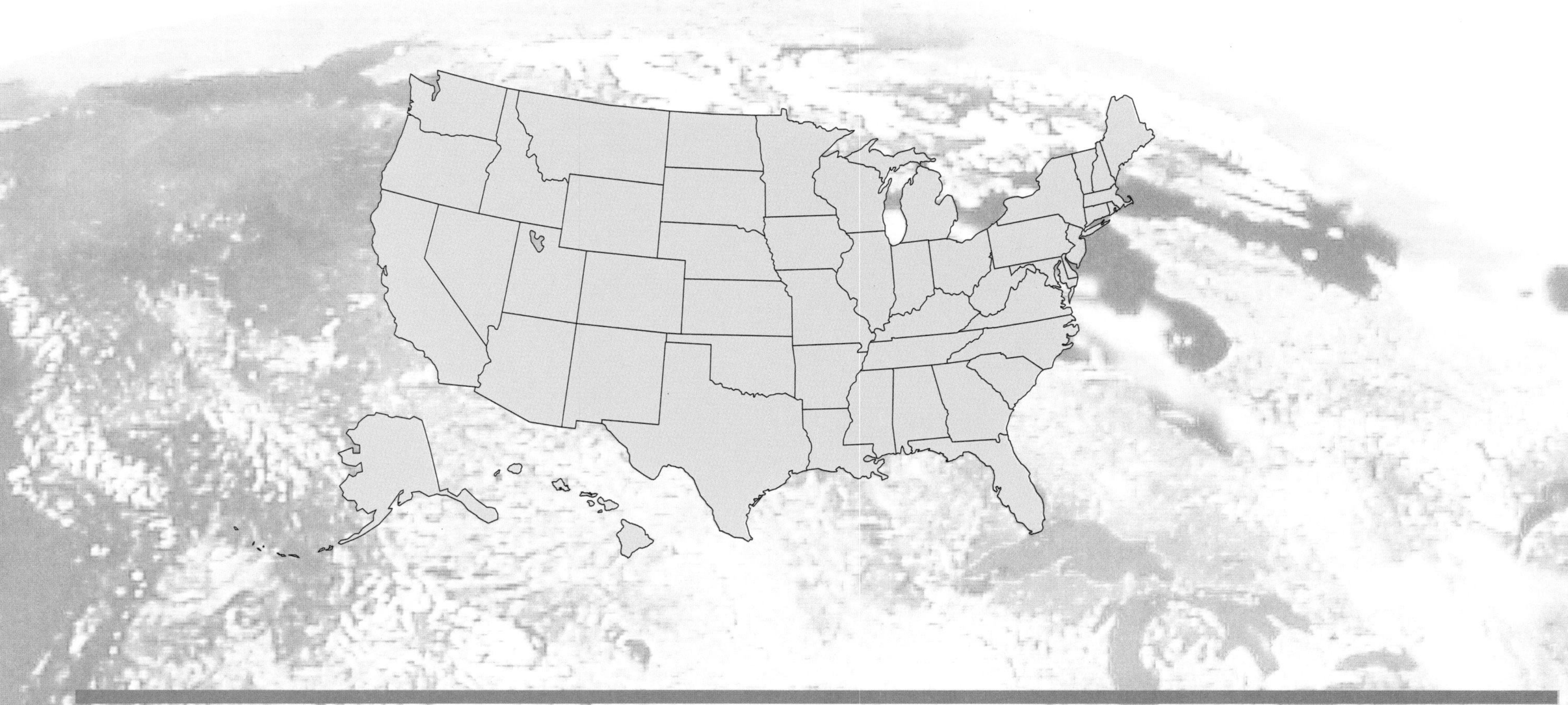

Legend

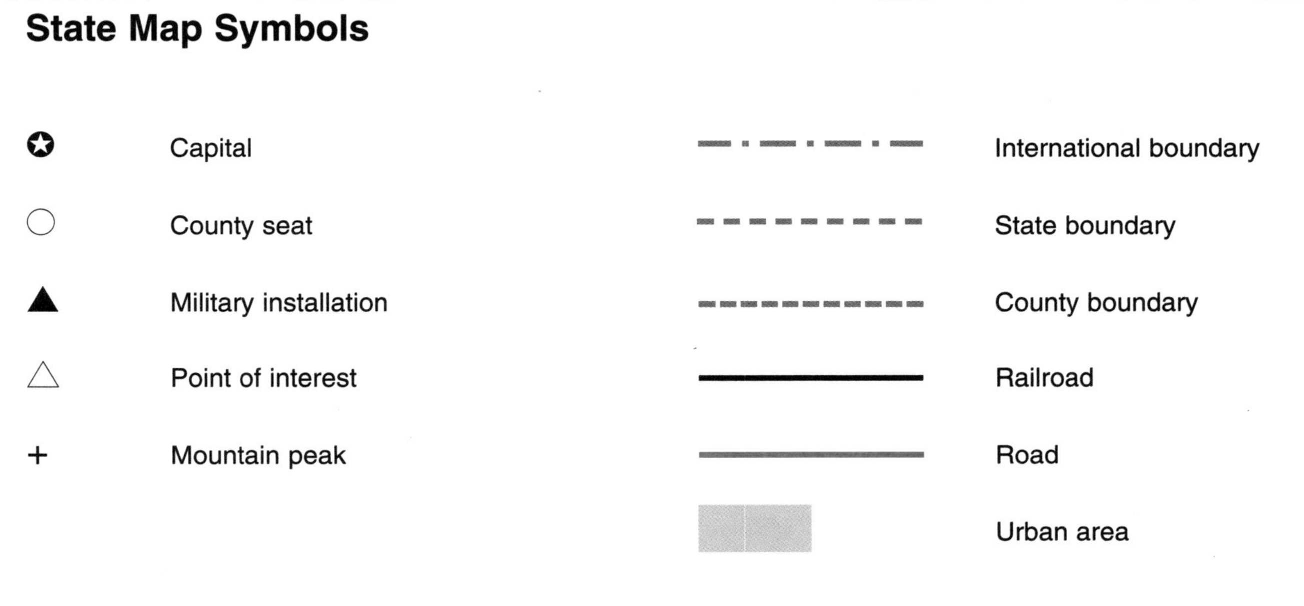

PACIFIC
OCEAN
CANADA
UNITED STATES
MEXICO
ROCKY MOUNTAINS
CASCADE RANGE
SIERRA NEVADA
COAST RANGES
GREAT BASIN
VANCOUVER ISLAND
BRITISH COLUMBIA
ALBERTA
SASKATCHEWAN
MANITOBA
WASHINGTON
OREGON
IDAHO
MONTANA
WYOMING
NEVADA
UTAH
COLORADO
CALIFORNIA
ARIZONA
NEW MEXICO
TEXAS
NORTH DAKOTA
SOUTH DAKOTA
NEBRASKA
KANSAS
OKLAHOMA
Edmonton
Calgary
Saskatoon
Regina
Winnipeg
Vancouver
Victoria
Seattle
Tacoma
Spokane
Portland
Salem
Eugene
Boise
Great Falls
Helena
Butte
Billings
Salt Lake City
Ogden
Provo
Reno
Sacramento
SAN FRANCISCO
Oakland
San Jose
Fresno
Bakersfield
Las Vegas
LOS ANGELES
Long Beach
Anaheim
Riverside
San Bernardino
Santa Ana
San Diego
Tijuana
Mexicali
Ensenada
Phoenix
Tucson
Albuquerque
Santa Fe
El Paso
Ciudad Juárez
Denver
Aurora
Colorado Springs
Pueblo
Cheyenne
Rapid City
Bismarck
Amarillo
Lubbock
Odessa
Midland
Wichita
Oklahoma City
Fort Worth
Austin
San Antonio
Laredo
Nuevo Laredo
Monclova
Reynosa
ARCTIC OCEAN
Beaufort Sea
Chukchi Sea
RUSSIA
Bering Strait
BROOKS RANGE
Arctic Circle
ALASKA
ALASKA RANGE
Mount McKinley 6194
Fairbanks
Anchorage
Juneau
Nome
BERING SEA
Gulf of Alaska
MACKENZIE MOUNTAINS
ALEUTIAN ISLANDS
Kilometers 0 200 Km.
Miles 0 200 Mi.
Copyright © by Rand McNally & Co.
OAHU
Honolulu
MOLOKAI
LANAI
MAUI
KAHOOLAWE
HAWAII
Hilo
Mauna Kea 4205
Mauna Loa 4169
KAUAI
NIIHAU
Kilometers 0 50 Km.
Miles 0 50 Mi.
Copyright © by Rand McNally & Co.
Map prepared by Rand McNally & Co.
A-520590-264

Kilometers 0 200 400 600 Km.

Statute Miles 0 200 400 600 Mi.

Scale 1:12,000,000

One centimeter represents 120 kilometers.
One inch represents approximately 190 miles.

Albers Conical Equal-Area Projection

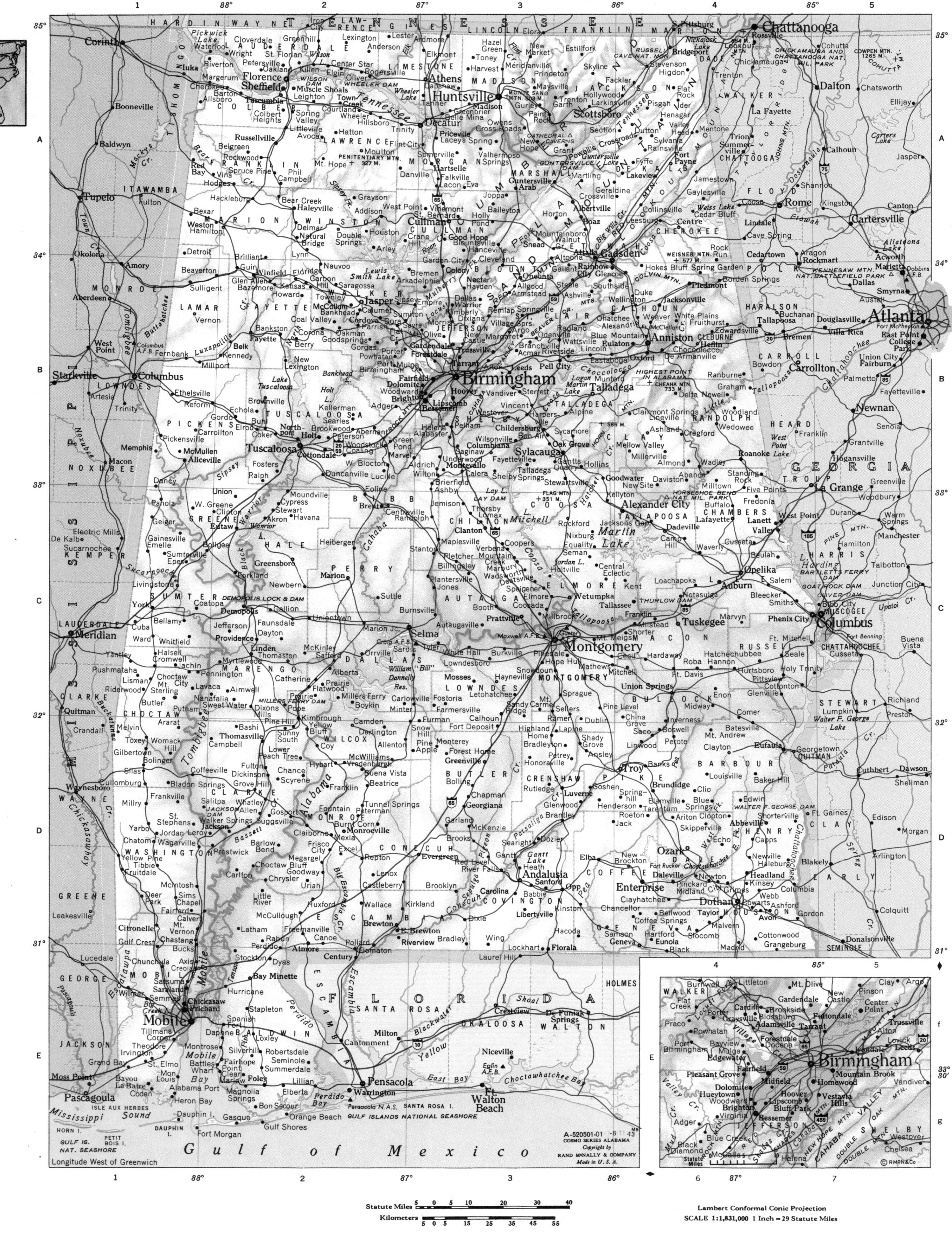
T E N N E S S E E
M I S S I S S I P P I
G E O R G I A
F L O R I D A
Gulf of Mexico
Birmingham
Montgomery
Mobile
Huntsville
Tuscaloosa
Gadsden
Anniston
Dothan
Selma
Florence
Decatur
Auburn
Tuskegee
Chattanooga
Atlanta
Columbus
Meridian
Pensacola
Longitude West of Greenwich
A-520501-01
COSMO SERIES ALABAMA
Copyright by
RAND McNALLY & COMPANY
Made in U. S. A.
Statute Miles 5 0 5 10 20 30 40
Kilometers 5 0 5 15 25 35 45 55
Lambert Conformal Conic Projection
SCALE 1:1,831,000 1 Inch = 29 Statute Miles

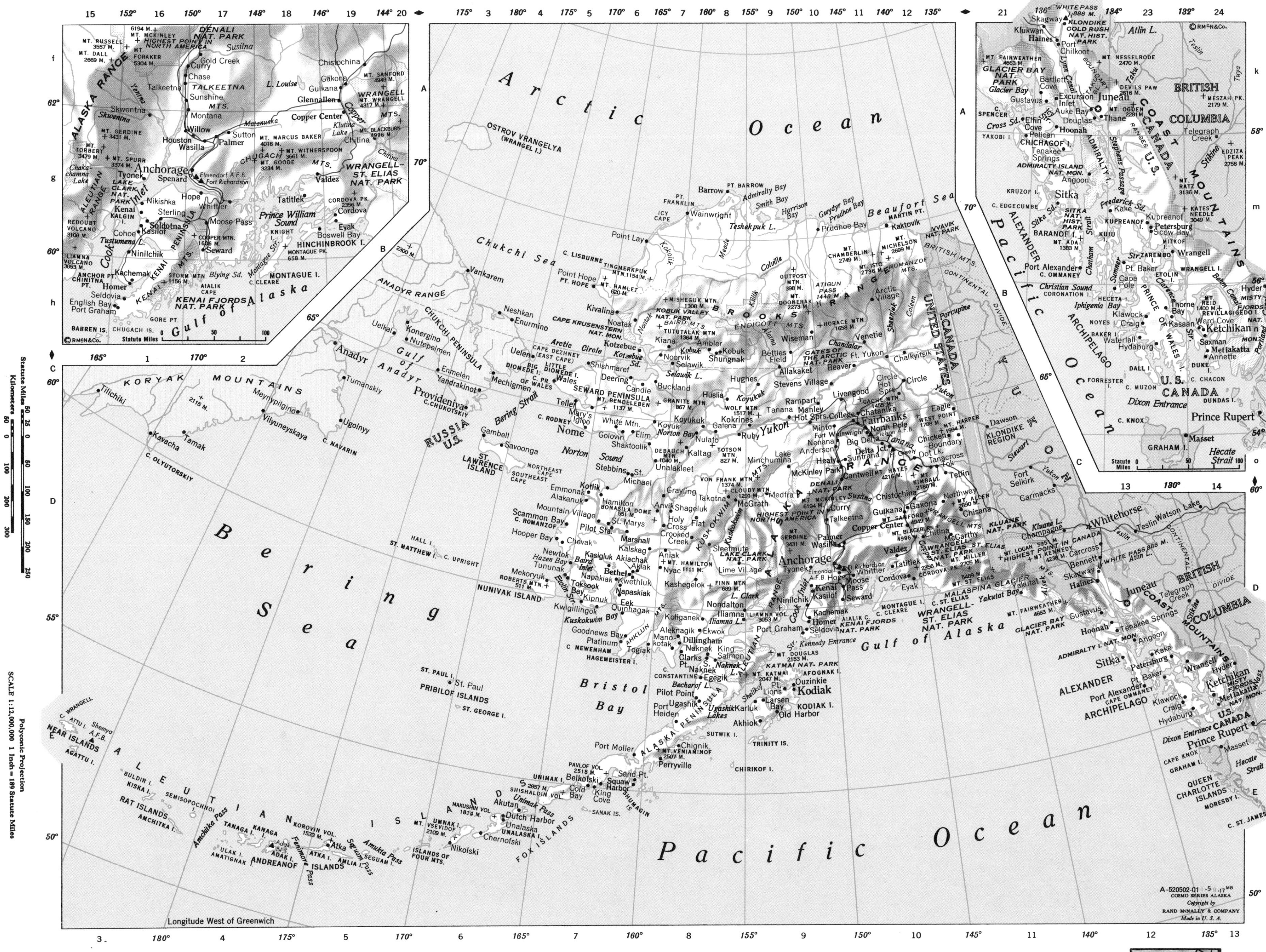
Arctic Ocean
Bering Sea
Pacific Ocean
Gulf of Alaska
Chukchi Sea
Beaufort Sea
Bristol Bay
Norton Sound
Gulf of Anadyr
UNITED STATES
CANADA
RUSSIA
U.S.
BRITISH COLUMBIA
YUKON
BROOKS RANGE
ALASKA RANGE
KORYAK MOUNTAINS
ANADYR RANGE
CHUKCHI PENINSULA
SEWARD PENINSULA
ALASKA PENINSULA
ALEUTIAN ISLANDS
ALEXANDER ARCHIPELAGO
COAST MOUNTAINS
KODIAK I.
NUNIVAK ISLAND
ST. LAWRENCE ISLAND
PRIBILOF ISLANDS
OSTROV VRANGELYA (WRANGEL I.)
Anchorage
Fairbanks
Juneau
Nome
Barrow
Kotzebue
Bethel
Sitka
Ketchikan
Kodiak
Valdez
Whitehorse
Prince Rupert
Dawson
Providenya
Anadyr
Statute Miles 50 25 0 50 100 150 200 250
Kilometers 50 0 100 200 300
Polyconic Projection
SCALE 1:12,000,000 1 Inch = 189 Statute Miles
Longitude West of Greenwich
A-520502-01 -5 -17 MB
COSMO SERIES ALASKA
Copyright by
RAND McNALLY & COMPANY
Made in U. S. A.

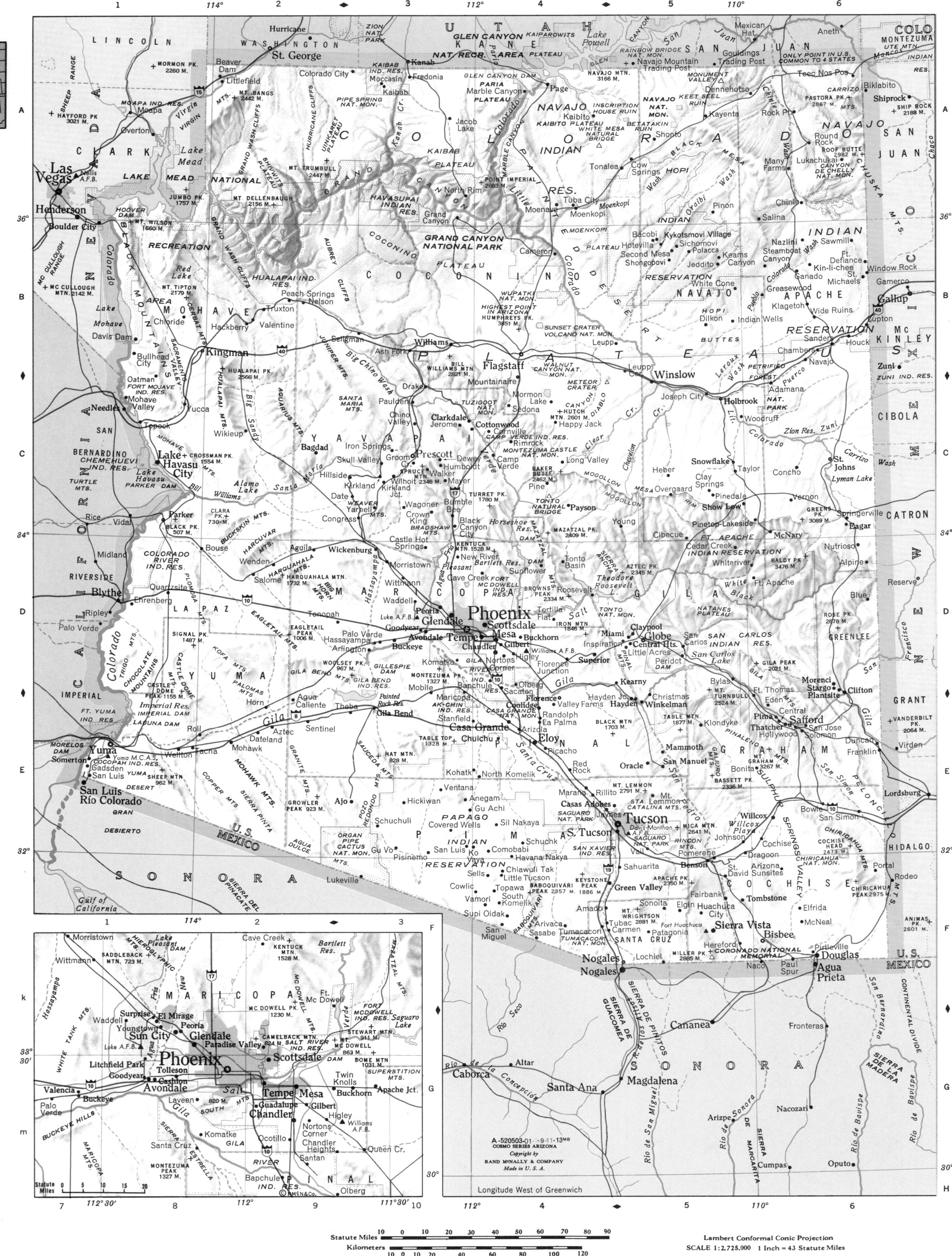

Statute Miles 10 0 10 20 30 40 50 60 70 80 90

Kilometers 10 0 10 20 40 60 80 100 120

Lambert Conformal Conic Projection

SCALE 1:2,725,000 1 Inch = 43 Statute Miles

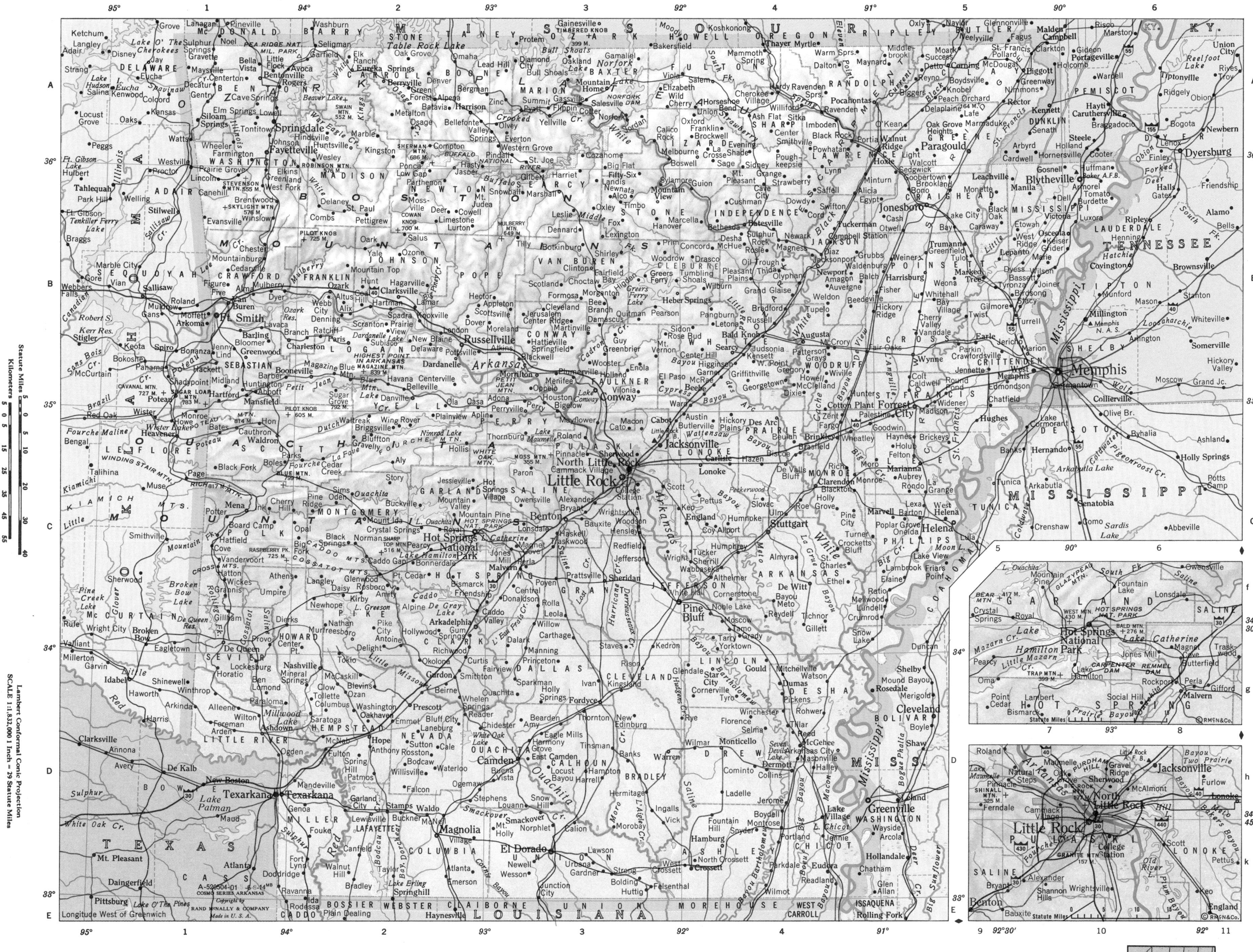
Statute Miles 5 0 5 10 20 30 40
Kilometers 5 0 5 15 25 35 45 55
Lambert Conformal Conic Projection
SCALE 1:1,832,000 1 Inch = 29 Statute Miles

A-520505-01-9-13-20MB
COSMO SERIES CALIFORNIA

Longitude West of Greenwich

Statute Miles 10 0 10 20 30 40 50 60 70 80 90

Kilometers 10 0 10 20 40 60 80 100 120

Lambert Conformal Conic Projection
SCALE 1:3,733,000 1 Inch = 59 Statute Miles

WYOMING
NEBRASKA
KANSAS
OKLAHOMA
NEW MEXICO
UTAH
Cheyenne
Laramie
Denver
Colorado Springs
Pueblo
Grand Junction
Ft. Collins
Boulder
Greeley
Durango
Trinidad
Longitude West of Greenwich
Statute Miles 5 0 5 10 20 30 40 50
Kilometers 5 0 5 15 25 35 45 55 65 75
Lambert Conformal Conic Projection
SCALE 1:2,186,000 1 Inch = 34.5 Statute Miles

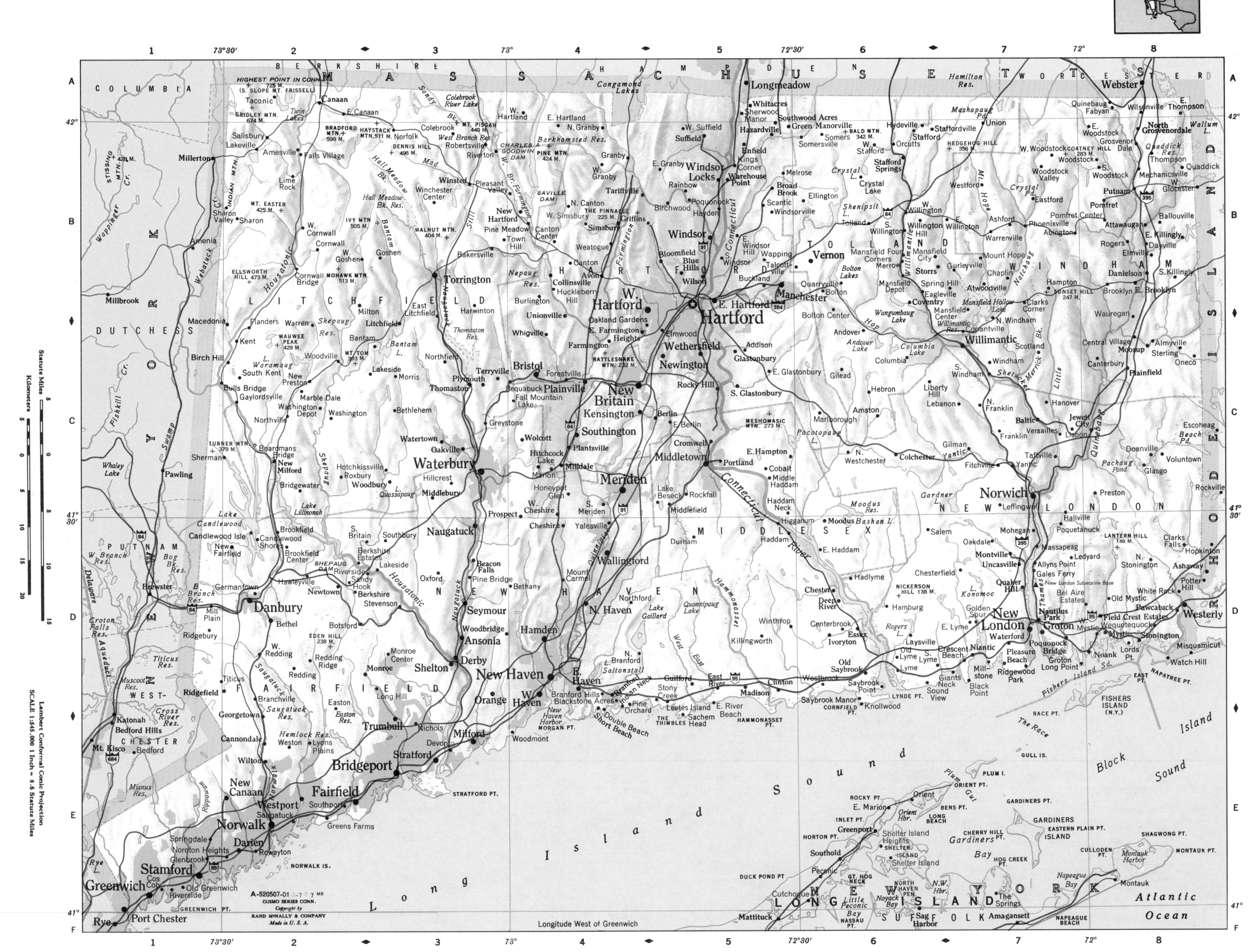
MASSACHUSETTS
RHODE ISLAND
NEW YORK
COLUMBIA
DUTCHESS
PUTNAM
WESTCHESTER
BERKSHIRE
HAMPDEN
WORCESTER
LITCHFIELD
HARTFORD
TOLLAND
WINDHAM
FAIRFIELD
NEW HAVEN
MIDDLESEX
NEW LONDON
SUFFOLK
LONG ISLAND
Long Island Sound
Block Island Sound
Atlantic Ocean
Hartford
W. Hartford
New Britain
Waterbury
New Haven
Bridgeport
Stamford
Norwalk
Danbury
Meriden
Middletown
Norwich
New London
Torrington
Bristol
Manchester
Willimantic
Greenwich
Fairfield
Stratford
Milford
Westerly
Webster
Longmeadow
HIGHEST POINT IN CONN. 725 M. (S. SLOPE MT. FRISSELL)
Connecticut River
Housatonic
Naugatuck
Thames
Quinebaug
A-520507-01
COSMO SERIES CONN.
Copyright by RAND McNALLY & COMPANY
Made in U. S. A.
Longitude West of Greenwich
Statute Miles 5 0 5 10 15
Kilometers 5 0 5 10 15 20
Lambert Conformal Conic Projection
SCALE 1:545,000 1 Inch = 8.6 Statute Miles

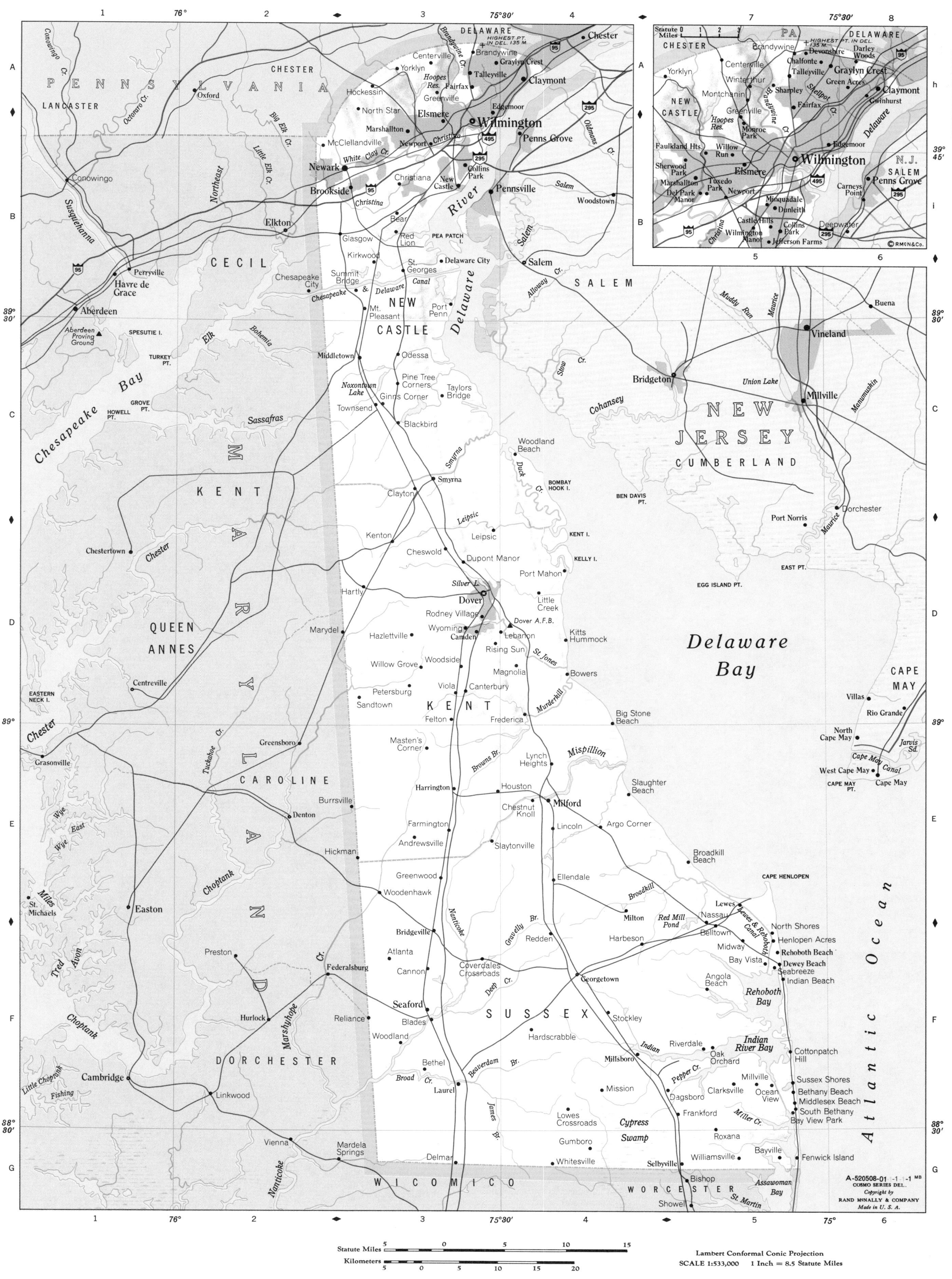

Statute Miles 5 0 5 10 15

Kilometers 5 0 5 10 15 20

Lambert Conformal Conic Projection

SCALE 1:533,000 1 Inch = 8.5 Statute Miles

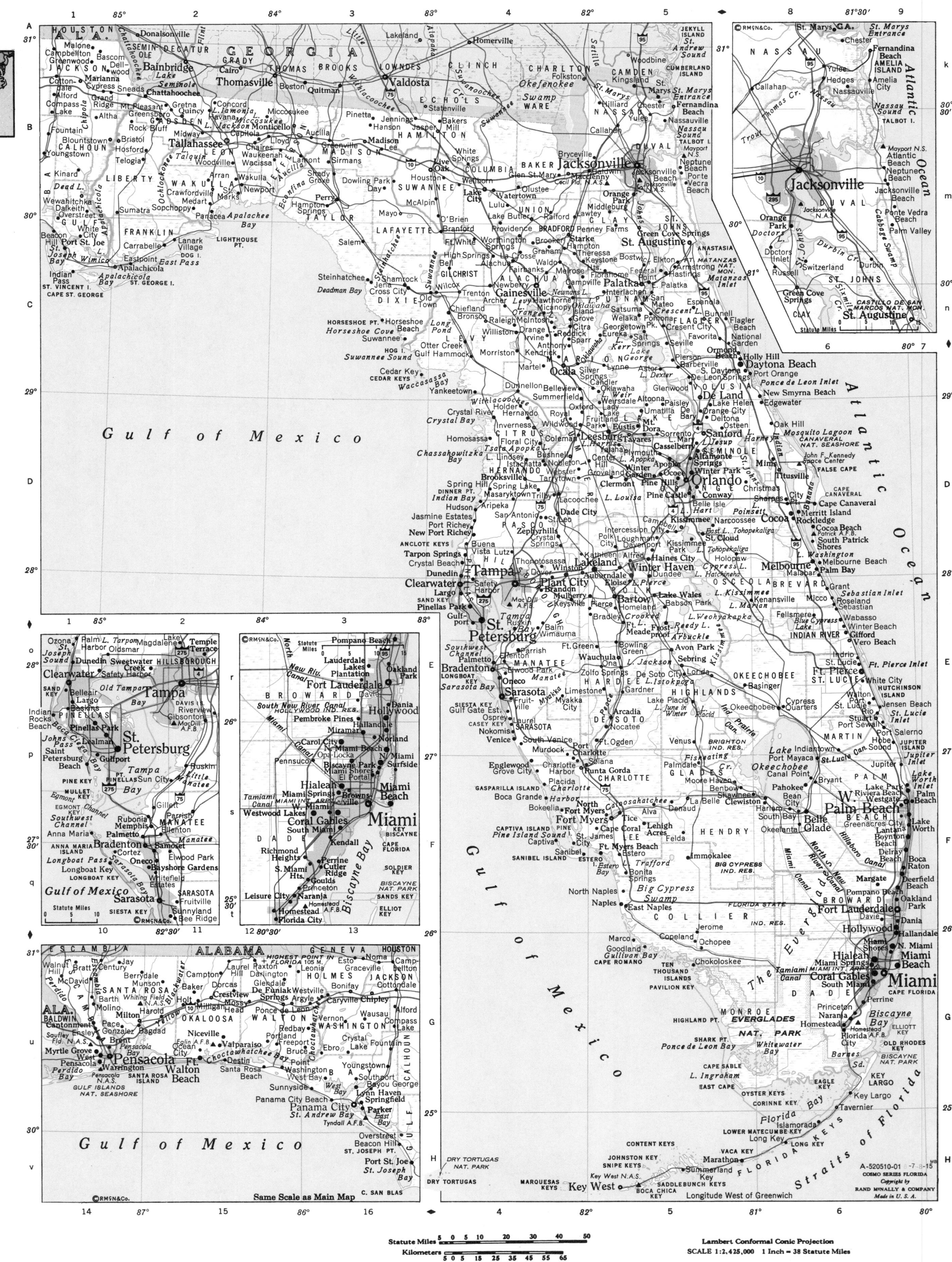

Statute Miles 5 0 5 10 20 30 40 50

Kilometers 5 0 5 15 25 35 45 55 65

Lambert Conformal Conic Projection

SCALE 1:2,425,000 1 Inch = 38 Statute Miles

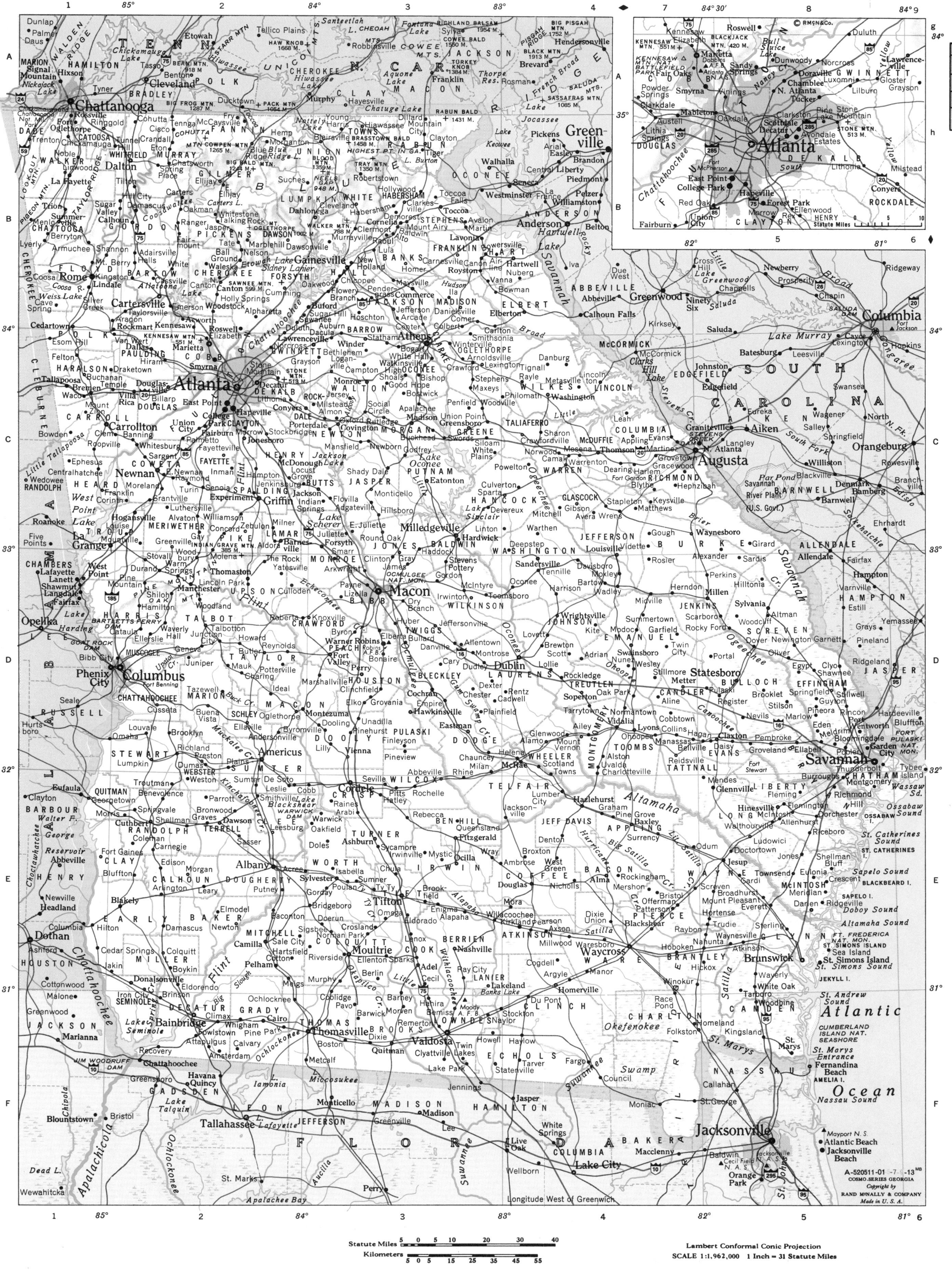
A-520511-01 -7-13
COSMO SERIES GEORGIA
Copyright by
RAND McNALLY & COMPANY
Made in U. S. A.
Longitude West of Greenwich
Statute Miles
Kilometers
Lambert Conformal Conic Projection
SCALE 1:1,962,000 1 Inch = 31 Statute Miles
Atlantic
Ocean

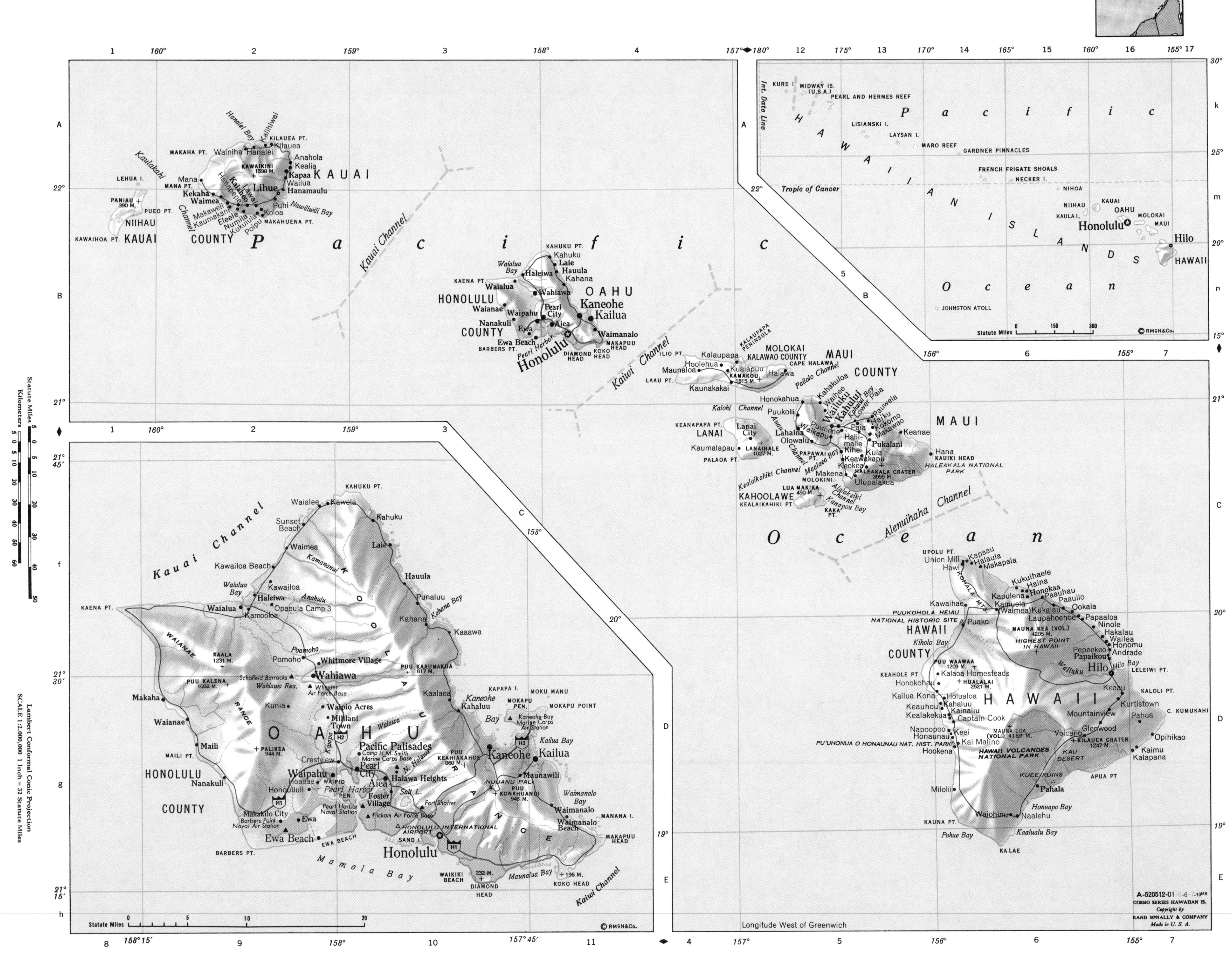
Pacific Ocean
HAWAIIAN ISLANDS
KAUAI
OAHU
MOLOKAI
LANAI
MAUI
KAHOOLAWE
HAWAII
NIIHAU
Honolulu
Hilo
Kauai Channel
Kaiwi Channel
Alenuihaha Channel
Kaulakahi Channel
Kalohi Channel
Pailolo Channel
KAUAI COUNTY
HONOLULU COUNTY
MAUI COUNTY
KALAWAO COUNTY
HAWAII COUNTY
Tropic of Cancer
Int. Date Line
Longitude West of Greenwich
Mamala Bay
Kaneohe Bay
Pearl Harbor
Kailua
Kaneohe
Wahiawa
Waipahu
Pearl City
Aiea
Ewa Beach
Waianae
Makaha
Haleiwa
Laie
Kahuku
WAIANAE RANGE
KOOLAU RANGE
DIAMOND HEAD
KOKO HEAD
MAKAPUU HEAD
BARBERS PT.
KAENA PT.
KAHUKU PT.
MOKAPU POINT
HONOLULU INTERNATIONAL AIRPORT
Lihue
Kapaa
Waimea
Hanalei
Koloa
Wailuku
Kahului
Lahaina
Kihei
Hana
Kaunakakai
Lanai City
Kailua Kona
Kamuela
Honokaa
Pahoa
Volcano
Naalehu
Captain Cook
MAUNA KEA (VOL.) 4205 M.
MAUNA LOA (VOL.) 4169 M.
HUALALAI 2521 M.
KILAUEA CRATER 1247 M.
HALEAKALA CRATER 3055 M.
HAWAII VOLCANOES NATIONAL PARK
HALEAKALA NATIONAL PARK
KA LAE
UPOLU PT.
C. KUMUKAHI
A-520512-01
COSMO SERIES HAWAIIAN IS.
Copyright by RAND McNALLY & COMPANY
Made in U. S. A.
© RMCN&Co.
Statute Miles 5 0 5 10 20 30 40 50
Kilometers 5 0 5 10 20 30 40 50 60
Lambert Conformal Conic Projection
SCALE 1:2,000,000 1 Inch = 32 Statute Miles

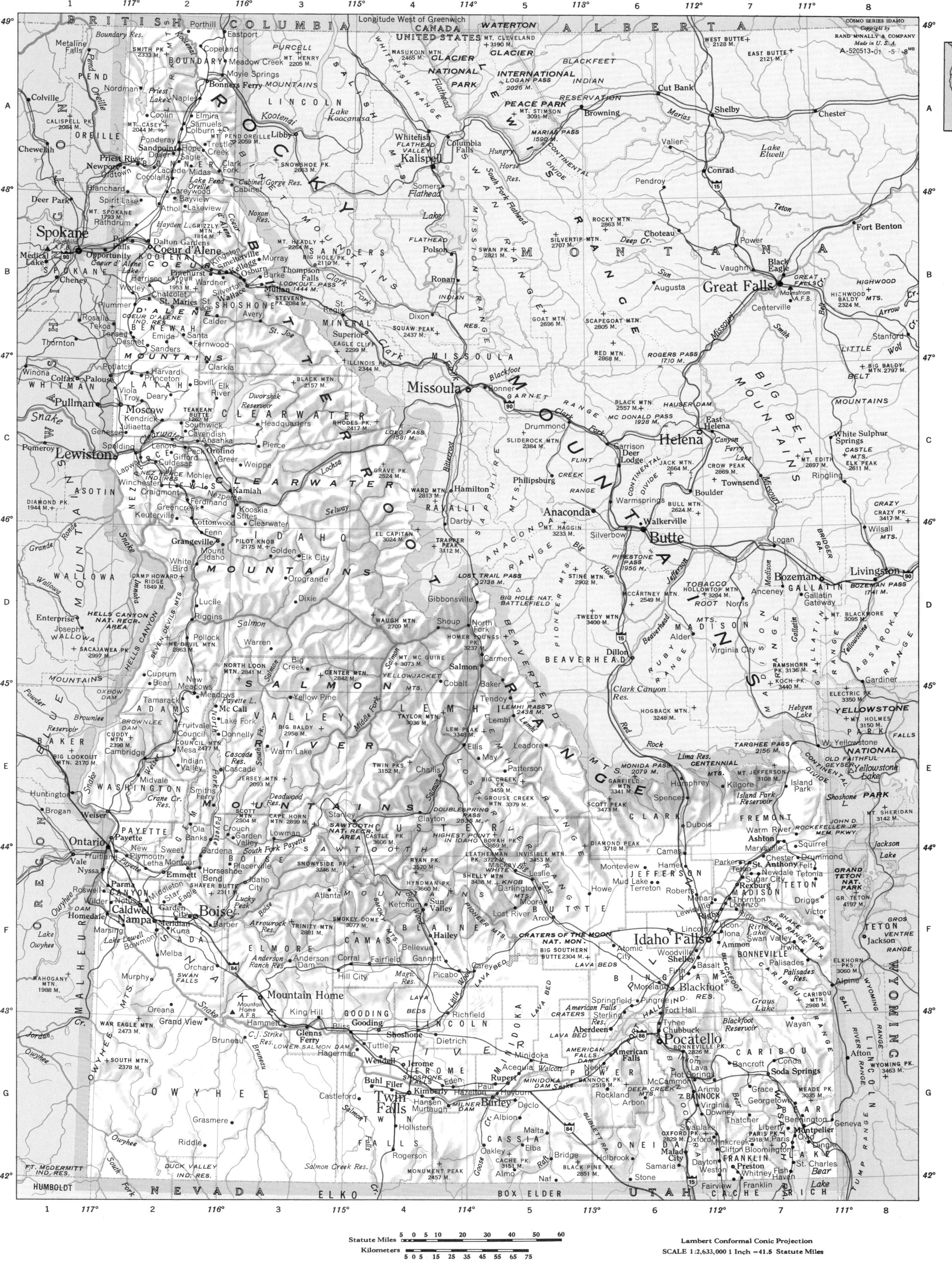
COSMO SERIES IDAHO
Copyright by RAND McNALLY & COMPANY
Made in U. S. A.
A-520513-01 -5-7-8
BRITISH COLUMBIA
ALBERTA
CANADA
UNITED STATES
Longitude West of Greenwich
MONTANA
IDAHO
WASHINGTON
OREGON
NEVADA
UTAH
WYOMING
ROCKY MOUNTAINS
BITTERROOT RANGE
SALMON RIVER MOUNTAINS
CLEARWATER MOUNTAINS
SAWTOOTH MOUNTAINS
LEMHI RANGE
BEAVERHEAD RANGE
GLACIER NATIONAL PARK
YELLOWSTONE NATIONAL PARK
GRAND TETON NAT. PARK
CRATERS OF THE MOON NAT. MON.
HELLS CANYON NAT. RECR. AREA
SAWTOOTH NAT. RECR. AREA
HIGHEST POINT IN IDAHO BORAH PK. 3859 M.
Spokane
Coeur d'Alene
Lewiston
Moscow
Boise
Nampa
Caldwell
Twin Falls
Pocatello
Idaho Falls
Mountain Home
Missoula
Helena
Butte
Great Falls
Kalispell
Bozeman
Snake
Salmon
Clearwater
Statute Miles 5 0 5 10 20 30 40 50 60
Kilometers 5 0 5 15 25 35 45 55 65 75
Lambert Conformal Conic Projection
SCALE 1:2,633,000 1 Inch =41.5 Statute Miles

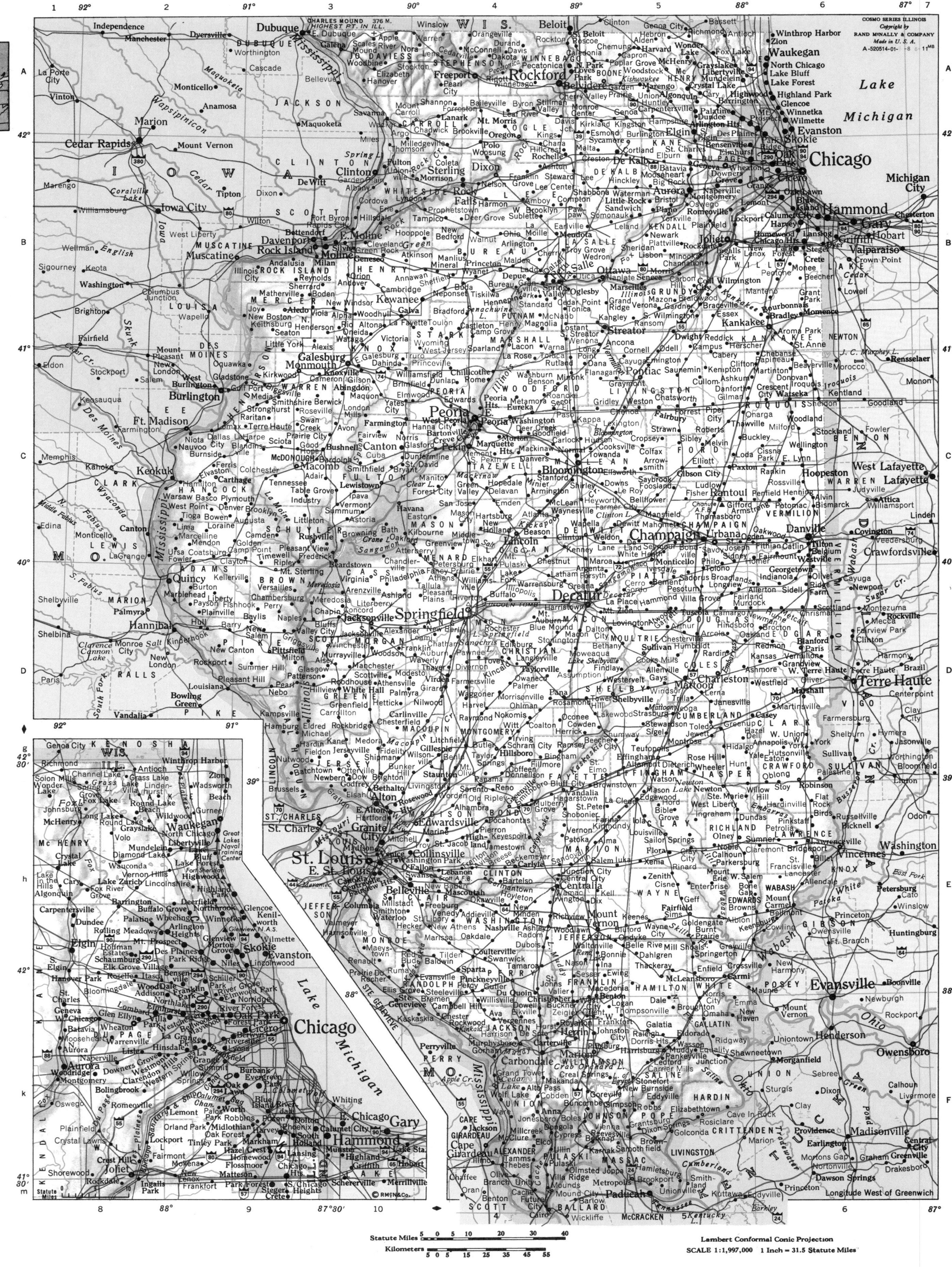
COSMO SERIES ILLINOIS
Copyright by
RAND McNALLY & COMPANY
Made in U. S. A.
CHARLES MOUND 376 M.
HIGHEST PT. IN ILL.
Lake Michigan
Chicago
Rockford
Peoria
Springfield
Decatur
Champaign
Urbana
Bloomington
Danville
St. Louis
Terre Haute
Evansville
Hammond
Gary
Waukegan
Evanston
Joliet
Aurora
Elgin
Kankakee
Quincy
Galesburg
Moline
Rock Island
Davenport
Dubuque
Burlington
Cedar Rapids
Iowa City
Keokuk
Hannibal
Paducah
Cairo
Carbondale
Belleville
Centralia
Mount Vernon
Alton
Jacksonville
Kewanee
Ottawa
La Salle
Streator
Pontiac
Dixon
Sterling
Freeport
Clinton
Muscatine
Vincennes
Henderson
Owensboro
Lafayette
West Lafayette
Crawfordsville
Michigan City
Valparaiso
I O W A
W I S.
M O.
K E N T U C K Y
Mississippi
Illinois
Ohio
Wabash
Lambert Conformal Conic Projection
SCALE 1:1,997,000 1 Inch = 31.5 Statute Miles
Statute Miles 5 0 5 10 20 30 40
Kilometers 5 0 5 15 25 35 45 55
Longitude West of Greenwich
© RMcN&Co.

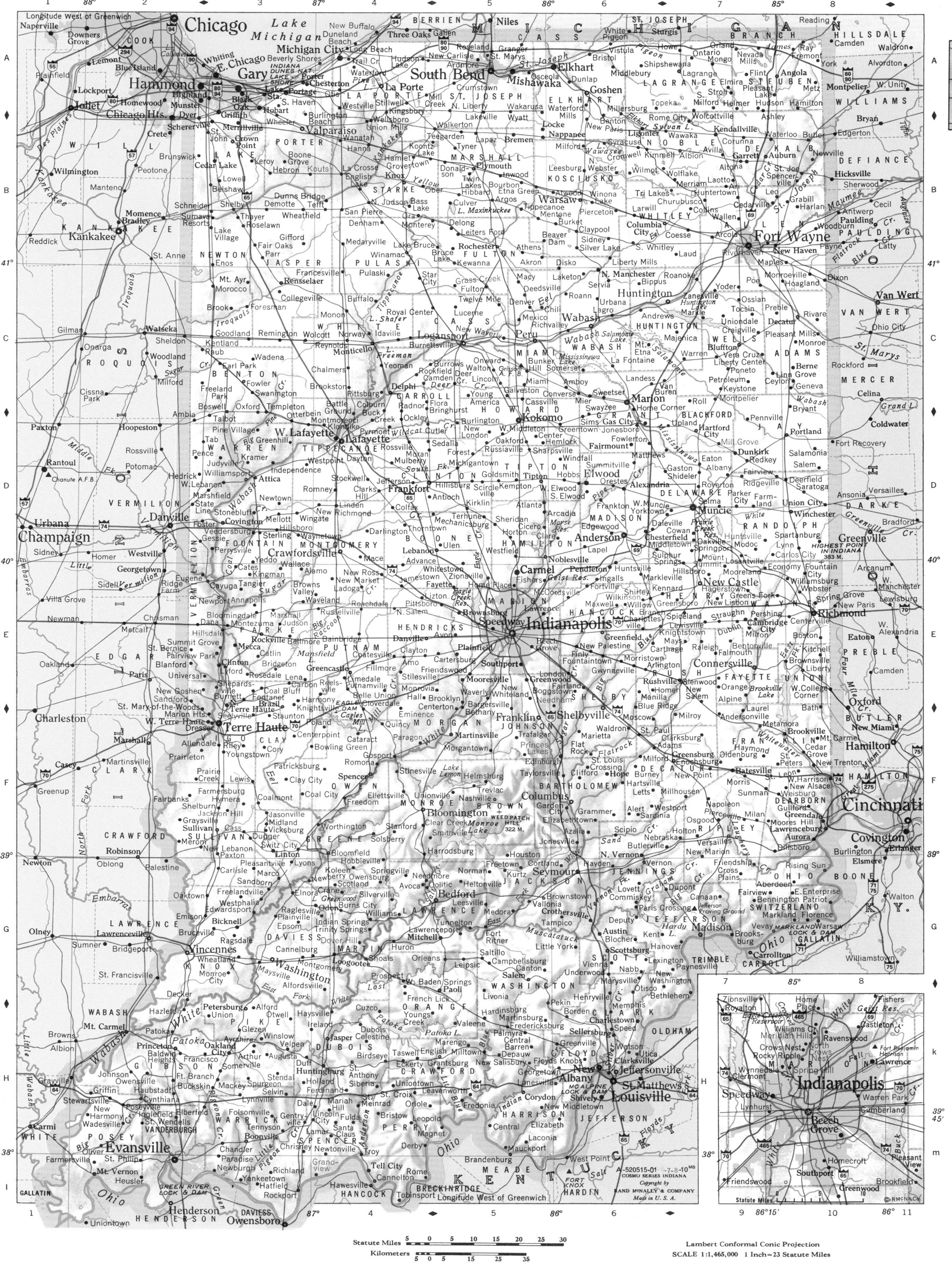
Chicago
Lake Michigan
Gary
Hammond
Michigan City
South Bend
Elkhart
Fort Wayne
Logansport
Kokomo
Lafayette
Marion
Muncie
Anderson
Richmond
Indianapolis
Terre Haute
Bloomington
Columbus
Vincennes
Evansville
New Albany
Jeffersonville
Louisville
Cincinnati
Champaign
Danville
Owensboro
Henderson
HIGHEST POINT IN INDIANA 383 M.
WEED PATCH HILL 322 M.
Longitude West of Greenwich
COSMO SERIES INDIANA
Copyright by RAND McNALLY & COMPANY
Made in U. S. A.
Statute Miles 5 0 5 10 15 20 25 30
Kilometers 5 0 5 15 25 35
Lambert Conformal Conic Projection
SCALE 1:1,465,000 1 Inch=23 Statute Miles

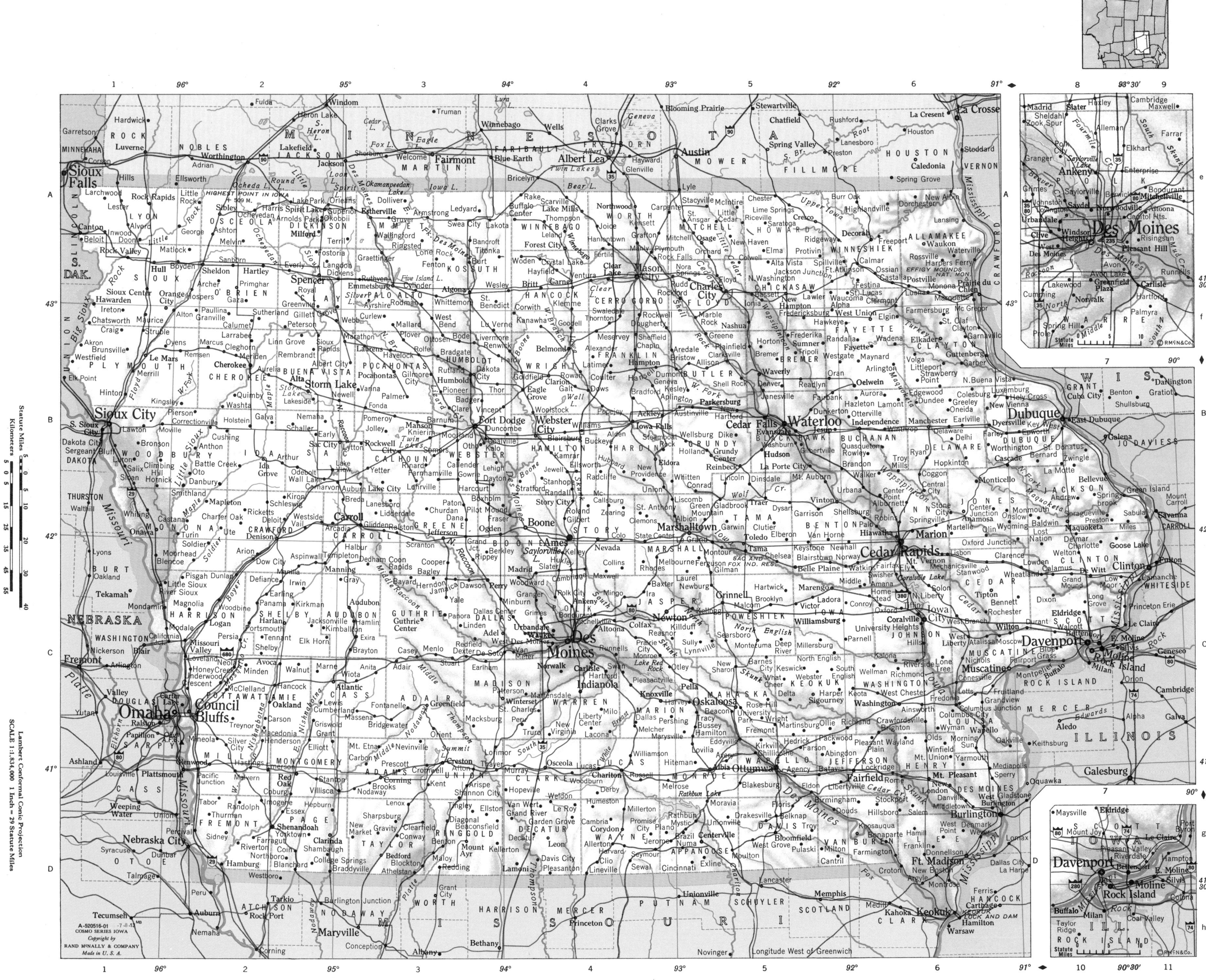
Statute Miles 5 0 5 10 20 30 40
Kilometers 5 0 5 15 25 35 45 55
Lambert Conformal Conic Projection
SCALE 1:1,834,000 1 Inch = 29 Statute Miles
A-520516-01
COSMO SERIES IOWA
Copyright by
RAND McNALLY & COMPANY
Made in U. S. A.

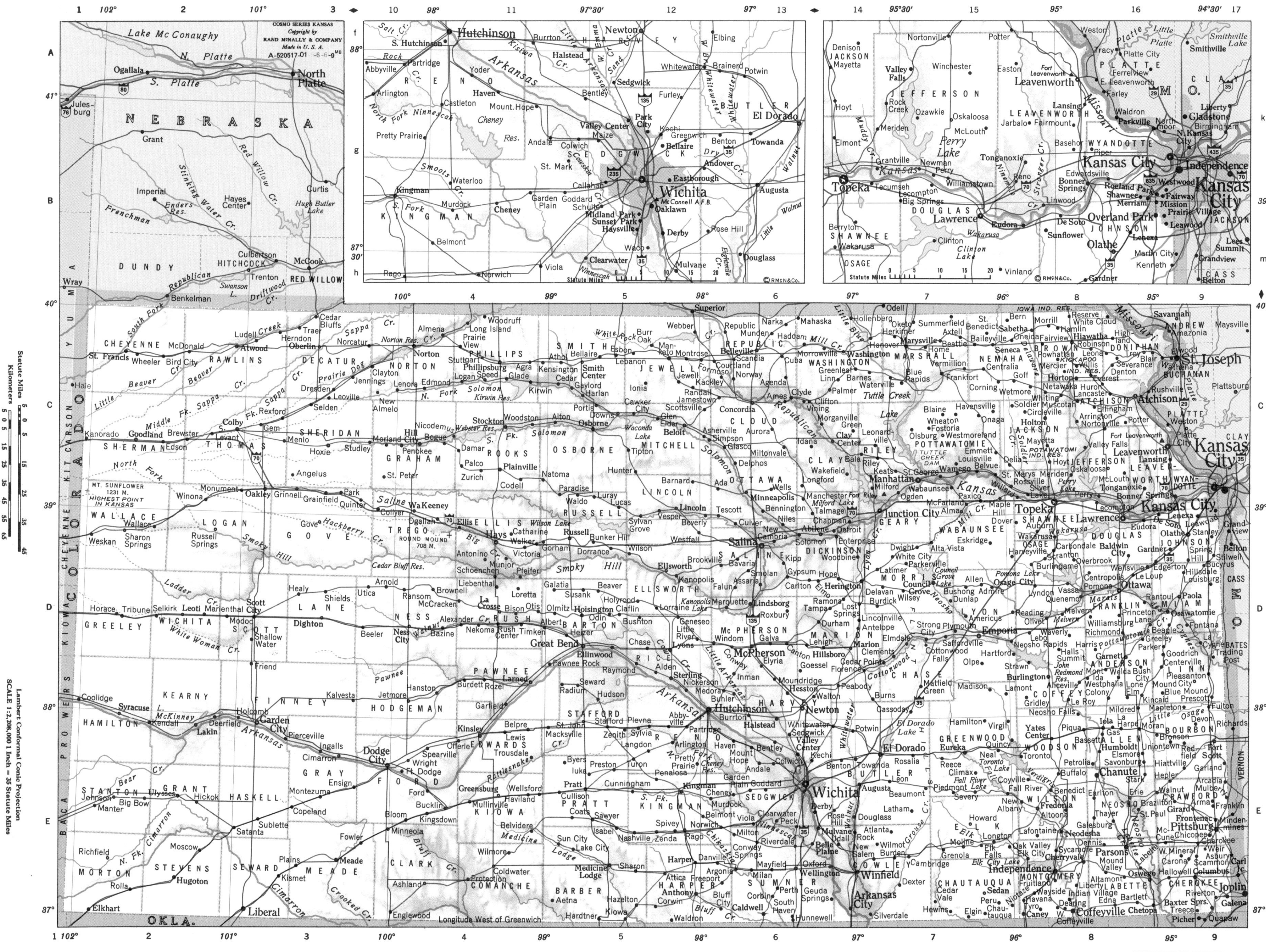
COSMO SERIES KANSAS
Copyright by
RAND McNALLY & COMPANY
Made in U. S. A.
A-520517-01
NEBRASKA
COLORADO
OKLA.
MO.
Wichita
Topeka
Kansas City
Hutchinson
Salina
Dodge City
Garden City
Liberal
Great Bend
Lawrence
Manhattan
Emporia
MT. SUNFLOWER 1231 M. HIGHEST POINT IN KANSAS
Longitude West of Greenwich
Statute Miles 5 0 5 15 25 35 45
Kilometers 5 0 5 15 25 35 45 55 65
Lambert Conformal Conic Projection
SCALE 1:2,208,000 1 Inch = 35 Statute Miles

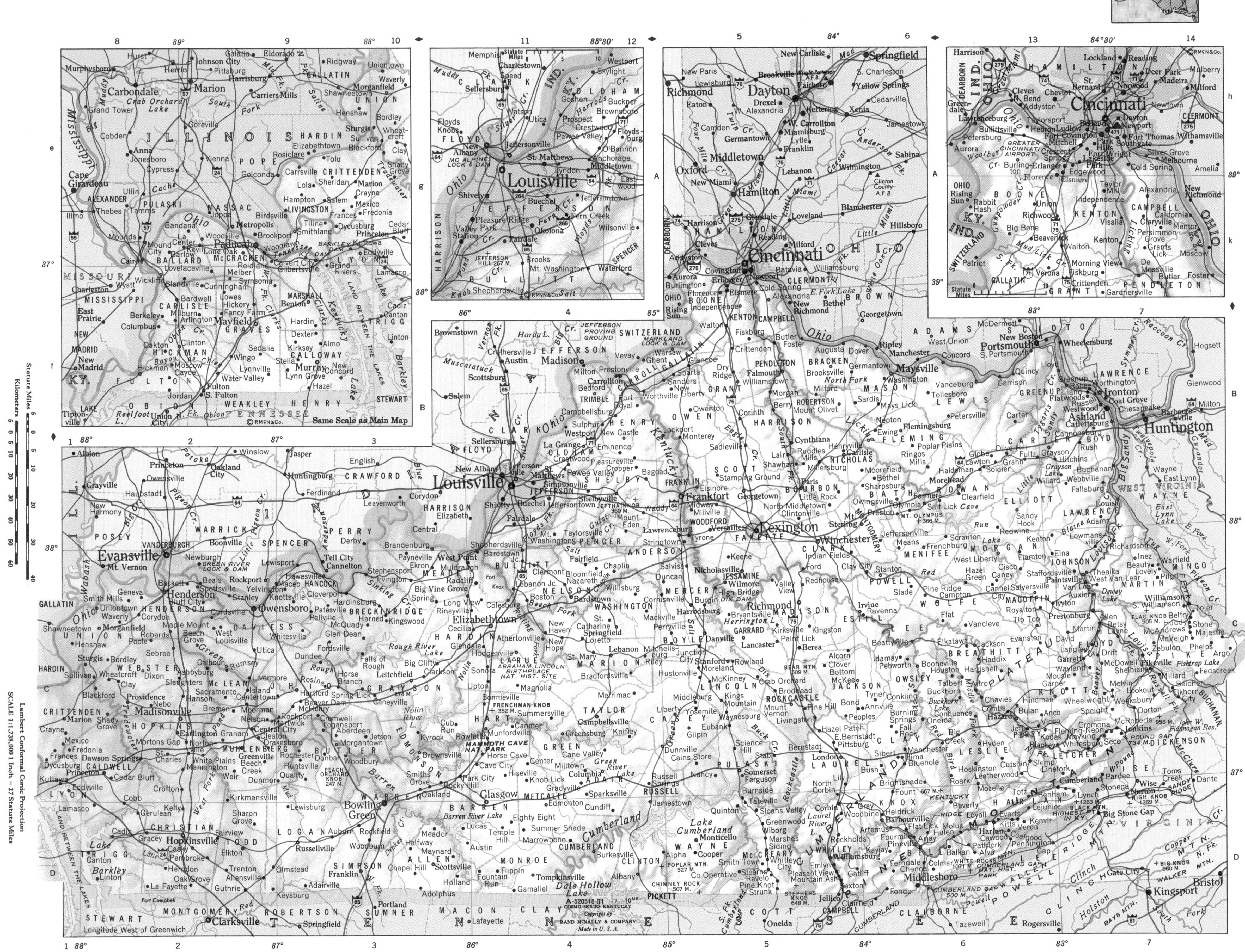
Louisville
Cincinnati
Dayton
Lexington
Frankfort
Evansville
Huntington
Ashland
Owensboro
Bowling Green
Paducah
Elizabethtown
Kingsport
Bristol
Portsmouth
Hamilton
Middletown
Richmond
ILLINOIS
OHIO
Ohio
Kentucky
Cumberland
Lake Cumberland
Barkley
LAND BETWEEN THE LAKES
Same Scale as Main Map
Longitude West of Greenwich
Copyright by RAND MCNALLY & COMPANY Made in U. S. A.
Statute Miles 5 0 5 10 20 30 40
Kilometers 5 0 5 10 20 30 40 50 60
Lambert Conformal Conic Projection
SCALE 1:1,738,000 1 Inch = 27 Statute Miles

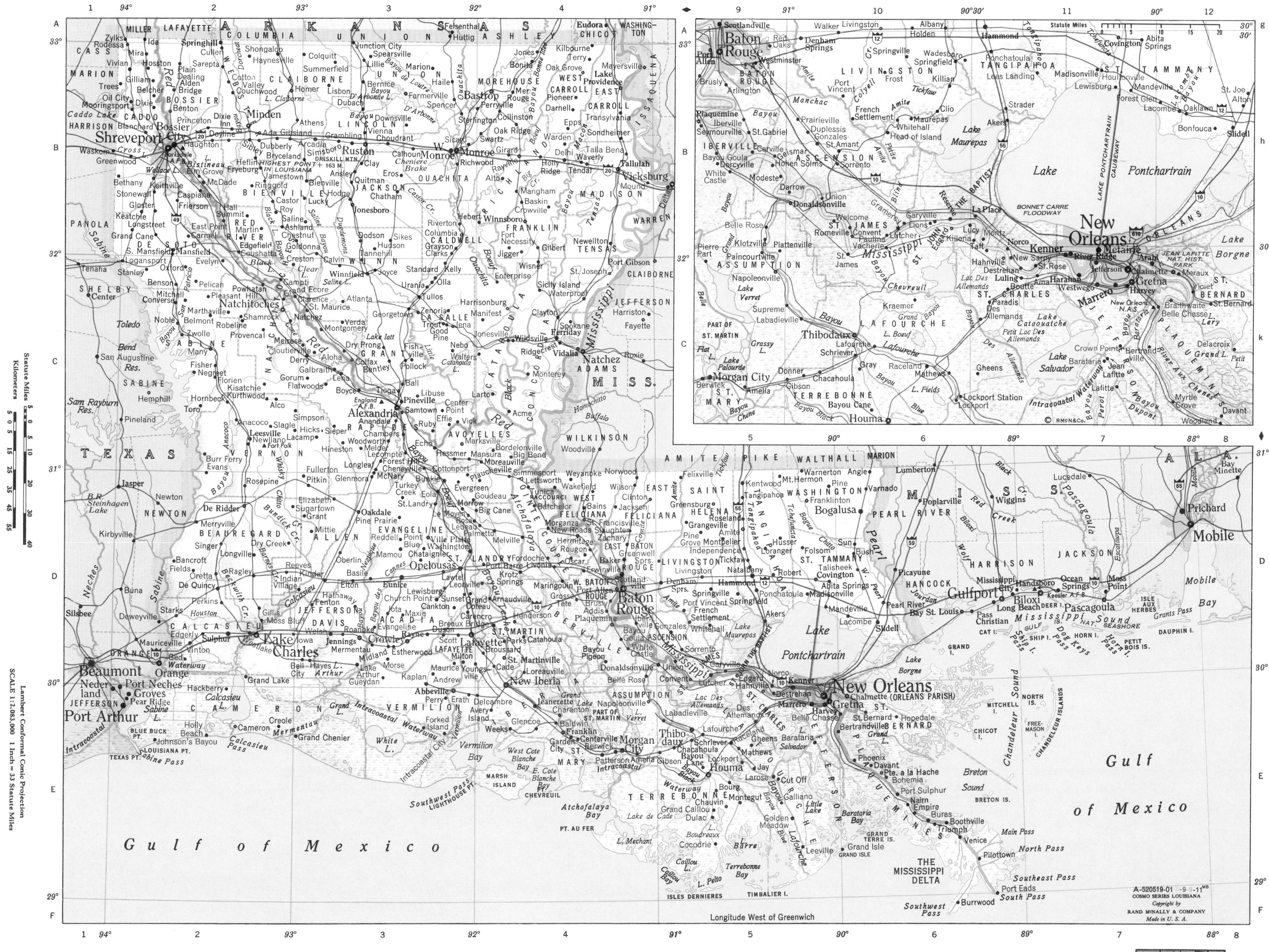
Gulf of Mexico
New Orleans
Baton Rouge
Shreveport
Monroe
Alexandria
Lake Charles
Lafayette
Mobile
Gulfport
Biloxi
Pascagoula
Beaumont
Port Arthur
Lake Pontchartrain
Mississippi
THE MISSISSIPPI DELTA
Chandeleur Sound
Breton Sound
Atchafalaya Bay
Vermilion Bay
Longitude West of Greenwich
A-520519-01
COSMO SERIES LOUISIANA
Copyright by RAND McNALLY & COMPANY
Made in U.S.A.
Statute Miles 5 0 5 10 20 30 40
Kilometers 5 0 5 15 25 35 45 55
Lambert Conformal Conic Projection
SCALE 1:2,083,000 1 Inch = 33 Statute Miles

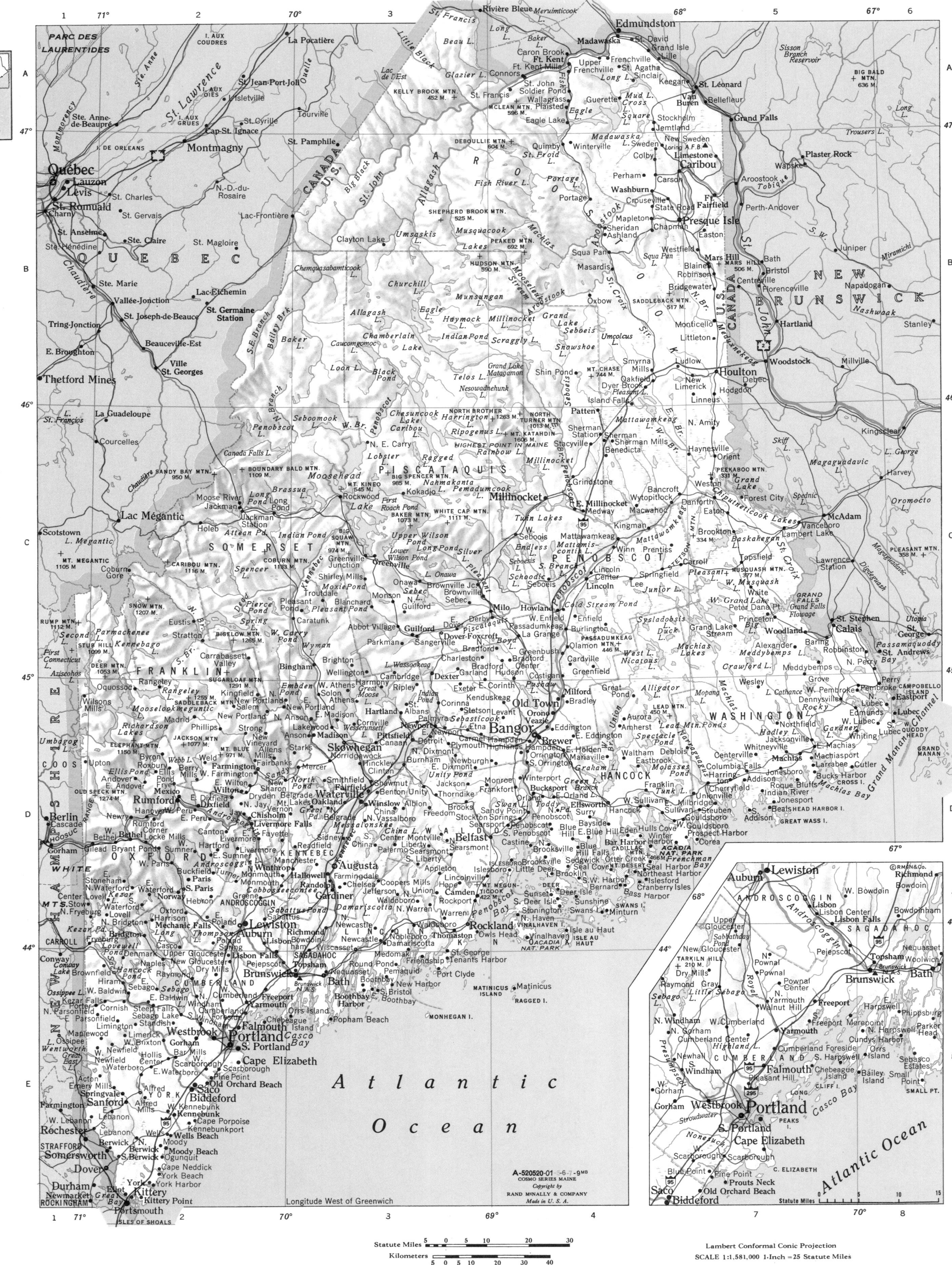
Atlantic Ocean
QUEBEC
NEW BRUNSWICK
CANADA
U.S.A.
AROOSTOOK
PISCATAQUIS
SOMERSET
PENOBSCOT
WASHINGTON
HANCOCK
FRANKLIN
OXFORD
KENNEBEC
WALDO
ANDROSCOGGIN
SAGADAHOC
LINCOLN
KNOX
CUMBERLAND
YORK
NEW HAMPSHIRE
PARC DES LAURENTIDES
St. Lawrence
Québec
Lévis
Lauzon
Montmagny
La Pocatière
Rivière Bleue
Edmundston
Madawaska
Ft. Kent
St. Francis
Van Buren
Grand Falls
Caribou
Presque Isle
Fort Fairfield
Mars Hill
Houlton
Woodstock
Washburn
Ashland
Patten
Millinocket
E. Millinocket
Lincoln
Milo
Dover-Foxcroft
Greenville
Jackman
Moosehead Lake
Chesuncook Lake
Rockwood
Lac Mégantic
Thetford Mines
Skowhegan
Waterville
Pittsfield
Newport
Bangor
Brewer
Old Town
Orono
Ellsworth
Bar Harbor
Calais
St. Stephen
Eastport
Lubec
Machias
Belfast
Camden
Rockland
Augusta
Gardiner
Hallowell
Lewiston
Auburn
Rumford
Farmington
Bethel
Brunswick
Bath
Topsham
Freeport
Yarmouth
Portland
S. Portland
Cape Elizabeth
Westbrook
Gorham
Saco
Biddeford
Old Orchard Beach
Sanford
Kennebunk
York
Kittery
Portsmouth
Dover
Rochester
Somersworth
Berlin
Conway
Penobscot Bay
Casco Bay
Passamaquoddy Bay
Grand Manan Channel
Machias Bay
Monhegan I.
Matinicus Island
HIGHEST POINT IN MAINE
MT. KATAHDIN 1606 M.
ACADIA NAT. PARK
Longitude West of Greenwich
A-520520-01 -6-7-9MB
COSMO SERIES MAINE
Copyright by RAND McNALLY & COMPANY
Made in U. S. A.
Statute Miles 5 0 5 10 20 30
Kilometers 5 0 5 10 20 30 40
Lambert Conformal Conic Projection
SCALE 1:1,581,000 1-Inch =25 Statute Miles

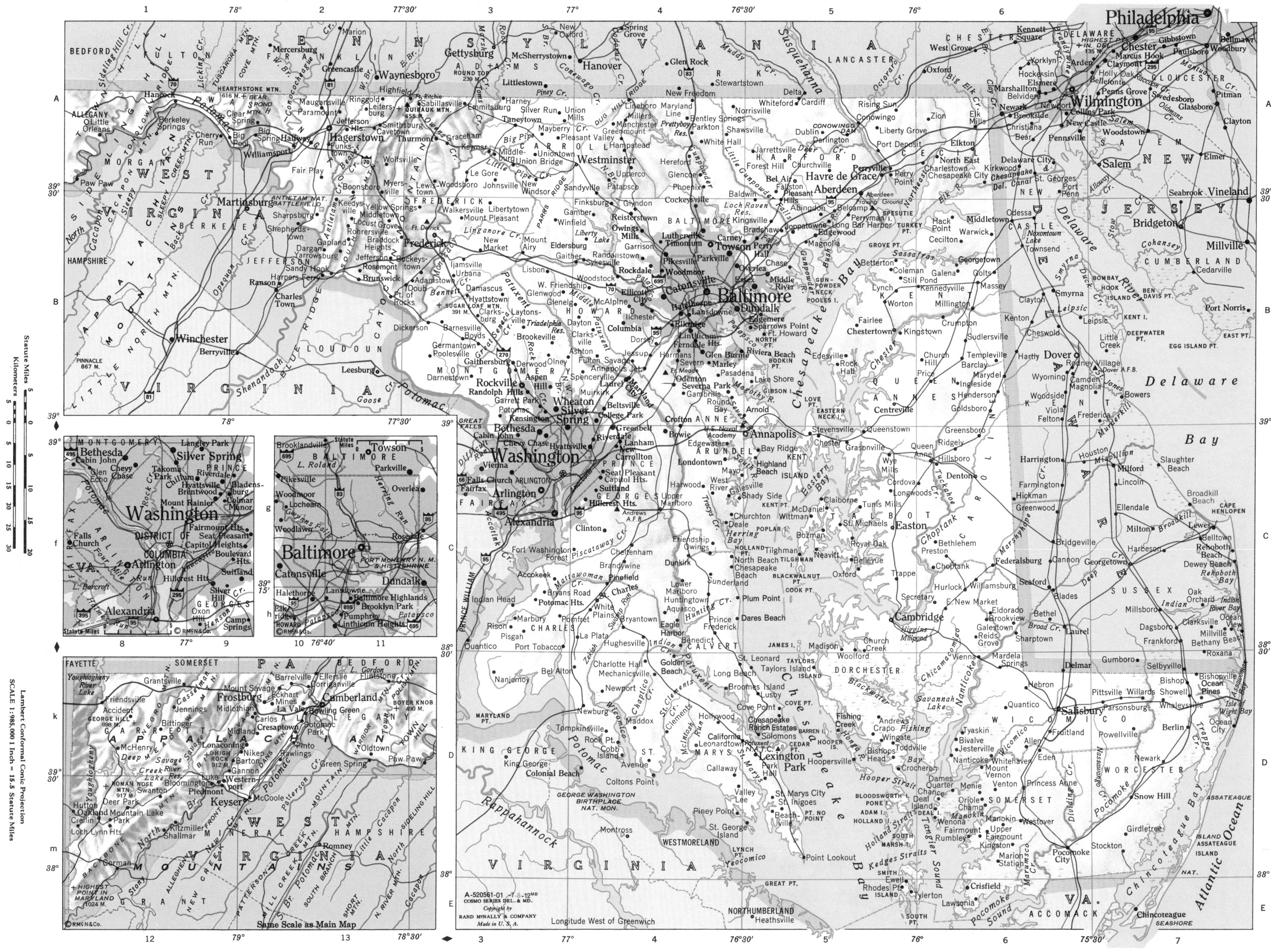
Statute Miles 5 0 5 10 15 20
Kilometers 5 0 5 10 15 20 25 30
Lambert Conformal Conic Projection
SCALE 1:985,000 1 Inch = 15.5 Statute Miles
Same Scale as Main Map
A-520561-01 -7-8-12MB
COSMO SERIES DEL. & MD.
Copyright by
RAND McNALLY & COMPANY
Made in U. S. A.
Longitude West of Greenwich

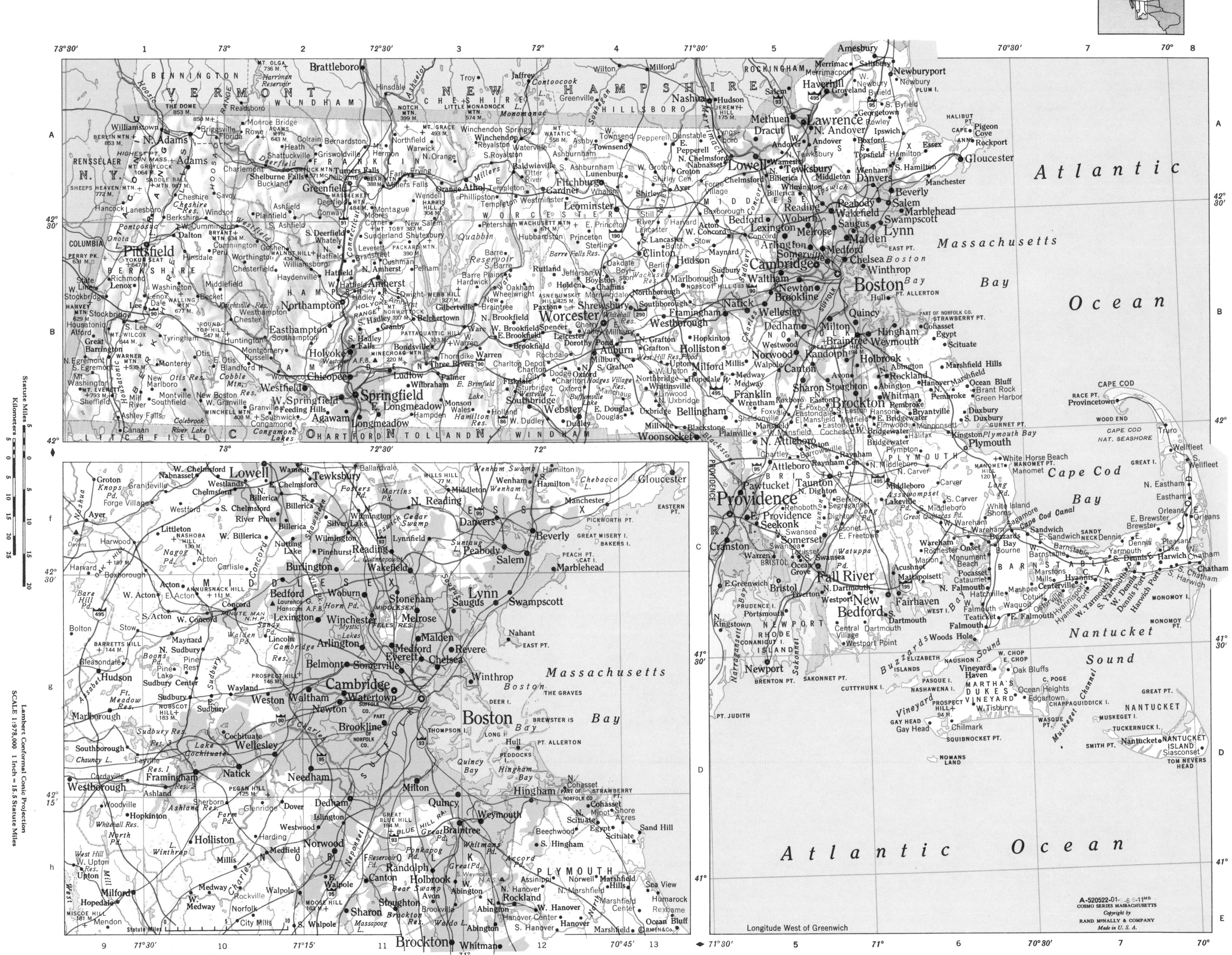

Atlantic Ocean
Massachusetts Bay
Cape Cod Bay
Nantucket Sound
Boston
Worcester
Springfield
Providence
Longitude West of Greenwich
A-520522-01-
COSMO SERIES MASSACHUSETTS
Copyright by
RAND McNALLY & COMPANY
Made in U. S. A.
Statute Miles 5 0 5 10 15 20
Kilometers 5 0 5 10 15 20 25
Lambert Conformal Conic Projection
SCALE 1:978,000 1 Inch = 15.5 Statute Miles

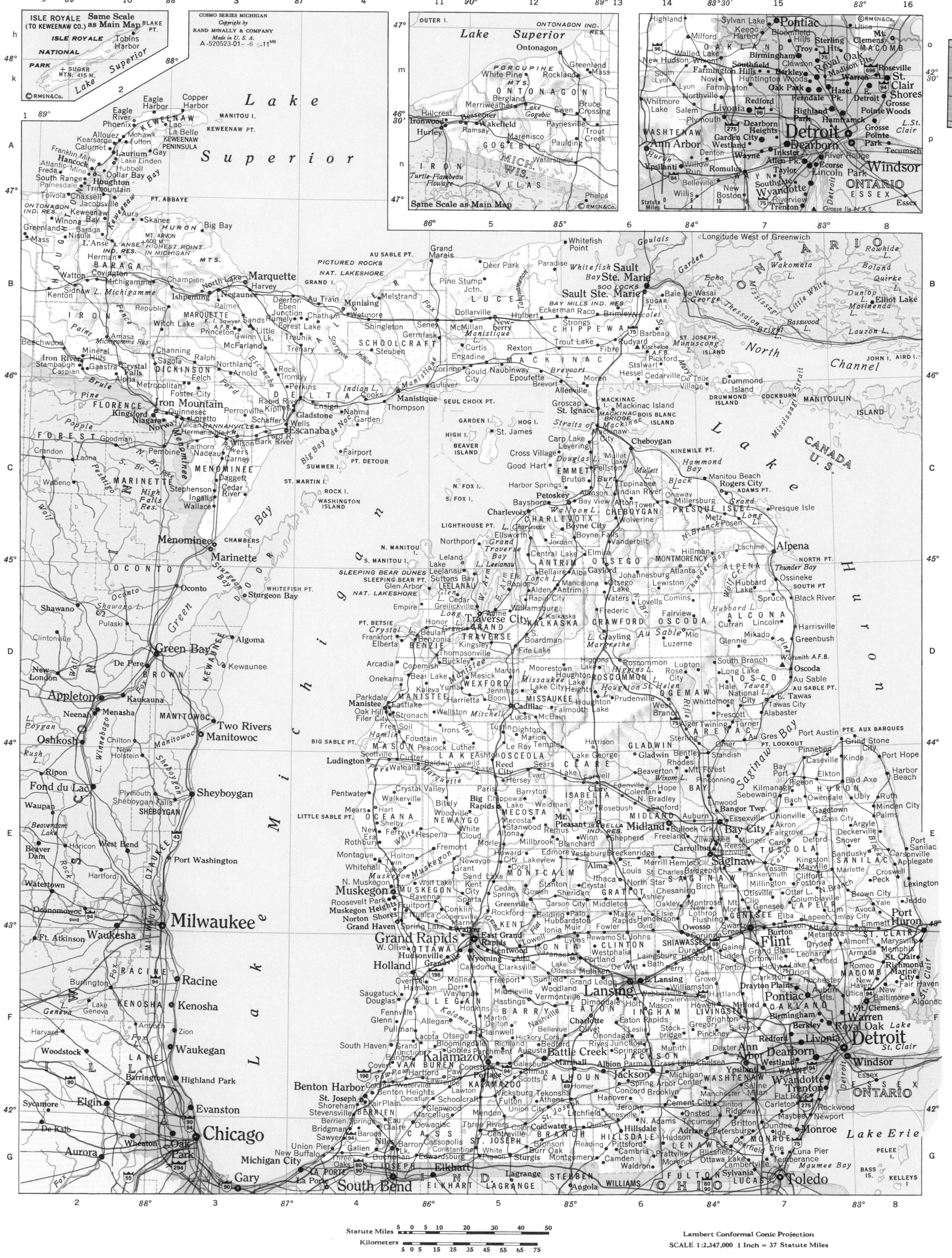
ISLE ROYALE (TO KEWEENAW CO.) Same Scale as Main Map
ISLE ROYALE NATIONAL PARK
COSMO SERIES MICHIGAN
Copyright by RAND McNALLY & COMPANY
Made in U. S. A.
A-520523-01- -6 -11
Lake Superior
Same Scale as Main Map
Lake Michigan
Lake Huron
Lake Erie
Green Bay
North Channel
Saginaw Bay
Grand Traverse Bay
Straits of Mackinac
ONTARIO
CANADA
U.S.
OHIO
Marquette
Sault Ste. Marie
Escanaba
Menominee
Marinette
Iron Mountain
Petoskey
Cheboygan
Alpena
Traverse City
Cadillac
Ludington
Muskegon
Grand Rapids
Holland
Kalamazoo
Battle Creek
Lansing
Jackson
Ann Arbor
Flint
Saginaw
Bay City
Midland
Port Huron
Pontiac
Detroit
Dearborn
Windsor
Monroe
Toledo
South Bend
Benton Harbor
Chicago
Milwaukee
Green Bay
Appleton
Oshkosh
Sheboygan
Racine
Kenosha
Waukegan
Gary
Statute Miles 5 0 5 10 20 30 40 50
Kilometers 5 0 5 15 25 35 45 55 65 75
Lambert Conformal Conic Projection
SCALE 1:2,347,000 1 Inch = 37 Statute Miles

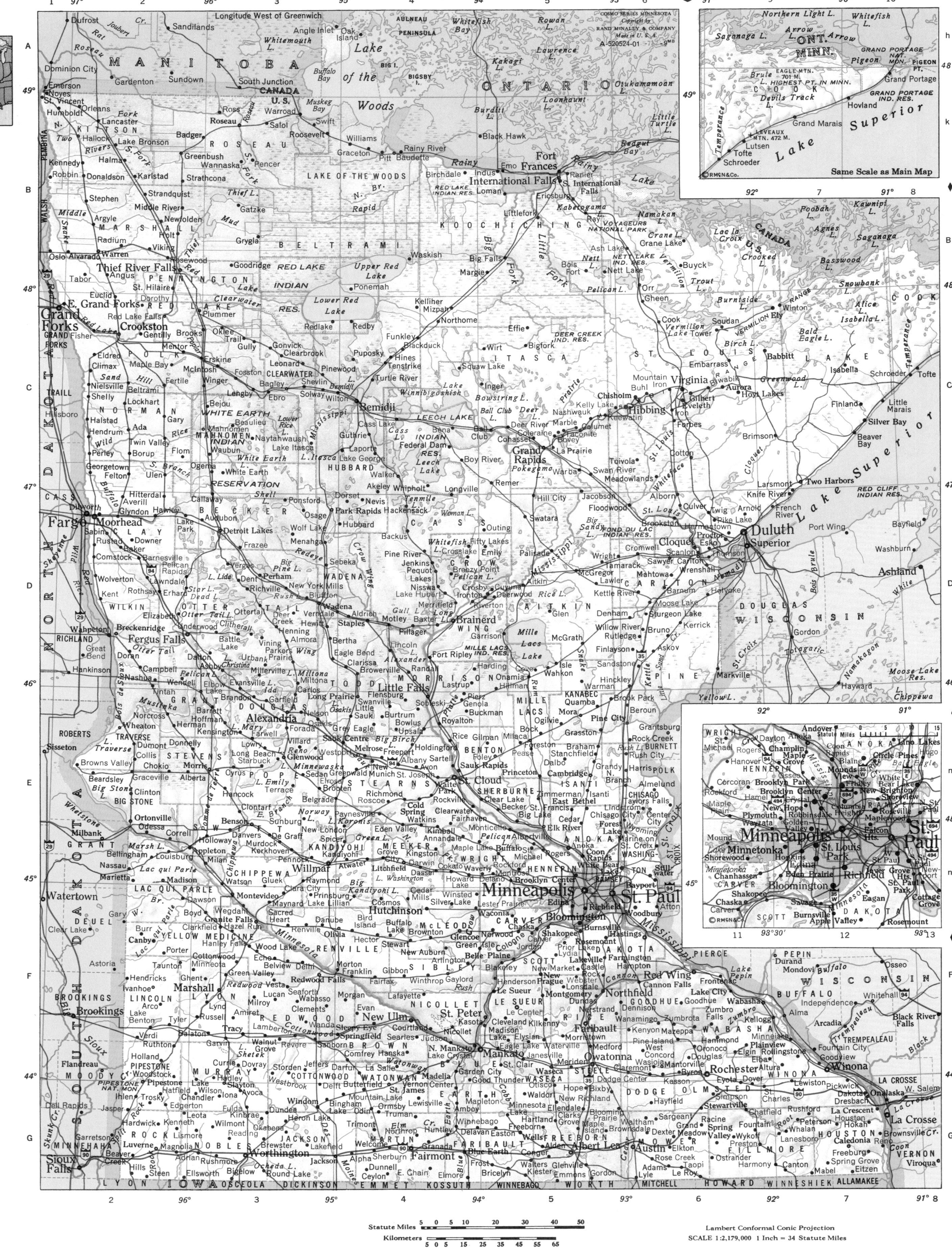
Longitude West of Greenwich
COSMO SERIES MINNESOTA
Copyright by RAND McNALLY & COMPANY
Made in U. S. A.
A-520524-01
M A N I T O B A
O N T A R I O
Lake of the Woods
CANADA
U.S.
NORTH DAKOTA
SOUTH DAKOTA
IOWA
WISCONSIN
Lake Superior
Minneapolis
St. Paul
Duluth
Superior
St. Cloud
Rochester
Mankato
Moorhead
Fargo
Grand Forks
International Falls
Bemidji
Brainerd
Hibbing
Virginia
Winona
La Crosse
Sioux Falls
Same Scale as Main Map
Statute Miles
Kilometers
Lambert Conformal Conic Projection
SCALE 1:2,179,000 1 Inch = 34 Statute Miles

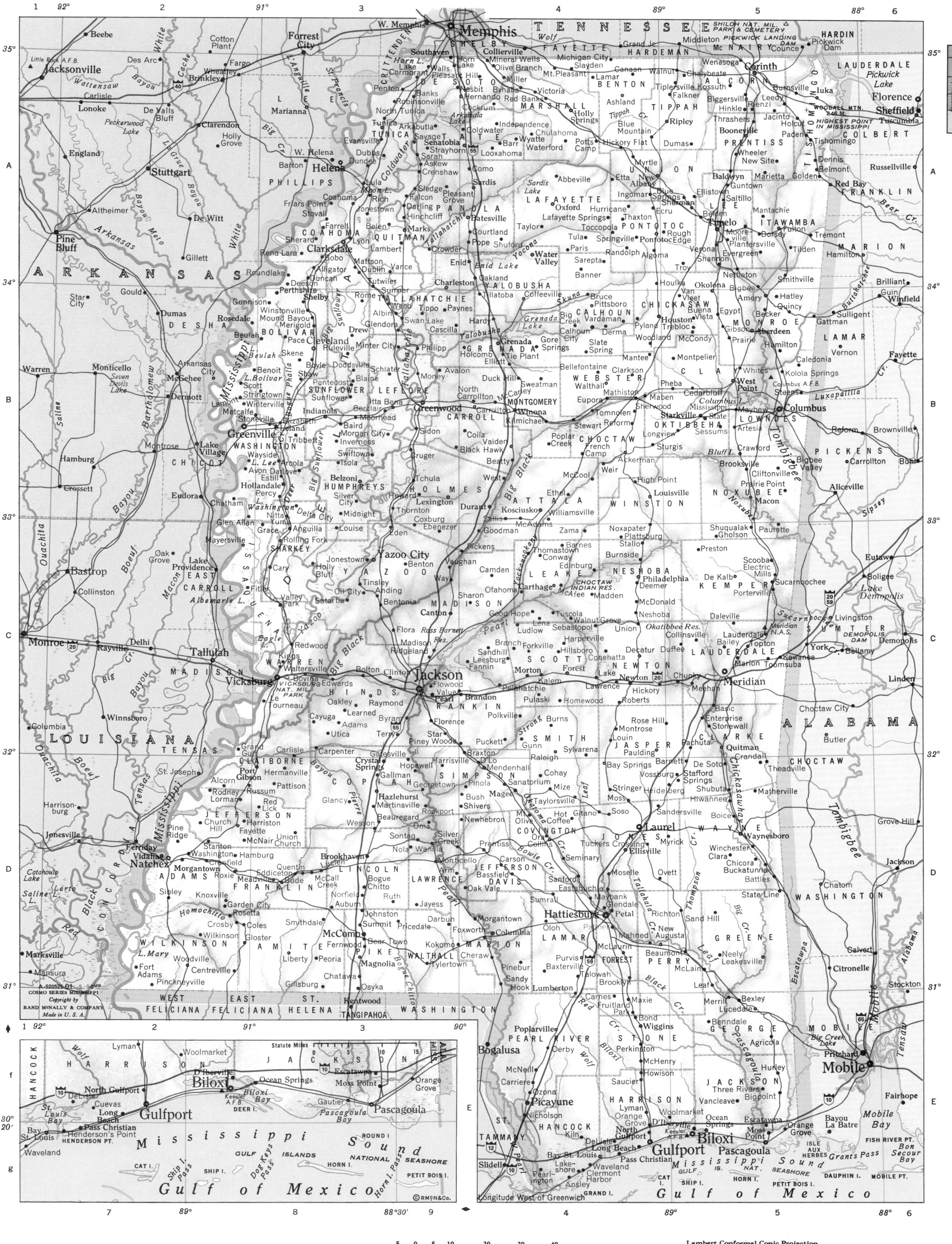
TENNESSEE
ARKANSAS
LOUISIANA
ALABAMA
Memphis
Jackson
Vicksburg
Greenville
Greenwood
Clarksdale
Yazoo City
Meridian
Hattiesburg
Laurel
Natchez
McComb
Columbus
Tupelo
Corinth
Oxford
Starkville
West Point
Grenada
Cleveland
Biloxi
Gulfport
Pascagoula
Picayune
Mobile
Monroe
Tallulah
Helena
Pine Bluff
Stuttgart
Jacksonville
Forrest City
Florence
Sheffield
Gulf of Mexico
Mississippi Sound
Lambert Conformal Conic Projection
SCALE 1:1,837,000 1 Inch = 29 Statute Miles
Statute Miles 5 0 5 10 20 30 40
Kilometers 5 0 5 15 25 35 45 55
COSMO SERIES MISSISSIPPI
Copyright by RAND McNALLY & COMPANY
Made in U. S. A.

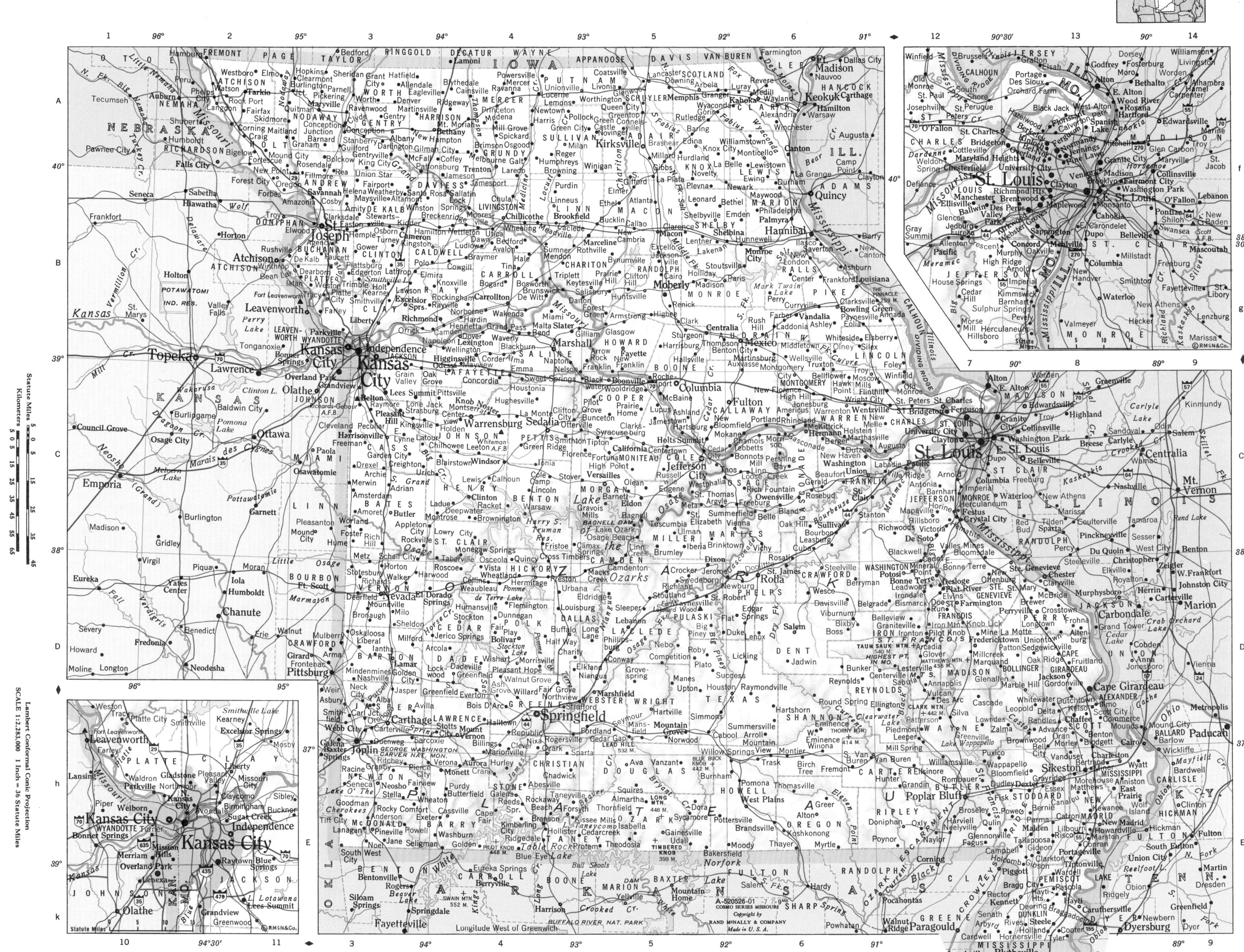

Statute Miles 5 0 5 15 25 35 45
Kilometers 5 0 5 15 25 35 45 55 65
Lambert Conformal Conic Projection
SCALE 1:2,283,000 1 Inch = 36 Statute Miles
Longitude West of Greenwich
A-520526-01
COSMO SERIES MISSOURI
Copyright by RAND McNALLY & COMPANY
Made in U. S. A.

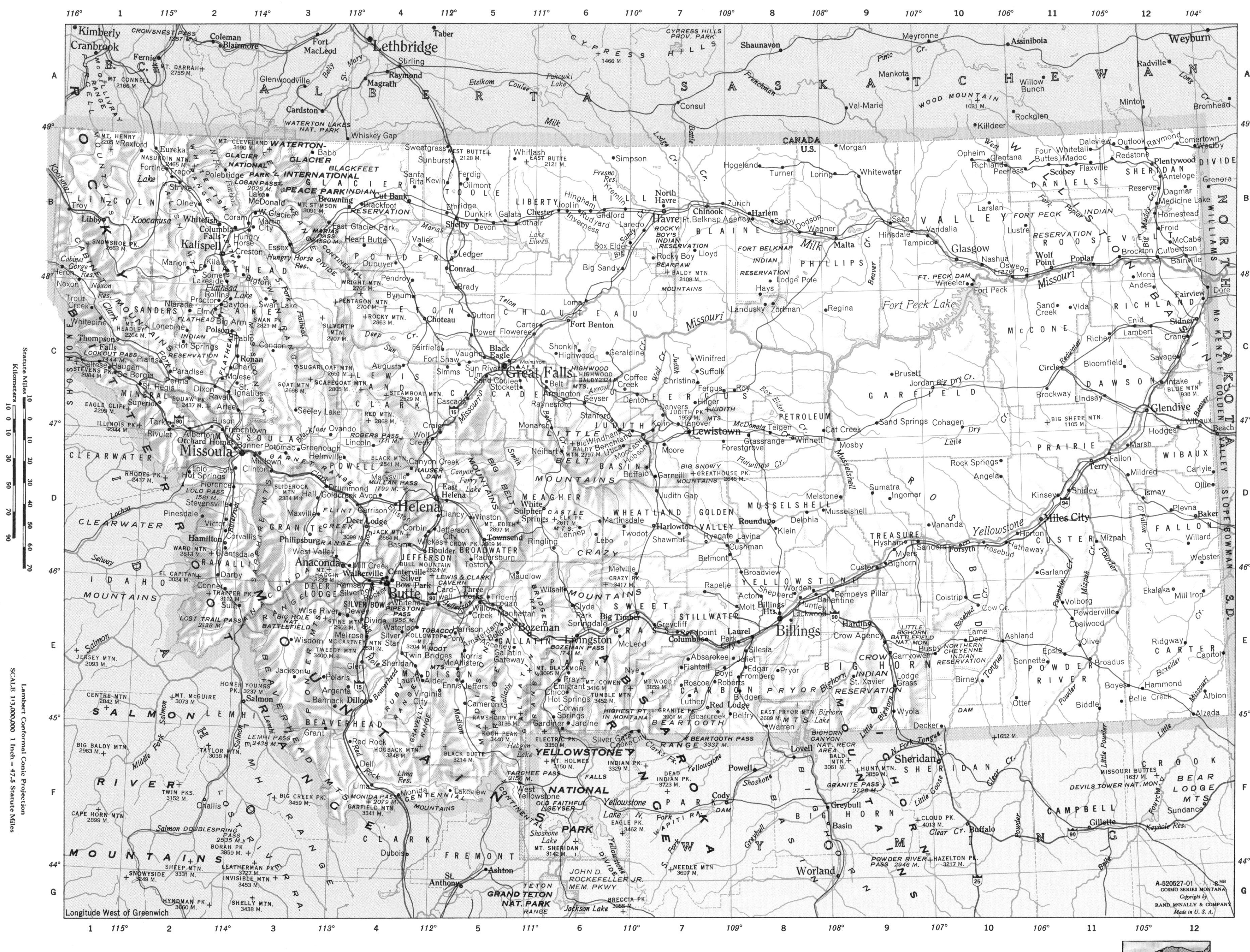
NORTH DAKOTA
S.D.
CANADA
U.S.
Billings
Great Falls
Helena
Butte
Missoula
Bozeman
Kalispell
Havre
Glasgow
Miles City
Lewistown
Livingston
Anaconda
Glendive
Sidney
Wolf Point
Lethbridge
Sheridan
Cody
YELLOWSTONE NATIONAL PARK
GRAND TETON NAT. PARK
Longitude West of Greenwich
A-520527-01 COSMO SERIES MONTANA Copyright by RAND McNALLY & COMPANY Made in U. S. A.
Statute Miles 10 0 10 20 30 40 50 60 70
Kilometers 10 0 10 30 50 70 90
Lambert Conformal Conic Projection
SCALE 1:3,000,000 1 Inch = 47.5 Statute Miles

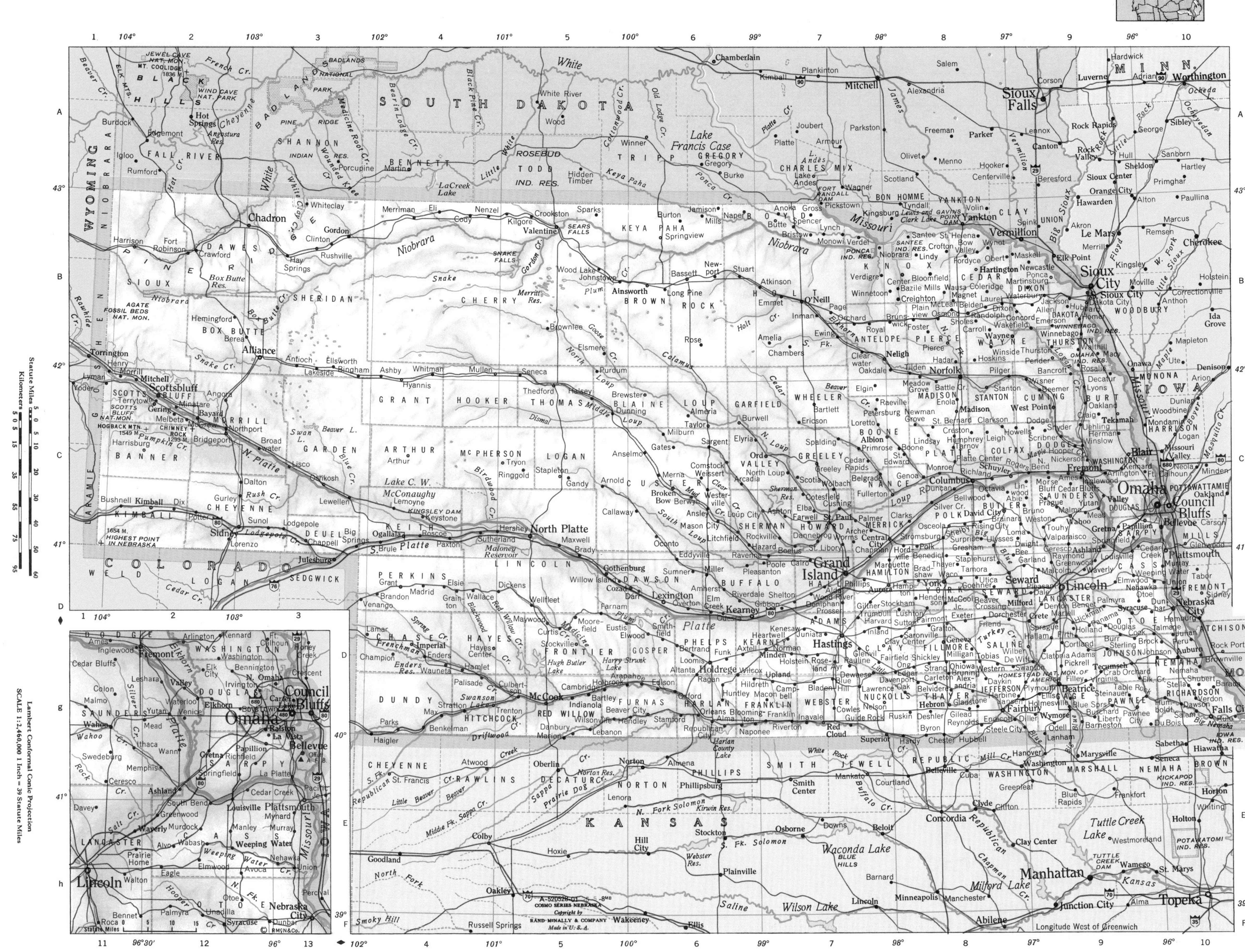
SOUTH DAKOTA
WYOMING
COLORADO
KANSAS
IOWA
MINN.
MO.
Omaha
Lincoln
Grand Island
North Platte
Sioux City
Council Bluffs
Sioux Falls
Topeka
Manhattan
A-520528-01-5-8MB
COSMO SERIES NEBRASKA
Copyright by RAND McNALLY & COMPANY
Made in U. S. A.
Longitude West of Greenwich
Statute Miles 5 0 5 10 20 30 40 50 60
Kilometers 5 0 5 15 35 55 75 95
Lambert Conformal Conic Projection
SCALE 1:2,460,000 1 Inch = 39 Statute Miles

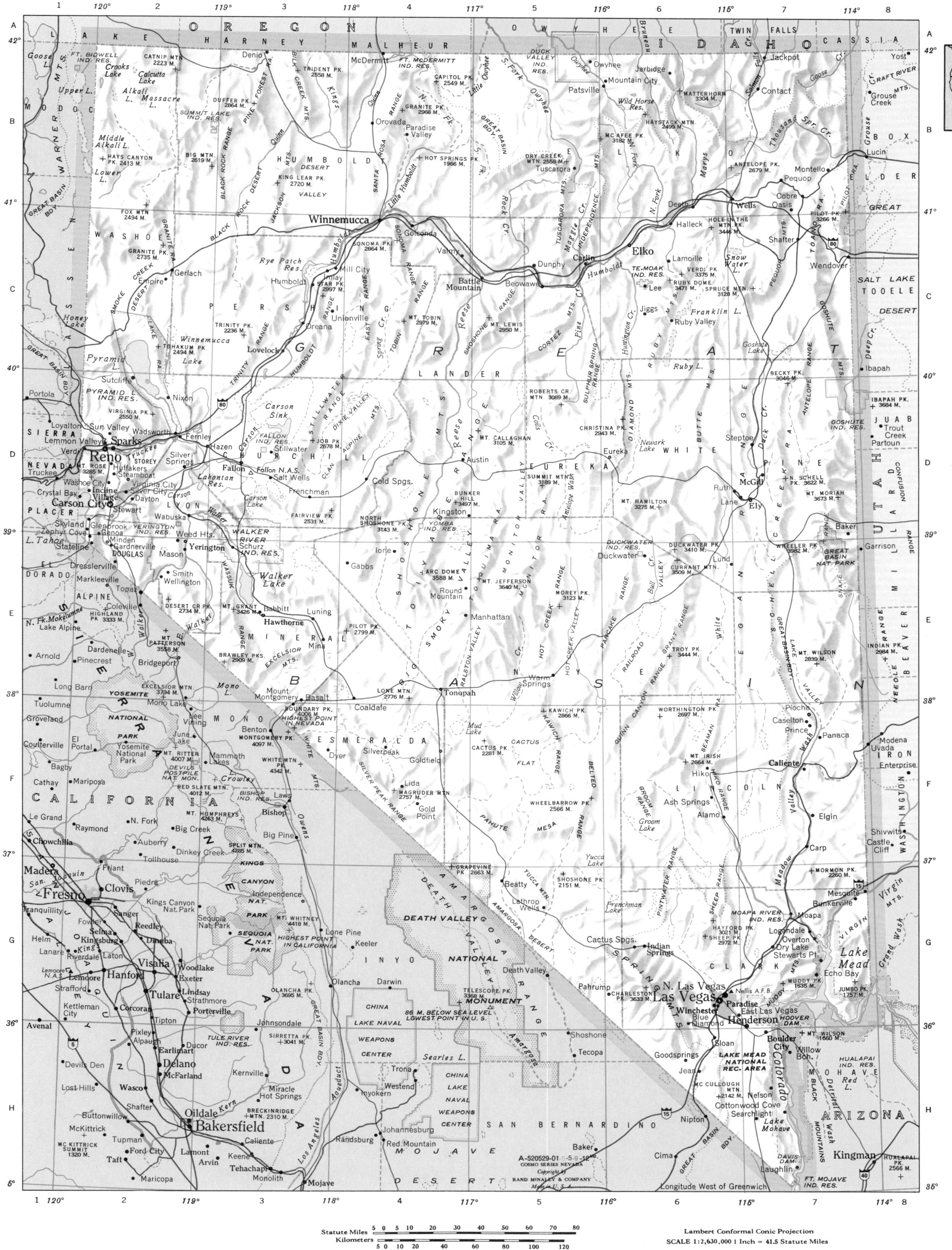

Statute Miles 5 0 5 10 20 30 40 50 60 70 80
Kilometers 5 0 10 20 40 60 80 100 120

Lambert Conformal Conic Projection
SCALE 1:2,630,000 1 Inch = 41.5 Statute Miles

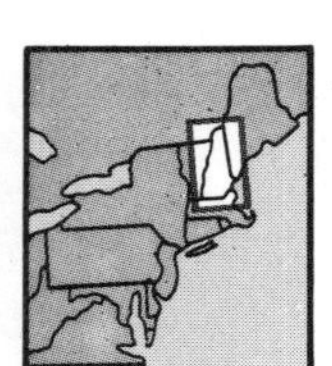

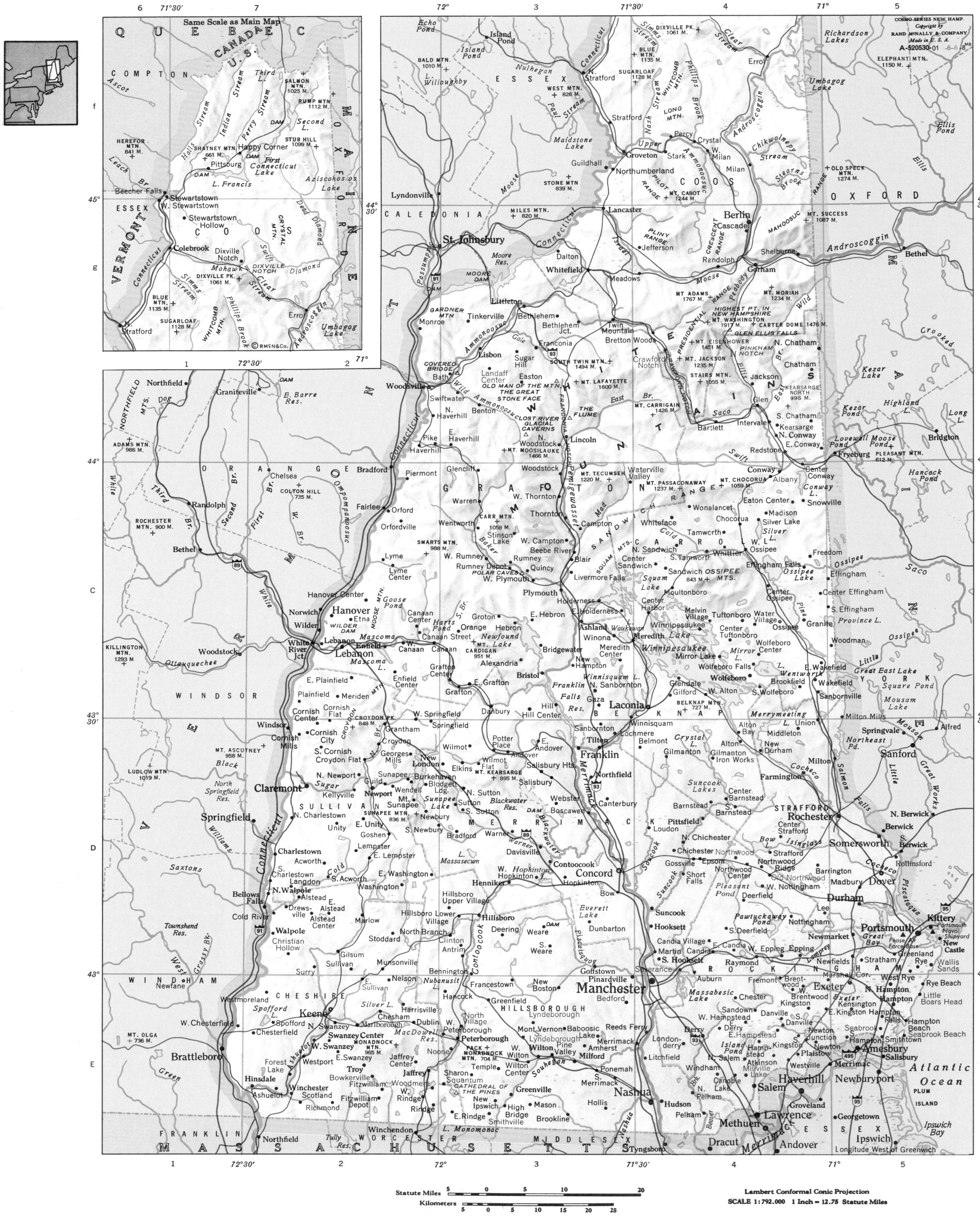

Same Scale as Main Map

Statute Miles 5 0 5 10 20

Kilometers 5 0 5 10 15 20 25

Lambert Conformal Conic Projection

SCALE 1:792,000 1 Inch = 12.75 Statute Miles

Longitude West of Greenwich

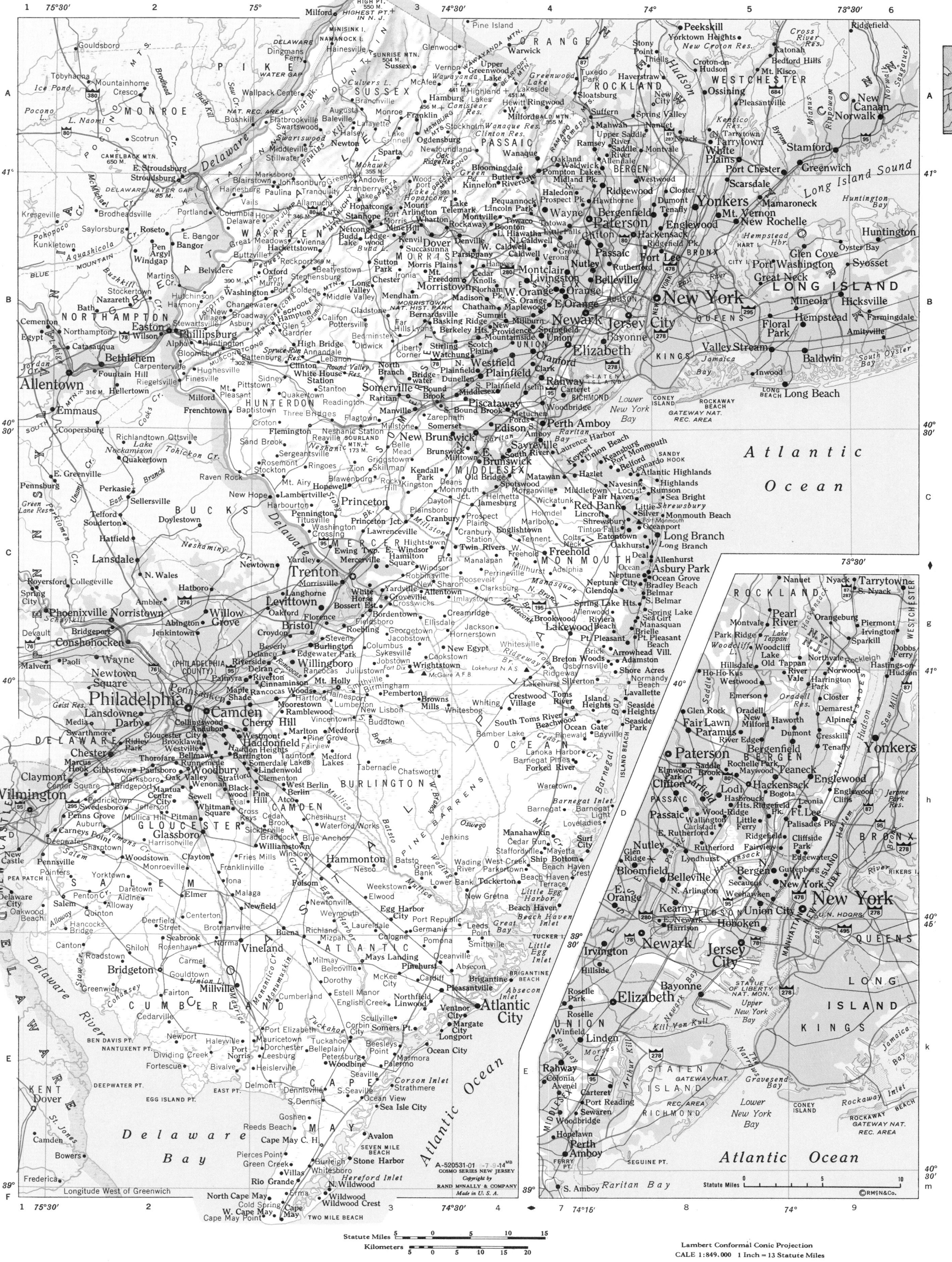
Atlantic Ocean
Delaware Bay
Long Island Sound
New York
Philadelphia
Newark
Jersey City
Paterson
Elizabeth
Trenton
Camden
Atlantic City
Allentown
Wilmington
Yonkers
Long Island
Lower New York Bay
Raritan Bay
Staten Island
SUSSEX
PASSAIC
BERGEN
MORRIS
WARREN
HUNTERDON
SOMERSET
MIDDLESEX
MONMOUTH
OCEAN
BURLINGTON
MERCER
CAMDEN
GLOUCESTER
SALEM
CUMBERLAND
ATLANTIC
CAPE MAY
UNION
ESSEX
HUDSON
Longitude West of Greenwich
A-520531-01 -7-9-14MB
COSMO SERIES NEW JERSEY
Copyright by RAND McNALLY & COMPANY
Made in U. S. A.
Statute Miles 5 0 5 10 15
Kilometers 5 0 5 10 15 20
Lambert Conformal Conic Projection
CALE 1:849,000 1 Inch = 13 Statute Miles

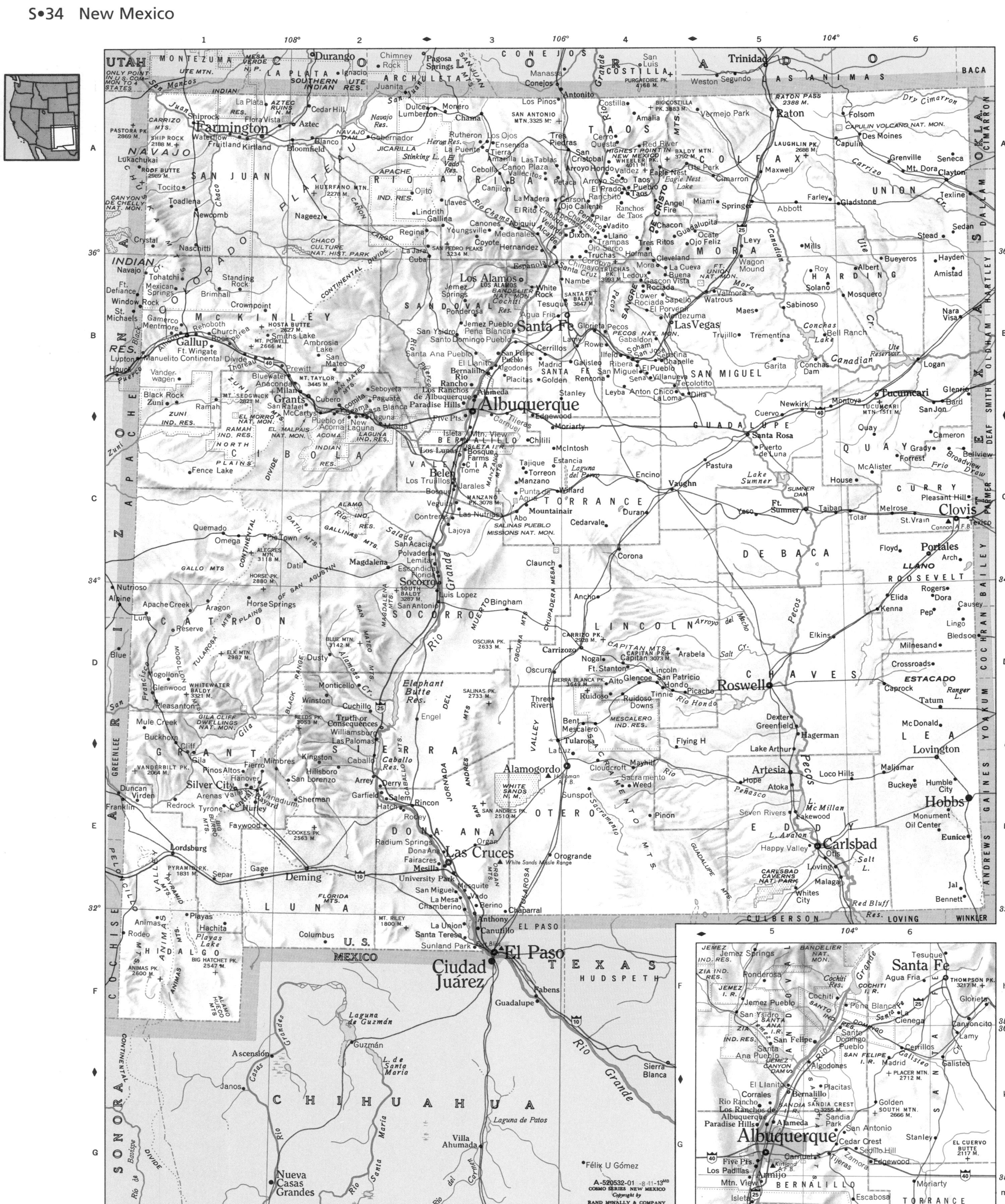

Statute Miles 10 0 10 20 30 40 50 60 70 80 90

Kilometers 10 0 10 20 40 60 80 100 120

Lambert Conformal Conic Projection

SCALE 1:2,600,000 1 Inch = 41 Statute Miles

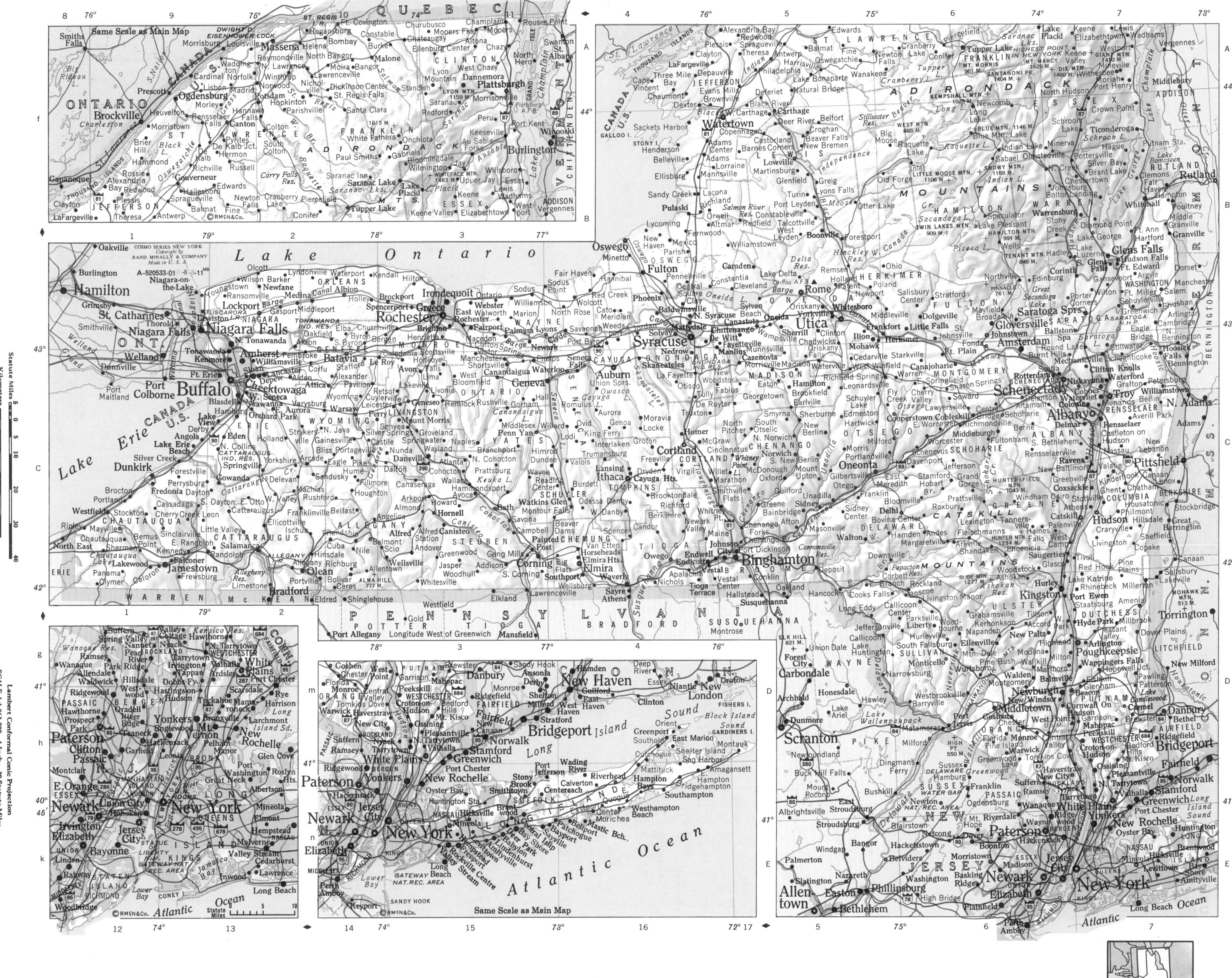

Statute Miles 5 0 5 10 20 30 40

Kilometers 5 0 5 15 25 35 45 55

Lambert Conformal Conic Projection

SCALE 1:1,862,000 1 Inch = 29 Statute Miles

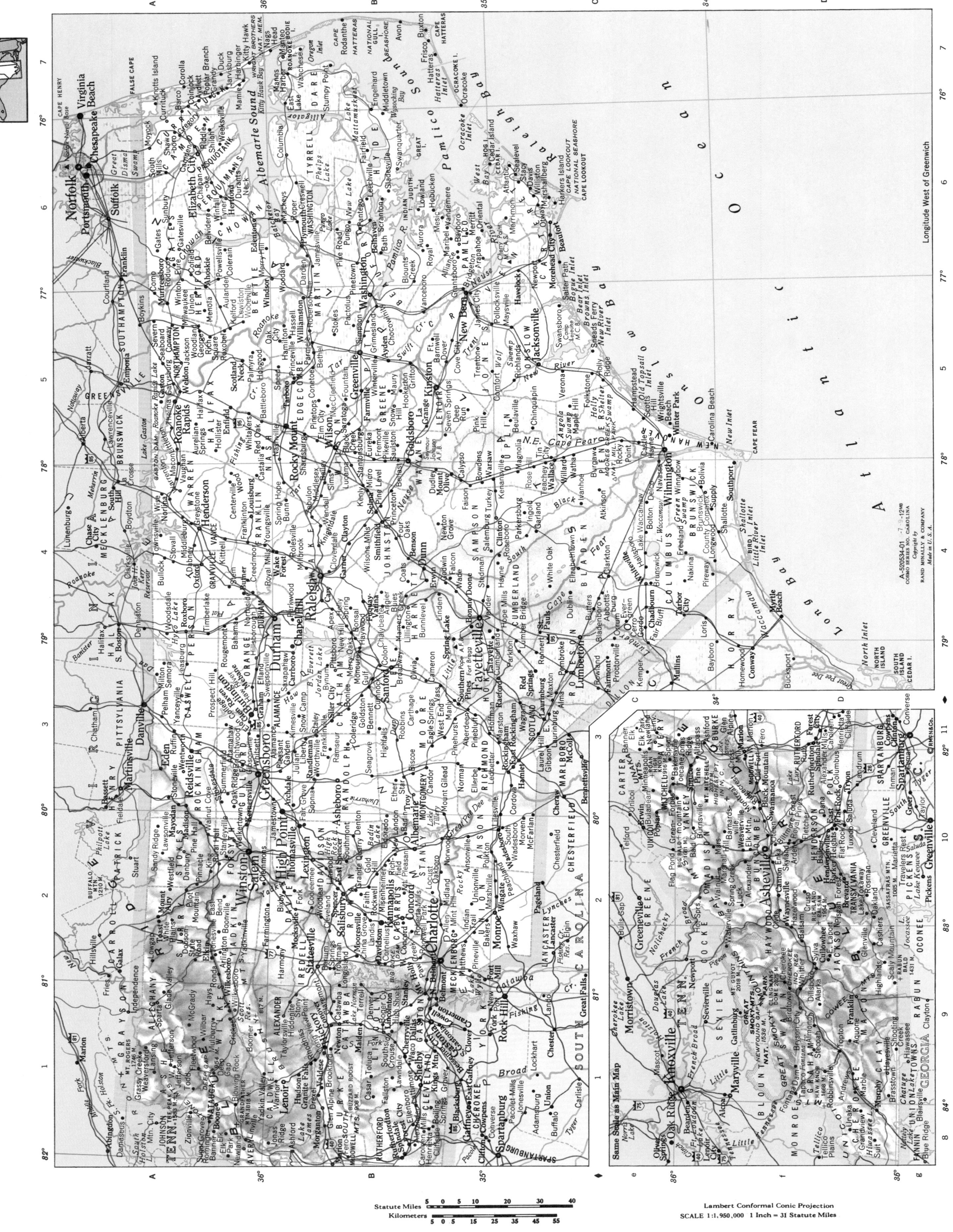

Statute Miles 5 0 5 10 20 30 40
Kilometers 5 0 5 15 25 35 45 55

Lambert Conformal Conic Projection
SCALE 1:1,950,000 1 Inch = 31 Statute Miles

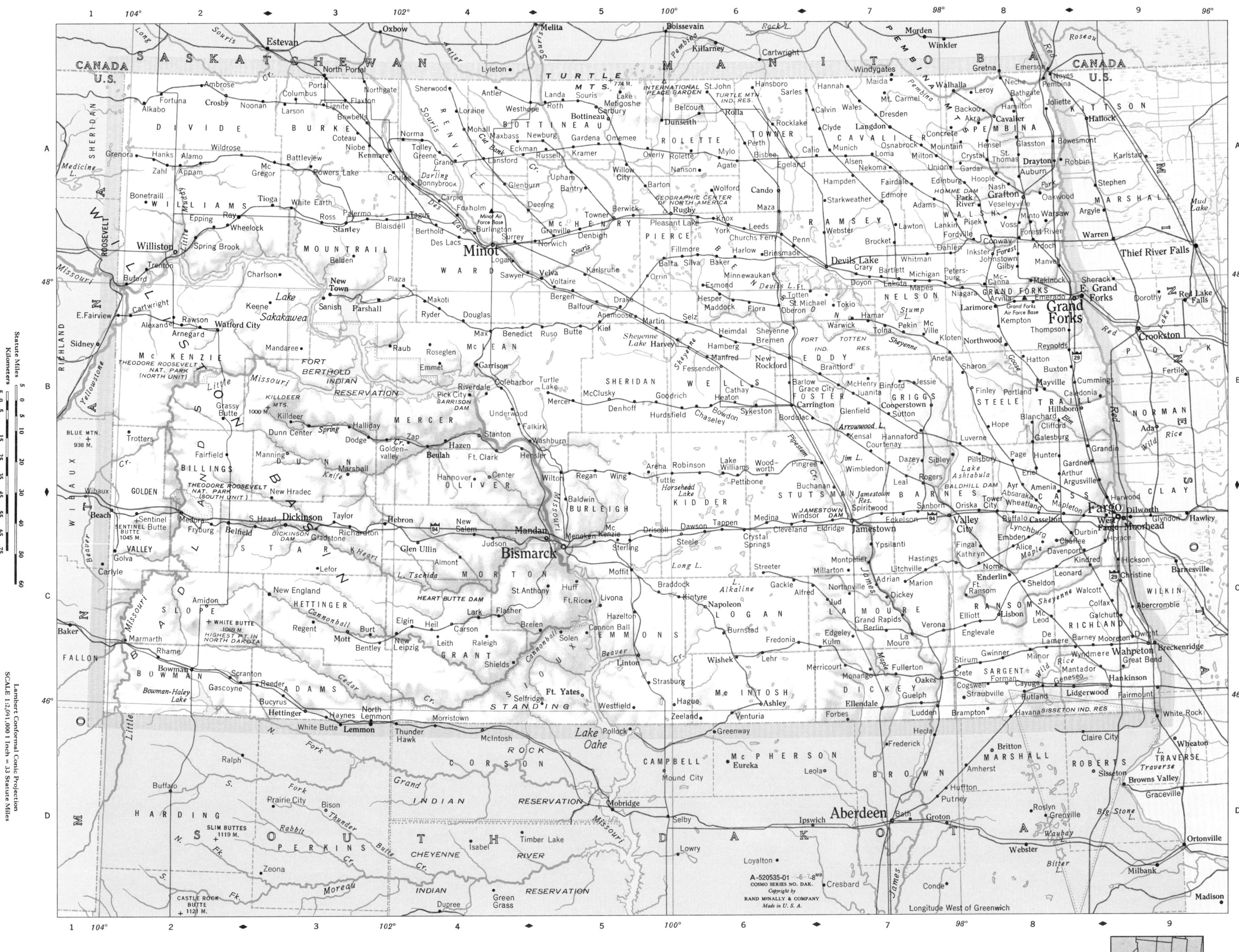

Statute Miles 5 0 5 10 20 30 40 50 60

Kilometers 5 0 5 15 25 35 45 55 65 75

Lambert Conformal Conic Projection
SCALE 1:2,091,000 1 Inch = 33 Statute Miles

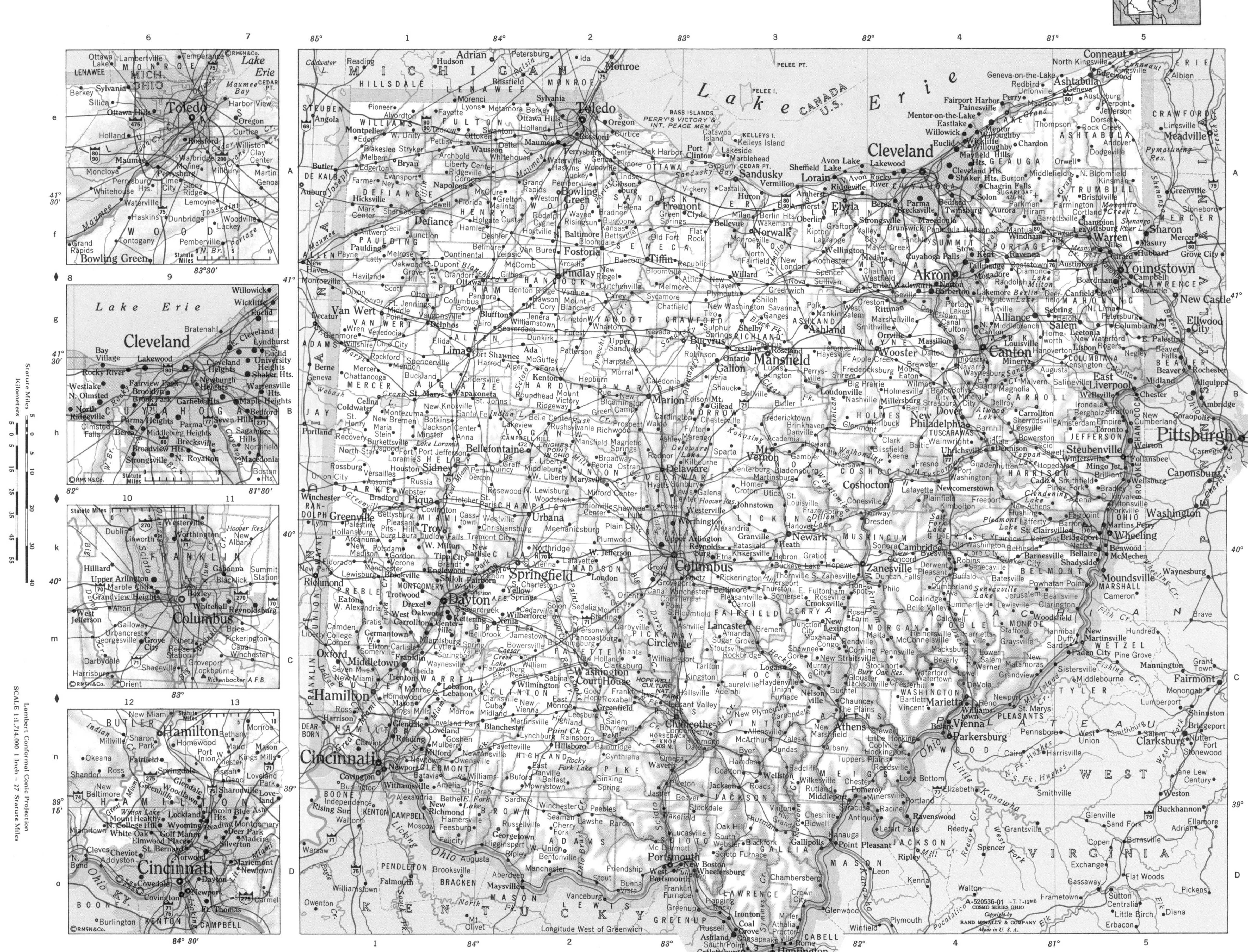
Lake Erie
CANADA
U.S.
MICHIGAN
PENNSYLVANIA
WEST VIRGINIA
KENTUCKY
INDIANA
Toledo
Cleveland
Akron
Youngstown
Canton
Mansfield
Columbus
Dayton
Springfield
Cincinnati
Hamilton
Zanesville
Marietta
Parkersburg
Portsmouth
Huntington
Pittsburgh
Wheeling
Steubenville
Sandusky
Lorain
Elyria
Findlay
Lima
Marion
Newark
Chillicothe
Athens
Longitude West of Greenwich
A-520536-01
COSMO SERIES OHIO
Copyright by RAND McNALLY & COMPANY
Made in U.S.A.
Statute Miles 5 0 5 10 20 30 40
Kilometers 5 0 5 15 25 35 45 55
Lambert Conformal Conic Projection
SCALE 1:1,714,000 1 Inch = 27 Statute Miles

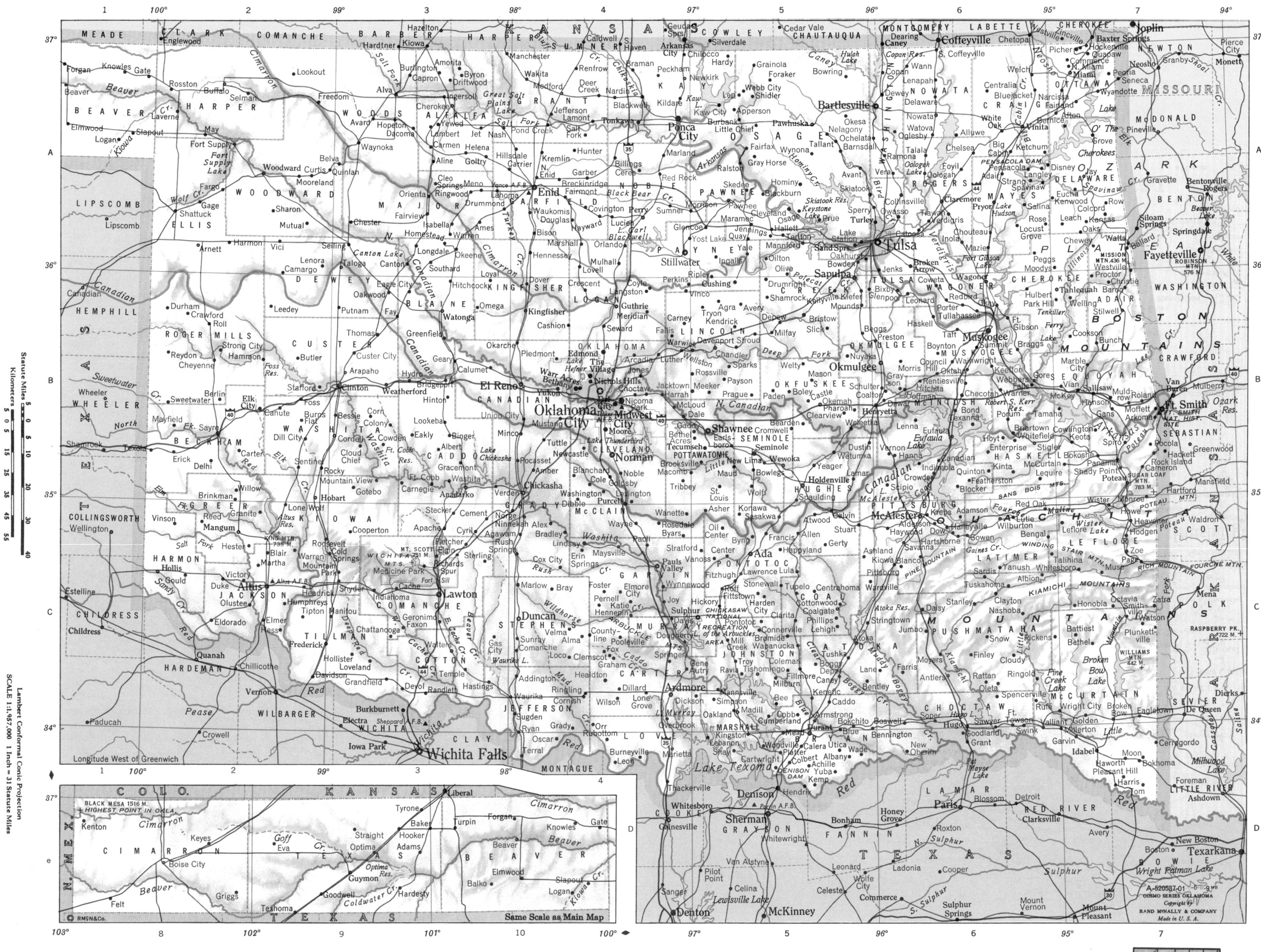
K A N S A S
T E X A S
Oklahoma City
Tulsa
Wichita Falls
Same Scale as Main Map
Longitude West of Greenwich
Statute Miles 5 0 5 10 20 30 40
Kilometers 5 0 5 15 25 35 45 55
Lambert Conformal Conic Projection
SCALE 1:1,957,000 1 Inch = 31 Statute Miles
A-520537-01
COSMO SERIES OKLAHOMA
Copyright by RAND McNALLY & COMPANY
Made in U. S. A.
© RMcN&Co.

Statute Miles 5 0 5 10 20 30 40 50

Kilometers 5 0 5 15 25 35 45 55 65 75

Lambert Conformal Conic Projection

SCALE 1:2,329,000 1 Inch = 37 Statute Miles

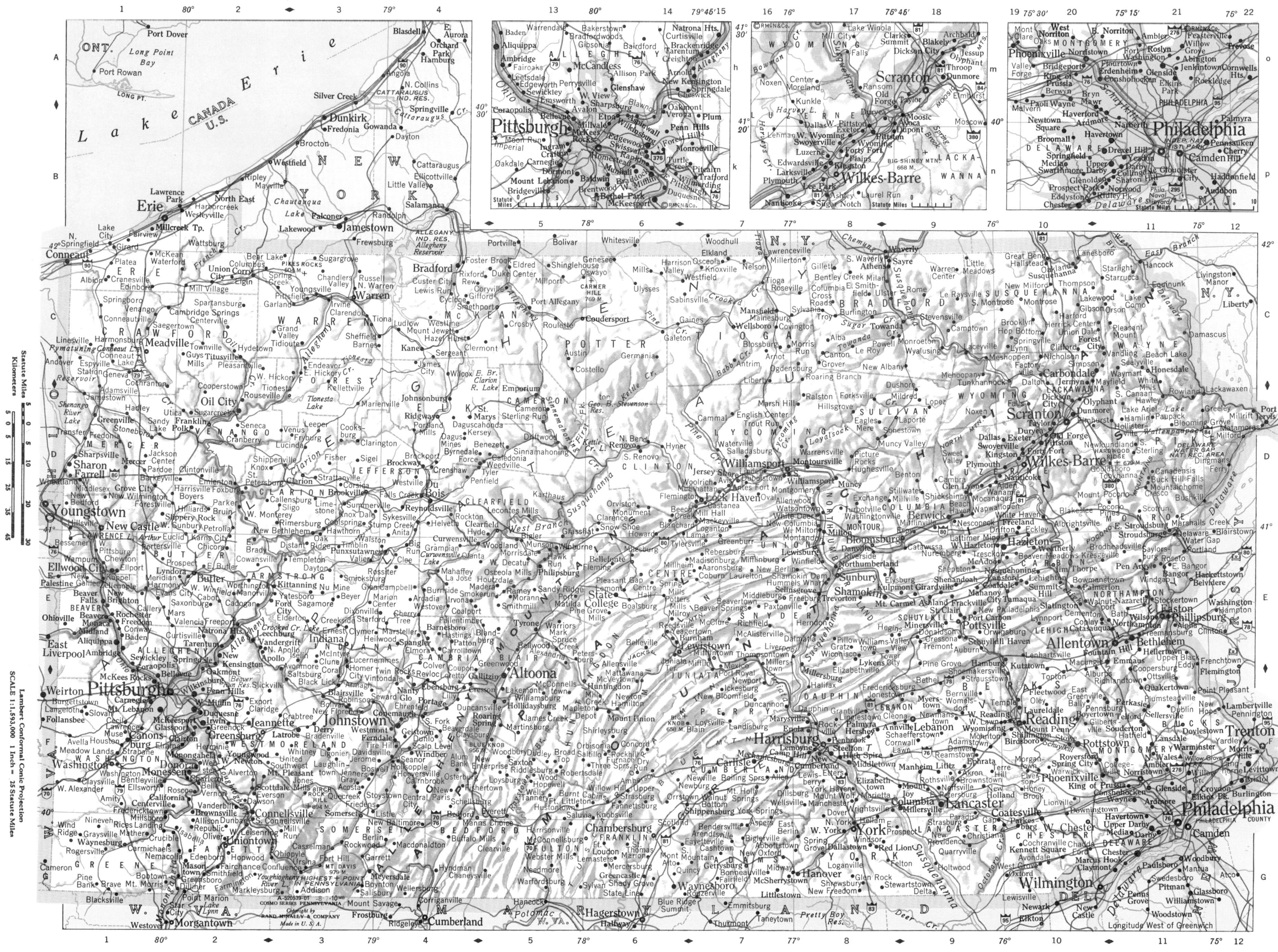
Lake Erie
CANADA
U.S.
NEW YORK
Pittsburgh
Scranton
Wilkes-Barre
Philadelphia
Erie
Youngstown
Altoona
Johnstown
Harrisburg
Allentown
Reading
Lancaster
York
Trenton
Wilmington
Camden
Statute Miles 5 0 5 10 20 30
Kilometers 5 0 5 15 25 35 45
Lambert Conformal Conic Projection
SCALE 1:1,593,000 1 Inch = 25 Statute Miles
Copyright by RAND McNALLY & COMPANY Made in U. S. A.

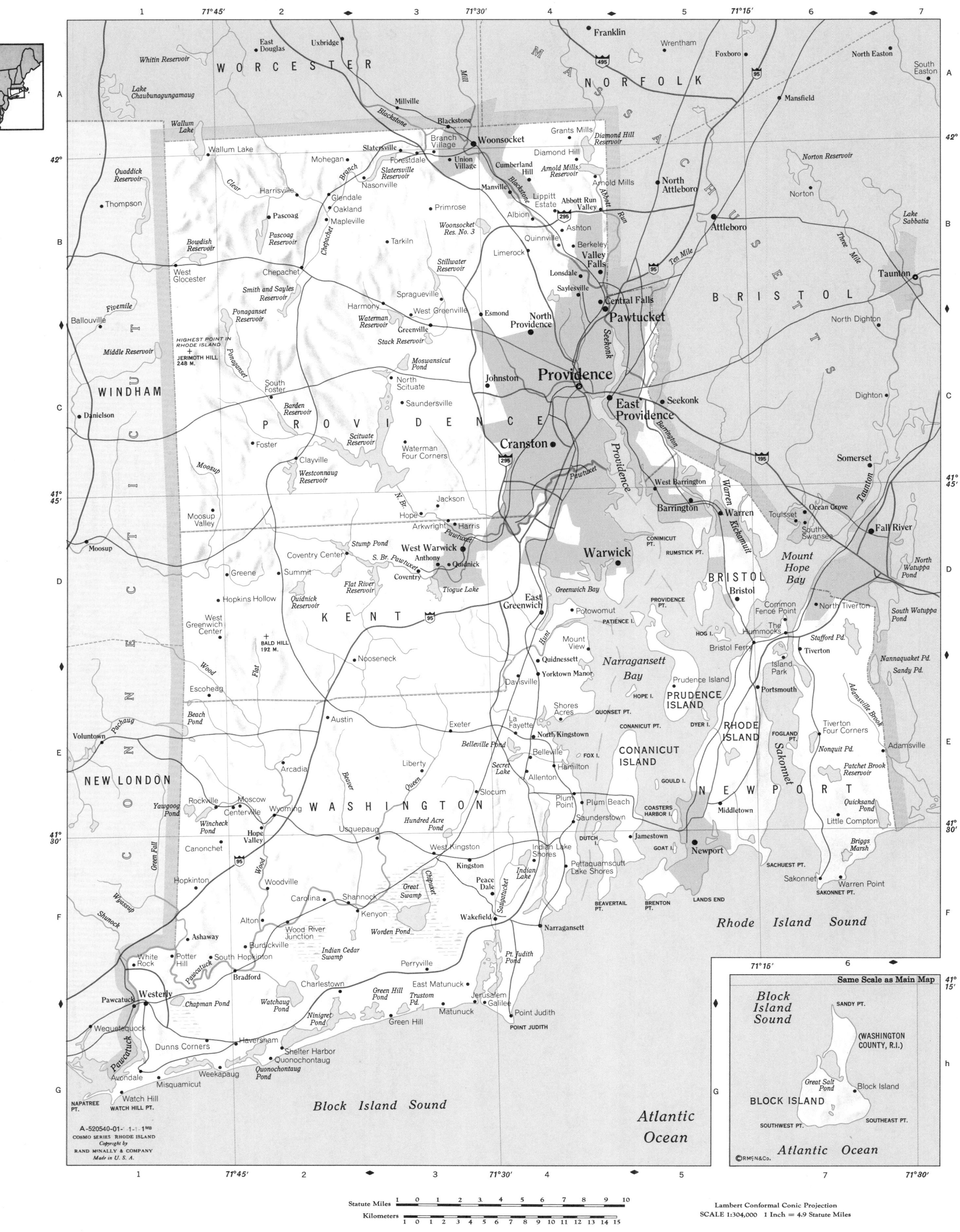
WORCESTER
NORFOLK
MASSACHUSETTS
BRISTOL
WINDHAM
CONNECTICUT
NEW LONDON
PROVIDENCE
KENT
WASHINGTON
NEWPORT
Providence
Pawtucket
Central Falls
East Providence
Cranston
Warwick
West Warwick
Woonsocket
North Providence
Johnston
Newport
Westerly
Bristol
Barrington
Warren
Fall River
Attleboro
Taunton
Franklin
Narragansett Bay
Rhode Island Sound
Block Island Sound
Atlantic Ocean
PRUDENCE ISLAND
CONANICUT ISLAND
RHODE ISLAND
Mount Hope Bay
HIGHEST POINT IN RHODE ISLAND
JERIMOTH HILL 248 M.
BALD HILL 192 M.
POINT JUDITH
WATCH HILL PT.
NAPATREE PT.
Same Scale as Main Map
Block Island Sound
BLOCK ISLAND
(WASHINGTON COUNTY, R.I.)
SANDY PT.
SOUTHWEST PT.
SOUTHEAST PT.
Atlantic Ocean
A-520540-01-1-1-1MB
COSMO SERIES RHODE ISLAND
Copyright by RAND McNALLY & COMPANY
Made in U. S. A.
©RM&Co.
Statute Miles
Kilometers
Lambert Conformal Conic Projection
SCALE 1:304,000 1 Inch = 4.9 Statute Miles

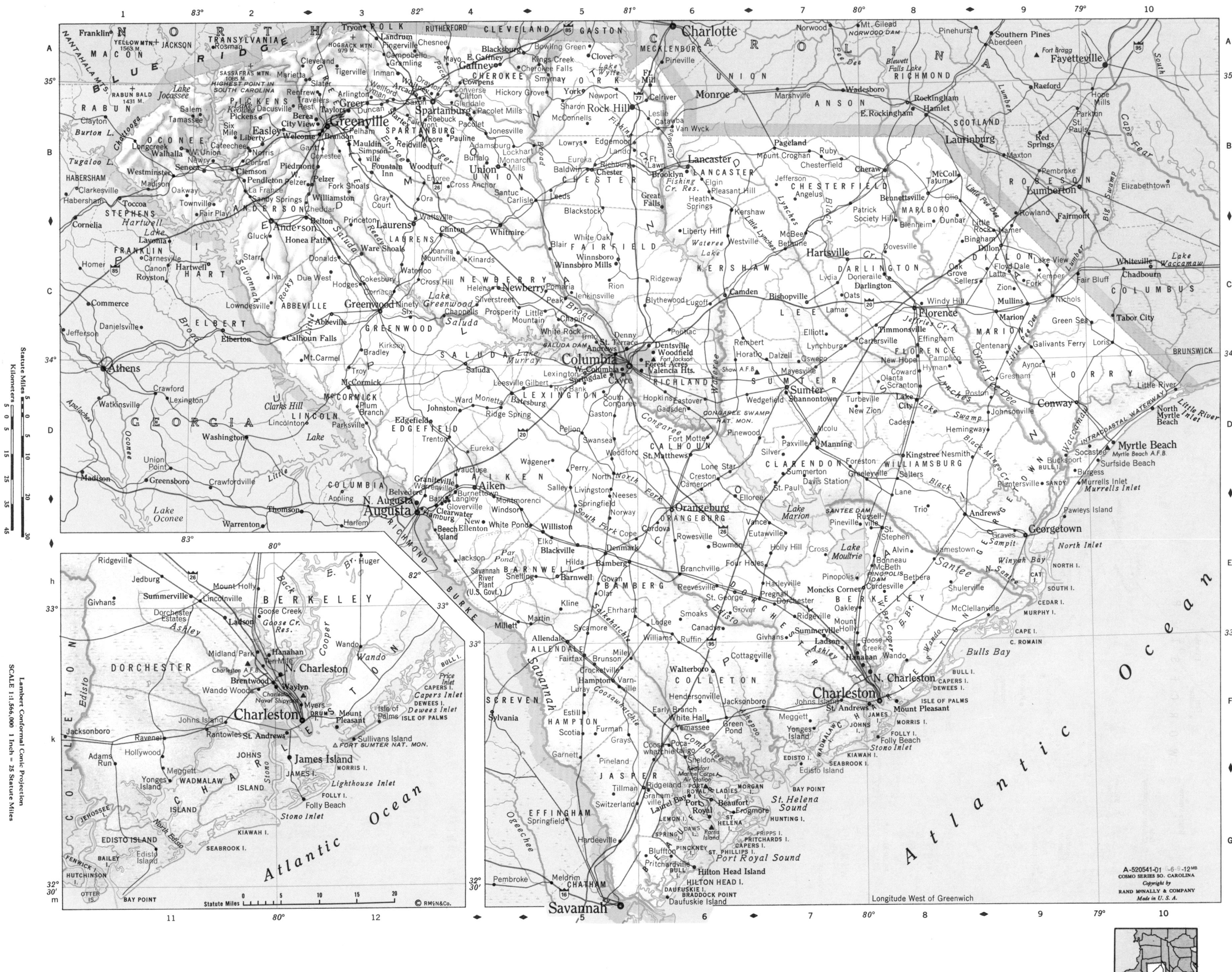
NORTH CAROLINA
GEORGIA
Atlantic Ocean
Charlotte
Columbia
Charleston
N. Charleston
Augusta
N. Augusta
Savannah
Greenville
Spartanburg
Anderson
Rock Hill
Florence
Sumter
Orangeburg
Aiken
Conway
Myrtle Beach
Georgetown
Fayetteville
Athens
Statute Miles 5 0 5 10 20 30
Kilometers 5 0 5 15 25 35 45
Lambert Conformal Conic Projection
SCALE 1:1,566,000 1 Inch = 25 Statute Miles
Longitude West of Greenwich
A-520541-01
COSMO SERIES SO. CAROLINA
Copyright by RAND McNALLY & COMPANY
Made in U. S. A.

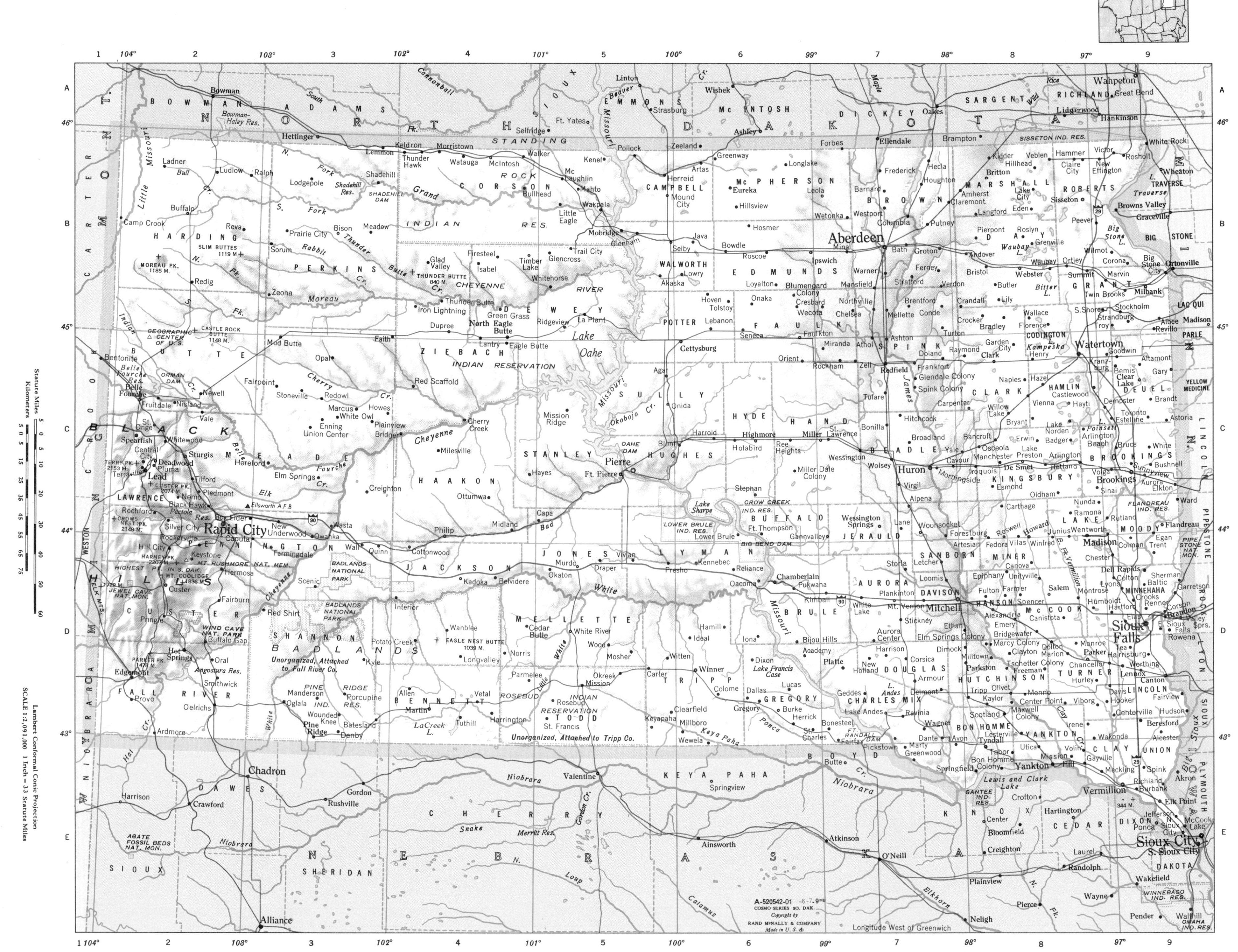

Statute Miles 5 0 5 10 20 30 40 50 60
Kilometers 5 0 5 15 25 35 45 55 65 75

Lambert Conformal Conic Projection
SCALE 1:2,091,000 1 Inch = 33 Statute Miles

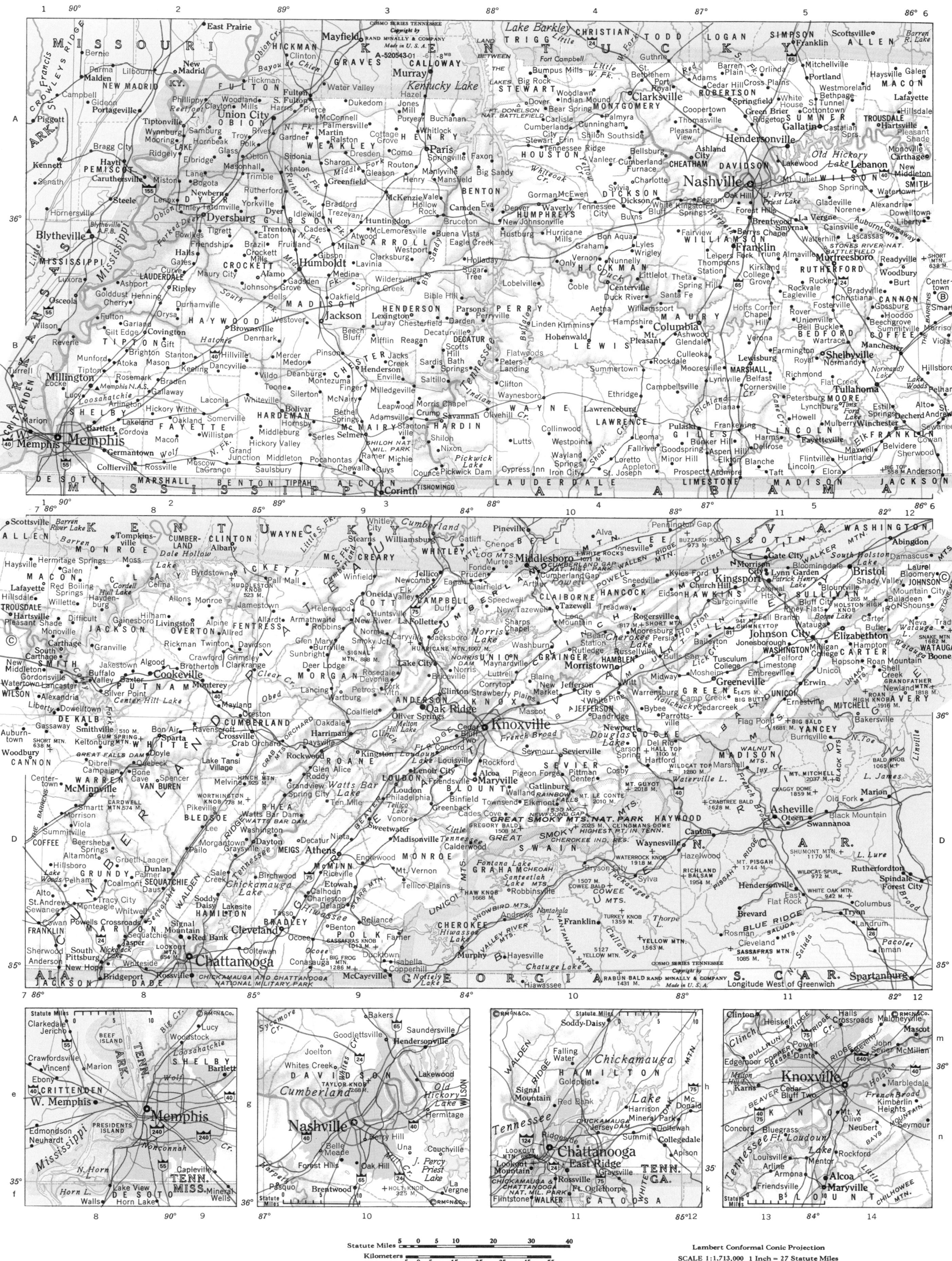
COSMO SERIES TENNESSEE
Copyright by RAND McNALLY & COMPANY
Made in U. S. A.
A-520543-01
MISSOURI
KENTUCKY
ARKANSAS
MISSISSIPPI
ALABAMA
GEORGIA
S. CAR.
N. CAR.
VIRGINIA
Memphis
Nashville
Knoxville
Chattanooga
Jackson
Clarksville
Murfreesboro
Franklin
Columbia
Kingsport
Bristol
Johnson City
Oak Ridge
Cleveland
Asheville
Kentucky Lake
Lake Barkley
Norris Lake
Cherokee Lake
Douglas Lake
Watts Bar Lake
Chickamauga Lake
Dale Hollow Lake
Center Hill Lake
Old Hickory Lake
J. Percy Priest Lake
Tennessee
Mississippi
Cumberland
GREAT SMOKY MTS. NAT. PARK
CUMBERLAND PLATEAU
Statute Miles
Kilometers
Lambert Conformal Conic Projection
SCALE 1:1,713,000 1 Inch = 27 Statute Miles
Longitude West of Greenwich

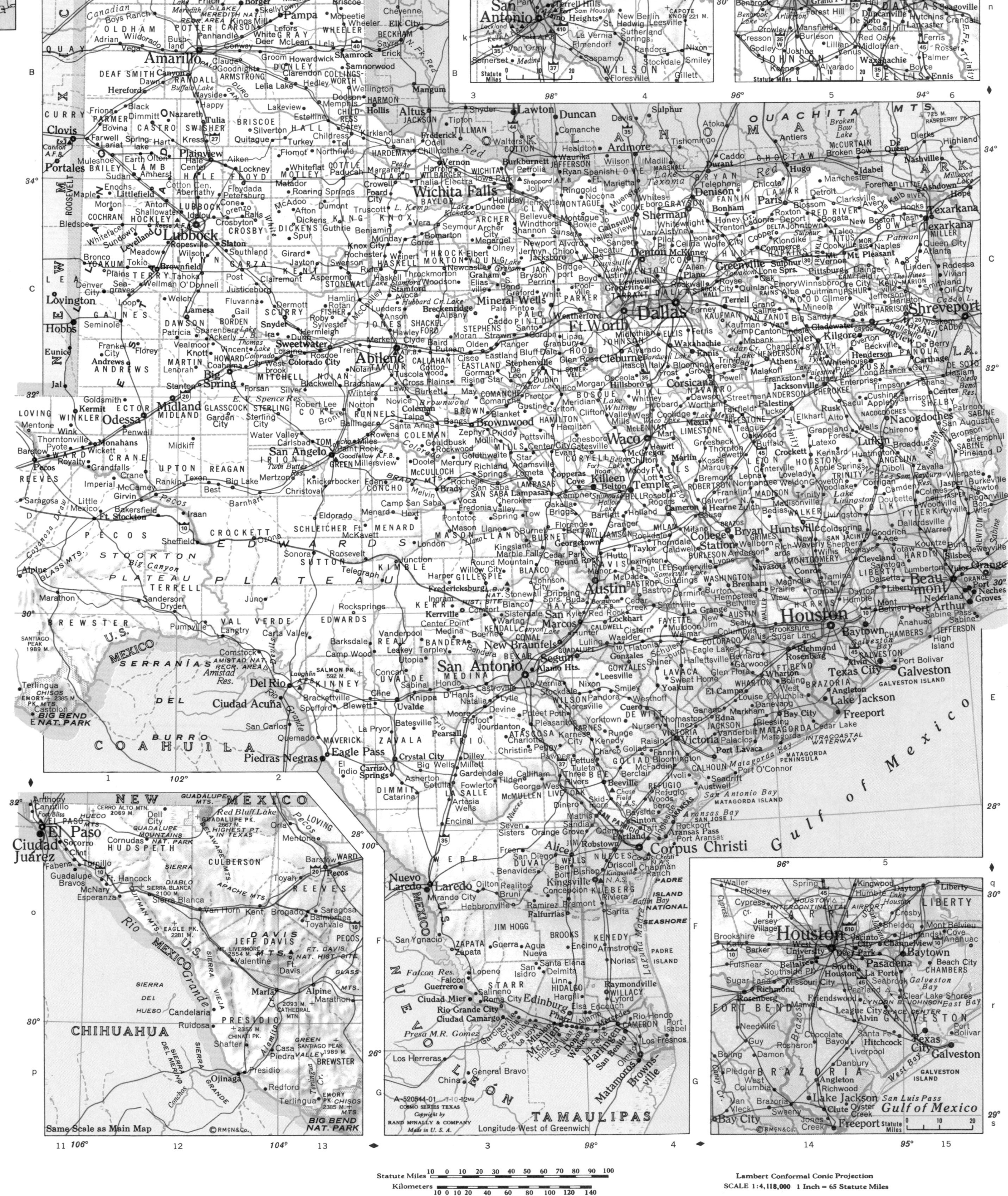

Statute Miles 10 0 10 20 30 40 50 60 70 80 90 100

Kilometers 10 0 10 20 40 60 80 100 120 140

Lambert Conformal Conic Projection

SCALE 1:4,118,000 1 Inch = 65 Statute Miles

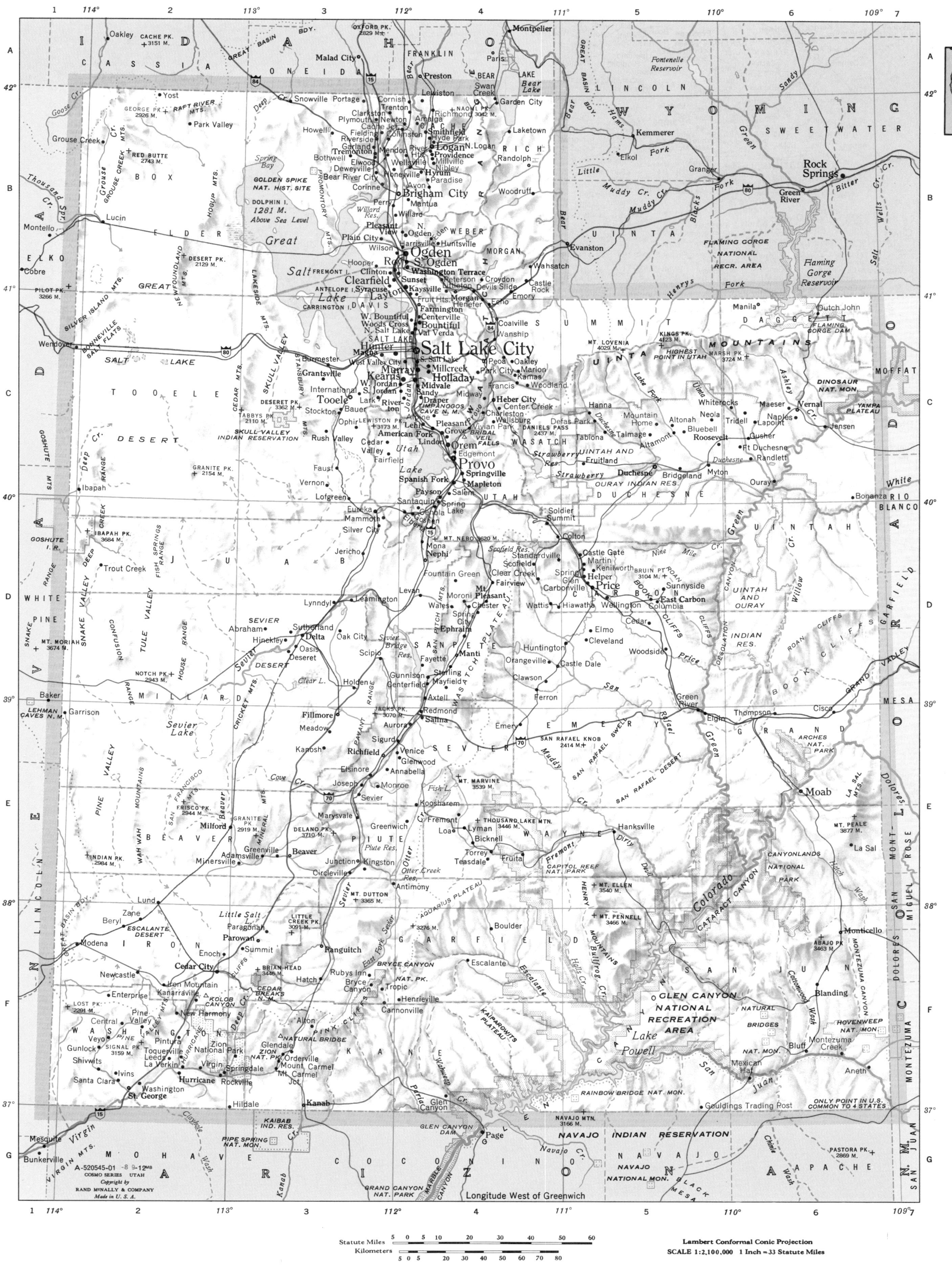

Statute Miles 5 0 5 10 20 30 40 50 60
Kilometers 5 0 5 20 30 40 50 60 70 80

Lambert Conformal Conic Projection
SCALE 1:2,100,000 1 Inch = 33 Statute Miles

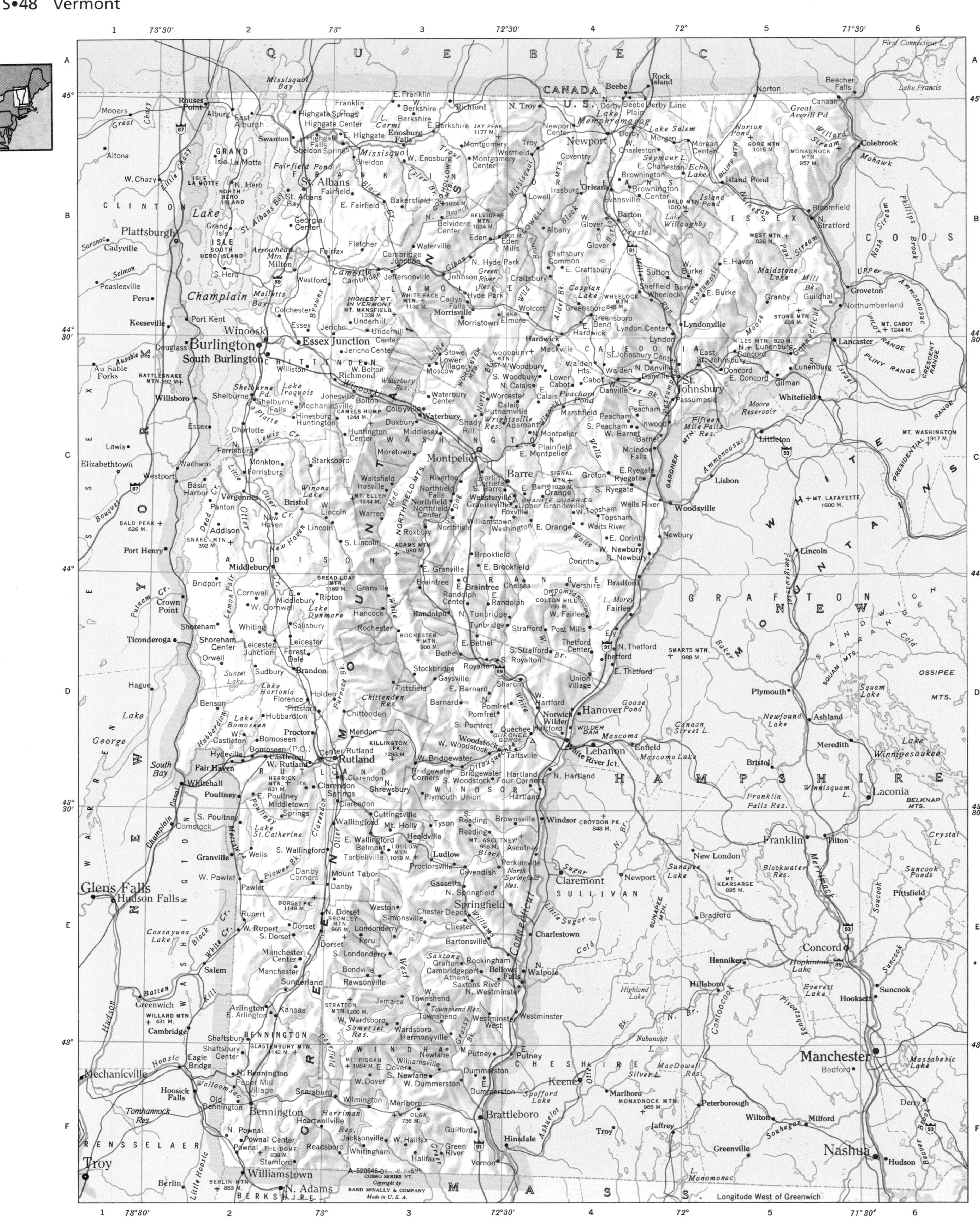

Statute Miles 5 0 5 10 20

Kilometers 5 0 5 10 15 20 25

Lambert Conformal Conic Projection

SCALE 1:903,000 1 Inch = 14.25 Statute Miles

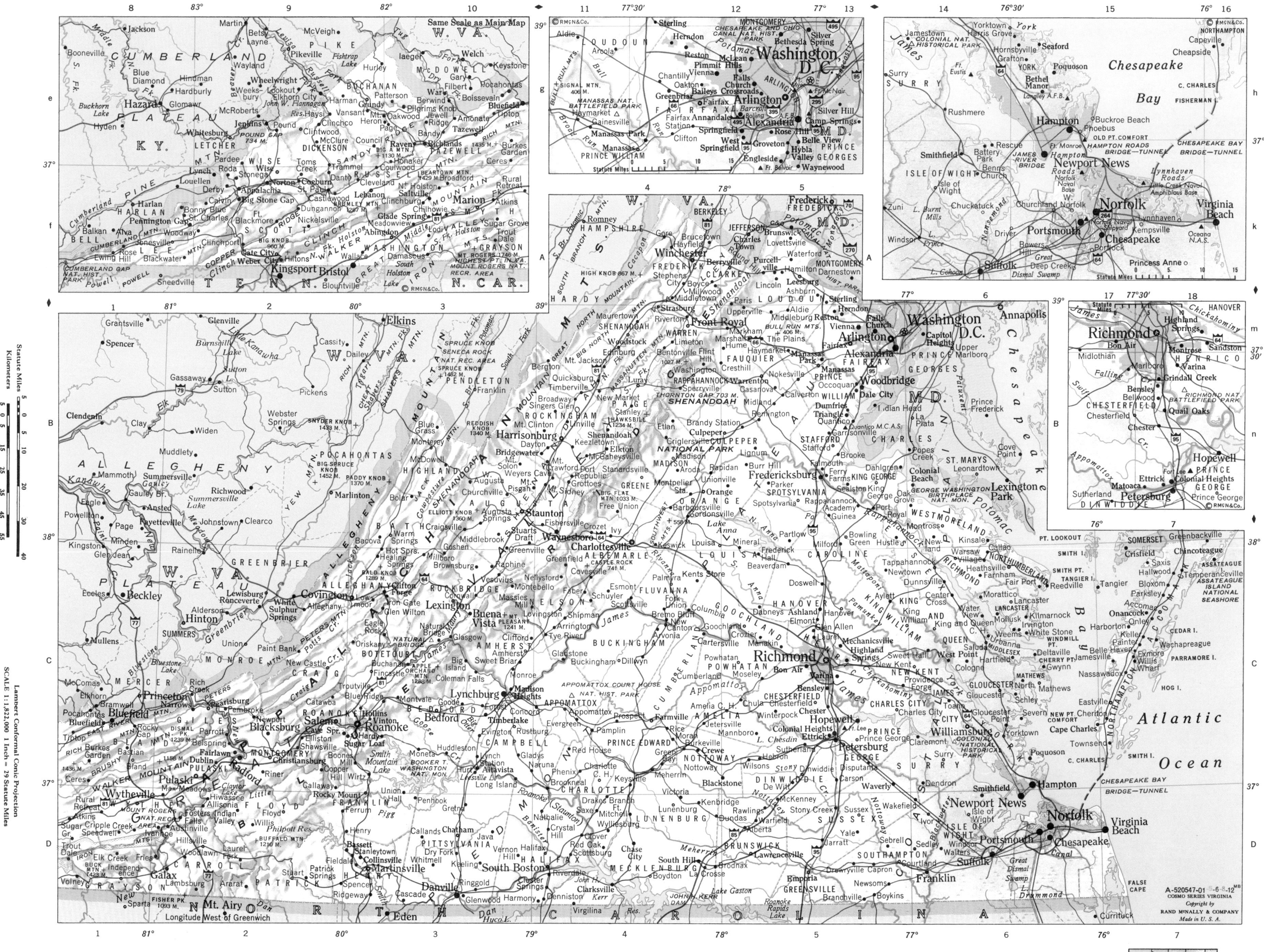
Same Scale as Main Map
Chesapeake Bay
Atlantic Ocean
Longitude West of Greenwich
Statute Miles
Kilometers
Lambert Conformal Conic Projection
SCALE 1:1,822,000 1 Inch = 29 Statute Miles
COSMO SERIES VIRGINIA
Copyright by
RAND McNALLY & COMPANY
Made in U. S. A.

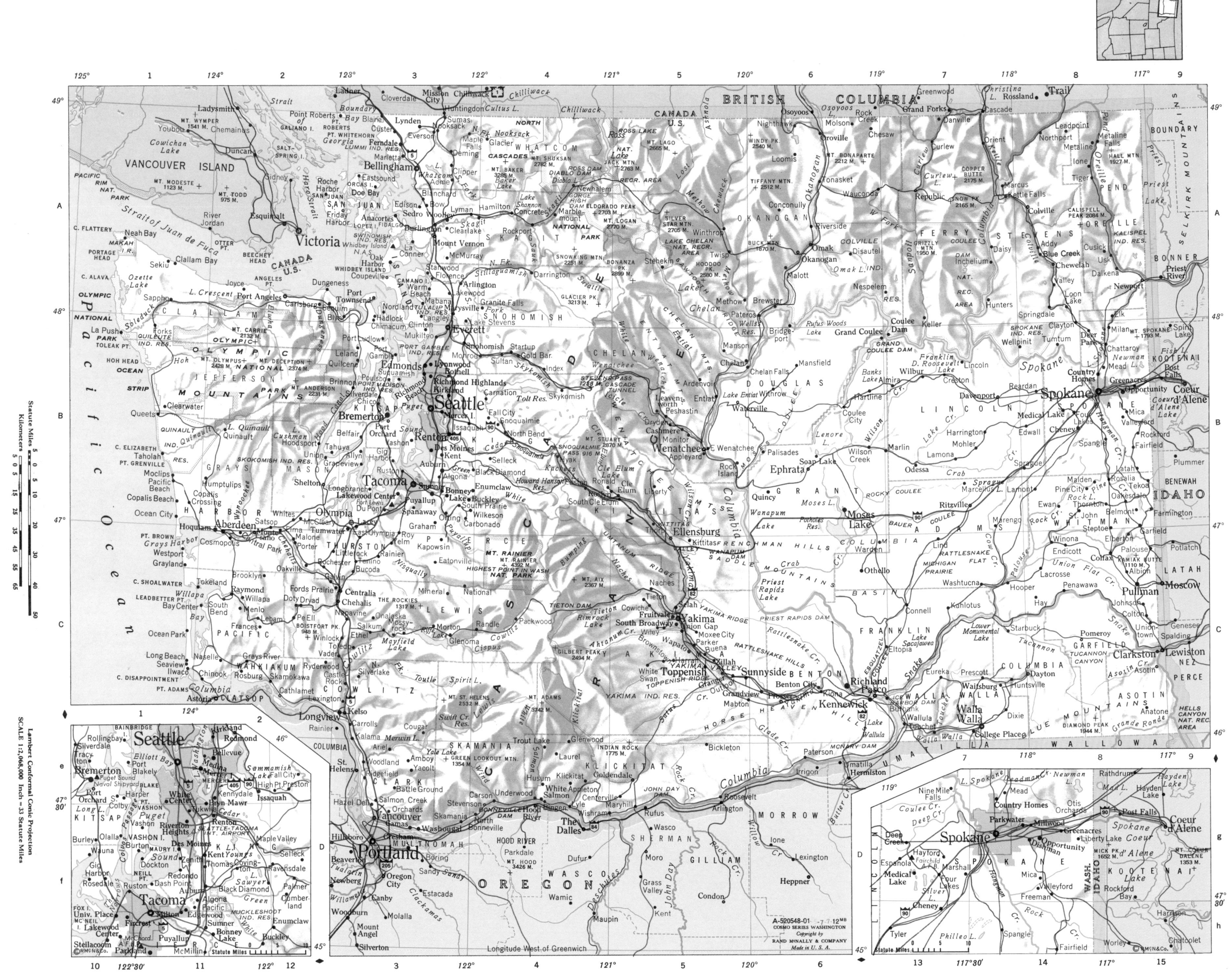
Statute Miles 5 0 5 10 20 30 40 50
Kilometers 5 0 5 15 25 35 45 55 65
Lambert Conformal Conic Projection
SCALE 1:2,068,000 Inch = 33 Statute Miles
Pacific Ocean
BRITISH COLUMBIA
CANADA
IDAHO
OREGON
VANCOUVER ISLAND
Seattle
Spokane
Tacoma
Olympia
Portland
Victoria
Longitude West of Greenwich

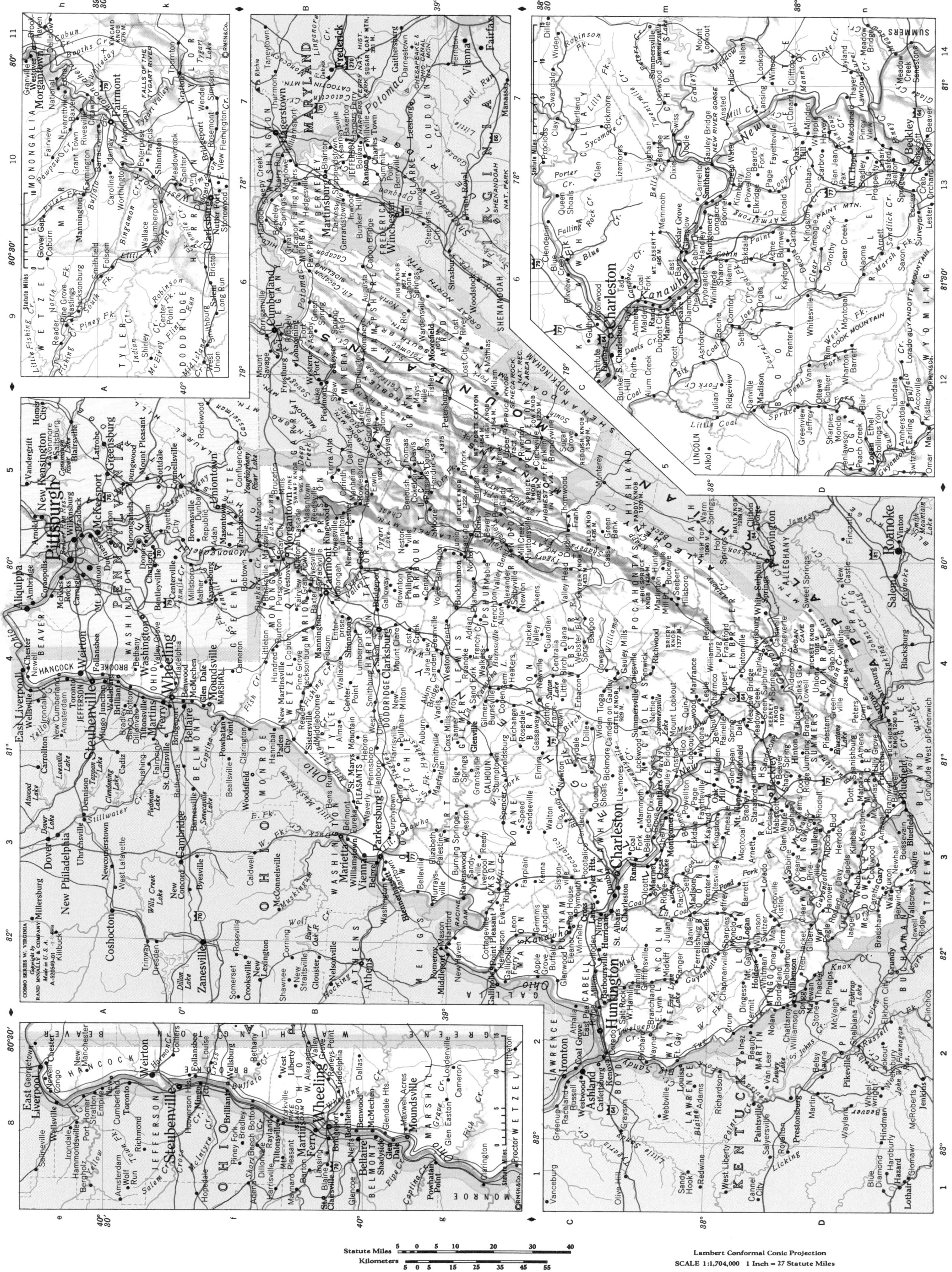
Statute Miles 5 0 5 10 20 30 40
Kilometers 5 0 5 15 25 35 45 55
Lambert Conformal Conic Projection
SCALE 1:1,704,000 1 Inch = 27 Statute Miles

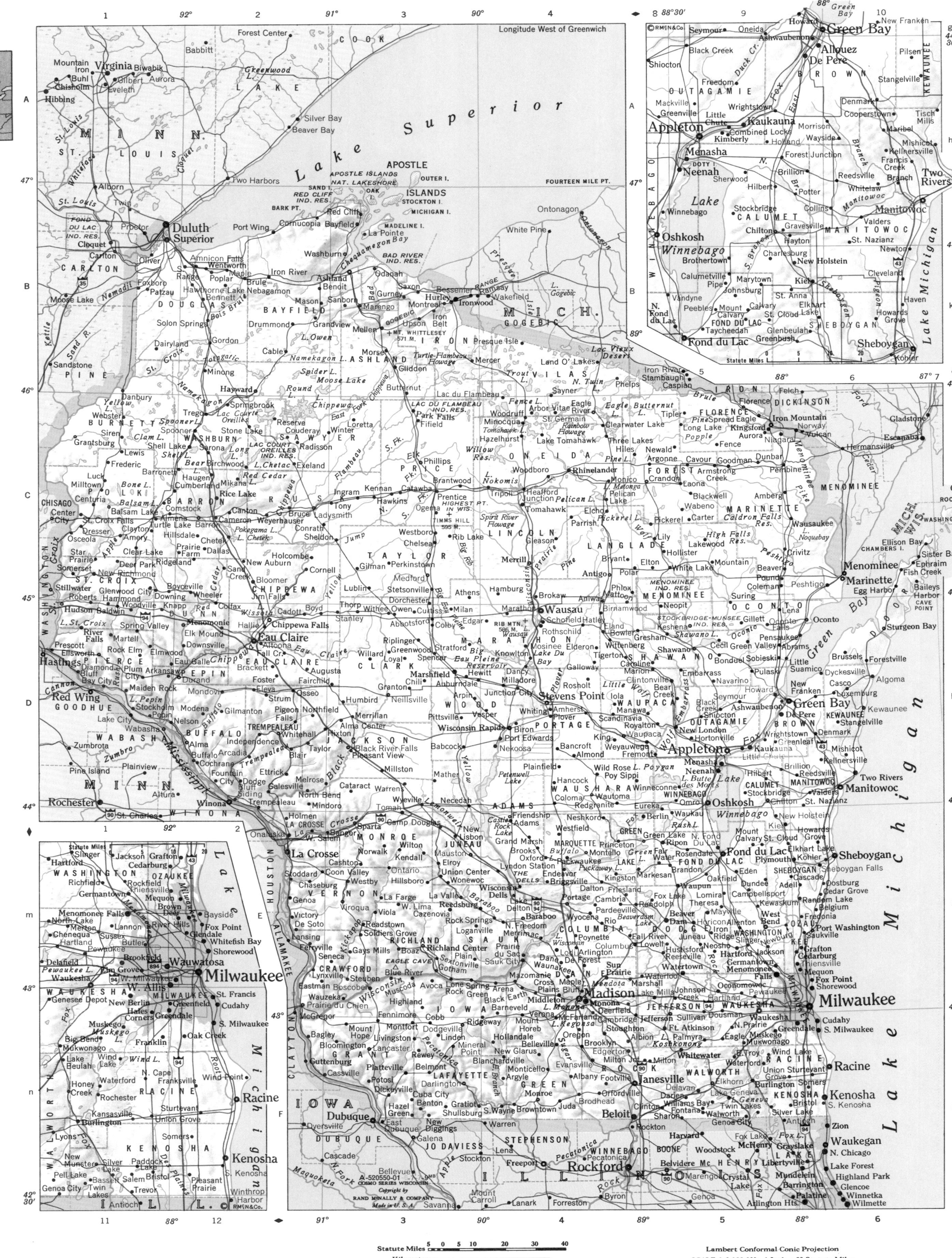
Longitude West of Greenwich
Lake Superior
APOSTLE ISLANDS
APOSTLE ISLANDS NAT. LAKESHORE
MINN.
MICH.
IOWA
ILL.
Lake Michigan
Green Bay
Lake Winnebago
Duluth
Superior
Ashland
Rhinelander
Wausau
Eau Claire
Chippewa Falls
La Crosse
Stevens Point
Wisconsin Rapids
Green Bay
Appleton
Oshkosh
Fond du Lac
Sheboygan
Manitowoc
Madison
Milwaukee
Racine
Kenosha
Janesville
Beloit
Rockford
Dubuque
Menominee
Marinette
Waukesha
Wauwatosa
W. Allis
TIMMS HILL 595 M. HIGHEST PT. IN WIS.
RIB MTN. 586 M.
Statute Miles 5 0 5 10 20 30 40
Kilometers 5 0 5 15 25 35 45 55
Lambert Conformal Conic Projection
SCALE 1:2,088,000 1 Inch = 33 Statute Miles
A-520550-01 COSMO SERIES WISCONSIN
Copyright by RAND McNALLY & COMPANY Made in U. S. A.

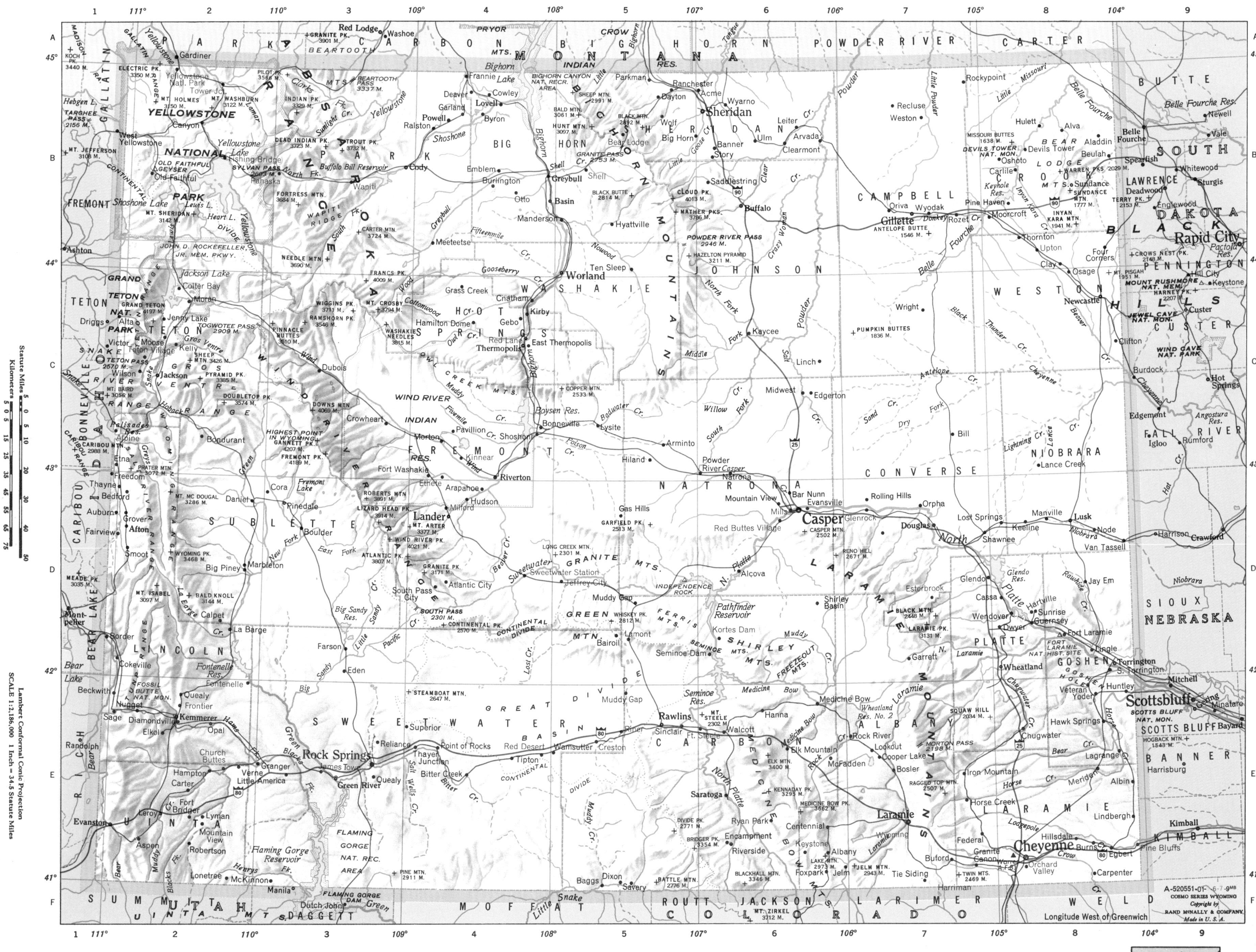
Statute Miles 5 0 5 10 20 30 40 50
Kilometers 5 0 5 15 25 35 45 55 65 75
Lambert Conformal Conic Projection
SCALE 1:2,186,000 1 Inch = 34.5 Statute Miles
Longitude West of Greenwich
A-520551-01-6-7-9MB
COSMO SERIES WYOMING
Copyright by
RAND McNALLY & COMPANY
Made in U. S. A.

Index to State Maps

In a single alphabetical list, this index includes the names of features that appear on the individual state maps. The names of cities and towns appear in regular type. The names of all other features appear in *italics.*

The names of physical features may be inverted, since they are always alphabetized under the proper, not the generic, part of the name. For example, Lake Erie is listed as *Erie, Lake.* Otherwise every entry, whether consisting of one word or more, is alphabetized as a single continuous entity. In the case of identical names, towns are listed first, then political divisions, then physical features. Entries that are completely identical are listed alphabetically by state name.

The map reference keys and page references are found in the last two columns of each entry. Each map reference key consists of a letter and a number. The letters correspond to letters along the sides of the maps. The numbers correspond to numbers that appear across the tops and bottoms of the maps.

List of Abbreviations

AK . . . . Alaska
AL . . . . Alabama
AR . . . . Arkansas
AZ . . . . Arizona
CA . . . . California
CO . . . . Colorado
CT . . . . Connecticut
DC . . . . District of Columbia
DE . . . . Delaware
FL . . . . Florida
GA . . . . Georgia
HI . . . . Hawaii
IA . . . . Iowa
ID . . . . Idaho
IL . . . . Illinois
IN . . . . Indiana
KS . . . . Kansas
KY . . . . Kentucky
LA . . . . Louisiana
MA . . . . Massachusetts
MD . . . . Maryland
ME . . . . Maine
MI . . . . Michigan
MN . . . . Minnesota
MO . . . . Missouri
MS . . . . Mississippi
MT . . . . Montana
NA . . . . North America
NC . . . . North Carolina
ND . . . . North Dakota
NE . . . . Nebraska
NH . . . . New Hampshire
NJ . . . . New Jersey
NM . . . . New Mexico
NV . . . . Nevada
NY . . . . New York
OH . . . . Ohio
OK . . . . Oklahoma
OR . . . . Oregon
PA . . . . Pennsylvania
r. . . . . river
RI . . . . Rhode Island
SC . . . . South Carolina
SD . . . . South Dakota
TN . . . . Tennessee
TX . . . . Texas
US . . . . United States
UT . . . . Utah
VA . . . . Virginia
VT . . . . Vermont
WA . . . . Washington
WI . . . . Wisconsin
WV . . . . West Virginia
WY . . . . Wyoming

A

Name	Map Ref.	Page
Abajo Peak, UT	F6	47
Abbaye, Point, MI	B2	25
Abbeville, AL	D4	4
Abbeville, LA	E3	21
Abbeville, SC	C3	43
Aberdeen, ID	G6	15
Aberdeen, MD	A5	23
Aberdeen, MS	B5	27
Aberdeen, SD	B7	44
Aberdeen, WA	C2	50
Abert, Lake, OR	E6	40
Abilene, KS	D6	19
Abilene, TX	C3	46
Abingdon, IL	C3	16
Abingdon, VA	f10	49
Abington, MA	B6	24
Abington [Township], PA	o21	41
Abraham Lincoln Birthplace National Historic Site, KY	C4	20
Absaroka Range, US	F7	53
Absarokee, MT	E7	29
Acadia National Park, ME	D4	22
Accokeek, MD	C3	23
Ackerman, MS	B4	27
Ackley, IA	B4	18
Acomita, NM	B2	34
Acworth, GA	B2	13
Ada, MN	C2	26
Ada, OK	C5	39
Adairsville, GA	B2	13
Adak Island, AK	E4	5
Adams, Mount, NH	B4	32
Adams, Mount, WA	C4	50
Adamsville, AL	f7	4
Addison, CT	C5	10
Addison, IL	k8	16
Adel, GA	E3	13
Adel, IA	C3	18
Adirondack Mountains, NY	A6	35
Admiralty Bay, AK	A9	5
Admiralty Island, AK	m22	5
Adrian, MI	G6	25
Afognak Island, AK	D9	5
Afton, MN	F6	26
Afton, WY	D2	53
Agawam, MA	B2	24
Agua Fria, NM	B3	34
Agua Fria, r., AZ	D3	6
Ahoskie, NC	A6	36
Aiea, HI	B4	14
Aiken, SC	D4	43
Ainsworth, NE	B6	30
Aitkin, MN	D5	26
Ajo, AZ	E3	6
Akiachak, AK	C7	5
Akron, CO	A7	9
Akron, IA	B1	18
Akron, OH	A4	38
Alabama, state, US	C3	4
Alabama, r., AL	D2	4
Alabaster, AL	B3	4
Alameda, CA	h8	8
Alameda, NM	B3	34
Alamo, TN	B2	45
Alamo, TX	F3	46
Alamogordo, NM	E4	34
Alamosa, CO	D5	9
Alamosa, r., CO	D4	9
Alamosa East, CO	D5	9
Alapaha, r., US	E3	13
Alaska, state, US	C9	5
Alaska, Gulf of, AK	D10	5
Alaska Peninsula, AK	D8	5
Alaska Range, AK	C9	5
Alava, Cape, WA	A1	50
Albany, GA	E2	13
Albany, IN	D7	17
Albany, KY	D4	20
Albany, MO	A3	28
Albany, NY	C7	35
Albany, OR	C3	40
Albemarle, NC	B2	36
Albemarle Sound, NC	A6	36
Albert Lea, MN	G5	26
Albertville, AL	A3	4
Albia, IA	C5	18
Albion, IN	B7	17
Albion, MI	F6	25
Albion, NE	C7	30
Albuquerque, NM	B3	34
Alcalde, NM	A3	34
Alcester, SD	D9	44
Alcoa, TN	D10	45
Alderson, WV	D4	51
Aldrich, AL	B3	4
Aledo, IL	B3	16
Alegres Mountain, NM	C2	34
Alenuihaha Channel, HI	C5	14
Aleutian Islands, AK	E3	5
Aleutian Range, AK	D9	5
Alexander City, AL	C4	4
Alexandria, IN	D6	17
Alexandria, KY	B5	20
Alexandria, LA	C3	21
Alexandria, MN	E3	26
Alexandria, VA	B5	49
Alfred, ME	E2	22
Algoma, WI	D6	52
Algona, IA	A3	18
Algonquin, IL	A5	16
Algood, TN	C8	45
Alhambra, CA	m12	8
Alice, TX	F3	46
Aliceville, AL	B1	4
Aliquippa, PA	E1	41
Allagash, r., ME	B3	22
Allatoona Lake, GA	B2	13
Allegheny, r., US	E2	41
Allegheny Mountain, US	B3	49
Allegheny Plateau, US	E1	41
Allegheny Reservoir, US	B4	41
Allemands, Lac Des, LA	E5	21
Allen, TX	C4	46
Allendale, SC	E5	43
Allen Park, MI	p15	25
Allentown, PA	E11	41
Alliance, NE	B3	30
Alliance, OH	B4	38
Alligator, r., NC	B6	36
Allison Park, PA	h14	41
Allouez, WI	h9	52
Alma, AR	B1	7
Alma, GA	E4	13
Alma, MI	E6	25
Alma, NE	D6	30
Aloha, OR	h12	40
Alpena, MI	C7	25
Alpharetta, GA	B2	13
Alstead, NH	D2	32
Alta, IA	B2	18
Altamaha, r., GA	E4	13
Altamont, OR	E5	40
Altamonte Springs, FL	D5	12
Altavista, VA	C3	49
Altheimer, AR	C4	7
Alton, IL	E3	16
Alton, MO	E6	28
Alton, NH	D4	32
Alton Bay, NH	D4	32
Altoona, IA	C4	18
Altoona, PA	E5	41
Altoona, WI	D2	52
Altus, OK	C2	39
Altus Reservoir, OK	C2	39
Alva, OK	A3	39
Alvin, TX	E5	46
Amargosa, r., US	D5	8
Amargosa Desert, US	G5	31
Amargosa Range, US	G5	31
Amarillo, TX	B2	46
Ambler, PA	F11	41
Ambridge, PA	E1	41
American Falls, ID	G6	15
American Falls Reservoir, ID	F5	15
American Fork, UT	C4	47
Americus, GA	D2	13
Amery, WI	C1	52
Ames, IA	B4	18
Amesbury, MA	A6	24
Amherst, MA	B2	24
Amherst, NH	E3	32
Amherst, NY	C2	35
Amherst, OH	A3	38
Amherstdale, WV	n12	51
Amite, LA	D5	21
Amite, r., LA	D5	21
Amityville, NY	E7	35
Ammon, ID	F7	15
Ammonoosuc, r., NH	B3	32
Amory, MS	B5	27
Amsterdam, NY	C6	35
Anaconda, MT	D4	29
Anaconda Range, MT	E3	29
Anacortes, WA	A3	50
Anacostia, r., US	C4	23
Anadarko, OK	B3	39
Anaheim, CA	F5	8
Anamosa, IA	B6	18
Anchorage, AK	C10	5
Anchorage, KY	g11	20
Anchor Point, AK	D9	5
Andalusia, AL	D3	4
Anderson, AK	C10	5
Anderson, IN	D6	17
Anderson, MO	E3	28
Anderson, SC	B2	43
Anderson Ranch Reservoir, ID	F3	15
Andover, KS	g12	19
Andover, MA	A5	24
Andover, MN	m12	26
Andreanof Islands, AK	E4	5
Andrews, NC	f9	36
Andrews, SC	E8	43
Andrews, TX	C1	46
Andrews Air Force Base, MD	C4	23
Androscoggin, r., ME	D2	22
Angle Inlet, MN	A3	26
Angleton, TX	E5	46
Angola, IN	A8	17
Animas, r., US	D3	9
Ankeny, IA	C4	18
Ann, Cape, MA	A6	24
Anna, IL	F4	16
Anna, Lake, VA	B5	49
Annandale, VA	g12	49
Annapolis, MD	C5	23
Ann Arbor, MI	F7	25
Anniston, AL	B4	4
Annville, PA	F8	41
Anoka, MN	E5	26
Anson, ME	D3	22
Ansonia, CT	D3	10
Ansted, WV	C3	51
Antelope Island, UT	B3	47
Antelope Peak, NV	B7	31
Anthony, KS	E5	19
Anthony, NM	F3	34
Anthony, RI	D3	42
Antietam National Battlefield, MD	B2	23
Antigo, WI	C4	52
Antioch, CA	h9	8
Antioch, IL	A5	16
Antlers, OK	C6	39
Antrim, NH	D3	32
Apache Junction, AZ	m9	6
Apalachee Bay, FL	B2	12
Apalachicola, r., FL	B1	12
Apalachicola Bay, FL	C2	12
Apex, NC	B4	36
Apopka, FL	D5	12
Apopka, Lake, FL	D5	12
Apostle Islands, WI	A3	52
Apostle Islands National Lakeshore, WI	A3	52
Appalachian Mountains, NA	C11	2
Apple, r., WI	C1	52
Apple Orchard Mountain, VA	C3	49
Appleton, MN	E2	26
Appleton, WI	D5	52
Apple Valley, CA	E5	8
Apple Valley, MN	n12	26
Appomattox, r., VA	C4	49
Appomattox Court House National Historical Park, VA	C4	49
Arab, AL	A3	4
Arabi, LA	k11	21
Aransas Bay, TX	E4	46
Arapahoe, NE	D6	30
Arbuckle Mountains, OK	C4	39
Arcadia, CA	m12	8
Arcadia, IN	D5	17
Arc Dome, NV	E4	31
Archbald, PA	m18	41
Archdale, NC	B3	36
Arches National Park, UT	E6	47
Arco, ID	F5	15
Ardmore, IN	A5	17
Ardmore, OK	C4	39
Ardmore, PA	F11	41
Arena, Point, CA	C2	8
Argos, IN	B5	17
Arizona, state, US	C4	6
Arkadelphia, AR	C2	7
Arkansas, state, US	C3	7
Arkansas, r., US	C9	2
Arkansas City, AR	D4	7
Arkansas City, KS	E6	19
Arkoma, OK	B7	39
Arlington, MA	B5	24
Arlington, NE	C9	30
Arlington, NY	D7	35
Arlington, SD	C8	44
Arlington, TX	n9	46
Arlington, VT	E2	48
Arlington, VA	B5	49
Arlington, WA	A3	50
Arlington Heights, IL	A5	16
Arma, KS	E9	19
Armijo, NM	k7	34
Armour, SD	D7	44
Arnold, MD	B5	23
Arnold, MO	C7	28
Arnold, NE	C5	30
Arnold, PA	h14	41
Artesia, NM	E5	34
Arthur, Lake, PA	E1	41
Arvada, CO	B5	9
Arvon, Mount, MI	B2	25
Asbury Park, NJ	C4	33
Ashburn, GA	E3	13
Ashdown, AR	D1	7
Asheboro, NC	B3	36
Asheville, NC	f10	36
Ashford, AL	D4	4
Ashland, AL	B4	4
Ashland, KY	B7	20
Ashland, NE	C9	30
Ashland, NH	C3	32
Ashland, OH	B3	38
Ashland, OR	E4	40
Ashland, VA	C5	49
Ashland, WI	B3	52
Ashland City, TN	A4	45
Ashley, ND	C6	37
Ashokan Reservoir, NY	D6	35
Ashtabula, OH	A5	38
Ashton, ID	E7	15
Ashuelot, r., NH	E2	32
Ashwaubenon, WI	D5	52
Aspen, CO	B4	9
Aspen Butte, OR	E4	40
Aspen Hill, MD	B3	23
Assateague Island, US	D7	23
Assateague Island National Seashore, US	D7	23
Astoria, OR	A3	40
Atchafalaya, r., LA	D4	21
Atchafalaya Bay, LA	E4	21
Atchison, KS	C8	19
Athens, AL	A3	4
Athens, GA	C3	13
Athens, OH	C3	38
Athens, TN	D9	45
Athens, TX	C5	46
Athol, MA	A3	24
Atkins, AR	B3	7
Atkinson, NE	B7	30
Atkinson, NH	E4	32
Atlanta, GA	C2	13
Atlantic, IA	C2	18
Atlantic Beach, FL	m9	12
Atlantic City, NJ	E4	33
Atlantic Peak, WY	D3	53
Atmore, AL	D2	4
Atoka, OK	C5	39
Attalla, AL	A3	4
Attica, IN	D3	17
Attleboro, MA	C5	24
Attu Island, AK	E2	5
Atwood, KS	C2	19
Auau Channel, HI	C5	14
Auburn, AL	C4	4
Auburn, GA	B3	13
Auburn, IL	D4	16
Auburn, IN	B7	17
Auburn, ME	D2	22
Auburn, MA	B4	24
Auburn, NE	D10	30
Auburn, NY	C4	35
Auburn, WA	B3	50
Auburn Heights, MI	F7	25
Audubon, IA	C3	18
Auglaize, r., OH	A1	38
Augusta, AR	B4	7
Augusta, GA	C5	13
Augusta, KS	E7	19
Augusta, ME	D3	22
Augusta, MT	C4	29
Ault, CO	A6	9
Aurora, CO	B6	9
Aurora, IL	B5	16
Aurora, IN	F8	17
Aurora, MN	C6	26
Aurora, MO	E4	28
Aurora, NE	D7	30
Aurora, OH	A4	38
Au Sable, r., MI	D6	25
Ausable, r., NY	f11	35
Au Sable Point, MI	D7	25
Austell, GA	h7	13
Austin, IN	G6	17
Austin, MN	G6	26
Austin, NV	D4	31
Austin, TX	D4	46
Austintown, OH	A5	38
Ava, MO	E5	28
Avalon, PA	h13	41
Avenel, NJ	k7	33
Avilla, IN	B7	17
Avoca, IA	C2	18
Avon, CT	B4	10
Avon, OH	A3	38
Avon, SD	E7	44
Avondale, AZ	D3	6
Avondale Estates, GA	h8	13
Avon Lake, OH	A3	38
Ayden, NC	B5	36
Azle, TX	n9	46
Aztec, NM	A2	34

B

Name	Map Ref.	Page
Babbitt, NV	E3	31
Baboquivari Mountains, AZ	F4	6
Baboquivari Peak, AZ	F4	6
Babylon, NY	n15	35
Backbone Mountain, US	m12	23
Bad, r., SD	C5	44
Bad Axe, MI	E8	25
Baden, PA	E1	41
Badlands, SD	D3	44
Badlands National Park, SD	D3	44
Bagley, MN	C3	26
Baileys Crossroads, VA	g12	49
Bainbridge, GA	F2	13
Bainbridge Island, WA	e10	50
Baker, LA	D4	21
Baker, MT	D12	29
Baker, OR	C9	40
Baker, Mount, WA	A4	50
Baker Mountain, ME	C3	22
Bakersfield, CA	E4	8
Bald Knob, AR	B4	7
Bald Knob, VA	c3	49
Bald Knob, WV	C5	51
Baldwin, PA	k14	41
Baldwin City, KS	D8	19
Baldwinsville, NY	B4	35
Baldwyn, MS	A5	27
Baldy Peak, AZ	D6	6
Ball, LA	C3	21
Ballwin, MO	f12	28
Baltimore, MD	B4	23
Baltimore Highlands, MD	h11	23
Bamberg, SC	E5	43
Banana River, FL	D6	12
Bangor, ME	D4	22
Bangor, PA	E11	41
Bangor Township, MI	E7	25
Bankhead Lake, AL	B2	4
Banks Lake, WA	B6	50
Bannock Peak, ID	F6	15
Baraboo, WI	E4	52
Baranof Island, AK	m22	5
Barataria Bay, LA	E6	21
Barbers Point, HI	B3	14
Barberton, OH	A4	38
Barboursville, WV	C2	51
Barbourville, KY	D6	20
Bardstown, KY	C4	20
Bargersville, IN	E5	17
Bar Harbor, ME	D4	22
Barkley, Lake, US	f10	20
Barling, AR	B1	7
Barnegat Bay, NJ	D4	33
Barnesville, GA	C2	13
Barnesville, MN	D2	26
Barnstable, MA	C7	24
Bar Nunn, WY	D6	53
Barnwell, SC	E5	43
Barques, Pointe aux, MI	D8	25
Barrackville, WV	B4	51
Barre, VT	C4	48
Barren, r., KY	C3	20
Barren River Lake, KY	D3	20
Barrington, IL	A5	16
Barrington, RI	D5	42
Barron, WI	C2	52
Barrow, AK	A8	5
Barrow, Point, AK	A8	5
Barstow, CA	E5	8
Bartlesville, OK	A6	39
Bartlett, NH	B4	32
Bartlett, TN	B2	45
Barton, VT	B4	48
Bartonville, IL	C4	16
Bartow, FL	E5	12
Basalt, CO	B3	9
Basehor, KS	k16	19
Basin, WY	B4	53
Bass Harbor, ME	D4	22
Bass Islands, OH	A3	38
Bass Lake, IN	B4	17
Basswood Lake, MN	B7	26
Bastrop, LA	B4	21
Batavia, IL	B5	16
Batavia, NY	C2	35
Batesburg, SC	D4	43
Batesville, AR	B4	7
Batesville, IN	F7	17
Batesville, MS	A4	27
Bath, ME	E3	22
Baton Rouge, LA	D4	21
Battle Creek, MI	F5	25
Battle Creek, NE	C8	30
Battle Ground, WA	D3	50
Battle Lake, MN	D3	26
Battle Mountain, NV	C5	31
Baxley, GA	E4	13
Baxter, MN	D4	26
Baxter Springs, KS	E9	19
Bay, AR	B5	7
Bayard, NE	C2	30
Bayard, NM	E1	34
Bay City, MI	E7	25
Bay City, TX	E5	46
Bayfield, CO	D3	9
Bay Minette, AL	E2	4
Bayonne, NJ	B4	33
Bayou Cane, LA	E5	21
Bayou D'Arbonne Lake, LA	B3	21
Bayou La Batre, AL	E1	4
Bayport, MN	E6	26
Bay Saint Louis, MS	E4	27
Bay Shore, NY	E7	35
Bayshore Gardens, FL	q10	12
Bayside, WI	m12	52
Bays Mountain, TN	C10	45
Bay Springs, MS	D4	27
Baytown, TX	E5	46
Bay Village, OH	h9	38
Beach, IL	h9	16
Beach, ND	C1	37
Beacon, NY	D7	35
Beals, ME	D5	22
Bearden, AR	D3	7
Beardstown, IL	C3	16
Bear Lake, US	A4	47
Bear Mountain, AR	f7	7
Beartooth Pass, WY	B3	53
Beartooth Range, US	E7	29
Beatrice, NE	D9	30
Beatty, NV	G5	31
Beaufort, NC	C6	36
Beaufort, SC	G6	43
Beaumont, TX	D5	46
Beaver, OK	A1	39
Beaver, PA	E1	41
Beaver, WV	D3	51
Beaver, r., US	A2	39
Beavercreek, OH	C1	38
Beaver Dam, KY	C3	20
Beaver Dam, WI	E5	52
Beaverdam Lake, WI	E5	52
Beaver Falls, PA	E1	41
Beaverhead, r., MT	E4	29
Beaverhead Mountains, US	D5	15
Beaver Island, MI	C5	25
Beaver Lake, AR	A2	7
Beavertail Point, RI	F4	42
Beaverton, OR	B4	40
Beckley, WV	D3	51
Bedford, IN	G5	17
Bedford, IA	D3	18
Bedford, MA	B5	24
Bedford, NH	E3	32
Bedford, OH	A4	38
Bedford, VA	C3	49
Beebe, AR	B4	7
Beech Grove, IN	E5	17
Beeville, TX	E4	46
Bel Air, MD	A5	23
Belen, NM	C3	34
Belfast, ME	D3	22
Belfield, ND	C2	37
Belgrade, MT	E5	29
Belington, WV	B5	51
Belknap Crater, OR	C5	40
Bellaire, KS	g12	19
Bellaire, OH	C5	38
Bellaire, TX	r14	46
Bella Vista, AR	A1	7
Bellbrook, OH	C1	38
Belle, WV	C3	51
Belle Chasse, LA	E5	21
Bellefontaine, OH	B2	38
Bellefonte, PA	E6	41
Belle Fourche, SD	C2	44
Belle Fourche, r., US	C3	44
Belle Glade, FL	F6	12
Belle Meade, TN	g10	45
Belle Plaine, IA	C5	18
Belle Plaine, KS	E6	19
Belle Plaine, MN	F5	26
Belle View, VA	g12	49
Belleville, IL	E4	16
Belleville, KS	C6	19
Belleville, NJ	B4	33
Bellevue, ID	F4	15
Bellevue, IA	B7	18
Bellevue, KY	h13	20
Bellevue, NE	C10	30
Bellevue, OH	A3	38
Bellevue, PA	F1	41
Bellevue, WA	e11	50
Bellflower, CA	n12	8
Bellingham, WA	A3	50
Bellmawr, NJ	D2	33
Bellows Falls, VT	E4	48
Bellwood, IL	k9	16
Bellwood, VA	n18	49
Belmond, IA	B4	18
Belmont, CA	h8	8
Belmont, MA	g11	24
Belmont, MS	A5	27
Belmont, NH	D4	32
Belmont, NC	B1	36
Beloit, KS	C5	19
Beloit, WI	F4	52
Belpre, OH	C4	38
Belton, MO	C3	28
Belton, SC	B3	43
Belton, TX	D4	46
Belton Lake, TX	D4	46
Beltsville, MD	B4	23
Belvedere, SC	D4	43
Belvidere, IL	A5	16
Belzoni, MS	B3	27
Bemidji, MN	C4	26
Benbrook, TX	n9	46
Bend, OR	C5	40
Benicia, CA	C2	8
Benkelman, NE	D4	30
Bennett, CO	B6	9
Bennettsville, SC	B8	43
Bennington, NH	D3	32
Bennington, VT	F2	48
Bensenville, IL	B6	16
Bensley, VA	C5	49
Benson, AZ	F5	6
Benson, MN	E3	26
Benton, AR	C3	7
Benton, IL	E5	16
Benton, KY	f9	20
Benton, TN	B7	45
Benton Harbor, MI	F4	25
Bentonville, AR	A1	7
Benwood, WV	f8	51
Berea, KY	C5	20
Berea, OH	A4	38
Berea, SC	B3	43
Beresford, SD	D9	44
Bergenfield, NJ	B4	33
Berkeley, CA	D2	8
Berkeley, MO	f13	28
Berkeley Heights, NJ	B4	33
Berkley, MI	F7	25

Name | Map Ref. | Page

Berkshire Hills, MA B1 24
Berlin, NH B4 32
Berlin, PA G4 41
Berlin, WI E5 52
Berlin Lake, OH A4 38
Bernalillo, NM B3 34
Berne, IN C8 17
Bernie, MO E8 28
Berryessa, Lake, CA C2 8
Berrys Chapel, TN B5 45
Berryville, AR A2 7
Berryville, VA A5 49
Berthoud, CO A5 9
Berthoud Pass, CO B5 9
Berwick, LA E4 21
Berwick, ME E2 22
Berwick, PA D9 41
Berwyn, IL k9 16
Berwyn, PA o20 41
Bessemer, AL B3 4
Bessemer, MI n11 25
Bessemer City, NC B1 36
Bethalto, IL E3 16
Bethany, MO A3 28
Bethany, OK B4 39
Bethany, WV A4 51
Bethel, AK C7 5
Bethel, CT D2 10
Bethel, VT D3 48
Bethel Acres, OK B5 39
Bethel Park, PA k14 41
Bethesda, MD C3 23
Bethlehem, NH B3 32
Bethlehem, PA E11 41
Bettendorf, IA C7 18
Beulah, ND B4 37
B. Everett Jordan Lake, NC B3 36
Beverly, MA A6 24
Beverly Hills, CA m12 8
Bexley, OH m11 38
Bickle Knob, WV C5 51
Bicknell, IN G3 17
Biddeford, ME E2 22
Big Bay De Noc, MI C4 25
Big Belt Mountains, MT D5 29
Big Bend National Park, TX E1 46
Big Black, r., ME B3 22
Big Black, r., MS C3 27
Big Butt, TN C11 45
Big Costilla Peak, NM A4 34
Big Cypress Swamp, FL F5 12
Big Eau Pleine, r., WI D3 52
Bigelow, Mount, ME C2 22
Bigfork, MT B2 29
Big Fork, r., MN B5 26
Bighorn, r., US B6 2
Bighorn Lake, US E8 29
Bighorn Mountains, US B5 53
Big Lake, MN E5 26
Big Lake, ME C5 22
Big Lost, r., ID F5 15
Big Muddy, r., IL F4 16
Big Nemaha, r., NE D10 30
Big Piney, WY D2 53
Big Rapids, MI E5 25
Big Sable Point, MI D4 25
Big Sandy, MT B6 29
Big Sandy, r., US C2 51
Big Sandy, r., AZ C2 6
Big Sandy, r., TN B3 45
Big Sandy, r., WY D3 53
Big Sandy Creek, r., CO C8 9
Big Sioux, r., US E9 44
Big Spring, TX C2 46
Big Spruce Knob, WV C4 51
Big Stone Gap, VA f9 49
Big Stone Lake, US E2 26
Big Sunflower, r., MS B3 27
Big Sur, CA D3 8
Big Thompson, r., CO A5 9
Big Timber, MT E7 29
Big Wood, r., ID F4 15
Bijou Creek, r., CO B6 9
Billerica, MA A5 24
Billings, MT E8 29
Biloxi, MS E5 27
Binghamton, NY C5 35
Birdsboro, PA F10 41
Birmingham, AL B3 4
Birmingham, MI F7 25
Bisbee, AZ F6 6
Biscayne, Key, FL s13 12
Biscayne Bay, FL G6 12
Biscayne National Monument, FL G6 12
Bishopville, SC C7 43
Bismarck, ND C5 37
Bistineau, Lake, LA B2 21
Bitter Creek, r., WY E4 53
Bitterroot, r., MT D2 29
Bitterroot Range, US B3 15
Bixby, OK B6 39
Black, r., AZ D5 6
Black, r., AR B4 7
Black, r., LA C4 21
Black, r., MI E8 25
Black, r., SC D8 43
Black, Bayou, r., LA E5 21
Blackburn, Mount, AK C11 5
Black Butte, MT F5 29
Black Canyon, CO C3 9
Black Canyon City, AZ C3 6
Black Canyon of the Gunnison National Monument, CO C3 9
Black Creek, r., SC B7 43
Blackduck, MN C4 26
Blackfoot, ID F6 15
Black Forest, CO C6 9
Black Hawk, SD C2 44
Black Hills, US C2 44
Black Lake, NY f9 35
Black Mesa, OK e8 39
Black Mountain, NC f10 36
Black Mountain, US D7 20
Black Mountain, MT D4 29
Black Mountains, AZ B1 6
Black River Falls, WI D3 52
Blacksburg, VA C2 49
Blacks Fork, r., US E3 53
Blackshear, GA E4 13
Blackstone, VA C5 49
Blackstone, r., RI B4 42
Black Warrior, r., AL C2 4
Blackwater, r., VA D6 49
Blackwell, OK A4 39
Bladensburg, MD f9 23
Blaine, MN m12 26
Blaine, WA A3 50
Blair, NE C9 30
Blakely, GA E2 13
Blakely, PA m18 41
Blake Point, MI h10 25
Blanca, Sierra, TX o12 46
Blanca Peak, CO D5 9
Blanco, Cape, OR E2 40
Blanding, UT F6 47
Blende, CO C6 9
Blennerhassett, WV B3 51
Block Island, RI h7 42
Block Island Sound, US G2 42
Bloodsworth Island, MD D5 23
Bloomer, WI C2 52
Bloomfield, CT B5 10
Bloomfield, IN F4 17
Bloomfield, IA D5 18
Bloomfield, NE B8 30
Bloomfield, NJ h8 33
Bloomfield, NM A2 34
Bloomfield Hills, MI o15 25
Bloomingdale, GA D5 13
Bloomingdale, IL k8 16
Bloomingdale, TN C11 45
Blooming Prairie, MN G5 26
Bloomington, IL C4 16
Bloomington, IN F4 17
Bloomington, MN F5 26
Bloomsburg, PA E9 41
Blountsville, AL A3 4
Blountville, TN C11 45
Blue Ash, OH o13 38
Blue Earth, MN G4 26
Blue Earth, r., MN G4 26
Bluefield, VA C1 49
Bluefield, WV D3 51
Blue Hills, CT B5 10
Blue Island, IL B6 16
Blue Mountain, NY B6 35
Blue Mountain, PA F6 41
Blue Mountains, US A4 2
Blue Ridge, US C11 2
Blue Springs, MO h11 28
Bluestone Lake, US D4 51
Bluewell, WV D3 51
Bluff Park, AL g7 4
Bluffton, IN C7 17
Blytheville, AR B6 7
Boardman, OH A5 38
Boaz, AL A3 4
Boca Chica Key, FL H5 12
Boca Raton, FL F6 12
Boeuf, r., LA C4 21
Boeuf, Bayou, r., LA D3 21
Bogalusa, LA D6 21
Bogue Chitto, r., US D5 21
Bois Blanc Island, MI C6 25
Boise, ID F2 15
Boise City, OK e8 39
Bolingbrook, IL k8 16
Bolivar, MO D4 28
Bolivar, TN B3 45
Bolivar, WV B7 51
Bomoseen, Lake, VT D2 48
Bon Air, VA C5 49
Bonanza Peak, WA A5 50
Bondurant, IA C4 18
Bonita Springs, FL F5 12
Bonners Ferry, ID A2 15
Bonner Springs, KS C9 19
Bonnet Carre Floodway, LA h11 21
Bonne Terre, MO D7 28
Bonneville Peak, ID F6 15
Bonneville Salt Flats, UT C2 47
Bonney Lake, WA B3 50
Bono, AR B5 7
Bon Secour, AL E2 4
Boomer, WV C3 51
Boone, IA B4 18
Boone, NC A1 36
Boone, r., IA B4 18
Booneville, AR B2 7
Booneville, MS A5 27
Boonville, IN H3 17
Boonville, MO C5 28
Boothbay, ME E3 22
Boothbay Harbor, ME E3 22
Borah Peak, ID E5 15
Borger, TX B2 46
Borgne, Lake, LA D6 21
Boscobel, WI E3 52
Bosque Farms, NM C3 34
Bossier City, LA B2 21
Boston, MA B5 24
Boston Bay, MA B6 24
Boston Mountains, AR B2 7
Bothell, WA B3 50
Bottineau, ND A5 37
Boulder, CO A5 9
Boulder City, NV H7 31
Boundary Bald Mountain, ME C2 22
Boundary Bay, WA A3 50
Boundary Peak, NV F3 31
Bountiful, UT C4 47
Bourbon, IN B5 17
Bourbonnais, IL B6 16
Bow, NH D3 32
Bowdon, GA C1 13
Bowie, MD C4 23
Bowling Green, KY D3 20
Bowling Green, MO B6 28
Bowling Green, OH A2 38
Bowman, ND C2 37
Bowman-Haley Lake, ND C2 37
Box Elder, SD C2 44
Box Elder Creek, r., CO A6 9
Boyer, r., IA C2 18
Boynton Beach, FL F6 12
Boysen Reservoir, WY C4 53
Boys Town, NE g12 30
Bozeman, MT E5 29
Brackenridge, PA h15 41
Braddock, PA k14 41
Braddock Heights, MD B2 23
Bradenton, FL E4 12
Bradford, PA C4 41
Bradford, VT D4 48
Bradley, IL B6 16
Bradley, WV D3 51
Braidwood, IL B5 16
Brainerd, MN D4 26
Braintree, MA B5 24
Brandenburg, KY C3 20
Brandon, FL E4 12
Brandon, MS C4 27
Brandon, SD D9 44
Brandon, VT D2 48
Branford, CT D4 10
Branford Hills, CT D4 10
Branson, MO E4 28
Brasstown Bald, GA B3 13
Brattleboro, VT F3 48
Brawley Peaks, NV E3 31
Brazil, IN E3 17
Brazos, r., TX D4 46
Brea, CA n13 8
Bread Loaf Mountain, VT D3 48
Breaux Bridge, LA D4 21
Breckenridge, CO B4 9
Breckenridge, MN D2 26
Brecksville, OH A4 38
Breese, IL E4 16
Bremen, GA C1 13
Bremen, IN B5 17
Bremerton, WA B3 50
Brenham, TX D4 46
Brent, FL u14 12
Brenton Point, RI F5 42
Brentwood, MO f13 28
Brentwood, NY E7 35
Brentwood, PA k14 41
Brentwood, TN A5 45
Breton Islands, LA E6 21
Breton Sound, LA E6 21
Brevard, NC f10 36
Brewer, ME D4 22
Brewster Islands, MA g12 24
Brewton, AL D2 4
Brick [Township], NJ C4 33
Bridgeport, AL A4 4
Bridgeport, CT E3 10
Bridgeport, MI E7 25
Bridgeport, NE C2 30
Bridgeport, PA o20 41
Bridgeport, WV B4 51
Bridgeton, MO C7 28
Bridgeton, NJ E2 33
Bridgeville, PA k13 41
Bridgewater, VA B4 49
Bridgton, ME D2 22
Briery Knob, WV C4 51
Brigantine, NJ E4 33
Brigham City, UT B3 47
Brighton, AL B3 4
Brighton, CO B6 9
Brighton, MI F7 25
Brighton, NY B3 35
Brillion, WI D5 52
Brinkley, AR C4 7
Bristol, CT C4 10
Bristol, NH C3 32
Bristol, RI D5 42
Bristol, TN C11 45
Bristol, VT C2 48
Bristol, VA f9 49
Bristol Bay, AK D7 5
Bristol [Township], PA F12 41
Bristow, OK B5 39
Britt, IA A4 18
Britton, SD B8 44
Broad, r., SC C5 43
Broadview Heights, OH h9 38
Brockport, NY B3 35
Brockton, MA B5 24
Brodhead, WI F4 52
Broken Arrow, OK A6 39
Broken Bow, NE C6 30
Broken Bow, OK C7 39
Broken Bow Lake, OK C7 39
Brookfield, IL k9 16
Brookfield, MA B3 24
Brookfield, MO B4 28
Brookfield, WI m11 52
Brookhaven, MS D3 27
Brookhaven, WV h11 51
Brookings, OR E2 40
Brookings, SD C9 44
Brookline, MA B5 24
Brooklyn, IA C5 18
Brooklyn, OH h9 38
Brooklyn Center, MN E5 26
Brooklyn Park, MD h11 23
Brooklyn Park, MN m12 26
Brook Park, OH h9 38
Brooks, KY g11 20
Brookside, AL f7 4
Brookside, DE B3 11
Brooks Range, AK B9 5
Brookston, IN C4 17
Brookville, IN F8 17
Brookville Lake, IN E7 17
Broomall, PA p20 41
Broomfield, CO B5 9
Browerville, MN D4 26
Brown Deer, WI m12 52
Brownfield, TX C1 46
Browning, MT B3 29
Brownlee Reservoir, US C10 40
Brownsburg, IN E5 17
Browns Mills, NJ D3 33
Brownstown, IN G5 17
Brownsville, FL s13 12
Brownsville, TN B2 45
Brownsville, TX G4 46
Brownville Junction, ME C3 22
Brownwood, TX D3 46
Bruce, MS B4 27
Brundidge, AL D4 4
Bruneau, r., US G3 15
Brunswick, GA E5 13
Brunswick, ME E3 22
Brunswick, MD B2 23
Brunswick, OH A4 38
Brush, CO A7 9
Bryan, OH A1 38
Bryan, TX D4 46
Bryant, AR C3 7
Bryant Pond, ME D2 22
Bryce Canyon National Park, UT F3 47
Buchanan, MI G4 25
Buckatunna, MS D5 27
Buckeye, AZ D3 6
Buckfield, ME D2 22
Buckhannon, WV C4 51
Buckley, WA B3 50
Buck Mountain, VA D1 49
Buckner, MO h11 28
Bucksport, ME D4 22
Bucyrus, OH B3 38
Buena Park, CA n12 8
Buena Vista, CO C4 9
Buena Vista, VA C3 49
Buffalo, MN E5 26
Buffalo, MO D4 28
Buffalo, NY C2 35
Buffalo, SD B2 44
Buffalo, WV C3 51
Buffalo, WY B6 53
Buffalo, r., AR B3 7
Buffalo, r., TN B4 45
Buffalo, r., WI D2 52
Buffalo Bill Reservoir, WY B3 53
Buffalo Grove, IL h9 16
Buford, GA B2 13
Buhl, ID G4 15
Buhler, KS D6 19
Bullhead City, AZ B1 6
Bull Run, r., VA g11 49
Bulls Bay, SC F8 43
Bull Shoals, AR A3 7
Bull Shoals Lake, US A3 7
Bunker Hill, NV D4 31
Bunkie, LA D3 21
Burbank, CA E4 8
Burbank, IL k9 16
Burkburnett, TX B3 46
Burke, SD D6 44
Burkesville, KY D4 20
Burleson, TX n9 46
Burley, ID G5 15
Burlington, CO B8 9
Burlington, IA D6 18
Burlington, KS D8 19
Burlington, KY A5 20
Burlington, MA f11 24
Burlington, NC A3 36
Burlington, ND A4 37
Burlington, VT C2 48
Burlington, WA A3 50
Burlington, WI F5 52
Burns, OR D7 40
Burnsville, MN F5 26
Burnt Mills, Lake, VA k14 49
Burt Lake, MI C6 25
Burton, MI F7 25
Burwell, NE C6 30
Bushnell, IL C3 16
Butler, AL C1 4
Butler, IN B8 17
Butler, MO C3 28
Butler, PA E2 41
Butner, NC A4 36
Butte, MT E4 29
Butte des Morts, Lake, WI D5 52
Buzzards Bay, MA C6 24
Buzzards Bay, MA C6 24
Byron, GA D3 13
Byron, MN F6 26
Byron, WY B4 53

C

Cabin Creek, WV m13 51
Cabinet Gorge Reservoir, US B1 29
Cabinet Mountains, MT B1 29
Cabool, MO D5 28
Cabot, AR C3 7
Cacapon, r., WV B6 51
Cache, OK C3 39
Cache, r., AR C4 7
Cache la Poudre, r., CO A5 9
Cache Peak, ID G5 15
Caddo, r., AR C2 7
Caddo Mountains, AR C2 7
Caddo Valley, AR C2 7
Cadillac, MI D5 25
Cadiz, KY D2 20
Caesar Creek Lake, OH C2 38
Cahaba, r., AL C2 4
Cahokia, IL E3 16
Cairo, GA F2 13
Cairo, IL F4 16
Calais, ME C5 22
Calcasieu, r., LA D2 21
Calcasieu Lake, LA E2 21
Calcasieu Pass, LA E2 21
Caldwell, ID F2 15
Caldwell, KS E6 19
Caledonia, MN G7 26
Calera, AL B3 4
Calera, OK D5 39
Calhoun, GA B2 13
Calhoun City, MS B4 27
Calhoun Falls, SC C2 43
Caliente, NV F7 31
California, MD D4 23
California, MO C5 28
California, PA F2 41
California, state, US D4 8
California Aqueduct, CA E4 8
Caloosahatchee, r., FL F5 12
Calumet, Lake, IL k9 16
Calumet City, IL B6 16
Calvert City, KY e9 20
Camanche, IA C7 18
Camano Island, WA A3 50
Camarillo, CA E4 8
Camas, WA D3 50
Cambridge, MD C5 23
Cambridge, MA B5 24
Cambridge, MN E5 26
Cambridge, NE D5 30
Cambridge, OH B4 38
Cambridge City, IN E7 17
Camden, AL D2 4
Camden, AR D3 7
Camden, DE D3 11
Camden, ME D3 22
Camden, NJ D2 33
Camden, SC C6 43
Camden, TN A3 45
Camdenton, MO D5 28
Camelback Mountain, AZ k9 6
Camels Hump, VT C3 48
Cameron, LA E2 21
Cameron, MO B3 28
Cameron, WV B4 51
Camilla, GA E2 13
Campbell, MO E7 28
Campbell, OH A5 38
Campbell Hill, OH B2 38
Campbellsville, KY C4 20
Camp Hill, AL C4 4
Camp Hill, PA F8 41
Camp Lejeune Marine Corps Base, NC C5 36
Camp Springs, MD f9 23
Campton, NH C3 32
Camp Verde, AZ C4 6
Canaan, NH C2 32
Canadian, r., US C7 2
Canandaigua, NY C3 35
Canandaigua Lake, NY C3 35
Canaveral, Cape, FL D6 12
Canaveral National Seashore, FL D6 12
Canby, MN F2 26
Canby, OR B4 40
Candlewood, Lake, CT D1 10
Cando, ND A6 37
Cane, r., LA C2 21
Caney, KS E8 19
Caney Fork, r., TN C8 45
Canisteo, r., NY C3 35
Cannelton, IN I4 17
Cannon, r., MN F5 26
Cannonball, r., ND C5 37
Cannon Falls, MN F6 26
Cannonsville Reservoir, NY C5 35
Canon City, CO C5 9
Canonsburg, PA F1 41
Canton, GA B2 13
Canton, IL C3 16
Canton, ME D2 22
Canton, MA B5 24
Canton, MS C3 27
Canton, MO A6 28
Canton, NC f10 36
Canton, OH B4 38
Canton, SD D9 44
Canyon, TX B2 46
Canyon de Chelly National Monument, AZ A6 6
Canyon Ferry Lake, MT D5 29
Canyon Lake, TX E3 46
Canyonlands National Park, UT E6 47
Cape Cod Bay, MA C7 24
Cape Cod Canal, MA C6 24
Cape Cod National Seashore, MA C7 24
Cape Coral, FL F5 12
Cape Elizabeth, ME E2 22
Cape Fear, r., NC C4 36
Cape Girardeau, MO D8 28
Cape Hatteras National Seashore, NC B7 36
Cape Lookout National Seashore, NC C6 36
Cape Porpoise, ME E2 22
Capitan, NM D4 34
Capitan Peak, NM D4 34
Capitol Reef National Park, UT E4 47
Caraway, AR B5 7
Carbondale, CO B3 9
Carbondale, IL F4 16
Carbondale, KS D8 19
Carbondale, PA C10 41
Carencro, LA D3 21
Caribou, ME B5 22
Caribou Mountain, ME C2 22
Carlin, NV C5 31
Carlinville, IL D4 16
Carlisle, AR C4 7
Carlisle, IA C4 18
Carlisle, KY B5 20
Carlisle, PA F7 41
Carl Junction, MO D3 28
Carlsbad, CA F5 8
Carlsbad, NM E5 34
Carlsbad Caverns National Park, NM E5 34
Carlyle, IL E4 16
Carlyle Lake, IL E4 16
Carmel, IN E5 17
Carmi, IL E5 16
Carnegie, PA F1 41
Carney, MD B4 23
Carol City, FL s13 12
Carolina Beach, NC C5 36
Carpentersville, IL A5 16
Carrboro, NC B3 36
Carrington, ND B6 37
Carrington Island, UT C3 47
Carrizozo, NM D4 34
Carroll, IA B3 18
Carrollton, AL B1 4
Carrollton, GA C1 13
Carrollton, KY B4 20
Carrollton, MO B4 28
Carrollton, TX n10 46
Carry Falls Reservoir, NY f10 35
Carson, r., NV D2 31
Carson City, NV D2 31
Carson Sink, NV D3 31
Carter Dome, NH B4 32
Carteret, NJ B4 33
Carter Lake, IA C2 18
Cartersville, GA B2 13
Carterville, IL F4 16
Carterville, MO D3 28
Carthage, MS C4 27
Carthage, MO D3 28
Carthage, TN C8 45
Caruthersville, MO E8 28
Cary, IL A5 16
Cary, NC B4 36
Casa Grande, AZ E4 6
Casas Adobes, AZ E5 6
Cascade, IA B6 18
Cascade Range, NA B3 2
Cascade Reservoir, ID E3 15
Casco, ME D2 22
Casco Bay, ME E3 22
Casey, Mount, ID A2 15
Cashion, AZ m8 6
Cashmere, WA B5 50
Casper, WY D6 53
Casselberry, FL D5 12
Casselton, ND C8 37
Cass Lake, MN C4 26
Cassopolis, MI G4 25
Cassville, MO E4 28
Castle Dome Peak, AZ D1 6
Castle Hills, DE i7 11
Castle Point, MO f13 28
Castle Rock, CO B6 9
Castle Rock Lake, WI E4 52
Castleton, VT D2 48
Castro Valley, CA h8 8
Catahoula Lake, LA C3 21
Catasauqua, PA E11 41
Catawba, r., SC B6 43
Cathedral City, CA F5 8
Catlettsburg, KY B7 20
Catoctin Mountain, US B2 23
Catonsville, MD B4 23
Catoosa, OK A6 39
Catskill, NY C7 35
Catskill Mountains, NY C6 35
Cavalier, ND A8 37
Cave City, AR B4 7
Cave City, KY C4 20
Cave Run Lake, KY B6 20
Cave Spring, VA C2 49
Cayce, SC D5 43
Cayuga Lake, NY C4 35
Cedar, r., US C6 18
Cedar Bluff, AL A4 4
Cedar Breaks National Monument, UT F3 47
Cedarburg, WI E6 52
Cedar City, UT F2 47
Cedar Creek, r., ND C3 37
Cedar Creek Lake, TX C4 46
Cedar Crest, NM k8 34
Cedaredge, CO C3 9
Cedar Falls, IA B5 18
Cedar Grove, NJ B4 33
Cedar Grove, WV C3 51
Cedar Hill, TX n10 46
Cedar Lake, IN B3 17
Cedar Point, OH A3 38
Cedar Rapids, IA C6 18
Cedar Springs, MI E5 25
Cedartown, GA B1 13
Celina, OH B1 38
Center, CO D4 9
Center, ND B4 37
Centereach, NY n15 35
Center Harbor, NH C4 32
Center Hill Lake, TN C8 45
Center Ossipee, NH C4 32
Center Point, AL f7 4
Center Point, IA B6 18
Center Rutland, VT D2 48
Centerville, IN E8 17
Centerville, IA D5 18
Centerville, MA C7 24
Centerville, OH C1 38
Centerville, SD D9 44
Centerville, TN B4 45
Centerville, UT C4 47
Central, NM E1 34
Central City, KY C2 20
Central City, NE C7 30
Central Falls, RI B4 42
Centralia, IL E4 16
Centralia, MO B5 28
Centralia, WA C3 50
Central Islip, NY n15 35
Central Park, WA C2 50
Central Point, OR E4 40
Centre, AL A4 4
Centreville, IL E3 16
Centreville, MS D2 27
Ceredo, WV C2 51
Ceresco, NE C9 30
Chacon, Cape, AK n24 5
Chadron, NE B3 30
Chaffee, MO D8 28
Chagrin Falls, OH A4 38
Chalfonte, DE h7 11
Chalmette, LA E6 21
Chama, NM A3 34
Chama, Rio, r., NM A3 34
Chamberlain, SD D6 44
Chamberlin, Mount, AK B10 5
Chambersburg, PA G6 41
Chambers Island, WI C6 52
Chamblee, GA h8 13
Champaign, IL C5 16
Champlin, MN m12 26
Chandalar, r., AK B10 5
Chandeleur Islands, LA E7 21
Chandeleur Sound, LA E6 21
Chandler, AZ D4 6
Chandler, IN H3 17
Chandler, OK B5 39
Chanhassen, MN n11 26
Channahon, IL B5 16
Channel Islands, CA F4 8
Channelview, TX r14 46
Chantilly, VA g12 49
Chanute, KS E8 19
Chaparral, NM E3 34
Chapel Hill, NC B3 36
Chapman, KS D6 19
Chapmanville, WV D2 51
Chappaquiddick Island, MA D7 24
Chappell, NE C3 30
Chariton, IA C4 18
Chariton, r., US A5 28
Charleroi, PA F2 41
Charles, r., MA B5 24
Charles, Cape, VA C6 49
Charles City, IA A5 18
Charles Mound, IL A3 16
Charleston, AR B1 7
Charleston, IL D5 16
Charleston, MS A3 27
Charleston, MO E8 28
Charleston, SC F8 43
Charleston, WV C3 51
Charleston Peak, NV G6 31
Charlestown, IN H6 17
Charlestown, NH D2 32
Charles Town, WV B7 51
Charlevoix, MI C5 25
Charlotte, MI F6 25
Charlotte, NC B2 36
Charlottesville, VA B4 49
Chase, Mount, ME B4 22
Chaska, MN F5 26
Chatfield, MN G6 26
Chatham, IL D4 16
Chatham Strait, AK m22 5
Chatsworth, GA B2 13
Chattahoochee, r., US E1 13
Chattanooga, TN D8 45
Chattaroy, WV D2 51
Chattooga, r., US B1 43
Chautauqua, NY C1 35
Chautauqua Lake, NY C1 35
Chauvin, LA E5 21
Cheaha Mountain, AL B4 4
Chebeague Island, ME E2 22
Cheboygan, MI C6 25
Checotah, OK B6 39
Cheektowaga, NY C2 35
Chehalis, WA C3 50
Chehalis, r., WA C2 50
Chelan, WA B5 50
Chelan Mountains, WA A5 50
Chelmsford, MA A5 24
Chelsea, AL g7 4
Chelsea, MA B5 24
Chelsea, MI F6 25
Chelsea, VT D4 48
Cheney, KS E6 19
Cheney, WA B8 50
Chenoweth, OR B5 40
Chequamegon Bay, WI B3 52
Cheraw, SC B8 43
Cherokee, AL A2 4
Cherokee, IA B2 18
Cherokee, OK A3 39
Cherokee Lake, TN C10 45
Cherokees, Lake O' The, OK A7 39
Cherokee Village, AR A4 7
Cherry Creek, r., SD C3 44
Cherry Hill, NJ D2 33
Cherryvale, KS E8 19
Cherryville, NC B1 36
Chesapeake, VA D6 49
Chesapeake, WV C3 51
Chesapeake Bay, US C12 2
Chesapeake Bay Bridge-Tunnel, VA D7 49
Cheshire, CT D4 10
Chester, IL F4 16
Chester, MT B6 29
Chester, NH E4 32
Chester, PA G11 41
Chester, SC B5 43
Chester, VT E3 48
Chester, VA C5 49
Chester, WV A4 51
Chester, r., MD B5 23
Chester Depot, VT E3 48
Chesterfield, IN D6 17
Chesterton, IN A3 17
Chetopa, KS E8 19
Cheviot, OH C1 38
Chevy Chase, MD C3 23
Cheyenne, WY E8 53
Cheyenne, r., US C4 44
Cheyenne Wells, CO C8 9
Chicago, IL B6 16
Chicago Heights, IL B6 16
Chicago Sanitary and Ship Canal, IL k8 16
Chickahominy, r., VA C5 49
Chickamauga, GA B1 13
Chickamauga Lake, TN D8 45
Chickasaw, AL E1 4
Chickasawhay, r., MS D5 27
Chickasha, OK B4 39
Chico, CA C3 8
Chicopee, MA B2 24
Childersburg, AL B3 4
Chillicothe, IL C4 16
Chillicothe, MO B4 28
Chillicothe, OH C3 38
Chillum, MD f9 23
Chilton, WI D5 52
Chimayo, NM A4 34
Chimney Rock, NE C2 30
China, ME D3 22
Chinati Peak, TX p12 46
Chincoteague, VA C7 49
Chincoteague Bay, US D7 23
Chinle, AZ A6 6
Chino, CA F5 8
Chinook, MT B7 29
Chinook, Lake, OR C5 40
Chino Valley, AZ C3 6
Chippewa, r., WI D2 52
Chippewa, Lake, WI C2 52
Chippewa Falls, WI D2 52
Chiricahua Peak, AZ F6 6
Chisago City, MN E6 26
Chisholm, MN C6 26
Chisos Mountains, TX E1 46
Chocolate Mountains, US F6 8
Choctaw, OK B4 39
Choctawhatchee Bay, FL u15 12
Choptank, r., MD C6 23
Choteau, MT C4 29
Chowan, r., NC A6 36
Christiansburg, VA C2 49
Christina, r., DE B3 11
Christina Peak, NV D6 31
Chubbuck, ID G6 15
Chula Vista, CA F5 8
Church Hill, TN C11 45
Church Point, LA D3 21
Churubusco, IN B7 17
Cicero, IL B6 16
Cicero, IN D5 17
Cimarron, KS E3 19
Cimarron, r., US C8 2
Cincinnati, OH C1 38
Cinnaminson, NJ D3 33
Circle, MT C11 29

Name	Map Ref.	Page
Circle Pines, MN	m12	26
Circleville, OH	C3	38
Citronelle, AL	D1	4
City of Refuge National Historical Park, HI	D5	14
C.J. Strike Reservoir, ID	G3	15
Clair Engle Lake, CA	B2	8
Clairton, PA	F2	41
Clanton, AL	C3	4
Clare, MI	E6	25
Claremont, NH	D2	32
Claremore, OK	A6	39
Clarence Strait, AK	n23	5
Clarendon, AR	C4	7
Clarendon Hills, IL	k9	16
Clarinda, IA	D2	18
Clarion, IA	B4	18
Clarion, PA	D3	41
Clarion, r., PA	D3	41
Clark, NJ	B4	33
Clark, SD	C8	44
Clark, Lake, AK	C9	5
Clarkdale, AZ	C3	6
Clark Fork, r., US	C1	29
Clarksburg, WV	B4	51
Clarksdale, MS	A3	27
Clarks Summit, PA	m18	41
Clarkston, GA	h8	13
Clarkston, WA	C8	50
Clarksville, AR	B2	7
Clarksville, IN	H6	17
Clarksville, IA	B5	18
Clarksville, TN	A4	45
Clawson, MI	o15	25
Claxton, GA	D5	13
Clay Center, KS	C6	19
Clay Center, NE	D7	30
Claymont, DE	A4	11
Claypool, AZ	D5	6
Clayton, MO	f13	28
Clayton, NM	A6	34
Clayton, NC	B4	36
Clear Boggy Creek, r., OK	C5	39
Cleare, Cape, AK	D10	5
Clearfield, PA	D5	41
Clearfield, UT	B3	47
Clear Lake, IA	A4	18
Clear Lake, SD	C9	44
Clearwater, FL	E4	12
Clearwater, KS	E6	19
Clearwater, SC	E4	43
Clearwater, r., ID	C2	15
Clearwater Mountains, ID	C2	15
Cleburne, TX	C4	46
Clemmons, NC	A2	36
Clemson, SC	B2	43
Clendenin, WV	C3	51
Cleveland, MS	B3	27
Cleveland, OH	A4	38
Cleveland, OK	A5	39
Cleveland, TN	D9	45
Cleveland, Mount, MT	B3	29
Cleveland Heights, OH	A4	38
Cliffside Park, NJ	h9	33
Clifton, AZ	D6	6
Clifton, CO	B2	9
Clifton, NJ	B4	33
Clifton Forge, VA	C3	49
Clinch, r., US	D9	45
Clinch Mountain, US	C10	45
Clingmans Dome, US	D10	45
Clinton, AR	B3	7
Clinton, CT	D5	10
Clinton, IL	C5	16
Clinton, IN	E3	17
Clinton, IA	C7	18
Clinton, KY	f9	20
Clinton, MD	C4	23
Clinton, MS	C3	27
Clinton, MO	C4	28
Clinton, NC	C4	36
Clinton, OK	B3	39
Clinton, SC	C4	43
Clinton, TN	C9	45
Clinton, UT	B3	47
Clinton, Lake, IL	C5	16
Clintonville, WI	D5	52
Clintwood, VA	e9	49
Clio, MI	E7	25
Clive, IA	e8	18
Cloquet, MN	D6	26
Cloud Peak, WY	B5	53
Clover, SC	A5	43
Cloverdale, IN	E4	17
Clovis, CA	D4	8
Clovis, NM	C6	34
Clute, TX	r14	46
Clyde, OH	A3	38
Coal City, IL	B5	16
Coal Fork, WV	C3	51
Coalgate, OK	C5	39
Coaling, AL	B2	4
Coast Ranges, US	B3	2
Coatesville, PA	G10	41
Cobble Mountain Reservoir, MA	B2	24
Cochran, GA	D3	13
Cockeysville, MD	B4	23
Cocoa, FL	D6	12
Cocoa Beach, FL	D6	12
Cod, Cape, MA	C7	24
Coden, AL	E1	4
Cody, WY	B3	53
Coeur d'Alene, ID	B2	15
Coeur d'Alene, r., ID	B2	15
Coeur d'Alene Lake, ID	B2	15
Coeur d'Alene Mountains, ID	B2	15
Coffeyville, KS	E8	19
Cohoes, NY	C7	35
Cokeville, WY	D2	53
Colbert Heights, AL	A2	4
Colby, KS	C2	19
Colchester, CT	C6	10
Cold Spring, KY	A5	20
Cold Spring, MN	E4	26
Coldwater, MI	G5	25
Coldwater, MS	A4	27
Colebrook, NH	g7	32
Colfax, IA	C4	18
Colfax, WA	C8	50
College, AK	B10	5
Collegedale, TN	h11	45
College Park, GA	C2	13
College Park, MD	C4	23
College Place, WA	C7	50
College Station, AR	C3	7
College Station, TX	D4	46
Collegeville, PA	F11	41
Collierville, TN	B2	45
Collingdale, PA	p20	41
Collingswood, NJ	D2	33
Collins, MS	D4	27
Collins Park, DE	B3	11
Collinsville, CT	B4	10
Collinsville, IL	E4	16
Collinsville, OK	A6	39
Colonial Beach, VA	B6	49
Colonial Heights, TN	C11	45
Colonial Heights, VA	C5	49
Colonial National Historical Park, VA	C6	49
Colonie, NY	C7	35
Colorado, state, US	B5	9
Colorado, r., NA	D5	2
Colorado, r., TX	D3	46
Colorado City, AZ	A3	6
Colorado City, CO	D6	9
Colorado Plateau, US	B4	6
Colorado River Aqueduct, CA	F6	8
Colorado Springs, CO	C6	9
Colquitt, GA	E2	13
Colstrip, MT	E10	29
Columbia, IL	E3	16
Columbia, KY	C4	20
Columbia, MD	B4	23
Columbia, MS	D4	27
Columbia, MO	C5	28
Columbia, PA	F9	41
Columbia, SC	C5	43
Columbia, TN	B4	45
Columbia, r., NA	A3	2
Columbia City, IN	B7	17
Columbia Falls, MT	B2	29
Columbia Heights, MN	m12	26
Columbiana, AL	B3	4
Columbus, GA	D2	13
Columbus, IN	F6	17
Columbus, KS	E9	19
Columbus, MS	B5	27
Columbus, MT	E7	29
Columbus, NE	C8	30
Columbus, OH	C2	38
Columbus, WI	E4	52
Columbus Junction, IA	C6	18
Colville, WA	A8	50
Colville, r., AK	B9	5
Colville, r., WA	A8	50
Colvos Passage, WA	f10	50
Combahee, r., SC	F6	43
Commerce, GA	B3	13
Commerce, OK	A7	39
Commerce City, CO	B6	9
Como, MS	A4	27
Compton, CA	n12	8
Conanicut Island, RI	E5	42
Conception, Point, CA	E3	8
Conchas Lake, NM	B5	34
Concord, CA	h8	8
Concord, MA	B5	24
Concord, NH	D3	32
Concord, NC	B2	36
Concord, TN	D9	45
Concordia, KS	C6	19
Concordia, MO	C4	28
Conecuh, r., US	D3	4
Congamond Lakes, US	A4	10
Congaree, r., SC	D6	43
Conneaut, OH	A5	38
Connecticut, state, US	C5	10
Connellsville, PA	F2	41
Connersville, IN	E7	17
Conover, NC	B1	36
Conrad, MT	B5	29
Conroe, TX	D5	46
Conshohocken, PA	F11	41
Contoocook, NH	D3	32
Contoocook, r., NH	D3	32
Conway, AR	B3	7
Conway, FL	D5	12
Conway, NH	C4	32
Conway, SC	D9	43
Conway Springs, KS	E6	19
Conyers, GA	C2	13
Cookes Peak, NM	E2	34
Cookeville, TN	C8	45
Cook Inlet, AK	D9	5
Cook Point, MD	C5	23
Coolidge, AZ	E4	6
Coon Rapids, MN	E5	26
Cooper Mountain, AK	g17	5
Cooperstown, NY	C6	35
Cooperstown, ND	B7	37
Coosa, r., US	C3	4
Coosawhatchie, r., SC	F5	43
Coos Bay, OR	D2	40
Copperas Cove, TX	D4	46
Copper Harbor, MI	A3	25
Coquille, OR	D2	40
Coral Gables, FL	G6	12
Coralville, IA	C6	18
Coralville Lake, IA	C5	18
Coraopolis, PA	E1	41
Corbin, KY	D5	20
Corcoran, MN	m11	26
Cordele, GA	E3	13
Cordell, OK	B3	39
Cordell Hull Lake, TN	C8	45
Cordova, AL	B2	4
Cordova, AK	C10	5
Corea, ME	D5	22
Corinth, MS	A5	27
Cornelia, GA	B3	13
Cornelius, OR	g11	40
Corning, AR	A5	7
Corning, IA	D3	18
Corning, NY	C3	35
Cornish, ME	E2	22
Corona, CA	F5	8
Coronado, CA	F5	8
Corpus Christi, TX	F4	46
Corrales, NM	k7	34
Corry, PA	C2	41
Corsicana, TX	C4	46
Cortez, CO	D2	9
Cortland, NY	C4	35
Cortland, OH	A5	38
Corvallis, OR	C3	40
Corydon, IN	H5	17
Corydon, IA	D4	18
Coshocton, OH	B4	38
Costa Mesa, CA	n13	8
Cottage Grove, MN	n13	26
Cottage Grove, OR	D3	40
Cottleville, MO	f12	28
Cottondale, AL	B2	4
Cotton Plant, AR	B4	7
Cottonwood, AZ	C3	6
Cottonwood, r., KS	D7	19
Coudersport, PA	C5	41
Coulee Dam National Recreation Area, WA	A7	50
Council Bluffs, IA	C2	18
Council Grove, KS	D7	19
Country Homes, WA	B8	50
Courtland, AL	A2	4
Covedale, OH	o12	38
Coventry, CT	B6	10
Coventry, RI	D3	42
Cove Point, MD	D5	23
Covina, CA	m13	8
Covington, GA	C3	13
Covington, IN	D3	17
Covington, KY	A5	20
Covington, LA	D5	21
Covington, TN	B2	45
Covington, VA	C3	49
Cowen, Mount, MT	E6	29
Coweta, OK	B6	39
Cowley, WY	B4	53
Cowlitz, r., WA	C3	50
Cowpasture, r., VA	B3	49
Cozad, NE	D6	30
Crab Orchard, WV	n13	51
Crab Orchard Lake, IL	F4	16
Crafton, PA	k13	41
Craig, CO	A3	9
Craigsville, WV	C4	51
Cranberry Lake, NY	A6	35
Crandon, WI	C5	52
Cranford, NJ	B4	33
Cranston, RI	C4	42
Crater Lake, OR	E4	40
Crater Lake National Park, OR	E4	40
Craters of the Moon National Monument, ID	F5	15
Crawford, NE	B2	30
Crawford Notch State Park, NH	B4	32
Crawfordsville, IN	D4	17
Creighton, NE	B8	30
Creola, AL	E1	4
Cresaptown, MD	k13	23
Crescent Springs, KY	h13	20
Cresco, IA	A5	18
Cresskill, NJ	h9	33
Crest Hill, IL	k8	16
Creston, IA	C3	18
Crestone Peak, CO	D5	9
Crestview, FL	u15	12
Crete, IL	B6	16
Crete, NE	D9	30
Creve Coeur, IL	C4	16
Crisfield, MD	E6	23
Crofton, MD	B4	23
Crofton, NE	B8	30
Croix, Lac la, MN	B6	26
Crooked, r., OR	C6	40
Crooked Lake, MN	B7	26
Crookston, MN	C2	26
Crosby, MN	D5	26
Crosby, ND	A2	37
Crossett, AR	D4	7
Cross Lanes, WV	C3	51
Crossville, AL	A4	4
Crossville, TN	D8	45
Croswell, MI	E8	25
Crothersville, IN	G6	17
Croton-on-Hudson, NY	D7	35
Crow Agency, MT	E9	29
Crowley, LA	D3	21
Crown Point, IN	B3	17
Crownpoint, NM	B1	34
Crows Nest Peak, SD	C2	44
Crow Wing, r., MN	D4	26
Croydon, PA	F12	41
Crystal, MN	m12	26
Crystal Bay, NV	D1	31
Crystal City, MO	C7	28
Crystal City, TX	E3	46
Crystal Falls, MI	B2	25
Crystal Lake, IL	A5	16
Crystal Lake, MI	D4	25
Crystal Springs, MS	D3	27
Cuba, MO	C6	28
Cudahy, WI	F6	52
Culebra Peak, CO	D5	9
Cullman, AL	A3	4
Culloden, WV	C2	51
Culpeper, VA	B4	49
Culver, IN	B5	17
Culver City, CA	m12	8
Cumberland, KY	D7	20
Cumberland, MD	k13	23
Cumberland, r., US	C11	2
Cumberland, Lake, KY	D5	20
Cumberland Foreside, ME	E2	22
Cumberland Gap, US	D6	20
Cumberland Gap National Historical Park, US	D6	20
Cumberland Hill, RI	B4	42
Cumberland Island National Seashore, GA	F5	13
Cumberland Mountain, TN	C9	45
Cumberland Plateau, US	D8	45
Cumbres Pass, CO	D4	9
Cumming, GA	B2	13
Currant Mountain, NV	E6	31
Current, r., US	A5	7
Cushing, OK	B5	39
Custer, SD	D2	44
Custer Battlefield National Monument, MT	E9	29
Custer Peak, SD	C2	44
Cut Bank, MT	B4	29
Cuthbert, GA	E2	13
Cutler Ridge, FL	s13	12
Cut Off, LA	E5	21
Cuyahoga, r., OH	A4	38
Cuyahoga Falls, OH	A4	38
C.W. McConaughy, Lake, NE	C4	30
Cynthiana, KY	B5	20

D

Name	Map Ref.	Page
Dacono, CO	A6	9
Dacula, GA	C3	13
Dadeville, AL	C4	4
Dahlonega, GA	B3	13
Dakota City, NE	B9	30
Dale, IN	H4	17
Dale City, VA	B5	49
Dale Hollow Lake, US	C8	45
Daleville, AL	D4	4
Daleville, IN	D6	17
Dalhart, TX	A1	46
Dall, Mount, AK	f15	5
Dallas, GA	C2	13
Dallas, NC	B1	36
Dallas, OR	C3	40
Dallas, TX	C4	46
Dallas Center, IA	C4	18
Dalton, GA	B2	13
Dalton Gardens, ID	B2	15
Daly City, CA	h8	8
Damariscotta, ME	D3	22
Damascus, MD	B3	23
Dan, r., US	D3	49
Danbury, CT	D2	10
Danforth, ME	C5	22
Dania, FL	F6	12
Danielson, CT	B8	10
Daniels Pass, UT	C4	47
Danvers, MA	A6	24
Danville, AR	B2	7
Danville, IL	C6	16
Danville, IN	E4	17
Danville, KY	C5	20
Danville, NH	E4	32
Danville, PA	E8	41
Danville, VA	D3	49
Daphne, AL	E2	4
D'Arbonne, Bayou, r., LA	B3	21
Darby, PA	G11	41
Dardanelle, AR	B2	7
Darien, CT	E2	10
Darling, Lake, ND	A4	37
Darlington, SC	C8	43
Dauphin Island, AL	E1	4
Davenport, IA	C7	18
David City, NE	C8	30
Davidson, NC	B2	36
Davie, FL	F6	12
Davis, CA	C3	8
Davis, OK	C4	39
Davis, Mount, PA	G3	41
Davis Mountains, TX	o12	46
Dawson, GA	E2	13
Dawson Springs, KY	C2	20
Dayton, KY	h14	20
Dayton, OH	C1	38
Dayton, TN	D8	45
Dayton, WA	C8	50
Dayton, WY	B5	53
Daytona Beach, FL	C5	12
Deadwood, SD	C2	44
Dearborn, MI	F7	25
Dearborn Heights, MI	p15	25
Death Valley, CA	D5	8
Death Valley National Park, US	D5	8
Decatur, AL	A3	4
Decatur, GA	C2	13
Decatur, IL	D5	16
Decatur, IN	C8	17
Decatur, Lake, IL	D5	16
Decherd, TN	B5	45
Decorah, IA	A6	18
Dedham, MA	B5	24
Deep Creek Lake, MD	K12	23
Deep Fork, r., OK	B5	39
Deep River, CT	D6	10
Deerfield, IL	h9	16
Deerfield, r., US	A2	24
Deerfield Beach, FL	F6	12
Deer Isle, ME	D4	22
Deer Lodge, MT	D4	29
Deer Park, NY	n15	35
Deer Park, OH	o13	38
Deer Park, TX	r14	46
Deer River, MN	C5	26
Defiance, OH	A1	38
De Forest, WI	E4	52
De Kalb, IL	B5	16
Delafield, WI	m11	52
De Land, FL	C5	12
Delano, MN	E5	26
Delano Peak, UT	E3	47
Delavan, WI	F5	52
Delaware, OH	B2	38
Delaware, state, US	D3	11
Delaware, r., US	E2	33
Delaware, r., KS	C8	19
Delaware Bay, US	C12	2
Delaware City, DE	B3	11
Delaware Water Gap National Recreation Area, US	B2	33
Del City, OK	B4	39
Dellenbaugh, Mount, AZ	A2	6
Dell Rapids, SD	D9	44
Delmar, DE	G3	11
Delmar, NY	C7	35
Del Norte, CO	D4	9
Del Park Manor, DE	i7	11
Delphi, IN	C4	17
Delphos, OH	B1	38
Delran, NJ	C3	33
Delray Beach, FL	F6	12
Del Rio, TX	E2	46
Delta, CO	C2	9
Delta, UT	D3	47
Delta, MS	B3	27
Deltona, FL	D5	12
Deming, NM	E2	34
Demopolis, AL	C2	4
Demotte, IN	B3	17
Denali National Park, AK	C9	5
Denham Springs, LA	D5	21
Denison, IA	B2	18
Denison, TX	C4	46
Denmark, SC	E5	43
Dennis, MA	C7	24
Dennis Port, MA	C7	24
Denton, MD	C6	23
Denton, TX	C4	46
Dentsville, SC	C6	43
Denver, CO	B6	9
Denver, IA	B5	18
Denville, NJ	B4	33
De Pere, WI	D5	52
Depew, NY	C2	35
De Queen, AR	C1	7
De Quincy, LA	D2	21
Derby, CT	D3	10
Derby, KS	E6	19
Derby, VT	B4	48
Derby Line, VT	A4	48
De Ridder, LA	D2	21
Dermott, AR	D4	7
Dernieres, Isles, LA	E5	21
Derry, NH	E4	32
Des Arc, AR	C4	7
Deschutes, r., OR	B6	40
Deseret Peak, UT	C3	47
Desert Creek Peak, NV	E2	31
Desert Hot Springs, CA	F5	8
Des Lacs, r., ND	A4	37
Desloge, MO	D7	28
De Smet, SD	C8	44
Des Moines, IA	C4	18
Des Moines, WA	B3	50
Des Moines, r., US	D5	18
De Soto, KS	D9	19
De Soto, MO	C7	28
De Soto, TX	n10	46
Despard, WV	k10	51
Des Peres, MO	f13	28
Des Plaines, IL	A6	16
Des Plaines, r., US	k8	16
Destrehan, LA	E5	21
Detroit, MI	F7	25
Detroit Lakes, MN	D3	26
DeView, Bayou, r., AR	B4	7
Devils Lake, ND	A7	37
Devils Tower National Monument, WY	B8	53
Devonshire, DE	h7	11
Dewey, OK	A6	39
De Witt, AR	C4	7
De Witt, IA	C7	18
De Witt, NY	B4	35
Dexter, ME	C3	22
Dexter, MO	E8	28
Dexter, NM	D5	34
Diablo, Canyon, AZ	C4	6
Diablo, Mount, CA	h9	8
Diamond Head, HI	B4	14
Diamondville, WY	E2	53
Diaz, AR	B4	7
D'Iberville, MS	E5	27
Dickinson, ND	C3	37
Dickson, TN	A4	45
Dickson City, PA	D10	41
Dierks, AR	C1	7
Dighton, KS	D3	19
Dillingham, AK	D8	5
Dillon, MT	E4	29
Dillon, SC	C9	43
Dillon Lake, OH	B3	38
Dilworth, MN	D2	26
Dinosaur National Monument, US	C6	47
Dirty Devil, r., UT	E5	47
Disappointment, Cape, WA	C1	50
Dishman, WA	g14	50
District of Columbia, US	f8	23
Dixfield, ME	D2	22
Dix Mountain, NY	A7	35
Dixon, IL	B4	16
Dixon, NM	A4	34
Dobbs Ferry, NY	g13	35
Docena, AL	f7	4
Dodge Center, MN	F6	26
Dodge City, KS	E3	19
Dodgeville, WI	F3	52
Dolomite, AL	B3	4
Dolton, IL	k9	16
Dona Ana, NM	E3	34
Donaldsonville, LA	D4	21
Donalsonville, GA	E2	13
Doniphan, MO	E7	28
Donna, TX	F3	46
Donner Pass, CA	C3	8
Donora, PA	F2	41
Dora, AL	B2	4
Doraville, GA	h8	13
Dormont, PA	k13	41
Dorset, VT	E2	48
Dorset Peak, VT	E2	48
Dothan, AL	D4	4
Double Springs, AL	A2	4
Douglas, AZ	F6	6
Douglas, GA	E4	13
Douglas, WY	D7	53
Douglas, Mount, AK	D9	5
Douglas Lake, TN	D10	45
Douglass, KS	E7	19
Douglasville, GA	C2	13
Dover, AR	B2	7
Dover, DE	D3	11
Dover, NH	D5	32
Dover, NJ	B3	33
Dover, OH	B4	38
Dover Air Force Base, DE	D4	11
Dover-Foxcroft, ME	C3	22
Dowagiac, MI	G4	25
Downers Grove, IL	B5	16
Downey, CA	n12	8
Downingtown, PA	F10	41
Doylestown, PA	F11	41
Dracut, MA	A5	24
Drake Peak, OR	E6	40
Draper, UT	C4	47
Drayton, ND	A8	37
Drayton Plains, MI	F7	25
Dresden, TN	A3	45
Drew, MS	B3	27
Driskill Mountain, LA	B3	21
Drummond Island, MI	C7	25
Drumright, OK	B5	39
Dryden, ME	D2	22
Dry Ridge, KY	B5	20
Dry Tortugas, FL	H5	12
Dublin, GA	D4	13
Dublin, NH	E2	32
Dublin, OH	k10	38
Du Bois, PA	D4	41
Dubois, WY	C3	53
Dubuque, IA	B7	18
Duck, r., TN	B4	45
Dudley, MA	B4	24
Dulce, NM	A2	34
Duluth, GA	B2	13
Duluth, MN	D6	26
Dumas, AR	D4	7
Dumas, TX	B2	46
Dumfries, VA	B5	49
Dumont, NJ	B5	33
Dunbar, WV	C3	51
Duncan, OK	C4	39
Duncanville, TX	n10	46
Dundalk, MD	B4	23
Dundee, IL	A5	16
Dundee, MI	G7	25
Dunedin, FL	D4	12
Dunkirk, IN	D7	17
Dunkirk, NY	C1	35
Dunlap, IN	A6	17
Dunlap, TN	D8	45
Dunleith, DE	i7	11
Dunmore, PA	D10	41
Dunn, NC	B4	36
Dunseith, ND	A5	37
Dunwoody, GA	h8	13
Du Page, r., IL	k8	16
Dupont, CO	B6	9
Dupont, PA	n18	41
Duquesne, PA	F2	41
Du Quoin, IL	E4	16
Durand, MI	F6	25
Durango, CO	D3	9
Durant, IA	C7	18
Durant, MS	B4	27
Durant, OK	D5	39
Durham, CT	D5	10
Durham, NH	D5	32
Durham, NC	B4	36
Duryea, PA	D10	41
Dwight, IL	B5	16
Dwight D. Eisenhower Lock, NY	f9	35
Dworshak Reservoir, ID	C3	15
Dyer, IN	A2	17
Dyer, TN	A3	45
Dyersburg, TN	A2	45
Dyersville, IA	B6	18

E

Name	Map Ref.	Page
Eagan, MN	n12	26
Eagar, AZ	C6	6
Eagle, CO	B4	9
Eagle, ID	F2	15
Eagle, NE	h12	30
Eagle Creek Reservoir, IN	E5	17
Eagle Grove, IA	B4	18
Eagle Lake, ME	A4	22
Eagle Mountain, MN	k9	26
Eagle Pass, TX	E2	46
Eagle Peak, TX	o12	46
Eagle Point, OR	E4	40
Earle, AR	B5	7
Earlington, KY	C2	20
Easley, SC	B2	43
East Alton, IL	E3	16
East Arlington, VT	E2	48
East Aurora, NY	C2	35
East Barre, VT	C4	48
East Bethel, MN	E5	26
East Brewton, AL	D2	4
East Bridgewater, MA	B6	24
East Brimfield Lake, MA	B3	24
East Brunswick, NJ	C4	33
East Chicago, IN	A3	17
East Cleveland, OH	g9	38
East Cote Blanche Bay, LA	E4	21
East Derry, NH	E4	32
East Detroit, MI	p16	25
Eastern Bay, MD	C5	23
Eastern Neck Island, MD	B5	23
East Flat Rock, NC	f10	36
East Grand Forks, MN	C2	26
East Grand Rapids, MI	F5	25
East Greenwich, RI	D4	42
East Hampstead, NH	E4	32
East Hampton, CT	C5	10
Easthampton, MA	B2	24
East Hartford, CT	B5	10
East Haven, CT	D4	10
East Helena, MT	D5	29
Eastlake, OH	A4	38
East Lansing, MI	F6	25
East Las Vegas, NV	G6	31
East Liverpool, OH	B5	38
East Longmeadow, MA	B2	24
East Los Angeles, CA	m12	8
East Lynn Lake, WV	C2	51
East Machias, ME	D5	22
Eastman, GA	D3	13
East Middlebury, VT	D2	48
East Moline, IL	B3	16
East Montpelier, VT	C4	48
East Naples, FL	F5	12
East Nishnabotna, r., IA	C2	18
East Norriton, PA	o20	41
Easton, MD	C5	23
Easton, PA	E11	41
East Orange, NJ	B4	33
East Pea Ridge, WV	C2	51
East Peoria, IL	C4	16
East Point, GA	C2	13
East Point, MA	B6	24
Eastport, ME	D6	22
East Poultney, VT	D2	48
East Prairie, MO	E8	28
East Providence, RI	C4	42
East Ridge, TN	h11	45
East River, CT	D5	10
East Rochester, NY	B3	35
East Rockingham, NC	C3	36
East Saint Louis, IL	E3	16
East Sebago, ME	E2	22
East Stroudsburg, PA	D11	41
East Troy, WI	F5	52
East View, WV	k10	51
East Wenatchee, WA	B5	50
East Windsor, NJ	C3	33
Eaton, CO	A6	9
Eaton, IN	D7	17
Eaton, OH	C1	38
Eaton Rapids, MI	F6	25
Eatonton, GA	C3	13
Eatontown, NJ	C4	33
Eau Claire, WI	D2	52
Eccles, WV	n13	51
Eclectic, AL	C3	4
Ecorse, MI	p15	25
Eddyville, KY	e9	20
Eden, NC	A3	36
Eden Prairie, MN	n12	26
Edenton, NC	A6	36
Edgeley, ND	C7	37
Edgemere, MD	B5	23
Edgemont, SD	D2	44
Edgemoor, DE	A3	11
Edgerton, KS	D8	19
Edgerton, WI	F4	52
Edgewater, AL	f7	4
Edgewater, FL	D6	12
Edgewood, IN	D6	17
Edgewood, KY	h13	20
Edgewood, MD	B5	23
Edgewood, WA	f11	50
Edina, MN	F5	26
Edina, MO	A5	28
Edinboro, PA	C1	41
Edinburg, TX	F3	46
Edinburgh, IN	F6	17
Edison, NJ	B4	33
Edisto, r., SC	E6	43
Edisto Island, SC	F7	43
Edmond, OK	B4	39
Edmonds, WA	B3	50
Edwardsville, IL	E4	16
Edwardsville, KS	k16	19
Edwardsville, PA	n17	41
Eel, r., IN	C6	17
Eel, r., IN	F3	17
Effingham, IL	D5	16
Egan Range, NV	E7	31
Egg Island Point, NJ	E2	33
Eglin Air Force Base, FL	u15	12
Egypt, Lake of, IL	F5	16
Elba, AL	D3	4
Elbert, Mount, CO	B4	9
Elberton, GA	B4	13
El Cajon, CA	F5	8
El Campo, TX	E4	46
El Cerrito, CA	h8	8
Eldersburg, MD	B4	23
Eldon, MO	C5	28
Eldora, IA	B4	18
El Dorado, AR	D3	7
Eldorado, IL	F5	16
El Dorado, KS	E7	19
Eldorado Peak, WA	A4	50
El Dorado Springs, MO	D3	28
Eldridge, IA	C7	18
Eleanor, WV	C3	51
Elephant Butte Reservoir, NM	D2	34
Elephant Mountain, ME	D2	22
Eleven Point, r., US	A4	7
Elgin, IL	A5	16
Elgin, ND	C4	37
Elizabeth, NJ	B4	33
Elizabeth City, NC	A6	36
Elizabeth Islands, MA	D6	24
Elizabethton, TN	C11	45
Elizabethtown, KY	C4	20
Elizabethtown, NC	C4	36
Elizabethtown, PA	F8	41
Elk, r., WV	C3	51
Elkader, IA	B6	18
Elk City, OK	B2	39
Elk Grove Village, IL	h9	16
Elkhart, IN	A6	17
Elkhart, KS	E2	19
Elkhorn, NE	g12	30
Elkhorn, WI	F5	52
Elkhorn, r., NE	B7	30
Elkin, NC	A2	36
Elkins, WV	C5	51
Elk Mountain, NM	D1	34
Elko, NV	C6	31
Elk Point, SD	E9	44
Elkridge, MD	B4	23
Elk River, MN	E5	26
Elkton, KY	D2	20
Elkton, MD	A6	23
Elkview, WV	m13	51
Ellen, Mount, UT	E5	47
Ellen, Mount, VT	C3	48
Ellendale, ND	C7	37
Ellensburg, WA	C5	50
Ellettsville, IN	F4	17
Ellicott City, MD	B4	23
Ellinwood, KS	D5	19
Ellis, KS	D4	19
Ellisville, MS	D4	27
Ellisville, MO	f12	28
Ellsworth, KS	D5	19
Ellsworth, ME	D4	22
Ellsworth, WI	D1	52
Ellwood City, PA	E1	41
Elma, WA	C2	50
Elm Creek, NE	D6	30
Elm Grove, WI	m11	52
Elmhurst, IL	B6	16
Elmira, NY	C4	35
El Mirage, AZ	k8	6
Elmont, NY	k13	35
El Monte, CA	m12	8
Elmwood Park, IL	k9	16
Elmwood Park, NJ	h8	33
Elon College, NC	A3	36
Eloy, AZ	E4	6
El Paso, TX	o11	46
El Reno, OK	B4	39
Elsberry, MO	B7	28
Elsmere, DE	B3	11
Elsmere, KY	B5	20
El Toro, CA	n13	8
Elwell, Lake, MT	B5	29

Name — Map Ref. — Page

Elwood, IN D6 17
Ely, MN C7 26
Ely, NV D7 31
Elyria, OH A3 38
Embarras, r., IL E6 16
Eminence, KY B4 20
Emmaus, PA E11 41
Emmetsburg, IA A3 18
Emmett, ID F2 15
Emory Peak, TX E1 46
Empire, NV C2 31
Emporia, KS D7 19
Emporia, VA D5 49
Encampment, WY E6 53
Encinitas, CA F5 8
Enderlin, ND C8 37
Endicott, NY C4 35
Endicott Mountains, AK B9 5
Endwell, NY C4 35
Enfield (Thompsonville), CT B5 10
Enfield, NH C2 32
Enfield, NC A5 36
England, AR C4 7
Engleside, VA g12 49
Englewood, CO B6 9
Englewood, FL F4 12
Englewood, NJ B5 33
Englewood, OH C1 38
Enid, OK A4 39
Enid Lake, MS A4 27
Enka, NC f10 36
Ennis, TX C4 46
Enola, PA F8 41
Enoree, r., SC B3 43
Enosburg Falls, VT B3 48
Ensley, FL u14 12
Enterprise, AL D4 4
Enterprise, WV B4 51
Entiat, r., WA B5 50
Entiat, Lake, WA B5 50
Enumclaw, WA B4 50
Ephrata, PA F9 41
Ephrata, WA B6 50
Epping, NH D4 32
Erie, CO A5 9
Erie, KS E8 19
Erie, PA B1 41
Erie, Lake, NA B11 2
Erie Canal, NY B5 35
Erlanger, KY A5 20
Erwin, TN C11 45
Escalante, UT F4 47
Escambia, r., FL u14 12
Escanaba, MI C3 25
Escanaba, r., MI B3 25
Escatawpa, MS E5 27
Escondido, CA F5 8
Esmond, RI B4 42
Espanola, NM B3 34
Essex, CT D6 10
Essex, MD B5 23
Essex, VT B2 48
Essex Junction, VT C2 48
Estes Park, CO A5 9
Estherville, IA A3 18
Etolin Island, AK m23 5
Etowah, TN D9 45
Etowah, r., GA B2 13
Ettrick, VA C5 49
Euclid, OH A4 38
Eudora, AR D4 7
Eudora, KS D8 19
Eufaula, AL D4 4
Eufaula, OK B6 39
Eufaula Lake, OK B6 39
Eugene, OR C3 40
Eunice, LA D3 21
Eunice, NM E6 34
Eupora, MS B4 27
Eureka, CA B1 8
Eureka, IL C4 16
Eureka, KS E7 19
Eureka, MO f12 28
Eureka, MT B1 29
Eureka, NV D6 31
Eureka, SD B6 44
Eureka Springs, AR A2 7
Eustis, FL D5 12
Evans, CO A6 9
Evans, GA C4 13
Evans, Mount, CO B5 9
Evansdale, IA B5 18
Evanston, IL A6 16
Evanston, WY E2 53
Evansville, IN I2 17
Evansville, WI F4 52
Evansville, WY D6 53
Eveleth, MN C6 26
Everett, MA g11 24
Everett, WA B3 50
Everett, Mount, MA B1 24
Everglades National Park, FL G5 12
Evergreen, AL D3 4
Evergreen, CO B5 9
Evergreen Park, IL k9 16
E.V. Spence Reservoir, TX D2 46
Ewa, HI B3 14
Ewa Beach, HI B3 14
Ewing Township, NJ C3 33
Excelsior Springs, MO B3 28
Exeter, NH E5 32
Exeter, PA D10 41
Experiment, GA C2 13

F

Fairbanks, AK C10 5
Fairborn, OH C1 38
Fairburn, GA C2 13
Fairbury, IL C5 16
Fairbury, NE D8 30
Fairdale, KY B4 20
Fairfax, DE A3 11
Fairfax, VA B5 49
Fairfield, AL B3 4
Fairfield, CA C2 8
Fairfield, CT E2 10
Fairfield, IL E5 16
Fairfield, IA C6 18
Fairfield, ME D3 22
Fairfield, OH n12 38
Fairfield Bay, AR B3 7
Fairhaven, MA C6 24
Fair Haven, VT D2 48
Fairhope, AL E2 4
Fair Lawn, NJ h8 33
Fairlea, WV D4 51
Fairmont, MN G4 26
Fairmont, WV B4 51
Fairmount, IN D6 17
Fair Oaks, GA h7 13
Fair Plain, MI F4 25
Fairview, NJ h8 33
Fairview, OK A3 39
Fairview, TN B4 45
Fairview Heights, IL E3 16
Fairview Park, IN E3 17
Fairview Park, OH g9 38
Fairway, KS k16 19
Falcon Heights, MN n12 26
Fallon, NV D3 31
Fall River, MA C5 24
Falls Church, VA g12 49
Falls City, NE D10 30
Fallston, MD A5 23
Falmouth, KY B5 20
Falmouth, ME E2 22
Falmouth, MA C6 24
Falmouth, VA B5 49
Fargo, ND C9 37
Faribault, MN F5 26
Farley, IA B6 18
Farmers Branch, TX n10 46
Farmerville, LA B3 21
Farmington, AR A1 7
Farmington, CT C4 10
Farmington, ME D2 22
Farmington, MI p15 25
Farmington, MN F5 26
Farmington, MO D7 28
Farmington, NH D4 32
Farmington, NM A1 34
Farmington, UT C4 47
Farmington, r., CT B4 10
Farmington Hills, MI o15 25
Farmland, IN D7 17
Farmville, NC B5 36
Farmville, VA C4 49
Farrell, PA D1 41
Faulkland Heights, DE i7 11
Faulkton, SD B6 44
Fayette, AL B2 4
Fayette, IA B6 18
Fayette, MS D2 27
Fayette, MO B5 28
Fayetteville, AR A1 7
Fayetteville, GA C2 13
Fayetteville, NC B4 36
Fayetteville, TN B5 45
Fayetteville, WV C3 51
Fear, Cape, NC D5 36
Feather, r., CA C3 8
Fennimore, WI F3 52
Fenton, MI F7 25
Fer, Point au, LA E4 21
Ferdinand, IN H4 17
Fergus Falls, MN D2 26
Ferguson, MO C7 28
Fern Creek, KY g11 20
Ferndale, MD B4 23
Ferndale, MI P15 25
Ferndale, WA A3 50
Fernley, NV D2 31
Ferriday, LA C4 21
Fessenden, ND B6 37
Festus, MO C7 28
Fidalgo Island, WA A3 50
Filer, ID G4 15
Findlay, OH A2 38
Fircrest, WA f10 50
Firestone, CO A6 9
First Connecticut Lake, NH f7 32
Fishers, IN E5 17
Fishers Island, NY m16 35
Fishing Bay, MD D5 23
Fitchburg, MA A4 24
Fitzgerald, GA E3 13
Fitzwilliam, NH E2 32
Five Points, NM B3 34
Flagstaff, AZ B4 6
Flaming Gorge Reservoir, US E3 53
Flandreau, SD C9 44
Flathead Lake, MT C2 29
Flat River, MO D7 28
Flat Rock, MI F7 25
Flattery, Cape, WA A1 50
Flatwoods, KY B7 20
Flemingsburg, KY B6 20
Flint, MI E7 25
Flint, r., GA E2 13
Flint City, AL A3 4
Flippin, AR A3 7
Flomaton, AL D2 4
Flora, IL E5 16
Flora, IN C4 17
Flora, MS C3 27
Florala, AL D3 4
Florence, AL A2 4
Florence, AZ D4 6
Florence, CO C5 9
Florence, KY A5 20
Florence, MS C3 27
Florence, OR D2 40
Florence, SC C8 43
Florida, state, US E5 12
Florida, Cape, FL G6 12
Florida Bay, FL H6 12
Florida Keys, FL H6 12
Florissant, MO f13 28
Flossmoor, IL k9 16
Flourtown, PA o21 41
Flowood, MS C3 27
Flushing, MI E7 25
Foley, AL E2 4
Folkston, GA F4 13
Follansbee, WV A4 51
Fond du Lac, WI E5 52
Fond du Lac Indian Reservation, MN D6 26
Fontana, CA m14 8
Fontenelle Reservoir, WY D2 53
Foraker, Mount, AK f16 5
Fords, NJ B4 33
Fords Prairie, WA C2 50
Fordyce, AR D3 7
Foreman, AR D1 7
Forest, MS C4 27
Forest Acres, SC C6 43
Forest City, IA A4 18
Forest City, NC B1 36
Forestdale, AL B3 4
Forest Grove, OR B3 40
Forest Hill, TX n9 46
Forest Hills, PA k14 41
Forest Hills, TN A5 45
Forest Lake, MN E6 26
Forest Park, GA h8 13
Forest Park, IL k9 16
Forked Deer, r., TN B2 45
Forks, WA B1 50
Forman, ND C8 37
Forrest City, AR B5 7
Forsyth, GA C3 13
Forsyth, MT D10 29
Fort Ashby, WV B6 51
Fort Atkinson, WI F5 52
Fort Belvoir, VA g12 49
Fort Benning, GA D2 13
Fort Benton, MT C6 29
Fort Bragg, NC B3 36
Fort Branch, IN H2 17
Fort Carson, CO C6 9
Fort Cobb Reservoir, OK B3 39
Fort Collins, CO A5 9
Fort Davis, TX o13 46
Fort Davis National Historic Site, TX o13 46
Fort Defiance, AZ B6 6
Fort Dix, NJ C3 33
Fort Dodge, IA B3 18
Fort Gibson, OK B6 39
Fort Gibson Lake, OK A6 39
Fort Gordon, GA C4 13
Fort Greely, AK C10 5
Fort Hall, ID F6 15
Fort Jefferson National Monument, FL H4 12
Fort Kent, ME A4 22
Fort Knox, KY B4 20
Fort Lauderdale, FL F6 12
Fort Leavenworth, KS C9 19
Fort Lee, NJ B5 33
Fort Loudoun Lake, TN D9 45
Fort Lupton, CO A6 9
Fort Madison, IA D6 18
Fort McHenry National Monument And Historic Shrine, MD g11 23
Fort Meade, MD B4 23
Fort Mill, SC A6 43
Fort Mitchell, KY h13 20
Fort Morgan, CO A7 9
Fort Myers, FL F5 12
Fort Myers Beach, FL F5 12
Fort Oglethorpe, GA B1 13
Fort Payne, AL A4 4
Fort Peck Lake, MT C9 29
Fort Pierce, FL E6 12
Fort Pierre, SD C5 44
Fort Richardson, AK C10 5
Fort Scott, KS E9 19
Fort Sill, OK C3 39
Fort Smith, AR B1 7
Fort Stewart, GA D5 13
Fort Stockton, TX D1 46
Fort Sumner, NM C5 34
Fort Sumter National Monument, SC k12 43
Fort Thomas, KY h14 20
Fort Totten, ND B7 37
Fort Valley, GA D3 13
Fortville, IN E6 17
Fort Wainwright, AK C10 5
Fort Walton Beach, FL u15 12
Fort Wayne, IN B7 17
Fort Wingate, NM B1 34
Fort Worth, TX C4 46
Fort Wright, KY h13 20
Forty Fort, PA D10 41
Fort Yukon, AK B10 5
Foss Reservoir, OK B2 39
Foster Village, HI g10 14
Fostoria, OH A2 38
Fountain, CO C6 9
Fountain Hill, PA E11 41
Fountain Inn, SC B3 43
Fourche Mountain, AR C2 7
Four Mountains, Islands of, AK E6 5
Fowler, CO C6 9
Fowler, IN C3 17
Fowlerville, MI F6 25
Fox, r., US B5 16
Fox, r., WI D5 52
Foxboro, MA B5 24
Fox Islands, AK E6 5
Fox Lake, IL A5 16
Fox Point, WI E6 52
Fox River Grove, IL h8 16
Frackville, PA E9 41
Framingham, MA B5 24
Francis Case, Lake, SD D6 44
Franconia, NH B3 32
Franconia Notch, NH B3 32
Francs Peak, WY C3 53
Frankenmuth, MI E7 25
Frankfort, IL m9 16
Frankfort, IN D4 17
Frankfort, KY B5 20
Frankfort, MI D4 25
Franklin, IN F5 17
Franklin, KY D3 20
Franklin, LA E4 21
Franklin, MA B5 24
Franklin, NE D7 30
Franklin, NH D3 32
Franklin, NC f9 36
Franklin, OH C1 38
Franklin, PA D2 41
Franklin, TN B5 45
Franklin, VA D6 49
Franklin, WI n11 52
Franklin D. Roosevelt Lake, WA B7 50
Franklin Falls Reservoir, NH C3 32
Franklin Park, IL k9 16
Franklinton, LA D5 21
Frankton, IN D6 17
Frederica, DE D4 11
Frederick, MD B3 23
Frederick, OK C2 39
Fredericksburg, VA B5 49
Fredericktown, MO D7 28
Fredonia, AZ A3 6
Fredonia, KS E8 19
Fredonia, NY C1 35
Freeburg, IL E4 16
Freedom, WY D2 53
Freehold, NJ C4 33
Freeman, SD D8 44
Freeport, IL A4 16
Freeport, NY n15 35
Freeport, TX E5 46
Fremont, CA D2 8
Fremont, IN A8 17
Fremont, NE C9 30
Fremont, OH A2 38
Fremont Peak, WY C3 53
French Broad, r., US D10 45
French Lick, IN G4 17
Frenchman Bay, ME D4 22
Frenchville, ME A4 22
Fresno, CA D4 8
Fridley, MN m12 26
Friend, NE D8 30
Friendswood, TX r14 46
Frio, r., TX E3 46
Frisco, CO B4 9
Frissell, Mount, US A2 10
Frontenac, KS E9 19
Front Range, CO A5 9
Front Royal, VA B4 49
Frostburg, MD k13 23
Fruita, CO B2 9
Fruit Heights, UT B4 47
Fruitland, ID F2 15
Fruitvale, WA C5 50
Fruitville, FL E4 12
Fullerton, CA n13 8
Fullerton, NE C8 30
Fulton, IL B3 16
Fulton, KY f9 20
Fulton, MS A5 27
Fulton, MO C6 28
Fulton, NY B4 35
Fultondale, AL f7 4
Fuquay-Varina, NC B4 36

G

Gadsden, AL A3 4
Gaffney, SC A4 43
Gahanna, OH k11 38
Gainesville, FL C4 12
Gainesville, GA B3 13
Gainesville, MO E5 28
Gainesville, TX C4 46
Gaithersburg, MD B3 23
Galax, VA D2 49
Galena, IL A3 16
Galena, KS E9 19
Galesburg, IL C3 16
Galion, OH B3 38
Gallatin, TN A5 45
Galliano, LA E5 21
Gallup, NM B1 34
Galveston, IN C5 17
Galveston, TX E5 46
Galveston Bay, TX E5 46
Galveston Island, TX E5 46
Ganado, AZ B6 6
Gannett Peak, WY C3 53
Gantt, SC B3 43
Gardena, CA n12 8
Garden City, GA D5 13
Garden City, ID F2 15
Garden City, KS E3 19
Garden City, MI p15 25
Gardendale, AL B3 4
Garden Grove, CA n13 8
Gardiner, ME D3 22
Gardiners Island, NY m16 35
Gardner, KS D9 19
Gardner, MA A4 24
Gardnerville, NV E2 31
Garfield, NJ h8 33
Garfield Heights, OH h9 38
Garfield Mountain, MT F4 29
Garland, TX n10 46
Garner, IA A4 18
Garner, NC B4 36
Garnett, KS D8 19
Garretson, SD D9 44
Garrett, IN B7 17
Garrison, MD B4 23
Garrison, ND B4 37
Gary, IN A3 17
Gary, WV D3 51
Gas City, IN D6 17
Gasconade, r., MO C6 28
Gassville, AR A3 7
Gaston, Lake, US A5 36
Gastonia, NC B1 36
Gates of the Arctic National Park, AK B9 5
Gatesville, TX D4 46
Gatlinburg, TN D10 45
Gauley, r., WV C3 51
Gautier, MS f8 27
Gay Head, MA D6 24
Gaylord, MI C6 25
Genesee, r., NY C2 35
Geneseo, IL B3 16
Geneseo, NY C3 35
Geneva, AL D4 4
Geneva, IL B5 16
Geneva, NE D8 30
Geneva, NY C4 35
Geneva, OH A5 38
Genoa, IL A5 16
Genoa, NE C8 30
Gentry, AR A1 7
George, Lake, FL C5 12
George, Lake, NY B7 35
Georgetown, DE F4 11
Georgetown, IL D6 16
Georgetown, IN H6 17
Georgetown, KY B5 20
Georgetown, OH D2 38
Georgetown, SC E9 43
Georgetown, TX D4 46
George Washington Birthplace National Monument, VA B6 49
Georgia, state, US D3 13
Georgiana, AL D3 4
Gering, NE C2 30
Germantown, MD B3 23
Germantown, TN B2 45
Germantown, WI E5 52
Gettysburg, PA G7 41
Gettysburg, SD C6 44
Gibbon, NE D7 30
Gibson City, IL C5 16
Gibsonton, FL p11 12
Gibsonville, NC A3 36
Gig Harbor, WA B3 50
Gila, r., US E3 6
Gila Bend, AZ E3 6
Gila Bend Mountains, AZ D2 6
Gilbert, AZ D4 6
Gilbert, MN C6 26
Gilbert Peak, WA C4 50
Gilcrest, CO A6 9
Gillespie, IL D4 16
Gillette, WY B7 53
Gilman, VT C5 48
Gilmanton, NH D4 32
Gilsum, NH D2 32
Girard, KS E9 19
Girard, OH A5 38
Glacier Bay, AK k21 5
Glacier Bay National Park, AK D12 5
Glacier National Park, MT B2 29
Glacier Peak, WA A4 50
Gladstone, MO h10 28
Gladstone, OR B4 40
Glasgow, KY C4 20
Glasgow, MO B5 28
Glasgow, MT B10 29
Glassboro, NJ D2 33
Glassport, PA F2 41
Glastenbury Mountain, VT F2 48
Glastonbury, CT C5 10
Glen Allen, VA C5 49
Glen Burnie, MD B4 23
Glen Canyon, US G4 47
Glencoe, AL B4 4
Glencoe, IL A6 16
Glencoe, MN F4 26
Glen Cove, NY h13 35
Glendale, AZ D3 6
Glendale, CA m12 8
Glen Dale, WV B4 51
Glendale, WI m12 52
Glendive, MT C12 29
Glendora, CA m13 8
Glendo Reservoir, WY D8 53
Glen Ellyn, IL k8 16
Glenns Ferry, ID G3 15
Glennville, GA E5 13
Glenolden, PA p20 41
Glenpool, OK B5 39
Glen Rock, NJ h8 33
Glenrock, WY D7 53
Glens Falls, NY B7 35
Glenside, PA F11 41
Glen Ullin, ND C4 37
Glenview, IL h9 16
Glenville, WV C4 51
Glenwood, AR C2 7
Glenwood, IA C2 18
Glenwood, MN E3 26
Glenwood Springs, CO B3 9
Globe, AZ D5 6
Gloucester, MA A6 24
Gloucester City, NJ D2 33
Gloucester Point, VA C6 49
Gloversville, NY B6 35
Goat Mountain, MT C3 29
Goddard, KS E6 19
Godfrey, IL E3 16
Goffstown, NH D3 32
Golden, CO B5 9
Goldendale, WA D5 50
Golden Gate Bridge, CA h7 8
Golden Spike National Historic Site, UT B3 47
Golden Valley, MN n12 26
Goldsboro, NC B5 36
Gonzales, LA D5 21
Good Hope, AL A3 4
Gooding, ID G4 15
Goodland, KS C2 19
Goodlettsville, TN g10 45
Goodview, MN F7 26
Goodwater, AL B3 4
Goodyear, AZ D3 6
Goose Creek, SC F7 43
Gordon, GA D3 13
Gordon, NE B3 30
Gorham, ME E2 22
Gorham, NH B4 32
Goshen, IN A6 17
Gosnell, AR B6 7
Gothenburg, NE D5 30
Gould, AR D4 7
Grafton, ND A8 37
Grafton, WV B4 51
Grafton, WI E6 52
Graham, NC A3 36
Graham, TX C3 46
Graham, Mount, AZ E6 6
Graham Lake, ME D4 22
Grain Valley, MO B3 28
Grambling, LA B3 21
Granby, CT B4 10
Granby, MO E3 28
Granby, Lake, CO A5 9
Grand, r., MI E5 25
Grand, r., MO A3 28
Grand, r., OH A4 38
Grand, r., SD B4 44
Grand Bay, AL E1 4
Grand Blanc, MI F7 25
Grand Canyon, AZ A3 6
Grand Canyon, AZ A3 6
Grand Canyon National Park, AZ B3 6
Grand Coulee Dam, WA B6 50
Grande, Rio, r., NA E7 2
Grande Ronde, r., US C8 50
Grand Falls, ME C5 22
Grandfather Mountain, NC A1 36
Grand Forks, ND B8 37
Grand Haven, MI E4 25
Grand Island, NE D7 30
Grand Island, MI B4 25
Grand Isle, LA E6 21
Grand Junction, CO B2 9
Grand Lake, LA E6 21
Grand Lake, LA E3 21
Grand Lake, OH B1 38
Grand Ledge, MI F6 25
Grand Portage Indian Reservation, MN k10 26
Grand Portage National Monument, MN h10 26
Grand Prairie, TX n10 46
Grand Rapids, MI F5 25
Grand Rapids, MN C5 26
Grand Teton, WY C2 53
Grand Teton National Park, WY C2 53
Grand Traverse Bay, MI C5 25
Grandview, MO C3 28
Grandview, WA C6 50
Grandview Heights, OH m10 38
Grandville, MI F5 25
Grand Wash Cliffs, AZ B2 6
Granger, IN A5 17
Grangeville, ID D2 15
Granite, OK C2 39
Granite City, IL E3 16
Granite Falls, MN F3 26
Granite Falls, NC B1 36
Granite Falls, WA A4 50
Granite Pass, WY B5 53
Granite Peak, MT E7 29
Granite Peak, NV B4 31
Graniteville, VT C4 48
Grant, NE D4 30
Grant, Mount, NV E3 31
Grants, NM B2 34
Grants Pass, OR E3 40
Grantsville, UT C3 47
Grapevine, TX C4 46
Gravel Ridge, AR h10 7
Gravette, AR A1 7
Gray, GA C3 13
Grayling, MI D6 25
Graylyn Crest, DE A3 11
Grays Harbor, WA C1 50
Grayslake, IL A5 16
Grayson, KY B7 20
Grays Peak, CO B5 9
Graysville, AL f7 4
Great Barrington, MA B1 24
Great Basin, US C4 2
Great Basin National Park, NV E7 31
Great Bay, NJ D4 33
Great Bend, KS D5 19
Great Dismal Swamp, US D6 49
Great Divide Basin, WY E4 53
Great Egg Harbor, r., NJ D3 33
Great Falls, MT C5 29
Great Falls, MD B3 23
Great Lakes Naval Training Center, IL h9 16
Great Miami, r., US C1 38
Great Pee Dee, r., US D9 43
Great Sacandaga Lake, NY C6 35
Great Salt Lake, UT B3 47
Great Salt Lake Desert, UT C2 47
Great Salt Plains Lake, OK A3 39
Great Sand Dunes National Monument, CO D5 9
Great Smoky Mountains, US D10 45
Great Smoky Mountains National Park, US D10 45
Great Valley, US C2 49
Greece, NY B3 35
Greeley, CO A6 9
Green, OR D3 40
Green, r., US C6 2
Green, r., US F3 48
Green, r., IL B4 16
Green, r., KY C2 20
Greenacres, WA B8 50
Greenacres City, FL F6 12
Green Bay, WI D6 52
Green Bay, US D3 25
Greenbelt, MD C4 23
Greenbriar, VA g12 49
Greenbrier, AR B3 7
Green Brier, TN A5 45
Greenbrier, r., WV D4 51
Greenbush, MN B2 26
Greencastle, IN E4 17
Greendale, IN F8 17
Greendale, WI F6 52
Greene, ME D2 22
Greeneville, TN C11 45
Greenfield, IN E6 17
Greenfield, IA C3 18
Greenfield, MA A2 24
Greenfield, MO D4 28
Greenfield, NH E3 32
Greenfield, TN A3 45
Greenfield, WI n12 52
Greenfield Plaza, IA e8 18
Green Forest, AR A2 7
Greenland, NH D5 32
Green Mountains, VT F2 48
Green Peter Lake, OR C4 40
Green River, UT E5 47
Green River, WY E3 53
Green River Lake, KY C4 20
Green River Reservoir, VT B3 48
Greensboro, AL C2 4
Greensboro, GA C3 13
Greensboro, NC A3 36
Greensburg, IN F7 17
Greensburg, KS E4 19
Greensburg, KY C4 20
Greensburg, PA F2 41
Greentown, IN D6 17
Green Valley, AZ F5 6
Greenville, AL D3 4
Greenville, IL E4 16
Greenville, KY C2 20
Greenville, ME C3 22
Greenville, MI E5 25
Greenville, MS B2 27
Greenville, NH E3 32
Greenville, NC B5 36
Greenville, OH B1 38
Greenville, PA D1 41
Greenville, RI C3 42
Greenville, SC B3 43
Greenville, TX C4 46
Greenwich, CT E1 10
Greenwood, AR B1 7
Greenwood, IN E5 17
Greenwood, MS B3 27
Greenwood, MO k11 28
Greenwood, SC C3 43
Greenwood, Lake, SC C4 43
Greer, SC B3 43
Greers Ferry Lake, AR B3 7
Gregory, SD D6 44
Grenada, MS B4 27
Grenada Lake, MS B4 27
Gresham, OR B4 40
Gretna, LA E5 21
Gretna, NE C9 30
Greybull, WY B4 53
Greybull, r., WY B4 53
Greylock, Mount, MA A1 24
Griffin, GA C2 13
Griffith, IN A3 17
Grimes, IA C4 18
Grinnell, IA C5 18
Grosse Pointe Park, MI p16 25
Grosse Pointe Woods, MI p16 25
Gros Ventre Range, WY C2 53
Groton, CT D7 10
Groton, SD B7 44
Grove, OK A7 39
Grove City, OH C2 38
Grove City, PA D1 41
Grove Point, MD B5 23
Groves, TX E6 46
Groveton, NH A3 32
Groveton, VA g12 49
Grovetown, GA C4 13
Grundy Center, IA B5 18
Guadalupe, AZ m9 6
Guadalupe Mountains, US E5 34
Guadalupe Mountains National Park, TX o12 46
Guadalupe Peak, TX o12 46
Guernsey, WY D8 53
Guilford, CT D5 10
Guilford, ME C3 22
Gulf Gate Estates, FL E4 12
Gulf Islands National Seashore, US E5 27
Gulfport, FL E4 12
Gulfport, MS E4 27
Gulf Shores, AL E2 4
Gunnison, CO C4 9
Gunnison, r., CO C2 9
Gunpowder Neck, MD B5 23
Gunpowder River, MD B5 23
Guntersville, AL A3 4
Guntersville Lake, AL A3 4
Gurdon, AR D2 7
Gurnee, IL h9 16
Guthrie, OK B4 39
Guthrie Center, IA C3 18
Guttenberg, IA B6 18
Guyandotte, r., WV C2 51
Guymon, OK e9 39
Guyot, Mount, US D10 45
Gwinhurst, DE h8 11
Gypsum, CO B4 9

H

Hackensack, NJ B4 33
Haddonfield, NJ D2 33
Hagerman, NM D5 34
Hagerstown, IN E7 17
Hagerstown, MD A2 23
Haggin, Mount, MT D3 29
Hailey, ID F4 15
Haines City, FL D5 12
Halawa, Cape, HI B5 14
Halawa Heights, HI g10 14
Haleakala Crater, HI C5 14
Haleakala National Park, HI C6 14
Hales Corners, WI n11 52
Halethorpe, MD B4 23
Haleyville, AL A2 4
Half Moon Bay, CA k8 8
Halfway, MD A2 23
Hallandale, FL G6 12
Hallock, MN B2 26
Hallowell, ME D3 22
Halls, TN B2 45
Halls Crossroads, TN m14 45
Halstead, KS E6 19
Hamburg, AR D4 7
Hamburg, NY C2 35
Hamden, CT D4 10
Hamilton, AL A2 4
Hamilton, IL C2 16
Hamilton, MT D2 29
Hamilton, OH C1 38
Hamilton, Mount, NV D6 31
Hamilton Square, NJ C3 33
Hamlet, NC C3 36
Hamlin, WV C2 51
Hammond, IN A2 17
Hammond, LA D5 21
Hammonton, NJ D3 33
Hampden, ME D4 22
Hampstead, NH E4 32
Hampton, AR D3 7
Hampton, GA C2 13
Hampton, IA B4 18
Hampton, NH E5 32
Hampton, SC F5 43
Hampton, TN C11 45
Hampton, VA C6 49
Hampton Bays, NY n16 35
Hampton Beach, NH E5 32
Hampton Falls, NH E5 32
Hams Fork, r., WY E2 53
Hamtramck, MI p15 25

Name	Map Ref.	Page
Hanahan, SC	F7	43
Hanamaulu, HI	B2	14
Hanceville, AL	A3	4
Hancock, ME	D4	22
Hancock, MI	A2	25
Hankinson, ND	C9	37
Hanna, WY	E6	53
Hannibal, MO	B6	28
Hanover, IN	G7	17
Hanover, NH	C2	32
Hanover, PA	G8	41
Hanover Park, IL	k8	16
Hapeville, GA	C2	13
Harahan, LA	k11	21
Harcuvar Mountains, AZ	D2	6
Hardeeville, SC	G5	43
Hardin, MT	E9	29
Hardinsburg, KY	C3	20
Hardwick, GA	C3	13
Hardwick, VT	B4	48
Harlan, IA	C2	18
Harlan, KY	D6	20
Harlan County Lake, NE	E6	30
Harlem, GA	C4	13
Harlem, MT	B8	29
Harlingen, TX	F4	46
Harlowton, MT	D7	29
Harney Lake, OR	D7	40
Harney Peak, SD	D2	44
Harper, KS	E5	19
Harpers Ferry National Historical Park, WV	B7	51
Harpersville, AL	B3	4
Harpeth, r., TN	A5	45
Harquahala Mountain, AZ	D2	6
Harrah, OK	B4	39
Harriman, TN	D9	45
Harriman Reservoir, VT	F3	48
Harrington, DE	E3	11
Harrington, ME	D5	22
Harrisburg, AR	B5	7
Harrisburg, IL	F5	16
Harrisburg, PA	F8	41
Harrisburg, SD	D9	44
Harrison, AR	A2	7
Harrison, ME	D2	22
Harrison, MI	D6	25
Harrison, NJ	k8	33
Harrison, NY	h13	35
Harrison, OH	C1	38
Harrison, TN	h11	45
Harrisonburg, VA	B4	49
Harrisonville, MO	C3	28
Harrisville, RI	B2	42
Harrisville, WV	B3	51
Harrodsburg, KY	C5	20
Harry S. Truman Reservoir, MO	C4	28
Hartford, AL	D4	4
Hartford, CT	B5	10
Hartford, KY	C3	20
Hartford, MI	F4	25
Hartford, SD	D9	44
Hartford, VT	D4	48
Hartford, WI	E5	52
Hartford City, IN	D7	17
Hartington, NE	B8	30
Hartland, VT	D4	48
Hartland, WI	E5	52
Hartley, IA	A2	18
Hartselle, AL	A3	4
Hartshorne, OK	C6	39
Hartsville, SC	C7	43
Hartsville, TN	A5	45
Hartwell, GA	B4	13
Hartwell Lake, US	B1	43
Harvard, IL	A5	16
Harvard, NE	D7	30
Harvard, Mount, CO	C4	9
Harvey, IL	B6	16
Harvey, LA	E5	21
Harvey, ND	B6	37
Harwinton, CT	B3	10
Harwood, ND	C9	37
Hasbrouck Heights, NJ	h8	33
Haskell, AR	C3	7
Haskell, OK	B6	39
Hastings, MI	F5	25
Hastings, MN	F6	26
Hastings, NE	D7	30
Hatch, NM	E2	34
Hatchie, r., TN	B2	45
Hatteras, Cape, NC	B7	36
Hattiesburg, MS	D4	27
Hatton, ND	B8	37
Haubstadt, IN	H2	17
Haut, Isle au, ME	D4	22
Hauula, HI	B4	14
Havana, IL	C3	16
Havasu, Lake, US	C1	6
Havelock, NC	C6	36
Haven, KS	E6	19
Haverford [Township], PA	o20	41
Haverhill, MA	A5	24
Haverstraw, NY	D7	35
Havre, MT	B7	29
Havre de Grace, MD	A5	23
Hawaii, state, US	C5	14
Hawaii, HI	D6	14
Hawaiian Islands, HI	m14	14
Hawaii Volcanoes National Park, HI	D6	14
Hawarden, IA	A1	18
Hawkinsville, GA	D3	13
Hawthorne, CA	n12	8
Hawthorne, NV	E3	31
Hawthorne, NJ	B4	33
Hayden, CO	A3	9
Hayden Lake, ID	B2	15
Hayes, Mount, AK	C10	5
Hayford Peak, NV	G6	31
Hays, KS	D4	19
Hays, MT	C8	29
Haysville, KS	g12	19
Hayti, MO	E8	28
Hayward, CA	h8	8
Hazard, KY	C6	20
Hazardville, CT	B5	10
Hazel Crest, IL	k9	16
Hazel Dell, WA	D3	50
Hazel Green, AL	A3	4
Hazel Park, MI	p15	25
Hazen, AR	C4	7
Hazen, ND	B4	37
Hazlehurst, GA	E4	13
Hazlehurst, MS	D3	27
Hazlet, NJ	C4	33
Hazleton, PA	E10	41
Headland, AL	D4	4
Healdton, OK	C4	39
Heart, r., ND	C3	37
Heath, OH	B3	38
Heavener, OK	C7	39
Heber City, UT	C4	47
Heber Springs, AR	B3	7
Hebron, IN	B3	17
Hebron, NE	D8	30
Hebron, ND	C3	37
He Devil, ID	D2	15
Heflin, AL	B4	4
Helena, AL	B3	4
Helena, AR	C5	7
Helena, MT	D4	29
Hellertown, PA	E11	41
Hells Canyon, US	B10	40
Hemet, CA	F5	8
Hemingford, NE	B2	30
Hempstead, NY	n15	35
Henagar, AL	A4	4
Henderson, KY	C2	20
Henderson, NE	D8	30
Henderson, NV	G7	31
Henderson, NC	A4	36
Henderson, TN	B3	45
Henderson, TX	C5	46
Hendersonville, NC	f10	36
Hendersonville, TN	A5	45
Henlawson, WV	n12	51
Henlopen, Cape, DE	E5	11
Hennessey, OK	A4	39
Henniker, NH	D3	32
Henning, MN	D3	26
Henryetta, OK	B6	39
Henry Mountains, UT	E5	47
Henrys Fork, r., US	E2	53
Hephzibah, GA	C4	13
Hereford, TX	B1	46
Herington, KS	D7	19
Herkimer, NY	B6	35
Hermann, MO	C6	28
Hermano Peak, CO	D2	9
Hermantown, MN	D6	26
Hermiston, OR	B7	40
Hernando, MS	A4	27
Herndon, VA	B5	49
Herrin, IL	F4	16
Hershey, PA	F8	41
Hesperia, CA	E5	8
Hesston, KS	D6	19
Hettinger, ND	D3	37
Hewitt, TX	D4	46
Heyburn, ID	G5	15
Hialeah, FL	G6	12
Hiawatha, IA	B6	18
Hiawatha, KS	C8	19
Hibbing, MN	C6	26
Hickam Air Force Base, HI	g10	14
Hickman, KY	f8	20
Hickman, NE	D9	30
Hickory, NC	B1	36
Hicksville, NY	E7	35
Hico, WV	C3	51
Higgins Lake, MI	D6	25
Higginsville, MO	B4	28
High Knob, US	A4	49
Highland, IL	E4	16
Highland, IN	A3	17
Highland Park, IL	A6	16
Highland Park, MI	p15	25
Highland Park, TX	n10	46
Highland Springs, VA	C5	49
Highmore, SD	C6	44
High Point, NC	B2	36
High Rock Lake, NC	B2	36
Highwood, IL	A6	16
Hill City, KS	C4	19
Hillcrest Heights, MD	C4	23
Hilliard, OH	k10	38
Hillsboro, IL	D4	16
Hillsboro, KS	D6	19
Hillsboro, NH	D3	32
Hillsboro, ND	B8	37
Hillsboro, OH	C2	38
Hillsboro, OR	B4	40
Hillsboro Canal, FL	F6	12
Hillsborough, NC	A3	36
Hillsdale, MI	G6	25
Hillside, NJ	k8	33
Hilo, HI	D6	14
Hilton Head Island, SC	G6	43
Hilton Head Island, SC	G6	43
Hinesville, GA	E5	13
Hingham, MA	B6	24
Hingham Bay, MA	g12	24
Hinsdale, IL	k9	16
Hinsdale, NH	E2	32
Hinton, WV	D4	51
Hiwassee, r., TN	D9	45
Hiwassee Lake, NC	f8	36
Hobart, IN	A3	17
Hobart, OK	B2	39
Hobbs, NM	E6	34
Hobe Sound, FL	E6	12
Hoboken, NJ	k8	33
Hockessin, DE	A3	11
Hocking, r., OH	C3	38
Hodgenville, KY	C4	20
Hoffman Estates, IL	h8	16
Hogansville, GA	C2	13
Hogback Mountain, MT	F4	29
Hohenwald, TN	B4	45
Hoisington, KS	D5	19
Hokes Bluff, AL	B4	4
Holbrook, AZ	C5	6
Holbrook, MA	B5	24
Holcomb, KS	E3	19
Holden, MO	C4	28
Holden, WV	D2	51
Holdenville, OK	B5	39
Holdrege, NE	D6	30
Hole in the Mountain Peak, NV	C6	31
Holladay, UT	C4	47
Holland, MI	F4	25
Hollandale, MS	B3	27
Hollidaysburg, PA	F5	41
Hollins, VA	C3	49
Hollis, OK	C2	39
Hollister, MO	E4	28
Holliston, MA	B5	24
Hollowtop Mountain, MT	E4	29
Holly Hill, FL	C5	12
Holly Springs, GA	B2	13
Holly Springs, MS	A4	27
Hollywood, AL	A4	4
Hollywood (part of Los Angeles), CA	m12	8
Hollywood, FL	F6	12
Holmen, WI	E2	52
Holstein, IA	B2	18
Holston, r., TN	C11	45
Holt, AL	B2	4
Holt, MI	F6	25
Holton, KS	C8	19
Holualoa, HI	D6	14
Holy Cross, Mountain of the, CO	B4	9
Holyoke, CO	A8	9
Holyoke, MA	B2	24
Holyoke Range, MA	B2	24
Homedale, ID	F2	15
Homer, AK	D9	5
Homer, LA	B2	21
Homerville, GA	E4	13
Homestead, FL	G6	12
Homestead National Monument of America, NE	D9	30
Homewood, AL	g7	4
Homewood, IL	B6	16
Hominy, OK	A5	39
Hondo, Rio, r., NM	D4	34
Honea Path, SC	C3	43
Honesdale, PA	C11	41
Honolulu, HI	B4	14
Hood, Mount, OR	B5	40
Hood Canal, WA	B2	50
Hoodoo Peak, WA	A5	50
Hood River, OR	B5	40
Hooker, OK	e9	39
Hooksett, NH	D4	32
Hooper, NE	C9	30
Hoopeston, IL	C6	16
Hoosac Range, US	A1	24
Hoover, AL	B3	4
Hoover Dam, US	G7	31
Hoover Reservoir, OH	B3	38
Hooverson Heights, WV	f8	51
Hopatcong, NJ	B3	33
Hopatcong, Lake, NJ	A3	33
Hope, AR	D2	7
Hope, IN	F6	17
Hope Mills, NC	C4	36
Hopewell, VA	C5	49
Hopi Indian Reservation, AZ	A5	6
Hopkins, MN	n12	26
Hopkinsville, KY	D2	20
Hoquiam, WA	C2	50
Horace, ND	C9	37
Horicon, WI	E5	52
Hornell, NY	C3	35
Horn Lake, MS	A3	27
Horse Cave, KY	C4	20
Horseheads, NY	C4	35
Horseshoe Bend, AR	A4	7
Horton, KS	C8	19
Hot Springs, SD	D2	44
Hot Springs National Park, AR	C2	7
Hot Springs National Park, AR	C2	7
Hot Springs Village, AR	C2	7
Houghton, MI	A2	25
Houghton Lake, MI	D6	25
Houghton Lake, MI	D6	25
Houlton, ME	B5	22
Houma, LA	E5	21
Housatonic, r., US	D3	10
Houston, MS	B4	27
Houston, MO	D6	28
Houston, TX	E5	46
Howard, SD	C8	44
Howard, WI	D5	52
Howards Grove-Millersville, WI	E6	52
Howell, MI	F7	25
Howland, ME	C4	22
Hoxie, AR	A5	7
Hoxie, KS	C3	19
Hoyt Lakes, MN	C6	26
Huachuca City, AZ	F5	6
Hualapai Mountains, AZ	C2	6
Hualapai Peak, AZ	B2	6
Hubbard, OH	A5	38
Hubbard Creek Lake, TX	C3	46
Hudson, IA	B5	18
Hudson, MA	B4	24
Hudson, NH	E4	32
Hudson, NY	C7	35
Hudson, WI	D1	52
Hudson, r., US	E7	35
Hudson, Lake, OK	A6	39
Hudson Falls, NY	B7	35
Hudson Lake, IN	A4	17
Hudsonville, MI	F5	25
Hueytown, AL	g6	4
Hugh Butler Lake, NE	D5	30
Hughes, AR	C5	7
Hugo, MN	m13	26
Hugo, OK	C6	39
Hugoton, KS	E2	19
Hull, IA	A1	18
Hull, MA	B6	24
Humble, TX	E5	46
Humboldt, IA	B3	18
Humboldt, KS	E8	19
Humboldt, NE	D10	30
Humboldt, TN	B3	45
Humboldt, r., NV	C3	31
Humphreys Peak, AZ	B4	6
Hungry Horse Reservoir, MT	B3	29
Hunter Mountain, NY	C6	35
Huntertown, IN	B7	17
Huntingburg, IN	H4	17
Huntingdon, PA	F6	41
Huntingdon, TN	A3	45
Huntington, IN	C7	17
Huntington, NY	E7	35
Huntington, WV	C2	51
Huntington Beach, CA	F4	8
Huntington Lake, IN	C7	17
Huntsville, AL	A3	4
Huntsville, AR	A2	7
Huntsville, MO	B5	28
Huntsville, TX	D5	46
Hurley, NM	E1	34
Huron, OH	A3	38
Huron, SD	C7	44
Huron, r., MI	p14	25
Huron, Lake, NA	B11	2
Huron Mountains, MI	B3	25
Hurricane, UT	F2	47
Hurricane, WV	C2	51
Hutchinson, KS	D6	19
Hutchinson, MN	F4	26
Huxley, IA	C4	18
Hyannis, MA	C7	24
Hyattsville, MD	C4	23
Hybla Valley, VA	g12	49
Hyco Lake, NC	A3	36
Hyde Park, VT	B3	48
Hydeville, VT	D2	48
Hyndman Peak, ID	F4	15
Hyrum, UT	B4	47

I

Name	Map Ref.	Page
Ibapah Peak, UT	D2	47
Icy Cape, AK	A7	5
Idabel, OK	D7	39
Ida Grove, IA	B2	18
Idaho, state, US	E3	15
Idaho Falls, ID	F6	15
Idaho Springs, CO	B5	9
Iliamna Lake, AK	D8	5
Iliamna Volcano, AK	C9	5
Ilion, NY	B5	35
Illinois, state, US	C4	16
Illinois, r., US	A7	39
Illinois, r., IL	B5	16
Immokalee, FL	F5	12
Imnaha, r., OR	B10	40
Imperial, NE	D4	30
Imperial Beach, CA	o15	8
Imperial Reservoir, US	E1	6
Imperial Valley, CA	F6	8
Incline Village, NV	D2	31
Independence, IA	B6	18
Independence, KS	E8	19
Independence, KY	B5	20
Independence, MO	B3	28
Independence, OR	C3	40
Independence National Historical Park, PA	p21	41
Independence Rock, WY	D5	53
Indiana, PA	E3	41
Indiana, state, US	E5	17
Indiana Dunes National Lakeshore, IN	A3	17
Indianapolis, IN	E5	17
Indian Neck, CT	D4	10
Indianola, IA	C4	18
Indianola, MS	B3	27
Indian River, FL	D6	12
Indian River Bay, DE	F5	11
Indio, CA	F5	8
Inglewood, CA	n12	8
Inkster, MI	p15	25
Institute, WV	m12	51
International Falls, MN	B5	26
Intracoastal Waterway, US	E4	21
Inver Grove Heights, MN	n12	26
Inwood, NY	k13	35
Inwood, WV	B6	51
Iola, KS	E8	19
Ionia, MI	F5	25
Iowa, state, US	C4	18
Iowa, r., IA	C6	18
Iowa City, IA	C6	18
Iowa Falls, IA	B4	18
Ipswich, SD	B6	44
Irmo, SC	C5	43
Irondale, AL	f7	4
Irondequoit, NY	B3	35
Iron Mountain, MI	C2	25
Iron Mountains, US	D1	49
Iron River, MI	B2	25
Ironton, OH	D3	38
Ironwood, MI	n11	25
Iroquois, r., US	C6	16
Irvine, CA	n13	8
Irvine, KY	C6	20
Irving, TX	n10	46
Irvington, NJ	k8	33
Irwin, PA	F2	41
Iselin, NJ	B4	33
Ishpeming, MI	B3	25
Island Pond, VT	B5	48
Isle of Palms, SC	k12	43
Isle of Wight Bay, MD	D7	23
Isle Royale National Park, MI	h9	25
Islesboro Island, ME	D4	22
Isleta, NM	C3	34
Issaquah, WA	B3	50
Isto, Mount, AK	B11	5
Istokpoga, Lake, FL	E5	12
Itasca, IL	k8	16
Ithaca, NY	C4	35
Itta Bena, MS	B3	27
Iuka, MS	A5	27
Ivanhoe, MN	F2	26
Ivoryton, CT	D6	10

J

Name	Map Ref.	Page
Jacinto City, TX	r14	46
Jackman, ME	C2	22
Jack Mountain, MT	D4	29
Jack Mountain, WA	A5	50
Jacks Mountain, PA	E6	41
Jackson, AL	D2	4
Jackson, GA	C3	13
Jackson, KY	C6	20
Jackson, LA	D4	21
Jackson, MI	F6	25
Jackson, MN	G4	26
Jackson, MS	C3	27
Jackson, MO	D8	28
Jackson, OH	C3	38
Jackson, TN	B3	45
Jackson, WI	E5	52
Jackson, WY	C2	53
Jackson Lake, WY	C2	53
Jackson Mountain, ME	D2	22
Jacksonville, AL	B4	4
Jacksonville, AR	C3	7
Jacksonville, FL	B5	12
Jacksonville, IL	D3	16
Jacksonville, NC	C5	36
Jacksonville, TX	D5	46
Jacksonville Beach, FL	B5	12
Jaffrey, NH	E2	32
Jal, NM	E6	34
Jamaica Bay, NY	k13	35
James, r., US	A8	2
James, r., MO	E4	28
James, r., VA	C5	49
James City, NC	B5	36
James Island, SC	k12	43
Jamestown, KY	D4	20
Jamestown, NY	C1	35
Jamestown, ND	C7	37
Jamestown, RI	F5	42
Janesville, WI	F4	52
Jasmine Estates, FL	D4	12
Jasonville, IN	F3	17
Jasper, AL	B2	4
Jasper, IN	H4	17
Jasper, TN	D8	45
Jay, OK	A7	39
Jay Peak, VT	B3	48
Jeanerette, LA	E4	21
Jeannette, PA	F2	41
Jefferson, GA	B3	13
Jefferson, IA	B3	18
Jefferson, LA	k11	21
Jefferson, WI	E5	52
Jefferson, r., MT	E5	29
Jefferson, Mount, ID	E7	15
Jefferson, Mount, NV	E5	31
Jefferson, Mount, OR	C5	40
Jefferson City, MO	C5	28
Jefferson City, TN	C10	45
Jefferson Farms, DE	i7	11
Jeffersontown, KY	B4	20
Jeffersonville, IN	H6	17
Jeffersonville, KY	C6	20
Jeffersonville, VT	B3	48
Jeffrey City, WY	D5	53
Jekyll Island, GA	E5	13
Jellico, TN	C9	45
Jemez Pueblo, NM	B3	34
Jenkins, KY	C7	20
Jenkintown, PA	o21	41
Jenks, OK	A6	39
Jennings, LA	D3	21
Jennings, MO	f13	28
Jensen Beach, FL	E6	12
Jericho, VT	B3	48
Jerimoth Hill, RI	C1	42
Jerome, ID	G4	15
Jersey City, NJ	B4	33
Jersey Shore, PA	D7	41
Jerseyville, IL	D3	16
Jessup, MD	B4	23
Jessup, PA	m18	41
Jesup, GA	E5	13
Jesup, IA	B5	18
Jesup, Lake, FL	D5	12
Jewett City, CT	C8	10
Jim Thorpe, PA	E10	41
Job Peak, NV	D3	31
Jocassee, Lake, US	B1	43
John Day, r., OR	C4	40
John F. Kennedy Space Center, FL	D6	12
John H. Kerr Reservoir, US	D4	49
John Martin Reservoir, CO	C7	9
John Redmond Reservoir, KS	D8	19
Johnson, KS	E2	19
Johnson, VT	B3	48
Johnson City, NY	C5	35
Johnson City, TN	C11	45
Johnston, IA	e8	18
Johnston, RI	C4	42
Johnston City, IL	F5	16
Johnstown, CO	A6	9
Johnstown, NY	B6	35
Johnstown, PA	F4	41
John W. Flannagan Reservoir, VA	e9	49
Joliet, IL	B5	16
Jones, OK	B4	39
Jonesboro, AR	B5	7
Jonesboro, GA	C2	13
Jonesboro, IN	D6	17
Jonesboro, LA	B3	21
Jonesborough, TN	C11	45
Jones Mill, AR	C3	7
Jonestown, MS	A3	27
Joplin, MO	D3	28
Joppatowne, MD	B5	23
Jordan, MT	C10	29
Jordan, r., UT	C4	47
Jornado del Muerto, NM	D3	34
J. Percy Priest Lake, TN	A5	45
Juan de Fuca, Strait of, NA	A1	50
Judsonia, AR	B4	7
Julesburg, CO	A8	9
Junction City, KS	C7	19
Junction City, KY	C5	20
Junction City, OR	C3	40
Juneau, AK	D13	5
June in Winter, Lake, FL	E5	12
Juniata, r., PA	F7	41
Jupiter, FL	F6	12
Jupiter Inlet, FL	F6	12

K

Name	Map Ref.	Page
Kaala, HI	f9	14
Kabetogama Lake, MN	B5	26
Kadoka, SD	D4	44
Kaena Point, HI	B3	14
Kahoka, MO	A6	28
Kahoolawe, HI	C5	14
Kahuku Point, HI	B4	14
Kahului, HI	C5	14
Kaibab Plateau, AZ	A3	6
Kailua, HI	B4	14
Kailua Kona, HI	D6	14
Kaiwi Channel, HI	B4	14
Ka Lae, HI	E6	14
Kalaheo, HI	B2	14
Kalamazoo, MI	F5	25
Kalamazoo, r., MI	F5	25
Kalispell, MT	B2	29
Kalona, IA	C6	18
Kamuela (Waimea), HI	C6	14
Kanab, UT	F3	47
Kanawha, r., WV	C3	51
Kane, PA	C4	41
Kaneohe, HI	B4	14
Kaneohe Bay, HI	g10	14
Kankakee, IL	B6	16
Kankakee, r., US	B5	16
Kannapolis, NC	B2	36
Kansas, state, US	D5	19
Kansas, r., KS	C7	19
Kansas City, KS	C9	19
Kansas City, MO	B3	28
Kapaa, HI	A2	14
Kaplan, LA	D3	21
Karns, TN	n13	45
Kaskaskia, r., IL	D5	16
Kasson, MN	F6	26
Katahdin, Mount, ME	C4	22
Kates Needle, AK	m24	5
Katmai, Mount, AK	D9	5
Katmai National Park, AK	D9	5
Katy, TX	r14	46
Kauai, HI	A2	14
Kauai Channel, HI	B3	14
Kauiki Head, HI	C6	14
Kaukauna, WI	D5	52
Kaulakahi Channel, HI	A2	14
Kawaikini, HI	A2	14
Kaw Lake, OK	A5	39
Kayenta, AZ	A5	6
Kaysville, UT	B4	47
Keahole Point, HI	D5	14
Keansburg, NJ	C4	33
Kearney, MO	B3	28
Kearney, NE	D6	30
Kearns, UT	C4	47
Kearny, AZ	D5	6
Kearny, NJ	h8	33
Keene, NH	E2	32
Keizer, OR	C3	40
Kekaha, HI	B2	14
Keller, TX	n9	46
Kellogg, ID	B2	15
Kelso, WA	C3	50
Kemmerer, WY	E2	53
Kenai, AK	C9	5
Kenai Fjords National Park, AK	D10	5
Kenai Mountains, AK	h16	5
Kenai Peninsula, AK	h16	5
Kendall, FL	s13	12
Kendallville, IN	B7	17
Kenduskeag, ME	D4	22
Kenesaw, NE	D7	30
Kenmare, ND	A3	37
Kenmore, NY	C2	35
Kennebec, r., ME	D3	22
Kennebunk, ME	E2	22
Kennebunkport, ME	E2	22
Kenner, LA	E5	21
Kennesaw, GA	B2	13
Kennett, MO	E7	28
Kennett Square, PA	G10	41
Kennewick, WA	C6	50
Kenosha, WI	F6	52
Kenova, WV	C2	51
Kensett, AR	B4	7
Kensington, CT	C4	10
Kent, OH	A4	38
Kent, WA	B3	50
Kent Island, MD	C5	23
Kentland, IN	C3	17
Kenton, OH	B2	38
Kent Point, MD	C5	23
Kentucky, state, US	C4	20
Kentucky, r., KY	B5	20
Kentucky Lake, US	C10	2
Kentwood, MI	F5	25
Keokuk, IA	D6	18
Keowee, Lake, SC	B2	43
Kern, r., CA	E4	8
Kernersville, NC	A2	36
Kerrville, TX	D3	46
Ketchikan, AK	D13	5
Ketchum, ID	F4	15
Kettering, OH	C1	38
Kettle Falls, WA	A7	50
Keuka Lake, NY	C3	35
Kewanee, IL	B4	16
Kewaskum, WI	E5	52
Kewaunee, WI	D6	52
Keweenaw Bay, MI	B2	25
Keweenaw Peninsula, MI	A3	25
Keweenaw Point, MI	A3	25
Keya Paha, r., US	A5	30
Keyhole Reservoir, WY	B8	53
Key Largo, FL	G6	12
Keyser, WV	B6	51
Keystone Lake, OK	A5	39
Key West, FL	H5	12
Kiamichi, r., OK	C6	39
Kiel, WI	E5	52
Kihei, HI	C5	14
Kilauea Crater, HI	D6	14
Kilgore, TX	C5	46
Killdeer, ND	B3	37
Killeen, TX	D4	46
Killen, AL	A2	4
Killington Peak, VT	D3	48
Kimball, NE	C2	30
Kimball, SD	D7	44
Kimberly, AL	B3	4
Kimberly, ID	G4	15
Kimberly, WI	h9	52
Kinchafoonee Creek, r., GA	E2	13
King, NC	A2	36
Kingfield, ME	D2	22
Kingfisher, OK	B4	39
Kingman, AZ	B1	6
Kingman, KS	E5	19
King of Prussia, PA	F11	41
Kings, r., CA	D4	8
King Salmon, AK	D8	5
Kings Canyon National Park, CA	D4	8
Kingsford, MI	C2	25
Kingsland, GA	F5	13
Kings Mountain, NC	B1	36
Kings Peak, UT	C5	47
Kingsport, TN	C11	45
Kingston, NH	E4	32
Kingston, NY	D6	35
Kingston, PA	D10	41
Kingston, RI	F3	42
Kingston, TN	D9	45
Kingstree, SC	D8	43
Kingsville, TX	F4	46
Kingwood, TX	q14	46
Kingwood, WV	B5	51
Kinsley, KS	E4	19
Kinston, NC	B5	36
Kiowa, KS	E5	19
Kiowa Creek, r., CO	B6	9
Kirkland, WA	B3	50
Kirksville, MO	A5	28
Kirkwood, MO	f13	28
Kirtland, NM	A1	34
Kissimmee, FL	D5	12
Kissimmee, r., FL	E5	12
Kissimmee, Lake, FL	E5	12
Kittanning, PA	E2	41
Kittatinny Mountain, US	B2	33
Kittery, ME	E2	22
Kitty Hawk, NC	A7	36
Klamath, r., US	B2	8
Klamath Falls, OR	E5	40
Klamath Mountains, US	E2	40
Klickitat, r., WA	C4	50
Klondike Gold Rush National Historical Park, AK	k22	5
Knife, r., ND	B3	37
Knightstown, IN	E6	17
Knob Noster, MO	C4	28
Knollwood, WV	m12	51
Knox, IN	B4	17
Knoxville, IL	C3	16
Knoxville, IA	C4	18
Knoxville, TN	D10	45
Koch Peak, MT	E5	29
Kodiak, AK	D9	5
Kodiak Island, AK	D9	5
Koko Head, HI	B4	14
Kokomo, IN	D5	17
Koolau Range, HI	f10	14
Koontz Lake, IN	B5	17
Korovin Volcano, AK	E5	5
Kosciusko, MS	B4	27
Koshkonong, Lake, WI	F5	52
Kotzebue, AK	B7	5
Kouts, IN	B3	17
Koyukuk, r., AK	B8	5
Kremmling, CO	A4	9
Kumukahi, Cape, HI	D7	14
Kuna, ID	F2	15
Kure Island, HI	k12	14
Kuskokwim, r., AK	C8	5
Kuskokwim Mountains, AK	C8	5
Kutztown, PA	E10	41

L

Name	Map Ref.	Page
Laau Point, HI	B4	14
La Barge, WY	D2	53
Lacey, WA	B3	50
Lackawanna, NY	C2	35
Lacombe, LA	D6	21
Laconia, NH	C4	32
La Crescent, MN	G7	26
La Crosse, KS	D4	19
La Crosse, WI	E2	52
Ladson, SC	F7	43
Ladysmith, WI	C2	52
Lafayette, AL	C4	4
Lafayette, CO	B5	9
Lafayette, GA	B1	13
Lafayette, IN	D4	17
Lafayette, LA	D3	21
Lafayette, NC	B3	36
Lafayette, TN	A5	45
Lafayette, Mount, NH	B3	32
La Follette, TN	C9	45
Lafourche, Bayou, r., LA	E5	21
La Grande, OR	B8	40
La Grange, GA	C1	13
La Grange, IL	B6	16
Lagrange, IN	A7	17
La Grange, KY	B4	20
La Grange, MO	A6	28
La Grange Park, IL	k9	16
Laguna Beach, CA	F5	8
La Habra, CA	n13	8
Lahaina, HI	C5	14
Lahontan Reservoir, NV	D2	31
Laie, HI	B4	14
La Junta, CO	D7	9
Lake Andes, SD	D7	44
Lake Bluff, IL	A6	16
Lake Charles, LA	D2	21
Lake Chelan National Recreation Area, WA	A5	50
Lake City, AR	B5	7
Lake City, FL	B4	12
Lake City, IA	B3	18
Lake City, MN	F6	26
Lake City, SC	D8	43
Lake City, TN	C9	45
Lake Elsinore, CA	F5	8
Lake Forest, IL	A6	16
Lake Geneva, WI	F5	52
Lake Hamilton, AR	g7	7
Lake Havasu City, AZ	C1	6
Lake in the Hills, IL	h8	16
Lake Jackson, TX	r14	46
Lakeland, FL	D5	12
Lakeland, GA	E3	13
Lake Magdalene, FL	o11	12
Lake Mead National Recreation Area, US	H7	31
Lake Mills, IA	A4	18
Lake Mills, WI	E5	52
Lake Orion, MI	F7	25
Lake Oswego, OR	B4	40
Lake Placid, NY	A7	35
Lake Pontchartrain Causeway, LA	h11	21

Name — Map Ref. — Page

Lake Providence, LA B4 21
Lake Shore, MD B5 23
Lakeside Park, KY h13 20
Lake Station, IN A3 17
Lake Stevens, WA A3 50
Lake View, IA B2 18
Lake Village, AR D4 7
Lakeville, MN F5 26
Lake Wales, FL E5 12
Lakewood, CA n12 8
Lakewood, CO B5 9
Lakewood, IA f8 18
Lakewood, NJ C4 33
Lakewood, OH A4 38
Lakewood, WA B3 50
Lake Worth, FL F6 12
Lake Zurich, IL h8 16
Lakin, KS E2 19
Lakota, ND A7 37
La Luz, NM E4 34
Lamar, CO C8 9
Lamar, MO D3 28
Lambertville, MI G7 25
Lame Deer, MT E10 29
La Mesa, CA F5 8
La Mesa, NM E3 34
Lamesa, TX C2 46
Lamoille, r., VT B3 48
La Moine, r., IL C3 16
Lamoni, IA D4 18
La Motte, Isle, VT B2 48
La Moure, ND C7 37
Lanai, HI C4 14
Lancaster, CA E4 8
Lancaster, KY C5 20
Lancaster, NH B3 32
Lancaster, NY C2 35
Lancaster, OH C3 38
Lancaster, PA F9 41
Lancaster, SC B6 43
Lancaster, TX n10 46
Lancaster, WI F3 52
Land Between the Lakes, US f9 20
Lander, WY D4 53
Landess, IN C6 17
Landrum, SC A3 43
Lanett, AL C4 4
Langdon, ND A7 37
Langley Park, MD f9 23
Lanham, MD C4 23
Lansdale, PA F11 41
Lansdowne, MD B4 23
L'Anse, MI B2 25
Lansford, PA E10 41
Lansing, IL B6 16
Lansing, KS C9 19
Lansing, MI F6 25
Lapeer, MI E7 25
Lapel, IN D6 17
La Place, LA h11 21
La Plata, MD C4 23
La Plata, MO A5 28
La Plata Peak, CO B4 9
Laporte, CO A5 9
La Porte, IN A4 17
La Porte, TX r14 46
La Porte City, IA B5 18
Laramie, WY E7 53
Laramie, r., US E7 53
Laramie Mountains, WY D7 53
Laredo, TX F3 46
Largo, FL E4 12
Largo, Key, FL G6 12
Larimore, ND B8 37
Larksville, PA n17 41
Larned, KS D4 19
Larose, LA E5 21
La Salle, CO A6 9
La Salle, IL B4 16
La Sal Mountains, UT E6 47
Las Animas, CO C7 9
Las Cruces, NM E3 34
Lassen Peak, CA B3 8
Lassen Volcanic National Park, CA B3 8
Las Vegas, NV G6 31
Las Vegas, NM B4 34
Lathrop, MO B3 28
Latrobe, PA F3 41
Lauderdale Lakes, FL r13 12
Laurel, DE F3 11
Laurel, MD B4 23
Laurel, MS D4 27
Laurel, MT E8 29
Laurel, NE B8 30
Laurel, VA C5 49
Laurel Bay, SC G6 43
Laurel River Lake, KY D5 20
Laurens, IA B3 18
Laurens, SC C3 43
Laurinburg, NC C3 36
Lavaca, AR B1 7
La Vale, MD k13 23
La Vergne, TN A5 45
La Vista, NE g12 30
Lawrence, IN E5 17
Lawrence, KS D8 19
Lawrence, MA A5 24
Lawrenceburg, IN F8 17
Lawrenceburg, KY B5 20
Lawrenceburg, TN B4 45
Lawrence Park, PA B1 41
Lawrenceville, GA C3 13
Lawrenceville, IL E6 16
Lawson, MO B3 28
Lawton, OK C3 39
Layton, UT B4 47
Leachville, AR B5 7
Lead, SD C2 44
Leadville, CO B4 9
Leaf, r., MS D5 27
League City, TX r14 46
Leakesville, MS D5 27
Lealman, FL p10 12
Leatherman Peak, ID E5 15
Leavenworth, KS C9 19
Leawood, KS D9 19
Lebanon, IL E4 16
Lebanon, IN D5 17
Lebanon, KY C4 20
Lebanon, MO D5 28
Lebanon, NH C2 32
Lebanon, OH C1 38
Lebanon, OR C4 40
Lebanon, PA F9 41
Lebanon, TN A5 45
Lebanon, VA f9 49
Lebanon Junction, KY C4 20
Le Claire, IA C7 18
Leconte, Mount, TN D10 45
Leech Lake, MN C4 26
Leech Lake Indian Reservation, MN C4 26
Leeds, AL B3 4
Leesburg, FL D5 12
Leesburg, VA A5 49
Lees Summit, MO C3 28
Leesville, LA C2 21
Lehi, UT C4 47
Lehigh, r., PA E10 41
Lehigh Acres, FL F5 12
Lehighton, PA E10 41
Leighton, AL A2 4
Leipsic, r., DE C3 11
Leisure City, FL s13 12
Leitchfield, KY C3 20
Leland, MS B3 27
Le Mars, IA B1 18
Lemhi, r., ID E5 15
Lemhi Range, ID E5 15
Lemmon, SD B3 44
Lemmon, Mount, AZ E5 6
Lemmon Valley, NV D2 31
Lemon Grove, CA o15 8
Lemont, IL B5 16
Lenexa, KS D9 19
Lennox, SD D9 44
Lenoir, NC B1 36
Lenoir City, TN D9 45
Lenox, IA D3 18
Leominster, MA A4 24
Leon, IA D4 18
Leonia, NJ h9 33
Leoti, KS D2 19
Lepanto, AR B5 7
Le Sueur, MN F5 26
Levelland, TX C1 46
Levisa Fork, r., US C7 20
Levittown, NY E7 35
Levittown, PA F12 41
Lewes, DE E5 11
Lewis, r., WA C4 50
Lewis, Mount, NV C5 31
Lewis and Clark Lake, US E8 44
Lewisburg, PA E8 41
Lewisburg, TN B5 45
Lewisburg, WV D4 51
Lewisport, KY C3 20
Lewis Smith Lake, AL B2 4
Lewiston, ID C1 15
Lewiston, ME D2 22
Lewistown, MT C7 29
Lewistown, PA E6 41
Lewisville, AR D2 7
Lewisville, TX C4 46
Lewisville Lake, TX C4 46
Lexington, KY B5 20
Lexington, MA B5 24
Lexington, MS B3 27
Lexington, MO B4 28
Lexington, NE D6 30
Lexington, NC B2 36
Lexington, TN B3 45
Lexington, VA C3 49
Lexington Park, MD D5 23
Libby, MT B1 29
Liberal, KS E3 19
Liberty, IN E8 17
Liberty, KY C5 20
Liberty, MO B3 28
Liberty, TX D5 46
Libertyville, IL A6 16
Licking, r., KY B6 20
Lidgerwood, ND C8 37
Lighthouse Point, MI C5 25
Ligonier, IN B6 17
Lihue, HI B2 14
Lilburn, GA h8 13
Lillinonah, Lake, CT C2 10
Lilly Grove, WV D3 51
Lima, OH B1 38
Limon, CO B7 9
Lincoln, AL B3 4
Lincoln, AR B1 7
Lincoln, IL C4 16
Lincoln, KS C5 19
Lincoln, ME C4 22
Lincoln, NE D9 30
Lincoln, NH B3 32
Lincoln City, OR C3 40
Lincoln Park, CO C5 9
Lincoln Park, MI p15 25
Lincolnshire, IL h9 16
Lincoln Tomb State Memorial, IL D4 16
Lincolnton, NC B1 36
Lincolnwood, IL h9 16
Lindale, GA B1 13
Linden, NJ k8 33
Lindenhurst, IL h8 16
Lindenhurst, NY n15 35
Lindenwold, NJ D3 33
Lindon, UT C4 47
Lindsay, OK C4 39
Lindsborg, KS D6 19
Lindstrom, MN E6 26
Lingle, WY D8 53
Lino Lakes, MN m12 26
Linton, IN F3 17
Linton, ND C5 37
Lipscomb, AL B3 4
Lisbon, IA C6 18
Lisbon, NH B3 32
Lisbon, OH B5 38
Lisbon Falls, ME E2 22
Lisburne, Cape, AK B6 5
Lisle, IL k8 16
Litchfield, IL D4 16
Litchfield, MN E4 26
Litchfield Park, AZ m8 6
Lithia Springs, GA h7 13
Lithonia, GA C2 13
Lititz, PA F9 41
Little, r., LA C3 21
Little Arkansas, r., KS D6 19
Little Belt Mountains, MT D6 29
Little Blue, r., US C6 19
Little Boars Head, NH E5 32
Little Chute, WI D5 52
Little Colorado, r., AZ B4 6
Little Diomede Island, AK B6 5
Little Egg Harbor, NJ D4 33
Little Falls, MN E4 26
Little Falls, NJ B4 33
Little Fork, r., MN B5 26
Little Gunpowder Falls, r., MD A4 23
Little Humboldt, r., NV B4 31
Little Kanawha, r., WV C4 51
Little Lake, LA E5 21
Little Missouri, r., US A7 2
Little Missouri, r., AR D2 7
Little Pee Dee, r., SC C9 43
Little Red, r., AR B4 7
Little Rock, AR C3 7
Little Sandy, r., KY B6 20
Little Sioux, r., US B2 18
Little Tennessee, r., US D9 45
Littleton, CO B6 9
Littleton, NH B3 32
Little Wabash, r., IL E5 16
Livermore, CA h9 8
Livermore, KY C2 20
Livermore, Mount, TX o12 46
Livermore Falls, ME D2 22
Livingston, AL C1 4
Livingston, MT E6 29
Livingston, NJ B4 33
Livingston, TN C8 45
Livonia, MI F7 25
Lizard Head Pass, CO D3 9
Lizard Head Peak, WY D3 53
Llano, r., TX D3 46
Lochearn, MD g10 23
Loch Raven Reservoir, MD B4 23
Lockhart, TX E4 46
Lock Haven, PA D7 41
Lockport, IL B5 16
Lockport, NY B2 35
Lockwood, MT E8 29
Lodi, CA C3 8
Lodi, NJ h8 33
Logan, IA C2 18
Logan, NM B6 34
Logan, OH C3 38
Logan, UT B4 47
Logan, WV D3 51
Logan Pass, MT B2 29
Logansport, IN C5 17
Loganville, GA C3 13
Lolo, MT D2 29
Lolo Pass, US C4 15
Lombard, IL k8 16
London, KY C5 20
London, OH C2 38
Londonderry, NH E4 32
Londontown, MD C4 23
Lone Grove, OK C4 39
Long Beach, CA F4 8
Long Beach, IN A4 17
Long Beach, MS g7 27
Long Beach, NY E7 35
Long Branch, NJ C5 33
Long Island, NY E7 35
Long Island Sound, US E7 35
Long Lake, ND C6 37
Longmeadow, MA B2 24
Longmont, CO A5 9
Long Prairie, MN E4 26
Longs Peak, CO A5 9
Long View, NC B1 36
Longview, TX C5 46
Longview, WA C3 50
Lonoke, AR C4 7
Lonsdale, RI B4 42
Loogootee, IN G4 17
Lookout, Cape, NC C6 36
Lookout Mountain, US D8 45
Lookout Pass, US B3 15
Loosahatchie, r., TN B2 45
Lopez Island, WA A3 50
Lorain, OH A3 38
Lordsburg, NM E1 34
Loris, SC C10 43
Los Alamos, NM B3 34
Los Altos, CA k8 8
Los Angeles, CA E4 8
Los Angeles Aqueduct, CA E4 8
Los Gatos, CA D2 8
Los Lunas, NM C3 34
Los Padillas, NM m7 34
Los Ranchos de Albuquerque, NM B3 34
Lost River Range, ID E5 15
Lost Trail Pass, US D5 15
Loudon, TN D9 45
Louisa, KY B7 20
Louisburg, KS D9 19
Louisburg, NC A4 36
Louisiana, MO B6 28
Louisiana, state, US C3 21
Louisiana Point, LA E2 21
Louisville, CO B5 9
Louisville, GA C4 13
Louisville, KY B4 20
Louisville, MS B4 27
Louisville, NE D9 30
Louisville, OH B4 38
Loup, r., NE C8 30
Loup City, NE C7 30
Loveland, CO A5 9
Loveland, OH n13 38
Loveland Pass, CO B5 9
Lovell, WY B4 53
Lovelock, NV C3 31
Lovenia, Mount, UT C5 47
Love Point, MD B5 23
Loves Park, IL A4 16
Loving, NM E5 34
Lovington, NM E6 34
Lowell, AR A1 7
Lowell, IN B3 17
Lowell, MA A5 24
Lower Klamath Lake, CA B3 8
Lower New York Bay, NJ B4 33
Lower Red Lake, MN C3 26
Loxley, AL E2 4
Lubbock, TX C2 46
Lubec, ME D6 22
Lucedale, MS E5 27
Lucky Peak Lake, ID F3 15
Ludington, MI E4 25
Ludlow, KY h13 20
Ludlow, MA B3 24
Ludlow, VT E3 48
Lufkin, TX D5 46
Lumberport, WV B4 51
Lumberton, MS D4 27
Lumberton, NC C3 36
Lund, NV E6 31
Luray, VA B4 49
Lusk, WY D8 53
Lutcher, LA D5 21
Lutherville-Timonium, MD B4 23
Lutz, FL D4 12
Luverne, AL D3 4
Luverne, MN G2 26
Luxora, AR B6 7
Lyman, WY E2 53
Lynchburg, TN B5 45
Lynchburg, VA C3 49
Lynches, r., SC D8 43
Lynden, WA A3 50
Lyndhurst, NJ h8 33
Lyndhurst, OH g9 38
Lyndon, KY g11 20
Lyndon, VT B4 48
Lyndon B. Johnson National Historical Site, TX D3 46
Lyndon B. Johnson Space Center, TX r14 46
Lyndonville, VT B4 48
Lynn, MA B6 24
Lynn, Lake, WV B5 51
Lynnfield, MA f11 24
Lynn Garden, TN C11 45
Lynn Haven, FL u16 12
Lynnwood, WA B3 50
Lynwood, CA n12 8
Lyons, CO A5 9
Lyons, GA D4 13
Lyons, IL k9 16
Lyons, KS D5 19
Lyons, NE C9 30

M

Mableton, GA h7 13
Mabscott, WV D3 51
Machias, ME D5 22
Machias Bay, ME D5 22
Mackinac, Straits of, MI C6 25
Mackinac Bridge, MI C6 25
Mackinac Island, MI C6 25
Mackinaw City, MI C6 25
Macomb, IL C3 16
Macon, GA D3 13
Macon, MS B5 27
Macon, MO B5 28
Madawaska, ME A4 22
Madeira, OH o13 38
Madelia, MN F4 26
Madeline Island, WI B3 52
Madill, OK C5 39
Madison, AL A3 4
Madison, AR B5 7
Madison, GA C3 13
Madison, IL E3 16
Madison, IN G7 17
Madison, ME D3 22
Madison, MN E2 26
Madison, MS C3 27
Madison, NE C8 30
Madison, NJ B4 33
Madison, SD D8 44
Madison, WV C3 51
Madison, WI E4 52
Madison, r., MT E5 29
Madison Heights, MI o15 25
Madison Heights, VA C3 49
Madisonville, KY C2 20
Madisonville, TN D9 45
Madras, OR C5 40
Madre, Laguna, TX F4 46
Madrid, IA C4 18
Magazine, AR B2 7
Magazine Mountain, AR B2 7
Magdalena, NM C2 34
Magee, MS D4 27
Magna, UT C3 47
Magnolia, AR D2 7
Magnolia, MS D3 27
Mahanoy City, PA E9 41
Mahomet, IL C5 16
Mahopac, NY D7 35
Maili, HI g9 14
Maine, state, US C3 22
Maize, KS g12 19
Makaha, HI g9 14
Makakilo City, HI g9 14
Makapuu Head, HI B4 14
Makawao, HI C5 14
Makushin Volcano, AK E6 5
Malad City, ID G6 15
Malden, MA B5 24
Malden, MO E8 28
Malheur, r., OR D9 40
Malheur Lake, OR D8 40
Malibu, CA m11 8
Malone, NY f10 35
Malta, MT B9 29
Malvern, AR C3 7
Malvern, PA o19 41
Malverne, NY k13 35
Mamaroneck, NY h13 35
Mammoth Cave National Park, KY C4 20
Mammoth Spring, AR A4 7
Mamou, LA D3 21
Manassas, VA B5 49
Manassas National Battlefield Park, VA g11 49
Manassas Park, VA B5 49
Manatee, r., FL E4 12
Manchester, CT B5 10
Manchester, GA D2 13
Manchester, IA B6 18
Manchester, KY C6 20
Manchester, MO f12 28
Manchester, NH E4 32
Manchester, TN B5 45
Manchester, VT E2 48
Manchester Center, VT E2 48
Mandan, ND C5 37
Mandeville, LA D5 21
Mangum, OK C2 39
Manhattan, KS C7 19
Manhattan Beach, CA n12 8
Manhattan Island, NY h13 35
Manheim, PA F9 41
Manila, AR B5 7
Manistee, MI D4 25
Manistee, r., MI D5 25
Manistique, MI C4 25
Manistique, r., MI B4 25
Manistique Lake, MI B5 25
Manitou Springs, CO C6 9
Manitowoc, WI D6 52
Mankato, MN F5 26
Manly, IA A4 18
Mannford, OK A5 39
Manning, IA C2 18
Manning, SC D7 43
Mannington, WV B4 51
Mansfield, AR B1 7
Mansfield, LA B2 21
Mansfield, OH B3 38
Mansfield, PA C7 41
Mansfield, TX n9 46
Mansfield, Mount, VT C3 48
Mansfield Hollow Lake, CT B7 10
Manson, IA B3 18
Manteno, IL B6 16
Manville, NJ B3 33
Manville, RI B4 42
Maple, r., IA B2 18
Maple, r., ND C8 37
Maple Grove, MN m12 26
Maple Heights, OH h9 38
Maple Shade, NJ D2 33
Mapleton, ND C8 37
Maplewood, MN n12 26
Maplewood, MO f13 28
Maplewood, NJ B4 33
Maquoketa, IA B7 18
Maquoketa, r., IA B6 18
Marana, AZ E4 6
Marble Canyon, AZ A4 6
Marblehead, MA B6 24
Marbleton, WY D2 53
Marceline, MO B5 28
Marco, FL G5 12
Marcus Baker, Mount, AK g18 5
Marcy, Mount, NY A7 35
Marengo, IL A5 16
Marengo, IA C5 18
Margaret, AL B3 4
Margate, FL F6 12
Marianna, AR C5 7
Marianna, FL B1 12
Marias Pass, MT B3 29
Maricopa, AZ E3 6
Maricopa Mountains, AZ m7 6
Marietta, GA C2 13
Marietta, OH C4 38
Marietta, OK D4 39
Marine City, MI F8 25
Marinette, WI C6 52
Marion, AL C2 4
Marion, AR B5 7
Marion, IL F5 16
Marion, IN C6 17
Marion, IA B6 18
Marion, KS D6 19
Marion, KY e9 20
Marion, MS C5 27
Marion, NC B1 36
Marion, OH B2 38
Marion, SC C9 43
Marion, SD D8 44
Marion, VA f10 49
Marion, Lake, SC E7 43
Marionville, MO D4 28
Marked Tree, AR B5 7
Markham, IL k9 16
Marks, MS A3 27
Marksville, LA C3 21
Mark Twain Lake, MO B6 28
Marlborough, CT C6 10
Marlborough, MA B4 24
Marlborough, NH E2 32
Marley, MD B4 23
Marlinton, WV C4 51
Marlow, OK C4 39
Marlton, NJ D3 33
Marmaduke, AR A5 7
Marmet, WV C3 51
Marquesas Keys, FL H4 12
Marquette, MI B3 25
Marquette Heights, IL C4 16
Marrero, LA E5 21
Marseilles, IL B5 16
Marshall, AR B3 7
Marshall, IL D6 16
Marshall, MI F6 25
Marshall, MN F3 26
Marshall, MO B4 28
Marshall, TX C5 46
Marshall, WI E4 52
Marshallton, DE B3 11
Marshalltown, IA B5 18
Marshfield, MA B6 24
Marshfield, MO D5 28
Marshfield, WI D3 52
Mars Hill, ME B5 22
Marsh Island, LA E4 21
Marsh Peak, UT C6 47
Martha's Vineyard, MA D6 24
Martin, SD D4 44
Martin, TN A3 45
Martin City, MT B3 29
Martinez, GA C4 13
Martin Lake, AL C4 4
Martinsburg, WV B7 51
Martins Ferry, OH B5 38
Martinsville, IN F5 17
Martinsville, VA D3 49
Marvell, AR C5 7
Marvine, Mount, UT E4 47
Maryland, state, US B4 23
Maryland City, MD B4 23
Maryland Heights, MO f13 28
Maryland Point, MD D3 23
Marys, r., NV B6 31
Marysville, KS C7 19
Marysville, MI F8 25
Marysville, OH B2 38
Marysville, WA A3 50
Maryville, MO A3 28
Maryville, TN D10 45
Mascoma, r., NH C2 32
Mascot, TN C10 45
Mascoutah, IL E4 16
Mason, OH C1 38
Mason, WV B2 51
Mason City, IA A4 18
Massachusetts, state, US B4 24
Massachusetts Bay, MA B6 24
Massena, NY f10 35
Massillon, OH B4 38
Massive, Mount, CO B4 9
Mastic Beach, NY n16 35
Matagorda Bay, TX E4 46
Matagorda Island, TX E4 46
Matagorda Peninsula, TX E5 46
Matanuska, r., AK g18 5
Mattapoisett, MA C6 24
Mattaponi, r., VA C5 49
Mattawamkeag, ME C4 22
Mattawamkeag, r., ME C4 22
Matterhorn, NV B6 31
Matteson, IL k9 16
Matthews, NC B2 36
Mattoon, IL D5 16
Maui, HI C6 14
Mauldin, SC B3 43
Maumee, OH A2 38
Maumee, r., US A2 38
Maumelle, AR h10 7
Maumelle, Lake, AR C3 7
Mauna Kea, HI D6 14
Mauna Loa, HI D6 14
Maunawili, HI g10 14
Maurepas, Lake, LA D5 21
Maurice, r., NJ E2 33
Mauston, WI E3 52
Maxwell Acres, WV g8 51
Mayfield, KY f9 20
Mayfield Heights, OH A4 38
Mayflower, AR C3 7
Maynard, MA B5 24
Maysville, KY B6 20
Mayville, ND B8 37
Mayville, WI E5 52
Maywood, IL k9 16
McAfee Peak, NV B6 31
McAlester, OK C6 39
McAllen, TX F3 46
McAlmont, AR h10 7
McCall, ID E2 15
McCandless, PA h13 41
McComb, MS D3 27
McCook, NE D5 30
McCormick, SC D3 43
McCrory, AR B4 7
McDonough, GA C2 13
McDowell Peak, AZ k9 6
McFarland, WI E4 52
McGehee, AR D4 7
McGill, NV D7 31
McGrath, AK C8 5
McGuire Air Force Base, NJ C3 33
McHenry, IL A5 16
McIntosh, MN C3 26
McKeesport, PA F2 41
McKees Rocks, PA F1 41
McKenzie, TN A3 45
McKenzie, r., OR C4 40
McKinley, Mount, AK C9 5
McKinney, TX C4 46
McLaughlin, SD B5 44
McLean, VA g12 49
McLoud, OK B4 39
McLoughlin, Mount, OR E4 40
McMechen, WV B4 51
McMillan, Lake, NM E5 34
McMinnville, OR B3 40
McMinnville, TN D8 45
McPherson, KS D6 19
McRae, GA D4 13
Mead, Lake, US A1 6
Meade, KS E3 19
Meade Peak, ID G7 15
Meadville, PA C1 41
Mebane, NC A3 36
Mechanic Falls, ME D2 22
Mechanicsburg, PA F7 41
Mechanicsville, VA C5 49
Medford, MA B5 24
Medford, OR E4 40
Medford, WI C3 52
Media, PA G11 41
Mediapolis, IA C6 18
Medical Lake, WA B8 50
Medicine Bow, r., WY E6 53
Medicine Bow Mountains, US E6 53
Medicine Bow Peak, WY E6 53
Medicine Lodge, KS E5 19
Medicine Lodge, r., US E4 19
Medina, NY B2 35
Medina, OH A4 38
Medina, WA e11 50
Medway, MA B5 24
Meeker, CO A3 9
Mehlville, MO f13 28
Melbourne, AR A4 7
Melbourne, FL D6 12
Melrose, MA B5 24
Melrose, MN E4 26
Melton Hill Lake, TN D9 45
Memphis, MO A5 28
Memphis, TN B1 45
Mena, AR C1 7
Menasha, WI D5 52
Mendenhall, MS D4 27
Mendota, IL B4 16
Mendota, Lake, WI E4 52
Menlo Park, CA k8 8
Menno, SD D8 44
Menominee, MI C3 25
Menominee, r., US C6 52
Menomonee Falls, WI E5 52
Menomonie, WI D2 52
Mentone, AL A4 4
Mentor, OH A4 38
Mentor-on-the-Lake, OH A4 38
Mequon, WI E6 52
Meramec, r., MO C7 28
Meraux, LA k12 21
Merced, CA D3 8
Merced, r., CA D3 8
Mercedes, TX F4 46
Mercer Island, WA B3 50
Mercerville, NJ C3 33
Meredith, NH C3 32
Meredith, Lake, TX B2 46
Meriden, CT C4 10
Meridian, ID F2 15
Meridian, MS C5 27
Meridian Hills, IN k10 17
Meridianville, AL A3 4
Merriam, KS k16 19
Merrill, WI C4 52
Merrillville, IN B3 17
Merrimac, MA A5 24
Merrimack, NH E4 32
Merrimack, r., US A5 24
Merritt Island, FL D6 12
Mesa, AZ D4 6
Mesabi Range, MN C6 26
Mesa Verde National Park, CO D2 9
Mescalero, NM D4 34
Mesilla, NM E3 34
Mesquite, NV G7 31
Mesquite, TX n10 46
Metairie, LA k11 21
Meteor Crater, AZ C4 6
Methow, r., WA A5 50
Methuen, MA A5 24
Meto, Bayou, r., AR C4 7
Metropolis, IL F5 16
Metter, GA D4 13
Metuchen, NJ B4 33
Metzger, OR h12 40
Mexico, ME D2 22
Mexico, MO B6 28
Miami, AZ D5 6
Miami, FL G6 12
Miami, OK A7 39
Miami Beach, FL G6 12
Miami Canal, FL F6 12
Miamisburg, OH C1 38
Miami Shores, FL G6 12
Miami Springs, FL G6 12
Michelson, Mount, AK B11 5
Michigamme Reservoir, MI B2 25
Michigan, state, US E6 25
Michigan, Lake, US B10 2
Michigan Center, MI F6 25
Michigan City, IN A4 17
Middleboro (Middleborough Center), MA C6 24
Middleburg Heights, OH h9 38
Middlebury, CT C3 10
Middlebury, IN A6 17
Middlebury, VT C2 48
Middle River, MD B5 23
Middlesboro, KY D6 20
Middlesex, NJ B4 33
Middleton, ID F2 15
Middleton, WI E4 52
Middletown, CT C5 10
Middletown, DE C3 11
Middletown, IN D6 17
Middletown, KY g11 20
Middletown, NJ C4 33
Middletown, NY D6 35
Middletown, OH C1 38
Middletown, PA F8 41
Middletown, RI E5 42
Midfield, AL g7 4
Midland, MI E6 25
Midland, TX D1 46
Midland City, AL D4 4
Midland Park, KS g12 19
Midlothian, IL k9 16
Midvale, UT C4 47
Midwest, WY C6 53
Midwest City, OK B4 39
Milan, IL B3 16
Milan, IN F7 17
Milan, MI F7 25
Milan, MO A4 28
Milan, NM B2 34
Milan, TN B3 45
Milbank, SD B9 44
Miles City, MT D11 29
Milford, CT E3 10
Milford, DE E4 11
Milford, IN B6 17
Milford, IA A2 18
Milford, ME D4 22
Milford, MA B4 24
Milford, MI F7 25
Milford, NE D8 30
Milford, NH E3 32
Milford, UT E2 47
Milford Lake, KS C6 19
Mililani Town, HI g9 14
Millbrook, AL C3 4
Millburn, NJ B4 33
Millcreek, UT C4 47
Millcreek Township, PA B1 41
Milledgeville, GA C3 13
Mille Lacs Lake, MN D5 26
Millen, GA D5 13
Miller, SD C7 44
Millersville, PA F9 41
Milliken, CO A6 9
Millington, TN B2 45
Millinocket, ME C4 22
Millinocket Lake, ME C4 22
Millport, AL B1 4
Mills, WY D6 53
Millsboro, DE F4 11
Millstone, r., NJ C3 33
Millvale, PA k14 41
Millville, NJ E2 33
Millville Lake, NH E4 32
Millwood Lake, AR D1 7
Milnor, ND C8 37
Milo, ME C4 22
Milpitas, CA k9 8
Milton, MA B5 24
Milton, NH D5 32

Name	Map Ref.	Page
Milton, PA	D8	41
Milton, VT	B2	48
Milton, WA	f11	50
Milton, WV	C2	51
Milton, WI	F5	52
Milton-Freewater, OR	B8	40
Milwaukee, WI	E6	52
Milwaukie, OR	B4	40
Mims, FL	D6	12
Minatare, NE	C2	30
Minden, LA	B2	21
Minden, NE	D7	30
Minden, WV	D3	51
Mineola, NY	E7	35
Mineral Point, WI	F3	52
Mineral Springs, AR	D2	7
Mineral Wells, TX	C3	46
Minersville, PA	E9	41
Minneapolis, KS	C6	19
Minneapolis, MN	F5	26
Minnesota, state, US	E4	26
Minnesota, r., MN	F2	26
Minnetonka, MN	n12	26
Minnetonka, Lake, MN	n11	26
Minot, ND	A4	37
Mint Hill, NC	B2	36
Minute Man National Historical Park, MA	g10	24
Miramar, FL	s13	12
Mishawaka, IN	A5	17
Mispillion, r., DE	E4	11
Mission, KS	m16	19
Mission, SD	D5	44
Mission, TX	F3	46
Mission Viejo, CA	n13	8
Missisquoi, r., VT	B3	48
Missisquoi Bay, VT	A2	48
Mississinewa, r., US	D7	17
Mississinewa Lake, IN	C6	17
Mississippi, state, US	C4	27
Mississippi, r., US	D9	2
Mississippi Delta, LA	E6	21
Mississippi Sound, US	E5	27
Mississippi State, MS	B5	27
Missoula, MT	D2	29
Missouri, state, US	C5	28
Missouri, r., US	B8	2
Missouri Buttes, WY	B8	53
Missouri City, TX	r14	46
Missouri Valley, IA	C2	18
Mitchell, IN	G5	17
Mitchell, NE	C2	30
Mitchell, SD	D7	44
Mitchell, Mount, NC	f10	36
Mitchellville, IA	C4	18
Moab, UT	E6	47
Moberly, MO	B5	28
Mobile, AL	E1	4
Mobile, r., AL	E1	4
Mobile Bay, AL	E1	9
Mobridge, SD	B5	44
Mocksville, NC	B2	36
Modesto, CA	D3	8
Moffat Tunnel, CO	B5	9
Mogollon Mesa, AZ	C4	6
Mogollon Rim, AZ	C5	6
Mohall, ND	A4	37
Mohave, Lake, US	H7	31
Mohawk, r., NY	C6	35
Mojave, r., CA	E5	8
Mojave Desert, CA	E5	8
Mokapu Peninsula, HI	g10	14
Mokelumne, r., CA	C3	8
Mokena, IL	k9	16
Molalla, OR	B4	40
Moline, IL	B3	16
Molokai, HI	B5	14
Momence, IL	B6	16
Monaca, PA	E1	41
Monadnock, Mount, NH	E2	32
Monahans, TX	D1	46
Monarch Pass, CO	C4	9
Moncks Corner, SC	E7	43
Mondovi, WI	D2	52
Monessen, PA	F2	41
Monett, MO	E4	28
Monette, AR	B5	7
Monida Pass, US	E6	15
Monmouth, IL	C3	16
Monmouth, ME	D2	22
Monmouth, OR	C3	40
Monocacy, r., MD	B3	23
Mono Lake, CA	D4	8
Monomoy Point, MA	C7	24
Monon, IN	C4	17
Monona, IA	A6	18
Monona, WI	E4	52
Monongah, WV	B4	51
Monongahela, PA	F2	41
Monongahela, r., US	G2	41
Monroe, GA	C3	13
Monroe, IA	C4	18
Monroe, LA	B3	21
Monroe, MI	G7	25
Monroe, NY	D6	35
Monroe, NC	C2	36
Monroe, WA	B4	50
Monroe, WI	F4	52
Monroe Center, CT	D3	10
Monroe City, MO	B6	28
Monroe Lake, IN	F5	17
Monroeville, AL	D2	4
Monroeville, PA	k14	41
Monrovia, CA	m13	8
Montague Island, AK	D10	5
Montana, state, US	D7	29
Montclair, NJ	B4	33
Montebello, CA	m12	8
Monterey, CA	D3	8
Monterey, TN	C8	45
Monterey Bay, CA	D2	8
Monterey Park, CA	m12	8
Montesano, WA	C2	50
Montevallo, AL	B3	4
Montevideo, MN	F3	26
Monte Vista, CO	D4	9
Montezuma, GA	D2	13
Montezuma, IA	C5	18
Montgomery, AL	C3	4
Montgomery, IL	B5	16
Montgomery, OH	o13	38
Montgomery, WV	C3	51
Montgomery City, MO	C6	28
Monticello, AR	D4	7
Monticello, GA	C3	13
Monticello, IL	C5	16
Monticello, IN	C4	17
Monticello, IA	B6	18
Monticello, KY	D5	20
Monticello, ME	B5	22
Monticello, MN	E5	26
Monticello, MS	D3	27
Monticello, NY	D6	35
Montoursville, PA	D8	41
Montpelier, ID	G7	15
Montpelier, IN	C7	17
Montpelier, VT	C3	48
Montrose, AL	E2	4
Montrose, CO	C3	9
Montrose, VA	m18	49
Montville, CT	D7	10
Monument Peak, ID	G4	15
Monument Valley, AZ	A5	6
Moorcroft, WY	B8	53
Moore, OK	B4	39
Moorefield, WV	B6	51
Moore Reservoir, US	B3	32
Moorestown, NJ	D3	33
Mooresville, IN	E5	17
Mooresville, NC	B2	36
Moorhead, MN	D2	26
Moorhead, MS	B3	27
Moosehead Lake, ME	C3	22
Mooselookmeguntic Lake, ME	D2	22
Moosic, PA	m18	41
Moosilauke, Mount, NH	B3	32
Moosup, CT	C8	10
Mora, MN	E5	26
Mora, NM	B4	34
Moreau, r., SD	B3	44
Morehead, KY	B6	20
Morehead City, NC	C6	36
Morenci, AZ	D6	6
Morgan City, LA	E4	21
Morganfield, KY	C2	20
Morganton, NC	B1	36
Morgantown, KY	C3	20
Morgantown, MS	D2	27
Morgantown, WV	B5	51
Moriah, Mount, NV	D7	31
Moriarty, NM	C3	34
Morrill, NE	C2	30
Morrilton, AR	B3	7
Morris, IL	B5	16
Morris, MN	E3	26
Morrison, IL	B4	16
Morristown, NJ	B4	33
Morristown, TN	C10	45
Morrisville, PA	F12	41
Morrisville, VT	B3	48
Morro Bay, CA	E3	8
Morrow, GA	C2	13
Morton, IL	C4	16
Morton, MS	C4	27
Morton Grove, IL	h9	16
Moscow, ID	C2	15
Moses Lake, WA	B6	50
Mosinee, WI	D4	52
Mosquito Creek Lake, OH	A5	38
Mosquito Lagoon, FL	D6	12
Moss Bluff, LA	D2	21
Moss Point, MS	E5	27
Mott, ND	C3	37
Moulton, AL	A2	4
Moultrie, GA	E3	13
Moultrie, Lake, SC	E7	43
Mound, MN	n11	26
Mound Bayou, MS	B3	27
Mound City, MO	A2	28
Moundridge, KS	D6	19
Mounds View, MN	m12	26
Moundsville, WV	B4	51
Mountainair, NM	C3	34
Mountain Brook, AL	g7	4
Mountain City, TN	C12	45
Mountain Grove, MO	D5	28
Mountain Home, AR	A3	7
Mountain Home, ID	F3	15
Mountain Iron, MN	C6	26
Mountain Lake, MN	G4	26
Mountain View, AR	B3	7
Mountain View, CA	k8	8
Mountain View, MO	D6	28
Mountain View, NM	C3	34
Mountain View, WY	E2	53
Mountain View, WY	D6	53
Mount Airy, NC	A2	36
Mount Angel, OR	B4	40
Mount Ayr, IA	D3	18
Mount Carmel, IL	E6	16
Mount Carmel, PA	E9	41
Mount Clemens, MI	F8	25
Mount Desert Island, ME	D4	22
Mount Gay, WV	D2	51
Mount Healthy, OH	o12	38
Mount Holly, NJ	D3	33
Mount Holly, NC	B1	36
Mount Hope, WV	D3	51
Mount Horeb, WI	E4	52
Mount Ida, AR	C2	7
Mount Joy, PA	F9	41
Mount Juliet, TN	A5	45
Mount Kisco, NY	D7	35
Mount Lebanon, PA	F1	41
Mount Olive, AL	B3	4
Mount Olive, NC	B4	36
Mount Olive, TN	n14	45
Mount Pleasant, IA	D6	18
Mount Pleasant, MI	E6	25
Mount Pleasant, PA	F2	41
Mount Pleasant, SC	F8	43
Mount Pleasant, TN	B4	45
Mount Pleasant, TX	C5	46
Mount Prospect, IL	A6	16
Mount Rainier, MD	f9	23
Mount Rainier National Park, WA	C4	50
Mount Rushmore National Memorial, SD	D2	44
Mount Sterling, KY	B6	20
Mount Vernon, AL	D1	4
Mount Vernon, IL	E5	16
Mount Vernon, IN	I2	17
Mount Vernon, IA	C6	18
Mount Vernon, KY	C5	20
Mount Vernon, MO	D4	28
Mount Vernon, NY	h13	35
Mount Vernon, OH	B3	38
Mount Vernon, WA	A3	50
Mount Washington, KY	B4	20
Mount Zion, IL	D5	16
Moville, IA	B1	18
Muddy Boggy Creek, r., OK	C6	39
Mukilteo, WA	B3	50
Mukwonago, WI	F5	52
Mulberry, AR	B1	7
Muldrow, OK	B7	39
Mullen, NE	B4	30
Mullens, WV	D3	51
Mullett Lake, MI	C6	25
Mullica, r., NJ	D3	33
Mullins, SC	C9	43
Mulvane, KS	E6	19
Muncie, IN	D7	17
Mundelein, IL	A5	16
Munford, AL	B4	4
Munford, TN	B2	45
Munfordville, KY	C4	20
Munhall, PA	k14	41
Munising, MI	B4	25
Munster, IN	A2	17
Murderkill, r., DE	D4	11
Murfreesboro, AR	C2	7
Murfreesboro, TN	B5	45
Murphy, MO	g13	28
Murphy, NC	f8	36
Murphysboro, IL	F4	16
Murray, KY	f9	20
Murray, UT	C4	47
Murray, Lake, SC	C5	43
Murrells Inlet, SC	D9	43
Muscatatuck, r., IN	G5	17
Muscatine, IA	C6	18
Muscle Shoals, AL	A2	4
Musconetcong, r., NJ	B4	33
Muskego, WI	F5	52
Muskegon, MI	E4	25
Muskegon, r., MI	E4	25
Muskegon Heights, MI	E4	25
Muskingum, r., OH	C4	38
Muskogee, OK	B6	39
Musselshell, r., MT	D9	29
Mustang, OK	B4	39
Myrtle Beach, SC	D10	43
Myrtle Grove, FL	u14	12
Myrtle Point, OR	D2	40
Mystic, CT	D8	10

N

Name	Map Ref.	Page
Naches, r., WA	C5	50
Nacogdoches, TX	D5	46
Nags Head, NC	B7	36
Nambe, NM	B4	34
Namekagon, r., WI	B2	52
Nampa, ID	F2	15
Nanakuli, HI	B3	14
Nanticoke, PA	D10	41
Nanticoke, r., US	D6	23
Nantucket, MA	D7	24
Nantucket Island, MA	D7	24
Nantucket Sound, MA	C7	24
Nanuet, NY	g12	35
Napa, CA	C2	8
Napatree Point, RI	G1	42
Naperville, IL	B5	16
Naples, FL	F5	12
Naples, ME	E2	22
Napoleon, ND	C6	37
Napoleon, OH	A1	38
Nappanee, IN	B5	17
Narberth, PA	p20	41
Narragansett, RI	F4	42
Narragansett Bay, RI	E5	42
Nashua, IA	B5	18
Nashua, NH	E4	32
Nashville, AR	D2	7
Nashville, GA	E3	13
Nashville, IL	E4	16
Nashville, NC	B5	36
Nashville, TN	A5	45
Nashwauk, MN	C5	26
Natchez, MS	D2	27
Natchitoches, LA	C2	21
Natick, MA	B5	24
National City, CA	F5	8
Natrona Heights, PA	E2	41
Natural Bridges National Monument, UT	F6	47
Naugatuck, CT	D3	10
Naugatuck, r., CT	D3	10
Naushon Island, MA	D6	24
Nautilus Park, CT	D7	10
Navajo, NM	B1	34
Navajo Indian Reservation, US	A4	6
Navajo Mountain, UT	F5	47
Navajo Reservoir, US	A2	34
Nazareth, PA	E11	41
Neah Bay, WA	A1	50
Nebo, Mount, UT	D4	47
Nebraska, state, US	C6	30
Nebraska City, NE	D10	30
Nederland, CO	B5	9
Nederland, TX	E6	46
Needham, MA	g11	24
Neenah, WI	D5	52
Neillsville, WI	D3	52
Nekoosa, WI	D4	52
Neligh, NE	B7	30
Nemadji, r., US	B1	52
Neodesha, KS	E8	19
Neosho, MO	E3	28
Nephi, UT	D4	47
Neponset, r., MA	h11	24
Neptune, NJ	C4	33
Ness City, KS	D4	19
Nett Lake Indian Reservation, MN	B6	26
Nettleton, MS	A5	27
Neuse, r., NC	B6	36
Nevada, IA	B4	18
Nevada, MO	D3	28
Nevada, state, US	D5	31
Nevada, Sierra, CA	D4	8
New, r., US	C3	51
New Albany, IN	H6	17
New Albany, MS	A4	27
Newark, AR	B4	7
Newark, CA	h8	8
Newark, DE	B3	11
Newark, NJ	B4	33
Newark, NY	B3	35
Newark, OH	B3	38
New Bedford, MA	C6	24
Newberg, OR	B4	40
New Berlin, WI	n11	52
New Bern, NC	B5	36
Newbern, TN	A2	45
Newberry, MI	B5	25
Newberry, SC	C4	43
New Braunfels, TX	E3	46
New Brighton, MN	m12	26
New Brighton, PA	E1	41
New Britain, CT	C4	10
New Brunswick, NJ	C4	33
Newburgh, IN	I3	17
Newburgh, NY	D6	35
Newburyport, MA	A6	24
New Canaan, CT	E2	10
New Carlisle, IN	A4	17
New Carrollton, MD	C4	23
New Castle, AL	B3	4
New Castle, DE	B3	11
New Castle, IN	E7	17
Newcastle, OK	B4	39
New Castle, PA	D1	41
Newcastle, WY	C8	53
New City, NY	D6	35
New Cumberland, PA	F8	41
New Cumberland, WV	A4	51
Newell, WV	A4	51
New England, ND	C3	37
Newenham, Cape, AK	D7	5
New Fairfield, CT	D2	10
Newfields, NH	D5	32
Newfound Gap, US	f9	36
Newfound Lake, NH	C3	32
New Gloucester, ME	E2	22
New Hampshire, state, US	C3	32
New Hampton, IA	A5	18
New Harbor, ME	E3	22
New Haven, CT	D4	10
New Haven, IN	B7	17
New Haven, WV	C3	51
New Holland, PA	F9	41
New Holstein, WI	E5	52
New Hope, AL	A3	4
New Hope, MN	m12	26
New Iberia, LA	D4	21
Newington, CT	C5	10
New Ipswich, NH	E3	32
New Jersey, state, US	C4	33
New Kensington, PA	E2	41
Newkirk, OK	A4	39
New Lenox, IL	B6	16
New London, CT	D7	10
New London, IA	D6	18
New London, NH	D3	32
New London, WI	D5	52
New Madrid, MO	E8	28
Newmarket, NH	D5	32
New Martinsville, WV	B4	51
New Mexico, state, US	C3	34
New Milford, CT	C2	10
New Milford, NJ	h8	33
Newnan, GA	C2	13
New Orleans, LA	E5	21
New Philadelphia, OH	B4	38
New Plymouth, ID	F2	15
New Point Comfort, VA	C6	49
Newport, AR	B4	7
Newport, KY	A5	20
Newport, ME	D3	22
Newport, MN	n13	26
Newport, NH	D2	32
Newport, OR	C2	40
Newport, RI	F5	42
Newport, TN	D10	45
Newport, VT	B4	48
Newport Beach, CA	n13	8
Newport News, VA	D6	49
New Port Richey, FL	D4	12
New Prague, MN	F5	26
New Providence, NJ	B4	33
New Richmond, OH	D1	38
New Richmond, WI	C1	52
New Roads, LA	D4	21
New Rochelle, NY	E7	35
New Rockford, ND	B6	37
New Salem, ND	C4	37
New Site, AL	B4	4
New Smyrna Beach, FL	C6	12
Newton, AL	D4	4
Newton, IL	E5	16
Newton, IA	C4	18
Newton, KS	D6	19
Newton, MA	B5	24
Newton, MS	C4	27
Newton, NJ	A3	33
Newton, NC	B1	36
New Town, ND	B3	37
Newtown Square, PA	p20	41
New Ulm, MN	F4	26
New Whiteland, IN	E5	17
New Windsor, NY	D6	35
New York, NY	E7	35
New York, state, US	C6	35
Niagara Falls, NY	B1	35
Niantic, CT	D7	10
Niceville, FL	u15	12
Nicholasville, KY	C5	20
Nichols Hills, OK	B4	39
Nickajack Lake, TN	D8	45
Nicoma Park, OK	B4	39
Niihau, HI	B1	14
Niles, IL	h9	16
Niles, MI	G4	25
Niles, OH	A5	38
Nimrod Lake, AR	C2	7
Ninnescah, r., KS	E6	19
Niobrara, r., US	B7	30
Nisqually, r., WA	C3	50
Nitro, WV	C3	51
Niwot, CO	A5	9
Nixa, MO	D4	28
Noble, OK	B4	39
Noblesville, IN	D6	17
Nogales, AZ	F5	6
Nolichucky, r., TN	C10	45
Nomans Land, MA	D6	24
Nome, AK	C6	5
Noorvik, AK	B7	5
No Point, Point, MD	D5	23
Nora Springs, IA	A5	18
Norco, LA	E5	21
Norcross, GA	C2	13
Norfolk, NE	B8	30
Norfolk, VA	D6	49
Norfork, AR	A3	7
Norfork Lake, US	A3	7
Norland, FL	s13	12
Normal, IL	C5	16
Norman, OK	B4	39
Norman, Lake, NC	B2	36
Normandy, MO	f13	28
Norridge, IL	k9	16
Norris Lake, TN	C10	45
Norristown, PA	F11	41
North Adams, MA	A1	24
North Albany, OR	k11	40
Northampton, MA	B2	24
Northampton, PA	E11	41
North Andover, MA	A5	24
North Arlington, NJ	h8	33
North Atlanta, GA	h8	13
North Attleboro, MA	C5	24
North Augusta, SC	D4	43
North Aurora, IL	k8	16
North Belmont, NC	B1	36
North Bend, NE	C9	30
North Bend, OR	D2	40
North Bend, WA	B4	50
North Bennington, VT	F2	48
North Bergen, NJ	h8	33
North Branch, NH	D3	32
North Branford, CT	D4	10
Northbridge, MA	B4	24
Northbrook, IL	h9	16
North Brother, ME	C4	22
North Brunswick, NJ	C4	33
North Canadian, r., OK	A5	39
North Canton, OH	B4	38
North Carolina, state, US	B3	36
North Cascades National Park, WA	A4	50
North Charleston, SC	F8	43
North Chicago, IL	A6	16
North Clarendon, VT	D3	48
North College Hill, OH	o12	38
North Conway, NH	B4	32
North Corbin, KY	D5	20
North Crossett, AR	D4	7
North Dakota, state, US	B5	37
North Eagle Butte, SD	B4	44
North East, PA	B2	41
Northeast Harbor, ME	D4	22
Northfield, MN	F5	26
Northfield, NH	D3	32
Northfield, VT	C3	48
Northfield Falls, VT	C3	48
North Fond du Lac, WI	E5	52
Northford, CT	D4	10
North Fort Myers, FL	F5	12
Northglenn, CO	B6	9
North Gulfport, MS	E4	27
North Hampton, NH	E5	32
North Haven, CT	D4	10
North Haven, ME	D4	22
North Hero Island, VT	B2	48
North Judson, IN	B4	17
North Kansas City, MO	h10	28
North Kingstown, RI	E4	42
Northlake, IL	k9	16
North Las Vegas, NV	G6	31
North Liberty, IN	A5	17
North Liberty, IA	C6	18
North Little Rock, AR	C3	7
North Manchester, IN	C6	17
North Manitou Island, MI	C4	25
North Mankato, MN	F4	26
North Miami, FL	G6	12
North Miami Beach, FL	s13	12
North Myrtle Beach, SC	D10	43
North Naples, FL	F5	12
North New River Canal, FL	F6	12
North Ogden, UT	B4	47
North Olmsted, OH	h9	38
North Park, IL	A4	16
North Pembroke, MA	B6	24
North Plainfield, NJ	B4	33
North Platte, NE	C5	30
North Platte, r., US	B7	2
North Point, MI	C7	25
North Pole, AK	C10	5
Northport, AL	B2	4
North Providence, RI	C4	42
North Raccoon, r., IA	C3	18
North Reading, MA	f11	24
North Richland Hills, TX	n9	46
Northridge, OH	C2	38
North Ridgeville, OH	A3	38
North Royalton, OH	h9	38
North Salem, NH	E4	32
North Salt Lake, UT	C4	47
North Sioux City, SD	E9	44
North Skunk, r., IA	C5	18
North Springfield, VT	E3	48
North St. Paul, MN	m13	26
North Stratford, NH	A3	32
North Sudbury, MA	g10	24
North Swanzey, NH	E2	32
North Syracuse, NY	B4	35
North Tarrytown, NY	D7	35
North Terre Haute, IN	E3	17
North Tonawanda, NY	B2	35
North Troy, VT	B4	48
North Turner Mountain, ME	C4	22
North Vernon, IN	F6	17
North Walpole, NH	D2	32
North Wilkesboro, NC	A1	36
North Windham, ME	E2	22
Northwood, IA	A4	18
Northwood, ND	B8	37
North Woodstock, NH	B3	32
Norton, KS	C4	19
Norton, OH	A4	38
Norton, VA	f9	49
Norton Shores, MI	E4	25
Norton Sound, AK	C6	5
Norwalk, CA	n12	8
Norwalk, CT	E2	10
Norwalk, IA	C4	18
Norwalk, OH	A3	38
Norwalk, r., CT	E2	10
Norway, ME	D2	22
Norwich, CT	C7	10
Norwich, NY	C5	35
Norwich, VT	D4	48
Norwood, MA	B5	24
Norwood, OH	o13	38
Norwood, PA	p20	41
Nottoway, r., VA	D5	49
Novato, CA	C2	8
Novi, MI	p15	25
Nowata, OK	A6	39
Nowood, r., WY	B5	53
Noxon Reservoir, MT	C1	29
Noxubee, r., US	B5	27
Nueces, r., TX	E3	46
Nulhegan, r., VT	B5	48
Nunivak Island, AK	D6	5
Nutley, NJ	B4	33
Nutter Fort, WV	k10	51

O

Name	Map Ref.	Page
Oahe, Lake, US	A7	2
Oahu, HI	B4	14
Oak Creek, WI	n12	52
Oakdale, LA	D3	21
Oakes, ND	C7	37
Oak Forest, IL	k9	16
Oak Grove, KY	D2	20
Oak Grove, OR	B4	40
Oak Harbor, WA	A3	50
Oak Hill, TN	A5	45
Oak Hill, WV	D3	51
Oakhurst, OK	A5	39
Oakland, CA	D2	8
Oakland, IA	C2	18
Oakland, ME	D3	22
Oakland, NE	C9	30
Oakland, NJ	A4	33
Oakland City, IN	H3	17
Oakland Park, FL	r13	12
Oak Lawn, IL	B6	16
Oaklawn, KS	g12	19
Oakley, KS	C3	19
Oakmont, PA	E2	41
Oak Park, IL	B6	16
Oak Park, MI	p15	25
Oakridge, OR	D4	40
Oak Ridge, TN	C9	45
Oakton, VA	g12	49
Oakville, CT	C3	10
Oakville, MO	g13	28
Oberlin, KS	C3	19
Oberlin, OH	A3	38
Obion, r., TN	A2	45
Ocala, FL	C4	12
Oceana, WV	D3	51
Ocean Bluff, MA	B6	24
Ocean City, MD	D7	23
Ocean City, NJ	E3	33
Oceanside, CA	F5	8
Ocean Springs, MS	E5	27
Ocean [Township], NJ	C4	33
Ochlockonee, r., FL	B2	12
Ocilla, GA	E3	13
Ocmulgee, r., GA	D3	13
Ocoee, FL	D5	12
Oconee, r., GA	C3	13
Oconee, Lake, GA	C3	13
Oconomowoc, WI	E5	52
Oconto, WI	D6	52
Oconto, r., WI	D5	52
Oconto Falls, WI	D5	52
Ocracoke Island, NC	B7	36
Odenton, MD	B4	23
Odessa, MO	C4	28
Odessa, TX	D1	46
Odon, IN	G4	17
Oelwein, IA	B6	18
O'Fallon, IL	E4	16
O'Fallon, MO	f12	28
Ogallala, NE	C4	30
Ogden, IA	B3	18
Ogden, KS	C7	19
Ogden, UT	B4	47
Ogdensburg, NY	f9	35
Ogeechee, r., GA	D5	13
Oglesby, IL	B4	16
Ohatchee, AL	B3	4
Ohio, state, US	B3	38
Ohio, r., US	C11	2
Oil City, PA	D2	41
Okeechobee, Lake, FL	F6	12
Okefenokee Swamp, US	F4	13
Okemah, OK	B5	39
Oklahoma, state, US	B4	39
Oklahoma City, OK	B4	39
Oklawaha, r., FL	C5	12
Oklawaha, Lake, FL	C5	12
Okmulgee, OK	B6	39
Okolona, KY	g11	20
Okolona, MS	B5	27
Ola, AR	B2	7
Olathe, CO	C3	9
Olathe, KS	D9	19
Old Bridge, NJ	C4	33
Old Faithful Geyser, WY	B2	53
Old Forge, PA	D10	41
Old Hickory Lake, TN	A5	45
Old Man of the Mountain, NH	B3	32
Old Orchard Beach, ME	E2	22
Old Point Comfort, VA	h15	49
Old Speck Mountain, ME	D2	22
Old Town, ME	D4	22
Olean, NY	C2	35
Olive Branch, MS	A4	27
Olive Hill, KY	B6	20
Oliver Springs, TN	C9	45
Olivia, MN	F4	26
Olmsted Falls, OH	h9	38
Olney, IL	E5	16
Olney, MD	B3	23
Olympia, WA	B3	50
Olympic Mountains, WA	B2	50
Olympic National Park, WA	B2	50
Olympus, Mount, WA	B2	50
Olyphant, PA	D10	41
Omaha, NE	C10	30
Omak, WA	A6	50
Omro, WI	D5	52
Onalaska, WI	E2	52
Onawa, IA	B1	18
Oneida, NY	B5	35
Oneida, TN	C9	45
Oneida Lake, NY	B5	35
O'Neill, NE	B7	30
Oneonta, AL	B3	4
Oneonta, NY	C5	35
Onida, SD	C5	44
Onslow Bay, NC	C5	36
Ontario, CA	E5	8
Ontario, OR	C10	40
Ontario, Lake, NA	B12	2
Ontonagon, MI	m12	25
Oolitic, IN	G4	17
Oologah Lake, OK	A6	39
Opa-Locka, FL	s13	12
Opelika, AL	C4	4
Opelousas, LA	D3	21
Opp, AL	D3	4
Opportunity, WA	B8	50
Optima Reservoir, OK	e9	39
Oracle, AZ	E5	6
Orange, CA	n13	8
Orange, CT	D3	10
Orange, NJ	B4	33
Orange, TX	D6	46
Orange Beach, AL	E2	4
Orangeburg, SC	E6	43
Orange City, IA	B1	18
Orange Grove, MS	E5	27
Orange Park, FL	B5	12
Orcas Island, WA	A3	50
Orchard City, CO	C3	9
Orchard Homes, MT	D2	29
Orchards, WA	D3	50
Orchard Valley, WY	E8	53
Ord, NE	C7	30
Oregon, IL	A4	16
Oregon, MO	B2	28
Oregon, OH	A2	38
Oregon, WI	F4	52
Oregon, state, US	C6	40
Oregon City, OR	B4	40
Orem, UT	C4	47
Orlando, FL	D5	12
Orland Park, IL	k9	16
Orleans, IN	G5	17
Orleans, VT	B4	48
Ormond Beach, FL	C5	12
Orofino, ID	C2	15
Orono, ME	D4	22
Oroville, Lake, CA	C3	8
Orrington, ME	D4	22
Orrville, OH	B4	38
Ortonville, MN	E2	26
Osage, IA	A5	18
Osage, r., MO	C3	28
Osage Beach, MO	C5	28
Osage City, KS	D8	19
Osawatomie, KS	D9	19
Osborne, KS	C5	19
Osburn, ID	B3	15
Osceola, AR	B6	7
Osceola, IN	A5	17
Osceola, IA	C4	18
Osceola, NE	C8	30
Osgood, IN	F7	17
Oshkosh, NE	C3	30
Oshkosh, WI	D5	52
Oskaloosa, IA	C5	18
Ossabaw Island, GA	E5	13
Ossian, IN	C7	17
Ossining, NY	D7	35
Ossipee, r., US	C5	32
Oswegatchie, r., NY	f9	35
Oswego, IL	B5	16
Oswego, KS	E8	19
Oswego, NY	B4	35
Othello, WA	C6	50
Otis Orchards, WA	g14	50
Ottawa, IL	B5	16
Ottawa, KS	D8	19
Ottawa Hills, OH	e6	38
Otter Creek, r., VT	C2	48
Otter Tail, r., MN	D2	26
Otter Tail Lake, MN	D3	26
Ottumwa, IA	C5	18
Ouachita, Lake, AR	C2	7
Ouachita Mountains, US	D9	2
Outer Island, WI	A3	52
Overland, MO	f13	28
Overland Park, KS	m16	19
Overlea, MD	B4	23
Owasco Lake, NY	C4	35
Owasso, OK	A6	39
Owatonna, MN	F5	26
Owens, r., CA	D4	8
Owensboro, KY	C2	20
Owens Lake, CA	D5	8
Owensville, MO	C6	28
Owings Mills, MD	B4	23
Owls Head, ME	D3	22
Owosso, MI	E6	25
Owyhee, NV	B5	31
Owyhee, r., US	E9	40
Owyhee, Lake, OR	D9	40
Owyhee Mountains, US	G2	15
Oxford, AL	B4	4
Oxford, KS	E6	19
Oxford, MA	B4	24
Oxford, MS	A4	27
Oxford, NE	D6	30
Oxford, NC	A4	36
Oxford, OH	C1	38
Oxnard, CA	E4	8
Oxon Hill, MD	f9	23
Oyster Bay, NY	E7	35
Ozark, AL	D4	4
Ozark, AR	B2	7
Ozark, MO	D4	28
Ozark Escarpment, US	B4	7
Ozark Plateau, US	C9	2
Ozark Reservoir, AR	B1	7
Ozarks, Lake of the, MO	C5	28

Name | Map Ref. | Page

P

Pacific, MO C7 28
Pacific, WA f11 50
Pacifica, CA h8 8
Pacific Grove, CA D3 8
Pacific Palisades, HI g10 14
Packwood, WA C4 50
Paddock Lake, WI n11 52
Paden City, WV B4 51
Padre Island, TX F4 46
Padre Island National Seashore, TX F4 46
Paducah, KY e9 20
Page, AZ A4 6
Pageland, SC B7 43
Pagoda Peak, CO A3 9
Pagosa Springs, CO D3 9
Pahrump, NV G6 31
Painesville, OH A4 38
Painted Desert, AZ B4 6
Painted Rock Reservoir, AZ D3 6
Paintsville, KY C7 20
Palatine, IL A5 16
Palatka, FL C5 12
Palestine, TX D5 46
Palisade, CO B2 9
Palisades Park, NJ h8 33
Palisades Reservoir, US F7 15
Palm Bay, FL D6 12
Palm Beach, FL F6 12
Palmdale, CA E4 8
Palm Desert, CA F5 8
Palmer, AK C10 5
Palmer, MS D4 27
Palmer Lake, CO B6 9
Palmerton, PA E10 41
Palmetto, GA C2 13
Palm Harbor, FL o10 12
Palm Springs, CA F5 8
Palm Valley, FL m9 12
Palmyra, MO B6 28
Palmyra, NJ C2 33
Palmyra, PA F8 41
Palo Alto, CA D2 8
Palos Park, IL k9 16
Palos Verdes Estates, CA n12 8
Palouse, r., WA C7 50
Pamlico, r., NC B6 36
Pamlico Sound, NC B6 36
Pampa, TX B2 46
Pamunkey, r., VA C5 49
Pana, IL D4 16
Panama City, FL u16 12
Paola, KS D9 19
Paoli, IN G5 17
Paoli, PA o20 41
Paonia, CO C3 9
Papillion, NE C9 30
Paradise, NV G6 31
Paradise Hills, NM B3 34
Paradise Valley, AZ k9 6
Paragould, AR A5 7
Paramus, NJ h8 33
Paris, AR B2 7
Paris, IL D6 16
Paris, KY B5 20
Paris, MO B5 28
Paris, TN A3 45
Paris, TX C5 46
Park City, KS g12 19
Park City, UT C4 47
Parker, AZ C1 6
Parker, CO B6 9
Parker, SD D8 44
Parker City, IN D7 17
Parkersburg, IA B5 18
Parkersburg, WV B3 51
Park Falls, WI C3 52
Park Forest, IL B6 16
Park Hills, KY h13 20
Parkin, AR B5 7
Parkland, WA f11 50
Park Range, CO A4 9
Park Rapids, MN D3 26
Park Ridge, IL B6 16
Park River, ND A8 37
Parkrose, OR B4 40
Parkston, SD D8 44
Parkville, MD B4 23
Parkville, MO B3 28
Parkwater, WA g14 50
Parkwood, NC B4 36
Parma, ID F2 15
Parma, OH A4 38
Parma Heights, OH h9 38
Parrish, AL B2 4
Parshall, ND B3 37
Parsons, KS E8 19
Parsons, WV B5 51
Pasadena, CA E4 8
Pasadena, MD B4 23
Pasadena, TX r14 46
Pascagoula, MS E5 27
Pascagoula, r., MS E5 27
Pasco, WA C6 50
Pascoag, RI B2 42
Passaic, NJ B4 33
Passaic, r., NJ h8 33
Passamaquoddy Bay, ME C6 22
Pass Christian, MS E4 27
Passumpsic, r., VT C4 48
Patapsco, r., MD B4 23
Patchogue, NY n15 35
Paterson, NJ B4 33
Pathfinder Reservoir, WY D6 53
Patoka, r., IN H2 17
Patoka Lake, IN H4 17
Patrick Air Force Base, FL D6 12
Patten, ME C4 22
Patterson, LA E4 21
Patuxent, r., MD D4 23
Paulina Peak, OR E5 40
Paulins Kill, r., NJ A3 33
Pauls Valley, OK C4 39
Pavlof Volcano, AK D7 5
Pawcatuck, CT D8 10
Pawcatuck, r., RI G1 42
Pawhuska, OK A5 39
Pawnee, OK A5 39
Pawnee City, NE D9 30
Paw Paw, MI F5 25
Pawtucket, RI C4 42
Pawtuxet, r., RI C4 42
Paxton, IL C5 16
Payette, ID E2 15
Paynesville, MN E4 26
Payson, AZ C4 6
Payson, UT C4 47
Pea, r., AL D3 4
Peabody, KS D6 19
Peabody, MA A6 24
Peace, r., FL E5 12
Peace Dale, RI F3 42
Peale, Mount, UT E6 47
Pea Ridge, AR A1 7
Pearl, MS C3 27
Pearl, r., US D3 27
Pearland, TX r14 46
Pearl City, HI B4 14
Pearl Harbor, HI B3 14
Pearl River, NY g12 35
Pecatonica, r., US A4 16
Pecos, NM B4 34
Pecos, TX D1 46
Pecos, r., US D7 2
Peekskill, NY D7 35
Pekin, IL C4 16
Pelahatchie, MS C4 27
Pelham, AL B3 4
Pelham, GA E2 13
Pelham, NH E4 32
Pelican Rapids, MN D2 26
Pella, IA C5 18
Pell City, AL B3 4
Peloncillo Mountains, US E1 34
Pemadumcook Lake, ME C3 22
Pembina, ND A8 37
Pembroke Pines, FL r13 12
Pemigewasset, r., NH C3 32
Pender, NE B9 30
Pendleton, IN E6 17
Pendleton, OR B8 40
Pendleton, SC B2 43
Pend Oreille, Lake, ID A2 15
Pennell, Mount, UT F5 47
Penn Hills, PA k14 41
Pennington Gap, VA f8 49
Pennsauken, NJ D2 33
Pennsboro, WV B4 51
Pennsville, NJ D1 33
Pennsylvania, state, US E7 41
Penobscot, r., ME C4 22
Penobscot Bay, ME D3 22
Pensacola, FL u14 12
Pentagon Mountain, MT C3 29
Peoria, AZ D3 6
Peoria, IL C4 16
Peoria Heights, IL C4 16
Peotone, IL B6 16
Pepin, Lake, US D1 52
Pepperell, MA A4 24
Pequannock, NJ B4 33
Pequot Lakes, MN D4 26
Perdido Bay, AL E2 4
Perham, MN D3 26
Perkasie, PA F11 41
Perrine, FL G6 12
Perry, FL B3 12
Perry, GA D3 13
Perry, IA C3 18
Perry, OK A4 39
Perry Hall, MD B5 23
Perry Lake, KS C8 19
Perrysburg, OH A2 38
Perryton, TX A2 46
Perryville, AR B3 7
Perryville, MO D8 28
Perth Amboy, NJ B4 33
Peru, IL B4 16
Peru, IN C5 17
Peru, NE D10 30
Peshtigo, WI C6 52
Peshtigo, r., WI C5 52
Petal, MS D4 27
Petenwell Lake, WI D4 52
Peterborough, NH E3 32
Petersburg, AK D13 5
Petersburg, IN H3 17
Petersburg, VA C5 49
Petersburg, WV B5 51
Petersville, AL A2 4
Petit Bois Island, MS E5 27
Petit Jean, r., AR B2 7
Petoskey, MI C6 25
Petrified Forest National Park, AZ B6 6
Pevely, MO g13 28
Pewaukee, WI E5 52
Pharr, TX F3 46
Phelps Lake, NC B6 36
Phenix City, AL C4 4
Philadelphia, MS C4 27
Philadelphia, PA G11 41
Phil Campbell, AL A2 4
Philip, SD C4 44
Philippi, WV B4 51
Philipsburg, MT D3 29
Phillips, ME D2 22
Phillipsburg, KS C4 19
Phillipsburg, NJ B2 33
Philomath, OR C3 40
Philpott Reservoir, VA D2 49
Phoenix, AZ D3 6
Phoenix, OR E4 40
Phoenixville, PA F10 41
Picayune, MS E4 27
Pickerington, OH C3 38
Pickwick Lake, US A6 27
Pico Rivera, CA n12 8
Pictured Rocks National Lakeshore, MI B4 25
Piedmont, AL B4 4
Piedmont, MO D7 28
Piedmont, OK B4 39
Piedmont, SC B3 43
Piedmont, WV B5 51
Pierce, NE B8 30
Pierce, Lake, FL E5 12
Pierce City, MO E3 28
Pierre, SD C5 44
Pierre Part, LA k9 21
Pigeon, MI E7 25
Pigeon Forge, TN D10 45
Pigeon Point, MN h10 26
Pigg, r., VA D3 49
Piggott, AR A5 7
Pikes Peak, CO C5 9
Pikesville, MD B4 23
Pikeville, KY C7 20
Pilot Peak, NV B7 31
Pima, AZ E6 6
Pimmit Hills, VA g12 49
Pinardville, NH E3 32
Pinckney, MI F7 25
Pinckneyville, IL E4 16
Pinconning, MI E7 25
Pine Barrens, NJ D3 33
Pine Bluff, AR C3 7
Pine Bluffs, WY E8 53
Pine City, MN E6 26
Pine Creek Lake, OK C6 39
Pinedale, WY D3 53
Pinefield, MD C4 23
Pine Hills, FL D5 12
Pinehurst, NC B3 36
Pine Island, MN F6 26
Pine Knot, KY D5 20
Pine Lawn, MO f13 28
Pinellas Park, FL E4 12
Pine Mountain, US D6 20
Pine Ridge, SD D3 44
Pines, Lake O' the, TX C5 46
Pineville, KY D6 20
Pineville, LA C3 21
Pineville, NC B2 36
Piney View, WV n13 51
Pinson, AL f7 4
Pioche, NV F7 31
Pipestone, MN G2 26
Pipestone National Monument, MN G2 26
Piqua, OH B1 38
Piscataway, NJ B4 33
Pisgah, AL A4 4
Pisgah, OH n13 38
Pismo Beach, CA E3 8
Pittsburg, KS E9 19
Pittsburgh, PA F1 41
Pittsfield, IL D3 16
Pittsfield, ME D3 22
Pittsfield, MA B1 24
Pittsfield, NH D4 32
Pittsford, VT D2 48
Pittston, PA D10 41
Placitas, NM B3 34
Plainfield, CT C8 10
Plainfield, IL B5 16
Plainfield, IN E5 17
Plainfield, NJ B4 33
Plainfield, VT C4 48
Plains, MT C2 29
Plains, PA n17 41
Plainview, MN F6 26
Plainview, NE B8 30
Plainview, TX B2 46
Plainville, CT C4 10
Plainville, KS C4 19
Plainwell, MI F5 25
Plaistow, NH E4 32
Plano, IL B5 16
Plano, TX C4 46
Plantation, FL r13 12
Plant City, FL D4 12
Plantsville, CT C4 10
Plaquemine, LA D4 21
Platte, SD D7 44
Platte, r., US B3 28
Platte, r., NE D6 30
Platte City, MO B3 28
Platteville, CO A6 9
Platteville, WI F3 52
Plattsburg, MO B3 28
Plattsburgh, NY f11 35
Plattsmouth, NE D10 30
Pleasant Grove, AL g7 4
Pleasant Grove, UT C4 47
Pleasant Hill, IA e8 18
Pleasant Hill, MO C3 28
Pleasanton, CA h9 8
Pleasanton, KS D9 19
Pleasant Prairie, WI n12 52
Pleasantville, IA C4 18
Pleasantville, NJ E3 33
Pleasantville, NY D7 35
Pleasure Ridge Park, KY g11 20
Plentywood, MT B12 29
Plover, WI D4 52
Plum, PA k14 41
Plum Bayou, r., AR k10 7
Plymouth, IN B5 17
Plymouth, MA C6 24
Plymouth, MI p15 25
Plymouth, MN m12 26
Plymouth, NH C3 32
Plymouth, NC B6 36
Plymouth, PA D10 41
Plymouth, WI E6 52
Plymouth Bay, MA C6 24
Pocahontas, AR A5 7
Pocahontas, IA B3 18
Pocatalico, WV C3 51
Pocatello, ID G6 15
Pocola, OK B7 39
Pocomoke, r., MD D7 23
Pocomoke Sound, MD E6 23
Pocono Mountains, PA E11 41
Point Clear, AL E2 4
Point Hope, AK B6 5
Point Pleasant, NJ C4 33
Point Pleasant, WV C2 51
Polk City, IA C4 18
Polson, MT C2 29
Pomme de Terre Lake, MO D4 28
Pomona, CA E5 8
Pompano Beach, FL F6 12
Pompton Lakes, NJ A4 33
Ponca, NE B9 30
Ponca City, OK A4 39
Ponchatoula, LA D5 21
Pontchartrain, Lake, LA D5 21
Pontiac, IL C5 16
Pontiac, MI F7 25
Pontotoc, MS A4 27
Pooler, GA D5 13
Poplar, MT B11 29
Poplar Bluff, MO E7 28
Poplarville, MS E4 27
Poquonock Bridge, CT D7 10
Poquoson, VA C6 49
Porcupine Mountains, MI m12 25
Portage, IN A3 17
Portage, ME B4 22
Portage, MI F5 25
Portage, WI E4 52
Portage Lakes, OH B4 38
Portageville, MO E8 28
Portales, NM C6 34
Port Allen, LA D4 21
Port Angeles, WA A2 50
Port Arthur, TX E6 46
Port Charlotte, FL F4 12
Port Chester, NY E7 35
Port Clinton, OH A3 38
Port Clyde, ME E3 22
Porte Crayon, Mount, WV C5 51
Porter, IN A3 17
Port Gibson, MS D3 27
Port Huron, MI F8 25
Port Jervis, NY D6 35
Portland, CT C5 10
Portland, IN D8 17
Portland, ME E2 22
Portland, MI F6 25
Portland, ND B8 37
Portland, OR B4 40
Portland, TN A5 45
Portland, TX F4 46
Port Lavaca, TX E4 46
Port Neches, TX E6 46
Port Orange, FL C6 12
Port Orchard, WA B3 50
Port Royal, SC G6 43
Port Royal Sound, SC G6 43
Port Saint Lucie, FL E6 12
Portsmouth, NH D5 32
Portsmouth, OH D3 38
Portsmouth, RI E6 42
Portsmouth, VA D6 49
Port Sulphur, LA E6 21
Port Townsend, WA A3 50
Port Washington, NY h13 35
Port Washington, WI E6 52
Port Wentworth, GA D5 13
Posen, IL k9 16
Post Falls, ID B2 15
Postville, IA A6 18
Poteau, OK B7 39
Potholes Reservoir, WA B6 50
Potomac, MD B3 23
Potomac, r., US D4 23
Potosi, MO D7 28
Potsdam, NY f10 35
Pottstown, PA F10 41
Pottsville, AR B2 7
Pottsville, PA E9 41
Poughkeepsie, NY D7 35
Poulsbo, WA B3 50
Poultney, VT D2 48
Pound Gap, US C7 20
Poway, CA F5 8
Powder, r., US A6 2
Powder Springs, GA h8 13
Powell, TN m13 45
Powell, WY B4 53
Powell, Lake, US F5 47
Powell Mountain, US C10 45
Powell's Crossroads, AL A4 4
Powellton, WV C3 51
Poygan, Lake, WI D5 52
Prairie City, IA C4 18
Prairie du Chien, WI E2 52
Prairie du Sac, WI E4 52
Prairie Grove, AR B1 7
Prairie Village, KS m16 19
Pratt, KS E5 19
Prattville, AL C3 4
Prentiss, MS D4 27
Prescott, AZ C3 6
Prescott, AR D2 7
Prescott, WI D1 52
Presidential Range, NH B4 32
Presidio, TX p12 46
Presque Isle, ME B5 22
Preston, ID G7 15
Prestonsburg, KY C7 20
Prettyboy Reservoir, MD A4 23
Pribilof Islands, AK D5 5
Price, UT D5 47
Priceville, AL A3 4
Prichard, AL E1 4
Priest Lake, ID A2 15
Priest Rapids Lake, WA C6 50
Priest River, ID A2 15
Prince of Wales, Cape, AK B6 5
Prince of Wales Island, AK n23 5
Princeton, IL B4 16
Princeton, IN H2 17
Princeton, KY C2 20
Princeton, MN E5 26
Princeton, MO A4 28
Princeton, NJ C3 33
Princeton, WV D3 51
Princeton, Mount, CO C4 9
Prince William Sound, AK g18 5
Prineville, OR C6 40
Prior Lake, MN F5 26
Proctor, MN D6 26
Proctor, VT D2 48
Proctorsville, VT E3 48
Prospect, CT C4 10
Prospect, KY g11 20
Prospect Harbor, ME D4 22
Prospect Park, PA p20 41
Prosperity, WV n13 51
Prosser, WA C6 50
Providence, KY C2 20
Providence, RI C4 42
Providence, r., RI C5 42
Provincetown, MA B7 24
Provo, UT C4 47
Provo, r., UT C4 47
Prudence Island, RI E5 42
Pryor, OK A6 39
Pueblo, CO C6 9
Pueblo Mountain, OR E8 40
Pueblo of Acoma, NM C2 34
Puerco, r., US C6 6
Puget Sound, WA B3 50
Pukalani, HI C5 14
Pulaski, TN B4 45
Pulaski, VA C2 49
Pullman, WA C8 50
Pumphrey, MD h11 23
Punta Gorda, FL F4 12
Punxsutawney, PA E4 41
Purcell, OK B4 39
Purgatoire Peak, CO D5 9
Purvis, MS D4 27
Putnam, CT B8 10
Putney, VT F3 48
Puyallup, WA B3 50
Pymatuning Reservoir, US C1 41
Pyramid Lake, NV C2 31

Q

Quabbin Reservoir, MA B3 24
Quakertown, PA F11 41
Quartzsite, AZ D1 6
Quechee, VT D4 48
Questa, NM A4 34
Quidnessett, RI E4 42
Quidnick, RI D3 42
Quinault, r., WA B1 50
Quincy, IL D2 16
Quincy, MA B5 24
Quincy, WA B6 50
Quinebaug, r., CT C8 10
Quinhagak, AK D7 5
Quinn, r., NV B3 31
Quinnipiac, r., CT D4 10
Quitman, GA F3 13
Quitman, MS C5 27

R

Raceland, KY B7 20
Raceland, LA E5 21
Race Point, MA B7 24
Racine, WI F6 52
Radcliff, KY C4 20
Radford, VA C2 49
Raeford, NC C3 36
Raft, r., ID G5 15
Raft River Mountains, UT B2 47
Rahway, NJ B4 33
Rainbow Bridge National Monument, UT F5 47
Rainelle, WV D4 51
Rainier, Mount, WA C4 50
Rainsville, AL A4 4
Rainy Lake, MN B5 26
Raleigh, NC B4 36
Raleigh Bay, NC C6 36
Ralston, NE g12 30
Ramapo, r., NJ A4 33
Ramsey, NJ A4 33
Ramshorn Peak, MT E5 29
Ranchester, WY B5 53
Ranchos de Taos, NM A4 34
Rand, WV C3 51
Randallstown, MD B4 23
Randolph, MA B5 24
Randolph, NE B8 30
Randolph, VT D3 48
Randolph Hills, MD B3 23
Rangeley, ME D2 22
Rangely, CO A2 9
Ranson, WV B7 51
Rantoul, IL C5 16
Rapid City, SD C2 44
Raquette, r., NY f10 35
Raritan, r., NJ C4 33
Raritan Bay, NJ C4 33
Rathbun Lake, IA D5 18
Rathdrum, ID B2 15
Raton, NM A5 34
Raton Pass, NM A5 34
Ravenna, NE C7 30
Ravenna, OH A4 38
Ravenswood, WV C3 51
Rawlins, WY E5 53
Ray, ND A2 37
Raymond, ME E2 22
Raymond, NH D4 32
Raymond, WA C2 50
Raymondville, TX F4 46
Raymore, MO C3 28
Rayne, LA D3 21
Raynham, MA C5 24
Raytown, MO h11 28
Rayville, LA B4 21
Readfield, ME D3 22
Reading, MA A5 24
Reading, OH C1 38
Reading, PA F10 41
Rector, AR A5 7
Red, r., NA A8 2
Red, r., US D9 2
Red, r., KY C6 20
Red, r., TN A4 45
Red Bank, NJ C4 33
Red Bank, SC D5 43
Red Bank, TN D8 45
Red Bay, AL A1 4
Red Bluff Lake, US o12 46
Red Cedar, r., WI C2 52
Red Cloud, NE D7 30
Redcloud Peak, CO D3 9
Redding, CA B2 8
Redfield, AR C3 7
Redfield, SD C7 44
Redford, MI F7 25
Redkey, IN D7 17
Red Lake, AZ B1 6
Red Lake, r., MN C2 26
Red Lake Indian Reservation, MN B3 26
Redlands, CA E5 8
Red Lion, PA G8 41
Red Lodge, MT E7 29
Redmond, OR C5 40
Redmond, WA e11 50
Red Mountain, MT C4 29
Red Oak, GA h7 13
Red Oak, IA D2 18
Redondo Beach, CA n12 8
Redoubt Volcano, AK g15 5
Red Rock, Lake, IA C4 18
Red Springs, NC C3 36
Red Wing, MN F6 26
Redwood City, CA D2 8
Redwood Falls, MN F3 26
Redwood National Park, CA B2 8
Reed City, MI E5 25
Reedsburg, WI E3 52
Reedsport, OR D2 40
Reelfoot Lake, TN A2 45
Reese, r., NV C4 31
Rehoboth Bay, DE F5 11
Rehoboth Beach, DE F5 11
Reidland, KY e9 20
Reidsville, GA D4 13
Reidsville, NC A3 36
Reinbeck, IA B5 18
Reisterstown, MD B4 23
Reliance, WY E3 53
Remsen, IA B2 18
Rend Lake, IL E5 16
Reno, NV D2 31
Rensselaer, IN C3 17
Rensselaer, NY C7 35
Renton, WA B3 50
Republic, MO D4 28
Republican, r., US C6 19
Reserve, LA h10 21
Reston, VA B5 49
Revere, MA g11 24
Rexburg, ID F7 15
Reyes, Point, CA C2 8
Reynoldsburg, OH C3 38
Rhinelander, WI C4 52
Rhode Island, state, US D3 42
Rhode Island, RI E5 42
Rhode Island Sound, US F5 42
Rialto, CA m14 8
Rib Mountain, WI D4 52
Rice Lake, WI C2 52
Richardson, TX n10 46
Richardson Lakes, ME D2 22
Richardton, ND C3 37
Richfield, MN F5 26
Richfield, UT E3 47
Richford, VT B3 48
Richland, MO D5 28
Richland, WA C6 50
Richland Balsam, NC f10 36
Richland Center, WI E3 52
Richlands, VA e10 49
Richmond, CA D2 8
Richmond, IN E8 17
Richmond, KY C5 20
Richmond, ME D3 22
Richmond, MO B4 28
Richmond, TX E5 46
Richmond, VT C3 48
Richmond, VA C5 49
Richmond Heights, MO f13 28
Richmond Hill, GA E5 13
Richwood, WV C4 51
Ridgefield, CT D2 10
Ridgefield Park, NJ B4 33
Ridgeland, MS C3 27
Ridgewood, NJ B4 33
Ridgway, PA D4 41
Ridley Park, PA p20 41
Riffe Lake, WA C3 50
Rifle, CO B3 9
Rigby, ID F7 15
Rincon, GA D5 13
Ringwood, NJ A4 33
Rio Grande 20 Grande, Rio, r., NA E7 2
Rio Grande City, TX F3 46
Rio Rancho, NM B3 34
Ripley, MS A5 27
Ripley, TN B2 45
Ripley, WV C3 51
Ripon, WI E5 52
Rising Sun, IN G8 17
Rison, AR D3 7
Ritter, Mount, CA D4 8
Rittman, OH B4 38
Rivanna, r., VA C4 49
Riverdale, IL k9 16
Riverdale, MD C4 23
River Edge, NJ h8 33
River Falls, WI D1 52
River Forest, IL k9 16
River Grove, IL k9 16
Riverhead, NY n16 35
River Pines, MA f10 24
River Ridge, LA k11 21
River Road, OR C3 40
River Rouge, MI p15 25
Riverside, AL B3 4
Riverside, CA F5 8
Riverside, IL k9 16
Riverton, UT C4 47
Riverton, WY C4 53
Riverton Heights, WA f11 50
Riverview, MI p15 25
Rivesville, WV B4 51
Riviera Beach, FL F6 12
Riviera Beach, MD B4 23
Roanoke, AL B4 4
Roanoke, VA C3 49
Roanoke, r., US A5 36
Roanoke Rapids, NC A5 36
Roaring Fork, r., CO C4 9
Robbins, IL k9 16
Robbinsdale, MN m12 26
Roberts, MT E7 29
Robertsdale, AL E2 4
Robert S. Kerr Reservoir, OK B6 39
Roberts Mountain, WY D3 53
Robinson, IL D6 16
Robstown, TX F4 46
Rochelle, IL B4 16
Rochester, IN B5 17
Rochester, MN F6 26
Rochester, NH D5 32
Rochester, NY B3 35
Rochester, VT D3 48
Rock, r., US B3 16
Rock, r., US A1 18
Rock Creek Butte, OR C8 40
Rockdale, MD B4 23
Rock Falls, IL B4 16
Rockford, IL A4 16
Rock Hill, SC B5 43
Rockingham, NC C3 36
Rock Island, IL B3 16
Rockland, ME D3 22
Rockland, MA B6 24
Rockledge, FL D6 12
Rockmart, GA B1 13
Rockport, IN I3 17
Rockport, MA A6 24
Rock Port, MO A2 28
Rock Rapids, IA A1 18
Rock Springs, WY E3 53
Rockton, IL A4 16
Rock Valley, IA A1 18
Rockville, IN E3 17
Rockville, MD B3 23
Rockville Centre, NY n15 35
Rockwall, TX C4 46
Rockwell City, IA B3 18
Rockwood, TN D9 45
Rocky Ford, CO C7 9
Rocky Hill, CT C5 10
Rocky Mount, NC B5 36
Rocky Mount, VA D3 49
Rocky Mountain, MT C4 29
Rocky Mountain National Park, CO A5 9
Rocky River, OH A4 38
Roderfield, WV D3 51
Rodney Village, DE D3 11
Roeland Park, KS k16 19
Rogers, AR A1 7
Rogers, Mount, VA f10 49
Rogersville, AL A2 4
Rogersville, TN C10 45
Rogue, r., OR E2 40
Rohnert Park, CA C2 8
Roland, OK B7 39
Rolette, ND A6 37
Rolla, MO D6 28
Rolla, ND A6 37
Rolling Fork, MS C3 27
Rolling Fork, r., KY C4 20
Rolling Meadows, IL h8 16
Rollinsford, NH D5 32
Roma, TX F3 46
Roman Nose Mountain, MD m12 23
Romanzof, Cape, AK C6 5
Rome, GA B1 13
Rome, NY B5 35
Romeo, MI F7 25
Romeoville, IL k8 16
Romney, WV B6 51
Romulus, MI p15 25
Ronan, MT C2 29
Ronceverte, WV D4 51
Roosevelt, UT C5 47
Rose, Mount, NV D2 31
Roseau, MN B3 26
Rosebud, SD D5 44
Roseburg, OR D3 40
Rosedale, MD g11 23
Rosedale, MS B2 27
Rose Hill, KS E6 19
Roselle, IL k8 16
Roselle, NJ k7 33
Roselle Park, NJ k7 33
Rosemount, MN F5 26
Rosenberg, TX E5 46
Roseville, MI o16 25
Roseville, MN m12 26
Rosewood Heights, IL E3 16
Ross Barnett Reservoir, MS C3 27
Rossford, OH A2 38
Ross Lake National Recreation Area, WA A5 50
Rossville, GA B1 13
Roswell, GA B2 13
Roswell, NM D5 34
Rothschild, WI D4 52
Rotterdam, NY C6 35
Rough River Lake, KY C3 20
Round Lake, IL h8 16
Round Lake Beach, IL h8 16
Round Rock, TX D4 46
Roundup, MT D8 29
Roxboro, NC A4 36
Roy, UT B3 47
Royale, Isle, MI h9 25
Royal Gorge, CO C5 9
Royal Oak, MI F7 25
Royersford, PA F10 41
Royston, GA B3 13
Rubidoux, CA n14 8
Ruby Dome, NV C6 31
Rufus Woods Lake, WA A6 50
Rugby, ND A6 37
Ruidoso, NM D4 34
Ruidoso Downs, NM D4 34
Ruleville, MS B3 27
Rumford, ME D2 22
Rupert, ID G5 15
Rupert, WV D4 51
Rushville, IL C3 16
Rushville, IN E7 17
Rushville, NE B3 30
Russell, KS D5 19
Russell, KY B7 20
Russell Springs, KY C4 20
Russellville, AL A2 4
Russellville, AR B2 7
Russellville, KY D3 20
Russian, r., CA C2 8
Ruston, LA B3 21
Rutherford, NJ B4 33
Rutherfordton, NC B1 36
Rutland, VT D3 48
Rye, NH D5 32
Rye, NY h13 35
Rye Beach, NH E5 32

S

Sabattus, ME D2 22
Sabetha, KS C8 19
Sabine, r., US D6 46
Sabine Lake, US E2 21
Sable, Cape, FL G5 12
Sacajawea, Lake, WA C7 50
Sacajawea Peak, OR B9 40
Sac City, IA B2 18
Saco, ME E2 22

Name	Map Ref.	Page
Saco, r., US	E2	22
Sacramento, CA	C3	8
Sacramento, r., CA	C3	8
Sacramento Mountains, NM	E4	34
Sacramento Valley, AZ	B1	6
Sacramento Valley, CA	C2	8
Saddle Ball Mountain, MA	A1	24
Saddle Brook, NJ	h8	33
Safety Harbor, FL	E4	12
Safford, AZ	E6	6
Saginaw, MI	E7	25
Saginaw, TX	n9	46
Saginaw Bay, MI	E7	25
Saint Agatha, ME	A4	22
Saint Albans, VT	B2	48
Saint Albans, WV	C3	51
Saint Andrews, SC	F7	43
Saint Anthony, ID	F7	15
Saint Augustine, FL	C5	12
Saint Bernard, AL	A3	4
Saint Catherines Island, GA	E5	13
Saint Charles, IL	B5	16
Saint Charles, MD	C4	23
Saint Charles, MN	G6	26
Saint Charles, MO	C7	28
Saint Clair, MI	F8	25
Saint Clair, MO	C6	28
Saint Clair Shores, MI	p16	25
Saint Cloud, FL	D5	12
Saint Cloud, MN	E4	26
Saint Croix, r., US	C1	52
Saint Edward, NE	C8	30
Saint Elias, Cape, AK	D11	5
Saint Francis, KS	C2	19
Saint Francis, SD	D5	44
Saint Francis, WI	n12	52
Saint Francis, r., US	A5	7
Saint Francois Mountains, MO	D7	28
Sainte Genevieve, MO	D7	28
Saint George, UT	F2	47
Saint George, Cape, FL	C1	12
Saint George Island, AK	D6	5
Saint Helena Island, SC	G6	43
Saint Helens, OR	B4	40
Saint Helens, Mount, WA	C3	50
Saint Ignace, MI	C6	25
Saint Ignatius, MT	C2	29
Saint James, MN	G4	26
Saint James, MO	D6	28
Saint Joe, r., ID	B3	15
Saint John, IN	B3	17
Saint John, KS	E5	19
Saint Johns, AZ	C6	6
Saint Johns, MI	F6	25
Saint Johns, r., FL	B5	12
Saint Johnsbury, VT	C4	48
Saint Johnsbury Center, VT	C4	48
Saint Jones, r., DE	D4	11
Saint Joseph, MI	F4	25
Saint Joseph, MN	E4	26
Saint Joseph, MO	B3	28
Saint Joseph, r., US	F5	25
Saint Joseph Bay, FL	C1	12
Saint Joseph Point, FL	v16	12
Saint Lawrence Island, AK	C5	5
Saint Louis, MI	E6	25
Saint Louis, MO	C7	28
Saint Louis, r., US	D6	26
Saint Louis Bay, MS	f7	27
Saint Louis Park, MN	n12	26
Saint Lucie Canal, FL	F6	12
Saint Maries, ID	B2	15
Saint Martinville, LA	D4	21
Saint Marys, GA	F5	13
Saint Marys, IN	A5	17
Saint Marys, KS	C7	19
Saint Marys, OH	B1	38
Saint Marys, PA	D4	41
Saint Marys, WV	B3	51
Saint Marys, r., US	F5	13
Saint Marys, r., US	C8	17
Saint Matthew Island, AK	C5	5
Saint Matthews, KY	B4	20
Saint Paul, MN	F5	26
Saint Paul, NE	C7	30
Saint Paul Island, AK	D5	5
Saint Paul Park, MN	n12	26
Saint Peter, MN	F5	26
Saint Peters, MO	C7	28
Saint Petersburg, FL	E4	12
Saint Simons Island, GA	E5	13
Saint Simons Island, GA	E5	13
Sakakawea, Lake, ND	B3	37
Sakonnet, r., RI	E6	42
Sakonnet Point, RI	F6	42
Salamonie, r., IN	C6	17
Salamonie Lake, IN	C6	17
Salem, AR	A4	7
Salem, IL	E5	16
Salem, IN	G5	17
Salem, MA	A6	24
Salem, MO	D6	28
Salem, NH	E4	32
Salem, OH	B5	38
Salem, OR	C4	40
Salem, SD	D8	44
Salem, VA	C2	49
Salem, WV	B4	51
Salida, CO	C5	9
Salina, KS	D6	19
Salina, UT	E4	47
Salinas, CA	D3	8
Saline, MI	F7	25
Saline, r., AR	D4	7
Saline, r., KS	C3	19
Salisbury, MD	D6	23
Salisbury, MA	A6	24
Salisbury, MO	B5	28
Salisbury, NC	B2	36
Salkehatchie, r., SC	E5	43
Sallisaw, OK	B7	39
Salmon, ID	D5	15
Salmon, r., ID	D3	15
Salmon Creek, WA	D3	50
Salmon Falls, r., US	D5	32
Salmon River Mountains, ID	E3	15
Salt, r., AZ	D4	6
Salt, r., KY	C4	20
Salt, r., MO	B6	28
Salt Fork Lake, OH	B4	38
Saltillo, MS	A5	27
Salt Lake, HI	g10	14
Salt Lake City, UT	C4	47
Salton Sea, CA	F5	8
Saluda, r., SC	C4	43
Salvador, Lake, LA	E5	21
Salyersville, KY	C6	20
Sam Rayburn Reservoir, TX	D5	46
Samson, AL	D3	4
Samtown, LA	C3	21
San Agustin, Plains of, NM	C2	34
San Angelo, TX	D2	46
San Antonio, TX	E3	46
San Antonio Bay, TX	E4	46
San Antonio Mountain, NM	A3	34
San Benito, TX	F4	46
San Bernardino, CA	E5	8
San Blas, Cape, FL	v16	12
Sanborn, IA	A2	18
Sanbornville, NH	C4	32
San Bruno, CA	D2	8
San Carlos, AZ	D5	6
San Clemente, CA	F5	8
San Clemente Island, CA	F4	8
Sandersville, GA	D4	13
Sandia Mountains, NM	k8	34
San Diego, CA	F5	8
Sand Island, HI	g10	14
Sand Mountain, US	A3	4
Sandpoint, ID	A2	15
Sand Springs, OK	A5	39
Sandston, VA	m18	49
Sandstone, MN	D6	26
Sandusky, OH	A3	38
Sandusky, r., OH	B2	38
Sandusky Bay, OH	A3	38
Sandwich, IL	B5	16
Sandwich, MA	C7	24
Sandy, OR	B4	40
Sandy, UT	C4	47
Sandy Hook, NJ	C5	33
Sandy Springs, GA	h8	13
San Felipe Pueblo, NM	B3	34
San Fernando, CA	m12	8
Sanford, FL	D5	12
Sanford, ME	E2	22
Sanford, NC	B3	36
Sanford, Mount, AK	C11	5
San Francisco, CA	D2	8
San Francisco Bay, CA	h8	8
San Gabriel Mountains, CA	m12	8
Sangamon, r., IL	C3	16
Sanibel Island, FL	F4	12
San Jacinto, CA	F5	8
San Joaquin, r., CA	D3	8
San Joaquin Valley, CA	D3	8
San Jose, CA	D3	8
San Jose Island, TX	E4	46
San Juan, TX	F3	46
San Juan, r., US	C6	2
San Juan Capistrano, CA	F5	8
San Juan Island, WA	A2	50
San Juan Mountains, CO	D3	9
San Leandro, CA	h8	8
San Luis, AZ	E1	6
San Luis Obispo, CA	E3	8
San Luis Valley, CO	D4	9
San Manuel, AZ	E5	6
San Marcos, TX	E4	46
San Mateo, CA	D2	8
San Pablo, CA	h8	8
San Pedro, r., AZ	E5	6
San Pedro Peaks, NM	A3	34
Sanpoil, r., WA	A7	50
San Rafael, CA	D2	8
San Rafael, r., UT	D5	47
San Simon, r., AZ	E6	6
Santa Ana, CA	F5	8
Santa Barbara, CA	E4	8
Santa Catalina Island, CA	F4	8
Santa Clara, CA	D2	8
Santa Cruz, CA	D2	8
Santa Cruz, NM	B3	34
Santa Cruz, r., AZ	E4	6
Santa Cruz Island, CA	F4	8
Santa Fe, NM	B4	34
Santa Fe, TX	r14	46
Santa Maria, CA	E3	8
Santa Maria, r., AZ	C2	6
Santa Monica, CA	m12	8
Santa Paula, CA	E4	8
Santa Rosa, CA	C2	8
Santa Rosa, NM	C5	34
Santa Rosa Island, CA	F3	8
Santa Teresa, NM	F3	34
Santee, CA	o16	8
Santee, r., SC	E8	43
Santiam Pass, OR	C4	40
Santo Domingo Pueblo, NM	B3	34
Sapelo Island, GA	E5	13
Sapulpa, OK	B5	39
Saraland, AL	E1	4
Saranac, r., NY	F11	35
Saranac Lake, NY	f10	35
Sarasota, FL	E4	12
Sarasota Bay, FL	E4	12
Saratoga, CA	k8	8
Saratoga, WY	E6	53
Saratoga National Historical Park, NY	B7	35
Saratoga Springs, NY	B7	35
Sarcoxie, MO	D3	28
Sardis, MS	A4	27
Sardis Lake, MS	A4	27
Sargent, NE	C6	30
Sartell, MN	E4	26
Sassafras Mountain, US	A2	43
Satilla, r., GA	E5	13
Satsuma, AL	E1	4
Saugus, MA	B5	24
Sauk, r., WA	A4	50
Sauk Centre, MN	E4	26
Sauk City, WI	E4	52
Sauk Rapids, MN	E4	26
Saukville, WI	E6	52
Sault Sainte Marie, MI	B6	25
Sausalito, CA	D2	8
Savage, r., MD	k12	23
Savanna, IL	A3	16
Savannah, GA	D5	13
Savannah, MO	B3	28
Savannah, TN	B3	45
Savannah, r., US	F5	43
Sawtooth Mountains, ID	F4	15
Saxtons River, VT	E3	48
Saydel, IA	e8	18
Saylesville, RI	B4	42
Saylorville Lake, IA	C4	18
Sayre, OK	B2	39
Sayre, PA	C8	41
Sayreville, NJ	C4	33
Sayville, NY	n15	35
Scapegoat Mountain, MT	C3	29
Scappoose, OR	B4	40
Scarborough, ME	E2	22
Scarsdale, NY	h13	35
Schaumburg, IL	h8	16
Schell Creek Range, NV	D7	31
Schenectady, NY	C7	35
Schererville, IN	B3	17
Schertz, TX	h7	46
Schiller Park, IL	k9	16
Schofield, WI	D4	52
Schofield Barracks, HI	g9	14
Schuyler, NE	C8	30
Schuylkill, r., PA	F10	41
Schuylkill Haven, PA	E9	41
Scioto, r., OH	B2	38
Scituate, MA	B6	24
Scituate Reservoir, RI	C3	42
Scobey, MT	B11	29
Scotch Plains, NJ	B4	33
Scotia, NY	C7	35
Scotland, SD	D8	44
Scotlandville, LA	D4	21
Scott, LA	D3	21
Scott, Mount, OR	E4	40
Scott City, KS	D3	19
Scott City, MO	D8	28
Scottdale, GA	h8	13
Scottdale, PA	F2	41
Scottsbluff, NE	C2	30
Scotts Bluff National Monument, NE	C2	30
Scottsboro, AL	A3	4
Scottsburg, IN	G6	17
Scottsdale, AZ	D4	6
Scottsville, KY	D3	20
Scranton, PA	D10	41
Scribner, NE	C9	30
Seabrook, NH	E5	32
Seaford, DE	F3	11
Seaford, VA	h15	49
Seagoville, TX	n10	46
Searcy, AR	B4	7
Seaside, OR	B3	40
Seat Pleasant, MD	C4	23
Seattle, WA	B3	50
Sebastian, FL	E6	12
Sebec Lake, ME	C3	22
Sebree, KY	C2	20
Secaucus, NJ	h8	33
Section, AL	A4	4
Security, CO	C6	9
Sedalia, MO	C4	28
Sedan, KS	E7	19
Sedgwick, KS	E6	19
Sedona, AZ	C4	6
Sedro Woolley, WA	A3	50
Seekonk, MA	C5	24
Seeley Lake, MT	C3	29
Seguin, TX	E4	46
Selah, WA	C5	50
Selby, SD	B5	44
Selbyville, DE	G5	11
Selinsgrove, PA	E8	41
Sellersburg, IN	H6	17
Sellersville, PA	F11	41
Sells, AZ	F4	6
Selma, AL	C2	4
Selma, NC	B4	36
Selmer, TN	B3	45
Selway, r., ID	C3	15
Seminoe Reservoir, WY	D6	53
Seminole, OK	B5	39
Seminole, Lake, US	F2	13
Semmes, AL	E1	4
Senath, MO	E7	28
Senatobia, MS	A4	27
Seneca, KS	C7	19
Seneca, MO	E3	28
Seneca, SC	B2	43
Seneca Falls, NY	C4	35
Seneca Lake, NY	C4	35
Sequatchie, r., TN	D8	45
Sequim, WA	A2	50
Sequoia National Park, CA	D4	8
Sergeant Bluff, IA	B1	18
Seven Devils Mountains, ID	D2	15
Seven Hills, OH	h9	38
Severn, MD	B4	23
Severna Park, MD	B4	23
Sevier, r., UT	D3	47
Sevier Bridge Reservoir, UT	D4	47
Sevier Lake, UT	E2	47
Sevierville, TN	D10	45
Sewanee, TN	D8	45
Seward, AK	C10	5
Seward, NE	D8	30
Seward Peninsula, AK	B7	5
Seymour, CT	D3	10
Seymour, IN	G6	17
Seymour, MO	D5	28
Seymour, TN	D10	45
Seymour, WI	D5	52
Seymourville, LA	h9	21
Shady Spring, WV	D3	51
Shaker Heights, OH	A4	38
Shakopee, MN	F5	26
Shamokin, PA	E8	41
Shannon, MS	A5	27
Shannon Hills, AR	k10	7
Shannontown, SC	D7	43
Sharon, PA	D1	41
Sharon Hill, PA	p20	41
Sharonville, OH	n13	38
Sharpe, Lake, SD	C6	44
Sharpsville, PA	D1	41
Shasta, Mount, CA	B2	8
Shasta Lake, CA	B2	8
Shattuck, OK	A2	39
Shaw, MS	B3	27
Shawangunk Mountains, NY	D6	35
Shawano, WI	D5	52
Shawnee, KS	k16	19
Shawnee, OK	B5	39
Sheboygan, WI	E6	52
Sheboygan Falls, WI	E6	52
Sheenjek, r., AK	B11	5
Sheffield, AL	A2	4
Sheffield Lake, OH	A3	38
Shelbina, MO	B5	28
Shelby, MI	E4	25
Shelby, MS	B3	27
Shelby, MT	B5	29
Shelby, NC	B1	36
Shelby, OH	B3	38
Shelbyville, IL	D5	16
Shelbyville, IN	F6	17
Shelbyville, KY	B4	20
Shelbyville, TN	B5	45
Shelbyville, Lake, IL	D5	16
Sheldon, IA	A2	18
Shelley, ID	F6	15
Shell Rock, IA	B5	18
Shelton, CT	D3	10
Shelton, NE	D7	30
Shelton, WA	B2	50
Shenandoah, IA	D2	18
Shenandoah, PA	E9	41
Shenandoah, r., US	A5	49
Shenandoah National Park, VA	B4	49
Shepherdstown, WV	B7	51
Shepherdsville, KY	C4	20
Sheridan, AR	C3	7
Sheridan, IN	D5	17
Sheridan, OR	B3	40
Sheridan, WY	B6	53
Sherman, TX	C4	46
Sherman Reservoir, NE	C7	30
Sherwood, AR	C3	7
Sherwood, OR	h12	40
Sherwood Manor, CT	A5	10
Sherwood Park, DE	i7	11
Shetucket, r., CT	C7	10
Sheyenne, r., ND	C8	37
Shillington, PA	F10	41
Shiloh, OH	C1	38
Shiloh National Military Park, TN	B3	45
Shinnston, WV	B4	51
Shippensburg, PA	F6	41
Shiprock, NM	A1	34
Ship Rock, NM	A1	34
Shishaldin Volcano, AK	E7	5
Shively, KY	B4	20
Shoreview, MN	m12	26
Shorewood, IL	k8	16
Shorewood, WI	E6	52
Short Beach, CT	D4	10
Shoshone, ID	G4	15
Shoshone, r., WY	B4	53
Shoshone Falls, ID	G4	15
Shoshone Mountains, NV	E4	31
Shoshoni, WY	C4	53
Show Low, AZ	C5	6
Shreveport, LA	B2	21
Shrewsbury, MA	B4	24
Shuksan, Mount, WA	A4	50
Sibley, IA	A2	18
Sidney, MT	C12	29
Sidney, NE	C3	30
Sidney, OH	B1	38
Sidney Lanier, Lake, GA	B2	13
Sierra Blanca Peak, NM	D4	34
Sierra Madre, CA	m12	8
Sierra Vista, AZ	F5	6
Signal Mountain, TN	D8	45
Sigourney, IA	C5	18
Sikeston, MO	E8	28
Siler City, NC	B3	36
Siloam Springs, AR	A1	7
Silt, CO	B3	9
Silver Bay, MN	C7	26
Silver City, NM	E1	34
Silverdale, WA	B3	50
Silver Lake, KS	C8	19
Silver Spring, MD	C3	23
Silver Springs, NV	D2	31
Silver Star Mountain, WA	A5	50
Silvertip Mountain, MT	C3	29
Silverton, OH	o13	38
Silverton, OR	C4	40
Silview, DE	B3	11
Silvis, IL	B3	16
Simi Valley, CA	E4	8
Simpsonville, SC	B3	43
Simsbury, CT	B4	10
Sinclair, WY	E5	53
Sinclair, Lake, GA	C3	13
Sioux Center, IA	A1	18
Sioux City, IA	B1	18
Sioux Falls, SD	D9	44
Siskiyou Mountains, US	F3	40
Siskiyou Pass, OR	E4	40
Sisseton, SD	B8	44
Sistersville, WV	B4	51
Sitka, AK	D12	5
Sitka National Historical Park, AK	m22	5
Sitka Sound, AK	m22	5
Skagway, AK	D12	5
Skaneateles Lake, NY	C4	35
Skiatook, OK	A5	39
Skokie, IL	A6	16
Skowhegan, ME	D3	22
Skunk, r., IA	D6	18
Skykomish, r., WA	B4	50
Slater, MO	B4	28
Slatersville, RI	A3	42
Slatington, PA	E10	41
Slayton, MN	G3	26
Sleeping Bear Dunes National Lakeshore, MI	D4	25
Sleepy Eye, MN	F4	26
Slidell, LA	D6	21
Slide Mountain, NY	D6	35
Slinger, WI	E5	52
Smackover, AR	D3	7
Smith Center, KS	C5	19
Smithers, WV	C3	51
Smithfield, NC	B4	36
Smithfield, UT	B4	47
Smithfield, VA	D6	49
Smith Mountain Lake, VA	C3	49
Smith Point, VA	C6	49
Smithtown, NY	n15	35
Smithville, MO	B3	28
Smithville, TN	D8	45
Smoky Hill, r., US	D5	19
Smyrna, DE	C3	11
Smyrna, GA	C2	13
Smyrna, TN	B5	45
Snake, r., US	A4	2
Snohomish, WA	B3	50
Snoqualmie, r., WA	B4	50
Snoqualmie Pass, WA	B4	50
Snowflake, AZ	C5	6
Snowmass Mountain, CO	B3	9
Snow Mountain, ME	C2	22
Snowshoe Peak, MT	B1	29
Snowy Mountain, NY	B6	35
Snyder, TX	C2	46
Socastee, SC	D9	43
Social Circle, GA	C3	13
Socorro, NM	C3	34
Socorro, TX	o11	46
Soda Springs, ID	G7	15
Soddy-Daisy, TN	D8	45
Soldotna, AK	g16	5
Solomon, r., KS	C6	19
Solon, OH	A4	38
Solvay, NY	B4	35
Somers, CT	B6	10
Somerset, KY	C5	20
Somerset, MA	C5	24
Somerset, NJ	B3	33
Somerset, PA	F3	41
Somerset Reservoir, VT	E3	48
Somers Point, NJ	E3	33
Somersworth, NH	D5	32
Somerton, AZ	E1	6
Somerville, MA	B5	24
Somerville, NJ	B3	33
Sonoma Peak, NV	C4	31
Soperton, GA	D4	13
Sophia, WV	D3	51
Souderton, PA	F11	41
Souris, r., NA	A7	2
Southaven, MS	A3	27
South Baldy, NM	D2	34
South Barre, VT	C3	48
South Beloit, IL	A4	16
South Bend, IN	A5	17
South Berwick, ME	E2	22
South Boston, VA	D4	49
Southbridge, MA	B3	24
South Bristol, ME	E3	22
South Broadway, WA	C5	50
South Burlington, VT	C2	48
Southbury, CT	D3	10
South Carolina, state, US	D6	43
South Charleston, WV	C3	51
South Chicago Heights, IL	m9	16
South Dakota, state, US	C5	44
South Dartmouth, MA	C6	24
South Daytona, FL	C5	12
South Elgin, IL	B5	16
Southern Pines, NC	B3	36
South Euclid, OH	g9	38
Southfield, MI	o15	25
South Fulton, TN	A3	45
South Gastonia, NC	B1	36
South Gate, CA	n12	8
Southgate, KY	h14	20
Southgate, MI	p15	25
South Haven, IN	A3	17
South Hero Island, VT	B2	48
South Hill, VA	D4	49
South Holland, IL	k9	16
South Hooksett, NH	D4	32
South Houston, TX	r14	46
South Hutchinson, KS	f11	19
Southington, CT	C4	10
South International Falls, MN	B5	26
South Jacksonville, IL	D3	16
South Jordan, UT	C3	47
South Lake Tahoe, CA	C4	8
South Manitou Island, MI	C4	25
South Marsh Island, MD	D5	23
South Miami, FL	G6	12
South Miami Heights, FL	s13	12
South Milwaukee, WI	F6	52
South Ogden, UT	B4	47
South Orange, NJ	B4	33
South Paris, ME	D2	22
South Pass, WY	D4	53
South Pass, LA	F6	21
South Patrick Shores, FL	D6	12
South Pittsburg, TN	D8	45
South Plainfield, NJ	B4	33
South Platte, r., US	B7	2
Southport, IN	E5	17
Southport, NY	C4	35
South Portland, ME	E2	22
South River, NJ	C4	33
South Royalton, VT	D3	48
South Ryegate, VT	C4	48
South Saint Paul, MN	n12	26
South San Francisco, CA	h8	8
Southside, AL	B3	4
South Sioux City, NE	B9	30
South Skunk, r., IA	C4	18
South Tucson, AZ	E5	6
South Venice, FL	E4	12
South Wellfleet, MA	C8	24
Southwest Harbor, ME	D4	22
Southwest Pass, LA	F6	21
Southwest Pass, LA	E3	21
South Whitley, IN	B6	17
South Williamsport, PA	D7	41
South Windsor, CT	B5	10
Southwood Acres, CT	A5	10
South Yarmouth, MA	C7	24
Spanaway, WA	B3	50
Spanish Fork, UT	C4	47
Spanish Fort, AL	E2	4
Spanish Lake, MO	f13	28
Sparks, NV	D2	31
Sparta, IL	E4	16
Sparta (Lake Mohawk), NJ	A3	33
Sparta, TN	D8	45
Sparta, WI	E3	52
Spartanburg, SC	B4	43
Spearfish, SD	C2	44
Speedway, IN	E5	17
Spencer, IN	F4	17
Spencer, IA	A2	18
Spencer, MA	B4	24
Spencer, NC	B2	36
Spencer, WV	C3	51
Spesutie Island, MD	B5	23
Spindale, NC	B1	36
Spirit Lake, IA	A2	18
Spiro, OK	B7	39
Spokane, WA	B8	50
Spokane, r., US	B8	50
Spoon, r., IL	C3	16
Spooner, WI	C2	52
Sprague, WV	n13	51
Spring, TX	q14	46
Spring, r., AR	A4	7
Springboro, OH	C1	38
Spring City, TN	D9	45
Springdale, AR	A1	7
Springdale, OH	n13	38
Springer, NM	A5	34
Springfield, CO	D8	9
Springfield, IL	D4	16
Springfield, KY	C4	20
Springfield, MA	B2	24
Springfield, MO	D4	28
Springfield, NE	C9	30
Springfield, NJ	B4	33
Springfield, OH	C2	38
Springfield, OR	C4	40
Springfield, PA	p20	41
Springfield, SD	E8	44
Springfield, TN	A5	45
Springfield, VT	E4	48
Springfield, VA	g12	49
Springfield, Lake, IL	D4	16
Spring Hill, FL	D4	12
Spring Hill, KS	D9	19
Springhill, LA	A2	21
Spring Lake, MI	E4	25
Spring Lake, NC	B4	36
Spring Lake, ME	C2	22
Spring Mountains, NV	G6	31
Springvale, ME	E2	22
Spring Valley, CA	o16	8
Spring Valley, IL	B4	16
Spring Valley, MN	G6	26
Spring Valley, NY	g12	35
Springville, UT	C4	47
Spruce Knob, WV	C6	51
Spruce Knob-Seneca Rocks National Recreation Area, WV	C5	51
Spruce Mountain, NV	C7	31
Spurr, Mount, AK	g15	5
Squam Lake, NH	C4	32
Square Lake, ME	A4	22
Squibnocket Point, MA	D6	24
Stafford, KS	E5	19
Stafford Springs, CT	B6	10
Stamford, CT	E1	10
Stamps, AR	D2	7
Stanaford, WV	D3	51
Stanberry, MO	A3	28
Standish, MI	E7	25
Stanford, KY	C5	20
Stanley, ND	A3	37
Stanleyville, NC	A2	36
Stanton, KY	C6	20
Stanton, MI	E5	25
Stanton, NE	C8	30
Staples, MN	D4	26
Stapleton, AL	E2	4
Star City, AR	D4	7
Star City, WV	B5	51
Starkville, MS	B5	27
Star Peak, NV	C3	31
State College, PA	E6	41
Stateline, NV	E2	31
Staten Island, NY	k12	35
Statesboro, GA	D5	13
Statesville, NC	B2	36
Statue of Liberty National Monument, NJ	k8	33
Staunton, IL	D4	16
Staunton, VA	B3	49
Stayton, OR	C4	40
Steamboat Springs, CO	A4	9
Stearns, KY	D5	20
Stebbins, AK	C7	5
Steele, AL	B3	4
Steele, MO	E8	28
Steele, ND	C6	37
Steelton, PA	F8	41
Steelville, MO	D6	28
Steens Mountain, OR	E8	40
Steep Falls, ME	E2	22
Steger, IL	B6	16
Steilacoom, WA	f10	50
Stephens, AR	D2	7
Stephenville, TX	C3	46
Sterling, AK	g16	5
Sterling, CO	A7	9
Sterling, IL	B4	16
Sterling, KS	D5	19
Sterling, VA	A5	49
Sterling Heights, MI	o15	25
Steubenville, OH	B5	38
Stevens Pass, WA	B4	50
Stevens Point, WI	D4	52
Stewartville, MN	G6	26
Stigler, OK	B6	39
Stikine, r., AK	D13	5
Stillhouse Hollow Lake, TX	D4	46
Stillwater, MN	E6	26
Stillwater, OK	A4	39
Stilwell, OK	B7	39
Stimson, Mount, MT	B3	29
Stockbridge, GA	C2	13
Stockton, CA	D3	8
Stockton, KS	C4	19
Stockton Lake, MO	D4	28
Stockton Springs, ME	D4	22
Stollings, WV	n12	51
Stoneham, MA	g11	24
Stone Mountain, GA	C2	13
Stone Mountains, US	A1	36
Stonewood, WV	k10	51
Stony Brook, NY	n15	35
Storm Lake, IA	B2	18
Storrs, CT	B7	10
Story, WY	B6	53
Story City, IA	B4	18
Stoughton, MA	B5	24
Stoughton, WI	F4	52
Stow, OH	A4	38
Stowe, VT	C3	48
Strasburg, PA	G9	41
Strasburg, VA	B4	49
Stratford, CT	E3	10
Stratford Point, CT	E3	10
Stratham, NH	D5	32
Stratton Mountain, VT	E3	48
Strawberry, r., UT	C5	47
Strawberry Mountain, OR	C8	40
Strawberry Point, IA	B6	18
Streator, IL	B5	16
Stromsburg, NE	C8	30
Strongsville, OH	A4	38
Stroud, OK	B5	39
Stroudsburg, PA	E11	41
Struthers, OH	A5	38
Stuart, FL	E6	12
Stuart, IA	C3	18
Stuart, Mount, WA	B5	50
Stuarts Draft, VA	B3	49
Sturgeon Bay, WI	D6	52
Sturgis, KY	e10	20
Sturgis, MI	G5	25
Sturgis, SD	C2	44
Sturtevant, WI	F6	52
Stuttgart, AR	C4	7
Sublette, KS	E3	19
Suffern, NY	D6	35
Suffolk, VA	D6	49
Sugar, r., NH	D2	32
Sugar City, ID	F7	15
Sugar Creek, MO	h11	28
Sugarcreek, PA	D2	41
Sugar Hill, GA	B2	13
Sugar Island, MI	B6	25
Sugar Land, TX	E5	46
Sugarloaf Mountain, ME	C2	22
Suiattle, r., WA	A4	50
Suitland, MD	C4	23
Sullivan, IL	D5	16
Sullivan, IN	F3	17
Sullivan, MO	C6	28
Sulphur, LA	D2	21
Sulphur, OK	C5	39
Sulphur Springs, TX	C5	46
Sulphur Springs Valley, AZ	E6	6
Sumiton, AL	B2	4
Summer Lake, OR	E6	40
Summersville, WV	C4	51
Summersville Lake, WV	C4	51
Summerville, GA	B1	13
Summerville, SC	E7	43
Summit, IL	k9	16
Summit, MS	D3	27
Summit, NJ	B4	33
Summit, TN	h11	45
Summit Mountain, NV	D5	31
Sumner, IA	B5	18
Sumner, WA	B3	50
Sumter, SC	D7	43
Sunapee, NH	D2	32
Sunapee Lake, NH	D2	32
Sunbury, PA	E8	41
Sun City, AZ	k8	6
Suncook, NH	D4	32
Sundance, WY	B8	53
Sunflower, Mount, KS	C2	19
Sunland Park, NM	F3	34
Sunnyside, WA	C5	50
Sunnyvale, CA	k8	8
Sun Prairie, WI	E4	52
Sunset, UT	B4	47
Sun Valley, NV	D2	31
Superior, AZ	D4	6
Superior, MT	C2	29
Superior, NE	D7	30
Superior, WI	B1	52
Superior, Lake, NA	A10	2
Superstition Mountains, AZ	m10	6
Suquamish, WA	B3	50
Surfside Beach, SC	D10	43
Surprise, AZ	k8	6
Surrey, ND	A4	37
Susquehanna, r., US	A5	23
Sussex, WI	m11	52
Sutherland, NE	C4	30
Sutherlin, OR	D3	40
Sutton, NE	D8	30
Sutton Lake, WV	C4	51
Suwanee, GA	B2	13
Suwannee, r., US	C4	12
Swainsboro, GA	D4	13
Swampscott, MA	B6	24
Swannanoa, NC	f10	36
Swan Peak, MT	C3	29
Swansea, IL	E4	16
Swanson Lake, NE	D4	30
Swanton, VT	B2	48
Swanzey Center, NH	E2	32
Swarthmore, PA	p20	41
Sweet Home, OR	C4	40
Sweetwater, TN	D9	45
Sweetwater, TX	C2	46
Sweetwater, r., WY	D4	53
Sweetwater Creek, FL	p10	12
Swissvale, PA	k14	41
Switzer, WV	D3	51
Swoyerville, PA	D10	41
Sycamore, IL	B5	16
Sylacauga, AL	B3	4
Sylvania, AL	A4	4
Sylvania, GA	D5	13
Sylvania, OH	A2	38
Sylvester, GA	E3	13
Syracuse, IN	B6	17
Syracuse, KS	E2	19
Syracuse, NE	D9	30
Syracuse, NY	B4	35
Syracuse, UT	B3	47

T

Name	Map Ref.	Page
Table Rock Lake, US	E4	28
Tacoma, WA	B3	50
Taconic Range, US	A1	24
Tahlequah, OK	B7	39
Tahoe, Lake, US	E1	31
Tahquamenon, r., MI	B5	25
Takoma Park, MD	f8	23
Talent, OR	E4	40
Talladega, AL	B3	4
Tallahassee, FL	B2	12
Tallahatchie, r., MS	B3	27
Tallapoosa, GA	C1	13

Name	Map Ref.	Page
Tallapoosa, r., AL	C3	4
Tallassee, AL	C4	4
Talleyville, DE	A3	11
Tallmadge, OH	A4	38
Tallulah, LA	B4	21
Tama, IA	C5	18
Tamalpais, Mount, CA	h7	8
Tamaqua, PA	E10	41
Tamiami Canal, FL	G6	12
Tampa, FL	E4	12
Tampa Bay, FL	E4	12
Tamworth, NH	C4	32
Tanana, r., AK	C10	5
Taneytown, MD	A3	23
Tangier Sound, MD	D6	23
Tangipahoa, r., LA	D5	21
Taos, NM	A4	34
Taos Pueblo, NM	A4	34
Tar, r., NC	B5	36
Tarboro, NC	B5	36
Tarentum, PA	E2	41
Targhee Pass, US	E7	15
Tarkio, MO	A2	28
Tarpon Springs, FL	D4	12
Tarrant, AL	B3	4
Tarrytown, NY	D7	35
Taum Sauk Mountain, MO	D6	28
Taunton, MA	C5	24
Tawakoni, Lake, TX	C4	46
Tawas City, MI	D7	25
Taylor, AZ	C5	6
Taylor, MI	p15	25
Taylor, PA	D10	41
Taylor, TX	D4	46
Taylor, Mount, NM	B2	34
Taylor Mill, KY	k14	20
Taylor Mountain, ID	E4	15
Taylors, SC	B3	43
Taylors Island, MD	D5	23
Taylorsville, MS	D4	27
Taylorville, IL	D4	16
Tazewell, TN	C10	45
Tazewell, VA	e10	49
Tchula, MS	B3	27
Tea, SD	D9	44
Teaneck, NJ	h8	33
Teaticket, MA	C6	24
Teche, Bayou, r., LA	D4	21
Tecumseh, MI	G7	25
Tecumseh, NE	D9	30
Tecumseh, OK	B5	39
Tekamah, NE	C9	30
Telescope Peak, CA	D5	8
Telford, PA	F11	41
Tell City, IN	I4	17
Telluride, CO	D3	9
Temecula, CA	F5	8
Tempe, AZ	D4	6
Temperance, MI	G7	25
Temple, TX	D4	46
Temple Terrace, FL	o11	12
Tenafly, NJ	B5	33
Tenants Harbor, ME	E3	22
Tenkiller Ferry Lake, OK	B6	39
Tennessee, state, US	B5	45
Tennessee, r., US	D10	2
Tennessee Pass, CO	B4	9
Tensas, r., LA	B4	21
Tensaw, r., AL	E2	4
Ten Thousand Islands, FL	G5	12
Terra Alta, WV	B5	51
Terrebonne Bay, LA	E5	21
Terre Haute, IN	F3	17
Terrell, TX	C4	46
Terrell Hills, TX	k7	46
Terry, MT	D11	29
Terry Peak, SD	C2	44
Terryville, CT	C3	10
Tesuque, NM	B4	34
Teton Range, WY	C2	53
Tewksbury, MA	A5	24
Texarkana, AR	D1	7
Texarkana, TX	C5	46
Texas, state, US	D3	46
Texas City, TX	E5	46
Texico, NM	C6	34
Texoma, Lake, US	D5	39
Thames, r., CT	D7	10
Thatcher, AZ	E6	6
Thayer, MO	E6	28
The Dalles, OR	B5	40
The Dells, WI	E4	52
The Everglades, FL	G6	12
The Flume, NH	B3	32
The Narrows, WA	f10	50
Theodore, AL	E1	4
Theodore Roosevelt Lake, AZ	D4	6
Theodore Roosevelt National Park (South Unit), ND	C2	37
Theodore Roosevelt National Park (North Unit), ND	B2	37
Thermopolis, WY	C4	53
The Village, OK	B4	39
Thibodaux, LA	E5	21
Thief River Falls, MN	B2	26
Thielsen, Mount, OR	D4	40
Thiensville, WI	E6	52
Thomaston, CT	C3	10
Thomaston, GA	D2	13
Thomaston, ME	D3	22
Thomasville, AL	D2	4
Thomasville, GA	F3	13
Thomasville, NC	B2	36
Thompson, ND	B8	37
Thompson Falls, MT	C1	29
Thomson, GA	C4	13
Thoreau, NM	B1	34
Thorntown, IN	D4	17
Thorsby, AL	C3	4
Thousand Islands, NY	A4	35
Thousand Lake Mountain, UT	E4	47
Three Forks, MT	E5	29
Three Rivers, MI	G5	25
Three Sisters, OR	C5	40
Thunder Bay, MI	D7	25
Thunder Bay, r., MI	D6	25
Thunderbolt, GA	D5	13
Tickfaw, r., LA	C5	21
Ticonderoga, NY	B7	35
Tierra Amarilla, NM	A3	34
Tiffin, OH	A2	38
Tifton, GA	E3	13
Tigard, OR	h12	40
Tilden, NE	B8	30
Tillamook, OR	B3	40
Tillery, Lake, NC	B2	36
Tillmans Corner, AL	E1	4
Tilton, NH	D3	32
Timberlake, VA	C3	49
Timms Hill, WI	C3	52
Tims Ford Lake, TN	B5	45
Tinley Park, IL	k9	16
Tinton Falls, NJ	C4	33
Tioga, ND	A3	37
Tioughnioga, r., NY	C4	35
Tippecanoe, r., IN	C4	17
Tipton, IN	D5	17
Tipton, IA	C6	18
Tipton, Mount, AZ	B1	6
Tiptonville, TN	A2	45
Tishomingo, OK	C5	39
Titusville, FL	D6	12
Titusville, PA	C2	41
Tiverton, RI	D6	42
Tobin, Mount, NV	C4	31
Toccoa, GA	B3	13
Toccoa, r., GA	B2	13
Togwotee Pass, WY	C2	53
Toiyabe Range, NV	D4	31
Tok, AK	C11	5
Toledo, IA	B5	18
Toledo, OH	A2	38
Toledo, OR	C3	40
Toledo Bend Reservoir, US	C2	21
Tolleson, AZ	m8	6
Tomah, WI	E3	52
Tomahawk, WI	C4	52
Tombigbee, r., US	D1	4
Tombstone, AZ	F5	6
Tom Nevers Head, MA	D8	24
Tompkinsville, KY	D4	20
Toms River, NJ	D4	33
Tonawanda, NY	B2	35
Tonganoxie, KS	C8	19
Tongue, r., MT	E10	29
Tonkawa, OK	A4	39
Tonopah, NV	E4	31
Tooele, UT	C3	47
Topeka, KS	C8	19
Toppenish, WA	C5	50
Topsham, ME	E3	22
Toronto, OH	B5	38
Torrance, CA	n12	8
Torrington, CT	B3	10
Torrington, WY	D8	53
Towanda, KS	E7	19
Towner, ND	A5	37
Townley, AL	B2	4
Townsend, MT	D5	29
Towson, MD	B4	23
Tracy, MN	F3	26
Tracyton, WA	e10	50
Tradewater, r., KY	C2	20
Traer, IA	B5	18
Trail Creek, IN	A4	17
Traverse, Lake, US	B9	44
Traverse City, MI	D5	25
Tremonton, UT	B3	47
Trenton, GA	B1	13
Trenton, MI	F7	25
Trenton, MO	A4	28
Trenton, NJ	C3	33
Trenton, OH	C1	38
Trenton, TN	B3	45
Triangle, VA	B5	49
Tri City, OR	E3	40
Tri Lakes, IN	B7	17
Trinidad, CO	D6	9
Trinity, r., CA	B2	8
Trinity, r., TX	D5	46
Trotwood, OH	C1	38
Troy, AL	D4	4
Troy, IL	E4	16
Troy, MI	o15	25
Troy, MT	B1	29
Troy, NH	E2	32
Troy, NY	C7	35
Troy, NC	B3	36
Troy, OH	B1	38
Troy Peak, NV	E6	31
Truchas Peak, NM	B4	34
Truckee, r., US	D2	31
Trumann, AR	B5	7
Trumbull, CT	E3	10
Trumbull, Mount, AZ	A2	6
Trussville, AL	B3	4
Truth or Consequences (Hot Springs), NM	D2	34
Tsala Apopka Lake, FL	D4	12
Tuba City, AZ	A4	6
Tucker, GA	h8	13
Tuckerman, AR	B4	7
Tucson, AZ	E5	6
Tucumcari, NM	B6	34
Tugaloo Lake, US	B1	43
Tug Fork, r., US	C2	51
Tukwila, WA	f11	50
Tulare, CA	D4	8
Tularosa, NM	D3	34
Tularosa Valley, NM	E3	34
Tullahoma, TN	B5	45
Tulsa, OK	A6	39
Tumwater, WA	B3	50
Tupelo, MS	A5	27
Turkey, r., IA	B6	18
Turlock, CA	D3	8
Turnbull, Mount, AZ	D5	6
Turrell, AR	B5	7
Turtle Creek, PA	k14	41
Turtle Lake, ND	B5	37
Tuscaloosa, AL	B2	4
Tuscola, IL	D5	16
Tuscumbia, AL	A2	4
Tuskegee, AL	C4	4
Tuttle, OK	B4	39
Tuttle Creek Lake, KS	C7	19
Tutwiler, MS	A3	27
Tuxedo Park, DE	i7	11
Tweedy Mountain, MT	E4	29
Twentynine Palms, CA	E5	8
Twin Falls, ID	G4	15
Twin Knolls, AZ	m9	6
Twin Lakes, WI	F5	52
Twinsburg, OH	A4	38
Twin Valley, MN	C2	26
Two Harbors, MN	C7	26
Two Rivers, WI	D6	52
Tybee Island, GA	D6	13
Tygart Lake, WV	B5	51
Tygart Valley, r., WV	B4	51
Tyger, r., SC	B4	43
Tyler, MN	F2	26
Tyler, TX	C5	46
Tyler Heights, WV	C3	51
Tylertown, MS	D3	27
Tyndall, SD	E8	44
Tyrone, NM	E1	34
Tyrone, PA	E5	41

U

Name	Map Ref.	Page
Ugashik Lakes, AK	D8	5
Uhrichsville, OH	B4	38
Uinta Mountains, UT	C5	47
Ulysses, KS	E2	19
Umatilla, OR	B7	40
Umnak Island, AK	E6	5
Umpqua, r., OR	D3	40
Unaka Mountains, US	C11	45
Unalaska, AK	E6	5
Unalaska Island, AK	E6	5
Uncompahgre Peak, CO	C3	9
Underwood, ND	B4	37
Unicoi Mountains, US	D9	45
Unimak Island, AK	D7	5
Union, KY	k13	20
Union, ME	D3	22
Union, MS	C4	27
Union, MO	C6	28
Union, SC	B4	43
Union City, CA	h8	8
Union City, GA	C2	13
Union City, IN	D8	17
Union City, NJ	h8	33
Union City, TN	A2	45
Union Gap, WA	C5	50
Union Grove, WI	F5	52
Union Springs, AL	C4	4
Uniontown, PA	G2	41
Union Village, RI	B3	42
Unionville, CT	B4	10
Unionville, MO	A4	28
United States, NA	C8	2
United States Air Force Academy, CO	B6	9
United States Military Academy, NY	C6	35
United States Naval Academy, MD	C4	23
University City, MO	C7	28
University Heights, OH	h9	38
University Park, NM	E3	34
University Park, TX	n10	46
University Place, WA	f10	50
Upland, CA	E5	8
Upland, IN	D7	17
Upolu Point, HI	C6	14
Upper Arlington, OH	B2	38
Upper Darby, PA	G11	41
Upper Iowa, r., IA	A5	18
Upper Klamath Lake, OR	E4	40
Upper Red Lake, MN	B4	26
Upper Sandusky, OH	B2	38
Upton, WY	B8	53
Urbana, IL	C5	16
Urbana, OH	B2	38
Urbandale, IA	C4	18
Utah, state, US	D4	47
Utah Lake, UT	C4	47
Ute Reservoir, NM	B6	34
Utica, NY	B5	35
Uvalde, TX	E3	46

V

Name	Map Ref.	Page
Vacaville, CA	C3	8
Vail, CO	B4	9
Valdese, NC	B1	36
Valdez, AK	C10	5
Valdosta, GA	F3	13
Valencia Heights, SC	D6	43
Valentine, NE	B5	30
Vallejo, CA	C2	8
Valley, NE	C9	30
Valley Center, KS	E6	19
Valley City, ND	C8	37
Valley Cottage, NY	g13	35
Valley Falls, KS	C8	19
Valley Falls, RI	B4	42
Valley Park, MO	f12	28
Valley Springs, SD	D9	44
Valley Station, KY	g11	20
Valley Stream, NY	n15	35
Valliant, OK	D6	39
Valparaiso, IN	B3	17
Van Buren, AR	B1	7
Van Buren, ME	A5	22
Vanceboro, ME	C5	22
Vanceburg, KY	B6	20
Vancleave, MS	E5	27
Vancouver, WA	D3	50
Vandalia, IL	E4	16
Vandalia, MO	B6	28
Vandergrift, PA	E2	41
Van Horn, TX	o12	46
Van Kull, Kill, r., NJ	k8	33
Van Wert, OH	B1	38
Vashon Island, WA	f11	50
Vaughn, MT	C5	29
Veedersburg, IN	D3	17
Velva, ND	A5	37
Veniaminof, Mount, AK	D8	5
Venice, FL	E4	12
Venice, IL	E3	16
Ventnor City, NJ	E4	33
Ventura (San Buenaventura), CA	E4	8
Verde, r., AZ	C4	6
Verdi, NV	D2	31
Verdigre, NE	B7	30
Verdigris, r., US	A6	39
Vergennes, VT	C2	48
Vermilion, OH	A3	38
Vermilion, r., IL	C5	16
Vermilion, r., LA	E3	21
Vermilion Bay, LA	E3	21
Vermilion Lake, MN	C6	26
Vermilion Range, MN	C7	26
Vermillion, SD	E9	44
Vermont, state, US	D3	48
Vernal, UT	C6	47
Vernon, AL	B1	4
Vernon, TX	B3	46
Vernon Hills, IL	h9	16
Vero Beach, FL	E6	12
Verona, MS	A5	27
Verona, WI	E4	52
Verret, Lake, LA	E4	21
Versailles, IN	F7	17
Versailles, KY	B5	20
Versailles, MO	C5	28
Vestavia Hills, AL	g7	4
Vevay, IN	G7	17
Viborg, SD	D8	44
Vicksburg, MS	C3	27
Victoria, KS	D4	19
Victoria, TX	E4	46
Victorville, CA	E5	8
Vidalia, GA	D4	13
Vidalia, LA	C4	21
Vidor, TX	D5	46
Vienna, GA	D3	13
Vienna, VA	B5	49
Vienna, WV	B3	51
Villa Park, IL	k8	16
Villa Rica, GA	C2	13
Ville Platte, LA	D3	21
Villisca, IA	D3	18
Vilonia, AR	B3	7
Vinalhaven, ME	D4	22
Vinalhaven Island, ME	D4	22
Vincennes, IN	G2	17
Vinegar Hill, OR	C8	40
Vine Grove, KY	C4	20
Vineland, NJ	E2	33
Vinita, OK	A6	39
Vinton, IA	B5	18
Vinton, VA	C3	49
Violet, LA	k12	21
Virden, IL	D4	16
Virgin, r., US	G8	31
Virginia, MN	C6	26
Virginia, state, US	C4	49
Virginia Beach, VA	D7	49
Virginia Peak, NV	D2	31
Virgin Mountains, US	A1	6
Viroqua, WI	E3	52
Visalia, CA	D4	8
Vista, CA	F5	8
Vivian, LA	B2	21
Volga, SD	C9	44
Voyageurs National Park, MN	B5	26
Vsevidof, Mount, AK	E6	5

W

Name	Map Ref.	Page
Wabash, IN	C6	17
Wabash, r., US	H2	17
Wabasha, MN	F6	26
Waccamaw, Lake, NC	C4	36
Wachusett Reservoir, MA	B4	24
Waco, TX	D4	46
Waconda Lake, KS	C5	19
Waconia, MN	F5	26
Wadena, MN	D3	26
Wadesboro, NC	C2	36
Wadley, GA	D4	13
Wadsworth, OH	A4	38
Wagner, SD	D7	44
Wagoner, OK	B6	39
Wahiawa, HI	B3	14
Wahoo, NE	C9	30
Wahpeton, ND	C9	37
Waialua, HI	B3	14
Waianae, HI	B3	14
Waikiki Beach, HI	g10	14
Wailuku, HI	C5	14
Waimanalo, HI	B4	14
Waimea, HI	B2	14
Wainwright, AK	A8	5
Waipahu, HI	B3	14
Waipio Acres, HI	g9	14
Waite Park, MN	E4	26
Wakarusa, IN	A5	17
WaKeeney, KS	C4	19
Wakefield, MA	B5	24
Wakefield, MI	n12	25
Wakefield, NE	B9	30
Wakefield, RI	F3	42
Wake Forest, NC	B4	36
Walbridge, OH	e6	38
Walcott, IA	C7	18
Walcott, Lake, ID	G5	15
Walden Pond, MA	g10	24
Walden Ridge, TN	D8	45
Waldo, AR	D2	7
Waldron, AR	C1	7
Walhalla, ND	A8	37
Walhalla, SC	B1	43
Walker, LA	g10	21
Walker, MI	E5	25
Walker, MN	C4	26
Walker Lake, NV	E3	31
Walkerton, IN	B5	17
Wall, SD	D3	44
Wallace, NC	B4	36
Walla Walla, WA	C7	50
Wallenpaupack, Lake, PA	D11	41
Wallingford, CT	D4	10
Wallingford, VT	E3	48
Wallington, NJ	h8	33
Wallowa Mountains, OR	B9	40
Wallula, Lake, US	C7	50
Walnut, r., KS	E6	19
Walnut Creek, CA	h8	8
Walnut Ridge, AR	A5	7
Walpole, MA	B5	24
Walpole, NH	D2	32
Walsenburg, CO	D6	9
Walterboro, SC	F6	43
Walter F. George Lake, US	D4	4
Walters, OK	C3	39
Waltham, MA	B5	24
Walthourville, GA	E5	13
Walton, KY	B5	20
Wamego, KS	C7	19
Wanapum Lake, WA	B6	50
Wanaque Reservoir, NJ	A4	33
Wando Woods, SC	k11	43
Wapakoneta, OH	B1	38
Wapato, WA	C5	50
Wapello, IA	C6	18
Wapsipinicon, r., IA	B6	18
War, WV	D3	51
Ward, AR	B4	7
Ward Mountain, MT	D2	29
Ware, r., MA	B3	24
Wareham, MA	C6	24
Warminster, PA	F11	41
Warm Springs Reservoir, OR	D8	40
Warner, NH	D3	32
Warner Peak, OR	E7	40
Warner Robins, GA	D3	13
Warr Acres, OK	B4	39
Warren, AR	D3	7
Warren, MI	F7	25
Warren, OH	A5	38
Warren, PA	C3	41
Warren, RI	D5	42
Warren Park, IN	k10	17
Warrensburg, MO	C4	28
Warrensville Heights, OH	h9	38
Warrenton, GA	C4	13
Warrenton, MO	C6	28
Warrenton, VA	B5	49
Warrenville, IL	k8	16
Warrington, FL	u14	12
Warrior, AL	B3	4
Warsaw, IN	B6	17
Warwick, RI	D4	42
Waseca, MN	F5	26
Washburn, IA	B5	18
Washburn, ME	B4	22
Washburn, ND	B5	37
Washington, DC	C3	23
Washington, GA	C4	13
Washington, IL	C4	16
Washington, IN	G3	17
Washington, IA	C6	18
Washington, KS	C6	19
Washington, MO	C6	28
Washington, NC	B5	36
Washington, PA	F1	41
Washington, UT	F2	47
Washington, state, US	B5	50
Washington, Lake, WA	e11	50
Washington, Mount, NH	B4	32
Washington Court House, OH	C2	38
Washington Island, WI	C7	52
Washington Park, IL	E3	16
Washington Terrace, UT	B4	47
Washita, r., OK	C4	39
Washougal, WA	D3	50
Wasilla, AK	C10	5
Watatic, Mount, MA	A4	24
Watauga Lake, TN	C12	45
Watch Hill, RI	G1	42
Waterboro, ME	E2	22
Waterbury, CT	C3	10
Waterbury, VT	C3	48
Waterbury Center, VT	C3	48
Wateree, r., SC	D6	43
Wateree Lake, SC	C6	43
Waterford, CT	D7	10
Waterford, WI	F5	52
Waterloo, IL	E3	16
Waterloo, IN	B7	17
Waterloo, IA	B5	18
Waterloo, WI	E5	52
Watertown, CT	C3	10
Watertown, MA	g11	24
Watertown, NY	B5	35
Watertown, SD	C8	44
Watertown, WI	E5	52
Water Valley, MS	A4	27
Waterville, ME	D3	22
Watervliet, NY	C7	35
Watford City, ND	B2	37
Wathena, KS	C9	19
Watkins Glen, NY	C4	35
Watonga, OK	B3	39
Watseka, IL	C6	16
Watts Bar Lake, TN	D9	45
Wauconda, IL	h8	16
Waukee, IA	C4	18
Waukegan, IL	A6	16
Waukesha, WI	F5	52
Waukon, IA	A6	18
Waunakee, WI	E4	52
Waupaca, WI	D4	52
Waupun, WI	E5	52
Waurika, OK	C4	39
Wausau, WI	D4	52
Wauseon, OH	A1	38
Wauwatosa, WI	m12	52
Waveland, MS	E4	27
Waverly, IA	B5	18
Waverly, NE	D9	30
Waverly, TN	A4	45
Waxahachie, TX	C4	46
Waycross, GA	E4	13
Wayne, MI	p15	25
Wayne, NE	B8	30
Wayne, NJ	B4	33
Wayne, WV	C2	51
Waynesboro, GA	C4	13
Waynesboro, MS	D5	27
Waynesboro, PA	G6	41
Waynesboro, VA	B4	49
Waynesburg, PA	G1	41
Waynesville, MO	D5	28
Waynesville, NC	f10	36
Waynewood, VA	g12	49
Weatherford, OK	B3	39
Weatherford, TX	C4	46
Weatogue, CT	B4	10
Weaver, AL	B4	4
Webb City, MO	D3	28
Webster, MA	B4	24
Webster, SD	B8	44
Webster City, IA	B4	18
Webster Groves, MO	f13	28
Websterville, VT	C4	48
Wedgewood, MO	f13	28
Wedowee, AL	B4	4
Weehawken, NJ	h8	33
Weeping Water, NE	D9	30
Weirton, WV	A4	51
Weiser, ID	E2	15
Weiss Lake, US	A4	4
Welch, WV	D3	51
Welcome, SC	B3	43
Wellesley, MA	B5	24
Wellington, CO	A5	9
Wellington, KS	E6	19
Wells, ME	E2	22
Wells, MN	G5	26
Wells, NV	B7	31
Wellsburg, WV	A4	51
Wellston, OH	C3	38
Wellsville, KS	D8	19
Wenatchee, WA	B5	50
Wenatchee, r., WA	B5	50
Wenatchee Mountains, WA	B5	50
Wendell, ID	G4	15
Wendover, UT	C1	47
Wentzville, MO	C7	28
Weslaco, TX	F4	46
Wessington Springs, SD	C7	44
Wesson, MS	D3	27
West Allis, WI	m11	52
West Bend, WI	E5	52
West Blocton, AL	B2	4
Westborough, MA	B4	24
West Bountiful, UT	C4	47
West Branch, IA	C6	18
Westbrook, ME	E2	22
West Burlington, IA	D6	18
West Buxton, ME	E2	22
West Carrollton, OH	C1	38
Westchester, IL	k9	16
West Chester, PA	G10	41
West Chicago, IL	k8	16
West Columbia, SC	D5	43
West Concord, NC	B2	36
West Cote Blanche Bay, LA	E4	21
West Covina, CA	m13	8
West Crossett, AR	D4	7
West Des Moines, IA	C4	18
West Enfield, ME	C4	22
Westerly, RI	F1	42
Western Springs, IL	k9	16
Westerville, OH	B3	38
West Fargo, ND	C9	37
Westfield, IN	D5	17
Westfield, MA	B2	24
Westfield, NJ	B4	33
West Fork, AR	B1	7
West Frankfort, IL	F5	16
West Freehold, NJ	C4	33
West Glacier, MT	B3	29
West Grand Lake, ME	C5	22
West Hartford, CT	B4	10
West Haven, CT	D4	10
West Helena, AR	C5	7
West Jordan, UT	C3	47
West Lafayette, IN	D4	17
Westlake, LA	D2	21
Westlake, OH	h9	38
Westland, MI	F7	25
West Laramie, WY	E7	53
West Liberty, IA	C6	18
West Liberty, KY	C6	20
West Liberty, WV	f8	51
West Linn, OR	B4	40
West Memphis, AR	B5	7
West Mifflin, PA	F2	41
West Milford, NJ	A4	33
West Milwaukee, WI	m12	52
Westminster, CA	n12	8
Westminster, CO	B5	9
Westminster, MD	A4	23
West Monroe, LA	B3	21
Westmont, IL	k9	16
Westmont, PA	F4	41
West Mystic, CT	D8	10
West New York, NJ	h8	33
West Nishnabotna, r., IA	C2	18
West Norriton, PA	o20	41
Weston, MA	g10	24
Weston, WV	B4	51
West Orange, NJ	B4	33
Westover, WV	B5	51
West Palm Beach, FL	F6	12
West Pensacola, FL	u14	12
West Peoria, IL	C4	16
West Pittston, PA	m17	41
West Plains, MO	E6	28
West Point, GA	D1	13
West Point, MS	B5	27
West Point, NE	C9	30
West Point, NY	D7	35
West Point Lake, US	C1	13
Westport, CT	E2	10
Westport, IN	F6	17
Westport, WA	C1	50
West Quoddy Head, ME	D6	22
West Rutland, VT	D2	48
West Saint Paul, MN	n12	26
West Salem, WI	E2	52
West Seneca, NY	C2	35
West Slope, OR	g12	40
West Springfield, MA	B2	24
West Springfield, VA	g12	49
West Swanzey, NH	E2	32
West Terre Haute, IN	F3	17
West Union, IA	B6	18
West University Place, TX	r14	46
West Valley City, UT	C4	47
West View, PA	h13	41
Westville, IL	C6	16
Westville, IN	A4	17
Westville, NH	E4	32
West Virginia, state, US	C4	51
West Warwick, RI	D3	42
Westwego, LA	k11	21
Westwood, KS	k16	19
Westwood, KY	B7	20
Westwood Lakes, FL	s13	12
West Yellowstone, MT	F5	29
West York, PA	G8	41
Wethersfield, CT	C5	10
Wet Mountains, CO	C5	9
Wetumpka, AL	C3	4
Wewoka, OK	B5	39
Weymouth, MA	B6	24
Wharton, TX	E4	46
Whatcom, Lake, WA	A3	50
Wheatland, WY	D8	53
Wheaton, IL	B5	16
Wheaton, MD	B3	23
Wheat Ridge, CO	B5	9
Wheeler Air Force Base, HI	g9	14
Wheeler Lake, AL	A2	4
Wheeler Peak, NV	E7	31
Wheeler Peak, NM	A4	34
Wheelersburg, OH	D3	38
Wheeling, IL	h9	16
Wheeling, WV	A4	51
Whidbey Island, WA	A3	50
Whitacres, CT	A5	10
White, r., US	D5	44
White, r., US	C7	47
White, r., IN	H2	17
White, r., NV	E6	31
White, r., TX	C2	46
White, r., VT	D4	48
White Bear Lake, MN	E5	26
White Butte, ND	C2	37
White Cap Mountain, ME	C3	22
White Center, WA	e11	50
White City, OR	E4	40
White Earth Indian Reservation, MN	C3	26
Whiteface Mountain, NY	f11	35
White Face Mountain, VT	B3	48
Whitefield, NH	B3	32
Whitefish, MT	B2	29
Whitefish Bay, WI	m12	52
Whitefish Bay, MI	B6	25
White Hall, AR	C3	7
Whitehall, OH	m11	38
White House, TN	A5	45
White Lake, LA	E3	21
White Mountain Peak, CA	D4	8
White Mountains, US	D4	8
White Mountains, NH	B3	32
White Oak, OH	o12	38
White Plains, NY	D7	35
Whiteriver, AZ	D6	6
White River Junction, VT	D4	48
White Rock, NM	B3	34
White Salmon, WA	D4	50
White Sands Missile Range, NM	E3	34
White Sands National Monument, NM	E3	34
Whitesburg, KY	C7	20
White Sulphur Springs, MT	D6	29
White Sulphur Springs, WV	D4	51
White Tank Mountains, AZ	k7	6
Whiteville, NC	C4	36
Whitewater, WI	F5	52
Whitewater, r., US	F7	17
Whitewood, SD	C2	44
Whiting, IN	A3	17
Whitman, MA	B6	24
Whitman, WV	D2	51
Whitmore Village, HI	f9	14
Whitney, SC	B4	43
Whitney, Mount, CA	D4	8
Whittier, CA	F4	8
Wichita, KS	E6	19
Wichita Falls, TX	C3	46
Wichita Mountains, OK	C3	39
Wickenburg, AZ	D3	6
Wickiup Reservoir, OR	E5	40
Wickliffe, OH	A4	38
Wicomico, r., MD	D6	23
Widefield, CO	C6	9
Wiggins, MS	E4	27
Wilber, NE	D9	30
Wilbraham, MA	B3	24
Wilburton, OK	C6	39
Wilder, VT	D4	48
Wilkes-Barre, PA	D10	41
Wilkinsburg, PA	F2	41
Willamette, r., OR	C3	40
Willamette Pass, OR	D4	40
Willapa Bay, WA	C1	50
Willard, MO	D4	28
Willard, OH	A3	38
Willcox, AZ	E6	6
Willcox Playa, AZ	E5	6
William Bill Dannelly Reservoir, AL	C2	4
Williams, AZ	B3	6
Williams, r., WV	C4	51
Williamsburg, IA	C5	18
Williamsburg, KY	D5	20
Williamsburg, VA	C6	49
Williamson, WV	D2	51
Williamsport, IN	D3	17
Williamsport, PA	D7	41
Williamston, MI	F6	25
Williamston, NC	B5	36
Williamston, SC	B3	43
Williamstown, KY	B5	20
Williamstown, NJ	D3	33
Williamstown, VT	C3	48
Williamstown, WV	B3	51
Willimantic, CT	C7	10
Willimantic, r., CT	B6	10
Willingboro, NJ	C3	33
Williston, ND	A2	37
Willmar, MN	E3	26
Willoughby, OH	A4	38
Willoughby Hills, OH	A4	38
Willow Grove, PA	F11	41
Willowick, OH	A4	38
Willow Run, DE	i7	11
Willow Run, MI	p14	25
Willow Springs, IL	k9	16
Willow Springs, MO	E6	28
Wilmette, IL	A6	16
Wilmington, DE	B3	11
Wilmington, IL	B5	16
Wilmington, MA	A5	24
Wilmington, NC	C5	36
Wilmington, OH	C2	38
Wilmington, VT	F3	48
Wilmington Manor, DE	i7	11
Wilmore, KY	C5	20
Wilmot, AR	D4	7
Wilson, AR	B5	7
Wilson, NC	B5	36

Name	Map Ref.	Page
Wilson, PA	E11	41
Wilson, WY	C2	53
Wilson, Mount, CA	m12	8
Wilson Lake, AL	A2	4
Wilsonville, OR	h12	40
Wilton, CT	E2	10
Wilton, IA	C6	18
Wilton, ME	D2	22
Wilton, NH	E3	32
Wilton, ND	B5	37
Winamac, IN	B4	17
Winchester, IN	D8	17
Winchester, KY	C5	20
Winchester, MA	g11	24
Winchester, NV	G6	31
Winchester, NH	E2	32
Winchester, TN	B5	45
Winchester, VA	A4	49
Wind, r., WY	C4	53
Windber, PA	F4	41
Winder, GA	C3	13
Wind Lake, WI	F5	52
Windmill Point, VA	C6	49
Windom, MN	G3	26
Window Rock, AZ	B6	6
Wind River Peak, WY	D3	53
Wind River Range, WY	C3	53
Windsor, CO	A6	9
Windsor, CT	B5	10
Windsor, MO	C4	28
Windsor, VT	E4	48
Windsor Heights, IA	e8	18
Windsor Locks, CT	B5	10
Winfield, AL	B2	4
Winfield, KS	E7	19
Winfield, WV	C3	51
Winnebago, r., IA	A4	18
Winnebago, Lake, WI	E5	52
Winnemucca, NV	C4	31
Winner, SD	D6	44
Winnetka, IL	A6	16
Winnfield, LA	C3	21
Winnibigoshish, Lake, MN	C4	26
Winnipesaukee, Lake, NH	C4	32
Winnisquam, NH	C3	32
Winnisquam Lake, NH	C3	32
Winnsboro, LA	B4	21
Winnsboro, SC	C5	43
Winona, MN	F7	26
Winona, MS	B4	27
Winona Lake, IN	B6	17
Winooski, VT	C2	48
Winooski, r., VT	C3	48
Winslow, AZ	C5	6
Winslow, ME	D3	22
Winsted, CT	B3	10
Winston, OR	D3	40
Winston-Salem, NC	A2	36
Winter Garden, FL	D5	12
Winter Harbor, ME	D4	22
Winter Haven, FL	D5	12
Winter Park, FL	D5	12
Winter Park, NC	C5	36
Winterset, IA	C4	18
Winthrop, ME	D3	22
Winthrop, MA	B6	24
Winthrop Harbor, IL	A6	16
Wiscasset, ME	D3	22
Wisconsin, state, US	D4	52
Wisconsin, r., WI	E3	52
Wisconsin, Lake, WI	E4	52
Wisconsin Dells, WI	E4	52
Wisconsin Rapids, WI	D4	52
Wise, VA	f9	49
Wishek, ND	C6	37
Wisner, NE	C9	30
Wister Lake, OK	C7	39
Withlacoochee, r., US	B3	12
Withlacoochee, r., FL	C4	12
Wixom, MI	o14	25
Woburn, MA	B5	24
Wolcott, CT	C4	10
Wolf, r., WI	C5	52
Wolfeboro, NH	C4	32
Wolfeboro Falls, NH	C4	32
Wolf Lake, IL	k9	16
Wolf Point, MT	B11	29
Wonder Lake, IL	A5	16
Wood, r., RI	F2	42
Wood, Mount, MT	E7	29
Woodall Mountain, MS	A5	27
Woodbine, IA	C2	18
Woodbridge, CT	D3	10
Woodbridge, VA	B5	49
Woodbridge [Township], NJ	B4	33
Woodburn, IN	B8	17
Woodburn, OR	B4	40
Woodbury, MN	F6	26
Woodbury, NJ	D2	33
Woodbury, TN	B5	45
Wood Dale, IL	k9	16
Woodfield, SC	C6	43
Woodland, ME	C5	22
Woodland, WA	D3	50
Woodland Park, CO	C5	9
Woodlawn, KY	e9	20
Woodlawn, MD	g10	23
Woodmoor, MD	B4	23
Woodridge, IL	k8	16
Wood River, IL	E3	16
Wood River, NE	D7	30
Woodruff, SC	B3	43
Woods Cross, UT	C4	47
Woods Hole, MA	C6	24
Woodstock, GA	B2	13
Woodstock, IL	A5	16
Woodstock, VT	D3	48
Woodstock, VA	B4	49
Woodsville, NH	B2	32
Woodville, MS	D2	27
Woodward, OK	A2	39
Woonsocket, RI	A3	42
Woonsocket, SD	C7	44
Wooster, OH	B4	38
Worcester, MA	B4	24
Worden Pond, RI	F3	42
Worland, WY	B5	53
Worth, IL	k9	16
Worthington, IN	F4	17
Worthington, KY	B7	20
Worthington, MN	G3	26
Worthington, OH	B2	38
Wrangell, AK	D13	5
Wrangell, Cape, AK	E2	5
Wrangell, Mount, AK	f19	5
Wrangell Island, AK	m24	5
Wrangell Mountains, AK	C11	5
Wrangell-Saint Elias National Park, AK	C11	5
Wray, CO	A8	9
Wrens, GA	C4	13
Wright, WY	B7	53
Wright, Mount, MT	C4	29
Wright Brothers National Memorial, NC	A7	36
Wright-Patterson Air Force Base, OH	C1	38
Wrightsville, AR	C3	7
Wrightsville, GA	D4	13
Wrightsville Beach, NC	C5	36
Wyandotte, MI	F7	25
Wylie, Lake, US	A5	43
Wymore, NE	D9	30
Wynne, AR	B5	7
Wyoming, MI	F5	25
Wyoming, MN	E6	26
Wyoming, OH	o13	38
Wyoming, state, US	C5	53
Wyomissing, PA	F10	41
Wytheville, VA	D1	49

X

Name	Map Ref.	Page
Xenia, OH	C2	38

Y

Name	Map Ref.	Page
Yadkin, r., NC	B2	36
Yakima, WA	C5	50
Yakima, r., WA	C6	50
Yakutat Bay, AK	D11	5
Yale, Mount, CO	C5	9
Yampa, r., CO	A2	9
Yamsay Mountain, OR	E5	40
Yankton, SD	E8	44
Yarmouth, ME	E2	22
Yates Center, KS	E8	19
Yazoo, r., MS	C3	27
Yazoo City, MS	C3	27
Yeadon, PA	p21	41
Yellow, r., US	u15	12
Yellow, r., GA	h8	13
Yellow, r., WI	D3	52
Yellow, r., WI	C3	52
Yellowstone, r., US	D10	29
Yellowstone Lake, WY	B2	53
Yellowstone National Park, US	B2	53
Yellville, AR	A3	7
Yerington, NV	E2	31
Yonkers, NY	E7	35
Yorba Linda, CA	n13	8
York, AL	C1	4
York, ME	E2	22
York, NE	D8	30
York, PA	G8	41
York, SC	B5	43
York, r., VA	C6	49
York Harbor, ME	E2	22
Yorktown, IN	D7	17
Yorktown Manor, RI	E4	42
Yorkville, IL	B5	16
Yosemite National Park, CA	D4	8
Youghiogheny, r., US	F2	41
Youghiogheny River Lake, US	G3	41
Youngstown, OH	A5	38
Youngtown, AZ	k8	6
Ypsilanti, MI	F7	25
Yuba, r., CA	C3	8
Yuba City, CA	C3	8
Yukon, OK	B4	39
Yuma, AZ	E1	6
Yuma, CO	A8	9

Z

Name	Map Ref.	Page
Zachary, LA	D4	21
Zanesville, OH	C4	38
Zeeland, MI	F5	25
Zephyr Cove, NV	E2	31
Zion, IL	A6	16
Zion National Park, UT	F3	47
Zionsville, IN	E5	17
Zumbrota, MN	F6	26
Zuni (Zuni Pueblo), NM	B1	34
Zuni, r., US	C6	6

Maps and Index of the World

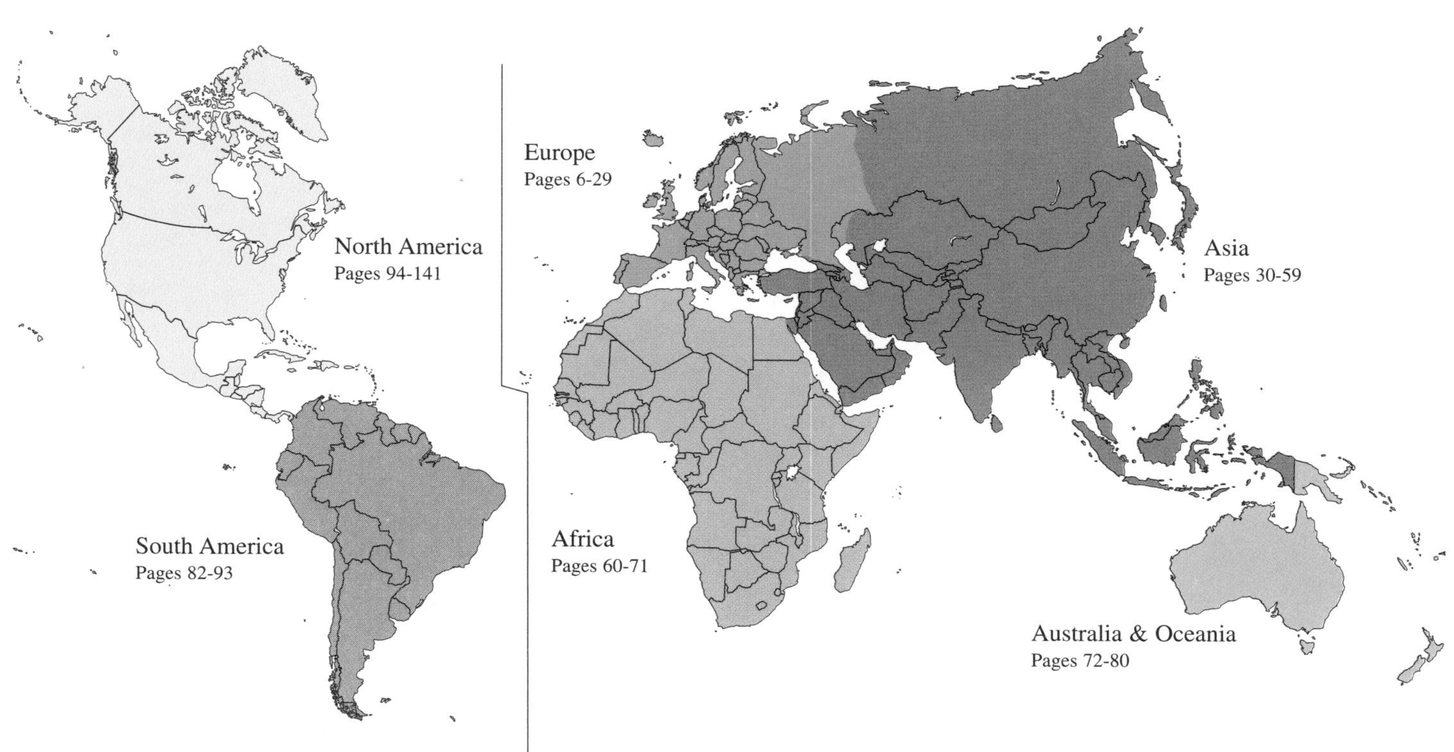

Legend

Hydrographic Features

- Perennial river
- Seasonal river
- Dam (Aswan High Dam)
- Falls (Salto Ángel)
- Aqueduct (Los Angeles Aqueduct)
- Lake, reservoir
- Seasonal lake
- Salt lake
- Seasonal salt lake
- Dry lake
- Lake surface elevation (395)
- Swamp, marsh
- Reef
- Glacier/ice sheet

Topographic Features

All elevations and depths are given in meters.

- 764 Depth of water
- 2278 Elevation above sea level
- 1700 Elevation below sea level
- Mountain pass
- Huo Shan 1774 Mountain peak/elevation

The highest elevation on each continent is underlined.

The highest elevation in each country is shown in boldface.

Transportation Features

- Motorway/Special Highway
- Major road
- Other road
- Trail
- Major railway
- Other railway
- Navigable canal
- Tunnel
- Ferry
- International airport
- Other airport

Political Features

International boundaries

- Demarcated
- Disputed (de facto)
- Disputed (de jure)
- Indefinite/undefined
- Demarcation line

Internal boundaries

- State/province
- Third-order (counties, oblasts, etc.)
- *NORMANDIE* Cultural/historic region
- (Denmark) Administering country

Cities and Towns

The size of symbol and type indicates the relative importance of the locality.

- **LONDON**
- **CHICAGO**
- **Milwaukee**
- Tacna
- Iquitos
- Old Crow
- Mettawa
- Urban area

Capitals

- MEXICO CITY / Bonn — Country, dependency
- RIO DE JANEIRO / Perth — State, province
- MANCHESTER / Chester — County

Cultural Features

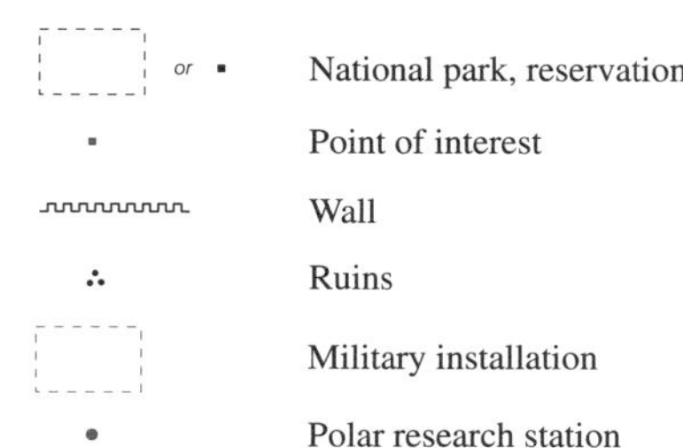

- National park, reservation
- Point of interest
- Wall
- Ruins
- Military installation
- Polar research station

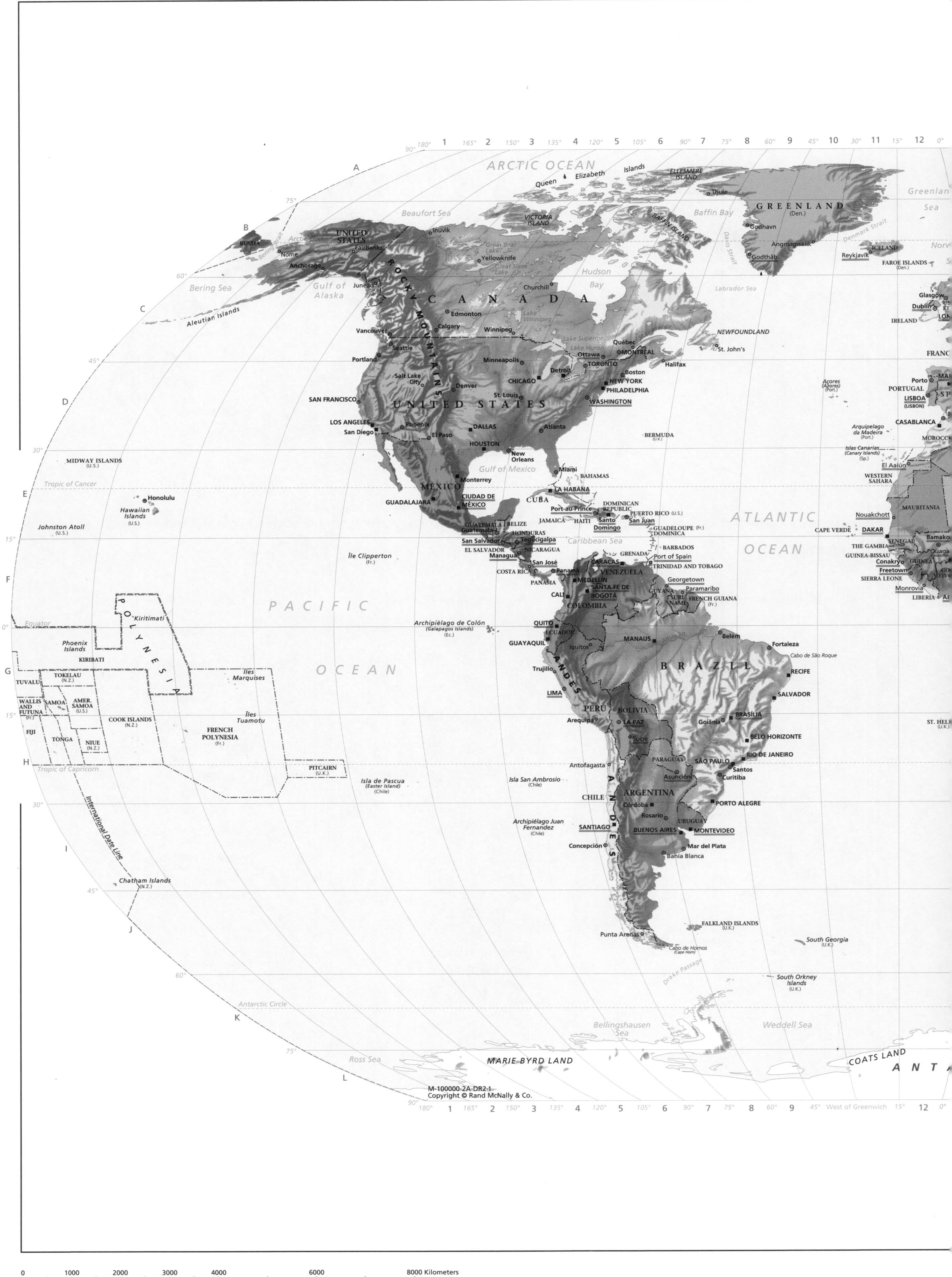

0 1000 2000 3000 4000 6000 8000 Kilometers

0 500 1000 1500 2000 3000 4000 5000 Miles

Scale 1 : 80,000,000

ARCTIC OCEAN
Zemlja Franca-Iosifa
Barents Sea
Novaja Zemlja
Karskoe more
more Laptevyh
Novosibirskie ostrova
Vostočno-Sibirskoe more
Hammerfest
Narvik
Murmansk
Arhangel'sk
Vorkuta
Igarka
Tiksi
SWEDEN
FINLAND
Helsinki
SANKT-PETERBURG (ST. PETERSBURG)
Stockholm
ESTONIA
LATVIA
LITH.
BERLIN
POLAND
BELARUS
WARSZAWA
MOSKVA (MOSCOW)
NIŽNIJ NOVGOROD
Perm'
Ekaterinburg
Čeljabinsk
Samara
Omsk
Novosibirsk
Krasnojarsk
RUSSIA
Jakutsk
Magadan
Sea of Okhotsk
ostrov Sahalin
Bering Sea
Aleutian Is. (U.S.)
Petropavlovsk-Kamčatskij
Kuril'skie ostrova
Irkutsk
Čita
Habarovsk
Ulaanbaatar
MONGOLIA
ALTAI
KYIV
UKRAINE
Volgograd
Astana (Akmola)
KAZAKSTAN
BUDAPEST
ROMANIA
MOLD.
Beograd
Sofija
BULGARIA
ITALY
ROMA
Napoli
GREECE
ATHINA (ATHENS)
Black Sea
ISTANBUL
ANKARA
TURKEY
İzmir
GEORGIA
ARM.
AZER.
BAKI
UZBEKISTAN
TAŠKENT
KYRGYZSTAN
ALMATY
TIEN SHAN
Ürümqi
TAJIKISTAN
TURKMENISTAN
GOBI DESERT
Hohhot
Harbin
SHENYANG
BEIJING
Dalian
TIANJIN
Qingdao
Vladivostok
Sapporo
Hokkaidō
NORTH KOREA
P'yongyang
Sea of Japan
SŎUL
SOUTH KOREA
PUSAN
HONSHŪ
JAPAN
TŌKYŌ
Sendai
ŌSAKA
Fukuoka
CHINA
Yellow Sea
Xi'an
Nanjing
SHANGHAI
WUHAN
Chengdu
Chongqing
Changsha
Kunming
GUANGZHOU
XIANGGANG (HONG KONG)
T'AIPEI
TAIWAN
Nansei-shotō
PACIFIC OCEAN
Tunis
TUNISIA
Mediterranean Sea
Tarābulus
Banghāzī
LIBYA
EL-ISKANDARIYA (ALEXANDRIA)
EL-QAHIRA (CAIRO)
EGYPT
CYPRUS
LEBANON
ISRAEL
Ammān
JORDAN
SYRIA
BAGHDAD
IRAQ
TEHRAN
Eşfahān
IRAN
Abadan
KUWAIT
KABOL
AFGHANISTAN
Islāmābād
Rawalpindi
LAHORE
PAKISTAN
KARĀCHI
HIMALAYAS
NEPAL
DELHI
New Delhi
Kāthmāndau
BHUTAN
BANG.
DHAKA
Lhasa
CALCUTTA
INDIA
Ahmadābād
MUMBAI (BOMBAY)
Pune
HYDERĀBĀD
BANGALORE
CHENNAI (MADRAS)
Kochi
SRI LANKA
Colombo
MALDIVES
Arabian Sea
Bay of Bengal
Andaman Islands (India)
Nicobar Islands (India)
MYANMAR (BURMA)
YANGON (RANGOON)
LAOS
HA NOI
Viangchan
THAILAND
KRUNG THEP (BANGKOK)
CAMBODIA
VIETNAM
Phnum Pénh
THANH-PHO HO CHI MINH (HO CHI MINH CITY) (SAIGON)
South China Sea
LUZON
PHILIPPINES
MANILA
Philippine Sea
Davao
MINDANAO
BRUNEI
Medan
MALAYSIA
Kuala Lumpur
SINGAPORE
BORNEO (KALIMANTAN)
SUMATERA (SUMATRA)
Banjarmasin
SULAWESI (CELEBES)
Ujungpandang
INDONESIA
JAKARTA
JAWA (JAVA)
Surabaya
AR-RIYĀD (RIYADH)
SAUDI ARABIA
BAHRAIN
QATAR
Abū Zaby
U.A.E.
Masqaț
OMAN
Red Sea
YEMEN
San'ā'
Adan
ERITREA
Asmera
DJIBOUTI
Djibouti
Gees Gwardafuy
ADIS ABEBA
ETHIOPIA
SOMALIA
Muqdisho
SAHARA
NIGER
CHAD
N'Djamena
Al-Khartūm (Khartoum)
SUDAN
Kano
NIGERIA
Abuja
LAGOS
CAMEROON
Yaoundé
CENTRAL AFRICAN REPUBLIC
Bangui
EQUAT. GUINEA
GABON
CONGO
DEM. REP. OF THE CONGO
Brazzaville
KINSHASA
UGANDA
Kampala
KENYA
NAIROBI
RWANDA
Kigali
BURUNDI
Bujumbura
TANZANIA
Dodoma
Zanzibar
Dar es Salaam
SEYCHELLES
BRITISH INDIAN OCEAN TERRITORY
LUANDA
ANGOLA
Lobito
Lubumbashi
ZAMBIA
Lusaka
MALAWI
Lilongwe
MOZAMBIQUE
Harare
ZIMBABWE
COMOROS
Mozambique Channel
MADAGASCAR
Antananarivo
MAURITIUS
REUNION (Fr.)
NAMIBIA
Windhoek
Walvis Bay
BOTSWANA
Gaborone
Pretoria
JOHANNESBURG
Maputo
SWAZILAND
Durban
LESOTHO
SOUTH AFRICA
Cape Town
Cape of Good Hope
Port Elizabeth
INDIAN OCEAN
NORTHERN MARIANAS (U.S.)
GUAM (U.S.)
WAKE ISLAND (U.S.)
MARSHALL ISLANDS
FEDERATED STATES OF MICRONESIA
PALAU
MICRONESIA
NAURU
KIRIBATI
PAPUA NEW GUINEA
NEW GUINEA
Port Moresby
Cape York
SOLOMON ISLANDS
TUVALU
MELANESIA
VANUATU
FIJI
Suva
Darwin
Cairns
Coral Sea
NEW CALEDONIA (Fr.)
Nouméa
Alice Springs
Rockhampton
AUSTRALIA
Brisbane
Perth
Adelaide
SYDNEY
Canberra
MELBOURNE
TASMANIA
Hobart
Tasman Sea
Auckland
NORTH ISLAND
NEW ZEALAND
Wellington
SOUTH ISLAND
Christchurch
International Date Line
Tropic of Cancer
Equator
Tropic of Capricorn
Antarctic Circle
SOUTHERN OCEAN
Archipel de Kerguelen (Fr.)
ENDERBY LAND
WILKES LAND
ANTARCTICA
East of Greenwich

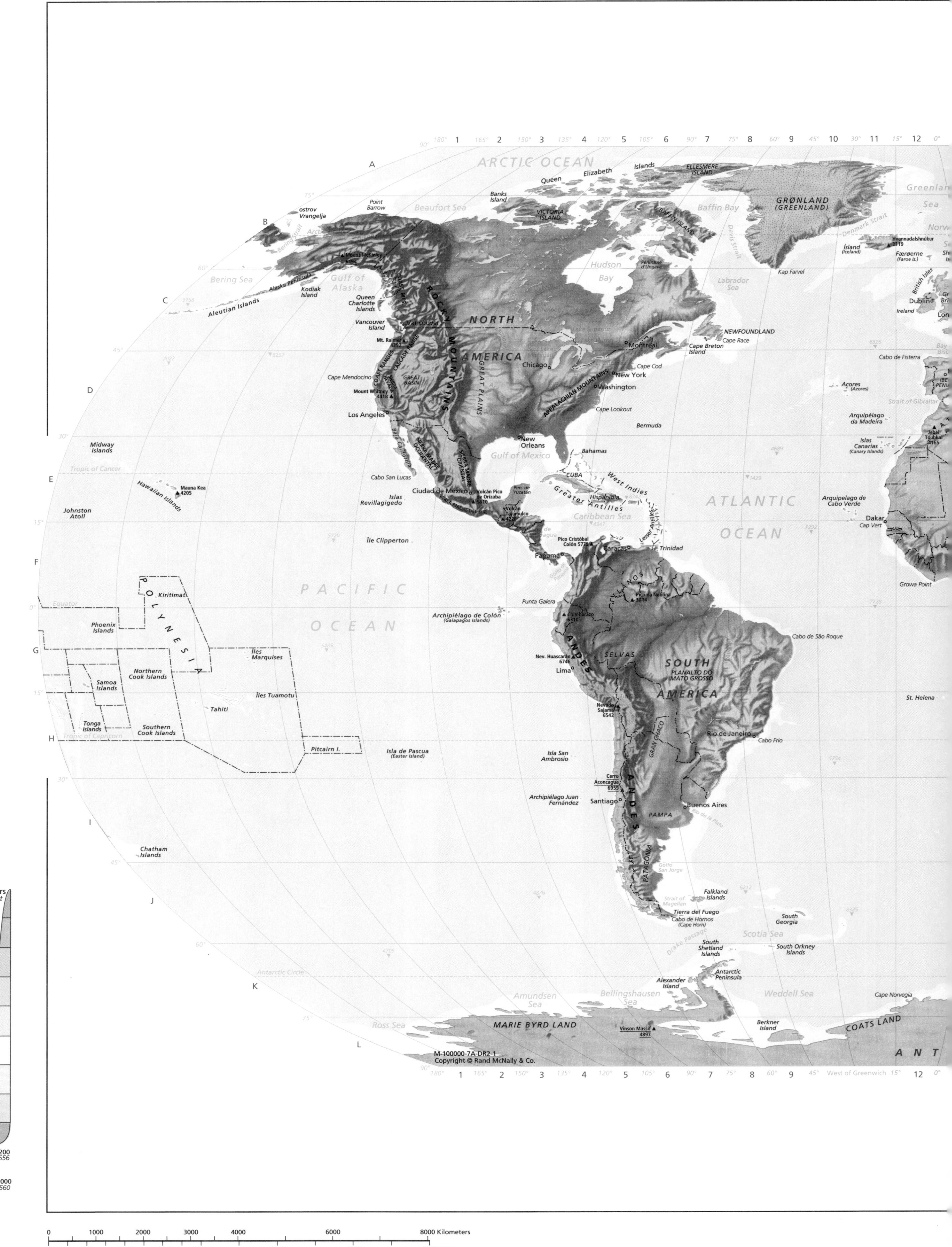

0 1000 2000 3000 4000 6000 8000 Kilometers

0 500 1000 1500 2000 3000 4000 5000 Miles

Scale 1 : 80,000,000 Robinson Projection

4 15 16 17 18 19 20 21 22 23 24

ARCTIC OCEAN
Zemlja Franca-Iosifa
Severnaja Zemlja
Novosibirskie ostrova
Barents Sea
Novaja Zemlja
Karskoe more
more Laptevyh
Vostočno-Sibirskoe more
Nordkapp
Kol'skij poluostrov
ZAPADNO-SIBIRSKAJA RAVNINA (WEST SIBERIAN LOWLAND)
URAL'SKIE GORY
Ekaterinberg
gora Kamen 1701
SIBIR' (SIBERIA)
gora Pobeda 3147
ASIA
Moskva (Moscow)
Berlin
Sea of Okhotsk
Bering Sea
ostrov Sahalin
mys Lopatka
Kuril'skie ostrova
Irkutsk
ALTAI
Ulaanbaatar
GOBI DESERT
CARPATHIANS
ALPS
gora El'brus 5642
CAUCASUS
Black Sea
Istanbul
Roma
BALKAN PENINSULA
Hokkaidō
HONSHŪ
Beijing
Sea of Japan
Tōkyō
TIEN SHAN
pik Pobedy 7439
pik Kommunizma 7495
Sicilia (Sicily)
Kriti
Mediterranean Sea
Cyprus
Tehran
Qolleh-ye Damāvand 5604
DASHT-E KAVIR
HINDU KUSH
KUNLUN SHAN
QING ZANG GAOYUAN
Yellow Sea
Fuji-san 3776
Shikoku
Kyūshū
El Qâhira (Cairo)
KUHHA-YE ZAGROS
Persian Gulf
HIMALAYAS
Delhi
Mount Everest 8848
Gongga Shan 7556
Shanghai
East China Sea
Nansei-shotō
PACIFIC OCEAN
SAHARA
TIBESTI
Emi Koussi 3415
NUBIAN DESERT
ARABIAN PENINSULA
Red Sea
Gulf of Oman
AR-RUB' AL-KHALI
Taiwan
Yü Shan 3997
Tropic of Cancer
Wake Island
Mariana Islands
Mumbai (Bombay)
WESTERN GHATS
EASTERN GHATS
Bay of Bengal
Arabian Sea
Hainan Dao
LUZON
PHILIPPINES
Philippine Sea
Manila
South China Sea
Krung Thep
INDOCHINA
Guam
Marshall Islands
Ras Dashen Terara 4620
Gulf of Aden
Suquṭrā
Gees Gwardafuy
Adis Abeba
Andaman Islands
Palawan
MICRONESIA
AFRICA
Cape Comorin
Pidurutalagala 2524
Sri Lanka
Nicobar Islands
Malay Peninsula
Gunong Kinabalu 4101
MINDANAO
Palau Islands
Maldive Islands
Celebes Sea
Caroline Islands
Margherita Peak 5109
CONGO BASIN
RIFT VALLEY
Kirinyaga 5199
SUMATERA (SUMATRA)
BORNEO (KALIMANTAN)
Halmahera
Equator
Kilimanjaro 5895
Zanzibar
Les Amirantes
Seychelles
SULAWESI (CELEBES)
Maluku
Seram
New Britain
NEW GUINEA
Mount Wilhelm 4509
Greater Sunda Islands
Jakarta
JAWA (JAVA)
Laut Banda
Solomon Islands
Timor
Arafura Sea
INDIAN OCEAN
Tanjona Bobaomby
Maromokotro 2876
Cape York
MELANESIA
Timor Sea
Kimberley Plateau
CAPE YORK PENINSULA
New Hebrides
Fiji Islands
Cape Fria
MADAGASCAR
Mozambique Channel
Tanami Desert
Coral Sea
Mauritius
Réunion
North West Cape
GREAT SANDY DESERT
Nouvelle-Calédonie
Tropic of Capricorn
NAMIB DESERT
KALAHARI DESERT
Tanjona Vohimena
Mount Meharry 1253
AUSTRALIA
Mount Woodroffe 1435
GREAT DIVIDING RANGE
GREAT VICTORIA DESERT
Thabana-Ntlenyana 3482
DRAKENSBERG
Sydney
Cape Town
Cape Leeuwin
Great Australian Bight
North Cape
Cape of Good Hope
Île Amsterdam
Melbourne
Mount Kosciusko 2229
Tasman Sea
NORTH ISLAND
Mount Ruapehu 2797
Mount Ossa 1617
TASMANIA
SOUTH ISLAND
Mount Cook 3754
South East Cape
Prince Edward Islands
Îles de Crozet
Îles Kerguélen
SOUTHERN OCEAN
South West Cape
Heard Island
Macquarie Island
Antarctic Circle
Cape Poinsett
ENDERBY LAND
WILKES LAND
Cape Adare
VICTORIA LAND
Ross Sea
N MAUD LAND
TICA

A B C D E F G H I J K L

st of Greenwich 16 17 18 19 20 21 22 23 24

0 200 400 800 1200 Kilometers
0 100 200 400 600 800 Miles

Scale 1 : 12,500,000   Conic Equidistant Projection

BARENTS SEA
Murmansk
KOL'SKIJ POLUOSTROV (KOLA PENINSULA)
BELOE MORE (WHITE SEA)
Arhangel'sk
FINLAND
Helsinki
Tallinn
ESTONIA
RIGA
LATVIA
LITHUANIA
Vilnius
MINSK
BELARUS
SANKT-PETERBURG (ST. PETERSBURG)
MOSKVA (MOSCOW)
NIŽNIJ NOVGOROD
KAZAN'
PERM'
EKATERINBURG
ČELJABINSK
UFA
SAMARA
SARATOV
VOLGOGRAD
ROSTOV-NA-DONU
R U S S I A
URAL'SKIE GORY (URAL MOUNTAINS)
ZAPADNO-SIBIRSKAJA RAVNINA (WEST SIBERIAN PLAIN)
OMSK
K A Z A K S T A N
UZBEKISTAN
TURKMENISTAN
KYÏV (KIEV)
KHARKIV
DNIPROPETROVS'K
DONETS'K
ODESA
U K R A I N E
Chişinău
MOLDOVA
ROMANIA
BUCUREŞTI (BUCHAREST)
BULGARIA
SOFIJA (SOFIA)
CASPIAN DEPRESSION (PRIKASPIJSKAJA NIZMENNOST')
C A S P I A N S E A
Sea of Azov
KRYMS'KYI PIVOSTRIV (CRIMEAN PENINSULA)
B L A C K S E A
C A U C A S U S
GEORGIA
Tbilisi
ARMENIA
AZERBAIJAN
BAKI (BAKU)
ISTANBUL
ANKARA
T U R K E Y
İZMIR
A N A T O L I A
TOROS DAĞLARI (TAURUS MOUNTAINS)
K U R D I S T A N
M E S O P O T A M I A
BAGHDĀD
I R A Q
S Y R I A
NORTH CYPRUS
CYPRUS
LEBANON
TEHRĀN
I R A N
RESHTEH-YE KŪHHĀ-YE ALBORZ
KŪHHĀ-YE ZĀGROS
EŞFAHĀN
ATHÍNA (ATHENS)
KIKLÁDHES
KRÍTI (CRETE)

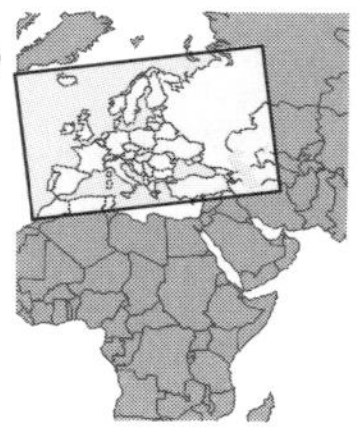

NORWEGIAN SEA
ATLANTIC OCEAN
NORTH SEA
BALTIC SEA
Skagerrak
Kattegat
Gulf of Bothnia
Gulf of Riga
Aland Sea
NORWAY
SWEDEN
DENMARK
GERMANY
LITHUANIA
Oslo
STOCKHOLM
KØBENHAVN (COPENHAGEN)
Tallinn
RIGA
Göteborg (Gothenburg)
Bergen
Trondheim
Stavanger
Kristiansand
Ålesund
Tromsø
Narvik
Bodø
Luleå
Umeå
Sundsvall
Uppsala
Malmö
Kiruna
NORDLAND
NORRBOTTEN
VÄSTERBOTTEN
JÄMTLAND
NORD-TRØNDELAG
SØR-TRØNDELAG
MØRE OG ROMSDAL
SOGN OG FJORDANE
HORDALAND
ROGALAND
OPPLAND
HEDMARK
BUSKERUD
AKERSHUS
TELEMARK
AUST-AGDER
VEST-AGDER
DALARNA
GÄVLEBORG
VÄRMLAND
UPPSALA
SÖDERMANLAND
ÖSTERGÖTLAND
GOTLAND
JÖNKÖPING
KALMAR
KRONOBERG
BLEKINGE
SKÅNE
HALLAND
ÄLVSBORG
SKARABORG
GÖTEBORG OCH BOHUS
ÖREBRO
VÄSTMANLAND
NORDJYLLAND
VIBORG
RINGKØBING
ÅRHUS
VEJLE
RIBE
SØNDERJYLLAND
FYN
BORNHOLM
LOFOTEN
VESTERÅLEN
Same scale as main map
a
ICELAND
GREENLAND SEA
ATLANTIC OCEAN
NORWEGIAN SEA
Reykjavík
Akureyri
Ísafjörður
Húsavík
Hvannadalshnúkur 2119
Same scale as main map
b
ATLANTIC OCEAN
FAROE ISLANDS
(Denmark)
Tórshavn
(Thorshavn)
Same scale as main map

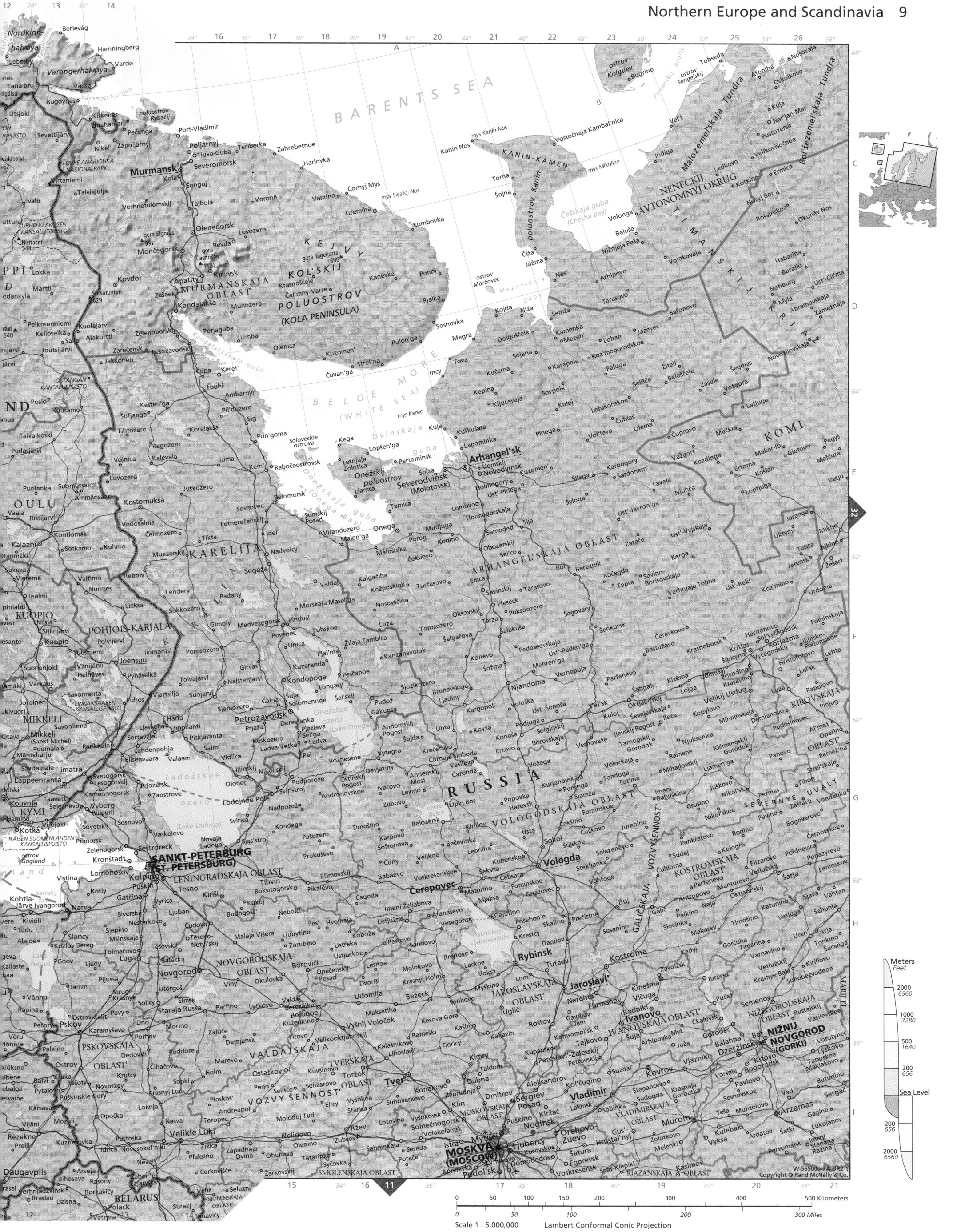

BARENTS SEA
BELOE MORE (WHITE SEA)
KOL'SKIJ POLUOSTROV (KOLA PENINSULA)
Češskaja guba (Chesha Bay)
poluostrov Kanin
NENECKIJ AVTONOMNYJ OKRUG
Malozemel'skaja Tundra
Bol'šezemel'skaja Tundra
TIMANSKIJ KRJAŽ
KOMI
MURMANSKAJA OBLAST'
KARELIJA
ARHANGEL'SKAJA OBLAST'
VOLOGODSKAJA OBLAST'
LENINGRADSKAJA OBLAST'
NOVGORODSKAJA OBLAST'
PSKOVSKAJA OBLAST'
TVERSKAJA OBLAST'
MOSKOVSKAJA OBLAST'
JAROSLAVSKAJA OBLAST'
KOSTROMSKAJA OBLAST'
IVANOVSKAJA OBLAST'
VLADIMIRSKAJA OBLAST'
NIŽEGORODSKAJA OBLAST'
KIROVSKAJA OBLAST'
SMOLENSKAJA OBLAST'
RJAZANSKAJA
VALDAJSKAJA VOZVYŠENNOST'
SEVERNYE UVALY
RUSSIA
OULU
KUOPIO
POHJOIS-KARJALA
MIKKELI
KYMI
BELARUS
Ladožskoe ozero (Lake Ladoga)
Onežskoe ozero (Lake Onega)
Rybinskoe vodohranilišče
Murmansk
Arhangel'sk
Severodvinsk (Molotovsk)
Petrozavodsk
SANKT-PETERBURG (ST. PETERSBURG)
Novgorod
Pskov
Vologda
Čerepovec
Rybinsk
Jaroslavl'
Kostroma
Ivanovo
Vladimir
Tver
MOSKVA (MOSCOW)
NIŽNIJ NOVGOROD (GORKI)
Dzeržinsk
Arzamas
Murom
Velikie Luki
Daugavpils
Narva
Vyborg (Viipuri)
Kuopio
Joensuu
Mikkeli (Sankt Michel)
Lappeenranta
Kotka
Meters Feet
2000 6560
1000 3280
500 1640
200 656
Sea Level
200 656
2000 6560
0 50 100 150 200 300 400 500 Kilometers
0 50 100 200 300 Miles
Scale 1 : 5,000,000
Lambert Conformal Conic Projection
W-565000-7A-DR2-1
Copyright © Rand McNally & Co.

SWEDEN
Sandhamn
Gotska Sandön (Sweden)
Fårön (Sweden)
BALTIC SEA
Gulf of Finland
Gulf of Riga
Gulf of Gdansk
ESTONIA
LATVIA
LITHUANIA
RUSSIA
KALININGRADSKAJA OBLAST'
POLAND
BELARUS
Tallinn
Narva
Tartu
Pärnu
HIIUMAA
SAAREMAA
Kuressaare
Lake Peipus
Lake Pskov
Pskov
PSKOVSKAJA OBL.
Riga
RIGA
Jūrmala
Ventspils
Liepāja
COURLAND (KURZEME)
VIDZEME
Daugavpils
Rēzekne
Jelgava
Klaipėda (Memel)
Šiauliai
Panevėžys
Kaunas
Vilnius
Kaliningrad (Königsberg)
Sovetsk
Curonian Lagoon
Kurshskaja kosa
Baltijsk
OSTPREUSSEN
ELBLĄG
OLSZTYN
MAZURY (MASURIA)
SUWAŁKI
Suwałki
Augustów
Ełk
Hrodna
HRODNA
Białystok
BIAŁYSTOK
ŁOMŻA
Łomża
OSTROŁĘKA
CIECHANÓW
SIEDLCE
PODLASIE
BIAŁA PODLASKA
Biała Podlaska
Brest
BREST
WARSZAWA (WARSAW)
KAMPINOSKI PARK NARODOWY
BIAŁOWIESKI PARK NARODOWY
Baranavičy
Slonim
Lida
Maladzečna
Barysaŭ
MINSK
Minsk
Polack
Navapolack
VICEBSK
Babrujsk
Pinsk
PRIPET
Suur Munamägi 318
Gaiziņa Kalns 312
Juozapinės kalnas 294
hara Dzjaržynskaja 345
Meters
Feet
200
656
Sea Level
200
656
2000
6560
0 25 50 100 Kilometers
0 25 50 Miles
Scale 1 : 2,500,000
Lambert Conformal Conic Projection

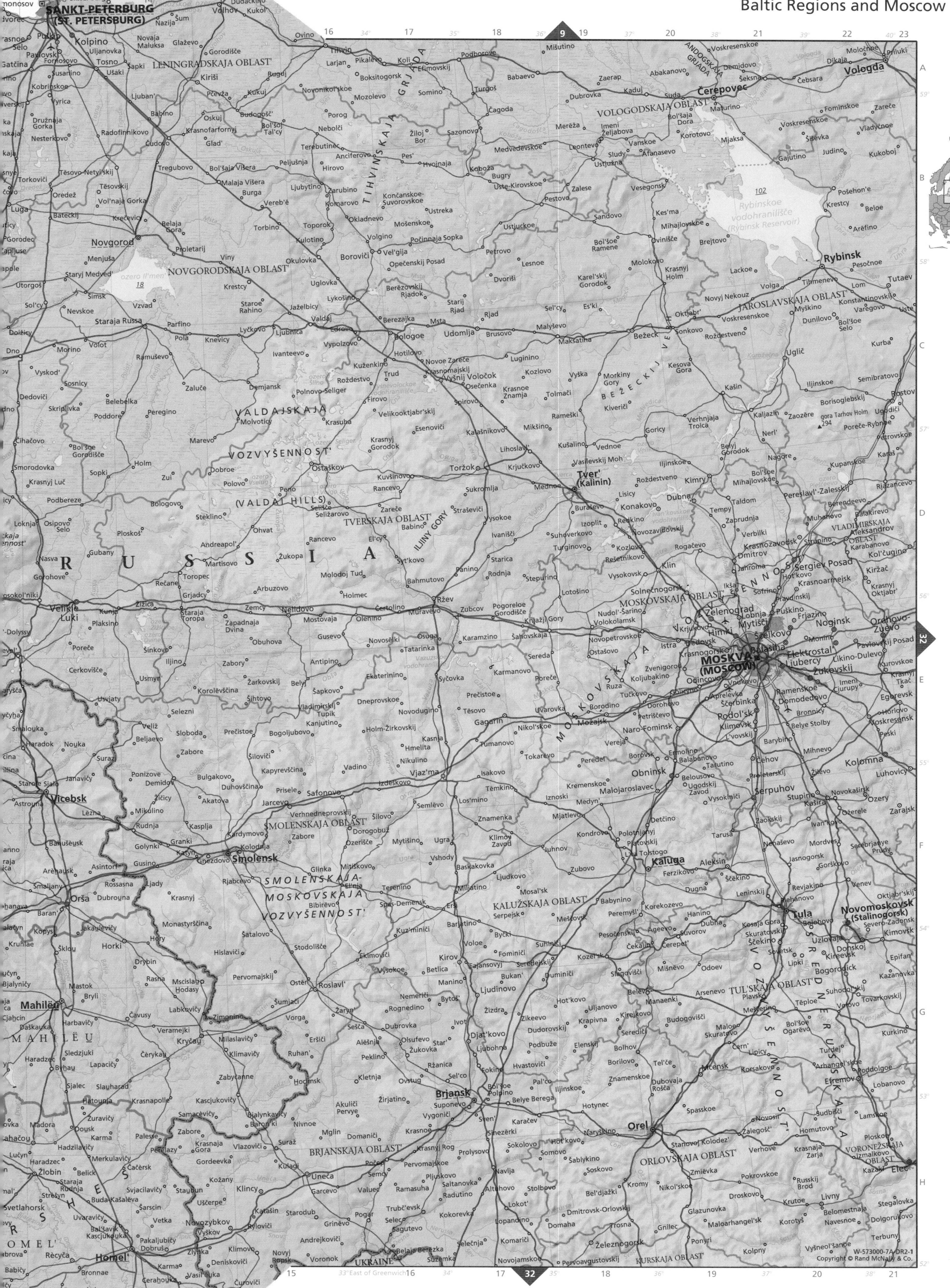

SANKT-PETERBURG
(ST. PETERSBURG)
Kronštadt
Šlissel'burg
Kolpino
Puškin
Pavlovsk
Tosno
Gatčina
LENINGRADSKAJA OBLAST'
Kiriši
Tihvin
Boksitogorsk
Podborov'e
Babaevo
Čerepovec
Vologda
VOLOGODSKAJA OBLAST'
ANDOGSKAJA GRJADA
TIHVINSKAJA GRJADA
Novgorod
ozero Il'men'
NOVGORODSKAJA OBLAST'
Staraja Russa
Boroviči
Ustjužna
Vesegonsk
Rybinskoe vodohranilišče
(Rybinsk Reservoir)
Rybinsk
JAROSLAVSKAJA OBLAST'
Valdaj
Bologoe
Udomlja
Vyšnij Voloček
VALDAJSKAJA VOZVYŠENNOST'
(VALDAI HILLS)
Ostaškov
Toržok
Tver'
(Kalinin)
TVERSKAJA OBLAST'
Kimry
Dubna
Uglič
Kašin
Kaljazin
Sergiev Posad
Dmitrov
Klin
R U S S I A
Velikie Luki
Ržev
Nelidovo
Toropec
MOSKOVSKAJA OBLAST'
Zelenograd
Mytišči
Himki
Noginsk
Elektrostal'
MOSKVA
(MOSCOW)
Ljubercy
Podol'sk
Kolomna
Serpuhov
Obninsk
Možajsk
Vjaz'ma
Safonovo
Jarcevo
SMOLENSKAJA OBLAST'
Smolensk
SMOLENSKAJA-MOSKOVSKAJA VOZVYŠENNOST'
Vicebsk
Orša
Mahilëu
MAHILËU
Kaluga
KALUŽSKAJA OBLAST'
Tula
TUL'SKAJA OBLAST'
Novomoskovsk
(Stalinogorsk)
Roslavl'
Ljudinovo
Brjansk
BRJANSKAJA OBLAST'
Orel
ORLOVSKAJA OBLAST'
Mcensk
Klincy
Novozybkov
Homel'
Žlobin
Rečyca
Elec
VORONEŽSKAJA OBLAST'
KURSKAJA OBLAST'
UKRAINE
SREDNERUSSKAJA VOZVYŠENNOST'
33° East of Greenwich
W-573000-7A-DR2-1
Copyright © Rand McNally & Co.

SHETLAND ISLANDS
ORKNEY ISLANDS
ATLANTIC OCEAN
NORTH SEA
Same scale as main map
To Aberdeen
To Stavanger
To Göteborg
To Esbjerg
Unst
Yell
Fetlar
Out Skerries
Whalsay
Lerwick
Bressay
Mainland
West Burra
Sumburgh Head
Sumburgh Roost
Hillswick
St. Magnus Bay
Papa Stour
Foula
Fair Isle
North Ronaldsay
Sanday
Stronsay
Eday
Shapinsay
Westray
Rousay
Kirkwall
Stromness
Ward Hill
Hoy
St. Margaret's Hope
South Ronaldsay
Pentland Firth
Duncansby Head
John o' Groats
Dunnet Head
Thurso
Castletown
Wick
Helmsdale
Brora
Golspie
Dornoch Firth
Moray Firth
Lossiemouth
Elgin
Buckie
Banff
Macduff
Portsoy
Fraserburgh
Kinnaird Head
Peterhead
Buchan Ness
Aberdeen
Stonehaven
Inverbervie
Montrose
Arbroath
Carnoustie
Dundee
Broughty Ferry
St. Andrews
Fife Ness
Isle of May
Firth of Forth
North Berwick
Dunbar
Haddington
EDINBURGH
Kirkcaldy
Dunfermline
Stirling
Falkirk
GLASGOW
Motherwell
Paisley
Greenock
Kilmarnock
Ayr
Troon
Irvine
Girvan
Stranraer
Dumfries
Carlisle
Berwick-upon-Tweed
Eyemouth
St. Abb's Head
Holy Island
Farne Islands
Alnwick
Amble
Morpeth
Ashington
Blyth
Tynemouth
NEWCASTLE UPON TYNE
Gateshead
Sunderland
Chester-le-Street
Durham
Hartlepool
Middlesbrough
Redcar
UNITED KINGDOM
SCOTLAND
GRAMPIAN MOUNTAINS
CAIRNGORM MTS.
MONADHLIATH MOUNTAINS
NORTHWEST HIGHLANDS
SOUTHERN UPLANDS
GALLOWAY
Glen Mor
Ben Nevis
Fort William
Inverness
Nairn
Aviemore
Perth
Oban
Mallaig
Ullapool
Durness
Cape Wrath
Scourie
Lochinver
Gairloch
Torridon
Stornoway
ISLE OF LEWIS
Butt of Lewis
Port of Ness
Harris
Tarbert
North Uist
Benbecula
South Uist
Barra
Mingulay
St. Kilda
Rona
The Minch
The Little Minch
Sea of the Hebrides
OUTER HEBRIDES
INNER HEBRIDES
HEBRIDES
ISLE OF SKYE
Portree
Dunvegan
Raasay
Canna
Rum
Eigg
Coll
Tiree
Mull
Tobermory
Iona
Colonsay
Jura
Islay
Port Ellen
Gigha Island
Kintyre
Campbeltown
Mull of Kintyre
Isle of Arran
Bute
Firth of Clyde
Skerryvore
Dubh Artach
Rathlin Island
North Channel
Larne
Bangor
Donaghadee
Ballymena
Coleraine
Portrush
Londonderry (Derry)
NORTHERN IRELAND
Omagh
Cookstown
Strabane
Malin Head
Inishowen
Buncrana
Carndonagh
Lough Swilly
Letterkenny
DONEGAL
Glenties
Tory Island
Bloody Foreland
Gweedore
Aran Island
Donegal Bay
Killybegs

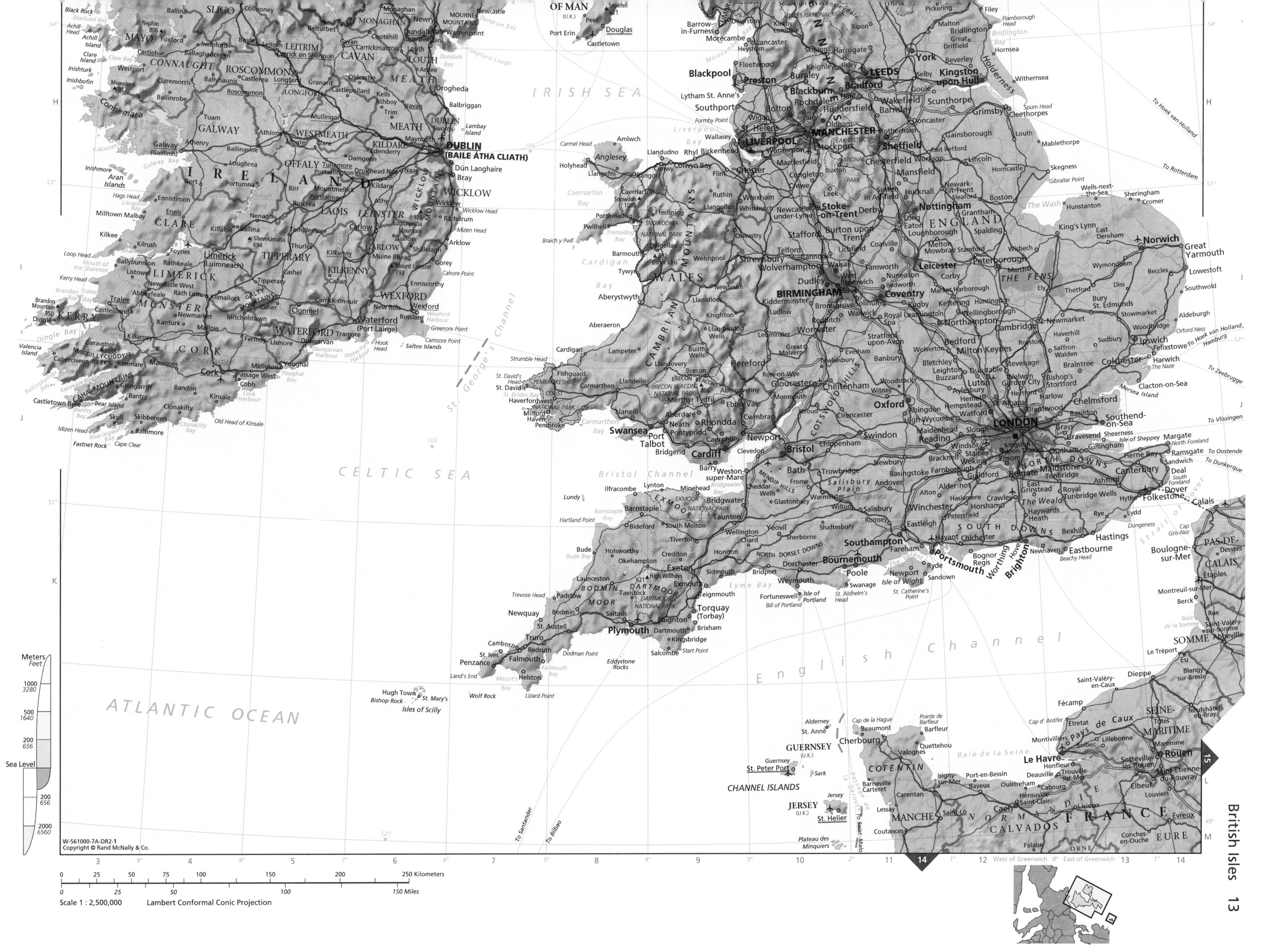
IRISH SEA
CELTIC SEA
ATLANTIC OCEAN
English Channel
Bristol Channel
St. George's Channel
IRELAND
ENGLAND
WALES
FRANCE
LONDON
BIRMINGHAM
MANCHESTER
LIVERPOOL
LEEDS
DUBLIN (BAILE ÁTHA CLIATH)
Cardiff
Bristol
Plymouth
Southampton
Portsmouth
Brighton
Norwich
Nottingham
Sheffield
Leicester
Coventry
Oxford
Swansea
Cork
Limerick
Galway
Waterford
Wexford
Le Havre
Rouen
Cherbourg
Calais
Dover
CHANNEL ISLANDS
GUERNSEY (U.K.)
JERSEY (U.K.)
St. Peter Port
St. Helier
Isles of Scilly
Isle of Wight
Anglesey
Douglas
OF MAN (U.K.)
Scale 1 : 2,500,000
Lambert Conformal Conic Projection
250 Kilometers
150 Miles
Meters
Feet
Sea Level
W-561000-7A-DR2-1
Copyright © Rand McNally & Co.

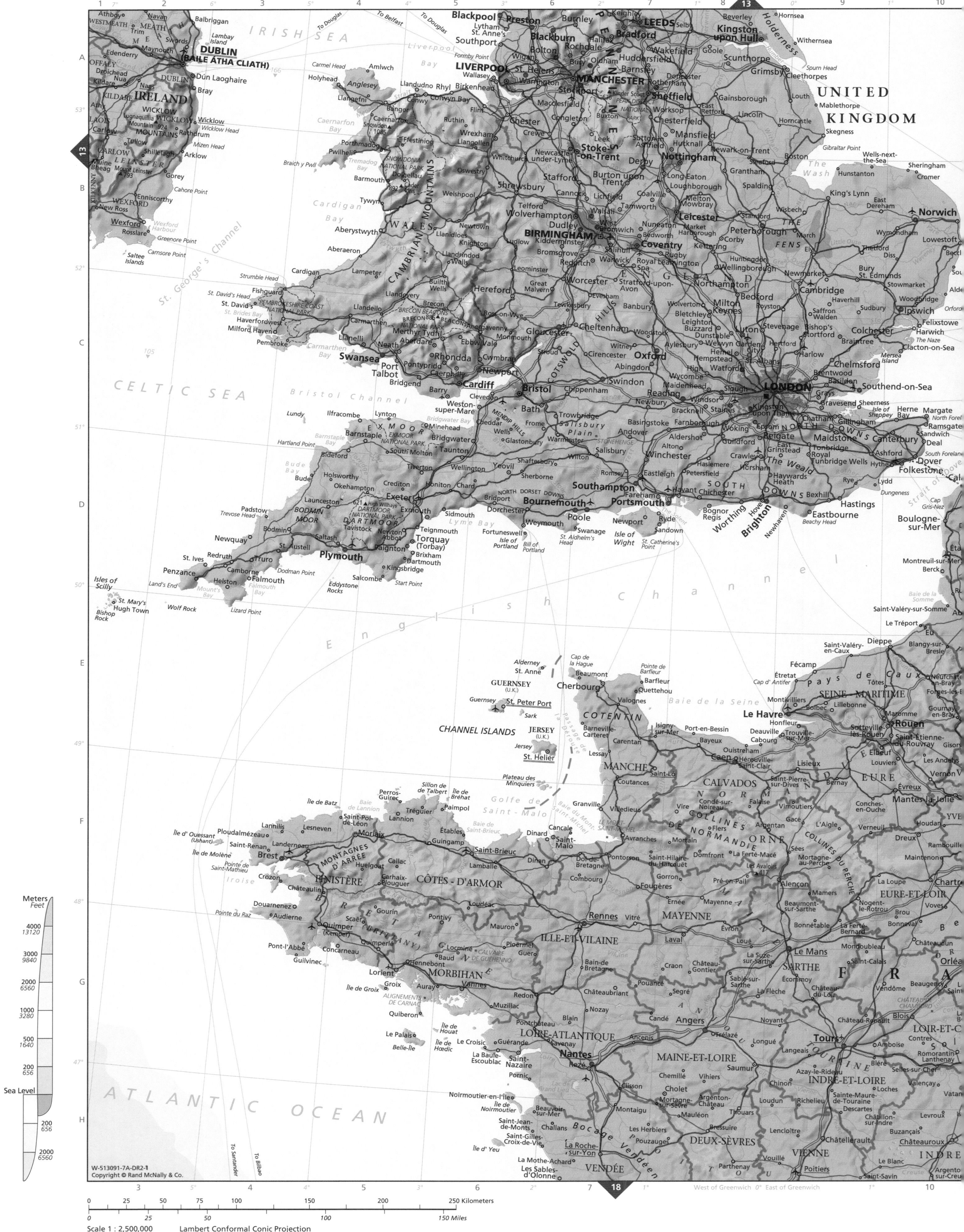
IRISH SEA
UNITED KINGDOM
IRELAND
DUBLIN (BAILE ÁTHA CLIATH)
Dún Laoghaire
Bray
Wicklow
Arklow
Gorey
Wexford
Rosslare
New Ross
Enniscorthy
WALES
CAMBRIAN MOUNTAINS
ENGLAND
Liverpool Bay
Cardigan Bay
St. George's Channel
Bristol Channel
CELTIC SEA
English Channel
ATLANTIC OCEAN
Blackpool
Preston
LEEDS
Bradford
Kingston upon Hull
LIVERPOOL
MANCHESTER
Sheffield
Nottingham
Stoke-on-Trent
Derby
Leicester
BIRMINGHAM
Coventry
Norwich
Cambridge
Ipswich
Colchester
Oxford
LONDON
Swindon
Bristol
Cardiff
Newport
Swansea
Bath
Reading
Southampton
Portsmouth
Bournemouth
Brighton
Hastings
Eastbourne
Canterbury
Dover
Folkestone
Exeter
Plymouth
Torquay (Torbay)
Falmouth
Penzance
Isles of Scilly
Weymouth
Poole
Isle of Wight
Boulogne-sur-Mer
Dieppe
Le Havre
Rouen
Cherbourg
Caen
CHANNEL ISLANDS
GUERNSEY (U.K.)
St. Peter Port
JERSEY (U.K.)
St. Helier
Alderney
COTENTIN
MANCHE
CALVADOS
SEINE-MARITIME
EURE
ORNE
MAYENNE
SARTHE
Le Mans
Brest
Quimper (Kemper)
Lorient
Vannes
Saint-Brieuc
Saint-Malo
Rennes
FINISTÈRE
CÔTES-D'ARMOR
ILLE-ET-VILAINE
MORBIHAN
LOIRE-ATLANTIQUE
Nantes
Saint-Nazaire
Angers
MAINE-ET-LOIRE
Tours
INDRE-ET-LOIRE
DEUX-SÈVRES
VENDÉE
La Roche-sur-Yon
Poitiers
VIENNE
Blois
FRANCE
Meters / Feet
4000 13120
3000 9840
2000 6560
1000 3280
500 1640
200 656
Sea Level
200 656
2000 6560
0 25 50 75 100 150 200 250 Kilometers
0 25 50 100 150 Miles
Scale 1 : 2,500,000
Lambert Conformal Conic Projection
W-513091-7A-DR2-1
Copyright © Rand McNally & Co.

NORTH SEA
FRISIAN ISLANDS
West Friese Eilanden
Ostfriesische Inseln
NETHERLANDS
BELGIUM
LUXEMBOURG
GERMANY
SWITZERLAND
ALPS
AMSTERDAM
ROTTERDAM
's-Gravenhage
(The Hague)
Utrecht
Arnhem
Groningen
Leeuwarden
Eindhoven
ANTWERPEN
(ANTWERP)
BRUXELLES
(BRUSSELS)
Gent
(Ghent)
Brugge
(Bruges)
Oostende
Liège (Luik)
Namur
(Namen)
Charleroi
LILLE
Luxembourg
PARIS
Reims
(Rheims)
Metz
Nancy
Strasbourg
Mulhouse
Basel
(Bâle)
Zürich
(Zurigo)
Bern
(Berne)
Luzern
Dijon
Besançon
HAMBURG
Bremen
Hannover
Braunschweig
(Brunswick)
Osnabrück
Bielefeld
Münster
Dortmund
ESSEN
Duisburg
DÜSSELDORF
Wuppertal
KÖLN
(COLOGNE)
Bonn
Aachen
Koblenz
Wiesbaden
FRANKFURT AM MAIN
Mainz
Darmstadt
Würzburg
MANNHEIM
Heidelberg
Karlsruhe
STUTTGART
Saarbrücken
Trier
Kassel
Göttingen
Freiburg im Breisgau
NIEDERSACHSEN
(SAXONY)
NORDRHEIN
WESTFALEN
RHEINLAND-PFALZ
HESSEN
SAARLAND
BADEN-WÜRTTEMBERG
BAYERN (BAVARIA)
THÜRINGEN
ARDENNES
EIFEL
HUNSRÜCK
SCHWARZWALD
(BLACK FOREST)
VOSGES
JURA
NORD
AISNE
MARNE
MEUSE
MOSELLE
BAS-RHIN
HAUT-RHIN
SEINE-ET-MARNE
AUBE
HAUTE-MARNE
YONNE
CÔTE-D'OR
HAUTE-SAÔNE
DOUBS
NIÈVRE
SAÔNE-ET-LOIRE
LOIRET
CHER
ALLIER
11
12
13
14
15
16
17
18
19
20
A
B
C
D
E
F
G
H
16
19
22

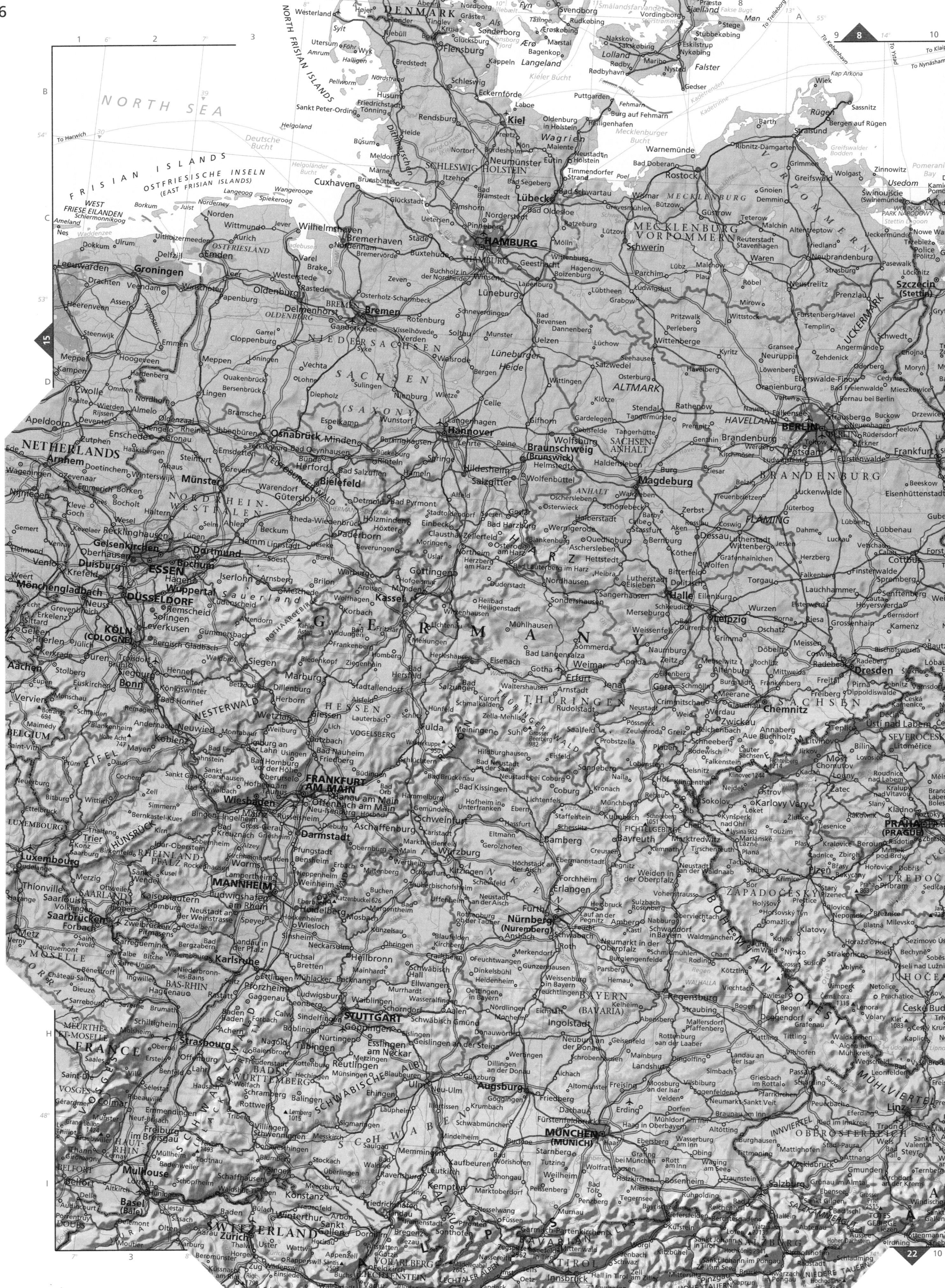
NORTH SEA
FRISIAN ISLANDS
OSTFRIESISCHE INSELN
(EAST FRISIAN ISLANDS)
NORTH FRISIAN ISLANDS
DENMARK
NETHERLANDS
BELGIUM
LUXEMBOURG
FRANCE
SWITZERLAND
GERMANY
SCHLESWIG-HOLSTEIN
MECKLENBURG-VORPOMMERN
NIEDERSACHSEN
SACHSEN (SAXONY)
SACHSEN-ANHALT
BRANDENBURG
NORDRHEIN-WESTFALEN
HESSEN
THÜRINGEN
SACHSEN
RHEINLAND-PFALZ
SAARLAND
BADEN-WÜRTTEMBERG
BAYERN (BAVARIA)
Lüneburger Heide
ALTMARK
HARZ
Sauerland
WESTERWALD
EIFEL
HUNSRÜCK
SCHWÄBISCHE ALB
SCHWARZWALD
BOHEMIAN FOREST
ZÁPADOČESKÝ
JIHOČESKÝ
STŘEDOČESKÝ
SEVEROČESKÝ
OBERÖSTERREICH
TIROL
ALPS
Kiel
Lübeck
HAMBURG
Bremen
Rostock
Schwerin
BERLIN
Potsdam
Hannover
Braunschweig (Brunswick)
Magdeburg
Osnabrück
Münster
Bielefeld
Dortmund
ESSEN
Duisburg
DÜSSELDORF
KÖLN (COLOGNE)
Bonn
Kassel
Göttingen
Halle
Leipzig
Dresden
Chemnitz
Erfurt
FRANKFURT AM MAIN
Wiesbaden
Mainz
Darmstadt
MANNHEIM
Heidelberg
Karlsruhe
STUTTGART
Würzburg
Nürnberg (Nuremberg)
Regensburg
Augsburg
MÜNCHEN (MUNICH)
Saarbrücken
Strasbourg
Basel (Bâle)
Zürich
Mulhouse
Luxembourg
Groningen
Szczecin (Stettin)
PRAHA (PRAGUE)
Plzeň
Linz
Salzburg
Innsbruck

BALTIC SEA
Gulf of Gdansk
RUSSIA
KALININGRADSKAJA OBLAST
Kaliningrad (Königsberg)
LITHUANIA
Gdańsk (Danzig)
Gdynia
POLAND
WARSZAWA (WARSAW)
Łódź
Poznań
Wrocław (Breslau)
Kraków
Katowice
Bydgoszcz
Toruń
Szczecin
Lublin
Białystok
Hrodna
BELARUS
Brest
UKRAINE
L'VIV
CZECH REPUBLIC
Brno
Ostrava
Olomouc
SLOVAKIA
Bratislava
Košice
CARPATHIAN MTS.
WIEN (VIENNA)
NIEDERÖSTERREICH
HUNGARY
BUDAPEST
Győr (Raab)
Miskolc
Debrecen
ROMANIA
Satu Mare
Meters
Feet
2000
6560
1000
3280
500
1640
200
656
Sea Level
200
656
2000
6560
Scale 1 : 2,500,000
Lambert Conformal Conic Projection
0 25 50 75 100 150 200 250 Kilometers
0 25 50 100 150 Miles
16° East of Greenwich
Copyright © Rand McNally & Co.
26
10

ATLANTIC OCEAN
Bay of Biscay
Iroise
To Portsmouth
To Plymouth
FRANCE
SPAIN
PARIS
Versailles
YVELINES
EURE
NORMANDIE (NORMANDY)
COLLINES DE NORMANDIE
COLLINES DU PERCHE
MANCHE
ORNE
Alençon
Dreux
Chartres
EURE-ET-LOIR
ESSONNE
Fontainebleau
Étampes
Orléans
LOIRET
Montargis
Pithiviers
Beauce
ORLÉANAIS
Brest
Saint-Renan
Île de Molène
Pointe de Saint-Mathieu
Crozon
Douarnenez
FINISTÈRE
Pointe du Raz
Audierne
Quimper (Kemper)
Pont-l'Abbé
Guilvinec
Concarneau
Quimperlé
Lorient
Hennebont
Île de Groix
Groix
MONTAGNES D'ARRÉE
Carhaix-Plouguer
Châteaulin
Huelgoat
Callac
Gourin
Scaër
Pontivy
Loudéac
Mauron
Ploërmel
Baud
Locminé
Guer
MORBIHAN
Auray
Vannes
Quiberon
Le Palais
Belle-Île
Île de Houat
Île de Hœdic
Muzillac
Redon
Saint-Brieuc
Lamballe
Dinan
Dol-de-Bretagne
CÔTES-D'ARMOR
BRETAGNE
Combourg
Fougères
Rennes
ILLE-ET-VILAINE
Vitré
Pontorson
Domfront
La Ferté-Macé
Gorron
Ernée
Mayenne
MAYENNE
Laval
Évron
Pré-en-Pail
Mamers
Mortagne-au-Perche
Sées
La Loupe
Nogent-le-Rotrou
Beaumont-sur-Sarthe
Bonnétable
La Ferté-Bernard
Le Mans
SARTHE
Sablé-sur-Sarthe
La Flèche
Loué
Mondoubleau
Saint-Calais
Vendôme
Écommoy
Château-du-Loir
Château-Renault
Blois
LOIR-ET-CHER
Châteaudun
Brou
Bonneval
Voves
Bain-de-Bretagne
Craon
Château-Gontier
Châteaubriant
Pouancé
Segré
Nozay
Candé
Blain
LOIRE-ATLANTIQUE
Angers
ANJOU
Noyant
Longué
Saumur
MAINE-ET-LOIRE
Ancenis
Pontchâteau
Guérande
Le Croisic
La Baule-Escoublac
Saint-Nazaire
Pornic
Nantes
Rezé
Noirmoutier-en-l'Île
Île de Noirmoutier
Beauvoir-sur-Mer
Saint-Jean-de-Monts
Saint-Gilles-Croix-de-Vie
Île d'Yeu
Challans
Bocage Vendéen
Montaigu
Clisson
Cholet
Chemillé
Vihiers
Mortagne-sur-Sèvre
Les Herbiers
Pouzauges
Mauléon
Bressuire
Argenton-Château
Thouars
Loudun
La Roche-sur-Yon
La Mothe-Achard
VENDÉE
Les Sables-d'Olonne
Luçon
Fontenay-le-Comte
La Châtaigneraie
Parthenay
DEUX-SÈVRES
Niort
Marans
La Rochelle
Pertuis Breton
Île de Ré
Île d'Aix
Rochefort
CHARENTE-MARITIME
Le Château-d'Oléron
Île d'Oléron
Marennes
Surgères
Saint-Jean-d'Angély
Matha
Saintes
Pointe de la Coubre
Royan
Soulac-sur-Mer
Saint-Vivien-de-Médoc
MÉDOC
Gironde
Pons
Jonzac
Mirambeau
Montguyon
Blaye-et-Sainte-Luce
Cognac
Jarnac
Châteauneuf-sur-Charente
Archiac
Barbezieux
SAINTONGE
ANGOUMOIS
Angoulême
CHARENTE
Ruffec
Mansle
Chef-Boutonne
Melle
Couhé
Civray
Charroux
Confolens
Chabanais
Rochechouart
La Rochefoucauld
Montbron
Nontron
Tours
Langeais
Azay-le-Rideau
Bléré
Amboise
Chinon
Sainte-Maure-de-Touraine
Loches
INDRE-ET-LOIRE
TOURAINE
Richelieu
Descartes
Lencloître
Châtellerault
Poitiers
POITOU
VIENNE
Vouillé
Montmorillon
Lussac-les-Châteaux
L'Isle-Jourdain
Le Blanc
Saint-Savin
Argenton-sur-Creuse
Châtillon-sur-Indre
Châteauroux
INDRE
BERRY
Valençay
Selles-sur-Cher
Romorantin-Lanthenay
Sologne
Vierzon
Bourges
CHER
Issoudun
Levroux
Buzançais
Vatan
Mehun-sur-Yèvre
Saint-Florent-sur-Cher
Lignières
La Châtre
Aigurande
Boussac
Guéret
CREUSE
Aubusson
Felletin
Bourganeuf
MARCHE
Plateau du Limousin
Limoges
HAUTE-VIENNE
Saint-Junien
Bellac
Le Dorat
Saint-Yrieix-la-Perche
Uzerche
Eymoutiers
Plateau de Millevaches
Égletons
Ussel
Tulle
CORRÈZE
Brive-la-Gaillarde
Thiviers
Brantôme
Périgueux
PÉRIGORD
Ribérac
Chalais
Montpon-Ménesterol
Mussidan
DORDOGNE
Montignac
Sarlat-la-Canéda
Bergerac
Sainte-Foy-la-Grande
Castillon-la-Bataille
Coutras
Libourne
Bordeaux
Mérignac
Pessac
Talence
GIRONDE
Lacanau
Étang de Lacanau
Lac de Carcans
Étang d'Hourtin
Saint-Laurent-et-Benon
Arès
Bassin d'Arcachon
Arcachon
Cap Ferret
La Teste-de-Buch
Audenge
Belin
Étang de Cazaux et de Sanguinet
Biscarrosse
Étang de Biscarrosse et de Parentis
Parentis-en-Born
Mimizan-les-Bains
Saint-Julien-en-Born
Côte d'Argent
LANDES
Sabres
Labrit
Morcenx
Castets
Mont-de-Marsan
Roquefort
Sore
Captieux
Villandraut
Langon
Cadillac
Bazas
La Réole
Marmande
Duras
Sauveterre-de-Guyenne
Targon
Tonneins
Grignols
LOT-ET-GARONNE
Villeneuve-sur-Lot
Fumel
Cancon
Agen
Nérac
Houeillès
Lauzerte
Moissac
Castelsarrasin
Montauban
TARN-ET-GARONNE
Cahors
LOT
Gourdon
Souillac
Martel
Gramat
Figeac
QUERCY
Decazeville
Villefranche-de-Rouergue
Caylus
Caussade
Najac
AVEYRON
Rodez
Aurillac
Mauriac
Salers
CANTAL
Plomb du Cantal
Bort-les-Orgues
Neuvic
Dax
Léon
Hossegor
Bayonne
Anglet
Biarritz
Saint-Jean-de-Luz
Irún
Aire-sur-l'Adour
Hagetmau
Nogaro
Eauze
Condom
Fleurance
GERS
Auch
Mirande
Masseube
Lectoure
Mézin
GASCOGNE
CHALOSSE
BÉARN
Orthez
Salies-de-Béarn
Sauveterre-de-Béarn
Pau
PYRÉNÉES-ATLANTIQUES
Mauléon-Licharre
Saint-Jean-Pied-de-Port
Oloron-Sainte-Marie
Tarbes
Lourdes
Argelès-Gazost
HAUTES-PYRÉNÉES
Lannemezan
Pic du Midi de Bigorre
Bagnères-de-Luchon
Saint-Gaudens
Comminges
Saint-Girons
Boulogne-sur-Gesse
Muret
HAUTE-GARONNE
Toulouse
Verdun-sur-Garonne
Grisolles
Gaillac
Albi
TARN
Graulhet
Lavaur
Castres
Mazamet
Castelnaudary
Carcassonne
AUDE
Limoux
Pamiers
Foix
ARIÈGE
Lavelanet
Quillan
Tarascon-sur-Ariège
Ax-les-Thermes
ANDORRA
Andorra la Vella
PYRÉNÉES-ORIENTALES
Prades
Mont-Louis
Puigcerdà
Llívia
La Seu d'Urgell
Sort
Vielha
Tremp
La Pobla de Segur
Benavarri
LLEIDA
Lleida (Lérida)
Balaguer
Tàrrega
Cervera
Solsona
Berga
Manresa
Igualada
Vic
Ripoll
Olot
GIRONA
Mataró
Badalona
Sabadell
Terrassa (Tarrassa)
Granollers
BARCELONA
L'Hospitalet de Llobregat
CATALUNYA
Montblanc
Les Borges Blanques
La Granadella
Fraga
Mequinenza
Monzón
Barbastro
Binéfar
Tamarite de Litera
Huesca
HUESCA
SIERRA DE GUARA
Sabiñánigo
Jaca
Canfranc
Boltaña
Aínsa
Monte Perdido
Grañén
Sariñena
Almudévar
ARAGÓN
Zaragoza (Saragossa)
ZARAGOZA
Zuera
Alagón
Gallur
Borja
Tarazona
Tudela
Ejea de los Caballeros
Sádaba
Bardenas Reales
Sos del Rey Católico
Sangüesa
NAVARRA
Pamplona
Puente la Reina
Estella
Tafalla
Olite
Lodosa
Calahorra
Alfaro
Logroño
LA RIOJA
Haro
Santo Domingo de la Calzada
Torrecilla en Cameros
Arnedo
Cervera del Río Alhama
SISTEMA IBÉRICO (IBERIAN MTS.)
Soria
SORIA
Almenar de Soria
Ágreda
Ólvega
Medinaceli
Calatayud
Cariñena
Belchite
Ateca
La Almunia de Doña Godina
Épila
Tierga
Burgo de Osma
San Esteban de Gormaz
Berlanga de Duero
Aranda de Duero
CASTILLA Y LEÓN
Burgos
BURGOS
Belorado
Briviesca
Miranda de Ebro
Vitoria-Gasteiz
ARABA
Sedano
Villadiego
Castrojeriz
Lerma
Salas de los Infantes
Barbadillo del Mercado
Tardajos
Palencia
PALENCIA
Torquemada
Baltanás
VALLADOLID
Peñafiel
Cuéllar
SEGOVIA
Sepúlveda
Riaza
Cantalejo
Puerto de Somosierra
MADRID
Atienza
Santander
CANTABRIA
San Vicente de la Barquera
Torrelavega
Laredo
Cabo de Ajo
Cabo Matxitxako
Bermeo
Gernika
Lekeitio
Bilbao
Barakaldo
Portugalete
Getxo
Algorta
BIZKAIA
Durango
Eibar
Zarautz
Azpeitia
GIPUZKOA
Donostia (San Sebastián)
Errenteria
Tolosa
Bergara
EUSKAL HERRIKO
Beasain
Altsasu
Reinosa
Aguilar de Campoo
Cervera de Pisuerga
Herrera de Pisuerga
Osorno
CORDILLERA CANTÁBRICA
Villarcayo
TIERRA DE CAMPOS
PYRENEES
West of Greenwich
East of Greenwich
Meters
Feet
4000
13120
3000
9840
2000
6560
1000
3280
500
1640
200
656
Sea Level
200
656
2000
6560
0 25 50 75 100 150 200 250 Kilometers
0 25 50 100 150 Miles
Scale 1 : 2,500,000
Lambert Conformal Conic Projection

GERMANY
SWITZERLAND
AUSTRIA
ITALY
FRANCE
LIECHTENSTEIN
MONACO
ALPS
LIGURIAN SEA
MEDITERRANEAN SEA
Golfe du Lion
Golfo di Genova
Strasbourg
Basel (Bâle)
Zürich (Zurigo)
Bern (Berne)
Genève (Geneva)
Lausanne
Luzern (Lucerne)
LYON
Saint-Étienne
Grenoble
MARSEILLE
Toulon
Nice
Cannes
Avignon
Montpellier
Dijon
Besançon
TORINO (TURIN)
MILANO (MILAN)
GENOVA (GENOA)
Bergamo
Brescia
Augsburg
Mulhouse
Colmar
Troyes
CORSE (CORSICA)
Bastia
Ajaccio
SARDEGNA (SARDINIA)
Isola d'Elba
Riviera di Ponente
Riviera di Levante
Côte d'Azur
W-513092-7A-DR2-1
Copyright © Rand McNally & Co.

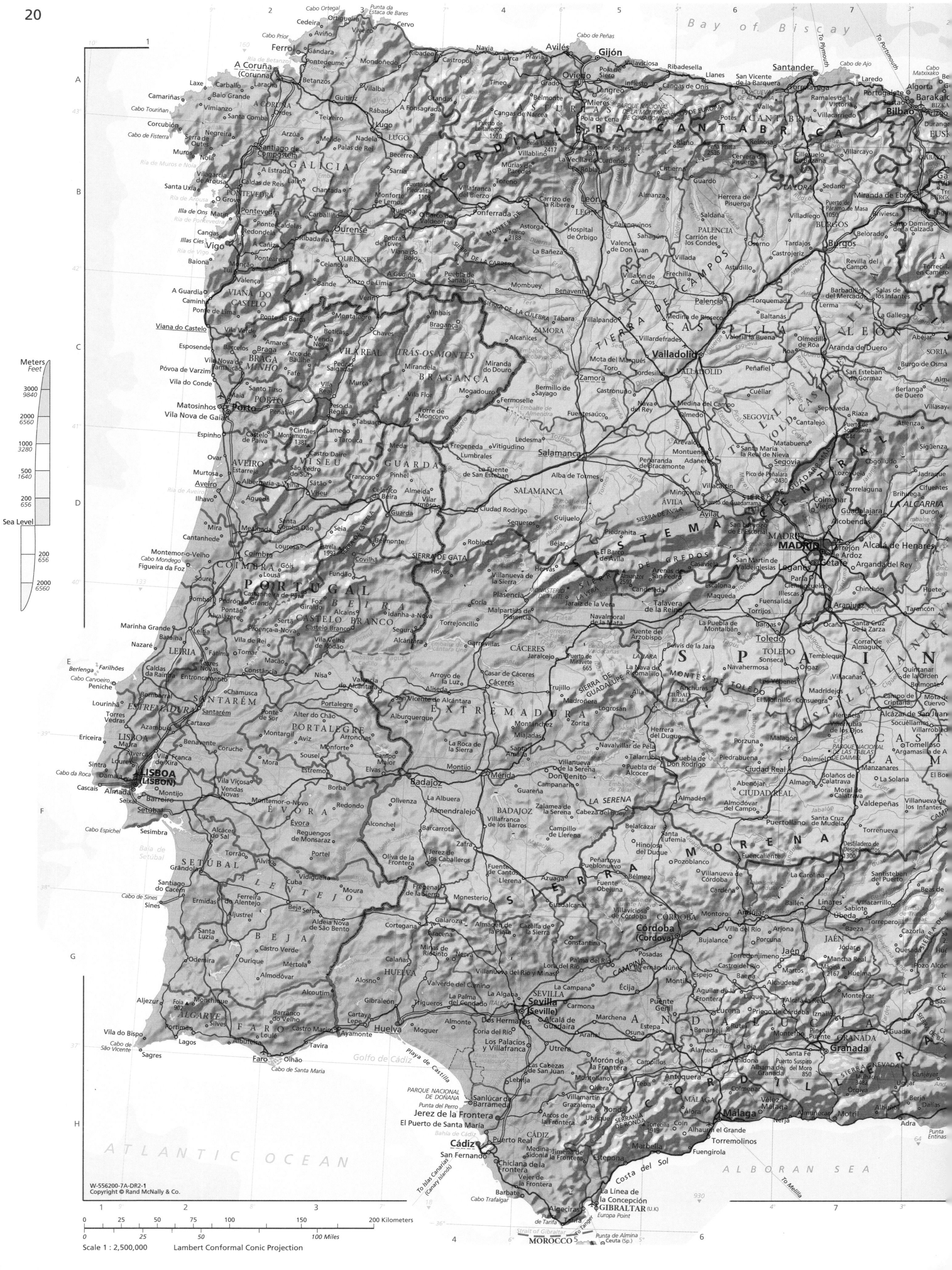

Bay of Biscay
ATLANTIC OCEAN
ALBORAN SEA
Golfo de Cádiz
PORTUGAL
SPAIN
GALICIA
CASTILLA Y LEÓN
EXTREMADURA
ANDALUCÍA
CORDILLERA CANTÁBRICA
SISTEMA CENTRAL
SIERRA MORENA
CORDILLERA PENIBÉTICA
Madrid
Lisboa (Lisbon)
Porto
Sevilla (Seville)
Córdoba (Cordova)
Granada
Málaga
Cádiz
Valladolid
Salamanca
Toledo
Badajoz
Bilbao
Santander
Gijón
Oviedo
A Coruña (Corunna)
Vigo
Faro
Gibraltar (U.K.)
Morocco
Ceuta (Sp.)
Strait of Gibraltar
To Islas Canarias (Canary Islands)
To Melilla
To Plymouth
To Portsmouth
Meters / Feet
3000 / 9840
2000 / 6560
1000 / 3280
500 / 1640
200 / 656
Sea Level
200 / 656
2000 / 6560
W-556200-7A-DR2-1
Copyright © Rand McNally & Co.
0 25 50 75 100 150 200 Kilometers
0 25 50 100 Miles
Scale 1 : 2,500,000
Lambert Conformal Conic Projection

FRANCE
PYRÉNÉES
Golfe du Lion
Perpignan
Donostia (San Sebastián)
Pamplona
NAVARRA
ARAGON
Zaragoza (Saragossa)
Huesca
Lleida
CATALUNYA
Girona
Costa Brava
BARCELONA
L'Hospitalet de Llobregat
Badalona
Mataró
Terrassa
Sabadell
Tarragona
Reus
Golf de Sant Jordi
Tortosa
Delta de l'Ebre
Teruel
Castelló de la Plana
Illes Columbretes
VALÈNCIA
Golf de València
Sagunt
Gandia
Dénia
Xàbia
Cap de la Nau
Benidorm
Alcoi
Elx
Alacant (Alicante)
Cap de Santa Pola
Murcia
Cartagena
Cabo de Palos
Mar Menor
Torrevella
Lorca
Albacete
Cuenca
ILLES BALEARS (BALEARIC ISLANDS)
MENORCA (Minorca)
Ciutadella de Menorca
Maó
MALLORCA (Majorca)
Palma de Mallorca
Manacor
Cap de Formentor
EIVISSA (IBIZA)
Sant Antoni de Portmany
Santa Eulària del Riu
FORMENTERA
Cap de Barbaria
Illa de Cabrera
BALEARS
MEDITERRANEAN SEA
EL DJAZAÏR (ALGIERS)
Cherchell
Tizi-Ouzou
Bordj Menaiel
Blida
ATLAS MOUNTAINS
Ech Cheliff
Ténès
Cabo de Gata
Águilas
Mojácar
To Marseille
West of Greenwich 0° East of Greenwich
18
64

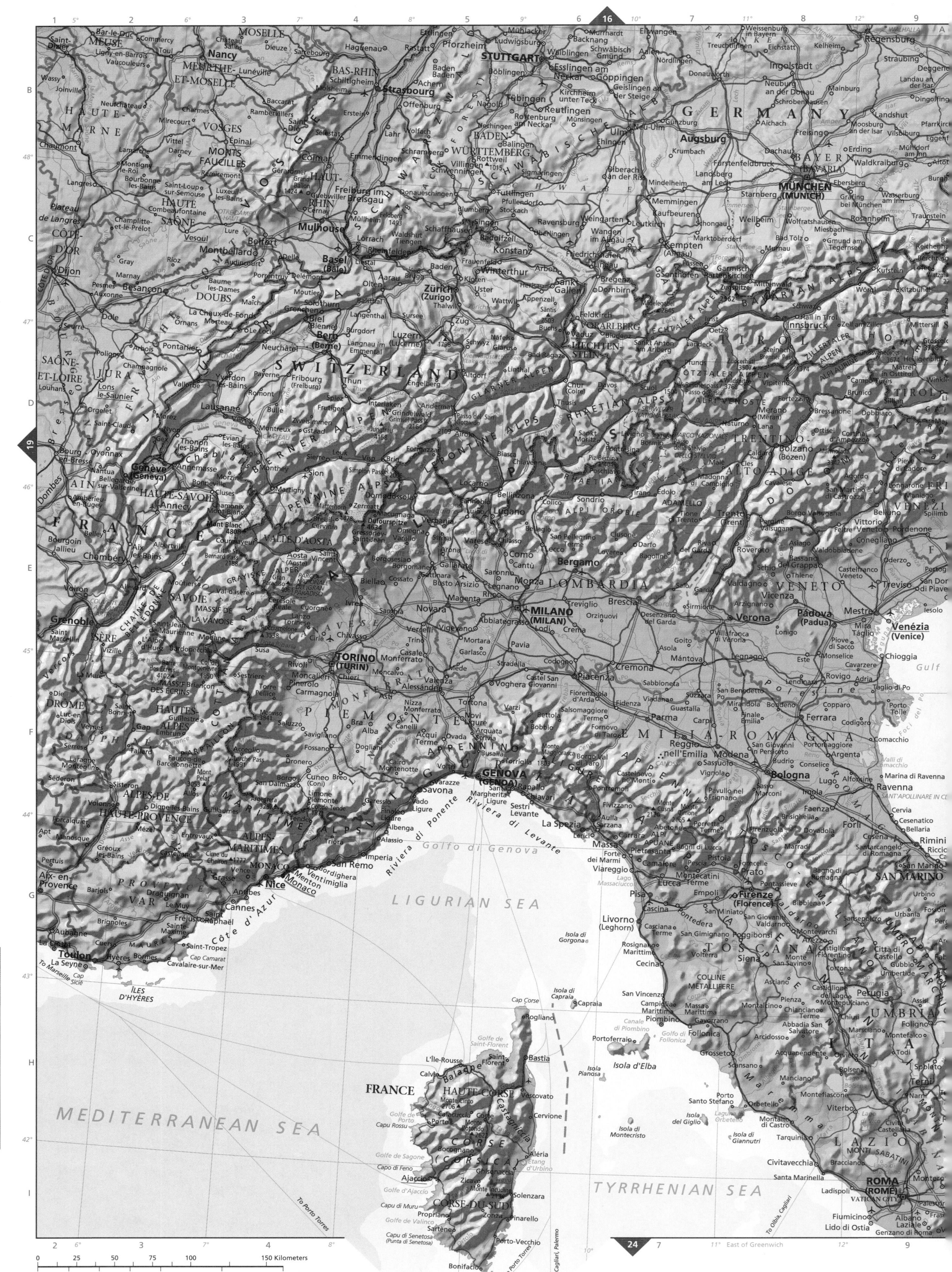

Scale 1 : 2,500,000 Lambert Conformal Conic Projection

0 25 50 75 100 150 Kilometers

0 25 50 100 Miles

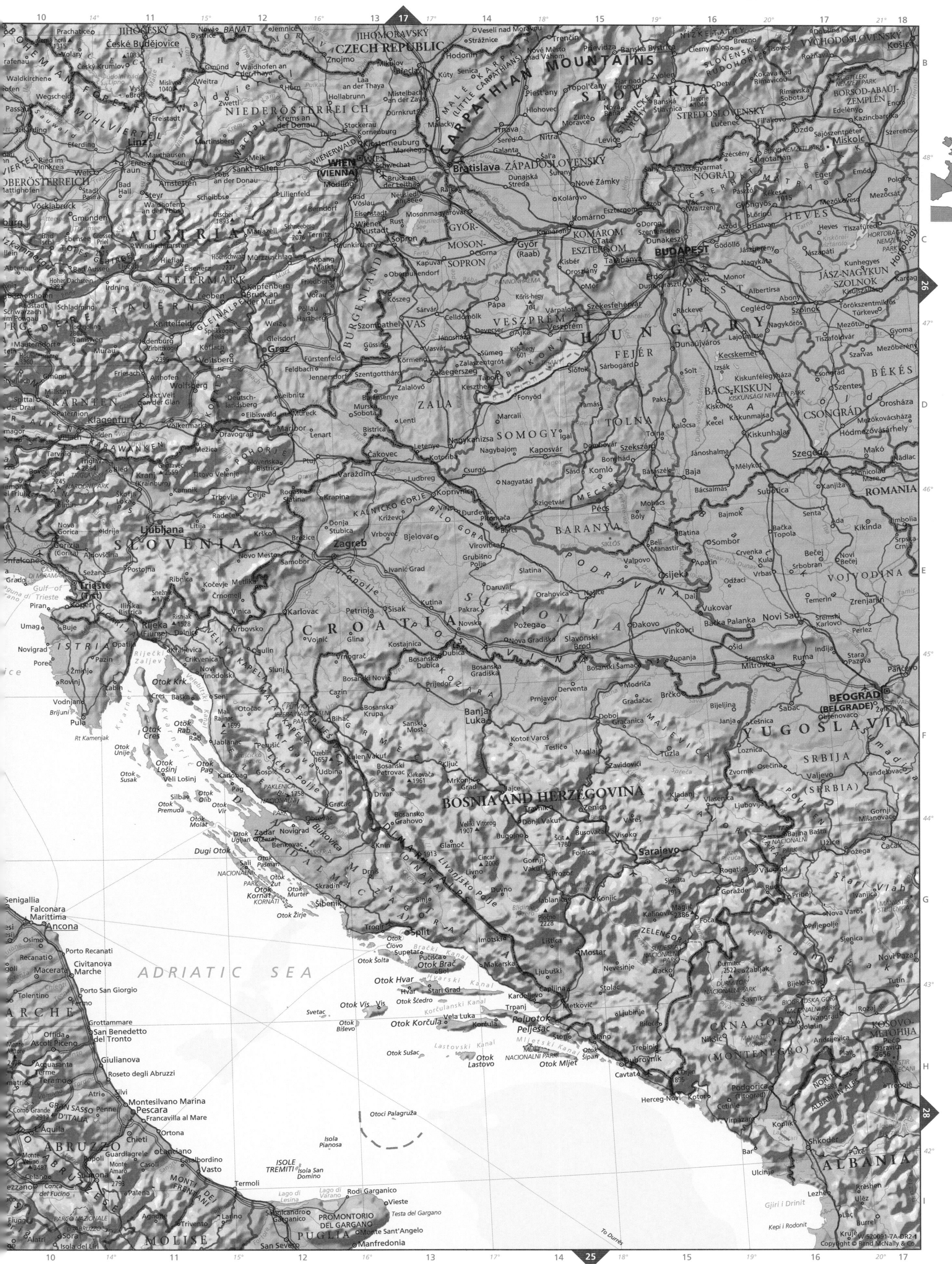
CZECH REPUBLIC
CARPATHIAN MOUNTAINS
SLOVAKIA
NIEDERÖSTERREICH
AUSTRIA
STEIERMARK
KÄRNTEN
WIEN (VIENNA)
Bratislava
BUDAPEST
HUNGARY
SLOVENIA
Ljubljana
Zagreb
CROATIA
BOSNIA AND HERZEGOVINA
Sarajevo
YUGOSLAVIA
BEOGRAD (BELGRADE)
ROMANIA
ALBANIA
ADRIATIC SEA
Trieste (Trst)
Rijeka (Fiume)
Split
Dubrovnik
Podgorica (Titograd)
Ancona
Pescara
Graz
Linz
Győr (Raab)
Szeged
Novi Sad
Osijek
Pécs
Kecskemét
Miskolc
Košice
Mostar
Zenica
Banja Luka
CRNA GORA (MONTENEGRO)
SRBIJA (SERBIA)
VOJVODINA
DINARIC ALPS
ABRUZZO
MOLISE
PUGLIA
MARCHE
Copyright © Rand McNally & Co.

FRANCE
HAUTE-CORSE
CORSE (CORSICA)
CORSE-DU-SUD
Cap Corse
Rogliano
Bastia
Saint-Florent
L'Île-Rousse
Calvi
Balagne
Monte Cinto
Vescovato
Castagniccia
Corte
Cervione
Calcatoggio
Golfe de Porto
Capu Rossu
Porto
Monte Rotondo
Golfe de Sagone
Capo di Feno
Ajaccio
Bocognano
Ghisonaccia
Aléria
Étang d' Urbino
Golfe d' Ajaccio
Zicavo
Monte Incudine
Solenzara
Capu di Muru
Golfe de Valinco
Propriano
Zonza
Pinarello
Sartène
Capu di Senetosa (Punta di Senetosa)
Porto-Vecchio
Bonifacio
Strait of Bonifacio
To Marseille
To Genova
To Nice
To Livorno
To Toulon
Isola di Capraia
Campiglia Marittima
Piombino
Follonica
Canale di Piombino
Golfo di Follonica
Portoferraio
Isola d' Elba
Isola Pianosa
Isola di Montecristo
Isola del Giglio
Santo Stefano
Porto
Orbetello
Laguna di Orbetello
Isola di Giannutri
Montalto di Castro
Massa Marittima
Gavorrano
Montalcino
Pienza
Chianciano Terme
Chiusi
Abbadia San Salvatore
Arcidosso
TOSCANA
Maremma
Grosseto
Scansano
Manciano
Acquapendente
Orvieto
Bolsena
Montefiascone
Viterbo
Tarquinia
Civitavecchia
Santa Marinella
Caprarola
Civita Castellana
Bracciano
Ladispoli
Fiumicino
Lido di Ostia
LAZIO
ROMA (ROME)
VATICAN CITY
MONTI SABATINI
Perugia
Assisi
Foligno
Marsciano
Todi
Spoleto
Norcia
UMBRIA
Terni
Narni
Rieti
Monte Terminillo 2216
Antrodoco
MONTI SABINI
Monterotondo
Tivoli
Palestrina
Frascati
Albano Laziale
Genzano di Roma
Velletri
Aprilia
Nettuno
Anzio
Latina
Agro Pontino
Sabaudia
Lago di Sabaudia
PARCO NAZIONALE DEL CIRCEO
Terracina
Fondi
Formia
Gaeta
Golfo di Gaeta
Mondragone
MONTI LEPINI
MONTI AURUNCI
Priverno
Ferentino
Frosinone
Subiaco
Fiuggi
Alatri
Avezzano
Sora
Isola del Liri
Cassino
Venafro
Camerino
MARCHE
Grottammare
San Benedetto del Tronto
Offida
Ascoli Piceno
Monte Vettore
Teramo
Amatrice
Giulianova
Roseto degli Abruzzi
Atri
Silvi
Montesilvano Marina
Pescara
Francavilla al Mare
Penne
Chieti
Ortona
Lanciano
GRAN SASSO D'ITALIA
Corno Grande
L'Aquila
ABRUZZO
Guardiagrele
Popoli
Sulmona
Conca del Fucino
Monte Amaro 2793
Casoli
Palena
MOLISE
ITALY
Isernia
Campobasso
Monte Miletto
Piedimonte Matese
Teano
Sessa Aurunca
Capua
Caserta
Benevento
Maddaloni
Aversa
Santa Maria Capua Vetere
Acerra
Nola
NAPOLI (NAPLES)
Pozzuoli
Ercolano
Isola di Procida
Ischia
Isola d' Ischia
Torre del Greco
Golfo di Napoli
Castellammare di Stabia
Sorrento
Salerno
Battipaglia
Isola di Capri
Capri
Golfo di Salerno
Isola Palmarola
Isola Zannone
Isola di Ponza
ISOLE PONZIANE (PONTINE ISLANDS)
Isola Ventotene
APPENNINO
3600
Isola Maddalena
Capo Testa
Isola Spargi
La Maddalena
Isola Caprera
Santa Teresa Gallura
Palau
Punta Caprara
Isola Asinara
Golfo dell' Asinara
Castelsardo
Gallura
Tempio Pausania
Calangianus
Costa Smeralda
Arzachena
Golfo Aranci
Golfo di Olbia
Olbia
Monte Limbara 1359
Isola Tavolara
Isola Molara
Porto Torres
Sorso
Sedini
Anglona
La Nurra
Sassari
Ittiri
Osilo
Logudoro
Capo Caccia
Alghero
Thiesi
Ozieri
Budduso
Siniscola
Capo Comino
Bitti
Bono
Bosa
Bonorva
Nuoro
Orosei
Macomer
SARDEGNA (SARDINIA)
Oliena
Dorgali
Golfo di Orosei
Orgosolo
Fonni
Santu Lussurgiu
Ghilarza
Isola di Mal di Ventre
MONTI DEL GENNARGENTU
Punta La Marmora 1834
Sorgono
Capo di Monte Santu
Baunei
SARDEGNA
Cabras
Oristano
Golfo di Oristano
Arborea
Laconi
Barbagia
Arbatax
Tortolì
Lanusei
Seui
Jerzu
ITALY
Terralba
Barumini
Mandas
Perdasdefogu
Campidano
Guspini
Sanluri
San Gavino Monreale
Senorbì
Villacidro
Fluminimaggiore
Iglesias
Dolianova
San Vito
Muravera
Assemini
Capo Ferrato
Isola di San Pietro
Carloforte
Carbonia
Cagliari
Quartu Sant'Elena
Villasimius
Sant'Antioco
Isola di Sant'Antioco
Sulcis
Teulada
Pula
Golfo di Cagliari
Capo Carbonara
Golfo di Palmas
Capo Teulada
Capo Spartivento
TYRRHENIAN SEA
710
To Marseille
Isola di Ustica
Isola Alicudi
Isola Filicudi
ISOLE EOLIE (ISOLE LIPARI)
Capo San Vito
Golfo di Castellammare
Capo Gallo
Golfo di Palermo
SICILIA
Palermo
Monreale
Bagheria
Golfo di Termini Imerese
Termini Imerese
Cefalù
Sant'Agata di Militello
Isola di Levanzo
Isola Marettimo
ISOLE EGADI
Trapani
Erice
Castellammare del Golfo
Partinico
Alcamo
Calatafimi
Isola Favignana
Capo Boeo
Marsala
Salemi
SEGESTA
Val di Mazara
Corleone
Castelbuono
Mistretta
MADONIE
NEBRODI
Castelvetrano
Partanna
Mazara del Vallo
Capo Granitola
SELINUNTE
Menfi
Sciacca
Ribera
Caltanissetta
Nicosia
Troina
Enna
Leonforte
San Cataldo
Agrigento
Favara
Canicattì
Aragona
Porto Empedocle
VALLE DEI TEMPLI
Piazza Armerina
Ravanusa
Riesi
Caltagirone
Palma di Montechiaro
Licata
Niscemi
Gela
Golfo di Gela
Vittoria
Comiso
Modica
Scicli
Pozzallo
MEDITERRANEAN SEA
Strait of Sicily
Malta Channel
Pantelleria
Isola di Pantelleria
La Galite
Canal de la Galite
Rass Ben Sekka
Cap Blanc
Cap Serrat
Bizerte (Binzert)
Ras Djebel
Menzel Bourguiba
Cap Rosa
Tabarka
El Qala
Nefza
Mateur
MEDJERDA MOUNTAINS
Aïn Draham
Golfe de Tunis
Île Zembra
Cap Bon
Tébourba
Ariana
La Marsa
Carthage
La Goulette
TUNIS
Ben Arous
Béja
ALGERIA
Bou Salem
Jendouba
Ghardimaou
Medjez el Bab
Testour
MONTS DE TÉBOURSOUK
Téboursouk
DOUGGA
Soliman
Menzel Bou Zelfa
Grombalia
Korba
Kelibia
Menzel Temime
Nabeul
Hammamet
Zaghouan
Jebel Zaghouan 1295
El Fahs
Gafour
Bou Ficha
Golfe de Hammamet
El Kef
Sakiet Sidi Youssef
TUNISIA
DORSALE
Siliana
Es Sers
Enfida
Dahmani
Tadjerouine
Maktar
Kalaa Kebira
Sousse
M'Saken
Monastir
Kairouan
Thala
Haffouz
Isola di Linosa
ISOLE PELAGIE (Italy)
Isolotto di Lampione
Isola di Lampedusa
Ghawdex (Gozo)
Kemmuna (Comino)
Rabat
MALTA
Sliema
Valletta
Malta
Birżebbuġa
Meters
Feet
3000
9840
2000
6560
1000
3280
500
1640
200
656
Sea Level
200
656
2000
6560
0
25
50
75
100
150
200
250 Kilometers
0
25
50
100
150 Miles
Scale 1 : 2,500,000
Lambert Conformal Conic Projection

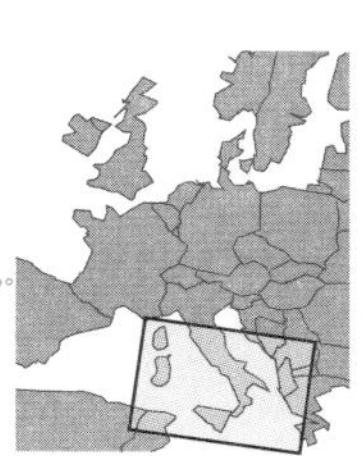

CROATIA
BOSNIA AND HERZEGOVINA
YUGOSLAVIA
CRNA GORA (MONTENEGRO)
SRBIJA (SERBIA)
KOSOVO-METOHIJA
ALBANIA
MACEDONIA
GREECE
PUGLIA
BASILICATA
CALABRIA
ADRIATIC SEA
IONIAN SEA
Golfo di Taranto
Strait of Otranto
IÓNIOI NÍSOI (IONIAN ISLANDS)
Penisola Salentina
PROMONTORIO DEL GARGANO
SILA GRANDE
NORTH ALBANIAN ALPS
SAR PLANINA
PELOPÓNNISOS
DYTIKÍ MAKEDONÍA
KENTRIKÍ MAKEDONÍA
THESSALÍA
ÍPEIROS
STERÉA ELLÁDA
DYTIKÍ ELLÁDA
Pelopónnisos (Peloponnesus)

Dubrovnik
Podgorica
Shkodër
Skopje
Priština
Tiranë
Durrës
Vlorë
Bari
Brindisi
Taranto
Lecce
Foggia
Manfredonia
Barletta
Trani
Molfetta
Monopoli
Gallipoli
Otranto
Potenza
Matera
Cosenza
Crotone
Catanzaro
Reggio di Calabria
Messina
Catania
Siracusa
Kérkyra (Corfu)
Ioánnina
Árta
Préveza
Lefkáda
Kefallinía
Zákynthos
Pátra
Pýrgos
Kalamáta

SLOVAKIA
HUNGARY
AUSTRIA
SLOVENIA
CROATIA
BOSNIA AND HERZEGOVINA
YUGOSLAVIA
SRBIJA (SERBIA)
CRNA GORA (MONTENEGRO)
KOSOVO-METOHIJA
VOJVODINA
ALBANIA
MACEDONIA
ITALY
ADRIATIC SEA
CARPATHIAN MOUNTAINS
WIEN (VIENNA)
Bratislava
BUDAPEST
Zagreb
Sarajevo
BEOGRAD (BELGRADE)
Novi Sad
Timişoara
Skopje
Tiranë
Podgorica (Titograd)
Split
Dubrovnik
Bari
Debrecen
Szeged
Pécs
Graz
Győr (Raab)
Kosice
Miskolc
Oradea
Arad
Niš
Priština
Banja Luka
Osijek
Maribor
Rijeka
Durrës
NIEDERÖSTERREICH
BURGENLAND
STEIERMARK
ZÁPADOSLOVENSKÝ
STREDOSLOVENSKÝ
VÝCHODOSLOVENSKÝ
BORSOD-ABAÚJ-ZEMPLÉN
GYŐR-MOSON-SOPRON
KOMÁROM-ESZTERGOM
PEST
FEJÉR
VESZPRÉM
VAS
ZALA
SOMOGY
TOLNA
BARANYA
BÁCS-KISKUN
CSONGRÁD
BÉKÉS
JÁSZ-NAGYKUN-SZOLNOK
HAJDÚ-BIHAR
SZABOLCS-SZATMÁR-BEREG
HEVES
NÓGRÁD
BIHOR
ARAD
TIMIŞ
CARAŞ-SEVERIN
PODRAVINA
POSAVINA
SLAVONIJA
BANAT
ŠUMADIJA
DINARA
DALMACIJA
ŠAR PLANINA
NORTH ALBANIAN ALPS
PROMONTORIO DEL GARGANO
PUGLIA
To Ancona
To Ortona
Meters
Feet
2000
6560
1000
3280
500
1640
200
656
Sea Level
200
656
2000
6560
W-560000-7A-DR2-1
Copyright © Rand McNally & Co.
0 25 50 75 100 150 200 250 Kilometers
0 25 50 100 150 Miles
Scale 1 : 2,500,000
Lambert Conformal Conic Projection

UKRAINE
MOLDOVA
ROMANIA
BULGARIA
TURKEY
GREECE
BLACK SEA
CARPATHIAN MOUNTAINS
TRANSYLVANIAN ALPS
BALKAN MOUNTAINS
RHODOPE MOUNTAINS
MOLDAVIA
WALACHIA
LUDOGORIE
DOBRUDŽA
Mouths of the Danube
Dobrudžansko plato
Chernivtsi
Chişinău
Tiraspol
Odesa
Iaşi
Suceava
Botoşani
Bacău
Cluj-Napoca
Târgu Mureş
Braşov
Sibiu
Piteşti
Ploieşti
Buzău
Brăila
Galaţi
Tulcea
Constanţa
Mangalia
Bucureşti
(Bucharest)
Craiova
Giurgiu
Ruse
Pleven
Veliko Târnovo
Varna
Burgas
Stara Zagora
Plovdiv
Haskovo
Kărdžali
Sofija
(Sofia)
Edirne
Kırklareli
İstanbul
İstanbul Boğazı
(Bosporus)
Sulina
Izmail
Reni
Bilhorod-Dnistrovs'kyi
ostriv Zmiïnyi
(Ukraine)
Bălţi
Cahul
Dobrič
Silistra
Šumen
Razgrad
Jambol
Sliven
Kazanlăk
Lovеč
Gabrovo

YUGOSLAVIA
CRNA GORA
(MONTENEGRO)
ALBANIA
Tiranë
Durrës
MACEDONIA
Skopje
B U L G A R I A
Plovdiv
ADRIATIC SEA
To Ancona
To Bari
To Brindisi
Strait of Otranto
IONIAN SEA
MEDITERRANEAN SEA
AEGEAN SEA
THRAKIKÓ PÉLAGOS
KRITIKÓN PÉLAGOS
(SEA OF CRETE)
MIRTÓON PÉLAGOS
IÓNIOI NÍSOI
Ionian Islands
GREECE
DYTIKÍ MAKEDONÍA
KENTRIKÍ MAKEDONÍA
ANATOLIKÍ MAKEDONÍA KAI THRÁKI
THESSALIA
ÍPEIROS
DYTIKÍ ELLÁDA
STERÉA ELLÁDA
PELOPÓNNISOS
ATTIKÍ
VÓREIO AIGAÍO
KRÍTI
Thessaloníki
(Salonika)
Thermaïkós Kólpos
(Gulf of Salonika)
ÁGIO ÓROS
Lárisa
Vólos
Pátra
Korinthiakós Kólpos
(Gulf of Corinth)
ATHÍNA
(ATHENS)
Peiraiás
(Piraeus)
Pelopónnisos
(Peloponnesus)
Kalamáta
Kerkyra
(Corfu)
Kefallinía
Zákynthos
Kýthira
Chaniá
Irákleio
Kríti
(Crete)
Kykládes
Vórioi Sporádhes
Évvoia
Límnos
Thásos
Náxos
Páros
Thíra
(Santoríni)
Meters
Feet
3000
9840
2000
6560
1000
3280
500
1640
200
656
Sea Level
200
656
2000
6560
W-516000-7A-DR2-1
Copyright © Rand McNally & Co.
0
25
50
75
100
150
200
250 Kilometers
0
25
50
100
150 Miles
Scale 1 : 2,500,000
Lambert Conformal Conic Projection

BLACK SEA
MEDITERRANEAN SEA
TURKEY
İSTANBUL
ANKARA
İzmir (Smyrna)
Bursa
Eskişehir
Kütahya
Konya
Antalya
Marmara Denizi (Sea of Marmara)
Antalya Körfezi (Gulf of Antalya)
Dhodhekánisos (Dodecanese)
TOROS DAĞLARI (TAURUS MOUNTAINS)
CYPRUS
Ródos (Rhodes)

Scale 1 : 30,000,000 Lambert Azimuthal Equal Area Projection

Bering Strait
St. Lawrence Island (U.S.)
ostrov Vrangelja
NOVOSIBIRSKIE OSTROVA
VOSTOČNO-SIBIRSKOE MORE
MORE LAPTEVYH (LAPTEV SEA)
BERING SEA
ALEUTIAN ISLANDS (U.S.)
KOMANDORSKIE OSTROVA
Attu Island
HREBET ČERSKOGO
VERHOJANSKIJ HREBET
SREDINNYJ HREBET
Petropavlovsk-Kamčatskij
SEA OF OKHOTSK
POLUOSTROV KAMČATKA
Magadan
HAWAIIAN ISLANDS (U.S.)
MIDWAY ISLANDS (U.S.)
Tropic of Cancer
KURIL'SKIE OSTROVA (KURIL ISLANDS)
OSTROV SAHALIN
Južno-Sahalinsk
STANOVOJ HREBET
CENTRAL SIBERIAN UPLANDS
Jakutsk
Komsomol'sk-na-Amure
Blagoveščensk
Habarovsk
SIHOTE-ALIN'
Tatarskij proliv
HOKKAIDŌ
Sapporo
Hakodate
Aomori
Sendai
HONSHŪ
PACIFIC OCEAN
WAKE ISLAND (U.S.)
Bratsk
Irkutsk
Angarsk
Čita
Ulan-Ude
Ulaanbaatar
Choybalsan
HANGAYN NURUU
MONGOLIA
GOBI DESERT
Qiqihar
HARBIN
Jilin
Vladivostok
Ch'ŏngjin
CHANGCHUN
FUSHUN
SHENYANG
Dandong
NORTH KOREA
P'YŎNGYANG
SEA OF JAPAN
Niigata
TŌKYŌ
YOKOHAMA
Kanazawa
KYŌTO
NAGOYA
ŌSAKA
JAPAN
HIROSHIMA
SHIKOKU
FUKUOKA
KYŪSHŪ
Kagoshima
SOUTH KOREA
SEOUL
PUSAN
Taegu
Mokp'o
Cheju-do
DALIAN
Zhangjiakou
BEIJING
TIANJIN
Hohhot
Baotou
TAIYUAN
Shijiazhuang
JINAN
Qingdao
Bo Hai
YELLOW SEA
Yinchuan
Xining
Lanzhou
Baoji
XI'AN
Zhengzhou
Xuzhou
Huainan
Nanjing
SHANGHAI
Ningbo
Hangzhou
EAST CHINA SEA
CHINA
WUHAN
Nanchang
Wenzhou
CHENGDU
CHONGQING
CHANGSHA
Zigong
Hengyang
Fuzhou
Xiamen
T'AIPEI
TAIWAN
Tainan
KAOHSIUNG
Guiyang
Kunming
Liuzhou
GUANGZHOU
XIANGGANG (HONG KONG)
MACAU
Nanning
Zhanjiang
Lhasa
NANSEI-SHOTŌ (RYUKYU ISLANDS)
Amami-Ō-shima
Okinawa-jima
Naha
IZU-SHOTŌ (Japan)
OGASAWARA-GUNTŌ (Japan)
KAZAN-RETTŌ (Japan)
Minami-Tori-Shima (Japan)
MARSHALL ISLANDS
Enewetak
Ujelang
Farallon de Pajaros
NORTHERN MARIANAS (U.S.)
Agrihan
Pagan
Alamagan
Guguan
Anatahan
MARIANA ISLANDS
Saipan
Tinian
Rota
Agana
GUAM (U.S.)
MICRONESIA
PHILIPPINE SEA
HALL ISLANDS
Oroluk
Pohnpei
Kolonia
SENYAVIN ISLANDS
MORTLOCK ISLANDS
CHUUK
Ulul
Gaferut
Lamotrek
Pulap
CAROLINE ISLANDS
FEDERATED STATES OF MICRONESIA
Kapingamarangi
Equator
YAP
Ngulu
Sorol
Woleai
Eauripik
Luzon Strait
Taiwan Strait
LUZON
Baguio
Quezon City
MANILA
PHILIPPINES
Mindoro
Samar
Leyte
Panay
Iloilo
Cebu
Palawan
MINDANAO
Zamboanga
Davao
SULU SEA
Koror
PALAU ISLANDS
PALAU
SONSOROL ISLANDS
ADMIRALTY ISLANDS
New Hanover
NEW IRELAND
Kavieng
Rabaul
Manus Island
BISMARCK SEA
BISMARCK ARCHIPELAGO
NEW BRITAIN
SOLOMON SEA
LADESH
DHAKA (DACCA)
TTAGONG
MYANMAR (BURMA)
Mandalay
HA NOI (HANOI)
Hai Phong
Gulf of Tonkin
Haikou
HAINAN DAO
LAOS
Sittwe
XISHA QUNDAO (PARACEL ISLANDS)
VIETNAM
Viangchan
Da Nang
YANGON (RANGOON)
Gulf of Martaban
THAILAND
KRUNG THEP (BANGKOK)
CAMBODIA
Phnum Penh
THANH PHO HO CHI MINH (HO CHI MINH CITY) (SAIGON)
Gulf of Thailand
Kâmpóng Saôm
Mui Ca Mau
COCO ISLANDS
Dawei
ANDAMAN ISLANDS (India)
ANDAMAN SEA
SOUTH CHINA SEA
SPRATLY ISLANDS
Balabac Island
Jolo Island
Moro Gulf
KEPULAUAN TALAUD
Tinaca Point
KEPULAUAN SANGIHE
Morotai
HALMAHERA
Pulau Waigeo
Biak
Pulau Yapen
Jayapura
Wewak
NEW GUINEA
PAPUA NEW GUINEA
Madang
Mount Wilhelm 4509
Lae
Port Moresby
Gulf of Papua
Puncak Jaya 5030
Gunong Kinabalu 4101
Bandar Seri Begawan
BRUNEI
Manado
CELEBES SEA
NICOBAR ISLANDS (India)
Phuket
MALAY PENINSULA
George Town (Penang)
MALAYSIA
KUALA LUMPUR
Banda Aceh
MEDAN
Strait of Malacca
SINGAPORE
KEPULAUAN NATUNA BESAR
Kuching
BORNEO (KALIMANTAN)
Pontianak
Balikpapan
Selat Makasar
SULAWESI (CELEBES)
Teluk Tomini
LAUT MALUKU
MALUKU (MOLUCCAS)
KEPULAUAN OBI
LAUT SERAM
SERAM (CERAM)
KEPULAUAN SULA
Buru
KEPULAUAN KAI
KEPULAUAN ARU
Pulau Yos Sudarso
Torres Strait
Cape York
CAPE YORK PENINSULA
CORAL SEA
Great Barrier Reef
KEPULAUAN TANIMBAR
ARAFURA SEA
Cape Wessel
Cape Arnhem
Gulf of Carpentaria
AUSTRALIA
Cairns
Melville Island
Pulau Buton
LAUT BANDA
Pulau Wetar
Dili
TIMOR
TIMOR SEA
Kupang
LAUT SAWU
LAUT FLORES
FLORES
Sumba
Sumbawa
Lombok
Bali
INDONESIA
Ujungpandang
Pulau Laut
Banjarmasin
LAUT JAWA
Madura
SURABAYA
JAWA (JAVA)
BANDUNG
JAKARTA
Selat Sunda
Tanjungkarang-Telukbetung
Palembang
Belitung
Pulau Bangka
Selat Karimata
SUMATERA (SUMATRA)
Padang
Pulau Nias
KEPULAUAN MENTAWAI
Pulau Siberut
M-600000-2A-DR2-1
Copyright © Rand McNally & Co.

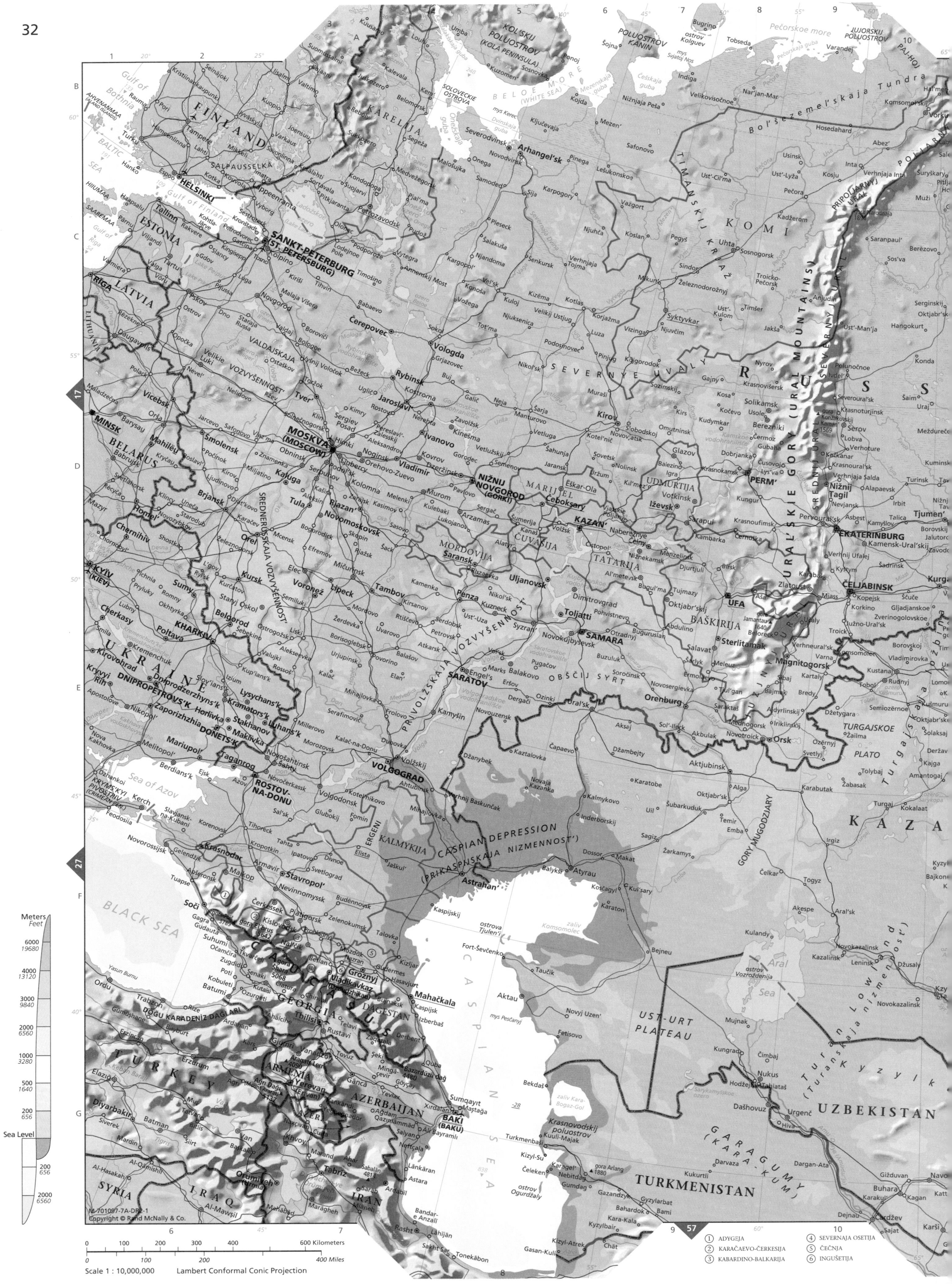
FINLAND
ESTONIA
LATVIA
LITHUANIA
BELARUS
UKRAINE
RUSSIA
KAZAKHSTAN
UZBEKISTAN
TURKMENISTAN
GEORGIA
ARMENIA
AZERBAIJAN
TURKEY
SYRIA
IRAQ
IRAN
HELSINKI
Tallinn
RIGA
MINSK
KYÏV (KIEV)
MOSKVA (MOSCOW)
SANKT-PETERBURG (ST. PETERSBURG)
NIŽNIJ NOVGOROD (GOR'KIJ)
KAZAN'
SAMARA
SARATOV
VOLGOGRAD
ROSTOV-NA-DONU
KHARKIV
DNIPROPETROVS'K
DONETS'K
PERM'
EKATERINBURG
ČELJABINSK
UFA
Tbilisi
Yerevan
BAKI (BAKU)
Gulf of Bothnia
Gulf of Finland
Gulf of Riga
BALTIC SEA
BELOE MORE (WHITE SEA)
Pečorskoe more
Sea of Azov
BLACK SEA
CASPIAN SEA
Aral Sea
KOL'SKIJ POLUOSTROV (KOLA PENINSULA)
POLUOSTROV KANIN
KARELIJA
KOMI
TIMANSKIJ KRJAŽ
SEVERNYE UVALY
VALDAJSKAJA VOZVYŠENNOST'
SREDNERUSSKAJA VOZVYŠENNOST'
PRIVOLŽSKAJA VOZVYŠENNOST'
URAL'SKIE GORY (URAL MOUNTAINS)
OBŠČIJ SYRT
CASPIAN DEPRESSION (PRIKASPIJSKAJA NIZMENNOST')
KALMYKIJA
CAUCASUS
DAGESTAN
UST-URT PLATEAU
GARAGUMY (KARA-KUM)
Turan Lowland (Turanskaja nizmennost')
Kyzylkum
TURGAJSKOE PLATO
GORY MUGODŽARY
Meters
Feet
6000
19680
4000
13120
3000
9840
2000
6560
1000
3280
500
1640
200
656
Sea Level
200
656
2000
6560
M-701097-7A-DR2-1
Copyright © Rand McNally & Co.
0 100 200 300 400 600 Kilometers
0 100 200 400 Miles
Scale 1 : 10,000,000
Lambert Conformal Conic Projection
① ADYGEJA
② KARAČAEVO-ČERKESIJA
③ KABARDINO-BALKARIJA
④ SEVERNAJA OSETIJA
⑤ ČEČNJA
⑥ INGUŠETIJA
17
27
57

12
13
14
15
16
17
18
19
20
B
C
D
E
F
G
POLUOSTROV
JAMAL
Tazovskij poluostrov
Obskaja guba
Novyj Port
Nahodka
Tazovskij
Jar-Sale
Nyda
Nori
Samburg
Sidorovsk
Igarka
Serkovo
Turuhansk
Farkovo
Kostino
Urengoj
Krasnosel'kup
Nadym
Tarko-Sale
Harampur
Tol'ka
Ratta
Numto
Haljasavėj
S I B I R'
Z A P A D N O -
(S I B E R I A)
SREDNESIBIRSKOE
PLOSKOGOR'E
(CENTRAL SIBERIAN PLATEAU)
CENTRALNO-
TUNGUSSKOE PLATO
Noginsk
Tutončana
Učami
Tura
Nidym
Verhneimbatsk
Surgutiha
Vereščagino
Bahta
Kellog
Komsa
Sumarokovo
Podkamennaja Tunguska
Vorogovo
Kuz'movka
Poligus
Bajkit
Mutoraj
Vanavara
Kujumba
Tajmba
Strelka-Čunja
Erbogačon
Dušekan
Nepa
Ika
Bur
Čemdal'sk
Lensk
Hamra
Peleduj
Vitim
Paršino
Čerkašina
Koršunovo
Kirensk
Nižnjaja Karelinao
Teja
Severo-Enisejskij
gora Enašimskij Polkan 1104
ENISEJSKIJ KRJAŽ
Noveorudinskij
Pit-Gorodok
Južno-Enisejskij
Brjanka
Kamenka
Bedoba
Jarohta
Klimino
Kova
Kežma
Panovo
Edarma
Keul'
Kirjanovskaja Kontora
Tokma
Ust'-Ilimsk
Badarma
Karamyševo
Nižneilimsk
Železnogorsk-Ilimskij
Ust'-Kut
Bratsk
Vihorevka
Zajarsk
Razdolinsk
Motygino
Karabula
Boguçany
Červjanka
Jarkino
Sedanovo
Vydrino
Pokateeva
Dolgij Most
Taseevo
Troick
Aban
Nižnjaja Pojma
Tajšet
Birjusinsk
Ilanskij
Kansk
Dzeržinskoe
Surgut
Neftejugansk
Megion
Niževartovsk
Larjak
Korliki
Hanty-Mansijsk
Aleksandrovskoe
Nazina
Brusovo
Sym
Nazimovo
Aleksandrovskij Šljuz
Kolmogorovo
Ust'-Pit
Podtesovo
Enisejsk
Lesosibirsk
Novoeniseijsk
Strelka
Kazačinskoe
Pirovskoe
Talovka
Bol'šaja Murta
Šila
Altaj
Kajmysovy
Prohorkino
Berëzovka
Ust'-Ozërnoe
Ždanova
Losinoborskaja
Maksimkin Jar
Kljukvenka
Belyj Jar
Kargasok
Narym
Parabel'
Srednij Vasjugan
Novyj Vasjugan
Nefëdovo
Togur
Kolpaševo
Baturino
Komsomol'sk
Asino
Krivošeino
Krasnyj Jar
Mogočin
Podgornoe
Tegul'det
Tjuhtet
Birilјussy
Bol'šoj Uluj
Ačinsk
Krasnojarsk
Nazarovo
Šadrino
Divnogorsk
Ujar
Zaozërnyj
Borodino
Irbejskoe
Aginskoe
Narva
Zamzor
Uk
Ataga
Nižneudinsk
Tulun
Ikej
Harik
Angaul
Ust'-Uda
Zima
Zalari
Čeremhovo
Svirsk
Ust'-Ordynskij
Bajandaj
Usole-Sibirskoe
Irkutsk
Angarsk
Šelehov
Kultuk
Sljudjanka
Mondy
Ulan
A
R A V N I N A
Sumkino
Dubrovnoe
Ust'-Išim
Tevriz
Moiseevka
Mirnoe Ozero
Kenga
Bakčar
Morjakovskij Zaton
Aleksandrovskoe
Zyrjanskoe
Mariinsk
Tomsk
Jaja
Anžero-Sudžensk
Bogotol
Tisul'
Šarypovo
Balahta
Novosëlovo
Uzur
Kopevo
Šira
Bellyk
Abakan
Minusinsk
Kuragino
Artëmovsk
Ermakovskoe
(WEST SIBERIAN PLAIN)
Znamenskoe
Bol'šie Uki
Tara
Sedel'nikovo
Severnoe
Vikulovo
Kolosovka
Muromcevo
Vorobevo
Kožemikovo
Bolotnoe
Jurga
Kemerovo
Topki
Tajga
Berëzovskij
Stancionno-Ojašinskij
Toguçin
Leninsk-Kuzneckij
Belovo
Gur'evsk
Kiselëvsk
Prokop'evsk
Novokuzneck
Osinniki
Meždurečensk
Taštagol
KUZNECKIJ ALATAU
SALAIRSKIJ KRJAŽ
ABAKANSKIJ HREBET
HAKASIJA
Sorsk
Černogorsk
Sajanogorsk
Askiz
Abaza
Olenja Rečka
Abatskij
Krutinka
Tjukalinsk
Išim
Bol'šereče
Vengerovo
Kujbyšev
Barabinsk
Kargat
Čulym
Ust'-Sumy
NOVOSIBIRSK
Berdsk
Iskitim
Čerepanovo
Maslјanino
Tal'menka
Suzun
Novoaltajsk
Barnaul
Troickoe
Bijsk
B a r a b i n s k a j a
Kazanskoe
Nazyvaevsk
Krasnyj Jar
Sargatskoe
Tatarsk
Čany
OMSK
Kalačinsk
Čistoozërnoe
Kupino
Karasuk
Krasnozërskoe
Kamen'-na-Obi
Habary
Pavlovsk
Petropavlovsk
Bulaevo
Isil'kul'
Marjanovka
Poltavka
Odesskoe
Irtyšsk
Čerlak
Železinka
s t e p'
Kulundinskaja
Slavgorod
Kulunda
r a v n i n a
Len'ki
Aleјsk
Borovljanka
Gorno-Altajsk
Turočak
Ust'-Ulagan
Onguday
Altajskij
Pospeliha
Rubcovsk
Zmeinogorsk
Čaryškoe
Čemal
Volčiha
Mihajlovka
ALTAJ
Kokčetav
Ščučinsk
Stepnjak
Ajsary
Kačiry
Tavolžan
Ščerbakty
Pavlodar
Ermak
Šaldaj
Krasnoarmejsk
Kzyltu
Makinsk
Aksu
Bestobe
Danilovka
Alekseevka
Žolymbet
Šortandy
Kamenka
Kolutor
Žaltyr
Bozšakol'
Ekibastuz
Ermentau
Majkain
Lebjažje
Sosnovka
Majskoe
Bajanaul
Moldary
Astana (Akmola)
Višnëvka
Kurgal'džinskij
Osakarovka
Aktau
Ul'janovskij
Semizbuga
Temirtau
Saran'
Kievka
Karaganda
Šahtinsk
Abaj
Baršino
Karkaralinsk
Kajnar
Enbek
Semipalatinsk
Ust'-Kamenogorsk
Glubokoe
Zyrjanovsk
Leninogorsk
Serebrjansk
Georgievka
Kaskabulak
Čarsk
Kokpekti
Akžal
Kurčum
Katon-Karagaj
Žarma
Karaul
Aksuat
Alekseevka
Karata
Zajsan
Priozërnyj
Bol'šoj Vladimirovka
Semonaiha
Gornjak
Ajaguz
Mount Belukha 4374
gora Tavan-Bogdo-Ula 4356
K A Z A H S K I J
M E L K O S O P O Č N I K
(KAZAKH HILLS)
T A N
Milybulak
gora Aksoran 1566
Atasu
Žarsuat
Nura
Agadyr'
Bosaga
Akčatau
Kzyltu
Karažal
Kyzylžar
Kiik
Kounradskij
Vostočno-Kounradskij
Balhaš
Žambyl
Gul'šad
Imeni Kirova
Sajak
Aktogaj
Makanči
Bahty
Rybač'e
Učaral
Lepsy
Kabanbaj
Sarkand
Matai
Mulaly
Kujgan
Ozero Balhaš (Lake Balkhash)
t p a k - D a l a
Mynaral
Akkol'
Bakanas
Ustobe
Kirovskij
Taldykorgan
Tekeli
Saryozek
Panfilov
DZHUNGARIAN ALATAU MTS.
Dzhungarian Gate
Družba
HREBET TARBAGATAJ
Urdžar
Tacheng
Emin
Toli
Karamay
JUNGGAR PENDI
Xiaoguai
PESKI MOJYNKUM
Hantau
Kapčagaj
Talgar
Čilik
Čundža
Čokpar
Novotroickoe
Šu
ALMATY
Suzak
Čulakkurgan
Akkol'
Žanatas
Kentau
Karatau
Lugovoj
Kara-Balta
Biškek
Tokmak
Žambyl
KIRGIZ RANGE
Issyk-Kul'
Narynkol
Karakol
HREBET KUNGEJ-ALATOO
HREBET TERSKEJ-ALATAU
Talas
Šymkent
Lenger
Arys
KYRGYZSTAN
Naryn
Čatyrtaš
Kazarman
Džalal-Abad
Namangan
Andižan
Uzgen
Oš
Kyzyl-Kija
Alajku
Margilan
Kokand
TAŠKENT
Angren
Almalyk
Čirčik
Jangijul
Syrdarja
Hudžand
Kanibadam
Havast
Ura-Tjube
Suljukta
ALAJSKIJ HREBET
TURKESTANSKIJ HREBET
ZERAVŠANSKIJ HREBET
TAJIKISTAN
pik Kommunizma (Communism Peak) 7495
Lenin Peak 7134
Garm
Ordžonikidzeabad
Dušanbe
Dangara
AFG.
Bartang
Murgab
PAMIR
Tohtamyš
Yining
Nilka
Tekes
Gongliu
BOROHORO SHAN
Wenquan
Bole
Jinghe
Usu
Shawan
Manas
Dushanzi
Changji
Ürümqi
Miquan
Fukang
Jimsar
Qitai
BOGDA SHAN
Turpan
Turpan Pendi (Turfan Depression)
154
Shanshan
Hami
Kushui
Barkol
Karlik Shan 4925
Santanghu
Yanqi
Hejing
Kümüx
Bosten Hu
Korla
KURUKTAG
Luntai
Kuqa
Baicheng
Wensu
Aksu
pik Pobedy 7439
Xayar
T I E N S H A N
C H I N A
XINJIANG
TARIM PENDI
Taklimakan Shamo (Takla Makan Desert)
Awat
Kalpin
Bachu
Artux
Kashi
Shule
Jiashi
Yopurga
Yengisar
Markit
Akto
Wuqia
Ulugqat
Shache
Zepu
Yecheng
Taxkorgan
Pishan
Hotan
Moyu
Lop
Yutian
Minfeng
Andirlang
Karasay
Qiemo
Tatrang
Waxxari
Ruoqiang
ALTUN SHAN
KUNLUN SHAN
Ulugh Muztagh
Muztag 7723
Mangya
QAIDAM PENDI
QINGHAI
Lenghu
GANSU
Dunhuang
Anxi
Subei
Mattanjing
BEI SHAN
Atas Bogd uul 3590
Hüren Tovon uul 3802
Yumt uul 2076
MONGOLIA
HANGAYN NURUU
MONGOL ALTAYN NURUU
Uliastay
Aldarhaan
Bulgan
Jargalant
Altay
Bichigt
Hovd
Ulaangom
Tsagaannuur
Ölgiy
Tolbo
Har-Us
Hyargas nuur
Har-Us nuur
Dörgön nuur
Buyant
Takanta
Tsetsegnuur
Uvs nuur
Erdenet
Bulgan
Ertai
Burenhayrhan
Fuhai
Hoxtolgay
Burqin
Ulungur Hu
T U V A
TANNU-OLA
HREBET
HREBET SANGILEN
Kyzyl
Čadan
Ak-Dovurak
Teeli
Šagonar
Turan
Hovu-Aksy
Samagaltaj
Erzin
Bajgazyn
Sarga-Sep
Toora-Hem
Systyg-Hem
Kuragino
ZAPADNYJ SAJAN
VOSTOČNYJ SAJAN
SAYAN MOUNTAINS
BURJATIJA
pik Grandioznyj
Alygdžer
Orlik
Mönh Saridag 3492
Hatgal
Mörön
Tosontsengel
gora Karagoš 2930
34
36
90° East of Greenwich 16

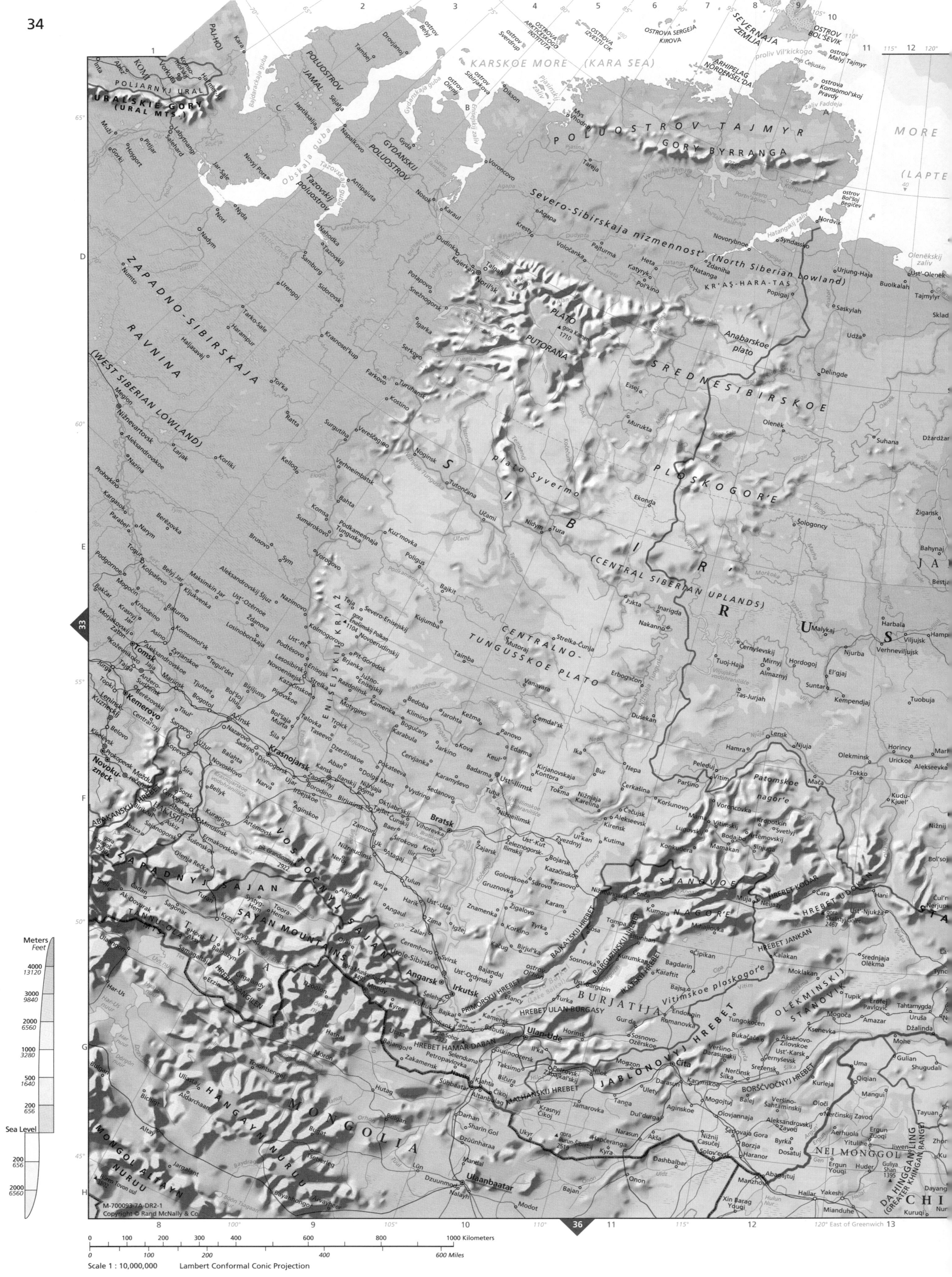
KARSKOE MORE (KARA SEA)
POLUOSTROV JAMAL
GYDANSKIJ POLUOSTROV
Tazovskij poluostrov
Obskaja guba
OSTROVA ARKTIČESKOGO INSTITUTA
OSTROVA IZVESTIJ CIK
OSTROVA SERGEJA KIROVA
SEVERNAJA ZEMLJA
OSTROV BOL'ŠEVIK
ARHIPELAG NORDENŠEL'DA
POLUOSTROV TAJMYR
GORY BYRRANGA
MORE (LAPTE
URAL'SKIE GORY (URAL MTS.)
POLJARNYJ URAL
PAJ-HOJ
KOMI
ZAPADNO-SIBIRSKAJA RAVNINA (WEST SIBERIAN LOWLAND)
Severo-Sibirskaja nizmennost' (North Siberian Lowland)
KR'AŠ-HARA-TAS
PLATO PUTORANA
Anabarskoe plato
SREDNESIBIRSKOE PLOSKOGOR'E (CENTRAL SIBERIAN UPLANDS)
plato Syverma
SIBIR' RUS
CENTRALNO-TUNGUSSKOE PLATO
ENISEJSKIJ KRJAŽ
Patomskoe nagor'e
STANOVOE NAGOR'E
HREBET KODAR
HREBET UDOKAN
OLEKMINSKIJ STANOVIK
Vitimskoe ploskogor'e
BURJATIJA
JABLONOVYJ HREBET
HREBET ULAN-BURGASY
PRIMORSKIJ HREBET
BAJKAL'SKIJ HREBET
HREBET HAMAR-DABAN
MALHANSKIJ HREBET
BORŠČOVOČNYJ HREBET
VOSTOČNYJ SAJAN
ZAPADNYJ SAJAN
SAYAN MOUNTAINS
ABAKANSKIJ HREBET
HAKASIJA
TUVA
TANNU-OLA
HREBET SANGILEN
HANGAYN NURUU
MONGOLIA
MONGOL ALTAYN NURUU
NEI MONGGOL
DA HINGGAN LING (GREATER KHINGAN RANGE)
CHI
Noril'sk
Tomsk
Kemerovo
Novokuzneck
Krasnojarsk
Bratsk
Irkutsk
Angarsk
Ulan-Ude
Čita
Ulaanbaatar
Mirnyj
Lensk
Ust'-Ilimsk
Dudinka
Igarka
Surgut
Nižnevartovsk
Abakan
Kyzyl
Salehard
Labytnangi
Vorkuta
Dikson
Hatanga
Nordvik
Tura
Vanavara
Kirensk
Bodajbo
Severobajkal'sk
Tajšet
Kansk
Ačinsk
Kyra
Nerčinsk
Sretensk
Borzja
Zabajkal'sk
Hajlar
Manzhouli
Darhan
Sühbaatar
Kjahta
gora Kamen 1710
pik Grandioznyj 2922
gora Barun-Šabartuj 2519
gora Enašimskij Polkan 1104
gora Skalistyj Golec 2467
Meters Feet
4000 13120
3000 9840
2000 6560
1000 3280
500 1640
200 656
Sea Level
200 656
2000 6560
M-700093-7A-DR2-1
Copyright © Rand McNally & Co.
120° East of Greenwich
0 100 200 300 400 600 800 1000 Kilometers
0 100 200 400 600 Miles
Scale 1 : 10,000,000 Lambert Conformal Conic Projection
33
36

NOVOSIBIRSKIE OSTROVA
OSTROVA ANŽU
OSTROVA DE-LONGA
ostrov Genrietty
ostrov Žannetty
ostrov Bennetta
ostrov Žohova
ostrov Vil'kickogo
OSTROV KOTEL'NYJ
OSTROV FADDEEVSKIJ
OSTROV NOVAJA SIBIR'
ostrov Bel'kovskij
proliv Sannikova
LJAHOVSKIJE OSTROV
OSTROV BOL'ŠOJ LJAHOVSKIJ
LJAHOVSKIJE OSTROVA
ostrov Stolbovoj
proliv Dmitrija Lapteva
mys Svjatoj Nos
VOSTOČNO-SIBIRSKOE MORE
(EAST SIBERIAN SEA)
MEDVEŽJI OSTROVA
ostrov Ajon
OSTROV VRANGELJA (WRANGEL ISLAND)
proliv Longa
CHUKCHI SEA
ČUKOTSKIJ POLUOSTROV (CHUKOTSK PEN.)
U.S. ALASKA
Bering Strait
Cape Prince of Wales
Teller
Wales
ostrov Ratmanova
mys Dežneva
Uelen
Enurmino
Vankarem
Lavrentija
Provideniya
Gambell
mys Čukotskij
Anadyrskij zaliv (Gulf of Anadyr)
zaliv Kresta
Egvekinot
Ušakovskoe
mys Šelagskij
Pevek
Krasnoarmejskij
Poljarnyj
Iultin
HREBET PEKUL'NEJ
ANADYRSKOE PLOSKOGOR'E
Bilibino
Ust'-Čaun
Čaunskaja guba
Ambarčik
Anadyr
Anadyrskij liman
Ugol'nye Kopi
Tumanskij
Beringovskij
Krasneno
Ust'-Belaja
Markovo
Mejnypil'gyno
mys Navarin
Hatyrka
KORJAKSKOE NAGOR'E
PENŽINSKIJ HREBET
Ajanka
Slautnoe
Kamenskoe
Manily
Talovka
Kamenskoe
Korf
Oljutorskij zaliv
mys Oljutorskij
Pahača
BERING SEA
Tabor
Logaškino
Pohodsk
Čerskij
Anjujsk
Ostrovnoe
ANJUJSKIJ HREBET
OLOJSKIJ HREBET
Omolon
Kolymskaja nizmennost' (Kolyma Plain)
Kolymskaja
Jukagirskoe ploskogor'e
Srednekolymsk
Svatai
Zyrjanka
Nelemnoe
Oroek
Balygyčan
Kedon
Paren'
POLUOSTROV TAJGONOS
Penžinskaja guba
Gižiga
Evensk
Gižiginskaja guba
mys Tajgonos
zaliv Šelihova
Omsukčan
Talaja
Tumany
Jano-Indigirskaja nizmennost'
Janskij zaliv
mys Buor-Haja
guba Buor-Haja
Bykovskij
Nižnejansk
Tiksi
Čokurdah
Kazačje
Tumat
Najba
Hajyr
Kular
Vlasovo
Tenkeli
Ust'-Kujda
Deputatskij
Kjusjur
HREBET KULAR
Namy
Sajdy
Janskij
Syagannah
Družina
Krest-Maer
Batagaj-Alyta
Verhojansk
Batagaj
VERHOJANSKIJ HREBET (VERKHOYANSK MOUNTAINS)
HREBET ČERSKOGO (CHERSKY MOUNTAINS)
MOMSKIJ HREBET
gora Pobeda 3147
Hanuu
Tomtor
Bala
Junkjur
Suordah
Barylas
Ust'-Nera
Artyk
Ojmjakon
Mjaundža
Susuman
Taskan
Jagodnoe
Sejmčan
Orotukan
Adygalak
Bol'ševik
Spornoe
gora Aborigen 2586
Mjakit
Atka
Tahtojamsk
HREBET SUNTAR-HAJATA
gora Mus-Haja 2959
Omčak
Ust'-Omčug
Palatka
Stekol'nyj
Ola
Jamsk
mys Tolstoj
Magadan
Sirlin
Arman'
Taujsk
Taujskaja guba
mys Alevina
Motyklejka
Inja
Ohotsk
mys Duga-Zapadnaja
Ulja
SIBERIA
Tompo
Sangar
Batamaj
Namtcy
Borogoncy
Ytyk-Kjuël
Handyga
HREBET SETTE-DABAN
Džebariki-Haja
Ohotskij Perevoz
rdigestjah
Kangalassy
Bestjah
Majja
Jakutsk
Čurapča
Pokrovsk
Myndagaj
Allah-Jun'
Ketanda
Arka
El'dikan
Amga
Bolugur
Ust'-Maja
Hajysardah
Ulu
Ynykčanskij
Ust'-Mil'
Imeni Kirova
Verhnjaja Amga
Ust'-Judoma
Aim
Čagda
ALDANSKOE NAGOR'E (ALDAN PLATEAU)
Nel'kan
gora Topko 1906
HREBET DŽUGDŽUR
Kemkara
Aldoma
Ajan
Gonam
Tomptokan
STANOVOJ HREBET
ŠANTARSKIE OSTROVA
Udskaja guba
zaliv Akademii
Čumikan
Torom
Udskoe
Bomnak
Zejskoe vodohranilišče
HREBET DŽAGDY
Baladek
Tugur
HREBET JAM-ALIN'
Zlatoustovsk
Ekimčan
Tokur
Stojba
Imeni Poliny Osipenko
Selemdžinsk
Sofijsk
Norsk
Majskij
Zeja
Ovsjanka
Jasnyj
Oktjabr'skij
Šimanovsk
Svobodnyj
Belogorsk
Ekaterinoslavka
Ivanovka
Blagoveščensk
Heihe
Bureja
Arhara
Poyarkovo
Raichihsk
HREBET TURANA
BUREINSKIJ HREBET
Ust'-Urgal
Čegdomyn
Ust'-Umal'ta
Tyrma
Sogda
Obluče
Kul'dur
Birakan
Bira
Birobidžan
Daotiandi
Paškovo
Smidovič
Pompejevka
Bidžan
Leninskoe
Zhaoxing
Tongjiang
Habarovsk
Fuyuan
Hor
Antun'
Vjazemskij
Muhen
Komsomol'sk-na-Amure
Amursk
Niženetambovskoe
Bolon'
Sel'gon
Troickoe
Litovko
Kukan
Sarapul'skoe
Pivan'
Gurskoe
Vysokogornyj
Innokentevka
Datta
Vanino
Sovetskaja Gavan'
gora Tardoki-Jani 2077
SIHOTE-ALIN'
Adžima
Nel'ma
Adimi
Lazarev
Bogorodskoe
Sulinskij
Mariinskoe
De-Kastri
Mgači
Aleksandrovsk-Sahalinskij
Herpuči
Guga
Mago
Nikolaevsk-na-Amure
Susanino
Moskal'vo
Oha
Nyvrovo
mys Elizavety
POLUOSTROV ŠMIDTA
Sahalinskij zaliv
Paromaj
Pogibi
Nogliki
Katangli
Nys
Tymovskoe
gora Lopatina 1609
OSTROV SAHALIN (SAKHALIN)
ZAPADNYJ HREBET
Širokaja Pad'
Pobedino
Smirnyh
Bošnjakovo
Lesogorsk
Šahtersk
Uglegorsk
Poronajsk
Kotikovo
zaliv Terpenija
mys Terpenija
Makarov
Krasnogorsk
Vostočnyj
Il'jinskij
Tomari
Čehovo
Holmsk
Dolinsk
Bykov
Južno-Sahalinsk
Nevel'sk
Aniva
Korsakov
Novikovo
zaliv Aniva
SEA OF OKHOTSK
ostrov Iony
POLUOSTROV KAMČATKA
SREDINNYJ HREBET
VOSTOČNYJ HREBET
Il'pyrskij
Karaginskij zaliv
ostrov Karaginskij
Ossora
Karaga
Tymlat
Lesnaja
Palana
Uka
Ivaška
zaliv Ozernoj
KAMČATSKIJ POLUOSTROV
Vojampolka
Tigil'
vulkan Šiveluč 3283
Ust'-Kamčatsk
Kamčatskij zaliv
Ključi
Kozyrevsk
Kljuchevskaja Sopka 4750
Esso
Atlasovo
mys Južnyj
Ust'-Hajrjuzovo
Hajrjuzovo
Morošečnoe
vulkan Ičinskaja Sopka 3621
Sobolevo
Mil'kovo
Kronoki
Kronockij zaliv
vulkan Kronockaja Sopka 3456
Pušino
mys Šipunskij
vulkan Korjakskaja Sopka 3456
Kirovskij
Malki
Elizovo
Paratunka
Petropavlovsk-Kamčatskij
Kihčik
Ust'-Bol'šereck
Oktjabr'skij
Bol'šereck
Ozernovskij
mys Lopatka
Pervyj Kuril'skij proliv
ostrov Atlasova
Severo-Kuril'sk
ostrov Šumšu
ostrov Paramušir
ostrov Onekotan
ostrov Šiaškotan
proliv Kruzenšterna
ostrov Matua
ostrov Rasšua
ostrov Ketoj
ostrov Simušir
KURIL'SKIE OSTROVA (KURIL ISLANDS)
Aleutka
ostrov Urup
KOMANDORSKIE OSTROVA
Nikol'skoe
ostrov Beringa
HEILONGJIANG

RUSSIA
KAZAKSTAN
MONGOLIA
CHINA
INDIA
BHUTAN
BANGLADESH
MYANMAR (BURMA)
LAOS
VIETNAM
XINJIANG
XIZANG (TIBET)
QINGHAI
GANSU
NINGXIA
NEI MONGGOL
SHAANXI
SHANXI
HENAN
HUBEI
HUNAN
SICHUAN
GUIZHOU
YUNNAN
GUANGXI
GUANGDONG
ASSAM
MEGHALAYA
NAGALAND
MANIPUR
MIZORAM
TRIPURA
ARUNACHAL PRADESH
ALTAI
MONGOL ALTAYN NURUU
HANGAYN NURUU
GOBI DESERT
GURVAN SAYHAN UUL
Junggar Pendi
BOGDA SHAN
KURUKTAG
BEI SHAN
ALTUN SHAN
QILIAN SHAN
KUNLUN SHAN
HOH XIL SHAN
QAIDAM PENDI
BURHAN BUDAI SHAN
QING ZANG GAOYUAN (PLATEAU OF TIBET)
TANGGULA SHAN
BAYAN HAR SHAN
QIN LING
DABA SHAN
MIN SHAN
DATONG SHAN
YIN SHAN
LULIANG SHAN
Tengger Shamo
MU US SHAMO
NU SHAN
SHALULI SHAN
WULIANG SHAN
AILAO SHAN
DALIANG SHAN
PATKAI RANGE
CHIN HILLS
ARAKAN YOMA
Ulaanbaatar
Ürümqi
Lanzhou
Xining
Hohhot
Baotou
Datong
TAIYUAN
XI'AN
Zhengzhou
Luoyang
CHENGDU
CHONGQING
Guiyang
Kunming
Nanning
CHANGSHA
Lhasa
Mandalay
HA NOI
Hai Phong
Gulf of Tonkin
SHENZHEN
Haikou
Meters / Feet
6000 19680
4000 13120
3000 9840
2000 6560
1000 3280
500 1640
200 656
Sea Level
200 656
2000 6560
0 100 200 300 400 600 Kilometers
0 100 200 400 Miles
Scale 1 : 10,000,000
Lambert Conformal Conic Projection

M-661000-7A-DR2-1

CHINA
NEI MONGGOL
DONG SAN SHEN
(MANCHURIA)
HEILONGJIANG
JILIN
LIAONING
HEBEI
SHANDONG
JIANGSU
ANHUI
ZHEJIANG
SHANGHAI
TIANJIN
BEIJING
NORTH KOREA
SOUTH KOREA
HARBIN
CHANGCHUN
Jilin
SHENYANG
(MUKDEN)
FUSHUN
Anshan
Benxi
Liaoyang
Fuxin
Jinzhou
Yingkou
Dandong
Siping
Liaoyuan
Tieling
Chaoyang
Beipiao
Chengde
BEIJING
(PEKING)
TIANJIN
(TIENTSIN)
Tangshan
Qinhuangdao
Tanggu
Dagu
Liaodong Wan
(Gulf of Liaotung)
Liaodong Bandao
(Liaotung Peninsula)
DALIAN
(DAIREN)
Lüshun
(Port Arthur)
Bohai Wan
Bo Hai
(Gulf of Chihli)
Bohai Haixia
Korea Bay
Yantai
Weihai
Shandong Bandao
(Shantung Peninsula)
Weifang
Zibo
Boshan
Qingdao(Tsingtao)
Jiaozhou Wan
Laizhou Wan
(Laizhou Bay)
Lianyungang
Haizhou Wan
YELLOW SEA
EAST CHINA SEA
Nantong
NANJING
(NANKING)
Zhenjiang
Yangzhou
Changzhou
Wuxi
Suzhou
SHANGHAI
Hangzhou
Jiaxing
Huzhou
Wuhu
Chongming Dao
Hangzhou Wan
Mudanjiang
Yanji
Tumen
Changbai Mts.
Paektu-san
2744
P'YŎNGYANG
Namp'o
Sinŭiju
Hamhŭng
Hŭngnam
Wŏnsan
Ch'ŏngjin
Kimch'aek
Haeju
Kaesŏng
SŎUL
(SEOUL)
INCH'ŎN
Suwŏn
Ch'ŏnan
Taejŏn
Taegu
Kunsan
Chŏnju
Kwangju
Mokp'o
P'ohang
Ulsan
PUSAN
(FUSAN)
Masan
Kangnŭng
Ch'unch'ŏn
Cheju
CHEJU-DO
(QUELPART ISLAND)
Halla-san
1950
TSUSHIMA
Korea Strait
KITAKYŪSHŪ
FUKUOKA
Nagasaki
Kumamoto
GOTŌ-RETTŌ
Kagoshima
Ullŭng
Meters
Feet
3000
9840
2000
6560
1000
3280
500
1640
200
656
Sea Level
200
656
2000
6560
0
50
100
150
200
300
400
500 Kilometers
0
50
100
200
300 Miles
Scale 1 : 5,000,000
Lambert Conformal Conic Projection

Japan, Korea, and Northeastern China

W-566400-7A-DR2-1

SEA OF JAPAN
(EAST SEA)
SOUTH KOREA
NORTH KOREA
JAPA
KYŪSHŪ
SHIKOKU
EAST CHINA SEA
Korea Strait
Western Channel
Tsushima-kaikyō (Eastern Channel)
Ullŭng-do (S. Korea)
Tok-to Take-shima (Claimed by S. Korea and Japan)
OKI-SHOTŌ
TSUSHIMA
GOTŌ-RETTŌ
Kangnŭng
Taegu
Ulsan
Changwŏn
PUSAN (FUSAN)
P'ohang
Andong
Shimonoseki
KITAKYŪSHŪ
FUKUOKA
Nagasaki
Kumamoto
Kagoshima
Miyazaki
Ōita
Beppu
HIROSHIMA
Okayama
Kurashiki
Matsue
Takamatsu
Matsuyama
Kōchi
Tokushima
CHŪGOKU-SANCHI
SHIKOKU-SANCHI
KYŪSHŪ-SANCHI
Suō-nada
Iyo-nada
Hyūga-nada
Amakusa-nada
Genkai-nada
Tosa-wan
To Okinawa
To Cheju-do
134° East of Greenwich

HONSHŪ
PACIFIC OCEAN
Sado-kaikyō
SADO
Toyama-wan
Wakasa-wan
Ise-wan
Enshū-nada
Kumano-nada
Suruga-wan
Sagami-nada
Tōkyō-wan
Kashima-nada
IZU-SHOTŌ (IZU ISLANDS)
Noto-hantō
Kii-hantō
Izu-hantō
Bōsō-hantō
Atsumi-hantō
Chita-hantō
Miura-hantō
Tango-hantō
YAMAGATA
MIYAGI
FUKUSHIMA
NIIGATA
TOCHIGI
GUMMA
IBARAKI
SAITAMA
CHIBA
TOKYO
KANAGAWA
YAMANASHI
NAGANO
SHIZUOKA
TOYAMA
ISHIKAWA
FUKUI
GIFU
AICHI
SHIGA
MIE
KYOTO
OSAKA
NARA
WAKAYAMA
IWATE
TŌKYŌ
Yokohama
Kawasaki
Chiba
Nagoya
Kyōto
Ōsaka
Kōbe
Niigata
Sendai
Shizuoka
Hamamatsu
Kanazawa
Toyama
Nagano
Maebashi
Utsunomiya
Mito
Fukushima
Kōfu
Gifu
Fukui
Wakayama
Fuji-san (Mount Fuji) 3776
Sado
Awa-shima
Ō-shima
To-shima
Nii-jima
Kōzu-shima
Miyake-jima
Mikura-jima
Hachijō-jima
Aoga-shima
Meters
Feet
3000 9840
2000 6560
1000 3280
500 1640
200 656
Sea Level
200 656
2000 6560
0 25 50 75 100 150 200 250 Kilometers
0 25 50 100 150 Miles
Scale 1 : 2,500,000
Lambert Conformal Conic Projection
W-561592-7A-DR2-1
Copyright © Rand McNally & Co.

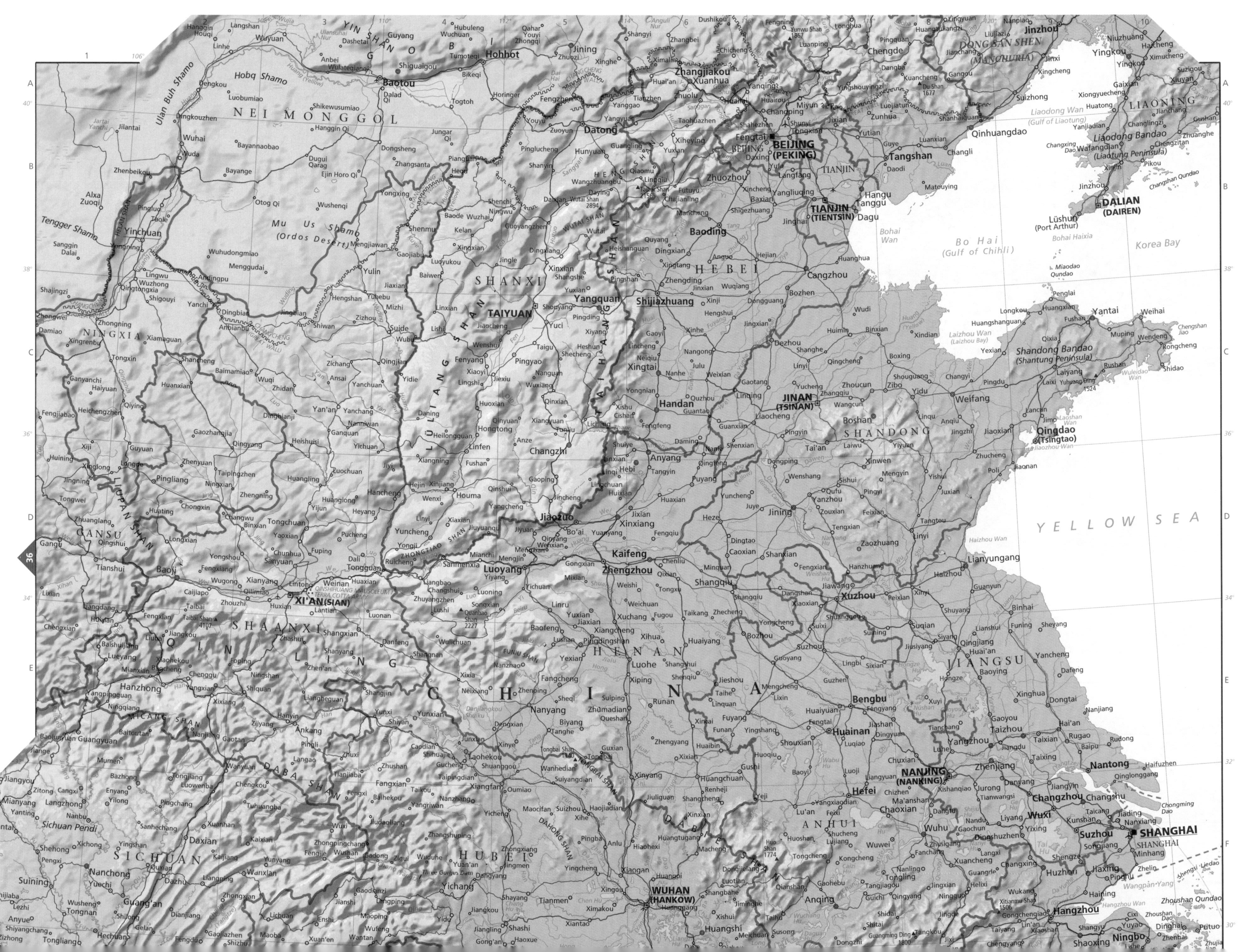
YELLOW SEA
Bo Hai
(Gulf of Chihli)
Korea Bay
Liaodong Wan
(Gulf of Liaotung)
Bohai Haixia
Bohai Wan
Laizhou Wan
(Laizhou Bay)
Liaodong Bandao
(Liaotung Peninsula)
Shandong Bandao
(Shantung Peninsula)
LIAONING
HEBEI
SHANDONG
JIANGSU
ANHUI
HENAN
SHANXI
SHAANXI
NEI MONGGOL
NINGXIA
GANSU
SICHUAN
HUBEI
BEIJING
(PEKING)
TIANJIN
(TIENTSIN)
SHANGHAI
NANJING
(NANKING)
DALIAN
(DAIREN)
JINAN
(TSINAN)
WUHAN
(HANKOW)
XI'AN (SIAN)
TAIYUAN
Shijiazhuang
Zhengzhou
Luoyang
Kaifeng
Qingdao
(Tsingtao)
Yantai
Lüshun
(Port Arthur)
Tangshan
Qinhuangdao
Baoding
Zhangjiakou
Datong
Hohhot
Baotou
Yinchuan
Yan'an
Baoji
Hanzhong
Nanchong
Suining
Hefei
Bengbu
Huainan
Xuzhou
Lianyungang
Weifang
Zibo
Nantong
Suzhou
Wuxi
Changzhou
Zhenjiang
Hangzhou
Ningbo
Jinzhou
Yingkou
Chengde
Handan
Xingtai
Anyang
Xinxiang
Jiaozuo
Changzhi
Yangquan
Nanyang
Xiangfan
Anqing
Wuhu
Huangshi
Shashi
Yichang
MU US SHAMO
(Ordos Desert)
Hobq Shamo
Tengger Shamo
Ulan Buh Shamo
YIN SHAN
LÜLIANG SHAN
TAIHANG SHAN
HENG SHAN
QINLING
DABA SHAN
DABIE SHAN
LIUPAN SHAN
HELAN SHAN
MICANG SHAN
Sichuan Pendi
Grand Canal
Huang (Yellow)

EAST CHINA SEA
SOUTH CHINA SEA
Taiwan Strait
Luzon Strait
Bashi Channel
Gulf of Tonkin
TAIWAN
PHILIPPINES
LUZON
BATAN ISLANDS
BABUYAN ISLANDS
HAINAN DAO (HAINAN ISLAND)
VIETNAM
BAC PHAN (TONKIN)
ZHEJIANG
FUJIAN
JIANGXI
HUNAN
GUANGDONG
GUANGXI
GUIZHOU
HAINAN
WUYI SHAN
NAN LING
XIANGGANG (HONG KONG)
MACAU
GUANGZHOU (CANTON)
T'AIPEI
KAOHSIUNG
CHANGSHA
Nanchang
Fuzhou
Xiamen (Amoy)
Shantou
Guilin
Liuzhou
Nanning
Guiyang
Zhanjiang
Haikou
Hai Phong
WENCHOW
Tungsha Tao (Pratas Island) (China/Taiwan)
P'enghu Ch'üntao (Pescadores)
Chinmen Tao (Quemoy)
Scale 1 : 5,000,000
500 Kilometers
300 Miles
Lambert Conformal Conic Projection
Meters Feet
3000 9840
2000 6560
1000 3280
500 1640
200 656
Sea Level
W-560898-7A-DR2-1
Copyright © Rand McNally & Co.

47

36

MYANMAR (BURMA)

THAILAND

LAOS

VIETNAM

CAMBODIA

CHINA

MALAYSIA

BRUNEI

SINGAPORE

I N D

INDOCHINA

SOUTH CHINA SEA

Gulf of Tonkin

Gulf of Thailand

Andaman Sea

Gulf of Martaban

Mouths of the Ayeyarwady

INDIAN OCEAN

LAUT JAWA (JAVA SEA)

GREATER SUNDA I

Strait of Malacca

Selat Karimata (Karimata Strait)

Selat Sunda

Selat Mentawai

Selat Bangka

Selat Gelasa

Selat Madura

Selat Berhala

Selat Lombok

Laut Bali (Bali Sea)

HAINAN DAO (HAINAN ISLAND)

XISHA QUNDAO (PARACEL ISLANDS) (Claimed by China, Taiwan and Vietnam)

SPRATLY ISLANDS (Claimed by Brunei, China, Malaysia, Philippines, Taiwan and Vietnam)

HA NOI

Hai Phong

Haikou

YANGON (RANGOON)

KRUNG THEP (BANGKOK)

Vientiane

Phnum Penh (Phnom Penh)

THANH PHO HO CHI MINH (HO CHI MINH CITY) (SAIGON)

KUALA LUMPUR

JAKARTA

Bandar Seri Begawan

MALAY PENINSULA

Isthmus of Kra

MERGUI ARCHIPELAGO

PEGU YOMA

DAWNA RA.

TAUNGNYO RANGE

BILAUKTAUNG RANGE

PHANOM DONGRAK RANGE

ANNAMITIQUE

SUMATERA (SUMATRA)

PEGUNUNGAN BARISAN

BORNEO (KALIMANTAN)

SARAWAK

SABAH

UPPER KAPUAS MTS.

IRAN MTS.

PEG. MULLER

JAWA (JAVA)

SEMENANJUNG MALAYSIA

KEPULAUAN NATUNA BESAR

KEPULAUAN ANAMBAS

KEPULAUAN NATUNA SELATAN

KEPULAUAN TAMBELAN

KEPULAUAN RIAU

KEPULAUAN LINGGA

KEPULAUAN BATU

KEPULAUAN MENTAWAI

Doi Inthanon 2600

Phou Bia 2819

Phnum Aôral 1813

Gunung Leuser 3381

Gunung Kerinci 3800

Gunung Tahan 2187

Gunung Kinabalu 4101

Gunung Semeru 3676

Gunung Rinjani 3726

Meters / Feet

4000 / 13120

3000 / 9840

2000 / 6560

1000 / 3280

500 / 1640

200 / 656

Sea Level

200 / 656

2000 / 6560

M-600098-7A-DR2-1

0 100 200 300 400 600 800 1000 Kilometers

0 100 200 400 600 Miles

Scale 1 : 10,000,000 Sinusoidal Projection

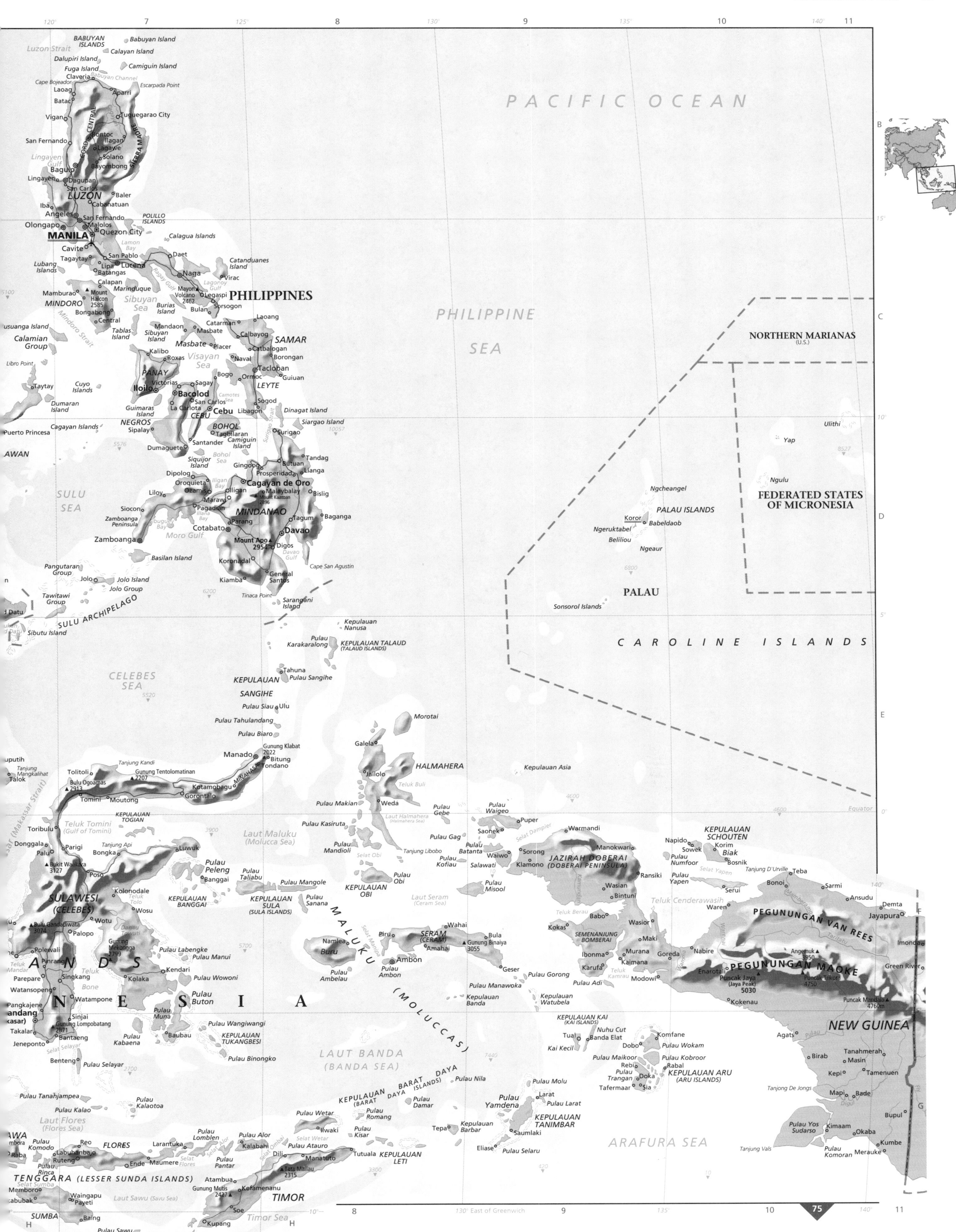
PACIFIC OCEAN
PHILIPPINES
PHILIPPINE SEA
NORTHERN MARIANAS (U.S.)
FEDERATED STATES OF MICRONESIA
PALAU
PALAU ISLANDS
CAROLINE ISLANDS
LUZON
MANILA
Quezon City
MINDORO
SAMAR
PANAY
NEGROS
CEBU
BOHOL
LEYTE
MINDANAO
Davao
Cagayan de Oro
Zamboanga
Cotabato
SULU SEA
SULU ARCHIPELAGO
CELEBES SEA
KEPULAUAN SANGIHE
KEPULAUAN TALAUD (TALAUD ISLANDS)
HALMAHERA
Morotai
Manado
SULAWESI (CELEBES)
Laut Maluku (Molucca Sea)
MALUKU (MOLUCCAS)
Laut Seram (Ceram Sea)
SERAM (CERAM)
Buru
Ambon
LAUT BANDA (BANDA SEA)
JAZIRAH DOBERAI (DOBERAI PENINSULA)
KEPULAUAN SCHOUTEN
Biak
Teluk Cenderawasih
PEGUNUNGAN VAN REES
PEGUNUNGAN MAOKE
Puncak Jaya (Jaya Peak) 5030
NEW GUINEA
Jayapura
KEPULAUAN KAI (KAI ISLANDS)
KEPULAUAN ARU (ARU ISLANDS)
KEPULAUAN TANIMBAR
ARAFURA SEA
KEPULAUAN BARAT DAYA (BARAT DAYA ISLANDS)
TIMOR
Timor Sea
FLORES
Laut Flores (Flores Sea)
SUMBA
Laut Sawu (Savu Sea)
TENGGARA (LESSER SUNDA ISLANDS)
INDONESIA
Equator
130° East of Greenwich

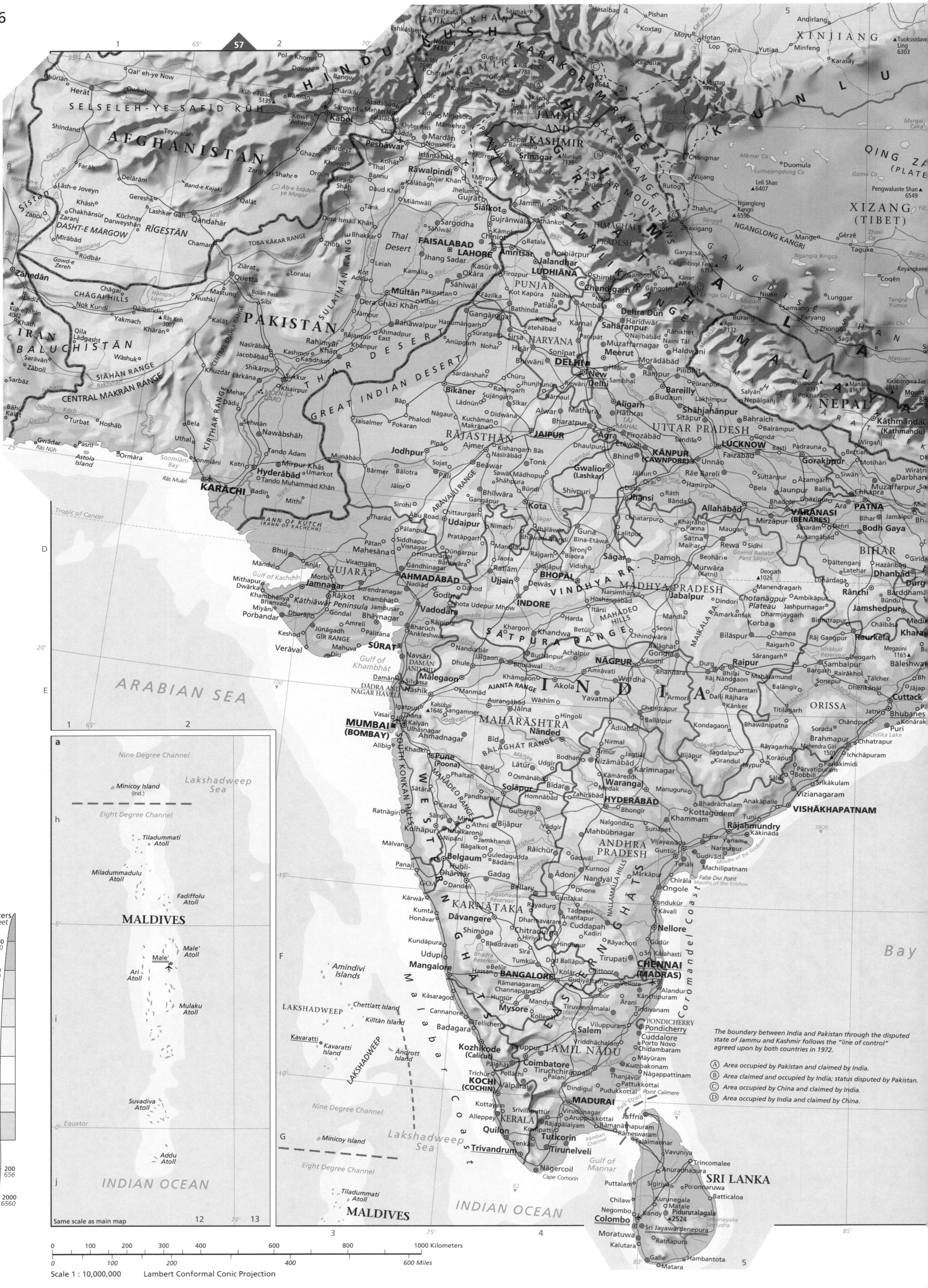

57
AFGHANISTAN
PAKISTAN
IRAN
INDIA
NEPAL
SRI LANKA
MALDIVES
XINJIANG
XIZANG (TIBET)
HINDU KUSH
SELSELEH-YE SAFĪD KŪH
KARAKORAM RANGE
KUNLUN
HIMALAYA
JAMMU AND KASHMIR
THAR DESERT
GREAT INDIAN DESERT
RANN OF KUTCH (RANN OF KACHCHH)
VINDHYA RA.
SATPURA RANGE
WESTERN GHATS
EASTERN GHATS
ARABIAN SEA
INDIAN OCEAN
Lakshadweep Sea
Bay
Tropic of Cancer
Kābol
Islāmābād
Rawalpindi
Lahore
Karāchi
Delhi
New Delhi
Jaipur
Āgra
Lucknow
Kānpur (Cawnpore)
Vārānasi (Benares)
Patna
Kāthmāndu
Ahmadābād
Bhopāl
Indore
Nāgpur
Mumbai (Bombay)
Pune (Poona)
Hyderābād
Vishākhapatnam
Bangalore
Chennai (Madras)
Kochi (Cochin)
Madurai
Colombo
Sri Jayawardenepura
The boundary between India and Pakistan through the disputed state of Jammu and Kashmir follows the "line of control" agreed upon by both countries in 1972.
Ⓐ Area occupied by Pakistan and claimed by India.
Ⓑ Area claimed and occupied by India; status disputed by Pakistan.
Ⓒ Area occupied by China and claimed by India.
Ⓓ Area occupied by India and claimed by China.
Meters / Feet
6000 19680
4000 13120
3000 9840
2000 6560
1000 3280
500 1640
200 656
Sea Level
200 656
2000 6560
Same scale as main map
0 100 200 300 400 600 800 1000 Kilometers
0 100 200 400 600 Miles
Scale 1 : 10,000,000
Lambert Conformal Conic Projection

CHINA
MYANMAR (BURMA)
THAILAND
LAOS
VIETNAM
CAMBODIA
BANGLADESH
BHUTAN
MALAYSIA
QINGHAI
SICHUAN
YUNNAN
GUIZHOU
GUANGXI
HUNAN
HUBEI
SHAANXI
GANSU
HENAN
SHANXI
NINGXIA
GUANGDONG
HAINAN
ASSAM
MEGHALAYA
TRIPURA
MIZORAM
MANIPUR
NAGALAND
ARUNACHAL PRADESH
Gulf of Tonkin
Gulf of Thailand
Gulf of Martaban
Andaman Sea
SOUTH CHINA SEA
ANDAMAN ISLANDS
NICOBAR ISLANDS
ANDAMAN AND NICOBAR ISLANDS (India)
MERGUI ARCHIPELAGO
HAINAN DAO (HAINAN ISLAND)
Isthmus of Kra
MALAY PENINSULA
INDOCHINA
Mouths of the Ganges
Mouths of the Ayeyarwady
Ten Degree Channel
KRUNG THEP (BANGKOK)
YANGON (RANGOON)
HA NOI
THANH PHO HO CHI MINH (HO CHI MINH CITY) (SAIGON)
Phnum Penh (Phnom Penh)
Viangchan
DHAKA
CHITTAGONG
Mandalay
CHENGDU
CHONGQING
Kunming
Nanning
XI'AN
Lanzhou
Zhengzhou
Luoyang
Guiyang
Haikou
Hai Phong
Da Nang
90° East of Greenwich
M-690000-7A-DR2-1
Copyright © Rand McNally & Co.

CHINA
YUNNAN
GUANGXI
Nanning
HAINAN DAO
(HAINAN ISLAND)
Gulf of Tonkin
SOUTH CHINA SEA
VIETNAM
HA NOI
Hai Phong
Da Nang
Hue
Quy Nhon
Nha Trang
LAOS
Louangphrabang
Viangchan
(Vientiane)
INDOCHINA
CAMBODIA
THAILAND
KRUNG THEP
(BANGKOK)
Chiang Mai
Nakhon Ratchasima
Khon Kaen
MYANMAR
(BURMA)
Mandalay
YANGON
(RANGOON)
Gulf of Martaban
Bay of Bengal
Moscos Islands
TANINTHARYI

ANDAMAN SEA
MERGUI ARCHIPELAGO
GULF OF THAILAND
SOUTH CHINA SEA
INDIAN OCEAN
Strait of Malacca
INDONESIA
MALAYSIA
SINGAPORE
RIAU
SUMATERA (SUMATRA)
ACEH
SUMATERA UTARA
KEPULAUAN ANAMBAS (ANAMBAS ISLANDS)
KEPULAUAN NATUNA BESAR
KEPULAUAN RIAU
Isthmus of Kra
Phnum Penh (Phnom Penh)
THANH PHO HO CHI MINH (HO CHI MINH CITY) (SAIGON)
Vung Tau
Bien Hoa
Phan Thiet
Can Tho
Long Xuyen
Rach Gia
Ca Mau
Kota Bharu
Kuala Terengganu
Kuantan
KUALA LUMPUR
Ipoh
Melaka
Johor Bahru
George Town (Penang)
Alor Setar
Hat Yai
Songkhla
Pattani
Nakhon Si Thammarat
Surat Thani
Phuket
Trang
MEDAN
Banda Aceh
Pekanbaru
PULAU SIMEULUE
PULAU NIAS
Lambert Conformal Conic Projection
Scale 1 : 5,000,000
W-566730-7A-DR2-1
Copyright © Rand McNally & Co.
Meters
Feet
Sea Level

SOUTH CHINA SEA
MALAY PENINSULA
MALAYSIA
SINGAPORE
KUALA LUMPUR
MEDAN
Pekanbaru
Padang
Palembang
Jambi
Bengkulu
JAKARTA
BANDUNG
Pontianak
Tanjungkarang-Telukbetung
SUMATERA (SUMATRA)
JAWA (JAVA)
INDIAN OCEAN
RIAU
JAMBI
LAMPUNG
SUMATERA UTARA
SUMATERA BARAT
SUMATERA SELATAN
BENGKULU
JAWA BARAT
JOHOR
PAHANG
PERAK
KELANTAN
TERENGGANU
SELANGOR
MELAKA
NEGERI SEMBILAN
KEPULAUAN RIAU
KEPULAUAN LINGGA (LINGGA ISLANDS)
KEPULAUAN ANAMBAS (ANAMBAS ISLANDS)
KEPULAUAN NATUNA BESAR
KEPULAUAN NATUNA SELATAN
KEPULAUAN MENTAWAI (MENTAWAI ISLANDS)
PULAU BANGKA
PULAU SIBERUT
Strait of Malacca
Selat Mentawai
Selat Karimata
Selat Bangka
Selat Berhala
GREATER S
I N D
LAUT
Meters Feet
3000 9840
2000 6560
1000 3280
500 1640
200 656
Sea Level
200 656
2000 6560
W-561194-7A-DR2-1l
Copyright © Rand McNally & Co.
0 50 100 150 200 300 400 500 Kilometers
0 50 100 200 300 Miles
Scale 1 : 5,000,000
Sinusoidal Projection

BRUNEI
Bandar Seri Begawan
SABAH
MALAYSIA
SARAWAK
PHILIPPINES
CELEBES SEA
SULU ARCHIPELAGO
TAWITAWI GROUP
BORNEO
(KALIMANTAN)
KALIMANTAN TIMUR
KALIMANTAN TENGAH
KALIMANTAN BARAT
KALIMANTAN SELATAN
Samarinda
Balikpapan
Banjarmasin
Palangkaraya
Tarakan
Tawau
Miri
Sibu
Bintulu
Kuching
Selat Makasar (Makassar Strait)
Equator
SULAWESI (CELEBES)
SULAWESI TENGAH
SULAWESI SELATAN
SULAWESI TENGGARA
Teluk Tomini (Gulf of Tomini)
Teluk Bone (Gulf of Bone)
Ujungpandang (Makasar)
Palu
Donggala
Poso
Watampone
Parepare
Palopo
SUNDA ISLANDS
INDONESIA
JAWA (JAVA SEA)
MADURA
SURABAYA
SEMARANG
Surakarta
Madiun
Malang
Kediri
Jember
Banyuwangi
JAWA TIMUR
BALI
Denpasar
Laut Bali (Bali Sea)
LOMBOK
Mataram
SUMBAWA
NUSA TENGGARA BARAT
NUSA TENGGARA TIMUR
NUSA TENGGARA (LESSER SUNDA ISLANDS)
FLORES
Laut Flores (Flores Sea)
Laut Sawu (Savu Sea)
SUMBA
Waingapu
Tanjung Selatan (Cape Selatan)
Pulau Laut
Kepulauan Sabalana
Pulau Selayar

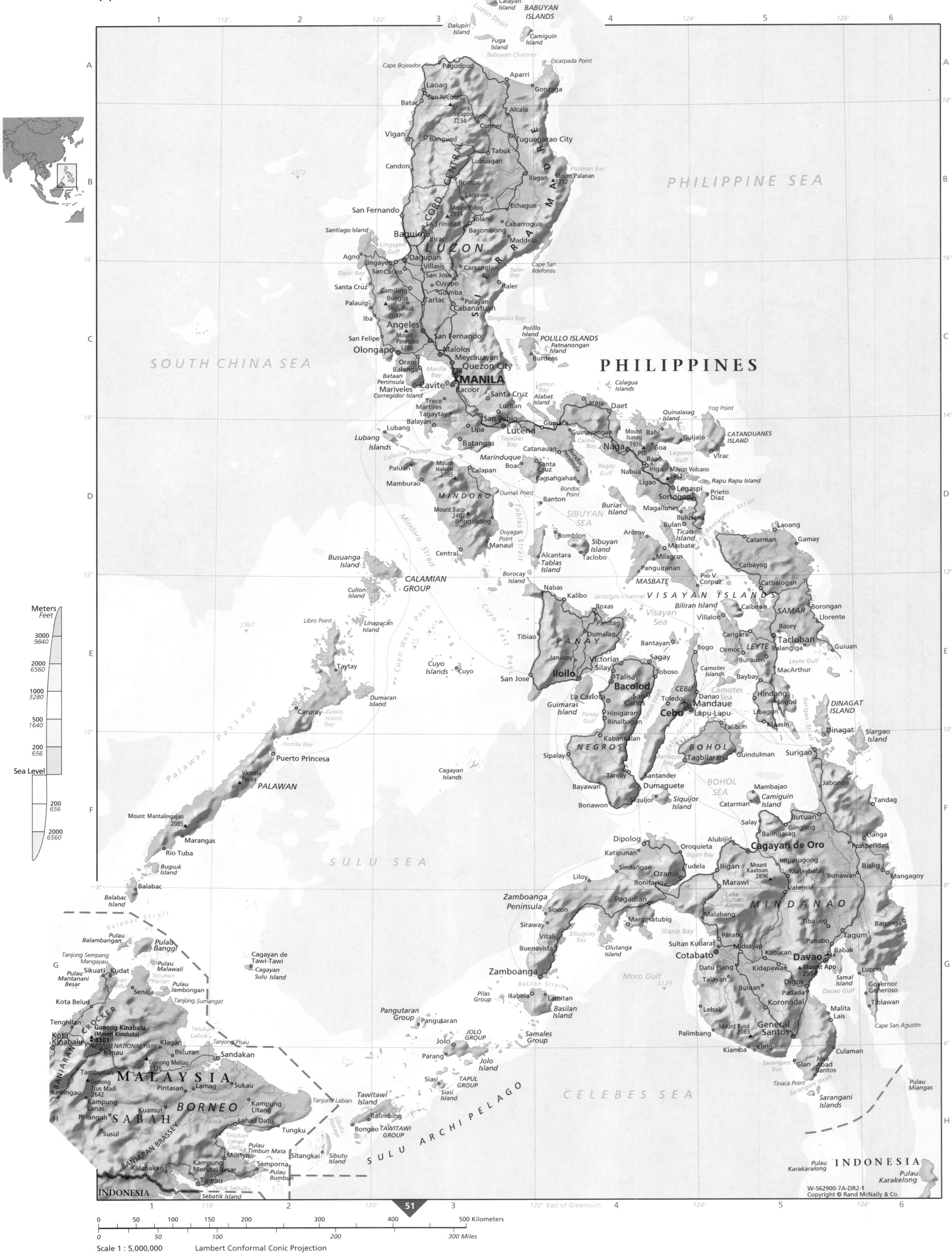

PHILIPPINES

PHILIPPINE SEA
SOUTH CHINA SEA
SULU SEA
CELEBES SEA
SIBUYAN SEA
BOHOL SEA
Visayan Sea
Camotes Sea
Moro Gulf
Luzon Strait
Babuyan Channel
Mindoro Strait
Cuyo East Pass
Cuyo West Pass
Tablas Strait
San Bernardino Strait
Surigao Strait
Basilan Strait
Balabac Strait
Palawan Passage
Polillo Strait
Calavite Passage
Jintotolo Channel
Tañon Strait
Cebu Strait

Babuyan Island
Calayan Island
BABUYAN ISLANDS
Dalupiri Island
Fuga Island
Camiguin Island
Escarpada Point
Cape Bojeador
Pagudpud
Aparri
Gonzaga
Laoag
San Nicolas
Batac
Mount Sicapoo 2234
Alcala
Conner
Vigan
Bangued
Tuguegarao City
Tabuk
Lubuagan
Candon
CORD. CENTRAL
Bontoc
Ilagan
Palanan Bay
Mount Palanan 1212
SIERRA MADRE
Lagawe
San Fernando
Mount Pulog 2934
Echague
Trinidad
Solano
Cabarroguis
Santiago Island
Baguio
Bayombong
Maddela
Lingayen Gulf
Birac
LUZON
Agno
Lingayen
Dagupan
Villasis
San Carlos
Dasol Bay
Carranglan
Baler Bay
Cape San Ildefonso
San Jose
Cuyapo
Santa Cruz
Camiling
Guimba
Baler
Burgos
Palauig
Tarlac
Palayan
High Peak 2037
Cabanatuan
Dingalan Bay
Iba
Angeles
Mount Pinatubo 1780
San Fernando
San Felipe
Malolos
Olongapo
Polillo Island
POLILLO ISLANDS
Patnanongan Island
Burdeos
Meycauayan
Quezon City
Orani
Balanga
Manila Bay
MANILA
Bataan Peninsula
Cavite
Bacoor
Mariveles
Corregidor Island
Lamon Bay
Santa Cruz
Alabat Island
Calagua Islands
Trece Martires
Tagaytay
Lucban
Laguna de Bay
Balayan
Taal
San Pablo
Lucena
Lubang
Lubang Islands
Lipa
Batangas
Tayabas Bay
Gumaca
Daet
Labo
Quinalasag Island
Yog Point
Guinayangan
Ragay Gulf
Mount Isarog 1976
Bahi
Caima Bay
Gujjalo
CATANDUANES ISLAND
Virac
Naga
Goa
Pili
Lagonoy Gulf
Baao
Iriga
Nabua
Ligao
Mayon Volcano 2462
Rapu Rapu Island
Legaspi
Sorsogon
Prieto Diaz
Marinduque
Boac
Catanauan
Bondoc Peninsula
Santa Cruz
Pagsangahan
Bondoc Point
Paluan
Mount Halcon 2585
Calapan
Mamburao
MINDORO
Dumali Point
Banton
Mount Baco 2487
Bongabong
Burias Island
Magallanes
Bulusan
Bulan
Ticao Island
Masbate
Duyagan Point
Manaul
Central
Romblon
Sibuyan Island
Aroroy
Alcantara
Tablas Island
Taclobo
Milagros
Laoang
Catarman
Gamay
Busuanga Island
CALAMIAN GROUP
Culion Island
Boracay Island
MASBATE
Panguiranan
Pio V. Corpuz
Calbayog
Catbalogan
Nabas
Kalibo
VISAYAN ISLANDS
Biliran Island
SAMAR
Borongan
Caibiran
Roxas
Villalon
Llorente
Libro Point
Linapacan Island
Pandan
PANAY
Dumalag
Carigara
Basey
Tibiao
Tacloban
Bantayan
Bogo
Ormoc
LEYTE
Balangiga
Guiuan
Januay
Victorias
Sagay
Burauen
Leyte Gulf
Cuyo Islands
Cuyo
Taytay
San Jose
Iloilo
Silay
Talisay
Bacolod
Toboso
Camotes Islands
Baybay
MacArthur
Dumaran Island
La Carlota
San Carlos
CEBU
Toledo
Danao
Mandaue
Cebu
Lapu-Lapu
Hindang
Sogod
Guimaras Island
Hinigaran
Binalbagan
Panay Gulf
Libagon
DINAGAT ISLAND
Caruray
Green Island Bay
Maasin
Talibon
Dinagat
Siargao Island
Kabankalan
NEGROS
BOHOL
Tagbilaran
Guindulman
Surigao
Honda Bay
Puerto Princesa
Sipalay
Maribojoc Bay
Cagayan Islands
Tanjay
Santander
Victoria Peaks
PALAWAN
Bayawan
Dumaguete
Siquijor
Siquijor Island
Mambajao
Camiguin Island
Jabonga
Catarman
Tandag
Bonawon
Butuan
Salay
Gingoog
Balingasag
Lianga
Mount Mantalingajan 2085
Marangas
Dipolog
Alubijid
Cagayan de Oro
Prosperidad
Katipunan
Oroquieta
Iligan Bay
Rio Tuba
Tudela
Iligan
Mount Kaatoan 2896
Impasugong
Sindangan
Ozamis
Bisliq
Bugsuk Island
Malaybalay
Bonifacio
Liloy
Marawi
Bunawan
Mangagoy
Balabac
Valencia
Balabac Island
Zamboanga Peninsula
Pagadian
Lake Sultan Alonto
MINDANAO
Siocon
Malabang
Margosatubig
Tibal-og
Baganga
Siraway
Illana Bay
Vitali
Sibuguey Bay
Parang
Tagum
Buenavista
Olutanga Island
Sultan Kudarat
Midsayap
Panabo
Cotabato
Kabacan
Babak
Davao
Mount Apo 2954
Kidapawan
Zamboanga
Datu Piang
Lupon
Talayan
Samal Island
Governor Generoso
Digos
Davao Gulf
Pilas Group
Isabela
Lamitan
Buluan
Padada
Basilan Island
Koronadal
Tiblawan
Lebak
Malita
Lais
Pangutaran Group
Pangutaran
Mount Busa 2083
Cape San Agustin
General Santos
Palimbang
JOLO GROUP
Samales Group
Jolo
Kiamba
Kling
Culaman
Parang
Jolo Island
Sarangani Bay
Glan
Jose Abad Santos
Siasi
TAPUL GROUP
Siasi Island
Tinaca Point
Sarangani Strait
Pulau Miangas
Tawitawi Island
Sarangani Islands
SULU ARCHIPELAGO
Balimbing
Bongao
TAWITAWI GROUP
Sibutu Passage
Sitangkai
Sibutu Island
Pulau Karakalong
INDONESIA
Pulau Karakelong
Cagayan de Tawi-Tawi
Cagayan Sulu Island

Pulau Balambangan
Pulau Banggi
Tanjong Sempang Mangayau
Pulau Malawali
Sikuati
Kudat
Pulau Mantanani Besar
Teluk Paitan
Pulau Jambongan
Senaja
Kota Belud
Tanjong Sumangat
Tenghilan
CROCKER
Gunong Kinabalu (Mount Kinabalu) 4101
Kota Kinabalu
KINABALU NATIONAL PARK
Teluk Labuk
Tanjong Pisau
Klagan
Ranau
Beluran
Sandakan
Gunong Meliau
Tambunan
BANJARAN
MALAYSIA
Gunong Trus Madi 2642
Lamag
Sukau
Keningau
Pintasan
Kinabatangan
Kampung Lanas
BORNEO
Kampung Litang
Tanjung Labian
SABAH
Pinangah
Kuamut
Lahad Datu
Tungku
Susul
BANJARAN BRASSEY
Teluk Lahad Datu
Pulau Timbun Mata
Mostyn
Kampung Merutai Besar
Semporna
Kalabakan
Pulau Bumbun
Tawau
Teluk Sebuku
Sebatik Island
INDONESIA

Meters / Feet
3000 / 9840
2000 / 6560
1000 / 3280
500 / 1640
200 / 656
Sea Level
200 / 656
2000 / 6560

W-562900-7A-DR2-1

0 50 100 150 200 300 400 500 Kilometers
0 50 100 200 300 Miles
Scale 1 : 5,000,000
Lambert Conformal Conic Projection
122° East of Greenwich

51

54
55
INDIA
MAHĀRĀSHTRA
ANDHRA PRADESH
KARNĀTAKA
TAMIL NĀDU
KERALA
ORISSA
MADHYA PRADESH
GOA
GUJARAT
DECCAN
WESTERN GHĀTS
EASTERN GHĀTS
NORTHERN CIRCARS
SOUTH KONKAN
COROMANDEL COAST
MALABAR COAST
LAKSHADWEEP
LAKSHADWEEP SEA
INDIAN OCEAN
Bay of Bengal
Gulf of Mannar
Palk Strait
SRI LANKA
MUMBAI (BOMBAY)
Pune (Poona)
Ahmadnagar
Nāshik
Aurangābād
Jālna
Nānded
Solāpur
Kolhāpur
Belgaum
Panaji
Hubli-Dhārwār
Bellary
Dāvangere
Shimoga
Mangalore
BANGALORE
Mysore
Kozhikode (Calicut)
Coimbatore (Koyambattur)
KOCHI (COCHIN)
Quilon
Trivandrum
Nāgercoil
Kanniyākumari
Cape Comorin
Tirunelveli
Tuticorin
MADURAI
Tiruchchirāppalli
Salem
Pondicherry (Puducheri)
Cuddalore
CHENNAI (MADRAS)
Vellore
Tirupati
Nellore
Ongole
Kurnool
Cuddapah
HYDERĀBĀD
Warangal
Vijayawāda
Rājahmundry
Kākināda (Cocanada)
Machilīpatnam (Bandar)
VISHĀKHAPATNAM
Vizianagaram
Brahmapur
Jaffna
Trincomalee
Anuradhapura
Kandy
Colombo
Sri Jayawardenepura (Kotte)
Dehiwala-Mount Lavinia
Moratuwa
Galle
Batticaloa
Pidurutalagala 2524
Anai Mudi 2695
Meters
Feet
2000
6560
1000
3280
500
1640
200
656
Sea Level
0
50
100
150
200
300
400
500 Kilometers
300 Miles
Scale 1 : 5,000,000
Lambert Conformal Conic Projection
W-561092-7A-DR2-1
Copyright © Rand McNally & Co.

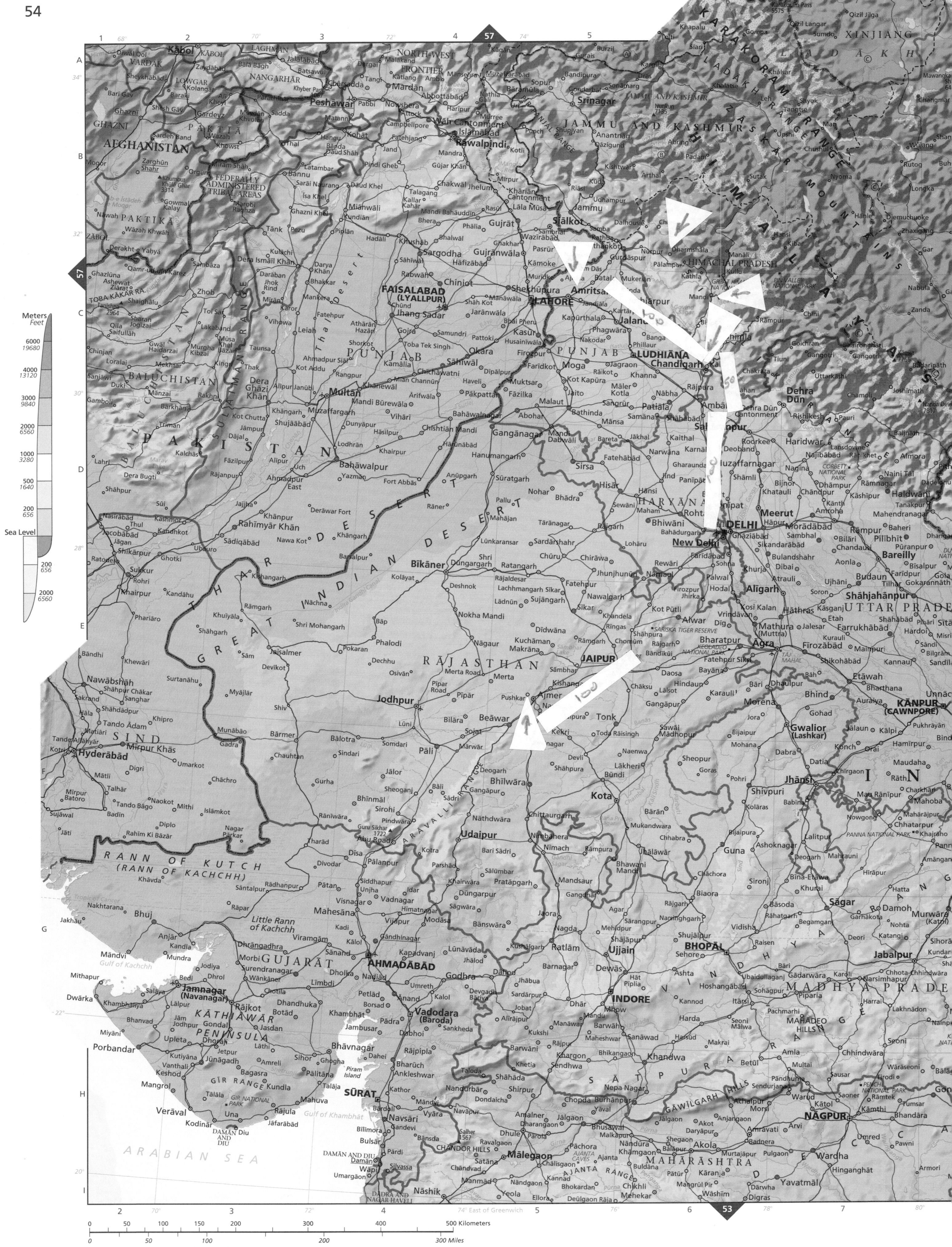
AFGHANISTAN
PAKISTAN
BALUCHISTAN
SIND
PUNJAB
JAMMU AND KASHMIR
HIMACHAL PRADESH
HARYANA
RĀJASTHAN
GUJARĀT
MADHYA PRADE
UTTAR PRADE
MAHĀRĀSHTRA
XINJIANG
NORTH-WEST FRONTIER
FEDERALLY ADMINISTERED TRIBAL AREAS
THAR DESERT
GREAT INDIAN DESERT
Thal Desert
RANN OF KUTCH
(RANN OF KACHCHH)
Little Rann of Kachchh
KĀTHIĀWĀR PENINSULA
Gulf of Kachchh
Gulf of Khambhāt
ARABIAN SEA
KARAKORAM RANGE
HIMALAYA
ZĀSKĀR MOUNTAINS
LADAKH RANGE
SULAIMAN RANGE
ARAVALLI RANGE
VINDHYA RANGE
SĀTPURA RANGE
GĀWILGARH HILLS
AJANTA RANGE
MAHADEO HILLS
GIR RANGE
Kābol
Peshāwar
Rawalpindi
Islāmābād
Srīnagar
Jammu
Lahore
Amritsar
FAISALABAD (LYALLPUR)
Multān
LUDHIĀNA
Chandīgarh
Shimla
DELHI
New Delhi
Meerut
Āgra
JAIPUR
Ajmer
Jodhpur
Bīkāner
Udaipur
Kota
Gwalior (Lashkar)
Jhānsi
KĀNPUR (CAWNPORE)
Bareilly
Hyderābād
AHMADĀBĀD
Vadodara (Baroda)
SŪRAT
INDORE
BHOPĀL
Ujjain
Jabalpur
NĀGPUR
Jamnagar (Navanagar)
Rājkot
Bhāvnagar
Porbandar
Dehra Dūn
Mālegaon
Meters
Feet
6000 19680
4000 13120
3000 9840
2000 6560
1000 3280
500 1640
200 656
Sea Level
200 656
2000 6560
0 50 100 150 200 300 400 500 Kilometers
0 50 100 200 300 Miles
Scale 1 : 5,000,000
Lambert Conformal Conic Projection
74° East of Greenwich
57
53

CHINA
XIZANG (TIBET)
QINGZANG GAOYUAN (PLATEAU OF TIBET)
QINGHAI
TANGGULA SHAN
NYAINQÊNTANGLHA SHAN
HIMALAYAS
NEPAL
BHUTAN
BANGLADESH
SIKKIM
ASSAM
MEGHALAYA
ARUNACHAL PRADESH
TRIPURA
MIZORAM
BIHAR
WEST BENGAL
ORISSA
MYANMAR
Lhasa
Kathmandu (Kathmandu)
Mount Everest (Qomolangma Feng) 8848
Gangtok
Thimphu
Guwāhāti
Shillong
Patna
Vārānasi (Benares)
Allahābād
Gorakhpur
Ranchi
Jamshedpur
Calcutta
Dhaka (Dacca)
Chittagong
Cuttack
Bhubaneshwar
Puri
Raipur
Sittwe
Mouths of the Ganges
Bay of Bengal
SUNDARBANS
Ⓐ Area occupied by Pakistan and claimed by India.
Ⓑ Area claimed and occupied by India; status disputed by Pakistan.
Ⓒ Area occupied by China and claimed by India.
Ⓓ Area occupied by India and claimed by China.
W-561091-7A-DR2-1
Copyright © Rand McNally & Co.

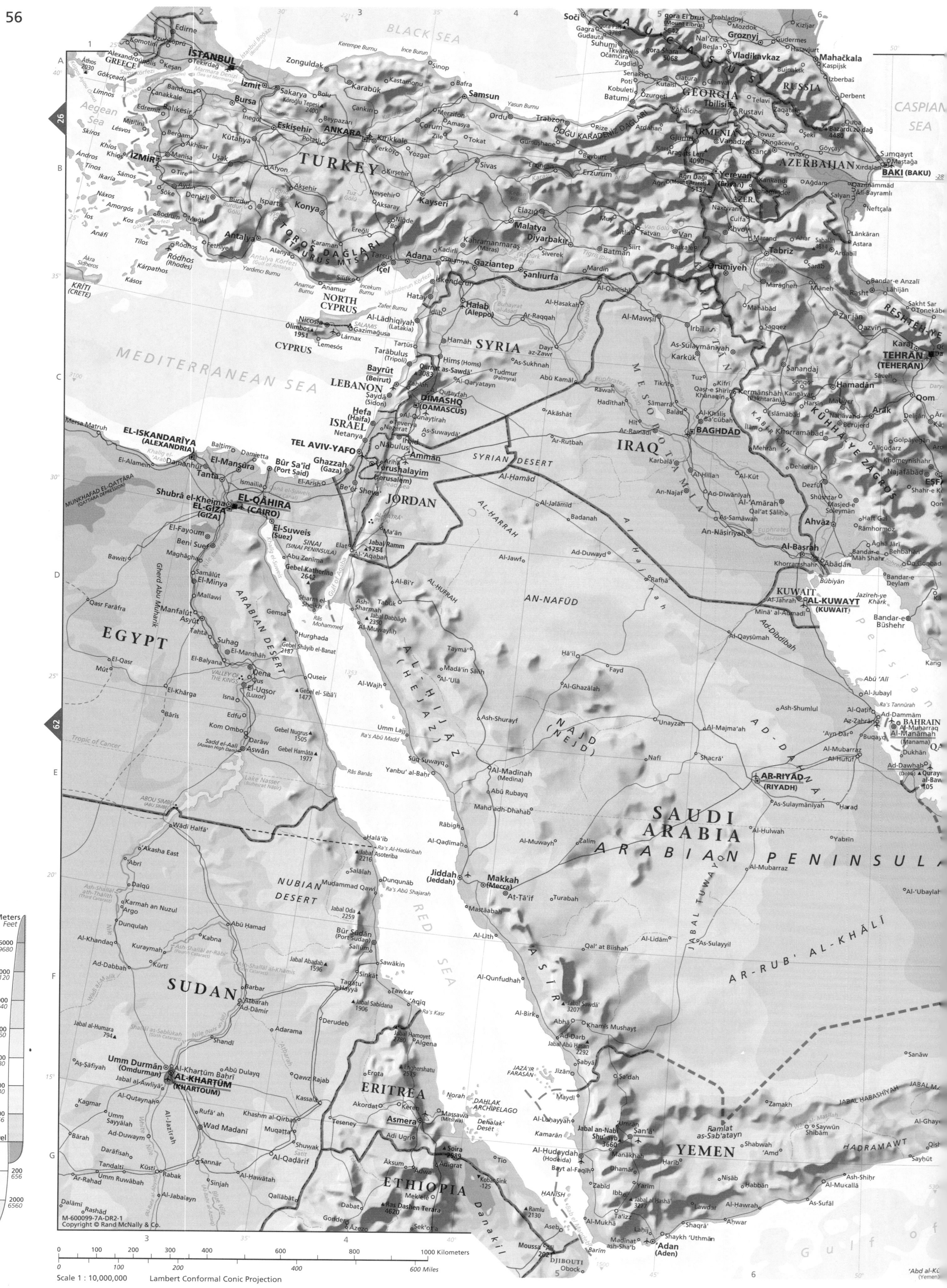
BLACK SEA
CASPIAN SEA
Aegean Sea
MEDITERRANEAN SEA
RED SEA
Persian Gulf
TURKEY
GEORGIA
ARMENIA
AZERBAIJAN
RUSSIA
SYRIA
LEBANON
ISRAEL
CYPRUS
NORTH CYPRUS
JORDAN
IRAQ
KUWAIT
SAUDI ARABIA
EGYPT
SUDAN
ERITREA
ETHIOPIA
YEMEN
DJIBOUTI
BAHRAIN
GREECE
ARABIAN PENINSULA
ARABIAN DESERT
NUBIAN DESERT
SYRIAN DESERT
AN-NAFŪD
AL-ḤIJĀZ (HEJAZ)
NAJD (NEJD)
AD-DAHNĀ'
AR-RUB' AL-KHĀLĪ
'ASĪR
AL-HARRAH
MESOPOTAMIA
TOROS DAĞLARI (TAURUS MTS.)
KŪHHĀ-YE ZĀGROS
KABĪR KŪH
CAUCASUS
DOĞU KARADENIZ DAĞLARI
JABAL ṬUWAYQ
ḤAḌRAMAWT
DAHLAK ARCHIPELAGO
SINAI (SINAI PENINSULA)
İSTANBUL
ANKARA
İzmir
Bursa
Konya
Kayseri
Samsun
Trabzon
Adana
Gaziantep
Antalya
Erzurum
Malatya
Diyarbakır
Şanlıurfa
Tbilisi
Yerevan
BAKI (BAKU)
TEHRĀN (TEHERAN)
Tabrīz
Hamadān
Qom
Arāk
Rasht
Ahvāz
Ābādān
Bandar-e Būshehr
Halab (Aleppo)
Ḥamāh
Ḥimṣ (Homs)
Ar-Raqqah
DIMASHQ (DAMASCUS)
Bayrūt (Beirut)
Ṣaydā (Sidon)
Ṭarābulus (Tripoli)
Al-Lādhiqīyah (Latakia)
Nicosia
Lárnax
Lemesós
TEL AVIV-YAFO
Yerushalayim (Jerusalem)
Hefa (Haifa)
Netanya
Ghazzah (Gaza)
Be'er Sheva'
'Ammān
Irbid
Al-'Aqabah
Elat
Al-Mawṣil
Irbīl
Karkūk
As-Sulaymānīyah
BAGHDĀD
Al-Ḥillah
Karbalā'
An-Najaf
Al-Kūt
Al-'Amārah
An-Nāṣirīyah
Al-Baṣrah
AL-KUWAYT (KUWAIT)
AR-RIYĀḌ (RIYADH)
Al-Madīnah (Medina)
Makkah (Mecca)
Jiddah (Jeddah)
Aṭ-Ṭā'if
Tabūk
Ḥā'il
Buraydah
Al-Hufūf
Ad-Dammām
Al-Manāmah (Manama)
Ad-Dawḥah (Doha)
Abhā
Jīzān
Najrān
Ṣan'ā'
Al-Ḥudaydah (Hodeida)
Ta'izz
'Adan (Aden)
Al-Mukallā
EL-QĀHIRA (CAIRO)
EL-GIZA (GIZA)
EL-ISKANDARĪYA (ALEXANDRIA)
Bûr Sa'îd (Port Said)
El-Suweis (Suez)
Ismailia
Tanta
El-Manṣûra
Asyûṭ
El-Minya
Sohag
Qena
El-Uqsur (Luxor)
Aswân
Hurghada
Wādī Ḥalfā'
Bûr Sūdān (Port Sudan)
Sawākin
Umm Durmān (Omdurman)
AL-KHARṬŪM (KHARTOUM)
Al-Kharṭūm Baḥrī
Wad Madanī
Kassalā
Atbarah
Asmera
Massawa
Keren
Aksum
Djibouti
Tropic of Cancer
Lake Nasser (Buheirat Nâṣir)
Meters / Feet
6000 19680
4000 13120
3000 9840
2000 6560
1000 3280
500 1640
200 656
Sea Level
200 656
2000 6560
0 100 200 300 400 600 800 1000 Kilometers
0 100 200 400 600 Miles
Scale 1 : 10,000,000
Lambert Conformal Conic Projection
M-600099-7A-DR2-1
Copyright © Rand McNally & Co.

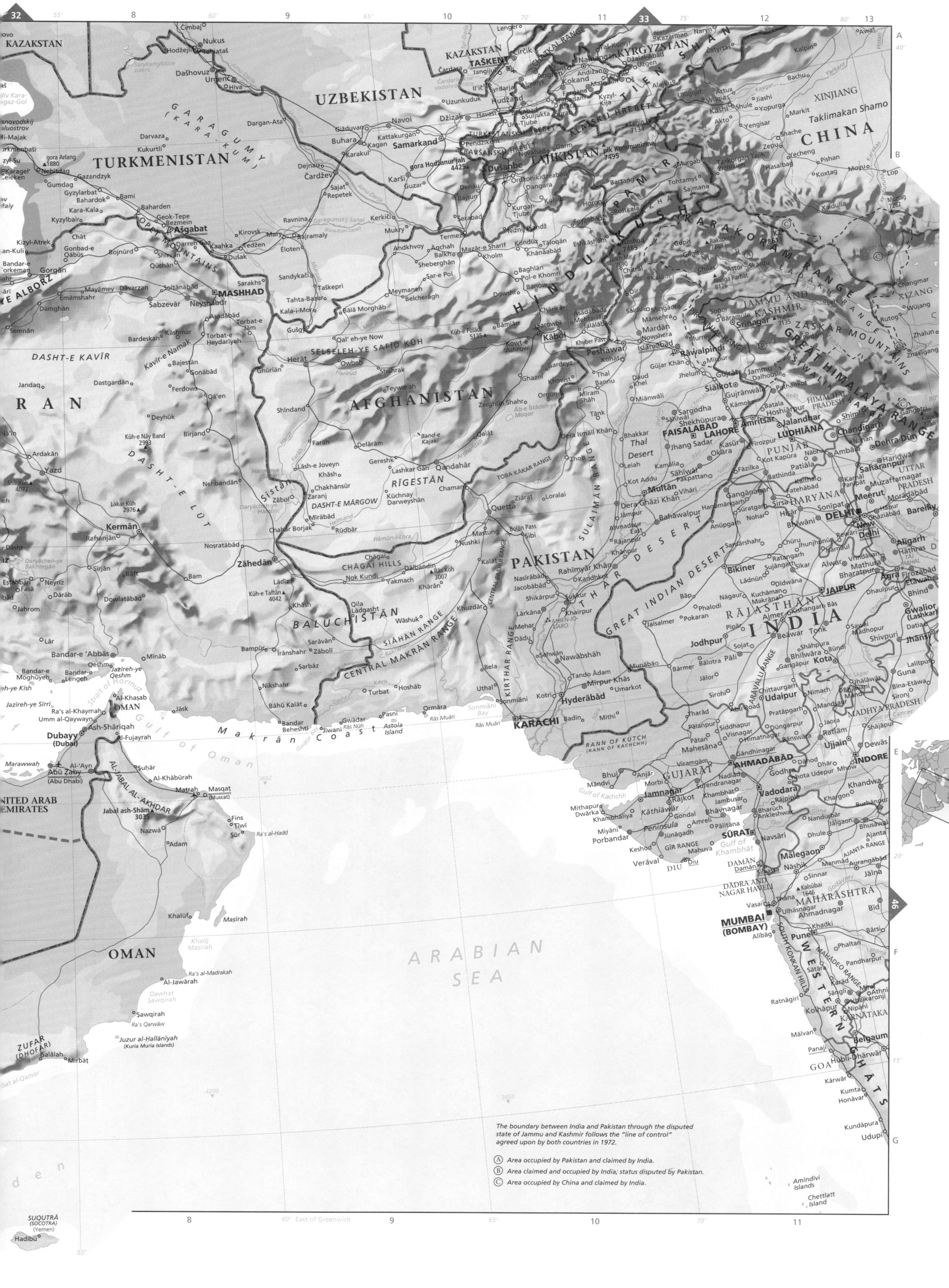

KAZAKSTAN
UZBEKISTAN
TURKMENISTAN
KYRGYZSTAN
TAJIKISTAN
AFGHANISTAN
PAKISTAN
INDIA
CHINA
XINJIANG
IRAN
OMAN
UNITED ARAB EMIRATES
ARABIAN SEA
Gulf of Oman
Makrān Coast
Taklimakan Shamo
TIEN SHAN
PAMIR
HINDU KUSH
KARAKORAM RANGE
GREAT HIMALAYA RANGE
ZASKAR MOUNTAINS
SIWALIK RANGE
JAMMU AND KASHMIR
GARAGUMY (KARA KUM)
KOPET MOUNTAINS
DASHT-E KAVĪR
DASHT-E LŪT
SELSELEH-YE SAFĪD KŪH
RĪGESTĀN
DASHT-E MĀRGOW
CHĀGAI HILLS
BALUCHISTĀN
SIĀHAN RANGE
CENTRAL MAKRĀN RANGE
TOBA KĀKAR RANGE
SULAIMĀN RANGE
KIRTHAR RANGE
THAR DESERT
GREAT INDIAN DESERT
RĀJASTHĀN
PUNJAB
HARYĀNA
HIMACHAL PRADESH
UTTAR PRADESH
MADHYA PRADESH
GUJARĀT
MAHĀRĀSHTRA
KARNĀTAKA
GOA
DIU
DAMĀN
DĀDRA AND NAGAR HAVELI
RANN OF KUTCH (RANN OF KACHCHH)
ARAVALLI RANGE
WESTERN GHATS
Gulf of Kachchh
Gulf of Khambhāt
ZUFAR (DHOFAR)
AL-JABAL AL-AKHDAR
Strait of Hormuz
Kābol
Islāmābād
Rāwalpindi
Lahore
Karāchi
Hyderābād
Quetta
Peshāwar
Multān
Faisalābād
Delhi
New Delhi
Jaipur
Ahmadābād
Mumbai (Bombay)
Pune
Vadodara
Sūrat
Indore
Ujjain
Srīnagar
Amritsar
Ludhiāna
Chandīgarh
Samarkand
Buhara
Taškent
Dušanbe
Ašgabat
Mashhad
Herāt
Qandahār
Zāhedān
Kermān
Yazd
Masqaṭ (Muscat)
Abū Ẓaby (Abu Dhabi)
Dubayy (Dubai)
Suquṭrā (Socotra) (Yemen)
Amīndīvi Islands
Chettlatt Island
Kuria Muria Islands
The boundary between India and Pakistan through the disputed state of Jammu and Kashmir follows the "line of control" agreed upon by both countries in 1972.
Ⓐ Area occupied by Pakistan and claimed by India.
Ⓑ Area claimed and occupied by India; status disputed by Pakistan.
Ⓒ Area occupied by China and claimed by India.
60° East of Greenwich

MEDITERRANEAN SEA
TURKEY
SYRIA
LEBANON
NORTH CYPRUS
CYPRUS
IRAQ
SYRIAN DESERT (BĀDIYAT ASH-SHĀM)
TOROS DAĞLARI (TAURUS MOUNTAINS)
Antalya Körfezi (Gulf of Antalya)
Antalya
Adana
İçel (Mersin)
İskenderun (Alexandretta)
Halab (Aleppo)
Gaziantep
Şanlıurfa (Urfa)
Kahramanmaraş (Maraş)
Al-Lādhiqīyah (Latakia)
Ḥamāh
Ḥims (Homs)
Ṭarṭūs
Ṭarābulus (Tripoli)
Bayrūt (Beirut)
DIMASHQ (DAMASCUS)
Nicosia (Lefkoşa) (Levkosía)
Gazimağusa (Famagusta)
Lemesós (Limassol)
Lárnax (Larnaca)
Néa Páfos (Paphos)
Girne (Kyrenia)
Hefa (Haifa)
Irbid
Ar-Raqqah
Tudmur (Palmyra)
In November 1983, Turkish Cypriots unilaterally declared their independence as the Turkish Republic of Northern Cyprus. A United Nations buffer zone now runs across the island.
Ⓐ Golan Heights area, occupied by Israel since 1967, was unilaterally annexed by Israel in 1981.
Ⓑ West Bank area has been occupied by Israel since 1967. Limited autonomy was granted to the Jericho area in 1994. The East Jerusalem portion was unilaterally annexed by Israel in 1980.
Ⓒ The Gaza Strip, occupied by Israel in 1967, was granted limited autonomy in 1994.

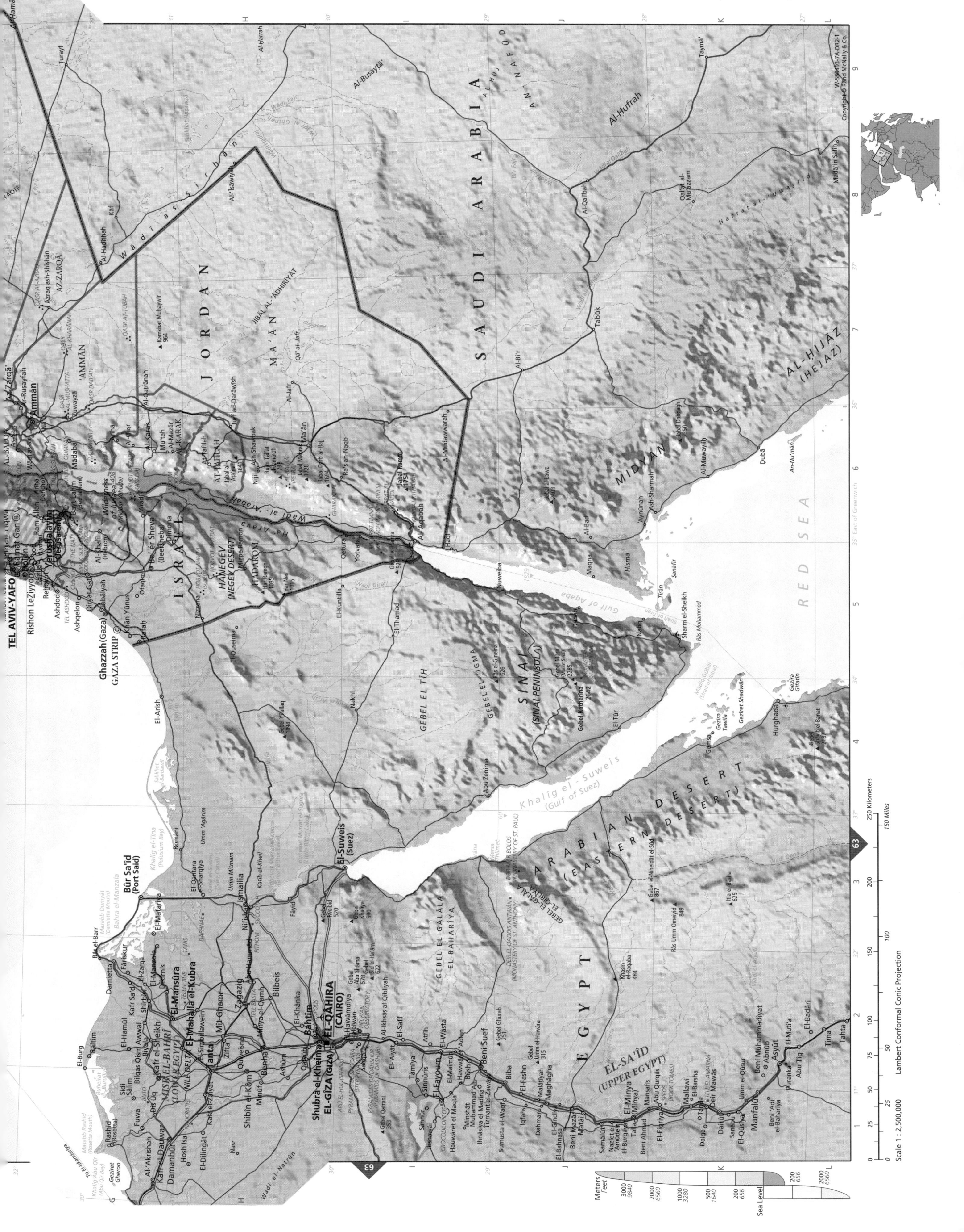

Scale 1 : 2,500,000

Lambert Conformal Conic Projection

0 25 50 75 100 150 200 250 Kilometers

0 25 50 100 150 Miles

Meters / Feet

3000 / 9840

2000 / 6560

1000 / 3280

500 / 1640

200 / 656

Sea Level

200 / 656

2000 / 6560

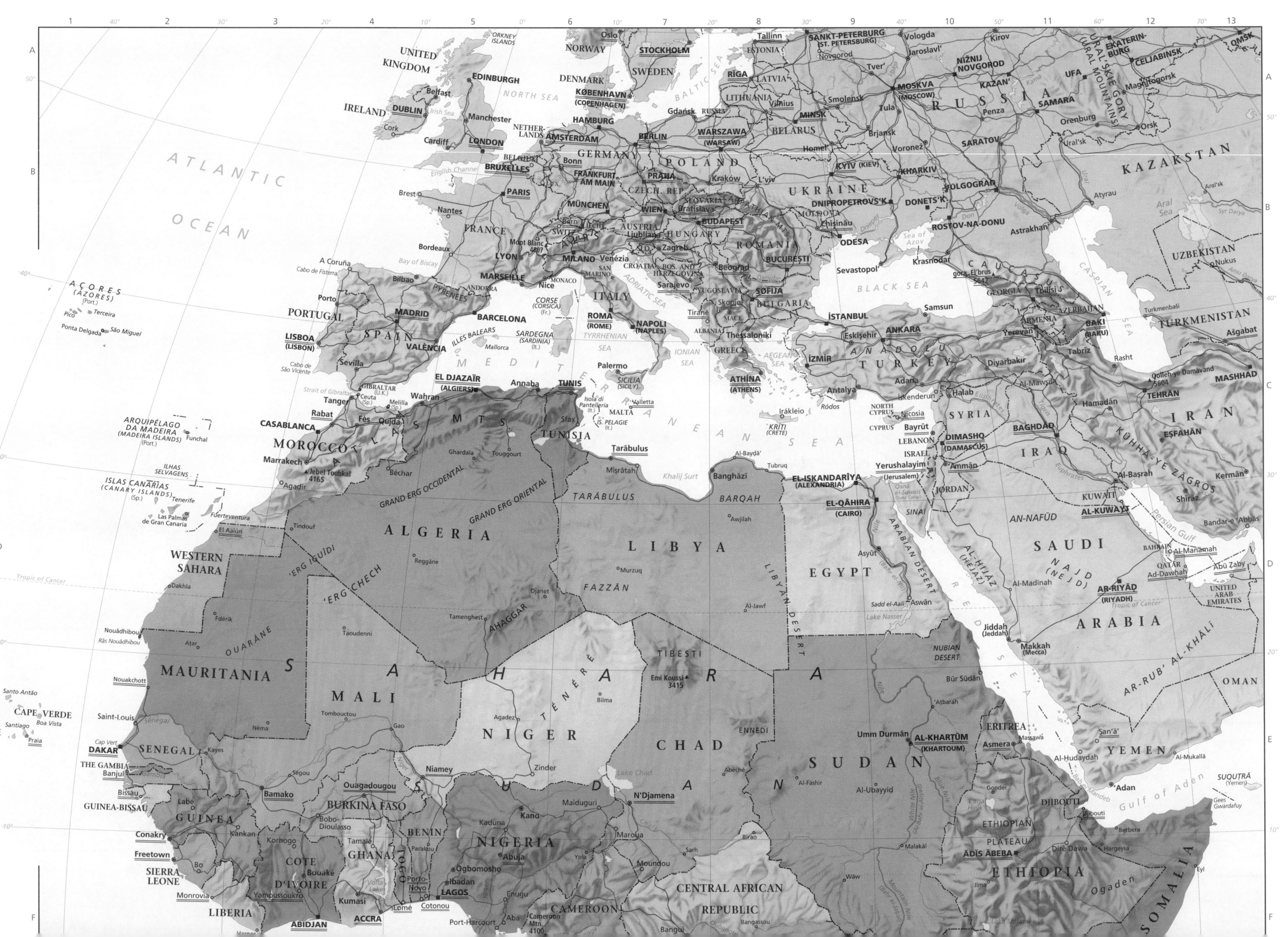
ATLANTIC OCEAN
UNITED KINGDOM
IRELAND
NORWAY
SWEDEN
DENMARK
NETHERLANDS
GERMANY
POLAND
FRANCE
SPAIN
PORTUGAL
ITALY
AUSTRIA
CZECH REP.
HUNGARY
ROMANIA
BULGARIA
GREECE
ESTONIA
LATVIA
LITHUANIA
BELARUS
UKRAINE
MOLDOVA
RUSSIA
KAZAKSTAN
UZBEKISTAN
TURKMENISTAN
GEORGIA
ARMENIA
AZERBAIJAN
TURKEY
CYPRUS
SYRIA
LEBANON
ISRAEL
JORDAN
IRAQ
IRAN
KUWAIT
SAUDI ARABIA
QATAR
UNITED ARAB EMIRATES
OMAN
YEMEN
EGYPT
LIBYA
TUNISIA
ALGERIA
MOROCCO
WESTERN SAHARA
MAURITANIA
MALI
NIGER
CHAD
SUDAN
ERITREA
DJIBOUTI
ETHIOPIA
SOMALIA
SENEGAL
THE GAMBIA
GUINEA-BISSAU
GUINEA
SIERRA LEONE
LIBERIA
CÔTE D'IVOIRE
BURKINA FASO
GHANA
TOGO
BENIN
NIGERIA
CAMEROON
CENTRAL AFRICAN REPUBLIC
CAPE VERDE
SAHARA
MEDITERRANEAN SEA
NORTH SEA
BALTIC SEA
BLACK SEA
CASPIAN SEA
RED SEA
Persian Gulf
Gulf of Aden
URAL'SKIE GORY (URAL MOUNTAINS)
AÇORES (AZORES) (Port.)
ARQUIPÉLAGO DA MADEIRA (MADEIRA ISLANDS) (Port.)
ISLAS CANARIAS (CANARY ISLANDS) (Sp.)
Tropic of Cancer

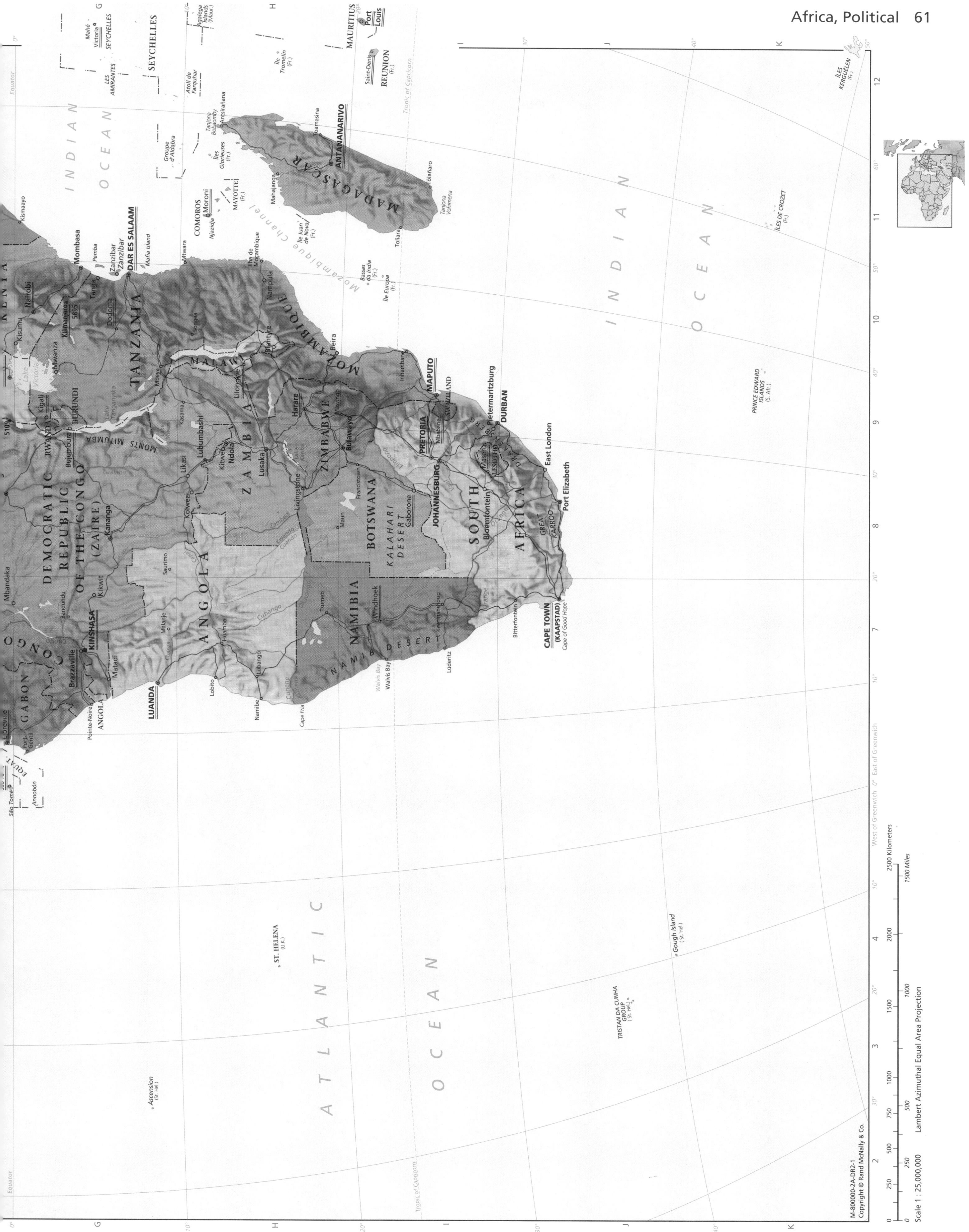

DEMOCRATIC REPUBLIC OF THE CONGO (ZAIRE)
CONGO
GABON
ANGOLA
ZAMBIA
TANZANIA
KENYA
RWANDA
BURUNDI
MALAWI
MOZAMBIQUE
ZIMBABWE
BOTSWANA
NAMIBIA
SOUTH AFRICA
LESOTHO
SWAZILAND
MADAGASCAR
COMOROS
MAYOTTE (Fr.)
SEYCHELLES
LES SEYCHELLES
LES AMIRANTES
MAURITIUS
REUNION (Fr.)
ST. HELENA (U.K.)
Ascension (St. Hel.)
TRISTAN DA CUNHA GROUP (St. Hel.)
Gough Island (St. Hel.)
PRINCE EDWARD ISLANDS (S. Afr.)
ÎLES CROZET (Fr.)
ÎLES KERGUELEN (Fr.)
Île Tromelin (Fr.)
Agalega Islands (Maur.)
Atoll de Farquhar
Groupe d'Aldabra
Îles Glorieuses (Fr.)
Île Juan de Nova (Fr.)
Bassas da India (Fr.)
Île Europa (Fr.)
Annobón
São Tomé

INDIAN OCEAN
ATLANTIC OCEAN
Mozambique Channel
KALAHARI DESERT
NAMIB DESERT
GREAT KARROO
DRAKENSBERG
MONTS MITUMBA
Lake Victoria
Lake Tanganyika
Lake Kariba
Kilimanjaro 5895
5109
Cape of Good Hope
Cape Fria
Walvis Bay
Tanjona Bobaomby
Tanjona Vohimena
Mafia Island
Pemba
Zanzibar
Equator
Tropic of Capricorn
West of Greenwich 0° East of Greenwich

LUANDA
KINSHASA
Brazzaville
Libreville
Port-Gentil
Pointe-Noire
Matadi
Mbandaka
Bandundu
Kikwit
Kananga
Kolwezi
Likasi
Lubumbashi
Kitwe
Ndola
Lusaka
Livingstone
Kasama
Mbeya
Bujumbura
Kigali
Mwanza
Kisumu
Nairobi
Mombasa
Tanga
Dodoma
DAR ES SALAAM
Kismaayo
Mtwara
Songea
Lilongwe
Blantyre
Nampula
Ilha de Moçambique
Beira
Harare
Bulawayo
Masvingo
Inhambane
MAPUTO
Mbabane
PRETORIA
JOHANNESBURG
Francistown
Maun
Gaborone
Bloemfontein
Maseru
Pietermaritzburg
DURBAN
East London
Port Elizabeth
CAPE TOWN (KAAPSTAD)
Bitterfontein
Lüderitz
Keetmanshoop
Windhoek
Tsumeb
Namibe
Lubango
Huambo
Lobito
Malanje
Saurimo
Moroni
Njazidja
Mahajanga
ANTANANARIVO
Toamasina
Antsiranana
Toliara
Tôlañaro
Victoria
Mahé
Port Louis
Saint-Denis

Zambezi
Congo
Cubango
Cuando
Okavango
Limpopo
Orange
Cunene

Scale 1 : 25,000,000
0 250 500 750 1000 1500 2000 2500 Kilometers
0 250 500 1000 1500 Miles
Lambert Azimuthal Equal Area Projection

M-800000-2A-DR2-1

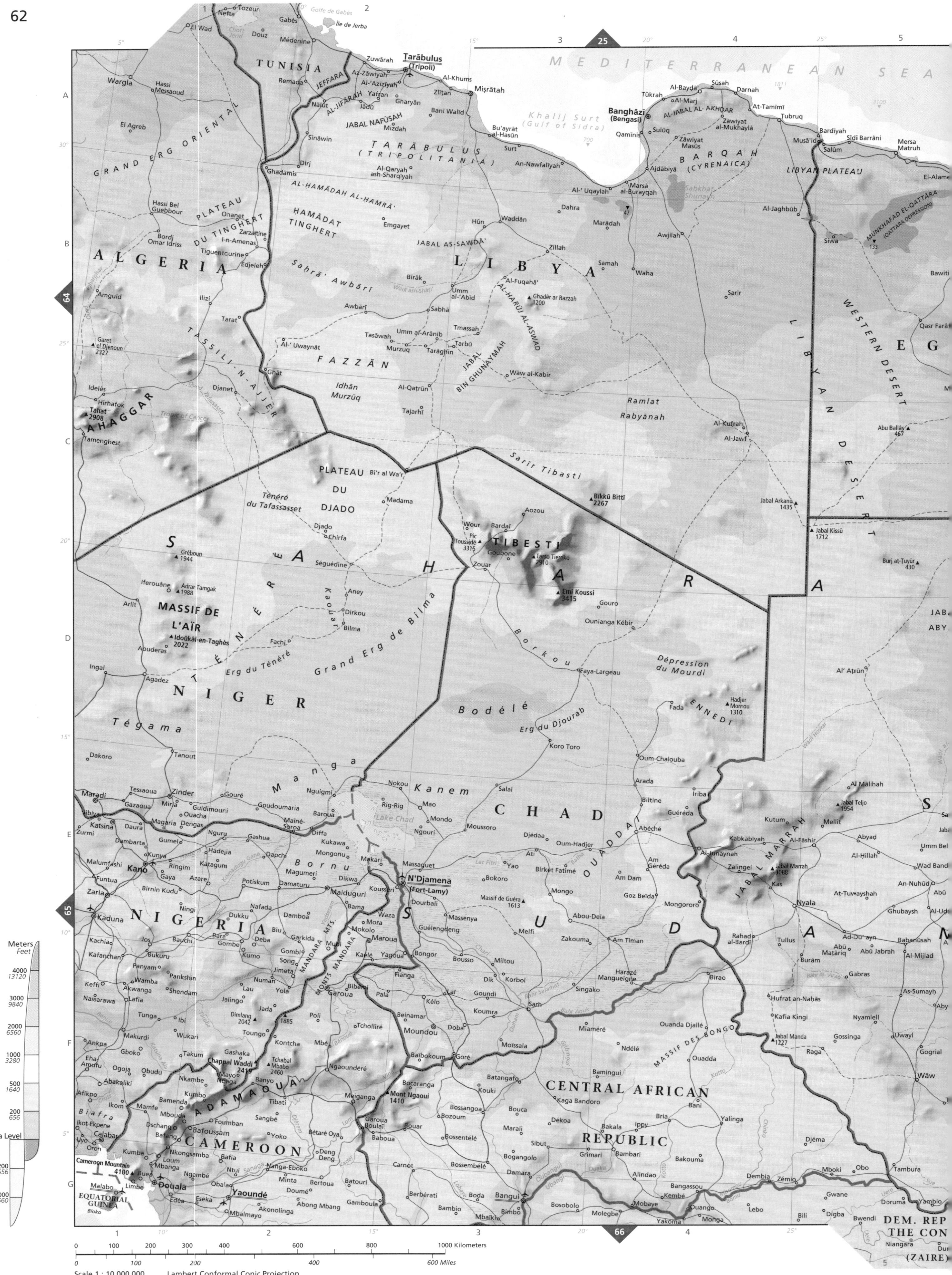
MEDITERRANEAN SEA
Golfe de Gabès
Île de Jerba
Khalīj Surt (Gulf of Sidra)
TUNISIA
Tozeur
Nefta
Gabès
Douz
Médenine
El Wad
Chott Jerid
JEFFARA
Remada
Zuwārah
Tarābulus (Tripoli)
Az-Zāwiyah
Al-'Azīziyah
Al-Khums
Zlīṭan
Miṣrātah
Nālūt
Yafran
Jādū
Gharyān
Banī Walīd
AL-JIFĀRAH
JABAL NAFŪSAH
Mizdah
Sīnāwin
Dirj
Ghadāmis
TARĀBULUS (TRIPOLITANIA)
Al-Qaryah ash-Sharqīyah
Bu'ayrāt al-Ḥasūn
Surt
An-Nawfalīyah
Al-'Uqaylah
Marsá al-Burayqah
Ajdābiyā
Banghāzī (Bengasi)
Qamīnis
Sulūq
Tūkrah
Al-Bayḍā'
Al-Marj
Sūsah
Darnah
AL-JABAL AL-AKHḌAR
At-Tamīmī
Tubruq
Zāwiyat al-Mukhaylá
Zāwiyat Masūs
BARQAH (CYRENAICA)
Sabkhat Shunayn
Bardīyah
Musā'id
Salūm
Sīdī Barrānī
Mersa Matruh
El-Alamein
LIBYAN PLATEAU
Al-Jaghbūb
Siwa
MUNKHAFAD EL-QATTARA (QATTARA DEPRESSION)
133
Bawiti
Wargla
Hassi Messaoud
GRAND ERG ORIENTAL
El Agreb
ALGERIA
Hassi Bel Guebbour
Ohanet
PLATEAU DU TINGHERT
Bordj Omar Idriss
Zarzaitine
I-n-Amenas
Tiguentourine
Edjeleh
Amguid
Illizi
Tarat
TASSILI-N-AJJER
Garet el Djenoun 2327
Idelès
Hirhafok
Tahat 2908
AHAGGAR
Tamenghest
Tropic of Cancer
Djanet
Ghāt
AL-ḤAMĀDAH AL-ḤAMRĀ'
ḤAMĀDAT TINGHERT
Emgayet
Hūn
Waddān
Dahra
Marādah
Awjilah
JABAL AS-SAWDĀ'
Zillah
LIBYA
Samah
Waha
Birāk
Umm al-'Abīd
Al-Fuqahā'
AL-HARŪJ AL-ASWAD
Ghadēr ar Razzah 1200
Ṣaḥrā' Awbārī
Awbārī
Sabhā
Tmassah
Umm al-Arānib
Tasāwah
Al-'Uwaynāt
Murzuq
Tarbū
Tarāghin
JABAL BIN GHUNAYMAH
FAZZĀN
Wāw al-Kabīr
Idhān Murzūq
Al-Qaṭrūn
Tajarhī
Ramlat Rabyānah
Al-Kufrah
Al-Jawf
Sarīr
LIBYAN DESERT
WESTERN DESERT
Qasr Farâfra
Abu Ballâs 467
Jabal Arkanū 1435
Jabal Kissū 1712
Burj at-Tuyūr 430
EGYPT
Sarīr Tibasti
Bikkū Bittī 2267
PLATEAU DU DJADO
Bi'r al Wa'r
Madama
Ténéré du Tafassasset
Djado
Chirfa
Aozou
Bardaï
Wour
Pic Toussidé 3315
TIBESTI
Tarso Tieroko 2910
Goubone
Zouar
Emi Koussi 3415
Gouro
Ounianga Kébir
SAHARA
Gréboun 1944
Iferouāne
Adrar Tamgak 1988
Arlit
MASSIF DE L'AÏR
Idoûkâl-en-Taghès 2022
Abuderas
Séguédine
Aney
Dirkou
Bilma
Kaouar
Fachi
TÉNÉRÉ
Erg du Ténéré
Grand Erg de Bilma
Ingal
Agadez
NIGER
Tégama
Borkou
Faya-Largeau
Dépression du Mourdi
Bodélé
Erg du Djourab
Fada
ENNEDI
Hadjer Morrou 1310
Koro Toro
Oum-Chalouba
Al' Atrūn
Dakoro
Tanout
Manga
Kanem
Maradi
Tessaoua
Zinder
Gouré
Goudoumaria
Nguigmi
Nokou
Rig-Rig
Mao
Lake Chad
Mondo
Ngouri
Moussoro
Salal
CHAD
Arada
Iriba
Biltine
Guéréda
Abéché
OUADDAÏ
Al Māliḥah
Jabal Teljo 1954
Kutum
Mellit
Kabkābīyah
Al-Fāshir
JABAL MARRAH
Jabal Marrah 3088
Al-Junaynah
Zalingei
Kas
Nyala
Abyad
Al-Ḥillah
Umm Bel
Wad Banda
An-Nuhūd
Abū
Aṭ-Ṭuwayshah
Ghubaysh
Ad-Du'ayn
Babanūsah
Al-Mijlad
Abū Maṭāriq
Abū Jabrah
Burām
Gabras
Tullus
As-Sumayh
Rahad al-Bardi
Hufrat an-Naḥās
Kafia Kingi
Nyamlell
Jabal Manda 1227
Gossinga
Uwayl
Raga
Gogrial
Wāw
Katsina
Daura
Magaria
Mirria
Guidimouri
Ouacha
Dengas
Maïné-Soroa
Diffa
Barouà
Zurmi
Dambarta
Gumel
Nguru
Gashua
Kukawa
Mongonu
Kunya
Hadejia
Malumfashi
Kano
Ringim
Katagum
Dapchi
Bornu
Magumeri
Makari
Massaguet
N'Djamena (Fort-Lamy)
Dikwa
Gaya
Azare
Potiskum
Damaturu
Maiduguri
Kousseri
Dourbali
Funtua
Zaria
Birnin Kudu
Ningi
Nafada
Bama
Massenya
Kaduna
NIGERIA
Dukku
Damboa
Waza
Mora
Mokolo
Maroua
Guélengdeng
Kachia
Jos
Bauchi
Bara
Gombe
Deba
Biu
Garkida
Gombi
Song
Kumo
Jimeta
Numan
Yola
MANDARA MTS.
MONTS MANDARA
Kaélé
Yagoua
Bongor
Bousso
Miltou
Dik
Korbol
Kafanchan
Bukuru
Panyam
Pankshin
Wamba
Akwanga
Shendam
Keffi
Nassarawa
Lafia
Lau
Jalingo
Jada
Dimlang 2042
1885
Tunga
Ibi
Wukari
Makurdi
Takum
Toungo
Kontcha
Poli
Tchollire
Garoua
Bibemi
Pala
Fianga
Kélo
Lai
Goundi
Koumra
Beinamar
Moundou
Doba
Sarh
Moïssala
Goré
Baïbokoum
Ankpa
Gboko
Eha-Amufu
Ogoja
Obudu
Abakaliki
Afikpo
Ikom
Mamfe
Kumbo
Nkambe
Chappal Waddi 2419
Gashaka
Mayo Ncaga
Tchabal Mbabo 2460
Banyo
Ngaoundéré
Meiganga
ADAMAOUA
Tibati
Bocaranga
Mont Ngaoui 1410
Bamenda
Mbouda
Dschang
Bafoussam
Foumban
Bangangté
Batang
Sangbé
Yoko
Bétaré Oya
Garoua Boulaï
Babaoua
Bouar
Kumba
Nkongsamba
Bafia
Loum
CAMEROON
Deng Deng
Ngambé
Ntui
Nanga-Eboko
Minta
Bertoua
Batouri
Douala
Edéa
Eséka
Yaoundé
Mbalmayo
Akonolinga
Doumé
Abong Mbang
Gamboula
Berbérati
Carnot
Bambio
Boda
Mbaïki
Bangui
Bimbo
Cameroon Mountain 4100
Buea
Limbe
Malabo
Bioko
EQUATORIAL GUINEA
Ikot-Ekpene
Calabar
Uyo
Oron
Biafra
CENTRAL AFRICAN REPUBLIC
Kaga Bandoro
Batangafo
Kouki
Bossangoa
Bozoum
Bouca
Dékoa
Marali
Sibut
Bossentélé
Bogangolo
Bossembélé
Damara
Grimari
Bambari
Bakala
Ippy
Bria
Yalinga
Bani
Ndélé
Ouadda
MASSIF DES BONGO
Ouanda Djallé
Miamére
Bamingui
Birao
Harazé Mangueigne
Singako
Bahr Salamat
Am Timan
Abou-Deïa
Zakouma
Mongo
Melfi
Massif de Guéra 1613
Bokoro
Yao
Ati
Djédaa
Oum-Hadjer
Birket Fatimé
Am Dam
Am Géréda
Goz Beïda
Mongororo
Lac Fitri
SUDAN
Djéma
Bakouma
Alindao
Bangassou
Kembé
Mobaye
Ouango
Monga
Yakoma
Mbomou
Dembia
Zémio
Mboki
Obo
Tambura
Gwane
Lebo
Bili
Digba
Bwendi
Doruma
Yambio
Niangara
DEM. REP. OF THE CONGO (ZAIRE)
Bosobolo
Molegbe
Meters Feet
4000 13120
3000 9840
2000 6560
1000 3280
500 1640
200 656
Sea Level
200 656
2000 6560
0 100 200 300 400 600 800 1000 Kilometers
0 100 200 400 600 Miles
Scale 1 : 10,000,000
Lambert Conformal Conic Projection
25
64
65
66
1 2 3 4 5
A B C D E F G

LEBANON
SYRIA
IRAQ
JORDAN
ISRAEL
KUWAIT
BAHRAIN
QATAR
UNITED ARAB EMIRATES
OMAN
SAUDI ARABIA
YEMEN
ERITREA
DJIBOUTI
ETHIOPIA
SOMALIA
KENYA
UGANDA
IRAN
DIMASHQ (DAMASCUS)
BAGHDĀD
EŞFAHĀN
AL-KUWAYT (KUWAIT)
AR-RIYĀD (RIYADH)
Al-Manāmah (Manama)
Ad-Dawhah (Doha)
EL-QÂHIRA (CAIRO)
EL-GÎZA (GIZA)
Yerushalayim (Jerusalem)
TEL AVIV-YAFO
'Ammān
Bûr Sa'îd (Port Said)
El-Suweis (Suez)
Makkah (Mecca)
Jiddah (Jeddah)
Al-Madīnah (Medina)
Bûr Sûdân (Port Sudan)
Umm Durmān (Omdurman)
AL-KHARŢŪM (KHARTOUM)
Asmera
Şan'ā'
'Adan (Aden)
Djibouti
ĀDĪS ĀBEBA (ADDIS ABABA)
Dirē Dawa
Hargeysa
Berbera
Aswân
El-Uqsor (Luxor)
Al-Başrah
Shīrāz
SYRIAN DESERT
AN-NAFŪD
ARABIAN DESERT
NUBIAN DESERT
ARABIAN PENINSULA
AR-RUB' AL-KHĀLĪ
AL-HIJAZ (HEJAZ)
NAJD (NEJD)
'ASĪR
HADRAMAWT
MESOPOTAMIA
KŪHHĀ-YE ZAGROS
ETHIOPIAN PLATEAU
DANAKIL
RIFT VALLEY
Ogaden
RED SEA
Persian Gulf
Gulf of Aden
INDIAN OCEAN
Lake Nasser
Lake Rudolf (Lake Turkana)
Tropic of Cancer
45° East of Greenwich
M-800096-7A-DR2-1
Copyright © Rand McNally & Co.

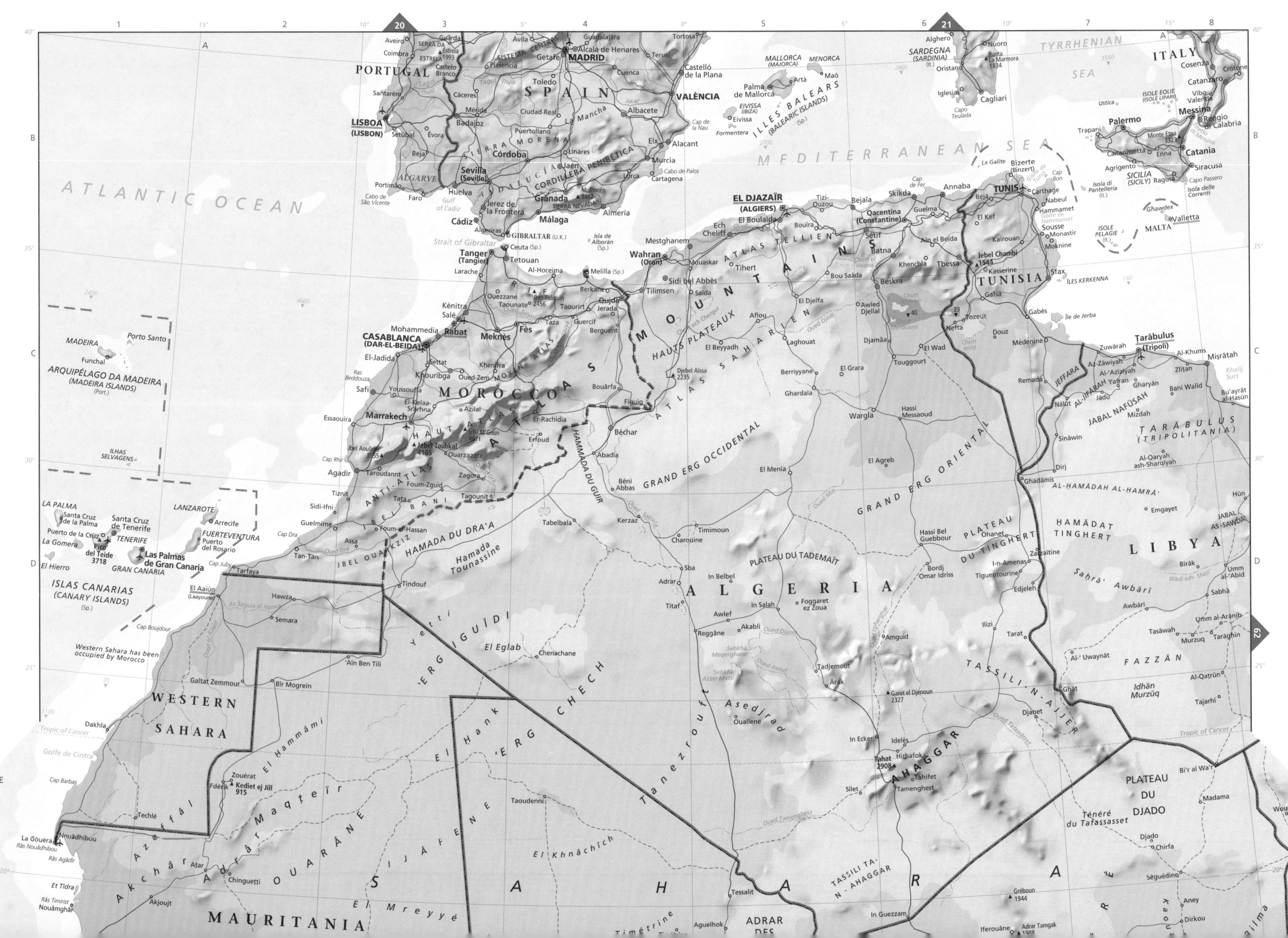

ATLANTIC OCEAN
MEDITERRANEAN SEA
TYRRHENIAN SEA
PORTUGAL
LISBOA (LISBON)
SPAIN
MADRID
VALÈNCIA
ITALY
SARDEGNA (SARDINIA) (It.)
SICILIA (SICILY)
MALTA
Valletta
ILLES BALEARS (BALEARIC ISLANDS) (Sp.)
MALLORCA (MAJORCA)
MENORCA
EIVISSA (IBIZA)
GIBRALTAR (U.K.)
Strait of Gibraltar
MOROCCO
Rabat
CASABLANCA (DAR-EL-BEIDA)
Marrakech
Fès
Meknès
Tanger (Tangier)
ALGERIA
EL DJAZAÏR (ALGIERS)
Wahran (Oran)
Qacentina (Constantine)
TUNISIA
TUNIS
LIBYA
Tarābulus (Tripoli)
WESTERN SAHARA
Western Sahara has been occupied by Morocco
El Aaiún (Laayoune)
MAURITANIA
ISLAS CANARIAS (CANARY ISLANDS) (Sp.)
ARQUIPÉLAGO DA MADEIRA (MADEIRA ISLANDS) (Port.)
Funchal
Las Palmas de Gran Canaria
Santa Cruz de Tenerife
Pico del Teide 3718
ILHAS SELVAGENS
ATLAS TELLIEN
HAUTS PLATEAUX
HAUT ATLAS
ANTI-ATLAS
Jebel Toubkal 4165
GRAND ERG OCCIDENTAL
GRAND ERG ORIENTAL
HAMMADA DU GUIR
HAMADA DU DRA'A
PLATEAU DU TADEMAÏT
TASSILI-N-AJJER
AHAGGAR
Tahat 2908
SAHARA
PLATEAU DU DJADO
FAZZĀN
Tropic of Cancer

a Same scale as main map

CAPE VERDE

Scale 1 : 10,000,000

Lambert Conformal Conic Projection

0 100 200 300 400 600 800 1000 Kilometers

0 100 200 400 600 Miles

Meters / Feet

4000 / 13120

3000 / 9840

2000 / 6560

1000 / 3280

500 / 1640

200 / 656

Sea Level

200 / 656

2000 / 6560

M-800097-7A-DR2-1

62
65
68
NIGER
CHAD
NIGERIA
CAMEROON
CENTRAL AFRICAN REPUBLIC
EQUATORIAL GUINEA
SAO TOME AND PRINCIPE
GABON
CONGO
DEMOCRATIC REPUBLIC OF THE CONGO (ZAIRE)
ANGOLA
SUDAN
ATLANTIC OCEAN
Gulf of Guinea
Bight of Biafra
Biafra
BIOKO
Príncipe
São Tomé
Lake Chad
Kanem
Manga
Bornu
MANDARA MTS.
ADAMAOUA
OUADDAI
JABAL MARRAH
MASSIF DES BONGO
MONTS DE CRISTAL
PLATEAUX BATÉKÉ
CONGO BASIN
KATANGA
MONTS MITUMBA
N'Djamena (Fort-Lamy)
Bangui
Yaoundé
Douala
Malabo
Libreville
Brazzaville
KINSHASA (LÉOPOLDVILLE)
LUANDA
Kisangani (Stanleyville)
Mbandaka (Coquilhatville)
Kananga (Luluabourg)
Mbuji-Mayi (Bakwanga)
Lubumbashi (Élisabethville)
Likasi (Jadotville)
Kolwezi
Kano
Kaduna
Zaria
Maiduguri
Garoua
Ngaoundéré
Port-Harcourt
Calabar
Enugu
Port-Gentil
Pointe-Noire
Cabinda
Matadi
Boma
Lobito
Benguela
Huambo
Kitwe
Cameroon Mtn. 4100
Pico de Santa Isabel 3008
Mont Ngaoui 1410
Morro de Môco 2620
Jabal Marrah 3088
PARC NATIONAL DE LA SALONGA
PARQUE NACIONAL DA QUIÇAMA
Meters / Feet
4000 13120
3000 9840
2000 6560
1000 3280
500 1640
200 656
Sea Level
200 656
2000 6560
M-80095-7A-DR2-1
Copyright © Rand McNally & Co.
0 100 200 300 400 600 800 1000 Kilometers
0 100 200 400 600 Miles
Scale 1 : 10,000,000 Sinusoidal Projection

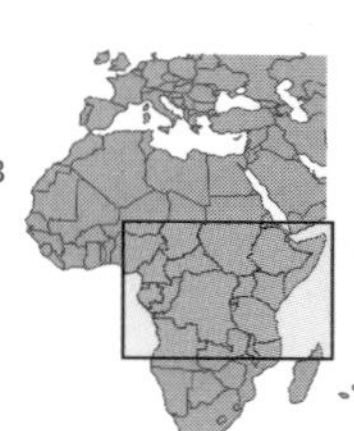

6 35° 7 40° 63 8 45° 9 50° 10

A B C D E F G

RED SEA
Asmera
ERITREA
Soira 2989
Adi Ugri
Teseney
Khashm al-Qirbah
Jabal al-Awliyā
Al-Qutaynah
Rufā'ah
Umm Sayyālah
Wad Madanī
Kagmar
Ad-Duwaym
Al-Jazīrah
Al-Kawah
Shuwak
Al-Qaḍārif
Aksum
Adigrat
Adwa
Ramlu 2130
125 Kobar Sink
Danakil
Kamarān
Jabal an-Nabī Shu'ayb 3660
Ṣan'ā'
Al-Ḥudaydah (Hodeida)
Tio
Bayt al-Faqih
Zabīd
Dhamār
Yarīm
Ibb
Jabal ad-Hasha' 3227
Ta'izz
Lahij
Al-Mukhā
Madīnat ash-Sha'b
Shaykh 'Uthmān
Adan (Aden)
HANĪSH
Barīm
Bab el Mandeb
Harib
Shabwah
'Amd
Qishn
Sayhūt
YEMEN
Niṣāb
Ḥabbān
Lawdar
Shaqrā'
Aḥwar
Al-Hawrah
Ash-Shiḥr
Al-Mukallā
As-Sufāl
Gulf of Aden
Bārah
Sannār
Darāfisah
Kūstī
Rabak
Sinjah
Al-Ḥawātah
Umm Ruwābah
Tandaltī
Ar-Rahad
Al-Jabalayn
Qallābāt
Gonder
Dabat
Ras Dashen Terara 4620
Mek'elē
Azezo
Sek'ot'a
Lalibela
K'obo
Weldiya
Tana Hāyk'
Bahir Dar
Debre Tabor
Mot'a
Amba Farīt 3975
Dese
ETHIOPIAN PLATEAU
CH'OK'E
Debre Mark'os
Rashād
Abū Jubayhah
Dalāmī
Ar-Rank
Ar-Ruṣayriṣ
Abu Mendi
Guba
Dangila
Agalak
Kaka
Kurmuk
Paloich
Talawdī
Tungaru
Malakāl
Kodok
Āsosa
Mendī
Bambesi
Beigi
Gimbī
Debre Sīna
Debre Birhan
Fichē
Āsendabo
Shambu
Tulu Welel 3001
Dembī Dolo
Nek'emtē
Āk'ak'ī Besek'a
ĀDĪS ĀBEBA (ADDIS ABEBA)
Debre Zeyit
Giyon
Mojo
Nazrēt
Welk'itē
Bedelē
Gorē
Gambēla
Tor
Akūbū
Jīma
Dembī
Mai Gudo 3100
Hosa'ina
Āsela
Shashemenē
Mizan Teferī
Wakā
Sodo
Awasa
Yirga'Alem
Agere Selam
Dīla
Gugē 4200
Arba Minch'
Bako
Ch'amo Hāyk'
Batu 4307
MENDEBO
Ādaba
Goba
Ginir
Lega Hida
Kibre Mengist
Negēlē
Filtu
Wabera
Denan
Īmī
Ēl Kerē
K'ebri Dehar
Werdēr
Shilabo
K'elafo
Mustahīl
ETHIOPIA
RIFT VALLEY
Āwash
Hārer
AHMAR MOUNTAINS
Jijiga
Dirē Dawa
Aysha
Trena
Lake Abe
Tendaho
Serdo
Moussa 'Ali 2021
Tadjoura
Obock
DJIBOUTI
Djibouti
Dikhil
Saylac
Berbera
Bullaxaar
Burco
Hargeysa
Caynabo
Degeh Bur
Āwarē
Sasabeneh
Daga Medo
El Fud
Ogaden
Domo
Geladī
Laascaanood
Garoowe
Eyl
Qooriga Neegro
Beyra
Gaalkacyo
Daborow
Dhuusamarreeb
Hobyo
Xalin
Bandarbeyla
Qardho
Maydh
Raas Surud
Raas Khansiir
Karin
Shimbiris 2407
Ceerigaabo
Boosaaso
Qandala
Baxaya 2200
Caluula
Gees Gwardafuy
Bargaal
Meeladeen
Hurdiyo
Raas Xaafuun
Xaafuun
Sudd
Fangak
Bentiu
Abwong
Daga Post
Nyerol
Nāṣir
Mogogh
Ayod
Duk Fadiat
Shambe
Kongor
Pibor Post
Yirol
Bor
Malik
Nelichu 1740
Tombe
Mongalla
Juba
Ngangala
Kapoeta
Yei
Torit
Jabal Lotuke 2795
Kinyeti 3187
Lokichokio
Lokitaung
Sabarei
Mēga
Moyale
Lake Rudolf (Lake Turkana)
North Horr
Chalbi Desert
Lodwar
Lokichar
Ng'iro 2805
South Horr
Marsabit
Baragoi
Laisamis
Kajo Kaji
Nimule
Atiak
Kitgum
Kaabong
Loyoro
Kotido
Arua
Gulu
Patonga
Moroto 3084
Okollo
Pakwach
Lira
Moroto
Amudat
Mahagi
Djugu
Butiaba
UGANDA
Masindi
Hoima
Soroti
Bunia
Nakasongola
Mount Elgon 4321
Mbale
Kaliro
Iganga
Tororo
Fort Portal
Mubende
Kampala
Jinja
Busia
Entebbe
Margherita Peak
Kasese
Lake George
Masaka
Bugala Island
Sese Islands
Lake Victoria
Kome Island
Rusinga Island
Mfangano Island
Homa Bay
Kisii
Kisumu
Kakamega
Butere
Eldoret
Chepkotet 3370
Kitale
Bungoma
Maralal
Lake Baringo
Solai
Nanyuki
Nyeri
Kirinyaga (Mount Kenya) 5199
Meru
Isiolo
Archer's Post
Merti
Mado Gashi
Tana
Garissa
Embu
Thika
Kitui
Kaningo
Bura
KENYA
Nakuru
Gilgil
Naivasha
Narok
NAIROBI
MASAI MARA GAME RESERVE
Kericho
Ngong
Kajiado
Machakos
Konza
Magadi
Namanga
Makindu
AMBOSELI NATIONAL PARK
Lake Amboseli
Kilimanjaro 5895
Moshi
Arusha
Taveta
Voi
Tsavo
Lugards Falls
Galana
Garsen
Lamu
Pate Island
Manda Island
Kipini
Raas Ngomeni
Malindi
Mariakani
Mackinnon Road
Mombasa
Kyaka
Bukoba
Ukara Island
Ukerewe Island
Rubondo Island
Musoma
Utegi
SERENGETI NATIONAL PARK
Ushashi
Serengeti Plain
Speke Gulf
Nyahanga
Loliondo
OLDUVAI GORGE
Lake Natron
Loolmalassin 3648
NGORONGORO CRATER CONSERVATION AREA
Ngorongoro Crater 3188
Lake Eyasi
Lake Manyara
Biharamulo
Mwanza
Ngara
Nyakanazi
Geita
Mwadui
Shinyanga
Kibondo
Kahama
Isaka
Lake Kitangiri
Mkalama
Kinyangiri
Bukene
Masai Steppe
Same
Lushoto
Kondoa
Singida
Tabora
Kaliua
Malagarasi
Usoke
Issuna
Kibaya
Korogwe
Wete
Tanga
Chake Chake
Pemba
Pangani
Lake Tanganyika
Sikonge
Ikungu
Manyoni
Meia Meia
Dodoma
Mpwapwa
Mkokotoni
Zanzibar
Zanzibar Channel
Kizimkazi
Bagamoyo
Morogoro
DAR ES SALAAM
TANZANIA
Mpanda
Uruwira
Inyonga
Karema
Kitunda
Rungwa
Kilosa
Kipili
Namanyere
Kipembawe
Great Ruaha
Mikumi
Kisiju
Mafia Island
Kilindoni
Iringa
Kidatu
Rufiji
Sumbawanga
Kasanga
Mpui
Makongolosi
Mgeta
Ifakara
Utete
Chunya
Usangu Flats
Sao Hill
Mbeya
Mkulwe
Mbala
Mpulungu
Mahenge
Njinjo
Kilwa Kivinje
Kilwa Masoko
Tukuyu
Mdandu
Njombe
KIPENGERE RANGE
Nakonde
Karonga
Chitipa
Zinga Mulike
Liwale
Lindi
Mbwemkuru
Isoka
Kasama
Nyika Plateau 2606
Chilumba
Chinsali
Livingstonia
Nyamtumbo
Nachingwea
Mikindani
Mtwara
Mtama
Masasi
Newala
Cabo Delgado
Palma
Rovuma
Manda
Songea
Mbinga
Mbamba Bay
Tunduru
Rumphi
Mzuzu
Nkhata Bay
Chitambo
Mpika
Chamba
Olivenèa
Cóbuè
Diaca
Quiterajo
Mueda
Mecula
Macomia
Mucojo
Quissanga
Lundazi
Lake Nyasa
Luangwa
Lugenda
Metangula
Nkhotakota
MOZAMBIQUE
Nantulo
Ancuabe
Montepuez
Marrupa
Pemba
Balama
Lúrio
Namapa
Niassa
Lichinga
Maúa
Muite
MALAWI
Chipata
Mchinji
Salima
Lilongwe
Katete
MUCHINGA MOUNTAINS
RIFT VALLEY
Ilemba
Wak
Doolow
Luuq
Ramu
Mandera
Lema Shilindi
Beledweyne
Ceelbuur
Xarardheere
SOMALIA
Totiyas
Waajid
Buulobarde
Ceeldheere
Mereeg
Baydhabo (Baidoa)
Buurhakaba
Weyne
Jawhar
Baardheere
Diinsor
Balcad
Afgooye
Muqdisho (Mogadiscio)
Dhoomadheere
Marka
Dujuuma
Shabeelle
Baraawe
Lak Dera
Afmadow
Jilib
Kamsuuma
Jamaame
Jumba
Kismaayo
Dif
Wajir
Lak Bor
Buna
El Wak
Kolbio
Buur Gaabo
Kiunga
Raas Jumbo
Equator
INDIAN OCEAN
SEYCHELLES
Groupe d'Aldabra
Assomption
Atoll de Cosmoledo
Astove
Atoll de Providence
St. Pierre
Atoll de Farquhar
COMOROS
Njazidja
Moroni
Kartala 2361
Nzwani
Mwali
Fomboni
Mutsamudu
Dzaoudzi
MAYOTTE (Fr.)
ARCHIPEL DES COMORES
Îles Glorieuses (Fr.)
Tanjona Bobaomby
Antsirañana
Nosy Mitsio
Ambohitra 1475
Nosy Be
Andoany
Ambilobe
Iharaña
Ambanja
MADAGASCAR
Maromokotro 2876

CONGO
ANGOLA
DEMOCRATIC REPUBLIC OF THE CONGO (ZAIRE)
ZAMBIA
NAMIBIA
BOTSWANA
SOUTH AFRICA
LESOTHO
ATLANTIC OCEAN
LUANDA
Windhoek
Gaborone
PRETORIA
JOHANNESBURG
Bloemfontein
CAPE TOWN (KAAPSTAD)
Port Elizabeth
Lusaka
Lubumbashi (Élisabethville)
Kolwezi
Mbuji-Mayi (Bakwanga)
Matadi
OVAMBOLAND
DAMARALAND
GREAT NAMAQUALAND
NAMIB DESERT
KALAHARI DESERT
KAOKOVELD
BUSHMAN LAND
LITTLE NAMAQUALAND
GREAT KARROO
LITTLE KARROO
Caprivi Strip
Okavango Delta
Etosha Pan
Tropic of Capricorn
Cape of Good Hope
Kaap Agulhas
Walvis Bay
Lüderitz
Swakopmund
Morro de Moco 2620
Brandberg 2579
East of Greenwich
Meters
Feet
3000
9840
2000
6560
1000
3280
500
1640
200
656
Sea Level
200
656
2000
6560
0
100
200
300
400
600
800
1000 Kilometers
0
100
200
400
600 Miles
Scale 1 : 10,000,000
Lambert Conformal Conic Projection
M-800092-7A-DR2-1

INDIAN OCEAN
TANZANIA
DAR ES SALAAM
Zanzibar
MOZAMBIQUE
MALAWI
MADAGASCAR
ANTANANARIVO
COMOROS
Moroni
ARCHIPEL DES COMORES
MAYOTTE (Fr.)
SEYCHELLES
Mozambique Channel
MAPUTO
DURBAN
Beira
Nampula
Quelimane
Toamasina
Mahajanga
Toliara
Antsiranana
Same scale as main map
MAURITIUS
Port Louis
REUNION (Fr.)
Saint-Denis
MASCARENE ISLANDS
LES AMIRANTES
Victoria
Mahé
Groupe d'Aldabra
Tropic of Capricorn
55° East of Greenwich
50° East of Greenwich

68
KAOKO VELD
KUNENE
Skeleton Coast
OTJOZONDJUPA
DAMARALAND
ERONGO
OMAHEKE
KHOMAS
Khomas Hochland
NAMIBIA
NAMIB-NAUKLUFT PARK
HARDAP
GREAT NAMAQUALAND (GROOT NAMALAND)
Schwarz-rand
NAMIB DESERT
HUIB-HOCH PLATEAU
KARAS
HUNSBERGE
GROOT KARASBERGE
NGAMILAND
MAKGADIKGADI PANS GAME RESERVE
GHANZI
CENTRAL KALAHARI GAME RESERVE
BOTS
KUTSE GAME RESERVE
KWENEN
KALAHARI
KGALAGADI
DESERT
GEMSBOK NATIONAL PARK
MABUASEHUBE GAME RESERVE
KALAHARI GEMSBOK NATIONAL PARK
BECHUANALAND
KURUMANHEUWELS
Ghaap plato
GRIQUALAND WEST
AUGRABIES FALLS NATIONAL PARK
LITTLE NAMAQUALAND (KLEIN NAMALAND)
BUSHMAN LAND
SOUTH A
NORTHERN CAPE
ASBESBERGE
ROGGEVELDBERGE
NUWEVELDBERGE
KAROO NATIONAL PARK
GREAT KARROO
GROOT KARROO
WESTERN CAPE
GROOT-SWARTBERGE
LITTLE KARROO (KLEIN KAROO)
LANGEBERG
KOUGABERGE
BONTEBOK NATIONAL PARK
ATLANTIC OCEAN
Tropic of Capricorn
Windhoek
Swakopmund
Walvis Bay (Walvisbaai)
Lüderitz
Keetmanshoop
Upington
Kimberley
CAPE TOWN (KAAPSTAD)
Cape of Good Hope (Kaap die Goeie Hoop)
Kaap Agulhas
Mosselbaai (Mossel Bay)
Meters Feet
3000 9840
2000 6560
1000 3280
500 1640
200 656
Sea Level
200 656
2000 6560
0 100 200 300 400 600 800 1000 Kilometer
0 100 200 400 600 Miles
Scale 1 : 5,000,000
Lambert Conformal Conic Projection
20° East of Greenwich

ZIMBABWE
MOZAMBIQUE
SWAZILAND
LESOTHO
MATABELELAND NORTH
MATABELELAND SOUTH
MIDLANDS
MASVINGO
MANICA
SOFALA
GAZA
INHAMBANE
CENTRAL
NORTHERN
GAUTENG
MPUMALANGA
KWAZULU-NATAL
FREE STATE
EASTERN CAPE
DRAKENSBERG
LEBOMBO MOUNTAINS
SOUTPANSBERG
WATERBERGE
WITWATERSRAND
TRANSKEI
KRUGER NATIONAL PARK
GONAREZHOU NATIONAL PARK
Bulawayo
Beira
Francistown
Gaborone
Mochudi
Molepolole
Serowe
Palapye
Mahalapye
Messina
Beitbridge
Pietersburg
Potgietersrus
Phalaborwa
Nelspruit
PRETORIA
JOHANNESBURG
Soweto
Germiston
Benoni
Springs
Vereeniging
Krugersdorp
Potchefstroom
Klerksdorp
Welkom
Kroonstad
Bethlehem
Harrismith
Newcastle
Ladysmith
Bloemfontein
Maseru
Mbabane
Manzini
MAPUTO
Xai-Xai
Inhambane
Maxixe
Vilankulo
Richard's Bay
Pietermaritzburg
DURBAN
Port Edward
Umtata
Port St. Johns
Queenstown
East London (Oos-Londen)
Grahamstown
Port Alfred
Port Elizabeth
Uitenhage
Algoabaai
Wild Coast
Mozambique Channel
Baia de Maputo
Ilha da Inhaca
Tropic of Capricorn
INDIAN OCEAN
W-847000-7A-DR2-1
Copyright © Rand McNally & Co.

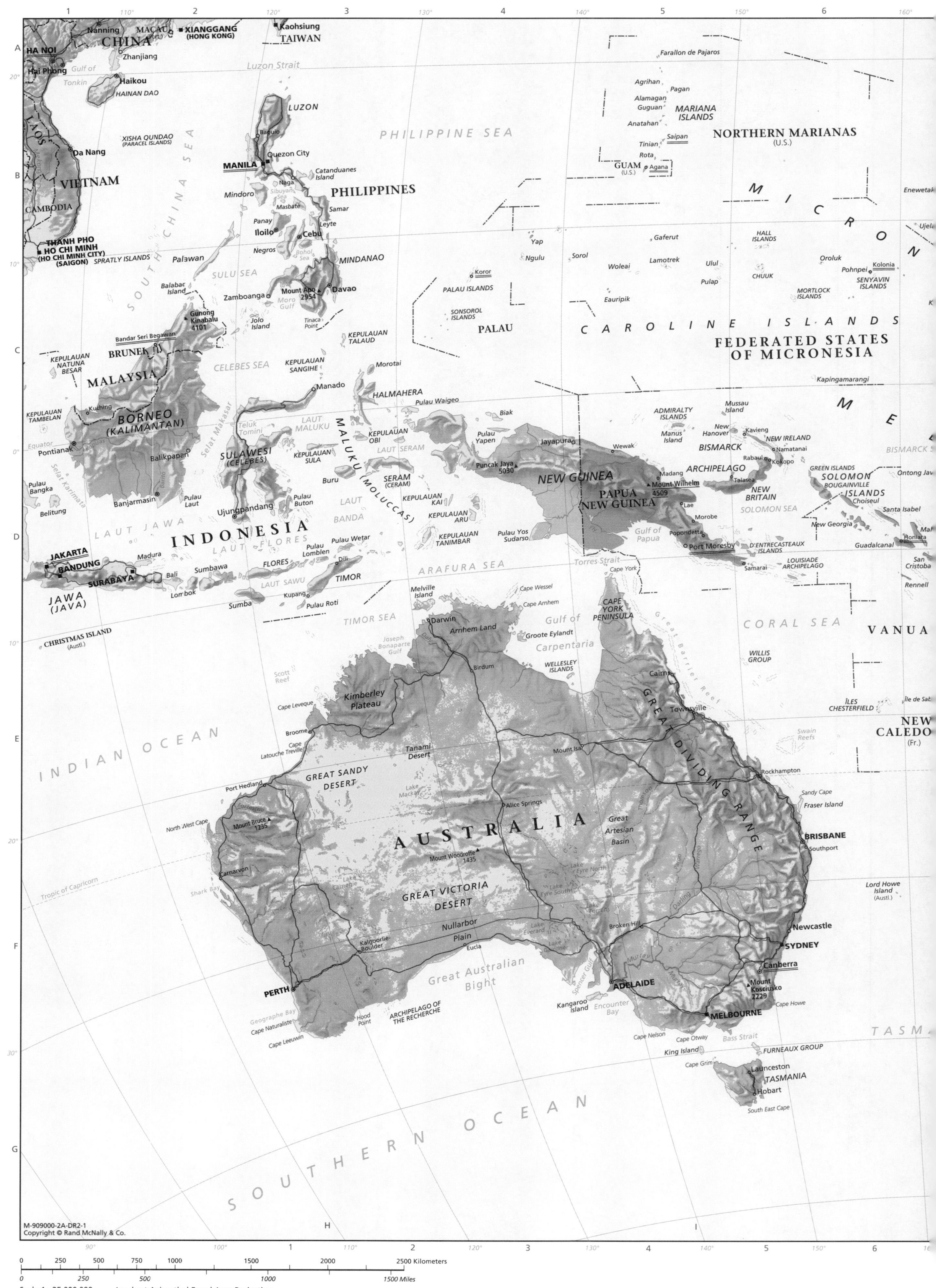

0 250 500 750 1000 1500 2000 2500 Kilometers

0 250 500 1000 1500 Miles

Scale 1 : 25,000,000 Lambert Azimuthal Equal Area Projection

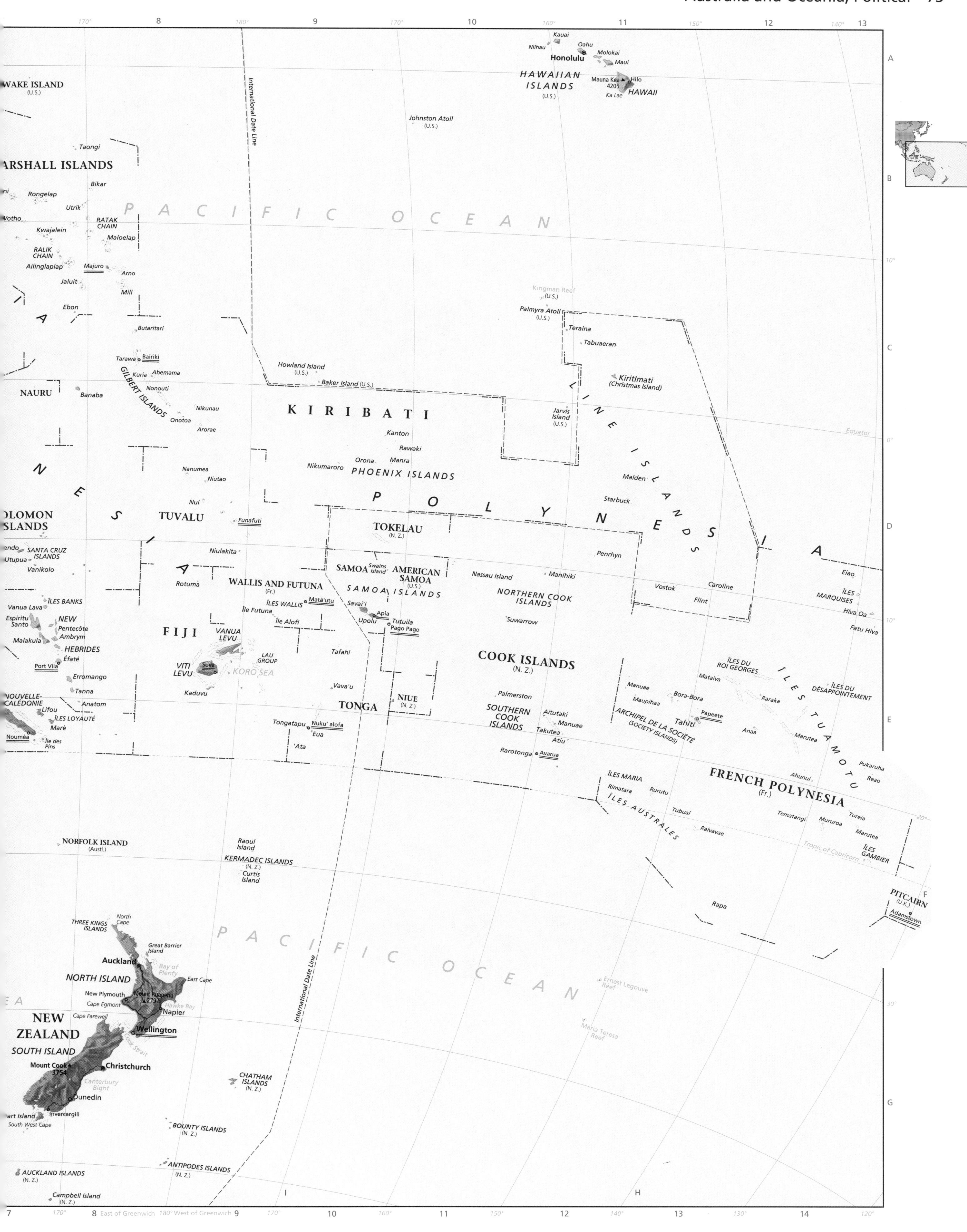

HAWAIIAN ISLANDS (U.S.)
Kauai
Niihau
Oahu
Honolulu
Molokai
Maui
Mauna Kea 4205
Hilo
HAWAII
Ka Lae
Johnston Atoll (U.S.)
WAKE ISLAND (U.S.)
International Date Line
Taongi
MARSHALL ISLANDS
Bikar
Rongelap
Utrik
RATAK CHAIN
Kwajalein
Maloelap
RALIK CHAIN
Ailinglaplap
Majuro
Arno
Jaluit
Mili
Ebon
PACIFIC OCEAN
Kingman Reef (U.S.)
Palmyra Atoll (U.S.)
Teraina
Tabuaeran
Butaritari
Tarawa
Bairiki
Abemama
Kuria
GILBERT ISLANDS
Nonouti
Howland Island (U.S.)
Baker Island (U.S.)
Kiritimati (Christmas Island)
NAURU
Banaba
Nikunau
Onotoa
Arorae
KIRIBATI
Jarvis Island (U.S.)
LINE ISLANDS
Equator
Kanton
Rawaki
Orona
Manra
Nikumaroro
PHOENIX ISLANDS
Nanumea
Niutao
Malden
Starbuck
Nui
TUVALU
Funafuti
POLYNESIA
TOKELAU (N. Z.)
SOLOMON ISLANDS
SANTA CRUZ ISLANDS
Utupua
Vanikolo
Niulakita
Penrhyn
SAMOA
Swains Island
AMERICAN SAMOA (U.S.)
Nassau Island
Manihiki
Rotuma
WALLIS AND FUTUNA (Fr.)
SAMOA ISLANDS
NORTHERN COOK ISLANDS
Vostok
Caroline
Eiao
ÎLES MARQUISES
Hiva Oa
Fatu Hiva
Flint
ÎLES BANKS
Vanua Lava
Espiritu Santo
NEW HEBRIDES
Pentecôte
Ambrym
Malakula
Éfaté
Port Vila
Erromango
Tanna
Anatom
ÎLES WALLIS
Matā'utu
Île Futuna
Île Alofi
Savai'i
Apia
Upolu
Tutuila
Pago Pago
Suwarrow
FIJI
VANUA LEVU
VITI LEVU
Suva
KORO SEA
LAU GROUP
Kaduvu
Tafahi
Vava'u
TONGA
NIUE (N. Z.)
COOK ISLANDS (N. Z.)
Palmerston
SOUTHERN COOK ISLANDS
Aitutaki
Manuae
Takutea
Atiu
Rarotonga
Avarua
ÎLES DU ROI GEORGES
Mataiva
ÎLES TUAMOTU
ÎLES DU DÉSAPPOINTEMENT
Manuae
Maupihaa
Bora-Bora
ARCHIPEL DE LA SOCIÉTÉ (SOCIETY ISLANDS)
Tahiti
Papeete
Raraka
Anaa
Marutea
Pukaruha
Reao
NOUVELLE-CALÉDONIE
Lifou
ÎLES LOYAUTÉ
Maré
Nouméa
Île des Pins
Tongatapu
Nuku'alofa
'Eua
'Ata
ÎLES MARIA
Rimatara
Rurutu
ÎLES AUSTRALES
Tubuai
Raivavae
FRENCH POLYNESIA (Fr.)
Ahunui
Tematangi
Mururoa
Tureia
Marutea
ÎLES GAMBIER
Tropic of Capricorn
NORFOLK ISLAND (Austl.)
Raoul Island
KERMADEC ISLANDS (N. Z.)
Curtis Island
Rapa
PITCAIRN (U.K.)
Adamstown
THREE KINGS ISLANDS
North Cape
Great Barrier Island
Auckland
Bay of Plenty
NORTH ISLAND
East Cape
New Plymouth
Mount Ruapehu 2797
Cape Egmont
Hawke Bay
Napier
Cape Farewell
NEW ZEALAND
Wellington
Cook Strait
SOUTH ISLAND
Mount Cook 3754
Christchurch
Canterbury Bight
Dunedin
Invercargill
Stewart Island
South West Cape
Ernest Legouve Reef
Maria Teresa Reef
CHATHAM ISLANDS (N. Z.)
BOUNTY ISLANDS (N. Z.)
ANTIPODES ISLANDS (N. Z.)
AUCKLAND ISLANDS (N. Z.)
Campbell Island (N. Z.)
East of Greenwich
180° West of Greenwich

0 100 200 300 400 600 800 1000 Kilometers

0 100 200 400 600 Miles

Scale 1 : 10,000,000 Lambert Conformal Conic Projection

PAPUA NEW GUINEA
SOLOMON ISLANDS
CORAL SEA
CORAL SEA ISLANDS TERRITORY (Austl.)
VANUATU
NEW CALEDONIA (Fr.)
PACIFIC OCEAN
TASMAN SEA
Gulf of Carpentaria
CAPE YORK PENINSULA
Great Barrier Reef
GREAT DIVIDING RANGE
QUEENSLAND
NEW SOUTH WALES
VICTORIA
Great Artesian Basin
Simpson Desert
Sturt Stony Desert
Barkly Tableland
Darling Downs
Louisiade Archipelago
Thursday Island
Cape York
Weipa
Cooktown
Cairns
Townsville
Mackay
Rockhampton
Bundaberg
Fraser Island
Gympie
BRISBANE
Southport (Gold Coast)
Toowoomba
Mount Isa
Cloncurry
Longreach
Charleville
Roma
Cunnamulla
Lismore
Coffs Harbour
Port Macquarie
Tamworth
Armidale
Dubbo
Broken Hill
Newcastle
SYDNEY
Wollongong
Canberra
Wagga Wagga
Albury
Mildura
Bendigo
Ballarat
Geelong
MELBOURNE
Mount Kosciusko 2229
SNOWY MTS.
JERVIS BAY TERRITORY
Mount Gambier
Port Augusta
Port Pirie
ADELAIDE
Kangaroo Island
Bass Strait
King Island
Flinders Island
Wilsons Promontory
TASMANIA
Launceston
Devonport
Burnie
Hobart
Port Arthur
Queenstown
SOUTHERN OCEAN
Same scale as main map
A.C.T. = AUSTRALIAN CAPITAL TERRITORY

CORAL SEA
ISLANDS TERRITORY
(Austl.)
C O R A L S E A
PACIFIC
OCEAN
GREAT BARRIER REEF
MARINE PARK
Capricorn Channel
Gulf of Carpentaria
QUEENSLAND
A U S T R A L I A
G R E A T D I V I D I N G R A N G E
GREGORY RANGE
LOLWORTH RA.
LEICHHARDT RANGE
DENHAM RA.
CLARKE RANGE
CONNORS RANGE
DRUMMOND RANGE
EXPEDITION RANGE
DAWSON RA.
AUBURN RANGE
CHESTERTON RA.
WARREGO RA.
GOWAN RA.
MCGREGOR RANGE
SELWYN RA.
FORSYTH RA.
Great Artesian Basin
Channel Country
Darling Downs
Diamond Islets
Tregosse Islets
Marion Reef
Swain Reefs
Fraser Island
Capricorn Group
Bunker Group
Lady Elliot Island
Whitsunday Island
Cumberland Islands
Northumberland Isles
Percy Isles
Hinchinbrook Island
Magnetic Island
Wellesley Islands
Moreton Island
North Stradbroke Island
Bribie Island
BRISBANE
Southport
Toowoomba
Ipswich
Redcliffe
Caloundra
Nambour
Tewantin-Noosa
Gympie
Maryborough
Bundaberg
Gladstone
Rockhampton
Yeppoon
Mackay
Bowen
Proserpine
Ayr
Townsville
Ingham
Cardwell
Tully
Innisfail
Babinda
Cairns
Atherton
Mareeba
Herberton
Charters Towers
Hughenden
Richmond
Julia Creek
Cloncurry
Mount Isa
Winton
Longreach
Barcaldine
Blackall
Emerald
Clermont
Moranbah
Charleville
Roma
Dalby
Miles
Chinchilla
Kingaroy
Normanton
Karumba
Burketown
Croydon
Georgetown
Birdsville
Bedourie
Boulia
Windorah
Quilpie
Tambo
Augathella
Injune
Taroom
Biloela
Moura
Monto
Gayndah
Mundubbera
Eidsvold

NEW SOUTH WALES
VICTORIA
SOUTH AUSTRALIA
TASMANIA
TASMAN SEA
SOUTHERN OCEAN
Bass Strait
Great Australian Bight
RIVERINA
LIVERPOOL RA.
AUSTRALIAN CAPITAL TERRITORY
SNOWY MOUNTAINS
SYDNEY
MELBOURNE
ADELAIDE
Canberra
Newcastle
Wollongong
Hobart
Same scale as main map
Meters
Feet
Sea Level
Scale 1 : 5,000,000
Lambert Conformal Conic Projection
W-590293-7A-DR2-1
Copyright © Rand McNally & Co.

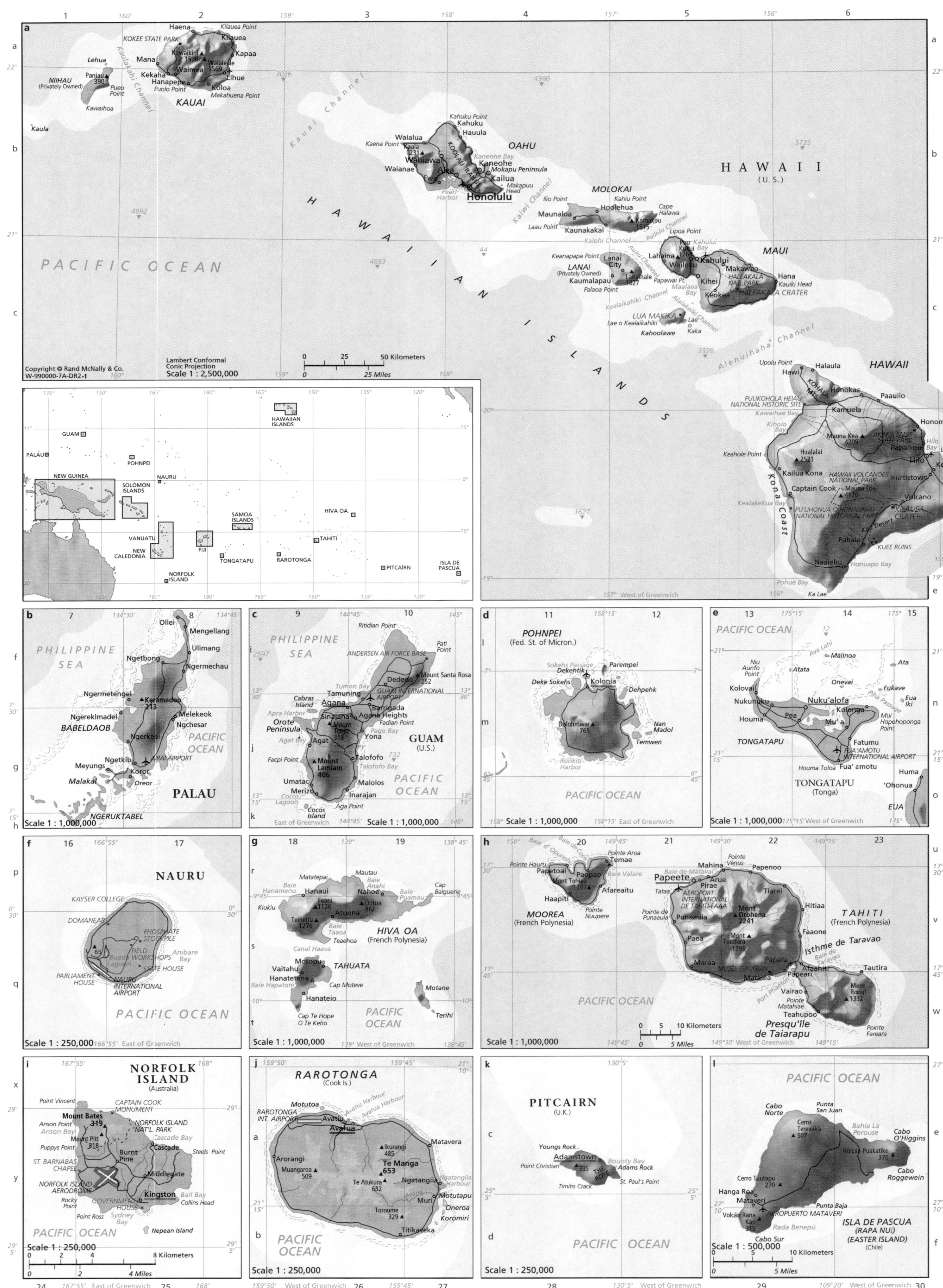

HAWAII (U.S.)
HAWAIIAN ISLANDS
PACIFIC OCEAN
KAUAI
NIIHAU (Privately Owned)
OAHU
Honolulu
MOLOKAI
LANAI
MAUI
HAWAII
Kahoolawe
Kauai Channel
Kaulakahi Channel
Kaiwi Channel
Pailolo Channel
Alenuihaha Channel
Copyright © Rand McNally & Co.
W-990000-7A-DR2-1
Lambert Conformal Conic Projection
Scale 1 : 2,500,000
PALAU
GUAM (U.S.)
POHNPEI (Fed. St. of Micron.)
TONGATAPU (Tonga)
NAURU
HIVA OA (French Polynesia)
TAHITI (French Polynesia)
MOOREA (French Polynesia)
NORFOLK ISLAND (Australia)
RAROTONGA (Cook Is.)
PITCAIRN (U.K.)
ISLA DE PASCUA (RAPA NUI) (EASTER ISLAND) (Chile)
PHILIPPINE SEA
Scale 1 : 1,000,000
Scale 1 : 250,000
Scale 1 : 500,000

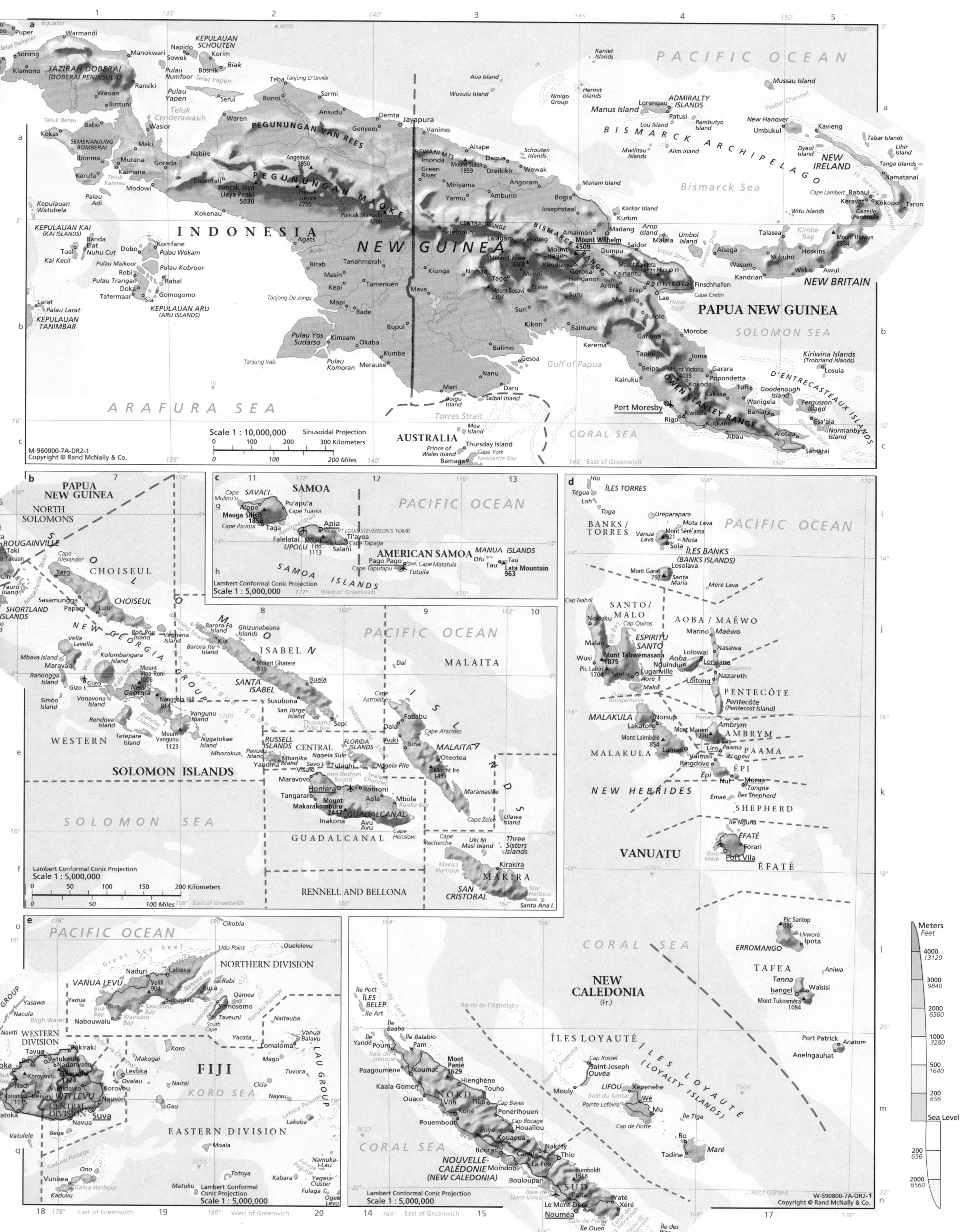
PACIFIC OCEAN
INDONESIA
NEW GUINEA
PAPUA NEW GUINEA
BISMARCK ARCHIPELAGO
Bismarck Sea
NEW IRELAND
NEW BRITAIN
SOLOMON SEA
CORAL SEA
ARAFURA SEA
AUSTRALIA
Gulf of Papua
Torres Strait
PEGUNUNGAN VAN REES
PEGUNUNGAN MAOKE
Puncak Jaya (Jaya Peak) 5030
OWEN STANLEY RANGE
BISMARCK RANGE
Mount Wilhelm 4509
Port Moresby
Jayapura
Lae
Madang
Rabaul
Kavieng
Manus Island
ADMIRALTY ISLANDS
D'ENTRECASTEAUX ISLANDS
JAZIRAH DOBERAI (DOBERAI PENINSULA)
KEPULAUAN KAI (KAI ISLANDS)
KEPULAUAN ARU (ARU ISLANDS)
KEPULAUAN TANIMBAR
Scale 1 : 10,000,000
Sinusoidal Projection
0 100 200 300 Kilometers
0 100 200 Miles
M-960000-7A-DR2-1
Copyright © Rand McNally & Co.
SAMOA
SAVAI'I
UPOLU
Apia
Mauga Silisili 1858
AMERICAN SAMOA
Pago Pago
Tutuila
MANUA ISLANDS
Lata Mountain 963
SAMOA ISLANDS
Lambert Conformal Conic Projection
Scale 1 : 5,000,000
PAPUA NEW GUINEA
NORTH SOLOMONS
BOUGAINVILLE
CHOISEUL
NEW GEORGIA GROUP
SANTA ISABEL
MALAITA
GUADALCANAL
Honiara
Mount Makarakomburu 2447
SAN CRISTOBAL
MAKIRA
SOLOMON ISLANDS
WESTERN
CENTRAL
RENNELL AND BELLONA
SOLOMON SEA
Lambert Conformal Conic Projection
Scale 1 : 5,000,000
0 50 100 150 200 Kilometers
0 50 100 Miles
ÎLES TORRES
ÎLES BANKS (BANKS ISLANDS)
BANKS / TORRES
SANTO / MALO
ESPIRITU SANTO
Mont Tabwémasana 1879
Luganville
AOBA / MAÉWO
PENTECÔTE
MALAKULA
AMBRYM
PAAMA
ÉPI
SHEPHERD
ÉFATÉ
Port Vila
NEW HEBRIDES
VANUATU
ERROMANGO
TAFEA
Tanna
Anatom
CORAL SEA
NEW CALEDONIA (Fr.)
ÎLES LOYAUTÉ
ÎLES LOYAUTÉ (LOYALTY ISLANDS)
Ouvéa
Lifou
Maré
NOUVELLE-CALÉDONIE (NEW CALEDONIA)
Mont Panié 1629
Humboldt 1618
Nouméa
NORD
SUD
Île des Pins
Lambert Conformal Conic Projection
Scale 1 : 5,000,000
W-590800-7A-DR2-1
Copyright © Rand McNally & Co.
FIJI
VANUA LEVU
VITI LEVU
Suva
Tomanivi 1323
NORTHERN DIVISION
WESTERN DIVISION
CENTRAL DIVISION
EASTERN DIVISION
KORO SEA
LAU GROUP
Taveuni
Kadavu
Lambert Conformal Conic Projection
Scale 1 : 5,000,000
Meters
Feet
4000 13120
3000 9840
2000 6560
1000 3280
500 1640
200 656
Sea Level
200 656
2000 6560

NEW ZEALAND

TASMAN SEA

PACIFIC OCEAN

NORTH ISLAND

SOUTH ISLAND

Three Kings Islands
Cape Reinga
North Cape
Rangaunu Bay
Doubtless Bay
Ahipara Bay
Tauroa Point
Cape Brett
Okaihau
Opua
Whangarei
Bream Bay
Dargaville
Great Barrier Island
Wellsford
Kaipara Harbour
Hauraki Gulf
Mercury Islands
Auckland
North Shore City
Coromandel Peninsula
Waitemata
Manukau
Manukau Harbour
Firth of Thames
Thames
Pukekohe
Waiuku
Mayor Island
Waihi
Bay of Plenty
White Island
Cape Runaway
Huntly
Morrinsville
Tauranga
Hamilton
Cambridge
East Cape
Te Awamutu
Whakatane
Kawhia Harbour
Opotiki
RAUKUMARA RA.
Hikurangi 1752
Te Kuiti
Rotorua
Tokoroa
UREWERA NATIONAL PARK
Murupara
HUIARAU RA.
Taupo
Lake Taupo
North Taranaki Bight
Waitara
Taumarunui
TONGARIRO NATIONAL PARK
Gisborne
New Plymouth
Mount Taranaki (Mount Egmont) 2518
EGMONT NATIONAL PARK
Cape Egmont
Tarawera
Wairoa
Stratford
Hawke Bay
Mahia Peninsula
Opunake
Hawera
Raetihi
Mount Ruapehu 2797
Napier
South Taranaki Bight
Taihape
Patea
Hastings
Cape Kidnappers
RUAHINE RANGE
Waitotara
Wanganui
Waipukurau
Palmerston North
Dannevirke
Woodville
TARARUA RA.
Levin
Otaki
Masterton
Lower Hutt
Wellington
Lake Wairarapa
Cape Palliser
Cook Strait

Cape Farewell
Golden Bay
D'Urville Island
Takaka
ABEL TASMAN NATIONAL PARK
Tasman Bay
Motueka
Nelson
Richmond
Mount Owen 1875
Karamea Bight
Seddonville
Picton
Blenheim
Cape Foulwind
Westport
NELSON LAKES NATIONAL PARK
Cape Campbell
Mount Uriah 1525
Mount Travers 2338
Tapuae-o-Uenuku 2885
Reefton
Manakau 2610
SPENSER MTS.
Runanga
Greymouth
Kaikoura
Waiau
Hokitika
ARTHURS PASS NATIONAL PARK
Culverden
Ross
Waipara
SOUTHERN ALPS
Mount Murchison 2400
Whataroa
Oxford
Pegasus Bay
Kaiapoi
WESTLAND NATIONAL PARK
MOUNT COOK NATIONAL PARK
Sheffield
Christchurch
Mount Cook 3754
Methven
Little River
Banks Peninsula
Haast
Mount Somers
Lake Tekapo
Canterbury Plains
Southbridge
Ashburton
Canterbury Bight
Cascade Point
MOUNT ASPIRING NATIONAL PARK
Fairlie
Mount Aspiring 3030
Timaru
Omarama
Milford Sound
Mount Tutoko 2746
Mount St. Bathans 2088
Waimate
Wanaka
Kurow
FIORDLAND NATIONAL PARK
LIVINGSTONE MTS.
Queenstown
Cromwell
Ranfurly
Oamaru
Doubtful Sound
Alexandra
Te Anau
Kingston
Roxburgh
Palmerston
Resolution Island
Mossburn
Edievale
Beaumont
Port Chalmers
Dunedin
Nightcaps
West Cape
Cape Providence
Otautau
Gore
Milton
Winton
Te Waewae Bay
Invercargill
Kaitangata
Riverton
Tahakopa
Tokanui
Foveaux Strait
Bluff
Ruapuke Island
Mount Anglem 980
STEWART ISLAND
South West Cape
Snares Islands
Bounty Islands

2491
549
112
677
3122
4870
33
2235
1500

Meters / Feet
3000 / 9840
2000 / 6560
1000 / 3280
500 / 1640
200 / 656
Sea Level
200 / 656
2000 / 6560

170° East of Greenwich

0 50 100 150 200 300 400 500 Kilometers
0 50 100 200 300 Miles

Scale 1 : 5,000,000

Lambert Conformal Conic Projection

W-591700-7A-DR2-1

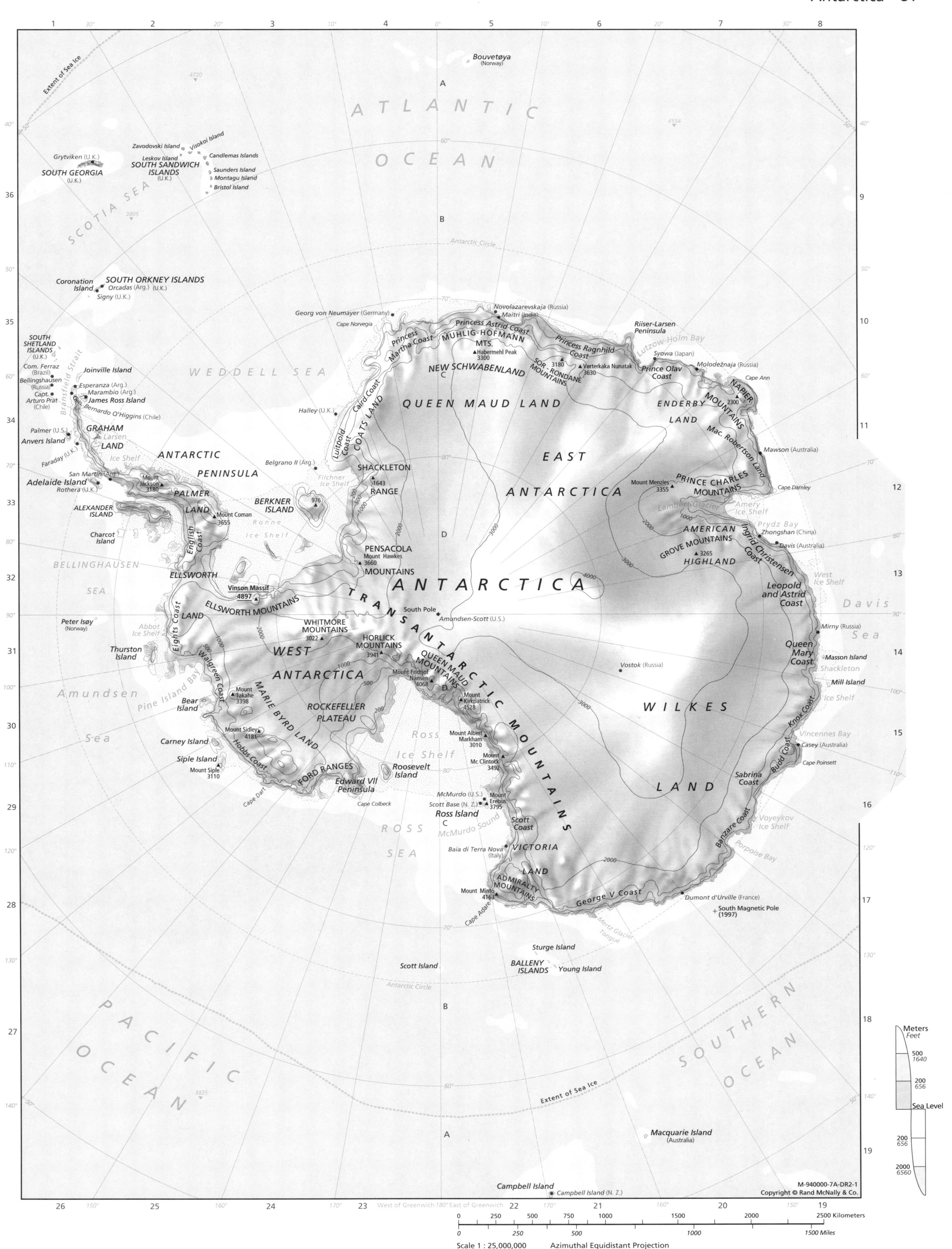
ATLANTIC OCEAN
Bouvetøya (Norway)
SOUTH GEORGIA (U.K.)
Grytviken (U.K.)
SOUTH SANDWICH ISLANDS (U.K.)
SCOTIA SEA
SOUTH ORKNEY ISLANDS (U.K.)
SOUTH SHETLAND ISLANDS (U.K.)
WEDDELL SEA
GRAHAM LAND
ANTARCTIC PENINSULA
PALMER LAND
ALEXANDER ISLAND
BERKNER ISLAND
Ronne Ice Shelf
Filchner Ice Shelf
BELLINGHAUSEN SEA
ELLSWORTH LAND
ELLSWORTH MOUNTAINS
Vinson Massif 4897
QUEEN MAUD LAND
NEW SCHWABENLAND
EAST ANTARCTICA
ENDERBY LAND
PRINCE CHARLES MOUNTAINS
AMERICAN HIGHLAND
ANTARCTICA
South Pole
Amundsen-Scott (U.S.)
TRANSANTARCTIC MOUNTAINS
WEST ANTARCTICA
MARIE BYRD LAND
ROCKEFELLER PLATEAU
Ross Ice Shelf
ROSS SEA
VICTORIA LAND
WILKES LAND
Vostok (Russia)
Davis Sea
Amundsen Sea
PACIFIC OCEAN
SOUTHERN OCEAN
Extent of Sea Ice
Antarctic Circle
BALLENY ISLANDS
Scott Island
Macquarie Island (Australia)
Campbell Island
South Magnetic Pole (1997)
Meters Feet
500 1640
200 656
Sea Level
2000 6560
M-940000-7A-DR2-1
Copyright © Rand McNally & Co.
Scale 1 : 25,000,000
Azimuthal Equidistant Projection
0 250 500 750 1000 1500 2000 2500 Kilometers
0 250 500 1000 1500 Miles

ATLANTIC OCEAN
AÇORES (AZORES) (Port.)
São Miguel
BERMUDA (U.K.)
Tropic of Cancer
Equator
UNITED STATES
APPALACHIAN MOUNTAINS
CHICAGO
CLEVELAND
PITTSBURGH
NEW YORK
PHILADELPHIA
BALTIMORE
WASHINGTON
Providence
Hartford
Richmond
Norfolk
Cape Hatteras
Cape Lookout
Cape Fear
Raleigh
Charlotte
Columbia
Charleston
Savannah
Jacksonville
Daytona Beach
Cape Canaveral
Orlando
Tampa
MIAMI
ATLANTA
Montgomery
Tallahassee
Birmingham
Jackson
Mobile
NEW ORLEANS
Baton Rouge
HOUSTON
SAN ANTONIO
Austin
DALLAS
Fort Worth
Shreveport
Little Rock
Oklahoma City
Wichita
KANSAS CITY
Omaha
Des Moines
ST. LOUIS
INDIANAPOLIS
CINCINNATI
Louisville
Charleston
Chattanooga
Corpus Christi
Brownsville
Matamoros
GULF OF MEXICO
MEXICO
Veracruz
Villahermosa
Campeche
Bahía de Campeche
Mérida
PENÍNSULA DE YUCATÁN
Cancún
Isla Cozumel
Cabo Catoche
Yucatan Channel
Golfo de Tehuantepec
BELIZE
Belmopan
Belize City
GUATEMALA
Guatemala
Tuxtla Gutiérrez
Volcán Tajumulco 4220
San Salvador
EL SALVADOR
HONDURAS
Tegucigalpa
San Pedro Sula
NICARAGUA
Managua
COSTA RICA
SAN JOSÉ
Cerro Chirripó 3819
Volcán Barú 3475
PANAMA
Panamá
Colón
Golfo de Panamá
Isla de Coiba
Isla del Coco (C.R.)
Isla de Malpelo (Col.)
Isla de San Andrés (Col.)
CARIBBEAN SEA
BAHAMAS
Grand Bahama
Abaco
Eleuthera
Andros
Nassau
Cat Island
Long Island
Acklins
Mayaguana
Great Inagua
TURKS AND CAICOS ISLANDS (U.K.)
Straits of Florida
Cape Sable
Lake Okeechobee
LA HABANA (HAVANA)
CUBA
Matanzas
Cienfuegos
Camagüey
Holguín
Santiago de Cuba
Isla de la Juventud
CAYMAN ISLANDS (U.K.)
JAMAICA
Kingston
WEST INDIES
GREATER ANTILLES
HISPANIOLA
HAITI
Port-au-Prince
DOMINICAN REPUBLIC
SANTO DOMINGO
Pico Duarte 3175
PUERTO RICO (U.S.)
SAN JUAN
LEEWARD ISLANDS
ANGUILLA (U.K.)
ANTIGUA AND BARBUDA
MONTSERRAT (U.K.)
GUADELOUPE (Fr.)
DOMINICA
MARTINIQUE (Fr.)
ST. LUCIA
BARBADOS
WINDWARD ISLANDS
ST. VINCENT AND THE GRENADINES
GRENADA
Lesser Antilles
TRINIDAD AND TOBAGO
Tobago
Trinidad
Port of Spain
ARUBA (Neth.)
NETHERLANDS ANTILLES
Punto Fijo
Punta Gallinas
Riohacha
Pico Cristóbal Colón 5775
Barranquilla
Cartagena
Sincelejo
Montería
Turbo
Quibdó
MEDELLÍN
Manizales
Ibagué
CALI
Buenaventura
Pasto
Tumaco
SANTA FE DE BOGOTÁ
Cúcuta
Bucaramanga
COLOMBIA
Mitú
CORDILLERA OCCIDENTAL
CORDILLERA CENTRAL
CORDILLERA ORIENTAL
MARACAIBO
Barquisimeto
Barinas
CARACAS
Maracay
San Fernando de Apure
VENEZUELA
LLANOS
Ciudad Bolívar
Ciudad Guayana
Puerto Ayacucho
Pico Bolívar 5007
San Cristóbal
Puerto la Cruz
Maturín
El Tigre
GUYANA
Georgetown
Roraima 2875
PAKARAIMA MTS.
SURINAME
Paramaribo
FRENCH GUIANA (Fr.)
Cayenne
TUMUC-HUMAC MOUNTAINS
Pico da Neblina 3014
ECUADOR
QUITO
Cayambe 5790
GUAYAQUIL
Chimborazo 6310
Cuenca
Esmeraldas
Punta Galera
Portoviejo
Isla Puná
ARCHIPIÉLAGO DE COLÓN (GALÁPAGOS ISLANDS) (Ec.)
Isla Fernandina
Isla Isabela
Isla Santiago
Isla Santa Cruz
Isla San Cristóbal
PERU
ANDES
LIMA
Iquitos
Piura
Talara
Chiclayo
Cajamarca
Trujillo
Chimbote
Huancayo
Huánuco
Ayacucho
Cusco
Pucallpa
Cruzeiro do Sul
Nevado Huascarán 6746
Nevado Yerupajá 6634
Cerro de Pasco
Puerto Maldonado
Leticia
BRAZIL
SELVAS
MANAUS
Manacapuru
Itacoatiara
BELÉM
Macapá
Amapá
Ilha de Marajó
Ilha Grande do Gurupá
Ilha Caviana de Fora
Ilha de Maracá
Bragança
Santarém
Óbidos
Itaituba
Altamira
Marabá
Boa Vista
Fonte Boa
Porto Velho
Rio Branco
Cobija
Riberalta
SERRA FORMOSA
PLANALTO DO
Ilha do Bananal
São Luís
Bacabal
Imperatriz
Teresina
Caxias
Parnaíba
Sobral
FORTALEZA
Mossoró
Natal
João Pessoa
RECIFE
Campina Grande
Caruaru
Maceió
Aracaju
SALVADOR
Alagoinhas
Feira de Santana
Juazeiro do Norte
Paulistana
Petrolina
Juazeiro
Senhor do Bonfim
Xique-Xique
Barra
Represa de Sobradinho
Atol das Rocas
Ilha Fernando de Noronha (Brazil)
Cabo de São Roque
Carolina
Palmas
Porto Nacional
Gurupi
Barreiras

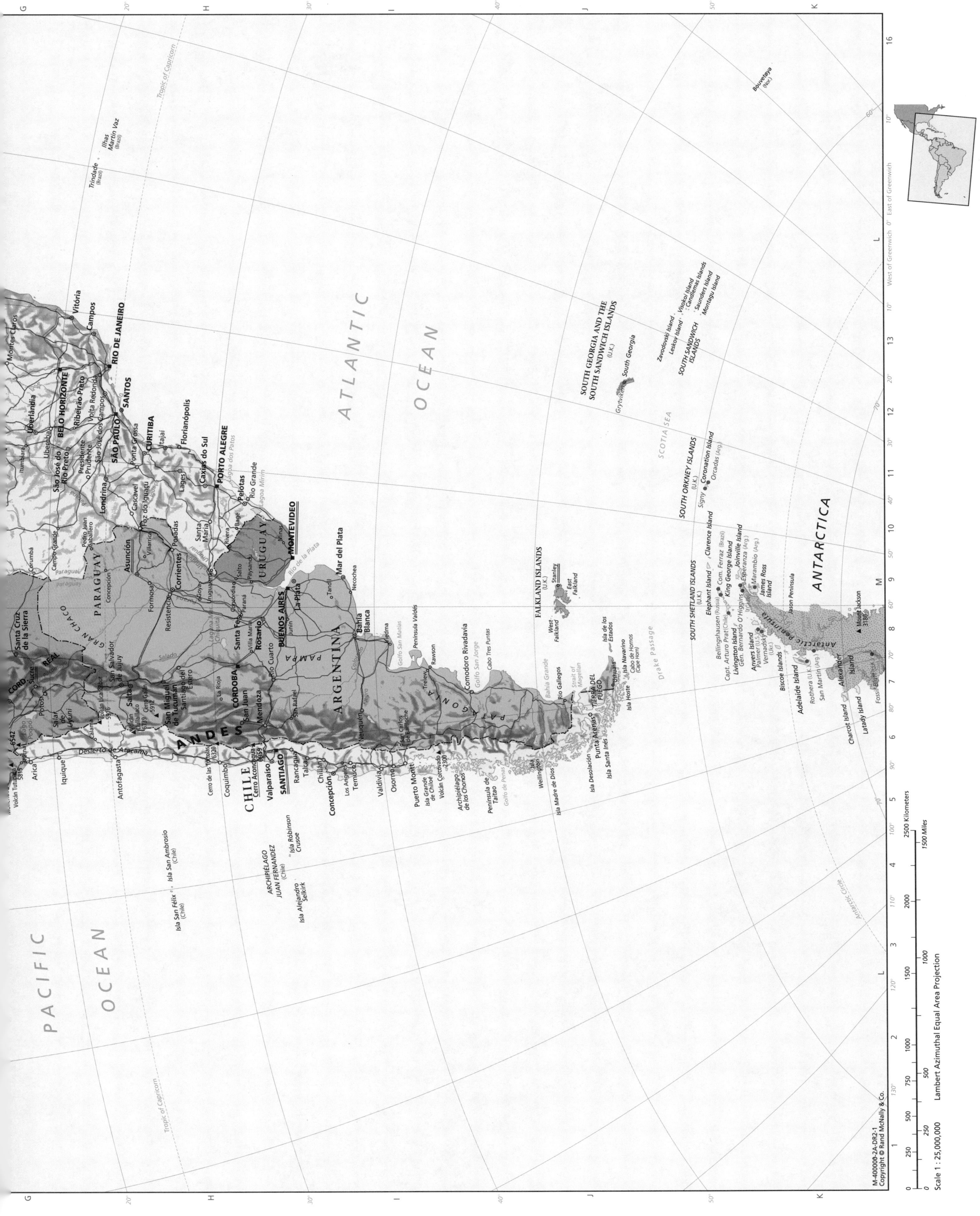

PACIFIC OCEAN

ATLANTIC OCEAN

ARGENTINA

CHILE

URUGUAY

PARAGUAY

ANTARCTICA

ANDES

PAMPA

PATAGONIA

GRAN CHACO

SCOTIA SEA

Drake Passage

FALKLAND ISLANDS (U.K.)

SOUTH GEORGIA AND THE SOUTH SANDWICH ISLANDS (U.K.)

SOUTH ORKNEY ISLANDS (U.K.)

SOUTH SHETLAND ISLANDS (U.K.)

SOUTH SANDWICH ISLANDS

ARCHIPIÉLAGO JUAN FERNANDEZ (Chile)

Isla San Félix (Chile)

Isla San Ambrosio (Chile)

Isla Robinson Crusoe

Isla Alejandro Selkirk

Trindade (Brazil)

Ilhas Martin Vaz (Brazil)

Bouvetøya (Nor.)

Antarctic Peninsula

Tropic of Capricorn

Antarctic Circle

West of Greenwich 0° East of Greenwich

BUENOS AIRES

MONTEVIDEO

SANTIAGO

RIO DE JANEIRO

SÃO PAULO

BELO HORIZONTE

CURITIBA

PORTO ALEGRE

SANTOS

CÓRDOBA

Asunción

Rosario

Mendoza

Valparaíso

Concepción

Mar del Plata

Bahía Blanca

Comodoro Rivadavia

Punta Arenas

Ushuaia

Stanley

Río de la Plata

M-400000-2A-DR2-1

Scale 1 : 25,000,000

0 250 500 750 1000 1500 2000 2500 Kilometers

0 250 500 1000 1500 Miles

Lambert Azimuthal Equal Area Projection

CARIBBEAN SEA
PANAMA
COLOMBIA
VENEZUELA
ECUADOR
PERU
BOLIVIA
CHILE
GUYANA
TRINIDAD AND TOBAGO
ARUBA (Neth.)
NETHERLANDS ANTILLES
PACIFIC OCEAN
AMAZONAS
SELVAS
ACRE
RONDÔNIA
RORAIMA
LLANOS
ANDES
ALTIPLANO
CORDILLERA OCCIDENTAL
CORDILLERA CENTRAL
CORDILLERA ORIENTAL
CORDILLERA REAL
CORD. DE MÉRIDA
SERRA PARIMA
SIERRA PARIMA
PAKARAIMA MTS.
SERRA DO DIVISOR
SERRA DOS PACAÁS NOVOS
SERRANÍA DE HUANCHACA
SERRA DO NORTE
KANUKU MOUNTAINS
LA GRAN SABANA
Barranquilla
Cartagena
Santa Marta
MARACAIBO
Barquisimeto
Valencia
CARACAS
Maracay
Barcelona
Cumaná
Ciudad Guayana
Ciudad Bolívar
Port of Spain
Panamá
Colón
Cúcuta
Bucaramanga
MEDELLÍN
Manizales
SANTA FE DE BOGOTÁ
CALI
Popayán
Pasto
QUITO
GUAYAQUIL
Cuenca
Chiclayo
Trujillo
Callao
LIMA
Arequipa
LA PAZ
Cochabamba
Santa Cruz de la Sierra
MANAUS
Porto Velho
Rio Branco
Boa Vista
Iquitos
Leticia
Pico Cristóbal Colón 5775
Pico Bolívar 5007
Chimborazo 6310
Nevado Huascarán 6746
Mount Roraima 2875
Pico da Neblina 3014
ARCHIPIÉLAGO DE COLÓN (GALAPAGOS ISLANDS) (Ec.)
Same scale as main map
Meters
Feet
Sea Level
0 100 200 300 400 600 Kilometers
0 100 200 400 Miles
Scale 1 : 10,000,000
Sinusoidal Projection

ATLANTIC
OCEAN
SURINAME
FRENCH GUIANA
BRAZIL
AMAPÁ
PARÁ
MARANHÃO
PIAUÍ
CEARÁ
RIO GRANDE DO NORTE
PARAÍBA
PERNAMBUCO
ALAGOAS
SERGIPE
BAHIA
TOCANTINS
GOIÁS
MATO GROSSO
MATO GROSSO DO SUL
MINAS GERAIS
DISTRITO FEDERAL
Paramaribo
New Amsterdam
Nieuw Nickerie
Totness
Groningen
Onverwacht
Brokopondo
Kwakoegron
Albina
Moengo
Nieuw Amsterdam
Saint-Laurent du Maroni
Iracoubo
Sinnamary
Île du Diable
Kourou
Cayenne
Rémiré
Tonate
Saint-Élie
Guisan Bourg
Cabo Orange
Ouanary
Saint-Georges
Oiapoque
Cabo Caciporé
Clevelândia do Norte
Saül
Juliana Top 1230
WILHELMINA GEBERGTE
ORANJE GEBERGTE
TUMUC-HUMAC MOUNTAINS
Vila Velha
Cunani
Calçoene
Amapá
Ilha de Maracá
Cabo Norte
Sucuriju
Aporema
Serra do Navio
Porto Grande
Ferreira Gomes
Ilha Bailique
Ilha do Curuá
Ilha Janaucu
Ilha Caviana de Fora
Ilha Mexiana
Macapá
Porto Santana
Mazagão
Cabo Maguari
ILHA DE MARAJÓ
Ilha Grande do Gurupá
Boca do Jari
Itatupã
Soure
Joanes
Salinópolis
Curuçá
Maracanã
Marajá
Igarapé-Açu
Bragança
Carutapera
Mosqueiro
BELÉM
Muaná
Capanema
Anajás
Curumu
São Miguel dos Macacos
Breves
Gurupá
Carrazedo
Ilha da Laguna
Porto de Moz
Veiros
Portel
Oriximiná
Óbidos
Alenquer
Prainha
Monte Alegre
Faro
Terra Santa
Juriti
Parintins
Barreirinha
Maués
Santarém
Vitória
Altamira
Abaetetuba
Acará
Curralinho
São Domingos do Capim
Irituia
Cametá
Curuçambaba
Carapajó
Juaba
Tomé-Açu
Baião
Tucuruí
Itaituba
Jacundá
Turiaçu
Cururupu
Camiranga
Santa Helena
Guimarães
Alcântara
Itamataré
Pinheiro
São Bento
Anil
São Luís
Rosário
Viana
Monção
Pindaré-Mirim
Paulino Neves
Tutóia
Parnaíba
Camocim
Granja
Barreirinhas
Urbano Santos
Acaraú
Marco
Paracuru
FORTALEZA
Itapecuru-Mirim
Cantanhede
Chapadinha
Brejo
Luzilândia
Piracuruca
Coroatá
Miguel Alves
Barras
União
Piripiri
Pedro II
Tianguá
Sobral
Ipu
Itapipoca
Maranguape
Maracanaú
Pacajus
Beberibe
Aracati
Canindé
Baturité
Itapiúna
Quixadá
Tamboril
Russas
Areia Branca
São Bento do Norte
Cabo de São Roque
Macau
Touros
Ceará-Mirim
Macaíba
Natal
Mossoró
Assu
Tabuleiro do Norte
Jaguaribe
Bacabal
Lago da Pedra
Pedreiras
Codó
Caxias
Teresina
Timon
Campo Maior
Crateús
Quixeramobim
Açailândia
Itupiranga
Marabá
São João do Araguaia
Imperatriz
Amarante do Maranhão
Barra do Corda
Presidente Dutra
São Miguel do Tapuio
Água Branca
Elesbão Veloso
Senador Pompeu
Piquet Carneiro
Tauá
Acopiara
Iguatu
Icó
Araguatins
Santa Isabel do Araguaia
Montes Altos
Sítio Novo
Grajaú
Bacatuba
Colinas
Amarante
Valença do Piauí
Carajás
Nazaré
Xambioá
Tocantinópolis
Mirador
Pastos Bons
São João dos Patos
Floriano
Oeiras
Picos
Pio IX
Campos Sales
Sousa
Pombal
Cajazeiras
Patos
Campina Grande
João Pessoa
Currais Novos
Caicó
São Raimundo das Mangabeiras
Babaçulândia
Araguaína
Carolina
Riachão
Balsas
Benedito Leite
Crato
Juazeiro do Norte
Itaporanga
Afogados da Ingazeira
Timbaúba
Goiana
Carpina
Olinda
RECIFE
SERRA DO CACHIMBO
Gradaús
Conceição do Araguaia
Itaporã de Goiás
Pequizeiro
Itacajá
Simplício Mendes
CHAPADA DO ARARIPE
Ouricuri
Parnamirim
Salgueiro
Serra Talhada
Flores
Sertânia
Arcoverde
Belo Jardim
Caruaru
Ribeirão
Palmares
Cachimbo
Araguacema
Pedro Afonso
Canto do Buriti
Paulistana
Santa Maria da Boa Vista
Belém de São Francisco
Garanhuns
União dos Palmares
Porto de Pedras
Rio Largo
Maceió
Dois Irmãos de Goiás
Miracema do Tocantins
Tocantínia
Alto Parnaíba
Santa Filomena
Cristino Castro
Bom Jesus
São Raimundo Nonato
Caracol
Remanso
Casa Nova
Petrolina
Juazeiro
Chorrochó
Paulo Afonso
Palmeira dos Índios
Arapiraca
Penedo
Junqueiro
Coruripe
SERRA DO ESTRONDO
CHAPADA DAS MANGABEIRAS
SA. DO PENITENTE
Palmas
Curupá
Monte Alegre do Piauí
Gilbués
Curimatá
Parnaguá
Uauá
Jaguarari
Senhor do Bonfim
Jeremoabo
Euclides da Cunha
Propriá
Brejo Grande
Pium
Cristalândia
Porto Nacional
Brejinho de Nazaré
Campo Formoso
Ribeira do Pombal
Itabaiana
Lagarto
Aracaju
Estância
Barra
Xique-Xique
Irecê
Jacobina
Queimadas
Tucano
Olindina
Rio Real
Esplanada
Ilha do Bananal
Dueré
Gurupi
Natividade
Dianópolis
Peixe
SERRA GERAL DE GOIÁS
Morro do Chapéu
Riachão do Jacuípe
Serrinha
Inhambupe
Alagoinhas
Feira de Santana
Porto dos Gaúchos
SERRA FORMOSA
PLANALTO DO MATO GROSSO
Paranã
Ponte Alta do Bom Jesus
Taguatinga
Arraias
Barreiras
Ibotirama
Ruy Barbosa
Itaberaba
Santo Amaro
Candeias
Camaçari
SALVADOR
Lençóis
Iaçu
Maragogipe
Santo Antônio de Jesus
Valença
Ilha de Tinharé
SERRA DO RONCADOR
São Miguel do Araguaia
Araguaçu
Porangatu
São Domingos
Santana
Correntina
Bom Jesus da Lapa
Paratinga
Ibitiara
Paramirim
Mucujê
Pico das Almas 1836
Maracás
Itiruçu
Jaguaquara
Gandu
Camamu
Itacaré
Parecis
Diamantino
Nobres
Rosário Oeste
Acorizal
Bandeirantes
SERRA DOURADA
Cavalcante
Nova Roma
Posse
Colinas
Riacho de Santana
Barra da Estiva
Caetité
Brumado
Poções
Jequié
Ipiaú
Ubatã
Coaraci
Ibicaraí
Ilhéus
Itabuna
Una
Cocos
Guanambi
Carinhanha
Caculé
Vitória da Conquista
Mozarlândia
Aruanã
Pilar de Goiás
São João da Aliança
São Gabriel de Goiás
Itapaci
Ceres
Goianésia
Britânia
Jeroaquara
Uruana
Formosa
Cabeceiras
Manga
Urandi
Monte Azul
SERRA DO ESPINHAÇO
Itambé
Itapetinga
Canavieiras
Belmonte
Várzea Grande
Cuiabá
Cáceres
Jaciara
Poxoréu
General Carneiro
Barra do Garças
Aragarças
Baliza
Itapirapuã
Jussara
Goiás
Jaraguá
Itaberaí
BRASÍLIA
Luziânia
Unaí
Januária
São Francisco
Janaúba
São João do Paraíso
Rio Pardo de Minas
Salinas
Pedra Azul
Jordânia
Salto da Divisa
Poconé
Barão de Melgaço
Rondonópolis
SERRA DE SÃO JERÔNIMO
Guiratinga
Piranhas
Iporá
Inhumas
Anápolis
Silvânia
GOIÂNIA
Aurilândia
São Romão
Grão Mogol
Coronel Murta
Jequitinhonha
Porto Seguro
Alto Garças
Alto Araguaia
Caiapônia
Jandaia
Cristianópolis
Cristalina
Paracatu
Caatinga
Montes Claros
Araçuaí
Itaobim
Águas Formosas
Itamaraju
Prado
Pirapora
Bocaiúva
Minas Novas
SERRA DO CAIAPÓ
Mineiros
Rio Verde
Pontalina
Pires do Rio
Campo Alegre de Goiás
João Pinheiro
Capelinha
Carlos Chagas
Alcobaça
Ponta da Baleia
Caravelas
Jataí
Santa Helena de Goiás
Morrinhos
Ipameri
Teófilo Otoni
Nanuque
Pedro Gomes
Equator
West of Greenwich
M-400091-7A-DR2-1
Copyright © Rand McNally & Co.

90

CARIBBEAN SEA
PACIFIC OCEAN
PANAMA
COLOMBIA
ECUADOR
PERU
Golfo de Panamá
Istmo de Panamá (Isthmus of Panama)
Colón
Panamá
Península de Azuero
Península de La Guajira
Golfo de Venezuela
Lago de Maracaibo
MARACAIBO
Santa Marta
Barranquilla
Cartagena
Riohacha
Valledupar
Montería
Sincelejo
Cúcuta
Bucaramanga
Barrancabermeja
MEDELLÍN
Quibdó
Manizales
Pereira
Armenia
Ibagué
SANTA FE DE BOGOTÁ
Villavicencio
Buenaventura
CALI
Neiva
Popayán
Pasto
Florencia
Mocoa
Tumaco
Esmeraldas
QUITO
Santo Domingo de los Colorados
Manta
Portoviejo
Ambato
Riobamba
GUAYAQUIL
Cuenca
Golfo de Guayaquil
Mérida
CORDILLERA OCCIDENTAL
CORDILLERA CENTRAL
CORDILLERA ORIENTAL
CORDILLERA DE MÉRIDA
SERRANÍA DE PERIJÁ
ANTIOQUIA
CHOCÓ
CÓRDOBA
SUCRE
BOLÍVAR
MAGDALENA
ATLÁNTICO
CESAR
LA GUAJIRA
NORTE DE SANTANDER
SANTANDER
BOYACÁ
CASANARE
ARAUCA
CUNDINAMARCA
META
TOLIMA
HUILA
CAUCA
NARIÑO
VALLE DEL CAUCA
PUTUMAYO
CAQUETÁ
GUAVIARE
VAUPÉS
AMAZONAS
ZULIA
TÁCHIRA
LORETO
NAPO
PASTAZA
SUCUMBÍOS
MORONA SANTIAGO
GUAYAS
MANABÍ
PICHINCHA
IMBABURA
COTOPAXI
Equator
Meters Feet
4000 13120
3000 9840
2000 6560
1000 3280
500 1640
200 656
Sea Level
200 656
2000 6560
W-544000-7A-DR2-1
Copyright © Rand McNally & Co.
72° West of Greenwich
0 50 100 150 200 300 400 500 Kilometers
0 50 100 200 300 Miles
Scale 1 : 5,000,000
Sinusoidal Projection

VENEZUELA
BRAZIL
GUYANA
TRINIDAD AND TOBAGO
NETHERLANDS ANTILLES
ATLANTIC OCEAN
GUIANA HIGHLANDS
(MACIZO DE GUAYANA)
BOLÍVAR
AMAZONAS
RORAIMA
DELTA AMACURO
MONAGAS
ANZOÁTEGUI
GUÁRICO
SUCRE
APURE
CARACAS
Ciudad Guayana
Ciudad Bolívar
Boa Vista
MANAUS
Port of Spain
Willemstad

ATLANTIC OCEAN
FORTALEZA
RECIFE
Natal
João Pessoa
Maceió
Aracaju
Teresina
São Luís
BELÉM
Imperatriz
Petrolina
Juazeiro do Norte
Campina Grande
Feira de Santana
Mossoró
Parnaíba
Caruaru
Olinda
CEARÁ
PIAUÍ
MARANHÃO
PERNAMBUCO
PARAÍBA
RIO GRANDE DO NORTE
ALAGOAS
SERGIPE
TOCANTINS
PARÁ
BAHIA
B R A Z I L
SERRA GRANDE
CHAPADA DO ARARIPE
CHAPADA DAS MANGABEIRAS
SERRA DA URUÇUÍ
SERRA DO PENITENTE
SERRA GERAL
SA. DO BOQUEIRÃO
SERRA DO ESTRONDO
PARQUE NACIONAL DOS LENÇÓIS MARANHENSES
PARQUE NACIONAL DA SERRA DA CAPIVARA
PARQUE NAC. DE SETE CIDADES
PARQUE NACIONAL DE UBAJARA
Ilha de Marajó
Ilha de Santana
Ilha do Gado Bravo
Ponta do Seixas
Cabo de São Roque
Ponta de Jericoacoara
85

ATLANTIC
OCEAN
GOIÁS
MINAS GERAIS
ESPÍRITO SANTO
SÃO PAULO
RIO DE JANEIRO
DISTRITO FEDERAL
BRASÍLIA
GOIÂNIA
BELO HORIZONTE
RIO DE JANEIRO
SÃO PAULO
CAMPINAS
SANTOS
Vitória
Campos
Uberlândia
Montes Claros
Juiz de Fora
Ilhéus
Vitória da Conquista
Governador Valadares
Tropic of Capricorn
42° West of Greenwich
Scale 1 : 5,000,000
Lambert Conformal Conic Projection
500 Kilometers
300 Miles
Meters
Feet
Sea Level
W-540393-7A-DR2-1
Copyright © Rand McNally & Co.
90
93

BRAZIL
BOLIVIA
PARAGUAY
PERU
ANDES
ALTIPLANO
CHACO BOREAL
GRAN CHACO
BAHIA
TOCANTINS
GOIÁS
MINAS GERAIS
MATO GROSSO
PLANALTO DO MATO GROSSO
MATO GROSSO DO SUL
SÃO PAULO
PARANÁ
SANTA CATARINA
RIO GRANDE DO SUL
ESPÍRITO SANTO
RIO DE JANEIRO
RONDÔNIA
ACRE
BRASÍLIA
DISTRITO FEDERAL
RIO DE JANEIRO
SÃO PAULO
BELO HORIZONTE
CURITIBA
PORTO ALEGRE
Florianópolis
Goiânia
Campo Grande
Cuiabá
Vitória
Santos
Asunción
LA PAZ
Santa Cruz de la Sierra
Cochabamba
Corrientes
Resistencia
Santa Fe
Córdoba
Salta
San Miguel de Tucumán
Antofagasta
Iquique
Arica
Pantanal
SERRA DO MAR
SERRA DA MANTIQUEIRA
SERRA DO ESPINHAÇO
SERRA DOS PACAÁS NOVOS
SERRA DO RONCADOR
Tropic of Capricorn
84
85

ATLANTIC OCEAN
PACIFIC OCEAN
ARGENTINA
CHILE
ANDES
PATAGONIA
BUENOS AIRES
MONTEVIDEO
SANTIAGO
FALKLAND ISLANDS (U.K.)
WEST FALKLAND
EAST FALKLAND
Stanley
SOUTH GEORGIA AND THE SOUTH SANDWICH ISLANDS (U.K.)
SOUTH GEORGIA
TIERRA DEL FUEGO
Cabo de Hornos (Cape Horn)
LA PAMPA
RÍO NEGRO
CHUBUT
SANTA CRUZ
NEUQUÉN
MENDOZA
SAN LUIS
Mar del Plata
Bahía Blanca
Comodoro Rivadavia
Punta Arenas
Río Gallegos
Ushuaia
Concepción
Valparaíso
Río de la Plata
Golfo San Jorge
Golfo San Matías
Bahía Grande
Scale 1 : 10,000,000
Lambert Conformal Conic Projection
M-400092-7A-DR2-1
Copyright © Rand McNally & Co.
Meters
Feet
Sea Level

PACIFIC OCEAN
Tropic of Capricorn
ANDES
CHILE
ARGENTINA
GRAN CHACO
PAMPA
ANTOFAGASTA
ATACAMA
COQUIMBO
VALPARAÍSO
REGIÓN METROPOLITANA
LIBERTADOR GENERAL BERNARDO O'HIGGINS
MAULE
BIOBÍO
LA ARAUCANÍA
JUJUY
SALTA
TUCUMÁN
CATAMARCA
SANTIAGO DEL ESTERO
LA RIOJA
SAN JUAN
CÓRDOBA
SAN LUIS
MENDOZA
LA PAMPA
NEUQUÉN
RÍO NEGRO
BUENOS AIRES
SANTA FE
CHACO
Antofagasta
Copiapó
La Serena
Coquimbo
Viña del Mar
Valparaíso
SANTIAGO
Rancagua
Talca
Chillán
Concepción
Talcahuano
Los Angeles
San Salvador de Jujuy
Salta
San Miguel de Tucumán
San Fernando del Valle de Catamarca
Santiago del Estero
La Rioja
San Juan
CÓRDOBA
Mendoza
San Luis
Río Cuarto
ROSARIO
Santa Fe
Paraná
Santa Rosa
Bahía Blanca
Cerro Aconcagua 6959
Volcán Llullaillaco 6739
Nevado Ojos del Salado 6893
Salar de Atacama
Salinas Grandes
Laguna Mar Chiquita
Desierto de Atacama
Puna de Atacama
Cordillera Domeyko
Valle Central
2
3
4
5
6
7
A
B
C
D
E
F
G
H
I
70°
68°
66°
64°
62°
60°
24°
26°
28°
30°
32°
34°
36°
38°

91

90
PARAGUAY
Asunción
Ciudad del Este
Foz do Iguaçu
Posadas
Encarnación
CORRIENTES
PARANÁ
CURITIBA
SÃO PAULO
Santos
Sorocaba
Joinville
Blumenau
Florianópolis
SANTA CATARINA
BRAZIL
SERRA GERAL
SERRA DO MAR
RIO GRANDE DO SUL
PORTO ALEGRE
Caxias do Sul
Novo Hamburgo
Pelotas
Rio Grande
Lagoa dos Patos
Lagoa Mirim
Uruguaiana
Santa Maria
Passo Fundo
URUGUAY
MONTEVIDEO
BUENOS AIRES
La Plata
Mar del Plata
Río de la Plata
Bahía Samborombón
Cabo San Antonio
Concordia
Salto
Paysandú
Rivera
Santana do Livramento
COXILHA DE SANTANA
CUCHILLA GRANDE
ATLANTIC OCEAN
Meters
Feet
6000
19680
4000
13120
3000
9840
2000
6560
1000
3280
500
1640
200
656
Sea Level
200
656
2000
6560
W-540195-7A-DR2-1
Copyright © Rand McNally & Co.
0 50 100 150 200 300 400 500 Kilometers
0 50 100 200 300 Miles
Scale 1 : 5,000,000
Lambert Conformal Conic Projection
52° West of Greenwich

ARCTIC OCEAN
ATLANTIC OCEAN
PACIFIC OCEAN
North Pole
GREENLAND
(Denmark)
ICELAND
Reykjavík
SVALBARD
(Nor.)
SWEDEN
NORWAY
Oslo
Göteborg
DENMARK
UNITED KINGDOM
FAROE ISLANDS
(Den.)
Shetland Islands
(U.K.)
Jan Mayen
(Nor.)
NORWEGIAN SEA
GREENLAND SEA
Denmark Strait
Davis Strait
Baffin Bay
LABRADOR SEA
BAFFIN ISLAND
ELLESMERE ISLAND
QUEEN ELIZABETH ISLANDS
VICTORIA ISLAND
BANKS ISLAND
Devon Island
Hudson Bay
Hudson Strait
Labrador
NEWFOUNDLAND
CANADA
ROCKY MOUNTAINS
MACKENZIE MOUNTAINS
COAST MOUNTAINS
BROOKS RANGE
ALASKA RANGE
Beaufort Sea
Chukchi Sea
Bering Strait
BERING SEA
Gulf of Alaska
ALEUTIAN ISLANDS
RUSSIA
International Date Line
VANCOUVER ISLAND
VANCOUVER
SEATTLE
PORTLAND
SACRAMENTO
SAN FRANCISCO
Anchorage
Fairbanks
Juneau
Edmonton
Calgary
Saskatoon
Regina
Winnipeg
MINNEAPOLIS
St. Paul
MILWAUKEE
CHICAGO
DETROIT
TORONTO
Ottawa
MONTREAL
Québec
BOSTON
NEW YORK
PHILADELPHIA
BUFFALO
CLEVELAND
PITTSBURGH
Halifax
St. John's
ST. PIERRE AND MIQUELON
(Fr.)

ATLANTIC OCEAN
PACIFIC OCEAN
GULF OF MEXICO
CARIBBEAN SEA
WEST INDIES
GREATER ANTILLES
LESSER ANTILLES
MEXICO
BAHAMAS
CUBA
HAITI
DOMINICAN REPUBLIC
JAMAICA
BELIZE
GUATEMALA
HONDURAS
EL SALVADOR
NICARAGUA
COSTA RICA
PANAMA
COLOMBIA
VENEZUELA
ECUADOR
PERU
BRAZIL
BOLIVIA
GUYANA
PARAGUAY
LOS ANGELES
SAN DIEGO
PHOENIX
DALLAS
HOUSTON
ATLANTA
NEW ORLEANS
MIAMI
SAN ANTONIO
MONTERREY
GUADALAJARA
CIUDAD DE MÉXICO
LA HABANA (HAVANA)
SANTO DOMINGO
SAN JUAN
SAN JOSÉ
MARACAIBO
CARACAS
MEDELLÍN
SANTA FE DE BOGOTÁ
CALI
QUITO
GUAYAQUIL
LIMA
LA PAZ
Tropic of Cancer
Equator
90° West of Greenwich
M-200000-2A-DR2-1
Copyright © Rand McNally & Co.
Scale 1 : 25,000,000
Lambert Azimuthal Equal Area Projection
2500 Kilometers
1500 Miles

Meters / Feet

Meters	Feet
4000	13120
3000	9840
2000	6560
1000	3280
500	1640
200	656
Sea Level	
200	656
2000	6560

0 100 200 300 400 600 800 1000 Kilometers

0 100 200 400 600 Miles

Scale 1 : 10,000,000   Lambert Conformal Conic Projection

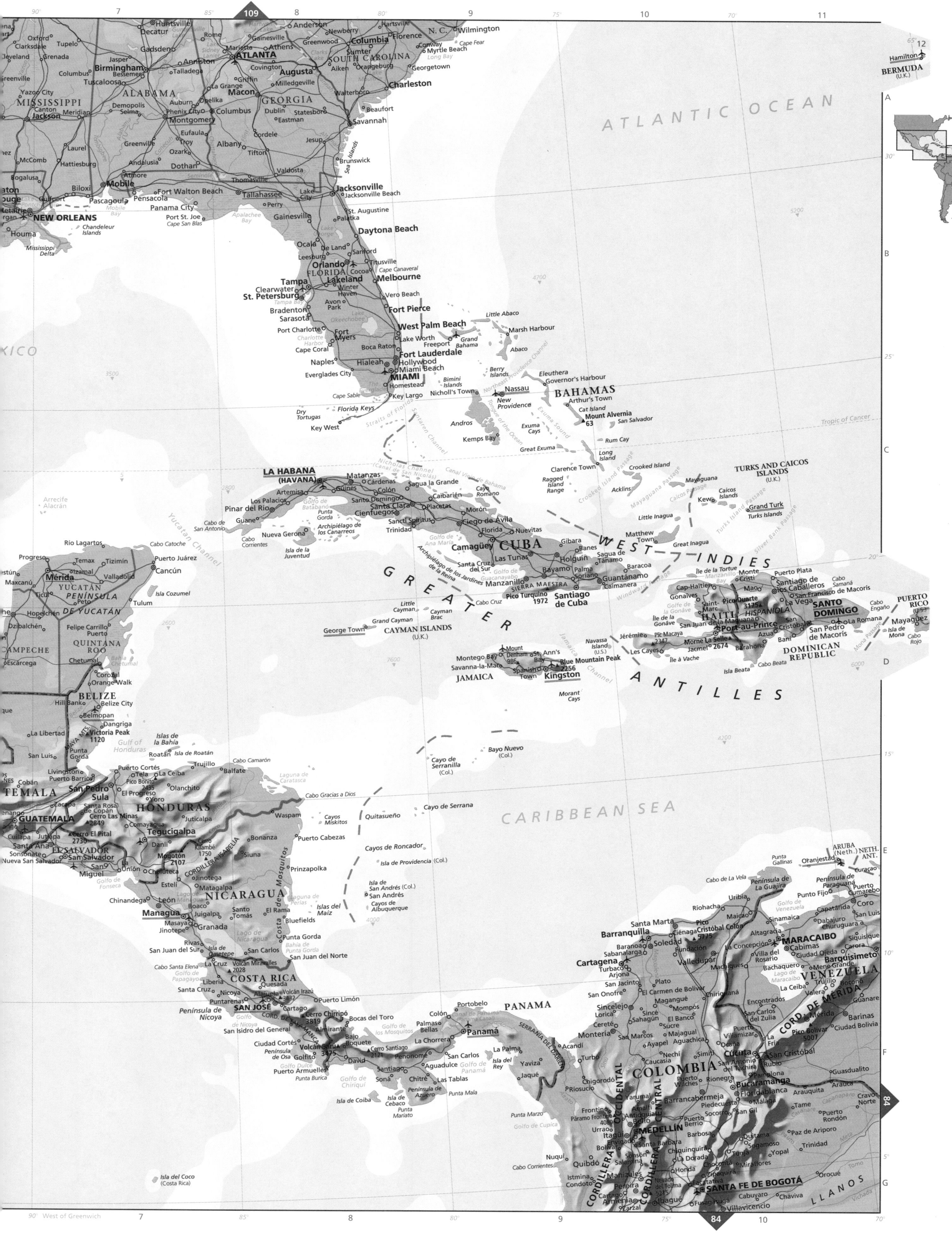
ATLANTIC OCEAN
CARIBBEAN SEA
GREATER ANTILLES
WEST INDIES
Tropic of Cancer
Hamilton
BERMUDA (U.K.)
MISSISSIPPI
ALABAMA
GEORGIA
SOUTH CAROLINA
N. C.
FLORIDA
Jackson
Birmingham
Montgomery
Mobile
NEW ORLEANS
ATLANTA
Columbia
Augusta
Macon
Columbus
Charleston
Savannah
Wilmington
Jacksonville
Tallahassee
Pensacola
Gainesville
Daytona Beach
Orlando
Tampa
St. Petersburg
Lakeland
Melbourne
Fort Pierce
West Palm Beach
Fort Lauderdale
Hollywood
Miami Beach
MIAMI
Key West
Straits of Florida
BAHAMAS
Nassau
Little Abaco
Marsh Harbour
Freeport
Grand Bahama
Andros
Eleuthera
Exuma Cays
Great Exuma
San Salvador
Rum Cay
Long Island
Crooked Island
Acklins
Mayaguana
Little Inagua
Great Inagua
TURKS AND CAICOS ISLANDS (U.K.)
Caicos Islands
Grand Turk
LA HABANA (HAVANA)
Matanzas
Pinar del Río
Cienfuegos
Santa Clara
Sancti Spíritus
Ciego de Ávila
Camagüey
CUBA
Las Tunas
Holguín
Bayamo
Manzanillo
Santiago de Cuba
Guantánamo
SIERRA MAESTRA
Pico Turquino 1972
Nueva Gerona
Isla de la Juventud
Archipiélago de los Canarreos
Archipiélago de los Jardines de la Reina
George Town
CAYMAN ISLANDS (U.K.)
Little Cayman
Cayman Brac
Grand Cayman
Montego Bay
JAMAICA
Kingston
Spanish Town
Blue Mountain Peak 2256
Morant Cays
Navassa Island (U.S.)
HAITI
HISPANIOLA
Port-au-Prince
Cap-Haïtien
Gonaïves
Jacmel
Les Cayes
Île de la Gonâve
Île de la Tortue
DOMINICAN REPUBLIC
SANTO DOMINGO
Santiago de los Caballeros
Puerto Plata
La Vega
San Pedro de Macorís
La Romana
Pico Duarte 3175
PUERTO RICO (U.S.)
Mayagüez
Isla de Mona
Mona Passage
Windward Passage
Jamaica Channel
Yucatan Channel
YUCATÁN
PENÍNSULA DE YUCATÁN
Mérida
Progreso
Cancún
Isla Cozumel
Tulum
CAMPECHE
QUINTANA ROO
Chetumal
Río Lagartos
Cabo Catoche
BELIZE
Belize City
Belmopan
Victoria Peak 1120
Gulf of Honduras
Islas de la Bahía
Roatán
HONDURAS
Tegucigalpa
San Pedro Sula
La Ceiba
Puerto Cortés
Trujillo
Choluteca
GUATEMALA
EL SALVADOR
San Salvador
San Miguel
NICARAGUA
Managua
León
Granada
Lago de Nicaragua
Bluefields
Puerto Cabezas
Costa de Mosquitos
Cabo Gracias a Dios
COSTA RICA
SAN JOSÉ
Puerto Limón
Puntarenas
Península de Nicoya
PANAMA
Panamá
Colón
David
Golfo de Panamá
Golfo de Chiriquí
Isla de Coiba
Península de Azuero
Isla del Coco (Costa Rica)
Cayos Miskitos
Quitasueño
Cayo de Serrana
Serranilla (Col.)
Bayo Nuevo (Col.)
Cayos de Roncador
Isla de Providencia (Col.)
Isla de San Andrés (Col.)
Islas del Maíz
COLOMBIA
Barranquilla
Cartagena
Santa Marta
MEDELLÍN
SANTA FE DE BOGOTÁ
Bucaramanga
Cúcuta
Villavicencio
Montería
Sincelejo
Valledupar
Riohacha
Quibdó
Manizales
Pereira
Ibagué
CORDILLERA OCCIDENTAL
CORDILLERA CENTRAL
Península de La Guajira
Punta Gallinas
Pico Cristóbal Colón 5775
VENEZUELA
MARACAIBO
Lago de Maracaibo
Golfo de Venezuela
Barquisimeto
Mérida
Barinas
CORD. DE MÉRIDA
Pico Bolívar 5007
Punto Fijo
Península de Paraguaná
Coro
ARUBA (Neth.)
NETH. ANT.
Oranjestad
Curaçao
LLANOS
West of Greenwich

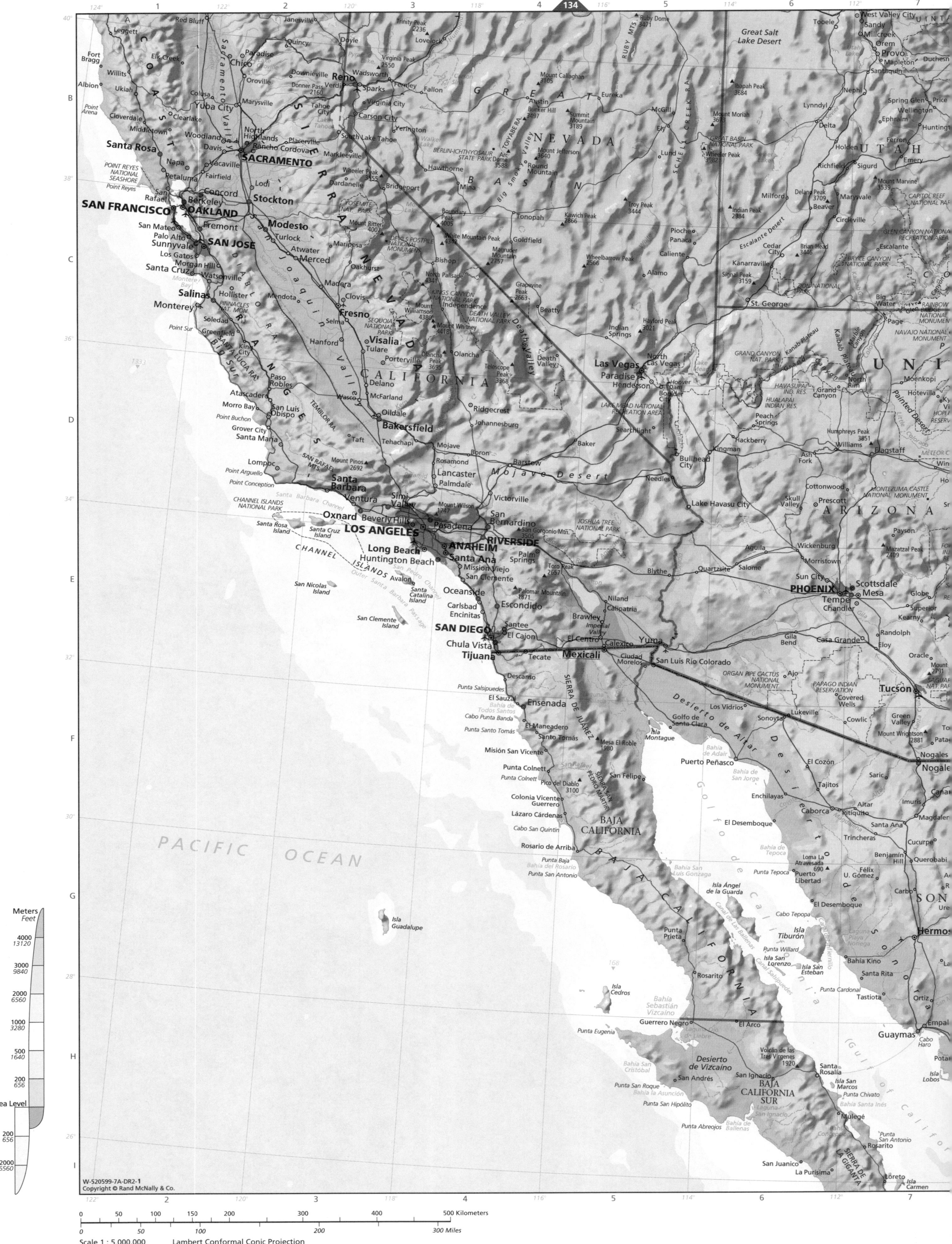
134
PACIFIC OCEAN
CALIFORNIA
NEVADA
UTAH
ARIZONA
BAJA CALIFORNIA
BAJA CALIFORNIA SUR
GREAT BASIN
SIERRA NEVADA
COAST RANGES
San Joaquin Valley
Sacramento Valley
Mojave Desert
Great Salt Lake Desert
Desierto de Altar
Desierto de Vizcaíno
Golfo de California
CHANNEL ISLANDS
SAN FRANCISCO
OAKLAND
SAN JOSE
SACRAMENTO
LOS ANGELES
ANAHEIM
RIVERSIDE
SAN DIEGO
PHOENIX
Santa Rosa
Stockton
Modesto
Fresno
Visalia
Bakersfield
Salinas
Monterey
Santa Cruz
Santa Barbara
Oxnard
Long Beach
Huntington Beach
Santa Ana
Oceanside
Escondido
Chula Vista
Tijuana
Mexicali
Ensenada
Reno
Carson City
Las Vegas
Henderson
Yuma
Tucson
Scottsdale
Mesa
Tempe
Provo
Nogales
Hermosillo
Guaymas
Santa Rosalía
Isla Guadalupe
Isla Cedros
Isla Tiburón
Point Conception
Scale 1 : 5,000,000
Lambert Conformal Conic Projection
0 50 100 150 200 300 400 500 Kilometers
0 50 100 200 300 Miles
Meters / Feet
4000 13120
3000 9840
2000 6560
1000 3280
500 1640
200 656
Sea Level
200 656
2000 6560
W-520599-7A-DR2-1
Copyright © Rand McNally & Co.

126
129
131
100
101
COLORADO
KANSAS
OKLAHOMA
TEXAS
NEW MEXICO
NEBRASKA
MEXICO
CHIHUAHUA
COAHUILA
NUEVO LEÓN
DURANGO
SINALOA
TAMAULIPAS
ROCKY MOUNTAINS
FRONT RANGE
GREAT PLAINS
SANGRE DE CRISTO MOUNTAINS
SAN JUAN MOUNTAINS
SACRAMENTO MTS.
GUADALUPE MTS.
DESIERTO DE CHIHUAHUA
SIERRA MADRE OCCIDENTAL
SIERRA MADRE ORIENTAL
Llano Estacado
Pecos Plains
Edwards Plateau
Balcones Escarpment
Stockton Plateau
Nueces Plains
Bolsón de Mapimí
San Luis Valley
Tularosa Valley
WICHITA MOUNTAINS
DAVIS MTS.
Gulf of Mexico
Padre Island
DENVER
Fort Collins
Greeley
Loveland
Longmont
Boulder
Lakewood
Aurora
Castle Rock
Colorado Springs
Pueblo
Cañon City
Grand Junction
Durango
Walsenburg
Trinidad
Raton
Wichita
Hutchinson
Salina
Manhattan
Dodge City
Garden City
Liberal
Enid
Oklahoma City
Norman
Lawton
Wichita Falls
Amarillo
Lubbock
Abilene
Midland
Odessa
Big Spring
San Angelo
Fort Worth
Arlington
Waco
Austin
SAN ANTONIO
Del Rio
Eagle Pass
Laredo
Nuevo Laredo
Corpus Christi
McAllen
Brownsville
Matamoros
Reynosa
Santa Fe
Albuquerque
Las Cruces
El Paso
Ciudad Juárez
Roswell
Carlsbad
Alamogordo
Clovis
Tucumcari
Las Vegas
Gallup
Farmington
Chihuahua
Delicias
Ciudad Camargo
Hidalgo del Parral
Monclova
Piedras Negras
Ciudad Acuña
San Nicolás de los Garza
Guadalupe
MONTERREY
Santa Catarina
Ciudad Obregón
Navojoa
Huatabampo
Nuevo Casas Grandes
Ojinaga
Saltillo
Pikes Peak 4301
Mount Elbert 4399
Blanca Peak 4372
Wheeler Peak 4011
Guadalupe Peak 2667
Emory Peak 2385
West of Greenwich

98
1
2
3
4
5
6
114°
112°
110°
108°
106°
104°
A
B
C
D
E
F
G
H
28°
26°
24°
22°
20°
18°
16°
Hermosillo
SONORA
Bahía Kino
Santa Rita
Tastiota
Ortiz
Guaymas
Cabo Haro
Empalme
Cumuripa
La Colorada
Sahuaripa
Guaycora
Mulatos
Onabas
Suaqui Grande
Yécora
San José de Batuc
Isla Ángel de la Guarda
Isla Tiburón
Punta Willard
Isla San Esteban
Isla San Lorenzo
Punta Cardonal
Canal de Ballenas
Canal Salsipuedes
Punta Prieta
Rosarito
Isla Cedros
BAJA CALIFORNIA
Bahía Sebastián Vizcaíno
Guerrero Negro
El Arco
Punta Eugenia
Bahía San Cristóbal
Desierto de Vizcaíno
Volcán de las Tres Vírgenes 1920
Santa Rosalía
Punta San Roque
San Andrés
San Ignacio
Punta San Hipólito
Isla San Marcos
Punta Chivato
Bahía Santa Inés
Mulegé
Punta Abreojos
Bahía de Ballenas
Punta San Antonio
Rosarito
San Juanico
La Purísima
BAJA CALIFORNIA SUR
La Poza Grande
Santo Domingo
Villa Insurgentes
Isla Santa Magdalena
Ciudad Constitución
Cabo San Lázaro
El Médano
Isla Santa Margarita
Bahía Almejas
Loreto
Isla Carmen
Ligui
Isla Santa Catalina
Punta San Pasqual
Isla San José
San Luis Gonzaga
SIERRA DE LA GIGANTA
BAJA CALIFORNIA
Isla del Espíritu Santo
La Paz
Isla Cerralvo
Punta Arena de la Ventana
Punta Pescadores
El Triunfo
Las Casitas 2164
Punta Arena
Todos Santos
Santiago
San José del Cabo
San Lucas
Cabo San Lucas
Tropic of Cancer
Golfo de California
Gulf of California
Vicam
Potam
San José de Bácum
Ciudad Obregón
Esperanza
Rosario
Isla Lobos
Pueblo Yaqui
Villa Juárez
Navojoa
Álamos
Etchojoa
Huatabampo
Yavaros
El Fuerte
Choix
Higuera de Zaragoza
Ahome
Los Mochis
Topolobampo
San Blas
General Juan José Ríos
Corerepe
Guasave
Guamúchil
Angostura
SINALOA
Isla San Ignacio
Bahía Santa María
Isla Altamura
Isla de Tachichilte
La Reforma
Pericos
Culiacancito
Culiacán
Navolato
Aguaruto
Altata
Ensenada del Pabellón
Costa Rica
Quila
Higuera de Abuya
Tamazula
Badiraguato
Tameapa
Chihuahua
CHIHUAHUA
SIERRA MADRE OCCIDENTAL
Madera
Gómez Farías
Santa Clara
Temosachic
Cerro Grande 2780
Bachiniva
Guerrero
Adolfo López Mateos
Cuauhtémoc
Cerro El Nopal 3060
Cusihuiriachic
Ocampo
Yepachic
Parque Nacional Cascadas Basaseachic
Creel
Carichic
San Francisco de Borja
Agua Caliente
Guazapares
Urique
Nonoava
Norogachi
Guazárachi
Guachochi
Morelos
Picacho Soledad 2752
Nabogame
Cerro las Iglesias 3110
Ciudad Camargo
Valle de Zaragoza
Valle de Olivos
Balleza
San Francisco del Oro
Hidalgo del Parral
Santa Bárbara
Jiménez
Delicias
Meoqui
Rosales
Saucillo
Naica
Julimes
Aldama
El Sauz
Aquiles Serdán
Las Chorreras
Coyame
Presidio
Ojinaga
Maclovio Herrera
Manuel Benavides
La Perla
Hércules
Jaco
Maravillas
Carrillo
Escalón
Ceballos
Bolsón de Mapimí
El Jaralito
Tlahualilo de Zaragoza
Orestes Pereyra
Las Nieves
San Bernardo
Santa María del Oro
La Zarca
Mapimí
Gómez Palacio
Lerdo
Guanaceví
Cerro Ocotes 3150
Cerro Tagarete 3020
General Escobedo
Tepehuanes
San Pedro del Gallo
Nazas
Abasolo
Rodeo
Pedriceña
Santiago Papasquiaro
DURANGO
Tejamén
San Juan del Río
Diez de Octubre
Francisco I. Madero
Guadalupe Victoria
Antonio Amaro
Canatlán
San Miguel de Cruces
Otinapa
Durango
Nombre de Dios
Vicente Guerrero
Súchil
Topia
Canelas
El Limón de Teachi
Coacoyole
Conitaca
Ajoya
Tayoltita
El Salto
La Ciudad
El Quelite
Agua Caliente
Cebollas
Mezquital
Concordia
Mazatlán
Villa Unión
Rosario
Mineral de Cucharas
Escuinapa de Hidalgo
Laguna del Caimanero
Teacapan
Acaponeta
Tecuala
Huazamota
Cerro Lechuguilla 2480
Valparaíso
Rosamorada
Ruiz
Tuxpan
Santiago Ixcuintla
NAYARIT
Tepic
San Blas
Compostela
Volcán Ceboruco 2280
Las Varas
Ahuacatlán
Ixtlán del Río
San Juan de Abajo
Punta de Mita
Bahía de Banderas
Puerto Vallarta
Cabo Corrientes
Mascota
Atenguillo
Cerro la Tetilla 2680
Ameca
Cocula
Ayutla
JALISCO
GUADALAJARA
Zapopan
Tlaquepaque
Magdalena
Tomatlán
Autlán de Navarro
Purificación
Cuautitlán
Parque Nacional del Nevado de Colima
Nevado de Colima 4240
Comala
COLIMA
Colima
Manzanillo
Armería
Tecomán
Punta Tejupan
Isla San Juanito
Isla María Madre
Isla María Magdalena
ISLAS TRES MARÍAS
Isla María Cleofas
PACIFIC OCEAN
Isla San Benedicto
Isla Roca Partida
Cerro Evermann 1050
ISLAS REVILLAGIGEDO
Isla Socorro
168
868
1668
4616
4134
Meters
Feet
4000
13120
3000
9840
2000
6560
1000
3280
500
1640
200
656
Sea Level
200
656
2000
6560
W-532095-7A-DR2-1
Copyright © Rand McNally & Co.
West of Greenwich
0
50
100
150
200
300
400
500 Kilometers
0
50
100
200
300 Miles
Scale 1 : 5,000,000
Lambert Conformal Conic Projection

SAN ANTONIO
UNITED STATES
TEXAS
Nueces Plains
Corpus Christi
Laredo
Nuevo Laredo
Piedras Negras
Monclova
COAHUILA
McAllen
Reynosa
Brownsville
Matamoros
NUEVO LEÓN
San Nicolás de los Garza
MONTERREY
Guadalupe
Saltillo
GULF OF MEXICO
TAMAULIPAS
Ciudad Victoria
SAN LUIS POTOSÍ
San Luis Potosí
Ciudad Madero
Tampico
Aguascalientes
León
Irapuato
Querétaro
Celaya
Morelia
MICHOACÁN
Uruapan del Progreso
Toluca
CIUDAD DE MÉXICO (MEXICO CITY)
Tlalnepantla
Ciudad Netzahualcóyotl
PUEBLA
Cuernavaca
Poza Rica de Hidalgo
VERACRUZ
Xalapa (Jalapa)
Veracruz
Bahía de Campeche
Orizaba
Córdoba
Coatzacoalcos
Minatitlán
Villahermosa
TABASCO
Ciudad del Carmen
CAMPECHE
Chilpancingo de los Bravo
GUERRERO
Acapulco
Oaxaca de Juárez
OAXACA
SIERRA MADRE DEL SUR
ISTMO DE TEHUANTEPEC
Golfo de Tehuantepec
Salina Cruz
Tuxtla Gutiérrez
CHIAPAS
SIERRA MADRE DE CHIAPAS
GUATEMALA
Tapachula
Puerto Escondido
SIERRA MADRE ORIENTAL
Tropic of Cancer
Cayo Arenas
Cayo Nuevo
Cayos Arcas

Gulf of Mexico
Yucatan Channel
Cayo Arenas
LA HABANA (HAVANA)
Matanzas
Cárdenas
San Antonio de los Baños
San José de las Lajas
Artemisa
Güines
Unión de Reyes
Colón
La Esperanza
Minas de Matahambre
Los Palacios
Pinar del Río
Consolación del Sur
Mantua
Guane
Golfo de Guanahacabibes
Ensenada de la Broa
Punta Gorda
Golfo de Batabanó
Península de Zapata
Jagüey Grande
Cienfuegos
Cabo de San Antonio
Bahía de Corrientes
Cabo Corrientes
Cayos de San Felipe
Nueva Gerona
Archipiélago de los Canarreos
La Fe
Isla de la Juventud (Isle of Pines)
Cayo Largo
Bahía de Cochinos (Bay of Pigs)
Río Lagartos
Punta Holohit
Cabo Catoche
Dzilam González
Progreso
Panabá
Motul de Felipe Carrillo Puerto
Tizimín
Isla Mujeres
Puerto Juárez
Punta Cancún
Temax
Kantunilkín
Cancún
Celestún
Umán
Mérida
Izamal
Espita
X-Can
Valladolid
Puerto Morelos
CHICHÉN ITZÁ
Halachó
Maxcanú
Playa del Carmen
Muna
Ticul
YUCATÁN
COBÁ
Cozumel
Isla Cozumel
Bahía de Campeche
Becal
Oxkutzcab
Dzitbalché
Chikindzonot
Tulum
Hecelchakán
Tekax
Peto
TULUM
Tenabo
Tzucacab
Campeche
Bolonchén de Rejón
PENÍNSULA DE YUCATÁN
Seybaplaya
Punta Morro
Hopelchén
Iturbide
ETZNÁ
Champotón
Dzibalchén
Chunhuhux
Felipe Carrillo Puerto
(YUCATAN PENINSULA)
CAYMAN ISLANDS (U.K.)
Sabancuy
MEXICO
QUINTANA ROO
George Town
Grand Cayman
Isla del Carmen
Ciudad del Carmen
CAMPECHE
Bahía Chetumal
Laguna de Términos
Escárcega
Chetumal
Corozal
Xcalak
Caledonia
Orange Walk
Ambergris Cay
Emiliano Zapata
San Pedro Tabasco
San Pedro
Indian Church
Hill Bank
Belize City
Turneffe Islands
Chuntuqui
Sierra de Agua
TABASCO
Tenosique
UAXACTÚN
TIKAL
PARQUE NACIONAL TIKAL
El Encanto
Belmopan
Islas Santanilla (Hond.)
Piedras Negras
Benque Viejo del Carmen
BELIZE
YAXCHILÁN
Middlesex
Dangriga
CHIAPAS
La Libertad
La Florida
MAYA MOUNTAINS
Victoria Peak 1120
Dolores
Sayaxché
Palmar Camp
Las Margaritas
ISLAS DE LA BAHÍA
Isla de Guanaja
Guanaja
Comitán de Domínguez
San Luis
Roatán
Isla de Roatán
Gulf of Honduras
Punta Negra
Punta Gorda
Utila
Isla de Utila
Cabo de Honduras
Barillas
Puerto Cortés
Trujillo
Cabo Camarón
GUATEMALA
Chahal
Livingston
Puerto Barrios
Colorado
La Ceiba
Limón
Punta Patuca
Concepción Huista
Cobán
El Estor
Tela
Balfate
Paya
Huehuetenango
San Pedro Carchá
Panzós
San Pedro Sula
Pico Bonito 2435
Tocoa
Brus Laguna
El Progreso
Olanchito
Volcán Tajumulco 4220
San Andrés Sajcabajá
La Lima
El Negrito
SIERRA MADRE
San Jerónimo
Santa Cruz del Quiché
Santa Rita
Yoro
Pico Pijol 2282
Arrecifes de la Media Luna
Quetzaltenango
Santa Bárbara
Chiquimula
HONDURAS
Cabo Gracias a Dios
Zacapa
Santa Rosa de Copán
Catacamas
Wampú
Chimaltenango
Jalapa
Mazatenango
San Luis Jilotepeque
Salamá
GUATEMALA
Minas de Oro
Juticalpa
Retalhuleu
Siguatepeque
Waspam
Bilwaskarma
Volcán de Fuego 3763
Barberena
Cerro El Pital 2730
Cerro Las Minas 2849
Comayagua
Guaimaca
Montaña El Chile 2256
Champerico
Cuilapa
Escuintla
Metapán
La Esperanza
La Paz
Cayos Miskitos
Quitasueño
Bocay
Puerto San José
Santa Ana
Chalatenango
Tegucigalpa
Punta Gorda
Yablis
Cayo de Serrana
Sonsonate
Nueva San Salvador
Cojutepeque
Sabanagrande
Yuscarán
Danlí
Bonanza
Puerto Cabezas
San Salvador
San Vicente
San Francisco
Güinope
Cerro Saslaya 1650
Punta Remedios
EL SALVADOR
San Miguel
Ocotal
Mogotón 2107
Cerro Kilambé 1750
Siuna
Somoto
COSTA DE MOSQUITOS
Usulután
Choluteca
La Unión
Condega
Wouhnta
Prinzapolka
El Corpus
San Rafael del Norte
CORDILLERA ISABELIA
Tungla
Isla de Providencia
Golfo de Fonseca
Estelí
Jinotega
La Cruzde Río Grande
Punta Cosigüina
Volcán Cosigüina 859
La Trinidad
Matagalpa
CORDILLERA DARIENSE
Barra de Río Grande
Volcán San Cristóbal 1745
Río Grande
Sébaco
El Viejo
Ciudad Darío
NICARAGUA
Isla de San Andrés
San Andrés
Chinandega
Volcán Momotombo 1280
Boaco
Cayos del Este Sudeste
León
La Paz Centro
Santo Domingo
Nagarote
Tipitapa
Managua
Juigalpa
El Rama
Islas del Maíz
Cayos de Albuquerque
SAN ANDRÉS Y PROVIDENCIA (Col.)
Masaya
Granada
Santo Tomás
Muelle de los Bueyes
Bluefields
El Bluff
Jinotepe
Masatepe
CORDILLERA CHONTALEÑA
Nandaime
Volcán Concepción 1610
Isla de Ometepe
Belén
Rivas
Lago de Nicaragua
Punta Gorda
San Juan del Sur
Bahía de Punta Gorda
San Carlos
San Juan del Norte
Cabo Santa Elena
Volcán Miravalles 2028
PACIFIC OCEAN
Golfo de Papagayo
CORDILLERA DE GUANACASTE
Barra del Colorado
Liberia
Bagaces
Cañas
Fortuna
Puerto Viejo
Venecia
Cabo Velas
Santa Cruz
Guápiles
Siquirres
Nicoya
Cerro Azul 1018
Puntarenas
Alajuela
Heredia
Puerto Limón
Península de Nicoya
SAN JOSÉ
Juan Viñas
Cartago
Golfo de Nicoya
Cabo Blanco
Cerro La Muerte 3491
Punta Mona
PARQUE INTERNACIONAL DE LA AMISTAD
Bocas del Toro
San Isidro del General
Cerro Chirripó 3819
Cerro Kámuk 3554
Almirante
COSTA RICA
Península Valiente
Buenos Aires
Bahía de Coronado
Ciudad Cortés
Volcán Barú 3475
Golfo de los Mosquitos
Bajo Boquete
Península de Osa
PARQUE NACIONAL CORCOVADO
Golfito
La Concepción
David
Dolega
Gualaca
Cerro Santiago 2121
PANAMA
Puerto Armuelles
Pedregal
Las Lajas
Remedios
Cañazas
Santiago
Punta Burica
Golfo de Chiriquí
Soná
Montijo
Isla de Coiba
Isla de Cebaco
Punta Mariato
Isla Jicarón
5578
3493
Meters Feet
3000 9840
2000 6560
1000 3280
500 1640
200 656
Sea Level
200 656
2000 6560
W-536000-7A-DR2-1
Copyright © Rand McNally & Co.
0 50 100 150 200 300 400 500 Kilometers
0 50 100 200 300 Miles
Scale 1 : 5,000,000
Lambert Conformal Conic Projection
101

BAHAMAS
TURKS AND CAICOS ISLANDS (U.K.)
ATLANTIC OCEAN
WEST INDIES
CUBA
HISPANIOLA
HAITI
DOMINICAN REPUBLIC
JAMAICA
GREATER ANTILLES
CARIBBEAN SEA
LESSER ANTILLES
ARUBA (Neth.)
NETHERLANDS ANTILLES (Neth.)
COLOMBIA
VENEZUELA

Deadman's Cay
Clarence Town
Long Island
Cape Verde
Crooked Island
Samana Cay
North East Point
Ragged Island Range
Long Cay
Acklins
Ragged Island
Salina Point
Mayaguana
Mayaguana Passage
Caicos Passage
Providenciales
Kew
Middle Caicos
North Caicos
East Caicos
West Caicos
Grand Turk
CAICOS ISLANDS
TURKS ISLANDS
Little Inagua
North East Point
Palacca Point
Great Inagua
Matthew Town
Seal Cays
Mouchoir Passage
Silver Bank Passage
Turks Island Passage

Caibarién
Yaguajay
Placetas
Sancti Spíritus
Ciego de Ávila
Morón
Cayo Coco
Cay Lobos
Cayo Romano
Cayo Guajaba
Cayo Sabinal
Esmeralda
Nuevitas
Júcaro
Florida
Minas
Camagüey
Vertientes
Puerto Manatí
Jesús Menéndez
Puerto Padre
Gibara
Rafael Freyre
Punta de Mulas
Banes
Antilla
Las Tunas
Holguín
Guayabal
Cueto
Mayarí
Santa Cruz del Sur
Bayamo
Jiguaní
Alto Cedro
Sagua de Tánamo
Baracoa
Manzanillo
Palma Soriano
San Luis
Guantánamo
Campechuela
Niquero
SIERRA MAESTRA
Pico Turquino 1972
Santiago de Cuba
Marea de Portillo
Caimanera
GUANTANAMO BAY NAVAL STATION (U.S.)
Imías
Punta de Quemado
Cabo Cruz
Golfo de Guacanayabo
Golfo de Ana María
Archipiélago de los Jardines de la Reina
Canal Viejo de Bahama
Cayman Brac

Île de la Tortue
Port-de-Paix
Cap du Môle
Cap-Haïtien
Limbé
Fort-Liberté
Monte Cristi
Cabo Isabela
Puerto Plata
Cabo Macorís
Cabo Francés Viejo
Pico Diego de Ocampo 1249
Mao
Dajabón
Santiago de los Caballeros
Moca
Nagua
Cabo Samaná
Samaná
San Francisco de Macorís
Cap à Foux
Gonaïves
Desdunes
Golfe de la Gonâve
Île de la Gonâve
Saint-Marc
Morne Bonhomme 1788
Pico Duarte 3175
La Vega
Bonao
Comendador
Sabana de la Mar
Miches
Hato Mayor del Rey
El Seibo
Higüey
Cabo Engaño
Alto Bandera 2630
San Juan de la Maguana
SANTO DOMINGO
Port-au-Prince
Jérémie
Grande Cayemite
Pointe Fanchon
Anse-d'Hainault
Pic Macaya 2347
Aquin
Léogâne
Pétion-Ville
Petit-Goâve
Jacmel
Morne La Selle 2674
Neiba
Azua
San Cristóbal
San Pedro de Macorís
La Romana
Baní
Punta Palenque
Isla Saona
Coteaux
Les Cayes
Pointe Abacou
Île à Vache
Pedernales
Barahona
Enriquillo
Cabo Falso
Isla Beata
Cabo Beata
Navassa Island (U.S.)
Windward Passage
Jamaica Channel

Montego Bay
Falmouth
Ocho Rios
Saint Ann's Bay
Port Maria
Port Antonio
South Negril Point
Savanna-la-Mar
Mount Denham 986
Kingston
Blue Mountain Peak 2256
Mandeville
Spanish Town
Morant Point
Morant Bay
Portland Point
Portland Bight
Morant Cays
Pedro Cays
Cayo de Serranilla (Col.)
Bajo Nuevo (Col.)
de Roncador

Oranjestad
Bonaire
Curaçao
Willemstad
Punta Gallinas
Bahía Honda
Puerto Bolívar
Cabo de La Vela
Península de La Guajira
Punta Espada
Cabo San Román
Pueblo Nuevo
Península de Paraguaná
Los Taques
Punto Fijo
Golfo de Venezuela
Punta Cardón
Puerto Cumarebo
Punta Zamuro
Uribia
Riohacha
Maicao
Paraguaipoa
Sinamaica
San Rafael
Coro
La Vela de Coro
Capatárida
Pedregal
Dabajuro
FALCÓN
Churuguara
Cabure
Santa Marta
Cabo de La Aguja
Ciénaga
Pico Cristóbal Colón 5775
LA GUAJIRA
Barrancas
Albania
Fonseca
San Juan del Cesar
Barranquilla
Soledad
ATLÁNTICO
Malambo
Baranoa
MARACAIBO
Altagracia
Mene de Mauroa
Santa Rita
Cabimas
Cerro Cerrón 1930
Siquisique
Yaritagua
San Felipe
YARACUY
Cartagena
Sabanalarga
Turbaco
Arjona
Islas del Rosario
Valledupar
Aracataca
Fundación
La Paz
Agustín Codazzi
Villa del Rosario
Tía Juana
Ciudad Ojeda
Machiques
Lago de Maracaibo
Carora
LARA
Barquisimeto
Bachaquero
Mene Grande
Quíbor
Sarare
Acarigua
Araure
Píritu
El Piñón
Calamar
Pivijay
Pedraza
Mahates
El Guamo
María La Baja
San Juan Nepomuceno
San Jacinto
San Onofre
Islas de San Bernardo
El Carmen de Bolívar
MAGDALENA
CESAR
ZULIA
Cerro Mu 2610
Chiriguaná
Chimichagua
Tolú
Ovejas
San Pedro
Sincelejo
Magangué
San Antero
Corozal
Mompós
Guamal
Lorica
COLOMBIA
Chinú
Sahagún
Pinillos
El Banco
San Pelayo
Cereté
Ciénaga de Oro
Sucre
SUCRE
Montería
San Marcos
BOLÍVAR
Achí
Majagual
Planeta Rica
CÓRDOBA
Ayapel
Tierralta
Alto de Quimari 2000
Montelíbano
Caucasia
ANTIOQUIA
Nechí
Simití
Apartadó
Turbo
Arboletes
Golfo de Morrosquillo
Golfo de Urabá
Tamalameque
Pailitas
La Gloria
El Carmen
Gamarra
Aguachica
Río de Oro
Ocaña
Ábrego
NORTE DE SANTANDER
SERRANÍA DE PERIJÁ
La Ceiba
Sabana de Mendoza
Bobures
Valera
TRUJILLO
Trujillo
Carache
San Timoteo
Boconó
PORTUGUESA
Guanare
Ospino
Biscucuy
Guanarito
San Carlos del Zulia
Encontrados
San Pedro
Casigua
Timotes
Mucuchíes
El Vigía
Mérida
Ejido
Barinitas
PARQUE NAC. SIERRA NEVADA
Pico Bolívar 5007
Barinas
Santa Rosa
Dolores
Libertad
Ciudad Bolivia
Ciudad de Nutrias
Bruzual
BARINAS
Tovar
Bailadores
La Grita
MÉRIDA
CORDILLERA DE MÉRIDA
Petrólea
Sardinata
La Fría
San Juan de Colón
TÁCHIRA
Cúcuta
San Antonio del Táchira
Rubio
San Cristóbal
Santa Bárbara
Palmarito
APURE
LLANOS

Istmo de Panamá (Isthmus of Panama)
Punta Manzanillo
Nombre de Dios
El Porvenir
Golfo de San Blas
Nidiatupo
Chepo
SERRANÍA DE SAN BLAS
Punta Mosquito
Mansucum
Panamá
Capira
Chimán
Bejuco
San Carlos
Bahía de Panamá
San Miguel
ARCHIPIÉLAGO DE LAS PERLAS
Isla del Rey
La Palma
Golfo de San Miguel
Isla San José
Garachiné
Yaviza
El Real de Santa María
Golfo de Panamá
PARQUE NACIONAL DARIÉN
Cabo Tiburón
Punta Caribana
Acandí
CHOCÓ

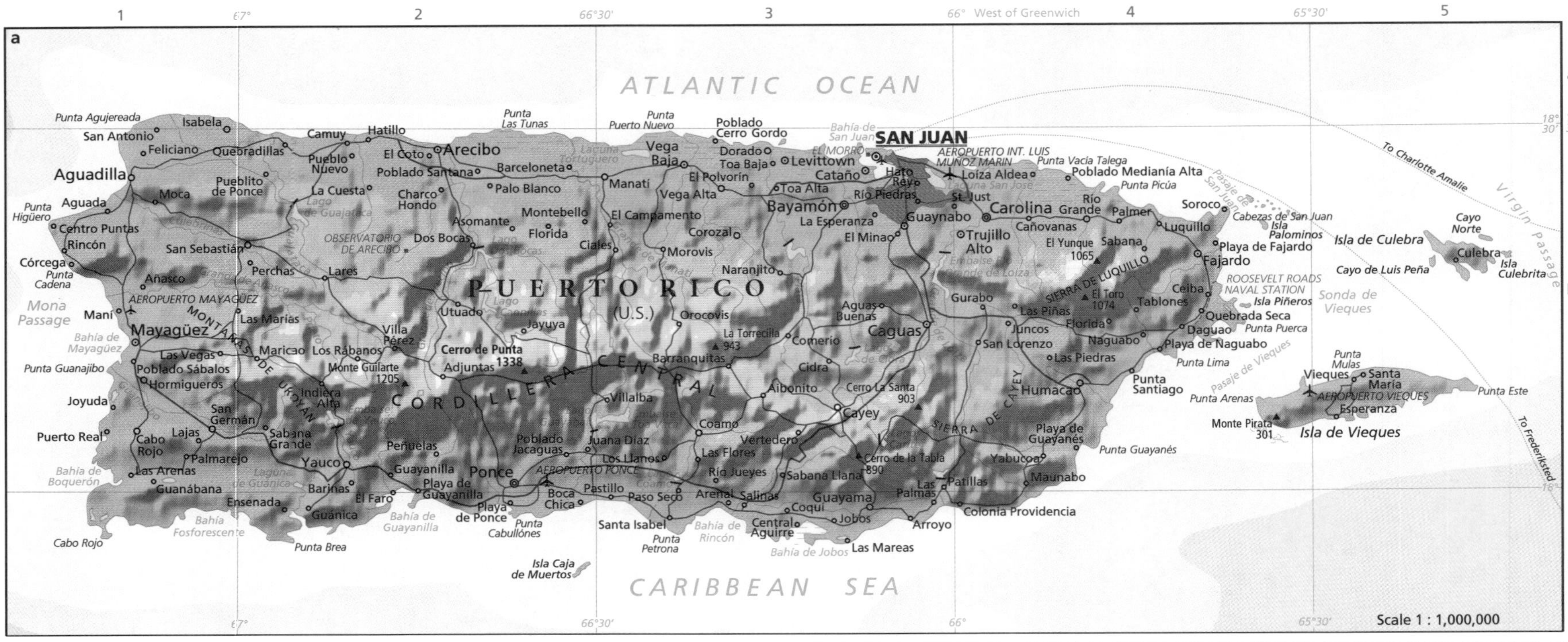

a

ATLANTIC OCEAN

PUERTO RICO (U.S.)

SAN JUAN

Aguadilla, Mayagüez, Arecibo, Bayamón, Carolina, Caguas, Ponce, Humacao, Fajardo, Vieques, Isla de Vieques, Isla de Culebra, Culebra, Mona Passage, Cordillera Central, Cerro de Punta 1338, El Yunque 1065, El Toro 1074, Monte Pirata 301

CARIBBEAN SEA

Scale 1 : 1,000,000

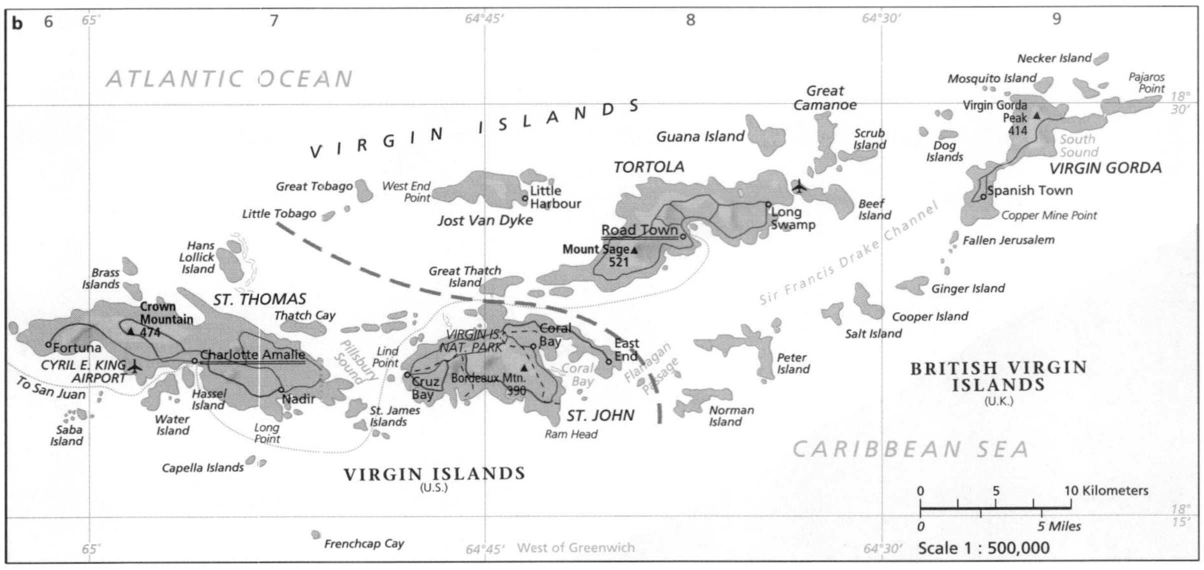

b

ATLANTIC OCEAN

VIRGIN ISLANDS

Great Camanoe, Guana Island, Tortola, Road Town, Mount Sage 521, Jost Van Dyke, Virgin Gorda, Virgin Gorda Peak 414, Spanish Town, St. Thomas, Crown Mountain 474, Charlotte Amalie, St. John, Cruz Bay, Bordeaux Mtn. 390, Sir Francis Drake Channel

BRITISH VIRGIN ISLANDS (U.K.)

VIRGIN ISLANDS (U.S.)

CARIBBEAN SEA

0 5 10 Kilometers

0 5 Miles

Scale 1 : 500,000

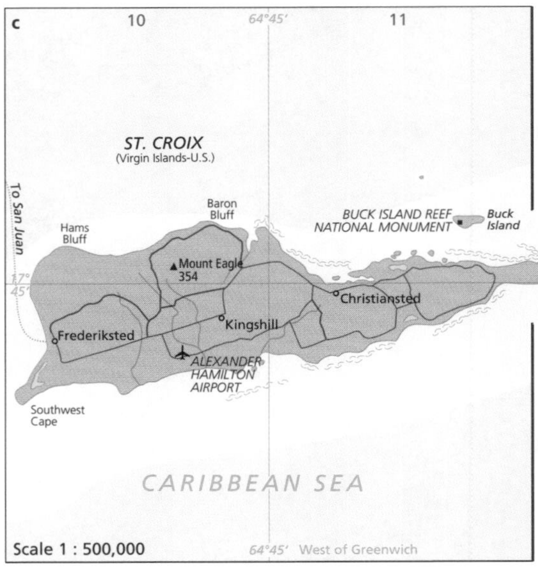

c

ST. CROIX (Virgin Islands-U.S.)

Frederiksted, Kingshill, Christiansted, Mount Eagle 354, Buck Island Reef National Monument, Alexander Hamilton Airport

CARIBBEAN SEA

Scale 1 : 500,000

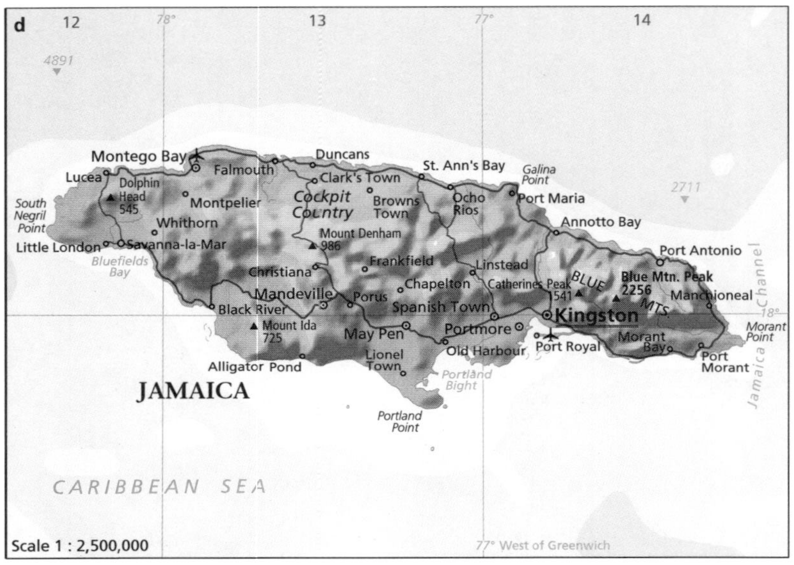

d

JAMAICA

Montego Bay, Falmouth, St. Ann's Bay, Port Maria, Mandeville, May Pen, Spanish Town, Kingston, Port Antonio, Blue Mtn. Peak 2256, Morant Point, Portland Point

CARIBBEAN SEA

Scale 1 : 2,500,000

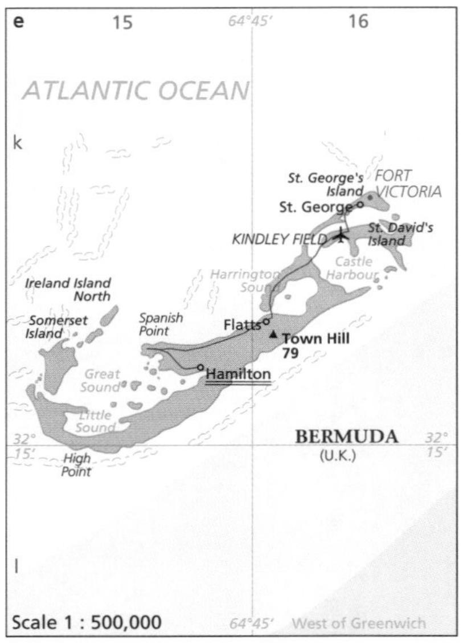

e

ATLANTIC OCEAN

BERMUDA (U.K.)

St. George's, Hamilton, Flatts, Town Hill 79

Scale 1 : 500,000

f

ATLANTIC OCEAN

NEW PROVIDENCE (Bahamas)

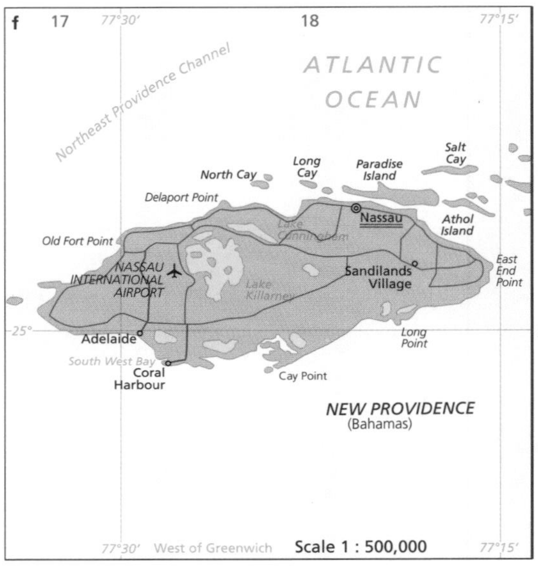

Nassau, Nassau International Airport, Adelaide, Coral Harbour, Sandilands Village

Scale 1 : 500,000

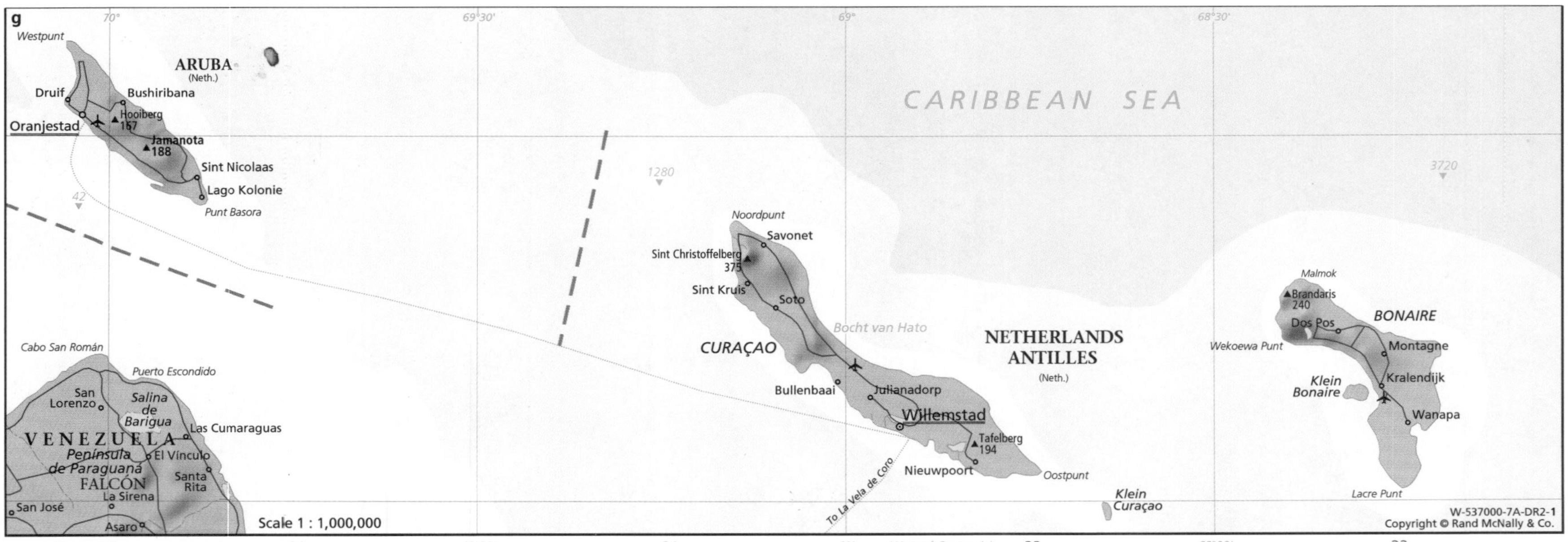

g

CARIBBEAN SEA

ARUBA (Neth.)

Oranjestad, Jamanota 188, Sint Nicolaas

CURAÇAO

Willemstad, Sint Christoffelberg 375, Klein Curaçao

NETHERLANDS ANTILLES (Neth.)

BONAIRE

Kralendijk, Brandaris 240, Klein Bonaire

VENEZUELA

Península de Paraguaná, FALCÓN

Scale 1 : 1,000,000

W-537000-7A-DR2-1

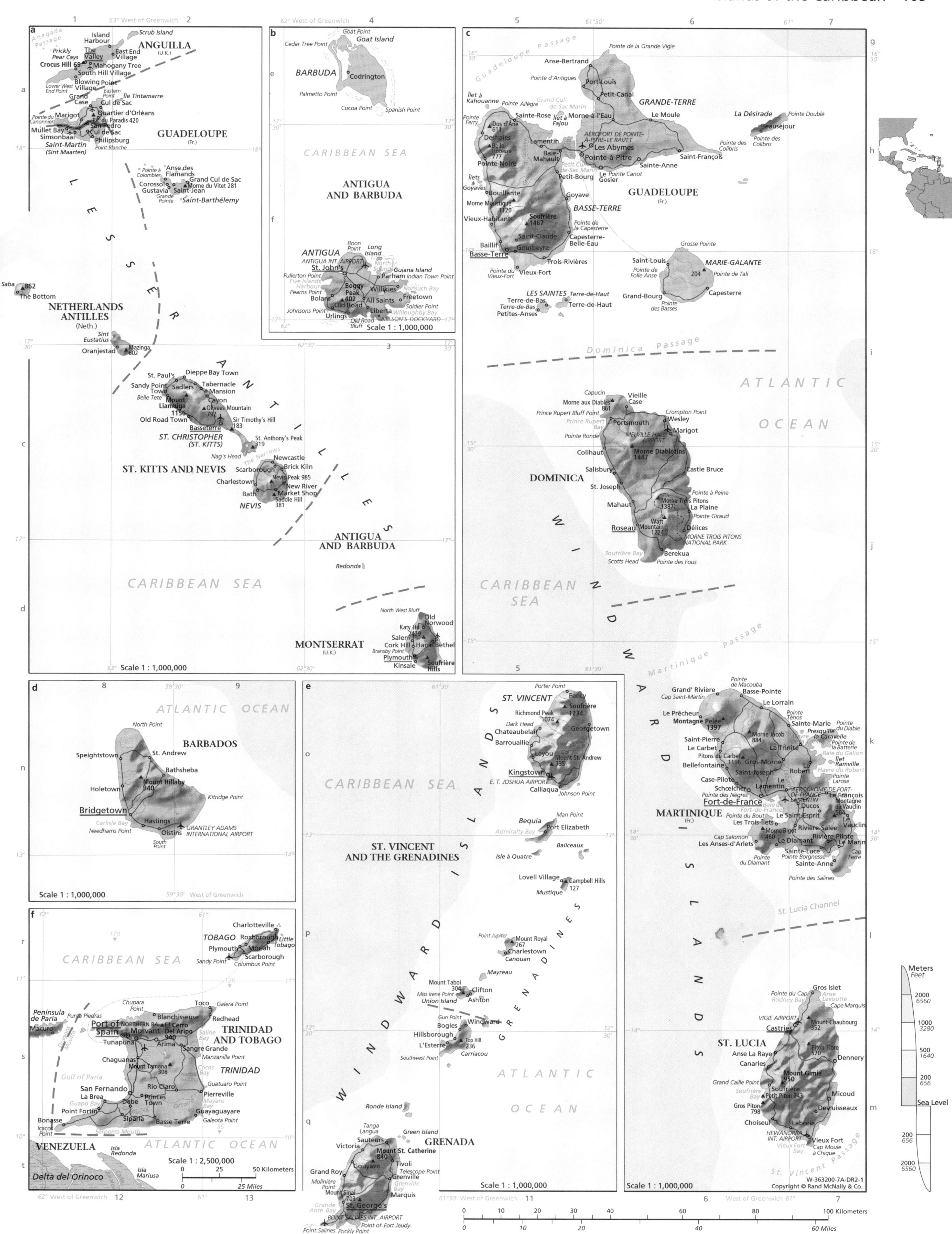
ANGUILLA
(U.K.)
Island Harbour
The Valley
East End Village
Crocus Hill 69
Mahogany Tree
South Hill Village
Blowing Point Village
Scrub Island
Prickly Pear Cays
Lower West End Point
Anegada Passage
Grand Case
Cul de Sac
Marigot
Quartier d'Orléans
Pic du Paradis 420
Mullet Bay
Simsonbaai
Saint-Martin
(Sint Maarten)
Philipsburg
Point Blanche
Île Tintamarre
GUADELOUPE
(Fr.)
Anse des Flamands
Grand Cul de Sac
Morne du Vitet 281
Corossol
Gustavia
Saint-Jean
Saint-Barthélemy
Saba
862
The Bottom
NETHERLANDS ANTILLES
(Neth.)
Sint Eustatius
Oranjestad
Mazinga 602
LESSER ANTILLES
BARBUDA
Goat Point
Goat Island
Cedar Tree Point
Codrington
Palmetto Point
Cocoa Point
Spanish Point
CARIBBEAN SEA
ANTIGUA AND BARBUDA
ANTIGUA
ANTIGUA INT. AIRPORT
St. John's
Boon Point
Long Island
Guiana Island
Parham
Indian Town Point
Fullerton Point
Five Islands Harbour
Pearns Point
Boggy Peak 402
Bolans
Willikies
Freetown
All Saints
Johnsons Point
Urlings
Old Road
Liberta
Soldier Point
Old Road Bluff
NELSON'S DOCKYARD
Scale 1 : 1,000,000
St. Paul's
Dieppe Bay Town
Sandy Point Town
Sadlers
Tabernacle
Mansion
Belle Tete
Mount Liamuiga 1156
Cayon
Olivees Mountain 792
Old Road Town
Basseterre
Sir Timothy's Hill 183
ST. CHRISTOPHER
(ST. KITTS)
St. Anthony's Peak 319
Nag's Head
The Narrows
ST. KITTS AND NEVIS
Newcastle
Brick Kiln
Scarborough
Nevis Peak 985
Charlestown
New River
Market Shop
Bath
Saddle Hill 381
NEVIS
Redonda
CARIBBEAN SEA
North West Bluff
Old Norwood
Katy Hill
Salem
Cork Hill
Harris
Bethel
Bransby Point
Plymouth
Kinsale
Soufrière Hills
MONTSERRAT
(U.K.)
Guadeloupe Passage
Pointe de la Grande Vigie
Anse-Bertrand
Pointe d'Antigues
Port-Louis
Petit-Canal
GRANDE-TERRE
Îlet à Kahouanne
Pointe Allègre
Grand Cul-de-Sac Marin
Sainte-Rose
Morne-à-l'Eau
Le Moule
La Désirade
Pointe Doublé
Beauséjour
Deshaies
Lamentin
AÉROPORT DE POINTE-À-PITRE-LE RAIZET
Les Abymes
Pointe-à-Pitre
Baie-Mahault
Pointe-Noire
Petit-Bourg
Le Gosier
Pointe Canot
Sainte-Anne
Saint-François
Pointe des Colibris
GUADELOUPE
(Fr.)
Bouillante
Goyave
BASSE-TERRE
Soufrière 1467
Vieux-Habitants
Saint-Claude
Capesterre-Belle-Eau
Baillif
Basse-Terre
Gourbeyre
Trois-Rivières
Vieux-Fort
Grosse Pointe
Saint-Louis
MARIE-GALANTE
Pointe de Tali
Capesterre
Grand-Bourg
Pointe des Basses
LES SAINTES
Terre-de-Haut
Terre-de-Bas
Petites-Anses
Dominica Passage
ATLANTIC OCEAN
Capucin
Vieille Case
Morne aux Diables 861
Prince Rupert Bluff Point
Crompton Point
Wesley
Portsmouth
Marigot
MELVILLE HALL AIRPORT
Pointe Ronde
Colihaut
Morne Diablotins 1447
DOMINICA
Salisbury
Castle Bruce
St. Joseph
Pointe à Peine
Morne Trois Pitons 1387
La Plaine
Mahaut
Pointe Giraud
Roseau
Watt Mountain 1224
Délices
MORNE TROIS PITONS NATIONAL PARK
Soufrière Bay
Scotts Head
Berekua
Pointe des Fous
CARIBBEAN SEA
WINDWARD ISLANDS
Martinique Passage
Pointe de Macouba
Grand' Rivière
Basse-Pointe
Cap Saint-Martin
Le Lorrain
Le Prêcheur
Montagne Pelée 1397
Sainte-Marie
Saint-Pierre
Morne Jacob 884
Le Carbet
La Trinité
Pitons du Carbet 1196
Gros-Morne
Bellefontaine
Saint-Joseph
Le Robert
Case-Pilote
Le Lamentin
Schœlcher
Le François
Fort-de-France
Ducos
MARTINIQUE
(Fr.)
Les Trois-Îlets
Le Saint-Esprit
Morne Bigot 460
Rivière-Salée
Vauclin
Les Anses-d'Arlets
Le Diamant
Rivière-Pilote
Sainte-Luce
Le Marin
Sainte-Anne
Pointe du Diamant
Pointe des Salines
St. Lucia Channel
Gros Islet
Cape Marquis
VIGIE AIRPORT
Castries
Mount Chaubourg 552
Piton Flore 570
ST. LUCIA
Anse La Raye
Dennery
Canaries
Mount Gimie 950
Soufrière
Micoud
Petit Piton 743
Gros Piton 798
Desruisseaux
Choiseul
Laborie
HEWANORRA INT. AIRPORT
Vieux Fort
Cap Moule à Chique
St. Vincent Passage
Scale 1 : 1,000,000
W-363200-7A-DR2-1
Copyright © Rand McNally & Co.
Meters
Feet
2000 6560
1000 3280
500 1640
200 656
Sea Level
200 656
2000 6560
ATLANTIC OCEAN
North Point
BARBADOS
Speightstown
St. Andrew
Bathsheba
Holetown
Mount Hillaby 840
Kitridge Point
Bridgetown
Hastings
Carlisle Bay
Needhams Point
Oistins
GRANTLEY ADAMS INTERNATIONAL AIRPORT
South Point
Scale 1 : 1,000,000
Porter Point
ST. VINCENT
Fancy
Soufrière 1234
Richmond Peak 1074
Georgetown
Chateaubelair
Barrouallie
Layou
Mount St. Andrew 735
Kingstown
E. T. JOSHUA AIRPORT
Calliaqua
Johnson Point
CARIBBEAN SEA
Bequia
Man Point
Port Elizabeth
Admiralty Bay
Baliceaux
Isle à Quatre
ST. VINCENT AND THE GRENADINES
Lovell Village
Campbell Hills 127
Mustique
GRENADINES
Point Jupiter
Mount Royal 267
Charlestown
Canouan
Mayreau
Mount Taboi 304
Clifton
Ashton
Union Island
Gun Point
Windward
Bogles
Hillsborough
L'Esterre
Top Hill 236
Carriacou
Southwest Point
ATLANTIC OCEAN
Ronde Island
Green Island
GRENADA
Sauteurs
Victoria
Mount St. Catherine 840
Tivoli
Grand Roy
Gouyave
Grenville
Marquis
St. George's
POINT SALINES INT. AIRPORT
Point Salines
Prickly Point
Scale 1 : 1,000,000
Charlotteville
TOBAGO
Roxborough
Little Tobago
Plymouth
Scarborough
Sandy Point
Columbus Point
CARIBBEAN SEA
Chupara Point
Toco
Galera Point
Peninsula de Paria
Blanchisseuse
Redhead
Port of Spain
El Cerro Del Aripo 940
TRINIDAD AND TOBAGO
Tunapuna
Arima
Sangre Grande
Manzanilla Point
Chaguanas
Mount Tamana 308
TRINIDAD
Gulf of Paria
San Fernando
Rio Claro
Guataro Point
La Brea
Princes Town
Pierreville
Point Fortin
Debe
Guayaguayare
Bonasse
Siparia
Basse Terre
Galeota Point
Icacos Point
Serpents Mouth
VENEZUELA
Isla Redonda
ATLANTIC OCEAN
Delta del Orinoco
Isla Mariusa
Scale 1 : 2,500,000
0 25 50 Kilometers
0 25 Miles
0 10 20 30 40 60 80 100 Kilometers
0 10 20 40 60 Miles
Scale 1 : 1,000,000
Lambert Conformal Conic Projection

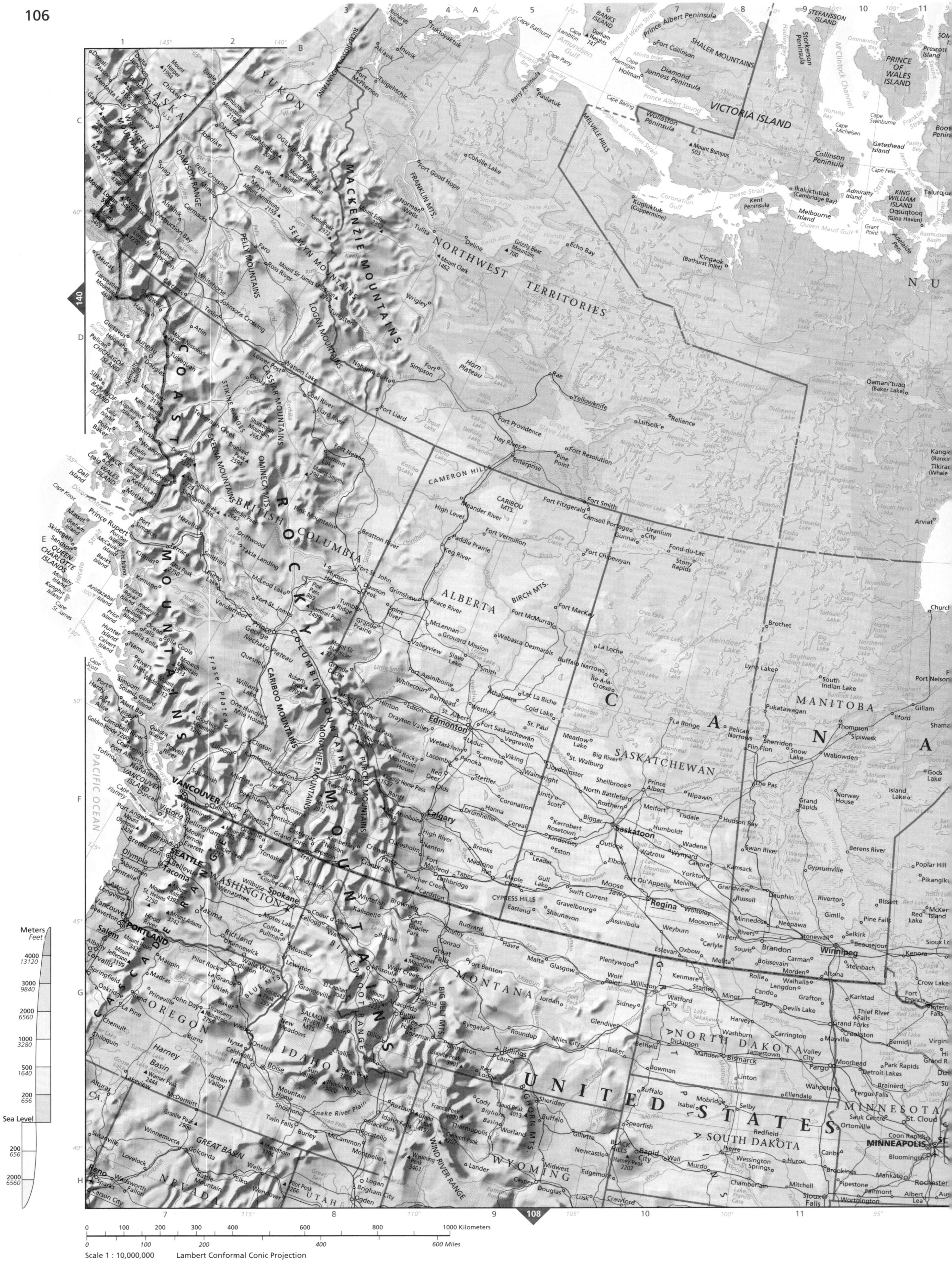

140

Meters / *Feet*
4000 / *13120*
3000 / *9840*
2000 / *6560*
1000 / *3280*
500 / *1640*
200 / *656*
Sea Level
200 / *656*
2000 / *6560*

108

0 100 200 300 400 600 800 1000 Kilometers
0 100 200 400 600 Miles

Scale 1 : 10,000,000   Lambert Conformal Conic Projection

BAFFIN ISLAND
GREENLAND (Den.)
Davis Strait
Foxe Basin
Foxe Peninsula
Hall Peninsula
Cumberland Peninsula
Melville Peninsula
SOUTHAMPTON ISLAND
PRINCE CHARLES ISLAND
COATS ISLAND
MANSEL ISLAND
Hudson Strait
Ungava Bay
PÉNINSULE D'UNGAVA
Hudson Bay
James Bay
AKIMISKI ISLAND
Belcher Islands
All islands within Hudson Bay, James Bay, and Ungava Bay lie within Nunavut
LABRADOR SEA
ATLANTIC OCEAN
Labrador
NEWFOUNDLAND
LONG RANGE MOUNTAINS
QUÉBEC
ONTARIO
MICHIGAN
NEW BRUNSWICK
NOVA SCOTIA
PRINCE EDWARD ISLAND
ÎLE D'ANTICOSTI
Gulf of St. Lawrence
Gulf of Maine
MAINE
VERMONT
N.H.
MASS.
NEW YORK
ADIRONDACK MTS.
MONTS NOTRE-DAME
Les Laurentides
MONTS OTISH
CAPE BRETON ISLAND
SAINT PIERRE AND MIQUELON (Fr.)
MONTRÉAL
Québec
Ottawa
TORONTO
BOSTON
BUFFALO
DETROIT
Halifax
Fredericton
Charlottetown
St. John's
Iqaluit
Same scale as main map

109

M-202000-7A-DR2-1

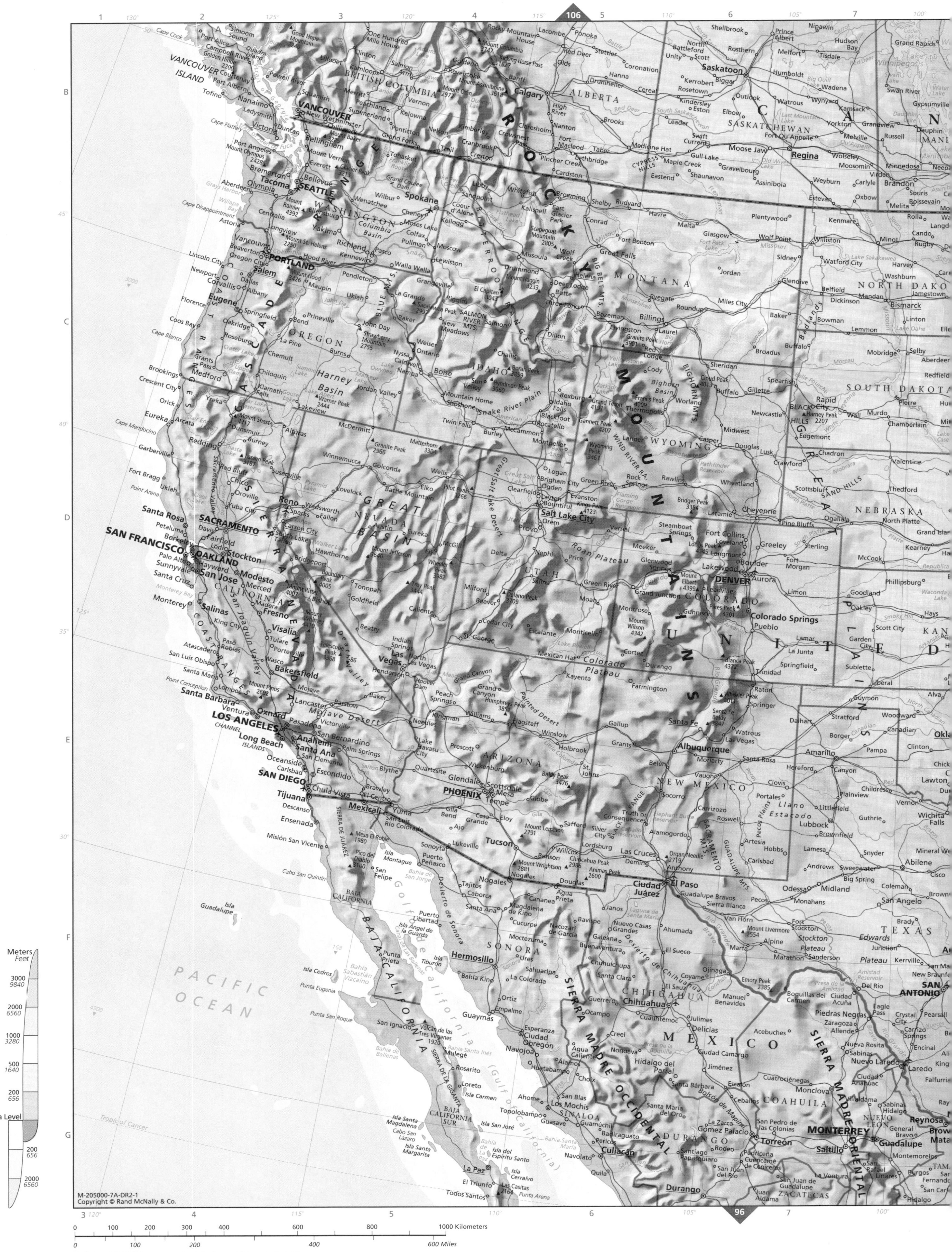

106
96
VANCOUVER ISLAND
BRITISH COLUMBIA
ALBERTA
SASKATCHEWAN
CANADA
ROCKY MOUNTAINS
Calgary
VANCOUVER
Victoria
Saskatoon
Regina
Moose Jaw
Medicine Hat
Lethbridge
Red Deer
Kamloops
Kelowna
Brandon
SEATTLE
Tacoma
Olympia
Spokane
WASHINGTON
Columbia Basin
Mount Rainier 4392
Mount St. Helens 2550
PORTLAND
Salem
Eugene
Mount Hood 3426
OREGON
CASCADE RANGE
Harney Basin
Boise
IDAHO
Snake River Plain
MONTANA
Great Falls
Missoula
Helena
Billings
Bozeman
Butte
NORTH DAKOTA
Bismarck
Minot
SOUTH DAKOTA
Rapid City
Pierre
BLACK HILLS
WYOMING
WIND RIVER RA.
Casper
Cheyenne
Laramie
Sheridan
Cody
NEBRASKA
North Platte
SAND HILLS
GREAT PLAINS
UTAH
Salt Lake City
Ogden
Provo
Great Salt Lake
Great Salt Lake Desert
COLORADO
DENVER
Colorado Springs
Pueblo
Boulder
Fort Collins
Grand Junction
Mount Elbert 4399
Colorado Plateau
NEVADA
GREAT BASIN
Reno
Carson City
Las Vegas
Death Valley
CALIFORNIA
SACRAMENTO
SAN FRANCISCO
OAKLAND
San Jose
Stockton
Modesto
Fresno
Bakersfield
Monterey
Santa Barbara
LOS ANGELES
Long Beach
Anaheim
Santa Ana
San Bernardino
SAN DIEGO
SIERRA NEVADA
San Joaquin Valley
Mojave Desert
Mount Whitney 4418
Mount Shasta 4317
ARIZONA
PHOENIX
Tucson
Flagstaff
Yuma
Grand Canyon
NEW MEXICO
Albuquerque
Santa Fe
Las Cruces
Roswell
Llano Estacado
TEXAS
El Paso
Amarillo
Lubbock
Midland
Odessa
Abilene
San Angelo
SAN ANTONIO
Laredo
Del Rio
MEXICO
Tijuana
Mexicali
Ensenada
Ciudad Juárez
Chihuahua
Hermosillo
Guaymas
Ciudad Obregón
Los Mochis
Culiacán
Durango
Torreón
Saltillo
MONTERREY
Nuevo Laredo
Reynosa
La Paz
SONORA
CHIHUAHUA
COAHUILA
DURANGO
SINALOA
NUEVO LEÓN
BAJA CALIFORNIA
BAJA CALIFORNIA SUR
SIERRA MADRE OCCIDENTAL
SIERRA MADRE ORIENTAL
Golfo de California (Gulf of California)
Tropic of Cancer
PACIFIC OCEAN
Meters
Feet
3000
9840
2000
6560
1000
3280
500
1640
200
656
Sea Level
200
656
2000
6560
M-205000-7A-DR2-1
Copyright © Rand McNally & Co.
0 100 200 300 400 600 800 1000 Kilometers
0 100 200 400 600 Miles
Scale 1 : 10,000,000
Lambert Conformal Conic Projection

107
97
ONTARIO
QUÉBEC
MINNESOTA
WISCONSIN
MICHIGAN
IOWA
ILLINOIS
INDIANA
OHIO
PENNSYLVANIA
NEW YORK
MAINE
VERMONT
N.H.
MASS.
CONN.
NEW JERSEY
DELAWARE
MARYLAND
WEST VIRGINIA
VIRGINIA
KENTUCKY
TENNESSEE
NORTH CAROLINA
SOUTH CAROLINA
GEORGIA
ALABAMA
MISSISSIPPI
LOUISIANA
ARKANSAS
MISSOURI
FLORIDA
NEW BRUNSWICK
NOVA SCOTIA
PRINCE EDWARD ISLAND
BAHAMAS
CUBA
ATLANTIC OCEAN
Gulf of Mexico
Gulf of Maine
James Bay
Lake Superior
Lake Michigan
Lake Huron
Lake Erie
Lake Ontario
Straits of Florida
Florida Keys
Sea Islands
Ozark Plateau
BOSTON MTS.
OUACHITA MTS.
ADIRONDACK MTS.
APPALACHIAN MOUNTAINS
BLUE RIDGE
MONTS NOTRE-DAME
Les Laurentides
MINNEAPOLIS
St. Paul
MILWAUKEE
CHICAGO
DETROIT
CLEVELAND
PITTSBURGH
BUFFALO
TORONTO
MONTRÉAL
Ottawa
Québec
NEW YORK
LONG ISLAND
PHILADELPHIA
BALTIMORE
WASHINGTON
BOSTON
Providence
INDIANAPOLIS
CINCINNATI
ST. LOUIS
KANSAS CITY
Des Moines
Nashville
Memphis
Louisville
Atlanta
Charlotte
Raleigh
Richmond
Norfolk
Virginia Beach
Columbia
Charleston
Savannah
Jacksonville
Orlando
Tampa
St. Petersburg
Miami
Fort Lauderdale
West Palm Beach
Nassau
LA HABANA (HAVANA)
NEW ORLEANS
Baton Rouge
Jackson
Birmingham
Montgomery
Mobile
Tallahassee
Little Rock
Tulsa
DALLAS
HOUSTON
Thunder Bay
Duluth
Sudbury
Halifax
Fredericton
Moncton
Bangor
Portland
Cape Cod
Cape Hatteras
Cape Canaveral
Cape Sable
Key West
Spruce Knob 1482
Mount Mitchell 2037
Mount Rogers 1746
Mt. Washington 1917
Mt. Carleton 820
Mount Alvernia 63
West of Greenwich

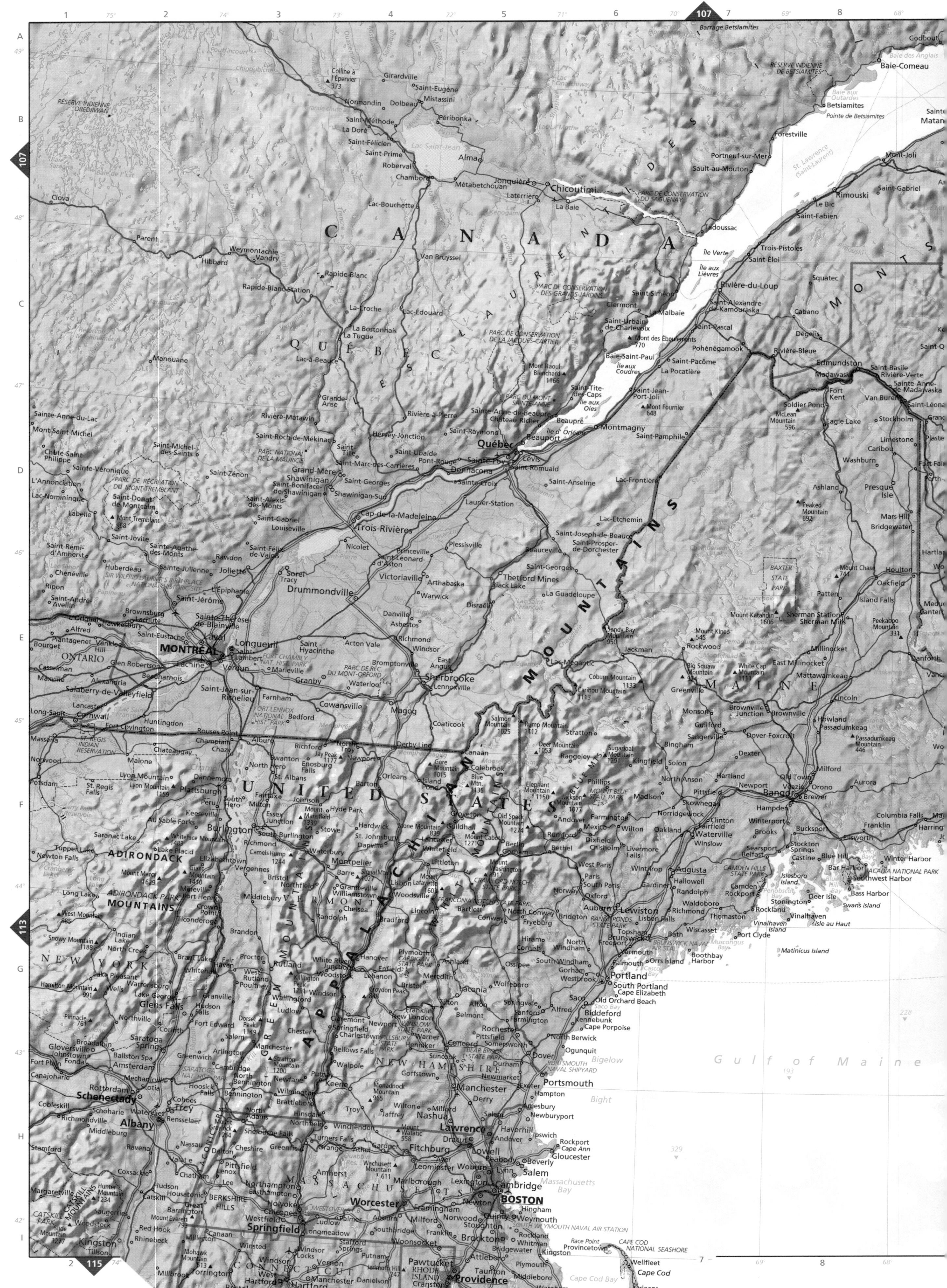

107
113
115
C A N A D A
Q U É B E C
L E S L A U R E N T I D E S
M O N T S
U N I T E D S T A T E S
APPALACHIAN MOUNTAINS
S H O C K MOUNTAINS
MOUNTAINS
GREEN MOUNTAINS
WHITE MOUNTAINS
ADIRONDACK MOUNTAINS
NEW YORK
VERMONT
NEW HAMPSHIRE
MAINE
MASSACHUSETTS
CONNECTICUT
RHODE ISLAND
ONTARIO
Gulf of Maine
Massachusetts Bay
Cape Cod Bay
Bigelow Bight
Lac Saint-Jean
St. Lawrence (Saint-Laurent)
RÉSERVE INDIENNE OBEDJIWAN
RÉSERVE INDIENNE DE BETSIAMITES
PARC DE CONSERVATION DU SAGUENAY
PARC DE CONSERVATION DES GRANDS-JARDINS
PARC DE CONSERVATION DE LA JACQUES-CARTIER
PARC NATIONAL DE LA MAURICIE
PARC DE RÉCRÉATION DU MONT-TREMBLANT
PARC DE RÉC. DU MONT-ORFORD
FORT CHAMBLY NAT. HIST. PARK
FORT LENNOX NATIONAL HIST. PARK
ST. REGIS INDIAN RESERVATION
BAXTER STATE PARK
ACADIA NATIONAL PARK
CAPE COD NATIONAL SEASHORE
SOUTH WEYMOUTH NAVAL AIR STATION
PORTSMOUTH NAVAL SHIPYARD
MONTRÉAL
Québec
BOSTON
Providence
Albany
Schenectady
Springfield
Worcester
Hartford
Portland
South Portland
Augusta
Bangor
Burlington
Montpelier
Concord
Manchester
Nashua
Lawrence
Lowell
Portsmouth
Sherbrooke
Trois-Rivières
Chicoutimi
Jonquière
Baie-Comeau
Rimouski
Rivière-du-Loup
Edmundston
Lévis
Longueuil
Laval
Granby
Drummondville
Saint-Jean-sur-Richelieu
Saint-Jérôme
Victoriaville
Thetford Mines
Plattsburgh
Glens Falls
Saratoga Springs
Pittsfield
Fitchburg
Salem
Cambridge
Brockton
Fall River
Pawtucket
Lewiston
Auburn
Waterville
Brunswick
Saco
Biddeford
Dover
Rochester
Keene
Rutland
Gulf of Maine

ÎLE D'ANTICOSTI
Rivière-de-la-Chaloupe
Pointe de l'Est
Pointe Heath
Pointe du Sud-Ouest
Détroit d' Honguedo
La Martre
Rivière-à-Claude
Madeleine-Centre
Pointe-à-la-Frégate
Saint-Yvon
Cap-Chat
Sainte-Anne-des-Monts
Mont Jacques-Cartier 1277
PARC PROVINCIAL DE LA GASPÉSIE
MONTS CHIC-CHOCS
Mont Blanc 1059
PÉNINSULE DE LA GASPÉSIE (GASPE PENINSULA)
PARC NATIONAL DE FORILLON
Fontenelle
Gaspé
Cap Gaspé
Baie de Gaspé
Matane
NOTRE DAME
Saint-Gabriel-de-Gaspé
La Malbaie
Percé
Île Bonaventure
Grande-Rivière
Chandler
Newport
Pointe au Maquereau
New Richmond
Nouvelle
Dalhousie
Caplan
Bonaventure
New Carlisle
Campbellton
Jacquet River
Chaleur Bay
Miscou Point
Miscou Island
Miscou Centre
Île Lamèque
Lamèque
Shippegan
Grande-Anse
Caraquet
Nepisiguit Bay
Squaw Cap Mountain 483
Lorne
Blue Mountain 528
Beresford
Bathurst
Saint-Isidore
Tracadie
Haut Sheila
MOUNT CARLETON PROVINCIAL PARK
Mount Carleton 820
Brantville
Lavillette
Neguac
Big Bald Mountain 672
Miramichi Bay
Point Escuminac
Newcastle
Chatham
Chatham Head
Point Sapin
Renous
KOUCHIBOUGUAC NATIONAL PARK
Saint-Louis de Kent
Richibucto
Rogersville
St.-Ignace
Upper Blackville
Rexton
Doaktown
Bouctouche
Boiestown
Saint-Antoine
Notre-Dame
Stanley
Shediac
NEW BRUNSWICK
Taymouth
Minto
Chipman
Moncton
Rothwell
Dieppe
Lewisville
Nashwaaksis
Marysville
Fredericton
Petitcodiac
Turtle Creek
Hillsborough
Oromocto
Geary
Gagetown
CANADIAN FORCES BASE GAGETOWN
Fredericton Junction
Sussex
Norton
Hampton
FUNDY NATIONAL PARK
Alma
Welsford
Mount Pleasant 358
Rothesay
St. Martins
Grand Bay
Saint John
Cape Spencer
Point Lepreau
St. George
St. Andrews
Passamaquoddy Bay
Deer Island
Wilsons Beach
ROOSEVELT CAMPOBELLO INTERNATIONAL PARK
West Quoddy Head
Grand Manan Island
Grand Manan
Bay of Fundy
Gulf of St. Lawrence
Île Brion
La Grosse Île
Grande-Entrée
Île de l' Est
ÎLES DE LA MADELEINE (Que.)
Île du Cap aux Meules
Cap-aux-Meules
Baie de Plaisance
Île du Havre Aubert
Havre-Aubert
North Cape
Tignish
Cape Kildare
Alberton
Cascumpec Bay
Campbellton
O'Leary
Conway
Malpeque Bay
Port Hill
Egmont Bay
West Point
Wellington Station
PRINCE EDWARD ISLAND NATIONAL PARK
Kensington
North Rustico
Summerside
Bedeque Bay
Hunter River
PRINCE EDWARD ISLAND
Morell
St. Peters Bay
Elmira
Souris
Mount Stewart
Charlottetown
Cardigan
Victoria
Borden
Port Borden
Bonshaw
FORT AMHERST NAT. HIST. PARK
Vernon River
Georgetown
Cardigan Bay
Montague
Hillsborough Bay
Murray River
Murray Head
Murray Harbour
Flat River
Wood Islands
Northumberland Strait
Cap-Pelé
Shemogue
Cape Tormentine
Port Elgin
Memramcook
Dorchester
Sackville
Amherst
FORT BEAUSÉJOUR NATIONAL HISTORIC PARK
Harvey
Joggins
River Hebert
Smith Point
Amet Sound
Pugwash
Malagash
Oxford
River John
Pictou Island
Caribou
Pictou
Westchester Station
Scotsburn
Trenton
Westville
New Glasgow
Stellarton
Springhill
Southampton
COBEQUID MTS.
Londonderry
Nuttby Mountain 367
Chignecto Bay
Port Greville
Five Islands
Bass River
Belmont
Truro
Parrsboro
Cobequid Bay
Cape Chignecto
Advocate Harbour
Greville Bay
Cape Split
Minas Basin
Minas Channel
Maitland
Brookfield
NOVA SCOTIA
Middle Stewiacke
Sunnybrae
GRAND PRÉ NATIONAL HISTORIC PARK
Walton
Kennetcook
Harbourville
Canning
Gore
Stewiacke
Upper Musquodoboit
Berwick
Kentville
Wolfville
Hantsport
Windsor
Milford Station
Middle Musquodoboit
Kingston
Waterville
Elmsdale
Middleton
Three Mile Plains
Meaghers Grant
Mosers River
Ecum Secum
Sheet Harbour
Tangier
Torbrook
Bridgetown
Mount Uniacke
CANADIAN FORCES BASE HALIFAX
New Road
Musquodoboit Harbour
PORT ROYAL NATIONAL HISTORIC PARK
Annapolis Royal
Annapolis Basin
FORT ANNE NAT. HIST. PARK
Springfield
New Ross
Hubbards
Halifax
Dartmouth
HALIFAX CITADEL NATIONAL HISTORIC PARK
Digby
Clementsport
Chester Basin
Hatchet Lake
Herring Cove
Halifax Harbour
Digby Neck
Bear River
New Germany
Western Shore
Hemford
Mahone Bay
Terence Bay
Pennant Point
Weymouth
KEJIMKUJIK NATIONAL PARK
Caledonia
Lunenburg
St. Margarets Bay
Long Island
South Brookfield
Bridgewater
Hell Point
Westport
Freeport
Brier Island
St. Marys Bay
Meteghan
Hectanooga
Cape St. Marys
Brooklyn
Port Maitland
Liverpool
Liverpool Bay
Yarmouth
Port Mouton
Chebogue Point
Wedgeport
Shelburne
Pubnico
Lockeport
Lower West Pubnico
Barrington
Lower Woods Harbour
Clark's Harbour
Cape Sable Island
Seal Island
Cape Sable
ATLANTIC OCEAN
Port au Port Peninsula
Cape St. George
NEWFOUNDLAND
Cape Anguille
Codroy
Doyle
Tompkins
Table Mountain
Cape Ray
Cabot Strait
To Channel-Port-aux-Basques
St. Paul Island
Cape St. Lawrence
Cape North
Aspy Bay
Dingwall
Long Point
Pleasant Bay
CAPE BRETON HIGHLANDS NATIONAL PARK
Ingonish
Chéticamp
Cape Smokey
Grand-Étang
East Point
Margaree Harbour
Margaree
Indian Brook
St. Anns Bay
Boularderie Island
New Waterford
Dominion
CAPE BRETON ISLAND
Inverness
Strathlorne
Sydney Mines
North Sydney
Sydney
Glace Bay
Port Morien
Baddeck
Mira Bay
Scatarie Island
Mabou
Iona
LOUISBOURG NAT. HIST. SITE
Louisbourg
Gabarus Bay
Gabarus
Port Hood
Whycocomagh
Judique
Bras d'Or Lake
Cape George
St. Georges Bay
West Bay
St. Peters
L'Ardoise
Fourchu
Lismore
Pomquet
Antigonish
Mulgrave
Port Hawkesbury
Louisdale
Arichat
Point Michaud
Isle Madame
Strait of Canso
Chedabucto Bay
Canso
Guysborough
Goshen
Queensport
Goldboro
Larrys River
Sherbrooke
Sable Island (N.S.)
To Sept-Îles
Meters Feet
1000 3280
500 1640
200 656
Sea Level
200 656
2000 6560
W-520298-7A-DR2-1
Copyright © Rand McNally & Co.
West of Greenwich
0 25 50 75 100 150 200 250 Kilometers
0 25 50 100 150 Miles
Scale 1 : 2,500,000
Lambert Conformal Conic Projection

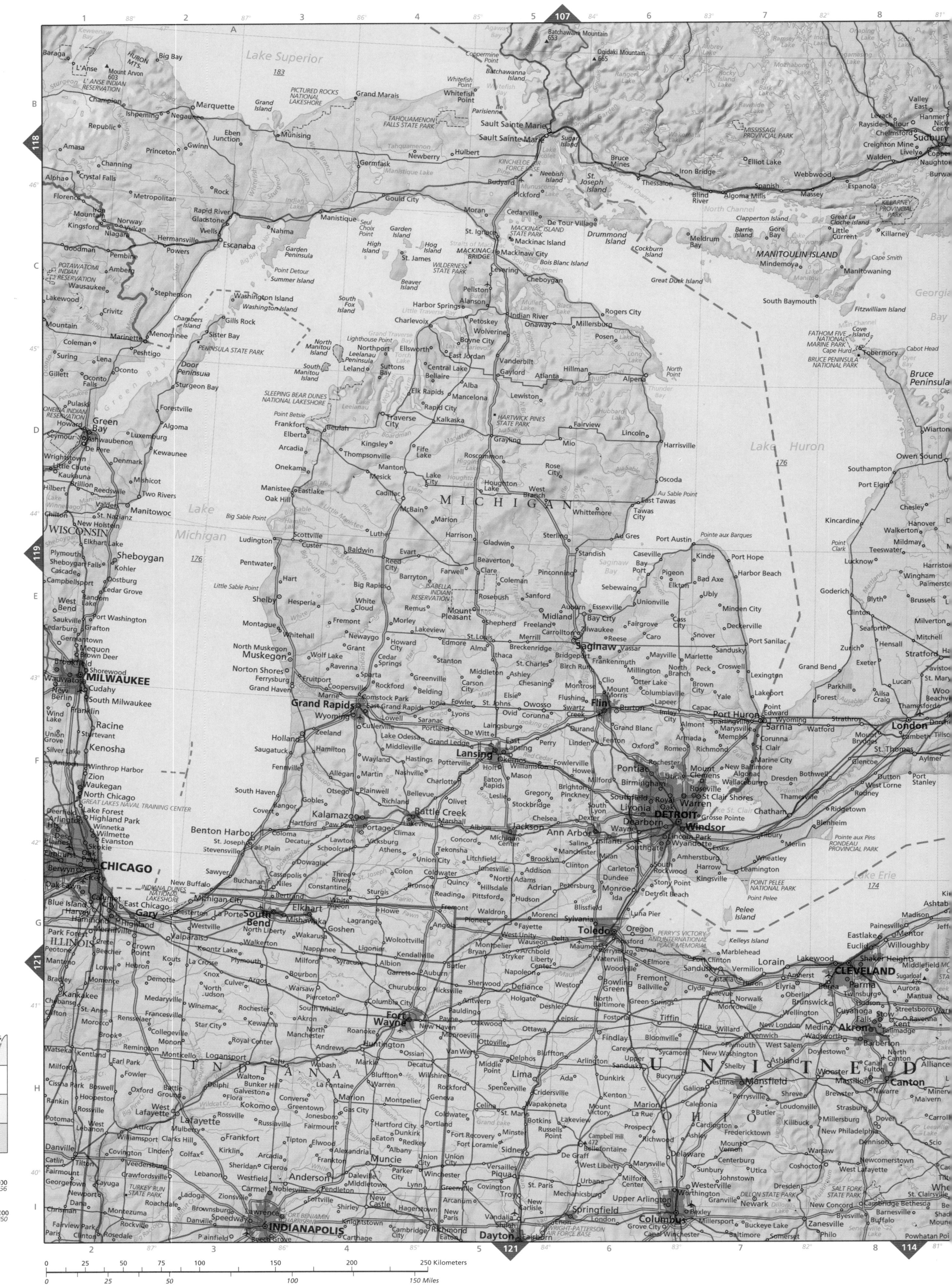

0 25 50 75 100 150 200 250 Kilometers

0 25 50 100 150 Miles

Scale 1 : 2,500,000 Lambert Conformal Conic Projection

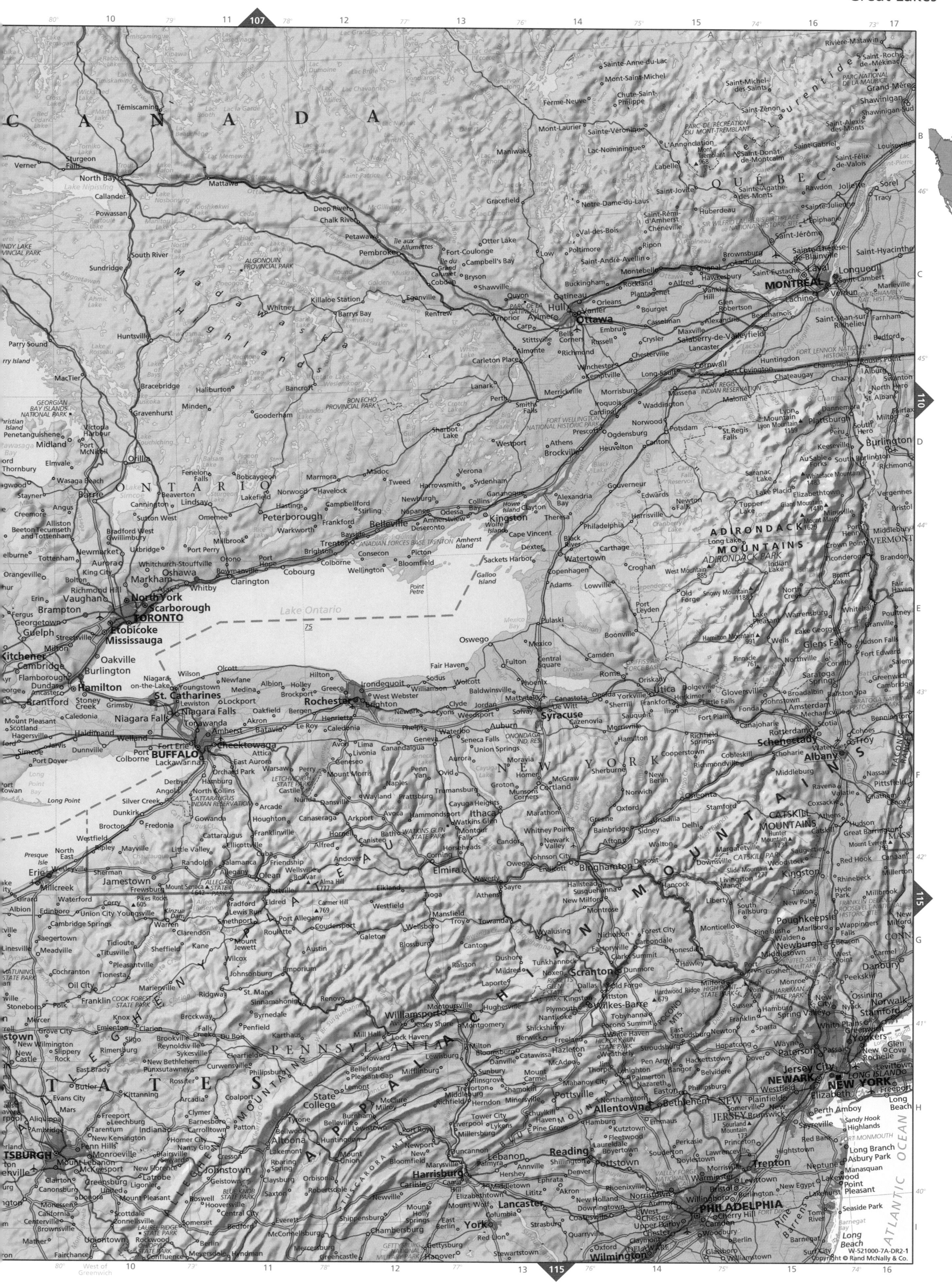
CANADA
ONTARIO
QUÉBEC
Madawaska Highlands
Laurentides
ADIRONDACK MOUNTAINS
ADIRONDACK PARK
CATSKILL MOUNTAINS
APPALACHIAN MOUNTAINS
ALLEGHENY PLATEAU
NEW YORK
PENNSYLVANIA
NEW JERSEY
UNITED STATES
VERMONT
MASS.
CONN.
ATLANTIC OCEAN
Lake Ontario
Lake Nipissing
MONTREAL
Ottawa
TORONTO
North York
Scarborough
Etobicoke
Mississauga
Hamilton
St. Catharines
Niagara Falls
BUFFALO
Cheektowaga
Rochester
Syracuse
Utica
Schenectady
Albany
Troy
Binghamton
Scranton
Wilkes-Barre
Allentown
Bethlehem
Reading
Harrisburg
Lancaster
York
PHILADELPHIA
Wilmington
Trenton
NEWARK
Jersey City
NEW YORK
Yonkers
Stamford
Norwalk
Poughkeepsie
Newburgh
Kingston
Burlington
Plattsburgh
Kingston
Belleville
Peterborough
Oshawa
Barrie
Orillia
Huntsville
North Bay
Pembroke
Hull
Gatineau
Cornwall
Brockville
Watertown
Oswego
Elmira
Ithaca
Erie
Jamestown
Williamsport
Altoona
State College
Johnstown
Hazleton
Pottsville
Camden
Cherry Hill
Long Branch
Asbury Park
W-521000-7A-DR2-1
Copyright © Rand McNally & Co.

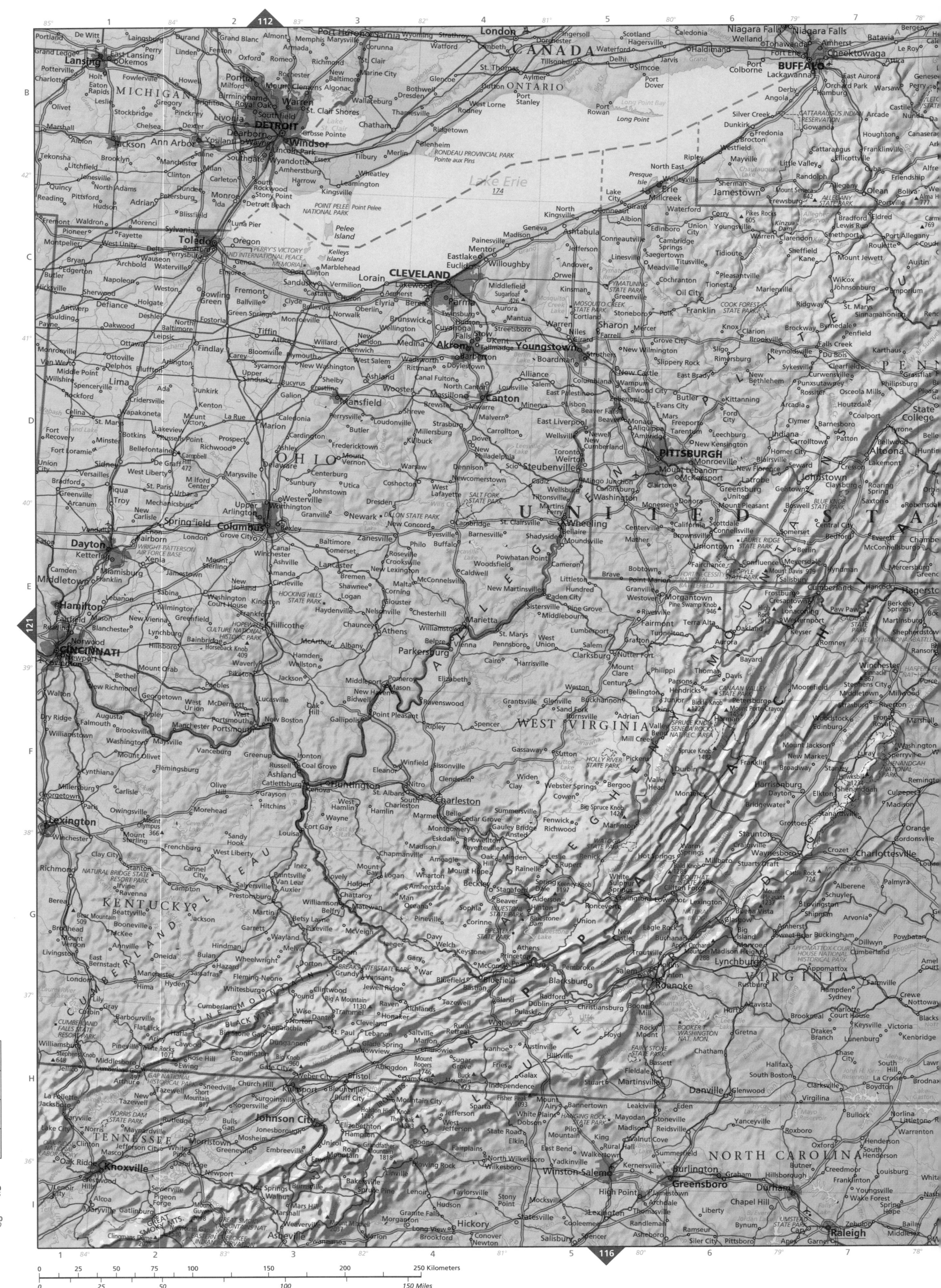

Meters / Feet
1000 / 3280
500 / 1640
200 / 656
Sea Level
200 / 656
2000 / 6560

0 25 50 75 100 150 200 250 Kilometers
0 25 50 100 150 Miles

Scale 1 : 2,500,000 Lambert Conformal Conic Projection

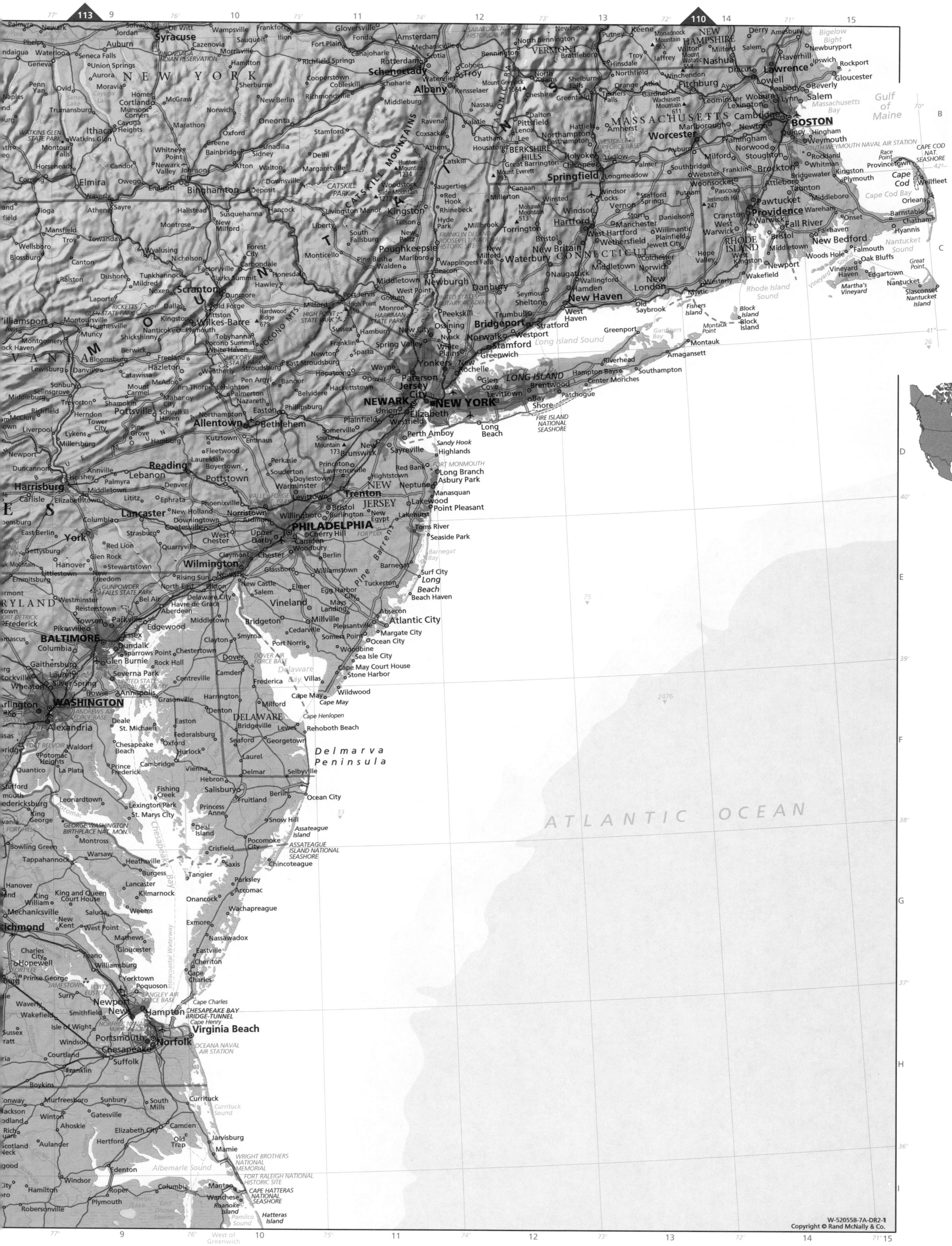

ATLANTIC OCEAN

Gulf of Maine

Long Island Sound

Delmarva Peninsula

NEW YORK

MASSACHUSETTS

CONNECTICUT

RHODE ISLAND

NEW JERSEY

DELAWARE

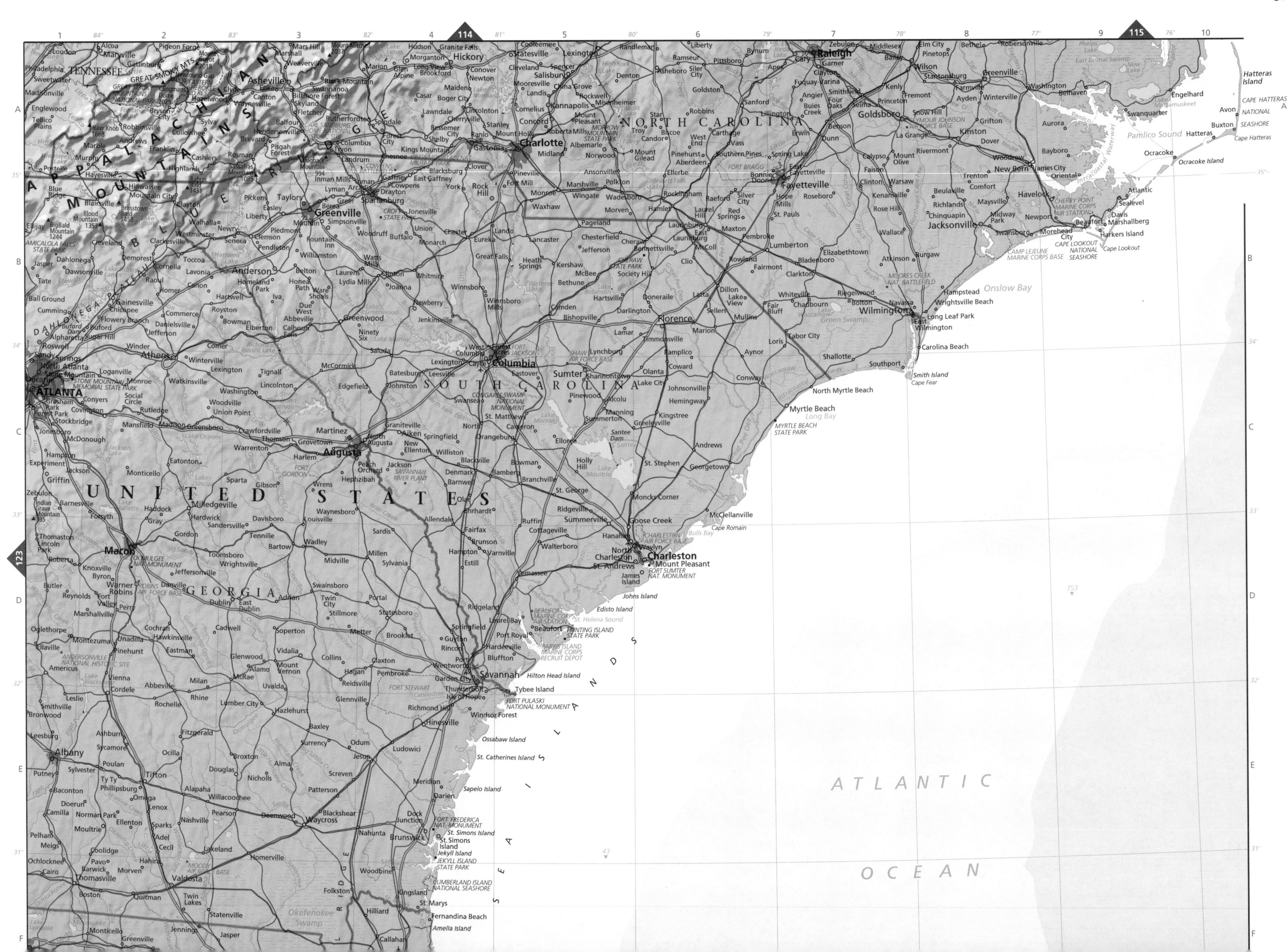
ATLANTIC
OCEAN
NORTH CAROLINA
SOUTH CAROLINA
GEORGIA
UNITED STATES
APPALACHIAN MOUNTAINS
BLUE RIDGE
SEA ISLANDS
DAHLONEGA PLATEAU
TENNESSEE
GREAT SMOKY MTS.
Raleigh
Charlotte
Columbia
Charleston
Savannah
Augusta
Macon
ATLANTA
Wilmington
Greenville
Fayetteville
Florence
Sumter
Myrtle Beach
Jacksonville
Goldsboro
Asheville
Hickory
Athens
Anderson
Albany
Valdosta
Waycross
Brunswick
Onslow Bay
Long Bay
Pamlico Sound
Okefenokee Swamp
Cape Hatteras
Cape Lookout
Cape Fear
Cape Romain
Hatteras Island
Ocracoke Island
Hilton Head Island
Tybee Island
Ossabaw Island
St. Catherines Island
Sapelo Island
Fernandina Beach
Amelia Island
114
115
123

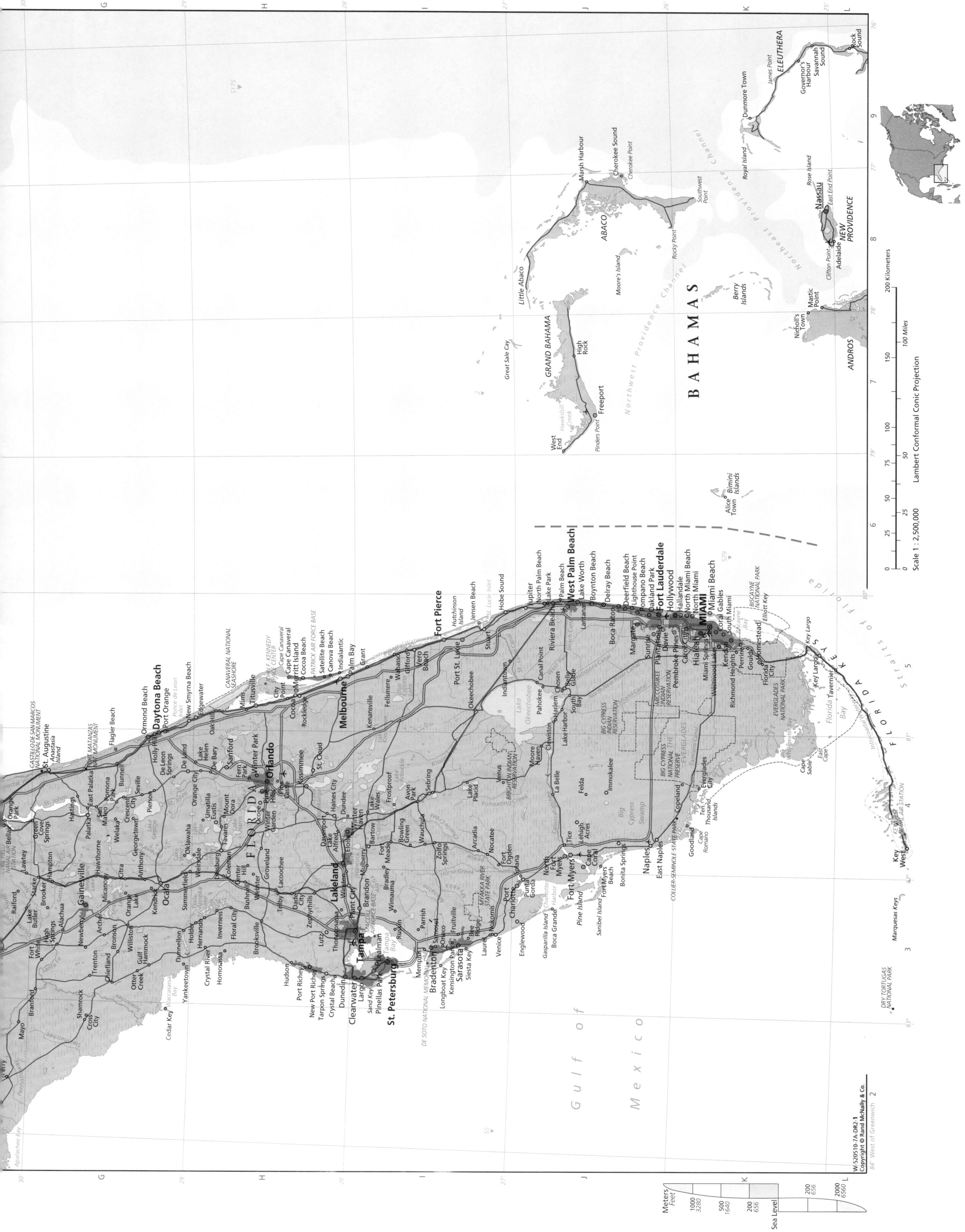

Scale 1 : 2,500,000

0 25 50 75 100 150 200 Kilometers

0 25 50 100 Miles

Lambert Conformal Conic Projection

Meters / Feet

1000 / 3280

500 / 1640

200 / 656

Sea Level

200 / 656

2000 / 6560

W-520510-7A-DR2-1

84° West of Greenwich 2

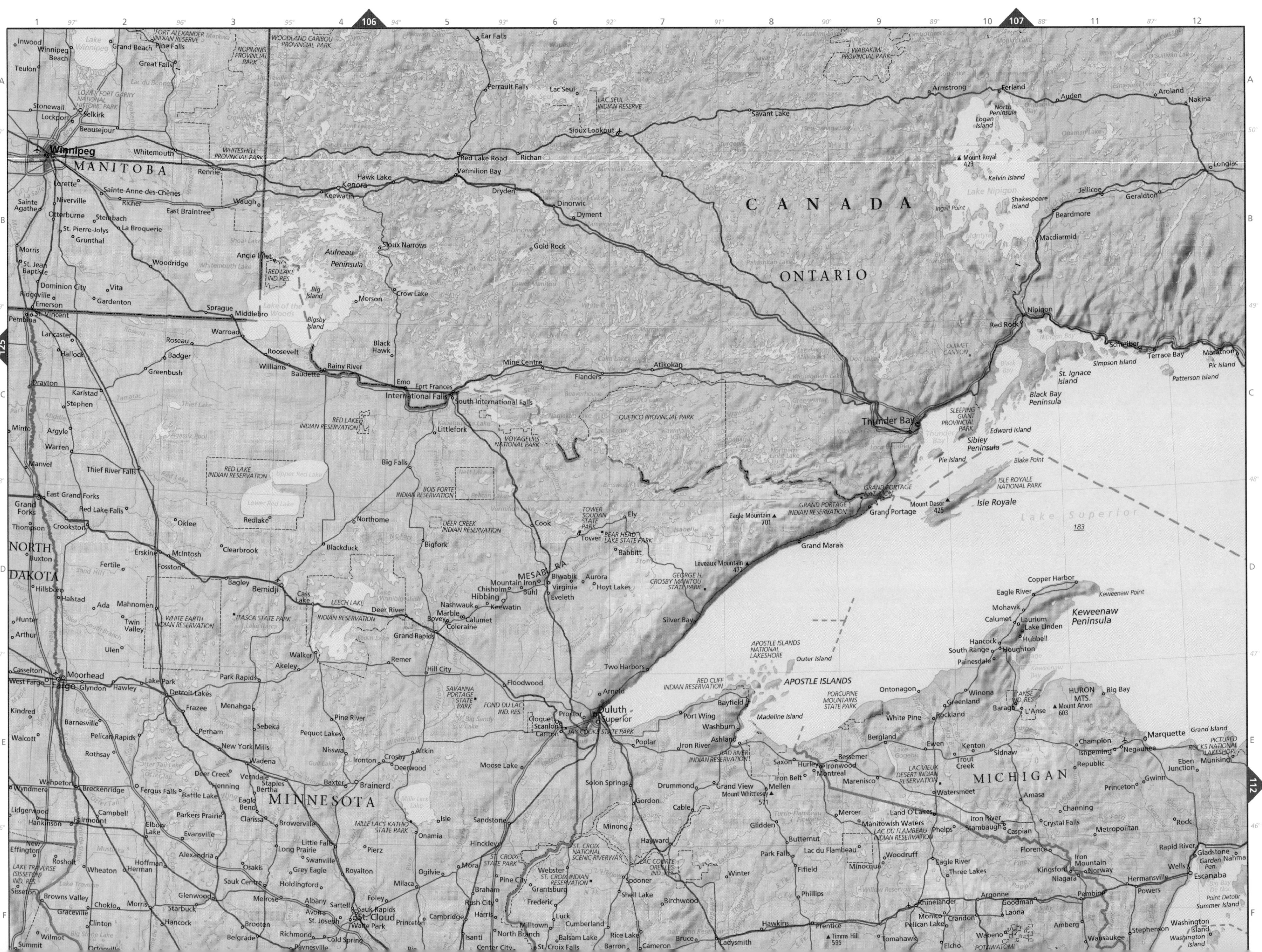
CANADA
ONTARIO
MANITOBA
MINNESOTA
MICHIGAN
NORTH DAKOTA
Lake Superior
Lake Nipigon
Isle Royale
ISLE ROYALE NATIONAL PARK
APOSTLE ISLANDS
Keweenaw Peninsula
Thunder Bay
Winnipeg
Duluth
Superior
Fargo
Moorhead
International Falls
Fort Frances
Kenora
Dryden
Sioux Lookout
Marquette
Escanaba
St. Cloud
Grand Marais
Hibbing
Bemidji
Grand Forks
VOYAGEURS NATIONAL PARK
QUETICO PROVINCIAL PARK
RED LAKE INDIAN RESERVATION
LEECH LAKE INDIAN RESERVATION
WHITE EARTH INDIAN RESERVATION
GRAND PORTAGE INDIAN RESERVATION
MESABI RA.
WOODLAND CARIBOU PROVINCIAL PARK
WHITESHELL PROVINCIAL PARK
WABAKIMI PROVINCIAL PARK
106
107
112
125
183

Scale 1 : 2,500,000

Lambert Conformal Conic Projection

W-520563-7A-DR2-1 Copyright © by Rand McNally & Co.

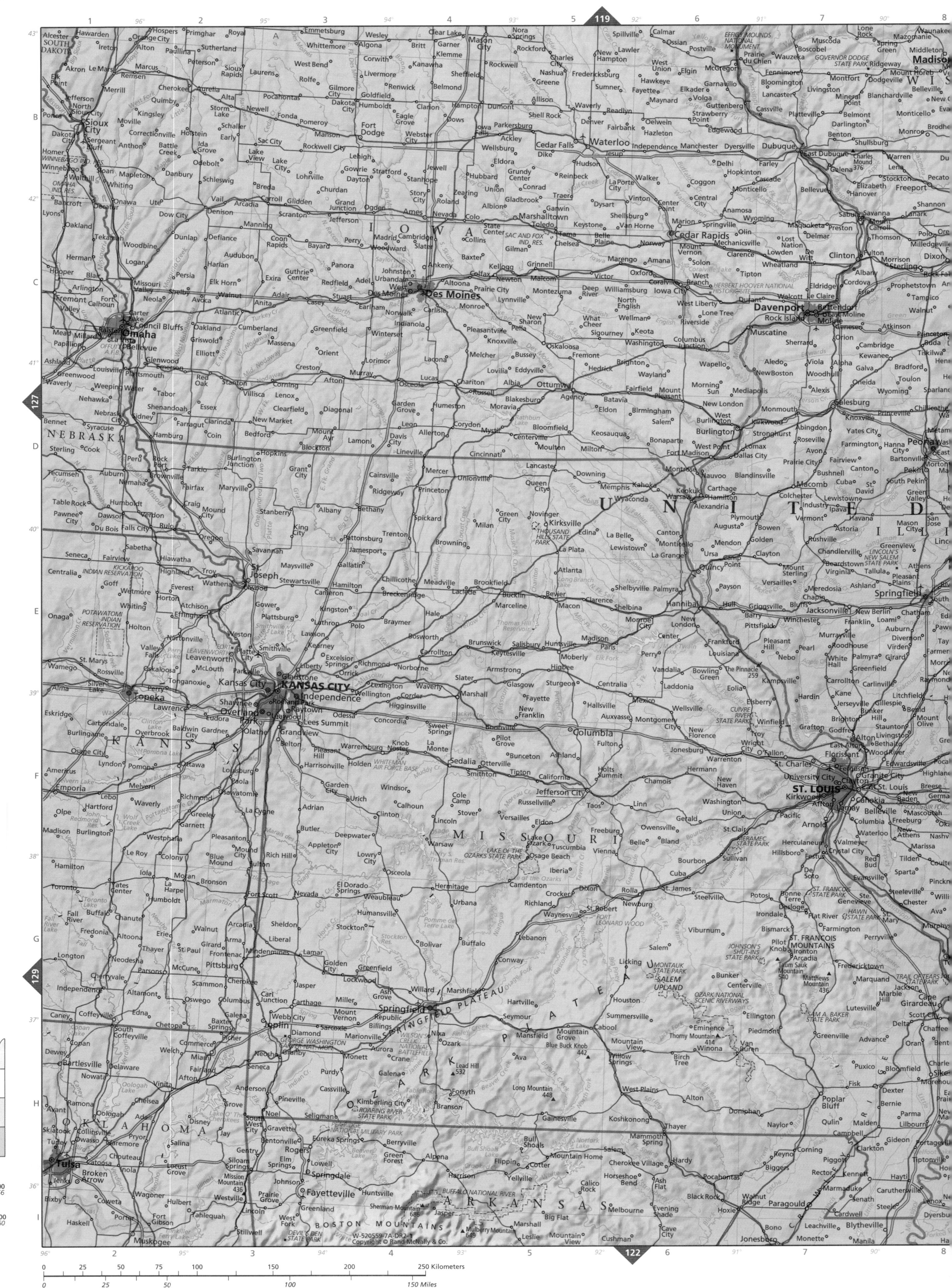

IOWA
NEBRASKA
KANSAS
MISSOURI
OKLAHOMA
ARKANSAS
SOUTH DAKOTA
UNITED
Des Moines
Omaha
Council Bluffs
Sioux City
Cedar Rapids
Iowa City
Davenport
Waterloo
Dubuque
Kansas City
KANSAS CITY
Independence
Topeka
St. Joseph
Jefferson City
Columbia
Springfield
Joplin
St. Louis
Tulsa
Fayetteville
Peoria
Springfield
Madison
OZARK PLATEAU
SPRINGFIELD PLATEAU
BOSTON MOUNTAINS
SALEM UPLAND
ST. FRANCOIS MOUNTAINS
LAKE OF THE OZARKS STATE PARK
HERBERT HOOVER NATIONAL HISTORIC SITE
WHITEMAN AIR FORCE BASE
BUFFALO NATIONAL RIVER
GEORGE WASHINGTON CARVER NAT'L MON.
Meters
Feet
1000
3280
500
1640
200
656
Sea Level
200
656
2000
6560
0 25 50 75 100 150 200 250 Kilometers
0 25 50 100 150 Miles
Scale 1 : 2,500,000
Lambert Conformal Conic Projection
W-520559-7A-DR2-1
Copyright © Rand McNally & Co.
119
122
127
129

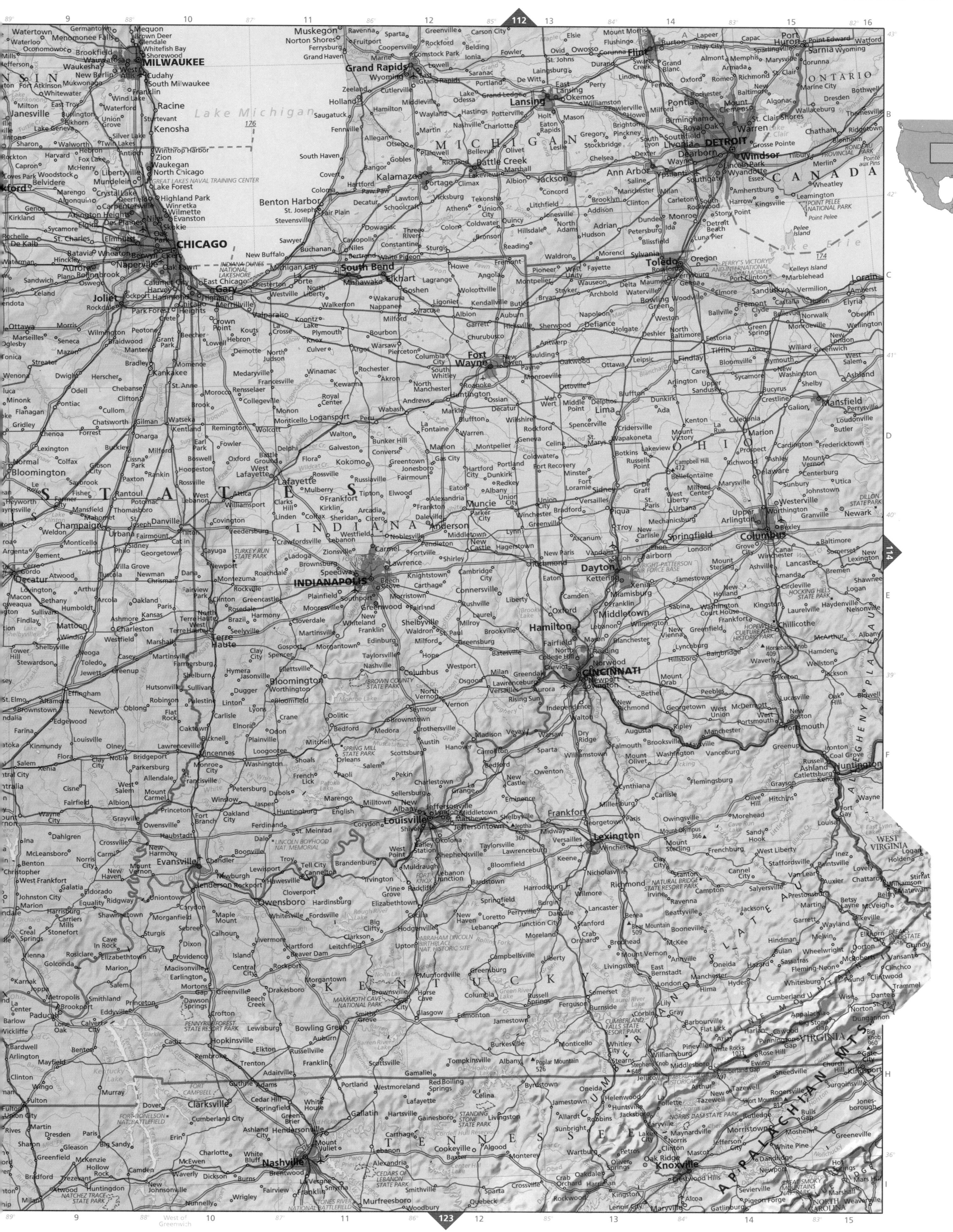
MILWAUKEE
CHICAGO
DETROIT
INDIANAPOLIS
CINCINNATI
Lake Michigan
MICHIGAN
INDIANA
OHIO
KENTUCKY
TENNESSEE
ONTARIO
CANADA
Lake Erie
Grand Rapids
Lansing
Kalamazoo
Ann Arbor
Toledo
Fort Wayne
South Bend
Gary
Joliet
Columbus
Dayton
Hamilton
Louisville
Lexington
Evansville
Nashville
Knoxville
Windsor
Flint
Muskegon
Racine
Kenosha
Champaign
Bloomington
Decatur
Terre Haute
Lafayette
Muncie
Anderson
Springfield
Lima
Mansfield
Frankfort
Owensboro
Bowling Green
Clarksville
Paducah
Huntington
Ashland
APPALACHIAN MTS.
112
113
114
123
West of Greenwich

Meters
Feet
2000
6560
1000
3280
500
1640
200
656
Sea Level
200
656
2000
6560

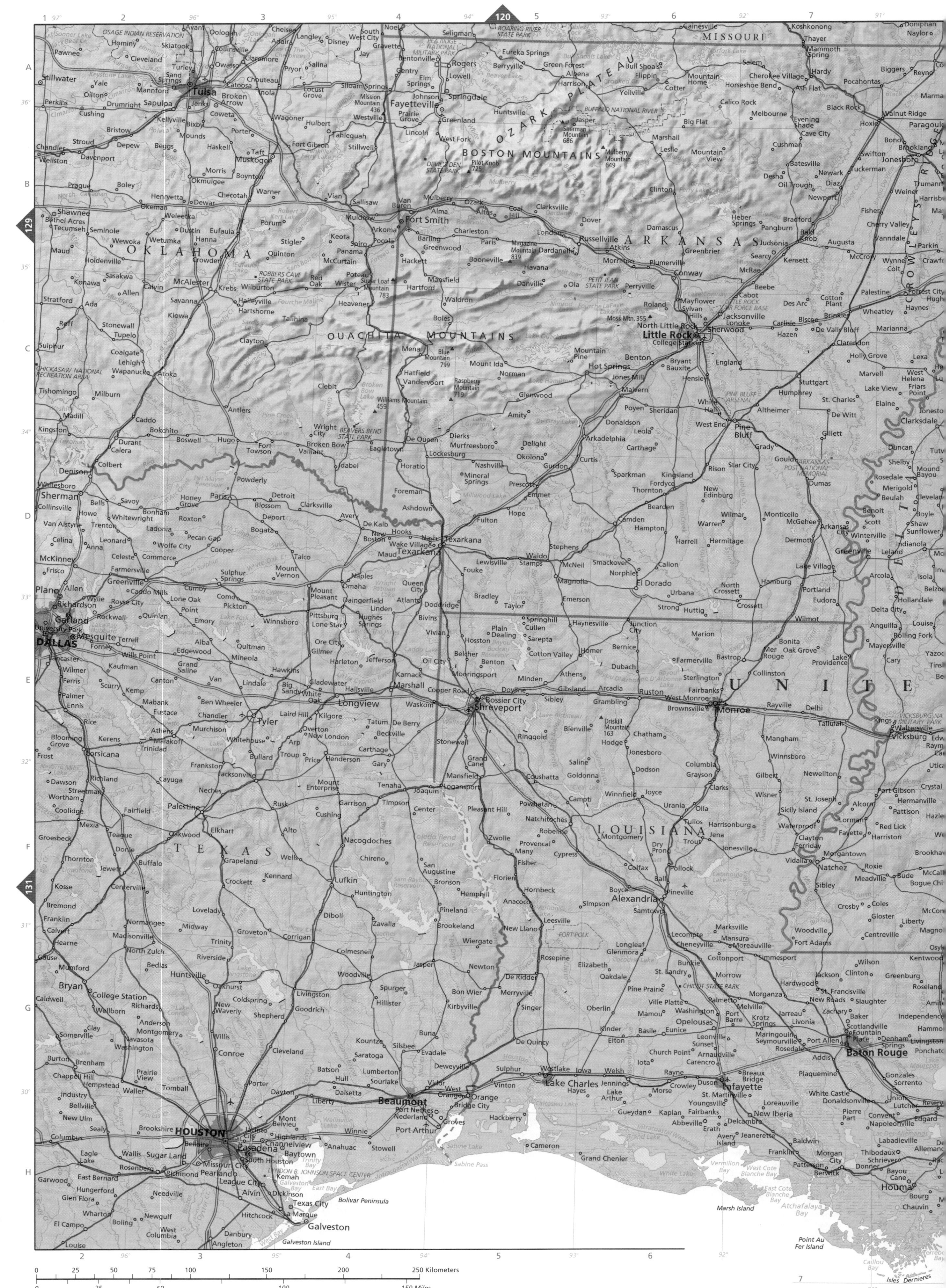

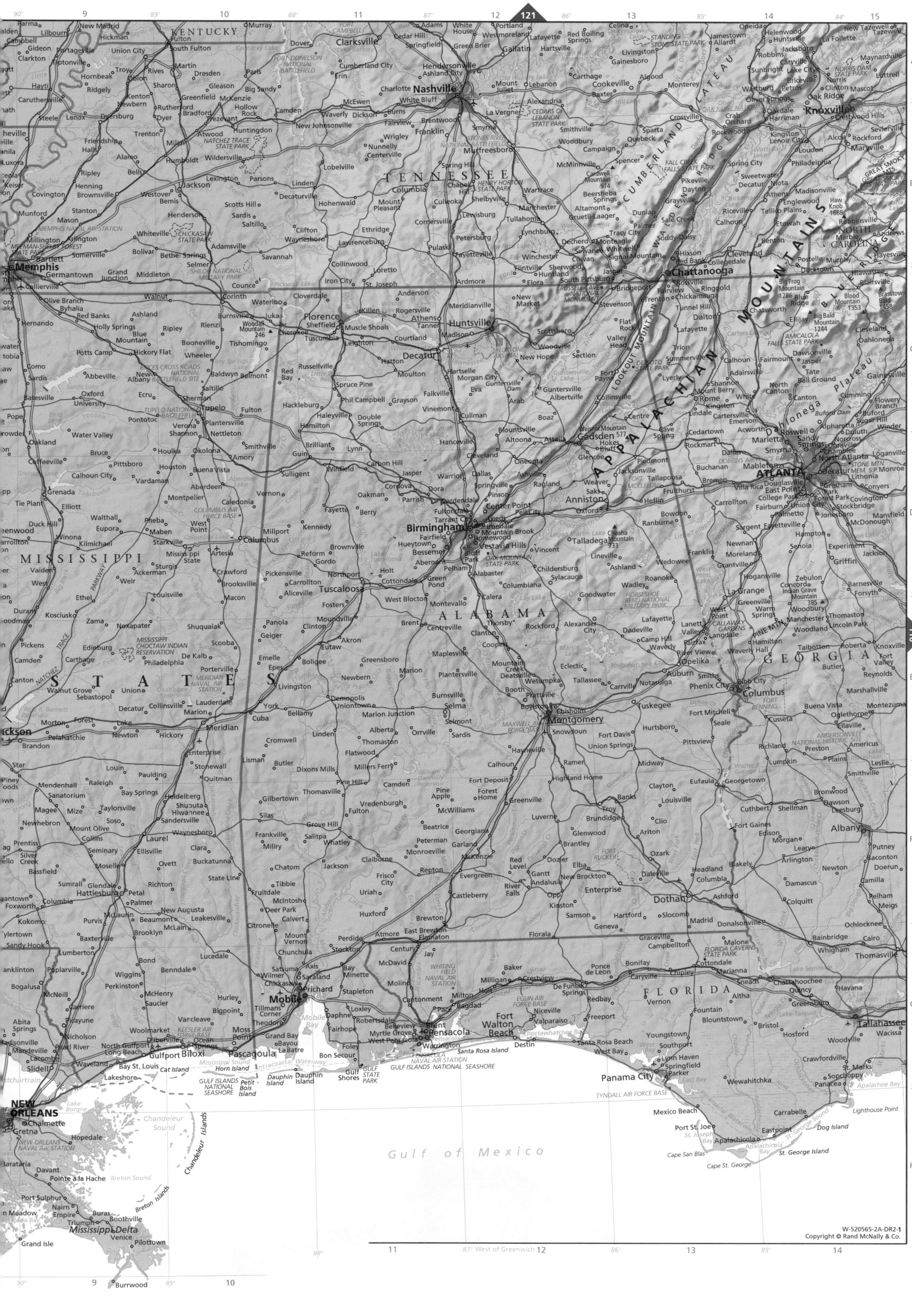

W-520565-2A-DR2-1

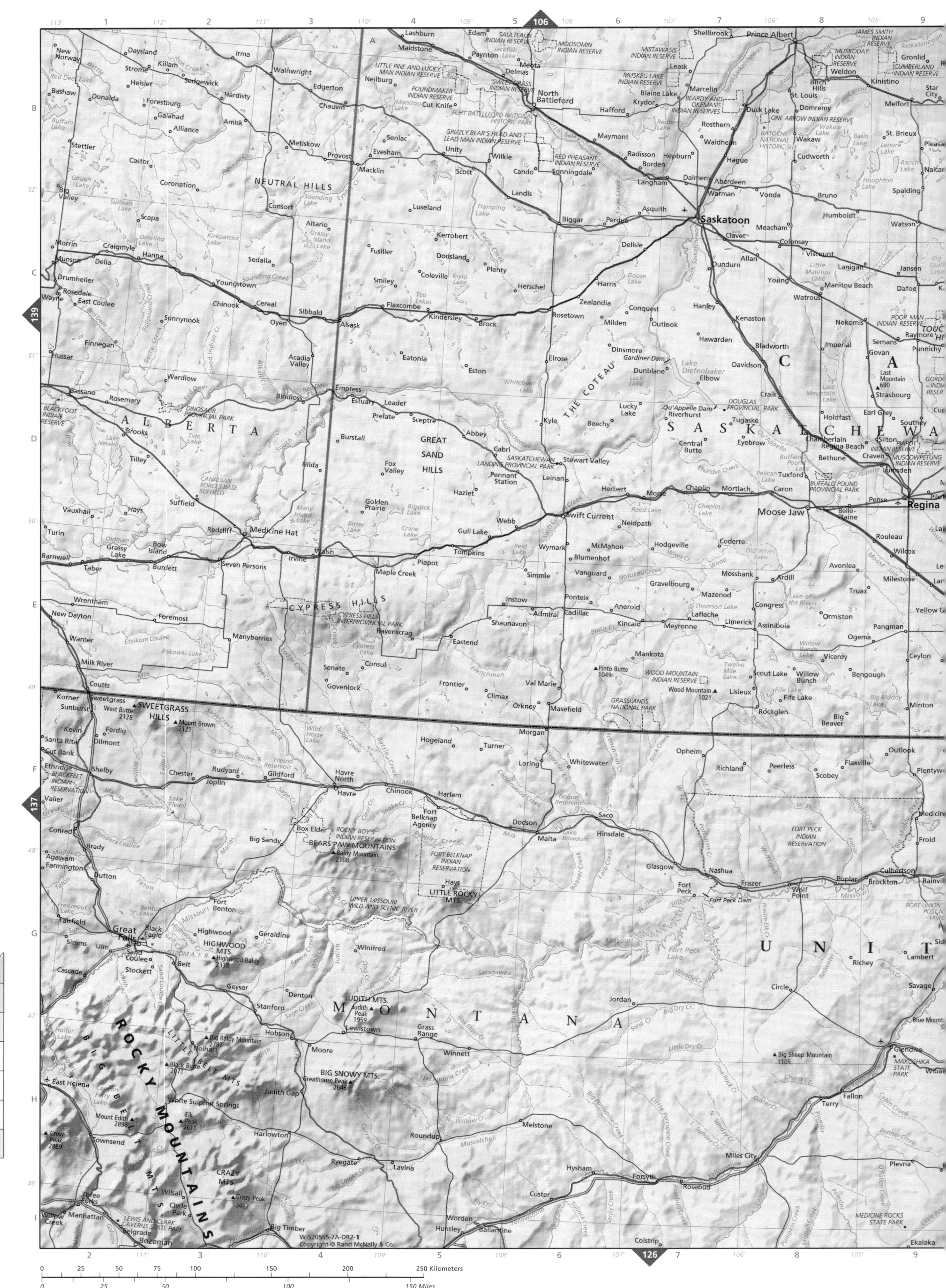

0 25 50 75 100 150 200 250 Kilometers

0 25 50 100 150 Miles

Scale 1 : 2,500,000 Lambert Conformal Conic Projection

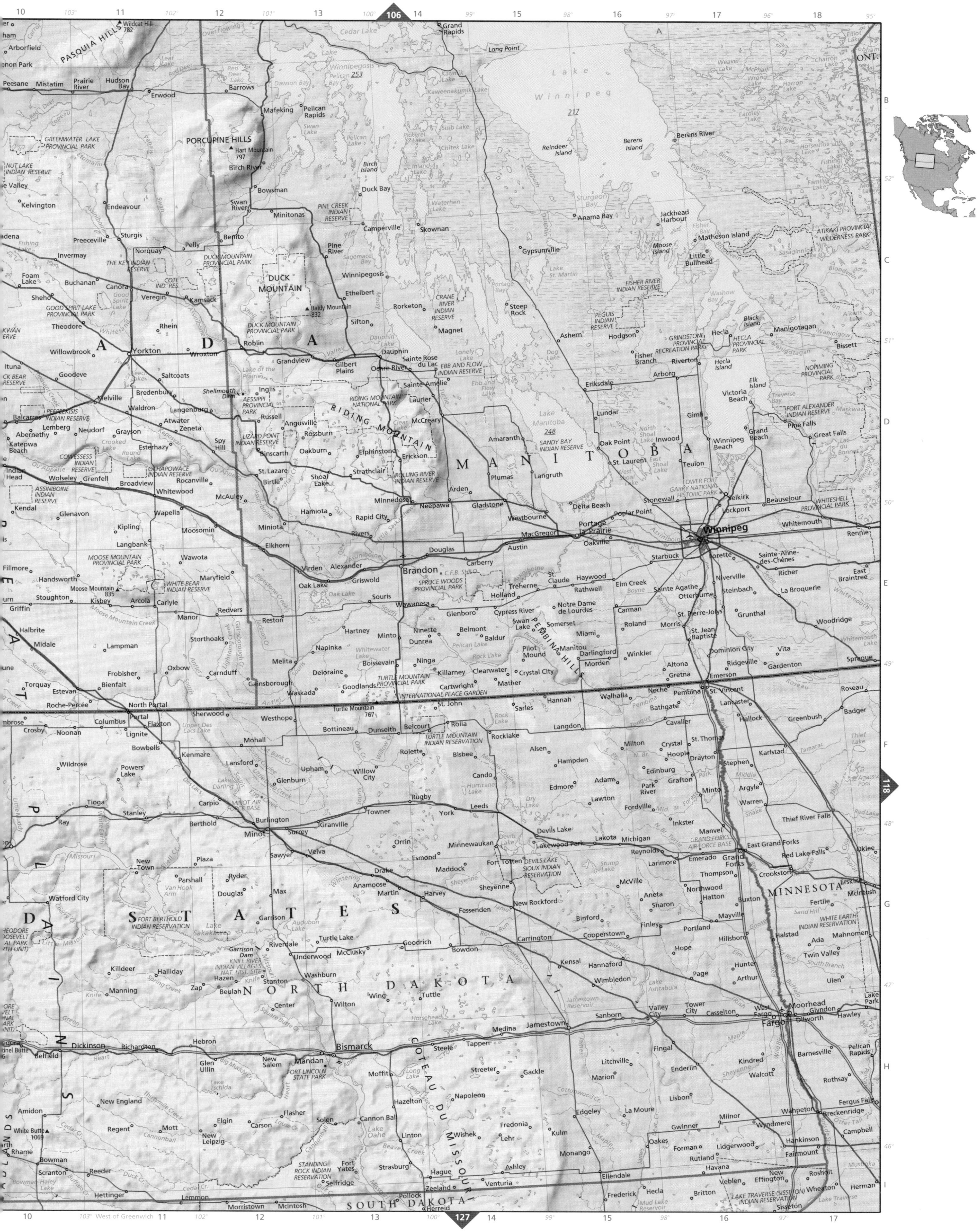

CANADA
MANITOBA
UNITED STATES
NORTH DAKOTA
MINNESOTA
SOUTH DAKOTA
ONT.

Lake Winnipeg
Lake Manitoba
Lake Winnipegosis
Cedar Lake
PORCUPINE HILLS
DUCK MOUNTAIN
RIDING MOUNTAIN
PEMBINA HILLS
COTEAU DU MISSOURI
PASQUIA HILLS

Winnipeg
Brandon
Portage la Prairie
Dauphin
Yorkton
Melville
Selkirk
Steinbach
Morden
Swan River
Grand Rapids
Gimli
Minot
Bismarck
Mandan
Fargo
Moorhead
Grand Forks
East Grand Forks
Jamestown
Valley City
Devils Lake
Dickinson
Williston
Wahpeton
Thief River Falls
Crookston
Fergus Falls
Wildcat Hill 782
Hart Mountain 797
Baldy Mountain 832
Moose Mountain 835
Turtle Mountain 767
White Butte 1069

106
118
127

10 11 12 13 14 15 16 17 18
103° West of Greenwich 102° 101° 100° 99° 98° 97° 96° 95°
B C D E F G H I
52° 51° 50° 49° 48° 47° 46°

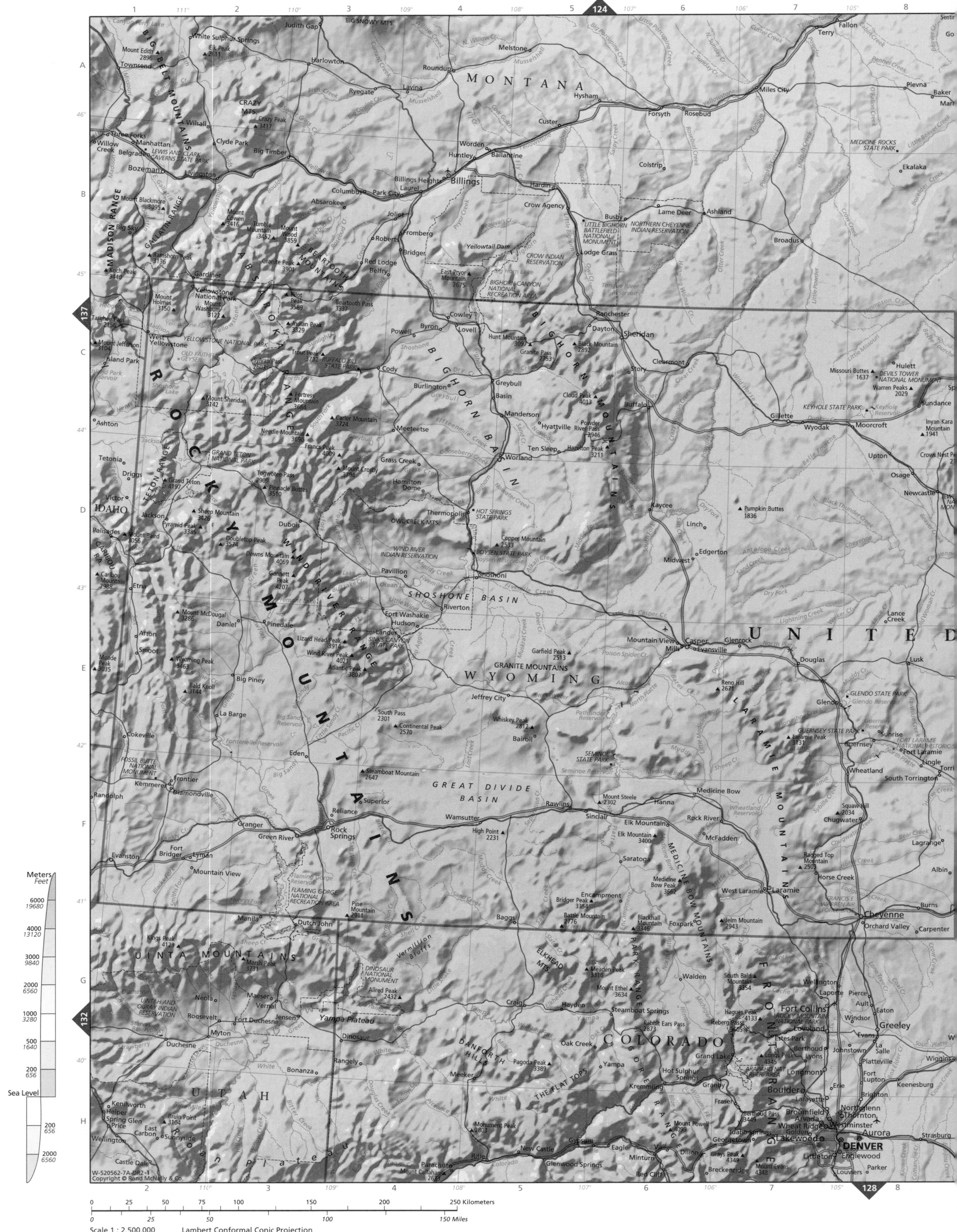

MONTANA
WYOMING
IDAHO
UTAH
COLORADO
UNITED
ROCKY MOUNTAINS
BIGHORN BASIN
BIGHORN MOUNTAINS
WIND RIVER RANGE
ABSAROKA RANGE
SHOSHONE BASIN
GREAT DIVIDE BASIN
GRANITE MOUNTAINS
LARAMIE MOUNTAINS
MEDICINE BOW MOUNTAINS
FRONT RANGE
PARK RANGE
GORE RANGE
UINTA MOUNTAINS
MADISON RANGE
GALLATIN RANGE
BIG BELT MOUNTAINS
CRAZY MTS.
BEARTOOTH MOUNTAINS
TETON RANGE
OWL CREEK MTS.
DANFORTH HILLS
THE FLAT TOPS
ELKHEAD MTS.
Roan Plateau
Yampa Plateau
YELLOWSTONE NATIONAL PARK
GRAND TETON NATIONAL PARK
WIND RIVER INDIAN RESERVATION
CROW INDIAN RESERVATION
NORTHERN CHEYENNE INDIAN RESERVATION
UINTAH AND OURAY INDIAN RESERVATION
FLAMING GORGE NATIONAL RECREATION AREA
DINOSAUR NATIONAL MONUMENT
ROCKY MOUNTAIN NATIONAL PARK
DEVILS TOWER NATIONAL MONUMENT
FOSSIL BUTTE NATIONAL MONUMENT
BIGHORN CANYON NATIONAL RECREATION AREA
LITTLE BIGHORN BATTLEFIELD NATIONAL MONUMENT
Billings
Bozeman
Livingston
Miles City
Sheridan
Buffalo
Gillette
Cody
Worland
Thermopolis
Riverton
Lander
Casper
Douglas
Rawlins
Rock Springs
Green River
Evanston
Laramie
Cheyenne
Fort Collins
Greeley
Loveland
Longmont
Boulder
DENVER
Aurora
Lakewood
Vernal
Craig
Steamboat Springs
Glenwood Springs
Rifle
Jackson
W-520562-7A-DR2-1
Copyright © Rand McNally & Co.
Meters / Feet
6000 19680
4000 13120
3000 9840
2000 6560
1000 3280
500 1640
200 656
Sea Level
200 656
2000 6560
0 25 50 75 100 150 200 250 Kilometers
0 25 50 100 150 Miles
Scale 1 : 2,500,000
Lambert Conformal Conic Projection

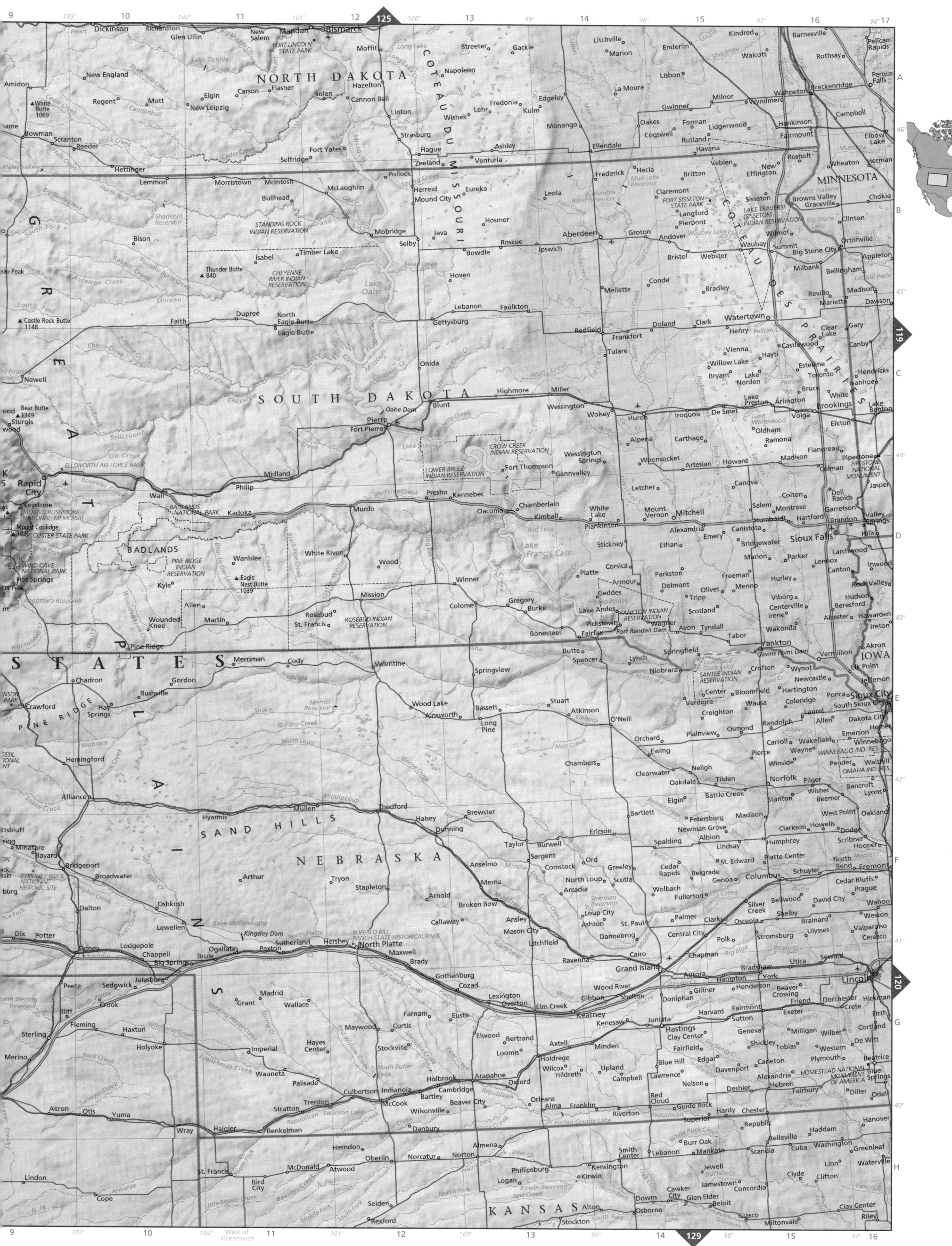
NORTH DAKOTA
SOUTH DAKOTA
NEBRASKA
KANSAS
MINNESOTA
IOWA
STATES
COTEAU DU MISSOURI
COTEAU DES PRAIRIES
SAND HILLS
PINE RIDGE
BADLANDS
125
119
120
129
Dickinson
Richardton
Glen Ullin
New Salem
Mandan
Bismarck
FORT LINCOLN STATE PARK
Moffit
Streeter
Gackle
Litchville
Marion
Enderlin
Kindred
Barnesville
Pelican Rapids
Rothsay
Fergus Falls
Walcott
Lisbon
New England
Flasher
Carson
Elgin
New Leipzig
Regent
Mott
Amidon
White Butte 1069
Hazelton
Napoleon
Solen
Cannon Ball
Linton
Strasburg
Wishek
Lehr
Fredonia
Kulm
Edgeley
La Moure
Gwinner
Milnor
Wyndmere
Wahpeton
Breckenridge
Campbell
Elbow Lake
Monango
Oakes
Cogswell
Forman
Lidgerwood
Rutland
Hankinson
Fairmount
Bowman
Scranton
Reeder
Hettinger
Selfridge
Fort Yates
Hague
Zeeland
Venturia
Ashley
Ellendale
Havana
Veblen
Rosholt
New Effington
Wheaton
Herman
Lemmon
Morristown
McIntosh
McLaughlin
Pollock
Herreid
Mound City
Eureka
Leola
Frederick
Hecla
Britton
Claremont
FORT SISSETON STATE PARK
Langford
Pierpont
Sisseton
LAKE TRAVERSE (SISSETON) INDIAN RESERVATION
Browns Valley
Graceville
Chokio
Bullhead
STANDING ROCK INDIAN RESERVATION
Mobridge
Selby
Java
Hosmer
Bowdle
Roscoe
Ipswich
Aberdeen
Groton
Andover
Bristol
Webster
Waubay
Wilmot
Summit
Big Stone City
Ortonville
Clinton
Appleton
Milbank
Bellingham
Bison
Isabel
Timber Lake
Thunder Butte 840
CHEYENNE RIVER INDIAN RESERVATION
Lake Oahe
Hoven
Mellette
Conde
Bradley
Revillo
Madison
Marietta
Dawson
Castle Rock Butte 1148
Faith
Dupree
North Eagle Butte
Eagle Butte
Lebanon
Gettysburg
Faulkton
Redfield
Frankfort
Doland
Clark
Watertown
Henry
Clear Lake
Gary
Tulare
Vienna
Hayti
Castlewood
Canby
Onida
Willow Lake
Bryant
Lake Norden
Estelline
Toronto
Bruce
Hendricks
Ivanhoe
Newell
Highmore
Miller
Wessington
Wolsey
Huron
Iroquois
De Smet
Lake Preston
Arlington
Brookings
White
Lake Benton
Bear Butte 1349
Sturgis
Oahe Dam
Blunt
Pierre
Fort Pierre
Alpena
Carthage
Oldham
Ramona
Volga
Elkton
CROW CREEK INDIAN RESERVATION
Wessington Springs
Woonsocket
Artesian
Howard
Madison
Flandreau
Pipestone
PIPESTONE NATIONAL MONUMENT
Colman
LOWER BRULE INDIAN RESERVATION
Fort Thompson
Gannvalley
Midland
ELLSWORTH AIR FORCE BASE
Rapid City
Philip
Wall
Letcher
Canova
Colton
Dell Rapids
Jasper
Keystone
MOUNT RUSHMORE NATIONAL MEMORIAL
BADLANDS NATIONAL PARK
Kadoka
Murdo
Presho
Kennebec
Chamberlain
Oacoma
Kimball
White Lake
Plankinton
Mount Vernon
Mitchell
Salem
Montrose
Hartford
Garretson
Brandon
Valley Springs
Mount Coolidge 1836
CUSTER STATE PARK
Alexandria
Emery
Canistota
Humboldt
Sioux Falls
Bridgewater
Stickney
Ethan
Marion
Parker
Larchwood
White River
Wood
Lake Francis Case
PINE RIDGE INDIAN RESERVATION
Wanblee
WIND CAVE NATIONAL PARK
Hot Springs
Eagle Nest Butte 1039
Kyle
Winner
Platte
Corsica
Parkston
Freeman
Hurley
Lennox
Canton
Inwood
Rock Valley
Mission
Armour
Delmont
Geddes
Olivet
Menno
Tripp
Viborg
Centerville
Hudson
Beresford
Allen
Colome
Gregory
Burke
Lake Andes
YANKTON INDIAN RESERVATION
Scotland
Irene
Alcester
Hawarden
Ireton
Wounded Knee
Martin
Rosebud
St. Francis
ROSEBUD INDIAN RESERVATION
Bonesteel
Pickstown
Fort Randall Dam
Wagner
Avon
Tyndall
Wakonda
Pine Ridge
Fairfax
Tabor
Yankton
Gavins Point Dam
Vermillion
Akron
Merriman
Cody
Valentine
Butte
Spencer
Lynch
Springfield
Springview
Niobrara
SANTEE INDIAN RESERVATION
Crofton
Wynot
Newcastle
Elk Point
Chadron
Gordon
Rushville
Hay Springs
Crawford
Wood Lake
Ainsworth
Bassett
Long Pine
Stuart
Atkinson
O'Neill
Center
Bloomfield
Hartington
Ponca
Sioux City
South Sioux City
Jefferson
Verdigre
Creighton
Wausa
Coleridge
Laurel
Allen
Dakota City
Plainview
Osmond
Randolph
Emerson
Homer
Orchard
Carroll
Wakefield
Winnebago
Ewing
Pierce
Wayne
WINNEBAGO IND. RES.
Hemingford
Chambers
Winside
Pender
Walthill
OMAHA IND. RES.
Clearwater
Neligh
Oakdale
Tilden
Norfolk
Pilger
Bancroft
Lyons
Alliance
Elgin
Battle Creek
Wisner
Beemer
Stanton
Hyannis
Mullen
Thedford
Brewster
Halsey
Dunning
Bartlett
Petersburg
Madison
West Point
Oakland
Ericson
Newman Grove
Clarkson
Howells
Dodge
Minatare
Bayard
Bridgeport
Broadwater
Arthur
Tryon
Stapleton
Taylor
Burwell
Sargent
Anselmo
Comstock
Ord
Spalding
Albion
Lindsay
Humphrey
Scribner
Hooper
Greeley
Cedar Rapids
Belgrade
Genoa
St. Edward
Platte Center
Columbus
Schuyler
North Bend
Fremont
CHIMNEY ROCK NATIONAL HISTORIC SITE
Merna
North Loup
Scotia
Arcadia
Wolbach
Fullerton
Cedar Bluffs
Prague
Oshkosh
Dalton
Lewellen
Arnold
Broken Bow
Loup City
Sherman Reservoir
Palmer
Silver Creek
Bellwood
David City
Wahoo
Callaway
Ansley
Mason City
Ashton
St. Paul
Dannebrog
Clarks
Osceola
Shelby
Brainard
Weston
Dix
Potter
Lake McConaughy
Kingsley Dam
BUFFALO BILL RANCH STATE HISTORICAL PARK
Central City
Polk
Stromsburg
Ulysses
Valparaiso
Ceresco
Sidney
Lodgepole
Chappell
Ogallala
Paxton
Sutherland
Hershey
North Platte
Maxwell
Brady
Litchfield
Ravenna
Cairo
Grand Island
Chapman
Bradshaw
Utica
Seward
Lincoln
Julesburg
Big Springs
Brule
Gothenburg
Cozad
Aurora
Hampton
York
Peetz
Sedgwick
Crook
Grant
Madrid
Wallace
Lexington
Overton
Elm Creek
Gibbon
Shelton
Wood River
Doniphan
Giltner
Henderson
Beaver Crossing
Friend
Dorchester
Crete
Hickman
Iliff
Fleming
Haxtun
Holyoke
Farnam
Eustis
Kearney
Kenesaw
Juniata
Harvard
Fairmont
Sutton
Exeter
Firth
Sterling
Maywood
Curtis
Elwood
Bertrand
Axtell
Hastings
Clay Center
Geneva
Milligan
Wilber
Cortland
De Witt
Imperial
Hayes Center
Stockville
Loomis
Holdrege
Minden
Fairfield
Shickley
Tobias
Western
Plymouth
Beatrice
Merino
Wauneta
Palisade
Hugh Butler Lake
Wilcox
Hildreth
Upland
Campbell
Blue Hill
Lawrence
Edgar
Davenport
Carleton
Alexandria
HOMESTEAD NATIONAL MONUMENT OF AMERICA
Blue Springs
Culbertson
Indianola
Holbrook
Arapahoe
Cambridge
Oxford
Bartley
Beaver City
Orleans
Alma
Franklin
Nelson
Hebron
Deshler
Fairbury
Diller
Odell
Akron
Otis
Yuma
Stratton
Trenton
McCook
Wilsonville
Danbury
Harlan County Lake
Riverton
Red Cloud
Guide Rock
Hardy
Chester
Superior
Republic
Hanover
Wray
Haigler
Benkelman
Herndon
Oberlin
Norcatur
Norton
Almena
Smith Center
Lebanon
Burr Oak
Mankato
Belleville
Scandia
Cuba
Haddam
Washington
Greenleaf
Waterville
St. Francis
McDonald
Atwood
Bird City
Phillipsburg
Kensington
Kirwin
Logan
Kirwin Reservoir
Jewell
Jamestown
Concordia
Clyde
Clifton
Linn
Lindon
Cope
Selden
Rexford
Alton
Stockton
Osborne
Downs
Cawker City
Glen Elder
Beloit
Glasco
Miltonvale
Clay Center
Riley
West of Greenwich

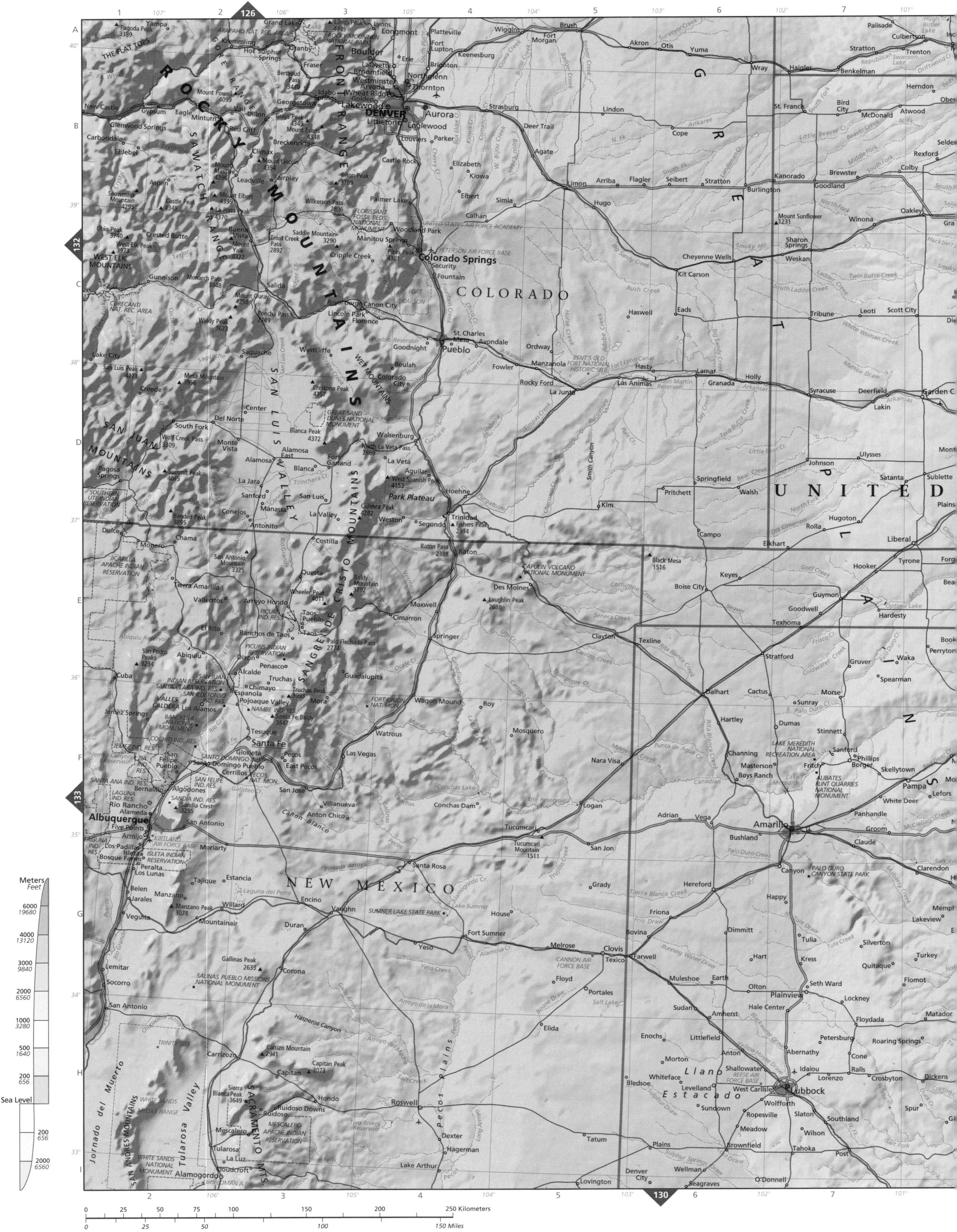

ROCKY MOUNTAINS
FRONT RANGE
SAWATCH RANGE
GORE RANGE
THE FLAT TOPS
WEST ELK MOUNTAINS
SAN JUAN MOUNTAINS
SAN LUIS VALLEY
WET MOUNTAINS
SANGRE DE CRISTO MOUNTAINS
SACRAMENTO MTS.
SAN ANDRES MOUNTAINS
Jornado del Muerto
Tularosa Valley
Llano Estacado
Pecos Plains
COLORADO
NEW MEXICO
GREAT PLAINS
UNITED
DENVER
Colorado Springs
Pueblo
Boulder
Aurora
Lakewood
Littleton
Englewood
Fort Collins
Longmont
Loveland
Greeley
Trinidad
Raton
Santa Fe
Albuquerque
Rio Rancho
Las Vegas
Roswell
Clovis
Tucumcari
Amarillo
Lubbock
Dalhart
Liberal
Goodland
Lamar
La Junta
Alamogordo
Socorro
Taos
Española
Los Alamos
Pikes Peak 4301
Mount Elbert 4399
Blanca Peak 4372
Wheeler Peak 4011
Sandia Crest 3255
Black Mesa 1516
Mount Sunflower 1231
Meters / Feet
6000 19680
4000 13120
3000 9840
2000 6560
1000 3280
500 1640
200 656
Sea Level
200 656
2000 6560
0 25 50 75 100 150 200 250 Kilometers
0 25 50 100 150 Miles
Scale 1 : 2,500,000
Lambert Conformal Conic Projection

NEBRASKA

KANSAS

MISSOURI

OKLAHOMA

TEXAS

ARKANSAS

OZARK PLATEAU

BOSTON MOUNTAINS

OUACHITA MOUNTAINS

FLINT HILLS

WICHITA MOUNTAINS

ARBUCKLE MTS.

Kansas City

St. Joseph

Topeka

Wichita

Tulsa

Oklahoma City

Fort Smith

Fayetteville

Springfield

Joplin

Wichita Falls

Dallas

Fort Worth

Texarkana

100° West of Greenwich

0 25 50 75 100 150 200 250 Kilometers

0 25 50 100 150 Miles

Scale 1 : 2,500,000 Lambert Conformal Conic Projection

TEXAS
LOUISIANA
TAMAULIPAS
EDWARDS PLATEAU
NUECES PLAINS
BALCONES ESCARPMENT
BRADY MOUNTAINS
Gulf of Mexico
DALLAS
Fort Worth
Arlington
Abilene
Waco
Killeen
Temple
Austin
SAN ANTONIO
HOUSTON
Pasadena
Galveston
Texas City
Beaumont
Port Arthur
Orange
Tyler
Longview
Shreveport
Bryan
College Station
Corpus Christi
Laredo
Nuevo Laredo
McAllen
Reynosa
Brownsville
Matamoros
Harlingen
Victoria
Lufkin
Nacogdoches
Palestine
Padre Island
PADRE ISLAND NATIONAL SEASHORE
Matagorda Island
Matagorda Peninsula
Galveston Island
Bolivar Peninsula
Mustang Island
San Jose Island
Laguna Madre
LYNDON B. JOHNSON SPACE CENTER
KINGSVILLE NAVAL AIR STATION
CORPUS CHRISTI NAVAL AIR STATION
FORT HOOD
129
122
W-520564-7A-DR2-4

A
B
C
D
E
F
1
2
3
4
5
6
7
8
9
10
137
126
134
128
ROCKY MOUNTAINS
WYOMING
GREAT DIVIDE BASIN
IDAHO
UTAH
NEVADA
COLORADO
GREAT BASIN
COLORADO PLATEAU
SAN JUAN MOUNTAINS
UINTA MOUNTAINS
WASATCH RANGE
BEAR RIVER RANGE
SAWATCH RANGE
GORE RANGE
PARK RA.
ELKHEAD MTS.
MEDICINE BOW MTS.
DANFORTH HILLS
THE FLAT TOPS
WEST ELK MOUNTAINS
RAFT RIVER MOUNTAINS
PEQUOP MTS.
TOANO RANGE
SCHELL CREEK RANGE
RUBY MOUNTAINS
BUTTE MTS.
HENRY MTS.
LA SAL MTS.
ABAJO MTS.
PAVANT RANGE
Uncompahgre Plateau
Yampa Plateau
San Rafael Swell
San Rafael Desert
Kaiparowits Plateau
Aquarius Plateau
Great Salt Lake Desert
Great Salt Lake
Bonneville Salt Flats
Sevier Desert
Escalante Desert
Snake Valley
Tule Valley
Pine Valley
Spring Valley
Railroad Valley
Coal Valley
Glen Canyon
Salt Lake City
Provo
Ogden
Logan
Rock Springs
Green River
Evanston
Vernal
Price
Moab
Grand Junction
Durango
Montrose
Rawlins
Wells
Elko
Ely
St. George
Cedar City
Kanab
Delta
Richfield
Tooele
Rifle
Gunnison
Cortez
Monticello
Blanding
Pioche
Caliente
Jackpot
Wendover
DINOSAUR NATIONAL MONUMENT
CAPITOL REEF NATIONAL PARK
ARCHES NATIONAL PARK
CANYONLANDS NATIONAL PARK
BRYCE CANYON NATIONAL PARK
ZION NAT. PARK
MESA VERDE NATIONAL PARK
GREAT BASIN NATIONAL PARK
GLEN CANYON NATIONAL RECREATION AREA
FLAMING GORGE NATIONAL RECREATION AREA
UINTAH AND OURAY INDIAN RESERVATION
GOSHUTE INDIAN RESERVATION
DUCK VALLEY INDIAN RESERVATION
UTE MOUNTAIN INDIAN RESERVATION
SOUTHERN UTE INDIAN RESERVATION
HILL AIR FORCE BASE
DUGWAY PROVING GROUND

UNITED STATES
ARIZONA
NEW MEXICO
CALIFORNIA
MEXICO
SONORA
CHIHUAHUA
BAJA CALIFORNIA
Golfo de California
PHOENIX
Tucson
Albuquerque
Flagstaff
Las Vegas
Yuma
Ciudad Juárez
El Paso
Nogales
Mogollon Rim
Painted Desert
Grand Canyon
Coconino Plateau
Defiance Plateau
Plains of San Agustin
Jornada del Muerto
Animas Valley
Sulphur Springs Valley
Desierto de Altar
Scale 1 : 2,500,000
Lambert Conformal Conic Projection
Meters
Feet
Sea Level
Copyright © Rand McNally & Co.

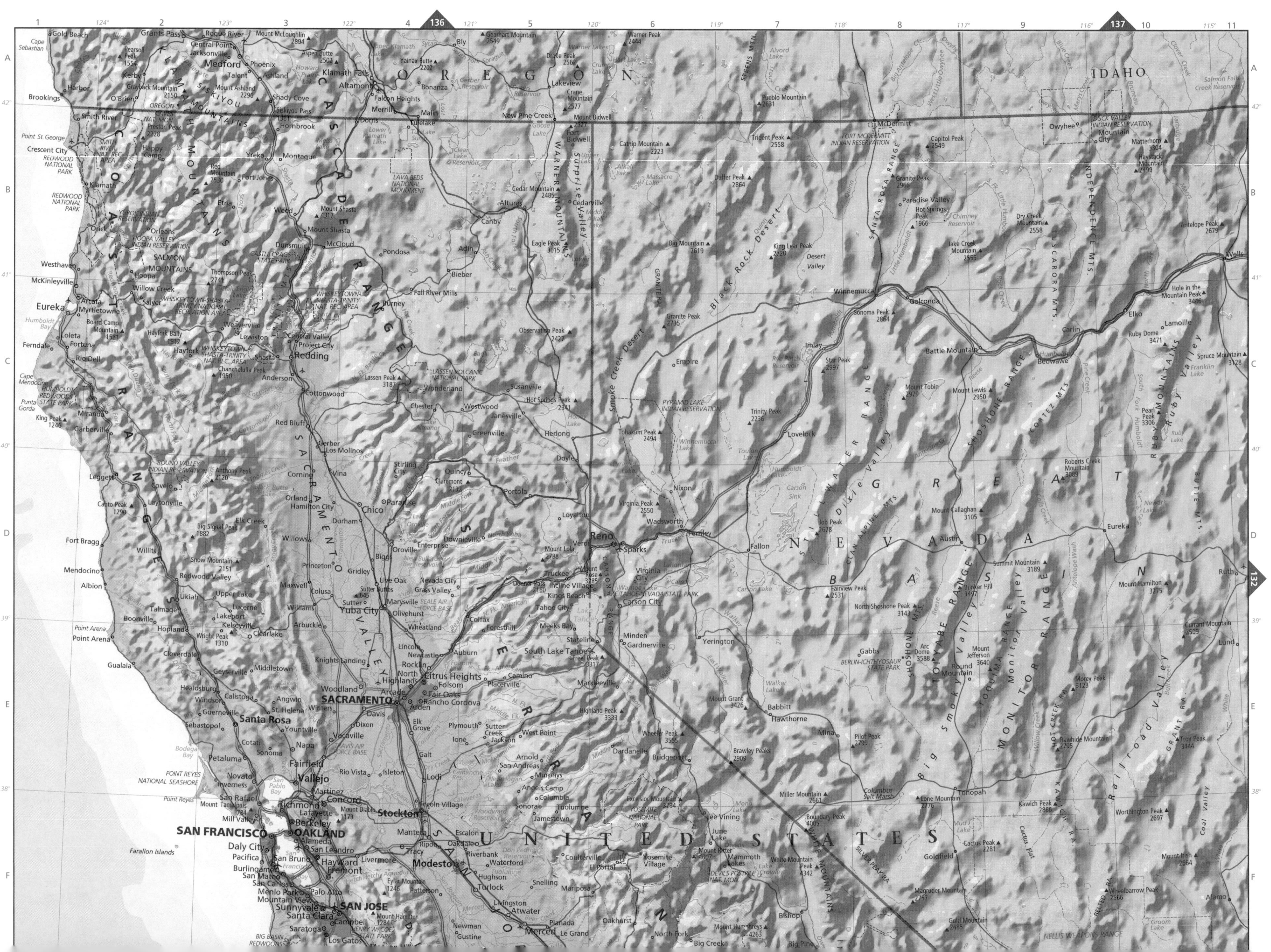
132
136
137
IDAHO
OREGON
NEVADA
CASCADE RANGE
COAST RANGES
SACRAMENTO VALLEY
SAN FRANCISCO
OAKLAND
SAN JOSE
SACRAMENTO
Stockton
Modesto
Reno
Carson City
Eureka
Elko
Winnemucca
Fallon
Redding
Chico
Medford
Black Rock Desert
Smoke Creek Desert
RUBY MOUNTAINS
TOIYABE RANGE
WHITE MOUNTAINS
Farallon Islands

PACIFIC OCEAN
COAST RANGES
MOJAVE DESERT
DEATH VALLEY
Salinas
Monterey
Fresno
Visalia
Bakersfield
Las Vegas
Santa Barbara
Ventura
Oxnard
LOS ANGELES
ANAHEIM
Santa Ana
RIVERSIDE
Long Beach
Santa Monica
San Bernardino
Lancaster
SAN DIEGO
Tijuana
Mexicali
CHANNEL ISLANDS
Gulf of Santa Catalina
MEXICO
BAJA CALIFORNIA
Ensenada
a
Same scale as main map
OAHU
Honolulu
MOLOKAI
LANAI
MAUI
KAHOOLAWE
HAWAII
HAWAII (U.S.)
HAWAIIAN ISLANDS
Kaiwi Channel
Alenuihaha Channel
Kona Coast
PACIFIC OCEAN
Meters
Feet
Sea Level
Scale 1 : 2,500,000
Lambert Conformal Conic Projection
250 Kilometers
150 Miles
W-520505-7A-DR2-4
Copyright © Rand McNally & Co.

Scale 1 : 2,500,000 Lambert Conformal Conic Projection

ALBERTA
SASKATCHEWAN
MONTANA
IDAHO
WYOMING
UTAH
ROCKY MOUNTAINS
BITTERROOT RANGE
SALMON RIVER MOUNTAINS
Snake River Plain
Great Falls
Helena
Missoula
Butte
Bozeman
Boise
Pocatello
Idaho Falls
Twin Falls
YELLOWSTONE NATIONAL PARK
West of Greenwich
WS20561-7A-OR2-1
Copyright © Rand McNally & Co.

BRITISH COLUMBIA
COAST MOUNTAINS
PACIFIC RANGES
KITIMAT RANGES
HAZELTON MOUNTAINS
BABINE RANGE
BULKLEY RANGES
NECHAKO PLATEAU
FRASER PLATEAU
CARIBOO MOUNTAINS
CASCADE RANGE
VANCOUVER ISLAND RANGES
VANCOUVER ISLAND
PACIFIC OCEAN
Queen Charlotte Sound
Queen Charlotte Strait
Strait of Georgia
Strait of Juan de Fuca
VANCOUVER
Victoria
Prince George
Burnaby
Richmond
North Vancouver
West Vancouver
Nanaimo
Campbell River
Port Alberni
Kamloops
Williams Lake
Quesnel
Bellingham
Hazelton
New Hazelton
Smithers
Houston
Terrace
Kitimat
Fort St. James
Vanderhoof
Fort Fraser
Burns Lake
Bella Coola
Port Hardy
Port McNeill
Tofino
Ucluelet
Powell River
Squamish
Whistler
Pemberton
Lillooet
Hope
Chilliwack
Abbotsford
Courtenay
Comox
Duncan
Sooke
Port Angeles
Mount Vernon
Anacortes
Tumbler Ridge
McLeod Lake
Mackenzie
Scale 1 : 2,500,000
Lambert Conformal Conic Projection
W-520299-7A-DR2-1
Copyright © Rand McNally & Co.
Meters
Feet
4000
13120
3000
9840
2000
6560
1000
3280
500
1640
200
656
Sea Level
200
656
2000
6560
0
25
50
75
100
150
200
250 Kilometers
0
25
50
100
150 Miles

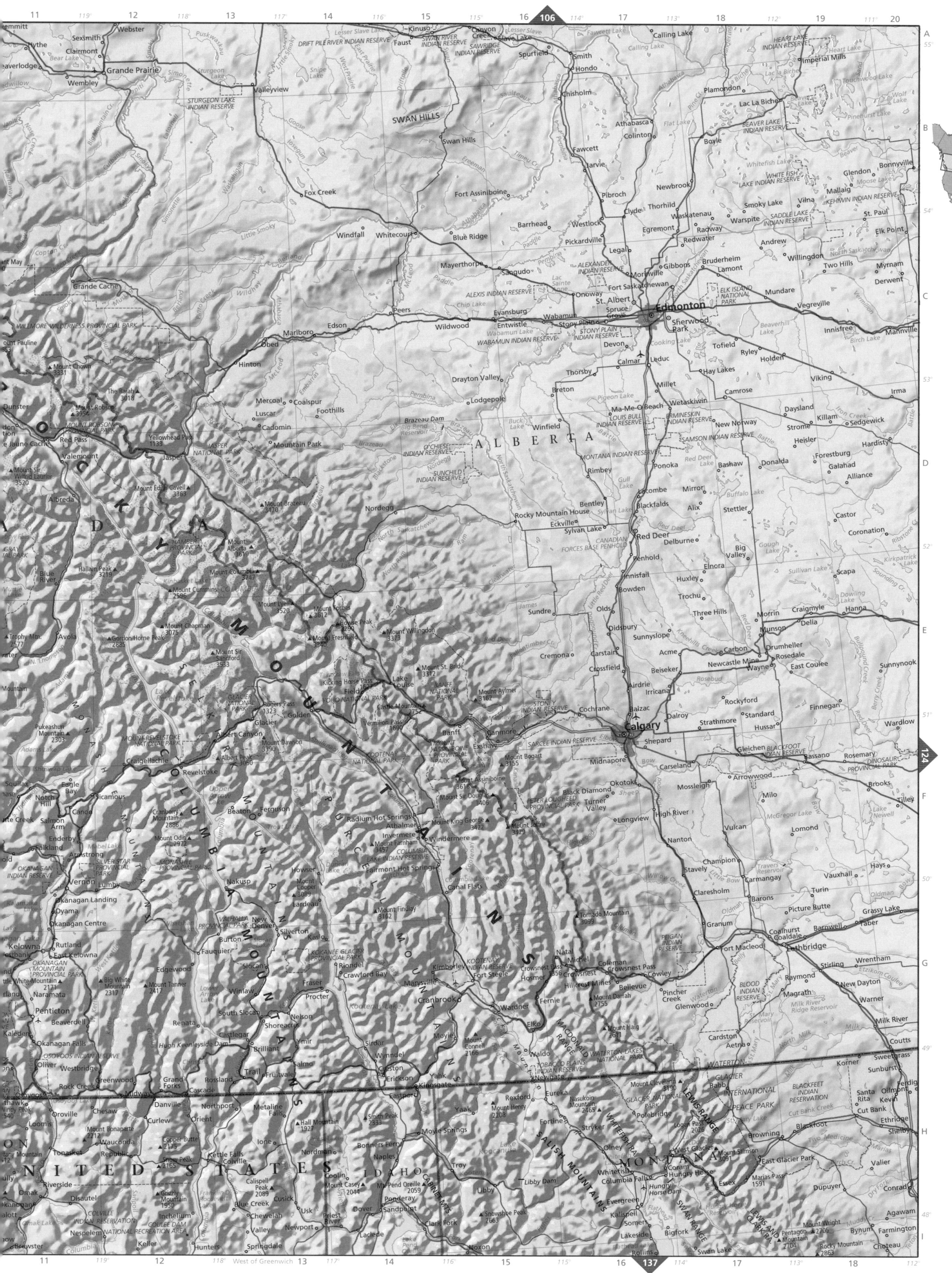
ALBERTA
ROCKY MOUNTAINS
COLUMBIA MOUNTAINS
SELKIRK MOUNTAINS
MONASHEE MOUNTAINS
PURCELL MOUNTAINS
SALISH MOUNTAINS
LEWIS RANGE
SWAN HILLS
UNITED STATES
IDAHO
MONTANA
Edmonton
Calgary
Red Deer
Lethbridge
Grande Prairie
Grande Cache
Fox Creek
Swan Hills
Whitecourt
Edson
Hinton
Jasper
Valemount
Blue River
Revelstoke
Golden
Banff
Canmore
Lake Louise
Field
Cochrane
Airdrie
Okotoks
High River
Nanton
Claresholm
Fort Macleod
Pincher Creek
Cardston
Drumheller
Three Hills
Olds
Innisfail
Sylvan Lake
Lacombe
Ponoka
Wetaskiwin
Leduc
Camrose
Stettler
Hanna
Brooks
Taber
Milk River
Coutts
Vegreville
Vermilion
St. Paul
Bonnyville
Cold Lake
Lac La Biche
Athabasca
Westlock
Barrhead
St. Albert
Spruce Grove
Stony Plain
Sherwood Park
Fort Saskatchewan
Drayton Valley
Rocky Mountain House
Sundre
Cranbrook
Kimberley
Fernie
Invermere
Radium Hot Springs
Nelson
Castlegar
Trail
Rossland
Grand Forks
Penticton
Kelowna
Vernon
Salmon Arm
Enderby
Nakusp
Kalispell
Whitefish
Columbia Falls
Shelby
Browning
Cut Bank
Sandpoint
Bonners Ferry
Libby
Colville
Oroville
Omak
Mount Robson 3954
Mount Columbia 3747
Mount Forbes 3612
Mount Assiniboine 3618
Mount Edith Cavell 3363
JASPER NATIONAL PARK
BANFF NATIONAL PARK
YOHO NATIONAL PARK
KOOTENAY NATIONAL PARK
GLACIER NATIONAL PARK
WATERTON LAKES NATIONAL PARK
MOUNT REVELSTOKE NATIONAL PARK
West of Greenwich

0 100 200 300 400 600 800 1000 Kilometers

0 100 200 400 600 Miles

Scale 1 : 10,000,000 Lambert Conformal Conic Projection

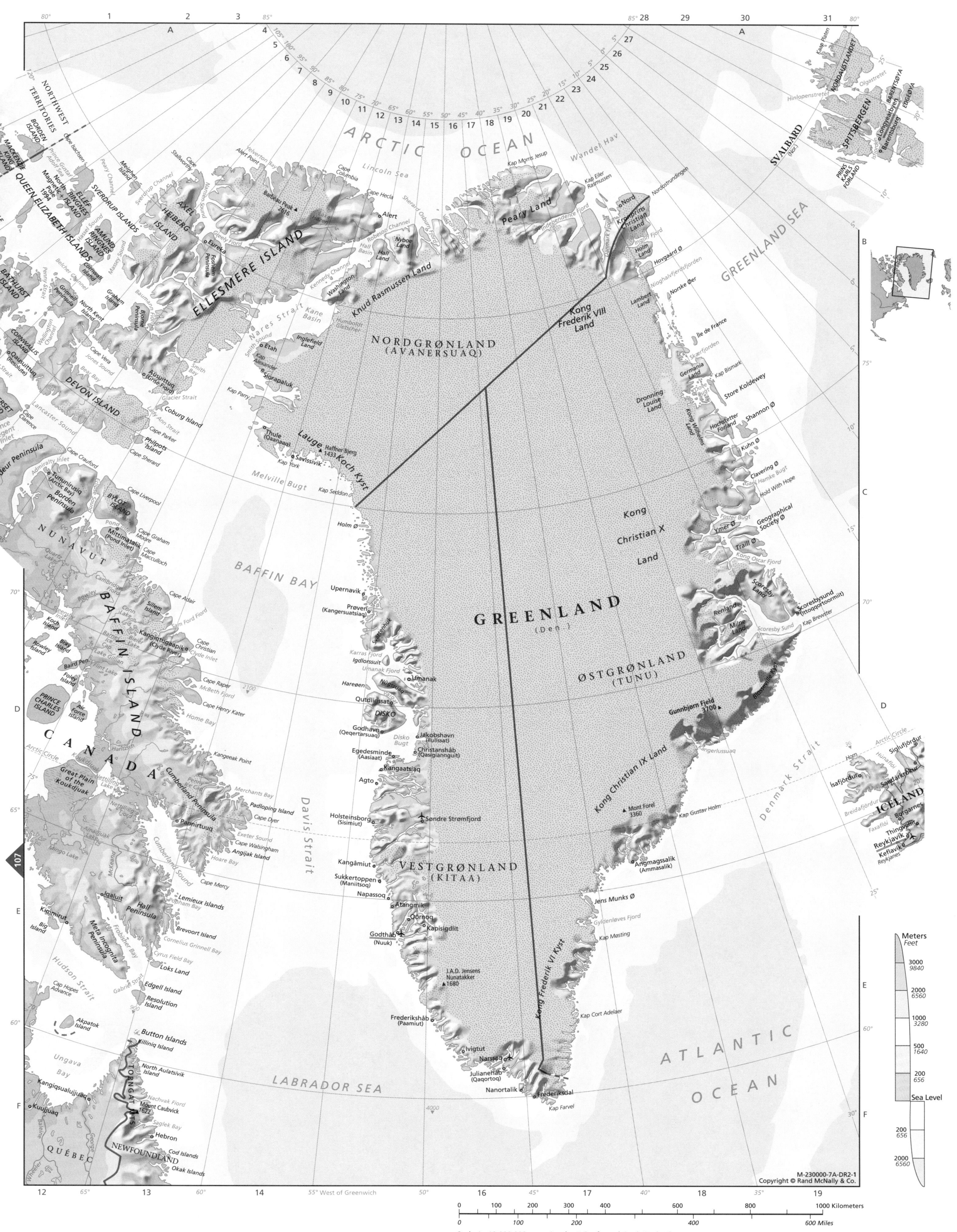
ARCTIC OCEAN
Lincoln Sea
Wandel Hav
GREENLAND SEA
GREENLAND
(Den.)
NORDGRØNLAND
(AVANERSUAQ)
ØSTGRØNLAND
(TUNU)
VESTGRØNLAND
(KITAA)
Peary Land
Kronprins Christian Land
Kong Frederik VIII Land
Knud Rasmussen Land
Dronning Louise Land
Kong Christian X Land
Kong Christian IX Land
Kong Frederik VI Kyst
Lauge Koch Kyst
Gunnbjørn Fjeld 3700
Mont Forel 3360
Kap Morris Jesup
Nord
Hovgaard Ø
Norske Øer
Île de France
Germania Land
Kap Bismark
Store Koldewey
Shannon Ø
Kuhn Ø
Clavering Ø
Geographical Society Ø
Ymer Ø
Traill Ø
Scoresby Land
Scoresbysund (Ittoqqortoormiit)
Kap Brewster
Scoresby Sund
Renland
Milne Land
Kap Gustav Holm
Angmagssalik (Ammasalik)
Jens Munks Ø
Kap Møsting
Kap Cort Adelaer
Kap Farvel
Frederiksdal
Nanortalik
Julianehåb (Qaqortoq)
Narssaq
Ivigtut
Frederikshåb (Paamiut)
J.A.D. Jensens Nunatakker 1680
Godthåb (Nuuk)
Kapisigdlit
Qôrnoq
Atangmik
Napassoq
Sukkertoppen (Maniitsoq)
Kangâmiut
Holsteinsborg (Sisimiut)
Søndre Strømfjord
Agto
Kangaatsiaq
Egedesminde (Aasiaat)
Christianshåb (Qasigiannguit)
Jakobshavn (Ilulissat)
Godhavn (Qeqertarsuaq)
Disko
Disko Bugt
Qutdligssat
Umanak
Hareøen
Nûgssuaq
Igdlorssuit
Prøven (Kangersuatsiaq)
Upernavik
Holm Ø
Kap Seddon
Melville Bugt
Savissivik
Kap York
Thule (Qaanaaq)
Haffner Bjerg 1433
Kap Parry
Etah
Siorapaluk
Inglefield Land
Washington Land
Hall Land
Nyboe Land
Alert
Cape Columbia
Barbeau Peak 2616
Eureka
Ausuittuq (Grise Fiord)
ELLESMERE ISLAND
AXEL HEIBERG ISLAND
QUEEN ELIZABETH ISLANDS
SVERDRUP ISLANDS
DEVON ISLAND
BYLOT ISLAND
BAFFIN BAY
BAFFIN ISLAND
NUNAVUT
CANADA
Davis Strait
LABRADOR SEA
ATLANTIC OCEAN
Denmark Strait
Nares Strait
Kane Basin
Humboldt Gletscher
Smith Sound
Lancaster Sound
Pond Inlet
Mittimatalik (Pond Inlet)
Clyde River
Cumberland Peninsula
Cumberland Sound
Pangnirtung
Padloping Island
Cape Dyer
Hall Peninsula
Iqaluit
Kimmirut
Meta Incognita Peninsula
Resolution Island
Button Islands
Killiniq Island
Hudson Strait
Ungava Bay
Kangiqsualujjuaq
Kuujjuaq
Akpatok Island
TORNGAT MTS.
Mount Caubvick 1622
Hebron
Cod Islands
Okak Islands
QUÉBEC
NEWFOUNDLAND
Great Plain of the Koukdjuak
Arctic Circle
SVALBARD (Nor.)
SPITSBERGEN
NORDAUSTLANDET
BARENTSØYA
EDGEØYA
PRINS KARLS FORLAND
Longyearbyen
Barentsburg
Hinlopenstretet
ICELAND
Ísafjörður
Siglufjörður
Sauðárkrókur
Borgarnes
Thingvellir
Reykjavík
Keflavík
Meters
Feet
3000 9840
2000 6560
1000 3280
500 1640
200 656
Sea Level
200 656
2000 6560
M-230000-7A-DR2-1
Copyright © Rand McNally & Co.
Scale 1 : 10,000,000
Lambert Conformal Conic Projection
0 100 200 300 400 600 800 1000 Kilometers
0 100 200 400 600 Miles
55° West of Greenwich
107

Scale 1 : 60,000,000 Robinson Projection

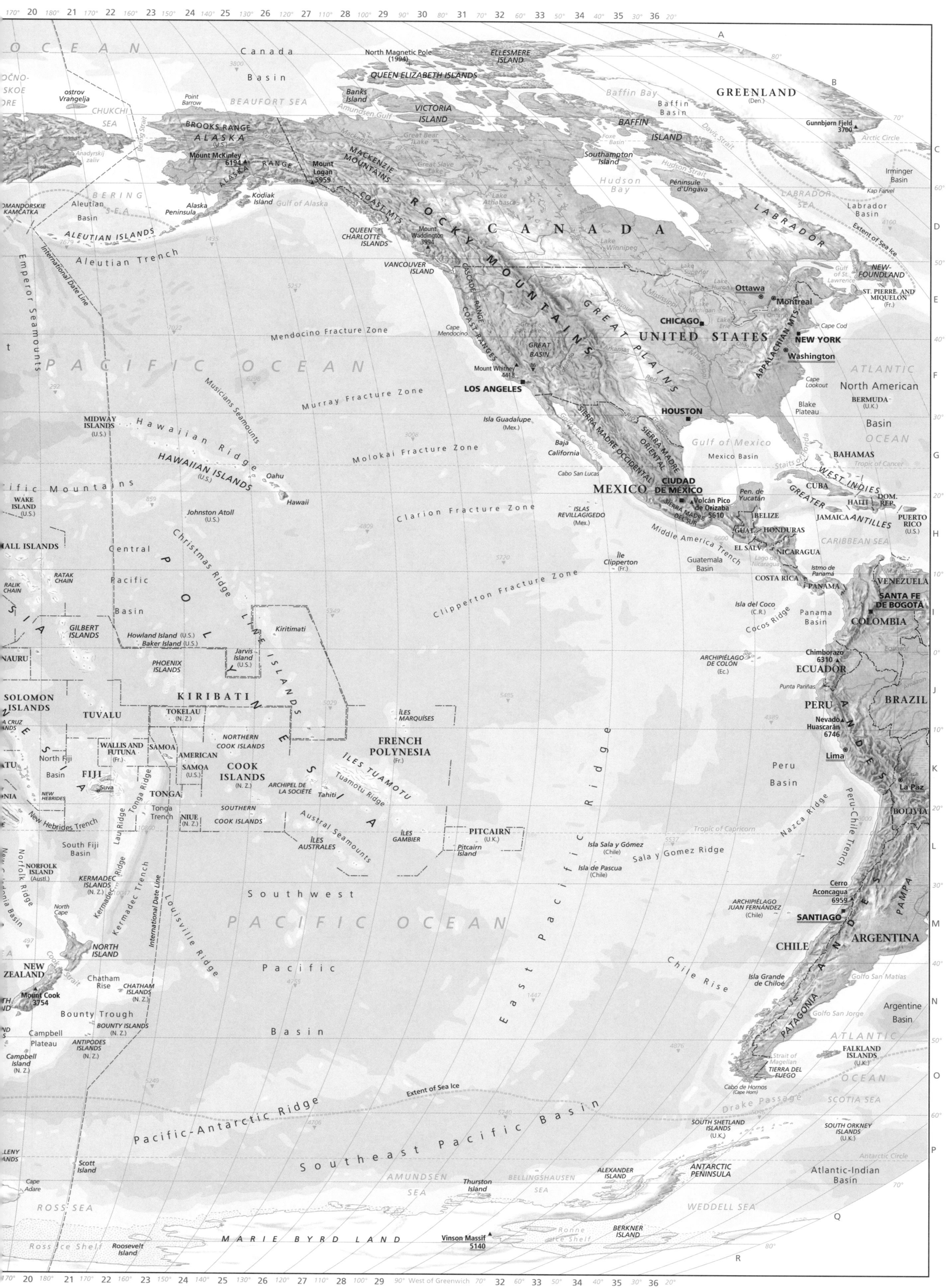

Canada Basin
North Magnetic Pole (1994)
ELLESMERE ISLAND
QUEEN ELIZABETH ISLANDS
GREENLAND (Den.)
Gunnbjørn Fjeld 3700
Baffin Bay
Baffin Basin
BAFFIN ISLAND
Banks Island
VICTORIA ISLAND
ostrov Vrangelja
CHUKCHI SEA
Point Barrow
BEAUFORT SEA
BROOKS RANGE
ALASKA (U.S.)
Mount McKinley 6194
ALASKA RANGE
Mount Logan 5959
MACKENZIE MOUNTAINS
Southampton Island
Hudson Bay
Péninsule d'Ungava
Irminger Basin
Kap Farvel
Labrador Basin
LABRADOR SEA
LABRADOR
BERING SEA
Aleutian Basin
Kodiak Island
Alaska Peninsula
Gulf of Alaska
COAST MTS.
ROCKY MOUNTAINS
CANADA
ALEUTIAN ISLANDS
Aleutian Trench
QUEEN CHARLOTTE ISLANDS
Mount Waddington 3994
VANCOUVER ISLAND
Emperor Seamounts
International Date Line
NEW-FOUNDLAND
ST. PIERRE AND MIQUELON (Fr.)
Ottawa
Montreal
Cape Cod
CHICAGO
UNITED STATES
NEW YORK
Washington
GREAT PLAINS
APPALACHIAN MTS.
Mendocino Fracture Zone
Cape Mendocino
CASCADE RANGE
COAST RANGES
GREAT BASIN
Mount Whitney 4418
LOS ANGELES
PACIFIC OCEAN
ATLANTIC
North American Basin
Cape Lookout
BERMUDA (U.K.)
Blake Plateau
Murray Fracture Zone
Musicians Seamounts
HOUSTON
MIDWAY ISLANDS (U.S.)
Hawaiian Ridge
HAWAIIAN ISLANDS (U.S.)
Isla Guadalupe (Mex.)
Baja California
SIERRA MADRE OCCIDENTAL
SIERRA MADRE ORIENTAL
Gulf of Mexico
Mexico Basin
BAHAMAS
Tropic of Cancer
Molokai Fracture Zone
Cabo San Lucas
MEXICO
CIUDAD DE MÉXICO
Volcán Pico de Orizaba 5610
SIERRA MADRE DEL SUR
Pen. de Yucatán
CUBA
WEST INDIES
GREATER ANTILLES
HAITI
DOM. REP.
JAMAICA
PUERTO RICO (U.S.)
Oahu
Hawaii
Mid-Pacific Mountains
WAKE ISLAND (U.S.)
Johnston Atoll (U.S.)
Clarion Fracture Zone
ISLAS REVILLAGIGEDO (Mex.)
BELIZE
GUAT.
HONDURAS
EL SALV.
NICARAGUA
CARIBBEAN SEA
Middle America Trench
Guatemala Basin
Île Clipperton (Fr.)
COSTA RICA
PANAMA
VENEZUELA
MARSHALL ISLANDS
Central Pacific Basin
Christmas Ridge
RATAK CHAIN
RALIK CHAIN
POLYNESIA
Clipperton Fracture Zone
Isla del Coco (C.R.)
Panama Basin
SANTA FE DE BOGOTÁ
COLOMBIA
Cocos Ridge
GILBERT ISLANDS
Howland Island (U.S.)
Baker Island (U.S.)
Kiritimati
LINE ISLANDS
Jarvis Island (U.S.)
NAURU
PHOENIX ISLANDS
ARCHIPIÉLAGO DE COLÓN (Ec.)
Chimborazo 6310
ECUADOR
Equator
SOLOMON ISLANDS
KIRIBATI
TUVALU
TOKELAU (N. Z.)
ÎLES MARQUISES
Punta Pariñas
PERU
BRAZIL
Nevado Huascarán 6746
WALLIS AND FUTUNA (Fr.)
SAMOA
AMERICAN SAMOA (U.S.)
NORTHERN COOK ISLANDS
FRENCH POLYNESIA (Fr.)
ÎLES TUAMOTU
North Fiji Basin
FIJI
Suva
COOK ISLANDS (N. Z.)
ARCHIPEL DE LA SOCIÉTÉ
Tahiti
Tuamotu Ridge
Lima
ANDES
Peru Basin
La Paz
NEW HEBRIDES
TONGA
Tonga Trench
Tonga Ridge
Lau Ridge
NIUE (N. Z.)
SOUTHERN COOK ISLANDS
New Hebrides Trench
Austral Seamounts
ÎLES GAMBIER
PITCAIRN (U.K.)
Pitcairn Island
ÎLES AUSTRALES
East Pacific Ridge
Nazca Ridge
Peru-Chile Trench
BOLIVIA
Tropic of Capricorn
South Fiji Basin
Isla Sala y Gómez (Chile)
Isla de Pascua (Chile)
Sala y Gomez Ridge
NORFOLK ISLAND (Austl.)
Norfolk Ridge
KERMADEC ISLANDS (N. Z.)
Kermadec Ridge
Kermadec Trench
Louisville Ridge
Southwest PACIFIC OCEAN
Cerro Aconcagua 6959
ARCHIPIÉLAGO JUAN FERNÁNDEZ (Chile)
SANTIAGO
PAMPA
ARGENTINA
CHILE
North Cape
NORTH ISLAND
NEW ZEALAND
Cook Strait
Mount Cook 3754
Chatham Rise
CHATHAM ISLANDS (N. Z.)
Pacific Basin
Chile Rise
Isla Grande de Chiloé
Golfo San Matías
Argentine Basin
Golfo San Jorge
PATAGONIA
Bounty Trough
BOUNTY ISLANDS (N. Z.)
Campbell Plateau
ANTIPODES ISLANDS (N. Z.)
Campbell Island (N. Z.)
ATLANTIC OCEAN
FALKLAND ISLANDS (U.K.)
Strait of Magellan
TIERRA DEL FUEGO
Cabo de Hornos (Cape Horn)
Extent of Sea Ice
Drake Passage
SCOTIA SEA
Pacific-Antarctic Ridge
Southeast Pacific Basin
SOUTH SHETLAND ISLANDS (U.K.)
SOUTH ORKNEY ISLANDS (U.K.)
Antarctic Circle
Scott Island
ALEXANDER ISLAND
ANTARCTIC PENINSULA
Atlantic-Indian Basin
Cape Adare
AMUNDSEN SEA
Thurston Island
BELLINGSHAUSEN SEA
ROSS SEA
WEDDELL SEA
Ronne Ice Shelf
BERKNER ISLAND
MARIE BYRD LAND
Vinson Massif 5140
Ross Ice Shelf
Roosevelt Island
West of Greenwich

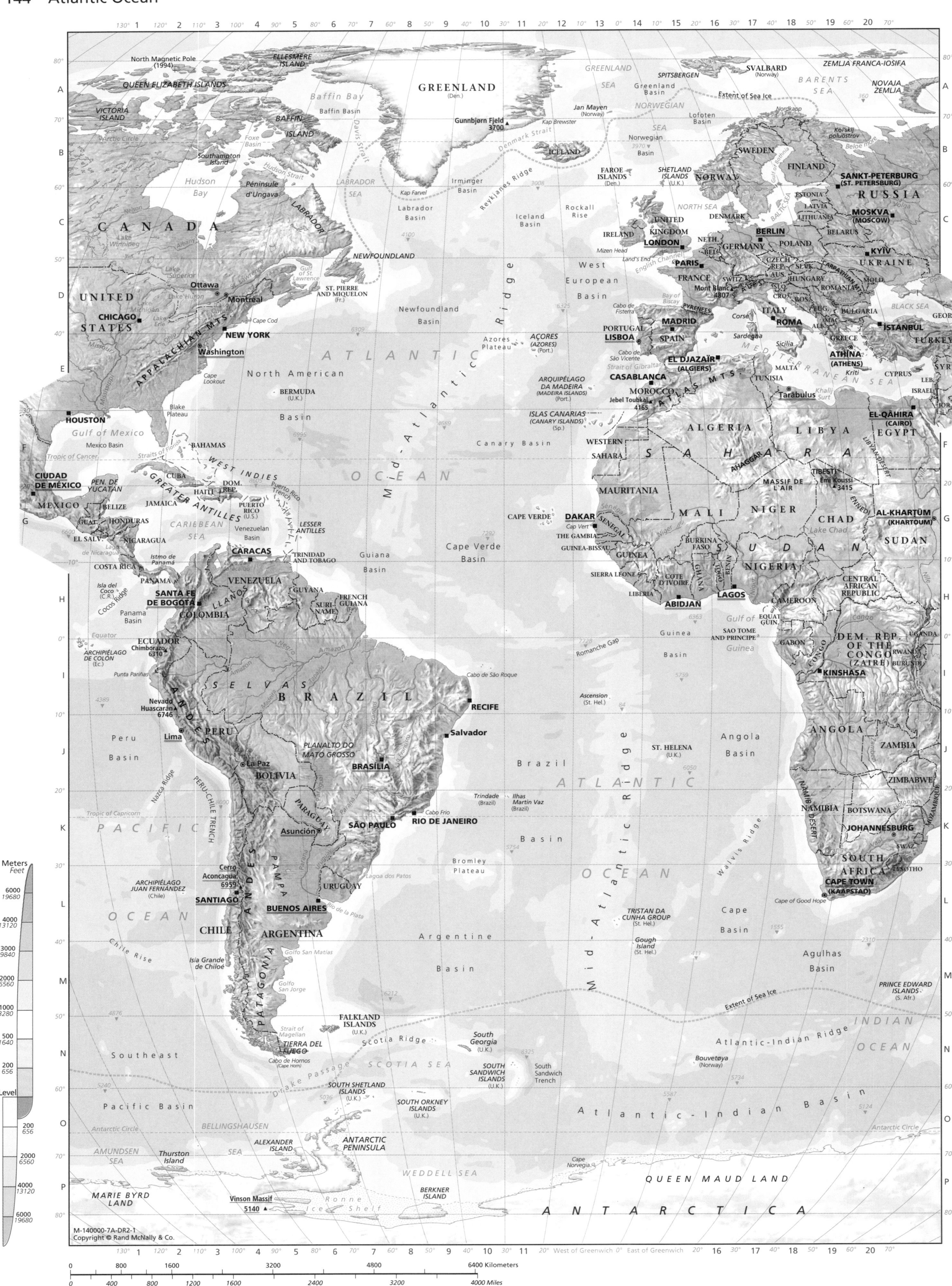

North Magnetic Pole (1994)
ELLESMERE ISLAND
QUEEN ELIZABETH ISLANDS
VICTORIA ISLAND
BAFFIN ISLAND
GREENLAND (Den.)
Baffin Bay
Baffin Basin
Davis Strait
Gunnbjørn Fjeld 3700
Kap Brewster
Denmark Strait
GREENLAND SEA
Greenland Basin
SPITSBERGEN
SVALBARD (Norway)
ZEMLJA FRANCA-IOSIFA
BARENTS SEA
NOVAJA ZEMLJA
Extent of Sea Ice
Jan Mayen (Norway)
NORWEGIAN SEA
Lofoten Basin
Nordkapp
Norwegian Basin
ICELAND
Southampton Island
Foxe Basin
Hudson Strait
Hudson Bay
Péninsule d'Ungava
LABRADOR
LABRADOR SEA
Kap Farvel
Irminger Basin
Reykjanes Ridge
Labrador Basin
Iceland Basin
Rockall Rise
FAROE ISLANDS (Den.)
SHETLAND ISLANDS (U.K.)
SWEDEN
NORWAY
FINLAND
SANKT-PETERBURG (ST. PETERSBURG)
RUSSIA
ESTONIA
LATVIA
LITHUANIA
MOSKVA (MOSCOW)
BELARUS
NORTH SEA
DENMARK
IRELAND
UNITED KINGDOM
LONDON
BERLIN
NETH.
POLAND
GERMANY
BEL.
KYIV
UKRAINE
PARIS
FRANCE
CZECH REP.
AUS.
SWITZ.
HUNGARY
ROMANIA
MOLD.
Mont Blanc 4807
ALPS
PYRENEES
BULGARIA
BLACK SEA
GEORGIA
ITALY
ROMA
ISTANBUL
TURKEY
GREECE
ATHINA (ATHENS)
CYPRUS
SYRIA
LEB.
ISRAEL
CANADA
NEWFOUNDLAND
ST. PIERRE AND MIQUELON (Fr.)
Ottawa
Montréal
UNITED STATES
CHICAGO
NEW YORK
Cape Cod
Washington
APPALACHIAN MTS.
Cape Lookout
Newfoundland Basin
West European Basin
Mizen Head
Land's End
English Channel
Bay of Biscay
Cabo de Finisterra
PORTUGAL
LISBOA
MADRID
SPAIN
Corse
Sardegna
Sicilia
Cabo de São Vicente
Strait of Gibraltar
EL DJAZAÏR (ALGIERS)
CASABLANCA
MOROCCO
Jebel Toubkal 4165
ATLAS MTS.
TUNISIA
MALTA
MEDITERRANEAN SEA
Kriti
Tarābulus
Khalīj Surt
Azores Plateau
AÇORES (AZORES) (Port.)
ARQUIPÉLAGO DA MADEIRA (MADEIRA ISLANDS) (Port.)
ISLAS CANARIAS (CANARY ISLANDS) (Sp.)
ATLANTIC OCEAN
North American Basin
Mid-Atlantic Ridge
BERMUDA (U.K.)
Blake Plateau
HOUSTON
Gulf of Mexico
Mexico Basin
BAHAMAS
Tropic of Cancer
Straits of Florida
Canary Basin
WESTERN SAHARA
ALGERIA
LIBYA
EGYPT
EL-QÂHIRA (CAIRO)
SAHARA
AHAGGAR
TIBESTI
Emi Koussi 3415
MASSIF DE L'AÏR
LIBYAN DESERT
CIUDAD DE MÉXICO
MEXICO
PEN. DE YUCATÁN
CUBA
WEST INDIES
GREATER ANTILLES
DOM. REP.
HAITI
Puerto Rico Trench
JAMAICA
PUERTO RICO (U.S.)
BELIZE
HONDURAS
GUAT.
EL SALV.
NICARAGUA
CARIBBEAN SEA
Venezuelan Basin
LESSER ANTILLES
MAURITANIA
MALI
NIGER
CHAD
AL-KHARṬŪM (KHARTOUM)
SUDAN
CAPE VERDE
DAKAR
Cap Vert
SENEGAL
THE GAMBIA
GUINEA-BISSAU
GUINEA
BURKINA FASO
Lake Chad
Cape Verde Basin
COSTA RICA
PANAMA
CARACAS
TRINIDAD AND TOBAGO
Guiana Basin
SIERRA LEONE
LIBERIA
CÔTE D'IVOIRE
GHANA
TOGO
BENIN
NIGERIA
ABIDJAN
LAGOS
CENTRAL AFRICAN REPUBLIC
CAMEROON
Isla del Coco (C.R.)
Cocos Ridge
SANTA FE DE BOGOTÁ
COLOMBIA
VENEZUELA
LLANOS
GUYANA
SURINAME
FRENCH GUIANA (Fr.)
Panama Basin
Equator
ECUADOR
Chimborazo 6310
ARCHIPIÉLAGO DE COLÓN (Ec.)
Punta Pariñas
Gulf of Guinea
EQUAT. GUIN.
SAO TOME AND PRINCIPE
Guinea Basin
Romanche Gap
GABON
CONGO
DEM. REP. OF THE CONGO (ZAIRE)
RWANDA
BURUNDI
UGANDA
KINSHASA
Amazon
Cabo de São Roque
SELVAS
BRAZIL
RECIFE
Ascension (St. Hel.)
Nevado Huascarán 6746
ANDES
PERU
Lima
Peru Basin
Salvador
PLANALTO DO MATO GROSSO
BRASÍLIA
La Paz
BOLIVIA
ST. HELENA (U.K.)
Angola Basin
ANGOLA
ZAMBIA
Brazil Basin
Nazca Ridge
PERU-CHILE TRENCH
ZIMBABWE
Trindade (Brazil)
Ilhas Martin Vaz (Brazil)
Tropic of Capricorn
PARAGUAY
Asunción
SÃO PAULO
RIO DE JANEIRO
Cabo Frio
NAMIBIA
NAMIB DESERT
BOTSWANA
JOHANNESBURG
MOZAMBIQUE
SWAZ.
PACIFIC OCEAN
Walvis Ridge
Bromley Plateau
Cerro Aconcagua 6959
PAMPA
Lagoa dos Patos
URUGUAY
SOUTH AFRICA
LESOTHO
CAPE TOWN (KAAPSTAD)
Cape of Good Hope
ARCHIPIÉLAGO JUAN FERNÁNDEZ (Chile)
SANTIAGO
BUENOS AIRES
Río de la Plata
TRISTAN DA CUNHA GROUP (St. Hel.)
Cape Basin
CHILE
ARGENTINA
Argentine Basin
Gough Island (St. Hel.)
Agulhas Basin
Chile Rise
Isla Grande de Chiloé
Golfo San Matías
PATAGONIA
Golfo San Jorge
PRINCE EDWARD ISLANDS (S. Afr.)
Extent of Sea Ice
FALKLAND ISLANDS (U.K.)
Strait of Magellan
TIERRA DEL FUEGO
Scotia Ridge
South Georgia (U.K.)
INDIAN OCEAN
Atlantic-Indian Ridge
Southeast Pacific Basin
Cabo de Hornos (Cape Horn)
SCOTIA SEA
Drake Passage
SOUTH SANDWICH ISLANDS (U.K.)
South Sandwich Trench
Bouvetøya (Norway)
SOUTH SHETLAND ISLANDS (U.K.)
SOUTH ORKNEY ISLANDS (U.K.)
Atlantic-Indian Basin
Antarctic Circle
BELLINGSHAUSEN SEA
ALEXANDER ISLAND
ANTARCTIC PENINSULA
AMUNDSEN SEA
Thurston Island
WEDDELL SEA
Cape Norvegia
QUEEN MAUD LAND
MARIE BYRD LAND
Vinson Massif 5140
Ronne Ice Shelf
BERKNER ISLAND
ANTARCTICA
Meters Feet
6000 19680
4000 13120
3000 9840
2000 6560
1000 3280
500 1640
200 656
Sea Level
200 656
2000 6560
4000 13120
6000 19680
M-140000-7A-DR2-1
Copyright © Rand McNally & Co.
West of Greenwich 0° East of Greenwich
0 800 1600 3200 4800 6400 Kilometers
0 400 800 1200 1600 2400 3200 4000 Miles
Scale 1 : 60,000,000
Robinson Projection

Index to World Reference Maps

Introduction to the Index

This index includes in a single alphabetical list approximately 54,000 names of places and geographical features that appear on the reference maps. Each name is followed by the name of the country or continent in which it is located, an alpha-numeric map reference key, and a page reference.

Names The names of cities and towns appear in the index in regular type. The names of all other features appear in *italics*, followed by descriptive terms (hill, mtn., state) to indicate their nature.

Abbreviations of names on the maps have been standardized as much as possible. Names that are abbreviated on the maps are generally spelled out in full in the index.

Country names and names of features that extend beyond the boundaries of one country are followed by the name of the continent in which each is located. Country designations follow the names of all other places in the index. The locations of places in the United States, Canada, and the United Kingdom are further defined by abbreviations that indicate the state, province, or other political division in which each is located.

All abbreviations used in the index are defined in the List of Abbreviations to the right.

Alphabetization Names are alphabetized in the order of the letters of the English alphabet. Spanish *ll* and *ch*, for example, are not treated as distinct letters. Furthermore, diacritical marks are disregarded in alphabetization—German or Scandinavian *ä* or *ö* are treated as *a* or *o*.

The names of physical features may appear inverted, since they are always alphabetized under the proper, not the generic, part of the name, thus: "Gibraltar, Strait of". Otherwise every entry, whether consisting of one word or more, is alphabetized as a single continuous entity. "Lakeland", for example, appears after "La Crosse" and before "La Salle". Names beginning with articles (Le Havre, Den Helder, Al-Manāmah) are not inverted. Names beginning "St.", "Ste." and "Sainte" are alphabetized as though spelled "Saint".

In the case of identical names, towns are listed first, then political divisions, then physical features. Entries that are completely identical are listed alphabetically by country name.

Map Reference Keys and Page References The map reference keys and page references are found in the last two columns of each entry.

Each map reference key consists of a letter and number. The letters correspond to letters along the sides of the maps. Lowercase letters refer to inset maps. The numbers correspond to numbers that appear across the tops and bottoms of the maps.

Map reference keys for point features, such as cities and mountain peaks, indicate the locations of the symbols for these features. For other features, such as countries, mountain ranges, or rivers, the map reference keys indicate the locations of the names.

The page number generally refers to the main map for the country in which the feature is located. Page references for two-page maps always refer to the left-hand page.

List of Abbreviations

Ab., Can.	Alberta, Can.
Afg.	Afghanistan
Afr.	Africa
Ak., U.S.	Alaska, U.S.
Al., U.S.	Alabama, U.S.
Alb.	Albania
Alg.	Algeria
Am. Sam.	American Samoa
anch.	anchorage
And.	Andorra
Ang.	Angola
Ant.	Antarctica
Antig.	Antigua and Barbuda
aq.	aqueduct
Ar., U.S.	Arkansas, U.S.
Arg.	Argentina
Arm.	Armenia
at.	atoll
Aus.	Austria
Austl.	Australia
Az., U.S.	Arizona, U.S.
Azer.	Azerbaijan
b.	bay, gulf, inlet, lagoon
B.C., Can.	British Columbia, Can.
Bah.	Bahamas
Bahr.	Bahrain
Barb.	Barbados
bas.	basin
Bdi.	Burundi
Bel.	Belgium
Bela.	Belarus
Ber.	Bermuda
Bhu.	Bhutan
B.I.O.T.	British Indian Ocean Territory
Blg.	Bulgaria
Bngl.	Bangladesh
Bol.	Bolivia
Bos.	Bosnia and Hercegovina
Bots.	Botswana
Braz.	Brazil
Bru.	Brunei
Br. Vir. Is.	British Virgin Islands
Burkina	Burkina Faso
c.	cape, point
Ca., U.S.	California, U.S.
Cam.	Cameroon
Camb.	Cambodia
Can.	Canada
can.	canal
C.A.R.	Central African Republic
Cay. Is.	Cayman Islands
Christ. I.	Christmas Island
C. Iv.	Cote d'Ivoire
clf.	cliff, escarpment
Co., U.S.	Colorado, U.S.
co.	county, district, etc.
Cocos Is.	Cocos (Keeling) Islands
Col.	Colombia
Com.	Comoros
cont.	continent
Cook Is.	Cook Islands
C.R.	Costa Rica
crat.	crater
Cro.	Croatia
cst.	coast, beach
Ct., U.S.	Connecticut, U.S.
ctry.	independent country
C.V.	Cape Verde
cv.	cave
Cyp.	Cyprus
Czech Rep.	Czech Republic
D.C., U.S.	District of Columbia, U.S.
De., U.S.	Delaware, U.S.
Den.	Denmark
dep.	dependency, colony
depr.	depression
des.	desert
Dji.	Djibouti
Dom.	Dominica
Dom. Rep.	Dominican Republic
D.R.C.	Democratic Republic of the Congo
Ec.	Ecuador
El Sal.	El Salvador
Eng., U.K.	England, U.K.
Eq. Gui.	Equatorial Guinea
Erit.	Eritrea
Est.	Estonia
est.	estuary
Eth.	Ethiopia
Eur.	Europe
Falk. Is.	Falkland Islands
Far. Is.	Faroe Islands
Fin.	Finland
Fl., U.S.	Florida, U.S.
for.	forest, moor
Fr.	France
Fr. Gu.	French Guiana
Fr. Poly.	French Polynesia
Ga., U.S.	Georgia, U.S.
Gam.	The Gambia
Gaza	Gaza Strip
Geor.	Georgia
Ger.	Germany
Gib.	Gibraltar
Golan	Golan Heights
Grc.	Greece
Gren.	Grenada
Grnld.	Greenland
Guad.	Guadeloupe
Guat.	Guatemala
Guern.	Guernsey
Gui.	Guinea
Gui.-B.	Guinea-Bissau
Guy.	Guyana
gysr.	geyser
Hi., U.S.	Hawaii, U.S.
hist.	historic site, ruins
hist. reg.	historic region
Hond.	Honduras
Hung.	Hungary
i.	island
Ia., U.S.	Iowa, U.S.
Ice.	Iceland
ice	ice feature, glacier
Id., U.S.	Idaho, U.S.
Il., U.S.	Illinois, U.S.
In., U.S.	Indiana, U.S.
Indon.	Indonesia
I. of Man	Isle of Man
Ire.	Ireland
is.	islands
Isr.	Israel
isth.	isthmus
Jam.	Jamaica
Jer.	Jericho Area
Jord.	Jordan
Kaz.	Kazakhstan
Kir.	Kiribati
Kor., N.	Korea, North
Kor., S.	Korea, South
Ks., U.S.	Kansas, U.S.
Kuw.	Kuwait
Ky., U.S.	Kentucky, U.S.
Kyrg.	Kyrgyzstan
l.	lake, pond
La., U.S.	Louisiana, U.S.
Lat.	Latvia
lav.	lava flow
Leb.	Lebanon
Leso.	Lesotho
Lib.	Liberia
Liech.	Liechtenstein
Lith.	Lithuania
Lux.	Luxembourg
Ma., U.S.	Massachusetts, U.S.
Mac.	Macedonia
Madag.	Madagascar
Malay.	Malaysia
Mald.	Maldives
Marsh. Is.	Marshall Islands
Mart.	Martinique
Maur.	Mauritania
May.	Mayotte
Mb., Can.	Manitoba, Can.
Md., U.S.	Maryland, U.S.
Me., U.S.	Maine, U.S.
Mex.	Mexico
Mi., U.S.	Michigan, U.S.
Micron.	Micronesia, Federated States of
Mid. Is.	Midway Islands
misc. cult.	miscellaneous cultural
Mn., U.S.	Minnesota, U.S.
Mo., U.S.	Missouri, U.S.
Mol.	Moldova
Mon.	Monaco
Mong.	Mongolia
Monts.	Montserrat
Mor.	Morocco
Moz.	Mozambique
Mrts.	Mauritius
Ms., U.S.	Mississippi, U.S.
Mt., U.S.	Montana, U.S.
mth.	river mouth or channel
mtn.	mountain
mts.	mountains
Mwi.	Malawi
Mya.	Myanmar
N.A.	North America
N.B., Can.	New Brunswick, Can.
N.C., U.S.	North Carolina, U.S.
N. Cal.	New Caledonia
N. Cyp.	North Cyprus
N.D., U.S.	North Dakota, U.S.
Ne., U.S.	Nebraska, U.S.
Neth.	Netherlands
Neth. Ant.	Netherlands Antilles
Nf., Can.	Newfoundland, Can.
ngh.	neighborhood
N.H., U.S.	New Hampshire, U.S.
Nic.	Nicaragua
Nig.	Nigeria
N. Ire., U.K.	Northern Ireland, U.K.
N.J., U.S.	New Jersey, U.S.
N.M., U.S.	New Mexico, U.S.
N. Mar. Is.	Northern Mariana Islands
Nmb.	Namibia
Nor.	Norway
Norf. I.	Norfolk Island
N.S., Can.	Nova Scotia, Can.
N.T., Can.	Northwest Territories, Can.
Nu., Can.	Nunavut, Can.
Nv., U.S.	Nevada, U.S.
N.Y., U.S.	New York, U.S.
N.Z.	New Zealand
Oc.	Oceania
Oh., U.S.	Ohio, U.S.
Ok., U.S.	Oklahoma, U.S.
On., Can.	Ontario, Can.
Or., U.S.	Oregon, U.S.
p.	pass
Pa., U.S.	Pennsylvania, U.S.
Pak.	Pakistan
Pan.	Panama
Pap. N. Gui.	Papua New Guinea
Para.	Paraguay
P.E., Can.	Prince Edward Island, Can.
pen.	peninsula
Phil.	Philippines
Pit.	Pitcairn
pl.	plain, flat
plat.	plateau, highland
p.o.i.	point of interest
Pol.	Poland
Port.	Portugal
P.R.	Puerto Rico
Qc., Can.	Quebec, Can.
r.	rock, rocks
reg.	physical region
res.	reservoir
Reu.	Reunion
rf.	reef, shoal
R.I., U.S.	Rhode Island, U.S.
Rom.	Romania
Rw.	Rwanda
S.A.	South America
S. Afr.	South Africa
Samoa	Samoa
sand	sand area
Sau. Ar.	Saudi Arabia
S.C., U.S.	South Carolina, U.S.
sci.	scientific station
Scot., U.K.	Scotland, U.K.
S.D., U.S.	South Dakota, U.S.
Sen.	Senegal
Sey.	Seychelles
S. Geor.	South Georgia
Sing.	Singapore
Sk., Can.	Saskatchewan, Can.
S.L.	Sierra Leone
Slov.	Slovakia
Slvn.	Slovenia
S. Mar.	San Marino
Sol. Is.	Solomon Islands
Som.	Somalia
Sp. N. Afr.	Spanish North Africa
Sri L.	Sri Lanka
state	state, province, etc.
St. Hel.	St. Helena
St. K./N.	St. Kitts and Nevis
St. Luc.	St. Lucia
stm.	stream (river, creek)
S. Tom./P.	Sao Tome and Principe
St. P./M.	St. Pierre and Miquelon
strt.	strait, channel, etc.
St. Vin.	St. Vincent and the Grenadines
Sur.	Suriname
sw.	swamp, marsh
Swaz.	Swaziland
Swe.	Sweden
Switz.	Switzerland
Tai.	Taiwan
Taj.	Tajikistan
Tan.	Tanzania
T./C. Is.	Turks and Caicos Islands
Thai.	Thailand
Tn., U.S.	Tennessee, U.S.
Tok.	Tokelau
Trin.	Trinidad and Tobago
Tun.	Tunisia
Tur.	Turkey
Turkmen.	Turkmenistan
Tx., U.S.	Texas, U.S.
U.A.E.	United Arab Emirates
Ug.	Uganda
U.K.	United Kingdom
Ukr.	Ukraine
unds.	undersea feature
Ur.	Uruguay
U.S.	United States
Ut., U.S.	Utah, U.S.
Uzb.	Uzbekistan
Va., U.S.	Virginia, U.S.
val.	valley, watercourse
Vat.	Vatican City
Ven.	Venezuela
Viet.	Vietnam
V.I.U.S.	Virgin Islands (U.S.)
vol.	volcano
Vt., U.S.	Vermont, U.S.
Wa., U.S.	Washington, U.S.
Wake I.	Wake Island
Wal./F.	Wallis and Futuna
W.B.	West Bank
well	well, spring, oasis
Wi., U.S.	Wisconsin, U.S.
W. Sah.	Western Sahara
wtfl.	waterfall, rapids
W.V., U.S.	West Virginia, U.S.
Wy., U.S.	Wyoming, U.S.
Yk., Can.	Yukon Territory, Can.
Yugo.	Yugoslavia
Zam.	Zambia
Zimb.	Zimbabwe

Index

A

Name	Map Ref.	Page
Å, Nor.	C5	8
Aachen, Ger.	F1	16
Aalen, Ger.	H6	16
Aali, Sadd el- (Aswan High Dam), dam, Egypt	C6	62
Aalst (Alost), Bel.	D13	14
Äänekoski, Fin.	E11	8
Aarau, Switz.	C4	22
Aare, stm., Switz.	C5	22
Aarlen see Arlon, Bel.	E14	14
Aarschot, Bel.	D14	14
Aasiaat see Egedesminde, Grnld.	D15	141
Aat see Ath, Bel.	D12	14
Aba, China	E5	36
Aba, D.R.C.	D6	66
Aba, Nig.	H6	64
Abā al-Bawl, Qurayn, hill, Qatar	E7	56
Abacaxis, stm., Braz.	E6	84
Abaco, i., Bah.	B9	96
Abacou, Pointe, c., Haiti	D10	102
Abadab, Jabal, mtn., Sudan	D7	62
Ābādān, Iran	C6	56
Ābādeh, Iran	C7	56
Abadla, Alg.	C4	64
Abaeté, Braz.	J3	88
Abaeté, stm., Braz.	J3	88
Abaetetuba, Braz.	A1	88
Abag Qi, China	C7	36
Abaí, Para.	C10	92
Abaj, Kaz.	E12	32
Abakaliki, Nig.	H6	64
Abakan, Russia	D16	32
Abakan, stm., Russia	D15	32
Abakanovo, Russia	A20	10
Abakanskij hrebet, mts., Russia	D15	32
Abala, Niger	G5	64
Abalak, Niger	F6	64
Aban, Russia	C17	32
Abancay, Peru	F3	84
Abashiri, Japan	B16	38
Abasolo, Mex.	C6	100
Abasolo, Mex.	I7	130
Abasolo, Mex.	G6	130
Abau, Pap. N. Gui.	c4	79a
Abay see Abaj, Kaz.	E12	32
Ābay see Blue Nile, stm., Afr.	E6	62
Abaya, Lake see Ābaya Hāyk', l., Eth.	F7	62
Ābaya Hāyk', l., Eth.	F7	62
Abaza, Russia	D15	32
Abbadia San Salvatore, Italy	H8	22
Abbé, Lac see Abe, Lake, l., Afr.	E8	62
Abbeville, Fr.	D10	14
Abbeville, Ga., U.S.	D2	116
Abbeville, La., U.S.	H6	122
Abbeville, S.C., U.S.	B3	116
Abbey, Sk., Can.	D5	124
Abbeyfeale, Ire.	I3	12
Abbiategrasso, Italy	E5	22
Abbot, Mount, mtn., Austl.	B6	76
Abbot Ice Shelf, ice, Ant.	C31	81
Abbotsford, B.C., Can.	G8	138
Abbottābād, Pak.	A4	54
'Abd al-Kūrī, i., Yemen	G7	56
Ábdēra, hist., Grc.	B7	28
Abdulino, Russia	D8	32
Abe, Lake, l., Afr.	E8	62
Abéché, Chad	E4	62
Abel Tasman National Park, p.o.i., N.Z.	E5	80
Abemama, at., Kir.	C8	72
Abengourou, C. Iv.	H4	64
Abenójar, Spain	F6	20
Åbenrå, Den.	I3	8
Abensberg, Ger.	H7	16
Abeokuta, Nig.	H5	64
Aberdare, Wales, U.K.	J9	12
Aberdeen, S. Afr.	H6	70
Aberdeen, Scot., U.K.	D10	12
Aberdeen, Id., U.S.	H14	136
Aberdeen, Md., U.S.	E9	114
Aberdeen, Ms., U.S.	D10	122
Aberdeen, N.C., U.S.	A6	116
Aberdeen, S.D., U.S.	B14	126
Aberdeen, Wa., U.S.	D3	136
Aberdeen Lake, l., Nu., Can.	C10	106
Aberdeen Lake, res., Ms., U.S.	D10	122
Aberfeldy, Scot., U.K.	E9	12
Abergavenny, Wales, U.K.	J9	12
Abernant, Al., U.S.	D11	122
Abernathy, Tx., U.S.	H7	128
Abernethy, Sk., Can.	D10	124
Abert, Lake, l., Or., U.S.	H6	136
Aberystwyth, Wales, U.K.	I8	12
Abez', Russia	A10	32
Abhā, Sau. Ar.	F5	56
Abidjan, C. Iv.	H4	64
Abilene, Tx., U.S.	B8	130
Abingdon, Eng., U.K.	J11	12
Abingdon, Il., U.S.	D7	120
Abingdon, Va., U.S.	H4	114
Abiquiu, N.M., U.S.	E2	128
Abiquiu Reservoir, res., N.M., U.S.	E2	128
Abisko, Swe.	B8	8
Abitibi, stm., On., Can.	E14	106
Abitibi, Lake, l., Can.	F15	106
Abja-Paluoja, Est.	B8	10
Abnûb, Egypt	K2	58
Åbo see Turku, Fin.	F9	8
Abohar, India	C5	54
Abomey, Benin	H5	64
Abongabong, Gunung, mtn., Indon.	J3	48
Abong Mbang, Cam.	D2	66
Abony, Hung.	B6	26
Aborigen, pik, mtn., Russia	D18	34
Abou-Deïa, Chad	E3	62
Abou Simbel (Abu Simbel), hist., Egypt	C6	62
Abraham Lake, res., Ab., Can.	D14	138
Abra Pampa, Arg.	D3	90
Abre Campo, Braz.	K4	88
Abreu e Lima, Braz.	D8	88
Abring, India	B6	54
Abrud, Rom.	C10	26
Abruzzo, state, Italy	H10	22
Abruzzo, Parco Nazionale d', p.o.i., Italy	C7	24
Absaroka Range, mts., U.S.	C3	126
Absarokee, Mt., U.S.	E17	136
Absecon, N.J., U.S.	E11	114
Abū 'Alī, i., Sau. Ar.	D6	56
Abu Ballâs, mtn., Egypt	C5	62
Abu Dhabi see Abū Ẓaby, U.A.E.	E7	56
Abū Dulayq, Sudan	D6	62
Abū el-Hul (Sphinx), hist., Egypt	I1	58
Abufari, Braz.	E5	84
Abū Ḥamad, Sudan	D6	62
Abu Hammâd, Egypt	H2	58
Abuja, Nig.	H6	64
Abū Jabrah, Sudan	E5	62
Abū Jubayhah, Sudan	E6	62
Abū Kamāl, Syria	C5	56
Abukuma, stm., Japan	B13	40
Abukuma-kōchi, plat., Japan	B13	40
Abū Madd, Ra's, c., Sau. Ar.	E4	56
Abu Mendi, Eth.	E7	62
Abunã, Braz.	E4	84
Abu Qîr, Khalîg, b., Egypt	G1	58
Abu Qurqâs, Egypt	K1	58
Ābu Road, India	F4	54
Abū Rubayq, Sau. Ar.	E4	56
Abū Shajarah Ra's, c., Sudan	C7	62
Abu Shâma, Gebel, mtn., Egypt	I2	58
Abu Simbel see Abou Simbel, hist., Egypt	C6	62
Abu Tîg, Egypt	K2	58
Abū Zabad, Sudan	E5	62
Abū Ẓaby (Abu Dhabi), U.A.E.	E7	56
Abwong, Sudan	F6	62
Abyei, Sudan	F5	62
Abyssinia see Ethiopia, ctry., Afr.	F7	62
Acacías, Col.	E5	86
Acadia National Park, p.o.i., Me., U.S.	F8	110
Acadia Valley, Ab., Can.	C3	124
Açailândia, Braz.	C2	88
Acajutiba, Braz.	F7	88
Acámbaro, Mex.	E8	100
Acandí, Col.	C3	86
Acaponeta, Mex.	D6	100
Acaponeta, stm., Mex.	D6	100
Acapulco de Juárez, Mex.	G8	100
Acará, Braz.	A1	88
Acará, stm., Braz.	A1	88
Acarai Mountains, mts., S.A.	C6	84
Acará-Mirim, stm., Braz.	B1	88
Acaraú, Braz.	B5	88
Acaraú, stm., Braz.	B5	88
Acaray, stm., Para.	B10	92
Acarí, Peru	G3	84
Acari, stm., Braz.	H3	88
Acarigua, Ven.	C7	86
Acatlán de Osorio, Mex.	F9	100
Acay, Nevado de, mtn., Arg.	B4	92
Acayucan, Mex.	F11	100
Acceglio, Italy	F3	22
Accomac, Va., U.S.	G10	114
Accra, Ghana	H5	64
Acebuches, Mex.	A7	100
Aceguá, Braz.	E10	92
Aceh, state, Indon.	J3	48
Acerra, Italy	D8	24
Achacachi, Bol.	C3	90
Achaguas, Ven.	D7	86
Achalpur, India	H6	54
Achar, Ur.	F9	92
Acharnés, Grc.	E6	28
Achelóos, stm., Grc.	E4	28
Acheng, China	B7	38
Achern, Ger.	H4	16
Achill Head, c., Ire.	G2	12
Achill Island, i., Ire.	H2	12
Achiras, Arg.	F5	92
Achit nuur, l., Mong.	E16	32
Achwa, stm., Afr.	D6	66
Acı Göl, l., Tur.	F12	28
Ačinsk, Russia	C16	32
Acıpayam, Tur.	F12	28
Acireale, Italy	G9	24
Ačisaj, Kaz.	F11	32
Ackerly, Tx., U.S.	B6	130
Ackley, Ia., U.S.	B4	120
Acklins, i., Bah.	C10	96
Acklins, Bight of, b., Bah.	A10	102
Acme, Ab., Can.	E17	138
Aconcagua, Cerro, mtn., Arg.	F3	92
Aconchi, Mex.	G7	98
Acopiara, Braz.	D6	88
Açores (Azores), is., Port.	C3	60
Acorizal, Braz.	G6	84
A Coruña (Corunna), Spain	A2	20
A Coruña, co., Spain	A2	20
Acquasanta Terme, Italy	H10	22
Acqui Terme, Italy	F5	22
Acre see 'Akko, Isr.	F6	58
Acre, state, Braz.	E4	84
Acre, stm., S.A.	F4	84
Acri, Italy	E10	24
Acton Vale, Qc., Can.	E4	110
Actopan, Mex.	E9	100
Açucena, Braz.	J4	88
Acuña, Arg.	D8	92
Ada, Mn., U.S.	D2	118
Ada, Oh., U.S.	D2	114
Ada, Ok., U.S.	C2	122
Ādaba, Eth.	F7	62
Adair, Ia., U.S.	C3	120
Adair, Bahía de, b., Mex.	F6	98
Adair, Cape, c., Nu., Can.	A16	106
Adairsville, Ga., U.S.	C14	122
Adairville, Ky., U.S.	H11	120
Adaja, stm., Spain	C6	20
Adak Island, i., Ak., U.S.	g23	140a
Adam, Oman	E8	56
Adamantina, Braz.	D6	90
Adamaoua, mts., Afr.	C2	66
Adamclisi, Rom.	E14	26
Adamello, mts., Italy	D7	22
Adaminaby, Austl.	K7	76
Adams, Mn., U.S.	H6	118
Adams, Ne., U.S.	K2	118
Adams, N.Y., U.S.	E13	112
Adams, N.D., U.S.	F15	124
Adams, stm., B.C., Can.	E11	138
Adams, Mount, vol., Wa., U.S.	D5	136
Adam's Bridge, rf., Asia	G4	53
Adams Lake, l., B.C., Can.	E11	138
Adams Peak, mtn., Sri L.	H5	53
Adams Rock, r., Pit.	c28	78k
Adamstown, Pit.	c28	78k
Adamsville, Tn., U.S.	B10	122
'Adan (Aden), Yemen	G6	56
Adana, Tur.	A6	58
Adana, state, Tur.	A6	58
Adanero, Spain	D6	20
Adarama, Sudan	D6	62
Adare, Cape, c., Ant.	C22	81
Adavale, Austl.	E5	76
Adda, stm., Italy	E6	22
Ad-Dabbah, Sudan	D6	62
Ad-Dahnā', des., Sau. Ar.	D6	56
Ad-Dāmir, Sudan	D6	62
Ad-Dammām, Sau. Ar.	D7	56
Ad-Dānā, Syria	B7	58
Ad-Dawḥah (Doha), Qatar	D7	56
Ad-Dibdibah, reg., Sau. Ar.	D6	56
Addis, La., U.S.	G7	122
Addis Ababa see Ādīs Ābeba, Eth.	F7	62
Addis Abeba see Ādīs Ābeba, Eth.	F7	62
Addison, Mi., U.S.	F5	112
Ad-Dīwānīyah, Iraq	C6	56
Addo Elephant National Park, p.o.i., S. Afr.	H7	70
Addu Atoll, at., Mald.	j12	46a
Ad-Du'ayn, Sudan	E5	62
Ad-Duwayd, Sau. Ar.	C5	56
Ad-Duwaym, Sudan	E6	62
Adel, Ga., U.S.	E2	116
Adelaide, Austl.	J2	76
Adelaide, Bah.	n18	104f
Adelaide Island, i., Ant.	B33	81
Adelaide Peninsula, pen., Nu., Can.	B11	106
Adelaide River, Austl.	B6	74
Adèle Island, i., Austl.	C4	74
Adélie, Terre, cst., Ant.	B18	81
Adelie Coast see Adélie, Terre, cst., Ant.	B18	81
Adelong, Austl.	J6	76
Aden see 'Adan, Yemen	G6	56
Aden, Gulf of, b.	E9	62
Adendorp, S. Afr.	H7	70
Adi, Pulau, i., Indon.	F9	44
Adiaké, C. Iv.	H4	64
Adige (Etsch), stm., Italy	E8	22
Ādīgrat, Eth.	E7	62
Adıgüzel Barajı, res., Tur.	E12	28
Ādilābād, India	B4	53
Adimi, Russia	G16	34
Adin, Ca., U.S.	B5	134
Adirondack Mountains, mts., N.Y., U.S.	E15	112
Ādīs Ābeba (Addis Abeba), Eth.	F7	62
Adi Ugri, Erit.	E7	62
Adıyaman, Tur.	A9	58
Adıyaman, state, Tur.	A9	58
Adjuntas, Presa de las see Vicente Guerrero, Presa, res., Mex.	D9	100
Admiral, Sk., Can.	E5	124
Admiralty Gulf, b., Austl.	B5	74
Admiralty Inlet, b., Nu., Can.	A13	106
Admiralty Island, i., Nu., Can.	B10	106
Admiralty Island, i., Ak., U.S.	E13	140
Admiralty Islands, is., Pap. N. Gui.	a4	79a
Admiralty Mountains, mts., Ant.	C21	81
Ado, Nig.	H5	64
Ado-Ekiti, Nig.	H6	64
Adolfo Gonzales Chaves, Arg.	H7	92
Adolfo López Mateos, Mex.	A5	100
Adolfo López Mateos, Presa, res., Mex.	C5	100
Adolfo Rodriguez Sáa see Santa Rosa del Conlara, Arg.	F5	92
Ādoni, India	D3	53
Adour, stm., Fr.	F4	18
Ādra, India	G11	54
Adra, Spain	H7	20
Adrano, Italy	G8	24
Adrar, Alg.	D4	64
Adrâr, reg., Maur.	E2	64
Adria, Italy	E9	22
Adrian, Mi., U.S.	C1	114
Adrian, Mo., U.S.	F3	120
Adrian, Or., U.S.	G9	136
Adrian, Tx., U.S.	F6	128
Adrian, W.V., U.S.	F5	114
Adriatic Sea, Eur.	G11	22
A Dun, stm., Viet.	F9	48
Adutiškis, Lith.	E9	10
Advance, Mo., U.S.	G7	120
Advocate Harbour, N.S., Can.	E11	110
Ādwa, Eth.	E7	62
Adyča, stm., Russia	C16	34
Adygea see Adygeja, state, Russia	F6	32
Adygeja, state, Russia	F6	32
Adygheya see Adygeja, state, Russia	F6	32
Adzopé, C. Iv.	H4	64
Aegean Sea	E7	28
Aegina see Aígina, i., Grc.	F6	28
Aegviidu, Est.	A8	10
Aën, ostrov, i., Russia	B22	34
Aerku Hu, l., China	C9	54
Ærø, i., Den.	I4	8
Ærøskøbing, Den.	B6	16
A Estrada, Spain	B2	20
Aetna, Ab., Can.	G17	138
Afaahiti, Fr. Poly.	v22	78h
Afadjoto, mtn., Ghana	H5	64
Afareaitu, Fr. Poly.	v20	78h
Afars and Issas see Djibouti, ctry., Afr.	E8	62
Affton, Mo., U.S.	F7	120
Afghanistan, ctry., Asia	C9	56
Afgooye, Som.	D8	66
Afikpo, Nig.	H6	64
Aflou, Alg.	C5	64
Afmadow, Som.	D8	66
Afogados da Ingazeira, Braz.	D7	88
Afognak Island, i., Ak., U.S.	E9	140
Afoniha, Russia	B25	8
A Fonsagrada, Spain	A3	20
Africa, cont.	F14	4
'Afrīn, Syria	B7	58
Afton, N.Y., U.S.	B10	114
Afton, Ok., U.S.	H2	120
Afton, Wy., U.S.	H16	136
'Afula, Isr.	F6	58
Afyon, Tur.	E13	28
Afyon, state, Tur.	E13	28
Agadez, Niger	F6	64
Agadir, Mor.	C2	64
Agâdîr, Râs, c., Maur.	E1	64
Agadyr', Kaz.	E12	32
Agalak, Sudan	E6	62
Agalega Islands, is., Mrts.	K8	142
Agan, stm., Russia	B13	32
Agana, Guam	j10	78c
Agana Heights, Guam	j10	78c
Agano, stm., Japan	B12	40
Agapa, Russia	B6	34
Aga Point, c., Guam	k10	78c
Agar, India	G5	54
Agartala, India	G13	54
Agassiz, B.C., Can.	G9	138
Agassiz Pool, res., Mn., U.S.	C3	118
Agate, Co., U.S.	B5	128
Agate Fossil Beds National Monument, p.o.i., Ne., U.S.	E9	126
Agattu Island, i., Ak., U.S.	g21	140a
Agawa Bay, b., On., Can.	A5	112
Agawam, Mt., U.S.	B14	136
Agboville, C. Iv.	H4	64
Ağdam, Azer.	B6	56
Ageevo, Russia	F19	10
Agen, Fr.	E6	18
Agency, Ia., U.S.	D5	120
Agency Lake, l., Or., U.S.	H5	136
Aggeneys, S. Afr.	F4	70
Aggteleki Nemzeti Park, p.o.i., Hung.	A7	26
Āghā Jārī, Iran	C6	56
Agía Marína, Grc.	F9	28
Agiásos, Grc.	D9	28
Aginskoe, Russia	F11	34
Ágio Óros, state, Grc.	C7	28
Ágio Óros, pen., Grc.	C7	28
Ágios Nikólaos, Grc.	H8	28
Ağlasun, Tur.	F13	28
Agnes Lake, l., On., Can.	C7	118
Agnew, Austl.	E4	74
Agnibilékrou, C. Iv.	H4	64
Agno, Phil.	B2	52
Agno, stm., Phil.	C3	52
Ago, Japan	E9	40
Agogna, stm., Italy	E5	22
Agou, Mont, mtn., Togo	H5	64
Agout, stm., Fr.	F8	18
Āgra, India	E6	54
Agraciada, Ur.	F8	92
Agreda, Spain	C8	20
Ağrı, Tur.	B5	56
Agri, stm., Italy	D9	24
Ağrı Dağı (Ararat, Mount), mtn., Tur.	B5	56
Agrigento, Italy	G7	24
Agrihan, i., N. Mar. Is.	B5	72
Agrínio, Grc.	E4	28
Agrio, stm., Arg.	H2	92
Agrópoli, Italy	D9	24
Agro Pontino, reg., Italy	C6	24
Agto, Grnld.	D15	141
Água Branca, Braz.	C4	88
Agua Caliente, Mex.	B4	100
Agua Caliente Grande, Mex.	B4	100
Aguachica, Col.	C5	86
Água Clara, Braz.	D6	90
Aguada Cecilio, Arg.	H3	90
Aguada de Guerra, Arg.	H3	90
Aguada de Pasajeros, Cuba	A7	102
Aguadas, Col.	E4	86
Aguadilla, P.R.	B1	104a
Água Doce, Braz.	C12	92
Aguadulce, Pan.	H7	102
Agua Dulce, Tx., U.S.	G9	130
Agua Fria, stm., Az., U.S.	I4	132
Aguaí, Braz.	L2	88
Agualeguas, Mex.	H8	130
Aguán, stm., Hond.	E4	102
Aguanaval, stm., Mex.	C7	100
Aguapey, stm., Arg.	D9	92
Água Preta, Igarapé, stm., Braz.	H9	86
Agua Prieta, Mex.	F8	98
Aguaray Guazú, stm., Para.	A9	92
A Guardia, Spain	C1	20
Aguarico, stm., S.A.	H3	86
Aguaro-Guariquito, Parque Nacional, p.o.i., Ven.	C8	86
Aguaruto, Mex.	C5	100
Aguasabon, stm., On., Can.	C11	118
Águas Belas, Braz.	E7	88
Aguas Buenas, P.R.	B3	104a
Aguascalientes, Mex.	E7	100
Aguascalientes, state, Mex.	D7	100
Águas Formosas, Braz.	I5	88
Água Vermelha, Represa de, res., Braz.	C6	90
Aguayo, Arg.	E4	92
Agu Bay, b., Nu., Can.	A13	106
Agudos, Braz.	L1	88
Águeda, stm., Eur.	D4	20
Aguelhok, Mali	F5	64
Aguilar, Co., U.S.	D4	128
Aguilar de la Frontera, Spain	G6	20
Aguilares, Arg.	C5	92
Águilas, Spain	G9	20
Aguililla, Mex.	F7	100
Agujereada, Punta, c., P.R.	A1	104a
Agujita, Mex.	G6	130
Agulhas, Kaap, c., S. Afr.	I5	70
Agulhas Basin, unds.	M15	144
Agulhas Negras, Pico das, mtn., Braz.	L3	88
Agung, Gunung, vol., Indon.	G6	44
Agusan, stm., Phil.	F5	52
Agustín Codazzi, Col.	C5	86
Ağva, Tur.	B12	28
Ahaggar, mts., Alg.	E6	64
Ahaggar, Tassili ta-n-, plat., Alg.	E5	64
Ahalcihe, Geor.	F6	32
Ahar, Iran	B6	56
Ahaus, Ger.	D3	16
Ahipara Bay, b., N.Z.	B5	80
Ahlen, Ger.	E3	16
Ahmadābād, India	G4	54
Ahmadnagar, India	B2	53
Ahmadpur East, Pak.	D3	54
Ahmadpur Siāl, Pak.	C3	54
Ahmar Mountains, mts., Eth.	F8	62
Ahmetli, Tur.	E10	28
Ahmic Lake, l., On., Can.	C10	112
Ahoskie, N.C., U.S.	H9	114
Ahousat, B.C., Can.	G4	138
Ahraura, India	F9	54
Ahtuba, stm., Russia	E7	32
Ahtubinsk, Russia	E7	32
Ahuacatlán, Mex.	E6	100
Ahumada, Mex.	D1	130
Ahunui, at., Fr. Poly.	E12	72
Ahvāz, Iran	C6	56
Ahvenanmaa (Åland), state, Fin.	F9	8
Ahvenanmaa (Aland Islands), is., Fin.	F8	8
Aḥwar, Yemen	G6	56
Ahwa-ri, Kor., S.	D2	40
Å i Åfjord, Nor.	D4	8
Aibonito, P.R.	B3	104a
Aichi, state, Japan	D10	40
Aidong, China	I2	42
Aiea, Hi., U.S.	B3	78a
Aígina, Grc.	F6	28
Aígina, i., Grc.	F6	28
Aígio, Grc.	E5	28
Aigle, Switz.	D3	22
Aigle, stm., Qc., Can.	A1	110
Aiguá, Ur.	G10	92
Aigüestortes i Estany Sant Maurici, Parque Nacional d', p.o.i., Spain	B11	20
Aigüestortes i Llac de Sant Maurici, Parc Nacional d' see Aigüestortes i Esta, p.o.i., Spain	B11	20
Aikawa, Japan	A11	40
Aiken, S.C., U.S.	C4	116
Aikens Lake, l., Mb., Can.	C18	124
Ailao Shan, mts., China	G5	36
Aileron, Austl.	D6	74
Ailinglaplap, at., Marsh. Is.	C7	72
Ailsa Craig, On., Can.	E8	112
Ailsa Craig, i., Scot., U.K.	F7	12
Aim, Russia	E15	34
Aimorés, Braz.	J5	88
Ain, state, Fr.	D11	18
Ain, stm., Fr.	D11	18
Aïn Benian, Alg.	H13	20
Aïn Bessem, Alg.	H14	20
Aïn Defla, Alg.	H12	20
Aïn Draham, Tun.	H2	24
Aïn el Beïda, Alg.	B6	64
Ainslie Lake, l., N.S., Can.	D15	110
Aioi, Japan	E7	40
Aiora, Spain	E9	20
Aipe, Col.	F4	86
Aïr, Massif de l', mts., Niger	F6	64
Airai Airport, Palau	g8	78b
Airbangis, Indon.	C1	50
Airdrie, Ab., Can.	E16	138
Aire, stm., Fr.	F14	14
Aire, stm., Eng., U.K.	H11	12
Aire-sur-l'Adour, Fr.	F5	18
Air Force Island, i., Nu., Can.	B16	106
Airhaji, Indon.	D2	50
Airlie Beach, Austl.	C7	76
Airolo, Switz.	D5	22
Airuoca, Braz.	L3	88
Aishihik, Yk., Can.	C3	106
Aishihik Lake, l., Yk., Can.	C3	106
Aisne, state, Fr.	E12	14
Aisne, stm., Fr.	E12	14
Aïssa, Djebel, mtn., Alg.	C4	64
Aitape, Pap. N. Gui.	a3	79a
Aitkin, Mn., U.S.	E5	118
Aitolikó, Grc.	E4	28
Aitutaki, at., Cook Is.	E11	72
Aiuaba, Braz.	D5	88
Aiud, Rom.	C10	26
Aix, Île d', i., Fr.	C4	18
Aix, Mount, mtn., Wa., U.S.	D5	136
Aix-en-Provence, Fr.	F11	18
Aix-la-Chapelle see Aachen, Ger.	F1	16
Aix-les-Bains, Fr.	D11	18
Āīzawl, India	G14	54
Aizkraukle, Lat.	D8	10
Aizu-bange, Japan	B12	40
Aizu-wakamatsu, Japan	B12	40
Ajaccio, Fr.	H14	18
Ajaccio, Golfe d', b., Fr.	H14	18
Ajaguz, Kaz.	E13	32
Ajaguz, stm., Kaz.	E13	32
Ajajú, stm., Col.	G5	86
Ajan, Russia	E16	34
Ajan, stm., Russia	C7	34
Ajanta, India	H5	54
Ajanta Caves, hist., India	H5	54
Ajanta Range, mts., India	H5	54
Ajarani, stm., Braz.	F11	86
Ajax, On., Can.	E10	112
Ajdābiyā, Libya	A4	62
Ajdyrlinskij, Russia	D9	32
Ajjer, Tassili-n-, plat., Alg.	D6	64
Ajka, Hung.	B4	26
'Ajlūn, Jord.	F6	58
Ajmer, India	E5	54
Ajnāla, India	C5	54
Ajo, Az., U.S.	K4	132
Ajtos, Blg.	G14	26
Ajusco, Mex.	L9	134
Akabira, Japan	C15	38
Akabli, Alg.	D5	64
Akademii, zaliv, b., Russia	F16	34
Akagi-san, vol., Japan	C12	40
Akaishi-sammyaku, mts., Japan	D11	40
Āk'ak'ī Besek'a, Eth.	F7	62
Akalkot, India	C2	53
Akámas, Akrotírion, c., Cyp.	C3	58
Akan-kokuritsu-kōen, p.o.i., Japan	C16	38
'Akasha East, Sudan	C6	62
'Akāshāt, Iraq	C5	56
Akashi, Japan	E7	40
Akbarpur, India	E9	54
Akbulak, Russia	D9	32
Akçakale, Tur.	B9	58
Akçakoca, Tur.	B14	28
Akçakoyunlu, Tur.	B8	58
Akçaova, Tur.	F11	28
Akçay, Tur.	G12	28
Akçay, stm., Tur.	F11	28
Akchâr, reg., Maur.	E2	64
Akdoğan, N. Cyp.	C4	58
Ak-Dovurak, Russia	D15	32
Akeley, Mn., U.S.	D4	118
Aken, Ger.	E8	16
Akershus, state, Nor.	F4	8
Aketi, D.R.C.	D4	66
Akhaltsikhe see Ahalcihe, Geor.	F6	32
Akhḍar, Al-Jabal al-, mts., Libya	A4	62
Akhḍar, Al-Jabal al-, mts., Oman	E8	56
Akhḍar, Wādī al-, stm., Sau. Ar.	J7	58
Akhisar, Tur.	E10	28
Akhtarīn, Syria	B8	58
Akhtubinsk see Ahtubinsk, Russia	E7	32
Aki, Japan	F6	40
Akimiski Island, i., Nu., Can.	E14	106
Akıncı Burun, c., Tur.	B6	58
Akita, Japan	E13	38
Akjoujt, Maur.	F2	64
Akkeshi, Japan	C16	38
'Akko, Isr.	F6	58
Akkol', Kaz.	E13	32
Akkol', Kaz.	F12	32
Akköy, Tur.	F10	28
Aklavik, N.T., Can.	B4	106
'Aklé 'Aouâna, reg., Afr.	F3	64
Akmenrags, c., Lat.	D3	10
Akmola see Astana, Kaz.	D12	32
Akō, Japan	E7	40
Ākobo (Akūbū), stm., Afr.	F6	62
Akola, India	H6	54
Akonolinga, Cam.	D2	66
Akordat, Erit.	D7	62
Akören, Tur.	F15	28
Akot, India	H6	54
Akpatok Island, i., Nu., Can.	C17	106
Akpınar, Tur.	A9	58
Akrítas, Ákra, c., Grc.	G4	28
Akrokórinthos, hist., Grc.	F5	28
Akron, Co., U.S.	A5	128
Akron, In., U.S.	G4	112
Akron, N.Y., U.S.	E11	112
Akron, Oh., U.S.	C4	114
Akron, Pa., U.S.	H13	112
Akrotíri, Cyp.	D3	58
Akša, Russia	F11	34
Aksaj, Kaz.	D8	32
Aksaray, Tur.	B3	56
Aksayqin Hu, l., China	A7	54
Akşehir, Tur.	E14	28
Akşehir Gölü, l., Tur.	E14	28
Akseki, Tur.	F14	28
Aksu, China	F14	32
Aksu, Kaz.	D12	32
Aksu, stm., Kaz.	E13	32
Aksu, stm., Tur.	F13	28
Aksu, stm., Tur.	A8	58
Aksuat, Kaz.	E14	32
Aksuat, Kaz.	E14	32
Āksum, Eth.	E7	62
Aktau, Kaz.	F8	32
Aktau, Kaz.	D12	32
Aktjubinsk, Kaz.	D9	32
Akto, China	B12	56
Akūbū, Sudan	F6	62
Akūbū (Ākobo), stm., Afr.	F6	62
Akuliči Pervye, Russia	G16	10
Akune, Japan	G3	40
Akure, Nig.	H5	64
Akureyri, Ice.	k30	8a
Akutan Island, i., Ak., U.S.	F6	140
Akwanga, Nig.	H6	64
Akyazı, Tur.	C13	28
Ål, Nor.	F3	8
Alabama, state, U.S.	E12	122
Alabama, stm., Al., U.S.	F11	122
Alabaster, Al., U.S.	D12	122
Alacant (Alicante), Spain	F10	20
Alacant, co., Spain	F10	20
Alaçatı, Tur.	E9	28
Alachua, Fl., U.S.	G3	116
Alacrán, Arrecife, rf., Mex.	C7	96
Alacranes, Presa, res., Cuba	A7	102
Aladağ, mtn., Tur.	A6	58
Alagoa Grande, Braz.	D8	88
Alagoas, state, Braz.	E7	88
Alagoinhas, Braz.	G6	88
Alagón, Spain	C9	20
Alagón, stm., Spain	E4	20
Alahanpanjang, Indon.	D2	50
Alaior, Spain	E15	20
Alajku, Kyrg.	F12	32
Alajskij hrebet, mts., Asia	B11	56
Alajuela, C.R.	H5	102
Alajuela, Lago, res., Pan.	H8	102
Alakanuk, Ak., U.S.	D7	140
Alakol', ozero, l., Kaz.	E14	32
Alaköl Köli see Alakol', ozero, l., Kaz.	E14	32
Al-'Akrīshah, Egypt	G1	58
Alaktara, India	H9	54
Alakurtti, Russia	C13	8
Alalakeiki Channel, strt., Hi., U.S.	C5	78a
Alalaú, stm., Braz.	H11	86
Alamagan, i., N. Mar. Is.	B5	72
Al-'Amārah, Iraq	C6	56
Alameda, Ca., U.S.	F3	134
Alameda, N.M., U.S.	H10	132
Alamo, Ga., U.S.	D3	116
Alamo, Tn., U.S.	B9	122
Alamo, stm., Ca., U.S.	K1	132
Alamogordo, N.M., U.S.	B2	130
Alamo Heights, Tx., U.S.	E9	130
Alamo Lake, res., Az., U.S.	I3	132
Álamos, Mex.	B4	100
Álamos, stm., Mex.	A8	100
Alamosa, Co., U.S.	D3	128
Alamosa East, Co., U.S.	D3	128
Álamos de Márquez, Mex.	A7	100
Aland, India	C3	53
Åland see Ahvenanmaa, state, Fin.	F9	8
Åland see Ahvenanmaa, is., Fin.	F8	8
Aland Islands see Ahvenanmaa, is., Fin.	F8	8
Aland Sea, Eur.	G8	8
Alandur, India	E5	53
Alanya, Tur.	G15	28
Alaotra, Farihy, l., Madag.	D8	68
Alapaevsk, Russia	C10	32
Alapaha, Ga., U.S.	E2	116
Alapaha, stm., U.S.	F2	116
Alaplı, Tur.	B14	28
Alappuzha see Alleppey, India	G3	53
Al-'Aqabah, Jord.	I6	58
Alarcón, Spain	E8	20
Alarcón, Embalse de, res., Spain	E9	20
Alas, stm., Indon.	K3	48
Alas, Selat, strt., Indon.	H10	50
Alaşehir, Tur.	E11	28
Alashanyouqi, China	C5	36
Alaska, state, U.S.	D9	140
Alaska, Gulf of, b., Ak., U.S.	E10	140
Alaska Peninsula, pen., Ak., U.S.	E7	140
Alaska Range, mts., Ak., U.S.	D9	140
Alassio, Italy	F5	22
Alatan'aola see Xin Barag Youqi, China	B8	36
Alatri, Italy	I10	22
Alatyr', Russia	D7	32
Alausí, Ec.	I2	86
Alava see Arabako, co., Spain	B8	20
Alava, Cape, c., Wa., U.S.	B2	136
Al-'Ayn, U.A.E.	E8	56
Alayor see Alaior, Spain	E15	20
Alazeja, stm., Russia	B19	34
Al-'Azīzīyah, Libya	A2	62
Alba, Italy	F5	22
Alba, Mi., U.S.	D5	112
Alba, Tx., U.S.	E3	122
Alba, state, Rom.	C10	26
Al-Bāb, Syria	B8	58
Albacete, Spain	E9	20
Albacete, co., Spain	F9	20
Al-Bad', Sau. Ar.	J6	58
Alba de Tormes, Spain	D5	20
Albaida, Spain	F10	20
Alba Iulia, Rom.	C10	26
Al-Balqā', state, Jord.	F6	58
Al-Bālū'ah, l., Syria	C7	58
Albanel, Lac, l., Qc., Can.	E16	106
Albania, Col.	B5	86
Albania, ctry., Eur.	C14	24
Albano Laziale, Italy	I9	22
Albany, Ga., U.S.	E1	116
Albany, In., U.S.	H4	112
Albany, Ky., U.S.	H12	120
Albany, Mn., U.S.	F4	118
Albany, Mo., U.S.	D3	120
Albany, N.Y., U.S.	B12	114
Albany, Oh., U.S.	E3	114
Albany, Or., U.S.	F3	136
Albany, Tx., U.S.	B8	130
Albany, stm., On., Can.	E14	106
Albarracín, Spain	D9	20
Al-Baṣrah, Iraq	C6	56
Al-Batrā' (Petra), hist., Jord.	H6	58
Albatross Bay, b., Austl.	B8	74
Al-Bayḍā', Libya	A4	62
Albemarle, N.C., U.S.	A5	116
Albemarle Island see Isabela, Isla, i., Ec.	i11	84a
Albemarle Sound, strt., N.C., U.S.	H9	114
Albenga, Italy	F5	22
Alberche, stm., Spain	D6	20
Alberdi, Para.	C8	92
Alberga Creek, stm., Austl.	E6	74
Alberni Inlet, b., B.C., Can.	G6	138
Alberobello, Italy	D11	24
Albert, Fr.	E11	14
Albert, Lake, l., Afr.	D6	66
Albert, Lake, l., Austl.	J2	76
Alberta, Al., U.S.	E11	122
Alberta, state, Can.	E8	106
Alberta, Mount, mtn., Ab., Can.	D13	138
Albert Canyon, B.C., Can.	E13	138
Albert City, Ia., U.S.	I3	118
Albert Edward Bay, b., Nu., Can.	B10	106
Alberti, Arg.	G7	92
Albertirsa, Hung.	B6	26
Albertkanaal, can., Bel.	D14	14
Albert Lea, Mn., U.S.	H5	118
Albert Markham, Mount, mtn., Ant.	D21	81
Albert Nile, stm., Afr.	D6	66
Alberton, P.E., Can.	D12	110
Albertville, Fr.	D12	18
Albertville, Al., U.S.	C12	122
Albi, Fr.	F8	18
Albia, Ia., U.S.	C5	120
Albin, Wy., U.S.	F8	126
Albina, Sur.	B7	84
Albina, Ponta, c., Ang.	D1	68
Albion, Ca., U.S.	D2	134
Albion, Id., U.S.	H13	136
Albion, Il., U.S.	F9	120
Albion, In., U.S.	G4	112
Albion, Mi., U.S.	B1	114
Albion, N.Y., U.S.	E11	112
Albion, Pa., U.S.	C5	114
Albion, Wa., U.S.	D9	136
Al-Biqā', state, Leb.	D7	58
Al-Biqā' (Bekaa Valley), val., Leb.	D7	58
Al-Bi'r, Sau. Ar.	J7	58
Albocàsser, Spain	D10	20
Alboran Sea	B4	64
Ålborg, Den.	H4	8
Ålborg Bugt, b., Den.	H4	8
Alborz, Reshteh-ye Kūhhā-ye, mts., Iran	B7	56
Albuñol, Spain	H7	20
Albuquerque, N.M., U.S.	H10	132
Albuquerque, Cayos de, is., Col.	F6	102
Alburg, Vt., U.S.	E3	110
Alburquerque, Spain	E3	20
Albury, Austl.	J6	76
Alcains, Port.	E3	20
Alcalá de Guadaira, Spain	G5	20
Alcalá de Henares, Spain	D7	20
Alcalá la Real, Spain	G7	20
Alcalde, N.M., U.S.	E2	128
Alcamo, Italy	G6	24
Alcanar, Spain	D11	20
Alcañices, Spain	C4	20
Alcañiz, Spain	C10	20
Alcântara, Braz.	B3	88
Alcántara, Spain	E3	20
Alcantarilla, Spain	G9	20
Alcaraz, Spain	F8	20
Alcaudete, Spain	G6	20
Alcázar de San Juan, Spain	E7	20
Alcester, S.D., U.S.	A1	120
Alcira, Arg.	F5	92
Alcira see Alzira, Spain	E10	20
Alcobaça, Braz.	I6	88
Alcobendas, Spain	D7	20
Alcoi, Spain	F10	20
Alcolea del Pinar, Spain	C8	20
Alcolu, S.C., U.S.	C5	116

Name — Map Ref. — Page

Alcorn, Ms., U.S. F7 122
Alcorta, Arg. F7 92
Alcoutim, Port. G3 20
Alcoy see Alcoi, Spain F10 20
Alcúdia, Spain E14 20
Alcúdia, Badia d', b., Spain E14 20
Aldabra, Groupe d', is., Sey. k11 69b
Aldama, Mex. D9 100
Aldama, Mex. A5 100
Aldan, Russia E14 34
Aldan, stm., Russia D15 34
Aldan Plateau see Aldanskoe nagor'e, plat., Russia E14 34
Aldanskoe nagor'e (Aldan Plateau), plat., Russia E14 34
Aldarchaan, Mong. B4 36
Aldeia Nova de São Bento, Port. G3 20
Alden, Mn., U.S. H5 118
Alderney, i., Guern. E6 14
Aldershot, Eng., U.K. J12 12
Alderson, W.V., U.S. G5 114
Aledo, Il., U.S. C7 120
Aleg, Maur. F2 64
Alegre, Braz. K5 88
Alegrete, Braz. D10 92
Alej, stm., Russia D14 32
Alejandro Roca, Arg. F5 92
Alejandro Selkirk, Isla, i., Chile I6 82
Alejsk, Russia D14 32
Aleksandrov, Russia D21 10
Aleksandrovskij Zavod, Russia F12 34
Aleksandrovskoe, Russia B13 32
Aleksandrovsk-Sahalinskij, Russia F17 34
Aleksandrów Kujawski, Pol. D14 16
Alekseevka, Kaz. D12 32
Alekseevka, Kaz. E14 32
Alekseevka, Russia D5 32
Alekseevsk, Russia C19 32
Aleksejevka see Alekseevka, Kaz. D12 32
Alekseyevka see Alekseevka, Kaz. D12 32
Aleksin, Russia F19 10
Aleksinac, Yugo. F8 26
Alemania, Arg. B5 92
Além Paraíba, Braz. K4 88
Alençon, Fr. F9 14
Alenquer, Braz. D7 84
Alentejo, hist. reg., Port. F3 20
Alenuihaha Channel, strt., Hi., U.S. C5 78a
Aleppo see Halab, Syria B8 58
Aléria, Fr. G15 18
Alert, Nu., Can. A13 141
Alert Bay, B.C., Can. F4 138
Alert Point, c., Nu., Can. A8 141
Alès, Fr. E10 18
Alëšnja, Russia G16 10
Alessándria, Italy F5 22
Ålesund, Nor. E1 8
Aleutian Basin, unds. D20 142
Aleutian Islands, is., Ak., U.S. g22 140a
Aleutian Range, mts., Ak., U.S. E8 140
Aleutian Trench, unds. E21 142
Aleutka, Russia G19 34
Alevina, mys, c., Russia E19 34
Alex, Ok., U.S. G11 128
Alexander, Mb., Can. E13 124
Alexander, N.D., U.S. G10 124
Alexander, Kap, c., Grnld. B11 141
Alexander Archipelago, is., Ak., U.S. E12 140
Alexander Bay, S. Afr. F3 70
Alexander City, Al., U.S. E12 122
Alexander Island, i., Ant. B33 81
Alexandra, N.Z. G3 80
Alexandra, stm., Austl. B3 76
Alexandra Falls, wtfl, N.T., Can. C7 106
Alexandretta see İskenderun, Tur. B6 58
Alexandretta, Gulf of see İskenderun Körfezi, b., Tur. B6 58
Alexandria, Braz. D6 88
Alexandria, B.C., Can. D8 138
Alexandria, On., Can. E2 110
Alexandria see El-Iskandarîya, Egypt A6 62
Alexandria, Rom. F12 26
Alexandria, La., U.S. F6 122
Alexandria, Mn., U.S. F3 118
Alexandria, Mo., U.S. D6 120
Alexandria, S.D., U.S. D15 126
Alexandria, Tn., U.S. H11 120
Alexandria, Va., U.S. F8 114
Alexandria Bay, N.Y., U.S. D14 112
Alexandrina, Lake, l., Austl. J2 76
Alexandroúpoli, Grc. C8 28
Alexis, Il., U.S. C7 120
Alfambra, Spain D9 20
Alfaro, Spain B9 20
Alfarràs, Spain C11 20
Alfarrás see Alfarràs, Spain C11 20
Al-Fāshir, Sudan E5 62
Alfeiós, stm., Grc. F4 28
Alfeld, Ger. D5 16
Alfenas, Braz. K3 88
Alföld, pl., Hung. C7 26
Alfonsine, Italy F9 22
Alfred, On., Can. E2 110
Alfred, Me., U.S. G6 110
Alfred, N.Y., U.S. B8 114
Al-Fujayrah, U.A.E. D8 56
Al-Fuqahā', Libya B3 62
Al-Furāt see Euphrates, stm., Asia C6 56
Alga, Kaz. E9 32
Ålgård, Nor. G1 8
Algarrobal, Chile D2 92
Algarrobo, Chile F2 92
Algarrobo del Águila, Arg. H4 92
Algarve, hist. reg., Port. G2 20
Algeciras, Col. F4 86
Algeciras, Spain H5 20
Algemesí, Spain E10 20
Algeria, ctry., Afr. D5 64
Algérie see Algeria, ctry., Afr. D5 64
Al-Ghāb, sw., Syria C7 58
Al-Ghaydah, Yemen F7 56
Al-Ghāzīyah, Leb. E6 58
Alghero, Italy D2 24
Algiers see El Djazaïr, Alg. B5 64
Alginet, Spain E10 20
Algoabaai, b., S. Afr. H7 70
Algoa Bay see Algoabaai, b., S. Afr. H7 70
Algodón, stm., Peru I5 86
Algodones, N.M., U.S. F2 128
Algoma Mills, On., Can. B7 112
Algona, Ia., U.S. A3 120
Algonac, Mi., U.S. B3 114
Algonquin, Il., U.S. B9 120
Algorta, Spain A7 20
Algorta, Ur. F9 92
Al-Haffah, Syria C7 58
Al-Hajarah, reg., Asia C5 56
Al-Hamād, pl., Sau. Ar. C4 56
Alhama de Murcia, Spain G9 20
Alhandra, Braz. D8 88
Al-Harrah, lav., Sau. Ar. C4 56
Al-Harūj al-Aswad, hills, Libya B3 62
Al-Hasakah, Syria B5 56
Alhaurín el Grande, Spain H6 20
Al-Hawātah, Sudan E7 62
Al-Hawrah, Yemen G6 56
Al-Hijāz (Hejaz), reg., Sau. Ar. D4 56
Al-Hillah, Iraq C5 56
Al-Hirmil, Leb. D7 58
Al-Hoceima, Mor. B4 64
Al-Hudaydah (Hodeida), Yemen G5 56
Al-Hufrah, reg., Sau. Ar. J9 58
Al-Hufūf, Sau. Ar. D6 56
Al Hūj, hills, Sau. Ar. J9 58
Al-Hulwah, Sau. Ar. E6 56
Alía, Spain E5 20
Aliağa, Tur. E9 28
Aliákmonas, stm., Grc. C4 28
Aliança, Braz. D8 88
Alībāg, India B1 53
Alibates Flint Quarries National Monument, p.o.i., Tx., U.S. F7 128
Äli Bayramlı, Azer. B6 56
Alibei, ozero, l., Ukr. D17 26
Alibey Adası, i., Tur. D9 28
Alibunar, Yugo. D7 26
Alicante see Alacant, Spain F10 20
Alicante see Alacant, co., Spain F10 20
Alice, S. Afr. H8 70
Alice, Tx., U.S. G9 130
Alice, stm., Austl. D5 76
Alice, Punta, c., Italy E11 24
Alice Springs, Austl. D6 74
Alice Town, Bah. K6 116
Aliceville, Al., U.S. D10 122
Alick Creek, stm., Austl. C4 76
Alīgarh, India E6 54
Alignements de Carnac, hist., Fr. G5 14
Alīgūdarz, Iran C6 56
'Alī Kheyl, Afg. B2 54
Al-Ikhşāş al-Qiblīyah, Egypt I2 58
Alima, stm., Congo E3 66
Alim Island, i., Pap. N. Gui. a4 79a
Alindao, C.A.R. C4 66
Alingsås, Swe. G5 8
Alīpur, Pak. D3 54
Ālīpur Duār, India E12 54
Aliquippa, Pa., U.S. D5 114
Alīrājpur, India G5 54
Aliseda, Spain E4 20
Alitak, Cape, c., Ak., U.S. E9 140
Alivéri, Grc. E7 28
Aliwal North, S. Afr. G8 70
Alix, Ab., Can. D17 138
Al-Jabalayn, Sudan E6 62
Al-Jafr, Jord. H7 58
Al-Jaghbūb, Libya B4 62
Al-Jahrah, Kuw. D6 56
Al-Jawārah, Oman F8 56
Al-Jawf, Libya C4 62
Al-Jawf, Sau. Ar. D4 56
Al-Jazaïr see El Djazaïr, Alg. B5 64
Al-Jazīrah, reg., Sudan E6 62
Al-Jifārah (Jeffara), pl., Afr. C7 64
Al-Jubayl, Sau. Ar. D6 56
Al-Junaynah, Sudan E4 62
Aljustrel, Port. G2 20
Al-Kafr, Syria F7 58
Al-Karak, Jord. G6 58
Al-Karak, state, Jord. G6 58
Al-Khalīl (Hebron), W.B. G5 58
Al-Khāliş, Iraq C5 56
Al-Khandaq, Sudan D6 62
Al-Kharṭām Baḥrī, Sudan D6 62
Al-Kharṭūm (Khartoum), Sudan D6 62
Al-Khaşab, Oman D8 56
Al-Khums, Libya A2 62
Alkmaar, Neth. B13 14
Al-Kufrah, Libya C4 62
Al-Kūt, Iraq C6 56
Al-Kuwayt (Kuwait), Kuw. D6 56
Al-Labwah, Leb. D7 58
Al-Lādhiqīyah (Latakia), Syria C6 58
Al-Lādhiqīyah, state, Syria C6 58
Allagash, stm., Me., U.S. D7 110
Allahābād, India F8 54
Allah-Jun', Russia D16 34
Allakaket, Ak., U.S. C9 140
Allan, Sk., Can. C7 124
Allanmyo, Mya. C2 48
Allanridge, S. Afr. E8 70
Allatoona Lake, res., Ga., U.S. C14 122
Alldays, S. Afr. C9 70
Allegan, Mi., U.S. F4 112
Allegany, N.Y., U.S. B7 114
Allegheny, stm., U.S. D6 114
Allegheny Mountains, mts., U.S. E6 114
Allegheny Plateau, plat., U.S. D5 114
Allegheny Reservoir, res., U.S. C7 114
Allemands, Lac des, l., La., U.S. H8 122
Allen, Ne., U.S. I2 118
Allen, Ok., U.S. C2 122
Allen, Tx., U.S. D2 122
Allen, Lough, l., Ire. G4 12
Allendale, Il., U.S. F10 120
Allendale, S.C., U.S. C4 116
Allende, Mex. A8 100
Allenstein see Olsztyn, Pol. C16 16
Allentown, Pa., U.S. D10 114
Alleppey, India G3 53
Aller, stm., Ger. D5 16
Allevard, Fr. D12 18
Allgäu see Kempten, Ger. I6 16
Allgäu, reg., Ger. I6 16
Alliance, Ab., Can. D19 138
Alliance, Ne., U.S. E10 126
Alliance, Oh., U.S. D4 114
Al-Lidām, Sau. Ar. E5 56
Allier, state, Fr. C9 18
Allier, stm., Fr. C9 18
Alligator Pond, Jam. j13 104d
Allinagaram, India F3 53
Allison, Ia., U.S. B5 120
Al-Līth, Sau. Ar. E5 56
Alloa, Scot., U.K. E9 12
Allos, Fr. E12 18
Allouez, Wi., U.S. G11 118
Allred Peak, mtn., Co., U.S. C8 132
All Saints, Antig. f4 105b
Al-Luhayyah, Yemen F5 56
Allumette Lake, l., Can. C12 112
Allumettes, Île aux, i., Qc., Can. C12 112
Alma, N.B., Can. E12 110
Alma, Qc., Can. B5 110
Alma, Ar., U.S. B4 122
Alma, Ga., U.S. E3 116
Alma, Ks., U.S. E1 120
Alma, Mi., U.S. E5 112
Alma, Wi., U.S. G7 118
Almada, Port. F1 20
Almaden, Austl. A5 76
Almadén, Spain F6 20
Al-Madīnah (Medina), Sau. Ar. E4 56
Al-Mafraq, Jord. F7 58
Al-Mafraq, state, Jord. F8 58
Almafuerte, Arg. F5 92
Almagro, Spain F7 20
Alma Hill, hill, N.Y., U.S. B8 114
Al Māliḥah, Sudan D5 62
Almalyk, Uzb. F11 32
Al-Manāmah (Manama), Bahr. D7 56
Almanor, Lake, res., Ca., U.S. C4 134
Almansa, Spain F9 20
Almanza, Spain B5 20
Almanzor, mtn., Spain D5 20
Al-Marj, Libya A4 62
Almas, Braz. F2 88
Almas, Pico das, mtn., Braz. G4 88
Al-Mashrafah, Syria D7 58
Almaty, Kaz. F13 32
Al-Mawşil, Iraq B5 56
Almeida, Port. D3 20
Almejas, Bahía, b., Mex. C3 100
Almelo, Neth. B15 14
Almena, Ks., U.S. B9 128
Almenara, Braz. I5 88
Almendra, Embalse de, res., Spain C4 20
Almendralejo, Spain F4 20
Almería, Spain H8 20
Almería, co., Spain G8 20
Almería, Golfo de, b., Spain H8 20
Al'metevsk, Russia D8 32
Al-Mijlad, Sudan E5 62
Al-Mīnā', Leb. D6 58
Almira, Wa., U.S. C7 136
Almirante, Pan. H6 102
Almirante Latorre, Chile D2 92
Almirós, Grc. D5 28
Almo, Id., U.S. A3 132
Almodóvar del Campo, Spain F6 20
Almont, Mi., U.S. B2 114
Almonte, On., Can. C13 112
Almonte, Spain G4 20
Almonte, stm., Spain E4 20
Almora, India D7 54
Al-Mubarraz, Sau. Ar. E6 56
Al-Mubarraz, Sau. Ar. D6 56
Al-Mudawwarah, Jord. I6 58
Almudévar, Spain B10 20
Al-Muharraq, Bahr. D7 56
Al-Mukallā, Yemen G6 56
Al-Mukhā, Yemen G5 56
Almuñécar, Spain H7 20
Al-Muwaylih, Sau. Ar. K6 58
Almyroú, Órmos, b., Grc. H7 28
Alnwick, Eng., U.K. F11 12
Alofi, Île, i., Wal./F. E9 72
Alónnisos, Grc. D6 28
Alónnisos, i., Grc. D6 28
Alor, Pulau, i., Indon. G7 44
Alor, Selat, strt., Indon. G7 44
Alor Setar, Malay. I5 48
Alosno, Spain G3 20
Alost see Aalst, Bel. D13 14
Alotau, Pap. N. Gui. c5 79a
Aloysius, Mount, mtn., Austl. E5 74
Alpachiri, Arg. H5 92
Alpaugh, Ca., U.S. H6 134
Alpena, Mi., U.S. C6 112
Alpena, S.D., U.S. C14 126
Alpercatas, stm., Braz. D3 88
Alpes-de-Haute-Provence, state, Fr. E12 18
Alpes-Maritimes, state, Fr. F13 18
Alpha, Austl. D6 76
Alpha, Il., U.S. C7 120
Alpha, Mi., U.S. B1 112
Alpharetta, Ga., U.S. B1 116
Alphonse, i., Sey. k12 69b
Alpine, Ca., U.S. K9 134
Alpine, Tx., U.S. D4 130
Alpine National Park, p.o.i., Austl. K6 76
Alpinópolis, Braz. K2 88
Alps, mts., Eur. D6 22
Al-Qaḍārif, Sudan E7 62
Al-Qaḍīmah, Sau. Ar. E4 56
Al-Qāmishlī, Syria B5 56
Al-Qaryah ash-Sharqīyah, Libya A2 62
Al-Qaryatayn, Syria D8 58
Al-Qaṭīf, Sau. Ar. D6 56
Al-Qaṭrānah, Jord. G7 58
Al-Qaṭrūn, Libya C2 62
Al-Qayṣūmah, Sau. Ar. D6 56
Al-Qunayṭirah, Syria E6 58
Al-Qunayṭirah, state, Syria E6 58
Al-Qunfudhah, Sau. Ar. F5 56
Al-Quṭayfah, Syria E7 58
Al-Quṭaynah, Sudan E6 62
Als, i., Den. I3 8
Alsace, hist. reg., Fr. F16 14
Al'šany, Bela. H10 10
Alsask, Sk., Can. C4 124
Alsasua, Spain B8 20
Alsea, Or., U.S. F3 136
Alsek, stm., N.A. D3 106
Alsen, N.D., U.S. F15 124
Alsfeld, Ger. F5 16
Alta, Nor. B10 8
Altaelva, stm., Nor. B10 8
Alta Gracia, Arg. E5 92
Altagracia, Ven. B6 86
Altagracia de Orituco, Ven. C8 86
Altai, mts., Asia E15 32
Altaj, state, Russia D15 32
Altajskij, Russia D14 32
Altamaha, stm., Ga., U.S. E4 116
Altamira, Braz. D7 84
Altamira, Chile B3 92
Altamirano, Mex. I10 130
Altamont, Ks., U.S. G2 120
Altamont, Or., U.S. A4 134
Altamont, Tn., U.S. B13 122
Altamura, Italy D10 24
Altamura, Isla, i., Mex. C4 100
Altanbulag, Mong. A6 36
Altar, Mex. F7 98
Altar, stm., Mex. F7 98
Altar, Desierto de, des., Mex. F6 98
Altar de Los Sacrificios, hist., Guat. D2 102
Altario, Ab., Can. C3 124
Altata, Mex. C4 100
Alta Vista, Ks., U.S. C12 128
Altay, China E15 32
Altay, Mong. B4 36
Altay see Altaj, state, Russia D15 32
Altay Mountains see Altai, mts., Asia E15 32
Altdorf, Switz. D5 22
Altenburg, Ger. E8 16
Altentreptow, Ger. C9 16
Alter do Chão, Port. E3 20
Altevatnet, l., Nor. B8 8
Altha, Fl., U.S. G13 122
Altheimer, Ar., U.S. C7 122
Altınekin, Tur. E15 28
Altinho, Braz. E7 88
Altınova, Tur. D9 28
Altıntaş, Tur. D13 28
Altiplano, plat., S.A. G4 84
Altmark, reg., Ger. D7 16
Altmühl, stm., Ger. G6 16
Alto, Tx., U.S. F3 122
Alto Araguaia, Braz. G7 84
Alto Chicapa, Ang. C2 68
Alto Garças, Braz. G7 84
Alto Longá, Braz. C4 88
Altomünster, Ger. H7 16
Alton, Eng., U.K. J11 12
Alton, Il., U.S. F7 120
Alton, Ia., U.S. B1 120
Alton, Ks., U.S. B9 128
Alton, N.H., U.S. G5 110
Altona, Mb., Can. E16 124
Altoona, Al., U.S. C12 122
Altoona, Ia., U.S. C4 120
Altoona, Pa., U.S. D7 114
Altoona, Wi., U.S. G7 118
Alto Paraguai, Braz. F6 84
Alto Paraíso de Goiás, Braz. G2 88
Alto Paraná, state, Para. B10 92
Alto Parnaíba, Braz. E2 88
Alto Río Mayo, Arg. I2 90
Alto Río Senguer, Arg. I2 90
Altos, Braz. C4 88
Alto Santo, Braz. C6 88
Altötting, Ger. H8 16
Altun Shan, mts., China D2 36
Alturas, Ca., U.S. B5 134
Altus, Ar., U.S. B5 122
Altus, Ok., U.S. G9 128
Alu see Shortland Island, i., Sol. Is. d6 79b
Al-'Ubaylah, Sau. Ar. E7 56
Al-Ubayyiḍ, Sudan E6 62
Alubijid, Phil. F5 52
Al-Uḍayyah, Sudan E5 62
Alūksne, Lat. C9 10
Al-'Ulā, Sau. Ar. D4 56
Al-'Uqaylah, Libya A3 62
Al-'Uwaynāt, Libya B2 62
Alva, Ok., U.S. E10 128
Alvaiázere, Port. E2 20
Alvarado, Mex. F11 100
Alvarado, Tx., U.S. B10 130
Álvaro Obregón, Presa, res., Mex. B4 100
Alvear, Arg. D9 92
Alverca, Port. F1 20
Alvernia, Mount, hill, Bah. C10 96
Alvesta, Swe. H6 8
Alvin, Tx., U.S. H3 122
Alvinópolis, Braz. K4 88
Älvkarleby, Swe. F7 8
Alvord, Tx., U.S. H11 128
Alvord Desert, des., Or., U.S. H8 136
Al-Wajh, Sau. Ar. D4 56
Alwar, India E6 54
Alwaye, India F3 53
Alxa Zuoqi, China B1 42
Alytus, Lith. F6 10
Alzey, Ger. G4 16
Alzira, Spain E10 20
Amacuro (Amakura), stm., S.A. C11 86
Amadeus, Lake, l., Austl. D6 74
Amadjuak Lake, l., Nu., Can. B16 106
Amagasaki, Japan E8 40
Amagi, Japan F3 40
Amahai, Indon. F8 44
Amaichá del Valle, Arg. C4 92
Amaimon, Pap. N. Gui. b4 79a
Amajac, stm., Mex. E9 100
Amakura (Amacuro), stm., S.A. D11 86
Amakusa-nada, Japan G2 40
Amakusa-shotō, is., Japan G2 40
Åmål, Swe. G5 8
Amalāpuram, India C6 53
Amalfi, Col. B2 84
Amaliáda, Grc. F4 28
Amalner, India H5 54
Amambaí, Braz. D5 90
Amami Islands see Amami-Ō-shima, i., Japan k19 39a
Amami-Ō-shima, i., Japan k19 39a
Amami-shotō, is., Japan I19 39a
Amana, Ia., U.S. C6 120
Amana, stm., Ven. C10 86
Amanã, Lago, l., Braz. I9 86
Amanda, Oh., U.S. E3 114
Amantea, Italy E9 24
Amapá, Braz. C7 84
Amapá, state, Braz. C7 84
Amarante, Braz. D4 88
Amaranth, Mb., Can. D15 124
Amarapura, Mya. B3 48
Amărăştii de Jos, Rom. F11 26
Amarāvati, stm., India F3 53
Amares, Port. C2 20
Amargosa, Braz. G6 88
Amargosa, stm., U.S. H9 134
Amarillo, Tx., U.S. F7 128
Amarkantak, India G8 54
Amaro, Monte, mtn., Italy H11 22
Amasra, Tur. B15 28
Amasya, Tur. A4 56
aMatikulu, S. Afr. F10 70
Amatsu-kominato, Japan D13 40
Amawbia Awka, Nig. H6 64
Amazar, Russia F13 34
Amazon (Amazonas) (Solimões), stm., S.A. D7 84
Amazonas, state, Braz. D4 84
Amazonas, state, Col. H6 86
Amazonas, state, Ven. F8 86
Ambājogāi, India B3 53
Ambāla, India C6 54
Ambalangoda, Sri L. H4 53
Ambalavao, Madag. E8 68
Ambam, Cam. D2 66
Ambanja, Madag. C8 68
Ambarčik, Russia C21 34
Ambargasta, Salinas de, pl., Arg. D5 92
Ambato, Ec. H2 86
Ambatolampy, Madag. D8 68
Ambatondrazaka, Madag. D8 68
Ambelau, Pulau, i., Indon. F8 44
Amberg, Ger. G7 16
Amberg, Wi., U.S. C2 112
Ambergris Cay, i., Belize C4 102
Ambérieu-en-Bugey, Fr. D11 18
Ambert, Fr. D9 18
Ambidédi, Mali G2 64
Ambikāpur, India G9 54
Ambilobe, Madag. C8 68
Ambla, Est. A8 10
Amble, Eng., U.K. F11 12
Ambo, Peru F2 84
Ambodifototra, Madag. D8 68
Ambohimahasoa, Madag. E8 68
Amboise, Fr. G10 14
Ambon, Indon. F8 44
Ambon, Pulau, i., Indon. F8 44
Amboseli, Lake, l., Afr. E7 66
Amboseli National Park, p.o.i., Kenya E7 66
Ambositra, Madag. E8 68
Ambovombe, Madag. F8 68
Amboy, Il., U.S. C8 120
Amboy, Mn., U.S. H4 118
Ambridge, Pa., U.S. D5 114
Ambriz, Ang. B1 68
Ambrosia Lake, N.M., U.S. H9 132
Ambrym, state, Vanuatu k17 79d
Ambrym, i., Vanuatu k17 79d
Ambuntentimur, Indon. G8 50
Ambunti, Pap. N. Gui. a3 79a
Āmbūr, India E4 53
Amchitka Island, i., Ak., U.S. g22 140a
Amchitka Pass, strt., Ak., U.S. g22 140a
Am Dam, Chad E4 62
Amdo, China B13 54
Ameagle, W.V., U.S. G4 114
Ameca, Mex. E6 100
Ameca, stm., Mex. E6 100
Ameghino, Arg. G6 92
Ameland, i., Neth. A14 14
Amelia Court House, Va., U.S. G8 114
Amelia Island, i., Fl., U.S. F4 116
Āmer, India E5 54
American, North Fork, stm., Ca., U.S. D5 134
American, South Fork, stm., Ca., U.S. E5 134
Americana, Braz. L2 88
American Falls Reservoir, res., Id., U.S. H13 136
American Fork, Ut., U.S. C5 132
American Highland, plat., Ant. C12 81
Americanos, Barra de los, i., Mex. C10 100
American Samoa, dep., Oc. h12 79c
Americus, Ga., U.S. D1 116
Americus, Ks., U.S. F1 120
Amersfoort, Neth. B14 14
Amery, Wi., U.S. F6 118
Amery Ice Shelf, ice, Ant. B12 81
Ames, Ia., U.S. B4 120
Amesbury, Ma., U.S. B14 114
Amfilochía, Grc. E4 28
Ámfissa, Grc. E5 28
Amga, Russia D15 34
Amga, stm., Russia D15 34
Amguema, stm., Russia C24 34
Amguid, Alg. D6 64
Amgun', stm., Russia F16 34
Amherst, N.S., Can. E12 110
Amherst, Ma., U.S. B13 114
Amherst, N.Y., U.S. A7 114
Amherst, Oh., U.S. C3 114
Amherst, Tx., U.S. G6 128
Amherst, Wi., U.S. G9 118
Amherstburg, On., Can. F6 112
Amherstdale, W.V., U.S. G4 114
Amherst Island, i., On., Can. D13 112
Amherstview, On., Can. D13 112
Amiens, Austl. G8 76
Amiens, Fr. E11 14
Amīndīvi Islands, is., India F3 46
Amino, Japan D8 40
Aminuis, Nmb. C4 70
Amirantes, Les, is., Sey. k12 69b
Amisk, Ab., Can. B2 124
Amisk Lake, l., Sk., Can. E10 106
Amistad, Parque Internacional de la, p.o.i., C.R. H6 102
Amistad, Presa de la (Amistad Reservoir), res., N.A. E6 130
Amistad National Recreation Area, p.o.i., Tx., U.S. E6 130
Amistad Reservoir (Amistad, Presa de la), res., N.A. E6 130
Amite, La., U.S. G8 122
Amite, stm., La., U.S. G8 122
Amity, Ar., U.S. C5 122
Amla, India H7 54
Åmli, Nor. G3 8
'Ammān, Jord. G6 58
'Ammān, state, Jord. G7 58
Ämmänsaari, Fin. D13 8
'Ammār, Tall, hill, Syria F7 58
Ammasalik see Angmagssalik, Grnld. D18 141
Ammon, Id., U.S. G15 136
Amnat Charoen, Thai. E7 48
Amnok-kang (Yalu), stm., Asia D7 38
Amo (Torsa), stm., Asia E12 54
Amo, stm., China A5 48
Āmol, Iran B7 56
Amorgós, i., Grc. G8 28
Amory, Ms., U.S. D10 122
Amos, Qc., Can. F15 106
Åmot, Nor. G2 8
Amoy see Xiamen, China I7 42
Ampanihy, Madag. E7 68
Amparo, Braz. L2 88
Ampasimanolotra, Madag. D8 68
Amposta, Spain D11 20
Amqui, Qc., Can. B9 110
Amrāvati, India H6 54
Amreli, India H3 54
Amritsar, India C5 54
Amroha, India D7 54
Amrum, i., Ger. B4 16
Amsterdam, Neth. B13 14
Amsterdam, S. Afr. E10 70
Amsterdam, N.Y., U.S. B11 114
Amsterdam, Île, i., Afr. M10 142
Amstetten, Aus. B11 22
Am Timan, Chad E4 62
Amu Darya, stm., Asia F10 32
Amugulang see Xin Barag Zuoqi, China B8 36
Amund Ringnes Island, i., Nu., Can. B6 141
Amundsen Gulf, b., Can. B14 140
Amundsen-Scott, sci., Ant. D19 81
Amundsen Sea, Ant. P27 142
Amuntai, Indon. E9 50
Amur (Heilong), stm., Asia F16 34
Amursk, Russia F16 34
Amuzhong, China C10 54
Amvrakikós Kólpos, b., Grc. E3 28
An, Mya. C2 48
Ana, Parque Nacional dedo see Doñana, Parque Nacional de, p.o.i., Spain H4 20
Anaa, at., Fr. Poly. E12 72
Anabar, stm., Russia B11 34
Anaco, Ven. C9 86
Anaconda, Mt., U.S. D14 136
Anaconda Range, mts., Mt., U.S. E13 136
Anacortes, Wa., U.S. B4 136
Anadarko, Ok., U.S. F10 128
Anadolu (Anatolia), hist. reg., Tur. H15 6
Anadyr', Russia D24 34
Anadyr, stm., Russia C23 34
Anadyr, Gulf of see Anadyrskij zaliv, b., Russia C21 142
Anadyr Mountains see Anadyrskoe ploskogor'e, plat., Russia C23 34
Anadyrskij liman, b., Russia D24 34
Anadyrskij zaliv, b., Russia C21 142
Anadyrskoe ploskogor'e, plat., Russia C23 34
Anáfi, i., Grc. G8 28
Anagni, Italy C7 24
Anaheim, Ca., U.S. J8 134
Anahim Lake, B.C., Can. D5 138
Anáhuac, Mex. I10 130
Ānai Mudi, mtn., India F3 53
Anajás, Braz. D8 84
Anakāpalle, India C6 53
Anaktuvuk Pass, Ak., U.S. C9 140
Analalava, Madag. C8 68
Anamã, Braz. D5 84
Anama Bay, Mb., Can. C15 124
Ana María, Golfo de, b., Cuba B8 102
Anambas, Kepulauan (Anambas Islands), is., Indon. B5 50
Anambas Islands see Anambas, Kepulauan, is., Indon. B5 50
Anamizu, Japan B9 40
Anamoose, N.D., U.S. G13 124
Anamur, Tur. B3 58
Anamur Burnu, c., Tur. B3 58
Anan, Japan F7 40
Ānand, India G4 54
Ānandapur, India H11 54
Ananindeua, Braz. A1 88
Anan'iv, Ukr. B16 26
Anantapur, India D3 53
Anantnāg, India B5 54
Anápolis, Braz. I1 88
Anapurus, Braz. B4 88
Añasco, P.R. B1 104a
Anastasia Island, i., Fl., U.S. G4 116
Anatahan, i., N. Mar. Is. B5 72
Anatolia see Anadolu, hist. reg., Tur. H15 6
Anatolikí Makedonía kai Thráki, state, Grc. B8 28
Anatom, i., Vanuatu m17 79d
Añatuya, Arg. D6 92
Anauá, stm., Braz. G11 86
Anavilhanas, Arquipélago das, is., Braz. I11 86
Anbei, China F17 32
Anbianbu, China C2 42
Anbyŏn-ŭp, Kor., N. E7 38
Ancaster, On., Can. E9 112
Ancasti, Sierra de, mts., Arg. D5 92
Anchiang see Qianyang, China H3 42
Anch'ing see Anqing, China F7 42
Anchorage, Ak., U.S. D10 140
Anchuras, Spain E6 20
Ancona, Italy G10 22
Ancón de Sardinas, Bahía de, b., S.A. G2 86
Ancuabe, Moz. C6 68
Ancud, Chile H2 90
Ancy-le-Franc, Fr. G13 14
Anda, China B10 36
Andacollo, Arg. H2 92
Andahuaylas, Peru F3 84
Andalgalá, Arg. C4 92
Andalucía, state, Spain G6 20
Andalusia see Jan Kempdorp, S. Afr. E7 70
Andalusia, Al., U.S. F12 122
Andalusia see Andalucía, state, Spain G6 20
Andaman and Nicobar Islands, state, India F7 46
Andaman Basin, unds. H12 142
Andaman Islands, is., India F7 46
Andaman Sea, Asia G8 46
Andamook, Austl. F7 74
Andapa, Madag. C8 68
Andenes, Nor. B6 8
Andéramboukane, Mali F5 64
Andernach, Ger. F3 16
Anderson, Ca., U.S. C3 134
Anderson, In., U.S. H4 112
Anderson, Mo., U.S. H3 120
Anderson, S.C., U.S. B3 116
Anderson, Tx., U.S. G3 122
Anderson, stm., N.T., Can. B5 106
Anderson, Mount, mtn., Wa., U.S. C3 136
Anderson Dam, Id., U.S. G11 136
Andes, Col. E4 86
Andes, mts., S.A. F7 82
Andfjorden, strt., Nor. B7 8
Andhra Lake, res., India B1 53
Andhra Pradesh, state, India C4 53
Andilamena, Madag. D8 68
Andingpu, China B2 42
Andirlang, China A5 46
Andižan, Uzb. F12 32
Andkhvoy, Afg. B10 56
Andoany, Madag. C8 68
Andoga, stm., Russia A19 10
Andong, Kor., S. C1 40
Andong-chŏsuji, res., Kor., S. C1 40
Andorra, ctry., Eur. B12 20
Andorra, ctry., Eur. B12 20
Andorra-la-Vella, And. B12 20
Andover, Eng., U.K. J11 12
Andover, Me., U.S. F6 110
Andover, Ma., U.S. H5 110
Andover, Oh., U.S. C5 114
Andover, S.D., U.S. B15 126
Andøya, i., Nor. B6 8
Andradina, Braz. D6 90
Andranopasy, Madag. E7 68
Andreanof Islands, is., Ak., U.S. g23 140a
Andreapol', Russia D15 10
Andrews, In., U.S. H4 112
Andrews, N.C., U.S. A2 116
Andrews, S.C., U.S. C6 116
Andrews, Tx., U.S. B5 130
Andria, Italy C10 24
Andriamena, Madag. D8 68
Andriievo-Ivanivka, Ukr. B17 26
Androka, Madag. F7 68
Andronovskoe, Russia F16 8
Andros, i., Bah. C9 96
Ándros, i., Grc. F7 28
Androscoggin, stm., Me., U.S. F6 110
Āndrott Island, i., India F1 53
Andrupene, Lat. D10 10
Andudu, D.R.C. D5 66
Andújar, Spain F6 20
Andulo, Ang. C2 68
Anduze, Fr. E9 18
Anegada, Bahía, b., Arg. H4 90
Anegada Passage, strt., N.A. h15 96a
Aného, Togo H5 64
Añelo, Arg. I3 92
Anemata, Passe d', strt., N. Cal. m16 79d
Anenii Noi, Mol. C16 26
Aneroid, Sk., Can. E6 124
Aneta, N.D., U.S. G16 124
Anétis, Mali F5 64
Aneto, mtn., Spain B11 20
Anfu, China H6 42
Angamos, Punta, c., Chile D2 90
Ang'angxi, China B9 36
Angara, stm., Russia E8 34
Angarsk, Russia D18 32
Angas Downs, Austl. D6 74
Angastaco, Arg. B4 92
Angaul, Russia D18 32
Ånge, Swe. E6 8
Ángel, Salto (Angel Falls), wtfl, Ven. E10 86
Ángel de la Guarda, Isla, i., Mex. G6 98
Angeles, Phil. C3 52
Angel Falls see Ángel, Salto, wtfl, Ven. E10 86
Ängelholm, Swe. H5 8
Angelina, stm., Tx., U.S. F4 122
Angellala Creek, stm., Austl. F6 76
Angels Camp, Ca., U.S. E5 134
Angemuk, mtn., Indon. F10 44
Ångermanälven, stm., Swe. E7 8
Angermünde, Ger. C9 16
Angers, Fr. G8 14
Angical, Braz. F3 88
Angical do Piauí, Braz. D4 88
Angicos, Braz. C7 88
Angijak Island, i., Nu., Can. D13 141
Angikuni Lake, l., Nu., Can. C11 106
Angkor Wat, hist., Camb. F6 48
Ângk Tasaôm, Camb. G7 48
Angle Inlet, Mn., U.S. B3 118
Anglem, Mount, mtn., N.Z. H2 80
Anglesey, i., Wales, U.K. H8 12
Anglet, Fr. F4 18
Angleton, Tx., U.S. H3 122
Anglona, reg., Italy D2 24
Angmagssalik (Ammasalik), Grnld. D18 141
Angoche, Moz. D6 68
Angol, Chile H1 92
Angola, In., U.S. G5 112
Angola, N.Y., U.S. B6 114
Angola, ctry., Afr. C2 68
Angola Basin, unds. J14 144
Angora see Ankara, Tur. D15 28
Angoram, Pap. N. Gui. a3 79a
Angostura, Presa de la, res., Mex. H12 100
Angoulême, Fr. D6 18

Name | Map Ref. | Page

Angoumois, hist. reg., Fr. D5 18
Angra dos Reis, Braz. L3 88
Angren, Uzb. F12 32
Angu, D.R.C. D4 66
Angualasto, Arg. D3 92
Anguilla, Ms., U.S. E8 122
Anguilla, dep., N.A. h15 96a
Anguille, Cape, c., Nf., Can. C17 110
Anguli Nur, l., China A6 42
Anguo, China B6 42
Angus, On., Can. D10 112
Angusville, Mb., Can. D13 124
Anhalt, hist. reg., Ger. D7 16
Anholt, i., Den. H4 8
Anhua, China G4 42
Anhui, state, China F7 42
Anhwei see Anhui, state, China F7 42
Aniak, Ak., U.S. D8 140
Anibare Bay, b., Nauru q17 78f
Anie, Pic d', mtn., Fr. F5 18
Anil, Braz. B3 88
Animas, N.M., U.S. L8 132
Animas, stm., U.S. G9 132
Animas Valley, val., N.A. L8 132
Anina, Rom. D8 26
Anita, Ia., U.S. C3 120
Anıtkaya, Tur. E13 28
Aniva, mys, c., Russia B13 36
Aniva, zaliv, b., Russia G17 34
Aniwa, i., Vanuatu I17 79d
Anjangaon, India H6 54
Anjār, India G2 54
'Anjar, Leb. E6 58
Anjou, hist. reg., Fr. G8 14
Anjouan see Nzwani, i., Com. C7 68
Anjudin, Russia B9 32
Anjujsk, Russia C21 34
Anjujskij hrebet, mts., Russia C21 34
Anju-ŭp, Kor., N. E6 38
Anka, Nig. G6 64
Ankaboa, Tanjona, c., Madag. E7 68
Ankang, China E3 42
Ankara, Tur. D15 28
Ankara, state, Tur. D15 28
Ankavandra, Madag. D8 68
Ankazoabo, Madag. E7 68
Ankazobe, Madag. D8 68
Ankeny, Ia., U.S. C4 120
Anking see Anqing, China F7 42
Ankleshwar, India H4 54
Ankoro, D.R.C. F5 66
Anlong, China F6 36
Ânlóng Vêng, Camb. E6 48
Anlu, China F5 42
An Muileann gCearr see Mullingar, Ire. H5 12
Ånn, l., Swe. E5 8
Ann, Cape, c., Ant. B10 81
Ann, Cape, pen., Ma., U.S. H6 110
Anna, Il., U.S. G8 120
Anna, Lake, res., Va., U.S. F8 114
Annaba, Alg. B6 64
An-Nabaṭīyah, state, Leb. E6 58
An-Nabaṭīyah at-Taḥtā, Leb. E6 58
Annaberg-Buchholz, Ger. F9 16
An-Nabk, Syria D7 58
An-Nafūd, des., Sau. Ar. D5 56
An-Najaf, Iraq C5 56
Annam see Trung Phan, hist. reg., Viet. D8 48
Annamitique, Chaîne, mts., Asia D8 48
Annan, Scot., U.K. G9 12
Annandale, Austl. C7 76
Annandale, Mn., U.S. F4 118
Annandale, val., Scot., U.K. F9 12
Anna Plains, Austl. C4 74
Annapolis, Md., U.S. F9 114
Annapolis Royal, N.S., Can. F11 110
Annapūrṇa, mtn., Nepal D9 54
Ann Arbor, Mi., U.S. B2 114
An Nás see Naas, Ire. H6 12
An-Nāṣirīyah, Iraq C6 56
An-Nāṣirīyah, Syria E7 58
An-Nawfalīyah, Libya A3 62
Annecy, Fr. D12 18
Annecy, Lac d', l., Fr. D12 18
Annemasse, Fr. C12 18
Annenkov Island, i., S. Geor. J9 90
An Nhon, Viet. F9 48
Anning, China G5 36
Anniston, Al., U.S. D13 122
Annobón, i., Eq. Gui. J6 64
Annonay, Fr. D10 18
An-Nuhūd, Sudan E5 62
Annville, Ky., U.S. G2 114
Annville, Pa., U.S. D9 114
Anoka, Mn., U.S. F5 118
Anori, Braz. D5 84
Anpu, China K3 42
Anqing, China F7 42
Anqiu, China C8 42
Anren, China H5 42
Ansai, China C3 42
Ansbach, Ger. G6 16
Anse-d'Hainault, Haiti C10 102
Anse La Raye, St. Luc. m6 105c
Anselmo, Ne., U.S. F13 126
Anserma, Col. E4 86
Anshan, China D5 38
Anshun, China H1 42
Ansina, Ur. E10 92
Ansley, Ne., U.S. F13 126
Anson Bay, b., Austl. B5 74
Anson Bay, b., Norf. I. y24 78i
Ansongo, Mali F5 64
Ansonville, N.C., U.S. A5 116
Ansted, W.V., U.S. F4 114
Antakya see Hatay, Tur. B7 58
Antalaha, Madag. C9 68
Antalieptė, Lith. E8 10
Antalya, Tur. G13 28
Antalya, state, Tur. F14 28
Antalya, Gulf of see Antalya Körfezi, b., Tur. G14 28
Antalya Körfezi (Antalya, Gulf of), b., Tur. G14 28
Antananarivo, Madag. D8 68
An tAonach see Nenagh, Ire. I4 12
Antarctica, cont. D11 81
Antarctic Peninsula, pen., Ant. C35 81
Antas, Braz. F6 88
Antas, stm., Braz. D12 92
Antelope Island, i., Ut., U.S. C4 132
Antelope Mine, Zimb. B9 70
Antelope Peak, mtn., Nv., U.S. B1 132
Antenor Navarro, Braz. D6 88
Antequera, Para. A9 92
Antequera, Spain H6 20
Anthon, Ia., U.S. B2 120
Anthony, Ks., U.S. D10 128
Anthony, N.M., U.S. K10 132
Anthony, Tx., U.S. E9 98
Anti-Atlas, mts., Mor. D3 64
Antibes, Fr. F13 18
Anticosti, Île d', i., Qc., Can. F18 106
Antifer, Cap d', c., Fr. E8 14
Antigonish, N.S., Can. E14 110
Antigua, i., Antig. f4 105b
Antigua and Barbuda, ctry., N.A. h15 96a
Antigua International Airport, Antig. f4 105b
Antiguo Morelos, Mex. D9 100
Antikýthira, i., Grc. H6 28
Anti-Lebanon (Sharqī, Al-Jabal ash-), mts., Asia E7 58
Antilla, Cuba B10 102
Antillen, Nederlandse see Netherlands Antilles, dep., N.A. i14 96a
Antimony, Ut., U.S. E5 132
Antioch see Hatay, Tur. B7 58
Antioch, Il., U.S. F1 112
Antioquia, Col. D4 86
Antioquia, state, Col. D4 86
Antipajuta, Russia C4 34
Antipodes Islands, is., N.Z. H9 72
Antisana, vol., Ec. H2 86
Antler, stm., N.A. E12 124
Antofagasta, Chile A2 92
Antofagasta, state, Chile B3 92
Antofagasta de la Sierra, Arg. C4 92
Antofalla, Salar de, pl., Arg. C3 92
Antofalla, Volcán, vol., Arg. B4 92
Antón, Pan. H7 102
Anton, Tx., U.S. H6 128
Anton Chico, N.M., U.S. F3 128
Antongila, Helodrano, b., Madag. D8 68
Antonina, Braz. B13 92
Antonina do Norte, Braz. D5 88
Antônio Prado, Braz. D12 92
Antonito, Co., U.S. D2 128
Antón Lizardo, Punta, c., Mex. F10 100
Antopal', Bela. H7 10
Antrim, N. Ire., U.K. G6 12
Antropovo, Russia G20 8
Antsalova, Madag. D7 68
Antsirabe, Madag. D8 68
Antsirañana, Madag. C8 68
Antsohihy, Madag. C8 68
Antulai, Gunong, mtn., Malay. A10 50
Antun', Russia G16 34
Antung see Dandong, China D5 38
Antwerp see Antwerpen, Bel. C13 14
Antwerp, Oh., U.S. C1 114
Antwerpen (Antwerp), Bel. C13 14
An Uaimh see Navan, Ire. H6 12
Anugul, India H10 54
Anūpgarh, India D4 54
Anuradhapura, Sri L. G5 53
Anvers see Antwerpen, Bel. C13 14
Anvers Island, i., Ant. B34 81
Anvik, Ak., U.S. D7 140
Anxi, China C4 36
Anxi, China I8 42
Anxiang, China G5 42
Anxious Bay, b., Austl. F6 74
Anyang, China C6 42
Anyang, Kor., S. F7 38
A'nyêmaqên Shan, mts., China D4 36
Anyer Kidul, Indon. G4 50
Anykščiai, Lith. E7 10
Anyuan, China I6 42
Anyuanyi see Tianzhu, China D5 36
Anyue, China F1 42
Anze, China C5 42
Anžero-Sudžensk, Russia C15 32
Anzio, Italy C6 24
Anzoátegui, state, Ven. C9 86
Anžu, ostrova, is., Russia A17 34
Aoba, i., Vanuatu j16 79d
Aoba / Maéwo, state, Vanuatu j17 79d
Aoga-shima, i., Japan G12 40
Aohan Qi, China C3 38
Aojiang, China H9 42
Aoji-ri, Kor., N. C9 38
Ao Luk, Thai. H4 48
Aomar, Alg. H14 20
Aomen see Macau, Macau J5 42
Aomen see Macau, dep., Asia J5 42
Aomori, Japan D14 38
Aonla, India D7 54
Aóös (Vjosës), stm., Eur. D13 24
A'opo, Samoa g11 79c
Aôral, Phnum, mtn., Camb. F7 48
Aore, i., Vanuatu j16 79d
Aosta (Aoste), Italy E4 22
Aoste see Aosta, Italy E4 22
Aouderas, Niger F6 64
Aouk, Bahr, stm., Afr. F3 62
Aoukâr, reg., Maur. F3 64
Aoya, Japan D7 40
Aozou, Chad C3 62
Apache Junction, Az., U.S. J5 132
Apache Peak, mtn., Az., U.S. L6 132
Apalachee, stm., Ga., U.S. C2 116
Apalachicola, Fl., U.S. H13 122
Apalachicola, stm., Fl., U.S. H14 122
Apalachicola Bay, b., Fl., U.S. H13 122
Apaporis, stm., S.A. H7 86
Aparados da Serra, Parque Nacional de, p.o.i., Braz. D12 92
Aparri, Phil. A3 52
Apartadó, Col. D3 86
Apatin, Yugo. D5 26
Apatity, Russia C15 8
Apatzingán de la Constitución, Mex. F7 100
Apaxtla de Castrejón, Mex. F8 100
Apeldoorn, Neth. B15 14
Apennines see Appennino, mts., Italy G11 6
Apex, N.C., U.S. I7 114
Api, mtn., Nepal D8 54
Apía, Col. E4 86
Apia, Samoa g12 79c
Apiacás, Serra dos, plat., Braz. E6 84
Apiaí, Braz. B13 92
Apiaú, stm., Braz. F11 86
Apishapa, stm., Co., U.S. D4 128
Apizaco, Mex. F9 100
Apo, Mount, mtn., Phil. G5 52
Apodi, Braz. C7 88
Apodi, stm., Braz. C7 88
Apolakkiá, Grc. G10 28
Apolda, Ger. E7 16
Apolinario Saravia, Arg. B6 92
Apolo, Bol. B3 90
Apón, stm., Ven. B5 86
Aponguao, stm., Ven. E11 86
Apopka, Lake, l., Fl., U.S. H4 116
Aporá, Braz. F6 88
Aporé, Braz. C6 90
Apostle Islands, is., Wi., U.S. E8 118
Apostle Islands National Lakeshore, p.o.i., Wi., U.S. D8 118
Apóstoles, Arg. C10 92
Apostolove, Ukr. E4 32
Appalaches, Les see Appalachian Mountains, mts., N.A. D12 108
Appalachia, Va., U.S. H3 114
Appalachian Mountains, mts., N.A. D12 108
Appennino see Apennines, mts., Italy G11 6
Appennino, Calabro, mts., Italy E10 24
Appennino Abruzzese, mts., Italy B7 24
Appennino Ligure, mts., Italy F6 22
Appennino Lucano, mts., Italy D9 24
Appennino Tosco-Emiliano, mts., Italy F8 22
Appennino Umbro-Marchigiano, mts., Italy G9 22
Appenzell, Switz. C6 22
Apple Orchard Mountain, mtn., Va., U.S. G6 114
Appleton, Mn., U.S. F3 118
Appleton, Wi., U.S. G10 118
Appleton City, Mo., U.S. F3 120
Apple Valley, Ca., U.S. I8 134
Appomattox, Va., U.S. G7 114
Appomattox, stm., Va., U.S. G7 114
Aprelevka, Russia E20 10
Aprilia, Italy C6 24
Apšeronsk, Russia F5 32
Apt, Fr. F11 18
Apucarana, Braz. A12 92
Apulia see Puglia, state, Italy C10 24
Apure, state, Ven. D7 86
Apure, stm., Ven. D8 86
Apurímac, stm., Peru F3 84
Apurito, Ven. D7 86
Aqaba, Gulf of, b. J5 58
Āqchah, Afg. B10 56
'Aqīq, Sudan D7 62
Aqtaū see Aktau, Kaz. F8 32
Aqtöbe see Aktjubinsk, Kaz. D9 32
Aquidabã, Braz. F7 88
Aquidauana, Braz. D5 90
Aquila, Mex. F7 100
Aquiles Serdán, Mex. A6 100
Aquiles Serdán, Mex. C9 100
Aquin, Haiti C11 102
Aquio, stm., Col. F8 86
Ara, India F10 54
Ara, stm., Japan D12 40
Arab, Al., U.S. C12 122
'Arab, Bahr al-, stm., Sudan E5 62
'Araba, Wadi ('Arabah, Wādī), stm., Egypt I3 58
'Arabah, Wādī al- (Ha'Arava), val., Asia H6 58
Arabako, co., Spain B8 20
Araban, Tur. A8 58
Arabian Basin, unds. H9 142
Arabian Desert (Eastern Desert), des., Egypt B6 62
Arabian Gulf see Persian Gulf, b., Asia D7 56
Arabian Peninsula, pen., Asia E6 56
Arabian Sea F9 56
Araçá, stm., Braz. G10 86
Aracaju, Braz. F7 88
Aracataca, Col. B4 86
Aracati, Braz. C7 88
Araçatuba, Braz. D6 90
Aracena, Spain G4 20
Araci, Braz. F6 88
Aracides, Cape, c., Sol. Is. e9 79b
Aracoiaba, Braz. C6 88
Aracruz, Braz. J5 88
Araçuaí, Braz. I4 88
Araçuaí, stm., Braz. I4 88
'Arad, Isr. G6 58
Arad, Rom. C8 26
Arad, state, Rom. C8 26
Aradhíppou, Cyp. D4 58
Arafura Sea J16 142
Arafura Shelf, unds. K16 142
Aragarças, Braz. G7 84
Aragats Lerr, mtn., Arm. A5 56
Aragón, state, Spain C10 20
Aragón, stm., Spain B9 20
Aragona, Italy G7 24
Aragua, state, Ven. B8 86
Araguacema, Braz. E8 84
Araguaçu, Braz. F8 84
Aragua de Barcelona, Ven. C9 86
Araguaia, stm., Braz. E8 84
Araguaína, Braz. D1 88
Araguao, Caño, stm., Ven. C11 86
Araguari, Braz. J1 88
Araguari, stm., Braz. C7 84
Araguari, stm., Braz. J1 88
Araguatins, Braz. C1 88
Arahal, Spain G5 20
Arai, Japan B11 40
Araioses, Braz. B4 88
Arak, Alg. D5 64
Arāk, Iran C6 56
Arakan see Rakhine, state, Mya. C1 48
Arakan Yoma, mts., Mya. C2 48
Arakkonam, India E4 53
Araks see Aras, stm., Asia B6 56
Araks see Araz, stm., Asia B6 56
Aral Sea, l., Asia E9 32
Aral'sk, Kaz. E10 32
Aralsk see Aral'sk, Kaz. E10 32
Aramac, Austl. D5 76
Aramac, stm., Austl. D5 76
Ārāmbāg, India G11 54
Aramberri, Mex. C8 100
Ārān, Iran C7 56
Aranda de Duero, Spain C7 20
Arandas, Mex. E7 100
Arandis, Nmb. C2 70
Arang, India H8 54
Ārani, India E4 53
Aran Island, i., Ire. G4 12
Aran Islands, is., Ire. H3 12
Aranjuez, Spain D7 20
Aranos, Nmb. D4 70
Aransas, stm., Tx., U.S. F10 130
Arantāngi, India F4 53
Aranyaprathet, Thai. F6 48
Arao, Japan G3 40
Araouane, Mali F4 64
Arapaho, Ok., U.S. F9 128
Arapahoe, Ne., U.S. A9 128
Arapey Grande, stm., Ur. E9 92
Arapiraca, Braz. E7 88
Arapongas, Braz. D6 90
Arapoti, Braz. B12 92
Araranguá, Braz. D13 92
Araraquara, Braz. K1 88
Araras, Braz. L2 88
Araras, Açude, res., Braz. C5 88
Ararat, Austl. K4 76
Ararat, Mount see Ağrı Dağı, mtn., Tur. B5 56
Arari, Braz. B3 88
Arāria, India E11 54
Araripe, Braz. D5 88
Araripe, Chapada do, plat., Braz. D6 88
Araripina, Braz. D5 88
Ararirá, stm., Braz. H10 86
Araruama, Lagoa de, b., Braz. L4 88
Araruna, Braz. D8 88
Aras (Araz), stm., Asia B6 56
Aratuípe, Braz. G6 88
Arauca, Col. D6 86
Arauca, state, Col. D6 86
Arauca, stm., S.A. D8 86
Araucária, Braz. B13 92
Arauquita, Col. D6 86
Araure, Ven. C7 86
Arāvalli Range, mts., India F4 54
Arawa, Pap. N. Gui. d6 79b
Araxá, Braz. J2 88
Araya, Ven. B9 86
Araya, Punta de, c., Ven. B9 86
Araz (Aras), stm., Asia B6 56
Ārba Minch', Eth. F7 62
Arbatax, Italy E3 24
Arboga, Swe. G6 8
Arboledas, Arg. H7 92
Arbon, Switz. C6 22
Arboréa, Italy E2 24
Arborea, reg., Italy E2 24
Arborfield, Sk., Can. A10 124
Arbroath, Scot., U.K. E10 12
Arbuckle, Ca., U.S. D3 134
Arc, stm., Fr. D12 18
Arcachon, Fr. E4 18
Arcachon, Bassin d', b., Fr. E4 18
Arcade, Ca., U.S. E4 134
Arcade, N.Y., U.S. B7 114
Arcadia, Ca., U.S. I7 134
Arcadia, Fl., U.S. I4 116
Arcadia, Ia., U.S. B2 120
Arcadia, Ks., U.S. G3 120
Arcadia, La., U.S. E6 122
Arcadia, Mi., U.S. D3 112
Arcadia, Mo., U.S. G7 120
Arcadia, S.C., U.S. B3 116
Arcadia, Wi., U.S. G7 118
Arcanum, Oh., U.S. D1 114
Arcas, Cayos, is., Mex. E12 100
Arcata, Ca., U.S. C1 134
Arc Dome, mtn., Nv., U.S. E8 134
Arcelia, Mex. F8 100
Arcevia, Italy G9 22
Archangel see Arhangel'sk, Russia D19 8
Archbold, Oh., U.S. C1 114
Archer, Fl., U.S. G3 116
Archer, stm., Austl. B8 74
Archer, Mount, mtn., Austl. D8 76
Archer City, Tx., U.S. H10 128
Archer's Post, Kenya D7 66
Arches National Park, p.o.i., Ut., U.S. E7 132
Archiac, Fr. D5 18
Archidona, Spain G6 20
Arcis-sur-Aube, Fr. F13 14
Arco, Id., U.S. G13 136
Arcola, Il., U.S. E9 120
Arcola, Ms., U.S. D8 122
Arcos, Braz. K3 88
Arcos de la Frontera, Spain H5 20
Arcot, India E4 53
Arcoverde, Braz. E7 88
Arctic Bay, Nu., Can. A14 106
Arctic Ocean A21 4
Arctic Red, stm., N.T., Can. B4 106
Arctic Village, Ak., U.S. C10 140
Arda, stm., Eur. H12 26
Ardabīl, Iran B6 56
Ardahan, Tur. A5 56
Ardakān, Iran C7 56
Ardatov, Russia I20 8
Ardèche, state, Fr. E10 18
Arden, Ca., U.S. E4 134
Ardennes, state, Fr. E13 14
Ardennes, reg., Eur. D14 14
Ardennes, Canal des, can., Fr. E13 14
Ardestān, Iran C7 56
Ardila, stm., Eur. F3 20
Ardill, Sk., Can. E8 124
Ardlethan, Austl. J6 76
Ardmore, Al., U.S. B12 122
Ardmore, Ok., U.S. G11 128
Ardmore, Pa., U.S. D10 114
Åre, Swe. E5 8
Areado, Braz. K2 88
Arecibo, P.R. B2 104a
Arecibo, Observatorio de, sci., P.R. B2 104a
Arecibo Observatory see Arecibo, Observatorio de, sci., P.R. B2 104a
Arèhausk, Bela. F13 10
Areia, Braz. D8 88
Areia, stm., Braz. H3 88
Areia Branca, Braz. C7 88
Arena, Point, c., Ca., U.S. E2 134
Arena, Punta, c., Mex. D4 100
Arena de la Ventana, Punta, c., Mex. C4 100
Arenal, P.R. C3 104a
Arenas, Cayo, i., Mex. D13 100
Arenas, Punta de, c., Arg. J3 90
Arenas de San Pedro, Spain D5 20
Arendal, Nor. G3 8
Arenys de Mar, Spain C13 20
Arequipa, Peru G3 84
Arequito, Arg. F7 92
Arévalo, Spain C6 20
Arezzo, Italy G8 22
Arga, stm., Spain B9 20
Argadargada, Austl. D7 74
Argamasilla de Alba, Spain E7 20
Arganda del Rey, Spain D7 20
Arga-Sala, stm., Russia C10 34
Argelès-Gazost, Fr. F5 18
Argens, stm., Fr. F12 18
Argent, Côte d', cst., Fr. F4 18
Argenta, Italy F8 22
Argentan, Fr. F8 14
Argentat, Fr. D7 18
Argenteuil, Fr. F11 14
Argentina, ctry., S.A. G3 90
Argentine Basin, unds. L10 144
Argentino, Lago, l., Arg. J2 90
Argenton-sur-Creuse, Fr. H10 14
Argeș, state, Rom. E11 26
Argeș, stm., Rom. E13 26
Arghandāb, stm., Afg. C10 56
Argolikós Kólpos (Argolis, Gulf of), b., Grc. F6 28
Argolis, Gulf of see Argolikós Kólpos, b., Grc. F6 28
Argonia, Ks., U.S. D11 128
Argonne, Wi., U.S. F10 118
Argonne, reg., Fr. E14 14
Árgos, Grc. F5 28
Argos, In., U.S. G3 112
Argostóli, Grc. E3 28
Arguello, Point, c., Ca., U.S. I5 134
Argun' (Ergun), stm., Asia F12 34
Argungu, Nig. G5 64
Argyle, Lake, l., Austl. C5 74
Arhangel'sk, Russia D19 8
Arhangel'skaja oblast', co., Russia E20 8
Arhangel'skoe, Russia G20 10
Arhara, Russia G15 34
Arhipovo, Russia C21 8
Århus, Den. H4 8
Århus, state, Den. H4 8
Ariake-kai, b., Japan F3 40
Ariana, Tun. H4 24
Ariano Irpino, Italy C9 24
Ariari, stm., Col. F5 86
Arias, Arg. F6 92
Ari Atoll, at., Mald. i12 46a
Arica, Chile C2 90
Arica, Col. I6 86
Arichat, N.S., Can. E16 110
Arichuna, Ven. D8 86
Arid, Cape, c., Austl. F4 74
Arida, Japan E8 40
Aridaía, Grc. C5 28
Ariège, state, Fr. G7 18
Ārifwāla, Pak. C4 54
Ariguaní, stm., Col. C5 86
Arīḥā (Jericho), Gaza G6 58
Arīḥā, Syria C7 58
Arikaree, stm., U.S. B6 128
Arima, Trin. s12 105f
Arinos, stm., Braz. F6 84
Ariogala, Lith. E6 10
Ariporo, stm., Col. D6 86
Aripuanã, Braz. E5 84
Aripuanã, stm., Braz. E5 84
Ariquemes, Braz. E5 84
Arisa, stm., Ven. D9 86
Arish, Wadi el- ('Arīsh, Wādī al-), stm., Egypt H4 58
Aristazabal Island, i., B.C., Can. E5 106
Ariton, Al., U.S. F13 122
Arivonimamo, Madag. D8 68
Ariyalūr, India F4 53
Arizaro, Salar de, pl., Arg. B4 92
Arizgoiti, Spain A8 20
Arizona, Arg. G5 92
Arizona, state, U.S. I5 132
Arizpe, Mex. F7 98
Arja, Russia H22 8
Arjasa, Indon. G9 50
Arjona, Col. B4 86
Arjona, Spain G6 20
Arka, Russia D17 34
Arkadelphia, Ar., U.S. C5 122
Arkalyk, Kaz. D11 32
Arkansas, state, U.S. B6 122
Arkansas, stm., U.S. E9 108
Arkansas, Salt Fork, stm., U.S. D7 122
Arkansas City, Ar., U.S. D7 122
Arkansas City, Ks., U.S. D11 128
Arkanū, Jabal, mtn., Libya C4 62
Arkhara see Arhara, Russia G15 34
Arklow, Ire. I6 12
Arkoma, Ok., U.S. B4 122
Arkona, Kap, c., Ger. B9 16
Arkport, N.Y., U.S. B8 114
Arktičeskogo Instituta, ostrova, is., Russia A5 34
Arlanza, stm., Spain B7 20
Arlanzón, stm., Spain B7 20
Arles, Fr. F10 18
Arlington, S. Afr. E8 70
Arlington, Ga., U.S. F14 122
Arlington, Ks., U.S. D10 128
Arlington, Ky., U.S. H9 120
Arlington, Ne., U.S. C1 120
Arlington, Oh., U.S. D2 114
Arlington, Or., U.S. E6 136
Arlington, Tn., U.S. B9 122
Arlington, Tx., U.S. B10 130
Arlington, Vt., U.S. G3 110
Arlington, Va., U.S. F8 114
Arlington, Wa., U.S. B4 136
Arlington Heights, Il., U.S. F2 112
Arlit, Niger F6 64
Arlon, Bel. E14 14
Arm, stm., Sk., Can. D8 124
Arma, Ks., U.S. G3 120
Armada, Mi., U.S. B3 114
Armadale, Austl. F3 74
Armageddon see Tel Megiddo, hist., Isr. F6 58
Armagh, N. Ire., U.K. G6 12
Armançon, stm., Fr. G13 14
Armavir, Russia E6 32
Armenia, Col. E4 86
Armenia, ctry., Asia A5 56
Armenija see Armenia, ctry., Asia A5 56
Armenistís, Grc. F9 28
Armentières, Fr. D11 14
Armería, Mex. F6 100
Armero, Col. E4 86
Armidale, Austl. H8 76
Armijo, N.M., U.S. H10 132
Armour, S.D., U.S. D14 126
Armstrong, Arg. F7 92
Armstrong, B.C., Can. F11 138
Armstrong, On., Can. A9 118
Armstrong, Mo., U.S. E5 120
Armstrong, Mount, mtn., Yk., Can. C4 106
Ārmūr, India B4 53
Armutlu, Tur. C11 28
Arnarfjörður, b., Ice. k27 8a
Arnaud, stm., Qc., Can. D16 106
Arnaudville, La., U.S. G6 122
Arnay-le-Duc, Fr. G13 14
Arnedo, Spain B8 20
Arneiros, Braz. D5 88
Arnhem, Neth. B14 14
Arnhem, Cape, c., Austl. B7 74
Arnhem Bay, b., Austl. B7 74
Arnhem Land, reg., Austl. B6 74
Arno, at., Marsh. Is. C8 72
Arno, stm., Italy G7 22
Arnold, Ca., U.S. E5 134
Arnold, Mn., U.S. E6 118
Arnold, Mo., U.S. F7 120
Arnold, Ne., U.S. F12 126
Arnolds Park, Ia., U.S. H3 118
Arnon, stm., Fr. C8 18
Arnprior, On., Can. C13 112
Arnsberg, Ger. E4 16
Arnstadt, Ger. F6 16
Aro, stm., Ven. D9 86
Aroa, Ven. B7 86
Aroa, Pointe, c., Fr. Poly. u20 78h
Aroab, Nmb. E4 70
Aroland, On., Can. A12 118
Arolsen, Ger. E5 16
Arona, Italy E5 22
Arona, Pap. N. Gui. b4 79a
Aroostook, stm., N.A. D8 110
Arop Island (Long Island), i., Pap. N. Gui. b4 79a
Arorae, i., Kir. D8 72
Aroroy, Phil. D4 52
Arosa, Ría de see Arousa, Ría de, est., Spain B1 20
Arousa, Ría de, est., Spain B1 20
Arp, Tx., U.S. E3 122
Arqalyq see Arkalyk, Kaz. D11 32
Arquata Scrivia, Italy F5 22
Arraga, Arg. D5 92
Ar-Rahad, Sudan E6 62
Arraial do Cabo, Braz. L5 88
Arraias, Braz. G2 88
Ar-Ramādī, Iraq C5 56
Ar-Ramthā, Jord. F7 58
Arran, Island of, i., Scot., U.K. F7 12
Ar-Rank, Sudan E6 62
Ar-Raqqah, Syria B9 58
Ar-Raqqah, state, Syria B9 58
Arras, Fr. D11 14
Ar-Rastan, Syria D7 58
Arrecifes, Arg. G7 92
Arrey, N.M., U.S. K9 132
Arriaga, Mex. G11 100
Ar-Riyāḍ (Riyadh), Sau. Ar. E6 56
Arroio Grande, Braz. F11 92
Arrojado, stm., Braz. G3 88
Arronches, Port. E3 20
Arros, stm., Fr. F6 18
Arroux, stm., Fr. B10 18
Arrowhead, Lake, res., Tx., U.S. H10 128
Arrowwood, Ab., Can. F17 138
Arroyito, Arg. E6 92
Arroyo, P.R. C3 104a
Arroyo de la Luz, Spain E4 20
Arroyo Grande, Ca., U.S. H5 134
Arroyo Hondo, N.M., U.S. E3 128
Arroyo Seco, Arg. F7 92
Arroyos y Esteros, Para. B9 92
Ar-Rub' al-Khālī, des., Asia E6 56
Ar-Ruqayyah, hist., Syria F8 58
Ar-Ruṣāfah, hist., Syria C9 58
Ar-Ruṣayfah, Jord. F7 58
Ar-Ruṣayriṣ, Sudan E6 62
Ar-Ruṭbah, Iraq C5 56
Arsenev, Russia B10 38
Arsenevka, stm., Russia B10 38
Arsikere, India E3 53
Ársoș, Cyp. D3 58
Art, Île, i., N. Cal. I14 79d
Árta, Grc. D3 28
Artà, Spain E14 20
Artá see Artà, Spain E14 20
Arteaga, Mex. F7 100
Art'em, Russia C9 38
Artemisa, Cuba A6 102
Artëmovsk, Russia D16 32
Artëmovskij, Russia E12 34
Artëmovskij, Russia C10 38
Artesia, Ms., U.S. D10 122
Artesia, N.M., U.S. B3 130
Arthabaska, ngh., Qc., Can. D5 110
Arthal, India B6 54
Arthur, On., Can. E9 112
Arthur, Il., U.S. E9 120
Arthur, N.D., U.S. D1 118
Arthur, Tn., U.S. H2 114
Arthur, stm., Austl. n12 77a
Arthur's Pass National Park, p.o.i., N.Z. F5 80
Arthur's Town, Bah. C9 96
Artibonite, stm., Haiti C11 102
Artigas, Ur. E9 92
Artillery Lake, l., N.T., Can. C9 106
Artois, hist. reg., Fr. D11 14
Artsyz, Ukr. D16 26
Artyk, Russia D18 34
Aru, Kepulauan (Aru Islands), is., Indon. G10 44
Aru, Tanjung, c., Indon. E10 50
Arua, Ug. D6 66
Aruanã, Braz. F7 84
Aruba, dep., N.A. F12 102
Aru Islands see Aru, Kepulauan, is., Indon. G10 44
Arunāchal Pradesh, state, India C7 46
Arun Qi, China B9 36
Aruppukkottai, India G4 53
Arurandeua, stm., Braz. C1 88
Arusha, Tan. E7 66
Arut, stm., Indon. E7 50
Aruvi, stm., Sri L. G5 53
Aruwimi, stm., D.R.C. D4 66
Arvada, Co., U.S. B3 128
Arvayheer, Mong. B5 36
Arvi, India H7 54
Arviat, Nu., Can. C12 106
Arvidsjaur, Swe. D8 8
Arvika, Swe. G5 8
Arvin, Ca., U.S. H7 134
Arvon, Mount, mtn., Mi., U.S. B1 112
Arvorezinha, Braz. D11 92
Arxan, China B8 36
Arys', Kaz. F11 32
Arys, ozero, l., Kaz. E11 32
Arzachena, Italy C3 24
Arzamas, Russia I20 8
Arzignano, Italy E8 22
Arz Lubnān, for., Leb. D7 58
Aš, Czech Rep. F8 16
Aša, Russia D9 32
Asa, stm., Ven. D10 86
Asaba, Nig. H6 64
Asad, Buḥayrat al- (Assad, Lake), res., Syria B9 58
Asadābād, Afg. C11 56
Asadābād, Iran B8 56
Aşağibostancı, N. Cyp. C3 58
Asahan, stm., Indon. B1 50
Asahi, Japan D13 40
Asahi, stm., Japan E6 40
Asahi-dake, vol., Japan C15 38
Asahigawa see Asahikawa, Japan C15 38
Asahikawa, Japan C15 38
Asama-yama, vol., Japan C11 40
Asan-man, b., Kor., S. F7 38
Āsānsol, India G11 54
Åsarna, Swe. E6 8
Asaro, Ven. q20 104g
Asbest, Russia C10 32
Asbestos, Qc., Can. E4 110
Asbestos Range National Park, p.o.i., Austl. n13 77a
Asbury Park, N.J., U.S. D12 114
Ascensión, Mex. F9 98
Ascension, i., St. Hel. G4 60
Aschaffenburg, Ger. G5 16
Aschersleben, Ger. E7 16
Ascoli Piceno, Italy H10 22
Ascoli Satriano, Italy C9 24
Ascör (Ostër), stm., Eur. G14 10
Āseb, Erit. E8 62
Åseda, Swe. H6 8
Āsela, Eth. F7 62
Åsele, Swe. D7 8
Āsendabo, Eth. F7 62
Asenovgrad, Blg. G11 26
Aseri, Est. A9 10
Ašgabat, Turkmen. B8 56
Ashāqif, Jabal al-, hills, Jord. F8 58
Ashburton, N.Z. F4 80
Ashburton, stm., Austl. D3 74
Ashcroft, B.C., Can. F9 138
Ashdod, Isr. G5 58
Ashdod, Tel, hist., Isr. G5 58
Ashdown, Ar., U.S. D4 122
Asheboro, N.C., U.S. I6 114
Ashern, Mb., Can. C15 124
Asheville, N.C., U.S. I3 114
Ash Flat, Ar., U.S. H6 120
Ashford, Eng., U.K. J13 12
Ashford, Al., U.S. F13 122
Ash Fork, Az., U.S. H4 132
Ashgabat see Ašgabat, Turkmen. B8 56
Ash Grove, Mo., U.S. G4 120
Ashibe, Japan F2 40
Ashikaga, Japan C12 40
Ashington, Eng., U.K. F11 12
Ashio, Japan C12 40
Ashizuri-misaki, c., Japan G6 40
Ashland, Al., U.S. D13 122
Ashland, Il., U.S. E7 120
Ashland, Ks., U.S. D9 128
Ashland, Ky., U.S. F3 114
Ashland, Mo., U.S. F5 120
Ashland, Mt., U.S. B6 126
Ashland, Ne., U.S. C1 120
Ashland, N.H., U.S. G5 110
Ashland, Oh., U.S. D3 114
Ashland, Or., U.S. A3 134
Ashland, Va., U.S. G8 114
Ashland, Wi., U.S. E7 118
Ashland, Mount, mtn., Or., U.S. A3 134
Ashley, Austl. G7 76
Ashley, Il., U.S. F8 120
Ashley, Mi., U.S. E5 112
Ashley, Oh., U.S. D3 114
Ashmore, Il., U.S. E9 120
Ashmore Islands, is., Austl. B4 74
Ashoknagar, India F6 54
Ashqelon, Isr. G5 58
Ash-Shamāl, state, Leb. D7 58
Ash-Shaqrā' see Shaqrā', Sau. Ar. D6 56
Ash-Shāriqah, U.A.E. D8 56
Ash-Shawbak, Jord. H6 58
Ash-Shiḥr, Yemen G6 56
Ash-Shurayf, Sau. Ar. D4 56
Ashta, India C2 53
Ashta, India G6 54
Ashtabula, Oh., U.S. C5 114
Ashtabula, Lake, res., N.D., U.S. G16 124
Ashton, St. Vin. p11 105e
Ashton, S. Afr. H5 70
Ashton, Id., U.S. F15 136
Ashton, Il., U.S. C8 120
Ashton, Ne., U.S. F14 126
Ashuanipi Lake, l., Nf., Can. E17 106
Ashuapmushuan, stm., Qc., Can. B3 110
Ashûm, Egypt H1 58
Ashville, Al., U.S. D12 122
Ashwaubenon, Wi., U.S. D1 112

Name	Map Ref.	Page
Asi see Orontes, stm., Asia	B7	58
Asia, cont.	C19	4
Asia, Kepulauan, is., Indon.	E9	44
Asia Minor, hist. reg., Tur.	E13	28
Āsika, India	I10	54
Asinara, Golfo dell', b., Italy	D2	24
Asinara, Isola, i., Italy	C2	24
Asino, Russia	C15	32
Asintorf, Bela.	F13	10
Asipovičy, Bela.	G11	10
'Asīr, reg., Sau. Ar.	F5	56
Askham, S. Afr.	E5	70
Askiz, Russia	D16	32
Askja, vol., Ice.	k31	8a
Aslanapa, Tur.	D12	28
Aslantaş Barajı, res., Tur.	A7	58
Asmara see Asmera, Erit.	D7	62
Asmera, Erit.	D7	62
Ašmjany, Bela.	F8	10
Asola, Italy	E7	22
Asomante, P.R.	B2	104a
Āsosa, Eth.	E6	62
Asoteriba, Jabal, mtn., Sudan	C7	62
Asotin, Wa., U.S.	D9	136
Asouf, Oued, stm., Alg.	D5	64
Asp, Spain	F10	20
Aspe see Asp, Spain	F10	20
Aspen, Co., U.S.	D10	132
Aspendos, hist., Tur.	G14	28
Aspermont, Tx., U.S.	A7	130
Aspiring, Mount, mtn., N.Z.	G3	80
Assad, Lake see Asad, Buḥayrat al-, res., Syria	B9	58
As-Safīrah, Syria	B8	58
Aṣ-Ṣāfiyah, Sudan	D6	62
As-Salṭ, Jord.	F6	58
Assam, state, India	C7	46
As-Samāwah, Iraq	C6	56
Aṣ-Ṣanamayn, Syria	E7	58
Aṣ-Ṣarafand, Leb.	E6	58
Assaré, Braz.	D6	88
Assateague Island, i., U.S.	F10	114
Assateague Island National Seashore, p.o.i., U.S.	G10	114
Assemini, Italy	E2	24
Assen, Neth.	A15	14
Asseria, hist., Cro.	F12	22
Assíni, hist., Grc.	F5	28
Assiniboia, Sk., Can.	E8	124
Assiniboine, stm., Can.	E16	124
Assiniboine, Mount, mtn., Can.	F15	138
Assis, Braz.	D6	90
Assis Chateaubriand, Braz.	B11	92
Assisi, Italy	G9	22
Assomption, i., Sey.	k11	69b
Assu, Braz.	C7	88
As-Sudd, reg., Sudan	F6	62
As-Sufāl, Yemen	G6	56
As-Sulaymānīyah, Iraq	B6	56
As-Sulaymānīyah, Sau. Ar.	E6	56
As-Sulayyil, Sau. Ar.	E6	56
Assumption, Il., U.S.	E8	120
As-Suwaydā', Syria	F7	58
As-Suwaydā', state, Syria	F7	58
Astakós, Grc.	E3	28
Astana (Akmola), Kaz.	D12	32
Astara, Azer.	B6	56
Asti, Italy	F5	22
Astica, Arg.	E4	92
Astola Island, i., Pak.	D9	56
Astorga, Spain	B4	20
Astoria, Il., U.S.	D7	120
Astoria, Or., U.S.	D3	136
Astove, i., Sey.	I11	69b
Astrahan', Russia	E7	32
Astrakhan see Astrahan', Russia	E7	32
Astrašycki Haradok, Bela.	F10	10
Astrolabe, Cape, c., Sol. Is.	e9	79b
Astrolabe, Récifs de l', rf., N. Cal.	I15	79d
Astrolabe Reefs see Astrolabe, Récifs de l', rf., N. Cal.	I15	79d
Astrouna, Bela.	E12	10
Astudillo, Spain	B6	20
Asturias, state, Spain	A5	20
Astypálaia, i., Grc.	G9	28
Asunción, Para.	B9	92
Asunción, Bahía la, b., Mex.	B1	100
Asunción Nochixtlán, Mex.	G10	100
Åsunden, l., Swe.	H5	8
Asveja, Bela.	E11	10
Asvejskae, vozero, l., Bela.	D10	10
Aswân, Egypt	C6	62
Aswan High Dam see Aali, Sadd el-, dam, Egypt	C6	62
Asyût, Egypt	K2	58
Asyûti, Wadi el- (Asyūṭī, Wādī al-), stm., Egypt	K2	58
'Ata, i., Tonga	F9	72
Atabapo, stm., S.A.	F8	86
Atacama, state, Chile	C3	92
Atacama, Desierto de, des., Chile	E2	90
Atacama, Puna de, plat., S.A.	B4	92
Atacama, Salar de, pl., Chile	D3	90
Atacama Desert see Atacama, Desierto de, des., Chile	B3	92
Ataco, Col.	F4	86
Atagaj, Russia	C17	32
Atakpamé, Togo	H5	64
Atalaia, Braz.	E7	88
Atambua, Indon.	G7	44
Atami, Japan	D12	40
Atangmik, Grnld.	E15	141
Aṭar, Maur.	E2	64
Atascadero, Ca., U.S.	H5	134
Atascosa, stm., Tx., U.S.	F9	130
Atasu, Kaz.	E12	32
Atata, i., Tonga	n14	78e
Atatürk Barajı, res., Tur.	A9	58
Atauro, Pulau, i., Indon.	G8	44
'Aṭbarah, Sudan	D6	62
'Aṭbarah, stm., Afr.	D7	62
Atbasar, Kaz.	D11	32
Atchafalaya, stm., La., U.S.	G7	122
Atchafalaya Bay, b., La., U.S.	H7	122
Atchison, Ks., U.S.	E2	120
Ateca, Spain	C9	20
Aterno, stm., Italy	H10	22
Aṭfīh, Egypt	I2	58
Ath, Bel.	D12	14
Athabasca, Ab., Can.	B17	138
Athabasca, stm., Ab., Can.	D8	106
Athabasca, Lake, l., Can.	D9	106
Athalmer, B.C., Can.	F14	138
Athboy, Ire.	H6	12
Athena, Or., U.S.	E8	136
Athens, On., Can.	D14	112
Athens see Athína, Grc.	E6	28
Athens, Al., U.S.	C11	122
Athens, Ga., U.S.	C2	116
Athens, Il., U.S.	E8	120
Athens, La., U.S.	E5	122
Athens, Mi., U.S.	F4	112
Athens, Oh., U.S.	E3	114
Athens, Pa., U.S.	C9	114
Athens, Tn., U.S.	B14	122
Athens, Tx., U.S.	E3	122
Athens, W.V., U.S.	G5	114
Atherton, Austl.	A5	76
Athi, stm., Kenya	E7	66
Athiaínou, Cyp.	C4	58
Athína (Athens), Grc.	E6	28
Athlone, Ire.	H4	12
Athni, India	C2	53
Athok, Mya.	D2	48
Athol, Ma., U.S.	B13	114
Áthos, mtn., Grc.	C7	28
Athos, Mount see Áthos, mtn., Grc.	C7	28
Ati, Chad	E3	62
Atiak, Ug.	D6	66
Atico, Peru	G3	84
Atienza, Spain	C8	20
Atikokan, On., Can.	C7	118
Atirāmpattinam, India	F4	53
Atiu, i., Cook Is.	F11	72
Atka, Russia	D19	34
Atka Island, i., Ak., U.S.	g24	140a
Atkarsk, Russia	D6	32
Atkins, Ar., U.S.	B6	122
Atkinson, Il., U.S.	C8	120
Atkinson, N.C., U.S.	B7	116
Atlanta, Ga., U.S.	C1	116
Atlanta, Il., U.S.	D8	120
Atlanta, Mi., U.S.	C5	112
Atlanta, Mo., U.S.	E5	120
Atlantic, Ia., U.S.	C2	120
Atlantic, N.C., U.S.	B9	116
Atlantic Beach, Fl., U.S.	F4	116
Atlantic City, N.J., U.S.	E11	114
Atlantic-Indian Basin, unds.	O5	142
Atlantic-Indian Ridge, unds.	N15	144
Atlántico, state, Col.	B4	86
Atlantic Ocean	E9	144
Atlantic Peak, mtn., Wy., U.S.	E3	126
Atlas Mountains, mts., Afr.	C4	64
Atlasova, ostrov, i., Russia	F20	34
Atlas Saharien, mts., Alg.	C4	64
Atlin, B.C., Can.	D4	106
Atlin Lake, l., Can.	D4	106
'Atlit, Isr.	F5	58
Ātmakūr, India	D4	53
Atmore, Al., U.S.	F11	122
Atnarko, stm., B.C., Can.	D5	138
Atocha, Bol.	D3	90
Atoka, Ok., U.S.	C2	122
Atotonilco, Cerro, mtn., Mex.	H3	130
Atoyac, stm., Mex.	F9	100
Atoyac de Álvarez, Mex.	G8	100
Atrak (Atrek), stm., Asia	B7	56
Ätran, stm., Swe.	H5	8
Atrato, stm., Col.	D3	86
Atrauli, India	D7	54
Atrek (Atrak), stm., Asia	B7	56
Atri, Italy	H10	22
Atsumi, Japan	E10	40
Atsumi-hantō, pen., Japan	E10	40
Aṭ-Ṭafīlah, Jord.	H6	58
Aṭ-Ṭafīlah, state, Jord.	H6	58
Aṭ-Ṭā'if, Sau. Ar.	E5	56
At-Tall, Syria	E7	58
Attalla, Al., U.S.	C12	122
Attapu, Laos	E8	48
Attawapiskat, On., Can.	E14	106
Attawapiskat, stm., On., Can.	E13	106
Attawapiskat Lake, l., On., Can.	E13	106
Aṭ-Ṭawīl, mts., Sau. Ar.	D4	56
Aṭ-Ṭayyibah, Syria	C9	58
Attendorn, Ger.	E3	16
Attersee, l., Aus.	C10	22
Attica, In., U.S.	H2	112
Attica, Ks., U.S.	D10	128
Attica, N.Y., U.S.	B7	114
Attica see Attikí, hist. reg., Grc.	E6	28
Attikí, state, Grc.	F6	28
Attikí, hist. reg., Grc.	E6	28
Attleboro, Ma., U.S.	C14	114
Attock, Pak.	B4	54
Attu, Ak., U.S.	g21	140a
Attu Island, i., Ak., U.S.	g21	140a
Āttūr, India	F4	53
Aṭ-Ṭuwayshah, Sudan	E5	62
Atuel, stm., Arg.	G3	92
Atuel, Bañados del, sw., Arg.	H4	92
Atuntaqui, Ec.	G2	86
Atuona, Fr. Poly.	s18	78g
Atwater, Ca., U.S.	F5	134
Atwater, Mn., U.S.	F4	118
Atwood, Il., U.S.	E9	120
Atwood, Ks., U.S.	B7	128
Atwood, Tn., U.S.	I9	120
Atyrau, Kaz.	E8	32
Aua Island, i., Pap. N. Gui.	a3	79a
Auari, stm., Braz.	F9	86
Auau Channel, strt., Hi., U.S.	C5	78a
Aubagne, Fr.	F11	18
Aube, state, Fr.	F13	14
Aube, stm., Fr.	F13	14
Aubigny-sur-Nère, Fr.	G11	14
Aubinadong, stm., On., Can.	A6	112
Aubrey Cliffs, clf, Az., U.S.	H3	132
Aubrey Lake, res., On., Can.	A6	112
Aubry Lake, l., N.T., Can.	B5	106
Auburn, Al., U.S.	E13	122
Auburn, Ca., U.S.	E4	134
Auburn, Il., U.S.	E8	120
Auburn, In., U.S.	G4	112
Auburn, Ky., U.S.	H11	120
Auburn, Me., U.S.	F6	110
Auburn, Ma., U.S.	B14	114
Auburn, Mi., U.S.	E5	112
Auburn, N.Y., U.S.	B9	114
Auburn, Wa., U.S.	C4	136
Auburn, stm., Austl.	E8	76
Aubusson, Fr.	D8	18
Auca Mahuida, Cerro, mtn., Arg.	H3	92
Auce, Lat.	D5	10
Auch, Fr.	F6	18
Auchi, Nig.	H6	64
Aucilla, stm., U.S.	F2	116
Auckland, N.Z.	C6	80
Auckland Islands, is., N.Z.	I7	72
Aude, state, Fr.	F8	18
Aude, stm., Fr.	F9	18
Auden, On., Can.	A11	118
Audenarde see Oudenaarde, Bel.	D12	14
Audierne, Fr.	F4	14
Audincourt, Fr.	G15	14
Audubon Lake, res., N.D., U.S.	G12	124
Aue, Ger.	F8	16
Augathella, Austl.	E6	76
Augrabies Falls National Park, p.o.i., S. Afr.	F4	70
Augrabiesvalle, wtfl, S. Afr.	F5	70
Augsburg, Ger.	H6	16
Augusta, Austl.	F2	74
Augusta, Italy	G9	24
Augusta, Ar., U.S.	B7	122
Augusta, Ga., U.S.	C3	116
Augusta, Il., U.S.	D6	120
Augusta, Ky., U.S.	F1	114
Augusta, Me., U.S.	F7	110
Augusta, Mt., U.S.	C14	136
Augusta, Wi., U.S.	G7	118
Augusto Severo, Braz.	C7	88
Augustów, Pol.	C18	16
Augustowski, Kanał, can., Eur.	C19	16
Augustus, Mount, mtn., Austl.	D3	74
Auki, Sol. Is.	e9	79b
Aukstaitijos nacionalnis parkas, p.o.i., Lith.	E8	10
Aulander, N.C., U.S.	H8	114
Auld, Lake, l., Austl.	D4	74
Aulla, Italy	F6	22
Aulne, stm., Fr.	F5	14
Aulneau Peninsula, pen., On., Can.	B4	118
Aumale, Fr.	E10	14
Auna, Nig.	G5	64
Auob, stm., Afr.	E5	70
Auraiya, India	E7	54
Aurangābād, India	B2	53
Aurangābād, India	F10	54
Aure, Nor.	E3	8
Aurelia, Ia., U.S.	B2	120
Aurich, Ger.	C3	16
Aurilândia, Braz.	G7	84
Aurillac, Fr.	E8	18
Aurine, Alpi (Zillertaler Alpen), mts., Eur.	C8	22
Aurora, On., Can.	D10	112
Aurora, Co., U.S.	B4	128
Aurora, Il., U.S.	C9	120
Aurora, In., U.S.	E13	120
Aurora, Me., U.S.	F8	110
Aurora, Mn., U.S.	D6	118
Aurora, N.Y., U.S.	B9	114
Aurora, N.C., U.S.	A9	116
Aurora, Oh., U.S.	C4	114
Aurora, Ut., U.S.	E4	132
Aurora, W.V., U.S.	E6	114
Aurora do Norte, Braz.	G2	88
Aursunden, l., Nor.	E4	8
Aurukun, Austl.	B8	74
Aus, Nmb.	E3	70
Ausable, stm., On., Can.	E8	112
Au Sable, stm., Mi., U.S.	D6	112
Au Sable Forks, N.Y., U.S.	F3	110
Au Sable Point, c., Mi., U.S.	D6	112
Auschwitz see Oświęcim, Pol.	F15	16
Aust-Agder, state, Nor.	G3	8
Austin, In., U.S.	F12	120
Austin, Mn., U.S.	H6	118
Austin, Nv., U.S.	D8	134
Austin, Pa., U.S.	C7	114
Austin, Tx., U.S.	D10	130
Austin, Lake, l., Austl.	E3	74
Australes, Îles, is., Fr. Poly.	F11	72
Australia, ctry., Oc.	D5	74
Australian Capital Territory, state, Austl.	J7	76
Austral Islands see Australes, Îles, is., Fr. Poly.	F11	72
Austral Seamounts, unds.	L24	142
Austria, ctry., Eur.	C11	22
Austvågøya, i., Nor.	B6	8
Autlán de Navarro, Mex.	F6	100
Autun, Fr.	H13	14
Auvergne, hist. reg., Fr.	D8	18
Auxerre, Fr.	G12	14
Auxier, Ky., U.S.	G3	114
Auxi-le-Château, Fr.	D11	14
Auxvasse, Mo., U.S.	E6	120
Auyán Tepuy, mtn., Ven.	E10	86
Auzances, Fr.	C8	18
Auzangate, Nevado, mtn., Peru	F3	84
Ava, Mo., U.S.	H5	120
Avaí, Braz.	L1	88
Avala, hist., Yugo.	E7	26
Avallon, Fr.	G12	14
Avalon, Ca., U.S.	J7	134
Ávalos, Mex.	A5	100
Avanersuaq see Nordgrønland, state, Grnld.	B14	141
Avant, Ok., U.S.	H1	120
Avaré, Braz.	L1	88
Avarua, Cook Is.	a26	78j
Avarua Harbour, b., Cook Is.	a26	78j
Avatiu Harbour, b., Cook Is.	a26	78j
'Avedat, Horvot, hist., Isr.	H5	58
Aveiro, Port.	D2	20
Aveiro, state, Port.	D2	20
Aveiro, Ria de, mth., Port.	D1	20
Avellaneda, Arg.	D8	92
Avellaneda, Arg.	G8	92
Avellino, Italy	D8	24
Averøya, i., Nor.	E2	8
Aversa, Italy	D8	24
Avery, Id., U.S.	C11	136
Avery, Tx., U.S.	D4	122
Avery Island, La., U.S.	H6	122
Aves, Islas de, is., Ven.	B8	86
Avesnes-sur-Helpe, Fr.	D12	14
Avesta, Swe.	F6	8
Aveyron, state, Fr.	E8	18
Aveyron, stm., Fr.	E7	18
Avezzano, Italy	H10	22
Avigliano, Italy	D9	24
Avignon, Fr.	F10	18
Ávila, Spain	D6	20
Ávila, co., Spain	D6	20
Ávila, Sierra de, mts., Spain	D5	20
Avilés, Spain	A4	20
Aviño, Spain	A2	20
Avinurme, Est.	B9	10
Avispa, Cerro, mtn., Ven.	G9	86
Avoca, Austl.	K4	76
Avoca, Ia., U.S.	C2	120
Avoca, N.Y., U.S.	B8	114
Avoca, stm., Austl.	K4	76
Avola, B.C., Can.	E11	138
Avola, Italy	H9	24
Avon, Il., U.S.	D7	120
Avon, Mn., U.S.	F4	118
Avon, N.Y., U.S.	B8	114
Avon, N.C., U.S.	A10	116
Avon, stm., Eng., U.K.	K11	12
Avon, stm., Eng., U.K.	I11	12
Avon, stm., Eng., U.K.	J10	12
Avondale, Az., U.S.	J4	132
Avondale, Co., U.S.	C4	128
Avon Downs, Austl.	D7	74
Avon Park, Fl., U.S.	I4	116
Avontuur, S. Afr.	H6	70
Avranches, Fr.	F7	14
Awaaso, Ghana	H4	64
Awaji, Japan	E8	40
Awaji-shima, i., Japan	E7	40
Awara, Japan	C9	40
Āwarē, Eth.	F8	62
Āwasa, Eth.	F7	62
Āwash, Eth.	F8	62
Āwash, stm., Eth.	E8	62
Awa-shima, i., Japan	A12	40
Awbārī, Libya	B2	62
Awbārī, Ṣaḥrā', reg., Libya	B2	62
Awe, Loch, l., Scot., U.K.	E7	12
Awegyun, Mya.	F4	48
Awjilah, Libya	B4	62
Awled Djellal, Alg.	C6	64
Awlef, Alg.	D5	64
Awul, Pap. N. Gui.	b5	79a
Axel Heiberg Island, i., Nu., Can.	A7	141
Axim, Ghana	I4	64
Axiós (Vardar), stm., Eur.	C5	28
Axis, Al., U.S.	G10	122
Axixá, Braz.	B3	88
Axtell, Ks., U.S.	L2	118
Axtell, Ne., U.S.	G13	126
Ayabe, Japan	D8	40
Ayacucho, Arg.	H8	92
Ayacucho, Peru	F3	84
Ayakkum Hu, l., China	D2	36
Ayakoz see Ajaguz, Kaz.	E13	32
Ayam, C. Iv.	H4	64
Ayamonte, Spain	G3	20
Ayapel, Col.	C4	86
Ayaş, Tur.	C15	28
Ayaviri, Peru	F3	84
Aydın, Tur.	F10	28
Aydın, state, Tur.	F11	28
Aydınkent, Tur.	F14	28
Ayer, Ma., U.S.	B14	114
Ayers Rock see Uluru, mtn., Austl.	E6	74
Ayeyarwady, state, Mya.	D2	48
Ayeyarwady (Irrawaddy), stm., Mya.	E8	46
Ayeyarwady, Mouths of the, mth., Mya.	E7	46
Ayíou Órous, Kólpos (Singitic Gulf), b., Grc.	C6	28
Aylesbury, Eng., U.K.	J12	12
Aylmer, On., Can.	F8	112
Aylmer, Qc., Can.	C14	112
Aylmer Lake, l., N.T., Can.	C9	106
Aylsham, Sk., Can.	A10	124
'Ayn Dār, Sau. Ar.	D6	56
Aynor, S.C., U.S.	B6	116
'Aynūnah, Sau. Ar.	J6	58
Ayon Island see Aën, ostrov, i., Russia	B22	34
Ayora see Aiora, Spain	E9	20
Ayorou, Niger	G5	64
'Ayoûn el 'Atroûs, Maur.	F3	64
Ayr, Austl.	B6	76
Ayr, Scot., U.K.	F8	12
Ayrancı, Tur.	A4	58
Ayre, Point of, c., I. of Man	G8	12
Āysha, Eth.	E8	62
Aytos see Ajtos, Blg.	G14	26
Ayutla, Mex.	E6	100
Ayutla de los Libres, Mex.	G9	100
Ayvacık, Tur.	D9	28
Ayvalık, Tur.	D9	28
Azaila, Spain	C10	20
Āzamgarh, India	E9	54
Azángaro, Peru	F3	84
Azaouâd, reg., Mali	F4	64
Azare, Nig.	G6	64
Azaryčy, Bela.	H12	10
A'zāz, Syria	B8	58
Azdavay, Tur.	B16	28
Azeffâl, sand, Afr.	E2	64
Azerbaijan, ctry., Asia	A6	56
Azëry, Bela.	G7	10
Āzezo, Eth.	E7	62
Azhikode, India	F2	53
Azilal, Mor.	C3	64
Azogues, Ec.	I2	86
Azores see Açores, is., Port.	C3	60
Azores Plateau, unds.	E10	144
Azov, Russia	E5	32
Azov, Sea of, Eur.	E5	32
Azovskoje more see Azov, Sea of, Eur.	E5	32
Azraq, Al-Bahr al- see Blue Nile, stm., Afr.	E6	62
Aztec, N.M., U.S.	G9	132
Aztec Peak, mtn., Az., U.S.	J5	132
Aztec Ruins National Monument, p.o.i., N.M., U.S.	G8	132
Azua, Dom. Rep.	C12	102
Azuaga, Spain	F5	20
Azuay, state, Ec.	I2	86
Azuer, stm., Spain	F7	20
Azuero, Península de, pen., Pan.	D1	86
Azufre, Volcán, vol., S.A.	B3	92
Azuga, Rom.	D12	26
Azul, Arg.	H8	92
Azur, Côte d', cst., Fr.	F13	18
Azurduy, Bol.	C4	90
Azure Lake, l., B.C., Can.	D10	138
Az-Zahrān, Sau. Ar.	D6	56
Az-Zarqā', Jord.	F7	58
Az-Zarqā', state, Jord.	G8	58
Az-Zāwiyah, Libya	A2	62
Azzel Matti, Sebkha, pl., Alg.	D5	64

B

Name	Map Ref.	Page
Ba, Fiji	p18	79e
Ba, stm., China	F6	42
Ba, stm., China	F2	42
Ba, stm., Viet.	F9	48
Baa, Indon.	H7	44
Baaba, Île, i., N. Cal.	I14	79d
Baao, Phil.	D4	52
Baardheere, Som.	D8	66
Baba Burnu, c., Tur.	D9	28
Babadağ, Tur.	F11	28
Babaeski, Tur.	B10	28
Babaevo, Russia	A18	10
Babahoyo, Ec.	H2	86
Babak, Phil.	G5	52
Babanango, S. Afr.	F10	70
Babanūsah, Sudan	E5	62
Babar, Kepulauan, is., Indon.	G8	44
Babbitt, Mn., U.S.	D7	118
Babbitt, Nv., U.S.	E7	134
B'abdā, Leb.	E6	58
Babeldaob, i., Palau	g7	78b
Bab el Mandeb see Mandeb, Bab el, strt.	E8	62
Babia, Arroyo de la, stm., Mex.	F5	130
Babian, stm., China	A5	48
Babičy, Bela.	H12	10
Babīna, India	F7	54
Babinda, Austl.	A5	76
Babine, stm., B.C., Can.	D5	106
Babine Lake, l., B.C., Can.	B5	138
Babine Range, mts., B.C., Can.	B4	138
Babino, Russia	A14	10
Babiogórski Park Narodowy, p.o.i., Pol.	G15	16
Babo, Indon.	F9	44
Bābol, Iran	B7	56
Baboquivari Peak, mtn., Az., U.S.	L5	132
Baborów, Pol.	F13	16
Babrujsk, Bela.	G12	10
Babuškin, Russia	F10	34
Babuyan Channel, strt., Phil.	A3	52
Babuyan Island, i., Phil.	A4	52
Babuyan Islands, is., Phil.	A3	52
Bacabal, Braz.	C3	88
Bacadéhuachi, Mex.	G8	98
Bacatuba, Braz.	C4	88
Bacău, Rom.	C13	26
Bacău, state, Rom.	C13	26
Bac Binh, Viet.	G9	48
Baccarat, Fr.	F15	14
Bačèjkava, Bela.	F12	10
Bac Giang, Viet.	B8	48
Bachaquero, Ven.	B6	86
Bachiniva, Mex.	A5	100
Bach Ma, Viet.	D8	48
Bach Thong, Viet.	A7	48
Bachu, China	B12	56
Back, stm., Nu., Can.	B11	106
Bačka, reg., Eur.	E16	22
Bačka Palanka, Yugo.	D6	26
Bačka Topola, Yugo.	D6	26
Back Creek, stm., Va., U.S.	F6	114
Backnang, Ger.	H5	16
Backstairs Passage, strt., Austl.	J1	76
Bac Lieu, Viet.	H7	48
Bac Ninh, Viet.	B8	48
Baco, Mount, mtn., Phil.	D3	52
Bacoachi, Mex.	F8	98
Bacolod, Phil.	E4	52
Baconton, Ga., U.S.	E1	116
Bacoor, Phil.	C3	52
Bac Phan, hist. reg., Viet.	A7	48
Bács-Kiskun, state, Hung.	C6	26
Bâcu, stm., Mol.	C15	26
Bacuri, Lago do, l., Braz.	B4	88
Bād, Iran	C7	56
Bad, stm., Mi., U.S.	E5	112
Bad, stm., S.D., U.S.	C12	126
Badagara, India	F2	53
Badajós, Lago, l., Braz.	D5	84
Badajoz, Spain	F4	20
Badajoz, co., Spain	F4	20
Badalona, Spain	C13	20
Bādāmi, India	D2	53
Badanah, Sau. Ar.	C5	56
Badarīnāth, India	C7	54
Badas, Bru.	A9	50
Badas, Kepulauan, is., Indon.	C5	50
Bad Axe, Mi., U.S.	E7	112
Bad Bergzabern, Ger.	G3	16
Bad Bevensen, Ger.	C6	16
Bad Bramstedt, Ger.	C5	16
Baddeck, N.S., Can.	D16	110
Bad Doberan, Ger.	B7	16
Bad Dürrenberg, Ger.	E8	16
Bad Ems, Ger.	F3	16
Baden, Switz.	C5	22
Baden-Baden, Ger.	H4	16
Badenoch, hist. reg., Scot., U.K.	E8	12
Badenweiler, Ger.	I3	16
Baden-Württemberg, state, Ger.	H4	16
Bad Freienwalde, Ger.	D9	16
Badgastein, Aus.	C10	22
Badger, Mn., U.S.	C3	118
Bad Hall, Aus.	B11	22
Bad Harzburg, Ger.	E6	16
Bad Hersfeld, Ger.	F5	16
Bad Homburg vor der Höhe, Ger.	F4	16
Bad Honnef, Ger.	F3	16
Badin Lake, res., N.C., U.S.	A5	116
Bad Ischl, Aus.	C10	22
Bad Kissingen, Ger.	F6	16
Bad Kreuznach, Ger.	G3	16
Badlands, hills, U.S.	A9	126
Badlands, hills, S.D., U.S.	D10	126
Badlands National Park, p.o.i., S.D., U.S.	D10	126
Bad Langensalza, Ger.	E6	16
Bad Lauterberg im Harz, Ger.	E6	16
Bad Mergentheim, Ger.	G5	16
Bad Muskau, Ger.	E10	16
Bad Nauheim, Ger.	F4	16
Badnera, India	H6	54
Bad Neustadt an der Saale, Ger.	F6	16
Bad Oeynhausen, Ger.	D4	16
Bad Oldesloe, Ger.	C6	16
Badong, China	F4	42
Bad Orb, Ger.	F5	16
Bad Pyrmont, Ger.	E5	16
Bad Reichenhall, Ger.	I8	16
Bad Salzuflen, Ger.	D4	16
Bad Salzungen, Ger.	F6	16
Bad Schwalbach, Ger.	F3	16
Bad Schwartau, Ger.	C6	16
Bad Segeberg, Ger.	C6	16
Bādshāhpur, India	F9	54
Bad Tölz, Ger.	I7	16
Badulla, Sri L.	H5	53
Badvel, India	D4	53
Bad Vöslau, Aus.	C13	22
Bad Waldsee, Ger.	I5	16
Bad Wildungen, Ger.	E4	16
Bad Wörishofen, Ger.	I6	16
Badžalskij hrebet, mts., Russia	F15	34
Baena, Spain	G6	20
Baependi, Braz.	K3	88
Baer, Russia	C17	32
Baeza, Spain	G7	20
Baezaeko, stm., B.C., Can.	D7	138
Bafang, Cam.	C1	66
Bafatá, Gui.-B.	G2	64
Baffin Basin, unds.	A7	144
Baffin Bay, b., N.A.	C12	141
Baffin Bay, b., Tx., U.S.	G10	130
Baffin Island, i., Nu., Can.	B16	106
Bafia, Cam.	D2	66
Bafing, stm., Afr.	G2	64
Bafoulabé, Mali	G2	64
Bafoussam, Cam.	C2	66
Bafra, Tur.	A4	56
Bāft, Iran	D8	56
Bafwaboli, D.R.C.	D5	66
Bafwasende, D.R.C.	D5	66
Bagaces, C.R.	G5	102
Bagagem, stm., Braz.	H1	88
Bagaha, India	E9	54
Bāgalkot, India	C2	53
Bagamoyo, Tan.	F7	66
Bagan Datuk, Malay.	K5	48
Baganga, Phil.	G6	52
Bagansiapiapi, Indon.	B2	50
Bagasra, India	H3	54
Bagdad, Az., U.S.	I3	132
Bagdad, Fl., U.S.	G11	122
Bagdarin, Russia	F11	34
Bagé, Braz.	E10	92
Bagenkop, Den.	B6	16
Bāgerhāt, Bngl.	G12	54
Bāgevādi, India	C2	53
Baghdād, Iraq	C5	56
Bagheria, Italy	F7	24
Baghlān, Afg.	B10	56
Bagley, Mn., U.S.	D3	118
Bagnères-de-Luchon, Fr.	G6	18
Bagni di Lucca, Italy	F7	22
Bagnols-sur-Cèze, Fr.	E10	18
Bago (Pegu), Mya.	D3	48
Bago, state, Mya.	C2	48
Bagodar, India	F10	54
Bagoé, stm., Afr.	G3	64
Bağpınar, Tur.	A9	58
Baguio, Phil.	B3	52
Bāh, India	E7	54
Bahādurgarh, India	D6	54
Bahama, Canal Viejo de, strt., N.A.	A8	102
Bahamas, ctry., N.A.	C9	96
Baharampur, India	F11	54
Bahau, Malay.	K6	48
Bahau, stm., Indon.	B9	50
Bahāwalnagar, Pak.	C4	54
Bahāwalpur, Pak.	D3	54
Bahçe, Tur.	A7	58
Baheri, India	D7	54
Bahi, Phil.	D4	52
Bahia see Salvador, Braz.	G6	88
Bahia, state, Braz.	G4	88
Bahía, Islas de la, is., Hond.	D4	102
Bahía Blanca, Arg.	I6	92
Bahía Bustamante, Arg.	I3	90
Bahía de Caráquez, Ec.	H1	86
Bahía Kino, Mex.	A3	100
Bahir Dar, Eth.	E7	62
Bahraich, India	E8	54
Bahrain, ctry., Asia	D7	56
Bahta, Russia	B15	32
Bahtîm, Egypt	H2	58
Bahty, Kaz.	E14	32
Bahušèusk, Bela.	F13	10
Bai, stm., China	A7	42
Bai, stm., China	E5	42
Baia de Aramă, Rom.	E9	26
Baia di Terra Nova, sci., Ant.	C21	81
Baía Farta, Ang.	C1	68
Baia Mare, Rom.	B10	26
Baião, Braz.	B1	88
Baicheng, China	F14	32
Baicheng, China	B9	36
Baidoa see Baydhabo, Som.	D8	66
Baie-Comeau, Qc., Can.	A8	110
Baiersbronn, Ger.	H4	16
Baie-Saint-Paul, Qc., Can.	C6	110
Baie-Trinité, Qc., Can.	A9	110
Baie Verte, Nf., Can.	j22	107a
Baihe, China	B11	46
Baijnāth, India	D7	54
Baikal, Lake see Bajkal, ozero, l., Russia	F10	34
Baikal Mountains see Bajkal'skij hrebet, mts., Russia	F10	34
Baikonur see Bajkonur, Kaz.	E11	32
Bailadores, Ven.	C6	86
Baile Átha Cliath see Dublin, Ire.	H6	12
Baile Átha Luain see Athlone, Ire.	H4	12
Băile Govora, Rom.	D11	26
Bailén, Spain	F7	20
Băileşti, Rom.	F10	26
Bailey, N.C., U.S.	I7	114
Bail Hongal, India	D2	53
Bailicun, China	I4	42
Bailique, Ilha, i., Braz.	C8	84
Baillie Islands, is., N.T., Can.	B14	140
Baillif, Guad.	h5	105c
Bailong, stm., China	E1	42
Bailu Hu, l., China	G5	42
Bailundo, Ang.	C2	68
Baimamiao, China	C2	42
Baima Shan, mtn., China	H4	42
Baimuru, Pap. N. Gui.	b3	79a
Bainbridge, Ga., U.S.	G14	122
Bainbridge, N.Y., U.S.	B10	114
Bain-de-Bretagne, Fr.	G7	14
Baing, Indon.	I12	50
Bainville, Mt., U.S.	F9	124
Baio Grande, Spain	A2	20
Baiona, Spain	B2	20
Baipeng, China	I3	42
Baipu, China	E9	42
Baiquan, China	B10	36
Baird, Tx., U.S.	B8	130
Baird Mountains, mts., Ak., U.S.	C7	140
Baird Peninsula, pen., Nu., Can.	B15	106
Bairiki, Kir.	C8	72
Bairin Zuoqi, China	C8	36
Bairnsdale, Austl.	K6	76
Baïse, stm., Fr.	F6	18
Baisha, China	G2	42
Baisha, China	L3	42
Baisha, China	I8	42
Baishe, China	H7	42
Baishuijiang, China	E2	42
Baisogala, Lith.	E6	10
Baiwang, China	I3	42
Baixingt, China	C4	38
Baixio, Braz.	D6	88
Baiyan Shan, mtn., China	H8	42
Baiyin, China	D5	36
Baiyü, China	E4	36
Baja, Hung.	C5	26
Baja, Punta, c., Chile	e29	78l
Baja California, state, Mex.	F5	98
Baja California, pen., Mex.	B2	96
Baja California Sur, state, Mex.	C2	100
Bajada del Agrio, Arg.	I2	92
Baján, Mex.	H6	130
Bajan, Mong.	B7	36
Bajanaul, Kaz.	D13	32
Bajangol, Russia	F9	34
Bajánsenye, Hung.	C3	26
Bajawa, Indon.	H12	50
Bajdarackaja guba, b., Russia	C2	34
Bajestān, Iran	C8	56
Bajkal, Russia	F9	34
Bajkal, ozero (Baikal, Lake), l., Russia	F10	34
Bajkal'skij hrebet, mts., Russia	F10	34
Bajkit, Russia	B17	32
Bajkonur, Kaz.	E11	32
Bajmak, Russia	D9	32
Bajmok, Yugo.	D6	26
Bajo, Indon.	H11	50
Bajo Boquete, Pan.	H6	102
Bajool, Austl.	D8	76
Bajramaly, Turkmen.	B9	56
Bajsun, Uzb.	G11	32
Bakacak, Tur.	C10	28
Bakala, C.A.R.	C4	66
Bakanas, Kaz.	F13	32
Bake, Indon.	E2	50
Bakel, Sen.	G2	64
Baker, Ca., U.S.	H9	134
Baker, Fl., U.S.	G12	122
Baker, La., U.S.	G7	122
Baker, Mt., U.S.	A8	126
Baker, Or., U.S.	F9	136
Baker, Mount, vol., Wa., U.S.	B5	136
Baker Butte, mtn., Az., U.S.	I5	132
Baker Island, i., Oc.	C9	72
Baker Lake, Nu., Can.	C11	106
Baker Lake, l., Austl.	E5	74
Baker Lake, l., Nu., Can.	C11	106
Bakersfield, Ca., U.S.	H7	134
Bâ Kêv, Camb.	F8	48
Bakharden, Turkmen.	B8	56
Bakhardok, Turkmen.	B8	56
Bakhtegān, Daryācheh-ye, l., Iran	D7	56
Bakı (Baku), Azer.	A6	56
Bakkafjörđur, Ice.	j32	8a
Bakkaflói, b., Ice.	j32	8a
Baklan, Tur.	F12	28
Bako, C. Iv.	H3	64
Bako, Eth.	F7	62
Bakony, mts., Hung.	C4	26
Bakouma, C.A.R.	C4	66
Baku see Bakı, Azer.	A6	56
Bakumpai, Indon.	D8	50
Bakung, Pulau, i., Indon.	C4	50
Bakungan, Indon.	K3	48
Bakwanga see Mbuji-Mayi, D.R.C.	F4	66
Balâ, Tur.	D16	28
Balabac, Phil.	F1	52
Balabac Island, i., Phil.	G1	52
Balabac Strait, strt., Asia	G1	52
Ba'labakk, Leb.	D7	58
Balabalagan, Kepulauan, is., Indon.	E10	50
Balabanovo, Russia	E19	10
Balabio, Île, i., N. Cal.	m15	79d
Balad, Iraq	C5	56
Baladëk, Russia	F15	34
Bālāghāt, India	H8	54
Bālāghāt Range, mts., India	B3	53
Balagne, reg., Fr.	G14	18
Balaguer, Spain	C11	20
Balahna, Russia	H20	8
Balaikarangan, Indon.	C7	50
Balaisepuah, Indon.	C7	50
Balakirevo, Russia	D21	10
Balaklava, Austl.	J2	76
Balakovo, Russia	D7	32
Balama, Moz.	C6	68
Balambangan, Pulau, i., Malay.	G1	52
Bālā Morghāb, Afg.	B9	56
Balanga, Phil.	C3	52
Balāngīr, India	H9	54
Balapulang, Indon.	G6	50
Balarāmpur, India	G11	54
Balašiha, Russia	E20	10
Balašov, Russia	D6	32
Balassagyarmat, Hung.	A6	26
Balatina, Mol.	B14	26
Balaton, Mn., U.S.	G3	118

Name	Map Ref.	Page
Balaton, l., Hung.	C4	26
Balayan, Phil.	D3	52
Balbieriškis, Lith.	F6	10
Balbina, Represa, res., Braz.	H12	86
Balcanoona, Austl.	H2	76
Balcarce, Arg.	H8	92
Balcarres, Sk., Can.	D10	124
Bălcești, Rom.	E10	26
Balcones Escarpment, clf, Tx., U.S.	D9	130
Balde, Arg.	F4	92
Bald Knob, Ar., U.S.	B7	122
Bald Knob, mtn., Va., U.S.	G6	114
Bald Mountain, mtn., Or., U.S.	G5	136
Bald Mountain, mtn., Or., U.S.	F3	136
Baldock Lake, l., Mb., Can.	D11	106
Baldone, Lat.	D7	10
Baldwin, La., U.S.	H7	122
Baldwin, Mi., U.S.	E4	112
Baldwin, Wi., U.S.	G6	118
Baldwinsville, N.Y., U.S.	E13	112
Baldwyn, Ms., U.S.	C10	122
Baldy Mountain, mtn., Mb., Can.	C13	124
Baldy Mountain, mtn., N.M., U.S.	E3	128
Baldy Peak, mtn., Az., U.S.	J7	132
Bâle see Basel, Switz.	C4	22
Baleares see Balears, state, Spain	E13	20
Baleares, Islas see Balears, Illes, is., Spain	E12	20
Balearic Islands see Balears, state, Spain	E13	20
Balearic Islands see Balears, Illes, is., Spain	E12	20
Balears, state, Spain	E13	20
Balears, Illes (Balearic Islands), is., Spain	E12	20
Balease, Gunung, mtn., Indon.	E12	50
Baleh, stm., Malay.	C8	50
Baleia, Ponta da, c., Braz.	I6	88
Baleine, stm., Qc., Can.	D17	106
Baleine, Grande rivière de la, stm., Qc., Can.	D15	106
Baleine, Petite rivière de la, stm., Qc., Can.	D15	106
Balej, Russia	F12	34
Baler, Phil.	C3	52
Baler Bay, b., Phil.	C3	52
Bāleshwar, India	H11	54
Balezino, Russia	C8	32
Balfate, Hond.	E4	102
Balfour, N.C., U.S.	A3	116
Balgazyn, Russia	D17	32
Balhaš, ozero (Balkhash, Lake), l., Kaz.	E13	32
Bāli, India	F4	54
Bali, state, Indon.	G9	50
Bali, i., Indon.	G9	50
Bali, Laut (Bali Sea), Indon.	G9	50
Bali, Selat, strt., Indon.	H9	50
Bali Barat National Park, p.o.i., Indon.	H9	50
Baliceaux, i., St. Vin.	p11	105e
Balige, Indon.	B1	50
Balıkesir, Tur.	D10	28
Balıkesir, state, Tur.	D10	28
Balīkh, stm., Syria	B10	58
Balikpapan, Indon.	D10	50
Balimbing, Indon.	F4	50
Balimbing, Phil.	H2	52
Balimo, Pap. N. Gui.	b3	79a
Balingen, Ger.	H4	16
Balingian, Malay.	B8	50
Balintang Channel, strt., Phil.	K9	42
Bali Sea see Bali, Laut, Indon.	G9	50
Bali Strait see Bali, Selat, strt., Indon.	H9	50
Baliza, Braz.	G7	84
Balkan Mountains, mts., Eur.	G11	26
Balkan Peninsula, pen., Eur.	B6	28
Balkaria see Kabardino-Balkarija, state, Russia	F6	32
Balkh, Afg.	B10	56
Balkhash, Lake see Balhaš, ozero, l., Kaz.	E13	32
Ballachulish, Scot., U.K.	E7	12
Balladonia, Austl.	F4	74
Ballālpur, India	B4	53
Ballangen, Nor.	B7	8
Ballantine, Mt., U.S.	B4	126
Ballarat, Austl.	K4	76
Ballard, Lake, l., Austl.	E4	74
Ballater, Scot., U.K.	D9	12
Ball Bay, b., Norf. I.	y25	78i
Ballenas, Bahía de, b., Mex.	B2	100
Ballenita, Punta, c., Chile	B2	92
Balleny Islands, is., Ant.	B21	81
Balleza, Mex.	B5	100
Balleza, stm., Mex.	B5	100
Ball Ground, Ga., U.S.	B1	116
Ballia, India	F10	54
Ballina, Austl.	G9	76
Ballina, Ire.	G3	12
Ballina, Ire.	I4	12
Ballinrobe, Ire.	H3	12
Ballston Spa, N.Y., U.S.	G2	110
Ballville, Oh., U.S.	C2	114
Ballybunnion, Ire.	I3	12
Ballyhaunis, Ire.	H4	12
Ballymena, N. Ire., U.K.	G6	12
Ballymoney, N. Ire., U.K.	F6	12
Ballyrogan, Lake, l., Austl.	I6	76
Balmaceda, Chile	I2	90
Balmoral, Austl.	K3	76
Balmorhea, Tx., U.S.	C4	130
Balnearia, Arg.	E6	92
Baloda Bāzār, India	H9	54
Balombo, Ang.	C1	68
Balong, Indon.	G7	50
Balonne, stm., Austl.	G7	76
Bālotra, India	F4	54
Balphakram National Park, p.o.i., India	F13	54
Balqash Köli see Balhaš, ozero, l., Kaz.	E13	32
Balrāmpur, India	E8	54
Balranald, Austl.	J4	76
Balș, Rom.	E11	26
Balsam Lake, Wi., U.S.	F6	118
Balsam Lake, l., On., Can.	D11	112
Balsas, Braz.	D2	88
Balsas, stm., Braz.	F2	88
Balsas, stm., Braz.	D3	88
Balsas, stm., Mex.	F8	100
Balsas, stm., Pan.	C3	86
Balsthal, Switz.	C4	22
Balta, Ukr.	B16	26
Baltasar Brum, Ur.	E9	92
Bălți, Mol.	B14	26
Baltic Sea, Eur.	D12	6
Baltijsk, Russia	F2	10
Baltijskaja kosa, spit, Eur.	F2	10
Baltijskoje more see Baltic Sea, Eur.	D12	6
Baltim, Egypt	G2	58
Baltimore, Ire.	J3	12
Baltimore, Md., U.S.	E9	114
Baltimore, Oh., U.S.	E3	114
Ba Lu, stm., Viet.	E9	48
Baluchistān, state, Pak.	C2	54
Baluchistan, hist. reg., Asia	D9	56
Balui, stm., Malay.	B8	50
Bālurghāt, India	F12	54
Balvi, Lat.	C10	10
Balygyčan, Russia	D19	34
Balykši, Kaz.	E8	32
Balzac, Ab., Can.	E16	138
Balzar, Ec.	H2	86
Bam, Iran	D8	56
Bama, China	I2	42
Bama, Nig.	G7	64
Bamaga, Austl.	B8	74
Bamako, Mali	G3	64
Bamba, Mali	F4	64
Bambamarca, Peru	E2	84
Bambana, stm., Nic.	F6	102
Bambari, C.A.R.	C4	66
Bambaroo, Austl.	B6	76
Bamberg, Ger.	G6	16
Bamberg, S.C., U.S.	C4	116
Bambio, C.A.R.	D3	66
Bambuí, Braz.	K2	88
Bam Co, l., China	C13	54
Bamenda, Cam.	C1	66
Bami, Turkmen.	B8	56
Bāmīān, Afg.	C10	56
Bamingui, C.A.R.	C4	66
Bampūr, Iran	D9	56
Bāmra Hills, hills, India	H10	54
Bamumo, China	B14	54
Banaba, i., Kir.	D7	72
Banabuiú, stm., Braz.	C6	88
Banabuiú, Açude, l., Braz.	C6	88
Banalia, D.R.C.	D5	66
Banamba, Mali	G3	64
Banana Islands, is., S.L.	H2	64
Bananal, stm., Braz.	E1	88
Bananal, Ilha do, i., Braz.	F7	84
Banarlı, Tur.	B10	28
Banās, stm., India	E6	54
Banâs, Râs, c., Egypt	C7	62
Banat, hist. reg., Eur.	D7	26
Banaz, Tur.	E12	28
Ban Ban, Laos	C6	48
Ban Bouang-nom, Laos	E8	48
Banbridge, N. Ire., U.K.	G6	12
Ban Bung Na Rang, Thai.	D5	48
Banbury, Eng., U.K.	I11	12
Ban Cha La, Laos	D7	48
Bancroft, On., Can.	C12	112
Bancroft, Id., U.S.	H15	136
Bancroft, Ia., U.S.	H4	118
Bancroft, Ne., U.S.	C1	120
Bānda, India	F8	54
Banda, Kepulauan, is., Indon.	F9	44
Banda, Laut (Banda Sea), Indon.	G8	44
Banda Aceh, Indon.	J2	48
Bānda Dāūd Shāh, Pak.	B3	54
Banda del Río Salí, Arg.	C5	92
Bandai-Asahi-kokuritsu-kōen, p.o.i., Japan	B12	40
Bandai-san, vol., Japan	B13	40
Bandama, stm., C. Iv.	H3	64
Bandama Blanc, stm., C. Iv.	H3	64
Ban Dan, Thai.	E7	48
Ban Dangtai, Laos	D7	48
Bandar Beheshtī, Iran	D9	56
Bandarbeyla, Som.	C10	66
Bandar-e ʿAbbās, Iran	D8	56
Bandar-e Anzalī, Iran	B6	56
Bandar-e Būshehr, Iran	D7	56
Bandar-e Deylam, Iran	D7	56
Bandar-e Lengeh, Iran	D7	56
Bandar-e Māh Shahr, Iran	C6	56
Bandar-e Moghūyeh, Iran	D7	56
Bandar-e Torkeman, Iran	B7	56
Bandar Seri Begawan, Bru.	A9	50
Banda Sea see Banda, Laut, Indon.	G8	44
Bandeira, Pico da, mtn., Braz.	K5	88
Bandeirantes, Braz.	F7	84
Bandelier National Monument, p.o.i., N.M., U.S.	F2	128
Bandera, Arg.	D6	92
Bandera, Alto, mtn., Dom. Rep.	C12	102
Banderas, Mex.	C2	130
Banderas, Bahía de, b., Mex.	E6	100
Bandhavgarh National Park, p.o.i., India	G8	54
Bāndhi, Pak.	E2	54
Bandiagara, Mali	G4	64
Bandiantaolehai, China	C5	36
Bāndīkūi, India	E6	54
Bandipura, India	A5	54
Bandipur Tiger Reserve, India	F3	53
Bandırma, Tur.	C11	28
Bandon, Or., U.S.	G2	136
Ban Don, Ao, b., Thai.	H4	48
Ban Donhiang, Laos	C5	48
Bandundu, D.R.C.	E3	66
Bandung, Indon.	G5	50
Banes, Cuba	B10	102
Banff, Ab., Can.	E15	138
Banff, Scot., U.K.	D10	12
Banff National Park, p.o.i., Ab., Can.	E15	138
Banfora, Burkina	G4	64
Banga, D.R.C.	F4	66
Banga, India	C6	54
Banga, stm., Phil.	G5	52
Bangalore, India	E3	53
Bangaon, India	G12	54
Bangassou, C.A.R.	D4	66
Bangdag Co, l., China	A8	54
Banggai, Indon.	F7	44
Banggai, Kepulauan, is., Indon.	F7	44
Banggi, Pulau, i., Malay.	G1	52
Banggong Co, l., China	B7	54
Banghāzī (Bengasi), Libya	A3	62
Banghiang, stm., Laos	D7	48
Bangil, Indon.	G8	50
Bangka, Pulau, i., Indon.	E5	50
Bangka, Selat, strt., Indon.	E4	50
Bangkalan, Indon.	G8	50
Bangkaru, Pulau, i., Indon.	L3	48
Bangkinang, Indon.	C2	50
Bangkir, Indon.	C12	50
Bangko, Indon.	E3	50
Bangkog Co, l., China	C12	54
Bangkok see Krung Thep, Thai.	F5	48
Bangladesh, ctry., Asia	G13	54
Bang Lamung, Thai.	F5	48
Bang Mun Nak, Thai.	D5	48
Bangor, N. Ire., U.K.	G7	12
Bangor, Wales, U.K.	H8	12
Bangor, Me., U.S.	F8	110
Bangor, Pa., U.S.	D10	114
Bangriposi, India	G11	54
Bangs, Tx., U.S.	C8	130
Bangs, Mount, mtn., Az., U.S.	G3	132
Bang Saphan, Thai.	G4	48
Bangued, Phil.	B3	52
Bangui, C.A.R.	D3	66
Bangweulu, Lake, l., Zam.	C4	68
Bangweulu Swamps, sw., Zam.	C5	68
Bangxu, China	J2	42
Ban Hatgnao, Laos	E8	48
Ban Hèt, Laos	E8	48
Ban Hom, Thai.	E4	48
Ban Hong Muang, Laos	D7	48
Ban Houayxay, Laos	B5	48
Bani, C.A.R.	C4	66
Baní, Dom. Rep.	C12	102
Bani, Jbel, mts., Mor.	D3	64
Baniara, Pap. N. Gui.	b4	79a
Bani Bangou, Niger	F5	64
Banihāl Pass, p., India	B4	46
Banī Walīd, Libya	A2	62
Bāniyās, Golan	E6	58
Bāniyās, Syria	C6	58
Banja Luka, Bos.	E4	26
Banjarmasin, Indon.	E9	50
Banjul (Bathurst), Gam.	G1	64
Bānka, India	F11	54
Banka Banka, Austl.	C6	74
Ban Katèp, Laos	D7	48
Ban Kèngkabao, Laos	D7	48
Ban Kèngtangan, Laos	D7	48
Ban Kheun, Laos	B5	48
Ban Khuan Mao, Thai.	I4	48
Ban Kruat, Thai.	E6	48
Banks, Al., U.S.	F13	122
Banks, Îles (Banks Islands), is., Vanuatu	i16	79d
Banks Island, i., B.C., Can.	E4	106
Banks Island, i., N.T., Can.	B15	140
Banks Islands see Banks, Îles, is., Vanuatu	i16	79d
Banks Lake, res., Wa., U.S.	C7	136
Banks Peninsula, pen., N.Z.	F5	80
Banks Strait, strt., Austl.	n13	77a
Banks / Torres, state, Vanuatu	i16	79d
Bānkura, India	G11	54
Ban Mae La Luang, Thai.	C3	48
Ban Mit, Laos	C5	48
Ban Muangngat, Laos	C6	48
Bann, stm., N. Ire., U.K.	F6	12
Ban Nadou, Laos	E7	48
Ban Nahin, Laos	C7	48
Ban Nalan, Laos	E7	48
Ban Nam Chan, Thai.	C6	48
Ban Namnga, Laos	B6	48
Ban Nam Thaeng, Thai.	E7	48
Ban Naxouang, Laos	C7	48
Bannertown, N.C., U.S.	H5	114
Banning, Ca., U.S.	J9	134
Ban Nong Lumphuk, Thai.	E6	48
Bannu, Pak.	B3	54
Bañolas see Banyoles, Spain	B13	20
Baños, Ec.	H2	86
Banow, Afg.	B10	56
Ban Pak Bong, Thai.	C4	48
Ban Pakkhop, Laos	C5	48
Ban Pak Nam, Thai.	G4	48
Ban Phai, Thai.	D6	48
Ban Phai, Thai.	D6	48
Ban Pho, Thai.	F5	48
Ban Phông Pho, Laos	E7	48
Ban Pong, Thai.	F4	48
Ban Sa-ang, Laos	D7	48
Ban Salik, Thai.	C5	48
Ban Sam Pong, Laos	C6	48
Ban Samrong, Thai.	E6	48
Bānsda, India	H4	54
Banshadhāra, stm., India	B6	53
Banská Bystrica, Slov.	H15	16
Banská Štiavnica, Slov.	H14	16
Bansko, Blg.	H10	26
Ban Songkhon, Laos	C7	48
Bānswāra, India	G5	54
Bantaeng, Indon.	F11	50
Ban Takhlo, Thai.	E5	48
Bantarkawung, Indon.	G6	50
Bantayan, Phil.	E4	52
Ban Thabôk, Laos	C6	48
Ban Thapayi, Laos	D7	48
Ban Tian Sa, Laos	C6	48
Bantry, Ire.	J3	12
Bantry Bay, b., Ire.	J3	12
Ban Van Hom, Laos	C7	48
Ban Xènkhalôk, Laos	C5	48
Banya, Testa de la, c., Spain	D11	20
Banyak, Kepulauan, is., Indon.	K3	48
Ban Ya Plong, Thai.	H4	48
Banyo, Cam.	C2	66
Banyoles, Spain	B13	20
Banyuwangi, Indon.	H9	50
Banzare Coast, cst., Ant.	B17	81
Baode, China	B4	42
Baoding, China	B6	42
Baofeng, China	E5	42
Bao Ha, Viet.	A7	48
Baoji, China	D2	42
Baojing, China	G3	42
Bao Lac, Viet.	G8	48
Bao Lac, Viet.	A7	48
Baolunyuan, China	E1	42
Baoqing, China	B11	36
Baoshan, China	F4	36
Baoting, China	L3	42
Baotou, China	A4	42
Baoulé, stm., Mali	G3	64
Baowei, China	A8	48
Baoyi, China	E7	42
Baoying, China	E8	42
Bāpatla, India	D5	53
Bapaume, Fr.	D11	14
Baptiste Lake, res., On., Can.	C12	112
Bāqa el Gharbiyya, Isr.	F6	58
Baqing, China	B14	54
Baʿqūbah, Iraq	C5	56
Baquedano, Chile	A3	92
Bar, Yugo.	G6	26
Bara, Nig.	G7	64
Baraawe, Som.	D8	66
Barabinsk, Russia	C13	32
Barabinskaja step', pl., Russia	C13	32
Baraboo, Wi., U.S.	H9	118
Baraboo, stm., Wi., U.S.	H8	118
Baracaldo see Barakaldo, Spain	A8	20
Baracoa, Cuba	B10	102
Baradero, Arg.	F8	92
Baradine, Austl.	H7	76
Baraga, Mi., U.S.	B1	112
Bārah, Sudan	E6	62
Barahona, Dom. Rep.	C12	102
Barak, Tur.	B8	58
Barāk, stm., India	F14	54
Barakaldo, Spain	A8	20
Baraki, Afg.	B2	54
Barakula, Austl.	F8	76
Baralaba, Austl.	E7	76
Baram, stm., Malay.	A9	50
Barama, stm., Guy.	D12	86
Bārāmati, India	B2	53
Bāramūla, India	A5	54
Baran', Bela.	F13	10
Bārān, India	F6	54
Baranagar, India	G12	54
Baranavičy, Bela.	G9	10
Barangbarang, Indon.	G12	50
Baranoa, Col.	B4	86
Baranof Island, i., Ak., U.S.	E12	140
Barany, Russia	C12	10
Baranya, state, Hung.	D5	26
Barão de Grajaú, Braz.	D4	88
Barão de Melgaço, Braz.	G6	84
Barão de Tromai, Braz.	A3	88
Baraški, Russia	D24	8
Barataria, La., U.S.	H8	122
Barataria Bay, b., La., U.S.	H8	122
Barat Daya, Kepulauan (Barat Daya Islands), is., Indon.	G8	44
Barat Daya Islands see Barat Daya, Kepulauan, is., Indon.	G8	44
Barauana, stm., Braz.	G11	86
Barauni, India	F10	54
Baraut, India	D6	54
Baraya, Col.	F4	86
Barbacena, Braz.	K4	88
Barbacoas, Col.	G2	86
Barbadillo del Mercado, Spain	B7	20
Barbados, ctry., N.A.	h16	96a
Barbalha, Braz.	D6	88
Barbar, Sudan	D6	62
Barbaria, Cap de, c., Spain	F12	20
Barbas, Cap, c., W. Sah.	E1	64
Barbaši, Russia	C11	10
Barbastro, Spain	B10	20
Barbate, Spain	H4	20
Barbeau Peak, mtn., Nu., Can.	A10	141
Barberena, Guat.	E2	102
Barberton, S. Afr.	D10	70
Barberton, Oh., U.S.	C4	114
Barbil, India	G10	54
Barbosa, Col.	E5	86
Barbuda, i., Antig.	e4	105b
Barby, Ger.	E7	16
Bârca, Rom.	F10	26
Barcaldine, Austl.	D5	76
Barcău (Berettyó), stm., Eur.	B8	26
Barcellona Pozzo di Gotto, Italy	F9	24
Barcelona, Mex.	B7	100
Barcelona, Spain	C13	20
Barcelona, Ven.	B9	86
Barcelona, co., Spain	C13	20
Barceloneta, P.R.	B2	104a
Barcelos, Braz.	H10	86
Barcelos, Port.	C2	20
Barcin, Pol.	D13	16
Barcoo, stm., Austl.	E4	76
Barczewo, Pol.	C16	16
Barda del Medio, Arg.	I3	92
Bardaï, Chad	C3	62
Bardawîl, Sabkhet el-, b., Egypt	G4	58
Barddhamān, India	G11	54
Bardejov, Slov.	G17	16
Bardeskan, Iran	B8	56
Bardīyah, Libya	A5	62
Bardo, Tun.	H4	24
Bārdoli, India	H4	54
Bardstown, Ky., U.S.	G12	120
Bardwell Lake, res., Tx., U.S.	E2	122
Bareilly, India	D7	54
Barentsburg, Nor.	B29	141
Barentsøya, i., Nor.	B30	141
Barents Sea, Eur.	B7	30
Bareta, India	D5	54
Barfleur, Fr.	E7	14
Bargaal, Som.	B10	66
Bargara, Austl.	E9	76
Bargarh, India	D5	46
Barguzin, stm., Russia	F11	34
Barguzinskij hrebet, mts., Russia	F11	34
Bar Harbor, Me., U.S.	F8	110
Barharwa, India	F11	54
Barhi, India	F10	54
Bāri, India	E6	54
Bari, Italy	C10	24
Baria, stm., Ven.	G8	86
Barī Gāv, Afg.	B1	54
Barigua, Salina de, pl., Ven.	p20	104g
Barillas, Guat.	E2	102
Barīm, i., Yemen	G5	56
Barima, stm., S.A.	C12	86
Barima-Waini, state, Guy.	D12	86
Barinas, P.R.	B2	104a
Barinas, Ven.	C6	86
Barinas, state, Ven.	C7	86
Baring, Cape, c., N.T., Can.	A7	106
Baringo, Lake, l., Kenya	D7	66
Bāripada, India	H11	54
Bariri, Braz.	L1	88
Bârîs, Egypt	C6	62
Bari Sādri, India	F5	54
Barisāl, Bngl.	G13	54
Barisāl, state, Bngl.	G13	54
Barisan, Pegunungan, mts., Indon.	E2	50
Barito, stm., Indon.	E9	50
Barjols, Fr.	F11	18
Barkam, China	E5	36
Barkava, Lat.	D9	10
Barkerville, B.C., Can.	C9	138
Bark Lake, l., On., Can.	C12	112
Barkley, Lake, res., U.S.	H10	120
Barkley Sound, strt., B.C., Can.	H5	138
Barkly East, S. Afr.	G8	70
Barkly Tableland, plat., Austl.	C7	74
Barkly West, S. Afr.	F7	70
Barkol, China	C3	36
Bârlad, Rom.	C14	26
Bârlad, stm., Rom.	D14	26
Bar-le-Duc, Fr.	F14	14
Barlee, Lake, l., Austl.	E3	74
Barletta, Italy	C10	24
Barlinek, Pol.	D11	16
Barling, Ar., U.S.	B4	122
Barlow, Ky., U.S.	G8	120
Barmedman, Austl.	J6	76
Bārmer, India	F3	54
Barmera, Austl.	J3	76
Barnagar, India	G5	54
Barnard Castle, Eng., U.K.	G11	12
Barnaul, Russia	D14	32
Barn Bluff, mtn., Austl.	n12	77a
Barnegat, N.J., U.S.	E11	114
Barnegat Bay, b., N.J., U.S.	E11	114
Barnes Ice Cap, ice, Nu., Can.	A16	106
Barnesville, Ga., U.S.	C1	116
Barnesville, Mn., U.S.	E2	118
Barnesville, Oh., U.S.	E4	114
Barneville-Carteret, Fr.	E7	14
Barnsdall, Ok., U.S.	E12	128
Barnsley, Eng., U.K.	H11	12
Barnstable, Ma., U.S.	C15	114
Barnstaple, Eng., U.K.	J8	12
Barnstaple Bay, b., Eng., U.K.	J8	12
Barnwell, Ab., Can.	G18	138
Barnwell, S.C., U.S.	C4	116
Baro, stm., Afr.	F7	62
Baron Bluff, clf, V.I.U.S.	g10	104c
Baron'ki, Bela.	G15	10
Barora Fa Island, i., Sol. Is.	d8	79b
Barora Ite Island, i., Sol. Is.	d8	79b
Baroua, Niger	G7	64
Barpeta, India	E13	54
Barqah (Cyrenaica), hist. reg., Libya	A4	62
Barques, Pointe aux, c., Mi., U.S.	D7	112
Barquisimeto, Ven.	B7	86
Barra, Braz.	F4	88
Barra, i., Scot., U.K.	D5	12
Barra, Ponta da, c., Moz.	C12	70
Barraba, Austl.	H8	76
Barra da Estiva, Braz.	G5	88
Barra del Colorado, C.R.	G6	102
Barra de Rio Grande, Nic.	F6	102
Barra do Corda, Braz.	C3	88
Barra do Cuanza, Ang.	B1	68
Barra do Garças, Braz.	G7	84
Barra do Mendes, Braz.	F4	88
Barra do Piraí, Braz.	L3	88
Barra do Ribeiro, Braz.	E12	92
Barra Falsa, Ponta da, c., Moz.	C12	70
Barra Mansa, Braz.	L3	88
Barranca, Peru	F2	84
Barrancabermeja, Col.	D4	86
Barrancas, Ven.	C10	86
Barrancas, Ven.	C7	86
Barrancas, stm., Arg.	H2	92
Barranco Azul, Mex.	E3	130
Barranco do Velho, Port.	G3	20
Barranqueras, Arg.	C8	92
Barranquilla, Col.	B4	86
Barranquitas, P.R.	B3	104a
Barras, Braz.	C4	88
Barre, Vt., U.S.	F4	110
Barreal, Arg.	E3	92
Barreiras, Braz.	G3	88
Barreirinha, Braz.	D6	84
Barreiro, Port.	F1	20
Barreiros, Braz.	E8	88
Barren, stm., Ky., U.S.	H11	120
Barren, Nosy, is., Madag.	D7	68
Barren Islands, is., Ak., U.S.	E9	140
Barren River Lake, res., Ky., U.S.	H11	120
Barretos, Braz.	K1	88
Barrhead, Ab., Can.	B16	138
Barrie, On., Can.	D10	112
Barrie Island, i., On., Can.	C7	112
Barrière, B.C., Can.	E10	138
Barrier Range, mts., Austl.	H3	76
Barrigada, Guam	j10	78c
Barrington, N.S., Can.	G11	110
Barrington Tops National Park, p.o.i., Austl.	I8	76
Barringun, Austl.	G5	76
Barrouallie, St. Vin.	o11	105e
Barrow, Arg.	I7	92
Barrow, Ak., U.S.	B8	140
Barrow, stm., Ire.	I5	12
Barrow, Point, c., Ak., U.S.	B8	140
Barrow Creek, Austl.	D6	74
Barrow-in-Furness, Eng., U.K.	G9	12
Barrow Island, i., Austl.	D2	74
Barrows, Mb., Can.	B12	124
Barrow Strait, strt., Nu., Can.	C6	141
Barry, Wales, U.K.	J9	12
Barry, Il., U.S.	E6	120
Barryton, Mi., U.S.	E4	112
Barsalpur, India	D4	54
Bārsi, India	B2	53
Barsinghausen, Ger.	D5	16
Barstow, Ca., U.S.	I8	134
Barstow, Tx., U.S.	C4	130
Bar-sur-Seine, Fr.	F13	14
Bartang, Taj.	B11	56
Barth, Ger.	B8	16
Barthélemy, Deo, p., Viet.	C6	48
Bartholomew, Bayou, stm., U.S.	E7	122
Bartibougou, Burkina	G5	64
Bartica, Guy.	B6	84
Bartın, Tur.	B15	28
Bartle Frere, mtn., Austl.	A5	76
Bartlesville, Ok., U.S.	H2	120
Bartlett, N.H., U.S.	F5	110
Bartlett, Tn., U.S.	B9	122
Bartlett, Tx., U.S.	D10	130
Bartley, Ne., U.S.	A8	128
Barton, Vt., U.S.	F4	110
Bartoszyce, Pol.	B16	16
Bartow, Fl., U.S.	I4	116
Bartow, Ga., U.S.	D3	116
Barú, Volcán, vol., Pan.	H6	102
Bārūk, Jabal al-, mtn., Leb.	E6	58
Barumini, Italy	E2	24
Barumun, stm., Indon.	C2	50
Barung, Nusa, i., Indon.	H8	50
Barus, Indon.	L4	48
Baruun-Urt, Mong.	B7	36
Barvas, Scot., U.K.	C6	12
Barview, Or., U.S.	G2	136
Barwāh, India	G5	54
Barwāni, India	H5	54
Barwick, Ga., U.S.	F2	116
Barwon, stm., Austl.	H6	76
Barybino, Russia	E20	10
Barycz, stm., Pol.	E13	16
Barysaŭ, Bela.	F11	10
Basail, Arg.	C8	92
Basalt, stm., Austl.	B5	76
Basankusu, D.R.C.	D3	66
Basarabeasca, Mol.	C15	26
Basatongwula Shan, mtn., China	B13	54
Basavakalyān, India	C3	53
Basavilbaso, Arg.	F8	92
Bascuñán, Cabo, c., Chile	D2	92
Basel (Bâle), Switz.	C4	22
Basella see Bassella, Spain	B12	20
Basey, Phil.	E5	52
Bashi Channel, strt., Asia	K9	42
Bashkortostan see Baškirija, state, Russia	D9	32
Basilan Island, i., Phil.	G4	52
Basilan Strait, strt., Phil.	G4	52
Basildon, Eng., U.K.	J13	12
Basile, La., U.S.	G6	122
Basilicata, state, Italy	D10	24
Basin, Mt., U.S.	D14	136
Basin, Wy., U.S.	C4	126
Basingstoke, Eng., U.K.	J11	12
Basin Lake, l., Sk., Can.	B8	124
Basīrhāt, India	G12	54
Baskahegan Lake, l., Me., U.S.	E8	110
Baskakovka, Russia	F17	10
Başkale, Tur.	B5	56
Baskatong, Réservoir, res., Qc., Can.	B13	112
Basket Lake, l., On., Can.	B6	118
Baškirija, state, Russia	D9	32
Baskomutan Milli Parkı, p.o.i., Tur.	E13	28
Basmat, India	B3	53
Bāsoda, India	G6	54
Basoko, D.R.C.	D4	66
Basora, Punt, c., Aruba	p20	104g
Basque Provinces see Euskal Herriko, state, Spain	A8	20
Basra see Al-Başrah, Iraq	C6	56
Bas-Rhin, state, Fr.	F16	14
Bassano, Ab., Can.	F18	138
Bassano del Grappa, Italy	E8	22
Bassari, Togo	H5	64
Bassas da India, rf., Reu.	E6	68
Bassein, stm., Mya.	D2	48
Bassella, Spain	B12	20
Basse Santa Su, Gam.	G2	64
Basse-Terre, Guad.	i5	105c
Basseterre, St. K./N.	C2	105a
Basse Terre, Trin.	s12	105f
Basse-Terre, i., Guad.	h5	105c
Bassett, Ne., U.S.	E13	126
Bassett, Va., U.S.	H6	114
Bassfield, Ms., U.S.	F9	122
Bassikounou, Maur.	F3	64
Bassila, Benin	H5	64
Bass River, N.S., Can.	E13	110
Bass Strait, strt., Austl.	L6	76
Basswood Lake, l., N.A.	C6	118
Båstad, Swe.	H5	8
Bastenaken see Bastogne, Bel.	D14	14
Bastersberge, hill, S. Afr.	G5	70
Basti, India	E9	54
Bastia, Fr.	G15	18
Bastogne, Bel.	D14	14
Bastrop, La., U.S.	E6	122
Bastrop, Tx., U.S.	D10	130
Basu, Pulau, i., Indon.	D3	50
Basutoland see Lesotho, ctry., Afr.	F9	70
Bata, Eq. Gui.	I6	64
Bataan Peninsula, pen., Phil.	C3	52
Batabanó, Golfo de, b., Cuba	A6	102
Batac, Phil.	A3	52
Batagaj, Russia	C15	34
Batagaj-Alyta, Russia	C15	34
Batak, Blg.	H11	26
Batala, India	C5	54
Batalha, Braz.	E7	88
Batalha, Port.	E2	20
Batam, Pulau, i., Indon.	C3	50
Batamaj, Russia	D14	34
Batang, China	E5	36
Batangafo, C.A.R.	C3	66
Batangas, Phil.	D3	52
Batangtoru, Indon.	C1	50
Batan Islands, is., Phil.	K9	42
Batanta, Pulau, i., Indon.	F9	44
Batatais, Braz.	K2	88
Batavia, Arg.	G5	92
Batavia see Jakarta, Indon.	G5	50
Batavia, Il., U.S.	C9	120
Batavia, Ia., U.S.	D5	120
Batavia, N.Y., U.S.	A7	114
Batchelor, Austl.	B6	74
Bătdâmbâng, Camb.	F6	48
Bateckij, Russia	B13	10
Batemans Bay, Austl.	J8	76
Bates, Mount, mtn., Norf. I.	y24	78i
Batesburg, S.C., U.S.	C4	116
Batesville, Ar., U.S.	B7	122
Batesville, Ms., U.S.	C9	122
Batesville, Tx., U.S.	F8	130
Bath, N.B., Can.	D9	110
Bath, Eng., U.K.	J10	12
Bath, Me., U.S.	G7	110
Bath, N.Y., U.S.	B8	114
Batha, stm., Chad	E3	62
Bathgate, N.D., U.S.	F16	124
Bathinda, India	C5	54
Bathsheba, Barb.	n8	105d
Bathurst, Austl.	I7	76
Bathurst, N.B., Can.	C11	110
Bathurst see Banjul, Gam.	G1	64
Bathurst, Cape, c., N.T., Can.	A5	106
Bathurst Inlet, Nu., Can.	B9	106
Bathurst Island, i., Austl.	B5	74
Bathurst Island, i., Nu., Can.	B5	141
Batlow, Austl.	J6	76
Batman, Tur.	B5	56
Batna, Alg.	B6	64
Ba To, Viet.	E9	48
Baton Rouge, La., U.S.	G7	122
Batouri, Cam.	D2	66
Batsawul, Afg.	A3	54
Batson, Tx., U.S.	G4	122
Batterie, Pointe de la, c., Mart.	k7	105c
Batticaloa, Sri L.	H5	53
Battipaglia, Italy	D8	24
Battle, stm., Can.	D19	138
Battle Creek, Mi., U.S.	F4	112
Battle Creek, Ne., U.S.	F15	126
Battle Creek, stm., N.A.	F4	124
Battle Ground, In., U.S.	H3	112
Battle Ground, Wa., U.S.	E4	136
Battle Harbour, Nf., Can.	i22	107a
Battle Mountain, Nv., U.S.	C8	134
Battle Mountain, mtn., Wy., U.S.	B9	132
Batu, mtn., Eth.	F7	62
Batu, Kepulauan, is., Indon.	F2	44
Batu-Batu, Indon.	F11	50
Batu Berincang, Gunong, mtn., Malay.	J5	48
Batubrok, Bukit, mtn., Indon.	C9	50
Batu Gajah, Malay.	J5	48
Batukelau, Indon.	C9	50
Batumi, Geor.	F6	32
Batu Pahat, Malay.	L6	48
Batupanjang, Indon.	C2	50
Baturaja, Indon.	F3	50
Baturino, Russia	C15	32
Baturité, Braz.	C6	88
Baturusa, Indon.	D5	50
Batusangkar, Indon.	D2	50
Batz, Île de, i., Fr.	F4	14
Bau, Malay.	C7	50
Baubau, Indon.	G7	44
Bauchi, Nig.	G6	64
Bauda, India	H10	54
Baudette, Mn., U.S.	C4	118
Baudó, stm., Col.	E3	86
Bauld, Cape, c., Nf., Can.	i22	107a
Bauman Fiord, b., Nu., Can.	B8	141
Baume-les-Dames, Fr.	G15	14
Baures, Bol.	B4	90
Bauru, Braz.	L1	88
Bauska, Lat.	D7	10
Bautzen, Ger.	E10	16
Bauxite, Ar., U.S.	C6	122
Bavaria see Bayern, state, Ger.	H7	16
Bavarian Alps, mts., Eur.	I7	16
Båven, l., Swe.	G7	8
Bavispe, Mex.	F8	98
Bavispe, stm., Mex.	F8	98
Bawang, Indon.	G6	50
Bawdwin, Mya.	A3	48
Bawean, Pulau, i., Indon.	F8	50
Bawiti, Egypt	B5	62
Bawmi, Mya.	D2	48
Baxaya, mtn., Som.	B9	66
Baxian, China	G2	42
Baxian, China	B7	42
Baxter, Ia., U.S.	C4	120
Baxter, Mn., U.S.	E4	118
Baxter, Tn., U.S.	H12	120
Baxterville, Ms., U.S.	F9	122
Bay, Ar., U.S.	B8	122
Bay, Laguna de, l., Phil.	C3	52
Bayamo, Cuba	B9	102
Bayamón, P.R.	B3	104a
Bayan, China	A7	38
Bayan, Indon.	H10	50
Bayāna, India	E6	54
Bayan Har Shan, mts., China	E4	36
Bayanhongor, Mong.	B5	36
Bayannaobao, China	B2	42
Bayano, Lago, res., Pan.	H8	102
Bayan Obo, China	C7	36
Bayard, Ia., U.S.	C3	120
Bayard, N.M., U.S.	K8	132
Bayard, W.V., U.S.	E6	114
Bayawan, Phil.	F4	52
Baybay, Phil.	E5	52
Bayboro, N.C., U.S.	A9	116
Bayburt, Tur.	A5	56
Bay City, Mi., U.S.	E6	112
Bay City, Or., U.S.	E3	136
Bay City, Tx., U.S.	F12	130
Baydhabo (Baidoa), Som.	D8	66
Baydrag, stm., Mong.	B4	36
Bayern (Bavaria), state, Ger.	H7	16
Bayeux, Braz.	D8	88
Bayeux, Fr.	E8	14
Bayfield, Co., U.S.	F9	132
Bayfield, Wi., U.S.	E8	118
Bayındır, Tur.	E10	28
Baykonur see Bajkonur, Kaz.	E11	32
Bay Minette, Al., U.S.	G11	122
Bayombong, Phil.	B3	52
Bayona see Baiona, Spain	B2	20
Bayonne, Fr.	F4	18
Bayou Bodcau Reservoir, res., La., U.S.	E5	122
Bayou Cane, La., U.S.	H8	122
Bayou D'Arbonne Lake, res., La., U.S.	E6	122
Bayovar, Peru	E1	84
Bay Port, Mi., U.S.	E6	112
Bayport, Mn., U.S.	F6	118
Bayramiç, Tur.	D9	28
Bayreuth, Ger.	G7	16

Name — Map Ref. — Page

Bayrūt (Beirut), Leb. E6 58
Bays, Lake of, l., On., Can. C10 112
Bay Saint Louis, Ms., U.S. G9 122
Bay Shore, N.Y., U.S. D12 114
Bayside, On., Can. D12 112
Bay Springs Lake, res., Ms., U.S. C10 122
Bayt ad-Dīn, Leb. E6 58
Bayt al-Faqīh, Yemen G3 56
Bayt Laḥm (Bethlehem), W.B. G6 58
Baytown, Tx., U.S. H4 122
Bayyāʿīyah al-Kabīrah, Syria C8 58
Baza, Spain G8 20
Bazardüzü dağ, mtn., Azer. A6 56
Bazaruto, Ilha do, i., Moz. B12 70
Bazhong, China F2 42
Baziège, Fr. F7 18
Bazine, Ks., U.S. C9 128
Be, stm., Viet. G8 48
Be, Nosy, i., Madag. C8 68
Beach Haven, N.J., U.S. E11 114
Beachport, Austl. K3 76
Beachville, On., Can. E9 112
Beachy Head, c., Eng., U.K. K13 12
Beacon, Austl. F3 74
Beacon, N.Y., U.S. C12 114
Beacon Hill, Wa., U.S. D3 136
Beaconsfield, Austl. n13 77a
Beagle Gulf, b., Austl. B5 74
Bealanana, Madag. C8 68
Bealdoaivi see Peäldoajvi, mtn., Fin. B12 8
Beale, Cape, c., B.C., Can. H5 138
Beals Creek, stm., Tx., U.S. B7 130
Bear, stm., U.S. I14 136
Bear, stm., Ca., U.S. D4 134
Bear Bay, b., Nu., Can. B8 141
Bear Creek, stm., U.S. C10 122
Bear Creek, stm., U.S. D6 128
Bearden, Ar., U.S. D6 122
Beardmore, On., Can. B11 118
Bear Island, i., Ant. C29 81
Bear Island, i., Ire. J3 12
Bear Island see Bjørnøya, i., Nor. B5 30
Bear Lake, l., Ab., Can. A11 138
Bear Lake, l., U.S. A5 132
Bear Mountain, mtn., Or., U.S. G3 136
Béarn, hist. reg., Fr. F5 18
Bear River, N.S., Can. F11 110
Bear River Range, mts., U.S. B5 132
Beartooth Pass, p., Wy., U.S. C3 126
Bear Town, Ms., U.S. F8 122
Beās, stm., India C6 54
Beasain, Spain A8 20
Beata, Cabo, c., Dom. Rep. D12 102
Beata, Isla, i., Dom. Rep. D12 102
Beaton, B.C., Can. F13 138
Beatrice, Al., U.S. F11 122
Beatrice, Ne., U.S. A12 128
Beatrice, Cape, c., Austl. B7 74
Beattie, Ks., U.S. L2 118
Beatton, stm., B.C., Can. D6 106
Beatty, Nv., U.S. G9 134
Beattyville, Ky., U.S. G2 114
Beaucaire, Fr. F10 18
Beauce, reg., Fr. F10 14
Beauceville, Qc., Can. D6 110
Beauchêne, Lac, l., Qc., Can. B11 112
Beauchêne Island, i., Falk. Is. J5 90
Beaudesert, Austl. F9 76
Beaufort, Malay. A9 50
Beaufort, S.C., U.S. D5 116
Beaufort Castle see Qal'at ash-Shaqīf, hist., Leb. E6 58
Beaufort Sea, N.A. B12 140
Beaufort West, S. Afr. H6 70
Beaugency, Fr. G10 14
Beauharnois, Qc., Can. E2 110
Beaujolais, hist. reg., Fr. C10 18
Beaumont, Fr. E7 14
Beaumont, N.Z. G3 80
Beaumont, Ca., U.S. J8 134
Beaumont, Ms., U.S. F9 122
Beaumont, Tx., U.S. G4 122
Beaumont Hill, hill, Austl. H5 76
Beaune, Fr. G13 14
Beauport, Qc., Can. D5 110
Beaupré, Qc., Can. C6 110
Beaurepaire, Fr. D11 18
Beausejour, Mb., Can. D17 124
Beauséjour, Guad. h6 105c
Beauvais, Fr. E11 14
Beauvoir-sur-Mer, Fr. H6 14
Beaver, Ak., U.S. C10 140
Beaver, Ok., U.S. E8 128
Beaver, Pa., U.S. D5 114
Beaver, Ut., U.S. E4 132
Beaver, stm., Can. E9 106
Beaver, stm., Can. C6 106
Beaver, stm., U.S. E9 128
Beaver, stm., Ut., U.S. E3 132
Beaver Creek, stm., U.S. G9 124
Beaver Creek, stm., U.S. D8 126
Beaver Creek, stm., U.S. A8 128
Beaver Creek, stm., Co., U.S. G9 126
Beaver Creek, stm., Mt., U.S. F6 124
Beaver Creek, stm., Ne., U.S. F14 126
Beaver Creek, stm., Ne., U.S. G14 126
Beaver Creek, stm., Ok., U.S. G10 128
Beaver Creek, stm., Tx., U.S. H9 128
Beaver Crossing, Ne., U.S. G15 126
Beaver Dam, Ky., U.S. G11 120
Beaver Dam, Wi., U.S. H9 118
Beaverdell, B.C., Can. G11 138
Beaver Falls, Pa., U.S. D5 114
Beaverhead, stm., Mt., U.S. E14 136
Beaverhead Mountains, mts., U.S. E13 136
Beaverhill Lake, l., Ab., Can. C18 138
Beaverhouse Lake, l., On., Can. C6 118
Beaver Island, i., Mi., U.S. C4 112
Beaver Lake, l., Ab., Can. B19 138
Beaver Lake, res., Ar., U.S. H4 120
Beaverlodge, Ab., Can. A11 138
Beaverton, On., Can. D10 112
Beaverton, Mi., U.S. E5 112
Beaverton, Or., U.S. E4 136
Beāwar, India E5 54
Beazley, Arg. F4 92
Bebedouro, Braz. K1 88
Becal, Mex. B2 102
Bécancour, stm., Qc., Can. D5 110
Beccles, Eng., U.K. I14 12
Bečej, Yugo. D6 26
Beceni, Rom. D13 26
Bečevinka, Russia G17 8
Béchar, Alg. C4 64
Becharof Lake, l., Ak., U.S. E8 140
Bechevin Bay, b., Ak., U.S. E7 140
Bechuanaland, hist. reg., S. Afr. E5 70
Bechuanaland see Botswana, ctry., Afr. E3 68
Bechyně, Czech Rep. G10 16
Beckley, W.V., U.S. G4 114
Beckum, Ger. E4 16
Bédarieux, Fr. F9 18
Bedelē, Eth. F7 62
Bedford, Qc., Can. E4 110
Bedford, S. Afr. H8 70
Bedford, Eng., U.K. I12 12
Bedford, In., U.S. F11 120
Bedford, Ia., U.S. D3 120
Bedford, Ky., U.S. F12 120
Bedford, Pa., U.S. D7 114
Bedford, Tx., U.S. B10 130
Bedi, India G3 54
Bedoba, Russia C17 32
Bedourie, Austl. E2 76
Bedworth, Eng., U.K. I11 12
Beebe, Ar., U.S. B7 122
Beechal Creek, stm., Austl. F5 76
Beech Creek, Ky., U.S. G10 120
Beech Fork, stm., Ky., U.S. G12 120
Beech Grove, In., U.S. I3 112
Beechworth, Austl. K6 76
Beechy, Sk., Can. D6 124
Beecroft Head, c., Austl. J8 76
Beemer, Ne., U.S. J2 118
Beenleigh, Austl. F9 76
Bee Ridge, Fl., U.S. I3 116
Beersheba see Be'ér Sheva', Isr. G6 58
Beersheba Springs, Tn., U.S. B13 122
Be'ér Sheva' (Beersheba), Isr. G6 58
Beeskow, Ger. D10 16
Beeville, Tx., U.S. F10 130
Befale, D.R.C. D4 66
Befandriana Avaratra, Madag. E7 68
Bega, Austl. K7 76
Bega, stm., Eur. D9 26
Begamganj, India G7 54
Begur, Cap de, c., Spain C14 20
Begusarai, India F11 54
Behbahān, Iran C7 56
Behshahr, Iran B7 56
Bei, stm., China J5 42
Bei'an, China B10 36
Beibei, China G2 42
Beicheng, China G5 36
Beigi, Eth. F6 62
Beihai, China K3 42
Beijing (Peking), China B7 42
Beijing, state, China B6 42
Beili, China L3 42
Beiliu, China J4 42
Beinamar, Chad F3 62
Beipa, Pap. N. Gui. b4 79a
Beipan, stm., China I1 42
Beipiao, China D4 38
Beira, Moz. A12 70
Beira, hist. reg., Port. E3 20
Beiru, stm., China D5 42
Beirut see Bayrūt, Leb. E6 58
Beiseker, Ab., Can. E17 138
Beishan, China I3 42
Bei Shan, mts., China C4 36
Beitbridge, Zimb. C10 70
Beizhen, China D4 38
Beja, Port. G3 20
Beja, Tun. H3 24
Beja, state, Port. G3 20
Bejaïa, Alg. B6 64
Béjar, Spain D5 20
Bejhi, stm., Pak. D2 54
Bejneu, Kaz. E9 32
Bejuco, Pan. H8 102
Bekaa Valley see Al-Biqā', val., Leb. D7 58
Bekabad, Uzb. F11 32
Bekdaš, Turkmen. A7 56
Békés, Hung. C8 26
Békés, state, Hung. C7 26
Békéscsaba, Hung. C7 26
Bekilli, Tur. E12 28
Bekily, Madag. E8 68
Bekodoka, Madag. D7 68
Bekopaka, Madag. D7 68
Bela, India F9 54
Bela, Pak. D10 56
Belaazërsk, Bela. H8 10
Bela Crkva, Yugo. E8 26
Belaga, Malay. B8 50
Bel Air, Md., U.S. E9 114
Belaja, stm., Russia C8 32
Belaja Gora, Russia B14 10
Belambanganumpu, Indon. F4 50
Belampalli, India B4 53
Bela Palanka, Yugo. F9 26
Belarus, ctry., Eur. E14 6
Belaruskaja hrada, mts., Bela. F10 10
Belau see Palau, ctry., Oc. g8 78b
Bela Vista, Braz. D5 90
Bela Vista, Moz. E11 70
Belawan, Indon. B1 50
Belayan, stm., Indon. C10 50
Bełchatów, Pol. E15 16
Belcher, La., U.S. E5 122
Belcheragh, Afg. B10 56
Belcher Channel, strt., Nu., Can. B6 141
Belcher Islands, is., Nu., Can. D14 106
Belding, Mi., U.S. E4 112
Belebelka, Russia C13 10
Beledweyne, Som. D8 66
Belém, Braz. A1 88
Belém, Moz. C6 68
Belém de São Francisco, Braz. E6 88
Belén, Arg. C4 92
Belén, Nic. G4 102
Belén, Para. D5 90
Belen, Tur. B7 58
Belen, N.M., U.S. I10 132
Belén, Ur. E9 92
Belén, stm., Arg. C4 92
Belep, Îles, is., N. Cal. I14 79d
Belesar, Embalse de, res., Spain B3 20
Belëv, Russia G19 10
Belfast, S. Afr. D9 70
Belfast, N. Ire., U.K. G6 12
Belfast, Me., U.S. F7 110
Belfield, N.D., U.S. H10 124
Belford, Eng., U.K. F11 12
Belfort, Fr. G15 14
Belfry, Mt., U.S. B3 126
Belgaum, India D2 53
Belgium, ctry., Eur. D13 14
Belgorod, Russia D5 32
Belgrade, Mt., U.S. E15 136
Belgrade, Ne., U.S. F14 126
Belgrade see Beograd, Yugo. E7 26
Belgrano II, sci., Ant. C36 81
Belhaven, N.C., U.S. A9 116
Belick, Bela. H13 10
Beliliou, i., Palau D9 44
Belin, Fr. E5 18
Belin-Béliet see Belin, Fr. E5 18
Belington, W.V., U.S. E5 114
Belinyu, Indon. D4 50
Belitung, i., Indon. E5 50
Belize, ctry., N.A. D3 102
Belize, stm., Belize D3 102
Belize City, Belize D3 102
Belkovskij, ostrov see Bel'kovskij, ostrov, i., Russia A16 34
Bel'kovskij, ostrov, i., Russia A16 34
Bella Bella, B.C., Can. D2 138
Bellac, Fr. C7 18
Bella Coola, B.C., Can. D4 138
Bella Coola, stm., B.C., Can. D4 138
Bellaire, Fl., U.S. F4 116
Bellaire, Oh., U.S. D5 114
Bellaire, Tx., U.S. H3 122
Bellamy, Al., U.S. E10 122
Bellaria, Italy F9 22
Bellary, India D3 53
Bellata, Austl. G7 76
Bella Unión, Ur. E9 92
Bella Vista, Arg. C5 92
Bella Vista, Arg. D8 92
Bellavista, Peru E2 84
Bellbrook, Austl. H9 76
Belle, W.V., U.S. F4 114
Bellefontaine, Mart. k6 105c
Bellefontaine, Oh., U.S. D2 114
Bellefonte, Pa., U.S. D8 114
Belle Fourche, S.D., U.S. C9 126
Belle Fourche, stm., U.S. C10 126
Bellegarde-sur-Valserine, Fr. C11 18
Belle Glade, Fl., U.S. J5 116
Belle Hôtesse, mtn., Guad. h5 105c
Belle-Île, i., Fr. G5 14
Belle Isle, i., Nf., Can. i22 107a
Belle Isle, Strait of, strt., Nf., Can. i22 107a
Bellenden Ker National Park, p.o.i., Austl. A5 76
Belle Plaine, Ia., U.S. C5 120
Belle Plaine, Ks., U.S. D11 128
Belle Plaine, Mn., U.S. G5 118
Belleview, Fl., U.S. G11 122
Belleville, On., Can. D12 112
Belleville, Il., U.S. F8 120
Belleville, Ks., U.S. B11 128
Belleville, Pa., U.S. D8 114
Belleville-sur-Saône, Fr. C10 18
Bellevue, Ab., Can. G16 138
Bellevue, Id., U.S. G12 136
Bellevue, Ia., U.S. B7 120
Bellevue, Mi., U.S. F4 112
Bellevue, Ne., U.S. C2 120
Bellevue, Oh., U.S. C3 114
Bellevue, Wa., U.S. C4 136
Belley, Fr. D11 18
Bellingham, Mn., U.S. F2 118
Bellingham, Wa., U.S. B4 136
Bellinghausen, sci., Ant. B35 81
Bellingshausen Sea, Ant. P29 142
Bellinzona, Switz. D6 22
Bell Lake, l., On., Can. B7 118
Bellmead, Tx., U.S. C10 130
Bello, Col. D4 86
Bellot Strait, strt., Nu., Can. A12 106
Bell Peninsula, pen., Nu., Can. C14 106
Bells, Tn., U.S. B9 122
Bells, Tx., U.S. D2 122
Bells Corners, On., Can. C14 112
Belluno, Italy D9 22
Bell Ville, Arg. F6 92
Bellville, S. Afr. H4 70
Bellwood, Ne., U.S. F15 126
Bellwood, Pa., U.S. D7 114
Belly, stm., N.A. G17 138
Bellyk, Russia D16 32
Belmond, Ia., U.S. B4 120
Belmont, N.S., Can. E13 110
Belmont, S. Afr. F7 70
Belmont, N.H., U.S. G5 110
Belmont, Wi., U.S. B7 120
Belmonte, Braz. H6 88
Belmonte, Port. D3 20
Belmonte, Spain A4 20
Belmopan, Belize D3 102
Beloe, Russia B22 10
Beloe, ozero, l., Russia F17 8
Beloe more (White Sea), Russia D18 8
Belogorsk, Russia F14 34
Belo Horizonte, Braz. J3 88
Beloit, Ks., U.S. B10 128
Beloit, Wi., U.S. B8 120
Belo Jardim, Braz. E7 88
Belomestnaja, Russia H20 10
Belomorsk, Russia D16 8
Beloreck, Russia D9 32
Belören, Tur. F15 28
Belorussia see Belarus, ctry., Eur. E14 6
Beloščele, Russia D22 8
Belo sur Mer, Madag. E7 68
Belot, Lac, l., N.T., Can. B5 106
Belo Tsiribihina, Madag. D7 68
Belousovo, Russia E19 10
Belovo, Russia D15 32
Belozërsk, Russia F17 8
Belpre, Oh., U.S. E4 114
Belt, Mt., U.S. C16 136
Beltana, Austl. H2 76
Belt Creek, stm., Mt., U.S. C16 136
Belton, Mo., U.S. F3 120
Belton, Tx., U.S. C10 130
Belton Lake, res., Tx., U.S. C10 130
Beltrán, Arg. C5 92
Belukha, Mount, mtn., Asia E15 32
Belūr, India E2 53
Beluran, Malay. H1 52
Belvedere Marittimo, Italy E9 24
Belvidere, Il., U.S. B9 120
Belvidere, N.J., U.S. D10 114
Belview, Mn., U.S. G3 118
Belvoir see Kokhav HaYarden, hist., Isr. F6 58
Belyando, stm., Austl. D6 76
Belye Berega, Russia G17 10
Belye Stolby, Russia E20 10
Belyj Gorodok, Russia C20 10
Belyj Jar, Russia C15 32
Bełżec, Pol. F19 16
Belzig, Ger. D8 16
Belzoni, Ms., U.S. D8 122
Bement, Il., U.S. E9 120
Bemidji, Mn., U.S. D3 118
Benaco see Garda, Lago di, l., Italy E7 22
Bena-Dibele, D.R.C. E4 66
Benagerie, Austl. H3 76
Benalla, Austl. K6 76
Benares see Vārānasi, India F9 54
Ben Arous, Tun. H4 24
Benavarri, Spain B11 20
Benavente, Spain B5 20
Benbecula, i., Scot., U.K. D5 12
Ben Bolt, Tx., U.S. G9 130
Ben Cat, Viet. G8 48
Bencha, Khao Phanom, mtn., Thai. H4 48
Ben-Chicao, Col de, p., Alg. H13 20
Bencubbin, Austl. F3 74
Bend, Or., U.S. F5 136
Bendemeer, Austl. H8 76
Bender Cassim see Boosaaso, Som. B9 66
Bendigo, Austl. K5 76
Bēne, Lat. D6 10
Benedito Leite, Braz. D3 88
Benepú, Rada, anch., Chile f29 78l
Benevento, Italy C8 24
Bèng, stm., Laos B5 48
Bengal, Bay of, b., Asia F6 46
Bengara, Indon. B10 50
Bengasi see Banghāzī, Libya A3 62
Bengbu, China E7 42
Benghazi see Banghāzī, Libya A3 62
Bengkalis, Indon. C3 50
Bengkalis, Pulau, i., Indon. C3 50
Bengkayang, Indon. C6 50
Bengkulu, Indon. E3 50
Bengkulu, state, Indon. E3 50
Bengough, Sk., Can. E8 124
Benguela, Ang. C1 68
Benguerua, Ilha, i., Moz. B12 70
Benha, Egypt H2 58
Beni, D.R.C. D5 66
Beni, stm., Bol. B3 90
Béni Abbas, Alg. C4 64
Beni'Adi el-Baharīya, Egypt K1 58
Beni Ahmad, Egypt J1 58
Benicarló, Spain D11 20
Benidorm, Spain F10 20
Beni Mazâr, Egypt J1 58
Beni Muhammadîyat, Egypt K2 58
Benin, ctry., Afr. G5 64
Benin, Bight of, b., Afr. I5 64
Benin City, Nig. H6 64
Benisa see Benissa, Spain F11 20
Benissa, Spain F11 20
Beni Suef, Egypt I2 58
Benito, Mb., Can. C12 124
Benito Juárez, Arg. H8 92
Benito Juárez, Presa, res., Mex. G10 100
Benjamin, Tx., U.S. H9 128
Benjamin, Isla, i., Chile H2 90
Benjamin Constant, Braz. D3 84
Benkelman, Ne., U.S. A7 128
Benkovac, Cro. F12 22
Benld, Il., U.S. E8 120
Ben Lomond, Ca., U.S. F3 134
Ben Lomond National Park, p.o.i., Austl. n13 77a
Benndale, Ms., U.S. G10 122
Bennetta, ostrov, i., Russia A18 34
Bennett Island see Bennetta, ostrov, i., Russia A18 34
Bennettsville, S.C., U.S. B6 116
Bennington, Ks., U.S. B11 128
Bennington, Vt., U.S. B12 114
Benoit, Ms., U.S. D7 122
Benoni, S. Afr. E9 70
Ben Sekka, Rass, c., Tun. G3 24
Bensheim, Ger. G4 16
Benson, Az., U.S. L6 132
Benson, Mn., U.S. F3 118
Benson, N.C., U.S. A7 116
Benteng, Indon. G12 50
Ben Thuy, Viet. C7 48
Bentinck Island, i., Austl. C7 74
Bentinck Island, i., Mya. G3 48
Bentiu, Sudan F6 62
Bento Gonçalves, Braz. D12 92
Benton, Ar., U.S. C6 122
Benton, Il., U.S. F9 120
Benton, Ky., U.S. H9 120
Benton, La., U.S. E5 122
Benton, Mo., U.S. G8 120
Benton, Tn., U.S. B14 122
Benton, Wi., U.S. B7 120
Benton Harbor, Mi., U.S. F3 112
Bentonia, Ms., U.S. E8 122
Bentonville, Ar., U.S. H3 120
Ben Tre, Viet. G8 48
Bentung, Malay. K5 48
Benua, Pulau, i., Indon. C5 50
Benue, stm., Afr. H6 64
Ben Wheeler, Tx., U.S. E3 122
Benxi, China D5 38
Beograd (Belgrade), Yugo. E7 26
Beohāri, India F8 54
Béoumi, C. Iv. H3 64
Beowawe, Nv., U.S. C9 134
Beppu, Japan F4 40
Bequia, i., St. Vin. o11 105e
Bequimão, Braz. B3 88
Berat, Alb. D13 24
Berati see Berat, Alb. D13 24
Berau, stm., Indon. B10 50
Berau, Teluk, b., Indon. F9 44
Berazino, Bela. F11 10
Berazino, Bela. G11 10
Berbera, Som. B9 66
Berbérati, C.A.R. D3 66
Berchtesgaden, Ger. I8 16
Berck, Fr. D10 14
Berclair, Tx., U.S. F10 130
Berdians'k, Ukr. E5 32
Berdigestjah, Russia D14 34
Berdsk, Russia D14 32
Berea, Oh., U.S. C4 114
Berea, S.C., U.S. B3 116
Berehomet, Ukr. A12 26
Berehove, Ukr. A9 26
Berekua, Dom. j6 105c
Berekum, Ghana H4 64
Berens, stm., Can. B17 124
Berens Island, i., Mb., Can. B16 124
Berens River, Mb., Can. B16 124
Beresford, N.B., Can. C11 110
Beresford, S.D., U.S. H2 118
Berești, Rom. C14 26
Berettyó (Barcău), stm., Eur. B8 26
Berettyóújfalu, Hung. B8 26
Berezivka, Ukr. B17 26
Bereznik, Russia E20 8
Berezniki, Russia C9 32
Berëzovo, Russia B10 32
Berëzovskij, Russia C15 32
Berëzovskij Rjadok, Russia B17 10
Berga, Spain B12 20
Bergama, Tur. D10 28
Bergamo, Italy E6 22
Bergantín, Ven. C9 86
Bergby, Swe. F7 8
Bergen see Mons, Bel. D12 14
Bergen, Ger. D5 16
Bergen, Nor. F1 8
Bergen, N.Y., U.S. A7 114
Bergen auf Rügen, Ger. B9 16
Bergen op Zoom, Neth. C13 14
Bergerac, Fr. E6 18
Bergisch Gladbach, Ger. F3 16
Bergoo, W.V., U.S. F5 114
Bergsjö, Swe. E7 8
Berguent, Mor. C4 64
Bergville, S. Afr. F9 70
Berhala, Selat, strt., Indon. D4 50
Beringa, ostrov, i., Russia F22 34
Bering Glacier, ice, Ak., U.S. D11 140
Beringovskij, Russia D24 34
Bering Sea D21 142
Bering Strait, strt. C6 140
Berja, Spain H8 20
Berkåk, Nor. E4 8
Berkakit, Russia E14 34
Berkane, Mor. C4 64
Berkeley, Ca., U.S. F3 134
Berkeley Springs, W.V., U.S. E7 114
Berkner Island, i., Ant. C35 81
Berkshire Hills, hills, Ma., U.S. B12 114
Berland, stm., Ab., Can. B13 138
Berlevåg, Nor. A13 8
Berlin, Ger. D9 16
Berlin, N.H., U.S. F5 110
Berlin, N.J., U.S. E11 114
Berlin, Pa., U.S. E7 114
Berlin, Wi., U.S. H9 118
Berlin, state, Ger. D9 16
Berlinguet Inlet, b., Nu., Can. A14 106
Bermagui, Austl. K8 76
Bermejillo, Mex. C7 100
Bermejito, stm., Arg. B7 92
Bermejo, stm., Arg. E4 92
Bermejo, stm., S.A. C8 92
Bermejo, Paso del, p., S.A. F2 92
Bermen, Lac, l., Qc., Can. E17 106
Bermeo, Spain A8 20
Bermuda, dep., N.A. k16 104e
Bern (Berne), Switz. C4 22
Bernalda, Italy D10 24
Bernasconi, Arg. H5 92
Bernau bei Berlin, Ger. D9 16
Bernay, Fr. E9 14
Bernburg, Ger. E7 16
Berndorf, Aus. C12 22
Berne see Bern, Switz. C4 22
Berner Alpen, mts., Switz. D4 22
Berneray, i., Scot., U.K. D5 12
Bernese Alps see Berner Alpen, mts., Switz. D4 22
Bernice, La., U.S. E6 122
Bernie, Mo., U.S. H8 120
Bernier Bay, b., Nu., Can. A12 106
Bernier Island, i., Austl. D2 74
Bernina, Piz, mtn., Eur. H18 14
Bernkastel-Kues, Ger. G3 16
Bernsdorf, Ger. E10 16
Berón de Astrada, Arg. C9 92
Beroroha, Madag. E8 68
Beroun, Czech Rep. G9 16
Berounka, stm., Czech Rep. F9 16
Berre, Étang de, l., Fr. F11 18
Berri, Austl. J3 76
Berriyyane, Alg. C5 64
Berry, Al., U.S. D11 122
Berry, hist. reg., Fr. H11 14
Berry, Canal du, can., Fr. G10 14
Berry Creek, stm., Ab., Can. E19 138
Berryessa, Lake, res., Ca., U.S. E3 134
Berry Islands, is., Bah. B9 96
Berseba, Nmb. D3 70
Bersenbrück, Ger. D3 16
Bershad', Ukr. A16 26
Bertha, Mn., U.S. E3 118
Berthold, N.D., U.S. F12 124
Berthoud, Co., U.S. G7 126
Berthoud Pass, p., Co., U.S. B3 128
Bertoua, Cam. D2 66
Bertrand, Mi., U.S. G3 112
Bertrand, Ne., U.S. G13 126
Beruri, Braz. D5 84
Berwick, La., U.S. H7 122
Berwick, Pa., U.S. C9 114
Berwick-upon-Tweed, Eng., U.K. F11 12
Berwyn, Il., U.S. G2 112
Besalampy, Madag. D7 68
Besançon, Fr. G14 14
Bešankovičy, Bela. E12 10
Besar, Gunong, mtn., Malay. K6 48
Besar, Gunung, vol., Indon. E9 50
Besedz', stm., Eur. H14 10
Beskid Mountains see Beskids, mts., Eur. G15 16
Beskids, mts., Eur. G15 16
Beskra, Alg. C6 64
Beslan, Russia F6 32
Besni, Tur. A8 58
Bessarabia, hist. reg., Eur. C15 26
Bessemer, Al., U.S. D11 122
Bessemer, Mi., U.S. E8 118
Bessemer City, N.C., U.S. A4 116
Bestjah, Russia D15 34
Bestobe, Kaz. D12 32
Bestuževo, Russia F20 8
Betafo, Madag. D8 68
Betanzos, Spain A2 20
Bétaré Oya, Cam. C2 66
Bétera, Spain E10 20
Bethal, S. Afr. E9 70
Bethalto, Il., U.S. F7 120
Bethanien, Nmb. E3 70
Bethany, Mo., U.S. D3 120
Bethany, Ok., U.S. F11 128
Bethel, Monts. D3 105a
Bethel, Ak., U.S. D7 140
Bethel, Me., U.S. F6 110
Bethel, N.C., U.S. I8 114
Bethel Acres, Ok., U.S. B2 122
Bethel Springs, Tn., U.S. B10 122
Bethlehem, S. Afr. F9 70
Bethlehem, Pa., U.S. D10 114
Bethlehem, W.V., U.S. H9 112
Bethlehem see Bayt Laḥm, W.B. G6 58
Bethune, Sk., Can. D8 124
Béthune, Fr. D11 14
Bethune, S.C., U.S. B5 116
Betong, Malay. C7 50
Betong, Thai. J5 48
Betoota, Austl. E3 76
Betpak-Dala, des., Kaz. E11 32
Betroka, Madag. E8 68
Bet She'arim, Ḥorbat, hist., Isr. F6 58
Betsiamites, stm., Qc., Can. A8 110
Betsiamites, Barrage, dam, Qc., Can. A7 110
Betsiamites, Pointe de, c., Qc., Can. B8 110
Betsiboka, stm., Madag. D8 68
Betsie, Point, c., Mi., U.S. D3 112
Betsy Layne, Ky., U.S. G3 114
Bettendorf, Ia., U.S. C7 120
Bettiah, India E10 54
Bettles Field, Ak., U.S. C9 140
Bettola, Italy F6 22
Betūl, India H6 54
Betung, Indon. E4 50
Betwa, stm., India F7 54
Betzdorf, Ger. F3 16
Beulah, Austl. J4 76
Beulah, Co., U.S. C4 128
Beulah, Mi., U.S. D3 112
Beulah, Ms., U.S. D8 122
Beulaville, N.C., U.S. B8 116
Beuvron, stm., Fr. G11 14
B. Everett Jordan Lake, res., N.C., U.S. I6 114
Beverley, Eng., U.K. H12 12
Beverly, Ma., U.S. B15 114
Beverly Hills, Ca., U.S. I7 134
Beverly Lake, l., Nu., Can. C10 106
Beverungen, Ger. E5 16
Beverwijk, Neth. B13 14
Bewani Mountains, mts., Pap. N. Gui. a3 79a
Bexhill, Eng., U.K. K13 12
Bexley, Oh., U.S. E3 114
Bey Dağları, mts., Tur. G13 28
Beydagları Olimpos Milli Parkı, p.o.i., Tur. G13 28
Beyla, Gui. H3 64
Beypazarı, Tur. C14 28
Beypore, India F2 53
Beyra, Som. C9 66
Beyşehir, Tur. F14 28
Beyşehir Gölü, l., Tur. F14 28
Bežanickaja vozvyšennost', plat., Russia D12 10
Bežanicy, Russia D12 10
Bežeck, Russia C19 10
Béziers, Fr. F9 18
Bezmein, Turkmen. B8 56
Bhadohi, India F9 54
Bhādra, India D5 54
Bhadrāchalam, India C5 53
Bhadrak, India H11 54
Bhadra Reservoir, res., India E2 53
Bhadrāvati, India E2 53
Bhāgalpur, India F11 54
Bhainsa, India B3 53
Bhāi Pheru, Pak. C4 54
Bhairab Bāzār, Bngl. F13 54
Bhaironghāti, India C7 54
Bhakkar, Pak. C3 54
Bhaktapur (Bhādgāon), Nepal E10 54
Bhālki, India C3 53
Bhalwāl, Pak. B4 54
Bhamo, Mya. D8 46
Bhandāra, India H7 54
Bhanvad, India H2 54
Bharatpur, India E6 54
Bharatpur, Nepal E10 54
Bharthana, India E7 54
Bharūch, India H4 54
Bhātāpāra, India H8 54
Bhātghar Lake, res., India B1 53
Bhatkal, India E2 53
Bhātpāra, India G12 54
Bhattiprolu, India C5 53
Bhavāni, India F3 53
Bhāvnagar, India H4 54
Bhawani Mandi, India F5 54
Bhawānipatna, India I9 54
Bhera, Pak. B4 54
Bhīkangaon, India H5 54
Bhilai, India H8 54
Bhīlwāra, India F5 54
Bhīma, stm., India C3 53
Bhīmavaram, India C5 53
Bhind, India E7 54
Bhīnmāl, India F4 54
Bhiwandi, India B1 53
Bhiwāni, India D6 54
Bhojpur, Nepal E11 54
Bhokardan, India H5 54
Bhongīr, India C4 53
Bhopāl, India G6 54
Bhuban, India H10 54
Bhubaneshwar, India H10 54
Bhuj, India G2 54
Bhusāwal, India H5 54
Bhutan, ctry., Asia E13 54
Bia, Phou, mtn., Laos C6 48
Biafra, Bight of, b., Afr. I6 64
Biak, i., Indon. F10 44
Biała Piska, Pol. C18 16
Biała Podlaska, Pol. D19 16
Biała Podlaska, state, Pol. E19 16
Białobrzegi, Pol. E16 16
Białogard, Pol. B12 16
Białowieski Park Narodowy, p.o.i., Pol. D19 16
Białystok, Pol. C19 16
Białystok, state, Pol. C19 16
Bianco, Monte see Blanc, Mont, mtn., Eur. D12 18
Biankouma, C. Iv. H3 64
Biaora, India F6 54
Biaro, Pulau, i., Indon. E8 44
Biarritz, Fr. F4 18
Biasca, Switz. D5 22
Biba, Egypt J2 58
Bibala, Ang. C1 68
Bibb City, Ga., U.S. E14 122
Bibbiena, Italy G8 22
Bibémi, Cam. C2 66
Bicas, Braz. K4 88
Bicaz, Rom. C13 26
Biche, Lac la, l., Ab., Can. B18 138
Bichigt, Mong. B4 36
Bicknell, In., U.S. F10 120
Bicknell, Ut., U.S. E5 132
Bicudo, stm., Braz. J3 88
Bičura, Russia F10 34
Bīd, India B2 53
Bida, Nig. H6 64
Bīdar, India C3 53
Biddeford, Me., U.S. G6 110
Bideford, Eng., U.K. J8 12
Bieber, Ca., U.S. B4 134
Biebrza, stm., Pol. C18 16
Biebrzański Park Narodowy, p.o.i., Pol. C18 16
Biecz, Pol. G17 16
Biedenkopf, Ger. F4 16
Biel (Bienne), Switz. C4 22
Bielawa, Pol. F12 16
Bielefeld, Ger. D4 16
Bieler Lake, l., Nu., Can. A15 106
Biella, Italy E4 22
Bielsko-Biała, Pol. G14 16
Bielsko-Biała, state, Pol. G15 16
Bielsk Podlaski, Pol. D19 16
Bienfait, Sk., Can. E11 124
Bien Hoa, Viet. G8 48
Bienne see Biel, Switz. C4 22
Bien Son, Viet. B7 48
Bienville, La., U.S. E5 122
Bienville, Lac, l., Qc., Can. D16 106
Bierutów, Pol. E13 16
Bieszczadzki Park Narodowy, p.o.i., Pol. G18 16
Bifoun, Gabon E2 66
Big, stm., Mo., U.S. F7 120
Biga, Tur. C10 28
Bigadiç, Tur. D11 28
Big A Mountain, mtn., Va., U.S. G3 114
Big Bald Mountain, mtn., Ga., U.S. B1 116
Big Baldy Mountain, mtn., Mt., U.S. D16 136
Big Bay, Mi., U.S. B2 112
Big Bay, b., Vanuatu j16 79d
Big Bay De Noc, b., Mi., U.S. C3 112
Big Bear Lake, Ca., U.S. I9 134
Big Beaver, Sk., Can. E8 124
Big Belt Mountains, mts., Mt., U.S. D15 136
Big Bend, Swaz. E10 70
Big Bend National Park, p.o.i., Tx., U.S. E4 130
Big Bend Reservoir, res., Ab., Can. D15 138
Big Black, stm., Ms., U.S. E8 122
Big Blue, stm., U.S. G16 126
Big Blue, West Fork, stm., Ne., U.S. G15 126
Big Bonito Creek, stm., Az., U.S. J7 132
Big Canyon, val., Tx., U.S. D5 130
Big Chino Wash, stm., Az., U.S. H4 132
Big Creek, B.C., Can. E7 138
Big Creek, Ca., U.S. F6 134
Big Creek, stm., B.C., Can. E8 138
Big Creek, stm., Ar., U.S. C8 122
Big Creek, stm., Ks., U.S. C9 128
Big Cypress National Preserve, Fl., U.S. J4 116
Big Cypress Swamp, sw., Fl., U.S. J4 116
Big Delta, Ak., U.S. D10 140
Big Desert, des., Austl. J3 76
Big Diomede Island see Ratmanova, ostrov, i., Russia C27 34
Big Dry Creek, stm., Mt., U.S. G7 124
Bigelow Bight, b., U.S. G6 110
Big Flat, Ar., U.S. I5 120
Bigfork, Mn., U.S. D5 118
Big Fork, stm., Mn., U.S. C5 118
Big Frog Mountain, mtn., Tn., U.S. C14 122
Biggar, Sk., Can. B6 124
Biggers, Ar., U.S. H7 120
Biggs, Ca., U.S. D4 134
Big Gull Lake, l., On., Can. D12 112
Big Hole, stm., Mt., U.S. E14 136
Bighorn, stm., U.S. A5 126
Bighorn Basin, bas., U.S. C4 126
Bighorn Canyon National Recreation Area, p.o.i., U.S. B4 126
Bighorn Lake, res., U.S. B4 126
Bighorn Mountains, mts., U.S. C5 126
Bight, Head of, b., Austl. F6 74
Big Island, Va., U.S. G6 114
Big Island, i., Nu., Can. C17 106
Big Lake, Mn., U.S. F5 118
Big Lake, l., Me., U.S. E9 110
Big Lookout Mountain, mtn., Or., U.S. F9 136
Big Lost, stm., Id., U.S. G13 136
Big Muddy, stm., Il., U.S. G8 120

Name | Map Ref. | Page

Big Muddy Creek, stm., Mt., U.S. F9 124
Big Nemaha, North Fork, stm., Ne., U.S. K2 118
Bignona, Sen. G1 64
Big Pine, Ca., U.S. F7 134
Big Pine Mountain, mtn., Ca., U.S. I6 134
Big Piney, Wy., U.S. H16 136
Big Piney, stm., Mo., U.S. G6 120
Bigpoint, Ms., U.S. G10 122
Big Porcupine Creek, stm., Mt., U.S. H6 124
Big Prairie Creek, stm., Al., U.S. E11 122
Big Quill Lake, l., Sk., Can. C9 124
Big Raccoon Creek, stm., In., U.S. I2 112
Big Rapids, Mi., U.S. E4 112
Big Rideau Lake, l., On., Can. D13 112
Big River, Sk., Can. E9 106
Big Sable Point, c., Mi., U.S. D3 112
Big Sand Lake, l., Mb., Can. D11 106
Big Sandy, Tn., U.S. H9 120
Big Sandy, Tx., U.S. E3 122
Big Sandy, stm., U.S. F3 114
Big Sandy, stm., Wy., U.S. F3 126
Big Sandy Creek, stm., Co., U.S. C6 128
Bigsby Island, i., On., Can. B4 118
Big Signal Peak, mtn., Ca., U.S. D2 134
Big Sioux, stm., U.S. E16 126
Big Sky, Mt., U.S. E15 136
Big Smoky Valley, val., Nv., U.S. E8 134
Big Spring, Tx., U.S. B6 130
Big Spruce Knob, mtn., W.V., U.S. F5 114
Big Stone City, S.D., U.S. F2 118
Big Stone Gap, Va., U.S. H3 114
Big Stone Lake, l., U.S. F2 118
Big Sunflower, stm., Ms., U.S. D8 122
Big Sur, reg., Ca., U.S. H4 134
Big Timber, Mt., U.S. E16 136
Big Trout Lake, l., On., Can. E12 106
Biguaçu, Braz. C13 92
Big Water, Ut., U.S. F5 132
Big Wells, Tx., U.S. F8 130
Big White Mountain, mtn., B.C., Can. G12 138
Big Wood, stm., Id., U.S. G12 136
Bihać, Bos. E2 26
Bīhar, India F10 54
Bihār, state, India F10 54
Biharamulo, Tan. E6 66
Bihor, state, Rom. C9 26
Bihor, Vârful, mtn., Rom. C9 26
Bihoro, Japan C16 38
Bihosava, Bela. E10 10
Bihu, China G8 42
Bija, stm., Russia D15 32
Bijagós, Arquipélago dos, is., Gui.-B. G1 64
Bijainagar, India F5 54
Bijaipur, India E6 54
Bijāpur, India C2 53
Bījāpur, India B5 53
Bijeljina, Bos. E6 26
Bijelo Polje, Yugo. F6 26
Bijie, China F6 36
Bijlikol', ozero, l., Kaz. F12 32
Bijnor, India D7 54
Bijsk, Russia D15 32
Bīkāner, India D4 54
Bikar, at., Marsh. Is. B8 72
Bikeqi, China A4 42
Bikin, Russia B11 36
Bikini, at., Marsh. Is. B7 72
Bīkkū Bīttī, mtn., Libya C3 62
Bikoro, D.R.C. E3 66
Bilāra, India E4 54
Bilāri, India D7 54
Bilāsipāra, India E13 54
Bilāspur, India C6 54
Bilāspur, India G9 54
Bila Tserkva, Ukr. F15 6
Bilauktaung Range, mts., Asia F4 48
Bilbao, Spain A7 20
Bilbeis, Egypt H2 58
Bilbilis, hist., Spain C9 20
Bileća, Bos. G5 26
Bilecik, Tur. C12 28
Bilecik, state, Tur. C13 28
Biłgoraj, Pol. F18 16
Bilgrām, India E8 54
Bilhorod-Dnistrovs'kyi, Ukr. C17 26
Bili, D.R.C. D5 66
Biliaïvka, Ukr. C17 26
Bīlimora, India H4 54
Bilin, Mya. D3 48
Bilin, stm., Mya. D3 48
Bílina, Czech Rep. F9 16
Biliran Island, i., Phil. E5 52
Billabong Creek, stm., Austl. J5 76
Billings, Mo., U.S. G4 120
Billings, Mt., U.S. B4 126
Billings Heights, Mt., U.S. B4 126
Billiton see Belitung, i., Indon. E5 50
Bill Williams, stm., Az., U.S. I3 132
Billy Chinook, Lake, res., Or., U.S. F5 136
Bilma, Niger F7 64
Biloela, Austl. E8 76
Biloxi, Ms., U.S. G10 122
Bilpa Morea Claypan, l., Austl. E2 76
Bilqas Qism Awwal, Egypt G2 58
Biltine, Chad E4 62
Biltmore Forest, N.C., U.S. A3 116
Bilugyun Island, i., Mya. D3 48
Bimbo, C.A.R. D3 66
Bimbowrie, Austl. H3 76
Bimini Islands, is., Bah. B9 96
Bīna-Etāwa, India F7 54
Binaiya, Gunung, mtn., Indon. F9 44
Binalbagan, Phil. E4 52
Bin'an, China B7 38
Bindki, India E8 54
Bindloss, Ab., Can. D3 124
Bindura, Zimb. D5 68
Binéfar, Spain C11 20
Binford, N.D., U.S. G15 124
Binga, D.R.C. D4 66
Binga, Monte, mtn., Afr. D5 68
Bingara, Austl. G8 76
Bingen, Ger. G3 16
Binger, Ok., U.S. F10 128
Binghamton, N.Y., U.S. B10 114
Bin Ghunaymah, Jabal, mts., Libya B3 62
Binhai, China D8 42
Binh Gia, Viet. B8 48
Binjai, Indon. K4 48
Binnaway, Austl. H7 76
Binongko, Pulau, i., Indon. G7 44
Binscarth, Mb., Can. D12 124
Bintan, Pulau, i., Indon. C4 50
Bintimani, mtn., S.L. H2 64
Bintuhan, Indon. F3 50
Bintulu, Malay. B8 50
Bintuni, Indon. F9 44
Binxian, China B7 38
Binxian, China C7 42
Binxian, China D3 42
Binyang, China J3 42
Bin-Yauri, Nig. G5 64
Biobío, state, Chile H1 92
Biobío, stm., Chile G2 90
Biogradska Gora Nacionalni Park, p.o.i., Yugo. G6 26
Bioko, i., Eq. Gui. I6 64
Bira, Russia G15 34
Birac, Phil. B3 52
Birāk, Libya B2 62
Birakan, Russia G15 34
Bi'r al Wa'r, Libya C2 62
Birao, C.A.R. B4 66
Birch, stm., Ab., Can. D8 106
Birch Creek, stm., Mt., U.S. B14 136
Birch Hills, Sk., Can. B8 124
Birch Island, B.C., Can. E10 138
Birch Island, i., Mb., Can. B13 124
Birch Mountains, hills, Ab., Can. D8 106
Birch Run, Mi., U.S. E6 112
Birch Tree, Mo., U.S. H6 120
Birchwood, Wi., U.S. F7 118
Bird Creek, stm., Ok., U.S. E13 128
Bird Island, Mn., U.S. G4 118
Bird Island, sci., S. Geor. J9 90
Birdsville, Austl. E2 76
Birdtail Creek, stm., Mb., Can. D13 124
Birdum, Austl. C6 74
Birecik, Tur. A9 58
Bireun, Indon. J3 48
Bir Ghbalou, Alg. H14 20
Birigui, Braz. D6 90
Biriljussy, Russia C16 32
Bīrjand, Iran C8 56
Birjul'ka, Russia D19 32
Birjusa, stm., Russia C17 32
Birjusinsk, Russia C17 32
Birken, B.C., Can. F8 138
Birkenfeld, Ger. G3 16
Birkenhead, Eng., U.K. H9 12
Birmingham, Eng., U.K. I10 12
Birmingham, Al., U.S. D11 122
Birmingham, Ia., U.S. D6 120
Birmingham, Mi., U.S. B2 114
Birmitrapur, India G10 54
Bîr Mogreïn, Maur. D2 64
Birnin Gaouré, Niger G5 64
Birnin-Kebbi, Nig. G5 64
Birnin Konni, Niger G5 64
Birnin Kudu, Nig. G6 64
Birobidžan, Russia G15 34
Birrie, stm., Austl. G6 76
Birsk, Russia C9 32
Birštonas, Lith. F7 10
Birtle, Mb., Can. D12 124
Birūr, India E2 53
Biržai, Lith. D7 10
Birżebbuġa, Malta I8 24
Bisaccia, Italy C9 24
Bīsalpur, India D7 54
Bisbee, Az., U.S. L7 132
Bisbee, N.D., U.S. F14 124
Biscarrosse et de Parentis, Étang de, l., Fr. E4 18
Biscay, Bay of, b., Eur. E2 18
Biscayne Bay, b., Fl., U.S. K5 116
Biscayne National Park, p.o.i., Fl., U.S. K5 116
Bisceglie, Italy C10 24
Bischofshofen, Aus. C10 22
Bischofswerda, Ger. E10 16
Biscoe, N.C., U.S. A6 116
Bishnupur, India G11 54
Bisho, S. Afr. H8 70
Bishop, Ca., U.S. F7 134
Bishop, Tx., U.S. G10 130
Bishop Auckland, Eng., U.K. G11 12
Bishop Rock, r., Eng., U.K. L6 12
Bishop's Falls, Nf., Can. j22 107a
Bishop's Stortford, Eng., U.K. J13 12
Bishopville, S.C., U.S. B5 116
Biškek, Kyrg. F12 32
Biskupiec, Pol. C16 16
Bislig, Phil. F6 52
Bismarck, Mo., U.S. G7 120
Bismarck, N.D., U.S. A12 126
Bismarck Archipelago, is., Pap. N. Gui. a4 79a
Bismarck Range, mts., Pap. N. Gui. b3 79a
Bismarck Sea, Pap. N. Gui. a4 79a
Bismark, Kap, c., Grnld. B22 141
Bissa, Djebel, mtn., Alg. H12 20
Bissau, Gui.-B. G1 64
Bissett, Mb., Can. C18 124
Bissikrima, Gui. G2 64
Bistcho Lake, l., Ab., Can. D7 106
Bistineau, Lake, res., La., U.S. E5 122
Bistrica, Slvn. D13 22
Bistrița, Rom. B11 26
Bistrița, stm., Rom. C13 26
Bistrița-Năsăud, state, Rom. B11 26
Biswān, India E8 54
Bitam, Gabon D2 66
Bitburg, Ger. G2 16
Bitche, Fr. E16 14
Bitlis, Tur. B5 56
Bitola, Mac. B4 28
Bitolj see Bitola, Mac. B4 28
Bitonto, Italy C10 24
Bitou, Burkina G4 64
Bitter Creek, stm., Wy., U.S. B8 132
Bitterfeld, Ger. E8 16
Bitterfontein, S. Afr. G4 70
Bitterroot, stm., Mt., U.S. D13 136
Bitterroot, West Fork, stm., Mt., U.S. E12 136
Bitterroot Range, mts., U.S. C11 136
Bitung, Indon. E8 44
Bitupitá, Braz. B5 88
Biu, Nig. G7 64
Bivins, Tx., U.S. E4 122
Biwabik, Mn., U.S. D6 118
Biwa-ko, l., Japan D8 40
Bixby, Ok., U.S. I2 120
Biyala, Egypt G2 58
Biyang, China E5 42
Bizana, S. Afr. G9 70
Bizen, Japan E7 40
Bizerte (Binzert), Tun. G3 24
Bizerte, Lac de, l., Tun. G3 24
Bizkaiko, co., Spain A8 20
Bjahoml', Bela. F10 10
Bjala, Blg. G14 26
Bjala Slatina, Blg. F10 26
Bjalyničy, Bela. F12 10
Bjarèzina, stm., Bela. H13 10
Bjarèzina, stm., Bela. G9 10
Bjaroza, Bela. H7 10
Bjarozauka, Bela. G8 10
Bjelovar, Cro. E13 22
Björna, Swe. E8 8
Björneborg see Pori, Fin. F9 8
Bjorne Peninsula, pen., Nu., Can. B8 141
Bjørnøya, i., Nor. B5 30
Bla, Mali G3 64
Blace, Yugo. F8 26
Black (Da, Song) (Lixian), stm., Asia D9 46
Black, stm., Mb., Can. D18 124
Black, stm., U.S. I6 120
Black, stm., Ak., U.S. C11 140
Black, stm., Az., U.S. J6 132
Black, stm., La., U.S. F7 122
Black, stm., Mi., U.S. E7 112
Black, stm., N.Y., U.S. E14 112
Black, stm., Wi., U.S. G7 118
Blackall, Austl. E5 76
Black Bay, b., On., Can. C10 118
Black Bay Peninsula, pen., On., Can. C10 118
Black Bear Creek, stm., Ok., U.S. E11 128
Blackburn, Eng., U.K. H10 12
Blackburn, Mount, mtn., Ak., U.S. D11 140
Black Butte, mtn., Mt., U.S. D15 136
Black Canyon of the Gunnison National Monument, p.o.i., Co., U.S. E9 132
Black Creek, stm., Ms., U.S. G9 122
Black Creek, stm., S.C., U.S. B6 116
Black Diamond, Ab., Can. F16 138
Black Diamond, Wa., U.S. C5 136
Blackdown Tableland National Park, p.o.i., Austl. D7 76
Blackduck, Mn., U.S. D4 118
Black Eagle, Mt., U.S. C15 136
Blackfoot, Id., U.S. G14 136
Blackfoot, Mt., U.S. B14 136
Blackfoot, stm., Id., U.S. G15 136
Blackfoot, stm., Mt., U.S. D13 136
Blackfoot Reservoir, res., Id., U.S. H15 136
Black Forest see Schwarzwald, mts., Ger. H4 16
Black Hills, mts., U.S. C9 126
Black Island, i., Mb., Can. C17 124
Black Lake, Qc., Can. D5 110
Black Lake, l., Sk., Can. D10 106
Black Lake, l., Mi., U.S. C5 112
Black Lake, l., N.Y., U.S. D14 112
Black Mesa, mtn., U.S. E6 128
Blackmore, Mount, mtn., Mt., U.S. E15 136
Black Mountain, N.C., U.S. A3 116
Black Mountain, mtn., Az., U.S. K5 132
Black Mountain, mtn., Ca., U.S. H5 134
Black Mountain, mtn., Mt., U.S. D14 136
Black Mountain, hill, Austl. C2 76
Black Mountain, mts., U.S. H2 114
Black Nossob, stm., Nmb. C4 70
Black Pine Peak, mtn., Id., U.S. A3 132
Blackpool, Eng., U.K. H9 12
Black Range, mts., N.M., U.S. J9 132
Black River, N.Y., U.S. D14 112
Black River Falls, Wi., U.S. G8 118
Black Rock, Ar., U.S. H6 120
Black Rock, r., Ire. G2 12
Black Rock, r., S. Geor. J8 90
Black Rock Desert, des., Nv., U.S. B7 134
Blacksburg, S.C., U.S. A4 116
Blacksburg, Va., U.S. G5 114
Black Sea G15 6
Blacks Fork, stm., U.S. B7 132
Blackshear, Lake, res., Ga., U.S. D2 116
Blackstone, Va., U.S. G8 114
Black Sturgeon Lake, l., On., Can. B9 118
Blackville, S.C., U.S. C4 116
Black Volta (Volta Noire) (Mouhoun), stm., Afr. H4 64
Blackwater, Austl. D7 76
Blackwater, stm., Ire. I4 12
Blackwater, stm., Mo., U.S. E4 120
Blackwater Creek, stm., Austl. E5 76
Blackwater Draw, stm., Tx., U.S. H7 128
Blackwater Lake, l., N.T., Can. C6 106
Blackwell, Tx., U.S. B7 130
Bladenboro, N.C., U.S. B7 116
Bladensburg National Park, p.o.i., Austl. D4 76
Bladgrond-Noord, S. Afr. F4 70
Bladworth, Sk., Can. C7 124
Bláfell, mtn., Ice. k30 8a
Blagoevgrad, Blg. G10 26
Blagoveščensk, Russia D16 34
Blaine, Mn., U.S. F5 118
Blaine, Wa., U.S. B4 136
Blair, Ne., U.S. C1 120
Blair, Ok., U.S. G9 128
Blair, Wi., U.S. G7 118
Blair Athol, Austl. D6 76
Blairsville, Ga., U.S. B2 116
Blairsville, Pa., U.S. D6 114
Blaj, Rom. C10 26
Blakely, Ga., U.S. F13 122
Blake Plateau, unds. E6 144
Blake Point, c., Mi., U.S. C10 118
Blalock Island, i., Wa., U.S. E7 136
Blanc, Mont, mtn., Eur. D12 18
Blanca, Co., U.S. D3 128
Blanca, Bahía, b., Arg. G4 90
Blanca, Laguna, l., Chile J2 90
Blanca, Punta, c., Chile B2 92
Blanca, Sierra, mtn., Tx., U.S. C2 130
Blanca Peak, mtn., Co., U.S. D3 128
Blanchard, Ok., U.S. F11 128
Blanchard, stm., Oh., U.S. D2 114
Blanche, Lake, l., Austl. G2 76
Blanche Channel, strt., Sol. Is. e7 79b
Blanchester, Oh., U.S. E1 114
Blanchisseuse, Trin. s12 105f
Blanco, Tx., U.S. D9 130
Blanco, stm., Arg. D3 92
Blanco, stm., Ec. G2 86
Blanco, stm., Tx., U.S. E9 130
Blanco, Cabo, c., C.R. H5 102
Blanco, Cañon, val., N.M., U.S. F3 128
Blanco, Cape, c., Or., U.S. H2 136
Blanco, Lago, l., Chile J3 90
Blanc-Sablon, Qc., Can. i22 107a
Bland, Va., U.S. G4 114
Blanda, stm., Ice. k30 8a
Blanding, Ut., U.S. F7 132
Blandinsville, Il., U.S. D7 120
Blanes, Spain C13 20
Blangkejeren, Indon. K3 48
Blangy-sur-Bresle, Fr. E10 14
Blankenburg, Ger. E6 16
Blanquilla, Isla, i., Ven. B9 86
Blansko, Czech Rep. G12 16
Blantyre, Mwi. D6 68
Blarney Castle, hist., Ire. J4 12
Błaszki, Pol. E14 16
Blaubeuren, Ger. H5 16
Blaufelden, Ger. G5 16
Błażowa, Pol. G18 16
Bledsoe, Tx., U.S. H5 128
Blega, Indon. G8 50
Bleik see Andenes, Nor. B6 8
Blekinge, state, Swe. H6 8
Blenheim, On., Can. F8 112
Blenheim, N.Z. E5 80
Blessing, Tx., U.S. F11 130
Bletchley, Eng., U.K. J12 12
Bligh Water, strt., Fiji p18 79e
Blind River, On., Can. B6 112
Blissfield, Mi., U.S. C2 114
Blitar, Indon. H8 50
Block Island, i., R.I., U.S. C14 114
Blockton, Ia., U.S. D3 120
Bloedel, B.C., Can. F5 138
Bloemfontein, S. Afr. F8 70
Bloemhof, S. Afr. E7 70
Bloemhofdam, res., S. Afr. E7 70
Blois, Fr. G10 14
Blönduós, Ice. k29 8a
Bloodvein, stm., Can. E11 106
Bloody Foreland, c., Ire. F4 12
Bloomer, Wi., U.S. F7 118
Bloomfield, On., Can. E12 112
Bloomfield, Ky., U.S. G12 120
Bloomfield, Mo., U.S. H8 120
Bloomfield, Ne., U.S. E15 126
Bloomfield, N.M., U.S. G9 132
Blooming Grove, Tx., U.S. E2 122
Blooming Prairie, Mn., U.S. H5 118
Bloomington, Il., U.S. D9 120
Bloomington, In., U.S. E11 120
Bloomington, Mn., U.S. G5 118
Bloomington, Tx., U.S. F11 130
Bloomington, Wi., U.S. B7 120
Bloomsburg, Pa., U.S. C9 114
Bloomsbury, Austl. C7 76
Bloomville, Oh., U.S. C2 114
Blora, Indon. G7 50
Blosseville Kyst, cst., Grnld. D20 141
Blossom, Tx., U.S. D3 122
Blouberg, mtn., S. Afr. C9 70
Blountstown, Fl., U.S. G13 122
Blountsville, Al., U.S. C12 122
Blowering Reservoir, res., Austl. J6 76
Blowing Point Village, Anguilla A1 105a
Blowing Rock, N.C., U.S. H4 114
Bludenz, Aus. C6 22
Blue, stm., Az., U.S. J7 132
Blue, stm., Ok., U.S. C2 122
Blue Creek, Wa., U.S. B8 136
Blue Cypress Lake, l., Fl., U.S. I5 116
Blue Earth, Mn., U.S. H4 118
Blue Earth, stm., U.S. H4 118
Bluefield, Va., U.S. G4 114
Bluefield, W.V., U.S. G4 114
Bluefields, Nic. F6 102
Blue Hill, Ne., U.S. A10 128
Blue Hill Bay, b., Me., U.S. F8 110
Blue Island, Il., U.S. G2 112
Blue Mound, Ks., U.S. F3 120
Blue Mountain, Ms., U.S. C9 122
Blue Mountain, mtn., Ar., U.S. C4 122
Blue Mountain, mtn., Mt., U.S. G9 124
Blue Mountain, mts., Pa., U.S. D8 114
Blue Mountain Peak, mtn., Jam. i14 104d
Blue Mountains, mts., Jam. i14 104d
Blue Mountains, mts., U.S. E8 136
Blue Mountains, mts., Me., U.S. F6 110
Blue Mountains National Park, p.o.i., Austl. J8 76
Blue Mud Bay, b., Austl. B7 74
Blue Nile (Azraq, Al-Baḩr al-) (Ābay), stm., Afr. E6 62
Bluenose Lake, l., Nu., Can. B6 106
Blue Ridge, Ab., Can. B15 138
Blue Ridge, Ga., U.S. B1 116
Blue Ridge, mts., U.S. H4 114
Blue River, B.C., Can. D11 138
Bluestone Dam, dam, W.V., U.S. G5 114
Bluestone Lake, res., W.V., U.S. G5 114
Bluewater, N.M., U.S. H9 132
Bluff, N.Z. H3 80
Bluff, Ut., U.S. F7 132
Bluff Cape, c., Mya. D2 48
Bluff Creek, stm., U.S. D11 128
Bluff Dale, Tx., U.S. B9 130
Bluff Park, Al., U.S. D12 122
Bluffs, Il., U.S. E7 120
Bluffton, In., U.S. H4 112
Bluffton, S.C., U.S. D5 116
Blumberg, Ger. I4 16
Blumenau, Braz. C13 92
Blumenhof, Sk., Can. D6 124
Bly, Or., U.S. A4 134
Blyth, On., Can. E8 112
Blyth, Eng., U.K. F11 12
Blythe, Ca., U.S. J2 132
Blytheville, Ar., U.S. I7 120
Bø, Nor. G3 8
Bo, S.L. H2 64
Boac, Phil. D3 52
Boaco, Nic. F5 102
Boa Esperança, Braz. K3 88
Boa Esperança, Represa, res., Braz. D3 88
Bo'ai, China D5 42
Boane, Moz. E11 70
Board Camp Mountain, mtn., Ca., U.S. C2 134
Boardman, Oh., U.S. C5 114
Boatman, Austl. F6 76
Boa Viagem, Braz. C5 88
Boa Vista, Braz. F11 86
Boa Vista, i., C.V. k10 65a
Boawai, Indon. H12 50
Boaz, Al., U.S. C12 122
Bobai, China J3 42
Bobaomby, Tanjona, c., Madag. C8 68
Bobbili, India B6 53
Bobcaygeon, On., Can. D11 112
Bobigny, Fr. F11 14
Böblingen, Ger. H4 16
Bobo-Dioulasso, Burkina G4 64
Bobolice, Pol. C12 16
Bobonaza, stm., Ec. H3 86
Bobonong, Bots. B9 70
Bobr, Bela. F12 10
Bobtown, Pa., U.S. E5 114
Bobures, Ven. C6 86
Boby, mtn., Madag. E8 68
Bôca da Mata, Braz. E7 88
Boca do Acre, Braz. E4 84
Boca do Jari, Braz. D7 84
Bocage, Cap, c., N. Cal. m15 79d
Boca Grande, Fl., U.S. J3 116
Bocaiúva, Braz. I3 88
Bocaranga, C.A.R. C3 66
Boca Raton, Fl., U.S. J5 116
Bocas del Toro, Pan. H6 102
Bocay, Nic. E5 102
Bochnia, Pol. G16 16
Bocholt, Ger. E2 16
Bochum, Ger. E3 16
Bocón, Caño, stm., Col. F7 86
Boconó, Ven. C6 86
Bocșa, Rom. D8 26
Boda, C.A.R. D3 66
Bodajbo, Russia E11 34
Bodalla, Austl. K8 76
Bodcau Creek, stm., Ar., U.S. D5 122
Bode, Ia., U.S. I4 118
Bodélé, reg., Chad D3 62
Boden, Swe. D9 8
Bodensee see Constance, Lake, l., Eur. I5 16
Bodhan, India B3 53
Bodh Gaya, India F10 54
Bodināyakkanūr, India G3 53
Bodmin, Eng., U.K. K8 12
Bodø, Nor. C6 8
Bodoquena, Serra da, plat., Braz. D5 90
Bodrum, Tur. F10 28
Bodzentyn, Pol. F16 16
Boende, D.R.C. E4 66
Bœng Lvea, Camb. F7 48
Boeo, Capo, c., Italy G6 24
Boesmans, stm., S. Afr. H7 70
Boeuf, stm., U.S. E7 122
Boffa, Gui. G2 64
Bogale, Mya. D2 48
Bogalusa, La., U.S. G9 122
Bogan, stm., Austl. H6 76
Bogan Gate, Austl. I6 76
Bogangolo, C.A.R. C3 66
Bogata, Tx., U.S. D3 122
Bogcang, stm., China C11 54
Bogda Shan, mts., China C2 36
Bogen, Ger. H8 16
Boger City, N.C., U.S. A4 116
Boggabilla, Austl. G8 76
Boggabri, Austl. H7 76
Boggy Peak, mtn., Antig. f4 105b
Bogles, Gren. p11 105e
Bognor Regis, Eng., U.K. K12 12
Bogo, Phil. E5 52
Bogoljubovo, Russia E15 10
Bogong, Mount, mtn., Austl. K6 76
Bogor, Indon. G5 50
Bogorodick, Russia G21 10
Bogorodsk, Russia H20 8
Bogorodskoe, Russia F17 34
Bogotá see Santa Fe de Bogotá, Col E4 86
Bogotol, Russia C15 32
Bogra, Bngl. F12 54
Bogučany, Russia C17 32
Bogué, Maur. F2 64
Bogue Chitto, stm., U.S. G8 122
Bogue Phalia, stm., Ms., U.S. D8 122
Böğürtlen, Tur. A8 58
Bo Hai (Chihli, Gulf of), b., China B8 42
Bohai Haixia, strt., China B9 42
Bohain-en-Vermandois, Fr. D12 14
Bohai Wan, b., China B8 42
Bohemian Forest, mts., Eur. G8 16
Böhmer Wald see Bohemian Forest, mts., Eur. G8 16
Bohol, i., Phil. F4 52
Bohol Sea, Phil. F5 52
Boiaçu, Braz. H11 86
Boiano, Italy C8 24
Boiestown, N.B., Can. D10 110
Boipeba, Ilha de, i., Braz. G6 88
Bois, stm., Braz. C6 90
Bois, Lac des, l., N.T., Can. B6 106
Bois Blanc Island, i., Mi., U.S. C5 112
Bois de Sioux, stm., U.S. F2 118
Boise, Id., U.S. G10 136
Boise, stm., Id., U.S. G10 136
Boise, Middle Fork, stm., Id., U.S. G11 136
Boise, South Fork, stm., Id., U.S. G11 136
Boise City, Ok., U.S. E6 128
Boissevain, Mb., Can. E13 124
Boistfort Peak, mtn., Wa., U.S. D3 136
Boizenburg, Ger. C6 16
Boja, Indon. G7 50
Bojadła, Pol. E11 16
Bojeador, Cape, c., Phil. A3 52
Bojnūrd, Iran B8 56
Bojonegoro, Indon. G7 50
Bojuru, Braz. E12 92
Bokāro Steel City, India G10 54
Bokchito, Ok., U.S. C2 122
Boké, Gui. G2 64
Bokhara, stm., Austl. G6 76
Bok Koŭ, Camb. G6 48
Boknafjorden, strt., Nor. G1 8
Boko, Congo E2 66
Bokoro, Chad E3 62
Bokote, D.R.C. E4 66
Boksitogorsk, Russia A16 10
Bokungu, D.R.C. E4 66
Bol, Cro. G13 22
Bolama, Gui.-B. G1 64
Bolaños, stm., Mex. E7 100
Bolaños de Calatrava, Spain F7 20
Bolān Pass, p., Pak. D10 56
Bolayır, Tur. C9 28
Bolbec, Fr. E9 14
Bole, China F14 32
Bole, Ghana H4 64
Boles, Ar., U.S. C4 122
Bolesławiec, Pol. E11 16
Boley, Ok., U.S. B2 122
Bolgatanga, Ghana G4 64
Bolhov, Russia G18 10
Bolhrad, Ukr. D15 26
Boli, China B11 36
Boligee, Al., U.S. E10 122
Bolingbrook, Il., U.S. C9 120
Bolishan, China C5 38
Bolívar, Col. G3 86
Bolívar, Col. G3 86
Bolivar, Mo., U.S. G4 120
Bolivar, N.Y., U.S. B7 114
Bolivar, Tn., U.S. B9 122
Bolívar, state, Col. C4 86
Bolívar, state, Ec. H2 86
Bolívar, state, Ven. D10 86
Bolívar, Cerro, mtn., Ven. D10 86
Bolívar, Pico (La Columna), mtn., Ven. C6 86
Bolivar Peninsula, pen., Tx., U.S. H4 122
Bolivia, ctry., S.A. G5 84
Bollnäs, Swe. F7 8
Bollon, Austl. G6 76
Bolmen, l., Swe. H5 8
Bolobo, D.R.C. E3 66
Bologna, Italy F8 22
Bolognesi, Peru F3 84
Bologoe, Russia C17 10
Bologovo, Russia D14 10
Bolohovo, Russia F20 10
Bol'ŏj Anjuj, stm., Russia C21 34
Bolomba, D.R.C. D3 66
Bolon', ozero, l., Russia G16 34
Bolotnoe, Russia C14 32
Bolovens, Plateau des, plat., Laos E8 48
Bol'šaja Balahnja, stm., Russia B9 34
Bol'šaja Heta, stm., Russia C5 34
Bol'šaja Kuonamka, stm., Russia C10 34
Bol'šaja Murta, Russia C16 32
Bol'šaja Ussurka, stm., Russia B11 38
Bol'šaja Višera, Russia B15 10
Bol'šakovo, Russia F4 10
Bolsena, Italy H8 22
Bolsena, Lago di, l., Italy H9 22
Bol'šereče, Russia C13 32
Bol'šereck, Russia F20 34
Bol'ševik, Russia D18 34
Bol'ševik, ostrov, i., Russia A10 34
Bol'šezemel'skaja Tundra, reg., Russia A9 32
Bolshevik see Bol'ševik, ostrov, i., Russia A10 34
Bol'šie Uki, Russia C12 32
Bol'šoe Mihajlovskoe, Russia D20 10
Bol'šoe Polpino, Russia G17 10
Bol'šoe Selo, Russia C21 10
Bol'šoj Begičev, ostrov, i., Russia B11 34
Bol'šoj Jugan, stm., Russia B12 32
Bol'šoj Kamen', Russia C10 38
Bol'šoj Ljahovskij, ostrov, i., Russia B17 34
Bol'šoj Tal'cy, Russia A15 10
Bolton, On., Can. E10 112
Bolton, Eng., U.K. H10 12
Bolton, Ms., U.S. E8 122
Bolton, N.C., U.S. B7 116
Bolu, Tur. C14 28
Bolu, state, Tur. C14 28
Bolva, stm., Russia G17 10
Bolvadin, Tur. E13 28
Bóly, Hung. C5 26
Bolzano (Bozen), Italy D8 22
Boma, D.R.C. F2 66
Bomaderry, Austl. J8 76
Bombala, Austl. K7 76
Bombay see Mumbai, India B1 53
Bomberai, Semenanjung, pen., Indon. F9 44
Bomboma, D.R.C. D3 66
Bom Conselho, Braz. E7 88
Bom Despacho, Braz. J3 88
Bomdila, India E14 54
Bom Jesus, Braz. E3 88
Bom Jesus da Lapa, Braz. G4 88
Bomnak, Russia F14 34
Bomokandi, stm., D.R.C. D5 66
Bomongo, D.R.C. D3 66
Bom Retiro, Braz. C13 92
Bomu, stm., Afr. D4 66
Bon, Cap, c., Tun. G5 24
Bon Air, Va., U.S. G8 114
Bonaire, i., Neth. Ant. p23 104g
Bonampak, hist., Mex. D2 102
Bonandolok, Indon. C1 50
Bonanza, Or., U.S. A4 134
Bonanza, Ut., U.S. C7 132
Bonanza Peak, mtn., Wa., U.S. B5 136
Bonao, Dom. Rep. C12 102
Bonaparte, Ia., U.S. D6 120
Bonaparte, stm., B.C., Can. F9 138
Bonaparte, Mount, mtn., Wa., U.S. B7 136
Bonaparte Lake, l., B.C., Can. E10 138
Bonar Bridge, Scot., U.K. D8 12
Bonasse, Trin. s12 105f
Bonaventure, Qc., Can. B11 110
Bonaventure, stm., Qc., Can. B11 110
Bonaventure, Île, i., Qc., Can. B12 110
Bonavista, Nf., Can. j23 107a
Bonavista Bay, b., Nf., Can. j23 107a
Bondeno, Italy F8 22
Bondo, D.R.C. E4 66
Bondo, D.R.C. D4 66
Bondoc Peninsula, pen., Phil. D4 52
Bondoukou, C. Iv. H4 64
Bondowoso, Indon. G8 50
Bonduel, Wi., U.S. G10 118
Bone, Teluk, b., Indon. F7 44
Bonebone, Indon. E12 50
Boneogeh, Indon. G12 50
Bonerate, Pulau, i., Indon. G12 50
Bonesteel, S.D., U.S. D13 126
Bonete Chico, Cerro, mtn., Arg. D3 92
Bonete Grande, Cerro, mtn., Arg. C3 92
Bongabong, Phil. D3 52
Bongaigaon, India E13 54
Bongandanga, D.R.C. D4 66
Bongka, Indon. F7 44
Bongo, Gabon E2 66
Bongo, Massif des, mts., C.A.R. C4 66
Bongor, Chad E3 62
Bonham, Tx., U.S. D2 122
Bonhomme, Morne, mtn., Haiti C11 102
Bonifacio, Fr. H15 18
Bonifacio, Strait of, strt., Eur. H15 18
Bonifati, Capo, c., Italy E9 24
Bonin Islands see Ogasawara-guntō, is., Japan G18 30
Bonita, La., U.S. E7 122
Bonita Springs, Fl., U.S. J4 116
Bonito, Braz. E8 88
Bonito, Braz. D5 90
Bonito de Santa Fé, Braz. D6 88
Bonn, Ger. F2 16
Bonners Ferry, Id., U.S. B10 136
Bonnet, Lac du, res., Mb., Can. D17 124
Bonnétable, Fr. F9 14
Bonne Terre, Mo., U.S. G7 120
Bonnet Plume, stm., Yk., Can. B3 106
Bonneville, Fr. C12 18
Bonneville Peak, mtn., Id., U.S. H14 136
Bonneville Salt Flats, pl., Ut., U.S. C2 132
Bonney SE, Lake, l., Austl. K3 76
Bonnie Rock, Austl. F3 74
Bonny, Nig. I6 64
Bonnyville, Ab., Can. B20 138
Bono, Ar., U.S. I7 120
Bonoi, Indon. F10 44
Bonshaw, P.E., Can. D13 110
Bontang, Indon. C10 50
Bontebok National Park, p.o.i., S. Afr. I5 70
Bonthe, S.L. H2 64
Bontoc, Phil. B3 52
Bon Wier, Tx., U.S. G5 122
Booker, Tx., U.S. E8 128
Booker T. Washington National Monument, p.o.i., Va., U.S. H6 114
Boola, Gui. H3 64
Boolaloo, Austl. D3 74
Booleroo Centre, Austl. I2 76
Boologooro, Austl. D2 74
Boomarra, Austl. B3 76
Boonah, Austl. F9 76
Boone, Ia., U.S. I5 118
Boone, N.C., U.S. H4 114
Boone, stm., Ia., U.S. B4 120
Booneville, Ar., U.S. B5 122
Booneville, Ky., U.S. G2 114
Booneville, Ms., U.S. C10 122
Böön Tsagaan nuur, l., Mong. B4 36
Boonville, Ca., U.S. D2 134
Boonville, Mo., U.S. F5 120
Boonville, N.Y., U.S. E14 112
Boorindal, Austl. H6 76
Booroorban, Austl. J5 76
Boosaaso, Som. B9 66
Booth, Al., U.S. E12 122
Boothbay Harbor, Me., U.S. G7 110
Boothia, Gulf of, b., Nu., Can. A12 106
Boothia Peninsula, pen., Nu., Can. A12 106
Boothville, La., U.S. H9 122
Booué, Gabon E2 66
Bophuthatswana, hist. reg., S. Afr. E7 70
Boping Ling, mts., China I7 42
Bopolu, Lib. H2 64
Boqueirão, Serra do, hills, Braz. F4 88
Boquilla, Presa de la, res., Mex. B6 100
Boquim, Braz. F7 88
Bor, Russia H20 8
Bor, Russia E20 8
Bor, Sudan F6 62
Bor, Tur. B3 56
Bor, Yugo. E9 26
Bor, Lak, stm., Kenya D7 66
Bora-Bora, i., Fr. Poly. E11 72
Borabu, Thai. E6 48
Borah Peak, mtn., Id., U.S. F13 136

Name	Map Ref.	Page
Borås, Swe.	H5	8
Borba, Braz.	D6	84
Bordeaux, Fr.	E5	18
Bordeaux Mountain, hill, V.I.U.S.	e8	104b
Borden, Sk., Can.	B6	124
Borden Peninsula, pen., Nu., Can.	A14	106
Bordertown, Austl.	K3	76
Bordesholm, Ger.	B6	16
Bordighera, Italy	G4	22
Bordj Menaïel, Alg.	H14	20
Bordj Omar Idriss, Alg.	D6	64
Borðoy, i., Far. Is.	m34	8b
Borgå see Porvoo, Fin.	F11	8
Borgarnes, Ice.	k28	8a
Børgefjell Nasjonalpark, p.o.i., Nor.	D5	8
Borger, Tx., U.S.	F7	128
Borgholm, Swe.	H7	8
Borgne, Lake, b., La., U.S.	G9	122
Borgnesse, Pointe, c., Mart.	I7	105c
Borgomanero, Italy	E5	22
Borgo San Dalmazzo, Italy	F4	22
Borgosesia, Italy	E5	22
Borgo Val di Taro, Italy	F6	22
Borgworm see Waremme, Bel.	D14	14
Borikhan, Laos	C6	48
Borisoglebsk, Russia	D6	32
Borisoglebskij, Russia	C21	10
Borjas Blancas see Les Borges Blanques, Spain	C11	20
Borkavičy, Bela.	E11	10
Borken, Ger.	E2	16
Borkou, reg., Chad	D3	62
Borkum, i., Ger.	C2	16
Borlänge, Swe.	F6	8
Bormes, Fr.	F12	18
Borna, Ger.	E9	16
Borneo (Kalimantan), i., Asia	E5	44
Bornholm, state, Den.	I6	8
Bornholm, i., Den.	I6	8
Borocay Island, i., Phil.	E3	52
Borodino, Russia	C17	32
Borogoncy, Russia	D15	34
Borohoro Shan, mts., China	F14	32
Boromo, Burkina	G4	64
Boron, Ca., U.S.	H8	134
Boronga Islands, is., Mya.	I14	54
Borongan, Phil.	E5	52
Borovan, Blg.	F10	26
Boroviči, Russia	B16	10
Borovljanka, Russia	D14	32
Borovsk, Russia	E19	10
Borovskij, Russia	C11	32
Borovskoj, Kaz.	D10	32
Borrachudo, stm., Braz.	J3	88
Borrazópolis, Braz.	A12	92
Borriana, Spain	E10	20
Borroloola, Austl.	C7	74
Borș, Rom.	B8	26
Borșa, Rom.	B11	26
Borsad, India	G4	54
Borščovočnyj hrebet, mts., Russia	F12	34
Borsod-Abaúj-Zemplén, state, Hung.	A8	26
Bort-les-Orgues, Fr.	D8	18
Borūjerd, Iran	C6	56
Borzja, Russia	F12	34
Bosa, Italy	D2	24
Bosanska Dubica, Bos.	D3	26
Bosanska Gradiška, Bos.	D4	26
Bosanska Krupa, Bos.	E3	26
Bosanski Novi, Bos.	D3	26
Bosanski Šamac, Bos.	D5	26
Bosavi, Mount, mtn., Pap. N. Gui.	b3	79a
Boscobel, Wi., U.S.	A7	120
Bose, China	J2	42
Boshan, China	C7	42
Boshof, S. Afr.	F7	70
Bosilegrad, Yugo.	G9	26
Bosna, stm., Bos.	E5	26
Bosnia and Herzegovina, ctry., Eur.	E3	26
Bosnik, Indon.	F10	44
Bošnjakovo, Russia	G17	34
Bosobolo, D.R.C.	D3	66
Bōsō-hantō, pen., Japan	D13	40
Bosporus see İstanbul Boğazı, strt., Tur.	B12	28
Bossangoa, C.A.R.	C3	66
Bossembélé, C.A.R.	C3	66
Bossey Bangou, Niger	G5	64
Bossier City, La., U.S.	E5	122
Bosten Hu, l., China	C2	36
Boston, Eng., U.K.	H12	12
Boston, Ga., U.S.	F2	116
Boston, Ma., U.S.	B14	114
Boston Bar, B.C., Can.	G9	138
Boston Mountains, mts., Ar., U.S.	B5	122
Boswell, In., U.S.	H2	112
Boswell, Ok., U.S.	C3	122
Bosworth, Mo., U.S.	E4	120
Botād, India	G3	54
Botany Bay, b., Austl.	J8	76
Boteti, stm., Bots.	E3	68
Bothaville, S. Afr.	E8	70
Bothnia, Gulf of, b., Eur.	E9	8
Bothwell, On., Can.	F8	112
Boticas, Port.	C3	20
Botna, stm., Mol.	C15	26
Botoșani, Rom.	B13	26
Botoșani, state, Rom.	B13	26
Bo Trach, Viet.	D8	48
Botrange, mtn., Bel.	D15	14
Botswana, ctry., Afr.	E3	68
Botte Donato, Monte, mtn., Italy	E10	24
Bottineau, N.D., U.S.	F13	124
Botucatu, Braz.	L1	88
Botwood, Nf., Can.	j22	107a
Bouaflé, C. Iv.	H3	64
Bouaké, C. Iv.	H3	64
Bouar, C.A.R.	C3	66
Bouârfa, Mor.	C4	64
Bouca, C.A.R.	C3	66
Boucher, stm., Qc., Can.	A7	110
Bouches-du-Rhône, state, Fr.	F11	18
Bouctouche, N.B., Can.	D12	110
Boufarik, Alg.	H13	20
Bou Ficha, Tun.	H4	24
Bougainville, i., Pap. N. Gui.	d7	79b
Bougainville, Détroit de, strt., Vanuatu	j16	79d
Bougainville Strait, strt., Oc.	d7	79b
Bougouni, Mali	G3	64
Bouillante, Guad.	h5	105c
Bouillon, Bel.	E14	14
Bouïra, Alg.	B5	64
Boujdour, Cap, c., W. Sah.	D2	64
Boularderie Island, i., N.S., Can.	D16	110
Boulder, Co., U.S.	A3	128
Boulder, Mt., U.S.	D14	136
Boulder, stm., Mt., U.S.	D15	136
Boulder City, Nv., U.S.	H2	132
Boulia, Austl.	D2	76
Boulogne-sur-Mer, Fr.	D10	14
Bouloupari, N. Cal.	m15	79d
Boulsa, Burkina	G4	64
Bou Medfaa, Alg.	H13	20
Bouna, C. Iv.	H4	64
Boundary Peak, mtn., Nv., U.S.	F7	134
Boundiali, C. Iv.	H3	64
Boun Nua, Laos	B5	48
Bountiful, Ut., U.S.	C4	132
Bounty Bay, b., Pit.	c28	78k
Bounty Islands, is., N.Z.	H8	80
Bounty Trough, unds.	N20	142
Bourail, N. Cal.	m15	79d
Bourbeuse, stm., Mo., U.S.	F6	120
Bourbon, In., U.S.	G3	112
Bourbonnais, hist. reg., Fr.	C9	18
Bourbonne-les-Bains, Fr.	G14	14
Bourem, Mali	F4	64
Bourg, La., U.S.	H8	122
Bourg-en-Bresse, Fr.	C11	18
Bourges, Fr.	G11	14
Bourget, On., Can.	E1	110
Bourget, Lac du, l., Fr.	D11	18
Bourgogne (Burgundy), hist. reg., Fr.	B10	18
Bourgogne, Canal de, can., Fr.	G13	14
Bourgoin-Jallieu, Fr.	D11	18
Bourke, Austl.	H5	76
Bournemouth, Eng., U.K.	K11	12
Bou Saâda, Alg.	B5	64
Bou Salem, Tun.	H2	24
Bouse Wash, stm., Az., U.S.	J3	132
Bou Smail, Alg.	H13	20
Boussac, Fr.	C8	18
Bousso, Chad	E3	62
Boutilimit, Maur.	F2	64
Bouvetøya, i., Ant.	A5	81
Bouza, Niger	G6	64
Bøvågen, Nor.	F1	8
Bovec, Slvn.	D10	22
Bovey, Mn., U.S.	D5	118
Bovill, Id., U.S.	D10	136
Bovina, Tx., U.S.	G6	128
Bow, stm., Ab., Can.	G19	138
Bo-Wadrif, S. Afr.	H4	70
Bowbells, N.D., U.S.	F11	124
Bow Creek, stm., Ks., U.S.	B9	128
Bowden, Ab., Can.	E16	138
Bowdle, S.D., U.S.	B13	126
Bowdon, N.D., U.S.	G14	124
Bowen, Arg.	G4	92
Bowen, Austl.	C7	76
Bowen, Il., U.S.	D7	120
Bowen, stm., Austl.	C6	76
Bowie, Az., U.S.	K7	132
Bowie, Md., U.S.	F9	114
Bowling Green, Fl., U.S.	I4	116
Bowling Green, Ky., U.S.	H11	120
Bowling Green, Mo., U.S.	E6	120
Bowling Green, Oh., U.S.	C2	114
Bowling Green, Va., U.S.	F8	114
Bowling Green, Cape, c., Austl.	B6	76
Bowling Green Bay National Park, p.o.i., Austl.	B6	76
Bowman, N.D., U.S.	A9	126
Bowman, S.C., U.S.	C5	116
Bowman, Mount, mtn., B.C., Can.	E9	138
Bowmanville, On., Can.	E11	112
Bowral, Austl.	J8	76
Bowraville, Austl.	H9	76
Bowron, stm., B.C., Can.	C9	138
Bowsman, Mb., Can.	B12	124
Boxelder Creek, stm., U.S.	B8	126
Box Elder Creek, stm., Mt., U.S.	G5	124
Boxelder Creek, stm., S.D., U.S.	C10	126
Boxing, China	C8	42
Boyacá, state, Col.	E5	86
Boyang, China	G7	42
Boyce, La., U.S.	F6	122
Boyceville, Wi., U.S.	F6	118
Boyd, Tx., U.S.	A10	130
Boyd, stm., Austl.	G9	76
Boydton, Va., U.S.	H7	114
Boyer, stm., Ia., U.S.	C2	120
Boyertown, Pa., U.S.	D10	114
Boykins, Va., U.S.	H8	114
Boyle, Ms., U.S.	D8	122
Boylston, Al., U.S.	E12	122
Boyne, stm., Austl.	E8	76
Boyne, stm., Mb., Can.	E16	124
Boyne, stm., Ire.	H5	12
Boyne City, Mi., U.S.	C5	112
Boynton Beach, Fl., U.S.	J5	116
Boysen Reservoir, res., Wy., U.S.	D4	126
Boys Ranch, Tx., U.S.	F6	128
Bozburun, Tur.	G11	28
Bozburun Yarımadası, pen., Tur.	G11	28
Boz Dağ, mtn., Tur.	E11	28
Boz Dağlar, mts., Tur.	E10	28
Bozdoğan, Tur.	F11	28
Bozeman, Mt., U.S.	E15	136
Bozen see Bolzano, Italy	D8	22
Bozhen, China	B7	42
Bozhou, China	E6	42
Bozkurt, Tur.	F12	28
Bozoum, C.A.R.	C3	66
Bozova, Tur.	A9	58
Bozovici, Rom.	E9	26
Bozšakol', Kaz.	D12	32
Bozüyük, Tur.	D13	28
Bra, Italy	F4	22
Brač, Otok, i., Cro.	G13	22
Bracciano, Italy	H9	22
Bracciano, Lago di, l., Italy	H9	22
Bracebridge, On., Can.	C10	112
Brackendale, B.C., Can.	G7	138
Brackettville, Tx., U.S.	E7	130
Bracknell, Eng., U.K.	J12	12
Braço do Norte, Braz.	D13	92
Brad, Rom.	C9	26
Bradano, stm., Italy	D10	24
Bradenton, Fl., U.S.	I3	116
Bradford, Eng., U.K.	H11	12
Bradford, Ar., U.S.	B7	122
Bradford, Pa., U.S.	C7	114
Bradford, Tn., U.S.	H9	120
Bradford, Vt., U.S.	G4	110
Bradford West Gwillimbury, On., Can.	D10	112
Bradley, Ar., U.S.	D5	122
Bradley, Fl., U.S.	I3	116
Bradley, Il., U.S.	G2	112
Bradley, S.D., U.S.	B15	126
Brady, Mt., U.S.	B15	136
Brady, Ne., U.S.	F12	126
Brady, Tx., U.S.	C8	130
Brady Creek, stm., Tx., U.S.	C8	130
Braga, Port.	C2	20
Braga, state, Port.	C2	20
Bragado, Arg.	G7	92
Bragança, Braz.	D8	84
Bragança, Port.	C4	20
Bragança, state, Port.	C4	20
Bragança Paulista, Braz.	L2	88
Brāhmanbāria, Bngl.	F13	54
Brāhmani, stm., India	H10	54
Brahmapur, India	B7	53
Brahmaputra (Yarlung), stm., Asia	C7	46
Braich y Pwll, c., Wales, U.K.	I8	12
Braidwood, Austl.	J7	76
Braidwood, Il., U.S.	C9	120
Brăila, Rom.	D14	26
Brăila, state, Rom.	D14	26
Brainard, Ne., U.S.	F15	126
Brainerd, Mn., U.S.	E4	118
Braintree, Eng., U.K.	J13	12
Brak, stm., S. Afr.	G6	70
Brake, Ger.	C4	16
Bralorne, B.C., Can.	F8	138
Brampton, On., Can.	E10	112
Bramsche, Ger.	D3	16
Branchville, S.C., U.S.	C5	116
Branco, stm., Braz.	H11	86
Branco, stm., Braz.	F3	88
Brandaris, hill, Neth. Ant.	p23	104g
Brandberg, mtn., Nmb.	B2	70
Brandbu, Nor.	F4	8
Brandenburg, Ger.	D8	16
Brandenburg, Ky., U.S.	G11	120
Brandenburg, state, Ger.	D9	16
Brandfort, S. Afr.	F8	70
Brandon, Mb., Can.	E14	124
Brandon, Fl., U.S.	I3	116
Brandon, Ms., U.S.	E9	122
Brandon, S.D., U.S.	H2	118
Brandon, Vt., U.S.	G3	110
Brandsen, Arg.	G8	92
Brandvlei, S. Afr.	G5	70
Brandy Peak, mtn., Or., U.S.	H3	136
Brandýs nad Labem-Stará Boleslav, Czech Rep.	F10	16
Branford, Fl., U.S.	G2	116
Braniewo, Pol.	B15	16
Bransby, Austl.	G4	76
Bransby Point, c., Monts.	D3	105a
Bransfield Strait, strt., Ant.	B35	81
Branson, Mo., U.S.	H4	120
Brantford, On., Can.	E9	112
Brantley, Al., U.S.	F12	122
Brantley Tank, res., N.M., U.S.	B3	130
Brantôme, Fr.	D6	18
Brantville, N.B., Can.	C12	110
Bras d'Or Lake, l., N.S., Can.	E16	110
Brasiléia, Braz.	F4	84
Brasília, Braz.	H1	88
Brasília, Parque Nacional de, p.o.i., Braz.	H1	88
Brasília de Minas, Braz.	I3	88
Braslau, Bela.	E9	10
Brașov, Rom.	D12	26
Brașov, state, Rom.	D12	26
Brassey, Banjaran, mts., Malay.	A10	50
Brass Islands, is., V.I.U.S.	e7	104b
Brasstown Bald, mtn., Ga., U.S.	B2	116
Bratca, Rom.	C9	26
Bratislava, Slov.	H13	16
Bratislava, state, Slov.	H13	16
Bratsk, Russia	C18	32
Bratskoe vodohranilišče, res., Russia	C18	32
Bratsk Reservoir see Bratskoe vodohranilišče, res., Russia	C18	32
Brattleboro, Vt., U.S.	B13	114
Braulio Carrillo, Parque Nacional, p.o.i., C.R.	G5	102
Braúnas, Braz.	J4	88
Braunau am Inn, Aus.	B10	22
Braunschweig (Brunswick), Ger.	D6	16
Brava, i., C.V.	I10	65a
Brava, Costa, cst., Spain	C14	20
Brava, Laguna, l., Arg.	D3	92
Brava, Punta, c., Ur.	G9	92
Brave, Pa., U.S.	E5	114
Bravo (Rio Grande), stm., N.A.	H13	98
Bravo, Cerro, mtn., Peru	E2	84
Bravo del Norte see Bravo, stm., N.A.	H13	98
Brawley, Ca., U.S.	K10	134
Bray, Ire.	H6	12
Bray Island, i., Nu., Can.	B15	106
Brazeau, stm., Ab., Can.	D15	138
Brazeau, Mount, mtn., Ab., Can.	D13	138
Brazeau Dam, dam, Ab., Can.	C15	138
Brazil, In., U.S.	E10	120
Brazil, ctry., S.A.	F9	82
Brazil Basin, unds.	J11	144
Brazoria, Tx., U.S.	E12	130
Brazos, stm., Tx., U.S.	E8	108
Brazos, Clear Fork, stm., Tx., U.S.	B8	130
Brazos, Double Mountain Fork, stm., Tx., U.S.	H8	128
Brazos, North Fork, stm., Tx., U.S.	H3	122
Brazzaville, Congo	E2	66
Brčko, Bos.	E5	26
Brda, stm., Pol.	C13	16
Bré see Bray, Ire.	H6	12
Brea, Ca., U.S.	J8	134
Bream Bay, b., N.Z.	B6	80
Brea Pozo, Arg.	D6	92
Breaux Bridge, La., U.S.	G7	122
Brebes, Indon.	G6	50
Brechin, Scot., U.K.	E10	12
Breckenridge, Mi., U.S.	E5	112
Breckenridge, Mn., U.S.	E2	118
Breckenridge, Mo., U.S.	E4	120
Brecknock, Península, pen., Chile	J2	90
Břeclav, Czech Rep.	H12	16
Brecon, Wales, U.K.	J9	12
Brecon Beacons, hills, Wales, U.K.	J9	12
Brecon Beacons National Park, p.o.i., Wales, U.K.	J9	12
Breda, Neth.	C13	14
Breda, Ia., U.S.	B3	120
Bredasdorp, S. Afr.	I5	70
Bredenbury, Sk., Can.	D11	124
Bredy, Russia	D9	32
Breë, stm., S. Afr.	I5	70
Breese, Il., U.S.	F8	120
Bregalnica, stm., Mac.	A5	28
Bregenz, Aus.	C6	22
Bregovo, Blg.	E9	26
Bréhat, Île de, i., Fr.	F6	14
Breiðafjörður, b., Ice.	k28	8a
Brejinho de Nazaré, Braz.	F1	88
Brejo, Braz.	B4	88
Brejo Grande, Braz.	F7	88
Brejo Santo, Braz.	D6	88
Brekstad, Nor.	E3	8
Bremen, Ger.	C4	16
Bremen, Ga., U.S.	D13	122
Bremen, Oh., U.S.	E3	114
Bremen, state, Ger.	C4	16
Bremer Bay, Austl.	F3	74
Bremer Bay, b., Austl.	F3	74
Bremerhaven, Ger.	C4	16
Bremerton, Wa., U.S.	C4	136
Bremervörde, Ger.	C4	16
Bremond, Tx., U.S.	F2	122
Brenham, Tx., U.S.	G2	122
Brenner Pass, p., Eur.	C8	22
Brent, Fl., U.S.	G11	122
Brenta, stm., Italy	D8	22
Brentwood, Eng., U.K.	J13	12
Brentwood, N.Y., U.S.	D12	114
Brentwood, Tn., U.S.	H11	120
Breo, Italy	F4	22
Brescia, Italy	E7	22
Breslau see Wrocław, Pol.	E13	16
Bressanone, Italy	D8	22
Bressay, i., Scot., U.K.	n18	12a
Bresse, reg., Fr.	C11	18
Bressuire, Fr.	H8	14
Brèst, Bela.	H6	10
Brest, Fr.	F4	14
Brèst, state, Bela.	H8	10
Bretagne (Brittany), hist. reg., Fr.	F5	14
Bretenoux, Fr.	E7	18
Breton, Ab., Can.	C16	138
Breton Islands, is., La., U.S.	H9	122
Breton Sound, strt., La., U.S.	H9	122
Brett, Cape, c., N.Z.	B6	80
Bretten, Ger.	G4	16
Breueh, Pulau, i., Indon.	J2	48
Breuil-Cervinia, Italy	E4	22
Brevard, N.C., U.S.	A3	116
Breves, Braz.	D7	84
Brevoort Island, i., Nu., Can.	E13	141
Brewarrina, Austl.	G6	76
Brewer, Me., U.S.	F8	110
Brewster, Mn., U.S.	H3	118
Brewster, Ne., U.S.	F13	126
Brewster, Wa., U.S.	B7	136
Brewster, Kap, c., Grnld.	C21	141
Brewton, Al., U.S.	F11	122
Breyten, S. Afr.	E10	70
Březnice, Czech Rep.	G9	16
Brezno, Slov.	H15	16
Bria, C.A.R.	C4	66
Brian Boru Peak, mtn., B.C., Can.	A3	138
Briançon, Fr.	E12	18
Brian Head, mtn., Ut., U.S.	F4	132
Briare, Canal de, can., Fr.	G11	14
Bribie Island, i., Austl.	F9	76
Bricelyn, Mn., U.S.	H5	118
Briceni, Mol.	A14	26
Briceville, Tn., U.S.	A14	122
Bri Chuallan see Bray, Ire.	H6	12
Bridge, stm., B.C., Can.	F7	138
Bridge City, Tx., U.S.	G5	122
Bridge Lake, B.C., Can.	E10	138
Bridgend, Wales, U.K.	J9	12
Bridgeport, Ca., U.S.	E6	134
Bridgeport, Ct., U.S.	C12	114
Bridgeport, Mi., U.S.	E6	112
Bridgeport, Ne., U.S.	F9	126
Bridgeport, Tx., U.S.	H11	128
Bridgeport, Wa., U.S.	C7	136
Bridgeport, Lake, res., Tx., U.S.	H10	128
Bridger, Mt., U.S.	B4	126
Bridger Peak, mtn., Wy., U.S.	B9	132
Bridgeton, N.J., U.S.	E10	114
Bridgetown, Austl.	F3	74
Bridgetown, Barb.	n8	105d
Bridgetown, N.S., Can.	F11	110
Bridgeville, De., U.S.	F10	114
Bridgewater, N.S., Can.	F12	110
Bridgewater, Ma., U.S.	B15	114
Bridgewater, S.D., U.S.	D15	126
Bridgewater, Va., U.S.	F6	114
Bridgwater, Eng., U.K.	J9	12
Bridgwater Bay, b., Eng., U.K.	J9	12
Bridlington, Eng., U.K.	G12	12
Bridport, Eng., U.K.	K10	12
Brie, reg., Fr.	F12	14
Brier Creek, stm., Ga., U.S.	C4	116
Brig, Switz.	D5	22
Briggs, Tx., U.S.	D10	130
Brigham City, Ut., U.S.	B4	132
Bright, Austl.	K6	76
Brighton, On., Can.	D12	112
Brighton, Eng., U.K.	K12	12
Brighton, Co., U.S.	A4	128
Brighton, Ia., U.S.	C6	120
Brighton, Mi., U.S.	B2	114
Brighton, N.Y., U.S.	E12	112
Brighton Downs, Austl.	D3	76
Brignoles, Fr.	F11	18
Brijuni, i., Cro.	F10	22
Brilliant, B.C., Can.	G13	138
Brilliant, Al., U.S.	C11	122
Brillion, Wi., U.S.	D1	112
Brilon, Ger.	E4	16
Brindisi, Italy	D11	24
Brinkworth, Austl.	I2	76
Brion, Île, i., Qc., Can.	C15	110
Brioude, Fr.	D9	18
Brisbane, Austl.	F9	76
Brisighella, Italy	F8	22
Bristol, Eng., U.K.	J10	12
Bristol, Ct., U.S.	C12	114
Bristol, Fl., U.S.	G14	122
Bristol, N.H., U.S.	G5	110
Bristol, Pa., U.S.	D11	114
Bristol, R.I., U.S.	C14	114
Bristol, Tn., U.S.	H3	114
Bristol, Vt., U.S.	F3	110
Bristol Bay, b., Ak., U.S.	E7	140
Bristol Channel, strt., U.K.	J8	12
Bristol Island, i., S. Geor.	A2	81
Bristol Lake, l., Ca., U.S.	I10	134
Bristow, Ok., U.S.	B2	122
Britannia Beach, B.C., Can.	G7	138
British Columbia, state, Can.	E5	106
British Guiana see Guyana, ctry., S.A.	C6	84
British Honduras see Belize, ctry., N.A.	D3	102
British Indian Ocean Territory, dep., Afr.	G17	2
British Isles, is., Eur.	C12	4
British Mountains, mts., N.A.	C11	140
British Solomon Islands see Solomon Islands, ctry., Oc.	D7	72
British Virgin Islands, dep., N.A.	h15	96a
Brits, S. Afr.	D8	70
Britstown, S. Afr.	G6	70
Britt, Ia., U.S.	A4	120
Brittany see Bretagne, hist. reg., Fr.	F5	14
Britton, S.D., U.S.	B15	126
Brive-la-Gaillarde, Fr.	D7	18
Brixen see Bressanone, Italy	D8	22
Brixham, Eng., U.K.	K9	12
Brixton, Austl.	D5	76
Brjanka, Russia	C16	32
Brjansk, Russia	G17	10
Brjanskaja oblast', co., Russia	H16	10
Brno, Czech Rep.	G12	16
Broa, Ensenada de la, b., Cuba	A6	102
Broad, stm., U.S.	B4	116
Broad, stm., Ga., U.S.	B2	116
Broadalbin, N.Y., U.S.	G2	110
Broad Sound, b., Austl.	D7	76
Broad Sound Channel, strt., Austl.	C8	76
Broadus, Mt., U.S.	B7	126
Broadwater, Ne., U.S.	F10	126
Broadway, Va., U.S.	F7	114
Brocēni, Lat.	D5	10
Brochet, Mb., Can.	D10	106
Brock, Sk., Can.	C5	124
Brockman, Mount, mtn., Austl.	D3	74
Brockton, Ma., U.S.	B14	114
Brockton, Mt., U.S.	F9	124
Brockville, On., Can.	D14	112
Brockway, Pa., U.S.	C7	114
Brocton, N.Y., U.S.	B6	114
Brodeur Peninsula, pen., Nu., Can.	A13	106
Brodhead, Wi., U.S.	B8	120
Brodick, Scot., U.K.	F7	12
Brodnax, Va., U.S.	H7	114
Brodnica, Pol.	C15	16
Brogan, Or., U.S.	F9	136
Brok, Pol.	D17	16
Broken Arrow, Ok., U.S.	H2	120
Broken Bay, b., Austl.	I8	76
Broken Bow, Ok., U.S.	C4	122
Broken Bow Lake, res., Ok., U.S.	C4	122
Broken Hill, Austl.	H3	76
Broken Hill see Kabwe, Zam.	C4	68
Broken Ridge, unds.	M12	142
Brokopondo, Sur.	B6	84
Brokopondo Stuwmeer, res., Sur.	C6	84
Bromley Plateau, unds.	K10	144
Bromptonville, Qc., Can.	E4	110
Bromsgrove, Eng., U.K.	I10	12
Bronkhorstspruit, S. Afr.	D9	70
Bronlund Peak, mtn., B.C., Can.	D5	106
Bronnae, Bela.	H13	10
Bronnicy, Russia	E21	10
Bronson, Fl., U.S.	G3	116
Bronson, Ks., U.S.	G2	120
Bronson, Mi., U.S.	G4	112
Bronte, Italy	G8	24
Bronte, Tx., U.S.	C7	130
Brook, In., U.S.	H2	112
Brookeland, Tx., U.S.	F5	122
Brooker, Fl., U.S.	G3	116
Brookfield, N.S., Can.	E13	110
Brookfield, Wi., U.S.	E1	112
Brookford, N.C., U.S.	I4	114
Brookhaven, Ms., U.S.	F8	122
Brookings, Or., U.S.	A1	134
Brookings, S.D., U.S.	G2	118
Brookland, Ar., U.S.	B8	122
Brooklyn, N.S., Can.	F12	110
Brooklyn, Ia., U.S.	J6	118
Brooklyn, Mi., U.S.	B1	114
Brooklyn Center, Mn., U.S.	F5	118
Brookmere, B.C., Can.	G10	138
Brookneal, Va., U.S.	G7	114
Brookport, Il., U.S.	G9	120
Brooks, Ab., Can.	F19	138
Brooks Bay, b., B.C., Can.	F2	138
Brookshire, Tx., U.S.	H3	122
Brooks Range, mts., Ak., U.S.	C8	140
Brooksville, Fl., U.S.	H3	116
Brooksville, Ms., U.S.	D10	122
Brookville, In., U.S.	E12	120
Brookville, Pa., U.S.	C6	114
Brookville Lake, res., In., U.S.	E13	120
Broome, Austl.	C4	74
Broomfield, Co., U.S.	B3	128
Brooten, Mn., U.S.	F3	118
Brora, Scot., U.K.	C9	12
Brosna, stm., Ire.	H5	12
Brotas de Macaúbas, Braz.	G4	88
Brou, Fr.	F10	14
Broughton, Mount, mtn., Austl.	K5	76
Broughty Ferry, Scot., U.K.	E10	12
Browerville, Mn., U.S.	E4	118
Brown, Mount, mtn., Mt., U.S.	B15	136
Brown, Point, c., Wa., U.S.	D2	136
Brown Deer, Wi., U.S.	E2	112
Browne Bay, b., Nu., Can.	A11	106
Brownfield, Tx., U.S.	A5	130
Browning, Mo., U.S.	D4	120
Browning, Mt., U.S.	B13	136
Brownlee Reservoir, res., U.S.	F9	136
Brownsburg, Qc., Can.	E2	110
Brownsburg, In., U.S.	I3	112
Brownsdale, Mn., U.S.	H5	118
Browns Town, Jam.	i13	104d
Brownstown, In., U.S.	F11	120
Brownsville, Ky., U.S.	G11	120
Brownsville, La., U.S.	E6	122
Brownsville, Or., U.S.	F4	136
Brownsville, Tn., U.S.	B9	122
Brownsville, Tx., U.S.	I10	130
Brownton, Mn., U.S.	G4	118
Brownville, Me., U.S.	E7	110
Brownville, Ne., U.S.	D2	120
Brownville Junction, Me., U.S.	E7	110
Brownwood, Tx., U.S.	C8	130
Brownwood, Lake, res., Tx., U.S.	C9	130
Browse Island, i., Austl.	B4	74
Broxton, Ga., U.S.	E3	116
Broža, Bela.	H12	10
Bruay-en-Artois, Fr.	D11	14
Bruce, S.D., U.S.	G2	118
Bruce, Wi., U.S.	F7	118
Bruce, Mount, mtn., Austl.	D3	74
Bruce Mines, On., Can.	B6	112
Bruce Peninsula, pen., On., Can.	C8	112
Bruce Peninsula National Park, p.o.i., On., Can.	C8	112
Bruce Rock, Austl.	F3	74
Bruchsal, Ger.	G4	16
Bruck an der Leitha, Aus.	B13	22
Bruck an der Mur, Aus.	C12	22
Bruges see Brugge, Bel.	C12	14
Brugg, Switz.	C5	22
Brugge (Bruges), Bel.	C12	14
Brühl, Ger.	F2	16
Bruit, Pulau, i., Malay.	B7	50
Brule, Ne., U.S.	F11	126
Brumado, Braz.	H5	88
Brundidge, Al., U.S.	F13	122
Bruneau, Id., U.S.	H11	136
Bruneau, stm., U.S.	H11	136
Bruneck see Brunico, Italy	D8	22
Brunei, ctry., Asia	A9	50
Brunico, Italy	D8	22
Brunsbüttel, Ger.	C4	16
Brunson, S.C., U.S.	D4	116
Brunswick see Braunschweig, Ger.	D6	16
Brunswick, Ga., U.S.	E4	116
Brunswick, Me., U.S.	G6	110
Brunswick, Md., U.S.	E8	114
Brunswick, Mo., U.S.	E4	120
Brunswick, Oh., U.S.	C4	114
Brunswick, Península, pen., Chile	J2	90
Bruntál, Czech Rep.	F13	16
Brus, Laguna de, b., Hond.	E5	102
Brush, Co., U.S.	A5	128
Brusovo, Russia	C18	10
Brusque, Braz.	C13	92
Brussel see Bruxelles, Bel.	D13	14
Brussels see Bruxelles, Bel.	D13	14
Brussels, On., Can.	E8	112
Bruthen, Austl.	K6	76
Bruxelles (Brussels), Bel.	D13	14
Bruzual, Ven.	D7	86
Bryan, Oh., U.S.	C1	114
Bryan, Tx., U.S.	G2	122
Bryan, Mount, mtn., Austl.	I2	76
Bryant, Ar., U.S.	C6	122
Bryce Canyon National Park, p.o.i., Ut., U.S.	F4	132
Bryli, Bela.	G13	10
Bryson, Qc., Can.	C13	112
Bryson, Tx., U.S.	A9	130
Brzeg, Pol.	F13	16
Brześć Kujawski, Pol.	D14	16
Brzesko, Pol.	F16	16
Brzeziny, Pol.	E15	16
Bsharrī, Leb.	D6	58
Bua, Fiji	p19	79e
Bua Bay, b., Fiji	p19	79e
Buada Lagoon, b., Nauru	q17	78f
Buala, Sol. Is.	e8	79b
Bua Yai, Thai.	E6	48
Bubanza, Bdi.	E5	66
Bubaque, Gui.-B.	G1	64
Bubi, stm., Zimb.	B10	70
Būbiyān, i., Kuw.	D6	56
Bubuduo, China	C10	54
Bucak, Tur.	F13	28
Bucaramanga, Col.	D5	86
Buccaneer Archipelago, is., Austl.	C4	74
Buchanan, Sk., Can.	C11	124
Buchanan, Lib.	H2	64
Buchanan, Ga., U.S.	D13	122
Buchanan, Mi., U.S.	G3	112
Buchanan, Lake, l., Austl.	C5	76
Buchanan, Lake, l., Tx., U.S.	D9	130
Buchan Ness, c., Scot., U.K.	D11	12
Buchans, Nf., Can.	j22	107a
Bucharest see București, Rom.	E13	26
Buchen, Ger.	G5	16
Buchholz in der Nordheide, Ger.	C5	16
Buchloe, Ger.	H6	16
Buchon, Point, c., Ca., U.S.	H4	134
Buchs, Switz.	C6	22
Buckatunna, Ms., U.S.	F10	122
Buckatunna Creek, stm., Ms., U.S.	F10	122
Bückeburg, Ger.	D5	16
Buckeye, Az., U.S.	J4	132
Buckeye Lake, Oh., U.S.	I7	112
Buckhaven, Scot., U.K.	E9	12
Buckholts, Tx., U.S.	D10	130
Buckhorn Draw, stm., Tx., U.S.	D7	130
Buckie, Scot., U.K.	D10	12
Buckingham, Qc., Can.	C14	112
Buckingham, Va., U.S.	G7	114
Buckingham Bay, b., Austl.	B7	74
Buck Island, i., V.I.U.S.	g11	104c
Buck Island Reef National Monument, p.o.i., V.I.U.S.	g11	104c
Buck Lake, l., Ab., Can.	D16	138
Buckland, Ak., U.S.	C7	140
Buckley, Wa., U.S.	C4	136
Bucklin, Ks., U.S.	D9	128
Bucklin, Mo., U.S.	E5	120
Buck Mountain, mtn., Wa., U.S.	B7	136
Bucovăț, Mol.	B15	26
Buco Zau, Ang.	A1	68
București (Bucharest), Rom.	E13	26
București, state, Rom.	E13	26
Bucyrus, Oh., U.S.	D3	114
Buda, Il., U.S.	C8	120
Buda, Tx., U.S.	D10	130
Budalin, Mya.	A2	48
Budapest, Hung.	B6	26
Budapest, state, Hung.	B6	26
Budaun, India	D7	54
Budd Coast, cst., Ant.	B16	81
Buddh Gaya see Bodh Gaya, India	F10	54
Buddusò, Italy	D3	24
Bude, Ms., U.S.	F8	122
Bude Bay, b., Eng., U.K.	K8	12
Buděnnovsk, Russia	F6	32
Budești, Rom.	E13	26
Büdingen, Ger.	F5	16
Budišov nad Budišovkou, Czech Rep.	G13	16
Budjala, D.R.C.	D3	66
Budogovišči, Russia	G19	10
Budrio, Italy	F8	22
Budweis see České Budějovice, Czech Rep.	H10	16
Buea, Cam.	D1	66
Buena Esperanza, Arg.	G5	92
Buenaventura, Col.	F3	86
Buenaventura, Mex.	G9	98
Buena Vista, Bol.	C4	90
Buena Vista, Mex.	K9	134
Buenavista, Phil.	G4	52
Buena Vista, Co., U.S.	C2	128
Buena Vista, Ga., U.S.	E14	122
Buena Vista, Va., U.S.	G6	114
Buena Vista Lake Bed, reg., Ca., U.S.	H6	134
Buendía, Embalse de, res., Spain	D8	20
Buenópolis, Braz.	I3	88
Buenos Aires, Arg.	G8	92
Buenos Aires, Col.	F3	86
Buenos Aires, C.R.	H6	102
Buenos Aires, state, Arg.	G5	90
Buenos Aires, Lago see General Carrera, Lago, l., S.A.	I2	90
Buen Pasto, Arg.	I3	90
Buerarema, Braz.	H6	88
Buffalo, Ks., U.S.	G2	120
Buffalo, Mn., U.S.	F5	118
Buffalo, Mo., U.S.	G4	120
Buffalo, N.Y., U.S.	B7	114
Buffalo, Oh., U.S.	E4	114
Buffalo, S.C., U.S.	B4	116
Buffalo, S.D., U.S.	B9	126
Buffalo, Tx., U.S.	F2	122
Buffalo, stm., Can.	C8	106
Buffalo, stm., Ar., U.S.	H4	120
Buffalo, stm., Tn., U.S.	B11	122
Buffalo Creek, stm., Mn., U.S.	G4	118
Buffalo Lake, Mn., U.S.	G4	118
Buffalo Lake, l., Ab., Can.	D18	138
Buffalo Lake, l., N.T., Can.	C7	106
Buffalo Narrows, Sk., Can.	D8	106
Buffalo Pound Lake, l., Sk., Can.	D8	124
Buffels, stm., S. Afr.	F10	70
Buffels, stm., S. Afr.	F3	70
Buford, Ga., U.S.	B2	116
Buford Dam, dam, Ga., U.S.	B1	116
Buftea, Rom.	E12	26
Bug (Buh) (Zakhidnyy Buh), stm., Eur.	D17	16
Buga, Col.	F3	86
Bugala Island, i., Ug.	E6	66
Bugeat, Fr.	D7	18
Bugojno, Bos.	E4	26
Bugrino, Russia	B23	8
Bugsuk Island, i., Phil.	F1	52
Bugt, China	C4	38
Bugul'ma, Russia	D8	32
Buguruslan, Russia	D8	32
Buh, stm., China	D4	36
Buh (Bug) (Zakhidnyy Buh), stm., Eur.	D19	16
Buhara, Uzb.	G10	32
Buhl, Mn., U.S.	D6	118
Buhler, Ks., U.S.	C11	128
Buhuși, Rom.	C13	26
Buies Creek, N.C., U.S.	A7	116
Builth Wells, Wales, U.K.	I9	12
Buin, Chile	F2	92
Buin, Pap. N. Gui.	d6	79b
Buíque, Braz.	E7	88
Buitsivango (Rietfontein), stm., Afr.	B4	70
Buj, Russia	G19	8
Bujalance, Spain	G6	20
Buje, Cro.	E10	22
Bujnaksk, Russia	F7	32
Bujumbura, Bdi.	E5	66
Bukačača, Russia	F12	34
Bukama, D.R.C.	F5	66
Bukan', Russia	G17	10
Bukavu, D.R.C.	E5	66
Bukeya, D.R.C.	G5	66
Bukhara see Buhara, Uzb.	G10	32
Bukittinggi, Indon.	D2	50
Bükki Nemzeti Park, p.o.i., Hung.	A7	26
Bukoba, Tan.	E6	66
Bukovica, reg., Cro.	F12	22
Bukovina, hist. reg., Eur.	B12	26
Bukuru, Nig.	H6	64
Bula, Indon.	F9	44
Bulaevo, Kaz.	C12	32
Bulajevo see Bulaevo, Kaz.	C12	32
Bulan, Phil.	D4	52
Bulandshahr, India	D6	54
Bulawayo, Zimb.	B9	70
Bulbul, Syria	B7	58

Name	Map Ref.	Page
Buldan, Tur.	E11	28
Buldāna, India	H6	54
Buldir Island, i., Ak., U.S.	g22	140a
Bulgan, Mong.	B3	36
Bulgan, Mong.	B5	36
Bulgaria, ctry., Eur.	G12	26
Bulkley, stm., B.C., Can.	B3	138
Bullard, Tx., U.S.	E3	122
Bulla Regia, hist., Tun.	H2	24
Bullas, Spain	F9	20
Bullaxaar, Som.	B8	66
Bulle, Switz.	D4	22
Buller, stm., N.Z.	E5	80
Buller, Mount, mtn., Austl.	K6	76
Bullfinch, Austl.	F3	74
Bull Harbour, B.C., Can.	F2	138
Bullhead, S.D., U.S.	B11	126
Bullhead City, Az., U.S.	H2	132
Bullock, N.C., U.S.	H7	114
Bullock Creek, Austl.	A5	76
Bullock Creek, stm., Austl.	C5	76
Bulloo, stm., Austl.	G4	76
Bullpound Creek, stm., Ab., Can.	E19	138
Bulls Gap, Tn., U.S.	H2	114
Bull Shoals, Ar., U.S.	H5	120
Bull Shoals Lake, res., U.S.	H5	120
Bulnes, Chile	H1	92
Bulolo, Pap. N. Gui.	b4	79a
Bulsār, India	H4	54
Buluan, Phil.	G5	52
Bulukumba, Indon.	F12	50
Bululawang, Indon.	H8	50
Bumba, D.R.C.	D4	66
Bumpus, Mount, hill, Nu., Can.	B8	106
Bumu Hu, l., China	C13	54
Buna, Kenya	D7	66
Bunawan, Phil.	F5	52
Bunbury, Austl.	F3	74
Bunceton, Mo., U.S.	F5	120
Bundaberg, Austl.	E9	76
Bundarra, Austl.	H8	76
Bünde, Ger.	D4	16
Būndi, India	F5	54
Bundoran, Ire.	G4	12
Būndu, India	G10	54
Bungamas, Indon.	E3	50
Bungo-suidō, strt., Japan	G5	40
Bungo-takada, Japan	F4	40
Bungtlang, India	G14	54
Bunia, D.R.C.	D6	66
Bunker, Mo., U.S.	G6	120
Bunker Group, is., Austl.	D9	76
Bunker Hill, In., U.S.	H3	112
Bunker Hill, Or., U.S.	G2	136
Bunker Hill, mtn., Nv., U.S.	D8	134
Bunkie, La., U.S.	G6	122
Bunnell, Fl., U.S.	G4	116
Buñol see Bunyolo, Spain	E10	20
Buntok, Indon.	D9	50
Bunyolo, Spain	E10	20
Bunyu, Pulau, i., Indon.	B10	50
Buolkalah, Russia	B12	34
Buolkalakh see Buolkalah, Russia	B12	34
Buon Ma Thuot, Viet.	F9	48
Buor-Haja, guba, b., Russia	B15	34
Buor-Haja, mys, c., Russia	B15	34
Bupul, Indon.	G11	44
Buqayq, Sau. Ar.	D6	56
Bura, Kenya	E7	66
Burām, Sudan	E5	62
Burang, China	C8	54
Buranhém, stm., Braz.	I6	88
Burāq, Syria	E7	58
Burauen, Phil.	E5	52
Burbank, Wa., U.S.	D8	136
Burç, Tur.	A8	58
Burcher, Austl.	I6	76
Burco, Som.	C9	66
Burdekin, stm., Austl.	C6	76
Burdekin Falls, wtfl, Austl.	C6	76
Burden, Ks., U.S.	D12	128
Burdett, Ks., U.S.	C9	128
Burdur, Tur.	F13	28
Burdur, state, Tur.	F13	28
Burdur Gölü, l., Tur.	F12	28
Bureinskij hrebet, mts., Russia	G15	34
Bureja, Russia	G15	34
Bureja, stm., Russia	F15	34
Büren, Ger.	E4	16
Bürenhayrhan, Mong.	B3	36
Burford, On., Can.	E9	112
Burg, Ger.	D7	16
Burg, Den see Den Burg, Neth.	A13	14
Burgas, Blg.	G14	26
Burgas, state, Blg.	G13	26
Burgas, Gulf of see Burgaski Zaliv, b., Blg.	G14	26
Burgaski Zaliv, b., Blg.	G14	26
Burg auf Fehmarn, Ger.	B7	16
Burgaw, N.C., U.S.	B8	116
Burgdorf, Switz.	C4	22
Burgenland, state, Aus.	C13	22
Burgeo, Nf., Can.	j22	107a
Burgersdorp, S. Afr.	G8	70
Burghausen, Ger.	H8	16
Burghead, Scot., U.K.	D9	12
Burgin, Ky., U.S.	G13	120
Burgo de Osma, Spain	C7	20
Burgos, Mex.	C9	100
Burgos, Phil.	C3	52
Burgos, Spain	B7	20
Burgos, co., Spain	B7	20
Burgstädt, Ger.	F8	16
Burgundy see Bourgogne, hist. reg., Fr.	B10	18
Burhan Budai Shan, mts., China	D4	36
Burhaniye, Tur.	D9	28
Burhānpur, India	H5	54
Burias Island, i., Phil.	D4	52
Burica, Punta, c., N.A.	I6	102
Burien, Wa., U.S.	C4	136
Burila Mare, Rom.	E9	26
Buri Ram, Thai.	E6	48
Buriti, Braz.	B4	88
Buriti Bravo, Braz.	C4	88
Buriticupu, stm., Braz.	C2	88
Buriti dos Lopes, Braz.	B5	88
Buritizeiro, Braz.	I3	88
Burjasot see Burjassot, Spain	E10	20
Burjassot, Spain	E10	20
Burjatija, state, Russia	F11	34
Burkburnett, Tx., U.S.	G10	128
Burke, S.D., U.S.	D13	126
Burke, stm., Austl.	D2	76
Burketown, Austl.	A2	76
Burkina Faso, ctry., Afr.	G4	64
Burleson, Tx., U.S.	B10	130
Burley, Id., U.S.	H13	136
Burlingame, Ca., U.S.	F3	134
Burlingame, Ks., U.S.	F2	120
Burlington, On., Can.	E10	112
Burlington, Co., U.S.	B6	128
Burlington, Ia., U.S.	D6	120
Burlington, Ks., U.S.	F2	120
Burlington, N.C., U.S.	H6	114
Burlington, Vt., U.S.	F3	110
Burlington, Wa., U.S.	B4	136
Burlington, Wi., U.S.	B9	120
Burlington, Wy., U.S.	C4	126
Burlington Junction, Mo., U.S.	D2	120
Burma see Myanmar, ctry., Asia	D8	46
Burnaby, B.C., Can.	G7	138
Burnet, Tx., U.S.	D9	130
Burnett, stm., Austl.	E8	76
Burnett Bay, b., N.T., Can.	B14	140
Burney, Ca., U.S.	C4	134
Burnie, Austl.	n12	77a
Burnley, Eng., U.K.	H10	12
Burns, Ks., U.S.	C12	128
Burns, Or., U.S.	G7	136
Burns, Tn., U.S.	H10	120
Burns, Wy., U.S.	F8	126
Burnside, Ky., U.S.	G13	120
Burnside, stm., Nu., Can.	B8	106
Burnside, Lake, l., Austl.	E4	74
Burns Lake, B.C., Can.	B5	138
Burnsville, Ms., U.S.	C10	122
Burnsville, N.C., U.S.	I3	114
Burnsville, W.V., U.S.	F5	114
Burnt, stm., Or., U.S.	F9	136
Burnt Pine, Norf. I.	y25	78i
Burntwood, stm., Mb., Can.	D11	106
Burqin, China	B2	36
Burra, Austl.	I2	76
Burragorang, Lake, res., Austl.	J7	76
Burrel, Alb.	C13	24
Burreli see Burrel, Alb.	C13	24
Burrendong, Lake, res., Austl.	I7	76
Burren Junction, Austl.	H7	76
Burriana see Borriana, Spain	E10	20
Burrinjuck Reservoir, res., Austl.	J7	76
Burr Oak, Ks., U.S.	B10	128
Burrton, Ks., U.S.	C11	128
Burruyacú, Arg.	E4	90
Bursa, Tur.	C11	28
Bursa, state, Tur.	C11	28
Bûr Sa'îd (Port Said), Egypt	G3	58
Burstall, Sk., Can.	D4	124
Būr Sūdān (Port Sudan), Sudan	D7	62
Burt, Ia., U.S.	H4	118
Burt Lake, l., Mi., U.S.	C5	112
Burtnieks ezers, l., Lat.	C8	10
Burton, Mi., U.S.	E6	112
Burton, Tx., U.S.	G2	122
Burton upon Trent, Eng., U.K.	I11	12
Buru, i., Indon.	F8	44
Burullus, Buheirat el-, l., Egypt	G1	58
Burundi, ctry., Afr.	E6	66
Burun-Šibertuj, gora, mtn., Russia	G10	34
Bururi, Bdi.	E5	66
Burwash, On., Can.	B9	112
Burwell, Ne., U.S.	F13	126
Bury, Eng., U.K.	H10	12
Buryatia see Burjatija, state, Russia	F11	34
Bury Saint Edmunds, Eng., U.K.	I13	12
Burzil, Pak.	A5	54
Busa, Mount, mtn., Phil.	G5	52
Busan see Pusan-jikhalsi, state, Kor., S.	D2	40
Busanga, D.R.C.	E4	66
Busby, Mt., U.S.	B5	126
Bûsh, Egypt	I2	58
Bushire see Bandar-e Būshehr, Iran	D7	56
Bushland, Tx., U.S.	F6	128
Bushman Land, reg., S. Afr.	F4	70
Bushnell, Fl., U.S.	H3	116
Bushnell, Il., U.S.	D7	120
Bushtyna, Ukr.	A10	26
Busia, Ug.	D6	66
Businga, D.R.C.	D4	66
Busira, stm., D.R.C.	E3	66
Buskerud, state, Nor.	F3	8
Busko-Zdrój, Pol.	F16	16
Buṣrá ash-Shām, Syria	F7	58
Busselton, Austl.	F3	74
Bussey, Ia., U.S.	C5	120
Bussum, Neth.	B14	14
Bustamante, Mex.	B8	100
Busto Arsizio, Italy	E5	22
Busuanga Island, i., Phil.	D2	52
Busu-Djanoa, D.R.C.	D4	66
Büsum, Ger.	B4	16
Buta, D.R.C.	D4	66
Buta Ranquil, Arg.	H2	92
Butare, Rw.	E5	66
Butaritari, at., Kir.	C8	72
Bute, Island of, i., Scot., U.K.	F7	12
Bute Inlet, b., B.C., Can.	F5	138
Butembo, D.R.C.	D5	66
Butera, Italy	G8	24
Butere, Kenya	D6	66
Butha-Buthe, Leso.	F9	70
Buthidaung, Mya.	D7	46
Butiá, Braz.	E11	92
Butler, Ga., U.S.	D1	116
Butler, In., U.S.	C1	114
Butler, Mo., U.S.	F3	120
Butler, Oh., U.S.	D3	114
Butler, Pa., U.S.	D6	114
Butner, N.C., U.S.	H7	114
Buto, hist., Egypt	G1	58
Buton, Pulau, i., Indon.	F7	44
Butrint, hist., Alb.	E14	24
Butru, Austl.	C2	76
Butte, Mt., U.S.	D14	136
Butte, Ne., U.S.	E14	126
Butte Creek, stm., Ca., U.S.	D4	134
Butte Falls, Or., U.S.	H4	136
Butternut, Wi., U.S.	E8	118
Butterworth, Malay.	J5	48
Butterworth, S. Afr.	H9	70
Buttle Lake, l., B.C., Can.	G5	138
Button Islands, is., Nu., Can.	C17	106
Buttonwillow, Ca., U.S.	H6	134
Butuan, Phil.	F5	52
Buturlino, Russia	I21	8
Butwal, Nepal	E9	54
Butzbach, Ger.	F4	16
Bützow, Ger.	C7	16
Buulobarde, Som.	D9	66
Buur Gaabo, Som.	E8	66
Buurgplaatz, mtn., Lux.	D15	14
Buxtehude, Ger.	C5	16
Buxton, S. Afr.	E7	70
Buxton, Eng., U.K.	H11	12
Buxton, N.C., U.S.	A10	116
Buxton, Mount, mtn., B.C., Can.	E2	138
Buyr nuur, l., Asia	B8	36
Büyükada, Tur.	C12	28
Büyükçekmece, Tur.	B11	28
Büyükkarıştıran, Tur.	B10	28
Büyükkemikli Burnu, c., Tur.	C9	28
Büyükmenderes, stm., Tur.	F10	28
Buzău, Rom.	D13	26
Buzău, state, Rom.	D13	26
Buzău, stm., Rom.	D13	26
Buzen, Japan	F4	40
Búzi, stm., Moz.	A12	70
Buziaș, Rom.	D8	26
Buzuluk, Russia	D8	32
Byādgi, India	D2	53
Byam Channel, strt., Nu., Can.	A19	140
Byam Martin Island, i., Nu., Can.	B19	140
Bycen', Bela.	H8	10
Byčki, Russia	F17	10
Byczyna, Pol.	E14	16
Bydgoszcz, Pol.	C13	16
Bydgoszcz, state, Pol.	C13	16
Byelorussia see Belarus, ctry., Eur.	E14	6
Byers, Tx., U.S.	G10	128
Byesville, Oh., U.S.	E4	114
Bygdin, l., Nor.	F3	8
Byhalia, Ms., U.S.	C9	122
Byhau, Bela.	G13	10
Bykle, Nor.	G2	8
Bylnice, Czech Rep.	G14	16
Bylot Island, i., Nu., Can.	A15	106
Byng Inlet, On., Can.	C9	112
Bynum, Mt., U.S.	C14	136
Bynum, N.C., U.S.	I6	114
Byrd, Lac, l., Qc., Can.	A13	112
Byrnedale, Pa., U.S.	C7	114
Byro, Austl.	E3	74
Byron, Ga., U.S.	D2	116
Byron, Il., U.S.	B8	120
Byron, Cape, c., Austl.	G9	76
Byron Bay, Austl.	G9	76
Byrranga, gory, mts., Russia	B8	34
Bystřice pod Hostýnem, Czech Rep.	G13	16
Bytantaj, stm., Russia	C15	34
Bytča, Slov.	G14	16
Bytom, Pol.	F14	16
Bytoš', Russia	G17	10
Bytów, Pol.	B13	16

C

Name	Map Ref.	Page
Ca, stm., Asia	C7	48
Caacupé, Para.	B9	92
Caaguazú, Para.	B9	92
Caaguazú, state, Para.	B10	92
Caála, Ang.	C2	68
Caapiranga, Braz.	I11	86
Caatinga, Braz.	I3	88
Caazapá, Para.	C9	92
Caazapá, state, Para.	C9	92
Cabaiguán, Cuba	A8	102
Caballana, Lago, l., Braz.	I11	86
Caballococha, Peru	D3	84
Caballo Reservoir, res., N.M., U.S.	K9	132
Cabanatuan, Phil.	C3	52
Cabano, Qc., Can.	C8	110
Cabarroguis, Phil.	B3	52
Cabedelo, Braz.	D8	88
Cabeza del Buey, Spain	F5	20
Cabezas, Bol.	C4	90
Cabildo, Arg.	I7	92
Cabimas, Ven.	B6	86
Cabinda, Ang.	B1	68
Cabinda, state, Ang.	B1	68
Cabinet Mountains, mts., U.S.	B10	136
Cable, Wi., U.S.	E7	118
Cabo, Braz.	E8	88
Cabo Blanco, Arg.	I3	90
Cabo Frio, Braz.	L4	88
Cabonga, Réservoir, res., Qc., Can.	F15	106
Cabool, Mo., U.S.	G5	120
Caboolture, Austl.	F9	76
Caborca, Mex.	F6	98
Cabo Rojo, P.R.	B1	104a
Cabot, Ar., U.S.	C7	122
Cabot Head, c., On., Can.	C8	112
Cabot Strait, strt., Can.	j21	107a
Cabourg, Fr.	E8	14
Cabra Corral, Embalse, res., Arg.	B5	92
Cabramurra, Austl.	J7	76
Cabrera, stm., Col.	F4	86
Cabrera, Illa de, i., Spain	E13	20
Cabri, Sk., Can.	D5	124
Cabriel, stm., Spain	E9	20
Cabrillo National Monument, p.o.i., Ca., U.S.	K8	134
Cabrobó, Braz.	E6	88
Cabruta, Ven.	D8	86
Cabullónes, Punta, c., P.R.	C2	104a
Cabusy, Bela.	H11	10
Cabuyaro, Col.	E5	86
Caçador, Braz.	C12	92
Čačak, Yugo.	F7	26
Caçapava, Braz.	L3	88
Caçapava do Sul, Braz.	E11	92
Cacapon, stm., W.V., U.S.	E7	114
Cacequi, Braz.	D10	92
Cáceres, Braz.	G6	84
Cáceres, Col.	D4	86
Cáceres, Spain	E4	20
Cáceres, co., Spain	E4	20
Cačèrsk, Bela.	H13	10
Cache, stm., Ar., U.S.	B7	122
Cache, stm., Il., U.S.	G8	120
Cache Creek, B.C., Can.	F9	138
Cache Creek, stm., Ca., U.S.	E3	134
Cache la Poudre, stm., Co., U.S.	G7	126
Cache Peak, mtn., Id., U.S.	A3	132
Cachi, Arg.	B4	92
Cachimbo, Braz.	E7	84
Cachimbo, Serra do, mts., Braz.	E6	84
Cachoeira Alta, Braz.	C6	90
Cachoeira de Manteiga, Braz.	I3	88
Cachoeira do Sul, Braz.	E11	92
Cachoeiro de Itapemirim, Braz.	K5	88
Cachos, Punta, c., Chile	C2	92
Cachuela Esperanza, Bol.	B3	90
Căciulați, Rom.	E13	26
Cacolo, Ang.	C2	68
Caconda, Ang.	C2	68
Cactus, Tx., U.S.	E6	128
Cactus Flat, pl., Nv., U.S.	F9	134
Cacuaco, Ang.	B1	68
Caculé, Braz.	H4	88
Cacuri, Ven.	E9	86
Čadan, Russia	D16	32
Čadca, Slov.	G14	16
Caddo, Ok., U.S.	C2	122
Caddo, stm., Ar., U.S.	C5	122
Caddo Lake, res., U.S.	E4	122
Caddo Mills, Tx., U.S.	D2	122
Cadell, stm., Austl.	D3	76
Cadena, Cerro, mtn., Mex.	I3	130
Cadena, Punta, c., P.R.	B1	104a
Cadillac, Sk., Can.	E6	124
Cadillac, Fr.	E5	18
Cadillac, Mi., U.S.	D4	112
Cádiz, Spain	H4	20
Cadiz, Ky., U.S.	H10	120
Cádiz, co., Spain	H5	20
Cádiz, Bahía de, b., Spain	H4	20
Cadiz Lake, l., Ca., U.S.	I1	132
Čadobec, stm., Russia	C17	32
Cadomin, Ab., Can.	C13	138
Cadore, reg., Italy	D9	22
Cadott, Wi., U.S.	G7	118
Cadwell, Ga., U.S.	D2	116
Čaek, Kyrg.	F12	32
Caen, Fr.	E8	14
Caengo (Kwenge), stm., Afr.	B2	68
Caernarfon, Wales, U.K.	H8	12
Caernarfon Bay, b., Wales, U.K.	H8	12
Caerphilly, Wales, U.K.	J9	12
Caesarea see Qesari, Horbat, hist., Isr.	F5	58
Caeté, Braz.	J4	88
Caetité, Braz.	H4	88
Cafayate, Arg.	C4	92
Cagayan, stm., Phil.	A3	52
Cagayan de Oro, Phil.	F5	52
Cagayan Islands, is., Phil.	F3	52
Cagayan Sulu Island, i., Phil.	G2	52
Čagda, Russia	E15	34
Çağış, Tur.	D10	28
Cagliari, Italy	E3	24
Cagliari, Golfo di, b., Italy	E3	24
Cagliari, Stagno di, l., Italy	E2	24
Cagnes-sur-Mer, Fr.	F13	18
Čagoda, stm., Russia	A17	10
Čagodošča, stm., Russia	A18	10
Caguán, stm., Col.	G4	86
Caguas, P.R.	B3	104a
Cahaba, stm., Al., U.S.	E11	122
Cahama, Ang.	D1	68
Caher, Ire.	I4	12
Cahokia, Il., U.S.	F7	120
Cahora Bassa, Albufeira, res., Moz.	D5	68
Cahors, Fr.	E7	18
Cahto Peak, mtn., Ca., U.S.	D2	134
Cahuinari, stm., Col.	H6	86
Cahul, Mol.	D15	26
Caí, stm., Braz.	D12	92
Caianda, Ang.	C3	68
Caiapó, Serra do, mts., Braz.	G7	84
Caibarién, Cuba	A8	102
Cai Bau, Dao, i., Viet.	B8	48
Caiçara, Braz.	D8	88
Caicara, Caño, stm., Ven.	D7	86
Caicara de Maturín, Ven.	C10	86
Caicara de Orinoco, Ven.	D8	86
Caicedonia, Col.	E4	86
Caicó, Braz.	D7	88
Caicos Islands, is., T./C. Is.	B11	102
Caicos Passage, strt., N.A.	B11	102
Caijiapo, China	D2	42
Caima Bay, b., Phil.	D4	52
Caimanera, Cuba	C10	102
Caimanero, Laguna del, l., Mex.	D5	100
Cain Creek, stm., S.D., U.S.	C14	126
Cai Nuoc, Viet.	H7	48
Cairari, Braz.	B1	88
Caird Coast, cst., Ant.	C3	81
Cairns, Austl.	A5	76
Cairo see El-Qâhira, Egypt	H2	58
Cairo, Ga., U.S.	F1	116
Cairo, Il., U.S.	G8	120
Cairo, Ne., U.S.	F14	126
Cairo, W.V., U.S.	E4	114
Cairo Montenotte, Italy	F5	22
Cairu, Braz.	G6	88
Caisleán an Bharraigh see Castlebar, Ire.	H3	12
Caiundo, Ang.	D2	68
Caiwan, China	I4	42
Caizi Hu, l., China	F7	42
Caja de Muertos, Isla, i., P.R.	C2	104a
Cajamarca, Peru	E2	84
Cajapió, Braz.	B3	88
Cajazeiras, Braz.	D6	88
Cajon Summit, p., Ca., U.S.	I8	134
Cajuru, Braz.	K2	88
Caka, China	D4	36
Çakmak, Tur.	A5	58
Čakovec, Cro.	D13	22
Calabar, Nig.	H6	64
Calabozo, Ven.	C8	86
Calabozo, Ensenada de, b., Ven.	B6	86
Calabria, state, Italy	F10	24
Calafat, Rom.	F9	26
Calagua Islands, is., Phil.	C4	52
Calahorra, Spain	B8	20
Calais, Fr.	C10	14
Calalaste, Sierra de, mts., Arg.	B4	92
Calama, Chile	D3	90
Calamar, Col.	B4	86
Calamar, Col.	F5	86
Calamian Group, is., Phil.	E3	52
Calamus, stm., Ne., U.S.	E13	126
Calañas, Spain	G4	20
Calang, Indon.	J2	48
Calapan, Phil.	D3	52
Călărași, Mol.	B15	26
Călărași, Rom.	E14	26
Călărași, state, Rom.	E14	26
Calarcá, Col.	E4	86
Calatafimi, Italy	G6	24
Calatayud, Spain	C9	20
Calau, Ger.	E9	16
Calavite Passage, strt., Phil.	D3	52
Calayan Island, i., Phil.	A3	52
Calbayog, Phil.	D5	52
Calbe, Ger.	E7	16
Calbuco, Chile	H2	90
Calcasieu, stm., La., U.S.	G5	122
Calcasieu Lake, l., La., U.S.	G5	122
Calceta, Ec.	H1	86
Calchaquí, Arg.	D7	92
Calchaquí, stm., Arg.	B4	92
Calçoene, Braz.	C7	84
Calcutta, India	G12	54
Caldaro, Italy	D8	22
Caldas, Col.	D4	86
Caldas, state, Col.	E4	86
Caldas da Rainha, Port.	E1	20
Caldas de Reis, Spain	B2	20
Caldas de Reyes see Caldas de Reis, Spain	B2	20
Caldas Novas, Braz.	I1	88
Caldera, Chile	C2	92
Caldwell, Id., U.S.	G10	136
Caldwell, Ks., U.S.	D11	128
Caldwell, Oh., U.S.	E4	114
Caldwell, Tx., U.S.	G2	122
Caledon, S. Afr.	I4	70
Caledon (Mohokare), stm., Afr.	F8	70
Caledonia, Belize	C3	102
Caledonia, N.S., Can.	F11	110
Caledonia, Ms., U.S.	D10	122
Caledonia, N.Y., U.S.	A8	114
Caledonia, Oh., U.S.	D3	114
Calella, Spain	C13	20
Calen, Austl.	C7	76
Calera, Al., U.S.	D12	122
Caleta Olivia, Arg.	I3	90
Caleufú, Arg.	G5	92
Calexico, Ca., U.S.	K10	134
Calgary, Ab., Can.	E16	138
Calhan, Co., U.S.	B4	128
Calhoun, Al., U.S.	E12	122
Calhoun, Ga., U.S.	C14	122
Calhoun, Mo., U.S.	F4	120
Calhoun, Tn., U.S.	B14	122
Calhoun City, Ms., U.S.	D9	122
Cali, Col.	F3	86
Calico Rock, Ar., U.S.	H5	120
Calicut see Kozhikode, India	F2	53
Caliente, Nv., U.S.	F2	132
California, Mo., U.S.	F5	120
California, state, U.S.	D3	108
California, Golfo de (California, Gulf of), b., Mex.	B2	96
California, Gulf of see California, Golfo de, b., Mex.	B2	96
California Aqueduct, aq., Ca., U.S.	I8	134
Calilegua, Parque Nacional, p.o.i., Arg.	A5	92
Calimere, Point, c., India	F4	53
Calingasta, Arg.	E3	92
Calion, Ar., U.S.	D6	122
Calipatria, Ca., U.S.	J10	134
Calispell Peak, mtn., Wa., U.S.	B9	136
Calistoga, Ca., U.S.	E3	134
Calitri, Italy	D9	24
Calitzdorp, S. Afr.	H5	70
Callabonna, Lake, l., Austl.	G2	76
Callabonna Creek, stm., Austl.	G3	76
Callahan, Mount, mtn., Co., U.S.	D8	132
Callan, Ire.	I5	12
Callander, On., Can.	B10	112
Callao, Peru	F2	84
Callaquén, Volcán, vol., Chile	H2	92
Callaway, Ne., U.S.	F12	126
Calliaqua, St. Vin.	o11	105e
Calling Lake, Ab., Can.	A17	138
Calling Lake, l., Ab., Can.	A17	138
Callosa de Segura, Spain	F9	20
Calmar, Ab., Can.	C17	138
Calmar, Ia., U.S.	A6	120
Calm Lake, l., On., Can.	C6	118
Čal'mny-Varre, Russia	C17	8
Čalna, Russia	F15	8
Caloundra, Austl.	F9	76
Calp, Spain	F11	20
Calpe see Calp, Spain	F11	20
Caltagirone, Italy	G8	24
Caltanissetta, Italy	G8	24
Călugăreni, Rom.	E12	26
Calulo, Ang.	B2	68
Calumet, Mn., U.S.	D5	118
Calumet City, Il., U.S.	G2	112
Calunda, Ang.	C3	68
Caluula, Som.	B10	66
Calvados, state, Fr.	E8	14
Calvert, Al., U.S.	F10	122
Calvert, Tx., U.S.	G2	122
Calvert Island, i., B.C., Can.	E2	138
Calvillo, Mex.	E7	100
Calvin, Ok., U.S.	C2	122
Calvinia, S. Afr.	G4	70
Calw, Ger.	H4	16
Calwa, Ca., U.S.	G6	134
Calypso, N.C., U.S.	A7	116
Camabatela, Ang.	B2	68
Camaçari, Braz.	G6	88
Camacupa, Ang.	C2	68
Camaguán, Ven.	C8	86
Camagüey, Cuba	B9	102
Camaiore, Italy	G7	22
Camajuaní, Cuba	A8	102
Camaná, Peru	G3	84
Camaná, stm., Peru	G3	84
Camanaú, stm., Braz.	H11	86
Camanche Reservoir, res., Ca., U.S.	E4	134
Camapuã, Braz.	C6	90
Camaquã, Braz.	E12	92
Camaquã, stm., Braz.	E11	92
Camará, Braz.	D5	84
Camarajibe, Braz.	D8	88
Camararé, stm., Braz.	F6	84
Camarat, Cap, c., Fr.	F12	18
Camarès, Fr.	F8	18
Camargo, Bol.	D3	90
Camargue, reg., Fr.	F10	18
Camarillo, Ca., U.S.	I6	134
Camarón, Arroyo, stm., Mex.	G7	130
Camarón, Cabo, c., Hond.	D5	102
Camarones, Arg.	H3	90
Camarones, Bahía, b., Arg.	H3	90
Camas Creek, stm., Id., U.S.	F14	136
Camatagua, Embalse de, l., Ven.	C8	86
Ca Mau, Viet.	H7	48
Ca Mau, Mui, c., Viet.	H7	48
Camba, Indon.	F11	50
Cambodia, ctry., Asia	C3	48
Camboon, Austl.	E8	76
Camboriú, Braz.	C13	92
Camborne, Eng., U.K.	K7	12
Cambrai, Fr.	D12	14
Cambria, Ca., U.S.	H4	134
Cambrian Mountains, mts., Wales, U.K.	I9	12
Cambridge, On., Can.	E9	112
Cambridge, N.Z.	C6	80
Cambridge, Eng., U.K.	I12	12
Cambridge, Il., U.S.	C7	120
Cambridge, Ia., U.S.	C4	120
Cambridge, Md., U.S.	F9	114
Cambridge, Ma., U.S.	B14	114
Cambridge, Mn., U.S.	F5	118
Cambridge, Ne., U.S.	A8	128
Cambridge, N.Y., U.S.	G3	110
Cambridge, Oh., U.S.	D4	114
Cambridge Bay, Nu., Can.	B10	106
Cambridge Fiord, b., Nu., Can.	A15	106
Cambridge Springs, Pa., U.S.	C5	114
Cambrils, Spain	C11	20
Cambuí, Braz.	L2	88
Cambulo, Ang.	B3	68
Cambundi-Catembo, Ang.	C2	68
Camden, Austl.	J8	76
Camden, Al., U.S.	F11	122
Camden, Ar., U.S.	D6	122
Camden, Me., U.S.	F7	110
Camden, N.J., U.S.	E10	114
Camden, N.Y., U.S.	E14	112
Camden, N.C., U.S.	H9	114
Camden, Oh., U.S.	E1	114
Camden, S.C., U.S.	B5	116
Camden, Tn., U.S.	H9	120
Camden Bay, b., Ak., U.S.	B11	140
Camdenton, Mo., U.S.	G5	120
Camels Hump, mtn., Vt., U.S.	F3	110
Camenca, Mol.	A15	26
Camerino, Italy	G10	22
Cameron, Mo., U.S.	E3	120
Cameron, Tx., U.S.	D10	130
Cameron, W.V., U.S.	E5	114
Cameron, Wi., U.S.	F7	118
Cameron Hills, hills, Can.	D7	106
Cameroon, ctry., Afr.	C2	66
Cameroon Mountain, vol., Cam.	D1	66
Camerota, Italy	D9	24
Cametá, Braz.	B1	88
Çamiçi Gölü, l., Tur.	F10	28
Camiguin Island, i., Phil.	F5	52
Camiguin Island, i., Phil.	A3	52
Camiling, Phil.	C3	52
Camilla, Ga., U.S.	E1	116
Camino, Ca., U.S.	E5	134
Camiranga, Braz.	A2	88
Camiri, Bol.	D4	90
Camissombo, Ang.	B3	68
Çamlıdere, Tur.	C15	28
Çamlıdere, Tur.	A10	58
Cam Lo, Viet.	D8	48
Camocim, Braz.	B5	88
Camooweal, Austl.	C7	74
Camorta Island, i., India	G7	46
Camotes Islands, is., Phil.	E5	52
Camotes Sea, Phil.	E5	52
Campagna di Roma, reg., Italy	C6	24
Campaign, Tn., U.S.	B13	122
Campana, Arg.	G8	92
Campana, Isla, i., Chile	I1	90
Campanario, Spain	F5	20
Campania, state, Italy	D8	24
Campano, Appennino, mts., Italy	C8	24
Campaspe, stm., Austl.	C6	76
Campbell, S. Afr.	F6	70
Campbell, Ca., U.S.	F4	134
Campbell, Mo., U.S.	H7	120
Campbell, Ne., U.S.	A10	128
Campbell, Cape, c., N.Z.	E6	80
Campbellford, On., Can.	D12	112
Campbell Hill, hill, Oh., U.S.	D2	114
Campbell Hills, hill, St. Vin.	p11	105e
Campbell Island, B.C., Can.	D2	138
Campbell Island, i., N.Z.	I7	72
Campbell Lake, l., B.C., Can.	G5	138
Campbell Plateau, unds.	O20	142
Campbellpore, Pak.	B4	54
Campbell River, B.C., Can.	F5	138
Campbell's Bay, Qc., Can.	C13	112
Campbellsport, Wi., U.S.	E1	112
Campbellton, N.B., Can.	C10	110
Campbellton, P.E., Can.	D12	110
Campbellton, Fl., U.S.	G13	122
Campbelltown, Austl.	J8	76
Campbell Town, Austl.	n13	77a
Campbeltown, Scot., U.K.	F7	12
Campeche, Mex.	C2	102
Campeche, state, Mex.	C2	102
Campeche, Bahía de, b., Mex.	D6	96
Campeche, Gulf of see Campeche, Bahía de, b., Mex.	E13	100
Campechuela, Cuba	B9	102
Câmpeni, Rom.	C10	26
Camperdown, Austl.	L4	76
Camperville, Mb., Can.	C13	124
Cam Pha, Viet.	B8	48
Camp Hill, Al., U.S.	E13	122
Camp Hill, Pa., U.S.	H12	112
Câmpia Turzii, Rom.	C10	26
Campidano, val., Italy	E2	24
Campiglia Marittima, Italy	G7	22
Campillos, Spain	G6	20
Câmpina, Rom.	D12	26
Campina, reg., Spain	G5	20
Campina Grande, Braz.	D7	88
Campinas, Braz.	L2	88
Campina Verde, Braz.	J1	88
Campoalegre, Col.	F4	86
Campo Alegre de Goiás, Braz.	I2	88
Campobasso, Italy	C8	24
Campo Belo, Braz.	K3	88
Campo de Criptana, Spain	E7	20
Campo Erê, Braz.	C11	92
Campo Florido, Braz.	J1	88
Campo Formoso, Braz.	F5	88
Campo Gallo, Arg.	C6	92
Campo Grande, Braz.	D6	90
Campo Largo, Arg.	C7	92
Campo Largo, Braz.	B13	92
Campo Maior, Braz.	C4	88
Campo Maior, Port.	F3	20
Campo Mourão, Braz.	A11	92
Campo Novo, Braz.	C11	92
Campos, Braz.	K5	88
Campos Altos, Braz.	J2	88
Campo Santo, Arg.	B5	92
Campos Belos, Braz.	G2	88
Campos do Jordão, Braz.	L3	88
Campos Gerais, Braz.	K2	88
Campos Novos, Braz.	C12	92
Campos Sales, Braz.	D5	88
Camp Point, Il., U.S.	D6	120
Campti, La., U.S.	F5	122
Campton, Ky., U.S.	G2	114
Câmpulung, Rom.	D11	26
Câmpulung Moldovenesc, Rom.	B12	26
Campuya, stm., Peru	H4	86
Camp Verde, Az., U.S.	I4	132
Cam Ranh, Viet.	G9	48
Cam Ranh, Vinh, b., Viet.	G9	48
Cam Ranh Bay see Cam Ranh, Vinh, b., Viet.	G9	48
Camrose, Ab., Can.	C18	138
Camsell, stm., N.T., Can.	B7	106
Camuy, P.R.	B2	104a
Çan, Tur.	C10	28
Canaan, Vt., U.S.	E5	110
Cana-brava, stm., Braz.	G1	88
Cana-brava, stm., Braz.	G1	88
Canada, ctry., N.A.	D9	106
Canada Basin, unds.	A25	142
Cañada de Gómez, Arg.	F7	92
Cañada Honda, Arg.	F3	92
Canadian, Tx., U.S.	F8	128
Canadian, stm., U.S.	F13	128
Canadian, Deep Fork, stm., Ok., U.S.	F13	128
Canaguá, stm., Ven.	D7	86
Canaima, Parque Nacional, p.o.i., Ven.	E10	86
Canajoharie, N.Y., U.S.	B11	114
Çanakkale, Tur.	C9	28
Çanakkale, state, Tur.	D9	28
Çanakkale Boğazı (Dardanelles), strt., Tur.	C9	28
Canala, N. Cal.	m15	79d
Canal Fulton, Oh., U.S.	D4	114
Canal Point, Fl., U.S.	J5	116
Canals, Arg.	F6	92
Canal Winchester, Oh., U.S.	E3	114
Canandaigua, N.Y., U.S.	B8	114
Cananea, Mex.	F7	98
Canápolis, Braz.	J1	88
Cañar, Ec.	I2	86
Cañar, state, Ec.	I2	86
Canarias, Islas (Canary Islands), is., Spain	D1	64
Canarreos, Archipiélago de los, is., Cuba	B6	102
Canary Basin, unds.	F11	144
Canary Islands see Canarias, Islas, is., Spain	D1	64
Cañas, C.R.	G5	102
Canaseraga, N.Y., U.S.	B8	114
Canastota, N.Y., U.S.	E14	112
Canatlán, Mex.	C6	100
Canaveral, Cape, c., Fl., U.S.	H5	116
Canaveral National Seashore, p.o.i., Fl., U.S.	H5	116
Cañaveras, Spain	D8	20
Canavese, hist. reg., Italy	E4	22
Canavieiras, Braz.	H6	88
Canbelego, Austl.	H6	76
Canberra, Austl.	J7	76
Canby, Ca., U.S.	B5	134
Canby, Mn., U.S.	G2	118
Canby, Or., U.S.	E4	136
Cancon, Fr.	E6	18
Cancún, Mex.	B4	102
Cancún, Punta, c., Mex.	B4	102
Çandarlı Körfezi, b., Tur.	E9	28
Candé, Fr.	G7	14
Candeias, Braz.	G6	88
Candeias, Braz.	K3	88
Candela, stm., Mex.	B8	100
Candelaria, Arg.	C10	92
Candelária, Braz.	D11	92
Candelaria, stm., Mex.	C2	102
Candelo, Austl.	K7	76
Cándido Aguilar, Mex.	C9	100
Cândido Mendes, Braz.	A3	88
Candlemas Islands, is., S. Geor.	K12	82
Candlestick, Ms., U.S.	E8	122
Cando, N.D., U.S.	F14	124
Candon, Phil.	B3	52
Candor, N.Y., U.S.	B9	114
Candor, N.C., U.S.	A6	116
Canea see Chaniá, Grc.	H7	28
Canela, Braz.	D12	92
Canelas, Mex.	C5	100
Canelli, Italy	F5	22
Canelones, Ur.	G9	92
Cañete, Chile	H1	92
Caney, stm., U.S.	E13	128
Caney Creek, stm., Tx., U.S.	F12	130
Canfranc, Spain	B10	20
Cangas de Narcea, Spain	A4	20
Cangas de Onís, Spain	A5	20

Name	Map Ref.	Page
Cangkuang, Tanjung, c., Indon.	G4	50
Cangombe, Ang.	C2	68
Canguaretama, Braz.	D8	88
Canguçu, Braz.	E11	92
Cangumbe, Ang.	C2	68
Cangxi, China	F1	42
Cangzhou, China	B7	42
Caniapiscau, stm., Qc., Can.	D17	106
Caniapiscau, Lac, res., Qc., Can.	E17	106
Canicattì, Italy	G7	24
Canim Lake, B.C., Can.	E10	138
Canim Lake, l., B.C., Can.	E9	138
Canindé, Braz.	C6	88
Canindé, stm., Braz.	D4	88
Canindeyú, state, Para.	B10	92
Canisteo, N.Y., U.S.	B8	114
Canistota, S.D., U.S.	D15	126
Cañitas de Felipe Pescador, Mex.	D7	100
Canjáyar, Spain	G8	20
Çankırı, Tur.	A3	56
Çankırı, state, Tur.	C15	28
Canmore, Ab., Can.	E15	138
Cannanore, India	F2	53
Cannelton, In., U.S.	G11	120
Cannes, Fr.	F13	18
Canning, N.S., Can.	E12	110
Cannington, On., Can.	D10	112
Cannock, Eng., U.K.	I10	12
Cannon, stm., Mn., U.S.	G5	118
Cannonball, stm., N.D., U.S.	A11	126
Cannon Beach, Or., U.S.	E2	136
Cannon Falls, Mn., U.S.	G6	118
Cannonvale, Austl.	C7	76
Cann River, Austl.	K7	76
Canoas, Braz.	D12	92
Canoas, stm., Braz.	C12	92
Canoe, B.C., Can.	F11	138
Canoe, stm., B.C., Can.	D12	138
Canoinhas, Braz.	C12	92
Canon City, Co., U.S.	C3	128
Cañon de Río Blanco, Parque Nacional, p.o.i., Mex.	F10	100
Canonsburg, Pa., U.S.	D5	114
Canoochee, stm., Ga., U.S.	E4	116
Canora, Sk., Can.	C11	124
Canosa di Púglia, Italy	C10	24
Canossa, hist., Italy	F7	22
Canouan, i., St. Vin.	p11	105e
Canova, S.D., U.S.	D15	126
Canova Beach, Fl., U.S.	H5	116
Canóvanas, P.R.	B4	104a
Canowindra, Austl.	I7	76
Canso, N.S., Can.	E16	110
Cantabria, state, Spain	A6	20
Cantabrian Mountains see Cantábrica, Cordillera, mts., Spain	A5	20
Cantábrica, Cordillera, mts., Spain	A5	20
Cantagalo, Braz.	K4	88
Cantal, state, Fr.	D8	18
Cantalejo, Spain	C7	20
Cantanhede, Braz.	B3	88
Cantaura, Ven.	C9	86
Canterbury, Eng., U.K.	J14	12
Canterbury Bight, b., N.Z.	G4	80
Canterbury Plains, pl., N.Z.	G4	80
Can Tho, Viet.	G7	48
Canton see Guangzhou, China	J5	42
Canton, Il., U.S.	D7	120
Canton, Ks., U.S.	C11	128
Canton, Mn., U.S.	H7	118
Canton, Ms., U.S.	E8	122
Canton, Mo., U.S.	D6	120
Canton, N.Y., U.S.	D14	112
Canton, Oh., U.S.	D4	114
Canton, Ok., U.S.	E10	128
Canton, Pa., U.S.	C9	114
Canton, S.D., U.S.	H2	118
Canton, Tx., U.S.	E3	122
Canton see Kanton, i., Kir.	D9	72
Canton Lake, res., Ok., U.S.	E10	128
Cantonment, Fl., U.S.	G11	122
Cantù, Italy	E6	22
Cantu, stm., Braz.	B11	92
Cantwell, Ak., U.S.	D10	140
Cañuelas, Arg.	G8	92
Canumã, Braz.	D6	84
Canutama, Braz.	E5	84
Čany, Russia	C13	32
Čany, ozero, l., Russia	D13	32
Canyon, Tx., U.S.	G7	128
Canyon City, Or., U.S.	F8	136
Canyon Creek, Ab., Can.	A15	138
Canyon de Chelly National Monument, p.o.i., Az., U.S.	G7	132
Canyon Ferry Lake, res., Mt., U.S.	D15	136
Canyon Lake, res., Tx., U.S.	E9	130
Canyonlands National Park, p.o.i., Ut., U.S.	E6	132
Canyonville, Or., U.S.	H3	136
Cao, stm., China	D5	38
Cao Bang, Viet.	A7	48
Cao Lanh, Viet.	G7	48
Caombo, Ang.	B2	68
Caorle, Italy	E9	22
Caoxian, China	D6	42
Cap, Pointe du, c., St. Luc.	I7	105c
Capac, Mi., U.S.	E7	112
Čapaevo, Kaz.	D8	32
Capanaparo, stm., S.A.	D8	86
Capanema, Braz.	D8	84
Capão Bonito, Braz.	L1	88
Capão Doce, Morro do, mtn., Braz.	C12	92
Caparaó, Parque Nacional do, p.o.i., Braz.	K4	88
Caparo Viejo, stm., Ven.	D6	86
Capatárida, Ven.	B6	86
Cap aux Meules, Île du, i., Qc., Can.	C14	110
Cap-Chat, Qc., Can.	A10	110
Cap-de-la-Madeleine, Qc., Can.	D4	110
Cape, stm., Austl.	C5	76
Cape Barren Island, i., Austl.	n13	77a
Cape Basin, unds.	L14	144
Cape Breton Highlands National Park, p.o.i., N.S., Can.	D16	110
Cape Breton Island, i., N.S., Can.	D16	110
Cape Charles, Va., U.S.	G9	114
Cape Coast, Ghana	H4	64
Cape Cod Bay, b., Ma., U.S.	C15	114
Cape Cod National Seashore, p.o.i., Ma., U.S.	B16	114
Cape Coral, Fl., U.S.	J4	116
Cape Dorset, Nu., Can.	C15	106
Cape Elizabeth, Me., U.S.	G6	110
Cape Fear, stm., N.C., U.S.	B8	116
Cape Girardeau, Mo., U.S.	G8	120
Cape Hatteras National Seashore, p.o.i., N.C., U.S.	A10	116
Capelinha, Braz.	I4	88
Cape Lisburne, Ak., U.S.	C6	140
Capel'ka, Russia	B11	10
Capella, Austl.	D7	76
Capelongo, Ang.	C2	68
Cape Lookout National Seashore, p.o.i., N.C., U.S.	B9	116
Cape May, N.J., U.S.	F10	114
Cape May Court House, N.J., U.S.	E11	114
Cape Porpoise, Me., U.S.	G6	110
Capernaum see Kefar Naḥum, hist., Isr.	F6	58
Cape Sable Island, i., N.S., Can.	G11	110
Capesterre, Guad.	i6	105c
Capesterre, Pointe de la, c., Guad.	h5	105c
Capesterre-Belle-Eau, Guad.	h5	105c
Cape Tormentine, N.B., Can.	D12	110
Cape Town (Kaapstad), S. Afr.	H4	70
Cape Verde, ctry., Afr.	k9	65a
Cape Verde Basin, unds.	G10	144
Cape Vincent, N.Y., U.S.	D13	112
Cape York Peninsula, pen., Austl.	B8	74
Cap-Haïtien, Haiti	C11	102
Capilla del Monte, Arg.	E5	92
Capim, stm., Braz.	A2	88
Capinota, Bol.	C3	90
Capira, Pan.	H8	102
Capitan, N.M., U.S.	H3	128
Capitán Arturo Prat, sci., Ant.	B34	81
Capitán Bado, Para.	D5	90
Capitán Bermúdez, Arg.	F7	92
Capitán Meza, Para.	C10	92
Capitão Enéas, Braz.	I4	88
Capitola, Ca., U.S.	G4	134
Capitol Peak, mtn., Nv., U.S.	B8	134
Capitol Reef National Park, p.o.i., Ut., U.S.	E5	132
Capivara, Represa de, res., Braz.	D6	90
Capivari, Braz.	L2	88
Capivari, stm., Braz.	G6	88
Cap-Pelé, N.B., Can.	D12	110
Cappella Islands, is., V.I.U.S.	e7	104b
Capraia, Italy	G6	22
Capraia, Isola di, i., Italy	G6	22
Caprara, Punta, c., Italy	C2	24
Caprarola, Italy	B6	24
Capreol, On., Can.	B9	112
Caprera, Isola, i., Italy	C3	24
Capri, Italy	D8	24
Capri, Isola di, i., Italy	D8	24
Capricorn Channel, strt., Austl.	D9	76
Capricorn Group, is., Austl.	D9	76
Caprivi Strip, hist. reg., Nmb.	D3	68
Capron, Il., U.S.	B9	120
Captain Cook, Hi., U.S.	D6	78a
Captain Cook Monument, hist., Norf. I.	x25	78i
Captains Flat, Austl.	J7	76
Capua, Italy	C8	24
Capucapu, stm., Braz.	H12	86
Capucin, c., Dom.	i5	105c
Capulin Volcano National Monument, p.o.i., N.M., U.S.	E5	128
Caquetá, state, Col.	G4	86
Caquetá (Japurá), stm., S.A.	H7	86
Čara, Russia	E12	34
Čara, stm., Russia	E12	34
Carabinani, stm., Braz.	I10	86
Carabobo, state, Ven.	B7	86
Caracal, Rom.	E11	26
Caracaraí, Braz.	G11	86
Caracas, Ven.	B8	86
Caracol, Braz.	E4	88
Caraguatatuba, Braz.	L3	88
Caraguatay, Para.	B9	92
Carajás, Braz.	E7	84
Carajás, Serra dos, hills, Braz.	E7	84
Carakol, hist., Belize	D3	102
Caranavi, Bol.	C3	90
Carandaí, Braz.	K4	88
Carangola, Braz.	K4	88
Caransebeş, Rom.	D9	26
Carapá, stm., Para.	B10	92
Carapajó, Braz.	B1	88
Cara-Paraná, stm., Col.	H5	86
Carapina, Braz.	K5	88
Caraquet, N.B., Can.	C11	110
Caraş-Severin, state, Rom.	D8	26
Caratasca, Laguna de, b., Hond.	E5	102
Caratinga, Braz.	J4	88
Carauari, Braz.	D4	84
Caraúbas, Braz.	C7	88
Caravaca de la Cruz, Spain	F8	20
Caravelas, Braz.	I6	88
Caraveli, Peru	G3	84
Caravelle, Presqu'île la, pen., Mart.	k7	105c
Caraway, Ar., U.S.	B8	122
Carayaó, Para.	B9	92
Carazinho, Braz.	D11	92
Carballiño, Spain	B2	20
Carballo, Spain	A2	20
Carberry, Mb., Can.	E14	124
Carbon, Ab., Can.	E17	138
Carbon, Tx., U.S.	B9	130
Carbonara, Capo, c., Italy	E3	24
Carbondale, Co., U.S.	D9	132
Carbondale, Il., U.S.	G8	120
Carbondale, Pa., U.S.	C10	114
Carbonear, Nf., Can.	j23	107a
Carboneras de Guadazaón, Spain	E9	20
Carbon Hill, Al., U.S.	D11	122
Carbonia, Italy	E2	24
Carcagente see Carcaixent, Spain	E10	20
Carcaixent, Spain	E10	20
Carcajou, stm., N.T., Can.	B5	106
Carcans, Lac de, b., Fr.	D4	18
Carcarañá, Arg.	F7	92
Carcarañá, stm., Arg.	F7	92
Carcassonne, Fr.	F8	18
Carchi, state, Ec.	G3	86
Carcross, Yk., Can.	C3	106
Çardak, Tur.	F12	28
Čardara, Kaz.	F11	32
Čardarinskoe vodohranilišče, res., Asia	A10	56
Cárdenas, Cuba	A7	102
Cárdenas, Mex.	F12	100
Cárdenas, Mex.	D9	100
Cárdenas, Bahía de, b., Cuba	A7	102
Cardiel, Lago, l., Arg.	I2	90
Cardiff, Wales, U.K.	J9	12
Cardigan, P.E., Can.	D14	110
Cardigan, Wales, U.K.	I8	12
Cardigan Bay, b., Wales, U.K.	I8	12
Cardinal, On., Can.	D14	112
Cardona, Ur.	F9	92
Cardonal, Punta, c., Mex.	A3	100
Cardoso, Ur.	F9	92
Cardston, Ab., Can.	G17	138
Cardwell, Austl.	B5	76
Cardwell, Mo., U.S.	H7	120
Cardwell Mountain, mtn., Tn., U.S.	B13	122
Čardžev, Turkmen.	B9	56
Carei, Rom.	B9	26
Careiro, Braz.	I12	86
Careiro, Ilha do, i., Braz.	I12	86
Carèja, Bela.	F12	10
Carencro, La., U.S.	G6	122
Carey, Oh., U.S.	D2	114
Carey, Lake, l., Austl.	E4	74
Carey Downs, Austl.	E3	74
Cargados Carajos Shoals, is., Mrts.	K9	142
Carhaix-Plouguer, Fr.	F5	14
Carhué, Arg.	H6	92
Cariacica, Braz.	K5	88
Cariaco, Golfo de, b., Ven.	B9	86
Caribbean Sea	D7	82
Cariboo, stm., B.C., Can.	D9	138
Cariboo Mountains, mts., B.C., Can.	D10	138
Caribou, Me., U.S.	D8	110
Caribou Lake, l., On., Can.	A9	118
Caribou Mountain, mtn., Me., U.S.	E6	110
Caribou Mountains, mts., Ab., Can.	D7	106
Carichic, Mex.	B5	100
Caridade, Braz.	C6	88
Carigara, Phil.	E5	52
Carignan, Fr.	E14	14
Carinda, Austl.	H6	76
Carinhanha, Braz.	H4	88
Carinhanha, stm., Braz.	H3	88
Carini, Italy	F7	24
Carinthia see Kärnten, state, Aus.	D10	22
Caripito, Ven.	B10	86
Carira, Braz.	F7	88
Cariré, Braz.	C5	88
Cariús, Braz.	D6	88
Carleton, Mi., U.S.	B2	114
Carleton, Mount, mtn., N.B., Can.	C10	110
Carleton Place, On., Can.	C13	112
Carletonville, S. Afr.	E8	70
Cârlibaba, Rom.	B12	26
Carlin, Nv., U.S.	C9	134
Carlingford Lough, b., Eur.	H7	12
Carlinville, Il., U.S.	E8	120
Carlisle, Eng., U.K.	G9	12
Carlisle, In., U.S.	F10	120
Carlisle, Ia., U.S.	C4	120
Carlisle, Ky., U.S.	F1	114
Carlisle, Pa., U.S.	D8	114
Carl Junction, Mo., U.S.	G3	120
Carlos, Isla, i., Chile	J2	90
Carlos Casares, Arg.	G7	92
Carlos Chagas, Braz.	I5	88
Carlos Pellegrini, Arg.	E6	92
Carlow, Ire.	I5	12
Carlow, state, Ire.	I6	12
Carloway, Scot., U.K.	C6	12
Carlsbad see Karlovy Vary, Czech Rep.	F8	16
Carlsbad, Ca., U.S.	J8	134
Carlsbad, N.M., U.S.	B3	130
Carlsbad, Tx., U.S.	C7	130
Carlsbad Caverns National Park, p.o.i., N.M., U.S.	B3	130
Carlsberg Ridge, unds.	I9	142
Carlton, Or., U.S.	E3	136
Carlton, Tx., U.S.	C9	130
Carlyle, Sk., Can.	E11	124
Carlyle Lake, res., Il., U.S.	F8	120
Carmacks, Yk., Can.	C3	106
Carmagnola, Italy	F4	22
Carman, Mb., Can.	E16	124
Carmangay, Ab., Can.	F17	138
Carmarthen, Wales, U.K.	J8	12
Carmarthen Bay, b., Wales, U.K.	J8	12
Carmel, Ca., U.S.	G3	134
Carmel, In., U.S.	I3	112
Carmel, N.Y., U.S.	G16	112
Carmel Head, c., Wales, U.K.	H8	12
Carmelo, Ur.	F8	92
Carmel Valley, Ca., U.S.	G4	134
Carmen see Ciudad del Carmen, Mex.	F12	100
Carmen, stm., Chile	D2	92
Carmen, Isla, i., Mex.	C3	100
Carmen, Isla del, i., Mex.	F13	100
Carmen de Areco, Arg.	G8	92
Carmen de Patagones, Arg.	H4	90
Carmi, Il., U.S.	F9	120
Carmila, Austl.	C7	76
Carmine, Tx., U.S.	D11	130
Carmo do Paranaíba, Braz.	J2	88
Carmona, Spain	G5	20
Carmópolis de Minas, Braz.	K3	88
Carnarvon, Austl.	D2	74
Carnarvon, S. Afr.	G5	70
Carnarvon National Park, p.o.i., Austl.	E6	76
Čarnaŭčycy, Bela.	H6	10
Carnduff, Sk., Can.	E12	124
Carnegie, Austl.	E4	74
Carnegie, Lake, l., Austl.	E4	74
Carney Island, i., Ant.	C29	81
Carnia, reg., Italy	D9	22
Carnic Alps, mts., Eur.	D9	22
Car Nicobar Island, i., India	G7	46
Carnot, C.A.R.	D3	66
Carnoustie, Scot., U.K.	E10	12
Carnsore Point, c., Ire.	I6	12
Carnwath, stm., N.T., Can.	B5	106
Caro, Mi., U.S.	E6	112
Carol City, Fl., U.S.	K5	116
Carolina, Braz.	D2	88
Carolina, P.R.	B4	104a
Carolina, S. Afr.	E10	70
Carolina Beach, N.C., U.S.	B8	116
Caroline, at., Kir.	D12	72
Caroline Islands, is., Oc.	C5	72
Caron, Sk., Can.	D8	124
Caroní, stm., Ven.	C10	86
Carora, Ven.	B6	86
Carpathian Mountains, mts., Eur.	B13	26
Carpații Meridionali (Transylvanian Alps), mts., Rom.	D11	26
Carpentaria, Gulf of, b., Austl.	B7	74
Carpenter, Wy., U.S.	F8	126
Carpenter Lake, res., B.C., Can.	F8	138
Carpentersville, Il., U.S.	B9	120
Carpentras, Fr.	E11	18
Carpi, Italy	F7	22
Carpina, Braz.	D8	88
Cărpineni, Mol.	C15	26
Carpinteria, Ca., U.S.	I6	134
Carpio, N.D., U.S.	F12	124
Carp Lake, l., B.C., Can.	B7	138
Carrabelle, Fl., U.S.	H14	122
Carranza, Cabo, c., Chile	G1	92
Carrara, Italy	F7	22
Carrauntoohil, mtn., Ire.	I3	12
Carreta, Punta, c., Peru	F2	84
Carriacou, i., Gren.	q11	105e
Carrick on Shannon, Ire.	H4	12
Carrick-on-Suir, Ire.	I5	12
Carrie, Mount, mtn., Wa., U.S.	C3	136
Carriers Mills, Il., U.S.	G9	120
Carrieton, Austl.	I2	76
Carrillo, Mex.	B6	100
Carrington, N.D., U.S.	G14	124
Carrión, stm., Spain	B6	20
Carrión de los Condes, Spain	B6	20
Carrizal Bajo, Chile	D2	92
Carrizo Creek, stm., U.S.	E5	128
Carrizo Mountain, mtn., N.M., U.S.	H3	128
Carrizo Springs, Tx., U.S.	F7	130
Carroll, Ia., U.S.	B3	120
Carroll, Ne., U.S.	E15	126
Carrollton, Al., U.S.	D10	122
Carrollton, Ga., U.S.	D13	122
Carrollton, Mi., U.S.	E5	112
Carrollton, Ms., U.S.	D8	122
Carrollton, Mo., U.S.	E4	120
Carrollton, Oh., U.S.	D4	114
Carrollton, Tx., U.S.	A10	130
Carrolltown, Pa., U.S.	D7	114
Carron, stm., Austl.	A3	76
Carrot, stm., Can.	E10	106
Carrot River, Sk., Can.	A10	124
Carry Falls Reservoir, res., N.Y., U.S.	F2	110
Carseland, Ab., Can.	F17	138
Čarsk, Kaz.	E14	32
Carson, N.D., U.S.	A11	126
Carson, Wa., U.S.	E5	136
Carson, East Fork, stm., U.S.	E6	134
Carson City, Nv., U.S.	D6	134
Carson Lake, res., Nv., U.S.	D7	134
Carson Range, mts., U.S.	D6	134
Carson Sink, l., Nv., U.S.	D7	134
Carstairs, Ab., Can.	E16	138
Cartagena, Chile	F2	92
Cartagena, Col.	B4	86
Cartagena, Spain	G9	20
Cartago, Col.	E3	86
Cartago, C.R.	H6	102
Cartaxo, Port.	E2	20
Cartaya, Spain	G3	20
Carter, Ok., U.S.	F9	128
Carter Lake, Ia., U.S.	C2	120
Cartersville, Ga., U.S.	C14	122
Carthage, Tun.	H4	24
Carthage, Ar., U.S.	C6	122
Carthage, Ms., U.S.	E9	122
Carthage, Mo., U.S.	G3	120
Carthage, N.C., U.S.	A6	116
Carthage, S.D., U.S.	C15	126
Carthage, Tn., U.S.	H11	120
Carthage, Tx., U.S.	E4	122
Carthage, hist., Tun.	H4	24
Cartier Islands, is., Austl.	B4	74
Cartwright, Mb., Can.	E14	124
Caruaru, Braz.	E8	88
Carúpano, Ven.	B10	86
Carutapera, Braz.	D8	84
Caruthersville, Mo., U.S.	H8	120
Carutu, stm., Ven.	E10	86
Carvoeiro, Braz.	H10	86
Carvoeiro, Cabo, c., Port.	E1	20
Cary, Ms., U.S.	E8	122
Cary, N.C., U.S.	I7	114
Čaryšskoe, Russia	D14	32
Caryville, Fl., U.S.	G13	122
Casablanca (Dar-el-Beida), Mor.	C3	64
Casa Branca, Braz.	K2	88
Casa de Piedra, Embalse, res., Arg.	I4	92
Casa Grande, Az., U.S.	K5	132
Casa Grande Ruins National Monument, p.o.i., Az., U.S.	K5	132
Casale Monferrato, Italy	E5	22
Casanare, state, Col.	E6	86
Casanare, stm., Col.	D6	86
Casa Nova, Braz.	E5	88
Casar, N.C., U.S.	A4	116
Casarano, Italy	D12	24
Casar de Cáceres, Spain	E4	20
Casas Adobes, Az., U.S.	K6	132
Casas Grandes, stm., Mex.	F9	98
Casavieja, Spain	D6	20
Casca, Braz.	D12	92
Cascadas Basaseachic, Parque Nacional, p.o.i., Mex.	A4	100
Cascade, B.C., Can.	G12	138
Cascade, Norf. I.	y25	78i
Cascade, Ia., U.S.	B6	120
Cascade, Mt., U.S.	C15	136
Cascade, Wi., U.S.	E1	112
Cascade Bay, b., Norf. I.	y25	78i
Cascade Mountains see Cascade Range, mts., N.A.	C3	108
Cascade Range, mts., N.A.	C3	108
Cascade Reservoir, res., Id., U.S.	F10	136
Cascais, Port.	F1	20
Cascapédia, stm., Qc., Can.	B10	110
Cascavel, Braz.	C6	88
Cascavel, Braz.	B11	92
Cascina, Italy	G7	22
Case-Pilote, Mart.	k6	105c
Caserta, Italy	C8	24
Caseville, Mi., U.S.	E6	112
Casey, Il., U.S.	E9	120
Casey, sci., Ant.	B16	81
Casey, Mount, mtn., Id., U.S.	B10	136
Cashel, Ire.	I5	12
Cashiers, N.C., U.S.	A2	116
Cashmere, Wa., U.S.	C6	136
Cashton, Wi., U.S.	H8	118
Casigua, Ven.	C5	86
Casilda, Arg.	F7	92
Casino, Austl.	G9	76
Casiquiare, stm., Ven.	F8	86
Čáslav, Czech Rep.	G11	16
Casma, Peru	E2	84
Časniki, Bela.	F12	10
Casoli, Italy	H11	22
Caspe, Spain	C10	20
Casper, Wy., U.S.	E6	126
Caspian Depression (Prikaspijskaja nizmennost'), pl.	E7	32
Caspian Sea	F7	32
Cass, stm., Mi., U.S.	E6	112
Cassano allo Ionio, Italy	E10	24
Cass City, Mi., U.S.	E6	112
Casselman, On., Can.	E1	110
Cássia, Braz.	K2	88
Cassiar, B.C., Can.	D5	106
Cassiar Mountains, mts., Can.	D5	106
Cassilândia, Braz.	C6	90
Cassinga, Ang.	D2	68
Cassino, Italy	C7	24
Cass Lake, Mn., U.S.	D4	118
Cass Lake, res., Mn., U.S.	D4	118
Cassongue, Ang.	C1	68
Cassopolis, Mi., U.S.	G3	112
Cassumba, Ilha, i., Braz.	I6	88
Cassville, Mo., U.S.	H4	120
Cassville, Wi., U.S.	B7	120
Castagniccia, reg., Fr.	G15	18
Castaños, Mex.	H6	130
Castelbuono, Italy	G8	24
Castelfranco Veneto, Italy	E8	22
Castellammare, Golfo di, b., Italy	F6	24
Castellammare del Golfo, Italy	F6	24
Castellammare di Stabia, Italy	D8	24
Castellana Grotte, Italy	D11	24
Castellane, Fr.	F12	18
Castellaneta, Italy	D10	24
Castelli, Arg.	B7	92
Castelli, Arg.	H9	92
Castelló, co., Spain	D10	20
Castelló de la Plana, Spain	E11	20
Castellón de la Plana see Castelló de la Plana, Spain	E11	20
Castellón de la Plana see Castelló, co., Spain	D10	20
Castelnaudary, Fr.	F7	18
Castelnau-Montratier, Fr.	E7	18
Castelo, Braz.	K5	88
Castelo Branco, Port.	E3	20
Castelo Branco, state, Port.	E3	20
Castelo de Paiva, Port.	C2	20
Castel San Giovanni, Italy	E6	22
Castelsarrasin, Fr.	E6	18
Casteltermini, Italy	G7	24
Castelvetrano, Italy	G6	24
Casterton, Austl.	K3	76
Castets, Fr.	F4	18
Castiglione del Lago, Italy	G8	22
Castile, N.Y., U.S.	B7	114
Castilla, Peru	E1	84
Castilla, Playa de, cst., Spain	G4	20
Castilla-La Mancha, state, Spain	E9	20
Castilla la Nueva, hist. reg., Spain	E7	20
Castilla la Vieja (Old Castile), hist. reg., Spain	C7	20
Castilla y León, state, Spain	C6	20
Castillo de San Marcos National Monument, p.o.i., Fl., U.S.	F5	116
Castillo Incaico de Ingapirca, hist., Ec.	I2	86
Castillon-la-Bataille, Fr.	E5	18
Castillos, Ur.	G11	92
Castillos, Laguna de, l., Ur.	G11	92
Castine, Me., U.S.	F8	110
Castlebar, Ire.	H3	12
Castle Bruce, Dom.	j6	105c
Castle Dome Peak, mtn., Az., U.S.	J2	132
Castlegar, B.C., Can.	G13	138
Castle Hills, Tx., U.S.	E9	130
Castleisland, Ire.	I3	12
Castlemaine, Austl.	K5	76
Castle Mountain, mtn., Yk., Can.	C3	106
Castle Peak, mtn., Co., U.S.	D9	132
Castlerea, Ire.	H4	12
Castlereagh, stm., Austl.	H7	76
Castle Rock, Co., U.S.	B3	128
Castle Rock, Wa., U.S.	D3	136
Castle Rock, mtn., Or., U.S.	F8	136
Castle Rock Butte, mtn., S.D., U.S.	B9	126
Castle Rock Lake, res., Wi., U.S.	H8	118
Castletown, I. of Man	G8	12
Castlewood, S.D., U.S.	G1	118
Castor, Ab., Can.	D19	138
Castor, stm., Mo., U.S.	G7	120
Castres, Fr.	F8	18
Castries, St. Luc.	I6	105c
Castro, Braz.	B13	92
Castro, Chile	H2	90
Castro Barros, Arg.	E5	92
Castro Daire, Port.	D3	20
Castro del Río, Spain	G6	20
Castronuño, Spain	C5	20
Castro Verde, Port.	G2	20
Castrovillari, Italy	E10	24
Castroville, Ca., U.S.	G4	134
Castroville, Tx., U.S.	E8	130
Catacamas, Hond.	E5	102
Catacaos, Peru	E1	84
Catacocha, Ec.	D2	84
Cataguases, Braz.	K4	88
Catahoula Lake, l., La., U.S.	F6	122
Çatalan, Tur.	A6	58
Catalão, Braz.	J2	88
Çatalca, Tur.	B11	28
Catalina, Chile	B3	92
Catalina see Santa Catalina Island, i., Ca., U.S.	J7	134
Catalina, Punta, c., Chile	J3	90
Catalonia see Catalunya, state, Spain	C12	20
Cataluña see Catalunya, state, Spain	C12	20
Catalunya, state, Spain	C12	20
Catamarca, state, Arg.	C4	92
Catamayo, Ec.	D2	84
Catanauan, Phil.	D4	52
Catanduanes Island, i., Phil.	D5	52
Catanduva, Braz.	K1	88
Catania, Italy	G9	24
Catania, Golfo di, b., Italy	G9	24
Cataño, P.R.	B3	104a
Catanzaro, Italy	F10	24
Cataract Canyon, val., Az., U.S.	H4	132
Catarina, Braz.	D6	88
Catarino Rodríguez, Mex.	C8	100
Catarman, Phil.	F5	52
Catarman, Phil.	D5	52
Catarroja, Spain	E10	20
Catatumbo, stm., Ven.	C5	86
Catawba, stm., U.S.	B5	116
Catawissa, Pa., U.S.	D9	114
Cat Ba, Dao, i., Viet.	B8	48
Catbalogan, Phil.	E5	52
Catedral, Cerro, hill, Ur.	G10	92
Catete, Ang.	B1	68
Cathcart, S. Afr.	H8	70
Cathedral City, Ca., U.S.	J9	134
Catherine, Mount see Katherina, Gebel, mtn., Egypt	J4	58
Catherines Peak, mtn., Jam.	i14	104d
Cat Island, i., Bah.	C9	96
Cat Lake, l., On., Can.	E12	106
Catlettsburg, Ky., U.S.	F3	114
Catlin, Il., U.S.	H2	112
Catoche, Cabo, c., Mex.	B4	102
Catolé do Rocha, Braz.	D7	88
Catoosa, Ok., U.S.	H2	120
Catriló, Arg.	H6	92
Catrimani, stm., Braz.	G11	86
Catskill, N.Y., U.S.	B12	114
Catskill Mountains, mts., N.Y., U.S.	B11	114
Catt, Mount, mtn., B.C., Can.	B2	138
Cattaraugus, N.Y., U.S.	B7	114
Cattolica, Italy	G9	22
Catu, Braz.	G6	88
Catuane, Moz.	E11	70
Catur, Moz.	C6	68
Catwick, Îles, is., Viet.	G9	48
Čatyrtaš, Kyrg.	F13	32
Cau, stm., Viet.	A7	48
Cauaburi, stm., Braz.	G8	86
Caubvick, Mount, mtn., Can.	F13	141
Cauca, state, Col.	F3	86
Cauca, stm., Col.	D4	86
Caucaia, Braz.	B6	88
Caucasia, Col.	D4	86
Caucasus, mts.	F6	32
Caucete, Arg.	E3	92
Cauchari, Salar de, pl., Arg.	D3	90
Caudry, Fr.	D12	14
Caungula, Ang.	B2	68
Čaunskaja guba, b., Russia	C22	34
Cauquenes, Chile	G1	92
Caura, stm., Ven.	D9	86
Caurés, stm., Braz.	H10	86
Căuşani, Mol.	C16	26
Causapscal, Qc., Can.	B9	110
Caussade, Fr.	E7	18
Cauto, stm., Cuba	B9	102
Caux, Pays de, reg., Fr.	E9	14
Cávado, stm., Port.	C3	20
Cavaillon, Fr.	F11	18
Cavalcante, Braz.	G2	88
Cavalese, Italy	D8	22
Cavalier, N.D., U.S.	F16	124
Cavalla (Cavally), stm., Afr.	H3	64
Cavalleria, Cap de, c., Spain	D15	20
Cavally (Cavalla), stm., Afr.	H3	64
Cavan, Ire.	H5	12
Cavan, state, Ire.	H5	12
Cavarzere, Italy	E9	22
Çavdır, Tur.	F12	28
Cave City, Ky., U.S.	G11	120
Cave In Rock, Il., U.S.	G9	120
Caveiras, stm., Braz.	C12	92
Cavendish, Austl.	K4	76
Cave Run Lake, res., Ky., U.S.	F2	114
Cave Spring, Ga., U.S.	C13	122
Caviana de Fora, Ilha, i., Braz.	C8	84
Cavite, Phil.	C3	52
Cavour, Canale, can., Italy	E5	22
Çavuş, Tur.	A2	58
Čavusy, Bela.	G14	10
Cawood, Ky., U.S.	H2	114
Cawston, B.C., Can.	G11	138
Caxambu, Braz.	K3	88
Caxias, Braz.	C4	88
Caxias do Sul, Braz.	D12	92
Caxito, Ang.	B1	68
Çay, Tur.	E13	28
Cayambe, Ec.	G2	86
Cayambe, vol., Ec.	G3	86
Cayce, S.C., U.S.	C4	116
Çaycuma, Tur.	B15	28
Cay Duong, Vinh, b., Viet.	G7	48
Cayenne, Fr. Gu.	C7	84
Cayey, P.R.	B3	104a
Caylus, Fr.	E7	18
Cayman Brac, i., Cay. Is.	C8	102
Cayman Islands, dep., N.A.	C7	102
Caynaba, Som.	C9	66
Cayon, St. K./N.	C2	105a
Cayuga, In., U.S.	I2	112
Cayuga, Tx., U.S.	F3	122
Cayuga Heights, N.Y., U.S.	B9	114
Cayuga Lake, res., N.Y., U.S.	B9	114
Cazalla de la Sierra, Spain	G5	20
Cazaux et de Sanguinet, Étang de, l., Fr.	E4	18
Cazères, Fr.	F6	18
Cazombo, Ang.	C3	68
Cazorla, Spain	G7	20
Cea, stm., Spain	B5	20
Ceanannas see Kells, Ire.	H6	12
Ceará, state, Braz.	C6	88
Ceará-Mirim, Braz.	C8	88
Ceará-Mirim, stm., Braz.	C8	88
Ceatharlach see Carlow, Ire.	I5	12
Cebaco, Isla de, i., Pan.	I7	102
Ceballos, Mex.	B6	100
Čeboksary, Russia	C7	32
Cebollar, Arg.	D4	92
Cebollas, Mex.	D6	100
Cebollatí, Ur.	F11	92
Cebollatí, stm., Ur.	F10	92
Céboruco, Volcán, vol., Mex.	E6	100
Cebu, Phil.	E4	52
Cebu, i., Phil.	E4	52
Cebu Strait, strt., Phil.	F4	52
Ceceda, Mex.	H4	130
Čechtice, Czech Rep.	G11	16
Čechy, hist. reg., Czech Rep.	G10	16
Cecilia, Ky., U.S.	G12	120
Cecil Plains, Austl.	F8	76
Cecina, Italy	G7	22
Čečnja, state, Russia	F7	32
Cedar, stm., U.S.	J7	118
Cedar, stm., Ne., U.S.	F14	126
Cedar Bluffs, Ne., U.S.	J2	118
Cedar Breaks National Monument, p.o.i., Ut., U.S.	F3	132
Cedarburg, Wi., U.S.	E1	112
Cedar City, Ut., U.S.	F3	132
Cedar Creek, stm., Id., U.S.	B2	132
Cedar Creek, stm., Ia., U.S.	C5	120
Cedar Creek, stm., N.D., U.S.	A11	126
Cedar Falls, Ia., U.S.	B5	120
Cedar Grove, Wi., U.S.	E2	112
Cedar Hill, Tn., U.S.	H10	120
Cedar Key, Fl., U.S.	G2	116
Cedar Lake, In., U.S.	J11	118
Cedar Lake, l., On., Can.	B11	112
Cedar Lake, res., Mb., Can.	E10	106
Cedar Mountain, mtn., Ca., U.S.	B5	134
Cedar Rapids, Ia., U.S.	C6	120
Cedars of Lebanon see Arz Lubnān, for., Leb.	D7	58
Cedar Springs, Mi., U.S.	E4	112
Cedartown, Ga., U.S.	C13	122
Cedar Tree Point, c., Antig.	e4	105b
Cedarvale, B.C., Can.	A2	138
Cedar Vale, Ks., U.S.	D12	128
Cedarville, Ca., U.S.	B5	134
Cedarville, Mi., U.S.	B5	112
Cedeira, Spain	A2	20
Cedillo, Embalse de, res., Eur.	E3	20
Cedro, Braz.	D6	88
Cedros, Mex.	C8	100
Cedros, Isla, i., Mex.	A1	100
Ceduna, Austl.	F6	74
Ceelbuur, Som.	D9	66
Ceepeecee, B.C., Can.	G4	138
Ceerigaabo, Som.	B9	66
Cefalonia see Kefallinía, i., Grc.	E3	28
Cefalù, Italy	F8	24
Cega, stm., Spain	C6	20
Čegdomyn, Russia	F15	34
Cegléd, Hung.	B6	26
Ceglie Messapico, Italy	D11	24
Cehegín, Spain	F9	20
Čehov, Russia	E20	10
Čehov, Russia	G17	34
Čekalin, Russia	F19	10
Čekuevo, Russia	E18	8
Čelákovice, Czech Rep.	F10	16
Celano, Italy	H10	22
Celaya, Mex.	E8	100
Celebes see Sulawesi, i., Indon.	F7	44
Celebes Basin, unds.	I15	142
Celebes Sea, Asia	E7	44
Čeleken, Turkmen.	B7	56
Celeste, Tx., U.S.	D2	122
Celestún, Mex.	B2	102
Celina, Tn., U.S.	H12	120
Celina, Tx., U.S.	D2	122
Čeljabinsk, Russia	C10	32
Čeljahany, Bela.	H8	10
Celje, Slvn.	D12	22
Čeljuskin, mys, c., Russia	A9	34
Čelkar, Kaz.	E9	32
Celle, Ger.	D6	16
Čelmozero, Russia	D14	8
Celtic Sea, Eur.	J6	12
Çeltikçi, Tur.	A1	58
Čemal, Russia	D15	32
Cement, Ok., U.S.	G10	128
Cenajo, Embalse del, res., Spain	F9	20
Cenderawasih, Teluk, b., Indon.	F10	44
Cenovo, Blg.	F12	26
Centenario, Arg.	I3	92
Center, Co., U.S.	D2	128
Center, Mo., U.S.	E6	120
Center, N.D., U.S.	G12	124
Center, Tx., U.S.	F4	122
Centerburg, Oh., U.S.	D3	114
Center Hill, Fl., U.S.	H3	116
Center Hill Lake, res., Tn., U.S.	H12	120
Center Moriches, N.Y., U.S.	D13	114
Center Point, Al., U.S.	D12	122
Center Point, Ia., U.S.	B6	120
Centerville, Ia., U.S.	D5	120
Centerville, Mo., U.S.	G7	120

Name	Map Ref.	Page
Centerville, Pa., U.S.	D5	114
Centerville, Tn., U.S.	B11	122
Centerville, Tx., U.S.	F2	122
Centerville, Ut., U.S.	C4	132
Central, Braz.	F4	88
Central, Phil.	D3	52
Central, Az., U.S.	K7	132
Central, N.M., U.S.	K8	132
Central, state, Bots.	C8	70
Central, state, Para.	B9	92
Central, state, Sol. Is.	e8	79b
Central, Cordillera, mts., Col.	E4	86
Central, Cordillera, mts., Peru	E2	84
Central, Cordillera, mts., Phil.	B3	52
Central, Cordillera, mts., P.R.	B2	104a
Central, Massif, mts., Fr.	D8	18
Central, Sistema, mts., Spain	D6	20
Central African Republic, ctry., Afr.	C4	66
Central Aguirre, P.R.	C3	104a
Central Arizona Project Aqueduct, aq., U.S.	J3	132
Central Bohemia see Středočeský, state, Czech Rep.	G10	16
Central Borneo see Kalimantan Tengah, state, Indon.	D8	50
Central Brāhui Range, mts., Pak.	D10	56
Central Celebes see Sulawesi Tengah, state, Indon.	D12	50
Central City, Il., U.S.	F8	120
Central City, Ia., U.S.	B6	120
Central City, Ky., U.S.	G10	120
Central City, Pa., U.S.	D7	114
Central Division, state, Fiji	q19	79e
Centralia, Il., U.S.	F8	120
Centralia, Ks., U.S.	E1	120
Centralia, Mo., U.S.	E5	120
Centralia, Wa., U.S.	D4	136
Centralina, Braz.	J1	88
Central Java see Jawa Tengah, state, Indon.	G7	50
Central Kalahari Game Reserve, Bots.	C6	70
Central Lake, Mi., U.S.	C4	112
Central Makrān Range, mts., Pak.	D9	56
Central'nyj, Russia	C15	32
Central Pacific Basin, unds.	I21	142
Central Point, Or., U.S.	A2	134
Central Range, mts., Pap. N. Gui.	a3	79a
Central Russian Upland see Srednerusskaja vozvyšennost', plat., Russia	H20	10
Central Siberian Plateau see Srednesibirskoe ploskogor'e, plat., Russia	C13	34
Central Siberian Uplands see Srednesibirskoe ploskogor'e, plat., Russia	C13	34
Central Slovakia see Stredoslovenský Kraj, state, Slov.	H15	16
Central Utah Canal, can., Ut., U.S.	D4	132
Central Valley, Ca., U.S.	C3	134
Central Valley see Longitudinal, Valle, val., Chile	H1	92
Centre, Canal du, can., Fr.	C10	18
Centreville, Al., U.S.	E11	122
Centreville, Md., U.S.	E9	114
Centreville, Ms., U.S.	F7	122
Centro Puntas, P.R.	B1	104a
Century, Fl., U.S.	G11	122
Çeos see Kéa, i., Grc.	F7	28
Čepelare, Blg.	H11	26
Cephalonia see Kefallinía, i., Grc.	E3	28
Cepu, Indon.	G7	50
Ceram see Seram, i., Indon.	F8	44
Ceram Sea see Seram, Laut, Indon.	F8	44
Čerčany, Czech Rep.	G10	16
Cerdas, Bol.	D3	90
Çereal, Ab., Can.	C3	124
Çereha, stm., Russia	C11	10
Çeremhovo, Russia	D18	32
Çeremšany, Russia	B11	38
Çerepanovo, Russia	D14	32
Çerepet', Russia	F19	10
Çerepovec, Russia	A20	10
Ceres, Arg.	D7	92
Ceres, Braz.	G8	84
Ceres, S. Afr.	H4	70
Ceresco, Ne., U.S.	J2	118
Ceresio see Lugano, Lago di, I., Eur.	D14	18
Çereté, Col.	C4	86
Čerevkovo, Russia	F21	8
Cerignola, Italy	C9	24
Cérilly, Fr.	H11	14
Çerkeş, Tur.	C15	28
Čerkessk, Russia	F6	32
Çerkezköy, Tur.	B10	28
Čerlak, Russia	D12	32
Çermei, Rom.	C8	26
Čermoz, Russia	C9	32
Çerna, Rom.	D15	26
Černá hora, mtn., Czech Rep.	G9	16
Cernavodă, Rom.	E15	26
Çernay, Fr.	G16	14
Çernigovka, Russia	B10	38
Çernjahovsk, Russia	F4	10
Çernogorsk, Russia	D16	32
Çernuška, Russia	C9	32
Çernyševsk, Russia	F12	34
Černyševskij, Russia	D11	34
Cerralvo, Isla, i., Mex.	C4	100
Cërrik, Alb.	C14	24
Cërriku see Cërrik, Alb.	C14	24
Cerrillos, Arg.	B5	92
Cerrillos, N.M., U.S.	F2	128
Cerritos, Mex.	D8	100
Cerro Azul, Arg.	C10	92
Cerro Azul, Mex.	E9	100
Cerro Azul, Peru	F2	84
Cerro Chato, Ur.	F10	92
Cerro de las Mesas, hist., Mex.	F10	100
Cerro de Pasco, Peru	F2	84
Cerro Gordo, Il., U.S.	E9	120
Cerro Largo, Braz.	D10	92
Cerro Moreno, Chile	A2	92
Cerrón, Cerro, mtn., Ven.	B6	86
Cerrón Grande, Embalse, res., El Sal.	E3	102
Cerro Prieto, Mex.	K10	134
Cerros Colorados, Embalse, res., Arg.	I3	92
Cerro Tololo, Observatorio Astronómico, sci., Chile	E2	92
Çerskij, Russia	C21	34
Čerskogo, hrebet (Cherskiy Mountains), mts., Russia	C17	34
Çertolino, Russia	D16	10
Çerven', Bela.	G11	10
Červen Brjag, Blg.	F11	26
Cervera, Spain	C12	20
Cervera de Pisuerga, Spain	B6	20
Cervia, Italy	F9	22
Cervialto, Monte, mtn., Italy	D9	24
Cervino see Matterhorn, mtn., Eur.	D13	18
Cervione, Fr.	G15	18
Cervo, Spain	A3	20
Cesar, state, Col.	C5	86
Cesar, stm., Col.	B5	86
Cesena, Italy	F9	22
Cesenatico, Italy	F9	22
Çēsis, Lat.	C8	10
Česká Kamenice, Czech Rep.	F10	16
Česká Lípa, Czech Rep.	F10	16
Česká Třebová, Czech Rep.	G12	16
České Budějovice, Czech Rep.	H10	16
Český Brod, Czech Rep.	F10	16
Çeşme, Tur.	E9	28
Čeŝskaja guba (Chesha Bay), b., Russia	C21	8
Cessnock, Austl.	I8	76
Cesvaine, Lat.	D9	10
Cetina, stm., Cro.	G13	22
Cetinje, Yugo.	G5	26
Ceuta, Sp. N. Afr.	B3	64
Cévennes, reg., Fr.	E9	18
Cévennes, Parc National des, p.o.i., Fr.	E9	18
Cevizli, Tur.	F14	28
Ceyhan, Tur.	A6	58
Ceyhan, stm., Tur.	B6	58
Ceylon, Mn., U.S.	H4	118
Ceylon see Sri Lanka, ctry., Asia	G5	53
Cèze, stm., Fr.	E10	18
Cha-am, Thai.	F5	48
Chabanais, Fr.	D6	18
Chabás, Arg.	F7	92
Chabjuwardoo Bay, b., Austl.	D2	74
Chablais, reg., Fr.	C12	18
Chacabuco, Arg.	G7	92
Chachani, Nevado, vol., Peru	G3	84
Chachapoyas, Peru	E2	84
Chāchora, India	F6	54
Chāchro, Pak.	F3	54
Chaco, state, Arg.	C7	92
Chaco, stm., N.M., U.S.	G8	132
Chaco, Parque Nacional, p.o.i., Arg.	C8	92
Chaco Austral, reg., Arg.	C7	92
Chaco Boreal, reg., Para.	D4	90
Chaco Central, reg., Arg.	D4	90
Chaco Mesa, mtn., N.M., U.S.	H9	132
Chad, ctry., Afr.	E3	62
Chad, Lake, I., Afr.	G7	64
Chadbourn, N.C., U.S.	B7	116
Chadian, China	H1	42
Chadron, Ne., U.S.	E10	126
Chadwick, Il., U.S.	I9	118
Chaem, stm., Thai.	C4	48
Chāgai, Pak.	D9	56
Chāgai Hills, hills, Asia	D9	56
Chagos Archipelago, is., B.I.O.T.	J10	142
Chagos-Lacadive Plateau, unds.	J10	142
Chaguanas, Trin.	s12	105f
Chaguaramas, Ven.	C8	86
Chahal, Guat.	E3	102
Chahanwusu see Dulan, China	D4	36
Chahār Borjak, Afg.	C9	56
Chahe, China	E4	36
Chāībāsa, India	G10	54
Chaihe, China	B8	38
Chai Nat, Thai.	E4	48
Chaiya, Thai.	H4	48
Chaiyaphum, Thai.	E6	48
Chajarí, Arg.	E8	92
Chakaria, Bngl.	H14	54
Chākdaha, India	G12	54
Chake Chake, Tan.	F7	66
Chākia, India	E10	54
Chakkarat, Thai.	E6	48
Chakradharpur, India	G10	54
Chāksu, India	E5	54
Chakwāl, Pak.	B4	54
Chala, Peru	G3	84
Chalais, Fr.	D6	18
Chalatenango, El Sal.	F3	102
Chalaxung, China	E4	36
Chalbi Desert, des., Kenya	D7	66
Chalcidice see Chalkidiki, hist. reg., Grc.	C6	28
Chalcis see Chalkída, Grc.	E6	28
Chaleur Bay, b., Can.	C11	110
Chalía, stm., Arg.	I2	90
Chālisgaon, India	H5	54
Chalke see Chálki, i., Grc.	G10	28
Chálki, i., Grc.	G10	28
Chalkída, Grc.	E6	28
Chalkidikí, hist. reg., Grc.	C6	28
Chalk River, On., Can.	B12	112
Challakere, India	D3	53
Challapata, Bol.	C3	90
Challenger Deep, unds.	H17	142
Chalmette, La., U.S.	H9	122
Châlons-sur-Marne, Fr.	F13	14
Chalon-sur-Saône, Fr.	H13	14
Chalosse, reg., Fr.	F5	18
Chaltel, Cerro (Fitz Roy, Monte), mtn., S.A.	I2	90
Chaluhe, China	C6	38
Cham, Ger.	G8	16
Chama, N.M., U.S.	G10	132
Chama, stm., U.S.	E2	128
Chama, stm., Ven.	C6	86
Chamaicó, Arg.	G5	92
Chaman, Pak.	C10	56
Chamba, India	B6	54
Chambal, stm., India	E6	54
Chamberlain, Sk., Can.	D8	124
Chamberlain, S.D., U.S.	D13	126
Chamberlain, stm., Austl.	C5	74
Chamberlain Lake, I., Me., U.S.	D7	110
Chambers, Ne., U.S.	E14	126
Chambersburg, Pa., U.S.	E8	114
Chambers Island, i., Wi., U.S.	C2	112
Chambéry, Fr.	D11	18
Chambi, Jebel, mtn., Tun.	B6	64
Chamblee, Ga., U.S.	D14	122
Chambord, Qc., Can.	B4	110
Chamdo see Qamdo, China	E4	36
Chamical, Arg.	E4	92
Chamo, Lake see Ch'amo Hāyk', I., Eth.	F7	62
Ch'amo Hāyk', I., Eth.	F7	62
Chamois, Mo., U.S.	F6	120
Chamoli, India	C7	54
Chamonix-Mont-Blanc, Fr.	D12	18
Chāmpa, India	G9	54
Champagne, hist. reg., Fr.	F13	14
Champagne Castle, mtn., S. Afr.	F9	70
Champagnole, Fr.	H14	14
Champaign, Il., U.S.	D9	120
Champaquí, Cerro, mtn., Arg.	F5	92
Champasak, Laos	E7	48
Champdoré, Lac, I., Qc., Can.	D17	106
Champion, Ab., Can.	F17	138
Champion, Mi., U.S.	B1	112
Champion, Oh., U.S.	G9	112
Champlain, Lake, I., N.A.	D16	112
Champlitte-et-le-Prélot, Fr.	G14	14
Champotón, Mex.	C2	102
Chāmrājnagar Rāmasamudram, India	F3	53
Chana, Thai.	I5	48
Chañar, Arg.	E4	92
Chañaral, Chile	C2	92
Chañaral, Isla, i., Chile	D2	92
Chancay, Peru	F2	84
Chanchiang see Zhanjiang, China	K4	42
Chanco, Chile	G1	92
Chandalar, Ak., U.S.	C10	140
Chandalar, stm., Ak., U.S.	C10	140
Chandannagar, India	G11	54
Chandausi, India	D7	54
Chāndbāli, India	H11	54
Chandeleur Islands, is., La., U.S.	H10	122
Chandeleur Sound, strt., La., U.S.	H9	122
Chandīgarh, India	C6	54
Chandler, Qc., Can.	B12	110
Chandler, Az., U.S.	J5	132
Chandler, In., U.S.	F10	120
Chandler, Tx., U.S.	E3	122
Chandlerville, Il., U.S.	D7	120
Chāndpur, Bngl.	G13	54
Chāndpur, Bngl.	G14	54
Chāndpur, India	D7	54
Chandrapur, India	B4	53
Chāndvad, India	H5	54
Chang (Yangtze), stm., China	F8	36
Chang, stm., China	G1	42
Chang, Ko, i., Thai.	F6	48
Changan see Xi'an, China	D3	42
Changanācheri, India	G3	53
Changane, stm., Moz.	D11	70
Changcheng, China	L3	42
Chang Cheng (Great Wall), misc. cult., China	D6	36
Chang Chenmo, stm., Asia	A7	54
Changchiak'ou see Zhangjiakou, China	A6	42
Ch'angchih see Changzhi, China	C5	42
Changchou see Changzhou, China	F8	42
Changchou see Zhangzhou, China	I7	42
Changchow see Changzhou, China	F8	42
Changchow see Zhangzhou, China	I7	42
Changchun, China	C6	38
Changde, China	G4	42
Chang Hu, I., China	F5	42
Changhua, Tai.	I9	42
Changhŭng, Kor., S.	G7	38
Changji, China	C2	36
Changjiang, China	L3	42
Changkiakow see Zhangjiakou, China	A6	42
Changli, China	B8	42
Changling, China	B5	38
Changlun, Malay.	I5	48
Changmar, China	A7	54
Changning, China	G4	36
Changning, China	H5	42
Ch'angnyŏng, Kor., S.	D1	40
Changping, China	A7	42
Changsa, China	L4	42
Changsan-got, c., Kor., N.	E6	38
Changsha, China	G5	42
Changshan Qundao, is., China	B10	42
Changshou, China	G2	42
Changshu, China	F9	42
Ch'angte see Changde, China	G4	42
Changteh see Anyang, China	C6	42
Changtien see Zibo, China	C8	42
Changting, China	B8	38
Changting, China	I7	42
Changwŏn, Kor., S.	D1	40
Changwu, China	D2	42
Changxing, China	F8	42
Changxing Dao, i., China	B9	42
Changyi, China	C8	42
Changyŏn-ŭp, Kor., N.	E6	38
Changzhi, China	C5	42
Changzhou, China	F8	42
Chaniá, Grc.	H7	28
Chanión, Kólpos, b., Grc.	H6	28
Chankiang see Zhanjiang, China	K4	42
Channagiri, India	D2	53
Channapatna, India	E3	53
Channel Country, reg., Austl.	E3	76
Channel Islands, is., Eur.	L10	12
Channel Islands, is., Ca., U.S.	J6	134
Channel Islands National Park, p.o.i., Ca., U.S.	J6	134
Channel-Port aux Basques, Nf., Can.	j22	107a
Channelview, Tx., U.S.	H3	122
Channing, Mi., U.S.	B1	112
Channing, Tx., U.S.	F6	128
Chan-si see Shanxi, state, China	B5	42
Chantada, Spain	B3	20
Chanthaburi, Thai.	F6	48
Chantilly, Fr.	E11	14
Chan-tong see Shandong, state, China	C7	42
Chantrey Inlet, b., Nu., Can.	B11	106
Chanute, Ks., U.S.	G2	120
Chao, stm., China	A7	42
Chao'an, China	J7	42
Ch'aochou see Chao'an, China	J7	42
Chaochow see Chao'an, China	J7	42
Chao Hu, I., China	F7	42
Chao Phraya, stm., Thai.	E5	48
Chaor, stm., China	B9	36
Chaoxian, China	F7	42
Chaoyang, China	D4	38
Chaoyang, China	B7	38
Chaoyang, China	J7	42
Chaoyangshan, China	C6	38
Chapada dos Veadeiros, Parque Nacional da, p.o.i., Braz.	H2	88
Chapadinha, Braz.	B4	88
Chapala, Mex.	E7	100
Chapala, Laguna de, I., Mex.	E7	100
Chāparmukh, India	E14	54
Chaparral, Col.	F4	86
Chapecó, Braz.	C11	92
Chapel Hill, N.C., U.S.	I6	114
Chapelton, Jam.	i13	104d
Chapéu, Morro do, mtn., Braz.	H4	88
Chapicuy, Ur.	E9	92
Chapin, Il., U.S.	E7	120
Chapleau, On., Can.	F14	106
Chaplin, Sk., Can.	D7	124
Chaplin Lake, I., Sk., Can.	D7	124
Chapman, Ne., U.S.	F14	126
Chapman, Cape, c., Nu., Can.	B13	106
Chapmanville, W.V., U.S.	G3	114
Chapo, Mex.	E3	130
Chappal, Waddi, mtn., Afr.	H7	64
Chappell Hill, Tx., U.S.	G2	122
Chapultepec, Mex.	L9	134
Chaquiago, Arg.	C4	92
Charadai, Arg.	C8	92
Charalá, Col.	D5	86
Charata, Arg.	C7	92
Charcas, Mex.	D8	100
Charco Hondo, P.R.	B2	104a
Charcos de Risa, Mex.	B7	100
Charcot Island, i., Ant.	B33	81
Chard, Eng., U.K.	K10	12
Charente, state, Fr.	D6	18
Charente, stm., Fr.	C6	18
Charente-Maritime, state, Fr.	C5	18
Chari, stm., Afr.	E3	62
Chārīkār, Afg.	B10	56
Chariton, Ia., U.S.	C4	120
Chariton, stm., U.S.	E5	120
Chariton, Mussel Fork, stm., Mo., U.S.	E5	120
Charity, Guy.	B6	84
Charkhāri, India	F7	54
Charkhlik see Ruoqiang, China	D2	36
Charleroi, Bel.	D13	14
Charles, Cape, c., Va., U.S.	G10	114
Charles, Peak, mtn., Austl.	F4	74
Charles City, Ia., U.S.	A5	120
Charles City, Va., U.S.	G8	114
Charles Island, i., Nu., Can.	C16	106
Charles Mound, hill, Il., U.S.	B7	120
Charles Point, c., Austl.	B6	74
Charleston, Ar., U.S.	B4	122
Charleston, Il., U.S.	E9	120
Charleston, Ms., U.S.	C8	122
Charleston, Mo., U.S.	H8	120
Charleston, S.C., U.S.	D6	116
Charleston, W.V., U.S.	F4	114
Charleston Peak, mtn., Nv., U.S.	G10	134
Charlestown, St. K./N.	C2	105a
Charlestown, St. Vin.	p11	105e
Charlestown, S. Afr.	E9	70
Charlestown, In., U.S.	F12	120
Charleville, Austl.	F5	76
Charleville-Mézières, Fr.	E13	14
Charlevoix, Lake, I., Mi., U.S.	C5	112
Charlieu, Fr.	C10	18
Charlotte, Mi., U.S.	B1	114
Charlotte, N.C., U.S.	A5	116
Charlotte, Tn., U.S.	H10	120
Charlotte, Tx., U.S.	F9	130
Charlotte Amalie, V.I.U.S.	e7	104b
Charlotte Harbor, b., Fl., U.S.	J3	116
Charlotte Lake, I., B.C., Can.	D5	138
Charlottesville, Va., U.S.	F7	114
Charlottetown, P.E., Can.	D13	110
Charlotteville, Trin.	r13	105f
Charlton Island, i., Nu., Can.	E14	106
Charouine, Alg.	D4	64
Charron Lake, I., Mb., Can.	B18	124
Charroux, Fr.	C6	18
Chārsadda, Pak.	A3	54
Charter Oak, Ia., U.S.	I3	118
Charters Towers, Austl.	C6	76
Chartres, Fr.	F10	14
Chascomús, Arg.	G8	92
Chase, B.C., Can.	F11	138
Chase, Mount, mtn., Me., U.S.	D8	110
Chase City, Va., U.S.	H7	114
Chaska, Mn., U.S.	G5	118
Chateaubelair, St. Vin.	o11	105e
Châteaubriant, Fr.	G7	14
Château-du-Loir, Fr.	G9	14
Châteaudun, Fr.	F10	14
Chateaugay (Châteauguay), stm., N.A.	D15	112
Châteaulin, Fr.	F4	14
Châteauneuf-sur-Charente, Fr.	D5	18
Château-Renault, Fr.	G9	14
Château-Richer, Qc., Can.	C5	110
Châteauroux, Fr.	H10	14
Château-Thierry, Fr.	E12	14
Châtellerault, Fr.	H9	14
Chatfield, Mn., U.S.	H6	118
Chatham, N.B., Can.	C11	110
Chatham, On., Can.	F7	112
Chatham, Eng., U.K.	J13	12
Chatham, Il., U.S.	E8	120
Chatham, La., U.S.	E6	122
Chatham, Ma., U.S.	C15	114
Chatham, N.Y., U.S.	B12	114
Chatham, Isla, i., Chile	J2	90
Chatham Islands, is., N.Z.	H9	72
Chatham Rise, unds.	N20	142
Chatham Strait, strt., Ak., U.S.	E13	140
Châtillon-en-Bazois, Fr.	G12	14
Châtillon-sur-Seine, Fr.	G13	14
Chatkal Range, mts., Asia	F12	32
Chatom, Al., U.S.	F10	122
Chatra, India	F10	54
Chatsworth, Austl.	C3	76
Chatsworth, Ga., U.S.	C14	122
Chatsworth, Il., U.S.	D9	120
Chattahoochee, stm., U.S.	G14	122
Chattanooga, Tn., U.S.	B13	122
Chattaroy, W.V., U.S.	G3	114
Chaturat, Thai.	E5	48
Chaubourg, Mount, hill, St. Luc.	I7	105c
Chaudière, stm., Qc., Can.	D5	110
Chau Doc, Viet.	G7	48
Chauk, Mya.	B2	48
Chaumont, Fr.	F13	14
Chauncey, Oh., U.S.	E3	114
Chaungwabyin, Mya.	F4	48
Chauny, Fr.	E12	14
Chaupāran, India	F10	54
Chautauqua Lake, I., N.Y., U.S.	B6	114
Chauvin, La., U.S.	H8	122
Chavakkad, India	F2	53
Chavarría, Arg.	D8	92
Chaves, Port.	C3	20
Cháviva, Col.	E5	86
Chawa'nanake, China	C12	54
Chay, stm., Viet.	A7	48
Chayuan, China	G9	42
Chazy, N.Y., U.S.	F3	110
Chbar, stm., Camb.	F8	48
Cheaha Mountain, mtn., Al., U.S.	D13	122
Cheat, stm., U.S.	E6	114
Cheat, Shavers Fork, stm., W.V., U.S.	E6	114
Cheb, Czech Rep.	F8	16
Chebanse, Il., U.S.	G2	112
Cheboygan, Mi., U.S.	C5	112
Chech, 'Erg, des., Afr.	E4	64
Chechnya see Čečnja, state, Russia	F7	32
Chech'on, Kor., S.	B1	40
Chęciny, Pol.	F16	16
Checleset Bay, b., B.C., Can.	F3	138
Checotah, Ok., U.S.	B3	122
Chedabucto Bay, b., N.S., Can.	E15	110
Cheduba Island, i., Mya.	C1	48
Cheduba Strait, strt., Mya.	C1	48
Cheektowaga, N.Y., U.S.	B7	114
Cheepie, Austl.	F5	76
Chef-Boutonne, Fr.	C5	18
Chefoo see Yantai, China	C9	42
Chehalis, Wa., U.S.	D4	136
Chehalis, stm., Wa., U.S.	D3	136
Cheju, Kor., S.	H7	38
Cheju-do (Quelpart Island), i., Kor., S.	H7	38
Chekiang see Zhejiang, state, China	G8	42
Chela, Serra da, mts., Ang.	D1	68
Chelan, Lake, res., Wa., U.S.	B6	136
Chelif, Oued, stm., Alg.	B5	64
Chełm, Pol.	E19	16
Chełm, state, Pol.	E19	16
Chełmno, Pol.	C14	16
Chelmsford, On., Can.	B8	112
Chelmsford, Eng., U.K.	J13	12
Chełmża, Pol.	C14	16
Chelsea, Ia., U.S.	C5	120
Chelsea, Mi., U.S.	B1	114
Chelsea, Vt., U.S.	F4	110
Cheltenham, Eng., U.K.	J10	12
Chelva see Xelva, Spain	E9	20
Chelyuskin, Cape see Čeljuskin, mys, c., Russia	A9	34
Chemainus, B.C., Can.	H7	138
Chemba, Moz.	D5	68
Chemnitz, Ger.	F8	16
Chemult, Or., U.S.	G5	136
Chenāb, stm., Asia	D3	54
Chenango, stm., N.Y., U.S.	B10	114
Chenchiang see Zhenjiang, China	E8	42
Chenderoh, Tasik, I., Malay.	J5	48
Chénéville, Qc., Can.	E1	110
Cheney, Wa., U.S.	C9	136
Cheney Reservoir, res., Ks., U.S.	D10	128
Cheneyville, La., U.S.	F6	122
Chengbu, China	H4	42
Chengchou see Zhengzhou, China	D5	42
Chengchow see Zhengzhou, China	D5	42
Chengde, China	A7	42
Chengdu, China	E5	36
Chenggu, China	E2	42
Chenghai, China	J7	42
Chengmai, China	L3	42
Chengshan Jiao, c., China	C10	42
Chengteh see Chengde, China	A7	42
Chengtu see Chengdu, China	E5	36
Chengxian, China	E1	42
Chengyang, China	G8	42
Chengzitan, China	B10	42
Ch'enhsien see Chenzhou, China	I5	42
Chen Hu, I., China	F5	42
Chenliu, China	D6	42
Chennai (Madras), India	E5	53
Chenoa, Il., U.S.	D9	120
Chen-si see Shaanxi, state, China	E3	42
Chentang, China	J4	42
Chenxi, China	H3	42
Chenxiangtun, China	D5	38
Chenyang see Shenyang, China	D5	38
Chenzhou, China	I5	42
Cheonan see Ch'ŏnan, Kor., S.	F7	38
Cheongju see Ch'ŏngju, Kor., S.	F7	38
Chepén, Peru	E2	84
Chepes, Arg.	E4	92
Chepkotet, mtn., Kenya	D7	66
Chepo, Pan.	H8	102
Cher, state, Fr.	B8	18
Cher, stm., Fr.	B7	18
Cheradi, Isole, i., Italy	D11	24
Cherbourg, Fr.	E7	14
Cherchell, Alg.	H13	20
Chergui, Chott ech, I., Alg.	C5	64
Cheriton, Va., U.S.	G10	114
Cheriyam Island, i., India	F1	53
Cherkassy see Cherkasy, Ukr.	E4	32
Cherkasy, Ukr.	E4	32
Cherkessia see Karačaevo-Čerkesija, state, Russia	F6	32
Chernihiv, Ukr.	D4	32
Chernivtsi, Ukr.	A12	26
Chernivtsi, co., Ukr.	A13	26
Chernobyl see Chornobyl', Ukr.	D4	32
Cherokee, Ia., U.S.	B2	120
Cherokee, Ks., U.S.	G3	120
Cherokee, Ok., U.S.	E10	128
Cherokee, Tx., U.S.	C9	130
Cherokee Lake, res., Tn., U.S.	H2	114
Cherokee Point, c., Bah.	J8	116
Cherokees, Lake O' The, res., Ok., U.S.	H2	120
Cherokee Sound, Bah.	J8	116
Cherrapunji, India	F13	54
Cherry Creek, stm., S.D., U.S.	C11	126
Cherry Hill, N.J., U.S.	E10	114
Cherryvale, Ks., U.S.	G2	120
Cherry Valley, Ar., U.S.	B8	122
Cherryville, N.C., U.S.	A4	116
Cherskiy Mountains see Čerskogo, hrebet, mts., Russia	C17	34
Chesapeake, Va., U.S.	H9	114
Chesapeake Bay, b., U.S.	F9	114
Chesapeake Bay Bridge-Tunnel, Va., U.S.	G9	114
Chesapeake Beach, Md., U.S.	F9	114
Chesaw, Wa., U.S.	B7	136
Chesha Bay see Čeŝskaja guba, b., Russia	C21	8
Cheshire, Ma., U.S.	B12	114
Cheslatta Lake, I., B.C., Can.	C5	138
Chesnee, S.C., U.S.	A4	116
Chest Creek, stm., Pa., U.S.	D7	114
Chester, Eng., U.K.	H10	12
Chester, Ca., U.S.	C4	134
Chester, Il., U.S.	G8	120
Chester, Mt., U.S.	B15	136
Chester, Ne., U.S.	A11	128
Chester, Ok., U.S.	E10	128
Chester, Pa., U.S.	E10	114
Chester, Va., U.S.	G8	114
Chester Basin, N.S., Can.	F12	110
Chesterfield, Eng., U.K.	H11	12
Chesterfield, S.C., U.S.	B5	116
Chesterfield, Îles, is., N. Cal.	E6	72
Chesterfield Inlet, Nu., Can.	C12	106
Chesterfield Inlet, b., Nu., Can.	C12	106
Chesterfield Islands see Chesterfield, Îles, is., N. Cal.	E6	72
Chesterhill, Oh., U.S.	E4	114
Chester-le-Street, Eng., U.K.	G11	12
Chestertown, Md., U.S.	E9	114
Chesterville, On., Can.	C14	112
Chesuncook Lake, I., Me., U.S.	E7	110
Chetek, Wi., U.S.	F7	118
Chéticamp, N.S., Can.	D16	110
Chetumal, Mex.	C3	102
Chetumal, Bahía, b., N.A.	C3	102
Chevelon Creek, stm., Az., U.S.	I6	132
Cheviot, Oh., U.S.	E13	120
Cheviot Hills, hills, U.K.	F10	12
Ch'ew Bahir see Stefanie, Lake, I., Afr.	G7	62
Chewelah, Wa., U.S.	B9	136
Cheyenne, Ok., U.S.	F9	128
Cheyenne, Wy., U.S.	F8	126
Cheyenne, stm., U.S.	C11	126
Cheyenne Wells, Co., U.S.	C6	128
Cheyne Bay, b., Austl.	F3	74
Chhabra, India	F6	54
Chhapra, India	F10	54
Chhātak, Bngl.	F13	54
Chhatarpur, India	F7	54
Chhatrapur, India	E6	46
Chhattīsgarh, pl., India	H9	54
Chhay Arêng, stm., Camb.	G6	48
Chhêb Kândal, Camb.	F7	48
Chhindwāra, India	H7	54
Chhlong, stm., Camb.	F8	48
Chhota-Chhindwāra, India	G7	54
Chhota Udepur Mhow, India	D3	46
Chi, stm., China	E7	42
Chi, stm., Thai.	E7	48
Chía, Col.	E4	86
Chiahsing see Jiaxing, China	F9	42
Chiai, Tai.	J9	42
Chiamussu see Jiamusi, China	B11	36
Chian see Ji'an, China	H6	42
Chiang Dao, Thai.	C4	48
Chiange, Ang.	D1	68
Chiang Kham, Thai.	C5	48
Chiang Khan, Thai.	D5	48
Chiang Mai, Thai.	C4	48
Chiangmen see Jiangmen, China	J5	42
Chiang Rai, Thai.	C4	48
Chiang Saen, Thai.	B4	48
Chiangtu see Yangzhou, China	E8	42
Chiangyin see Jiangyin, China	F9	42
Chiaohsien see Jiaoxian, China	C8	42
Chiaotso see Jiaozuo, China	D5	42
Chiapas, state, Mex.	D6	96
Chiavari, Italy	F6	22
Chiavenna, Italy	D6	22
Chiba, Japan	D13	40
Chiba, state, Japan	D13	40
Chibabava, Moz.	B11	70
Chibemba, Ang.	D1	68
Chibougamau, Qc., Can.	F15	106
Chibuto, Moz.	D11	70
Chibuzhangchu Hu, I., China	B13	54
Chicago, Il., U.S.	G2	112
Chicago Heights, Il., U.S.	C10	120
Chicapa, stm., Afr.	B3	68
Chichagof Island, i., Ak., U.S.	E12	140
Chīchāwatni, Pak.	C4	54
Chicheng, China	A6	42
Chichén Itzá, hist., Mex.	B3	102
Chichester, Eng., U.K.	K12	12
Chichibu, Japan	C11	40
Ch'ich'ihaerh see Qiqihar, China	B9	36
Chichiriviche, Ven.	B7	86
Chickamauga, Ga., U.S.	C13	122
Chickamauga Lake, res., Tn., U.S.	B14	122
Chickasaw, Al., U.S.	G10	122
Chickasawhay, stm., Ms., U.S.	F10	122
Chickasaw National Recreation Area, p.o.i., Ok., U.S.	G12	128
Chickasha, Ok., U.S.	F11	128
Chicken, Ak., U.S.	D11	140
Chiclana de la Frontera, Spain	H4	20
Chiclayo, Peru	E2	84
Chico, Ca., U.S.	D4	134
Chico, Tx., U.S.	H11	128
Chico, stm., Arg.	I2	90
Chico, stm., Arg.	I3	90
Chico, stm., Phil.	B3	52
Chicomba, Ang.	C2	68
Chicopee, Ga., U.S.	B2	116
Chicopee, Ma., U.S.	B13	114
Chicoutimi, Qc., Can.	B5	110
Chicoutimi, stm., Qc., Can.	B5	110
Chicuma, Ang.	C1	68
Chidambaram, India	F4	53
Chidenguele, Moz.	D12	70
Chiefland, Fl., U.S.	G3	116
Chiehyang see Jieyang, China	J7	42
Chiemsee, I., Ger.	I8	16
Chieo Lan Reservoir, res., Thai.	H4	48
Chieri, Italy	F4	22
Chiese, stm., Italy	E7	22
Chieti, Italy	H11	22
Chifeng, China	C3	38
Chigasaki, Japan	D12	40
Chignahuapan, Mex.	F9	100
Chignecto, Cape, c., N.S., Can.	E11	110
Chignecto Bay, b., Can.	E12	110
Chignik, Ak., U.S.	E8	140
Chigoubiche, Lac, I., Qc., Can.	A3	110
Chigubo, Moz.	C11	70
Chigu Co, I., China	D13	54
Ch'ihfeng see Chifeng, China	C3	38
Chihli, Gulf of see Bo Hai, b., China	B8	42
Chihsi see Jixi, China	B9	38
Chihuahua, Mex.	A5	100
Chihuahua, state, Mex.	B3	96
Chihuahua, Desierto de, des., N.A.	F6	108
Chihuahuan Desert see Chihuahua, Desierto de, des., N.A.	F6	108
Chii-san, mtn., Kor., S.	G7	38
Chikaskia, stm., U.S.	E11	128
Chik Ballāpur, India	E3	53
Chikhli, India	H6	54
Chikmagalūr, India	E2	53
Chiknāyakanhalli, India	E3	53
Chikodi, India	C2	53
Chikrêng, stm., Camb.	F7	48
Chikuma, stm., Japan	C11	40
Chi-kyaw, Mya.	B1	48
Chilakalūrupet, India	C4	53
Chilako, stm., B.C., Can.	C7	138
Chilanko Forks, B.C., Can.	D6	138
Chilapa de Álvarez, Mex.	G9	100
Chilās, Pak.	B11	56
Chilcotin, stm., B.C., Can.	E8	138
Childers, Austl.	E9	76
Childersburg, Al., U.S.	D12	122
Childress, Tx., U.S.	G8	128
Chile, ctry., S.A.	F2	90
Chile Chico, Chile	I2	90
Chilecito, Arg.	F3	92
Chilecito, Arg.	D4	92
Chile Rise, unds.	M5	144
Chilhowie, Va., U.S.	H4	114
Chilia, Bratul, stm., Eur.	D16	26
Chilika Lake, I., India	I10	54
Chililabombwe, Zam.	C4	68
Chilin see Jilin, China	C7	38
Chilko, stm., B.C., Can.	D7	138
Chilko Lake, I., B.C., Can.	E6	138
Chillagoe, Austl.	C8	74
Chillán, Chile	H1	92
Chillicothe, Mo., U.S.	E4	120
Chillicothe, Oh., U.S.	E3	114
Chillicothe, Tx., U.S.	G9	128
Chilliwack, B.C., Can.	G9	138
Chiloé, Isla Grande de, i., Chile	H2	90
Chilón, Mex.	G12	100
Chiloquin, Or., U.S.	H5	136
Chilpancingo de los Bravo, Mex.	G9	100
Chiluage, Ang.	B3	68
Chilumba, Mwi.	C5	68
Chilung, Tai.	I9	42
Chilwa, Lake, I., Afr.	D6	68
Chimaltenango, Guat.	E2	102
Chimán, Pan.	H8	102

Name	Map Ref.	Page
Chimayo, N.M., U.S.	E3	128
Chimbarongo, Chile	G2	92
Chimbas, Arg.	E3	92
Chimborazo, state, Ec.	H2	86
Chimborazo, vol., Ec.	H2	86
Chimbote, Peru	E2	84
Chimoio, Moz.	D5	68
Chimpay, Arg.	G3	90
Chin, state, Mya.	B1	48
China, Mex.	C9	100
China, ctry., Asia	B8	46
Chinan see Jinan, China	C7	42
Chinandega, Nic.	F4	102
Chinati Peak, mtn., Tx., U.S.	E3	130
Chincha Alta, Peru	F2	84
Chinchaga, stm., Can.	D7	106
Chinchilla, Austl.	F8	76
Chinchilla de Monte-Aragón, Spain	F9	20
Chinchiná, Col.	E4	86
Chinchou see Jinzhou, China	A9	42
Chinchow see Jinzhou, China	A9	42
Chincolco, Chile	F2	92
Chincoteague, Va., U.S.	G10	114
Chinde, Moz.	D6	68
Chindo, Kor., S.	G7	38
Chin-do, i., Kor., S.	G7	38
Chindong, Kor., S.	D1	40
Chindwinn, stm., Mya.	D7	46
Ch'ingchiang see Qingjiang, China	E8	42
Chingleput, India	E4	53
Chingola, Zam.	C4	68
Chingshih see Jinshi, China	G4	42
Ch'ingtao see Qingdao, China	C9	42
Chingtechen see Jingdezhen, China	G7	42
Chinguetti, Maur.	E2	64
Chinhae, Kor., S.	D1	40
Chin Hills, hills, Mya.	D7	46
Chinhoyi, Zimb.	D5	68
Chinhsien see Jinzhou, China	B9	42
Chinhua see Jinhua, China	G8	42
Ch'inhuangtao see Qinhuangdao, China	B8	42
Chining see Jining, China	D7	42
Chining see Jining, China	A5	42
Chiniot, Pak.	C4	54
Chinit, stm., Camb.	F7	48
Chinjan, Pak.	C1	54
Chinju, Kor., S.	G7	38
Chinkiang see Zhenjiang, China	E8	42
Chinko, stm., C.A.R.	C4	66
Chinle, Az., U.S.	G7	132
Chinle Wash, stm., Az., U.S.	G7	132
Chinmen Tao (Quemoy), i., Tai.	I8	42
Chino, Ca., U.S.	J8	134
Chinon, Fr.	G9	14
Chinook, Ab., Can.	C2	124
Chinook Cove, B.C., Can.	E10	138
Chino Valley, Az., U.S.	I4	132
Chinquapin, N.C., U.S.	B8	116
Chinsali, Zam.	C5	68
Chintāmani, India	E4	53
Chinú, Col.	C4	86
Chinwangtao see Qinhuangdao, China	B8	42
Chioco, Moz.	D5	68
Chioggia, Italy	E9	22
Chíos, Grc.	E9	28
Chíos, i., Grc.	E8	28
Chios see Chíos, i., Grc.	E8	28
Chipata, Zam.	C5	68
Chip Lake, l., Ab., Can.	C15	138
Chiplūn, India	C1	53
Chipman, N.B., Can.	D11	110
Chipola, stm., Fl., U.S.	G13	122
Chippenham, Eng., U.K.	J10	12
Chippewa, stm., Mn., U.S.	F3	118
Chippewa, stm., Wi., U.S.	G6	118
Chippewa, East Fork, stm., Wi., U.S.	F8	118
Chippewa Falls, Wi., U.S.	G7	118
Chiquimula, Guat.	E3	102
Chiquinquirá, Col.	E4	86
Chīrāla, India	D5	53
Chirāwa, India	D5	54
Chiredzi, Zimb.	B10	70
Chireno, Tx., U.S.	F4	122
Chirfa, Niger	E7	64
Chīrgaon, India	F7	54
Chiribiquete, Parque Nacional, p.o.i., Col.	G5	86
Chiricahua Mountains, mts., Az., U.S.	L7	132
Chiricahua National Monument, p.o.i., Az., U.S.	L7	132
Chiricahua Peak, mtn., Az., U.S.	L7	132
Chiriguaná, Col.	C5	86
Chirikof Island, i., Ak., U.S.	E8	140
Chiriquí, Golfo de, b., Pan.	H6	102
Chiriquí, Laguna de, b., Pan.	H6	102
Chiromo, Mwi.	D5	68
Chirpan see Čirpan, Blg.	G12	26
Chirripó, Cerro, mtn., C.R.	H6	102
Chirripó, Parque Nacional, p.o.i., C.R.	H6	102
Chisago City, Mn., U.S.	F5	118
Chisamba, Zam.	C4	68
Chisasibi, Qc., Can.	E15	106
Chisep'o, Kor., S.	E1	40
Ch'ishan, Tai.	J9	42
Chisholm, Ab., Can.	B16	138
Chisholm, Me., U.S.	F6	110
Chisholm, Mn., U.S.	D5	118
Chishtiān Mandi, Pak.	D4	54
Chishui, China	G1	42
Chishui, stm., China	F6	36
Chisimayu see Kismaayo, Som.	E8	66
Chişinău, Mol.	B15	26
Chişineu-Criş, Rom.	C8	26
Chita, Col.	D5	86
Chitado, Ang.	D1	68
Chitagá, Col.	D5	86
Chita-hantō, pen., Japan	E9	40
Chitato, Ang.	B3	68
Chitek Lake, l., Mb., Can.	B14	124
Chitembo, Ang.	C2	68
Chitina, Ak., U.S.	D11	140
Chitina, stm., Ak., U.S.	D11	140
Chitipa, Mwi.	B5	68
Chitokoloki, Zam.	C3	68
Chitose, Japan	C14	38
Chitradurga, India	D3	53
Chitrakūt Dham, India	F8	54
Chitrāl, Pak.	B11	56
Chitrāvati, stm., India	D3	53
Chitré, Pan.	H7	102
Chittagong, Bngl.	G13	54
Chittagong, state, Bngl.	G13	54
Chīttāpur, India	C3	53
Chittaurgarh, India	F5	54
Chittoor, India	E4	53
Chittūr, India	F3	53
Chitungwiza, Zimb.	D5	68
Chiuchiang see Jiujiang, China	G6	42
Chiumbe (Tshumbe), stm., Afr.	B3	68
Chiume, Ang.	D3	68
Chiusi, Italy	G8	22
Chiva see Xiva, Spain	E10	20
Chivacoa, Ven.	B7	86
Chivasso, Italy	E4	22
Chivi, Zimb.	B10	70
Chivilcoy, Arg.	G7	92
Chivirira Falls, wtfl, Zimb.	B11	70
Chizu, Japan	D7	40
Chloride, Az., U.S.	H2	132
Chmielnik, Pol.	F16	16
Chŏâm Khsant, Camb.	E7	48
Choapa, stm., Chile	E2	92
Choceň, Czech Rep.	F12	16
Chochis, Cerro, mtn., Bol.	C5	90
Choch'iwŏn, Kor., S.	F7	38
Chociwel, Pol.	C11	16
Chocó, state, Col.	E3	86
Chocolate Mountains, mts., U.S.	J1	132
Chocontá, Col.	E5	86
Chocope, Peru	E2	84
Choctawhatchee, West Fork, stm., Al., U.S.	G13	122
Choctawhatchee Bay, b., Fl., U.S.	G12	122
Chodzież, Pol.	D12	16
Choele Choel, Arg.	G3	90
Choiseul, St. Luc.	m6	105c
Choiseul, state, Sol. Is.	d7	79b
Choiseul, i., Sol. Is.	d7	79b
Chojna, Pol.	D10	16
Chojnice, Pol.	C13	16
Chojnów, Pol.	E11	16
Ch'ok'ē, mts., Eth.	E7	62
Choke Canyon Reservoir, res., Tx., U.S.	F9	130
Chokio, Mn., U.S.	F2	118
Chókwe, Moz.	D11	70
Cholet, Fr.	G8	14
Choluteca, Hond.	F4	102
Choluteca, stm., Hond.	F4	102
Choma, Zam.	D4	68
Chomo Lhāri, mtn., Asia	E12	54
Chomūm, India	E5	54
Chomutov, Czech Rep.	F9	16
Ch'ŏnan, Kor., S.	F7	38
Chon Buri, Thai.	F5	48
Chon Daen, Thai.	D5	48
Chone, Ec.	H1	86
Chong'an, China	H8	42
Ch'ŏngdo, Kor., S.	D1	40
Ch'ŏngjin, Kor., N.	D8	38
Ch'ŏngju, Kor., S.	F7	38
Chŏng Kal, Camb.	E6	48
Chongming, China	I4	38
Chongming Dao, i., China	F9	42
Chongoroi, Ang.	C1	68
Chongqing (Chungking), China	G2	42
Chŏngsŏn, Kor., S.	B1	40
Chŏngŭp, Kor., S.	G7	38
Chongxin, China	D2	42
Chongzuo, China	A8	48
Chŏnju, Kor., S.	G7	38
Chonos, Archipiélago de los, is., Chile	I1	90
Ch'ŏnsu-ri, Kor., N.	D8	38
Chontaleña, Cordillera, mts., Nic.	G5	102
Cho Oyu see Chopu, mtn., Asia	D11	54
Cho Oyu see Qowowuyag, mtn., Asia	D11	54
Chop, Ukr.	A9	26
Chopda, India	H5	54
Chopim, stm., Braz.	C11	92
Chopinzinho, Braz.	B11	92
Chopu (Qowowuyag), mtn., Asia	D11	54
Chorna, Ukr.	B16	26
Chornobyl', Ukr.	D4	32
Choros, Isla, i., Chile	D2	92
Ch'ŏrwŏn, Kor., S.	E7	38
Chorzele, Pol.	C16	16
Chosen, Fl., U.S.	J5	116
Chōshi, Japan	D13	40
Chosica, Peru	F2	84
Chos Malal, Arg.	H2	92
Choszczno, Pol.	C11	16
Choteau, Mt., U.S.	C14	136
Chotila, India	G3	54
Chouchiak'ou see Shangshui, China	E6	42
Chouk'ou see Shangshui, China	E6	42
Choushan Islands see Zhoushan Qundao, is., China	F10	42
Chowchilla, Ca., U.S.	F5	134
Chown, Mount, mtn., Ab., Can.	C11	138
Choya, Arg.	D5	92
Choybalsan, Mong.	B7	36
Choyr, Mong.	B6	36
Chrisman, Il., U.S.	I2	112
Christanshåb (Qasigiannguit), Grnld.	D15	141
Christchurch, N.Z.	F5	80
Christian, Cape, c., Nu., Can.	A17	106
Christian, Point, c., Pit.	c28	78k
Christiana, Jam.	i13	104d
Christiana, S. Afr.	E7	70
Christian Island, i., On., Can.	D9	112
Christiansburg, Va., U.S.	G5	114
Christian Sound, strt., Ak., U.S.	E12	140
Christianstad, V.I.U.S.	h11	104c
Christmas Island, dep., Oc.	K13	142
Christmas Island, i., Christ. I.	E1	72
Christmas Island see Kiritimati, at., Kir.	C11	72
Christmas Ridge, unds.	I22	142
Christoval, Tx., U.S.	C7	130
Chrudim, Czech Rep.	G11	16
Chrzanów, Pol.	F15	16
Chu (Xam), stm., Asia	B7	48
Chuādanga, Bngl.	G12	54
Chuanchou see Quanzhou, China	I8	42
Chubbuck, Id., U.S.	H14	136
Chūbu-Sangaku-kokuritsu-kōen, p.o.i., Japan	C10	40
Chubut, state, Arg.	H3	90
Chubut, stm., Arg.	H3	90
Ch'üchiang see Shaoguan, China	I5	42
Chuchi Lake, l., B.C., Can.	A6	138
Chuchou see Zhuzhou, China	H5	42
Chuchow see Zhuzhou, China	H5	42
Chu Chua, B.C., Can.	E10	138
Chucunaque, stm., Pan.	H9	102
Chugach Mountains, mts., Ak., U.S.	D10	140
Chuginadak Island, i., Ak., U.S.	g25	140a
Chūgoku-sanchi, mts., Japan	D6	40
Chugwater Creek, stm., Wy., U.S.	F8	126
Chuhuichupa, Mex.	G8	98
Chuí, Braz.	F11	92
Chukchi Sea	C5	94
Chuke Hu, l., China	C11	54
Chukotsk Peninsula see Čukotskij poluostrov, pen., Russia	C26	34
Chula Vista, Ca., U.S.	K8	134
Chulucanas, Peru	E1	84
Chumbicha, Arg.	D4	92
Chum Phae, Thai.	D6	48
Chumphon, Thai.	G4	48
Chumphon Buri, Thai.	E6	48
Chum Saeng, Thai.	E5	48
Chumunjin, Kor., S.	B1	40
Chun'an, China	G8	42
Chunan, Tai.	I9	42
Chuncheon see Ch'unch'ŏn, Kor., S.	F7	38
Chunchi, Ec.	I2	86
Ch'unch'ŏn, Kor., S.	F7	38
Chunchula, Al., U.S.	G10	122
Ch'ungch'ŏng-bukto, state, Kor., S.	B1	40
Ch'ungju, Kor., S.	F7	38
Chungking see Chongqing, China	G2	42
Ch'ungmu, Kor., S.	E1	40
Chungshan see Zhongshan, China	J5	42
Chungyang Shanmo, mts., Tai.	J9	42
Chunhua, China	D3	42
Chunhuhux, Mex.	C3	102
Chuquibamba, Peru	G3	84
Chuquicamata, Chile	D3	90
Chur (Coire), Switz.	D6	22
Church Hill, Tn., U.S.	H3	114
Churchill, Mb., Can.	D12	106
Churchill, stm., Can.	D11	106
Churchill, stm., Nf., Can.	E18	106
Churchill, Mount, mtn., B.C., Can.	G7	138
Churchill, Mount, vol., Ak., U.S.	D11	140
Churchill Falls, wtfl, Nf., Can.	E17	106
Churchill Lake, l., Sk., Can.	D9	106
Church Point, La., U.S.	G6	122
Church Rock, N.M., U.S.	H8	132
Chūru, India	D5	54
Churubusco, In., U.S.	G4	112
Churuguara, Ven.	B7	86
Chushul, India	B7	54
Chute-Saint-Philippe, Qc., Can.	D1	110
Chutung, Tai.	I9	42
Chuuk, is., Micron.	C6	72
Chuvashia see Čuvašija, state, Russia	C7	32
Chuxian, China	E8	42
Chuxiong, China	F5	36
Ci, stm., China	B6	42
Ci, stm., China	E6	42
Ciadâr Lunga, Mol.	C15	26
Ciales, P.R.	B3	104a
Ciamis, Indon.	G6	50
Cianjur, Indon.	G5	50
Cianorte, Braz.	A11	92
Čiatura, Geor.	F6	32
Ciawi, Indon.	G5	50
Cibaliung, Indon.	G4	50
Cibatu, Indon.	G6	50
Cibinong, Indon.	G5	50
Cibolo Creek, stm., Tx., U.S.	E3	130
Cibolo Creek, stm., Tx., U.S.	E10	130
Cicero, Il., U.S.	G2	112
Cicero, In., U.S.	H3	112
Cícero Dantas, Braz.	F6	88
Cicurug, Indon.	G5	50
Cidra, P.R.	B3	104a
Ciechanów, Pol.	D16	16
Ciechanów, state, Pol.	C16	16
Ciechanowiec, Pol.	D18	16
Ciego de Ávila, Cuba	B8	102
Ciempozuelos, Spain	D7	20
Ciénaga, Col.	B4	86
Ciénega de Flores, Mex.	H7	130
Cienfuegos, Cuba	A7	102
Cíes, Illas, is., Spain	B1	20
Cies, Islas see Cíes, Illas, is., Spain	B1	20
Cieszanów, Pol.	F19	16
Cieszyn, Pol.	G14	16
Cieza, Spain	F9	20
Çifteler, Tur.	D13	28
Cifuentes, Spain	D8	20
Cigüela, stm., Spain	E7	20
Cihanbeyli, Tur.	E15	28
Čiili, Kaz.	F11	32
Cijara, Embalse de, res., Spain	E6	20
Cijulang, Indon.	G6	50
Cikampek, Indon.	G5	50
Čikobia, i., Fiji	o20	79e
Čikoj, Russia	F10	34
Cilacap, Indon.	G6	50
Cilamaya, Indon.	G5	50
Cilento, reg., Italy	D9	24
Cili, China	G4	42
Cilician Gates see Gülek Boğazı, p., Tur.	A5	58
Čilik, Kaz.	F13	32
Cill Chainnigh see Kilkenny, Ire.	I5	12
Cilleruelo de Bezana, Spain	B7	20
Cil'ma, stm., Russia	D24	8
Cimarron, N.M., U.S.	E4	128
Cimarron, stm., U.S.	F12	128
Cimarron, North Fork, stm., U.S.	D7	128
Čimbaj, Uzb.	F9	32
Cimişlia, Mol.	C15	26
Cimljanskoe vodohranilišče, res., Russia	E6	32
Cimone, Monte, mtn., Italy	F7	22
Cimpu, Indon.	E12	50
Cina, Tanjung, c., Indon.	G4	50
Cinaruco, stm., Ven.	D7	86
Cinaruco-Capanaparo Santos Luzardo, Parque Nacional, p.o.i., Ven.	D8	86
Cinca, stm., Spain	C11	20
Cincinnati, Ia., U.S.	D4	120
Cincinnati, Oh., U.S.	E1	114
Cinco, Canal Numero, can., Arg.	H9	92
Cinco de Mayo, Mex.	I3	130
Cinco Saltos, Arg.	I3	92
Çine, Tur.	F10	28
Ciney, Bel.	D14	14
Cinfães, Port.	C2	20
Cinişeuţi, Mol.	B15	26
Cintalapa, Mex.	G12	100
Cinto, Monte, mtn., Fr.	G14	18
Cintra, Golfe de, b., W. Sah.	E1	64
Ciociaria, reg., Italy	I10	22
Cipa, stm., Russia	F11	34
Cipatujah, Indon.	G5	50
Cipó, Braz.	F6	88
Cipó, stm., Braz.	J4	88
Cipolletti, Arg.	G3	90
Circeo, Parco Nazionale del, p.o.i., Italy	C6	24
Čirčik, Uzb.	F11	32
Circle, Ak., U.S.	C11	140
Circle, Mt., U.S.	G8	124
Circleville, Oh., U.S.	E3	114
Circleville, Ut., U.S.	E4	132
Circleville Mountain, mtn., Ut., U.S.	E4	132
Cirebon, Indon.	G6	50
Ciremay, Gunung, vol., Indon.	G6	50
Cirencester, Eng., U.K.	J11	12
Čirgalandy, Russia	D17	32
Ciriè, Italy	E4	22
Cirò Marina, Italy	E11	24
Čirpan, Blg.	G12	26
Ciskei, hist. reg., S. Afr.	H8	70
Cisnădie, Rom.	D11	26
Cisne, Il., U.S.	F9	120
Cisne, Islas del see Santanilla, Islas, is., Hond.	D6	102
Cisneros, Col.	D4	86
Cisolok, Indon.	G5	50
Cissna Park, Il., U.S.	H2	112
Čistoozërnoe, Russia	D13	32
Čistopol', Russia	C8	32
Čita, Russia	F11	34
Citlaltépetl, Volcán see Pico de Orizaba, Volcán, vol., Mex.	F10	100
Citra, Fl., U.S.	G3	116
Citrus Heights, Ca., U.S.	E4	134
Città di Castello, Italy	G9	22
Cittanova, Italy	F10	24
City of Sunrise see Sunrise, Fl., U.S.	J5	116
City Point, Fl., U.S.	H5	116
Ciudad Acuña, Mex.	A8	100
Ciudad Altamirano, Mex.	F8	100
Ciudad Anáhuac, Mex.	B8	100
Ciudad Bolívar, Ven.	C10	86
Ciudad Bolivia, Ven.	C6	86
Ciudad Camargo, Mex.	B6	100
Ciudad Camargo, Mex.	B9	100
Ciudad Constitución, Mex.	C3	100
Ciudad Cortés, C.R.	H6	102
Ciudad Darío, Nic.	F4	102
Ciudad del Carmen, Mex.	F12	100
Ciudad del Este, Para.	B10	92
Ciudad de Libertador General San Martín, Arg.	A5	92
Ciudad de México (Mexico City), Mex.	F9	100
Ciudad de Nutrias, Ven.	C7	86
Ciudadela see Ciutadella de Menorca, Spain	D14	20
Ciudad Guayana, Ven.	C10	86
Ciudad Hidalgo, Mex.	F8	100
Ciudad Jiménez see Jiménez, Mex.	B6	100
Ciudad Juárez, Mex.	C1	130
Ciudad Lerdo see Lerdo, Mex.	C7	100
Ciudad Madero, Mex.	D10	100
Ciudad Mante, Mex.	D9	100
Ciudad Miguel Alemán, Mex.	B9	100
Ciudad Morelos, Mex.	E5	98
Ciudad Netzahualcóyotl, Mex.	F9	100
Ciudad Obregón, Mex.	B4	100
Ciudad Ojeda, Ven.	B6	86
Ciudad Piar, Ven.	D10	86
Ciudad Real, Spain	F6	20
Ciudad Real, co., Spain	F6	20
Ciudad Rodrigo, Spain	D4	20
Ciudad Valles, Mex.	E9	100
Ciudad Victoria, Mex.	D9	100
Ciutadella de Menorca, Spain	D14	20
Civita Castellana, Italy	H9	22
Civitanova Marche, Italy	G10	22
Civitavecchia, Italy	H8	22
Çivril, Tur.	E12	28
Cixi, China	F9	42
Čiža, Russia	C21	8
Cjaluša, Bela.	G12	10
Čkalovsk, Russia	H20	8
Clackamas, stm., Or., U.S.	E4	136
Clacton-on-Sea, Eng., U.K.	J14	12
Claflin, Ks., U.S.	C10	128
Claiborne, Al., U.S.	F11	122
Clain, stm., Fr.	C6	18
Claire, Lake, l., Ab., Can.	D8	106
Clair Engle Lake, res., Ca., U.S.	C3	134
Clairton, Pa., U.S.	D6	114
Clallam Bay, Wa., U.S.	B2	136
Clanton, Al., U.S.	E12	122
Clanwilliam, S. Afr.	H4	70
Clapperton Island, i., On., Can.	B7	112
Clara, Ire.	H5	12
Clara, Ms., U.S.	F10	122
Clara, stm., Austl.	B4	76
Clara, Punta, c., Arg.	H4	90
Clare, Austl.	I4	76
Clare, Mi., U.S.	E5	112
Clare, state, Ire.	I3	12
Clare Island, i., Ire.	H2	12
Claremont, N.H., U.S.	G4	110
Claremont, S.D., U.S.	B15	126
Claremont, mtn., Ca., U.S.	D4	134
Claremore, Ok., U.S.	H2	120
Clarence, Mo., U.S.	E5	120
Clarence, stm., Austl.	G9	76
Clarence, stm., N.Z.	F5	80
Clarence, Cape, c., Nu., Can.	A13	106
Clarence, Isla, i., Chile	J2	90
Clarence Strait, strt., Austl.	B6	74
Clarence Strait, strt., Ak., U.S.	E13	140
Clarence Town, Bah.	C9	96
Clarendon, Ar., U.S.	C7	122
Clarendon, Tx., U.S.	G8	128
Clarenville, Nf., Can.	j23	107a
Claresholm, Ab., Can.	F17	138
Clarinda, Ia., U.S.	D2	120
Clarines, Ven.	C9	86
Clarington, On., Can.	E11	112
Clarion, Ia., U.S.	B4	120
Clarion, Pa., U.S.	C6	114
Clarion, stm., Pa., U.S.	C6	114
Clarion Fracture Zone, unds.	H25	142
Clarissa, Mn., U.S.	E3	118
Clark, Mount, mtn., N.T., Can.	C6	106
Clarke, stm., Austl.	B5	76
Clarke Island, i., Austl.	n14	77a
Clarkesville, Ga., U.S.	B2	116
Clarkfield, Mn., U.S.	G3	118
Clark Fork, Id., U.S.	B10	136
Clark Fork, stm., U.S.	C11	136
Clarks, La., U.S.	E6	122
Clarksburg, W.V., U.S.	E5	114
Clarksdale, Ms., U.S.	C8	122
Clark's Harbour, N.S., Can.	G11	110
Clarks Hill, In., U.S.	H3	112
Clarkson, Ky., U.S.	G11	120
Clarks Summit, Pa., U.S.	C10	114
Clarkston, Wa., U.S.	D9	136
Clark's Town, Jam.	i13	104d
Clarksville, Ar., U.S.	B5	122
Clarksville, Ia., U.S.	I6	118
Clarksville, Tn., U.S.	H10	120
Clarksville, Va., U.S.	H7	114
Clarkton, Mo., U.S.	H7	120
Clarkton, N.C., U.S.	B7	116
Claro, stm., Braz.	G7	84
Claude, Tx., U.S.	F7	128
Clausthal-Zellerfeld, Ger.	E5	16
Claveria, Phil.	B7	44
Clavering Ø, i., Grnld.	C22	141
Clavet, Sk., Can.	B7	124
Claxton, Ga., U.S.	D4	116
Clay, Ky., U.S.	G10	120
Clay, Tx., U.S.	G2	122
Clay Center, Ne., U.S.	G14	126
Clay City, Il., U.S.	F9	120
Clay City, In., U.S.	E10	120
Clay City, Ky., U.S.	G1	114
Claymont, De., U.S.	E10	114
Claypool, Az., U.S.	J6	132
Claysburg, Pa., U.S.	D7	114
Clayton, Al., U.S.	F13	122
Clayton, Ga., U.S.	B2	116
Clayton, Il., U.S.	D7	120
Clayton, La., U.S.	F7	122
Clayton, Mo., U.S.	F7	120
Clayton, N.M., U.S.	E5	128
Clayton, N.Y., U.S.	D13	112
Clayton, Ok., U.S.	C3	122
Clayton, Wa., U.S.	B9	136
Clear, Cape, c., Ire.	J3	12
Clear Boggy Creek, stm., Ok., U.S.	C2	122
Clearbrook, Mn., U.S.	D3	118
Clear Creek, stm., Wy., U.S.	C6	126
Clearfield, Pa., U.S.	C7	114
Clearfield, Ut., U.S.	B4	132
Clearlake, Ca., U.S.	E3	134
Clear Lake, Ia., U.S.	A4	120
Clear Lake, S.D., U.S.	G2	118
Clear Lake, Wi., U.S.	F6	118
Clear Lake, l., Mb., Can.	D14	124
Clear Lake, l., Ca., U.S.	D3	134
Clear Lake, res., La., U.S.	F5	122
Clear Lake Reservoir, res., Ca., U.S.	B4	134
Clearmont, Wy., U.S.	C6	126
Clearwater, B.C., Can.	E10	138
Clearwater, Mb., Can.	E14	124
Clearwater, Fl., U.S.	I3	116
Clearwater, Ne., U.S.	E14	126
Clearwater, stm., Can.	D8	106
Clearwater, stm., Ab., Can.	D15	138
Clearwater, stm., B.C., Can.	D10	138
Clearwater, stm., Id., U.S.	D10	136
Clearwater, stm., Mn., U.S.	D3	118
Clearwater, stm., Mt., U.S.	C13	136
Clearwater, Middle Fork, stm., Id., U.S.	D11	136
Clearwater, North Fork, stm., Id., U.S.	D11	136
Clearwater Lake, l., B.C., Can.	D10	138
Clearwater Mountains, mts., Id., U.S.	D11	136
Clebit, Ok., U.S.	C4	122
Cleburne, Tx., U.S.	B10	130
Cle Elum, stm., Wa., U.S.	C5	136
Cle Elum Lake, res., Wa., U.S.	C6	136
Cleethorpes, Eng., U.K.	H12	12
Clementsport, N.S., Can.	F11	110
Clemson, S.C., U.S.	B3	116
Clermont, Austl.	D6	76
Clermont, Qc., Can.	C6	110
Clermont, Fr.	E11	14
Clermont-Ferrand, Fr.	D9	18
Clevedon, Eng., U.K.	J10	12
Cleveland, Al., U.S.	D12	122
Cleveland, Ms., U.S.	D8	122
Cleveland, N.C., U.S.	A5	116
Cleveland, Oh., U.S.	C4	114
Cleveland, Ok., U.S.	A2	122
Cleveland, Tn., U.S.	B14	122
Cleveland, Tx., U.S.	G3	122
Cleveland, Va., U.S.	H3	114
Cleveland, Cape, c., Austl.	B6	76
Cleveland, Mount, mtn., Mt., U.S.	B13	136
Clevelândia, Braz.	C11	92
Cleves see Kleve, Ger.	E2	16
Clew Bay, b., Ire.	H3	12
Clewiston, Fl., U.S.	J4	116
Clifton, St. Vin.	p11	105e
Clifton, Az., U.S.	J7	132
Clifton, Tn., U.S.	B11	122
Clifton, Tx., U.S.	C10	130
Clifton Forge, Va., U.S.	G6	114
Clifton Hills, Austl.	F2	76
Climax, Sk., Can.	E5	124
Climax, Co., U.S.	B2	128
Clinch, stm., U.S.	I13	120
Clinchco, Va., U.S.	G15	120
Clingmans Dome, mtn., U.S.	I2	114
Clinton, B.C., Can.	E9	138
Clinton, On., Can.	E8	112
Clinton, Al., U.S.	E11	122
Clinton, Ar., U.S.	B6	122
Clinton, In., U.S.	I2	112
Clinton, Ia., U.S.	C7	120
Clinton, Ky., U.S.	H9	120
Clinton, La., U.S.	G7	122
Clinton, Mi., U.S.	B2	114
Clinton, Mn., U.S.	F2	118
Clinton, Ms., U.S.	E8	122
Clinton, N.C., U.S.	A7	116
Clinton, Ok., U.S.	F9	128
Clinton, S.C., U.S.	B4	116
Clinton, Wi., U.S.	B9	120
Clinton, Cape, c., Austl.	D8	76
Clinton, Lake, res., Il., U.S.	D9	120
Clinton-Colden Lake, l., N.T., Can.	C9	106
Clinton Lake, res., Ks., U.S.	F2	120
Clintonville, Wi., U.S.	G10	118
Clintwood, Va., U.S.	G3	114
Clio, Mi., U.S.	E6	112
Clio, S.C., U.S.	B6	116
Clipperton, Île, at., Oc.	H28	142
Clipperton Fracture Zone, unds.	I25	142
Clipperton Island see Clipperton, Île, at., Oc.	H28	142
Clisson, Fr.	G7	14
Clodomira, Arg.	C5	92
Cloete, Mex.	G6	130
Cloncurry, Austl.	C3	76
Cloncurry, stm., Austl.	B3	76
Clonmel, Ire.	I5	12
Clo-oose, B.C., Can.	H6	138
Cloppenburg, Ger.	D3	16
Cloquet, Mn., U.S.	E6	118
Clorinda, Arg.	B9	92
Cloud Peak, mtn., Wy., U.S.	C5	126
Clova, Qc., Can.	B1	110
Clover, S.C., U.S.	A4	116
Cloverdale, Ca., U.S.	E2	134
Cloverdale, In., U.S.	E11	120
Cloverport, Ky., U.S.	G11	120
Clovis, Ca., U.S.	G6	134
Clovis, N.M., U.S.	G5	128
Cluain Meala see Clonmel, Ire.	I5	12
Cluj, state, Rom.	C10	26
Cluj-Napoca, Rom.	C10	26
Clunes, Austl.	K4	76
Cluny, Austl.	E2	76
Cluny, Fr.	C10	18
Clusone, Italy	E7	22
Clute, Tx., U.S.	E12	130
Clutha, stm., N.Z.	H3	80
Clyde, Ks., U.S.	B11	128
Clyde, N.C., U.S.	A3	116
Clyde, Oh., U.S.	C3	114
Clyde, Tx., U.S.	B8	130
Clyde, stm., Scot., U.K.	F9	12
Clyde, Firth of, b., Scot., U.K.	F7	12
Clyde Inlet, b., Nu., Can.	A17	106
Clyde Park, Mt., U.S.	E16	136
Clyde River, Nu., Can.	A16	106
Clymer, Pa., U.S.	D6	114
Ćmielów, Pol.	F17	16
Cna, stm., Russia	C17	10
Cna, stm., Russia	D6	32
Cnossus see Knosós, hist., Grc.	H8	28
Côa, stm., Port.	D3	20
Coachella, Ca., U.S.	J9	134
Coachella Canal, can., Ca., U.S.	K1	132
Coahoma, Tx., U.S.	B6	130
Coahuila, state, Mex.	B7	100
Coal City, Il., U.S.	J10	118
Coalcomán de Matamoros, Mex.	F7	100
Coal Creek, stm., Wa., U.S.	C8	136
Coaldale, Ab., Can.	G18	138
Coalgate, Ok., U.S.	C2	122
Coal Grove, Oh., U.S.	F3	114
Coal Hill, Ar., U.S.	B5	122
Coalinga, Ca., U.S.	G5	134
Coalmont, B.C., Can.	G10	138
Coalport, Pa., U.S.	D7	114
Coal River, B.C., Can.	D5	106
Coal Valley, val., Nv., U.S.	F1	132
Coalville, Eng., U.K.	I11	12
Coalville, Ut., U.S.	C5	132
Coamo, P.R.	B3	104a
Coaraci, Braz.	H6	88
Coari, Braz.	D5	84
Coari, stm., Braz.	D5	84
Coast Mountains, mts., N.A.	D4	106
Coast Ranges, mts., U.S.	C2	134
Coatbridge, Scot., U.K.	F9	12
Coatesville, Pa., U.S.	E10	114
Coaticook, Qc., Can.	E5	110
Coats Island, i., Nu., Can.	C14	106
Coats Land, reg., Ant.	C2	81
Coatzacoalcos, Mex.	F11	100
Cobá, hist., Mex.	B4	102
Cobalt, On., Can.	F14	106
Cobán, Guat.	E2	102
Cobar, Austl.	H5	76
Cobberas, Mount, mtn., Austl.	K6	76
Cobden, On., Can.	C13	112
Cobequid Bay, b., N.S., Can.	E13	110
Cobh, Ire.	J4	12
Cobham, stm., Can.	B18	124
Cobija, Bol.	B3	90
Coblence see Koblenz, Ger.	F3	16
Coblenz see Koblenz, Ger.	F3	16
Cobleskill, N.Y., U.S.	B11	114
Cobourg, On., Can.	E11	112
Cobquecura, Chile	H1	92
Cobram, Austl.	J5	76
Cobre, Barranca del (Copper Canyon), misc. cult., Mex.	B5	100
Cóbuè, Moz.	C5	68
Coburg, Ger.	F6	16
Coburg Island, i., Nu., Can.	B10	141
Coburg Peninsula, pen., Austl.	B6	74
Coca, stm., Ec.	H3	86
Cocal, Braz.	B5	88
Cocentaina, Spain	F10	20
Cöch, stm., Asia	B6	36
Cochabamba, Bol.	C3	90
Coche, Isla, i., Ven.	B10	86
Cochem, Ger.	F3	16
Cochin see Kochi, India	G3	53
Cochin China see Nam Phan, hist. reg., Viet.	G8	48
Cochinos, Bahía de (Pigs, Bay of), b., Cuba	B7	102
Cochise Head, mtn., Az., U.S.	K7	132
Cochrane, Ab., Can.	E16	138
Cochrane, On., Can.	F14	106
Cochrane, Wi., U.S.	G7	118
Cochrane, Lago (Pueyrredón, Lago), l., S.A.	I2	90
Cochranton, Pa., U.S.	C5	114
Cockburn, Austl.	I3	76
Cockburn, Mount, mtn., Austl.	E5	74
Cockburn, Mount, mtn., Austl.	D5	74
Cockburn Island, i., On., Can.	C6	112
Cockermouth, Eng., U.K.	G9	12
Cockpit Country, reg., Jam.	i13	104d
Côco, stm., Braz.	F1	88
Coco, stm., N.A.	E6	102
Coco, Cayo, i., Cuba	A8	102
Coco, Isla del, i., C.R.	F7	96
Cocoa, Fl., U.S.	H5	116
Cocoa Beach, Fl., U.S.	H5	116
Coco Channel, strt., Asia	F7	46
Cocodrie Lake, res., La., U.S.	G6	122
Coco Islands, is., Mya.	F7	46
Coconino Plateau, plat., Az., U.S.	H4	132
Cocos, Braz.	H3	88
Cocos Islands, dep., Oc.	K12	142
Cocos Lagoon, b., Guam	k9	78c
Cocos Ridge, unds.	H5	144
Cocula, Mex.	E7	100
Cod, Cape, pen., Ma., U.S.	C15	114
Codajás, Braz.	D5	84
Codera, Cabo, c., Ven.	B8	86
Coderre, Sk., Can.	D7	124
Codigoro, Italy	F9	22
Cod Island, i., Nf., Can.	F13	141
Codlea, Rom.	D12	26
Codó, Braz.	C3	88
Codogno, Italy	E6	22
Codòzinho, Braz.	C3	88
Codroy, Nf., Can.	C17	110
Cody, Ne., U.S.	E11	126
Cody, Wy., U.S.	C3	126
Coelho Neto, Braz.	C4	88
Coen, Austl.	B8	74
Coëtivy, i., Sey.	k13	69b
Coeur d'Alene, Id., U.S.	C10	136
Coeur d'Alene, stm., Id., U.S.	C10	136
Coeur d'Alene Lake, res., Id., U.S.	C10	136
Coffeeville, Ms., U.S.	D9	122
Coffeyville, Ks., U.S.	G2	120
Coffs Harbour, Austl.	H9	76
Cofre de Perote, Cerro, mtn., Mex.	F10	100
Cofre de Perote, Parque Nacional, p.o.i., Mex.	F10	100
Cofrentes see Cofrents, Spain	E9	20
Cofrents, Spain	E9	20
Cogâlnic (Kohyl'nyk), stm., Eur.	C15	26
Coggon, Ia., U.S.	B6	120
Cognac, Fr.	D5	18
Cogolludo, Spain	D7	20
Cogoon, stm., Austl.	F7	76
Cogswell, N.D., U.S.	A15	126
Cohocton, stm., N.Y., U.S.	F12	112
Cohoes, N.Y., U.S.	B12	114
Cohuna, Austl.	J5	76
Coiba, Isla de, i., Pan.	I6	102
Coig, stm., Arg.	J3	90
Coihaique, Chile	I2	90
Coimbatore (Koyambattur), India	F3	53
Coimbra, Braz.	K4	88
Coimbra, Port.	D2	20
Coimbra, state, Port.	D2	20
Coín, Spain	H6	20
Coipasa, Lago, l., Bol.	C3	90
Coipasa, Salar de, pl., S.A.	C3	90
Coire see Chur, Switz.	D6	22
Cojedes, state, Ven.	C7	86
Cojudo Blanco, Cerro, mtn., Arg.	I3	90
Cojutepeque, El Sal.	F3	102
Cokato, Mn., U.S.	F4	118
Cokeville, Wy., U.S.	A6	132
Čokpar, Kaz.	F12	32
Čokurdah, Russia	B18	34
Colac, Austl.	L4	76
Colatina, Braz.	J5	88
Colbeck, Cape, c., Ant.	C25	81
Colbert, Ok., U.S.	D2	122
Colbinabbin, Austl.	K5	76
Colbún, Chile	G2	92
Colbún, Embalse, res., Chile	G2	92
Colby, Ks., U.S.	B7	128
Colby, Wi., U.S.	G8	118
Colchester, Eng., U.K.	J13	12
Colchester, Il., U.S.	D7	120
Cold Bay, Ak., U.S.	E7	140
Cold Lake, Ab., Can.	E8	106
Cold Spring, Mn., U.S.	F4	118
Coldstream, Scot., U.K.	F10	12
Coldwater, Ks., U.S.	D9	128

Name — Map Ref. — Page

Coldwater, Mi., U.S. G4 112
Coldwater, Oh., U.S. H5 112
Coldwater, stm., Ms., U.S. C8 122
Coldwater Creek, stm., U.S. E7 128
Coleambally, Austl. J5 76
Colebrook, N.H., U.S. F15 110
Cole Camp, Mo., U.S. F4 120
Coleman, Ab., Can. G16 138
Coleman, Fl., U.S. H3 116
Coleman, Mi., U.S. E5 112
Coleman, Wi., U.S. C1 112
Coleman, stm., Austl. B8 74
Colenso, S. Afr. F9 70
Coleraine, Austl. K3 76
Coleraine, N. Ire., U.K. F6 12
Coleridge, Ne., U.S. E15 126
Coles, Ms., U.S. F7 122
Colesberg, S. Afr. G7 70
Coleville, Sk., Can. C4 124
Colfax, In., U.S. H3 112
Colfax, Ia., U.S. C4 120
Colfax, La., U.S. F6 122
Colfax, Wa., U.S. D9 136
Colfax, Wi., U.S. F7 118
Colgong, India F11 54
Colhué Huapi, Lago, l., Arg. I3 90
Colibris, Pointe des, c., Guad. h6 105c
Colico, Italy D6 22
Coligny, S. Afr. E8 70
Colihaut, Dom. j5 105c
Colima, Mex. F7 100
Colima, state, Mex. F7 100
Colima, Nevado de, vol., Mex. F7 100
Colinas, Braz. D3 88
Colinas, Braz. H1 88
Colinton, Ab., Can. B17 138
Coll, i., Scot., U.K. E6 12
Collarenebri, Austl. G7 76
College, Ak., U.S. D10 140
Collegedale, Tn., U.S. B13 122
College Park, Ga., U.S. D14 122
College Place, Wa., U.S. D8 136
College Station, Ar., U.S. C6 122
College Station, Tx., U.S. G2 122
Collerina, Austl. G6 76
Colleymount, B.C., Can. B4 138
Collie, Austl. F3 74
Collier Bay, b., Austl. C4 74
Collierville, Tn., U.S. B9 122
Collingwood, On., Can. D9 112
Collins, Ga., U.S. D3 116
Collins, Ms., U.S. F9 122
Collins Bay, On., Can. D13 112
Collins Head, c., Norf. I. y25 78i
Collinston, La., U.S. E7 122
Collinsville, Austl. C6 76
Collinsville, Al., U.S. C13 122
Collinsville, Ok., U.S. H2 120
Collinsville, Tx., U.S. D2 122
Collinwood, Tn., U.S. B11 122
Collipulli, Chile H1 92
Colman, S.D., U.S. H2 118
Colmar, Fr. F16 14
Colmenar, Spain H6 20
Colmenar Viejo, Spain D7 20
Colmeneros, Mex. F8 100
Colmesneil, Tx., U.S. G4 122
Colnett, Punta, c., Mex. F4 98
Cologne see Köln, Ger. F2 16
Cologne, Mn., U.S. G5 118
Coloma, Mi., U.S. F3 112
Coloma, Wi., U.S. G9 118
Colomb-Béchar see Béchar, Alg. C4 64
Colombia, Col. F4 86
Colombia, ctry., S.A. C3 84
Colombie-Britannique see British Columbia, state, Can. E5 106
Colombo, Braz. B13 92
Colombo, Sri L. H4 53
Colome, S.D., U.S. D13 126
Colomiers, Fr. F7 18
Colón, Arg. F8 92
Colón, Arg. F7 92
Colón, Cuba A7 102
Colón, Pan. H7 102
Colon, Mi., U.S. G4 112
Colón, Ur. F10 92
Colón, Archipiélago de (Galapagos Islands), is., Ec. h12 84a
Colona, Austl. F6 74
Colonelganj, India E8 54
Colônia, stm., Braz. H6 88
Colonia Alvear Norte see General Alvear, Arg. G3 92
Colonia del Sacramento, Ur. G9 92
Colonia Dora, Arg. D6 92
Colonia Elisa, Arg. C8 92
Colonia Lavalleja, Ur. E9 92
Colonial Heights, Va., U.S. G8 114
Colonia Providencia, P.R. C4 104a
Colonia Suiza, Ur. G9 92
Colonias Unidas, Arg. C8 92
Colonne, Capo, c., Italy E11 24
Colonsay, Sk., Can. B8 124
Colonsay, i., Scot., U.K. E6 12
Colony, Ks., U.S. F2 120
Colorada Grande, Salina, pl., Arg. I5 92
Coloradas, Lomas, hills, Arg. H3 90
Colorado, Hond. E4 102
Colorado, state, U.S. D6 108
Colorado, stm., Arg. G4 90
Colorado, stm., N.A. E5 98
Colorado, stm., Tx., U.S. F11 130
Colorado, Cerro, mtn., Arg. H3 90
Colorado City, Co., U.S. C4 128
Colorado City, Tx., U.S. B7 130
Colorado Kolonie see Lago Kolonie, Aruba p20 104g
Colorado National Monument, p.o.i., Co., U.S. D8 132
Colorado Plateau, plat., U.S. E7 132
Colorado River Aqueduct, aq., Ca., U.S. E5 98
Colorado Springs, Co., U.S. C4 128
Colotlán, Mex. D7 100
Colquechaca, Bol. C3 90
Colstrip, Mt., U.S. B6 126
Colt, Ar., U.S. B8 122
Coltauco, Chile G2 92
Colton, Ca., U.S. I8 134
Colton, S.D., U.S. H2 118
Columbia, Ca., U.S. E5 134
Columbia, Il., U.S. F7 120
Columbia, Ky., U.S. G12 120
Columbia, La., U.S. E6 122
Columbia, Md., U.S. E9 114
Columbia, Mo., U.S. F5 120
Columbia, N.C., U.S. I9 114
Columbia, Pa., U.S. D9 114
Columbia, S.C., U.S. C4 116
Columbia, Tn., U.S. B11 122
Columbia, stm., N.A. D3 136
Columbia, Cape, c., Nu., Can. A11 141
Columbia, Mount, mtn., Ab., Can. D13 138
Columbia Basin, bas., Wa., U.S. C8 136
Columbia City, In., U.S. G4 112
Columbia Falls, Me., U.S. F9 110
Columbia Icefield, ice, Can. D13 138
Columbia Mountains, mts., N.A. G13 138
Columbiana, Al., U.S. D12 122
Columbiana, Oh., U.S. D5 114
Columbine, Cape, c., S. Afr. H3 70
Columbretes, Illes, is., Spain E11 20
Columbus, Ga., U.S. E14 122
Columbus, In., U.S. E12 120
Columbus, Ks., U.S. G3 120
Columbus, Ms., U.S. D10 122
Columbus, Ne., U.S. F15 126
Columbus, N.M., U.S. L9 132
Columbus, N.C., U.S. A3 116
Columbus, N.D., U.S. F11 124
Columbus, Oh., U.S. E2 114
Columbus, Tx., U.S. H2 122
Columbus, Wi., U.S. H9 118
Columbus Point, c., Trin. r13 105f
Columbus Salt Marsh, pl., Nv., U.S. E8 134
Colusa, Ca., U.S. D3 134
Colville, Wa., U.S. B9 136
Colville, stm., Ak., U.S. C9 140
Colville Lake, l., N.T., Can. B5 106
Colwyn Bay, Wales, U.K. H9 12
Comacchio, Italy F9 22
Comacchio, Valli di, l., Italy F9 22
Comala, Mex. F7 100
Comalcalco, Mex. F12 100
Comales, Mex. H9 130
Coman, Mount, mtn., Ant. C34 81
Comana, Rom. F15 26
Comanche, Ok., U.S. G10 128
Comandante Ferraz, sci., Ant. B35 81
Comandante Fontana, Arg. B7 92
Comandante Leal, Arg. E5 92
Comandante Luis Piedra Buena, Arg. I3 90
Comănești, Rom. C13 26
Comayagua, Hond. E4 102
Combarbalá, Chile E2 92
Combermere Bay, b., Mya. C1 48
Combourg, Fr. F7 14
Comboyne, Austl. H9 76
Comendador, Dom. Rep. C12 102
Comer, Ga., U.S. B2 116
Comercinho, Braz. I5 88
Comet, stm., Austl. E7 76
Cometela, Moz. B12 70
Comfort, N.C., U.S. B8 116
Comfort, Tx., U.S. E8 130
Comfort, Cape, c., Nu., Can. B14 106
Comfrey, Mn., U.S. G4 118
Comilla, Bngl. G13 54
Comino see Kemmuna, i., Malta H8 24
Comiso, Italy H8 24
Comitán de Domínguez, Mex. G12 100
Commerce, Ga., U.S. B2 116
Commerce, Ok., U.S. H3 120
Commercy, Fr. F14 14
Comminges, reg., Fr. F6 18
Committee Bay, b., Nu., Can. B13 106
Communism Peak see Kommunizma, pik, mtn., Taj. B11 56
Como, Italy E6 22
Como, Tx., U.S. D3 122
Como, Lago di, l., Italy D6 22
Comodoro Rivadavia, Arg. I3 90
Comores, Archipel des, is., Afr. C7 68
Comorin, Cape, c., India G3 53
Comoros, ctry., Afr. C7 68
Comox, B.C., Can. G6 138
Compiègne, Fr. E11 14
Compostela, Mex. E6 100
Compton, Ca., U.S. J7 134
Comrat, Mol. C15 26
Comstock, Ne., U.S. F13 126
Comstock, Tx., U.S. E6 130
Comstock Park, Mi., U.S. E4 112
Con, stm., Viet. C7 48
Cona, stm., Russia B19 32
Co Nag, l., China B13 54
Conakry, Gui. H2 64
Conambo, stm., Ec. H3 86
Cona Niyeo, Arg. H3 90
Conasauga, stm., U.S. C14 122
Concarán, Arg. F5 92
Concarneau, Fr. G5 14
Conceição, Braz. D6 88
Conceição da Barra, Braz. J6 88
Conceição das Alagoas, Braz. J1 88
Conceição do Araguaia, Braz. E1 88
Conceição do Canindé, Braz. D5 88
Conceição do Coité, Braz. F6 88
Conceição do Mato Dentro, Braz. J4 88
Conceição do Norte, Braz. G2 88
Concepción, Arg. D9 92
Concepción, Arg. C5 92
Concepción, Bol. C4 90
Concepción, Chile H1 92
Concepción, Col. D5 86
Concepción, Para. D5 90
Concepción, Bahía, b., Mex. B2 100
Concepción, Canal, strt., Chile J2 90
Concepción, Laguna, l., Bol. C4 90
Concepción, Volcán, vol., Nic. G5 102
Concepción de la Sierra, Arg. D10 92
Concepción del Oro, Mex. C8 100
Concepción del Uruguay, Arg. F8 92
Conception, Point, c., Ca., U.S. I5 134
Conception Bay, b., Nf., Can. j23 107a
Conception Bay, b., Nmb. C2 70
Conchas, stm., Arg. B5 92
Conchas Dam, N.M., U.S. F4 128
Conchas Lake, res., N.M., U.S. F4 128
Concho, Az., U.S. I7 132
Concho, stm., Tx., U.S. C8 130
Conchos, stm., Mex. A6 100
Conchos, stm., Mex. C10 100
Conconully, Wa., U.S. B7 136
Concord, Ca., U.S. E4 134
Concord, Ga., U.S. D14 122
Concord, N.H., U.S. G5 110
Concord, N.C., U.S. A5 116
Concordia, Arg. E8 92
Concórdia, Braz. C11 92
Concordia, Mex. D5 100
Concordia, Mex. I4 130
Concordia, Mo., U.S. F4 120
Concrete, Wa., U.S. B5 136
Con Cuong, Viet. C7 48
Conda, Ang. C1 68
Condamine, Austl. F7 76
Condamine, stm., Austl. F8 76
Condat, Fr. D8 18
Conde, S.D., U.S. B14 126
Condeúba, Braz. H5 88
Condobolin, Austl. I6 76
Condom, Fr. F6 18
Condon, Or., U.S. E6 136
Condoto, Col. E3 86
Condroz, hist. reg., Bel. D14 14
Cone, Tx., U.S. H7 128
Conecuh, stm., U.S. F12 122
Conegliano, Italy E9 22
Conejos, Co., U.S. D2 128
Conejos, stm., Co., U.S. D3 128
Confuso, stm., Para. B8 92
Congaree Swamp National Monument, p.o.i., S.C., U.S. C5 116
Congaz, Mol. C15 26
Conghua, China J5 42
Congjiang, China I3 42
Congleton, Eng., U.K. H10 12
Congo, ctry., Afr. E3 66
Congo (Zaire), stm., Afr. F2 66
Congo, Democratic Republic of the (Zaire), ctry., Afr. E4 66
Congo, République démocratique du see Congo, Democratic Republic of the, ctry., Afr. E4 66
Congo Basin, bas., Afr. E4 66
Congonhinhas, Braz. A12 92
Congress, Sk., Can. E8 124
Conitaca, Mex. C5 100
Conn, Lough, l., Ire. G3 12
Connacht see Connaught, hist. reg., Ire. H3 12
Connaught, hist. reg., Ire. H3 12
Conneaut, Oh., U.S. C5 114
Conneautville, Pa., U.S. C5 114
Connecticut, state, U.S. C13 114
Connecticut, stm., U.S. H4 110
Connellsville, Pa., U.S. D6 114
Connemara, reg., Ire. H3 12
Connersville, In., U.S. E12 120
Conn Lake, l., Nu., Can. A15 106
Connors Range, mts., Austl. C7 76
Cononaco, stm., Ec. H3 86
Conorochite, stm., Ven. F8 86
Conover, N.C., U.S. I4 114
Conquest, Sk., Can. C6 124
Conquista, Braz. J2 88
Conrad, Ia., U.S. B5 120
Conroe, Tx., U.S. G3 122
Conroe, Lake, res., Tx., U.S. G3 122
Consecon, On., Can. D12 112
Conselheiro Lafaiete, Braz. K4 88
Conselheiro Pena, Braz. J5 88
Conselice, Italy F8 22
Consett, Eng., U.K. G10 12
Consolación del Sur, Cuba A6 102
Con Son, is., Viet. H8 48
Consort, Ab., Can. B3 124
Constance see Konstanz, Ger. I4 16
Constance, Lake (Bodensee), l., Eur. I5 16
Constância, Port. E2 20
Constanța, Rom. E15 26
Constanța, state, Rom. E15 26
Constantina, Spain G5 20
Constantine see Qacentina, Alg. B6 64
Constantine, Mi., U.S. G4 112
Constantine, Cape, c., Ak., U.S. E8 140
Constantinople see İstanbul, Tur. B12 28
Constitución, Chile G1 92
Constitución, Ur. E9 92
Constitución de 1857, Parque Nacional, p.o.i., Mex. K10 134
Consuegra, Spain E7 20
Contai, India H11 54
Contas, stm., Braz. H6 88
Contentnea Creek, stm., N.C., U.S. A8 116
Continental Peak, mtn., Wy., U.S. E4 126
Contratación, Col. D5 86
Contreras, Embalse de, res., Spain E9 20
Contreras, Isla, i., Chile J1 90
Contursi, Italy D9 24
Contwoyto Lake, l., Can. B8 106
Convent, La., U.S. G8 122
Conversano, Italy D10 24
Converse, In., U.S. H4 112
Conway, Ar., U.S. B6 122
Conway, Mo., U.S. G5 120
Conway, N.H., U.S. F5 110
Conway, N.C., U.S. H8 114
Conway, S.C., U.S. C6 116
Conway, Lake, res., Ar., U.S. C6 122
Conway National Park, p.o.i., Austl. C7 76
Conway Springs, Ks., U.S. D11 128
Conwy, Wales, U.K. H9 12
Coober Pedy, Austl. E6 74
Cook, Austl. F6 74
Cook, Mn., U.S. D6 118
Cook, Ne., U.S. D1 120
Cook, Cape, c., B.C., Can. F2 138
Cook, Mount, mtn., N.Z. F4 80
Cook, Récif de, rf., N. Cal. I14 79d
Cookeville, Tn., U.S. H12 120
Cooking Lake, l., Ab., Can. C17 138
Cook Inlet, b., Ak., U.S. D9 140
Cook Islands, dep., Oc. E10 72
Cook Strait, strt., N.Z. E6 80
Cooktown, Austl. C9 74
Coolabah, Austl. H6 76
Cooladdi, Austl. F5 76
Coolamon, Austl. J6 76
Coolangatta, Austl. G9 76
Cooleemee, N.C., U.S. I5 114
Coolgardie, Austl. F4 74
Coolidge, Ga., U.S. E2 116
Coolidge, Tx., U.S. F2 122
Coolidge, Mount, mtn., S.D., U.S. D9 126
Coolidge Dam, dam, Az., U.S. J6 132
Coolin, Id., U.S. B10 136
Cooloola National Park, p.o.i., Austl. F9 76
Cooma, Austl. K7 76
Coonabarabran, Austl. H7 76
Coonalpyn, Austl. J2 76
Coonamble, Austl. H7 76
Coonoor, India F3 53
Coon Rapids, Mn., U.S. F5 118
Coon Valley, Wi., U.S. H8 118
Cooper, Tx., U.S. D3 122
Cooper Creek, stm., Austl. G2 76
Cooper Road, La., U.S. E5 122
Coopers, Al., U.S. E12 122
Cooperstown, N.Y., U.S. B11 114
Coopersville, Mi., U.S. E4 112
Coopracambra National Park, p.o.i., Austl. K7 76
Coorong National Park, p.o.i., Austl. K2 76
Coorow, Austl. E3 74
Cooroy, Austl. F9 76
Coosa, stm., U.S. E12 122
Coos Bay, Or., U.S. G2 136
Cootamundra, Austl. J7 76
Cootehill, Ire. G5 12
Copacabana, Arg. D4 92
Copacabana, Col. D4 86
Copainalá, Mex. G12 100
Copan, Ok., U.S. H2 120
Copán, hist., Hond. E3 102
Copatana, Braz. I8 86
Copeland, Fl., U.S. K4 116
Copenhagen see København, Den. I4 8
Copenhagen, N.Y., U.S. E14 112
Copertino, Italy D11 24
Copiapó, Chile C2 92
Copiapó, stm., Chile C2 92
Copley, Austl. H2 76
Copparo, Italy F8 22
Copper, stm., Ak., U.S. D11 140
Copperas Cove, Tx., U.S. C9 130
Copper Butte, mtn., Wa., U.S. B8 136
Copper Canyon see Cobre, Barranca del, misc. cult., Mex. B5 100
Copper Center, Ak., U.S. D10 140
Copper Harbor, Mi., U.S. D10 118
Coppermine, stm., Can. B7 106
Copper Mine Point, c., Br. Vir. Is. e9 104b
Copper Mountain, B.C., Can. G10 138
Coquí, P.R. C3 104a
Coquilhatville see Mbandaka, D.R.C. D3 66
Coquimbo, Chile E2 92
Coquimbo, state, Chile E2 92
Corabia, Rom. F11 26
Coração de Jesus, Braz. I3 88
Coradi, Isole see Cheradi, Isole, i., Italy D11 24
Coral Gables, Fl., U.S. K5 116
Coral Harbour, Bah. n18 104f
Coral Harbour, Nu., Can. C14 106
Coral Sea, Oc. E6 72
Coral Sea Basin, unds. K18 142
Coral Sea Islands Territory, dep., Oc. B9 76
Coralville, Ia., U.S. C6 120
Coram, Mt., U.S. B12 136
Corangamite, Lake, l., Austl. K4 76
Corato, Italy C10 24
Corbeil-Essonnes, Fr. F11 14
Corbett National Park, p.o.i., India D7 54
Corbigny, Fr. G12 14
Corbin, Ky., U.S. H1 114
Corbones, stm., Spain G5 20
Corby, Eng., U.K. I12 12
Corcaigh see Cork, Ire. J4 12
Córcega, P.R. B1 104a
Corcoran, Ca., U.S. G6 134
Corcovado, Golfo, b., Chile H2 90
Corcovado, Parque Nacional, p.o.i., C.R. H6 102
Corcovado, Volcán, vol., Chile H2 90
Corcubión, Spain B1 20
Cordeiro, Braz. L4 88
Cordele, Ga., U.S. E2 116
Cordell Hull Reservoir, res., Tn., U.S. H12 120
Corder, Mo., U.S. E4 120
Cordillera, state, Para. B9 92
Cordillo Downs, Austl. F3 76
Córdoba, Arg. E5 92
Córdoba, Mex. F10 100
Córdoba (Cordova), Spain G6 20
Córdoba, state, Arg. E5 92
Córdoba, state, Col. C4 86
Córdoba, co., Spain F6 20
Córdova, Peru F2 84
Cordova see Córdoba, Spain G6 20
Cordova, Al., U.S. D11 122
Cordova, Ak., U.S. D10 140
Cordova, Il., U.S. C7 120
Cordova Peak, mtn., Ak., U.S. D10 140
Coreaú, Braz. B5 88
Coreaú, stm., Braz. B5 88
Corentyne, stm., S.A. C6 84
Corfield, Austl. C4 76
Corfu see Kérkyra, Grc. D2 28
Corfu see Kérkyra, i., Grc. D2 28
Coria, Spain D4 20
Coria del Río, Spain G4 20
Coribe, Braz. G3 88
Coricudgy, Mount, mtn., Austl. I8 76
Corigliano Calabro, Italy E10 24
Corinne, Ut., U.S. B4 132
Corinne, W.V., U.S. G4 114
Corinth see Kórinthos, Grc. F5 28
Corinth, Ms., U.S. C10 122
Corinth, N.Y., U.S. G3 110
Corinth, Gulf of see Korinthiakós Kólpos, b., Grc. E5 28
Corinto, Braz. J3 88
Corisco, Isla de, i., Eq. Gui. I6 64
Corjeuți, Mol. A14 26
Cork, Ire. J4 12
Cork, state, Ire. I4 12
Corleone, Italy G7 24
Çorlu, Tur. B10 28
Cornelia, Ga., U.S. B2 116
Cornélio Procópio, Braz. D6 90
Cornelius, N.C., U.S. A5 116
Cornelius Grinnell Bay, b., Nu., Can. E13 141
Cornell, Wi., U.S. F7 118
Corner Brook, Nf., Can. j22 107a
Cornești, Mol. B14 26
Corneta, Punta, c., Mex. H10 100
Corning, Ar., U.S. H7 120
Corning, Ca., U.S. D3 134
Corning, Ia., U.S. D3 120
Corning, Ks., U.S. B12 128
Corning, N.Y., U.S. B8 114
Cornish, Me., U.S. G6 110
Cornoe more see Black Sea G15 6
Corno Grande, mtn., Italy H10 22
Cornwall, On., Can. E2 110
Cornwallis Island, i., Nu., Can. B7 141
Cornwall Island, i., Nu., Can. B6 141
Coro, Ven. B7 86
Coro, Golfete de, b., Ven. B6 86
Coroaci, Braz. J4 88
Coroatá, Braz. C3 88
Corocoro, Bol. C3 90
Corocoro, Isla, i., S.A. C11 86
Coroico, Bol. C3 90
Coromandel, Braz. J2 88
Coromandel Coast, cst., India E5 53
Coromandel Peninsula, pen., N.Z. C6 80
Corona, Ca., U.S. J8 134
Corona, N.M., U.S. G3 128
Coronado, Mex. D8 100
Coronado, Bahía de, b., C.R. H6 102
Coronado, Islas, is., Mex. K8 134
Coronation, Ab., Can. D19 138
Coronation Gulf, b., Nu., Can. B8 106
Coronation Island, i., Ant. B36 81
Coronda, Arg. E7 92
Coronel, Chile H1 92
Coronel Bogado, Para. C9 92
Coronel Dorrego, Arg. I7 92
Coronel Fabriciano, Braz. J4 88
Coronel Moldes, Arg. B5 92
Coronel Moldes, Arg. F5 92
Coronel Oviedo, Para. B9 92
Coronel Pringles, Arg. H7 92
Coronel Suárez, Arg. H6 92
Coronel Vidal, Arg. H9 92
Coronel Vivida, Braz. C11 92
Corongo, Peru E2 84
Coropuna, Nevado, vol., Peru G3 84
Corossol, Guad. B2 105a
Çorovodë, Alb. D14 24
Corowa, Austl. J6 76
Corozal, Belize C3 102
Corozal, Col. C4 86
Corozal, P.R. B3 104a
Corpus Christi, Tx., U.S. G10 130
Corpus Christi, Lake, res., Tx., U.S. F9 130
Corpus Christi Bay, b., Tx., U.S. G10 130
Corral, Chile H2 90
Corral de Almaguer, Spain E7 20
Corral de Bustos, Arg. F6 92
Corrales, Cerro, mtn., Mex. H2 130
Corralito, Arg. F5 92
Correctionville, Ia., U.S. B2 120
Corregidor Island, i., Phil. C3 52
Corrente, Braz. F3 88
Corrente, stm., Braz. G4 88
Correntes, Cabo das, c., Moz. D12 70
Correntina, Braz. G3 88
Corrèze, state, Fr. D7 18
Corrib, Lough, l., Ire. H3 12
Corrientes, Arg. C8 92
Corrientes, state, Arg. D9 92
Corrientes, stm., Arg. D8 92
Corrientes, stm., S.A. D2 84
Corrientes, Bahía de, b., Cuba B5 102
Corrientes, Cabo, c., Arg. I9 92
Corrientes, Cabo, c., Col. E3 86
Corrientes, Cabo, c., Mex. E6 100
Corrigan, Tx., U.S. F4 122
Corrigin, Austl. F3 74
Corriverton, Guy. B6 84
Corrumpa Creek, stm., U.S. E5 128
Corry, Pa., U.S. C6 114
Corse (Corsica), i., Fr. G15 18
Corse, Cap, c., Fr. F15 18
Corse-du-Sud, state, Fr. H15 18
Corsica see Corse, i., Fr. G15 18
Corsicana, Tx., U.S. E2 122
Cort Adelaer, Kap, c., Grnld. E17 141
Cortazar, Mex. E8 100
Corte, Fr. G15 18
Cortés, Mar de see California, Golfo de, b., Mex. B2 96
Cortez, Co., U.S. F8 132
Cortez, Sea of see California, Golfo de, b., Mex. B2 96
Cortina d'Ampezzo, Italy D8 22
Cortland, Ne., U.S. K2 118
Cortland, N.Y., U.S. B9 114
Cortland, Oh., U.S. C5 114
Cortona, Italy G8 22
Corubal, stm., Afr. G2 64
Coruche, Port. F2 20
Çorum, Tur. A4 56
Corumbá, Braz. C5 90
Corumbá, stm., Braz. I1 88
Corumbaíba, Braz. J1 88
Corumbataí, stm., Braz. B11 92
Corumo, stm., Ven. D11 86
Corunna see A Coruña, Spain A2 20
Corunna, Mi., U.S. F5 112
Coruripe, Braz. F7 88
Corvallis, Mt., U.S. D12 136
Corvallis, Or., U.S. F3 136
Corwith, Ia., U.S. B3 120
Corydon, In., U.S. F11 120
Corydon, Ky., U.S. G10 120
Corzu, Rom. E10 26
Corzuela, Arg. C7 92
Cos see Kos, i., Grc. G10 28
Cosamaloapan de Carpio, Mex. F10 100
Coscomate, Mex. I2 130
Cosenza, Italy E10 24
Coshocton, Oh., U.S. D4 114
Cosigüina, Punta, c., Nic. F4 102
Cosigüina, Volcán, vol., Nic. F4 102
Cosmoledo, Atoll de, i., Sey. k11 69b
Cosmos, Mn., U.S. G4 118
Cosne-sur-Loire, Fr. G11 14
Cosquín, Arg. E5 92
Cossato, Italy E5 22
Cossatot, stm., Ar., U.S. C4 122
Costa Mesa, Ca., U.S. J8 134
Costa Rica, Mex. C5 100
Costa Rica, ctry., N.A. H5 102
Coswig, Ger. E9 16
Coswig, Ger. E8 16
Cotabato, Phil. G4 52
Cotahuasi, Peru G3 84
Cotati, Ca., U.S. E3 134
Coteaux, Haiti C10 102
Cote d'Ivoire, ctry., Afr. H3 64
Côte-d'Or, state, Fr. G13 14
Cotegipe, Braz. F3 88
Cotentin, pen., Fr. E7 14
Côtes-d'Armor, state, Fr. F6 14
Cotingo, stm., Braz. E11 86
Cotiujeni, Mol. B15 26
Cotonou, Benin H5 64
Cotopaxi, state, Ec. H2 86
Cotopaxi, vol., Ec. H2 86
Cotopaxi, Parque Nacional, p.o.i., Ec. H2 86
Cotswold Hills, hills, Eng., U.K. J10 12
Cottage Grove, Or., U.S. G3 136
Cottbus, Ger. E10 16
Cotter, Ar., U.S. H5 120
Cottian Alps, mts., Eur. E12 18
Cottondale, Fl., U.S. G13 122
Cotton Plant, Ar., U.S. C7 122
Cottonport, La., U.S. G6 122
Cotton Valley, La., U.S. E5 122
Cottonwood, Az., U.S. I5 132
Cottonwood, Ca., U.S. C3 134
Cottonwood, Mn., U.S. G3 118
Cottonwood, stm., Ks., U.S. C12 128
Cottonwood, stm., Mn., U.S. G3 118
Cottonwood Creek, stm., Mt., U.S. F5 124
Cottonwood Falls, Ks., U.S. C12 128
Coubre, Pointe de la, c., Fr. D4 18
Couchiching, Lake, l., On., Can. D10 112
Coudersport, Pa., U.S. C8 114
Coudres, Île aux, i., Qc., Can. C6 110
Coulee City, Wa., U.S. C7 136
Coulee Dam, Wa., U.S. B8 136
Coulommiers, Fr. F12 14
Coulonge, stm., Qc., Can. C13 112
Coulterville, Il., U.S. F8 120
Counce, Tn., U.S. B10 122
Council, Id., U.S. F10 136
Council Bluffs, Ia., U.S. C2 120
Council Grove, Ks., U.S. C12 128
Coupeville, Wa., U.S. B4 136
Courantyne see Corentyne, stm., S.A. C6 84
Courland (Kurzeme), hist. reg., Lat. C5 10
Courland Lagoon, b., Eur. E3 10
Courmayeur, Italy E3 22
Courtenay, B.C., Can. G5 138
Courtland, Al., U.S. C11 122
Courtland, Va., U.S. H8 114
Courtrai see Kortrijk, Bel. D12 14
Coutras, Fr. D5 18
Coutts, Ab., Can. G19 138
Couture, Lac, l., Qc., Can. C16 106
Covasna, state, Rom. C12 26
Cove, Or., U.S. E9 136
Cove Island, i., On., Can. C8 112
Covelo, Ca., U.S. D2 134
Coventry, Eng., U.K. I11 12
Covert, Mi., U.S. F3 112
Covilhã, Port. D3 20
Covington, Ga., U.S. C2 116
Covington, In., U.S. H2 112
Covington, Ky., U.S. E1 114
Covington, La., U.S. G8 122
Covington, Oh., U.S. H5 112
Covington, Ok., U.S. E11 128
Covington, Tn., U.S. B9 122
Covington, Va., U.S. G5 114
Cowal, pen., Scot., U.K. E7 12
Cowal, Lake, l., Austl. I6 76
Cowan, Tn., U.S. B13 122
Cowan, Lake, l., Austl. F4 74
Cowansville, Qc., Can. E4 110
Cowarie, Austl. E7 74
Cow Creek, stm., Ks., U.S. C10 128
Cow Creek, stm., Or., U.S. H3 136
Cowdenbeath, Scot., U.K. E9 12
Cowell, Austl. F7 74
Cowen, W.V., U.S. F5 114
Coweta, Ok., U.S. I2 120
Cowhouse Creek, stm., Tx., U.S. C10 130
Cowichan Bay, B.C., Can. H7 138
Cowichan Lake, l., B.C., Can. H6 138
Cowley, Austl. F5 76
Cowley, Wy., U.S. C4 126
Cowlic, Az., U.S. L4 132
Cowlitz, stm., Wa., U.S. D4 136
Cowpasture, stm., Va., U.S. F6 114
Cowpens, S.C., U.S. A4 116
Cowra, Austl. I7 76
Coxá, stm., Braz. H3 88
Coxim, Braz. C6 90
Cox's Bāzār, Bngl. H13 54
Coyaguaima, Cerro, mtn., Arg. D3 90
Coyame, Mex. A6 100
Coyle see Coig, stm., Arg. J3 90
Coyote, stm., Mex. F6 98
Coyote Wash, stm., N.M., U.S. G8 132
Coyuca de Benítez, Mex. G8 100
Coyuca de Catalán, Mex. F8 100
Cozad, Ne., U.S. G13 126
Cozumel, Mex. B4 102
Cozumel, Isla, i., Mex. B4 102
Crab Orchard, Tn., U.S. I13 120
Crab Orchard Lake, res., Il., U.S. G9 120
Cradle Mountain-Lake Saint Clair National Park, p.o.i., Austl. n12 77a
Cradock, S. Afr. H7 70
Craig, Co., U.S. C9 132
Craig, Mo., U.S. D2 120
Craig, Ne., U.S. J2 118
Craigellachie, B.C., Can. E12 138
Craigmont, Id., U.S. D10 136
Craigsville, Va., U.S. F6 114
Craik, Sk., Can. C8 124
Crailsheim, Ger. G6 16
Craiova, Rom. E10 26
Cranberry Lake, l., N.Y., U.S. F1 110
Cranbrook, Austl. F3 74
Cranbrook, B.C., Can. G15 138
Crandon, Wi., U.S. F9 118
Crane, Az., U.S. K2 132
Crane, In., U.S. F11 120
Crane, Tx., U.S. C5 130
Crane Lake, l., Sk., Can. D4 124
Crane Mountain, mtn., Or., U.S. A5 134
Crângeni, Rom. E11 26
Cranston, R.I., U.S. C14 114
Crasna, Rom. D13 26
Crasna, stm., Eur. I18 16
Crasnoe, Mol. C16 26
Crater Lake, l., Or., U.S. H4 136
Crater Lake National Park, p.o.i., Or., U.S. H5 136
Craters of the Moon National Monument, p.o.i., Id., U.S. G13 136
Crateús, Braz. C5 88
Crato, Braz. D6 88
Crauford, Cape, c., Nu., Can. A14 106
Cravo Norte, Col. D6 86
Cravo Norte, stm., Col. D6 86
Cravo Sur, stm., Col. E6 86
Crawford, Co., U.S. E9 132
Crawford, Ms., U.S. D10 122
Crawford, Tx., U.S. C10 130
Crawford Bay, B.C., Can. G14 138
Crawfordsville, Ar., U.S. B8 122
Crawfordsville, In., U.S. H2 112
Crawfordville, Ga., U.S. C3 116
Crawley, Eng., U.K. J12 12
Crazy Woman Creek, stm., Wy., U.S. C6 126
Creal Springs, Il., U.S. G9 120
Cree, stm., Sk., Can. D9 106
Creede, Co., U.S. F10 132
Creedmoor, N.C., U.S. H7 114
Cree Lake, l., Sk., Can. D9 106
Creemore, On., Can. D9 112
Creighton, Ne., U.S. E15 126
Creighton Mine, On., Can. B8 112
Creil, Fr. E11 14
Crema, Italy E6 22
Cremona, Italy E7 22
Crenshaw, Ms., U.S. C8 122
Crepori, stm., Braz. E6 84
Crépy-en-Valois, Fr. E11 14
Cres, Cro. E11 22
Cres, Otok, i., Cro. F11 22
Cresaptown, Md., U.S. E7 114
Crescent, Or., U.S. G5 136
Crescent City, Ca., U.S. B1 134
Crescent City, Fl., U.S. G4 116
Crescent Spur, B.C., Can. C10 138
Cresco, Ia., U.S. H6 118
Crespo, Arg. F7 92
Cresson, Tx., U.S. B10 130
Cressy, Austl. K4 76
Crested Butte, Co., U.S. E9 132
Crestline, Ca., U.S. I8 134
Creston, B.C., Can. G14 138
Creston, Ia., U.S. C3 120
Crestone Peak, mtn., Co., U.S. D3 128
Crestview, Fl., U.S. G12 122
Crestwood Hills, Tn., U.S. I1 114
Creswell, Or., U.S. G3 136
Creswell Bay, b., Nu., Can. A12 106
Crete, Il., U.S. G2 112
Crete, Ne., U.S. G16 126
Crete see Kríti, i., Grc. H7 28
Crete, Sea of see Kritikón Pélagos, Grc. H8 28
Créteil, Fr. F11 14
Cretin, Cape, c., Pap. N. Gui. b4 79a
Creus, Cap de, c., Spain B14 20
Creuse, state, Fr. C8 18
Creuse, stm., Fr. C6 18
Creussen, Ger. G7 16
Creve Coeur, Il., U.S. K9 118
Crevillent, Spain F10 20
Crevillente see Crevillent, Spain F10 20
Crewe, Eng., U.K. H10 12
Crewe, Va., U.S. G7 114
Cricaré, stm., Braz. J5 88
Criciúma, Braz. D13 92
Crikvenica, Cro. E11 22
Crimea see Kryms'kyi pivostriv, pen., Ukr. E4 32
Crimean Peninsula see Kryms'kyi pivostriv, pen., Ukr. E4 32
Crimmitschau, Ger. F8 16
Cripple Creek, Co., U.S. C3 128
Crisfield, Md., U.S. F10 114
Criss Creek, B.C., Can. E10 138
Crissiumal, Braz. C10 92
Cristal, Monts de, mts., Afr. I7 64
Cristalândia, Braz. F1 88

Name	Map Ref.	Page
Cristália, Braz.	I4	88
Cristalina, Braz.	I2	88
Cristinápolis, Braz.	F7	88
Cristino Castro, Braz.	E3	88
Cristóbal Colón, Pico, mtn., Col.	B5	86
Crişul Alb, stm., Eur.	C8	26
Crişul Negru, stm., Eur.	C8	26
Crişul Repede (Sebes Körös), stm., Eur.	B8	26
Crivitz, Wi., U.S.	C1	112
Crna, stm., Mac.	B4	28
Crna Gora (Montenegro), state, Yugo.	G6	26
Crni Drim (Drinit të Zi), stm., Eur.	C14	24
Črnomelj, Slvn.	E12	22
Croajingolong National Park, p.o.i., Austl.	K7	76
Croatia, ctry., Eur.	E13	22
Croche, stm., Qc., Can.	C4	110
Crocker, Mo., U.S.	G5	120
Crocker, Banjaran, mts., Malay.	H1	52
Crockett, Tx., U.S.	F3	122
Crocodilopilos, hist., Egypt	I1	58
Crocus Hill, hill, Anguilla	A1	105a
Crofton, Ky., U.S.	G10	120
Croghan, N.Y., U.S.	E14	112
Croix, Lac la, I., N.A.	C6	118
Croker, Cape, c., Austl.	B6	74
Croker, Cape, c., On., Can.	D9	112
Croker Island, i., Austl.	B6	74
Cromer, Eng., U.K.	I14	12
Cromínia, Braz.	I1	88
Crompton Point, c., Dom.	i6	105c
Cromwell, N.Z.	G3	80
Cromwell, Al., U.S.	E10	122
Crooked, stm., Or., U.S.	F5	136
Crooked Creek, Ak., U.S.	D8	140
Crooked Creek, stm., U.S.	D8	128
Crooked Island, i., Bah.	A10	102
Crooked Island Passage, strt., Bah.	A10	102
Crooked River, Sk., Can.	B10	124
Crookston, Mn., U.S.	D2	118
Crooksville, Oh., U.S.	E3	114
Crosby, Mn., U.S.	E5	118
Crosby, N.D., U.S.	F10	124
Crosby, Mount, mtn., Wy., U.S.	D3	126
Crosbyton, Tx., U.S.	H7	128
Cross, stm., Afr.	H6	64
Crossett, Ar., U.S.	D7	122
Cross Lake, res., Mb., Can.	E11	106
Crossman Peak, mtn., Az., U.S.	I2	132
Cross Plains, Tx., U.S.	B8	130
Cross Plains, Wi., U.S.	H9	118
Cross Sound, strt., Ak., U.S.	E12	140
Crossville, Il., U.S.	F9	120
Crossville, Tn., U.S.	I12	120
Croswell, Mi., U.S.	E7	112
Crotone, Italy	E11	24
Crow, North Fork, stm., Mn., U.S.	F5	118
Crow, South Fork, stm., Mn., U.S.	G4	118
Crow Agency, Mt., U.S.	B5	126
Crow Creek, stm., U.S.	G8	126
Crowder, Ms., U.S.	C8	122
Crowduck Lake, I., Mb., Can.	A3	118
Crowdy Head, c., Austl.	H9	76
Crowell, Tx., U.S.	H9	128
Crow Lake, On., Can.	B5	118
Crowley, La., U.S.	G6	122
Crowleys Ridge, mts., U.S.	B8	122
Crown Mountain, mtn., V.I.U.S.	e7	104b
Crown Point, In., U.S.	G2	112
Crownpoint, N.M., U.S.	H8	132
Crown Point, N.Y., U.S.	G3	110
Crown Prince Frederik Island, i., Nu., Can.	A13	106
Crowsnest Pass, Ab., Can.	G16	138
Crowsnest Pass, p., Can.	G16	138
Crows Nest Peak, mtn., S.D., U.S.	C8	126
Crow Wing, stm., Mn., U.S.	E4	118
Croydon, Austl.	B4	76
Croydon Station, B.C., Can.	C11	138
Crozet, Va., U.S.	F7	114
Crozet, Îles, is., Afr.	J16	4
Crozet Basin, unds.	M9	142
Crucea, Rom.	E15	26
Cruces, Cuba	A7	102
Cruger, Ms., U.S.	D8	122
Crump Lake, I., Or., U.S.	A6	134
Cruz, Cabo, c., Cuba	C9	102
Cruz Alta, Arg.	F6	92
Cruz Alta, Braz.	D11	92
Cruz Bay, V.I.U.S.	e7	104b
Cruz del Eje, Arg.	E5	92
Cruzeiro, Braz.	L3	88
Cruzeiro do Oeste, Braz.	A11	92
Cruzeiro do Sul, Braz.	E3	84
Cruzeta, Braz.	D7	88
Cruz Grande, Chile	D2	92
Crysler, On., Can.	C14	112
Crystal, Mn., U.S.	F5	118
Crystal, N.D., U.S.	F16	124
Crystal Brook, Austl.	I2	76
Crystal City, Mb., Can.	E15	124
Crystal City, Mo., U.S.	F7	120
Crystal City, Tx., U.S.	F8	130
Crystal Falls, Mi., U.S.	B1	112
Crystal Lake, Il., U.S.	B9	120
Crystal Lake, I., Mi., U.S.	D3	112
Crystal Springs, Ms., U.S.	E8	122
Csongrád, Hung.	C7	26
Csongrád, state, Hung.	C7	26
Csorna, Hung.	B4	26
Cu, stm., Asia	F11	32
Cúa, Ven.	B8	86
Cuajinicuilapa, Mex.	G9	100
Cuamba, Moz.	C6	68
Cuando (Kwando), stm., Afr.	D3	68
Cuangar, Ang.	D2	68
Cuango, Ang.	B2	68
Cuango see Kwango, stm., Afr.	F3	66
Cuanza, stm., Ang.	C2	68
Cuao, stm., Ven.	E8	86
Cuareim (Quaraí), stm., S.A.	E9	92
Cuaró, Ur.	E9	92
Cuarto, stm., Arg.	F5	92
Cuatrociénegas, Mex.	B7	100
Cuauhtémoc, Mex.	A5	100
Cuautitlán, Mex.	F6	100
Cuba, Port.	F3	20
Cuba, Al., U.S.	E10	122
Cuba, Il., U.S.	D7	120
Cuba, Mo., U.S.	F6	120
Cuba, N.M., U.S.	G10	132
Cuba, ctry., N.A.	C9	96
Cubagua, Isla, i., Ven.	B9	86
Cubal, Ang.	C1	68
Cubango (Okavango), stm., Afr.	D2	68
Çubati, Braz.	D7	88
Čublas, Russia	D21	8
Çubuk, Tur.	C15	28
Cuchi, stm., Ang.	C2	68
Cuchillo Co, Arg.	I5	92
Cuchivero, stm., Ven.	D9	86
Cucuí, Braz.	G8	86
Cucurpe, Mex.	F7	98
Cúcuta, Col.	D5	86
Cucuy, Piedra de, hill, Ven.	G8	86
Cudahy, Wi., U.S.	F2	112
Cuddalore, India	F4	53
Cuddapah, India	D4	53
Čudovo, Russia	A14	10
Çudworth, Sk., Can.	B8	124
Čudzin, Bela.	H9	10
Cue, Austl.	E3	74
Cuemba, Ang.	C2	68
Cuenca, Ec.	I2	86
Cuenca, Spain	D8	20
Cuenca, co., Spain	E9	20
Cuencamé de Ceniceros, Mex.	C7	100
Cuernavaca, Mex.	F9	100
Cuero, Tx., U.S.	E10	130
Cuers, Fr.	F12	18
Cuervo, Laguna del, I., Mex.	A6	100
Cuesta Pass, p., Ca., U.S.	H5	134
Cueto, Cuba	B9	102
Çugir, Rom.	D10	26
Čuguevka, Russia	B10	38
Čuhlomskoe, ozero, I., Russia	G19	8
Cuiabá, Braz.	G6	84
Cuiabá, stm., Braz.	G6	84
Cuiari, Braz.	G7	86
Cuicatlán, Mex.	G10	100
Cuilapa, Guat.	E2	102
Cuilco see Grijalva, stm., N.A.	G12	100
Cuilo (Kwilu), stm., Afr.	F3	66
Cuité, Braz.	D7	88
Cuíto, stm., Ang.	D2	68
Cuito Cuanavale, Ang.	D2	68
Cuitzeo, Lago de, I., Mex.	F8	100
Cuiuni, stm., Braz.	H10	86
Cukai, Malay.	J6	48
Çukas, Indon.	D4	50
Čukotskij, mys, c., Russia	D26	34
Čukotskij poluostrov (Chukotsk Peninsula), pen., Russia	C26	34
Čulakkurgan, Kaz.	F11	32
Culbertson, Mt., U.S.	F9	124
Cul de Sac, Guad.	A1	105a
Cul de Sac, Neth. Ant.	A1	105a
Culebra, P.R.	B5	104a
Culebra, Isla de, i., P.R.	B5	104a
Culebra Peak, mtn., Co., U.S.	D3	128
Culfa, Azer.	B6	56
Culgoa, stm., Austl.	G6	76
Culiacán, Mex.	C5	100
Culiacán, Mex.	C5	100
Culion Island, i., Phil.	E2	52
Cúllar, Spain	G8	20
Cullen, La., U.S.	E5	122
Culleoka, Tn., U.S.	B12	122
Cullera, Spain	E10	20
Cullman, Al., U.S.	C12	122
Çullom, Il., U.S.	D9	120
Čul'man, Russia	E13	34
Culpeper, Va., U.S.	F7	114
Culpina, Bol.	D4	90
Culuene, stm., Braz.	F7	84
Culver, In., U.S.	G3	112
Culver, Or., U.S.	F5	136
Çulverden, N.Z.	F5	80
Čulym, Russia	C14	32
Čulym, stm., Russia	C14	32
Čum, Russia	C1	34
Cumaná, Ven.	B9	86
Cumare, Cerro, hill, Col.	G5	86
Cumari, Braz.	J1	88
Cumbal, Nevado, vol., Col.	G2	86
Cumbe, Braz.	F7	88
Cumberland, B.C., Can.	G5	138
Cumberland, Ky., U.S.	G2	114
Cumberland, Md., U.S.	E7	114
Cumberland, Va., U.S.	G7	114
Cumberland, Wi., U.S.	F6	118
Cumberland, stm., U.S.	H2	114
Cumberland, Lake, res., Ky., U.S.	H13	120
Cumberland, South Fork, stm., U.S.	H13	120
Cumberland Gap, p., U.S.	H2	114
Cumberland Island National Seashore, p.o.i., Ga., U.S.	F4	116
Cumberland Islands, is., Austl.	C7	76
Cumberland Lake, I., Sk., Can.	E10	106
Cumberland Peninsula, pen., Nu., Can.	B17	106
Cumberland Plateau, plat., U.S.	G14	120
Cumberland Sound, strt., Nu., Can.	B17	106
Cumbernauld, Scot., U.K.	F9	12
Cumbrian Mountains, mts., Eng., U.K.	G9	12
Çumby, Tx., U.S.	D3	122
Čumikan, Russia	F16	34
Cumming, Ga., U.S.	B1	116
Cummins, Austl.	F7	74
Cumnock, Scot., U.K.	F8	12
Cumpas, Mex.	F8	98
Çumra, Tur.	F15	28
Čumyš, stm., Russia	D15	32
Čuna, stm., Russia	C17	32
Cunani, Braz.	C7	84
Cunaviche, Ven.	D8	86
Cunco, Chile	G2	90
Çundinamarca, state, Col.	E4	86
Čundža, Kaz.	F13	32
Cunene (Kunene), stm., Afr.	D1	68
Cuneo (Coni), Italy	F4	22
Çunha Porã, Braz.	C11	92
Čunja, stm., Russia	B17	32
Cunnamulla, Austl.	G5	76
Çunningham, Ks., U.S.	D10	128
Čunskij, Russia	C17	32
Çunucunuma, stm., Ven.	F9	86
Čuny, Russia	G17	8
Cuorgnè, Italy	E4	22
Cupar, Sk., Can.	D9	124
Cupar, Scot., U.K.	E9	12
Çupica, Golfo de, b., Col.	D3	86
Čuprovo, Russia	D22	8
Cuquenán, stm., Ven.	E11	86
Curaçá, Braz.	E6	88
Curaçao, i., Neth. Ant.	p21	104g
Curacautín, Chile	I2	92
Curanilahue, Chile	H1	92
Çuranipe, Chile	G1	92
Čurapča, Russia	D15	34
Curaray, stm., S.A.	H4	86
Curepipe, Mrts.	i10	69a
Curepto, Chile	G1	92
Curicó, Chile	G2	92
Curicuriari, stm., Braz.	H8	86
Curimatá, Braz.	E3	88
Curitiba, Braz.	B13	92
Curitibanos, Braz.	C12	92
Curiuaú, stm., Braz.	H11	86
Curiúva, Braz.	B12	92
Curlew, Wa., U.S.	B8	136
Çurnamona, Austl.	H2	76
Čurovići, Russia	H15	10
Currais Novos, Braz.	D7	88
Curralinho, Braz.	D8	84
Currant Mountain, mtn., Nv., U.S.	E1	132
Current, stm., U.S.	H7	120
Currie, Austl.	m12	77a
Currituck, N.C., U.S.	H9	114
Currituck Sound, strt., N.C., U.S.	H10	114
Curtea de Argeş, Rom.	D11	26
Curtina, Ur.	F9	92
Curtis, Ar., U.S.	D5	122
Curtis, Ne., U.S.	G12	126
Curtis, Port, b., Austl.	D8	76
Curtis Channel, strt., Austl.	D8	76
Curtis Island, i., Austl.	D8	76
Curtis Island, i., N.Z.	G9	72
Curu, stm., Braz.	B6	88
Curuá, stm., Braz.	D7	84
Curuá, stm., Braz.	E7	84
Curuá, Ilha do, i., Braz.	C7	84
Curuá-Una, stm., Braz.	D7	84
Curuçá, Braz.	D8	84
Curumu, Braz.	D7	84
Curup, Indon.	E3	50
Curupá, Braz.	E2	88
Cururupu, Braz.	A3	88
Curuzú Cuatiá, Arg.	D8	92
Curvelo, Braz.	J3	88
Cusco, Peru	F3	84
Cushing, Ok., U.S.	B2	122
Cushing, Tx., U.S.	F4	122
Cushman, Ar., U.S.	I6	120
Cusiana, stm., Col.	E5	86
Çusihuiriachic, Mex.	A5	100
Čusovaja, stm., Russia	C9	32
Čusovoj, Russia	C9	32
Cusset, Fr.	C9	18
Çusseta, Ga., U.S.	E14	122
Čust, Uzb.	F12	32
Custer, Mi., U.S.	E3	112
Custer, Mt., U.S.	A5	126
Custer, S.D., U.S.	D9	126
Custódia, Braz.	E7	88
Cut, Nuhu, i., Indon.	G9	44
Cut Bank, Mt., U.S.	B14	136
Cutbank, stm., Ab., Can.	B12	138
Cut Bank Creek, stm., U.S.	F12	124
Cut Bank Creek, stm., Mt., U.S.	B14	136
Cutervo, Peru	E2	84
Cuthbert, Ga., U.S.	F14	122
Cutler, Ca., U.S.	G6	134
Cutler, Me., U.S.	F9	110
Cutlerville, Mi., U.S.	F4	112
Cutral-Có, Arg.	G3	90
Cutro, Italy	E10	24
Cuttack, India	H10	54
Çutzamalá, stm., Mex.	F8	100
Čuvašija, state, Russia	C7	32
Cuvier, Cape, c., Austl.	D2	74
Cuvo, stm., Ang.	C1	68
Cuxhaven, Ger.	C4	16
Cuyahoga Falls, Oh., U.S.	C4	114
Cuyama, stm., Ca., U.S.	I6	134
Cuyamaca Peak, mtn., Ca., U.S.	J9	134
Cuyarí, stm., S.A.	G7	86
Cuyo, Phil.	E3	52
Cuyo East Pass, strt., Phil.	E3	52
Cuyo Islands, is., Phil.	E3	52
Cuyo West Pass, strt., Phil.	E3	52
Cuyubini, stm., Ven.	D11	86
Cuyuni, stm., S.A.	B6	84
Cuyuni-Mazaruni, state, Guy.	D11	86
Cwmbran, Wales, U.K.	J10	12
Cyclades see Kikládhes, is., Grc.	F7	28
Cypress, La., U.S.	F5	122
Cypress Hills, hills, Can.	E4	124
Cypress River, Mb., Can.	E14	124
Cypress Springs, Lake, res., Tx., U.S.	D3	122
Cyprus, ctry., Asia	C4	58
Cyprus, i., Asia	D15	4
Cyprus, North, ctry., Asia	C4	58
Cyrenaica see Barqah, hist. reg., Libya	A4	62
Cyril, Ok., U.S.	G10	128
Cyril E. King Airport, V.I.U.S.	e7	104b
Cyrus Field Bay, b., Nu., Can.	E13	141
Čyrvonae, vozero, I., Bela.	H10	10
Cythera see Kýthira, i., Grc.	G5	28
Czaplinek, Pol.	C12	16
Czarna Woda, Pol.	C14	16
Czarnków, Pol.	D12	16
Czechoslovakia see Czech Republic, ctry., Eur.	G11	16
Czechowice-Dziedzice, Pol.	G15	16
Czech Republic, ctry., Eur.	G11	16
Czerniejewo, Pol.	D13	16
Czerwieńsk, Pol.	D11	16
Częstochowa, Pol.	F15	16
Częstochowa, state, Pol.	F15	16
Człuchów, Pol.	C13	16

D

Name	Map Ref.	Page
Da, stm., China	G8	42
Da, Song see Black, stm., Asia	D9	46
Da'an, China	J4	42
Dabajuro, Ven.	B6	86
Daba Ling, mtn., China	I5	42
Daba Shan, mts., China	E3	42
Dabat, Eth.	E7	62
Dabeiba, Col.	D3	86
Dabhoi, India	G4	54
Dąbie, Pol.	D14	16
Dabie Shan, mts., China	F6	42
Dabnou, Niger	G5	64
Dabola, Gui.	G2	64
Dabou, C. Iv.	H4	64
Daboya, Ghana	H4	64
Dabra, India	F7	54
Dąbrowa Białostocka, Pol.	C19	16
Dabu, China	I7	42
Dacca see Dhaka, Bngl.	G13	54
Dac Glei, Viet.	E8	48
Dachau, Ger.	H7	16
Dačice, Czech Rep.	G11	16
Dacoma, Ok., U.S.	E10	128
Dadanawa, Guy.	F12	86
Dade City, Fl., U.S.	H3	116
Dadeldhurā, Nepal	D8	54
Dadeville, Al., U.S.	E13	122
Dādra and Nagar Haveli, state, India	I4	54
Dādu, Pak.	D10	56
Daegu see Taegu, Kor., S.	D1	40
Daejeon see Taejŏn, Kor., S.	F7	38
Daerhanwangfu, China	B5	38
Daet, Phil.	C4	52
Dafang, China	F6	36
Dafeng, China	E9	42
Dáfni, Grc.	F5	28
Dafoe, Sk., Can.	C9	124
Dafu, stm., China	F5	42
Dagā, stm., Mya.	D2	48
Dagana, Sen.	F1	64
Daga Post, Sudan	F6	62
Dağardı, Tur.	D12	28
Dagda, Lat.	D10	10
Dagestan, state, Russia	F7	32
Daglung, China	D13	54
Dagu, China	B7	42
Dagua, Pap. N. Gui.	a3	79a
Daguan, China	F5	36
Daguan Hu, I., China	F7	42
Daguao, P.R.	B4	104a
Dagujia, China	C6	38
Dagupan, Phil.	B3	52
Dagzê Co, I., China	B11	54
Dahab, Egypt	J5	58
Dahei, India	H4	54
Daheiding Shan, mtn., China	B10	36
Da Hinggan Ling (Greater Khingan Range), mts., China	B9	36
Dahlak Archipelago, is., Erit.	D8	62
Dahlonega, Ga., U.S.	B1	116
Dahlonega Plateau, plat., U.S.	C14	122
Dahmani, Tun.	I2	24
Dahme, Ger.	E9	16
Dāhod, India	G5	54
Dahomey see Benin, ctry., Afr.	G5	64
Dahra, Libya	B3	62
Dahra, mts., Alg.	H11	20
Dahshur, Pyramides de (Dashur, Pyramids of), hist., Egypt	I1	58
Dai, i., Sol. Is.	d9	79b
Daia, Rom.	E12	26
Dai Hai, I., China	A5	42
Daik-u, Mya.	D3	48
Dā'il, Syria	F7	58
Daimiel, Spain	E7	20
Daingean, Ire.	H5	12
Daingerfield, Tx., U.S.	D4	122
Dainkog, China	E4	36
Daireaux, Arg.	H7	92
Dairen see Dalian, China	B9	42
Dairût, Egypt	K1	58
Dai-sen, vol., Japan	D6	40
Daisetta, Tx., U.S.	G4	122
Daixian, China	B5	42
Daiyun Shan, mts., China	I8	42
Dajarra, Austl.	C2	76
Dajian Shan, mtn., China	F5	36
Dakar, Sen.	G1	64
Dakeng, China	H6	42
Dakhin Shāhbāzpur Island, i., Bngl.	G13	54
Dakhla, W. Sah.	E1	64
Dākoānk, India	G7	46
Dakoro, Niger	G6	64
Dakota City, Ia., U.S.	B3	120
Dakota City, Ne., U.S.	B1	120
Đakovica, Yugo.	G7	26
Đakovo, Cro.	E15	22
Dala, Sol. Is.	e9	79b
Dalaba, Gui.	G2	64
Dalad Qi, China	A4	42
Dalälven, stm., Swe.	F7	8
Dalaman, stm., Tur.	G11	28
Dalāmī, Sudan	E6	62
Dalandzadgad, Mong.	C5	36
Dalarna, state, Swe.	F6	8
Da Lat, Viet.	F9	48
Dālbandin, Pak.	D9	56
Dalbosjön, b., Swe.	G5	8
Dalby, Austl.	F8	76
Dale, Nor.	F1	8
Dale, In., U.S.	F10	120
Dale Hollow Lake, res., U.S.	H12	120
Dalet, Mya.	B1	48
Daleville, In., U.S.	H4	112
Dalga, Egypt	K1	58
Dalhart, Tx., U.S.	E6	128
Dalhousie, N.B., Can.	B10	110
Dalhousie, India	B5	54
Dalhousie, Cape, c., N.T., Can.	B14	140
Dali, China	F5	36
Dali, China	D3	42
Dalian (Dairen), China	B9	42
Daliang Shan, mts., China	F5	36
Dalin, China	C5	38
Daling, stm., China	D4	38
Dalj, Cro.	E15	22
Dālkola, India	F11	54
Dallas, Ga., U.S.	D14	122
Dallas, Or., U.S.	F3	136
Dallas, Pa., U.S.	C9	114
Dallas, Tx., U.S.	B11	130
Dallas, Wi., U.S.	F7	118
Dallas Center, Ia., U.S.	J4	118
Dallas City, Il., U.S.	D6	120
Dalli Rājhara, India	H8	54
Dall Island, i., Ak., U.S.	F13	140
Dall Lake, I., Ak., U.S.	D7	140
Dalmacija see Dalmatia, hist. reg., Eur.	G12	22
Dalmatia, hist. reg., Eur.	G12	22
Dalmau, India	E8	54
Dal'negorsk, Russia	B11	38
Dal'nerečensk, Russia	B11	36
Dal'nyk, Ukr.	C17	26
Daloa, C. Iv.	H3	64
Dalqū, Sudan	C6	62
Dalroy, Ab., Can.	E17	138
Dalrymple, Mount, mtn., Austl.	C7	76
Dalsing Sarai, India	F10	54
Dāltenganj, India	F10	54
Dalton, Ga., U.S.	C13	122
Dalton, Ma., U.S.	B12	114
Dalton, Ne., U.S.	F10	126
Daludalu, Indon.	C2	50
Dalupiri Island, i., Phil.	A3	52
Dalwallinu, Austl.	F3	74
Daly, stm., Austl.	B6	74
Daly Bay, b., Nu., Can.	C13	106
Daly City, Ca., U.S.	F3	134
Daly Lake, I., Sk., Can.	D9	106
Daly Waters, Austl.	C6	74
Dam, stm., China	B14	54
Damaia, Port.	F1	20
Damān, India	H4	54
Damān and Diu, state, India	H4	54
Damanhûr, Egypt	G1	58
Damar, Pulau, i., Indon.	G8	44
Damaraland, hist. reg., Nmb.	E2	68
Damascus see Dimashq, Syria	E7	58
Damascus, Ar., U.S.	B6	122
Damascus, Ga., U.S.	F14	122
Damascus, Md., U.S.	E8	114
Damaturu, Nig.	G7	64
Damāvand, Qolleh-ye, vol., Iran	B7	56
Damba, Ang.	B2	68
Dambarta, Nig.	G6	64
Damboa, Nig.	G7	64
Dâmboviţa, state, Rom.	E12	26
Dâmboviţa, stm., Rom.	D12	26
Dam Doi, Viet.	H7	48
Damen Dao, i., China	H9	42
Dāmghān, Iran	B7	56
Damiao, China	C1	42
Damietta, Egypt	G2	58
Damietta Mouth see Dumyât, Masabb, mth., Egypt	G3	58
Daming, China	C6	42
Dāmodar, stm., India	G11	54
Damoh, India	G7	54
Damongo, Ghana	H4	64
Dampier, Austl.	D3	74
Dampier, Selat, strt., Indon.	F9	44
Dampier Land, pen., Austl.	C4	74
Dampier Strait, strt., Pap. N. Gui.	b4	79a
Dâmrei, Chuŏr Phnum, mts., Camb.	G7	48
Damxung, China	C13	54
Dan, stm., China	E4	42
Dan, stm., U.S.	H6	114
Dana, In., U.S.	I2	112
Danai, Indon.	C3	50
Danakil, reg., Afr.	E8	62
Danané, C. Iv.	H3	64
Da Nang, Viet.	D9	48
Danao, Phil.	E5	52
Dānāpur, India	F10	54
Danba, China	E5	36
Danbury, Ct., U.S.	C12	114
Danbury, Ia., U.S.	B2	120
Danbury, Ne., U.S.	A8	128
Danby Lake, I., Ca., U.S.	I1	132
Dandeli, India	D2	53
Dandenong, Austl.	K5	76
Dandong, China	D5	38
Dandridge, Tn., U.S.	H2	114
Danfeng, China	E4	42
Danforth, Me., U.S.	E9	110
Dang, stm., China	F16	32
Dangan Liedao, is., China	K6	42
Dangara, Taj.	B10	56
Dangchang, China	E5	36
Danger Point, c., S. Afr.	I4	70
Danggali Conservation Park, p.o.i., Austl.	I3	76
Dangila, Eth.	E7	62
Dangriga, Belize	D3	102
Dangshan, China	D7	42
Dangtu, China	F8	42
Dan-Gulbi, Nig.	G6	64
Dangyang, China	F4	42
Daniel, Wy., U.S.	H16	136
Daniel-Johnson, Barrage, dam, Qc., Can.	E17	106
Daniëlskuil, S. Afr.	F6	70
Danielson, Ct., U.S.	C13	114
Daniels Pass, p., Ut., U.S.	C5	132
Danielsville, Ga., U.S.	B2	116
Danilov, Russia	G18	8
Danilovka, Kaz.	D12	32
Daning, China	I4	42
Danjiangkou Shuiku, res., China	E4	42
Danjo-guntō, is., Japan	G1	40
Danlí, Hond.	F4	102
Danmark Fjord, b., Grnld.	A22	141
Dannebrog, Ne., U.S.	F14	126
Dannenberg, Ger.	C6	16
Dannevirke, N.Z.	E7	80
Danshui, China	J6	42
Dansville, N.Y., U.S.	B8	114
Dante, Va., U.S.	H3	114
Dantewāra, India	B5	53
Danube, stm., Eur.	F11	6
Danube, Mouths of the, mth., Eur.	E16	26
Danubyu, Mya.	D2	48
Danvers, Il., U.S.	D8	120
Danville, Qc., Can.	E4	110
Danville, Ga., U.S.	D2	116
Danville, Il., U.S.	H2	112
Danville, Ky., U.S.	G13	120
Danville, Pa., U.S.	D9	114
Danville, Vt., U.S.	F4	110
Danville, Va., U.S.	H6	114
Danville, Wa., U.S.	B8	136
Danxian, China	L3	42
Danyang, China	F8	42
Danzig see Gdańsk, Pol.	B14	16
Danzig, Gulf of see Gdansk, Gulf of, b., Eur.	B15	16
Daocheng, China	F5	36
Daodi, China	B8	42
Daohu, China	G7	42
Daosa, India	E6	54
Daotiandi, China	B10	36
Daoukro, C. Iv.	H4	64
Daoxian, China	I4	42
Daozhen, China	G2	42
Dapaong, Togo	G5	64
Dapchi, Nig.	G7	64
Daphnae, hist., Egypt	H3	58
Daphne, Al., U.S.	G11	122
Dapingshan, China	I3	42
Da Qaidam, China	D4	36
Daqiu, China	I8	42
Dara, Sen.	F1	64
Dar'ā, Syria	F7	58
Dar'ā, state, Syria	F7	58
Dārāb, Iran	D7	56
Darāban, Pak.	C3	54
Darabani, Rom.	A13	26
Darasun, Russia	F11	34
Đaravica, mtn., Yugo.	G7	26
Darâw, Egypt	C6	62
Dārayyā, Syria	E7	58
Darb al-Ḥajj, Jabal, mtn., Jord.	H6	58
Darbhanga, India	E10	54
D'Arbonne, Bayou, stm., La., U.S.	E6	122
Darby, Mt., U.S.	D12	136
Dardanelle, Ar., U.S.	B5	122
Dardanelle Lake, res., Ar., U.S.	B5	122
Dardanelles see Çanakkale Boğazı, strt., Tur.	C9	28
Dar-el-Beida see Casablanca, Mor.	C3	64
Dar es Salaam, Tan.	F7	66
Darfo, Italy	E7	22
Dargai, Pak.	A3	54
Dargan-Ata, Turkmen.	A9	56
Dargaville, N.Z.	B5	80
Dargol, Niger	G5	64
Darhan, Mong.	B6	36
Darıca, Tur.	C12	28
Darién, Col.	F3	86
Darien, Ga., U.S.	E4	116
Darien, Parque Nacional, p.o.i., Pan.	D2	86
Darién, Serranía del, mts.	C3	86
Dārjiling, India	E12	54
Dark Head, c., St. Vin.	o11	105e
Darlag, China	E4	36
Darling, S. Afr.	H4	70
Darling, Ms., U.S.	C8	122
Darling, stm., Austl.	I4	76
Darling Downs, reg., Austl.	F8	76
Darlingford, Mb., Can.	E15	124
Darling Range, mts., Austl.	F3	74
Darlington, Eng., U.K.	G11	12
Darlington, Wi., U.S.	B7	120
Darlington Dam, res., S. Afr.	H7	70
Darlot, Lake, I., Austl.	E4	74
Darłowo, Pol.	B12	16
Darmstadt, Ger.	G4	16
Darnah, Libya	A4	62
Darnall, S. Afr.	F10	70
Darney, Fr.	F15	14
Darnley, Cape, c., Ant.	B11	81
Darnley Bay, b., N.T., Can.	B6	106
Darr, stm., Austl.	D4	76
Darregueira, Arg.	H6	92
Darreh Gaz, Iran	B8	56
Darrington, Wa., U.S.	B5	136
Darrouzett, Tx., U.S.	E8	128
Dart, Cape, c., Ant.	C27	81
Dartmoor, Austl.	K3	76
Dartmoor, for., Eng., U.K.	K9	12
Dartmoor National Park, p.o.i., Eng., U.K.	K9	12
Dartmouth, N.S., Can.	F13	110
Dartmouth, Eng., U.K.	K9	12
Dartmouth, Lake, I., Austl.	E5	76
Dartmouth Reservoir, res., Austl.	K6	76
Daru, Pap. N. Gui.	b3	79a
Daruvar, Cro.	E14	22
Darvaza, Turkmen.	A8	56
Dārwha, India	H6	54
Darwin, Austl.	B6	74
Darwin, Bahía, b., Chile	I2	90
Darya Khān, Pak.	C3	54
Dashbalbar, Mong.	B7	36
Dashitou, China	C8	38
Dašhovuz, Turkmen.	A8	56
Dasht, stm., Pak.	D9	56
Dashur, Pyramids of see Dahshur, Pyramides de, hist., Egypt	I1	58
Dashutang, China	A6	48
Dasol Bay, b., Phil.	C2	52
Dastgardān, Iran	C8	56
Datang, China	I3	42
Datça, Tur.	G10	28
Date, Japan	C14	38
Datia, India	F7	54
Datian, China	I7	42
Datian Ding, mtn., China	J4	42
Datong, China	D5	36
Datong, China	B9	36
Datong, China	A5	42
Datong Shan, mts., China	D4	36
Datu, Cape, c., Asia	E4	44
Datumakuta, Indon.	B10	50
Datu Piang, Phil.	G5	52
Daua (Dawa), stm., Afr.	G8	62
Daudnagar, India	F10	54
Daugai, Lith.	F7	10
Daugavpils, Lat.	E9	10
Dauhinava, Bela.	F10	10
Daule, Ec.	H2	86
Daule, stm., Ec.	H1	86
Daund, India	B2	53
Daung Kyun, i., Mya.	F3	48
Dauphin, Mb., Can.	C13	124
Dauphin, stm., Mb., Can.	C15	124
Dauphiné, hist. reg., Fr.	E11	18
Dauphin Island, Al., U.S.	G10	122
Dauphin Island, i., Al., U.S.	G10	122
Dauphin Lake, I., Mb., Can.	C13	124
Daura, Nig.	G6	64
Dāvangere, India	D2	53
Davant, La., U.S.	H9	122
Davao, Phil.	G5	52
Davao Gulf, b., Phil.	G5	52
Dāvarzan, Iran	B8	56
Davenport, Fl., U.S.	H4	116
Davenport, Ia., U.S.	C7	120
Davenport, Ok., U.S.	B2	122
Davenport, Wa., U.S.	C8	136
Davenport Downs, Austl.	E3	76
Davey, Port, b., Austl.	o12	77a
David, Pan.	H6	102
David City, Ne., U.S.	F15	126
Davidson, Sk., Can.	C7	124
Davidson Mountains, mts., Ak., U.S.	C11	140
Davie, Fl., U.S.	J5	116
Davis, Ca., U.S.	E4	134
Davis, N.C., U.S.	B9	116
Davis, Ok., U.S.	G11	128
Davis, W.V., U.S.	E6	114
Davis, stm., Austl.	D4	74
Davis, sci., Ant.	B12	81
Davis, Mount, mtn., Pa., U.S.	E6	114
Davisboro, Ga., U.S.	C3	116
Davis Dam, dam, U.S.	H2	132
Davis Inlet, Nf., Can.	D18	106
Davis Mountains, mts., Tx., U.S.	D3	130
Davis Sea, Ant.	P11	142
Davis Strait, strt., N.A.	D14	141
Davos, Switz.	D6	22
Davy, W.V., U.S.	G4	114
Davyd-Haradok, Bela.	H9	10
Dawa (Daua), stm., Afr.	G7	62
Dawei (Tavoy), Mya.	E4	48
Dawen, stm., China	D7	42
Dawlan, Mya.	D4	48
Dawna Range, mts., Mya.	D4	48
Dawson, Yk., Can.	C3	106
Dawson, Ga., U.S.	F14	122
Dawson, Ne., U.S.	D2	120
Dawson, Tx., U.S.	F2	122
Dawson, stm., Austl.	D7	76
Dawson, Isla, i., Chile	J2	90
Dawson Bay, b., Mb., Can.	B13	124
Dawson Creek, B.C., Can.	D7	106
Dawson Inlet, b., Nu., Can.	C12	106
Dawson Range, mts., Yk., Can.	C3	106
Dawsonville, Ga., U.S.	B1	116
Dax, Fr.	F4	18
Daxian, China	F2	42
Daxing, China	B7	42
Daxu, China	I4	42
Daxue Shan, mts., China	F5	36
Dayang, stm., China	D5	38
Dayangshu, China	B9	36
Dayao, China	F5	36
Daye, China	F6	42
Daying, China	B5	42
Daylesford, Austl.	K5	76
Daymán, stm., Ur.	E9	92
Dayong, China	G4	42
Dayr az-Zawr, Syria	B4	56
Dayr Ḥāfir, Syria	B8	58
Daysland, Ab., Can.	D18	138
Dayton, Oh., U.S.	E1	114
Dayton, Or., U.S.	E3	136
Dayton, Tn., U.S.	B13	122
Dayton, Tx., U.S.	G4	122
Dayton, Wa., U.S.	D9	136
Dayton, Wy., U.S.	C5	126
Daytona Beach, Fl., U.S.	G5	116
Dayu, China	I6	42
Dayu Ling, mts., China	I6	42
Da Yunhe (Grand Canal), can., China	E8	42
Dayville, Or., U.S.	F7	136
Dazhu, China	F2	42
Dazkırı, Tur.	F12	28
De Aar, S. Afr.	G7	70
Deadhorse, Ak., U.S.	B10	140
Deadman's Cay, Bah.	A10	102
Dead Sea, I., Asia	G6	58
Deadwood, S.D., U.S.	C9	126
Deakin, Austl.	F5	74
Deal, Eng., U.K.	J14	12
Dealesville, S. Afr.	F7	70
Deal Island, Md., U.S.	F10	114
De'an, China	G6	42
Dean, stm., B.C., Can.	D4	138
Deán Funes, Arg.	E5	92
Deans Dundas Bay, b., N.T., Can.	B16	140
Dearborn, Mi., U.S.	B2	114
Dearg, Beinn, mtn., Scot., U.K.	D8	12
Dease, stm., B.C., Can.	D5	106
Dease Arm, b., N.T., Can.	B6	106
Dease Strait, strt., Nu., Can.	B9	106
Death Valley, Ca., U.S.	G9	134
Death Valley, val., Ca., U.S.	G9	134
Death Valley National Park, p.o.i., U.S.	G8	134
Deatsville, Al., U.S.	E12	122
Deauville, Fr.	E8	14
Deba, Nig.	G7	64
Debao, China	J2	42
Debar, Mac.	B3	28
De Bary, Fl., U.S.	H4	116
Debe, Trin.	s12	105f
De Berry, Tx., U.S.	E4	122
Dębica, Pol.	F17	16
Dęblin, Pol.	E17	16
Débo, Lac, I., Mali	F4	64
Deborah West, Lake, I., Austl.	F3	74
Deboyne Islands, is., Pap. N. Gui.	B10	74
Debre Birhan, Eth.	F7	62
Debrecen, Hung.	B8	26
Debre Mark'os, Eth.	E7	62
Debre Tabor, Eth.	E7	62
Debre Zeyit, Eth.	F7	62
Debrzno, Pol.	C13	16
Decatur, Al., U.S.	C11	122
Decatur, Ga., U.S.	C1	116
Decatur, Il., U.S.	E9	120
Decatur, In., U.S.	H4	112
Decatur, Mi., U.S.	F3	112
Decatur, Ne., U.S.	C1	120
Decatur, Tn., U.S.	B14	122
Decaturville, Tn., U.S.	B10	122
Decazeville, Fr.	E8	18
Deccan, plat., India	B4	53
Decelles, Réservoir, res., Qc., Can.	F15	106
Deception, stm., Bots.	B6	70

Name	Map Ref.	Page
Deception, Mount, mtn., Wa., U.S.	C3	136
Decherd, Tn., U.S.	B12	122
Dechhu, India	E4	54
Děčín, Czech Rep.	F10	16
Decize, Fr.	H12	14
Decker Lake, B.C., Can.	B5	138
Decorah, Ia., U.S.	H7	118
Dedaye, Mya.	D2	48
Dededo, Guam	i10	78c
Dedegöl Tepesi, mtn., Tur.	F14	28
De Doorns, S. Afr.	H4	70
Dédougou, Burkina	G4	64
Dedoviči, Russia	C12	10
Dedovsk, Russia	E20	10
Deduru, stm., Sri L.	H5	53
Dee, stm., U.K.	I9	12
Dee, stm., Scot., U.K.	D10	12
Deenwood, Ga., U.S.	E3	116
Deep, stm., N.C., U.S.	A6	116
Deep Creek, stm., U.S.	H14	136
Deep River, On., Can.	B12	112
Deep River, Ia., U.S.	C5	120
Deepwater, Mo., U.S.	F4	120
Deep Well, Austl.	D6	74
Deer Creek, stm., Ms., U.S.	D8	122
Deerfield, Il., U.S.	F2	112
Deerfield, Ks., U.S.	C7	128
Deerfield Beach, Fl., U.S.	J5	116
Deering, Ak., U.S.	C7	140
Deer Island, i., N.B., Can.	F10	110
Deer Isle, Me., U.S.	F8	110
Deer Lake, Nf., Can.	j22	107a
Deer Lodge, Mt., U.S.	D14	136
Deer Park, Al., U.S.	F10	122
Deer Park, Wa., U.S.	C9	136
Deerpass Bay, b., N.T., Can.	B6	106
Deer Trail, Co., U.S.	B4	128
Defiance, Ia., U.S.	C2	120
Defiance, Oh., U.S.	C1	114
Defiance, Mount, mtn., Or., U.S.	E5	136
De Forest, Wi., U.S.	H9	118
De Funiak Springs, Fl., U.S.	G12	122
Dêgê, China	E4	36
Degeh Bur, Eth.	F8	62
Dégelis, Qc., Can.	C8	110
Degerfors, Swe.	G6	8
Deggendorf, Ger.	H8	16
Degh, stm., Asia	B5	54
Değirmendere, Tur.	E10	28
De Gray Lake, res., Ar., U.S.	C5	122
De Grey, stm., Austl.	D3	74
Dehalak' Desēt, i., Erit.	D8	62
Dehiwala-Mount Lavinia, Sri L.	H4	53
Dehlorān, Iran	C6	56
Dehra Dūn, India	C7	54
Dehra Dūn Cantonment, India	C6	54
Dehri, India	F10	54
Dehu, India	B1	53
Dehua, China	I8	42
Dehui, China	B6	38
Deinze, Bel.	D12	14
Deir Mawâs, Egypt	K1	58
Dej, Rom.	B10	26
Dejnau, Turkmen.	B9	56
De Kalb, Il., U.S.	C9	120
De Kalb, Ms., U.S.	E10	122
De Kalb, Tx., U.S.	D4	122
Dekese, D.R.C.	E4	66
Deke Sokehs, i., Micron.	m11	78d
Dékoa, C.A.R.	C3	66
De Land, Fl., U.S.	G4	116
Delanggu, Indon.	G7	50
Delano, Ca., U.S.	H6	134
Delano, Mn., U.S.	F5	118
Delaport Point, c., Bah.	m18	104f
Delapu, China	C13	54
Delarof Islands, is., Ak., U.S.	g23	140a
Delaware, Oh., U.S.	D2	114
Delaware, Ok., U.S.	H2	120
Delaware, state, U.S.	F10	114
Delaware, stm., U.S.	D10	114
Delaware, stm., Ks., U.S.	E2	120
Delaware, East Branch, stm., N.Y., U.S.	B10	114
Delaware, West Branch, stm., U.S.	B11	114
Delaware Bay, b., U.S.	E10	114
Delaware City, De., U.S.	E10	114
Delburne, Ab., Can.	D17	138
Del Campillo, Arg.	G5	92
Del City, Ok., U.S.	F11	128
Delegate, Austl.	K7	76
Delémont, Switz.	C4	22
De Leon, Tx., U.S.	B9	130
Delfinópolis, Braz.	K2	88
Délfoi, hist., Grc.	E5	28
Delft, Neth.	B13	14
Delft Island, i., Sri L.	G4	53
Delfzijl, Neth.	A15	14
Delgado, Cabo, c., Moz.	C7	68
Delger, stm., Mong.	G8	34
Delgerhet, Mong.	B7	36
Delhi, On., Can.	F9	112
Delhi, India	D6	54
Delhi, Ia., U.S.	B6	120
Delhi, La., U.S.	E7	122
Delhi, N.Y., U.S.	B11	114
Delhi, state, India	D6	54
Delia, Ab., Can.	E18	138
Deliblato, Yugo.	E8	26
Delicias, Mex.	A6	100
Delight, Ar., U.S.	C5	122
Delījān, Iran	C7	56
Deline, N.T., Can.	B6	106
Delingde, Russia	B11	34
Delingha, China	D4	36
Dēliņkalns, hill, Lat.	C9	10
Delisle, Sk., Can.	C6	124
Delitzsch, Ger.	E8	16
Dell City, Tx., U.S.	C2	130
Delle, Fr.	G16	14
Dellys, Alg.	H14	20
Del Mar, Ca., U.S.	K8	134
Delmar, Ia., U.S.	C7	120
Delmar, Md., U.S.	F10	114
Delmarva Peninsula, pen., U.S.	F10	114
Delmas, Sk., Can.	B5	124
Delmenhorst, Ger.	C4	16
Delmiro Gouveia, Braz.	E7	88
Delnice, Cro.	E11	22
Del Norte, Co., U.S.	D2	128
De-Longa, ostrova, is., Russia	A19	34
De Long Mountains, mts., Ak., U.S.	C7	140
Deloraine, Mb., Can.	E13	124
Delorme, Lac, l., Qc., Can.	E16	106
Delos see Dílos, hist., Grc.	F8	28
Delphi, In., U.S.	H3	112
Delphi see Délfoi, hist., Grc.	E5	28
Delphos, Ks., U.S.	B11	128
Delportshoop, S. Afr.	F7	70
Delray Beach, Fl., U.S.	J5	116
Del Rio, Tx., U.S.	E7	130
Delta, Co., U.S.	E8	132
Delta, Mo., U.S.	G8	120
Delta, Ut., U.S.	D4	132
Delta Amacuro, state, Ven.	C11	86
Delta Beach, Mb., Can.	D15	124
Delta City, Ms., U.S.	D8	122
Delta Downs, Austl.	C8	74
Delta Junction, Ak., U.S.	D10	140
Delta Peak, mtn., B.C., Can.	D4	106
Del Valle, Tx., U.S.	D10	130
Del Verme Falls, wtfl, Eth.	F8	62
Delvinë, Alb.	E14	24
Demak, Indon.	G7	50
Demarcation Point, c., Ak., U.S.	C11	140
Demavend, Mount see Damāvand, Qolleh-ye, vol., Iran	B7	56
Demba, D.R.C.	F4	66
Dembī, Eth.	F7	62
Dembia, C.A.R.	C4	66
Dembī Dolo, Eth.	F6	62
Demidov, Russia	E14	10
Deming, N.M., U.S.	K9	132
Demini, stm., Braz.	H10	86
Demirci, Tur.	D11	28
Demirköprü Barajı, res., Tur.	E11	28
Demirköy, Tur.	B10	28
Demjanka, stm., Russia	C12	32
Demjanovo, Russia	F22	8
Demjanskoe, Russia	C11	32
Demmin, Ger.	C8	16
Demmitt, Ab., Can.	A11	138
Demopolis, Al., U.S.	E11	122
Demorest, Ga., U.S.	B2	116
Dempo, Gunung, vol., Indon.	F3	50
Demta, Indon.	F11	44
Denain, Fr.	D12	14
Denali, Ak., U.S.	D10	140
Denali National Park, Ak., U.S.	D10	140
Denan, Eth.	F8	62
Denau, Uzb.	G11	32
Den Burg, Neth.	A13	14
Dendang, Indon.	E5	50
Dendermonde (Termonde), Bel.	C12	14
Deng Deng, Cam.	C2	66
Dengkou, China	A2	42
Dêngqên, China	E4	36
Dengxian, China	E5	42
Denham, Austl.	E2	74
Denham, Mount, mtn., Jam.	i13	104d
Denham Range, mts., Austl.	C6	76
Denham Springs, La., U.S.	G8	122
Den Helder (Helder), Neth.	B13	14
Dénia, Spain	F11	20
Deniliquin, Austl.	J5	76
Deniskoviči, Russia	H14	10
Denison, Tx., U.S.	D2	122
Denison, Mount, vol., Ak., U.S.	E9	140
Denizli, Tur.	F12	28
Denizli, state, Tur.	F12	28
Denkanikota, India	E3	53
Denmark, Austl.	F3	74
Denmark, S.C., U.S.	C4	116
Denmark, Wi., U.S.	D2	112
Denmark, ctry., Eur.	D10	6
Denmark Strait, strt.	C20	94
Dennery, St. Luc.	m7	105c
Denpasar, Indon.	H9	50
Denton, Md., U.S.	F10	114
Denton, Mt., U.S.	C17	136
Denton, N.C., U.S.	A5	116
Denton, Tx., U.S.	H11	128
Denton Creek, stm., Tx., U.S.	H11	128
D'Entrecasteaux, Point, c., Austl.	F3	74
D'Entrecasteaux Islands, is., Pap. N. Gui.	D6	72
Denver, Co., U.S.	B3	128
Denver, Pa., U.S.	D9	114
Denver City, Tx., U.S.	A5	130
Deoband, India	D6	54
Deogarh, India	F4	54
Deogarh, India	F7	54
Deogarh, mtn., India	G9	54
Deogarh Hills, hills, India	G9	54
Deoghar, India	F11	54
Deori, India	G7	54
Deoria, India	E9	54
De Pere, Wi., U.S.	D1	112
Depew, Ok., U.S.	B2	122
Depoe Bay, Or., U.S.	F2	136
Depok, Indon.	G5	50
Deposit, N.Y., U.S.	B10	114
Depue, Il., U.S.	C8	120
Dêqên, China	F4	36
Deqing, China	J4	42
De Queen, Ar., U.S.	C4	122
De Quincy, La., U.S.	G5	122
Dera, Lach, stm., Afr.	D8	66
Dera Bugti, Pak.	D2	54
Dera Ghāzi Khān, Pak.	C3	54
Dera Ismāīl Khān, Pak.	C3	54
Derāwar Fort, Pak.	D3	54
Derbent, Russia	F7	32
Derby, Austl.	C4	74
Derby, Austl.	n13	77a
Derby, Eng., U.K.	I11	12
Derby, Ks., U.S.	D11	128
Derby, N.Y., U.S.	B6	114
Dereköy, Tur.	B10	28
Derg, Lough, l., Ire.	I4	12
Dergači, Russia	D7	32
De Ridder, La., U.S.	G5	122
Dermott, Ar., U.S.	D7	122
Dernieres, Isles, is., La., U.S.	H8	122
Dêrong, China	F4	36
Derrame, Mex.	H3	130
Derry see Londonderry, N. Ire., U.K.	F6	12
Derry, N.H., U.S.	B14	114
Derudeb, Sudan	D7	62
Derventa, Bos.	E4	26
Derwent, Ab., Can.	C19	138
Derwent, stm., Austl.	o13	77a
Derwent, stm., Eng., U.K.	G12	12
Derwent Water, l., Eng., U.K.	G9	12
Deržavinsk, Kaz.	D11	32
Desaguadero, stm., Arg.	F4	92
Desaguadero, stm., S.A.	G4	84
Désappointement, Îles du, is., Fr. Poly.	E12	72
Des Arc, Ar., U.S.	C7	122
Descabezado Grande, Volcán, vol., Chile	G2	92
Descalvado, Braz.	C11	92
Descanso, Ca., U.S.	K9	134
Descanso, Punta, c., Mex.	K8	134
Descartes, Fr.	G9	14
Deschambault Lake, l., Sk., Can.	E10	106
Deschutes, stm., Or., U.S.	E6	136
Desdunes, Haiti	C11	102
Desē, Eth.	E7	62
Deseado, stm., Arg.	I3	90
Desengaño, Punta, c., Arg.	I3	90
Desenzano del Garda, Italy	E7	22
Deseret Peak, mtn., Ut., U.S.	C4	132
Deseronto, On., Can.	D12	112
Désert, stm., Qc., Can.	B13	112
Désert, Lac, l., Qc., Can.	B13	112
Desert Hot Springs, Ca., U.S.	J9	134
Desert Lake, l., Nv., U.S.	F1	132
Desert Peak, mtn., Ut., U.S.	B3	132
Desert Valley, val., Nv., U.S.	B7	134
Desha, Ar., U.S.	B7	122
Deshaies, Guad.	h5	105c
Deshler, Oh., U.S.	C1	114
Deshnok, India	E4	54
Desiderio Tello, Arg.	E4	92
Deskáti, Grc.	D4	28
Desloge, Mo., U.S.	G7	120
Des Moines, Ia., U.S.	C4	120
Des Moines, N.M., U.S.	E5	128
Des Moines, stm., U.S.	K7	118
Des Moines, East Fork, stm., U.S.	H4	118
Desna, stm., Eur.	D4	32
Desolación, Isla, i., Chile	J2	90
De Soto, Il., U.S.	G8	120
De Soto, Mo., U.S.	F7	120
Despatch, S. Afr.	H7	70
Despeñaperros, Desfiladero de, p., Spain	F7	20
Des Plaines, Il., U.S.	F1	112
Des Plaines, stm., U.S.	C9	120
Desroches, i., Sey.	k12	69b
Desruisseaux, St. Luc.	m7	105c
Dessau, Ger.	E8	16
Destruction Bay, Yk., Can.	C3	106
Desvres, Fr.	D10	14
Detčino, Russia	F19	10
Dete, Zimb.	D4	68
Detmold, Ger.	E4	16
Detour, Point, c., Mi., U.S.	C3	112
De Tour Village, Mi., U.S.	C5	112
Detrital Wash, stm., Az., U.S.	H2	132
Detroit, Mi., U.S.	B2	114
Detroit, Or., U.S.	F4	136
Detroit, Tx., U.S.	D3	122
Detroit Beach, Mi., U.S.	C2	114
Dettifoss, wtfl, Ice.	k31	8a
Det Udom, Thai.	E7	48
Detva, Slov.	H15	16
Deua National Park, p.o.i., Austl.	J7	76
Deūlgaon Rāja, India	H5	54
Deutsche Bucht, b., Ger.	C4	16
Deutschlandsberg, Aus.	D12	22
Deux-Sèvres, state, Fr.	C5	18
Deva, Rom.	D9	26
Devakottai, India	G4	53
Dévaványa, Hung.	B7	26
Deventer, Neth.	B15	14
Deveron, stm., Scot., U.K.	D10	12
Devgadh Bāriva, India	G4	54
De View, Bayou, stm., Ar., U.S.	B8	122
Devīkot, India	E3	54
Devils, stm., Tx., U.S.	E6	130
Devils Island see Diable, Île du, i., Fr. Gu.	B7	84
Devils Lake, N.D., U.S.	F15	124
Devils Lake, l., N.D., U.S.	F14	124
Devils Postpile National Monument, p.o.i., Ca., U.S.	F6	134
Devils Tower National Monument, p.o.i., Wy., U.S.	C8	126
Devine, B.C., Can.	F8	138
Devine, Tx., U.S.	E9	130
Devjatiny, Russia	F17	8
Devli, India	F5	54
Devoll, stm., Alb.	D14	24
Devon, Ab., Can.	C17	138
Devon Island, i., Nu., Can.	B8	141
Devonport, Austl.	n13	77a
Devoto, Arg.	E6	92
Devrek, Tur.	B14	28
Dewakang-lompo, Pulau, i., Indon.	F11	50
Dewar, Ok., U.S.	B3	122
Dewās, India	G5	54
Dewey, Ok., U.S.	H1	120
Deweyville, Tx., U.S.	G5	122
De Witt, Ar., U.S.	C7	122
De Witt, Ia., U.S.	C7	120
De Witt, Ne., U.S.	G16	126
De Witt, N.Y., U.S.	A9	114
Dexing, China	G7	42
Dexter, Me., U.S.	E7	110
Dexter, Mi., U.S.	B2	114
Dexter, N.M., U.S.	H4	128
Dexter, N.Y., U.S.	D13	112
Dexterity Fiord, b., Nu., Can.	A16	106
Deyang, China	E5	36
Dey-Dey, Lake, l., Austl.	E6	74
Dezfūl, Iran	C6	56
Dezhou, China	C7	42
Dežneva, mys, c., Russia	C27	34
Dezong, China	B13	54
Dhahran see Az-Zahrān, Sau. Ar.	D6	56
Dhaka (Dacca), Bngl.	G13	54
Dhaka, state, Bngl.	F13	54
Dhamār, Yemen	G5	56
Dhāmpur, India	D7	54
Dhamtari, India	H8	54
Dhanbād, India	G11	54
Dhandhuka, India	G3	54
Dhangaḍhī, Nepal	D8	54
D'Hanis, Tx., U.S.	E8	130
Dhankuṭa, Nepal	E11	54
Dhār, India	G5	54
Dharān, Nepal	E11	54
Dhārāpuram, India	F3	53
Dharmābād, India	B3	53
Dharmapuri, India	E4	53
Dharmavaram, India	D3	53
Dharmjaygarh, India	G9	54
Dharmshāla, India	B6	54
Dhaulpur, India	E6	54
Dhawalāgiri, mtn., Nepal	D9	54
Dhenkānāl, India	H10	54
Dherínia, Cyp.	C4	58
Dhodhekánisos (Dodecanese), is., Grc.	G10	28
Dhodhóni, hist., Grc.	D3	28
Dhofar see Zufar, reg., Oman	F7	56
Dholka, India	G4	54
Dhone, India	D3	53
Dhoomadheere, Som.	D8	66
Dhorāji, India	H3	54
Dhrāngadhra, India	G3	54
Dhrol, India	G3	54
Dhuburi, India	E13	54
Dhule, India	H5	54
Dhuliān, India	F12	54
Dhupgāri, India	E12	54
Dhuusamarreeb, Som.	C9	66
Diable, Île du (Devils Island), i., Fr. Gu.	B7	84
Diable, Pointe du, c., Mart.	k7	105c
Diables, Morne aux, vol., Dom.	i5	105c
Diablo, Canyon, val., Az., U.S.	H5	132
Diablo, Mount, mtn., Ca., U.S.	F4	134
Diablo, Pico del, mtn., Mex.	F4	98
Diablo Range, mts., Ca., U.S.	G4	134
Diablotins, Morne, vol., Dom.	j6	105c
Diaca, Moz.	C6	68
Dialakoto, Sen.	G2	64
Diamante, Arg.	F7	92
Diamante, stm., Arg.	G4	92
Diamantina, Braz.	J4	88
Diamantina, stm., Austl.	E2	76
Diamantina Lakes, Austl.	D3	76
Diamantino, Braz.	F6	84
Diamond, Mo., U.S.	G3	120
Diamond Harbour, India	G12	54
Diamond Islets, is., Austl.	A8	76
Diamond Peak, mtn., Id., U.S.	F13	136
Diamond Peak, mtn., Wa., U.S.	D9	136
Diamondville, Wy., U.S.	B6	132
Diana Bay, b., Can.	C16	106
Dianbai, China	K4	42
Dian Chi, l., China	G5	36
Dianjiang, China	F2	42
Dianópolis, Braz.	F2	88
Diapaga, Burkina	G5	64
Diaz, Ar., U.S.	B7	122
Diaz Point, c., Nmb.	E2	70
Dibai, India	D7	54
Dibaya, D.R.C.	F4	66
Dibeng, S. Afr.	E6	70
D'Iberville, Ms., U.S.	G9	122
Dibete, Bots.	C8	70
Dibrugarh, India	C7	46
Dickens, Tx., U.S.	H8	128
Dickinson, N.D., U.S.	A10	126
Dickinson, Tx., U.S.	H3	122
Dickson, Tn., U.S.	H10	120
Didao, China	B9	38
Didsbury, Ab., Can.	E16	138
Dīdwāna, India	E5	54
Didymóteicho, Grc.	B9	28
Dieburg, Ger.	G4	16
Dieciocho de Julio, Ur.	F11	92
Diefenbaker, Lake, res., Sk., Can.	C7	124
Diego de Almagro, Chile	C2	92
Diego de Almagro, Isla, i., Chile	J1	90
Diego de Ocampo, Pico, mtn., Dom. Rep.	C12	102
Diégo-Suarez see Antsiranana, Madag.	C8	68
Diemuchuoke, China	B7	54
Dien Bien, Viet.	B6	48
Dien Bien Phu see Dien Bien, Viet.	B6	48
Diepholz, Ger.	D4	16
Dieppe, N.B., Can.	D12	110
Dieppe, Fr.	E9	14
Dieppe Bay Town, St. K./N.	C2	105a
Dierks, Ar., U.S.	C4	122
Di'er Songhua, stm., China	B6	38
Diest, Bel.	D14	14
Dieulefit, Fr.	E10	18
Dieveniškės, Lith.	F8	10
Diez de Octubre, Mex.	C6	100
Dif, Kenya	D8	66
Diffa, Niger	G7	64
Differdange, Lux.	E14	14
Dīg, India	E6	54
Digba, D.R.C.	D5	66
Digboi, India	C8	46
Digby, N.S., Can.	F11	110
Digby Neck, pen., N.S., Can.	F10	110
Digges Islands, is., Nu., Can.	C15	106
Dighton, Ks., U.S.	C8	128
Dīglūr, India	B3	53
Digne-les-Bains, Fr.	E12	18
Digoin, Fr.	C9	18
Digos, Phil.	G5	52
Digras, India	H6	54
Digul, stm., Indon.	G10	44
Diinsor, Som.	D8	66
Dijon, Fr.	G14	14
Dikaja, Russia	A22	10
Dike, Ia., U.S.	B5	120
Dikhil, Dji.	E8	62
Dikili, Tur.	D9	28
Dikirnis, Egypt	G2	58
Dikodougou, C. Iv.	H3	64
Diksmuide, Bel.	C11	14
Dikson, Russia	B5	34
Dikwa, Nig.	G7	64
Dīla, Eth.	F7	62
Dilek Yarımdası Milli Parkı, p.o.i., Tur.	F10	28
Dili, Indon.	G8	44
Dillenburg, Ger.	F4	16
Diller, Ne., U.S.	A12	128
Dilley, Tx., U.S.	F8	130
Dilling, Sudan	E5	62
Dillingen an der Donau, Ger.	H6	16
Dillingham, Ak., U.S.	E8	140
Dillon, Mt., U.S.	E14	136
Dillon, S.C., U.S.	B6	116
Dillon Mountain, mtn., N.M., U.S.	J8	132
Dillwyn, Va., U.S.	G7	114
Dilolo, D.R.C.	G4	66
Dílos, hist., Grc.	F8	28
Dilworth, Mn., U.S.	H17	124
Dimāpur, India	C7	46
Dimashq (Damascus), Syria	E7	58
Dimashq, state, Syria	E7	58
Dimbelenge, D.R.C.	F4	66
Dimbokro, C. Iv.	H4	64
Dimbulah, Austl.	A5	76
Dimitrovgrad, Blg.	G12	26
Dimitrovgrad, Russia	D8	32
Dimitsána, Grc.	F4	28
Dimlang, mtn., Nig.	H7	64
Dimmitt, Tx., U.S.	G6	128
Dimona, Isr.	G6	58
Dinagat, Phil.	E5	52
Dinagat Island, i., Phil.	E5	52
Dinājpur, Bngl.	F12	54
Dinan, Fr.	F6	14
Dinant, Bel.	D13	14
Dinar, Tur.	E13	28
Dinard, Fr.	F6	14
Dinaric Alps (Dinara), mts., Eur.	G13	22
Dindi, stm., India	C4	53
Dindigul, India	F4	53
Dindori, India	G8	54
Dingalan Bay, b., Phil.	C3	52
Ding'an, China	L4	42
Dingbian, China	C2	42
Dingbianji, China	C3	42
Dinggyê, China	D11	54
Dinghai, China	F9	42
Dingle, Ire.	I2	12
Dingle Bay, b., Ire.	I2	12
Dingnan, China	I6	42
Dingo, Austl.	D7	76
Dingolfing, Ger.	H8	16
Dingshuzhen, China	F8	42
Dingtao, China	D6	42
Dinguiraye, Gui.	G2	64
Dingwall, N.S., Can.	D16	110
Dingxian, China	B6	42
Dingxiang, China	B5	42
Dingyuan, China	E7	42
Dinhāta, India	E12	54
Dinh Hoa, Viet.	B7	48
Dinh Lap, Viet.	B8	48
Dinkelsbühl, Ger.	G6	16
Dinnebito Wash, stm., Az., U.S.	H5	132
Dinorwic, On., Can.	B6	118
Dinorwic Lake, l., On., Can.	B6	118
Dinosaur National Monument, p.o.i., U.S.	C8	132
Dinsmore, Sk., Can.	C6	124
Dinuba, Ca., U.S.	G6	134
Dinwiddie, Va., U.S.	G8	114
Dionísio Cerqueira, Braz.	C11	92
Diouloulou, Sen.	G1	64
Diourbel, Sen.	G1	64
Dīpālpur, Pak.	C4	54
Diplo, Pak.	F2	54
Dipolog, Phil.	F4	52
Dippoldiswalde, Ger.	F9	16
Dīr, Pak.	B11	56
Diré, Mali	F4	64
Dirē Dawa, Eth.	F8	62
Dirico, Ang.	D3	68
Dirj, Libya	A2	62
Dirk Hartog Island, i., Austl.	E2	74
Dirkou, Niger	F7	64
Dirranbandi, Austl.	G7	76
Dīsa, India	F4	54
Disappointment, Cape, c., S. Geor.	J9	90
Disappointment, Cape, c., Wa., U.S.	D2	136
Disappointment, Lake, l., Austl.	D4	74
Disaster Bay, b., Austl.	K8	76
Disautel, Wa., U.S.	B7	136
Discovery Bay, b., Austl.	L3	76
Dishman, Wa., U.S.	C9	136
Disko, i., Grnld.	D15	141
Disko Bugt, b., Grnld.	D15	141
Dismal, stm., Ne., U.S.	F12	126
Dispur, India	E13	54
Disraëli, Qc., Can.	E5	110
Distrito Capital, state, Col.	E4	86
Distrito Federal, state, Braz.	H2	88
Distrito Federal, state, Mex.	F9	100
Distrito Federal, state, Ven.	B8	86
Dis Ûq, Egypt	G1	58
Dithmarschen, reg., Ger.	B5	16
Diu, India	H3	54
Dive, can., Fr.	B5	18
Divenskaja, Russia	A12	10
Divernon, Il., U.S.	E8	120
Divinhe, Moz.	B12	70
Divinópolis, Braz.	K3	88
Divi Point, c., India	D5	53
Divisor, Serra do, plat., S.A.	E3	84
Divnoe, Russia	E6	32
Divnogorsk, Russia	C16	32
Divo, C. Iv.	H3	64
Dīwāl Qol, Afg.	A1	54
Dix, Ne., U.S.	F9	126
Dixie Valley, val., Nv., U.S.	D8	134
Dixon, Ca., U.S.	E4	134
Dixon, Il., U.S.	C8	120
Dixon, Ky., U.S.	G10	120
Dixon, Mo., U.S.	G5	120
Dixon, N.M., U.S.	E3	128
Dixon Entrance, strt., N.A.	E4	106
Diyarbakır, Tur.	B4	56
Dizhou, China	J2	42
Djado, Niger	E7	64
Djado, Plateau du, plat., Niger	E7	64
Djakarta see Jakarta, Indon.	G5	50
Djamâa, Alg.	C6	64
Djambala, Congo	E2	66
Djanet, Alg.	E6	64
Djaret, Oued, stm., Alg.	D5	64
Djat'kovo, Russia	G17	10
Djedi, Oued, stm., Alg.	C5	64
Djéma, C.A.R.	C5	66
Djenné, Mali	G4	64
Djenoun, Garet el, mtn., Alg.	D6	64
Djérem, stm., Cam.	C2	66
Djibo, Burkina	G4	64
Djibouti, Dji.	E8	62
Djibouti, ctry., Afr.	E8	62
Djoku-Punda, D.R.C.	F4	66
Djolu, D.R.C.	D4	66
Djougou, Benin	H5	64
Djourab, Erg du, sand, Chad	D3	62
Djugu, D.R.C.	D6	66
Djurås, Swe.	F6	8
Djurtjuli, Russia	C8	32
Dmitrija Lapteva, proliv, strt., Russia	B16	34
Dmitrov, Russia	D20	10
Dneprovskoe, Russia	E16	10
Dnieper, stm., Eur.	F15	6
Dniester (Dnister), stm., Eur.	G19	16
Dniprodzerzhyns'k, Ukr.	E5	32
Dnipropetrovs'k, Ukr.	E4	32
Dnistrovs'kyi lyman, l., Ukr.	C17	26
Dnjaprouska Buhski, kanal, can., Bela.	I8	10
Dno, Russia	C12	10
Do, Lac, l., Mali	F4	64
Dôa, Moz.	D5	68
Doaktown, N.B., Can.	D10	110
Doangdoangan-Besar, Pulau, i., Indon.	F10	50
Doba, Chad	F3	62
Dobczyce, Pol.	G15	16
Dobele, Lat.	D6	10
Döbeln, Ger.	E8	16
Doberai, Jazirah (Doberai Peninsula), pen., Indon.	F9	44
Doberai Peninsula see Doberai, Jazirah, pen., Indon.	F9	44
Dobo, Indon.	G9	44
Doboj, Bos.	E4	26
Dobra, Pol.	E14	16
Dobre Miasto, Pol.	C16	16
Dobrič, Blg.	F14	26
Dobříš, Czech Rep.	G10	16
Dobrjanka, Russia	C9	32
Dobroe, Russia	C15	10
Dobroteasa, Rom.	E11	26
Dobruja, hist. reg., Eur.	E15	26
Dobruš, Bela.	H14	10
Dobruška, Czech Rep.	F12	16
Dobrzyń nad Wisłą, Pol.	D15	16
Dobson, N.C., U.S.	H5	114
Dobzha, China	D12	54
Doce, stm., Braz.	J6	88
Dock Junction, Ga., U.S.	E4	116
Doctor Cecilio Báez, Para.	B9	92
Doctor Coss, Mex.	I8	130
Doctor González, Mex.	I8	130
Dod Ballāpur, India	E3	53
Doddridge, Ar., U.S.	D4	122
Dodecanese see Dhodhekánisos, is., Grc.	G10	28
Dodge Center, Mn., U.S.	G5	118
Dodge City, Ks., U.S.	D9	128
Dodgeville, Wi., U.S.	B7	120
Dodoma, Tan.	F7	66
Dodsland, Sk., Can.	C5	124
Dodson, Mt., U.S.	F5	124
Dodson, Tx., U.S.	G8	128
Doerun, Ga., U.S.	E1	116
Doetinchem, Neth.	C15	14
Dogai Coring, l., China	A12	54
Doğanbey, Tur.	E9	28
Doğanhisar, Tur.	E14	28
Dog Island, i., Fl., U.S.	H14	122
Dog Islands, is., Br. Vir. Is.	e9	104b
Dog Lake, l., Mb., Can.	C15	124
Dog Lake, l., On., Can.	C9	118
Dogliani, Italy	F4	22
Dōgo, i., Japan	C6	40
Do Gonbadān, Iran	C7	56
Dogondoutchi, Niger	G5	64
Doğu Karadeniz Dağları, mts., Tur.	A5	56
Doha see Ad-Dawḥah, Qatar	D7	56
Dohrīghāt, India	E9	54
Doiran, Lake, l., Eur.	B5	28
Dois Irmãos de Goiás, Braz.	E1	88
Doi Suthep-Pui National Park, p.o.i., Thai.	C4	48
Doka, Indon.	G9	44
Dokkum, Neth.	A14	14
Doksy, Czech Rep.	F10	16
Doland, S.D., U.S.	C14	126
Dolbeau, Qc., Can.	B4	110
Dol-de-Bretagne, Fr.	F7	14
Dole, Fr.	G14	14
Dolega, Pan.	H6	102
Dolgeville, N.Y., U.S.	E15	112
Dolgij Most, Russia	C17	32
Dolgoščele, Russia	C20	8
Dolinsk, Russia	G17	34
Dolj, state, Rom.	E10	26
Dolni Dăbnik, Blg.	F11	26
Dolný Kubín, Slov.	G15	16
Dolomites see Dolomiti, mts., Italy	D8	22
Dolomiti, mts., Italy	D8	22
Dolores, Arg.	H9	92
Dolores, Col.	F4	86
Dolores, Guat.	D3	102
Dolores, Mex.	H6	130
Dolores, Ur.	F8	92
Dolores, stm., U.S.	E7	132
Dolores Hidalgo, Mex.	E8	100
Dolphin, Cape, c., Falk. Is.	J5	90
Dolphin and Union Strait, strt., Nu., Can.	B7	106
Dolphin Head, mtn., Jam.	i12	104d
Dolsk, Pol.	D13	16
Dolžicy, Russia	C12	10
Domaniči, Russia	G16	10
Domažlice, Czech Rep.	G8	16
Dombås, Nor.	E3	8
Dombes, reg., Fr.	D11	18
Dombóvár, Hung.	C4	26
Dom Cavati, Braz.	J4	88
Dôme, Puy de, mtn., Fr.	D8	18
Dome Creek, B.C., Can.	C9	138
Domeyko, Chile	D2	92
Domeyko, Cordillera, mts., Chile	D3	90
Domfront, Fr.	F8	14
Domiciano Ribeiro, Braz.	I2	88
Domingo M. Irala, Para.	B10	92
Dominica, ctry., N.A.	j5	105c
Dominica Channel see Martinique Passage, strt., N.A.	k6	105c
Dominicana, República see Dominican Republic, ctry., N.A.	D10	96
Dominican Republic, ctry., N.A.	D10	96
Dominica Passage, strt., N.A.	i6	105c
Dominion, Cape, c., Nu., Can.	B15	106
Dominion City, Mb., Can.	E16	124
Dom Joaquim, Braz.	J4	88
Domo, Eth.	F9	62
Domodedovo, Russia	E20	10
Domodossola, Italy	D5	22
Dom Pedrito, Braz.	E10	92
Dom Pedro, Braz.	C3	88
Dompu, Indon.	H11	50
Domremy, Sk., Can.	B8	124
Domuyo, Volcán, vol., Arg.	H2	92
Dom Yai, stm., Thai.	E7	48
Don, stm., India	C2	53
Don, stm., Laos	E7	48
Don, stm., Russia	E6	32
Don, stm., Scot., U.K.	D10	12
Donadeu, Arg.	C6	92
Donaghadee, N. Ire., U.K.	G7	12
Donald, Austl.	K4	76
Donalda, Ab., Can.	D18	138
Donaldson, Ar., U.S.	C6	122
Donaldsonville, La., U.S.	G7	122
Doñana, Parque Nacional de, p.o.i., Spain	H4	20
Donau, stm., Eur.	F11	6
Donaueschingen, Ger.	I4	16
Donauwörth, Ger.	H6	16
Don Benito, Spain	F5	20
Doncaster, Eng., U.K.	H11	12
Dondaicha, India	H5	54
Dondo, Ang.	B1	68
Dondo, Moz.	A12	70
Dondo, Teluk, b., Indon.	C12	50
Dondra Head, c., Sri L.	I5	53
Donduşeni, Mol.	A14	26
Donegal, Ire.	G4	12
Donegal, state, Ire.	G5	12
Donegal Bay, b., Ire.	G4	12
Doneraile, S.C., U.S.	B6	116
Donets'k, Ukr.	E5	32
Dong, stm., China	J6	42
Dong'an, China	B11	36
Dong'an, China	H4	42
Dongara, Austl.	E3	74
Dongchuan, China	F5	36
Dongfang, China	L3	42
Dongfeng, China	C6	38
Donggala, Indon.	D11	50
Donggi Cona, l., China	D4	36
Donggong Shan, mts., China	H8	42
Dongguan, China	J5	42
Dongguang, China	C7	42
Dong Ha, Viet.	D8	48
Donghai Dao, i., China	K4	42
Dong Hoi, Viet.	D8	48
Dong Hu, l., China	B10	54
Dongjielang, China	F6	42
Dongjingcheng, China	B8	38
Donglan, China	I2	42
Dongliao, stm., China	C5	38
Dong Nai, stm., Viet.	G8	48
Dongning, China	B9	38
Dongo, D.R.C.	D3	66
Dongou, Congo	D3	66
Dongping, China	K5	42
Dongping, China	D7	42
Dong San Shen (Manchuria), hist. reg., China	B5	38
Dongshan, China	L4	42
Dongshan Dao, i., China	J7	42
Dongsheng, China	B4	42
Dongtai, China	E9	42
Dongting Hu, l., China	G5	42
Dong Trieu, Viet.	B8	48
Dongwe, stm., Zam.	C3	68
Dongxi, China	G2	42
Dongxiang, China	G7	42
Dongyang, China	G9	42
Dongzhi, China	F7	42
Donie, Tx., U.S.	F2	122
Doniphan, Ne., U.S.	G14	126
Donja Stubica, Cro.	E12	22
Donjek, stm., Yk., Can.	C3	106
Don Martín, Mex.	G7	130
Donna, Tx., U.S.	H9	130
Donnacona, Qc., Can.	D5	110
Donnelly, Id., U.S.	F10	136
Donner, La., U.S.	H7	122
Donner Pass, p., Ca., U.S.	D5	134
Donner und Blitzen, stm., Or., U.S.	G8	136
Donnybrook, Austl.	F3	74
Donora, Pa., U.S.	D6	114
Donostia (San Sebastián), Spain	A9	20
Donostia-San Sebastián see Donostia, Spain	A9	20
Don Pedro Reservoir, res., Ca., U.S.	F5	134
Don Peninsula, pen., B.C., Can.	D2	138
Donskoj, Russia	G21	10
Doolow, Som.	D8	66
Doonerak, Mount, mtn., Ak., U.S.	C9	140
Doornik see Tournai, Bel.	D12	14
Door Peninsula, pen., Wi., U.S.	D2	112
Dor, Isr.	F5	58
Dora, Al., U.S.	D11	122
Dora, Lake, l., Austl.	D4	74
Dora Baltea, stm., Italy	E4	22
Dorado, P.R.	B3	104a
Doraville, Ga., U.S.	D14	122
Dorcheat, Bayou, stm., U.S.	D5	122
Dorchester, N.B., Can.	E12	110
Dorchester, On., Can.	F8	112
Dorchester, Eng., U.K.	K10	12
Dorchester, Ne., U.S.	G15	126
Dorchester, Cape, c., Nu., Can.	B15	106
Dordabis, Nmb.	C3	70
Dordogne, state, Fr.	D6	18
Dordogne, stm., Fr.	D8	18
Dordrecht, Neth.	C13	14
Dordrecht, S. Afr.	G8	70
Dore Lake, l., Sk., Can.	E9	106
Dorena, Or., U.S.	G4	136
Dores do Indaiá, Braz.	J3	88
Dorfen, Ger.	H8	16
Dorgali, Italy	D3	24

Name — **Map Ref.** — **Page**

Dörgön nuur, l., Mong. B3 36
Dori, Burkina G4 64
Doring, stm., S. Afr. G4 70
Dornbirn, Aus. C6 22
Dornoch, Scot., U.K. D8 12
Dorog, Hung. B5 26
Dorogobuž, Russia F16 10
Dorohoi, Rom. A13 26
Dorokempo, Indon. H11 50
Dorre Island, i., Austl. E2 74
Dorrigo, Austl. H9 76
Dorris, Ca., U.S. B4 134
Dorsale, mts., Tun. I3 24
Dort see Dordrecht, Neth. C13 14
Dortmund, Ger. E3 16
Dorton, Ky., U.S. G3 114
Dörtyol, Tur. B7 58
Doruma, D.R.C. D5 66
Dos, Canal Numero, can., Arg. H9 92
Dosatuj, Russia A8 36
Dos Bahías, Cabo, c., Arg. H3 90
Dos Bocas, P.R. B2 104a
Döşemealtı, Tur. F13 28
Dos Hermanas, Spain G4 20
Do Son, Viet. B8 48
Dos Pos, Neth. Ant. p23 104g
Dos Quebradas, Col. E4 86
Dosso, Niger G5 64
Dossor, Kaz. E8 32
Dothan, Al., U.S. F13 122
Dotnuva, Lith. E6 10
Dou, stm., China B8 42
Douai, Fr. D11 14
Douala, Cam. D1 66
Douarnenez, Fr. F4 14
Doublé, Pointe, c., Guad. h7 105c
Double Island Point, c., Austl. E9 76
Double Springs, Al., U.S. C11 122
Doubletop Peak, mtn., Wy., U.S. G16 136
Doubs, state, Fr. G15 14
Doubs, stm., Eur. H14 14
Doubtful Sound, strt., N.Z. G2 80
Doubtless Bay, b., N.Z. B5 80
Douentza, Mali F4 64
Dougga, hist., Tun. H3 24
Douglas, Mb., Can. E14 124
Douglas, I. of Man G8 12
Douglas, S. Afr. F6 70
Douglas, Ak., U.S. E13 140
Douglas, Az., U.S. L7 132
Douglas, Ga., U.S. E3 116
Douglas, Wy., U.S. E7 126
Douglas Channel, strt., B.C., Can. C1 138
Douglas Lake, B.C., Can. F10 138
Douglas Lake, res., Tn., U.S. H2 114
Douglasville, Ga., U.S. D14 122
Doullens, Fr. D11 14
Dourada, Serra, plat., Braz. G1 88
Dourados, Braz. D6 90
Dourbali, Chad E3 62
Douro (Duero), stm., Eur. C2 20
Doųsk, Bela. G13 10
Douz, Tun. C6 64
Dove Bugt, strt., Grnld. B21 141
Dove Creek, Co., U.S. F7 132
Dover, Austl. o13 77a
Dover, Eng., U.K. J14 12
Dover, De., U.S. E10 114
Dover, Id., U.S. B10 136
Dover, N.H., U.S. G6 110
Dover, N.J., U.S. D11 114
Dover, N.C., U.S. A8 116
Dover, Oh., U.S. D4 114
Dover, Ok., U.S. E11 128
Dover, Tn., U.S. H10 120
Dover, Strait of, strt., Eur. K14 12
Dover-Foxcroft, Me., U.S. E7 110
Dovrefjell Nasjonalpark, p.o.i., Nor. E3 8
Dow City, Ia., U.S. C2 120
Dowlatābād, Iran D8 56
Downey, Id., U.S. H14 136
Downieville, Ca., U.S. D5 134
Downing, Mo., U.S. D5 120
Downingtown, Pa., U.S. D10 114
Downpatrick, N. Ire., U.K. G7 12
Downs, Ks., U.S. B10 128
Downton, Mount, mtn., B.C., Can. D6 138
Dows, Ia., U.S. B4 120
Dowshī, Afg. B10 56
Doyle, Ca., U.S. C5 134
Doyles, Nf., Can. C17 110
Doylestown, Pa., U.S. D10 114
Doyline, La., U.S. E5 122
Dōzen, is., Japan C5 40
Dozier, Al., U.S. F12 122
Dra, Cap, c., Mor. D2 64
Dra'a, Hamada du, des., Alg. D3 64
Drâa, Oued, stm., Afr. D2 64
Drac, stm., Fr. E2 22
Dracena, Braz. D6 90
Drachten, Neth. A15 14
Dracut, Ma., U.S. B14 114
Dragalina, Rom. E14 26
Drăgănești-Vlașca, Rom. E12 26
Drăgășani, Rom. E11 26
Dragonera, Sa, i., Spain E13 20
Dragons Mouths, strt. s12 105f
Dragoon, Az., U.S. K6 132
Draguignan, Fr. F12 18
Drahičyn, Bela. H8 10
Drake, N.D., U.S. G13 124
Drakensberg, mts., Afr. F9 70
Drake Passage, strt. K8 82
Drakesboro, Ky., U.S. G10 120
Drakes Branch, Va., U.S. H7 114
Dráma, Grc. B7 28
Drammen, Nor. G3 8
Drang, stm., Asia F8 48
Drangajökull, ice, Ice. j28 8a
Dranov, Ostrovul, i., Rom. E16 26
Drau (Dráva), stm., Eur. D11 22
Dráva (Drau), stm., Eur. D14 22
Dravograd, Slvn. D12 22
Drawsko Pomorskie, Pol. C11 16
Drayton, N.D., U.S. C1 118
Drayton, S.C., U.S. B4 116
Drayton Valley, Ab., Can. C15 138
Dresden, On., Can. F7 112
Dresden, Ger. E9 16
Dresden, Oh., U.S. D3 114
Drètun', Bela. E12 10
Dreux, Fr. F10 14
Drew, Ms., U.S. D8 122
Drienov, Slov. H17 16
Driftwood, B.C., Can. D5 106
Driftwood, stm., In., U.S. E12 120
Driggs, Id., U.S. G15 136
Drin, stm., Alb. C13 24
Drina, stm., Eur. F16 22
Drinit, Gjiri i, b., Alb. C13 24
Drinit të Zi (Crni Drim), stm., Eur. C14 24
Driskill Mountain, hill, La., U.S. E6 122
Drissa (Drysa), stm., Eur. E11 10
Drniš, Cro. G13 22
Drobeta-Turnu Severin, Rom. E9 26
Drochia, Mol. A14 26
Drogheda, Ire. H6 12
Droichead Átha see Drogheda, Ire. H6 12
Droichead Nua, Ire. H6 12
Drôme, state, Fr. E11 18
Dronero, Italy F4 22
Dronne, stm., Fr. D6 18
Dronning Louise Land, reg., Grnld. B20 141
Druc', stm., Bela. G12 10
Druif, Aruba o19 104g
Druja, Bela. E10 10
Drūkšiai, l., Eur. E9 10
Drumheller, Ab., Can. E18 138
Drummond, Mt., U.S. D13 136
Drummond, Wi., U.S. E7 118
Drummond Island, i., Mi., U.S. C6 112
Drummondville, Qc., Can. E4 110
Druskininkai, Lith. F7 10
Družba, Kaz. E14 32
Druzhba see Družba, Kaz. E14 32
Družina, Russia C18 34
Drvar, Bos. E3 26
Dry Arm, b., Mt., U.S. G7 124
Dry Bay, b., Ak., U.S. E12 140
Dryberry Lake, l., On., Can. B4 118
Dry Cimarron, stm., U.S. B2 122
Dry Creek Mountain, mtn., Nv., U.S. B9 134
Dryden, On., Can. B6 118
Dry Devils, stm., Tx., U.S. D7 130
Dry Prong, La., U.S. F6 122
Dry Ridge, Ky., U.S. F1 114
Drysdale, stm., Austl. C5 74
Dry Tortugas, is., Fl., U.S. G11 108
Dry Tortugas National Park, p.o.i., Fl., U.S. L3 116
Drzewica, Pol. E16 16
Dschang, Cam. C1 66
Du, stm., China E4 42
Du'an, China I3 42
Duaringa, Austl. D7 76
Duarte, Pico, mtn., Dom. Rep. C12 102
Duartina, Braz. L1 88
Ḍubā, Sau. Ar. K6 58
Ḍubach, La., U.S. E6 122
Dubai see Dubayy, U.A.E. D8 56
Dubăsari, Mol. B16 26
Dubăsari, Lacul, res., Mol. B15 26
Dubawnt, stm., Can. C10 106
Dubawnt Lake, l., Can. C10 106
Dubayy (Dubai), U.A.E. D8 56
Dubbo, Austl. I7 76
Dubh Artach, r., Scot., U.K. E6 12
Dublin (Baile Átha Cliath), Ire. H6 12
Dublin, Ga., U.S. D3 116
Dublin, Tx., U.S. B9 130
Dublin, Va., U.S. G5 114
Dublin, state, Ire. H6 12
Dubna, Russia F19 10
Dubna, Russia D20 10
Dubna, stm., Russia D21 10
Dubnica nad Váhom, Slov. H14 16
Dubois, In., U.S. F11 120
Du Bois, Ne., U.S. D1 120
Du Bois, Pa., U.S. C7 114
Dubois, Wy., U.S. D3 126
Dubossary Reservoir see Dubăsari, Lacul, res., Mol. B15 26
Dubovka, Russia E6 32
Dubrājpur, India G11 54
Dubréka, Gui. H2 64
Dubroųna, Bela. F13 10
Dubrovka, Russia G16 10
Dubrovnik, Cro. H15 22
Dubrovnoe, Russia C11 32
Dubuque, Ia., U.S. B7 120
Dubysa, stm., Lith. E6 10
Duchang, China G7 42
Duchesne, Ut., U.S. C6 132
Duchesne, stm., Ut., U.S. C7 132
Duchess, Austl. C2 76
Duck, stm., Tn., U.S. B11 122
Duck Creek, stm., Nv., U.S. D2 132
Duck Hill, Ms., U.S. D9 122
Duck Lake, Sk., Can. B7 124
Ducktown, Tn., U.S. B14 122
Duda, stm., Col. F4 86
Dudačkino, Russia A15 10
Duderstadt, Ger. E6 16
Dudinka, Russia C6 34
Dudley, Eng., U.K. I10 12
Dudleyville, Az., U.S. K6 132
Dudna, stm., India B2 53
Dudorovskij, Russia G18 10
Dudwa National Park, p.o.i., India D8 54
Dueré, stm., Braz. F1 88
Duero (Douro), stm., Eur. C2 20
Due West, S.C., U.S. B3 116
Dufourspitze, mtn., Eur. D13 18
Dufur, Or., U.S. E5 136
Duga-Zapadnaja, mys, c., Russia E18 34
Dugdemona, stm., La., U.S. F6 122
Dugi Otok, i., Cro. F11 22
Dugna, Russia F19 10
Du Gué, stm., Qc., Can. D16 106
Duhovščina, Russia E15 10
Duida, Cerro, mtn., Ven. F9 86
Duisburg, Ger. E2 16
Duitama, Col. E5 86
Duiwelskloof, S. Afr. C10 70
Dujuuma, Som. D8 66
Duke, Ok., U.S. G9 128
Duke of York Bay, b., Nu., Can. B13 106
Duk Fadiat, Sudan F6 62
Dukhān, Qatar D7 56
Duki, Pak. C2 54
Dukla Pass, p., Eur. G17 16
Dukou, China F5 36
Dūkštas, Lith. E9 10
Dulan, China D4 36
Dulce, N.M., U.S. G9 132
Dulce, stm., Arg. D6 92
Dulce, Golfo, b., C.R. H6 102
Dul'durga, Russia F11 34
Dulgalah, stm., Russia C15 34
Dullstroom, S. Afr. D10 70
Dulovka, Russia C11 10
Dulq Maghār, Syria B9 58
Duluth, Ga., U.S. C14 122
Duluth, Mn., U.S. E6 118
Dūmā, Syria E7 58
Dumaguete, Phil. F4 52
Dumai, Indon. C2 50
Dumalag, Phil. E4 52
Dumali Point, c., Phil. D3 52
Dumaran Island, i., Phil. E2 52
Dumaresq, stm., Austl. G8 76
Dumaring, Indon. C11 50
Dumas, Tx., U.S. F7 128
Dumbarton, Scot., U.K. F8 12
Dumbrăveni, Rom. C11 26
Dume, Point, c., Ca., U.S. J7 134
Dumfries, Scot., U.K. F9 12
Dumka, India F11 54
Dumlupınar, Tur. E12 28
Dummar, Syria E7 58
Dumoine, Lac, l., Qc., Can. B12 112
Dumont, Ia., U.S. B4 120
Dumont d'Urville, sci., Ant. B18 81
Dumpu, Pap. N. Gui. b4 79a
Dumraon, India F10 54
Dumyât, Masabb (Damietta Mouth), mth., Egypt G3 58
Duna see Danube, stm., Eur. F11 6
Dunaharaszti, Hung. B6 26
Dunaj see Danube, stm., Eur. F11 6
Dunajec, stm., Eur. F16 16
Dunajská Streda, Slov. H13 16
Dunakeszi, Hung. B6 26
Dunărea Veche, Brațul, stm., Rom. E15 26
Dunaújváros, Hung. C5 26
Dunavățu de Sus, Rom. E16 26
Duna-völgyi-főcsatorna, can., Hung. C6 26
Dunav-Tisa-Dunav, Kanal, can., Yugo. D6 26
Dunbar, Scot., U.K. E10 12
Dunblane, Sk., Can. C6 124
Duncan, B.C., Can. H7 138
Duncan, Az., U.S. K7 132
Duncan, Ok., U.S. G11 128
Duncan, stm., B.C., Can. F13 138
Duncan Lake, res., B.C., Can. F14 138
Duncannon, Pa., U.S. D8 114
Duncan Passage, strt., India F7 46
Duncans, Jam. i13 104d
Duncansby Head, c., Scot., U.K. C9 12
Dundaga, Lat. C5 10
Dundalk, On., Can. D9 112
Dundalk (Dún Dealgan), Ire. G6 12
Dundalk, Md., U.S. E9 114
Dundalk Bay, b., Ire. H6 12
Dundas, On., Can. E9 112
Dundas, Lake, l., Austl. F4 74
Dundas Peninsula, pen., Can. B17 140
Dundas Strait, strt., Austl. B6 74
Dún Dealgan see Dundalk, Ire. G6 12
Dundee, S. Afr. F10 70
Dundee, Scot., U.K. E10 12
Dundee, Fl., U.S. H4 116
Dundee, Mi., U.S. C2 114
Dundurn, Sk., Can. C7 124
Dunedin, N.Z. G4 80
Dunedin, Fl., U.S. H3 116
Dunedoo, Austl. I7 76
Dunfermline, Scot., U.K. E9 12
Dungannon, N. Ire., U.K. G6 12
Dūngarpur, India G4 54
Dungarvan, Ire. I5 12
Dungeness, c., Eng., U.K. K13 12
Dungog, Austl. I8 76
Dungu, D.R.C. D5 66
Dungun, Malay. J6 48
Dunhua, China C8 38
Dunhuang, China C3 36
Dunilovo, Russia C21 10
Dunkerque (Dunkirk), Fr. C11 14
Dunkirk see Dunkerque, Fr. C11 14
Dunkirk, In., U.S. H4 112
Dunkirk, N.Y., U.S. B6 114
Dunkirk, Oh., U.S. D2 114
Dunkwa, Ghana H4 64
Dún Laoghaire, Ire. H6 12
Dunlap, Tn., U.S. B13 122
Dunmore, Pa., U.S. C10 114
Dunmore Town, Bah. K9 116
Dunn, N.C., U.S. A7 116
Dunnellon, Fl., U.S. G3 116
Dunnet Head, c., Scot., U.K. C9 12
Dunning, Ne., U.S. F12 126
Dunnville, On., Can. F10 112
Dunoon, Scot., U.K. F8 12
Dunqulah, Sudan D5 62
Dunqunāb, Sudan C7 62
Duns, Scot., U.K. F10 12
Dunseith, N.D., U.S. F13 124
Dunsmuir, Ca., U.S. B3 134
Dunstable, Eng., U.K. J12 12
Dunster, B.C., Can. C11 138
Dunyāpur, Pak. D3 54
Duolun, China C2 38
Duolundabohuer, China B14 54
Duomula, China A9 54
Duozhu, China J6 42
Dupang Ling, mts., China I4 42
Dupnica, Blg. G10 26
Dupnitsa see Dupnica, Blg. G10 26
Dupuyer, Mt., U.S. B14 136
Duque Bacelar, Braz. C4 88
Duque de Caxias, Braz. L4 88
Duque de York, Isla, i., Chile J1 90
Duran, N.M., U.S. G3 128
Durance, stm., Fr. F11 18
Durand, Il., U.S. B8 120
Durand, Wi., U.S. G7 118
Durand, Récif, rf., N. Cal. n17 79d
Durand Reef see Durand, Récif, rf., N. Cal. n17 79d
Durango, Mex. C6 100
Durango, Spain A8 20
Durango, Co., U.S. F9 132
Durango, state, Mex. C6 100
Durant, Ia., U.S. C6 120
Durant, Ms., U.S. D9 122
Durant, Ok., U.S. D2 122
Duras, Fr. E6 18
Durazno, Ur. F9 92
Durban, S. Afr. F10 70
Đurđevac, Cro. D14 22
Düren, Ger. F2 16
Durg, India H8 54
Durgāpur, India G11 54
Durham, On., Can. D9 112
Durham, Eng., U.K. G11 12
Durham, Ca., U.S. D4 134
Durham, N.H., U.S. G5 110
Durham, N.C., U.S. H6 114
Durham Downs, Austl. F3 76
Durham Heights, mtn., N.T., Can. A6 106
Durlas éile see Thurles, Ire. I5 12
Durlești, Mol. B15 26
Durmitor, mtn., Yugo. F5 26
Durmitor Nacionalni Park, p.o.i., Yugo. F6 26
Dürnkrut, Aus. B13 22
Durrës, Alb. C13 24
Durrësi see Durrës, Alb. C13 24
Durrie, Austl. E3 76
Dursunbey, Tur. D11 28
Duru Gölü, l., Tur. B11 28
Durūz, Jabal ad-, mtn., Syria F7 58
D'Urville, Tanjung, c., Indon. F10 44
D'Urville Island, i., N.Z. E5 80
Dušak, Turkmen. B9 56
Dusa Marreb see Dhuusamarreeb, Som. C9 66
Dušanbe, Taj. B10 56
Dušekan, Russia B19 32
Dusetos, Lith. E8 10
Dushan, China I2 42
Du Shan, mtn., China A8 42
Dushanzi, China C1 36
Duson, La., U.S. G6 122
Düsseldorf, Ger. E2 16
Dustin, Ok., U.S. B2 122
Dutch John, Ut., U.S. C7 132
Dutton, Mt., U.S. C15 136
Dutton, stm., Austl. C4 76
Duvno, Bos. F4 26
Duxun, China J7 42
Duyfken Point, c., Austl. B8 74
Duyun, China H2 42
Düzce, Tur. C14 28
Dve Mogili, Blg. F12 26
Dvine, ozero, l., Russia D14 10
Dvinskaja guba, b., Russia D17 8
Dvuh Cirkov, gora, mtn., Russia C22 34
Dvůr Králové nad Labem, Czech Rep. F11 16
Dwārka, India G2 54
Dwight, Il., U.S. C9 120
Dworshak Reservoir, res., Id., U.S. D11 136
Dwyka, stm., S. Afr. H5 70
Dyer, Tn., U.S. H8 120
Dyer, Cape, c., Nu., Can. D13 141
Dyer Bay, b., On., Can. C8 112
Dyersburg, Tn., U.S. H8 120
Dyje (Thaya), stm., Eur. H12 16
Dyment, On., Can. B6 118
Dynów, Pol. G18 16
Dysart, Sk., Can. D9 124
Dysart, Ia., U.S. B5 120
Dysna (Dzisna), stm., Eur. E9 10
Dytikí Elláda, state, Grc. E4 28
Dytikí Makedonía, state, Grc. C4 28
Džagdy, hrebet, mts., Russia F15 34
Džalal-Abad, Kyrg. F12 32
Džalinda, Russia F13 34
Džambejty, Kaz. D8 32
Džanybek, Kaz. E7 32
Dzaoudzi, May. C8 68
Džardžan, Russia C13 34
Dzavhan, stm., Mong. B3 36
Dzeržinsk, Russia H20 8
Dzeržinskoe, Russia C16 32
Džetygara, Kaz. D10 32
Dzhankoi, Ukr. E4 32
Dzhugdzhur Mountains see Džugdžur, hrebet, mts., Russia E16 34
Dzhungarian Alatau Mountains, mts., Asia E14 32
Działoszyce, Pol. F16 16
Dzibilchaltún, hist., Mex. B3 102
Dzierżoniów, Pol. F12 16
Dzilam González, Mex. B3 102
Dzisna, Bela. E11 10
Dzisna (Dysna), stm., Eur. E9 10
Dzitbalché, Mex. B2 102
Dziwnów, Pol. B10 16
Džizak, Uzb. F11 32
Dzjarėčyn, Bela. G7 10
Dzjaršynskaja, hara, hill, Bela. G9 10
Dzjaržynsk, Bela. G9 10
Dzjatlavičy, Bela. H9 10
Dzöölön, Mong. F8 34
Džugdžur, hrebet, mts., Russia E16 34
Dzūkijos nacionalinis parkas, p.o.i., Lith. F7 10
Dzungarian Basin see Junggar Pendi, bas., China B2 36
Dzungarian Gate, p., Asia E14 32
Džusaly, Kaz. E10 32
Dzüünharaa, Mong. B6 36
Dzuunmod, Mong. B6 36
Dzyhivka, Ukr. A15 26

E

Eads, Co., U.S. C6 128
Eagle, Ak., U.S. D11 140
Eagle, Co., U.S. D10 132
Eagle, stm., Co., U.S. B2 128
Eagle Bay, B.C., Can. F11 138
Eagle Butte, S.D., U.S. C11 126
Eagle Creek, stm., Sk., Can. B6 124
Eagle Grove, Ia., U.S. B4 120
Eaglehawk, Austl. K4 76
Eagle Lake, Tx., U.S. H2 122
Eagle Lake, l., On., Can. B5 118
Eagle Lake, l., Ca., U.S. C5 134
Eagle Lake, l., Me., U.S. D7 110
Eagle Mountain, Ca., U.S. J1 132
Eagle Mountain, mtn., Id., U.S. D11 136
Eagle Mountain, mtn., Mn., U.S. D8 118
Eagle Mountain Lake, res., Tx., U.S. A10 130
Eagle Pass, Tx., U.S. F7 130
Eagle Peak, mtn., Ca., U.S. B5 134
Eagle River, Mi., U.S. D10 118
Eagle River, Wi., U.S. F9 118
Eagletown, Ok., U.S. C4 122
Ear Falls, On., Can. A5 118
Earle, Ar., U.S. B8 122
Earl Grey, Sk., Can. D9 124
Earlham, Ia., U.S. C3 120
Earlimart, Ca., U.S. H6 134
Earlville, Il., U.S. C8 120
Early, Ia., U.S. B2 120
Early, Tx., U.S. C9 130
Eas, Vanuatu k17 79d
Easley, S.C., U.S. B3 116
East Alton, Il., U.S. F7 120
East Angus, Qc., Can. E5 110
East Antarctica, reg., Ant. C8 81
East Aurora, N.Y., U.S. B7 114
East Bay, b., Tx., U.S. H4 122
East Bend, N.C., U.S. H5 114
East Bernard, Tx., U.S. H2 122
East Bernstadt, Ky., U.S. G1 114
East Borneo see Kalimantan Timur, state, Indon. C10 50
Eastbourne, Eng., U.K. K13 12
East Brady, Pa., U.S. D6 114
East Brewton, Al., U.S. F11 122
East Cache Creek, stm., Ok., U.S. G10 128
East Caicos, i., T./C. Is. B12 102
East Cape, c., N.Z. C8 80
East Cape, c., Fl., U.S. K4 116
East Carbon, Ut., U.S. D6 132
East Caroline Basin, unds. I17 142
East Chicago, In., U.S. G2 112
East China Sea, Asia F9 36
East Cote Blanche Bay, b., La., U.S. H7 122
East Coulee, Ab., Can. E18 138
East Dereham, Eng., U.K. I13 12
East Dismal Swamp, sw., N.C., U.S. A9 116
East Dubuque, Il., U.S. B7 120
East Ely, Nv., U.S. D2 132
East End, V.I.U.S. e8 104b
Easter Island see Pascua, Isla de, i., Chile f30 78l
Eastern Cape, state, S. Afr. G8 70
Eastern Channel see Tsushima-kaikyō, strt., Japan F2 40
Eastern Creek, stm., Austl. C3 76
Eastern Desert see Arabian Desert, des., Egypt B6 62
Eastern Division, state, Fiji q20 79e
Eastern Ghāts, mts., India E4 53
Eastern Point, c., Guad. A1 105a
Eastern Sayans see Vostočnyj Sajan, mts., Russia D17 32
East Falkland, i., Falk. Is. J5 90
East Fayetteville, N.C., U.S. A7 116
East Frisian Islands see Ostfriesische Inseln, is., Ger. C3 16
East Gaffney, S.C., U.S. A4 116
East Germany see Germany, ctry., Eur. E6 16
East Glacier Park, Mt., U.S. B13 136
East Grand Forks, Mn., U.S. D2 118
East Grand Rapids, Mi., U.S. F4 112
East Grinstead, Eng., U.K. J12 12
Easthampton, Ma., U.S. B13 114
East Java see Jawa Timur, state, Indon. G8 50
East Jordan, Mi., U.S. C4 112
East Kelowna, B.C., Can. G11 138
East Kilbride, Scot., U.K. F8 12
Eastlake, Mi., U.S. D3 112
Eastlake, Oh., U.S. C4 114
Eastland, Tx., U.S. B9 130
East Lansing, Mi., U.S. B1 114
East Laurinburg, N.C., U.S. B6 116
Eastleigh, Eng., U.K. K11 12
East Liverpool, Oh., U.S. D5 114
East London (Oos-Londen), S. Afr. H9 70
Eastmain, Qc., Can. E15 106
Eastmain, stm., Qc., Can. E15 106
Eastmain-Opinaca, Réservoir, res., Qc., Can. E15 106
Eastman, Ga., U.S. D2 116
East Mariana Basin, unds. H18 142
East Matagorda Bay, b., Tx., U.S. F11 130
East Missoula, Mt., U.S. D13 136
East Moline, Il., U.S. C7 120
East Naples, Fl., U.S. J4 116
East Nishnabotna, stm., Ia., U.S. C2 120
East Nusa Tenggara see Nusa Tenggara Timur, state, Indon. H12 50
East Olympia, Wa., U.S. D3 136
Easton, Md., U.S. F9 114
Easton, Pa., U.S. D10 114
East Pacific Rise, unds. N27 142
East Palatka, Fl., U.S. G4 116
East Pecos, N.M., U.S. F3 128
East Peoria, Il., U.S. D8 120
Eastpoint, Fl., U.S. H14 122
East Point, Ga., U.S. D14 122
East Point, c., P.E., Can. D15 110
East Point, c., V.I.U.S. g11 104c
Eastport, Id., U.S. B10 136
Eastport, Me., U.S. F9 110
East Prairie, Mo., U.S. H8 120
East Prairie, stm., Ab., Can. A14 138
East Pryor Mountain, mtn., Mt., U.S. B4 126
East Retford, Eng., U.K. H12 12
East Saint Louis, Il., U.S. F7 120
East Sea (Japan, Sea of), Asia D11 38
East Shoal Lake, l., Mb., Can. D16 124
East Siberian Sea see Vostočno-Sibirskoe more, Russia B20 34
East Sister Island, i., Austl. L6 76
East Slovakia see Východoslovenský Kraj, state, Slov. H17 16
East Stroudsburg, Pa., U.S. D11 114
East Troy, Wi., U.S. B9 120
Eastville, Va., U.S. G10 114
East Wenatchee, Wa., U.S. C6 136
East Wilmington, N.C., U.S. B8 116
Eaton, In., U.S. H4 112
Eaton, Oh., U.S. E1 114
Eaton Rapids, Mi., U.S. B1 114
Eatonton, Ga., U.S. C2 116
Eatonville, Wa., U.S. D4 136
Eau Claire, Wi., U.S. G7 118
Eau Claire, Lac à l', l., Qc., Can. D16 106
Eauripik, at., Micron. C5 72
Eauripik Rise, unds. I17 142
Eauze, Fr. F6 18
Ebano, Mex. D9 100
Ebb and Flow Lake, l., Mb., Can. D14 124
Ebbw Vale, Wales, U.K. J9 12
Ebebiyín, Eq. Gui. I7 64
Eben Junction, Mi., U.S. B2 112
Ebensee, Aus. C10 22
Eberbach, Ger. G4 16
Eber Gölü, l., Tur. E14 28
Ebern, Ger. F6 16
Ebersbach, Ger. E10 16
Eberswalde-Finow, Ger. D9 16
Ebetsu, Japan C14 38
Ebino, Japan G3 40
Ebinur Hu, l., China F14 32
Eboli, Italy D9 24
Ebolowa, Cam. D2 66
Ebon, at., Marsh. Is. C7 72
Ebre see Ebro, stm., Spain C11 20
Ebre, Delta de l', Spain D11 20
Ebro (Ebre), stm., Spain C11 20
Ebro, Delta del see Ebre, Delta de l', Spain D11 20
Ebro, Embalse del, res., Spain B7 20
Eceabat, Tur. C9 28
Ech Cheliff, Alg. B5 64
Echeng, China E7 36
Echínos, Grc. B7 28
Echt, Neth. E1 16
Echuca, Austl. K5 76
Écija, Spain G5 20
Eckernförde, Ger. B5 16
Eckerö, i., Fin. F8 8
Eckville, Ab., Can. D16 138
Eclectic, Al., U.S. E12 122
Eclipse Sound, strt., Nu., Can. A14 106
Ecoporanga, Braz. J5 88
Écorce, Lac de l', res., Qc., Can. B13 112
Écrins, Barre des, mtn., Fr. E12 18
Écrins, Massif des, plat., Fr. E12 18
Ecru, Ms., U.S. C9 122
Ecuador, ctry., S.A. D2 84
Ed, Swe. G4 8
Edam, Sk., Can. A5 124
Eddrachillis Bay, b., Scot., U.K. C7 12
Eddystone Rocks, r., Eng., U.K. K8 12
Eddyville, Ia., U.S. C5 120
Eddyville, Ky., U.S. G9 120
Ede, Neth. B14 14
Ede, Nig. H5 64
Edéa, Cam. D2 66
Edehon Lake, l., Nu., Can. C11 106
Edelény, Hung. A7 26
Eden, Austl. K7 76
Eden, Ms., U.S. D8 122
Eden, N.C., U.S. H6 114
Eden, Wy., U.S. A7 132
Eden, stm., Eng., U.K. G10 12
Edendale, S. Afr. F10 70
Eden Valley, Mn., U.S. F4 118
Edenville, S. Afr. E8 70
Eder, stm., Ger. E4 16
Édessa, Grc. C4 28
Edfu, Egypt C6 62
Edgar, Ne., U.S. G14 126
Edgar, Wi., U.S. G8 118
Edgard, La., U.S. H8 122
Edgartown, Ma., U.S. C15 114
Edgeley, N.D., U.S. A14 126
Edgell Island, i., Grnld. E13 141
Edgemont, S.D., U.S. D9 126
Edgeøya, i., Nor. B30 141
Edgeroi, Austl. H7 76
Edgerton, Ab., Can. B3 124
Edgerton, Mn., U.S. H2 118
Edgerton, Oh., U.S. C1 114
Edgerton, Wi., U.S. B8 120
Edgewater, Fl., U.S. H5 116
Edgewood, Il., U.S. F9 120
Edgewood, Ia., U.S. B6 120
Edgewood, Md., U.S. E9 114
Edgewood, Tx., U.S. E3 122
Edina, Mn., U.S. G5 118
Edina, Mo., U.S. D5 120
Edinburg, Il., U.S. E8 120
Edinburg, In., U.S. E11 120
Edinburg, Ms., U.S. E9 122
Edinburg, Tx., U.S. H9 130
Edinburg, Va., U.S. F7 114
Edinburgh, Scot., U.K. F9 12
Edincik, Tur. C10 28
Edineț, Mol. A14 26
Edirne, Tur. B9 28
Edirne, state, Tur. B9 28
Edison, Ga., U.S. F14 122
Edisto, stm., S.C., U.S. D5 116
Edisto, North Fork, stm., S.C., U.S. C4 116
Edisto Island, i., S.C., U.S. D5 116
Edith, Mount, mtn., Mt., U.S. D15 136
Edith Cavell, Mount, mtn., Ab., Can. D12 138
Edjeleh, Alg. D6 64
Edmond, Ok., U.S. F11 128
Edmonds, Wa., U.S. C4 136
Edmonton, Austl. A5 76
Edmonton, Ab., Can. C17 138
Edmonton, Ky., U.S. G12 120
Edmore, N.D., U.S. F15 124
Edmundston, N.B., Can. C8 110
Edna, Ks., U.S. G2 120
Edna, Tx., U.S. E11 130
Edremit, Tur. D10 28
Edremit Körfezi, b., Tur. D9 28
Edrovo, Russia C16 10
Edson, Ab., Can. C14 138
Eduardo Castex, Arg. G5 92
Eduni, Mount, mtn., N.T., Can. C5 106
Edward, stm., Austl. J5 76
Edward, Lake, l., Afr. E5 66
Edward Island, i., On., Can. C10 118
Edwards, Ms., U.S. E8 122
Edwards Air Force Base, Ca., U.S. I8 134
Edwards Plateau, plat., Tx., U.S. D7 130
Edwardsville, Il., U.S. F8 120
Edward VII Peninsula, pen., Ant. C25 81
Eek, Ak., U.S. D7 140
Eeklo, Bel. C12 14
Eel, stm., Ca., U.S. D2 134
Eel, stm., In., U.S. G4 112
Eel, stm., In., U.S. E10 120
Eems (Ems), stm., Eur. A16 14
Éfaté, state, Vanuatu k17 79d
Éfaté, i., Vanuatu k17 79d
Eferding, Aus. B10 22
Efes (Ephesus), hist., Tur. F10 28
Effigy Mounds National Monument, p.o.i., Ia., U.S. A6 120
Effingham, Il., U.S. E9 120
Effingham, Ks., U.S. E2 120
Eflâni, Tur. B15 28
Eforie Nord, Rom. E15 26
Eforie Sud, Rom. F15 26
Efremov, Russia G20 10
Eg, stm., Mong. F9 34
Egadi, Isole, is., Italy G5 24
Egaña, Arg. H8 92
Egan Range, mts., Nv., U.S. D2 132
Egedesminde (Aasiaat), Grnld. D15 141
Egegik, Ak., U.S. E8 140
Eger, Hung. B7 26
Egersund, Nor. G1 8
Eggenfelden, Ger. H8 16
Egg Harbor City, N.J., U.S. E11 114
Égletons, Fr. D7 18
Egmont, Cape, c., N.Z. D5 80
Egmont, Mount see Taranaki, Mount, vol., N.Z. D6 80
Egmont Bay, b., P.E., Can. D12 110
Egmont National Park, p.o.i., N.Z. D5 80
Egorevsk, Russia E22 10
Egremont, Ab., Can. B17 138
Eğridir, Tur. F13 28
Eğridir Gölü, l., Tur. E13 28
Éguas, stm., Braz. G3 88
Egvekinot, Russia C25 34
Egypt, ctry., Afr. B5 62
Eha-Amufu, Nig. H6 64
Ehime, state, Japan F5 40
Ehingen, Ger. H5 16
Ehrhardt, S.C., U.S. C4 116
Eibar, Spain A8 20
Eibiswald, Aus. D12 22
Eichstätt, Ger. H7 16
Eidsvold, Austl. E8 76
Eifel, mts., Ger. F2 16
Eigg, i., Scot., U.K. E6 12
Eight Degree Channel, strt., Asia h12 46a
Eights Coast, cst., Ant. C31 81
Eighty Mile Beach, cst., Austl. C4 74
Eildon, Austl. K5 76
Eildon, Lake, res., Austl. K5 76
Eilenburg, Ger. E8 16
Eiler Rasmussen, Kap, c., Grnld. A21 141
Einasleigh, Austl. B5 76
Einasleigh, stm., Austl. A4 76
Einbeck, Ger. E5 16
Eindhoven, Neth. C14 14
Einme, Mya. D2 48
Eirunepé, Braz. E4 84
Eiseb, stm., Afr. B4 70
Eisenach, Ger. E6 16
Eisenberg, Ger. F7 16
Eisenerz, Aus. C11 22
Eisenhüttenstadt, Ger. D10 16
Eisenstadt, Aus. C13 22
Eisfeld, Ger. F6 16
Eišiškės, Lith. F7 10
Eislingen, Ger. H5 16
Eitorf, Ger. F3 16
Eivissa (Iviza), Spain F12 20
Eivissa (Ibiza), i., Spain F12 20
Ejea de los Caballeros, Spain B9 20
Ejeda, Madag. E7 68
Ejido Jaboncillos, Mex. A7 100
Ejin Horo Qi, China B3 42
Ejin Qi, China C5 36
Ejsk, Russia E5 32
Ejura, Ghana H4 64
Ejutla de Crespo, Mex. G10 100
Ekaterinburg, Russia C10 32
Ekaterinino, Russia E16 10
Ekateriny, proliv, strt., Russia B17 38
Ekenäs see Tammisaari, Fin. G10 8
Ekibastuz, Kaz. D13 32
Ekimčan, Russia F15 34
Ekonda, Russia C10 34
Ekwan, stm., On., Can. E14 106
Ela, Mya. C3 48
El Aaiún (Laayoune), W. Sah. D2 64
El 'Açâba, plat., Maur. F2 64
El Affroun, Alg. H13 20
El Agreb, Alg. C6 64
El Ahijadero, Cerro, mtn., Mex. E1 130
Elaine, Ar., U.S. C8 122
El-'Aiyât, Egypt I2 58
El-Alamein, Egypt A5 62
El Álamo, Mex. G7 130
El Álamo, Mex. H8 130
El Álamo, Mex. L9 134
El Alto, Arg. D5 92
Elan', Russia D6 32
Elancy, Russia F10 34
El Ángel, Ec. G2 86
El-Arish, Egypt G4 58
Elat, Isr. I5 58

Name — **Map Ref.** — **Page**

Elat, Gulf of see Aqaba, Gulf of, b. J5 58
El Ávila, Parque Nacional, p.o.i., Ven. B8 86
Elazığ, Tur. B4 56
Elba, Isola d', i., Italy H7 22
El-Badâri, Egypt K2 58
El-Bahnasa, Egypt J1 58
El-Balyana, Egypt B6 62
El'ban, Russia F16 34
El Banco, Col. C4 86
El Barco de Ávila, Spain D5 20
Elbasan, Alb. C13 24
Elbasani see Elbasan, Alb. C13 24
El Baúl, Ven. C7 86
El Baúl, Cerro, mtn., Mex. G11 100
Elbe (Labe), stm., Eur. C5 16
Elbe-Havel-Kanal, can., Ger. D8 16
Elbert, Co., U.S. B4 128
Elbert, Mount, mtn., Co., U.S. D10 132
Elberta, Mi., U.S. D3 112
Elberton, Ga., U.S. B3 116
Elbeuf, Fr. E10 14
Elbeyli, Tur. B8 58
El Beyyadh, Alg. C5 64
Elbląg, Pol. B15 16
Elbląg, state, Pol. B15 16
El Bluff, Nic. G6 102
El Bonillo, Spain F8 20
El Boulaïda, Alg. B5 64
Elbow, stm., Ab., Can. E16 138
Elbow Lake, Mn., U.S. E3 118
El'brus, gora, mtn., Russia F6 32
Elbrus, Mount see El'brus, gora, mtn., Russia F6 32
El-Burg, Egypt G1 58
El-Burgâya, Egypt J1 58
Elburs see Alborz, Reshteh-ye Kūhhā-ye, mts., Iran B7 56
Elburz Mountains see Alborz, Reshteh-ye Kūhhā-ye, mts., Iran B7 56
El Cadilla, Embalse, res., Arg. C5 92
El Cajon, Ca., U.S. K9 134
El Calafate, Arg. J2 90
El Callao, Ven. D11 86
El Calvario, Ven. C8 86
El Campamento, P.R. B3 104a
El Campo, Tx., U.S. H2 122
El Capitan, mtn., Mt., U.S. D12 136
El Carmen, Arg. B5 92
El Carmen, Col. C5 86
El Carmen, stm., Mex. F9 98
El Carmen de Bolívar, Col. C4 86
El Carricito, Mex. A7 100
El Carril, Arg. B5 92
El Centinela, Mex. K10 134
El Centro, Ca., U.S. K10 134
El Cerrito, Col. F3 86
El Cerro Del Aripo, mtn., Trin. s12 105f
Elche see Elx, Spain F10 20
El Chile, Montaña, mtn., Nic. E4 102
Elcho, Wi., U.S. F9 118
Elcho Island, i., Austl. B7 74
El Cocuy, Col. D5 86
El Colorado, Arg. C8 92
El Cóndor, Cerro, vol., Arg. C3 92
El Corazón, Ec. H2 86
El Corpus, Hond. F4 102
El Coto, P.R. B2 104a
El'cy, Russia D16 10
Elda, Spain F10 20
El Desemboque, Mex. G6 98
El Desemboque, Mex. F6 98
El'dikan, Russia D16 34
El-Dilingât, Egypt H1 58
El Diviso, Col. G2 86
El Djazaïr (Algiers), Alg. B5 64
El Djelfa, Alg. C5 64
Eldon, Ia., U.S. D5 120
Eldora, Ia., U.S. B4 120
Eldorado, Arg. C10 92
Eldorado, Braz. B13 92
El Dorado, Ar., U.S. D6 122
Eldorado, Il., U.S. G9 120
El Dorado, Ks., U.S. D12 128
Eldorado, Ok., U.S. G9 128
El Dorado, Ven. D11 86
El Dorado Springs, Mo., U.S. G3 120
Eldoret, Kenya D7 66
Eldred, Pa., U.S. C7 114
Eldridge, Ia., U.S. C7 120
Eleanor, W.V., U.S. F3 114
Elec, Russia H21 10
Electric City, Wa., U.S. C7 136
Elefantes (Olifants), stm., Afr. D10 70
Elefsína, Grc. E6 28
Eleftheroúpoli, Grc. C7 28
Elektrostal', Russia E21 10
Elena, Blg. G12 26
El Encanto, Col. H5 86
Elephant Butte Reservoir, res., N.M., U.S. J9 132
Elephant Mountain, mtn., Me., U.S. F6 110
Elesbão Veloso, Braz. D4 88
El Estor, Guat. E3 102
Eleuthera, i., Bah. B9 96
Eleva, Wi., U.S. G7 118
Eleven Point, stm., U.S. H6 120
El Fahs, Tun. H3 24
El Faro, P.R. C2 104a
El-Fashn, Egypt J1 58
El-Fayoum, Egypt I1 58
El Ferrol del Caudillo see Ferrol, Spain A2 20
El-Fiqriya, Egypt K1 58
Elfrida, Az., U.S. L7 132
El Fuerte, Mex. B4 100
El Galpón, Arg. B5 92
Elgin, Scot., U.K. D9 12
Elgin, Il., U.S. B9 120
Elgin, Ia., U.S. B6 120
Elgin, Mn., U.S. G6 118
Elgin, Ne., U.S. F14 126
Elgin, N.D., U.S. A11 126
Elgin, Ok., U.S. G10 128
Elgin, Or., U.S. E8 136
El-Gindîya, Egypt J1 58
El-Gîza (Giza), Egypt H1 58
Elgon, Mount, mtn., Afr. D6 66
El Grara, Alg. C5 64
El Grove see O Grove, Spain B2 20
El Guaje, Mex. A7 100
El Guamo, Col. B4 86
El Guapo, Ven. B9 86
El Hachero, Cerro, mtn., Mex. H2 130
El Ḥammâmi, reg., Maur. E2 64
El-Hamûl, Egypt G2 58
El Ḥank, clf, Afr. E3 64
El-Hawâmdîya, Egypt I2 58
Elhovo, Blg. G13 26
El Huisache, Mex. D8 100
Eliase, Indon. G9 44
Elida, N.M., U.S. H5 128
Elila, stm., D.R.C. E5 66
Elim, Ak., U.S. D7 140
Elisenvaara, Russia F13 8
Eliseu Martins, Braz. E4 88
El-Iskandarîya (Alexandria), Egypt A6 62
Elista, Russia E6 32
Elizabeth, Austl. J2 76
Elizabeth, Co., U.S. B4 128
Elizabeth, Il., U.S. B7 120
Elizabeth, N.J., U.S. D11 114
Elizabeth, W.V., U.S. E4 114
Elizabeth City, N.C., U.S. H9 114
Elizabethton, Tn., U.S. H3 114
Elizabethtown, Il., U.S. G9 120
Elizabethtown, Ky., U.S. G11 120
Elizabethtown, N.Y., U.S. F3 110
Elizabethtown, Pa., U.S. D9 114
Elizavety, mys, c., Russia F17 34
Elizovo, Russia F20 34
El-Jadida, Mor. C3 64
El Jaralito, Mex. B6 100
El Jebel, Co., U.S. D9 132
Ełk, Pol. C18 16
Elk, stm., B.C., Can. F16 138
Elk, stm., U.S. C12 122
Elk, stm., Ks., U.S. D12 128
Elk, stm., W.V., U.S. F4 114
Elkader, Ia., U.S. B6 120
Elk City, Ok., U.S. F9 128
Elk Creek, Ca., U.S. D3 134
Elk Creek, stm., S.D., U.S. C10 126
El Kef, Tun. H2 24
El-Kelaa-Srarhna, Mor. C3 64
Ēl Kerē, Eth. F8 62
Elk Grove, Ca., U.S. E4 134
El-Khânka, Egypt H2 58
El-Khârga, Egypt B6 62
Elkhart, In., U.S. G4 112
Elkhart, Ks., U.S. D7 128
Elkhart, Tx., U.S. F3 122
El Khnâchîch, clf, Mali E4 64
Elkhorn, Mb., Can. D12 124
Elk Horn, Ia., U.S. C2 120
Elkhorn, Wi., U.S. B9 120
Elkhorn, stm., Ne., U.S. F16 126
Elkhorn City, Ky., U.S. G3 114
Elkhorn Mountain, mtn., B.C., Can. G4 138
Elkhovo see Elhovo, Blg. G13 26
Elkins, W.V., U.S. F6 114
Elk Island, i., Mb., Can. D17 124
Elk Island National Park, p.o.i., Ab., Can. C18 138
Elkland, Pa., U.S. C8 114
Elk Mountain, mtn., Wy., U.S. B10 132
Elko, B.C., Can. G15 138
Elko, Nv., U.S. C1 132
Elk Point, Ab., Can. C19 138
Elk Point, S.D., U.S. B1 120
Elk Rapids, Mi., U.S. D4 112
Elk River, Mn., U.S. F5 118
Elkton, Md., U.S. E10 114
Elkton, Mi., U.S. E6 112
Elkton, S.D., U.S. G2 118
Elkton, Va., U.S. F7 114
Ellaville, Ga., U.S. D1 116
Ellef Ringnes Island, i., Nu., Can. B5 141
Ellen, Mount, mtn., Ut., U.S. E6 132
Ellendale, Mn., U.S. H5 118
Ellendale, N.D., U.S. A14 126
Ellensburg, Wa., U.S. C6 136
Ellenton, Ga., U.S. E2 116
Ellesmere, Lake, l., N.Z. F5 80
Ellesmere Island, i., Nu., Can. B9 141
Ellettsville, In., U.S. E11 120
Ellice, stm., Nu., Can. B10 106
Ellice Islands see Tuvalu, ctry., Oc. D8 72
Ellicottville, N.Y., U.S. B7 114
Ellijay, Ga., U.S. B1 116
Ellinwood, Ks., U.S. C10 128
Elliot, S. Afr. G8 70
Elliot, Mount, mtn., Austl. B6 76
Elliot Lake, On., Can. B7 112
Elliot Lake, l., Mb., Can. B18 124
Elliott, Ia., U.S. C2 120
Elliott, Ms., U.S. D9 122
Ellisras, S. Afr. C8 70
Elliston, Austl. F6 74
Elliston, Mt., U.S. D14 136
Ellisville, Ms., U.S. F9 122
Ellon, Scot., U.K. D10 12
Ellora, India H5 54
Ellora Caves, hist., India A2 53
Elloree, S.C., U.S. C5 116
Ellsworth, Ks., U.S. C10 128
Ellsworth, Me., U.S. F8 110
Ellsworth, Mi., U.S. C4 112
Ellsworth, Mn., U.S. H3 118
Ellsworth, Wi., U.S. G6 118
Ellsworth Land, reg., Ant. C32 81
Ellsworth Mountains, mts., Ant. C32 81
El Lucero, Mex. I4 130
Ellwangen, Ger. H5 16
Ellwood City, Pa., U.S. D5 114
Elm, stm., U.S. B14 126
Elma, Wa., U.S. D3 136
El-Mahalla el-Kubra, Egypt H2 58
El-Maimûn, Egypt I2 58
Elmalı, Tur. G12 28
El Maneadero, Mex. L9 134
El-Mansûra, Egypt G2 58
El Manteco, Ven. D10 86
El-Manzala, Egypt G2 58
El-Matariya, Egypt G3 58
Elm Creek, Mb., Can. E16 124
Elm Creek, Ne., U.S. G13 126
El Médano, Mex. C3 100
El Menia, Alg. C5 64
Elmer, N.J., U.S. E10 114
Elmhurst, Il., U.S. G2 112
El-Minya (Minya), Egypt J1 58
Elmira, On., Can. E9 112
Elmira, P.E., Can. D14 110
Elmira, N.Y., U.S. B9 114
El Moral, Mex. F7 130
Elmore, Austl. K5 76
Elmore, Mn., U.S. H4 118
Elmore, Oh., U.S. C2 114
Elmore City, Ok., U.S. G11 128
El Morro, hist., P.R. B3 104a
El Morro National Monument, p.o.i., N.M., U.S. H8 132
El Mreyyé, reg., Maur. F3 64
Elmshorn, Ger. C5 16
Elm Springs, Ar., U.S. H3 120
El Mulato, Mex. E3 130
El-Mutî'a, Egypt K2 58
Elmvale, On., Can. D10 112
Elmwood, Il., U.S. K8 118
Elmwood, Ne., U.S. K2 118
El Negrito, Hond. E4 102
Elnora, Ab., Can. D17 138
Elnora, In., U.S. F10 120
Eloguj, stm., Russia B15 32
Eloise, Fl., U.S. H4 116
Elora, On., Can. E9 112
Elorza, Ven. D7 86
El Otate, Cerro, mtn., Mex. F1 130
Èloten, Turkmen. B9 56
Eloy, Az., U.S. K5 132
Eloy Alfaro, Ec. I2 86
El Palmar, Ven. D10 86
El Palmar de los Sepúlveda, Mex. C5 100
El Palmito, Mex. I8 130
El Palqui, Chile E2 92
El Pao, Ven. C7 86
El Paso, Il., U.S. D8 120
El Paso, Tx., U.S. L10 132
El Paso de Robles see Paso Robles, Ca., U.S. H5 134
El Paso Peaks, mtn., Ca., U.S. H8 134
El Perú, Ven. D11 86
Elphinstone, Mb., Can. D13 124
El Piñón, Col. B4 86
El Pintado, Arg. B7 92
El Pital, Cerro, mtn., N.A. E3 102
El Planchón, Volcán (Planchón, Cerro del), vol., S.A. G2 92
El Polvorín, P.R. B3 104a
El Portal, Ca., U.S. F6 134
El Porvenir, Mex. G3 130
El Porvenir, Mex. K9 134
El Porvenir, Pan. H8 102
El Potrero, Mex. H7 130
El Potro, Cerro (Potro, Cerro del), mtn., S.A. D3 92
El Prat de Llobregat, Spain C12 20
El Progreso, Hond. E4 102
El Puerto de Santa María, Spain H4 20
El Puesto, Arg. C4 92
El-Qâhira (Cairo), Egypt H2 58
El-Qantara el-Sharqîya, Egypt H3 58
El-Qasr, Egypt B5 62
El Quebrachal, Arg. B5 92
El Quelite, Mex. D5 100
Elqui, stm., Chile D2 92
El-Qûsîya, Egypt K1 58
El Real de Santa María, Pan. H9 102
El Remolino, Mex. F6 130
El Reno, Ok., U.S. F10 128
El Rio, Ca., U.S. I6 134
El Roble, Mesa, mtn., Mex. L10 134
Elroy, Wi., U.S. H8 118
Elsa, Yk., Can. C3 106
Elsa, Tx., U.S. H9 130
El-Saff, Egypt I2 58
El-Sa'îd (Upper Egypt), hist. reg., Egypt J2 58
El Salado, Chile C2 92
El Salado, Parque Nacional, p.o.i., Ec. I1 86
El Salto, Mex. D6 100
El Salvador, Chile C3 92
El Salvador, ctry., N.A. F3 102
El Samán de Apure, Ven. D7 86
El Sauz, Mex. A5 100
El Sauzal, Mex. L9 134
Elsberry, Mo., U.S. E7 120
El Seibo, Dom. Rep. C13 102
Elsen Nur, l., China D3 36
El-Simbillawein, Egypt H2 58
Elsinore see Helsingør, Den. H5 8
Elsinore, Ut., U.S. E4 132
El Sombrero, Ven. C8 86
Elsterwerda, Ger. E9 16
El Sueco, Mex. E1 130
El-Suweis (Suez), Egypt I3 58
El Tajín, hist., Mex. E10 100
El Tala, Arg. C5 92
El Tanque, Mex. H8 130
El Tecuán, Mex. C5 100
El-Thamad, Egypt I5 58
El Tigre, Ven. C9 86
Eltmann, Ger. G6 16
El Toco, Chile D3 90
El Tocuyo, Ven. C7 86
Elton, La., U.S. G6 122
El Tránsito, Chile D2 92
El Trébol, Arg. F7 92
El Tule, Mex. G1 130
El Tuparro, Parque Nacional, p.o.i., Col. E7 86
El-Tûr, Egypt J4 58
El Turbio, Arg. J2 90
El-Uqsor (Luxor), Egypt B6 62
Elūru, India C5 53
El Valle, Pan. H7 102
Elvas, Port. F3 20
El Vendrell, Spain C12 20
Elverum, Nor. F4 8
El Viejo, Nic. F4 102
El Vigía, Ven. C6 86
El Vínculo, Ven. p20 104g
Elvira, Arg. G8 92
El Volcán, Chile F2 92
El Wad, Alg. C6 64
El-Wâsta, Egypt I2 58
Elwell, Lake, res., Mt., U.S. B15 136
Elwood, In., U.S. H4 112
Elwood, Ne., U.S. G13 126
Elx, Spain F10 20
Ely, Eng., U.K. I13 12
Ely, Mn., U.S. D7 118
Ely, Nv., U.S. D2 132
El Yagual, Ven. D7 86
Elyria, Oh., U.S. C3 114
El Yunque, mtn., P.R. B4 104a
El-Zarqa, Egypt G2 58
Émaé, i., Vanuatu k17 79d
Emajõgi, stm., Est. B9 10
Emāmshahr, Iran B8 56
Emba, Kaz. E9 32
Emba, stm., Kaz. E9 32
Embarras, stm., Il., U.S. F10 120
Embarrass, Wi., U.S. G10 118
Emborcação, Represa da, res., Braz. J2 88
Embreeville, Tn., U.S. H3 114
Embrun, Fr. E12 18
Embu, Kenya E7 66
Emca, stm., Russia E19 8
Emden, Ger. C3 16
Emden, Il., U.S. K9 118
Emelle, Al., U.S. E10 122
Emerado, N.D., U.S. G16 124
Emerald, Austl. D6 76
Emerson, Mb., Can. E16 124
Emerson, Ar., U.S. D5 122
Emerson, Ia., U.S. C2 120
Emery, S.D., U.S. D15 126
Emery, Ut., U.S. E5 132
Emet, Tur. D12 28
Emiliano Zapata, Mex. G13 100
Emilia-Romagna, state, Italy F8 22
Emin, China B1 36
Emine, nos, c., Blg. G14 26
Eminence, Mo., U.S. G6 120
Emirdağ, Tur. D14 28
Emır Dağları, mts., Tur. E14 28
Emita, Austl. m13 77a
Emlembe, mtn., Afr. D10 70
Emlenton, Pa., U.S. G10 112
Emmaste, Est. B5 10
Emmaus, Pa., U.S. D10 114
Emmaville, Austl. G8 76
Emmen, Neth. B15 14
Emmendingen, Ger. H3 16
Emmerich, Ger. E2 16
Emmet, Ar., U.S. D5 122
Emmetsburg, Ia., U.S. A3 120
Emmiganūru, India D3 53
Emmitsburg, Md., U.S. E8 114
Emmonak, Ak., U.S. D7 140
Emo, On., Can. C5 118
Emory Peak, mtn., Tx., U.S. E4 130
Empalme, Mex. A3 100
Empangeni, S. Afr. F10 70
Empedrado, Arg. C8 92
Emperor Seamounts, unds. E19 142
Empire, La., U.S. H9 122
Empire, Nv., U.S. C6 134
Empoli, Italy G7 22
Emporia, Ks., U.S. F1 120
Emporia, Va., U.S. H8 114
Emporium, Pa., U.S. C7 114
Empty Quarter see Ar-Rub' al-Khālī, des., Asia E6 56
Ems, stm., Eur. C3 16
Emsdetten, Ger. D3 16
Emu, China C8 38
Emu Park, Austl. D8 76
Enarotali, Indon. F10 44
Enašimskij Polkan, gora, mtn., Russia C16 32
Encampment, Wy., U.S. B10 132
Encantado, Braz. D11 92
Encarnación, Para. C9 92
Enchi, Ghana H4 64
Enchilayas, Mex. F6 98
Encinal, Tx., U.S. F8 130
Encinitas, Ca., U.S. J8 134
Encino, N.M., U.S. G3 128
Encontrados, Ven. C5 86
Encounter Bay, b., Austl. J2 76
Encruzilhada, Braz. H5 88
Encruzilhada do Sul, Braz. E11 92
Encs, Hung. A8 26
Endako, B.C., Can. B5 138
Ende, Indon. G7 44
Endeavor, Wi., U.S. H9 118
Endeavour Strait, strt., Austl. B8 74
Enderby, B.C., Can. F11 138
Enderby Land, reg., Ant. B10 81
Enderlin, N.D., U.S. A15 126
Endicott, N.Y., U.S. B9 114
Endicott, Wa., U.S. D9 136
Endicott Mountains, mts., Ak., U.S. C9 140
Ene, stm., Peru F3 84
Enewetak, at., Marsh. Is. B7 72
Enez, Tur. C9 28
Enfield, N.C., U.S. H8 114
Engaño, Cabo, c., Dom. Rep. C13 102
Engcobo, S. Afr. G9 70
Engelhard, N.C., U.S. A10 116
Engel's, Russia D7 32
Engen, B.C., Can. B6 138
Engenheiro Navarro, Braz. I3 88
Enggano, Pulau, i., Indon. F2 50
England, state, U.K. I12 12
Englefield, Cape, c., Nu., Can. B13 106
Englehart, On., Can. F15 106
Englewood, B.C., Can. F3 138
Englewood, Co., U.S. B4 128
Englewood, Fl., U.S. J3 116
Englewood, Ks., U.S. D8 128
Englewood, Tn., U.S. A1 116
English, stm., On., Can. A4 118
English Channel, strt., Eur. D7 14
English Coast, cst., Ant. C33 81
Engure, Lat. C6 10
Engures ezers, l., Lat. C6 10
Enid, Ok., U.S. E11 128
Enid Lake, res., Ms., U.S. C9 122
Enisej, stm., Russia C6 34
Enisejsk, Russia C16 32
Enisejskij krjaž, mts., Russia C16 32
Enisejskij zaliv, b., Russia B5 34
Eniwetok see Enewetak, at., Marsh. Is. B7 72
Enka, N.C., U.S. A3 116
Enkhuizen, Neth. B14 14
Enköping, Swe. G7 8
Enmedio, Mex. E4 130
Enmedio, Cerro de, mtn., Mex. F8 100
Enna, Italy G8 24
Ennadai Lake, l., Nu., Can. C10 106
Ennedi, plat., Chad D4 62
Ennis, Ire. I3 12
Ennis, Mt., U.S. E15 136
Ennis, Tx., U.S. E2 122
Enniscorthy, Ire. I6 12
Enniskillen, N. Ire., U.K. G5 12
Enns, Aus. B11 22
Enns, stm., Aus. B11 22
Enon, Oh., U.S. E2 114
Enontekiö, Fin. B10 8
Enoree, stm., S.C., U.S. B3 116
Enosburg Falls, Vt., U.S. F4 110
Enping, China J5 42
Enrekang, Indon. E11 50
Enrique Urien, Arg. C7 92
Enriquillo, Dom. Rep. D12 102
Enriquillo, Lago, l., Dom. Rep. C12 102
Enschede, Neth. B15 14
Ensenada, Arg. G9 92
Ensenada, Mex. L9 134
Enshi, China F3 42
Enshū-nada, Japan E10 40
Entebbe, Ug. D6 66
Enterprise, N.T., Can. C7 106
Enterprise, Al., U.S. F13 122
Enterprise, Ca., U.S. D4 134
Enterprise, Ms., U.S. E10 122
Enterprise, Or., U.S. E9 136
Enterprise, Ut., U.S. F3 132
Entrepeñas, Embalse de, res., Spain D8 20
Entre Ríos, Bol. D4 90
Entre Rios, Braz. G7 88
Entre Ríos, state, Arg. F8 92
Entrevaux, Fr. F12 18
Entroncamento, Port. E2 20
Entwistle, Ab., Can. C16 138
Enugu, Nig. H6 64
Enurmino, Russia C26 34
Envalira, Port d', p., And. B12 20
Envigado, Col. D4 86
Envira, stm., Braz. E3 84
Enyamba, D.R.C. E5 66
Enyellé, Congo D3 66
Eolia, Mo., U.S. E6 120
Eolie, Isole (Lipari, Isole), is., Italy F8 24
Epanomí, Grc. C5 28
Epecuén, Lago, l., Arg. H6 92
Épernay, Fr. E12 14
Epes, Al., U.S. E10 122
Ephesus see Efes, hist., Tur. F10 28
Ephraim, Ut., U.S. D5 132
Ephrata, Pa., U.S. D9 114
Ephrata, Wa., U.S. C7 136
Épi, state, Vanuatu k17 79d
Épi, i., Vanuatu k17 79d
Epídavros, hist., Grc. F6 28
Épila, Spain C9 20
Épinal, Fr. F15 14
Epirus see Ípeiros, hist. reg., Grc. D3 28
Epsom, Eng., U.K. J12 12
Epukiro, Nmb. B4 70
Epukiro, stm., Nmb. B4 70
Eqlīd, Iran C7 56
Equatorial Guinea, ctry., Afr. I6 64
Erap, Pap. N. Gui. b4 79a
Erath, La., U.S. H6 122
Erave, Pap. N. Gui. b3 79a
Erawan National Park, p.o.i., Thai. E4 48
Erbach, Ger. G5 16
Erbogačon, Russia B19 32
Ercevo, Russia F18 8
Ercolano, Italy D8 24
Érd, Hung. B5 26
Erdao, stm., China C8 38
Erdaohezi, China B8 38
Erdek, Tur. C10 28
Erdemli, Tur. B5 58
Erding, Ger. H7 16
Erebato, stm., Ven. E9 86
Erebus, Mount, mtn., Ant. C21 81
Erechim, Braz. C11 92
Ereğli, Tur. B14 28
Ereğli, Tur. A4 58
Erenhot, China C7 36
Erepecuru, Lago do, l., Braz. D6 84
Erfoud, Mor. C4 64
Erft, stm., Ger. E2 16
Erfurt, Ger. F7 16
Ergene, stm., Tur. B10 28
Ergeni, hills, Russia E6 32
Ērgļi, Lat. D8 10
Ergun Youqi, China A9 36
Ergun Zuoqi, China F13 34
Er Hai, l., China F5 36
Erice, Italy F6 24
Ericeira, Port. F1 20
Erichsen Lake, l., Nu., Can. A14 106
Erick, Ok., U.S. F9 128
Erickson, Mb., Can. D14 124
Ericson, Ne., U.S. F14 126
Erie, Co., U.S. A3 128
Erie, Il., U.S. C7 120
Erie, Pa., U.S. B5 114
Erie, Lake, l., N.A. B4 114
Erie Canal see New York State Barge Canal, can., N.Y., U.S. E12 112
Eriksdale, Mb., Can. D15 124
Erimo-misaki, c., Japan D15 38
Erin, On., Can. E9 112
Erin, Tn., U.S. H10 120
Eriskay, i., Scot., U.K. D5 12
Eritrea, ctry., Afr. D7 62
Erivan see Yerevan, Arm. A5 56
Erkelenz, Ger. E2 16
Erkner, Ger. D9 16
Erlangen, Ger. G7 16
Ermak, Kaz. D13 32
Ermelo, S. Afr. E10 70
Ermenek, Tur. B3 58
Ermenek, stm., Tur. B3 58
Ermentau, Kaz. D12 32
Ermica, Russia C25 8
Ermolaevo, Russia D9 32
Ermolino, Russia E19 10
Ermoúpoli, Grc. F7 28
Erne, Lower Lough, l., N. Ire., U.K. G4 12
Erne, Upper Lough, l., Eur. G5 12
Ernée, Fr. F8 14
Erode, India F3 53
Erofej Pavlovič, Russia F13 34
Eromanga, Austl. F4 76
Erongo, state, Nmb. C2 70
Erongo, mtn., Nmb. B2 70
Eropol, Russia C22 34
Erota, Erit. D7 62
Er-Rachidia, Mor. C4 64
Errego, Moz. D6 68
Errigal Mountain, mtn., Ire. F4 12
Errinundra National Park, p.o.i., Austl. K7 76
Erris Head, c., Ire. G2 12
Errol Heights, Or., U.S. E4 136
Erromango, i., Vanuatu l17 79d
Erši, Russia F17 10
Eršov, Russia D7 32
Erstein, Fr. F16 14
Ertai, China B3 36
Ertix see Irtysh, stm., Asia E15 32
Ertoma, Russia E22 8
Erval, Braz. F11 92
Ervy-le-Châtel, Fr. F12 14
Erwin, N.C., U.S. A7 116
Erwin, Tn., U.S. H3 114
Erwood, Sk., Can. B11 124
Erýmanthos, mtn., Grc. F4 28
Eryuan, China F4 36
Erzhan, China B8 38
Erzin, Russia D17 32
Erzincan, Tur. B4 56
Erzurum, Tur. B5 56
Esa'ala, Pap. N. Gui. b5 79a
Esashi, Japan D13 38
Esbjerg, Den. I3 8
Esbo see Espoo, Fin. F11 8
Escada, Braz. E8 88
Escalante, stm., Ut., U.S. F6 132
Escalante, stm., Ven. C5 86
Escalón, Mex. B6 100
Escalon, Ca., U.S. F5 134
Escambia, stm., Fl., U.S. G11 122
Escanaba, Mi., U.S. C2 112
Escanaba, stm., Mi., U.S. B2 112
Escandón, Puerto, p., Spain D10 20
Escárcega, Mex. C2 102
Escarpada Point, c., Phil. A4 52
Escatawpa, stm., U.S. G10 122
Esch-sur-Alzette, Lux. E15 14
Escobedo, Mex. G6 130
Escocesa, Bahía, b., Dom. Rep. C13 102
Escondido, Ca., U.S. J8 134
Escondido, stm., Mex. F7 130
Escondido, stm., Nic. F6 102
Escuinapa de Hidalgo, Mex. D5 100
Escuintla, Guat. E2 102
Escuintla, Mex. H12 100
Eséka, Cam. D2 66
Eşen, Tur. G12 28
Eşfahān, Iran C7 56
Esgueva, stm., Spain C6 20
Eshkāshem, Afg. B11 56
Eshowe, S. Afr. F10 70
Esil', Kaz. D11 32
Esil see Ishim, stm., Asia C12 32
Esk, Austl. F9 76
Ěškar-Ola, Russia C7 32
Eskdale, W.V., U.S. F4 114
Es'ki, Russia C19 10
Eskilstrup, Den. B7 16
Eskilstuna, Swe. G7 8
Eskimo Lakes, l., N.T., Can. B4 106
Eskimo Point see Arviat, Nu., Can. C12 106
Eskişehir, Tur. D13 28
Eskişehir, state, Tur. D13 28
Eskridge, Ks., U.S. F1 120
Esla, stm., Spain C5 20
Eslāmābād, Iran C6 56
Eşme, Tur. E11 28
Esmeralda, Austl. B4 76
Esmeralda, Cuba B8 102
Esmeralda, Isla, i., Chile I1 90
Esmeraldas, Ec. G2 86
Esmeraldas, state, Ec. G2 86
Esmeraldas, stm., Ec. G2 86
Esnagami Lake, l., On., Can. A11 118
Espada, Punta, c., Col. A6 86
Espalion, Fr. E8 18
Espanola, On., Can. B8 112
Espanola, N.M., U.S. F2 128
Espejo, Spain G6 20
Espelkamp, Ger. D4 16
Espera Feliz, Braz. K5 88
Esperança, Braz. D4 84
Esperança, Braz. D7 88
Esperance, Austl. F4 74
Esperantina, Braz. B4 88
Esperanza, Arg. E7 92
Esperanza, Mex. B4 100
Esperanza, P.R. B5 104a
Esperanza, sci., Ant. B35 81
Espichel, Cabo, c., Port. F1 20
Espinal, Col. E4 86
Espinazo, Mex. H6 130
Espinhaço, Serra do, mts., Braz. I4 88
Espinho, Port. D2 20
Espinillo, Arg. B8 92
Espino, Ven. C9 86
Espinosa, Braz. H4 88
Espírito Santo, state, Braz. J5 88
Espiritu Santo, i., Vanuatu j16 79d
Espíritu Santo, Isla del, i., Mex. C3 100
Espita, Mex. B3 102
Esplanada, Braz. F7 88
Espoo, Fin. F11 8
Espungabera, Moz. B11 70
Esquel, Arg. H2 90
Esquimalt, B.C., Can. H7 138
Esquina, Arg. D8 92
Esquiú, Arg. D5 92
Essaouira, Mor. C3 64
Essej, Russia C9 34
Essen, Ger. E3 16
Essendon, Mount, mtn., Austl. D3 74
Essequibo, stm., Guy. C6 84
Es Sers, Tun. H2 24
Essex, On., Can. F7 112
Essex, Md., U.S. E9 114
Essex, Mt., U.S. B13 136
Essex Junction, Vt., U.S. F3 110
Essexville, Mi., U.S. E6 112
Esslingen am Neckar, Ger. H5 16
Essonne, state, Fr. F11 14
Est, Pointe de l', c., Qc., Can. A15 110
Estacada, Or., U.S. E4 136
Estaca de Bares, Punta da, c., Spain A3 20
Estaca de Bares, Punta de la see Estaca de Bares, Punta da, c., Spain A3 20
Estacado, Llano, pl., U.S. H6 128
Estación Adolfo Rodriguez Sáa see Santa Rosa del Conlara, Arg. F5 92
Estación Colonia Alvear Norte see General Alvear, Arg. G3 92
Estación Foguista J. F. Juárez see El Galpón, Arg. B5 92
Estación Gobernador Vera see Vera, Arg. D7 92
Estación J. J. Castelli see Castelli, Arg. B7 92
Estación Justino Solari see Mariano I. Loza, Arg. D8 92
Estación Manuel F. Mantilla see Pedro R. Fernández, Arg. D8 92
Estación Vela see María Ignacia, Arg. H8 92
Estados, Isla de los, i., Arg. J4 90
Eşṭahbān, Iran D7 56
Estância, Braz. F7 88
Estancia, N.M., U.S. G2 128
Estanislao del Campo, Arg. B7 92
Estarreja, Port. D2 20
Estats, Pic d' (Estats, Pique d'), mtn., Eur. G7 18
Estats, Pico de see Estats, Pic d', mtn., Eur. G7 18
Estats, Pique d' (Estats, Pic d'), mtn., Eur. G7 18
Estcourt, S. Afr. F9 70
Este, Italy E8 22
Esteio, Braz. D12 92
Estelí, Nic. F4 102
Estella, Spain B8 20
Estelline, S.D., U.S. G2 118
Estelline, Tx., U.S. G8 128
Estepa, Spain G6 20
Estepona, Spain H5 20
Estes Park, Co., U.S. G7 126
Este Sudeste, Cayos del, is., Col. F7 102
Estevan, Sk., Can. E10 124
Estevan Point, B.C., Can. G4 138
Estherville, Ia., U.S. H4 118
Estill, S.C., U.S. D4 116
Estiva, stm., Braz. G3 88
Eston, Sk., Can. C5 124
Estonia, ctry., Eur. G11 8
Estrela, Braz. D11 92
Estrela, mtn., Port. D3 20
Estrela do Sul, Braz. J2 88
Estremadura, hist. reg., Port. E1 20
Estremoz, Port. F3 20
Estrondo, Serra do, plat., Braz. E1 88
Esztergom, Hung. B5 26
Etadunna, Austl. G2 76
Etah, Grnld. B11 141
Etah, India E7 54
Étain, Fr. E14 14
Étampes, Fr. F11 14
Etamunbanie, Lake, l., Austl. F2 76
Étaples, Fr. D10 14
Etāwah, India E7 54
Etchojoa, Mex. B4 100
Ethan, S.D., U.S. D14 126
Ethel, Ms., U.S. D9 122
Ethel, Mount, mtn., Co., U.S. C10 132
Ethiopia, ctry., Afr. F7 62
Ethiopian Plateau, plat., Eth. E7 62
Ethridge, Mt., U.S. B14 136
Ethridge, Tn., U.S. B11 122
Etigo-heiya, pl., Japan B12 40
Etive, Loch, l., Scot., U.K. E7 12
E. T. Joshua Airport, St. Vin. o11 105e
Etna, Ca., U.S. B3 134
Etna, Monte, vol., Italy G8 24
Etobicoke, ngh., On., Can. E10 112
Etolin Island, i., Ak., U.S. E13 140
Etolin Strait, strt., Ak., U.S. D6 140
Etomami, stm., Sk., Can. B11 124
Eton, Austl. C7 76
Etorofu-tō (Iturup, ostrov), i., Russia B17 38
Etosha Pan, pl., Nmb. D2 68
Etoumbi, Congo D2 66
Etowah, Tn., U.S. B14 122
Etowah, stm., Ga., U.S. C14 122
Étretat, Fr. E9 14
Etsch see Adige, stm., Italy E8 22
Et Tîdra, i., Maur. F1 64
Ettlingen, Ger. H4 16
Etzikom Coulee, stm., Ab., Can. E2 124
Etzná, hist., Mex. C2 102
Eu, Fr. D10 14
Eua, i., Tonga F9 72
Eua Iki, i., Tonga n15 78e
Euboea see Évvoia, i., Grc. E6 28
Euboea, Gulf of see Vórios Evvoïkós Kólpos, b., Grc. E5 28
Eucla, Austl. F5 74
Euclid, Oh., U.S. C4 114
Euclides da Cunha, Braz. F6 88
Eucumbene, Lake, res., Austl. K7 76
Eudora, Ar., U.S. D7 122
Eudora, Ks., U.S. F2 120
Eufaula, Al., U.S. F13 122
Eufaula Lake, res., Ok., U.S. B3 122
Eugene, Or., U.S. F3 136
Eugenia, Punta, c., Mex. B1 100
Eugenio Bustos, Arg. F3 92
Eugowra, Austl. I7 76
Eumungerie, Austl. H7 76
Eunápolis, Braz. I6 88
Eungella National Park, p.o.i., Austl. C7 76
Eunice, La., U.S. G6 122
Eunice, N.M., U.S. B4 130
Euphrates (Al-Furāt), stm., Asia C6 56
Eupora, Ms., U.S. D9 122
Eure, state, Fr. E9 14
Eure, stm., Fr. E10 14
Eure-et-Loir, state, Fr. F10 14
Eureka, Can. A8 141
Eureka, Ca., U.S. C1 134
Eureka, Il., U.S. K9 118
Eureka, Ks., U.S. D12 128
Eureka, Mt., U.S. B11 136
Eureka, Nv., U.S. D10 134

Name | Map Ref. | Page

Eureka, S.C., U.S. B4 116
Eureka Springs, Ar., U.S. H4 120
Eurinilla Creek, stm., Austl. H3 76
Euroa, Austl. K5 76
Europa, Île, i., Reu. E7 68
Europa, Picos de, mts., Spain A6 20
Europa Island see Europa, Île, i., Reu. E7 68
Europa Point, c., Gib. H5 20
Europe, cont. C13 4
Euskal Herriko, state, Spain A8 20
Euskirchen, Ger. F2 16
Eustace, Tx., U.S. G4 122
Eustis, Fl., U.S. H4 116
Eustis, Lake, l., Fl., U.S. H4 116
Euston, Austl. J4 76
Eutaw, Al., U.S. E11 122
Eutin, Ger. B6 16
Eutsuk Lake, l., B.C., Can. C4 138
Eva, Al., U.S. C12 122
Evadale, Tx., U.S. G4 122
Evandale, Austl. n13 77a
Evans, Lac, l., Qc., Can. E15 106
Evans, Mount, mtn., Co., U.S. B3 128
Evansburg, Ab., Can. C15 138
Evans City, Pa., U.S. D5 114
Evansdale, Ia., U.S. I6 118
Evans Strait, strt., Nu., Can. C14 106
Evanston, Il., U.S. F2 112
Evanston, Wy., U.S. B6 132
Evansville, In., U.S. F10 120
Evansville, Mn., U.S. E3 118
Evansville, Wi., U.S. B8 120
Evansville, Wy., U.S. E6 126
Evart, Mi., U.S. E4 112
Eveleth, Mn., U.S. D6 118
Evening Shade, Ar., U.S. H6 120
Evensk, Russia D20 34
Everard, Lake, l., Austl. F6 74
Everest, Mount (Qomolangma Feng), mtn., Asia D11 54
Everett, Pa., U.S. E7 114
Everett, Wa., U.S. C4 136
Everett, Mount, mtn., Ma., U.S. B12 114
Everglades, The, sw., Fl., U.S. K4 116
Everglades City, Fl., U.S. K4 116
Everglades National Park, p.o.i., Fl., U.S. K5 116
Evergreen, Al., U.S. F12 122
Evergreen, Mt., U.S. B12 136
Evermann, Cerro, vol., Mex. F3 100
Evesham, Sk., Can. B4 124
Evesham, Eng., U.K. I11 12
Évian-les-Bains, Fr. C12 18
Evje, Nor. G2 8
Évora, Port. F3 20
Évora, state, Port. F3 20
Evoron, ozero, l., Russia F16 34
Évreux, Fr. E10 14
Évry, Fr. F11 14
E. V. Spence Reservoir, res., Tx., U.S. C7 130
Évvoia, i., Grc. E6 28
Ewa, Hi., U.S. B3 78a
Ewing, Ne., U.S. E14 126
Ewing, Va., U.S. H2 114
Ewo, Congo E2 66
Exaltación, Bol. B3 90
Excelsior Mountain, mtn., Ca., U.S. E6 134
Excelsior Springs, Mo., U.S. E3 120
Exeter, On., Can. E8 112
Exeter, Eng., U.K. K9 12
Exeter, Ca., U.S. G6 134
Exeter, N.H., U.S. G6 110
Exeter Sound, strt., Nu., Can. D13 141
Exira, Ia., U.S. C3 120
Exmoor, plat., Eng., U.K. J9 12
Exmoor National Park, p.o.i., Eng., U.K. J9 12
Exmore, Va., U.S. G10 114
Exmouth, Austl. D2 74
Exmouth, Eng., U.K. K9 12
Exmouth Gulf, b., Austl. D2 74
Exshaw, Ab., Can. E15 138
Extremadura, state, Spain E4 20
Exuma Cays, is., Bah. C9 96
Exuma Sound, strt., Bah. C9 96
Eyasi, Lake, l., Tan. E6 66
Eyebrow, Sk., Can. D7 124
Eyemouth, Scot., U.K. F10 12
Eye Peninsula, pen., Scot., U.K. C6 12
Eyjafjördur, b., Ice. j30 8a
Eyl, Som. C9 66
Eyl, val., Som. C9 66
Eylar Mountain, mtn., Ca., U.S. F4 134
Eyota, Mn., U.S. H6 118
Eyrarbakki, Ice. I29 8a
Eyre, Austl. F5 74
Eyre Creek, stm., Austl. F2 76
Eyre North, Lake, l., Austl. E7 74
Eyre Peninsula, pen., Austl. F7 74
Eyre South, Lake, l., Austl. E7 74
Ezequiel Ramos Mexía, Embalse, res., Arg. G3 90
Ežerėlis, Lith. F6 10
Ezine, Tur. D9 28

F

Faaone, Fr. Poly. v22 78h
Faber Lake, l., N.T., Can. C7 106
Fabriano, Italy G9 22
Facatativá, Col. E4 86
Fachi, Niger F7 64
Facpi Point, c., Guam j9 78c
Factoryville, Pa., U.S. C10 114
Fada, Chad D4 62
Fada-Ngourma, Burkina G5 64
Faddeevskij, ostrov, i., Russia A18 34
Fadeša, zaliv, b., Russia A10 34
Fadiffolu Atoll, at., Mald. h12 46a
Faenza, Italy F8 22
Fafe, Port. C2 20
Făgăraș, Rom. D11 26
Fagernes, Nor. F3 8
Fagersta, Swe. F6 8
Faguibine, Lac, l., Mali F4 64
Fagurhólsmýri, Ice. I31 8a
Fairbank, Ia., U.S. B5 120
Fairbanks, Ak., U.S. D10 140
Fairbanks, La., U.S. E6 122
Fair Bluff, N.C., U.S. B6 116
Fairborn, Oh., U.S. E1 114
Fairbury, Il., U.S. K10 118
Fairbury, Ne., U.S. A11 128
Fairchance, Pa., U.S. E6 114
Fairchild, Wi., U.S. G8 118
Fairfax, Mn., U.S. G4 118
Fairfax, Mo., U.S. D2 120
Fairfax, S.C., U.S. D4 116
Fairfax, S.D., U.S. D14 126
Fairfax, Vt., U.S. F3 110
Fairfax, Va., U.S. F8 114
Fairfield, Al., U.S. D11 122
Fairfield, Ca., U.S. E3 134
Fairfield, Id., U.S. G12 136
Fairfield, Il., U.S. F9 120
Fairfield, Me., U.S. F7 110
Fairfield, Ne., U.S. G14 126
Fairfield, Oh., U.S. E1 114
Fairfield, Tx., U.S. F2 122
Fairgrove, Mi., U.S. E6 112
Fairhaven, Ma., U.S. C15 114
Fair Haven, N.Y., U.S. E13 112
Fair Head, c., N. Ire., U.K. F6 12
Fairhope, Al., U.S. G11 122
Fair Isle, i., Scot., U.K. B11 12
Fairland, In., U.S. E12 120
Fairlie, N.Z. G4 80
Fairmont, Mn., U.S. H4 118
Fairmont, Ne., U.S. G15 126
Fairmont, N.C., U.S. B6 116
Fairmont, W.V., U.S. E5 114
Fairmont Hot Springs, B.C., Can. F14 138
Fairmount, Il., U.S. H2 112
Fairmount, In., U.S. H4 112
Fairmount, N.D., U.S. E2 118
Fair Ness, c., Nu., Can. C16 106
Fair Oaks, Ca., U.S. E4 134
Fair Plain, Mi., U.S. F3 112
Fairplay, Co., U.S. B3 128
Fairview, Ga., U.S. C13 122
Fairview, Il., U.S. D7 120
Fairview, Mi., U.S. D5 112
Fairview, Mt., U.S. G9 124
Fairview, Tn., U.S. I10 120
Fairview, Ut., U.S. D5 132
Fairview Park, In., U.S. I2 112
Fairview Peak, mtn., Nv., U.S. D7 134
Fairweather Mountain, mtn., N.A. D3 106
Faisalabad (Lyallpur), Pak. C4 54
Faison, N.C., U.S. A7 116
Faistós, hist., Grc. H7 28
Faith, S.D., U.S. B10 126
Faizābād, India E9 54
Fajardo, P.R. B4 104a
Fajou, Îlet à, i., Guad. h5 105c
Fajr, Bi'r, well, Sau. Ar. J8 58
Fajr, Wādī, stm., Sau. Ar. H8 58
Fakse Bugt, b., Den. A8 16
Faku, China C5 38
Falaba, S.L. H2 64
Falaise, Fr. F8 14
Fālākāta, India E12 54
Falam, Mya. A1 48
Falcón, state, Ven. B7 86
Falcón, Presa (Falcon Reservoir), res., N.A. H8 130
Falconara Marittima, Italy G10 22
Falcon Reservoir (Falcón, Presa), res., N.A. H8 130
Falealai, Samoa g11 79c
Falémé, stm., Afr. G2 64
Fălești, Mol. B14 26
Falfurrias, Tx., U.S. G9 130
Falkenberg, Ger. E9 16
Falkenberg, Swe. H5 8
Falkensee, Ger. D9 16
Falkenstein, Ger. F8 16
Falkirk, Scot., U.K. E9 12
Falkland, B.C., Can. F11 138
Falkland Islands, dep., S.A. J4 90
Falkland Sound, strt., Falk. Is. J5 90
Falköping, Swe. G5 8
Falkville, Al., U.S. C11 122
Fall, stm., Ks., U.S. D13 128
Fallbrook, Ca., U.S. J8 134
Fallon, Nv., U.S. D7 134
Fall River, Ks., U.S. G1 120
Fall River, Ma., U.S. C14 114
Fall River, Wi., U.S. H9 118
Fall River Mills, Ca., U.S. B4 134
Falls City, Ne., U.S. D2 120
Falls City, Or., U.S. F3 136
Falls Creek, Pa., U.S. C7 114
Falls Lake, res., N.C., U.S. I7 114
Falmouth, Jam. i13 104d
Falmouth, Eng., U.K. K7 12
Falmouth, Me., U.S. G6 110
Falmouth, Ma., U.S. C15 114
False Bay, b., S. Afr. I4 70
False Divi Point, c., India D5 53
False Pass, Ak., U.S. F7 140
Falset, Spain C11 20
Falso, Cabo, c., Dom. Rep. D12 102
Falster, i., Den. I4 8
Fălticeni, Rom. B13 26
Falun, Swe. F6 8
Famagusta see Gazimağusa, N. Cyp. C4 58
Famaillá, Arg. C5 92
Famatina, Sierra de, mts., Arg. D4 92
Famenne, reg., Bel. D14 14
Family Lake, l., Mb., Can. B18 124
Fanchang, China F8 42
Fanch'eng see Xiangfan, China F4 42
Fanchon, Pointe, c., Haiti C10 102
Fancy, St. Vin. o11 105e
Fang, Thai. C4 48
Fangak, Sudan F6 62
Fangcheng, China E5 42
Fangxian, China E4 42
Fangzheng, China B10 36
Fanipal', Bela. G10 10
Fanjiatun, China C6 38
Fanny Bay, B.C., Can. G6 138
Fano, Italy G10 22
Fan Si Pan, mtn., Viet. A6 48
Faraday, sci., Ant. B34 81
Faradje, D.R.C. D5 66
Farafangana, Madag. E8 68
Farāh, Afg. C9 56
Farāh, stm., Afg. C9 56
Farallon de Pajaros, i., N. Mar. Is. A5 72
Farallon Islands, is., Ca., U.S. F2 134
Faranah, Gui. G2 64
Farasān, Jazā'ir, is., Sau. Ar. F5 56
Fareham, Eng., U.K. K11 12
Farewell, Ak., U.S. D9 140
Farewell, Cape, c., N.Z. E5 80
Fargo, N.D., U.S. E2 118
Faribault, Mn., U.S. G5 118
Faribault, Lac, l., Qc., Can. D16 106
Farīdābād, India D6 54
Farīdkot, India C5 54
Farīdpur, Bngl. G12 54
Farīdpur, India D7 54
Farilhões, is., Port. E1 20
Farim, Gui.-B. G2 64
Farina, Il., U.S. F9 120
Farinha, stm., Braz. D2 88
Fāriskūr, Egypt G2 58
Farit, Amba, mtn., Eth. E7 62
Färjestaden, Swe. H7 8
Farley, Ia., U.S. B7 120
Farmer City, Il., U.S. D9 120
Farmersville, Il., U.S. E8 120
Farmersville, Tx., U.S. D2 122
Farmerville, La., U.S. E6 122
Farmington, Il., U.S. D7 120
Farmington, Me., U.S. F6 110
Farmington, Mn., U.S. G5 118
Farmington, Mo., U.S. G7 120
Farmington, Mt., U.S. C14 136
Farmington, N.H., U.S. G5 110
Farmington, N.M., U.S. G8 132
Farmington, Ut., U.S. C5 132
Far Mountain, mtn., B.C., Can. D5 138
Farmville, N.C., U.S. A8 116
Farmville, Va., U.S. G7 114
Farnborough, Eng., U.K. J12 12
Farne Islands, is., Eng., U.K. F11 12
Farnham, Qc., Can. E3 110
Faro, Braz. D6 84
Faro, Yk., Can. C4 106
Faro, Port. H3 20
Faro, state, Port. G3 20
Faroe Islands, dep., Eur. n34 8b
Fårön, i., Swe. H8 8
Farquhar, Atoll de, i., Sey. I12 69b
Farquhar, Cape, c., Austl. D2 74
Farragut, Ia., U.S. D2 120
Farrars Creek, stm., Austl. E3 76
Farrell, Pa., U.S. C5 114
Farrukhābād, India E7 54
Fársala, Grc. D5 28
Fartak, Ra's, c., Yemen F7 56
Farvel, Kap, c., Grnld. F17 141
Farwell, Mi., U.S. E5 112
Fasā, Iran D7 56
Fasano, Italy D11 24
Fastnet Rock, r., Ire. J3 12
Fatehābād, India D5 54
Fatehjang, Pak. B4 54
Fatehpur, India F8 54
Fatehpur, India E5 54
Fatehpur Sīkri, India E6 54
Fathom Five National Marine Park, p.o.i., On., Can. C8 112
Fatick, Sen. G1 64
Fátima, Port. E2 20
Fatshan see Foshan, China J5 42
Fatu Hiva, i., Fr. Poly. E13 72
Fatumu, Tonga n14 78e
Fatwā, India F10 54
Fauabu, Sol. Is. e9 79b
Faucilles, Monts, mts., Fr. F15 14
Faulkton, S.D., U.S. B13 126
Fauquier, B.C., Can. G12 138
Făurei, Rom. D14 26
Fauresmith, S. Afr. F7 70
Fauro Island, i., Sol. Is. d6 79b
Fauske, Nor. C6 8
Faust, Ab., Can. A15 138
Favara, Italy G7 24
Fawcett Lake, l., Ab., Can. A17 138
Fawn, stm., On., Can. E13 106
Fawnie Nose, mtn., B.C., Can. C5 138
Faxaflói, b., Ice. k28 8a
Faxinal do Soturno, Braz. D11 92
Faya-Largeau, Chad D3 62
Fayette, Al., U.S. D11 122
Fayette, Ia., U.S. B6 120
Fayette, Ms., U.S. F7 122
Fayette, Mo., U.S. E5 120
Fayette, Lake, res., Tx., U.S. E2 122
Fayetteville, Ar., U.S. H3 120
Fayetteville, Ga., U.S. D14 122
Fayetteville, N.C., U.S. A7 116
Fayetteville, W.V., U.S. F4 114
Fāyid, Egypt H3 58
Fāzilka, India C5 54
Fāzilpur, Pak. D3 54
Fazzān, hist. reg., Libya B2 62
Fdérik, Maur. E2 64
Fear, Cape, c., N.C., U.S. C8 116
Feather, stm., Ca., U.S. D4 134
Feather, Middle Fork, stm., Ca., U.S. D5 134
Feather, North Fork, East Branch, stm., Ca., U.S. C5 134
Fécamp, Fr. E9 14
Federación, Arg. E8 92
Federal, Arg. E8 92
Federally Administered Tribal Areas, state, Pak. B2 54
Federal Republic of Germany see Germany, ctry., Eur. E6 16
Federalsburg, Md., U.S. F10 114
Federated States of Micronesia see Micronesia, Federated States of, ctry., Oc. C6 72
Fehérgyarmat, Hung. A9 26
Fehmarn, i., Ger. B7 16
Feia, Lagoa, b., Braz. L5 88
Fei Huang, stm., China D8 42
Feijó, Braz. E3 84
Feiketu, China B7 38
Feira de Santana, Braz. G6 88
Feixi, China F7 42
Feixian, China D7 42
Fejér, state, Hung. B5 26
Felanitx, Spain E14 20
Felda, Fl., U.S. J4 116
Feldbach, Aus. D12 22
Feldberg, mtn., Ger. I4 16
Feldkirch, Aus. C6 22
Feliciano, P.R. B1 104a
Feliciano, Arroyo, stm., Arg. E8 92
Felipe Carrillo Puerto, Mex. C4 102
Felix, Cape, c., Nu., Can. B11 106
Felixlândia, Braz. J3 88
Felixstowe, Eng., U.K. I14 12
Felletin, Fr. D8 18
Fellsmere, Fl., U.S. I5 116
Feltre, Italy E8 22
Femunden, l., Nor. E4 8
Femundsmarka Nasjonalpark, p.o.i., Nor. E4 8
Fen, stm., China D4 42
Fenelon Falls, On., Can. D11 112
Fengcheng, China D6 38
Fengcheng, China G6 42
Fengdu, China G2 42
Fengfeng, China C6 42
Fenggang, China G2 42
Fenghuang, China H3 42
Fengjiabao, China C1 42
Fengjie, China F3 42
Fengning, China A7 42
Fengqing, China G4 36
Fengqiu, China D6 42
Fengrun, China B7 42
Fengtai, China E7 42
Fengtien see Shenyang, China D5 38
Fengxi, China F3 42
Fengxian, China D7 42
Fengxiang, China D2 42
Fengyang, China E7 42
Fengyüan, Tai. I9 42
Fengzhen, China A5 42
Feni, Bngl. G13 54
Fennimore, Wi., U.S. B7 120
Fenoarivo Atsinanana, Madag. D8 68
Fenton, Mi., U.S. B2 114
Fentress, Tx., U.S. E10 130
Fenwick, W.V., U.S. F5 114
Fenyang, China C4 42
Fenyi, China H6 42
Feodosija, Ukr. F5 32
Fer, Cap de, c., Alg. B6 64
Ferdinand, In., U.S. F10 120
Ferdows, Iran C8 56
Ferentino, Italy I10 22
Fergana, Uzb. F12 32
Fergana Mountains see Ferganskij hrebet, mts., Kyrg. F12 32
Ferganskij hrebet, mts., Kyrg. F12 32
Fergus, On., Can. E9 112
Fergus Falls, Mn., U.S. E2 118
Ferguson, B.C., Can. F13 138
Ferguson, Ky., U.S. G13 120
Ferguson, Mo., U.S. F7 120
Fergusson Island, i., Pap. N. Gui. b5 79a
Ferkéssédougou, C. Iv. H4 64
Ferlo, reg., Sen. F2 64
Ferme-Neuve, Qc., Can. B14 112
Fermo, Italy G10 22
Fermont, Qc., Can. E17 106
Fermoselle, Spain C4 20
Fernández, Arg. C6 92
Fernandina, Isla, i., Ec. I11 84a
Fernandina Beach, Fl., U.S. F4 116
Fernando de Noronha, Ilha, i., Braz. F11 82
Fernandópolis, Braz. D6 90
Fernando Póo see Bioko, i., Eq. Gui. I6 64
Fernán-Núñez, Spain G6 20
Ferndale, Ca., U.S. C1 134
Fernie, B.C., Can. G15 138
Fernley, Nv., U.S. D6 134
Fern Park, Fl., U.S. H4 116
Fern Ridge Lake, res., Or., U.S. F3 136
Fernwood, Id., U.S. C10 136
Ferokh, India F2 53
Ferrandina, Italy D10 24
Ferrara, Italy F8 22
Ferrato, Capo, c., Italy E3 24
Ferreira Gomes, Braz. C7 84
Ferreñafe, Peru E2 84
Ferret, Cap, c., Fr. E4 18
Ferrières, Fr. F11 14
Ferris, Tx., U.S. E2 122
Ferrol, Spain A2 20
Ferron, Ut., U.S. D5 132
Ferrysburg, Mi., U.S. E3 112
Fertő-tavi Nemzeti Park, p.o.i., Hung. B3 26
Fès, Mor. C3 64
Feshi, D.R.C. F3 66
Fessenden, N.D., U.S. G14 124
Festus, Mo., U.S. F7 120
Fetești, Rom. E14 26
Fethiye, Tur. G12 28
Fetisovo, Kaz. F8 32
Fetlar, i., Scot., U.K. n19 12a
Feucht, Ger. G7 16
Feuchtwangen, Ger. G6 16
Feuilles, stm., Qc., Can. D16 106
Feuilles, Baie aux, b., Qc., Can. D16 106
Feurs, Fr. D10 18
Feyzābād, Afg. B11 56
Fez see Fès, Mor. C3 64
Fezzan see Fazzān, hist. reg., Libya B2 62
Ffestiniog, Wales, U.K. I9 12
Fianarantsoa, Madag. E8 68
Fianga, Chad F3 62
Fichē, Eth. F7 62
Fichtelgebirge, mts., Eur. F7 16
Ficksburg, S. Afr. F8 70
Fidalgo, stm., Braz. E5 88
Fidenza, Italy F7 22
Field, B.C., Can. E14 138
Fier, Alb. D13 24
Fieri see Fier, Alb. D13 24
Fiery Creek, stm., Austl. B2 76
Fierzës, Liqeni i, res., Alb. B14 24
Fife Lake, Sk., Can. E8 124
Fife Lake, Mi., U.S. D4 112
Fife Lake, l., Sk., Can. E8 124
Fife Ness, c., Scot., U.K. E10 12
Fifield, Wi., U.S. F8 118
Fifth Cataract see Khāmis, Ash-Shallāl al-, wtfl, Sudan D6 62
Figeac, Fr. E7 18
Figtree, Zimb. B9 70
Figueira da Foz, Port. D1 20
Figueras see Figueres, Spain B13 20
Figueres, Spain B13 20
Figuig, Mor. C4 64
Fiji, ctry., Oc. E8 72
Filabusi, Zimb. B9 70
Filadelfia, Italy F10 24
Filchner Ice Shelf, ice, Ant. C1 81
Filey, Eng., U.K. G12 12
Fili, hist., Grc. E6 28
Filiatrá, Grc. F4 28
Filingué, Niger G5 64
Filippoi, hist., Grc. C7 28
Fillmore, Sk., Can. E10 124
Fillmore, Ca., U.S. I7 134
Filtu, Eth. F8 62
Fimi, stm., D.R.C. E3 66
Finale Emilia, Italy F8 22
Finale Ligure, Italy F5 22
Finca El Rey, Parque Nacional, p.o.i., Arg. B5 92
Findlay, Il., U.S. E9 120
Findlay, Oh., U.S. C2 114
Findlay, Mount, mtn., B.C., Can. F14 138
Fingal, N.D., U.S. H16 124
Fingoè, Moz. D5 68
Finistère, state, Fr. F5 14
Finisterre, Cabo de see Fisterra, Cabo de, c., Spain B1 20
Finke, Austl. E6 74
Finland, ctry., Eur. C12 8
Finland, Gulf of, b., Eur. G11 8
Finlay, stm., B.C., Can. D5 106
Finley, Austl. J5 76
Finley, N.D., U.S. G16 124
Finmoore, B.C., Can. C7 138
Finnegan, Ab., Can. E18 138
Finnis, Cape, c., Austl. F6 74
Finnmark, state, Nor. B11 8
Finnsnes, Nor. B8 8
Finschhafen, Pap. N. Gui. b4 79a
Finse, Nor. F2 8
Finspång, Swe. G6 8
Finsterwalde, Ger. E9 16
Fiordland National Park, p.o.i., N.Z. G2 80
Fiorenzuola d'Arda, Italy F6 22
Fire Island National Seashore, p.o.i., N.Y., U.S. D12 114
Firenze (Florence), Italy G8 22
Firmat, Arg. F7 92
Firminy, Fr. D10 18
Firovo, Russia C16 10
Fīrozābād, India E7 54
Fīrozpur, India C5 54
Fīrozpur Jhirka, India E6 54
First Cataract, wtfl, Egypt C6 62
Firūzābād, Iran D7 56
Fish, stm., N.A. C11 140
Fish, stm., Namibia E4 70
Fisher, Ar., U.S. B7 122
Fisher, Il., U.S. D9 120
Fisher Bay, b., Mb., Can. C17 124
Fisher Branch, Mb., Can. C16 124
Fisher Peak, mtn., Va., U.S. H5 114
Fishers Island, i., N.Y., U.S. C14 114
Fisher Strait, strt., Nu., Can. C14 106
Fishing Creek, Md., U.S. F9 114
Fishing Creek, stm., N.C., U.S. H8 114
Fishing Lake, l., Mb., Can. B18 124
Fisk, Mo., U.S. H7 120
Fiskárdo, Grc. E3 28
Fisterra, Cabo de, c., Spain B1 20
Fitchburg, Ma., U.S. B14 114
Fito, Mount, vol., Samoa g12 79c
Fitri, Lac, l., Chad E3 62
Fitzgerald, Ga., U.S. I3 90
Fitzroy, stm., Austl. C4 74
Fitzroy, stm., Austl. D8 76
Fitz Roy, Monte (Chaltel, Cerro), mtn., S.A. I2 90
Fitzroy Crossing, Austl. C5 74
Fitzwilliam Island, i., On., Can. C8 112
Fiuggi, Italy I10 22
Fiume see Rijeka, Cro. E11 22
Fiumicino, Italy I9 22
Fivizzano, Italy E12 110
Five Islands, N.S., Can. f4 105b
Five Islands Harbour, b., Antig.
Fivemile Creek, stm., Wy., U.S. D4 126
Five Points, N.M., U.S. H10 132
Fivizzano, Italy F7 22
Fizi, D.R.C. E5 66
Fjällåsen, Swe. C8 8
Flagler, Co., U.S. B5 128
Flagstaff, Az., U.S. H5 132
Flagstaff Lake, res., Me., U.S. E6 110
Flamands, Anse des, Guad. B2 105a
Flambeau, stm., Wi., U.S. F8 118
Flamborough, On., Can. E9 112
Flamborough Head, c., Eng., U.K. G12 12
Fläming, reg., Ger. E8 16
Flaming Gorge National Recreation Area, p.o.i., U.S. B7 132
Flaming Gorge Reservoir, res., U.S. B7 132
Flanagan, Il., U.S. D9 120
Flanders, On., Can. C6 118
Flasher, N.D., U.S. A11 126
Flåsjön, l., Swe. D6 8
Flat, Ak., U.S. D8 140
Flat, Tx., U.S. C10 130
Flat, stm., N.T., Can. C5 106
Flat, stm., Mi., U.S. E4 112
Flatey, Ice. k28 8a
Flathead (Flathead, North Fork), stm., N.A. H16 138
Flathead, stm., Mt., U.S. C12 136
Flathead, Middle Fork, stm., Mt., U.S. B13 136
Flathead, North Fork (Flathead), stm., N.A. H16 138
Flathead, South Fork, stm., Mt., U.S. B13 136
Flathead Lake, l., Mt., U.S. C12 136
Flat Lake, l., Ab., Can. B17 138
Flatonia, Tx., U.S. E10 130
Flat River, P.E., Can. D13 110
Flat River, Mo., U.S. G7 120
Flat Rock, Al., U.S. C13 122
Flattery, Cape, c., Wa., U.S. B2 136
Flatts, Ber. k15 104e
Flatwillow Creek, stm., Mt., U.S. H5 124
Flatwood, U.S. E11 122
Flaxton, N.D., U.S. F11 124
Flaxville, Mt., U.S. F8 124
Fleetwood, Eng., U.K. H10 12
Fleetwood, Pa., U.S. D10 114
Flekkefjord, Nor. G2 8
Fleming-Neon, Ky., U.S. G3 114
Flemingsburg, Ky., U.S. F2 114
Flen, Swe. G7 8
Flensburg, Ger. B5 16
Fletcher, N.C., U.S. A3 116
Fletcher Pond, l., Mi., U.S. D5 112
Fleurance, Fr. F6 18
Flinders, stm., Austl. A3 76
Flinders Bay, b., Austl. F3 74
Flinders Island, i., Austl. m14 77a
Flinders Ranges National Park, p.o.i., Austl. H2 76
Flinders Reefs, rf., Austl. A7 76
Flin Flon, Mb., Can. E10 106
Flint, Wales, U.K. H9 12
Flint, Mi., U.S. E6 112
Flint, i., Kir. E11 72
Flint, stm., Oc. C12 122
Flint, stm., Ga., U.S. G14 122
Flint Lake, l., Nu., Can. B16 106
Flinton, Austl. F7 76
Flintville, Tn., U.S. B12 122
Flippin, Ar., U.S. H5 120
Flix, Pantà de, res., Spain C11 20
Flomaton, Al., U.S. F11 122
Floodwood, Mn., U.S. E6 118
Flora, Il., U.S. F9 120
Flora, In., U.S. H3 112
Florac, Fr. E9 18
Floral City, Fl., U.S. H3 116
Floral Park, Mt., U.S. E14 136
Flora Vista, N.M., U.S. G8 132
Flore, Piton, mtn., St. Luc. m7 105c
Florence see Firenze, Italy G8 22
Florence, Al., U.S. C11 122
Florence, Az., U.S. J5 132
Florence, Co., U.S. C3 128
Florence, Ks., U.S. C12 128
Florence, S.C., U.S. B6 116
Florence, Tx., U.S. D10 130
Florence, Wi., U.S. C1 112
Florencia, Col. G4 86
Florentino Ameghino, Embalse, res., Arg. H3 90
Flores, Braz. D7 88
Flores, i., Indon. G7 44
Flores, Laut (Flores Sea), Indon. G11 50
Flores, Selat, strt., Indon. G7 44
Flores de Goiás, Braz. H2 88
Flores Island, i., B.C., Can. G4 138
Flores Sea see Flores, Laut, Indon. G11 50
Floresta, Braz. E6 88
Florești, Mol. B15 26
Floresville, Tx., U.S. E9 130
Floriano, Braz. D4 88
Floriano Peixoto, Braz. E4 84
Florianópolis, Braz. C13 92
Florida, Col. F3 86
Florida, Cuba B8 102
Florida, P.R. B4 104a
Florida, Ur. G9 92
Florida, state, U.S. F11 108
Florida, Straits of, strt., N.A. G11 108
Florida Bay, b., Fl., U.S. K5 116
Floridablanca, Col. D5 86
Florida City, Fl., U.S. K5 116
Florida Islands, is., Sol. Is. e9 79b
Florida Keys, is., Fl., U.S. L4 116
Florida, Italy G9 24
Florido, stm., Mex. B6 100
Florien, La., U.S. F5 122
Flórina, Grc. C4 28
Florissant, Mo., U.S. F7 120
Florissant Fossil Beds National Monument, p.o.i., Co., U.S. B3 128
Florø, Nor. F1 8
Flotte, Cap de, c., N. Cal. m16 79d
Floyd, N.M., U.S. G5 128
Floyd, Va., U.S. H5 114
Floyd, stm., Ia., U.S. I2 118
Floydada, Tx., U.S. G7 128
Flumendosa, stm., Italy E3 24
Fluminimaggiore, Italy E2 24
Flushing see Vlissingen, Neth. C12 14
Fluvanna, Tx., U.S. B6 130
Fly, stm. b3 79a
Foam Lake, Sk., Can. C10 124
Foča, Bos. F5 26
Foça, Tur. E9 28
Focșani, Rom. D14 26
Fogang, China J5 42
Foggaret ez Zoua, Alg. D5 64
Foggia, Italy C9 24
Fogo, i., C.V. k10 65a
Fogo Island, i., Nf., Can. j23 107a
Foguista J. F. Juárez see El Galpón, Arg. B5 92
Föhr, i., Ger. B4 16
Fóia, mtn., Port. G2 20
Foix, Fr. G7 18
Foix, hist. reg., Fr. F7 18
Fojnica, Bos. F4 26
Fokino, Russia G17 10
Folda, b., Nor. C6 8
Foley, Al., U.S. G11 122
Foleyet, On., Can. F14 106
Foley Island, i., Nu., Can. B15 106
Folgefonni, ice, Nor. G2 8
Foligno, Italy H9 22
Folkestone, Eng., U.K. J14 12
Folkston, Ga., U.S. F3 116
Follett, Tx., U.S. E8 128
Föllinge, Swe. E6 8
Follonica, Italy H7 22
Follonica, Golfo di, b., Italy H7 22
Folsom, Ca., U.S. E4 134
Folsom Lake, res., Ca., U.S. E4 134
Fomboni, Com. C7 68
Fominiči, Russia F17 10
Fominskoe, Russia A22 10
Fonda, N.Y., U.S. B11 114
Fond-du-Lac, Sk., Can. D9 106
Fond du Lac, Wi., U.S. H10 118
Fond du Lac, stm., Sk., Can. D9 106
Fondi, Italy C7 24
Fonni, Italy D3 24
Fonseca, Col. B5 86
Fonseca, Golfo de, b., N.A. F4 102
Fontainebleau, Fr. F11 14
Fontana, Arg. C8 92
Fontana, Ca., U.S. I8 134
Fontana Lake, res., N.C., U.S. A2 116
Fontanelle, Ia., U.S. J4 118
Fontas, stm., Can. D6 106
Fonte Boa, Braz. I8 86
Fontenay-le-Comte, Fr. C5 18
Fontenelle, Qc., Can. B12 110
Fontenelle Reservoir, res., Wy., U.S. A6 132
Fontur, c., Ice. j32 8a
Fonyód, Hung. C4 26
Foochow see Fuzhou, China H8 42
Foothills, Ab., Can. C14 138
Forari, Vanuatu k17 79d
Forbach, Fr. E15 14
Forbach, Ger. H4 16
Forbes, Austl. I7 76
Forbes, Mount, mtn., Ab., Can. E14 138
Forbesganj, India E11 54
Forchheim, Ger. G7 16
Ford, Ks., U.S. D9 128
Ford, stm., Mi., U.S. B2 112
Ford City, Ca., U.S. H6 134
Ford City, Pa., U.S. D6 114
Førde, Nor. F1 8
Ford Ranges, mts., Ant. C26 81
Fords Bridge, Austl. G5 76
Fordville, N.D., U.S. F16 124
Fordyce, Ar., U.S. D6 122
Forécariah, Gui. H2 64
Forel, Mont, mtn., Grnld. D18 141
Foreman, Ar., U.S. D4 122
Forest, On., Can. E8 112
Forest, Ms., U.S. E9 122
Forest Acres, S.C., U.S. B4 116
Forestburg, Ab., Can. D18 138
Forest City, N.C., U.S. A4 116
Forest City, Pa., U.S. C10 114
Forest Grove, B.C., Can. E9 138
Foresthill, Ca., U.S. D5 134
Forestier Peninsula, pen., Austl. o14 77a
Forest Lake, Mn., U.S. F5 118
Forest Park, Ga., U.S. C1 116
Forestville, Qc., Can. B7 110
Forgan, Ok., U.S. E8 128
Forges-les-Eaux, Fr. E10 14
Forillon, Parc national de, p.o.i., Qc., Can. B12 110
Forked Deer, stm., Tn., U.S. I8 120
Forks, Wa., U.S. C2 136
Forlì, Italy F9 22
Formby Point, c., Eng., U.K. H9 12
Formentera, i., Spain F12 20
Formentor, Cap de, c., Spain E14 20
Formia, Italy C7 24
Formiga, Braz. K3 88
Formosa, Arg. C8 92
Formosa, Braz. H2 88
Formosa, state, Arg. D4 90
Formosa see Taiwan, ctry., Asia J9 42
Formosa, Serra, plat., Braz. F6 84
Formosa Strait see Taiwan Strait, strt., Asia I8 42
Formoso, stm., Braz. G3 88
Fornacelle, Italy G8 22
Forney, Tx., U.S. E2 122
Fornosovo, Russia A13 10
Forres, Scot., U.K. D9 12
Forrest, Austl. F5 74
Forrest, Il., U.S. D9 120
Forrest City, Ar., U.S. B8 122
Forreston, Il., U.S. I9 118
Forsayth, Austl. B4 76
Forst, Ger. E10 16
Forster, Austl. I9 76
Forsyth, Ga., U.S. C2 116
Forsyth, Mo., U.S. H4 120
Forsyth, Mt., U.S. A6 126
Fort Abbās, Pak. D4 54
Fort Albany, On., Can. E14 106
Fortaleza, Braz. B6 88
Fortaleza do Ituxi, Braz. E4 84
Fort Assiniboine, Ab., Can. B15 138
Fort Atkinson, Wi., U.S. B9 120
Fort Bayard see Zhanjiang, China K4 42
Fort Beaufort, S. Afr. H8 70
Fort Belknap Agency, Mt., U.S. F5 124
Fort Benton, Mt., U.S. C16 136
Fort Bragg, Ca., U.S. D2 134
Fort Branch, In., U.S. F10 120
Fort Bridger, Wy., U.S. B6 132
Fort Calhoun, Ne., U.S. C1 120
Fort Chipewyan, Ab., Can. D8 106
Fort Collins, Co., U.S. G7 126
Fort-Coulonge, Qc., Can. C13 112
Fort Covington, N.Y., U.S. E2 110
Fort Davis, Al., U.S. E13 122
Fort Davis, Tx., U.S. D4 130
Fort-de-France, Mart. k6 105c
Fort-de-France-Lamentin, Aérodrome de, Mart. k7 105c
Fort Deposit, Al., U.S. F12 122
Fort Dodge, Ia., U.S. B3 120
Fort Duchesne, Ut., U.S. C7 132
Forte dei Marmi, Italy G7 22
Fort Edward, N.Y., U.S. G3 110
Fort Erie, On., Can. F10 112
Fortescue, stm., Austl. D3 74
Fortezza, Italy D8 22
Fort Frances, On., Can. C5 118
Fort Fraser, B.C., Can. B6 138
Fort Frederica National Monument, p.o.i., Ga., U.S. E4 116
Fort Gaines, Ga., U.S. F13 122
Fort Garland, Co., U.S. D3 128
Fort Gibson, Ok., U.S. I2 120
Fort Good Hope, N.T., Can. B5 106
Forth, Firth of, b., Scot., U.K. E10 12

Name — Map Ref. — Page

Fort Hall, Id., U.S. G14 136
Fortine, Mt., U.S. B12 136
Fortín Uno, Arg. I5 92
Fort Jones, Ca., U.S. B3 134
Fort Klamath, Or., U.S. H4 136
Fort Knox, Ky., U.S. G12 120
Fort-Lamy see N'Djamena, Chad E3 62
Fort Laramie, Wy., U.S. E8 126
Fort Lauderdale, Fl., U.S. J5 116
Fort Liard, N.T., Can. C6 106
Fort Loramie, Oh., U.S. D1 114
Fort Loudoun Lake, res., Tn., U.S. B15 122
Fort Lyon Canal, can., Co., U.S. C5 128
Fort MacKay, Ab., Can. D8 106
Fort Macleod, Ab., Can. G17 138
Fort Madison, Ia., U.S. D6 120
Fort Matanzas National Monument, p.o.i., Fl., U.S. G4 116
Fort McMurray, Ab., Can. D8 106
Fort McPherson, N.T., Can. B4 106
Fort Meade, Fl., U.S. I4 116
Fort Mill, S.C., U.S. A5 116
Fort Morgan, Co., U.S. A5 128
Fort Myers, Fl., U.S. J3 116
Fort Myers Beach, Fl., U.S. J3 116
Fort Nelson, B.C., Can. D6 106
Fort Nelson, stm., B.C., Can. D6 106
Fort Ogden, Fl., U.S. I4 116
Fort Payne, Al., U.S. C13 122
Fort Peck, Mt., U.S. F7 124
Fort Peck Dam, dam, Mt., U.S. G7 124
Fort Peck Lake, res., Mt., U.S. G7 124
Fort Pierce, Fl., U.S. I5 116
Fort Plain, N.Y., U.S. B11 114
Fort Portal, Ug. D6 66
Fort Providence, N.T., Can. C7 106
Fort Pulaski National Monument, p.o.i., Ga., U.S. E5 116
Fort Qu'Appelle, Sk., Can. D10 124
Fort Randall Dam, dam, S.D., U.S. D14 126
Fort Recovery, Oh., U.S. D1 114
Fort Resolution, N.T., Can. C8 106
Fort Rixon, Zimb. B9 70
Fort Saint James, B.C., Can. B6 138
Fort Saint John, B.C., Can. D6 106
Fort Saskatchewan, Ab., Can. C17 138
Fort Scott, Ks., U.S. G3 120
Fort-Ševčenko, Kaz. F7 32
Fort Severn, On., Can. D13 106
Fort Simpson, N.T., Can. C6 106
Fort Smith, N.T., Can. C8 106
Fort Smith, Ar., U.S. B4 122
Fort Stockton, Tx., U.S. D4 130
Fort Sumner, N.M., U.S. G4 128
Fort Sumter National Monument, p.o.i., S.C., U.S. D6 116
Fort Supply, Ok., U.S. E9 128
Fort Thomas, Az., U.S. J7 132
Fort Totten, N.D., U.S. G14 124
Fort Towson, Ok., U.S. D3 122
Fortuna, Arg. G5 92
Fortuna, C.R. G5 102
Fortuna, Ca., U.S. C1 134
Fortuna, V.I.U.S. e6 104b
Fortune Bay, b., Nf., Can. j22 107a
Fortuneswell, Eng., U.K. K10 12
Fort Union National Monument, p.o.i., N.M., U.S. F3 128
Fort Valley, Ga., U.S. D2 116
Fort Vermilion, Ab., Can. D7 106
Fort Victoria, hist., Ber. k16 104e
Fort Walton Beach, Fl., U.S. G12 122
Fort Wayne, In., U.S. G4 112
Fort White, Fl., U.S. G3 116
Fort William, Scot., U.K. E7 12
Fort Worth, Tx., U.S. B10 130
Fort Yates, N.D., U.S. A12 126
Fort Yukon, Ak., U.S. C10 140
Foshan, China J5 42
Fosheim Peninsula, pen., Nu., Can. B9 141
Foso, Ghana H4 64
Fossano, Italy F4 22
Fossil, Or., U.S. F6 136
Fossil Butte National Monument, p.o.i., Wy., U.S. B6 132
Fossil Lake, l., Or., U.S. G6 136
Fossombrone, Italy G9 22
Fosston, Mn., U.S. D3 118
Foster, Austl. L6 76
Foster Bugt, strt., Grnld. C21 141
Fosters, Al., U.S. D11 122
Fostoria, Oh., U.S. C2 114
Fougamou, Gabon E2 66
Fougères, Fr. F7 14
Fouhsin see Fuxin, China C4 38
Fou-kien see Fujian, state, China I7 42
Foula, i., Scot., U.K. n17 12a
Fouling see Fuling, China G2 42
Foulwind, Cape, c., N.Z. E4 80
Foumban, Cam. C2 66
Foum-el-Hassan, Mor. D3 64
Foum-Zguid, Mor. C3 64
Foundiougne, Sen. G1 64
Fountain, Co., U.S. C4 128
Fountain, Fl., U.S. G13 122
Fountain City, Wi., U.S. G7 118
Fountain Green, Ut., U.S. D5 132
Fountain Peak, mtn., Ca., U.S. I1 132
Fountain Place, La., U.S. G7 122
Fourche LaFave, stm., Ar., U.S. C6 122
Fourchu, N.S., Can. E16 110
Four Corners, Or., U.S. F4 136
Fourmies, Fr. D13 14
Four Mountains, Islands of, is., Ak., U.S. g24 140a
Four Oaks, N.C., U.S. A7 116
Fourth Cataract see Rābi', Ash-Shallāl ar-, wtfl, Sudan D6 62
Fous, Pointe des, c., Dom. j6 105c
Fouta Djalon, reg., Gui. G2 64
Foux, Cap à, c., Haiti C11 102
Fouyang see Fuyang, China E6 42
Foveaux Strait, strt., N.Z. H3 80
Fowler, Co., U.S. C4 128
Fowler, In., U.S. H2 112
Fowler, Mi., U.S. E5 112
Fowlers Bay, Austl. F6 74
Fowlerville, Mi., U.S. B1 114
Fox, stm., U.S. C9 120
Fox, stm., U.S. D5 120
Fox, stm., Wi., U.S. H10 118
Fox Creek, Ab., Can. B14 138
Foxe Basin, b., Nu., Can. B15 106
Foxe Channel, strt., Nu., Can. C15 106
Foxe Peninsula, pen., Nu., Can. C15 106
Foxford, Ire. H3 12
Fox Islands, is., Ak., U.S. g25 140a
Fox Lake, Il., U.S. B9 120
Foxpark, Wy., U.S. B10 132
Fox Valley, Sk., Can. D4 124
Foxworth, Ms., U.S. F9 122
Foyle, Lough, b., Eur. F5 12
Foz do Areia, Represa de, res., Braz. B12 92
Foz do Cunene, Ang. D1 68
Foz do Iguaçu, Braz. B10 92
Foz do Jordão, Braz. E3 84
Foz Giraldo, Port. E3 20
Fraga, Spain C11 20
Fraile Muerto, Ur. F10 92
Framingham, Ma., U.S. B14 114
França, Braz. F5 88
Franca, Braz. K2 88
Franca-Iosifa, Zemlja, is., Russia B9 30
Francavilla al Mare, Italy H11 22
Francavilla Fontana, Italy D11 24
France, ctry., Eur. C8 18
Frances, stm., Yk., Can. C5 106
Frances Lake, l., Yk., Can. C4 106
Francés Viejo, Cabo, c., Dom. Rep. C13 102
Franceville, Gabon E2 66
Franche-Comté, hist. reg., Fr. B12 18
Francis, Sk., Can. D10 124
Francis Case, Lake, res., S.D., U.S. D13 126
Francisco Beltrão, Braz. B11 92
Francisco I. Madero, Mex. C6 100
Francisco I. Madero, Mex. I4 130
Francisco Murguía, Mex. C7 100
Francisco Sá, Braz. I4 88
Francistown, Bots. B8 70
Francofonte, Italy G8 24
François Lake, B.C., Can. B5 138
Francois Lake, l., B.C., Can. C5 138
Francs Peak, mtn., Wy., U.S. C3 126
Frankel City, Tx., U.S. B5 130
Franken, hist. reg., Ger. G6 16
Frankenberg, Ger. F9 16
Frankenberg, Ger. E4 16
Frankenmuth, Mi., U.S. E6 112
Frankford, On., Can. D12 112
Frankford, Mo., U.S. E6 120
Frankfort, S. Afr. E9 70
Frankfort, In., U.S. H3 112
Frankfort, Ks., U.S. B12 128
Frankfort, Ky., U.S. F13 120
Frankfort, N.Y., U.S. A10 114
Frankfort, Oh., U.S. E2 114
Frankfort, S.D., U.S. C14 126
Frankfurt, Ger. D10 16
Frankfurt am Main, Ger. F4 16
Franklin, Az., U.S. K7 132
Franklin, Ga., U.S. D13 122
Franklin, Id., U.S. A5 132
Franklin, Il., U.S. E7 120
Franklin, In., U.S. E11 120
Franklin, Ma., U.S. B14 114
Franklin, Ne., U.S. A9 128
Franklin, N.H., U.S. G5 110
Franklin, N.J., U.S. C11 114
Franklin, N.C., U.S. A2 116
Franklin, Oh., U.S. E1 114
Franklin, Pa., U.S. C6 114
Franklin, Tn., U.S. I11 120
Franklin, Tx., U.S. F2 122
Franklin, Va., U.S. H9 114
Franklin, Wi., U.S. F2 112
Franklin Bay, b., N.T., Can. B5 106
Franklin D. Roosevelt Lake, res., Wa., U.S. B4 108
Franklin Gordon Wild Rivers National Park, p.o.i., Austl. o12 77a
Franklin Grove, Il., U.S. C8 120
Franklin Lake, l., Nu., Can. B12 106
Franklin Mountains, mts., N.T., Can. B5 106
Franklin Strait, strt., Nu., Can. A11 106
Franklinton, La., U.S. G8 122
Franklinville, N.Y., U.S. B7 114
Frankston, Tx., U.S. E3 122
Frankton, In., U.S. H4 112
Fransfontein, Nmb. B2 70
Franzensfeste see Fortezza, Italy D8 22
Franz Josef Land see Franca-Iosifa, Zemlja, is., Russia B9 30
Frascati, Italy I9 22
Fraser, B.C., Can. G13 138
Fraser, Co., U.S. B3 128
Fraser, stm., B.C., Can. G9 138
Fraser, Mount, mtn., Austl. E3 74
Fraserburgh, Scot., U.K. D11 12
Fraser Island, i., Austl. E9 76
Fraser Lake, B.C., Can. B6 138
Fraser Lake, l., B.C., Can. B6 138
Fraser Plateau, plat., B.C., Can. E8 138
Fraser Range, Austl. F4 74
Frauenfeld, Switz. C5 22
Fray Bentos, Ur. F8 92
Fray Jorge, Parque Nacional, p.o.i., Chile E2 92
Fray Marcos, Ur. G10 92
Frazer, Mt., U.S. F7 124
Frederic, Wi., U.S. F6 118
Frederica, De., U.S. E10 114
Fredericia, Den. I3 8
Frederick, Md., U.S. E8 114
Frederick, S.D., U.S. B14 126
Frederick Hills, hills, Austl. B7 74
Frederick Reef, rf., Austl. C10 76
Fredericksburg, Ia., U.S. B5 120
Fredericksburg, Tx., U.S. D9 130
Fredericksburg, Va., U.S. F8 114
Fredericktown, Oh., U.S. D3 114
Frederico Westphalen, Braz. C11 92
Fredericton, N.B., Can. E10 110
Fredericton Junction, N.B., Can. E10 110
Frederiksborg, state, Den. H5 8
Frederiksdal, Grnld. E17 141
Frederikshåb (Paamiut), Grnld. E15 141
Frederikshavn, Den. H4 8
Frederiksted, V.I.U.S. h10 104c
Fredonia, Ks., U.S. G2 120
Fredonia, N.Y., U.S. B6 114
Fredonia, N.D., U.S. A13 126
Fredrika, Swe. D8 8
Fredrikstad, Nor. G4 8
Freeburg, Il., U.S. F8 120
Freeland, Mi., U.S. E5 112
Freeland, Pa., U.S. C9 114
Freel Peak, mtn., Ca., U.S. E5 134
Freels, Cape, c., Nf., Can. j23 107a
Freeman, S.D., U.S. D15 126
Freeport, Bah. B9 96
Freeport, N.S., Can. F10 110
Freeport, Fl., U.S. G12 122
Freeport, Il., U.S. B8 120
Freeport, N.Y., U.S. H16 112
Freeport, Pa., U.S. D6 114
Freeport, Tx., U.S. F12 130
Free State, state, S. Afr. F8 70
Freetown, Antig. f4 105b
Freetown, S.L. H2 64
Fregenal de la Sierra, Spain F4 20
Freiberg, Ger. F9 16
Freiburg see Fribourg, Switz. D4 22
Freiburg im Breisgau, Ger. I3 16
Freirina, Chile D2 92
Freising, Ger. H7 16
Freistadt, Aus. B11 22
Freital, Ger. F9 16
Fréjus, Fr. F12 18
Fremantle, Austl. F3 74
Fremont, Ca., U.S. F4 134
Fremont, In., U.S. C1 114
Fremont, Ia., U.S. C5 120
Fremont, Mi., U.S. E4 112
Fremont, Ne., U.S. C1 120
Fremont, Oh., U.S. C2 114
Fremont, Wi., U.S. G10 118
Fremont, stm., Ut., U.S. E6 132
French, stm., On., Can. B9 112
French Broad, stm., U.S. I3 114
Frenchcap Cay, i., V.I.U.S. f7 104b
French Guiana, dep., S.A. C7 84
French Island, i., Austl. L5 76
French Lick, In., U.S. F11 120
Frenchman (Frenchman Creek), stm., N.A. E5 124
Frenchman Creek (Frenchman), stm., N.A. E5 124
Frenchman Creek, stm., U.S. G11 126
Frenchmans Cap, mtn., Austl. o12 77a
French Polynesia, dep., Oc. K24 142
French Somaliland see Djibouti, ctry., Afr. E8 62
Fresco, C. Iv. H3 64
Fresco, stm., Braz. E7 84
Fresnillo, Mex. D7 100
Fresno, Ca., U.S. G6 134
Fresno, stm., Ca., U.S. F6 134
Fresno Reservoir, res., Mt., U.S. B16 136
Freu, Cap des, c., Spain E14 20
Freudenstadt, Ger. H4 16
Frewena, Austl. C7 74
Frewsburg, N.Y., U.S. B6 114
Freycinet National Park, p.o.i., Austl. o14 77a
Freycinet Peninsula, pen., Austl. o14 77a
Freyre, Arg. E6 92
Fria, Gui. G2 64
Fria, Cape, c., Nmb. D1 68
Friant, Ca., U.S. G6 134
Friars Point, Ms., U.S. C8 122
Frías, Arg. D5 92
Fribourg (Freiburg), Switz. D4 22
Fridley, Mn., U.S. F5 118
Fridtjof Nansen, Mount, mtn., Ant. D25 81
Friedberg, Aus. C12 22
Friedberg, Ger. F4 16
Friedberg, Ger. H7 16
Friedland, Ger. C9 16
Friedrichshafen, Ger. I5 16
Friend, Ne., U.S. G15 126
Friendship, N.Y., U.S. B7 114
Friendship, Tn., U.S. I8 120
Fries, Va., U.S. H4 114
Friesach, Aus. D11 22
Frio, stm., Tx., U.S. F9 130
Frio, Cabo, c., Braz. L5 88
Frio Draw, stm., U.S. G6 128
Friona, Tx., U.S. G6 128
Frisco, Tx., U.S. D2 122
Frisian Islands, is., Eur. A14 14
Fritch, Tx., U.S. F7 128
Fritzlar, Ger. E5 16
Friuli, hist. reg., Italy E9 22
Friuli-Venezia Giulia, state, Italy D9 22
Frjazino, Russia E21 10
Frobisher, Sk., Can. E11 124
Frobisher Bay, b., Nu., Can. C17 106
Frobisher Lake, l., Sk., Can. D9 106
Froid, Mt., U.S. F9 124
Frolovo, Russia E6 32
Frome, Eng., U.K. J10 12
Frome, stm., Austl. G2 76
Frome, Lake, l., Austl. H2 76
Fronteiras, Braz. D5 88
Frontenac, Ks., U.S. G3 120
Frontera, Mex. F12 100
Frontera, Mex. B8 100
Frontier, Sk., Can. E5 124
Frontier, Wy., U.S. B6 132
Frontino, Col. B2 84
Frontino, Páramo, mtn., Col. D3 86
Front Range, mts., Co., U.S. H7 126
Front Royal, Va., U.S. F7 114
Frosinone, Italy C7 24
Frostburg, Md., U.S. E6 114
Frostproof, Fl., U.S. I4 116
Frøya, i., Nor. E3 8
Fruges, Fr. D11 14
Fruita, Co., U.S. D8 132
Fruitdale, Or., U.S. H3 136
Fruithurst, Al., U.S. D13 122
Fruitland, Id., U.S. F10 136
Fruitport, Mi., U.S. E3 112
Fruitvale, B.C., Can. G13 138
Fruitvale, Wa., U.S. D6 136
Frunzivka, Ukr. B16 26
Frutal, Braz. J1 88
Frutigen, Switz. D4 22
Frýdek-Místek, Czech Rep. G14 16
Fryeburg, Me., U.S. G6 110
Fu, stm., China G7 42
Fu, stm., China F2 42
Fu, stm., China G6 42
Fua'amotu International Airport, Tonga n14 78e
Fu'an, China H8 42
Fuchou see Fuzhou, China H8 42
Fuchow see Fuzhou, China G7 42
Fuchū, Japan E6 40
Fuchun, stm., China G8 42
Fuding, China H9 42
Fuego, Volcán de, vol., Guat. E2 102
Fuencaliente, Spain F6 20
Fuengirola, Spain H6 20
Fuensalida, Spain D6 20
Fuente, Mex. F7 130
Fuente de Cantos, Spain F4 20
Fuente de Oro, Col. F5 86
Fuentes de Ebro, Spain C10 20
Fuerte, stm., Mex. B4 100
Fuerte Olimpo, Para. D5 90
Fuga Island, i., Phil. A3 52
Fugou, China D6 42
Fuhai, China B2 36
Fuhsien see Wafangdian, China B9 42
Fuji, Japan D11 40
Fuji, Mount see Fuji-san, vol., Japan D11 40
Fujian, state, China I7 42
Fujieda, Japan E11 40
Fujin, China B11 36
Fujinomiya, Japan D11 40
Fuji-san (Fuji, Mount), vol., Japan D11 40
Fujisawa, Japan D12 40
Fujiyama see Fuji-san, vol., Japan D11 40
Fuji-yoshida, Japan D11 40
Fukagawa, Japan C14 38
Fukang, China C2 36
Fukave, i., Tonga n14 78e
Fukaya, Japan C12 40
Fukien see Fujian, state, China I7 42
Fukuchiyama, Japan D8 40
Fukue, Japan G1 40
Fukue-jima, i., Japan G1 40
Fukui, Japan C9 40
Fukui, state, Japan D9 40
Fukuoka, Japan F3 40
Fukuoka, state, Japan F3 40
Fukuroi, Japan E10 40
Fukushima, Japan B13 40
Fukushima, state, Japan B12 40
Fukuyama, Japan E6 40
Fūlādī, Kūh-e, mtn., Afg. C10 56
Fulaga Passage, strt., Fiji q20 79e
Fulda, Ger. F5 16
Fulda, Mn., U.S. H3 118
Fulda, stm., Ger. E5 16
Fuling, China G2 42
Fullarton, stm., Austl. C3 76
Fullerton, Ca., U.S. J8 134
Fullerton Point, c., Antig. f4 105b
Fulong, China J2 42
Fulton, Al., U.S. F11 122
Fulton, Ar., U.S. D5 122
Fulton, Il., U.S. C7 120
Fulton, Ks., U.S. F3 120
Fulton, Ky., U.S. H9 120
Fulton, Mo., U.S. F5 120
Fulton, N.Y., U.S. E13 112
Fulton, Tx., U.S. F10 130
Fumay, Fr. D13 14
Funabashi, Japan D12 40
Funafuti, i., Tuvalu D8 72
Funan, China E6 42
Funchal, Port. C1 64
Fundación, Col. B4 86
Fundão, Port. D3 20
Fundy, Bay of, b., Can. F10 110
Fundy National Park, p.o.i., N.B., Can. E11 110
Funhalouro, Moz. C12 70
Funing, China E8 42
Funiu Shan, mts., China E5 42
Funsi, Ghana G4 64
Funtua, Nig. G6 64
Fuping, China D3 42
Fuqing, China I8 42
Fuquay-Varina, N.C., U.S. A7 116
Furculeşti, Rom. F12 26
Furmanov, Russia H19 8
Furnas, Represa de, res., Braz. K2 88
Furneaux Group, is., Austl. m13 77a
Furnes see Veurne, Bel. C11 14
Fürstenberg / Havel, Ger. C9 16
Fürstenfeld, Aus. C12 22
Fürstenfeldbruck, Ger. H7 16
Fürstenwalde, Ger. D9 16
Fürth, Ger. G6 16
Furth im Wald, Ger. G8 16
Furukawa, Japan C10 40
Furukawa, Japan A13 40
Fury and Hecla Strait, strt., Nu., Can. B14 106
Fusagasugá, Col. E4 86
Fusan see Pusan, Kor., S. D2 40
Fushan, China C9 42
Fushan, China D4 42
Fushih see Yan'an, China C3 42
Fushun, China D5 38
Fushun, China G1 42
Fusilier, Sk., Can. C4 124
Fusong, China C7 38
Füssen, Ger. I6 16
Fuste, Picacho del, mtn., Mex. G5 130
Fusui, China J2 42
Futun, stm., China H7 42
Futuna, Île, i., Wal./F. E9 72
Futuyu, China B6 42
Fuwa, Egypt G1 58
Fuxian Hu, l., China G5 36
Fuxin, China C4 38
Fuyang, China E6 42
Fuyang, stm., China C6 42
Fuyu, China B9 36
Fuyu, China B6 38
Fuyuan see Tongjiang, China B11 36
Fuyuan, China F5 36
Fuyuan, China B11 36
Fuzhou, China G7 42
Fuzhou, China H8 42
Fyn, state, Den. I4 8
Fyn, i., Den. I4 8
Fyne, Loch, b., Scot., U.K. E7 12
Fyresvatnet, l., Nor. G2 8

G

Gaalkacyo, Som. C9 66
Gabare, Blg. F10 26
Gabarus, N.S., Can. E16 110
Gabela, Ang. C1 68
Gaberones see Gaborone, Bots. D7 70
Gabès, Tun. C7 64
Gabiarra, Braz. I6 88
Gabon, ctry., Afr. E2 66
Gaborone, Bots. D7 70
Gabras, Sudan E5 62
Gabriel Strait, strt., Nu., Can. C17 106
Gabriel y Galán, Embalse de, res., Spain D4 20
Gabrovo, Blg. G12 26
Gacé, Fr. F9 14
Gackle, N.D., U.S. A13 126
Gadag, India D2 53
Gādarwāra, India G7 54
Gäddede, Swe. D6 8
Gado Bravo, Ilha do, i., Braz. F4 88
Gádor, Spain H8 20
Gadsden, Al., U.S. C12 122
Gadsden, Az., U.S. K2 132
Gadwāl, India C3 53
Gael Hamke Bugt, b., Grnld. C22 141
Găeşti, Rom. E12 26
Gaeta, Italy C7 24
Gaeta, Golfo di, b., Italy C7 24
Gaferut, i., Micron. C5 72
Gaffney, S.C., U.S. A4 116
Gafour, Tun. H3 24
Gafsa, Tun. C6 64
Gag, Pulau, i., Indon. F8 44
Gagarin, Russia E17 10
Gage, Ok., U.S. E9 128
Gaggenau, Ger. H4 16
Gagliano del Capo, Italy E12 24
Gagnoa, C. Iv. H3 64
Gagra, Geor. F5 32
Gaibandha, Bngl. F12 54
Gail, Tx., U.S. B6 130
Gaillac, Fr. F7 18
Gaillimh see Galway, Ire. H3 12
Gaimán, Arg. H3 90
Gainesboro, Tn., U.S. H12 120
Gainesville, Fl., U.S. G3 116
Gainesville, Ga., U.S. B2 116
Gainesville, Mo., U.S. H5 120
Gainesville, Tx., U.S. H11 128
Gainsborough, Eng., U.K. H12 12
Gainsborough Creek, stm., Can. E12 124
Gairdner, Lake, l., Austl. F7 74
Gaithersburg, Md., U.S. E8 114
Gaixian, China A10 42
Gaizina Kalns, hill, Lat. D8 10
Gajendragarh, India D2 53
Gajny, Russia B8 32
Gajuapara, stm., Braz. C2 88
Gajutino, Russia B21 10
Gakarosa, mtn., S. Afr. E6 70
Gakona, Ak., U.S. D10 140
Galahad, Ab., Can. D19 138
Galâla el Baharîya, Gebel el-, mts., Egypt I3 58
Galâla el-Qiblîya, Gebel el-, mts., Egypt J3 58
Galán, Cerro, mtn., Arg. C4 92
Galana, stm., Kenya E7 66
Galanta, Slov. H13 16
Galapagos Islands see Colón, Archipiélago de, is., Ec. h12 84a
Galashiels, Scot., U.K. F9 12
Galaţi, Rom. D14 26
Galaţi, state, Rom. D14 26
Galatia, Il., U.S. G9 120
Galatina, Italy D12 24
Galaxídi, Grc. E5 28
Galdhøpiggen, mtn., Nor. F2 8
Galeana, Mex. F9 98
Galeana, Mex. C8 100
Galela, Indon. E8 44
Galena, Ak., U.S. D8 140
Galena, Il., U.S. B7 120
Galena, Mo., U.S. H4 120
Galena Park, Tx., U.S. E12 130
Galeota Point, c., Trin. s13 105f
Galera, Punta, c., Chile G2 90
Galera, Punta, c., Ec. G1 86
Galera Point, c., Trin. s13 105f
Galeras, Volcán, vol., Col. G3 86
Galesburg, Il., U.S. D7 120
Galesville, Wi., U.S. G7 118
Galeton, Pa., U.S. C8 114
Galiano Island, i., B.C., Can. H7 138
Galič, Russia G20 8
Galicia, state, Spain B3 20
Galicia, hist. reg., Eur. G18 16
Galičica Nacionalni Park, p.o.i., Mac. C3 28
Galičskaja vozvyšennost', hills, Russia G20 8
Galičskoe, ozero, l., Russia G20 8
Galilee, Lake, l., Austl. D5 76
Galilee, Sea of see Kinneret, Yam, l., Isr. F6 58
Galiléia, Braz. J5 88
Galina Point, c., Jam. i14 104d
Galion, Oh., U.S. D3 114
Galite, Canal de la, strt., Tun. G3 24
Gallarate, Italy E5 22
Gallatin, Tn., U.S. H11 120
Gallatin, stm., U.S. E15 136
Galle, Sri L. H5 53
Gállego, stm., Spain B10 20
Gallegos, stm., Arg. J3 90
Galliano, La., U.S. H8 122
Gallinas, stm., N.M., U.S. F4 128
Gallinas, Punta, c., Col. A6 86
Gallipoli, Italy D11 24
Gallipoli see Gelibolu, Tur. C9 28
Gallipoli Peninsula see Gelibolu Yarımadası, pen., Tur. C9 28
Gallipolis, Oh., U.S. F3 114
Gällivare, Swe. C9 8
Gallo, Capo, c., Italy F7 24
Gallo Arroyo, stm., N.M., U.S. G3 128
Galloo Island, i., N.Y., U.S. E13 112
Galloway, hist. reg., Scot., U.K. G8 12
Galloway, Mull of, c., Scot., U.K. G8 12
Gallup, N.M., U.S. H8 132
Gallura, reg., Italy C3 24
Galoa Harbour, b., Fiji q19 79e
Galt, Ca., U.S. E4 134
Galtat Zemmour, W. Sah. D2 64
Galty Mountains, mts., Ire. I4 12
Galva, Il., U.S. C7 120
Galva, Ks., U.S. C11 128
Galveston, In., U.S. H3 112
Galveston, Tx., U.S. H4 122
Galveston Bay, b., Tx., U.S. H4 122
Galveston Island, i., Tx., U.S. E13 130
Gálvez, Arg. F7 92
Galway (Gaillimh), Ire. H3 12
Galway, state, Ire. H4 12
Galway Bay, b., Ire. H3 12
Gam (Jin), stm., Asia A7 48
Gama, Isla, i., Arg. H4 90
Gamagōri, Japan E10 40
Gamarra, Col. C5 86
Gamay, Phil. D5 52
Gamba, China D12 54
Gambaga, Ghana G4 64
Gambēla, Eth. F6 62
Gambell, Ak., U.S. D5 140
Gambia (Gambie), stm., Afr. G1 64
Gambia, The, ctry., Afr. G1 64
Gambie (Gambia), stm., Afr. G2 64
Gambier, Îles, is., Fr. Poly. F13 72
Gamboa, Pan. C2 86
Gamboma, Congo E3 66
Gamboula, C.A.R. D2 66
Gamka, stm., S. Afr. H5 70
Gamlakarleby see Kokkola, Fin. E10 8
Gamleby, Swe. H7 8
Gammon Ranges National Park, p.o.i., Austl. H2 76
Ga-Mogara, stm., S. Afr. E6 70
Gan, stm., China B10 36
Gan, stm., China G6 42
Ganado, Az., U.S. H7 132
Ganado, Tx., U.S. E11 130
Gananoque, On., Can. D13 112
Gäncä, Azer. A6 56
Gand see Gent, Bel. C12 14
Ganda, Ang. C1 68
Gandadiwata, Bulu, mtn., Indon. E11 50
Gandajika, D.R.C. F4 66
Gandak (Nārāyani), stm., Asia E10 54
Gándara, Spain A2 20
Gander, Nf., Can. j23 107a
Ganderkesee, Ger. C4 16
Gandesa, Spain C11 20
Gandevi, India H4 54
Gāndhinagar, India G4 54
Gandhi Reservoir see Gāndhi Sāgar, res., India F5 54
Gāndhi Sāgar, res., India F5 54
Gandia, Spain F10 20
Gandu, Braz. G6 88
Ganga see Ganges, stm., Asia F11 54
Gan Gan, Arg. H3 90
Gangānagar, India D4 54
Gangāpur, India B2 53
Gangāpur, India F5 54
Gangāpur, India E6 54
Gangārāmpur, India F12 54
Gangaw, Mya. A2 48
Gangāwati, India D3 53
Gangdhār, India G5 54
Gangdisê Shan, mts., China C9 54
Ganges, B.C., Can. H7 138
Ganges (Ganga) (Padma), stm., Asia G13 54
Ganges, Mouths of the, mth., Asia H12 54
Ganghu, China B11 54
Gangmar Co, l., China B10 54
Gangneung see Kangnŭng, Kor., S. B1 40
Gangoa, China D5 36
Gangotri, India C7 54
Gangotri, India C7 54
Gangoumen, China D2 38
Gangtok, India E12 54
Gangu, China D1 42
Gangweon see Kangwŏn-do, state, Kor., S. B1 40
Gannan, China B9 36
Gannett Peak, mtn., Wy., U.S. D3 126
Gannvalley, S.D., U.S. C14 126
Ganquan, China C3 42
Gansbaai, S. Afr. I4 70
Gansu, state, China D5 36
Gantang, China H8 42
Gantt, Al., U.S. F12 122
Gantung, Indon. E6 50
Ganyanchi, China C1 42
Ganyesa, S. Afr. E7 70
Ganzê, China E4 36
Ganzhou, China I6 42
Gao, Mali F4 64
Gao'an, China G6 42
Gaochun, China F8 42
Gaohebu, China F7 42
Gaojian, China F9 36
Gaolan, China D5 36
Gaolong, China H5 42
Gaona, Arg. B5 92
Gaoping, China D5 42
Gaotan, China E3 42
Gaotang, China C7 42
Gaoua, Burkina G4 64
Gaoual, Gui. G2 64
Gaoxian, China F5 36
Gaoyi, China C6 42
Gaoyou, China E8 42
Gaoyou Hu, l., China E8 42
Gaozhou, China K4 42
Gap, Fr. E12 18
Gar, China B8 54
Gar, stm., China C8 54
Gara, Lough, l., Ire. H4 12
Garagumskij kanal (Kara-Kum Canal), can., Turkmen. B9 56
Garagumy (Kara-Kum), des., Turkmen. A8 56
Garaina, Pap. N. Gui. b4 79a
Garanhuns, Braz. E7 88
Garapan, N. Mar. Is. B5 72
Garara, Pap. N. Gui. b4 79a
Garber, Ok., U.S. E11 128
Garberville, Ca., U.S. C2 134
Gârbovu, Rom. E10 26
Garça, Braz. L1 88
García, Mex. G8 98
García de Sola, Embalse de, res., Spain E5 20
Gard, state, Fr. F10 18
Garda, Italy E7 22
Garda, Lago di, l., Italy E7 22
Gardelegen, Ger. D7 16
Garden City, Ks., U.S. C8 128
Garden City, Mo., U.S. F3 120
Garden City, Tx., U.S. C6 130
Gardendale, Al., U.S. D12 122
Garden Grove, Ca., U.S. J7 134
Garden Grove, Ia., U.S. D4 120
Garden Island, i., Mi., U.S. C4 112
Garden Peninsula, pen., Mi., U.S. C3 112
Garden Reach, India G11 54
Gardenton, Mb., Can. E17 124
Gardey, Arg. H8 92
Gardeyz, Afg. C10 56
Gardiner, Mt., U.S. E16 136
Gardiner, Or., U.S. G2 136
Gardiner Dam, dam, Sk., Can. C6 124
Gardner, Ks., U.S. F2 120
Gardner, Ma., U.S. B13 114
Gardner Canal, b., B.C., Can. C2 138
Gardnerville, Nv., U.S. E6 134
Garessio, Italy F5 22
Garet, Mont, vol., Vanuatu j16 79d
Garfield, Ks., U.S. C9 128
Garfield, N.M., U.S. K9 132
Garfield Mountain, mtn., Mt., U.S. F14 136
Gargano, Promontorio del, mts., Italy I12 22
Gargano, Testa del, c., Italy I13 22
Gargždai, Lith. E4 10
Garhākota, India G7 54
Garibaldi, Braz. D12 92
Garibaldi, B.C., Can. G7 138
Garibaldi, Or., U.S. E2 136
Garibaldi, Mount, vol., B.C., Can. G8 138
Gariep Dam, res., S. Afr. G7 70
Garies, S. Afr. G4 70
Garigliano, stm., Italy C7 24
Gariglione, Monte, mtn., Italy E10 24
Garissa, Kenya E7 66
Garland, Tx., U.S. E2 122
Garland, Ut., U.S. B4 132
Garlasco, Italy E5 22
Garlin, Fr. F5 18
Garm, Taj. B11 56
Garmisch-Partenkirchen, Ger. I7 16
Garnavillo, Ia., U.S. B6 120
Garner, Ia., U.S. A4 120
Garner, N.C., U.S. I7 114
Garnpung Lake, l., Austl. I4 76
Garona (Garonne), stm., Eur. E5 18
Garonne (Garona), stm., Eur. E5 18
Garoowe, Som. C9 66
Garoua, Cam. C2 66
Garoua Boulaï, Cam. C2 66
Garqu Yan, China B14 54
Garqu Yan, China A14 54
Garrel, Ger. D3 16
Garretson, S.D., U.S. H2 118
Garrett, In., U.S. G4 112
Garrett, Ky., U.S. G3 114
Garrison, N.D., U.S. G12 124
Garrison, Tx., U.S. F4 122
Garrison Dam, dam, N.D., U.S. G12 124
Garry Bay, b., Nu., Can. B13 106
Garry Lake, l., Nu., Can. B10 106
Garsen, Kenya E7 66
Garson, On., Can. B9 112
Garut, Indon. G5 50
Garwolin, Pol. E17 16
Garwood, Tx., U.S. H2 122
Gary, In., U.S. G2 112
Gary, Tx., U.S. E4 122
Gary, W.V., U.S. G4 114
Garyarsa, China C8 54
Garza, Arg. D6 92
Garza Ayala, Mex. H7 130
Garzón, Col. F4 86
Garzón, Ur. G10 92
Gasan-Kuli, Turkmen. B7 56
Gas City, In., U.S. H4 112
Gascogne (Gascony), hist. reg., Fr. F6 18
Gasconade, stm., Mo., U.S. F6 120
Gasconade, Osage Fork, stm., Mo., U.S. G5 120
Gascony see Gascogne, hist. reg., Fr. F6 18
Gascoyne, stm., Austl. D2 74
Gashaka, Nig. H7 64
Gashua, Nig. G7 64
Gaspar, Braz. C13 92
Gasparilla Island, i., Fl., U.S. J3 116
Gaspé, Qc., Can. B12 110
Gaspé, Baie de, b., Qc., Can. B12 110
Gaspé, Cap, c., Qc., Can. B12 110
Gaspe Peninsula see Gaspésie, Péninsule de la, pen., Qc., Can. B11 110
Gaspésie, Péninsule de la (Gaspe Peninsula), pen., Qc., Can. B11 110
Gassaway, W.V., U.S. F5 114
Gasteiz (Vitoria), Spain B8 20
Gaston, Lake, res., U.S. H7 114
Gastonia, N.C., U.S. A4 116
Gastre, Arg. H3 90
Gata, Cabo de, c., Spain H8 20

Name | Map Ref. | Page

Gata, Sierra de, mts., Spain D4 20
Gătaia, Rom. D8 26
Gátas, Akrotírion, c., Cyp. D4 58
Gatčina, Russia A12 10
Gate City, Va., U.S. H3 114
Gateshead, Eng., U.K. G11 12
Gateshead Island, i., Nu., Can. A11 106
Gatesville, N.C., U.S. H9 114
Gatesville, Tx., U.S. C10 130
Gateway, Co., U.S. E8 132
Gatineau, Qc., Can. C14 112
Gatineau, stm., Qc., Can. C14 112
Gatineau, Parc de la, p.o.i., Qc., Can. C13 112
Gatlinburg, Tn., U.S. I2 114
Gattinara, Italy E5 22
Gatton, Austl. F9 76
Gatún, Lago, res., Pan. H7 102
Gatun Lake see Gatún, Lago, res., Pan. H7 102
Gauer Lake, l., Mb., Can. D11 106
Gauja (Koiva), stm., Eur. C7 10
Gaujiena, Lat. C9 10
Gauley, stm., W.V., U.S. F4 114
Gauley Bridge, W.V., U.S. F4 114
Gaurela, India G8 54
Gauribidanūr, India E3 53
Gause, Tx., U.S. G2 122
Gaustatoppen, mtn., Nor. G3 8
Gauteng, state, S. Afr. D9 70
Gavà, Spain C12 20
Gávdos, i., Grc. I7 28
Gavião, stm., Braz. H5 88
Gavins Point Dam, dam, U.S. E15 126
Gävle, Swe. F7 8
Gävleborg, state, Swe. F7 8
Gavorrano, Italy H7 22
Gavrilov-Jam, Russia H18 8
Gawachab, Nmb. E3 70
Gāwān, India F10 54
Gawler, Austl. J2 76
Gawler Ranges, mts., Austl. F7 74
Gaya, India F10 54
Gaya, Niger G5 64
Gaya, Nig. G6 64
Gaylord, Mn., U.S. G4 118
Gayndah, Austl. E8 76
Gays Mills, Wi., U.S. H8 118
Gaza see Ghazzah, Gaza G5 58
Gaza, state, Moz. C11 70
Gazandzhyk see Gazandzyk, Turkmen. B8 56
Gazandzyk, Turkmen. B8 56
Gazaoua, Niger G6 64
Gaza Strip, dep., Asia G5 58
Gazelle Peninsula, pen., Pap. N. Gui. a5 79a
Gaziantep, Tur. A8 58
Gaziantep, state, Tur. B8 58
Gazimağusa (Famagusta), N. Cyp. C4 58
Gazimağusa Körfezi, b., N. Cyp. C4 58
Gazipaşa, Tur. G15 28
Gazivoda Jezero, res., Yugo. G7 26
Gbanga, Lib. H3 64
Gboko, Nig. H6 64
Gdańsk (Danzig), Pol. B14 16
Gdańsk, state, Pol. B14 16
Gdansk, Gulf of, b., Eur. B15 16
Gdov, Russia B10 10
Gdynia, Pol. B14 16
Gearhart Mountain, mtn., Or., U.S. A5 134
Geary, N.B., Can. E10 110
Geary, Ok., U.S. F10 128
Gebe, Pulau, i., Indon. E8 44
Gebze, Tur. C12 28
Geçitkale, N. Cyp. C4 58
Gediz, Tur. D12 28
Gediz (Hermus), stm., Tur. E10 28
Gedser, Den. B7 16
Geel, Bel. C13 14
Geelong, Austl. L5 76
Geelvink Channel, strt., Austl. E2 74
Geesthacht, Ger. C6 16
Geeveston, Austl. o13 77a
Ge Hu, l., China F8 42
Geiger, Al., U.S. E10 122
Geikie, stm., Sk., Can. D9 106
Geisenfeld, Ger. H7 16
Geislingen an der Steige, Ger. H5 16
Geistown, Pa., U.S. D7 114
Geita, Tan. E6 66
Gejiu, China G5 36
Gela, Italy G8 24
Gela, Golfo di, b., Italy H7 24
Gelādī, Eth. F9 62
Gelang, Tanjong, c., Malay. K6 48
Gelasa, Selat, strt., Indon. E5 50
Geleen, Neth. D14 14
Gelembe, Tur. D10 28
Gelendžik, Russia F5 32
Gelgaudiškis, Lith. E6 10
Gelibolu, Tur. C9 28
Gelibolu Yarımadası (Gallipoli Peninsula), pen., Tur. C9 28
Gellibrand River, Austl. L4 76
Gelsenkirchen, Ger. E2 16
Gemas, Malay. K6 48
Gemena, D.R.C. D3 66
Gemert, Neth. E1 16
Gemlik, Tur. C12 28
Gemlik Körfezi, b., Tur. C11 28
Gemona del Friuli, Italy D10 22
Gemsa, Egypt K4 58
Gemsbok National Park, p.o.i., Bots. D5 70
Gemünden, Ger. F5 16
Gen, stm., China A9 36
Genalē (Jubba), stm., Afr. C8 66
Gending, Indon. G8 50
General Acha, Arg. H5 92
General Alvear, Arg. G3 92
General Alvear, Arg. H8 92
General Belgrano, Arg. G8 92
General Bernardo O'Higgins, sci., Ant. B35 81
General Bravo, Mex. C9 100
General Cabrera, Arg. F6 92
General Campos, Arg. E8 92
General Carrera, Lago, l., S.A. I2 90
General Conesa, Arg. H4 90
General Conesa, Arg. H9 92
General Daniel Cerri, Arg. I6 92
General Elizardo Aquino, Para. C9 92
General Enrique Martínez, Ur. F10 92
General Escobedo, Mex. I7 130
General Eugenio A. Garay, Para. D4 90
General Galarza, Arg. F8 92
General Güemes, Arg. B5 92
General Guido, Arg. H8 92
General José de San Martín, Arg. C8 92
General Juan José Ríos, Mex. C4 100
General Juan Madariaga, Arg. H9 92
General La Madrid, Arg. H7 92
General Lavalle, Arg. H9 92
General Levalle, Arg. G5 92
General Manuel Belgrano, Cerro, mtn., Arg. D4 92
General Pico, Arg. G6 92
General Pinedo, Arg. C7 92
General Pizarro, Arg. B6 92
General Ramírez, Arg. F7 92
General Roca, Arg. G3 90
General San Martín, Arg. G8 92
General Santos, Phil. G5 52
General Terán, Mex. C9 100
General Toševo, Blg. F14 26
General Toshevo see General Toševo, Blg. F14 26
General Treviño, Mex. H8 130
General Trias, Mex. F1 130
General Viamonte, Arg. G7 92
General Villegas, Arg. G6 92
Genesee, Id., U.S. D9 136
Genesee, stm., U.S. F12 112
Geneseo, Il., U.S. C7 120
Geneseo, Ks., U.S. C10 128
Geneseo, N.Y., U.S. B8 114
Geneva see Genève, Switz. D3 22
Geneva, Il., U.S. J10 118
Geneva, In., U.S. H5 112
Geneva, Ne., U.S. G15 126
Geneva, N.Y., U.S. B8 114
Geneva, Oh., U.S. C4 114
Geneva, Lake, l., Eur. C12 18
Genève (Geneva), Switz. D3 22
Genève, Lac de see Geneva, Lake, l., Eur. C12 18
Genf see Genève, Switz. D3 22
Gengma, China G4 36
Genil, stm., Spain G5 20
Genk, Bel. C14 14
Genkai-nada, Japan F2 40
Genoa, Austl. K7 76
Genoa see Genova, Italy F5 22
Genoa, Ne., U.S. F15 126
Genoa, Oh., U.S. C2 114
Genoa, Wi., U.S. H7 118
Genova (Genoa), Italy F5 22
Genova, Golfo di, b., Italy G5 22
Genrietty, ostrov, i., Russia A20 34
Gens de Terre, stm., Qc., Can. B13 112
Genshiryoku-kenkyūsho, sci., Japan C13 40
Gent (Ghent), Bel. C12 14
Genteng, Gili, i., Indon. G8 50
Genthin, Ger. D8 16
Gentio do Ouro, Braz. F4 88
Genzano di Roma, Italy I9 22
Geographe Bay, b., Austl. F3 74
Geographical Society Ø, i., Grnld. C21 141
Geok-Tepe, Turkmen. B8 56
George, S. Afr. H6 70
George, Ia., U.S. H2 118
George, stm., Qc., Can. D17 106
George, Lake, l., Austl. D4 74
George, Lake, l., Austl. J7 76
George, Lake, l., Ug. E6 66
George, Lake, l., Fl., U.S. G4 116
George, Lake, res., N.Y., U.S. G3 110
Georgetown, Austl. B4 76
George Town, Austl. n13 77a
Georgetown, On., Can. E9 112
Georgetown, P.E., Can. D14 110
George Town, Cay. Is. C7 102
Georgetown, Gam. G2 64
Georgetown, Guy. B6 84
George Town (Penang), Malay. J4 48
Georgetown, St. Vin. o11 105e
Georgetown, Co., U.S. B3 128
Georgetown, De., U.S. F10 114
Georgetown, Fl., U.S. G4 116
Georgetown, Id., U.S. H15 136
Georgetown, Ky., U.S. F1 114
Georgetown, Ms., U.S. F8 122
Georgetown, Oh., U.S. F2 114
Georgetown, S.C., U.S. C6 116
Georgetown, Tx., U.S. D10 130
George V Coast, cst., Ant. B19 81
George Washington Birthplace National Monument, p.o.i., Va., U.S. F9 114
George Washington Carver National Monument, p.o.i., Mo., U.S. H3 120
George West, Tx., U.S. F9 130
Georgia, ctry., Asia F6 32
Georgia, state, U.S. E11 108
Georgia, Strait of, strt., N.A. G7 138
Georgian Bay, b., On., Can. C8 112
Georgian Bay Islands National Park, p.o.i., On., Can. D9 112
Georgievka, Kaz. E14 32
Georgina, stm., Austl. D2 76
Georg von Neumayer, sci., Ant. B3 81
Gera, Ger. F7 16
Geral, Serra, mts., Braz. C12 92
Geral, Serra, clf, Braz. F2 88
Gerald, Mo., U.S. F6 120
Geral de Goiás, Serra, clf, Braz. G2 88
Geraldine, Mt., U.S. C16 136
Geraldton, Austl. E2 74
Geraldton, On., Can. B11 118
Gérardmer, Fr. F15 14
Gerber, Ca., U.S. C3 134
Gerdine, Mount, mtn., Ak., U.S. D9 140
Gerede, Tur. C15 28
Gereshk, Afg. C9 56
Gérgal, Spain G8 20
Gerik, Malay. J5 48
Gerlachovský štít, mtn., Slov. G16 16
German Democratic Republic see Germany, ctry., Eur. E6 16
Germania Land, reg., Grnld. B21 141
Germantown, Il., U.S. F8 120
Germantown, Tn., U.S. B9 122
Germantown, Wi., U.S. E1 112
Germany, ctry., Eur. E6 16
Germany, Federal Republic of see Germany, ctry., Eur. E6 16
Germencik, Tur. F10 28
Germfask, Mi., U.S. B4 112
Germiston, S. Afr. E9 70
Gernika, Spain A8 20
Gero, Japan D10 40
Geroliménas, Grc. G5 28
Gerona see Girona, Spain B13 20
Geronimo, Ok., U.S. G10 128
Gers, state, Fr. F6 18
Gers, stm., Fr. F6 18
Gêrzê, China B10 54
Geseke, Ger. E4 16
Geser, Indon. F9 44
Getafe, Spain D7 20
Gettysburg, Pa., U.S. E8 114
Getúlio Vargas, Braz. C11 92
Geumpang, Indon. J2 48
Gevgelija, Mac. B5 28
Geyikli, Tur. D9 28
Geyser, Mt., U.S. C16 136
Geyserville, Ca., U.S. E3 134
Geyve, Tur. C13 28
Ghaapplato, plat., S. Afr. E7 70
Ghadāmis, Libya B1 62
Ghagghar, stm., India D5 54
Ghāghara (Kauriālā), stm., Asia E9 54
Ghāghra see Ghāghara, stm., Asia E9 54
Ghakhar, Pak. B4 54
Ghana, ctry., Afr. H4 64
Ghanzi, Bots. B5 70
Ghanzi, state, Bots. C6 70
Gharandal, hist., Jord. H6 58
Gharaunda, India D6 54
Ghardaïa, Alg. C5 64
Ghardimaou, Tun. H2 24
Gharyān, Libya A2 62
Ghāt, Libya C2 62
Ghatere, Mount, mtn., Sol. Is. d8 79b
Ghātprabha, stm., India C2 53
Ghātsīla, India G11 54
Għawdex (Gozo), i., Malta H8 24
Ghazāl, Baḥr al-, stm., Sudan F6 62
Ghāziābād, India D6 54
Ghāzīpur, India F9 54
Ghazlūna, Pak. C1 54
Ghaznī, Afg. C10 56
Ghaznī, state, Afg. B1 54
Ghaznī, stm., Afg. B2 54
Ghazzah (Gaza), Gaza G5 58
Ghazzah, Leb. E6 58
Ghent see Gent, Bel. C12 14
Gheorgheni, Rom. C12 26
Gherla, Rom. C10 26
Gheroo, Geziret, i., Egypt G1 58
Ghīnah, Wādī al-, stm., Sau. Ar. H9 58
Ghisonaccia, Fr. H15 18
Ghizo see Gizo Island, i., Sol. Is. e7 79b
Ghizunabeana Islands, is., Sol. Is. d8 79b
Ghotki, Pak. E2 54
Ghubaysh, Sudan E5 62
Ghūriān, Afg. C9 56
Gianh, stm., Viet. C7 48
Giannitsá, Grc. C5 28
Giant Mountain, mtn., N.Y., U.S. F3 110
Giant's Castle, mtn., S. Afr. F9 70
Giant's Castle Game Reserve, S. Afr. F9 70
Gia Rai, Viet. H7 48
Giarre, Italy G9 24
Gibara, Cuba B9 102
Gibbon, Mn., U.S. G4 118
Gibbons, Ab., Can. C17 138
Gibbonsville, Id., U.S. E13 136
Gibb River, Austl. C5 74
Gibeon, Nmb. D3 70
Gibraleón, Spain G3 20
Gibraltar, Gib. H5 20
Gibraltar, dep., Eur. H5 20
Gibraltar, Strait of, strt. B3 64
Gibraltar Point, c., Eng., U.K. H13 12
Gibsland, La., U.S. E5 122
Gibson City, Il., U.S. D9 120
Gibson Desert, des., Austl. D4 74
Gibsons, B.C., Can. G7 138
Giddalūr, India D4 53
Giddings, Tx., U.S. D11 130
Gidgi, Lake, l., Austl. E5 74
Giedraičiai, Lith. E8 10
Gien, Fr. G11 14
Giessen, Ger. F4 16
Gifatîn, Gezira, is., Egypt K4 58
Gifford, Fl., U.S. I5 116
Gifford, stm., Nu., Can. A14 106
Gifford Creek, Austl. D3 74
Gifgâfa, Bîr, well, Egypt H4 58
Gifhorn, Ger. D6 16
Gifu, Japan D9 40
Gifu, state, Japan D10 40
Giganta, Sierra de la, mts., Mex. C3 100
Gigena see Alcira, Arg. F5 92
Gigha Island, i., Scot., U.K. F7 12
Giglio, Isola del, i., Italy H7 22
Gihu see Gifu, Japan D9 40
Gijón, Spain A5 20
Gila, stm., U.S. K2 132
Gila Bend, Az., U.S. K4 132
Gila Cliff Dwellings National Monument, p.o.i., N.M., U.S. J8 132
Gilbert, La., U.S. E7 122
Gilbert, stm., Austl. C8 74
Gilbert Islands see Kiribati, ctry., Oc. D9 72
Gilbert Islands, is., Kir. D8 72
Gilbert Peak, mtn., Wa., U.S. D5 136
Gilbert Plains, Mb., Can. C13 124
Gilbués, Braz. E3 88
Gildford, Mt., U.S. B16 136
Gilford Island, i., B.C., Can. F4 138
Gilgandra, Austl. H7 76
Gilgil, Kenya E7 66
Gil Gil Creek, stm., Austl. G8 76
Gilgit, Pak. B11 56
Gilirang, Indon. E12 50
Gil Island, i., B.C., Can. C1 138
Giljuj, stm., Russia F14 34
Gillam, Mb., Can. D12 106
Gillen, Lake, l., Austl. E5 74
Gillespie, Il., U.S. E8 120
Gillett, Ar., U.S. C7 122
Gillette, Wy., U.S. C7 126
Gillian, Lake, l., Nu., Can. B16 106
Gillingham, Eng., U.K. J13 12
Gills Rock, Wi., U.S. C3 112
Gilman, Il., U.S. D10 120
Gilman, Wi., U.S. F8 118
Gilmer, Tx., U.S. E4 122
Gilmore City, Ia., U.S. B3 120
Gilroy, Ca., U.S. F4 134
Giltner, Ne., U.S. G14 126
Giluwe, Mount, mtn., Pap. N. Gui. b3 79a
Gīmbī, Eth. F7 62
Gimcheon see Kimch'ŏn, Kor., S. F8 38
Gimie, Mount, vol., St. Luc. m6 105c
Gimli, Mb., Can. D16 124
Gimpu, Indon. D12 50
Gineina, Râs el-, mtn., Egypt I4 58
Gin Gin, Austl. E8 76
Gingoog, Phil. F5 52
Gīnīr, Eth. F8 62
Ginosa, Italy D10 24
Gioia, Golfo di, b., Italy F9 24
Gioia del Colle, Italy D10 24
Gioia Tauro, Italy F9 24
Giong Rieng, Viet. H7 48
Gipuzkoako, co., Spain A8 20
Girafi, Wadi (Paran, Naḥal), stm. I5 58
Giralia, Austl. D2 74
Girard, Il., U.S. E8 120
Girard, Ks., U.S. G3 120
Girard, Oh., U.S. C5 114
Girard, Pa., U.S. C5 114
Girardot, Col. E4 86
Giraud, Pointe, c., Dom. j6 105c
Girgarre, Austl. K5 76
Girīdīh, India F11 54
Girna, stm., India H5 54
Gir National Park, p.o.i., India H3 54
Girne (Kyrenia), N. Cyp. C4 58
Girón, Ec. D2 84
Girona, Spain B13 20
Girona, co., Spain B13 20
Gironde, state, Fr. E5 18
Gironde, est., Fr. D5 18
Gīr Range, mts., India H3 54
Giru, Austl. B6 76
Giruá, Braz. D10 92
Girvan, Scot., U.K. F8 12
Gisborne, N.Z. D8 80
Giscome, B.C., Can. B8 138
Gislaved, Swe. H5 8
Gisors, Fr. E10 14
Gitarama, Rw. E5 66
Gitega, Bdi. E5 66
Giulianova, Italy H10 22
Giurgiu, Rom. F12 26
Giurgiu, state, Rom. E13 26
Giuvala, Pasul, p., Rom. D12 26
Givet, Fr. D13 14
Givors, Fr. D10 18
Giyon, Eth. F7 62
Giza see El-Gîza, Egypt H1 58
Gižduvan, Uzb. F10 32
Gižiga, Russia D21 34
Gižiginskaja guba, b., Russia D20 34
Gizo, Sol. Is. e7 79b
Gizo Island, i., Sol. Is. e7 79b
Giżycko, Pol. B17 16
Gjirokastër, Alb. D14 24
Gjirokastra see Gjirokastër, Alb. D14 24
Gjoa Haven, Nu., Can. B11 106
Gjøvik, Nor. F4 8
Gjuhëzës, Kepi i, c., Alb. D13 24
Gjumri, Arm. A5 56
Glace Bay, N.S., Can. D17 110
Glacier, B.C., Can. E13 138
Glacier Bay, b., Ak., U.S. E12 140
Glacier National Park, p.o.i., B.C., Can. E13 138
Glacier National Park, p.o.i., Mt., U.S. B12 136
Glacier Peak, vol., Wa., U.S. B5 136
Glacier Strait, strt., Nu., Can. B10 141
Glad', Russia A15 10
Gladbrook, Ia., U.S. B5 120
Gladewater, Tx., U.S. E4 122
Gladstone, Austl. D8 76
Gladstone, Mb., Can. D14 124
Gladstone, Mi., U.S. C2 112
Gladstone, Mo., U.S. E3 120
Glåma, stm., Nor. F4 8
Glan, Phil. H5 52
Glaris see Glarus, Switz. C5 22
Glarner Alpen, mts., Switz. D6 22
Glarus, Switz. C5 22
Glarus Alps see Glarner Alpen, mts., Switz. D6 22
Glasco, Ks., U.S. B11 128
Glasgow, Scot., U.K. F8 12
Glasgow, Ky., U.S. G12 120
Glasgow, Mo., U.S. E5 120
Glasgow, Mt., U.S. F7 124
Glasgow, Va., U.S. G6 114
Glassboro, N.J., U.S. E10 114
Glastonbury, Eng., U.K. J10 12
Glauchau, Ger. F8 16
Glazov, Russia C8 32
Glazunovka, Russia H19 10
Gleichen, Ab., Can. F17 138
Glen Alpine, N.C., U.S. A4 116
Glenavon, Sk., Can. D10 124
Glenboro, Mb., Can. E14 124
Glenburn, N.D., U.S. F12 124
Glen Burnie, Md., U.S. E9 114
Glen Canyon, val., U.S. F6 132
Glen Canyon Dam, dam, Az., U.S. G5 132
Glen Canyon National Recreation Area, p.o.i., U.S. F6 132
Glencoe, On., Can. F8 112
Glencoe, S. Afr. F9 70
Glencoe, Mn., U.S. G4 118
Glen Cove, N.Y., U.S. D12 114
Glendale, Az., U.S. J4 132
Glendale, Ca., U.S. I7 134
Glendale, Ms., U.S. F9 122
Glendale, Ut., U.S. F4 132
Glendale, Wi., U.S. A10 120
Glendive, Mt., U.S. G9 124
Glendo, Wy., U.S. E7 126
Glendon, Ab., Can. B19 138
Glendo Reservoir, res., Wy., U.S. E8 126
Glen Elder, Ks., U.S. B10 128
Glenelg, stm., Austl. K3 76
Glengarriff, Ire. J3 12
Glengyle, Austl. E2 76
Glen Innes, Austl. G8 76
Glenmora, La., U.S. G6 122
Glennallen, Ak., U.S. D10 140
Glenns Ferry, Id., U.S. H11 136
Glenoma, Wa., U.S. D4 136
Glenormiston, Austl. D7 74
Glenreagh, Austl. G9 76
Glen Robertson, On., Can. E2 110
Glen Rock, Pa., U.S. E9 114
Glenrock, Wy., U.S. E7 126
Glen Rose, Tx., U.S. B10 130
Glenrothes, Scot., U.K. E9 12
Glens Falls, N.Y., U.S. G3 110
Glenville, Mn., U.S. H5 118
Glenwood, Ab., Can. G17 138
Glenwood, Al., U.S. F12 122
Glenwood, Ar., U.S. C5 122
Glenwood, Ga., U.S. D3 116
Glenwood, Ia., U.S. C2 120
Glenwood, Mn., U.S. F3 118
Glenwood, Va., U.S. H6 114
Glenwood City, Wi., U.S. F6 118
Glenwood Springs, Co., U.S. D9 132
Glidden, Wi., U.S. E8 118
Glide, Or., U.S. G3 136
Glina, Cro. E13 22
Glittertind see Glittertinden, mtn., Nor. F3 8
Glittertinden, mtn., Nor. F3 8
Gliwice, Pol. F14 16
Gljadjanskoe, Russia D10 32
Globe, Az., U.S. J6 132
Glodeni, Mol. B14 26
Głogów, Pol. E11 16
Głogów Małopolski, Pol. F17 16
Glomma see Glåma, stm., Nor. F4 8
Glommersträsk, Swe. D8 8
Glorieta, N.M., U.S. F3 128
Glorieuses. Îles, is., Reu. C8 68
Glorioso Islands see Glorieuses. Îles, is., Reu. C8 68
Gloucester, Austl. H9 76
Gloucester, Eng., U.K. J10 12
Gloucester, Ma., U.S. B15 114
Gloucester, Va., U.S. G9 114
Gloucester Island, i., Austl. B7 76
Glouster, Oh., U.S. E3 114
Gloversville, N.Y., U.S. A11 114
Głowno, Pol. E15 16
Głubczyce, Pol. F13 16
Glubokoe, Kaz. D14 32
Glubokoje see Glubokoe, Kaz. D14 32
Głuchołazy, Pol. F13 16
Glücksburg, Ger. B5 16
Glückstadt, Ger. C5 16
Glucomanka, gora, mtn., Russia B11 38
Glyndon, Mn., U.S. E2 118
Gmünd, Aus. D10 22
Gmünd, Aus. B12 22
Gmunden, Aus. C10 22
Gnalta, Austl. H4 76
Gnezdovo, Russia F14 10
Gniew, Pol. C14 16
Gniezno, Pol. D13 16
Gnilec, Russia H19 10
Gnjilane, Yugo. G8 26
Gnowangerup, Austl. F3 74
Gō, stm., Japan E5 40
Goa, state, India D2 53
Goālpāra, India E13 54
Goaso, Ghana H4 64
Goat Island, i., Antig. e4 105b
Goat Point, c., Antig. e4 105b
Goba, Eth. F8 62
Gobabis, Nmb. C4 70
Göbel, Tur. D11 28
Gobernador Gregores, Arg. I2 90
Gobernador Ingeniero Valentín Virasoro, Arg. D9 92
Gobernador Juan E. Martínez, Arg. D8 92
Gobernador Vera see Vera, Arg. D7 92
Gobi Desert, des., Asia C5 36
Gobō, Japan F8 40
Goce Delčev, Blg. H10 26
Goch, Ger. E2 16
Goðafoss, wtfl, Ice. k31 8a
Godāvari, stm., India C5 53
Godāvari, Mouths of the, mth., India C5 53
Godbout, Qc., Can. A9 110
Goderich, On., Can. E8 112
Godfrey, Il., U.S. F7 120
Godhavn (Qeqertarsuaq), Grnld. D15 141
Godhra, India G4 54
Gödöllő, Hung. B6 26
Godoy Cruz, Arg. F3 92
Gods, stm., Mb., Can. D12 106
Gods Lake, Mb., Can. E12 106
Gods Lake, l., Mb., Can. E12 106
Gods Mercy, Bay of, b., Nu., Can. C13 106
Godthåb (Nuuk), Grnld. E15 141
Godwin Austen see K2, mtn., Asia B12 56
Goeie Hoop, Kaap die see Good Hope, Cape of, c., S. Afr. I4 70
Goéland, Lac au, l., Qc., Can. E15 106
Goes, Neth. C12 14
Goffstown, N.H., U.S. G5 110
Gogebic, Lake, res., Mi., U.S. E9 118
Gogoi, Moz. B11 70
Gogrial, Sudan F5 62
Gohad, India E7 54
Gohpur, India E14 54
Goiana, Braz. D8 88
Goianésia, Braz. H1 88
Goiânia, Braz. I1 88
Goianinha, Braz. D8 88
Goiás, Braz. G7 84
Goiás, state, Braz. C7 90
Goiatuba, Braz. J1 88
Goio-Erê, Braz. B11 92
Goio-Erê, stm., Braz. B11 92
Góis, Port. D2 20
Gojō, Japan E8 40
Gojra, Pak. C4 54
Gokāk, India C2 53
Gökçeada, i., Tur. C8 28
Gökova Körfezi (Kerme, Gulf of), b., Tur. G10 28
Göksu, stm., Tur. B4 58
Göksu, stm., Tur. A6 58
Göktepe, Tur. F11 28
Gokwe, Zimb. D4 68
Golāghāt, India C7 46
Gola Gokarannāth, India D8 54
Gołańcz, Pol. D13 16
Gölbaşı, Tur. D15 28
Gölbası, Tur. A8 58
Golcanda, hist., India C4 53
Golconda, Il., U.S. G9 120
Golconda, Nv., U.S. C8 134
Gölcük, Tur. C12 28
Gołdap, Pol. B18 16
Gold Bridge, B.C., Can. F8 138
Gold Coast see Southport, Austl. F9 76
Gold Coast, cst., Ghana I4 64
Golden, B.C., Can. E13 138
Golden, Co., U.S. B3 128
Golden, Il., U.S. D7 120
Golden Bay, b., N.Z. E5 80
Golden City, Mo., U.S. G3 120
Goldendale, Wa., U.S. E6 136
Golden Gate Highlands National Park, p.o.i., S. Afr. F9 70
Golden Hinde, mtn., B.C., Can. G5 138
Golden Lake, l., On., Can. C12 112
Golden Meadow, La., U.S. H8 122
Goldfield, Ia., U.S. B3 120
Goldfield, Nv., U.S. F8 134
Gold Mountain, mtn., Nv., U.S. F8 134
Goldonna, La., U.S. E5 122
Gold River, B.C., Can. G4 138
Gold Rock, On., Can. B6 118
Goldsboro, N.C., U.S. A7 116
Goldston, N.C., U.S. A6 116
Goldsworthy, Austl. D3 74
Goldthwaite, Tx., U.S. C9 130
Goleniów, Pol. C10 16
Goleta, Ca., U.S. I6 134
Golfito, C.R. H6 102
Golfo de Santa Clara, Mex. F5 98
Gölhisar, Tur. F12 28
Goliad, Tx., U.S. F10 130
Golicyno, Russia E19 10
Golina, Pol. D13 16
Golin Baixing, China B4 38
Gölmarmara, Tur. E10 28
Golmud, China D3 36
Golmud, stm., China A7 46
Golodnaja Guba, ozero, l., Russia C24 8
Golovin, Ak., U.S. D7 140
Golpāyegān, Iran C7 56
Gölpazarı, Tur. C13 28
Golub-Dobrzyń, Pol. C14 16
Golva, N.D., U.S. A8 126
Golyšmanovo, Russia C11 32
Goma, D.R.C. E5 66
Gomang Co, l., China C12 54
Gomati, stm., India E8 54
Gombe, Nig. G7 64
Gombi, Nig. G7 64
Gómez Farías, Mex. A5 100
Gómez Palacio, Mex. C7 100
Gómez Plata, Col. D4 86
Gomo Co, l., China B10 54
Gomogomo, Indon. b1 79a
Gomoh, India G10 54
Gonābād, Iran C8 56
Gonaïves, Haiti C11 102
Gonam, Russia E15 34
Gonam, stm., Russia E14 34
Gonarezhou National Park, p.o.i., Zimb. B10 70
Gonâve, Golfe de la, b., Haiti C11 102
Gonâve, Île de la, i., Haiti C11 102
Gonbad-e Qābūs, Iran B8 56
Gonda, India E8 54
Gondal, India G3 54
Gondar see Gonder, Eth. E7 62
Gondarbal, India A5 54
Gonder, Eth. E7 62
Gondia, India H8 54
Gönen, Tur. C10 28
Gong, stm., China I6 42
Gong'an, China F4 42
Gongcheng, China I4 42
Gongchenqiao, China F8 42
Gonggar, China D13 54
Gonghe, China D5 36
Gongliu, China F14 32
Gongola, stm., Nig. G7 64
Gongshiya, China C10 54
Gongxi, China H6 42
Gongxian, China D5 42
Gongzhuling, China C6 38
Goñi, Ur. F9 92
Goniądz, Pol. C18 16
Gōnoura, Japan F2 40
Gonzales, Ca., U.S. G4 134
Gonzales, La., U.S. G8 122
González, Mex. D9 100
González Moreno, Arg. G6 92
Goochland, Va., U.S. G8 114
Goodenough Island, i., Pap. N. Gui. b5 79a
Gooderham, On., Can. D11 112
Goodeve, Sk., Can. C10 124
Good Hope, Cape of (Goeie Hoop, Kaap die), c., S. Afr. I4 70
Good Hope Mountain, mtn., B.C., Can. E6 138
Goodhue, Mn., U.S. G6 118
Goodland, Fl., U.S. K4 116
Goodland, In., U.S. K11 118
Goodland, Ks., U.S. B7 128
Goodlands, Mb., Can. E13 124
Goodman, Wi., U.S. C1 112
Goodnews Bay, Ak., U.S. E7 140
Goodnight, Co., U.S. C4 128
Goodooga, Austl. G6 76
Goodrich, N.D., U.S. G13 124
Good Spirit Lake, l., Sk., Can. C11 124
Goodview, Mn., U.S. G7 118
Goodwater, Al., U.S. D12 122
Goodyear, Az., U.S. J4 132
Goole, Eng., U.K. H12 12
Goolgowi, Austl. I5 76
Goonda, Moz. A11 70
Goondiwindi, Austl. G8 76
Goongarrie, Austl. F4 74
Goose, stm., N.D., U.S. G17 124
Goose Creek, S.C., U.S. C6 116
Goose Island, i., B.C., Can. E2 138
Goose Lake, l., Sk., Can. C6 124
Goose Lake, l., U.S. B5 134
Gooty, India D3 53
Gopālganj, Bngl. G12 54
Gopālganj, India E10 54
Gopichettipālaiyam, India F3 53
Göppingen, Ger. H5 16
Goqên, China F4 36
Go Quao, Viet. H7 48
Góra Kalwaria, Pol. E17 16
Gorakhpur, India E9 54
Goražde, Bos. F5 26
Gorda, Punta, c., Cuba A6 102
Gorda, Punta, c., Nic. E6 102
Gordeevka, Russia H14 10
Gordion, hist., Tur. D15 28
Gordo, Al., U.S. D11 122
Gordon, Ga., U.S. D2 116
Gordon, Wi., U.S. E7 118
Gordon, Lake, res., Austl. o13 77a
Gordon Creek, stm., Ne., U.S. E11 126
Gordon Downs, Austl. C5 74
Gordon Horne Peak, mtn., B.C., Can. E12 138
Gordonsville, Va., U.S. F7 114
Gordonvale, Austl. A5 76
Gore, N.S., Can. E13 110
Goré, Chad F3 62
Gorē, Eth. F7 62
Gore, N.Z. H3 80
Goreda, Indon. F9 44
Goree, Tx., U.S. H9 128
Gore Range, mts., Co., U.S. H6 126
Goreville, Il., U.S. G8 120
Gorgān, Iran B7 56
Gorgona, Isla, i., Col. F2 86
Gorgota, Rom. E13 26
Gorham, Me., U.S. G6 110
Gori, Geor. F6 32
Gorica see Gorizia, Italy E10 22
Goricy, Russia C19 10
Gorinchem, Neth. C14 14
Gorizia (Gorica), Italy E10 22
Gorj, state, Rom. E10 26
Gorkhā, Nepal E10 54
Gorki see Nižnij Novgorod, Russia H21 8
Gorki, Russia A11 32
Gorkiy Reservoir see Gor'kovskoe vodohranilišče, res., Russia H20 8
Gor'kovskoe vodohranilišče (Gorkiy Reservoir), res., Russia H20 8
Gorlice, Pol. G17 16
Görlitz, Ger. E10 16
Gorman, Tx., U.S. B9 130
Gorna Orjahovica, Blg. F12 26
Gornjak, Russia D14 32
Gornji Vakuf, Bos. F4 26
Gorno-Altajsk, Russia D15 32
Gornozavodsk, Russia B13 36
Gornye Ključi, Russia B10 38
Gorodec, Russia H20 8
Gorodec, Russia B12 10
Gorodno, Russia C12 10
Goroka, Pap. N. Gui. b4 79a
Gorong, Pulau, i., Indon. F9 44
Gorongosa, stm., Moz. B12 70
Gorongosa, Serra da, mtn., Moz. D5 68
Gorontalo, Indon. E7 44
Górowo Iławeckie, Pol. B16 16
Gorškovo, Russia F20 10
Görükle, Tur. C11 28
Gorutuba, stm., Braz. H4 88
Gorzów, state, Pol. D11 16
Gorzów Śląski, Pol. E14 16
Gorzów Wielkopolski (Landsberg), Pol. D11 16
Goschen Strait, strt., Pap. N. Gui. c5 79a
Gosen, Japan B12 40
Gosford, Austl. I8 76
Goshen, N.S., Can. E15 110
Goshen, Ca., U.S. G6 134
Goshen, In., U.S. G4 112
Goshen, N.Y., U.S. C11 114
Goshute Lake, l., Nv., U.S. C2 132
Goshute Valley, val., Nv., U.S. C2 132
Goslar, Ger. E6 16
Gosnells, Austl. F3 74
Gossinga, Sudan F5 62
Gostivar, Mac. B3 28
Gostynin, Pol. D15 16
Göta, stm., Swe. G5 8
Gotebo, Ok., U.S. F10 128
Göteborg (Gothenburg), Swe. H4 8
Gotemba, Japan D11 40
Gotești, Mol. C15 26
Gotha, Ger. F6 16
Gothenburg see Göteborg, Swe. H4 8
Gothenburg, Ne., U.S. G12 126
Gothèye, Niger G5 64
Gotland, state, Swe. G8 8
Gotland, i., Swe. H8 8
Gotō-rettō, is., Japan F1 40
Gotska Sandön, i., Swe. G8 8
Gōtsu, Japan D5 40
Göttingen, Ger. E5 16
Goubangzi, China D4 38

Name	Map Ref.	Page
Gouda, Neth.	B13	14
Goudge, Arg.	G3	92
Goudiri, Sen.	G2	64
Gough Island, i., St. Hel.	K5	60
Gough Lake, l., Ab., Can.	D18	138
Gouin, Réservoir, res., Qc., Can.	B1	110
Goulais, stm., On., Can.	B6	112
Goulburn, Austl.	J7	76
Goulburn Islands, is., Austl.	B6	74
Goulburn River National Park, p.o.i., Austl.	I7	76
Gould, Ar., U.S.	D7	122
Goulds, Fl., U.S.	K5	116
Goumbou, Mali	G3	64
Goundam, Mali	F4	64
Goundi, Chad	F3	62
Gourbeyre, Guad.	h5	105c
Gourdon, Fr.	E7	18
Gouré, Niger	G7	64
Gourma-Rharous, Mali	F4	64
Gournay-en-Bray, Fr.	E10	14
Gouro, Chad	D3	62
Gouverneur, N.Y., U.S.	D14	112
Govan, Sk., Can.	C9	124
Gove, Ks., U.S.	C8	128
Govena, mys, c., Russia	E22	34
Govenlock, Sk., Can.	E4	124
Governador Valadares, Braz.	J5	88
Govind Ballabh Pant Reservoir see Govind Ballabh Pant Sāgar, res., India	F9	54
Govind Ballabh Pant Sāgar, res., India	F9	54
Govind Reservoir see Govind Sāgar, res., India	C6	54
Govind Sāgar, res., India	C6	54
Gowanda, N.Y., U.S.	B7	114
Gower, Mo., U.S.	E3	120
Gowmal (Gumal), stm., Asia	B2	54
Gowmal Kalay, Afg.	B2	54
Gowrie, Ia., U.S.	B3	120
Goya, Arg.	D8	92
Goyaves, Îlets à, is., Guad.	h5	105c
Göyçay, Azer.	A6	56
Goz Beïda, Chad	E4	62
Gozdnica, Pol.	E11	16
Gozha Co, l., China	A5	46
Gozo see Għawdex, i., Malta	H8	24
Graaff-Reinet, S. Afr.	H7	70
Grabo, C. Iv.	I3	64
Grabow, Ger.	C7	16
Grabów nad Prosną, Pol.	E13	16
Gračac, Cro.	F12	22
Gračanica, Bos.	E5	26
Grace, Id., U.S.	H15	136
Gracefield, Qc., Can.	B13	112
Graceville, Fl., U.S.	G13	122
Gracias a Dios, Cabo, c., N.A.	E6	102
Gradaús, Braz.	E7	84
Grado, Italy	E10	22
Grado, Spain	A4	20
Grad Sofija, state, Blg.	G10	26
Grady, Ar., U.S.	C7	122
Grady, N.M., U.S.	G5	128
Graettinger, Ia., U.S.	H4	118
Grafenau, Ger.	H9	16
Gräfenhainichen, Ger.	E8	16
Grafing bei München, Ger.	H7	16
Grafton, Austl.	G9	76
Grafton, Il., U.S.	F7	120
Grafton, N.D., U.S.	F16	124
Grafton, W.V., U.S.	E5	114
Grafton, Wi., U.S.	E2	112
Grafton, Cape, c., Austl.	A5	76
Graham, N.C., U.S.	H6	114
Graham, Mount, mtn., Az., U.S.	K7	132
Graham Island, i., B.C., Can.	E4	106
Graham Island, i., Nu., Can.	B7	141
Graham Lake, res., Me., U.S.	F8	110
Graham Land, reg., Ant.	B34	81
Graham Moore, Cape, c., Nu., Can.	A15	106
Grahamstad see Grahamstown, S. Afr.	H8	70
Grahamstown, S. Afr.	H8	70
Grain Coast, cst., Lib.	I3	64
Grainfield, Ks., U.S.	B8	128
Grajaú, Braz.	C2	88
Grajaú, stm., Braz.	B3	88
Grajewo, Pol.	C18	16
Gramada, Blg.	F9	26
Grambling, La., U.S.	E6	122
Gramilla, Arg.	C5	92
Grammichele, Italy	G8	24
Grampian Mountains, mts., Scot., U.K.	E9	12
Grampians National Park, p.o.i., Austl.	K3	76
Gramsh, Alb.	D14	24
Granada, Col.	F5	86
Granada, Nic.	G5	102
Granada, Spain	G7	20
Granada, Co., U.S.	C6	128
Granada, co., Spain	G7	20
Granadella see La Granadella, Spain	C11	20
Granbury, Tx., U.S.	B10	130
Granbury, Lake, res., Tx., U.S.	B10	130
Granby, Qc., Can.	E4	110
Granby, Co., U.S.	A3	128
Granby, Mo., U.S.	H3	120
Granby, stm., B.C., Can.	G12	138
Granby, Lake, res., Co., U.S.	A2	128
Gran Chaco, reg., S.A.	D5	90
Grand, stm., On., Can.	E9	112
Grand, stm., U.S.	E4	120
Grand, stm., Mi., U.S.	E3	112
Grand, stm., Oh., U.S.	C4	114
Grand, stm., S.D., U.S.	B12	126
Grand, East Fork, stm., U.S.	D3	120
Grand, Lac, l., Qc., Can.	A12	112
Grand, North Fork, stm., U.S.	B10	126
Grand, South Fork, stm., S.D., U.S.	B9	126
Grandas, Spain	A4	20
Grand Bahama, i., Bah.	B9	96
Grand Ballon, mtn., Fr.	G16	14
Grand Bank, Nf., Can.	j22	107a
Grand-Bassam, C. Iv.	H4	64
Grand Bay, Al., U.S.	G10	122
Grand Beach, Mb., Can.	D17	124
Grand Bend, On., Can.	E8	112
Grand-Bourg, Guad.	i6	105c
Grand Caille Point, c., St. Luc.	m6	105c
Grand Calumet, Île du, i., Qc., Can.	C13	112
Grand Canal see Da Yunhe, can., China	E8	42
Grand Canal, can., Ire.	H6	12
Grand Cane, La., U.S.	E5	122
Grand Canyon, Az., U.S.	G4	132
Grand Canyon, val., Az., U.S.	G4	132
Grand Canyon National Park, p.o.i., Az., U.S.	G4	132
Grand Case, Guad.	A1	105a
Grand Cayman, i., Cay. Is.	C7	102
Grand Cess, Lib.	I3	64
Grand Chenier, La., U.S.	H6	122
Grand Coulee Dam, dam, Wa., U.S.	C8	136
Grand Cul de Sac, Guad.	B2	105a
Grande, stm., Arg.	H3	92
Grande, stm., Arg.	A5	92
Grande, stm., Bol.	C4	90
Grande, stm., Braz.	F4	88
Grande, stm., Braz.	C7	90
Grande, stm., S.A.	J3	90
Grande, stm., Ven.	C11	86
Grande, Arroyo, stm., Ur.	F9	92
Grande, Bahía, b., Arg.	J3	90
Grande, Boca, mth., Ven.	C11	86
Grande, Cerro, mtn., Mex.	E7	100
Grande, Cerro, mtn., Mex.	G2	130
Grande, Ilha, i., Braz.	L3	88
Grande, Ilha, i., Braz.	A11	92
Grande, Ponta, c., Braz.	I6	88
Grande, Rio see Rio Grande, stm., N.A.	H13	98
Grande, Serra, mts., Braz.	D5	88
Grande-Anse, Qc., Can.	C4	110
Grande Cache, Ab., Can.	C11	138
Grande Cayemite, i., Haiti	C11	102
Grande de Manacapuru, Lago, l., Braz.	I11	86
Grande de Matagalpa, stm., Nic.	F6	102
Grande de Santiago, stm., Mex.	E6	100
Grande do Gurupá, Ilha, i., Braz.	D7	84
Grande-Entrée, Qc., Can.	C15	110
Grande Prairie, Ab., Can.	A12	138
Grand Erg de Bilma, des., Niger	F7	64
Grand Erg Occidental, des., Alg.	C5	64
Grand Erg Oriental, des., Alg.	C6	64
Grande-Rivière, Qc., Can.	B12	110
Grande Rivière, La, stm., Qc., Can.	E15	106
Grande Ronde, stm., U.S.	E9	136
Grandes, Salinas, pl., Arg.	A4	92
Grandes, Salinas, pl., Arg.	D5	92
Grand-Étang, N.S., Can.	D15	110
Grande-Terre, i., Guad.	h6	105c
Grande Vigie, Pointe de la, c., Guad.	g6	105c
Grand Falls, N.B., Can.	C9	110
Grandfather Mountain, mtn., N.C., U.S.	H4	114
Grandfield, Ok., U.S.	G10	128
Grand Forks, B.C., Can.	G12	138
Grand Forks, N.D., U.S.	D1	118
Grand Haven, Mi., U.S.	E3	112
Grandin, Lac, l., N.T., Can.	C7	106
Grand Island, Ne., U.S.	G14	126
Grand Island, i., Mi., U.S.	B3	112
Grand Isle, La., U.S.	H9	122
Grand Junction, Co., U.S.	D8	132
Grand Junction, Ia., U.S.	B3	120
Grand Lake, Co., U.S.	A3	128
Grand Lake, l., N.B., Can.	D11	110
Grand Lake, l., N.A.	E9	110
Grand Lake, l., La., U.S.	H6	122
Grand Lake, l., Mi., U.S.	C6	112
Grand Lake, res., Oh., U.S.	D1	114
Grand Ledge, Mi., U.S.	B1	114
Grand Manan, N.B., Can.	F10	110
Grand Manan Island, i., N.B., Can.	F10	110
Grand Marais, Mi., U.S.	B4	112
Grand Meadow, Mn., U.S.	H6	118
Grand-Mère, Qc., Can.	D4	110
Grand Morin, stm., Fr.	F12	14
Grand Portage, Mn., U.S.	D9	118
Grand Portage National Monument, p.o.i., Mn., U.S.	C9	118
Grand Prairie, Tx., U.S.	B11	130
Grand Rapids, Mb., Can.	A14	124
Grand Rapids, Mi., U.S.	F4	112
Grand Rapids, Mn., U.S.	D5	118
Grand Rhône, stm., Fr.	F10	18
Grand Saline, Tx., U.S.	E3	122
Grand Staircase--Escalante National Monument, p.o.i., Ut., U.S.	F5	132
Grand Teton, mtn., Wy., U.S.	G16	136
Grand Teton National Park, p.o.i., Wy., U.S.	F16	136
Grand Tower, Il., U.S.	G8	120
Grand Traverse Bay, b., Mi., U.S.	C4	112
Grand Turk, T./C. Is.	B12	102
Grandview, Mb., Can.	C13	124
Grandview, Mo., U.S.	F3	120
Grandview, Tx., U.S.	B10	130
Grandview, Wa., U.S.	D6	136
Grand View, Wi., U.S.	E7	118
Grand Wash Cliffs, clf, Az., U.S.	H3	132
Grañén, Spain	C10	20
Graneros, Chile	G2	92
Granger, Wa., U.S.	D6	136
Granger, Wy., U.S.	B6	132
Granger Draw, stm., Tx., U.S.	D7	130
Granger Lake, res., Tx., U.S.	D10	130
Granges see Grenchen, Switz.	C4	22
Grangeville, Id., U.S.	E10	136
Granite City, Il., U.S.	F7	120
Granite Falls, Mn., U.S.	G3	118
Granite Falls, N.C., U.S.	I4	114
Granite Falls, Wa., U.S.	B5	136
Granite Pass, p., Wy., U.S.	C5	126
Granite Peak, Austl.	E4	74
Granite Peak, mtn., Mt., U.S.	E14	136
Granite Peak, mtn., Mt., U.S.	E17	136
Granite Peak, mtn., Nv., U.S.	C6	134
Graniteville, S.C., U.S.	C4	116
Granitola, Capo, c., Italy	G6	24
Granja, Braz.	B5	88
Gran Laguna Salada, l., Arg.	H3	90
Gränna, Swe.	G6	8
Granollers, Spain	C13	20
Gran Paradiso, mtn., Italy	E4	22
Gran Paradiso, Parco Nazionale del, p.o.i., Italy	E4	22
Gran Rio, stm., Sur.	C6	84
Gran Sasso d'Italia, mts., Italy	H10	22
Gransee, Ger.	C9	16
Grant, Fl., U.S.	I5	116
Grant, Mi., U.S.	E4	112
Grant City, Mo., U.S.	D3	120
Grantham, Eng., U.K.	I12	12
Grantley Adams International Airport, Barb.	n9	105d
Grant Park, Il., U.S.	C10	120
Grant Point, c., Nu., Can.	B11	106
Grants, N.M., U.S.	H9	132
Grantsburg, Wi., U.S.	F6	118
Grants Pass, Or., U.S.	A2	134
Grant-Suttie Bay, b., Nu., Can.	B15	106
Grantsville, W.V., U.S.	F4	114
Grantville, Ga., U.S.	D14	122
Granum, Ab., Can.	G17	138
Granville, Fr.	F7	14
Granville, Il., U.S.	J9	118
Granville, N.D., U.S.	F13	124
Granville, W.V., U.S.	E5	114
Granville Lake, l., Mb., Can.	D10	106
Granvin, Nor.	F2	8
Grão Mogol, Braz.	I4	88
Grapeland, Tx., U.S.	F3	122
Grapevine Lake, res., Tx., U.S.	B10	130
Grapevine Peak, mtn., Nv., U.S.	G8	134
Gras, Lac de, l., N.T., Can.	C8	106
Gräsö, i., Swe.	F8	8
Grasonville, Md., U.S.	F9	114
Grass, stm., N.Y., U.S.	D15	112
Grass Creek, Wy., U.S.	D4	126
Grasse, Fr.	F12	18
Grassflat, Pa., U.S.	D7	114
Grasslands National Park, p.o.i., Sk., Can.	E6	124
Grass Valley, Ca., U.S.	D4	134
Grass Valley, Or., U.S.	E6	136
Grassy, Austl.	n12	77a
Grassy Plains, B.C., Can.	C4	138
Graulhet, Fr.	F7	18
Gravelbourg, Sk., Can.	E7	124
Gravelines, Fr.	D11	14
Gravelotte, S. Afr.	C10	70
Gravenhage, 's- see 's-Gravenhage, Neth.	B12	14
Gravenhurst, On., Can.	D10	112
Gravesend, Eng., U.K.	J13	12
Gravette, Ar., U.S.	H3	120
Gravina in Puglia, Italy	D10	24
Gray, Fr.	G14	14
Gray, Ga., U.S.	D2	116
Grayback Mountain, mtn., Or., U.S.	A2	134
Grayiske alper, mts., Eur.	D13	18
Grayling, Mi., U.S.	D5	112
Grays, Eng., U.K.	J13	12
Grays Harbor, b., Wa., U.S.	D2	136
Grays Lake, sw., Id., U.S.	G15	136
Grayson, Sk., Can.	D11	124
Grayson, Al., U.S.	C11	122
Grayson, La., U.S.	E6	122
Grays Peak, mtn., Co., U.S.	B3	128
Graysville, Tn., U.S.	B13	122
Grayville, Il., U.S.	F9	120
Graz, Aus.	C12	22
Grdelica, Yugo.	G9	26
Great Artesian Basin, bas., Austl.	E3	76
Great Australian Bight, b., Austl.	F5	74
Great Barrier Island, i., N.Z.	C6	80
Great Barrier Reef, rf., Austl.	C9	74
Great Basin, bas., U.S.	C4	108
Great Basin National Park, p.o.i., Nv., U.S.	E2	132
Great Bear, stm., N.T., Can.	B6	106
Great Bear Lake, l., N.T., Can.	B6	106
Great Beaver Lake, l., B.C., Can.	B7	138
Great Belt see Storebælt, strt., Den.	I4	8
Great Bend, Ks., U.S.	C10	128
Great Bitter Lake see Murrat el-Kubra, Buheirat, l., Egypt	H3	58
Great Britain see United Kingdom, ctry., Eur.	D8	6
Great Camanoe, i., Br. Vir. Is.	e8	104b
Great Central, B.C., Can.	G6	138
Great Channel, strt., Asia	G7	46
Great Dismal Swamp, sw., U.S.	H9	114
Great Divide Basin, bas., Wy., U.S.	F4	126
Great Dividing Range, mts., Austl.	C8	74
Great Driffield, Eng., U.K.	G12	12
Greater Antilles, is., N.A.	H15	94
Greater Khingan Range see Da Hinggan Ling, mts., China	B9	36
Greater Sunda Islands, is., Asia	F4	44
Great Exuma, i., Bah.	C9	96
Great Falls, Mb., Can.	D18	124
Great Falls, Mt., U.S.	C15	136
Great Falls, S.C., U.S.	B4	116
Great Himalayan National Park, p.o.i., India	C6	54
Great Inagua, i., Bah.	B11	102
Great Indian Desert (Thar Desert), des., Asia	D3	54
Great Karroo (Groot Karroo), plat., S. Afr.	H6	70
Great La Cloche Island, i., On., Can.	B8	112
Great Lake, res., Austl.	n13	77a
Great Malvern, Eng., U.K.	I10	12
Great Miami, stm., U.S.	E13	120
Great Namaqualand (Groot Namaland), hist. reg., Nmb.	D3	70
Great Nicobar, i., India	G7	46
Great Ouse, stm., Eng., U.K.	I13	12
Great Palm Island, i., Austl.	B6	76
Great Pee Dee, stm., S.C., U.S.	C6	116
Great Plain of the Koukdjuak, pl., Nu., Can.	B16	106
Great Plains, pl., N.A.	C4	108
Great Point, c., Ma., U.S.	C15	114
Great Ruaha, stm., Tan.	F7	66
Great Sacandaga Lake, res., N.Y., U.S.	G2	110
Great Sale Cay, i., Bah.	I7	116
Great Salt Lake, l., Ut., U.S.	B4	132
Great Salt Lake Desert, des., Ut., U.S.	C3	132
Great Salt Plains Lake, res., Ok., U.S.	E10	128
Great Sand Dunes National Monument, p.o.i., Co., U.S.	D3	128
Great Sand Hills, hills, Sk., Can.	D4	124
Great Sandy Desert, des., Austl.	D4	74
Great Sandy National Park, p.o.i., Austl.	E9	76
Great Scarcies, stm., Afr.	H2	64
Great Sea Reef, rf., Fiji	p19	79e
Great Slave Lake, l., N.T., Can.	C8	106
Great Smoky Mountains, mts., U.S.	A2	116
Great Smoky Mountains National Park, p.o.i., U.S.	A2	116
Great Tenasserim, stm., Mya.	F4	48
Great Thatch Island, i., Br. Vir. Is.	e7	104b
Great Tobago, i., Br. Vir. Is.	e7	104b
Great Victoria Desert, des., Austl.	E5	74
Great Wall see Chang Cheng, misc. cult., China	D6	36
Great Yarmouth, Eng., U.K.	I14	12
Gréboun, mtn., Niger	F6	64
Grecco, Ur.	F9	92
Gredos, Sierra de, mts., Spain	D5	20
Greece, N.Y., U.S.	E12	112
Greece, ctry., Eur.	H13	6
Greeley, Co., U.S.	G8	126
Greeley, Ks., U.S.	F2	120
Greeleyville, S.C., U.S.	C6	116
Greely Fiord, b., Nu., Can.	A9	141
Green, stm., U.S.	E7	132
Green, stm., Il., U.S.	C8	120
Green, stm., Ky., U.S.	G10	120
Green, stm., N.D., U.S.	G17	136
Green, stm., Wa., U.S.	C5	136
Green Bay, Wi., U.S.	D1	112
Green Bay, b., U.S.	D2	112
Greenbrier, Ar., U.S.	B6	122
Green Brier, Tn., U.S.	H11	120
Greenbrier, stm., W.V., U.S.	F5	114
Greenburg, La., U.S.	G8	122
Greenbush, Mn., U.S.	C2	118
Greencastle, In., U.S.	E10	120
Greencastle, Pa., U.S.	E8	114
Green Cove Springs, Fl., U.S.	G4	116
Greendale, In., U.S.	E13	120
Greene, Ia., U.S.	B5	120
Greeneville, Tn., U.S.	H3	114
Greenfield, Ca., U.S.	B13	114
Greenfield, Il., U.S.	E7	120
Greenfield, Ia., U.S.	C3	120
Greenfield, Ma., U.S.	H4	110
Greenfield, Mo., U.S.	G4	120
Greenfield, Oh., U.S.	E2	114
Greenfield, Ok., U.S.	F10	128
Green Forest, Ar., U.S.	H4	120
Green Island Bay, b., Phil.	E2	52
Green Islands, is., Pap. N. Gui.	D6	72
Green Lake, Wi., U.S.	H10	118
Green Lake, l., B.C., Can.	E9	138
Green Lake, l., Wi., U.S.	H9	118
Greenland, Ar., U.S.	I3	120
Greenland, dep., N.A.	B19	94
Greenland Basin, unds.	A14	144
Greenland Sea	B21	94
Greenleaf, Ks., U.S.	B11	128
Green Lookout Mountain, mtn., Wa., U.S.	E4	136
Green Mountains, mts., N.A.	G4	110
Greenock, Scot., U.K.	F8	12
Greenore Point, c., Ire.	I6	12
Greenough, stm., Austl.	E3	74
Greenport, N.Y., U.S.	C13	114
Green River, Pap. N. Gui.	a3	79a
Green River, Ut., U.S.	D7	132
Green River, Wy., U.S.	B7	132
Green River Lake, res., Ky., U.S.	G12	120
Greensboro, Fl., U.S.	G14	122
Greensboro, Ga., U.S.	C2	116
Greensboro, N.C., U.S.	H6	114
Greensburg, In., U.S.	E12	120
Greensburg, Ks., U.S.	D9	128
Greensburg, Pa., U.S.	D6	114
Green Springs, Oh., U.S.	C2	114
Green Swamp, sw., N.C., U.S.	B7	116
Greentown, In., U.S.	H4	112
Greenup, Il., U.S.	E9	120
Greenup, Ky., U.S.	F3	114
Greenvale, Austl.	B5	76
Green Valley, Az., U.S.	L6	132
Greenville, Lib.	H3	64
Greenville, Al., U.S.	F12	122
Greenville, Ga., U.S.	D14	122
Greenville, Il., U.S.	F8	120
Greenville, Ky., U.S.	G10	120
Greenville, Me., U.S.	E7	110
Greenville, Mi., U.S.	E4	112
Greenville, Ms., U.S.	D7	122
Greenville, Mo., U.S.	G7	120
Greenville, N.C., U.S.	A8	116
Greenville, Oh., U.S.	D1	114
Greenville, Pa., U.S.	C5	114
Greenville, S.C., U.S.	B3	116
Greenville, Tx., U.S.	D2	122
Greenwater Lake, l., On., Can.	C8	118
Greenwich, Ct., U.S.	C12	114
Greenwich, Oh., U.S.	C3	114
Greenwood, B.C., Can.	G12	138
Greenwood, Ar., U.S.	B4	122
Greenwood, In., U.S.	E11	120
Greenwood, Ms., U.S.	D8	122
Greenwood, S.C., U.S.	B3	116
Greenwood, Wi., U.S.	G8	118
Greenwood, Lake, res., S.C., U.S.	B4	116
Greer, S.C., U.S.	B3	116
Greers Ferry Lake, res., Ar., U.S.	B6	122
Greeson, Lake, res., Ar., U.S.	C5	122
Gregório, stm., Braz.	E3	84
Gregory, Mi., U.S.	B1	114
Gregory, S.D., U.S.	D13	126
Gregory, Tx., U.S.	G10	130
Gregory, stm., Austl.	C7	74
Gregory, Lake, l., Austl.	E3	74
Gregory, Lake, l., Austl.	D5	74
Gregory, Lake, l., Austl.	G2	76
Gregory Range, mts., Austl.	B4	76
Greifswald, Ger.	B9	16
Greifswalder Bodden, b., Ger.	B9	16
Greiz, Ger.	F8	16
Gremiha, Russia	B18	8
Grenå, Den.	H4	8
Grenada, Ms., U.S.	D9	122
Grenada, ctry., N.A.	q11	105e
Grenada Lake, res., Ms., U.S.	D9	122
Grenadines, is., N.A.	p11	105e
Grenchen, Switz.	C4	22
Grenen, c., Den.	H4	8
Grenfell, Austl.	I7	76
Grenoble, Fr.	D11	18
Grenola, Ks., U.S.	D12	128
Grenora, N.D., U.S.	F10	124
Grenville, Gren.	q10	105e
Gresham, Or., U.S.	E4	136
Gresik, Indon.	G8	50
Gresik, Indon.	E3	50
Gressåmoen Nasjonalpark, p.o.i., Nor.	D5	8
Gretna, Mb., Can.	E16	124
Gretna, La., U.S.	H8	122
Gretna, Va., U.S.	H6	114
Gretna Green, Scot., U.K.	F9	12
Greven, Ger.	D3	16
Grevená, Grc.	C4	28
Grevenbroich, Ger.	E2	16
Grevesmühlen, Ger.	C7	16
Greybull, stm., Wy., U.S.	C4	126
Grey Eagle, Mn., U.S.	F4	118
Grey Islands, is., Nf., Can.	i22	107a
Greylock, Mount, mtn., Ma., U.S.	B12	114
Greymouth, N.Z.	F4	80
Grey Range, mts., Austl.	F4	76
Greytown, S. Afr.	F10	70
Gribbel Island, i., B.C., Can.	C1	138
Gribingui, stm., C.A.R.	C3	66
Gridley, Ca., U.S.	D4	134
Gridley, Il., U.S.	D9	120
Griesheim, Ger.	G4	16
Griffin, Sk., Can.	E10	124
Griffin, Ga., U.S.	C1	116
Griffin, Lake, l., Fl., U.S.	H4	116
Griffith, Austl.	J5	76
Griggsville, Il., U.S.	E7	120
Grignols, Fr.	E5	18
Grigoriopol, Mol.	B16	26
Grijalva (Cuilco), stm., N.A.	G12	100
Grim, Cape, c., Austl.	n12	77a
Grimari, C.A.R.	C3	66
Grimma, Ger.	E8	16
Grimmen, Ger.	B9	16
Grimsby, On., Can.	E10	112
Grimsby, Eng., U.K.	H12	12
Grimsel Pass, p., Switz.	D5	22
Grímsey, i., Ice.	j30	8a
Grimshaw, Ab., Can.	D7	106
Grimstad, Nor.	G3	8
Grímsvötn, vol., Ice.	k31	8a
Grindelwald, Switz.	D5	22
Grinnell, Ia., U.S.	C5	120
Grinnell Peninsula, pen., Nu., Can.	B7	141
Grintavec, mtn., Slvn.	D11	22
Griqualand East, hist. reg., S. Afr.	G9	70
Griqualand West, hist. reg., S. Afr.	F6	70
Grise Fiord, Nu., Can.	B9	141
Gris-Nez, Cap, c., Fr.	D10	14
Griswold, Mb., Can.	E13	124
Griswold, Ia., U.S.	C2	120
Grizzly Bear Mountain, mtn., N.T., Can.	B6	106
Grizzly Mountain, mtn., Id., U.S.	C10	136
Grjadcy, Russia	D14	10
Grjazovec, Russia	G18	8
Groaíras, Braz.	B5	88
Groblersdal, S. Afr.	D9	70
Grodków, Pol.	F13	16
Grodzisk Mazowiecki, Pol.	D16	16
Groen, stm., S. Afr.	G6	70
Groesbeck, Tx., U.S.	F2	122
Grofa, hora, mtn., Ukr.	A10	26
Groix, Fr.	G5	14
Groix, Île de, i., Fr.	G5	14
Grójec, Pol.	E16	16
Grombalia, Tun.	H4	24
Gronau, Ger.	D3	16
Grong, Nor.	D5	8
Groningen, Neth.	A15	14
Groningen, Sur.	B6	84
Groom, Tx., U.S.	F7	128
Groot, stm., S. Afr.	H7	70
Groot-Berg, stm., S. Afr.	H4	70
Groot-Brakrivier, S. Afr.	I6	70
Grootdraaidam, res., S. Afr.	E9	70
Groote Eylandt, i., Austl.	B7	74
Grootfontein, Nmb.	D2	68
Grootgeluk, S. Afr.	C8	70
Groot Karasberge, mts., Nmb.	E4	70
Groot Karroo see Great Karroo, plat., S. Afr.	H6	70
Groot-Kei, stm., S. Afr.	H9	70
Groot Laagte, stm., Afr.	B5	70
Groot Namaland see Great Namaqualand, hist. reg., Nmb.	D3	70
Groot-Swartberge, mts., S. Afr.	H6	70
Groot-Vis, stm., S. Afr.	H8	70
Grootvloer, pl., S. Afr.	F5	70
Gros Islet, St. Luc.	I7	105c
Gros-Morne, Mart.	k6	105c
Gros Morne, mtn., Nf., Can.	j22	107a
Gros Piton, vol., St. Luc.	m6	105c
Grossenhain, Ger.	E9	16
Grosse Pointe, Mi., U.S.	B3	114
Grosse Pointe, c., Guad.	h6	105c
Grosser Beerberg, mtn., Ger.	F6	16
Grosseto, Italy	H7	22
Gross-Gerau, Ger.	G4	16
Grossglockner, mtn., Aus.	C9	22
Grossos, Braz.	C7	88
Grossvenediger, mtn., Aus.	C9	22
Groton, N.Y., U.S.	F13	112
Groton, S.D., U.S.	B14	126
Grottaglie, Italy	D11	24
Grottammare, Italy	G11	22
Grottoes, Va., U.S.	F7	114
Grouard Mission, Ab., Can.	D7	106
Groundhog, stm., On., Can.	F14	106
Grove City, Mn., U.S.	F4	118
Grove City, Oh., U.S.	E2	114
Grove City, Pa., U.S.	C5	114
Grove Hill, Al., U.S.	F11	122
Grove Mountains, mts., Ant.	C12	81
Grover City, Ca., U.S.	H5	134
Groves, Tx., U.S.	H5	122
Groveton, N.H., U.S.	F5	110
Groveton, Tx., U.S.	F3	122
Grovetown, Ga., U.S.	C3	116
Growa Point, c., Lib.	I3	64
Growler Peak, mtn., Az., U.S.	K3	132
Groznyj, Russia	F7	32
Grubišno Polje, Cro.	E14	22
Grudziądz, Pol.	C14	16
Grulla, Tx., U.S.	H9	130
Grumo Appula, Italy	D10	24
Grundy, Va., U.S.	G3	114
Grundy Center, Ia., U.S.	B5	120
Grušino, Russia	G21	8
Gruver, Tx., U.S.	E7	128
Gruznovka, Russia	E10	34
Gryfice, Pol.	C11	16
Gryfino, Pol.	C10	16
Grytviken, S. Geor.	J9	90
Guacanayabo, Golfo de, b., Cuba	B9	102
Guacara, Ven.	B7	86
Guacarí, Col.	F3	86
Gu Achi, Az., U.S.	K4	132
Guachiría, stm., Col.	E6	86
Guachochi, Mex.	B5	100
Guadajoz, stm., Spain	G6	20
Guadalajara, Mex.	E7	100
Guadalajara, Spain	D7	20
Guadalajara, co., Spain	D8	20
Guadalcanal, state, Sol. Is.	f8	79b
Guadalcanal, i., Sol. Is.	e9	79b
Guadalete, stm., Spain	H4	20
Guadalhorce, stm., Spain	G6	20
Guadalimar, stm., Spain	F7	20
Guadalmena, stm., Spain	F8	20
Guadalope, stm., Spain	D10	20
Guadalquivir, stm., Spain	H4	20
Guadalquivir, Marismas del, sw., Spain	G4	20
Guadalupe, Mex.	D7	100
Guadalupe, Mex.	C8	100
Guadalupe, Ca., U.S.	I5	134
Guadalupe, stm., Tx., U.S.	F11	130
Guadalupe, Isla, i., Mex.	G3	98
Guadalupe Bravos, Mex.	C1	130
Guadalupe Mountains, mts., U.S.	B3	130
Guadalupe Mountains National Park, p.o.i., Tx., U.S.	C3	130
Guadalupe Peak, mtn., Tx., U.S.	C3	130
Guadalupe Victoria, Mex.	C6	100
Guadalupe Victoria, Mex.	G6	130
Guadarrama, Puerto de, p., Spain	D6	20
Guadarrama, Sierra de, mts., Spain	D6	20
Guadeloupe, dep., N.A.	h15	96a
Guadeloupe Passage, strt., N.A.	g5	105c
Guadiana, stm., Eur.	G3	20
Guadiana Menor, stm., Spain	G7	20
Guadiato, stm., Spain	F5	20
Guadiela, stm., Spain	D8	20
Guadix, Spain	G7	20
Guafo, Isla, i., Chile	H1	90
Guaíba, Braz.	E12	92
Guaíba, est., Braz.	E12	92
Guaimaca, Hond.	E4	102
Guainía, state, Col.	F7	86
Guainía, stm., S.A.	F8	86
Guaiquinima, Cerro, mtn., Ven.	E10	86
Guaíra, Braz.	K1	88
Guaíra, Braz.	B10	92
Guairá, state, Para.	B9	92
Guairá, Salto del (Sete Quedas, Salto das), wtfl, S.A.	B10	92
Guáitara, stm., Col.	G3	86
Guaitecas, Islas, is., Chile	H2	90
Guajaba, Cayo, i., Cuba	B9	102
Guajará-Açu, Braz.	A1	88
Guajará-Mirim, Braz.	F4	84
Guaje, Laguna del, l., Mex.	B7	100
Gualaca, Pan.	H6	102
Gualaceo, Ec.	I2	86
Gualala, Ca., U.S.	E2	134
Gualdo Tadino, Italy	G9	22
Gualeguay, Arg.	F8	92
Gualeguay, stm., Arg.	F8	92
Gualeguaychú, Arg.	F8	92
Gualicho, Salina del, pl., Arg.	H4	90
Guam, dep., Oc.	j10	78c
Guamá, stm., Braz.	A1	88
Guamal, Col.	F5	86
Guamal, Col.	C4	86
Guaminí, Arg.	H6	92
Guam International Airport, Guam	i10	78c
Guamote, Ec.	H2	86
Guamúchil, Mex.	C4	100
Guamués, stm., Col.	G3	86
Gua Musang, Malay.	J5	48
Guanacaste, Cordillera de, mts., C.R.	G5	102
Guanaceví, Mex.	C6	100
Guanahacabibes, Golfo de, b., Cuba	A5	102
Guana Island, i., Br. Vir. Is.	e8	104b
Guanaja, Hond.	D5	102
Guanaja, Isla de, i., Hond.	D5	102
Guanajuato, Mex.	E8	100
Guanajuato, state, Mex.	E8	100
Guanambi, Braz.	H4	88
Guanaparo, Caño, stm., Ven.	C7	86
Guañape, Islas, is., Peru	E2	84
Guanare, Ven.	C7	86
Guanare, stm., Ven.	C7	86
Guanarito, Ven.	C7	86
Guandacol, Arg.	D3	92
Guandu, China	I5	42
Guane, Cuba	A5	102
Guang'an, China	F2	42
Guangchang, China	H7	42
Guangde, China	F8	42
Guangdong, state, China	J6	42
Guangfeng, China	G8	42
Guangji, China	G6	42
Guangling, China	B6	42
Guangming Ding, mtn., China	F7	42
Guangnan, China	G5	36
Guangxi, state, China	G6	36
Guangxi Zhuangzu Zizhiqu see Guangxi, state, China	G6	36
Guangyuan, China	E1	42
Guangze, China	H7	42
Guangzhou (Canton), China	J5	42
Guanhães, Braz.	J4	88
Guánica, P.R.	C2	104a
Guanipa, stm., Ven.	C10	86
Guanta, Ven.	B9	86
Guantánamo, Cuba	B10	102
Guantao, China	C6	42
Guanting Shuiku, res., China	A6	42
Guanxian, China	E5	36
Guanxian, China	C6	42
Guanyun, China	D8	42
Guapí, Col.	F3	86
Guapiara, Braz.	B13	92
Guápiles, C.R.	G6	102
Guaporé, Braz.	D11	92
Guaporé (Iténez), stm., S.A.	F5	84
Guaqui, Bol.	C3	90
Guará, stm., Braz.	G3	88
Guarabira, Braz.	D8	88
Guaraciaba do Norte, Braz.	C5	88
Guaraciana, Braz.	I4	88
Guaranda, Ec.	H2	86
Guaraniaçu, Braz.	B11	92
Guarapari, Braz.	K5	88
Guarapuava, Braz.	B12	92
Guaraqueçaba, Braz.	B13	92
Guaratinguetá, Braz.	L3	88
Guaratuba, Braz.	B13	92
Guarda, Port.	D3	20
Guarda, state, Port.	D3	20
Guardafui, Cape see Gwardafuy, Gees, c., Som.	B10	66
Guardia Escolta, Arg.	D6	92
Guardiagrele, Italy	H11	22
Guardia Mitre, Arg.	H4	90
Guardo, Spain	B6	20
Guareña, Spain	F4	20
Guarenas, Ven.	B8	86
Guárico, state, Ven.	C8	86
Guárico, stm., Ven.	C8	86
Guárico, Embalse del, l., Ven.	C8	86
Guariquito, stm., Ven.	C8	86
Guarulhos, Braz.	L2	88
Guasare, stm., Ven.	B5	86
Guasave, Mex.	C4	100
Guasdualito, Ven.	D6	86
Guasipati, Ven.	D11	86
Guastalla, Italy	F7	22
Guatemala, Guat.	E2	102
Guatemala, ctry., N.A.	E2	102
Guatemala Basin, unds.	H29	142
Guateque, Col.	E5	86
Guatimozín, Arg.	F6	92
Guatopo, Parque Nacional, p.o.i., Ven.	B8	86
Guatuaro Point, c., Trin.	s13	105f
Guaviare, state, Col.	G5	86
Guaviare, stm., Col.	E8	86
Guaxupé, Braz.	K2	88
Guayabal, Cuba	B9	102
Guayabal, Ven.	D8	86
Guayabero, stm., Col.	F5	86
Guayacán, Chile	D2	92
Guayaguayare, Trin.	s12	105f
Guayama, P.R.	C3	104a
Guayana see Guyana, ctry., S.A.	C6	84
Guayana, Macizo de (Guiana Highlands), mts., S.A.	E10	86
Guayaneco, Archipiélago, is., Chile	I1	90
Guayanilla, P.R.	B2	104a
Guayape, stm., Hond.	E4	102
Guayapo, stm., Ven.	E8	86
Guayaquil, Ec.	I1	86
Guayaquil, Golfo de, b., S.A.	D1	84
Guayaramerín, Bol.	B3	90
Guayas, state, Ec.	H1	86
Guayas, stm., Ec.	I2	86
Guaymallén, Arg.	F3	92
Guaymas, Mex.	B3	100
Guaynabo, P.R.	B3	104a
Guayquiraró, stm., Arg.	E8	92
Guazapares, Mex.	B4	100
Guazárachi, Mex.	B5	100
Guba, D.R.C.	G5	66
Gubaha, Russia	C9	32
Gûbâl, Madîq (Jubal, Strait of), strt., Egypt	K4	58
Gubavica, wtfl, Cro.	G13	22
Gubbi, India	E3	53
Gubbio, Italy	G9	22
Guben, Ger.	E10	16
Gubin, Pol.	E10	16
Gucheng, China	E4	42
Gūdalūr, India	G3	53
Gúdar, Sierra de, mts., Spain	D10	20
Gudauta, Geor.	F6	32
Gudermes, Russia	F7	32
Gudivāda, India	C5	53

Name	Map Ref.	Page
Gudiyāttam, India	E4	53
Güdül, Tur.	C15	28
Gūdūr, India	D4	53
Guebwiller, Fr.	G16	14
Güejar, stm., Col.	F5	86
Guékédou, Gui.	H2	64
Guélengdeng, Chad	E3	62
Guelma, Alg.	B6	64
Guelmime, Mor.	D2	64
Guelph, On., Can.	E9	112
Guérande, Fr.	G6	14
Guercif, Mor.	C4	64
Guerdjoumane, Djebel, mtn., Alg.	H13	20
Güere, stm., Ven.	C9	86
Guéréda, Chad	E4	62
Guéret, Fr.	C7	18
Guerla Mandata Shan, mtn., China	C8	54
Guernesey see Guernsey, dep., Eur.	L10	12
Guerneville, Ca., U.S.	E3	134
Guernica see Gernika, Spain	A8	20
Guernica y Luno see Gernika, Spain	A8	20
Guernsey, dep., Eur.	E6	14
Guernsey, i., Guern.	E6	14
Guerrero, Mex.	A5	100
Guerrero, Mex.	F7	130
Guerrero, state, Mex.	G8	100
Guerrero Negro, Mex.	B1	100
Gueydan, La., U.S.	G6	122
Guga, Russia	F16	34
Gugē, mtn., Eth.	F7	62
Guguan, i., N. Mar. Is.	B5	72
Gui, stm., China	I4	42
Guiana Basin, unds.	G9	144
Guiana Highlands (Guayana, Macizo de), mts., S.A.	E10	86
Güicán, Col.	D5	86
Guichi, China	F7	42
Guide, China	D5	36
Guidimouni, Niger	G6	64
Guiding, China	H2	42
Guier, Lac de, l., Sen.	F1	64
Guijuelo, Spain	D5	20
Guilarte, Monte, mtn., P.R.	B2	104a
Guildford, Eng., U.K.	J12	12
Guildhall, Vt., U.S.	F5	110
Guilford, Me., U.S.	E7	110
Guilin, China	I4	42
Guillaume-Delisle, Lac, l., Qc., Can.	D15	106
Guillestre, Fr.	E12	18
Guimarães, Braz.	B3	88
Guimaras Island, i., Phil.	E4	52
Guimba, Phil.	C3	52
Guin, Al., U.S.	D11	122
Guinan, China	D5	36
Guindulman, Phil.	F5	52
Guinea, ctry., Afr.	G2	64
Guinea, Gulf of, b., Afr.	I6	64
Guinea Basin, unds.	H13	144
Guinea-Bissau, ctry., Afr.	G1	64
Güines, Cuba	A7	102
Guingamp, Fr.	F5	14
Güinope, Hond.	F4	102
Guiping, China	J4	42
Guipúzcoa see Gipuzkoako, co., Spain	A8	20
Guiratinga, Braz.	G7	84
Güiria, Ven.	B10	86
Guitry, C. Iv.	H3	64
Guiuan, Phil.	E5	52
Guixian, China	J3	42
Guiyang, China	I5	42
Guiyang, China	H2	42
Güiza, stm., Col.	G2	86
Guizhou, state, China	F6	36
Gujarāt, state, India	G3	54
Gūjar Khān, Pak.	B4	54
Gujrānwāla, Pak.	B4	54
Gujrāt, Pak.	B4	54
Gukou, China	H8	42
Gulargambone, Austl.	H7	76
Gulbarga, India	C3	53
Gulbene, Lat.	C9	10
Güldüzü, Tur.	B8	58
Guledagudda, India	C2	53
Gülek Boğazı, p., Tur.	A5	58
Gulf Islands National Seashore, p.o.i., U.S.	G10	122
Gulfport, Ms., U.S.	G9	122
Gulf Shores, Al., U.S.	G11	122
Gulgong, Austl.	I7	76
Gulian, China	F13	34
Gulistan, Uzb.	F11	32
Gulkana, Ak., U.S.	D10	140
Gull, stm., On., Can.	B9	118
Gullfoss, wtfl, Ice.	k29	8a
Gull Lake, Sk., Can.	D5	124
Gull Lake, l., Ab., Can.	D17	138
Gull Lake, l., Mn., U.S.	E4	118
Güllük, Tur.	F10	28
Güllük Körfezi, b., Tur.	F10	28
Gülpınar, Tur.	D9	28
Gulu, Ug.	D6	66
Guluogongba, China	A10	54
Gumaca, Phil.	D4	52
Gumal (Gowmal), stm., Asia	B2	54
Gumbalie, Austl.	G5	76
Gumdag, Turkmen.	B7	56
Gumel, Nig.	G6	64
Gumla, India	G10	54
Gumma, state, Japan	C11	40
Gummersbach, Ger.	E3	16
Gümüşhane, Tur.	A4	56
Gümüşsü, Tur.	E12	28
Guna, India	F6	54
Gundagai, Austl.	J7	76
Gundji, D.R.C.	D4	66
Gundlupet, India	F3	53
Gündoğdu, Tur.	C9	28
Güney, Tur.	E12	28
Gungu, D.R.C.	F3	66
Gunmi, Nig.	G6	64
Gunnar, Sk., Can.	D9	106
Gunnarn, Swe.	D7	8
Gunnbjørn Fjeld, mtn., Grnld.	D19	141
Gunnedah, Austl.	H7	76
Gunnison, Ut., U.S.	D5	132
Gunnison, stm., Co., U.S.	E8	132
Gunong Mulu National Park, p.o.i., Malay.	A9	50
Gun Point, c., Gren.	p11	105e
Gunpowder Creek, stm., Austl.	B2	76
Gunsan see Kunsan, Kor., S.	F7	38
Guntakal, India	D3	53
Guntersville, Al., U.S.	C12	122
Guntersville Dam, dam, Al., U.S.	C12	122
Guntersville Lake, res., Al., U.S.	C12	122
Guntūr, India	C5	53
Gunungkencana, Indon.	G4	50
Gunungsahilan, Indon.	C2	50
Gunungsitoli, Indon.	L3	48
Gunupur, India	B6	53
Günzburg, Ger.	H6	16
Gunzenhausen, Ger.	G6	16
Guo, stm., China	E7	42
Guoyang, China	E7	42
Guoyangzhen, China	B5	42
Gupis, Pak.	B11	56
Gurabo, P.R.	B4	104a
Gura Humorului, Rom.	B12	26
Gurais, India	A5	54
Gurdāspur, India	B5	54
Gurdon, Ar., U.S.	D5	122
Güre, Tur.	E12	28
Gurevsk, Russia	D15	32
Gurgueia, stm., Braz.	D4	88
Gurha, India	F3	54
Guri, Embalse de, res., Ven.	D10	86
Gurskoe, Russia	F16	34
Gurskøya, i., Nor.	E1	8
Gürsu, Tur.	C12	28
Gurupá, Braz.	D7	84
Gurupi, Braz.	F1	88
Gurupi, stm., Braz.	D8	84
Guru Sikhar, mtn., India	F4	54
Gurvan Sayhan uul, mts., Mong.	C5	36
Gusau, Nig.	G6	64
Gusev, Russia	F5	10
Gušgy, Turkmen.	B9	56
Gushan, China	B10	42
Gushi, China	E6	42
Gus'-Hrustal'nyj, Russia	I19	8
Gusino, Russia	F14	10
Gusinoozersk, Russia	F10	34
Gus'-Khrustal'nyy see Gus'-Hrustal'nyj, Russia	I19	8
Guspini, Italy	E2	24
Güssing, Aus.	C13	22
Gustav Holm, Kap, c., Grnld.	D19	141
Gustavus, Ak., U.S.	E12	140
Gustine, Ca., U.S.	F5	134
Gustine, Tx., U.S.	C9	130
Güstrow, Ger.	C8	16
Gütersloh, Ger.	E4	16
Guthrie, Ok., U.S.	F11	128
Guthrie, Tx., U.S.	H8	128
Guthrie Center, Ia., U.S.	C3	120
Gutian, China	H8	42
Gutiérrez Zamora, Mex.	E10	100
Guttenberg, Ia., U.S.	B6	120
Guwāhāti, India	E13	54
Guxian, China	E5	42
Guyana, ctry., S.A.	C6	84
Guyang, China	A4	42
Guye, China	B8	42
Guy Fawkes River National Park, p.o.i., Austl.	H9	76
Guymon, Ok., U.S.	E7	128
Guyot, Mount, mtn., U.S.	I2	114
Guyra, Austl.	H8	76
Guyton, Ga., U.S.	D4	116
Guyuan, China	D2	42
Guzar, Uzb.	G11	32
Güzelyurt, N. Cyp.	C3	58
Güzelyurt Körfezi, b., N. Cyp.	C3	58
Guzhen, China	E7	42
Guzmán, Mex.	F9	98
Guzmán, Mex.	F7	100
Gvardejsk, Russia	F4	10
Gwa, Mya.	D2	48
Gwaai, Zimb.	D4	68
Gwādar, Pak.	D9	56
Gwalia, Austl.	E4	74
Gwalior (Lashkar), India	E7	54
Gwanda, Zimb.	B9	70
Gwane, D.R.C.	D5	66
Gwangju see Kwangju, Kor., S.	G7	38
Gwardafuy, Gees, c., Som.	B10	66
Gwātar Bay, b., Asia	E9	56
Gwayi, stm., Zimb.	D4	68
Gwda, stm., Pol.	C12	16
Gweedore, Ire.	F4	12
Gweru, Zimb.	D4	68
Gwinn, Mi., U.S.	B2	112
Gwydir, stm., Austl.	G7	76
Gyangtse see Gyangzê, China	D12	54
Gyangzê, China	D12	54
Gyaring Co, l., China	C12	54
Gyaring Hu, l., China	E4	36
Gyda, Russia	B4	34
Gydanskaja guba, b., Russia	B4	34
Gydanskij poluostrov, pen., Russia	B4	34
Gyeongju see Kyŏngju, Kor., S.	D2	40
Gyirong, China	D10	54
Gyldenløves Fjord, b., Grnld.	E17	141
Gym Peak, mtn., N.M., U.S.	K9	132
Gympie, Austl.	F9	76
Gyobingauk, Mya.	C2	48
Gyoma, Hung.	C7	26
Gyöngyös, Hung.	B6	26
Győr (Raab), Hung.	B4	26
Győr-Moson-Sopron, state, Hung.	B4	26
Gypsum, Co., U.S.	D10	132
Gypsum, Ks., U.S.	C11	128
Gypsumville, Mb., Can.	C15	124
Gyula, Hung.	C8	26
Gyulafehérvár see Alba Iulia, Rom.	C10	26
Gyzylarbat, Turkmen.	B8	56

H

Name	Map Ref.	Page
Haag in Oberbayern, Ger.	H8	16
Haaksbergen, Neth.	D2	16
Haapiti, Fr. Poly.	v20	78h
Haapsalu, Est.	G10	8
Haar, Ger.	H7	16
Ha'Arava ('Arabah, Wādī al-), val., Asia	H6	58
Ha'Arava (Jayb, Wādī al-), stm., Asia	H6	58
Haarlem, Neth.	B13	14
Habaqila, China	C6	36
Habarovsk, Russia	G16	34
Habary, Russia	D13	32
Ḥabashīyah, Jabal, mts., Yemen	F7	56
Ḥabbān, Yemen	G6	56
Habermehl Peak, mtn., Ant.	C6	81
Habiganj, Bngl.	F13	54
Habomai Islands see Malaja Kuril'skaja Grjada, is., Russia	C17	38
Hachijō-jima, i., Japan	F12	40
Hachiman, Japan	D9	40
Hachinohe, Japan	D14	38
Hachiōji, Japan	D12	40
Hackberry, La., U.S.	H5	122
Hackberry Creek, stm., Ks., U.S.	C8	128
Hackett, Ar., U.S.	B4	122
Hackettstown, N.J., U.S.	D11	114
Hadāli, Pak.	B4	54
HaDarom, state, Isr.	H5	58
Ḥadd, Ra's al-, c., Oman	E8	56
Haddam, Ks., U.S.	B11	128
Haddington, Scot., U.K.	F10	12
Haddock, Ga., U.S.	C2	116
Haddon Downs, Austl.	F3	76
Hadejia, Nig.	G7	64
Hadejia, stm., Nig.	G6	64
Haden, Austl.	F8	76
Hadera, Isr.	F5	58
Haderslev, Den.	I3	8
Hadībū, Yemen	G7	56
Ḥadīthah, Iraq	C5	56
Hadley Bay, b., Nu., Can.	A9	106
Hadlock, Wa., U.S.	B4	136
Ha Dong, Viet.	B7	48
Ḥaḍramawt, reg., Yemen	F6	56
Hadrian's Wall, misc. cult., Eng., U.K.	G10	12
Hadzilavičy, Bela.	G13	10
Haeju, Kor., N.	E6	38
Haenam, Kor., S.	G7	38
Haerhpin see Harbin, China	B7	38
Haffner Bjerg, mtn., Grnld.	B13	141
Hafford, Sk., Can.	B6	124
Haffouz, Tun.	I3	24
Hāfizābād, Pak.	B4	54
Hāflong, India	F14	54
Hafnarfjörður, Ice.	k28	8a
Haft Gel, Iran	C6	56
Hagan, Ga., U.S.	D3	116
Hagari, stm., India	D3	53
Hagemeister Island, i., Ak., U.S.	E7	140
Hagen, Ger.	E3	16
Hagenow, Ger.	C7	16
Hagensborg, B.C., Can.	D4	138
Hagerman, N.M., U.S.	A3	130
Hagerstown, In., U.S.	I4	112
Hagerstown, Md., U.S.	E8	114
Hagersville, On., Can.	F9	112
Hagfors, Swe.	F5	8
Haggin, Mount, mtn., Mt., U.S.	D13	136
Hagi, Japan	E4	40
Ha Giang, Viet.	A7	48
Hagondange, Fr.	E15	14
Hags Head, c., Ire.	I3	12
Hague, Sk., Can.	B7	124
Hague, Cap de la, c., Fr.	E7	14
Haguenau, Fr.	F16	14
Hagues Peak, mtn., Co., U.S.	G7	126
Hahira, Ga., U.S.	F2	116
Hai'an, China	E9	42
Haibei, China	B10	36
Haicheng, China	A10	42
Haichow Bay see Haizhou Wan, b., China	D8	42
Haidargarh, India	E8	54
Hai Duong, Viet.	B8	48
Haifa see Ḥefa, Isr.	F5	58
Haifa see Ḥefa, state, Isr.	F5	58
Haifeng, China	J6	42
Haig, Austl.	F5	74
Haigler, Ne., U.S.	A7	128
Haikang, China	K3	42
Haikou, China	K4	42
Haikou, China	G9	42
Ḥā'il, Sau. Ar.	D5	56
Hailākāndi, India	F14	54
Hailar, China	B8	36
Hailar, stm., China	B8	36
Haileyville, Ok., U.S.	C3	122
Hailin, China	B8	38
Hailun, China	B10	36
Hailuoto, i., Fin.	D11	8
Haimen, China	J7	42
Haimen, China	G9	42
Hainan, state, China	L3	42
Hainan Dao (Hainan Island), i., China	L4	42
Hainan Island see Hainan Dao, i., China	L4	42
Hainan Strait see Qiongzhou Haixia, strt., China	K4	42
Haines, Ak., U.S.	E12	140
Haines, Or., U.S.	F8	136
Haines City, Fl., U.S.	H4	116
Haines Junction, Yk., Can.	C3	106
Haining, China	F9	42
Hai Ninh, Viet.	B8	48
Hai Phong, Viet.	B8	48
Haiphong see Hai Phong, Viet.	B8	48
Haiti, ctry., N.A.	C11	102
Haitun, China	D4	36
Haivoron, Ukr.	A16	26
Haiyuan, China	C1	42
Haizhou, China	D8	42
Haizhou Wan, b., China	D8	42
Hajdú-Bihar, state, Hung.	B8	26
Hajdúböszörmény, Hung.	B8	26
Hajdúnánás, Hung.	B8	26
Hajdúszoboszló, Hung.	B8	26
Hājīpur, India	F10	54
Hajnówka, Pol.	D19	16
Hakasija, state, Russia	D16	32
Hakha, Mya.	A1	48
Hakken-san, mtn., Japan	E8	40
Hakodate, Japan	D14	38
Hakone-yama, vol., Japan	D12	40
Hakui, Japan	C9	40
Haku-san, vol., Japan	C9	40
Haku-san-kokuritsu-kōen, p.o.i., Japan	C9	40
Hal see Halle, Bel.	D13	14
Ḥalab (Aleppo), Syria	B8	58
Ḥalab, state, Syria	B8	58
Halachó, Mex.	B2	102
Halahai, China	B6	38
Ḥalā'ib, Sudan	C7	62
Halawa, Cape, c., Hi., U.S.	B5	78a
Halberstadt, Ger.	E7	16
Halbrite, Sk., Can.	E10	124
Halcon, Mount, mtn., Phil.	D3	52
Halden, Nor.	G4	8
Haldensleben, Ger.	D7	16
Haldimand, On., Can.	F10	112
Haldwāni, India	D7	54
Hale, Mo., U.S.	E4	120
Haleakala Crater, crat., Hi., U.S.	C5	78a
Haleakala National Park, p.o.i., Hi., U.S.	C5	78a
Hale Center, Tx., U.S.	G7	128
Halenkov, Czech Rep.	G14	16
Halfmoon Bay, B.C., Can.	G6	138
Halfway, Md., U.S.	E8	114
Halfway, Or., U.S.	F9	136
Halicarnassus, hist., Tur.	F10	28
Halifax, Austl.	B6	76
Halifax, N.S., Can.	F13	110
Halifax, Eng., U.K.	H11	12
Halifax, N.C., U.S.	H8	114
Halifax, Va., U.S.	H6	114
Halifax Bay, b., Austl.	B6	76
Haliyāl, India	D2	53
Haljala, Est.	A9	10
Halkapınar, Tur.	A5	58
Halland, state, Swe.	H5	8
Hallandale, Fl., U.S.	K5	116
Ḥallānīyah, Juzur al- (Kuria Muria Islands), is., Oman	F8	56
Halla-san, mtn., Kor., S.	H7	38
Hall Basin, b., N.A.	A13	141
Halle, Bel.	D13	14
Halle, Ger.	E7	16
Hällefors, Swe.	G6	8
Hallein, Aus.	C10	22
Hallettsville, Tx., U.S.	E11	130
Halley, sci., Ant.	C2	81
Halligen, is., Ger.	B4	16
Hall in Tirol, Aus.	C8	22
Hall Islands, is., Micron.	C6	72
Hall Lake, l., Nu., Can.	B14	106
Hall Land, reg., Grnld.	A14	141
Hall Mountain, mtn., Wa., U.S.	B9	136
Hallock, Mn., U.S.	C2	118
Hallowell, Me., U.S.	F7	110
Hall Peninsula, pen., Nu., Can.	C17	106
Halls, Tn., U.S.	I8	120
Hallsberg, Swe.	G6	8
Halls Creek, Austl.	C5	74
Hallstahammar, Swe.	G7	8
Hallstavik, Swe.	F8	8
Hallstead, Pa., U.S.	C10	114
Hallsville, Mo., U.S.	E5	120
Halmahera, i., Indon.	E8	44
Halmahera, Laut (Halmahera Sea), Indon.	F8	44
Halmahera Sea see Halmahera, Laut, Indon.	F8	44
Hal'mer-Ju, Russia	A10	32
Halmstad, Swe.	H5	8
Haloučyn, Bela.	F12	10
Hal'šany, Bela.	F8	10
Halsey, Ne., U.S.	F12	126
Halsey, Or., U.S.	F3	136
Halstead, Ks., U.S.	D11	128
Haltern, Ger.	E3	16
Haltiatunturi, mtn., Eur.	B9	8
Haltom City, Tx., U.S.	B10	130
Halton Hills see Georgetown, On., Can.	E9	112
Halvorson, Mount, mtn., B.C., Can.	C10	138
Ham, stm., Nmb.	F4	70
Hamada, Japan	E4	40
Hamadān, Iran	C6	56
Ḥamāh, Syria	C7	58
Ḥamāh, state, Syria	C8	58
Hamamatsu, Japan	E10	40
Haman, Kor., S.	D1	40
Hamana-ko, l., Japan	E10	40
Hamar, Nor.	F4	8
Ha Marakabei, Leso.	F9	70
Hamar-Daban, hrebet, mts., Russia	F9	34
Hamburg, Ger.	C6	16
Hamburg, Ar., U.S.	D7	122
Hamburg, Ia., U.S.	D2	120
Hamburg, N.J., U.S.	C11	114
Hamburg, N.Y., U.S.	B7	114
Hamburg, state, Ger.	C6	16
Hamden, Ct., U.S.	C13	114
Hamden, Oh., U.S.	E3	114
Häme, state, Fin.	F11	8
Hämeenlinna (Tavastehus), Fin.	F10	8
Hamelin, Austl.	E2	74
Hameln, Ger.	D5	16
HaMerkaz, state, Isr.	F5	58
Hamersley Range, mts., Austl.	D3	74
Hamgyŏng-sanjulgi, mts., Kor., N.	D8	38
Hamhŭng, Kor., N.	E7	38
Hami, China	C3	36
Hamilton, Austl.	K4	76
Hamilton, Ber.	k15	104e
Hamilton, On., Can.	E10	112
Hamilton, N.Z.	C6	80
Hamilton, Scot., U.K.	F8	12
Hamilton, Al., U.S.	C11	122
Hamilton, Ga., U.S.	E14	122
Hamilton, Il., U.S.	D6	120
Hamilton, Mi., U.S.	F4	112
Hamilton, Mo., U.S.	E3	120
Hamilton, Mt., U.S.	D12	136
Hamilton, N.Y., U.S.	B10	114
Hamilton, Oh., U.S.	E1	114
Hamilton, stm., Austl.	D3	76
Hamilton, Lake, res., Ar., U.S.	C5	122
Hamilton, Mount, mtn., Ca., U.S.	F4	134
Hamilton City, Ca., U.S.	D3	134
Hamilton Dome, Wy., U.S.	D4	126
Hamilton Hotel, Austl.	D3	76
Hamilton Mountain, mtn., N.Y., U.S.	G2	110
Hamina, Fin.	F12	8
Hamiota, Mb., Can.	D13	124
Hamīrpur, India	F7	54
Hamlin, Tx., U.S.	B7	130
Hamlin, W.V., U.S.	F3	114
Hamlin Valley Wash, stm., U.S.	E3	132
Hamm, Ger.	E3	16
Hammamet, Tun.	H4	24
Hammamet, Golfe de, b., Tun.	H4	24
Hammam Lif, Tun.	H4	24
Hammelburg, Ger.	F5	16
Hammerdal, Swe.	E6	8
Hammerfest, Nor.	A10	8
Hammon, Ok., U.S.	F9	128
Hammond, In., U.S.	G2	112
Hammond, La., U.S.	G8	122
Hammondsport, N.Y., U.S.	F12	112
Hampden, Me., U.S.	F8	110
Hampden, N.D., U.S.	F15	124
Hampi, India	D3	53
Hampshire, Il., U.S.	I10	118
Hampstead, N.C., U.S.	B8	116
Hampton, N.B., Can.	E11	110
Hampton, Ar., U.S.	D6	122
Hampton, Fl., U.S.	G3	116
Hampton, Ga., U.S.	C1	116
Hampton, Ne., U.S.	G15	126
Hampton, N.H., U.S.	H6	110
Hampton, Tn., U.S.	H3	114
Hampton, Va., U.S.	G9	114
Hampton Butte, mtn., Or., U.S.	G6	136
Hampton Tableland, plat., Austl.	F5	74
Hamra, Swe.	F6	8
Ḥamrā',Al-Ḥamādah al-, des., Libya	B2	62
Hamra, As Saquia al, stm., W. Sah.	D2	64
Hamsara, stm., Russia	D16	32
Hams Fork, stm., Wy., U.S.	F2	126
Hamṭa, Gebel (Ḥamāṭah, Jabal), mtn., Egypt	C6	62
Ham Tan, Viet.	G8	48
Hāmūn, Daryācheh-ye, l., Iran	C9	56
Han, stm., China	I7	42
Han, stm., China	F6	42
Han, Nong, l., Thai.	D7	48
Hana, Hi., U.S.	C6	78a
Hanahan, S.C., U.S.	D5	116
Hanamaki, Japan	E14	38
Hananui see Anglem, Mount, mtn., N.Z.	H2	80
Hanapepe, Hi., U.S.	B2	78a
Hanateio, Fr. Poly.	s18	78g
Hanatetena, Fr. Poly.	s18	78g
Hanau am Main, Ger.	F4	16
Hanbury, stm., N.T., Can.	C9	106
Hancavičy, Bela.	H9	10
Hâncești, Mol.	C15	26
Hanceville, Al., U.S.	C12	122
Hancheng, China	D7	36
Hancheng, China	D4	42
Hanchung see Hanzhong, China	E2	42
Hancock, Md., U.S.	E7	114
Hancock, Mi., U.S.	D10	118
Hancock, Mn., U.S.	F3	118
Hancock, N.Y., U.S.	C10	114
Handa, Japan	E9	40
Handan, China	C6	42
Handlová, Slov.	H14	16
Handsworth, Sk., Can.	E10	124
Handyga, Russia	D16	34
HaNegev (Negev Desert), reg., Isr.	H5	58
Hanford, Ca., U.S.	G6	134
Hanga Roa, Chile	e29	78l
Hangayn nuruu, mts., Mong.	B4	36
Hangchou see Hangzhou, China	F9	42
Hangchow see Hangzhou, China	F9	42
Hangchow Bay see Hangzhou Wan, b., China	F9	42
Hanggin Houqi, China	A2	42
Hanggin Qi, China	B3	42
Hangman Creek, stm., U.S.	C9	136
Hangö see Hanko, Fin.	G10	8
Hangokurt, Russia	B10	32
Hangu, China	B7	42
Hangu, Pak.	B3	54
Hanguang, China	I5	42
Hangzhou, China	F9	42
Hangzhou Wan, b., China	F9	42
Hanino, Russia	F19	10
Ḥanīsh, is., Yemen	G5	56
Hanish Islands see Ḥanīsh, is., Yemen	G5	56
Hanjiang, China	I8	42
Hankinson, N.D., U.S.	E2	118
Hanko, Fin.	G10	8
Hankow see Wuhan, China	F6	42
Hanku see Hangu, China	B7	42
Hānle, India	B7	54
Hanley, Sk., Can.	C7	124
Hanna, Ab., Can.	E19	138
Hanna, Ok., U.S.	B3	122
Hanna, Wy., U.S.	B10	132
Hanna City, Il., U.S.	D8	120
Hannah, N.D., U.S.	F15	124
Hannah Bay, b., On., Can.	E14	106
Hannibal, Mo., U.S.	E6	120
Hannover, Ger.	D5	16
Ha Noi (Hanoi), Viet.	B7	48
Hanoi see Ha Noi, Viet.	B7	48
Hanover, On., Can.	D8	112
Hanover see Hannover, Ger.	D5	16
Hanover, S. Afr.	G7	70
Hanover, Il., U.S.	B7	120
Hanover, In., U.S.	F12	120
Hanover, N.H., U.S.	G4	110
Hanover, N.M., U.S.	K8	132
Hanover, Pa., U.S.	E9	114
Hanover, Va., U.S.	G8	114
Hanover, Isla, i., Chile	J2	90
Hansdiha, India	F11	54
Hānsi, India	D5	54
Hanska, Mn., U.S.	G4	118
Hantajskoe, ozero, l., Russia	C6	34
Hantan see Handan, China	C6	42
Hantau, Kaz.	F12	32
Hantsport, N.S., Can.	E12	110
Hanty-Mansijsk, Russia	B11	32
Hantzsch, stm., Nu., Can.	B16	106
Hanumāngarh, India	C3	46
Hanumangarh, India	D4	54
Hanuy, stm., Mong.	B5	36
Hanyin, China	E3	42
Hanzhong, China	E2	42
Hanzhuang, China	D7	42
Haojiadian, China	F5	42
Haoli see Hegang, China	B11	36
Hāora, India	G12	54
Haparanda, Swe.	D10	8
Hapčeranga, Russia	G11	34
Happy, Tx., U.S.	G7	128
Happy Jack, Az., U.S.	I5	132
Happy Valley-Goose Bay, Nf., Can.	E18	106
Hāpur, India	D6	54
Ḥaql, Sau. Ar.	I5	58
Ḥaraḍ, Sau. Ar.	E6	56
Haradok, Bela.	E13	10
Haradzec, Bela.	H7	10
Haradzec, Bela.	G13	10
Haradzišča, Bela.	G9	10
Haramachi, Japan	B13	40
Haranor, Russia	A8	36
Harar see Hārer, Eth.	F8	62
Harare, Zimb.	D5	68
Harazé Mangueigne, Chad	E4	62
Harbala, Russia	D13	34
Harbavičy, Bela.	G13	10
Harbin, China	B7	38
Harbiye, Tur.	B7	58
Harbor, Or., U.S.	A1	134
Harbor Beach, Mi., U.S.	E7	112
Harbour Breton, Nf., Can.	j22	107a
Harbourville, N.S., Can.	E12	110
Harda, India	G6	54
Hardangerfjorden, b., Nor.	F2	8
Hardangerjøkulen, ice, Nor.	F2	8
Hardangervidda Nasjonalpark, p.o.i., Nor.	F2	8
Hardap, state, Nmb.	D3	70
Hardeeville, S.C., U.S.	D4	116
Harderwijk, Neth.	B14	14
Hardin, Il., U.S.	E7	120
Hardin, Mt., U.S.	B5	126
Harding, S. Afr.	G9	70
Harding, Lake, res., U.S.	E13	122
Hardinsburg, Ky., U.S.	G11	120
Hardisty Lake, l., N.T., Can.	C7	106
Hardoi, India	E7	54
Hardtner, Ks., U.S.	D10	128
Hardwick, Ga., U.S.	C2	116
Hardwick, Vt., U.S.	F4	110
Hardy, Ar., U.S.	H6	120
Hardy, Ne., U.S.	G15	126
Hardy Bay, b., N.T., Can.	B16	140
Hare Bay, b., Nf., Can.	i22	107a
Hare Indian, stm., N.T., Can.	B5	106
Hareøen, i., Grnld.	C14	141
Hārer, Eth.	F8	62
Hargeysa, Som.	C8	66
Harghita, state, Rom.	C12	26
Har Hu, l., China	D4	36
Hari, stm., Indon.	D3	50
Ḥarīb, Yemen	G6	56
Haridwār, India	D7	54
Harihar, India	D2	53
Ḥārim, Syria	B7	58
Harīpur, Pak.	B4	54
Harīrūd (Tedžen), stm., Asia	C9	56
Harischandra Range, mts., India	B1	53
Haritonovo, Russia	F22	8
Harkers Island, N.C., U.S.	B9	116
Harlan, Ky., U.S.	H2	114
Harlan County Lake, res., Ne., U.S.	A9	128
Harlem, Fl., U.S.	J5	116
Harlem, Ga., U.S.	C3	116
Harleton, Tx., U.S.	E4	122
Harlingen, Neth.	A14	14
Harlingen, Tx., U.S.	H10	130
Harlovka, Russia	B17	8
Harlow, Eng., U.K.	J13	12
Harlowton, Mt., U.S.	D17	136
Harman, W.V., U.S.	F6	114
Harmancık, Tur.	D12	28
Harmanli, Blg.	H12	26
Harmony, In., U.S.	E10	120
Harnai, India	C1	53
Harney Basin, bas., Or., U.S.	G8	136
Harney Lake, l., Or., U.S.	G7	136
Harney Peak, mtn., S.D., U.S.	D9	126
Härnösand, Swe.	E8	8
Har nuur, l., Mong.	B3	36
Haro, Spain	B8	20
Haro, Cabo, c., Mex.	B3	100
Harovsk, Russia	F18	8
Harpanahalli, India	D3	53
Harper, Lib.	I3	64
Harper, Ks., U.S.	D10	128
Harper, Tx., U.S.	D8	130
Harper, Mount, mtn., Ak., U.S.	D11	140
Harqin Qi, China	D3	38
Harrai, India	G7	54
Harricana, stm., Can.	E15	106
Harriman, Tn., U.S.	I13	120
Harrington, De., U.S.	F10	114
Harrington, Me., U.S.	F9	110
Harris, Sk., Can.	C6	124
Harris, Monts.	D3	105a
Harris, Mn., U.S.	F5	118
Harris, reg., Scot., U.K.	D6	12
Harris, Lake, l., Fl., U.S.	H4	116
Harrisburg, Ar., U.S.	B8	122
Harrisburg, Ne., U.S.	F9	126
Harrisburg, Or., U.S.	F3	136
Harrisburg, Pa., U.S.	D8	114
Harrismith, S. Afr.	F9	70
Harrison, Ar., U.S.	H4	120
Harrison, Mi., U.S.	D5	112
Harrison, Ne., U.S.	E9	126
Harrison Bay, b., Ak., U.S.	B9	140
Harrisonburg, La., U.S.	F7	122
Harrisonburg, Va., U.S.	F6	114
Harrison Islands, is., Nu., Can.	B13	106
Harrison Lake, l., B.C., Can.	G9	138
Harriston, On., Can.	E9	112
Harriston, Ms., U.S.	F7	122
Harrisville, N.Y., U.S.	D14	112
Harrisville, W.V., U.S.	E4	114
Harrodsburg, Ky., U.S.	G13	120
Harrogate, Eng., U.K.	H11	12
Harrold, Tx., U.S.	G9	128
Harrowsmith, On., Can.	D13	112
Harry S. Truman Reservoir, res., Mo., U.S.	F4	120
Har Sai Shan, mtn., China	D4	36
Harsīn, Iran	C6	56
Hârșova, Rom.	E14	26
Harstad, Nor.	B7	8
Harsūd, India	G6	54
Hart, Mi., U.S.	E3	112
Hart, Tx., U.S.	G6	128
Hart, stm., Yk., Can.	B3	106
Hartbees, stm., S. Afr.	F5	70
Hartberg, Aus.	C12	22
Hartford, Ar., U.S.	C4	122
Hartford, Ct., U.S.	C13	114
Hartford, Ks., U.S.	F2	120
Hartford, Mi., U.S.	F3	112
Hartford, S.D., U.S.	H2	118
Hartford, Wi., U.S.	H10	118
Hartford City, In., U.S.	H4	112
Hartland, N.B., Can.	D9	110
Hartland, Me., U.S.	F7	110
Hartlepool, Eng., U.K.	G11	12
Hartley, Ia., U.S.	H3	118
Hartley Bay, B.C., Can.	C1	138
Hart Mountain, mtn., Mb., Can.	B12	124
Hartney, Mb., Can.	E13	124
Harts, stm., S. Afr.	E7	70
Hartselle, Al., U.S.	C12	122
Hartshorne, Ok., U.S.	C3	122
Hartsville, S.C., U.S.	B5	116
Hartville, Mo., U.S.	G5	120
Hartwell, Ga., U.S.	B3	116
Hartwell Lake, res., U.S.	B2	116
Hartz Mountains National Park, p.o.i., Austl.	o13	77a
Hārūnābād, Pak.	D4	54
Haruniye, Tur.	A7	58
Harūr, India	E4	53
Har-Us nuur, l., Mong.	B3	36
Hārūt, stm., Afg.	C9	56
Harvard, Ne., U.S.	G14	126
Harvey, N.B., Can.	E12	110
Harvey, Il., U.S.	G2	112
Harvey, N.D., U.S.	G14	124
Harwich, Eng., U.K.	J14	12
Haryāna, state, India	D6	54
Haryn', stm., Eur.	H10	10
Harz, mts., Ger.	E6	16
Hasavjurt, Russia	F7	32
Hasdo, stm., India	G9	54
Hase, stm., Ger.	D3	16
Hasenkamp, Arg.	E8	92
Hashima, Japan	D9	40
Hashimoto, Japan	E8	40
Hāsilpur, Pak.	D4	54
Haskell, Ok., U.S.	I2	120
Haskell, Tx., U.S.	A8	130
Haskovo, Blg.	H12	26
Haskovo, state, Blg.	G12	26
Haslemere, Eng., U.K.	J12	12
Hasperos Canyon, val., N.M., U.S.	H3	128
Ḥaṣṣ, Jabal al-, hill, Syria	C8	58
Hassa, Tur.	B7	58
Hassan, India	E3	53
Hassayampa, stm., Az., U.S.	J4	132
Hassel Sound, strt., Nu., Can.	B6	141
Hasselt, Bel.	D14	14
Hassfurt, Ger.	F6	16
Hassi Messaoud, Alg.	C6	64
Hässleholm, Swe.	H5	8
Hastings, Barb.	n8	105d
Hastings, On., Can.	D11	112
Hastings, N.Z.	D7	80
Hastings, Eng., U.K.	K13	12
Hastings, Mi., U.S.	F4	112
Hastings, Mn., U.S.	G6	118
Hastings, Ne., U.S.	G14	126
Haswell, Co., U.S.	C5	128
Hatanga, Russia	B9	34
Hatanga, stm., Russia	B9	34
Hatangskij zaliv, b., Russia	B10	34
Hatay (Antioch), Tur.	B7	58
Hatay, state, Tur.	B7	58
Hatch, N.M., U.S.	K9	132
Hatch, Ut., U.S.	F4	132
Hat Chao Mai National Park, p.o.i., Thai.	I4	48
Hatchie, stm., U.S.	B9	122
Hatfield, Austl.	I4	76
Hatfield, Ar., U.S.	C4	122
Hatfield, Ma., U.S.	B13	114
Hatgal, Mong.	F9	34
Hāthras, India	E7	54
Ha Tien, Viet.	G7	48
Hatillo, P.R.	A2	104a
Ha Tinh, Viet.	C7	48
Hatip, Tur.	F15	28
Hato, Bocht van, b., Neth. Ant.	p21	104g
Hato Mayor del Rey, Dom. Rep.	C13	102
Hāt Pīplia, India	G6	54
Hatta, India	F7	54
Hatteras, N.C., U.S.	A10	116
Hatteras, Cape, c., N.C., U.S.	A10	116
Hatteras Island, i., N.C., U.S.	A10	116
Hattiesburg, Ms., U.S.	F9	122
Hatton, Al., U.S.	C11	122
Hatton, N.D., U.S.	G16	124
Hatunsaray, Tur.	A3	58
Hatvan, Hung.	B6	26
Hat Yai, Thai.	I5	48
Hatyrka, Russia	D24	34
Haugesund, Nor.	G1	8
Haukeligrend, Nor.	G2	8
Haukivesi, l., Fin.	E12	8
Hauraki Gulf, b., N.Z.	C6	80
Hausach, Ger.	H4	16
Haut, Isle au, i., Me., U.S.	F8	110
Haut Atlas, mts., Mor.	C3	64
Haute-Corse, state, Fr.	G15	18
Haute-Garonne, state, Fr.	F7	18
Haute-Loire, state, Fr.	D9	18
Haute-Marne, state, Fr.	F14	14
Hautes-Alpes, state, Fr.	E12	18
Haute-Saône, state, Fr.	G14	14
Haute-Savoie, state, Fr.	C12	18
Hautes-Pyrénées, state, Fr.	F6	18
Haute-Vienne, state, Fr.	D7	18
Haut-Rhin, state, Fr.	G16	14
Haut Sheila, N.B., Can.	C11	110
Hauts Plateaux, reg., Afr.	C5	64
Hauula, Hi., U.S.	B4	78a
Hauwâret el-Maqta', Egypt	I1	58
Havana see La Habana, Cuba	A6	102
Havana, Fl., U.S.	G14	122
Havana, Il., U.S.	D7	120
Havana, N.D., U.S.	B15	126
Havannah, Canal de la, strt., N. Cal.	n16	79d
Havant, Eng., U.K.	K12	12

Name	Map Ref.	Page
Havast, Uzb.	F11	32
Havasu, Lake, res., U.S.	I2	132
Havasu Creek, stm., Az., U.S.	H4	132
Havel, stm., Ger.	D8	16
Havelberg, Ger.	D8	16
Haveli, Pak.	C4	54
Havelland, reg., Ger.	D8	16
Havelock, On., Can.	D12	112
Havelock, N.C., U.S.	B8	116
Haverfordwest, Wales, U.K.	J7	12
Haverhill, Eng., U.K.	I13	12
Haverhill, Ma., U.S.	B14	114
Hāveri, India	D2	53
Haviland, Ks., U.S.	D9	128
Havířov, Czech Rep.	G14	16
Havlíčkův Brod, Czech Rep.	G11	16
Havre see Le Havre, Fr.	E8	14
Havre, Mt., U.S.	B17	136
Havre-Aubert, Qc., Can.	C15	110
Havre Aubert, Île du, i., Qc., Can.	C14	110
Havre de Grace, Md., U.S.	E9	114
Havre North, Mt., U.S.	B17	136
Havsa, Tur.	B9	28
Haw, stm., N.C., U.S.	A7	116
Hawaii, state, U.S.	B5	78a
Hawaii, i., Hi., U.S.	C6	78a
Hawaiian Islands, is., Hi., U.S.	C4	78a
Hawaiian Ridge, unds.	G21	142
Hawaii Volcanoes National Park, p.o.i., Hi., U.S.	D6	78a
Hawarden, Sk., Can.	C7	124
Hawea, Lake, l., N.Z.	G3	80
Hawera, N.Z.	D6	80
Hawesville, Ky., U.S.	G11	120
Hawi, Hi., U.S.	C6	78a
Hawick, Scot., U.K.	F10	12
Hawke, Cape, c., Austl.	I9	76
Hawke Bay, b., N.Z.	D7	80
Hawker, Austl.	H2	76
Hawkes, Mount, mtn., Ant.	D36	81
Hawkesbury, On., Can.	E2	110
Hawkesbury Island, i., B.C., Can.	C1	138
Hawkeye, Ia., U.S.	B6	120
Hawkins, Tx., U.S.	E3	122
Hawkins, Wi., U.S.	F8	118
Haw Knob, mtn., U.S.	A1	116
Hawksbill Creek, b., Bah.	J7	116
Hawkwood, Austl.	E8	76
Hawley, Mn., U.S.	E2	118
Hawley, Pa., U.S.	C10	114
Hawthorne, Fl., U.S.	G3	116
Hawthorne, Nv., U.S.	E7	134
Hawwâret'Adlan, Egypt	I1	58
Hay, Austl.	J5	76
Hay, stm., Austl.	D7	74
Hay, stm., Can.	D7	106
Hay, Cape, c., N.T., Can.	B17	140
Hayang, Kor., S.	D1	40
Hayange, Fr.	E14	14
Haybān, Jabal, mtn., Sudan	E6	62
Haydarlı, Tur.	E13	28
Hayden, Co., U.S.	C9	132
Haydenville, Oh., U.S.	E3	114
Hayes, La., U.S.	G6	122
Hayes, stm., Mb., Can.	D12	106
Hayes, stm., Nu., Can.	B11	106
Hayes, Mount, mtn., Ak., U.S.	D10	140
Hayes Center, Ne., U.S.	G11	126
Hayesville, Or., U.S.	F4	136
Hayfield, Mn., U.S.	H6	118
Hayford Peak, mtn., Nv., U.S.	G1	132
Hayfork, Ca., U.S.	C2	134
Hay Lakes, Ab., Can.	C17	138
Haynes, Ar., U.S.	C8	122
Hayneville, Al., U.S.	E12	122
Hayrabolu, Tur.	B10	28
Hay River, N.T., Can.	C7	106
Hays, Ab., Can.	F19	138
Hays, Ks., U.S.	C9	128
Hays, Mt., U.S.	F5	124
Hay Springs, Ne., U.S.	E10	126
Haystack Mountain, mtn., Nv., U.S.	B1	132
Hayti, Mo., U.S.	H8	120
Hayti, S.D., U.S.	C15	126
Hayward, Ca., U.S.	F3	134
Hayward, Wi., U.S.	E7	118
Haywards Heath, Eng., U.K.	J13	12
HaZafon, state, Isr.	F6	58
Hazard, Ky., U.S.	G2	114
Hazārībāg, India	G10	54
Hazawzā, Sabkhat, l., Sau. Ar.	H9	58
Hazebrouck, Fr.	D11	14
Hazel Green, Wi., U.S.	I8	118
Hazelton, B.C., Can.	A3	138
Hazelton, N.D., U.S.	A12	126
Hazelton Mountains, mts., B.C., Can.	B3	138
Hazelwood, N.C., U.S.	A2	116
Hazen, Ar., U.S.	C7	122
Hazen, N.D., U.S.	G12	124
Hazen, Lake, l., Nu., Can.	A11	141
Hazlehurst, Ms., U.S.	F8	122
Hazlet, Sk., Can.	D5	124
Hazleton, Ia., U.S.	B6	120
Hazleton, Pa., U.S.	D9	114
Hazlett, Lake, l., Austl.	D5	74
Hazor HaGelilit, Isr.	E6	58
He, stm., China	H6	42
He, stm., China	I4	42
Healdsburg, Ca., U.S.	E2	134
Healdton, Ok., U.S.	G11	128
Healesville, Austl.	K5	76
Healy, Ks., U.S.	C8	128
Heard Island, i., Austl.	O10	142
Hearst, On., Can.	F14	106
Heart, stm., N.D., U.S.	H12	124
Heart Lake, l., Ab., Can.	A19	138
Heath, Pointe, c., Qc., Can.	A15	110
Heathcote, Austl.	K5	76
Heath Springs, S.C., U.S.	B5	116
Heathsville, Va., U.S.	G9	114
Heavener, Ok., U.S.	C4	122
Hebei, state, China	D8	36
Hebel, Austl.	G6	76
Heber, Az., U.S.	I6	132
Heber City, Ut., U.S.	C5	132
Heber Springs, Ar., U.S.	B6	122
Hebgen Lake, res., Mt., U.S.	F15	136
Hebi, China	D6	42
Hebrides, is., Scot., U.K.	D5	12
Hebrides, Sea of the, Scot., U.K.	D6	12
Hebron, Nf., Can.	F13	141
Hebron, Il., U.S.	B9	120
Hebron, Ne., U.S.	A11	128
Hebron, N.D., U.S.	H11	124
Hebron see Al-Khalīl, W.B.	G5	58
Hecate Strait, strt., B.C., Can.	E4	106
Hecelchakán, Mex.	B2	102
Hechi, China	I3	42
Hechiceros, Mex.	F4	130
Hechingen, Ger.	H4	16
Hechuan, China	G2	42
Hecla, Mb., Can.	C17	124
Hecla, Cape, c., Nu., Can.	A13	141
Hecla Island, i., Mb., Can.	D17	124
Hectanooga, N.S., Can.	F10	110
Hector, Mn., U.S.	G4	118
Hede, Swe.	E5	8
Hedemora, Swe.	F6	8
He Devil, mtn., Id., U.S.	E10	136
Hedley, Tx., U.S.	G8	128
Hedmark, state, Nor.	F4	8
Hedrick, Ia., U.S.	C5	120
Heerenveen, Neth.	B14	14
Heerlen, Neth.	D15	14
Hefa (Haifa), Isr.	F5	58
Hefa, state, Isr.	F5	58
Hefei, China	F7	42
Heflin, Al., U.S.	D13	122
Hegang, China	B11	36
Heho, Mya.	B3	48
Hei, stm., China	A7	42
Heide, Ger.	B5	16
Heidelberg, Ger.	G4	16
Heidelberg, S. Afr.	E9	70
Heidelberg, Ms., U.S.	F10	122
Heidenheim, Ger.	G6	16
Heihe, China	A10	36
Heilbad Heiligenstadt, Ger.	E6	16
Heilbron, S. Afr.	E8	70
Heilbronn, Ger.	G5	16
Heiligenhafen, Ger.	B6	16
Heilong (Amur), stm., Asia	F14	34
Heilongguan, China	C4	42
Heilongjiang, state, China	B10	36
Heilungkiang see Heilongjiang, state, China	B8	38
Heimaey, i., Ice.	I29	8a
Heinola, Fin.	F12	8
Heishan, China	D4	38
Heishuisi, China	C3	42
Hejaz see Al-Ḥijāz, reg., Sau. Ar.	D4	56
Hejian, China	B7	42
Hejiang, China	G1	42
Hejing, China	C2	36
Hekla, vol., Ice.	k30	8a
Hekou, China	G4	42
Hekou, China	A6	48
Helagsfjället, mtn., Swe.	E5	8
Helan Mountains see Helan Shan, mts., China	B1	42
Helan Shan, mts., China	B1	42
Helbra, Ger.	E7	16
Helder see Den Helder, Neth.	B13	14
Helder, Den see Den Helder, Neth.	B13	14
Helen, Mount, hill, Austl.	C3	76
Helena, Ar., U.S.	C8	122
Helena, Mt., U.S.	D14	136
Helena, Ok., U.S.	E10	128
Helensburgh, Scot., U.K.	E8	12
Helenwood, Tn., U.S.	H13	120
Helgoland, i., Ger.	B3	16
Helgoländer Bucht, b., Ger.	C4	16
Heli, China	B11	36
Heliopolis, hist., Egypt	H2	58
Helixi, China	F8	42
Hellesylt, Nor.	E2	8
Hellín, Spain	F9	20
Hells Canyon, val., U.S.	E10	136
Hells Canyon National Recreation Area, p.o.i., Or., U.S.	E10	136
Hells Gate, val., B.C., Can.	G9	138
Helmand, stm., Asia	C9	56
Helmcken Falls, wtfl, B.C., Can.	E10	138
Helmond, Neth.	C14	14
Helmstedt, Ger.	D6	16
Helong, China	C8	38
Helper, Ut., U.S.	D6	132
Helsingborg, Swe.	H5	8
Helsingfors see Helsinki, Fin.	F11	8
Helsingør, Den.	H5	8
Helsinki (Helsingfors), Fin.	F11	8
Helska, Mierzeja, pen., Pol.	B14	16
Helston, Eng., U.K.	K7	12
Helvecia, Arg.	E7	92
Helwan, Egypt	I2	58
Helwan Observatory, sci., Egypt	I2	58
Hemau, Ger.	G7	16
Hemāvati, stm., India	E2	53
Hemel Hempstead, Eng., U.K.	J12	12
Hemet, Ca., U.S.	J9	134
Hemingford, Ne., U.S.	E9	126
Hemingway, S.C., U.S.	C6	116
Hemphill, Tx., U.S.	F5	122
Hemsön, i., Swe.	E8	8
Henan, state, China	E5	42
Henares, stm., Spain	D7	20
Henbury, Austl.	D6	74
Hendek, Tur.	C13	28
Henderson, Ky., U.S.	G10	120
Henderson, Mn., U.S.	G5	118
Henderson, Ne., U.S.	G15	126
Henderson, Nv., U.S.	G1	132
Henderson, N.C., U.S.	H7	114
Henderson, Tn., U.S.	B10	122
Henderson, Tx., U.S.	E4	122
Hendersonville, Tn., U.S.	H11	120
Hendricks, Mn., U.S.	G2	118
Hendricks, W.V., U.S.	E6	114
Henefer, Ut., U.S.	B5	132
Henganofi, Pap. N. Gui.	b4	79a
Hengchow see Hengyang, China	H5	42
Hengdaozi, China	C7	38
Hengelo, Neth.	B15	14
Hengfeng, China	G7	42
Henglu, China	D7	38
Hengshan, China	C3	42
Hengshan, China	H5	42
Heng Shan, mts., China	B5	42
Hengshui, China	C6	42
Hengxian, China	J3	42
Hengyang, China	H5	42
Hénin-Beaumont, Fr.	D11	14
Henlopen, Cape, c., De., U.S.	F10	114
Hennebont, Fr.	G5	14
Hennef, Ger.	F3	16
Hennessey, Ok., U.S.	E11	128
Henniker, N.H., U.S.	G5	110
Henning, Mn., U.S.	E3	118
Henrietta, N.Y., U.S.	A8	114
Henrietta, Tx., U.S.	H10	128
Henrietta Island see Genrietty, ostrov, i., Russia	A20	34
Henrietta Maria, Cape, c., On., Can.	D14	106
Henri Pittier, Parque Nacional, p.o.i., Ven.	B8	86
Henry, Il., U.S.	C8	120
Henry, Cape, c., Va., U.S.	H10	114
Henry, Mount, mtn., Mt., U.S.	B11	136
Henryetta, Ok., U.S.	B2	122
Henry Kater, Cape, c., Nu., Can.	B17	106
Henrys Fork, stm., Id., U.S.	F15	136
Hensall, On., Can.	E8	112
Hensley, Ar., U.S.	C6	122
Henslow, Cape, c., Sol. Is.	e9	79b
Hentiesbaai, Nmb.	C2	70
Hentiyn nuruu, mts., Mong.	G10	34
Henzada, Mya.	D2	48
Hephzibah, Ga., U.S.	C3	116
Heping, China	H7	42
Heppenheim, Ger.	G4	16
Heppner, Or., U.S.	E7	136
Hepu, China	K3	42
Hequ, China	B4	42
Héraðsflói, b., Ice.	k32	8a
Herāt, Afg.	C9	56
Hérault, state, Fr.	F9	18
Hérault, stm., Fr.	F9	18
Herbert, Sk., Can.	D6	124
Herberton, Austl.	A5	76
Herbertsdale, S. Afr.	H5	70
Herborn, Ger.	F4	16
Herceg-Novi, Yugo.	G5	26
Hércules, Mex.	A7	100
Herðubreið, vol., Ice.	k31	8a
Heredia, C.R.	G5	102
Hereford, Eng., U.K.	I10	12
Hereford, Az., U.S.	L6	132
Hereford, Tx., U.S.	G6	128
Hereke, Tur.	C12	28
Herencia, Spain	E7	20
Herford, Ger.	D4	16
Herington, Ks., U.S.	C11	128
Herisau, Switz.	C6	22
Herkimer, N.Y., U.S.	E15	112
Hermagor, Aus.	D10	22
Herman, Mn., U.S.	F2	118
Herman, Ne., U.S.	C1	120
Hermanas, Mex.	G6	130
Hermanns-Denkmal, hist., Ger.	E4	16
Hermansverk, Nor.	F2	8
Hermansville, Mi., U.S.	C2	112
Hermanus, S. Afr.	I4	70
Hermanville, Ms., U.S.	F8	122
Hermiston, Or., U.S.	E7	136
Hermitage, Ar., U.S.	D6	122
Hermit Islands, is., Pap. N. Gui.	a4	79a
Hermleigh, Tx., U.S.	B7	130
Hermon, Mount (Shaykh, Jabal ash-), mtn., Asia	E6	58
Hermosillo, Mex.	A3	100
Hermyingyi, Mya.	E4	48
Hernád (Hornad), stm., Eur.	H17	16
Hernandarias, Arg.	E8	92
Hernandarias, Para.	B10	92
Hernando, Arg.	F6	92
Hernando, Fl., U.S.	H3	116
Hernando, Ms., U.S.	C9	122
Herndon, Pa., U.S.	D9	114
Herne Bay, Eng., U.K.	J14	12
Herning, Den.	H3	8
Heroica Zitácuaro, Mex.	F8	100
Heron Island, i., Austl.	D8	76
Heron Lake, Mn., U.S.	H3	118
Hérouville-Saint-Clair, Fr.	E8	14
Herradura, Arg.	C8	92
Herreid, S.D., U.S.	B12	126
Herrera de Pisuerga, Spain	B6	20
Herrick, Austl.	n13	77a
Herrin, Il., U.S.	G8	120
Hersbruck, Ger.	G7	16
Herschel, Sk., Can.	C5	124
Herschel, S. Afr.	G8	70
Herschel Island, i., Yk., Can.	C12	140
Herscher, Il., U.S.	C9	120
Hershey, Ne., U.S.	F11	126
Hershey, Pa., U.S.	D9	114
Herstal, Bel.	D14	14
Hertford, Eng., U.K.	J12	12
Hertogenbosch, 's- see 's-Hertogenbosch, Neth.	C14	14
Herval d'Oeste, Braz.	C12	92
Hervás, Spain	D5	20
Hervey Bay, b., Austl.	E9	76
Hervey-Jonction, Qc., Can.	D4	110
Herzberg, Ger.	E9	16
Herzberg am Harz, Ger.	E6	16
Heshan, China	J3	42
Heshui, China	J4	42
Heshun, China	C5	42
Hesperia, Mi., U.S.	E3	112
Hesperus Mountain, mtn., Co., U.S.	F8	132
Hess, stm., Yk., Can.	C4	106
Hessen, state, Ger.	F5	16
Hesston, Ks., U.S.	C11	128
Het, stm., Laos	B6	48
Heta, stm., Russia	B8	34
Hetang, China	H8	42
Hetaunḍā, Nepal	E10	54
Hetch Hetchy Aqueduct, aq., Ca., U.S.	F4	134
Hetögeln, l., Swe.	D6	8
Hettstedt, Ger.	E7	16
Heuvelton, N.Y., U.S.	D14	112
Heves, Hung.	B7	26
Heves, state, Hung.	A7	26
Hewanorra International Airport, St. Luc.	m6	105c
Hewu, China	H5	42
Hexham, Eng., U.K.	F11	12
Hexian, China	I4	42
Heyang, China	D3	42
Heyburn, Id., U.S.	H13	136
Heysham, Eng., U.K.	G10	12
Heyuan, China	J6	42
Heywood, Austl.	L3	76
Heyworth, Il., U.S.	D9	120
Heze, China	D6	42
Hezheng, China	D5	36
Hialeah, Fl., U.S.	K5	116
Hiawatha, Ks., U.S.	E2	120
Hiawatha, Ut., U.S.	D6	132
Hibbard, Qc., Can.	C2	110
Hibbing, Mn., U.S.	D5	118
Hickman, Ky., U.S.	H8	120
Hickory, Ms., U.S.	E9	122
Hickory, N.C., U.S.	I4	114
Hickory Flat, Ms., U.S.	C9	122
Hicks, Point, c., Austl.	K7	76
Hico, Tx., U.S.	C9	130
Hida see Hita, Japan	F3	40
Hidalgo, Mex.	B8	100
Hidalgo, Mex.	C9	100
Hidalgo, Mex.	B9	100
Hidalgo, state, Mex.	E9	100
Hidalgo del Parral, Mex.	B6	100
Hida-sammyaku, mts., Japan	C10	40
Hidrolândia, Braz.	I1	88
Hieflau, Aus.	C11	22
Hienghène, N. Cal.	m15	79d
Hierapolis see Pamukkale, hist., Tur.	F12	28
Higashīhiroshima, Japan	E5	40
Higashiichiki, Japan	H3	40
Higashine, Japan	A13	40
Higashiōsaka, Japan	E8	40
Higgins, Tx., U.S.	E8	128
Higgins Lake, l., Mi., U.S.	D5	112
Higginsville, Mo., U.S.	E4	120
Highbury, Austl.	C8	74
Highland, Il., U.S.	F8	120
Highland, In., U.S.	G2	112
Highland, Ks., U.S.	E2	120
Highland Park, Il., U.S.	F2	112
Highlands, N.J., U.S.	D12	114
Highlands, N.C., U.S.	A2	116
Highlands, Tx., U.S.	H3	122
High Level, Ab., Can.	D7	106
High Point, N.C., U.S.	I5	114
High Point, mtn., N.J., U.S.	C11	114
High Point, mtn., Wy., U.S.	B9	132
High Point, c., Ber.	I15	104e
High River, Ab., Can.	F17	138
Highrock Lake, l., Mb., Can.	D10	106
Highrock Lake, l., Sk., Can.	D9	106
High Rock Lake, res., N.C., U.S.	A5	116
High Springs, Fl., U.S.	G3	116
Hightstown, N.J., U.S.	D11	114
High Willhays, mtn., Eng., U.K.	K9	12
Highwood, Mt., U.S.	C16	136
Highwood, stm., Ab., Can.	F17	138
Highwood Baldy, mtn., Mt., U.S.	C16	136
High Wycombe, Eng., U.K.	J11	12
Higuera de Abuya, Mex.	C5	100
Higueras, Mex.	I8	130
Higüero, Punta, c., P.R.	B1	104a
Higüey, Dom. Rep.	C13	102
Hiiumaa, i., Est.	G10	8
Hikari, Japan	F4	40
Hikone, Japan	D9	40
Hilbert, Wi., U.S.	D1	112
Hilda, Ab., Can.	D3	124
Hildburghausen, Ger.	F6	16
Hildesheim, Ger.	D5	16
Hiliotaluwa, Indon.	L3	48
Hillaby, Mount, mtn., Barb.	n8	105d
Hill Bank, Belize	D3	102
Hill City, Ks., U.S.	B9	128
Hill City, S.D., U.S.	D9	126
Hillcrest Mines, Ab., Can.	G16	138
Hillerød, Den.	I4	8
Hilliard, Fl., U.S.	F4	116
Hill Island Lake, l., N.T., Can.	C9	106
Hillister, Tx., U.S.	G4	122
Hills, Mn., U.S.	H2	118
Hillsboro, Il., U.S.	E8	120
Hillsboro, Ks., U.S.	C11	128
Hillsboro, Mo., U.S.	F7	120
Hillsboro, N.D., U.S.	D1	118
Hillsboro, Oh., U.S.	E2	114
Hillsboro, Or., U.S.	E3	136
Hillsboro, Wi., U.S.	H8	118
Hillsboro Canal, can., Fl., U.S.	J5	116
Hillsborough, Gren.	q10	105e
Hillsborough, N.C., U.S.	H6	114
Hillsborough, stm., Fl., U.S.	H3	116
Hillsborough, Cape, c., Austl.	C7	76
Hillsborough Bay, b., P.E., Can.	D13	110
Hillsdale, Mi., U.S.	G5	112
Hillston, Austl.	I5	76
Hillsville, Va., U.S.	H5	114
Hillswick, Scot., U.K.	n18	12a
Hilo, Hi., U.S.	D6	78a
Hilok, Russia	F11	34
Hilok, stm., Russia	F10	34
Hilton, N.Y., U.S.	E12	112
Hilton Head Island, i., S.C., U.S.	D5	116
Hilvan, Tur.	A9	58
Hilversum, Neth.	B14	14
Himāchal Pradesh, state, India	B6	54
Himalayas, mts., Asia	F10	142
Himarë, Alb.	D13	24
Himatnagar, India	G4	54
Himeji, Japan	E7	40
Himi, Japan	C9	40
Himki, Russia	E20	10
Ḥimṣ (Homs), Syria	D7	58
Ḥimṣ, state, Syria	D8	58
Hinchinbrook Island, i., Austl.	B6	76
Hinchinbrook Island, i., Ak., U.S.	D10	140
Hinchinbrook Island National Park, p.o.i., Austl.	B6	76
Hinckley, Il., U.S.	C9	120
Hinckley, Mn., U.S.	E5	118
Hinckley, Ut., U.S.	D4	132
Hindang, Phil.	E5	52
Hindaun, India	E6	54
Hindmarsh, Lake, l., Austl.	J3	76
Hindu Kush, mts., Asia	B10	56
Hindupur, India	E3	53
Hines, Or., U.S.	G7	136
Hinesville, Ga., U.S.	E4	116
Hinganghāt, India	H7	54
Hingham, Ma., U.S.	B15	114
Hingol, stm., Pak.	D10	56
Hingoli, India	B3	53
Hinigaran, Phil.	E4	52
Hinnøya, i., Nor.	B6	8
Hinojosa del Duque, Spain	F5	20
Hinokage, Japan	G4	40
Hinsdale, Mt., U.S.	F6	124
Hinterrhein, stm., Switz.	D6	22
Hinton, Ab., Can.	C13	138
Hinton, Ok., U.S.	F10	128
Hinton, W.V., U.S.	G5	114
Hipólito, Mex.	C8	100
Hipólito Yrigoyen, Arg.	F4	92
Hirado, Japan	F2	40
Hirado-shima, i., Japan	F2	40
Hīrākud, India	H9	54
Hīrākud Reservoir, res., India	H10	54
Hirara, Japan	G10	36
Hirata, Japan	D5	40
Hiratsuka, Japan	D12	40
Hiriyūr, India	E3	53
Hirosaki, Japan	D14	38
Hiroshima, Japan	E5	40
Hiroshima, state, Japan	E5	40
Hirosima see Hiroshima, Japan	E5	40
Hirovo, Russia	B16	10
Hirson, Fr.	E13	14
Hisār, India	D5	54
Hisarönü, Tur.	B14	28
Hispaniola, i., N.A.	D10	96
Hisua, India	F10	54
Ḥisyah, Syria	D7	58
Hita, Japan	F3	40
Hitachi, Japan	C13	40
Hitachi-ōta, Japan	C13	40
Hitchcock, Tx., U.S.	H3	122
Hitchins, Ky., U.S.	F3	114
Hitiaa, Fr. Poly.	v22	78h
Hitoyoshi, Japan	G3	40
Hitra, i., Nor.	E3	8
Hiuchiga-take, vol., Japan	C12	40
Hiuchi-nada, Japan	E6	40
Hiva, Uzb.	F10	32
Hiva Oa, i., Fr. Poly.	s19	78g
Hiwannee, Ms., U.S.	F10	122
Hiwasa, Japan	F7	40
Hiwassee, stm., U.S.	B14	122
Hiwassee Lake, res., N.C., U.S.	A1	116
Hixson, Tn., U.S.	B13	122
Hjälmaren, l., Swe.	G6	8
Hjo, Swe.	G6	8
Hjørring, Den.	H3	8
Hkakabo Razi, mtn., Mya.	C8	46
Hkok (Kok), stm., Asia	B4	48
Hlaingbwe, Mya.	D3	48
Hlathikulu, Swaz.	E10	70
Hlinsko, Czech Rep.	G11	16
Hlohovec, Slov.	H13	16
Hlotse, Leso.	F9	70
Hluhluwe, S. Afr.	F11	70
Hluhluwe Game Reserve, S. Afr.	F10	70
Hluša, Bela.	G11	10
Hlyboka, Ukr.	A12	26
Hlybokae, Bela.	E10	10
Hmelita, Russia	E16	10
H. Neely Henry Lake, res., Al., U.S.	D12	122
Ho, Ghana	H5	64
Hoa Binh, Viet.	B7	48
Hoare Bay, b., Nu., Can.	D13	141
Hobart, Austl.	o13	77a
Hobart, Ok., U.S.	F9	128
Hobbs, N.M., U.S.	B4	130
Hobbs Coast, cst., Ant.	C28	81
Hobe Sound, Fl., U.S.	I5	116
Hobgood, N.C., U.S.	H8	114
Hobq Shamo, des., China	A2	42
Hobson Lake, l., B.C., Can.	D10	138
Hobyo, Som.	C9	66
Hochalmspitze, mtn., Aus.	C10	22
Hochfeld, Nmb.	B3	70
Ho Chi Minh City see Thanh Pho Ho Chi Minh, Viet.	G8	48
Hochkönig, mtn., Aus.	C10	22
Höchstadt an der Aisch, Ger.	G6	16
Hochstetter Forland, pen.	B21	141
Hoch'uan see Hechuan, China	G2	42
Hocimsk, Bela.	G15	10
Hockenheim, Ger.	G4	16
Hocking, stm., Oh., U.S.	E15	120
Hôḍ, reg., Maur.	F3	64
Hodal, India	E6	54
Hodeida see Al-Ḥudaydah, Yemen	G5	56
Hodge, La., U.S.	E6	122
Hodgenville, Ky., U.S.	G12	120
Hodgeville, Sk., Can.	D7	124
Hódmezővásárhely, Hung.	C7	26
Hodna, Chott el, l., Alg.	B6	64
Hodonín, Czech Rep.	H12	16
Hodžanur'jah, gora, mtn., Uzb.	G11	32
Hodžejli, Uzb.	F9	32
Hœdic, Île de, i., Fr.	G6	14
Hoehne, Co., U.S.	D4	128
Hoei see Huy, Bel.	D14	14
Hoek van Holland, Neth.	C12	14
Hoeryŏng-ŭp, Kor., N.	C8	38
Hoeyang-ŭp, Kor., N.	E7	38
Hof, Ger.	F7	16
Hof, Ice.	k32	8a
Hofei see Hefei, China	F7	42
Hoffman, Mn., U.S.	F3	118
Hofgeismar, Ger.	E5	16
Hofheim am Taunus, Ger.	F4	16
Hofheim in Unterfranken, Ger.	F6	16
Hofors, Swe.	F7	8
Hofsjökull, ice, Ice.	k30	8a
Hōfu, Japan	E4	40
Hofuf see Al-Hufūf, Sau. Ar.	D6	56
Hogansville, Ga., U.S.	D14	122
Hogback Mountain, mtn., Ne., U.S.	F9	126
Hogback Mountain, mtn., S.C., U.S.	A3	116
Högsby, Swe.	H6	8
Hohenwald, Tn., U.S.	B11	122
Hoher Dachstein, mtn., Aus.	C10	22
Hohe Tauern, mts., Aus.	C9	22
Hohhot, China	A4	42
Hohoe, Ghana	H5	64
Hōhoku, Japan	E3	40
Hoh Xil Hu, l., China	D3	36
Hoh Xil Shan, mts., China	D2	36
Hoi An, Viet.	E9	48
Hoihong see Haikang, China	K3	42
Hoihow see Haikou, China	K4	42
Hoima, Ug.	D6	66
Hoisington, Ks., U.S.	C10	128
Hojāi, India	E14	54
Højer, Den.	B4	16
Hōjō, Japan	F5	40
Hokah, Mn., U.S.	H7	118
Hokang see Hegang, China	B11	36
Hokitika, N.Z.	F4	80
Hokkaidō, i., Japan	C15	38
Holalkere, India	D3	53
Holberg, B.C., Can.	F2	138
Holbrook, Austl.	J6	76
Holbrook, Az., U.S.	I6	132
Holbrook, Ne., U.S.	A8	128
Holden, Ab., Can.	C18	138
Holden, Mo., U.S.	F4	120
Holden, W.V., U.S.	G3	114
Holden Village, Wa., U.S.	B6	136
Holder, Fl., U.S.	H3	116
Holderness, pen., Eng., U.K.	H12	12
Holdfast, Sk., Can.	D8	124
Holdingford, Mn., U.S.	F4	118
Hold With Hope, reg., Grnld.	C22	141
Hole in the Mountain Peak, mtn., Nv., U.S.	C1	132
Hole Narsipur, India	E2	53
Holetown, Barb.	n8	105d
Holgate, Oh., U.S.	C1	114
Holguín, Cuba	B9	102
Holíč, Slov.	H13	16
Hollabrunn, Aus.	B13	22
Holland, Mi., U.S.	F3	112
Holland, Tx., U.S.	D10	130
Holland, hist. reg., Neth.	B13	14
Holland see Netherlands, ctry., Eur.	B15	14
Hollandale, Ms., U.S.	D8	122
Hollandia see Jayapura, Indon.	F11	44
Hollandsbird Island, i., Nmb.	D2	70
Holley, N.Y., U.S.	E11	112
Holliday, Tx., U.S.	H10	128
Hollins, Va., U.S.	G6	114
Hollister, Ca., U.S.	G4	134
Hollow Rock, Tn., U.S.	H9	120
Holly, Co., U.S.	C6	128
Holly Grove, Ar., U.S.	C7	122
Holly Hill, Fl., U.S.	G4	116
Holly Springs, Ms., U.S.	C9	122
Hollywood, Fl., U.S.	J5	116
Holm, Russia	C14	10
Holman, N.T., Can.	A7	106
Hólmavík, Ice.	k28	8a
Holmen, Wi., U.S.	H7	118
Holmes, Mount, mtn., Wy., U.S.	F16	136
Holm Land, pen., Grnld.	A22	141
Holm Ø, i., Grnld.	C14	141
Holmogorskaja, Russia	E19	8
Holmsk, Russia	G17	34
Holmsund, Swe.	E9	8
Holon, Isr.	F5	58
Holoog, Nmb.	E4	70
Holovanivs'k, Ukr.	A17	26
Holstebro, Den.	H3	8
Holstein, Ia., U.S.	B2	120
Holsteinsborg (Sisimiut), Grnld.	D15	141
Holston, stm., Tn., U.S.	H2	114
Holston, North Fork, stm., U.S.	H3	114
Holsworthy, Eng., U.K.	K8	12
Holt, Fl., U.S.	G12	122
Holt, Mi., U.S.	B1	114
Holton, Ks., U.S.	E2	120
Holts Summit, Mo., U.S.	F5	120
Holy Cross, Ak., U.S.	D8	140
Holy Cross Mountain, mtn., B.C., Can.	C10	138
Holyhead, Wales, U.K.	H8	12
Holy Island, i., Eng., U.K.	F11	12
Holyoke, Co., U.S.	G10	126
Holyoke, Ma., U.S.	B13	114
Holyrood, Ks., U.S.	C10	128
Holzkirchen, Ger.	I7	16
Holzminden, Ger.	E5	16
Hom, stm., Nmb.	F4	70
Homa Bay, Kenya	E6	66
Homalin, Mya.	D7	46
Homathko, stm., B.C., Can.	E6	138
Homathko Icefield, ice, B.C., Can.	E6	138
Homberg, Ger.	E5	16
Hombori Tondo, mtn., Mali	F4	64
Hombre Muerto, Salar del, pl., Arg.	B4	92
Homburg, Ger.	G3	16
Home Bay, b., Nu., Can.	B17	106
Home Hill, Austl.	B6	76
Homel', Bela.	H13	10
Homel', state, Bela.	H12	10
Homeland Park, S.C., U.S.	B3	116
Homer, Ak., U.S.	E9	140
Homer, Ga., U.S.	B2	116
Homer, La., U.S.	E5	122
Homer, Ne., U.S.	B1	120
Homer City, Pa., U.S.	D6	114
Homerville, Ga., U.S.	E3	116
Homestead, Fl., U.S.	K5	116
Homestead National Monument of America, p.o.i., Ne., U.S.	A11	128
Homewood, Al., U.S.	D12	122
Hommura, Japan	E12	40
Homnābād, India	C3	53
Homochitto, stm., Ms., U.S.	F7	122
Homoíne, Moz.	C12	70
Homosassa, Fl., U.S.	H3	116
Homs see Al-Khums, Libya	A2	62
Homs see Ḥimṣ, Syria	D7	58
Honaker, Va., U.S.	H4	114
Honan see Luoyang, China	D5	42
Honan see Henan, state, China	E5	42
Honāvar, India	D2	53
Hon Chong, Viet.	G7	48
Honda, Col.	E4	86
Honda, Bahía, b., Col.	A5	86
Honda Bay, b., Phil.	F2	52
Hondeklipbaai, S. Afr.	G3	70
Hon Dien, Nui, mtn., Viet.	G9	48
Hondo, Ab., Can.	A16	138
Hondo, Japan	G3	40
Hondo, N.M., U.S.	H3	128
Hondo, stm., N.A.	C3	102
Hondo Creek, stm., Tx., U.S.	E8	130
Honduras, ctry., N.A.	E4	102
Honduras, Cabo de, c., Hond.	D5	102
Honduras, Gulf of, b., N.A.	D4	102
Honea Path, S.C., U.S.	B3	116
Hønefoss, Nor.	F4	8
Honesdale, Pa., U.S.	C10	114
Honey Grove, Tx., U.S.	D3	122
Honey Lake, l., Ca., U.S.	C5	134
Honeyville, Ut., U.S.	B4	132
Honfleur, Fr.	E9	14
Hong, stm., China	E6	42
Hong, Song see Red, stm., Asia	D9	46
Hon Gai, Viet.	B8	48
Hong Hu, l., China	F5	42
Hongjiang, China	H4	42
Hong Kong see Xianggang, China	J6	42
Hongliuyuan, China	F17	32
Hong Ngu, Viet.	G7	48
Hongqi, China	B7	38
Hongshi, China	C7	38
Hongshui, stm., China	J3	42
Hongtong, China	C4	42
Honguedo, Détroit d', strt., Qc., Can.	A12	110
Hongze, China	E8	42
Hongze Hu, l., China	E8	42
Honiara, Sol. Is.	e8	79b
Honjō, Japan	E13	38
Honningsvåg, Nor.	A11	8
Honokaa, Hi., U.S.	C6	78a
Honolulu, Hi., U.S.	B4	78a
Honomu, Hi., U.S.	D6	78a
Hon Quan, Viet.	G8	48
Honshū, i., Japan	G12	38
Honuu, Russia	C17	34
Hood, stm., Nu., Can.	B9	106
Hood, Mount, vol., Or., U.S.	E5	136
Hood Canal, b., Wa., U.S.	C4	136
Hoodoo Peak, mtn., Wa., U.S.	B6	136
Hood Point, c., Austl.	F3	74
Hoodsport, Wa., U.S.	C3	136
Hoogeveen, Neth.	B15	14
Hoogeveense Vaart, can., Neth.	B15	14
Hooker, Ok., U.S.	E7	128
Hook Head, c., Ire.	I6	12
Hookina, Austl.	H2	76
Hook Island, i., Austl.	C7	76
Hook Point, c., Austl.	E9	76
Hooks, Tx., U.S.	D4	122
Hoonah, Ak., U.S.	E12	140
Hoopa, Ca., U.S.	B2	134
Hooper, Ne., U.S.	C1	120
Hooper Bay, Ak., U.S.	D6	140
Hoople, N.D., U.S.	F16	124
Hoopstad, S. Afr.	E7	70
Hoorn, Neth.	B14	14
Hoosick Falls, N.Y., U.S.	H3	110
Hoover Dam, dam, U.S.	G2	132
Hooversville, Pa., U.S.	H11	112
Hopatcong, N.J., U.S.	D11	114
Hope, B.C., Can.	G9	138
Hope, Ar., U.S.	D5	122
Hope, In., U.S.	E12	120
Hope, Ben, mtn., Scot., U.K.	C8	12
Hope, Point, c., Ak., U.S.	C6	140
Hopedale, La., U.S.	H9	122
Hopeh see Hebei, state, China	D8	36
Ho-pei see Hebei, state, China	D8	36
Hopelchén, Mex.	C3	102
Hope Mills, N.C., U.S.	B7	116
Hopër, stm., Russia	E17	6
Hopes Advance, Cap, c., Qc., Can.	C17	106
Hopetoun, Austl.	F4	74
Hopetoun, Austl.	J4	76
Hopetown, S. Afr.	F6	70
Hope Valley, R.I., U.S.	C14	114
Hopewell, Va., U.S.	G8	114
Hopewell Culture National Historic Park, p.o.i., Oh., U.S.	E2	114
Hopewell Islands, is., Nu., Can.	D14	106
Hopi see Hebi, China	D6	42
Hopkins, Mo., U.S.	D3	120
Hopkins, stm., Austl.	K4	76
Hopkinsville, Ky., U.S.	H10	120
Hopkinton, Ia., U.S.	B6	120
Hopólite Bouchard, Arg.	G6	92
Hoppo see Hepu, China	K3	42
Hopwood, Mount, hill, Austl.	C5	76
Hoquiam, Wa., U.S.	C2	136
Hor, Russia	G16	34
Hor, stm., Russia	G16	34
Hor, stm., Russia	B12	36
Horatio, Ar., U.S.	D4	122
Hordaland, state, Nor.	F2	8
Horezu, Rom.	D10	26
Horicon, Wi., U.S.	H10	118
Horinger, China	A4	42
Horinsk, Russia	F10	34
Horizontina, Braz.	C10	92
Horlick Mountains, mts., Ant.	D29	81
Horlivka, Ukr.	E5	32
Horlovo, Russia	E21	10
Hormigueros, P.R.	B1	104a
Hormuz, Strait of, strt., Asia	D8	56
Horn, Aus.	B12	22
Horn, c., Ice.	j28	8a
Horn, stm., N.T., Can.	C7	106
Horn, Cape see Hornos, Cabo de, c., Chile	K3	90
Hornad (Hernád), stm., Eur.	H17	16
Hornaday, stm., Can.	B6	106
Hornafjörður, b., Ice.	k32	8a
Hornavan, l., Swe.	C7	8
Hornbeck, La., U.S.	F5	122
Hornbrook, Ca., U.S.	B3	134
Hornby Bay, b., N.T., Can.	B7	106
Hornell, N.Y., U.S.	B8	114
Hornepayne, On., Can.	F13	106
Horn Island, i., Ms., U.S.	G10	122
Horn Lake, Ms., U.S.	C8	122
Hornos, Cabo de (Horn Cape), c., Chile	K3	90
Horn Plateau, plat., N.T., Can.	C6	106

Name	Map Ref.	Page
Hornsea, Eng., U.K.	H12	12
Horodkivka, Ukr.	A15	26
Horodok, Ukr.	G19	16
Horog, Taj.	B11	56
Horol', Russia	B10	38
Horqin Youyi Qianqi, China	B9	36
Horqin Youyi Zhongqi, China	B4	38
Horqin Zuoyi Houqi, China	C4	38
Horqin Zuoyi Zhongqi, China	B5	38
Horqueta, Para.	D5	90
Horse Cave, Ky., U.S.	G12	120
Horse Creek, stm., U.S.	F8	126
Horse Creek, stm., Co., U.S.	C5	128
Horsefly, B.C., Can.	D9	138
Horsefly Lake, l., B.C., Can.	D10	138
Horseheads, N.Y., U.S.	B9	114
Horse Islands, is., Nf., Can.	i22	107a
Horsens, Den.	I3	8
Horseshoe Bend, Id., U.S.	G10	136
Horsham, Austl.	K4	76
Horsham, Eng., U.K.	J12	12
Horšovský Týn, Czech Rep.	G8	16
Horten, Nor.	G4	8
Hortobágy, reg., Hung.	B8	26
Hortobágyi Nemzeti Park, p.o.i., Hung.	B8	26
Horton, Ks., U.S.	E2	120
Horton, stm., N.T., Can.	B6	106
Horton Lake, l., N.T., Can.	B6	106
Hortonville, Wi., U.S.	G10	118
Hory, Bela.	F14	10
Hosa'ina, Eth.	F7	62
Hösbach, Ger.	F5	16
Hosedahard, Russia	A9	32
Hosford, Fl., U.S.	G14	122
Hoshāb, Pak.	D9	56
Hoshangābād, India	G6	54
Hoshiārpur, India	C5	54
Hosh Isa, Egypt	H1	58
Hosmer, B.C., Can.	G15	138
Hospers, Ia., U.S.	A2	120
Hospet, India	D3	53
Hospitalet see L'Hospitalet de Llobregat, Spain	C13	20
Hossegor, Fr.	F4	18
Hosston, La., U.S.	E5	122
Hosta Butte, mtn., N.M., U.S.	H8	132
Hoste, Isla, i., Chile	K3	90
Hosūr, India	E3	53
Hotagen, l., Swe.	E5	8
Hotaka-dake, mtn., Japan	C10	40
Hotamış, Tur.	A4	58
Hotan, China	A5	46
Hotazel, S. Afr.	E6	70
Hotevilla, Az., U.S.	H6	132
Hotilovo, Russia	C17	10
Hot'kovo, Russia	G18	10
Hot'kovo, Russia	D21	10
Hot Springs, Ar., U.S.	C5	122
Hot Springs, N.C., U.S.	I3	114
Hot Springs, S.D., U.S.	D9	126
Hot Springs, Va., U.S.	F6	114
Hot Springs National Park see Hot Springs, Ar., U.S.	C5	122
Hot Springs Peak, mtn., Nv., U.S.	B8	134
Hot Sulphur Springs, Co., U.S.	A2	128
Hottah Lake, l., N.T., Can.	B7	106
Hottentotsbaai, b., Nmb.	E2	70
Hotynec, Russia	G18	10
Houaïlou, N. Cal.	m15	79d
Houat, Île de, i., Fr.	G6	14
Houdan, Fr.	F10	14
Houghton, Mi., U.S.	D10	118
Houghton, N.Y., U.S.	B7	114
Houghton Lake, l., Mi., U.S.	D4	112
Houlka, Ms., U.S.	C10	122
Houlton, Me., U.S.	D9	110
Houma, China	D4	42
Houma, Tonga	n13	78e
Houma, La., U.S.	H8	122
Hou-pei see Hubei, state, China	F5	42
Hourtin, Étang d', l., Fr.	D4	18
Housatonic, Ma., U.S.	B12	114
House, N.M., U.S.	G5	128
Houston, B.C., Can.	B4	138
Houston, Mn., U.S.	H7	118
Houston, Mo., U.S.	G6	120
Houston, Tx., U.S.	H3	122
Houston, Lake, res., Tx., U.S.	H3	122
Hout, stm., S. Afr.	C9	70
Houtman Abrolhos, is., Austl.	E2	74
Houxinqiu, China	C5	38
Hovd, Mong.	B3	36
Hovd, Mong.	C5	36
Hovd, stm., Mong.	E16	32
Hove, Eng., U.K.	K12	12
Hoven, S.D., U.S.	B13	126
Hovenweep National Monument, p.o.i., U.S.	F7	132
Hoverla, hora, mtn., Ukr.	A11	26
Hovgaard Ø, i., Grnld.	A22	141
Hövsgöl nuur, l., Mong.	F9	34
Hovu-Aksy, Russia	D16	32
Howar, Wādī, val., Afr.	D5	62
Howard, Austl.	E9	76
Howard, Ks., U.S.	D12	128
Howard, Pa., U.S.	D8	114
Howard, S.D., U.S.	C15	126
Howard City, Mi., U.S.	E4	112
Howard Draw, stm., Tx., U.S.	D6	130
Howard Lake, Mn., U.S.	F4	118
Howe, In., U.S.	G4	112
Howe, Cape, c., Austl.	K7	76
Howe Island, i., On., Can.	D13	112
Howell, Mi., U.S.	B2	114
Howells, Ne., U.S.	F15	126
Howick, S. Afr.	F10	70
Howitt, Mount, mtn., Austl.	K6	76
Howland Island, i., Oc.	C9	72
Howser, B.C., Can.	F13	138
Howson Peak, mtn., B.C., Can.	B3	138
Hoxie, Ar., U.S.	H6	120
Hoxie, Ks., U.S.	B8	128
Höxter, Ger.	E5	16
Hoxtolgay, China	B2	36
Hoy, i., Scot., U.K.	C9	12
Hoyerswerda, Ger.	E10	16
Hoyos, Spain	D4	20
Höytiäinen, l., Fin.	E13	8
Hoyt Lakes, Mn., U.S.	D6	118
Hradec Králové, Czech Rep.	F11	16
Hradzjanka, Bela.	G11	10
Hranice, Czech Rep.	G13	16
Hrèsk, Bela.	G10	10
Hristoforovo, Russia	F22	8
Hrodna, Bela.	G6	10
Hrodna, state, Bela.	G7	10
Hroma, stm., Russia	B17	34
Hron, stm., Slov.	H14	16
Hronov, Czech Rep.	F12	16
Hrubieszów, Pol.	F19	16
Hrustal'nyj, Russia	B11	38
Hsiakuan see Dali, China	F5	36
Hsiamen see Xiamen, China	I7	42
Hsian see Xi'an, China	D3	42
Hsiangt'an see Xiangtan, China	H5	42
Hsiangyang see Xiangfan, China	F4	42
Hsienyang see Xianyang, China	D3	42
Hsi-hseng, Mya.	B3	48
Hsilo, Tai.	J9	42
Hsim, stm., Mya.	B4	48
Hsinchu, Tai.	I9	42
Hsinghua see Xinghua, China	E8	42
Hsingt'ai see Xingtai, China	C6	42
Hsinhailien see Lianyungang, China	D8	42
Hsinhsiang see Xinxiang, China	D5	42
Hsining see Xining, China	D5	36
Hsinking see Changchun, China	C6	38
Hsinp'u see Lianyungang, China	D8	42
Hsintien, Tai.	I9	42
Hsinyang see Xinyang, China	E6	42
Hsipaw, Mya.	A3	48
Hsüanhua see Xuanhua, China	A6	42
Hsüch'ang see Xuchang, China	D5	42
Hsüchou see Xuzhou, China	D7	42
Hua'an, China	I7	42
Huab, stm., Nmb.	B2	70
Huacaraje, Bol.	B4	90
Huacho, Peru	F2	84
Huachuca City, Az., U.S.	L6	132
Huadian, China	C7	38
Huading Shan, mtn., China	G9	42
Hua Hin, Thai.	F4	48
Huai, stm., China	C6	42
Huai, stm., China	E8	42
Huai'an, China	E8	42
Huai'an, China	A6	42
Huaibin, China	E6	42
Huaicheng see Huai'an, China	E8	42
Huaidezhen, China	C6	38
Huaiji, China	I5	42
Huailai, China	A6	42
Huainan, China	E7	42
Huairou, China	A7	42
Huaite see Gongzhuling, China	C6	38
Huaiyang, China	E6	42
Huai Yot, Thai.	I4	48
Huaiyuan, China	E7	42
Huajuapan de León, Mex.	G10	100
Hualahuises, Mex.	C9	100
Hualalai, vol., Hi., U.S.	D6	78a
Hualañé, Chile	G2	92
Hualfín, Arg.	C4	92
Hualien, Tai.	J9	42
Huallaga, stm., Peru	E2	84
Huallanca, Peru	E2	84
Hualong, China	D5	36
Huambo, Ang.	C2	68
Huamei Shan, mtn., China	I5	42
Huan, stm., China	F6	42
Huanan, China	B11	36
Huancabamba, Peru	E2	84
Huancané, Peru	G4	84
Huancavelica, Peru	F2	84
Huancayo, Peru	F2	84
Huang (Yellow), stm., China	D8	36
Huangchuan, China	E6	42
Huanggai Hu, l., China	G5	42
Huanggang, China	F6	42
Huanggangliang, mtn., China	C2	38
Huanghua, China	B7	42
Huangjinbu, China	G7	42
Huangling, China	D3	42
Huanglong, China	D3	42
Huangnihe, China	C7	38
Huangpi, China	F6	42
Huangqi, China	H8	42
Huangshahe, China	H4	42
Huangshan, China	G8	42
Huangshan see Guangming Ding, mtn., China	F7	42
Huangshi, China	F6	42
Huangshi, China	G4	42
Huangtang Hu, l., China	G6	42
Huangtuliangzi, China	A8	42
Huanguelén, Arg.	H6	92
Huangxian, China	C9	42
Huangyan, China	G9	42
Huangyuan, China	D5	36
Huangzhong, China	D5	36
Huangzhu, China	L4	42
Huanjiang, China	I3	42
Huanren, China	D6	38
Huánuco, Peru	E2	84
Huanuni, Bol.	C3	90
Huanxian, China	C2	42
Huara, Chile	C3	90
Huaral, Peru	F2	84
Huaraz, Peru	E2	84
Huariaca, Peru	F2	84
Huarmey, Peru	F2	84
Huarong, China	G5	42
Huasaga, stm., S.A.	I3	86
Hua Sai, Thai.	H5	48
Huascarán, Nevado, mtn., Peru	E2	84
Huasco, Chile	D2	92
Huasco, stm., Chile	D2	92
Huatabampo, Mex.	B4	100
Huating, China	D2	42
Huatong, China	A9	42
Huauchinango, Mex.	E9	100
Huautla, Mex.	C5	96
Huaxian, China	J5	42
Huaxian, China	D3	42
Huaxian, China	D6	42
Huaynamota, stm., Mex.	D6	100
Huazamota, Mex.	D6	100
Huazhou, China	K4	42
Hubbard, Ia., U.S.	B4	120
Hubbard Creek Reservoir, l., Tx., U.S.	B8	130
Hubbard Lake, l., Mi., U.S.	D6	112
Hubbards, N.S., Can.	F12	110
Hubbell, Mi., U.S.	D10	118
Hubei, state, China	F5	42
Huberdeau, Qc., Can.	E2	110
Hubli-Dhārwār, India	D2	53
Hubuleng, China	A4	42
Huchow see Huzhou, China	F9	42
Huckleberry Mountain, mtn., Or., U.S.	G4	136
Hucknall, Eng., U.K.	H11	12
Huddersfield, Eng., U.K.	H11	12
Huddinge, Swe.	G8	8
Huder, China	A9	36
Hudiksvall, Swe.	F7	8
Hudson, Fl., U.S.	H3	116
Hudson, Ia., U.S.	B5	120
Hudson, N.Y., U.S.	H3	110
Hudson, N.C., U.S.	I4	114
Hudson, Oh., U.S.	C4	114
Hudson, S.D., U.S.	H2	118
Hudson, Wy., U.S.	E4	126
Hudson, stm., U.S.	G16	112
Hudson, Baie d' see Hudson Bay, b., Can.	C13	106
Hudson Bay, Sk., Can.	B11	124
Hudson Bay, b., Can.	C13	106
Hudson Falls, N.Y., U.S.	G3	110
Hudson's Hope, B.C., Can.	D6	106
Hudson Strait, strt., Can.	C16	106
Hudžand, Taj.	A10	56
Hue, Viet.	D8	48
Huebra, stm., Spain	D4	20
Huehuetenango, Guat.	E2	102
Huejutla de Reyes, Mex.	E9	100
Huelgoat, Fr.	F5	14
Huelva, Spain	G3	20
Huelva, co., Spain	G4	20
Huentelauquén, Chile	E2	92
Huércal-Overa, Spain	G8	20
Huerfano, stm., Co., U.S.	C4	128
Huerlumada, China	B13	54
Huerva, stm., Spain	C9	20
Huesca, Spain	B10	20
Huesca, co., Spain	B10	20
Huéscar, Spain	G8	20
Huetamo de Núñez, Mex.	F8	100
Hueytown, Al., U.S.	D11	122
Hufrat an-Nahās, Sudan	F4	62
Hughenden, Austl.	C4	76
Hughes, Ak., U.S.	C9	140
Hughes, Ar., U.S.	C8	122
Hughes Springs, Tx., U.S.	E4	122
Hugh Keenleyside Dam, dam, B.C., Can.	G12	138
Hughson, Ca., U.S.	F5	134
Hugh Town, Eng., U.K.	L6	12
Hugli, stm., India	G12	54
Hugo, Co., U.S.	B5	128
Hugo, Ok., U.S.	C3	122
Hugoton, Ks., U.S.	D7	128
Huhar, stm., China	B4	38
Huhehaote see Hohhot, China	A4	42
Huhehot see Hohhot, China	A4	42
Huichang, China	I6	42
Huicheng see Huilai, China	J7	42
Hŭich'ŏn, Kor., N.	D7	38
Huichou see Huizhou, China	J6	42
Huila, state, Col.	F4	86
Huila, Nevado del, vol., Col.	F3	86
Huilai, China	J7	42
Huili, China	F5	36
Huillapima, Arg.	D4	92
Huimin, China	C7	42
Huinan, China	C7	38
Huisachal, Mex.	H6	130
Huishui, China	H2	42
Huisne, stm., Fr.	F9	14
Huitong, China	H3	42
Huitzo, Mex.	G10	100
Huitzuco de los Figueroa, Mex.	F9	100
Huixian, China	E2	42
Huixian, China	D5	42
Huixtla, Mex.	H12	100
Huize, China	F5	36
Huizhou, China	J6	42
Hŭksan-chedo, is., Kor., S.	G6	38
Hukuntsi, Bots.	D5	70
Hulan, China	B7	38
Hulan Ergi, China	B9	36
Hulbert, Mi., U.S.	B4	112
Hulett, Wy., U.S.	C8	126
Hulga, stm., Russia	B10	32
Hulin, China	B11	36
Hulin, stm., China	B4	38
Huliu, stm., China	A6	42
Hull, Qc., Can.	C14	112
Hull, Il., U.S.	E6	120
Hull, Ia., U.S.	H2	118
Hullo, Est.	A6	10
Hulun see Hailar, China	B8	36
Hulun Nur, l., China	B8	36
Huma, China	F14	34
Huma, Tonga	o15	78e
Humacao, P.R.	B4	104a
Humahuaca, Arg.	D3	90
Humaitá, Braz.	E5	84
Humaitá, Para.	C8	92
Humansdorp, S. Afr.	I7	70
Humansville, Mo., U.S.	G4	120
Humara, Jabal al-, hill, Sudan	D6	62
Humbe, Ang.	D1	68
Humber, stm., Eng., U.K.	H12	12
Humbird, Wi., U.S.	G8	118
Humboldt, Sk., Can.	B8	124
Humboldt, Az., U.S.	I4	132
Humboldt, Il., U.S.	E9	120
Humboldt, Ia., U.S.	B3	120
Humboldt, Ne., U.S.	D2	120
Humboldt, S.D., U.S.	D15	126
Humboldt, stm., Nv., U.S.	C7	134
Humboldt, North Fork, stm., Nv., U.S.	B1	132
Humboldt, South Fork, stm., Nv., U.S.	C1	132
Humboldt Gletscher, ice, Grnld.	B13	141
Humboldt Lake, l., Nv., U.S.	D7	134
Hume, Ca., U.S.	G7	134
Hume, Lake, res., Austl.	J6	76
Humeburn, Austl.	F5	76
Humenné, Slov.	H17	16
Humeston, Ia., U.S.	D4	120
Hummi, ozero, l., Russia	F16	34
Humphrey, Ne., U.S.	F15	126
Humphreys, Mount, mtn., Ca., U.S.	F7	134
Humphreys Peak, mtn., Az., U.S.	H5	132
Humpoiec, Czech Rep.	G11	16
Humpty Doo, Austl.	B6	74
Hūn, Libya	B3	62
Hun, stm., China	D5	38
Hun, stm., China	D6	38
Húnaflói, b., Ice.	j29	8a
Hunan, state, China	H4	42
Hunchun, China	C9	38
Hundred, W.V., U.S.	E5	114
Hunedoara, Rom.	D9	26
Hunedoara, state, Rom.	C9	26
Hünfeld, Ger.	F5	16
Hungary, ctry., Eur.	B6	26
Hungchiang see Hongjiang, China	H4	42
Hŭngdŏki-dong, Kor., N.	E7	38
Hungerford, Austl.	G5	76
Hungerford, Tx., U.S.	H2	122
Hungry Horse Dam, dam, Mt., U.S.	B13	136
Hungry Horse Reservoir, res., Mt., U.S.	B12	136
Hung Yen, Viet.	B8	48
Hunjiang, China	C7	38
Hunlen Falls, wtfl, B.C., Can.	D5	138
Hunsberge, mts., Nmb.	E3	70
Hunsrück, mts., Ger.	G3	16
Hunsūr, India	E3	53
Hunte, stm., Ger.	D4	16
Hunter, N.D., U.S.	D1	118
Hunter, stm., Austl.	I8	76
Hunter Island, i., Austl.	n12	77a
Hunter Island, i., B.C., Can.	E2	138
Hunter Mountain, mtn., N.Y., U.S.	B11	114
Hunter River, P.E., Can.	D13	110
Hunters, Wa., U.S.	B8	136
Hunters Bay, b., Mya.	C1	48
Huntingdon, Qc., Can.	E2	110
Huntingdon, Eng., U.K.	I12	12
Huntingdon, Pa., U.S.	D7	114
Huntingdon, Tn., U.S.	I9	120
Huntington, In., U.S.	H4	112
Huntington, Tx., U.S.	F4	122
Huntington, Ut., U.S.	D5	132
Huntington, W.V., U.S.	F3	114
Huntington Beach, Ca., U.S.	J7	134
Huntland, Tn., U.S.	B12	122
Huntley, Mt., U.S.	B4	126
Huntly, N.Z.	C6	80
Huntly, Scot., U.K.	D10	12
Huntsville, On., Can.	C10	112
Huntsville, Al., U.S.	C12	122
Huntsville, Mo., U.S.	E5	120
Huntsville, Tn., U.S.	H13	120
Huntsville, Tx., U.S.	G3	122
Huntsville, Ut., U.S.	B5	132
Hunyuan, China	B5	42
Huong Hoa, Viet.	D8	48
Huon Gulf, b., Pap. N. Gui.	b4	79a
Huon Peninsula, pen., Pap. N. Gui.	b4	79a
Huonville, Austl.	o13	77a
Huoqiu, China	E7	42
Huoshan, China	F7	42
Huoxian, China	C4	42
Hurd, Cape, c., On., Can.	C8	112
Hüren Tovon uul, mtn., Mong.	C4	36
Hure Qi, China	C4	38
Hurghada, Egypt	K4	58
Hurley, N.M., U.S.	K8	132
Hurley, S.D., U.S.	D15	126
Hurley, Wi., U.S.	E8	118
Huron, Ca., U.S.	G5	134
Huron, Oh., U.S.	C3	114
Huron, S.D., U.S.	C14	126
Huron, stm., Mi., U.S.	B2	114
Huron, Lake, l., N.A.	D7	112
Huron Mountains, hills, Mi., U.S.	B2	112
Hurricane, Ut., U.S.	F3	132
Hurstbridge, Austl.	K5	76
Hurtado, stm., Chile	E2	92
Hurtsboro, Al., U.S.	E13	122
Hurunui, stm., N.Z.	F5	80
Husainīwāla, India	C5	54
Húsavík, Far. Is.	n34	8b
Húsavík, Ice.	j31	8a
Hushitai, China	C5	38
Huşi, Rom.	C15	26
Huslia, Ak., U.S.	C8	140
Hussar, Ab., Can.	E18	138
Husum, Ger.	B4	16
Hutag, Mong.	B5	36
Hutanopan, Indon.	C1	50
Hutchinson, S. Afr.	G6	70
Hutchinson, Ks., U.S.	C11	128
Hutchinson, Mn., U.S.	G4	118
Hutch Mountain, mtn., Az., U.S.	I5	132
Hutsonville, Il., U.S.	E10	120
Huttig, Ar., U.S.	D6	122
Hutto, Tx., U.S.	D10	130
Hutuo, stm., China	B5	42
Huwei, Tai.	J9	42
Huxi, China	H6	42
Huxian, China	D3	42
Huxley, Ab., Can.	E17	138
Huy, Bel.	D14	14
Huzhen, China	G9	42
Huzhou, China	F9	42
Hvannadalshnúkur, mtn., Ice.	k31	8a
Hvar, Cro.	G13	22
Hvar, Otok, i., Cro.	G13	22
Hveragerđi, Ice.	k29	8a
Hvolsvöllur, Ice.	l29	8a
Hwainan see Huainan, China	E7	42
Hwange, Zimb.	D4	68
Hwang Ho see Huang, stm., China	D8	36
Hwangju-ŭp, Kor., N.	E6	38
Hwangshih see Huangshi, China	F6	42
Hyannis, Ma., U.S.	C15	114
Hyannis, Ne., U.S.	F11	126
Hyargas nuur, l., Mong.	B3	36
Hyattville, Wy., U.S.	C5	126
Hyden, Austl.	F3	74
Hyden, Ky., U.S.	G2	114
Hyde Park, Guy.	B6	84
Hyde Park, N.Y., U.S.	C12	114
Hyde Park, Vt., U.S.	F4	110
Hyderābād, India	C4	53
Hyderābād, Pak.	F2	54
Hydra see Ýdra, i., Grc.	F6	28
Hydraulic, B.C., Can.	D9	138
Hydro, Ok., U.S.	F10	128
Hydrographers Passage, strt., Austl.	C8	76
Hyères, Fr.	F12	18
Hyères, Îles d', is., Fr.	G12	18
Hyesan, Kor., N.	D8	38
Hyland, stm., Can.	C5	106
Hyndman, Pa., U.S.	E7	114
Hyndman Peak, mtn., Id., U.S.	G12	136
Hyōgo, state, Japan	D7	40
Hyrum, Ut., U.S.	B5	132
Hysham, Mt., U.S.	A5	126
Hythe, Eng., U.K.	J13	12
Hyūga, Japan	G4	40
Hyūga-nada, Japan	G4	40
Hyvinge see Hyvinkää, Fin.	F11	8
Hyvinkää, Fin.	F11	8
I		
Iaciara, Braz.	H2	88
Iaco (Yaco), stm., S.A.	F4	84
Iaçu, Braz.	G5	88
Iaeger, W.V., U.S.	G4	114
Ialomiţa, state, Rom.	E14	26
Ialomiţa, stm., Rom.	E13	26
Ialomiţei, Balta, sw., Rom.	E14	26
Iamonia, Lake, l., Fl., U.S.	F1	116
Iapu, Braz.	J4	88
Iargara, Mol.	C15	26
Iaşi, Rom.	B14	26
Iaşi, state, Rom.	B14	26
Iatt, Lake, res., La., U.S.	F6	122
Ib, stm., India	G10	54
Iba, Phil.	C2	52
Ibadan, Nig.	H5	64
Ibagué, Col.	E4	86
Ibaiti, Braz.	A12	92
Ibăneşti, Rom.	A13	26
Ibapah Peak, mtn., Ut., U.S.	D3	132
Ibar, stm., Yugo.	F7	26
Ibaraki, state, Japan	C13	40
Ibarra, Ec.	G2	86
Ibarreta, Arg.	B8	92
Ibb, Yemen	G5	56
Ibbenbüren, Ger.	D3	16
Ibembo, D.R.C.	D4	66
Iberá, Esteros del, sw., Arg.	D8	92
Iberia, Mo., U.S.	F5	120
Iberian Mountains see Ibérico, Sistema, mts., Spain	D8	20
Iberian Peninsula, pen., Eur.	D12	4
Ibérico, Sistema (Iberian Mountains), mts., Spain	D8	20
Ibiá, Braz.	J2	88
Ibiapina, Braz.	B5	88
Ibicaraí, Braz.	H6	88
Ibicuí, Braz.	H5	88
Ibicuí, stm., Braz.	D9	92
Ibiquera, Braz.	G5	88
Ibiraçu, Braz.	J5	88
Ibirapuã, Braz.	I5	88
Ibirapuitã, stm., Braz.	D10	92
Ibirataia, Braz.	H6	88
Ibirubá, Braz.	D11	92
Ibitiara, Braz.	G4	88
Ibitinga, Braz.	K1	88
Ibiza see Eivissa, Spain	F12	20
Ibiza see Eivissa, i., Spain	F12	20
Ibotirama, Braz.	G4	88
İbriktepe, Tur.	B9	28
Ibshawâi, Egypt	I1	58
Ibusuki, Japan	H3	40
Ica, Peru	F2	84
Içá (Putumayo), stm., S.A.	D4	84
Icabarú, stm., Ven.	E10	86
Icacos Point, c., Trin.	s11	105f
Icamaquã, stm., Braz.	D10	92
Icamole, Mex.	I7	130
Içana, Braz.	G8	86
Içana (Isana), stm., S.A.	G7	86
Icaño, Arg.	D5	92
Icatu, Braz.	B3	88
Iceberg Pass, p., Co., U.S.	G7	126
İçel (Mersin), Tur.	B5	58
İçel, state, Tur.	B4	58
Iceland, ctry., Eur.	k30	8a
Iceland Basin, unds.	C11	144
Ice Mountain, mtn., B.C., Can.	B9	138
Ichaikaronji, India	C2	53
Ichchāpuram, India	B7	53
Ichikawa, Japan	D12	40
Ichinomiya, Japan	D9	40
Ichkeul, Lac, l., Tun.	G3	24
Ichnia, Ukr.	D4	32
Ich'un see Yichun, China	B10	36
Ičinskaja Sopka, vulkan, vol., Russia	E20	34
Icó, Braz.	D6	88
Icy Cape, c., Ak., U.S.	B7	140
Ida, Mount see Ídhi Óros, mtn., Grc.	H7	28
Idabel, Ok., U.S.	D4	122
Ida Grove, Ia., U.S.	B2	120
Idah, Nig.	H6	64
Idaho, state, U.S.	G12	136
Idaho City, Id., U.S.	G11	136
Idaho Falls, Id., U.S.	G14	136
Idaho National Engineering Laboratory, sci., Id., U.S.	G14	136
Idalou, Tx., U.S.	H7	128
Idanha-a-Nova, Port.	E3	20
Idāppādi, India	F3	53
Idar, India	G4	54
Idar-Oberstein, Ger.	G3	16
Idelès, Alg.	E6	64
Ídhi Óros, mtn., Grc.	H7	28
Idi, Indon.	J3	48
Idiofa, D.R.C.	F3	66
Idku, Bahra el-, l., Egypt	G1	58
Idlib, Syria	C7	58
Idlib, state, Syria	C7	58
Ídolo, Isla del, i., Mex.	E10	100
Idoûkâl-en-Taghès, mtn., Niger	F6	64
Idre, Swe.	F5	8
Idrija, Slvn.	D11	22
Idutywa, S. Afr.	H9	70
Iecava, stm., Lat.	D7	10
Ieper, Bel.	D11	14
Ierápetra, Grc.	H8	28
Ierzu, Italy	E3	24
Iesolo, Italy	E9	22
Ifakara, Tan.	F7	66
Ife, Nig.	H5	64
Iferouâne, Niger	F6	64
Iferten see Yverdon-les-Bains, Switz.	D3	22
Ifôghas, Adrar des, mts., Afr.	F5	64
Igan, Malay.	B7	50
Igan, stm., Malay.	B7	50
Iganga, Ug.	D6	66
Igaporã, Braz.	G4	88
Igara, Braz.	F5	88
Igara Paraná, stm., Col.	H5	86
Igarapé-Açu, Braz.	D8	84
Igarapé-Miri, Braz.	B1	88
Igarka, Russia	A15	32
Igatpuri, India	B1	53
Igboho, Nig.	H5	64
Igharghar, Oued, stm., Alg.	D6	64
Igiugig, Ak., U.S.	E8	140
Iglesias, Italy	E2	24
Iglesias, Cerro las, mtn., Mex.	B5	100
Iglesiente, reg., Italy	E2	24
Igloolik, Nu., Can.	B14	106
'Igma, Gebel el-, mts., Egypt	I4	58
Ignacio, Co., U.S.	F9	132
Ignalina, Lith.	E9	10
Ignaţei, Mol.	B15	26
Igoumenítsa, Grc.	D3	28
Igra, Russia	C8	32
Iguaçu (Iguazú), stm., S.A.	B10	92
Iguaçu, Parque Nacional do, p.o.i., Braz.	B11	92
Iguaí, Braz.	H5	88
Iguala, Mex.	F9	100
Igualada, Spain	C12	20
Iguana, stm., Ven.	D9	86
Iguape, Braz.	B14	92
Iguape, stm., Braz.	B13	92
Iguassu Falls, wtfl, S.A.	B10	92
Iguatemi, stm., Braz.	A10	92
Iguatu, Braz.	D6	88
Iguazú (Iguaçu), stm., S.A.	B10	92
Iguazú, Parque Nacional, p.o.i., S.A.	B10	92
Iguéla, Gabon	E1	66
Iguéla, Lagune, b., Gabon	E1	66
Iguîdi, 'Erg, sand, Afr.	D3	64
Igžej, Russia	D18	32
Iharaña, Madag.	C9	68
Iheya-shima, i., Japan	I18	39a
Ihnâsiya el-Madina, Egypt	I1	58
Ihosy, Madag.	E8	68
Ihtiman, Blg.	G10	26
Iida, Japan	D10	40
Iisalmi, Fin.	E12	8
Iiyama, Japan	C11	40
Iizuka, Japan	F3	40
Ijâfene, des., Maur.	E3	64
Ijebu-Ode, Nig.	H5	64
IJmuiden, Neth.	B13	14
IJssel, stm., Neth.	B15	14
IJsselmeer, l., Neth.	B14	14
Ijuí, Braz.	D11	92
Ijuí, stm., Braz.	D10	92
Ika, Russia	C19	32
Ikali, D.R.C.	E4	66
Ikaría, i., Grc.	F9	28
Ikatskij hrebet, mts., Russia	F11	34
Ikeda, Japan	E6	40
Ikej, Russia	D17	32
Ikeja, Nig.	H5	64
Ikela, D.R.C.	E4	66
Ikerre, Nig.	H6	64
İkizce, Tur.	D15	28
Ikom, Nig.	H6	64
Ikot-Ekpene, Nig.	H6	64
Ikuno, Japan	D7	40
Ikurangi, hill, Cook Is.	a26	78j
Ila, Nig.	H6	64
Ilagan, Phil.	B3	52
Ilaiyānkudi, India	G4	53
Īlām, Iran	C6	56
Ilām, Nepal	E11	54
Ilan, Tai.	I9	42
Ilanskij, Russia	C17	32
Ilaro, Nig.	H5	64
Iława, Pol.	C15	16
Ilbenge, Russia	D13	34
Île-à-la-Crosse, Sk., Can.	D9	106
Ilebo, D.R.C.	E4	66
Île-de-France, hist. reg., Fr.	E11	14
Île de France, i., Grnld.	B22	141
Île-du-Prince-Édouard see Prince Edward Island, state, Can.	D13	110
Ilek, stm., Asia	D8	32
Ilesha, Nig.	H5	64
Îles Loyauté, state, N. Cal.	m16	79d
Île Tintamarre, i., Anguilla	A2	105a
Ilevskij Pogost, Russia	F20	8
Ileza, Russia	F20	8
Ilfracombe, Austl.	D5	76
Ilfracombe, Eng., U.K.	J8	12
Ilhabela, Braz.	L3	88
Ilha Grande, Baía da, b., Braz.	L3	88
Ilha Solteira, Represa de, res., Braz.	D6	90
Ilhea Point, c., Nmb.	C2	70
Ilhéus, Braz.	H6	88
Ilia, Rom.	D9	26
Iliamna, Ak., U.S.	E8	140
Iliamna Lake, l., Ak., U.S.	D9	140
Il'ič, Kaz.	F11	32
Ilicinea, Braz.	K3	88
Iliff, Co., U.S.	G9	126
Iligan, Phil.	F5	52
Iligan Bay, b., Phil.	F4	52
Iliniza, vol., Ec.	H2	86
Ilion, N.Y., U.S.	A10	114
Ilir, Russia	C18	32
Ilizi, Alg.	D6	64
Il'ja, Bela.	F10	10
Iljino, Russia	E14	10
Iljinskij, Russia	G17	34
Iljinskoe, Russia	D19	10
Iljinsko-Podomskoe, Russia	F23	8
Iljiny gory, hills, Russia	D17	10
Ilkal, India	D2	53
Ilkley, Eng., U.K.	H11	12
Illampu, Nevado, mtn., Bol.	C3	90
Illana Bay, b., Phil.	G4	52
Illapel, Chile	E2	92
Ille-et-Vilaine, state, Fr.	F7	14
Illéla, Niger	G6	64
Iller, stm., Ger.	I6	16
Illertissen, Ger.	H6	16
Illescas, Mex.	D7	100
Illichivs'k, Ukr.	C17	26
Illimani, Nevado, mtn., Bol.	C3	90
Illinois, state, U.S.	D8	120
Illinois, stm., U.S.	B3	122
Illinois, stm., Il., U.S.	E7	120
Illinois, stm., Or., U.S.	H3	136
Il'men', ozero, l., Russia	B14	10
Ilo, Peru	G3	84
Iloilo, Phil.	E4	52
Ilomantsi, Fin.	E14	8
Ilorin, Nig.	H5	64
Il'pyrskij, Russia	D21	34
Ilūkste, Lat.	E9	10
Ilulissat see Jakobshavn, Grnld.	D15	141
Ilwaki, Indon.	G8	44
Ilwŏl-san, mtn., Kor., S.	C1	40
Imabari, Japan	E5	40
Imaichi, Japan	C12	40
Imandra, ozero, l., Russia	C14	8
Imari, Japan	F2	40
Imaruí, Braz.	D13	92
Imaruí, Lagoa do, l., Braz.	D13	92
Imatra, Fin.	F13	8
Imavere, Est.	B8	10
Imbabura, state, Ec.	G2	86
Imbituba, Braz.	D13	92
Imeni Cjurupy, Russia	E21	10
Imeni Kirova, Russia	E14	34
Imeni Poliny Osipenko, Russia	F16	34
Imeni Stepana Razina, Russia	I21	8
Imeni Željabova, Russia	A19	10
Īmī, Eth.	F8	62
Imías, Cuba	B10	102
Imilac, Chile	B3	92
Imlay, Nv., U.S.	C7	134
Imlay City, Mi., U.S.	E6	112
Immenstadt, Ger.	I6	16
Immokalee, Fl., U.S.	J4	116
Imnaha, stm., Or., U.S.	E10	136
Imola, Italy	F8	22
Imonda, Pap. N. Gui.	a3	79a
Impasugong, Phil.	F5	52
Imperatriz, Braz.	C2	88
Imperia, Italy	G5	22
Imperial, Sk., Can.	C8	124
Imperial, Ca., U.S.	K10	134
Imperial, Tx., U.S.	C5	130
Imperial Beach, Ca., U.S.	K8	134
Imperial Dam, dam, U.S.	K2	132
Imperial de Aragón, Canal, can., Spain	C9	20
Imperial Valley, val., Ca., U.S.	E5	98
Impfondo, Congo	D3	66
Imphāl, India	D7	46
Imroz, Tur.	C8	28
Imst, Aus.	C7	22
Imuris, Mex.	F7	98
Ina, Japan	D10	40
Ina, Il., U.S.	F9	120
Inajá, Braz.	E7	88
I-n-Amenas, Alg.	D6	64
Iñapari, Peru	F4	84
Inarajan, Guam	j10	78c
Inari, Fin.	B12	8
Inarigda, Russia	B19	32
Inarijärvi, l., Fin.	B12	8
Inawashiro-ko, l., Japan	B12	40
Inca, Spain	E13	20
Inca de Oro, Chile	C3	92
Incahuasi, Cerro de, mtn., S.A.	C3	92
İnce Burun, c., Tur.	C10	28
İncekum Burnu, c., Tur.	B4	58
Inchelium, Wa., U.S.	B8	136
Inch'ŏn, Kor., S.	F7	38
İncirliova, Tur.	F10	28
Incomati (Komati), stm., Afr.	E10	70
Incudine, Monte, mtn., Fr.	H15	18
Incy, Russia	D19	8
Indaiá, stm., Braz.	J3	88
Indalsälven, stm., Swe.	E6	8
Indé, Mex.	I2	130
Independence, Ca., U.S.	G7	134
Independence, Ia., U.S.	B6	120
Independence, Ks., U.S.	G2	120
Independence, Ky., U.S.	F13	120
Independence, La., U.S.	G8	122
Independence, Mo., U.S.	E3	120
Independence, Va., U.S.	H4	114
Independence, Wi., U.S.	G7	118
Independence Fjord, b., Grnld.	A20	141
Independencia, Bol.	C3	90
Independência, Braz.	C5	88
Inderborskij, Kaz.	E8	32
Indi, India	C2	53
India, ctry., Asia	D4	46
Indialantic, Fl., U.S.	H5	116
Indiana, Pa., U.S.	D6	114
Indiana, state, U.S.	D11	120
Indiana Dunes National Lakeshore, p.o.i., In., U.S.	G2	112
Indianapolis, In., U.S.	I3	112
Indian Bayou, stm., Ar., U.S.	C7	122
Indian Church, Belize	D3	102
Indian Head, Sk., Can.	D10	124
Indian Lake, N.Y., U.S.	G2	110
Indian Lake, l., On., Can.	A7	112
Indian Lake, l., Mi., U.S.	B3	112
Indian Ocean	K11	142
Indianola, Ia., U.S.	C4	120
Indianola, Ms., U.S.	D8	122
Indianola, Ne., U.S.	A8	128
Indian Peak, mtn., Ut., U.S.	E3	132
Indian River, Mi., U.S.	C5	112
Indian Rock, mtn., Wa., U.S.	E6	136
Indiantown, Fl., U.S.	I5	116
Indiera Alta, P.R.	B2	104a
Indiga, Russia	C23	8
Indigirka, stm., Russia	C18	34
Indin, Mya.	H14	54
Indio, Ca., U.S.	J9	134
Indira Gandhi Canal, can., India	E4	54
Indispensable Strait, strt., Sol. Is.	e9	79b
Indochina, reg., Asia	D7	48
Indonesia, ctry., Asia	J16	30
Indore, India	G5	54
Indragiri, stm., Indon.	D2	50
Indramayu, Indon.	G6	50
Indrāvati, stm., India	B5	53

Name | Map Ref. | Page

Indravati Tiger Reserve, p.o.i., India B5 53
Indre, state, Fr. C7 18
Indre, stm., Fr. G10 14
Indre-et-Loire, state, Fr. G9 14
Indus, stm., Asia D2 46
Industry, Tx., U.S. H2 122
İnece, Tur. B10 28
In Ecker, Alg. E6 64
İnegöl, Tur. C12 28
Ineu, Rom. C8 26
Inez, Ky., U.S. G3 114
Inez, Tx., U.S. F11 130
Inferior, Laguna, b., Mex. G11 100
Infiernillo, Canal del, strt., Mex. G6 98
Infiernillo, Presa del, res., Mex. F7 100
Ing, stm., Thai. C5 48
Ingá, Braz. D8 88
Ingabu, Mya. D2 48
Ingal, Niger F6 64
Ingall Point, c., On., Can. B10 118
Ingelheim, Ger. G4 16
Ingende, D.R.C. E3 66
Ingeniero Jacobacci, Arg. H3 90
Ingeniero Luiggi, Arg. G5 92
Ingham, Austl. B6 76
Inglefield Land, reg., Grnld. B12 141
Ingleside, Tx., U.S. G10 130
Inglewood, Austl. G8 76
Inglewood, Austl. K4 76
Inglewood, Ca., U.S. J7 134
Inglis, Mb., Can. D12 124
Ingolf Fjord, b., Grnld. A22 141
Ingolstadt, Ger. H7 16
Ingonish, N.S., Can. D16 110
Ingrāj Bāzār, India F12 54
Ingrid Christensen Coast, cst., Ant. B12 81
In Guezzam, Alg. F6 64
Ingušetija, state, Russia F6 32
Ingushetia see Ingušetija, state, Russia F6 32
Inhaca, Ilha da, i., Moz. E11 70
Inhambane, Moz. C12 70
Inhambane, state, Moz. C12 70
Inhambane, Baía de, b., Moz. C12 70
Inhambupe, Braz. F6 88
Inhaminga, Moz. D5 68
Inhapim, Braz. J4 88
Inharrime, Moz. D12 70
Inhassoro, Moz. B12 70
Inhuma, Braz. D5 88
Inhumas, Braz. I1 88
Inimutaba, Braz. J3 88
Ining see Yining, China F14 32
Inírida, stm., Col. F7 86
Inis see Ennis, Ire. I3 12
Inis Córthaidh see Enniscorthy, Ire. I6 12
Inishbofin, i., Ire. H2 12
Inishmore, i., Ire. H3 12
Inishowen, pen., Ire. F5 12
Inishturk, i., Ire. H2 12
Inja, Russia E17 34
Inja, stm., Russia D18 34
Injune, Austl. E7 76
Inkom, Id., U.S. H14 136
Inkster, N.D., U.S. F16 124
Inland Lake, l., Mb., Can. B14 124
Inland Sea see Seto-naikai, Japan E5 40
Inle Lake, l., Mya. B3 48
Inman, Ks., U.S. C11 128
Inman Mills, S.C., U.S. A3 116
Inn, stm., Eur. B10 22
Innamincka, Austl. F3 76
Inner Channel, strt., Belize D3 102
Inner Hebrides, is., Scot., U.K. E6 12
Inner Mongolia see Nei Monggol, state, China C7 36
Inner Sister Island, i., Austl. m13 77a
Innisfail, Austl. A6 76
Innisfail, Ab., Can. D17 138
Innisfree, Ab., Can. C19 138
Innokentevka, Russia G16 34
Innoko, stm., Ak., U.S. D8 140
Innoshima, Japan E6 40
Innsbruck, Aus. C8 22
Innviertel, reg., Aus. B10 22
Inola, Ok., U.S. H2 120
Inongo, D.R.C. E3 66
İnönü, Tur. D13 28
Inowrocław, Pol. D14 16
In Salah, Alg. D5 64
Instow, Sk., Can. E5 124
Inta, Russia A10 32
Intendente Alvear, Arg. G6 92
İntepe, Tur. D9 28
Interlaken, Switz. D4 22
Interlândia, Braz. I1 88
International Falls, Mn., U.S. C5 118
Inthanon, Doi, mtn., Thai. C4 48
Intiyaco, Arg. D7 92
Intracoastal Waterway, strt., U.S. L5 116
Intracoastal Waterway, strt., U.S. H10 130
Intu, Indon. D9 50
Inubō-saki, c., Japan D13 40
Inukjuak, Qc., Can. D15 106
Inuvik, N.T., Can. B4 106
Inverbervie, Scot., U.K. E10 12
Invercargill, N.Z. H3 80
Inverell, Austl. G8 76
Inverloch, Austl. L5 76
Invermay, Sk., Can. C10 124
Invermere, B.C., Can. F14 138
Inverness, N.S., Can. D15 110
Inverness, Scot., U.K. D8 12
Inverness, Ca., U.S. E3 134
Inverness, Fl., U.S. H3 116
Inverurie, Scot., U.K. D10 12
Inverway, Austl. C5 74
Investigator Strait, strt., Austl. G7 74
Inwood, Mb., Can. D16 124
Inyangani, mtn., Zimb. D5 68
Inyathi, Zimb. D4 68
Inyo, Mount, mtn., Ca., U.S. G8 134
Inyokern, Ca., U.S. H8 134
Inyo Mountains, mts., Ca., U.S. G7 134
Inzana Lake, l., B.C., Can. B6 138
Ioánnina, Grc. D3 28
Iokanga, stm., Russia C18 8
Iola, Ks., U.S. G2 120
Ioma, Pap. N. Gui. b4 79a
Iona, Ang. D1 68
Iona, N.S., Can. D16 110
Iona, Id., U.S. G15 136
Iona, i., Scot., U.K. E6 12
Ione, Ca., U.S. E5 134
Ione, Wa., U.S. B9 136
Ionia, Mi., U.S. E4 112
Ionian Islands see Iónioi Nísoi, is., Grc. E3 28
Ionian Sea, Eur. F11 24
Iónioi Nísoi, state, Grc. E3 28
Iónioi Nísoi (Ionian Islands), is., Grc. E3 28
Iony, ostrov, i., Russia E17 34
Íos, i., Grc. G8 28
Iosegun Lake see Fox Creek, Ab., Can. B14 138
Iowa, La., U.S. G5 122
Iowa, state, U.S. I5 118
Iowa, stm., Ia., U.S. C6 120
Iowa City, Ia., U.S. C6 120
Iowa Falls, Ia., U.S. B4 120
Iowa Park, Tx., U.S. H10 128
Ipameri, Braz. I1 88
Ipanema, stm., Braz. E7 88
Ipanguaçu, Braz. C7 88
Ipatinga, Braz. J4 88
Ipatovo, Russia E6 32
Ipaumirim, Braz. D6 88
Ípeiros, state, Grc. D3 28
Ípeiros, hist. reg., Grc. D3 28
Ipel' (Ipoly), stm., Eur. I14 16
Ipiales, Col. G3 86
Ipiaú, Braz. H6 88
Ipin see Yibin, China F5 36
Ipirá, Braz. G6 88
Ipixuna, Braz. C3 88
Ipoh, Malay. J5 48
Ipojuca, stm., Braz. E7 88
Ipoly (Ipel'), stm., Eur. I14 16
Iporã, Braz. G7 84
Iporã, Braz. A11 92
Ipota, Vanuatu I17 79d
İpsala, Tur. C9 28
Ipswich, Austl. F9 76
Ipswich, Eng., U.K. I14 12
Ipswich, Ma., U.S. B15 114
Ipswich, S.D., U.S. B13 126
Ipu, Braz. C5 88
Ipubi, Braz. D5 88
Ipuc' (Iput'), stm., Eur. H14 10
Ipueiras, Braz. C5 88
Iput' (Ipuc'), stm., Eur. H14 10
Iqaluit, Nu., Can. C17 106
Iqfahs, Egypt J1 58
Iquique, Chile D2 90
Iquitos, Peru D3 84
Ira, Tx., U.S. B7 130
Iracema, Braz. C6 88
Irákleia, i., Grc. G8 28
Irákleio, Grc. H8 28
Iran, ctry., Asia C7 56
Iran Mountains, mts., Asia C9 50
Īrānshahr, Iran D9 56
Irapa, Ven. B10 86
Irapuato, Mex. E8 100
Iraq, ctry., Asia C5 56
Irará, Braz. F6 88
Irati, Braz. B12 92
Irazú, Volcán, vol., C.R. G6 102
Irbejskoe, Russia C17 32
Irbid, Jord. F6 58
Irbid, state, Jord. F6 58
Irbīl, Iraq B5 56
Irbit, Russia C10 32
Irdning, Aus. C11 22
Irebu, D.R.C. E3 66
Irecê, Braz. F5 88
Ireland, ctry., Eur. H4 12
Ireland Island North, i., Ber. k15 104e
Irene, S.D., U.S. D15 126
Ireng (Maú), stm., S.A. F12 86
Ireton, Ia., U.S. B1 120
Irgiz, Kaz. E10 32
Iri, Kor., S. G7 38
Iriba, Chad E4 62
Iriga, Phil. D4 52
Irígui, reg., Afr. F3 64
Iringa, Tan. F7 66
Irinjālakuda, India F3 53
Iriomote-jima, i., Japan G9 36
Iriri, stm., Braz. D7 84
Irish, Mount, mtn., Nv., U.S. F1 132
Irish Sea, Eur. H7 12
Irituia, Braz. A2 88
Irkutsk, Russia D18 32
Irma, Ab., Can. D19 138
Irminger Basin, unds. B10 144
Irnijärvi, l., Fin. D13 8
Iroise, b., Fr. F4 14
Iron Bottom Sound, strt., Sol. Is. e8 79b
Iron Bridge, On., Can. B6 112
Iron City, Tn., U.S. B11 122
Irondale, Al., U.S. D12 122
Irondale, Mo., U.S. G7 120
Irondequoit, N.Y., U.S. E12 112
Iron Gate, val., Eur. E9 26
Iron Knob, Austl. F7 74
Iron Mountain, Mi., U.S. C1 112
Iron Range, Austl. B8 74
Iron River, Mi., U.S. E10 118
Ironton, Mn., U.S. E4 118
Ironton, Mo., U.S. G7 120
Ironton, Oh., U.S. F3 114
Ironwood, Mi., U.S. E8 118
Iroquois, On., Can. D14 112
Iroquois, stm., U.S. H2 112
Iroquois Falls, On., Can. F14 106
Irō-zaki, c., Japan E11 40
Irrawaddy see Ayeyarwady, stm., Mya. E8 46
Irricana, Ab., Can. E17 138
Irrigon, Or., U.S. E7 136
Irshava, Ukr. A10 26
Irsina, Italy D10 24
Irtyš see Irtysh, stm., Asia C11 32
Irtysh (Irtyš) (Ertix), stm., Asia C11 32
Irtyšsk, Kaz. D12 32
Irún, Spain A9 20
Iruña see Pamplona, Spain B9 20
Irurzun, Spain B9 20
Irú Tepuy, mtn., Ven. E11 86
Irvine, Ab., Can. E3 124
Irvine, Scot., U.K. F8 12
Irvines Landing, B.C., Can. G6 138
Irving, Tx., U.S. B10 130
Irvington, Ky., U.S. G11 120
Isa, Nig. G6 64
Isaac, stm., Austl. D7 76
Isaac Lake, l., B.C., Can. C10 138
Isabel, state, Sol. Is. d8 79b
Isabela, Phil. G3 52
Isabela, P.R. A1 104a
Isabela, Cabo, c., Dom. Rep. C12 102
Isabela, Isla, i., Ec. i11 84a
Isabelia, Cordillera, mts., Nic. F5 102
Isaccea, Rom. D15 26
Isachsen, Nu., Can. B5 141
Isachsen, Cape, c., Nu., Can. B4 141
Ísafjarđardjúp, b., Ice. j28 8a
Ísafjörđur, Ice. j28 8a
Isahaya, Japan G3 40
Isak, Indon. J3 48
Isaka, Tan. E6 66
Īsa Khel, Pak. B3 54
Işalniţa, Rom. E10 26
Isana (Içana), stm., S.A. G7 86
Isangel, Vanuatu I17 79d
Isanti, Mn., U.S. F5 118
Isar, stm., Eur. H8 16
Isarog, Mount, vol., Phil. D4 52
İscehisar, Tur. E13 28
Ischia, Italy D7 24
Ischia, Isola d', i., Italy D7 24
Ise, Japan E9 40
Iseo, Lago d', l., Italy E6 22
Isère, state, Fr. D11 18
Isère, stm., Fr. D11 18
Iserlohn, Ger. E3 16
Isernia, Italy C8 24
Isesaki, Japan C12 40
Ise-shima-kokuritsu-kōen, p.o.i., Japan E9 40
Ise-wan, b., Japan E9 40
Iseyin, Nig. H5 64
Isezaki see Isesaki, Japan C12 40
Isfahan see Eşfahān, Iran C7 56
Isfara, Taj. A11 56
Isherton, Guy. F12 86
Ishigaki, Japan G9 36
Ishikari, stm., Japan C14 38
Ishikari-wan, b., Japan C14 38
Ishikawa, state, Japan C9 40
Ishim (Išim), stm., Asia C12 32
Ishinomaki, Japan A14 40
Ishioka, Japan C13 40
Ishizuchi-san, mtn., Japan F5 40
Ishpeming, Mi., U.S. B2 112
Ishurdi, Bngl. F12 54
Isigny-sur-Mer, Fr. E7 14
Işıklı, Tur. E12 28
Isil'kul', Russia C12 32
Išim, Russia C11 32
Išimskaja ravnina, pl., Asia C11 32
Isiolo, Kenya D7 66
Isipingo, ngh., S. Afr. G10 70
Isiro, D.R.C. D5 66
Isis, Austl. E9 76
Iskăr, stm., Blg. F11 26
Iskăr, Jazovir, res., Blg. G10 26
İskenderun (Alexandretta), Tur. B6 58
İskenderun Körfezi, b., Tur. B6 58
Iskitim, Russia D14 32
Iskut, stm., B.C., Can. D4 106
Isla, Mex. G11 100
Isla, Salar de la, pl., Chile B3 92
İslâhiye, Tur. A7 58
Islāmābād, Pak. B4 54
Islāmkot, Pak. F3 54
Islāmpur, India C2 53
Islāmpur, India F10 54
Islāmpur, India E12 54
Island, Ky., U.S. G10 120
Island Falls, Me., U.S. E8 110
Island Harbour, Anguilla A1 105a
Island Lake, l., Mb., Can. E12 106
Island Park, Id., U.S. F15 136
Island Pond, Vt., U.S. F5 110
Islands, Bay of, b., Nf., Can. j22 107a
Isla Patrulla, Ur. F10 92
Isla Vista, Ca., U.S. I5 134
Islay, i., Scot., U.K. F6 12
Isle, Mn., U.S. E5 118
Isle, stm., Fr. E5 18
Isle of Man, dep., Eur. G8 12
Isle of Wight, Va., U.S. H9 114
Isle Royale National Park, p.o.i., Mi., U.S. C10 118
Islesboro Island, i., Me., U.S. F8 110
Isleta, N.M., U.S. I10 132
Isleton, Ca., U.S. E4 134
Islón, Chile D2 92
Ismailia (Al-Ismā'īlīyah), Egypt H3 58
Isna, Egypt B6 62
Isny, Ger. I5 16
Isoka, Zam. C5 68
Isola del Liri, Italy I10 22
Isola di Capo Rizzuto, Italy F11 24
Isonzo, stm., Eur. E10 22
Isparta, Tur. F13 28
Isparta, state, Tur. F13 28
Ispica, Italy H8 24
Israel, ctry., Asia G5 58
Isrā'īl see Israel, ctry., Asia G5 58
Issa, stm., Russia D11 10
Isser, Oued, stm., Alg. H14 20
Issia, C. Iv. H3 64
Issoire, Fr. D9 18
Issoudun, Fr. H10 14
Issuna, Tan. F6 66
Issyk-Kul', Kyrg. F13 32
Issyk-Kul, Lake see Issyk-Kul', ozero, l., Kyrg. F13 32
Issyk-Kul', ozero, l., Kyrg. F13 32
Īstādeh-ye Moqor, Āb-e, l., Afg. B2 54
İstanbul, Tur. B12 28
İstanbul, state, Tur. B11 28
İstanbul Boğazı (Bosporus), strt., Tur. B12 28
Istiaía, Grc. E6 28
Istmina, Col. E3 86
Isto, Mount, mtn., Ak., U.S. C11 140
Istra, Russia E19 10
Istria, pen., Eur. E10 22
Itá, Para. B9 92
Itabaiana, Braz. D8 88
Itabaiana, Braz. F7 88
Itabaianinha, Braz. F7 88
Itabapoana, Braz. K5 88
Itaberaba, Braz. G5 88
Itaberaí, Braz. G8 84
Itabi, Braz. F7 88
Itabira, Braz. J4 88
Itabuna, Braz. H6 88
Itacajá, Braz. E2 88
Itacambiruçu, stm., Braz. I4 88
Itacoatiara, Braz. D6 84
Itacurubí del Rosario, Para. B9 92
Itaeté, Braz. G5 88
Itaguajé, Braz. D6 90
Itaguara, Braz. K3 88
Itaguari, stm., Braz. H3 88
Itagüí, Col. D4 86
Itaí, Braz. A13 92
Itaiçaba, Braz. C7 88
Itaim, stm., Braz. D5 88
Itainópolis, Braz. D5 88
Itaipu Reservoir, res., S.A. B10 92
Itäisen Suomenlahden kansallispuisto, p.o.i., Fin. F12 8
Itaituba, Braz. D6 84
Itajaí, Braz. C13 92
Itajubá, Braz. L3 88
Itaju do Colônia, Braz. H6 88
Itajuípe, Braz. H6 88
Itala Game Reserve, S. Afr. E10 70
Itálica, hist., Spain G4 20
Italy, Tx., U.S. B11 130
Italy, ctry., Eur. G11 6
Itamaraju, Braz. I6 88
Itamarandiba, Braz. I4 88
Itamarandiba, stm., Braz. I4 88
Itamari, Braz. G6 88
Itambacuri, Braz. I5 88
Itambé, Braz. H5 88
Itami, Japan E8 40
Itampolo, Madag. E7 68
Itānagar, India E14 54
Itanhaém, Braz. B14 92
Itanhém, Braz. I5 88
Itaobim, Braz. I5 88
Itapagipe, Braz. J1 88
Itapajé, Braz. B6 88
Itaparica, Ilha de, i., Braz. G6 88
Itaparica, Represa de, res., Braz. E6 88
Itapebi, Braz. H6 88
Itapecerica, Braz. K3 88
Itapecuru-Mirim, Braz. B3 88
Itapemirim, Braz. K5 88
Itaperuna, Braz. K5 88
Itapetim, Braz. D7 88
Itapetinga, Braz. H5 88
Itapetininga, Braz. L1 88
Itapetininga, stm., Braz. A14 92
Itapeva, Braz. L1 88
Itapicuru, Braz. F6 88
Itapicuru, stm., Braz. B3 88
Itapicuru, stm., Braz. F6 88
Itapipoca, Braz. B6 88
Itapiranga, Braz. D6 84
Itapirapuã, Braz. G7 84
Itapiúna, Braz. C6 88
Itápolis, Braz. K1 88
Itaporã de Goiás, Braz. D1 88
Itaporanga, Braz. D6 88
Itaporanga d'Ajuda, Braz. F7 88
Itapúa, state, Para. C10 92
Itaquara, Braz. G6 88
Itaquari, Braz. K5 88
Itaqui, Braz. D9 92
Itarantim, Braz. H5 88
Itararé, Braz. B13 92
Itararé, stm., Braz. A13 92
Itārsi, India G6 54
Itarumã, Braz. C6 90
Itasca, Tx., U.S. B10 130
Itasca, Lake, l., Mn., U.S. D3 118
Itata, stm., Chile H1 92
Itatinga, Braz. L1 88
Itatira, Braz. C6 88
Itatupã, Braz. D7 84
Itaueira, Braz. D4 88
Itaueira, stm., Braz. D4 88
Itaúna, Braz. K3 88
Itbayat Island, i., Phil. K9 42
Itéa, Grc. E5 28
Iténez (Guaporé), stm., S.A. F5 84
Ithaca, Mi., U.S. E5 112
Ithaca, N.Y., U.S. B9 114
Ithaca see Itháki, i., Grc. E3 28
Itháki, i., Grc. E3 28
Itimbiri, stm., D.R.C. D4 66
Itinga, Braz. I5 88
Itiquira, stm., Braz. G6 84
Itiruçu, Braz. G5 88
Itiúba, Braz. F5 88
Itla el-Bâsha, hill, Egypt K3 58
Itō, Japan E12 40
Itoigawa, Japan B10 40
Iton, stm., Fr. F9 14
Itororó, Braz. H5 88
Itsuki, Japan G3 40
Ittiri, Italy D2 24
Ittoqqortoormiit see Scoresbysund, Grnld. C21 141
Itu, Braz. L2 88
Itu, stm., Braz. D10 92
Ituaçu, Braz. G5 88
Ituango, Col. D4 86
Ituberá, Braz. G6 88
Itueta, Braz. J5 88
Ituí, stm., Braz. E3 84
Ituiutaba, Braz. J1 88
Itumbiara, Braz. J1 88
Ituna, Sk., Can. C10 124
Itupiranga, Braz. E8 84
Ituporanga, Braz. C13 92
Iturama, Braz. C6 90
Iturbide, Mex. C3 102
Iturup, ostrov (Etorofu-tō), i., Russia B17 38
Ituverava, Braz. K2 88
Ituxi, stm., Braz. E4 84
Ituzaingó, Arg. C9 92
Itzehoe, Ger. C5 16
Iuka, Ms., U.S. C10 122
Iul'tin, Russia C25 34
Iúna, Braz. K5 88
Ivacėvičy, Bela. H8 10
Ivačovo, Russia F17 8
Ivaí, stm., Braz. D6 90
Ivaiporã, Braz. B12 92
Ivalo, Fin. B12 8
Ivalojoki, stm., Fin. B12 8
Ivanava, Bela. H8 10
Ivančice, Czech Rep. G12 16
Ivangorod, Russia A11 10
Ivangrad, Yugo. G6 26
Ivanhoe, Austl. I5 76
Ivanhoe, Ca., U.S. G6 134
Ivanhoe, Mn., U.S. G2 118
Ivanhoe, Va., U.S. H4 114
Ivanišči, Russia D18 10
Ivanjica, Yugo. F7 26
Ivan'kovo, Russia F20 10
Ivan'kovskoe vodohranilišče, res., Russia D19 10
Ivano-Frankivs'k, Ukr. F13 6
Ivano-Frankivs'k, co., Ukr. A11 26
Ivanovka, Russia F14 34
Ivanovo, Russia H19 8
Ivanovskaja oblast', co., Russia H19 8
Ivanovskoe, Russia A11 10
Ivanpah Lake, l., Ca., U.S. H1 132
Ivdel', Russia B9 32
Ivigtut, Grnld. E16 141
Ivindo, stm., Gabon D2 66
Ivinheíma, stm., Braz. D6 90
Iviza see Eivissa, Spain F12 20
Ivjanec, Bela. G9 10
Ivohibe, Madag. E8 68
Ivory Coast see Cote d'Ivoire, ctry., Afr. H3 64
Ivory Coast, cst., C. Iv. I3 64
Ivrea, Italy E4 22
İvrindi, Tur. D10 28
Ivujivik, Qc., Can. C15 106
Iwaki, Japan B13 40
Iwaki-san, vol., Japan D14 38
Iwakuni, Japan E5 40
Iwami, Japan D7 40
Iwanuma, Japan A13 40
Iwata, Japan E10 40
Iwate, state, Japan A14 40
Iwate-san, vol., Japan E14 38
'Iweibid, Gebel, mtn., Egypt H3 58
Iwo, Nig. H5 64
Ixmiquilpan, Mex. E9 100
Ixopo, S. Afr. G10 70
Ixtapa, Mex. G8 100
Ixtepec, Mex. G11 100
Ixtlán del Río, Mex. E6 100
Iyang see Yiyang, China G5 42
Iyo, Japan F5 40
Iyo-mishima, Japan F6 40
Iyo-nada, Japan F5 40
Izabal, Lago de, l., Guat. E3 102
Izamal, Mex. B3 102
Izapa, hist., Mex. H12 100
Izberbaš, Russia F7 32
Izbica, Pol. F19 16
Izegem, Bel. D12 14
Iževsk, Russia C8 32
Izium, Ukr. E5 32
Ižma, stm., Russia B8 32
Izmaïl, Ukr. D15 26
Izmalkovo, Russia H21 10
Izmayil see Izmaïl, Ukr. D15 26
İzmir (Smyrna), Tur. E10 28
İzmir, state, Tur. E10 28
İzmir Körfezi, b., Tur. E9 28
İzmit (Kocaeli), Tur. C12 28
İzmit Körfezi, b., Tur. C12 28
İznik, Tur. C12 28
İznik Gölü, l., Tur. C12 28
Iznoski, Russia E18 10
Izozog, Bañados del, sw., Bol. C4 90
Izra', Syria F7 58
Izsák, Hung. C6 26
Iztaccíhuatl, Volcán, vol., Mex. F9 100
Iztaccíhuatl y Popocatéptl, Parques Nacionales, p.o.i., Mex. F9 100
Izucar de Matamoros, Mex. F9 100
Izu-hantō, pen., Japan E11 40
Izuhara, Japan E2 40
Izu Islands see Izu-shotō, is., Japan E12 40
Izumi, Japan G3 40
Izumi, Japan A13 40
Izumi, Japan E8 40
Izumo, Japan D5 40
Izu-shotō (Izu Islands), is., Japan E12 40
Izu Trench, unds. G17 142
Izvestij CIK, ostrova, is., Russia A5 34
Izvorul Muntelui, Lacul, l., Rom. C12 26

J

Jabal, Bahr al- see Mountain Nile, stm., Afr. F6 62
Jabal al-Awliyā', Sudan D6 62
Jabal Lubnān, state, Leb. D6 58
Jabalón, stm., Spain F7 20
Jabalpur, India G7 54
Jabālyah, Gaza G5 58
Jabbūl, Sabkhat al-, l., Syria C8 58
Jabiru, Austl. B6 74
Jablah, Syria C6 58
Jablanica, Bos. F4 26
Jablaničko jezero, res., Bos. F4 26
Jablonec nad Nisou, Czech Rep. F11 16
Jabłonka, Pol. G15 16
Jablonovyj hrebet, mts., Russia F11 34
Jablunkov, Czech Rep. G14 16
Jaboticabal, Braz. K1 88
Jaca, Spain B10 20
Jacala, Mex. E9 100
Jacaré, stm., Braz. F5 88
Jacareí, Braz. L2 88
Jacarezinho, Braz. D7 90
Jáchal, stm., Arg. E4 92
Jaciara, Braz. G6 84
Jacinto, Braz. I5 88
Jacinto Aráuz, Arg. I6 92
Jacinto City, Tx., U.S. H3 122
Jackfish Lake, l., Sk., Can. A5 124
Jackhead Harbour, Mb., Can. C16 124
Jack Mountain, mtn., Mt., U.S. D14 136
Jackpot, Nv., U.S. B2 132
Jacksboro, Tn., U.S. H1 114
Jacksboro, Tx., U.S. H10 128
Jackson, Ca., U.S. E5 134
Jackson, Ky., U.S. G2 114
Jackson, La., U.S. G7 122
Jackson, Mi., U.S. B1 114
Jackson, Mn., U.S. H4 118
Jackson, Ms., U.S. E8 122
Jackson, N.C., U.S. H8 114
Jackson, Oh., U.S. E3 114
Jackson, S.C., U.S. C4 116
Jackson, Tn., U.S. B10 122
Jackson, Wy., U.S. G16 136
Jackson, stm., Va., U.S. G6 114
Jackson, Mount, mtn., Ant. C34 81
Jackson, Mount, mtn., Austl. F3 74
Jackson Creek, stm., Can. E12 124
Jackson Lake, l., Wy., U.S. G16 136
Jacksonville, Al., U.S. D13 122
Jacksonville, Ar., U.S. C6 122
Jacksonville, Fl., U.S. F4 116
Jacksonville, Il., U.S. E7 120
Jacksonville, N.C., U.S. B8 116
Jacksonville, Or., U.S. A2 134
Jacksonville, Tx., U.S. F3 122
Jacksonville Beach, Fl., U.S. F4 116
Jacmel, Haiti C11 102
Jaco, Mex. B6 100
Jacobābād, Pak. D2 54
Jacobina, Braz. F5 88
Jacobsdal, S. Afr. F7 70
Jacques-Cartier, Mont, mtn., Qc., Can. A11 110
Jacu, stm., Braz. D8 88
Jacuí, stm., Braz. D11 92
Jacuípe, stm., Braz. F5 88
Jacumba, Ca., U.S. K9 134
Jacundá, Braz. D8 84
Jacupiranga, Braz. B13 92
Jacuriaí, stm., Braz. F6 88
Jadebusen, b., Ger. C4 16
J.A.D. Jensens Nunatakker, mtn., Grnld. E16 141
Jadraque, Spain D8 20
Jādū, Libya A2 62
Jaén, Peru E2 84
Jaén, Spain G7 20
Jaén, co., Spain G7 20
Jāfarābād, India H3 54
Jaffa, Cape, c., Austl. K2 76
Jaffna, Sri L. G4 53
Jaffna Lagoon, b., Sri L. G4 53
Jaffrey, N.H., U.S. B13 114
Jafr, Qā' al-, depr., Jord. H7 58
Jagalūr, India D3 53
Jagannāthganj Ghāt, Bngl. F12 54
Jagatsingpur, India H11 54
Jagdalpur, India B6 53
Jageljurta, gora, hill, Russia C17 8
Jagersfontein, S. Afr. F7 70
Jaggayyapeta, India C5 53
Jagodnoe, Russia D18 34
Jagraon, India C5 54
Jagtiāl, India B4 53
Jaguaquara, Braz. G6 88
Jaguarão, Braz. F11 92
Jaguarão (Yaguarón), stm., S.A. F11 92
Jaguarari, Braz. F5 88
Jaguari, Braz. D10 92
Jaguariaíva, Braz. B13 92
Jaguaribara, Braz. C6 88
Jaguaribe, Braz. C6 88
Jaguaribe, stm., Braz. C7 88
Jaguaruna, Braz. D13 92
Jagüey Grande, Cuba A7 102
Jahānābād, India F10 54
Jahrom, Iran D7 56
Jahroma, Russia D20 10
Jaicós, Braz. D5 88
Jailolo, Indon. E8 44
Jaintiāpur, Bngl. F14 54
Jaipur, India E5 54
Jaipur Hāt, Bngl. F12 54
Jais, India E8 54
Jaisalmer, India E3 54
Jaito, India C5 54
Jaja, Russia C15 32
Jājapur, India H11 54
Jajce, Bos. E4 26
Jakarta, Indon. G5 50
Jakarta, Teluk, b., Indon. F5 50
Jakaulevičy, Bela. F13 10
Jakhāu, India G2 54
Jakobshavn (Ilulissat), Grnld. D15 141
Jakobstad see Pietarsaari, Fin. E10 8
Jakovlevka, Russia B10 38
Jakša, Russia B9 32
Jakutija, state, Russia C14 34
Jakutsk, Russia D14 34
Jal, N.M., U.S. B4 130
Jalaid Qi, China B9 36
Jalālābād, Afg. C11 56
Jalālpur, India E9 54
Jalandhar, India C5 54
Jalapa, Guat. E3 102
Jalapa see Xalapa, Mex. F10 100
Jālaun, India E7 54
Jales, Braz. D6 90
Jalesar, India E7 54
Jaleshwar, India H11 54
Jālgaon, India H5 54
Jālgaon, India H6 54
Jalingo, Nig. H7 64
Jalisco, state, Mex. E6 100
Jālna, India B2 53
Jalón, stm., Spain C9 20
Jālor, India F4 54
Jalostotitlán, Mex. E7 100
Jalpa, Mex. E7 100
Jalpāiguri, India E12 54
Jaluit, at., Marsh. Is. C7 72
Jalutorovsk, Russia C11 32
Jamaame, Som. E8 66
Jamaica, ctry., N.A. D8 102
Jamaica Channel, strt., N.A. D9 102
Jamal, poluostrov, pen., Russia B2 34
Jam-Alin', hrebet, mts., Russia F15 34
Jamālpur, Bngl. F12 54
Jamālpur, India F11 54
Jamanota, hill, Aruba o20 104g
Jamantau, gora, mtn., Russia D9 32
Jamanxim, stm., Braz. E6 84
Jamari, stm., Braz. E5 84
Jamarovka, Russia F11 34
Jambelí, Canal de, strt., Ec. I2 86
Jambi, Indon. D3 50
Jambi, state, Indon. D3 50
Jamboaye, stm., Indon. J3 48
Jambol, Blg. G13 26
Jambongan, Pulau, i., Malay. G1 52
Jambuair, Tanjung, c., Indon. J3 48
Jambusar, India G4 54
James, stm., U.S. C8 108
James, stm., Mo., U.S. H4 120
James, stm., Va., U.S. G8 114
James, Isla, i., Chile H2 90
James Bay, b., Can. E14 106
James City, N.C., U.S. A8 116
James Craik, Arg. F6 92
James Island, S.C., U.S. D5 116
James Point, c., Bah. K9 116
Jamesport, Mo., U.S. E4 120
James Ross, Cape, c., N.T., Can. B17 140
James Ross Island, i., Ant. B35 81
James Ross Strait, strt., Nu., Can. A11 106
Jamestown, Austl. I2 76
Jamestown, S. Afr. G8 70
Jamestown, Ca., U.S. F5 134
Jamestown, Ky., U.S. H12 120
Jamestown, N.Y., U.S. B6 114
Jamestown, N.C., U.S. I6 114
Jamestown, N.D., U.S. H15 124
Jamestown, Tn., U.S. H13 120
Jamestown, misc. cult., Va., U.S. G9 114
Jām Jodhpur, India H3 54
Jamkhandi, India C2 53
Jamm, Russia B10 10
Jammerbugten, b., Den. H3 8
Jammu, India B5 54
Jammu and Kashmir see Kashmir, hist. reg., Asia B4 46
Jamnagar (Navanagar), India G3 54
Jampang-kulon, Indon. G5 50
Jāmpur, Pak. D3 54
Jämsä, Fin. F11 8
Jamshedpur, India G10 54
Jamsk, Russia E19 34
Jämtland, state, Swe. E6 8
Jamūi, India F11 54
Jamuna, stm., Bngl. F12 54
Jana, stm., Russia C16 34
Janaúba, Braz. H4 88
Janaucu, Ilha, i., Braz. C7 84
Jand, Pak. B4 54
Jandaia, Braz. G7 84
Jandiāla, India C5 54
Jandowae, Austl. F8 76
Jándula, stm., Spain F7 20
Janeiro, stm., Braz. F3 88
Janesville, Ca., U.S. C5 134
Janesville, Mn., U.S. G5 118
Janesville, Wi., U.S. B9 120
Jangamo, Moz. D12 70
Jangeru, Indon. E10 50
Jangijul', Uzb. F11 32
Jangīpur, India F11 54
Jangoon, India C4 53
Janīn, W.B. F6 58
Janisjarvi, ozero, l., Russia E14 8
Janiuay, Phil. E4 52
Jankan, hrebet, mts., Russia E12 34
Jan Kempdorp, S. Afr. E7 70
Janlohong, Indon. B10 50
Jan Mayen, i., Nor. B22 94
Janos, Mex. F8 98
Jánosháza, Hung. B4 26
Janowiec Wielkopolski, Pol. D13 16
Janskij, Russia C15 34
Janskij zaliv, b., Russia B16 34
Jantra, stm., Blg. F12 26
Januária, Braz. H3 88
Januário Cicco, Braz. D8 88
Jaora, India G5 54
Japan, ctry., Asia E12 38
Japan, Sea of (East Sea), Asia D11 38
Japan Basin, unds. E16 142
Japan Trench, unds. F17 142
Japaratinga, Braz. E8 88
Japi, Braz. D7 88
Japonskoje more see East Sea, Asia D11 38
Japonskoje more see Japan, Sea of, Asia D11 38
Japtiksalja, Russia C3 34
Japurá, Braz. H8 86
Japurá (Caquetá), stm., S.A. D5 84
Jaqué, Pan. D2 86
Jarābulus, Syria B9 58
Jaraguá, Braz. H1 88
Jaraguá do Sul, Braz. C13 92
Jaraíz de la Vera, Spain D5 20
Jarales, N.M., U.S. I10 132
Jarama, stm., Spain D7 20
Jaramānah, Syria E7 58
Jaransk, Russia C7 32
Jarānwāla, Pak. C4 54
Jarash, Jord. F6 58
Jarash, hist., Jord. F6 58
Jarcevo, Russia E15 10
Jardim, Braz. D6 88
Jardim, Braz. D5 90
Jardim de Piranhas, Braz. D7 88
Jardín América, Arg. C10 92
Jardines de la Reina, Archipiélago de los, is., Cuba B8 102
Jardinópolis, Braz. K1 88
Jarej-Uliga-Delap, Marsh. Is. C8 72
Jarenga, Russia E23 8
Jarensk, Russia E23 8
Jargalant, Mong. B4 36
Jari, stm., Braz. C7 84
Jaridih, India G11 54
Jarkand see Shache, China B12 56
Jarkino, Russia C17 32
Jarocin, Pol. D13 16
Jarohta, Russia C17 32
Jaroměř, Czech Rep. F11 16
Jaroslavl', Russia H19 8
Jaroslavskaja oblast', co., Russia H18 8
Jarosław, Pol. F18 16
Jarratt, Va., U.S. H8 114
Jar-Sale, Russia A12 32
Jartai Yanchi, l., China B1 42
Jarud Qi, China B4 38
Järvakandi, Est. G11 8
Järvenpää, Fin. F11 8
Jarvie, Ab., Can. B17 138
Jarvis, On., Can. F9 112
Jarvisburg, N.C., U.S. H10 114
Jarvis Island, i., Oc. D10 72
Jasdan, India G3 54
Jasel'da, stm., Bela. H8 10
Jashpurnagar, India D5 46
Jasień, Pol. E11 16
Jāsk, Iran D8 56
Jaškul', Russia E7 32

Name	Map Ref.	Page
Jasło, Pol.	G17	16
Jasnogorsk, Russia	F20	10
Jasnyj, Russia	F14	34
Jason Islands, is., Falk. Is.	J4	90
Jasper, Ab., Can.	D12	138
Jasper, Al., U.S.	D11	122
Jasper, Ar., U.S.	I4	120
Jasper, Fl., U.S.	F3	116
Jasper, Ga., U.S.	B1	116
Jasper, In., U.S.	F10	120
Jasper, Mn., U.S.	H2	118
Jasper, Mo., U.S.	G3	120
Jasper, Tn., U.S.	B13	122
Jasper Lake, l., Ab., Can.	C13	138
Jasper National Park, p.o.i., Ab., Can.	D13	138
Jastarnia, Pol.	B14	16
Jászapáti, Hung.	B7	26
Jászberény, Hung.	B6	26
Jász-Nagykun-Szolnok, state, Hung.	B7	26
Jataí, Braz.	G7	84
Jatapu, stm., Braz.	D6	84
Jataté, stm., Mex.	G13	100
Jati, Braz.	D6	88
Jāti, Pak.	F2	54
Játiva see Xàtiva, Spain	F10	20
Jatni, India	H10	54
Jaú, Braz.	L1	88
Jaú, stm., Braz.	H11	86
Jaú, Parque Nacional do, p.o.i., Braz.	I10	86
Jauaperi, stm., Braz.	H11	86
Jauá Sarisariñama, Parque Nacional, p.o.i., Ven.	E9	86
Jauja, Peru	F2	84
Jaunjelgava, Lat.	D7	10
Jaunpiebalga, Lat.	C9	10
Jaunpur, India	F9	54
Java see Jawa, i., Indon.	H6	50
Javalambre, mtn., Spain	D9	20
Java Sea see Jawa, Laut, Indon.	F6	50
Java Trench, unds.	J13	142
Jávea see Xàbia, Spain	F11	20
Javorník, Czech Rep.	F13	16
Javorová skála, mtn., Czech Rep.	G10	16
Jawa (Java), i., Indon.	H6	50
Jawa, Laut (Java Sea), Indon.	F6	50
Jawa Barat, state, Indon.	G5	50
Jawa Tengah, state, Indon.	G7	50
Jawa Timur, state, Indon.	G8	50
Jawhar, Som.	D9	66
Jawi, Indon.	D6	50
Jawor, Pol.	E12	16
Jaworzno, Pol.	F15	16
Jay, Fl., U.S.	G11	122
Jay, Ok., U.S.	H3	120
Jaya, Puncak (Jaya Peak), mtn., Indon.	F10	44
Jaya Peak see Jaya, Puncak, mtn., Indon.	F10	44
Jayapura, Indon.	F11	44
Jayb, Wādī al- (HaʿArava), stm., Asia	H6	58
Jaynes, Az., U.S.	K5	132
Jaypur, India	B6	53
Jayuya, P.R.	B2	104a
Jaželbicy, Russia	B15	10
Jažma, Russia	C21	8
Jeanerette, La., U.S.	H7	122
Jeannette Island see Žannetty, ostrov, i., Russia	A20	34
Jebba, Nig.	H5	64
Jebel, Rom.	D8	26
Jedburgh, Scot., U.K.	F10	12
Jeddah see Jiddah, Sau. Ar.	E4	56
Jędrzejów, Pol.	F16	16
Jeffara (Al-Jifārah), pl., Afr.	C7	64
Jeffers, Mn., U.S.	G3	118
Jefferson, Ga., U.S.	B2	116
Jefferson, Oh., U.S.	C5	114
Jefferson, Or., U.S.	F3	136
Jefferson, S.C., U.S.	B5	116
Jefferson, S.D., U.S.	B1	120
Jefferson, Wi., U.S.	A9	120
Jefferson, Mount, mtn., U.S.	F15	136
Jefferson, Mount, mtn., Nv., U.S.	E8	134
Jefferson, Mount, vol., Or., U.S.	F5	136
Jefferson City, Mo., U.S.	F5	120
Jefferson City, Tn., U.S.	H2	114
Jeffersontown, Ky., U.S.	F12	120
Jeffersonville, Ga., U.S.	D2	116
Jeffersonville, In., U.S.	F12	120
Jeffrey City, Wy., U.S.	E5	126
Jega, Nig.	G5	64
Jehol see Chengde, China	A7	42
Jejsk see Ejsk, Russia	E5	32
Jeju see Cheju, Kor., S.	H7	38
Jēkabpils, Lat.	D8	10
Jekyll Island, i., Ga., U.S.	E4	116
Jelai, stm., Indon.	E7	50
Jelenia Góra, Pol.	F11	16
Jelenia Góra, state, Pol.	E11	16
Jelgava, Lat.	D6	10
Jelgavkrasti, Lat.	C7	10
Jellicoe, On., Can.	B11	118
Jelm Mountain, mtn., Wy., U.S.	F7	126
Jemaja, Pulau, i., Indon.	B4	50
Jember, Indon.	H8	50
Jemez Canyon Reservoir, res., N.M., U.S.	H9	132
Jemez Springs, N.M., U.S.	H10	132
Jemnice, Czech Rep.	H11	16
Jempang, Kenohan, l., Indon.	D9	50
Jena, Ger.	F7	16
Jena, La., U.S.	F6	122
Jendouba, Tun.	H2	24
Jeneponto, Indon.	F11	50
Jenks, Ok., U.S.	H2	120
Jennings, Fl., U.S.	F2	116
Jennings, La., U.S.	G6	122
Jensen, Ut., U.S.	C7	132
Jens Munk Island, i., Nu., Can.	B14	106
Jens Munks Ø, i., Grnld.	E17	141
Jenu, Indon.	D6	50
Jeonju see Chŏnju, Kor., S.	G7	38
Jepara, Indon.	G7	50
Jeparit, Austl.	K4	76
Jeptha Knob, hill, Ky., U.S.	F12	120
Jequié, Braz.	G5	88
Jequitinhonha, Braz.	I5	88
Jequitinhonha, stm., Braz.	H5	88
Jerada, Mor.	C4	64
Jerba, Île de, i., Tun.	C7	64
Jerécuaro, Mex.	E8	100
Jérémie, Haiti	C10	102
Jeremoabo, Braz.	F6	88
Jerevan see Yerevan, Arm.	A5	56
Jerez de García Salinas, Mex.	D7	100
Jerez de la Frontera, Spain	H4	20
Jerez de los Caballeros, Spain	F4	20
Jericho, Austl.	D5	76
Jericho see Arīḥā, Gaza	G6	58
Jericó, Braz.	D7	88
Jerid, Chott, l., Tun.	C6	64
Jerimoth Hill, hill, R.I., U.S.	C14	114
Jeroaquara, Braz.	G7	84
Jerome, Az., U.S.	I4	132
Jerome, Id., U.S.	H12	136
Jersey, dep., Eur.	E6	14
Jersey, i., Jersey	E6	14
Jersey City, N.J., U.S.	D11	114
Jerseyville, Il., U.S.	E7	120
Jerumenha, Braz.	D4	88
Jerusalem see Yerushalayim, Isr.	G6	58
Jervis, Cape, c., Austl.	J1	76
Jervis Bay, b., Austl.	J8	76
Jervis Bay Territory, co., Austl.	J8	76
Jervis Inlet, b., B.C., Can.	F7	138
Jesenice, Czech Rep.	F9	16
Jeseník, Czech Rep.	F13	16
Jesi (Iesi), Italy	G10	22
Jessen, Ger.	E9	16
Jessore, Bngl.	G12	54
Jesup, Ga., U.S.	E4	116
Jesup, Ia., U.S.	B5	120
Jesús Carranza, Mex.	G11	100
Jesús María, Arg.	E5	92
Jesús Menéndez, Cuba	B9	102
Jet, Ok., U.S.	E10	128
Jetmore, Ks., U.S.	C9	128
Jetpur, India	H3	54
Jeune Landing, B.C., Can.	F3	138
Jever, Ger.	C3	16
Jewel Cave National Monument, p.o.i., S.D., U.S.	D8	126
Jewell, Ks., U.S.	B10	128
Jewell Ridge, Va., U.S.	G4	114
Jewett, Il., U.S.	E9	120
Jewett City, Ct., U.S.	C13	114
Jezercës, maja e, mtn., Alb.	B13	24
Jeziorany, Pol.	B16	16
Jhābua, India	G5	54
Jha Jha, India	F11	54
Jhālakāti, Bngl.	G13	54
Jhālāwār, India	F6	54
Jhang Sadar, Pak.	C4	54
Jhānsi, India	F7	54
Jhārgrām, India	G11	54
Jharia, India	G11	54
Jhārsuguda, India	H10	54
Jhelum, Pak.	B4	54
Jhelum, stm., Asia	C4	54
Jhinkpāni, India	G10	54
Jhok Rind, Pak.	C3	54
Jhunjhunūn, India	D5	54
Jiaban, China	I2	42
Jiading, China	F9	42
Jiāganj, India	F12	54
Jiahe, China	I5	42
Jiali, China	C14	54
Jialing, stm., China	G2	42
Jialu, stm., China	E5	42
Jiamusi, China	B11	36
Ji'an, China	D7	38
Ji'an, China	H6	42
Jian, stm., China	H8	42
Jianchang, China	A8	42
Jianchang, China	B10	42
Jianchuan, China	F4	36
Jiande, China	G8	42
Jiang'an, China	G1	42
Jiangcheng, China	A5	48
Jiangdu, China	E8	42
Jiange, China	E1	42
Jianghua, China	I4	42
Jiangjin, China	G2	42
Jiangkou, China	J4	42
Jiangkou, China	H3	42
Jiangkou, China	F4	42
Jiangle, China	H7	42
Jiangling, China	F4	42
Jiangmen, China	J5	42
Jiangmifeng, China	B7	38
Jiangshan, China	G8	42
Jiangsu, state, China	E8	42
Jiangtun, China	J5	42
Jiangxi, state, China	H6	42
Jiangya, China	G4	42
Jiangyin, China	F9	42
Jiangyou, China	F1	42
Jiangzhong, China	D14	54
Jianli, China	G5	42
Jianning, China	H7	42
Jian'ou, China	H8	42
Jianping, China	D3	38
Jianshi, China	F3	42
Jianshui, China	G5	36
Jianyang, China	E5	36
Jianyang, China	H8	42
Jiaocheng, China	C4	42
Jiaohe, China	C7	38
Jiaolai, stm., China	C4	38
Jiaonan, China	D8	42
Jiaoxian, China	C8	42
Jiaozhou Wan, b., China	C9	42
Jiaozuo, China	D5	42
Jiashan, China	E7	42
Jiashi, China	B12	56
Jiashun Hu, l., China	A10	54
Jiawang, China	D7	42
Jiaxian, China	D5	42
Jiaxian, China	B4	42
Jiaxing, China	F9	42
Jiazi, China	J6	42
Jibuti see Djibouti, Dji.	E8	62
Jicarón, Isla, i., Pan.	I7	102
Jičín, Czech Rep.	F11	16
Jiddah (Jeddah), Sau. Ar.	E4	56
Jidingxilin, China	B14	54
Jieshi Wan, b., China	J6	42
Jieshou, China	E6	42
Jiexi, China	J6	42
Jiexiu, China	C4	42
Jieyang, China	J7	42
Jieznas, Lith.	F7	10
Jiguaní, Cuba	B9	102
Jigüey, Bahía de, strt., Cuba	A8	102
Jigzhi, China	E5	36
Jihlava, Czech Rep.	G11	16
Jihlava, stm., Czech Rep.	G12	16
Jihočeský kraj, state, Czech Rep.	G10	16
Jihomoravský kraj, state, Czech Rep.	G12	16
Jijia, stm., Rom.	B14	26
Jijiga, Eth.	F8	62
Jilantai, China	B1	42
Jilib, Som.	D8	66
Jili Hu, l., China	B2	36
Jilin, China	C7	38
Jilin, state, China	C10	36
Jill, Kediet ej, mtn., Maur.	E2	64
Jiloca, stm., Spain	C9	20
Jīma, Eth.	F7	62
Jimbolia, Rom.	D7	26
Jimena de la Frontera, Spain	H5	20
Jiménez, Mex.	B6	100
Jiménez, Mex.	A8	100
Jiménez del Téul, Mex.	D7	100
Jimeta, Nig.	H7	64
Jim Ned Creek, stm., Tx., U.S.	C8	130
Jimo, China	C9	42
Jimsar, China	C2	36
Jim Thorpe, Pa., U.S.	D10	114
Jin (Gam), stm., Asia	A7	48
Jin, stm., China	H7	42
Jinan (Tsinan), China	C7	42
Jincang, China	C9	38
Jincheng, China	D5	42
Jīnd, India	D6	54
Jindabyne, Austl.	K7	76
Jindřichův Hradec, Czech Rep.	G11	16
Jing, stm., China	D3	42
Jing'an, China	G6	42
Jingbian, China	C3	42
Jingbohu, res., China	C8	38
Jingde, China	F8	42
Jingdezhen, China	G7	42
Jinggangshan, China	H6	42
Jinghai, China	B7	42
Jinghe, China	F14	32
Jinghong, China	B5	48
Jingle, China	B4	42
Jingmen, China	F5	42
Jingning, China	D1	42
Jingxi, China	J2	42
Jingxian, China	F8	42
Jingxian, China	C7	42
Jingxian, China	H3	42
Jingxin, China	I6	42
Jingyu, China	C7	38
Jingzhi, China	C8	42
Jinhae see Chinhae, Kor., S.	D1	40
Jinhua, China	G8	42
Jining, China	D7	42
Jining, China	A5	42
Jinja, Ug.	D6	66
Jinjiazhen, China	C5	38
Jinju see Chinju, Kor., S.	G7	38
Jinmu Jiao, c., China	L3	42
Jinning, China	G5	36
Jinotega, Nic.	F5	102
Jinotepe, Nic.	G4	102
Jinping, China	H3	42
Jinqian, stm., China	E3	42
Jinsha, China	H1	42
Jinsha (Yangtze), stm., China	F5	36
Jinshi, China	G4	42
Jintian, China	H6	42
Jintotolo Channel, strt., Phil.	E4	52
Jinxi, China	A9	42
Jinxi, China	H7	42
Jinxian, China	G7	42
Jinxian, China	B6	42
Jinzhou, China	B9	42
Jinzhou, China	A9	42
Ji-Paraná, Braz.	F5	84
Jipijapa, Ec.	H1	86
Jiquiriçá, stm., Braz.	G6	88
Jiri, stm., India	F14	54
Jirkov, Czech Rep.	F9	16
Jishou, China	G3	42
Jisr ash-Shughūr, Syria	C7	58
Jitaúna, Braz.	G6	88
Jiu, stm., Rom.	F10	26
Jiudaoliang, China	F4	42
Jiufeng, China	I7	42
Jiujiang, China	G6	42
Jiulian Shan, mts., China	I6	42
Jiuliguan, China	F6	42
Jiuling Shan, mts., China	G6	42
Jiulong, China	J5	42
Jiulong, stm., China	I7	42
Jiuquan, China	D4	36
Jiutai, China	B6	38
Jiuyuanqu, China	D4	42
Jiuzhan, China	C7	38
Jiuzhen, China	I7	42
Jiwen, China	A9	36
Jixi, China	B9	38
Jixi, China	F8	42
Jixian, China	A7	42
Jixian, China	D6	42
Jiyi, China	D4	42
Jiyuan, China	D5	42
Jiyun, stm., China	B7	42
Jīzān, Sau. Ar.	F5	56
Jizl, Wādī al-, stm., Sau. Ar.	K8	58
J. J. Castelli see Castelli, Arg.	B7	92
J.M. Lencinas see Las Catitas, Arg.	F3	92
Joaçaba, Braz.	C12	92
Joana Coeli, Braz.	A1	88
Joanes, Braz.	D8	84
João Câmara, Braz.	C8	88
João Monlevade, Braz.	J4	88
João Pessoa, Braz.	D8	88
João Pinheiro, Braz.	I2	88
Joaquim Távora, Braz.	A12	92
Joaquin, Tx., U.S.	F4	122
Joaquín V. González, Arg.	B5	92
Jobos, P.R.	C3	104a
Job Peak, mtn., Nv., U.S.	D7	134
Jocolí, Arg.	F3	92
Jódar, Spain	G7	20
Jodhpur, India	E4	54
Jodiya, India	G3	54
Joensuu, Fin.	E13	8
Joetsu, Japan	B11	40
Jõgeva, Est.	G12	8
Jog Falls, wtfl, India	D2	53
Joggins, N.S., Can.	E12	110
Jogjakarta see Yogyakarta, Indon.	G7	50
Jōhana, Japan	C9	40
Johannesburg, S. Afr.	E8	70
John Day, Or., U.S.	F8	136
John Day, stm., Or., U.S.	E6	136
John Day, Middle Fork, stm., Or., U.S.	F8	136
John Day, North Fork, stm., Or., U.S.	F8	136
John Day Fossil Beds National Monument, p.o.i., Or., U.S.	F7	136
John F. Kennedy Space Center, sci., Fl., U.S.	H5	116
John H. Kerr Reservoir, res., U.S.	H7	114
John Martin Reservoir, res., Co., U.S.	C6	128
John o' Groats, Scot., U.K.	C9	12
John Redmond Reservoir, res., Ks., U.S.	F1	120
Johns Island, i., S.C., U.S.	D5	116
Johnson, Ar., U.S.	H3	120
Johnson, Ks., U.S.	D7	128
Johnsonburg, Pa., U.S.	C7	114
Johnson City, N.Y., U.S.	B10	114
Johnson City, Tn., U.S.	H3	114
Johnson City, Tx., U.S.	D9	130
Johnsondale, Ca., U.S.	H7	134
Johnson Draw, stm., Tx., U.S.	D6	130
Johnson Point, c., St. Vin.	o11	105e
Johnsonville, S.C., U.S.	C6	116
Johnston, Ia., U.S.	C4	120
Johnston, S.C., U.S.	C4	116
Johnston, Lake, l., Austl.	F4	74
Johnston Atoll, at., Oc.	B10	72
Johnstown, Co., U.S.	G8	126
Johnstown, N.Y., U.S.	G2	110
Johnstown, Oh., U.S.	D3	114
Johnstown, Pa., U.S.	D7	114
Johor, state, Malay.	L6	48
Johor Bahru, Malay.	L6	48
Joigny, Fr.	G12	14
Joiner, Ar., U.S.	B8	122
Joinville, Braz.	C13	92
Joinville Island, i., Ant.	B35	81
Jojogan, Indon.	G7	50
Jokkmokk, Swe.	C8	8
Jökulsá á Brú, stm., Ice.	k32	8a
Jökulsårgljúfur Nasjonalpark, p.o.i., Ice.	k32	8a
Joliet, Il., U.S.	C9	120
Joliette, Qc., Can.	D3	110
Jolo, Phil.	G3	52
Jolo Group, is., Phil.	G3	52
Jolo Island, i., Phil.	H3	52
Jombang, Indon.	G8	50
Jomda, China	E4	36
Jonava, Lith.	E7	10
Jones, Ok., U.S.	F11	128
Jonesboro, Ar., U.S.	I7	120
Jonesboro, Ga., U.S.	C1	116
Jonesboro, Il., U.S.	G8	120
Jonesboro, La., U.S.	E6	122
Jonesborough, Tn., U.S.	H3	114
Jones Mill, Ar., U.S.	C6	122
Jonesport, Me., U.S.	F9	110
Jones Sound, strt., Nu., Can.	B8	141
Jonestown, Ms., U.S.	C8	122
Jonesville, La., U.S.	F7	122
Jonesville, Mi., U.S.	B1	114
Jonglei Canal, can., Sudan	F6	62
Joniškėlis, Lith.	D6	10
Joniškis, Lith.	D6	10
Jönköping, Swe.	H6	8
Jönköping, state, Swe.	H6	8
Jonquière, Qc., Can.	B5	110
Jonuta, Mex.	F12	100
Jonzac, Fr.	D5	18
Joplin, Mo., U.S.	G3	120
Joplin, Mt., U.S.	B16	136
Joppa, Il., U.S.	G9	120
Jora, India	E6	54
Jordan, Mn., U.S.	G5	118
Jordan, Mt., U.S.	G6	124
Jordan, ctry., Asia	H7	58
Jordan (Al-Urdunn) (HaYarden), stm., Asia	F6	58
Jordan, stm., Ut., U.S.	C5	132
Jordan Creek, stm., U.S.	H10	136
Jordânia, Braz.	H5	88
Jordan Valley, Or., U.S.	G10	136
Jordão, stm., Braz.	B12	92
Jorge Montt, Isla, i., Chile	J2	90
Jorhāt, India	C7	46
Jornado del Muerto, des., N.M., U.S.	J10	132
Joroinen, Fin.	E12	8
Jos, Nig.	G6	64
Jose Abad Santos, Phil.	H5	52
José Batlle y Ordóñez, Ur.	F10	92
José Bonifácio, Braz.	K1	88
José de Freitas, Braz.	C4	88
José de San Martín, Arg.	H2	90
José Pedro Varela, Ur.	F10	92
Joseph, Or., U.S.	E9	136
Joseph, Lac, l., Nf., Can.	E17	106
Joseph Bonaparte Gulf, b., Austl.	B5	74
Joshīmath, India	C7	54
Jōshin-Etsu-kōgen-kokuritsu-kōen, p.o.i., Japan	C11	40
Joshua, Tx., U.S.	B10	130
Joshua Tree, Ca., U.S.	I9	134
Joshua Tree National Park, p.o.i., Ca., U.S.	J10	134
Jostedalsbreen, ice, Nor.	F2	8
Jostedalsbreen Nasjonalpark, p.o.i., Nor.	F2	8
Jotunheimen Nasjonalpark, p.o.i., Nor.	F2	8
Joubertina, S. Afr.	H6	70
Jourdanton, Tx., U.S.	F9	130
Joutsijärvi, Fin.	C13	8
Joviânia, Braz.	I1	88
Jowai, India	F14	54
Joya, Mex.	H6	130
Joyce, La., U.S.	F6	122
Joyuda, P.R.	B1	104a
J. Percy Priest Lake, res., Tn., U.S.	H11	120
J. Strom Thurmond Reservoir, res., U.S.	C3	116
Juami, stm., Braz.	I7	86
Juana Díaz, P.R.	B2	104a
Juan Aldama, Mex.	C7	100
Juan Bautista Alberdi, Arg.	C5	92
Juan de Fuca, Strait of, strt., N.A.	B2	136
Juan de Garay, Arg.	I5	92
Juan de Nova, Île, i., Reu.	D7	68
Juan E. Barra, Arg.	H7	92
Juan Fernández, Archipiélago, is., Chile	I6	82
Juanjuí, Peru	E2	84
Juan N. Fernández, Arg.	I8	92
Juan Viñas, C.R.	H6	102
Juárez see Benito Juárez, Arg.	H8	92
Juárez, Mex.	F8	98
Juárez, Mex.	B8	100
Juatinga, Ponta de, c., Braz.	L3	88
Juazeirinho, Braz.	D7	88
Juazeiro, Braz.	E5	88
Juazeiro do Norte, Braz.	D6	88
Juba, Sudan	G6	62
Juba see Genalē, stm., Afr.	C8	66
Juba see Jubba, stm., Afr.	D8	66
Jubal, Strait of see Gûbâl, Madîq, strt., Egypt	K4	58
Jubayl, Leb.	D6	58
Jubba (Genalē), stm., Afr.	D8	66
Juby, Cap, c., Mor.	D2	64
Júcar (Xúquer), stm., Spain	E10	20
Juchipila, Mex.	E7	100
Juchitán de Zaragoza, Mex.	G11	100
Jucurucu, stm., Braz.	I5	88
Jucurutu, Braz.	C7	88
Judenburg, Aus.	C11	22
Judino, Russia	B22	10
Judique, N.S., Can.	E15	110
Judith, stm., Mt., U.S.	C17	136
Judith Gap, Mt., U.S.	D17	136
Judith Peak, mtn., Mt., U.S.	C17	136
Judoma, stm., Russia	E16	34
Jufari, stm., Braz.	H10	86
Jug, stm., Russia	G21	8
Jugorskij poluostrov, pen., Russia	A10	32
Juhnov, Russia	F18	10
Juidongshan, China	J7	42
Juigalpa, Nic.	F5	102
Juist, i., Ger.	C2	16
Juiz de Fora, Braz.	K4	88
Jujuy, state, Arg.	D3	90
Jukagirskoe ploskogor'e, plat., Russia	C19	34
Jukta, Russia	B19	32
Jula, stm., Russia	E21	8
Julesburg, Co., U.S.	G10	126
Juliaca, Peru	G3	84
Julia Creek, Austl.	C3	76
Julia Creek, stm., Austl.	C3	76
Julianadorp, Neth. Ant.	p22	104g
Julian Alps, mts., Eur.	D10	22
Juliana Top, mtn., Sur.	C6	84
Julianehåb (Qaqortoq), Grnld.	E16	141
Jülich, Ger.	F2	16
Juliette, Lake, res., Ga., U.S.	D2	116
Julimes, Mex.	A6	100
Júlio de Castilhos, Braz.	D11	92
Juma, Russia	D15	8
Juma, stm., China	B6	42
Jumba, Som.	E8	66
Jumilla, Spain	F9	20
Jumlā, Nepal	D9	54
Jūnāgadh, India	H3	54
Juncos, P.R.	B4	104a
Junction, Tx., U.S.	D8	130
Junction City, Ar., U.S.	E6	122
Junction City, Ks., U.S.	B12	128
Junction City, Ky., U.S.	G13	120
Jundah, Austl.	E4	76
Jundiaí, Braz.	L2	88
Juneau, Ak., U.S.	E13	140
Juneau, Wi., U.S.	H10	118
Junee, Austl.	J6	76
June Lake, Ca., U.S.	F6	134
Jungar Qi, China	B4	42
Jungfrau, mtn., Switz.	D4	22
Junggar Pendi, bas., China	B2	36
Juniata, Ne., U.S.	G14	126
Juniata, stm., Pa., U.S.	D8	114
Junín, Arg.	G7	92
Junín, Ec.	H1	86
Junín de los Andes, Arg.	G2	90
Juniper, N.B., Can.	D9	110
Junipero Serra Peak, mtn., Ca., U.S.	G4	134
Jūniyah, Leb.	E6	58
Junlian, China	F5	36
Junnar, India	B1	53
Junqueiro, Braz.	E7	88
Junxian, China	E4	42
Juodkrantė, Lith.	E3	10
Juozapinės kalnas, hill, Lith.	F8	10
Juparanã, Lagoa, l., Braz.	J5	88
Jupiter, Fl., U.S.	J5	116
Juquiá, Braz.	B14	92
Juquiá, Ponta do, c., Braz.	B14	92
Jur, Russia	E16	34
Jur, stm., Sudan	F5	62
Jura, Mol.	B16	26
Jura, state, Fr.	C11	18
Jura, mts., Eur.	B12	18
Jura, i., Scot., U.K.	F7	12
Jūra, stm., Lith.	E5	10
Jurbarkas, Lith.	E5	10
Jurenino, Russia	G20	8
Jurevec, Russia	H20	8
Jurga, Russia	C15	32
Juriti, Braz.	D6	84
Jūrmala, Lat.	C6	10
Jurong, China	F8	42
Juruá, stm., S.A.	D4	84
Juruena, stm., Braz.	E6	84
Jurumirim, Represa de, res., Braz.	L1	88
Jusepín, Ven.	C10	86
Juškovo, Russia	G21	8
Justiniano Posse, Arg.	F6	92
Justino Solari see Mariano I. Loza, Arg.	D8	92
Justo Daract, Arg.	F5	92
Jutaí, stm., Braz.	D4	84
Jüterbog, Ger.	D9	16
Jutiapa, Guat.	E3	102
Juticalpa, Hond.	E4	102
Jutland see Jylland, reg., Den.	H3	8
Jutrosin, Pol.	E13	16
Juventud, Isla de la (Pines, Isle of), i., Cuba	B6	102
Juxian, China	D8	42
Juye, China	D6	42
Juža, Russia	H20	8
Južna Morava, stm., Yugo.	F8	26
Južno-Enisejskij, Russia	C17	32
Južno-Sahalinsk, Russia	G17	34
Južno-Ural'sk, Russia	D10	32
Južnyj, mys, c., Russia	E20	34
Južnyj Ural, mts., Russia	D9	32
Jwayyā, Leb.	E6	58
Jyekundo see Yushu, China	E4	36
Jylland (Jutland), reg., Den.	H3	8
Jyväskylä, Fin.	E11	8

K

Name	Map Ref.	Page
K2, mtn., Asia	B12	56
Kaabong, Ug.	D6	66
Kaahka, Turkmen.	B8	56
Kaala, mtn., Hi., U.S.	B3	78a
Kaala-Gomen, N. Cal.	m15	79d
Kaapstad see Cape Town, S. Afr.	H4	70
Kaarli, Est.	A9	10
Kaatoan, Mount, mtn., Phil.	F5	52
Kabacan, Phil.	G5	52
Kabaena, Pulau, i., Indon.	G7	44
Kabah, hist., Mex.	B3	102
Kabala, S.L.	H2	64
Kabale, Ug.	E5	66
Kabalega Falls, wtfl, Ug.	D6	66
Kabalo, D.R.C.	F5	66
Kabambare, D.R.C.	E5	66
Kabanjahe, Indon.	K4	48
Kabankalan, Phil.	F4	52
Kabardin-Balkaria see Kabardino-Balkarija, state, Russia	F6	32
Kabardino-Balkarija, state, Russia	F6	32
Kabba, Nig.	H6	64
Kabbani, stm., India	F3	53
Kåbdalis, Swe.	C8	8
Kabetogama Lake, l., Mn., U.S.	C5	118
Kab-hegy, mtn., Hung.	B4	26
Kabinda, D.R.C.	F4	66
Kabinu, Indon.	A9	50
Kabīr Kūh, mts., Iran	C6	56
Kabna, Sudan	D6	62
Kābol, Afg.	C10	56
Kābol, state, Afg.	A2	54
Kabompo, Zam.	C3	68
Kabompo, stm., Zam.	C3	68
Kabongo, D.R.C.	F5	66
Kābul see Kābol, Afg.	C10	56
Kabul (Kābol), stm., Asia	A4	54
Kabwe, Zam.	C4	68
Kabylie, reg., Alg.	H14	20
Kačanik, Yugo.	G8	26
Kačerginė, Lith.	F6	10
Kachchh, Gulf of, b., India	G2	54
Kačiry, Kaz.	D13	32
Kačkanar, Russia	C10	32
Kačug, Russia	D19	32
Kadaiyanallūr, India	G3	53
Kadaň, Czech Rep.	F9	16
Kadan Kyun, i., Mya.	F4	48
Kadapongan, Pulau, i., Indon.	F9	50
Kaddam, res., India	B4	53
Kade, Ghana	H4	64
Kadéï, stm., Afr.	G2	62
Kadi, India	G4	54
Kadina, Austl.	F7	74
Kading, stm., Laos	C7	48
Kadınhanı, Tur.	E15	28
Kadiolo, Mali	G3	64
Kādīpur, India	E9	54
Kadiri, India	D4	53
Kadirli, Tur.	A7	58
Kadoka, S.D., U.S.	D11	126
Kadoma, Zimb.	D4	68
Kaduj, Russia	A20	10
Kaduna, Nig.	G6	64
Kaduna, stm., Nig.	G6	64
Kāduqlī, Sudan	E5	62
Kadūr, India	E3	53
Kaduvu, i., Fiji	q19	79e
Kaduvu Passage, strt., Fiji	q18	79e
Kadyj, Russia	H20	8
Kadžerom, Russia	B9	32
Kaédi, Maur.	F2	64
Kaélé, Cam.	B2	66
Kaena Point, c., Hi., U.S.	B3	78a
Kaesŏng, Kor., N.	F7	38
Kafanchan, Nig.	H6	64
Kaffrine, Sen.	G1	64
Kafia Kingi, Sudan	F4	62
Kafr el-Dauwar, Egypt	G1	58
Kafr el-Sheikh, Egypt	G1	58
Kafr el-Zaiyât, Egypt	H1	58
Kafr Saʿd, Egypt	G2	58
Kafue, Zam.	D4	68
Kafue, stm., Zam.	D4	68
Kaga, Japan	C9	40
Kaga Bandoro, C.A.R.	C3	66
Kāgān, Pak.	A4	54
Kagan, Uzb.	G10	32
Kagawa, state, Japan	E6	40
Kagawong, Lake, l., On., Can.	C7	112
Kagaznagar, India	B4	53
Kagera, stm., Afr.	E6	66
Kagmar, Sudan	E6	62
Kagoshima, Japan	H3	40
Kagoshima, state, Japan	H3	40
Kagoshima-wan, b., Japan	H3	40
Kahama, Tan.	E6	66
Kahayan, stm., Indon.	D8	50
Ka-Hem see Malyj Enisej, stm., Russia	F8	34
Kahemba, D.R.C.	F3	66
Kahiu Point, c., Hi., U.S.	B5	78a
Kahoka, Mo., U.S.	D6	120
Kahoolawe, i., Hi., U.S.	C5	78a
Kahouanne, Îlet à, i., Guad.	h5	105c
Kahramanmaraş (Maraş), Tur.	A7	58
Kahraman Maraş, state, Tur.	A7	58
Kahuku Point, c., Hi., U.S.	B4	78a
Kahului, Hi., U.S.	C5	78a
Kai, Kepulauan (Kai Islands), is., Indon.	G9	44
Kaiapoi, N.Z.	F5	80
Kaibab Plateau, plat., Az., U.S.	G4	132
Kaidu, stm., China	F15	32
Kaieteur Fall, wtfl, Guy.	E12	86
Kaieteur National Park, p.o.i., Guy.	E12	86
Kaifeng, China	D6	42
Kaihua, China	G8	42
Kai Islands see Kai, Kepulauan, is., Indon.	G9	44
Kaijian, China	J4	42
Kaijiang, China	F2	42
Kai Kecil, i., Indon.	G9	44
Kaikoura, N.Z.	F5	80
Kailahun, S.L.	H2	64
Kailas see Kangrinboqê Feng, mtn., China	C8	54
Kailāshahar, India	F14	54
Kailas Range see Gangdisê Shan, mts., China	C9	54
Kaili, China	H2	42
Kailu, China	C4	38
Kailua, Hi., U.S.	B4	78a
Kailua Kona, Hi., U.S.	D6	78a
Kaïmaktsalán (Kajmakčalan), mtn., Eur.	C15	24
Kaimana, Indon.	F9	44
Kaimon-dake, vol., Japan	H3	40
Kainabrivier, stm., Nmb.	E4	70
Kainan, Japan	E8	40
Kainantu, Pap. N. Gui.	b4	79a
Kainji Reservoir, res., Nig.	G5	64
Kaipara Harbour, b., N.Z.	C5	80
Kaiparowits Plateau, plat., Ut., U.S.	F5	132
Kaiping, China	J5	42
Kairouan, Tun.	I3	24
Kairuku, Pap. N. Gui.	b4	79a
Kaiserslautern, Ger.	G3	16
Kaišiadorys, Lith.	F7	10
Kait, Tanjung, c., Indon.	E5	50
Kaitangata, N.Z.	H3	80
Kaithal, India	D6	54
Kaituma, stm., Guy.	D12	86
Kaiwi Channel, strt., Hi., U.S.	B4	78a
Kaixian, China	F3	42
Kaiyang, China	H2	42
Kaiyuan, China	G5	36
Kaiyuan, China	C6	38
Kaiyuancheng, China	C6	38
Kaiyuh Mountains, mts., Ak., U.S.	D8	140
Kajaani, Fin.	D12	8
Kajabbi, Austl.	B2	76
Kajakī, Band-e, res., Afg.	C10	56
Kajang, Malay.	K5	48
Kajga, Kaz.	D10	32
Kajmysovy, Russia	C13	32
Kajo Kaji, Sudan	G6	62
Kaka, Sudan	E6	62
Kakabeka Falls, wtfl, On., Can.	C9	118
Kakagi Lake, l., On., Can.	B5	118
Kakamas, S. Afr.	F5	70
Kakamega, Kenya	D6	66
Kakamigahara, Japan	D9	40
Kakata, Lib.	H2	64
Kākdwīp, India	H12	54
Kakegawa, Japan	E10	40
Kakhonak, Ak., U.S.	E9	140
Kakhovka Reservoir see Kakhovs'ke vodoskhovyshche, res., Ukr.	E4	32
Kakhovs'ke vodoskhovyshche, res., Ukr.	E4	32
Kākināda (Cocanada), India	C6	53
Kakisa Lake, l., N.T., Can.	C7	106
Kakizaki, Japan	B11	40
Kakogawa, Japan	E7	40
Kakšaal-Too, hrebet, mts., Asia	F13	32
Kaktovik, Ak., U.S.	B11	140
Kakuda, Japan	B13	40
Kakus, stm., Malay.	B8	50
Kakwa, stm., Ab., Can.	B12	138
Kala, stm., Sri L.	G4	53
Kalaa Kebira, Tun.	I4	24
Kalabahi, Indon.	G7	44
Kalabakan, Malay.	A10	50
Kalabo, Zam.	D3	68
Kalač, Russia	D6	32
Kalačinsk, Russia	D12	32
Kalač-na-Donu, Russia	E6	32
Kaladan, stm., Asia	G14	54
Ka Lae, c., Hi., U.S.	E6	78a
Kalahari Desert, des., Afr.	C5	70
Kalahari Gemsbok National Park, p.o.i., S. Afr.	D5	70
Kalajoki, Fin.	D10	8
Kalakan, Russia	E12	34
Kalām, Pak.	B11	56
Kalama, Wa., U.S.	D4	136
Kalamalka Lake, l., B.C., Can.	F11	138
Kalamáta, Grc.	F5	28
Kalamazoo, Mi., U.S.	F4	112
Kalamazoo, stm., Mi., U.S.	F4	112
Kalamb, India	B1	53
Kalampising, Indon.	B10	50
Kalao, Pulau, i., Indon.	G12	50
Kalaotoa, Pulau, i., Indon.	G7	44
Kalar, stm., Russia	E12	34
Kalasin, Thai.	D6	48
Kalašnikovo, Russia	C18	10
Kalāt, Pak.	D10	56
Kalávryta, Grc.	E5	28
Kalaw, Mya.	B3	48
Kalbarri, Austl.	E2	74
Kale, Tur.	F11	28
Kale, Tur.	G12	28
Kaleden, B.C., Can.	G11	138
Kalegauk Island, i., Mya.	E3	48
Kalehe, D.R.C.	E5	66
Kalemie, D.R.C.	F5	66
Kalemyo, Mya.	D7	46
Kaletwa, Mya.	H14	54
Kalevala, Russia	D14	8
Kalewa, Mya.	D7	46
Kálfafell, Ice.	k31	8a
Kalgan see Zhangjiakou, China	A6	42
Kalgoorlie-Boulder, Austl.	F4	74
Kaliakra, nos, c., Blg.	F15	26
Kalianda, Indon.	F4	50
Kalibo, Phil.	E4	52
Kalima, D.R.C.	E5	66
Kalimantan (Borneo), i., Asia	F5	44

Name	Map Ref.	Page
Kalimantan Barat, state, Indon.	D7	50
Kalimantan Selatan, state, Indon.	E9	50
Kalimantan Tengah, state, Indon.	D8	50
Kalimantan Timur, state, Indon.	C10	50
Kālimpang, India	E12	54
Kālīnadi, stm., India	D2	53
Kalinin see Tver', Russia	D18	10
Kaliningrad (Königsberg), Russia	F3	10
Kaliningradskaja oblast', co., Russia	F4	10
Kalinkavičy, Bela.	H12	10
Kaliro, Ug.	D6	66
Kalisat, Indon.	H8	50
Kāli Sindh, stm., India	F6	54
Kalispell, Mt., U.S.	B12	136
Kalisz, Pol.	E14	16
Kalisz, state, Pol.	E13	16
Kalisz Pomorski, Pol.	C11	16
Kaliua, Tan.	E6	66
Kaliveli Tank, l., India	E4	53
Kalixälven, stm., Swe.	C9	8
Kaljazin, Russia	C20	10
Kālka, India	C6	54
Kalkaska, Mi., U.S.	D4	112
Kalkfonteindam, res., S. Afr.	F7	70
Kalkım, Tur.	D10	28
Kalkrand, Nmb.	D3	70
Kallar Kahār, Pak.	B4	54
Kallavesi, l., Fin.	E12	8
Kallsjön, l., Swe.	E5	8
Kalmar, Swe.	H6	8
Kalmar, state, Swe.	H7	8
Kalmarsund, strt., Swe.	H7	8
Kalmykia see Kalmykija, state, Russia	E7	32
Kalmykija, state, Russia	E7	32
Kalmykovo, Kaz.	E8	32
Kālna, India	G12	54
Kalocsa, Hung.	C5	26
Kalofer, Blg.	G12	26
Kalohi Channel, strt., Hi., U.S.	B4	78a
Kalol, India	G4	54
Kālol, India	G4	54
Kalomo, Zam.	D4	68
Kalona, Ia., U.S.	J7	118
Kalone Peak, mtn., B.C., Can.	D4	138
Kalpeni Island, i., India	F1	53
Kālpi, India	E7	54
Kalpin, China	A12	56
Kalsūbai, mtn., India	B1	53
Kaltag, Ak., U.S.	D8	140
Kaluga, Russia	F19	10
Kalukalukuang, Pulau, i., Indon.	F10	50
Kalumburu, Austl.	B5	74
Kałuszyn, Pol.	D17	16
Kalutara, Sri L.	H4	53
Kalužskaja oblast', co., Russia	F18	10
Kalyān, India	B1	53
Kalyāndurg, India	D3	53
Kálymnos, Grc.	G9	28
Kálymnos, i., Grc.	F9	28
Kama, stm., Russia	C8	32
Kamae, Japan	G4	40
Kamaishi, Japan	E14	38
Kamakou, mtn., Hi., U.S.	B5	78a
Kamakura, Japan	D12	40
Kamālia, Pak.	C4	54
Kamamaung, Mya.	D3	48
Kaman, stm., Laos	E8	48
Kamanjab, Nmb.	D1	68
Kamarān, i., Yemen	F5	56
Kāmāreddi, India	B4	53
Kama Reservoir see Kamskoe vodohranilišče, res., Russia	C9	32
Kamas, Ut., U.S.	C5	132
Kamay, Tx., U.S.	H10	128
Kambalda, Austl.	F4	74
Kambam, India	G3	53
Kambarka, Russia	C8	32
Kambja, Est.	B9	10
Kambove, D.R.C.	G5	66
Kamčatka, stm., Russia	E21	34
Kamčatka, poluostrov, pen., Russia	E19	34
Kamčatskij poluostrov, pen., Russia	E21	34
Kamčatskij zaliv, b., Russia	E21	34
Kamchatka Peninsula see Kamčatka, poluostrov, pen., Russia	E20	34
Kameda, Japan	B12	40
Kamen', gora, mtn., Russia	C8	34
Kameng, stm., India	E14	54
Kamenjak, Rt, c., Cro.	F10	22
Kamenka, Kaz.	D11	32
Kamenka, Russia	D21	8
Kamenka, Russia	D6	32
Kamen'-na-Obi, Russia	D14	32
Kameno, Blg.	G14	26
Kamen-Rybolov, Russia	B9	38
Kamenskoe, Russia	D22	34
Kamensk-Ural'skij, Russia	C10	32
Kamenz, Ger.	E10	16
Kāmet, mtn., Asia	C7	54
Kam'ians'ke, Ukr.	D16	26
Kamień Krajeński, Pol.	C13	16
Kamienna Góra, Pol.	F12	16
Kamieńsk, Pol.	E15	16
Kamieskroon, S. Afr.	G3	70
Kamiiso, Japan	D14	38
Kamilukuak Lake, l., Can.	C10	106
Kamina, D.R.C.	F4	66
Kaminak Lake, l., Nu., Can.	C12	106
Kaminoyama, Japan	A13	40
Kaminuriak Lake, l., Nu., Can.	C12	106
Kamioka, Japan	C10	40
Kámiros, hist., Grc.	G10	28
Kamjanec, Bela.	H6	10
Kamkhat Muḥaywir, hill, Jord.	G7	58
Kamloops, B.C., Can.	F10	138
Kamnik, Slvn.	D11	22
Kamo, Japan	B12	40
Kamoa Mountains, mts., Guy.	C6	84
Kamojima, Japan	E7	40
Kāmoke, Pak.	B5	54
Kampala, Ug.	D6	66
Kampar, Malay.	J5	48
Kampar, stm., Indon.	C3	50
Kamparkalns, hill, Lat.	C5	10
Kampar Kanan, stm., Indon.	C2	50
Kampen, Neth.	B14	14
Kamphaeng Phet, Thai.	D4	48
Kampinoski Park Narodowy, p.o.i., Pol.	D16	16
Kâmpóng Cham, Camb.	F7	48
Kâmpóng Chhnăng, Camb.	F7	48
Kâmpóng Kântuŏt, Camb.	G7	48
Kâmpóng Saôm, Camb.	G6	48
Kâmpóng Saôm, Chhâk, b., Camb.	G6	48
Kâmpóng Thum, Camb.	F7	48
Kampong Ulu, Mya.	G4	48
Kâmpôt, Camb.	G7	48
Kampsville, Il., U.S.	E7	120
Kampti, Burkina	G4	64
Kampuchea see Cambodia, ctry., Asia	C3	48
Kampungbaru, Indon.	D3	50
Kampung Litang, Malay.	A11	50
Kamrau, Teluk, b., Indon.	F9	44
Kamsack, Sk., Can.	C12	124
Kamskoe vodohranilišče, res., Russia	C9	32
Kāmthi, India	H7	54
Kamuela, Hi., U.S.	D6	78a
Kámuk, Cerro, mtn., C.R.	H6	102
Kamundan, stm., Indon.	F9	44
Kamyšin, Russia	D7	32
Kamyšlov, Russia	C10	32
Kan, stm., Russia	C17	32
Kanaaupscow, stm., Qc., Can.	E15	106
Kanab, Ut., U.S.	F4	132
Kanab Creek, stm., U.S.	G4	132
Kanaga Island, i., Ak., U.S.	g23	140a
Kanagawa, state, Japan	D12	40
Kanakapura, India	E3	53
Kananga (Luluabourg), D.R.C.	F4	66
Kananggar, Indon.	I12	50
Kanangra-Boyd National Park, p.o.i., Austl.	I7	76
Kanaš, Russia	C7	32
Kanawha, Ia., U.S.	B4	120
Kanawha, stm., W.V., U.S.	F4	114
Kanazawa, Japan	C9	40
Kanbauk, Mya.	E3	48
Kanchanaburi, Thai.	F4	48
Kanchanjanggā (Kānchenjunga), mtn., Asia	E11	54
Kānchenjunga (Kanchanjanggā), mtn., Asia	E11	54
Kānchipuram, India	E4	53
Kanchow see Ganzhou, China	I6	42
Kańczuga, Pol.	F18	16
Kanda, Japan	F3	40
Kandahar, Sk., Can.	C9	124
Kandalakša, Russia	C15	8
Kandalakšskaja guba, b., Russia	C15	8
Kandale, D.R.C.	F3	66
Kandang, Indon.	K3	48
Kandangan, Indon.	E9	50
Kandanghaur, Indon.	G6	50
Kandé, Togo	H5	64
Kandhkot, Pak.	D2	54
Kandi, India	G12	54
Kandi, Tanjung, c., Indon.	E7	44
Kandıra, Tur.	B13	28
Kandla, India	G3	54
Kandos, Austl.	I7	76
Kandreho, Madag.	D8	68
Kandy, Sri L.	H5	53
Kane, Pa., U.S.	C7	114
Kane Basin, b., N.A.	B12	141
Kanem, state, Chad	E3	62
Kaneohe, Hi., U.S.	B4	78a
Kanëvka, Russia	C18	8
Kang, Bots.	C6	70
Kangaba, Mali	G3	64
Kangalassy, Russia	D15	34
Kangâmiut, Grnld.	D15	141
Kangān, Iran	D7	56
Kangar, Malay.	I5	48
Kangaroo Island, i., Austl.	G7	74
Kangāvar, Iran	C6	56
Kangbao, China	C7	36
Kangding, China	C9	46
Kangean, Kepulauan (Kangean Islands), is., Indon.	G9	50
Kangean, Pulau, i., Indon.	G9	50
Kangean Islands see Kangean, Kepulauan, is., Indon.	G9	50
Kangeeak Point, c., Nu., Can.	B18	106
Kangerlussuaq, b., Grnld.	D19	141
Kangersuatsiaq see Prøven, Grnld.	C14	141
Kanger Valley National Park, p.o.i., India	B6	53
Kanggye, Kor., N.	D7	38
Kanghwa-do, i., Kor., S.	F7	38
Kangiqsualujjuaq, Qc., Can.	D17	106
Kangiqsujuaq, Qc., Can.	C16	106
Kangirsuk, Qc., Can.	C17	106
Kangmar, China	D12	54
Kangnŭng, Kor., S.	B1	40
Kango, Gabon	D2	66
Kangping, China	C5	38
Kangpu, China	F4	36
Kangrinboqê Feng, mtn., China	C8	54
Kangshan, Tai.	J9	42
Kangsŏ, Kor., N.	E6	38
Kangto, mtn., Asia	D14	54
Kangwŏn-do, state, Kor., S.	B1	40
Kanha National Park, p.o.i., India	G8	54
Kanhar, stm., India	F9	54
Kanhsien see Ganzhou, China	I6	42
Kani, Mya.	A2	48
Kaniama, D.R.C.	F4	66
Kanibadam, Taj.	A11	56
Kaniet Islands, is., Pap. N. Gui.	a4	79a
Kanigiri, India	D4	53
Kanin, poluostrov, pen., Russia	C21	8
Kanin-Kamen', mts., Russia	B21	8
Kanin Nos, Russia	B20	8
Kanin Nos, mys, c., Russia	B20	8
Kaniva, Austl.	K3	76
Kanjiža, Yugo.	C7	26
Kankaanpää, Fin.	F10	8
Kankakee, Il., U.S.	G2	112
Kankan, Gui.	G3	64
Kānker, India	H8	54
Kankunskij, Russia	E14	34
Kanmaw Kyun, i., Mya.	G4	48
Kannack, Viet.	E9	48
Kannad, India	H5	54
Kannapolis, N.C., U.S.	A5	116
Kannauj, India	E7	54
Kanniyākumari, India	G3	53
Kannod, India	G6	54
Kannur see Cannanore, India	F2	53
Kannus, Fin.	E10	8
Kano, Nig.	G6	64
Kanonji, Japan	E6	40
Kanopolis, Ks., U.S.	C10	128
Kanorado, Ks., U.S.	B6	128
Kanosh, Ut., U.S.	E4	132
Kanoya, Japan	H3	40
Kanpetlet, Mya.	B1	48
Kānpur (Cawnpore), India	E7	54
Kansas, state, U.S.	C10	128
Kansas, stm., Ks., U.S.	B13	128
Kansas City, Ks., U.S.	E3	120
Kansas City, Mo., U.S.	E3	120
Kansk, Russia	C17	32
Kansŏng, Kor., S.	A1	40
Kan-sou see Gansu, state, China	D5	36
Kansu see Gansu, state, China	D5	36
Kantang, Thai.	I4	48
Kantchari, Burkina	G5	64
Kānth, India	D7	54
Kantishna, stm., Ak., U.S.	D9	140
Kantō-heiya, pl., Japan	D12	40
Kanton, i., Kir.	D9	72
Kantō-sanchi, mts., Japan	D11	40
Kantu-long, Mya.	C3	48
Kantunilkin, Mex.	B4	102
Kanuku Mountains, mts., Guy.	F12	86
Kanuma, Japan	C12	40
Kanye, Bots.	D7	70
Kanyutkwin, Mya.	C3	48
Kaohiung see Kaohsiung, Tai.	J8	42
Kaohsiung, Tai.	J8	42
Kaohsiunghsien, Tai.	J9	42
Kaoka Bay, b., Sol. Is.	e9	79b
Kaoko Veld, plat., Nmb.	D1	68
Kaolack, Sen.	G1	64
Kaolinovo, Blg.	F14	26
Kaoma, Zam.	C3	68
Kaouar, reg., Niger	F7	64
Kapaa, Hi., U.S.	A2	78a
Kapadvanj, India	G4	54
Kapanga, D.R.C.	F4	66
Kapaonik, mts., Yugo.	G8	26
Kapatkevičy, Bela.	H11	10
Kapčagaj, Kaz.	F13	32
Kapčagajskoe vodohranilišče, res., Kaz.	F13	32
Kapchagay Reservoir see Kapčagajskoe vodohranilišče, res., Kaz.	F13	32
Kapfenberg, Aus.	C12	22
Kapıdağ Yarımadası, pen., Tur.	C10	28
Kapikotongwa, stm., On., Can.	A11	118
Kapingamarangi, at., Micron.	C6	72
Kapiri Mposhi, Zam.	C4	68
Kapisigdlit, Grnld.	E16	141
Kapiskau, stm., On., Can.	E14	106
Kapit, Malay.	C8	50
Kaplan, La., U.S.	G6	122
Kaplice, Czech Rep.	H10	16
Kapoeta, Sudan	G6	62
Kapona, D.R.C.	F5	66
Kapos, stm., Hung.	C5	26
Kaposvár, Hung.	C4	26
Kaposvar Creek, stm., Sk., Can.	D11	124
Kappeln, Ger.	B5	16
Kaptai, Bngl.	G14	54
Kaptai Lake see Karnaphuli Reservoir, res., Bngl.	G14	54
Kapuas, stm., Indon.	D6	50
Kapuas, stm., Indon.	E9	50
Kapunda, Austl.	J2	76
Kapūrthala, India	C5	54
Kapuskasing, On., Can.	F14	106
Kapuvár, Hung.	B4	26
Kapyl', Bela.	G9	10
Kara, Russia	C1	34
Kara-Balta, Kyrg.	F12	32
Karabanovo, Russia	D21	10
Karabaš, Russia	C9	32
Kara-Bogaz-Gol, zaliv, b., Turkmen.	A7	56
Kara-Bogaz-Gol Gulf see Kara-Bogaz-Gol, zaliv, b., Turkmen.	A7	56
Karabük, Tur.	B15	28
Karabula, Russia	C17	32
Karaburun, Tur.	E9	28
Karabutak, Kaz.	D10	32
Karacabey, Tur.	C11	28
Karačaevo-Čerkesija, state, Russia	F6	32
Karacasu, Tur.	F11	28
Karačev, Russia	G17	10
Karachay see Karačaevo-Čerkesija, state, Russia	F6	32
Karachay-Cherkessia see Karačaevo-Čerkesija, state, Russia	F6	32
Karāchi, Pak.	E10	56
Karād, India	C2	53
Karaftit, Russia	F11	34
Karaganda, Kaz.	E12	32
Karagayly see Karkaralinsk, Kaz.	E13	32
Karaginskij, ostrov, i., Russia	E21	34
Karaginskij zaliv, b., Russia	E21	34
Karagoš, gora, mtn., Russia	D15	32
Karahallı, Tur.	E12	28
Kāraikkudi, India	F4	53
Karaisalı, Tur.	A6	58
Karaj, Iran	B7	56
Kara-Kala, Turkmen.	B8	56
Karakaralong, Pulau, is., Indon.	E8	44
Karakax, stm., China	A7	54
Karakojyn, ozero, l., Kaz.	E11	32
Karakol, Kyrg.	F13	32
Karakoram Pass, p., Asia	A6	54
Karakoram Range, mts., Asia	A4	46
Karakul', Uzb.	G10	32
Kara-Kum Canal see Garagumskij kanal, can., Turkmen.	B9	56
Karama, stm., Indon.	E11	50
Karamai see Karamay, China	B1	36
Karaman, Tur.	A4	58
Karaman, state, Tur.	A4	58
Karamanlı, Tur.	F12	28
Karamay, China	B1	36
Karamea Bight, b., N.Z.	E4	80
Karamürsel, Tur.	C12	28
Karamyševo, Russia	C18	32
Karamzino, Russia	D17	10
Karangasem, Indon.	H9	50
Karangnunggal, Indon.	G6	50
Kāranja, India	H6	54
Karanjia, India	H10	54
Karapınar, Tur.	A4	58
Karas, state, Nmb.	E3	70
Karaşar, Tur.	C14	28
Karasburg, Nmb.	F4	70
Kara Sea see Karskoe more, Russia	B10	30
Karasjok, Nor.	B11	8
Karasu, Tur.	B13	28
Karasu, stm., Tur.	B4	56
Karasuk, Russia	D13	32
Karatal, Kaz.	E15	32
Karatal, stm., Kaz.	E13	32
Karataş Burun, c., Tur.	B6	58
Karatau, Kaz.	F11	32
Karatau, hrebet, mts., Kaz.	F11	32
Karatau Range see Karatau, hrebet, mts., Kaz.	F11	32
Karatobe, Kaz.	E8	32
Karaton, Kaz.	E8	32
Karatsu, Japan	F2	40
Karaul, Kaz.	E13	32
Karaul, Russia	B5	34
Karauli, India	E6	54
Karawa, D.R.C.	D4	66
Karawang, Indon.	G5	50
Karawang, Tanjung, c., Indon.	F5	50
Karawanken, mts., Eur.	D11	22
Karažal, Kaz.	E12	32
Karbalā', Iraq	C5	56
Kårböle, Swe.	E6	8
Karcag, Hung.	B7	26
Kardámaina, Grc.	G9	28
Kardeljevo, Cro.	G14	22
Kárditsa, Grc.	D4	28
Kärdla, Est.	G10	8
Kărdžali, Blg.	H12	26
Karelia see Karelija, state, Russia	D15	8
Karelia, hist. reg., Eur.	E14	8
Karelija, state, Russia	D15	8
Karelija see Karelia, hist. reg., Eur.	E14	8
Karel'skij Gorodok, Russia	B19	10
Karema, Tan.	F6	66
Karen, India	F7	46
Karesuando, Swe.	B9	8
Kärevere, Est.	B9	10
Kargasok, Russia	C14	32
Kargat, Russia	C14	32
Kargil, India	A5	54
Kargopol', Russia	F18	8
Kariba, Zimb.	D4	68
Kariba, Lake, res., Afr.	D4	68
Karibib, Nmb.	B2	70
Kariega, stm., S. Afr.	H6	70
Karimata, Kepulauan, is., Indon.	D6	50
Karimata, Selat, strt., Indon.	E6	50
Karīmganj, India	F14	54
Karīmnagar, India	B4	53
Karimunjawa, Kepulauan, is., Indon.	F7	50
Karimunjawa, Pulau, i., Indon.	F7	50
Karisimbi, vol., Afr.	E5	66
Káristos, Grc.	E7	28
Kariya, Japan	D10	40
Kārkal, India	E2	53
Karkaralinsk, Kaz.	E13	32
Karkar Island, i., Pap. N. Gui.	a4	79a
Karkonoski Park Narodowy, p.o.i., Pol.	F11	16
Karkūk, Iraq	B5	56
Karleby see Kokkola, Fin.	E10	8
Karlino, Pol.	B11	16
Karl-Marx-Stadt see Chemnitz, Ger.	F8	16
Karlovac, Cro.	E12	22
Karlovo, Blg.	G11	26
Karlovy Vary, Czech Rep.	F8	16
Karlsborg, Swe.	D10	8
Karlsburg see Alba Iulia, Rom.	C10	26
Karlshamn, Swe.	H6	8
Karlskoga, Swe.	G6	8
Karlskrona, Swe.	H6	8
Karlsruhe, Ger.	G4	16
Karlstad, Swe.	G5	8
Karlstadt, Ger.	G5	16
Karluk, Ak., U.S.	E9	140
Karma, Bela.	H14	10
Karma, Niger	G5	64
Karmah an Nuzul, Sudan	D6	62
Karmāla, India	B2	53
Karmøy, i., Nor.	G1	8
Karnack, Tx., U.S.	E4	122
Karnak, Il., U.S.	G9	120
Karnāl, India	D6	54
Karṇālī, stm., Asia	D8	54
Karnāli, stm., Nepal	D8	54
Karnaphuli Reservoir, res., Bngl.	G14	54
Karnātaka, state, India	D2	53
Karnobat, Blg.	G13	26
Kärnten, state, Aus.	D10	22
Karoli, India	G7	54
Karonga, Mwi.	B5	68
Karoo National Park, p.o.i., S. Afr.	H6	70
Karoonda, Austl.	J2	76
Karor, Pak.	C3	54
Kárpathos, Grc.	H10	28
Kárpathos, i., Grc.	H10	28
Karpats'kyi Pryrodnyi Natsional'nyi Park, p.o.i., Ukr.	A11	26
Karpenísi, Grc.	E4	28
Karpogory, Russia	D21	8
Karpuzlu, Tur.	F10	28
Karratha, Austl.	D3	74
Karrats Fjord, b., Grnld.	C14	141
Kars, Tur.	A5	56
Karsakpaj, Kaz.	E11	32
Karsantı, Tur.	A6	58
Karši, Uzb.	G11	32
Karsin, Pol.	C13	16
Karskoe more (Kara Sea), Russia	B10	30
Kartala, vol., Com.	C7	68
Kartaly, Russia	D10	32
Kartārpur, India	C5	54
Karthaus, Pa., U.S.	C7	114
Kartuzy, Pol.	B14	16
Karufa, Indon.	F9	44
Karumba, Austl.	A3	76
Karungi, Swe.	C10	8
Karunjie, Austl.	C5	74
Karūr, India	F4	53
Karviná, Czech Rep.	G14	16
Kārwār, India	D1	53
Karyés, Grc.	C7	28
Karymskoe, Russia	F11	34
Kasai (Cassai), stm., Afr.	E3	66
Kasaji, D.R.C.	G4	66
Kasama, Japan	C13	40
Kasama, Zam.	C5	68
Kasane, Bots.	D3	68
Kasanga, Tan.	F6	66
Kasangulu, D.R.C.	E3	66
Kasaoka, Japan	E6	40
Kāsaragod, India	E2	53
Kasba, India	F11	54
Kasba Lake, l., Can.	C10	106
Kascjukouka, Bela.	H13	10
Kascjukovičy, Bela.	G14	10
Kaseda, Japan	H3	40
Kasempa, Zam.	C4	68
Kasenga, D.R.C.	G5	66
Kasenye, D.R.C.	D6	66
Kasese, D.R.C.	E5	66
Kasese, Ug.	D6	66
Kaset Sombun, Thai.	D5	48
Kāsganj, India	E7	54
Kāshān, Iran	C7	56
Kashgar see Kashi, China	B12	56
Kashi, China	B12	56
Kashihara, Japan	E8	40
Kashima, Japan	F3	40
Kashima-nada, Japan	C13	40
Kashing see Jiaxing, China	F9	42
Kāshīpur, India	D7	54
Kashiwazaki, Japan	B11	40
Kāshmar, Iran	B8	56
Kashmir, hist. reg., Asia	A3	46
Kasia, India	E9	54
Kasimbar, Indon.	D12	50
Kasimov, Russia	I19	8
Kašin, Russia	C20	10
Kaširа, Russia	F21	10
Kasiruta, Pulau, i., Indon.	F8	44
Kaskaskia, stm., Il., U.S.	E9	120
Kaskinen, Fin.	E9	8
Kaslo, B.C., Can.	G13	138
Kasnja, Russia	E17	10
Kasongo, D.R.C.	E5	66
Kasongo-Lunda, D.R.C.	F3	66
Kásos, i., Grc.	H9	28
Kasota, Mn., U.S.	G5	118
Kaspijsk, Russia	F7	32
Kaspijskij, Russia	E7	32
Kaspijskoje more see Caspian Sea	F7	32
Kasplja, stm., Eur.	E13	10
Kasr, Ra's, c., Afr.	D7	62
Kassab, Syria	C6	58
Kassalā, Sudan	D7	62
Kassándra, pen., Grc.	C6	28
Kassandra, Gulf of see Kassándras, Kólpos, b., Grc.	C6	28
Kassándras, Kólpos, b., Grc.	C6	28
Kassel, Ger.	E5	16
Kasserine, Tun.	B6	64
Kastamonu, Tur.	A3	56
Kastamonu, state, Tur.	B16	28
Kastélli, Grc.	H6	28
Kastoría, Grc.	C4	28
Kastorías, Límni, l., Grc.	C4	28
Kastrakíou, Technití Límni, res., Grc.	E4	28
Kasugai, Japan	D9	40
Kasulu, Tan.	E6	66
Kasumi, Japan	D7	40
Kasumiga-ura, l., Japan	C13	40
Kasungan, Indon.	E8	50
Kasūr, Pak.	C5	54
Kaszuby, hist. reg., Pol.	B13	16
Kataba, Zam.	D4	68
Katahdin, Mount, mtn., Me., U.S.	E7	110
Katako-Kombe, D.R.C.	E4	66
Katanga, hist. reg., D.R.C.	F4	66
Katanga, stm., Russia	C18	32
Katangi, India	G7	54
Katangli, Russia	F17	34
Katanning, Austl.	F3	74
Katchall Island, i., India	G7	46
Katepwa Beach, Sk., Can.	D10	124
Kateríni, Grc.	C5	28
Kates Needle, mtn., N.A.	D4	106
Katete, Zam.	C5	68
Katha, Mya.	D8	46
Katherîna, Gebel, mtn., Egypt	J4	58
Katherine, Austl.	B6	74
Katherine, stm., Austl.	B6	74
Katherine Creek, stm., Austl.	D4	76
Kāthiāwār Peninsula, pen., India	H3	54
Kathla, India	C6	54
Kāṭhmāṇḍau (Kathmandu), Nepal	E10	54
Kathmandu see Kāṭhmāṇḍau, Nepal	E10	54
Kathor, India	H4	54
Kathua, India	B5	54
Kati, Mali	G3	64
Katibas, stm., Malay.	C8	50
Katihār, India	F11	54
Katimik Lake, l., Mb., Can.	B14	124
Katiola, C. Iv.	H4	64
Katipunan, Phil.	F4	52
Ka Tiriti o te Moana see Southern Alps, mts., N.Z.	F4	80
Katmai, Mount, vol., Ak., U.S.	E8	140
Káto Achaía, Grc.	E4	28
Kātol, India	H7	54
Katoomba, Austl.	I8	76
Katowice, Pol.	F14	16
Katowice, state, Pol.	F15	16
Katrineholm, Swe.	G7	8
Katsina, Nig.	G6	64
Katsina Ala, stm., Afr.	H6	64
Katsuta, Japan	C13	40
Katsuura, Japan	D13	40
Katsuyama, Japan	C9	40
Katsuyama, Japan	D6	40
Kattakurgan, Uzb.	G11	32
Kattegat, strt., Eur.	H4	8
Katul, Jabal, mtn., Sudan	E5	62
Katun', stm., Russia	D15	32
Katunino, Russia	G21	8
Kātwa, India	G11	54
Katwijk aan Zee, Neth.	B13	14
Katyn, Russia	F14	10
Katzenbuckel, mtn., Ger.	G5	16
Kauai, i., Hi., U.S.	B2	78a
Kauai Channel, strt., Hi., U.S.	B3	78a
Kaufbeuren, Ger.	I6	16
Kaufman, Tx., U.S.	E2	122
Kaukauna, Wi., U.S.	D1	112
Kaukau Veld, plat., Afr.	D3	68
Kaulakahi Channel, strt., Hi., U.S.	B2	78a
Kaumalapau, Hi., U.S.	C4	78a
Kaunas, Lith.	F6	10
Kaura-Namoda, Nig.	G6	64
Kauriālā (Ghāghara), stm., Asia	D8	54
Kautokeino, Nor.	B10	8
Kau-ye Kyun, i., Mya.	G4	48
Kavača, Russia	D23	34
Kavadarci, Mac.	B5	28
Kavaja see Kavajë, Alb.	C13	24
Kavajë, Alb.	C13	24
Kavaklıdere, Tur.	F11	28
Kavála, Grc.	C7	28
Kavalerovo, Russia	B11	38
Kāvali, India	D4	53
Kavaratti, India	F3	46
Kavaratti Island, i., India	F3	46
Kāveri (Cauvery), stm., India	F4	53
Kāveri Falls, wtfl, India	E3	53
Kavieng, Pap. N. Gui.	a5	79a
Kavīr, Dasht-e, des., Iran	C8	56
Kaw, Ok., U.S.	E12	128
Kawa, Mya.	D3	48
Kawagama Lake, l., On., Can.	C10	112
Kawagoe, Japan	D12	40
Kawaguchi, Japan	D12	40
Kawaihoa, c., Hi., U.S.	B1	78a
Kawaikini, mtn., Hi., U.S.	A2	78a
Kawambwa, Zam.	B4	68
Kawanoe, Japan	E6	40
Kawardha, India	H8	54
Kawasaki, Japan	D12	40
Kawatana, Japan	F2	40
Kawdut, Mya.	E3	48
Kaweenakumik Lake, l., Mb., Can.	B14	124
Kawhia Harbour, b., N.Z.	D6	80
Kawich Peak, mtn., Nv., U.S.	F9	134
Kawkareik, Mya.	D4	48
Kaw Lake, res., Ok., U.S.	E12	128
Kawludo, Mya.	C3	48
Kawnipi Lake, l., On., Can.	C7	118
Kawthaung, Mya.	H4	48
Kaxgar, stm., China	B12	56
Kaya, Burkina	G4	64
Kayah, state, Mya.	C3	48
Kayak Island, i., Ak., U.S.	E11	140
Kāyalpattinam, India	G4	53
Kayan, Mya.	D3	48
Kayan, stm., Indon.	B10	50
Kāyankulam, India	G3	53
Kaycee, Wy., U.S.	D6	126
Kayenta, Az., U.S.	G6	132
Kayes, Mali	G2	64
Kayin, state, Mya.	D3	48
Kaymaz, Tur.	D14	28
Kayseri, Tur.	B4	56
Kaysville, Ut., U.S.	B4	132
Kayuadi, Pulau, i., Indon.	G12	50
Kayuagung, Indon.	E4	50
Kayumas, Indon.	G9	50
Kazače, Russia	B16	34
Kazačinskoe, Russia	C19	32
Kazačinskoe, Russia	E7	34
Kazahskij melkosopočnik (Kazakh Hills), hills, Kaz.	D12	32
Kazakh Hills see Kazahskij melkosopočnik, hills, Kaz.	D12	32
Kazaki, Russia	H21	10
Kazakstan, ctry., Asia	E10	32
Kazalinsk, Kaz.	E10	32
Kazan', Russia	C7	32
Kazan, stm., Can.	C11	106
Kazanlăk, Blg.	G12	26
Kazanlı, Tur.	B5	58
Kazan-rettō, is., Japan	G18	30
Kazanskoe, Russia	C11	32
Kāzerūn, Iran	D7	56
Kazimierza Wielka, Pol.	F16	16
Kazincbarcika, Hung.	A7	26
Kaziranga National Park, p.o.i., India	E14	54
Kazlų Rūda, Lith.	F6	10
Kaztalovka, Kaz.	E7	32
Kazula, Moz.	D5	68
Kazym, Russia	B11	32
Kazym, stm., Russia	B11	32
Kazyr, stm., Russia	D16	32
Kbal Dâmrei, Camb.	E7	48
Kdyně, Czech Rep.	G9	16
Kéa, Grc.	F7	28
Kéa, i., Grc.	F7	28
Keahole Point, c., Hi., U.S.	D5	78a
Kealaikahiki Channel, strt., Hi., U.S.	C5	78a
Keams Canyon, Az., U.S.	H6	132
Keanapapa Point, c., Hi., U.S.	C4	78a
Kearney, Mo., U.S.	E3	120
Kearney, Ne., U.S.	G13	126
Kearns, Ut., U.S.	C4	132
Kearny, Az., U.S.	J6	132
Keban Barajı, res., Tur.	B4	56
Keban Reservoir see Keban Barajı, res., Tur.	B4	56
Kébèmer, Sen.	F1	64
Kebnekaise, mtn., Swe.	B8	8
K'ebrī Dehar, Eth.	F8	62
Kech, stm., Pak.	D9	56
Kechika, stm., B.C., Can.	D5	106
Keçiborlu, Tur.	F13	28
Kecskemét, Hung.	C6	26
Kedah, state, Malay.	J5	48
Kėdainiai, Lith.	E6	10
Kediri, Indon.	G8	50
Kedon, Russia	D20	34
Kédougou, Sen.	G2	64
Kędzierzyn-Koźle, Pol.	F14	16
Keefers, B.C., Can.	F9	138
Keele, stm., N.T., Can.	C5	106
Keele Peak, mtn., Yk., Can.	C4	106
Keeling Islands see Cocos Islands, dep., Oc.	K12	142
Keelung see Chilung, Tai.	I9	42
Keene, Ky., U.S.	G13	120
Keene, N.H., U.S.	B13	114
Keene, Tx., U.S.	B10	130
Keeney Knob, mtn., W.V., U.S.	G5	114
Keer-Weer, Cape, c., Austl.	B8	74
Keeseville, N.Y., U.S.	F3	110
Keetmanshoop, Nmb.	E3	70
Keewatin, On., Can.	B4	118
Keewatin, Mn., U.S.	D5	118
Kefallinía, i., Grc.	E3	28
Kefamenanu, Indon.	G7	44
Kefar Naḥum (Capernaum), hist., Isr.	F6	58
Kefar Sava, Isr.	F5	58
Keffi, Nig.	H6	64
Keflavík, Ice.	k28	8a
Ke Ga, Mui, c., Viet.	F9	48
Kegalla, Sri L.	H5	53
Keg River, Ab., Can.	D7	106
Kegums, Lat.	D7	10
Ke-hsi Mānsām, Mya.	B3	48
Keighley, Eng., U.K.	H10	12
Keila, Est.	G11	8
Keimoes, S. Afr.	F5	70
Keith, Scot., U.K.	D9	12
Keith Arm, b., N.T., Can.	B6	106
Keithley Creek, B.C., Can.	D9	138
Keithsburg, Il., U.S.	J8	118
Keiyasi, Fiji	p18	79e
Keizer, Or., U.S.	F3	136
Kejimkujik National Park, p.o.i., N.S., Can.	F11	110
Kejvy, mts., Russia	C17	8
Kekaha, Hi., U.S.	B2	78a
Kékes, mtn., Hung.	B7	26
Kekri, India	E5	54
K'elafo, Eth.	F8	62
Kelai, stm., Indon.	C10	50
Kelani, stm., Sri L.	H5	53
Kelantan, state, Malay.	J6	48
Kelantan, stm., Malay.	J6	48
Kelapa, Indon.	D4	50
Kelbia, Sebkhet, l., Tun.	I4	24
Kelheim, Ger.	H7	16
Kelibia, Tun.	H5	24
Kéllé, Congo	E2	66
Kellerberrin, Austl.	F3	74
Keller Lake, l., N.T., Can.	C6	106
Kellett, Cape, c., N.T., Can.	B14	140
Kelleys Island, i., Oh., U.S.	C3	114
Kellogg, Id., U.S.	C10	136
Kellogg, Ia., U.S.	C5	120
Kellogg, Mn., U.S.	G6	118
Kelloselkä, Fin.	C13	8
Kells, Ire.	H6	12
Kelmė, Lith.	E5	10
Kélo, Chad	F3	62
Kelolokan, Indon.	C10	50
Kelowna, B.C., Can.	G11	138
Kelsey Bay, B.C., Can.	F5	138
Kelseyville, Ca., U.S.	D3	134
Kelso, Scot., U.K.	F10	12
Kelso, Wa., U.S.	D4	136
Keluang, Malay.	K6	48
Kelvington, Sk., Can.	B10	124
Kelvin Island, i., On., Can.	B10	118
Kem', Russia	D16	8
Kem', stm., Russia	D15	8
Kemano, B.C., Can.	C2	138
Kemena, stm., Malay.	B8	50
Kemer, Tur.	F13	28
Kemer Barajı, res., Tur.	F11	28
Kemerhisar, Tur.	A5	58
Kemerovo, Russia	C15	32
Kemi, Fin.	D11	8
Kemijärvi, Fin.	C12	8
Kemijärvi, l., Fin.	C12	8
Kemijoki, stm., Fin.	C12	8
Kemmerer, Wy., U.S.	B6	132
Kemmuna (Comino), i., Malta	H8	24
Kemnath, Ger.	G7	16
Kemp, Tx., U.S.	E2	122
Kemp, Lake, res., Tx., U.S.	H9	128
Kempner, Tx., U.S.	C9	130
Kempsey, Austl.	H9	76
Kempt, Lac, l., Qc., Can.	F16	106
Kempten, Ger.	I6	16
Kemptville, On., Can.	C14	112
Kemujan, Pulau, i., Indon.	F7	50
Kemul, Kong, mtn., Indon.	C9	50
Ken, stm., India	F8	54
Kenai, Ak., U.S.	D9	140
Kenai Mountains, mts., Ak., U.S.	E9	140
Kenai Peninsula, pen., Ak., U.S.	E9	140
Kenansville, Fl., U.S.	I5	116
Kenansville, N.C., U.S.	B7	116
Kenbridge, Va., U.S.	H7	114
Kendal, Sk., Can.	D10	124
Kendal, Indon.	G7	50
Kendal, Eng., U.K.	G10	12
Kendall, Austl.	H9	76
Kendall, Fl., U.S.	K5	116
Kendall, Wi., U.S.	H8	118
Kendall, Cape, c., Nu., Can.	C13	106
Kendari, Indon.	F7	44
Kendawangan, Indon.	E7	50
Kendrāparha, India	H11	54
Kendrew, S. Afr.	H7	70
Kendrick, Fl., U.S.	G3	116
Kendrick, Id., U.S.	D10	136
Kendujhargarh, India	H10	54
Kenedy, Tx., U.S.	F10	130
Kenema, S.L.	H2	64
Kenga, Russia	C14	32
Kenge, D.R.C.	E3	66
Keng Hkam, Mya.	B3	48
Kēng Tung, Mya.	B4	48
Kenhardt, S. Afr.	F5	70

Name Map Ref. Page

Kenilworth, Ut., U.S. D6 132
Kénitra, Mor. C3 64
Kenly, N.C., U.S. A7 116
Kenmare, Ire. J3 12
Kenmare, N.D., U.S. F11 124
Kennard, Tx., U.S. F3 122
Kennebec, stm., Me., U.S. F7 110
Kennebecasis Bay, b., N.B., Can. E11 110
Kennebunk, Me., U.S. G6 110
Kennedy, Al., U.S. D11 122
Kennedy, Cape see Canaveral, Cape, c., Fl., U.S. H5 116
Kennedy, Mount, mtn., B.C., Can. F5 138
Kennedy, Mount, mtn., Yk., Can. C3 106
Kennedy Lake, l., B.C., Can. G5 138
Kenner, La., U.S. G8 122
Kennetcook, N.S., Can. E13 110
Kennett, Mo., U.S. H7 120
Kennewick, Wa., U.S. D7 136
Kenney Dam, dam, B.C., Can. C6 138
Kenogami, stm., On., Can. E13 106
Kénogami, Lac, res., Qc., Can. B5 110
Keno Hill, Yk., Can. C3 106
Kenora, On., Can. B4 118
Kenosha, Wi., U.S. F2 112
Kenozero, ozero, l., Russia E18 8
Kensal, N.D., U.S. G15 124
Kensett, Ar., U.S. B7 122
Kensington, Ks., U.S. B9 128
Kensington Park, Fl., U.S. I3 116
Kent, Oh., U.S. C4 114
Kent, Wa., U.S. C4 136
Kentau, Kaz. F11 32
Kent Group, is., Austl. L6 76
Kentland, In., U.S. H2 112
Kenton, Mi., U.S. E10 118
Kenton, Tn., U.S. H8 120
Kent Peninsula, pen., Nu., Can. B9 106
Kentrikí Makedonía, state, Grc. C6 28
Kentucky, state, U.S. G12 120
Kentucky, stm., Ky., U.S. F13 120
Kentucky, Middle Fork, stm., Ky., U.S. G2 114
Kentucky, North Fork, stm., Ky., U.S. G2 114
Kentucky Lake, res., U.S. H9 120
Kentville, N.S., Can. E12 110
Kentwood, La., U.S. G8 122
Kenya, ctry., Afr. D7 66
Kenya, Mount see Kirinyaga, mtn., Kenya E7 66
Kenyon, Mn., U.S. G6 118
Keokuk, Ia., U.S. D6 120
Keoladeo National Park, p.o.i., India E6 54
Keo Nua, Deo, p., Asia C7 48
Keosauqua, Ia., U.S. D5 120
Keota, Ia., U.S. C6 120
Keota, Ok., U.S. B4 122
Keowee, Lake, res., S.C., U.S. B2 116
Kepi, Indon. G10 44
Kepina, Russia D19 8
Kępno, Pol. E13 16
Keppel Bay, b., Austl. D8 76
Kepsut, Tur. D11 28
Kerala, state, India F3 53
Keramadoo, mtn., Palau f8 78b
Keramian, Pulau, i., Indon. F9 50
Kerang, Austl. J4 76
Keratéa, Grc. F6 28
Keravat, Pap. N. Gui. a5 79a
Kerch, Ukr. E5 32
Kerec, mys, c., Russia D18 8
Kerema, Pap. N. Gui. b4 79a
Keremeos, B.C., Can. G11 138
Keren, Erit. D7 62
Kerens, Tx., U.S. E2 122
Keret', Russia C15 8
Keret', ozero, l., Russia D15 8
Kerewan, Gam. G1 64
Kerguelen, Îles, is., Afr. J17 4
Kerguelen Plateau, unds. O10 142
Keri, Grc. F3 28
Kericho, Kenya E7 66
Kerinci, Gunung, vol., Indon. D2 50
Kerkenna, Îles, is., Tun. C7 64
Kerkhoven, Mn., U.S. F3 118
Kerkiči, Turkmen. B10 56
Kerkrade, Neth. F2 16
Kérkyra (Corfu), Grc. D2 28
Kérkyra (Corfu), i., Grc. D2 28
Kermadec Islands, is., N.Z. F9 72
Kermadec Ridge, unds. M20 142
Kermadec Trench, unds. M21 142
Kermān, Iran C8 56
Kermānshāh (Bākhtarān), Iran C6 56
Kerme, Gulf of see Gökova Körfezi, b., Tur. G10 28
Kermit, Tx., U.S. C4 130
Kern, stm., Ca., U.S. H7 134
Kern, South Fork, stm., Ca., U.S. H7 134
Kernersville, N.C., U.S. H5 114
Kernville, Ca., U.S. H7 134
Kérouané, Gui. H3 64
Kerrobert, Sk., Can. C4 124
Kerrville, Tx., U.S. D8 130
Kerry, state, Ire. I2 12
Kerry Head, c., Ire. I2 12
Kershaw, S.C., U.S. B5 116
Kersley, B.C., Can. D8 138
Kertamulia, Indon. D6 50
Kerulen, stm., Asia B7 36
Kesagami Lake, l., On., Can. E14 106
Keşan, Tur. C9 28
Kesennuma, Japan E14 38
Keshan, China B10 36
Keshod, India H3 54
Keski-Suomi, state, Fin. E11 8
Kes'ma, Russia B20 10
Kesova Gora, Russia C20 10
Kestell, S. Afr. F9 70
Keswick, Eng., U.K. G9 12
Keszthely, Hung. C4 26
Ket', stm., Russia C14 32
Keta, Ghana H5 64
Keta, ozero, l., Russia C6 34
Ketapang, Indon. F4 50
Ketapang, Indon. D6 50
Ketchikan, Ak., U.S. E13 140
Ketchum, Id., U.S. G12 136
Kete-Krachi, Ghana H4 64
Ketoj, ostrov, i., Russia G19 34
Kętrzyn, Pol. B17 16
Kettering, Eng., U.K. I12 12
Kettering, Oh., U.S. E1 114
Kettle, stm., N.A. H12 138
Kettle Falls, Wa., U.S. B8 136
Kęty, Pol. G15 16
Keudeteunom, Indon. J2 48
Keuka Lake, l., N.Y., U.S. B8 114
Keukenhof, misc. cult., Neth. B13 14
Keul', Russia C18 32
Kevelaer, Ger. E2 16
Kevin, Mt., U.S. B14 136
Kew, T./C. Is. A12 102
Kewanee, Il., U.S. C7 120
Kewaunee, Wi., U.S. D2 112
Keweenaw Bay, b., Mi., U.S. E10 118
Keweenaw Peninsula, pen., Mi., U.S. D11 118
Keweenaw Point, c., Mi., U.S. D11 118
Key, Lough, l., Ire. G4 12
Keya Paha, stm., U.S. E13 126
Keyes, Ok., U.S. E6 128
Keyhole Reservoir, res., Wy., U.S. C8 126
Key Largo, Fl., U.S. K5 116
Key Largo, i., Fl., U.S. K5 116
Keyser, W.V., U.S. E7 114
Keystone, S.D., U.S. D9 126
Keystone, W.V., U.S. G4 114
Keystone Lake, res., Ok., U.S. A2 122
Keystone Peak, mtn., Az., U.S. L5 132
Keysville, Va., U.S. G7 114
Keytesville, Mo., U.S. E5 120
Key West, Fl., U.S. L4 116
Kezi, Zimb. B9 70
Kežma, Russia C18 32
Kežmarok, Slov. G16 16
Kgalagadi, state, Bots. D5 70
Kgatleng, state, Bots. D8 70
Khadki, India B1 53
Khadzhybeis'kyi lyman, l., Ukr. C17 26
Khagaria, India F11 54
Khairāgarh, India H8 54
Khairpur, Pak. E2 54
Khairpur, Pak. D4 54
Khajrāho, India F8 54
Khakassia see Hakasija, state, Russia D16 32
Kha Khaeng, stm., Thai. E4 48
Khakhea, Bots. D6 70
Khalatse, India A6 54
Khālidī, Khirbat al-, hist., Jord. I6 58
Khalīya, Gebel, mtn., Egypt I3 58
Khalūf, Oman E8 56
Khambhāliya, India G2 54
Khambhāt, India G4 54
Khambhāt, Gulf of, b., India H3 54
Khāmgaon, India H6 54
Khamīs, Ash-Shallāl al- (Fifth Cataract), wtfl, Sudan D6 62
Khamīs Mushayt, Sau. Ar. F5 56
Khammam, India C5 53
Khan, stm., Laos C6 48
Khan, stm., Nmb. C2 70
Khānābād, Afg. B10 56
Khān Abū Shāmāt, Syria E7 58
Khānaqīn, Iraq C6 56
Khancoban, Austl. K7 76
Khandela, India E5 54
Khandwa, India H6 54
Khānewāl, Pak. C3 54
Khāngarh, Pak. D3 54
Khangchendzonga National Park, p.o.i., India E12 54
Khangkhai, Laos C6 48
Khaniá, Gulf of see Chaniōn, Kólpos, b., Grc. H6 28
Khanka, Lake, l., Asia B10 38
Khanna, India C6 54
Khānpur, Pak. D3 54
Khansiir, Raas, c., Som. B9 66
Khān Yūnus, Gaza G5 58
Khao Laem Reservoir, res., Thai. E4 48
Khao Sok National Park, p.o.i., Thai. H4 48
Khao Yoi, Thai. F4 48
Kharagpur, India G11 54
Khārān, Pak. D10 56
Kharāyij, Sabkhat al-, l., Syria C8 58
Kharg Island see Khārk, Jazīreh-ye, i., Iran D7 56
Khargon, India H5 54
Khāriān Cantonment, Pak. B4 54
Khārk, Jazīreh-ye, i., Iran D7 56
Kharkiv, Ukr. D5 32
Kharmanli see Harmanli, Blg. H12 26
Khartoum see Al-Kharṭūm, Sudan D6 62
Khartoum North see Al-Kharṭūm Baḥrī, Sudan D6 62
Khasebake, Bots. B7 70
Khāsh, Afg. C9 56
Khāsh, Iran D9 56
Khashm al-Qirbah, Sudan D7 62
Khaskovo see Haskovo, Blg. H12 26
Khatanga see Hatanga, Russia B9 34
Khatanga see Hatanga, stm., Russia B9 34
Khatauli, India D6 54
Khatt, Oued al, stm., W. Sah. D2 64
Khavast see Havast, Uzb. F11 32
Khawsa, Mya. E3 48
Khayung, stm., Thai. E7 48
Khed, India C1 53
Kheil, Katīb el-, sand, Egypt H3 58
Khemis el Khechna, Alg. H14 20
Khemis Melyana, Alg. H13 20
Khemmarat, Thai. D7 48
Khenchla, Alg. B6 64
Khenifra, Mor. C3 64
Kherson, Ukr. F15 6
Kheta see Heta, stm., Russia B8 34
Khetia, India H5 54
Khimki see Himki, Russia E20 10
Khipro, Pak. F2 54
Khisfīn, Golan F5 58
Khiva see Hiva, Uzb. F10 32
Khlong Thom, Thai. I4 48
Khlung, Thai. F6 48
Khok Kloi, Thai. H4 48
Khok Samrong, Thai. E5 48
Kholm, Afg. B10 56
Khomas, state, Nmb. C3 70
Khomeynīshahr, Iran C7 56
Khondmāl Hills, hills, India H10 54
Khong see Mekong, stm., Asia E10 46
Khon Kaen, Thai. D6 48
Khordha, India H10 54
Khorixas, Nmb. B2 70
Khorog see Horog, Taj. B11 56
Khorramābād, Iran C6 56
Khorramshahr, Iran C6 56
Khotyn, Ukr. A13 26
Khouribga, Mor. C3 64
Khowai, India F13 54
Khowst, Afg. C10 56
Khrisokhoús, Kólpos, b., Cyp. C3 58
Khuis, Bots. E5 70
Khulyāla, India E3 54
Khulna, Bngl. G12 54
Khulna, state, Bngl. G12 54
Khun Tan, Doi, mtn., Thai. C4 48
Khunti, India G10 54
Khurai, India F7 54
Khurja, India D6 54
Khushāb, Pak. B4 54
Khust, Ukr. A10 26
Khuzdār, Pak. D10 56
Khvoy, Iran B6 56
Khwae Noi, stm., Thai. E4 48
Khyber Pass, p., Asia A3 54
Khyriv, Ukr. G18 16
Kiama, Austl. J8 76
Kiamba, D.R.C. F3 66
Kiamba, Phil. H5 52
Kiambi, D.R.C. F5 66
Kiamichi, stm., Ok., U.S. C3 122
Kiamusze see Jiamusi, China B11 36
Kian see Ji'an, China H6 42
Kiangarow, Mount, mtn., Austl. F8 76
Kiang-si see Jiangxi, state, China H6 42
Kiangsi see Jiangxi, state, China H6 42
Kiang-sou see Jiangsu, state, China E8 42
Kiangsu see Jiangsu, state, China E8 42
Kiaohsien see Jiaoxian, China C8 42
Kibangou, Congo E2 66
Kibombo, D.R.C. E5 66
Kibondo, Tan. E6 66
Kibre Mengist, Eth. F7 62
Kıbrıs see Cyprus, ctry., Asia C4 58
Kıbrısçık, Tur. C14 28
Kibuye, Rw. E5 66
Kičevo, Mac. B3 28
Kickapoo, stm., Wi., U.S. H8 118
Kicking Horse Pass, p., Can. E14 138
Kidal, Mali F5 64
Kidapawan, Phil. G5 52
Kidatu, Tan. F7 66
Kidderminster, Eng., U.K. I10 12
Kidira, Sen. G2 64
Kidnappers, Cape, c., N.Z. D7 80
Kidston, Austl. B5 76
Kiefersfelden, Ger. I8 16
Kiel, Ger. B6 16
Kiel, Wi., U.S. H10 118
Kiel Bay see Kieler Bucht, b., Ger. B6 16
Kiel Canal see Nord-Ostsee-Kanal, can., Ger. B5 16
Kielce, Pol. F16 16
Kielce, state, Pol. F16 16
Kieler Bucht, b., Ger. B6 16
Kiester, Mn., U.S. H5 118
Kiev see Kyïv, Ukr. D4 32
Kievka, Kaz. D12 32
Kiev Reservoir see Kyïvs'ke vodoskhovyshche, res., Ukr. D4 32
Kiffa, Maur. F2 64
Kifisiá, Grc. E6 28
Kigali, Rw. E6 66
Kigoma, Tan. E5 66
Kihčik, Russia F20 34
Kihei, Hi., U.S. C5 78a
Kihniö, Fin. E10 8
Kihnu, i., Est. G10 8
Kii-hantō, pen., Japan F8 40
Kiik, Kaz. E12 32
Kii-suidō, strt., Japan F7 40
Kikerino, Russia A12 10
Kikinda, Yugo. D7 26
Kikládhes (Cyclades), is., Grc. F7 28
Kikori, Pap. N. Gui. b3 79a
Kikori, stm., Pap. N. Gui. b3 79a
Kikuchi, Japan G3 40
Kikwit, D.R.C. F3 66
Kilakkarai, India G4 53
Kilauea, Hi., U.S. A2 78a
Kilauea Crater, crat., Hi., U.S. D6 78a
Kilbasan, Tur. A4 58
Kilbuck Mountains, mts., Ak., U.S. D8 140
Kilchu-ŭp, Kor., N. D8 38
Kilcoy, Austl. F9 76
Kildare, state, Ire. H6 12
Kildare, Cape, c., P.E., Can. D13 110
Kildurk, Austl. C5 74
Kilembe, D.R.C. F3 66
Kilgore, Tx., U.S. E4 122
Kilian Island, i., Nu., Can. B18 140
Kılıç, Tur. C12 28
Kilija, Ukr. D16 26
Kilikollūr, India G3 53
Kilimanjaro, mtn., Tan. E7 66
Kilimli, Tur. B14 28
Kilindoni, Tan. F7 66
Kilis, Tur. B8 58
Kilkee, Ire. I3 12
Kilkenny, Ire. I5 12
Kilkenny, state, Ire. I5 12
Kilkís, Grc. C5 28
Killaloe, Ire. I4 12
Killaloe Station, On., Can. C12 112
Killam, Ab., Can. D19 138
Killarney, Austl. G9 76
Killarney, Mb., Can. E14 124
Killarney, On., Can. C8 112
Killarney, Ire. I3 12
Killdeer, N.D., U.S. G11 124
Killeen, Tx., U.S. C10 130
Killen, Al., U.S. C11 122
Killington Peak, mtn., Vt., U.S. G4 110
Killiniq Island, i., Can. E13 141
Killybegs, Ire. G4 12
Kilmarnock, Scot., U.K. F8 12
Kilmarnock, Va., U.S. G9 114
Kilmore, Austl. K5 76
Kilo, Indon. H11 50
Kilombero, stm., Tan. F7 66
Kilomines, D.R.C. D6 66
Kilosa, Tan. F7 66
Kilrush, Ire. I3 12
Kilttān Island, i., India F3 46
Kilwa, D.R.C. F5 66
Kilwa Kivinje, Tan. F7 66
Kim, Co., U.S. D5 128
Kimba, Austl. F7 74
Kimball, Ne., U.S. F9 126
Kimball, S.D., U.S. D13 126
Kimbe Bay, b., Pap. N. Gui. b5 79a
Kimberley, B.C., Can. G15 138
Kimberley, S. Afr. F7 70
Kimberley Downs, Austl. C4 74
Kimberley Plateau, plat., Austl. C5 74
Kimberling City, Mo., U.S. H4 120
Kimberly, Id., U.S. H12 136
Kimberly, Wi., U.S. G10 118
Kimch'aek, Kor., N. D8 38
Kimch'ŏn, Kor., S. F8 38
Kimhae, Kor., S. D1 40
Kimito, Fin. F10 8
Kim-me-ni-oli Wash, stm., N.M., U.S. H8 132
Kimmirut, Nu., Can. C17 106
Kímolos, i., Grc. G7 28
Kimovsk, Russia F21 10
Kimpō-zan, mtn., Japan D11 40
Kimry, Russia D20 10
Kinabalu, Gunong (Kinabalu, Mount), mtn., Malay. G1 52
Kinabalu National Park, p.o.i., Malay. H1 52
Kinabatangan, stm., Malay. H2 52
Kinbasket Lake, res., B.C., Can. D12 138
Kincaid, Sk., Can. E6 124
Kincardine, On., Can. D8 112
Kinchafoonee Creek, stm., Ga., U.S. F14 122
Kinchega National Park, p.o.i., Austl. I4 76
Kinda, D.R.C. F4 66
Kinde, Mi., U.S. E7 112
Kinder, La., U.S. G6 122
Kindersley, Sk., Can. C4 124
Kindia, Gui. G2 64
Kindu, D.R.C. E5 66
Kinel', Russia D8 32
Kinešma, Russia H19 8
King, N.C., U.S. H5 114
King and Queen Court House, Va., U.S. G9 114
Kingaroy, Austl. F8 76
King City, On., Can. E10 112
King City, Ca., U.S. G4 134
Kingfield, Me., U.S. F6 110
Kingfisher, Ok., U.S. F10 128
King George, Va., U.S. F8 114
King George, Mount, mtn., B.C., Can. F15 138
King George Islands, is., Nu., Can. D14 106
King George Sound, strt., Austl. G3 74
King Hill, Id., U.S. G11 136
Kingisepp, Russia A11 10
King Island, i., Austl. m12 77a
King Island, i., B.C., Can. D3 138
King Leopold Ranges, mts., Austl. C4 74
Kingman, Az., U.S. H2 132
Kingman, Ks., U.S. D10 128
Kingman Reef, rf., Oc. C10 72
King Mountain, mtn., Or., U.S. H3 136
Kingombe, D.R.C. E5 66
Kingoonya, Austl. F7 74
King Peak, mtn., Ca., U.S. C1 134
Kings, stm., Ca., U.S. G6 134
Kings Beach, Ca., U.S. D5 134
Kingsbridge, Eng., U.K. K9 12
Kingsburg, Ca., U.S. G6 134
Kings Canyon National Park, p.o.i., Ca., U.S. G7 134
Kingsford, Mi., U.S. C1 112
Kingshill, V.I.U.S. h10 104c
Kingsland, Ar., U.S. D6 122
Kingsland, Ga., U.S. F4 116
Kingsley, S. Afr. E10 70
Kingsley, Ia., U.S. B2 120
Kingsley, Mi., U.S. D4 112
Kingsley Dam, dam, Ne., U.S. F11 126
King's Lynn, Eng., U.K. I13 12
Kings Mountain, N.C., U.S. A4 116
King Solomon's Mines see Mikhrot Timna', hist., Isr. I5 58
King Sound, strt., Austl. C4 74
Kings Peak, mtn., Ut., U.S. C6 132
Kingsport, Tn., U.S. H3 114
Kingston, N.S., Can. E11 110
Kingston, On., Can. D13 112
Kingston, Jam. I14 104d
Kingston, N.Z. G3 80
Kingston, Norf. I. y25 78i
Kingston, Ga., U.S. C14 122
Kingston, Mo., U.S. E3 120
Kingston, N.Y., U.S. C11 114
Kingston, Ok., U.S. C2 122
Kingston, Pa., U.S. C9 114
Kingston, Tn., U.S. I13 120
Kingston Southeast, Austl. K2 76
Kingston upon Hull, Eng., U.K. H12 12
Kingston upon Thames, Eng., U.K. J12 12
Kingstown, St. Vin. o11 105e
Kingstree, S.C., U.S. C6 116
Kingsville, On., Can. G7 112
Kingsville, Tx., U.S. G10 130
Kingtechen see Jingdezhen, China G7 42
King William Island, i., Nu., Can. B11 106
King William's Town, S. Afr. H8 70
Kinhwa see Jinhua, China G8 42
Kınık, Tur. D10 28
Kinira, stm., S. Afr. G9 70
Kinistino, Sk., Can. B9 124
Kinkala, Congo E2 66
Kinlochleven, Scot., U.K. E8 12
Kinnaird Head, c., Scot., U.K. D10 12
Kinneret, Yam (Galilee, Sea of), l., Isr. F6 58
Kinosaki, Japan D7 40
Kinpoku-san, mtn., Japan A11 40
Kinross, Scot., U.K. E9 12
Kinsale, Monts. D3 105a
Kinsale, Old Head of, c., Ire. J4 12
Kinsarvik, Nor. F2 8
Kinshasa (Léopoldville), D.R.C. E3 66
Kinsley, Ks., U.S. D9 128
Kinsman, Oh., U.S. C5 114
Kinston, N.C., U.S. A8 116
Kintampo, Ghana H4 64
Kintyre, pen., Scot., U.K. F7 12
Kintyre, Mull of, c., Scot., U.K. F7 12
Kinuseo Falls, wtfl, B.C., Can. B9 138
Kinuso, Ab., Can. A15 138
Kinyangiri, Tan. E6 66
Kinyeti, mtn., Sudan G6 62
Kinzia, D.R.C. E3 66
Kinzua, Or., U.S. E7 136
Kinzua Dam, dam, Pa., U.S. C6 114
Kiowa, Co., U.S. B4 128
Kiowa, Ok., U.S. C3 122
Kiowa Creek, stm., Co., U.S. A4 128
Kipawa, stm., Qc., Can. B11 112
Kipawa, Lac, res., Qc., Can. A10 112
Kipembawe, Tan. F6 66
Kipengere Range, mts., Tan. F6 66
Kipili, Tan. F6 66
Kipini, Kenya E8 66
Kipling, Sk., Can. D11 124
Kipnuk, Ak., U.S. E7 140
Kipushi, D.R.C. G5 66
Kirakira, Sol. Is. f9 79b
Kirandul, India B5 53
Kiraŭsk, Bela. G12 10
Kirazlı, Tur. C9 28
Kirbla, Est. B6 10
Kirbyville, Tx., U.S. G5 122
Kirchmöser, Ger. D8 16
Kireevsk, Russia G20 10
Kirejkovo, Russia G18 10
Kirenga, stm., Russia C19 32
Kirensk, Russia C19 32
Kirghizia see Kyrgyzstan, ctry., Asia F12 32
Kirgiz Range, mts., Asia F12 32
Kirgiz Soviet Socialist Republic see Kyrgyzstan, ctry., Asia F12 32
Kiri, D.R.C. E3 66
Kiribati, ctry., Oc. D9 72
Kırıkhan, Tur. B7 58
Kırıkkale, Tur. B3 56
Kirillovo, Russia H21 8
Kirin see Jilin, China C7 38
Kirin see Jilin, state, China C10 36
Kirinyaga (Kenya, Mount), mtn., Kenya E7 66
Kirishima-Yaku-kokuritsu-kōen, p.o.i., Japan H3 40
Kirishima-yama, vol., Japan H3 40
Kiriši, Russia A15 10
Kiritimati (Christmas Island), at., Kir. C11 72
Kiriwina Islands (Trobriand Islands), is., Pap. N. Gui. b5 79a
Kırka, Tur. D13 28
Kırkağaç, Tur. D10 28
Kirkcaldy, Scot., U.K. E9 12
Kirkcudbright, Scot., U.K. G8 12
Kirkenes, Nor. B14 8
Kirkland, Il., U.S. B9 120
Kirkland, Wa., U.S. C4 136
Kirkland Lake, On., Can. F14 106
Kırklareli, Tur. B10 28
Kırklareli, state, Tur. B10 28
Kirklin, In., U.S. H3 112
Kirkpatrick, Mount, mtn., Ant. D21 81
Kirksville, Mo., U.S. D5 120
Kirkwall, Scot., U.K. B9 12
Kirkwood, S. Afr. H7 70
Kirkwood, Mo., U.S. F7 120
Kirmir, stm., Tur. C15 28
Kirn, Ger. G3 16
Kirov, Russia F17 10
Kirov, Russia C7 32
Kirovakan see Vanadzor, Arm. A5 56
Kirovohrad, Ukr. E4 32
Kirovohrad, co., Ukr. A17 26
Kirovsk, Russia C15 8
Kirovsk, Turkmen. B9 56
Kirovskaja oblast', co., Russia F22 8
Kirovskij, Kaz. F13 32
Kirovskij, Russia F20 34
Kirovskij, Russia B10 38
Kirriemuir, Scot., U.K. E9 12
Kirs, Russia C8 32
Kirsanov, Russia D6 32
Kırşehir, Tur. B3 56
Kīrthar Range, mts., Pak. D10 56
Kirtland, N.M., U.S. G8 132
Kiruna, Swe. C8 8
Kirundu, D.R.C. E5 66
Kirwin, Ks., U.S. B9 128
Kiryū, Japan C12 40
Kirżač, Russia D21 10
Kisa, Swe. G6 8
Kisangani (Stanleyville), D.R.C. D5 66
Kisar, Pulau, i., Indon. G8 44
Kisaran, Indon. B1 50
Kisarazu, Japan D12 40
Kisbey, Sk., Can. E11 124
Kiselëvsk, Russia D15 32
Kīsh, Jazīreh-ye, i., Iran D7 56
Kishanganj, India E11 54
Kishangarh, India E3 54
Kishangarh Bās, India E5 54
Kishi, Nig. H5 64
Kishinev see Chişinău, Mol. B15 26
Kishiwada, Japan E8 40
Kishorganj, Bngl. F13 54
Kisii, Kenya E6 66
Kisiju, Tan. F7 66
Kisiwada see Kishiwada, Japan E8 40
Kiska Island, i., Ak., U.S. g22 140a
Kiskatinaw, stm., B.C., Can. A10 138
Kiska Volcano, vol., Ak., U.S. g22 140a
Kiskőrei-víztároló, res., Hung. B7 26
Kiskőrös, Hung. C6 26
Kiskunfélegyháza, Hung. C6 26
Kiskunhalas, Hung. C6 26
Kiskunmajsa, Hung. C6 26
Kiskunsági Nemzeti Park, p.o.i., Hung. C6 26
Kislovodsk, Russia F6 32
Kismaayo, Som. E8 66
Kiso, stm., Japan D9 40
Kiso-sammyaku, mts., Japan D10 40
Kissidougou, Gui. H2 64
Kissimmee, Fl., U.S. H4 116
Kissimmee, stm., Fl., U.S. I4 116
Kissimmee, Lake, l., Fl., U.S. I4 116
Kississing Lake, l., Mb., Can. D10 106
Kisújszállás, Hung. B7 26
Kisuki, Japan D5 40
Kisumu, Kenya E6 66
Kisvárda, Hung. A9 26
Kita, Mali G3 64
Kitaa see Vestgrønland, state, Grnld. D16 141
Kitaibaraki, Japan C13 40
Kitakami, stm., Japan E14 38
Kitakata, Japan B12 40
Kitakyūshū, Japan F3 40
Kitale, Kenya D7 66
Kitami, Japan C15 38
Kitangiri, Lake, l., Tan. E6 66
Kitchener, On., Can. E9 112
Kitharah, Khirbat, hist., Jord. I6 58
Kitimat, B.C., Can. B2 138
Kitimat Ranges, mts., B.C., Can. C2 138
Kitinen, stm., Fin. C12 8
Kitiou, Akrotírion, c., Cyp. D4 58
Kitridge Point, c., Barb. n9 105d
Kitsuki, Japan F4 40
Kittanning, Pa., U.S. D6 114
Kittitas, Wa., U.S. D6 136
Kitt Peak National Observatory, sci., Az., U.S. K5 132
Kitui, Kenya E7 66
Kitunda, Tan. F6 66
Kitwanga, B.C., Can. A4 138
Kitwe, Zam. C4 68
Kityang see Jieyang, China J7 42
Kitzbühel, Aus. C9 22
Kitzingen, Ger. G6 16
Kiukiang see Jiujiang, China G6 42
Kiunga, Pap. N. Gui. b3 79a
Kiuruvesi, Fin. E12 8
Kivalina, Ak., U.S. C7 140
Kivijärvi, l., Fin. E11 8
Kiviõli, Est. G12 8
Kivu, Lake, l., Afr. E5 66
Kıyıköy, Tur. B11 28
Kiyiu Lake, l., Sk., Can. C5 124
Kızıl Adalar, is., Tur. C11 28
Kızılcabölük, Tur. F11 28
Kızılcahamam, Tur. C15 28
Kızıldağ Milli Parkı, p.o.i., Tur. F14 28
Kızılırmak, stm., Tur. A4 56
Kızılören, Tur. F15 28
Kizimkazi, Tan. F7 66
Kızkalesi, hist., Tur. B4 58
Kizljar, Russia F7 32
Kizyl-Atrek, Turkmen. B7 56
Kizyl-Su, Turkmen. B7 56
Kjahta, Russia F10 34
Kjungej-Ala-Too, hrebet, mts., Asia F13 32
Kjusjur, Russia B14 34
Kjustendil, Blg. G9 26
Klabat, Gunung, vol., Indon. E8 44
Kladno, Czech Rep. F10 16
Kladovo, Yugo. E9 26
Klagan, Malay. G1 52
Klagenfurt, Aus. D11 22
Klaipėda (Memel), Lith. E3 10
Klakah, Indon. G8 50
Klamath, stm., U.S. B2 134
Klamath Falls, Or., U.S. A3 134
Klamath Marsh, sw., Or., U.S. H5 136
Klamath Mountains, mts., U.S. B2 134
Klamono, Indon. F9 44
Klang, Malay. K5 48
Klangenan, Indon. G6 50
Klangenang, Indon. G6 50
Klangpi, Mya. G14 54
Klatovy, Czech Rep. G9 16
Klawer, S. Afr. G4 70
Kleck, Bela. G9 10
Kleczew, Pol. D14 16
Kleena Kleene, B.C., Can. E5 138
Klein Curaçao, i., Neth. Ant. q22 104g
Klein Karroo see Little Karroo, plat., S. Afr. H5 70
Klein Namaland see Little Namaqualand, hist. reg., S. Afr. F3 70
Klekovača, mtn., Bos. E3 26
Klemme, Ia., U.S. A4 120
Klemtu, B.C., Can. D2 138
Klerksdorp, S. Afr. E8 70
Kletnja, Russia G16 10
Kleve, Ger. E2 16
Klickitat, stm., Wa., U.S. E5 136
Klimavičy, Bela. G14 10
Klimino, Russia C17 32
Klimovo, Russia H15 10
Klimovsk, Russia E20 10
Klimpfjäll, Swe. D6 8
Klin, Russia D19 10
Klinaklini, stm., B.C., Can. E5 138
Klincy, Russia H15 10
Klingenthal, Ger. F8 16
Klínovec, mtn., Czech Rep. F8 16
Klintehamn, Swe. H8 8
Klip, stm., S. Afr. E9 70
Klipdale, S. Afr. I4 70
Klipplaat, S. Afr. H7 70
Klisura, Blg. G11 26
Kljazma, stm., Russia E21 10
Ključ, Bos. E3 26
Ključevskaja Sopka, vulkan, vol., Russia E21 34
Ključi, Russia E21 34
Kljukvenka, Russia C15 32
Kłobuck, Pol. F14 16
Kłodawa, Pol. D14 16
Kłodzko, Pol. F12 16
Klondike, hist. reg., Yk., Can. C3 106
Klooga, Est. A7 10
Klosterneuburg, Aus. B13 22
Kloten, Switz. C5 22
Klotz, Lac, l., Qc., Can. C16 106
Klötze, Ger. D7 16
Kluane Lake, l., Yk., Can. C3 106
Kluczbork, Pol. F14 16
Klungkung, Indon. H9 50
Knaddah, Syria C7 58
Knapp, Wi., U.S. G6 118
Kneehills Creek, stm., Ab., Can. E17 138
Knee Lake, l., Mb., Can. D12 106
Kneža, Blg. F11 26
Knić, Yugo. F7 26
Knickerbocker, Tx., U.S. C7 130
Knife, stm., N.D., U.S. G12 124
Knight Inlet, b., B.C., Can. F4 138
Knights Landing, Ca., U.S. E4 134
Knin, Cro. F13 22
Knippa, Tx., U.S. E8 130
Knittelfeld, Aus. C11 22
Knjaževac, Yugo. F9 26
Knob Noster, Mo., U.S. F4 120
Knokke-Heist, Bel. C12 14
Knossós, hist., Grc. H8 28
Knox, Pa., U.S. C6 114
Knox, Cape, c., B.C., Can. E4 106
Knox City, Tx., U.S. H9 128
Knox Coast, cst., Ant. B15 81
Knoxville, Ga., U.S. D2 116
Knoxville, Il., U.S. D7 120
Knoxville, Tn., U.S. I2 114
Knuckles, mtn., Sri L. H5 53
Knud Rasmussen Land, reg., Grnld. A14 141
Knysna, S. Afr. I6 70
Knyszyn, Pol. C18 16
Kob', Russia C18 32
Kobar Sink, depr., Eth. E8 62
Kobayashi, Japan H3 40
Kōbe, Japan E8 40
København (Copenhagen), Den. I4 8
København, state, Den. I5 8
Kobjaj, Russia D14 34
Koblenz, Ger. F3 16
K'obo, Eth. E7 62
Koboža, Russia B18 10
Koboža, stm., Russia A18 10
Kobroor, Pulau, i., Indon. G10 44
Kobryn, Bela. H7 10
Kobuk, Ak., U.S. C8 140
Kobuk, stm., Ak., U.S. C8 140
Kobuleti, Geor. F6 32
Kobylin, Pol. E13 16
Kocaali, Tur. B13 28
Kocaavşar, stm., Tur. D10 28
Kocaeli, state, Tur. C12 28
Kočani, Mac. B5 28
Koçarlı, Tur. F10 28
Kočečum, stm., Russia C8 34
Kočevje, Slvn. E11 22
Kočevo, Russia C8 32
Koch'ang, Kor., S. G7 38
Koch Bihār, India E12 54
Kocher, stm., Ger. G5 16
Kochi (Cochin), India G3 53
Kōchi, Japan F6 40
Kōchi, state, Japan F6 40
Koch Island, i., Nu., Can. B15 106
Kochiu see Gejiu, China G5 36
Kodaikānal, India F3 53
Kodar, hrebet, mts., Russia E12 34
Kodāri, Nepal E10 54
Kodarma, India F10 54
Kodiak, Ak., U.S. E9 140
Kodiak Island, i., Ak., U.S. E9 140
Kodinār, India H3 54
Kodok, Sudan F6 62
Kodyma, Ukr. A16 26
Kodyma, stm., Ukr. B17 26
Koës, Nmb. D4 70
Köflach, Aus. C11 22
Koforidua, Ghana H4 64
Kōfu, Japan D11 40
Koga, Japan C12 40
Kogaluc, stm., Qc., Can. D15 106
Kogaluc, Baie, b., Qc., Can. D15 106
Kogan, Austl. F8 76
Køge, Den. I5 8
Kogon, stm., Gui. G2 64
Koḫanava, Bela. F12 10
Kohāt, Pak. B3 54
Kohīma, India C7 46
Kohler, Wi., U.S. E2 112
Kohtla-Järve, Est. G12 8
Kohyl'nyk (Cogâlnic), stm., Eur. C15 26
Koide, Japan B11 40
Koigi, Est. B8 10
Koindu, S.L. H2 64
Koiva (Gauja), stm., Eur. C7 10
Kojda, Russia C20 8
Koje-do, i., Kor., S. E1 40
Kojgorodok, Russia B8 32
Kojonup, Austl. F3 74
Kok (Hkok), stm., Asia B4 48
Kokalaat, Kaz. E10 32
Kokand, Uzb. F12 32
Kokas, Indon. F9 44
Kokčetav, Kaz. D12 32
Kokemäki, Fin. F9 8
Kokenau, Indon. F10 44
Kokhav HaYarden, hist., Isr. F6 58
Kokiu see Gejiu, China G5 36
Kokkilai Lagoon, b., Sri L. G5 53
Kokkola, Fin. E10 8
Kokoda, Pap. N. Gui. b4 79a
Kokomo, In., U.S. H3 112
Kokomo, Ms., U.S. F8 122
Kokong, Bots. D6 70
Kokopo, Pap. N. Gui. a5 79a
Kokorevka, Russia H17 10
Koksan-ŭp, Kor., N. E7 38
Kökshetaū see Kokčetav, Kaz. D12 32

Name	Map Ref.	Page
Koksoak, stm., Qc., Can.	D17	106
Kokstad, S. Afr.	G9	70
Kokubu, Japan	H3	40
Kola, Russia	B15	8
Kolachel, India	G3	53
Kolaka, Indon.	F7	44
Kolangār, Afg.	A2	54
Kola Peninsula see Kol'skij poluostrov, pen., Russia	C17	8
Kolār, India	E3	53
Kolāras, India	F6	54
Kolār Gold Fields, India	E4	53
Kolárovo, Slov.	I13	16
Kolašin, Yugo.	G6	26
Kolbio, Kenya	E8	66
Kolbuszowa, Pol.	F17	16
Kol'čugino, Russia	D22	10
Kolda, Sen.	G2	64
Kolding, Den.	I3	8
Kole, D.R.C.	E4	66
Kolea, Alg.	H13	20
Kolguev, ostrov, i., Russia	B18	6
Kolhāpur, India	C4	53
Kolhāpur, India	C1	53
Koli, Russia	A17	10
Kolín, Czech Rep.	F11	16
Koljubakino, Russia	E19	10
Kollam see Quilon, India	G3	53
Kollegāl, India	E3	53
Kolleru Lake, l., India	C5	53
Kolmogorovo, Russia	C16	32
Köln (Cologne), Ger.	E2	16
Kolno, Pol.	C17	16
Koło, Pol.	D14	16
Koloa, Hi., U.S.	B2	78a
Kołobrzeg, Pol.	B11	16
Kolodnja, Russia	F15	10
Kolokani, Mali	G3	64
Kolombangara Island, i., Sol. Is.	d7	79b
Kolomna, Russia	E21	10
Kolomyia, Ukr.	A12	26
Kolonga, Tonga	n14	78e
Kolonia, Micron.	m11	78d
Kolonodale, Indon.	F7	44
Kolosib, India	F14	54
Kolosovka, Russia	C12	32
Kolovai, Tonga	n13	78e
Kolozsvár see Cluj-Napoca, Rom.	C10	26
Kolp', stm., Russia	A19	10
Kolpaševo, Russia	C14	32
Kolpino, Russia	A13	10
Kolpny, Russia	H19	10
Kol'skij poluostrov (Kola Peninsula), pen., Russia	C17	8
Koluton, Kaz.	D11	32
Kolwezi, D.R.C.	G5	66
Kolyma, stm., Russia	C20	34
Kolyma Plain see Kolymskaja nizmennost', pl., Russia	C19	34
Kolymskaja, Russia	C20	34
Kolymskaja nizmennost' (Kolyma Plain), pl., Russia	C19	34
Kom, mtn., Blg.	F10	26
Koma, Mya.	E4	48
Komadugu Gana, stm., Nig.	G7	64
Komagane, Japan	D10	40
Komandorskie ostrova, is., Russia	D20	30
Komandorski Islands see Komandorskie ostrova, is., Russia	D20	30
Komárno, Slov.	I13	16
Komarnyky, Ukr.	G19	16
Komárom, Hung.	B5	26
Komárom-Esztergom, state, Hung.	B5	26
Komati (Incomati), stm., Afr.	E10	70
Komatipoort, S. Afr.	D10	70
Komatsu, Japan	C9	40
Komatsushima, Japan	E7	40
Kome Island, i., Ug.	E6	66
Komering, stm., Indon.	E4	50
Komfane, Indon.	G9	44
Komi, state, Russia	B8	32
Komissarovo, Russia	B9	38
Komló, Hung.	C5	26
Kommunizma, pik, mtn., Taj.	B11	56
Komodo, Pulau, i., Indon.	H11	50
Komodo National Park, p.o.i., Indon.	H11	50
Komoé, stm., Afr.	H4	64
Kom Ombo, Egypt	C6	62
Komoran, Pulau, i., Indon.	G10	44
Komoro, Japan	C11	40
Komotiní, Grc.	B8	28
Kompasberg, mtn., S. Afr.	G7	70
Komsomolec, Kaz.	D10	32
Komsomolec, zaliv, b., Kaz.	E8	32
Komsomol'sk, Russia	H18	8
Komsomol'sk, Russia	C15	32
Komsomol'sk-na-Amure, Russia	F16	34
Komsomol'skoj Pravdy, ostrova, is., Russia	A10	34
Konakovo, Russia	D19	10
Konakpınar, Tur.	D10	28
Konar, stm., Asia	A3	54
Konārak, India	I11	54
Konawa, Ok., U.S.	C2	122
Konch, India	F7	54
Konda, stm., Russia	B10	32
Kondagaon, India	B5	53
Kondega, Russia	F15	8
Kondinin, Austl.	F3	74
Kondoa, Tan.	E7	66
Kondopoga, Russia	E16	8
Kondrovo, Russia	F18	10
Kondukūr, India	D4	53
Kondūz, Afg.	B10	56
Koné, N. Cal.	m15	79d
Kong, stm., Asia	F8	48
Kŏng, Kaôh, i., Camb.	G6	48
Kongcheng, China	F7	42
Kong Christian IX Land, reg., Grnld.	D18	141
Kong Christian X Land, reg., Grnld.	C19	141
Kong Frederik VIII Land, reg., Grnld.	B19	141
Kong Frederik VI Kyst, cst., Grnld.	E17	141
Kongjiawopeng, China	B5	38
Kongju, Kor., S.	F7	38
Kongmoon see Jiangmen, China	J5	42
Kongolo, D.R.C.	F5	66
Kongor, Sudan	F6	62
Kong Oscar Fjord, strt., Grnld.	C21	141
Kongsvinger, Nor.	F5	8
Kongur Shan, mtn., China	G13	32
Kong Wilhelms Land, reg., Grnld.	B21	141
Konice, Czech Rep.	G12	16
Königsberg see Kaliningrad, Russia	F3	10
Königswinter, Ger.	F3	16
Konin, Pol.	D14	16
Konin, state, Pol.	D14	16
Konispol, Alb.	E14	24
Kónitsa, Grc.	C3	28
Konjic, Bos.	F4	26
Konkiep, stm., Nmb.	E3	70
Konkouré, stm., Gui.	G2	64
Konna, Mali	G4	64
Konnevesi, l., Fin.	E12	8
Konnur, India	C2	53
Konoša, Russia	F18	8
Kōnosu, Japan	C12	40
Konotop, Ukr.	E15	6
Końskie, Pol.	E16	16
Konstantinovskij, Russia	C22	10
Konstanz, Ger.	I4	16
Kontagora, Nig.	G5	64
Kontcha, Cam.	C2	66
Kontha, Mya.	C3	48
Kontseba, Ukr.	A16	26
Kon Tum, Viet.	E8	48
Konya, Tur.	F15	28
Konya, state, Tur.	E15	28
Konz, Ger.	G2	16
Konza, Kenya	E7	66
Konžakovskij Kamen', gora, mtn., Russia	C9	32
Koocanusa, Lake, res., N.A.	B11	136
Kookynie, Austl.	E4	74
Koolatah, Austl.	C8	74
Kooloonong, Austl.	J4	76
Koontz Lake, In., U.S.	G3	112
Koorawatha, Austl.	J7	76
Koosa, Est.	B9	10
Kooskia, Id., U.S.	D11	136
Kootenai (Kootenay), stm., N.A.	G13	138
Kootenay (Kootenai), stm., N.A.	G13	138
Kootenay Lake, l., B.C., Can.	G14	138
Kootenay National Park, p.o.i., B.C., Can.	F14	138
Kopāganj, India	E9	54
Kopargaon, India	B2	53
Kópavogur, Ice.	k29	8a
Kopejsk, Russia	C10	32
Koper, Slvn.	E10	22
Kopervik, Nor.	G1	8
Kopet Mountains, mts., Asia	B8	56
Köping, Swe.	G6	8
Koplik, Alb.	B13	24
Koppal, India	D3	53
Koppang, Nor.	F4	8
Koppies, S. Afr.	E8	70
Koprivnica, Cro.	D13	22
Köprü, stm., Tur.	F14	28
Köprülü Kanyon Milli Parkı, p.o.i., Tur.	F14	28
Kopylovo, Russia	F21	8
Korab (Korabit, Maja e), mtn., Eur.	C14	24
Korabit, Maja e (Korab), mtn., Eur.	C14	24
Korāput, India	B6	53
Korarou, Lac, l., Mali	F4	64
Koratla, India	B4	53
Korba, India	G9	54
Korba, Tun.	H4	24
Korbach, Ger.	E4	16
Korça see Korçë, Alb.	D14	24
Korçë, Alb.	D14	24
Korčula, Cro.	H14	22
Korčula, Otok, i., Cro.	H13	22
Korea, North, ctry., Asia	D7	38
Korea, South, ctry., Asia	G8	38
Korea Bay, b., Asia	E5	38
Korea Strait, strt., Asia	E2	40
Korelakša, Russia	D15	8
Korenovsk, Russia	E5	32
Korf, Russia	D22	34
Korhogo, C. Iv.	H3	64
Korientzé, Mali	F4	64
Korim, Indon.	F10	44
Korinthiakós Kólpos (Corinth, Gulf of), b., Grc.	E5	28
Kórinthos, Grc.	F5	28
Kōriyama, Japan	B13	40
Korjakskaja Sopka, vulkan, vol., Russia	F20	34
Korjakskoe nagor'e, mts., Russia	D22	34
Korjažma, Russia	F22	8
Korkino, Russia	D10	32
Korkuteli, Tur.	F13	28
Korla, China	C2	36
Korliki, Russia	B14	32
Körmend, Hung.	C3	26
Kornat, Otok, i., Cro.	G12	22
Kornati, Nacionalni Park, p.o.i., Cro.	G12	22
Korner, Mt., U.S.	A14	136
Korneuburg, Aus.	B13	22
Koro, i., Fiji	p19	79e
Köroğlu Tepesi, mtn., Tur.	C14	28
Korogwe, Tan.	F7	66
Koroleve, Ukr.	H19	16
Koromere see East Cape, c., N.Z.	C8	80
Koronadal, Phil.	G5	52
Koróni, Grc.	G4	28
Korónia, Límni, l., Grc.	C6	28
Korópi, Grc.	F6	28
Koror, Palau	g8	78b
Körös, stm., Hung.	C7	26
Koro Sea, Fiji	p20	79e
Korosten', Ukr.	E14	6
Koro Toro, Chad	D3	62
Korotyš, Russia	H20	10
Korovin Volcano, vol., Ak., U.S.	g24	140a
Korovou, Fiji	p19	79e
Koroyanitu, mtn., Fiji	p18	79e
Korsakov, Russia	G17	34
Korsakovo, Russia	G20	10
Korsør, Den.	I4	8
Koršunovo, Russia	C20	32
Kortrijk, Bel.	D12	14
Korucam, Cape see Koruçam Burnu, c., N. Cyp.	C3	58
Koruçam Burnu, c., N. Cyp.	C3	58
Korucu, Tur.	D10	28
Korumburra, Austl.	L5	76
Koryak Mountains see Korjakskoe nagor'e, mts., Russia	D22	34
Koryŏng, Kor., S.	D1	40
Kos (Cos), i., Grc.	G10	28
Kosa, Russia	C8	32
Kosa, Russia	F10	34
Kosai, Japan	E10	40
Kosaja Gora, Russia	F20	10
Koščagyl, Kaz.	E8	32
Kościan, Pol.	D12	16
Kościerzyna, Pol.	B14	16
Kosciusko, Ms., U.S.	D9	122
Kosciusko, Mount, mtn., Austl.	K6	76
Kosciusko National Park, p.o.i., Austl.	K6	76
Kose, Est.	A8	10
Koshikijima-rettō, is., Japan	H2	40
Koshkonong, Lake, l., Wi., U.S.	B9	120
Kōshoku, Japan	C11	40
Košice, Slov.	H17	16
Kosi Kalan, India	E6	54
Kosimeer, l., S. Afr.	E11	70
Kosiv, Ukr.	A12	26
Köşk, Tur.	F11	28
Koslan, Russia	E23	8
Kosŏng, Kor., S.	E1	40
Kosŏng-ŭp, Kor., N.	E8	38
Kosovo-Metohija, co., Yugo.	G7	26
Kosovska Mitrovica, Yugo.	G7	26
Kosrae, i., Micron.	C7	72
Kösreli, Tur.	A6	58
Kosse, Tx., U.S.	F2	122
Kossou, Lac de, res., C. Iv.	H3	64
Kostenec, Blg.	G10	26
Koster, S. Afr.	D8	70
Kostomukša, Russia	D14	8
Kostonjärvi, l., Fin.	D12	8
Kostroma, Russia	H19	8
Kostroma, stm., Russia	G19	8
Kostromskaja oblast', co., Russia	G20	8
Kostrzyn, Pol.	D10	16
Kosum Phisai, Thai.	D6	48
Koszalin, Pol.	B12	16
Koszalin, state, Pol.	C12	16
Kőszeg, Hung.	B3	26
Kota, India	G9	54
Kota, India	F5	54
Kotaagung, Indon.	F4	50
Kotabangun, Indon.	D10	50
Kotabaru, Indon.	E10	50
Kota Belud, Malay.	G1	52
Kota Bharu, Malay.	I6	48
Kotabumi, Indon.	F4	50
Kotadabok, Indon.	D4	50
Kot Addu, Pak.	C3	54
Kota Kinabalu, Malay.	G1	52
Kotamobagu, Indon.	E7	44
Kotapinang, Indon.	C1	50
Kota Tinggi, Malay.	L6	48
Kotawaringin, Indon.	E7	50
Kotcho Lake, l., B.C., Can.	D6	106
Kot Chutta, Pak.	D3	54
Kotel'nič, Russia	C7	32
Kotel'nikovo, Russia	E6	32
Kotel'nyj, ostrov, i., Russia	A16	34
Kotelnyj, ostrov, i., Russia	B3	34
Köthen, Ger.	E7	16
Kotikovo, Russia	G17	34
Kotka, Fin.	F12	8
Kot Kapūra, India	C5	54
Kotlas, Russia	F22	8
Kotli, Pak.	B4	54
Kotlik, Ak., U.S.	D7	140
Kôtomo, Île, i., N. Cal.	n16	79d
Kotor, Yugo.	G5	26
Kotoriba, Cro.	D13	22
Kotovs'k, Ukr.	B16	26
Kot Pūtli, India	E6	54
Kotri, Pak.	F2	54
Kottagūdem, India	C5	53
Kottayam, India	G3	53
Kotto, stm., C.A.R.	C4	66
Kottūru, India	D3	53
Kotuj, stm., Russia	B9	34
Kotzebue, Ak., U.S.	C7	140
Kotzebue Sound, strt., Ak., U.S.	C7	140
Kötzting, Ger.	G8	16
Kouang-si see Guangxi, state, China	G6	36
Kouang-tong see Guangdong, state, China	J6	42
Kouaoua, N. Cal.	m15	79d
Kouchibouguac National Park, p.o.i., N.B., Can.	D11	110
Koudougou, Burkina	G4	64
Kouei-tcheou see Guizhou, state, China	H2	42
Kouga, stm., S. Afr.	H7	70
Kougaberge, mts., S. Afr.	H6	70
Koukdjuak, stm., Nu., Can.	B16	106
Kouki, C.A.R.	C3	66
Koúklia, Cyp.	D3	58
Koulamoutou, Gabon	E2	66
Koulikoro, Mali	G3	64
Koumala, Austl.	C7	76
Koumbia, Gui.	G2	64
Koumpentoum, Sen.	G2	64
Koumra, Chad	F3	62
Koundâra, Gui.	G2	64
Kounradskij, Kaz.	E12	32
Kourou, Fr. Gu.	B7	84
Kouroussa, Gui.	G3	64
Kousséri, Cam.	B2	66
Koussi, Emi, mtn., Chad	D3	62
Koutiala, Mali	G3	64
Kouts, In., U.S.	G2	112
Kouvola, Fin.	F12	8
Kova, Russia	C18	32
Kovada Milli Parkı, p.o.i., Tur.	F13	28
Kovarskas, Lith.	E7	10
Kovdor, Russia	C14	8
Kovdozero, ozero, res., Russia	C14	8
Kovilpatti, India	G3	53
Kovrov, Russia	H19	8
Kovūr, India	D5	53
Kovža, Russia	F18	8
Kowalewo Pomorskie, Pol.	C14	16
Kowloon see Jiulong, China	J5	42
Kowŏn-ŭp, Kor., N.	E7	38
Kowt-e'Ashrow, Afg.	C10	56
Koxtag, China	A4	46
Köyceğiz Gölü, l., Tur.	G11	28
Koyna Reservoir, res., India	C1	53
Koyuk, Ak., U.S.	D7	140
Koyukuk, Ak., U.S.	D8	140
Koyukuk, stm., Ak., U.S.	C8	140
Kō-zaki, c., Japan	E2	40
Kozan, Tur.	A6	58
Kozáni, Grc.	C4	28
Kožany, Russia	H14	10
Kozel'sk, Russia	F18	10
Koževnikovo, Russia	C14	32
Kozhikode (Calicut), India	F2	53
Kozienice, Pol.	E17	16
Kozlov Bereg, Russia	B10	10
Kozlovo, Russia	D19	10
Kozlu, Tur.	B14	28
Koz'mino, Russia	F22	8
Kožposëlok, Russia	E17	8
Kōzu-shima, i., Japan	E12	40
Kpalimé, Togo	H5	64
Kra, Isthmus of, isth., Asia	H4	48
Kraai, stm., S. Afr.	G8	70
Krabi, Thai.	H4	48
Krâchéh, Camb.	F8	48
Kraeva, Russia	B9	38
Kragan, Indon.	G7	50
Kragujevac, Yugo.	F7	26
Krajenka, Pol.	C13	16
Krakatoa see Rakata, Pulau, i., Indon.	G4	50
Krakovets', Ukr.	G19	16
Kraków, Pol.	F15	16
Kraków, state, Pol.	G15	16
Kralendijk, Neth. Ant.	p23	104g
Kraljevo, Yugo.	F7	26
Kralovice, Czech Rep.	G9	16
Kralupy nad Vltavou, Czech Rep.	F10	16
Kramators'k, Ukr.	E5	32
Kramfors, Swe.	E7	8
Kranídi, Grc.	F6	28
Kranj (Krainburg), Slvn.	D11	22
Kranskop, S. Afr.	F10	70
Krapivna, Russia	G18	10
Krasavino, Russia	F22	8
Krasieo, stm., Thai.	E4	48
Krasivaja Meča, stm., Russia	G20	10
Krāslava, Lat.	E10	10
Krasnae, Bela.	F10	10
Krasnaja Gorbatka, Russia	I19	8
Krasnaja Slabada, Bela.	H9	10
Krasnaluki, Bela.	F11	10
Krasneno, Russia	D23	34
Kraśnik, Pol.	F18	16
Kraśnik Fabryczny, Pol.	F18	16
Krasni Okny, Ukr.	B16	26
Krasnoarmejsk, Russia	D21	10
Krasnoarmejskij, Russia	C23	34
Krasnobród, Pol.	F19	16
Krasnodar, Russia	E5	32
Krasnoe, ozero, l., Russia	D23	34
Krasnoe Selo, Russia	A12	10
Krasnoe Znamja, Russia	C18	10
Krasnogorodskoe, Russia	D11	10
Krasnogorsk, Russia	E20	10
Krasnogorsk, Russia	G17	34
Krasnojarovo, Russia	F14	34
Krasnojarsk, Russia	C16	32
Krasnojarskoe vodohranilišče, res., Russia	D16	32
Krasnokamsk, Russia	C8	32
Krasnomajskij, Russia	C17	10
Krasnoščele, Russia	C17	8
Krasnosel'kup, Russia	A14	32
Krasnoturjinsk, Russia	C10	32
Krasnoufimsk, Russia	C9	32
Krasnoural'sk, Russia	C10	32
Krasnovišersk, Russia	B9	32
Krasnovodskij poluostrov, pen., Turkmen.	A7	56
Krasnozavodsk, Russia	D20	10
Krasnozërskoe, Russia	D14	32
Krasnoznamensk, Russia	F5	10
Krasnoznamenskoe, Kaz.	D11	32
Krasnye Gory, Russia	B12	10
Krasnyj Čikoj, Russia	F10	34
Krasnyj Gorodok, Russia	C16	10
Krasnyj Jar, Russia	C12	32
Krasnyj Luč, Russia	C13	10
Krasnyj Oktjabr', Russia	D21	10
Krasnyj Tkač, Russia	E22	10
Krasnystaw, Pol.	E19	16
Kratovo, Mac.	A5	28
Krâvanh, Chuŏr Phnum, mts., Camb.	F6	48
Krbava, reg., Cro.	F12	22
Krečetovo, Russia	F18	8
Krefeld, Ger.	E2	16
Kremastón, Technití Límni, res., Grc.	E4	28
Kremenchug Reservoir see Kremenchuts'ke vodoskhovyshche, res., Ukr.	E4	32
Kremenchuk, Ukr.	E4	32
Kremenchuts'ke vodoskhovyshche, res., Ukr.	E4	32
Kremenskoe, Russia	E18	10
Kremmling, Co., U.S.	C10	132
Krems an der Donau, Aus.	B12	22
Kress, Tx., U.S.	G7	128
Kresta, zaliv, b., Russia	C25	34
Krestcy, Russia	B22	10
Krestcy, Russia	B15	10
Krest-Maër, Russia	C17	34
Kretinga, Lith.	E4	10
Kribi, Cam.	D1	66
Křimice, Czech Rep.	G9	16
Krishna, stm., India	C5	53
Krishna, Mouths of the, mth., India	D5	53
Krishnagiri, India	E4	53
Krishnanagar, India	G12	54
Krishnarāja Sāgara, res., India	E3	53
Krishnarājpet, India	E3	53
Kristiansand, Nor.	G3	8
Kristianstad, Swe.	I6	8
Kristiansund, Nor.	E2	8
Kristiinankaupunki (Kristinestad), Fin.	E9	8
Kristinehamn, Swe.	G6	8
Kristinestad see Kristiinankaupunki, Fin.	E9	8
Kríti, state, Grc.	H7	28
Kríti (Crete), i., Grc.	H7	28
Kritikón Pélagos (Crete, Sea of), Grc.	H8	28
Kriva Palanka, Mac.	A5	28
Krivodol, Blg.	F10	26
Križevci, Cro.	D13	22
Krjukovo, Russia	E20	10
Krjukovo, Russia	C20	34
Krk, Otok, i., Cro.	E11	22
Krnov, Czech Rep.	F13	16
Krobia, Pol.	E12	16
Krøderen, l., Nor.	F3	8
Krokodil, stm., S. Afr.	D8	70
Krom, stm., S. Afr.	G4	70
Kroměříž, Czech Rep.	G13	16
Kromy, Russia	H18	10
Kronach, Ger.	F7	16
Krŏng Kaôh Kŏng, Camb.	G6	48
Krŏng Kêb, Camb.	G7	48
Kronoberg, state, Swe.	H6	8
Kronockaja Sopka, vulkan, vol., Russia	F21	34
Kronockij zaliv, b., Russia	F21	34
Kronoki, Russia	F21	34
Kronprins Christian Land, reg., Grnld.	A22	141
Kronštadt, Russia	A12	10
Kroonstad, S. Afr.	E8	70
Kropotkin, Russia	E6	32
Kropotkin, Russia	E12	34
Krośniewice, Pol.	D14	16
Krosno, Pol.	G17	16
Krosno, state, Pol.	G17	16
Krotoszyn, Pol.	E13	16
Krotz Springs, La., U.S.	G7	122
Kroya, Indon.	G6	50
Krško, Slvn.	E12	22
Kruger National Park, p.o.i., S. Afr.	C10	70
Krugersdorp, S. Afr.	E8	70
Kruhlae, Bela.	F12	10
Krui, Indon.	F3	50
Kruisfontein, S. Afr.	H7	70
Kruja see Krujë, Alb.	C13	24
Krujë, Alb.	C13	24
Krumbach, Ger.	H6	16
Krumovgrad, Blg.	H12	26
Krung Thep (Bangkok), Thai.	F5	48
Kruså, Den.	B5	16
Kruševac, Yugo.	F8	26
Krušinovka, Bela.	G12	10
Krutcy, Russia	C12	10
Krutoe, Russia	H20	10
Kruzenšterna, proliv, strt., Russia	G19	34
Kruzof Island, i., Ak., U.S.	E12	140
Kryčau, Bela.	G14	10
Kryms'kyi pivostriv (Crimean Peninsula), pen., Ukr.	E4	32
Krynica, Pol.	G16	16
Krynychne, Ukr.	D15	26
Kryve Ozero, Ukr.	B17	26
Kryvošyn, Bela.	H8	10
Kryvyj Rih, Ukr.	E4	32
Kryzhopil', Ukr.	A15	26
Krzeszowice, Pol.	F15	16
Krzyż, Pol.	D11	16
Ksenevka, Russia	F12	34
Kstovo, Russia	H20	8
Kuah, Malay.	I4	48
Kuai, stm., China	E7	42
Kualacenako, Indon.	D3	50
Kuala Kangsar, Malay.	J5	48
Kualakapuas, Indon.	E9	50
Kuala Krai, Malay.	J6	48
Kuala Kubu Baharu, Malay.	K5	48
Kualakurun, Indon.	D8	50
Kualalangsa, Indon.	J4	48
Kuala Lipis, Malay.	J5	48
Kuala Lumpur, Malay.	K5	48
Kuala Nerang, Malay.	I5	48
Kualapesaguan, Indon.	E6	50
Kuala Pilah, Malay.	K6	48
Kuala Rompin, Malay.	K6	48
Kuala Sepetang, Malay.	J5	48
Kualasimpang, Indon.	J3	48
Kuala Terengganu, Malay.	J6	48
Kualu, stm., Indon.	B1	50
Kuamut, stm., Malay.	A10	50
Kuancheng, China	A8	42
Kuandian, China	D6	38
Kuan Shan, mtn., Tai.	J9	42
Kuantan, Malay.	K6	48
Kuanyün see Guanyun, China	D8	42
Kuban', stm., Russia	E6	32
Kubenskoe, ozero, l., Russia	G18	8
Kubokawa, Japan	F6	40
Kubrat, Blg.	F13	26
Kučema, Russia	D20	8
Kuchaiburi, India	G11	54
Kuchāman, India	E5	54
Kuching, Malay.	C7	50
Kūchnay Darweyshān, Afg.	C9	56
Kuchurhan, stm., Eur.	B16	26
Kuçova see Kuçovë, Alb.	D13	24
Kuçovë, Alb.	D13	24
Kūd, India	B5	54
Kudamatsu, Japan	F4	40
Kudat, Malay.	G1	52
Kudever', Russia	D12	10
Kudirkos Naumiestis, Lith.	F5	10
Kudus, Indon.	G7	50
Kudymkar, Russia	C8	32
Kuee Ruins, hist., Hi., U.S.	D6	78a
Kueisui see Hohhot, China	A4	42
Kueiyang see Guiyang, China	H2	42
K'uerhlo see Korla, China	C2	36
Kufstein, Aus.	C9	22
Kugluktuk, Nu., Can.	B8	106
Kugmallit Bay, b., N.T., Can.	C13	140
Kuhësi see Kukës, Alb.	B14	24
Kuhmoinen, Fin.	F11	8
Kuhn Ø, i., Grnld.	C22	141
Kuial'nyts'kyi lyman, l., Ukr.	C17	26
Kuiseb, stm., S. Afr.	C2	70
Kuitan, China	J7	42
Kuito, Ang.	C2	68
Kuiu Island, i., Ak., U.S.	E13	140
Kuivastu, Est.	G10	8
Kuja, Russia	D18	8
Kujang-ŭp, Kor., N.	E7	38
Kujawy, reg., Pol.	D14	16
Kujbyšev, Russia	C13	32
Kujbyševskoe vodohranilišče, res., Russia	D7	32
Kujgan, Kaz.	E12	32
Kujū-san, vol., Japan	F4	40
Kukalaya, stm., Nic.	F6	102
Kukawa, Nig.	G7	64
Kukës, Alb.	B14	24
Kukoboj, Russia	B22	10
Kükong see Shaoguan, China	I5	42
Kukshi, India	G5	54
Kukuj, Russia	A15	10
Kukukus Lake, l., On., Can.	B7	118
Kukurtli, Turkmen.	B8	56
Kula, Blg.	F9	26
Kula, Tur.	E11	28
Kula, Yugo.	D6	26
Kulagi, Russia	H15	10
Kula Gulf, strt., Sol. Is.	e7	79b
Kulai, Malay.	L6	48
Kula Kangri, mtn., Bhu.	E13	54
Kular, Russia	B15	34
Kulaura, Bngl.	F13	54
Kuldīga, Lat.	D5	10
Kuldja see Yining, China	F14	32
Kule, Bots.	C5	70
Kulebaki, Russia	I20	8
Kulen Vakuf, Bos.	E3	26
Kulim, Malay.	J5	48
Kuljab, Taj.	B10	56
Kulkyne Creek, stm., Austl.	H5	76
Kullu, India	B6	54
Kulm, N.D., U.S.	A13	126
Kulmbach, Ger.	F7	16
Kuloj, Russia	D20	8
Kuloj, Russia	F20	8
Kuloj, stm., Russia	D20	8
Kul'sary, Kaz.	E8	32
Kulti, India	G11	54
Kultuk, Russia	D18	32
Kulu, Tur.	D16	28
Kulunda, Russia	D13	32
Kulundinskaja ravnina, pl., Asia	D13	32
Kulundinskoe, ozero, l., Russia	D13	32
Kulwin, Austl.	J4	76
Kumagaya, Japan	C12	40
Kumai, Indon.	E8	50
Kumai, Teluk, b., Indon.	E7	50
Kumajri see Gjumri, Arm.	A5	56
Kumamoto, Japan	G3	40
Kumamoto, state, Japan	G3	40
Kumano, Japan	F9	40
Kumano-nada, Japan	F9	40
Kumanovo, Mac.	A4	28
Kumara, Russia	F14	34
Kumārghāt, India	F14	54
Kumasi, Ghana	H4	64
Kumba, Cam.	D1	66
Kumbakonam, India	F4	53
Kumbarilla, Austl.	F8	76
Kumdanlı, Tur.	E13	28
Kume-jima, i., Japan	I18	39a
Kŭm-gang, stm., Kor., S.	F7	38
Kumla, Swe.	G6	8
Kumluca, Tur.	B15	28
Kumluca, Tur.	G13	28
Kumo, Nig.	H7	64
Kumon Range, mts., Mya.	C8	46
Kumora, Russia	E11	34
Kumta, India	D2	53
Kumu, D.R.C.	D5	66
Kumukahi, Cape, c., Hi., U.S.	o16	135a
Kümüx, China	C2	36
Kŭmya-ŭp, Kor., N.	E7	38
Kuna, Id., U.S.	G10	136
Kunašir, ostrov (Kunashiri-tō), i., Russia	C16	38
Kunda, Est.	G12	8
Kunda Hills, hills, India	F3	53
Kundāpura, India	E2	53
Kundar, stm., Asia	C2	54
Kunderu, stm., India	D4	53
Kundiān, Pak.	B3	54
Kundiawa, Pap. N. Gui.	b3	79a
Kundla, India	H3	54
Kundur, Pulau, i., Indon.	C3	50
Kunene, state, Nmb.	B2	70
Kunene (Cunene), stm., Afr.	D1	68
Kunes, Nor.	A12	8
Kungchuling see Gongzhuling, China	C6	38
Kunggyü Yumco, l., China	C9	54
Kunghit Island, i., B.C., Can.	E4	106
Kungrad, Uzb.	F9	32
Kungsbacka, Swe.	H4	8
Kungur, Russia	C9	32
Kunhegyes, Hung.	B7	26
Kuningan, Indon.	G6	50
Kunisaki, Japan	F4	40
Kunisaki-hantō, pen., Japan	F4	40
Kunja, Russia	D13	10
Kunja, stm., Russia	D13	10
Kunlong, Mya.	D8	46
Kunlun Mountains see Kunlun Shan, mts., China	A5	46
Kunlun Shan, mts., China	A5	46
Kunming, China	F5	36
Kunnamkulam, India	F2	53
Kunsan, Kor., S.	F7	38
Kunshan, China	F9	42
Kunting, China	G9	42
Kununurra, Austl.	C5	74
Kunwi, Kor., S.	C1	40
Kunya, Nig.	G6	64
Künzelsau, Ger.	G5	16
Kuopio, Fin.	E12	8
Kuopio, state, Fin.	E12	8
Kupa, stm., Eur.	E12	22
Kupang, Indon.	H7	44
Kupanskoe, Russia	D21	10
Kup'ians'k, Ukr.	E5	32
Kupino, Russia	D13	32
Kupiškis, Lith.	E7	10
Kupreanof Island, i., Ak., U.S.	E13	140
Kuqa, China	F14	32
Kuqa, China	F14	32
Kuragino, Russia	D16	32
Kuranec, Bela.	F9	10
Kurashiki, Japan	E6	40
Kurasiki see Kurashiki, Japan	E6	40
Kurauli, India	E7	54
Kuraymah, Sudan	D6	62
Kurayoshi, Japan	D6	40
Kurčatov, Russia	D5	32
Kurčum, Kaz.	E14	32
Kurdistān, hist. reg., Asia	B5	56
Kurdistan see Kurdistān, hist. reg., Asia	B5	56
Kurdufān, state, Sudan	E6	62
Kurduvādi, India	B2	53
Kure, Japan	E5	40
Kurejka, stm., Russia	C7	34
Kuresaare, Est.	G10	8
Kurgal'džinskij, Kaz.	D12	32
Kurgan, Russia	C11	32
Kurgan-Tjube, Taj.	B10	56
Kuria, i., Kir.	C8	72
Kuria Muria Islands see Ḥallānīyah, Juzur al-, is., Oman	F8	56
Kuridala, Austl.	C3	76
Kurīgrām, Bngl.	F12	54
Kurikka, Fin.	E10	8
Kuril Islands see Kuril'skie ostrova, is., Russia	E19	30
Kuril'sk, Russia	B14	36
Kuril'skie ostrova (Kuril Islands), is., Russia	E19	30
Kuril Strait see Pervyj Kuril'skij proliv, strt., Russia	F20	34
Kuril Trench, unds.	E18	142
Kurinjippadi, India	F4	53
Kurinwás, stm., Nic.	F5	102
Kurjanovskaja, Russia	F19	8
Kurkliai, Lith.	E8	10
Kurmuk, Sudan	E6	62
Kurnool, India	D3	53
Kurobe, Japan	C10	40
Kurort Schmalkalden, Ger.	F6	16
Kurovskoe, Russia	E21	10
Kurow, N.Z.	G4	80
Kuršėnai, Lith.	D6	10
Kurseong, India	E12	54
Kuršiu nerija (Kurššskaja kosa), spit, Eur.	E3	10
Kursk, Russia	D5	32
Kurskaja oblast', co., Russia	H19	10
Kurššskaja kosa (Kuršiu nerija), spit, Eur.	E3	10
Kuršumlija, Yugo.	F8	26
Kurşunlu, Tur.	C16	28
Kūrtī, Sudan	D6	62
Kurtistown, Hi., U.S.	D6	78a
Kurtoğlu Burnu, c., Tur.	G11	28
Kuruktag, mts., China	C2	36
Kuruman, S. Afr.	E6	70
Kuruman, stm., S. Afr.	E5	70
Kurumanheuwels, mts., S. Afr.	E6	70
Kurume, Japan	F3	40
Kurumkan, Russia	F11	34
Kurunegala, Sri L.	H5	53
Kuruqi, China	B9	36
Kuryongp'o, Kor., S.	C2	40
Kuşadası, Tur.	F10	28
Kuşadası Körfezi, b., Tur.	F9	28
Kusan-ni, Kor., S.	B1	40
Kusawa Lake, l., Yk., Can.	D12	140
Kuş Gölü, l., Tur.	C10	28
Kuş Gölü Milli Parkı, p.o.i., Tur.	C10	28
Kushālgarh, India	G5	54
Kusheriki, Nig.	G6	64
Kushikino, Japan	H3	40
Kushima, Japan	H4	40
Kushiro, Japan	C16	38
Kushnytsia, Ukr.	A10	26
Kushtia, Bngl.	G12	54
Kushui, China	C3	36
Kusiro see Kushiro, Japan	C16	38
Kusiyāra, stm., Bngl.	F13	54
Kuskokwim, stm., Ak., U.S.	D7	140
Kuskokwim Bay, b., Ak., U.S.	E7	140
Kuskokwim Mountains, mts., Ak., U.S.	D8	140
Kuśmā, Nepal	D9	54
Kušmurun, Kaz.	D10	32
Kušmurun, ozero, l., Kaz.	D10	32
Kustanaj, Kaz.	D10	32
Kūstī, Sudan	E6	62
Kusu, Japan	F4	40
Kut, Ko, i., Thai.	G6	48
Kutabaru, Indon.	D3	50
Kutacane, Indon.	K3	48
Kütahya, Tur.	D13	28
Kütahya, state, Tur.	D12	28
Kutaisi, Geor.	F6	32
Kutch, Rann of (Kachchh, Rann of), reg., Asia	D2	46
Kutima, Russia	C19	32
Kutina, Cro.	E13	22
Kutiyāna, India	H3	54
Kutná Hora, Czech Rep.	G11	16
Kutno, Pol.	D15	16
Kutse Game Reserve, Bots.	C7	70
Kutu, D.R.C.	E3	66
Kutubdia Island, i., Bngl.	H13	54
Kutum, Sudan	E4	62
Kúty, Slov.	H13	16
Kuujjuaq, Qc., Can.	D17	106
Kuuli-Majak, Turkmen.	A7	56
Kuusamo, Fin.	D13	8
Kuusankoski, Fin.	F12	8
Kuvango, Ang.	C2	68
Kuvšinovo, Russia	C16	10
Kuwait see Al-Kuwayt, Kuw.	D6	56
Kuwait, ctry., Asia	D6	56
Kuwana, Japan	D9	40
Kuybyshev Reservoir see Kujbyševskoe vodohranilišče, res., Russia	D7	32
Kuye, stm., China	B4	42
Kuženkino, Russia	C16	10
Kuz'miniči, Russia	F16	10
Kuz'movka, Russia	B16	32
Kuzneck, Russia	D7	32
Kuzneckij Alatau, mts., Russia	D15	32
Kuznecovka, Russia	D11	10
Kuznetsk see Kuzneck, Russia	D7	32
Kuzomen', Russia	C17	8
Kvænangen, b., Nor.	A9	8
Kvaløya, i., Nor.	B8	8
Kvaløya, i., Nor.	A10	8
Kvam, Nor.	F3	8
Kvarnbergsvattnet, l., Swe.	D5	8
Kvarner, b., Cro.	F11	22
Kvarnerić, b., Cro.	F11	22
Kverkfjöll, vol., Ice.	k31	8a
Kvichak Bay, b., Ak., U.S.	E8	140
Kwa, stm., D.R.C.	E3	66
Kwai see Khwae Noi, stm., Thai.	E4	48

Name | Map Ref. | Page

Kwajalein, at., Marsh. Is. C7 72
Kwakoegron, Sur. B6 84
Kwamisa, mtn., Ghana H4 64
Kwamouth, D.R.C. E3 66
Kwando (Cuando), stm., Afr. D3 68
Kwangchow see Guangzhou, China J5 42
Kwangju, Kor., S. G7 38
Kwango (Cuango), stm., Afr. E3 66
Kwangsi Chuang see Guangxi, state, China G6 36
Kwangtung see Guangdong, state, China J6 42
KwaZulu-Natal, state, S. Afr. F10 70
Kweichow see Guizhou, state, China F6 36
Kweihwa see Hohhot, China A4 42
Kweilin see Guilin, China I4 42
Kweisui see Hohhot, China A4 42
Kweiyang see Guiyang, China H2 42
Kwekwe, Zimb. D4 68
Kweneng, state, Bots. C7 70
Kwenge (Caengo), stm., Afr. B2 68
Kwethluk, Ak., U.S. D7 140
Kwidzyn, Pol. C14 16
Kwigillingok, Ak., U.S. E7 140
Kwilu (Cuilo), stm., Afr. F3 66
Kyabra, Austl. F4 76
Kyabra Creek, stm., Austl. E4 76
Kyabram, Austl. K5 76
Kyaikkami, Mya. D3 48
Kyaiklat, Mya. D2 48
Kyaikto, Mya. D3 48
Kya-in, Mya. D4 48
Kyalite, Austl. J4 76
Kyancutta, Austl. F7 74
Ky Anh, Viet. C8 48
Kyaukhnyat, Mya. C3 48
Kyaukme, Mya. A3 48
Kyaukpa, Mya. F4 48
Kyaukpyu, Mya. C1 48
Kyaukse, Mya. B2 48
Kyauktaw, Mya. D7 46
Kyaunggon, Mya. D2 48
Kybartai, Lith. F5 10
Kyebang-san, mtn., Kor., S. B1 40
Kyeikdon, Mya. E4 48
Kyidaunggan, Mya. C3 48
Kyïv (Kiev), Ukr. D4 32
Kyïvs'ke vodoskhovyshche, res., Ukr. D4 32
Kyjov, Czech Rep. G13 16
Kykotsmovi Village, Az., U.S. H6 132
Kyle, Sk., Can. D5 124
Kyle, S.D., U.S. D10 126
Kyle, Lake, res., Zimb. B10 70
Kyllini, Grc. F4 28
Kymi, state, Fin. F12 8
Kyneton, Austl. K5 76
Kynšperk nad Ohří, Czech Rep. F8 16
Kyoga, Lake, l., Ug. D6 66
Kyogle, Austl. G9 76
Kyŏngju, Kor., S. D2 40
Kyŏngsan, Kor., S. D1 40
Kyŏngsang-bukto, state, Kor., S. C1 40
Kyŏngsang-namdo, state, Kor., S. D1 40
Kyŏngsŏng-ŭp, Kor., N. D8 38
Kyonkadun, Mya. D2 48
Kyonpyaw, Mya. D2 48
Kyōto, Japan D8 40
Kyōto, state, Japan D8 40
Kyparissía, Grc. F4 28
Kyparissiakós Kólpos, b., Grc. F4 28
Kyra, Russia G11 34
Kyren, Russia D18 32
Kyrgyzstan, ctry., Asia F12 32
Kyritz, Ger. D8 16
Kyrönjoki, stm., Fin. E10 8
Kyrösjärvi, l., Fin. F10 8
Kyštym, Russia C10 32
Kythira, Grc. G5 28
Kýthira, i., Grc. G5 28
Kýthnos, i., Grc. F7 28
Kyundon, Mya. B2 48
Kyungyi, i., Mya. E3 48
Kyuquot, B.C., Can. F3 138
Kyūshū, i., Japan G2 40
Kyushu-Palau Ridge, unds. H16 142
Kyūshū-sanchi, mts., Japan G4 40
Kywong, Austl. J6 76
Kyyjärvi, Fin. E11 8
Kyyvesi, l., Fin. E12 8
Kyzyl, Russia D16 32
Kyzylbair, Turkmen. B8 56
Kyzyl-Kija, Kyrg. F12 32
Kyzylkum, des., Asia F10 32
Kyzyluj, Kaz. E11 32
Kzyl-Orda, Kaz. F11 32
Kzyltu, Kaz. D12 32

L

La Aguja, Cabo de, c., Col. B4 86
La Albuera, Spain F4 20
La Alcarria, reg., Spain D8 20
La Algaba, Spain G4 20
La Almunia de Doña Godina, Spain C9 20
La Antigua, Salina, pl., Arg. D4 92
La Araucanía, state, Chile I1 92
Laascaanood, Som. C9 66
La Ascención, hill, Mex. C8 100
La Asunción, Ven. B10 86
Laau Point, c., Hi., U.S. B4 78a
Laayoune see El Aaiún, W. Sah. D2 64
La Azufrosa, Mex. F7 130
La Babia, Mex. A7 100
Labadieville, La., U.S. H8 122
La Baie, Qc., Can. B6 110
La Banda, Arg. C5 92
La Bandera, Cerro, mtn., Mex. C6 100
La Bañeza, Spain B4 20
La Barca, Mex. E7 100
La Barge, Wy., U.S. H16 136
Labasa, Fiji p19 79e
La Baule-Escoublac, Fr. G6 14
Labé, Gui. G2 64
Labe (Elbe), stm., Eur. C5 16
Labelle, Qc., Can. D2 110
La Belle, Mo., U.S. D5 120
Laberge, Lake, l., Yk., Can. C4 106
Labi, Bru. A9 50
Labian, Tanjong, c., Malay. A11 50
La Biche, stm., Ab., Can. B18 138
Labis, Malay. K6 48
La Bisbal d'Empordà, Spain C13 20
Łabiszyn, Pol. D13 16
La Blanca Grande, Laguna, l., Arg. I5 92
Labná, hist., Mex. B3 102
Laboe, Ger. B6 16
Laborde, Arg. F6 92
Laborie, St. Luc. m7 105c
La Bostonnais, Qc., Can. C4 110
Laboulaye, Arg. G6 92
Labrador, reg., Nf., Can. E18 106
Labrador Basin, unds. C9 144
Labrador City, Nf., Can. E17 106
Labrador Sea, N.A. D17 94
Lábrea, Braz. E5 84
La Brea, Trin. s12 105f
Labuan, Malay. A9 50
Labuan, state, Malay. A9 50
Labuan, Pulau, i., Malay. A9 50
Labuchongshan, mts., China C10 54
La Bufadora, Mex. L9 134
Labuhan, Indon. G4 50
Labuhanbajo, Indon. H11 50
Labuhanbilik, Indon. B2 50
Labuhanpandan, Indon. H10 50
Labuhanruku, Indon. B1 50
Labuk, stm., Malay. H1 52
Labuk, Telukan, b., Malay. G1 52
Labu Kananga, Indon. H10 50
Labutta, Mya. D2 48
Labytnangi, Russia A11 32
Laç, Alb. C13 24
Laća, ozero, l., Russia F18 8
Lac-à-Beauce, Qc., Can. C4 110
La Cadena, Mex. I3 130
La Calera, Chile F2 92
La Campana, Spain G5 20
La Canada Flintridge, Ca., U.S. I7 134
La Candelaria, Arg. C5 92
La Candelaria, Mex. C1 130
Lacantum, stm., Mex. D2 102
La Capelle-en-Thiérache, Fr. D12 14
La Carlota, Arg. F6 92
La Carlota, Phil. E4 52
La Carolina, Spain F7 20
Lacaune, Fr. F8 18
Laccadive Islands see Lakshadweep, is., India F3 46
Lac-Édouard, Qc., Can. C4 110
La Ceiba, Hond. E4 102
Lacepede Bay, b., Austl. K2 76
Lac-Etchemin, Qc., Can. D6 110
Lacey, Wa., U.S. C4 136
Lac-Frontière, Qc., Can. D6 110
La Chapelle-d'Angillon, Fr. G11 14
La Châtaigneraie, Fr. C5 18
La Chaux-de-Fonds, Switz. C3 22
Lachhmangarh Sīkar, India E5 54
Lachine, Qc., Can. E3 110
Lachlan, stm., Austl. J5 76
La Chorrera, Col. H5 86
La Chorrera, Pan. H8 102
Lachute, Qc., Can. E2 110
Laçi see Laç, Alb. C13 24
La Ciénaga, Arg. C4 92
La Ciotat, Fr. F11 18
La Citadelle, hist., Haiti C11 102
La Ciudad, Mex. D6 100
Lackawanna, N.Y., U.S. B6 114
Lac La Biche, Ab., Can. B18 138
Lac la Hache, B.C., Can. E9 138
Laclede, Id., U.S. B10 136
Laclede, Mo., U.S. E4 120
La Clotilde, Arg. C7 92
Lac-Mégantic, Qc., Can. E6 110
La Colorada, Mex. A3 100
La Coma, Mex. C9 100
Lacombe, Ab., Can. D17 138
Lacombe, La., U.S. G9 122
Lacona, Ia., U.S. C4 120
La Concepción, Pan. H6 102
La Concepción, Ven. B5 86
Laconi, Italy E2 24
Laconia, N.H., U.S. G5 110
Laconia, Gulf of see Lakonikós Kólpos, b., Grc. G5 28
La Consulta, Arg. F3 92
Lacoochee, Fl., U.S. H3 116
La Coruña see A Coruña, Spain A2 20
La Coruña see A Coruña, co., Spain A2 20
La Coste, Tx., U.S. E9 130
La Courtine, Fr. D8 18
La Crescent, Mn., U.S. H7 118
La Crosse, Ks., U.S. C9 128
La Crosse, Va., U.S. H7 114
Lacrosse, Wa., U.S. D9 136
La Crosse, Wi., U.S. H7 118
La Cruz, Arg. D9 92
La Cruz, Col. G3 86
La Cruz, C.R. E7 96
La Cruz, Mex. G2 130
La Cruz de Río Grande, Nic. F5 102
Lac Seul, On., Can. A6 118
La Cuesta, P.R. B2 104a
La Cumbre, Arg. E5 92
La Cygne, Ks., U.S. F3 120
Ladākh, hist. reg., Pak. A6 54
Ladākh Range, mts., Asia A6 54
Ladder Creek, stm., Ks., U.S. C7 128
Laddonia, Mo., U.S. E6 120
La Désirade, i., Guad. h6 105c
La Digue, i., Sey. j13 69b
Ladismith, S. Afr. H5 70
Ladispoli, Italy I8 22
Lādīz, Iran D9 56
Ladner, B.C., Can. G7 138
Lādnūn, India E5 54
Ladoga, In., U.S. I3 112
Ladoga, Lake see Ladožskoe ozero, l., Russia F14 8
La Dorada, Col. E4 86
La Dormida, Arg. F4 92
Ladožskoe ozero (Ladoga, Lake), l., Russia F14 8
Laduškin, Russia F3 10
Ladva-Vetka, Russia F15 8
Lady Ann Strait, strt., Nu., Can. B10 141
Lady Barron, Austl. n14 77a
Ladybrand, S. Afr. F8 70
Lady Elliot Island, i., Austl. E9 76
Ladysmith, B.C., Can. H7 138
Ladysmith, S. Afr. F9 70
Ladysmith, Wi., U.S. F7 118
Lae, Pap. N. Gui. b4 79a
La Encantada, Mex. C8 100
La Escondida, Mex. H8 130
La Esmeralda, Mex. B7 100
Læsø, i., Den. H4 8
La Esperanza, Cuba A5 102
La Esperanza, Hond. E3 102
La Esperanza, Mex. H4 130
La Esperanza, P.R. B3 104a
La Estrada see A Estrada, Spain B2 20
Lafa, China C7 38
La Falda, Arg. E5 92
La Farge, Wi., U.S. H8 118
Lafayette, Al., U.S. E13 122
Lafayette, Ca., U.S. F3 134
Lafayette, Co., U.S. A3 128
Lafayette, Ga., U.S. C13 122
Lafayette, In., U.S. H3 112
Lafayette, La., U.S. G6 122
Lafayette, Tn., U.S. H11 120
Lafayette, Mount, mtn., N.H., U.S. F5 110
La Feria, Tx., U.S. H10 130
La Ferté-Bernard, Fr. F9 14
La Ferté-Saint-Aubin, Fr. G10 14
Lafia, Nig. H6 64
Lafiagi, Nig. H6 64
Lafleche, Sk., Can. E7 124
La Flèche, Fr. G8 14
La Florida, Guat. D2 102
La Foa, N. Cal. m15 79d
La Follette, Tn., U.S. H1 114
Lafourche, Bayou, stm., La., U.S. H8 122
La Fragua, Arg. C5 92
La Fria, Ven. C5 86
La Fuente de San Esteban, Spain D4 20
La Galite, i., Tun. G2 24
La Gallareta, Arg. D7 92
Lagan, stm., Swe. E3 8
Lagarto, Braz. F7 88
Lagawe, Phil. B3 52
Lage, China D10 54
Lågen, stm., Nor. F4 8
Lages, Braz. C12 92
Laghmān, state, Afg. A3 54
Laghouat, Alg. C5 64
Lagkadás, Grc. C5 28
Lagoa da Prata, Braz. K3 88
Lagoa Vermelha, Braz. D12 92
Lago da Pedra, Braz. C3 88
Lago Kolonie, Aruba p20 104g
Lagolândia, Braz. H1 88
Lagonegro, Italy D9 24
Lagonoy Gulf, b., Phil. D4 52
Lago Posadas, Arg. I2 90
Lagos, Nig. H5 64
Lagos, Port. G2 20
Lagos de Moreno, Mex. E8 100
La Gouèra, W. Sah. E1 64
La Goulette, Tun. H4 24
Lago Viedma, Arg. I2 90
La Granadella, Spain C11 20
La Grande, Or., U.S. E8 136
La Grande Deux, Réservoir, res., Qc., Can. E15 106
La Grande Quatre, Réservoir, res., Qc., Can. E16 106
LaGrange, Austl. C4 74
La Grange, Ga., U.S. D13 122
La Grange, Ky., U.S. F12 120
La Grange, Mo., U.S. D6 120
La Grange, Tx., U.S. E11 130
Lagrange, Wy., U.S. F8 126
Lagrange Bay, b., Austl. C4 74
La Gran Sabana, pl., Ven. E10 86
La Guadeloupe, Qc., Can. E6 110
La Guajira, state, Col. G11 102
La Guajira, Peninsula de, pen., S.A. A6 86
La Guardia, Arg. D5 92
La Guardia, Bol. C4 90
La Guardia see A Guardia, Spain C1 20
La Guerche-sur-l'Aubois, Fr. G11 14
Laguiole, Fr. E8 18
Laguna, Braz. D13 92
Laguna, N.M., U.S. H9 132
Laguna, Ilha da, i., Braz. D7 84
Laguna Beach, Ca., U.S. J8 134
Laguna Dam, dam, U.S. K2 132
Laguna de Jaco, Mex. G4 130
Laguna Larga, Arg. E6 92
Laguna Paiva, Arg. E7 92
Lagunas, Peru E2 84
Lagunas de Chacagua, Parque Nacional, p.o.i., Mex. H9 100
Lagunillas, Bol. C4 90
Laha, China B9 36
La Habana (Havana), Cuba A6 102
Lahad Datu, Malay. A11 50
Lahad Datu, Telukan, b., Malay. A11 50
La Harpe, Il., U.S. K7 118
La Harpe, Ks., U.S. G2 120
Lahat, Indon. E3 50
Lahdenpohja, Russia F14 8
Lahemaa rahvus, p.o.i., Est. G11 8
Lahewa, Indon. L3 48
Laḥfān, Bi'r, well, Egypt G4 58
Lahij, Yemen G5 56
Lāhījān, Iran B7 56
Lahnstein, Ger. F3 16
Laholm, Swe. H5 8
Lahontan Reservoir, res., Nv., U.S. D6 134
Lahore, Pak. C5 54
La Horqueta, Col. F5 86
Lahr, Ger. H3 16
Lahti, Fin. F11 8
La Huerta, N.M., U.S. B3 130
Laï, Chad F3 62
Laiagam, Pap. N. Gui. b3 79a
Laibin, China J3 42
Lai Chau, Viet. A6 48
Laichow Bay see Laizhou Wan, b., China C8 42
Laifeng, China G3 42
L'Aigle, Fr. F9 14
Laihia, Fin. E9 8
Laïmbélé, Mont, mtn., Vanuatu k16 79d
Laingsburg, S. Afr. H5 70
Laingsburg, Mi., U.S. B1 114
Lainioälven, stm., Swe. C10 8
Lainsitz see Lužnice, stm., Eur. G10 16
Laird Hill, Tx., U.S. E3 122
Lais, Indon. C12 50
Lais, Indon. E3 50
Lais, Phil. G5 52
Laitila, Fin. F9 8
Laiwu, China C7 42
Laixi, China C9 42
Laiyang, China C9 42
Laizhou Bay see Laizhou Wan, b., China C8 42
Laizhou Wan (Laizhou Bay), b., China C8 42
Laja, stm., Chile H2 92
Laja, Laguna de la, l., Chile H2 92
Laja, Salto del, wtfl, Chile H2 92
La Jara, Co., U.S. D2 128
La Jara, reg., Spain E5 20
La Jara Canyon, val., N.M., U.S. G9 132
La Jarita, Mex. F4 130
Lajas, P.R. B1 104a
Laje, Braz. G6 88
Lajeado, Braz. D11 92
Lajedo, Braz. E7 88
Lajes, Braz. C7 88
Lajinha, Braz. K5 88
Laji Shan, mts., China D5 36
Lajosmizse, Hung. B6 26
Lajta (Leitha), stm., Eur. H12 16
La Junta, Co., U.S. D5 128
Lakar Kūh, mtn., Iran C8 56
Lakatoro, Vanuatu k16 79d
Lake, Ms., U.S. E9 122
Lake Alfred, Fl., U.S. H4 116
Lake Andes, S.D., U.S. D14 126
Lake Arthur, La., U.S. G6 122
Lakeba, i., Fiji q20 79e
Lakeba Passage, strt., Fiji q20 79e
Lake Benton, Mn., U.S. G2 118
Lake Brownwood, Tx., U.S. C8 130
Lake Cargelligo, Austl. I6 76
Lake Charles, La., U.S. G5 122
Lake Chelan National Recreation Area, p.o.i., Wa., U.S. B6 136
Lake City, Ar., U.S. B8 122
Lake City, Co., U.S. E9 132
Lake City, Fl., U.S. F3 116
Lake City, Mi., U.S. D4 112
Lake City, Pa., U.S. B5 114
Lake City, S.C., U.S. C6 116
Lake City, Tn., U.S. H1 114
Lake Cowichan, B.C., Can. H6 138
Lake Crystal, Mn., U.S. G4 118
Lake Dallas, Tx., U.S. A10 130
Lake Delton, Wi., U.S. H9 118
Lake District National Park, p.o.i., Eng., U.K. G9 12
Lake Elsinore, Ca., U.S. J8 134
Lakefield, On., Can. D11 112
Lakefield, Mn., U.S. H3 118
Lake Forest, Il., U.S. F2 112
Lake Fork Reservoir, res., Tx., U.S. E3 122
Lake Geneva, Wi., U.S. B9 120
Lake George, N.Y., U.S. G3 110
Lake Harbor, Fl., U.S. J5 116
Lake Havasu City, Az., U.S. I2 132
Lake Helen, Fl., U.S. H4 116
Lakehurst, N.J., U.S. D11 114
Lake Jackson, Tx., U.S. E12 130
Lake King, Austl. F3 74
Lakeland, Fl., U.S. H3 116
Lakeland, Ga., U.S. E2 116
Lake Linden, Mi., U.S. D10 118
Lake Louise, Ab., Can. E14 138
Lake Mead National Recreation Area, p.o.i., U.S. G2 132
Lake Mills, Wi., U.S. A8 120
Lake Minchumina, Ak., U.S. D9 140
Lake Mohawk see Sparta, N.J., U.S. C11 114
Lake Nash, Austl. D7 74
Lake Norden, S.D., U.S. C15 126
Lake Oswego, Or., U.S. E4 136
Lake Ozark, Mo., U.S. F5 120
Lake Park, Fl., U.S. J5 116
Lake Park, Ia., U.S. H3 118
Lake Placid, Fl., U.S. I4 116
Lake Placid, N.Y., U.S. F3 110
Lake Pleasant, N.Y., U.S. G2 110
Lakeport, Ca., U.S. D3 134
Lakeport, Mi., U.S. E7 112
Lake Preston, S.D., U.S. C15 126
Lakes Entrance, Austl. K7 76
Lakeshore, Ms., U.S. G9 122
Lakeside, Ca., U.S. K8 134
Lakeside, Mt., U.S. B12 136
Lake Stevens, Wa., U.S. B4 136
Laketown, Ut., U.S. B5 132
Lake View, Ar., U.S. C8 122
Lake View, Ia., U.S. B2 120
Lakeview, Mi., U.S. E4 112
Lakeview, Mi., U.S. F4 112
Lakeview, Oh., U.S. D2 114
Lakeview, Or., U.S. A5 134
Lake Village, Ar., U.S. D7 122
Lakeville, Mn., U.S. G5 118
Lake Wales, Fl., U.S. I4 116
Lake Wilson, Mn., U.S. G2 118
Lakewood, Co., U.S. B3 128
Lakewood, N.J., U.S. D11 114
Lakewood, Oh., U.S. C4 114
Lakewood, Wa., U.S. C4 136
Lakewood, Wi., U.S. C1 112
Lakewood Park, N.D., U.S. F15 124
Lake Worth, Fl., U.S. J5 116
Lakhdaria, Alg. H14 20
Lākheri, India F5 54
Lakhīmpur, India D8 54
Lakhipur, India F14 54
Lakhnādon, India G7 54
Lakinsk, Russia H18 8
Lakonikós Kólpos (Laconia, Gulf of), b., Grc. G5 28
Lakota, N.D., U.S. F15 124
Laksefjorden, b., Nor. A12 8
Lakshadweep, state, India F3 46
Lakshadweep, is., India F3 46
Lakshadweep Sea, Asia G3 46
Lāksām, Bngl. G13 54
Lakshmeshwar, India D2 53
La Laja, Chile H1 92
Lāla Mūsa, Pak. B4 54
Lâlapaşa, Tur. B9 28
L'Albufera, l., Spain E10 20
Laleham, Austl. D7 76
La Leona, Mex. I6 130
La Leonesa, Arg. C8 92
Lālganj, India F10 54
Lalibela, Eth. E7 62
La Libertad, Guat. D2 102
La Ligua, Chile F2 92
La Lima, Hond. E3 102
Lalin, stm., China B7 38
Lalindi, Indon. I12 50
La Línea de la Concepción, Spain H5 20
Lalitpur, India F7 54
Lalitpur, Nepal E10 54
Lalla Khedidja, Tamgout de, mtn., Alg. H14 20
Lālmanir Hāt, Bngl. F12 54
La Loche, Sk., Can. D9 106
La Lora, plat., Spain B7 20
La Louvière, Bel. D13 14
L'Alpe-d'Huez, Fr. D12 18
Lālpur, India G2 54
Lālsot, India E6 54
La Luz, Mex. C10 100
La Luz, Mex. I10 130
Lama, ozero, l., Russia C7 34
La Macarena, Parque Nacional, p.o.i., Col. F5 86
La Macarena, Serranía de, mts., Col. F5 86
La Maddalena, Italy C3 24
La Madrid, Arg. C5 92
Lamadrid, Mex. G6 130
La Magdalena, Mex. H1 130
Lama-Kara, Togo H5 64
La Malbaie, Qc., Can. C6 110
La Mancha, reg., Spain E8 20
Lamandau, stm., Indon. E7 50
Lamap, Vanuatu k16 79d
Lamar, Co., U.S. C6 128
Lamar, Mo., U.S. G3 120
Lamarche, Fr. F14 14
La Mármora, Punta, mtn., Italy D3 24
La Maroma, Mex. F7 130
La Marque, Tx., U.S. H4 122
La Marsa, Tun. H4 24
La Martre, Qc., Can. A10 110
Lamas, Peru E2 84
Lamballe, Fr. F6 14
Lambaréné, Gabon E2 66
Lambari, stm., Braz. J3 88
Lambayeque, Peru E2 84
Lambay Island, i., Ire. H7 12
Lambert, Ms., U.S. C8 122
Lambert, Mt., U.S. G9 124
Lambert, Cape, c., Pap. N. Gui. a5 79a
Lambert Glacier, ice, Ant. C11 81
Lambert Land, reg., Grnld. B21 141
Lamberton, Mn., U.S. G3 118
Lambertsbaai see Lambert's Bay, S. Afr. H3 70
Lambert's Bay, S. Afr. H3 70
Lambton, Cape, c., N.T., Can. A6 106
Lame Deer, Mt., U.S. B6 126
La Media Luna, Arrecifes de, rf., Hond. E6 102
Lamentin, Guad. h5 105c
Lamèque, N.B., Can. C12 110
Lamèque, Île, i., N.B., Can. C12 110
La Merced, Arg. B5 92
La Merced, Arg. D3 92
Lameroo, Austl. J3 76
La Mesa, Ca., U.S. K8 134
Lamesa, Tx., U.S. B6 130
Lamia, Grc. E5 28
Lamington National Park, p.o.i., Austl. G9 76
La Misión, Mex. K9 134
Lamitan, Phil. G4 52
Lamlam, Mount, hill, Guam j9 78c
Lammeulo, Indon. J2 48
La Moille, Il., U.S. C8 120
Lamoille, Nv., U.S. C1 132
Lamoille, stm., Vt., U.S. F4 110
Lamon Bay, b., Phil. C4 52
Lamone, stm., Italy F9 22
Lamongan, Indon. G8 50
Lamoni, Ia., U.S. D3 120
Lamont, Ca., U.S. H6 134
Lamont, Ia., U.S. I7 118
Lamont, Ok., U.S. E11 128
La Monte, Mo., U.S. F4 120
La Mothe, Lac, l., Qc., Can. B5 110
La Mothe-Achard, Fr. H7 14
Lamotrek, at., Micron. C5 72
Lamotte-Beuvron, Fr. G10 14
Lampang, Thai. C4 48
Lampasas, Tx., U.S. C9 130
Lampasas, stm., Tx., U.S. C9 130
Lampazos de Naranjo, Mex. B8 100
Lampedusa, Isola di, i., Italy I6 24
Lampertheim, Ger. G4 16
Lamphun, Thai. C4 48
Lampman, Sk., Can. E11 124
Lampung, state, Indon. F4 50
Lamskoe, Russia H21 10
Lamu, Kenya E8 66
La Mure, Fr. E11 18
Lan', stm., Bela. H10 10
Lana, Italy D8 22
Lanai, i., Hi., U.S. C4 78a
Lanai City, Hi., U.S. C4 78a
Lanaihale, mtn., Hi., U.S. C5 78a
Lanalhue, Lago, l., Chile I1 92
Lanark, On., Can. C13 112
Lanark, Scot., U.K. F9 12
Lanbi Kyun, i., Mya. G4 48
Lancang, China A4 48
Lancang see Mekong, stm., Asia D9 46
Lancaster, Eng., U.K. G10 12
Lancaster, Ca., U.S. I7 134
Lancaster, Mn., U.S. C2 118
Lancaster, Mo., U.S. D5 120
Lancaster, N.H., U.S. F5 110
Lancaster, Oh., U.S. E3 114
Lancaster, Pa., U.S. D9 114
Lancaster, S.C., U.S. B5 116
Lancaster, Tx., U.S. E2 122
Lancaster, Va., U.S. G9 114
Lancaster, Wi., U.S. B7 120
Lancaster Sound, strt., Nu., Can. C8 141
Lance Creek, Wy., U.S. D8 126
Lancelin, Austl. F2 74
Lanchou see Lanzhou, China D5 36
Lanchow see Lanzhou, China D5 36
Lanciano, Italy H11 22
Lancun, China C9 42
Łańcut, Pol. F18 16
Lândana, Ang. B1 68
Landau an der Isar, Ger. H8 16
Landau in der Pfalz, Ger. G4 16
Landeck, Aus. C7 22
Lander, Wy., U.S. E4 126
Landerneau, Fr. F4 14
Landes, state, Fr. F5 18
Landes, reg., Fr. E5 18
Landete, Spain E9 20
Landis, Sk., Can. B5 124
Landis, N.C., U.S. B4 116
Land O'Lakes, Wi., U.S. E9 118
Landösjön, l., Swe. E5 8
Landri Sales, Braz. D3 88
Landrum, S.C., U.S. A3 116
Landsborough Creek, stm., Austl. D5 76
Land's End, c., Eng., U.K. K7 12
Landshut, Ger. H7 16
Landskrona, Swe. I5 8
Lane, mth., Fr. G9 14
Lanesboro, Mn., U.S. H6 118
Lanett, Al., U.S. E13 122
Lanezi Lake, l., B.C., Can. C10 138
La'nga Co, l., China C8 54
Langa-Langa, D.R.C. E3 66
Langbank, Sk., Can. D11 124
Lang Bay, B.C., Can. G6 138
Langdale, Al., U.S. E13 122
Langdon, N.D., U.S. F15 124
Langeac, Fr. D9 18
Langeberg, mts., S. Afr. H5 70
Langeland, i., Den. I4 8
Langenhagen, Ger. D5 16
Langenthal, Switz. C4 22
Langfang, China B7 42
Langford, S.D., U.S. B15 126
Langgam, Indon. C2 50
Langham, Sk., Can. B6 124
Langhe, hist. reg., Italy F5 22
Langholm, Scot., U.K. F9 12
Langjökull, ice, Ice. k29 8a
Langkawi, Pulau, i., Malay. I4 48
Langley, B.C., Can. G8 138
Langley, Ok., U.S. A3 122
Langlo, stm., Austl. E5 76
Langnau im Emmental, Switz. C4 22
Langogne, Fr. E9 18
Langøya, i., Nor. B6 8
Langping, China F4 42
Langreo, Spain A5 20
Langres, Fr. G14 14
Langruth, Mb., Can. D15 124
Langsa, Indon. J3 48
Langsa, Teluk, b., Indon. J4 48
Langshan, China A2 42
Lang Son, Viet. B8 48
Langtry, Tx., U.S. E6 130
Languedoc, hist. reg., Fr. F9 18
L'Anguille, stm., Ar., U.S. C8 122
Langxi, China F8 42
Langzhong, China F1 42
Lanigan, Sk., Can. C8 124
Lanigan Creek, stm., Sk., Can. C9 124
Lanín, Volcán, vol., S.A. G2 90
Länkäran, Azer. B6 56
Länkipohja, Fin. F11 8
Lannemezan, Fr. F6 18
Lannion, Fr. F5 14
Lanping, China F4 36
Lansdowne, India D7 54
Lansdowne House, On., Can. E13 106
L'Anse, Mi., U.S. B1 112
Lansing, Ia., U.S. H7 118
Lansing, Mi., U.S. B1 114
Lantana, Fl., U.S. J5 116
Lantau Island, i., China J6 42
Lanta Yai, Ko, i., Thai. I4 48
Lantian, China D3 42
La Nurra, reg., Italy D2 24
Lanusei, Italy E3 24
Lanxi, China G8 42
Lan Yü, i., Tai. J9 42
Lanzhou, China D5 36
Lanzo Torinese, Italy E4 22
Lao, stm., Thai. C4 48
Laoag, Phil. A3 52
Laoang, Phil. D5 52
Lao Cai, Viet. A6 48
Laodao, stm., China G5 42
Laofu, China C3 38
Laoha, stm., China C4 38
Laohekou, China E4 42
Laohokow see Laohekou, China E4 42
Laois, state, Ire. I5 12
Lao Ling, mtn., China C9 38
Laon, Fr. E12 14
Laona, Wi., U.S. F10 118
La Orchila, Isla, i., Ven. B8 86
La Oroya, Peru F2 84
Laos, ctry., Asia C6 48
Laoshan Wan, b., China C9 42
Lapa, Braz. B13 92
Lapai, Nig. H6 64
Lapalisse, Fr. C9 18
La Palma, Col. E4 86
La Palma, Pan. H8 102
La Palma, Pan. I7 102
La Palma del Condado, Spain G4 20
La Paloma, Ur. G10 92
La Pampa, state, Arg. G3 90
La Paragua, Ven. D10 86
La Pasión, stm., Guat. D2 102
La Paya, Parque Nacional, p.o.i., Col. G4 86
La Paz, Arg. E8 92
La Paz, Arg. F4 92
La Paz, Bol. C3 90
La Paz, Col. B5 86
La Paz, Hond. E4 102
La Paz, Mex. C3 100
La Paz, Mex. D8 100
La Paz, Ur. G9 92
La Paz, Bahía de, b., Mex. C3 100
La Perla, Mex. A6 100
La Perouse, Bahía, b., Chile e30 78l
La Perouse Strait, strt., Asia B13 36
La Pesca, Mex. D10 100
La Piedad de Cabadas, Mex. E7 100
La Pine, Or., U.S. G5 136
La Place, La., U.S. G8 122
Lap Lae, Thai. D4 48
Lapland, hist. reg., Eur. C11 8
La Plata, Arg. G8 92
La Plata, Col. F4 86
La Plata, Md., U.S. F9 114
La Plata, Mo., U.S. D5 120
La Plata Peak, mtn., Co., U.S. D10 132
La Pobla de Segur, Spain B11 20
La Pocatière, Qc., Can. C6 110
Lapominka, Russia D19 8
Laporte, Co., U.S. G7 126
La Porte, In., U.S. G3 112
Laporte, Pa., U.S. C9 114
La Porte City, Ia., U.S. B5 120
La Potherie, Lac, l., Qc., Can. D16 106
La Poza Grande, Mex. C2 100
Lappajärvi, l., Fin. E10 8
Lappeenranta, Fin. F12 8
Lappi, state, Fin. C12 8
Laprida, Arg. D5 92
Laprida, Arg. H7 92
La Pryor, Tx., U.S. F8 130
Lapta, N. Cyp. C4 58
Laptev Sea see Laptevyh, more, Russia B4 32
Laptevyh, more, Russia B4 32
La Puebla de Montalbán, Spain E6 20
La Puerta, Arg. D5 92
La Puerta de Cabrera, Mex. H2 130
Lapu-Lapu, Phil. E4 52
La Purísima, Mex. B2 100
Lăpuş, Rom. B11 26
Lapwai, Id., U.S. D10 136
La Quiaca, Arg. D3 90
L'Aquila, Italy H10 22
Lār, Iran D7 56
Lara, state, Ven. B7 86
Laracha, Spain A2 20
Larache, Mor. B3 64
Laramie, Wy., U.S. F7 126
Laramie, stm., U.S. E8 126
Laramie Mountains, mts., Wy., U.S. F7 126
Laramie Peak, mtn., Wy., U.S. E7 126
Laranjal, Braz. K4 88
Laranjeiras, Braz. F7 88
Laranjeiras do Sul, Braz. B11 92
Larantuka, Indon. G7 44
Larap, Phil. C4 52
Larat, Indon. G9 44
Larat, Pulau, i., Indon. G9 44
Larche Pass, p., Eur. E12 18
Larchwood, Ia., U.S. H2 118
Larde, Moz. D6 68
L'Ardoise, N.S., Can. E16 110
Laredo, Spain A7 20
Laredo, Tx., U.S. G8 130
La Reforma, Mex. C4 100
Lares, P.R. B2 104a
Larga, Mol. A13 26
Larga, Laguna, l., Tx., U.S. G10 130
Largo, Fl., U.S. I3 116
Largo, Cañon, val., N.M., U.S. G9 132
Largo, Cayo, i., Cuba B7 102
Largs, Scot., U.K. F8 12
Lariang, stm., Indon. D11 50
Larimore, N.D., U.S. G16 124
Larino, Italy I11 22
Lario see Como, Lago di, l., Italy D6 22
La Rioja, Arg. D4 92
La Rioja, state, Arg. E4 92
La Rioja, state, Spain B8 20
Lárisa, Grc. D5 28
Larjak, Russia B14 32
Lārkāna, Pak. D10 56
Lárnakos, Kólpos, b., Cyp. D4 58
Larne, N. Ire., U.K. G7 12
Larned, Ks., U.S. C9 128
La Robla, Spain B5 20
La Rochefoucauld, Fr. D6 18
La Rochelle, Fr. C4 18
La Roche-sur-Yon, Fr. H7 14
La Roda, Spain E8 20
La Romaine, Qc., Can. i21 107a
La Romana, Dom. Rep. C13 102
La Ronge, Sk., Can. D10 106
Laroquebrou, Fr. D8 18
Larose, Pointe, c., Mart. k7 105c
Larroque, Arg. F8 92
Larrys River, N.S., Can. E15 110
Larsen Ice Shelf, ice, Ant. B34 81
La Rubia, Arg. E7 92
La Rue, Oh., U.S. D2 114
Larvik, Nor. G3 8
Larzac, Causse du, plat., Fr. F9 18
La Sabanilla, Mex. C8 100
La Sal, Ut., U.S. E7 132
La Salle, Co., U.S. G8 126
La Salle, Il., U.S. C8 120
La Salle, stm., Mb., Can. E16 124
Lasan, Indon. C9 50
Las Animas, Co., U.S. C5 128
Las Arenas, P.R. B1 104a
La Sarre, Qc., Can. F15 106
Las Arrias, Arg. E6 92
Las Ballenas, Canal de, strt., Mex. G6 98
Las Breñas, Arg. C7 92
Las Cabezas de San Juan, Spain G5 20
Las Cabras, Chile G2 92
Lascano, Ur. F10 92
Las Casitas, mtn., Mex. D4 100
Las Catitas, Arg. F3 92
Las Choapas, Mex. G11 100
Las Chorreras, Mex. A6 100
Las Cruces, N.M., U.S. K10 132
Las Cuatas, Mex. D1 130
Las Cuevas, Mex. A8 100
Las Cumaraguas, Ven. p20 104g
La Selle, Morne, mtn., Haiti C11 102
La Serena, Chile D2 92
La Serena, reg., Spain F5 20
La Seu d'Urgell, Spain B12 20
La Seyne, Fr. F11 18
La Seyne, Fr. F11 18
Las Flores, Arg. G8 92

Name	Map Ref.	Page
Las Flores, P.R.	B3	104a
Las Flores, Arroyo, stm., Arg.	H7	92
Las Garcitas, Arg.	C7	92
Las Guayabas, Mex.	C10	100
Lashburn, Sk., Can.	A4	124
Las Heras, Arg.	I3	92
Las Heras, Arg.	F3	92
Lashio, Mya.	A3	48
Lashkar Gāh, Afg.	C9	56
Las Hormigas, Mex.	C9	100
Lasia, Pulau, i., Indon.	K3	48
Łasin, Pol.	C15	16
La Sirena, Ven.	p20	104g
Łaskarzew, Pol.	E17	16
Las Lajas, Arg.	I2	92
Las Lajas, Pan.	H7	102
Las Lomitas, Arg.	B7	92
Las Malvinas, Arg.	G3	92
Las Mareas, P.R.	C3	104a
Las Margaritas, Mex.	G13	100
Las Marianas, Arg.	G8	92
Las Marías, P.R.	B1	104a
Las Minas, Cerro, mtn., Hond.	E3	102
Las Nopaleras, Cerro, mtn., Mex.	C7	100
La Solana, Spain	F7	20
Las Ovejas, Arg.	H2	92
Las Palmas, Arg.	C8	92
Las Palmas, P.R.	C3	104a
Las Palomas, Mex.	F9	98
La Spezia, Italy	F6	22
Las Piedras, P.R.	B4	104a
Las Piedras, Ur.	G9	92
Las Piedras, stm., Peru	F3	84
Las Plumas, Arg.	H3	90
Lasqueti Island, i., B.C., Can.	G6	138
Las Rosas, Arg.	F7	92
Las Rosas, Mex.	G12	100
Lassance, Braz.	I3	88
Lassen Peak, vol., Ca., U.S.	C4	134
Lassen Volcanic National Park, p.o.i., Ca., U.S.	C4	134
L'Assomption, stm., Qc., Can.	D3	110
Las Tablas, Pan.	I7	102
Las Tinajas, Arg.	C6	92
Last Mountain Lake, l., Sk., Can.	C8	124
Las Tórtolas, Cerro (Tórtolas, Cerro de las), mtn., S.A.	D2	92
Lastoursville, Gabon	E2	66
Las Tunas, Cuba	B9	102
Las Tunas Grandes, Laguna, l., Arg.	H6	92
Las Varas, Mex.	G8	98
Las Varas, Mex.	E6	100
Las Varillas, Arg.	E6	92
Las Vegas, P.R.	B1	104a
Las Vegas, Nv., U.S.	G1	132
Las Vegas, N.M., U.S.	F3	128
Las Vegas, Ven.	C7	86
Latacunga, Ec.	H2	86
La Tagua, Col.	H4	86
Latakia see Al-Lādhiqīyah, Syria	C6	58
Lata Mountain, vol., Am. Sam.	h13	79c
Latehar, India	G10	54
La Teste-de-Buch, Fr.	E4	18
Lāthi, India	H3	54
Lathrop, Mo., U.S.	E3	120
Latimer, Ia., U.S.	I5	118
Latina, Italy	C6	24
Latisana, Italy	E10	22
Latium see Lazio, state, Italy	B6	24
Latjuga, Russia	D23	8
La Torrecilla, mtn., P.R.	B3	104a
La Tortuga, Isla, i., Ven.	B9	86
Latouche Treville, Cape, c., Austl.	C4	74
La Tour-d'Auvergne, Fr.	D8	18
La Trimouille, Fr.	C7	18
La Trinidad, Nic.	F4	102
La Trinidad, Phil.	B3	52
La Trinidad de Orichuna, Ven.	D7	86
La Trinité, Mart.	k6	105c
Latrobe, Pa., U.S.	D6	114
Latta, S.C., U.S.	B6	116
La Tuque, Qc., Can.	C4	110
Lātūr, India	B3	53
Latvia, ctry., Eur.	D7	10
Lau, Nig.	H7	64
Lauchhammer, Ger.	E9	16
Lauenburg, Ger.	C6	16
Lauf an der Pegnitz, Ger.	G7	16
Lauge Koch Kyst, cst., Grnld.	B13	141
Laughlin, Nv., U.S.	H2	132
Laughlin Peak, mtn., N.M., U.S.	E4	128
Lau Group, is., Fiji	p20	79e
Lauis see Lugano, Switz.	D5	22
Laukaa, Fin.	E11	8
Laun, Thai.	G4	48
Launceston, Austl.	n13	77a
Launceston, Eng., U.K.	K8	12
La Unión, Chile	H2	90
La Unión, El Sal.	F4	102
La Unión, Mex.	G8	100
La Unión, Spain	G10	20
La Unión, N.M., U.S.	L10	132
La Unión, Ven.	C8	86
Laupheim, Ger.	H5	16
Laura, Austl.	C6	74
La Urbana, Ven.	D8	86
Laurel, Fl., U.S.	I3	116
Laurel, In., U.S.	E12	120
Laurel, Md., U.S.	E9	114
Laurel, Ms., U.S.	F9	122
Laurel, Mt., U.S.	B4	126
Laurel, Ne., U.S.	E15	126
Laurel Bay, S.C., U.S.	D5	116
Laureldale, Pa., U.S.	D10	114
Laureles, Ur.	E9	92
Laurel River Lake, res., Ky., U.S.	G1	114
Laurelville, Oh., U.S.	E15	120
Laurencekirk, Scot., U.K.	E10	12
Laurens, S.C., U.S.	B3	116
Laurentides, Les, plat., Qc., Can.	F16	106
Lau Ridge, unds.	L21	142
Laurier, Mb., Can.	D14	124
Laurier-Station, Qc., Can.	D5	110
Laurinburg, N.C., U.S.	B6	116
Laurium, Mi., U.S.	D10	118
Lausanne, Switz.	D3	22
Lausitzer Neisse (Nysa Łużycka), stm., Eur.	F10	16
Laut, Pulau, i., Indon.	A5	50
Laut, Pulau, i., Indon.	E10	50
Laut, Selat, strt., Indon.	E9	50
Lauta, Ger.	E9	16
Lautaro, Chile	I1	92
Lauterbach, Ger.	F5	16
Lauter Sachsen, Ger.	F8	16
Laut Kecil, Kepulauan, is., Indon.	F9	50
Lautoka, Fiji	p18	79e
Lauzerte, Fr.	E7	18
Lava (Łyna), stm., Eur.	B16	16
Lava Beds National Monument, p.o.i., Ca., U.S.	B4	134
Lavaca, stm., Tx., U.S.	E11	130
Laval, Qc., Can.	E3	110
Laval, Fr.	F8	14
La Vall d'Uixó, Spain	E10	20
Lavalle, Arg.	D5	92
Lavalle, Arg.	D8	92
Lavapié, Punta, c., Chile	H1	92
Lavassaare, Est.	G11	8
La Vega, Dom. Rep.	C12	102
La Vela de Coro, Ven.	B7	86
Lavelanet, Fr.	G7	18
Lavello, Italy	C9	24
La Venada, Mex.	I10	130
La Venta, hist., Mex.	F11	100
La Ventura, Mex.	C8	100
La Vera, reg., Spain	D5	20
La Vergne, Tn., U.S.	H11	120
Laverne, Ok., U.S.	E9	128
Laverton, Austl.	E4	74
La Veta, Co., U.S.	D4	128
Lavieille, Lake, l., On., Can.	C11	112
La Vila Joiosa, Spain	F10	20
Lavillette, N.B., Can.	C11	110
La Viña, Arg.	B5	92
Lavina, Mt., U.S.	A4	126
La Vista, Ne., U.S.	C1	120
La Voulte-sur-Rhône, Fr.	E10	18
Lavras, Braz.	K3	88
Lávrio, Grc.	F7	28
Lavumisa, Swaz.	E10	70
Lawang, Indon.	G8	50
Lawas, Malay.	A9	50
Lawdar, Yemen	G6	56
Lawers, Ben, mtn., Scot., U.K.	E8	12
Lawgi, Austl.	E8	76
Lawksawk, Mya.	B3	48
Lawler, Ia., U.S.	A5	120
Lawn, Tx., U.S.	B8	130
Lawndale, N.C., U.S.	A4	116
Lawn Hill, Austl.	C7	74
Lawn Hill Creek, stm., Austl.	C7	74
Lawrence, In., U.S.	I3	112
Lawrence, Ks., U.S.	F2	120
Lawrence, Ma., U.S.	B14	114
Lawrenceburg, In., U.S.	E12	120
Lawrenceburg, Ky., U.S.	F12	120
Lawrenceburg, Tn., U.S.	B11	122
Lawrenceville, Il., U.S.	F10	120
Lawrenceville, N.J., U.S.	D11	114
Lawson, Mo., U.S.	E3	120
Lawtey, Fl., U.S.	F3	116
Lawton, N.D., U.S.	F15	124
Lawton, Ok., U.S.	G10	128
Lawu, Gunung, vol., Indon.	G7	50
Lawz, Jabal al-, mtn., Sau. Ar.	J6	58
Laxå, Swe.	G6	8
Laxe, Spain	A1	20
Lay Lake, res., Al., U.S.	D12	122
Layou, St. Vin.	o11	105e
Layton, Ut., U.S.	B4	132
Laytonville, Ca., U.S.	D2	134
La Zarca, Mex.	C6	100
Lazarev, Russia	F17	34
Lázaro Cárdenas, Mex.	G7	100
Lázaro Cárdenas, Presa, res., Mex.	C6	100
Lazdijai, Lith.	F6	10
Lazio, state, Italy	B6	24
Léach, Camb.	F6	48
Leachville, Ar., U.S.	I7	120
Lead, S.D., U.S.	C9	126
Leadbetter Point, c., Wa., U.S.	D2	136
Leader, Sk., Can.	D4	124
Lead Hill, hill, Mo., U.S.	H4	120
Leadore, Id., U.S.	F13	136
Leadville, Co., U.S.	D10	132
Leaf, stm., Ms., U.S.	F10	122
Leaf Lake, l., Sk., Can.	A11	124
Leaghur, Lake, l., Austl.	I4	76
League City, Tx., U.S.	H3	122
Leakey, Tx., U.S.	E8	130
Leaksville, N.C., U.S.	H5	114
Lealman, Fl., U.S.	I3	116
Leamington, On., Can.	F7	112
Le'an, China	H6	42
Leandro, Braz.	C3	88
Leandro N. Alem, Arg.	C10	92
Leary, Ga., U.S.	F14	122
Leatherman Peak, mtn., Id., U.S.	F13	136
Leavenworth, Ks., U.S.	E2	120
Leavenworth, Wa., U.S.	C6	136
Leawood, Ks., U.S.	F3	120
Lebak, Phil.	G5	52
Lebam, Wa., U.S.	D3	136
Lebanon, In., U.S.	H3	112
Lebanon, Ks., U.S.	B10	128
Lebanon, Ky., U.S.	G12	120
Lebanon, N.H., U.S.	G4	110
Lebanon, Oh., U.S.	E1	114
Lebanon, Or., U.S.	F3	136
Lebanon, Pa., U.S.	D9	114
Lebanon, S.D., U.S.	B13	126
Lebanon, Tn., U.S.	H11	120
Lebanon, Va., U.S.	H3	114
Lebanon, ctry., Asia	E6	58
Le Bic, Qc., Can.	B8	110
Lebesby, Nor.	A12	8
Lebjaže, Kaz.	D13	32
Le Blanc, Fr.	H10	14
Lebo, D.R.C.	D4	66
Lebo, Ks., U.S.	F2	120
Lębork, Pol.	B13	16
Lebrija, Spain	H4	20
Lebrija, stm., Col.	D5	86
Łebsko, Jezioro, l., Pol.	B13	16
Lebu, Chile	H1	92
Le Carbet, Mart.	k6	105c
Lecce, Italy	D12	24
Lecco, Italy	E6	22
Le Center, Mn., U.S.	G5	118
Lech, stm., Eur.	H6	16
Lechainá, Grc.	F4	28
Lechang, China	I5	42
Le Chesne, Fr.	E13	14
Lechiguanas, Islas de las, is., Arg.	F8	92
Lechuguilla, Cerro, mtn., Mex.	D6	100
Lecompte, La., U.S.	F6	122
Le Creusot, Fr.	H13	14
Le Croisic, Fr.	G6	14
Łęczyca, Pol.	D15	16
Ledesma, Spain	C4	20
Le Diamant, Mart.	l6	105c
Ledjanaja, gora, mtn., Russia	D23	34
Ledo, India	C8	46
Ledo, Indon.	C6	50
Ledong, China	L3	42
Le Dorat, Fr.	C7	18
Ledu, China	D5	36
Leduc, Ab., Can.	C17	138
Leechburg, Pa., U.S.	D6	114
Leech Lake, l., Mn., U.S.	D4	118
Leedey, Ok., U.S.	F9	128
Leeds, Eng., U.K.	H11	12
Leeds, Al., U.S.	D12	122
Leek, Eng., U.K.	H10	12
Leelanau, Lake, l., Mi., U.S.	D4	112
Leelanau Peninsula, pen., Mi., U.S.	C4	112
Leer, Ger.	C3	16
Leesburg, Fl., U.S.	H4	116
Leesburg, Ga., U.S.	E1	116
Leesburg, Va., U.S.	E8	114
Lees Summit, Mo., U.S.	F3	120
Leesville, La., U.S.	F5	122
Leesville, Tx., U.S.	E10	130
Leeton, Austl.	J6	76
Leeu-Gamka, S. Afr.	H6	70
Leeuwarden, Neth.	A14	14
Leeuwin, Cape, c., Austl.	F2	74
Lee Vining, Ca., U.S.	F6	134
Leeward Islands, is., N.A.	h15	96a
Lefkáda, Grc.	E3	28
Lefkáda, i., Grc.	E3	28
Lefke, N. Cyp.	C3	58
Lefkosía see Nicosia, Cyp.	C4	58
Lefors, Tx., U.S.	F8	128
Le François, Mart.	k7	105c
Lefroy, Lake, l., Austl.	F4	74
Legal, Ab., Can.	C17	138
Leganés, Spain	D7	20
Legaspi, Phil.	D4	52
Leggett, Ca., U.S.	D2	134
Leghorn see Livorno, Italy	G7	22
Legion, Zimb.	B9	70
Legionowo, Pol.	D16	16
Legnago, Italy	E8	22
Legnano, Italy	E5	22
Legnica, Pol.	E12	16
Legnica, state, Pol.	E12	16
Le Gosier, Guad.	h6	105c
Le Grand, Ca., U.S.	F5	134
Le Guelta, Alg.	H11	20
Legume, Austl.	G9	76
Leh, India	A6	54
Le Havre, Fr.	E8	14
Lehčevo, Blg.	F10	26
Lehigh, Ia., U.S.	B3	120
Lehigh, Ok., U.S.	C2	122
Lehigh Acres, Fl., U.S.	J4	116
Lehighton, Pa., U.S.	D10	114
Lehrte, Ger.	D5	16
Lehtse, Est.	A8	10
Lehua, i., Hi., U.S.	A1	78a
Lehututu, Bots.	C5	70
Lei, stm., China	H5	42
Leiah, Pak.	C3	54
Leibnitz, Aus.	D12	22
Leicester, Eng., U.K.	I11	12
Leichhardt, stm., Austl.	A2	76
Leichhardt Falls, wtfl, Austl.	B2	76
Leiden (Leyden), Neth.	B13	14
Leigh Creek South, Austl.	H2	76
Leighton, Al., U.S.	C11	122
Leighton Buzzard, Eng., U.K.	J12	12
Leinan, Sk., Can.	D6	124
Leine, stm., Ger.	D5	16
Leinster, hist. reg., Ire.	I6	12
Leinster, Mount, mtn., Ire.	I6	12
Leipalingis, Lith.	F6	10
Leipsic, Oh., U.S.	C2	114
Leipzig, Ger.	E8	16
Leiria, Port.	E2	20
Leiria, state, Port.	E2	20
Leisler, Mount, mtn., Austl.	D6	74
Leitariegos, Puerto de, p., Spain	A4	20
Leitha (Lajta), stm., Eur.	H12	16
Leitrim, Ire.	H4	12
Leitrim, state, Ire.	H5	12
Leivádia, Grc.	E5	28
Leiyang, China	H5	42
Leizhou Bandao, pen., China	K3	42
Lejasciems, Lat.	C9	10
Lekeitio, Spain	A8	20
Leksozero, ozero, l., Russia	E14	8
Le Lamentin, Mart.	k6	105c
Leland, Il., U.S.	C9	120
Leland, Mi., U.S.	C4	112
Leland, Ms., U.S.	D8	122
Leleiwi Point, c., Hi., U.S.	D7	78a
Leleque, Arg.	H2	90
Leles, Indon.	G5	50
Leli Shan, mtn., China	A8	54
Le Locle, Switz.	C3	22
Lelystad, Neth.	B14	14
Le Maire, Estrecho de, strt., Arg.	J4	90
Le Mans, Fr.	G9	14
Le Marin, Mart.	l7	105c
Le Mars, Ia., U.S.	B1	120
Lema Shilindi, Eth.	G8	62
Lemay, Mo., U.S.	F7	120
Lembak, Indon.	C10	50
Lemdiyya, Alg.	H13	20
Leme, Braz.	L2	88
Lemesós (Limassol), Cyp.	D4	58
Lemhi, stm., Id., U.S.	F13	136
Lemhi Pass, p., U.S.	F13	136
Lemhi Range, mts., Id., U.S.	F13	136
Lemieux Islands, is., Nu., Can.	E13	141
Lemitar, N.M., U.S.	I10	132
Lemmatsi, Est.	B9	10
Lemmenjoen kansallispuisto, p.o.i., Fin.	B11	8
Lemmon, S.D., U.S.	B10	126
Lemmon, Mount, mtn., Az., U.S.	K6	132
Lemnos see Límnos, i., Grc.	D8	28
Lemoncove, Ca., U.S.	G7	134
Le Mont-Dore, N. Cal.	n16	79d
Lemoore, Ca., U.S.	G6	134
Le Moule, Guad.	h6	105c
Lempa, stm., N.A.	F3	102
Lempe, Indon.	D12	50
Lemro, stm., Mya.	B1	48
Le Murge, hills, Italy	D10	24
Le Muy, Fr.	F12	18
Lemyethna, Mya.	D2	48
Lena, Il., U.S.	B8	120
Lena, Wi., U.S.	D1	112
Lena, stm., Russia	B14	34
Lenart, Slvn.	D12	22
Lençóis, Braz.	G5	88
Lençóis Maranhenses, Parque Nacional dos, p.o.i., Braz.	B4	88
Lendery, Russia	E14	8
Lendinara, Italy	E8	22
Lenger, Kaz.	F12	32
Lenggor, stm., Malay.	K6	48
Lenghu, China	D3	36
Lengshuitan, China	H4	42
Lenhovda, Swe.	H6	8
Leningrad see Sankt-Peterburg, Russia	A13	10
Leningradskaja oblast', co., Russia	A13	10
Leninogor see Leninogorsk, Kaz.	D14	32
Leninogorsk, Kaz.	D14	32
Lenin Peak, mtn., Asia	B11	56
Leninsk, Kaz.	E10	32
Leninsk, Uzb.	F12	32
Leninskij, Russia	F20	10
Leninsk-Kuzneckij, Russia	D15	32
Leninskoe, Russia	G15	34
Lennonville, Austl.	E3	74
Lennox, S.D., U.S.	H2	118
Lennox, Isla, i., Chile	K3	90
Lennoxville, Qc., Can.	E5	110
Lenoir, N.C., U.S.	I4	114
Lenora, Czech Rep.	H9	16
Lenore Lake, l., Sk., Can.	B9	124
Lenox, Ga., U.S.	E2	116
Lenox, Ia., U.S.	D3	120
Lenox, Tn., U.S.	H8	120
Lens, Fr.	D11	14
Lensk, Russia	B20	32
Lenti, Hung.	C3	26
Lentini, Italy	G9	24
Lentua, l., Fin.	D13	8
Lentvaris, Lith.	F8	10
Lenya, stm., Mya.	G4	48
Léo, Burkina	G4	64
Leoben, Aus.	C12	22
Léogâne, Haiti	C11	102
Leola, Ar., U.S.	C6	122
Leola, S.D., U.S.	B14	126
Leominster, Eng., U.K.	I10	12
Leominster, Ma., U.S.	B14	114
Léon, Fr.	F4	18
León, Mex.	E8	100
León, Nic.	F4	102
León, Spain	B5	20
Leon, Ks., U.S.	D12	128
León, co., Spain	B5	20
Leon, stm., Tx., U.S.	C10	130
León, Montes de, mts., Spain	B4	20
Leona, stm., Tx., U.S.	F8	130
Leonard, Tx., U.S.	D2	122
Leonardtown, Md., U.S.	F9	114
Leonardville, Ks., U.S.	B11	128
Leonberg, Ger.	H4	16
Leones, Arg.	F6	92
Leonforte, Italy	G8	24
Leongatha, Austl.	L5	76
Leonīha, Russia	G18	8
Leonora, Austl.	E4	74
Leopold and Astrid Coast, cst., Ant.	B13	81
Leopoldina, Braz.	K4	88
Leopoldo de Bulhões, Braz.	I1	88
Léopoldville see Kinshasa, D.R.C.	E3	66
Leoti, Ks., U.S.	C7	128
Leova, Mol.	C15	26
Lepanto see Náfpaktos, Grc.	E4	28
Lepanto, Ar., U.S.	B8	122
Lepar, Pulau, i., Indon.	E5	50
Lepe, Spain	G3	20
Lepel', Bela.	F11	10
Leping, China	G7	42
L'Épiphanie, Qc., Can.	E3	110
Lepontine Alps, mts., Eur.	C14	18
Lepreau, Point, c., N.B., Can.	E10	110
Le Prêcheur, Mart.	k6	105c
Lepsi see Lepsy, Kaz.	E13	32
Lepsy, Kaz.	E13	32
Le Puy, Fr.	D9	18
Lequeitio see Lekeitio, Spain	A8	20
Lercara Friddi, Italy	G7	24
Lerdo, Mex.	C7	100
Lerici, Italy	F6	22
Lérida, Col.	G6	86
Lérida see Lleida, Spain	C11	20
Lerma, stm., Mex.	E8	100
Le Roy, Il., U.S.	D9	120
Le Roy, Ks., U.S.	F2	120
Le Roy, N.Y., U.S.	B7	114
Lerum, Swe.	H5	8
Lerwick, Scot., U.K.	n18	12a
Les Abymes, Guad.	h5	105c
Le Saint-Esprit, Mart.	k7	105c
Les Andelys, Fr.	E10	14
Les Anses-d'Arlets, Mart.	l6	105c
Les Borges Blanques, Spain	C11	20
Lesbos see Lésvos, i., Grc.	D9	28
Les Cayes, Haiti	C11	102
Leshan, China	F5	36
Les Herbiers, Fr.	H7	14
Lesina, Lago di, b., Italy	I12	22
Lesko, Pol.	G18	16
Leskovac, Yugo.	F8	26
Leskov Island, i., S. Geor.	K12	82
Les Laurentides see Laurentides, Les, plat., Qc., Can.	F16	106
Leslie, Ar., U.S.	I5	120
Leslie, Mi., U.S.	B1	114
Leslie, W.V., U.S.	F5	114
Lesneven, Fr.	F4	14
Lesnoe, Russia	B8	10
Lesogorsk, Russia	G17	34
Lesosibirsk, Russia	E7	34
Lesotho, ctry., Afr.	F9	70
Lesozavodsk, Russia	B10	38
Lesozavodskij, Russia	C15	8
Les Sables-d'Olonne, Fr.	H7	14
Les Saintes, is., Guad.	i5	105c
Lesser Antilles, is.	D8	82
Lesser Khingan Range see Xiao Hinggan Ling, mts., China	B10	36
Lesser Slave, stm., Ab., Can.	A16	138
Lesser Slave Lake, l., Ab., Can.	D8	106
Lesser Sunda Islands see Tenggara, Nusa, is., Indon.	G6	44
L'Esterre, Gren.	q10	105e
Lestock, Sk., Can.	C9	124
Le Sueur, Mn., U.S.	G4	118
Le Sueur, stm., Mn., U.S.	G5	118
Lešukonskoe, Russia	D21	8
Lésvos (Lesbos), i., Grc.	D9	28
Leszno, Pol.	E12	16
Leszno, state, Pol.	E12	16
Letaba, stm., S. Afr.	C10	70
Letcher, S.D., U.S.	D14	126
Letea, Ostrovul, i., Rom.	D16	26
Letenye, Hung.	C3	26
Lethbridge, Ab., Can.	G18	138
Lethem, Guy.	F12	86
Le Thillot, Fr.	G15	14
Leti, Kepulauan, is., Indon.	G8	44
Leticia, Col.	D4	84
Letlhakane, Bots.	B7	70
Letlhakeng, Bots.	D7	70
Letnjaja Zolotica, Russia	D17	8
Letpadan, Mya.	D2	48
Le Tréport, Fr.	D10	14
Letsôk-aw Kyun, i., Mya.	G3	48
Letung, Indon.	B4	50
Leucas see Lefkáda, i., Grc.	E3	28
Leucate, Étang de, l., Fr.	G9	18
Leuk, Switz.	D4	22
Leuser, Gunung, mtn., Indon.	K3	48
Leutkirch, Ger.	I6	16
Leuven, Bel.	D13	14
Levack, On., Can.	B8	112
Levan, Ut., U.S.	D5	132
Levanger, Nor.	E4	8
Levante, Riviera di, cst., Italy	F6	22
Levanzo, Isola di, i., Italy	F6	24
Le Vauclin, Mart.	k7	105c
Levelland, Tx., U.S.	H6	128
Levêque, Cape, c., Austl.	C4	74
Leverkusen, Ger.	E3	16
Levice, Slov.	H14	16
Levin, N.Z.	E6	80
Lévis, Qc., Can.	D5	110
Levisa Fork, stm., U.S.	G3	114
Levittown, P.R.	B3	104a
Levittown, N.Y., U.S.	D12	114
Levittown, Pa., U.S.	D11	114
Levkosía see Nicosia, Cyp.	C4	58
Levoča, Slov.	H16	16
Levski, Blg.	F12	26
Levuka, Fiji	p19	79e
Lévuo, stm., Lith.	E7	10
Lewe, Mya.	C2	48
Lewellen, Ne., U.S.	F10	126
Lewer, stm., Nmb.	D3	70
Lewes, De., U.S.	F10	114
Lewin Brzeski, Pol.	F13	16
Lewis, Ia., U.S.	J3	118
Lewis, Butt of, c., Scot., U.K.	C6	12
Lewis, Isle of, i., Scot., U.K.	C6	12
Lewis, Mount, mtn., Nv., U.S.	C8	134
Lewis and Clark Lake, res., U.S.	E15	126
Lewis and Clark Range, mts., Mt., U.S.	C13	136
Lewisburg, Ky., U.S.	H10	120
Lewisburg, Pa., U.S.	D8	114
Lewisburg, Tn., U.S.	B12	122
Lewis Range, mts., N.A.	B13	136
Lewis Run, Pa., U.S.	C7	114
Lewis Smith Lake, res., Al., U.S.	C11	122
Lewiston, Ca., U.S.	C3	134
Lewiston, Id., U.S.	D10	136
Lewiston, Me., U.S.	F6	110
Lewiston, Mi., U.S.	D5	112
Lewiston, Mn., U.S.	H7	118
Lewiston, Ut., U.S.	B5	132
Lewiston Orchards, Id., U.S.	D10	136
Lewistown, Il., U.S.	D7	120
Lewistown, Mt., U.S.	C17	136
Lewistown, Pa., U.S.	D8	114
Lewisville, N.B., Can.	D12	110
Lewisville, Ar., U.S.	D5	122
Lewisville, Tx., U.S.	A10	130
Lewisville Lake, res., Tx., U.S.	H12	128
Lewvan, Sk., Can.	D9	124
Lexa, Ar., U.S.	C8	122
Lexington, Ga., U.S.	C2	116
Lexington, Il., U.S.	D9	120
Lexington, Ky., U.S.	F1	114
Lexington, Ma., U.S.	B14	114
Lexington, Mi., U.S.	E7	112
Lexington, Ms., U.S.	D8	122
Lexington, N.C., U.S.	I5	114
Lexington, Ok., U.S.	F11	128
Lexington, Or., U.S.	E7	136
Lexington, S.C., U.S.	C4	116
Lexington, Tx., U.S.	D10	130
Lexington, Va., U.S.	G6	114
Lexington Park, Md., U.S.	F9	114
Leyden see Leiden, Neth.	B13	14
Leye, China	I2	42
Leyte, i., Phil.	E5	52
Leyte Gulf, b., Phil.	E5	52
Lezhë, Alb.	C13	24
Lezhi, China	F1	42
Lëzna, Bela.	E13	10
L'gov, Russia	D5	32
Lhasa, China	D13	54
Lhasa, stm., China	C13	54
Lhazê, China	D11	54
Lhoknga, Indon.	J2	48
Lhokseumawe, Indon.	J3	48
Lhoksukon, Indon.	J3	48
Lhorong, China	E4	36
L'Hospitalet de Llobregat, Spain	C13	20
Lhuntsi Dzong, Bhu.	E13	54
Li, Thai.	D4	48
Li, stm., China	G4	42
Li, stm., Thai.	D4	48
Liamuiga, Mount, vol., St. K./N.	C2	105a
Lian, stm., China	I5	42
Liancheng, China	I7	42
Lianga, Phil.	F6	52
Liangbao, China	D4	42
Liangbuaya, Indon.	C10	50
Liangdang, China	E1	42
Lianghekou, China	G3	42
Liangmentou, China	G9	42
Liangping, China	F2	42
Liangyuan, China	E7	42
Liangzi Hu, l., China	F6	42
Lianhuapao, China	B8	38
Lianhua Shan, mts., China	J6	42
Lianjiang, China	K4	42
Liannan, China	I5	42
Lianshui, China	E8	42
Lianxian, China	I5	42
Lianyuan, China	H4	42
Lianyungang, China	D8	42
Liao, stm., China	D5	38
Liaocheng, China	C7	42
Liaodong Bandao (Liaotung Peninsula), pen., China	D5	38
Liaodong Wan (Liaotung, Gulf of), b., China	A9	42
Liaoning, state, China	D5	38
Liaotung, Gulf of see Liaodong Wan, b., China	A9	42
Liaotung Peninsula see Liaodong Bandao, pen., China	E5	38
Liaoyang, China	D5	38
Liaoyuan, China	C6	38
Liaozhong, China	D5	38
Liard, stm., Can.	C6	106
Liat, Pulau, i., Indon.	E5	50
Libagon, Phil.	E5	52
Líbano, Col.	E4	86
Libby, Mt., U.S.	B11	136
Libby Dam, dam, Mt., U.S.	B11	136
Libenge, D.R.C.	D3	66
Liberal, Ks., U.S.	D7	128
Liberal, Mo., U.S.	G3	120
Liberec, Czech Rep.	F11	16
Liberia, C.R.	G5	102
Liberia, ctry., Afr.	H3	64
Liberta, Antig.	f4	105b
Libertad, Ven.	C7	86
Libertad, Ven.	C7	86
Libertador General Bernardo O'Higgins, state, Chile	G2	92
Liberty, Ms., U.S.	F8	122
Liberty, Mo., U.S.	E3	120
Liberty, N.Y., U.S.	C11	114
Liberty, N.C., U.S.	I6	114
Liberty, S.C., U.S.	B3	116
Liberty, Tx., U.S.	G4	122
Liberty Center, Oh., U.S.	G5	112
Libertyville, Il., U.S.	B9	120
Libo, China	I2	42
Libobo, Tanjung, c., Indon.	F8	44
Libode, S. Afr.	G9	70
Libourne, Fr.	E5	18
Librazhd, Alb.	C14	24
Libres, Mex.	F10	100
Libreville, Gabon	D1	66
Librung, Indon.	F12	50
Libya, ctry., Afr.	B3	62
Libyan Desert, des., Afr.	C5	62
Libyan Plateau, plat., Afr.	A4	62
Licancábur, Volcán, vol., S.A.	D3	90
Licantén, Chile	G1	92
Licata, Italy	G7	24
Lich, Ger.	F4	16
Licheng, China	C5	42
Licheng see Liyang, China	F8	42
Lichfield, Eng., U.K.	I11	12
Lichinga, Moz.	C6	68
Lichtenau, Ger.	E5	16
Lichtenburg, S. Afr.	E7	70
Lichtenfels, Ger.	F7	16
Lichuan, China	H7	42
Lichuan, China	F3	42
Licking, Mo., U.S.	G6	120
Licking, stm., Ky., U.S.	F1	114
Ličko Polje, val., Cro.	F12	22
Lida, Bela.	G8	10
Liddon Gulf, b., N.T., Can.	B17	140
Liden, Swe.	E7	8
Lidgerwood, N.D., U.S.	E1	118
Lidköping, Swe.	G5	8
Lido di Ostia, Italy	I9	22
Lidzbark, Pol.	C15	16
Lidzbark Warmiński, Pol.	B16	16
Liebenbergsvlei, stm., S. Afr.	E9	70
Liebig, Mount, mtn., Austl.	D6	74
Liechtenstein, ctry., Eur.	C6	22
Liège (Luik), Bel.	D14	14
Lielais Liepu kalns, hill, Lat.	D10	10
Lielvārde, Lat.	D7	10
Lienchou see Hepu, China	K3	42
Lienz, Aus.	D9	22
Liepāja, Lat.	D3	10
Liepājas ezers, l., Lat.	D4	10
Lier, Bel.	C13	14
Lierre see Lier, Bel.	C13	14
Liestal, Switz.	C4	22
Liesti, Rom.	D14	26
Liévin, Fr.	D11	14
Lièvre, stm., Qc., Can.	C14	112
Liezen, Aus.	C11	22
Liffey, stm., Ire.	H6	12
Lifford, Ire.	G5	12
Lifou, i., N. Cal.	m16	79d
Līgatne, Lat.	C7	10
Lighthouse Point, Fl., U.S.	J5	116
Lighthouse Point, c., Fl., U.S.	H14	122
Lighthouse Point, c., Mi., U.S.	C4	112
Lightning Creek, stm., Wy., U.S.	D7	126
Lightning Ridge, Austl.	G6	76
Lignite, N.D., U.S.	F11	124
Ligny-en-Barrois, Fr.	F14	14
Ligonha, stm., Moz.	D6	68
Ligonier, In., U.S.	G4	112
Ligonier, Pa., U.S.	H10	112
Liguria, state, Italy	F5	22
Ligurian Sea, Eur.	G5	22
Lihir Island, i., Pap. N. Gui.	a5	79a
Lihoslavl', Russia	C18	10
Lihou Reefs and Cays, rf., Austl.	A8	76
Lihue, Hi., U.S.	B2	78a
Lihuel Calel, Parque Nacional, p.o.i., Arg.	H5	92
Lihula, Est.	B6	10
Lijiang, China	F5	36
Lik, stm., Laos	C6	48
Likasi (Jadotville), D.R.C.	G5	66
Likati, D.R.C.	D4	66
Likely, B.C., Can.	D9	138
Liki, Indon.	D2	50
Likino-Dulevo, Russia	E21	10
Lilbourn, Mo., U.S.	H8	120
Lilibeo, Capo see Boeo, Capo, c., Italy	G6	24
Lilienfeld, Aus.	B12	22
Liling, China	H5	42
Lille, Fr.	D12	14
Lillebælt, strt., Den.	I3	8
Lillebonne, Fr.	E9	14
Lillehammer, Nor.	F3	8
Lillers, Fr.	D11	14
Lillestrøm, Nor.	F4	8
Lillhärdal, Swe.	F6	8
Lillington, N.C., U.S.	A7	116
Lillooet, B.C., Can.	F9	138
Lillooet, stm., B.C., Can.	G8	138
Lillooet Lake, l., B.C., Can.	F8	138
Lilongwe, Mwi.	C5	68
Liloy, Phil.	F4	52
Lilydale, Austl.	n13	77a
Lim, stm., Eur.	G16	22
Lima, Para.	A9	92
Lima, Peru	F2	84
Lima, Mt., U.S.	F14	136
Lima, N.Y., U.S.	B8	114
Lima, Oh., U.S.	D1	114
Lima (Limia), stm., Eur.	C2	20
Limarí, stm., Chile	E2	92
Limas, Indon.	C4	50
Limassol see Lemesós, Cyp.	D4	58
Limavady, N. Ire., U.K.	F6	12
Limay, stm., Arg.	G3	90
Limay Mahuida, Arg.	H4	92
Limbang, Malay.	A9	50
Limbang, stm., Malay.	A9	50
Līmbdi, India	G3	54
Limbe, Cam.	D1	66
Limbé, Haiti	C11	102
Limbujan see Pio V. Corpuz, Phil.	E5	52
Limburg an der Lahn, Ger.	F4	16
Limeira, Braz.	L2	88
Limerick, Sk., Can.	E7	124
Limerick (Luimneach), Ire.	I4	12
Limerick, state, Ire.	I4	12
Limestone, Me., U.S.	D9	110
Limestone, Lake, res., Tx., U.S.	F2	122
Limfjorden, l., Den.	H3	8
Limia (Lima), stm., Eur.	C2	20
Limingen, l., Nor.	D5	8
Limmared, Swe.	H5	8
Limmen Bight, b., Austl.	B7	74
Límnos, i., Grc.	D8	28
Limoeiro, Braz.	D8	88
Limoeiro do Norte, Braz.	C6	88
Limoges, Fr.	D7	18
Limón, Hond.	E5	102
Limone Piemonte, Italy	F4	22
Limoux, Fr.	F8	18
Limpopo, stm., Afr.	D8	70
Linahamari, Russia	B14	8
Lin'an, China	F8	42
Linapacan Island, i., Phil.	E2	52
Linares, Chile	G2	92
Linares, Mex.	C9	100
Linares, Spain	F7	20
Linch, Wy., U.S.	D6	126
Lincheng, China	C6	42
Linch'ing see Linqing, China	C6	42
Lincoln, Arg.	G7	92
Lincoln, Eng., U.K.	H12	12
Lincoln, Ar., U.S.	I3	120
Lincoln, Ca., U.S.	E4	134
Lincoln, Il., U.S.	D8	120
Lincoln, Mi., U.S.	D6	112
Lincoln, Mo., U.S.	F4	120
Lincoln, Mt., U.S.	D14	136
Lincoln, Ne., U.S.	K2	118
Lincoln, N.H., U.S.	F5	110
Lincoln, Mount, mtn., Co., U.S.	B2	128
Lincoln City, Or., U.S.	F2	136
Lincoln Creek, stm., Ne., U.S.	F15	126
Lincoln Park, Co., U.S.	C3	128
Lincoln Park, Mi., U.S.	B2	114
Lincoln Sea, N.A.	A13	141
Lincolnton, Ga., U.S.	C3	116
Lincolnton, N.C., U.S.	A4	116
Lincoln Village, Ca., U.S.	E4	134
Lindale, Ga., U.S.	C13	122
Lindale, Tx., U.S.	E3	122
Lindau, Ger.	I5	16
Linde, stm., Russia	C13	34
Linden, Guy.	B6	84
Linden, Al., U.S.	E11	122
Linden, In., U.S.	H3	112
Linden, Mi., U.S.	B2	114
Linden, Tn., U.S.	B11	122
Lindesnes, c., Nor.	H2	8
Lindi, Tan.	F7	66
Lindi, stm., D.R.C.	D5	66
Líndos, hist., Grc.	G10	28
Lind Point, c., V.I.U.S.	e7	104b
Lindsay, On., Can.	D11	112
Lindsay, Ca., U.S.	G6	134
Lindsay, Ne., U.S.	F15	126
Lindsay, Ok., U.S.	G11	128
Line Islands, is., Oc.	D11	72
Linesville, Pa., U.S.	C5	114
Lineville, Al., U.S.	D13	122
Lineville, Ia., U.S.	D4	120
Linfen, China	C4	42
Linganamakki Reservoir, res., India	D2	53
Lingao, China	L3	42
Lingayen, Phil.	B3	52
Lingayen Gulf, b., Phil.	B3	52
Lingbi, China	E7	42
Lingbo, Swe.	F7	8
Lingchuan, China	D5	42

Name	Map Ref.	Page
Lingen, Ger.	D3	16
Lingfengwei, China	I6	42
Lingga, Kepulauan, is., Indon.	C4	50
Lingga, Pulau, i., Indon.	D4	50
Lingomo II, D.R.C.	D4	66
Lingqiu, China	B6	42
Lingshan, China	J3	42
Lingshi, China	C4	42
Lingshui, China	L4	42
Linguère, Sen.	F2	64
Lingwu, China	B2	42
Lingxian, China	H5	42
Lingyuan, China	A8	42
Linh, Ngoc, mtn., Viet.	E9	48
Linhai, China	G9	42
Linhares, Braz.	J5	88
Linhe, China	A2	42
Linhsia see Linxia, China	D5	36
Linli see Linyi, China	D8	42
Linjiang, China	D7	38
Linköping, Swe.	G6	8
Linkou, China	B9	38
Linksmakalnis, Lith.	F6	10
Linkuva, Lith.	D6	10
Linn, Ks., U.S.	B11	128
Linn, Mo., U.S.	F6	120
Linnansaaren kansallispuisto, p.o.i., Fin.	E13	8
Linnhe, Loch, b., Scot., U.K.	E7	12
Linqi, China	D5	42
Linqing, China	C6	42
Linqu, China	C8	42
Linquan, China	E6	42
Linru, China	D5	42
Lins, Braz.	K1	88
Linstead, Jam.	i13	104d
Lintan, China	E5	36
Linton, In., U.S.	E10	120
Linton, N.D., U.S.	A12	126
Lintong, China	D3	42
Linwu, China	I5	42
Linxi, China	C8	36
Linxi, China	C3	38
Linxia, China	D5	36
Linxian, China	C4	42
Linxian, China	C5	42
Linyi, China	D8	42
Linyi, China	C7	42
Linyü see Shanhaiguan, China	A8	42
Linz, Aus.	B11	22
Lio Matoh, Malay.	B9	50
Lion, Golfe du, b., Fr.	G10	18
Lion, Gulf of see Lion, Golfe du, b., Fr.	G10	18
Lionel Town, Jam.	j13	104d
Liouesso, Congo	D3	66
Lipa, Phil.	D3	52
Lipan, Tx., U.S.	B9	130
Lipari, Italy	F8	24
Lipari, Isola, i., Italy	F9	24
Lipari, Isole see Eolie, Isole, is., Italy	F8	24
Lipcani, Mol.	A13	26
Lipeck, Russia	D6	32
Lípez, Cerro, mtn., Bol.	D3	90
Lipicy, Russia	G20	10
Liping, China	H3	42
Lipki, Russia	G20	10
Lipník nad Bečvou, Czech Rep.	G13	16
Lipno, Pol.	D15	16
Lipno, údolní nádrž, res., Czech Rep.	H10	16
Lipova, Rom.	C8	26
Lipovcy, Russia	B9	38
Lippe, stm., Ger.	E2	16
Lippstadt, Ger.	E4	16
Lipscomb, Tx., U.S.	E8	128
Lipsoí, i., Grc.	F9	28
Liptovská Teplička, Slov.	G15	16
Liptovský Mikuláš, Slov.	G15	16
Liptrap, Cape, c., Austl.	L5	76
Lipu, China	I4	42
Lira, Ug.	D6	66
Liri, stm., Italy	C7	24
Liria see Llíria, Spain	E10	20
Liro, Vanuatu	k17	79d
Lisala, D.R.C.	D4	66
Lisboa (Lisbon), Port.	F1	20
Lisboa, state, Port.	E1	20
Lisbon see Lisboa, Port.	F1	20
Lisbon, N.H., U.S.	F5	110
Lisbon, N.D., U.S.	A15	126
Lisbon, Oh., U.S.	D5	114
Lisburn, N. Ire., U.K.	G6	12
Lisburne, Cape, c., Ak., U.S.	C6	140
Lishi, China	C4	42
Lishu, China	C6	38
Lishui, China	G8	42
Lishuzhen, China	B9	38
Lisicy, Russia	D19	10
Lisieux, Sk., Can.	E7	124
Lisieux, Fr.	E9	14
Liski, Russia	D5	32
L'Isle-Jourdain, Fr.	C6	18
Lisman, Al., U.S.	E10	122
Lismore, Austl.	G9	76
Lismore, N.S., Can.	E14	110
Lišov, Czech Rep.	G10	16
Listowel, On., Can.	E9	112
Listowel, Ire.	I3	12
Litang, China	F5	36
Litang, China	J3	42
Litchfield, Il., U.S.	E8	120
Litchfield, Mn., U.S.	F4	118
Litchfield, Ne., U.S.	F13	126
Litchville, N.D., U.S.	A14	126
Lithgow, Austl.	I8	76
Líthinon, Ákra, c., Grc.	I7	28
Lithonia, Ga., U.S.	D14	122
Lithuania, ctry., Eur.	E7	10
Litija, Slvn.	D11	22
Lititz, Pa., U.S.	D9	114
Litoměřice, Czech Rep.	F10	16
Litomyšl, Czech Rep.	G12	16
Litovko, Russia	G16	34
Little, stm., U.S.	D5	122
Little, stm., U.S.	B8	122
Little, stm., Ga., U.S.	C3	116
Little, stm., N.C., U.S.	A7	116
Little, stm., Ok., U.S.	F11	128
Little, stm., Tx., U.S.	D11	130
Little, Mountain Fork, stm., U.S.	C4	122
Little Abaco, i., Bah.	B9	96
Little Andaman, i., India	F7	46
Little Arkansas, stm., Ks., U.S.	C11	128
Little Beaver Creek, stm., U.S.	A8	126
Little Beaver Creek, stm., U.S.	B7	128
Little Belt see Lillebælt, strt., Den.	I3	8
Little Belt Mountains, mts., Mt., U.S.	D16	136
Little Bighorn, stm., U.S.	B5	126
Little Bighorn Battlefield National Monument, p.o.i., Mt., U.S.	B5	126
Little Blue, stm., U.S.	G15	126
Little Buffalo, stm., Can.	C8	106
Little Carpathians see Malé Karpaty, mts., Slov.	H13	16
Little Cayman, i., Cay. Is.	C7	102
Little Chute, Wi., U.S.	D1	112
Little Colorado, stm., Az., U.S.	H5	132
Little Current, On., Can.	C8	112
Little Current, stm., On., Can.	A12	118
Little Deep Creek, stm., N.D., U.S.	F12	124
Little Deschutes, stm., Or., U.S.	G5	136
Little Desert, des., Austl.	K3	76
Little Desert National Park, p.o.i., Austl.	K3	76
Little Dry Creek, stm., Mt., U.S.	G7	124
Little Falls, Mn., U.S.	E4	118
Little Falls, N.Y., U.S.	E15	112
Littlefork, Mn., U.S.	C5	118
Little Fork, stm., Mn., U.S.	C5	118
Little Hurricane Creek, stm., Ga., U.S.	E3	116
Little Inagua, i., Bah.	B11	102
Little Kanawha, stm., W.V., U.S.	E4	114
Little Karroo (Klein Karroo), plat., S. Afr.	H5	70
Little Lake, l., La., U.S.	H8	122
Little London, Jam.	i12	104d
Little Lost, stm., Id., U.S.	F13	136
Little Mexico, Tx., U.S.	D4	130
Little Missouri, stm., U.S.	B7	108
Little Missouri, stm., Ar., U.S.	D5	122
Little Namaqualand (Klein Namaland), hist. reg., S. Afr.	F3	70
Little Nicobar, i., India	G7	46
Little Osage, stm., U.S.	G3	120
Little Pee Dee, stm., S.C., U.S.	B6	116
Little Pic, stm., On., Can.	C12	118
Little Powder, stm., U.S.	B7	126
Little Quill Lake, l., Sk., Can.	C10	124
Little Rann of Kachchh, reg., India	G3	54
Little Red, stm., Ar., U.S.	B7	122
Little Red, Middle Fork, stm., Ar., U.S.	B6	122
Little Red Deer, stm., Ab., Can.	E16	138
Little River, Ks., U.S.	C10	128
Little Rock, Ar., U.S.	C6	122
Little Rock, stm., U.S.	H2	118
Little Sable Point, c., Mi., U.S.	E3	112
Little Saint Bernard Pass, p., Eur.	D12	18
Little Sandy Creek, stm., Wy., U.S.	E3	126
Little Sioux, stm., U.S.	J3	118
Little Sioux, West Fork, stm., Ia., U.S.	B2	120
Little Smoky, stm., Ab., Can.	A14	138
Little Snake, stm., U.S.	C8	132
Littlestown, Pa., U.S.	E8	114
Little Tallapoosa, stm., U.S.	D13	122
Little Tennessee, stm., U.S.	A1	116
Little Tobago, i., Trin.	r13	105f
Littleton, Co., U.S.	B3	128
Littleton, N.H., U.S.	F5	110
Littleton, W.V., U.S.	E5	114
Little Valley, N.Y., U.S.	B7	114
Little Wabash, stm., Il., U.S.	F9	120
Little White, stm., S.D., U.S.	D12	126
Little Wood, stm., Id., U.S.	G12	136
Litvínov, Czech Rep.	F9	16
Liu, stm., China	C6	38
Liu, stm., China	C5	38
Liu, stm., China	I3	42
Liuaniua see Ontong Java, at., Sol. Is.	D7	72
Liuba, China	E2	42
Liuboml', Ukr.	E20	16
Liuchen, China	J4	42
Liucheng, China	I3	42
Liugou see Liuzhou, China	I3	42
Liucura, Chile	I2	92
Liufang, China	H7	42
Liuhe, China	C6	38
Liuheng Dao, i., China	G10	42
Liujiazi, China	A9	42
Liupan Shan, mts., China	D2	42
Liushuquan, China	F16	32
Liuxi, stm., China	J5	42
Liuyang, China	G5	42
Liuyang, stm., China	G5	42
Liuzhou, China	I3	42
Livada, Rom.	B10	26
Livadija, Russia	C10	38
Līvāni, Lat.	D9	10
Livanjsko Polje, val., Bos.	F3	26
Lively, On., Can.	B8	112
Lively Island, i., Falk. Is.	J5	90
Live Oak, Ca., U.S.	D4	134
Live Oak, Fl., U.S.	F2	116
Liveringa, Austl.	C4	74
Livermore, Ca., U.S.	F4	134
Livermore, Ia., U.S.	B3	120
Livermore, Ky., U.S.	G10	120
Livermore, Mount, mtn., Tx., U.S.	D3	130
Livermore Falls, Me., U.S.	F6	110
Liverpool, N.S., Can.	F12	110
Liverpool, Eng., U.K.	H10	12
Liverpool, Cape, c., Nu., Can.	C10	141
Liverpool Bay, b., N.T., Can.	A5	106
Liverpool Bay, b., Eng., U.K.	H9	12
Livingston, Gua.	E3	102
Livingston, Al., U.S.	E10	122
Livingston, Il., U.S.	F8	120
Livingston, La., U.S.	G8	122
Livingston, Mt., U.S.	E16	136
Livingston, Tn., U.S.	H12	120
Livingston, Tx., U.S.	G4	122
Livingston, Wi., U.S.	B7	120
Livingston, Lake, res., Tx., U.S.	G3	122
Livingstone, Zam.	D4	68
Livingstone Falls, wtfl, Afr.	A1	68
Livingstonia, Mwi.	C5	68
Livingston Manor, N.Y., U.S.	C11	114
Livno, Bos.	F4	26
Livny, Russia	H20	10
Livonia, La., U.S.	G7	122
Livonia, Mi., U.S.	B2	114
Livonia, N.Y., U.S.	B8	114
Livorno (Leghorn), Italy	G7	22
Livramento do Brumado, Braz.	G5	88
Liwale, Tan.	F7	66
Lixi, China	G6	42
Lixian, China	G4	42
Lixian, China	D2	42
Lixian see Black, stm., Asia	D9	56
Lixin, China	E7	42
Lixoúri, Grc.	E3	28
Liyang, China	F8	42
Lizarda, Braz.	E2	88
Lizard Point, c., Eng., U.K.	L7	12
Lizarra see Estella, Spain	B8	20
Ljady, Bela.	F14	10
Ljakavičy, Bela.	G9	10
Ljahovskie ostrova, is., Russia	B17	34
Ljamca, Russia	D17	8
Ljaskavičy, Bela.	H11	10
Ljasnaja, Bela.	G8	10
Ljuban', Bela.	H10	10
Ljuban', Russia	A13	10
Ljubercy, Russia	E20	10
Ljubimec, Blg.	H12	26
Ljubljana, Slvn.	D11	22
Ljubnica, Russia	C15	10
Ljubohna, Russia	G17	10
Ljubuški, Bos.	F4	26
Ljudinovo, Russia	G17	10
Ljudkovo, Russia	F17	10
Ljungan, stm., Swe.	E5	8
Ljungby, Swe.	H5	8
Ljusdal, Swe.	F7	8
Ljusina, Bela.	H9	10
Ljusnan, stm., Swe.	F6	8
Llancanelo, Laguna, l., Arg.	G3	92
Llandeilo, Wales, U.K.	J8	12
Llandrindod Wells, Wales, U.K.	I9	12
Llandudno, Wales, U.K.	H9	12
Llanelli, Wales, U.K.	J8	12
Llangefni, Wales, U.K.	H8	12
Llanidloes, Wales, U.K.	I9	12
Llano, stm., Tx., U.S.	D8	130
Llano Colorado, Mex.	L9	134
Llanos, pl., S.A.	E7	86
Llanquihue, Lago, l., Chile	H2	90
Lleida, Spain	C11	20
Lleida, co., Spain	B12	20
Llera de Canales, Mex.	D9	100
Llerena, Spain	F4	20
Lleulleu, Lago, l., Chile	I1	92
Llico, Chile	G1	92
Llíria, Spain	E10	20
Llivia, Spain	B12	20
Llobregat, stm., Spain	C12	20
Lloydminster, Sk., Can.	E9	106
Llucena, Spain	D10	20
Llucmayor see Llucmajor, Spain	E13	20
Llucmajor, Spain	E13	20
Llullaillaco, Volcán, vol., S.A.	B3	92
Lo (Panlong), stm., Asia	A7	48
Loa, Ut., U.S.	E5	132
Loa, stm., Chile	D3	90
Loanda, Braz.	D6	90
Loange (Luangue), stm., Afr.	F3	66
Lobamba, Swaz.	E10	70
Lobanovo, Russia	G21	10
Lobatse, Bots.	D7	70
Löbau, Ger.	E10	16
Lobaye, stm., C.A.R.	D3	66
Lobelville, Tn., U.S.	B11	122
Lobería, Arg.	I8	92
Lobnja, Russia	D20	10
Lobos, Arg.	G8	92
Lobos, Cay, i., Bah.	A9	102
Lobos, Isla, i., Mex.	B3	100
Lobskoe, Russia	E16	8
Łobżenica, Pol.	C13	16
Locarno, Switz.	D5	22
Loches, Fr.	G10	14
Loch Garman see Wexford, Ire.	I6	12
Lochinver, Scot., U.K.	C7	12
Lochsa, stm., Id., U.S.	D12	136
Lock, Austl.	F7	74
Lockeport, N.S., Can.	G11	110
Lockerbie, Scot., U.K.	F9	12
Lockesburg, Ar., U.S.	D4	122
Lockhart, Austl.	J6	76
Lock Haven, Pa., U.S.	C8	114
Lockney, Tx., U.S.	G7	128
Lockport, Il., U.S.	C9	120
Lockport, La., U.S.	H8	122
Lockport, N.Y., U.S.	E11	112
Lockwood, Mo., U.S.	G4	120
Locminé, Fr.	G6	14
Loc Ninh, Viet.	G8	48
Locust Creek, stm., U.S.	D4	120
Locust Fork, stm., Al., U.S.	D11	122
Locust Grove, Ok., U.S.	H2	120
Lod (Lydda), Isr.	G5	58
Lodalskåpa, mtn., Nor.	F2	8
Loddon, stm., Austl.	K4	76
Lodejnoe Pole, Russia	F15	8
Lodève, Fr.	F9	18
Lodge Creek, stm., N.A.	F4	124
Lodge Grass, Mt., U.S.	B5	126
Lodgepole, Ab., Can.	C15	138
Lodgepole, Ne., U.S.	F10	126
Lodgepole Creek, stm., U.S.	F10	126
Lodhrān, Pak.	D3	54
Lodi, Italy	E6	22
Lodi, Ca., U.S.	E4	134
Lodi, Wi., U.S.	H9	118
Lodja, D.R.C.	E4	66
Lodwar, Kenya	D7	66
Łódź, Pol.	E15	16
Łódź, state, Pol.	E15	16
Loei, Thai.	D6	48
Loei, stm., Thai.	D5	48
Loeriesfontein, S. Afr.	G4	70
Lofer, Aus.	C9	22
Lofoten, is., Nor.	B5	8
Lofoten Basin, unds.	A14	144
Loga, Niger	G5	64
Logan, Ia., U.S.	C2	120
Logan, Ks., U.S.	B9	128
Logan, Oh., U.S.	E3	114
Logan, Ut., U.S.	B5	132
Logan, W.V., U.S.	G4	114
Logan, Mount, mtn., Yk., Can.	C2	106
Logan Creek, stm., Ne., U.S.	E15	126
Logan Island, i., On., Can.	A10	118
Logan Martin Lake, res., Al., U.S.	D12	122
Logan Mountains, mts., Yk., Can.	C5	106
Logan Pass, p., Mt., U.S.	B13	136
Logansport, In., U.S.	H3	112
Logansport, La., U.S.	F5	122
Loganville, Ga., U.S.	C2	116
Logone, stm., Afr.	F3	62
Logroño, Spain	B8	20
Løgstør, Den.	H3	8
Logudoro, reg., Italy	D2	24
Lohārdaga, India	G10	54
Lohiniva, Fin.	C11	8
Lohne, Ger.	D4	16
Loho see Luohe, China	E6	42
Lohrville, Ia., U.S.	B3	120
Loi (Nanlei), stm., Asia	B4	48
Loi, Phou, mtn., Laos	B6	48
Loi-kaw, Mya.	C3	48
Loi Mwe, Mya.	B4	48
Loing, stm., Fr.	F11	14
Loing, Canal du, can., Fr.	F11	14
Loir, stm., Fr.	G8	14
Loire, state, Fr.	D10	18
Loire, stm., Fr.	B4	18
Loire, Canal latéral à la, can., Fr.	C9	18
Loire-Atlantique, state, Fr.	G7	14
Loiret, state, Fr.	F11	14
Loir-et-Cher, state, Fr.	G10	14
Loja, Ec.	D2	84
Loja, Spain	G6	20
Lokandu, D.R.C.	E5	66
Lokan Reservoir see Lokan tekojärvi, res., Fin.	C12	8
Lokan tekojärvi, res., Fin.	C12	8
Lokeren, Bel.	C13	14
Loket, Czech Rep.	F8	16
Lokichar, Kenya	D7	66
Lokichokio, Kenya	D6	66
Loknja, Russia	D13	10
Lokoja, Nig.	H6	64
Lokolama, D.R.C.	E3	66
Lokot', Russia	H17	10
Loksa, Est.	A8	10
Loks Land, i., Nu., Can.	E13	141
Lola, Gui.	H3	64
Loleta, Ca., U.S.	C1	134
Loliondo, Tan.	E7	66
Lolita, Tx., U.S.	F11	130
Lolland, i., Den.	I4	8
Lolo, Mt., U.S.	D12	136
Lolodorf, Cam.	D2	66
Lolo Pass, p., U.S.	D12	136
Lolowai, Vanuatu	j16	79d
Loltong, Vanuatu	j16	79d
Lolvavana, Passage, strt., Vanuatu	j16	79d
Lom, Blg.	F10	26
Lom, Nor.	F3	8
Lom, stm., Afr.	F2	62
Lomami, stm., D.R.C.	D4	66
Lomas de Zamora, Arg.	G8	92
Lomax, Il., U.S.	D6	120
Łomazy, Pol.	E19	16
Lombardia, state, Italy	E6	22
Lombardy see Lombardia, state, Italy	E6	22
Lomblen, Pulau, i., Indon.	G7	44
Lombok, Indon.	H10	50
Lombok, i., Indon.	H10	50
Lombok, Selat, strt., Indon.	H9	50
Lomé, Togo	H5	64
Lomela, D.R.C.	E4	66
Lomela, stm., D.R.C.	E4	66
Lomié, Cam.	D2	66
Lomira, Wi., U.S.	H10	118
Lommel, Bel.	C14	14
Lomond, Loch, l., Scot., U.K.	E8	12
Lomonosov, Russia	A12	10
Lomonosovka, Kaz.	D11	32
Lomovoe, Russia	D19	8
Lompobatang, Gunung, mtn., Indon.	F11	50
Lompoc, Ca., U.S.	I5	134
Lom Sak, Thai.	D5	48
Łomża, Pol.	C18	16
Łomża, state, Pol.	C18	16
Lonaconing, Md., U.S.	E7	114
Lonāvale, India	B1	53
Loncoche, Chile	G2	90
Loncopué, Arg.	I2	92
London, On., Can.	F8	112
London, Eng., U.K.	J12	12
London, Ar., U.S.	B5	122
London, Ky., U.S.	G1	114
London, Tx., U.S.	D8	130
Londonderry, N.S., Can.	E13	110
Londonderry (Derry), N. Ire., U.K.	F6	12
Londonderry, Cape, c., Austl.	B5	74
Londonderry, Isla, i., Chile	K2	90
Londrina, Braz.	D6	90
Lone Grove, Ok., U.S.	G11	128
Lone Oak, Ky., U.S.	G9	120
Lone Pine, Ca., U.S.	G7	134
Lone Rock, Wi., U.S.	A7	120
Lone Tree, Ia., U.S.	C6	120
Lone Wolf, Ok., U.S.	G9	128
Long, stm., China	I3	42
Longa, Ang.	C2	68
Longá, stm., Braz.	B5	88
Longa, proliv, strt., Russia	B24	34
Long Akah, Malay.	B9	50
Longana, Vanuatu	j17	79d
Longarone, Italy	D9	22
Longavi, Chile	G2	92
Longbangun, Indon.	C9	50
Long Bay, b., U.S.	C7	116
Long Beach, Ca., U.S.	J7	134
Long Beach, Ms., U.S.	G9	122
Long Beach, N.Y., U.S.	D12	114
Long Beach, Wa., U.S.	D2	136
Longboat Key, Fl., U.S.	I3	116
Long Branch, N.J., U.S.	D12	114
Long Cay, i., Bah.	m18	104f
Longchang, China	G1	42
Longchuan, China	I6	42
Long Creek, stm., N.A.	E10	124
Longde, China	D2	42
Long Eaton, Eng., U.K.	I11	12
Longford, Austl.	L6	76
Longford, Ire.	H5	12
Longford, state, Ire.	H5	12
Long Hu, l., China	F6	42
Longhua, China	A7	42
Longhui, China	H4	42
Longiram, Indon.	C9	50
Long Island, i., Antig.	f4	105b
Long Island, i., Austl.	D7	76
Long Island, i., Bah.	A10	102
Long Island, i., Nu., Can.	E14	106
Long Island, i., N.S., Can.	F10	110
Long Island, i., N.Y., U.S.	D12	114
Long Island Sound, strt., U.S.	D12	114
Longitudinal, Valle, val., Chile	H1	92
Longjiang, China	B9	36
Longkou, China	C9	42
Long Lake, N.Y., U.S.	G2	110
Long Lake, l., On., Can.	B11	118
Longleaf, La., U.S.	F6	122
Long Leaf Park, N.C., U.S.	B8	116
Longli, China	H2	42
Longlin, China	G6	36
Longling, China	G4	36
Longmeadow, Ma., U.S.	B13	114
Long Moc, Viet.	C7	48
Longmont, Co., U.S.	A3	128
Long Mountain, mtn., Mo., U.S.	H5	120
Longnan, China	I6	42
Longnawan, Indon.	C9	50
Long Pine, Ne., U.S.	E13	126
Long Point, c., Bah.	n18	104f
Long Point, c., N.S., Can.	D16	110
Long Point, pen., Mb., Can.	A15	124
Long Point, pen., On., Can.	F9	112
Long Point Bay, b., On., Can.	F9	112
Longquan, China	G8	42
Long Range Mountains, mts., Nf., Can.	j22	107a
Longreach, Austl.	D5	76
Long-Sault, On., Can.	E2	110
Longsegah, Indon.	B10	50
Longshan, China	G3	42
Longsheng, China	I3	42
Longs Peak, mtn., Co., U.S.	A3	128
Long Swamp, Br. Vir. Is.	e8	104b
Long Thanh, Viet.	G8	48
Longton, Ks., U.S.	G1	120
Longtown, Eng., U.K.	F10	12
Longueuil, Qc., Can.	E3	110
Longuyon, Fr.	E14	14
Longview, Ab., Can.	F16	138
Long View, N.C., U.S.	I4	114
Longview, Tx., U.S.	E4	122
Longview, Wa., U.S.	D4	136
Longwai, Indon.	C10	50
Longwy, Fr.	E14	14
Longxi, China	E5	36
Longxian, China	D2	42
Long Xuyen, Viet.	G7	48
Longyan, China	I7	42
Longyou, China	G8	42
Longzhen, China	B10	36
Longzhou, China	J2	42
Lonigo, Italy	E8	22
Löningen, Ger.	D3	16
Lonja, stm., Cro.	E13	22
Lonoke, Ar., U.S.	C7	122
Lonquimay, Volcán, vol., Chile	I2	92
Lonsdale, Mn., U.S.	G5	118
Lons-le-Saunier, Fr.	H14	14
Lontra, stm., Braz.	D1	88
Loogootee, In., U.S.	F11	120
Lookout, Cape, c., N.C., U.S.	B9	116
Lookout Mountain, mts., U.S.	C13	122
Lookout Pass, p., U.S.	C11	136
Lookout Ridge, mts., Ak., U.S.	C8	140
Loolmalasin, vol., Tan.	E7	66
Loomis, Ne., U.S.	G13	126
Loomis, Wa., U.S.	B7	136
Loop, Tx., U.S.	B5	130
Loop Head, c., Ire.	I2	12
Lop, China	A5	46
Lop, stm., Viet.	F8	48
Lopatina, gora, mtn., Russia	F17	34
Lopatka, mys, c., Russia	F20	34
Lopatovo, Russia	D12	10
Lop Buri, Thai.	E5	48
Lopévi, i., Vanuatu	k17	79d
Lopez, Cap, c., Gabon	E1	66
Lop Nur, l., China	C3	36
Loptjuga, Russia	E22	8
Lora, Hāmūn-i-, l., Asia	D9	56
Lora del Río, Spain	G5	20
Lorain, Oh., U.S.	C3	114
Loraine, Tx., U.S.	B7	130
Loralai, Pak.	C2	54
Lorca, Spain	G9	20
Lord Howe Island, i., Austl.	G6	72
Lord Howe Rise, unds.	L19	142
Lord Mayor Bay, b., Nu., Can.	B12	106
Lordsburg, N.M., U.S.	K8	132
Loreauville, La., U.S.	G7	122
Loreley, misc. cult., Ger.	F3	16
Lorena, Braz.	L3	88
Lorengau, Pap. N. Gui.	a4	79a
Lorenzo, Tx., U.S.	H7	128
Lorenzo Geyres, Ur.	F9	92
Loreto, Arg.	C9	92
Loreto, Mex.	D8	100
Loreto, Mex.	B3	100
Loreto, state, Peru	H4	86
Loretto, Ky., U.S.	G12	120
Loretto, Tn., U.S.	B11	122
Lorica, Col.	C4	86
Lorient, Fr.	G5	14
Lorimor, Ia., U.S.	C3	120
Loriol-sur-Drôme, Fr.	E10	18
Loris, S.C., U.S.	B7	116
Lorman, Ms., U.S.	F7	122
Lorn, Firth of, b., Scot., U.K.	E7	12
Lorne, Austl.	L5	76
Lorne, N.B., Can.	C10	110
Lörrach, Ger.	I3	16
Lorraine, hist. reg., Fr.	F14	14
Los, Îles de, is., Gui.	H2	64
Losada, stm., Col.	F4	86
Los Alamos, N.M., U.S.	F2	128
Los Aldamas, Mex.	B9	100
Los Andes, Chile	F2	92
Los Angeles, Chile	H1	92
Los Angeles, Ca., U.S.	I7	134
Los Angeles Aqueduct, aq., Ca., U.S.	H7	134
Los Antiguos, Arg.	I2	90
Los Banos, Ca., U.S.	F5	134
Los Blancos, Arg.	D4	90
Los Bolones, Cerro, mtn., Mex.	G12	100
Los Cerrillos, Arg.	E5	92
Los Conquistadores, Arg.	E8	92
Los Fresnos, Tx., U.S.	H10	130
Los Garza, Mex.	H8	130
Los Gatos, Ca., U.S.	F4	134
Loshan see Leshan, China	F5	36
Los Hermanos, Islas, is., Ven.	B9	86
Łosice, Pol.	D18	16
Los Idolos, Parque Arquelógico de, hist., Col.	G3	86
Lošinj, Otok, i., Cro.	F11	22
Losinoborskaja, Russia	C15	32
Los Juríes, Arg.	D6	92
Los Lagos, Chile	G2	90
Los Llanos, P.R.	B3	104a
Los López, Mex.	H8	130
Los Lunas, N.M., U.S.	I10	132
Los Mochis, Mex.	C4	100
Los Nogales, Mex.	H8	130
Losolava, Vanuatu	j16	79d
Los Padillas, N.M., U.S.	I10	132
Los Palacios, Arg.	D3	92
Los Palacios, Cuba	A6	102
Los Palacios y Villafranca, Spain	G4	20
Los Picachos, Parque Nacional, p.o.i., Col.	F4	86
Los Rábanos, P.R.	B2	104a
Los Ríos, state, Ec.	H2	86
Los Roques, Islas, is., Ven.	B8	86
Los Sauces, Chile	H1	92
Lossiemouth, Scot., U.K.	D9	12
Lost, stm., U.S.	A4	134
Los Taques, Ven.	B6	86
Los Teques, Ven.	B8	86
Los Testigos, Islas, is., Ven.	B10	86
Lost Hills, Ca., U.S.	H6	134
Lost Nation, Ia., U.S.	C7	120
Lost River Range, mts., Id., U.S.	F13	136
Lost Trail Pass, p., U.S.	E13	136
Losuia, Pap. N. Gui.	b5	79a
Los Vidrios, Mex.	F6	98
Los Vilos, Chile	E2	92
Los Yébenes, Spain	E6	20
Lot, state, Fr.	E7	18
Lot, stm., Fr.	E7	18
Lota, Chile	H1	92
Lot-et-Garonne, state, Fr.	E6	18
Lothair, S. Afr.	E10	70
Lotošino, Russia	D18	10
Lotsane, stm., Bots.	C8	70
Lotta, stm., Eur.	B13	8
Lotuke, Jabal, mtn., Sudan	G6	62
Lotung, Tai.	I9	42
Louang Namtha, Laos	B5	48
Louangphrabang, Laos	C6	48
Loubomo, Congo	E2	66
Loudon, Tn., U.S.	A1	116
Loudonville, Oh., U.S.	D3	114
Loudun, Fr.	G9	14
Loue, stm., Fr.	H14	14
Louga, Sen.	F1	64
Louge, Arg.	H7	92
Loughborough, Eng., U.K.	I11	12
Loughrea, Ire.	H4	12
Louhi, Russia	C15	8
Louin, Ms., U.S.	E9	122
Louisa, Ky., U.S.	F3	114
Louisbourg, N.S., Can.	E16	110
Louisburg, Ks., U.S.	F3	120
Louisburg, N.C., U.S.	H7	114
Louise, Ms., U.S.	D8	122
Louise, Tx., U.S.	H2	122
Louiseville, Qc., Can.	D3	110
Louisiade Archipelago, is., Pap. N. Gui.	B10	74
Louisiana, Mo., U.S.	E6	120
Louisiana, state, U.S.	F6	122
Louis Trichardt, S. Afr.	C9	70
Louisville, Al., U.S.	F13	122
Louisville, Ga., U.S.	C3	116
Louisville, Ky., U.S.	F12	120
Louisville, Ms., U.S.	D9	122
Louisville, Ne., U.S.	D1	120
Louisville, Oh., U.S.	D4	114
Louisville Ridge, unds.	M22	142
Louis-XIV, Pointe, c., Qc., Can.	E14	106
Loulé, Port.	G2	20
Loum, Cam.	D1	66
Lount Lake, l., On., Can.	A4	118
Louny, Czech Rep.	F9	16
Loup, stm., Ne., U.S.	F14	126
Loup City, Ne., U.S.	F14	126
Loups Marins, Lacs des, l., Qc., Can.	D16	106
Lourdes, Fr.	F5	18
Lourenço Marques see Maputo, Moz.	D11	70
Lourinhã, Port.	E1	20
Lousã, Port.	D2	20
Louth, Austl.	H5	76
Louth, Ire.	H6	12
Louth, Eng., U.K.	H13	12
Louth, state, Ire.	H6	12
Loutrá Aidhipsoú, Grc.	E6	28
Louvain see Leuven, Bel.	D13	14
Louviers, Fr.	E10	14
Louviers, Co., U.S.	B4	128
Lovat', stm., Russia	B14	10
Loveč, Blg.	F11	26
Loveč, state, Blg.	F11	26
Loveland, Co., U.S.	G7	126
Lovell, Wy., U.S.	C4	126
Lovell Village, St. Vin.	p11	105e
Lovelock, Nv., U.S.	C7	134
Lovely, Ky., U.S.	G3	114
Lovere, Italy	E6	22
Loves Park, Il., U.S.	B8	120
Loving, N.M., U.S.	B3	130
Loving, Tx., U.S.	H10	128
Lovingston, Va., U.S.	G7	114
Lovington, N.M., U.S.	B4	130
Lovosice, Czech Rep.	F9	16
Lovozero, Russia	D13	8
Lovozero, ozero, l., Russia	C16	8
Lóvua, Ang.	B3	68
Low, Qc., Can.	C14	112
Low, Cape, c., Nu., Can.	C13	106
Lowa, D.R.C.	E5	66
Lowa, stm., D.R.C.	E5	66
Lowden, Ia., U.S.	C7	120
Lowell, Ar., U.S.	H3	120
Lowell, In., U.S.	G2	112
Lowell, Ma., U.S.	B14	114
Lowell, Or., U.S.	G4	136
Lowell, Lake, res., Id., U.S.	G10	136
Löwen, stm., Nmb.	E3	70
Löwenberg, Ger.	D8	16
Lower Arrow Lake, res., B.C., Can.	G12	138
Lower Austria see Niederösterreich, state, Aus.	B12	22
Lower California see Baja California, pen., Mex.	B2	96
Lower Egypt see Misr el-Bahrî, hist. reg., Egypt	G2	58
Lower Glenelg National Park, p.o.i., Austl.	L3	76
Lower Hutt, N.Z.	E6	80
Lower Lake, l., U.S.	B5	134
Lower Manitou Lake, l., On., Can.	B6	118
Lower Post, B.C., Can.	D5	106
Lower Red Lake, l., Mn., U.S.	D3	118
Lower Saxony see Niedersachsen, state, Ger.	D4	16
Lower Trajan's Wall, misc. cult., Eur.	D15	26
Lower West End Point, c., Anguilla	A1	105a
Lower Woods Harbour, N.S., Can.	G10	110
Lowestoft, Eng., U.K.	I14	12
Lowgar, state, Afg.	A2	54
Łowicz, Pol.	D15	16
Lowmoor, Va., U.S.	G6	114
Low Rocky Point, c., Austl.	o12	77a
Lowry City, Mo., U.S.	F4	120
Lowville, N.Y., U.S.	E14	112
Loxton, Austl.	J3	76
Loyal, Wi., U.S.	G8	118
Loyalton, Ca., U.S.	D5	134
Loyalty Islands see Loyauté, Îles, is., N. Cal.	m16	79d
Loyang see Luoyang, China	D5	42
Loyauté, Îles (Loyalty Islands), is., N. Cal.	m16	79d
Loyoro, Ug.	D6	66
Lozère, state, Fr.	E9	18
Loznica, Yugo.	E6	26
Lualaba, stm., Afr.	E5	66
Luama, stm., D.R.C.	E5	66
Lu'an, China	F7	42
Luan, stm., China	E3	38
Luancheng, China	J3	42
Luanda, Ang.	B1	68
Luando, stm., Ang.	C2	68
Luang, Khao (Maw Taung), mtn., Asia	G4	48
Luang, Thale, l., Thai.	I5	48
Luang Chiang Dao, Doi, mtn., Thai.	C4	48
Luanginga, stm., Afr.	G4	66
Luang Prabang see Louangphrabang, Laos	C6	48
Luangue (Loange), stm., Afr.	F3	66
Luangwa, stm., Afr.	C5	68
Luanping, China	A7	42
Luanshya, Zam.	C4	68
Luan Toro, Arg.	H5	92
Luanxian, China	B8	42
Luapula, stm., Afr.	C4	68
Luar, Danau, l., Indon.	C8	50
Luarca, Spain	A4	20
Luba, Eq. Gui.	I6	64
Lubaantun, hist., Belize	D3	102
Lubań, Pol.	E11	16
Lubāna, Lat.	D9	10
Lubang Islands, is., Phil.	D3	52
Lubango, Ang.	C1	68
Lubāns, l., Lat.	D9	10
Lubartów, Pol.	E18	16
Lübben, Ger.	E9	16
Lübbenau, Ger.	E9	16
Lubbock, Tx., U.S.	H7	128
Lübeck, Ger.	C6	16
Lubefu, D.R.C.	E4	66
Lubefu, stm., D.R.C.	E4	66
Lubień Kujawski, Pol.	D15	16
Lubilash, stm., D.R.C.	F4	66
Lubin, Pol.	E12	16
Lublin, Pol.	E18	16
Lublin, state, Pol.	E18	16
Lubliniec, Pol.	F14	16
Lubny, Ukr.	E4	32
Luboń, Pol.	D12	16
Lubsko, Pol.	E10	16
Lübtheen, Ger.	C7	16
Lubuagan, Phil.	B3	52
Lubudi, D.R.C.	G5	66
Lubukbatang, Indon.	F3	50
Lubuklinggau, Indon.	E3	50
Lubukpakam, Indon.	B1	50
Lubuksikaping, Indon.	C1	50
Lubumbashi (Élisabethville), D.R.C.	G5	66
Lubutu, D.R.C.	E5	66
Lübz, Ger.	C7	16
Lucan, On., Can.	E8	112
Lucanas, Peru	F3	84
Lucania, hist. reg., Italy	D10	24
Lucania, Mount, mtn., Yk., Can.	C3	106
Lucapa, Ang.	B3	68
Lucas, Ia., U.S.	C4	120
Lucas, Ks., U.S.	B10	128
Lucban, Phil.	C3	52
Lucca, Italy	G7	22
Lucea, Jam.	i12	104d
Luce Bay, b., Scot., U.K.	G8	12
Lucedale, Ms., U.S.	G10	122
Lucena, Phil.	D3	52
Lucena, Spain	G6	20
Lucena del Cid see Llucena, Spain	D10	20
Lučenec, Slov.	H15	16
Lucera, Italy	C9	24

Name — Map Ref. — Page

Lucerne see Luzern, Switz. C5 22
Lucerne, Ca., U.S. D3 134
Lucerne, Lake of see Vierwaldstätter See, l., Switz. D5 22
Luchou see Luzhou, China G1 42
Luchow see Luzhou, China G1 42
Lüchow, Ger. C7 16
Luchuan, China J4 42
Lucinda, Austl. B6 76
Lucira, Ang. C1 68
Luckau, Ger. E9 16
Luckenwalde, Ger. D9 16
Luckhoff, S. Afr. F7 70
Luck Lake, l., Sk., Can. C6 124
Lucknow, On., Can. E8 112
Lucknow, India E8 54
Lucky Lake, Sk., Can. D6 124
Luçon, Fr. C4 18
Lucusse, Ang. C3 68
Luda Kamčija, stm., Blg. G14 26
Ludao, China C8 38
Lüdenscheid, Ger. E3 16
Lüderitz, Nmb. E2 70
Ludhiāna, India C5 54
Ludian, China F5 36
Ludington, Mi., U.S. E3 112
Ludlow, Eng., U.K. I10 12
Ludlow, Ma., U.S. B13 114
Ludogorie, reg., Blg. F13 26
Ludowici, Ga., U.S. E4 116
Luduș, Rom. C11 26
Ludvika, Swe. F6 8
Ludwigsburg, Ger. H4 16
Ludwigsfelde, Ger. D9 16
Ludwigshafen am Rhein, Ger. G4 16
Ludwigslust, Ger. C7 16
Ludza, Lat. D10 10
Luebo, D.R.C. F4 66
Lueders, Tx., U.S. B8 130
Luena, Ang. C3 68
Luena, D.R.C. F5 66
Luena, stm., Ang. C3 68
Luepa, Ven. E11 86
Lueyang, China E2 42
Lufeng, China J6 42
Lufico, Ang. B1 68
Lufira, stm., D.R.C. F5 66
Lufkin, Tx., U.S. F4 122
Luga, Russia B12 10
Luga, stm., Russia A11 10
Lugano, Switz. D5 22
Lugano, Lago di, l., Eur. D14 18
Luganville, Vanuatu j16 79d
Lugards Falls, wtfl, Kenya E7 66
Lugenda, stm., Moz. C6 68
Luggarus see Locarno, Switz. D5 22
Lugnaquillia Mountain, mtn., Ire. I6 12
Lugo, Italy F8 22
Lugo, Spain A3 20
Lugo, co., Spain B3 20
Lugoj, Rom. D8 26
Lugovoj, Kaz. F12 32
Lugovskij, Russia E11 34
Luhans'k, Ukr. E5 32
Luhe, China E8 42
Luhovicy, Russia F21 10
Luhsien see Luzhou, China G1 42
Luiana, Ang. D3 68
Luido, Moz. B12 70
Luik see Liège, Bel. D14 14
Luimneach see Limerick, Ire. I4 12
Luino, Italy D5 22
Luishia, D.R.C. G5 66
Luis L. León, Presa, res., Mex. F2 130
Luis Muñoz Marin, Aeropuerto Internacional, P.R. B3 104a
Luitpold Coast, cst., Ant. C1 81
Luiza, D.R.C. F4 66
Luján, Arg. F4 92
Luján de Cuyo, Arg. F3 92
Lujiang, China F7 42
Lukang, Tai. I9 42
Lukenie, stm., D.R.C. E3 66
Lukeville, Az., U.S. L4 132
Lukojanov, Russia I21 8
Lukolela, D.R.C. E3 66
Lukolela, D.R.C. F4 66
Lukovit, Blg. F11 26
Łuków, Pol. E18 16
Lukuga, stm., D.R.C. F5 66
Lukula, D.R.C. F2 66
Lukulu, Zam. C3 68
Lulaka, stm., D.R.C. E4 66
Luleå, Swe. D10 8
Luleälven, stm., Swe. C9 8
Lüleburgaz, Tur. B10 28
Lules, Arg. C5 92
Luliang, China G5 36
Lüliang Shan, mts., China C4 42
Luling, Tx., U.S. E10 130
Lulonga, stm., D.R.C. D3 66
Lulua, stm., D.R.C. F4 66
Luluabourg see Kananga, D.R.C. F4 66
Lumajang, Indon. H8 50
Lumajangdong Co, l., China B8 54
Lumaku, Gunong, mtn., Malay. A9 50
Lumana, D.R.C. E5 66
Lumbala Kaquengue, Ang. C3 68
Lumbala N'guimbo, Ang. C3 68
Lumber, stm., U.S. B6 116
Lumber City, Ga., U.S. E3 116
Lumberport, W.V., U.S. E5 114
Lumberton, N.C., U.S. B7 116
Lumberton, Tx., U.S. G4 122
Lumbis, Indon. A10 50
Lumbrales, Spain D4 20
Lumby, B.C., Can. F12 138
Lumding, India F14 54
Lumpkin, Ga., U.S. E14 122
Lumu, Indon. E11 50
Lumut, Malay. J5 48
Lumut, Tanjung, c., Indon. E4 50
Luna Pier, Mi., U.S. C2 114
Lūnāvāda, India G4 54
Lund, B.C., Can. G6 138
Lund, Swe. I5 8
Lund, Nv., U.S. E2 132
Lundazi, Zam. C5 68
Lundy, i., Eng., U.K. J8 12
Lüneburg, Ger. C6 16
Lüneburger Heide, reg., Ger. D6 16
Lunel, Fr. F10 18
Lünen, Ger. E3 16
Lunenburg, N.S., Can. F12 110
Lunenburg, Va., U.S. H7 114
Lunéville, Fr. F15 14
Lungch'i see Zhangzhou, China I7 42
Lunge'nake, China C10 54
Lunglei, India G14 54
Lungtsin see Longzhou, China J2 42
Lungué-Bungo (Lungwebungu), stm., Afr. C3 68
Lungwebungu (Lungué-Bungo), stm., Afr. C3 68
Lūni, India E4 54
Lūni, stm., India F4 54
Luninec, Bela. H9 10
Luninets see Luninec, Bela. H9 10
Lūnkaransar, India D4 54
Luntai, China F14 32
Luo, stm., China D4 42
Luo, stm., China D4 42
Luobei, China B11 36
Luobu, China I3 42
Luocheng, China I3 42
Luoding, China J4 42
Luofu, D.R.C. E5 66
Luohe, China E6 42
Luoji, China E7 42
Luonan, China D4 42
Luoning, China D4 42
Luoqi, China G2 42
Luotian, China F6 42
Luowenba, China F2 42
Luoxiao Shan, mts., China H6 42
Luoyang, China D5 42
Luoyuan, China H8 42
Luozi, D.R.C. F2 66
Lupanshui, China F5 36
Lupar, stm., Malay. C7 50
Łupawa, Pol. B13 16
Lupeni, Rom. D10 26
Lupin see Manzhouli, China B8 36
Luputa, D.R.C. F4 66
Luqiao, China E7 42
Luqiao, China G9 42
Luqu, China E5 36
Luque, Spain G6 20
Luquillo, P.R. B4 104a
Lure, Fr. G15 14
Luremo, Ang. B2 68
Lurgan, N. Ire., U.K. G6 12
Luribay, Bol. C3 90
Lurín, Peru F2 84
Lúrio, Moz. C7 68
Lúrio, stm., Moz. C6 68
Lusaka, Zam. D4 68
Lusambo, D.R.C. E4 66
Lusanga, D.R.C. E3 66
Lusangi, D.R.C. E5 66
Luscar, Ab., Can. C13 138
Luseland, Sk., Can. B4 124
Lushan, China E5 42
Lu Shan, mtn., China G6 42
Lushnja see Lushnjë, Alb. D13 24
Lushnjë, Alb. D13 24
Lushoto, Tan. E7 66
Lüshun (Port Arthur), China E4 38
Lusk, Wy., U.S. E8 126
Lussac-les-Châteaux, Fr. C6 18
Lūt, Dasht-e, des., Iran C8 56
Lü-ta see Dalian, China B9 42
Lü Tao, i., Tai. J9 42
Lutembo, Ang. C3 68
Lutesville, Mo., U.S. G7 120
Luther, Mi., U.S. D4 112
Luther, Ok., U.S. F11 128
Lutherstadt Eisleben, Ger. E7 16
Lutherstadt Wittenberg, Ger. E8 16
Luti, Sol. Is. d7 79b
Luton, Eng., U.K. J12 12
Lutong, Malay. A8 50
Łutselk'e, N.T., Can. C8 106
Lutz, Fl., U.S. H3 116
Lützow, Ger. C7 16
Lutzow-Holm Bay, b., Ant. B8 81
Luuq, Som. D8 66
Luverne, Al., U.S. F12 122
Lu Verne, Ia., U.S. I4 118
Luverne, Mn., U.S. H2 118
Luvua, stm., D.R.C. F5 66
Luvuvhu, stm., S. Afr. C10 70
Luwegu, stm., Tan. F7 66
Luwingu, Zam. C4 68
Luwuk, Indon. F7 44
Luxapallila Creek, stm., U.S. D11 122
Luxembourg, Lux. E14 14
Luxembourg, ctry., Eur. E15 14
Luxemburg, Wi., U.S. D2 112
Luxeuil-les-Bains, Fr. G15 14
Luxi, China G4 36
Luxor see El-Uqsor, Egypt B6 62
Luz, Braz. J3 88
Luza, Russia F22 8
Luža, Russia A14 10
Luzern (Lucerne), Switz. C5 22
Luzhai, China I3 42
Luzhou, China G1 42
Luziânia, Braz. I2 88
Luzilândia, Braz. B4 88
Lužki, Bela. E10 10
Lužnice, stm., Eur. G10 16
Luzon, i., Phil. B3 52
Luzon Strait, strt., Asia G16 30
L'viv, Ukr. F13 6
L'viv, co., Ukr. G19 16
L'vovskij, Russia E20 10
Lwówek, Pol. D12 16
Lyallpur see Faisalabad, Pak. C4 54
Lyčkovo, Russia C15 10
Lycksele, Swe. D8 8
Lydenburg, S. Afr. D10 70
Lydia Mills, S.C., U.S. B3 116
Lyell, Mount, mtn., Can. E13 138
Lyerly, Ga., U.S. C13 122
Lyford, Tx., U.S. H10 130
Lykošino, Russia B16 10
Lyle, Mn., U.S. H6 118
Lyman, Ne., U.S. F8 126
Lyman, S.C., U.S. B3 116
Lymans'ke, Ukr. C17 26
Lyme Bay, b., Eng., U.K. K9 12
Łyna (Lava), stm., Eur. B16 16
Lynch, Ne., U.S. E14 126
Lynchburg, Oh., U.S. E2 114
Lynchburg, S.C., U.S. B5 116
Lynchburg, Tn., U.S. B12 122
Lynchburg, Va., U.S. G6 114
Lynd, stm., Austl. A4 76
Lynden, Wa., U.S. B4 136
Lyndhurst, Austl. B5 76
Lyndon, Ks., U.S. F2 120
Lyndon, Ky., U.S. F12 120
Lyndon, stm., Austl. D2 74
Lyndon B. Johnson, Lake, res., Tx., U.S. D9 130
Lyndon B. Johnson Space Center, sci., Tx., U.S. H3 122
Lyngen, b., Nor. B9 8
Lyngseidet, Nor. B8 8
Lynn, Al., U.S. C11 122
Lynn, Ma., U.S. B14 114
Lynndyl, Ut., U.S. D4 132
Lynn Haven, Fl., U.S. G13 122
Lynn Lake, Mb., Can. D10 106
Lyntupy, Bela. E9 10
Lynx Lake, l., N.T., Can. C9 106
Lyon, Fr. D10 18
Lyon Inlet, b., Nu., Can. B14 106
Lyon Mountain, N.Y., U.S. F2 110
Lyonnais, hist. reg., Fr. D10 18
Lyons, In., U.S. F10 120
Lyons, Ks., U.S. C10 128
Lyons, Mi., U.S. F5 112
Lyons, Ne., U.S. C1 120
Lyons, N.Y., U.S. E13 112
Lyons, stm., Austl. D3 74
Lysa Hora, Ukr. A18 26
Łysica, mtn., Pol. F16 16
Lyskovo, Russia H21 8
Lys'va, Russia C9 32
Lysychans'k, Ukr. E5 32
Lytham Saint Anne's, Eng., U.K. H9 12
Lytle, Tx., U.S. E9 130

M

Ma, stm., Asia C7 48
Ma'ān, Jord. H6 58
Ma'ān, state, Jord. H7 58
Ma'anshan, China F8 42
Maardu, Est. G11 8
Maarianhamina (Mariehamn), Fin. F9 8
Ma'arrat an-Nu'mān, Syria C7 58
Maas (Meuse), stm., Eur. D14 14
Maasin, Phil. E5 52
Maastricht, Neth. D14 14
Mabalane, Moz. C11 70
Mabank, Tx., U.S. E2 122
Mabaruma, Guy. C12 86
Mabeleapodi, Bots. B6 70
Mabel Lake, l., B.C., Can. F12 138
Maben, Ms., U.S. D9 122
Mablethorpe, Eng., U.K. H13 12
Mableton, Ga., U.S. D14 122
Mabton, Wa., U.S. D6 136
Mabuasehube Game Reserve, Bots. D6 70
Mača, Russia E12 34
Maca, Cerro, vol., Chile H2 90
Macachín, Arg. H6 92
Macaé, Braz. L5 88
Macaíba, Braz. C8 88
Macajuba, Braz. G5 88
Macalister, B.C., Can. D8 138
Macalister, stm., Austl. K6 76
Macalister, Mount, mtn., Austl. J7 76
MacAlpine Lake, l., Nu., Can. B10 106
Macan, Kepulauan, is., Indon. G12 50
Macao see Macau, dep., Asia J5 42
Macapá, Braz. C7 84
Macará, Ec. D2 84
Macareo, Caño, stm., Ven. C11 86
MacArthur, Phil. E5 52
Macas, Ec. I2 86
Macau, Braz. C7 88
Macau, Macau J5 42
Macau, dep., Asia J5 42
Macaúbas, Braz. G4 88
MacClenny, Fl., U.S. F3 116
Macclesfield, Eng., U.K. H10 12
Macdhui, Ben, mtn., Afr. G9 70
Macdonald, Lake, l., Austl. D5 74
MacDonald Pass, p., Mt., U.S. D14 136
MacDonnell Ranges, mts., Austl. D6 74
Macdui, Ben, mtn., Scot., U.K. D9 12
Macedonia, hist. reg., Eur. H10 26
Macedonia, ctry., Eur. B4 28
Maceió, Braz. E8 88
Macenta, Gui. H3 64
Maceo, Col. D4 86
Macerata, Italy G10 22
MacFarlane, stm., Sk., Can. D9 106
Macgillycuddy's Reeks, mts., Ire. J3 12
MacGregor, Mb., Can. D15 124
Machado, Braz. K3 88
Machado, stm., Braz. F5 84
Machagai, Arg. C7 92
Machaíla, Moz. C11 70
Machakos, Kenya E7 66
Machala, Ec. D2 84
Machalí, Chile G2 92
Machalilla, Parque Nacional, p.o.i., Ec. H1 86
Machanga, Moz. B12 70
Machaquilá, stm., Guat. D3 102
Machattie, Lake, l., Austl. E2 76
Machaze, Moz. B11 70
Macheng, China F6 42
Mācherla, India C4 53
Machias, Me., U.S. F9 110
Machilīpatnam (Bandar), India C5 53
Machiques, Ven. B5 86
Machkund, res., India B6 53
Macho, Arroyo del, stm., N.M., U.S. H4 128
Machu Picchu see Machupicchu, hist., Peru F3 84
Machupicchu, hist., Peru F3 84
Maciá, Arg. F8 92
Macia, Moz. D11 70
Măcin, Rom. D15 26
Macintyre, stm., Austl. G7 76
Mackay, Austl. C7 76
Mackay, Id., U.S. G13 136
Mackay, Lake, l., Austl. D5 74
MacKay Lake, l., N.T., Can. C8 106
Mackenzie, stm., Austl. D7 76
Mackenzie, stm., N.T., Can. B4 106
Mackenzie Bay, b., Can. C12 140
Mackenzie King Island, i., Can. B3 141
Mackenzie Mountains, mts., Can. C4 106
Mackinac, Straits of, strt., Mi., U.S. C4 112
Mackinac Bridge, Mi., U.S. C5 112
Mackinac Island, Mi., U.S. C5 112
Mackinaw, stm., Il., U.S. D9 120
Mackinaw City, Mi., U.S. C5 112
Mackinnon Road, Kenya E7 66
Macklin, Sk., Can. B4 124
Macksville, Austl. H9 76
Macksville, Ks., U.S. C9 128
Maclean, Austl. G9 76
Maclear, S. Afr. G9 70
Macleay, stm., Austl. H9 76
Macleod, Lake, l., Austl. D2 74
Macmillan, stm., Yk., Can. C4 106
Macomb, Il., U.S. D7 120
Macomer, Italy D2 24
Mâcon, Fr. C10 18
Macon, Ga., U.S. D2 116
Macon, Il., U.S. E9 120
Macon, Ms., U.S. D10 122
Macon, Mo., U.S. E5 120
Macon, Bayou, stm., U.S. E7 122
Macondo, Ang. C3 68
Macorís, Cabo, c., Dom. Rep. C12 102
Macoupin Creek, stm., Il., U.S. E8 120
Macovane, Moz. B12 70
Macquarie, stm., Austl. H6 76
Macquarie, stm., Austl. n13 77a
Macquarie, Lake, l., Austl. I8 76
Macquarie Harbour, b., Austl. o12 77a
Macquarie Island, i., Austl. A20 81
Macquarie Marshes, sw., Austl. H6 76
Macquarie Ridge, unds. O18 142
Mac. Robertson Land, reg., Ant. B10 81
Macucuau, stm., Braz. H11 86
Macugnaga, Italy E4 22
Macumba, stm., Austl. E7 74
Macuro, Ven. B10 86
Macusani, Peru F3 84
Macuspana, Mex. G12 100
Mad, stm., Ca., U.S. C2 134
Mādabā, Jord. G6 58
Madagascar, ctry., Afr. D8 68
Madagascar Basin, unds. L8 142
Madagascar Plateau, unds. M7 142
Madan, Blg. H11 26
Madanapalle, India E4 53
Madang, Pap. N. Gui. b4 79a
Madaoua, Niger G6 64
Mādārīpur, Bngl. G13 54
Madawaska, Me., U.S. C8 110
Madawaska, stm., On., Can. C13 112
Madawaska Highlands, plat., On., Can. C12 112
Madaya, Mya. A3 48
Maddalena, Isola, i., Italy C3 24
Maddaloni, Italy C8 24
Maddock, N.D., U.S. G14 124
Madeira, i., Port. C1 64
Madeira, stm., S.A. E5 84
Madeira, Arquipélago da (Madeira Islands), is., Port. C1 64
Madeira Islands see Madeira, Arquipélago da, is., Port. C1 64
Mädelegabel, mtn., Eur. I6 16
Madeleine, Îles de la, is., Qc., Can. C15 110
Madeleine-Centre, Qc., Can. A11 110
Madeline Island, i., Wi., U.S. E8 118
Madera, Mex. A4 100
Madera, Ca., U.S. G5 134
Madera see Madeira, stm., S.A. E5 84
Madgaon, India D1 53
Madhepura, India F11 54
Madhubani, India E10 54
Madhugiri, India E3 53
Madhupur, India F11 54
Madhya Pradesh, state, India D4 46
Madibogo, S. Afr. E7 70
Madida, China C9 38
Madidi, stm., Bol. B3 90
Madill, Ok., U.S. C2 122
Madimba, D.R.C. E3 66
Madīnat ash-Sha'b, Yemen G5 56
Madingo-Kayes, Congo E2 66
Madingou, Congo E2 66
Madirovalo, Madag. D8 68
Madison, Al., U.S. C12 122
Madison, Fl., U.S. F2 116
Madison, Ga., U.S. C2 116
Madison, In., U.S. F12 120
Madison, Me., U.S. F6 110
Madison, Mn., U.S. F2 118
Madison, Mo., U.S. E5 120
Madison, Ne., U.S. F15 126
Madison, N.C., U.S. H5 114
Madison, S.D., U.S. C15 126
Madison, W.V., U.S. F4 114
Madison, Wi., U.S. A8 120
Madison, stm., U.S. E15 136
Madison Heights, Va., U.S. G6 114
Madison Range, mts., Mt., U.S. E15 136
Madisonville, Ky., U.S. G10 120
Madisonville, La., U.S. G8 122
Madisonville, Tn., U.S. A1 116
Madisonville, Tx., U.S. G2 122
Madiun, Indon. G7 50
Madiyi, China G4 42
Mado Gashi, Kenya D7 66
Madoi, China E4 36
Madona, Lat. D9 10
Madora, Bela. G13 10
Madrakah, Ra's al-, c., Oman F8 56
Madras see Chennai, India E5 53
Madras, Or., U.S. F5 136
Madre, Laguna, b., Mex. C10 100
Madre, Laguna, b., Tx., U.S. H10 130
Madre, Sierra, mts., Phil. B3 52
Madre de Chiapas, Sierra, mts., N.A. G12 100
Madre de Dios, stm., S.A. F4 84
Madre de Dios, Isla, i., Chile J1 90
Madre del Sur, Sierra, mts., Mex. G9 100
Madre Occidental, Sierra, mts., Mex. B3 96
Madre Oriental, Sierra, mts., Mex. C8 100
Madrid, Spain D7 20
Madrid, Al., U.S. F13 122
Madrid, Ne., U.S. G11 126
Madrid, state, Spain D7 20
Madridejos, Spain E7 20
Madura, i., Indon. G8 50
Madura, Selat, strt., Indon. G8 50
Madurai, India G4 53
Madurāntakam, India E4 53
Maduru, stm., Sri L. H5 53
Maebashi, Japan C11 40
Mae Hong Son, Thai. C3 48
Mae Klong, stm., Thai. E4 48
Mae Ping Mae Hat Mae Kor National Park, p.o.i., Thai. D4 48
Mae Ramat, Thai. D4 48
Mae Sariang, Thai. C3 48
Maeser, Ut., U.S. C7 132
Mae Sot, Thai. D4 48
Maestra, Sierra, mts., Cuba B9 102
Maestu, Spain B8 20
Mae Tha, Thai. C4 48
Maevatanana, Madag. D8 68
Maéwo, i., Vanuatu j17 79d
Mafeking, Mb., Can. B12 124
Mafeking see Mafikeng, S. Afr. D7 70
Mafeteng, Leso. F8 70
Maffra, Austl. K6 76
Mafia Island, i., Tan. F8 66
Mafikeng, S. Afr. D7 70
Mafra, Braz. C13 92
Magadan, Russia E19 34
Magadi, Kenya E7 66
Magaguadavic Lake, l., N.B., Can. E9 110
Magalhães de Almeida, Braz. B4 88
Magallanes, Phil. D4 52
Magangué, Col. C4 86
Magaria, Niger G6 64
Magazine Mountain, mtn., Ar., U.S. B5 122
Magdagači, Russia F14 34
Magdalena, Arg. G9 92
Magdalena, Bol. B4 90
Magdalena, Mex. E7 100
Magdalena, N.M., U.S. I9 132
Magdalena, state, Col. B4 86
Magdalena, stm., Col. B4 86
Magdalena, stm., Mex. F7 98
Magdalena, Bahía, b., Mex. C2 100
Magdalena, Isla, i., Chile H2 90
Magdalena, Punta, c., Col. F3 86
Magdalena de Kino, Mex. F7 98
Magdeburg, Ger. D7 16
Magelang, Indon. G7 50
Magellen, Strait of, strt., S.A. J2 90
Magenta, Italy E5 22
Magetan, Indon. G7 50
Maggiore, Lago, l., Eur. C14 18
Maghâgha, Egypt J1 58
Maghama, Maur. F2 64
Mágina, mtn., Spain G7 20
Maglaj, Bos. E5 26
Maglić, mtn., Bos. F5 26
Maglie, Italy D12 24
Magnet, Mb., Can. C14 124
Magnetawan, stm., On., Can. C10 112
Magnetic Island, i., Austl. B6 76
Magnitogorsk, Russia D9 32
Magnolia, Ar., U.S. D5 122
Magnolia, Ms., U.S. F8 122
Mago, i., Fiji p20 79e
Magog, Qc., Can. E4 110
Magozal, Mex. E10 100
Magrath, Ab., Can. G18 138
Maguan, China A7 48
Maguari, Cabo, c., Braz. D8 84
Magumeri, Nig. G7 64
Māgura, Bngl. G12 54
Maguse Lake, l., Nu., Can. C12 106
Magway, Mya. B2 48
Magway, state, Mya. B2 48
Mahābād, Iran B6 56
Mahābaleshwar, India C1 53
Mahabe, Madag. D8 68
Mahābhārat Lek, mts., Nepal E11 54
Mahabharat Range see Mahābhārat Lek, mts., Nepal E11 54
Mahabo, Madag. E7 68
Mahačkala, Russia F7 32
Mahād, India B1 53
Mahādeo Range, mts., India C2 53
Mahagi, D.R.C. D6 66
Mahajamba, stm., Madag. D8 68
Mahājan, India D4 54
Mahajanga, Madag. D8 68
Mahākālī (Sārda), stm., Asia D8 54
Mahakam, stm., Indon. D9 50
Mahalapye, Bots. E4 68
Maham, India D6 54
Mahānadi, stm., India H10 54
Mahanoro, Madag. D8 68
Mahanoy City, Pa., U.S. D9 114
Maharagama, Sri L. H4 53
Mahārājganj, India E10 54
Mahārājpur, India F7 54
Mahārāshtra, state, India E4 46
Mahāsamund, India H9 54
Maha Sarakham, Thai. D6 48
Mahaut, Dom. j6 105c
Mahaweli, stm., Sri L. H5 53
Mahaxai, Laos D7 48
Mahbūbābād, India C4 53
Mahbūbnagar, India C4 53
Mahd adh-Dhahab, Sau. Ar. E5 56
Mahdia, Guy. E12 86
Mahe, India F2 53
Mahé, i., Sey. j13 69b
Mahébourg, Mrts. i10 69a
Mahendra Giri, mtn., India B7 53
Mahendranagar, Nepal D7 54
Mahenge, Tan. F7 66
Mahesāna, India G4 54
Maheshwar, India G5 54
Mahi, stm., India G4 54
Mahia Peninsula, pen., N.Z. D7 80
Mahilëu, Bela. G13 10
Mahilëu, state, Bela. G13 10
Mahina, Fr. Poly. u21 78h
Mahlabatini, S. Afr. F10 70
Mahmūdābād, India E8 54
Mahmudiye, Tur. D14 28
Mahoba, India F7 54
Mahogany Mountain, mtn., Or., U.S. G9 136
Mahogany Tree, Anguilla A1 105a
Mahomet, Il., U.S. D9 120
Mahón see Maó, Spain E15 20
Mahone Bay, N.S., Can. F12 110
Mahone Bay, b., N.S., Can. F12 110
Mahood Lake, l., B.C., Can. E10 138
Mahora, Spain E9 20
Mahrāt, Jabal, plat., Yemen F7 56
Mahrauni, India F7 54
Mahuva, India H3 54
Maiaky, Ukr. C17 26
Maicao, Col. B5 86
Maichen, China K3 42
Maicuru, stm., Braz. D7 84
Maiden, N.C., U.S. A4 116
Maidenhead, Eng., U.K. J12 12
Maidstone, Sk., Can. A4 124
Maidstone, Eng., U.K. J13 12
Maiduguri, Nig. G7 64
Maihar, India F8 54
Maijoma, Mex. F3 130
Maikala Range, mts., India G8 54
Maikoor, Pulau, i., Indon. G9 44
Mailāni, India D8 54
Main, stm., Ger. F4 16
Maināguri, India E12 54
Mainburg, Ger. H7 16
Main Channel, strt., On., Can. C8 112
Mai-Ndombe, Lac, l., D.R.C. E3 66
Main-Donau-Kanal, can., Ger. G7 16
Maine, state, U.S. E7 110
Maine, hist. reg., Fr. F8 14
Maine, Gulf of, b., N.A. G8 110
Maine-et-Loire, state, Fr. G8 14
Maïné-Soroa, Niger G7 64
Mainhardt, Ger. G5 16
Mainland, i., Scot., U.K. B9 12
Mainland, i., Scot., U.K. n18 12a
Mainpuri, India E7 54
Maintirano, Madag. D7 68
Mainz, Ger. G4 16
Maio, i., C.V. k10 65a
Maipo, stm., Chile F2 92
Maipo, Volcán, vol., S.A. G3 92
Maipú, Arg. F3 92
Maipú, Arg. H8 92
Maipú, ngh., Chile F2 92
Maiqihamiao, China C4 38
Maiquetía, Ven. B8 86
Maišiagala, Lith. F8 10
Maiskhāl Island, i., Bngl. H13 54
Maitembge, Bots. E4 68
Maitland, Austl. F7 74
Maitland, Austl. I8 76
Maitland, stm., On., Can. E8 112
Maitri, sci., Ant. C6 81
Maíz, Islas del, is., Nic. F6 102
Maizuru, Japan D8 40
Maja, stm., Russia E15 34
Majari, stm., Braz. F11 86
Majene, Indon. E11 50
Majī, Eth. F7 62
Majia, stm., China C7 42
Majiang, China J4 42
Majiangzong, China C12 54
Majja, Russia D15 34
Majkain, Kaz. D13 32
Majkop, Russia F6 32
Major, Puig, mtn., Spain E13 20
Majorca see Mallorca, i., Spain E13 20
Majskij, Russia F14 34
Majskoe, Kaz. D13 32
Majuro, at., Marsh. Is. C8 72
Maka, Sen. G2 64
Makabana, Congo E2 66
Makale, Indon. E11 50
Makallé, Arg. C8 92
Makālu, mtn., Asia E11 54
Makanči, Kaz. E14 32
Makapuu Head, c., Hi., U.S. B4 78a
Makarakomburu, Mount, mtn., Sol. Is. e8 79b
Makarev, Russia H20 8
Makarov, Russia G17 34
Makasar, Selat (Makassar Strait), strt., Indon. D11 50
Makassar Strait see Makasar, Selat, strt., Indon. D11 50
Makat, Kaz. E8 32
Makawao, Hi., U.S. C5 78a
Makeni, S.L. H2 64
Makgadikgadi, pl., Bots. E4 68
Makgadikgadi Pans Game Reserve, Bots. B7 70
Makhaleng, stm., Afr. G8 70
Makham, Thai. F5 48
Maki, Indon. F9 44
Makiivka, Ukr. E5 32
Makindu, Kenya E7 66
Makinsk, Kaz. D11 32
Makira, state, Sol. Is. f10 79b
Makira Harbour, b., Sol. Is. f9 79b
Makkah (Mekka), Sau. Ar. E4 56
Makkovik, Nf., Can. D19 106
Makó, Hung. C7 26
Makokou, Gabon D2 66
Makongolosi, Tan. F6 66
Makoua, Congo E3 66
Maków Mazowiecki, Pol. D16 16
Makrai, India G6 54
Makrāna, India E5 54
Makrān Coast, cst., Asia D9 56
Maksatiha, Russia C18 10
Maksimkin Jar, Russia C15 32
Maktar, Tun. I3 24
Makumbi, D.R.C. F4 66
Makung, Tai. J8 42
Makurdi, Nig. H6 64
Makushin Volcano, vol., Ak., U.S. F6 140
Makušino, Russia C11 32
Makwassie, S. Afr. E8 70
Māl, India E12 54
Mala see Mallow, Ire. I4 12
Mala, Punta, c., Pan. I8 102
Malabang, Phil. G5 52
Malabar Coast, cst., India F2 53
Malabo, Eq. Gui. I6 64
Malacacheta, Braz. I4 88
Malacca see Melaka, Malay. K6 48
Malacca, Strait of, strt., Asia B2 50
Malacky, Slov. H13 16
Malad, stm., U.S. H14 136
Malad City, Id., U.S. A4 132
Maladzečna, Bela. F9 10
Málaga, Col. D5 86
Málaga, Spain H6 20
Málaga, co., Spain H6 20
Malagarasi, Tan. F6 66
Malagash, N.S., Can. E13 110
Malagasy Republic see Madagascar, ctry., Afr. D8 68
Malagón, Spain E7 20
Malaimbandy, Madag. E8 68
Malaita, state, Sol. Is. d9 79b
Malaita, i., Sol. Is. e9 79b
Malaja Kuril'skaja Grjada (Habomai-shotō), is., Russia C17 38
Malaja Višera, Russia B15 10
Malaka, Sempitan, strt., Indon. J2 48
Malakāl, Sudan F6 62
Malākand, Pak. A3 54
Malakoff, Tx., U.S. E3 122
Malakula, state, Vanuatu k16 79d
Malakula, i., Vanuatu k16 79d
Malambo, Col. B4 86
Malang, Indon. H8 50
Malanggwā, Nepal E10 54
Malanje, Ang. B2 68
Malanville, Benin G5 64
Malanzán, Arg. E4 92
Mała Panew, stm., Pol. F14 16
Mälaren, l., Swe. G7 8
Malargüe, Arg. G3 92
Malaspina, Arg. H3 90
Malaspina Glacier, ice, Ak., U.S. E11 140
Malatya, Tur. B4 56
Malau, Vanuatu j16 79d
Malaut, India C5 54
Malavalli, India E3 53
Malawali, Pulau, i., Malay. G1 52
Malawi, ctry., Afr. C5 68
Malaŵi, Lake see Nyasa, Lake, l., Afr. C5 68
Malaya see Semenanjung Malaysia, hist. reg., Malay. K6 48
Malayagiri, mtn., India H10 54
Malaybalay, Phil. F5 52
Malāyer, Iran C6 56
Malay Peninsula, pen., Asia J5 48
Malay Reef, rf., Austl. B7 76
Malaysia, ctry., Asia E3 44
Malbon, Austl. C3 76
Malbork, Pol. B15 16
Malbrán, Arg. D6 92
Malchin, Ger. C8 16
Malchow, Ger. C8 16
Malcolm, Austl. E4 74
Malcolm Island, i., B.C., Can. F4 138
Malcom, Ia., U.S. C5 120
Malczyce, Pol. E12 16
Malden, i., Kir. D11 72
Mal di Ventre, Isola di, i., Italy E2 24
Maldives, ctry., Asia I11 30
Maldonado, Ur. G10 92
Male', Mald. i12 46a
Male, Mya. A2 48
Maléas, Ákra, c., Grc. G6 28
Male' Atoll, at., Mald. i12 46a
Mālegaon, India H5 54
Malé Karpaty (Little Carpathians), mts., Slov. H13 16
Malema, Moz. C6 68
Malente, Ger. B6 16
Māler Kotla, India C5 54
Malesherbes, Fr. F11 14
Malgomaj, l., Swe. D6 8
Malhanskij hrebet, mts., Russia F10 34
Malheur, stm., Or., U.S. F9 136
Malheur, South Fork, stm., Or., U.S. G8 136
Malheur Lake, l., Or., U.S. G8 136
Mali, Gui. G2 64
Mali, ctry., Afr. F4 64
Mali, stm., Mya. C8 46
Malīk, Sudan F6 62
Malik, Wādī al-, val., Sudan D5 62
Mali Kyun, i., Mya. F4 48
Malili, Indon. E12 50
Malin, Or., U.S. A4 134
Malinaltepec, Mex. G9 100
Malinau, Indon. B10 50
Malindi, Kenya E8 66
Malines see Mechelen, Bel. C13 14
Malingping, Indon. G4 50
Malin Head, c., Ire. F5 12
Malino, Bukit, mtn., Indon. C12 50
Malita, Phil. G5 52
Malizhen, China A7 48
Maljamar, N.M., U.S. B4 130
Malka, Russia F20 34
Malkāpur, India H5 54
Malkara, Tur. C9 28
Mallāḥ, Syria F7 58
Mallan luonnonpuisto, p.o.i., Fin. B9 8
Mallawi, Egypt K1 58
Mallersdorf-Pfaffenberg, Ger. H8 16
Mallery Lake, l., Nu, Can. C11 106
Mallet, Braz. B12 92
Malligasta, Arg. D4 92
Mallorca (Majorca), i., Spain E13 20
Mallow, Ire. I4 12
Malm, Nor. D4 8
Malmberget, Swe. C8 8
Malmesbury, S. Afr. H4 70
Malmö, Swe. I5 8
Malmok, c., Neth. Ant. p23 104g
Malo, i., Vanuatu j16 79d
Maloelap, at., Marsh. Is. C8 72
Maloe Skuratovo, Russia G19 10
Malojaroslavec, Russia E19 10
Malolos, Phil. C3 52
Malone, Fl., U.S. G13 122
Malone, N.Y., U.S. F2 110
Malonga, D.R.C. G4 66
Małopolska, reg., Pol. F17 16
Malošujka, Russia E17 8
Malott, Wa., U.S. B7 136

Name | Map Ref. | Page

Małowice, Pol. E11 16
Måløy, Nor. E1 8
Malozemel'skaja Tundra, reg., Russia C24 8
Malpas, Austl. J3 76
Malpe, India E2 53
Malpeque Bay, b., P.E., Can. D13 110
Malprabha, stm., India D2 53
Mālpura, India E5 54
Malta, Braz. D7 88
Malta, Lat. D10 10
Malta, Mt., U.S. F6 124
Malta, ctry., Eur. I8 24
Malta, i., Malta I8 24
Malta Channel, strt., Eur. H8 24
Maltahöhe, Nmb. D3 70
Maluku (Moluccas), is., Indon. F8 44
Maluku, Laut (Molucca Sea), Indon. F8 44
Ma'lūlā, Syria E7 58
Malu Mare, Rom. E10 26
Malunda, Indon. E11 50
Mālvan, India C1 53
Malvern, Ar., U.S. C6 122
Malvern, Ia., U.S. K3 118
Malvern, Oh., U.S. D4 114
Malvérnia, Moz. C10 70
Malvinas Sur, Arg. D8 92
Malý Dunaj, stm., Slov. H13 16
Malyja Haradzjacičy, Bela. H11 10
Malyj Anjuj, stm., Russia C21 34
Malyj Enisej, stm., Russia F8 34
Malyj Tajmyr, ostrov, i., Russia A10 34
Mama, Russia E11 34
Mamaia, Rom. E15 26
Mamanguape, Braz. D8 88
Mamasa, Indon. E11 50
Mamasa, stm., Indon. E11 50
Mambajao, Phil. F5 52
Mambasa, D.R.C. D5 66
Mamberamo, stm., Indon. F10 44
Mamburao, Phil. D3 52
Mamehaktebo, Indon. C9 50
Mameigwess Lake, l., On., Can. B6 118
Ma-Me-O Beach, Ab., Can. C17 138
Mamfe, Cam. C1 66
Mamljutka, Kaz. D11 32
Mammoth, Az., U.S. K6 132
Mammoth Cave National Park, p.o.i., Ky., U.S. G11 120
Mammoth Lakes, Ca., U.S. F7 134
Mammoth Spring, Ar., U.S. H6 120
Mamonovo, Russia F2 10
Mamoré, stm., S.A. F4 84
Mamou, Gui. G2 64
Mampikony, Madag. D8 68
Mamry, Jezioro, l., Pol. B17 16
Mamuju, Indon. E11 50
Mamuno, Bots. C5 70
Man, C. Iv. H3 64
Man, W.V., U.S. G4 114
Man, Isle of see Isle of Man, dep., Eur. G8 12
Mana, Hi., U.S. A2 78a
Manabí, state, Ec. H2 86
Manacacías, stm., Col. F5 86
Manacapuru, Braz. I11 86
Manacapuru, stm., Braz. I11 86
Manacor, Spain E14 20
Manado (Menado), Indon. E7 44
Manaenki, Russia G19 10
Managua, Nic. F4 102
Managua, Lago de, l., Nic. F4 102
Manakara, Madag. E8 68
Manakau, mtn., N.Z. F5 80
Manāli, India B6 54
Manama see Al-Manāmah, Bahr. D7 56
Manam Island, i., Pap. N. Gui. a4 79a
Mánamo, Caño, stm., Ven. C10 86
Mananara Avaratra, Madag. D8 68
Mananjary, Madag. E8 68
Manantenina, Madag. E8 68
Manapire, stm., Ven. D8 86
Manappārai, India F4 53
Manār, stm., India B3 53
Manas, China C2 36
Manās, stm., Asia E13 54
Manasarowar Lake see Mapam Yumco, l., China C8 54
Manas Hu, l., China B2 36
Manāslu, mtn., Nepal D10 54
Manasquan, N.J., U.S. D11 114
Manassas, Va., U.S. F8 114
Mânăstirea, Rom. E13 26
Manatí, Col. B4 86
Manatí, P.R. B3 104a
Manatuto, Indon. G8 44
Manaung, Mya. C1 48
Manaus, Braz. D5 84
Manavgat, Tur. G14 28
Manawa, Wi., U.S. G10 118
Manāwar, India G5 54
Manawoka, Pulau, i., Indon. F9 44
Manban, China A6 48
Manbij, Syria B8 58
Mancelona, Mi., U.S. D4 112
Mancha Real, Spain G7 20
Manche, state, Fr. E7 14
Mancheng, China B6 42
Mancherāl, India B4 53
Manchester, Eng., U.K. H10 12
Manchester, Ct., U.S. C13 114
Manchester, Ga., U.S. E14 122
Manchester, Ia., U.S. B6 120
Manchester, Ky., U.S. G2 114
Manchester, N.H., U.S. H5 110
Manchester, Oh., U.S. F2 114
Manchester, Vt., U.S. G3 110
Manchioneal, Jam. i14 104d
Manchouli see Manzhouli, China B8 36
Manchuria see Dong San Shen, hist. reg., China B5 38
Manciano, Italy H8 22
Mancos, Co., U.S. F8 132
Mancos, stm., U.S. F8 132
Mānd, stm., India G9 54
Mand, stm., Iran D7 56
Manda, Tan. G6 66
Manda, Jabal, mtn., Sudan F4 62
Mandabe, Madag. E7 68
Mandaguari, Braz. A12 92
Manda Island, i., Kenya E8 66
Mandal, Mong. B6 36
Mandala, Puncak, mtn., Indon. F10 44
Mandalay, Mya. A2 48
Mandalay, state, Mya. B2 48
Mandan, N.D., U.S. A11 126
Mandar, Teluk, b., Indon. E11 50
Mandara, Monts (Mandara Mountains), mts., Afr. G7 64
Mandara Mountains (Mandara, Monts), mts., Afr. G7 64
Mandas, Italy E3 24
Mandaue, Phil. E4 52
Mandeb, Bab el, strt. E8 62
Mandera, Kenya D8 66
Manderson, Wy., U.S. C5 126
Mandeville, Jam. i13 104d
Mandi, India C6 54
Mandi Bahāuddīn, Pak. B4 54
Mandi Būrewāla, Pak. C4 54
Mandi Dabwāli, India D5 54
Mandimba, Moz. C6 68
Mandioli, Pulau, i., Indon. F8 44
Mandioré, Lagoa (Mandioré, Laguna), l., S.A. G6 84
Mandioré, Laguna (Mandioré, Lagoa), l., S.A. G6 84
Mandla, India G8 54
Mandlakazi, Moz. D11 70
Mandora, Austl. C4 74
Mandra, Pak. B4 54
Mandritsara, Madag. D8 68
Mandsaur, India F5 54
Mandun, China A4 48
Manduria, Italy D11 24
Māndvi, India H4 54
Māndvi, India G2 54
Mandya, India E3 53
Manendragarh, India G9 54
Manfalût, Egypt K1 58
Manfredonia, Italy I12 22
Manfredonia, Golfo di, b., Italy C10 24
Manga, Braz. H3 88
Manga, reg., Niger F7 64
Mangabeiras, Chapada das, hills, Braz. E2 88
Mangagoy, Phil. F6 52
Mangai, D.R.C. E3 66
Mangalagiri, India C5 53
Mangaldai, India E14 54
Mangalia, Rom. F15 26
Mangalore, India E2 53
Mangalvedha, India C2 53
Mangchang, China I2 42
Mange, China B9 54
Mangela, Mount see Nanggala Hill, mtn., Sol. Is. e7 79b
Manggar, Indon. E6 50
Mangham, La., U.S. E7 122
Mangin Range, mts., Mya. C8 46
Mangkalihat, Tanjung, c., Indon. C11 50
Manglares, Cabo, c., Col. G2 86
Mangla Reservoir, res., Pak. B4 54
Mangnai, China G16 32
Mangochi, Mwi. C6 68
Mangoky, stm., Madag. E7 68
Mangole, Pulau, i., Indon. F8 44
Mangrol, India H2 54
Mangrūl Pīr, India H6 54
Mangsang, Indon. E4 50
Mangshi see Luxi, China G4 36
Mangueira, Lagoa, b., Braz. F11 92
Mangueirinha, Braz. B11 92
Mangum, Ok., U.S. G9 128
Mangya, China D3 36
Manhattan, Ks., U.S. B12 128
Manhattan, Mt., U.S. E15 136
Manhiça, Moz. D11 70
Mān Hpāng, Mya. A4 48
Manhuaçu, Braz. K4 88
Manhuaçu, stm., Braz. J5 88
Manhumirim, Braz. K4 88
Maniago, Italy D9 22
Manica, Moz. D5 68
Manica, state, Moz. B11 70
Manicaland, state, Zimb. B11 70
Manic Deux, Réservoir, res., Qc., Can. A8 110
Manicoré, Braz. E5 84
Manicouagan, stm., Qc., Can. E17 106
Manicouagan, Réservoir, res., Qc., Can. E17 106
Maniganggo, China E4 36
Manigotagan, Mb., Can. C17 124
Manigotagan, stm., Can. C17 124
Manihiki, at., Cook Is. E10 72
Maniitsoq see Sukkertoppen, Grnld. D15 141
Mānikganj, Bngl. G13 54
Mānikpur, India F8 54
Manila, Phil. C3 52
Manila, Ar., U.S. I7 120
Manila, Ut., U.S. C7 132
Manila Bay, b., Phil. C3 52
Manilla, Austl. H8 76
Manily, Russia D22 34
Maningrida, Austl. B6 74
Maninjau, Danau, l., Indon. D1 50
Manipa, Selat, strt., Indon. F8 44
Manipur, state, India C7 46
Manipur, stm., Asia A1 48
Manisa, Tur. E10 28
Manisa, state, Tur. E11 28
Manistee, Mi., U.S. D3 112
Manistee, stm., Mi., U.S. D3 112
Manistique, Mi., U.S. C3 112
Manistique Lake, l., Mi., U.S. B4 112
Manito, Il., U.S. K9 118
Manitoba, state, Can. D11 106
Manitoba, Lake, l., Mb., Can. D15 124
Manitou, stm., On., Can. B5 118
Manitou, Lake, l., On., Can. C7 112
Manitou Beach, Sk., Can. C8 124
Manitou Lake, l., Sk., Can. B4 124
Manitoulin Island, i., On., Can. C7 112
Manitou Springs, Co., U.S. C3 128
Manitowaning, On., Can. C8 112
Manitowoc, Wi., U.S. D2 112
Maniwaki, Qc., Can. B13 112
Manizales, Col. E4 86
Manja, Madag. E7 68
Manjakandriana, Madag. D8 68
Manjeri, India F3 53
Mānjra, stm., India B3 53
Mankanza, D.R.C. D3 66
Mankato, Ks., U.S. B10 128
Mankato, Mn., U.S. G4 118
Mankera, Pak. C3 54
Mankota, Sk., Can. E6 124
Manley Hot Springs, Ak., U.S. D9 140
Manlleu, Spain B13 20
Manmād, India H5 54
Manna, Indon. F3 50
Mannahill, Austl. I3 76
Mannar, Sri L. G4 53
Mannar, Gulf of, b., Asia G4 53
Mannārgudi, India F4 53
Mannford, Ok., U.S. A2 122
Mannheim, Ger. G4 16
Manning, N.D., U.S. G11 124
Manning, S.C., U.S. C5 116
Manning Strait, strt., Sol. Is. d7 79b
Mannum, Austl. J2 76
Mannville, Ab., Can. C19 138
Manoharpur, India G10 54
Manokwari, Indon. F9 44
Manombo Atsimo, Madag. E7 68
Manono, D.R.C. F5 66
Manor, Sk., Can. E11 124
Manor, Tx., U.S. D10 130
Manosque, Fr. F11 18
Manouane, Lac, l., Qc., Can. C2 110
Manouane, Lac, res., Qc., Can. E16 106
Manp'o, Kor., N. D7 38
Mānpur, India H8 54
Manra, at., Kir. D9 72
Manresa, Spain C12 20
Mānsa, India C5 54
Mansa, Zam. C4 68
Mansafīs, Egypt J1 58
Mānsehra, Pak. A4 54
Mansel Island, i., Nu., Can. C14 106
Mansfield, Eng., U.K. H11 12
Mansfield, Ga., U.S. C2 116
Mansfield, Il., U.S. D9 120
Mansfield, La., U.S. E5 122
Mansfield, Mo., U.S. G5 120
Mansfield, Oh., U.S. D3 114
Mansfield, Pa., U.S. C8 114
Mansfield, Tx., U.S. B10 130
Mansfield, Mount, mtn., Vt., U.S. F4 110
Mansion, St. K./N. C2 105a
Mansôa, Gui.-B. G1 64
Manson, Ia., U.S. B3 120
Mansucum, Pan. H9 102
Mansura, La., U.S. F6 122
Manta, Ec. H1 86
Manta, Bahía de, b., Ec. H1 86
Mantagao, stm., Mb., Can. C16 124
Mantalingajan, Mount, mtn., Phil. F1 52
Mantanani Besar, Pulau, i., Malay. G1 52
Manteca, Ca., U.S. F4 134
Mantecal, Ven. D7 86
Mantena, Braz. J5 88
Manteo, N.C., U.S. I10 114
Mantes-la-Jolie, Fr. F10 14
Manti, Ut., U.S. D5 132
Mantiqueira, Serra da, mts., Braz. L3 88
Manton, Mi., U.S. D4 112
Mántova, Italy E7 22
Mantua, Cuba A5 102
Mantua see Mántova, Italy E7 22
Mantua, Oh., U.S. C4 114
Manturovo, Russia G21 8
Mäntyharju, Fin. F12 8
Manu, Peru F3 84
Manuae, at., Cook Is. E11 72
Manuae, at., Fr. Poly. E11 72
Manua Islands, is., Am. Sam. h13 79c
Manuel, Mex. D9 100
Manuel Alves, stm., Braz. F2 88
Manuel Alves Grande, stm., Braz. D2 88
Manuel Benavides, Mex. A6 100
Manuel F. Mantilla see Pedro R. Fernández, Arg. D8 92
Manuguru, India B5 53
Manui, Pulau, i., Indon. F7 44
Manukau, N.Z. C6 80
Manukau Harbour, b., N.Z. C6 80
Manus Island, i., Pap. N. Gui. a4 79a
Mānwat, India B3 53
Many, La., U.S. F5 122
Manyara, Lake, l., Tan. E7 66
Manyberries, Ab., Can. E3 124
Many Island Lake, l., Can. D3 124
Manyoni, Tan. F6 66
Many Peaks, Austl. E8 76
Manza, D.R.C. F5 66
Manzala, Bahra el-, l., Egypt G3 58
Manzanares, Spain E7 20
Manzanilla Point, c., Trin. s13 105f
Manzanillo, Cuba B9 102
Manzanillo, Mex. F6 100
Manzanillo Bay, b., N.A. C11 102
Manzano, N.M., U.S. G2 128
Manzano Peak, mtn., N.M., U.S. G2 128
Manzhouli, China B8 36
Manzini, Swaz. E10 70
Mao, Chad E3 62
Mao, Dom. Rep. C12 102
Maó, Spain E15 20
Maoba, China F3 42
Maoke, Pegunungan, mts., Indon. a2 79a
Maolin, China C5 38
Maoming, China K4 42
Mapaga, Indon. D11 50
Mapam Yumco, l., China C8 54
Mapane, Indon. D12 50
Mapari, stm., Braz. I8 86
Mapastepec, Mex. H12 100
Mapi, Indon. G10 44
Mapimí, Mex. C6 100
Mapimí, Bolsón de, des., Mex. B6 100
Mapire, Ven. D9 86
Mapiri, Bol. C3 90
Mapixari, Ilha, i., Braz. I9 86
Maple, stm., Ia., U.S. B2 120
Maple, stm., Mi., U.S. E5 112
Maple, stm., N.D., U.S. H16 124
Maple Creek, Sk., Can. E4 124
Maple Lake, Mn., U.S. F4 118
Maple Mount, Ky., U.S. G10 120
Maple Ridge, B.C., Can. G8 138
Mapleton, Ia., U.S. B2 120
Mapleton, Or., U.S. F3 136
Mapleton, Ut., U.S. C5 132
Mapuera, stm., Braz. C6 84
Maputo, Moz. D11 70
Maputo, state, Moz. D11 70
Maputo, stm., Afr. E11 70
Maqên Gangri, mtn., China E4 36
Maqna, Sau. Ar. J5 58
Maquan, stm., China D10 54
Maquela do Zombo, Ang. B2 68
Maquereau, Pointe au, c., Qc., Can. B12 110
Maquinchao, Arg. H3 90
Maquoketa, Ia., U.S. B7 120
Maquoketa, stm., Ia., U.S. B7 120
Maquoketa, North Fork, stm., Ia., U.S. B7 120
Mar, Serra do, mts., Braz. B13 92
Mara, stm., Afr. E7 66
Maraã, Braz. H9 86
Maraa, Fr. Poly. v21 78h
Marabá, Braz. C1 88
Marabahan, Indon. E9 50
Maraboon, Lake, res., Austl. D6 76
Maracá, Ilha de, i., Braz. C7 84
Maracá, Ilha de, i., Braz. F11 86
Maracaçumé, stm., Braz. A3 88
Maracaibo, Ven. B5 86
Maracaibo, Lago de, l., Ven. C6 86
Maracaju, Braz. D5 90
Maracanaú, Braz. B6 88
Maracás, Braz. G5 88
Maracay, Ven. B8 86
Marādah, Libya B3 62
Maradi, Niger G6 64
Marāghah, Sabkhat al-, l., Syria C8 58
Marāgheh, Iran B6 56
Maragogipe, Braz. G6 88
Maragoji, Braz. E8 88
Marahuaca, Cerro, mtn., Ven. F9 86
Maraial, Braz. E8 88
Marais des Cygnes, stm., U.S. F3 120
Marajó, Baía de, b., Braz. D8 84
Marajó, Ilha de, i., Braz. D8 84
Maralal, Kenya D7 66
Marali, C.A.R. C3 66
Maralinga, Austl. F6 74
Marambio, sci., Ant. B35 81
Marampa, S.L. H2 64
Maramsilli Reservoir, res., India H8 54
Maramureș, state, Rom. B10 26
Maran, Malay. K6 48
Marana, Az., U.S. K5 132
Marand, Iran B6 56
Marang, Malay. J6 48
Marangas, Phil. F1 52
Maranguape, Braz. B6 88
Maranhão, state, Braz. C3 88
Maranhão, stm., Braz. D9 84
Marano, Laguna di, b., Italy E10 22
Maranoa, stm., Austl. F7 76
Marañón, stm., Peru D2 84
Marasende, Pulau, i., Indon. F10 50
Mărășești, Rom. D14 26
Marataså, stm., Braz. C4 88
Marathon, Austl. C4 76
Marathon, On., Can. C12 118
Marathon, Tx., U.S. D4 130
Marathon, Wi., U.S. G9 118
Marathónas, Grc. E6 28
Maratua, Pulau, i., Indon. B11 50
Maraú, Braz. H6 88
Marau, Braz. D11 92
Marauiá, stm., Braz. H9 86
Maravilha, Braz. C11 92
Maravillas, Mex. B6 100
Maravillas Creek, stm., Tx., U.S. E4 130
Marav Lake, l., Pak. D2 54
Maravovo, Sol. Is. e8 79b
Marawi, Phil. F5 52
Marawwah, i., U.A.E. E7 56
Marayes, Arg. E4 92
Marbella, Spain H6 20
Marble, N.C., U.S. A2 116
Marble Bar, Austl. D3 74
Marble Canyon, val., Az., U.S. G5 132
Marble Falls, Tx., U.S. D9 130
Marble Hall, S. Afr. D9 70
Marble Hill, Mo., U.S. G8 120
Marblemount, Wa., U.S. B5 136
Marble Rock, Ia., U.S. I6 118
Marburg, Ger. F4 16
Marburg, S. Afr. G10 70
Marca, Ponta da, c., Ang. D1 68
Marcal, stm., Hung. B4 26
Marcelin, Sk., Can. B7 124
Marceline, Mo., U.S. E5 120
March, Eng., U.K. I12 12
March (Morava), stm., Eur. H12 16
Marche, state, Italy G10 22
Marche, hist. reg., Fr. C8 18
Marche-en-Famenne, Bel. D14 14
Marchena, Spain G5 20
Marches see Marche, state, Italy G10 22
Mar Chiquita, Laguna, b., Arg. H9 92
Mar Chiquita, Laguna, l., Arg. E6 92
Marcigny, Fr. C10 18
Marco, Braz. B5 88
Marcos Juárez, Arg. F6 92
Marcus, Ia., U.S. B2 120
Marcus Baker, Mount, mtn., Ak., U.S. D10 140
Marcus Island see Minami-Tori-shima, i., Japan G19 30
Marcy, Mount, mtn., N.Y., U.S. F2 110
Mardān, Pak. A4 54
Mardarivka, Ukr. B16 26
Mar del Plata, Arg. H9 92
Mardin, Tur. B5 56
Maré, i., N. Cal. m17 79d
Mare a Brăilei, Insula, i., Rom. D14 26
Marea de Portillo, Cuba C9 102
Marechal Cândido Rondon, Braz. B10 92
Marechal Deodoro, Braz. E8 88
Maree, Loch, l., Scot., U.K. D7 12
Mareeba, Austl. A5 76
Maremma, reg., Italy H8 22
Marengo, Il., U.S. B9 120
Marengo, Ia., U.S. C5 120
Marenisco, Mi., U.S. E9 118
Marennes, Fr. D4 18
Marettimo, Isola, i., Italy G5 24
Marfa, Tx., U.S. D3 130
Margai Caka, l., China A6 46
Margaree Harbour, N.S., Can. D15 110
Margaret, stm., Austl. C5 74
Margaret Bay, B.C., Can. E3 138
Margaret River, Austl. F2 74
Margaretville, N.Y., U.S. B11 114
Margarita, Isla de, i., Ven. B9 86
Margate, S. Afr. G10 70
Margate, Eng., U.K. J14 12
Margate, Fl., U.S. J5 116
Margecany, Slov. H16 16
Margelan see Margilan, Uzb. F12 32
Margherita di Savoia, Italy C10 24
Margherita Peak, mtn., Afr. D5 66
Margilan, Uzb. F12 32
Margonin, Pol. D13 16
Margosatubig, Phil. G4 52
Mārgow, Dasht-e, des., Afg. C9 56
Marha, Russia D13 34
Marha, stm., Russia C12 34
Maria, Îles, is., Fr. Poly. F11 72
María Cleofas, Isla, i., Mex. E5 100
María Elena, Chile D3 90
María Grande, Arg. E8 92
María Ignacia, Arg. H8 92
Maria Island, i., Austl. B7 74
Maria Island National Park, p.o.i., Austl. o14 77a
Mariakani, Kenya E7 66
María Madre, Isla, i., Mex. E5 100
María Magdalena, Isla, i., Mex. E5 100
Mariana, Braz. K4 88
Mariana Islands, is., Oc. B5 72
Mariana Ridge, unds. H17 142
Mariana Trench, unds. H17 142
Marian Lake, l., N.T., Can. C7 106
Marianna, Ar., U.S. C8 122
Marianna, Fl., U.S. G13 122
Mariano I. Loza, Arg. D8 92
Mariánské Lázně, Czech Rep. G8 16
Marias, stm., Mt., U.S. B16 136
Marias Pass, p., Mt., U.S. B13 136
María Teresa, Arg. G6 92
Mariato, Punta, c., Pan. I7 102
Maribo, Den. B7 16
Maribor, Slvn. D12 22
Maricao, P.R. B2 104a
Marico, stm., Afr. D8 70
Maricopa, Az., U.S. J4 132
Maricunga, Salar de, pl., Chile C3 92
Marié, stm., Braz. H8 86
Marie Byrd Land, reg., Ant. C29 81
Marie-Galante, i., Guad. i6 105c
Mariehamn see Maarianhamina, Fin. F9 8
Mariental, Nmb. D4 70
Marienville, Pa., U.S. C6 114
Mariestad, Swe. G5 8
Marieta, stm., Ven. E8 86
Marietta, Ga., U.S. D14 122
Marietta, Mn., U.S. G2 118
Marietta, Oh., U.S. E4 114
Marieville, Qc., Can. E3 110
Marignane, Fr. F11 18
Marigot, Dom. i6 105c
Marigot, Guad. A1 105a
Mariinsk, Russia C15 32
Mariinskoe, Russia F17 34
Marijampolė, Lith. F6 10
Marij El, state, Russia C7 32
Marília, Braz. D7 90
Marimba, Ang. B2 68
Marín, Mex. I7 130
Marín, Spain B2 20
Marina di Ravenna, Italy F9 22
Marina Fall, wtfl, Guy. E12 86
Mar''ina Horka, Bela. G11 10
Marinduque, i., Phil. D3 52
Marine City, Mi., U.S. B3 114
Marinette, Wi., U.S. C2 112
Maringá, Braz. D6 90
Marino, Vanuatu j16 79d
Marintu, Indon. C6 50
Marion, Al., U.S. E11 122
Marion, Ar., U.S. B8 122
Marion, Il., U.S. G9 120
Marion, In., U.S. H4 112
Marion, Ia., U.S. B6 120
Marion, Ks., U.S. C12 128
Marion, Ky., U.S. G9 120
Marion, La., U.S. E6 122
Marion, Ms., U.S. E10 122
Marion, N.C., U.S. I4 114
Marion, N.D., U.S. A14 126
Marion, Oh., U.S. D2 114
Marion, S.C., U.S. B6 116
Marion, Va., U.S. H4 114
Marion, Lake, res., S.C., U.S. C5 116
Marion Bay, b., Austl. o13 77a
Marion County Lake, res., Ks., U.S. C11 128
Marion Downs, Austl. D2 76
Marion Junction, Al., U.S. E11 122
Marion Reef, rf., Austl. B9 76
Marionville, Mo., U.S. G4 120
Maripa, Ven. D9 86
Mariposa, Ca., U.S. F5 134
Mariquita, Col. E4 86
Mariscal Estigarribia, Para. D4 90
Maritime Alps, mts., Eur. E12 18
Maritsa (Évros) (Marica) (Meriç), stm., Eur. C9 28
Mariupol', Ukr. E5 32
Mariusa, Caño, stm., Ven. C11 86
Mariveles, Phil. C3 52
Mariyampole see Marijampolė, Lith. F6 10
Marjanovka, Russia D12 32
Marka, Som. D8 66
Markakol', ozero, l., Kaz. E15 32
Mārkāpur, India D4 53
Markaryd, Swe. H5 8
Markdale, On., Can. D9 112
Marked Tree, Ar., U.S. B8 122
Markesan, Wi., U.S. H10 118
Market Harborough, Eng., U.K. I12 12
Markham, On., Can. E10 112
Markham, Tx., U.S. F11 130
Markham Bay, b., Nu., Can. C16 106
Markit, China B12 56
Markle, In., U.S. H4 112
Markleeville, Ca., U.S. E6 134
Markovo, Russia D23 34
Marks, Russia D7 32
Marks, Ms., U.S. C8 122
Marktheidenfeld, Ger. G5 16
Marktoberdorf, Ger. I6 16
Marktredwitz, Ger. G8 16
Mark Twain Lake, res., Mo., U.S. E6 120
Marlboro, Ab., Can. C14 138
Marlboro, N.Y., U.S. C11 114
Marlborough, Austl. D7 76
Marlborough, Guy. B6 84
Marlborough, Ma., U.S. B14 114
Marlette, Mi., U.S. E6 112
Marlinton, W.V., U.S. F5 114
Marlow, Ok., U.S. G11 128
Marmaduke, Ar., U.S. H7 120
Marmande, Fr. E6 18
Marmara, Sea of see Marmara Denizi, Tur. C11 28
Marmara Adası, i., Tur. C10 28
Marmara Denizi (Marmara, Sea of), Tur. C11 28
Marmara Ereğlisi, Tur. C10 28
Marmara Gölü, l., Tur. E10 28
Marmaris, Tur. G11 28
Marmaton, stm., U.S. G3 120
Marmelos, stm., Braz. E5 84
Marmet, W.V., U.S. F4 114
Marmion Lake, l., On., Can. C7 118
Marmolada, mtn., Italy D8 22
Marmora, On., Can. D12 112
Marnay, Fr. G14 14
Marne, Ger. C4 16
Marne, Mi., U.S. E4 112
Marne, state, Fr. E13 14
Marne, stm., Fr. E11 14
Marne à la Saône, Canal de la, can., Fr. F14 14
Maroa, Ven. F8 86
Maroantsetra, Madag. D8 68
Maromandia, Madag. C8 68
Maromme, Fr. E10 14
Maromokotro, mtn., Madag. C8 68
Marondera, Zimb. D5 68
Maroni (Marowijne), stm., S.A. C7 84
Maros, Indon. F11 50
Maros (Mureș), stm., Eur. C7 26
Maroua, Cam. B2 66
Marovoay, Madag. D8 68
Marowijne (Maroni), stm., S.A. C7 84
Marquand, Mo., U.S. G7 120
Marquard, S. Afr. F8 70
Marquesas Islands see Marquises, Îles, is., Fr. Poly. D12 72
Marquesas Keys, is., Fl., U.S. L3 116
Marquette, Ks., U.S. C11 128
Marquette, Mi., U.S. B2 112
Marquis, Gren. q10 105e
Marquises, Îles, is., Fr. Poly. D12 72
Marradi, Italy F8 22
Marrah, Jabal, hill, Sudan E4 62
Marrakech, Mor. C3 64
Marrakesh see Marrakech, Mor. C3 64
Marrawah, Austl. n12 77a
Marree, Austl. E7 74
Marrero, La., U.S. H8 122
Marromeu, Moz. D6 68
Marrupa, Moz. C6 68
Marsá al-Burayqah, Libya A3 62
Marsabit, Kenya D7 66
Marsala, Italy G6 24
Marsciano, Italy H9 22
Marseille, Fr. F11 18
Marseilles, Il., U.S. C9 120
Marsfjället, mtn., Swe. D6 8
Marshall, Lib. H2 64
Marshall, Ak., U.S. D7 140
Marshall, Ar., U.S. I5 120
Marshall, Mi., U.S. B1 114
Marshall, Mn., U.S. G3 118
Marshall, Mo., U.S. E4 120
Marshall, N.C., U.S. I3 114
Marshall, Tx., U.S. E4 122
Marshall, Va., U.S. F8 114
Marshall, stm., Austl. D7 74
Marshallberg, N.C., U.S. B9 116
Marshall Islands, ctry., Oc. H19 142
Marshall Islands, is., Marsh. Is. B7 72
Marshalltown, Ia., U.S. B5 120
Marshfield, Mo., U.S. G4 120
Marshfield, Wi., U.S. G8 118
Mars Hill, Me., U.S. D9 110
Mars Hill, N.C., U.S. I3 114
Marsh Island, i., La., U.S. H7 122
Marshville, N.C., U.S. A5 116
Marsing, Id., U.S. G10 136
Märsta, Swe. G7 8
Marstal, Den. B6 16
Martaban, Gulf of, b., Mya. D3 48
Martapura, Indon. E9 50
Martapura, Indon. F4 50
Marte R. Gómez, Presa, res., Mex. H9 130
Marthaguy Creek, stm., Austl. H6 76
Martha's Vineyard, i., Ma., U.S. C15 114
Martí, Cuba B9 102
Martigny, Switz. D4 22
Martigues, Fr. F11 18
Martin, Slov. G14 16
Martin, Ky., U.S. G3 114
Martin, Mi., U.S. F4 112
Martin, N.D., U.S. G13 124
Martin, Tn., U.S. H9 120
Martín, stm., Spain C10 20
Martina Franca, Italy D11 24
Martindale, Tx., U.S. E10 130
Mărtinești, Rom. D14 26
Martinez, Ca., U.S. E3 134
Martinez, Ga., U.S. C3 116
Martínez de la Torre, Mex. E10 100
Martinho Campos, Braz. J3 88
Martinique, dep., N.A. i15 96a
Martinique Passage, strt., N.A. k6 105c
Martin Lake, res., Al., U.S. E12 122
Martinópole, Braz. B5 88
Martinsberg, Aus. B12 22
Martinsburg, W.V., U.S. E7 114
Martins Ferry, Oh., U.S. D5 114
Martinsville, Il., U.S. E10 120
Martinsville, In., U.S. E11 120
Martinsville, Va., U.S. H5 114
Martin Vaz, Ilhas, is., Braz. H12 82
Martos, Spain G7 20
Martre, Lac la, l., N.T., Can. C7 106
Martti, Fin. C13 8
Marudi, Malay. A9 50
Marudu, Telukan, b., Malay. G1 52
Marugame, Japan E6 40
Maruim, Braz. F7 88
Maruoka, Japan C9 40
Marutea, at., Fr. Poly. E12 72
Marv Dasht, Iran D7 56
Marvine, Mount, mtn., Ut., U.S. E5 132
Mārwār, India F4 54
Mary, Turkmen. B9 56
Mary, stm., Austl. E9 76
Maryborough, Austl. E9 76
Maryborough, Austl. K4 76
Marydale, S. Afr. F5 70
Maryfield, Sk., Can. E12 124
Mary Kathleen, Austl. C2 76
Maryland, state, U.S. E8 114
Maryneal, Tx., U.S. B7 130
Maryport, Eng., U.K. G9 12
Marysvale, Ut., U.S. E4 132
Marysville, N.B., Can. D10 110
Marysville, Ca., U.S. D4 134
Marysville, Ks., U.S. L2 118
Marysville, Mi., U.S. B3 114
Marysville, Oh., U.S. D2 114
Marysville, Wa., U.S. B4 136
Maryville, Mo., U.S. D3 120
Maryville, Tn., U.S. I2 114
Marzagão, Braz. I1 88
Marzo, Punta, c., Col. D3 86
Masada see Mezada, Horvot, hist., Isr. G6 58
Masai Mara Game Reserve, Kenya E7 66
Masai Steppe, plat., Tan. E7 66
Masaka, Ug. E6 66
Masalembu Besar, Pulau, i., Indon. F9 50
Masamba, Indon. E12 50
Masan, Kor., S. D1 40
Masasi, Tan. G7 66
Masatepe, Nic. G4 102
Masaya, Nic. G4 102
Masbate, Phil. D4 52
Masbate, i., Phil. E4 52
Mascarene Basin, unds. K8 142
Mascarene Islands, is., Afr. i10 69a
Mascarene Plateau, unds. J8 142
Mascot, Tn., U.S. H2 114
Mascota, Mex. E6 100
Mascoutah, Il., U.S. F8 120
Maseru, Leso. F8 70
Mashan, China J3 42
Mashava, Zimb. D5 68
Mashhad, Iran B8 56
Mashi, China G6 42
Mashiko, Japan C13 40
Mashra'ar Raqq, Sudan F5 62
Masi-Manimba, D.R.C. E3 66
Masindi, Ug. D6 66
Masira, Gulf of see Maṣīrah, Khalīj, b., Oman F8 56
Maṣīrah, i., Oman E8 56
Maṣīrah, Khalīj, b., Oman F8 56
Masisea, Peru E3 84
Masjed-e Soleymān, Iran C6 56
Mask, Lough, l., Ire. H3 12
Maskanah, Syria B8 58
Masljanino, Russia D14 32
Mason, Mi., U.S. F5 112
Mason, Oh., U.S. E1 114
Mason, Tx., U.S. D8 130
Mason, W.V., U.S. E3 114
Mason City, Il., U.S. D8 120
Mason City, Ia., U.S. A4 120
Mason City, Ne., U.S. F13 126
Masqaṭ (Muscat), Oman E8 56
Massa, Italy F7 22
Massachusetts, state, U.S. B14 114
Massachusetts Bay, b., Ma., U.S. B15 114
Massafra, Italy D11 24
Massaguet, Chad E3 62
Massa Marittima, Italy G7 22
Massangena, Moz. B11 70
Massawa (Mitsiwa), Erit. D7 62
Massena, Ia., U.S. C3 120
Massena, N.Y., U.S. F2 110
Massenya, Chad E3 62
Massey, On., Can. B7 112
Massey Sound, strt., Nu., Can. B7 141
Massiac, Fr. D9 18
Massillon, Oh., U.S. D4 114
Massina, reg., Mali G4 64
Massinga, Moz. C12 70
Massingir, Moz. C11 70
Massive, Mount, mtn., Co., U.S. D10 132
Masson Island, i., Ant. B14 81
Mastābah, Sau. Ar. E4 56
Masterson, Tx., U.S. F6 128
Masterton, N.Z. E6 80
Mastic Point, Bah. K8 116
Mastung, Pak. D10 56
Masty, Bela. G7 10
Masuda, Japan E4 40
Masurai, Gunung, mtn., Indon. E2 50
Masuria see Mazury, reg., Pol. C16 16
Masvingo, Zimb. E5 68
Masvingo, state, Zimb. B10 70
Maṣyāf, Syria C7 58
Mata Amarilla, Arg. I2 90
Matabeleland North, state, Zimb. A9 70
Matabeleland South, state, Zimb. B9 70
Matabuena, Spain C7 20
Matacuni, stm., Ven. F9 86
Mata de São João, Braz. G6 88
Matadi, D.R.C. F2 66
Matagalpa, Nic. F5 102
Matagami, Qc., Can. F15 106
Matagorda, Tx., U.S. F12 130

Name | Map Ref. | Page

Matagorda Island, i., Tx., U.S. F11 130
Matagorda Peninsula, pen., Tx., U.S. F11 130
Matahiae, Pointe, c., Fr. Poly. w22 78h
Matâi, Egypt J1 58
Mataiea, Fr. Poly. w22 78h
Mataiva, at., Fr. Poly. E12 72
Matak, Pulau, i., Indon. B5 50
Matakana, Austl. I5 76
Matale, Sri L. H5 53
Matam, Sen. F2 64
Matamoros, Mex. C10 100
Matamoros, Mex. C7 100
Matan, Indon. D7 50
Matandu, stm., Tan. F7 66
Matane, Qc., Can. B9 110
Matanni, Pak. B3 54
Matanzas, Cuba A7 102
Matanzas, Mex. E8 100
Matapan, Cape see Taínaro, Ákra, c., Grc. G5 28
Matape, stm., Mex. A3 100
Matapédia, Qc., Can. C9 110
Matapédia, Lac, l., Qc., Can. B9 110
Mataquito, stm., Chile G2 92
Matara, Sri L. I5 53
Mataram, Indon. H9 50
Mataranka, Austl. B6 74
Mataró, Spain C13 20
Matasiri, Pulau, i., Indon. F9 50
Matatiele, S. Afr. G9 70
Matatula, Cape, c., Am. Sam. h12 79c
Matā'utu, Wal./F. E9 72
Matavera, Cook Is. a27 78j
Mataveri, Chile e29 78l
Mataveri, Aeropuerto, Chile f29 78l
Mataveri Airstrip see Mataveri, Aeropuerto, Chile f29 78l
Matehuala, Mex. D8 100
Mateke Hills, hills, Zimb. B10 70
Matera, Italy D10 24
Mateur, Tun. G3 24
Matha, Fr. D5 18
Mather, Mb., Can. E14 124
Mather, Pa., U.S. E5 114
Matheson, On., Can. F14 106
Mathews, Va., U.S. G9 114
Mathis, Tx., U.S. F10 130
Mathura (Muttra), India E6 54
Matias Barbosa, Braz. K4 88
Matías Romero, Mex. G11 100
Maticora, stm., Ven. B6 86
Matinha, Braz. B3 88
Matipó, Braz. K4 88
Matiyure, stm., Ven. D7 86
Mātli, Pak. F2 54
Mato, Cerro, mtn., Ven. D9 86
Mato Grosso, state, Braz. F6 84
Mato Grosso, Planalto do, plat., Braz. B5 90
Mato Grosso, Plateau of see Mato Grosso, Planalto do, plat., Braz. B5 90
Mato Grosso do Sul, state, Braz. C6 90
Matola Rio, Moz. D11 70
Matopos, Zimb. B9 70
Matosinhos, Port. C2 20
Matouying, China B8 42
Matozinhos, Braz. J3 88
Matrah, Oman E8 56
Matsudo, Japan D12 40
Matsue, Japan D6 40
Matsumoto, Japan C10 40
Matsusaka, Japan E9 40
Matsu Tao, i., Tai. H8 42
Matsutō, Japan C9 40
Matsuura, Japan F2 40
Matsuyama, Japan F5 40
Mattagami, stm., On., Can. F14 106
Mattamuskeet, Lake, l., N.C., U.S. A9 116
Mattaponi, stm., Va., U.S. G8 114
Mattawa, On., Can. B11 112
Mattawa, Wa., U.S. D7 136
Mattawamkeag, stm., Me., U.S. E8 110
Matterhorn, mtn., Eur. D13 18
Matterhorn, mtn., Nv., U.S. B1 132
Matthews Mountain, hill, Mo., U.S. G7 120
Matthew Town, Bah. C10 96
Mattighofen, Aus. B10 22
Mattoon, Il., U.S. E9 120
Mattoon, Wi., U.S. F9 118
Mattydale, N.Y., U.S. E13 112
Matua, Indon. E7 50
Matudo see Matsudo, Japan D12 40
Matue see Matsue, Japan D6 40
Matuku, i., Fiji q19 79e
Matumoto see Matsumoto, Japan C10 40
Maturín, Ven. C10 86
Matutina, Braz. J2 88
Matuzaka see Matsusaka, Japan E9 40
Maú (Ireng), stm., S.A. F12 86
Maúa, Moz. C6 68
Mau Aimma, India F8 54
Maubeuge, Fr. D12 14
Maud, Tx., U.S. D4 122
Maudaha, India F7 54
Maude, Austl. J5 76
Maués, Braz. D6 84
Maués, stm., Braz. D6 84
Mauganj, India F8 54
Maui, i., Hi., U.S. C5 78a
Mauk, Indon. F5 50
Mauldin, S.C., U.S. B3 116
Maule, state, Chile G2 92
Maule, stm., Chile G1 92
Maule, Laguna del, l., Chile G2 92
Mauléon-Licharre, Fr. F5 18
Maumee, Oh., U.S. G6 112
Maumee, stm., U.S. G6 112
Maumelle, Lake, res., Ar., U.S. C6 122
Maumere, Indon. G7 44
Maun, Bots. D3 68
Maunabo, P.R. B4 104a
Mauna Kea, vol., Hi., U.S. D6 78a
Maunaloa, Hi., U.S. B4 78a
Mauna Loa, vol., Hi., U.S. D6 78a
Maunath Bhanjan, India F9 54
Maungdaw, Mya. H14 54
Maungmagan, Mya. E3 48
Maunoir, Lac, l., N.T., Can. B6 106
Maupihaa, at., Fr. Poly. E11 72
Mau Rānīpur, India F7 54
Maurepas, Lake, l., La., U.S. G8 122
Maurice, Lake, l., Austl. E6 74
Mauricie, Parc national de la, p.o.i., Qc., Can. D3 110
Mauritania, ctry., Afr. F2 64
Mauritanie see Mauritania, ctry., Afr. F2 64
Mauritius, ctry., Afr. h10 69a
Mauron, Fr. F6 14
Mauston, Wi., U.S. H8 118
Mautau, c., Fr. Poly. r19 78g
Mauterndorf, Aus. C10 22
Mauthen, Aus. D9 22
Mauvais Coulee, stm., N.D., U.S. F14 124
Mava, Pap. N. Gui. b3 79a
Maverick, Az., U.S. J7 132
Mavinga, Ang. D3 68
Mavrovo Nacionalni Park, p.o.i., Mac. B3 28
Mavuradonha Mountains, mts., Zimb. D5 68
Mawchi, Mya. C3 48
Mawlaik, Mya. D7 46
Mawlamyine (Moulmein), Mya. D3 48
Mawson, sci., Ant. B11 81
Maw Taung (Luang, Khao), mtn., Asia G4 48
Max, N.D., U.S. G12 124
Maxaranguape, Braz. C8 88
Maxcanú, Mex. B3 102
Maxixe, Moz. C12 70
Maxville, On., Can. E2 110
Maxwell, Ca., U.S. D3 134
Maxwell, Ne., U.S. F12 126
Maxwell, N.M., U.S. E4 128
May, Tx., U.S. C9 130
May, Cape, pen., N.J., U.S. F11 114
May, Mount, mtn., Ab., Can. B11 138
Maya, Pulau, i., Indon. D6 50
Mayaguana, i., Bah. A11 102
Mayaguana Passage, strt., Bah. A11 102
Mayagüez, P.R. B1 104a
Mayang, China H3 42
Mayarí, Cuba B10 102
Maybole, Scot., U.K. F8 12
Maydena, Austl. o13 77a
Maydh, Som. B9 66
Mayen, Ger. F3 16
Mayenne, Fr. F8 14
Mayenne, state, Fr. F8 14
Mayenne, stm., Fr. F8 14
Mayer, Az., U.S. I4 132
Mayerthorpe, Ab., Can. C15 138
Mayfield, Ky., U.S. H9 120
Mayfield, Ut., U.S. D5 132
Mayflower, Ar., U.S. C6 122
Māyir, Syria B8 58
Maykain see Majkain, Kaz. D13 32
Maymyo, Mya. A3 48
Maynard, Ia., U.S. B6 120
Maynardville, Tn., U.S. H2 114
Mayne, stm., Austl. D3 76
Mayo, Yk., Can. C3 106
Mayo, Fl., U.S. F2 116
Mayo, state, Ire. H3 12
Mayo, stm., Arg. I3 90
Mayo, stm., Mex. B4 100
Mayon Volcano, vol., Phil. D4 52
Mayor Buratovich, Arg. G4 90
Mayotte, dep., Afr. C8 68
Mayoyoque, Col. G4 86
May Pen, Jam. j13 104d
Mayreau, i., St. Vin. p11 105e
Mays Landing, N.J., U.S. E11 114
Maysville, Ky., U.S. F2 114
Maysville, Mo., U.S. E3 120
Maysville, N.C., U.S. B8 116
Maysville, Ok., U.S. G11 128
Mayumba, Gabon E2 66
Māyūram, India F4 53
Mayville, Mi., U.S. E6 112
Mayville, N.Y., U.S. B6 114
Mayville, N.D., U.S. G16 124
Maywood, Ne., U.S. G12 126
Maza, Arg. H6 92
Mazabuka, Zam. D4 68
Mazagão, Braz. D7 84
Mazamet, Fr. F8 18
Mazān, stm., Peru I4 86
Mazara, Val di, reg., Italy G7 24
Mazara del Vallo, Italy G6 24
Mazār-e Sharīf, Afg. B10 56
Mazarrón, Golfo de, b., Spain G9 20
Mazaruni, stm., Guy. D11 86
Mazatenango, Guat. E2 102
Mazatlán, Mex. D5 100
Mažeikiai, Lith. D5 10
Mazenod, Sk., Can. E7 124
Mazinga, mtn., Neth. Ant. C2 105a
Mazirbe, Lat. C5 10
Mazon, Il., U.S. C9 120
Mazowe, stm., Afr. D5 68
Mazury (Masuria), reg., Pol. C16 16
Mazyr, Bela. D3 32
Mbabane, Swaz. E10 70
M'bahiakro, C. Iv. H4 64
Mbaïki, C.A.R. D3 66
Mbaké, Sen. G1 64
Mbala, Zam. B5 68
Mbalabala, Zimb. B9 70
Mbale, Ug. D6 66
Mbalmayo, Cam. D2 66
Mbamba Bay, Tan. G7 66
Mbandaka (Coquilhatville), D.R.C. D3 66
Mbanga, Cam. D1 66
Mbanika Island, i., Sol. Is. e8 79b
M'banza Congo, Ang. B1 68
Mbanza-Ngungu, D.R.C. F3 66
Mbarara, Ug. E6 66
Mbashe, stm., S. Afr. H9 70
Mbava Island, i., Sol. Is. d7 79b
Mbé, Cam. C2 66
Mberengwa, Zimb. B9 70
Mbeya, Tan. F6 66
Mbigou, Gabon E2 66
Mbinda, Congo E2 66
Mbini, Eq. Gui. I6 64
Mbini, stm., Afr. I6 64
Mboi, D.R.C. F4 66
Mboki, C.A.R. C5 66
Mbola, Sol. Is. e9 79b
Mborokua, i., Sol. Is. e8 79b
Mborong, Indon. H12 50
Mbouda, Cam. C2 66
Mbour, Sen. G1 64
Mbout, Maur. F2 64
Mbuji-Mayi (Bakwanga), D.R.C. F4 66
Mbuluzi, stm., Swaz. E10 70
Mbwemkuru, stm., Tan. F7 66
McAdam, N.B., Can. E9 110
McAdoo, Pa., U.S. D9 114
McAlester, Ok., U.S. C3 122
McAllen, Tx., U.S. H9 130
McArthur, Oh., U.S. E3 114
McArthur, stm., Austl. C7 74
McArthur River, Austl. C7 74
McBain, Mi., U.S. D4 112
McBee, S.C., U.S. B5 116
McBeth Fjord, b., Nu., Can. B17 106
McBride, B.C., Can. C10 138
McCall Creek, Ms., U.S. F8 122
McCamey, Tx., U.S. C5 130
McCammon, Id., U.S. H14 136
McCauley Island, i., B.C., Can. E4 106
McCleary, Wa., U.S. C3 136
McClellan Creek, stm., Tx., U.S. F8 128
McClellanville, S.C., U.S. C6 116
McClintock, Mount, mtn., Ant. D21 81
McCloud, Ca., U.S. B3 134
McCloud, stm., Ca., U.S. B3 134
McClure, Il., U.S. G8 120
McClusky, N.D., U.S. G13 124
McColl, S.C., U.S. B6 116
McComb, Ms., U.S. F8 122
McConaughy, Lake, res., Ne., U.S. F11 126
McConnellsburg, Pa., U.S. E7 114
McConnelsville, Oh., U.S. E4 114
McCook, Ne., U.S. A8 128
McCormick, S.C., U.S. C3 116
McCreary, Mb., Can. D14 124
McCullough Mountain, mtn., Nv., U.S. H1 132
McCune, Ks., U.S. G2 120
McCurtain, Ok., U.S. B4 122
McDade, Tx., U.S. D10 130
McDermitt, Nv., U.S. B8 134
McDermott, Oh., U.S. F2 114
McDonald, Ks., U.S. B7 128
McDonald, Lake, l., Mt., U.S. B12 136
McDowell Peak, mtn., Az., U.S. J4 132
Mcensk, Russia G19 10
McEwen, Tn., U.S. H10 120
McFadden, Wy., U.S. B10 132
McFarland, Ca., U.S. H6 134
McGehee, Ar., U.S. D7 122
McGill, Nv., U.S. D2 132
McGrath, Ak., U.S. D8 140
McGraw, N.Y., U.S. B9 114
McGregor, Tx., U.S. C10 130
McGregor, stm., B.C., Can. B9 138
McGregor Lake, l., Ab., Can. F18 138
McHenry, Il., U.S. B9 120
McHenry, Ms., U.S. G9 122
Mchinji, Mwi. C5 68
McIntosh, Al., U.S. F10 122
McIntosh, Mn., U.S. D3 118
McIntyre Bay, b., On., Can. B10 118
McKeand, stm., Nu., Can. C17 106
McKee, Ky., U.S. G2 114
McKeesport, Pa., U.S. D6 114
McKenzie, Tn., U.S. H9 120
McKenzie, stm., Or., U.S. F4 136
McKenzie Bridge, Or., U.S. F4 136
McKenzie Island, On., Can. E12 106
McKinlay, Austl. C3 76
McKinlay, stm., Austl. C3 76
McKinley, Mount, mtn., Ak., U.S. D9 140
McKinleyville, Ca., U.S. C1 134
McKinney, Tx., U.S. D2 122
McKittrick Summit, mtn., Ca., U.S. H6 134
McLain, Ms., U.S. F10 122
McLaurin, Ms., U.S. F9 122
McLean, Il., U.S. D8 120
McLean, Tx., U.S. F8 128
McLeansboro, Il., U.S. F9 120
McLennan, Ab., Can. D7 106
McLeod, stm., Ab., Can. C15 138
McLeod Bay, b., N.T., Can. C8 106
McLeod Lake, B.C., Can. B7 138
M'Clintock Channel, strt., Nu., Can. A10 106
McLoughlin, Mount, mtn., Or., U.S. A3 134
McLouth, Ks., U.S. E2 120
M'Clure Strait, strt., N.T., Can. B16 140
McMahon, Sk., Can. D6 124
McMinnville, Or., U.S. E3 136
McMinnville, Tn., U.S. B13 122
McMurdo, sci., Ant. C22 81
McMurdo Sound, strt., Ant. C22 81
McNary, Az., U.S. I7 132
McNeil, Ar., U.S. D5 122
McPherson, Ks., U.S. C11 128
McQueeney, Tx., U.S. E9 130
McRae, Ar., U.S. B7 122
McRae, Ga., U.S. D3 116
McVeigh, Ky., U.S. G3 114
McVille, N.D., U.S. G15 124
McWilliams, Al., U.S. F11 122
Mdantsane, S. Afr. H8 70
M'drak, Viet. F9 48
Mead, Ne., U.S. C1 120
Mead, Lake, res., U.S. G2 132
Meade, Ks., U.S. D8 128
Meaden Peak, mtn., Co., U.S. C9 132
Meadow, Ut., U.S. E4 132
Meadow Lake, Sk., Can. E9 106
Meadow Valley Wash, stm., Nv., U.S. F2 132
Meadowview, Va., U.S. H3 114
Meadville, Ms., U.S. F7 122
Meadville, Mo., U.S. E4 120
Meadville, Pa., U.S. C5 114
Meaford, On., Can. D9 112
Mealhada, Port. D2 20
Meandarra, Austl. F7 76
Meander River, Ab., Can. D7 106
Mearim, stm., Braz. B3 88
Meath, state, Ire. H6 12
Meath, hist. reg., Ire. H6 12
Meaux, Fr. F11 14
Mecaya, stm., Col. G4 86
Mecca see Makkah, Sau. Ar. E4 56
Mechanicsburg, Oh., U.S. D2 114
Mechanicsville, Ia., U.S. C6 120
Mechanicsville, Va., U.S. G8 114
Mechanicville, N.Y., U.S. B12 114
Mechelen (Malines), Bel. C13 14
Mecklenburg, hist. reg., Ger. C7 16
Mecklenburger Bucht, b., Ger. B7 16
Mecklenburg-Vorpommern, state, Ger. C8 16
Mecubúri, Moz. C6 68
Mecula, Moz. C6 68
Meda, Port. D3 20
Medak, India B4 53
Medan, Indon. B1 50
Medanosa, Punta, c., Arg. I3 90
Mede, Italy E5 22
Medeiros Neto, Braz. I5 88
Medellín, Col. D4 86
Médenine, Tun. C6 64
Mederdra, Maur. F1 64
Medford, Ok., U.S. E11 128
Medford, Or., U.S. A2 134
Medford, Wi., U.S. F8 118
Medgidia, Rom. E15 26
Mediapolis, Ia., U.S. C6 120
Mediaș, Rom. C11 26
Medicine Bow, Wy., U.S. B10 132
Medicine Bow, stm., Wy., U.S. A10 132
Medicine Bow Mountains, mts., U.S. F6 126
Medicine Creek, stm., Mo., U.S. E4 120
Medicine Hat, Ab., Can. D3 124
Medicine Lake, Mt., U.S. F9 124
Medicine Lodge, Ks., U.S. D10 128
Medicine Lodge, stm., U.S. D10 128
Medina, Braz. I5 88
Medina see Al-Madīnah, Sau. Ar. E4 56
Medina, N.Y., U.S. E11 112
Medina, Oh., U.S. C4 114
Medina, Tx., U.S. E8 130
Medina, stm., Tx., U.S. E9 130
Medinaceli, Spain C8 20
Medina del Campo, Spain C6 20
Medina de Rioseco, Spain C5 20
Medina-Sidonia, Spain H5 20
Medinīpur, India G11 54
Medio, Punta, c., Chile C2 92
Medio Creek, stm., Tx., U.S. F10 130
Mediterranean Sea A4 62
Medje, D.R.C. D5 66
Medjez el Bab, Tun. H3 24
Medkovec, Blg. F10 26
Mednogorsk, Russia D9 32
Médoc, reg., Fr. D4 18
Medora, N.D., U.S. H10 124
Médouneu, Gabon D2 66
Meductic, N.B., Can. E9 110
Medveda, Yugo. G8 26
Medvedica, stm., Russia C19 10
Medvedica, stm., Russia D6 32
Medvėgalis, hill, Lith. E5 10
Medvežegorsk, Russia E15 8
Medvežji ostrova, is., Russia B21 34
Medyn', Russia F18 10
Meekatharra, Austl. E3 74
Meeker, Co., U.S. C8 132
Meeks Bay, Ca., U.S. D5 134
Meeladeen, Som. B9 66
Meerane, Ger. F8 16
Meersburg, Ger. I5 16
Meerut, India D6 54
Mēga, Eth. G7 62
Mega, Pulau, i., Indon. E2 50
Megalópoli, Grc. F4 28
Mégantic, Lac, l., Qc., Can. E5 110
Mégara, Grc. E6 28
Megargel, Tx., U.S. H9 128
Meghālaya, state, India F13 54
Meghna, stm., Bngl. G13 54
Megísti, i., Grc. G12 28
Megra, Russia C19 8
Mehakit, Indon. E9 50
Meharry, Mount, mtn., Austl. D3 74
Mehedinți, state, Rom. E10 26
Mehekar, India H6 54
Meherrin, stm., U.S. H7 114
Mehidpur, India G5 54
Mehikoorma, Est. B10 10
Mehndāwal, India E9 54
Mehren'ga, Russia F19 8
Mehrenga, stm., Russia E19 8
Mehtarlām, Afg. C11 56
Mehun-sur-Yèvre, Fr. G11 14
Mei, stm., China I7 42
Mei, stm., China H7 42
Meia Meia, Tan. F7 66
Meia Ponte, stm., Braz. I1 88
Meichuan, China F6 42
Meiganga, Cam. C2 66
Meighen Island, i., Nu., Can. A5 141
Meigs, Ga., U.S. E1 116
Meihekou, China C6 38
Meihsien see Meizhou, China I7 42
Meikeng, China J6 42
Meiktila, Mya. B2 48
Meiners Oaks, Ca., U.S. I6 134
Meiningen, Ger. F6 16
Meishan, China E5 36
Meissen, Ger. E9 16
Meitan, China H2 42
Meizhou, China I7 42
Mejillones, Chile D2 90
Mejillones, Peninsula, pen., Chile A2 92
Mejnypil'gyno, Russia D24 34
Mékambo, Gabon D2 66
Mek'elē, Eth. E7 62
Mékhé, Sen. F1 64
Mekhtar, Pak. C2 54
Mekka see Makkah, Sau. Ar. E4 56
Meknès, Mor. C3 64
Mekong (Mékôngk) (Khong) (Lancang), stm., Asia F9 46
Mekongga, Gunung, mtn., Indon. F7 44
Mékôngk see Mekong, stm., Asia F10 46
Melado, stm., Chile H2 92
Melaka, Malay. K6 48
Melaka, state, Malay. K6 48
Melanesia, is., Oc. D7 72
Melawi, stm., Indon. D8 50
Melbourne, Austl. K5 76
Melbourne, Ar., U.S. H6 120
Melbourne, Fl., U.S. H5 116
Melbourne, Ia., U.S. J5 118
Melbourne Island, i., Nu., Can. B10 106
Melcher, Ia., U.S. C4 120
Melchor, Isla, i., Chile I2 90
Melchor Múzquiz, Mex. B8 100
Meldorf, Ger. B4 16
Meldrum Bay, On., Can. C6 112
Meldrum Creek, B.C., Can. D8 138
Mélé, Baie, b., Vanuatu k17 79d
Melekeok, Palau g8 78b
Melenki, Russia I19 8
Meleuz, Russia D9 32
Mélèzes, stm., Qc., Can. D16 106
Melfi, Chad E3 62
Melfi, Italy C9 24
Melfort, Sk., Can. B9 124
Meliane, Oued, stm., Tun. H4 24
Meliau, Indon. D7 50
Meligalás, Grc. F4 28
Melilla, Sp. N. Afr. B4 64
Melimoyu, Cerro, vol., Chile H2 90
Melincué, Arg. F7 92
Melita, Mb., Can. E12 124
Melitopol', Ukr. E5 32
Melívoia, Grc. D5 28
Mellansel, Swe. E7 8
Mellen, Wi., U.S. E8 118
Mellerud, Swe. G5 8
Mellish Reef, at., Austl. C11 74
Mellit, Sudan E5 62
Mělník, Czech Rep. F10 16
Melo, Ur. F10 92
Melolo, Indon. H12 50
Melos see Mílos, i., Grc. G7 28
Melrhir, Chott, l., Alg. C6 64
Melrose, Austl. E4 74
Melrose, Austl. I6 76
Melrose, Mn., U.S. F4 118
Melrose, N.M., U.S. G5 128
Melrose, Wi., U.S. G8 118
Melsungen, Ger. E5 16
Meltaus, Fin. C11 8
Melton Mowbray, Eng., U.K. I12 12
Melun, Fr. F11 14
Melūr, India F4 53
Melvern, Ks., U.S. F2 120
Melvern Lake, res., Ks., U.S. F2 120
Melville, Sk., Can. D11 124
Melville, La., U.S. G7 122
Melville, Cape, c., Austl. B9 74
Melville Bugt, b., Grnld. B12 141
Melville Hall Airport, Dom. i6 105c
Melville Hills, hills, Can. B7 106
Melville Island, i., Austl. B6 74
Melville Island, i., Can. A17 140
Melville Peninsula, pen., Nu., Can. B14 106
Melvin, Ky., U.S. G3 114
Melvin, Tx., U.S. C8 130
Melyana, Alg. H13 20
Mélykút, Hung. C6 26
Mêmar Co, l., China A9 54
Memba, Moz. C7 68
Membalong, Indon. E5 50
Memboro, Indon. H11 50
Memel see Klaipėda, Lith. E3 10
Memel, S. Afr. E9 70
Mēmele (Nemunėlis), stm., Eur. D7 10
Memmingen, Ger. I5 16
Mempawah, Indon. C6 50
Memphis, Fl., U.S. I3 116
Memphis, Mi., U.S. B3 114
Memphis, Tn., U.S. B8 122
Memphis, Tx., U.S. G8 128
Memphrémagog, Lac (Memphremagog, Lake), l., N.A. E4 110
Memphremagog, Lake (Memphrémagog, Lac), l., N.A. E4 110
Memramcook, N.B., Can. D12 110
Mena, Ar., U.S. C4 122
Menado see Manado, Indon. E7 44
Ménaka, Mali F5 64
Menan, Id., U.S. G15 136
Menard, Tx., U.S. D8 130
Menasha, Wi., U.S. G10 118
Menate, Indon. D8 50
Mendawai, Indon. E8 50
Mendawai, stm., Indon. E8 50
Mende, Fr. E9 18
Mendebo, mts., Eth. F7 62
Mendenhall, Ms., U.S. F9 122
Mendī, Eth. F7 62
Mendi, Pap. N. Gui. b3 79a
Mendocino, Ca., U.S. D2 134
Mendocino, Cape, c., Ca., U.S. C1 134
Mendocino Fracture Zone, unds. E24 142
Mendon, Il., U.S. D6 120
Mendota, Ca., U.S. G5 134
Mendoza, Arg. F3 92
Mendoza, state, Arg. G3 92
Mendoza, stm., Arg. F3 92
Mene de Mauroa, Ven. B6 86
Mene Grande, Ven. C6 86
Menemen, Tur. E9 28
Menen, Bel. D12 14
Menfi, Italy G6 24
Mengban, China A5 48
Mengcheng, China E7 42
Mengellang, Palau f8 78b
Menggala, Indon. F4 50
Menggudai, China B2 42
Menghai, China B5 48
Mengjiawan, China B3 42
Mengla, China B5 48
Menglian, China A4 48
Mengxian, China D5 42
Mengyin, China D7 42
Mengzi, China A6 48
Menihek Lakes, l., Nf., Can. E17 106
Menin see Menen, Bel. D12 14
Menindee, Austl. I4 76
Menjuša, Russia B13 10
Menlo Park, Ca., U.S. F3 134
Menno, S.D., U.S. D15 126
Meno, Ok., U.S. E10 128
Menominee, Mi., U.S. C2 112
Menominee, stm., U.S. C2 112
Menomonee Falls, Wi., U.S. A9 120
Menomonie, Wi., U.S. G7 118
Menongue, Ang. C2 68
Menor, Mar, b., Spain G10 20
Menorca (Minorca), i., Spain D15 20
Mentasta Lake, Ak., U.S. D11 140
Mentawai, Kepulauan, is., Indon. E1 50
Mentawai, Selat, strt., Indon. D2 50
Menton, Fr. F13 18
Mentor, Oh., U.S. C4 114
Menyapa, Gunung, mtn., Indon. C9 50
Menzel Bourguiba, Tun. G3 24
Menzel Bou Zelfa, Tun. H4 24
Menzelinsk, Russia C8 32
Menzel Temime, Tun. H5 24
Menzies, Austl. E4 74
Menzies, Mount, mtn., Ant. C10 81
Meobbaai, b., Nmb. D2 70
Meoqui, Mex. A6 100
Meota, Sk., Can. A5 124
Meppel, Neth. B15 14
Meppen, Ger. D3 16
Meqerghane, Sebkha, pl., Alg. D5 64
Mequinenza, Embalse de, res., Spain C10 20
Mequon, Wi., U.S. E2 112
Merah, Indon. C10 50
Meramec, stm., Mo., U.S. F7 120
Meran see Merano, Italy D8 22
Merangin, stm., Indon. E3 50
Merano (Meran), Italy D8 22
Meratus, Pegunungan, mts., Indon. E9 50
Merauke, Indon. G11 44
Merbau, Indon. C3 50
Merbein, Austl. J4 76
Mercaderes, Col. G3 86
Mercāra, India E2 53
Merced, Ca., U.S. F5 134
Merced, stm., Ca., U.S. F5 134
Mercedario, Cerro, mtn., Arg. E2 92
Mercedes, Arg. D8 92
Mercedes, Arg. G8 92
Mercedes, Tx., U.S. H10 130
Mercedes, Ur. F8 92
Mercer, Mo., U.S. D4 120
Mercer, Pa., U.S. C5 114
Mercersburg, Pa., U.S. E7 114
Merchants Bay, b., Nu., Can. D13 141
Mercoal, Ab., Can. C13 138
Mercury, Nv., U.S. G10 134
Mercury Islands, is., N.Z. C6 80
Mercy, Cape, c., Nu., Can. E13 141
Mercy Bay, b., N.T., Can. B16 140
Meredith, Lake, res., Tx., U.S. F7 128
Meredosia, Il., U.S. E7 120
Mereeg, Som. D9 66
Méré Lava, i., Vanuatu j17 79d
Merevari, stm., Ven. E9 86
Merëža, Russia A19 10
Mergui, Mya. F4 48
Mergui Archipelago, is., Mya. G3 48
Meribah, Austl. J3 76
Mérida, Mex. B3 102
Mérida, Spain F4 20
Mérida, Ven. C6 86
Mérida, state, Ven. C6 86
Mérida, Cordillera de, mts., Ven. C6 86
Meridian, Ga., U.S. E4 116
Meridian, Ms., U.S. E10 122
Meridian, Tx., U.S. C10 130
Meridianville, Al., U.S. C12 122
Mérignac, Fr. E5 18
Merigold, Ms., U.S. D8 122
Merikarvia, Fin. F9 8
Merimbula, Austl. K7 76
Merín, Laguna (Mirim, Lagoa), b., S.A. F11 92
Merinda, Austl. B6 76
Merino, Co., U.S. G9 126
Merinos, Ur. F9 92
Merizo, Guam j9 78c
Merkinė, Lith. F7 10
Merkys, stm., Lith. F8 10
Merlin, On., Can. F7 112
Merlin, Or., U.S. H3 136
Merna, Ne., U.S. F13 126
Meron, Har (Meron, Mount), mtn., Isr. E6 58
Meron, Mount see Meron, Har, mtn., Isr. E6 58
Merouane, Chott, l., Alg. C6 64
Merredin, Austl. F3 74
Merrick, mtn., Scot., U.K. F8 12
Merrill, Ia., U.S. B1 120
Merrill, Mi., U.S. E5 112
Merrill, Or., U.S. A4 134
Merrillan, Wi., U.S. G8 118
Merrillville, In., U.S. G2 112
Merrimack, stm., U.S. H5 110
Merriman, Ne., U.S. E11 126
Merritt, B.C., Can. F10 138
Merritt Island, Fl., U.S. H5 116
Merriwa, Austl. I8 76
Mer Rouge, La., U.S. E7 122
Merrygoen, Austl. H7 76
Merryville, La., U.S. G5 122
Mersa Matruh, Egypt A5 62
Mersea Island, i., Eng., U.K. J13 12
Merseburg, Ger. E7 16
Mersey, stm., Austl. n13 77a
Mersey, stm., N.S., Can. F12 110
Mersing, Malay. K6 48
Mērsrags, Lat. C6 10
Merta, India E5 54
Merthyr Tydfil, Wales, U.K. J9 12
Mértola, Port. G3 20
Mertz Glacier Tongue, ice, Ant. B19 81
Méru, Fr. E11 14
Meru, Kenya D7 66
Meruoca, Braz. B5 88
Merweville, S. Afr. H5 70
Merzifon, Tur. A4 56
Merzig, Ger. G2 16
Mesa, Az., U.S. J5 132
Mesabi Range, hills, Mn., U.S. D6 118
Mesagne, Italy D11 24
Mesáras, Órmos, b., Grc. I7 28
Mesa Verde National Park, p.o.i., Co., U.S. F8 132
Mescalero, N.M., U.S. H3 128
Meščerino, Russia G20 10
Meschede, Ger. E4 16
Meščura, Russia E24 8
Mesewa see Massawa, Erit. D7 62
Mesgouez, Lac, l., Qc., Can. E16 106
Mesick, Mi., U.S. D4 112
Mesilla, N.M., U.S. K10 132
Meškuičiai, Lith. D6 10
Mesolóngi, Grc. E4 28
Mesopotamia, hist. reg., Asia C5 56
Mesquite, Tx., U.S. E2 122
Messalo, stm., Moz. C6 68
Messina, Italy F9 24
Messina, S. Afr. C9 70
Messina, Gulf of see Messiniakós Kólpos, b., Grc. G5 28
Messina, Stretto di, strt., Italy F9 24
Messíni, Grc. F4 28
Messíni, hist., Grc. F4 28
Messiniakós Kólpos, b., Grc. G5 28
Messix Peak, mtn., Ut., U.S. B4 132
Messkirch, Ger. H5 16
Messojaha, stm., Russia C4 34
Mesta (Néstos), stm., Eur. B6 28
Mestghanem, Alg. B4 64
Mestre, ngh., Italy E9 22
Mesuji, stm., Indon. E4 50
Meta, state, Col. F5 86
Meta, stm., S.A. D7 86
Métabetchouan, Qc., Can. B5 110
Métabetchouane, stm., Qc., Can. B4 110
Meta Incognita Peninsula, pen., Nu., Can. C17 106
Metairie, La., U.S. H8 122
Metaline Falls, Wa., U.S. B9 136
Metamora, Il., U.S. D8 120
Metán, Arg. B5 92
Metangula, Moz. C5 68
Metapán, El Sal. E3 102
Metaponto, hist., Italy D10 24
Metapontum see Metaponto, hist., Italy D10 24
Meteor Crater, crat., Az., U.S. H6 132
Metharaw, Mya. D4 48
Methow, Wa., U.S. B7 136
Methow, stm., Wa., U.S. B6 136
Methven, N.Z. F4 80
Metica, stm., Col. E5 86
Metiskow, Ab., Can. B3 124
Metlakatla, Ak., U.S. E13 140
Metlika, Slvn. E12 22
Meto, Bayou, stm., Ar., U.S. C7 122
Metropolis, Il., U.S. G9 120
Metropolitan, Mi., U.S. C2 112
Metter, Ga., U.S. D3 116
Mettuppālaiyam, India F3 53
Mettūr, India F3 53
Metz, Fr. E15 14
Metzingen, Ger. H5 16
Meu, stm., Fr. F7 14
Meulaboh, Indon. J2 48
Meureudu, Indon. J3 48
Meurthe, stm., Fr. F15 14
Meurthe-et-Moselle, state, Fr. F15 14
Meuse, state, Fr. E14 14
Meuse (Maas), stm., Eur. D14 14
Meuselwitz, Ger. E8 16
Mexiana, Ilha, i., Braz. C8 84
Mexicali, Mex. K10 134
Mexican Hat, Ut., U.S. F7 132
México see Ciudad de México, Mex. F9 100
Mexico, Me., U.S. F6 110
Mexico, Mo., U.S. E6 120
Mexico, N.Y., U.S. E13 112
México, state, Mex. F9 100
Mexico, ctry., N.A. C4 96
Mexico, Gulf of, b., N.A. B6 96
Mexico Basin, unds. F5 144
Mexico Bay, b., N.Y., U.S. E13 112
Mexico City see Ciudad de México, Mex. F9 100
Meycauayan, Phil. C3 52
Meydān Khvolah, Afg. B2 54
Meyersdale, Pa., U.S. E6 114
Meymaneh, Afg. B9 56
Meyronne, Sk., Can. E7 124
Meyungs, Palau g7 78b
Mëža (M'oža), stm., Eur. E14 10
Mezada, Horvot (Masada), hist., Isr. G6 58
Mezcala, Mex. G9 100
Mezcalapa, stm., Mex. G12 100
Meždurečensk, Russia D15 32
Meždurečenskij, Russia C10 32
Mèze, Fr. F9 18
Mezen', Russia D21 8
Mezen', stm., Russia D21 8
Mezenskaja guba, b., Russia C20 8
Mežica, Slvn. D11 22
Mezőberény, Hung. C8 26
Mezőcsát, Hung. B7 26
Mezőkövesd, Hung. B7 26
Mezőtúr, Hung. B7 26
Mezquital, stm., Mex. D6 100
Mfangano Island, i., Kenya E6 66
Mgači, Russia F17 34
M'Goun, Irhil, mtn., Mor. C3 64
M'hai, B'nom, mtn., Viet. G8 48
Mhasvād, India C2 53
Mhow, India G5 54
Mi, stm., China H5 42
Mi, stm., China C8 42
Mia, Oued, stm., Alg. D5 64
Miahuatlán de Porfirio Díaz, Mex. G10 100
Miajadas, Spain E4 20
Miaméré, C.A.R. C4 66
Miami, Mb., Can. E15 124
Miami, Az., U.S. J6 132
Miami, Fl., U.S. K5 116
Miami, Ok., U.S. H3 120
Miami, Tx., U.S. F8 128
Miami Beach, Fl., U.S. K5 116
Miami Canal, can., Fl., U.S. J5 116
Miamisburg, Oh., U.S. E1 114
Miami Springs, Fl., U.S. K5 116
Miān Channūn, Pak. C4 54
Mianchi, China D4 42
Miandrivazo, Madag. D8 68
Mianduhe, China B9 36
Mīāneh, Iran B6 56
Miang, Phu, mtn., Thai. D5 48
Mianning, China F5 36
Miānwāli, Pak. B3 54

Name Map Ref. Page

Mianxian, China E2 42
Mianyang, China F1 42
Mianzhu, China E5 36
Miaodao Qundao, is., China B9 42
Miaoli, Tai. I9 42
Miao Ling, mts., China H2 42
Miass, Russia C10 32
Miass, stm., Russia C10 32
Miastko, Pol. B12 16
Micang Shan, mts., China E2 42
Michalovce, Slov. H17 16
Michaud, Point, c., N.S., Can. E16 110
Micheal Peak, mtn., B.C., Can. C4 138
Michel, B.C., Can. G16 138
Miches, Dom. Rep. C13 102
Michigan, N.D., U.S. F15 124
Michigan, state, U.S. C10 108
Michigan, stm., Co., U.S. G6 126
Michigan, Lake, l., U.S. E2 112
Michigan City, In., U.S. G3 112
Michipicoten Island, i., On., Can. F13 106
Michoacán, state, Mex. F8 100
Micoud, St. Luc. m7 105c
Micronesia, is., Oc. B6 72
Micronesia, Federated States of, ctry., Oc. C6 72
Mičurinsk, Russia D6 32
Midai, Pulau, i., Indon. B5 50
Midale, Sk., Can. E10 124
Mid-Atlantic Ridge, unds. F9 144
Middelburg, Neth. C12 14
Middelburg, S. Afr. G7 70
Middelburg, S. Afr. D9 70
Middle, stm., B.C., Can. B5 138
Middle, stm., Ia., U.S. C3 120
Middle, stm., Mn., U.S. C2 118
Middle Alkali Lake, l., Ca., U.S. B5 134
Middle America Trench, unds. H29 142
Middle Andaman, i., India F7 46
Middleboro, Ma., U.S. C15 114
Middlebourne, W.V., U.S. E5 114
Middleburg, N.Y., U.S. B11 114
Middleburg, Pa., U.S. D8 114
Middlebury, Vt., U.S. F3 110
Middle Caicos, i., T./C. Is. B12 102
Middle Fabius, stm., Mo., U.S. D5 120
Middlefield, Oh., U.S. C4 114
Middlegate, Norf. I. y25 78i
Middle Loup, stm., Ne., U.S. F14 126
Middlemount, Austl. D7 76
Middle Musquodoboit, N.S., Can. E13 110
Middleport, Oh., U.S. E3 114
Middle Raccoon, stm., Ia., U.S. J4 118
Middlesboro, Ky., U.S. H2 114
Middlesbrough, Eng., U.K. G11 12
Middlesex, Belize D3 102
Middle Stewiacke, N.S., Can. E13 110
Middleton, N.S., Can. F11 110
Middleton, Mi., U.S. E5 112
Middleton, Wi., U.S. A8 120
Middleton Island, i., Ak., U.S. E10 140
Middleton Reef, at., Austl. E11 74
Middletown, Ca., U.S. E3 134
Middletown, Ct., U.S. C13 114
Middletown, Il., U.S. K9 118
Middletown, In., U.S. H4 112
Middletown, Ky., U.S. F12 120
Middletown, Md., U.S. E8 114
Middletown, N.Y., U.S. C11 114
Middletown, Oh., U.S. E1 114
Middletown, Pa., U.S. D9 114
Middletown, R.I., U.S. C14 114
Middleville, Mi., U.S. F4 112
Midgic, N.B., Can. E12 110
Midi, Canal du, can., Fr. F9 18
Midi de Bigorre, Pic du, mtn., Fr. G5 18
Mid-Indian Basin, unds. J10 142
Mid-Indian Ridge, unds. L10 142
Midland, On., Can. D9 112
Midland, Ca., U.S. J2 132
Midland, Mi., U.S. E5 112
Midland, S.D., U.S. C11 126
Midland, Tx., U.S. C5 130
Midlands, state, Zimb. B10 70
Midleton, Ire. J4 12
Midlothian, Tx., U.S. B11 130
Midnapore, Ab., Can. F16 138
Midongy Atsimo, Madag. E8 68
Mid-Pacific Mountains, unds. G19 142
Midsayap, Phil. G5 52
Midville, Ga., U.S. D3 116
Midway, B.C., Can. G12 138
Midway, Al., U.S. E13 122
Midway, Ky., U.S. F13 120
Midway, Tx., U.S. F3 122
Midway Islands, dep., Oc. G22 30
Midway Park, N.C., U.S. B8 116
Midwest City, Ok., U.S. F11 128
Midyan, reg., Sau. Ar. J6 58
Midžur (Midžor), mtn., Eur. F9 26
Mie, Japan G4 40
Mie, state, Japan E9 40
Międzybórz, Pol. E13 16
Międzylesie, Pol. F12 16
Międzyrzec Podlaski, Pol. D18 16
Międzyrzecz, Pol. D11 16
Mielan, Fr. F6 18
Mielec, Pol. F17 16
Mier, Mex. B9 100
Miercurea-Ciuc, Rom. C12 26
Mieres, Spain A5 20
Mieroszów, Pol. F12 16
Mier y Noriega, Mex. D8 100
Miesbach, Ger. I7 16
Mī'ēso, Eth. F8 62
Mieszkowice, Pol. D10 16
Mifflinburg, Pa., U.S. H12 112
Miguel Alemán, Presa, res., Mex. F10 100
Miguel Alves, Braz. C4 88
Miguel Auza, Mex. C7 100
Miguel Calmon, Braz. F5 88
Miguel Hidalgo, Presa, res., Mex. B4 100
Miguelópolis, Braz. K1 88
Miguel Riglos, Arg. H6 92
Mihăești, Rom. D12 26
Mihajlovka, Russia D6 32
Mihajlovka, Russia D14 32
Mihajlovka, Russia C10 38
Mihajlovskij, Russia F20 8
Mihalgazi, Tur. C13 28
Mihanavičy, Bela. G10 10
Mihara, Japan E5 40
Mihara-yama, vol., Japan E12 40
Mihninskaja, Russia F21 8
Mikame, Japan F5 40
Mikasa, Japan C14 38
Mikaševičy, Bela. H10 10
Mikhrot Timna' (King Solomon's Mines), hist., Isr. I5 58
Mikindani, Tan. G8 66
Mikkeli (Sankt Michel), Fin. F12 8
Mikkeli, state, Fin. F12 8
Mikołajki, Pol. C17 16
Mikołów, Pol. F14 16
Mikrá Préspa, Límni, l., Eur. D15 24
Mikšino, Russia C18 10
Mikulino, Russia E18 10
Mikumi, Tan. F7 66
Mikun', Russia E23 8
Mikuni, Japan C9 40
Miladummadulu Atoll, at., Mald. h12 46a
Milagro, Arg. E5 92
Milagro, Ec. I2 86
Milagros, Phil. D4 52
Milan see Milano, Italy E6 22
Milan, Ga., U.S. D2 116
Milan, In., U.S. E12 120
Milan, Mi., U.S. B2 114
Milan, Mn., U.S. F3 118
Milan, Mo., U.S. D4 120
Milan, N.M., U.S. H8 132
Milang, Austl. J2 76
Milange, Moz. D6 68
Milano (Milan), Italy E6 22
Milâs, Tur. F10 28
Milavidy, Bela. H8 10
Milazzo, Italy F9 24
Milazzo, Golfo di, b., Italy F9 24
Milbank, S.D., U.S. F2 118
Milburn, Ok., U.S. C2 122
Milden, Sk., Can. C6 124
Mildmay, On., Can. D8 112
Mildura, Austl. J4 76
Mile, China G5 36
Miles, Austl. F8 76
Miles, Tx., U.S. C7 130
Miles City, Mt., U.S. A7 126
Milestone, Sk., Can. E9 124
Milet, hist., Tur. F10 28
Milford, De., U.S. F10 114
Milford, Ia., U.S. H3 118
Milford, Me., U.S. F8 110
Milford, Ma., U.S. B14 114
Milford, Mi., U.S. B2 114
Milford, N.H., U.S. B14 114
Milford, Pa., U.S. C11 114
Milford, Ut., U.S. E4 132
Milford Center, Oh., U.S. D2 114
Milford Haven, Wales, U.K. J7 12
Milford Lake, res., Ks., U.S. B11 128
Milford Sound, strt., N.Z. G2 80
Mili, at., Marsh. Is. C8 72
Milian, stm., Malay. A10 50
Milicz, Pol. E13 16
Miljatino, Russia F17 10
Milk, stm., N.A. B6 108
Milk, North Fork (North Milk), stm., N.A. B13 136
Mil'kovo, Russia F20 34
Milk River, Ab., Can. G18 138
Millard, Ne., U.S. C1 120
Millau, Fr. E9 18
Millboro, Va., U.S. F6 114
Millbrook, N.Y., U.S. C12 114
Mill City, Or., U.S. F4 136
Millcreek, Pa., U.S. B5 114
Millcreek, Ut., U.S. C5 132
Mill Creek, W.V., U.S. F5 114
Milledgeville, Ga., U.S. C2 116
Milledgeville, Il., U.S. C8 120
Mille Lacs, Lac des, l., On., Can. C8 118
Mille Lacs Lake, l., Mn., U.S. E5 118
Millen, Ga., U.S. D4 116
Miller, Mo., U.S. G4 120
Miller, S.D., U.S. C14 126
Miller Mountain, mtn., Nv., U.S. E7 134
Millerovo, Russia E6 32
Millersburg, Ky., U.S. F1 114
Millersburg, Mi., U.S. C5 112
Millersburg, Oh., U.S. D4 114
Millersport, Oh., U.S. I7 112
Millerton, N.Y., U.S. C12 114
Millet, Ab., Can. C17 138
Millevaches, Plateau de, plat., Fr. D7 18
Millicent, Austl. K3 76
Milligan, Fl., U.S. G12 122
Milligan, Ne., U.S. G15 126
Millington, Mi., U.S. E6 112
Millington, Tn., U.S. B9 122
Millinocket, Me., U.S. E8 110
Mill Island, i., Ant. B15 81
Mill Island, i., Nu., Can. C15 106
Millry, Al., U.S. F10 122
Mills, Wy., U.S. E6 126
Mills Creek, stm., Austl. D4 76
Mills Lake, l., N.T., Can. C7 106
Millstream, Austl. D3 74
Milltown, Mt., U.S. D13 136
Milltown, Wi., U.S. F6 118
Milltown Malbay, Ire. I3 12
Mill Valley, Ca., U.S. F3 134
Millville, N.J., U.S. E10 114
Millwood, Va., U.S. E7 114
Millwood Lake, res., Ar., U.S. D4 122
Milne Land, i., Grnld. C20 141
Milnor, N.D., U.S. A15 126
Milo, Ab., Can. F18 138
Mílos, i., Grc. G7 28
Miłosław, Pol. D13 16
Milparinka, Austl. G3 76
Milroy, In., U.S. E12 120
Milroy, Pa., U.S. D8 114
Miltenberg, Ger. G5 16
Milton, On., Can. E10 112
Milton, N.Z. H4 80
Milton, Fl., U.S. G11 122
Milton, Ia., U.S. D5 120
Milton, Pa., U.S. G13 112
Milton, Wi., U.S. B9 120
Milton-Freewater, Or., U.S. E8 136
Milton Keynes, Eng., U.K. I12 12
Miltonvale, Ks., U.S. B11 128
Miltou, Chad E3 62
Miluo, stm., China G5 42
Milwaukee, Wi., U.S. E2 112
Milwaukee, stm., Wi., U.S. H11 118
Milwaukie, Or., U.S. E4 136
Mimbres, stm., N.M., U.S. K9 132
Mimizan-les-Bains, Fr. E4 18
Mimoň, Czech Rep. F10 16
Mimoso do Sul, Braz. K5 88
Mims, Fl., U.S. H5 116
Min, stm., China F5 36
Min, stm., China I8 42
Mina, Mex. H7 130
Mina, Nv., U.S. E7 134
Mīnā' al-Aḥmadī, Kuw. D6 56
Mīnāb, Iran D8 56
Minahasa, pen., Indon. E7 44
Minakuchi, Japan E9 40
Minamata, Japan G3 40
Minami-Alps-kokuritsu-kōen, p.o.i., Japan D11 40
Minami-Tori-shima, i., Japan G19 30
Minas, Cuba B9 102
Minas, Indon. C2 50
Minas, Ur. G10 92
Minas Basin, b., N.S., Can. E12 110
Minas de Barroterán, Mex. B8 100
Minas de Corrales, Ur. E10 92
Minas de Matahambre, Cuba A5 102
Minas Gerais, state, Braz. C8 90
Minas Novas, Braz. I4 88
Minatare, Ne., U.S. F9 126
Minatitlán, Mex. F11 100
Minbu, Mya. B2 48
Minbya, Mya. B1 48
Minbyin, Mya. C1 48
Mincio, stm., Italy E7 22
Minco, Ok., U.S. F10 128
Minčol, mtn., Slov. G17 16
Mindanao, i., Phil. G5 52
Mindanao, stm., Phil. G5 52
Mindelheim, Ger. H6 16
Mindelo, C.V. k10 65a
Mindemoya, On., Can. C7 112
Minden, On., Can. D11 112
Minden, Ger. D4 16
Minden, La., U.S. E5 122
Minden, Ne., U.S. G14 126
Minden, Nv., U.S. E6 134
Minden City, Mi., U.S. E7 112
Mindoro, i., Phil. D3 52
Mindoro Strait, strt., Phil. D3 52
Mine, Japan E4 40
Mine Centre, On., Can. C6 118
Minehead, Eng., U.K. J9 12
Mineiros, Braz. G7 84
Mineola, Tx., U.S. E3 122
Mineral, Wa., U.S. D4 136
Mineral Point, Wi., U.S. B7 120
Mineral Springs, Ar., U.S. D5 122
Mineral Wells, Tx., U.S. B9 130
Minersville, Pa., U.S. H13 112
Minerva, Oh., U.S. D4 114
Minervino Murge, Italy C9 24
Mineville, N.Y., U.S. F3 110
Minfeng, China A5 46
Minga, D.R.C. G5 66
Mingäçevir, Azer. A6 56
Mingãora, Pak. C11 56
Mingary, Austl. I3 76
Mingene, Austl. E3 74
Mingin, Mya. A2 48
Minglanilla, Spain E9 20
Mingo Junction, Oh., U.S. D5 114
Mingo Lake, l., Nu., Can. C16 106
Mingshui, China B10 36
Mingulay, i., Scot., U.K. E5 12
Mingyuegou, China C8 38
Minhang, China F9 42
Minh Hai, Viet. H7 48
Minhla, Mya. B2 48
Minhla, Mya. C2 48
Minho, hist. reg., Port. C2 20
Minho (Miño), stm., Eur. B2 20
Minićevo, Yugo. F9 26
Minicoy Island, i., India G3 46
Miningwal, Lake, l., Austl. E4 74
Minija, stm., Lith. E4 10
Minilya, Austl. D2 74
Minilya, stm., Austl. D2 74
Miniota, Mb., Can. D12 124
Minitonas, Mb., Can. B12 124
Minle, China D5 36
Minna, Nig. H6 64
Minneapolis, Ks., U.S. B11 128
Minneapolis, Mn., U.S. G5 118
Minnedosa, Mb., Can. D13 124
Minneola, Ks., U.S. D8 128
Minneota, Mn., U.S. G2 118
Minnesota, state, U.S. E4 118
Minnesota, stm., Mn., U.S. G5 118
Minnesota Lake, Mn., U.S. H5 118
Minnewanka, Lake, res., Ab., Can. E15 138
Minnitaki Lake, l., On., Can. B6 118
Mino, Japan D9 40
Miño (Minho), stm., Eur. B2 20
Minocqua, Wi., U.S. F9 118
Minong, Wi., U.S. E7 118
Minonk, Il., U.S. D8 120
Minorca see Menorca, i., Spain D15 20
Minot, N.D., U.S. F12 124
Minqing, China H8 42
Minquan, China D6 42
Minquiers, Plateau des, is., Jersey E6 14
Min Shan, mts., China E5 36
Minsk, Bela. G10 10
Minsk, state, Bela. G10 10
Minskae uzvyšša, plat., Bela. G10 10
Mińsk Mazowiecki, Pol. D17 16
Minta, Cam. D2 66
Minto, Mb., Can. E13 124
Minto, Yk., Can. C3 106
Minto, N.D., U.S. C1 118
Minto, Lac, l., Qc., Can. D16 106
Minto, Mount, mtn., Ant. C22 81
Minto Inlet, b., N.T., Can. A7 106
Minton, Sk., Can. E9 124
Minturn, Co., U.S. D10 132
Minûf, Egypt H1 58
Minusinsk, Russia D16 32
Minvoul, Gabon D2 66
Minxian, China E5 36
Minya see El-Minya, Egypt J1 58
Minya el-Qamh, Egypt H2 58
Mio, Mi., U.S. D5 112
Miquan, China F15 32
Mir, Bela. G9 10
Mira, stm., Col. G2 86
Mīrābād, Afg. C9 56
Mirabella, Gulf of see Mirampéllou, Kólpos, b., Grc. H8 28
Miracema do Tocantins, Braz. E1 88
Mirador, Braz. D3 88
Miradouro, Braz. K4 88
Miraflores, Col. E5 86
Miraflores, Col. G5 86
Miraj, India C2 53
Miramar, Arg. I9 92
Miramar, Moz. C12 70
Miramas, Fr. F10 18
Miramichi Bay, b., N.B., Can. C11 110
Mirampéllou, Kólpos, b., Grc. H8 28
Mīrān, Pak. C3 54
Miranda, Braz. D5 90
Miranda, Col. F3 86
Miranda, state, Ven. B8 86
Miranda, stm., Braz. D5 90
Miranda de Ebro, Spain B7 20
Mirande, Fr. F6 18
Mirando City, Tx., U.S. G8 130
Mirandola, Italy F8 22
Mira Táglio, Italy E4 24
Miravalles, Volcán, vol., C.R. G5 102
Miravete, Puerto de, p., Spain E5 20
Mirbāṭ, Oman F7 56
Mirecourt, Fr. F14 14
Miri, Malay. A9 50
Miria, Niger G6 64
Miriam Vale, Austl. E8 76
Mirim, Lagoa (Merín, Laguna), b., S.A. F11 92
Mirinay, stm., Arg. D9 92
Miritiparaná, stm., Col. H6 86
Miriyama, Pap. N. Gui. a3 79a
Mirnoe Ozero, Russia C13 32
Mirny, sci., Ant. B14 81
Mirnyj, Russia D11 34
Mirnyy, sci., Ant. B14 81
Miroslav, Czech Rep. H12 16
Mirow, Ger. C8 16
Mīrpur, Bngl. G13 54
Mīrpur, Pak. B4 54
Mīrpur Batoro, Pak. F2 54
Mīrpur Khās, Pak. F2 54
Mirror, Ab., Can. D17 138
Mirtóon Pélagos, Grc. G6 28
Miryang, Kor., S. D1 40
Mirzāpur, India F9 54
Misantla, Mex. F10 100
Misawa, Japan D14 38
Miscou Centre, N.B., Can. C12 110
Miscou Island, i., N.B., Can. C12 110
Miscou Point, c., N.B., Can. B12 110
Mishan, China B9 38
Mishawaka, In., U.S. G3 112
Mishicot, Wi., U.S. D2 112
Misima Island, i., Pap. N. Gui. B10 74
Misiones, state, Arg. C10 92
Misiones, state, Para. C9 92
Misión Santa Rosa, Para. D4 90
Misión San Vicente, Mex. F4 98
Miskitos, Cayos, is., Nic. E6 102
Miskolc, Hung. A7 26
Mišněvo, Russia G19 10
Misool, Pulau, i., Indon. F9 44
Misrātah, Libya A3 62
Misr el-Bahrî (Lower Egypt), hist. reg., Egypt G2 58
Misrikh, India E8 54
Missinaibi, stm., On., Can. E14 106
Missinaibi Lake, l., On., Can. F14 106
Mission, B.C., Can. G8 138
Mission, S.D., U.S. D12 126
Mission, Tx., U.S. H9 130
Mission Mountain, hill, Ok., U.S. H3 120
Mission Viejo, Ca., U.S. J8 134
Missisagi, stm., On., Can. B6 112
Mississauga, On., Can. E10 112
Mississinewa, stm., U.S. H4 112
Mississippi, state, U.S. D9 122
Mississippi, stm., On., Can. C13 112
Mississippi, stm., U.S. E9 108
Mississippi Lake, l., On., Can. C13 112
Mississippi River Delta, La., U.S. H9 122
Mississippi Sound, strt., U.S. G10 122
Mississippi State, Ms., U.S. D10 122
Missoula, Mt., U.S. D12 136
Missouri, state, U.S. F5 120
Missouri, stm., U.S. D9 108
Missouri City, Tx., U.S. H3 122
Mistake Creek, stm., Austl. D6 76
Mistassibi, stm., Qc., Can. A4 110
Mistassini, Qc., Can. E16 106
Mistassini, Qc., Can. B4 110
Mistassini, stm., Qc., Can. B4 110
Mistassini, Lac, l., Qc., Can. E16 106
Mistatim, Sk., Can. B10 124
Mistelbach an der Zaya, Aus. B13 22
Misterbianco, Italy G9 24
Misti, Volcán, vol., Peru G3 84
Misumi, Japan E4 40
Mišutino, Russia A19 10
Mita, Punta de, c., Mex. E6 100
Mitchell, Austl. F6 76
Mitchell, On., Can. E8 112
Mitchell, In., U.S. F11 120
Mitchell, Or., U.S. F6 136
Mitchell, S.D., U.S. D14 126
Mitchell, stm., Austl. C8 74
Mitchell, stm., Austl. K6 76
Mitchell, Mount, mtn., N.C., U.S. I3 114
Mitchinamecus, stm., Qc., Can. C2 110
Mitchinamecus, Réservoir, res., Qc., Can. C1 110
Mīt Ghamr, Egypt H2 58
Mithapur, India G2 54
Mithi, Pak. F2 54
Mitidja, Plaine de la, pl., Alg. H14 20
Mitiškovo, Russia F16 10
Mitla, hist., Mex. G10 100
Mito, Japan C13 40
Mitsio, Nosy, i., Madag. C8 68
Mitsukaidō, Japan C13 40
Mitsuke, Japan B11 40
Mittellandkanal, can., Ger. D5 16
Mittenwald, Ger. I7 16
Mittersill, Aus. C9 22
Mittweida, Ger. F8 16
Mitú, Col. G6 86
Mitumba, Monts, mts., D.R.C. F5 66
Mitwaba, D.R.C. F5 66
Mitzic, Gabon D2 66
Miura, Japan D12 40
Miura-hantō, pen., Japan D12 40
Mixian, China D5 42
Miyagi, state, Japan A13 40
Miyake-jima, i., Japan E12 40
Miyako, Japan E14 38
Miyako-jima, i., Japan G10 36
Miyakonojō, Japan H4 40
Miyama, Japan E9 40
Miyanojō, Japan H3 40
Miyazaki, Japan H4 40
Miyazaki, state, Japan G4 40
Miyazu, Japan D8 40
Miyoshi, Japan E5 40
Miyun, China A7 42
Miyun Shuiku, res., China A7 42
Mīzan Teferī, Eth. F7 62
Mizdah, Libya A2 62
Mize, Ms., U.S. F9 122
Mizen Head, c., Ire. I6 12
Mizen Head, c., Ire. J3 12
Mizhhir'ia, Ukr. A10 26
Mizhi, China C4 42
Mizil, Rom. E13 26
Mizoram, state, India G14 54
Mizpah Creek, stm., Mt., U.S. A7 126
Mizque, Bol. C3 90
Mizukaidō see Mitsukaidō, Japan C13 40
Mizusawa, Japan E14 38
Mjadzel, Bela. F9 10
Mjakit, Russia D19 34
Mjaksa, Russia B21 10
Mjölby, Swe. G6 8
Mjøsa, l., Nor. F4 8
Mkalama, Tan. E6 66
Mkhondvo, stm., Afr. E10 70
Mkokotoni, Tan. F7 66
Mkomazi, stm., S. Afr. G10 70
Mkulwe, Tan. F6 66
Mkuze, S. Afr. E10 70
Mkuze, stm., S. Afr. E11 70
Mkuze Game Reserve, S. Afr. E11 70
Mladá Boleslav, Czech Rep. F11 16
Mladenovac, Yugo. E7 26
Mława, Pol. C16 16
Mljet, Otok, i., Cro. H14 22
Mljet Nacionalni Park, p.o.i., Cro. H14 22
Mmabatho, S. Afr. D7 70
Mmadinare, Bots. B8 70
Moa, stm., Afr. H2 64
Moab, Ut., U.S. E7 132
Moala, i., Fiji q18 79e
Moama, Austl. K5 76
Moamba, Moz. D11 70
Moanda, Gabon E2 66
Moar Lake, l., Can. C18 124
Moate, Ire. H5 12
Moba, D.R.C. F5 66
Mobara, Japan D13 40
Mobaye, C.A.R. D4 66
Mobeetie, Tx., U.S. F8 128
Moberly, Mo., U.S. E5 120
Mobile, Al., U.S. G10 122
Mobile, Az., U.S. J4 132
Mobile, stm., Al., U.S. G11 122
Mobile Bay, b., Al., U.S. G10 122
Mobridge, S.D., U.S. B12 126
Moca, Dom. Rep. C12 102
Mocajuba, Braz. B1 88
Mo Cay, Viet. G8 48
Mocha see Al-Mukhā, Yemen G5 56
Mochudi, Bots. D8 70
Mocksville, N.C., U.S. I5 114
Moclips, Wa., U.S. C2 136
Môco, Morro de, mtn., Ang. C2 68
Mocoa, Col. G3 86
Mococa, Braz. K2 88
Mocodoene, Moz. C12 70
Mocoretá, Arg. E8 92
Moctezuma, Mex. G8 98
Moctezuma, stm., Mex. G8 98
Moctezuma, stm., Mex. E9 100
Mocuba, Moz. D6 68
Modane, Fr. D12 18
Modāsa, India G4 54
Modder, stm., S. Afr. F7 70
Módena, Italy F7 22
Modeste, Mount, mtn., B.C., Can. H6 138
Modesto, Ca., U.S. F4 134
Modica, Italy H8 24
Mödling, Aus. B13 22
Modowi, Indon. F9 44
Modra, Slov. H13 16
Moe, Austl. L6 76
Moeda, Braz. K3 88
Moei (Thaungyin), stm., Asia D3 48
Moema, Braz. J3 88
Moengo, Sur. B7 84
Moen-jo-Daro, hist., Pak. D10 56
Moenkopi, Az., U.S. G5 132
Moenkopi Wash, stm., Az., U.S. G6 132
Moeris, Lake see Qârûn, Birket, l., Egypt I1 58
Moeskroen see Mouscron, Bel. D12 14
Moffat, Scot., U.K. F9 12
Moga, India C5 54
Mogadiscio see Muqdisho, Som. D9 66
Mogadishu see Muqdisho, Som. D9 66
Mogalakwena, stm., S. Afr. C9 70
Mogami, stm., Japan A13 40
Mogaung, Mya. C8 46
Mogdy, Russia F15 34
Mogilno, Pol. D13 16
Mogincual, Moz. D7 68
Mogoča, Russia F12 34
Mogočin, Russia C14 32
Mogogh, Sudan F6 62
Mogok, Mya. A3 48
Mogollon Rim, clf, Az., U.S. I6 132
Mogor, Afg. B1 54
Mogotes, Col. D5 86
Mogotón, mtn., N.A. F4 102
Moguer, Spain G4 20
Mogzon, Russia F11 34
Mohács, Hung. C5 26
Mohall, N.D., U.S. F12 124
Mohammed, Râs, c., Egypt K5 58
Mohammedia, Mor. C3 64
Mohania, India F9 54
Mohawk, Mi., U.S. D10 118
Mohawk, stm., N.Y., U.S. B11 114
Mohe, China F13 34
Mohéli see Mwali, i., Com. C7 68
Mohnyin, Mya. D8 46
Mohokare (Caledon), stm., Afr. F8 70
Mohyliv-Podil's'kyi, Ukr. A14 26
Moi, Nor. G2 8
Moinești, Rom. C13 26
Moira, stm., On., Can. D12 112
Moiraba, Braz. B1 88
Mo i Rana, Nor. C5 8
Moiseevka, Russia C13 32
Moisés Ville, Arg. E7 92
Moisie, Qc., Can. E17 106
Moisie, stm., Qc., Can. E17 106
Moitaco, Ven. C9 86
Mojácar, Spain G9 20
Mojave, Ca., U.S. H7 134
Mojave, stm., Ca., U.S. H9 134
Mojave Desert, des., Ca., U.S. D4 98
Mojero, stm., Russia C9 34
Mojiguaçu, stm., Braz. K2 88
Mojikit Lake, res., On., Can. A10 118
Moji-Mirim, Braz. L2 88
Moju, Eth. F7 62
Moju, Braz. A1 88
Moju, stm., Braz. D8 84
Mōka, Japan C12 40
Mokāma, India F10 54
Mokapu Peninsula, pen., Hi., U.S. B4 78a
Mokau, stm., N.Z. D6 80
Mokelumne, stm., Ca., U.S. E5 134
Moknine, Tun. B7 64
Mokochu, Khao, mtn., Thai. E4 48
Mokokchūng, India C7 46
Mokolo, Cam. B2 66
Mokolo, stm., S. Afr. C8 70
Mokpalin, Mya. D3 48
Mokp'o, Kor., S. G7 38
Mokša, stm., Russia D6 32
Mokwa, Nig. H5 64
Mol, Bel. C14 14
Mola di Bari, Italy C11 24
Molat, Otok, i., Cro. F11 22
Moldary, Kaz. D13 32
Moldau see Vltava, stm., Czech Rep. F10 16
Moldavia, hist. reg., Rom. C13 26
Molde, Nor. E2 8
Moldova, ctry., Eur. B15 26
Moldova, stm., Rom. C13 26
Moldoveanu, Vârful, mtn., Rom. D11 26
Môle, Cap du, c., Haiti C11 102
Molega Creek, Austl. n13 77a
Molega Lake, l., N.S., Can. F12 110
Molène, Île de, i., Fr. F3 14
Molepolole, Bots. D7 70
Molėtai, Lith. E8 10
Molfetta, Italy C10 24
Molina, Chile G2 92
Molina de Aragón, Spain D9 20
Molina de Segura, Spain F9 20
Moline, Il., U.S. C7 120
Moline, Ks., U.S. D12 128
Molino, Fl., U.S. G11 122
Molino de Valdo de Piedras, Mex. E3 130
Molinos, Arg. B4 92
Molise, state, Italy C8 24
Mollendo, Peru G3 84
Mölln, Ger. C6 16
Mölndal, Swe. H4 8
Molodežnaja, sci., Ant. B9 81
Molodogvardejskoe, Kaz. D11 32
Mologa, stm., Russia B19 10
Molokai, i., Hi., U.S. B5 78a
Molokai Fracture Zone, unds. G24 142
Molokovo, Russia B19 10
Molong, Austl. I7 76
Molopo, stm., Afr. E5 70
Moloundou, Cam. D3 66
Molson Lake, l., Mb., Can. E11 106
Molu, Pulau, i., Indon. G9 44
Moluccas see Maluku, is., Indon. F8 44
Molucca Sea see Maluku, Laut, Indon. F8 44
Molvotitsy, Russia C15 10
Moma, Moz. D6 68
Moma, stm., Russia C17 34
Mombaça, Braz. C6 88
Mombasa, Kenya E7 66
Mombetsu, Japan B15 38
Momčilgrad, Blg. H12 26
Momi, Fiji p18 79e
Momotombo, Volcán, vol., Nic. F4 102
Mompono, D.R.C. D4 66
Mompós, Col. C4 86
Momskij hrebet, mts., Russia C18 34
Mon, state, Mya. E3 48
Møn, i., Den. I5 8
Mona, Ut., U.S. D5 132
Mona, Isla de, i., P.R. h14 96a
Mona, Punta, c., C.R. H6 102
Monaca, Pa., U.S. D5 114
Monach Islands, is., Scot., U.K. D5 12
Monaco, Mon. G4 22
Monaco, ctry., Eur. F13 18
Monadnock Mountain, mtn., N.H., U.S. B13 114
Monagas, state, Ven. C10 86
Monaghan, Ire. G6 12
Monaghan, state, Ire. G6 12
Monahans, Tx., U.S. C5 130
Monakino, Russia C10 38
Mona Passage, strt., N.A. C13 102
Monapo, Moz. C7 68
Monarch, S.C., U.S. B4 116
Monarch Mountain, mtn., B.C., Can. E5 138
Monarch Pass, p., Co., U.S. E10 132
Monashee Mountains, mts., B.C., Can. F12 138
Monastir, Tun. I4 24
Moncalieri, Italy F4 22
Moncalvo, Italy E5 22
Monção, Braz. B3 88
Mončegorsk, Russia B15 8
Mönchengladbach, Ger. E2 16
Monchique, Port. G2 20
Moncks Corner, S.C., U.S. C5 116
Monclova, Mex. B8 100
Moncton, N.B., Can. D12 110
Monday, stm., Para. B10 92
Mondego, stm., Port. D3 20
Mondjamboli, D.R.C. D4 66
Mondoubleau, Fr. F9 14
Mondovi, Wi., U.S. G7 118
Mondragone, Italy C7 24
Monemvasía, Grc. G6 28
Monessen, Pa., U.S. D5 114
Monesterio, Spain F4 20
Monett, Mo., U.S. H4 120
Monette, Ar., U.S. I7 120
Monfalcone, Italy E10 22
Monferrato, hist. reg., Italy F5 22
Monforte de Lemos, Spain B3 20
Monga, D.R.C. D4 66
Mongaguá, Braz. B14 92
Mongalla, Sudan F6 62
Mongers Lake, l., Austl. E3 74
Monggon Qulu, China B8 36
Möng Hai, Mya. B4 48
Möng Hsat, Mya. B4 48
Mongibello see Etna, Monte, vol., Italy G8 24
Möng Küng, Mya. B3 48
Möng Ma, Mya. B4 48
Möng Nai, Mya. B3 48
Mongo, Chad E3 62
Mongol Altayn nuruu, mts., Asia E16 32
Mongolia, ctry., Asia E14 30
Mongonu, Nig. G7 64
Möng Pai, Mya. C3 48
Möng Pawn, Mya. B3 48
Mongu, Zam. D3 68
Möng Yai, Mya. A4 48
Monico, Wi., U.S. F9 118
Monida Pass, p., U.S. F14 136
Monino, Russia E21 10
Moniquirá, Col. E5 86
Mõniste, Est. H12 8
Monitor Valley, val., Nv., U.S. E9 134
Mońki, Pol. C18 16
Monkira, Austl. E3 76
Monmouth, Wales, U.K. J10 12
Monmouth, Or., U.S. F3 136
Monmouth Mountain, mtn., B.C., Can. E7 138
Mono, stm., Afr. H5 64
Mono, Caño, stm., Col. E7 86
Mono Island, i., Sol. Is. d6 79b
Mono Lake, l., Ca., U.S. E7 134
Monon, In., U.S. H3 112
Monona, Ia., U.S. H7 118
Monona, Wi., U.S. A8 120
Monongahela, stm., U.S. E6 114
Monopoli, Italy D11 24
Monor, Hung. B6 26
Monreal del Campo, Spain D9 20
Monreale, Italy F7 24
Monroe, La., U.S. E6 122
Monroe, Mi., U.S. C2 114
Monroe, N.Y., U.S. C11 114
Monroe, N.C., U.S. B5 116
Monroe, Or., U.S. F3 136
Monroe, Ut., U.S. E4 132
Monroe, Va., U.S. G6 114
Monroe, Wa., U.S. C4 136
Monroe, Wi., U.S. B8 120
Monroe City, In., U.S. F10 120
Monroe City, Mo., U.S. E6 120
Monroe Lake, res., In., U.S. E11 120
Monroeville, Al., U.S. F11 122
Monroeville, In., U.S. D1 114
Monroeville, Oh., U.S. C3 114
Monroeville, Pa., U.S. D6 114
Monrovia, Lib. H2 64
Mons, Bel. D12 14
Monsefú, Peru E2 84
Monselice, Italy E8 22
Monsenhor Hipólito, Braz. D5 88
Monsenhor Tabosa, Braz. C5 88
Mönsterås, Swe. H7 8
Montabaur, Ger. F3 16
Montagne, Neth. Ant. p23 104g
Montagu, S. Afr. H5 70
Montague, P.E., Can. D14 110
Montague, Mi., U.S. E3 112
Montague, Tx., U.S. H11 128
Montague, Isla, i., Mex. F5 98
Montague Island, i., Ak., U.S. E10 140
Montagu Island, i., S. Geor. K12 82
Montaigu, Fr. H7 14
Montalbano Ionico, Italy D10 24
Montalegre, Port. C3 20
Montana, Blg. F10 26
Montana, state, Blg. F10 26
Montana, state, U.S. B6 108
Montaña de Covadonga, Parque Nacional de la, p.o.i., Spain A5 20
Montánchez, Spain E4 20
Montanha, Braz. J5 88
Montargis, Fr. G11 14
Montauban, Fr. E7 18
Montauk Point, c., N.Y., U.S. C14 114
Montbard, Fr. G13 14
Montbéliard, Fr. G15 14
Mont Belvieu, Tx., U.S. H3 122
Montblanc, Spain C11 20
Montblanch see Montblanc, Spain C11 20
Montbrison, Fr. D9 18
Montbron, Fr. D6 18
Montceau-les-Mines, Fr. H13 14
Montclair, Ca., U.S. I8 134
Mont-de-Marsan, Fr. F5 18
Montdidier, Fr. E11 14
Monte, Laguna del, l., Arg. H6 92
Monteagudo, Bol. C4 90
Monte Albán, hist., Mex. G10 100
Monte Alegre, Braz. D7 84
Monte Alegre de Goiás, Braz. G2 88

Name | Map Ref. | Page

Monte Alegre de Minas, Braz. J1 88
Monte Alegre de Sergipe, Braz. F7 88
Monte Azul, Braz. H4 88
Montebello, Qc., Can. C14 112
Montebello, P.R. B2 104a
Montecarlo, Arg. C10 92
Monte Carmelo, Braz. J2 88
Monte Caseros, Arg. E8 92
Montecassino, Abbazia di, Italy C7 24
Montecatini Terme, Italy G7 22
Montecito, Ca., U.S. I6 134
Monte Comán, Arg. G4 92
Monte Creek, B.C., Can. F11 138
Monte Cristi, Dom. Rep. C12 102
Monte Cristo, Bol. B4 90
Montecristo, Isola di, i., Italy H7 22
Monte do Carmo, Braz. F1 88
Monte Escobedo, Mex. D7 100
Montefalco, Italy H9 22
Montefiascone, Italy H8 22
Montego Bay, Jam. i12 104d
Monteiro, Braz. D7 88
Montejicar, Spain G7 20
Montejinni, Austl. C6 74
Montelíbano, Col. C4 86
Montélimar, Fr. E10 18
Monte Lindo, stm., Para. A9 92
Montellano, Spain H5 20
Montello, Nv., U.S. B2 132
Montello, Wi., U.S. H9 118
Monte Maíz, Arg. F6 92
Montemayor, Meseta de, plat., Arg. H3 90
Montemorelos, Mex. C9 100
Montemor-o-Velho, Port. D2 20
Montemuro, mtn., Port. C2 20
Montenegro, Braz. D12 92
Montenegro see Crna Gora, state, Yugo. G6 26
Monte Pascoal, Parque Nacional de, p.o.i., Braz. I5 88
Monte Patria, Chile E2 92
Montepuez, Moz. C6 68
Montepulciano, Italy G8 22
Monte Quemado, Arg. B6 92
Montereau-Faut-Yonne, Fr. F11 14
Monterey, Ca., U.S. G3 134
Monterey, Va., U.S. F6 114
Monterey Bay, b., Ca., U.S. G3 134
Montería, Col. C3 86
Monteros, Arg. C5 92
Monterotondo, Italy H9 22
Monterrey, Mex. C8 100
Montesano, Wa., U.S. C3 136
Monte Sant'Angelo, Italy I12 22
Monte Santu, Capo di, c., Italy D3 24
Montes Claros, Braz. I3 88
Montesilvano Marina, Italy H11 22
Montevallo, Al., U.S. D12 122
Montevarchi, Italy G8 22
Montevideo, Mn., U.S. G3 118
Montevideo, Ur. G9 92
Monte Vista, Co., U.S. D2 128
Montezuma, Ga., U.S. D1 116
Montezuma, In., U.S. I2 112
Montezuma, Ks., U.S. D8 128
Montezuma Castle National Monument, p.o.i., Az., U.S. I4 132
Montgenèvre, Col de, p., Fr. E12 18
Montgomery, Al., U.S. E12 122
Montgomery, La., U.S. F6 122
Montgomery, Mn., U.S. G5 118
Montgomery, Pa., U.S. C8 114
Montgomery, Tx., U.S. G3 122
Montgomery City, Mo., U.S. E6 120
Montguyon, Fr. D5 18
Monthey, Switz. D3 22
Monticello, Ar., U.S. D7 122
Monticello, Fl., U.S. F2 116
Monticello, Il., U.S. D9 120
Monticello, In., U.S. H3 112
Monticello, Ky., U.S. H13 120
Monticello, Mn., U.S. F5 118
Monticello, Ms., U.S. F8 122
Monticello, Mo., U.S. D6 120
Monticello, N.Y., U.S. C11 114
Monticello, Ut., U.S. F7 132
Monticello, hist., Va., U.S. G7 114
Montigny-le-Roi, Fr. G14 14
Montigny-lès-Metz, Fr. E15 14
Montijo, Pan. I7 102
Montijo, Port. F2 20
Montijo, Spain F4 20
Montijo, Golfo de, b., Pan. I7 102
Montilla, Spain G6 20
Montivilliers, Fr. E9 14
Mont-Joli, Qc., Can. B8 110
Mont-Laurier, Qc., Can. B14 112
Montluçon, Fr. C8 18
Montmagny, Qc., Can. D6 110
Montmédy, Fr. E14 14
Montmorillon, Fr. C6 18
Monto, Austl. E8 76
Montoro, Spain F6 20
Montour Falls, N.Y., U.S. B9 114
Montpelier, Jam. i13 104d
Montpelier, Id., U.S. H15 136
Montpelier, In., U.S. H4 112
Montpelier, Oh., U.S. C1 114
Montpelier, Vt., U.S. F4 110
Montpellier, Fr. F9 18
Montréal, Qc., Can. E3 110
Montreal, Wi., U.S. E8 118
Montreal, stm., On., Can. A10 112
Montreal Lake, l., Sk., Can. E9 106
Montreuil-sur-Mer, Fr. D10 14
Montreux, Switz. D3 22
Montrose, Scot., U.K. E10 12
Montrose, Co., U.S. E9 132
Montrose, Mi., U.S. E6 112
Montrose, Pa., U.S. C10 114
Montrose, S.D., U.S. D15 126
Montross, Va., U.S. F9 114
Monts, Pointe des, c., Qc., Can. A9 110
Mont-Saint-Michel, Qc., Can. D1 110
Mont-Saint-Michel, Baie du, b., Fr. F7 14
Mont-Saint-Michel, Le, Fr. F7 14
Montserrat, dep., N.A. h15 96a
Mont-Tremblant, Parc de récréation du, p.o.i., Qc., Can. D2 110
Monument, Or., U.S. F7 136
Monument Draw, stm., U.S. B5 130
Monument Peak, mtn., Co., U.S. D9 132
Monument Valley, val., U.S. F6 132
Monviso, mtn., Italy F4 22
Monyo, Mya. C2 48
Monywa, Mya. A2 48
Monza, Italy E6 22
Monze, Zam. D4 68
Monzen, Japan B9 40
Monzón, Spain C11 20
Mooi, stm., S. Afr. F10 70
Moolawatana, Austl. G2 76
Moon, Mountains of the see Ruwenzori, mts., Afr. D6 66
Moonie, Austl. F8 76
Moonie, stm., Austl. G7 76
Moora, Austl. F3 74
Moorcroft, Wy., U.S. C8 126
Moore, Id., U.S. G13 136
Moore, Ok., U.S. F11 128
Moore, Tx., U.S. E8 130
Moore, Lake, l., Austl. E3 74
Moorea, i., Fr. Poly. v20 78h
Moorefield, W.V., U.S. E7 114
Moore Haven, Fl., U.S. J4 116
Mooreland, Ok., U.S. E9 128
Mooresville, N.C., U.S. A5 116
Moorhead, Mn., U.S. E2 118
Moorhead, Ms., U.S. D8 122
Mooringsport, La., U.S. E5 122
Moornanyah Lake, l., Austl. I4 76
Moorreesburg, S. Afr. H4 70
Moosburg an der Isar, Ger. H7 16
Moosehead Lake, l., Me., U.S. E7 110
Moose Island, i., Mb., Can. C16 124
Moose Jaw, Sk., Can. D8 124
Moose Jaw, stm., Sk., Can. D8 124
Moose Lake, Mn., U.S. E6 118
Moose Lake, l., Ab., Can. B19 138
Mooselookmeguntic Lake, l., Me., U.S. F5 110
Moose Mountain, mtn., Sk., Can. E11 124
Moose Mountain Creek, stm., Sk., Can. E11 124
Moose Pass, Ak., U.S. D10 140
Moosomin, Sk., Can. D12 124
Moosonee, On., Can. E14 106
Mootwingee National Park, p.o.i., Austl. H4 76
Mopane, S. Afr. C9 70
Mopipi, Bots. B7 70
Moppo see Mokp'o, Kor., S. G7 38
Mopti, Mali G4 64
Moquegua, Peru G3 84
Mór, Hung. B5 26
Mór, Glen, val., Scot., U.K. D8 12
Mora, Cam. B2 66
Mora, Port. F2 20
Mora, Swe. F6 8
Mora, Mn., U.S. F5 118
Mora, stm., N.M., U.S. F4 128
Morač, stm., Bela. H10 10
Morādābād, India D7 54
Morada Nova, Braz. C6 88
Morada Nova de Minas, Braz. J3 88
Morag, Pol. C15 16
Moral de Calatrava, Spain F7 20
Moraleda, Canal, strt., Chile H2 90
Morales, Laguna de, b., Mex. D10 100
Moramanga, Madag. D8 68
Moran, Ks., U.S. G2 120
Moran, Mi., U.S. B5 112
Moran, Tx., U.S. B8 130
Morant Bay, Jam. j14 104d
Morant Cays, is., Jam. D10 102
Morant Point, c., Jam. j14 104d
Morar, Loch, l., Scot., U.K. E7 12
Moratalla, Spain F9 20
Moratuwa, Sri L. H4 53
Morava, hist. reg., Czech Rep. G13 16
Morava (March), stm., Eur. H12 16
Moravia, N.Y., U.S. B9 114
Moravské Budějovice, Czech Rep. G11 16
Morawa, Austl. E3 74
Morawhanna, Guy. C12 86
Moray Firth, b., Scot., U.K. D9 12
Morbi, India G3 54
Morbihan, state, Fr. G6 14
Morcenx, Fr. E5 18
Morden, Mb., Can. E15 124
Mordovia see Mordovija, state, Russia D6 32
Mordovija, state, Russia D6 32
Mordves, Russia F21 10
Mordvinia see Mordovija, state, Russia D6 32
Mordy, Pol. D18 16
More, Ben, mtn., Scot., U.K. E7 12
Moreau, stm., S.D., U.S. B12 126
Moreau, North Fork, stm., S.D., U.S. B9 126
Moreau, South Fork, stm., S.D., U.S. B9 126
Moreau Peak, mtn., S.D., U.S. B9 126
Moreauville, La., U.S. F7 122
Morecambe, Eng., U.K. G9 12
Morecambe Bay, b., Eng., U.K. H9 12
Moree, Austl. G7 76
Morehead, Ky., U.S. F2 114
Morehead City, N.C., U.S. B9 116
Moreland, Ga., U.S. D14 122
Moreland, Ky., U.S. G13 120
Morelia, Mex. F8 100
Morell, P.E., Can. D14 110
Morella, Austl. D4 76
Morelos, Mex. B5 100
Morelos, Mex. I2 130
Morelos, state, Mex. F9 100
Morena, India E6 54
Morena, Sierra, mts., Spain F5 20
Morenci, Az., U.S. J7 132
Moreni, Rom. D12 26
Moreno, Bahía, b., Chile A2 92
Møre og Romsdal, state, Nor. E2 8
Moresby Island, i., B.C., Can. E4 106
Moreton, Austl. B8 74
Moreton Island, i., Austl. F9 76
Moreuil, Fr. E11 14
Morez, Fr. H14 14
Morgan, Mn., U.S. G3 118
Morgan, Mt., U.S. F6 124
Morgan, Tx., U.S. B10 130
Morgan, Ut., U.S. B5 132
Morgan City, Al., U.S. C12 122
Morgan City, La., U.S. H7 122
Morganfield, Ky., U.S. G10 120
Morgan Hill, Ca., U.S. F4 134
Morganito, Ven. E8 86
Morganton, N.C., U.S. I4 114
Morgantown, In., U.S. E11 120
Morgantown, Ms., U.S. F8 122
Morgantown, Ms., U.S. F7 122
Morgantown, W.V., U.S. E6 114
Morgenzon, S. Afr. E9 70
Morghāb (Murgab), stm., Asia B9 56
Moriah, Mount, mtn., Nv., U.S. D2 132
Moriarty, N.M., U.S. G2 128
Morice, stm., B.C., Can. B4 138
Morice Lake, l., B.C., Can. B3 138
Morichal Largo, stm., Ven. C10 86
Moricsala rezervāts, Lat. C5 10
Moriki, Nig. G6 64
Morino, Russia C13 10
Morinville, Ab., Can. C17 138
Morioka, Japan E14 38
Morir, Tso, l., India B6 54
Morisset, Austl. I8 76
Morjakovskij Zaton, Russia C14 32
Morkoka, stm., Russia D11 34
Morlaix, Fr. F5 14
Morley, Mi., U.S. E4 112
Mormal', Bela. H12 10
Mormugao, India D1 53
Morne-à-l'Eau, Guad. h5 105c
Morne du Vitet, hill, Guad. B2 105a
Morne Trois Pitons National Park, p.o.i., Dom. j6 105c
Morney, Austl. E3 76
Morning Sun, Ia., U.S. C6 120
Mornington, Austl. L5 76
Mornington, Isla, i., Chile I1 90
Mornington Island, i., Austl. C7 74
Morobe, Pap. N. Gui. b4 79a
Morocco, In., U.S. H2 112
Morocco, ctry., Afr. C3 64
Moro Creek, stm., Ar., U.S. D6 122
Morogoro, Tan. F7 66
Moro Gulf, b., Phil. G4 52
Moroleón, Mex. E8 100
Morombe, Madag. E7 68
Morón, Arg. G8 92
Morón, Cuba A8 102
Mörön, Mong. B5 36
Morón, Ven. B7 86
Morona, stm., S.A. I3 86
Morona Santiago, state, Ec. I3 86
Morondava, Madag. E7 68
Morón de Almazán, Spain C8 20
Morón de la Frontera, Spain G5 20
Moroni, Com. C7 68
Moroni, Ut., U.S. D5 132
Moron Us, stm., China E3 36
Morošečnoe, Russia E20 34
Morotai, i., Indon. E8 44
Moroto, Ug. D6 66
Moroto, mtn., Ug. D6 66
Morovis, P.R. B3 104a
Morozovsk, Russia E6 32
Morpeth, Eng., U.K. F11 12
Morrilton, Ar., U.S. B6 122
Morrin, Ab., Can. E18 138
Morrinhos, Braz. B5 88
Morrinhos, Braz. I1 88
Morrinsville, N.Z. C6 80
Morris, Mb., Can. E16 124
Morris, Il., U.S. C9 120
Morris, Mn., U.S. F2 118
Morrisburg, On., Can. D14 112
Morris Jesup, Kap, c., Grnld. A19 141
Morrison, Arg. F6 92
Morrison, Il., U.S. C8 120
Morrisonville, Il., U.S. E8 120
Morristown, Az., U.S. J4 132
Morristown, In., U.S. E12 120
Morristown, S.D., U.S. B11 126
Morristown, Tn., U.S. H2 114
Morrisville, Pa., U.S. H15 112
Morro, Punta, c., Mex. C2 102
Morro Bay, Ca., U.S. H5 134
Morro do Chapéu, Braz. F5 88
Morros, Braz. B3 88
Morrosquillo, Golfo de, b., Col. C3 86
Morrow, La., U.S. G6 122
Morrumbala, Moz. D6 68
Morrumbene, Moz. C12 70
Morse, La., U.S. G6 122
Morse, Tx., U.S. E7 128
Morsi, India H6 54
Mörskom see Myrskylä, Fin. F11 8
Morson, On., Can. B4 118
Mortagne-sur-Sèvre, Fr. H8 14
Mortara, Italy E5 22
Morteau, Fr. G15 14
Morteros, Arg. E6 92
Mortes, stm., Braz. F7 84
Mortlach, Sk., Can. D7 124
Mortlock Islands, is., Micron. C6 72
Morton, Il., U.S. D8 120
Morton, Mn., U.S. G4 118
Morton, Tx., U.S. H6 128
Morton, Wa., U.S. D4 136
Morton National Park, p.o.i., Austl. J7 76
Morua, Vanuatu k17 79d
Moruya, Austl. J7 76
Morvan, mts., Fr. G13 14
Morvant, Trin. s12 105f
Morven, Austl. F6 76
Morven, Ga., U.S. F2 116
Morven, N.C., U.S. B5 116
Morwell, Austl. L6 76
Moryń, Pol. D10 16
Moržovec, ostrov, i., Russia C20 8
Mosal'sk, Russia F17 10
Mosbach, Ger. G5 16
Moscos Islands, is., Mya. E3 48
Moscow see Moskva, Russia E20 10
Moscow, Id., U.S. D10 136
Moscow see Moskva, stm., Russia E21 10
Mosel (Moselle), stm., Eur. G2 16
Moselebe, stm., Bots. D7 70
Moselle, Ms., U.S. F9 122
Moselle, state, Fr. F15 14
Moselle (Mosel), stm., Eur. G2 16
Moses Lake, Wa., U.S. C7 136
Moses Point, Ak., U.S. D7 140
Moshaweng, stm., S. Afr. E6 70
Mosheim, Tn., U.S. H3 114
Moshi, Tan. E7 66
Mosinee, Wi., U.S. G9 118
Mosjøen, Nor. D5 8
Moskalvo, Russia F17 34
Moskenesøya, i., Nor. C5 8
Moskovskaja oblast', co., Russia D19 10
Moskovskaja vozvyšennost', plat., Russia E19 10
Moskva (Moscow), Russia E20 10
Moskva, stm., Russia E21 10
Moskvy, kanal imeni, can., Russia D20 10
Mosomane, Bots. C8 70
Mosonmagyaróvár, Hung. B4 26
Mosopa, Bots. D7 70
Mosqueiro, Braz. D8 84
Mosquera, Col. F2 86
Mosquito Coast see Mosquitos, Costa de, hist. reg., Nic. F6 102
Mosquitos, Costa de, hist. reg., Nic. F6 102
Mosquitos, Golfo de los, b., Pan. H7 102
Moss, Nor. G4 8
Mossaka, Congo E3 66
Mossbank, Sk., Can. E7 124
Mossburn, N.Z. G3 80
Mosselbaai (Mossel Bay), S. Afr. I6 70
Mossel Bay see Mosselbaai, S. Afr. I6 70
Mossleigh, Ab., Can. F17 138
Mossman, Austl. C9 74
Moss Mountain, mtn., Ar., U.S. C6 122
Mossoró, Braz. C7 88
Moss Point, Ms., U.S. G10 122
Moss Vale, Austl. J8 76
Mossy, stm., Mb., Can. C13 124
Most, Czech Rep. F9 16
Mostaganem, Alg. B4 64
Mostar, Bos. F4 26
Mostardas, Braz. E12 92
Møsting, Kap, c., Grnld. E17 141
Mostovaja, Russia D16 10
Mostyn, Malay. A11 50
Mosul see Al-Mawṣil, Iraq B5 56
Møsvatnet, l., Nor. G2 8
Mot'a, Eth. E7 62
Mota del Cuervo, Spain E8 20
Mota del Marqués, Spain C5 20
Motagua, stm., N.A. E3 102
Motal', Bela. H8 10
Motala, Swe. G6 8
Mota Lava, i., Vanuatu i16 79d
Motaze, Moz. D11 70
Moteve, Cap, c., Fr. Poly. s18 78g
Motherwell, Scot., U.K. F9 12
Motīhāri, India E10 54
Motloutse, stm., Bots. B9 70
Motopu, Fr. Poly. s18 78g
Motozintla de Mendoza, Mex. H12 100
Motril, Spain H7 20
Motru, Rom. E10 26
Mott, N.D., U.S. A10 126
Motu, stm., N.Z. C7 80
Motueka, N.Z. E5 80
Motul de Felipe Carrillo Puerto, Mex. B3 102
Motutapu, i., Cook Is. a27 78j
Motygino, Russia C17 32
Motyklejka, Russia E18 34
Mouaskar, Alg. B5 64
Mouchoir Passage, strt., N.A. B12 102
Moudjéria, Maur. F2 64
Moúdros, Grc. D8 28
Mouila, Gabon E2 66
Mould Bay, N.T., Can. A16 140
Moule à Chique, Cap, c., St. Luc. m7 105c
Moulins, Fr. H12 14
Moulmein see Mawlamyine, Mya. D3 48
Moulmeingyun, Mya. D2 48
Moulouya, Oued, stm., Mor. C4 64
Moulton, Al., U.S. C11 122
Moulton, Ia., U.S. D5 120
Moulton, Tx., U.S. E10 130
Moultrie, Ga., U.S. E2 116
Moultrie, Lake, res., S.C., U.S. C5 116
Mouly, N. Cal. m16 79d
Mounana, Gabon E2 66
Mound City, Ks., U.S. F3 120
Mound City, Mo., U.S. D2 120
Mound City, S.D., U.S. B12 126
Moundou, Chad F3 62
Moundridge, Ks., U.S. C11 128
Mounds, Ok., U.S. B2 122
Moundsville, W.V., U.S. E5 114
Moundville, Al., U.S. E11 122
Mounlapamôk, Laos E7 48
Mountain, Wi., U.S. C1 112
Mountain, stm., N.T., Can. C5 106
Mountainair, N.M., U.S. G2 128
Mountainaire, Az., U.S. H5 132
Mountain Brook, Al., U.S. D12 122
Mountain City, Ga., U.S. B2 116
Mountain City, Nv., U.S. F1 132
Mountain Creek, Al., U.S. E12 122
Mountain Grove, Mo., U.S. G5 120
Mountain Home, Ar., U.S. H5 120
Mountain Home, Id., U.S. G11 136
Mountain Iron, Mn., U.S. D6 118
Mountain Lake, Mn., U.S. H3 118
Mountain Nile, stm., Afr. F6 62
Mountain Park, Ab., Can. D13 138
Mountain Pine, Ar., U.S. C5 122
Mountain View, Ar., U.S. I5 120
Mountain View, Ca., U.S. F3 134
Mountain View, Ok., U.S. F10 128
Mountain View, Wy., U.S. E6 126
Mountain Village, Ak., U.S. D7 140
Mountain Zebra National Park, p.o.i., S. Afr. H7 70
Mount Airy, N.C., U.S. H5 114
Mount Alida, S. Afr. F10 70
Mount Angel, Or., U.S. E4 136
Mount Aspiring National Park, p.o.i., N.Z. G3 80
Mount Athos see Ágio Óros, state, Grc. C7 28
Mount Ayliff, S. Afr. G9 70
Mount Ayr, Ia., U.S. D3 120
Mount Barker, Austl. F3 74
Mount Barker, Austl. J2 76
Mount Berry, Ga., U.S. C13 122
Mount Buffalo National Park, p.o.i., Austl. K5 76
Mount Calm, Tx., U.S. C11 130
Mount Carmel, Il., U.S. F10 120
Mount Carmel, Pa., U.S. D9 114
Mount Carroll, Il., U.S. B7 120
Mount Clemens, Mi., U.S. B3 114
Mount Cook National Park, p.o.i., N.Z. F4 80
Mount Dora, Fl., U.S. H4 116
Mount Enterprise, Tx., U.S. F4 122
Mount Field National Park, p.o.i., Austl. o13 77a
Mount Forest, On., Can. D9 112
Mount Frere, S. Afr. G9 70
Mount Gambier, Austl. K3 76
Mount Garnet, Austl. A5 76
Mount Gay, W.V., U.S. G3 114
Mount Hagen, Pap. N. Gui. b3 79a
Mount Holly, N.C., U.S. A4 116
Mount Holly Springs, Pa., U.S. H12 112
Mount Hope, Austl. F7 74
Mount Hope, Ks., U.S. D11 128
Mount Horeb, Wi., U.S. B8 120
Mount Ida, Ar., U.S. C5 122
Mount Isa, Austl. C2 76
Mount Jackson, Va., U.S. F7 114
Mount Juliet, Tn., U.S. H11 120
Mount Kaputar National Park, p.o.i., Austl. H8 76
Mount Lebanon, Pa., U.S. D6 114
Mount Lofty Ranges, mts., Austl. I2 76
Mount Magnet, Austl. E3 74
Mount Manara, Austl. I4 76
Mount Margaret, Austl. F4 76
Mount Morgan, Austl. D8 76
Mount Morris, Il., U.S. I9 118
Mount Morris, Mi., U.S. E6 112
Mount Olive, Il., U.S. E8 120
Mount Olive, Ms., U.S. F9 122
Mount Olive, N.C., U.S. A7 116
Mount Orab, Oh., U.S. E2 114
Mount Perry, Austl. E8 76
Mount Pleasant, On., Can. E9 112
Mount Pleasant, Ia., U.S. D6 120
Mount Pleasant, Mi., U.S. E5 112
Mount Pleasant, Pa., U.S. D6 114
Mount Pleasant, S.C., U.S. D6 116
Mount Pleasant, Tn., U.S. B11 122
Mount Pleasant, Tx., U.S. D4 122
Mount Pleasant, Ut., U.S. D5 132
Mount Pulaski, Il., U.S. D8 120
Mount Rainier National Park, p.o.i., Wa., U.S. D5 136
Mount Revelstoke National Park, p.o.i., B.C., Can. E12 138
Mount Riddock, Austl. D6 74
Mount Saint Helens National Volcanic Monument, p.o.i., Wa., U.S. D5 136
Mount Selinda, Zimb. B11 70
Mount Somers, N.Z. F4 80
Mount Sterling, Il., U.S. E7 120
Mount Sterling, Ky., U.S. F2 114
Mount Sterling, Oh., U.S. E3 114
Mount Uniacke, N.S., Can. F12 110
Mount Union, Pa., U.S. D8 114
Mount Vernon, Austl. D3 74
Mount Vernon, Al., U.S. F10 122
Mount Vernon, Ga., U.S. D3 116
Mount Vernon, Il., U.S. F8 120
Mount Vernon, Ia., U.S. C6 120
Mount Vernon, Ky., U.S. G1 114
Mount Vernon, Mo., U.S. G4 120
Mount Vernon, Oh., U.S. D3 114
Mount Vernon, Or., U.S. F7 136
Mount Vernon, Tx., U.S. D4 122
Mount Vernon, Wa., U.S. B4 136
Mount Vernon, hist., Va., U.S. F8 114
Mount William National Park, p.o.i., Austl. n13 77a
Mount Willoughby, Austl. E6 74
Mount Wolf, Pa., U.S. H13 112
Moura, Austl. E7 76
Moura, Braz. H11 86
Moura, Port. F3 20
Mourdi, Dépression du, depr., Chad D4 62
Mourdiah, Mali G3 64
Mourne Mountains, mts., N. Ire., U.K. G6 12
Mouscron, Bel. D12 14
Moussa 'Ali, mtn., Afr. B8 66
Moussoro, Chad E3 62
Moutier, Switz. C4 22
Moutong, Indon. E7 44
Mouzáki, Grc. D4 28
Movenda, D.R.C. D4 66
Moweaqua, Il., U.S. E8 120
Moxotó, stm., Braz. E7 88
Moyahua, Mex. E7 100
Moyale, Kenya D7 66
Moyamba, S.L. H2 64
Moyen Atlas, mts., Mor. C4 64
Moyeuvre-Grande, Fr. E14 14
Moyie, B.C., Can. G15 138
Moyie, stm., N.A. H14 138
Moyo, Pulau, i., Indon. H10 50
Moyobamba, Peru E2 84
Moyu, China A4 46
M'oža (Mēža), stm., Eur. E14 10
Možajsk, Russia E18 10
Mozambique, ctry., Afr. D5 68
Mozambique Channel, strt., Afr. D7 68
Mozambique Plateau, unds. M6 142
Mozdok, Russia F6 32
Mozolevo, Russia A16 10
Mpala, D.R.C. F5 66
Mpanda, Tan. F6 66
Mphoengs, Zimb. B8 70
Mpika, Zam. C5 68
Mporokoso, Zam. B5 68
Mpui, Tan. F6 66
Mpumalanga, state, S. Afr. E9 70
Mpwapwa, Tan. F7 66
Mqanduli, S. Afr. G9 70
Mragowo, Pol. C17 16
Mrkonjić Grad, Bos. E3 26
M'Saken, Tun. I4 24
Mscislau, Bela. F14 10
Msciž, Bela. F11 10
Msta, Russia C17 10
Msta, stm., Russia B15 10
Mszczonów, Pol. E16 16
Mtama, Tan. G7 66
Mtamvuna, stm., S. Afr. G9 70
Mtwara, Tan. G8 66
Mu, N. Cal. m16 79d
Mu, stm., Mya. A2 48
Mu, Cerro, mtn., S.A. C5 86
Mu'a, Tonga n14 78e
Mualang, Indon. C7 50
Muanda, D.R.C. F2 66
Muang Hay, Laos B5 48
Muang Hôngsa, Laos C5 48
Muang Hounxianghoung, Laos B6 48
Muang Khammouan, Laos D7 48
Muang Khao, Laos C6 48
Muang Không, Laos E7 48
Muang Khôngxédôn, Laos E7 48
Muang La, Laos B6 48
Muang Long, Laos B5 48
Muang Ngoy, Laos B6 48
Muang Nông, Laos D8 48
Muang Ou Tai, Laos A5 48
Muang Pak-Lay, Laos C5 48
Muang Paktha, Laos B5 48
Muang Pakxan, Laos C6 48
Muang Phalan, Laos D7 48
Muang Phônthong, Laos E7 48
Muang Sam Sip, Thai. E7 48
Muang Sing, Laos B5 48
Muang Souvannakhili, Laos E7 48
Muang Sung, Laos B6 48
Muang Thateng, Laos E8 48
Muang Va, Laos B6 48
Muang Vangviang, Laos C6 48
Muang Xaignabouri, Laos C5 48
Muang Xamtong, Laos C6 48
Muang Xépôn, Laos D7 48
Muang Yo, Laos B5 48
Muar, Malay. L6 48
Muar, stm., Malay. K6 48
Muara, Bru. A9 50
Muaraancalung, Indon. C10 50
Muarabenangin, Indon. D9 50
Muarabungo, Indon. D2 50
Muaradua, Indon. F4 50
Muaraenim, Indon. E3 50
Muarajuloi, Indon. D8 50
Muarakelingi, Indon. E3 50
Muaralabuh, Indon. D2 50
Muaralakitan, Indon. E3 50
Muaralembu, Indon. D2 50
Muarapangean, Indon. B10 50
Muarapayang, Indon. D9 50
Muarasabak, Indon. D3 50
Muarasiberut, Indon. D1 50
Muaratebo, Indon. D3 50
Muarateladang, Indon. E4 50
Muaratembesi, Indon. D3 50
Muaratewe, Indon. D9 50
Muaratunan, Indon. D10 50
Mubārakpur, India E9 54
Mubende, Ug. D6 66
Mubi, Nig. G7 64
Mubur, Pulau, i., Indon. B5 50
Mucaitá, stm., Braz. D4 88
Mucajaí, stm., Braz. F11 86
Muchinga Escarpment, clf, Zam. C4 68
Muchinga Mountains, mts., Zam. C5 68
Muckadilla, Austl. F7 76
Mučkas, Russia D23 8
Mucojo, Moz. C7 68
Muconda, Ang. C3 68
Mucujê, Braz. G5 88
Muçum, Braz. D11 92
Mucuri, Braz. J6 88
Mucuri, stm., Braz. J6 88
Muda, stm., Malay. J5 48
Mudan, stm., China B10 36
Mudanjiang, China B8 38
Mudanya, Tur. C11 28
Mud Creek, stm., Ne., U.S. F13 126
Mud Creek, stm., Tx., U.S. E3 122
Muddus Nationalpark, p.o.i., Swe. C9 8
Muddy, stm., Nv., U.S. G2 132
Muddy Boggy Creek, stm., Ok., U.S. C3 122
Muddy Creek, stm., Ut., U.S. E6 132
Mudgee, Austl. I7 76
Mudhol, India C2 53
Mudjuga, Russia E18 8
Mud Lake, l., Nv., U.S. F8 134
Mudon, Mya. D3 48
Mudurnu, Tur. C14 28
Muelle de los Bueyes, Nic. G5 102
Muenster, Tx., U.S. H11 128
Muerto, Mar, l., Mex. G11 100
Mufulira, Zam. C4 68
Mufu Shan, mts., China G5 42
Mufu Shan, mts., China G6 42
Mughal Sarāi, India F9 54
Mugi, Japan F7 40
Mu Gia, Deo, p., Asia D7 48
Muğla, Tur. F11 28
Muğla, state, Tur. F11 28
Muhammad Qawl, Sudan C7 62
Muhanovo, Russia D21 10
Muhavec, stm., Bela. H7 10
Muhino, Russia F14 34
Mühlacker, Ger. H4 16
Mühldorf am Inn, Ger. H8 16
Mühlhausen, Ger. E6 16
Muhlig-Hofmann Mountains, mts., Ant. C5 81
Mühlviertel, reg., Aus. B11 22
Muhradah, Syria C7 58
Muhu, i., Est. G10 8
Muié, Ang. C3 68
Mui Hopohoponga Point, c., Tonga n14 78e
Muineachán see Monaghan, Ire. G6 12
Muine Bheag, Ire. I6 12
Muite, Moz. C6 68
Muja, Russia E12 34
Mujnak, Uzb. F9 32
Mukah, Malay. B8 50
Mukalla see Al-Mukallā, Yemen G6 56
Mukatsjeve, Ukr. A9 26
Mukāwir, hist., Jord. G6 58
Mukdahan, Thai. D7 48
Mukden see Shenyang, China D5 38
Mukeriān, India C5 54
Mukharram al-Fawqānī, Syria D7 58
Mukilteo, Wa., U.S. C4 136
Mukinbudin, Austl. F3 74
Mukomuko, Indon. E2 50
Mukry, Turkmen. B10 56
Muktsar, India C5 54
Mūl, India A4 53
Mula, China F5 36
Mula, Spain F9 20
Mula, stm., India B2 53
Mula, stm., India B1 53
Mulaku Atoll, at., Mald. i12 46a
Mulan, China B10 36
Mulas, Punta de, c., Cuba B10 102
Mulatos, Mex. A4 100
Mulbāgal, India E4 53
Mulberry, Ar., U.S. B4 122
Mulberry, Fl., U.S. I4 116
Mulberry Fork, stm., Al., U.S. D12 122
Mulberry Mountain, mtn., Ar., U.S. I5 120
Mulchatna, stm., Ak., U.S. D8 140
Mulchén, Chile H1 92
Mulde, stm., Ger. E8 16
Muldoon, Tx., U.S. E10 130
Muldraugh, Ky., U.S. G12 120
Muldrow, Ok., U.S. B4 122
Muleshoe, Tx., U.S. G6 128
Mulgowie, Austl. F9 76
Mulgrave, N.S., Can. E15 110
Mulhacén, mtn., Spain G7 20
Mulhall, Ok., U.S. E11 128
Mulhouse, Fr. G16 14
Muling, China B8 38
Muling, China B9 38
Muling, stm., China B9 38
Mulinu'u, Cape, c., Samoa g11 79c
Mülki, India E2 53
Mull, Island of, i., Scot., U.K. E6 12
Mullengudgery, Austl. H6 76
Muller, Pegunungan, mts., Indon. C8 50
Mullet Peninsula, pen., Ire. G2 12
Mullet Pond Bay, Neth. Ant. A1 105a
Mullett Lake, l., Mi., U.S. C5 112
Mullewa, Austl. E3 74
Müllheim, Ger. I3 16
Mullin, Tx., U.S. C9 130
Mullingar, Ire. H5 12
Mullins, S.C., U.S. B6 116
Mulobezi, Zam. D4 68
Mulongo, D.R.C. F5 66
Mulshi Lake, res., India B1 53
Multai, India H7 54
Multān, Pak. C3 54
Multé, Mex. D2 102
Mulumbe, Monts, mts., D.R.C. F5 66
Mulvane, Ks., U.S. D11 128
Mumbai (Bombay), India B1 53
Mumbwa, Zam. C4 68
Mumen, China E2 42
Mumeng, Pap. N. Gui. b4 79a
Mumford, Tx., U.S. G2 122
Mun, stm., Thai. E7 48
Muna, stm., Russia C13 34
Muna, Pulau, i., Indon. F7 44
Muncar, Indon. H9 50
Münchberg, Ger. F7 16
München (Munich), Ger. H7 16
Munchique, Cerro, mtn., Col. F3 86
Munchique, Parque Nacional, p.o.i., Col. F3 86
Muncie, In., U.S. H4 112
Muncy, Pa., U.S. C9 114
Mundare, Ab., Can. C18 138
Munday, Tx., U.S. H9 128
Mundelein, Il., U.S. B9 120
Münden, Ger. E5 16
Mundra, India G2 54
Mundrabilla, Austl. F5 74
Mundubbera, Austl. E8 76
Mundfordville, Ky., U.S. G12 120
Mungallala Creek, stm., Austl. F6 76
Mungana, Austl. C8 74
Mungar Junction, Austl. E9 76
Mungbere, D.R.C. D5 66
Mungeli, India G8 54
Munger, India F11 54
Mungindi, Austl. G7 76
Mungo, Ang. C2 68
Mungo National Park, p.o.i., Austl. I4 76
Munhango, Ang. C2 68
Munich see München, Ger. H7 16
Muniesa, Spain C10 20
Munim, stm., Braz. B3 88
Munising, Mi., U.S. B3 112
Muniz Freire, Braz. K5 88
Munku-Sardyk, gora, mtn., Asia D17 32
Münsingen, Ger. H5 16
Munson, Ab., Can. E18 138
Münster, Ger. D3 16
Munster, Ger. C6 16
Munster, hist. reg., Ire. I3 12
Munte, Indon. C11 50
Muntok, Indon. E4 50
Munuscong Lake, l., N.A. B5 112
Muong Hinh, Viet. C7 48
Muong Saiapoun, Laos C6 48
Muonio, Fin. C10 8
Muping, China C9 42
Muqdisho (Mogadiscio), Som. D9 66
Muqui, Braz. K5 88
Mur (Mura), stm., Eur. D12 22
Mura (Mur), stm., Eur. D12 22
Murajá, Braz. D8 84
Murakami, Japan A12 40
Murana, Indon. F9 44
Murashi, Russia C7 32
Murat, Fr. D8 18
Murat, stm., Tur. H17 6
Murat Dağı, mtn., Tur. E12 28
Muratlı, Tur. B10 28
Muravera, Italy E3 24
Murayama, Japan A13 40
Murça, Port. C3 20
Murchison, Tx., U.S. E3 122
Murchison, stm., Austl. E2 74
Murchison, Mount, mtn., N.Z. F4 80
Murcia, Spain G9 20
Murcia, state, Spain G9 20
Mur-de-Barrez, Fr. E8 18

Name	Map Ref.	Page
Murdo, S.D., U.S.	D12	126
Mürefte, Tur.	C10	28
Mureș, state, Rom.	C11	26
Mureș (Maros), stm., Eur.	C7	26
Muret, Fr.	F7	18
Murewa, Zimb.	D5	68
Murfreesboro, Ar., U.S.	C5	122
Murfreesboro, Tn., U.S.	I11	120
Murgab, Taj.	B11	56
Murgab (Morghāb), stm., Asia	B9	56
Murgha Kibzai, Pak.	C2	54
Murgon, Austl.	F8	76
Muri, Cook Is.	a27	78j
Muriaé, Braz.	K4	88
Muriaé, stm., Braz.	K5	88
Muribeca dos Guararapes, Braz.	E8	88
Murici, Braz.	E8	88
Muricizal, stm., Braz.	D1	88
Murīdke, Pak.	C5	54
Muriege, Ang.	C3	68
Müritz, l., Ger.	C8	16
Murmansk, Russia	B15	8
Murmanskaja oblast', co., Russia	C16	8
Murnau, Ger.	I7	16
Muro Lucano, Italy	D9	24
Murom, Russia	I19	8
Muromcevo, Russia	C13	32
Muroran, Japan	C14	38
Muroto, Japan	F7	40
Muroto-zaki, c., Japan	F7	40
Murowana Goślina, Pol.	D13	16
Murphy, Id., U.S.	G10	136
Murphy, N.C., U.S.	A1	116
Murphys, Ca., U.S.	E5	134
Murra Murra, Austl.	G6	76
Murrat el-Kubra, Buheirat (Great Bitter Lake), l., Egypt	H3	58
Murray, Ia., U.S.	C3	120
Murray, Ky., U.S.	H9	120
Murray, Ut., U.S.	C5	132
Murray, stm., Austl.	J2	76
Murray, stm., B.C., Can.	B9	138
Murray, Lake, l., Pap. N. Gui.	b3	79a
Murray, Lake, res., S.C., U.S.	B4	116
Murray Bridge, Austl.	J2	76
Murray Fracture Zone, unds.	F24	142
Murray Harbour, P.E., Can.	E14	110
Murray Maxwell Bay, b., Nu., Can.	A14	106
Murray River, P.E., Can.	D14	110
Murraysburg, S. Afr.	G6	70
Murree, Pak.	B4	54
Murrhardt, Ger.	H5	16
Murrumbidgee, stm., Austl.	J4	76
Murrumburrah, Austl.	J7	76
Murrupula, Moz.	D6	68
Mursala, Pulau, i., Indon.	L4	48
Murshidābād, India	F12	54
Murska Sobota, Slvn.	D13	22
Murtajāpur, India	H6	54
Murtee, Austl.	H4	76
Murter, Otok, i., Cro.	G12	22
Murtle Lake, l., B.C., Can.	D11	138
Murtoa, Austl.	K4	76
Murtosa, Port.	D2	20
Muru, Capu di, c., Fr.	H14	18
Murud, India	B1	53
Murud, Gunong, mtn., Malay.	B9	50
Murukta, Russia	C9	34
Murung, stm., Indon.	C9	50
Mururoa, at., Fr. Poly.	F13	72
Murwāra (Katni), India	G8	54
Murwillumbah, Austl.	G9	76
Murzuq, Libya	B2	62
Murzūq, Idhān, des., Libya	C2	62
Mürzzuschlag, Aus.	C12	22
Muş, Tur.	B5	56
Mūsa (Mūša), stm., Eur.	D6	10
Mūša (Mūsa), stm., Eur.	D6	10
Mûsa, Gebel (Sinai, Mount), mtn., Egypt	J5	58
Musadi, D.R.C.	E4	66
Musā'id, Libya	A4	62
Musala, mtn., Blg.	G10	26
Musan-ŭp, Kor., N.	C8	38
Muscat see Masqaṭ, Oman	E8	56
Muscat and Oman see Oman, ctry., Asia	F8	56
Muscatine, Ia., U.S.	C6	120
Muscle Shoals, Al., U.S.	C11	122
Musclow, Mount, mtn., B.C., Can.	C3	138
Muscoda, Wi., U.S.	A7	120
Musgrave, Austl.	B8	74
Mus-Haja, gora, mtn., Russia	D17	34
Mushie, D.R.C.	E3	66
Mushin, Nig.	H5	64
Mūsi, stm., India	C4	53
Musi, stm., Indon.	E4	50
Musicians Seamounts, unds.	F22	142
Muskegon, Mi., U.S.	E3	112
Muskegon, stm., Mi., U.S.	E4	112
Muskingum, stm., Oh., U.S.	E4	114
Muskogee, Ok., U.S.	I2	120
Muskoka, Lake, l., On., Can.	D10	112
Musoma, Tan.	E6	66
Musquodoboit Harbour, N.S., Can.	F13	110
Mussau Island, i., Pap. N. Gui.	a4	79a
Musselshell, stm., Mt., U.S.	G6	124
Mussende, Ang.	C2	68
Mussidan, Fr.	D6	18
Mussomeli, Italy	G7	24
Mussuma, Ang.	C3	68
Mustafakemalpaşa, Tur.	C11	28
Mustafa Kemal Paşa, stm., Tur.	D11	28
Mustahīl, Eth.	F8	62
Mustāng, Nepal	D9	54
Mustang Draw, stm., Tx., U.S.	B5	130
Mustang Island, i., Tx., U.S.	G10	130
Musters, Lago, l., Arg.	I3	90
Mustla, Est.	B8	10
Mustvee, Est.	B9	10
Muswellbrook, Austl.	I8	76
Mût, Egypt	B5	62
Mut, Tur.	B4	58
Mutá, Ponta do, c., Braz.	G6	88
Mutanchiang see Mudanjiang, China	B8	38
Mutankiang see Mudanjiang, China	B8	38
Mutare, Zimb.	D5	68
Mutlu (Rezovska), stm., Eur.	G14	26
Mutoko, Zimb.	D5	68
Mutoraj, Russia	B17	32
Mutsamudu, Com.	C7	68
Mutshatsha, D.R.C.	G4	66
Mutsu, Japan	D14	38
Mutsu-wan, b., Japan	D14	38
Mutton Bay, Qc., Can.	i22	107a
Mutuípe, Braz.	G6	88
Mutum, Braz.	J5	88
Mu Us Shamo (Ordos Desert), des., China	B3	42
Mūvattupula, India	F3	53
Muxima, Ang.	B1	68
Muyinga, Bdi.	E6	66
Muyumba, D.R.C.	F5	66
Muzaffarābād, Pak.	A4	54
Muzaffargarh, Pak.	C3	54
Muzaffarnagar, India	D6	54
Muzaffarpur, India	E10	54
Muzat, stm., China	C2	36
Muži, Russia	A10	32
Muzillac, Fr.	G6	14
Muztag, mtn., China	D2	36
Muztag, mtn., China	A5	46
Mvolo, Sudan	F6	62
Mvoti, stm., S. Afr.	F10	70
Mvuma, Zimb.	D5	68
Mwadui, Tan.	E6	66
Mwali, i., Com.	C7	68
Mwanza, Tan.	E6	66
Mweelrea, mtn., Ire.	H3	12
Mweka, D.R.C.	E4	66
Mwene-Ditu, D.R.C.	F4	66
Mwenezi, Zimb.	B10	70
Mwenezi, stm., Afr.	B10	70
Mweru, Lake, l., Afr.	B4	68
Mweru Wantipa, Lake, l., Zam.	B4	68
Mwilitau Islands (Purdy Islands), is., Pap. N. Gui.	a4	79a
Mwinilunga, Zam.	C3	68
Myājlār, India	E3	54
Myall Lakes National Park, p.o.i., Austl.	I9	76
Myanaung, Mya.	C2	48
Myanmar (Burma), ctry., Asia	D8	46
Myaungmya, Mya.	D2	48
Mycenae see Mykínes, hist., Grc.	F5	28
Myebon, Mya.	B1	48
Myingyan, Mya.	B2	48
Myitkyinā, Mya.	C8	46
Myitnge, stm., Mya.	B3	48
Myitta, Mya.	E4	48
Myittha, Mya.	B2	48
Myittha, stm., Mya.	B2	48
Myjava, Slov.	H13	16
Mykines, i., Far. Is.	m34	8b
Mykínes, hist., Grc.	F5	28
Mykolaïv, Ukr.	F15	6
Mykolaïv, co., Ukr.	B17	26
Mykolaïvka, Ukr.	C16	26
Mýkonos, i., Grc.	F8	28
Myla, Russia	D24	8
Mymensingh (Nasirābād), Bngl.	F13	54
Mynaral, Kaz.	E12	32
Mynfontein, S. Afr.	G6	70
Myohaung, Mya.	B1	48
Myohyang-san, mtn., Kor., N.	D7	38
Myōkō-san, vol., Japan	C11	40
Myra, hist., Tur.	G12	28
Mýrdalsjökull, ice, Ice.	I30	8a
Myrskylä, Fin.	F11	8
Myrtle Beach, S.C., U.S.	C7	116
Myrtle Creek, Or., U.S.	G3	136
Myrtle Grove, Fl., U.S.	G11	122
Myrtle Point, Or., U.S.	G2	136
Myrtletowne, Ca., U.S.	C1	134
Myškino, Russia	C21	10
Myślenice, Pol.	G15	16
Myślibórz, Pol.	D10	16
Mysłowice, Pol.	F15	16
Mysore, India	E3	53
Mysore see Karnātaka, state, India	F4	46
Mystic, Ct., U.S.	C14	114
Mystrás, hist., Grc.	F5	28
Mys Vhodnoj, Russia	B6	34
Myszków, Pol.	F15	16
Myt, Russia	H20	8
My Tho, Viet.	G8	48
Mytilíni, Grc.	D9	28
Mytišči, Russia	E20	10
Myton, Ut., U.S.	C6	132
Mývatn, l., Ice.	k31	8a
Mzimba, Mwi.	C5	68
Mzimvubu, stm., S. Afr.	G9	70
Mzintlava, stm., S. Afr.	G9	70
Mzuzu, Mwi.	C5	68

N

Name	Map Ref.	Page
Na (Tengtiao), stm., Asia	A6	48
Naab, stm., Ger.	G7	16
Naalehu, Hi., U.S.	D6	78a
Naas, Ire.	H6	12
Nababeep, S. Afr.	F3	70
Nabari, Japan	E9	40
Nabberu, Lake, l., Austl.	E4	74
Nabburg, Ger.	G8	16
Naberežnye Čelny, Russia	C8	32
Nabeul, Tun.	H4	24
Nābha, India	C6	54
Nabire, Indon.	F10	44
Nabī Shu'ayb, Jabal an-, mtn., Yemen	F5	56
Nabouwalu, Fiji	p19	79e
Nabq, Egypt	J5	58
Nabula, China	C7	54
Nābulus, W.B.	F6	58
Nacala-a-Velha, Moz.	C7	68
Nachingwea, Tan.	G7	66
Nāchna, India	E3	54
Náchod, Czech Rep.	F12	16
Nachvak Fiord, b., Nf., Can.	F13	141
Nacimiento, Chile	H1	92
Nacimiento, Lake, res., Ca., U.S.	H5	134
Naco, Mex.	F8	98
Naco, Az., U.S.	L6	132
Nacogdoches, Tx., U.S.	F4	122
Nácori Chico, Mex.	G8	98
Nacozari de García, Mex.	F8	98
Ñacunday, Para.	B10	92
Nadarivatu, Fiji	p18	79e
Nadela, Spain	B3	20
Nadiād, India	G4	54
Nadi Bay, b., Fiji	p18	79e
Nădlac, Rom.	C7	26
Naduri, Fiji	p19	79e
Nadvoicy, Russia	E16	8
Nadym, Russia	A12	32
Nadym, stm., Russia	A12	32
Naenwa, India	F5	54
Nærbø, Nor.	G1	8
Næstved, Den.	I4	8
Nafada, Nig.	G7	64
Nafī, Sau. Ar.	D5	56
Náfpaktos, Grc.	E4	28
Náfplio, Grc.	F5	28
Nafūsah, Jabal, hills, Libya	A2	62
Naga, Phil.	D4	52
Nagahama, Japan	D9	40
Nagahama, Japan	F5	40
Naga Hills, mts., Asia	C7	46
Nagai, Japan	A12	40
Nagai Island, i., Ak., U.S.	F7	140
Nāgāland, state, India	C7	46
Nagano, Japan	C11	40
Nagano, state, Japan	C11	40
Nagaoka, Japan	B11	40
Nagaon, India	E14	54
Nāgappattinam, India	F4	53
Nagara, stm., Japan	D9	40
Nagarhole Tiger Reserve, India	E2	53
Nāgārjuna Sāgar, res., India	C4	53
Nagarote, Nic.	F4	102
Nagasaki, Japan	G2	40
Nagasaki, state, Japan	G2	40
Nagato, Japan	E4	40
Nāgaur, India	E4	54
Nāgāvali, stm., India	B6	53
Nagda, India	G5	54
Nāgercoil, India	G3	53
Nagīna, India	D7	54
Nagłowice, Pol.	F15	16
Nago, Japan	I19	39a
Nagold, Ger.	H4	16
Nagornyj, Russia	E13	34
Nagoya, Japan	D9	40
Nāgpur, India	H7	54
Nagqu, China	C14	54
Nagua, Dom. Rep.	C12	102
Naguabo, P.R.	B4	104a
Nagyatád, Hung.	C4	26
Nagybánya see Baia Mare, Rom.	B10	26
Nagyecsed, Hung.	B9	26
Nagykanizsa, Hung.	C4	26
Nagykáta, Hung.	B6	26
Nagykőrös, Hung.	B6	26
Naha, Japan	I18	39a
Nahabuan, Indon.	C9	50
Nāhan, India	C6	54
Nahanni Butte, N.T., Can.	C6	106
Nahariyya, Isr.	E5	58
Nahāvand, Iran	C6	56
Nahe, China	B9	36
Nahe, stm., Ger.	G3	16
Nahma, Mi., U.S.	C3	112
Nahodka, Russia	A13	32
Nahodka, Russia	C10	38
Nahoe, Fr. Poly.	r19	78g
Nahoï, Cap, c., Vanuatu	j16	79d
Nahuel Huapi, Lago, l., Arg.	H2	90
Nahuel Niyeu, Arg.	H3	90
Naica, Mex.	B6	100
Naicam, Sk., Can.	B9	124
Naila, Ger.	F7	16
Naiman Qi, China	C4	38
Nā'īn, Iran	C7	56
Naini Tāl, India	D7	54
Nainpur, India	G8	54
Nairai, i., Fiji	p19	79e
Nairn, La., U.S.	H9	122
Nairobi, Kenya	E7	66
Naitauba, i., Fiji	p20	79e
Naivasha, Kenya	E7	66
Naizishan, China	C7	38
Najac, Fr.	E8	18
Najafābād, Iran	C7	56
Najasa, stm., Cuba	B9	102
Najd (Nejd), hist. reg., Sau. Ar.	D5	56
Najībābād, India	D7	54
Najin, Kor., N.	C9	38
Naka, stm., Japan	C13	40
Nakajō, Japan	A12	40
Nakama, Japan	F3	40
Nakaminato, Japan	C13	40
Nakamura, Japan	G5	40
Nakano, Japan	C11	40
Nakano-shima, i., Japan	k19	39a
Nakasongola, Ug.	D6	66
Nakatsu, Japan	F4	40
Nakatsugawa, Japan	D10	40
Nakhl, Egypt	I4	58
Nakhon Nayok, Thai.	E5	48
Nakhon Pathom, Thai.	F5	48
Nakhon Phanom, Thai.	D7	48
Nakhon Ratchasima, Thai.	E6	48
Nakhon Sawan, Thai.	E4	48
Nakhon Si Thammarat, Thai.	H5	48
Nakhon Thai, Thai.	D5	48
Nakina, On., Can.	A12	118
Nakło nad Notecią, Pol.	C13	16
Nakodar, India	C5	54
Nakonde, Zam.	B5	68
Nakskov, Den.	I4	8
Naktong-gang, stm., Kor., S.	C1	40
Nakuru, Kenya	E7	66
Nakusp, B.C., Can.	F13	138
Nālanda, India	F10	54
Nalayh, Mong.	B6	36
Nalbāri, India	E13	54
Nal'čik, Russia	F6	32
Nałęczów, Pol.	E18	16
Nalgonda, India	C4	53
Nallamalla Hills, mts., India	D4	53
Nallıhan, Tur.	C14	28
Nalón, stm., Spain	A5	20
Nalong, China	J2	42
Nālūt, Libya	A2	62
Nam (Nan'a), stm., Asia	B4	48
Namaacha, Moz.	D10	70
Namacurra, Moz.	D6	68
Namadgi National Park, p.o.i., Austl.	J7	76
Namak, Daryācheh-ye, l., Iran	C7	56
Namakan Lake, l., N.A.	C6	118
Nāmakkal, India	F4	53
Namangan, Uzb.	F12	32
Namanyere, Tan.	F6	66
Namapa, Moz.	C6	68
Namarrói, Moz.	D6	68
Namatanai, Pap. N. Gui.	a5	79a
Nambour, Austl.	F9	76
Nam Co, l., China	C13	54
Nam Dinh, Viet.	B7	48
Nam Du, Quan Dao, is., Viet.	H6	48
Nameh, Indon.	B10	50
Namen see Namur, Bel.	D13	14
Namerikawa, Japan	C10	40
Nametil, Moz.	D6	68
Nam-gang, stm., Kor., N.	E7	38
Namhae-do, i., Kor., S.	G8	38
Namhan-gang, stm., Kor., S.	F7	38
Namhkam, Mya.	D8	46
Namib Desert, des., Nmb.	E1	68
Namibe, Ang.	D1	68
Namibia, ctry., Afr.	E2	68
Namib Naukluft Park, p.o.i., Nmb.	D2	70
Namie, Japan	B14	40
Namies, S. Afr.	F4	70
Namji-ri, Kor., S.	D1	40
Namlea, Indon.	F8	44
Namling, China	D12	54
Nam Nao National Park, p.o.i., Thai.	D5	48
Nam Ngum Reservoir, res., Laos	C6	48
Namnoi, Khao, mtn., Mya.	G4	48
Namoi, stm., Austl.	H7	76
Nampa, Id., U.S.	G10	136
Nampala, Mali	F3	64
Nam Pat, Thai.	D5	48
Nampawng, Mya.	A3	48
Nam Phan (Cochin China), hist. reg., Viet.	G8	48
Namp'o, Kor., N.	E6	38
Nampula, Moz.	D6	68
Namsang, Mya.	B3	48
Namsen, stm., Nor.	D5	8
Namsos, Nor.	D4	8
Nam Tok, Thai.	E4	48
Nam Tok Mae Surin National Park, p.o.i., Thai.	C4	48
Namtu, Mya.	A3	48
Namu, B.C., Can.	E3	138
Namuka-I-Lau, i., Fiji	q20	79e
Namúli, Serra, mts., Moz.	D6	68
Namur (Namen), Bel.	D13	14
Namutoni, Nmb.	D2	68
Namwala, Zam.	D4	68
Namwŏn, Kor., S.	G7	38
Namysłów, Pol.	E13	16
Nan, Thai.	C5	48
Nan, stm., Thai.	D5	48
Nan'a (Nam), stm., Asia	B4	48
Nanaimo, B.C., Can.	G6	138
Nanam, Kor., N.	D8	38
Nan'an, China	I8	42
Nanango, Austl.	F8	76
Nanao, Japan	B9	40
Nanatsu-jima, is., Japan	B9	40
Nanbu, China	F1	42
Nancha, China	B10	36
Nanchang, China	G6	42
Nancheng, China	H7	42
Nancheng see Hanzhong, China	E2	42
Nanching see Nanjing, China	E8	42
Nanchong, China	F2	42
Nanchuan, China	G2	42
Nanch'ung see Nanchong, China	F2	42
Nancowry Island, i., India	G7	46
Nancy, Fr.	F15	14
Nanda Devi, mtn., India	C8	54
Nandaime, Nic.	G4	102
Nandan, Japan	E7	40
Nānded, India	B3	53
Nāndgaon, India	H5	54
Nandi Drug, mtn., India	E3	53
Nandikotkūr, India	D4	53
Nandu, China	F8	42
Nandu, stm., China	L4	42
Nāndūra, India	H6	54
Nandurbār, India	H4	54
Nandyāl, India	D4	53
Nanfen, China	D5	38
Nanfeng, China	H7	42
Nanga-Eboko, Cam.	D2	66
Nangakelawit, Indon.	C8	50
Nangamau, Indon.	D7	50
Nangaobat, Indon.	C8	50
Nanga Parbat, mtn., Pak.	B11	56
Nangapinoh, Indon.	D7	50
Nangarhār, state, Afg.	A3	54
Nangatayap, Indon.	D7	50
Nanggala Hill, mtn., Sol. Is.	e7	79b
Nangin, Mya.	G4	48
Nangnim-ŭp, Kor., N.	D7	38
Nangong, China	C6	42
Nang Rong, Thai.	E6	48
Nanguan, China	C5	42
Nanhua, China	F5	36
Nan Hulsan Hu, l., China	D4	36
Nanika Lake, l., B.C., Can.	C3	138
Nanjangūd, India	E3	53
Nanjiang, China	E2	42
Nanjing, China	I7	42
Nanjing (Nanking), China	E8	42
Nankang, China	I6	42
Nanking see Nanjing, China	E8	42
Nankoku, Japan	F6	40
Nankye, Mya.	E3	48
Nanle, China	C6	42
Nanlei (Loi), stm., Asia	A4	48
Nanling, China	F8	42
Nan Ling, mts., China	I5	42
Nanliu, stm., China	J3	42
Nanlou Shan, mtn., China	C7	38
Nannine, Austl.	E3	74
Nanning, China	J3	42
Na Noi, Thai.	C5	48
Nanortalik, Grnld.	E16	141
Nanpan, stm., China	G5	36
Nānpāra, India	E8	54
Nanpiao, China	A9	42
Nanping, China	E5	36
Nanping, China	H8	42
Nansei, Japan	E9	40
Nansei-shotō (Ryukyu Islands), is., Japan	k19	39a
Nan Shan see Qilian Shan, mts., China	D4	36
Nanshan Island, i., Asia	C6	44
Nantais, Lac, l., Qc., Can.	C16	106
Nantai-zan, vol., Japan	C12	40
Nanterre, Fr.	F11	14
Nantes, Fr.	G7	14
Nantes à Brest, Canal de, can., Fr.	F5	14
Nanticoke, Pa., U.S.	C9	114
Nanto, Japan	E9	40
Nanton, Ab., Can.	F17	138
Nantong, China	E9	42
Nant'ou, Tai.	J9	42
Nantucket, Ma., U.S.	C15	114
Nantucket Island, i., Ma., U.S.	C15	114
Nantucket Sound, strt., Ma., U.S.	C15	114
Nantulo, Moz.	C6	68
Nantung see Nantong, China	E9	42
Nanty Glo, Pa., U.S.	H11	112
Nanu, Pap. N. Gui.	b3	79a
Nanuku Passage, strt., Fiji	p20	79e
Nanumea, at., Tuvalu	D8	72
Nanuque, Braz.	I5	88
Nanusa, Kepulauan, is., Indon.	E8	44
Nanxi, China	G1	42
Nanxian, China	G5	42
Nanxiang, China	F9	42
Nanxiong, China	I6	42
Nanyang, China	E5	42
Nanyang Hu, l., China	D7	42
Nanyi Hu, l., China	F8	42
Nan-yō, Japan	A13	40
Nanyuki, Kenya	D7	66
Nanzamu, China	C6	38
Nanzhao, China	E5	42
Nao, Cabo de la see Nau, Cap de la, c., Spain	F11	20
Naococane, Lac, l., Qc., Can.	E16	106
Naogaon, Bngl.	F12	54
Naokot, Pak.	F2	54
Náousa, Grc.	C5	28
Napa, Ca., U.S.	E3	134
Napa, stm., Ca., U.S.	E3	134
Napaku, Indon.	B9	50
Napalkovo, Russia	C3	34
Napanee, On., Can.	D12	112
Napassoq, Grnld.	D15	141
Naperville, Il., U.S.	C9	120
Napido, Indon.	F10	44
Napier, N.Z.	D7	80
Napier, Mount, hill, Austl.	C5	74
Napier Mountains, mts., Ant.	B10	81
Naples see Napoli, Italy	D8	24
Naples, Fl., U.S.	J4	116
Naples, Id., U.S.	B10	136
Naples, N.Y., U.S.	B8	114
Naples, Tx., U.S.	D4	122
Napo, state, Ec.	H3	86
Napo, stm., S.A.	D3	84
Napoleon, N.D., U.S.	A13	126
Napoleonville, La., U.S.	H7	122
Napoli (Naples), Italy	D8	24
Napoli, Golfo di, b., Italy	D8	24
Nappamerrie, Austl.	F3	76
Nappanee, In., U.S.	G4	112
Napu, Indon.	H11	50
Nara, Japan	E8	40
Nara, Mali	F3	64
Nara, state, Japan	E8	40
Nāra, stm., Pak.	F2	54
Nara, stm., Russia	E20	10
Narač, vozero, l., Bela.	F9	10
Naracoorte, Austl.	K3	76
Naradhan, Austl.	I6	76
Naraini, India	F8	54
Naramata, B.C., Can.	G11	138
Naranjal, Ec.	I2	86
Naranjito, P.R.	B3	104a
Narasannapeta, India	B7	53
Narasapur, India	C5	53
Narasaraopet, India	C4	53
Narasun, Russia	A7	36
Narathiwat, Thai.	I5	48
Narau (Narew), stm., Eur.	D17	16
Nārāyanganj, Bngl.	G13	54
Nārāyani (Gandak), stm., Asia	E10	54
Nārāyanpet, India	C3	53
Narbonne, Fr.	F8	18
Nardò, Italy	D11	24
Nares Strait, strt., N.A.	B11	141
Narew (Narau), stm., Eur.	D17	16
Nargund, India	D2	53
Nariño, state, Col.	G3	86
Narita, Japan	D13	40
Nariva Swamp, sw., Trin.	s12	105f
Nar'jan-Mar, Russia	C25	8
Narkatiāganj, India	E10	54
Narlı, Tur.	A8	58
Narmada, stm., India	H4	54
Nārnaul, India	D6	54
Narodnaja, gora, mtn., Russia	B10	32
Narodnaya, Mount see Narodnaja, gora, mtn., Russia	B10	32
Naro-Fominsk, Russia	E19	10
Narol, Pol.	F19	16
Narooma, Austl.	K8	76
Nārowāl, Pak.	B5	54
Narrabri, Austl.	H7	76
Narran, stm., Austl.	G7	76
Narrandera, Austl.	J6	76
Narraway, stm., Can.	B11	138
Narrogin, Austl.	F3	74
Narromine, Austl.	I6	76
Narsaq see Narssaq, Grnld.	E16	141
Narsimhapur, India	G7	54
Narsinghgarh, India	G6	54
Narsīpatnam, India	C6	53
Narssaq, Grnld.	E16	141
Naru, Japan	G1	40
Naruto, Japan	E7	40
Narva, Est.	G13	8
Narva, Russia	C16	32
Narva, stm., Eur.	A11	10
Narvik, Nor.	B7	8
Narvskij zaliv, b., Eur.	A10	10
Narvskoe vodohranilišče, l., Eur.	A10	10
Narwāna, India	D6	54
Narwietooma, Austl.	D6	74
Narym, Russia	C14	32
Naryn, Kyrg.	F13	32
Naryn, stm., Asia	F13	32
Narynkol, Kaz.	F13	32
Näsåker, Swe.	E7	8
Na San, Thai.	H4	48
Nasawa, Vanuatu	j17	79d
Nasbinals, Fr.	E9	18
Nasca, Peru	F2	84
Nase see Naze, Japan	k19	39a
Nash, Tx., U.S.	D4	122
Nāshik, India	H4	54
Nashua, Ia., U.S.	B5	120
Nashua, N.H., U.S.	B14	114
Nashville, Ar., U.S.	D5	122
Nashville, Il., U.S.	F8	120
Nashville, In., U.S.	E11	120
Nashville, Mi., U.S.	F4	112
Nashville, N.C., U.S.	I8	114
Nashville, Tn., U.S.	H11	120
Nashwaak, stm., N.B., Can.	D10	110
Nashwauk, Mn., U.S.	D5	118
Nasielsk, Pol.	D16	16
Näsijärvi, l., Fin.	F10	8
Nāṣir, Sudan	F6	62
Nāṣir, Buheirat see Nasser, Lake, res., Afr.	C6	62
Nasīrābād, India	E5	54
Nasr, Egypt	H1	58
Nass, stm., B.C., Can.	E5	106
Nassarawa, Nig.	H6	64
Nassau, Bah.	m18	104f
Nassau, N.Y., U.S.	B12	114
Nassau International Airport, Bah.	m18	104f
Nassau Island, i., Cook Is.	E10	72
Nassawadox, Va., U.S.	G10	114
Nasser, Lake (Nâsir, Buheirat), res., Afr.	C6	62
Nässjö, Swe.	H6	8
Nastapoka Islands, is., Nu., Can.	D15	106
Nasu, Japan	B13	40
Nasu-dake, vol., Japan	B12	40
Nasukoin Mountain, mtn., Mt., U.S.	B12	136
Nasva, Russia	D13	10
Nata, Bots.	E4	68
Nata, stm., Afr.	B8	70
Natal, Braz.	C8	88
Natal, B.C., Can.	G16	138
Natal, Indon.	C1	50
Natal see KwaZulu-Natal, state, S. Afr.	F10	70
Natalia, Tx., U.S.	E9	130
Natalkuz Lake, res., B.C., Can.	C5	138
Natanes Plateau, plat., Az., U.S.	J6	132
Natashquan, stm., Can.	i21	107a
Natchez, Ms., U.S.	F7	122
Natchez Trace Parkway, p.o.i., U.S.	E9	122
Natchitoches, La., U.S.	F5	122
Natewa Bay, b., Fiji	p19	79e
Nāthdwāra, India	F4	54
Natimuk, Austl.	K3	76
Nation, stm., B.C., Can.	A7	138
National City, Ca., U.S.	K8	134
Natitingou, Benin	G5	64
Native Bay, b., Nu., Can.	C14	106
Natividade, Braz.	F2	88
Natkyizin, Mya.	E3	48
Natoma, Ks., U.S.	B9	128
Nator, Bngl.	F12	54
Natori, Japan	A13	40
Natron, Lake, l., Afr.	E7	66
Natrûn, Wadi el-, val., Egypt	H1	58
Nattaung, mtn., Mya.	C3	48
Natuna Besar, i., Indon.	A6	50
Natuna Besar, Kepulauan, is., Indon.	A5	50
Natuna Selatan, Kepulauan, is., Indon.	B6	50
Natural Bridge, misc. cult., Va., U.S.	G6	114
Natural Bridges National Monument, p.o.i., Ut., U.S.	F6	132
Naturaliste, Cape, c., Austl.	F2	74
Naturno, Italy	D7	22
Nau, Cap de la, c., Spain	F11	20
Naucelle, Fr.	E8	18
Naucratis, hist., Egypt	H1	58
Nauen, Ger.	D8	16
Naugatuck, Ct., U.S.	C12	114
Naughton, On., Can.	B8	112
Naujamiestis, Lith.	E6	10
Naujan, Lake, l., Phil.	D3	52
Naujoji Akmenė, Lith.	D5	10
Naumburg, Ger.	E7	16
Naunglon, Mya.	D3	48
Nā'ūr, Jord.	G6	58
Nauru, state, Oc.	p17	78f
Nauru International Airport, Nauru	q17	78f
Nauški, Russia	F10	34
Nausori, Fiji	p19	79e
Nauta, Peru	D3	84
Nautanwa, India	E9	54
Nautla, Mex.	E10	100
Nauvoo, Il., U.S.	D6	120
Nava, Mex.	A8	100
Navadwip, India	G12	54
Navael'nja, Bela.	G8	10
Navahrudak, Bela.	G8	10
Navajo, N.M., U.S.	H7	132
Navajo Mountain, mtn., Ut., U.S.	F6	132
Navajo National Monument, p.o.i., Az., U.S.	G6	132
Navajo Reservoir, res., U.S.	G9	132
Naval, Phil.	C7	44
Navalmoral de la Mata, Spain	E5	20
Navan, Ire.	H6	12
Navapolack, Bela.	E11	10
Navāpur, India	H4	54
Navarin, mys, c., Russia	D24	34
Navarino, Isla, i., Chile	K3	90
Navarra, state, Spain	B9	20
Navarro Mills Lake, res., Tx., U.S.	F2	122
Navasëlki, Bela.	H7	10
Navasota, Tx., U.S.	G2	122
Navasota, stm., Tx., U.S.	D11	130
Navassa, N.C., U.S.	B7	116
Navassa Island, i., N.A.	C10	102
Navesnoe, Russia	H20	10
Navia, Arg.	G4	92
Navia, stm., Spain	A4	20
Navidad, Chile	F1	92
Navidad, stm., Tx., U.S.	E11	130
Navio, Riacho do, stm., Braz.	E6	88
Naviti, i., Fiji	p18	79e
Navlja, Russia	H17	10
Năvodari, Rom.	E15	26
Navoi, Uzb.	F11	32
Navojoa, Mex.	B4	100
Navolato, Mex.	C5	100
Navsāri, India	H4	54
Nawa see Naha, Japan	I18	39a
Nawābganj, Bngl.	F12	54
Nawābganj, India	E8	54
Nawābshāh, Pak.	E2	54
Nawāda, India	F10	54
Nāwah, Afg.	B1	54
Nawalgarh, India	E5	54
Nawāpāra, India	H8	54
Naxçıvan, Azer.	B6	56
Naxi, China	G1	42
Náxos, i., Grc.	F8	28
Nayāgarh, India	H10	54
Nayarit, state, Mex.	E6	100
Nāy Band, Kūh-e, mtn., Iran	C8	56
Naylor, Mo., U.S.	H7	120
Nayoro, Japan	B15	38
Nazaré, Braz.	D2	88
Nazaré, Port.	E1	20
Nazaré da Mata, Braz.	D8	88
Nazaré do Piauí, Braz.	D4	88
Nazareth see Nazerat, Isr.	F6	58
Nazarovo, Russia	C16	32
Nazas, Mex.	C6	100
Nazas, stm., Mex.	C6	100
Nazca Ridge, unds.	K5	144
Naze, Japan	k19	39a
Naze, The see Lindesnes, c., Nor.	H2	8
Nazerat (Nazareth), Isr.	F6	58
Nazerat'Illit, Isr.	F6	58
Nazija, Russia	A14	10
Nazilli, Tur.	F11	28
Nazina, Russia	B13	32
Nazko, stm., B.C., Can.	D7	138
Nazlet el-'Amûdein, Egypt	J1	58
Nazran', Russia	F7	32
Nazrēt, Eth.	F7	62
Nazwá, Oman	E8	56
Nazyvaevsk, Russia	C12	32
N'dalatando, Ang.	B1	68
Ndali, Benin	H5	64
Ndélé, C.A.R.	C4	66
Ndendé, Gabon	E2	66
N'Djamena (Fort-Lamy), Chad	E3	62
Ndjolé, Gabon	E2	66
Ndogo, Lagune, l., Gabon	E2	66
Ndola, Zam.	C4	68
Ndumu Game Reserve, S. Afr.	E11	70
Neabul Creek, stm., Austl.	F6	76
Neagh, Lough, l., N. Ire., U.K.	G6	12
Neah Bay, Wa., U.S.	B2	136
Neale, Lake, l., Austl.	D6	74
Neamt, state, Rom.	B13	26
Néa Páfos (Paphos), Cyp.	D3	58
Neápoli, Grc.	G6	28
Near Islands, is., Ak., U.S.	g21	140a
Neath, Wales, U.K.	J9	12
Nebine Creek, stm., Austl.	G6	76
Nebitdag, Turkmen.	B7	56
Neblina, Cerro de la see Neblina, Pico da, mtn., S.A.	G9	86
Neblina, Pico da, mtn., S.A.	G9	86
Nebo, Il., U.S.	E7	120
Nebo, Mount, mtn., Ut., U.S.	D5	132
Nebolči, Russia	A16	10
Nebraska, state, U.S.	C7	108
Nebraska City, Ne., U.S.	D1	120
Necedah, Wi., U.S.	G8	118
Nechako, stm., B.C., Can.	C7	138
Nechako Reservoir, res., B.C., Can.	C5	138
Neches, Tx., U.S.	F3	122
Neches, stm., Tx., U.S.	G4	122
Nechí, Col.	C4	86
Nechí, stm., Col.	D4	86
Nechranice, vodní nádrž, res., Czech Rep.	F9	16
Neckarsulm, Ger.	G5	16
Necker Island, i., Br. Vir. Is.	d9	104b
Necochea, Arg.	I8	92
Nederland, Tx., U.S.	H4	122
Nêdong, China	D13	54
Needhams Point, c., Barb.	n8	105d
Needle Mountain, mtn., Wy., U.S.	F17	136
Needles, Ca., U.S.	I2	132
Needville, Tx., U.S.	H3	122
Neegro, Qooriga, b., Som.	C10	66
Ñeembucú, state, Para.	C8	92
Neenah, Wi., U.S.	G10	118
Neepawa, Mb., Can.	D14	124
Nefëdovo, Russia	C12	32
Nefta, Tun.	C6	64
Neftçala, Azer.	B6	56
Neftejugansk, Russia	B12	32
Nefza, Tun.	H3	24
Negage, Ang.	B2	68
Negara, Indon.	H9	50
Negara, stm., Indon.	E9	50
Negaunee, Mi., U.S.	B2	112
Negēlē, Eth.	F7	62
Negeribatin, Indon.	F4	50
Negeri Sembilan, state, Malay.	K6	48
Negev Desert see HaNegev, reg., Isr.	H5	58
Negombo, Sri L.	H4	53
Negra, Laguna, l., Ur.	G11	92
Negreira, Spain	B2	20
Nègres, Pointe des, c., Mart.	k6	105c
Negrești-Oaș, Rom.	B10	26
Negritos, Peru	D1	84
Negro, stm., Arg.	H4	90
Negro, stm., Braz.	C13	92
Negro, stm., Col.	E4	86
Negro, stm., Para.	B9	92
Negro, stm., S.A.	I11	86
Negro, stm., S.A.	F9	92
Negros, i., Phil.	F4	52
Nehalem, stm., Or., U.S.	E3	136
Neharèlae, Bela.	G9	10
Nehawka, Ne., U.S.	D1	120
Nehbandān, Iran	C8	56
Nehe see Nahe, China	B9	36
Néhoué, Baie de, b., N. Cal.	m14	79d
Neiba, Dom. Rep.	C12	102

Name	Map Ref.	Page
Neichiang see Neijiang, China	G1	42
Neidpath, Sk., Can.	D6	124
Neiges, Piton des, mtn., Reu.	i10	69a
Neijiang, China	G1	42
Neikiang see Neijiang, China	G1	42
Neilburg, Sk., Can.	B4	124
Neillsville, Wi., U.S.	G8	118
Nei Monggol, state, China	C7	36
Nei Mongol see Nei Monggol, state, China	C7	36
Neiqiu, China	C6	42
Neira, Col.	E4	86
Neisse see Lausitzer Neisse, stm., Eur.	F10	16
Neisse see Nysa Łużycka, stm., Eur.	E10	16
Neiva, Col.	F4	86
Neixiang, China	E4	42
Neja, Russia	G20	8
Nejapa de Madero, Mex.	G11	100
Nejd see Najd, hist. reg., Sau. Ar.	D5	56
Nejdek, Czech Rep.	F8	16
Nek'emtē, Eth.	F7	62
Nelichu, mtn., Sudan	F6	62
Nelidovo, Russia	D15	10
Neligh, Ne., U.S.	E14	126
Neljaty, Russia	E12	34
Nel'kan, Russia	E16	34
Nellikuppam, India	F4	53
Nellore, India	D4	53
Nel'ma, Russia	G16	34
Nelson, B.C., Can.	G13	138
Nelson, N.Z.	E5	80
Nelson, Ne., U.S.	A10	128
Nelson, stm., Mb., Can.	D12	106
Nelson, Cape, c., Austl.	L3	76
Nelson, Estrecho, strt., Chile	J2	90
Nelson Lakes National Park, p.o.i., N.Z.	E5	80
Nelson's Dockyard, hist., Antig.	f4	105b
Nelsonville, Oh., U.S.	E3	114
Nelspoort, S. Afr.	H6	70
Nelspruit, S. Afr.	D10	70
Néma, Maur.	F3	64
Nemadji, stm., U.S.	E6	118
Neman, Russia	E4	10
Neman (Nemunas), stm., Eur.	E4	10
Nembe, Nig.	I6	64
Nemenčinė, Lith.	F8	10
Nemeriči, Russia	G16	10
Nemours, Fr.	F11	14
Nemunas (Neman), stm., Eur.	E4	10
Nemunėlis (Mēmele), stm., Eur.	D7	10
Nemuro, Japan	C16	38
Nemuro Strait, strt., Asia	C16	38
Nen, stm., China	B9	36
Nenagh, Ire.	I4	12
Nenana, Ak., U.S.	D10	140
Nenana, stm., Ak., U.S.	D10	140
Nendo, i., Sol. Is.	E7	72
Nene, stm., Eng., U.K.	I13	12
Neneckij avtonomnyj okrug, Russia	C23	8
Nenets see Neneckij avtonomnyj okrug, Russia	C23	8
Nenetsia see Neneckij avtonomnyj okrug, Russia	C23	8
Nenggiri, stm., Malay.	J5	48
Neodesha, Ks., U.S.	G2	120
Neoga, Il., U.S.	E9	120
Néo Karlovási, Grc.	F9	28
Neola, Ut., U.S.	C6	132
Neopit, Wi., U.S.	G10	118
Neosho, Mo., U.S.	H3	120
Neosho, stm., U.S.	H2	120
Nepa, stm., Russia	C19	32
Nepal, ctry., Asia	E9	54
Nepālgañj, Nepal	D8	54
Nepa Nagar, India	H6	54
Nepeña, Peru	E2	84
Nephin, mtn., Ire.	G3	12
Nepisiguit, stm., N.B., Can.	C10	110
Nepisiguit Bay, b., N.B., Can.	C11	110
Neptune, N.J., U.S.	D11	114
Neptune Beach, Fl., U.S.	F4	116
Nérac, Fr.	E6	18
Nerča, stm., Russia	F12	34
Nerčinsk, Russia	F12	34
Nerčinskij Zavod, Russia	F12	34
Nerehta, Russia	H19	8
Neretva, stm., Eur.	G15	22
Neriquinha, Ang.	D3	68
Neris (Vilija), stm., Eur.	F6	10
Nerja, Spain	H7	20
Nerjungri, Russia	E13	34
Nerl', Russia	C20	10
Nerl', stm., Russia	D22	10
Nerópolis, Braz.	I1	88
Nerussa, stm., Russia	H16	10
Nerva, Spain	G4	20
Nes, Neth.	C1	16
Nesbyen, Nor.	F3	8
Neščarda, vozero, l., Bela.	E12	10
Neskaupstaður, Ice.	k32	8a
Nesna, Nor.	C5	8
Nespelem, Wa., U.S.	B7	136
Ness, Loch, l., Scot., U.K.	D8	12
Ness City, Ks., U.S.	C8	128
Nesselrode, Mount, mtn., N.A.	D4	106
Nesterkovo, Russia	A13	10
Nestoïta, Ukr.	B16	26
Netanya, Isr.	F5	58
Netherdale, Austl.	C7	76
Netherlands, ctry., Eur.	B14	14
Netherlands Antilles, dep., N.A.	i14	96a
Netherlands Guiana see Surinam, ctry., S.A.	C6	84
Netrakona, Bngl.	F13	54
Nettilling Fiord, b., Nu., Can.	B17	106
Nettilling Lake, l., Nu., Can.	B17	106
Nett Lake, l., Mn., U.S.	C5	118
Nettuno, Italy	C6	24
Neubrandenburg, Ger.	C9	16
Neuburg an der Donau, Ger.	H7	16
Neuchâtel, Switz.	D3	22
Neuchâtel, Lac de, l., Switz.	D3	22
Neudorf, Sk., Can.	D11	124
Neuenburg see Neuchâtel, Switz.	D3	22
Neuenhagen, Ger.	D9	16
Neuerburg, Ger.	F2	16
Neufchâteau, Fr.	F14	14
Neufchâtel-en-Bray, Fr.	E10	14
Neu-Isenburg, Ger.	F4	16
Neumarkt in der Oberpfalz, Ger.	G7	16
Neumünster, Ger.	B6	16
Neun, stm., Laos	C6	48
Neunkirchen, Aus.	C13	22
Neuquén, Arg.	G3	90
Neuquén, state, Arg.	G2	90
Neuquén, stm., Arg.	G3	90
Neurara, Chile	B3	92
Neuruppin, Ger.	D8	16
Neuse, stm., N.C., U.S.	A8	116
Neusiedl am See, Aus.	C13	22
Neuss, Ger.	E2	16
Neustadt, Ger.	F7	16
Neustadt an der Aisch, Ger.	G6	16
Neustadt an der Weinstrasse, Ger.	G3	16
Neustadt bei Coburg, Ger.	F6	16
Neustadt in Holstein, Ger.	B6	16
Neustrelitz, Ger.	C9	16
Neutral Hills, hills, Ab., Can.	B3	124
Neu-Ulm, Ger.	H6	16
Neuvic, Fr.	D8	18
Neuwied, Ger.	F3	16
Neva, stm., Russia	A13	10
Nevada, Ia., U.S.	B4	120
Nevada, Mo., U.S.	G3	120
Nevada, state, U.S.	D4	108
Nevada, Sierra, mts., Spain	G7	20
Nevada, Sierra, mts., Ca., U.S.	F6	134
Nevada City, Ca., U.S.	D4	134
Nevado, Cerro, mtn., Arg.	G3	92
Nevado, Cerro, mtn., Col.	E4	86
Nevado de Colima, Parque Nacional del, p.o.i., Mex.	F7	100
Nevado de Toluca, Parque Nacional, p.o.i., Mex.	F8	100
Neve, Serra da, mts., Ang.	C1	68
Nevel', Russia	D12	10
Nevel'sk, Russia	G17	34
Nevel'skogo, proliv, strt., Russia	F17	34
Never, Russia	F13	34
Nevers, Fr.	G12	14
Nevesinje, Bos.	F5	26
Nevinnomyssk, Russia	F6	32
Nevis, i., St. K./N.	C2	105a
Nevis, Ben, mtn., Scot., U.K.	E7	12
Nevis Peak, vol., St. K./N.	C2	105a
Nevjansk, Russia	C10	32
Nevşehir, Tur.	B3	56
New, stm., Belize	D3	102
New, stm., Guy.	C6	84
New, stm., U.S.	F4	114
New, stm., S.C., U.S.	D4	116
Newala, Tan.	G7	66
New Albany, In., U.S.	F12	120
New Albany, Ms., U.S.	C9	122
New Amsterdam, Guy.	B6	84
New Angledool, Austl.	G6	76
Newark, Ar., U.S.	B7	122
Newark, De., U.S.	E10	114
Newark, N.J., U.S.	D11	114
Newark, N.Y., U.S.	A8	114
Newark, Oh., U.S.	D3	114
Newark Lake, l., Nv., U.S.	D1	132
Newark-on-Trent, Eng., U.K.	H12	12
Newark Valley, N.Y., U.S.	B9	114
New Athens, Il., U.S.	F8	120
New Augusta, Ms., U.S.	F9	122
New Baden, Il., U.S.	F8	120
New Bedford, Ma., U.S.	C15	114
Newberg, Or., U.S.	E4	136
New Berlin, Il., U.S.	E7	120
New Berlin, N.Y., U.S.	B10	114
New Berlin, Wi., U.S.	F1	112
Newbern, Al., U.S.	E11	122
New Bern, N.C., U.S.	A8	116
Newbern, Tn., U.S.	H8	120
Newberry, Fl., U.S.	G3	116
Newberry, S.C., U.S.	B4	116
Newberry National Volcanic Monument, p.o.i., Or., U.S.	G5	136
New Bethlehem, Pa., U.S.	D6	114
New Bloomfield, Pa., U.S.	H12	112
New Boston, Oh., U.S.	F3	114
New Boston, Tx., U.S.	D4	122
New Braunfels, Tx., U.S.	E9	130
New Britain, Ct., U.S.	C13	114
New Britain, i., Pap. N. Gui.	b5	79a
New Brockton, Al., U.S.	F12	122
Newbrook, Ab., Can.	B17	138
New Brunswick, N.J., U.S.	D11	114
New Brunswick, state, Can.	D10	110
Newburg, Mo., U.S.	G6	120
Newburgh, In., U.S.	G10	120
Newburgh, N.Y., U.S.	C11	114
Newbury, Eng., U.K.	J11	12
Newburyport, Ma., U.S.	B15	114
New Caledonia, dep., Oc.	F7	72
New Caledonia see Nouvelle-Calédonie, i., N. Cal.	m15	79d
New Caledonia Basin, unds.	L19	142
New Carlisle, Qc., Can.	B11	110
New Carlisle, Oh., U.S.	E2	114
New Castille see Castilla la Nueva, hist. reg., Spain	E7	20
Newcastle, Austl.	I8	76
Newcastle, N.B., Can.	C11	110
Newcastle, St. K./N.	C2	105a
Newcastle, S. Afr.	E9	70
Newcastle, N. Ire., U.K.	G7	12
New Castle, Co., U.S.	D9	132
New Castle, De., U.S.	E10	114
New Castle, In., U.S.	I4	112
Newcastle, Ne., U.S.	I2	118
Newcastle, Ok., U.S.	F11	128
New Castle, Pa., U.S.	D5	114
Newcastle, Tx., U.S.	A9	130
New Castle, Va., U.S.	G5	114
Newcastle, Wy., U.S.	D8	126
Newcastle Bay, b., Austl.	B8	74
Newcastle-under-Lyme, Eng., U.K.	I10	12
Newcastle upon Tyne, Eng., U.K.	G10	12
Newcastle Waters, Austl.	C6	74
Newcastle West, Ire.	I3	12
New City, N.Y., U.S.	C11	114
Newcomerstown, Oh., U.S.	D4	114
New Concord, Oh., U.S.	D4	114
New Cumberland, W.V., U.S.	D5	114
Newdegate, Austl.	F3	74
New Delhi, India	D6	54
New Denver, B.C., Can.	F13	138
New Edinburg, Ar., U.S.	D6	122
New Effington, S.D., U.S.	F1	118
Newell, Ia., U.S.	B2	120
Newell, W.V., U.S.	D5	114
Newell, Lake, l., Ab., Can.	F19	138
New Ellenton, S.C., U.S.	C4	116
Newellton, La., U.S.	E7	122
New England, N.D., U.S.	A10	126
New England National Park, p.o.i., Austl.	H9	76
Newfane, N.Y., U.S.	E11	112
Newfane, Vt., U.S.	A13	114
New Florence, Pa., U.S.	D6	114
Newfound Gap, p., U.S.	I2	114
Newfoundland, state, Can.	j22	107a
Newfoundland, i., Nf., Can.	j22	107a
Newfoundland Basin, unds.	D9	144
New Franklin, Mo., U.S.	E5	120
New Freedom, Pa., U.S.	E9	114
New Galloway, Scot., U.K.	F8	12
Newgate, B.C., Can.	G15	138
New Georgia, i., Sol. Is.	e7	79b
New Georgia Group, is., Sol. Is.	d7	79b
New Georgia Sound, strt., Sol. Is.	e8	79b
New Germany, N.S., Can.	F12	110
New Glasgow, N.S., Can.	E14	110
New Guinea, i.	b3	79a
Newhalem, Wa., U.S.	B5	136
New Hamburg, On., Can.	E9	112
New Hampshire, state, U.S.	G5	110
New Hampton, Ia., U.S.	A5	120
New Hanover, S. Afr.	F10	70
New Hanover, i., Pap. N. Gui.	a4	79a
New Harmony, In., U.S.	F10	120
New Hartford, Ia., U.S.	I6	118
Newhaven, Eng., U.K.	K13	12
New Haven, Ct., U.S.	C13	114
New Haven, Il., U.S.	G9	120
New Haven, Ky., U.S.	G12	120
New Haven, Mo., U.S.	F6	120
New Hazelton, B.C., Can.	A3	138
New Hebrides see Vanuatu, ctry., Oc.	k16	79d
New Hebrides, is., Vanuatu	k16	79d
New Hebrides Trench, unds.	L20	142
Newhebron, Ms., U.S.	F9	122
New Holland, Oh., U.S.	E2	114
New Holland, Pa., U.S.	D9	114
New Holstein, Wi., U.S.	E1	112
New Hope, Al., U.S.	C12	122
New Iberia, La., U.S.	G7	122
New Ireland, i., Pap. N. Gui.	a5	79a
New Jersey, state, U.S.	D11	114
New Johnsonville, Tn., U.S.	H10	120
New Kensington, Pa., U.S.	D6	114
New Kent, Va., U.S.	G9	114
Newkirk, Ok., U.S.	E11	128
New Kowloon see Xinjiulong, China	J6	42
Newlands, Austl.	C6	76
New Lexington, Oh., U.S.	E3	114
New Lisbon, Wi., U.S.	H8	118
New Liskeard, On., Can.	F14	106
New Llano, La., U.S.	F5	122
New London, Ct., U.S.	C13	114
New London, Mo., U.S.	E6	120
New London, N.H., U.S.	G5	110
New London, Oh., U.S.	C3	114
New London, Tx., U.S.	E4	122
New London, Wi., U.S.	G10	118
New Madrid, Mo., U.S.	H8	120
Newman, Austl.	D3	74
Newman, Ca., U.S.	F4	134
Newman Grove, Ne., U.S.	F15	126
Newmarket, On., Can.	D10	112
Newmarket, Eng., U.K.	I13	12
New Market, Al., U.S.	C12	122
New Market, Ia., U.S.	D3	120
Newmarket, N.H., U.S.	G5	110
New Market, Va., U.S.	F7	114
New Martinsville, W.V., U.S.	E4	114
New Mexico, state, U.S.	D9	98
New Milford, Ct., U.S.	C12	114
New Milford, Pa., U.S.	C10	114
Newnan, Ga., U.S.	D14	122
New Norfolk, Austl.	o13	77a
New Norway, Ab., Can.	D18	138
New Orleans, La., U.S.	G8	122
New Paris, Oh., U.S.	I5	112
New Philadelphia, Oh., U.S.	D4	114
New Pine Creek, Or., U.S.	A5	134
New Plymouth, N.Z.	D5	80
New Plymouth, Id., U.S.	G10	136
Newport, Eng., U.K.	K11	12
Newport, Wales, U.K.	J10	12
Newport, Ar., U.S.	B7	122
Newport, Ky., U.S.	E1	114
Newport, Me., U.S.	F7	110
Newport, N.H., U.S.	G4	110
Newport, N.C., U.S.	B8	116
Newport, Or., U.S.	F2	136
Newport, Pa., U.S.	D8	114
Newport, R.I., U.S.	C14	114
Newport, Tn., U.S.	I2	114
Newport, Vt., U.S.	F4	110
Newport Beach, Ca., U.S.	J7	134
Newport News, Va., U.S.	G9	114
New Port Richey, Fl., U.S.	H3	116
New Providence, i., Bah.	C9	96
Newquay, Eng., U.K.	K7	12
New Richland, Mn., U.S.	H5	118
New Richmond, Qc., Can.	B10	110
New Richmond, Wi., U.S.	F6	118
New River, St. K./N.	C2	105a
New Road, N.S., Can.	F13	110
New Roads, La., U.S.	G7	122
New Rochelle, N.Y., U.S.	D12	114
New Ross, N.S., Can.	F12	110
New Ross, Ire.	I6	12
Newry, N. Ire., U.K.	G6	12
Newry, S.C., U.S.	B3	116
New Salem, N.D., U.S.	A11	126
New Schwabenland, reg., Ant.	C5	81
New Sharon, Ia., U.S.	C5	120
New Siberian Islands see Novosibirskie ostrova, is., Russia	A18	34
New Smyrna Beach, Fl., U.S.	G5	116
New South Wales, state, Austl.	I6	76
New Tazewell, Tn., U.S.	H2	114
New Tecumseth, On., Can.	D9	112
Newton, Ga., U.S.	F14	122
Newton, Il., U.S.	F9	120
Newton, Ia., U.S.	C4	120
Newton, Ks., U.S.	C11	128
Newton, Ma., U.S.	B14	114
Newton, Ms., U.S.	E9	122
Newton, N.J., U.S.	C11	114
Newton, Tx., U.S.	G5	122
Newton Falls, N.Y., U.S.	F2	110
Newton Stewart, Scot., U.K.	G8	12
New Town, N.D., U.S.	F11	124
Newtownabbey, N. Ire., U.K.	G6	12
Newtownards, N. Ire., U.K.	G7	12
New Ulm, Mn., U.S.	G4	118
New Ulm, Tx., U.S.	H2	122
New Washington, Oh., U.S.	D3	114
New Waterford, N.S., Can.	D16	110
New Waverly, Tx., U.S.	G3	122
New Westminster, B.C., Can.	G8	138
New Whiteland, In., U.S.	E11	120
New York, N.Y., U.S.	D12	114
New York, state, U.S.	C12	108
New York Mills, Mn., U.S.	E3	118
New York State Barge Canal, can., N.Y., U.S.	E12	112
New Zealand, ctry., Oc.	D4	80
Neyrīz, Iran	D7	56
Neyshābūr, Iran	B8	56
Neyveli, India	F4	53
Neyyāttinkara, India	G3	53
Nezahualcóyotl, Presa, res., Mex.	G12	100
Nezavertailovca, Mol.	C16	26
Nezperce, Id., U.S.	D10	136
Ngabang, Indon.	C6	50
Ngabé, Congo	E3	66
Ngambé, Cam.	D2	66
Ngami, Lake, l., Bots.	B6	70
Ngamiland, state, Bots.	B6	70
Ngan-chouei see Anhui, state, China	F7	42
Ngangla Ringco, l., China	C9	54
Nganglong Kangri, mts., China	B9	54
Ngangzê Co, l., China	C11	54
Nganjuk, Indon.	G7	50
Ngao, Thai.	C5	48
Ngaoui, Mont, mtn., Afr.	F3	62
Ngaoundéré, Cam.	C2	66
Ngape, Mya.	B2	48
Ngaputaw, Mya.	D2	48
Ngara, Tan.	E6	66
Ngatangiia, Cook Is.	a27	78j
Ngatangiia Harbour, b., Cook Is.	a27	78j
Ngawi, Indon.	G7	50
Ngay Nua, Laos	B5	48
Ngcheangel, is., Palau	D9	44
Ngeaur, i., Palau	D9	44
Ngereklmadel, Palau	g7	78b
Ngerkeai, Palau	g8	78b
Ngermetengel, Palau	f7	78b
Ngeruktabel, i., Palau	h7	78b
Ngetbong, Palau	f8	78b
Nggatokae Island, i., Sol. Is.	e8	79b
Nggela Pile, i., Sol. Is.	e9	79b
Nghia Hanh, Viet.	E9	48
Ngiap, stm., Laos	C6	48
Ngidinga, D.R.C.	F3	66
Ng'iro, mtn., Kenya	D7	66
Ngiro, Ewaso, stm., Kenya	D7	66
Ngo, Congo	E3	66
Ngoko, stm., Afr.	D3	66
Ngom, stm., China	B8	46
Ngomeni, Ras, c., Kenya	E8	66
Ngong, Kenya	E7	66
Ngoring Hu, l., China	E4	36
Ngounié, stm., Gabon	E2	66
Ngouri, Chad	E3	62
Nguigmi, Niger	G7	64
Ngulu, at., Micron.	C4	72
Ngum, stm., Laos	C6	48
Nguna, Île, i., Vanuatu	k17	79d
Nguru, Nig.	G7	64
Nhacoongo, Moz.	D12	70
Nhamundá, stm., Braz.	D6	84
Nha Trang, Viet.	F9	48
Nhill, Austl.	K3	76
Nhoma, stm., Afr.	D2	68
Niafounké, Mali	F4	64
Niagara, Wi., U.S.	C1	112
Niagara Falls, On., Can.	E10	112
Niagara Falls, N.Y., U.S.	A6	114
Niagara Falls, wtfl, N.A.	E10	112
Niagara-on-the-Lake, On., Can.	E10	112
Niagassola, Gui.	G3	64
Niah, Malay.	B8	50
Niamey, Niger	G5	64
Niangara, D.R.C.	D5	66
Niangay, Lac, l., Mali	F4	64
Niangoloko, Burkina	G4	64
Niangua, stm., Mo., U.S.	G5	120
Nia-Nia, D.R.C.	D5	66
Niantic, Il., U.S.	E8	120
Nianyushan, China	G7	42
Nianzishan, China	B9	36
Niari, stm., Congo	E2	66
Nias, Pulau, i., Indon.	L3	48
Nicaragua, ctry., N.A.	F5	102
Nicaragua, Lago de, l., Nic.	G5	102
Nicaragua, Lake see Nicaragua, Lago de, l., Nic.	G5	102
Nicastro, Italy	F10	24
Nice, Fr.	F13	18
Niceville, Fl., U.S.	G12	122
Nichinan, Japan	H4	40
Nicholas Channel (San Nicolás, Canal de), strt., N.A.	G11	108
Nicholasville, Ky., U.S.	G13	120
Nicholls, Ga., U.S.	E3	116
Nicholl's Town, Bah.	B9	96
Nicholson, Pa., U.S.	C10	114
Nickel Centre, On., Can.	B8	112
Nickerson, Ks., U.S.	C10	128
Nicobar Islands, is., India	G7	46
Nicola, B.C., Can.	F10	138
Nicola, stm., B.C., Can.	F9	138
Nicolae Bălcescu, Rom.	B13	26
Nicolet, Qc., Can.	D4	110
Nicolet, Lake, l., Mi., U.S.	B5	112
Nicolet Sud-Ouest, stm., Qc., Can.	E5	110
Nicollet, Mn., U.S.	G4	118
Nicosia (Levkosía), Cyp.	C4	58
Nicosia, Italy	G8	24
Nicoya, Golfo de, b., C.R.	H5	102
Nicoya, Península de, pen., C.R.	H5	102
Nida, Lith.	E3	10
Nida, stm., Pol.	F16	16
Nidadavole, India	C5	53
Nidzica, Pol.	C16	16
Niebüll, Ger.	B4	16
Niedere Tauern, mts., Aus.	C10	22
Niederösterreich, state, Aus.	B12	22
Niedersachsen, state, Ger.	D4	16
Niekerkshoop, S. Afr.	F6	70
Niemba, D.R.C.	F5	66
Niemodlin, Pol.	F13	16
Nienburg, Ger.	D5	16
Niers, stm., Eur.	C15	14
Niesky, Ger.	E10	16
Nieszawa, Pol.	D14	16
Nieu-Bethesda, S. Afr.	G7	70
Nieuport see Nieuwpoort, Bel.	C11	14
Nieuw Amsterdam, Sur.	B6	84
Nieuw Nickerie, Sur.	B6	84
Nieuwpoort, Bel.	C11	14
Nieuwpoort, Neth. Ant.	p22	104g
Nièvre, state, Fr.	G12	14
Nifisha, Egypt	H3	58
Niğde, Tur.	H15	6
Niğde, state, Tur.	A5	58
Nigei Island, i., B.C., Can.	F3	138
Nigel, S. Afr.	E9	70
Niger, ctry., Afr.	F6	64
Niger, stm., Afr.	H6	64
Niger Delta, Nig.	I6	64
Nigeria, ctry., Afr.	H6	64
Nightcaps, N.Z.	G3	80
Nighthawk, Wa., U.S.	B7	136
Nigríta, Grc.	C6	28
Niheidât el-Sûd, Gebel el-, mtn., Egypt	J3	58
Nihommatsu, Japan	B13	40
Nihuil, Embalse del, res., Arg.	G3	92
Niigata, Japan	B11	40
Niigata, state, Japan	B11	40
Niihama, Japan	F6	40
Niihau, i., Hi., U.S.	B1	78a
Nii-jima, i., Japan	E12	40
Niitsu, Japan	B12	40
Níjar, Spain	H8	20
Nijmegen, Neth.	C14	14
Nijvel see Nivelles, Bel.	D13	14
Nikel', Russia	B14	8
Nikki, Benin	G5	64
Nikkō, Japan	C12	40
Nikkō-kokuritsu-kōen, p.o.i., Japan	B12	40
Nikolaevo, Russia	B12	10
Nikolaevsk-na-Amure, Russia	F17	34
Nikol'sk, Russia	G21	8
Nikol'sk, Russia	C6	32
Nikolski, Ak., U.S.	F6	140
Nikol'skij, Russia	F15	8
Nikol'skoe, Russia	H19	10
Nikol'skoe, Russia	E22	34
Nikopol', Ukr.	E4	32
Nīkshahr, Iran	D9	56
Nikšić, Yugo.	G5	26
Nikumaroro, at., Kir.	D9	72
Nikunau, i., Kir.	D8	72
Nīl, Bahr el- see Nile, stm., Afr.	B6	62
Nīl, Nahr an- see Nile, stm., Afr.	D6	62
Nila, Pulau, i., Indon.	G9	44
Nilakka, l., Fin.	E12	8
Nile, stm., Afr.	D6	62
Nile Delta, Egypt	H1	58
Niles, Il., U.S.	B10	120
Niles, Mi., U.S.	G3	112
Niles, Oh., U.S.	C5	114
Nīlgiri, India	H11	54
Nilka, China	F14	32
Nilsiä, Fin.	E12	8
Nīmach, India	F5	54
Nimba, Mount, mtn., Afr.	H3	64
Nimbāhera, India	F5	54
Nîmes, Fr.	F10	18
Nimpkish Lake, l., B.C., Can.	F3	138
Nimule, Sudan	G6	62
Ninda, Ang.	C3	68
Nindigully, Austl.	G7	76
Nine Degree Channel, strt., India	G3	46
Ninette, Mb., Can.	E14	124
Ninetyeast Ridge, unds.	K11	142
Ninety Mile Beach, cst., Austl.	L6	76
Ninety Six, S.C., U.S.	B3	116
Ninfas, Punta, c., Arg.	H4	90
Ninga, Mb., Can.	E14	124
Ning'an, China	B8	38
Ningbo, China	G9	42
Ningcheng, China	D3	38
Ningde, China	H8	42
Ningdu, China	H6	42
Ningguo, China	F8	42
Ninghai, China	G9	42
Ning-hia see Ningxia, state, China	D6	36
Ninghua, China	H7	42
Ningi, Nig.	G6	64
Ningjing Shan, mts., China	F4	36
Ningming, China	J2	42
Ningnan, China	F5	36
Ningpo see Ningbo, China	G9	42
Ningqiang, China	E2	42
Ningshan, China	E3	42
Ningsia see Yinchuan, China	B2	42
Ningsia Hui see Ningxia, state, China	D6	36
Ningsia Hui Autonomous Region see Ningxia, state, China	D6	36
Ningwu, China	B4	42
Ningxia, state, China	D6	36
Ningxiang, China	G5	42
Ningyuan, China	I4	42
Ninh Binh, Viet.	B7	48
Ninh Hoa, Viet.	F9	48
Ninhue, Chile	H1	92
Ninigo Group, is., Pap. N. Gui.	a3	79a
Ninnescah, North Fork, stm., Ks., U.S.	D10	128
Ninnescah, South Fork, stm., Ks., U.S.	D10	128
Ninohe, Japan	D14	38
Nioaque, Braz.	D5	90
Niobrara, stm., U.S.	E14	126
Nioghalvfjerdsfjorden, ice, Grnld.	B22	141
Nioki, D.R.C.	E3	66
Niono, Mali	G3	64
Nioro, Mali	F3	64
Niort, Fr.	C5	18
Niota, Tn., U.S.	B14	122
Nipāni, India	C2	53
Nipawin, Sk., Can.	E10	106
Nipe, Bahía de, b., Cuba	B10	102
Nipigon, On., Can.	B10	118
Nipigon, Lake, res., On., Can.	B10	118
Nipigon Bay, b., On., Can.	C10	118
Nipissing, Lake, l., On., Can.	B10	112
Nipomo, Ca., U.S.	H5	134
Niquelândia, Braz.	H1	88
Niquero, Cuba	B9	102
Niquivil, Arg.	E3	92
Nīra, stm., India	B2	53
Nirasaki, Japan	D11	40
Nirgua, Ven.	B7	86
Nirmal, India	B4	53
Nirmāli, India	E11	54
Niš, Yugo.	F8	26
Nişāb, Yemen	G6	56
Nišava, stm., Eur.	F9	26
Niscemi, Italy	G8	24
Nishio, Japan	E10	40
Nishiwaki, Japan	E7	40
Nisporeni, Mol.	B15	26
Nisqually, stm., Wa., U.S.	D4	136
Nisswa, Mn., U.S.	E4	118
Nītaure, Lat.	C8	10
Niterói, Braz.	L4	88
Nith, stm., On., Can.	E9	112
Nitinat Lake, l., B.C., Can.	H6	138
Nitra, Slov.	H14	16
Nitra, stm., Slov.	H14	16
Nitro, W.V., U.S.	F4	114
Niue, dep., Oc.	E10	72
Niulakita, i., Tuvalu	E8	72
Niut, Gunung, mtn., Indon.	C6	50
Niutao, i., Tuvalu	D8	72
Niutoushan, China	B7	38
Niutou Shan, i., China	G9	42
Niuzhuang, China	A10	42
Nive, stm., Austl.	E6	76
Nivelles, Bel.	D13	14
Nivernais, hist. reg., Fr.	G12	14
Niverville, Mb., Can.	E16	124
Nixa, Mo., U.S.	G4	120
Nixon, Nv., U.S.	D6	134
Niža, Russia	C20	8
Nizāmābād, India	B4	53
Nizām Sāgar, res., India	C3	53
Nižegorodskaja oblast', co., Russia	H21	8
Nizip, Tur.	A8	58
Nízke Tatry, Narodny Park, p.o.i., Slov.	H15	16
Nižneangarsk, Russia	E10	34
Nižnee Kujto, ozero, l., Russia	D14	8
Nižneilimsk, Russia	C18	32
Nižnekamsk, Russia	C8	32
Nižnekamskoe vodohranilišče, res., Russia	C8	32
Nižneudinsk, Russia	D17	32
Nižnevartovsk, Russia	B13	32
Nižnij Casučej, Russia	F12	34
Nižnij Kuranah, Russia	E14	34
Nižnij Novgorod (Gorki), Russia	H21	8
Nižnij Pjandž, Taj.	B10	56
Nižnij Tagil, Russia	C10	32
Nižnjaja Peša, Russia	C22	8
Nižnjaja Pojma, Russia	C17	32
Nižnjaja Tavda, Russia	C11	32
Nižnjaja Tunguska, stm., Russia	B16	32
Nizza Monferrato, Italy	F5	22
Njandoma, Russia	F19	8
Njasviž, Bela.	G9	10
Njazidja, i., Com.	C7	68
Njesuthi, mtn., Afr.	F9	70
Njombe, stm., Tan.	F7	66
Njuhča, Russia	E22	8
Njuja, Russia	D12	34
Njuja, stm., Russia	B20	32
Njuk, ozero, l., Russia	D14	8
Njuksenica, Russia	F21	8
Njurba, Russia	D12	34
Njuvčim, Russia	B8	32
Nkambe, Cam.	C2	66
Nkawkaw, Ghana	H4	64
Nkayi, Zimb.	D4	68
Nkhata Bay, Mwi.	C5	68
Nkhotakota, Mwi.	C5	68
Nkomi, Lagune, l., Gabon	E1	66
Nkongsamba, Cam.	D2	66
Nkwalini, S. Afr.	F10	70
Nmai, stm., Mya.	C8	46
Noākhāli, Bngl.	G13	54
Noatak, Ak., U.S.	C7	140
Noatak, stm., Ak., U.S.	C8	140
Nobeoka, Japan	G4	40
Noble, Il., U.S.	F9	120
Noblesville, In., U.S.	H3	112
Noboribetsu, Japan	C14	38
Nobres, Braz.	F6	84
Nocatee, Fl., U.S.	I4	116
Noce, stm., Italy	D8	22
Nocera Inferiore, Italy	D8	24
Nockatunga, Austl.	F4	76
Nocona, Tx., U.S.	H11	128
Nocupétaro, Mex.	F8	100
Noetinger, Arg.	F6	92
Nogales, Mex.	F7	98
Nogales, Az., U.S.	L5	132
Nogent-le-Rotrou, Fr.	F9	14
Nogent-sur-Seine, Fr.	F12	14
Noginsk, Russia	E21	10
Nogliki, Russia	F17	34
Nogoa, stm., Austl.	E6	76
Nogoyá, Arg.	F7	92
Nógrád, state, Hung.	B6	26
Noguera Pallaresa, stm., Spain	B12	20
Noguera Ribagorçana, stm., Spain	B11	20
Nohar, India	D5	54
Noia, Spain	B2	20
Noir, Causse, plat., Fr.	E9	18
Noir, Isla, i., Chile	J2	90
Noire, stm., Qc., Can.	B13	112
Noirmoutier, Île de, i., Fr.	H6	14
Noirmoutier-en-l'Île, Fr.	H6	14
Nojima-zaki, c., Japan	E12	40
Nokha Mandi, India	E4	54
Nokia, Fin.	F10	8
Nokomis, Sk., Can.	C8	124
Nokomis, Fl., U.S.	I3	116
Nokomis, Il., U.S.	E8	120
Nokou, Chad	E2	62
Nokuku, Vanuatu	j16	79d
Nola, C.A.R.	D3	66
Nola, Italy	D8	24
Nolichucky, stm., U.S.	H2	114
Nolin, stm., Ky., U.S.	G11	120
Nolin Lake, res., Ky., U.S.	G11	120
Nolinsk, Russia	C8	32
Nólsoy, i., Far. Is.	n34	8b
Nombre de Dios, Pan.	H8	102
Nome, Ak., U.S.	D6	140
Nomozaki, Japan	G2	40
Nomtsas, Nmb.	D3	70
Nonacho Lake, l., N.T., Can.	C8	106
Nonburg, Russia	D24	8
Nondalton, Ak., U.S.	D8	140
Nong'an, China	B6	38
Nong Han, Thai.	D6	48
Nong Khai, Thai.	D6	48
Nongoma, S. Afr.	E10	70
Nongpoh, India	F13	54
Nongstoin, India	F13	54
Nonoava, Mex.	B5	100
Nonogasta, Arg.	D4	92
Nonouti, at., Kir.	D8	72
Nonsuch Bay, b., Antig.	f4	105b
Nonthaburi, Thai.	F5	48
Nooksack, Wa., U.S.	B4	136
Noonkanbah, Austl.	C4	74
Noordoostpolder, reg., Neth.	B14	14
Noordpunt, c., Neth. Ant.	p21	104g
Noordwijk aan Zee, Neth.	B13	14
Noorvik, Ak., U.S.	C7	140
Nootka Island, i., B.C., Can.	G4	138
Nóqui, Ang.	B1	68
Norah, is., Erit.	D7	62
Nora Islands see Norah, is., Erit.	D7	62
Noralee, B.C., Can.	B4	138
Nora Springs, Ia., U.S.	A5	120
Norcatur, Ks., U.S.	B8	128
Norcia, Italy	H10	22
Norcross, Ga., U.S.	D14	122
Nord, Grnld.	A22	141
Nord, state, Fr.	D12	14
Nord, state, N. Cal.	m15	79d
Nord, Canal du, can., Fr.	D12	14
Nord, Canal du, can., Fr.	E11	14
Nordaustlandet, i., Nor.	B29	141
Nordborg, Den.	A5	16
Nordegg, Ab., Can.	D14	138
Nordegg, stm., Ab., Can.	D15	138
Norden, Ger.	C3	16
Nordenham, Ger.	C4	16
Nordenšel'da, arhipelag, is., Russia	A8	34
Nordenskjold Archipelago see Nordenšel'da, arhipelag, is., Russia	A8	34
Norderstedt, Ger.	C6	16
Nordfjord, b., Nor.	F1	8
Nordfold, Nor.	C6	8
Nordgrønland (Avanersuaq), state, Grnld.	B15	141
Nordhausen, Ger.	E6	16
Nordhorn, Ger.	D2	16
Nordjylland, state, Den.	H4	8
Nordkapp (North Cape), c., Nor.	A11	8
Nordkinnhalvøya, pen., Nor.	A12	8
Nordland, state, Nor.	C6	8
Nördlingen, Ger.	H6	16
Nordmaling, Swe.	E8	8
Nordman, Id., U.S.	B9	136
Nordostrundingen, c., Grnld.	A23	141
Nord-Ostsee-Kanal (Kiel Canal), can., Ger.	B5	16
Nordrhein-Westfalen, state, Ger.	E4	16
Nordstrand, i., Ger.	B4	16
Nord-Trøndelag, state, Nor.	D5	8
Nordvik, Russia	B11	34
Norfolk, Ne., U.S.	E15	126
Norfolk, Va., U.S.	H9	114
Norfolk Island, dep., Norf. I.	x25	78i
Norfolk Island National Park, p.o.i., Norf. I.	y25	78i
Norfolk Ridge, unds.	L19	142
Norfork Lake, res., U.S.	H5	120
Norikura-dake, vol., Japan	C10	40
Noril'sk, Russia	C6	34
Norlina, N.C., U.S.	H7	114
Normal, Il., U.S.	D9	120
Norman, Ar., U.S.	C5	122
Norman, Ok., U.S.	F11	128
Norman, stm., Austl.	B3	76
Norman, Lake, res., N.C., U.S.	A4	116
Normanby Island, i., Pap. N. Gui.	c5	79a
Normandes, Îles see Channel Islands, is., Eur.	L10	12
Normandie, hist. reg., Fr.	F8	14
Normandie, Collines de, hills, Fr.	F8	14
Normandin, Qc., Can.	B4	110
Normandy see Normandie, hist. reg., Fr.	F8	14
Normandy, Hills of see Normandie, Collines de, hills, Fr.	F8	14
Normangee, Tx., U.S.	F2	122
Norman Island, i., Br. Vir. Is.	e8	104b
Normanton, Austl.	A3	76
Norman Wells, N.T., Can.	B5	106
Norogachi, Mex.	B5	100
Norquay, Sk., Can.	C11	124
Ñorquinco, Arg.	H2	90
Norra Storfjället, mtn., Swe.	D6	8
Norrbotten, state, Swe.	C9	8
Nørresundby, Den.	H3	8
Norridgewock, Me., U.S.	F7	110
Norris, Tn., U.S.	H1	114
Norris Lake, res., Tn., U.S.	H2	114
Norristown, Pa., U.S.	D10	114
Norrköping, Swe.	G7	8
Norrtälje, Swe.	G8	8
Norseman, Austl.	F4	74
Norsjö, Swe.	D8	8
Norsjø, l., Nor.	G3	8
Norsk, Russia	F15	34
Norske Øer, is., Grnld.	B22	141

Name	Map Ref.	Page
Norsup, Vanuatu	k16	79d
Norte, Cabo, c., Braz.	C8	84
Norte, Serra do, plat., Braz.	F6	84
Norte de Santander, state, Col.	C5	86
Nortelândia, Braz.	F6	84
North, S.C., U.S.	C4	116
North, stm., Ia., U.S.	C3	120
North, Cape, c., N.S., Can.	C16	110
North Adams, Ma., U.S.	B12	114
North Adams, Mi., U.S.	C1	114
North Albany, Or., U.S.	F3	136
Northallerton, Eng., U.K.	G11	12
Northam, Austl.	F3	74
North America, cont.	C5	4
North American Basin, unds.	E7	144
Northampton, Austl.	E2	74
Northampton, Eng., U.K.	I12	12
Northampton, Ma., U.S.	B13	114
North Andaman, i., India	F7	46
North Atlanta, Ga., U.S.	C1	116
North Augusta, S.C., U.S.	C4	116
North Aulatsivik Island, i., Nf., Can.	F13	141
North Australian Basin, unds.	K14	142
North Baltimore, Oh., U.S.	C2	114
North Battleford, Sk., Can.	B5	124
North Bay, On., Can.	B10	112
North Bend, B.C., Can.	G9	138
North Bend, Ne., U.S.	J2	118
North Bennington, Vt., U.S.	B12	114
North Berwick, Scot., U.K.	E10	12
North Berwick, Me., U.S.	G6	110
North Borneo see Sabah, state, Malay.	H1	52
North Bourke, Austl.	H5	76
North Branch, Mi., U.S.	E6	112
North Caicos, i., T./C. Is.	B11	102
North Canadian, stm., Ok., U.S.	F12	128
North Canton, Ga., U.S.	C14	122
North Canton, Oh., U.S.	D4	114
North Cape, c., P.E., Can.	C13	110
North Cape, c., N.Z.	B5	80
North Cape see Nordkapp, c., Nor.	A11	8
North Caribou Lake, l., On., Can.	E12	106
North Carolina, state, U.S.	D11	108
North Cascades National Park, p.o.i., Wa., U.S.	B5	136
North Channel, strt., On., Can.	B7	112
North Channel, strt., U.K.	F7	12
North Charleston, S.C., U.S.	D5	116
North Chicago, Il., U.S.	F2	112
North Chungcheong see Ch'ungch'ŏng-bukto, state, Kor., S.	B1	40
Northcliffe, Austl.	F3	74
North College Hill, Oh., U.S.	E13	120
North Collins, N.Y., U.S.	F11	112
North Concho, stm., Tx., U.S.	C7	130
North Conway, N.H., U.S.	F5	110
North Crossett, Ar., U.S.	D6	122
North Cyprus see Cyprus, North, ctry., Asia	C4	58
North Dakota, state, U.S.	G13	124
North Downs, hills, Eng., U.K.	J13	12
North Eagle Butte, S.D., U.S.	B11	126
North East, Md., U.S.	E9	114
North-East, state, Bots.	B8	70
Northeast Cape, Ak., U.S.	D6	140
Northeast Cape Fear, stm., N.C., U.S.	B8	116
North East Point, c., Bah.	A11	102
Northeast Providence Channel, strt., Bah.	B9	96
Northeim, Ger.	E6	16
North English, Ia., U.S.	C5	120
Northern see HaZafon, state, Isr.	F6	58
Northern, state, S. Afr.	C9	70
Northern Cape, state, S. Afr.	G5	70
Northern Cook Islands, is., Cook Is.	E10	72
Northern Division, state, Fiji	p20	79e
Northern Donets, stm., Eur.	F16	6
Northern Dvina see Severnaja Dvina, stm., Russia	E19	8
Northern Indian Lake, l., Mb., Can.	D11	106
Northern Ireland, state, U.K.	G6	12
Northern Marianas, dep., Oc.	B6	72
Northern Sporades see Vórioi Sporádhes, is., Grc.	D6	28
Northern Territory, state, Austl.	D6	74
North Fabius, stm., U.S.	D6	120
Northfield, Ma., U.S.	B13	114
Northfield, Mn., U.S.	G5	118
Northfield, Vt., U.S.	F4	110
North Fiji Basin, unds.	K20	142
North Flinders Range, mts., Austl.	H2	76
North Fond du Lac, Wi., U.S.	H10	118
North Foreland, c., Eng., U.K.	J14	12
North Fork, Ca., U.S.	F6	134
North Fork, stm., U.S.	H5	120
North Fort Myers, Fl., U.S.	J4	116
North Frisian Islands, is., Eur.	B3	16
Northglenn, Co., U.S.	B4	128
North Gulfport, Ms., U.S.	G9	122
North Gyeongsang see Kyŏngsang-bukto, state, Kor., S.	C1	40
North Henik Lake, l., Nu., Can.	C11	106
North Hero, Vt., U.S.	F3	110
North Highlands, Ca., U.S.	E4	134
North Horr, Kenya	D7	66
North Island, i., N.Z.	C5	80
North Judson, In., U.S.	G3	112
North Kent Island, i., Nu., Can.	B7	141
North Kingsville, Oh., U.S.	C5	114
North Knife Lake, l., Mb., Can.	D11	106
North Korea see Korea, North, ctry., Asia	D7	38
North Lakhimpur, India	C7	46
North Las Vegas, Nv., U.S.	G1	132
North La Veta Pass, p., Co., U.S.	D3	128
North Little Rock, Ar., U.S.	C6	122
North Llano, stm., Tx., U.S.	D8	130
North Logan, Ut., U.S.	B5	132
North Loup, Ne., U.S.	F14	126
North Loup, stm., Ne., U.S.	F14	126
North Magnetic Pole, misc. cult.	B4	141
North Mamm Peak, mtn., Co., U.S.	D9	132
North Manchester, In., U.S.	H4	112
North Manitou Island, i., Mi., U.S.	C3	112
North Mankato, Mn., U.S.	G4	118
North Miami, Fl., U.S.	K5	116
North Miami Beach, Fl., U.S.	K5	116
North Milk (Milk, North Fork), stm., N.A.	B13	136
North Myrtle Beach, S.C., U.S.	C7	116
North New River Canal, can., Fl., U.S.	J5	116
North Newton, Ks., U.S.	C11	128
North Ogden, Ut., U.S.	B5	132
North Ossetia see Severnaja Osetija, state, Russia	F6	32
North Palisade, mtn., Ca., U.S.	F7	134
North Palm Beach, Fl., U.S.	J5	116
North Park, Il., U.S.	B8	120
North Peninsula, pen., On., Can.	A10	118
North Plains, pl., N.M., U.S.	I8	132
North Platte, Ne., U.S.	F12	126
North Platte, stm., U.S.	F11	126
North Point, c., Barb.	n8	105d
North Pole, misc. cult.	A4	94
Northport, Al., U.S.	D11	122
Northport, Mi., U.S.	C4	112
Northport, Wa., U.S.	B9	136
North Portal, Sk., Can.	E11	124
North Raccoon, stm., Ia., U.S.	C3	120
North Rhine-Westphalia see Nordrhein-Westfalen, state, Ger.	E4	16
North Richland Hills, Tx., U.S.	B10	130
North Rim, Az., U.S.	G4	132
North Ronaldsay, i., Scot., U.K.	B10	12
North Rustico, P.E., Can.	D13	110
North Salt Lake, Ut., U.S.	C5	132
North Saskatchewan, stm., Can.	E9	106
North Sea, Eur.	D9	6
North Shoal Lake, l., Mb., Can.	D16	124
North Shore City, N.Z.	C6	80
North Shoshone Peak, mtn., Nv., U.S.	D8	134
North Siberain Lowland see Severo-Sibirskaja nizmennost', pl., Russia	B6	34
North Skunk, stm., Ia., U.S.	C5	120
North Solitary Island, i., Austl.	G9	76
North Solomons, state, Pap. N. Gui.	d7	79b
North Spicer Island, i., Nu., Can.	B15	106
North Stradbroke Island, i., Austl.	F9	76
North Sumatra see Sumatera Utara, state, Indon.	K4	48
North Sydney, N.S., Can.	D16	110
North Taranaki Bight, b., N.Z.	D5	80
North Terre Haute, In., U.S.	E10	120
North Thompson, stm., B.C., Can.	F10	138
North Troy, Vt., U.S.	F4	110
North Tunica, Ms., U.S.	C8	122
North Uist, i., Scot., U.K.	D5	12
Northumberland Isles, is., Austl.	C7	76
Northumberland National Park, p.o.i., Eng., U.K.	F10	12
Northumberland Strait, strt., Can.	D12	110
North Umpqua, stm., Or., U.S.	G4	136
North Vancouver, B.C., Can.	G7	138
North Vietnam see Vietnam, ctry., Asia	E9	48
Northville, N.Y., U.S.	G2	110
North-West, state, S. Afr.	E7	70
North West Bluff, c., Monts.	D3	105a
North West Cape, c., Austl.	D2	74
North-West Frontier, state, Pak.	A4	54
Northwest Miramichi, stm., N.B., Can.	C10	110
Northwest Pacific Basin, unds.	F18	142
Northwest Providence Channel, strt., Bah.	m17	104f
Northwest Territories, state, Can.	B10	106
North Wichita, stm., Tx., U.S.	H9	128
North Wilkesboro, N.C., U.S.	H4	114
North Windham, Me., U.S.	G6	110
Northwood, Ia., U.S.	H5	118
Northwood, N.D., U.S.	G16	124
North York, ngh., On., Can.	E10	112
North York Moors National Park, p.o.i., Eng., U.K.	G12	12
North Zulch, Tx., U.S.	G2	122
Norton, Ks., U.S.	B9	128
Norton, Va., U.S.	H3	114
Norton Shores, Mi., U.S.	E3	112
Norton Sound, strt., Ak., U.S.	D6	140
Nortonville, Ks., U.S.	E2	120
Norvegia, Cape, c., Ant.	C3	81
Norwalk, Ct., U.S.	C12	114
Norwalk, Ia., U.S.	C4	120
Norwalk, Oh., U.S.	C3	114
Norway, Ia., U.S.	C6	120
Norway, Me., U.S.	F6	110
Norway, ctry., Eur.	E3	8
Norway Bay, b., Nu., Can.	A10	106
Norway House, Mb., Can.	E11	106
Norwegian Basin, unds.	B13	144
Norwegian Sea, Eur.	C3	30
Norwich, On., Can.	E9	112
Norwich, Eng., U.K.	I14	12
Norwich, Ct., U.S.	C13	114
Norwich, N.Y., U.S.	B10	114
Norwood, On., Can.	D11	112
Norwood, Co., U.S.	E8	132
Norwood, Ma., U.S.	B14	114
Norwood, Mn., U.S.	G5	118
Norwood, N.C., U.S.	A5	116
Norwood, Oh., U.S.	E1	114
Noshiro, Japan	D13	38
Nosop (Nossob), stm., Afr.	D5	70
Nosovaja, Russia	B26	8
Nosovščina, Russia	E17	8
Nossa Senhora das Dores, Braz.	F7	88
Nossob (Nosop), stm., Afr.	D5	70
Nosy-Varika, Madag.	E8	68
Notasulga, Al., U.S.	E13	122
Notch Hill, B.C., Can.	F11	138
Noteć, stm., Pol.	D11	16
Nótio Aigaío, state, Grc.	G9	28
Noto, Italy	H9	24
Noto, Japan	B10	40
Noto, Golfo di, b., Italy	H9	24
Noto-hantō, pen., Japan	B10	40
Notozero, ozero, l., Russia	C14	8
Notre-Dame, N.B., Can.	D12	110
Notre-Dame, Monts, mts., Qc., Can.	B9	110
Notre Dame Bay, b., Nf., Can.	j22	107a
Notre-Dame-du-Laus, Qc., Can.	B14	112
Notrees, Tx., U.S.	C5	130
Nottawasaga, stm., On., Can.	D10	112
Nottawasaga Bay, b., On., Can.	D9	112
Nottaway, stm., Qc., Can.	E15	106
Nottingham, Eng., U.K.	I11	12
Nottingham Island, i., Nu., Can.	C15	106
Nottoway, stm., Va., U.S.	H8	114
Notukeu Creek, stm., Sk., Can.	E6	124
Notwane, stm., Afr.	D8	70
Nouâdhibou, Maur.	E1	64
Nouâdhibou, Râs, c., Afr.	E1	64
Nouakchott, Maur.	F1	64
Nouâmghâr, Maur.	F1	64
Nouméa, N. Cal.	n16	79d
Noupoort, S. Afr.	G7	70
Nouveau-Québec, Cratère du, crat., Qc., Can.	C16	106
Nouvelle, Qc., Can.	B10	110
Nouvelle-Calédonie (New Caledonia), i., N. Cal.	m15	79d
Nouvelle-Écosse see Nova Scotia, state, Can.	G18	106
Nouvelle-France, Cap de, c., Qc., Can.	C16	106
Nova Andradina, Braz.	D6	90
Nová Baňa, Slov.	H14	16
Nova Caipemba, Ang.	B1	68
Nova Era, Braz.	J4	88
Nova Friburgo, Braz.	L4	88
Nova Gorica, Slvn.	D10	22
Nova Gradiška, Cro.	E14	22
Nova Granada, Braz.	K1	88
Nova Iguaçu, Braz.	L4	88
Novaja Kazanka, Kaz.	E7	32
Novaja Ladoga, Russia	F14	8
Novaja Maluksa, Russia	A14	10
Novaja Sibir', ostrov, i., Russia	B19	34
Novaja Zemlja, is., Russia	B8	30
Nova Kakhovka, Ukr.	E4	32
Nova Lamego, Gui.-B.	G2	64
Nova Lima, Braz.	K4	88
Novalukoml', Bela.	F11	10
Nova Mambone, Moz.	B12	70
Nova Olinda, Braz.	D6	88
Nová Paka, Czech Rep.	F11	16
Nova Ponte, Braz.	J2	88
Nova Prata, Braz.	D12	92
Novara, Italy	E5	22
Nova Roma, Braz.	G2	88
Nova Russas, Braz.	C5	88
Nova Scotia, state, Can.	G18	106
Nova Soure, Braz.	F6	88
Novato, Ca., U.S.	E3	134
Nova Venécia, Braz.	J5	88
Nova Vida, Braz.	F5	84
Novaya Zemlya see Novaja Zemlja, is., Russia	B8	30
Nova Zagora, Blg.	G13	26
Nové Hrady, Czech Rep.	H10	16
Novelda, Spain	F10	20
Nové Město nad Váhom, Slov.	H13	16
Nové Město na Moravě, Czech Rep.	G12	16
Nové Zámky, Slov.	I14	16
Novgorod, Russia	B14	10
Novgorodskaja oblast', co., Russia	B15	10
Novi Bečej, Yugo.	D7	26
Novi Beograd, Yugo.	E7	26
Novice, Tx., U.S.	C8	130
Novigrad, Cro.	E10	22
Novikovo, Russia	G17	34
Novi Ligure, Italy	F5	22
Novinger, Mo., U.S.	D5	120
Novi Pazar, Blg.	F14	26
Novi Pazar, Yugo.	F7	26
Novi Sad, Yugo.	D6	26
Novo, Lago, l., Braz.	C7	84
Novo Airão, Braz.	H11	86
Novoaltajsk, Russia	D14	32
Novo Aripuanã, Braz.	E5	84
Novočerkassk, Russia	E6	32
Novodvinsk, Russia	D19	8
Novoe, Russia	C11	32
Novoenisejsk, Russia	C16	32
Novo Hamburgo, Braz.	D12	92
Novo Horizonte, Braz.	K1	88
Novoizborsk, Russia	C10	10
Novokačalinsk, Russia	B10	38
Novokaširsk, Russia	F21	10
Novokazalinsk, Kaz.	F10	32
Novokujbyševsk, Russia	D7	32
Novokuzneck, Russia	D15	32
Novolazarevskaja, sci., Ant.	C6	81
Novo Mesto, Slvn.	E12	22
Novomoskovsk (Stalinogorsk), Russia	F21	10
Novo Oriente, Braz.	C5	88
Novopetrovskoe, Russia	E19	10
Novorossijsk, Russia	F5	32
Novorybnoe, Russia	B10	34
Novoržev, Russia	C12	10
Novošahtinsk, Russia	E6	32
Novošelovo, Russia	E7	34
Novoselytsia, Ukr.	A13	26
Novosergievka, Russia	D8	32
Novosibirsk, Russia	C14	32
Novosibirskie ostrova, is., Russia	A18	34
Novosibirskoe vodohranilišče, res., Russia	D14	32
Novosil's'ke, Ukr.	D15	26
Novosokol'niki, Russia	D12	10
Novotroick, Russia	D9	32
Novotroickoe, Kaz.	F12	32
Novouzensk, Russia	D7	32
Novovjatsk, Russia	C7	32
Novozavidovskij, Russia	D19	10
Novozybkov, Russia	H14	10
Novska, Cro.	E13	22
Nový Bohumín, Czech Rep.	G14	16
Nový Bor, Czech Rep.	F10	16
Novyja Valosavičy, Bela.	F11	10
Nový Jičín, Czech Rep.	G13	16
Novyj Nekouz, Russia	C20	10
Novyj Port, Russia	A12	32
Novyj Uzen', Kaz.	F8	32
Novyj Vasjugan, Russia	C13	32
Novy Pahost, Bela.	E10	10
Nowa Ruda, Pol.	F12	16
Nowa Sól, Pol.	E11	16
Nowe, Pol.	C14	16
Nowe Miasto nad Pilicą, Pol.	E16	16
Nowendoc, Austl.	H8	76
Nowgong, India	F7	54
Nowitna, stm., Ak., U.S.	D9	140
Nowogard, Pol.	C11	16
Nowogrodziec, Pol.	E11	16
Nowood, stm., Wy., U.S.	C5	126
Nowra, Austl.	J8	76
Nowrangapur, India	B6	53
Nowshāk, mtn., Asia	B11	56
Nowshera, Pak.	B4	54
Nowshera, Pak.	C11	56
Nowy Dwór Mazowiecki, Pol.	D16	16
Nowy Sącz, Pol.	G16	16
Nowy Sącz, state, Pol.	G16	16
Nowy Staw, Pol.	B15	16
Nowy Targ, Pol.	G15	16
Noxapater, Ms., U.S.	E9	122
Noxen, Pa., U.S.	C9	114
Noxon, Mt., U.S.	B11	136
Noxubee, stm., U.S.	D10	122
Noy, stm., Laos	D7	48
Noya see Noia, Spain	B2	20
Noyant, Fr.	G9	14
Noyon, Fr.	E11	14
Nsanje, Mwi.	D6	68
Nsawam, Ghana	H4	64
Nsok, Eq. Gui.	I7	64
Nsukka, Nig.	H6	64
Nsuta, Ghana	H4	64
Ntwetwe Pan, pl., Bots.	B7	70
Nu see Salween, stm., Asia	C8	46
Nūbah, Jibāl an-, mts., Sudan	E6	62
Nubian Desert, des., Sudan	C6	62
Ñuble, stm., Chile	H2	92
Nucet, Rom.	C9	26
Nudol'-Šarino, Russia	D19	10
Nueces, stm., Tx., U.S.	G10	130
Nueces Plains, pl., Tx., U.S.	F8	130
Nueltin Lake, l., Can.	C11	106
Nuestra Señora de Talavera, Arg.	B6	92
Nueva, Isla, i., Chile	K3	90
Nueva Antioquia, Col.	D7	86
Nueva Ciudad Guerrero, Mex.	B9	100
Nueva Esparta, state, Ven.	B9	86
Nueva Galia, Arg.	G5	92
Nueva Germania, Para.	A9	92
Nueva Gerona, Cuba	B6	102
Nueva Imperial, Chile	G2	90
Nueva Italia de Ruiz, Mex.	F7	100
Nueva Loja, Ec.	G3	86
Nueva Palmira, Ur.	F8	92
Nueva Rosita, Mex.	A8	100
Nueva San Salvador, El Sal.	F3	102
Nueva Toltén, Chile	G2	90
Nueve, Canal Numero, can., Arg.	H8	92
Nueve de Julio, Arg.	G7	92
Nuevitas, Cuba	B9	102
Nuevo, Bajo, unds., Col.	E8	102
Nuevo, Cayo, i., Mex.	E12	100
Nuevo, Golfo, b., Arg.	H4	90
Nuevo Camarón, Mex.	G8	130
Nuevo Casas Grandes, Mex.	F9	98
Nuevo Delicias, Mex.	B7	100
Nuevo Laredo, Mex.	B9	100
Nuevo León, state, Mex.	B8	100
Nuevo Primero de Mayo, Mex.	H9	130
Nuevo Progreso, Mex.	F12	100
Nuevo Rocafuerte, Ec.	H4	86
Nuevo San Lucas, Mex.	F2	130
Nûgssuaq, pen., Grnld.	C15	141
Nugu, res., India	F3	53
Nui, at., Tuvalu	D8	72
Nuku'alofa, Tonga	n14	78e
Nukuhu, Pap. N. Gui.	b4	79a
Nukus, Uzb.	F9	32
Nul, Vanuatu	k17	79d
Nulato, Ak., U.S.	D8	140
Nullagine, Austl.	D4	74
Nullarbor, Austl.	F6	74
Nullarbor Plain, pl., Austl.	F5	74
Numan, Nig.	H7	64
Numancia (Numantia), hist., Spain	C8	20
Numantia see Numancia, hist., Spain	C8	20
Numata, Japan	C12	40
Numazu, Japan	D11	40
Numfoor, Pulau, i., Indon.	F10	44
Nunavut, state, Canada	B11	106
Nunda, N.Y., U.S.	B7	114
Nuneaton, Eng., U.K.	I11	12
Nuñez, Cape, c., S. Geor.	J9	90
Nunivak Island, i., Ak., U.S.	D6	140
Nunjiang, China	B10	36
Nunkun, mtn., India	A6	54
Nunnelly, Tn., U.S.	I10	120
Nuomin, stm., China	B10	36
Nuoro, Italy	D3	24
Nuquí, Col.	E3	86
Nura, Kaz.	E12	32
Nura, stm., Kaz.	E12	32
Nur Dağları, mts., Tur.	B7	58
Nuremberg see Nürnberg, Ger.	G6	16
Nuremburg see Nürnberg, Ger.	G6	16
Nuriootpa, Austl.	J2	76
Nürnberg (Nuremberg), Ger.	G6	16
Nūrpur, India	B5	54
Nürtingen, Ger.	H5	16
Nusa Tenggara Barat, state, Indon.	G10	50
Nusa Tenggara Timur, state, Indon.	H12	50
Nuṣayrīyah, Jabal an-, mts., Syria	C7	58
Nu Shan, mts., China	F4	36
Nüshan Hu, l., China	E8	42
Nushki, Pak.	D10	56
Nutrioso, Az., U.S.	J7	132
Nutter Fort, W.V., U.S.	E5	114
Nuuk see Godthåb, Grnld.	E15	141
Nuwerus, S. Afr.	G4	70
Nuweveldberge, mts., S. Afr.	H5	70
Nūzvīd, India	C5	53
Nyabéssan, Cam.	D2	66
Nyabing, Austl.	F3	74
Nyack, N.Y., U.S.	C12	114
Nyahanga, Tan.	E6	66
Nyainqêntanglha Feng, mtn., China	C13	54
Nyainqêntanglha Shan, mts., China	C6	46
Nyainrong, China	B14	54
Nyakanazi, Tan.	E6	66
Nyala, Sudan	E5	62
Nyalam, China	D10	54
Nyamlell, Sudan	F5	62
Nyamtumbo, Tan.	G7	66
Nyang, stm., China	D14	54
Nyanga, stm., Afr.	J7	64
Nyasa, Lake, l., Afr.	C5	68
Nyaunglebin, Mya.	C3	48
Nyboe Land, reg., Grnld.	A14	141
Nyborg, Den.	I4	8
Nybro, Swe.	H6	8
Nyda, Russia	A12	32
Nyêmo, China	C7	46
Nyeri, Kenya	E7	66
Nyerol, Sudan	F6	62
Nyimba, Zam.	C5	68
Nyingchi, China	F3	36
Nyírbátor, Hung.	B9	26
Nyíregyháza, Hung.	B8	26
Nykøbing, Den.	I4	8
Nyköping, Swe.	G7	8
Nyland see Uusimaa, state, Fin.	F11	8
Nylstroom, S. Afr.	D9	70
Nymboida, stm., Austl.	G9	76
Nymburk, Czech Rep.	F11	16
Nynäshamn, Swe.	G7	8
Nyngan, Austl.	H6	76
Nyon, Switz.	D3	22
Nyons, Fr.	E11	18
Nýrsko, Czech Rep.	G9	16
Nyš, Russia	F17	34
Nysa, Pol.	F13	16
Nysa Kłodzka, stm., Pol.	F12	16
Nysa Łużycka (Lausitzer Neisse), stm., Eur.	E10	16
Nyslott see Savonlinna, Fin.	F13	8
Nysted, Den.	B7	16
Nyunzu, D.R.C.	F5	66
Nyūzen, Japan	C10	40
Nyvrovo, Russia	F17	34
Nzébéla, Gui.	H3	64
Nzérékoré, Gui.	H3	64
N'zeto, Ang.	B1	68
Nzwani, i., Com.	C7	68
O		
Oahe, Lake, res., U.S.	A12	126
Oahe Dam, dam, S.D., U.S.	C12	126
Oahu, i., Hi., U.S.	B4	78a
Oakbank, Austl.	I3	76
Oak Bay, B.C., Can.	H7	138
Oak Bluffs, Ma., U.S.	C15	114
Oakburn, Mb., Can.	D13	124
Oak City, N.C., U.S.	I8	114
Oak City, Ut., U.S.	D4	132
Oakdale, Ca., U.S.	F5	134
Oakdale, La., U.S.	G6	122
Oakdale, Ne., U.S.	E14	126
Oakes, N.D., U.S.	A14	126
Oakesdale, Wa., U.S.	C9	136
Oakey, Austl.	F8	76
Oakfield, Me., U.S.	D8	110
Oakfield, Wi., U.S.	H10	118
Oak Grove, La., U.S.	E7	122
Oak Harbor, Wa., U.S.	B4	136
Oak Hill, Fl., U.S.	H5	116
Oak Hill, Oh., U.S.	F3	114
Oak Hill, W.V., U.S.	G4	114
Oakhurst, Ca., U.S.	F6	134
Oak Knolls, Ca., U.S.	I5	134
Oak Lake, Mb., Can.	E13	124
Oak Lake, l., Mb., Can.	E13	124
Oak Lake, l., On., Can.	A5	118
Oakland, Ca., U.S.	F3	134
Oakland, Ia., U.S.	C2	120
Oakland, Me., U.S.	F7	110
Oakland, Md., U.S.	E6	114
Oakland, Ms., U.S.	C9	122
Oakland, Ne., U.S.	C1	120
Oakland, Or., U.S.	G3	136
Oakland City, In., U.S.	F10	120
Oakland Park, Fl., U.S.	J5	116
Oak Lawn, Il., U.S.	G2	112
Oakley, Id., U.S.	H13	136
Oakley, Ks., U.S.	B8	128
Oakman, Al., U.S.	D11	122
Oakohay Creek, stm., Ms., U.S.	F9	122
Oakover, stm., Austl.	D4	74
Oak Park, Il., U.S.	G2	112
Oak Ridge, Tn., U.S.	H1	114
Oak Ridge National Laboratory, sci., Tn., U.S.	H1	114
Oaktown, In., U.S.	F10	120
Oak View, Ca., U.S.	I6	134
Oakville, Mb., Can.	E15	124
Oakville, On., Can.	E10	112
Oakwood, Oh., U.S.	C1	114
Oamaru, N.Z.	G4	80
Oancea, Rom.	D14	26
Ōarai, Japan	C13	40
Oatman, Az., U.S.	H2	132
Oaxaca, state, Mex.	G10	100
Oaxaca de Juárez, Mex.	G10	100
Ob', stm., Russia	A11	32
Obabika Lake, l., On., Can.	A9	112
Obal', stm., Bela.	E12	10
Obala, Cam.	D2	66
Obama, Japan	D8	40
Obama, Japan	G3	40
Oban, Austl.	C2	76
Oban, Scot., U.K.	E7	12
Obanazawa, Japan	A13	40
O Barco de Valdeorras, Spain	B3	20
Ob Bay see Obskaja guba, b., Russia	A12	32
Obed, Ab., Can.	C13	138
Obeliai, Lith.	E8	10
Oberá, Arg.	C10	92
Oberhausen, Ger.	E2	16
Oberlin, La., U.S.	G6	122
Oberlin, Oh., U.S.	C3	114
Oberösterreich, state, Aus.	B10	22
Oberpullendorf, Aus.	C13	22
Oberursel, Ger.	F4	16
Oberviechtach, Ger.	G8	16
Ob Gulf see Obskaja guba, b., Russia	A12	32
Obi, Kepulauan, is., Indon.	F8	44
Obi, Pulau, i., Indon.	F8	44
Obi, Selat, strt., Indon.	F8	44
Óbidos, Braz.	D6	84
Obihiro, Japan	C15	38
Obi Islands see Obi, Kepulauan, is., Indon.	F8	44
Obion, Tn., U.S.	H8	120
Obion, stm., Tn., U.S.	H8	120
Obion, Middle Fork, stm., Tn., U.S.	H9	120
Oblačnaja, gora, mtn., Russia	C11	38
Oblong, Il., U.S.	F9	120
Obluče, Russia	G15	34
Obninsk, Russia	E19	10
Obnova, Blg.	F12	26
Obo, C.A.R.	C5	66
Obock, Dji.	E8	62
Obokote, D.R.C.	E5	66
Obozërskij, Russia	E19	8
O'Brien, Or., U.S.	A2	134
Obrovac, Cro.	F12	22
Obša, stm., Russia	E16	10
Obščij syrt, mts., Eur.	D8	32
Obskaja guba, b., Russia	A12	32
Obuasi, Ghana	H4	64
Obudu, Nig.	H6	64
Ocala, Fl., U.S.	G3	116
Ocamo, stm., Ven.	F9	86
Ocampo, Mex.	A4	100
Ocaña, Col.	C5	86
Ocaña, Spain	E7	20
Occhito, Lago di, res., Italy	C8	24
Occidental, Cordillera, mts., Col.	E3	86
Oceana, W.V., U.S.	G4	114
Ocean Cape, c., Ak., U.S.	E12	140
Ocean City, Md., U.S.	F10	114
Ocean City, N.J., U.S.	E11	114
Ocean Falls, B.C., Can.	D3	138
Ocean Island see Banaba, i., Kir.	D7	72
Ocean Park, Wa., U.S.	D2	136
Oceanside, Ca., U.S.	J8	134
Ocean Springs, Ms., U.S.	G10	122
Ocheyedan, Ia., U.S.	H3	118
Ōchi, Japan	E7	40
Ochlocknee, Ga., U.S.	F1	116
Ochlockonee, stm., U.S.	G14	122
Ocho Rios, Jam.	i13	104d
Ochsenfurt, Ger.	G5	16
Ocilla, Ga., U.S.	E2	116
Ockelbo, Swe.	F7	8
Ocmulgee National Monument, p.o.i., Ga., U.S.	D2	116
Ocnița, Mol.	A14	26
Ocoa, Bahía de, b., Dom. Rep.	C12	102
Ocoee, Fl., U.S.	H4	116
Ocoña, stm., Peru	G3	84
Oconee, stm., Ga., U.S.	D3	116
Oconee, Lake, res., Ga., U.S.	C2	116
Oconomowoc, Wi., U.S.	A9	120
Oconto, Wi., U.S.	D2	112
Oconto Falls, Wi., U.S.	D1	112
Ocosingo, Mex.	G12	100
Ocotal, Nic.	F4	102
Ocotes, Cerro, mtn., Mex.	B5	100
Ocotlán, Mex.	E7	100
Ocotlán de Morelos, Mex.	G10	100
Ocozocuautla, Mex.	G12	100
Ocracoke Island, i., N.C., U.S.	A10	116
Ocumare del Tuy, Ven.	B8	86
Oda, Ghana	H4	64
Ōda, Japan	D5	40
Oda, Jabal, mtn., Sudan	C7	62
Odaka, Japan	B14	40
Ōdate, Japan	D14	38
Odawara, Japan	D12	40
Odebolt, Ia., U.S.	B2	120
Odell, Il., U.S.	D9	120
Odell, Tx., U.S.	G9	128
Odem, Tx., U.S.	G10	130
Odemira, Port.	G2	20
Ödemiş, Tur.	E10	28
Odendaalsrus, S. Afr.	E8	70
Odense, Den.	I3	8
Odenwald, mts., Ger.	G4	16
Oder (Odra), stm., Eur.	D10	16
Oderzo, Italy	E9	22
Odesa, Ukr.	C17	26
Odesa, co., Ukr.	C16	26
Odessa see Odesa, Ukr.	C17	26
Odessa, Mo., U.S.	F3	120
Odessa, Tx., U.S.	C5	130
Odessa, Wa., U.S.	C8	136
Odesskoe, Russia	D12	32
Odiel, stm., Spain	G4	20
Odienné, C. Iv.	H3	64
Odin, Mount, mtn., B.C., Can.	F12	138
Odincovo, Russia	E20	10
Odobeşti, Rom.	D13	26
Odolanów, Pol.	E13	16
Odon, In., U.S.	F11	120
O'Donnell, Tx., U.S.	B6	130
Odorheiu Secuiesc, Rom.	C12	26
Odra (Oder), stm., Eur.	D10	16
Odrzywół, Pol.	E16	16
Odum, Ga., U.S.	E3	116
Odžaci, Yugo.	D6	26
Oebisfelde, Ger.	D6	16
Oeiras, Braz.	D4	88
Oelsnitz, Ger.	F8	16
Oelwein, Ia., U.S.	B6	120
Oenpelli, Austl.	B6	74
Oetz, Aus.	C7	22
O'Fallon, Mo., U.S.	F7	120
Ofanto, stm., Italy	D9	24
Ofaqim, Isr.	G5	58
Offa, Nig.	H5	64
Offaly, state, Ire.	H5	12
Offenbach am Main, Ger.	F4	16
Offenburg, Ger.	H3	16
Oficina Alemania, Chile	B3	92
Ofu, i., Am. Sam.	h13	79c
Ogaden, reg., Afr.	F8	62
Ōgaki, Japan	D9	40
Ogallala, Ne., U.S.	F11	126
Ogan, stm., Indon.	E4	50
Ogasawara-guntō, is., Japan	G18	30
Ogatsu, Japan	A14	40
Ogawa, Japan	G3	40
Ogbomosho, Nig.	H5	64
Ogden, Ks., U.S.	B12	128
Ogden, Ut., U.S.	B5	132
Ogdensburg, N.Y., U.S.	D14	112
Ogeechee, stm., Ga., U.S.	D4	116
Ogema, Sk., Can.	E8	124
Ogidaki Mountain, hill, On., Can.	A6	112
Ogilvie, Mn., U.S.	F5	118
Ogilvie Mountains, mts., Yk., Can.	C3	106
Oglesby, Il., U.S.	C8	120
Oglethorpe, Ga., U.S.	D1	116
Ogliastra, reg., Italy	E3	24
Oglio, stm., Italy	E6	22
Ogmore, Austl.	D7	76
Ognon, stm., Fr.	G15	14
Ogoja, Nig.	H6	64
Ogoki, stm., On., Can.	E13	106
Ogooué, stm., Afr.	I7	64
Ogōri, Japan	E4	40
Ogosta, stm., Blg.	F10	26
Ogre, Lat.	D7	10
Ogre, stm., Lat.	D8	10
O Grove, Spain	B2	20
Ogulin, Cro.	E12	22
Ogunquit, Me., U.S.	G6	110
Ogurdžaly, ostrov, i., Turkmen.	B7	56
Oğuzeli, Tur.	B8	58
Oha, Russia	F17	34
Ohanet, Alg.	D6	64
Ōhara, Japan	D13	40
O'Higgins, Cabo, c., Chile	e30	78l
O'Higgins, Lago (San Martín, Lago), l., S.A.	I2	90
Ohio, state, U.S.	D3	114
Ohio, stm., U.S.	G9	120
Ohio Peak, mtn., Co., U.S.	E9	132
'Ohonua, Tonga	o15	78e
Ohoopee, stm., Ga., U.S.	D3	116
Ohota, stm., Russia	E17	34
Ohotsk, Russia	E17	34
Ohře, stm., Eur.	F9	16
Ohrid, Mac.	B3	28
Ohrid, Lake, l., Eur.	D14	24
Ohrigstad, S. Afr.	D10	70
Öhringen, Ger.	G5	16
Ohuira, Bahía de, l., Mex.	C4	100
Ōi, stm., Japan	E11	40
Oiapoque, Braz.	C7	84
Oiapoque (Oyapok), stm., S.A.	C7	84
Oies, Île aux, i., Qc., Can.	C6	110
Oil Center, N.M., U.S.	B4	130
Oil City, La., U.S.	E4	122
Oil City, Pa., U.S.	C6	114
Oildale, Ca., U.S.	H7	134
Oilton, Ok., U.S.	A2	122
Oilton, Tx., U.S.	G9	130
Oil Trough, Ar., U.S.	B7	122
Oise, state, Fr.	E11	14
Oise, stm., Eur.	E11	14
Oistins, Barb.	n8	105d
Ōita, Japan	F4	40
Ōita, state, Japan	F4	40
Oituz, Pasul, p., Rom.	C13	26
Ojat', stm., Russia	F16	8
Öje, Swe.	F5	8
Ojinaga, Mex.	A6	100
Ojiya, Japan	B11	40
Ojmjakon, Russia	D17	34
Ojocaliente, Mex.	D7	100
Ojo de la Casa, Mex.	C1	130
Ojo del Carrizo, Mex.	E2	130
Ojo de Liebre, Laguna, b., Mex.	B1	100
Ojos del Salado, Nevado, mtn., S.A.	C3	92
Ojos Negros, Mex.	L9	134
Oka, stm., Russia	D6	32
Oka, stm., Russia	D18	32
Okaba, Indon.	G10	44
Okahandja, Nmb.	B3	70
Okaihau, N.Z.	B5	80
Okak Islands, is., Nf., Can.	F13	141
Okanagan (Okanogan), stm., N.A.	G11	138
Okanagan Falls, B.C., Can.	G11	138
Okanagan Lake, l., B.C., Can.	G10	138
Okanagan Landing, B.C., Can.	F11	138
Okanogan, Wa., U.S.	B7	136
Okanogan (Okanagan), stm., N.A.	G11	138
Okanogan Range, mts., Can.	A6	136
Okāra, Pak.	C4	54
Okaukuejo, Nmb.	D2	68
Okavango (Cubango), stm., Afr.	D2	68
Okavango Delta, Bots.	D3	68
Ōkawa, Japan	F3	40
Okawville, Il., U.S.	F8	120
Okaya, Japan	C11	40
Okayama, Japan	E6	40
Okayama, state, Japan	E6	40
Okazaki, Japan	E10	40
Okeechobee, Fl., U.S.	I5	116
Okeechobee, Lake, l., Fl., U.S.	J5	116

Name Map Ref. Page

Okeene, Ok., U.S. E10 128
Okefenokee Swamp, sw., U.S. F3 116
Okemos, Mi., U.S. B1 114
Okene, Nig. H6 64
Okhaldunggā, Nepal E11 54
Okhotsk, Sea of, Asia D18 30
Okhotsk Basin, unds. D17 142
Okhtyrka, Ukr. D4 32
Okiep, S. Afr. F3 70
Okinawa, Japan I18 39a
Okinawa Island see Okinawa-jima, i., Japan I19 39a
Okinawa-jima, i., Japan I19 39a
Okinawa-shotō, is., Japan I18 39a
Okino-Erabu-shima, i., Japan I19 39a
Oki-shotō, is., Japan C6 40
Okitipupa, Nig. H5 64
Oklahoma, state, U.S. F11 128
Oklahoma City, Ok., U.S. F11 128
Oklawaha, Fl., U.S. G4 116
Oklee, Mn., U.S. D3 118
Okmulgee, Ok., U.S. B3 122
Okollo, Ug. D6 66
Okolona, Ar., U.S. D5 122
Okolona, Ky., U.S. F12 120
Okondja, Gabon E2 66
Okonek, Pol. C12 16
Okotoks, Ab., Can. F16 138
Okoyo, Congo E2 66
Oktjabr', Russia C20 10
Oktjabr'sk, Kaz. E9 32
Oktjabr'skij, Russia F20 8
Oktjabr'skij, Russia G21 8
Oktjabr'skij, Russia D8 32
Oktjabr'skij, Russia F14 34
Oktjabr'skoe, Kaz. D11 32
Oktjabr'skoe, Russia B10 32
Ōkuchi, Japan G3 40
Okulovka, Russia B16 10
Okunëv Nos, Russia C25 8
Okushiri-tō, i., Japan C13 38
Okuta, Nig. H5 64
Okwa, stm., Afr. C6 70
Ola, Russia E19 34
Ola, Ar., U.S. B5 122
Ólafsfjörður, Ice. j30 8a
Olancha, Ca., U.S. G8 134
Olancha Peak, mtn., Ca., U.S. G7 134
Olanchito, Hond. E4 102
Öland, i., Swe. H7 8
Olanta, S.C., U.S. C6 116
Olary, Austl. I3 76
Olathe, Co., U.S. E8 132
Olathe, Ks., U.S. F3 120
Olavarría, Arg. H7 92
Oława (Ohlau), Pol. F13 16
Olbia, Italy D3 24
Olcott, N.Y., U.S. E11 112
Old Castille see Castilla la Vieja, hist. reg., Spain C7 20
Old Cork, Austl. D3 76
Old Crow, Yk., Can. C12 140
Old Crow, stm., N.A. C11 140
Olden, Tx., U.S. B9 130
Oldenburg, Ger. C3 16
Oldenburg, hist. reg., Ger. C4 16
Oldenburg in Holstein, Ger. B6 16
Oldenzaal, Neth. B15 14
Old Faithful Geyser, gysr., Wy., U.S. F16 136
Old Forge, Pa., U.S. C10 114
Old Fort Bay see Vieux-Fort, Qc., Can. i22 107a
Oldham, Eng., U.K. H10 12
Oldham, S.D., U.S. C15 126
Old Harbor, Ak., U.S. E9 140
Old Harbour, Jam. j13 104d
Old Hickory Lake, res., Tn., U.S. H11 120
Oldman, stm., Ab., Can. G19 138
Old Mkushi, Zam. C4 68
Old Norwood, Monts. D3 105a
Old Road, Antig. f4 105b
Old Road Bluff, c., Antig. f4 105b
Old Road Town, St. K./N. C2 105a
Olds, Ab., Can. E16 138
Old Saybrook, Ct., U.S. C13 114
Old Speck Mountain, mtn., Me., U.S. F5 110
Old Tate, Bots. B8 70
Old Town, Me., U.S. F8 110
Olduvai Gorge, val., Tan. E7 66
Old Wives Lake, l., Sk., Can. D8 124
Olean, N.Y., U.S. B7 114
O'Leary, P.E., Can. D12 110
Olecko, Pol. B18 16
Olëkma, stm., Russia E13 34
Olekminsk, Russia D13 34
Olëkminskij Stanovik, mts., Russia F12 34
Ølen, Nor. G1 8
Olenegorsk, Russia B15 8
Olenëk, Russia C11 34
Olenëk, stm., Russia C12 34
Olenëkskij zaliv, b., Russia B13 34
Olenij, ostrov, i., Russia B4 34
Olenino, Russia D16 10
Oléron, Île d', i., Fr. D4 18
Oleśnica, Pol. E13 16
Olesno, Pol. F14 16
Ol'ga, Russia C11 38
Olga, Mount, mtn., Austl. D6 74
Olgastretet, strt., Nor. B30 141
Ölgiy, Mong. E16 32
Olhão, Port. G3 20
Olho d'Água das Flores, Braz. E7 88
Ol'hon, ostrov, i., Russia F10 34
Olib, Otok, i., Cro. F11 22
Olifants (Elefantes), stm., Afr. D10 70
Olifants, stm., S. Afr. H6 70
Olifants, stm., S. Afr. H4 70
Olifantshoek, S. Afr. E6 70
Ólimbos (Olympus), mtn., Cyp. C3 58
Olímpia, Braz. K1 88
Olin, Ia., U.S. B6 120
Olinda, Braz. D8 88
Olio, Austl. C4 76
Olite, Spain B9 20
Oliva, Arg. F6 92
Oliva, Spain F10 20
Oliva de la Frontera, Spain F3 20
Olivares, Cerro de, mtn., S.A. E2 92
Olive Branch, Ms., U.S. C9 122
Olivees Mountain, mtn., St. K./N. C2 105a
Olive Hill, Ky., U.S. F2 114
Olivehurst, Ca., U.S. D4 134
Oliveira, Braz. K3 88
Oliveira dos Brejinhos, Braz. G4 88
Olivenza, Spain F3 20
Oliver Springs, Tn., U.S. H13 120
Olivet, Mi., U.S. B1 114
Olivet, S.D., U.S. D15 126
Olji Moron, stm., China B4 38
Oljutorskij, mys, c., Russia E23 34
Oljutorskij zaliv, b., Russia D22 34
Olla, La., U.S. F6 122
Ollagüe, Chile D3 90
Ollagüe, Volcán, vol., S.A. D3 90
Ollei, Palau f8 78b
Olmedo, Spain C6 20
Olmos, Peru E2 84
Olney, Mt., U.S. B12 136
Olney, Tx., U.S. H10 128
Olomouc, Czech Rep. G13 16
Olonec, Russia F15 8
Olongapo, Phil. C2 52
Oloron-Sainte-Marie, Fr. F5 18
Olot, Spain B13 20
Olovjannaja, Russia F12 34
Olpe, Ger. E3 16
Olpe, Ks., U.S. F1 120
Olsufevo, Russia G16 10
Olsztyn, Pol. C16 16
Olsztyn, state, Pol. C16 16
Olt, state, Rom. E11 26
Olt, stm., Rom. D11 26
Olta, Arg. E4 92
Olten, Switz. C4 22
Olteni, Rom. E12 26
Oltenița, Rom. E13 26
Olteț, stm., Rom. E10 26
Olton, Tx., U.S. G6 128
Oluan Pi, c., Tai. K9 42
Olustee, Fl., U.S. F3 116
Olutanga Island, i., Phil. G4 52
Olvera, Spain H5 20
Olympia, Wa., U.S. C3 136
Olympiá, hist., Grc. F4 28
Olympia see Olympiá, hist., Grc. F4 28
Olympic Mountains, mts., Wa., U.S. C3 136
Olympic National Park, p.o.i., Wa., U.S. C3 136
Ólympos (Olympus, Mount), mtn., Grc. C5 28
Olympus see Ólimbos, mtn., Cyp. C3 58
Olympus, Mount see Ólympos, mtn., Grc. C5 28
Olympus, Mount, mtn., Wa., U.S. C3 136
Om', stm., Russia D13 32
Ōmachi, Japan C10 40
Omae-zaki, c., Japan E11 40
Ōmagari, Japan E14 38
Omagh, N. Ire., U.K. G5 12
Omaha, Ne., U.S. C2 120
Omaha, Tx., U.S. D4 122
Omaheke, state, Nmb. C4 70
Omak, Wa., U.S. B7 136
Oman, ctry., Asia F8 56
Oman, Gulf of, b., Asia E8 56
Omaruru, Nmb. B3 70
Omaruru, stm., Nmb. B2 70
Omatako, mtn., Nmb. B3 70
Omatako, stm., Nmb. B3 70
Omate, Peru G3 84
Omboué, Gabon E1 66
Ombrone, stm., Italy H8 22
Omčak, Russia D18 34
Omdurman see Umm Durmān, Sudan D6 62
Ōme, Japan D12 40
Omega, Ga., U.S. E2 116
Omegna, Italy E5 22
Omemee, On., Can. D11 112
Omeo, Austl. K6 76
Ömerköy, Tur. D10 28
Ömerli Barajı, res., Tur. C12 28
Ometepe, Isla de, i., Nic. G5 102
Ometepec, Mex. G9 100
Ōmi-hachiman, Japan D8 40
Omineca, stm., B.C., Can. D6 106
Omineca Mountains, mts., B.C., Can. D5 106
Ōmiya, Japan D12 40
Ommaney, Cape, c., Ak., U.S. E13 140
Ommanney Bay, b., Nu., Can. A10 106
Omo, stm., Afr. F7 62
Omoloj, stm., Russia B15 34
Omolon, stm., Russia C20 34
Omsk, Russia C12 32
Omsukčan, Russia D20 34
Omul, Vârful, mtn., Rom. D12 26
Ōmura, Japan G2 40
Omurtag, Blg. F13 26
Ōmuta, Japan F3 40
Omutinskij, Russia C11 32
Omutninsk, Russia C8 32
Onabas, Mex. A4 100
Onaga, Ks., U.S. E1 120
Onaman Lake, l., On., Can. A11 118
Onamia, Mn., U.S. E5 118
Onangué, Lac, l., Gabon E1 66
Onaping Lake, l., On., Can. A8 112
Onarga, Il., U.S. D10 120
Onatchiway, Lac, res., Qc., Can. A5 110
Onawa, Ia., U.S. B1 120
Onaway, Mi., U.S. C5 112
Oncativo, Arg. E6 92
Once, Canal Numero, can., Arg. H8 92
Oncócua, Ang. D1 68
Onda, Spain E10 20
Ondangwa, Nmb. D2 68
Ondas, stm., Braz. G3 88
Ondava, stm., Slov. H17 16
Ondjiva, Ang. D2 68
Ondo, Japan E5 40
Ondo, Nig. H5 64
Öndörhaan, Mong. B7 36
Ondozero, ozero, l., Russia E15 8
Oneco, Fl., U.S. I3 116
Onega, Russia E17 8
Onega, stm., Russia E18 8
Onega, Lake see Onežskoe ozero, l., Russia F16 8
Onega Bay see Onežskaja guba, b., Russia D17 8
One Hundred and Two, stm., Mo., U.S. D3 120
One Hundred Fifty Mile House, B.C., Can. D9 138
One Hundred Mile House, B.C., Can. E9 138
Oneida, Il., U.S. C7 120
Oneida, N.Y., U.S. E14 112
Oneida, Tn., U.S. H13 120
Oneida Lake, l., N.Y., U.S. E14 112
O'Neill, Ne., U.S. E14 126
Onekama, Mi., U.S. D3 112
Onekotan, ostrov, i., Russia G20 34
Oneonta, Al., U.S. D12 122
Oneonta, N.Y., U.S. B10 114
Onești, Rom. C13 26
Onevai, i., Tonga n14 78e
Onežskaja guba (Onega Bay), b., Russia D17 8
Onežskij poluostrov, pen., Russia D17 8
Onežskoe ozero (Onega, Lake), l., Russia F16 8
Ongjin-ŭp, Kor., N. F6 38
Ongniud Qi, China C3 38
Ongole, India D5 53
Onilahy, stm., Madag. F7 68
Onion Creek, stm., Tx., U.S. D10 130
Onitsha, Nig. H6 64
Ōno, Japan D9 40
Onoda, Japan F4 40
Onomichi, Japan E6 40
Onon, Mong. B7 36
Onon Gol, stm., Asia G11 34
Onoto, Ven. C9 86
Onotoa, at., Kir. D8 72
Onoway, Ab., Can. C16 138
Ons, Illa de, i., Spain B1 20
Onset, Ma., U.S. C15 114
Onslow, Austl. D3 74
Onslow Bay, b., N.C., U.S. B8 116
On-take, vol., Japan H3 40
Ontake-san, vol., Japan D10 40
Ontario, Ca., U.S. I8 134
Ontario, Or., U.S. F10 136
Ontario, state, Can. E13 106
Ontario, Lake, l., N.A. E11 112
Ontinyent, Spain F10 20
Ontojärvi, l., Fin. D13 8
Ontonagon, Mi., U.S. E9 118
Ontong Java, at., Sol. Is. D7 72
Onverwacht, Sur. B6 84
Oodnadatta, Austl. E7 74
Ooldea, Austl. F6 74
Oologah, Ok., U.S. H2 120
Oologah Lake, res., Ok., U.S. H2 120
Oorlogskloof, stm., S. Afr. G4 70
Oos-Londen see East London, S. Afr. H8 70
Oostburg, Wi., U.S. E2 112
Oostelijk Flevoland, reg., Neth. B14 14
Oostende, Bel. C11 14
Oosterhout, Neth. C13 14
Oosterschelde, est., Neth. C12 14
Ootsa Lake, B.C., Can. C4 138
Ootsa Lake, res., B.C., Can. C4 138
Opaka, Blg. F13 26
Opala, D.R.C. E4 66
Oparino, Russia G22 8
Opatija, Cro. E11 22
Opava, Czech Rep. G13 16
Opawica, stm., Qc., Can. A2 110
Opečenskij Posad, Russia B17 10
Opelika, Al., U.S. E13 122
Opelousas, La., U.S. G6 122
Opeongo, stm., On., Can. C12 112
Opeongo Lake, l., On., Can. C11 112
Ophir, Ak., U.S. D8 140
Ophir, Or., U.S. H2 136
Opihikao, Hi., U.S. D7 78a
Opinaca, stm., Qc., Can. E15 106
Opiscotéo, Lac, l., Qc., Can. E17 106
Opobo, Nig. I6 64
Opočka, Russia D11 10
Opoczno, Pol. E16 16
Opole, Pol. F13 16
Opole, state, Pol. F13 16
Opotiki, N.Z. D7 80
Oppdal, Nor. E3 8
Oppland, state, Nor. F3 8
Opportunity, Mt., U.S. D14 136
Opportunity, Wa., U.S. C9 136
Optima Lake, res., Ok., U.S. E7 128
Opua, N.Z. B6 80
Opunake, N.Z. D5 80
Opuwo, Nmb. D1 68
Oquawka, Il., U.S. K7 118
Or, Côte d', mts., Fr. G13 14
Oracle, Az., U.S. K6 132
Oradea, Rom. B8 26
Öræfajökull, ice, Ice. k31 8a
Orahovica, Cro. E14 22
Orai, India F7 54
Oraibi Wash, stm., Az., U.S. H6 132
Oral see Ural'sk, Kaz. D8 32
Oran see Wahran, Alg. B4 64
Orange, Austl. I7 76
Orange, Fr. E10 18
Orange, Ma., U.S. B13 114
Orange, Tx., U.S. G5 122
Orange, Va., U.S. F7 114
Orange (Oranje) (Senqu), stm., Afr. F3 70
Orange, Cabo, c., Braz. C7 84
Orangeburg, S.C., U.S. C4 116
Orange City, Ia., U.S. A1 120
Orange Cove, Ca., U.S. G6 134
Orange Free State see Free State, state, S. Afr. F8 70
Orange Grove, Tx., U.S. G9 130
Orange Lake, Fl., U.S. G3 116
Orange Lake, l., Fl., U.S. G3 116
Orangeville, On., Can. E9 112
Orangeville, Ut., U.S. D5 132
Orange Walk, Belize C3 102
Orango, Ilha de, i., Gui.-B. G1 64
Orani, Phil. C3 52
Oranienburg, Ger. D8 16
Oranje see Orange, stm., Afr. F3 70
Oranje Gebergte, mts., Sur. C6 84
Oranjemund, Nmb. F3 70
Oranjestad, Aruba o19 104g
Oranjestad, Neth. Ant. C1 105a
Oranje Vrijstaat see Free State, state, S. Afr. F8 70
Orăștie, Rom. D10 26
Orba Co, l., China A8 54
Orbetello, Italy H8 22
Órbigo, stm., Spain B5 20
Orbisonia, Pa., U.S. D8 114
Orbost, Austl. K7 76
Örbyhus, Swe. F7 8
Orcadas, sci., Ant. B36 81
Orchard City, Co., U.S. E8 132
Orchard Homes, Mt., U.S. D12 136
Orchard Mesa, Co., U.S. E8 132
Orchard Park, N.Y., U.S. B7 114
Ord, Ne., U.S. F14 126
Ord, stm., Austl. C5 74
Ord, Mount, mtn., Austl. C5 74
Ordenes see Ordes, Spain A2 20
Orderville, Ut., U.S. F4 132
Ordes, Spain A2 20
Ordesa y Monte Perdido, Parque Nacional de, p.o.i., Spain B10 20
Ord Mountain, mtn., Ca., U.S. I9 134
Ordos Desert see Mu Us Shamo, des., China B3 42
Ord River, Austl. C5 74
Ordu, Tur. A4 56
Ordway, Co., U.S. C5 128
Ordžonikidzeabad, Taj. B10 56
Örebro, Swe. G6 8
Örebro, state, Swe. G6 8
Oredež, Russia B13 10
Oredež, stm., Russia B13 10
Oregon, Il., U.S. B8 120
Oregon, Mo., U.S. D2 120
Oregon, Oh., U.S. C2 114
Oregon, state, U.S. G6 136
Oregon Caves National Monument, p.o.i., Or., U.S. A2 134
Oregon City, Or., U.S. E4 136
Oregon Dunes National Recreation Area, p.o.i., Or., U.S. G2 136
Orehovo-Zuevo, Russia E21 10
Orel, Russia G18 10
Orel', ozero, l., Russia F16 34
Orellana, Peru E2 84
Orellana, Embalse de, res., Spain E5 20
Orem, Ut., U.S. C5 132
Ore Mountains, mts., Eur. F8 16
Orenburg, Russia D8 32
Örencik, Tur. D12 28
Orense, Arg. I8 92
Orense see Ourense, Spain B3 20
Orense see Ourense, co., Spain B3 20
Oreor, i., Palau g8 78b
Orestes Pereyra, Mex. B6 100
Orestiáda, Grc. B9 28
Orford Ness, c., Eng., U.K. I14 12
Organ Pipe Cactus National Monument, p.o.i., Az., U.S. K4 132
Orgelet, Fr. H14 14
Orgosolo, Italy D3 24
Orgūn, Afg. C10 56
Orhangazi, Tur. C12 28
Orhei, Mol. B15 26
Orhon, stm., Mong. B5 36
Orichuna, stm., Ven. D7 86
Orick, Ca., U.S. B1 134
Orient, Ia., U.S. C3 120
Orient, Wa., U.S. B8 136
Oriental, Cordillera, mts., Col. E5 86
Oriental, Cordillera, mts., Peru F3 84
Orientos, Austl. G3 76
Orihuela see Oriola, Spain F10 20
Orillia, On., Can. D10 112
Orimattila, Fin. F11 8
Orinduik, Guy. E11 86
Orinoco, stm., S.A. C10 86
Orinoco, Delta del, Ven. C11 86
Oriola, Spain F10 20
Orion, Il., U.S. C7 120
Oriskany, N.Y., U.S. E14 112
Orissa, state, India D5 46
Orissaare, Est. B5 10
Oristano, Italy E2 24
Oristano, Golfo di, b., Italy E2 24
Orituco, stm., Ven. C8 86
Orivesi, l., Fin. E13 8
Oriximiná, Braz. D6 84
Orizaba, Mex. F10 100
Orjahovo, Blg. F10 26
Orjen, mtn., Yugo. G5 26
Orkney, Sk., Can. E5 124
Orkney, S. Afr. E8 70
Orkney Islands, is., Scot., U.K. C10 12
Orlândia, Braz. K1 88
Orlando, Fl., U.S. H4 116
Orléanais, hist. reg., Fr. F11 14
Orleans, On., Can. C14 112
Orléans, Fr. G10 14
Orleans, Ca., U.S. B2 134
Orleans, Ma., U.S. C15 114
Orleans, Ne., U.S. A9 128
Orleans, Vt., U.S. F4 110
Orléans, Canal d', can., Fr. G11 14
Orléans, Île d', i., Qc., Can. D6 110
Orlik, Russia D18 32
Orlovskaja oblast', co., Russia H19 10
Orly, Fr. F11 14
Ormāra, Pak. D9 56
Ormiston, Sk., Can. E8 124
Ormoc, Phil. E5 52
Ormond Beach, Fl., U.S. G4 116
Ornain, stm., Fr. F14 14
Ornans, Fr. G15 14
Orne, state, Fr. F8 14
Orne, stm., Fr. E14 14
Orne, stm., Fr. F8 14
Ornö, i., Swe. G8 8
Örnsköldsvik, Swe. E8 8
Oročen, Russia E14 34
Orocovis, P.R. B3 104a
Orocué, Col. E6 86
Orofino, Id., U.S. D10 136
Orog nuur, l., Mong. B5 36
Orohena, Mont, mtn., Fr. Poly. v22 78h
Oroluk, at., Micron. C6 72
Oromocto, N.B., Can. E10 110
Oromocto Lake, l., N.B., Can. E10 110
Oron, Nig. I6 64
Orona, at., Kir. D9 72
Orono, On., Can. D11 112
Orono, Me., U.S. F8 110
Orontes (Asi), stm., Asia B7 58
Oroquieta, Phil. F4 52
Orós, Braz. D6 88
Orós, Açude, res., Braz. D6 88
Orosei, Italy D3 24
Orosei, Golfo di, b., Italy D3 24
Orosháza, Hung. C7 26
Oroszlány, Hung. B5 26
Orote Peninsula, pen., Guam j9 78c
Oroville, Ca., U.S. D4 134
Oroville, Lake, res., Ca., U.S. D4 134
Orpheus Island, i., Austl. B6 76
Orrick, Mo., U.S. E3 120
Orrin, N.D., U.S. F13 124
Orroroo, Austl. I2 76
Orrs Island, Me., U.S. G7 110
Orša, Bela. F13 10
Orsk, Russia D9 32
Orșova, Rom. E9 26
Ortaca, Tur. G11 28
Ortakent, Tur. F10 28
Ortaklar, Tur. F10 28
Orta Nova, Italy C9 24
Ortega, Col. F4 86
Ortegal, Cabo, c., Spain A2 20
Orteguaza, stm., Col. G4 86
Orthon, stm., Bol. B3 90
Ortigueira, Spain A3 20
Orting, Wa., U.S. C4 136
Ortiz, Mex. A3 100
Ortiz, Ven. C8 86
Ortona, Italy H11 22
Ortonville, Mn., U.S. F2 118
Orūmīyeh, Iran B6 56
Orūmīyeh, Daryācheh-ye (Urmia, Lake), l., Iran B6 56
Orust, i., Swe. G4 8
Orvieto, Italy H9 22
Orwell, Oh., U.S. C5 114
Orxon, stm., China B8 36
Orzinuovi, Italy E6 22
Orzyc, stm., Pol. D17 16
Oš, Kyrg. F12 32
Os, Nor. E4 8
Osa, Península de, pen., C.R. H6 102
Osage, Ia., U.S. H6 118
Osage, Wy., U.S. D8 126
Osage, stm., Mo., U.S. F5 120
Osage Beach, Mo., U.S. F5 120
Osage City, Ks., U.S. F2 120
Ōsaka, Japan E8 40
Ōsaka, state, Japan E8 40
Osakarovka, Kaz. D12 32
Ōsaka-wan, b., Japan E8 40
Osăm, stm., Blg. F11 26
Osawatomie, Ks., U.S. F3 120
Osborne, Ks., U.S. B10 128
Osburn, Id., U.S. C11 136
Osceola, Ar., U.S. B8 122
Osceola, Ia., U.S. C4 120
Osceola, Mo., U.S. F4 120
Osceola, Wi., U.S. F6 118
Osceola Mills, Pa., U.S. D7 114
Oschatz, Ger. E8 16
Oschersleben, Ger. D7 16
Osečina, Yugo. E6 26
Osëtr, stm., Russia F21 10
Osetrovo, Russia E10 34
Osgood, In., U.S. E12 120
Oshawa, On., Can. E11 112
Oshika, Japan A14 40
Oshika-hantō, pen., Japan A14 40
Ō-shima, i., Japan E12 40
Oshima-hantō, pen., Japan C14 38
Oshkosh, Ne., U.S. F10 126
Oshkosh, Wi., U.S. G10 118
Oshogbo, Nig. H5 64
Oshwe, D.R.C. E3 66
Osica de Jos, Rom. E11 26
Osijek, Cro. E15 22
Osilo, Italy D2 24
Osimo, Italy G10 22
Osinniki, Russia D15 32
Osipovo Selo, Russia D13 10
Osire Süd, Nmb. B3 70
Oskaloosa, Ia., U.S. C5 120
Oskaloosa, Ks., U.S. E2 120
Oskarshamn, Swe. H7 8
Oskolkovo, Russia B26 8
Oslo, Nor. G4 8
Oslo, state, Nor. F4 8
Oslofjorden, b., Nor. G4 8
Osmānābād, India B3 53
Osmaneli, Tur. C12 28
Osmaniye, Tur. A7 58
Os'mino, Russia A11 10
Osmussaar, i., Est. A6 10
Osnabrück, Ger. D4 16
Osorno, Chile H2 90
Osorno, Spain B6 20
Osoyoos, B.C., Can. G11 138
Oss, Neth. C14 14
Ossa, Mount, mtn., Austl. n13 77a
Ossabaw Island, i., Ga., U.S. E4 116
Osseo, Wi., U.S. G7 118
Ossian, Ia., U.S. A6 120
Ossining, N.Y., U.S. C12 114
Ossipee, N.H., U.S. G5 110
Ossjøen, l., Nor. F4 8
Ossora, Russia E21 34
Ostaškov, Russia C16 10
Ostašovo, Russia E18 10
Ostende see Oostende, Bel. C11 14
Ostër (Ascör), stm., Eur. G15 10
Osterburg, Ger. D7 16
Östergötland, state, Swe. G7 8
Osterholz-Scharmbeck, Ger. C4 16
Osterode am Harz, Ger. E6 16
Osterøyni, i., Nor. F1 8
Östersund, Swe. E6 8
Osterwieck, Ger. E6 16
Østfold, state, Nor. G4 8
Ostfriesische Inseln (East Frisian Islands), is., Ger. C3 16
Ostfriesland, hist. reg., Ger. C3 16
Østgrønland (Tunu), state, Grnld. C18 141
Östhammar, Swe. F8 8
Ostpreussen, hist. reg., Eur. F4 10
Ostrava, Czech Rep. G14 16
Ostróda, Pol. C15 16
Ostrogožsk, Russia D5 32
Ostrołęka, Pol. C17 16
Ostrołęka, state, Pol. D17 16
Ostroróg, Pol. D12 16
Ostrov, Czech Rep. F8 16
Ostrov, Russia C11 10
Ostrov, i., Slov. I13 16
Ostrov-Zalit, Russia B11 10
Ostrowiec Świętokrzyski, Pol. F17 16
Ostrów Mazowiecka, Pol. D17 16
Ostrów Wielkopolski, Pol. E13 16
Ostrzeszów, Pol. E13 16
Ostuni, Italy D11 24
O'Sullivan Lake, l., On., Can. A11 118
Osum, stm., Alb. D14 24
Ōsumi-hantō, pen., Japan H3 40
Osumi Islands see Ōsumi-shotō, is., Japan I9 38
Ōsumi-kaikyō, strt., Japan I9 38
Ōsumi-shotō, is., Japan I9 38
Osuna, Spain G5 20
Oswego, Il., U.S. C9 120
Oswego, Ks., U.S. G2 120
Oswego, N.Y., U.S. E13 112
Oswestry, Eng., U.K. I9 12
Oświęcim (Auschwitz), Pol. F15 16
Osyka, Ms., U.S. F8 122
Ōta, Japan C12 40
Otaci, Mol. A14 26
Ōtake, Japan E5 40
Otaki, N.Z. E6 80
Otaru, Japan C14 38
Otautau, N.Z. H2 80
Otava, Fin. F12 8
Otava, stm., Czech Rep. G9 16
Otavalo, Ec. G2 86
Otavi, Nmb. D2 68
Ōtawara, Japan C12 40
Otego Creek, stm., N.Y., U.S. G3 110
Oteotea, Sol. Is. e9 79b
Oteros, stm., Mex. B4 100
Otinapa, Mex. C6 100
Otis, Co., U.S. A6 128
Otis, Ks., U.S. C9 128
Otish, Monts, mts., Qc., Can. E16 106
Otjimbingwe, Nmb. C2 70
Otjinene, Nmb. B4 70
Otjiwarongo, Nmb. B3 70
Otjozondjou, stm., Nmb. B5 70
Otjozondjupa, state, Nmb. B3 70
Otočac, Cro. F12 22
Otoskwin, stm., On., Can. E13 106
Otra, stm., Nor. G2 8
Otradnyj, Russia D8 32
Otranto, Italy D12 24
Otranto, Strait of, strt., Eur. D12 24
Otrokovice, Czech Rep. G13 16
Otrøya, i., Nor. E2 8
Ötscher, mtn., Aus. C12 22
Ōtsu, Japan D8 40
Otta, Nor. F3 8
Ottawa, On., Can. C14 112
Ottawa, Il., U.S. C9 120
Ottawa, Ks., U.S. F2 120
Ottawa, Oh., U.S. C1 114
Ottawa (Outaouais), stm., Can. C15 112
Ottawa Islands, is., Nu., Can. D14 106
Otterburne, Mb., Can. E16 124
Otter Creek, Fl., U.S. G3 116
Otter Creek, stm., Vt., U.S. F3 110
Otter Lake, Mi., U.S. E6 112
Otterøya see Otrøya, i., Nor. E2 8
Otter Tail, stm., Mn., U.S. E2 118
Otter Tail Lake, l., Mn., U.S. E2 118
Otterville, Mo., U.S. F5 120
Ottosdal, S. Afr. E7 70
Ottoshoop, S. Afr. D8 70
Ottoville, Oh., U.S. D1 114
Ottumwa, Ia., U.S. C5 120
Ottweiler, Ger. G3 16
Otway, Cape, c., Austl. L4 76
Otwock, Pol. D17 16
Ötztaler Alpen (Venoste, Alpi), mts., Eur. D7 22
Ou, stm., China G9 42
Ou, stm., China I5 42
Ou, stm., Laos B6 48
Ouacha, Niger G6 64
Ouachita, stm., U.S. F7 122
Ouachita, Lake, res., Ar., U.S. C5 122
Ouachita Mountains, mts., U.S. C4 122
Ouaco, N. Cal. m15 79d
Ouadda, C.A.R. C4 66
Ouagadougou, Burkina G4 64
Ouahigouya, Burkina G4 64
Ouahran see Wahran, Alg. B4 64
Ouaka, stm., C.A.R. C4 66
Oualâta, Maur. F3 64
Ouallene, Alg. E5 64
Ouanary, Fr. Gu. C7 84
Ouanda Djallé, C.A.R. C4 66
Ouango, C.A.R. D4 66
Ouangolodougou, C. Iv. H3 64
Ouarâne, reg., Maur. E2 64
Ouarkziz, Jbel, mts., Afr. D3 64
Ouarzazate, Mor. C3 64
Ouasiemsca, stm., Qc., Can. A4 110
Oubangui (Ubangi), stm., Afr. E3 66
Oudenaarde, Bel. D12 14
Oudtshoorn, S. Afr. H6 70
Oued Fodda, Alg. H12 20
Oued-Zem, Mor. C3 64
Ouémé, stm., Benin H5 64
Ouen, Île, i., N. Cal. n16 79d
Ouessant, Île d' (Ushant), i., Fr. F3 14
Ouesso, Congo D3 66
Ouezzane, Mor. C3 64
Ouham, stm., Afr. F3 62
Ouidah, Benin H5 64
Ouimet Canyon, misc. cult., On., Can. C10 118
Ouistreham, Fr. E8 14
Oujda, Mor. C4 64
Oulangan kansallispuisto, p.o.i., Fin. C13 8
Oulu (Uleåborg), Fin. D11 8
Oulu, state, Fin. D12 8
Oulujärvi, l., Fin. D12 8
Oum-Chalouba, Chad D4 62
Oumé, C. Iv. H3 64
Oum-Hadjer, Chad E3 62
Oumiao, China F5 42
Ounasjoki, stm., Fin. C11 8
Ounianga Kébir, Chad D3 62
Ourém, Braz. A2 88
Ourense, Spain B3 20
Ourense, co., Spain B3 20
Ouricuri, Braz. D5 88
Ourinhos, Braz. D7 90
Ouro Branco, Braz. D7 88
Ouro Fino, Braz. L2 88
Ouro Preto, Braz. K4 88
Ours, Grande chute à l', wtfl, Qc., Can. B4 110
Ourthe, stm., Bel. D14 14
Ōu-sammyaku, mts., Japan E14 38
Oust, can., Fr. F6 14
Outaouais (Ottawa), stm., Can. C15 112
Outardes, stm., Qc., Can. E17 106
Outer Hebrides, is., Scot., U.K. D5 12
Outer Island, i., Wi., U.S. D8 118
Outer Santa Barbara Passage, strt., Ca., U.S. J7 134
Outjo, Nmb. B3 70
Outlook, Sk., Can. C6 124
Outlook, Mt., U.S. F9 124
Out Skerries, is., Scot., U.K. n19 12a
Ouvéa, i., N. Cal. m16 79d
Ouyen, Austl. J4 76
Ovacık, Tur. B15 28
Ovada, Italy F5 22
Ovalle, Chile E2 92
Ovana, Cerro, mtn., Ven. E8 86
Ovar, Port. D2 20
Ovejas, Col. C4 86
Overbrook, Ks., U.S. F2 120
Overflowing, stm., Can. A12 124
Overland Park, Ks., U.S. F3 120
Overton, Ne., U.S. G13 126
Overton, Tx., U.S. E4 122
Overton Arm, b., Nv., U.S. G2 132
Övertorneå, Swe. C10 8
Ovett, Ms., U.S. F9 122
Ovid, N.Y., U.S. B9 114
Ovidiopol', Ukr. C17 26
Oviedo, Spain A5 20
Oviniščе, Russia B20 10
Ovīši, Lat. C4 10
Ovoot, Mong. B7 36
Øvre Anárjohka Nasjonalpark, p.o.i., Nor. B13 8
Øvre Dividal Nasjonalpark, p.o.i., Nor. B8 8
Ovstug, Russia G16 10
Owando, Congo E3 66
Owase, Japan E9 40
Owasso, Ok., U.S. H2 120
Owatonna, Mn., U.S. G5 118
Owbeh, Afg. C9 56
Owego, N.Y., U.S. B9 114
Owen, Wi., U.S. G8 118
Owendo, Gabon D1 66
Owens, stm., Ca., U.S. F7 134
Owensboro, Ky., U.S. G10 120
Owens Lake, l., Ca., U.S. G8 134
Owen Sound, On., Can. D8 112
Owen Sound, b., On., Can. D9 112
Owen Stanley Range, mts., Pap. N. Gui. b4 79a
Owensville, In., U.S. F10 120
Owensville, Mo., U.S. F6 120
Owerri, Nig. H6 64
Owikeno Lake, l., B.C., Can. E3 138
Owingsville, Ky., U.S. F2 114
Owl, stm., Ab., Can. A19 138
Owl, stm., Mb., Can. D12 106
Owo, Nig. H6 64
Owosso, Mi., U.S. E5 112
Owyhee, Nv., U.S. B9 134
Owyhee, stm., U.S. G9 136
Owyhee, Lake, res., Or., U.S. G9 136
Owyhee, South Fork, stm., U.S. H10 136
Öxarfjörður, b., Ice. j31 8a
Oxbow, Sk., Can. E11 124
Oxelösund, Swe. G7 8
Oxford, N.S., Can. E13 110
Oxford, N.Z. F5 80
Oxford, Eng., U.K. J11 12
Oxford, Al., U.S. D13 122
Oxford, In., U.S. H2 112
Oxford, Ks., U.S. D11 128
Oxford, Me., U.S. F6 110
Oxford, Md., U.S. F9 114
Oxford, Ms., U.S. C9 122
Oxford, N.Y., U.S. B10 114
Oxford, N.C., U.S. H7 114
Oxford, Oh., U.S. E13 120
Oxford, Pa., U.S. I14 112
Oxford, Wi., U.S. H9 118
Oxford Junction, Ia., U.S. J8 118
Oxford Lake, l., Mb., Can. E11 106
Oxford Peak, mtn., Id., U.S. H14 136
Oxkutzcab, Mex. B3 102
Oxley Downs, Austl. J4 76
Oxley Wild Rivers National Park, p.o.i., Austl. H8 76
Oxnard, Ca., U.S. I6 134
Oxus see Amu Darya, stm., Asia F10 32
Oya, stm., Malay. B8 50
Oyabe, Japan C9 40
Oyama, Japan C12 40
Ōyano, Japan G3 40
Oyapok (Oiapoque), stm., S.A. C7 84
Oyem, Gabon D2 66
Oyen, Ab., Can. C3 124
Oyo, Nig. H5 64
Oyonnax, Fr. C11 18
Oyster Creek, mth., Tx., U.S. E12 130
Ozamis, Phil. F4 52
Ozark, Al., U.S. F13 122
Ozark, Ar., U.S. B5 122
Ozark, Mo., U.S. G4 120
Ozark Plateau, plat., U.S. H4 120
Ozarks, Lake of the, res., Mo., U.S. F5 120
Ózd, Hung. A7 26
Ožerele, Russia F21 10
Ozernovskij, Russia F20 34
Ozërnyj, Russia D10 32
Ozery, Russia F21 10
Ozette Lake, l., Wa., U.S. B2 136
Ozieri, Italy D2 24
Ozimek, Pol. F14 16
Ozinki, Russia D7 32
Ozorków, Pol. E15 16

Name | Map Ref. | Page

Ōzu, Japan F5 40
Ozuluama, Mex. E9 100
Ozurgeti, Geor. F6 32

P

Paagoumène, N. Cal. m14 79d
Paama, state, Vanuatu k17 79d
Paama, i., Vanuatu k17 79d
Paamiut see Frederikshåb, Grnld. E15 141
Paarl, S. Afr. H4 70
Paauilo, Hi., U.S. C6 78a
Pabbay, i., Scot., U.K. D5 12
Pabbiring, Kepulauan, is., Indon. F11 50
Pabean, Indon. G9 50
Pabellón, Ensenada del, b., Mex. C4 100
Pabianice, Pol. E15 16
Pablo, Mt., U.S. C12 136
Pābna, Bngl. G12 54
Pabradė, Lith. F8 10
Pacaás Novos, Serra dos, mts., Braz. F5 84
Pacajus, Braz. C6 88
Pacasmayo, Peru E2 84
Pacatuba, Braz. C6 88
Pachino, Italy H9 24
Pachitea, stm., Peru E3 84
Pachmarhi, India G7 54
Pāchora, India H5 54
Pachuca de Soto, Mex. E9 100
Pacific, B.C., Can. B2 138
Pacific, Mo., U.S. F7 120
Pacifica, Ca., U.S. F3 134
Pacific-Antarctic Ridge, unds. P22 142
Pacific Grove, Ca., U.S. G3 134
Pacific Ocean F20 142
Pacific Ranges, mts., B.C., Can. E5 138
Pacific Rim National Park, p.o.i., B.C., Can. H5 138
Paciran, Indon. G8 50
Pacitan, Indon. H7 50
Pacora, Pan. C2 86
Pacov, Czech Rep. G11 16
Pacuí, stm., Braz. I3 88
Padada, Phil. G5 52
Padamo, stm., Ven. F9 86
Padampur, India H9 54
Padang, Indon. D6 50
Padang, Indon. G12 50
Padang, Indon. D2 50
Padang, Pulau, i., Indon. C3 50
Padang Endau, Malay. K6 48
Padangpanjang, Indon. D2 50
Padangsidempuan, Indon. C1 50
Padany, Russia E15 8
Padas, stm., Malay. A9 50
Padauari, stm., Braz. G9 86
Paddle, stm., Ab., Can. B16 138
Paddle Prairie, Ab., Can. D7 106
Paderborn, Ger. E4 16
Padjelanta Nationalpark, p.o.i., Swe. C7 8
Padloping Island, i., Nu., Can. D13 141
Padma see Ganges, stm., Asia G13 54
Pádova (Padua), Italy E8 22
Pādra, India G4 54
Padrauna, India E9 54
Padre Bernardo, Braz. H1 88
Padre Island, i., Tx., U.S. G10 130
Padre Island National Seashore, p.o.i., Tx., U.S. G10 130
Padre Paraíso, Braz. I5 88
Padstow, Eng., U.K. K8 12
Padua see Pádova, Italy E8 22
Paducah, Ky., U.S. G9 120
Paducah, Tx., U.S. G8 128
Paea, Fr. Poly. v21 78h
Paedun, Kor., S. D1 40
Paektu-san, mtn., Asia C10 36
Paestum, hist., Italy D8 24
Páez, stm., Col. F4 86
Pafúri, Moz. C10 70
Pag, Otok, i., Cro. F11 22
Pagadenbaru, Indon. G5 50
Pagadian, Phil. G4 52
Pagai Selatan, Pulau, i., Indon. E2 50
Pagai Utara, Pulau, i., Indon. E2 50
Pagan, Mya. B2 48
Pagan, i., N. Mar. Is. B5 72
Pagaralam, Indon. E3 50
Pagasitikós Kólpos, b., Grc. D5 28
Page, Az., U.S. G5 132
Page, N.D., U.S. G16 124
Pagėgiai, Lith. E4 10
Pagerdewa, Indon. E4 50
Paget, Mount, mtn., S. Geor. J9 90
Pagoda Peak, mtn., Co., U.S. C9 132
Pagoda Point, c., Mya. E2 48
Pagon, Bukit, mtn., Asia A9 50
Pago Pago, Am. Sam. h12 79c
Pagosa Springs, Co., U.S. F9 132
Paguate, N.M., U.S. H9 132
Pagudpud, Phil. A3 52
Pahača, Russia D22 34
Pahala, Hi., U.S. D6 78a
Pahang, state, Malay. K6 48
Pahang, stm., Malay. K6 48
Pahokee, Fl., U.S. J5 116
Pahost, Bela. G12 10
Pahrump, Nv., U.S. G10 134
Pai, Thai. C4 48
Pai, stm., Asia C3 48
Paico, Peru F3 84
Paide, Est. B8 10
Paige, Tx., U.S. D10 130
Paignton, Eng., U.K. K9 12
Paiguano, Chile E2 92
Päijänne, l., Fin. F11 8
Paikü Co, l., China D10 54
Pailolo Channel, strt., Hi., U.S. B5 78a
Paimpol, Fr. F5 14
Painan, Indon. D2 50
Painesdale, Mi., U.S. D10 118
Painesville, Oh., U.S. C4 114
Paint, stm., Mi., U.S. E10 118
Paint Creek, stm., Oh., U.S. E14 120
Painted Desert, des., Az., U.S. H5 132
Painted Rock Reservoir, res., Az., U.S. K3 132
Paintsville, Ky., U.S. G3 114
Paisley, Scot., U.K. F8 12
Paisley, Or., U.S. H6 136
Païta, N. Cal. n16 79d
Paita, Peru E1 84
Paitan, Telukan, b., Malay. G1 52
Paiton, Indon. G8 50
Pajala, Swe. C10 8
Paján, Ec. H1 86
Pajares, Puerto de, p., Spain B5 20
Pajaros Point, c., Br. Vir. Is. d9 104b
Pajęczno, Pol. E14 16
Pajer, gora, mtn., Russia C1 34
Pajeú, stm., Braz. E6 88
Paj-Hoj, hills, Russia A10 32
Paka, Malay. J6 48
Pākāla, India E4 53
Pakaraima Mountains, mts., S.A. E11 86
Pakashkan Lake, l., On., Can. B8 118
Pākaur, India F11 54
Pak Chong, Thai. E5 48
Pākhāl, l., India C5 53
Pákhna, Cyp. D3 58
Pakhoi see Beihai, China K3 42
Pakistan, ctry., Asia C2 46
Paklenica Nacionalni Park, p.o.i., Cro. F12 22
Pakokku, Mya. B2 48
Pakowki Lake, l., Ab., Can. E2 124
Pākpattan, Pak. C4 54
Pak Phanang, Thai. H5 48
Pak Phayun, Thai. I5 48
Pak Phraek, Thai. H5 48
Pakrac, Cro. E14 22
Pakruojis, Lith. E6 10
Paks, Hung. C5 26
Paktīā, state, Afg. B2 54
Paktīkā, state, Afg. B2 54
Pakwash Lake, l., On., Can. A5 118
Pakxé, Laos E7 48
Pala, Chad F2 62
Pala, Mya. F4 48
Palacios, Tx., U.S. F11 130
Palagruža, Otoci, is., Cro. H13 22
Palai, India G3 53
Palaiochóra, Grc. H6 28
Pālakodu, India C5 53
Palamós, Spain C14 20
Pālampur, India B6 54
Palamu National Park, p.o.i., India G10 54
Palamut, Tur. D10 28
Palana, Russia E20 34
Palanan Bay, b., Phil. B4 52
Palanga, Lith. E3 10
Palangkaraya, Indon. E8 50
Palani, India F3 53
Pālanpur, India F4 54
Palaoa Point, c., Hi., U.S. C4 78a
Palapye, Bots. C8 70
Pālār, stm., India E4 53
Palas de Rei, Spain B3 20
Palatka, Russia D19 34
Palatka, Fl., U.S. G4 116
Palau, Italy C3 24
Palau, ctry., Oc. g8 78b
Palau Islands, is., Palau D10 44
Palauk, Mya. F4 48
Palaw, Mya. F4 48
Palawan, i., Phil. F2 52
Palawan Passage, strt., Phil. F1 52
Palayan, Phil. C3 52
Pālayankottai, India G3 53
Palembang, Indon. E4 50
Palena, Italy I11 22
Palena, stm., S.A. H2 90
Palencia, Spain B6 20
Palencia, co., Spain B6 20
Palen Lake, l., Ca., U.S. J1 132
Palenque, Mex. G13 100
Palenque, hist., Mex. G12 100
Palermo, Col. F4 86
Palermo, Italy F7 24
Palermo, Ur. F10 92
Palestina, Mex. E6 130
Palestine, Ar., U.S. B7 122
Palestine, Il., U.S. E10 120
Palestine, Tx., U.S. F3 122
Palestine, hist. reg., Asia G6 58
Palestine, Lake, res., Tx., U.S. E3 122
Palestrina, Italy I9 22
Paletwa, Mya. D7 46
Pālghāt, India F3 53
Palgrave Point, c., Nmb. E1 68
Palhano, stm., Braz. C6 88
Pāli, India F4 54
Palima, Indon. F12 50
Palinuro, Capo, c., Italy D9 24
Palisade, Ne., U.S. A7 128
Palisades, Id., U.S. G15 136
Palisades Reservoir, res., U.S. G15 136
Pālitāna, India H3 54
Palivere, Est. A6 10
Palizada, Mex. F12 100
Palk Bay, b., Asia G4 53
Palkino, Russia G20 8
Pālkonda, India B6 53
Pālkonda Range, mts., India D4 53
Palk Strait, strt., Asia G4 53
Pallastunturi, mtn., Fin. B11 8
Palliser, Cape, c., N.Z. E6 80
Palma, Braz. K4 88
Palma, Moz. C7 68
Palma, stm., Braz. G2 88
Palma, Badia de, b., Spain E13 20
Palmácia, Braz. C6 88
Palma del Río, Spain G5 20
Palma de Mallorca, Spain E13 20
Palma di Montechiaro, Italy G7 24
Palmar, stm., Ven. B6 86
Palmar, Lago Artificial del, res., Ur. F9 92
Palmar Camp, Belize D3 102
Palmarejo, P.R. B1 104a
Palmares, Braz. E8 88
Palmarito, Ven. D6 86
Palmarola, Isola, i., Italy D6 24
Palmas, Braz. F1 88
Palmas, Braz. C12 92
Palmas Bellas, Pan. H7 102
Palmas de Monte Alto, Braz. H4 88
Palma Soriano, Cuba B9 102
Palm Bay, Fl., U.S. H5 116
Palm Beach, Fl., U.S. J5 116
Palmdale, Ca., U.S. I7 134
Palm Desert, Ca., U.S. J9 134
Palmeira, Braz. B13 92
Palmeira das Missões, Braz. C11 92
Palmeira dos Índios, Braz. E7 88
Palmeiras, stm., Braz. F2 88
Palmeirinhas, Ponta das, c., Ang. B1 68
Palmelo, Braz. I1 88
Palmer, P.R. B4 104a
Palmer, Ak., U.S. D10 140
Palmer, Ma., U.S. B13 114
Palmer, Ne., U.S. F14 126
Palmer, Tn., U.S. B13 122
Palmer, sci., Ant. B34 81
Palmer Lake, Co., U.S. B3 128
Palmer Land, reg., Ant. C34 81
Palmerston, N.Z. G4 80
Palmerston, at., Cook Is. E10 72
Palmerston, Cape, c., Austl. C7 76
Palmerston North, N.Z. E6 80
Palmerton, Pa., U.S. D10 114
Palmetto, Ga., U.S. D14 122
Palmetto, La., U.S. G6 122
Palmetto Point, c., Antig. e4 105b
Palmi, Italy F9 24
Palmira, Col. F3 86
Palmira, Cuba A7 102
Palmira, Ec. I2 86
Palmitas, Ur. F9 92
Palm Springs, Ca., U.S. J9 134
Palmyra see Tudmur, Syria D9 58
Palmyra, Il., U.S. E7 120
Palmyra, Mo., U.S. E6 120
Palmyra, N.Y., U.S. A8 114
Palmyra, Va., U.S. G7 114
Palmyra, hist., Syria D9 58
Palmyra Atoll, at., Oc. C10 72
Palo Alto, Mex. H8 130
Palo Alto, Ca., U.S. F3 134
Palo Blanco, P.R. B2 104a
Palo Flechado Pass, p., N.M., U.S. E3 128
Paloh, Malay. B7 50
Paloich, Sudan E6 62
Palojoensuu, Fin. B10 8
Palomar Mountain, mtn., Ca., U.S. J9 134
Palomas, Mex. F4 130
Palo Pinto, Tx., U.S. B9 130
Palopo, Indon. E12 50
Palos, Cabo de, c., Spain G10 20
Palo Santo, Arg. B8 92
Palos Verdes Point, c., Ca., U.S. J7 134
Palouse, stm., U.S. D8 136
Palo Verde, Ca., U.S. J2 132
Palpa, Peru F2 84
Palpalá, Arg. B5 92
Palu, Indon. D11 50
Palu, Teluk, b., Indon. D11 50
Paluga, Russia D21 8
Palwal, India D6 54
Pama, Burkina G5 64
Pamanukan, Indon. G5 50
Pāmban Channel, strt., India G4 53
Pāmban Island, i., India G4 53
Pamekasan, Indon. G8 50
Pamenang, Indon. E3 50
Pameungpeuk, Indon. G5 50
Pamiers, Fr. F7 18
Pamir, mts., Asia B11 56
Pamlico Sound, strt., N.C., U.S. A10 116
Pampa, Tx., U.S. F8 128
Pampã, stm., Braz. I5 88
Pampa (Pampas), reg., Arg. G4 90
Pampa Almirón, Arg. C8 92
Pampa del Chañar, Arg. E3 92
Pampa del Indio, Arg. B7 92
Pampanga, stm., Phil. C3 52
Pampanua, Indon. F12 50
Pampas, Peru F3 84
Pampas, stm., Peru F3 84
Pampas see Pampa, reg., Arg. F4 90
Pamplico, S.C., U.S. B6 116
Pamplona, Col. D5 86
Pamplona, Spain B9 20
Pamukkale (Hierapolis), hist., Tur. F12 28
Pamukova, Tur. C13 28
Pana, Il., U.S. E8 120
Panabá, Mex. B3 102
Panabo, Phil. G5 52
Panacea, Fl., U.S. G14 122
Panadura, Sri L. H4 53
Panagjurište, Blg. G11 26
Panaitan, Pulau, i., Indon. G4 50
Panaji, India D1 53
Panamá, Pan. H8 102
Panama, Ok., U.S. B4 122
Panama, ctry., N.A. F9 96
Panamá, Bahía de, b., Pan. H8 102
Panamá, Canal de (Panama Canal), can., Pan. H8 102
Panamá, Golfo de, b., Pan. D2 86
Panama, Gulf of see Panamá, Golfo de, b., Pan. D2 86
Panama, Isthmus of see Panamá, Istmo de, isth., Pan. H8 102
Panamá, Istmo de (Panama, Isthmus of), isth., Pan. H8 102
Panama Basin, unds. H5 144
Panama Canal see Panamá, Canal de, can., Pan. H8 102
Panama City, Fl., U.S. G13 122
Panambi, Braz. D11 92
Panamint Range, mts., Ca., U.S. G8 134
Panamint Valley, val., Ca., U.S. G8 134
Panao, Peru E2 84
Panarea, Isola, i., Italy F9 24
Panaro, stm., Italy F8 22
Panay, i., Phil. E4 52
Panay Gulf, b., Phil. E4 52
Pančevo, Yugo. E7 26
Panciu, Rom. D14 26
Panda, Moz. D12 70
Pandaria, India G8 54
Pan de Azúcar, Ur. G10 92
Pandėlys, Lith. D8 10
Pāndharkawada, India A4 53
Pandharpur, India C2 53
Pāndhurna, India H7 54
Pando, Ur. G10 92
Panevėžys, Lith. E7 10
Panfilov, Kaz. F13 32
Pāng, stm., Mya. B4 48
Panga, D.R.C. D5 66
Pangala, Congo E2 66
Pangandaran, Indon. G6 50
Pangani, Tan. F7 66
Pangani, stm., Tan. E7 66
Pangburn, Ar., U.S. B7 122
Pangfou see Bengbu, China E7 42
Panghkam, Mya. D8 46
Pangi, D.R.C. E5 66
Pangkajene, Indon. F11 50
Pangkalanbrandan, Indon. J4 48
Pangkalanbuun, Indon. E7 50
Pangkalpinang, Indon. E5 50
Pangnirtung, Nu., Can. B17 106
Pango Aluquem, Ang. B1 68
Pangŏjin, Kor., S. D2 40
Pangong Tso, l., Asia B7 54
Panguiranan, Phil. D4 52
Panguitch, Ut., U.S. F4 132
Pangutaran, Phil. G3 52
Pangutaran Group, is., Phil. G3 52
Panhandle, Tx., U.S. F7 128
Paniau, mtn., Hi., U.S. B1 78a
Panié, Mont, mtn., N. Cal. m15 79d
Panīpāt, India D6 54
Panitan, Phil. E4 52
Panj (Pjandž), stm., Asia B11 56
Panjang, Indon. F4 50
Panjang, Selat, strt., Indon. C3 50
Pankshin, Nig. H6 64
Panlong (Lo), stm., Asia A7 48
P'anmunjŏm-ni, Kor., N. E7 38
Panna, India F8 54
Panna National Park, p.o.i., India F7 54
Pannawonica, Austl. D3 74
Panola, U.S. E10 122
Páno Lévkara, Cyp. D4 58
Panopah, Indon. D7 50
Panorama, Braz. D6 90
Panovo, Russia C18 32
Panruti, India F4 53
Panshan, China D4 38
Pantanal, reg., S.A. C5 90
Pantanaw, Mya. D2 48
Pantar, Pulau, i., Indon. G7 44
Pantelleria, Isola di, i., Italy H6 24
Pantonlabu, Indon. J3 48
Pánuco, Mex. E10 100
Pánuco, stm., Mex. E9 100
Panxian, China F5 36
Panyam, Nig. H6 64
Panzós, Guat. E3 102
Pao, stm., Thai. D6 48
Pao, stm., Ven. C8 86
Pao, stm., Ven. C9 86
Paochi see Baoji, China D2 42
Paoki see Baoji, China D2 42
Paola, Italy E9 24
Paola, Ks., U.S. F3 120
Paoli, In., U.S. F11 120
Paopao, Fr. Poly. v20 78h
Paoting see Baoding, China B6 42
Paotou see Baotou, China A4 42
Paotow see Baotou, China A4 42
Pápa, Hung. B4 26
Papagaio, stm., Braz. I10 86
Papagaios, Braz. D3 88
Papagayo, Golfo de, b., C.R. G4 102
Papaikou, Hi., U.S. D6 78a
Papantla de Olarte, Mex. E10 100
Papara, Fr. Poly. v22 78h
Papa Stour, i., Scot., U.K. n18 12a
Papeari, Fr. Poly. w22 78h
Papeete, Fr. Poly. v21 78h
Papenburg, Ger. C3 16
Papetoai, Fr. Poly. v20 78h
Paphos see Néa Páfos, Cyp. D3 58
Papigochic, stm., Mex. G8 98
Papillion, Ne., U.S. C1 120
Paposo, Chile B2 92
Papua, Gulf of, b., Pap. N. Gui. D5 72
Papua New Guinea, ctry., Oc. D5 72
Papulovo, Russia F23 8
Papun, Mya. C3 48
Papunáua, stm., Col. G6 86
Papurí (Papuri), stm., S.A. G6 86
Papuri (Papurí), stm., S.A. G6 86
Pará, state, Braz. D7 84
Pará, stm., Braz. A1 88
Pará, stm., Braz. J3 88
Parabel', Russia C14 32
Paraburdoo, Austl. D3 74
Paracatu, Braz. I2 88
Paracatu, stm., Braz. I3 88
Paracel Islands see Xisha Qundao, is., China B5 50
Pārachinār, Pak. B3 54
Paracho de Verduzco, Mex. F7 100
Parachute, Co., U.S. D8 132
Paraćin, Yugo. F8 26
Paracuru, Braz. B6 88
Parada, Punta, c., Peru G2 84
Paradise, Ca., U.S. D4 134
Paradise, Mt., U.S. C12 136
Paradise, Nv., U.S. G1 132
Paradise Island, i., Bah. m18 104f
Paradise Valley, Az., U.S. J5 132
Paradise Valley, Nv., U.S. B8 134
Pāradwīp, India H11 54
Paragonah, Ut., U.S. F4 132
Paragould, Ar., U.S. H7 120
Paraguá, stm., Bol. B4 90
Paragua, stm., Ven. D10 86
Paraguaçu, stm., Braz. G6 88
Paraguai (Paraguay), stm., S.A. D5 90
Paraguaipoa, Ven. B6 86
Paraguaná, Península de, pen., Ven. A6 86
Paraguarí, Para. B9 92
Paraguarí, state, Para. C9 92
Paraguay, ctry., S.A. D5 90
Paraguay (Paraguai), stm., S.A. E5 90
Paraíba, state, Braz. D7 88
Paraíba do Sul, stm., Braz. K5 88
Paraibano, Braz. D3 88
Parainen, Fin. F9 8
Paraíso, Mex. F12 100
Paraiso, Pan. H8 102
Parakou, Benin H5 64
Paramakkudi, India G4 53
Paramaribo, Sur. B6 84
Parambu, Braz. D5 88
Paramillo, Parque Nacional, p.o.i., Col. D3 86
Paramirim, Braz. G4 88
Paramirim, stm., Braz. F4 88
Páramo de Masa, Puerto de, p., Spain B7 20
Paramušir, ostrov, i., Russia F20 34
Paramythiá, Grc. D3 28
Paran, Naḥal (Girafi, Wadi), stm. I5 58
Paraná, Arg. E7 92
Paranã, Braz. G1 88
Paraná, state, Braz. D6 90
Paranã, stm., Braz. G1 88
Paraná, stm., S.A. F5 90
Paranaguá, Braz. B13 92
Paranaguá, Baía de, b., Braz. B13 92
Paranaíba, Braz. C6 90
Paranaíba, stm., Braz. C6 90
Paranaidji, Braz. D2 88
Paranapanema, stm., Braz. D6 90
Paranapiacaba, Serra do, mts., Braz. B13 92
Paranavaí, Braz. D6 90
Parang, Phil. G5 52
Parang, Pulau, i., Indon. F7 50
Parângu Mare, Vârful, mtn., Rom. D10 26
Paranhos, Braz. A10 92
Paranoá, Lago do, res., Braz. H2 88
Paraopeba, Braz. J3 88
Parapetí, stm., Bol. C4 90
Parara, Indon. E12 50
Paratinga, Braz. G4 88
Paratoo, Austl. I2 76
Paray-le-Monial, Fr. C9 18
Pārbati, stm., India F6 54
Pārbatipur, Bngl. F12 54
Parbhani, India B3 53
Parchim, Ger. C7 16
Pardeeville, Wi., U.S. H9 118
Pārdi, India H4 54
Parding, China B12 54
Pardo, stm., Braz. K1 88
Pardo, stm., Braz. H6 88
Pardo, stm., Braz. L1 88
Pardo, stm., Braz. D6 90
Pardo, stm., Braz. D11 92
Pardubice, Czech Rep. F11 16
Paredón, Mex. C8 100
Parelhas, Braz. D7 88
Paren', Russia D21 34
Paren', stm., Russia D21 34
Parent, Qc., Can. C2 110
Parentis-en-Born, Fr. E4 18
Parepare, Indon. E11 50
Parera, Arg. G5 92
Parfenevo, Russia F20 8
Párga, Grc. D3 28
Parham, Antig. f4 105b
Paria, Gulf of, b. B10 86
Paria, Península de, pen., Ven. B10 86
Pariaguán, Ven. C9 86
Pariaman, Indon. D1 50
Paricutín, vol., Mex. F7 100
Parigi, Indon. D12 50
Parika, Guy. B6 84
Parikkala, Fin. F13 8
Parima, stm., Braz. F10 86
Parima, Serra (Parima, Sierra), mts., S.A. F9 86
Parima, Sierra (Parima, Serra), mts., S.A. F9 86
Parima Tapirapecó, Parque Nacional, p.o.i., Ven. F9 86
Parintins, Braz. D6 84
Paris, On., Can. E9 112
Paris, Fr. F11 14
Paris, Ar., U.S. B5 122
Paris, Il., U.S. I2 112
Paris, Ky., U.S. F1 114
Paris, Mo., U.S. E5 120
Paris, Tn., U.S. H9 120
Paris, Tx., U.S. D3 122
Parisienne, Ile, i., On., Can. B5 112
Parita, Bahía de, b., Pan. H7 102
Parit Buntar, Malay. J5 48
Parkano, Fin. E10 8
Park City, Mt., U.S. B3 126
Park City, Ut., U.S. C5 132
Parkdale, Or., U.S. E5 136
Parker, Az., U.S. I2 132
Parker, Co., U.S. B4 128
Parker, Fl., U.S. G13 122
Parker, Cape, c., Nu., Can. B10 141
Parker City, In., U.S. H4 112
Parker Dam, Ca., U.S. I2 132
Parker Dam, dam, U.S. I2 132
Parkersburg, Il., U.S. F9 120
Parkersburg, Ia., U.S. B5 120
Parkersburg, W.V., U.S. E4 114
Parkes, Austl. I7 76
Park Falls, Wi., U.S. F8 118
Park Forest, Il., U.S. G2 112
Parkhill, On., Can. E8 112
Parkland, Wa., U.S. C4 136
Park Range, mts., Co., U.S. C10 132
Park Rapids, Mn., U.S. E3 118
Parkrose, Or., U.S. E4 136
Park Rynie, S. Afr. G10 70
Parksley, Va., U.S. G10 114
Parkston, S.D., U.S. D14 126
Parksville, B.C., Can. G6 138
Parkville, Md., U.S. E9 114
Parkville, Mo., U.S. E3 120
Parla, Spain D7 20
Parlākimidi, India B7 53
Parli, India B3 53
Parma, Italy F7 22
Parma, Mo., U.S. H8 120
Parma, Oh., U.S. C4 114
Parnaguá, Braz. F3 88
Parnaíba, Braz. B5 88
Parnaíba, stm., Braz. B5 88
Parnaibinha, stm., Braz. E2 88
Parnamirim, Braz. E6 88
Parnassós, mtn., Grc. E5 28
Párnitha, mtn., Grc. E6 28
Pärnu, Est. G11 8
Pärnu laht, b., Est. G11 8
Paro, Bhu. E12 54
Pārola, India H5 54
Paromaj, Russia F17 34
Paroo, stm., Austl. G5 76
Páros, i., Grc. F8 28
Parowan, Ut., U.S. F4 132
Parque Nacional da Chapada da Diamantina, p.o.i., Braz. G4 88
Parral, Chile H2 92
Parral, stm., Mex. B6 100
Parramatta, Austl. I8 76
Parras de la Fuente, Mex. C7 100
Parrish, Fl., U.S. I3 116
Parrsboro, N.S., Can. E12 110
Parry, Cape, c., N.T., Can. A6 106
Parry Bay, b., Nu., Can. B14 106
Parry Island, i., On., Can. C9 112
Parry Peninsula, pen., N.T., Can. B6 106
Parry Sound, On., Can. C9 112
Parsberg, Ger. G7 16
Parsęta, stm., Pol. B11 16
Parshall, N.D., U.S. G11 124
Paršino, Russia C20 32
Parsnip, stm., B.C., Can. A8 138
Parsons, Ks., U.S. G2 120
Parsons, Tn., U.S. B10 122
Pärsti, Est. B8 10
Partanna, Italy G6 24
Parthenay, Fr. H8 14
Partinico, Italy F7 24
Partizansk, Russia C10 38
Partizánske, Slov. H14 16
Paru, stm., Braz. D7 84
Parú, stm., Ven. E9 86
Paru de Oeste, stm., Braz. C6 84
Parūr, India F3 53
Pārvatīpuram, India B6 53
Paryang, China C9 54
Parys, S. Afr. E8 70
Pasadena, Ca., U.S. I7 134
Pasadena, Tx., U.S. H3 122
Pasaje, Ec. D2 84
Pa Sak, stm., Thai. E5 48
Paşaköy, N. Cyp. C4 58
Pasarbantal, Indon. E2 50
Pasawng, Mya. C3 48
Pascagoula, Ms., U.S. G10 122
Pascagoula, stm., Ms., U.S. G10 122
Paşcani, Rom. B13 26
Pasco, Wa., U.S. D7 136
Pascoag, R.I., U.S. C14 114
Pascua, Isla de (Easter Island) (Rapa Nui), i., Chile f30 78l
Pas-de-Calais, state, Fr. D11 14
Pasewalk, Ger. C10 16
Pasir Mas, Malay. J6 48
Pasirpengarayan, Indon. C2 50
Pasir Puteh, Malay. J6 48
Paškovo, Russia G15 34
Pasłęka, stm., Pol. C16 16
Pasley Bay, b., Nu., Can. A11 106
Pašman, Otok, i., Cro. G12 22
Pasmore, stm., Austl. H2 76
Pasni, Pak. D9 56
Paso de Indios, Arg. H3 90
Paso del Cerro, Ur. E9 92
Paso de los Libres, Arg. D9 92
Paso de los Toros, Ur. F9 92
Paso de Patria, Para. C8 92
Paso de San Antonio, Mex. E3 130
Paso Hondo, Mex. H13 100
Paso Robles, Ca., U.S. H5 134
Pašozero, Russia F16 8
Pasquia Hills, hills, Sk., Can. A11 124
Pasrūr, Pak. B5 54
Passadumkeag, Me., U.S. E8 110
Passadumkeag Mountain, hill, Me., U.S. E8 110
Passage Point, c., N.T., Can. B16 140
Passaic, N.J., U.S. H15 112
Passamaquoddy Bay, b., N.A. E10 110
Passau, Ger. H9 16
Passero, Capo, c., Italy H9 24
Passo Fundo, Braz. D11 92
Passo Real, Represa do, res., Braz. D11 92
Passos, Braz. K2 88
Pastavy, Bela. E9 10
Pastaza, state, Ec. H3 86
Pastaza, stm., S.A. D2 84
Pastillo, P.R. B3 104a
Pasto, Col. G3 86
Pastos Bons, Braz. D3 88
Pasuruan, Indon. G8 50
Pasvalys, Lith. D7 10
Pásztó, Hung. B6 26
Patacamaya, Bol. C3 90
Patadkal, hist., India C3 53
Patagonia, Az., U.S. L6 132
Patagonia, reg., Arg. I2 90
Pātan, India G3 54
Patchogue, N.Y., U.S. D13 114
Patea, N.Z. D6 80
Pategi, Nig. H6 64
Pate Island, i., Kenya E8 66
Patensie, S. Afr. H7 70
Paterna, Spain E10 20
Paternion, Aus. D10 22
Paternò, Italy G8 24
Paterson, N.J., U.S. D11 114
Pathānkot, India B5 54
Pathein, Mya. D2 48
Pathfinder Reservoir, res., Wy., U.S. E5 126
Pathiu, Thai. G4 48
Pathum Thani, Thai. E5 48
Pati, Indon. G7 50
Patía, Col. F3 86
Patía, stm., Col. F2 86
Patiāla, India C6 54
Patillas, P.R. B3 104a
Pati Point, c., Guam i10 78c
Pativilca, Peru F2 84
Pātkai Range, mts., Asia F4 36
Pat Mayse Lake, res., Tx., U.S. D3 122
Pátmos, i., Grc. F9 28
Patna, India F10 54
Patna, India H11 54
Patnāgarh, India H9 54
Patnanongan Island, i., Phil. C4 52
Pato Branco, Braz. C11 92
Patoka, Il., U.S. F8 120
Patoka, stm., In., U.S. F10 120
Patoka Lake, res., In., U.S. F11 120
Patomskoe nagor'e, plat., Russia E12 34
Patonga, Ug. D6 66
Patos, Braz. D7 88
Patos, stm., Arg. E3 92
Patos, Lagoa dos, b., Braz. E12 92
Patos de Minas, Braz. J2 88
Patquía, Arg. D4 92
Pátra, Grc. E4 28
Patrai, Gulf of see Patraikós Kólpos, b., Grc. E4 28
Patraikós Kólpos, b., Grc. E4 28
Patricio Lynch, Isla, i., Chile I1 90
Patrocínio, Braz. J2 88
Pattani, Thai. I5 48
Pattaya, Thai. F5 48
Patten, Me., U.S. D8 110
Patterson, Ca., U.S. F4 134
Patterson, Ga., U.S. E3 116
Patterson, Mount, mtn., Yk., Can. C4 106
Patti, Golfo di, b., Italy F9 24
Pattison, Ms., U.S. F8 122
Pattoki, Pak. C4 54
Pattonsburg, Mo., U.S. D3 120
Pattukkottai, India F4 53
Pattullo, Mount, mtn., B.C., Can. D5 106
Patuākhāli, Bngl. G13 54
Patuca, stm., Hond. E5 102
Pātūr, India H6 54
Patusi, Pap. N. Gui. a4 79a
Patuxent, stm., Md., U.S. F9 114
Pátzcuaro, Mex. F8 100
Pau, Fr. F5 18
Pau, Gave de, stm., Fr. F5 18
Pau Brasil, Braz. H6 88
Pau dos Ferros, Braz. D6 88
Pauh, Indon. E3 50
Pauini, stm., Braz. E4 84
Pauini, stm., Braz. H10 86
Pauk, Mya. B2 48
Pauksa Taung, mtn., Mya. C2 48
Paul, Id., U.S. H13 136
Paulding, Ms., U.S. E9 122
Paulicéia, Braz. D6 90
Paulina Peak, mtn., Or., U.S. G5 136
Pauline, Mount, mtn., Can. C11 138
Paulino Neves, Braz. B4 88
Paulistana, Braz. E5 88
Paulistas, Braz. J4 88
Paullina, Ia., U.S. B2 120
Paulo Afonso, Braz. E6 88
Paulo Afonso, Cachoeira de, wtfl, Braz. E6 88
Paulpietersburg, S. Afr. E10 70
Pauls Valley, Ok., U.S. G11 128
Paung, Mya. D3 48
Paungde, Mya. C2 48
Pauri, India C7 54
Paute, Ec. I2 86
Paute, stm., Ec. I2 86
Pauto, stm., Col. E6 86
Pavia, Italy E6 22
Pavilion, B.C., Can. F9 138
Pāvilosta, Lat. D4 10
Pavlikeni, Blg. F12 26
Pavlodar, Kaz. D13 32
Pavlof Volcano, vol., Ak., U.S. E7 140
Pavlovo, Russia I20 8
Pavlovsk, Russia A13 10
Pavlovsk, Russia D14 32
Pavlovskij Posad, Russia E21 10
Pavo, Ga., U.S. F2 116
Pavullo nel Frignano, Italy F7 22
Pavuvu Island, i., Sol. Is. e8 79b
Pawan, stm., Indon. D7 50
Pawhuska, Ok., U.S. E12 128
Pawn, stm., Mya. C3 48
Pawnee, Il., U.S. E8 120
Pawnee, Ok., U.S. A2 122
Pawnee, stm., Ks., U.S. C9 128
Pawnee Rock, Ks., U.S. C9 128
Pawni, India H7 54
Pawota, Mya. D3 48
Paw Paw, Il., U.S. C8 120
Paw Paw, Mi., U.S. F4 112
Pawtucket, R.I., U.S. C14 114
Paxoí, i., Grc. D3 28
Paxson, Ak., U.S. D10 140
Paxton, Ne., U.S. F11 126
Paya, Hond. E5 102
Payakumbuh, Indon. D2 50
Payamlı, Tur. A9 58
Payerne, Switz. D3 22
Payeti, Indon. H12 50
Payette, Id., U.S. F10 136
Payette, stm., Id., U.S. G10 136
Payette, North Fork, stm., Id., U.S. F11 136
Payette, South Fork, stm., Id., U.S. F11 136
Payne, Oh., U.S. C1 114
Payne, Lac, l., Can. D16 106
Paynes Find, Austl. E3 74
Paynton, Sk., Can. A5 124
Paysandú, Ur. F8 92
Payson, Az., U.S. I5 132
Payson, Il., U.S. E6 120
Payson, Ut., U.S. C5 132
Payún, Cerro, mtn., Arg. H3 92
Pazarbaşı Burnu, c., Tur. B13 28
Pazarcık, Tur. A8 58
Pazardžik, Blg. G11 26
Pazaryeri, Tur. D12 28
Paz de Ariporo, Col. E6 86
Pčevža, Russia A15 10
Pe, Mya. F4 48
Pea, stm., U.S. F12 122
Peabody, Ks., U.S. C11 128
Peabody, Ma., U.S. B14 114
Peace, stm., Can. D8 106
Peace, stm., Fl., U.S. I4 116
Peace River, Ab., Can. D7 106
Peachland, B.C., Can. G11 138
Peach Orchard, Ga., U.S. C3 116
Peach Springs, Az., U.S. H3 132
Peak District National Park, p.o.i., Eng., U.K. H11 12
Peak Downs, Austl. D7 76
Peak Hill, Austl. E3 74
Peak Hill, Austl. I7 76
Peäldoajvi, mtn., Fin. B12 8
Peale, Mount, mtn., Ut., U.S. E7 132
Pearisburg, Va., U.S. G5 114
Pearl, Il., U.S. E7 120
Pearl, Ms., U.S. E8 122
Pearl, stm., U.S. G9 122
Pearland, Tx., U.S. H3 122
Pearl Harbor, b., Hi., U.S. B3 78a
Pearl Peak, mtn., Nv., U.S. C1 132
Pearl River, La., U.S. G9 122
Pearson, Ga., U.S. E3 116

Name | Map Ref. | Page

Peary Land, reg., Grnld. A18 141
Pease, stm., Tx., U.S. G9 128
Pebane, Moz. D6 68
Pebas, Peru D3 84
Pebble Island, i., Falk. Is. J5 90
Peć, Yugo. G7 26
Pecan Gap, Tx., U.S. D3 122
Peçanha, Braz. J4 88
Peças, Ilha das, i., Braz. B13 92
Pecatonica, Il., U.S. B8 120
Pecatonica, stm., U.S. B8 120
Pečenga, Russia B14 8
Pechenizhyn, Ukr. A11 26
Pechora see Pečora, stm., Russia C25 8
Pechora Bay see Pečorskaja guba, b., Russia A8 32
Pečora, Russia A9 32
Pečora (Pechora), stm., Russia A8 32
Pecoraro, Monte, mtn., Italy F10 24
Pečorskaja guba, b., Russia A8 32
Pečorskoe more, Russia A8 32
Pečory, Russia C10 10
Pecos, N.M., U.S. F3 128
Pecos, Tx., U.S. C4 130
Pecos, stm., U.S. F12 98
Pecos National Monument, p.o.i., N.M., U.S. F3 128
Pécs, Hung. C5 26
Pedana, India C5 53
Pedasí, Pan. I7 102
Pedder, Lake, res., Austl. o12 77a
Peddie, S. Afr. H8 70
Pededze, stm., Eur. C10 10
Pedernales, Dom. Rep. C12 102
Pedernales, Ven. C10 86
Pedernales, stm., Tx., U.S. D9 130
Pedernales, Salar de, pl., Chile C3 92
Pedra Azul, Braz. I5 88
Pedra Branca, Braz. C6 88
Pedra Lume, C.V. k10 65a
Pedras de Fogo, Braz. D8 88
Pedras Salgadas, Port. C3 20
Pedraza, Col. B4 86
Pedregal, Ven. B6 86
Pedreiras, Braz. C3 88
Pedriceña, Mex. C6 100
Pedro, Point, c., Sri L. G5 53
Pedro Afonso, Braz. E1 88
Pedro Avelino, Braz. C7 88
Pedro Cays, is., Jam. D9 102
Pedro Gomes, Braz. G7 84
Pedro II, Braz. C5 88
Pedro II, Ilha, i., S.A. G8 86
Pedro Juan Caballero, Para. D5 90
Pedro Leopoldo, Braz. J3 88
Pedro Osório, Braz. E11 92
Pedro R. Fernández, Arg. D8 92
Pedro Velho, Braz. D8 88
Peebles, Scot., U.K. F9 12
Peebles, Oh., U.S. F2 114
Pee Dee, stm., U.S. A6 116
Peekskill, N.Y., U.S. C12 114
Peel, I. of Man G8 12
Peel, stm., Can. B4 106
Peel Point, c., N.T., Can. B17 140
Peel Sound, strt., Nu., Can. A11 106
Peene, stm., Ger. C9 16
Peerless, Mt., U.S. F8 124
Peesane, Sk., Can. B10 124
Peetz, Co., U.S. G9 126
Pegasus Bay, b., N.Z. F5 80
Pegnitz, Ger. G7 16
Pegu, stm., Mya. D3 48
Pegu Yoma, mts., Mya. C2 48
Pegyš, Russia E24 8
Pehlivanköy, Tur. B9 28
Pehuajó, Arg. G7 92
Peian see Bei'an, China B10 36
Peiching see Beijing, China B7 42
Peihai see Beihai, China K3 42
Peikang, Tai. J9 42
Peine, Ger. D6 16
Peine, Pointe à, c., Dom. j6 105c
Peinnechaung, i., Mya. I14 54
Peip'ing see Beijing, China B7 42
Peipus, Lake, l., Eur. B10 10
Peiraiás (Piraeus), Grc. F6 28
Peissenberg, Ger. I7 16
Peixe, Braz. G1 88
Peixe, stm., Braz. D6 90
Peixian, China D7 42
Peixoto, Represa de, res., Braz. K2 88
Pekalongan, Indon. G6 50
Pekan, Malay. K6 48
Pekanbaru, Indon. C2 50
Pekin, Il., U.S. D8 120
Pekin, In., U.S. F11 120
Peking see Beijing, China B7 42
Peklino, Russia G16 10
Pekul'nej, hrebet, mts., Russia C24 34
Pelabohan Klang, Malay. K5 48
Pelabuhanratu, Indon. G5 50
Pelagie, Isole, is., Italy I6 24
Pelaihari, Indon. E9 50
Pelat, Mont, mtn., Fr. E12 18
Pełczyce, Pol. C11 16
Peleduj, Russia C20 32
Pelée, Montagne, vol., Mart. k6 105c
Pelee, Point, c., On., Can. G7 112
Pelee Island, i., On., Can. G7 112
Pelega, Vârful, mtn., Rom. D9 26
Peleliu see Beliliou, i., Palau D9 44
Peleng, Pulau, i., Indon. F7 44
Pelham, Al., U.S. D12 122
Pelham, Ga., U.S. E1 116
Pelhřimov, Czech Rep. G11 16
Pelican, Ak., U.S. E12 140
Pelican Bay, b., Mb., Can. B13 124
Pelican Lake, Wi., U.S. F9 118
Pelican Lake, l., Mb., Can. E14 124
Pelican Lake, l., Mb., Can. B13 124
Pelican Lake, l., Mn., U.S. C5 118
Pelican Rapids, Mb., Can. B13 124
Pelican Rapids, Mn., U.S. E2 118
Pelister Nacionalni Park, p.o.i., Mac. B4 28
Peljekaise Nationalpark see Pieljekaise Nationalpark, p.o.i., Swe. C6 8
Pelješac, Poluotok, pen., Cro. H14 22
Peljušnja, Russia B15 10
Pella, Ia., U.S. C5 120
Pélla, hist., Grc. C5 28
Pell City, Al., U.S. D12 122
Pellegrini, Arg. H6 92
Pellegrini, Lago, l., Arg. I4 92
Pello, Fin. C11 8
Pellworm, i., Ger. B4 16
Pelly, Sk., Can. C12 124
Pelly, stm., Yk., Can. C4 106
Pelly Bay, b., Nu., Can. B12 106
Pelly Crossing, Yk., Can. C3 106
Pelly Lake, l., Nu., Can. B10 106
Pelly Mountains, mts., Yk., Can. C4 106
Pelón de Nado, mtn., Mex. E9 100
Peloponnesus see Pelopónnisos, pen., Grc. F5 28
Pelopónnisos, state, Grc. F5 28
Pelopónnisos (Peloponnesus), pen., Grc. F5 28
Pelotas, Braz. E11 92
Pelotas, stm., Braz. C12 92
Pelusium Bay see Tina, Khalîg el-, b., Egypt G3 58
Pemadumcook Lake, l., Me., U.S. E7 110
Pemalang, Indon. G6 50
Pemangkat, Indon. C6 50
Pematangsiantar, Indon. B1 50
Pemba, Moz. C7 68
Pemba, Zam. D4 68
Pemba, i., Tan. F7 66
Pemberton, Austl. F3 74
Pemberton, B.C., Can. F8 138
Pembina, N.D., U.S. C1 118
Pembina, stm., Ab., Can. B16 138
Pembina, stm., N.A. F16 124
Pembina Hills, hills, N.A. E15 124
Pembroke, On., Can. C12 112
Pembroke, Wales, U.K. J7 12
Pembroke, Ga., U.S. D4 116
Pembroke, Ky., U.S. H10 120
Pembroke, Me., U.S. F9 110
Pembroke, N.C., U.S. B6 116
Pembroke, Cape, c., Nu., Can. C14 106
Pembroke Pines, Fl., U.S. K5 116
Pembrokeshire Coast National Park, p.o.i., Wales, U.K. J7 12
Pembuang, Indon. E7 50
Pembuang, stm., Indon. D8 50
Pemigewasset, stm., N.H., U.S. G5 110
Pemuco, Chile H1 92
Penafiel, Port. C2 20
Peñalara, Pico de, mtn., Spain D6 20
Penalva, Braz. B3 88
Penang see George Town, Malay. J4 48
Peñaranda de Bracamonte, Spain D5 20
Pen Argyl, Pa., U.S. D10 114
Peñarroya-Pueblonuevo, Spain F5 20
Peñas, Cabo de, c., Spain A5 20
Penas, Golfo de, b., Chile I2 90
Penasco, N.M., U.S. E3 128
Pench National Park, p.o.i., India H7 54
Pendembu, S.L. H2 64
Pendembu, S.L. H2 64
Pendências, Braz. C7 88
Pendleton, In., U.S. H4 112
Pendleton, Or., U.S. E8 136
Pendleton, S.C., U.S. B3 116
Pendolo, Indon. E12 50
Pend Oreille, stm., N.A. B9 136
Pend Oreille, Lake, l., Id., U.S. B10 136
Pendžikent, Taj. B10 56
Penebel, Indon. H9 50
Penedo, Braz. F7 88
Penetanguishene, On., Can. D9 112
Peneus see Pineiós, stm., Grc. D5 28
Penfield, Pa., U.S. C7 114
Penganga, stm., India H6 54
Penghu, China I8 42
P'enghu Ch'üntao (Pescadores), is., Tai. J8 42
P'enghu Shuitao, strt., Tai. J8 42
Pengkou, China I7 42
Penglai, China C9 42
Pengpu see Bengbu, China E7 42
Pengshui, China G2 42
Pengwaluote Shan, mtn., China B11 54
Pengxi, China F1 42
Pengxian, China E5 36
Pengze, China G7 42
Penha, Braz. C13 92
Penhsi see Benxi, China D5 38
Penibética, Cordillera, mts., Spain G8 20
Peniche, Port. E1 20
Penicuik, Scot., U.K. F9 12
Penida, Nusa, i., Indon. H9 50
Peninsular Malaysia see Semenanjung Malaysia, hist. reg., Malay. K6 48
Peñíscola, Spain D11 20
Penki see Benxi, China D5 38
Pennant Station, Sk., Can. D5 124
Penne, Italy H10 22
Penneru, stm., India D4 53
Penn Hills, Pa., U.S. H10 112
Pennine Alps, mts., Eur. C13 18
Pennines, mts., Eng., U.K. G10 12
Pennington Gap, Va., U.S. H2 114
Pennsboro, W.V., U.S. E4 114
Pennsylvania, state, U.S. C8 114
Penn Yan, N.Y., U.S. B8 114
Penny Ice Cap, ice, Nu., Can. B17 106
Penny Strait, strt., Nu., Can. B6 141
Peno, Russia D15 10
Penobscot, stm., Me., U.S. F8 110
Penobscot, East Branch, stm., Me., U.S. D8 110
Penobscot, West Branch, stm., Me., U.S. D7 110
Penobscot Bay, b., Me., U.S. F7 110
Penola, Austl. K3 76
Peñón de Ifac see Penyal d'Ifac, misc. cult., Spain F11 20
Penong, Austl. F6 74
Penonomé, Pan. H7 102
Penrhyn, at., Cook Is. D11 72
Penrith, Austl. I8 76
Penrith, Eng., U.K. G10 12
Pensacola, Fl., U.S. G11 122
Pensacola Bay, b., Fl., U.S. G11 122
Pensacola Mountains, mts., Ant. D36 81
Pense, Sk., Can. D9 124
Pensilvania, Col. E4 86
Pentagon Mountain, mtn., Mt., U.S. C13 136
Pentecostes, Braz. B6 88
Pentecost Island see Pentecôte, i., Vanuatu j17 79d
Pentecôte, state, Vanuatu j17 79d
Pentecôte (Pentecost Island), i., Vanuatu j17 79d
Penticton, B.C., Can. G11 138
Pentland, Austl. C5 76
Pentland Firth, strt., Scot., U.K. C9 12
Pentwater, Mi., U.S. E3 112
Penuba, Indon. D4 50
Peñuelas, P.R. B2 104a
Penuguan, Indon. E4 50
Penukonda, India D3 53
Penyal d'Ifac, misc. cult., Spain F11 20
Penza, Russia D7 32
Penzance, Eng., U.K. K7 12
Penzberg, Ger. I7 16
Penžina, stm., Russia D22 34
Penžinskaja guba, b., Russia D21 34
Penžinskij hrebet, mts., Russia D22 34
Peoples Creek, stm., Mt., U.S. F5 124
People's Democratic Republic of Korea see Korea, North, ctry., Asia D7 38
Peoria, Az., U.S. J4 132
Peoria, Il., U.S. D8 120
Peoria Heights, Il., U.S. K9 118
Peotone, Il., U.S. G2 112
Pepel, S.L. H2 64
Pepin, Wi., U.S. G6 118
Pepin, Lake, l., U.S. G7 118
Peqin, Alb. C13 24
Perabumulih, Indon. E4 50
Perak, state, Malay. J5 48
Perak, stm., Malay. J5 48
Perak, Kuala, b., Malay. J5 48
Perales de Alfambra, Spain D9 20
Peralillo, Chile G2 92
Peralta, N.M., U.S. I10 132
Perambalur, India F4 53
Percé, Qc., Can. B12 110
Perchas, P.R. B2 104a
Perche, Collines du, hills, Fr. F9 14
Percival Lakes, l., Austl. D4 74
Percy Isles, is., Austl. C8 76
Perdida, stm., Braz. E2 88
Perdido, stm., U.S. G11 122
Perdido, Monte, mtn., Spain B10 20
Perdizes, Braz. J2 88
Perdue, Sk., Can. B6 124
Perechyn, Ukr. H18 16
Pereež'na, Russia G22 8
Pereira, Col. E4 86
Perelazy, Russia G14 10
Peremyšl', Russia F18 10
Pereslavl'-Zalesskij, Russia D21 10
Pérez, Arg. F7 92
Pergamino, Arg. F7 92
Pergamum, hist., Tur. D10 28
Pergine Valsugana, Italy D8 22
Perham, Mn., U.S. E3 118
Péribonka, Qc., Can. B4 110
Péribonka, stm., Qc., Can. B5 110
Péribonka, Lac, l., Qc., Can. E16 106
Perico, Arg. B5 92
Pericumã, stm., Braz. B3 88
Peridot, Az., U.S. J6 132
Perigiraja, Indon. D3 50
Périgord, hist. reg., Fr. D6 18
Périgueux, Fr. D6 18
Perijá, Serranía de, mts., S.A. C5 86
Perim see Barīm, i., Yemen G5 56
Peri-Mirim, Braz. B3 88
Perito Moreno, Arg. I2 90
Peritoró, Braz. C3 88
Periyār, stm., India F3 53
Periyar Tiger Reserve, India G3 53
Perkasie, Pa., U.S. D10 114
Perkins, Ok., U.S. A2 122
Perlas, Archipiélago de las, is., Pan. H8 102
Perlas, Laguna de, b., Nic. F6 102
Perleberg, Ger. C7 16
Perlez, Yugo. D7 26
Perlis, state, Malay. I5 48
Perm', Russia C9 32
Përmet, Alb. D14 24
Pernambuco, state, Braz. E6 88
Pernik, Blg. G10 26
Péronne, Fr. E11 14
Perote, Mex. F10 100
Perow, B.C., Can. B4 138
Perpignan, Fr. G8 18
Perrault Falls, On., Can. A5 118
Perrin, Tx., U.S. A9 130
Perrine, Fl., U.S. K5 116
Perris, Ca., U.S. J8 134
Perro, Laguna del, l., N.M., U.S. G3 128
Perro, Punta del, c., Spain H4 20
Perros, Bahía de, strt., Cuba A8 102
Perros-Guirec, Fr. F5 14
Perry, Fl., U.S. F2 116
Perry, Ia., U.S. C3 120
Perry, Ks., U.S. E2 120
Perry, Mi., U.S. B1 114
Perry, Mo., U.S. E6 120
Perry, N.Y., U.S. B7 114
Perry, Kap, c., Grnld. B11 141
Perry Lake, res., Ks., U.S. E2 120
Perrysburg, Oh., U.S. C2 114
Perry's Victory and International Peace Memorial, hist., Oh., U.S. C2 114
Perrysville, Oh., U.S. D3 114
Perryton, Tx., U.S. E8 128
Perryville, Ak., U.S. E8 140
Perryville, Ar., U.S. B6 122
Perryville, Ky., U.S. G12 120
Perseverancia, Bol. B4 90
Persia, Ia., U.S. C2 120
Persia see Iran, ctry., Asia C7 56
Persian Gulf, b., Asia D7 56
Perth, Austl. F3 74
Perth, On., Can. D13 112
Perth, Scot., U.K. E9 12
Perth Amboy, N.J., U.S. D11 114
Perth Basin, unds. L13 142
Pertominsk, Russia D18 8
Pertuis, Fr. F11 18
Peru, Il., U.S. C8 120
Peru, In., U.S. H3 112
Peru, Ne., U.S. D2 120
Peru, N.Y., U.S. F3 110
Peru, ctry., S.A. E2 84
Peru Basin, unds. J5 144
Perućac, Jezero, res., Eur. G16 22
Peru-Chile Trench, unds. K6 144
Perugia, Italy G9 22
Perugorría, Arg. D8 92
Peruíbe, Braz. B14 92
Perušić, Cro. F12 22
Pervomais'k, Ukr. A17 26
Pervomajsk, Russia I20 8
Pervomajskij, Russia F15 10
Pervoural'sk, Russia C9 32
Pervyj Kuril'skij proliv, strt., Russia F20 34
Pes', Russia B17 10
Pesaro, Italy G9 22
Pescadores see P'enghu Ch'üntao, is., Tai. J8 42
Pescadores Channel see P'enghu Shuitao, strt., Tai. J8 42
Pescara, Italy H11 22
Pescara, stm., Italy H11 22
Pescasseroli, Italy C7 24
Pescia, Italy G7 22
Pesé, Pan. D1 86
Peshāwar, Pak. B3 54
Peshkopi, Alb. C14 24
Peshkopija see Peshkopi, Alb. C14 24
Peshtigo, Wi., U.S. C2 112
Peshtigo, stm., Wi., U.S. F10 118
Peski, Bela. G7 10
Pesočnoe, Russia B22 10
Peso da Régua, Port. C3 20
Pesquería, stm., Mex. I8 130
Pessac, Fr. E5 18
Pest, state, Hung. B6 26
Peštera, Blg. G11 26
Pestovo, Russia B18 10
Pëstraja Dresva, Russia D20 34
Petacalco, Bahía, b., Mex. G7 100
Petah Tiqwa, Isr. F5 58
Petal, Ms., U.S. F9 122
Petalcingo, Mex. G12 100
Petalión, Kólpos, b., Grc. F7 28
Petaluma, Ca., U.S. E3 134
Petare, Ven. B8 86
Petatlán, Mex. G8 100
Petawawa, On., Can. C12 112
Petén Itzá, Lago, l., Guat. D2 102
Petenwell Lake, res., Wi., U.S. G8 118
Peterborough, Austl. I2 76
Peterborough, On., Can. D11 112
Peterborough, Eng., U.K. I12 12
Peterhead, Scot., U.K. D11 12
Peter Island, i., Br. Vir. Is. e8 104b
Peter Isøy, i., Ant. B31 81
Peter Lake, l., Nu., Can. C12 106
Peterlee, Eng., U.K. G11 12
Peterman, Al., U.S. F11 122
Peter Pond Lake, l., Sk., Can. D9 106
Petersburg, Ak., U.S. E13 140
Petersburg, Il., U.S. K9 118
Petersburg, In., U.S. F10 120
Petersburg, Tn., U.S. B12 122
Petersburg, Tx., U.S. H7 128
Petersburg, Va., U.S. G8 114
Petersburg, W.V., U.S. F6 114
Petersfield, Eng., U.K. J12 12
Peterson, Ia., U.S. B2 120
Peter the Great Bay see Petra Velikogo, zaliv, b., Russia C9 38
Petilia Policastro, Italy E10 24
Pétion-Ville, Haiti C11 102
Petit-Bourg, Guad. h5 105c
Petitcodiac, N.B., Can. E11 110
Petite Rivière Noire, Piton de la, mtn., Mrts. i10 69a
Petites-Anses, Guad. i5 105c
Petit-Goâve, Haiti C11 102
Petit Jean, stm., Ar., U.S. B5 122
Petitot, stm., Can. D6 106
Petit Piton, vol., St. Luc. m6 105c
Petitsikapau Lake, l., Nf., Can. E17 106
Petlād, India G4 54
Peto, Mex. B3 102
Petoskey, Mi., U.S. C5 112
Petra see Al-Batrā', hist., Jord. H6 58
Petra Velikogo, zaliv (Peter the Great Bay), b., Russia C9 38
Petre, Point, c., On., Can. E12 112
Petrič, Blg. H10 26
Petrified Forest National Park, p.o.i., Az., U.S. I7 132
Petrila, Rom. D10 26
Petrinja, Cro. E13 22
Petriščevo, Russia E19 10
Petrodvorec, Russia A12 10
Petrolândia, Braz. E6 88
Petrolea, Col. C5 86
Petrolia, Tx., U.S. G10 128
Petrolina, Braz. E5 88
Petrolina de Goiás, Braz. I1 88
Petrona, Punta, c., P.R. C3 104a
Petropavl see Petropavlovsk, Kaz. D11 32
Petropavlovka, Russia F10 34
Petropavlovsk, Kaz. D11 32
Petropavlovsk-Kamčatskij, Russia F20 34
Petrópolis, Braz. L4 88
Petroşani, Rom. D10 26
Petros, Tn., U.S. H13 120
Petrovac, Yugo. E8 26
Petrovsk, Russia D6 32
Petrovskij, Russia H18 8
Petrovsk-Zabajkal'skij, Russia F10 34
Petrozavodsk, Russia F15 8
Petrusburg, S. Afr. F7 70
Petrusville, S. Afr. G7 70
Petrykau, Bela. H11 10
Pettus, Tx., U.S. F10 130
Petuhovo, Russia C11 32
Peuetsagoe, Gunung, vol., Indon. J3 48
Peureulak, Indon. J3 48
Peusangan, stm., Indon. J3 48
Pevek, Russia C23 34
Peza, stm., Russia D23 8
Pezawa Taung, mtn., Mya. C2 48
Pézenas, Fr. F9 18
Pezinok, Slov. H13 16
Pfarrkirchen, Ger. H8 16
Pforzheim, Ger. H4 16
Pfronten, Ger. I6 16
Pfunds, Aus. D7 22
Pfungstadt, Ger. G4 16
Pha-an, Mya. D3 48
Phagwāra, India C5 54
Phalaborwa, S. Afr. C10 70
Phalodi, India E4 54
Phaltan, India C2 53
Phan, Thai. C4 48
Phanat Nikhom, Thai. F5 48
Phangan, Ko, i., Thai. H5 48
Phangnga, Thai. H4 48
Phaniang, stm., Thai. D6 48
Phanom Dongrak Range (Dângrêk, Chuŏr Phnum), mts., Asia C3 44
Phan Rang, Viet. G9 48
Phan Thiet, Viet. G9 48
Phan Thong, Thai. F5 48
Pharenda, India E9 54
Pharr, Tx., U.S. H9 130
Phat Diem, Viet. B8 48
Phatthalung, Thai. I5 48
Phayao, Thai. C4 48
Phelps, N.Y., U.S. B8 114
Phelps, Wi., U.S. E9 118
Phelps Lake, l., N.C., U.S. I9 114
Phenix City, Al., U.S. E13 122
Phepane, stm., S. Afr. E6 70
Phet Buri, stm., Thai. F4 48
Phetchabun, Thai. D5 48
Phetchabun, Thiu Khao, mts., Thai. D5 48
Phetchaburi, Thai. F4 48
Phibun Mangsahan, Thai. E7 48
Phichai, Thai. D5 48
Phichit, Thai. D5 48
Philadelphia, Ms., U.S. E9 122
Philadelphia, N.Y., U.S. D14 112
Philadelphia, Pa., U.S. E10 114
Phil Campbell, Al., U.S. C11 122
Philip, S.D., U.S. C11 126
Philippeville see Skikda, Alg. B6 64
Philippeville, Bel. D13 14
Philippi, W.V., U.S. E5 114
Philippi see Fílippoi, hist., Grc. B7 28
Philippi, Lake, l., Austl. D2 76
Philippine Basin, unds. H15 142
Philippines, ctry., Asia C4 52
Philippine Sea H15 142
Philippine Trench, unds. H15 142
Philippolis, S. Afr. G7 70
Philipsburg, Mt., U.S. D13 136
Philipsburg, Pa., U.S. D7 114
Philip Smith Mountains, mts., Ak., U.S. C10 140
Philipstown, S. Afr. G7 70
Phillaur, India C5 54
Phillip Island, i., Austl. L5 76
Phillips, Me., U.S. F6 110
Phillips, Tx., U.S. F7 128
Phillips, Wi., U.S. F8 118
Phillipsburg, Ga., U.S. E2 116
Phillipsburg, N.J., U.S. D10 114
Philo, Il., U.S. D9 120
Philo, Oh., U.S. E4 114
Philpots Island, i., Nu., Can. C16 141
Phimai, Thai. E6 48
Phitsanulok, Thai. D5 48
Phnom Penh see Phnum Pénh, Camb. G7 48
Phnum Pénh (Phnom Penh), Camb. G7 48
Phoenix, Az., U.S. J4 132
Phoenix, N.Y., U.S. E13 112
Phoenix, Or., U.S. A3 134
Phoenix Islands, is., Kir. D9 72
Phoenixville, Pa., U.S. D10 114
Phofung (Sources, Mont-aux-), mtn., Afr. F9 70
Phon, Thai. E6 48
Phong, stm., Thai. D6 48
Phôngsali, Laos B6 48
Phon Phisai, Thai. D6 48
Phra Chedi Sam Ong, p., Asia E4 48
Phrae, Thai. C5 48
Phra Nakhon Si Ayutthaya, Thai. E5 48
Phran Kratai, Thai. D4 48
Phrom Phiram, Thai. D5 48
Phu Cat, Viet. E9 48
Phuket, Thai. I4 48
Phuket, Ko, i., Thai. I4 48
Phu Ly, Viet. B7 48
Phum Duang, stm., Thai. H4 48
Phumĭ Bâ Kham, Camb. F8 48
Phumĭ Béng, Camb. F7 48
Phumĭ Châmbák, Camb. G7 48
Phumĭ Chhuk, Camb. G7 48
Phumĭ Chruŏy Slêng, Camb. F8 48
Phumĭ Kâmpóng Srâlau, Camb. E7 48
Phumĭ Kâmpóng Trâbêk, Camb. F7 48
Phumĭ Kaôh Kért, Camb. F7 48
Phumĭ Khpŏb, Camb. G7 48
Phumĭ Lvéa Kraŏm, Camb. F6 48
Phumĭ Narŭng, Camb. F7 48
Phumĭ Prêk Kák, Camb. F7 48
Phumĭ Puŏk Chás, Camb. F6 48
Phumĭ Sâmraông, Camb. E6 48
Phumĭ Srê Kôkir, Camb. F8 48
Phumĭ Tbêng, Camb. F7 48
Phumĭ Thmâ Pôk, Camb. F6 48
Phumĭ Toek Choŭ, Camb. F6 48
Phu My, Viet. E9 48
Phuoc Long, Viet. G8 48
Phuoc Long, Viet. H7 48
Phu Pan National Park, p.o.i., Thai. D6 48
Phu Quoc, Dao, i., Viet. G6 48
Phu Tho, Viet. B7 48
Phu Vang, Viet. D8 48
Pi, stm., China F7 42
Piaçabuçu, Braz. F7 88
Piacenza, Italy E6 22
Pialba, Austl. E9 76
Piancó, Braz. D7 88
Pianosa, Isola, i., Italy H12 22
Pianosa, Isola, i., Italy H6 22
Piapot, Sk., Can. E4 124
Piaseczno, Pol. D16 16
Piaski, Pol. E18 16
Piatã, Braz. G5 88
Piatra-Neamţ, Rom. B13 26
Piauí, state, Braz. D4 88
Piauí, stm., Braz. D4 88
Piauí, Morro do, mtn., Braz. H2 88
Piave, stm., Italy E9 22
Piaxtla, stm., Mex. D5 100
Piazza Armerina, Italy G8 24
Pibor Post, Sudan F6 62
Pic, stm., On., Can. B12 118
Picacho, Az., U.S. K5 132
Picardie, hist. reg., Fr. E11 14
Picardy see Picardie, hist. reg., Fr. E11 14
Picayune, Ms., U.S. G9 122
Pichanal, Arg. D4 90
Picher, Ok., U.S. H3 120
Pichilemu, Chile G1 92
Pichimá, Col. E3 86
Pichi Mahuida, Arg. I5 92
Pichincha, state, Ec. H2 86
Pichucalco, Mex. G12 100
Pickardville, Ab., Can. B16 138
Pickens, Ms., U.S. E9 122
Pickens, S.C., U.S. B3 116
Pickensville, Al., U.S. D10 122
Pickerel Lake, l., Mb., Can. B14 124
Pickering, Eng., U.K. G12 12
Pickle Lake, On., Can. E12 106
Pickstown, S.D., U.S. D14 126
Pickton, Tx., U.S. D3 122
Pickwick Lake, res., U.S. B10 122
Pico, mtn., C.V. I10 65a
Pico, i., Port. C3 60
Pico de Neblina, Parque Nacional, p.o.i., Braz. G9 86
Pico de Orizaba, Parque Nacional, p.o.i., Mex. F10 100
Pico de Orizaba, Volcán (Citlaltépetl, Volcán), vol., Mex. F10 100
Picos, Braz. D5 88
Picquigny, Fr. E11 14
Picton, On., Can. D12 112
Picton, N.Z. E6 80
Picton, Isla, i., Chile K3 90
Pictou, N.S., Can. E14 110
Pictou Island, i., N.S., Can. E14 110
Picture Butte, Ab., Can. G18 138
Pictured Rocks National Lakeshore, p.o.i., Mi., U.S. B3 112
Picuí, Braz. D7 88
Picún Leufú, Arg. G3 90
Pidálion, Akrotírion, c., Cyp. D5 58
Pidhorodna, Ukr. A17 26
Pidurutalagala, mtn., Sri L. H5 53
Piedecuesta, Col. D5 86
Piedimonte Matese, Italy C8 24
Piedmont, Al., U.S. D13 122
Piedmont, Mo., U.S. G7 120
Piedmont see Piemonte, state, Italy F5 22
Piedra, stm., Co., U.S. F9 132
Piedra, Cerro, mtn., Chile H1 92
Piedra del Águila, Arg. H3 90
Piedrafita, Puerto de, p., Spain B3 20
Piedrahita, Spain D5 20
Piedras, Punta, c., Arg. G9 92
Piedras, Punta, c., Ven. B11 86
Piedras Blancas, Arg. E8 92
Piedras Negras, Guat. D2 102
Piedras Negras, Mex. A8 100
Pieksämäki, Fin. E12 8
Pielinen, l., Fin. E13 8
Pieljekaise Nationalpark, p.o.i., Swe. C6 8
Piemonte, state, Italy F5 22
Pienaarsrivier, S. Afr. D8 70
Pieniężno, Pol. B16 16
Pieniński Park Narodowy, p.o.i., Pol. G16 16
Pienza, Italy G8 22
Pierce, Co., U.S. G8 126
Pierce, Id., U.S. D11 136
Pierce City, Mo., U.S. E14 128
Pierpont, S.D., U.S. B15 126
Pierre, S.D., U.S. C12 126
Pierre, Bayou, stm., La., U.S. F5 122
Pierre, Bayou, stm., Ms., U.S. E8 122
Pierre Part, La., U.S. G7 122
Pierreville, Trin. s13 105f
Pierz, Mn., U.S. F4 118
Piešťany, Slov. H13 16
Pietarsaari, Fin. E10 8
Pietermaritzburg, S. Afr. F10 70
Pietersburg, S. Afr. C9 70
Pietrasanta, Italy F7 22
Piet Retief, S. Afr. E10 70
Pietrosu, Vârful, mtn., Rom. B12 26
Pigeon, Mi., U.S. E6 112
Pigeon, stm., Mb., Can. B17 124
Pigeon Forge, Tn., U.S. I2 114
Pigeon Lake, l., Ab., Can. C16 138
Pigeon Lake, l., On., Can. D11 112
Piggs Peak, Swaz. E10 70
Pigs, Bay of see Cochinos, Bahía de, b., Cuba B7 102
Pigüé, Arg. H6 92
Pihāri, India E8 54
Pihlajavesi, l., Fin. F13 8
Pihtipudas, Fin. E11 8
Pijijiapan, Mex. H12 100
Pikalëvo, Russia A17 10
Pikangikum, On., Can. E12 106
Pikes Peak, mtn., Co., U.S. C3 128
Pikes Rocks, hill, Pa., U.S. C6 114
Pikesville, Md., U.S. E9 114
Piketberg, S. Afr. H4 70
Piketon, Oh., U.S. E2 114
Pikeville, Tn., U.S. B13 122
Pikou, China B10 42
Pikounda, Congo D3 66
Piła, Pol. C12 16
Piła, state, Pol. C12 16
Pilanesberg Game Reserve, p.o.i., S. Afr. D8 70
Pilão Arcado, Braz. E4 88
Pilar, Arg. E5 92
Pilar, Braz. E8 88
Pilar, Para. C8 92
Pilar de Goiás, Braz. H1 88
Pilar do Sul, Braz. A14 92
Pilares, Mex. D3 130
Pilas Group, is., Phil. G3 52
Pilawa, Pol. D17 16
Pilcomayo, stm., S.A. D4 90
Pilcomayo, Brazo Norte, stm., Para. B8 92
Pilcomayo, Brazo Sur del, stm., S.A. B8 92
Pilcomayo, Parque Nacional, p.o.i., Arg. B8 92
Pilger, Ne., U.S. E15 126
Pilgrim's Rest, S. Afr. D10 70
Pili, Phil. D4 52
Pīlībhīt, India D7 54
Pilica, stm., Pol. E16 16
Pilliga, Austl. H7 76
Pilot, The, mtn., Austl. K7 76
Pilot Butte, Sk., Can. D9 124
Pilot Knob, Mo., U.S. G7 120
Pilot Knob, mtn., Id., U.S. E11 136
Pilot Mound, Mb., Can. E15 124
Pilot Mountain, N.C., U.S. H5 114
Pilot Peak, mtn., Nv., U.S. E8 134
Pilot Peak, mtn., Wy., U.S. F16 136
Pilot Rock, Or., U.S. E8 136
Pilottown, La., U.S. H9 122
Pilsen see Plzeň, Czech Rep. G9 16
Pilu, stm., Mya. B3 48
Pilzno, Pol. G17 16
Pima, Az., U.S. K7 132
Pimba, Austl. F7 74
Pimenteira, Vereda, stm., Braz. F4 88
Pimentel, Braz. B3 88
Pinang, Pulau, i., Malay. J4 48
Pınarbaşı, Tur. B16 28
Pinar del Río, Cuba A5 102
Pinarello, Fr. H15 18
Pınarhisar, Tur. B10 28
Pinas, Arg. E5 92
Pinatubo, Mount, vol., Phil. C3 52
Pincher Creek, Ab., Can. G17 138
Pinchi Lake, l., B.C., Can. B6 138
Pinckneyville, Il., U.S. F8 120
Pinconning, Mi., U.S. E5 112
Pindale, Mya. B2 48
Pindamonhangaba, Braz. L3 88
Pindaré, stm., Braz. B3 88
Pindaré-Mirim, Braz. B3 88
Pindhos Óros (Pindus Mountains), mts., Grc. D4 28
Pindi Gheb, Pak. B4 54
Pindobaçu, Braz. F5 88
Pindus Mountains see Pindhos Óros, mts., Grc. D4 28
Pindwāra, India F4 54
Pine, stm., Mi., U.S. E5 112
Pine Apple, Al., U.S. F11 122
Pine Barrens, reg., N.J., U.S. E11 114
Pine Bluff, Ar., U.S. C7 122
Pine Bush, N.Y., U.S. C11 114
Pine Castle, Fl., U.S. H4 116
Pine City, Mn., U.S. F6 118
Pine Creek, Austl. B6 74
Pine Creek, stm., Nv., U.S. C9 134
Pine Creek, stm., Pa., U.S. C8 114
Pine Falls, Mb., Can. D17 124
Pinega, Russia D20 8
Pinega, stm., Russia D20 8
Pine Grove, W.V., U.S. E5 114
Pine Hill, Austl. D6 76
Pine Hill, Al., U.S. F11 122
Pine Hills, Fl., U.S. H4 116
Pinehouse Lake, l., Sk., Can. D9 106
Pinehurst, Ga., U.S. D2 116
Pinehurst, Id., U.S. E10 136
Pinehurst, N.C., U.S. A6 116
Pinehurst Lake, l., Ab., Can. B19 138
Pineiós (Peneus), stm., Grc. D5 28
Pine Island, Mn., U.S. G6 118
Pine Island, i., Fl., U.S. J3 116
Pine Island Bay, b., Ant. C30 81
Pinellas Park, Fl., U.S. I3 116
Pine Mountain, mtn., Ca., U.S. H4 134
Pine Pass, p., B.C., Can. A8 138
Pine Point, N.T., Can. C8 106
Pine Ridge, S.D., U.S. D10 126
Pine River, Mb., Can. C13 124
Pine River, Mn., U.S. E4 118
Pinerolo, Italy F4 22
Piñeros, Isla, i., P.R. B4 104a
Pines, Isle of see Juventud, Isla de la, i., Cuba B6 102
Pines, Lake O' The, res., Tx., U.S. E4 122
Pine Swamp Knob, mtn., W.V., U.S. E6 114
Pinetop-Lakeside, Az., U.S. I6 132
Pinetops, N.C., U.S. I8 114
Pinetown, S. Afr. F10 70
Pine Valley, val., Ut., U.S. E3 132
Pineville, Ky., U.S. H2 114
Pineville, La., U.S. F6 122
Pineville, Mo., U.S. H3 120
Pineville, W.V., U.S. G4 114
Pinewood, S.C., U.S. C5 116
Ping, stm., Thai. E5 48
Ping'an, China B5 38
Pingba, China H2 42
Pingchang, China F2 42
Pingding, China C5 42
Pingdingshan, China E5 42
Pingdu, China C8 42
Pingelly, Austl. F3 74
Pinghe, China A6 48
Pinghu, China F9 42
Pingjiang, China G5 42
Pingle, China I4 42
Pingli, China E3 42
Pingliang, China D2 42
Pingluo, China B2 42
Pingnan, China H8 42
Pingnan, China J4 42
Pingquan, China A8 42
Pingshi, China I5 42
Pingtan, China I8 42
Pingtan Dao, i., China I8 42
P'ingtung, Tai. J9 42
Pingwu, China E5 36
Pingxiang, China H5 42
Pingxiang, China J2 42
Pingyang, China H9 42
Pingyao, China C5 42
Pingyi, China D7 42
Pingyin, China C7 42
Pingyuan, China I6 42

Name — Map Ref. — Page

Pinhão, Braz. F7 88
Pinheiro, Braz. B3 88
Pinheiros, Braz. J5 88
Pinhel, Port. D3 20
Pini, Pulau, i., Indon. E2 44
Pinillos, Col. C4 86
Pinjarra, Austl. F3 74
Pinjug, Russia F22 8
Pinkiang see Harbin, China B7 38
Pink Mountain, B.C., Can. D6 106
Pinnacle, mtn., Va., U.S. E7 114
Pinnacle Buttes, mtn., Wy., U.S. G17 136
Pinnacles National Monument, p.o.i., Ca., U.S. G4 134
Pinnaroo, Austl. J3 76
Pinneberg, Ger. C5 16
Pinos, Mex. D8 100
Pinos, Isla de see Juventud, Isla de la, i., Cuba B6 102
Pinos, Mount, mtn., Ca., U.S. I6 134
Pinos Puente, Spain G7 20
Pinrang, Indon. E11 50
Pins, Île des, i., N. Cal. n16 79d
Pins, Pointe aux, c., On., Can. F8 112
Pinsk, Bela. H9 10
Pinsk Marshes see Pripet Marshes, reg., Eur. H12 10
Pinson, Al., U.S. D12 122
Pinta, Isla, i., Ec. h11 84a
Pintada Arroyo, stm., N.M., U.S. G3 128
Pintados, Chile D3 90
Pintasan, Malay. A10 50
Pinto Butte, mtn., Sk., Can. E6 124
Pintoyacu, stm., Ec. H3 86
Pin Valley National Park, p.o.i., India C6 54
Pioche, Nv., U.S. F2 132
Piombino, Italy H7 22
Pioneer Mine, B.C., Can. F8 138
Pionerskij, Russia F3 10
Pionki, Pol. E17 16
Piorini, stm., Braz. D5 84
Piorini, Lago, l., Braz. D5 84
Piotrków, state, Pol. E15 16
Piotrków Trybunalski, Pol. E15 16
Pio V. Corpuz, Phil. E5 52
Piove di Sacco, Italy E8 22
Pio XII, Braz. B3 88
Pipanaco, Salar de, pl., Arg. D4 92
Pīpār, India E4 54
Piparia, India G7 54
Pīpar Road, India E4 54
Pipe Spring National Monument, p.o.i., Az., U.S. G4 132
Pipestem Creek, stm., N.D., U.S. G14 124
Pipestone, Mn., U.S. H2 118
Pipestone, stm., On., Can. E12 106
Pipestone Creek, stm., Can. E12 124
Pipestone National Monument, p.o.i., Mn., U.S. G2 118
Pipinas, Arg. G9 92
Piplān, Pak. B3 54
Pipmuacan, Réservoir, res., Qc., Can. A6 110
Piqua, Oh., U.S. D1 114
Piquet Carneiro, Braz. C6 88
Piquiri, stm., Braz. B11 92
Piracanjuba, Braz. I1 88
Piracanjuba, stm., Braz. I1 88
Piracicaba, Braz. L2 88
Piracicaba, stm., Braz. L1 88
Piracuruca, Braz. B5 88
Pirae, Fr. Poly. v21 78h
Piraeus see Peiraiás, Grc. F6 28
Piraí do Sul, Braz. B12 92
Piraju, Braz. L1 88
Pirajuí, Braz. L1 88
Piram Island, i., India H4 54
Piran, Slvn. E10 22
Pirané, Arg. B8 92
Piranga, Braz. K4 88
Piranhas, Braz. G7 84
Piranhas, stm., Braz. E1 88
Piranhas, stm., Braz. C7 88
Piranji, stm., Braz. C6 88
Pirapemas, Braz. B3 88
Pirapora, Braz. I3 88
Piraquara, Braz. B13 92
Pirassununga, Braz. K2 88
Pirata, Monte, hill, P.R. B4 104a
Piratinga, stm., Braz. H2 88
Piratini, Braz. E11 92
Piratini, stm., Braz. D10 92
Piratuba, Braz. C11 92
Pires do Rio, Braz. I1 88
Piriápolis, Ur. G10 92
Pirin, Parki Narodowe, p.o.i., Blg. H10 26
Piripiri, Braz. C5 88
Píritu, Ven. C7 86
Pirmasens, Ger. G3 16
Pirna, Ger. F9 16
Pirojpur, Bngl. G12 54
Pirot, Yugo. F9 26
Pirovano, Arg. H7 92
Pirovskoe, Russia C16 32
Pīr Panjāl Range, mts., Asia B5 54
Pirtleville, Az., U.S. L7 132
Pirttikylä, Fin. E9 8
Piru, Indon. F8 44
Pisa, Italy G7 22
Pisagua, Chile C2 90
Pisco, Peru F2 84
Pişcolt, Rom. B9 26
Písek, Czech Rep. G10 16
Pishan, China A4 46
Pishchanka, Ukr. A15 26
Pisinemo, Az., U.S. K4 132
Pismo Beach, Ca., U.S. H5 134
Pisticci, Italy D10 24
Pistoia, Italy G7 22
Pisuerga, stm., Spain C6 20
Pit, stm., Ca., U.S. B4 134
Pit, North Fork, stm., Ca., U.S. B5 134
Pita, Gui. G2 64
Pitalito, Col. G4 86
Pitanga, Braz. B12 92
Pitangui, Braz. J3 88
Pitcairn, dep., Pit. c28 78k
Piteå, Swe. D9 8
Piteälven, stm., Swe. D8 8
Pitești, Rom. E11 26
Pithāpuram, India C6 53
Pithiviers, Fr. F11 14
Pithom, hist., Egypt H2 58
Pithorāgarh, India D8 54
Pitinga, stm., Braz. H12 86
Pitiquito, Mex. F6 98
Pitkjaranta, Russia F14 8
Pitljar, Russia C2 34
Pitomača, Cro. D14 22
Pitrufquén, Chile G2 90
Pitt Island, i., B.C., Can. E5 106
Pitt Lake, l., B.C., Can. G8 138
Pittsboro, N.C., U.S. I6 114
Pittsburg, Ks., U.S. G3 120
Pittsburg, Tx., U.S. E4 122
Pittsburgh, Pa., U.S. D6 114
Pittsfield, Il., U.S. E7 120
Pittsfield, Me., U.S. F7 110
Pittsfield, Ma., U.S. B12 114
Pittsford, Mi., U.S. C1 114
Pittston, Pa., U.S. C10 114
Pittsview, Al., U.S. E13 122
Pittsworth, Austl. F8 76
Pituil, Arg. D4 92
Pium, Braz. F1 88
Piura, Peru E1 84
Piute Peak, mtn., Ca., U.S. H7 134
Pivan', Russia F16 34
Pivdennyy Buh, stm., Ukr. A17 26
Pizarro, Col. E3 86
Pizzo, Italy F10 24
Pjakupur, stm., Russia B13 32
Pjalka, Russia C19 8
Pjandž (Panj), stm., Asia B11 56
Pjaozero, ozero, l., Russia C14 8
Pjasina, stm., Russia B6 34
Pjasino, ozero, l., Russia B6 34
Pjasinskij zaliv, b., Russia B5 34
Pjatigorsk, Russia F6 32
Pjatovskij, Russia F19 10
Pjažieva Sel'ga, Russia F16 8
Placentia Bay, b., Nf., Can. j23 107a
Placerville, Ca., U.S. E5 134
Placetas, Cuba A8 102
Plácido Rosas, Ur. F11 92
Plai Mat, stm., Thai. E6 48
Plain City, Ut., U.S. B4 132
Plain Dealing, La., U.S. E5 122
Plainfield, Ct., U.S. C13 114
Plainfield, In., U.S. I3 112
Plainfield, N.J., U.S. D11 114
Plains, Ga., U.S. E14 122
Plains, Ks., U.S. D8 128
Plains, Mt., U.S. C12 136
Plainview, Mn., U.S. G6 118
Plainview, Ne., U.S. E15 126
Plainview, Tx., U.S. G7 128
Plainville, In., U.S. F10 120
Plainwell, Mi., U.S. F4 112
Plakhtiïvka, Ukr. C16 26
Plamondon, Ab., Can. B18 138
Plampang, Indon. H10 50
Planá, Czech Rep. G8 16
Plana, L'Illa, i., Spain F10 20
Planada, Ca., U.S. F5 134
Planalto, Braz. C11 92
Planchón, Cerro del (El Planchón, Volcán), vol., S.A. G2 92
Planeta Rica, Col. C4 86
Plano, Il., U.S. C9 120
Plano, Tx., U.S. D2 122
Plantagenet, On., Can. E2 110
Plantation, Fl., U.S. J5 116
Plant City, Fl., U.S. I3 116
Plantersville, Ms., U.S. C10 122
Plantsite, Az., U.S. J7 132
Plaquemine, La., U.S. G7 122
Plasencia, Spain D4 20
Plaster Rock, N.B., Can. D9 110
Plasy, Czech Rep. G9 16
Plata, Isla de la, i., Ec. H1 86
Plata, Río de la, est., S.A. G9 92
Plato, Col. C4 86
Platte, stm., U.S. E3 120
Platte, stm., Ne., U.S. C7 108
Platte, Île, i., Sey. k13 69b
Platte Center, Ne., U.S. F15 126
Platte City, Mo., U.S. E3 120
Platteville, Co., U.S. A4 128
Platteville, Wi., U.S. B7 120
Plattsburgh, N.Y., U.S. F3 110
Plattsmouth, Ne., U.S. D2 120
Plau, Ger. C8 16
Plauen, Ger. F8 16
Plav, Yugo. G6 26
Plavsk, Russia G20 10
Playa Azul, Mex. G7 100
Playa de Fajardo, P.R. B4 104a
Playa de Guayanilla, P.R. B2 104a
Playa de Naguabo, P.R. B4 104a
Playa de Ponce, P.R. C2 104a
Playa Noriega, Laguna, l., Mex. A3 100
Playa Vicente, Mex. G11 100
Playgreen Lake, l., Mb., Can. E11 106
Play Ku, Viet. F8 48
Plaza, N.D., U.S. F12 124
Pleasant, Mount, hill, N.B., Can. E9 110
Pleasant Bay, N.S., Can. D16 110
Pleasantdale, Sk., Can. B9 124
Pleasant Grove, Ut., U.S. C5 132
Pleasant Hill, Il., U.S. E7 120
Pleasant Hill, La., U.S. F5 122
Pleasant Hill, Mo., U.S. F3 120
Pleasanton, Ks., U.S. F3 120
Pleasanton, Tx., U.S. F9 130
Pleasantville, N.J., U.S. E11 114
Pleasantville, Pa., U.S. C6 114
Pleaux, Fr. D8 18
Plehanovo, Russia F20 10
Plenty, Sk., Can. C5 124
Plenty, Bay of, b., N.Z. C7 80
Plentywood, Mt., U.S. F9 124
Pleščeevo, ozero, l., Russia D21 10
Pleseck, Russia E19 8
Plessisville, Qc., Can. D5 110
Pleszew, Pol. E13 16
Plétipi, Lac, l., Qc., Can. E16 106
Plettenbergbaai, S. Afr. I6 70
Pleven, Blg. F11 26
Plevna, Mt., U.S. A8 126
Plitvička Jezera Nacionalni Park, p.o.i., Cro. F12 22
Pljevlja, Yugo. F6 26
Pljuskovo, Russia H16 10
Pljussa, stm., Russia A11 10
Płock, Pol. D15 16
Płock, state, Pol. D15 16
Ploërmel, Fr. G6 14
Ploiești, Rom. E12 26
Plomb du Cantal, mtn., Fr. D8 18
Plomer, Point, c., Austl. H9 76
Plön, Ger. B6 16
Płońsk, Pol. D16 16
Ploskoe, Russia H21 10
Plotnica, Bela. H9 10
Ploudalmézeau, Fr. F4 14
Plovdiv, Blg. G11 26
Plovdiv, state, Blg. G11 26
Plumerville, Ar., U.S. B6 122
Plummer, Id., U.S. C9 136
Plumridge Lakes, l., Austl. E5 74
Plumtree, Zimb. B8 70
Plungė, Lith. E4 10
Plutarco Elías Calles, Presa, res., Mex. G8 98
Plymouth, Monts. D3 105a
Plymouth, Eng., U.K. K8 12
Plymouth, Ca., U.S. E5 134
Plymouth, Il., U.S. D6 120
Plymouth, Ma., U.S. C15 114
Plymouth, Ne., U.S. A11 128
Plymouth, N.H., U.S. G5 110
Plymouth, N.C., U.S. I9 114
Plymouth, Oh., U.S. C3 114
Plymouth, Pa., U.S. C10 114
Plzeň, Czech Rep. G9 16
Pô, Burkina G4 64
Po, stm., Italy F8 22
Po, Foci del, mth., Italy F9 22
Po, Mouths of the see Po, Foci del, mth., Italy F9 22
Poarta Orientală, Pasul, p., Rom. D9 26
Pobè, Benin H5 64
Pobeda, gora, mtn., Russia C18 34
Pobedino, Russia G17 34
Pobedy, pik, mtn., Asia F14 32
Poblado Cerro Gordo, P.R. A3 104a
Poblado Jacaguas, P.R. B2 104a
Poblado Medianía Alta, P.R. B4 104a
Poblado Santana, P.R. B2 104a
Pobra de Trives, Spain B3 20
Pocahontas, Ar., U.S. H6 120
Pocahontas, Ia., U.S. B3 120
Poção, Braz. E7 88
Pocatello, Id., U.S. H14 136
Počep, Russia H16 10
Počinok, Russia D4 32
Pocitos, Salar, pl., Arg. B4 92
Poço da Cruz, Açude, res., Braz. E7 88
Poções, Braz. H5 88
Pocola, Ok., U.S. B4 122
Pocomoke City, Md., U.S. F10 114
Poconé, Braz. G6 84
Pocono Mountains, hills, Pa., U.S. C10 114
Pocono Summit, Pa., U.S. C10 114
Poço Redondo, Braz. E7 88
Poços de Caldas, Braz. K2 88
Pocrane, Braz. J5 88
Podbereze, Russia D13 10
Podborove, Russia A18 10
Poddębice, Pol. E14 16
Poddore, Russia C13 10
Poděbrady, Czech Rep. F11 16
Podgorica (Titograd), Yugo. G6 26
Podjuga, Russia F19 8
Podkamennaja Tunguska, Russia B16 32
Podkamennaja Tunguska, stm., Russia B16 32
Podlasie, reg., Pol. D19 16
Podol'sk, Russia E20 10
Podor, Sen. F2 64
Podporože, Russia F16 8
Podravina, reg., Cro. E15 22
Podtësovo, Russia C16 32
Podujevo, Yugo. G8 26
Poel, i., Ger. B7 16
Poelela, Lagoa, l., Moz. D12 70
Pofadder, S. Afr. F4 70
Pogar, Russia H16 10
Poggibonsi, Italy G8 22
Pogoanele, Rom. E13 26
Pogoreloe Gorodišče, Russia D17 10
Pogradec, Alb. D14 24
Pogradeci see Pogradec, Alb. D14 24
Pograničnyj, Russia B9 38
P'ohang, Kor., S. C2 40
Pohjanmaa, reg., Fin. D11 8
Pohjois-Karjala, state, Fin. E14 8
Pohnpei, i., Micron. I11 78d
Pohri, India F6 54
Pohvistnevo, Russia D8 32
Pöide, Est. B6 10
Poinsett, Cape, c., Ant. B16 81
Poinsett, Lake, l., S.D., U.S. C15 126
Point, Tx., U.S. E3 122
Point Arena, Ca., U.S. E2 134
Point Au Fer Island, i., La., U.S. H7 122
Point Baker, Ak., U.S. E13 140
Pointe-à-la-Garde, Qc., Can. B10 110
Pointe a la Hache, La., U.S. H9 122
Pointe-à-Pitre, Guad. h5 105c
Pointe-à-Pitre-le Raizet, Aéroport de, Guad. h5 105c
Pointe du Canonnier, c., Guad. A1 105a
Point Edward, On., Can. E7 112
Pointe-Noire, Congo E2 66
Pointe-Noire, Guad. h5 105c
Point Fortin, Trin. s12 105f
Point Hope, Ak., U.S. C6 140
Point Jupiter, c., St. Vin. p11 105e
Point Lake, l., N.T., Can. B8 106
Point Marion, Pa., U.S. E5 114
Point Pelee National Park, p.o.i., On., Can. G7 112
Point Pleasant, N.J., U.S. D11 114
Point Reyes National Seashore, p.o.i., Ca., U.S. E2 134
Point Roberts, Wa., U.S. B3 136
Point Salines International Airport, Gren. q10 105e
Point Sapin, N.B., Can. D12 110
Poisson Blanc, Lac du, res., Qc., Can. B14 112
Poissy, Fr. F10 14
Poitiers, Fr. H9 14
Poitou, hist. reg., Fr. C5 18
Poivre Atoll, i., Sey. k12 69b
Pojarkovo, Russia G14 34
Pojoaque Valley, N.M., U.S. F2 128
Pojuca, Braz. G6 88
Pojuca, stm., Braz. G6 88
Pokaran, India E3 54
Pokataroo, Austl. G7 76
Pokharā, Nepal D10 54
Poko, D.R.C. D5 66
Pokrovsk, Russia D14 34
Pokrovskoe, Russia H19 10
Pola, stm., Russia C14 10
Polacca Wash, stm., Az., U.S. H6 132
Polack, Bela. E11 10
Pola de Lena, Spain A5 20
Pola de Siero, Spain A5 20
Poland, ctry., Eur. D15 16
Polanów, Pol. B12 16
Polatlı, Tur. D15 28
Polcura, Chile H2 92
Poldnevica, Russia G22 8
Polebridge, Mt., U.S. B12 136
Pol-e Khomrī, Afg. B10 56
Polese see Pripet Marshes, reg., Eur. H12 10
Polesine, reg., Italy E8 22
Polewali, Indon. E11 50
Polgár, Hung. B8 26
Poli, Cam. C2 66
Poli, China D8 42
Policastro, Golfo di, b., Italy E9 24
Police (Pölitz), Pol. C10 16
Polička, Czech Rep. G12 16
Polillo Island, i., Phil. C3 52
Polillo Islands, is., Phil. C4 52
Pólis, Cyp. C3 58
Polist', stm., Russia C14 10
Polistena, Italy F10 24
Poljarnyj, Russia B15 8
Poljarnyj, Russia C24 34
Poljarnyj Ural, mts., Russia A10 32
Polk, Ne., U.S. F15 126
Polk, Pa., U.S. C6 114
Pol'kino, Russia B8 34
Pollāchi, India F3 53
Pöllau, Aus. C12 22
Pollino, Monte, mtn., Italy E10 24
Pollock, La., U.S. F6 122
Pollock, S.D., U.S. B12 126
Polnovo-Seliger, Russia C15 10
Polo, Il., U.S. B8 120
Polomet', stm., Russia C15 10
Polonnaruwa, Sri L. H5 53
Polonnaruwa, hist., Sri L. H5 53
Polotnjanyj, Russia F19 10
Polotsk see Polack, Bela. E11 10
Polski Trămbeš, Blg. F12 26
Polson, Mt., U.S. C12 136
Poltava, Ukr. E4 32
Poltimore, Qc., Can. C14 112
Põltsamaa, Est. G12 8
Poluj, stm., Russia A11 32
Polunočnoe, Russia B10 32
Polur, India E4 53
Polvijärvi, Fin. E13 8
Polýaigos, i., Grc. G7 28
Polynesia, is., Oc. J22 142
Polysajevo, Russia F6 34
Pomarkku, Fin. F9 8
Pombal, Braz. D7 88
Pomerania, hist. reg., Eur. C11 16
Pomeranian Bay, b., Eur. B10 16
Pomerene, Az., U.S. K6 132
Pomerode, Braz. C13 92
Pomeroy, Ia., U.S. B3 120
Pomeroy, Wa., U.S. D9 136
Pomfret, S. Afr. D6 70
Pomi, Rom. B10 26
Pomme de Terre, stm., Mn., U.S. F3 118
Pomme de Terre, stm., Mo., U.S. G4 120
Pomme de Terre Lake, res., Mo., U.S. G4 120
Pomona, Ca., U.S. I8 134
Pomona, Ks., U.S. F2 120
Pomona Lake, res., Ks., U.S. F2 120
Pomorskij proliv, strt., Russia B24 8
Pompano Beach, Fl., U.S. J5 116
Pompei, hist., Italy D8 24
Pompejevka, Russia G15 34
Pompéu, Braz. J3 88
Pomquet, N.S., Can. E15 110
Ponass Lakes, l., Sk., Can. B9 124
Ponazyrevo, Russia G22 8
Ponca, Ne., U.S. B1 120
Ponca City, Ok., U.S. E11 128
Ponca Creek, stm., U.S. E14 126
Ponce, P.R. B2 104a
Ponce, Aeropuerto, P.R. B2 104a
Ponce de Leon, Fl., U.S. G12 122
Poncha Pass, p., Co., U.S. C2 128
Pond Creek, Ok., U.S. E11 128
Ponderay, Id., U.S. B10 136
Pondicherry (Puduchcheri), India F4 53
Pondicherry, state, India E5 53
Pond Inlet, Nu., Can. A15 106
Pond Inlet, b., Nu., Can. A15 106
Pondosa, Ca., U.S. B4 134
Ponente, Riviera di, cst., Italy F5 22
Ponérihouen, N. Cal. m15 79d
Ponferrada, Spain B4 20
Pongolo, stm., S. Afr. E10 70
Poniatowa, Pol. E17 16
Ponizove, Russia E14 10
Ponnaiyār, stm., India E4 53
Ponnāni, India F2 53
Ponnūru Nidubrolu, India C5 53
Ponoj, Russia C19 8
Ponoj, stm., Russia C18 8
Ponoka, Ab., Can. D17 138
Ponorogo, Indon. G7 50
Pons, Fr. D5 18
Ponta Delgada, Port. C3 60
Ponta Grossa, Braz. B12 92
Pontalina, Braz. I1 88
Ponta Porã, Braz. D5 90
Pontarlier, Fr. H15 14
Pontas de Pedra, Braz. D8 88
Pontassieve, Italy G8 22
Pontchartrain, Lake, l., La., U.S. G8 122
Pontchâteau, Fr. G6 14
Pont-de-Vaux, Fr. C10 18
Ponte Alta do Bom Jesus, Braz. G2 88
Ponte-Caldelas, Spain B2 20
Ponte de Lima, Port. C2 20
Pontedera, Italy G7 22
Pontedeume, Spain A2 20
Ponte do Púngoè, Moz. A12 70
Ponteix, Sk., Can. E6 124
Ponte Nova, Braz. K4 88
Ponte Serrada, Braz. C12 92
Pontevedra, Spain B2 20
Pontevedra, co., Spain B2 20
Pontiac, Il., U.S. D9 120
Pontiac, Mi., U.S. B2 114
Pontianak, Indon. C6 50
Pontine Islands see Ponziane, Isole, is., Italy D6 24
Pontivy, Fr. F5 14
Pontoise, Fr. E11 14
Pontotoc, Ms., U.S. C9 122
Pontotoc, Tx., U.S. D9 130
Pontremoli, Italy F6 22
Pontresina, Switz. D6 22
Pont-Rouge, Qc., Can. D5 110
Ponts, Spain C12 20
Pont-sur-Yonne, Fr. F12 14
Pontus Mountains see Doğu Karadeniz Dağları, mts., Tur. A5 56
Pontypridd, Wales, U.K. J9 12
Ponyri, Russia H19 10
Ponziane, Isole (Pontine Islands), is., Italy D6 24
Poole, Eng., U.K. K11 12
Pooley Island, i., B.C., Can. D2 138
Poolville, Tx., U.S. B10 130
Pooncarie, Austl. I4 76
Poopó, Bol. C3 90
Poopó, Lago, l., Bol. C3 90
Popayán, Col. F3 86
Pope, Ms., U.S. C8 122
Popești-Leordeni, Rom. E13 26
Popham Bay, b., Nu., Can. C17 106
Popigaj, Russia B11 34
Popigaj, stm., Russia B10 34
Popiltah Lake, l., Austl. I3 76
Poplar, Mt., U.S. F8 124
Poplar, stm., Can. B16 124
Poplar, stm., N.A. F8 124
Poplar, West Fork (West Poplar), stm., N.A. F8 124
Poplar Bluff, Mo., U.S. H7 120
Poplar Hill, On., Can. E12 106
Poplar Point, Mb., Can. D16 124
Poplarville, Ms., U.S. G9 122
Popocatépetl, Volcán, vol., Mex. F9 100
Popoh, Indon. H7 50
Popokabaka, D.R.C. F3 66
Popoli, Italy H10 22
Popondetta, Pap. N. Gui. b4 79a
Popovo, Blg. F13 26
Poprad, Slov. G16 16
Poprad, stm., Eur. G16 16
Popricani, Rom. B14 26
Pŏptong-ŭp, Kor., N. E7 38
Poquoson, Va., U.S. G9 114
Porangatu, Braz. G1 88
Porbandar, India H2 54
Porce, stm., Col. D4 86
Porcher Island, i., B.C., Can. E4 106
Porco, Bol. C3 90
Porcos, stm., Braz. G3 88
Porcuna, Spain G6 20
Porcupine, stm., N.A. B3 106
Pordenone, Italy D9 22
Pordim, Blg. F11 26
Poreče, Russia E18 10
Poreče-Rybnoe, Russia C22 10
Porhov, Russia C12 10
Pori (Björneborg), Fin. F9 8
Porjaguba, Russia C15 8
Porlamar, Ven. B10 86
Porog, Russia E18 8
Poronajsk, Russia G17 34
Poroshkove, Ukr. H18 16
Porpoise Bay, b., Ant. B17 81
Porrentruy, Switz. C3 22
Porretta Terme, Italy F7 22
Porsangen, b., Nor. A11 8
Porsangerhalvøya, pen., Nor. A11 8
Porsgrunn, Nor. G3 8
Porsuk, stm., Tur. D13 28
Portachuelo, Bol. C4 90
Port Adelaide, Austl. J2 76
Portadown, N. Ire., U.K. G6 12
Portage, Mi., U.S. F4 112
Portage, Ut., U.S. B4 132
Portage Bay, b., Mb., Can. C15 124
Portage Lake, l., Mi., U.S. D10 118
Portage la Prairie, Mb., Can. E15 124
Portageville, Mo., U.S. H8 120
Portal, Ga., U.S. D4 116
Portal, N.D., U.S. F11 124
Port Alberni, B.C., Can. G6 138
Portalegre, Port. E3 20
Portalegre, state, Port. E3 20
Portales, N.M., U.S. G5 128
Port Alfred, S. Afr. H8 70
Port Alice, B.C., Can. F3 138
Port Allen, La., U.S. G7 122
Port Alma, Austl. D8 76
Port Angeles, Wa., U.S. B3 136
Port Antonio, Jam. i14 104d
Port Aransas, Tx., U.S. G10 130
Portarlington, Ire. H5 12
Port Arthur, Austl. o13 77a
Port Arthur see Lüshun, China E4 38
Port Arthur, Tx., U.S. H4 122
Port Askaig, Scot., U.K. F6 12
Port Augusta, Austl. F7 74
Port au Port Peninsula, pen., Nf., Can. B17 110
Port-au-Prince, Haiti C11 102
Port-au-Prince, Baie de, b., Haiti C11 102
Port Austin, Mi., U.S. D6 112
Port Blair, India F7 46
Port Borden, P.E., Can. D13 110
Port Byron, Il., U.S. J8 118
Port Canning, India G12 54
Port-Cartier, Qc., Can. E17 106
Port Chalmers, N.Z. G4 80
Port Charlotte, Fl., U.S. J3 116
Port Clinton, Oh., U.S. C3 114
Port Clyde, Me., U.S. G7 110
Port Colborne, On., Can. F10 112
Port Coquitlam, B.C., Can. G8 138
Port-de-Paix, Haiti C11 102
Port Dickson, Malay. K5 48
Porte Crayon, Mount, mtn., W.V., U.S. F6 114
Port Edward see Weihai, China C10 42
Port Edward, S. Afr. G10 70
Port Edwards, Wi., U.S. G9 118
Porteirinha, Braz. H4 88
Portel, Braz. D7 84
Port Elgin, N.B., Can. D12 110
Port Elgin, On., Can. D8 112
Port Elizabeth, S. Afr. H7 70
Port-en-Bessin, Fr. E8 14
Porter, Tx., U.S. G3 122
Port Erin, I. of Man G8 12
Porter Point, c., St. Vin. o11 105e
Porterville, S. Afr. H4 70
Porterville, Ca., U.S. G7 134
Porterville, Ms., U.S. E10 122
Portete, Bahía, b., Col. A6 86
Port Fairy, Austl. L4 76
Port Gamble, Wa., U.S. C4 136
Port-Gentil, Gabon E1 66
Port Gibson, Ms., U.S. F8 122
Port Graham, Ak., U.S. E9 140
Port-Harcourt, Nig. I6 64
Port Hardy, B.C., Can. F3 138
Port Hawkesbury, N.S., Can. E15 110
Port Hedland, Austl. D3 74
Port Heiden, Ak., U.S. E8 140
Port Hill, P.E., Can. D13 110
Porthmadog, Wales, U.K. I8 12
Port Hood, N.S., Can. D15 110
Port Hope, On., Can. E11 112
Port Hope, Mi., U.S. E7 112
Port Huron, Mi., U.S. B3 114
Portimão, Port. G2 20
Port Isabel, Tx., U.S. H10 130
Port Jervis, N.Y., U.S. C11 114
Port Kembla, Austl. J8 76
Port Lairge see Waterford, Ire. I5 12
Portland, Austl. I7 76
Portland, Austl. L3 76
Portland, Ar., U.S. D7 122
Portland, In., U.S. H5 112
Portland, Me., U.S. G6 110
Portland, N.D., U.S. G16 124
Portland, Or., U.S. E4 136
Portland, Tn., U.S. H11 120
Portland, Tx., U.S. G10 130
Portland, Bill of, c., Eng., U.K. K10 12
Portland, Cape, c., Austl. n13 77a
Portland, Isle of, i., Eng., U.K. K10 12
Portland Bay, b., Austl. L3 76
Portland Bight, b., Jam. j13 104d
Portland Point, c., Jam. j13 104d
Portlaoise, Ire. H5 12
Port Lavaca, Tx., U.S. F11 130
Port Leyden, N.Y., U.S. E14 112
Port Lincoln, Austl. F7 74
Port Loko, S.L. H2 64
Port-Louis, Guad. h5 105c
Port Louis, Mrts. h10 69a
Port-Lyautey see Kénitra, Mor. C3 64
Port MacDonnell, Austl. L3 76
Port Macquarie, Austl. H9 76
Port Maria, Jam. i14 104d
Port McNeill, B.C., Can. F3 138
Port McNicoll, On., Can. D10 112
Port Moller, Ak., U.S. E7 140
Port Morant, Jam. j14 104d
Portmore, Jam. j13 104d
Port Moresby, Pap. N. Gui. b4 79a
Port Morien, N.S., Can. D17 110
Port Neches, Tx., U.S. H4 122
Port Nelson, Mb., Can. D12 106
Portneuf, stm., Qc., Can. B7 110
Portneuf, stm., Id., U.S. H14 136
Port Neville, B.C., Can. F4 138
Port Nolloth, S. Afr. F3 70
Port Norris, N.J., U.S. E10 114
Porto, Port. C2 20
Porto, state, Port. C2 20
Porto Acre, Braz. E4 84
Porto Alegre, Braz. E12 92
Porto Alegre, S. Tom./P. J6 64
Porto Amboim, Ang. C1 68
Portobelo, Pan. H8 102
Porto Calvo, Braz. E8 88
Porto de Moz, Braz. D7 84
Porto de Pedras, Braz. E8 88
Porto dos Gaúchos, Braz. F6 84
Porto Empedocle, Italy G7 24
Porto Esperança, Braz. C5 90
Porto Esperidião, Braz. G6 84
Porto Feliz, Braz. L2 88
Portoferraio, Italy H7 22
Porto Ferreira, Braz. K2 88
Port of Ness, Scot., U.K. C6 12
Porto Franco, Braz. D2 88
Port of Spain, Trin. s12 105f
Portogruaro, Italy E9 22
Portola, Ca., U.S. D5 134
Portomaggiore, Italy F8 22
Porto Mendes, Braz. B10 92
Porto Murtinho, Braz. D5 90
Porto Nacional, Braz. F1 88
Porto-Novo, Benin H5 64
Porto Novo, India F4 53
Port Orange, Fl., U.S. G5 116
Port Orchard, Wa., U.S. C4 136
Port Orford, Or., U.S. H2 136
Porto San Giorgio, Italy G10 22
Porto Santana, Braz. D7 84
Porto Santo, i., Port. C1 64
Porto Santo Stefano, ngh., Italy H7 22
Porto Seguro, Braz. I6 88
Porto Tolle, Italy F9 22
Porto Torres, Italy D2 24
Porto União, Braz. C12 92
Porto Válter, Braz. E3 84
Porto-Vecchio, Fr. H15 18
Porto Velho, Braz. E5 84
Portoviejo, Ec. H1 86
Port Patrick, Vanuatu m17 79d
Port Perry, On., Can. D11 112
Port Phillip Bay, b., Austl. L5 76
Port Pirie, Austl. F7 74
Portree, Scot., U.K. D6 12
Port Renfrew, B.C., Can. H6 138
Port Rowan, On., Can. F9 112
Port Royal, Jam. j14 104d
Port Royal, Pa., U.S. D8 114
Port Royal, S.C., U.S. D5 116
Port Said see Bûr Sa'îd, Egypt G3 58
Port Saint Joe, Fl., U.S. H13 122
Port Saint Johns, S. Afr. G9 70
Port Saint Lucie, Fl., U.S. I5 116
Port Sanilac, Mi., U.S. E7 112
Port Saunders, Nf., Can. i22 107a
Portsea, Austl. L5 76
Portsmouth, Dom. i6 105c
Portsmouth, Eng., U.K. K11 12
Portsmouth, N.H., U.S. G6 110
Portsmouth, Oh., U.S. F2 114
Portsmouth, Va., U.S. H9 114
Portsoy, Scot., U.K. D10 12
Port Stanley, On., Can. F8 112
Port Sudan see Būr Sūdān, Sudan D7 62
Port Sulphur, La., U.S. H9 122
Port Talbot, Wales, U.K. J9 12
Porttipahdan tekojärvi, l., Fin. B12 8
Port Townsend, Wa., U.S. B4 136
Portugal, ctry., Eur. D3 20
Portugalete, Spain A7 20
Portuguesa, state, Ven. C7 86
Portuguesa, stm., Ven. C8 86
Portuguese Guinea see Guinea-Bissau, ctry., Afr. G1 64
Port Vila, Vanuatu k17 79d
Portville, N.Y., U.S. B7 114
Port-Vladimir, Russia B15 8
Port Wentworth, Ga., U.S. D4 116
Port Wing, Wi., U.S. E7 118
Porus, Jam. i13 104d
Porvenir, Chile J2 90
Porvoo, Fin. F11 8
Porzuna, Spain E6 20
Posadas, Arg. C9 92
Posadas, Spain G5 20
Posavina, val., Eur. E14 22
Pošehon'e, Russia B22 10
Poseidon, Temple of, hist., Grc. F6 28
Posen, Mi., U.S. C6 112
Poshan see Boshan, China C7 42
Posio, Fin. C12 8
Poso, Indon. D12 50
Poso, Danau, l., Indon. D12 50
Poso, Teluk, b., Indon. D12 50
Pospeliha, Russia D14 32
Posse, Braz. H2 88
Possession Island, i., Nmb. E2 70
Pössneck, Ger. F7 16
Possum Kingdom Lake, res., Tx., U.S. B9 130
Post, Tx., U.S. A6 130
Posta de Jihuites, Mex. I2 130
Postelle, Tn., U.S. A1 116
Postmasburg, S. Afr. F6 70
Postojna, Slvn. E11 22
Postrervalle, Bol. C4 90
Postville, Ia., U.S. A6 120
Potaro, stm., Guy. E12 86
Potaro-Siparuni, state, Guy. E12 86
Potchefstroom, S. Afr. E8 70
Poté, Braz. I5 88
Poteau, Ok., U.S. B4 122
Poteet, Tx., U.S. E9 130
Potenza, Italy D9 24
Potgietersrus, S. Afr. D9 70
Poth, Tx., U.S. E9 130
Potholes Reservoir, res., Wa., U.S. D7 136
Poti, Geor. F6 32
Poti, stm., Braz. C4 88
Potiraguá, Braz. H6 88
Potiskum, Nig. G7 64
Potomac, Il., U.S. H2 112
Potomac, stm., U.S. F9 114
Potomac, North Fork South Branch, stm., U.S. F6 114
Potomac, South Branch, stm., U.S. E7 114
Potomac Heights, Md., U.S. F8 114
Potosí, Bol. C3 90
Potosi, Mo., U.S. G7 120
Potrerillos, Chile C3 92
Potro, Cerro del (El Potro, Cerro), mtn., S.A. D3 92
Potsdam, Ger. D9 16
Potsdam, N.Y., U.S. F2 110
Pott, Île, i., N. Cal. I14 79d
Potter, Ne., U.S. F9 126
Potterville, Mi., U.S. B1 114
Potts Camp, Ms., U.S. C9 122
Pottstown, Pa., U.S. D10 114
Pottsville, Pa., U.S. D9 114
Pouancé, Fr. G7 14
Poughkeepsie, N.Y., U.S. C11 114
Poulan, Ga., U.S. E2 116
Poulsbo, Wa., U.S. C4 136
Poultney, Vt., U.S. G3 110
Poum, N. Cal. m14 79d
Pouso Alegre, Braz. L3 88
Poŭthĭsăt, Camb. F6 48
Poŭthĭsăt, stm., Camb. F6 48
Poutini see Westland National Park, p.o.i., N.Z. F3 80
Poutrincourt, Lac, l., Qc., Can. A2 110
Považská Bystrica, Slov. G14 16
Povenec, Russia E16 8
Póvoa de Varzim, Port. C2 20
Povorino, Russia D6 32
Povorotnyj, mys, c., Russia C10 38
Povungnituk, Qc., Can. C15 106
Povungnituk, stm., Qc., Can. C15 106
Powassan, On., Can. B10 112
Poway, Ca., U.S. K9 134
Powder, stm., U.S. A7 126
Powder, stm., Or., U.S. F9 136
Powder, South Fork, stm., Wy., U.S. D6 126
Powderly, Tx., U.S. D3 122
Powder River Pass, p., Wy., U.S. C5 126
Powell, Wy., U.S. C4 126
Powell, stm., U.S. H2 114
Powell, Lake, res., U.S. F5 132
Powell Creek, stm., Austl. E5 76
Powellhurst, Or., U.S. E4 136
Powell Lake, l., B.C., Can. F6 138
Powell River, B.C., Can. G6 138
Powers, Mi., U.S. C2 112
Powers, Or., U.S. H2 136
Powers Lake, N.D., U.S. F11 124
Powhatan, Va., U.S. G7 114
Powhatan Point, Oh., U.S. E4 114
Poxoréu, Braz. G7 84

Name	Map Ref.	Page
Poya, N. Cal.	m15	79d
Poyang Hu, l., China	G7	42
Poyen, Ar., U.S.	C6	122
Poygan, Lake, l., Wi., U.S.	G9	118
Požarevac, Yugo.	E8	26
Poza Rica de Hidalgo, Mex.	E10	100
Požega, Cro.	E14	22
Požega, Yugo.	F7	26
Poznań, Pol.	D12	16
Poznań, state, Pol.	D12	16
Pozoblanco, Spain	F6	20
Pozo-Cañada, Spain	F9	20
Pozo del Molle, Arg.	F6	92
Pozo del Tigre, Arg.	B7	92
Pozuelos, Ven.	B9	86
Pozzallo, Italy	H8	24
Pozzuoli, Italy	D8	24
Prachatice, Czech Rep.	G10	16
Prachin Buri, Thai.	E5	48
Prachuap Khiri Khan, Thai.	G4	48
Pradera, Col.	F3	86
Prado, Braz.	I6	88
Prados, Braz.	K3	88
Præstø, Den.	A8	16
Prague see Praha, Czech Rep.	F10	16
Prague, Ne., U.S.	F16	126
Prague, Ok., U.S.	B2	122
Praha (Prague), Czech Rep.	F10	16
Praha, state, Czech Rep.	F10	16
Praha, mtn., Czech Rep.	G9	16
Prahova, state, Rom.	D13	26
Prahova, stm., Rom.	E13	26
Praia, C.V.	I10	65a
Praia Grande, Braz.	D13	92
Prainha Nova, Braz.	E5	84
Prairie, Austl.	C5	76
Prairie, stm., Mi., U.S.	G4	112
Prairie City, Il., U.S.	D7	120
Prairie City, Ia., U.S.	C4	120
Prairie Creek, stm., Ne., U.S.	F15	126
Prairie Dog Creek, stm., Ks., U.S.	B8	128
Prairie du Chien, Wi., U.S.	A6	120
Prairie du Sac, Wi., U.S.	H9	118
Prairie River, Sk., Can.	B11	124
Prairies, Coteau des, hills, U.S.	C16	126
Prairies, Lake of the, res., Can.	C12	124
Prairie View, Tx., U.S.	G3	122
Prairie Village, Ks., U.S.	B14	128
Pran Buri, Thai.	F4	48
Pran Buri, stm., Thai.	F4	48
Prānhita, stm., India	B5	53
Praslin, i., Sey.	j13	69b
Prasonísi, Ákra, c., Grc.	H10	28
Praszka, Pol.	E14	16
Prata, Braz.	J1	88
Prata, stm., Braz.	J1	88
Prata, stm., Braz.	I2	88
Pratāpgarh, India	F5	54
Pratápolis, Braz.	K2	88
Pratas Island see Tungsha Tao, i., Tai.	K7	42
Prat de Llobregat see El Prat de Llobregat, Spain	C12	20
Prato, Italy	G8	22
Pratt, Ks., U.S.	D10	128
Prattville, Al., U.S.	E12	122
Pratudão, stm., Braz.	H3	88
Pravdinskij, Russia	D20	10
Pravia, Spain	A4	20
Praya, Indon.	H10	50
Preajba, Rom.	E12	26
Prečistoe, Russia	G19	8
Predeal, Rom.	D12	26
Preeceville, Sk., Can.	C11	124
Preetz, Ger.	B6	16
Pregolja, stm., Russia	F3	10
Pregonero, Ven.	D6	86
Preguiças, stm., Braz.	B4	88
Preila, Lith.	E4	10
Prĕk Poŭthĭ, Camb.	G7	48
Prelate, Sk., Can.	D4	124
Premnitz, Ger.	D8	16
Premont, Tx., U.S.	G9	130
Premuda, Otok, i., Cro.	F11	22
Prenjasi see Prrenjas, Alb.	C14	24
Prentiss, Ms., U.S.	F9	122
Prenzlau, Ger.	C9	16
Preobraženie, Russia	C10	38
Preparis Island, i., Mya.	F7	46
Preparis North Channel, strt., Mya.	E7	46
Preparis South Channel, strt., Mya.	F7	46
Přerov, Czech Rep.	G13	16
Prescott, On., Can.	D14	112
Prescott, Az., U.S.	I4	132
Prescott, Ar., U.S.	D5	122
Prescott, Wi., U.S.	G6	118
Prescott Island, i., Nu., Can.	A11	106
Presidencia de la Plaza, Arg.	C7	92
Presidencia Roca, Arg.	C8	92
Presidencia Roque Sáenz Peña, Arg.	C7	92
Presidente Dutra, Braz.	C3	88
Presidente Epitácio, Braz.	D6	90
Presidente Hayes, state, Para.	B8	92
Presidente Prudente, Braz.	D6	90
Presidio, Tx., U.S.	E3	130
Presidio, stm., Mex.	D6	100
Presnogor'kovka, Kaz.	D11	32
Prešov, Slov.	H17	16
Prespa, Lake, l., Eur.	D14	24
Presque Isle, Me., U.S.	D8	110
Presque Isle, pen., Pa., U.S.	B5	114
Prestea, Ghana	H4	64
Preston, Eng., U.K.	H10	12
Preston, Id., U.S.	A5	132
Preston, Ia., U.S.	B7	120
Preston, Ks., U.S.	D10	128
Preston, Mn., U.S.	H6	118
Prestonsburg, Ky., U.S.	G3	114
Prestwick, Scot., U.K.	F8	12
Preto, stm., Braz.	I9	86
Preto, stm., Braz.	I2	88
Preto, stm., Braz.	F3	88
Preto, stm., Braz.	B4	88
Preto, stm., Braz.	G1	88
Preto, stm., Braz.	K1	88
Preto, stm., Braz.	L4	88
Preto do Igapó-açu, stm., Braz.	E5	84
Pretoria, S. Afr.	D9	70
Pretty Prairie, Ks., U.S.	D10	128
Préveza, Grc.	E3	28
Prey Lvéa, Camb.	G7	48
Prey Vêng, Camb.	G7	48
Pribilof Islands, is., Ak., U.S.	E5	140
Priboj, Yugo.	F6	26
Příbram, Czech Rep.	G10	16
Price, Ut., U.S.	D6	132
Price, stm., Ut., U.S.	D6	132
Price Island, i., B.C., Can.	D2	138
Prichard, Al., U.S.	G10	122
Prickly Pear Cays, is., Anguilla	A1	105a
Priddy, Tx., U.S.	C9	130
Priego de Córdoba, Spain	G6	20
Priekule, Lat.	D4	10
Priekule, Lith.	E4	10
Prieska, S. Afr.	F6	70
Priest, stm., Id., U.S.	B10	136
Priest Lake, res., Id., U.S.	B9	136
Priest River, Id., U.S.	B10	136
Prieta, Peña, mtn., Spain	A6	20
Prieto Diaz, Phil.	D5	52
Prievidza, Slov.	H14	16
Prijedor, Bos.	E3	26
Prilep, Mac.	B4	28
Priluki, Russia	A22	10
Primeira Cruz, Braz.	B4	88
Primera, Tx., U.S.	H10	130
Primero, stm., Arg.	E6	92
Primghar, Ia., U.S.	A2	120
Primorsk, Russia	F13	8
Primorskij, Russia	C9	38
Primorskij hrebet, mts., Russia	F10	34
Primo Tapia, Mex.	K8	134
Primrose Lake, l., Can.	E9	106
Prince Albert, Sk., Can.	A8	124
Prince Albert, S. Afr.	H6	70
Prince Albert Sound, strt., N.T., Can.	A7	106
Prince Alfred, Cape, c., N.T., Can.	B15	140
Prince Charles Island, i., Nu., Can.	B15	106
Prince Charles Mountains, mts., Ant.	C11	81
Prince Edward Island, state, Can.	D13	110
Prince Edward Island, i., P.E., Can.	F18	106
Prince Edward Island National Park, p.o.i., P.E., Can.	D13	110
Prince Frederick, Md., U.S.	F9	114
Prince George, B.C., Can.	C8	138
Prince George, Va., U.S.	G8	114
Prince Gustaf Adolf Sea, Can.	B4	141
Prince of Wales Island, i., Austl.	B8	74
Prince of Wales Island, i., Nu., Can.	A11	106
Prince of Wales Island, i., Ak., U.S.	E13	140
Prince of Wales Strait, strt., N.T., Can.	B15	140
Prince Olav Coast, cst., Ant.	B9	81
Prince Patrick Island, i., N.T., Can.	A16	140
Prince Regent Inlet, b., Nu., Can.	A12	106
Prince Rupert, B.C., Can.	E4	106
Prince Rupert Bluff Point, c., Dom.	i5	105c
Princes Islands see Kızıl Adalar, is., Tur.	C11	28
Princess Anne, Md., U.S.	F10	114
Princess Astrid Coast, cst., Ant.	C6	81
Princess Charlotte Bay, b., Austl.	B8	74
Princess Martha Coast, cst., Ant.	C4	81
Princess Ragnhild Coast, cst., Ant.	C7	81
Princess Royal Island, i., B.C., Can.	C1	138
Princes Town, Trin.	s12	105f
Princeton, B.C., Can.	G10	138
Princeton, Ca., U.S.	D3	134
Princeton, In., U.S.	F10	120
Princeton, Ky., U.S.	G9	120
Princeton, Me., U.S.	E9	110
Princeton, Mi., U.S.	B2	112
Princeton, N.J., U.S.	D11	114
Princeton, N.C., U.S.	A7	116
Princeton, W.V., U.S.	G4	114
Princeton, Wi., U.S.	H9	118
Princeville, Qc., Can.	D4	110
Princeville, Il., U.S.	D8	120
Prince William Sound, strt., Ak., U.S.	D10	140
Príncipe, i., S. Tom./P.	I6	64
Príncipe da Beira, Braz.	F5	84
Prineville, Or., U.S.	F6	136
Pringsewu, Indon.	F4	50
Prinses Margrietkanaal, can., Neth.	A14	14
Prins Karls Forland, i., Nor.	B27	141
Prinzapolka, stm., Nic.	F5	102
Priozërnyj, Kaz.	E14	32
Priozersk, Russia	F14	8
Pripet (Prypjac'), stm., Eur.	H10	10
Pripet Marshes, reg., Eur.	H12	10
Pripoljarnyj Ural, mts., Russia	A9	32
Priština, Yugo.	G8	26
Pritchett, Co., U.S.	D6	128
Pritzwalk, Ger.	C8	16
Privas, Fr.	E10	18
Priverno, Italy	C7	24
Privodino, Russia	F22	8
Prizren, Yugo.	G7	26
Prjaža, Russia	F15	8
Probolinggo, Indon.	G8	50
Probstzella, Ger.	F7	16
Procida, Isola di, i., Italy	D7	24
Procter, B.C., Can.	G13	138
Proctor, Mn., U.S.	E6	118
Proctor Lake, res., Tx., U.S.	C9	130
Proddatūr, India	D4	53
Proença-a-Nova, Port.	E2	20
Progreso, Mex.	B8	100
Progreso, Mex.	B3	102
Progreso, Mex.	K10	134
Progreso, Ur.	G9	92
Prohladnyj, Russia	F6	32
Project City, Ca., U.S.	C3	134
Prokopevsk, Russia	D15	32
Prokuplje, Yugo.	F8	26
Prokuševo, Russia	G16	8
Proletarskij, Russia	E20	10
Prome (Pyè), Mya.	C2	48
Pronja, stm., Bela.	G14	10
Pronja, stm., Russia	F21	10
Prony, Baie de, b., N. Cal.	n16	79d
Prophet, stm., B.C., Can.	D6	106
Prophetstown, Il., U.S.	C8	120
Propriá, Braz.	F7	88
Propriano, Fr.	H14	18
Proserpine, Austl.	C7	76
Prosna, stm., Pol.	E14	16
Prospect, Oh., U.S.	D2	114
Prosperidad, Phil.	F5	52
Prosser, Wa., U.S.	D7	136
Prostějov, Czech Rep.	G12	16
Prostki, Pol.	C18	16
Proston, Austl.	F8	76
Proszowice, Pol.	F16	16
Protection, Ks., U.S.	D9	128
Protem, S. Afr.	I5	70
Protva, stm., Russia	F20	10
Provadija, Blg.	F14	26
Prøven (Kangersuatsiaq), Grnld.	C14	141
Provence, hist. reg., Fr.	F12	18
Providence, Ky., U.S.	G10	120
Providence, R.I., U.S.	C14	114
Providence, Ut., U.S.	B5	132
Providence, Atoll de, i., Sey.	k12	69b
Providence, Cape, c., N.Z.	H2	80
Providencia, Mex.	G4	130
Providencia, Isla de, i., Col.	F7	102
Providenciales, i., T./C. Is.	B11	102
Providenija, Russia	D26	34
Provincetown, Ma., U.S.	B15	114
Provins, Fr.	F12	14
Provo, Ut., U.S.	C5	132
Provo, stm., Ut., U.S.	C5	132
Provost, Ab., Can.	B3	124
Prrenjas, Alb.	C14	24
Prudentópolis, Braz.	B12	92
Prudhoe Bay, Ak., U.S.	B10	140
Prudhoe Island, i., Austl.	C7	76
Prudnik, Pol.	F13	16
Pruszków, Pol.	D16	16
Prut, stm., Eur.	D15	26
Pružany, Bela.	H7	10
Prydz Bay, b., Ant.	B12	81
Pryluky, Ukr.	D4	32
Pryor, Ok., U.S.	H2	120
Przasnysz, Pol.	D16	16
Przedbórz, Pol.	E15	16
Przemyśl, Pol.	G18	16
Przemyśl, state, Pol.	F18	16
Przeworsk, Pol.	F18	16
Psachná, Grc.	E6	28
Pskov, Russia	C11	10
Pskov, Lake, l., Eur.	B11	10
Pskovskaja oblast', co., Russia	C11	10
Pszczyna, Pol.	G14	16
Ptarmigan, Cape, c., N.T., Can.	A7	106
Ptolemaïda, Grc.	C4	28
Ptuj, Slvn.	D12	22
Puakatike, Volcán, vol., Chile	e30	78l
Puán, Arg.	H6	92
Pucallpa, Peru	E3	84
Pucará, Bol.	C4	90
Pučeveem, stm., Russia	C23	34
Pučež, Russia	H20	8
Pucheng, China	H8	42
Pucheng, China	D3	42
Púchov, Slov.	G14	16
Pučišća, Cro.	G13	22
Pudasjärvi, Fin.	D12	8
Pudož, Russia	F17	8
Puduari, stm., Braz.	I11	86
Puduchcheri see Pondicherry, India	F4	53
Pudukkottai, India	F4	53
Puebla, state, Mex.	F10	100
Puebla de Don Fadrique, Spain	G8	20
Puebla de Sanabria, Spain	B4	20
Puebla de Zaragoza, Mex.	F9	100
Pueblito, Mex.	E2	130
Pueblito de Ponce, P.R.	B1	104a
Pueblo, Co., U.S.	C4	128
Pueblonuevo, Col.	C4	86
Pueblo Nuevo, P.R.	B2	104a
Pueblo Nuevo, Ven.	B7	86
Pueblo Viejo, Laguna, l., Mex.	D10	100
Pueblo Yaqui, Mex.	B4	100
Puente-Caldelas see Ponte-Caldelas, Spain	B2	20
Puente del Arzobispo, Spain	E5	20
Puentedeume see Pontedeume, Spain	A2	20
Puente Genil, Spain	G6	20
Puerca, Punta, c., P.R.	B4	104a
Puerco, stm., U.S.	I7	132
Puerco, stm., N.M., U.S.	I10	132
Puerto Acosta, Bol.	C3	90
Puerto Adela, Para.	B10	92
Puerto Aisén, Chile	I2	90
Puerto Alegre, Bol.	B4	90
Puerto Ángel, Mex.	H10	100
Puerto Arista, Mex.	H11	100
Puerto Armuelles, Pan.	H6	102
Puerto Asís, Col.	G3	86
Puerto Ayacucho, Ven.	E8	86
Puerto Baquerizo Moreno, Ec.	i12	84a
Puerto Barrios, Guat.	E3	102
Puerto Bermúdez, Peru	F3	84
Puerto Berrío, Col.	D4	86
Puerto Bolívar, Col.	A5	86
Puerto Boyacá, Col.	E4	86
Puerto Cabello, Ven.	B7	86
Puerto Cabezas, Nic.	F6	102
Puerto Carreño, Col.	D8	86
Puerto Chicama, Peru	E2	84
Puerto Colombia, Col.	B4	86
Puerto Cortés, Hond.	E3	102
Puerto Cumarebo, Ven.	B7	86
Puerto Deseado, Arg.	I3	90
Puerto Escondido, Mex.	H10	100
Puerto Escondido, c., Ven.	p20	104g
Puerto Esperanza, Arg.	B10	92
Puerto Fonciere, Para.	D5	90
Puerto Francisco de Orellana, Ec.	H3	86
Puerto Heath, Bol.	B3	90
Puerto Iguazú, Arg.	B10	92
Puerto Ingeniero Ibáñez, Chile	I2	90
Puerto Inírida, Col.	F7	86
Puerto Juárez, Mex.	B4	102
Puerto la Cruz, Ven.	B9	86
Puerto Leguízamo, Col.	H4	86
Puerto Libertad, Mex.	G6	98
Puerto Limón, Col.	F5	86
Puerto Limón, C.R.	G6	102
Puertollano, Spain	F6	20
Puerto Lobos, Arg.	H4	90
Puerto López, Col.	E5	86
Puerto Madero, Mex.	H12	100
Puerto Madryn, Arg.	H3	90
Puerto Maldonado, Peru	F4	84
Puerto Montt, Chile	H2	90
Puerto Morelos, Mex.	B4	102
Puerto Natales, Chile	J2	90
Puerto Padre, Cuba	B9	102
Puerto Páez, Ven.	D8	86
Puerto Palmer, Pico, mtn., Mex.	G6	130
Puerto Peñasco, Mex.	F6	98
Puerto Pinasco, Para.	D5	90
Puerto Pirámides, Arg.	H4	90
Puerto Piray, Arg.	C10	92
Puerto Píritu, Ven.	B9	86
Puerto Plata, Dom. Rep.	C12	102
Puerto Princesa, Phil.	F2	52
Puerto Real, P.R.	B1	104a
Puerto Real, Spain	H4	20
Puerto Rico, Arg.	C10	92
Puerto Rico, Bol.	B3	90
Puerto Rico, Col.	G4	86
Puerto Rico, dep., N.A.	b3	104a
Puerto Rico Trench, unds.	G7	144
Puerto Rondón, Col.	D6	86
Puerto San José, Guat.	F2	102
Puerto San Julián, Arg.	I3	90
Puerto Santa Cruz, Arg.	J3	90
Puerto Sastre, Para.	D5	90
Puerto Suárez, Bol.	C5	90
Puerto Tejada, Col.	F3	86
Puerto Tolosa, Col.	H4	86
Puerto Umbría, Col.	G3	86
Puerto Vallarta, Mex.	E6	100
Puerto Varas, Chile	H2	90
Puerto Victoria, Arg.	C10	92
Puerto Viejo, C.R.	G5	102
Puerto Villamil, Ec.	i11	84a
Puerto Villamizar, Col.	C5	86
Puerto Wilches, Col.	D5	86
Puerto Ybapobó, Para.	D5	90
Pueyrredón, Lago (Cochrane, Lago), l., S.A.	I2	90
Pugačov, Russia	D7	32
Puget Sound, strt., Wa., U.S.	C4	136
Puglia, state, Italy	C10	24
Pugŏ-ri, Kor., N.	D9	38
Puhi-waero see South West Cape, c., N.Z.	H2	80
Puhja, Est.	B9	10
Puiești, Rom.	C14	26
Puigcerdá, Spain	B12	20
Puigmal d' Err (Puigmal), mtn., Eur.	G8	18
Pujiang, China	G8	42
Pujilí, Ec.	H2	86
Puka see Pukë, Alb.	B13	24
Pukaki, Lake, l., N.Z.	F3	80
Pukch'ŏng-ŭp, Kor., N.	D8	38
Pukë, Alb.	B13	24
Pukekohe, N.Z.	C6	80
Pukhrāyān, India	E7	54
Pukou, China	H8	42
Puksoozero, Russia	E19	8
Pula, Cro.	F10	22
Pula, Italy	F3	24
Pulacayo, Bol.	D3	90
Pulantien see Xinjin, China	B9	42
Pulap, at., Micron.	C5	72
Púlar, Cerro, vol., Chile	B3	92
Pulaski, N.Y., U.S.	E13	112
Pulaski, Tn., U.S.	B11	122
Pulaski, Va., U.S.	G5	114
Pulau, stm., Indon.	G10	44
Pulaukida, Indon.	E3	50
Pulau Pinang, state, Malay.	J5	48
Puławy, Pol.	E18	16
Pulgaon, India	H7	54
Puli, Tai.	J9	42
Pulicat, India	E5	53
Pulicat Lake, l., India	E4	53
Puliyangudi, India	G3	53
Pullman, Wa., U.S.	D9	136
Pulog, Mount, mtn., Phil.	B3	52
Pulon'ga, Russia	C18	8
Pułtusk, Pol.	D16	16
Puma Yumco, l., China	D13	54
Pumei, China	A7	48
Pumpkin Buttes, mtn., Wy., U.S.	D7	126
Pumpkin Creek, stm., Mt., U.S.	B7	126
Pumpkin Creek, stm., Ne., U.S.	F10	126
Puná, Isla, i., Ec.	I1	86
Punaauia, Fr. Poly.	v21	78h
Punakha, Bhu.	E12	54
Punan, Indon.	B10	50
Punata, Bol.	C3	90
Pūnch, India	B5	54
Punchaw, B.C., Can.	C7	138
Pune (Poona), India	B1	53
Punganūru, India	E4	53
P'ungsan-ŭp, Kor., N.	D7	38
Pungué, stm., Afr.	A12	70
Punia, D.R.C.	E5	66
Punilla, Sierra de la, mts., Arg.	D3	92
Punitaqui, Chile	E2	92
Punjab, state, India	C5	54
Punjab, state, Pak.	C4	54
Punnichy, Sk., Can.	C9	124
Puno, Peru	G3	84
Punta, Cerro de, mtn., P.R.	B2	104a
Punta Alta, Arg.	I6	92
Punta Arenas, Chile	J2	90
Punta Banda, Cabo, c., Mex.	L9	134
Punta Cardón, Ven.	B6	86
Punta Colnett, Mex.	F4	98
Punta de Agua Creek (Tramperos Creek), stm., U.S.	E5	128
Punta de Díaz, Chile	C2	92
Punta del Cobre, Chile	C2	92
Punta del Este, Ur.	G10	92
Punta Delgada, Arg.	H4	90
Punta de los Llanos, Arg.	E4	92
Punta de Piedras, Ven.	B9	86
Punta Gorda, Nic.	G6	102
Punta Gorda, Fl., U.S.	J3	116
Punta Gorda, Bahía de, b., Nic.	G6	102
Punta Negra, Salar de, pl., Chile	B3	92
Punta Prieta, Mex.	A1	100
Puntarenas, C.R.	G5	102
Punta Santiago, P.R.	B4	104a
Punto Fijo, Ven.	B6	86
Punung, Indon.	H7	50
Puper, Indon.	F9	44
Puppy's Point, c., Norf. I.	y24	78i
Puqi, China	G5	42
Puqian, China	L4	42
Puquio, Peru	F3	84
Pur, stm., Russia	A13	32
Puracé, Volcán, vol., Col.	F3	86
Pūranpur, India	D7	54
Purcell, Ok., U.S.	F11	128
Purcell Mountains, mts., N.A.	F14	138
Purcellville, Va., U.S.	E8	114
Purdy, Mo., U.S.	H3	120
Puré (Puruí), stm., S.A.	I6	86
Purgatoire, stm., Co., U.S.	D5	128
Puri, India	I10	54
Purificación, Col.	F4	86
Purificación, stm., Mex.	C9	100
Purísima, Mex.	E7	130
Purmerend, Neth.	B13	14
Pūrna, stm., India	H5	54
Pūrna, stm., India	H6	54
Pūrnia, India	F11	54
Puronga, Russia	F19	8
Puruí (Puré), stm., S.A.	I6	86
Puruliya, India	G11	54
Puruni, stm., Guy.	D12	86
Purús, stm., S.A.	E4	84
Puruvesi, l., Fin.	F13	8
Purvis, Ms., U.S.	F9	122
Purwakarta, Indon.	G5	50
Purwodadi, Indon.	G6	50
Purwodadi, Indon.	G7	50
Purwokerto, Indon.	G6	50
Purworejo, Indon.	G6	50
Pusa, Malay.	C7	50
Pusad, India	B3	53
Pusan (Fusan), Kor., S.	D2	40
Pusan-jikhalsi, state, Kor., S.	D2	40
Pusat Gayo, Pegunungan, mts., Indon.	J3	48
Pushkar, India	E5	54
Puškin, Russia	A13	10
Puškino, Russia	D20	10
Püspökladány, Hung.	B8	26
Püssi, Est.	A10	10
Pustozersk, Russia	C25	8
Putaendo, Chile	F2	92
Putao, Mya.	C8	46
Putian, China	G6	42
Putian, China	I8	42
Putignano, Italy	D10	24
Puting, Tanjung, c., Indon.	E7	50
Putla de Guerrero, Mex.	D5	96
Putnam, Ct., U.S.	C14	114
Putney, Ga., U.S.	E1	116
Putney, Vt., U.S.	B13	114
Putorana, plato, plat., Russia	C7	34
Puttalam, Sri L.	G4	53
Puttalam Lagoon, b., Sri L.	G4	53
Puttūr, India	E4	53
Putú, Chile	G1	92
Putumayo, state, Col.	G4	86
Putumayo (Içá), stm., S.A.	D3	84
Putuo, China	F10	42
Putussibau, Indon.	C8	50
Putyla, Ukr.	B12	26
Puula, l., Fin.	F12	8
Puurmani, Est.	B9	10
Puyallup, Wa., U.S.	C4	136
Puyang, China	D6	42
Puy-de-Dôme, state, Fr.	D9	18
Puymorens, Col de, p., Fr.	G7	18
Puyo, Ec.	H3	86
Pweto, D.R.C.	F5	66
Pwinbyu, Mya.	B2	48
Pyalo, Mya.	C2	48
Pyapon, Mya.	D2	48
Pyawbwe, Mya.	B3	48
Pyhäjärvi, l., Fin.	E11	8
Pyhäjärvi, l., Fin.	F9	8
Pyhäjoki, Fin.	D10	8
Pyhäjoki, stm., Fin.	D11	8
Pyhäselkä, l., Fin.	E13	8
Pyhätunturi, mtn., Fin.	C12	8
Pyinbongyi, Mya.	D3	48
Pyinmana, Mya.	C3	48
Pyin Oo Lwin see Maymyo, Mya.	A3	48
Pýlos, Grc.	G4	28
Pymatuning Reservoir, res., U.S.	C5	114
Pyŏktong-ŭp, Kor., N.	D6	38
P'yŏngch'ang, Kor., S.	B1	40
P'yonghae, Kor., S.	C2	40
P'yŏngt'aek, Kor., S.	F7	38
P'yŏngyang, Kor., N.	E6	38
Pyote, Tx., U.S.	C4	130
Pyramid Lake, l., Nv., U.S.	D6	134
Pyramid Peak, mtn., Wy., U.S.	G16	136
Pyrenees, mts., Eur.	G6	18
Pyrénées-Atlantiques, state, Fr.	F5	18
Pyrénées Occident, Parc National des, p.o.i., Fr.	G5	18
Pyrénées-Orientales, state, Fr.	G8	18
Pýrgos, Grc.	F4	28
Pytalovo, Russia	C10	10
Pyu, Mya.	C3	48
Pyūṭhān, Nepal	D9	54
Q		
Qaanaaq see Thule, Grnld.	B12	141
Qabbāsīn, Syria	B8	58
Qacentina (Constantine), Alg.	B6	64
Qā'en, Iran	C8	56
Qagan Moron, stm., China	C3	38
Qagan Nur, l., China	C7	36
Qahar Youyi Zhongqi, China	A5	42
Qaidam, stm., China	D4	36
Qaidam Pendi, bas., China	D3	36
Qalāt, Afg.	C10	56
Qalʿat ash-Shaqīf (Beaufort Castle), hist., Leb.	E6	58
Qalʿat Bīshah, Sau. Ar.	E5	56
Qalʿat Ṣāliḥ, Iraq	C6	56
Qalʿeh-ye Now, Afg.	C9	56
Qallābāt, Sudan	E7	62
Qalyûb, Egypt	H2	58
Qamar, Ghubbat al-, b., Yemen	F7	56
Qamdo, China	E4	36
Qamea, i., Fiji	p20	79e
Qamīnis, Libya	A3	62
Qānā, Leb.	E6	58
Qandahār, Afg.	C10	56
Qandala, Som.	B9	66
Qaqortoq see Julianehåb, Grnld.	E16	141
Qārah, Syria	D7	58
Qarazhal see Karažal, Kaz.	E12	32
Qardho, Som.	C9	66
Qarqan, stm., China	G15	32
Qârûn, Birket (Moeris, Lake), l., Egypt	I1	58
Qarwāw, Ra's, c., Oman	F8	56
Qasigiannguit see Christanshåb, Grnld.	D15	141
Qaṣr al-Azraq, hist., Jord.	G7	58
Qaṣr al-Kharānah, hist., Jord.	G7	58
Qaṣr al-Mushattá, hist., Jord.	G7	58
Qaṣr aṭ-Ṭūbah, hist., Jord.	G7	58
Qaṣr Ḍabʿah, hist., Jord.	G7	58
Qaṣr-e Shīrīn, Iran	C6	56
Qasr Farâfra, Egypt	B5	62
Qaṭanā, Syria	E6	58
Qatar, ctry., Asia	D7	56
Qatrani, Gebel, hill, Egypt	I1	58
Qattâra, Munkhafad el- (Qattara Depression), depr., Egypt	B5	62
Qattara Depression see Qattâra, Munkhafad el-, depr., Egypt	B5	62
Qaṭṭīnah, Buḥayrat, res., Syria	D7	58
Qāzigund, India	B5	54
Qazımämmäd, Azer.	B6	56
Qazvīn, Iran	B6	56
Qena, Egypt	B6	62
Qena, Wadi (Qinā, Wādī), stm., Egypt	K3	58
Qeqertarsuaq see Godhavn, Grnld.	D15	141
Qesari, Ḥorbat (Caesarea), hist., Isr.	F5	58
Qeshm, Jazīreh-ye, i., Iran	D8	56
Qetura, Isr.	I5	58
Qezel Owzan, stm., Iran	B6	56
Qian, stm., China	J3	42
Qian'an, China	B6	38
Qian Gorlos, China	B6	38
Qianning, China	E5	36
Qianshan, China	F7	42
Qianwei, China	F5	36
Qianxi, China	H1	42
Qianyang, China	H3	42
Qiaolima, China	A8	54
Qiaowan, China	C4	36
Qidong, China	H5	42
Qiemo, China	G15	32
Qigong, China	F5	36
Qijiang, China	G2	42
Qila Saifullāh, Pak.	C2	54
Qilian Shan, mtn., China	D4	36
Qilian Shan, mts., China	D4	36
Qimen, China	G7	42
Qin, stm., China	D5	42
Qing, stm., China	F4	42
Qingcheng, China	C7	42
Qingchengzi, China	D5	38
Qingdao (Tsingtao), China	C9	42
Qingfeng, China	D6	42
Qinggang, China	B10	36
Qinghai, state, China	D4	36
Qinghai Hu, l., China	D5	36
Qingjiang, China	G6	42
Qingjiang, China	E8	42
Qinglong, China	F6	36
Qinglonggang, China	F9	42
Qingshen, China	F5	36
Qingshui, China	D4	36
Qingshui, China	D2	42
Qingshui, stm., China	H3	42
Qingshui, stm., China	C2	42
Qingtang, China	I5	42
Qingyang, China	B8	38
Qingyang, China	F7	42
Qingyang, China	C2	42
Qingyuan, China	C6	38
Qingyuan, China	J5	42
Qingyuan, China	H8	42
Qingyuan, China	I3	42
Qing Zang Gaoyuan (Tibet, Plateau of), plat., China	B6	46
Qingzhen, China	H2	42
Qinhuangdao, China	B8	42
Qin Ling, mts., China	E3	42
Qinshihuang Mausoleum (Terra Cotta Army), hist., China	D3	42
Qinshui, China	D5	42
Qinxian, China	C5	42
Qinyang, China	D5	42
Qinyuan, China	C5	42
Qinzhou, China	J3	42
Qionghai, China	L4	42
Qionglai, China	E5	36
Qionglaishan, mts., China	E5	36
Qiongzhong, China	L3	42
Qiongzhou Haixia, strt., China	K4	42
Qiqian, China	F13	34
Qiqihar, China	B9	36
Qira, China	A5	46
Qiryat Ata, Isr.	F6	58
Qiryat Gat, Isr.	G5	58
Qiryat Shemona, Isr.	E6	58
Qishn, Yemen	F7	56
Qitai, China	C2	36
Qitaihe, China	B11	36
Qitamu, China	B7	38
Qixia, China	C9	42
Qixian, China	D6	42
Qiyang, China	H4	42
Qizhou, China	F6	42
Qizil Jilga, China	A7	54
Qom, Iran	C7	56
Qomsheh, Iran	C7	56
Qonggyai, China	D13	54
Qôrnoq, Grnld.	E15	141
Qostanay see Kustanaj, Kaz.	D10	32
Qowowuyag (Chopu), mtn., Asia	D11	54
Qu, stm., China	F2	42
Qu, stm., China	G8	42
Quabbin Reservoir, res., Ma., U.S.	B13	114
Quadra Island, i., B.C., Can.	F5	138
Quadros, Lagoa dos, l., Braz.	D12	92
Quakenbrück, Ger.	D3	16
Qualicum Beach, B.C., Can.	G6	138
Quambatook, Austl.	J4	76
Quang Ngai, Viet.	E9	48
Quang Trach, Viet.	D8	48
Quantico, Va., U.S.	F8	114
Quanyang, China	C7	38
Quanzhou, China	I8	42
Qu'Appelle, Sk., Can.	D10	124
Qu'Appelle, stm., Can.	D12	124
Qu'Appelle Dam, dam, Sk., Can.	D7	124
Quaraí, Braz.	E9	92
Quaraí (Cuareim), stm., S.A.	E9	92
Quarles, Pegunungan, mts., Indon.	E11	50
Quarryville, Pa., U.S.	E9	114
Quartier d'Orléans, Guad.	A1	105a
Quartu Sant'Elena, Italy	E3	24
Quartz Lake, l., Nu., Can.	A14	106
Quartz Mountain, mtn., Or., U.S.	G4	136
Quartzsite, Az., U.S.	J2	132
Quba, Azer.	A6	56
Qūchān, Iran	B8	56
Quchijie, China	G4	42
Queanbeyan, Austl.	J7	76
Québec, Qc., Can.	D5	110
Québec, state, Can.	E16	106
Quebeck, Tn., U.S.	I12	120
Quebra-Anzol, stm., Braz.	J2	88
Quebracho, Ur.	E9	92
Quebrada Seca, P.R.	B4	104a
Quedal, Cabo, c., Chile	H2	90
Quedlinburg, Ger.	E7	16
Queen Charlotte Islands, is., B.C., Can.	E4	106
Queen Charlotte Sound, strt., B.C., Can.	E2	138
Queen Charlotte Strait, strt., B.C., Can.	F3	138
Queen City, Mo., U.S.	D5	120
Queen City, Tx., U.S.	D4	122
Queen Elizabeth Islands, is., Can.	B13	94
Queen Mary Coast, cst., Ant.	B14	81
Queen Maud Gulf, b., Nu., Can.	B10	106
Queen Maud Land, reg., Ant.	C4	81
Queen Maud Mountains, mts., Ant.	D23	81
Queenscliff, Austl.	L5	76
Queensland, state, Austl.	D8	74
Queensport, N.S., Can.	E15	110
Queenstown, Austl.	o12	77a
Queenstown, N.Z.	G3	80
Queenstown, S. Afr.	G8	70
Queguay Grande, stm., Ur.	F9	92
Queimada Nova, Braz.	E5	88
Queimadas, Braz.	F6	88
Queimados, Braz.	L4	88
Quela, Ang.	B2	68
Quelelevu, i., Fiji	p20	79e
Quelimane, Moz.	D6	68
Quelpart Island see Cheju-do, i., Kor., S.	H7	38
Quemado, Tx., U.S.	F7	130
Quemado, Punta de, c., Cuba	B10	102
Quemoy see Chinmen Tao, i., Tai.	I8	42
Quemú Quemú, Arg.	H6	92
Quequén, Arg.	I8	92
Querary, stm., Col.	G6	86
Quercy, hist. reg., Fr.	E7	18
Querétaro, Mex.	E8	100
Querétaro, state, Mex.	E8	100
Querobabi, Mex.	F7	98
Quesada, C.R.	E8	96
Quesada, Spain	G7	20
Queshan, China	E5	42
Quesnel, B.C., Can.	C8	138
Quesnel, stm., B.C., Can.	D8	138
Quesnel Lake, l., B.C., Can.	D9	138
Que Son, Viet.	E9	48
Questa, N.M., U.S.	E3	128
Quetico Lake, l., On., Can.	C7	118
Quetta, Pak.	C10	56
Quetzaltenango, Guat.	E2	102
Quevedo, Ec.	H2	86
Quezon City, Phil.	C3	52
Qufu, China	D7	42
Quibala, Ang.	C2	68
Quibdó, Col.	E3	86
Quiberon, Fr.	G5	14
Quíbor, Ven.	C7	86
Quiculungo, Ang.	B2	68
Quila, Mex.	C5	100
Quilengues, Ang.	C1	68
Quilimarí, Chile	F2	92
Quillabamba, Peru	F3	84
Quillacollo, Bol.	C3	90
Quill Lake, Sk., Can.	B9	124
Quillota, Chile	F2	92
Quilon, India	G3	53
Quilpie, Austl.	F5	76
Quilpué, Chile	F2	92
Quimarí, Alto de, mtn., Col.	C3	86
Quimaria, Ang.	B1	68
Quimby, Ia., U.S.	B2	120
Quimilí, Arg.	C6	92
Quimper (Kemper), Fr.	F5	14
Quimperlé, Fr.	G5	14
Quinault, stm., Wa., U.S.	C3	136
Quince Mil, Peru	F3	84
Quincy, Ca., U.S.	D4	134
Quincy, Fl., U.S.	G14	122
Quincy, Il., U.S.	E6	120
Quincy, Ma., U.S.	B14	114
Quincy, Wa., U.S.	C7	136
Quindío, state, Col.	E4	86
Quines, Arg.	F5	92
Quinhagak, Ak., U.S.	E7	140
Quinlan, Tx., U.S.	E2	122
Quinn, stm., Nv., U.S.	B7	134

Name	Map Ref.	Page
Quintanar de la Orden, Spain	E7	20
Quintana Roo, state, Mex.	C3	102
Quinte, Bay of, b., On., Can.	D12	112
Quinto, Spain	C10	20
Quinto, stm., Arg.	G5	92
Quinton, Ok., U.S.	B3	122
Quipapá, Braz.	E7	88
Quirauk Mountain, mtn., Md., U.S.	E8	114
Quiriguá, hist., Guat.	E3	102
Quirihue, Chile	H1	92
Quirindi, Austl.	H8	76
Quirinópolis, Braz.	C6	90
Quiriquire, Ven.	C10	86
Quiroga, Mex.	F8	100
Quiros, Cap, c., Vanuatu	j16	79d
Quissanga, Moz.	C7	68
Quissico, Moz.	D12	70
Quitaque, Tx., U.S.	G7	128
Quitasueño, unds., Col.	E7	102
Quitasueño, Banco see Quitasueño, unds., Col.	E7	102
Quita Sueno Bank see Quitasueño, unds., Col.	E7	102
Quiterajo, Moz.	C7	68
Quitilipi, Arg.	C7	92
Quitman, Ga., U.S.	F2	116
Quitman, Tx., U.S.	E3	122
Quito, Ec.	H2	86
Quixadá, Braz.	C6	88
Quixeramobim, Braz.	C6	88
Qujiadian, China	C5	38
Qujing, China	F5	36
Qujiu, China	J2	42
Qulin, Mo., U.S.	H7	120
Qumarlêb, China	E4	36
Qumrān, Khirbat, hist., W.B.	G6	58
Quoich, stm., Nu., Can.	C12	106
Quorn, Austl.	F7	74
Quoxo, stm., Bots.	C7	70
Qurdūd, Sudan	E5	62
Qus, Egypt	B6	62
Quseir, Egypt	B6	62
Qutdligssat, Grnld.	C15	141
Quthing, Leso.	G8	70
Quweisna, Egypt	H2	58
Quxian, China	F2	42
Qüxü, China	D13	54
Quyang, China	B6	42
Quy Nhon, Viet.	F9	48
Quyon, Qc., Can.	C13	112
Quyquyó, Para.	C9	92
Quzhou, China	G8	42
Quzhou, China	C6	42
Qyzylorda see Kzyl-Orda, Kaz.	F11	32
R		
Raab (Rába), stm., Eur.	D12	22
Raalte, Neth.	B15	14
Ra'ananna, Isr.	F5	58
Raas, Pulau, i., Indon.	G9	50
Raasay, i., Scot., U.K.	D6	12
Raasiku, Est.	A8	10
Rab, Otok, i., Cro.	F11	22
Raba, Indon.	H11	50
Rába (Raab), stm., Eur.	D12	22
Rábade, Spain	A3	20
Rabak, Sudan	E6	62
Rabat, Malta	I8	24
Rabat, Malta	H8	24
Rabat, Mor.	C3	64
Rabaul, Pap. N. Gui.	a5	79a
Rabbit Creek, stm., S.D., U.S.	B10	126
Rabbit Ears Pass, p., Co., U.S.	C10	132
Rabi, i., Fiji	p20	79e
Rābi', Ash-Shallāl ar- (Fourth Cataract), wtfl, Sudan	D6	62
Rābigh, Sau. Ar.	E4	56
Rabka, Pol.	G15	16
Rabkavi Banhatti, India	C2	53
Râbnița, Mol.	B16	26
Raboč̌eostrovsk, Russia	D16	8
Rabwāh, Pak.	C4	54
Rabyānah, Ramlat, des., Libya	C4	62
Raccoon, stm., Ia., U.S.	C4	120
Raccoon Creek, stm., Oh., U.S.	E15	120
Race, Cape, c., Nf., Can.	j23	107a
Race Point, c., Ma., U.S.	B15	114
Rach Gia, Viet.	G7	48
Rach Gia, Vinh, b., Viet.	H7	48
Raciąż, Pol.	D16	16
Racibórz, Pol.	F14	16
Racine, Wi., U.S.	F2	112
Radaškovičy, Bela.	F10	10
Rădăuți, Rom.	B12	26
Radcliff, Ky., U.S.	G12	120
Radeberg, Ger.	E9	16
Radebeul, Ger.	E9	16
Radford, Va., U.S.	G5	114
Rādhanpur, India	G3	54
Rădinești, Rom.	E10	26
Radisson, Sk., Can.	B6	124
Radium Hot Springs, B.C., Can.	F14	138
Radnice, Czech Rep.	G9	16
Radofinnikovo, Russia	A13	10
Radom, Pol.	E17	16
Radom, state, Pol.	E16	16
Radomsko, Pol.	E15	16
Radomyśl Wielki, Pol.	F17	16
Radoviš, Mac.	B5	28
Radstadt, Aus.	C10	22
Radutino, Russia	H17	10
Radviliškis, Lith.	E6	10
Radville, Sk., Can.	E9	124
Radymno, Pol.	G18	16
Radzyń Chełmiński, Pol.	C14	16
Rae, N.T., Can.	C7	106
Rae, stm., Nu., Can.	B7	106
Rāe Bareli, India	E8	54
Raeford, N.C., U.S.	B6	116
Rae Isthmus, isth., Nu., Can.	B13	106
Rae Strait, strt., Nu., Can.	B12	106
Rafaela, Arg.	E7	92
Rafael Freyre, Cuba	B10	102
Rafaḥ, Gaza	G5	58
Rafḥā', Sau. Ar.	D5	56
Rafsanjān, Iran	C8	56
Raft, stm., U.S.	H13	136
Raga, Sudan	F5	62
Ragay Gulf, b., Phil.	D4	52
Ragged Island, i., Bah.	A10	102
Ragged Island Range, is., Bah.	A10	102
Ragged Top Mountain, mtn., Wy., U.S.	F7	126
Ragland, Al., U.S.	D12	122
Raguva, Lith.	E7	10
Rahačou, Bela.	G12	10
Rahad al-Bardī, Sudan	E4	62
Rāhatgarh, India	G7	54
Rahimatpur, India	C1	53
Rahīm Ki Bāzār, Pak.	F2	54
Rahīmyār Khān, Pak.	D3	54
Rāichūr, India	C3	53
Raiganj, India	F12	54
Raigarh, India	H9	54
Rāikot, India	C5	54
Railroad Valley, val., Nv., U.S.	E10	134
Railton, Austl.	n13	77a
Rainbow Bridge National Monument, p.o.i., Ut., U.S.	F6	132
Rainbow Falls, wtfl, B.C., Can.	D11	138
Rainelle, W.V., U.S.	G5	114
Rainier, Mount, vol., Wa., U.S.	D5	136
Rainy, stm., N.A.	C4	118
Rainy Lake, l., N.A.	C5	118
Rainy River, On., Can.	C4	118
Raipur, India	H8	54
Raipur Uplands, plat., India	H9	54
Raisen, India	G6	54
Raisin, stm., Mi., U.S.	G6	112
Raivavae, i., Fr. Poly.	F12	72
Rajabasa, Indon.	F4	50
Rājahmundry, India	C5	53
Rājaldesar, India	E5	54
Rājampet, India	D4	53
Rajang, stm., Malay.	B7	50
Rājapālaiyam, India	G3	53
Rājāpur, India	C1	53
Rājasthān, state, India	E4	54
Rājbāri, Bngl.	G12	54
Rajčihinsk, Russia	G14	34
Rāj Gangpur, India	G10	54
Rājgarh, India	E6	54
Rājgarh, India	G6	54
Rājgarh, India	D5	54
Rajik, Indon.	E4	50
Rājkot, India	G3	54
Rāj Nāndgaon, India	H8	54
Rājpipla, India	H4	54
Rājpur, India	G5	54
Rājpura, India	C6	54
Rājshāhi, Bngl.	F12	54
Rājshāhi, state, Bngl.	F12	54
Rājula, India	H3	54
Raka, stm., China	D11	54
Rakamaz, Hung.	A8	26
Rakaposhi, mtn., Pak.	B11	56
Rakata, Pulau (Krakatoa), i., Indon.	G4	50
Rakhine, state, Mya.	C1	48
Rakhiv, Ukr.	A11	26
Rakitnoe, Russia	B11	36
Rakiura see Stewart Island, i., N.Z.	H3	80
Rakoniewice, Pol.	D12	16
Rakops, Bots.	B7	70
Rakovník, Czech Rep.	F9	16
Råkvåg see Råkvågen, Nor.	E4	8
Råkvågen, Nor.	E4	8
Rakvere, Est.	G12	8
Raleigh, Ms., U.S.	E9	122
Raleigh, N.C., U.S.	I7	114
Ralik Chain, is., Marsh. Is.	C7	72
Ralls, Tx., U.S.	H7	128
Ralston, Pa., U.S.	C9	114
Ramah, N.M., U.S.	H8	132
Rām Allāh, W.B.	G6	58
Rāmanagaram, India	E3	53
Rāmanāthapuram, India	G4	53
Rāmānuj Ganj, India	G9	54
Ramat Gan, Isr.	F5	58
Ramat HaSharon, Isr.	F5	58
Ramatlabama, Bots.	D7	70
Rambervillers, Fr.	F15	14
Rambouillet, Fr.	F10	14
Rambutyo Island, i., Pap. N. Gui.	a4	79a
Rām Dās, India	B5	54
Rāmdurg, India	C2	53
Ramea, Nf., Can.	j22	107a
Ramene, Russia	F20	8
Ramenskoe, Russia	E21	10
Rāmeswaram, India	G4	53
Rāmgarh, Bngl.	G13	54
Rāmgarh, India	E5	54
Rāmgarh, India	G10	54
Ram Head, c., V.I.U.S.	e8	104b
Rāmhormoz, Iran	C6	56
Ramírez, Mex.	I10	130
Ramírez, Mex.	G7	130
Ramla, Isr.	G5	58
Ramlu, mtn., Afr.	E8	62
Ramm, Jabal, mtn., Jord.	I6	58
Rāmnagar, India	F9	54
Rāmnagar, India	D7	54
Râmnicu Sărat, Rom.	D14	26
Râmnicu Vâlcea, Rom.	D11	26
Ramona, Ca., U.S.	J9	134
Ramona, S.D., U.S.	C15	126
Ramos, Mex.	D8	100
Ramos, stm., Mex.	C6	100
Ramotswa, Bots.	D7	70
Rampart, Ak., U.S.	C9	140
Ramparts, stm., N.T., Can.	B4	106
Rāmpur, India	D7	54
Rāmpur, India	C6	54
Rāmpura, India	F5	54
Rāmpur Hāt, India	F11	54
Ramree Island, i., Mya.	C1	48
Ramseur, N.C., U.S.	I6	114
Ramsey, I. of Man	G8	12
Ramsey Lake, l., On., Can.	A7	112
Ramsgate, Eng., U.K.	J14	12
Ramshorn Peak, mtn., Mt., U.S.	E15	136
Rāmtek, India	H7	54
Rāmu, Bngl.	H14	54
Ramu, stm., Pap. N. Gui.	a3	79a
Ramville, Îlet, i., Mart.	k7	105c
Ramygala, Lith.	E7	10
Rānāghāt, India	G12	54
Rana Kao, Volcán, vol., Chile	f29	78l
Rāna Pratāp Sāgar, res., India	F5	54
Ranau, Malay.	H1	52
Ranau, Danau, l., Indon.	F3	50
Ranburne, Al., U.S.	D13	122
Rancagua, Chile	G2	92
Rancah, Indon.	G6	50
Rancevo, Russia	D16	10
Rancharia, Braz.	D6	90
Ranchería, stm., Col.	B5	86
Ranchester, Wy., U.S.	C5	126
Rānchi, India	G10	54
Ranchillos, Arg.	C5	92
Ranch Lake, l., Sk., Can.	B9	124
Rancho Cordova, Ca., U.S.	E4	134
Rancho Nuevo, Mex.	H7	130
Ranchos, Arg.	G8	92
Ranco, Lago, l., Chile	H2	90
Rancul, Arg.	G5	92
Randazzo, Italy	G8	24
Randers, Den.	H4	8
Randleman, N.C., U.S.	I6	114
Randlett, Ok., U.S.	G10	128
Randolph, Az., U.S.	K5	132
Randolph, Me., U.S.	F7	110
Randolph, Ne., U.S.	E15	126
Randolph, N.Y., U.S.	B7	114
Randolph, Ut., U.S.	B5	132
Random Lake, Wi., U.S.	E2	112
Randsfjorden, l., Nor.	F3	8
Ranfurly, N.Z.	G4	80
Rāngāmāti, Bngl.	G13	54
Rangantemiang, Indon.	D8	50
Rangas, Tanjung, c., Indon.	E11	50
Rangasa, Tanjung, c., Indon.	E11	50
Rangaunu Bay, b., N.Z.	B5	80
Rangeley, Me., U.S.	E6	110
Ranger, Tx., U.S.	B9	130
Rangia, India	E13	54
Rangitaiki, stm., N.Z.	D7	80
Rangitata, stm., N.Z.	F4	80
Rangitikei, stm., N.Z.	D7	80
Rangkasbitung, Indon.	G4	50
Rangoon see Yangon, Mya.	D2	48
Rangoon, stm., Mya.	D3	48
Rangpur, Bngl.	F12	54
Rangpur, Pak.	C3	54
Rangsang, Pulau, i., Indon.	C3	50
Rānībennur, India	D2	53
Rānīganj, India	G11	54
Rānikhet, India	D7	54
Rankamhaeng National Park, p.o.i., Thai.	D4	48
Ranken, stm., Austl.	D7	74
Ranken Store, Austl.	C7	74
Rankin, Il., U.S.	H2	112
Rankin, Tx., U.S.	C6	130
Rankin Inlet, Nu., Can.	C12	106
Rankins Springs, Austl.	I6	76
Rann of Kutch see Kutch, Rann of, reg., Asia	D2	46
Ranong, Thai.	H4	48
Ranongga Island, i., Sol. Is.	e7	79b
Ranot, Thai.	I5	48
Ransiki, Indon.	F9	44
Ransom, Ks., U.S.	C8	128
Ranson, W.V., U.S.	E8	114
Rantabe, Madag.	D8	68
Rantaukampar, Indon.	C2	50
Rantaupanjang, Indon.	D2	50
Rantauprapat, Indon.	B1	50
Rantekombola, Bulu, mtn., Indon.	E12	50
Rantepao, Indon.	E11	50
Rantoul, Il., U.S.	D9	120
Raohe, China	B11	36
Raoping, China	J7	42
Raoul, Ga., U.S.	B2	116
Raoul-Blanchard, Mont, mtn., Qc., Can.	C6	110
Raoul Island, i., N.Z.	F9	72
Rapa, i., Fr. Poly.	F12	72
Rapallo, Italy	F6	22
Rapang, Indon.	E11	50
Rapa Nui see Pascua, Isla de, i., Chile	f30	78l
Rāpar, India	G3	54
Rapel, stm., Chile	F2	92
Rapel, Embalse, res., Chile	G2	92
Rapelli, Arg.	C5	92
Raper, Cape, c., Nu., Can.	B17	106
Rapidan, stm., Va., U.S.	F7	114
Rapid City, Mb., Can.	D13	124
Rapid City, S.D., U.S.	C9	126
Rapid Creek, stm., S.D., U.S.	D9	126
Rapide-Blanc, Qc., Can.	C4	110
Rapid River, Mi., U.S.	C2	112
Räpina, Est.	G12	8
Rappahannock, stm., Va., U.S.	G9	114
Rāpti, stm., Asia	E9	54
Rapu Rapu Island, i., Phil.	D5	52
Raraka, at., Fr. Poly.	E12	72
Rarotonga, i., Cook Is.	a26	78j
Rarotonga International Airport, Cook Is.	a26	78j
Rasa, Punta, c., Arg.	H9	92
Ra's al-Khaymah, U.A.E.	D8	56
Ra's Ba'labakk, Leb.	D7	58
Râșcani, Mol.	B14	26
Rașcov, Mol.	B15	26
Ras Dashen Terara, mtn., Eth.	E7	62
Ras Dejen see Ras Dashen Terara, mtn., Eth.	E7	62
Ras Djebel, Tun.	G4	24
Raseiniai, Lith.	E5	10
Râs el-Barr, Egypt	G2	58
Rashād, Sudan	E6	62
Rashid (Rosetta), Egypt	G1	58
Rashid, Masabb (Rosetta Mouth), mth., Egypt	G1	58
Rasht, Iran	B6	56
Raška, Yugo.	F7	26
Rās Koh, mtn., Pak.	D10	56
Rasm al-Arwām, Sabkhat, l., Syria	C8	58
Râșnov, Rom.	D12	26
Rasra, India	F9	54
Rassua, ostrov, i., Russia	G19	34
Rast, Rom.	F10	26
Rastatt, Ger.	H4	16
Rastede, Ger.	C4	16
Rastenburg see Kętrzyn, Pol.	B17	16
Rásttigáisá, mtn., Nor.	A12	8
Ratak Chain, is., Marsh. Is.	C8	72
Ratamka, Bela.	G10	10
Ratangarh, India	D5	54
Rat Buri, Thai.	F4	48
Rāth, India	F7	54
Rathbun Lake, res., Ia., U.S.	D4	120
Rathdrum, Id., U.S.	C9	136
Rathenow, Ger.	D8	16
Rathkeale, Ire.	I3	12
Ráth Luirc, Ire.	I4	12
Rathwell, Mb., Can.	E15	124
Rat Island, i., Ak., U.S.	g22	140a
Rat Islands, is., Ak., U.S.	g22	140a
Ratlām, India	G5	54
Ratmanova, ostrov, i., Russia	C27	34
Ratnāgiri, India	C1	53
Ratnapura, Sri L.	H5	53
Raton, N.M., U.S.	E4	128
Raton Pass, p., N.M., U.S.	E4	128
Rats, stm., Qc., Can.	A4	110
Rattanaburi, Thai.	E6	48
Rattaphum, Thai.	I5	48
Rattlesnake, Mt., U.S.	D13	136
Rattlesnake Creek, stm., Ks., U.S.	D10	128
Ratz, Mount, mtn., B.C., Can.	D4	106
Ratzeburg, Ger.	C6	16
Rau, Indon.	C2	50
Raub, Malay.	K5	48
Rauch, Arg.	H8	92
Raul Soares, Braz.	K4	88
Rauma, Fin.	F9	8
Rauma, stm., Nor.	E2	8
Rauna, Lat.	C8	10
Raung, Gunung, vol., Indon.	H9	50
Raurkela, India	G10	54
Răut, stm., Mol.	B14	26
Ravalgaon, India	H5	54
Ravanusa, Italy	G7	24
Ravena, N.Y., U.S.	B12	114
Ravenna, Italy	F9	22
Ravenna, Ky., U.S.	G2	114
Ravenna, Ne., U.S.	F13	126
Ravenna, Oh., U.S.	G8	112
Ravensburg, Ger.	I5	16
Ravenscrag, Sk., Can.	E4	124
Ravenshoe, Austl.	A5	76
Ravensthorpe, Austl.	F4	74
Ravenswood, W.V., U.S.	F4	114
Rāvi, stm., Asia	C4	54
Ravnina, Turkmen.	B9	56
Rāwah, Iraq	C5	56
Rawaki, at., Kir.	D9	72
Rāwalpindi, Pak.	B4	54
Rawas, stm., Indon.	E3	50
Rawdon, Qc., Can.	D3	110
Rawicz, Pol.	E12	16
Rawlinna, Austl.	F4	74
Rawlins, Wy., U.S.	B9	132
Rawson, Arg.	H4	90
Rawson, Arg.	G7	92
Raxāul, India	E10	54
Ray, Cape, c., Nf., Can.	C17	110
Raya, Indon.	C11	50
Raya, Bukit, mtn., Indon.	D8	50
Rāyachoti, India	D4	53
Rāyadurg, India	D3	53
Rāyagarha, India	B6	53
Ray Hubbard, Lake, res., Tx., U.S.	E2	122
Raymond, Ab., Can.	G18	138
Raymond, Il., U.S.	E8	120
Raymond, Mn., U.S.	F3	118
Raymond, Wa., U.S.	D3	136
Raymond Terrace, Austl.	I8	76
Raymondville, Tx., U.S.	H10	130
Raymore, Sk., Can.	C9	124
Rayne, La., U.S.	G6	122
Rayones, Mex.	C8	100
Rayong, Thai.	F5	48
Rayside-Balfour, On., Can.	B8	112
Raytown, Mo., U.S.	E3	120
Rayville, La., U.S.	E7	122
Raz, Pointe du, c., Fr.	F4	14
Războieni, Rom.	B13	26
Razdolinsk, Russia	C16	32
Răzeni, Mol.	C15	26
Razgrad, Blg.	F13	26
Razim, Lacul, l., Rom.	E15	26
Rāznas ezers, l., Lat.	D10	10
Razorback Mountain, mtn., B.C., Can.	E6	138
Răzvani, Rom.	E13	26
Ré, Île de, i., Fr.	C4	18
Reading, Eng., U.K.	J11	12
Reading, Mi., U.S.	C1	114
Reading, Oh., U.S.	E1	114
Reading, Pa., U.S.	D9	114
Readlyn, Ia., U.S.	B5	120
Readstown, Wi., U.S.	H8	118
Real, stm., Braz.	F6	88
Real, Cordillera, mts., S.A.	G4	84
Real del Castillo, Mex.	L9	134
Real del Padre, Arg.	G4	92
Realicó, Arg.	G5	92
Reardan, Wa., U.S.	C8	136
Reata, Mex.	B8	100
Reay, Scot., U.K.	C9	12
Rebecca, Lake, l., Austl.	F4	74
Rebiana Sand Sea see Rabyānah, Ramlat, des., Libya	C4	62
Reboly, Russia	E14	8
Rebouças, Braz.	B12	92
Rebun-tō, i., Japan	B14	38
Recanati, Italy	G10	22
Recherche, Archipelago of the, is., Austl.	F4	74
Recife, Braz.	E8	88
Recinto, Chile	H2	92
Recklinghausen, Ger.	E2	16
Reconquista, Arg.	D8	92
Recreio, Braz.	K4	88
Recreo, Arg.	D5	92
Rector, Ar., U.S.	H7	120
Rèčyča, Bela.	H13	10
Recz, Pol.	C11	16
Red (Hong, Song) (Yuan), stm., Asia	D9	46
Red, stm., N.A.	A2	118
Red, stm., U.S.	E9	108
Red, stm., U.S.	H10	120
Red, Elm Fork, stm., U.S.	F8	128
Red, North Fork, stm., U.S.	G9	128
Red, Prairie Dog Town Fork, stm., U.S.	H7	122
Red, Salt Fork, stm., U.S.	G9	128
Redang, Pulau, i., Malay.	J6	48
Red Bank, N.J., U.S.	D11	114
Red Bank, Tn., U.S.	B13	122
Red Bay, Nf., Can.	i22	107a
Red Bay, Al., U.S.	C10	122
Redbay, Fl., U.S.	G12	122
Redberry Lake, l., Sk., Can.	B6	124
Red Bluff, Ca., U.S.	C3	134
Red Bluff Reservoir, res., U.S.	C4	130
Red Boiling Springs, Tn., U.S.	H12	120
Red Canyon, val., S.D., U.S.	D9	126
Redcar, Eng., U.K.	G11	12
Red Cedar, stm., Mi., U.S.	F5	112
Red Cedar Lake, l., On., Can.	B9	112
Redcliff, Ab., Can.	D3	124
Red Cliff, Co., U.S.	D10	132
Redcliff see Red Cliff, Co., U.S.	D10	132
Redcliffe, Austl.	F9	76
Redcliffe, Mount, mtn., Austl.	E4	74
Red Cliffs, Austl.	J3	76
Red Cloud, Ne., U.S.	A10	128
Red Creek, stm., Ms., U.S.	G10	122
Red Deer, Ab., Can.	D17	138
Red Deer, stm., Can.	B12	124
Red Deer, stm., Can.	F19	138
Red Deer Lake, l., Mb., Can.	B12	124
Reddersburg, S. Afr.	F8	70
Red Devil, Ak., U.S.	D8	140
Redding, Ca., U.S.	C3	134
Redditch, Eng., U.K.	I10	12
Redenção, Braz.	C6	88
Redfield, S.D., U.S.	C14	126
Redford, Tx., U.S.	E3	130
Redhead, Trin.	s13	105f
Redja, stm., Russia	C14	10
Redkey, In., U.S.	H4	112
Redkino, Russia	D19	10
Red Lake, On., Can.	E12	106
Red Lake, l., On., Can.	E12	106
Red Lake, l., Az., U.S.	H2	132
Red Lake, stm., Mn., U.S.	D2	118
Red Lake Falls, Mn., U.S.	D2	118
Red Lake Road, On., Can.	B5	118
Redlands, Ca., U.S.	I8	134
Redlands, Co., U.S.	D8	132
Red Level, Al., U.S.	F12	122
Red Lion, Pa., U.S.	E9	114
Red Lodge, Mt., U.S.	B3	126
Redmond, Or., U.S.	F5	136
Redmond, Ut., U.S.	D5	132
Redmond, Wa., U.S.	C4	136
Red Mountain, mtn., Mt., U.S.	C14	136
Red Mountain Pass, p., Co., U.S.	F9	132
Red Oak, Ia., U.S.	D2	120
Redon, Fr.	G6	14
Redonda, Isla, i., Ven.	t12	105f
Redonda Islands, is., B.C., Can.	F6	138
Redondela, Spain	B2	20
Redondo, Port.	F3	20
Redondo Beach, Ca., U.S.	J7	134
Redoubt Volcano, vol., Ak., U.S.	D9	140
Red Pass, B.C., Can.	D11	138
Red Rock, B.C., Can.	C8	138
Red Rock, On., Can.	C10	118
Red Rock, stm., Mt., U.S.	F14	136
Red Rock, Lake, res., Ia., U.S.	C4	120
Redruth, Eng., U.K.	K7	12
Red Sea	C7	62
Redvers, Sk., Can.	E12	124
Redwater, Ab., Can.	C17	138
Redwater, stm., Mt., U.S.	G8	124
Redwillow, stm., Can.	A11	138
Red Willow Creek, stm., Ne., U.S.	G12	126
Red Wing, Mn., U.S.	G6	118
Redwood, stm., Mn., U.S.	G3	118
Redwood Falls, Mn., U.S.	G3	118
Redwood National Park, p.o.i., Ca., U.S.	B1	134
Ree, Lough, l., Ire.	H5	12
Reed City, Mi., U.S.	E4	112
Reeder, N.D., U.S.	A10	126
Reed Lake, l., Sk., Can.	D6	124
Reedley, Ca., U.S.	G6	134
Reedsburg, Wi., U.S.	H8	118
Reedsville, Wi., U.S.	D2	112
Reefton, N.Z.	F4	80
Reelfoot Lake, l., Tn., U.S.	H8	120
Rees, Ger.	E2	16
Reese, Mi., U.S.	E6	112
Reese, stm., Nv., U.S.	C9	134
Reeseville, Wi., U.S.	H10	118
Refuge Cove, B.C., Can.	F6	138
Refugio, Tx., U.S.	F10	130
Rega, stm., Pol.	C11	16
Regência, Braz.	J6	88
Regeneração, Braz.	D4	88
Regensburg, Ger.	H8	16
Regent, N.D., U.S.	A10	126
Reggâne, Alg.	D5	64
Reggio di Calabria, Italy	F9	24
Reggio nell'Emilia, Italy	F7	22
Reghin, Rom.	C11	26
Regina, Sk., Can.	D9	124
Región Metropolitana, state, Chile	F2	92
Registan see Rīgestān, reg., Afg.	C9	56
Registro, Braz.	B14	92
Regozero, Russia	D14	8
Rehau, Ger.	F7	16
Rehoboth, Nmb.	C3	70
Rehoboth Beach, De., U.S.	F10	114
Reḥovot, Isr.	G5	58
Reichenbach, Ger.	F8	16
Reidsville, Ga., U.S.	D3	116
Reidsville, N.C., U.S.	H6	114
Reigate, Eng., U.K.	J12	12
Reihoku, Japan	G2	40
Reims (Rheims), Fr.	E12	14
Rein Anteriur (Vorderrhein), stm., Switz.	D6	22
Reinbeck, Ia., U.S.	B5	120
Reindeer Lake, l., Can.	D10	106
Reinga, Cape, c., N.Z.	B5	80
Reinosa, Spain	A6	20
Reisa Nasjonalpark, p.o.i., Nor.	B10	8
Reisterstown, Md., U.S.	E9	114
Reitz, S. Afr.	E9	70
Reliance, N.T., Can.	C9	106
Remada, Tun.	C7	64
Remagen, Ger.	F3	16
Remanso, Braz.	E4	88
Rembang, Indon.	G7	50
Remedios, Col.	D4	86
Remedios, Pan.	H7	102
Remedios, Punta, c., El Sal.	F2	102
Remer, Mn., U.S.	D5	118
Remington, Va., U.S.	F8	114
Rémire, Fr. Gu.	C7	84
Remiremont, Fr.	G15	14
Remoulins, Fr.	F10	18
Rempang, Pulau, i., Indon.	C3	50
Remscheid, Ger.	E3	16
Remsen, Ia., U.S.	B1	120
Remus, Mi., U.S.	E4	112
Renaix see Ronse, Bel.	D12	14
Renata, B.C., Can.	G12	138
Rencēni, Lat.	C8	10
Rende, Italy	E10	24
Rend Lake, res., Il., U.S.	F8	120
Rendova Island, i., Sol. Is.	e7	79b
Rendsburg, Ger.	B5	16
Renfrew, On., Can.	C13	112
Rengat, Indon.	D3	50
Rengel, Indon.	G8	50
Rengo, Chile	G2	92
Reng Tlāng, mtn., Asia	H14	54
Renheji, China	F6	42
Renhuai, China	H2	42
Reni, Ukr.	D15	26
Renland, reg., Grnld.	C20	141
Renmark, Austl.	J3	76
Rennell, i., Sol. Is.	E7	72
Rennell, Islas, is., Chile	J2	90
Rennell and Bellona, state, Sol. Is.	f9	79b
Rennes, Fr.	F7	14
Rennie, Mb., Can.	E18	124
Reno, Nv., U.S.	D6	134
Reno, stm., Italy	F8	22
Reno Hill, mtn., Wy., U.S.	E6	126
Renoster, stm., S. Afr.	G5	70
Renous, N.B., Can.	D11	110
Renovo, Pa., U.S.	C8	114
Rensjön, Swe.	B8	8
Rensselaer, In., U.S.	H2	112
Rensselaer, N.Y., U.S.	B12	114
Rentería, Spain	A9	20
Renton, Wa., U.S.	C4	136
Renville, Mn., U.S.	G3	118
Renwick, Ia., U.S.	B4	120
Reo, Indon.	H12	50
Repetek, Turkmen.	B9	56
Repton, Al., U.S.	F11	122
Republic, Mi., U.S.	B1	112
Republic, Mo., U.S.	G4	120
Republic, Wa., U.S.	B8	136
Republican, stm., U.S.	B11	128
Republican, North Fork, stm., U.S.	A6	128
Republican, South Fork, stm., U.S.	B7	128
Republic of Korea see Korea, South, ctry., Asia	G8	38
Repulse Bay, Nu., Can.	B13	106
Repulse Bay, b., Austl.	C7	76
Repvåg, Nor.	A11	8
Requena, Spain	E9	20
Reriutaba, Braz.	C5	88
Reşadiye Yarımadası, pen., Tur.	G10	28
Reschenpass (Resia, Passo di), p., Eur.	C16	18
Reschenscheideck see Reschenpass, p., Eur.	C16	18
Reschenscheideck see Resia, Passo di, p., Eur.	C16	18
Resen, Mac.	B4	28
Reserva, Braz.	B12	92
Reserve, La., U.S.	G8	122
Reserve, N.M., U.S.	J8	132
Resia, Passo di (Reschenpass), p., Eur.	C16	18
Resistencia, Arg.	C8	92
Reșița, Rom.	D8	26
Resko, Pol.	C11	16
Resolute (Kaujuitoq), Nu., Can.	C7	141
Resolution Island, i., Nu., Can.	E12	141
Resolution Island, i., N.Z.	G2	80
Resplendor, Braz.	J5	88
Restigouche, stm., Can.	C9	110
Restinga Seca, Braz.	D11	92
Reston, Mb., Can.	E12	124
Retalhuleu, Guat.	E2	102
Retamosa, Ur.	F10	92
Retezat, Parcul Național, p.o.i., Rom.	D9	26
Rethel, Fr.	E13	14
Réthymno, Grc.	H7	28
Rettihovka, Russia	B10	38
Reunion, dep., Afr.	I11	60
Reus, Spain	C12	20
Reuss, stm., Switz.	C5	22
Reuterstadt Stavenhagen, Ger.	C8	16
Reutlingen, Ger.	H5	16
Revda, Russia	C16	8
Revelstoke, B.C., Can.	F12	138
Revelstoke, Lake, res., B.C., Can.	E12	138
Reventazón, Peru	E1	84
Revilla del Campo, Spain	B7	20
Revillagigedo, Islas, is., Mex.	F2	100
Revillagigedo Island, i., Ak., U.S.	E13	140
Revillagigedo Islands see Revillagigedo, Islas, is., Mex.	F2	100
Revin, Fr.	E13	14
Revolución, Mex.	H2	130
Rewa, India	F8	54
Rewāri, India	D6	54
Rexburg, Id., U.S.	G15	136
Rexford, Ks., U.S.	B8	128
Rexford, Mt., U.S.	B11	136
Rey, Isla del, i., Pan.	H8	102
Rey, Laguna del, l., Mex.	B7	100
Reyes, Bol.	B3	90
Reyes, Point, c., Ca., U.S.	F2	134
Reyhanlı, Tur.	B7	58
Reykjanes Ridge, unds.	C10	144
Reykjavík, Ice.	k28	8a
Reyno, Ar., U.S.	H7	120
Reynolds, Ga., U.S.	D1	116
Reynolds, N.D., U.S.	G16	124
Reynosa, Mex.	B9	100
Rezé, Fr.	G7	14
Rēzekne, Lat.	D10	10
Rezina, Mol.	B15	26
Rezovo, Blg.	G15	26
Rezovska (Mutlu), stm., Eur.	G14	26
Rhaetian Alps, mts., Eur.	C15	18
Rhame, N.D., U.S.	A9	126
Rheda-Wiedenbrück, Ger.	E4	16
Rheims see Reims, Fr.	E12	14
Rhein, Sk., Can.	C11	124
Rhein see Rhine, stm., Eur.	C15	14
Rheine, Ger.	D3	16
Rheinland-Pfalz, state, Ger.	G3	16
Rhine, Ga., U.S.	E2	116
Rhine (Rhein) (Rhin), stm., Eur.	C15	14
Rhinelander, Wi., U.S.	F9	118
Rhineland-Palatinate see Rheinland-Pfalz, state, Ger.	G3	16
Rhinns Point, c., Scot., U.K.	F6	12
Rhir, Cap, c., Mor.	C2	64
Rho, Italy	E5	22
Rhode Island, state, U.S.	C14	114
Rhode Island Sound, strt., U.S.	C14	114
Rhodes see Ródos, Grc.	G11	28
Rhodes see Ródos, i., Grc.	G10	28
Rhodesia see Zimbabwe, ctry., Afr.	D4	68
Rhodes Matopos National Park, p.o.i., Zimb.	B8	70
Rhodes' Tomb, hist., Zimb.	B9	70
Rhodope Mountains, mts., Eur.	H11	26
Rhön, mts., Ger.	F5	16
Rhondda, Wales, U.K.	J9	12
Rhône, state, Fr.	D10	18
Rhône, stm., Eur.	F10	18
Rhyl, Wales, U.K.	H9	12
Riachão, Braz.	D2	88
Riachão do Jacuípe, Braz.	F6	88
Riacho de Santana, Braz.	G4	88
Riachos, Islas de los, is., Arg.	H4	90
Riamkanan, Waduk, res., Indon.	E9	50
Riaño, Spain	A6	20
Riau, state, Indon.	D2	50
Riau, Kepulauan, is., Indon.	C4	50
Riaza, Spain	C7	20
Ribadeo, Spain	A3	20
Ribas do Rio Pardo, Braz.	D6	90
Ribáuè, Moz.	C6	68
Ribe, Den.	I3	8
Ribe, state, Den.	I3	8
Ribeira, Braz.	B13	92
Ribeira do Pombal, Braz.	F6	88
Ribeirão, Braz.	E8	88
Ribeirão Preto, Braz.	K2	88
Ribeirão Vermelho, Braz.	K3	88
Ribeiro Gonçalves, Braz.	D3	88
Ribera, Italy	G7	24
Riberalta, Bol.	B3	90
Rib Lake, Wi., U.S.	F8	118
Ribnica, Slvn.	E11	22
Ribnitz-Damgarten, Ger.	B8	16
Ribstone Creek, stm., Ab., Can.	D19	138
Ricardo Flores Magón, Mex.	F9	98
Riccione, Italy	F9	22
Rice, Tx., U.S.	E2	122
Rice Lake, l., On., Can.	D11	112
Riceville, Ia., U.S.	H6	118
Riceville, Tn., U.S.	B14	122
Richan, On., Can.	B6	118
Richard B. Russell Lake, res., U.S.	B3	116
Richard Collinson Inlet, b., N.T., Can.	B17	140
Richards, Tx., U.S.	G3	122
Richards Bay, S. Afr.	F11	70
Richards Bay, b., S. Afr.	F11	70
Richards Island, i., N.T., Can.	C13	140
Richardson, Tx., U.S.	E2	122
Richardson, Wa., U.S.	B4	136
Richardson Mountains, mts., Can.	B3	106
Richard Toll, Sen.	F1	64
Riche, Pointe, c., Nf., Can.	i22	107a
Richelieu, Fr.	G9	14
Richelieu, stm., Qc., Can.	E3	110
Richer, Mb., Can.	E17	124
Richey, Mt., U.S.	G8	124
Richfield, Mn., U.S.	G5	118
Richfield, Pa., U.S.	D8	114
Richfield, Ut., U.S.	E4	132
Richfield Springs, N.Y., U.S.	B11	114
Richford, Vt., U.S.	F4	110
Rich Hill, Mo., U.S.	F3	120
Richibucto, N.B., Can.	D12	110
Richland, Ga., U.S.	E14	122
Richland, Mi., U.S.	F4	112
Richland, Mt., U.S.	F7	124
Richland, Wa., U.S.	D7	136
Richland Center, Wi., U.S.	H8	118
Richland Creek, stm., Tx., U.S.	C11	130
Richlands, Va., U.S.	G4	114
Richland Springs, Tx., U.S.	C9	130
Richmond, Austl.	C4	76
Richmond, Austl.	I8	76
Richmond, B.C., Can.	G7	138
Richmond, On., Can.	C14	112
Richmond, Qc., Can.	E4	110
Richmond, N.Z.	E5	80
Richmond, S. Afr.	G6	70
Richmond, S. Afr.	F10	70
Richmond, Eng., U.K.	G11	12
Richmond, Ca., U.S.	F3	134
Richmond, In., U.S.	I5	112
Richmond, Ky., U.S.	G1	114
Richmond, Me., U.S.	F7	110
Richmond, Mi., U.S.	B3	114
Richmond, Mn., U.S.	F4	118
Richmond, Mo., U.S.	E4	120
Richmond, Tx., U.S.	H3	122
Richmond, Ut., U.S.	B5	132
Richmond, Va., U.S.	G8	114
Richmond Heights, Fl., U.S.	K5	116
Richmond Highlands, Wa., U.S.	C4	136
Richmond Hill, On., Can.	E10	112
Richmond Hill, Ga., U.S.	E4	116
Richmond Peak, mtn., St. Vin.	o11	105e
Richton, Ms., U.S.	F9	122
Richwood, Oh., U.S.	D2	114
Richwood, W.V., U.S.	F5	114

Name — Map Ref. — Page

Ricobayo, Embalse de, res., Spain C4 20
Riddle, Or., U.S. H3 136
Rideau, stm., On., Can. C14 112
Ridgecrest, Ca., U.S. H8 134
Ridgedale, Sk., Can. A9 124
Ridgeland, Ms., U.S. E8 122
Ridgeland, S.C., U.S. D4 116
Ridgetown, On., Can. F8 112
Ridgeville, Mb., Can. E16 124
Ridgeville, S.C., U.S. C5 116
Ridgeway, Mo., U.S. D4 120
Ridgway, Co., U.S. E9 132
Ridgway, Il., U.S. G9 120
Ridgway, Pa., U.S. C7 114
Riding Mountain National Park, p.o.i., Mb., Can. D13 124
Riegelwood, N.C., U.S. B7 116
Riesa, Ger. E9 16
Riesco, Isla, i., Chile J2 90
Riesi, Italy G8 24
Riet, stm., S. Afr. F7 70
Riet, stm., S. Afr. H5 70
Rietavas, Lith. E4 10
Rietfontein (Buitsivango), stm., Afr. B4 70
Rieti, Italy H9 22
Rif, mts., Mor. C4 64
Riffe Lake, res., Wa., U.S. D4 136
Rifle, Co., U.S. D9 132
Rifstangi, c., Ice. j31 8a
Rift Valley, val., Afr. F7 62
Rīga, Lat. D7 10
Riga, Gulf of, b., Eur. C6 10
Rigaih, Indon. J2 48
Rigby, Id., U.S. G14 136
Rīgestān, reg., Afg. C9 56
Riggins, Id., U.S. E10 136
Rigi, mtn., Switz. C5 22
Rigo, Pap. N. Gui. b4 79a
Rig-Rig, Chad E2 62
Riihimäki, Fin. F11 8
Riiser-Larsen Peninsula, pen., Ant. B8 81
Riječki Zaljev, b., Cro. E11 22
Rijeka (Fiume), Cro. E11 22
Rijssen, Neth. D2 16
Rillito, Az., U.S. K5 132
Rimatara, i., Fr. Poly. F11 72
Rimavská Sobota, Slov. H15 16
Rimbey, Ab., Can. D16 138
Rimersburg, Pa., U.S. C6 114
Rimini, Italy F9 22
Rimouski, Qc., Can. B8 110
Rimouski, stm., Qc., Can. B8 110
Rinbung, China C7 46
Rinca, Pulau, i., Indon. H11 50
Rincon, Ga., U.S. D4 116
Rincon, N.M., U.S. K9 132
Rinconada, Arg. D3 90
Rincón del Bonete, Lago Artificial de, res., Ur. F9 92
Rincón de Romos, Mex. D7 100
Rīngas, India E5 54
Ringdove, Vanuatu k16 79d
Ringebu, Nor. F4 8
Ringgold, Ga., U.S. C13 122
Ringim, Nig. G6 64
Ringkøbing, Den. H2 8
Ringkøbing, state, Den. H3 8
Ringkøbing Fjord, b., Den. H2 8
Ringling, Ok., U.S. G11 128
Ringsted, Ia., U.S. H4 118
Ringvassøya, i., Nor. A8 8
Rinjani, Gunung, vol., Indon. H10 50
Rinteln, Ger. D5 16
Rio, Wi., U.S. H9 118
Riobamba, Ec. H2 86
Río Blanco, Chile F2 92
Rio Branco, Braz. E4 84
Río Branco, Ur. F11 92
Río Bravo, Mex. C9 100
Río Bravo, Parque Internacional del, p.o.i., Mex. F5 130
Rio Brilhante, Braz. D6 90
Río Bueno, Chile H2 90
Rio Casca, Braz. K4 88
Río Ceballos, Arg. E5 92
Río Chico, Ven. B9 86
Rio Claro, Braz. L2 88
Rio Claro, Trin. s12 105f
Río Colorado, Arg. I5 92
Río Cuarto, Arg. F5 92
Rio das Pedras, Moz. C12 70
Rio de Janeiro, Braz. L4 88
Rio de Janeiro, state, Braz. L4 88
Rio Dell, Ca., U.S. C1 134
Río de Oro, Col. C5 86
Rio do Sul, Braz. C13 92
Rio Espera, Braz. K4 88
Rio Felix, stm., N.M., U.S. H3 128
Río Gallegos, Arg. J3 90
Río Grande, Arg. J3 90
Rio Grande, Braz. F11 92
Río Grande, Mex. D7 100
Río Grande, Nic. F4 102
Río Grande, P.R. B4 104a
Rio Grande (Bravo), stm., N.A. H13 98
Rio Grande do Norte, state, Braz. C7 88
Rio Grande do Sul, state, Braz. D11 92
Ríohacha, Col. B5 86
Río Hato, Pan. H7 102
Rio Hondo, Tx., U.S. H10 130
Rio Hondo, stm., N.M., U.S. H3 128
Rio Hondo, Embalse, res., Arg. C5 92
Río Jueyes, P.R. B3 104a
Riolândia, Braz. D6 90
Rio Largo, Braz. E8 88
Riom, Fr. D9 18
Río Mayo, Arg. I2 90
Río Mulatos, Bol. C3 90
Riondel, B.C., Can. G14 138
Rio Negro, Braz. C13 92
Ríonegro, Col. D5 86
Río Negro, state, Arg. G3 90
Rio Negro, Pantanal do, sw., Braz. C5 90
Rionero in Vulture, Italy D9 24
Riópar, Spain F8 20
Rio Pardo, Braz. E11 92
Rio Pardo de Minas, Braz. H4 88
Río Piedras, P.R. B3 104a
Rio Piracicaba, Braz. J4 88
Rio Pomba, Braz. K4 88
Rio Preto, Braz. L3 88
Rio Rancho, N.M., U.S. H10 132
Rio Real, Braz. F6 88
Río Segundo, Arg. E5 92
Ríosucio, Col. E4 86
Río Tercero, Arg. F5 92
Rio Tinto, Braz. D8 88
Rio Verde, Braz. G7 84
Ríoverde, Mex. E8 100
Rio Verde de Mato Grosso, Braz. C6 90
Rio Vista, Ca., U.S. E4 134
Riozinho, stm., Braz. D4 84
Riozinho, stm., Braz. E3 88
Ripley, N.Y., U.S. B6 114
Ripley, Oh., U.S. F2 114
Ripley, Tn., U.S. B9 122
Ripoll, Spain B13 20
Ripon, Qc., Can. E1 110
Ripon, Eng., U.K. G11 12
Ripon, Ca., U.S. F4 134
Ripon, Wi., U.S. H10 118
Riposto, Italy G9 24
Risaralda, state, Col. E3 86
Risbäck, Swe. D6 8
Rishīkesh, India C7 54
Rishiri-suidō, strt., Japan B14 38
Rishiri-tō, i., Japan B14 38
Rishon LeZiyyon, Isr. G5 58
Rising Star, Tx., U.S. B9 130
Rising Sun, In., U.S. F12 120
Rising Sun, Md., U.S. E9 114
Risle, stm., Fr. E9 14
Risnjak, mtn., Cro. E11 22
Risti, Est. A7 10
Ristna, Est. G9 8
Rita Blanca Creek, stm., Tx., U.S. F6 128
Ritchie, S. Afr. F7 70
Ritidian Point, c., Guam i10 78c
Ritter, Mount, mtn., Ca., U.S. F6 134
Rittman, Oh., U.S. D4 114
Ritzville, Wa., U.S. C8 136
Rivadavia, Arg. E3 92
Rivadavia, Arg. G6 92
Rivadavia, Chile D2 92
Riva del Garda, Italy E7 22
Rivas, Nic. G5 102
Rive-de-Gier, Fr. D10 18
Rivera, Arg. H6 92
Rivera, Ur. E10 92
River Cess, Lib. H3 64
Riverdale, Ca., U.S. G6 134
Riverdale, N.D., U.S. G12 124
River Falls, Al., U.S. F12 122
River Falls, Wi., U.S. G6 118
Riverhead, N.Y., U.S. D13 114
Riverhurst, Sk., Can. D7 124
Riverina, reg., Austl. J5 76
River John, N.S., Can. E13 110
River Jordan, B.C., Can. H6 138
River Road, Or., U.S. F3 136
Rivers, Mb., Can. D13 124
Riversdale, S. Afr. I5 70
Riverside, Ca., U.S. J8 134
Riverside, Ia., U.S. C6 120
Riverside, Tx., U.S. G3 122
Riverside, Wa., U.S. B7 136
Rivers Inlet, B.C., Can. E3 138
Riversleigh, Austl. C7 74
Riverton, N.Z. H2 80
Riverton, Il., U.S. E8 120
Riverton, Ne., U.S. A10 128
Riverton, Ut., U.S. C4 132
Riverton, Va., U.S. F7 114
Riverton, Wy., U.S. D4 126
Riverton Heights, Wa., U.S. C4 136
River View, Al., U.S. E13 122
Rives, Tn., U.S. H8 120
Rivesville, W.V., U.S. E5 114
Riviera, Tx., U.S. G10 130
Riviera Beach, Fl., U.S. J5 116
Rivière-à-Pierre, Qc., Can. C5 110
Rivière-Bleue, Qc., Can. C7 110
Rivière-de-la-Chaloupe, Qc., Can. A14 110
Rivière-du-Loup, Qc., Can. C7 110
Rivière-Matawin, Qc., Can. D3 110
Rivière-Pilote, Mart. I7 105c
Rivière-Salée, Mart. k7 105c
Rivne, Ukr. E14 6
Rivoli, Italy E4 22
Rivoli Bay, b., Austl. K2 76
Riyadh see Ar-Riyāḍ, Sau. Ar. E6 56
Rīyāq, Leb. E7 58
Rize, Tur. A5 56
Rizzuto, Capo, c., Italy F11 24
Rjad, Russia C18 10
Rjazan', Russia D5 32
Rjazancevo, Russia D22 10
Rjazanskaja oblast', co., Russia I19 8
Rjažsk, Russia D6 32
Rjukan, Nor. G3 8
Ro, N. Cal. m16 79d
Roachdale, In., U.S. I3 112
Road Town, Br. Vir. Is. e8 104b
Roan Mountain, Tn., U.S. H3 114
Roanne, Fr. C9 18
Roanoke, Al., U.S. D13 122
Roanoke, Il., U.S. D8 120
Roanoke, Va., U.S. G6 114
Roanoke, stm., U.S. H8 114
Roanoke Island, i., N.C., U.S. I10 114
Roanoke Rapids, N.C., U.S. H8 114
Roanoke Rapids Lake Dam, dam, N.C., U.S. H8 114
Roan Plateau, plat., U.S. D7 132
Roaring Spring, Pa., U.S. D7 114
Roaring Springs, Tx., U.S. H7 128
Roatán, Isla de, i., Hond. D4 102
Robbins, N.C., U.S. A6 116
Robbins, Tn., U.S. H13 120
Robbins Island, i., Austl. n12 77a
Robbinsville, N.C., U.S. A2 116
Robe, Austl. K2 76
Robe, Mount, hill, Austl. H3 76
Röbel, Ger. C8 16
Robersonville, N.C., U.S. I8 114
Roberta, Ga., U.S. D1 116
Robert Lee, Tx., U.S. C7 130
Robert Louis Stevenson's Tomb, hist., Samoa g12 79c
Roberts, Id., U.S. G14 136
Roberts, Mt., U.S. B3 126
Robertsdale, Al., U.S. G11 122
Robertsfors, Swe. D9 8
Robert S. Kerr Lake, res., Ok., U.S. B3 122
Robertson, S. Afr. H4 70
Roberts Peak, mtn., B.C., Can. D10 138
Roberts Port, Lib. H2 64
Roberval, Qc., Can. B4 110
Robinson, Il., U.S. E10 120
Robinson, Tx., U.S. C10 130
Róbinson Crusoe, Isla, i., Chile I7 82
Robinvale, Austl. J4 76
Robledo, Spain F8 20
Roblin, Mb., Can. C12 124
Roboré, Bol. C5 90
Rob Roy Island, i., Sol. Is. d7 79b
Robson, Mount, mtn., B.C., Can. C11 138
Robstown, Tx., U.S. G10 130
Roby, Tx., U.S. B7 130
Roca, Cabo da, c., Port. F1 20
Roçado, Braz. D3 88
Rocafuerte, Ec. H1 86
Roca Partida, Isla, i., Mex. F2 100
Rocas, Atol das, at., Braz. F11 82
Rocciamelone, mtn., Italy E4 22
Rocha, Ur. G10 92
Rochdale, Eng., U.K. H10 12
Rochechouart, Fr. D6 18
Rochefort, Fr. D5 18
Rochelle, Ga., U.S. E2 116
Rochelle, Il., U.S. C8 120
Roche-Percée, Sk., Can. E10 124
Rochester, In., U.S. G3 112
Rochester, Mi., U.S. B2 114
Rochester, Mn., U.S. G6 118
Rochester, N.H., U.S. G5 110
Rochester, N.Y., U.S. E12 112
Rochester, Tx., U.S. H9 128
Rochlitz, Ger. E8 16
Rock, stm., U.S. H2 118
Rock, stm., U.S. J8 118
Rockall, i., Scot., U.K. D6 6
Rockall Rise, unds. C12 144
Rock Bay, B.C., Can. F5 138
Rock Creek, B.C., Can. G11 138
Rock Creek, stm., N.A. F7 124
Rock Creek, stm., Mt., U.S. D13 136
Rock Creek, stm., Nv., U.S. C9 134
Rock Creek Butte, mtn., Or., U.S. F8 136
Rockdale, Il., U.S. C9 120
Rockdale, Tx., U.S. D11 130
Rockefeller Plateau, plat., Ant. D27 81
Rockenhausen, Ger. G3 16
Rock Falls, Il., U.S. C8 120
Rockford, Il., U.S. B8 120
Rockford, Ia., U.S. A5 120
Rockford, Oh., U.S. D1 114
Rockford, Tn., U.S. B15 122
Rockglen, Sk., Can. E8 124
Rockhampton, Austl. D8 76
Rockhampton Downs, Austl. C7 74
Rock Hill, S.C., U.S. B4 116
Rockingham, N.C., U.S. B6 116
Rockingham Bay, b., Austl. B6 76
Rock Island, Il., U.S. C7 120
Rocklake, N.D., U.S. F14 124
Rockland, On., Can. C14 112
Rockland, Id., U.S. H14 136
Rockland, Me., U.S. F7 110
Rockland, Ma., U.S. B15 114
Rocklands Reservoir, l., Austl. K3 76
Rockledge, Fl., U.S. H5 116
Rocklin, Ca., U.S. E4 134
Rockmart, Ga., U.S. D13 122
Rockport, In., U.S. G10 120
Rockport, Ky., U.S. G11 120
Rockport, Me., U.S. F7 110
Rockport, Ma., U.S. B15 114
Rock Port, Mo., U.S. D2 120
Rock Rapids, Ia., U.S. H2 118
Rock River, Wy., U.S. F6 126
Rocksprings, Tx., U.S. E7 130
Rock Springs, Wy., U.S. B7 132
Rockstone, Guy. B6 84
Rock Tombs see Speos, hist., Egypt K1 58
Rock Valley, Ia., U.S. H2 118
Rockville, In., U.S. I2 112
Rockville, Md., U.S. E8 114
Rockwall, Tx., U.S. E2 122
Rockwell, Ia., U.S. B4 120
Rockwell, N.C., U.S. A5 116
Rockwood, Me., U.S. E7 110
Rockwood, Pa., U.S. I10 112
Rockwood, Tn., U.S. I13 120
Rocky Cape National Park, p.o.i., Austl. n12 77a
Rockyford, Ab., Can. E17 138
Rocky Ford, Co., U.S. C5 128
Rocky Mount, N.C., U.S. I8 114
Rocky Mount, Va., U.S. H5 114
Rocky Mountain, mtn., Mt., U.S. C14 136
Rocky Mountain House, Ab., Can. D16 138
Rocky Mountain National Park, p.o.i., Co., U.S. G7 126
Rocky Mountains, mts., N.A. D6 106
Rocky Mountain Trench, val., N.A. G15 138
Rocky Point, c., Bah. K8 116
Rodalben, Ger. G3 16
Rødbyhavn, Den. I4 8
Rodeo, Arg. E3 92
Rodeo, Mex. C6 100
Rodeo, N.M., U.S. L7 132
Roderick Island, i., B.C., Can. D2 138
Rodewisch, Ger. F8 16
Rodez, Fr. E8 18
Roding, Ger. G8 16
Rodino, Russia G21 8
Rodney, On., Can. F8 112
Rodney, Cape, c., Ak., U.S. D6 140
Rodniki, Russia H19 8
Ródos (Rhodes), Grc. G11 28
Ródos (Rhodes), i., Grc. G10 28
Rodrigues, i., Mrts. K9 142
Roebourne, Austl. D3 74
Roebuck Bay, b., Austl. C4 74
Roeland Park, Ks., U.S. E3 120
Roermond, Neth. C14 14
Roeselare, Bel. D11 14
Roes Welcome Sound, strt., Nu., Can. C13 106
Roff, Ok., U.S. C2 122
Rogačevo, Russia D20 10
Rogagua, Laguna, l., Bol. B3 90
Rogaguado, Laguna, l., Bol. B3 90
Rogaland, state, Nor. G2 8
Rogaška Slatina, Slvn. D12 22
Rogers, Ar., U.S. H3 120
Rogers, Tx., U.S. D10 130
Rogers, Mount, mtn., Va., U.S. H4 114
Rogers Lake, l., Ca., U.S. I8 134
Rogers Pass, p., B.C., Can. E13 138
Rogersville, N.B., Can. D11 110
Rogersville, Al., U.S. C11 122
Rogersville, Tn., U.S. H3 114
Roggewein, Cabo, c., Chile e30 78l
Rogliano, Fr. G15 18
Rognedino, Russia G16 10
Rogue, stm., Or., U.S. H2 136
Rohri, Pak. E2 54
Rohtak, India D6 54
Roi Et, Thai. E6 48
Roi Georges, Îles du, is., Fr. Poly. E12 72
Roilianka, Ukr. C16 26
Rojas, Arg. G7 92
Rojo, Cabo, c., Mex. E10 100
Rojo, Cabo, c., P.R. C1 104a
Rokan, Indon. C2 50
Rokan, stm., Indon. C2 50
Rokel, stm., S.L. H2 64
Rokiškis, Lith. E8 10
Rokycany, Czech Rep. G9 16
Roland, Mb., Can. E16 124
Roland, Ar., U.S. C6 122
Roland, Ia., U.S. B4 120
Rolândia, Braz. D6 90
Roldanillo, Col. E3 86
Rolfe, Ia., U.S. B3 120
Roll, Az., U.S. K2 132
Rolla, Mo., U.S. G6 120
Rolla, N.D., U.S. F14 124
Rolling Fork, Ms., U.S. E8 122
Rolling Fork, stm., Ky., U.S. G12 120
Rollingstone, Austl. B6 76
Rollins, Mt., U.S. C12 136
Rolvsøya, i., Nor. A10 8
Roma, Austl. F7 76
Roma (Rome), Italy I9 22
Roma, Leso. F8 70
Roma, Tx., U.S. H8 130
Romagna, hist. reg., Italy F9 22
Roman, Rom. C13 26
Romanche Gap, unds. I12 144
Romang, Pulau, i., Indon. G8 44
Romania, ctry., Eur. D11 26
Roman Nose Mountain, mtn., Or., U.S. G3 136
Romano, Cape, c., Fl., U.S. K4 116
Romano, Cayo, i., Cuba A9 102
Romans-sur-Isère, Fr. D10 18
Romanzof Mountains, mts., Ak., U.S. C11 140
Romblon, Phil. D4 52
Rome see Roma, Italy I9 22
Rome, Ga., U.S. C13 122
Rome, N.Y., U.S. E14 112
Romeo, Mi., U.S. B2 114
Romilly-sur-Seine, Fr. F12 14
Romney, W.V., U.S. E7 114
Romny, Ukr. D4 32
Romont, Switz. D3 22
Romorantin-Lanthenay, Fr. G10 14
Rompin, stm., Malay. K6 48
Romsey, Eng., U.K. J11 12
Ron, Mui, c., Viet. C8 48
Rona, i., Scot., U.K. D7 12
Rona, i., Scot., U.K. B7 12
Ronan, Mt., U.S. C12 136
Roncador, Banco see Roncador, Cayos de, unds., Col. F7 102
Roncador, Cayos de, unds., Col. F7 102
Roncador, Serra do, plat., Braz. F7 84
Roncador Bank see Roncador, Cayos de, unds., Col. F7 102
Ronda, Spain H5 20
Ronda, Serranía de, mts., Spain H5 20
Rondane Nasjonalpark, p.o.i., Nor. F3 8
Ronde, Pointe, c., Dom. i5 105c
Rondônia, state, Braz. F5 84
Rondonópolis, Braz. G7 84
Rong, stm., China I3 42
Rong'an, China I3 42
Rongcheng, China C10 42
Ronge, Lac la, l., Sk., Can. D10 106
Rongelap, at., Marsh. Is. B7 72
Rongjiang, China I3 42
Rongkop, Indon. H7 50
Rongshui, China I3 42
Rongxian, China J4 42
Rønne, Den. I6 8
Ronneby, Swe. H6 8
Ronne Ice Shelf, ice, Ant. C34 81
Ronse, Bel. D12 14
Ronuro, stm., Braz. F7 84
Roodhouse, Il., U.S. E7 120
Roof Butte, mtn., Az., U.S. G7 132
Rooiboklaagte, stm., Nmb. B5 70
Roorkee, India D6 54
Roosendaal, Neth. C13 14
Roosevelt, Mn., U.S. C3 118
Roosevelt, Ok., U.S. G9 128
Roosevelt, Ut., U.S. C6 132
Roosevelt, stm., Braz. E5 84
Roosevelt Campobello International Park, p.o.i., N.B., Can. F10 110
Roosevelt Island, i., Ant. C24 81
Root, stm., Mn., U.S. H7 118
Ropaži, Lat. C7 10
Roper, N.C., U.S. I9 114
Roper, stm., Austl. B6 74
Roper Valley, Austl. B6 74
Ropesville, Tx., U.S. H6 128
Roque, Braz. B3 88
Roquefort, Fr. E5 18
Roraima, state, Braz. C5 84
Roraima, Mount, mtn., S.A. E11 86
Røros, Nor. E4 8
Rosa, Lake, l., Bah. B11 102
Rosales, Mex. A6 100
Rosalia, Wa., U.S. C9 136
Rosamond, Ca., U.S. I7 134
Rosamond Lake, l., Ca., U.S. I7 134
Rosario, Arg. F7 92
Rosário, Braz. B3 88
Rosario, Mex. B4 100
Rosario, Mex. D5 100
Rosario, Para. B9 92
Rosario, Ur. G9 92
Rosario, stm., Arg. B5 92
Rosario, Bahía del, b., Mex. G4 98
Rosario, Islas del, is., Col. B4 86
Rosario de Arriba, Mex. F4 98
Rosario de la Frontera, Arg. B5 92
Rosario de Lerma, Arg. B5 92
Rosario del Tala, Arg. F8 92
Rosário do Sul, Braz. E10 92
Rosário Oeste, Braz. F6 84
Rosarito, Mex. A2 100
Rosarito, Mex. K8 134
Rosarno, Italy F9 24
Rosas, Mex. H4 130
Roscoe, S.D., U.S. B13 126
Roscoe, Tx., U.S. B7 130
Roscommon, Ire. H4 12
Roscommon, state, Ire. H4 12
Roscrea, Ire. I5 12
Rose, Mount, mtn., Nv., U.S. D5 134
Roseau, Dom. j6 105c
Roseau, Mn., U.S. C3 118
Roseau, stm., N.A. C2 118
Roseberth, Austl. E2 76
Rosebery, Austl. n12 77a
Roseboro, N.C., U.S. B7 116
Rosebud, Mt., U.S. A6 126
Rosebud, S.D., U.S. D12 126
Rosebud, Tx., U.S. C11 130
Rosebud, stm., Ab., Can. E17 138
Rosebud Creek, stm., Mt., U.S. A6 126
Roseburg, Or., U.S. G3 136
Rosebush, Mi., U.S. E5 112
Rose City, Mi., U.S. D5 112
Rosedale, Austl. E8 76
Rosedale, Ab., Can. E18 138
Rosedale, La., U.S. G7 122
Rosedale, Ms., U.S. D7 122
Rose Hill, N.C., U.S. B7 116
Rose Hill, Va., U.S. H2 114
Rose Island, i., Bah. K8 116
Rosemary, Ab., Can. F18 138
Rosenberg, Tx., U.S. H3 122
Rosenheim, Ger. I8 16
Rosepine, La., U.S. G5 122
Roses, Golf de, b., Spain B14 20
Roses, Golfo de see Roses, Golf de, b., Spain B14 20
Roseto degli Abruzzi, Italy H11 22
Rosetown, Sk., Can. C6 124
Rosetta see Rashid, Egypt G1 58
Rosetta Mouth see Rashid, Masabb, mth., Egypt G1 58
Rose Valley, Sk., Can. B10 124
Roseville, Il., U.S. D7 120
Roseville, Mi., U.S. F7 112
Roseville, Mn., U.S. F5 118
Rosholt, S.D., U.S. F2 118
Rosholt, Wi., U.S. G9 118
Rosica, stm., Blg. F12 26
Rosiclare, Il., U.S. G9 120
Rosignol, Guy. B6 84
Roșiori de Vede, Rom. E12 26
Roskilde, Den. I4 8
Roskilde, state, Den. I5 8
Roslavl', Russia G15 10
Rosman, N.C., U.S. A3 116
Rosmead, S. Afr. G7 70
Ros Mhic Thriúin see New Ross, Ire. I6 12
Ross, Austl. o13 77a
Ross, stm., Yk., Can. C4 106
Rossano, Italy E10 24
Rossasna, Bela. F13 10
Rossburn, Mb., Can. D13 124
Rosseau, Lake, l., On., Can. C10 112
Rossel, Cap, c., N. Cal. m16 79d
Rossell y Rius, Ur. F10 92
Rossford, Oh., U.S. C2 114
Ross Ice Shelf, ice, Ant. D23 81
Rossignol, Lake, l., N.S., Can. F11 110
Ross Island, i., Ant. C22 81
Ross Lake, res., N.A. B5 136
Rossland, B.C., Can. G13 138
Rosslau, Ger. E8 16
Rosso, Maur. F1 64
Ross-on-Wye, Eng., U.K. J10 12
Rossoš', Russia D5 32
Ross R. Barnett Reservoir, res., Ms., U.S. E9 122
Ross River, Yk., Can. C4 106
Ross Sea, Ant. C23 81
Røssvatnet, l., Nor. D5 8
Rossville, Ga., U.S. C13 122
Rossville, Il., U.S. H2 112
Rossville, Ks., U.S. E2 120
Røst, is., Nor. C4 8
Rosthern, Sk., Can. B7 124
Roštkala, Taj. B11 56
Rostock, Ger. B7 16
Rostov, Russia C22 10
Rostov-na-Donu, Russia E6 32
Rosvinskoe, Russia C24 8
Roswell, Ga., U.S. B1 116
Roswell, N.M., U.S. H4 128
Rota, i., N. Mar. Is. B5 72
Rotan, Tx., U.S. B7 130
Rotenburg, Ger. C5 16
Roth, Ger. G7 16
Rothenburg ob der Tauber, Ger. G6 16
Rothera, sci., Ant. B34 81
Rotherham, Eng., U.K. H11 12
Rothesay, N.B., Can. E11 110
Rothesay, Scot., U.K. F7 12
Rothsay, Mn., U.S. E2 118
Rothwell, N.B., Can. D10 110
Roti, Pulau, i., Indon. H7 44
Roto, Austl. I5 76
Rotondella, Italy D10 24
Rotorua, N.Z. D7 80
Rottenburg, Ger. H4 16
Rottenburg an der Laaber, Ger. H8 16
Rotterdam, Neth. C13 14
Rotterdam, N.Y., U.S. B11 114
Rottweil, Ger. H4 16
Rotuma, i., Fiji E8 72
Roubaix, Fr. D12 14
Roudnice nad Labem, Czech Rep. F9 16
Rouen, Fr. E10 14
Rouge, stm., Qc., Can. E2 110
Rough, stm., Ky., U.S. G11 120
Rough River Lake, res., Ky., U.S. G11 120
Rouleau, Sk., Can. D9 124
Roulers see Roeselare, Bel. D11 14
Roulette, Pa., U.S. C7 114
Round Hill Head, c., Austl. E8 76
Round Lake, Mn., U.S. H3 118
Round Lake, l., On., Can. C12 112
Round Mound, hill, Ks., U.S. C9 128
Round Mountain, Nv., U.S. E8 134
Round Mountain, mtn., Austl. H9 76
Round Rock, Tx., U.S. D10 130
Roundup, Mt., U.S. A4 126
Rousay, i., Scot., U.K. B9 12
Rouses Point, N.Y., U.S. E3 110
Roussillon, hist. reg., Fr. G8 18
Routhierville, Qc., Can. B9 110
Rouyn-Noranda, Qc., Can. F15 106
Rovaniemi, Fin. C11 8
Rovenskaja Slabada, Bela. H13 10
Rovereto, Italy E8 22
Roversi, Arg. C6 92
Rovigo, Italy E8 22
Rovuma (Ruvuma), stm., Afr. C6 68
Rowan Lake, l., On., Can. B5 118
Rowena, Austl. G7 76
Rowland, N.C., U.S. B6 116
Rowley, stm., Nu., Can. A15 106
Rowley Island, i., Nu., Can. B14 106
Roxas, Phil. E4 52
Roxboro, N.C., U.S. H7 114
Roxborough, Trin. r13 105f
Roxburgh, N.Z. G3 80
Roxton, Tx., U.S. D3 122
Roy, N.M., U.S. F4 128
Roy, Ut., U.S. B4 132
Roy, Wa., U.S. C4 136
Royal Bardiyā Wild Life Reserve, India D8 54
Royal Canal, can., Ire. H6 12
Royal Center, In., U.S. H3 112
Royal Chitwan National Park, p.o.i., Nepal E10 54
Royal City, Wa., U.S. D7 136
Royale, Isle, i., Mi., U.S. D10 118
Royal Gorge, val., Co., U.S. C3 128
Royal Leamington Spa, Eng., U.K. I11 12
Royal Natal National Park, p.o.i., S. Afr. F9 70
Royal Oak, Mi., U.S. B2 114
Royalton, Mn., U.S. F4 118
Royal Tunbridge Wells, Eng., U.K. J13 12
Royan, Fr. D5 18
Roye, Fr. E11 14
Royston, Eng., U.K. I12 12
Royston, Ga., U.S. B2 116
Różan, Pol. D17 16
Roždestveno, Russia C20 10
Rozdil'na, Ukr. C17 26
Rozewie, Przylądek, c., Pol. B14 16
Rožňava, Slov. H16 16
Roznov, Rom. C13 26
Rożnów, Pol. G16 16
Roztocze, hills, Eur. F19 16
Roztoky, Czech Rep. F10 16
Rrogozhina see Rrogozhinë, Alb. C13 24
Rrogozhinë, Alb. C13 24
Rtiščevo, Russia D6 32
Ru, stm., China E6 42
Ruacana Falls, wtfl, Afr. D1 68
Ruahine Range, mts., N.Z. D7 80
Ruapehu, Mount, vol., N.Z. D6 80
Ruapuke Island, i., N.Z. H3 80
Rubbestadneset, Nor. G1 8
Rubcovsk, Russia D14 32
Rubi, stm., D.R.C. D5 66
Rubio, Ven. D5 86
Rubondo Island, i., Tan. E6 66
Ruby, Ak., U.S. D8 140
Ruby, stm., Mt., U.S. E14 136
Ruby Dome, mtn., Nv., U.S. C1 132
Ruby Lake, sw., Nv., U.S. C1 132
Ruby Mountains, mts., Nv., U.S. C1 132
Ruby Valley, val., Nv., U.S. C1 132
Rucheng, China I5 42
Ruciane-Nida, Pol. C17 16
Ruda Śląska, Pol. F14 16
Rudauli, India E8 54
Rūdbār, Afg. C9 56
Rüdersdorf, Ger. D9 16
Rudkøbing, Den. B6 16
Rudnaja Pristan', Russia B11 38
Rudnja, Russia F14 10
Rudnyj, Kaz. D10 32
Rudnyj, Russia B11 38
Rūdnyy see Rudnyj, Kaz. D10 32
Rudo, Bos. F6 26
Rudolf, Lake (Turkana, Lake), l., Afr. D7 66
Rudolf Hāyk' see Rudolf, Lake, l., Afr. D7 66
Rudolstadt, Ger. F7 16
Rudong, China E9 42
Rudozem, Blg. H11 26
Rudyard, Mi., U.S. B5 112
Rue, Fr. D10 14
Rufā'ah, Sudan E6 62
Ruffin, S.C., U.S. C5 116
Rufiji, stm., Tan. F7 66
Rufino, Arg. G6 92
Rufisque, Sen. G1 64
Rufunsa, Zam. D4 68
Rufus, Or., U.S. E6 136
Rugāji, Lat. D10 10
Rugao, China E9 42
Rugby, Eng., U.K. I11 12
Rugby, N.D., U.S. F14 124
Rügen, i., Ger. B9 16
Rugged Mountain, mtn., B.C., Can. F4 138
Ruhan', Russia G15 10
Ruhengeri, Rw. E5 66
Ruhpolding, Ger. I8 16
Ruhr, stm., Ger. E3 16
Ruhunu National Park, p.o.i., Sri L. H5 53
Rui'an, China H9 42
Ruidoso, N.M., U.S. H3 128
Ruidoso, stm., N.M., U.S. H3 128
Ruihong, China G7 42
Ruijin, China I6 42
Ruiz, Mex. D6 100
Ruiz, Nevado del, vol., Col. E4 86
Ruiz de Montoya, Arg. C10 92
Ruki, stm., D.R.C. E3 66
Rukwa, Lake, l., Tan. F6 66
Rule, Tx., U.S. A8 130
Ruleville, Ms., U.S. D8 122
Rulo, Ne., U.S. D2 120
Rúm, i., Scot., U.K. D6 12
Rum, stm., Mn., U.S. F5 118
Ruma, Yugo. D6 26
Rumbek, Sudan F5 62
Rum Cay, i., Bah. C10 96
Rumia, Pol. B14 16
Rumigny, Fr. E13 14
Rum Jungle, Austl. B6 74
Rumoi, Japan B14 38
Runan, China E6 42
Runanga, N.Z. F4 80
Runde, stm., Zimb. B10 70
Rundēni, Lat. D10 10
Rundu, Nmb. D2 68
Rŭng, Kaôh, i., Camb. G6 48
Runge, Tx., U.S. F10 130
Rungwa, Tan. F6 66
Rungwa, stm., Tan. F6 66
Running Water Draw, stm., U.S. G6 128
Ruo, stm., China C4 36
Ruoqiang, China D2 36
Ruoxi, China G6 42
Rupat, Pulau, i., Indon. C2 50
Rupert, Id., U.S. H13 136
Rupert, W.V., U.S. G5 114
Rupert, stm., Qc., Can. E15 106
Rupert Creek, stm., Austl. C4 76
Rupununi, stm., Guy. F12 86
Rur, stm., Eur. D15 14
Rural Retreat, Va., U.S. H4 114
Rurrenabaque, Bol. B3 90
Rurutu, i., Fr. Poly. F11 72
Rusape, Zimb. D5 68
Ruṣayriṣ, Khazzān ar-, res., Afr. E6 62
Ruse, Blg. F12 26
Ruse, state, Blg. F13 26
Rusera, India F11 54
Rushan, China C9 42
Rush Center, Ks., U.S. C9 128
Rush City, Mn., U.S. F5 118
Rush Creek, stm., Co., U.S. C5 128
Rushford, Mn., U.S. H7 118
Rushmore, Mn., U.S. H3 118
Rushville, Il., U.S. D7 120
Rushville, In., U.S. E12 120
Rusinga Island, i., Kenya E6 66
Rusizi, stm., Afr. E5 66
Rusk, Tx., U.S. F3 122
Ruskin, Fl., U.S. I3 116
Rusnė, Lith. E4 10
Russas, Braz. C6 88
Russell, Mb., Can. D12 124
Russell, Ia., U.S. D4 120
Russell, Ks., U.S. C10 128
Russell, Ky., U.S. F3 114
Russell, Cape, c., N.T., Can. A16 140
Russell Cave National Monument, p.o.i., Al., U.S. C13 122
Russell Islands, is., Sol. Is. e8 79b
Russellkonda, India I10 54
Russells Point, Oh., U.S. D2 114
Russell Springs, Ky., U.S. G12 120
Russellville, Al., U.S. C11 122
Russellville, Ar., U.S. B5 122
Russellville, Ky., U.S. H11 120
Rüsselsheim, Ger. G4 16
Russia, ctry., Eur. B18 2
Russian, stm., Ca., U.S. E2 134
Russiaville, In., U.S. H3 112
Russkij, Russia C9 38
Rust, Aus. C13 22
Rustavi, Geor. F7 32
Rustburg, Va., U.S. G6 114
Rustenburg, S. Afr. D8 70
Ruston, La., U.S. E6 122
Rutana, Bdi. E6 66
Rute, Spain G6 20
Ruteng, Indon. H12 50
Ruth, Nv., U.S. D1 132
Rutherford, Tn., U.S. H8 120
Rutherfordton, N.C., U.S. A3 116
Ruthin, Wales, U.K. H9 12
Ruthven, Ia., U.S. H4 118
Rutland, B.C., Can. G11 138
Rutland, N.D., U.S. A15 126
Rutland, Vt., U.S. G4 110
Rutledge, Ga., U.S. C2 116
Rutog, China B7 54
Rutshuru, D.R.C. E5 66
Rutter, On., Can. B9 112
Ruvuma (Rovuma), stm., Afr. C6 68
Ruwenzori, mts., Afr. D6 66
Ruwenzori Range see Ruwenzori, mts., Afr. D6 66
Ruy Barbosa, Braz. G5 88
Ruza, Russia E19 10
Ruza, stm., Russia E18 10
Ruzaevka, Russia D7 32
Ružany, Bela. H7 10
Ružomberok, Slov. G15 16
Rwanda, ctry., Afr. E6 66
Ryan, Ok., U.S. G11 128
Ryan Peak, mtn., Id., U.S. G12 136
Rybače, Kaz. E14 32
Rybačij, poluostrov, pen., Russia B15 8
Rybinsk, Russia B21 10
Rybinskoe vodohranilišče (Rybinsk Reservoir), res., Russia B21 10
Rybinsk Reservoir see Rybinskoe vodohranilišče, res., Russia B21 10
Rybnik, Pol. F14 16
Rybnoje, Russia E7 34
Ryde, Eng., U.K. K11 12
Ryderwood, Wa., U.S. D3 136
Rydzyna, Pol. E12 16
Ryegate, Mt., U.S. A3 126
Rye Patch Reservoir, res., Nv., U.S. C7 134
Ryfoss, Nor. F3 8
Ryley, Ab., Can. C18 138
Rylovići, Russia H15 10
Ryl'sk, Russia D4 32
Rýmařov, Czech Rep. G13 16
Ryōhaku-sanchi, mts., Japan C9 40
Ryōtsu, Japan A11 40
Rysy, mtn., Eur. G15 16

Name	Map Ref.	Page
Ryūgasaki, Japan	D13	40
Ryukyu Islands see Nansei-shotō, is., Japan	k19	39a
Ryukyu Trench, unds.	G15	142
Ržanica, Russia	G16	10
Rzeszów, Pol.	F18	16
Rzeszów, state, Pol.	F17	16
Ržev, Russia	D17	10

S

Name	Map Ref.	Page
Sa, Thai.	C5	48
Saale, stm., Ger.	E7	16
Saalfeld, Ger.	F7	16
Saar see Saarland, state, Ger.	G2	16
Saarbrücken, Ger.	G2	16
Saarburg, Ger.	G2	16
Saaremaa, i., Est.	G9	8
Saarijärvi, Fin.	E11	8
Saaristomeren kansallispuisto, p.o.i., Fin.	G9	8
Saarland, state, Ger.	G2	16
Saarlouis, Ger.	G2	16
Saavedra, Arg.	H6	92
Saba, i., Neth. Ant.	B1	105a
Šabac, Yugo.	E6	26
Sabadell, Spain	C13	20
Sabae, Japan	D9	40
Sabah, state, Malay.	H1	52
Sabah, hist. reg., Malay.	D6	44
Sabak, Malay.	K5	48
Sabalana, Kepulauan, is., Indon.	G11	50
Sabana, Archipiélago de, is., Cuba	A7	102
Sabana de la Mar, Dom. Rep.	C13	102
Sabana de Mendoza, Ven.	C6	86
Sabanagrande, Hond.	F4	102
Sabana Grande, P.R.	B2	104a
Sabanalarga, Col.	B4	86
Sabana Llana, P.R.	B3	104a
Sabang, Indon.	J2	48
Sabang, Indon.	C11	50
Sabarei, Kenya	D7	66
Sābari, stm., India	C5	53
Sābarmati, stm., India	G4	54
Sab'atayn, Ramlat as-, sand, Yemen	F6	56
Sabbioneta, Italy	E7	22
Şāberī, Hāmūn-e, l., Asia	C9	56
Sabetha, Ks., U.S.	E2	120
Sabhā, Libya	B2	62
Sabidana, Jabal, mtn., Sudan	D7	62
Sabie, S. Afr.	D10	70
Sabiè, stm., Afr.	D10	70
Sabile, Lat.	C5	10
Sabina, Oh., U.S.	E2	114
Sabina, hist. reg., Italy	H9	22
Sabinal, Tx., U.S.	E8	130
Sabinal, stm., Tx., U.S.	E8	130
Sabinal, Cayo, i., Cuba	B9	102
Sabiñánigo, Spain	B10	20
Sabinas, Mex.	B8	100
Sabinas, stm., Mex.	B8	100
Sabinas, stm., Mex.	B9	100
Sabinas Hidalgo, Mex.	B8	100
Sabine, stm., U.S.	G5	122
Sabine Bay, b., Can.	A17	140
Sabine Lake, l., U.S.	H5	122
Sabine Pass, strt., U.S.	H5	122
Sabinópolis, Braz.	J4	88
Şabiote, Spain	F7	20
Šabla, Blg.	F15	26
Sable, Cape, c., N.S., Can.	G11	110
Sable, Cape, pen., Fl., U.S.	K4	116
Sable Island, i., N.S., Can.	G16	110
Sablūkah, Shallāl as- (Sixth Cataract), wtfl, Sudan	D6	62
Šablykino, Russia	H18	10
Sabor, stm., Port.	C4	20
Sabou, Burkina	G4	64
Sabrina Coast, cst., Ant.	B16	81
Şabyā, Sau. Ar.	F5	56
Sabyin, Mya.	C2	48
Sabzevār, Iran	B8	56
Sac, stm., Mo., U.S.	G4	120
Sacaton, Az., U.S.	J5	132
Sac City, Ia., U.S.	B3	120
Săcele, Rom.	D12	26
Sachayoj, Arg.	C6	92
Sachsen, state, Ger.	F9	16
Sachsen (Saxony), hist. reg., Ger.	D5	16
Sachsen-Anhalt, state, Ger.	D7	16
Sachs Harbour, N.T., Can.	B14	140
Šack, Bela.	G10	10
Sackets Harbor, N.Y., U.S.	E13	112
Sackville, N.B., Can.	E12	110
Saco, Me., U.S.	G6	110
Saco, stm., U.S.	F5	110
Sacramento, Braz.	J2	88
Sacramento, Ca., U.S.	E4	134
Sacramento, stm., Ca., U.S.	E4	134
Sacramento Mountains, mts., N.M., U.S.	E10	98
Sacramento Valley, val., Ca., U.S.	D3	134
Sacramento Wash, stm., Az., U.S.	H2	132
Sacred Heart, Mn., U.S.	G3	118
Sádaba, Spain	B9	20
Şa'dah, Yemen	F5	56
Sadaik Taung, mtn., Mya.	E4	48
Sada-misaki, c., Japan	F4	40
Sada-misaki-hantō, pen., Japan	F5	40
Sadang, stm., Indon.	E11	50
Sa Dao, Thai.	I5	48
Sadda, Pak.	B3	54
Saddle Mountain, mtn., Co., U.S.	C3	128
Saddle Mountain, mtn., Or., U.S.	E3	136
Saddle Peak, mtn., India	F7	46
Sa Dec, Viet.	G7	48
Sādiqābād, Pak.	D3	54
Sadiya, India	C8	46
Sadlers, St. K./N.	C2	105a
Sado, i., Japan	A11	40
Sado, stm., Port.	F2	20
Sado-kaikyō, strt., Japan	B11	40
Sadowara, Japan	G4	40
Şādri, India	F4	54
Šadrinsk, Russia	C10	32
Sädvaluspen, Swe.	C7	8
Saegertown, Pa., U.S.	C5	114
Şaerluojia Hu, l., China	B11	54
Šafárikovo, Slov.	H16	16
Säffle, Swe.	G5	8
Saffron Walden, Eng., U.K.	I13	12
Safi, Mor.	C3	64
Safīd Kūh, Selseleh-ye, mts., Afg.	C9	56
Safonovo, Russia	D22	8
Safonovo, Russia	E16	10
Safranbolu, Tur.	B15	28
Saga, China	D10	54
Saga, Japan	F3	40
Saga, state, Japan	F3	40
Sagae, Japan	A13	40
Sagaing, Mya.	B2	48
Sagaing, state, Mya.	A2	48
Sagamihara, Japan	D12	40
Sagami-nada, b., Japan	D12	40
Saganaga Lake, l., N.A.	C7	118
Saganoseki, Japan	F4	40
Saganthit Kyun, i., Mya.	F4	48
Sāgar, India	D2	53
Sāgar, India	G7	54
Sagara, Japan	E11	40
Sagaranten, Indon.	G5	50
Sagavanirktok, stm., Ak., U.S.	C10	140
Sagay, Phil.	E4	52
Sage, Mount, mtn., Br. Vir. Is.	e8	104b
Sage Creek, stm., Mt., U.S.	B16	136
Sagerton, Tx., U.S.	A8	130
Saginaw, Mi., U.S.	E6	112
Saginaw, stm., Mi., U.S.	E5	112
Saginaw Bay, b., Mi., U.S.	E6	112
Sağkaya, Tur.	A6	58
Sagleipie, Lib.	H3	64
Saglek Bay, b., Nf., Can.	F13	141
Šagonar, Russia	D16	32
Şagu, Rom.	C8	26
Saguache, Co., U.S.	C2	128
Saguache Creek, stm., Co., U.S.	C2	128
Sagua de Tánamo, Cuba	B10	102
Sagua la Grande, Cuba	A7	102
Saguaro National Park, p.o.i., Az., U.S.	K5	132
Saguenay, stm., Qc., Can.	B7	110
Sagunt, Spain	E10	20
Sagunto see Sagunt, Spain	E10	20
Sāgwāra, India	G4	54
Sa'gya, China	D12	54
Sahagún, Col.	C4	86
Sahagún, Spain	B5	20
Sahalin, ostrov, i., Russia	F17	34
Sahalinskij zaliv, b., Russia	F17	34
Sahara, des., Afr.	E5	64
Sahāranpur, India	C6	54
Saharsa, India	F11	54
Sahel see Sudan, reg., Afr.	E4	62
Sāhibganj, India	F11	54
Sāhīwāl, Pak.	C4	54
Sāhīwāl, Pak.	C4	54
Şahovskaja, Russia	D18	10
Şahrisabz, Uzb.	G11	32
Şahtinsk, Kaz.	E12	32
Şahtjorsk, Russia	G17	34
Šahty, Russia	E6	32
Sahuaripa, Mex.	A4	100
Sahuarita, Az., U.S.	L5	132
Sahuayo de José María Morelos, Mex.	E7	100
Şahunja, Russia	H22	8
Šahy, Slov.	H14	16
Sai Buri, Thai.	I5	48
Sai Buri, stm., Thai.	I5	48
Saidor, Pap. N. Gui.	b4	79a
Saidpur, Bngl.	F12	54
Saidu, Pak.	C11	56
Saigō, Japan	C6	40
Saigon see Thanh Pho Ho Chi Minh, Viet.	G8	48
Saijō, Japan	F6	40
Şaiki, Japan	G4	40
Šaim, Russia	B10	32
Saimaa, l., Fin.	F13	8
Sainte Agathe, Mb., Can.	E16	124
Sainte-Agathe-des-Monts, Qc., Can.	D2	110
Saint-Agrève, Fr.	D10	18
Saint Alban's, Nf., Can.	j22	107a
Saint Albans, Eng., U.K.	J12	12
Saint Albans, Vt., U.S.	F3	110
Saint Albans, W.V., U.S.	F4	114
Saint Albert, Ab., Can.	C17	138
Saint Aldhelm's Head, c., Eng., U.K.	K10	12
Saint-Alexis-des-Monts, Qc., Can.	D3	110
Saint-Amand-Mont-Rond, Fr.	H11	14
Saint-André-Avellin, Qc., Can.	E1	110
Saint Andrew, Barb.	n8	105d
Saint Andrew, Mount, mtn., St. Vin.	o11	105e
Saint Andrews, N.B., Can.	E9	110
Saint Andrews, Scot., U.K.	E10	12
Saint Andrews, S.C., U.S.	D5	116
Sainte-Anne, Guad.	h6	105c
Sainte-Anne, Mart.	I7	105c
Sainte Anne, Lac, l., Ab., Can.	C16	138
Sainte-Anne-de-Beaupré, Qc., Can.	C5	110
Sainte-Anne-de-Madawaska, N.B., Can.	C8	110
Sainte-Anne-des-Monts, Qc., Can.	A10	110
Sainte-Anne-du-Lac, Qc., Can.	D1	110
Saint Ann's Bay, Jam.	i13	104d
Saint-Anselme, Qc., Can.	D6	110
Saint Ansgar, Ia., U.S.	H5	118
Saint Anthony, Nf., Can.	i22	107a
Saint Anthony, Id., U.S.	G15	136
Saint Arnaud, Austl.	K4	76
Saint Augustin, Qc., Can.	i22	107a
Saint Augustine, Fl., U.S.	G4	116
Saint Austell, Eng., U.K.	K8	12
Saint-Avold, Fr.	E15	14
Saint-Barthélemy, i., Guad.	B2	105a
Saint-Basile, N.B., Can.	C8	110
Saint Bathans, Mount, mtn., N.Z.	G3	80
Saint Bees Head, c., Eng., U.K.	G9	12
Saint-Boniface-de-Shawinigan, Qc., Can.	D3	110
Saint-Bonnet, Fr.	E11	18
Saint Brides Bay, b., Wales, U.K.	J7	12
Saint-Brieuc, Fr.	F6	14
Saint-Brieuc, Baie de, b., Fr.	F6	14
Saint Catharines, On., Can.	E10	112
Saint Catherine, Mount, vol., Gren.	q10	105e
Saint Catherines Island, i., Ga., U.S.	E4	116
Saint Catherine's Point, c., Eng., U.K.	K11	12
Saint-Céré, Fr.	E7	18
Saint-Chamond, Fr.	D10	18
Saint Charles, Id., U.S.	A5	132
Saint Charles, Il., U.S.	C9	120
Saint Charles, Mi., U.S.	E5	112
Saint Charles, Mn., U.S.	H6	118
Saint Charles, Mo., U.S.	F7	120
Saint Charles Mesa, Co., U.S.	C4	128
Saint Christopher (Saint Kitts), i., St. K./N.	C2	105a
Saint Christopher and Nevis see Saint Kitts and Nevis, ctry., N.A.	C2	105a
Saint Clair, Mi., U.S.	B3	114
Saint Clair, Mo., U.S.	F6	120
Saint Clair, stm., N.A.	B3	114
Saint Clair, Lake, l., N.A.	B3	114
Saint Clair Shores, Mi., U.S.	B3	114
Saint-Claud, Fr.	D6	18
Saint Claude, Mb., Can.	E15	124
Saint-Claude, Fr.	C11	18
Saint-Claude, Guad.	h5	105c
Saint Cloud, Fl., U.S.	H4	116
Saint Cloud, Mn., U.S.	F4	118
Sainte-Croix, Qc., Can.	D5	110
Saint Croix, i., V.I.U.S.	g10	104c
Saint Croix, stm., N.A.	E9	110
Saint Croix, stm., U.S.	G6	118
Saint Croix Falls, Wi., U.S.	F6	118
Saint Croix Island National Monument, p.o.i., Me., U.S.	E10	110
Saint-Cyr, stm., Qc., Can.	A1	110
Saint David, Az., U.S.	L6	132
Saint David's, Wales, U.K.	J7	12
Saint David's Head, c., Wales, U.K.	J7	12
Saint David's Island, i., Ber.	k16	104e
Saint-Denis, Fr.	E11	14
Saint-Denis, Reu.	i10	69a
Saint-Dié, Fr.	F15	14
Saint-Dizier, Fr.	F13	14
Saint-Donat-de-Montcalm, Qc., Can.	D2	110
Saint Edward, Ne., U.S.	F15	126
Saint Elias, Cape, c., Ak., U.S.	E11	140
Saint Elias, Mount, mtn., N.A.	C2	106
Saint Elias Mountains, mts., N.A.	D12	140
Saint-Élie, Fr. Gu.	C7	84
Saint Elmo, Il., U.S.	E9	120
Saint-Étienne, Fr.	D10	18
Saint-Étienne-du-Rouvray, Fr.	E10	14
Saint-Eugène, Qc., Can.	B4	110
Saint-Eustache, Qc., Can.	E2	110
Saint-Fabien, Qc., Can.	B8	110
Saint-Félicien, Qc., Can.	B4	110
Saint-Félix-de-Valois, Qc., Can.	D3	110
Saint-Florent-sur-Cher, Fr.	G11	14
Saint-Flour, Fr.	D9	18
Sainte-Foy, Qc., Can.	D5	110
Sainte-Foy-la-Grande, Fr.	E6	18
Saint Francis, Ks., U.S.	B7	128
Saint Francis, Wi., U.S.	I11	118
Saint Francis, stm., N.A.	C7	110
Saint Francis, stm., U.S.	C8	122
Saint Francis, Cape, c., S. Afr.	I7	70
Saint Francis Bay, b., S. Afr.	I7	70
Saint Francisville, Il., U.S.	F10	120
Saint Francisville, La., U.S.	G7	122
Saint-François, Guad.	h6	105c
Saint-François, stm., Qc., Can.	D4	110
Saint-François, Lac, l., Can.	E2	110
Saint-François, Lac, res., Qc., Can.	E5	110
Saint-Gabriel, Can.	B8	110
Saint-Gabriel-de-Gaspé, Qc., Can.	B12	110
Saint-Gall see Sankt Gallen, Switz.	C6	22
Saint-Gaudens, Fr.	F6	18
Sainte Genevieve, Mo., U.S.	G7	120
Saint George, Austl.	G7	76
Saint George, Ber.	k16	104e
Saint George, N.B., Can.	E10	110
Saint George, On., Can.	E9	112
Saint George, Ut., U.S.	F3	132
Saint George, Cape, c., Fl., U.S.	H13	122
Saint George, Point, c., Ca., U.S.	B1	134
Saint George Island, i., Fl., U.S.	H14	122
Saint-Georges, Qc., Can.	D4	110
Saint-Georges, Qc., Can.	D6	110
Saint-Georges, Fr. Gu.	C7	84
Saint George's, Gren.	q10	105e
Saint George's Bay, b., Nf., Can.	j22	107a
Saint Georges Bay, b., N.S., Can.	E15	110
Saint George's Channel, strt., Eur.	J7	12
Saint George's Channel, strt., Pap. N. Gui.	a5	79a
Saint-Gilles-Croix-de-Vie, Fr.	H6	14
Saint Gotthard Pass see San Gottardo, Passo del, p., Switz.	D5	22
Saint Helena, Ca., U.S.	E3	134
Saint Helena, dep., Afr.	H5	60
Saint Helena Bay see Sint Helenabaai, b., S. Afr.	H3	70
Saint Helens, Eng., U.K.	H10	12
Saint Helens, Or., U.S.	E4	136
Saint Helens, Mount, vol., Wa., U.S.	D4	136
Saint Helier, Jersey	E6	14
Saint-Hilaire-du-Harcouët, Fr.	F7	14
Saint-Hyacinthe, Qc., Can.	E4	110
Saint Ignace Island, i., On., Can.	C11	118
Saint Ignatius, Guy.	F12	86
Saint Ignatius, Mt., U.S.	C12	136
Saint-Isidore, N.B., Can.	C11	110
Saint Ives, Eng., U.K.	K7	12
Saint James, Mi., U.S.	C4	112
Saint James, Mn., U.S.	G4	118
Saint James, Mo., U.S.	G6	120
Saint James, Cape, c., B.C., Can.	E4	106
Saint James Islands, is., V.I.U.S.	e7	104b
Saint-Jean, Guad.	B2	105a
Saint-Jean, Lac, res., Qc., Can.	B4	110
Saint Jean Baptiste, Mb., Can.	E16	124
Saint-Jean-d'Angély, Fr.	C5	18
Saint-Jean-de-Luz, Fr.	F4	18
Saint-Jean-de-Maurienne, Fr.	D12	18
Saint-Jean-du-Gard, Fr.	E9	18
Saint-Jean-Port-Joli, Qc., Can.	C6	110
Saint-Jean-sur-Richelieu, Qc., Can.	E3	110
Saint-Jérôme, Qc., Can.	E3	110
Saint Jo, Tx., U.S.	H11	128
Saint Joe, stm., Id., U.S.	C11	136
Saint John, N.B., Can.	E10	110
Saint John, N.D., U.S.	F14	124
Saint John, Wa., U.S.	C9	136
Saint John, i., V.I.U.S.	e8	104b
Saint John, stm., N.A.	E10	110
Saint John, Cape, c., Nf., Can.	E19	106
Saint John's, Antig.	f4	105b
Saint John's, Nf., Can.	j23	107a
Saint Johns, Az., U.S.	I7	132
Saint Johns, Mi., U.S.	E5	112
Saint Johns, stm., Fl., U.S.	G4	116
Saint Johnsbury, Vt., U.S.	F4	110
Saint Joseph, Dom.	j6	105c
Saint Joseph, Il., U.S.	D9	120
Saint Joseph, Mi., U.S.	F3	112
Saint Joseph, Mn., U.S.	F4	118
Saint Joseph, Mo., U.S.	E3	120
Saint Joseph, stm., U.S.	G3	112
Saint Joseph, stm., U.S.	G5	112
Saint Joseph, Lake, l., On., Can.	E12	106
Saint-Joseph-de-Beauce, Qc., Can.	D6	110
Saint Joseph Island, i., On., Can.	B6	112
Saint-Jovite, Qc., Can.	D2	110
Saint-Julien-en-Born, Fr.	E4	18
Sainte-Julienne, Qc., Can.	E3	110
Saint-Junien, Fr.	D6	18
Saint Just, P.R.	B4	104a
Saint Kilda, i., Scot., U.K.	D4	12
Saint Kitts see Saint Christopher, i., St. K./N.	C2	105a
Saint Kitts and Nevis, ctry., N.A.	C2	105a
Saint-Lambert, Qc., Can.	E3	110
Saint Landry, La., U.S.	G6	122
Saint Laurent, Mb., Can.	D16	124
Saint-Laurent (Saint Lawrence), stm., N.A.	B8	110
Saint-Laurent du Maroni, Fr. Gu.	B7	84
Saint Lawrence, Austl.	D7	76
Saint Lawrence (Saint-Laurent), stm., N.A.	B8	110
Saint Lawrence, Gulf of, b., Can.	F18	106
Saint Lawrence Island, i., Ak., U.S.	D5	140
Saint-Léandre, Qc., Can.	B9	110
Saint-Léonard, N.B., Can.	C9	110
Saint-Lô, Fr.	E7	14
Saint Louis, Sk., Can.	B8	124
Saint-Louis, Guad.	i6	105c
Saint-Louis, Sen.	F1	64
Saint Louis, Mi., U.S.	E5	112
Saint Louis, Mo., U.S.	F7	120
Saint Louis, stm., U.S.	E6	118
Saint-Louis, Lac, l., Qc., Can.	E3	110
Saint-Louis de Kent, N.B., Can.	D12	110
Saint Louis Park, Mn., U.S.	G5	118
Saint-Loup-sur-Semouse, Fr.	G14	14
Sainte-Luce, Mart.	I7	105c
Saint Lucia, ctry., N.A.	m6	105c
Saint Lucia, Cape, c., S. Afr.	F11	70
Saint Lucia, Lake, l., S. Afr.	E11	70
Saint Lucia Channel, strt., N.A.	I6	105c
Saint Lucia Game Reserve, S. Afr.	F11	70
Saint Lucie Canal, can., Fl., U.S.	J5	116
Saint Magnus Bay, b., Scot., U.K.	n18	12a
Saint-Malo, Fr.	F7	14
Saint-Malo, Golfe de, b., Fr.	F6	14
Saint-Marc, Haiti	C11	102
Saint-Marc, Canal de, strt., Haiti	C11	102
Saint-Marc-des-Carrières, Qc., Can.	D4	110
Sainte-Marie, Mart.	k7	105c
Sainte Marie, Nosy, i., Madag.	D9	68
Saint Maries, Id., U.S.	C10	136
Saint Marks, stm., Fl., U.S.	F1	116
Saint-Martin (Sint Maarten), i., N.A.	A1	105a
Saint-Martin, Cap, c., Mart.	k6	105c
Saint Martin, Lake, l., Mb., Can.	C15	124
Saint Martins, N.B., Can.	E11	110
Saint Martinville, La., U.S.	G7	122
Saint Mary, Mo., U.S.	G8	120
Saint Mary, stm., N.A.	G18	138
Saint Mary Peak, mtn., Austl.	H2	76
Saint Mary Reservoir, res., Ab., Can.	G17	138
Saint Marys, Austl.	n14	77a
Saint Marys, Ak., U.S.	D7	140
Saint Marys, Ga., U.S.	F4	116
Saint Marys, Ks., U.S.	E1	120
Saint Marys, Pa., U.S.	C7	114
Saint Marys, W.V., U.S.	E4	114
Saint Mary's, i., Eng., U.K.	L6	12
Saint Marys, stm., U.S.	H5	112
Saint Marys, stm., U.S.	F4	116
Saint Mary's Bay, b., Nf., Can.	j23	107a
Saint Marys Bay, b., N.S., Can.	F10	110
Saint Marys City, Md., U.S.	F9	114
Saint-Mathieu, Fr.	D6	18
Saint Matthew Island, i., Ak., U.S.	D5	140
Saint Matthews, Ky., U.S.	F12	120
Saint-Maurice, stm., Qc., Can.	D4	110
Sainte-Maxime, Fr.	F12	18
Saint Meinrad, In., U.S.	F11	120
Saint Michael, Ak., U.S.	D7	140
Saint Michaels, Md., U.S.	F9	114
Saint-Michel-des-Saints, Qc., Can.	D2	110
Saint-Mihiel, Fr.	F14	14
Saint Moritz see Sankt Moritz, Switz.	D6	22
Saint-Nazaire, Fr.	G6	14
Saint-Nicolas see Sint-Niklaas, Bel.	C12	14
Saint-Omer, Fr.	D11	14
Saintonge, hist. reg., Fr.	D5	18
Saint-Pacôme, Qc., Can.	C7	110
Saint-Pamphile, Qc., Can.	D7	110
Saint Paris, Oh., U.S.	D2	114
Saint-Patrice, Lac, l., Qc., Can.	B12	112
Saint Paul, Ab., Can.	B19	138
Saint-Paul, Reu.	i10	69a
Saint Paul, In., U.S.	E12	120
Saint Paul, Ks., U.S.	G2	120
Saint Paul, Mn., U.S.	G5	118
Saint Paul, Va., U.S.	H3	114
Saint Paul, stm., Lib.	H2	64
Saint-Paul, Île, i., Afr.	M10	142
Saint Paul Island, i., Ak., U.S.	E6	140
Saint Paul's, St. K./N.	C2	105a
Saint Pauls, N.C., U.S.	B7	116
Saint Paul's Point, c., Pit.	c28	78k
Saint Peter, Mn., U.S.	G4	118
Saint Peter Port, Guern.	E6	14
Saint Peters, N.S., Can.	E16	110
Saint Peters Bay, P.E., Can.	D14	110
Saint Petersburg see Sankt-Peterburg, Russia	A13	10
Saint Petersburg, Fl., U.S.	I3	116
Saint-Pierre, Mart.	k6	105c
Saint-Pierre, Reu.	i10	69a
Saint-Pierre, St. P./M.	j22	107a
Saint Pierre, i., Sey.	k12	69b
Saint-Pierre, Lac, l., Qc., Can.	D3	110
Saint Pierre and Miquelon, dep., N.A.	j22	107a
Saint Pierre-Jolys, Mb., Can.	E16	124
Saint-Pierre-sur-Dives, Fr.	E8	14
Saint-Pol-sur-Ternoise, Fr.	D11	14
Saint-Pons-de-Thomères, Fr.	F8	18
Saint-Prime, Qc., Can.	B4	110
Saint-Prosper-de-Dorchester, Qc., Can.	D6	110
Saint-Quentin, N.B., Can.	C9	110
Saint-Quentin, Fr.	E12	14
Saint-Raphaël, Fr.	F12	18
Saint-Raymond, Qc., Can.	D5	110
Saint Regis Falls, N.Y., U.S.	F2	110
Saint-Rémy-de-Provence, Fr.	F10	18
Saint Robert, Mo., U.S.	G5	120
Saint-Roch-de-Mékinac, Qc., Can.	D3	110
Saint-Romuald, Qc., Can.	D5	110
Sainte-Rose-du-dégelis see Dégelis, Can.	C8	110
Sainte Rose du Lac, Mb., Can.	C14	124
Saintes, Fr.	D5	18
Saint-Savin, Fr.	H9	14
Saint-Siméon, Qc., Can.	C6	110
Saint Simons Island, Ga., U.S.	E4	116
Saint Simons Island, i., Ga., U.S.	E4	116
Saintes-Maries-de-la-Mer, Fr.	F10	18
Saint Stephen, S.C., U.S.	C6	116
Sainte-Thérèse-de-Blainville, Qc., Can.	E3	110
Saint Thomas, On., Can.	F8	112
Saint Thomas, N.D., U.S.	F16	124
Saint Thomas, i., V.I.U.S.	e7	104b
Saint-Tite, Qc., Can.	D4	110
Saint-Trond see Sint-Truiden, Bel.	D14	14
Saint-Tropez, Fr.	F12	18
Saint-Ubalde, Qc., Can.	D4	110
Saint-Urbain-de-Charlevoix, Qc., Can.	C6	110
Saint-Valéry-en-Caux, Fr.	E9	14
Saint-Vallier, Fr.	D10	18
Sainte-Véronique, Qc., Can.	D2	110
Saint Vincent, Mn., U.S.	C1	118
Saint Vincent, i., St. Vin.	o11	105e
Saint-Vincent, Baie de, b., N. Cal.	n15	79d
Saint Vincent, Gulf, b., Austl.	J2	76
Saint Vincent and the Grenadines, ctry., N.A.	p10	105e
Saint Vincent Passage, strt., N.A.	m7	105c
Saint-Vith, Bel.	D14	14
Saint Walburg, Sk., Can.	E9	106
Saint-Yrieix-la-Perche, Fr.	D7	18
Saint-Yvon, Qc., Can.	A12	110
Saipan, i., N. Mar. Is.	B5	72
Saiqi, China	H8	42
Saitama, state, Japan	C12	40
Saito, Japan	G4	40
Sai Yok National Park, p.o.i., Thai.	E4	48
Sajama, Nevado, mtn., Bol.	C3	90
Sajanogorsk, Russia	D16	32
Şajat, Turkmen.	B9	56
Šajman, Taj.	B11	56
Sajószentpéter, Hung.	A7	26
Sak, stm., S. Afr.	G5	70
Sa Kaeo, Thai.	F6	48
Sakai, Japan	E8	40
Sakaide, Japan	E6	40
Sakaiminato, Japan	D6	40
Sakakawea, Lake, res., N.D., U.S.	G12	124
Sakala, Pulau, i., Indon.	G10	50
Sakami, stm., Qc., Can.	E15	106
Sakami, Lac, l., Qc., Can.	E15	106
Sakania, D.R.C.	G5	66
Sakaraha, Madag.	E7	68
Sakarya, Tur.	C13	28
Sakarya, state, Tur.	C13	28
Sakarya (Sangarius), stm., Tur.	B13	28
Sakata, Japan	A12	40
Sakawa, Japan	F6	40
Sakchu-ŭp, Kor., N.	D6	38
Sakété, Benin	H5	64
Sakhalin see Sahalin, ostrov, i., Russia	F17	34
Sakhnin, Isr.	F6	58
Şakht Sar, Iran	B7	56
Šakiai, Lith.	E6	10
Sakiet Sidi Youssef, Tun.	H2	24
Sakishima-shotō, is., Japan	G9	36
Sakon Nakhon, Thai.	D6	48
Sakrand, Pak.	E2	54
Saks, Al., U.S.	D13	122
Sakti, India	H9	54
Saku, Japan	C11	40
Sakuma, Japan	D10	40
Sakurai, Japan	E8	40
Sal, i., C.V.	k10	65a
Šal'a, Slov.	H13	16
Sala, Swe.	F7	8
Salaberry-de-Valleyfield, Qc., Can.	E2	110
Salacgrīva, Lat.	C7	10
Sala Consilina, Italy	D9	24
Salada, Laguna, l., Mex.	F5	98
Saladas, Arg.	D8	92
Saladillo, Arg.	G8	92
Saladillo, stm., Arg.	D6	92
Saladillo Dulce, Arroyo, stm., Arg.	E7	92
Salado, stm., Arg.	D4	92
Salado, stm., Arg.	E7	92
Salado, stm., Arg.	I5	92
Salado, stm., Arg.	G9	92
Salado, stm., Cuba	B9	102
Salado, stm., Mex.	B9	100
Salado, stm., N.M., U.S.	I9	132
Salaga, Ghana	H4	64
Salairskij krjaž, mts., Russia	D14	32
Şălaj, state, Rom.	B10	26
Šalakuša, Russia	E19	8
Salal, Chad	E3	62
Şalālah, Oman	F7	56
Salālah, Sudan	C7	62
Salamanca, Chile	E2	92
Salamanca, Mex.	E8	100
Salamanca, Spain	D5	20
Salamanca, N.Y., U.S.	F11	112
Salamanca, co., Spain	D4	20
Salamanga, Moz.	E11	70
Salamat, Bahr, stm., Chad	F3	62
Salamina, Col.	E4	86
Salamína, Grc.	F6	28
Salamína, i., Grc.	F6	28
Salamis, hist., N. Cyp.	C4	58
Salamīyah, Syria	C8	58
Salamonie, stm., In., U.S.	H4	112
Salantai, Lith.	D4	10
Salaquí, Col.	D3	86
Salaquí, stm., Col.	D3	86
Salas, Peru	E2	84
Salas de los Infantes, Spain	B7	20
Salatiga, Indon.	G7	50
Salavat, Russia	D9	32
Salaverry, Peru	E2	84
Salawati, i., Indon.	F9	44
Salāya, India	G2	54
Sala y Gómez, Isla, i., Chile	L28	142
Sala y Gomez Ridge, unds.	L29	142
Şalbani, India	G11	54
Šalčininkai, Lith.	F8	10
Salcombe, Eng., U.K.	K9	12
Saldaña, Spain	B6	20
Saldaña, stm., Col.	F4	86
Saldanha, S. Afr.	H3	70
Saldungaray, Arg.	I7	92
Saldus, Lat.	D5	10
Sale, Austl.	L6	76
Salé, Mor.	C3	64
Sale Creek, Tn., U.S.	B13	122
Saleh, Teluk, b., Indon.	H10	50
Salehard, Russia	A11	32
Salem, India	F4	53
Salem, Monts.	D3	105a
Salem, Ar., U.S.	H6	120
Salem, Il., U.S.	F9	120
Salem, Ia., U.S.	D6	120
Salem, Ma., U.S.	B15	114
Salem, Mo., U.S.	G6	120
Salem, N.H., U.S.	B14	114
Salem, N.J., U.S.	E10	114
Salem, N.Y., U.S.	G3	110
Salem, Oh., U.S.	D5	114
Salem, Or., U.S.	F3	136
Salem, S.D., U.S.	D15	126
Salem, Va., U.S.	G5	114
Salem, W.V., U.S.	E5	114
Salemi, Italy	G6	24
Salem Upland, plat., Mo., U.S.	G6	120
Salentina, Penisola, pen., Italy	D12	24
Salerno, Italy	D8	24
Salerno, Golfo di, b., Italy	D8	24
Salers, Fr.	D8	18
Salgar, Col.	D4	86
Salgótarján, Hung.	A6	26
Salgueiro, Braz.	E6	88
Salher, mtn., India	H4	54
Sali, Cro.	G12	22
Salida, Co., U.S.	C3	128
Salihli, Tur.	E11	28
Salihorsk, Bela.	H10	10
Salima, Mwi.	C5	68
Salimbatu, Indon.	B10	50
Salin, Mya.	B2	48
Salina, Ks., U.S.	C11	128
Salina, Ut., U.S.	E5	132
Salina Cruz, Mex.	G11	100
Salina Point, c., Bah.	A10	102
Salinas, Braz.	I4	88
Salinas, Ec.	I1	86
Salinas, Mex.	G5	130
Salinas, P.R.	C3	104a
Salinas, Ca., U.S.	G4	134
Salinas, stm., Braz.	I4	88
Salinas, stm., N.A.	D2	102
Salinas, stm., Ca., U.S.	G4	134
Salinas, Pampa de las, pl., Arg.	E4	92
Salinas de Hidalgo, Mex.	D8	100
Salinas Pueblo Missions National Monument, p.o.i., N.M., U.S.	G2	128
Salinas Victoria, Mex.	I7	130
Saline, Mi., U.S.	B2	114
Saline, stm., Ar., U.S.	D6	122
Saline, stm., Ar., U.S.	C4	122
Saline, stm., Ks., U.S.	C11	128
Saline Bayou, stm., La., U.S.	E6	122
Saline Lake, l., La., U.S.	F6	122
Salines, Cap de ses, c., Spain	E14	20
Salines, Point, c., Gren.	r10	105e
Salines, Pointe des, c., Mart.	I7	105c
Salinópolis, Braz.	D8	84
Salipolo, Indon.	E11	50
Salisbury, Austl.	J2	76
Salisbury, Eng., U.K.	J11	12
Salisbury, Md., U.S.	F10	114
Salisbury, Mo., U.S.	E5	120
Salisbury, N.C., U.S.	I5	114
Salisbury, Pa., U.S.	E6	114
Salisbury see Harare, Zimb.	D5	68
Salisbury Island, i., Nu., Can.	C15	106
Salisbury Plain, pl., Eng., U.K.	J11	12
Salish Mountains, mts., Mt., U.S.	B12	136
Salitpa, Al., U.S.	F10	122
Salitre, stm., Braz.	E5	88
Şalkhad, Syria	F7	58
Salles-Curan, Fr.	E8	18
Sallisaw, Ok., U.S.	B4	122
Salluit, Qc., Can.	C15	106
Salmi, Russia	F14	8
Salmo, B.C., Can.	G13	138
Salmon, stm., B.C., Can.	B8	138
Salmon, stm., N.B., Can.	D11	110
Salmon, stm., Id., U.S.	E10	136
Salmon, Middle Fork, stm., Id., U.S.	E12	136
Salmon, South Fork, stm., Id., U.S.	E11	136
Salmon Arm, B.C., Can.	F11	138
Salmon Falls Creek, stm., U.S.	H12	136
Salmon Gums, Austl.	F4	74
Salmon Peak, mtn., Tx., U.S.	E7	130
Salmon River Mountains, mts., Id., U.S.	F12	136
Salmon Valley, B.C., Can.	B8	138
Salo, Fin.	F10	8
Salò, Italy	E7	22
Salome, Az., U.S.	J3	132
Salomon, Cap, c., Mart.	I6	105c
Salon-de-Provence, Fr.	F11	18
Salonga, Parc National de la, p.o.i., D.R.C.	E4	66
Salonika see Thessaloníki, Grc.	C6	28
Salonika, Gulf of see Thermaïkós Kólpos, b., Grc.	C6	28
Salonta, Rom.	C8	26
Salor, stm., Spain	E4	20
Salpaussel'kja, mts., Eur.	B3	32
Sal Rei, C.V.	k10	65a
Salsacate, Arg.	E5	92
Salsipuedes, Canal, strt., Mex.	A2	100
Sal'sk, Russia	E6	32
Salsomaggiore Terme, Italy	F6	22
Salt, stm., Az., U.S.	J4	132
Salt, stm., Mo., U.S.	E6	120
Salt, Middle Fork, stm., Mo., U.S.	E5	120
Salt, North Fork, stm., Mo., U.S.	E5	120
Salta, Arg.	B5	92
Salta, state, Arg.	D4	90
Saltanovka, Russia	H17	10
Saltash, Eng., U.K.	K8	12
Salt Basin, l., Tx., U.S.	C2	130
Salt Cay, i., Bah.	m18	104f
Saltcoats, Sk., Can.	C11	124
Salt Creek, stm., Il., U.S.	D8	120
Saltee Islands, is., Ire.	I6	12
Saltfjellet Svartisen Nasjonalpark, p.o.i., Nor.	C6	8
Saltillo, Mex.	C8	100
Saltillo, Tn., U.S.	B10	122
Salt Lake City, Ut., U.S.	C4	132
Salto, Arg.	G7	92
Salto, Ur.	E9	92
Salto del Guairá, Para.	A10	92
Salto Grande, Embalse, res., S.A.	E8	92
Salton City, Ca., U.S.	J9	134
Salton Sea, l., Ca., U.S.	J10	134
Salto Santiago, Represa de, res., Braz.	B11	92
Saltspring Island, i., B.C., Can.	H7	138
Saltville, Va., U.S.	H4	114
Saluda, Va., U.S.	G9	114
Saluda, stm., S.C., U.S.	B4	116
Salûm, Egypt	A5	62
Sālūmbar, India	F5	54
Sālūr, India	B6	53
Saluzzo, Italy	F4	22
Salvador, Braz.	G6	88
Salvador, El see El Salvador, ctry., N.A.	F3	102
Salvador, Lake, l., La., U.S.	H8	122
Salvatierra, Mex.	E8	100
Salviac, Fr.	E7	18
Salween (Nu) (Khong) (Thanlwin), stm., Asia	E8	46
Salyan, Azer.	B6	56
Salyān, Nepal	D9	54
Salyer, Ca., U.S.	C2	134
Salyersville, Ky., U.S.	G2	114
Salzach, stm., Eur.	B9	22
Salzburg, Aus.	C10	22
Salzburg, state, Aus.	C10	22
Salzgitter, Ger.	D6	16
Salzkammergut, reg., Aus.	C10	22
Salzwedel, Ger.	D7	16
Samacá, Col.	E5	86
Samacèvičy, Bela.	G14	10
Samagaltaj, Russia	D16	32
Samah, Libya	B3	62
Samales Group, is., Phil.	G3	52
Samalga Pass, strt., Ak., U.S.	g25	140a
Samal Island, i., Phil.	G5	52
Sāmalkot, India	C6	53
Samâlût, Egypt	J1	58
Samaná, Dom. Rep.	C13	102
Samāna, India	C5	54

Name	Map Ref.	Page
Samaná, Bahía de, b., Dom. Rep.	C13	102
Samaná, Cabo, c., Dom. Rep.	C13	102
Samana Cay, i., Bah.	A11	102
Samandağı, Tur.	B6	58
Samaniego, Col.	G3	86
Samaqua, stm., Qc., Can.	A4	110
Samar, i., Phil.	E5	52
Samara, Russia	D8	32
Samara, stm., Russia	D8	32
Samarai, Pap. N. Gui.	c5	79a
Samaria, Id., U.S.	A4	132
Samaria Gorge see Samariás, Farángi, val., Grc.	H6	28
Samariapo, Ven.	E8	86
Samariás, Farángi (Samaria Gorge), val., Grc.	H6	28
Samarinda, Indon.	D10	50
Samarka, Russia	B10	38
Samarkand, Uzb.	G11	32
Sāmarrā', Iraq	C5	56
Samastīpur, India	F10	54
Samaúna, Braz.	E5	84
Samba Caju, Ang.	B2	68
Sambaíba, Braz.	D3	88
Sambalpur, India	H9	54
Sambar, Tanjung, c., Indon.	E7	50
Sambas, Indon.	C6	50
Sambava, Madag.	C9	68
Şambayat, Tur.	A9	58
Sambhal, India	D7	54
Sāmbhar, India	E5	54
Sāmbhar Lake, l., India	E5	54
Sambir, Ukr.	G19	16
Sambit, Pulau, i., Indon.	C11	50
Sambito, stm., Braz.	D5	88
Samboja, Indon.	D10	50
Sâmbor, Camb.	F7	48
Samborombón, stm., Arg.	G9	92
Samborombón, Bahía, b., Arg.	G9	92
Sambre, stm., Eur.	D12	14
Sambre à l'Oise, Canal de la, can., Fr.	E12	14
Sambriāl, Pak.	B5	54
Samch'ŏk, Kor., S.	B2	40
Sam Chom, Khao, mtn., Thai.	H4	48
Same, Tan.	E7	66
Sam Ford Fiord, b., Nu., Can.	A16	106
Samfya, Zam.	C4	68
Samka, Mya.	B3	48
Samnangjin, Kor., S.	D1	40
Sam Ngao, Thai.	D4	48
Samoa, ctry., Oc.	g12	79c
Samoa Islands, is., Oc.	h12	79c
Samo Alto, Chile	E2	92
Samobor, Cro.	E12	22
Samoded, Russia	E19	8
Samokov, Blg.	G10	26
Sámos, i., Grc.	F9	28
Samoset, Fl., U.S.	I3	116
Samosir, Pulau, i., Indon.	B1	50
Samothrace see Samothráki, i., Grc.	C8	28
Samothráki, Grc.	C8	28
Samothráki (Samothrace), i., Grc.	C8	28
Sampacho, Arg.	F5	92
Sampanahan, Indon.	E10	50
Sampang, Indon.	G8	50
Sampit, Indon.	E8	50
Sampit, stm., Indon.	E8	50
Sampit, Teluk, b., Indon.	E8	50
Sampwe, D.R.C.	F5	66
Sam Rayburn Reservoir, res., Tx., U.S.	F4	122
Samro, ozero, l., Russia	B11	10
Sam Son, Viet.	C7	48
Samsun, Tur.	A4	56
Samsu-ŭp, Kor., N.	D7	38
Samtown, La., U.S.	F6	122
Samuhú, Arg.	C7	92
Samui, Ko, i., Thai.	H5	48
Samundri, Pak.	C4	54
Samut Prakan, Thai.	F5	48
Samut Sakhon, Thai.	F5	48
Samut Songkhram, Thai.	F5	48
San, Mali	G3	64
San (Xan), stm., Asia	F8	48
San, stm., China	E8	42
San (Syan), stm., Eur.	F18	16
Saña, Peru	E2	84
Şan'ā', Yemen	F5	56
Sana, stm., Bos.	E3	26
Sanaa see Şan'ā', Yemen	F5	56
Sanabu, Egypt	K1	58
Sanaga, stm., Cam.	D2	66
San Agustín, Arg.	E5	92
San Agustín, Arg.	I8	92
San Agustín, Mex.	C1	130
San Agustin, Cape, c., Phil.	G6	52
Sanak Islands, is., Ak., U.S.	F7	140
San Alberto, Mex.	G6	130
San Ambrosio, Isla, i., Chile	H7	82
Sanana, Pulau, i., Indon.	F8	44
Sānand, India	G4	54
Sanandaj, Iran	B6	56
San Andreas, Ca., U.S.	E5	134
San Andrés, Col.	F7	102
San Andrés, Isla de, i., Col.	F7	102
San Andres Mountains, mts., N.M., U.S.	H2	128
San Andrés Sajcabajá, Guat.	E2	102
San Andrés Tuxtla, Mex.	F11	100
San Andrés y Providencia, state, Col.	F7	102
Sananduva, Braz.	C12	92
San Angelo, Tx., U.S.	C7	130
San Antero, Col.	C4	86
San Antonio, Arg.	D5	92
San Antonio, Chile	F2	92
San Antonio, Col.	F4	86
San Antonio, N.M., U.S.	F2	128
San Antonio, N.M., U.S.	J9	132
San Antonio, Tx., U.S.	E9	130
San Antonio, Ur.	E9	92
San Antonio, stm., Tx., U.S.	F10	130
San Antonio, Cabo, pen., Arg.	H9	92
San Antonio, Cabo de, c., Cuba	B5	102
San Antonio, Lake, res., Ca., U.S.	H4	134
San Antonio, Mount, mtn., Ca., U.S.	I8	134
San Antonio, Punta, c., Mex.	B3	100
San Antonio Abad see Sant Antoni de Portmany, Spain	F12	20
San Antonio Bay, b., Tx., U.S.	F11	130
San Antonio de Bravo, Mex.	D3	130
San Antonio de La Paz see San Antonio, Arg.	D5	92
San Antonio de los Baños, Cuba	A6	102
San Antonio de los Cobres, Arg.	B4	92
San Antonio del Táchira, Ven.	D5	86
San Antonio de Tamanaco, Ven.	C8	86
San Antonio el Grande, Mex.	F2	130
San Antonio Mountain, mtn., N.M., U.S.	E2	128
San Antonio Oeste, Arg.	H4	90
Sanatorium, Ms., U.S.	F9	122
San Augustine, Tx., U.S.	F4	122
San Augustin Pass, p., N.M., U.S.	K10	132
Sanāw, Yemen	F7	56
Sanāwad, India	G6	54
San Bartolomeo in Galdo, Italy	C9	24
San Benedetto del Tronto, Italy	H10	22
San Benedetto Po, Italy	E7	22
San Benedicto, Isla, i., Mex.	F3	100
San Benito, Tx., U.S.	H10	130
San Benito, stm., Ca., U.S.	G4	134
San Benito Mountain, mtn., Ca., U.S.	G5	134
San Bernard, stm., Tx., U.S.	E12	130
San Bernardino, Ca., U.S.	I8	134
San Bernardino Mountains, mts., Ca., U.S.	I9	134
San Bernardino Strait, strt., Phil.	D5	52
San Bernardo, Chile	F2	92
San Bernardo, Islas de, is., Col.	C3	86
San Bernardo del Viento, Col.	C3	86
Sanbe-yama, vol., Japan	D5	40
San Blas, Mex.	E6	100
San Blas, Mex.	B4	100
San Blas, Cape, c., Fl., U.S.	H13	122
San Blas, Golfo de, b., Pan.	H8	102
San Blas, Serranía de, mts., Pan.	H8	102
San Borja, Bol.	B3	90
Sanborn, Ia., U.S.	H3	118
Sanborn, N.D., U.S.	H15	124
San Bruno, Ca., U.S.	F3	134
San Buenaventura, Bol.	B3	90
San Buenaventura, Mex.	B8	100
San Buenaventura see Ventura, Ca., U.S.	I6	134
San Carlos, Chile	H2	92
San Carlos, Mex.	C9	100
San Carlos, Mex.	A8	100
San Carlos, Nic.	G5	102
San Carlos, Phil.	E4	52
San Carlos, Phil.	C3	52
San Carlos, Az., U.S.	J6	132
San Carlos, Ca., U.S.	F3	134
San Carlos, Ur.	G10	92
San Carlos, Ven.	C7	86
San Carlos, stm., C.R.	G5	102
San Carlos, stm., Ven.	C7	86
San Carlos Centro, Arg.	E7	92
San Carlos de Bariloche, Arg.	H2	90
San Carlos de Bolívar, Arg.	H7	92
San Carlos de Guaroa, Col.	F5	86
San Carlos del Zulia, Ven.	C5	86
San Carlos de Río Negro, Ven.	G8	86
San Carlos Reservoir, res., Az., U.S.	J6	132
San Cataldo, Italy	G7	24
San Cayetano, Arg.	I8	92
Sancha, stm., China	H1	42
Sanchahe, China	B7	38
Sanchenglong, China	B4	38
San Ciro de Acosta, Mex.	E9	100
San Clemente, Spain	E8	20
San Clemente, Ca., U.S.	J8	134
San Clemente Island, i., Ca., U.S.	K7	134
San Cristóbal, Arg.	E7	92
San Cristóbal, Dom. Rep.	C12	102
San Cristóbal, Ven.	D5	86
San Cristobal, i., Sol. Is.	f9	79b
San Cristóbal, Bahía, b., Mex.	B1	100
San Cristóbal, Isla, i., Ec.	i12	84a
San Cristóbal, Volcán, vol., Nic.	F4	102
San Cristóbal de las Casas, Mex.	G12	100
Sancti Spíritus, Cuba	A8	102
Sancy, Puy de, mtn., Fr.	D8	18
Sand, Nor.	G2	8
Sand, stm., Ab., Can.	B19	138
Sand, stm., S. Afr.	F8	70
Sand, stm., S. Afr.	C9	70
Sandai, Indon.	D7	50
Sandakan, Malay.	H2	52
Sândăn, Camb.	F8	48
Sandaré, Mali	G2	64
Sand Arroyo, stm., U.S.	D7	128
Sanday, i., Scot., U.K.	B10	12
Sandefjord, Nor.	G4	8
Sanderson, Tx., U.S.	D5	130
Sandersville, Ga., U.S.	D3	116
Sandersville, Ms., U.S.	F9	122
Sand Fork, W.V., U.S.	F5	114
Sand Hill, stm., Mn., U.S.	D2	118
Sand Hills, hills, Ne., U.S.	F11	126
Sāndi, India	E8	54
Sandia, Peru	F4	84
San Diego, Ca., U.S.	K8	134
San Diego, Tx., U.S.	G9	130
San Diego, Cabo, c., Arg.	J3	90
San Diego Aqueduct, aq., Ca., U.S.	J8	134
Sandıklı, Tur.	E13	28
Sandīla, India	E8	54
Sandilands Village, Bah.	m18	104f
Sand Key, i., Fl., U.S.	I3	116
Sand Lake, l., On., Can.	A4	118
Sandnes, Nor.	G1	8
Sandoa, D.R.C.	F4	66
Sandomierz, Pol.	F17	16
Sandoná, Col.	G3	86
San Donà di Piave, Italy	E9	22
Sandovo, Russia	B19	10
Sandoway, Mya.	C2	48
Sandown, Eng., U.K.	K11	12
Sand Point, Ak., U.S.	E7	140
Sandpoint, Id., U.S.	B10	136
Sandringham, Austl.	E2	76
Sandspit, B.C., Can.	E4	106
Sand Springs, Ok., U.S.	A2	122
Sand Springs, Tx., U.S.	B6	130
Sandstone, Austl.	E3	74
Sandstone, Mn., U.S.	E5	118
Sandu Ao, b., China	H8	42
Sandusky, Mi., U.S.	E7	112
Sandusky, Oh., U.S.	C3	114
Sandvika, Nor.	G4	8
Sandviken, Swe.	F7	8
Sandwich, Eng., U.K.	J14	12
Sandwich Bay, b., Nmb.	C2	70
Sandwick, B.C., Can.	G5	138
Sandwīp Island, i., Bngl.	G13	54
Sandy, Or., U.S.	E4	136
Sandy, Ut., U.S.	C5	132
Sandy Bay Mountain, mtn., Me., U.S.	E6	110
Sandy Cape, c., Austl.	E9	76
Sandy Cape, c., Austl.	n12	77a
Sandy Creek, stm., Austl.	I5	76
Sandy Hook, Ky., U.S.	F2	114
Sandy Hook, spit, N.J., U.S.	D12	114
Sandykači, Turkmen.	B9	56
Sandy Lake, l., On., Can.	E12	106
Sandy Point, c., Trin.	r13	105f
Sandy Point Town, St. K./N.	C2	105a
Sandy Springs, Ga., U.S.	C1	116
Sandžak, reg., Yugo.	F6	26
San Elizario, Tx., U.S.	C1	130
San Enrique, Arg.	G7	92
San Estanislao, Para.	B9	92
San Esteban, Isla, i., Mex.	A2	100
San Esteban de Gormaz, Spain	C7	20
San Felipe, Chile	F2	92
San Felipe, Col.	G8	86
San Felipe, Mex.	F5	98
San Felipe, Mex.	E8	100
San Felipe, Ven.	B7	86
San Felipe, Cayos de, is., Cuba	B6	102
San Felipe Nuevo Mercurio, Mex.	C7	100
San Felipe Pueblo, N.M., U.S.	F2	128
San Felíu de Guixols see Sant Feliu de Guíxols, Spain	C14	20
San Félix, Isla, i., Chile	H6	82
San Fernando, Chile	G2	92
San Fernando, Mex.	C9	100
San Fernando, Mex.	F6	130
San Fernando, Phil.	B2	52
San Fernando, Phil.	C3	52
San Fernando, Spain	H4	20
San Fernando, Trin.	s12	105f
San Fernando, Ca., U.S.	I7	134
San Fernando de Apure, Ven.	D8	86
San Fernando de Atabapo, Ven.	E8	86
San Fernando del Valle de Catamarca, Arg.	D4	92
Sånfjällets Nationalpark, p.o.i., Swe.	E5	8
Sanford, Co., U.S.	D2	128
Sanford, Fl., U.S.	H4	116
Sanford, Me., U.S.	G6	110
Sanford, N.C., U.S.	A6	116
Sanford, Tx., U.S.	F7	128
Sanford, stm., Austl.	E3	74
Sanford, Mount, vol., Ak., U.S.	D11	140
San Francisco, Arg.	E6	92
San Francisco, El Sal.	F3	102
San Francisco, Ca., U.S.	F3	134
San Francisco, stm., Arg.	B5	92
San Francisco, stm., U.S.	J8	132
San Francisco, Paso de, p., S.A.	C3	92
San Francisco Bay, b., Ca., U.S.	F3	134
San Francisco Creek, stm., Tx., U.S.	E5	130
San Francisco de Borja, Mex.	B5	100
San Francisco de Horizonte, Mex.	I4	130
San Francisco del Chañar, Arg.	D5	92
San Francisco del Oro, Mex.	B5	100
San Francisco del Rincón, Mex.	E7	100
San Francisco de Macorís, Dom. Rep.	C12	102
San Francisco de Mostazal, Chile	F2	92
San Gabriel, Ec.	G3	86
San Gabriel Chilac, Mex.	F10	100
San Gabriel Mountains, mts., Ca., U.S.	I8	134
Sangamankanda Point, c., Sri L.	H5	53
Sangamner, India	B1	53
Sangamon, stm., Il., U.S.	D7	120
Sangar, Russia	D14	34
Sangasanga-dalam, Indon.	D10	50
San Gavino Monreale, Italy	E2	24
Sangay, vol., Ec.	I2	86
Sangay, Parque Nacional, p.o.i., Ec.	H3	86
Sange, D.R.C.	F5	66
Sangeang, Pulau, i., Indon.	H11	50
Sanger, Ca., U.S.	G6	134
Sanger, Tx., U.S.	H11	128
Sângera, Mol.	B15	26
Sangerhausen, Ger.	E7	16
San Germán, P.R.	B1	104a
Sangerville, Me., U.S.	E7	110
Sanggan, stm., China	A6	42
Sanggau, Indon.	C7	50
Sangha, stm., Afr.	E3	66
Sanghar, Pak.	E2	54
Sangihe, Kepulauan, is., Indon.	E7	44
Sangihe, Pulau, i., Indon.	E8	44
San Gil, Col.	D5	86
Sangilen, hrebet, mts., Russia	D17	32
San Gimignano, Italy	G7	22
San Giovanni in Fiore, Italy	E10	24
San Giovanni in Persiceto, Italy	F8	22
San Giovanni Rotondo, Italy	C9	24
San Giovanni Valdarno, Italy	G8	22
Sangiyn Dalay nuur, l., Mong.	B4	36
Sangju, Kor., S.	F8	38
Sangkapura, Indon.	F8	50
Sângkê, stm., Camb.	F6	48
Sangkulirang, Indon.	C10	50
Sāngli, India	C2	53
Sangmélima, Cam.	D2	66
Sāngole, India	C2	53
Sangolquí, Ec.	H2	86
San Gorgonio Mountain, mtn., Ca., U.S.	I9	134
San Gottardo, Passo del, p., Switz.	D5	22
Sangre de Cristo Mountains, mts., U.S.	E3	128
San Gregorio, Arg.	G6	92
Sangre Grande, Trin.	s12	105f
Sangro, stm., Italy	H11	22
Sangrūr, India	C5	54
Sangsang, China	D11	54
Sangue, stm., Braz.	F6	84
Sangutane, stm., Moz.	C11	70
Sangya, China	C13	54
San Hipólito, Punta, c., Mex.	B1	100
Sanhu, China	H6	42
Sânhûr, Egypt	I1	58
Sanibel Island, i., Fl., U.S.	J3	116
San Ignacio, Arg.	C10	92
San Ignacio, Mex.	D8	100
San Ignacio, Mex.	B2	100
San Ignacio, Para.	C9	92
San Ignacio, Isla, i., Mex.	C4	100
San Ignacio, Laguna, b., Mex.	B2	100
San Ignacio de Moxo, Bol.	B3	90
San Ignacio de Velasco, Bol.	C4	90
San Isidro, Arg.	D5	92
San Isidro, Arg.	G8	92
San Isidro del General, C.R.	H5	102
San Jacinto, Col.	C4	86
San Jacinto, Ca., U.S.	J9	134
San Jacinto Peak, mtn., Ca., U.S.	J9	134
San Jaime, Arg.	E8	92
San Javier, Arg.	C10	92
San Javier, Arg.	E8	92
San Javier, Bol.	C4	90
San Javier, Chile	G2	92
San Javier, Mex.	H8	130
San Javier, Ur.	F8	92
San Javier, stm., Arg.	E8	92
Sanjay National Park, p.o.i., India	G8	54
San Jerónimo, Guat.	E2	102
Sanjiang, China	I3	42
Sanjō, Japan	B11	40
San Joaquín, Bol.	B4	90
San Joaquín, stm., Bol.	B4	90
San Joaquin, stm., Ca., U.S.	E4	134
San Joaquín de Omaguas, Peru	D3	84
San Joaquin Valley, val., Ca., U.S.	G5	134
San Jorge, Arg.	E6	92
San Jorge, stm., Col.	C4	86
San Jorge, Bahía de, b., Mex.	F6	98
San Jorge, Golfo, b., Arg.	I3	90
San Jorge Island, i., Sol. Is.	e8	79b
San José, C.R.	H5	102
San José, Mex.	F7	130
San Jose, Phil.	E3	52
San Jose, Ca., U.S.	F4	134
San Jose, Il., U.S.	D8	120
San Jose, N.M., U.S.	F3	128
San José, Ven.	q19	104g
San Jose, stm., N.M., U.S.	I9	132
San José, Cerro, mtn., Mex.	H2	130
San José, Isla, i., Mex.	C3	100
San José, Isla, i., Pan.	H8	102
San José, Laguna, b., P.R.	B3	104a
San José de Bácum, Mex.	B3	100
San José de Batuc, Mex.	A3	100
San José de Chiquitos, Bol.	C4	90
San José de Feliciano, Arg.	E8	92
San José de Guanipa, Ven.	C9	86
San José de Jáchal, Arg.	E3	92
San José de la Popa, Mex.	H7	130
San José de las Lajas, Cuba	A6	102
San José del Cabo, Mex.	D4	100
San José del Guaviare, Col.	F5	86
San José de Mayo, Ur.	G9	92
San José de Ocuné, Col.	E6	86
San José de Tiznados, Ven.	C8	86
San Jose Island, i., Tx., U.S.	G11	130
San Juan, Arg.	E3	92
San Juan, Mex.	E3	130
San Juan, P.R.	B3	104a
San Juan, state, Arg.	E3	92
San Juan, stm., Arg.	F4	92
San Juan, stm., Col.	E3	86
San Juan, stm., Mex.	H8	130
San Juan, stm., N.A.	G5	102
San Juan, stm., U.S.	F6	132
San Juan, stm., Ven.	B10	86
San Juan, Cabezas de, c., P.R.	B4	104a
San Juan, Cabo, c., Arg.	J4	90
San Juan Basin, bas., N.M., U.S.	G8	132
San Juan Bautista, Mex.	H6	130
San Juan Bautista, Para.	C9	92
San Juan Bautista see Sant Joan de Labritja, Spain	E12	20
San Juan Bautista, Ca., U.S.	G4	134
San Juan Creek, stm., Ca., U.S.	H5	134
San Juan de Colón, Ven.	C5	86
San Juan de Guadalupe, Mex.	C7	100
San Juan de la Maguana, Dom. Rep.	C12	102
San Juan del Norte, Nic.	G6	102
San Juan de los Cayos, Ven.	B7	86
San Juan de los Morros, Ven.	C8	86
San Juan del Río, Mex.	C6	100
San Juan del Río, Mex.	E8	100
San Juan del Sur, Nic.	G4	102
San Juan de Micay, stm., Col.	F3	86
San Juan de Payara, Ven.	D8	86
San Juan de Sabinas, Mex.	G6	130
San Juanico, Mex.	B2	100
San Juan Islands, is., Wa., U.S.	B3	136
San Juanito, Isla, i., Mex.	E5	100
San Juan Mountains, mts., Co., U.S.	C9	98
San Juan Nepomuceno, Col.	C4	86
San Juan Nepomuceno, Para.	C9	92
San Justo, Arg.	E7	92
Sankarani, stm., Afr.	G3	64
Sankeshwar, India	C2	53
Sankh, stm., India	G10	54
Sankheda, India	G4	54
Sankosh, stm., Asia	E13	54
Sankt Anton am Arlberg, Aus.	C7	22
Sankt Gallen, Switz.	C6	22
Sankt Goarshausen, Ger.	F3	16
Sankt Ingbert, Ger.	G3	16
Sankt Michel see Mikkeli, Fin.	F12	8
Sankt Moritz, Switz.	D6	22
Sankt-Peterburg (Saint Petersburg), Russia	A13	10
Sankt Peter-Ording, Ger.	B4	16
Sankt Pölten, Aus.	B12	22
Sankt Veit an der Glan, Aus.	D11	22
Sankt-Vith see Saint-Vith, Bel.	D14	14
Sankt Wendel, Ger.	G3	16
Sankuru, stm., D.R.C.	E4	66
San Lázaro, Cabo, c., Mex.	C2	100
San Leandro, Ca., U.S.	F3	134
San Leonardo, Mex.	G3	130
Şanlıurfa (Urfa), Tur.	A9	58
Şanlıurfa, state, Tur.	A9	58
San Lorenzo, Arg.	D8	92
San Lorenzo, Arg.	F7	92
San Lorenzo, Bol.	D4	90
San Lorenzo, Ec.	G2	86
San Lorenzo, Mex.	C7	100
San Lorenzo, P.R.	B4	104a
San Lorenzo, stm., Mex.	C5	100
San Lorenzo, Cabo, c., Ec.	H1	86
San Lorenzo, Isla, i., Mex.	A2	100
San Lorenzo, Monte (Cochrane, Cerro), mtn., S.A.	I2	90
San Lorenzo de la Parrilla, Spain	E8	20
Sanlúcar de Barrameda, Spain	H4	20
San Lucas, Bol.	D3	90
San Lucas, Mex.	D3	100
San Lucas, Cabo, c., Mex.	D4	100
San Luis, Arg.	F4	92
San Luis, Cuba	B10	102
San Luis, Guat.	D3	102
San Luis, Co., U.S.	D3	128
San Luis, Ven.	B7	86
San Luis, state, Arg.	F5	92
San Luís, Laguna, l., Bol.	B4	90
San Luis, Sierra de, mts., Arg.	F5	92
San Luis Creek, stm., Co., U.S.	C3	128
San Luis de la Paz, Mex.	E8	100
San Luis Gonzaga, Mex.	C3	100
San Luis Gonzaga, Bahía, b., Mex.	G5	98
San Luis Jilotepeque, Guat.	E3	102
San Luis Obispo, Ca., U.S.	H5	134
San Luis Potosí, Mex.	D8	100
San Luis Potosí, state, Mex.	D8	100
San Luis Reservoir, res., Ca., U.S.	F4	134
San Luis Río Colorado, Mex.	E5	98
San Luis Valley, val., Co., U.S.	D3	128
San Manuel, Arg.	H8	92
San Manuel, Az., U.S.	K6	132
San Marcial, stm., Mex.	A3	100
San Marcos, Col.	C4	86
San Marcos, Mex.	G9	100
San Marcos, Tx., U.S.	E9	130
San Marcos, Isla, i., Mex.	B2	100
San Marino, S. Mar.	G9	22
San Marino, ctry., Eur.	G9	22
San Martín, Arg.	D5	92
San Martín, Arg.	F3	92
San Martín, Col.	F5	86
San Martín, stm., Bol.	B4	90
San Martin, sci., Ant.	B34	81
San Martín, Lago (O'Higgins, Lago), l., S.A.	I2	90
San Martín de los Andes, Arg.	H2	90
San Martino di Castrozza, ngh., Italy	D8	22
San Mateo, Mex.	G1	130
San Mateo see Sant Mateu del Maestrat, Spain	D10	20
San Mateo, Ca., U.S.	F3	134
San Mateo, Fl., U.S.	G4	116
San Mateo, N.M., U.S.	H9	132
San Matías, Bol.	C5	90
San Matías, Golfo, b., Arg.	H4	90
Sanmen, China	G9	42
Sanmenhsia see Sanmenxia, China	D4	42
Sanmenxia, China	D4	42
San Miguel, Ec.	H2	86
San Miguel, El Sal.	F3	102
San Miguel, Mex.	A8	100
San Miguel, Pan.	H8	102
San Miguel, stm., Bol.	B4	90
San Miguel, stm., S.A.	G3	86
San Miguel, stm., Co., U.S.	E8	132
San Miguel, Golfo de, b., Pan.	H8	102
San Miguel de Allende, Mex.	E8	100
San Miguel de Cruces, Mex.	C6	100
San Miguel del Monte, Arg.	G8	92
San Miguel de Salcedo, Ec.	H2	86
San Miguel de Tucumán, Arg.	C4	92
San Miguel Island, i., Ca., U.S.	I5	134
Sanming, China	H7	42
San Miniato, Italy	G7	22
Sannār, Sudan	E6	62
Sannicandro Garganico, Italy	I12	22
San Nicolás, Peru	G2	84
San Nicolas, Phil.	A3	52
San Nicolás de los Arroyos, Arg.	F7	92
San Nicolás de los Garza, Mex.	C8	100
San Nicolas Island, i., Ca., U.S.	J6	134
Sânnicolau Mare, Rom.	C7	26
Sannieshof, S. Afr.	E7	70
Sannikova, proliv, strt., Russia	B16	34
Sano, Japan	C12	40
Sanok, Pol.	G18	16
Sânon, stm., Fr.	F15	14
San Pablo, Phil.	C3	52
San Pablo Bay, b., Ca., U.S.	E3	134
San Pasqual, Punta, c., Mex.	C3	100
San Pedro, Arg.	B5	92
San Pedro, Arg.	C5	92
San Pedro, Arg.	F8	92
San Pedro, Chile	F2	92
San Pedro, Col.	C4	86
San-Pédro, C. Iv.	I3	64
San Pedro, Neth. Ant.	A1	105a
San Pedro, state, Para.	B9	92
San Pedro, stm., Mex.	F8	98
San Pedro, stm., Mex.	G2	130
San Pedro, stm., N.A.	D2	102
San Pedro, stm., N.A.	K6	132
San Pedro, Punta, c., Chile	B2	92
San Pedro, Volcán, vol., Chile	D3	90
San Pedro Carchá, Guat.	E2	102
San Pedro de Jujuy see San Pedro, Arg.	B5	92
San Pedro de las Colonias, Mex.	C7	100
San Pedro del Gallo, Mex.	C6	100
San Pedro del Paraná, Para.	C9	92
San Pedro de Macorís, Dom. Rep.	C13	102
San Pedro de Ycuamandiyú, Para.	B9	92
San Pedro Peaks, mtn., N.M., U.S.	G10	132
San Pedro Sula, Hond.	E3	102
San Pedro Tabasco, Mex.	D2	102
San Pellegrino Terme, Italy	E6	22
San Pietro, Isola di, i., Italy	E2	24
San Pitch, stm., Ut., U.S.	D5	132
Sanquhar, Scot., U.K.	F9	12
Sanquianga, Parque Nacional, p.o.i., Col.	F2	86
San Quintín, Cabo, c., Mex.	F4	98
San Rafael, Arg.	G3	92
San Rafael, Chile	G2	92
San Rafael, Mex.	C8	100
San Rafael, Ca., U.S.	E3	134
San Rafael, N.M., U.S.	H8	132
San Rafael, Ven.	B6	86
San Rafael, stm., Mex.	F5	98
San Rafael, stm., Ut., U.S.	E6	132
San Rafael del Norte, Nic.	F4	102
San Rafael Swell, plat., Ut., U.S.	E6	132
San Ramón, Arg.	C5	92
San Ramón, Bol.	B4	90
San Ramón de la Nueva Orán, Arg.	D4	90
San Remo, Italy	G4	22
San Rodrigo, stm., Mex.	F6	130
San Roque, Arg.	D8	92
San Roque, Punta, c., Mex.	B1	100
San Saba, Tx., U.S.	C9	130
San Saba, stm., Tx., U.S.	C9	130
San Salvador, Arg.	E8	92
San Salvador, El Sal.	F3	102
San Salvador, i., Bah.	C10	96
San Salvador de Jujuy, Arg.	A5	92
Sansanné-Mango, Togo	G5	64
San Sebastián, P.R.	B1	104a
San Sebastián see Donostia, Spain	A9	20
San Sebastián, Bahía, b., Arg.	J3	90
Sansepolcro, Italy	G9	22
San Severo, Italy	I12	22
Sansha, China	H9	42
San Simon, Az., U.S.	K7	132
San Simon, stm., Az., U.S.	K7	132
San Simon Wash, stm., Az., U.S.	K4	132
Sanski Most, Bos.	E3	26
San Solano, Arg.	E4	92
Sans-Souci, hist., Haiti	C11	102
Santa, stm., Peru	E2	84
Santa Adélia, Braz.	K1	88
Santa Amalia, Spain	E4	20
Santa Ana, Bol.	B3	90
Santa Ana, Ec.	H1	86
Santa Ana, El Sal.	E3	102
Santa Ana, Mex.	F7	98
Santa Ana, Mex.	C8	100
Santa Ana, Ca., U.S.	J8	134
Santa Ana, Ven.	C9	86
Santa Ana del Alto Beni, Bol.	C3	90
Santa Anna, Tx., U.S.	C8	130
Santa Bárbara, Chile	H2	92
Santa Barbara, Col.	E4	86
Santa Bárbara, Hond.	E3	102
Santa Bárbara, Mex.	B6	100
Santa Barbara, Ca., U.S.	I6	134
Santa Bárbara, Ven.	D6	86
Santa Barbara Channel, strt., Ca., U.S.	I6	134
Santa Barbara Island, i., Ca., U.S.	J7	134
Santa Catalina, Gulf of, b., Ca., U.S.	J7	134
Santa Catalina, Isla, i., Mex.	C3	100
Santa Catalina Island, i., Ca., U.S.	J7	134
Santa Catarina, Mex.	C8	100
Santa Catarina, Mex.	L10	134
Santa Catarina, state, Braz.	C12	92
Santa Catarina, Ilha de, i., Braz.	C13	92
Santa Cecília, Braz.	C12	92
Santa Clara, Col.	I7	86
Santa Clara, Cuba	A7	102
Santa Clara, Ca., U.S.	F3	134
Santa Clara, Ut., U.S.	F3	132
Santa Clara, stm., Ca., U.S.	I7	134
Santa Clarita, Ca., U.S.	I7	134
Santa Clotilde, Peru	D3	84
Santa Coloma de Farners, Spain	C13	20
Santa Coloma de Farnés see Santa Coloma de Farners, Spain	C13	20
Santa Comba, Spain	A2	20
Santa Cruz, Braz.	J5	88
Santa Cruz, Braz.	D8	88
Santa Cruz, C.R.	G5	102
Santa Cruz, Phil.	C2	52
Santa Cruz, Phil.	D4	52
Santa Cruz, Phil.	C3	52
Santa Cruz, Ca., U.S.	G3	134
Santa Cruz, state, Arg.	I2	90
Santa Cruz, stm., Arg.	J3	90
Santa Cruz, stm., N.A.	J4	132
Santa Cruz, Isla, i., Ec.	i11	84a
Santa Cruz Cabrália, Braz.	I6	88
Santa Cruz de la Sierra, Bol.	C4	90
Santa Cruz del Quiché, Guat.	E2	102
Santa Cruz del Sur, Cuba	B9	102
Santa Cruz de Mudela, Spain	F7	20
Santa Cruz do Capibaribe, Braz.	D7	88
Santa Cruz do Piauí, Braz.	D5	88
Santa Cruz do Rio Pardo, Braz.	L1	88
Santa Cruz do Sul, Braz.	D11	92
Santa Cruz Island, i., Ca., U.S.	J6	134
Santa Cruz Islands, is., Sol. Is.	E7	72
Santa Elena, Arg.	E8	92
Santa Elena, Ec.	I1	86
Santa Elena, Mex.	B7	100
Santa Elena, Bahía de, b., Ec.	H1	86
Santa Elena, Cabo, c., C.R.	G4	102
Santa Eufemia, Spain	F6	20
Santa Eulalia, Spain	D9	20
Santa Eulalia del Río see Santa Eulària del Riu, Spain	E12	20
Santa Eulària del Riu, Spain	E12	20
Santa Fe, Arg.	E7	92
Santa Fe, Spain	G7	20
Santa Fe, N.M., U.S.	F3	128
Santa Fe, state, Arg.	D7	92
Santa Fe, stm., Fl., U.S.	G3	116
Santa Fe Baldy, mtn., N.M., U.S.	F3	128
Santa Fe de Bogotá, Col.	E4	86
Santa Fe de Minas, Braz.	I3	88
Santa Fé do Sul, Braz.	D6	90
Santa Filomena, Braz.	E3	88
Sant'Agata di Militello, Italy	F8	24
Santa Gertrudis, Mex.	G2	130
Santa Helena, Braz.	B3	88
Santa Helena de Goiás, Braz.	G7	84
Santai, China	F1	42
Santa Inês, Braz.	G5	88
Santa Inés, Bahía, b., Mex.	B3	100
Santa Inés, Isla, i., Chile	J2	90
Santa Isabel, Arg.	H4	92
Santa Isabel, P.R.	C3	104a
Santa Isabel, i., Sol. Is.	e8	79b
Santa Isabel, stm., Mex.	F1	130
Santa Isabel, Pico de, mtn., Eq. Gui.	I6	64
Santa Isabel Creek, stm., Tx., U.S.	G8	130
Santa Juliana, Braz.	J2	88
Santal, Baie du, b., N. Cal.	m16	79d
Santa Lucía, Arg.	D8	92
Santa Lucía, Ur.	G9	92
Santa Lucia Range, mts., Ca., U.S.	G4	134
Santaluz, Braz.	F6	88
Santa Luzia, Braz.	D7	88
Santa Magdalena, Arg.	G6	92
Santa Magdalena, Isla, i., Mex.	C2	100
Santa Margarita, Ca., U.S.	H5	134
Santa Margarita, Isla, i., Mex.	C2	100
Santa Margherita Ligure, Italy	F6	22
Santa María, Arg.	C4	92
Santa Maria, Braz.	D10	92
Santa María, Mex.	F6	130
Santa Maria, Ca., U.S.	I5	134
Santa Maria, i., Vanuatu	j16	79d
Santa Maria, stm., Braz.	E10	92
Santa María, stm., Mex.	F9	98
Santa María, stm., Mex.	E8	100
Santa Maria, stm., Az., U.S.	I3	132
Santa María, Bahía, b., Mex.	C4	100
Santa María, Cabo, c., Ur.	G10	92
Santa Maria, Cabo de, c., Ang.	C1	68
Santa Maria, Cabo de, c., Port.	H3	20
Santa María, Isla, i., Chile	H1	92
Santa María, Isla, i., Ec.	i11	84a
Santa María, Laguna de, l., Mex.	F9	98
Santa María Asunción Tlaxiaco, Mex.	G10	100
Santa Maria Capua Vetere, Italy	C7	24
Santa María Colotepec, Mex.	H10	100
Santa Maria da Boa Vista, Braz.	E5	88
Santa Maria da Vitória, Braz.	G3	88
Santa Maria de Itabira, Braz.	J4	88
Santa María del Oro, Mex.	C6	100
Santa María del Río, Mex.	E8	100
Santa Maria di Leuca, Capo, c., Italy	E12	24
Santa Maria do Suaçuí, Braz.	J4	88
Santa María la Real de Nieva, Spain	C6	20
Santa Marinella, Italy	H8	22
Santa Marta, Col.	B4	86
Santa Marta, Cabo de, c., Ang.	C1	68
Santa Marta, Ciénaga Grande, b., Col.	B4	86
Santa Mónica, Mex.	F7	130
Santa Monica, Ca., U.S.	I7	134
Santa Monica Bay, b., Ca., U.S.	J7	134
Santan, Indon.	D10	50
Santana, Braz.	G3	88
Santana, Coxilha de (Santa Ana, Cuchilla de), hills, S.A.	E10	92
Santana, Ilha de, i., Braz.	B4	88
Santana da Boa Vista, Braz.	E11	92
Santana do Ipanema, Braz.	E7	88
Santana do Livramento, Braz.	E9	92

Name	Map Ref.	Page
Santander, Col.	F3	86
Santander, Phil.	F4	52
Santander, Spain	A7	20
Santander, state, Col.	D5	86
Santander Jiménez, Mex.	C9	100
Sant'Andrea, Isola, i., Italy	D11	24
Santanghu, China	C3	36
Santanilla, Islas, is., Hond.	D6	102
Sant'Antine, Nuraghe, hist., Italy	D2	24
Sant'Antioco, Italy	E2	24
Sant'Antioco, Isola di, i., Italy	E2	24
Sant Antoni de Portmany, Spain	F12	20
Santanyí, Spain	E14	20
Santa Paula, Ca., U.S.	I6	134
Santaquin, Ut., U.S.	D5	132
Santa Quitéria, Braz.	C5	88
Santa Quitéria do Maranhão, Braz.	B4	88
Santarcangelo di Romagna, Italy	F9	22
Santarém, Braz.	D7	84
Santarém, Port.	E2	20
Santarém, state, Port.	E2	20
Santaren Channel, strt., Bah.	C9	96
Santa Rita, Braz.	D8	88
Santa Rita, Col.	G5	86
Santa Rita, Hond.	E3	102
Santa Rita, Mex.	G7	130
Santa Rita, Mt., U.S.	B14	136
Santa Rita, Ven.	B6	86
Santa Rosa, Arg.	H5	92
Santa Rosa, Braz.	H2	88
Santa Rosa, Braz.	C10	92
Santa Rosa, Col.	F7	86
Santa Rosa, Ec.	D2	84
Santa Rosa, Ca., U.S.	E3	134
Santa Rosa, Tx., U.S.	H10	130
Santa Rosa, Ven.	C7	86
Santa Rosa, Ven.	D7	86
Santa Rosa, Mount, hill, Guam	i10	78c
Santa Rosa Beach, Fl., U.S.	G12	122
Santa Rosa de Copán, Hond.	E3	102
Santa Rosa del Conlara, Arg.	F5	92
Santa Rosa de Leales, Arg.	C5	92
Santa Rosa de Osos, Col.	D4	86
Santa Rosa de Sucumbíos, Ec.	G3	86
Santa Rosa de Viterbo, Col.	E5	86
Santa Rosa Island, i., Ca., U.S.	J5	134
Santa Rosalía, Mex.	B2	100
Santa Rosalía, Mex.	H9	130
Santa Rosalía, Ven.	C7	86
Santa Rosa Wash, stm., Az., U.S.	K5	132
Šantarskie ostrova, is., Russia	E16	34
Santa Sylvina, Arg.	C7	92
Santa Teresa, Braz.	J5	88
Santa Teresa, Mex.	C9	100
Santa Teresa, stm., Braz.	G1	88
Santa Teresa, Embalse de, res., Spain	D5	20
Santa Teresa, Fortaleza de, hist., Ur.	F11	92
Santa Uxía, Spain	B1	20
Santa Vitória do Palmar, Braz.	F11	92
Santee, Ca., U.S.	K8	134
Santee, stm., S.C., U.S.	C6	116
Santee Dam, dam, S.C., U.S.	C5	116
Sant'Eufemia, Golfo di, b., Italy	F9	24
Sant Feliu de Guíxols, Spain	C14	20
Santhià, Italy	E5	22
Santiago, Braz.	D10	92
Santiago, Chile	F2	92
Santiago, Mex.	D4	100
Santiago, Pan.	H7	102
Santiago, Para.	C9	92
Santiago, i., C.V.	I10	65a
Santiago, stm., Mex.	C6	100
Santiago, stm., S.A.	D2	84
Santiago, Isla, i., Ec.	i11	84a
Santiago de Compostela, Spain	B2	20
Santiago de Cuba, Cuba	C9	102
Santiago del Estero, Arg.	C5	92
Santiago del Estero, state, Arg.	C5	92
Santiago de los Caballeros, Dom. Rep.	C12	102
Santiago Island, i., Phil.	B2	52
Santiago Ixcuintla, Mex.	E6	100
Santiago Jamiltepec, Mex.	G10	100
Santiago Larre, Arg.	G8	92
Santiago Papasquiaro, Mex.	C6	100
Santiago Peak, mtn., Ca., U.S.	J8	134
Santiago Peak, mtn., Tx., U.S.	E4	130
Santiaguillo, Laguna, l., Mex.	C6	100
Santiam Pass, p., Or., U.S.	F5	136
Säntis, mtn., Switz.	C6	22
Santisteban del Puerto, Spain	F7	20
Sant Joan de Labritja, Spain	E12	20
Sant Jordi, Golf de, b., Spain	D11	20
Sant Mateu del Maestrat, Spain	D10	20
Santo Amaro, Braz.	G6	88
Santo Amaro, Braz.	B4	88
Santo André, Braz.	L2	88
Santo Ângelo, Braz.	D10	92
Santo Antão, i., C.V.	k10	65a
Santo Antônio, Braz.	D8	88
Santo António, S. Tom./P.	I6	64
Santo Antônio, stm., Braz.	I3	88
Santo Antônio, stm., Braz.	F1	88
Santo Antônio da Patrulha, Braz.	D12	92
Santo Antônio de Jesus, Braz.	G6	88
Santo Antônio de Pádua, Braz.	K4	88
Santo Antônio do Amparo, Braz.	K3	88
Santo Antônio do Içá, Braz.	D4	84
Santo Augusto, Braz.	C11	92
Santo Domingo, Cuba	C8	96
Santo Domingo, Dom. Rep.	C13	102
Santo Domingo, Mex.	D8	100
Santo Domingo, Mex.	C2	100
Santo Domingo, Mex.	I3	130
Santo Domingo, Ven.	D5	86
Santo Domingo de la Calzada, Spain	B7	20
Santo Domingo de los Colorados, Ec.	H1	86
Santo Domingo Pueblo, N.M., U.S.	F2	128
Santo Domingo Tehuantepec, Mex.	G11	100
Santo Domingo Zanatepec, Mex.	G11	100
Santo Estêvão, Braz.	G6	88
Santo / Malo, state, Vanuatu	j16	79d
San Tomé, Ven.	C9	86
Santo Onofre, stm., Braz.	G4	88
Santorini see Thíra, i., Grc.	G8	28
Santos, Braz.	L2	88
Santos Dumont, Braz.	K4	88
Santo Tirso, Port.	C2	20
Santo Tomás, Mex.	L9	134
Santo Tomás, Punta, c., Mex.	L9	134
Santo Tomé, Arg.	E7	92
Santo Tomé, Arg.	D9	92
San Vicente de Alcántara, Spain	E3	20
San Vicente de Baracaldo see Barakaldo, Spain	A8	20
San Vicente del Caguán, Col.	F4	86
San Vincente, Arg.	D5	92
San Vincenzo, Italy	G7	22
San Vito, Capo, c., Italy	F6	24
Sanya, China	L3	42
Sanyati, stm., Zimb.	D4	68
Sanyō, Japan	E4	40
Sanyuan, China	D3	42
Sanzao Dao, i., China	K5	42
Sanza Pombo, Ang.	B2	68
São Benedito, Braz.	C5	88
São Benedito do Rio Preto, Braz.	B3	88
São Bento, Braz.	B3	88
São Bento do Norte, Braz.	C7	88
São Bento do Sul, Braz.	C13	92
São Bento do Una, Braz.	E7	88
São Borja, Braz.	D10	92
São Caetano do Sul, Braz.	L2	88
São Carlos, Braz.	L2	88
São Cristóvão, Braz.	F7	88
São Domingos, Braz.	G2	88
São Domingos, Braz.	C11	92
São Domingos, Gui.-B.	G1	64
São Domingos do Maranhão, Braz.	C3	88
São Felipe, Braz.	H5	88
São Félix de Balsas, Braz.	D3	88
São Francisco, Braz.	H3	88
São Francisco, stm., Braz.	E6	88
São Francisco, stm., Braz.	H5	88
São Francisco, Baía de, b., Braz.	C13	92
São Francisco, Ilha de, i., Braz.	C13	92
São Francisco de Assis, Braz.	D10	92
São Francisco de Goiás, Braz.	H1	88
São Francisco de Paula, Braz.	D12	92
São Francisco do Maranhão, Braz.	D4	88
São Francisco do Sul, Braz.	C13	92
São Gabriel, Braz.	F5	88
São Gabriel, Braz.	E10	92
São Gabriel da Palha, Braz.	J5	88
São Gabriel de Goiás, Braz.	H2	88
São Gonçalo do Sapucaí, Braz.	K3	88
São Gonçalo dos Campos, Braz.	G6	88
Sao Hill, Tan.	F7	66
São Jerônimo, Braz.	E12	92
São Jerônimo da Serra, Braz.	A12	92
São João da Aliança, Braz.	H2	88
São João da Barra, Braz.	K5	88
São João da Boa Vista, Braz.	L2	88
São João de Cortês, Braz.	B3	88
São João Del Rei, Braz.	K3	88
São João do Araguaia, Braz.	C1	88
São João do Jaguaribe, Braz.	C6	88
São João do Piauí, Braz.	E4	88
São João dos Patos, Braz.	D4	88
São Joaquim, Braz.	D12	92
São Joaquim, Parque Nacional de, p.o.i., Braz.	D13	92
São Joaquim da Barra, Braz.	K1	88
São José, Braz.	C13	92
São José, stm., Braz.	J5	88
São José da Laje, Braz.	E7	88
São José das Piranhas, Braz.	D6	88
São José de Anauá, Braz.	G11	86
São José do Cedro, Braz.	C11	92
São José do Egito, Braz.	D7	88
São José do Gurupi, Braz.	A2	88
São José do Mipibu, Braz.	D8	88
São José do Peixe, Braz.	D4	88
São José do Rio Preto, Braz.	K1	88
São José dos Campos, Braz.	L3	88
São José dos Pinhais, Braz.	B13	92
São Leopoldo, Braz.	D12	92
São Lourenço, Braz.	L3	88
São Lourenço, Pantanal de, sw., Braz.	C5	90
São Lourenço do Sul, Braz.	E12	92
São Luís, Braz.	B3	88
São Luís do Curu, Braz.	B6	88
São Luís do Quitunde, Braz.	E8	88
São Luís Gonzaga, Braz.	D10	92
São Manuel, Braz.	L1	88
São Manuel, stm., Braz.	E6	84
São Marcos, stm., Braz.	I2	88
São Marcos, Baía de, b., Braz.	B3	88
São Mateus, Braz.	J6	88
São Mateus, Braço Norte, stm., Braz.	J5	88
São Mateus do Sul, Braz.	B12	92
São Miguel, Braz.	D6	88
São Miguel, i., Port.	C3	60
São Miguel do Araguaia, Braz.	F7	84
São Miguel d'Oeste, Braz.	C11	92
São Miguel do Guamá, Braz.	A2	88
São Miguel dos Campos, Braz.	E7	88
São Miguel do Tapuio, Braz.	C5	88
Saona, Isla, i., Dom. Rep.	C13	102
Saône, stm., Fr.	C10	18
Saône-et-Loire, state, Fr.	C10	18
Saoner, India	H7	54
São Nicolau, i., C.V.	k10	65a
São Nicolau, stm., Braz.	C5	88
São Paulo, Braz.	L2	88
São Paulo, state, Braz.	D7	90
São Paulo de Olivença, Braz.	D4	84
São Paulo do Potengi, Braz.	C7	88
São Pedro do Piauí, Braz.	C4	88
São Pedro do Sul, Port.	D2	20
São Raimundo das Mangabeiras, Braz.	D3	88
São Raimundo Nonato, Braz.	E4	88
São Romão, Braz.	I3	88
São Roque, Braz.	L2	88
São Roque, Cabo de, c., Braz.	C8	88
São Sebastião, Braz.	L3	88
São Sebastião, Ilha de, i., Braz.	L3	88
São Sebastião, Ponta, c., Moz.	C12	70
São Sebastião do Paraíso, Braz.	K2	88
São Sepé, Braz.	E11	92
São Simão, Braz.	K2	88
São Simão, Represa de, res., Braz.	C7	90
São Timóteo, Braz.	G4	88
São Tomé, Braz.	C7	88
São Tomé, S. Tom./P.	I6	64
São Tomé, i., S. Tom./P.	I6	64
São Tomé, Cabo de, c., Braz.	L5	88
São Tomé, Pico de, mtn., S. Tom./P.	I6	64
Sao Tome and Principe, ctry., Afr.	I6	64
Saoura, Oued, stm., Alg.	D4	64
São Valério, stm., Braz.	F1	88
São Vicente, Braz.	M2	88
São Vicente, i., C.V.	k9	65a
São Vicente, Cabo de, c., Port.	H1	20
Sapanca, Tur.	C13	28
Sape, Selat, strt., Indon.	H11	50
Sapele, Nig.	H6	64
Sapelo Island, i., Ga., U.S.	E4	116
Sápes, Grc.	B8	28
Şapitwa, mtn., Mwi.	D6	68
Šapki, Russia	A14	10
Šapkina, stm., Russia	C26	8
Sapockin, Bela.	G6	10
Sappa Creek, stm., U.S.	A9	128
Sappa Creek, South Fork, stm., Ks., U.S.	B8	128
Sappho, Wa., U.S.	B2	136
Sapporo, Japan	C14	38
Sap Songkhla, Thale, l., Thai.	I5	48
Saptakośī, stm., Nepal	E11	54
Sapudi, Pulau, i., Indon.	G9	50
Sapulpa, Ok., U.S.	A2	122
Sapwe, D.R.C.	G5	66
Saqqâra, Egypt	I2	58
Saqqâra, Pyramides de (Step Pyramid), hist., Egypt	I1	58
Saqqez, Iran	B6	56
Saraana, Baie, b., Qc., Can.	B1	110
Sarāb, Iran	B6	56
Saraburi, Thai.	E5	48
Saracura, stm., Braz.	G5	88
Saraféré, Mali	F4	64
Saragosa, Tx., U.S.	C4	130
Saragossa see Zaragoza, Spain	C10	20
Sarāi Naurang, Pak.	B3	54
Saraipāli, India	H9	54
Sarajevo, Bos.	F5	26
Saraji, Austl.	D7	76
Sarakhs, Iran	B9	56
Saraktaš, Russia	D9	32
Saraland, Al., U.S.	G10	122
Saran', Kaz.	E12	32
Saran, Gunung, mtn., Indon.	D7	50
Saranac, Mi., U.S.	F4	112
Saranac, stm., N.Y., U.S.	F3	110
Saranda see Sarandë, Alb.	E13	24
Sarandë, Alb.	E13	24
Sarandi, Braz.	C11	92
Sarandí del Yi, Ur.	F10	92
Sarandí Grande, Ur.	F9	92
Sarangani Bay, b., Phil.	H5	52
Sarangani Islands, is., Phil.	H5	52
Sarangani Strait, strt., Phil.	H5	52
Sārangarh, India	H9	54
Sārangpur, India	G6	54
Saranpaul', Russia	B10	32
Saransk, Russia	D6	32
Saraphi, Thai.	C4	48
Sarapul, Russia	C8	32
Sarāqib, Syria	C7	58
Sarare, stm., Ven.	D6	86
Sarasota, Fl., U.S.	I3	116
Sarata, Ukr.	C16	26
Saratoga, Ca., U.S.	F3	134
Saratoga, Tx., U.S.	G4	122
Saratoga, Wy., U.S.	B10	132
Saratoga Springs, N.Y., U.S.	G2	110
Saratov, Russia	D7	32
Saratov Reservoir see Saratovskoe vodohranilišče, res., Russia	D7	32
Saratovskoe vodohranilišče, res., Russia	D7	32
Sarāvān, Iran	D9	56
Saravan, Laos	E8	48
Saravena, Col.	D5	86
Sarawak, state, Malay.	B8	50
Sarawak, hist. reg., Malay.	E5	44
Saray, Tur.	B10	28
Saraya, Gui.	G2	64
Sarayevo see Sarajevo, Bos.	F5	26
Sarayköy, Tur.	F11	28
Sarayönü, Tur.	E15	28
Sarbāz, Iran	D9	56
Sarcelle, Passe de la, strt., N. Cal.	n16	79d
Sarcidano, reg., Italy	E3	24
Sarcoxie, Mo., U.S.	G3	120
Sārda (Mahākālī), stm., Asia	D8	54
Sardah, Bngl.	F12	54
Sardārpur, India	G5	54
Sardārshahr, India	D5	54
Sardegna, state, Italy	D4	24
Sardegna (Sardinia), i., Italy	D3	24
Sardinata, Col.	H11	102
Sardinia see Sardegna, state, Italy	D4	24
Sardinia see Sardegna, i., Italy	D3	24
Sardis, Al., U.S.	E12	122
Sardis, Ga., U.S.	D4	116
Sardis, Tn., U.S.	B10	122
Sardis, hist., Tur.	E10	28
Sardis Lake, res., Ms., U.S.	C9	122
Sardis Lake, res., Ok., U.S.	C3	122
Šardonem', Russia	E21	8
Sarek, mtn., Swe.	C7	8
Sareks Nationalpark, p.o.i., Swe.	C7	8
Sar-e Pol, Afg.	B10	56
Sarepta, La., U.S.	E5	122
Sargent, Ga., U.S.	D14	122
Sargent, Ne., U.S.	F13	126
Sargodha, Pak.	B4	54
Sarh, Chad	F3	62
Sārī, Iran	B7	56
Saría, i., Grc.	H10	28
Sarıgöl, Tur.	E11	28
Sarıkaya, Tur.	E15	28
Sarikei, Malay.	B7	50
Sarina, Austl.	C7	76
Sariñena, Spain	C10	20
Sariska Tiger Reserve, India	E6	54
Sarita, Tx., U.S.	G10	130
Sariwŏn, Kor., N.	E6	38
Şarıyar Barajı, res., Tur.	D14	28
Šarja, Russia	G21	8
Sark, i., Guern.	E6	14
Şarkand, Kaz.	E13	32
Šarkaŭščyna, Bela.	E10	10
Şarkikaraağaç, Tur.	E14	28
Şarköy, Tur.	C10	28
Šarles, N.D., U.S.	F15	124
Šarlyk, Russia	D9	32
Sarmi, Indon.	F10	44
Sarmiento, Arg.	I3	90
Särna, Swe.	F5	8
Sarnia, On., Can.	F7	112
Sarno, Italy	D8	24
Sarolangun, Indon.	E3	50
Saronic Gulf see Saronikós Kólpos, b., Grc.	F6	28
Saronikós Kólpos, b., Grc.	F6	28
Saronno, Italy	E6	22
Saros Körfezi, b., Tur.	C9	28
Sárospatak, Hung.	A8	26
Sarowbī, Afg.	C10	56
Sarpsborg, Nor.	G4	8
Sarralbe, Fr.	E15	14
Sarre (Saar), stm., Eur.	E15	14
Sarrebourg, Fr.	F16	14
Şarreguemines, Fr.	E16	14
Šarscin, Bela.	H14	10
Sartang, stm., Russia	C15	34
Sartell, Mn., U.S.	F4	118
Sartène, Fr.	H14	18
Sarthe, state, Fr.	G9	14
Sarthe, stm., Fr.	G8	14
Saruhanlı, Tur.	E10	28
Sárvár, Hung.	B3	26
Sárvíz, can., Hung.	C5	26
Saryg-Sep, Russia	D17	32
Sarykamyšskoe ozero, l., Asia	A8	56
Sarykopa, ozero, l., Kaz.	E10	32
Şaryozek, Kaz.	F13	32
Šarypovo, Russia	C15	32
Sarysu, stm., Kaz.	E11	32
Sary-Taš, Kyrg.	G12	32
Sarzana, Italy	F6	22
Sasabeneh, Eth.	F8	62
Sasaginnigak Lake, l., Mb., Can.	C17	124
Sasakwa, Ok., U.S.	C2	122
Sasamungga, Sol. Is.	d7	79b
Sāsarām, India	F9	54
Sasayama, Japan	D8	40
Sásd, Hung.	C5	26
Sasebo, Japan	F2	40
Saseginaga, Lac, l., Qc., Can.	A11	112
Saskatchewan, state, Can.	E9	106
Saskatchewan, stm., Can.	E10	106
Saskatoon, Sk., Can.	B7	124
Saskylah, Russia	B11	34
Sasolburg, S. Afr.	E8	70
Sasovo, Russia	D6	32
Saspamco, Tx., U.S.	E9	130
Sassafras, Ky., U.S.	G2	114
Sassafras Mountain, mtn., U.S.	A3	116
Sassandra, C. Iv.	I3	64
Sassandra, stm., C. Iv.	I3	64
Sassari, Italy	D2	24
Sassnitz, Ger.	B9	16
Sasso Marconi, Italy	F8	22
Sassuolo, Italy	F7	22
Sasyk, ozero, l., Ukr.	D16	26
Sasykkol', ozero, l., Kaz.	E14	32
Satadougou, Mali	G2	64
Satah Mountain, vol., B.C., Can.	D6	138
Sata-misaki, c., Japan	H3	40
Satāna, India	H5	54
Sátão, Port.	D3	20
Sātāra, India	C1	53
Satara Ruskamp, S. Afr.	D10	70
Satélite, Mex.	C1	130
Satellite Beach, Fl., U.S.	H5	116
Satengar, Pulau, i., Indon.	G10	50
Satevó, Mex.	G1	130
Satevó, stm., Mex.	G1	130
Satilla, stm., Ga., U.S.	E4	116
Sátiro Dias, Braz.	F6	88
Şatīt (Tekezē), stm., Afr.	E7	62
Šatki, Russia	I20	8
Satluj see Sutlej, stm., Asia	C5	54
Satna, India	F8	54
Sátoraljaújhely, Hung.	A8	26
Sātpura Range, mts., India	H6	54
Satsuma-hantō, pen., Japan	H3	40
Satsunan-shotō, is., Japan	k19	39a
Sattahip, Thai.	F5	48
Satui, Indon.	E9	50
Satu Mare, Rom.	B9	26
Satu Mare, state, Rom.	B10	26
Şatun, Thai.	I4	48
Šatura, Russia	I18	8
Saturnino M. Laspiur, Arg.	E6	92
Satyamangalam, India	F3	53
Sauce, Arg.	E8	92
Sauce Corto, Arroyo, stm., Arg.	H7	92
Saucier, Ms., U.S.	G9	122
Saucillo, Mex.	A6	100
Sauđárkrókur, Ice.	k30	8a
Saudi Arabia, ctry., Asia	E5	56
Sauerland, reg., Ger.	E4	16
Saueruiná, stm., Braz.	F6	84
Saugatuck, Mi., U.S.	F3	112
Saugeen, stm., On., Can.	D8	112
Saugerties, N.Y., U.S.	B12	114
Saugstad, Mount, mtn., B.C., Can.	D4	138
Saujil, Arg.	D4	92
Sauk, stm., Mn., U.S.	F4	118
Sauk Centre, Mn., U.S.	F3	118
Sauk City, Wi., U.S.	H9	118
Sauk Rapids, Mn., U.S.	F4	118
Saukville, Wi., U.S.	E1	112
Saül, Fr. Gu.	C7	84
Sauldre, Canal de la, can., Fr.	B8	18
Saulgau, Ger.	I5	16
Saulieu, Fr.	G13	14
Sault aux Cochons, stm., Qc., Can.	A7	110
Sault-de-Vaucluse, Fr.	E11	18
Saulteaux, stm., Ab., Can.	B16	138
Sault Sainte Marie, On., Can.	B5	112
Sault Sainte Marie, Mi., U.S.	B5	112
Saumarez Reef, rf., Austl.	C9	76
Saumlaki, Indon.	G9	44
Saumur, Fr.	G8	14
Saunders Island, i., Falk. Is.	J4	90
Saunders Island, i., S. Geor.	K12	82
Sauquoit, N.Y., U.S.	B10	114
Saurimo, Ang.	B3	68
Sausar, India	H7	54
Sausu, Indon.	D12	50
Sautar, Ang.	C2	68
Sauteurs, Gren.	q10	105e
Sauveterre-de-Guyenne, Fr.	E5	18
Sauwald, for., Aus.	B10	22
Sauzal, Mex.	C1	130
Sava, stm., Eur.	F16	22
Savai'i, i., Samoa	g11	79c
Savalou, Benin	H5	64
Savanna, Il., U.S.	B7	120
Savanna, Ok., U.S.	C3	122
Savannah, Ga., U.S.	D4	116
Savannah, Tn., U.S.	B10	122
Savannah, stm., U.S.	D4	116
Savannah River Plant, sci., S.C., U.S.	C4	116
Savannah Sound, Bah.	K9	116
Savannakhét, Laos	D7	48
Savanna-la-Mar, Jam.	i12	104d
Savant Lake, On., Can.	A8	118
Savant Lake, l., On., Can.	A8	118
Sāvantvādi, India	D1	53
Savanūr, India	D2	53
Savaştepe, Tur.	D10	28
Savè, Benin	H5	64
Save (Sabi), stm., Afr.	E5	68
Sāveh, Iran	B7	56
Savelugu, Ghana	H4	64
Savenay, Fr.	G7	14
Saverdun, Fr.	F7	18
Savigliano, Italy	F4	22
Savino-Borisovskaja, Russia	E21	8
Savinskij, Russia	E19	8
Şavissik, Grnld.	B13	141
Šavnik, Yugo.	G6	26
Savoie, state, Fr.	D12	18
Savoie, hist. reg., Fr.	D12	18
Savo Island, i., Sol. Is.	e8	79b
Savona, B.C., Can.	F10	138
Savona, Italy	F5	22
Savonlinna, Fin.	F13	8
Savoy, Tx., U.S.	D2	122
Savoy see Savoie, hist. reg., Fr.	D12	18
Savran', Ukr.	A17	26
Savusavu Bay, b., Fiji	p19	79e
Savu Sea see Sawu, Laut, Indon.	G7	44
Sawah, Indon.	B9	50
Sawahlunto, Indon.	D2	50
Sawāi Mādhopur, India	E6	54
Sawākin, Sudan	D7	62
Sawankhalok, Thai.	D4	48
Sawara, Japan	D13	40
Sawata, Japan	A11	40
Sawatch Range, mts., Co., U.S.	B2	128
Sawdā', Jabal, mtn., Sau. Ar.	F5	56
Sawdā', Jabal as-, hills, Libya	A4	62
Sawdā', Qurnat as-, mtn., Leb.	D7	58
Sawdirī, Sudan	E5	62
Şawqirah, Oman	F8	56
Şawqirah, Dawḥat, b., Oman	F8	56
Sawtooth National Recreation Area, p.o.i., Id., U.S.	F12	136
Sawu, Laut (Savu Sea), Indon.	G7	44
Sawu, Pulau, i., Indon.	H7	44
Sawyer, Mi., U.S.	G3	112
Sawyer, N.D., U.S.	F12	124
Saxby, stm., Austl.	B3	76
Saxon, Wi., U.S.	E8	118
Saxony see Sachsen, state, Ger.	F9	16
Saxony see Sachsen, hist. reg., Ger.	D5	16
Saxony-Anhalt see Sachsen-Anhalt, state, Ger.	D7	16
Saxton, Pa., U.S.	D7	114
Say, Niger	G5	64
Sayan Mountains, mts., Asia	D17	32
Sayaxché, Guat.	D2	102
Şaydā (Sidon), Leb.	E6	58
Şaydā, state, Leb.	E6	58
Sayhūt, Yemen	F7	56
Sayil, hist., Mex.	B3	102
Saylac, Som.	B8	66
Saylūn, Khirbat (Shiloh), hist., W.B.	F6	58
Saynshand, Mong.	C7	36
Sayram Hu, l., China	F14	32
Sayre, Ok., U.S.	F9	128
Sayre, Pa., U.S.	C9	114
Sayreville, N.J., U.S.	D11	114
Sayward, B.C., Can.	F5	138
Saywūn, Yemen	F6	56
Saza, Japan	F2	40
Sazan, i., Alb.	D13	24
Şba, Alg.	D4	64
Ščadryn, Bela.	H12	10
Scafell Pike, mtn., Eng., U.K.	G9	12
Scalea, Italy	E9	24
Scammon Bay, Ak., U.S.	D6	140
Scandia, Ks., U.S.	B11	128
Scanlon, Mn., U.S.	E6	118
Scapa Flow, b., Scot., U.K.	C9	12
Scapegoat Mountain, mtn., Mt., U.S.	C14	136
Ščapino, Russia	E20	34
Şcappoose, Or., U.S.	E3	136
Ščara, stm., Bela.	G8	10
Scarborough, St. K./N.	C2	105a
Scarborough, Trin.	r13	105f
Scarborough, Eng., U.K.	G12	12
Scarborough, ngh., On., Can.	E10	112
Scărișoara, Rom.	F11	26
Scarp, i., Scot., U.K.	C5	12
Şcawfell Island, i., Austl.	C7	76
Šćedro, Otok, i., Cro.	G13	22
Ščekino, Russia	F20	10
Ščelkovo, Russia	E20	10
Şceptre, Sk., Can.	D4	124
Ščerbakovo, Russia	C21	34
Ščerbakty, Kaz.	D13	32
Ščerbinka, Russia	E20	10
Schaffhausen, Switz.	C5	22
Schaffhouse see Schaffhausen, Switz.	C5	22
Schärding, Aus.	B10	22
Schefferville, Qc., Can.	E17	106
Scheinfeld, Ger.	G6	16
Schelde, stm., Eur.	C13	14
Schell Creek Range, mts., Nv., U.S.	D2	132
Schenectady, N.Y., U.S.	B11	114
Schenevus Creek, stm., N.Y., U.S.	B11	114
Schertz, Tx., U.S.	E9	130
Schiedam, Neth.	C13	14
Schiermonnikoog, i., Neth.	C2	16
Schiltigheim, Fr.	F16	14
Schio, Italy	E8	22
Schkeuditz, Ger.	E8	16
Schladming, Aus.	C10	22
Schlater, Ms., U.S.	D8	122
Schleiden, Ger.	F2	16
Schleswig, Ger.	B5	16
Schleswig, Ia., U.S.	B2	120
Schleswig-Holstein, state, Ger.	B6	16
Schlitz, Ger.	F5	16
Schlüchtern, Ger.	F5	16
Schmölln, Ger.	F8	16
Schneeberg, Ger.	F8	16
Schneeberg, mtn., Ger.	F7	16
Schneverdingen, Ger.	C5	16
Schœlcher, Mart.	k6	105c
Schofield, Wi., U.S.	G9	118
Schoharie, N.Y., U.S.	B11	114
Schoharie Creek, stm., N.Y., U.S.	B11	114
Schönebeck, Ger.	D7	16
Schongau, Ger.	I6	16
Schopfheim, Ger.	I3	16
Schorndorf, Ger.	H5	16
Schouten, Kepulauan, is., Indon.	F10	44
Schouten Island, i., Austl.	o14	77a
Schouten Islands, is., Pap. N. Gui.	a3	79a
Schramberg, Ger.	H4	16
Schreiber, On., Can.	C11	118
Schriever, La., U.S.	H8	122
Schrobenhausen, Ger.	H7	16
Schulenburg, Tx., U.S.	E11	130
Schultz Lake, l., Nu., Can.	C11	106
Schuyler, Va., U.S.	G7	114
Schuylkill, stm., Pa., U.S.	D10	114
Schuylkill Haven, Pa., U.S.	D9	114
Schwabach, Ger.	G7	16
Schwaben, hist. reg., Ger.	H5	16
Schwäbische Alb, mts., Ger.	H5	16
Schwäbisch Gmünd, Ger.	H5	16
Schwäbisch Hall, Ger.	G5	16
Schwabmünchen, Ger.	H6	16
Schwandorf in Bayern, Ger.	G7	16
Schwaner, Pegunungan, mts., Indon.	D8	50
Schwarzach im Pongau, Aus.	C10	22
Schwarzwald (Black Forest), mts., Ger.	H4	16
Schwatka Mountains, mts., Ak., U.S.	C8	140
Schwaz, Aus.	C8	22
Schwechat, Aus.	B13	22
Schwedt, Ger.	C10	16
Schweinfurt, Ger.	F5	16
Schweizer Nationalpark, p.o.i., Switz.	D7	22
Schweizer-Reineke, S. Afr.	E7	70
Schwerin, Ger.	C7	16
Schweriner See, l., Ger.	C7	16
Schwyz, Switz.	C5	22
Sciacca, Italy	G6	24
Scicli, Italy	H8	24
Scilly, Isles of, is., Eng., U.K.	L6	12
Scio, Oh., U.S.	D4	114
Scio, Or., U.S.	F4	136
Şcioto, stm., Oh., U.S.	E3	114
Šćit, mtn., Bos.	E4	26
Scobey, Mt., U.S.	F8	124
Scone, Austl.	I8	76
Scooba, Ms., U.S.	E10	122
Scordia, Italy	G8	24
Scoresby Land, reg., Grnld.	C21	141
Scoresbysund (Ittoqqortoormiit), Grnld.	C21	141
Scoresby Sund, strt., Grnld.	C21	141
Scotia, N.Y., U.S.	B12	114
Scotia Ridge, unds.	N8	144
Scotia Sea	K10	82
Scotland, On., Can.	E9	112
Scotland, S.D., U.S.	D15	126
Scotland, Tx., U.S.	H10	128
Scotland, state, U.K.	E8	12
Scotlandville, La., U.S.	G7	122
Scotsburn, N.S., Can.	E14	110
Scott, Sk., Can.	B5	124
Scott, Ms., U.S.	D7	122
Scott, stm., Ca., U.S.	B3	134
Scott, Cape, c., B.C., Can.	F2	138
Scott, Mount, mtn., Or., U.S.	H4	136
Scott Base, sci., Ant.	C22	81
Scott City, Mo., U.S.	G8	120
Scott Coast, cst., Ant.	C20	81
Scottdale, Pa., U.S.	D6	114
Scott Island, i., Ant.	B23	81
Scott Islands, is., B.C., Can.	F2	138
Scott Peak, mtn., Id., U.S.	F14	136
Scott Reef, rf., Austl.	B4	74
Scottsbluff, Ne., U.S.	F9	126
Scotts Bluff National Monument, p.o.i., Ne., U.S.	F9	126
Scottsboro, Al., U.S.	C12	122
Scottsdale, Austl.	n13	77a
Scottsdale, Az., U.S.	J5	132
Scotts Head, c., Dom.	j6	105c
Scotts Hill, Tn., U.S.	B10	122
Scottsville, Ky., U.S.	H11	120
Scottville, Mi., U.S.	E3	112
Scourie, Scot., U.K.	C7	12
Scout Lake, Sk., Can.	E8	124
Scranton, N.D., U.S.	A9	126
Scranton, Pa., U.S.	C10	114
Screven, Ga., U.S.	E3	116
Scribner, Ne., U.S.	J2	118
Şcrub Island, i., Anguilla	A2	105a
Ščuče, Russia	C10	32
Ščučinsk, Kaz.	D12	32
Ščučyn, Bela.	G7	10
Scugog, Lake, l., On., Can.	D11	112
Scunthorpe, Eng., U.K.	H12	12
Şcutari, Lake, l., Eur.	H16	22
Ščytkavičy, Bela.	G10	10
Seabrook, Lake, l., Austl.	F3	74
Seaford, De., U.S.	F10	114
Seaforth, On., Can.	E8	112
Seahorse Point, c., Nu., Can.	C15	106
Sea Islands, is., U.S.	E5	116
Sea Isle City, N.J., U.S.	E11	114
Seal, stm., Mb., Can.	D11	106
Seal, Cape, c., S. Afr.	I6	70
Sea Lake, Austl.	J4	76
Sealark Channel, strt., Sol. Is.	e9	79b
Seal Cays, is., T./C. Is.	B12	102
Seale, Al., U.S.	E13	122
Sealevel, N.C., U.S.	B9	116
Seal Island, i., N.S., Can.	G10	110
Sealy, Tx., U.S.	H2	122
Seara, Braz.	C11	92
Searcy, Ar., U.S.	B7	122
Searles Lake, l., Ca., U.S.	H8	134
Searsport, Me., U.S.	F7	110
Seaside, Ca., U.S.	G4	134
Seaside, Or., U.S.	D3	136
Seaside Park, N.J., U.S.	E11	114
Seattle, Wa., U.S.	C4	136
Sebago Lake, l., Me., U.S.	G6	110
Se Bai, stm., Thai.	E7	48
Sebakung, Indon.	D10	50
Sebangan, Teluk, b., Indon.	E8	50
Sebangka, Pulau, i., Indon.	C4	50
Sebastian, Tx., U.S.	H10	130
Sebastian, Cape, c., Or., U.S.	A1	134
Sebastián Vizcaíno, Bahía, b., Mex.	A1	100
Sebastopol, Ca., U.S.	E3	134
Sebastopol, Ms., U.S.	E9	122
Şebec Lake, l., Me., U.S.	E7	110
Šebekino, Russia	D5	32
Seben, Tur.	C14	28
Sebeș, Rom.	D10	26
Sebes Körös (Crișul Repede), stm., Eur.	B8	26
Sebewaing, Mi., U.S.	E6	112
Sebež, Russia	D11	10
Sebino see Iseo, Lago d', l., Italy	E6	22
Sebnitz, Ger.	F10	16
Sebree, Ky., U.S.	G10	120
Sebring, Fl., U.S.	I4	116
Sebuku, Indon.	A10	50
Sebuku, Teluk, b., Indon.	A11	50
Sebuyau, Malay.	C7	50
Secchia, stm., Italy	F7	22
Sechura, Peru	E1	84
Sechura, Desierto de, des., Peru	E1	84
Seclantás, Arg.	B4	92
Sečovská Polianka, Slov.	H17	16
Section, Al., U.S.	C13	122
Security, Co., U.S.	C4	128
Seda, China	E5	36
Seda, Lith.	D5	10
Sedah, Indon.	B4	74
Sedalia, Ab., Can.	C3	124
Sedalia, Mo., U.S.	F4	120
Sedan, Fr.	E13	14
Sedanovo, Russia	C18	32
Sedayu, Indon.	G8	50
Seddon, Kap, c., Grnld.	B14	141
Sedel'nikovo, Russia	C13	32
Séderon, Fr.	E11	18
Sedgewick, Ab., Can.	D19	138
Sedgwick, Co., U.S.	G10	126
Sedgwick, Ks., U.S.	D11	128
Sédhiou, Sen.	G1	64
Sedlčany, Czech Rep.	G10	16
Sedom (Sodom), hist., Isr.	G6	58
Şedro Woolley, Wa., U.S.	B4	136
Šeduva, Lith.	E6	10
Seehausen, Ger.	D7	16
Seeheim, Nmb.	E3	70
Seeis, Nmb.	C3	70
Seekoei, stm., S. Afr.	G7	70
Seeley Lake, Mt., U.S.	C13	136
Seelyville, In., U.S.	E10	120
Sées, Fr.	F9	14
Seesen, Ger.	E6	16
Sefadu, S.L.	H2	64
Seferihisar, Tur.	E9	28
Segama, stm., Malay.	A11	50
Segamat, Malay.	K6	48
Ségbana, Benin	G5	64
Segeri, Indon.	F11	50
Segesta, hist., Italy	G6	24
Segeža, Russia	E15	8
Segorbe, Spain	E10	20

Name | Map Ref. | Page

Ségou, Mali G3 64
Segovary, Russia E20 8
Segovia, Spain D6 20
Segovia, co., Spain C6 20
Segozero, ozero, l., Russia E15 8
Segre, stm., Eur. H6 18
Seguam Island, i., Ak., U.S. g24 140a
Séguédine, Niger E7 64
Séguéla, C. Iv. H3 64
Seguí, Arg. E7 92
Seguin, Tx., U.S. E10 130
Segundo, stm., Arg. E6 92
Seguntur, Indon. C10 50
Segura, stm., Spain F10 20
Segura, Sierra de, mts., Spain G8 20
Sehithwa, Bots. B6 70
Sehore, India G6 54
Sehwān, Pak. D10 56
Seibert, Co., U.S. B6 128
Seikpyu, Mya. B2 48
Seiland, i., Nor. A10 8
Seiling, Ok., U.S. E9 128
Seim, stm., Eur. D4 32
Seinäjoki, Fin. E10 8
Seine, stm., Mb., Can. E17 124
Seine, stm., On., Can. C6 118
Seine, stm., Fr. E9 14
Seine, Baie de la, b., Fr. E8 14
Seine, Bay of the see Seine, Baie de la, b., Fr. E8 14
Seine-et-Marne, state, Fr. F12 14
Seine-Maritime, state, Fr. E9 14
Seixal, Port. F1 20
Seixas, Ponta do, c., Braz. D8 88
Sejmčan, Russia D19 34
Sejny, Pol. B19 16
Sekayam, stm., Indon. C7 50
Sekayu, Indon. E3 50
Sekeladi, Indon. E3 50
Şeki, Azer. A6 56
Seki, Japan D9 40
Sekiu, Wa., U.S. B2 136
Sekoma, Bots. D6 70
Şekondi, Ghana I4 64
Šeksna, Russia A21 10
Šelagskij, mys, c., Russia B23 34
Selama, Malay. J5 48
Selangor, state, Malay. K5 48
Selaru, Pulau, i., Indon. G9 44
Selatan, Tanjung, c., Indon. F9 50
Selatpanjang, Indon. C3 50
Selawik, Ak., U.S. C8 140
Selawik Lake, l., Ak., U.S. C7 140
Selayar, Pulau, i., Indon. G12 50
Selayar, Selat, strt., Indon. F12 50
Selb, Ger. F8 16
Selbusjøen, l., Nor. E4 8
Selby, Eng., U.K. H11 12
Selby, S.D., U.S. B12 126
Selbyville, De., U.S. F10 114
Sel'co, Russia E19 8
Sel'co, Russia G17 10
Selçuk, Tur. F10 28
Seldovia, Ak., U.S. E9 140
Selebi-Phikwe, Bots. C9 70
Šelečnja, Russia H17 10
Šelehov, Russia D18 32
Selemdža, stm., Russia F14 34
Selemdžinsk, Russia F15 34
Selenduma, Russia F10 34
Selenge, D.R.C. E3 66
Selenge, stm., Asia G9 34
Selenicë, Alb. D13 24
Selennjah, stm., Russia C16 34
Sélestat, Fr. F16 14
Seleznëvo, Russia F13 8
Selfoss, Ice. I29 8a
Selfridge, N.D., U.S. A11 126
Sel'gon, Russia G16 34
Sélibabi, Maur. F2 64
Seliger, ozero, l., Russia C15 10
Seligman, Az., U.S. H4 132
Šelihova, zaliv, b., Russia D20 34
Selimbau, Indon. C8 50
Selinsgrove, Pa., U.S. D8 114
Selinunte, hist., Italy G6 24
Seliŝče, Russia D16 10
Seližarovo, Russia D16 10
Selkirk, Mb., Can. D17 124
Selkirk, Scot., U.K. F10 12
Selkirk Mountains, mts., N.A. F13 138
Sellers, S.C., U.S. B6 116
Sellersburg, In., U.S. F12 120
Selles-sur-Cher, Fr. G10 14
Selm, Ger. E3 16
Selma, Al., U.S. E11 122
Selma, Ca., U.S. G6 134
Selma, N.C., U.S. A7 116
Selmer, Tn., U.S. B10 122
Şelmont, Al., U.S. E11 122
Šelon', stm., Russia B13 10
Selong, Indon. H10 50
Selva, Arg. D6 92
Selvagens, Ilhas, is., Port. C1 64
Selvas, for., Braz. F8 82
Selway, stm., Id., U.S. D11 136
Selwyn, Austl. C3 76
Selwyn, Passage, strt., Vanuatu k16 79d
Selwyn Lake, l., Can. D10 106
Selwyn Mountains, mts., Can. C4 106
Selwyn Range, mts., Austl. C3 76
Seman, stm., Alb. D13 24
Semangka, Teluk, b., Indon. F4 50
Semara, W. Sah. D2 64
Semarang, Indon. G7 50
Semayang, Kenohan, l., Indon. D10 50
Sembakung, stm., Indon. B10 50
Semcy, Russia H16 10
Semenanjung Malaysia, hist. reg., Malay. K6 48
Semenov, Russia H21 8
Semeru, Gunung, vol., Indon. H8 50
Semey see Semipalatinsk, Kaz. D13 32
Semežava, Bela. H10 10
Semichi Islands, is., Ak., U.S. g21 140a
Semiluki, Russia D5 32
Semily, Czech Rep. F11 16
Seminary, Ms., U.S. F9 122
Seminoe Reservoir, res., Wy., U.S. A9 132
Seminole, Ok., U.S. B2 122
Seminole, Tx., U.S. B5 130
Seminole, Lake, res., U.S. G14 122
Seminole Draw, stm., U.S. B5 130
Semiozërnoe, Kaz. D10 32
Semipalatinsk, Kaz. D13 32
Semitau, Indon. C7 50
Semizbuga, Kaz. D13 32
Semliki, stm., Afr. D6 66
Semnān, Iran B7 56
Şemois, stm., Eur. E13 14
Šemonaiha, Kaz. D14 32
Semporna, Malay. A11 50
Semuda, Indon. E8 50
Semža, Russia C21 8
Sên, stm., Camb. F7 48
Sena, Bol. B3 90
Senador Canedo, Braz. I1 88
Senador Pompeu, Braz. C6 88
Senaki, Geor. F6 32
Sena Madureira, Braz. E4 84
Senanayake Samudra, res., Sri L. H5 53
Senanga, Zam. D3 68
Senath, Mo., U.S. H7 120
Şenatobia, Ms., U.S. C8 122
Šenber, Kaz. E11 32
Sendai, Japan H3 40
Sendai, Japan A13 40
Sendelingsdrif, Nmb. F3 70
Sendhwa, India H5 54
Sendurjana, India H7 54
Senduruhan, Indon. D7 50
Senebui, Tanjung, c., Indon. B2 50
Seneca, Il., U.S. C9 120
Seneca, Ks., U.S. E1 120
Seneca, Mo., U.S. H3 120
Seneca, S.C., U.S. B3 116
Seneca, Mount, mtn., N.Y., U.S. B7 114
Seneca Falls, N.Y., U.S. B9 114
Seneca Lake, l., N.Y., U.S. B8 114
Senegal, ctry., Afr. G2 64
Sénégal, stm., Afr. F2 64
Senekal, S. Afr. F8 70
Senetosa, Capu di (Senetosa, Punta di), c., Fr. H14 18
Senetosa, Punta di see Senetosa, Capu di, c., Fr. H14 18
Senftenberg, Ger. E10 16
Sengés, Braz. B13 92
Sênggê, stm., China B8 54
Senhor do Bonfim, Braz. F5 88
Senica, Slov. H13 16
Senigallia, Italy G10 22
Senirkent, Tur. E13 28
Senise, Italy D10 24
Senja, i., Nor. B7 8
Senkaku-shotō, is., Japan F9 36
Şenköy, Tur. B7 58
Senkursk, Russia E20 8
Senlis, Fr. E11 14
Senmonorom, Camb. F8 48
Senneterre, Qc., Can. F15 106
Senoia, Ga., U.S. D14 122
Şenpazar, Tur. B16 28
Sens, Fr. F12 14
Senta, Yugo. D7 26
Sentarum, Danau, l., Indon. C7 50
Sentinel, Ok., U.S. F9 128
Sentinel Butte, mtn., N.D., U.S. A8 126
Senyavin Islands, is., Micron. C6 72
Seo de Urgel see La Seu d'Urgell, Spain B12 20
Seonāth, stm., India H8 54
Seoni, India G7 54
Seoni Mālwa, India G6 54
Seoul see Sŏul, Kor., S. F7 38
Sepanjang, Pulau, i., Indon. G9 50
Sepasu, Indon. C10 50
Sepetiba, Baía de, b., Braz. L4 88
Sepi, Sol. Is. e8 79b
Sepik, stm., Pap. N. Gui. a3 79a
Sepopol, Pol. B17 16
Sept-Îles, Qc., Can. E17 106
Sepúlveda, Spain C7 20
Seputih, stm., Indon. F4 50
Sequatchie, stm., Tn., U.S. B13 122
Sequillo, stm., Spain C5 20
Sequim, Wa., U.S. B3 136
Sequoia National Park, p.o.i., Ca., U.S. G7 134
Šerabad, Uzb. B10 56
Serafimovič, Russia E6 32
Seraing, Bel. D14 14
Seram (Ceram), i., Indon. F8 44
Seram, Laut (Ceram Sea), Indon. F8 44
Serang, Indon. G5 50
Serasan, Pulau, i., Indon. B6 50
Serasan, Selat, strt., Indon. B6 50
Serayevo see Sarajevo, Bos. F5 26
Serbeulangit, Pegunungan, mts., Indon. K3 48
Serbia see Srbija, state, Yugo. E7 26
Serdo, Eth. E8 62
Serdobsk, Russia D6 32
Séré'ama, Mont, mtn., Vanuatu i16 79d
Serebrjansk, Kaz. E14 32
Serebrjanye Prudy, Russia F21 10
Sered', Slov. H13 16
Seredejskij, Russia F18 10
Serëdka, Russia B11 10
Seremban, Malay. K5 48
Serengeti National Park, p.o.i., Tan. E6 66
Serengeti Plain, pl., Tan. E6 66
Serengka, Indon. D7 50
Serenje, Zam. C5 68
Seret (Siret), stm., Eur. A12 26
Sergač, Russia I21 8
Sergeevka, Kaz. D11 32
Sergeevka, Russia C10 38
Sergeja Kirova, ostrova, is., Russia A6 34
Sergen, Tur. B10 28
Sergiev Posad, Russia D21 10
Serginskij, Russia B10 32
Sergipe, state, Braz. F7 88
Sergozero, ozero, l., Russia C17 8
Seria, Bru. A9 50
Serian, Malay. C7 50
Seribudolok, Indon. B1 50
Seridó, stm., Braz. D7 88
Sérifos, i., Grc. F7 28
Serik, Tur. G14 28
Serinyol, Tur. B7 58
Serio, stm., Italy E6 22
Şerkovo, Russia A15 32
Serkovaja Gora, Russia F12 34
Serov, Russia C10 32
Serowe, Bots. C8 70
Serpejsk, Russia F17 10
Serpentine Lakes, l., Austl. E5 74
Serpents Mouth, strt. C11 86
Serpuhov, Russia F20 10
Serra, Braz. K5 88
Serra Branca, Braz. D7 88
Serra da Canastra, Parque Nacional da, p.o.i., Braz. K2 88
Serra da Capivara, Parque Nacional da, p.o.i., Braz. E4 88
Serra de Outes, Spain B1 20
Serra do Navio, Braz. C7 84
Serra do Salitre, Braz. J2 88
Serra dos Órgãos, Parque Nacional da, p.o.i., Braz. L4 88
Serrana, Braz. K2 88
Serrana, Cayo de, unds., Col. E7 102
Serrana Bank see Serrana, Cayo de, unds., Col. E7 102
Serrania, Braz. K2 88
Serranía de la Neblina, Parque Nacional, p.o.i., Ven. G8 86
Serranilla, Banco see Serranilla, Cayo de, unds., Col. E8 102
Serranilla, Cayo de, unds., Col. E8 102
Serranilla Bank see Serranilla, Cayo de, unds., Col. E8 102
Serrano, Banco see Serrana, Cayo de, unds., Col. E7 102
Serra Talhada, Braz. E6 88
Serres, Fr. E11 18
Sérres, Grc. B6 28
Serrezuela, Arg. E5 92
Serrinha, Braz. F6 88
Serrita, Braz. D6 88
Sertânia, Braz. E7 88
Sertãozinho, Braz. K1 88
Serui, Indon. F10 44
Serule, Bots. B8 70
Serutu, Pulau, i., Indon. D6 50
Seruwai, Indon. J4 48
Sêrxü, China E4 36
Seryševo, Russia F14 34
Sesayap, stm., Indon. B10 50
Sesayap Lama, Indon. B10 50
Seseganaga Lake, l., On., Can. A8 118
Sese Islands, is., Ug. E6 66
Sesfontein, Nmb. D1 68
Sesheke, Zam. D3 68
Sesia, stm., Italy E5 22
Sesibu, Indon. A10 50
Sessa Aurunca, Italy C7 24
Sestao, Spain A7 20
Sestri Levante, Italy F6 22
Şestroreck, Russia F14 8
Šešupė, stm., Eur. F5 10
Šeta, Lith. E7 10
Sète, Fr. F9 18
Sete Barras, Braz. B13 92
Sete Cidades, Parque Nacional de, p.o.i., Braz. C5 88
Sete Lagoas, Braz. J3 88
Sete Quedas, Parque Nacional de, p.o.i., Braz. A11 92
Sete Quedas, Salto das (Guairá, Salto del), wtfl, S.A. B10 92
Seth Ward, Tx., U.S. G7 128
Seto, Japan D10 40
Seto-naikai (Inland Sea), Japan E5 40
Seton Portage, B.C., Can. F8 138
Settat, Mor. C3 64
Setté Cama, Gabon E1 66
Sette-Daban, hrebet, mts., Russia D16 34
Settlers, S. Afr. D9 70
Setúbal, Port. F1 20
Setúbal, state, Port. F2 20
Setúbal, Baía de, b., Port. F2 20
Seul, Lac, l., On., Can. A6 118
Seul Choix Point, c., Mi., U.S. C4 112
Seulimeum, Indon. J2 48
Sevan, Lake see Sevana Lich, l., Arm. A6 56
Sevana Lich, l., Arm. A6 56
Sevastopol', Ukr. G15 6
Ševelevskaja, Russia F20 8
Seven Persons, Ab., Can. E3 124
Seven Sisters Peaks, mtn., B.C., Can. B2 138
Seventy Mile House, B.C., Can. E9 138
Severn, stm., On., Can. E12 106
Severn, stm., U.K. J10 12
Severnaja Dvina (Northern Dvina), stm., Russia E19 8
Severnaja Osetija, state, Russia F6 32
Severnaja Sos'va, stm., Russia B10 32
Severnaja Zemlja, is., Russia B12 30
Severna Park, Md., U.S. E9 114
Severnoe, Russia C13 32
Severnye uvaly, hills, Russia G22 8
Severnyj Ural, mts., Russia B9 32
Severočeský, state, Czech Rep. F10 16
Severodvinsk (Molotovsk), Russia D18 8
Severo-Enisejskij, Russia B16 32
Severo-Kuril'sk, Russia F20 34
Severomoravský, state, Czech Rep. G13 16
Severomorsk, Russia B15 8
Severo-Sibirskaja nizmennost' (North Siberain Lowland), pl., Russia B6 34
Severoural'sk (Severouralsk), Russia B9 32
Severo-Zadonsk, Russia F21 10
Severy, Ks., U.S. D12 128
Sevettijärvi, Fin. B13 8
Sevier, stm., Ut., U.S. D4 132
Sevier, East Fork, stm., Ut., U.S. F5 132
Sevier Desert, des., Ut., U.S. D4 132
Sevier Lake, l., Ut., U.S. B6 98
Sevierville, Tn., U.S. I2 114
Sevilla, Col. E4 86
Sevilla (Seville), Spain G5 20
Sevilla, co., Spain G5 20
Seville see Sevilla, Spain G5 20
Seville, Fl., U.S. G4 116
Sevlievo, Blg. F12 26
Sewāni, India D5 54
Seward, Ak., U.S. D10 140
Seward, Ne., U.S. G15 126
Seward, Pa., U.S. D7 114
Seward Peninsula, pen., Ak., U.S. C7 140
Sexsmith, Ab., Can. A12 138
Sextín, stm., Mex. B6 100
Seybaplaya, Mex. C2 102
Seychelles, ctry., Afr. k12 69b
Seychelles, is., Sey. k13 69b
Seydişehir, Tur. F14 28
Seyðisfjörður, Ice. k32 8a
Seyhan (Sarus), stm., Tur. B6 58
Seyhan Barajı, res., Tur. A6 58
Seymour, Austl. K5 76
Seymour, S. Afr. H8 70
Seymour, Ct., U.S. C12 114
Seymour, In., U.S. F12 120
Seymour, Mo., U.S. G5 120
Seymour, Tx., U.S. H9 128
Seymour, Wi., U.S. D1 112
Sežana, Slvn. E10 22
Sézanne, Fr. F12 14
Sfântu Gheorghe, Rom. D12 26
Sfântu Gheorghe, Braţul, stm., Rom. E16 26
Sfântu Gheorghe, Ostrovul, i., Rom. D16 26
Sfax, Tun. C7 64
's-Gravenhage (The Hague), Neth. B13 14
Sha, stm., China H7 42
Sha, stm., China H8 42
Shaanxi, state, China E3 42
Shabeelle (Shebelē Wenz, Wabē), stm., Afr. D8 66
Shabunda, D.R.C. E5 66
Shabwah, Yemen F6 56
Shache (Yarkant), China B12 56
Shackleton Ice Shelf, ice, Ant. B14 81
Shackleton Range, mts., Ant. D2 81
Shady Cove, Or., U.S. A3 134
Shady Grove, Fl., U.S. F2 116
Shadyside, Oh., U.S. E5 114
Shageluk, Ak., U.S. D8 140
Shag Rocks, r., S. Geor. J8 90
Shāhābād, India C3 53
Shāhābād, India C6 54
Shāhābād, India E7 54
Shāhāda, India H5 54
Shah Alam, Malay. K5 48
Shāhdādpur, Pak. F2 54
Shahdol, India G8 54
Shahe, China C7 42
Shahezhen, China A7 42
Shāhjahānpur, India E7 54
Shāh Kot, Pak. C4 54
Shāhpur, India C3 53
Shāhpur, Pak. D2 54
Shāhpura, India G8 54
Shāhpura, India E5 54
Shāhpura, India F5 54
Shahr-e Kord, Iran C7 56
Shaighālu, Pak. C2 54
Shājāpur, India G6 54
Shakawe, Bots. D3 68
Shaker Heights, Oh., U.S. G8 112
Shakespeare Island, i., On., Can. B10 118
Shaki, Nig. H5 64
Shakopee, Mn., U.S. G5 118
Shakotan-hantō, pen., Japan C14 38
Shaktoolik, Ak., U.S. D7 140
Shala, Lake see Shala Hāyk', l., Eth. F7 62
Shala Hāyk', l., Eth. F7 62
Shalalth, B.C., Can. F8 138
Shaler Mountains, mts., Can. A8 106
Shallowater, Tx., U.S. H6 128
Shaluli Shan, mts., China E4 36
Shām, Jabal ash-, mtn., Oman E8 56
Shamattawa, Mb., Can. D12 106
Shambe, Sudan F6 62
Shambu, Eth. F7 62
Shāmli, India D6 54
Shamokin, Pa., U.S. D9 114
Shamrock, Fl., U.S. G2 116
Shamrock, Tx., U.S. F8 128
Shamva, Zimb. D5 68
Shan, state, Mya. B4 48
Shancheng, China C2 42
Shandan, China D5 36
Shandī, Sudan D6 62
Shandong, state, China C7 42
Shandong Bandao (Shantung Peninsula), pen., China C9 42
Shangani, stm., Mong. C5 36
Shangani, Zimb. A9 70
Shangani, stm., Zimb. D4 68
Shangbahe, China F6 42
Shangcheng, China F6 42
Shangch'iu see Shangqiu, China D6 42
Shangchuan Dao, i., China K5 42
Shangdu, China C7 36
Shanghai, China F9 42
Shanghai, state, China F9 42
Shanghai Shih see Shanghai, state, China I4 38
Shanghang, China I7 42
Shanghe, China C7 42
Shangjao see Shangrao, China G7 42
Shangjin, China E4 42
Shanglin, China J3 42
Shangqing, China I8 42
Shangqiu, China D6 42
Shangqiu, China D6 42
Shangrao, China G7 42
Shangshui, China E6 42
Shangsi, China J2 42
Shangxian, China E3 42
Shangyi, China A6 42
Shangying, China B7 38
Shangyou Shuiku, res., China I6 42
Shangyu, China F9 42
Shangzhi, China B8 38
Shanhaiguan, China A8 42
Shanhaiwan see Shanhaiguan, China A8 42
Shanhetun, China B7 38
Shankou, China K3 42
Shannon, Il., U.S. B8 120
Shannon, Ms., U.S. C10 122
Shannon, stm., Ire. I3 12
Shannon Ø, i., Grnld. B22 141
Shannontown, S.C., U.S. C5 116
Shanshan, China C3 36
Shansi see Shanxi, state, China B5 42
Shantar Islands see Šantarskie ostrova, is., Russia E16 34
Shāntipur, India G12 54
Shantou, China J7 42
Shantung see Shandong, state, China C7 42
Shantung Peninsula see Shandong Bandao, pen., China C9 42
Shanwei, China J6 42
Shanxi, state, China B5 42
Shanxian, China D7 42
Shanyang, China E3 42
Shanyin, China B5 42
Shaoguan, China I5 42
Shaohing see Shaoxing, China G9 42
Shaohsing see Shaoxing, China G9 42
Shaokuan see Shaoguan, China I5 42
Shaoleng, stm., China C3 38
Shaowu, China H7 42
Shaoxing, China G9 42
Shaoyang, China H4 42
Shaqqā, Syria F7 58
Shaqrā', Sau. Ar. D6 56
Şhaqrā', Yemen G6 56
Shara, gora, mtn., Asia A5 56
Shari-dake, mtn., Japan C16 38
Sharīn Gol, Mong. B6 36
Sharjah see Ash-Shāriqah, U.A.E. D8 56
Shark Bay, b., Austl. E2 74
Sharktooth Mountain, mtn., B.C., Can. D5 106
Sharm el-Sheikh, Egypt K5 58
Sharon, N.D., U.S. G16 124
Sharon, Pa., U.S. C5 114
Sharon, Tn., U.S. H9 120
Sharon, Wi., U.S. B9 120
Sharpe, Lake, res., S.D., U.S. C12 126
Shashe, stm., Afr. B9 70
Shashemenē, Eth. F7 62
Shashi, China F5 42
Shasi see Shashi, China F5 42
Shasta, Ca., U.S. C3 134
Shasta, Mount, vol., Ca., U.S. B3 134
Shasta Lake, res., Ca., U.S. C3 134
Shāṭi', Wādī ash-, stm., Libya B2 62
Shats'k, Ukr. E19 16
Shats'kyi Pryrodnyi Natsional'nyi Park, p.o.i., Ukr. E19 16
Shattuck, Ok., U.S. E9 128
Shaunavon, Sk., Can. E5 124
Shaw, Ms., U.S. D8 122
Shawan, China C2 36
Shawinigan, Qc., Can. D4 110
Shawinigan-Sud, Qc., Can. D4 110
Shawnee, Ks., U.S. E3 120
Shawnee, Oh., U.S. E3 114
Shawnee, Ok., U.S. B2 122
Shawneetown, Il., U.S. G9 120
Shawville, Qc., Can. C13 112
Shaxian, China H7 42
Shayang, China F5 42
Shay Gap, Austl. D4 74
Shaykh Miskīn, Syria F7 58
Shaykh 'Uthmān, Yemen G6 56
Shchūchinsk see Ščučinsk, Kaz. D12 32
She, stm., China F6 42
Shebelē Wenz, Wabē (Shabeelle), stm., Afr. C8 66
Sheberghān, Afg. B10 56
Sheboygan, Wi., U.S. E2 112
Sheboygan, stm., Wi., U.S. E1 112
Sheboygan Falls, Wi., U.S. E1 112
Shechem, hist., W.B. F6 58
Shediac, N.B., Can. D12 110
Shedin Peak, mtn., B.C., Can. D5 106
Sheenjek, stm., Ak., U.S. C11 140
Sheep Mountain, mtn., Az., U.S. K2 132
Sheerness, Eng., U.K. J13 12
Sheet Harbour, N.S., Can. F14 110
Sheffield, N.Z. F4 80
Sheffield, Eng., U.K. H11 12
Sheffield, Al., U.S. C11 122
Sheffield, Il., U.S. J9 118
Sheffield, Ia., U.S. B4 120
Sheffield, Pa., U.S. C6 114
Shegaon, India H6 54
Sheho, Sk., Can. C10 124
Shehong, China F1 42
Sheikhpura, India F10 54
Shekhūpura, Pak. C5 54
Shekki see Zhongshan, China J5 42
Shelagyote Peak, mtn., B.C., Can. D5 106
Shelbina, Mo., U.S. E5 120
Shelburne, N.S., Can. G11 110
Shelburne, On., Can. D9 112
Shelburne Falls, Ma., U.S. B13 114
Shelby, Ia., U.S. C2 120
Shelby, Mi., U.S. E3 112
Shelby, Ms., U.S. D8 122
Shelby, Mt., U.S. B15 136
Shelby, Ne., U.S. F15 126
Shelby, N.C., U.S. A4 116
Shelbyville, Il., U.S. E9 120
Shelbyville, In., U.S. E12 120
Shelbyville, Mo., U.S. E5 120
Shelbyville, Tn., U.S. B12 122
Shelbyville, Lake, res., Il., U.S. E8 120
Sheldon, Ia., U.S. H3 118
Sheldon, Mo., U.S. G3 120
Shelek see Čilik, Kaz. F13 32
Shelekhov, Gulf of see Šelihova, zaliv, b., Russia D20 34
Shelikof Strait, strt., Ak., U.S. E9 140
Shell, stm., Mb., Can. C12 124
Shellbrook, Sk., Can. A7 124
Shell Creek, stm., Ne., U.S. F15 126
Shelley, B.C., Can. C8 138
Shellharbour, Austl. J8 76
Shell Lake, Wi., U.S. F7 118
Shellman, Ga., U.S. F14 122
Shellmouth Dam, dam, Mb., Can. D12 124
Shell Rock, Ia., U.S. B5 120
Shell Rock, stm., U.S. I6 118
Shellsburg, Ia., U.S. B5 120
Shelton, Ct., U.S. C12 114
Shelton, Ne., U.S. G14 126
Shemogue, N.B., Can. D12 110
Shemonaikha see Šemonaiha, Kaz. D14 32
Shenandoah, Ia., U.S. D2 120
Shenandoah, Va., U.S. F7 114
Shenandoah, stm., U.S. E8 114
Shenandoah, North Fork, stm., Va., U.S. F7 114
Shenandoah, South Fork, stm., Va., U.S. F7 114
Shenandoah National Park, p.o.i., Va., U.S. F7 114
Shenchi, China B4 42
Shencottah, India G3 53
Shendam, Nig. H6 64
Shenge, S.L. H2 64
Shengsi Liedao, is., China I5 38
Shengxian, China G9 42
Shengze, China F9 42
Shenjing, China J5 42
Shenmu, China B4 42
Shenqiu, China E6 42
Shensi see Shaanxi, state, China E3 42
Shenton, Mount, mtn., Austl. E4 74
Shenxian, China C6 42
Shenyang (Mukden), China D5 38
Shenzhen, China J6 42
Sheoganj, India F4 54
Sheopur, India F6 54
Shepard, Ab., Can. E17 138
Shepherd, Mi., U.S. E5 112
Shepherd, state, Vanuatu k17 79d
Shepherd, Îles, is., Vanuatu k17 79d
Shepherdstown, W.V., U.S. E7 114
Shepherdsville, Ky., U.S. F12 120
Shepparton, Austl. K5 76
Sheppey, Isle of, i., Eng., U.K. J13 12
Sheqi, China E5 42
Sherard, Cape, c., Nu., Can. C10 141
Sherard Osburn Fjord, b., Grnld. A14 141
Sherborne, Eng., U.K. K10 12
Sherbro Island, i., S.L. H2 64
Sherbrooke, N.S., Can. E14 110
Sherbrooke, Qc., Can. E5 110
Sherburn, Mn., U.S. H4 118
Sherburne, N.Y., U.S. B10 114
Sheridan, Ar., U.S. C6 122
Sheridan, In., U.S. H3 112
Sheridan, Or., U.S. E3 136
Sheridan, Tx., U.S. E11 130
Sheridan, Wy., U.S. C6 126
Sherman, N.Y., U.S. B6 114
Sherman, Tx., U.S. D2 122
Sherman Mills, Me., U.S. E8 110
Sherman Mountain, mtn., Ar., U.S. I4 120
Sherman Station, Me., U.S. E8 110
Sherpur, Bngl. F12 54
Sherpur, Bngl. F13 54
Sherridon, Mb., Can. E10 106
Sherrill, N.Y., U.S. E14 112
Shertallai, India G3 53
's-Hertogenbosch, Neth. C14 14
Sherwood, Ar., U.S. C6 122
Sherwood, Oh., U.S. C1 114
Sherwood, Tn., U.S. B12 122
Sherwood Park, Ab., Can. C17 138
Sherwood Shores, Tx., U.S. D9 130
Shesh Gāv, Afg. B2 54
Shetland Islands, is., Scot., U.K. n17 12a
Shetrunji, stm., India H3 54
Shexian, China G8 42
Sheyang, China E9 42
Sheyenne, N.D., U.S. G14 124
Sheyenne, stm., N.D., U.S. H16 124
Sheykhābād, Afg. A2 54
Shiant Islands, is., Scot., U.K. D6 12
Shibām, Yemen F6 56
Shibata, Japan B12 40
Shibîn el-Kôm, Egypt H1 58
Shibing, China H2 42
Shibukawa, Japan C12 40
Shicheng, China H7 42
Shickley, Ne., U.S. G15 126
Shidai, China F7 42
Shidao, China C10 42
Shidler, Ok., U.S. E12 128
Shiga, state, Japan D9 40
Shigezhuang, China B6 42
Shigouyi, China C2 42
Shiguaigou, China A4 42
Shihch'i see Zhongshan, China J5 42
Shihchiachuang see Shijiazhuang, China C6 42
Shihkiachwang see Shijiazhuang, China C6 42
Shijiaba, China F1 42
Shijiazhuang, China C6 42
Shijiu Hu, l., China F8 42
Shikārpur, India D2 53
Shikārpur, Pak. E2 54
Shikohābād, India E7 54
Shikoku, i., Japan F6 40
Shikoku-sanchi, mts., Japan F6 40
Shikotsu-ko, l., Japan C14 38
Shiliguri, India E12 54
Shillelagh, Ire. I6 12
Shillington, Pa., U.S. H13 112
Shillong, India F13 54
Shiloh, Oh., U.S. I5 112
Shiloh see Saylūn, Khirbat, hist., W.B. F6 58
Shilong, China J5 42
Shima, Japan E9 40
Shimabara, Japan G3 40
Shimada, Japan E11 40
Shimane, state, Japan D5 40
Shimbiris, mtn., Som. B9 66
Shimen, China G4 42
Shimian, China F5 36
Shimizu, Japan D11 40
Shimla, India C6 54
Shimminato, Japan C10 40
Shimoda, Japan E11 40
Shimodate, Japan C13 40
Shimoga, India E2 53
Shimonoseki, Japan F3 40
Shimono-shima, i., Japan E2 40
Shin, Loch, l., Scot., U.K. C8 12
Shinano, stm., Japan B11 40
Shīndand, Afg. C9 56
Shingbwiyang, Mya. C8 46
Shingū, Japan F9 40
Shingū, Japan E7 40
Shingwidzi, S. Afr. C10 70
Shingwidzi (Singuédeze), stm., Afr. C10 70
Shinji-ko, l., Japan D5 40
Shinjō, Japan A13 40
Shinyanga, Tan. E6 66
Shiocton, Wi., U.S. G10 118
Shiogama, Japan A14 40
Shiojiri, Japan C10 40
Shiono-misaki, c., Japan F8 40
Shioya-zaki, c., Japan C13 40
Shiping, China G5 36
Shiping, China G2 42
Shipka Pass see Šipčenski Prohod, p., Blg. G12 26
Shipman, Va., U.S. G7 114
Shippegan, N.B., Can. C12 110
Shippensburg, Pa., U.S. D8 114
Shiprock, N.M., U.S. G8 132
Ship Rock, mtn., N.M., U.S. G8 132
Shipshaw, stm., Qc., Can. B6 110
Shipu, China G9 42
Shiquan, China E3 42
Shirahama, Japan F8 40
Shirakawa, Japan B13 40
Shīrāz, Iran D7 56
Shirbîn, Egypt G2 58
Shiretoko-misaki, c., Japan B16 38
Shīr Kūh, mtn., Iran C7 56
Shirley, In., U.S. I4 112
Shiroishi, Japan A13 40
Shirone, Japan B11 40
Shirpur, India H5 54
Shīrvān, Iran B8 56
Shisanzhan, China F14 34
Shishaldin Volcano, vol., Ak., U.S. F7 140
Shishi, China I8 42
Shishmaref, Ak., U.S. C6 140
Shishou, China G5 42
Shitang, China I4 42
Shiv, India E3 54
Shively, Ky., U.S. F12 120
Shivpuri, India F6 54
Shivta, Ḥorvot (Subeita), hist., Isr. H5 58
Shivwits Plateau, plat., Az., U.S. G3 132
Shiwu, China C6 38
Shiyan, China E4 42
Shizhu, China G8 42
Shizugawa, Japan A14 40
Shizui, China C6 38
Shizunai, Japan C15 38
Shizuoka, Japan E11 40
Shizuoka, state, Japan E10 40
Shkodër, Alb. B13 24
Shkodra see Shkodër, Alb. B13 24
Shkumbin, stm., Alb. C14 24
Shō, stm., Japan C10 40
Shoal, stm., Fl., U.S. G12 122
Shoal Creek, stm., U.S. H3 120
Shoal Creek, stm., Mo., U.S. E4 120
Shoalhaven, stm., Austl. J8 76
Shoal Lake, l., Can. B3 118
Shoals, In., U.S. F11 120
Shoalwater Bay, b., Austl. D8 76
Shōbara, Japan E6 40
Shōdo-shima, i., Japan E7 40
Sholingnur, India E4 53
Shorāpur, India C3 53
Shoreacres, B.C., Can. G13 138
Shorewood, Wi., U.S. E2 112
Shorkot, Pak. C3 54
Shortland Island, i., Sol. Is. d6 79b
Shortland Islands, is., Sol. Is. d6 79b
Shoshone, Id., U.S. H12 136
Shoshone, stm., Wy., U.S. C4 126
Shoshone, South Fork, stm., Wy., U.S. G17 136
Shoshone Lake, l., Wy., U.S. F15 136
Shoshone Mountains, mts., Nv., U.S. E8 134
Shoshone Peak, mtn., Nv., U.S. G9 134
Shoshone Range, mts., Nv., U.S. C9 134
Shoshong, Bots. C8 70
Shostka, Ukr. D4 32
Shouchang, China G8 42
Shouguang, China C8 42
Shouning, China H8 42
Shouxian, China E7 42
Shouyang, China C5 42
Show Low, Az., U.S. I6 132
Shqipëria see Albania, ctry., Eur. C14 24
Shreve, Oh., U.S. D4 114
Shreveport, La., U.S. E5 122
Shrewsbury, Eng., U.K. I10 12
Shri Dūngargarh, India D4 54
Shri Mohangarh, India E3 54
Shū see Şu, Kaz. F12 32
Shū see Ču, stm., Asia F11 32
Shu, stm., China D8 42
Shuajingsi, China B9 46
Shuangcheng, China B7 38
Shuangfeng, China H5 42
Shuanggou, China E5 42
Shuanggou, China D7 42
Shuangji, stm., China D5 42
Shuangjiang, China G4 36
Shuangliao, China C5 38
Shuangpai, China I4 42

Name | Map Ref. | Page

Shuangshutai, China C4 38
Shuangyang, China C6 38
Shuangyashan, China B11 36
Shubrâ el-Kheima, Egypt H1 58
Shubuta, Ms., U.S. F10 122
Shucheng, China F7 42
Shuibatang, China G2 42
Shuiji, China H8 42
Shuijingtang, China G2 42
Shuikoushan, China H5 42
Shuitou, China I8 42
Shuiye, China C5 42
Shujāābād, Pak. D3 54
Shujālpur, India G6 54
Shuksan, Mount, mtn., Wa., U.S. B5 136
Shulan, China B7 38
Shulaps Peak, mtn., B.C., Can. F8 138
Shule, China B12 56
Shule, stm., China C4 36
Shumagin Islands, is., Ak., U.S. F7 140
Shunchang, China H7 42
Shunde, China J5 42
Shungnak, Ak., U.S. C8 140
Shunyi, China A7 42
Shuqualak, Ms., U.S. E10 122
Shurkhua, Mya. A1 48
Shurugwi, Zimb. D5 68
Shūshtar, Iran C6 56
Shuswap, stm., B.C., Can. F12 138
Shuswap Lake, l., B.C., Can. F11 138
Shuwak, Sudan E7 62
Shuyak Island, i., Ak., U.S. E9 140
Shuyang, China D8 42
Shwangliao see Liaoyuan, China C6 38
Shwebo, Mya. A2 48
Shwegun, Mya. D3 48
Shwegyin, Mya. D3 48
Shymkent see Šymkent, Kaz. F11 32
Shyok, India A7 54
Shyok, stm., Asia B4 46
Si, stm., China D7 42
Sia, Indon. G9 44
Siāhān Range, mts., Pak. D9 56
Siak, stm., Indon. C2 50
Siak Sri Indrapura, Indon. C3 50
Siālkot, Pak. B5 54
Siam see Thailand, ctry., Asia E5 48
Siam, Gulf of see Thailand, Gulf of, b., Asia G5 48
Sian see Xi'an, China D3 42
Siangtan see Xiangtan, China H5 42
Sianów, Pol. B12 16
Siantan, Pulau, i., Indon. B4 50
Siapa, stm., Ven. G9 86
Siargao Island, i., Phil. F6 52
Siasconset, Ma., U.S. C15 114
Siasi, Phil. H3 52
Siasi Island, i., Phil. H3 52
Siaškotan, ostrov, i., Russia G19 34
Siau, Pulau, i., Indon. E7 44
Šiauliai, Lith. E6 10
Sibaj, Russia D9 32
Sibayi, Lake, l., S. Afr. E11 70
Šibenik, Cro. G12 22
Siberia see Sibir', reg., Russia C12 34
Siberut, Pulau, i., Indon. D1 50
Sibi, Pak. D10 56
Sibigo, Indon. K2 48
Sibir', reg., Russia C12 34
Sibircevo, Russia B10 38
Sibirjakova, ostrov, i., Russia B4 34
Sibiti, Congo E2 66
Sibiu, Rom. D11 26
Sibiu, state, Rom. D11 26
Sibley, Ia., U.S. H3 118
Sibley, La., U.S. E5 122
Sibley, Ms., U.S. F7 122
Sibley Peninsula, pen., On., Can. C10 118
Sibolga, Indon. C1 50
Sibsāgar, India C7 46
Sibu, Malay. B7 50
Sibuguey Bay, b., Phil. G4 52
Sibut, C.A.R. C3 66
Sibutu Island, i., Phil. H2 52
Sibutu Passage, strt., Asia H2 52
Sibuyan Island, i., Phil. D4 52
Sibuyan Sea, Phil. D4 52
Sicapoo, Mount, mtn., Phil. B3 52
Siccus, stm., Austl. H2 76
Sichang see Xichang, China F5 36
Si Chon, Thai. H4 48
Sichuan, state, China E5 36
Sichuan Pendi, bas., China F1 42
Sichuanzhai, China A5 48
Sicilia, state, Italy F8 24
Sicilia (Sicily), i., Italy G7 24
Sicily see Sicilia, state, Italy F8 24
Sicily see Sicilia, i., Italy G7 24
Sicily, Strait of, strt. G5 24
Sicily Island, La., U.S. F7 122
Sicuani, Peru F3 84
Sidareja, Indon. G6 50
Sidas, Indon. C6 50
Siddhapur, India G4 54
Siddipet, India B4 53
Sidéradougou, Burkina G4 64
Siderno, Italy F10 24
Sideropolis, Braz. D13 92
Síderos, Ákra, c., Grc. H9 28
Sidhauli, India E8 54
Sidhi, India F8 54
Sîdi Barrâni, Egypt A5 62
Sidi bel Abbès, Alg. B4 64
Sidi-Ifni, Mor. D2 64
Siding Spring Mountain, mtn., Austl. H7 76
Sidirókastro, Grc. B6 28
Sidi Sâlim, Egypt G1 58
Sidlaghatta, India E3 53
Sidley, Mount, mtn., Ant. C28 81
Sidmouth, Eng., U.K. K9 12
Sidnaw, Mi., U.S. E10 118
Sidney, B.C., Can. H7 138
Sidney, Il., U.S. D9 120
Sidney, Mt., U.S. G9 124
Sidney, Ne., U.S. F10 126
Sidney, N.Y., U.S. B10 114
Sidney, Oh., U.S. D1 114
Sidney Lanier, Lake, res., Ga., U.S. B2 116
Sidon see Ṣaydā, Leb. E6 58
Sidon, Ms., U.S. D8 122
Sidorovsk, Russia A14 32
Sidra, Gulf of see Surt, Khalīj, b., Libya A3 62
Sidrolândia, Braz. D6 90
Siedlce, Pol. D18 16
Siedlce, state, Pol. D17 16
Siegburg, Ger. F3 16
Siegen, Ger. F4 16
Siemianowice Śląskie, Pol. F15 16
Siĕmpang, Camb. E8 48
Siĕmréab, Camb. F6 48
Siena, Italy G8 22
Sienyang see Xianyang, China D3 42
Sieradz, Pol. E14 16
Sieradz, state, Pol. E14 16
Sieraków, Pol. D12 16
Sierpc, Pol. D15 16
Sierra Blanca, Tx., U.S. C2 130
Sierra Blanca Peak, mtn., N.M., U.S. H3 128
Sierra Chica, Arg. H7 92
Sierra Colorada, Arg. H3 90
Sierra Gorda, Chile D3 90
Sierra Leone, ctry., Afr. H2 64
Sierra Mojada, Mex. G4 130
Sierra Nevada see Nevada, Sierra, mts., Ca., U.S. F6 134
Sierra Nevada, Parque Nacional, p.o.i., Ven. C6 86
Sierra Vista, Az., U.S. L6 132
Sierre, Switz. D4 22
Siesta Key, Fl., U.S. I3 116
Sífnos, i., Grc. F7 28
Sifón Villanueva, Mex. G7 130
Sig, Russia D16 8
Sigatoka, Fiji q18 79e
Sigep, Indon. D1 50
Sighetu Marmației, Rom. B10 26
Sighișoara, Rom. C11 26
Siglan, Russia E19 34
Sigli, Indon. J2 48
Siglufjörður, Ice. j30 8a
Sigmaringen, Ger. H5 16
Signal Mountain, Tn., U.S. B13 122
Signal Mountain, mtn., Vt., U.S. F4 110
Signy, sci., Ant. B36 81
Sigourney, Ia., U.S. C5 120
Sigsig, Ec. D2 84
Siguanea, Ensenada de la, b., Cuba B6 102
Siguatepeque, Hond. E3 102
Sigüenza, Spain C8 20
Siguiri, Gui. G3 64
Sigulda, Lat. C7 10
Sigurd, Ut., U.S. E5 132
Siguri Falls, wtfl, Tan. F7 66
Sihabuhabu, Dolok, mtn., Indon. B1 50
Sihanoukville see Kâmpóng Saôm, Camb. G6 48
Sihor, India H3 54
Sihorā, India G8 54
Sihote-Alin', mts., Russia E17 30
Sihtovo, Russia E15 10
Sihui, China J5 42
Siirt, Tur. B5 56
Sija, Russia E19 8
Sijunjung, Indon. D2 50
Sikandarābād, India D6 54
Sikanni Chief, stm., B.C., Can. D6 106
Sikao, Thai. I4 48
Sīkar, India E5 54
Sikasso, Mali G3 64
Sikeston, Mo., U.S. H8 120
Sikhote-Alin Mountains see Sihote-Alin', mts., Russia E17 30
Sikiang see Xi, stm., China J5 42
Siking see Xi'an, China D3 42
Síkinos, i., Grc. G8 28
Sikkim, state, India E12 54
Sikonge, Tan. F6 66
Sikotan, ostrov (Shikotan-tō), i., Russia C17 38
Siktjah, Russia B13 34
Sikuati, Malay. G1 52
Sikyón, hist., Grc. F5 28
Sil, stm., Spain B3 20
Šila, Russia E7 34
Šilalė, Lith. E5 10
Silao, Mex. E8 100
Silas, Al., U.S. F10 122
Silaut, Indon. E2 50
Silay, Phil. E4 52
Silchar, India F14 54
Şile, Tur. B12 28
Siler City, N.C., U.S. I6 114
Sileru, stm., India C5 53
Silesia, hist. reg., Eur. F13 16
Siletyteniz, ozero, l., Kaz. D12 32
Siletz, Or., U.S. F3 136
Siletz, stm., Or., U.S. F3 136
Silgaḍhī, Nepal D8 54
Silghāt, India E14 54
Silhouette, i., Sey. j13 69b
Siliana, Tun. H3 24
Siliana, Oued, stm., Tun. I3 24
Silifke, Tur. B4 58
Siling Co, l., China C12 54
Silistra, Blg. E14 26
Silivri, Tur. B11 28
Siljan, l., Swe. F6 8
Šilka, Russia F12 34
Šilka, stm., Russia F12 34
Silkeborg, Den. H3 8
Sillamäe, Est. A10 10
Sillem Island, i., Nu., Can. A16 106
Sillian, Aus. D9 22
Sillon de Talbert, pen., Fr. F5 14
Šilovići, Russia E15 10
Silsbee, Tx., U.S. G4 122
Silton, Sk., Can. D9 124
Siluas, Indon. C6 50
Šilutė, Lith. E4 10
Silvânia, Braz. I1 88
Silvassa, India H4 54
Silver, Tx., U.S. B7 130
Silver Bank Passage, strt., N.A. B12 102
Silver Bell, Az., U.S. K5 132
Silver City, N.M., U.S. K8 132
Silver City, N.C., U.S. B6 116
Silver Creek, Ms., U.S. F9 122
Silver Creek, Ne., U.S. F15 126
Silver Creek, stm., Az., U.S. I6 132
Silver Creek, stm., Or., U.S. G7 136
Silverdale, Wa., U.S. C4 136
Silver Lake, Ks., U.S. E2 120
Silver Lake, Mn., U.S. G4 118
Silver Lake, Wi., U.S. F1 112
Silver Lake, l., Or., U.S. G7 136
Silver Lake, l., Or., U.S. G5 136
Silver Spring, Md., U.S. E8 114
Silver Star Mountain, mtn., Wa., U.S. B6 136
Silverthrone Mountain, vol., B.C., Can. E4 138
Silverton, Austl. H3 76
Silverton, B.C., Can. G13 138
Silverton, Co., U.S. F9 132
Silverton, Tx., U.S. G7 128
Silvi, Italy H11 22
Silvia, Col. F3 86
Silvies, stm., Or., U.S. G7 136
Šimanovsk, Russia F14 34
Simao, China A5 48
Simão Dias, Braz. F6 88
Simav, Tur. D11 28
Simav, stm., Tur. C11 28
Simbach, Ger. H8 16
Simbo Island, i., Sol. Is. e7 79b
Simcoe, On., Can. F9 112
Simcoe, Lake, l., On., Can. D10 112
Simdega, India G10 54
Simeria, Rom. D10 26
Simeulue, Pulau, i., Indon. K2 48
Simferopol', Ukr. G15 6
Simikot, Nepal C8 54
Similkameen, stm., N.A. G10 138
Simití, Col. D4 86
Simi Valley, Ca., U.S. I7 134
Simizu see Shimizu, Japan D11 40
Simla, Co., U.S. B4 128
Simmern, Ger. G3 16
Simmie, Sk., Can. E5 124
Simms, Mt., U.S. C15 136
Simnas, Lith. F6 10
Simoca, Arg. C5 92
Simões, Braz. D5 88
Simojärvi, l., Fin. C12 8
Simojovel, Mex. G12 100
Simon, Lac, l., Qc., Can. E1 110
Simonette, stm., Ab., Can. A12 138
Simonoseki see Shimonoseki, Japan F3 40
Simonstad see Simon's Town, S. Afr. I4 70
Simon's Town, S. Afr. I4 70
Simoom Sound, B.C., Can. F4 138
Simpang, Indon. D3 50
Simpang-kiri, stm., Indon. K3 48
Simplon Pass, p., Switz. D4 22
Simpson Desert, des., Austl. D7 74
Simpson Island, i., On., Can. C11 118
Simpson Peninsula, pen., Nu., Can. B13 106
Simpson Strait, strt., Nu., Can. B11 106
Simpsonville, S.C., U.S. B3 116
Simrishamn, Swe. I6 8
Simsonbaai, Neth. Ant. A1 105a
Simunjan, Malay. C7 50
Simušir, ostrov, i., Russia G19 34
Sīna, stm., India B2 53
Sinabang, Indon. K3 48
Sinabung, Gunung, vol., Indon. K4 48
Sinai (Sinai Peninsula), pen., Egypt J4 58
Sinai, Mount see Mûsa, Gebel, mtn., Egypt J5 58
Sinai, Mount, vol., Gren. q10 105e
Sinaia, Rom. D12 26
Sinai Peninsula see Sinai, pen., Egypt J4 58
Sinajana, Guam j10 78c
Sinaloa, state, Mex. C5 100
Sinaloa, stm., Mex. C5 100
Sinamaica, Ven. B6 86
Sinan, China H3 42
Sinanpaşa, Tur. E13 28
Sīnāwin, Libya A2 62
Sincan, Tur. D15 28
Sincé, Col. B2 84
Sincelejo, Col. C4 86
Sinch'ang-ŭp, Kor., N. D8 38
Sin-ch'on, Kor., N. E6 38
Sinclair, Wy., U.S. B9 132
Sinclair, Lake, res., Ga., U.S. C2 116
Sinclair Mills, B.C., Can. B9 138
Sind, state, Pak. F2 54
Sind, stm., India F7 54
Sindañgan, Phil. F4 52
Sindangbarang, Indon. G5 50
Sindara, Gabon E2 66
Sindari, India F3 54
Sindelfingen, Ger. H4 16
Sindhnūr, India D3 53
Sindhulī Māṅdi, Nepal E10 54
Sindingale, Mya. C2 48
Sindor, Russia B8 32
Sines, Port. G2 20
Sinfra, C. Iv. H3 64
Singalamwe, Nmb. D3 68
Singapore, Sing. C3 50
Singapore, ctry., Asia L6 48
Singapore, Strait of, strt., Asia C4 50
Singaraja, Indon. H9 50
Sing Buri, Thai. E5 48
Singen, Ger. I4 16
Singida, Tan. E6 66
Singitic Gulf see Ayíou Órous, Kólpos, b., Grc. C6 28
Singkaling Hkāmti, Mya. C8 46
Singkang, Indon. F11 50
Singkawang, Indon. C6 50
Singkep, Pulau, i., Indon. D4 50
Singkil, Indon. K3 48
Singkuang, Indon. C1 50
Singleton, Austl. I8 76
Singleton, Mount, mtn., Austl. E3 74
Singuédeze (Shingwidzi), stm., Afr. C10 70
Sining see Xining, China D5 36
Sinj, Cro. G13 22
Sinjah, Sudan E6 62
Sinjai, Indon. F12 50
Sinjaja, stm., Eur. D11 10
Sinjaja, stm., Russia D14 34
Sinjuga, Russia E12 34
Sinkāt, Sudan D7 62
Sinkiang see Xinjiang, state, China A5 46
Sinnamahoning, Pa., U.S. C7 114
Sinnamary, Fr. Gu. B7 84
Sinnar, India B2 53
Sinnûris, Egypt I1 58
Sinnyŏng, Kor., S. C1 40
Sinoie, Lacul, l., Rom. E15 26
Sinop, Tur. A4 56
Sinsheim, Ger. G4 16
Sinsiang see Xinxiang, China D5 42
Sinskoe, Russia D14 34
Sintang, Indon. C7 50
Sint Christoffelberg, hill, Neth. Ant. p21 104g
Sint Eustatius, i., Neth. Ant. B1 105a
Sint Helenabaai, b., S. Afr. H3 70
Sint Kruis, Neth. Ant. p21 104g
Sint Maarten (Saint-Martin), i., N.A. A1 105a
Sint Nicolaas, Aruba p20 104g
Sint-Niklaas, Bel. C12 14
Sintra, Port. F1 20
Sint-Truiden, Bel. D14 14
Sinú, stm., Col. C4 86
Sinŭiju, Kor., N. D6 38
Sió, stm., Hung. C5 26
Siocon, Phil. G4 52
Siófok, Hung. C5 26
Sion, Switz. D4 22
Siorapaluk, Grnld. B12 141
Sioux Center, Ia., U.S. H2 118
Sioux City, Ia., U.S. B1 120
Sioux Falls, S.D., U.S. H2 118
Sioux Lookout, On., Can. A6 118
Sioux Narrows, On., Can. B4 118
Sioux Rapids, Ia., U.S. B2 120
Sipalay, Phil. F4 52
Šipan, Otok, i., Cro. H14 22
Sipapo, stm., Ven. E8 86
Siparia, Trin. s12 105f
Šipčenski Prohod (Shipka Pass), p., Blg. G12 26
Šipicyno, Russia F22 8
Siping, China C6 38
Sipiwesk Lake, l., Mb., Can. D11 106
Siple, Mount, mtn., Ant. C28 81
Siple Island, i., Ant. C28 81
Si Prachan, Thai. E4 48
Sipsey, stm., Al., U.S. D10 122
Šipunskij, mys, c., Russia F21 34
Sipura, Pulau, i., Indon. E1 50
Siqueira Campos, Braz. A12 92
Siquia, stm., Nic. F5 102
Siquijor, Phil. F4 52
Siquijor Island, i., Phil. F4 52
Siquirres, C.R. G6 102
Şīra, India E3 53
Šira, Russia D16 32
Sira, stm., Nor. G2 8
Si Racha, Thai. F5 48
Siracusa, Italy G9 24
Sirāhā, Nepal E11 54
Sirājganj, Bngl. F12 54
Şīr Banī Yās, i., U.A.E. E7 56
Sirdar, B.C., Can. G14 138
Sir Douglas, Mount, mtn., Can. F15 138
Sir Edward Pellew Group, is., Austl. C7 74
Siret, Rom. B12 26
Siret (Seret), stm., Eur. A12 26
Sirḥān, Wādī as-, val., Sau. Ar. H8 58
Sirik, Tanjong, c., Malay. B7 50
Sirikit Reservoir, res., Thai. D5 48
Sirino, Monte, mtn., Italy D9 24
Sir James MacBrien, Mount, mtn., N.T., Can. C4 106
Sīrjān, Iran D8 56
Sirkeli, Tur. C15 28
Sirocina, Bela. E12 10
Şirohi, India F4 54
Širokovo, Russia C17 32
Sironj, India F6 54
Sırpsındığı, Tur. B9 28
Sīrrī, Jazīreh-ye, i., Iran D7 56
Sirsa, India D5 54
Sir Sandford, Mount, mtn., B.C., Can. E13 138
Sirsi, India D2 53
Sirsilla, India B4 53
Sirte, Gulf of see Surt, Khalīj, b., Libya A3 62
Sir Timothy's Hill, hill, St. K./N. C2 105a
Şirupa, stm., Mex. G8 98
Širvintos, Lith. E7 10
Sir Wilfrid Laurier, Mount, mtn., B.C., Can. D11 138
Sisaba, mtn., Tan. F6 66
Sisak, Cro. E13 22
Si Sa Ket, Thai. E7 48
Sishen, S. Afr. E6 70
Sishilijie, China G7 42
Sishui, China D7 42
Sisib Lake, l., Mb., Can. B14 124
Sisimiut see Holsteinsborg, Grnld. D15 141
Siskiyou Pass, p., Or., U.S. A3 134
Sisseton, S.D., U.S. F1 118
Sīstān, reg., Asia C9 56
Sister Bay, Wi., U.S. C2 112
Sisteron, Fr. E11 18
Sisters, Or., U.S. F5 136
Sistersville, W.V., U.S. E5 114
Sit', stm., Russia B20 10
Sītāmarhi, India E10 54
Sītāpur, India E8 54
Siteia, Grc. H9 28
Siteki, Swaz. E10 70
Si Thep, hist., Thai. E5 48
Sithoniá, pen., Grc. C6 28
Sitidgi Lake, l., N.T., Can. B4 106
Sítio d'Abadia, Braz. H2 88
Sitka, Ak., U.S. E12 140
Sitkalidak Island, i., Ak., U.S. E9 140
Sittard, Neth. C14 14
Sitten see Sion, Switz. D4 22
Sittoung, stm., Mya. C3 48
Sittwe, Mya. D7 46
Siuri, India G11 54
Siuslaw, stm., Or., U.S. G3 136
Sivaganga, India G4 53
Sivakāsi, India G3 53
Sivaki, Russia F14 34
Sivas, Tur. B4 56
Ševeluč, vulkan, vol., Russia E21 34
Siverek, Tur. B4 56
Siverskij, Russia A12 10
Sivrihisar, Tur. D14 28
Siwa, Egypt B5 62
Siwalik Range, mts., India C6 54
Siwān, India E10 54
Sixian, China E7 42
Sixth Cataract see Sablūkah, Shallāl as-, wtfl, Sudan D6 62
Siyang, China E8 42
Sizuoka see Shizuoka, Japan E11 40
Sjælland, i., Den. I4 8
Sjalec, Bela. G13 10
Sjamža, Russia F19 8
Sjarheevičy, Bela. G10 10
Sjas', stm., Russia A15 10
Sjas'stroj, Russia F15 8
Sjenica, Yugo. F7 26
Sjuzikozero, Russia F17 8
Skærfjorden, b., Grnld. B22 141
Skaftafell Nasjonalpark, p.o.i., Ice. k31 8a
Skagafjörður, b., Ice. j31 8a
Skagen, Den. H4 8
Skagerrak, strt., Eur. H3 8
Skagit, stm., N.A. H8 138
Skagway, Ak., U.S. E12 140
Skaistkalne, Lat. D7 10
Skalbmierz, Pol. F16 16
Skalino, Russia G18 8
Skalistyj Golec, gora, mtn., Russia E12 34
Skalka, l., Swe. C8 8
Skåne, state, Swe. H5 8
Skārdu, Pak. B12 56
Skarszewy, Pol. B14 16
Skarżysko-Kamienna, Pol. E16 16
Skaudvilė, Lith. E5 10
Skawina, Pol. F15 16
Skeena, stm., B.C., Can. B1 138
Skeena Crossing, B.C., Can. A3 138
Skeena Mountains, mts., B.C., Can. D5 106
Skegness, Eng., U.K. H13 12
Skei, Nor. F2 8
Skeleton Coast, cst., Nmb. B1 70
Skellefteå, Swe. D9 8
Skellefteälven, stm., Swe. D8 8
Skellytown, Tx., U.S. F7 128
Skerryvore, r., Scot., U.K. E5 12
Ski, Nor. G4 8
Skiatook, Ok., U.S. H1 120
Skibbereen, Ire. J3 12
Skidal', Bela. G7 10
Skiddaw, mtn., Eng., U.K. G9 12
Skidmore, Tx., U.S. F10 130
Skien, Nor. G3 8
Skierniewice, Pol. E16 16
Skierniewice, state, Pol. D16 16
Skikda, Alg. B6 64
Skilak Lake, l., Ak., U.S. D9 140
Skillet Fork, stm., Il., U.S. F9 120
Skinnastaðir, Ice. j31 8a
Skipton, Austl. K4 76
Skipton, Eng., U.K. H10 12
Skive, Den. H3 8
Skjálfandafljót, stm., Ice. k31 8a
Šklad, Russia B13 34
Šklou, Bela. F13 10
Škofja Loka, Slvn. D11 22
Skoganvarre, Nor. B11 8
Skoganvarri see Skoganvarre, Nor. B11 8
Skokie, Il., U.S. F2 112
Skón, Camb. F7 48
Skópelos, i., Grc. D6 28
Skopin, Russia D5 32
Skopje, Mac. A4 28
Skoplje see Skopje, Mac. A4 28
Skórcz, Pol. C14 16
Skövde, Swe. G5 8
Skowhegan, Me., U.S. F7 110
Skownan, Mb., Can. C14 124
Skriplivka, Russia C13 10
Skrudaliena, Lat. E9 10
Skudeneshavn, Nor. G1 8
Skukuza, S. Afr. D10 70
Skull Valley, Az., U.S. I4 132
Skuna, can., Ms., U.S. D9 122
Skunk, stm., Ia., U.S. D6 120
Skuodas, Lith. D4 10
Skuratovskij, Russia F20 10
Skwierzyna, Pol. D11 16
Skye, Island of, i., Scot., U.K. D6 12
Skyland, N.C., U.S. A3 116
Skyring, Península, pen., Chile I1 90
Skyring, Seno, strt., Chile J2 90
Skýros, i., Grc. E7 28
Slabada, Bela. G11 10
Slagelse, Den. I4 8
Slagnäs, Swe. D8 8
Slamet, Gunung, vol., Indon. G6 50
Slancy, Russia A11 10
Slaney, stm., Ire. H6 12
Slănic, Rom. D12 26
Slano, Cro. H14 22
Slaný, Czech Rep. F10 16
Slater, Ia., U.S. C4 120
Slater, Mo., U.S. E4 120
Slatina, Cro. E14 22
Slatina, Rom. E11 26
Slaughter, La., U.S. G7 122
Slaunae, Bela. F12 10
Slautnoe, Russia D22 34
Slave, stm., Can. C8 106
Slave Coast, cst., Afr. H5 64
Slave Lake, Ab., Can. A16 138
Slavgorod, Russia D13 32
Slavjanka, Russia C9 38
Slavjansk-na-Kubani, Russia E5 32
Slavkoviči, Russia C12 10
Slavonia see Slavonija, hist. reg., Cro. E14 22
Slavonija, hist. reg., Cro. E14 22
Slavonski Brod, Cro. E15 22
Slavsk, Russia E4 10
Sławno, Pol. B12 16
Slayton, Mn., U.S. G3 118
Sleaford, Eng., U.K. H12 12
Sledge, Ms., U.S. C8 122
Sledzjuki, Bela. G13 10
Sleeper Islands, is., Nu., Can. D14 106
Sleeping Bear Dunes National Lakeshore, p.o.i., Mi., U.S. D3 112
Sleepy Eye, Mn., U.S. G4 118
Ślesin, Pol. D14 16
Slidell, La., U.S. G9 122
Slide Mountain, mtn., N.Y., U.S. B11 114
Sliema, Malta I8 24
Slievekimalta, mtn., Ire. I4 12
Sligeach see Sligo, Ire. G4 12
Sligo, Ire. G4 12
Sligo, Pa., U.S. C6 114
Sligo, state, Ire. G4 12
Sligo Bay, b., Ire. G4 12
Slinger, Wi., U.S. H10 118
Šlino, ozero, l., Russia C16 10
Slippery Rock, Pa., U.S. C5 114
Šlissel'burg, Russia A13 10
Slīteres Rezervāts, Lat. C5 10
Sliven, Blg. G13 26
Sljudjanka, Russia D18 32
Sloan, Nv., U.S. H1 132
Slobidka, Ukr. B16 26
Slobodskoj, Russia C8 32
Slobozia, Mol. C16 26
Slobozia, Rom. E14 26
Slobozia, Rom. F12 26
Slocan, B.C., Can. G13 138
Slocan Lake, l., B.C., Can. G13 138
Slocomb, Al., U.S. F13 122
Słomniki, Pol. F15 16
Slonim, Bela. G8 10
Slough, Eng., U.K. J12 12
Slovakia, ctry., Eur. H14 16
Slovenia, ctry., Eur. E11 22
Slovenija see Slovenia, ctry., Eur. E11 22
Slovenské rudohorie, mts., Slov. H15 16
Slov'ians'k, Ukr. E5 32
Slovinka, Russia G20 8
Słowiński Park Narodowy, p.o.i., Pol. B13 16
Słubice, Pol. D10 16
Sluč, stm., Bela. H10 10
Sluck, Bela. G10 10
Šluknov, Czech Rep. E10 16
Słupca, Pol. D13 16
Słupia, stm., Pol. B13 16
Słupsk (Stolp), Pol. B13 16
Słupsk, state, Pol. B13 16
Slutsk see Sluck, Bela. G10 10
Smålandsfarvandet, b., Den. I4 8
Smalininkai, Lith. E5 10
Smaljavičy, Bela. F10 10
Smallwood Reservoir, res., Nf., Can. E18 106
Smalouka, Bela. E13 10
Smarhon', Bela. F9 10
Smederevo, Yugo. E7 26
Smeralda, Costa, cst., Italy C3 24
Smethport, Pa., U.S. C7 114
Smidovič, Russia G15 34
Šmidta, poluostrov, pen., Russia F17 34
Śmigiel, Pol. D12 16
Smila, Ukr. E4 32
Smiley, Sk., Can. C4 124
Smiley, Tx., U.S. E10 130
Smiltene, Lat. C8 10
Smith, Ab., Can. A16 138
Smith, stm., U.S. H5 114
Smith, stm., Ca., U.S. B2 134
Smith, stm., Mt., U.S. C15 136
Smith, stm., Or., U.S. G2 136
Smith Arm, b., N.T., Can. B6 106
Smith Bay, b., Nu., Can. B10 141
Smith Bay, b., Ak., U.S. B9 140
Smith Canyon, val., Co., U.S. D5 128
Smithers, B.C., Can. B3 138
Smithfield, S. Afr. G8 70
Smithfield, N.C., U.S. A7 116
Smithfield, Va., U.S. G9 114
Smith Island see Sumisu-jima, i., Japan E13 36
Smith Island, i., N.C., U.S. C8 116
Smithland, Ky., U.S. G9 120
Smith Mountain Lake, res., Va., U.S. G6 114
Smith Point, c., N.S., Can. E13 110
Smith River, Ca., U.S. B1 134
Smiths, Al., U.S. E13 122
Smiths Falls, On., Can. D13 112
Smiths Grove, Ky., U.S. G11 120
Smithton, Austl. n12 77a
Smithville, Ga., U.S. E1 116
Smithville, Ms., U.S. C10 122
Smithville, Tn., U.S. I12 120
Smithville, Tx., U.S. D10 130
Smithville Lake, res., Mo., U.S. E3 120
Smoke Creek Desert, des., Nv., U.S. C6 134
Smokey, Cape, c., N.S., Can. D16 110
Smoky, stm., Ab., Can. A12 138
Smoky Cape, c., Austl. H9 76
Smoky Dome, mtn., Id., U.S. G12 136
Smoky Hill, stm., U.S. B12 128
Smoky Hill, North Fork, stm., U.S. B7 128
Smoky Lake, Ab., Can. B18 138
Smøla, i., Nor. E2 8
Smolensk, Russia F15 10
Smolenskaja-Moskovskaja vozvyšennost', plat., Eur. F16 10
Smolenskaja oblast', co., Russia F15 10
Smoljan, Blg. H11 26
Smoot, Wy., U.S. H16 136
Smoothrock Lake, l., On., Can. A9 118
Smorodovka, Russia C12 10
Smyrna see İzmir, Tur. E10 28
Smyrna, De., U.S. E10 114
Smyrna, Ga., U.S. D14 122
Smyrna, Tn., U.S. I11 120
Smythe, Mount, mtn., B.C., Can. D6 106
Snæfell, mtn., Ice. k32 8a
Snaefell, mtn., I. of Man G8 12
Snæfellsnes, pen., Ice. k28 8a
Snag, Yk., Can. C3 106
Snake, stm., Yk., Can. B4 106
Snake, stm., U.S. D8 136
Snake, stm., Mn., U.S. E5 118
Snake, stm., Ne., U.S. E11 126
Snake Creek, stm., S.D., U.S. B14 126
Snake River Plain, pl., Id., U.S. G13 136
Snake Valley, val., U.S. D3 132
Snares Islands, is., N.Z. H2 80
Snåsavatnet, l., Nor. D4 8
Sneads, Fl., U.S. G13 122
Sneedville, Tn., U.S. H2 114
Sneek, Neth. A14 14
Sněžka, mtn., Czech Rep. F11 16
Śniardwy, Jezioro, l., Pol. C17 16
Sniatyn, Ukr. A12 26
Snina, Slov. G18 16
Snipe Lake, l., Ab., Can. A14 138
Snjadin, Bela. H11 10
Snøhetta, mtn., Nor. E3 8
Snohomish, Wa., U.S. C4 136
Snoqualmie Pass, p., Wa., U.S. C5 136
Snøtinden, mtn., Nor. C5 8
Snov, stm., Eur. H15 10
Snover, Mi., U.S. E7 112
Snowbird Lake, l., N.T., Can. C10 106
Snowdon, mtn., Wales, U.K. H8 12
Snowdonia National Park, p.o.i., Wales, U.K. I8 12
Snowflake, Az., U.S. I6 132
Snow Hill, Md., U.S. F10 114
Snow Hill, N.C., U.S. A8 116
Snow Lake, Mb., Can. E10 106
Snowmass Mountain, mtn., Co., U.S. D9 132
Snow Mountain, mtn., Ca., U.S. D3 134
Snowtown, Austl. I2 76
Snowy, stm., Austl. K7 76
Snowy Mountain, mtn., N.Y., U.S. G2 110
Snowy Mountains, mts., Austl. K7 76
Snowy River National Park, p.o.i., Austl. K6 76
Snuŏl, Camb. F8 48
Snyder, Ok., U.S. G10 128
Snyder, Tx., U.S. B7 130
Soacha, Col. E4 86
Soalala, Madag. D8 68
Soap Lake, Wa., U.S. C7 136
Soavinandriana, Madag. D8 68
Sobaek-sanmaek, mts., Kor., S. C1 40
Soběslav, Czech Rep. G10 16
Sobinka, Russia I19 8
Sobradinho, Braz. D11 92
Sobradinho, Represa de, res., Braz. E5 88
Sobral, Braz. B5 88
Sobrance, Slov. H18 16
Sobrarbe, hist. reg., Spain B10 20
Sochaczew, Pol. D16 16
Soch'e see Shache, China B12 56
Soči, Russia F5 32
Société, Archipel de la (Society Islands), is., Fr. Poly. E11 72
Society Hill, S.C., U.S. B6 116
Society Islands see Société, Archipel de la, is., Fr. Poly. E11 72
Soco, stm., Dom. Rep. C13 102
Socompa, Paso (Socompa, Portezuelo de), p., S.A. B3 92
Socompa, Portezuelo de (Socompa, Paso), p., S.A. B3 92
Soconusco, Sierra de see Madre de Chiapas, Sierra, mts., N.A. G12 100
Socorro, Col. D5 86
Socorro, N.M., U.S. I10 132
Socorro, Tx., U.S. C1 130
Socorro, Isla, i., Mex. F3 100
Socotra see Suquṭrā, i., Yemen G7 56
Soc Trang, Viet. H8 48
Socuéllamos, Spain E8 20
Soda Creek, B.C., Can. D8 138
Soda Lake, l., Ca., U.S. H9 134
Sodankylä, Fin. C12 8
Soda Springs, Id., U.S. H15 136
Söderhamn, Swe. F7 8
Södermanland, state, Swe. G7 8
Södertälje, Swe. G7 8
Sodo, Eth. F7 62
Sodom see Sedom, hist., Isr. G6 58
Sodus, N.Y., U.S. E12 112
Sodwana Bay National Park, p.o.i., S. Afr. E11 70
Soe, Indon. G7 44
Soekmekaar, S. Afr. C9 70
Soest, Ger. E4 16
Soest, Neth. B14 14
Sofala, Moz. B12 70
Sofala, state, Moz. B12 70
Sofia see Sofija, Blg. G10 26
Sofija (Sofia), Blg. G10 26
Sofija, state, Blg. G10 26
Sofijsk, Russia F16 34
Sofjanga, Russia D14 8
Sofrino, Russia D20 10
Sogamoso, Col. E5 86
Sogamoso, stm., Col. D5 86
Soğanlı, stm., Tur. C15 28
Sogcho see Sokch'o, Kor., S. A1 40
Sogda, Russia F15 34
Sognefjorden, b., Nor. F1 8
Sogn og Fjordane, state, Nor. F2 8
Sogod, Phil. E5 52
Sogo Nur, l., China C5 36
Sogoža, stm., Russia B22 10
Soğuksu Milli Parkı, p.o.i., Tur. C15 28
Söğüt Gölü, l., Tur. F12 28
Söğütlü, Tur. C13 28
Sog Xian, China E3 36
Sohāgpur, India G6 54
Sohna, India D6 54
Sohor, gora, mtn., Russia F10 34
Soignies, Bel. D12 14
Sointula, B.C., Can. F4 138
Soira, mtn., Erit. E7 62
Soissons, Fr. E12 14
Sojana, Russia D20 8
Şojat, India F4 54
Šojna, Russia C20 8
Sŏjosŏn-man, b., Kor., N. E6 38
Sokch'o, Kor., S. A1 40
Söke, Tur. F10 28

Name	Map Ref.	Page
Sokele, D.R.C.	F4	66
Sokodé, Togo	H5	64
Sokol, Russia	G19	8
Sokol, Russia	B14	34
Sokółka, Pol.	C19	16
Sokolov, Czech Rep.	F8	16
Sokołów Małopolski, Pol.	F18	16
Sokone, Sen.	G1	64
Sokoto, Nig.	G5	64
Sokoto, stm., Nig.	G5	64
Sokyriany, Ukr.	A14	26
Sol, Costa del, cst., Spain	H5	20
Sola, Vanuatu	i16	79d
Solacolu, Rom.	E13	26
Solai, Kenya	D7	66
Solan, India	C6	54
Solana, Fl., U.S.	J3	116
Solânea, Braz.	D8	88
Solano, Phil.	B3	52
Solāpur, India	C2	53
Solca, Rom.	B12	26
Sol'cy, Russia	B13	10
Solda Gölü, l., Tur.	F12	28
Sol de Julio, Arg.	D6	92
Soldiers Grove, Wi., U.S.	H8	118
Soldotna, Ak., U.S.	D9	140
Soledad, Col.	B4	86
Soledad, Ca., U.S.	G4	134
Soledad, Ven.	C10	86
Soledad, Picacho, mtn., Mex.	B5	100
Soledad Díez Gutiérrez, Mex.	D8	100
Soledade, Braz.	D11	92
Soledad Pass, p., Ca., U.S.	I7	134
Solen, N.D., U.S.	A12	126
Solenzara, Fr.	H15	18
Soleure see Solothurn, Switz.	C4	22
Solihull, Eng., U.K.	I11	12
Solikamsk, Russia	C9	32
Sol'-Ileck, Russia	D8	32
Soliman, Tun.	H4	24
Solingen, Ger.	E3	16
Solís de Mataojo, Ur.	G10	92
Sollefteå, Swe.	E7	8
Sollentuna, Swe.	G7	8
Sóller, Spain	E13	20
Solnečnogorsk, Russia	D19	10
Sologne, reg., Fr.	G10	14
Sologoncy, Russia	C11	34
Solok, Indon.	D2	50
Solomennoe, Russia	F16	8
Solomon, Az., U.S.	K7	132
Solomon, stm., Ks., U.S.	B11	128
Solomon, North Fork, stm., Ks., U.S.	B10	128
Solomon, South Fork, stm., Ks., U.S.	B10	128
Solomon Basin, unds.	J18	142
Solomon Islands, ctry., Oc.	D7	72
Solomon Islands, is., Oc.	d7	79b
Solomon Sea, Oc.	D6	72
Solomon's Pools see Sulaymān, Birak, hist., W.B.	G5	58
Solon, China	B9	36
Solon, Ia., U.S.	C6	120
Solon, Me., U.S.	F7	110
Solothurn, Switz.	C4	22
Soloveckie ostrova, is., Russia	D16	8
Solov'evsk, Russia	F12	34
Solov'evsk, Russia	F13	34
Solsona, Spain	C12	20
Šolta, Otok, i., Cro.	G13	22
Solṭānābād, Iran	B8	56
Soltau, Ger.	C5	16
Solvang, Ca., U.S.	I5	134
Solvay, N.Y., U.S.	A9	114
Sol'vyčegodsk, Russia	F22	8
Solway Firth, b., U.K.	G9	12
Solwezi, Zam.	C4	68
Solza, Russia	D18	8
Sōma, Japan	B13	40
Soma, Tur.	D10	28
Somabhula, Zimb.	D4	68
Somalia, ctry., Afr.	D9	66
Somali Basin, unds.	I8	142
Somaliland see Somalia, ctry., Afr.	D9	66
Somali Republic see Somalia, ctry., Afr.	D9	66
Sombo, Ang.	B3	68
Sombor, Yugo.	D6	26
Sombrerete, Mex.	D7	100
Sombreretillo, Mex.	H7	130
Sombrero Channel, strt., India	G7	46
Sombrio, Braz.	D13	92
Sombrio, Lagoa do, l., Braz.	D13	92
Somdari, India	F4	54
Somerset, Austl.	n12	77a
Somerset, Co., U.S.	E9	132
Somerset, Ky., U.S.	G13	120
Somerset, Oh., U.S.	E3	114
Somerset, Pa., U.S.	D6	114
Somerset, Tx., U.S.	E9	130
Somerset East, S. Afr.	H7	70
Somerset Island, i., Nu., Can.	A12	106
Somerset West, S. Afr.	I4	70
Somers Point, N.J., U.S.	E11	114
Somersworth, N.H., U.S.	G5	110
Somerton, Az., U.S.	K2	132
Somerville, N.J., U.S.	D11	114
Somerville, Tn., U.S.	B9	122
Somerville, Tx., U.S.	G2	122
Somerville Lake, res., Tx., U.S.	D11	130
Someș (Szamos), stm., Eur.	B9	26
Somino, Russia	A17	10
Somme, state, Fr.	D11	14
Somme, stm., Fr.	E11	14
Somme, Baie de la, b., Fr.	D10	14
Sommen, l., Swe.	H6	8
Sömmerda, Ger.	E7	16
Somogy, state, Hung.	C4	26
Somosierra, Puerto de, p., Spain	C7	20
Somosomo, Fiji	p20	79e
Somosomo Strait, strt., Fiji	p19	79e
Somoto, Nic.	F4	102
Somovo, Russia	H17	10
Somport, Col du (Somport, Puerto de), p., Eur.	G5	18
Somport, Puerto de (Somport, Col du), p., Eur.	G5	18
Sompuis, Fr.	F13	14
Son, stm., India	F10	54
Sonāmarg, India	A5	54
Sonāmukhi, India	G11	54
Sŏnch'ŏn-ŭp, Kor., N.	E6	38
Sønderborg, Den.	I3	8
Sønderjylland, state, Den.	I3	8
Sondershausen, Ger.	E6	16
Søndre Strømfjord, Grnld.	D15	141
Sondrio, Italy	D6	22
Sonepur, India	H9	54
Song, Nig.	H7	64
Song, Thai.	C5	48
Song Bay Hap, Cua, b., Viet.	H7	48
Song Cau, Viet.	F9	48
Song Da see Black, stm., Asia	D9	46
Songe, Nor.	G3	8
Songea, Tan.	G7	66
Song Hong see Red, stm., Asia	D9	46
Songhua, stm., China	B11	36
Songhua Hu, res., China	C7	38
Songjiang, China	F9	42
Songjŏng, Kor., S.	G7	38
Sŏngju, Kor., S.	D1	40
Songkhla, Thai.	I5	48
Songkhram, stm., Thai.	D6	48
Songlinba, China	I6	42
Sŏngnam, Kor., S.	F7	38
Songnim, Kor., N.	E6	38
Songpan, China	E5	36
Song Phi Nong, Thai.	E4	48
Songtao, China	G3	42
Songxi, China	H8	42
Songxian, China	D4	42
Sonid Youqi, China	C7	36
Sonid Zuoqi, China	C7	36
Sonīpat, India	D6	54
Son La, Viet.	B6	48
Sonmiāni, Pak.	D10	56
Sonmiāni Bay, b., Pak.	D10	56
Sonneberg, Ger.	F7	16
Sonningdale, Sk., Can.	B6	124
Sono, stm., Braz.	I3	88
Sono, stm., Braz.	E1	88
Sonoma, Ca., U.S.	E3	134
Sonora, Ca., U.S.	F5	134
Sonora, Tx., U.S.	D7	130
Sonora, state, Mex.	G7	98
Sonora, stm., Mex.	G7	98
Sonora, Desierto de, des., N.A.	F6	98
Sonoyta, Mex.	F6	98
Sonqor, Iran	C6	56
Sŏnsan, Kor., S.	C1	40
Sonseca, Spain	E6	20
Sonsón, Col.	E4	86
Sonsonate, El Sal.	F3	102
Sonsorol Islands, is., Palau	D9	44
Sonstraal, S. Afr.	E6	70
Son Tay, Viet.	B7	48
Sonthofen, Ger.	I6	16
Soochow see Suzhou, China	F9	42
Sooke, B.C., Can.	H7	138
Sooner Lake, res., Ok., U.S.	A1	122
Sopchoppy, Fl., U.S.	G14	122
Soperton, Ga., U.S.	D3	116
Sopki, Russia	C13	10
Sopot, Pol.	B14	16
Sop Pong, Laos	A6	48
Sopron, Hung.	B3	26
Sopur, India	A5	54
Sora, Italy	I10	22
Sorada, India	I10	54
Sorata, Bol.	C3	90
Sorbhog, India	E13	54
Sorel, Qc., Can.	D3	110
Sorell, Cape, c., Austl.	o12	77a
Sørfold, Nor.	C6	8
Sorgues, Fr.	E10	18
Soria, Spain	C8	20
Soria, co., Spain	C8	20
Soriano, Ur.	F8	92
Sørli, Nor.	D5	8
Sorø, Den.	I4	8
Soro, India	H11	54
Soro, Monte, mtn., Italy	G8	24
Soroca, Mol.	A15	26
Sorocaba, Braz.	L2	88
Soročinsk, Russia	D8	32
Soroco, P.R.	B4	104a
Sorol, at., Micron.	C5	72
Soron, India	E7	54
Sorong, Indon.	F9	44
Sororó, stm., Braz.	C1	88
Sorot', stm., Russia	C12	10
Soroti, Ug.	D6	66
Sørøya, i., Nor.	A10	8
Sorrento, Italy	D8	24
Sorrento, La., U.S.	G8	122
Sorris-Sorris, Nmb.	B2	70
Sor Rondane Mountains, mts., Ant.	C7	81
Sorsk, Russia	D16	32
Sorso, Italy	D2	24
Sorsogon, Phil.	D4	52
Sort, Spain	B12	20
Sortandy, Kaz.	D12	32
Sortavala, Russia	F14	8
Sør-Trøndelag, state, Nor.	E4	8
Sõrve neem, c., Est.	C4	10
Šoša, stm., Russia	D18	10
Sos del Rey Católico, Spain	B9	20
Soskovo, Russia	H18	10
Sosna, stm., Russia	H21	10
Sosneado, Cerro, mtn., Arg.	G3	92
Sosnogorsk, Russia	B8	32
Sosnovec, Russia	D15	8
Sosnovka, Kaz.	D13	32
Sosnovka, Russia	C19	8
Sosnovo-Ozërskoe, Russia	F11	34
Sosnovskoe, Russia	I20	8
Sosnovyj Bor, Russia	A11	10
Sosnowiec, Pol.	F15	16
Soso, Ms., U.S.	F9	122
Sos'va, Russia	B10	32
Sotkamo, Fin.	D13	8
Soto, Mex.	F1	130
Soto la Marina, Mex.	D9	100
Soto la Marina, Barra, i., Mex.	C10	100
Sotra see Store Sotra, i., Nor.	F1	8
Sotteville-lès-Rouen, Fr.	E9	14
Souanké, Congo	D2	66
Soubré, C. Iv.	H3	64
Soudan, Austl.	D7	74
Souderton, Pa., U.S.	D10	114
Soufrière, St. Luc.	m6	105c
Soufrière, vol., Guad.	h5	105c
Soufrière, vol., St. Vin.	o11	105e
Soufrière Hills, vol., Monts.	d3	105a
Souillac, Fr.	E7	18
Sŏul (Seoul), Kor., S.	F7	38
Soulac-sur-Mer, Fr.	D4	18
Sound, The, strt., Eur.	I5	8
Sounding Creek, stm., Ab., Can.	E19	138
Sounding Lake, l., Ab., Can.	B3	124
Sources, Mont-aux- (Phofung), mtn., Afr.	F9	70
Soure, Braz.	D8	84
Sour el Ghozlane, Alg.	H14	20
Souris, Mb., Can.	E13	124
Souris, stm., N.A.	E13	124
Sourlake, Tx., U.S.	G4	122
Sourland Mountain, hill, N.J., U.S.	D11	114
Sousa, Braz.	D6	88
Sousel, Port.	F3	20
Sousse, Tun.	I4	24
Sout, stm., S. Afr.	H6	70
South, stm., N.C., U.S.	B7	116
South Africa, ctry., Afr.	F7	70
South America, cont.	G9	4
Southampton, On., Can.	D8	112
Southampton, Eng., U.K.	K11	12
Southampton, N.Y., U.S.	D13	114
Southampton, Cape, c., Nu., Can.	C13	106
Southampton Island, i., Nu., Can.	C14	106
South Andaman, i., India	F7	46
South Anna, stm., Va., U.S.	G8	114
South Antler Creek see Antler, stm., N.A.	E12	124
South Australia, state, Austl.	E6	74
South Australian Basin, unds.	M15	142
Southaven, Ms., U.S.	B8	122
South Baldy, mtn., N.M., U.S.	J9	132
Southbank, B.C., Can.	C5	138
South Bay, Fl., U.S.	J5	116
South Bay, b., Nu., Can.	C14	106
South Bay, b., On., Can.	C8	112
South Baymouth, On., Can.	C7	112
South Bend, In., U.S.	G3	112
South Bend, Wa., U.S.	D3	136
South Bohemia see Jihočeský kraj, state, Czech Rep.	G10	16
South Borneo see Kalimantan Selatan, state, Indon.	E9	50
South Boston, Va., U.S.	H6	114
Southbridge, N.Z.	F5	80
Southbridge, Ma., U.S.	B13	114
South Brookfield, N.S., Can.	F11	110
South Bruny Island, i., Austl.	o13	77a
South Burlington, Vt., U.S.	F3	110
South Carolina, state, U.S.	C5	116
South Celebes see Sulawesi Selatan, state, Indon.	E11	50
South Charleston, W.V., U.S.	F4	114
South China Basin, unds.	H14	142
South China Sea, Asia	H15	30
South Dakota, state, U.S.	C12	126
South Downs, hills, Eng., U.K.	K12	12
South East, state, Bots.	D7	70
South East Cape, c., Austl.	o13	77a
Southeast Indian Ridge, unds.	N12	142
Southeast Pacific Basin, unds.	P25	142
South East Point, c., Austl.	L6	76
Southend-on-Sea, Eng., U.K.	J13	12
Southern, state, Bots.	D7	70
Southern see HaDarom, state, Isr.	H5	58
Southern Alps, mts., N.Z.	F4	80
Southern Bug see Pivdennyy Buh, stm., Ukr.	A17	26
Southern Cook Islands, is., Cook Is.	E10	72
Southern Cross, Austl.	F3	74
Southern Ghāts, mts., India	G3	53
Southern Indian Lake, l., Mb., Can.	D10	106
Southern Ocean	N13	142
Southern Pines, N.C., U.S.	A6	116
South Esk, stm., Austl.	n13	77a
South Fabius, stm., Mo., U.S.	E6	120
South Fallsburg, N.Y., U.S.	C11	114
Southfield, Mi., U.S.	B2	114
South Fiji Basin, unds.	L20	142
South Foreland, c., Eng., U.K.	J14	12
South Fork, Co., U.S.	F10	132
South Fulton, Tn., U.S.	H8	120
Southgate, Mi., U.S.	B2	114
South Georgia, i., S. Geor.	J9	90
South Georgia and the South Sandwich Islands, dep., S.A.	K11	82
South Grand, stm., Mo., U.S.	F3	120
South Hātia Island, i., Bngl.	G13	54
South Haven, Mi., U.S.	F3	112
South Henderson, N.C., U.S.	H7	114
South Henik Lake, l., Nu., Can.	C11	106
South Hero, Vt., U.S.	F3	110
South Hill Village, Anguilla	A1	105a
South Holston Lake, res., U.S.	H3	114
South Honshu Ridge, unds.	G16	142
South Houston, Tx., U.S.	H3	122
South Indian Basin, unds.	O12	142
South Indian Lake, Mb., Can.	D11	106
South International Falls, Mn., U.S.	C5	118
South Island, i., N.Z.	G5	80
South Konkan Hills, hills, India	C1	53
South Korea see Korea, South, ctry., Asia	G8	38
South Lake Tahoe, Ca., U.S.	E5	134
Southland, Tx., U.S.	H7	128
Southlawn, Il., U.S.	E8	120
South Llano, stm., Tx., U.S.	D8	130
South Loup, stm., Ne., U.S.	F13	126
South Lyon, Mi., U.S.	F6	112
South Magnetic Pole, misc. cult.	B18	81
South Manitou Island, i., Mi., U.S.	C3	112
South Miami, Fl., U.S.	K5	116
South Milwaukee, Wi., U.S.	F2	112
South Moravia see Jihomoravský kraj, state, Czech Rep.	G12	16
South Nahanni, stm., N.T., Can.	C5	106
South Nation, stm., On., Can.	C14	112
South Negril Point, c., Jam.	i12	104d
South Ogden, Ut., U.S.	B5	132
South Orkney Islands, is., Ant.	B36	81
South Paris, Me., U.S.	F6	110
South Pass, p., Wy., U.S.	E4	126
South Pekin, Il., U.S.	D8	120
South Pittsburg, Tn., U.S.	B13	122
South Platte, stm., U.S.	F11	126
South Point, c., Barb.	n8	105d
South Pole, misc. cult., Ant.	D1	81
Southport (Gold Coast), Austl.	F9	76
Southport, Austl.	o13	77a
Southport, Eng., U.K.	H9	12
Southport, In., U.S.	E11	120
Southport, N.C., U.S.	C7	116
South Portland, Me., U.S.	G6	110
South Range, Mi., U.S.	D10	118
South River, On., Can.	C10	112
South Ronaldsay, i., Scot., U.K.	C10	12
South Sandwich Islands, is., S. Geor.	K11	82
South Sandwich Trench, unds.	N11	144
South Saskatchewan, stm., Can.	A8	124
South Shetland Islands, is., Ant.	B35	81
South Sioux City, Ne., U.S.	I2	118
South Skunk, stm., Ia., U.S.	C5	120
South Slocan, B.C., Can.	G13	138
South Sound, b., Br. Vir. Is.	e9	104b
South Spicer Island, i., Nu., Can.	B15	106
South Sulphur, stm., Tx., U.S.	D3	122
South Sumatra see Sumatera Selatan, state, Indon.	E4	50
South Taranaki Bight, b., N.Z.	D5	80
South Tasman Rise, unds.	N17	142
South Thompson, stm., B.C., Can.	F11	138
South Torrington, Wy., U.S.	E8	126
South Uist, i., Scot., U.K.	D5	12
South Umpqua, stm., Or., U.S.	G3	136
South Ventana Cone, mtn., Ca., U.S.	G4	134
South Vietnam see Vietnam, ctry., Asia	E9	48
South West Africa see Namibia, ctry., Afr.	E2	68
South West Cape, c., Austl.	o12	77a
South West Cape, c., N.Z.	H2	80
South West City, Mo., U.S.	H3	120
Southwest Harbor, Me., U.S.	F8	110
Southwest Indian Ridge, unds.	M8	142
Southwest Miramichi, stm., N.B., Can.	D10	110
Southwest National Park, p.o.i., Austl.	o12	77a
Southwest Pacific Basin, unds.	M23	142
Southwest Point, c., Bah.	K8	116
South Whitley, In., U.S.	G4	112
South Wichita, stm., Tx., U.S.	H9	128
South Windham, Me., U.S.	G6	110
Southwold, Eng., U.K.	I14	12
Soutpansberg, mts., S. Afr.	C9	70
Sovata, Rom.	C11	26
Sovetsk, Russia	G20	10
Sovetsk, Russia	E4	10
Sovetsk, Russia	C7	32
Sovetskaja Gavan', Russia	G17	34
Sovetskij, Russia	F13	8
Sovpole, Russia	D20	8
Sowa Pan, pl., Bots.	B7	70
Soweto, S. Afr.	E8	70
Sōya-misaki, c., Japan	B14	38
Soyang-chŏsuji, res., Kor., S.	F7	38
Soyo, Ang.	B1	68
Sož, stm., Eur.	H13	10
Sozimskij, Russia	C8	32
Sozopol, Blg.	G14	26
Spa, Bel.	D14	14
Spain, ctry., Eur.	E7	20
Spalding, Sk., Can.	B9	124
Spalding, Eng., U.K.	I12	12
Spanish, On., Can.	B7	112
Spanish, stm., On., Can.	B8	112
Spanish Fork, Ut., U.S.	C5	132
Spanish Point, c., Ber.	k15	104e
Spanish Sahara see Western Sahara, dep., Afr.	E2	64
Spanish Town, Br. Vir. Is.	e9	104b
Spanish Town, Jam.	i13	104d
Spánta, Ákra, c., Grc.	H6	28
Sparkman, Ar., U.S.	D6	122
Sparks, Nv., U.S.	D6	134
Sparland, Il., U.S.	C8	120
Sparlingville, Mi., U.S.	F7	112
Sparrows Point, Md., U.S.	E9	114
Sparta see Spárti, Grc.	F5	28
Sparta, Ga., U.S.	C3	116
Sparta, Il., U.S.	F8	120
Sparta, Ky., U.S.	F13	120
Sparta, N.J., U.S.	C11	114
Sparta, N.C., U.S.	H4	114
Sparta, Tn., U.S.	I12	120
Sparta, Wi., U.S.	H8	118
Spartanburg, S.C., U.S.	B4	116
Spárti, Grc.	F5	28
Spartivento, Capo, c., Italy	F2	24
Spartivento, Capo, c., Italy	G10	24
Spas-Klepiki, Russia	I19	8
Spassk-Dal'nij, Russia	B10	38
Spearfish, S.D., U.S.	C8	126
Spearville, Ks., U.S.	D9	128
Spednic Lake, l., N.A.	E9	110
Speedway, In., U.S.	I3	112
Speightstown, Barb.	n8	105d
Speikkogel, mtn., Aus.	C12	22
Speke Gulf, b., Tan.	E6	66
Spencer, In., U.S.	E11	120
Spencer, Ia., U.S.	H3	118
Spencer, Ne., U.S.	E14	126
Spencer, W.V., U.S.	F4	114
Spencer, Wi., U.S.	G8	118
Spencer, Cape, c., Austl.	G7	74
Spencer, Cape, c., N.B., Can.	E11	110
Spencer Gulf, b., Austl.	F7	74
Spencerville, Oh., U.S.	D1	114
Spences Bridge, B.C., Can.	F9	138
Speos (Rock Tombs), hist., Egypt	K1	58
Sperryville, Va., U.S.	F7	114
Spétses, i., Grc.	F6	28
Spey, stm., Scot., U.K.	D9	12
Speyer, Ger.	G4	16
Spezia see La Spezia, Italy	F6	22
Spezzano Albanese, Italy	E10	24
Sphinx see Abū el-Ḥul, hist., Egypt	I1	58
Spickard, Mo., U.S.	D4	120
Spilimbergo, Italy	D9	22
Spillville, Ia., U.S.	A5	120
Spinazzola, Italy	D10	24
Spindale, N.C., U.S.	A4	116
Spires see Speyer, Ger.	G4	16
Spirit Lake, Ia., U.S.	H3	118
Spirit River, Ab., Can.	D7	106
Spiro, Ok., U.S.	B4	122
Spišská Nová Ves, Slov.	H16	16
Spitsbergen, i., Nor.	B4	30
Spitsbergen Bank, unds.	B5	142
Spittal an der Drau, Aus.	D10	22
Split, Cro.	G13	22
Split Lake, res., Mb., Can.	D11	106
Špogi, Lat.	D9	10
Spokane, Wa., U.S.	C9	136
Spokane, stm., U.S.	C8	136
Spoleto, Italy	H9	22
Spoon, stm., Il., U.S.	D7	120
Spooner, Wi., U.S.	F7	118
Sporava, Bela.	H8	10
Spornoe, Russia	D19	34
Spotsylvania, Va., U.S.	F8	114
Sprague, Wa., U.S.	C9	136
Spratly Islands, is., Asia	D5	44
Spray, Or., U.S.	F7	136
Spree, stm., Ger.	E10	16
Spremberg, Ger.	E10	16
Spring, stm., U.S.	H3	120
Spring, stm., Ar., U.S.	H6	120
Spring, South Fork, stm., U.S.	H6	120
Springbok, S. Afr.	F3	70
Spring City, Tn., U.S.	B14	122
Spring City, Ut., U.S.	D5	132
Spring Creek, stm., Austl.	D3	76
Spring Creek, stm., N.D., U.S.	G11	124
Spring Creek, stm., S.D., U.S.	C8	134
Springdale, Nf., Can.	j22	107a
Springdale, Ar., U.S.	H3	120
Springdale, Ut., U.S.	F4	132
Springdale, Wa., U.S.	B9	136
Springe, Ger.	D5	16
Springerville, Az., U.S.	I7	132
Springfield, N.S., Can.	F12	110
Springfield, Co., U.S.	D6	128
Springfield, Fl., U.S.	G13	122
Springfield, Ga., U.S.	D4	116
Springfield, Il., U.S.	E8	120
Springfield, Ma., U.S.	B13	114
Springfield, Mn., U.S.	G4	118
Springfield, Mo., U.S.	G4	120
Springfield, Oh., U.S.	E2	114
Springfield, Or., U.S.	F3	136
Springfield, S.C., U.S.	C4	116
Springfield, S.D., U.S.	E14	126
Springfield, Tn., U.S.	H10	120
Springfontein, S. Afr.	G7	70
Spring Glen, Ut., U.S.	D5	132
Spring Green, Wi., U.S.	A7	120
Spring Grove, Mn., U.S.	H7	118
Springhill, N.S., Can.	E12	110
Springhill, La., U.S.	D5	122
Spring Hope, N.C., U.S.	I7	114
Springhouse, B.C., Can.	E8	138
Spring Lake, N.C., U.S.	A7	116
Springs, S. Afr.	E9	70
Springsure, Austl.	E7	76
Springvale, Austl.	D3	76
Springvale, Me., U.S.	G6	110
Spring Valley, Ca., U.S.	K9	134
Spring Valley, Il., U.S.	J9	118
Spring Valley, N.Y., U.S.	C11	114
Spring Valley, Wi., U.S.	G6	118
Spring Valley, val., Nv., U.S.	D2	132
Springview, Ne., U.S.	E13	126
Springville, Al., U.S.	D12	122
Springville, Ca., U.S.	G7	134
Springville, Ut., U.S.	C5	132
Sproat Lake, l., B.C., Can.	G5	138
Spruce Grove, Ab., Can.	C17	138
Spruce Knob, mtn., W.V., U.S.	F6	114
Spruce Mountain, mtn., Az., U.S.	I4	132
Spruce Pine, Al., U.S.	C11	122
Spruce Pine, N.C., U.S.	I3	114
Spulico, Capo, c., Italy	E10	24
Spurfield, Ab., Can.	A16	138
Spurger, Tx., U.S.	G4	122
Spurn Head, c., Eng., U.K.	H13	12
Spuzzum, B.C., Can.	G9	138
Squamish, B.C., Can.	G7	138
Squamish, stm., B.C., Can.	F7	138
Squam Lake, l., N.H., U.S.	G5	110
Square Lake, l., Me., U.S.	D8	110
Squatec, Qc., Can.	C8	110
Squaw Cap Mountain, mtn., N.B., Can.	C10	110
Squaw Peak, mtn., Mt., U.S.	C12	136
Squilax, B.C., Can.	F11	138
Squillace, Golfo di, b., Italy	F10	24
Squinzano, Italy	D12	24
Sragen, Indon.	G7	50
Srbija (Serbia), state, Yugo.	E7	26
Srbobran, Yugo.	D6	26
Srê Âmbĕl, Camb.	G6	48
Sredinnyj hrebet, mts., Russia	E20	34
Sredna Gora, mts., Blg.	G11	26
Srednee Kujto, ozero, l., Russia	D14	8
Srednekolymsk, Russia	C19	34
Srednerusskaja vozvyšennost', plat., Russia	D5	32
Srednesibirskoe ploskogor'e (Central Siberian Uplands), plat., Russia	C10	34
Srednij Ural, mts., Russia	C9	32
Srednij Vasjugan, Russia	C13	32
Srednjaja Olëkma, Russia	E13	34
Śrem, Pol.	D13	16
Srê Moăt, Camb.	F8	48
Sremska Mitrovica, Yugo.	E6	26
Sremski Karlovci, Yugo.	D6	26
Srêng, stm., Camb.	F6	48
Srêpŏk, stm., Camb.	F8	48
Sretensk, Russia	F12	34
Sri Aman, Malay.	C7	50
Sri Jayawardenepura (Kotte), Sri L.	H5	53
Srīkākulam, India	B6	53
Sri Kālahasti, India	E4	53
Sri Lanka, ctry., Asia	G5	53
Srīnagar, India	A5	54
Srīrampur, India	B2	53
Srīrangam, India	F4	53
Srīvardhan, India	B1	53
Srīvilliputtūr, India	G3	53
Środa Śląska, Pol.	E12	16
Środa Wielkopolska, Pol.	D13	16
Sseu-tch'ouan see Sichuan, state, China	E5	36
Ssup'ing see Siping, China	C6	38
Staaten, stm., Austl.	C8	74
Stacyville, Ia., U.S.	H6	118
Stade, Ger.	C5	16
Stadlandet, pen., Nor.	E1	8
Stadl-Paura, Aus.	B10	22
Stadskanaal, Neth.	A16	14
Stadtallendorf, Ger.	F5	16
Stadtoldendorf, Ger.	E5	16
Stafford, Eng., U.K.	I10	12
Stafford, Ks., U.S.	D10	128
Stafford Springs, Ct., U.S.	C13	114
Staffordsville, Ky., U.S.	G14	120
Stagen, Indon.	E10	50
Staines, Eng., U.K.	J12	12
Staked Plain see Estacado, Llano, pl., U.S.	H6	128
Stakhanov, Ukr.	E5	32
Stalać, Yugo.	F8	26
Stalowa Wola, Pol.	F18	16
Stamford, Austl.	C4	76
Stamford, Eng., U.K.	I12	12
Stamford, Ct., U.S.	C12	114
Stamford, N.Y., U.S.	B11	114
Stamford, Tx., U.S.	B8	130
Stamford, Lake, res., Tx., U.S.	A8	130
Stamps, Ar., U.S.	D5	122
Stanaford, W.V., U.S.	G4	114
Stanberry, Mo., U.S.	D3	120
Stancionno-Ojašinskij, Russia	C14	32
Standard, Ab., Can.	E18	138
Standerton, S. Afr.	E9	70
Standish, Mi., U.S.	E6	112
Stanfield, Or., U.S.	E7	136
Stanford, Ky., U.S.	G13	120
Stanford, Mt., U.S.	C16	136
Stanger, S. Afr.	F10	70
Stanislaus, stm., Ca., U.S.	F5	134
Stanley, Austl.	n12	77a
Stanley, N.B., Can.	D10	110
Stanley, Falk. Is.	J5	90
Stanley, N.C., U.S.	A4	116
Stanley, N.D., U.S.	F11	124
Stanley, Wi., U.S.	G7	118
Stanley Falls, wtfl, D.R.C.	D4	66
Stanley Reservoir, res., India	F3	53
Stanleyville see Kisangani, D.R.C.	D5	66
Stanovoe nagor'e, mts., Russia	E11	34
Stanovoj hrebet, mts., Russia	E14	34
Stanovoy Mountains see Stanovoe nagor'e, mts., Russia	E11	34
Stanthorpe, Austl.	G8	76
Stanton, Ky., U.S.	G2	114
Stanton, Mi., U.S.	E4	112
Stanton, Ne., U.S.	F15	126
Stanton, N.D., U.S.	G12	124
Stanton, Tn., U.S.	B9	122
Stantonsburg, N.C., U.S.	A8	116
Stanwood, Wa., U.S.	B4	136
Staples, Mn., U.S.	E4	118
Stapleton, Al., U.S.	G11	122
Stąporków, Pol.	E16	16
Star, Ms., U.S.	E8	122
Star, N.C., U.S.	A6	116
Starachowice, Pol.	E17	16
Staraja Rudnja, Bela.	H13	10
Staraja Russa, Russia	B14	10
Stara Pazova, Yugo.	D7	26
Stara Zagora, Blg.	G12	26
Starbuck, Mb., Can.	E16	124
Starbuck, Wa., U.S.	D8	136
Starbuck, i., Kir.	D11	72
Star City, Sk., Can.	B9	124
Star City, Ar., U.S.	D7	122
Stargard Szczeciński, Pol.	C11	16
Stargo, Az., U.S.	J7	132
Star Harbour, b., Sol. Is.	f10	79b
Starica, Russia	D17	10
Stari Grad, Cro.	G13	22
Starij Rjad, Russia	B17	10
Stari Vlah, reg., Yugo.	F7	26
Starke, Fl., U.S.	G3	116
Starkville, Ms., U.S.	D10	122
Starnberg, Ger.	H7	16
Starnberger See, l., Ger.	I7	16
Starodub, Russia	H15	10
Staroe Rahino, Russia	B15	10
Starogard Gdański, Pol.	C14	16
Starokozache, Ukr.	C16	26
Star Peak, mtn., Nv., U.S.	C7	134
Start Point, c., Eng., U.K.	K9	12
Staryja Darohi, Bela.	G11	10
Staryj Medved', Russia	B13	10
Staryj Oskol, Russia	D5	32
Stary Sącz, Pol.	G16	16
Stassfurt, Ger.	E7	16
State College, Pa., U.S.	D7	114
State Line, Ms., U.S.	F10	122
Stateline, Nv., U.S.	E5	134
Staten Island see Estados, Isla de los, i., Arg.	J4	90
State Road, N.C., U.S.	H4	114
Statesboro, Ga., U.S.	D4	116
Statesville, N.C., U.S.	I5	114
Staubun, Bela.	H14	10
Staunton, Il., U.S.	E8	120
Staunton, Va., U.S.	F6	114
Staunton see Roanoke, stm., U.S.	H8	114
Stavanger, Nor.	G1	8
Stave Lake, l., B.C., Can.	G8	138
Stavely, Ab., Can.	F17	138
Stavne, Ukr.	G18	16
Stavropol', Russia	E6	32
Stawell, Austl.	K4	76
Stawell, stm., Austl.	C4	76
Stawiszyn, Pol.	E14	16
Stayner, On., Can.	D9	112
Steamboat Springs, Co., U.S.	C10	132
Stearns, Ky., U.S.	H13	120
Stębark, Pol.	C16	16
Steele, Mo., U.S.	H8	120
Steele, N.D., U.S.	H14	124
Steele, Mount, mtn., Wy., U.S.	B9	132
Steels Point, c., Norf. I.	y25	78i
Steelville, Mo., U.S.	G6	120
Steensby Inlet, b., Nu., Can.	A15	106
Steenwijk, Neth.	B15	14
Steep Rock, Mb., Can.	C15	124
Stefanie, Lake, l., Afr.	G7	62
Stefansson Island, i., Nu., Can.	A9	106
Ștefan Vodă, Rom.	E14	26
Stege, Den.	B8	16
Stehekin, Wa., U.S.	B6	136
Steiermark, state, Aus.	C11	22
Steinach, Aus.	C8	22
Steinbach, Mb., Can.	E17	124
Steinfurt, Ger.	D3	16
Steinhausen, Nmb.	B4	70
Steinkjer, Nor.	D4	8
Stekljanka, Russia	G19	8
Stella, S. Afr.	E7	70
Stellarton, N.S., Can.	E14	110
Stellenbosch, S. Afr.	H4	70
Stelvio, Parco Nazionale dello, p.o.i., Italy	D7	22
Stelvio, Passo dello, p., Italy	D7	22
Stendal, Ger.	D7	16
Stende, Lat.	C5	10
Stephen, Mn., U.S.	C2	118
Stephens, Ar., U.S.	D5	122
Stephens, Port, b., Austl.	I9	76
Stephens City, Va., U.S.	E7	114
Stephens Creek, Austl.	H3	76
Stephens Lake, res., Mb., Can.	D11	106
Stephenville, Nf., Can.	j22	107a
Stephenville, Tx., U.S.	B9	130
Stepnjak, Kaz.	D12	32
Step Pyramid see Saqqâra, Pyramides de, hist., Egypt	I1	58
Steptoe Valley, val., Nv., U.S.	D2	132
Stepurino, Russia	D18	10
Steréa Elláda, state, Grc.	E5	28
Sterkstroom, S. Afr.	G8	70
Sterling, Co., U.S.	G9	126
Sterling, Il., U.S.	C8	120
Sterling, Ks., U.S.	C10	128
Sterling, Mi., U.S.	D5	112
Sterling, Ne., U.S.	D1	120
Sterling City, Tx., U.S.	C7	130
Sterlington, La., U.S.	E6	122
Šterlitamak, Russia	D9	32
Šternberk, Czech Rep.	G13	16
Sterzing see Vipiteno, Italy	D8	22
Stettin Lagoon, b., Eur.	C10	16
Stettler, Ab., Can.	D18	138
Steubenville, Oh., U.S.	D5	114
Stevenage, Eng., U.K.	J12	12
Stevenson, Al., U.S.	C13	122
Stevenson Entrance, strt., Ak., U.S.	E9	140
Stevens Pass, p., Wa., U.S.	C5	136
Stevens Peak, mtn., Id., U.S.	C11	136
Stevens Point, Wi., U.S.	G9	118
Stevensville, Mi., U.S.	F3	112
Stevensville, Mt., U.S.	D12	136
Stewardson, Il., U.S.	E9	120
Stewart, B.C., Can.	D4	106
Stewart, stm., Yk., Can.	C3	106
Stewart, Isla, i., Chile	J2	90
Stewart Island, i., N.Z.	H3	80
Stewartstown, Pa., U.S.	E9	114
Stewartsville, Mo., U.S.	E3	120
Stewart Valley, Sk., Can.	D6	124
Stewartville, Mn., U.S.	H6	118
Stewiacke, N.S., Can.	E13	110
Steyr, Aus.	B11	22
Steytlerville, S. Afr.	H7	70
Stickney, S.D., U.S.	D14	126
Stiene, Lat.	C7	10
Stif, Alg.	B6	64
Stigler, Ok., U.S.	B3	122
Stih, hora, mtn., Ukr.	A10	26
Stikine, stm., N.A.	D4	106
Stikine Ranges, mts., B.C., Can.	D4	106
Stilbaai, S. Afr.	I5	70
Stilfontein, S. Afr.	E8	70
Stilís, Grc.	E5	28
Stillhouse Hollow Lake, res., Tx., U.S.	D10	130
Stillwater, B.C., Can.	G6	138
Stillwater, Mn., U.S.	F6	118
Stillwater, Ok., U.S.	A1	122
Stillwell, Ok., U.S.	I3	120
Stînca-Costești, Lacul, res., Eur.	B14	26
Stine Mountain, mtn., Mt., U.S.	E13	136
Stinking Water Creek, stm., Ne., U.S.	G11	126
Stinnett, Tx., U.S.	F7	128
Štip, Mac.	B5	28
Stirling, Austl.	F3	74
Stirling, On., Can.	D12	112
Stirling, Scot., U.K.	E8	12
Stirling City, Ca., U.S.	D4	134
Stirrat, W.V., U.S.	G15	120
Stjernøya, i., Nor.	A9	8
Stobi, hist., Mac.	B4	28
Stockach, Ger.	I5	16
Stockbridge, Ga., U.S.	C1	116
Stockbridge, Mi., U.S.	B1	114
Stockdale, Tx., U.S.	E9	130
Stockerau, Aus.	B13	22

Name	Map Ref.	Page
Stockholm, Swe.	G8	8
Stockholm, Me., U.S.	C8	110
Stockholm, state, Swe.	G8	8
Stockport, Eng., U.K.	H10	12
Stockton, Al., U.S.	G11	122
Stockton, Ca., U.S.	F4	134
Stockton, Il., U.S.	B8	120
Stockton, Ks., U.S.	B9	128
Stockton, Mo., U.S.	G4	120
Stockton-on-Tees, Eng., U.K.	G11	12
Stockton Plateau, plat., Tx., U.S.	D5	130
Stockton Reservoir, res., Mo., U.S.	G4	120
Stockton Springs, Me., U.S.	F8	110
Stoczek Łukowski, Pol.	D18	16
Stœng Trêng, Camb.	F8	48
Stoffberg, S. Afr.	D9	70
Stojba, Russia	F15	34
Stoke-on-Trent, Eng., U.K.	I11	12
Stokes Point, c., Austl.	n11	77a
Stolberg, Ger.	F2	16
Stolbovo, Russia	H17	10
Stolbovoj, ostrov, i., Russia	B16	34
Stoneboro, Pa., U.S.	C5	114
Stone Harbor, N.J., U.S.	E11	114
Stonehaven, Scot., U.K.	E10	12
Stonehenge, Austl.	E4	76
Stonehenge, hist., Eng., U.K.	J11	12
Stone Mountain, Ga., U.S.	C1	116
Stone Mountain, mtn., Vt., U.S.	F5	110
Stoner, B.C., Can.	C8	138
Stoneville, N.C., U.S.	H6	114
Stonewall, Mb., Can.	D16	124
Stonewall, Ms., U.S.	E10	122
Stonewall, Ok., U.S.	C2	122
Stoney Creek, On., Can.	E10	112
Stonington, Il., U.S.	E8	120
Stonington, Me., U.S.	F8	110
Stony Creek, stm., Ca., U.S.	D3	134
Stony Lake, l., Mb., Can.	D11	106
Stony Lake, l., On., Can.	D11	112
Stony Plain, Ab., Can.	C16	138
Stony Point, N.C., U.S.	I4	114
Stony Rapids, Sk., Can.	D9	106
Stony River, Ak., U.S.	D8	140
Stopnica, Pol.	F16	16
Stora Lulevatten, l., Swe.	C8	8
Storavan, l., Swe.	D8	8
Stord, i., Nor.	G1	8
Storebælt, strt., Den.	I4	8
Store Koldewey, i., Grnld.	B22	141
Støren, Nor.	E4	8
Store Sotra, i., Nor.	F1	8
Storkerson Bay, b., N.T., Can.	B14	140
Storkerson Peninsula, pen., Nu., Can.	A9	106
Storlien, Swe.	E5	8
Storm Bay, b., Austl.	o13	77a
Storm Lake, Ia., U.S.	B2	120
Stornoway, Scot., U.K.	C6	12
Storozhynets', Ukr.	A12	26
Storrs, Ct., U.S.	C13	114
Storsjøen, l., Nor.	F4	8
Storsjön, l., Swe.	E5	8
Storstrøm, state, Den.	I5	8
Storthoaks, Sk., Can.	E12	124
Storuman, Swe.	D7	8
Storuman, l., Swe.	D6	8
Storvindeln, l., Swe.	D7	8
Storvreta, Swe.	F7	8
Story City, Ia., U.S.	B4	120
Stosch, Isla, i., Chile	I1	90
Stoubcy, Bela.	G9	10
Stoughton, Sk., Can.	E10	124
Stoughton, Ma., U.S.	B14	114
Stoughton, Wi., U.S.	B8	120
Stoŭng, stm., Camb.	F7	48
Stow, Oh., U.S.	C4	114
Stowe, Vt., U.S.	F4	110
Stowell, Tx., U.S.	H4	122
Stowmarket, Eng., U.K.	I14	12
Stoyoma Mountain, mtn., B.C., Can.	G9	138
Stradella, Italy	E6	22
Stradzečy, Bela.	I6	10
Strahan, Austl.	o12	77a
Strakonice, Czech Rep.	G9	16
Stralsund, Ger.	B9	16
Strand, S. Afr.	I4	70
Stranraer, Scot., U.K.	G8	12
Strasbourg, Sk., Can.	C9	124
Strasbourg, Fr.	F16	14
Strasburg, Ger.	C9	16
Strasburg, N.D., U.S.	A12	126
Strasburg, Oh., U.S.	D4	114
Strasburg, Pa., U.S.	E9	114
Strășeni, Mol.	B15	26
Stratford, On., Can.	E8	112
Stratford, N.Z.	D6	80
Stratford, Ca., U.S.	G6	134
Stratford, Ct., U.S.	C12	114
Stratford, Ia., U.S.	B4	120
Stratford, Ok., U.S.	C2	122
Stratford, Wi., U.S.	G8	118
Stratford-upon-Avon, Eng., U.K.	I11	12
Strathalbyn, Austl.	J2	76
Strathclair, Mb., Can.	D13	124
Strathgordon, Austl.	o12	77a
Strathlorne, N.S., Can.	D15	110
Strathmore, Ab., Can.	E17	138
Strathmore, val., Scot., U.K.	E9	12
Strathroy, On., Can.	F8	112
Strathy Point, c., Scot., U.K.	C8	12
Stratton, Co., U.S.	B6	128
Stratton, Me., U.S.	E6	110
Stratton, Ne., U.S.	A7	128
Straubing, Ger.	H8	16
Strausberg, Ger.	D9	16
Strawberry, stm., Ar., U.S.	H6	120
Strawberry, stm., Ut., U.S.	C6	132
Strawberry Mountain, mtn., Or., U.S.	F8	136
Strawberry Reservoir, res., Ut., U.S.	C5	132
Strawn, Tx., U.S.	B9	130
Strážnice, Czech Rep.	H13	16
Streaky Bay, b., Austl.	F6	74
Streatham, B.C., Can.	C4	138
Streator, Il., U.S.	C9	120
Středočeský, state, Czech Rep.	G10	16
Stredoslovenský Kraj, state, Slov.	H15	16
Streeter, N.D., U.S.	A13	126
Streetsboro, Oh., U.S.	C4	114
Streetsville, On., Can.	E10	112
Strehaia, Rom.	E10	26
Strelka-Čunja, Russia	B18	32
Strel'na, stm., Russia	C18	8
Strel'skaja, Russia	G22	8
Strenči, Lat.	C8	10
Strèšyn, Bela.	H13	10
Strickland, stm., Pap. N. Gui.	b3	79a
Strimon, Gulf of see Strymonikós Kólpos, b., Grc.	C6	28
Strjama, stm., Blg.	G11	26
Stroeder, Arg.	H4	90
Strofádes, is., Grc.	F3	28
Stromboli, Isola, i., Italy	F9	24
Strome, Ab., Can.	D18	138
Stromeferry, Scot., U.K.	D7	12
Stromsburg, Ne., U.S.	F15	126
Strömstad, Swe.	G4	8
Strömsund, Swe.	E6	8
Strong City, Ks., U.S.	C12	128
Stronghurst, Il., U.S.	D7	120
Stronsay, i., Scot., U.K.	B10	12
Stropkov, Slov.	G17	16
Stroud, Austl.	I8	76
Stroud, Eng., U.K.	J10	12
Stroud, Ok., U.S.	B2	122
Stroudsburg, Pa., U.S.	D10	114
Struga, Mac.	B3	28
Struma, stm., Eur.	H10	26
Strumble Head, c., Wales, U.K.	I7	12
Strumica, Mac.	B5	28
Strunino, Russia	D21	10
Struthers, Oh., U.S.	C5	114
Stryi, stm., Ukr.	H19	16
Stryker, Mt., U.S.	B12	136
Stryker, Oh., U.S.	G5	112
Stryków, Pol.	E15	16
Strymonikós Kólpos (Strimon, Gulf of), b., Grc.	C6	28
Strzegom, Pol.	F12	16
Strzelce Krajeńskie, Pol.	D11	16
Strzelce Opolskie, Pol.	F14	16
Strzelecki Creek, stm., Austl.	G3	76
Strzelecki Desert, des., Austl.	F3	76
Strzelecki National Park, p.o.i., Austl.	n13	77a
Strzelin, Pol.	F12	16
Strzyżów, Pol.	G17	16
Stuart, Fl., U.S.	I5	116
Stuart, Ia., U.S.	C3	120
Stuart, Va., U.S.	H5	114
Stuart, stm., B.C., Can.	B7	138
Stuart Island, i., Ak., U.S.	D7	140
Stuart Lake, l., B.C., Can.	B5	138
Stuarts Draft, Va., U.S.	G6	114
Studen Kladenec, Jazovir, res., Blg.	H12	26
Stuie, B.C., Can.	D4	138
Stupino, Russia	F20	10
Stura di Demonte, stm., Italy	F4	22
Sturge Island, i., Ant.	B21	81
Sturgeon, stm., On., Can.	B9	112
Sturgeon, stm., Mi., U.S.	E10	118
Sturgeon Bay, Wi., U.S.	D2	112
Sturgeon Bay, b., Mb., Can.	B15	124
Sturgeon Falls, On., Can.	B10	112
Sturgeon Lake, l., Ab., Can.	A13	138
Sturgeon Lake, l., On., Can.	D11	112
Sturgeon Lake, l., On., Can.	A7	118
Sturgis, Sk., Can.	C11	124
Sturgis, Ky., U.S.	G10	120
Sturgis, Mi., U.S.	G4	112
Sturgis, S.D., U.S.	C9	126
Štúrovo, Slov.	I14	16
Sturt, Mount, mtn., Austl.	G3	76
Sturtevant, Wi., U.S.	F2	112
Sturt National Park, p.o.i., Austl.	G3	76
Sturt Stony Desert, des., Austl.	G3	76
Stutterheim, S. Afr.	H8	70
Stuttgart, Ger.	H5	16
Stuttgart, Ar., U.S.	C7	122
Styr, stm., Eur.	H9	10
Styria see Steiermark, state, Aus.	C11	22
Šu, Kaz.	F12	32
Suaçuí Grande, stm., Braz.	J4	88
Suai, Malay.	B8	50
Suaita, Col.	D5	86
Suapure, stm., Ven.	D8	86
Suaqui Grande, Mex.	A4	100
Subah, Indon.	G6	50
Subang, Indon.	G5	50
Subansiri, stm., Asia	D14	54
Šubarkuduk, Kaz.	E9	32
Subarnarekha, stm., India	G11	54
Sūbāṭ, stm., Sudan	F6	62
Subate, Lat.	D8	10
Subei, China	D3	36
Subeita see Shivta, Ḥorvot, hist., Isr.	H5	58
Subiaco, Italy	I10	22
Sublette, Ks., U.S.	D8	128
Sublett Range, mts., Id., U.S.	H14	136
Subotica, Yugo.	C6	26
Sucarnoochee, stm., U.S.	E10	122
Succotah, hist., Egypt	H3	58
Suceava, Rom.	B13	26
Suceava, state, Rom.	B12	26
Suchań, Pol.	C11	16
Suchou see Suzhou, China	F9	42
Süchow see Xuzhou, China	D7	42
Sucio, stm., Col.	D3	86
Sucre, Bol.	C3	90
Sucre, Col.	C4	86
Sucre, state, Col.	C4	86
Sucre, state, Ven.	B10	86
Sucuaro, Col.	E7	86
Sucumbíos, state, Ec.	H3	86
Sucuriju, Braz.	C8	84
Sucuriú, stm., Braz.	C6	90
Sud, state, N. Cal.	m16	79d
Sud, Canal du, strt., Haiti	C11	102
Suda, Russia	A20	10
Suda, stm., Russia	A20	10
Sudan, Tx., U.S.	G6	128
Sudan, ctry., Afr.	E5	62
Sudan, reg., Afr.	E4	62
Sudbišči, Russia	H20	10
Sudbury, On., Can.	B8	112
Sudbury, Eng., U.K.	I13	12
Sudd see As-Sudd, reg., Sudan	F6	62
Sudetes, mts., Eur.	F11	16
Sudogda, Russia	H19	8
Sudomskaja vozvyšennost', plat., Russia	C12	10
Sudost', stm., Eur.	H16	10
Südtirol see Trentino-Alto Adige, state, Italy	D8	22
Suðuroy, i., Far. Is.	n34	8b
Sue, stm., Sudan	F5	62
Sueca, Spain	E10	20
Suez see El-Suweis, Egypt	I3	58
Suez, Gulf of see Suweis, Khalîg el-, b., Egypt	J4	58
Suez Canal see Suweis, Qanâ el-, can., Egypt	H3	58
Suffield, Ab., Can.	D2	124
Suffolk, Va., U.S.	H9	114
Sufu see Kashi, China	B12	56
Sugar City, Id., U.S.	G15	136
Sugar Hill, Ga., U.S.	B1	116
Sugar Island, i., Mi., U.S.	B5	112
Sugar Land, Tx., U.S.	H3	122
Sugarloaf, hill, Oh., U.S.	C4	114
Sugarloaf Mountain, mtn., Me., U.S.	E6	110
Sugarloaf Point, c., Austl.	I9	76
Suğla Gölü, l., Tur.	F14	28
Sugoj, stm., Russia	D20	34
Sugut, stm., Malay.	G1	52
Suhag, Egypt	B6	62
Suhai Hu, l., China	G16	32
Suhana, Russia	C12	34
Ṣuḥār, Oman	E8	56
Sühbaatar, Mong.	A6	36
Suhindol, Blg.	F12	26
Suhiniči, Russia	F18	10
Suhl, Ger.	F6	16
Suhodol'skij, Russia	G21	10
Suhona, stm., Russia	F22	8
Suhoverkovo, Russia	D18	10
Suhumi, Geor.	F6	32
Şuhut, Tur.	E13	28
Suiá-Miçu, stm., Braz.	F7	84
Suichuan, China	H6	42
Suide, China	C4	42
Suifu see Yibin, China	F5	36
Suihua, China	B10	36
Suijiang, China	F5	36
Suileng, China	B10	36
Suining, China	E7	42
Suining, China	F1	42
Suipacha, Arg.	G8	92
Suiping, China	E5	42
Suippes, Fr.	E13	14
Suir, stm., Ire.	I5	12
Suixi, China	E7	42
Suiyang, China	B9	38
Suiyang, China	H2	42
Suiyangdian, China	E5	42
Suizhong, China	A9	42
Suizhou, China	F5	42
Šuja, Russia	H19	8
Šuja, stm., Russia	E15	8
Sujāngarh, India	E5	54
Sujāwal, Pak.	F2	54
Sukabumi, Indon.	G5	50
Sukadana, Indon.	D6	50
Sukadana, Indon.	F4	50
Sukadana, Teluk, b., Indon.	D6	50
Sukagawa, Japan	B13	40
Sukamara, Indon.	E7	50
Sukaraja, Indon.	E7	50
Sukau, Malay.	A11	50
Sukhothai, Thai.	D4	48
Sukhumi see Suhumi, Geor.	F6	32
Sukkertoppen (Maniitsoq), Grnld.	D15	141
Sukkozero, Russia	E14	8
Sukkur, Pak.	E2	54
Sukoharjo, Indon.	G7	50
Sukromlja, Russia	D17	10
Sukses, Nmb.	B3	70
Sukumo, Japan	G5	40
Sukunka, stm., B.C., Can.	A9	138
Sul, Baía, b., Braz.	C13	92
Sula, i., Nor.	F1	8
Sula, stm., Russia	C23	8
Sula, Kepulauan (Sula Islands), is., Indon.	F8	44
Sulaimān Range, mts., Pak.	C3	54
Sula Islands see Sula, Kepulauan, is., Indon.	F8	44
Sulawesi (Celebes), i., Indon.	F7	44
Sulawesi Selatan, state, Indon.	E11	50
Sulawesi Tengah, state, Indon.	D12	50
Sulawesi Tenggara, state, Indon.	E12	50
Sulaymān, Birak (Solomon's Pools), hist., W.B.	G5	58
Sulcis, reg., Italy	E2	24
Sulechów, Pol.	D11	16
Sulęcin, Pol.	D11	16
Sulejówek, Pol.	D17	16
Sulen, Mount, mtn., Pap. N. Gui.	a3	79a
Sulina, Rom.	D16	26
Sulina, Braţul, stm., Rom.	D16	26
Sulingen, Ger.	D4	16
Sulitelma, mtn., Eur.	C7	8
Sullana, Peru	D1	84
Sulligent, Al., U.S.	D10	122
Sullivan, Il., U.S.	E9	120
Sullivan, In., U.S.	E10	120
Sullivan Lake, l., Ab., Can.	E18	138
Sulmona, Italy	H10	22
Sulphur, La., U.S.	G5	122
Sulphur, Ok., U.S.	C2	122
Sulphur, stm., U.S.	D5	122
Sulphur Springs, Tx., U.S.	D3	122
Sulphur Springs Draw, stm., U.S.	H6	128
Sulphur Springs Valley, val., Az., U.S.	L7	132
Sultan, Wa., U.S.	C5	136
Sultan Alonto, Lake, l., Phil.	G5	52
Sultandağı, Tur.	E14	28
Sultanhisar, Tur.	F11	28
Sultan Kudarat, Phil.	G4	52
Sultānpur, India	E8	54
Sulu Archipelago, is., Phil.	H3	52
Sulu Chi, l., China	C11	54
Sulūq, Libya	A4	62
Sulu Sea, Asia	F2	52
Sulzbach-Rosenberg, Ger.	G7	16
Šum, Russia	A14	10
Šumadija, reg., Yugo.	E7	26
Sumangat, Tanjong, c., Malay.	G1	52
Sumatera (Sumatra), i., Indon.	E3	44
Sumatera Barat, state, Indon.	D2	50
Sumatera Selatan, state, Indon.	E4	50
Sumatera Utara, state, Indon.	K4	48
Sumatra see Sumatera, i., Indon.	E3	44
Sumba, Far. Is.	n34	8b
Sumba, i., Indon.	H11	50
Sumba, Selat, strt., Indon.	H11	50
Sumbawa, i., Indon.	H10	50
Sumbawa Besar, Indon.	H10	50
Sumbawanga, Tan.	F6	66
Sumbe, Ang.	C1	68
Sumburgh Head, c., Scot., U.K.	o18	12a
Sumé, Braz.	D7	88
Sumedang, Indon.	G5	50
Sümeg, Hung.	B4	26
Šumen, Blg.	F13	26
Sumenep, Indon.	G8	50
Šumerlja, Russia	C7	32
Sumisu-jima (Smith Island), i., Japan	E13	36
Šumjači, Russia	G15	10
Summerfield, Fl., U.S.	G3	116
Summerfield, N.C., U.S.	H6	114
Summer Lake, l., Or., U.S.	H6	136
Summerland, B.C., Can.	G11	138
Summerside, P.E., Can.	D13	110
Summersville, Mo., U.S.	G6	120
Summerton, S.C., U.S.	C5	116
Summerville, Ga., U.S.	C13	122
Summerville, S.C., U.S.	C5	116
Summit, S.D., U.S.	F1	118
Summit Lake, B.C., Can.	B8	138
Summit Mountain, mtn., Nv., U.S.	D9	134
Sumner, Ia., U.S.	B5	120
Sumner, Ms., U.S.	D8	122
Sumner, Wa., U.S.	C4	136
Sumoto, Japan	E7	40
Sumpangbinangae, Indon.	F11	50
Šumperk, Czech Rep.	G13	16
Sumpiuh, Indon.	G6	50
Sumqayıt, Azer.	A6	56
Šumšu, ostrov, i., Russia	F20	34
Sumter, S.C., U.S.	C5	116
Sumusta el-Waqf, Egypt	J1	58
Sumy, Ukr.	D4	32
Sumzom, China	F4	36
Sun, stm., Mt., U.S.	C14	136
Sunāmganj, Bngl.	F13	54
Sunbright, Tn., U.S.	H13	120
Sunburst, Mt., U.S.	B14	136
Sunbury, Austl.	K5	76
Sunbury, Oh., U.S.	D3	114
Sunbury, Pa., U.S.	D9	114
Sunchales, Arg.	E7	92
Suncho Corral, Arg.	C6	92
Sunch'ŏn, Kor., S.	G7	38
Sunch'ŏn-ŭp, Kor., N.	E6	38
Sun City, Az., U.S.	J4	132
Suncook, N.H., U.S.	G5	110
Sunda, Selat (Sunda Strait), strt., Indon.	G4	50
Sundance, Wy., U.S.	C8	126
Sundarbans, reg., Asia	H12	54
Sundargarh, India	G9	54
Sunda Shelf, unds.	I13	142
Sunda Strait see Sunda, Selat, strt., Indon.	G4	50
Sundays, stm., S. Afr.	H7	70
Sunde, Nor.	G1	8
Sunderland, Eng., U.K.	G11	12
Sundown, Tx., U.S.	H6	128
Sundridge, On., Can.	C10	112
Sundsvall, Swe.	E7	8
Sunflower, Ms., U.S.	D8	122
Sunflower, Mount, mtn., Ks., U.S.	B7	128
Sungaianyar, Indon.	E10	50
Sungaibuntu, Indon.	F5	50
Sungaidareh, Indon.	D2	50
Sungaiguntung, Indon.	C3	50
Sungai Kolok, Thai.	I5	48
Sungailangsat, Indon.	D2	50
Sungailimau, Indon.	D1	50
Sungaipenuh, Indon.	E2	50
Sungai Petani, Malay.	J5	48
Sungaipinang, Indon.	D8	50
Sungairotan, Indon.	E4	50
Sungaiselan, Indon.	E5	50
Sungari see Songhua, stm., China	B11	36
Sungari Reservoir see Songhua Hu, res., China	C7	38
Sungchiang see Songjiang, China	F9	42
Sungguminasa, Indon.	F11	50
Sungsang, Indon.	E4	50
Sunland Park, N.M., U.S.	L10	132
Sunne, Swe.	G5	8
Sunnynook, Ab., Can.	E19	138
Sunnyside, Ut., U.S.	D6	132
Sunnyside, Wa., U.S.	D7	136
Sunnyslope, Ab., Can.	E17	138
Sunnyvale, Ca., U.S.	F3	134
Sun Prairie, Wi., U.S.	A8	120
Sunrise, Fl., U.S.	J5	116
Sunrise, Wy., U.S.	E8	126
Sunrise Manor, Nv., U.S.	G1	132
Sunset, La., U.S.	G6	122
Sunset, Tx., U.S.	H11	128
Sunset Country, reg., Austl.	J3	76
Sunset Crater National Monument, p.o.i., Az., U.S.	H5	132
Sunshine, Austl.	K5	76
Suntar, Russia	D12	34
Suntar-Hajata, hrebet, mts., Russia	D17	34
Sun Valley, Id., U.S.	G12	136
Sunwu, China	B10	36
Sunwui see Jiangmen, China	J5	42
Sunyani, Ghana	H4	64
Suojarvi, Russia	E15	8
Suomussalmi, Fin.	D13	8
Suō-nada, Japan	F4	40
Suordah, Russia	C15	34
Supamo, stm., Ven.	D10	86
Supaul, India	E11	54
Superí see La Merced, Arg.	D5	92
Superior, Az., U.S.	J5	132
Superior, Mt., U.S.	C12	136
Superior, Wi., U.S.	E6	118
Superior, Wy., U.S.	B7	132
Superior, Laguna, b., Mex.	G11	100
Superior, Lake, l., N.A.	B10	108
Supetar, Cro.	G13	22
Suphan Buri, Thai.	E4	48
Suphan Buri, stm., Thai.	E5	48
Suponevo, Russia	G17	10
Supung Reservoir, res., Asia	D6	38
Suqian, China	E8	42
Sūq Suwayq, Sau. Ar.	E4	56
Suquṭrā (Socotra), i., Yemen	G7	56
Ṣūr (Tyre), Leb.	E6	58
Ṣūr, Oman	E8	56
Sur, Point, c., Ca., U.S.	G4	134
Sura, stm., Russia	C7	32
Surabaya, Indon.	G8	50
Surakarta, Indon.	G7	50
Şūrān, Syria	C7	58
Šurany, Slov.	H14	16
Surat, Austl.	F7	76
Sūrat, India	H4	54
Sūratgarh, India	D4	54
Surat Thani, Thai.	H4	48
Suraž, Bela.	E13	10
Suraž, Russia	G15	10
Surendranagar, India	G3	54
Surf City, N.J., U.S.	E11	114
Surfers Paradise, Austl.	G9	76
Surgères, Fr.	C5	18
Surgoinsville, Tn., U.S.	H3	114
Surgut, Russia	B12	32
Suriāpet, India	C4	53
Surigao, Phil.	F5	52
Surin, Thai.	E6	48
Surinam, ctry., S.A.	C6	84
Suring, Wi., U.S.	D1	112
Surprise Valley, val., U.S.	B5	134
Surrency, Ga., U.S.	E3	116
Surrey, N.D., U.S.	F12	124
Surry, Va., U.S.	G9	114
Sursee, Switz.	C5	22
Surt, Libya	A3	62
Surt, Khalīj (Sidra, Gulf of), b., Libya	A3	62
Surtanāhu, Pak.	E2	54
Surtsey, i., Ice.	I29	8a
Suru, Pap. N. Gui.	b3	79a
Sürüç, Tur.	A9	58
Suruga-wan, b., Japan	E11	40
Surulangun, Indon.	E3	50
Surumu, stm., Braz.	F11	86
Šuryškary, Russia	A10	32
Susa, Italy	E4	22
Sušac, Otok, i., Cro.	H13	22
Sūsah, Libya	A4	62
Susaki, Japan	F6	40
Susanino, Russia	G19	8
Susanino, Russia	F17	34
Susanville, Ca., U.S.	C5	134
Šušenskoe, Russia	D16	32
Susitna, stm., Ak., U.S.	D9	140
Susleni, Mol.	B15	26
Susoh, Indon.	K3	48
Susong, China	F7	42
Suspiro del Moro, Puerto, p., Spain	G7	20
Susquehanna, Pa., U.S.	C10	114
Susquehanna, stm., U.S.	E9	114
Susquehanna, West Branch, stm., Pa., U.S.	C8	114
Susques, Arg.	D3	90
Sussex, N.B., Can.	E11	110
Sussex, N.J., U.S.	C11	114
Sussex, Va., U.S.	H8	114
Susuman, Russia	D18	34
Susurluk, Tur.	D11	28
Şusuzmüsellim, Tur.	B9	28
Šušvė, stm., Lith.	E6	10
Sutak, India	B6	54
Sutherland, S. Afr.	H5	70
Sutherland, Ia., U.S.	A2	120
Sutherlin, Or., U.S.	G3	136
Sutjeska Nacionalni Park, p.o.i., Bos.	F5	26
Sutlej (Langqên) (Satluj), stm., Asia	D3	54
Sutter, Ca., U.S.	D4	134
Sutter Buttes, mtn., Ca., U.S.	D4	134
Sutter Creek, Ca., U.S.	E5	134
Sutton, Ak., U.S.	D10	140
Sutton, W.V., U.S.	F5	114
Sutton, Monts see Green Mountains, mts., N.A.	G4	110
Sutton in Ashfield, Eng., U.K.	H11	12
Sutton West, On., Can.	D10	112
Suttor, stm., Austl.	C6	76
Sutwik Island, i., Ak., U.S.	E8	140
Suure-Jaani, Est.	B8	10
Suur Munamägi, hill, Est.	C9	10
Suur Pakri, i., Est.	A6	10
Suva, Fiji	q19	79e
Suvadiva Atoll, at., Mald.	i12	46a
Suvarlı, Tur.	A8	58
Suvasvesi, l., Fin.	E12	8
Suvorov, Russia	F19	10
Suwa, Japan	C11	40
Suwałki, Pol.	B18	16
Suwałki, state, Pol.	C18	16
Suwannaphum, Thai.	E6	48
Suwannee, stm., U.S.	G2	116
Suwanose-jima, i., Japan	k19	39a
Suwarrow, at., Cook Is.	E10	72
Suweis, Khalîg el- (Suez, Gulf of), b., Egypt	J4	58
Suweis, Qanâ el- (Suez Canal), can., Egypt	H3	58
Suwŏn, Kor., S.	F7	38
Suzak, Kaz.	F11	32
Suzaka, Japan	C11	40
Suzdal', Russia	H19	8
Suzhou, China	F9	42
Suzhou, China	E7	42
Suzigou, China	A10	42
Suzuka, Japan	E9	40
Suzuka-sammyaku, mts., Japan	D9	40
Suzu-misaki, c., Japan	B10	40
Suzun, Russia	D14	32
Suzzara, Italy	F7	22
Svalbard, dep., Eur.	B6	30
Svaliava, Ukr.	A10	26
Svapa, stm., Russia	H18	10
Svappavaara, Swe.	C9	8
Svärdsjö, Swe.	F6	8
Svartenhuk, pen., Grnld.	C15	141
Svartisen, ice, Nor.	C5	8
Svataj, Russia	C19	34
Svay Riĕng, Camb.	G7	48
Svėdasai, Lith.	E8	10
Svegssjön, l., Swe.	E5	8
Švėkšna, Lith.	E4	10
Svelvik, Nor.	G4	8
Švenčionėliai, Lith.	E8	10
Švenčionys, Lith.	E9	10
Svendborg, Den.	A6	16
Šventoji, Lith.	D3	10
Šventoji, stm., Lith.	E7	10
Sverdlovsk see Ekaterinburg, Russia	C10	32
Sverdrup, ostrov, i., Russia	B4	34
Sverdrup Channel, strt., Nu., Can.	A6	141
Sverdrup Islands, is., Nu., Can.	B5	141
Sveti Nikole, Mac.	B4	28
Svetlahorsk, Bela.	H12	10
Svetlaja, Russia	B12	36
Svetlogorsk, Russia	F2	10
Svetlograd, Russia	E6	32
Svetlyj, Russia	F3	10
Svetlyj, Russia	D10	32
Svetlyj, Russia	E12	34
Svetogorsk, Russia	F13	8
Svetozarevo, Yugo.	F8	26
Svidník, Slov.	G17	16
Svilengrad, Blg.	H13	26
Svínoy, i., Far. Is.	m34	8b
Svir, Bela.	F9	10
Svir', stm., Russia	F16	8
Svirica, Russia	F15	8
Svirsk, Russia	D18	32
Svislač, stm., Bela.	G11	10
Svištov, Blg.	F12	26
Svit, Slov.	G16	16
Svitavy, Czech Rep.	G12	16
Svjacilavičy, Bela.	H14	10
Svjatoj Nos, mys, c., Russia	B18	8
Svjatoj Nos, mys, c., Russia	B17	34
Svobodnyj, Russia	F14	34
Svolvær, Nor.	B6	8
Svratka, stm., Czech Rep.	G12	16
Swabia see Schwaben, hist. reg., Ger.	H5	16
Swain Reefs, rf., Austl.	C9	76
Swainsboro, Ga., U.S.	D3	116
Swains Island, at., Am. Sam.	E9	72
Swakop, stm., Nmb.	C2	70
Swakopmund, Nmb.	C2	70
Swale, stm., Eng., U.K.	G11	12
Swan, stm., Can.	B13	124
Swan, stm., Ab., Can.	A15	138
Swan, stm., Mt., U.S.	C13	136
Swanage, Eng., U.K.	K11	12
Swanee see Suwannee, stm., U.S.	G2	116
Swan Hill, Austl.	J4	76
Swan Hills, Ab., Can.	B15	138
Swan Islands see Santanilla, Islas, is., Hond.	D6	102
Swan Lake, Mb., Can.	E15	124
Swan Lake, l., Mb., Can.	B13	124
Swan Lake, l., Mn., U.S.	G4	118
Swannanoa, N.C., U.S.	I3	114
Swan Peak, mtn., Mt., U.S.	C13	136
Swanquarter, N.C., U.S.	A9	116
Swan Range, mts., Mt., U.S.	C13	136
Swan Reach, Austl.	J2	76
Swan River, Mb., Can.	B12	124
Swansboro, N.C., U.S.	B8	116
Swansea, Austl.	o13	77a
Swansea, Wales, U.K.	J8	12
Swanton, Vt., U.S.	F3	110
Swanville, Mn., U.S.	F4	118
Swart-Mfolozi, stm., S. Afr.	F10	70
Swartz Creek, Mi., U.S.	F6	112
Swarzędz, Pol.	D13	16
Swāt, stm., Pak.	A3	54
Swatow see Shantou, China	J7	42
Swaziland, ctry., Afr.	E10	70
Sweden, ctry., Eur.	E6	8
Swedish Knoll, mtn., Ut., U.S.	D5	132
Swedru, Ghana	H4	64
Sweeny, Tx., U.S.	E12	130
Sweet Briar, Va., U.S.	G6	114
Sweetgrass, Mt., U.S.	A15	136
Sweet Grass Hills, hills, Mt., U.S.	B15	136
Sweet Home, Tx., U.S.	E10	130
Sweet Springs, Mo., U.S.	F4	120
Sweetwater, Tn., U.S.	A1	116
Sweetwater, Tx., U.S.	B7	130
Sweetwater, stm., Wy., U.S.	E5	126
Swellendam, S. Afr.	H5	70
Świdnica, Pol.	F12	16
Świdnik, Pol.	E18	16
Świdwin, Pol.	C11	16
Świebodzice, Pol.	F12	16
Świebodzin, Pol.	D11	16
Świecie, Pol.	C14	16
Świerzawa, Pol.	E11	16
Świętokrzyski Park Narodowy, p.o.i., Pol.	F16	16
Swift Current, Sk., Can.	D6	124
Swift Current Creek, stm., Sk., Can.	D6	124
Swinburne, Cape, c., Nu., Can.	A11	106
Swindle Island, i., B.C., Can.	D2	138
Swindon, Eng., U.K.	J11	12
Swinford, Ire.	H4	12
Świnoujście (Swinemünde), Pol.	C9	16
Switzerland, ctry., Eur.	C14	18
Swords, Ire.	H6	12
Syalah, Russia	C13	34
Syan (San), stm., Eur.	F18	16
Sycamore, Ga., U.S.	E2	116
Sycamore, Il., U.S.	C9	120
Sycamore, Oh., U.S.	D2	114
Syčovka, Russia	E17	10
Sydenham, stm., On., Can.	F7	112
Sydney, Austl.	I8	76
Sydney, N.S., Can.	D16	110
Sydney Bay, b., Norf. I.	y25	78i
Sydney Lake, l., On., Can.	A4	118
Sydney Mines, N.S., Can.	D16	110
Syičy, Bela.	H12	10
Syke, Ger.	D4	16
Sykesville, Pa., U.S.	C7	114
Syktyvkar, Russia	B8	32
Sylacauga, Al., U.S.	D12	122
Sylhet, Bngl.	F13	54
Syloga, Russia	E20	8
Sylt, i., Ger.	B4	16
Sylva, N.C., U.S.	A2	116
Sylvan Grove, Ks., U.S.	C10	128
Sylvania, Ga., U.S.	D4	116
Sylvania, Oh., U.S.	C2	114
Sylvan Lake, Ab., Can.	D16	138
Sylvan Lake, l., Ab., Can.	D16	138
Sylvan Pass, p., Wy., U.S.	F16	136
Sylvester, Ga., U.S.	E2	116
Sylvester, Tx., U.S.	B7	130
Sym, Russia	B15	32
Syme see Sými, i., Grc.	G10	28
Sými, i., Grc.	G10	28
Šymkent, Kaz.	F11	32
Synevir, Ukr.	A10	26
Syowa, sci., Ant.	C9	81
Syracuse, In., U.S.	G4	112
Syracuse, Ks., U.S.	C7	128
Syracuse, Ne., U.S.	D1	120
Syracuse, N.Y., U.S.	A9	114
Syrdarja, Uzb.	A10	56
Syr Darya (Syrdar'ja), stm., Asia	F11	32
Syria, ctry., Asia	B4	56
Syriam, Mya.	D3	48
Syrian Desert (Shām, Bādiyat ash-), des., Asia	C4	56
Sýrna, i., Grc.	G9	28
Sýros, i., Grc.	F7	28
Sysmä, Fin.	F11	8
Sysola, stm., Russia	B8	32
Syt'kovo, Russia	D16	10
Syväri, l., Fin.	E13	8
Syzran', Russia	D7	32
Szabolcs-Szatmár-Bereg, state, Hung.	A9	26
Szamos (Someș), stm., Eur.	B9	26
Szamotuły, Pol.	D12	16
Szarvas, Hung.	C7	26
Szczawnica, Pol.	G16	16
Szczecin (Stettin), Pol.	C10	16
Szczecin, state, Pol.	C11	16
Szczecinek, Pol.	C12	16
Szczuczyn, Pol.	C18	16
Szczytno, Pol.	C17	16
Szechwan see Sichuan, state, China	E5	36
Szechwan Basin see Sichuan Pendi, bas., China	F1	42
Szeged, Hung.	C7	26
Szeghalom, Hung.	B8	26
Székesfehérvár, Hung.	B5	26
Szekszárd, Hung.	C5	26
Szentendre, Hung.	B5	26
Szentes, Hung.	C7	26
Szeping see Siping, China	C6	38
Szerencs, Hung.	A8	26
Szob, Hung.	B5	26
Szolnok, Hung.	B7	26
Szombathely, Hung.	B3	26
Szprotawa, Pol.	E11	16
Szubin, Pol.	C13	16
Szypliszki, Pol.	B19	16

T

Name	Map Ref.	Page
Taal, Lake, l., Phil.	D3	52
Tábara, Spain	C5	20
Tabar Islands, is., Pap. N. Gui.	a5	79a
Tabarka, Tun.	H2	24
Tabasco, state, Mex.	D6	96
Tabelbala, Alg.	D4	64
Taber, Ab., Can.	G18	138
Tabernes de Valldigna see Tavernes de la Valldigna, Spain	E10	20
Tabira, Braz.	D7	88
Tablas de Daimiel, Parque Nacional de las, p.o.i., Spain	E7	20
Tablas Island, i., Phil.	D4	52
Tablas Strait, strt., Phil.	D3	52
Tablat, Alg.	H14	20
Table Mountain, mtn., Az., U.S.	K6	132
Table Rock, Ne., U.S.	D1	120
Table Rock Lake, res., U.S.	H4	120
Table Top, mtn., Az., U.S.	K4	132
Tablones, P.R.	B4	104a
Taboi, Mount, hill, St. Vin.	p11	105e
Tábor, Czech Rep.	G10	16
Tabor, Russia	B19	34
Tabor, Ia., U.S.	D2	120
Tabora, Tan.	E6	66
Tabor City, N.C., U.S.	B7	116
Tabou, C. Iv.	I3	64
Tabrīz, Iran	B6	56
Tabuaeran, at., Kir.	C11	72
Tabu-dong, Kor., S.	C1	40
Tabuk, Phil.	B3	52
Tabūk, Sau. Ar.	J7	58
Tabuleiro do Norte, Braz.	C6	88
Tabwémasana, Mont, mtn., Vanuatu	j16	79d
Tacámbaro de Codallos, Mex.	F8	100
Tacaná, Volcán, vol., N.A.	H12	100
Tacañitas, Arg.	D6	92
Taché, Lac, l., N.T., Can.	C7	106
Tacheng, China	B1	36
Tachia, stm., Tai.	I9	42
Tachichitlte, Isla de, i., Mex.	C4	100
Tachie, stm., B.C., Can.	B6	138
Táchira, state, Ven.	D6	86
Tachoshui, Tai.	I9	42
Tacima, Braz.	D8	88
Tacloban, Phil.	E5	52
Taclobo, Phil.	D4	52
Tacna, Peru	G3	84
Tacna, Az., U.S.	K3	132
Tacoma, Wa., U.S.	C4	136
Taconic Range, mts., U.S.	B12	114
Taco Pozo, Arg.	B6	92
Tacuarembó, Ur.	E9	92
Tacuarembó, stm., Ur.	E10	92
Tacuarí, stm., Ur.	F10	92
Tacutu (Takutu), stm., S.A.	F11	86
Tademaït, Plateau du, plat., Alg.	D5	64
Tādepallegūdem, India	C5	53
Tadjemout, Alg.	D5	64
Tadjerouine, Tun.	I2	24
Tadjoura, Dji.	E8	62
Tadotsu, Japan	E6	40
Tadoule Lake, l., Mb., Can.	D11	106
Tadoussac, Qc., Can.	B7	110

Name	Map Ref.	Page
Tādpatri, India	D4	53
T'aean, Kor., S.	F7	38
T'aebaek-sanmaek, mts., Asia	F8	38
Taech'ŏn, Kor., S.	F7	38
Taedong-gang, stm., Kor., N.	E6	38
Taegu, Kor., S.	D1	40
Taejin, Kor., S.	C2	40
Taejŏn, Kor., S.	F7	38
Taeng, stm., Thai.	C4	48
Tafahi, i., Tonga	E9	72
Tafalla, Spain	B9	20
Tafanlieh, Tai.	J9	42
Tafassâsset, Oued, stm., Afr.	E6	64
Tafassasset, Ténéré du, des., Niger	E7	64
Taféa, state, Vanuatu	I17	79d
Tafelberg, hill, Neth. Ant.	p22	104g
Tafí Viejo, Arg.	C5	92
Tafo, Ghana	H4	64
Taft, Ca., U.S.	H6	134
Taft, Tx., U.S.	F10	130
Taftān, Kūh-e, vol., Iran	D9	56
Taga, Samoa	g11	79c
Tagajō, Japan	A14	40
Taganrog, Russia	E5	32
Tagânt, reg., Maur.	F2	64
Tagawa, Japan	F3	40
Tagaytay, Phil.	C3	52
Tagbilaran, Phil.	F4	52
Tage, Pap. N. Gui.	b3	79a
Tagish Lake, l., Can.	C3	106
Tagliamento, stm., Italy	E9	22
Taglio di Po, Italy	E9	22
Taguatinga, Braz.	G2	88
Taguke, China	B10	54
Tagula Island, i., Pap. N. Gui.	B10	74
Tagum, Phil.	G5	52
Tagus (Tajo) (Tejo), stm., Eur.	E2	20
Tahakopa, N.Z.	H3	80
Tahan, Gunong, mtn., Malay.	J6	48
Tahat, mtn., Alg.	E6	64
Tahiataš, Uzb.	F9	32
Tahifet, Alg.	E6	64
Tahiryuak Lake, l., N.T., Can.	A8	106
Tahiti, i., Fr. Poly.	v23	78h
Tahiti-Faaa, Aéroport International de, Fr. Poly.	v21	78h
Tahkuna nina, c., Est.	A5	10
Tahlequah, Ok., U.S.	I3	120
Tahoe, Lake, l., U.S.	E5	134
Tahoe City, Ca., U.S.	D5	134
Tahoe Lake, l., Nu., Can.	A8	106
Tahoka, Tx., U.S.	A6	130
Tahoua, Niger	F5	64
Tahquamenon, stm., Mi., U.S.	B4	112
Tahta, Egypt	L2	58
Tahta, Russia	E6	32
Tahta-Bazar, Turkmen.	B9	56
Tahtaköprü, Tur.	D12	28
Tahtamygda, Russia	F13	34
Tahtsa Lake, res., B.C., Can.	C3	138
Tahtsa Peak, mtn., B.C., Can.	C3	138
Tahuata, i., Fr. Poly.	s18	78g
Tahulandang, Pulau, i., Indon.	E7	44
Tahuna, Indon.	E8	44
Tai'an, China	C7	42
Taiarapu, Presqu'île de, pen., Fr. Poly.	w22	78h
Taibai Shan, mtn., China	E2	42
Taibilla, Sierra de, mts., Spain	F8	20
Taibus Qi, China	C8	36
Taicang, China	F9	42
T'aichou see Taizhou, China	E8	42
T'aichung, Tai.	I9	42
Taieri, stm., N.Z.	G4	80
Taigu, China	C5	42
Taihang Shan, mts., China	C5	42
Taihape, N.Z.	D6	80
Taihe, China	H6	42
Taihe, China	E6	42
Taihezhen, China	B5	38
T'aihsien see Taizhou, China	E8	42
Taihu, China	F7	42
Tai Hu, l., China	F9	42
Taikang, China	D6	42
Taikou, China	F4	42
Tailai, China	B9	36
Tai Lake see Tai Hu, l., China	F9	42
Tailem Bend, Austl.	J2	76
Taimba, Russia	B17	32
T'ainan, Tai.	J8	42
Taínaro, Ákra, c., Grc.	G5	28
Taining, China	H7	42
Taiobeiras, Braz.	H4	88
T'aipei, Tai.	I9	42
T'aipeihsien, Tai.	I9	42
Taiping, China	J2	42
Taiping, Malay.	J5	48
Taipingdian, China	E4	42
Taipu, Braz.	C8	88
Tais, Indon.	F3	50
Taisha, Japan	D5	40
Taishan, China	J5	42
Tai Shan see Yuhuang Ding, mtn., China	C9	42
Taishun, China	H8	42
Taitao, Península de, pen., Chile	I2	90
T'aitung, Tai.	J9	42
Taivalkoski, Fin.	D12	8
Taiwan, ctry., Asia	J9	42
Taiwan Strait, strt., Asia	I8	42
Taixian, China	E9	42
Taixing, China	E9	42
Ṭaiyiba, Isr.	F6	58
Taiyuan, China	C5	42
Taizhao, China	D14	54
Taizhou, China	E8	42
Taizi, stm., China	D5	38
Tajbola, Russia	B15	8
Tajga, Russia	C15	32
Tajgonos, mys, c., Russia	D21	34
Tajgonos, poluostrov, pen., Russia	D21	34
Tajikistan, ctry., Asia	B11	56
Tajima, Japan	B12	40
Tajimi, Japan	D10	40
Tajique, N.M., U.S.	G2	128
Tajitos, Mex.	F6	98
Tāj Mahal, hist., India	E7	54
Tajmura, stm., Russia	B18	32
Tajmyr, ozero, l., Russia	B9	34
Tajmyr, poluostrov, pen., Russia	B7	34
Tajšet, Russia	C17	32
Tajumulco, Volcán, vol., Guat.	E2	102
Tajuña, stm., Spain	D7	20
Tak, Thai.	D4	48
Takachu, Bots.	C5	70
Takahagi, Japan	C13	40
Takahashi, Japan	E6	40
Takahe, Mount, mtn., Ant.	C29	81
Takaka, N.Z.	E5	80
Takakkaw Falls, wtfl, B.C., Can.	E14	138
Takalar, Indon.	F11	50
Takamatsu, Japan	E7	40
Takanabe, Japan	G4	40
Takaoka, Japan	C9	40
Takasago, Japan	E7	40
Takasaki, Japan	C11	40
Takatsuki, Japan	E8	40
Ta-kaw, Mya.	B4	48
Takayama, Japan	C10	40
Takefu, Japan	D9	40
Takenake, China	A8	54
Takengon, Indon.	J3	48
Takeo, Japan	F3	40
Take-shima, is., Asia	B4	40
Taketa, Japan	G4	40
Takêv, Camb.	G7	48
Takhatpur, India	G8	54
Takhli, Thai.	E5	48
Takhta-Bazar see Tahta-Bazar, Turkmen.	B9	56
Takijuq Lake, l., Nu., Can.	B8	106
Takikawa, Japan	C14	38
Takla Lake, l., B.C., Can.	A5	138
Takla Landing, B.C., Can.	D5	106
Takla Makan Desert see Taklimakan Shamo, des., China	G14	32
Taklimakan Shamo (Takla Makan Desert), des., China	G14	32
Takolekaju, Pegunungan, mts., Indon.	E11	50
Taksimo, Russia	F10	34
Taku, Japan	F3	40
Takuan, Mount, vol., Pap. N. Gui.	d6	79b
Takum, Nig.	H7	64
Takutea, i., Cook Is.	E11	72
Takutu (Tacutu), stm., S.A.	F11	86
Talačyn, Bela.	F12	10
Talagang, Pak.	B4	54
Talagante, Chile	F2	92
Talaimannar, Sri L.	G4	53
Talāja, India	H4	54
Talak, reg., Niger	F6	64
Tālāla, India	H3	54
Talang, Gunung, vol., Indon.	D2	50
Talangbetutu, Indon.	E4	50
Talangpadang, Indon.	F4	50
Talangrimbo, Indon.	E4	50
Talara, Peru	D1	84
Talas, Kyrg.	F12	32
Talasea, Pap. N. Gui.	b4	79a
Tal'at al-Jamā'ah, Rujm, mtn., Jord.	H6	58
Talata Mafara, Nig.	G6	64
Talaud, Kepulauan (Talaud Islands), is., Indon.	E8	44
Talaud Islands see Talaud, Kepulauan, is., Indon.	E8	44
Talavera de la Reina, Spain	D5	20
Talawanta, Austl.	B3	76
Talawdī, Sudan	E6	62
Talayan, Phil.	G5	52
Talbotton, Ga., U.S.	E14	122
Talbragar, stm., Austl.	I7	76
Talca, Chile	G2	92
Talcahuano, Chile	H1	92
Tālcher, India	H10	54
Talco, Tx., U.S.	D3	122
Taldom, Russia	D20	10
Taldykorgan, Kaz.	F13	32
Taldyqorghan see Taldykorgan, Kaz.	F13	32
Talence, Fr.	E5	18
Talent, Or., U.S.	A3	134
Talgar, Kaz.	F13	32
Talghar see Talgar, Kaz.	F13	32
Talhār, Pak.	F2	54
Taliabu, Pulau, i., Indon.	F7	44
Talibon, Phil.	E5	52
Talibong, Ko, i., Thai.	I4	48
Talica, Russia	C10	32
Talien see Dalian, China	B9	42
Tālīkota, India	C3	53
Taliparamba, India	E2	53
Talisay, Phil.	E4	52
Taliwang, Indon.	H10	50
Talkeetna, Ak., U.S.	D9	140
Talkeetna Mountains, mts., Ak., U.S.	D10	140
Talla, Egypt	J1	58
Talladega, Al., U.S.	D12	122
Tallahala Creek, stm., Ms., U.S.	F9	122
Tallahassee, Fl., U.S.	F1	116
Tallahatchie, stm., Ms., U.S.	D8	122
Tallangatta, Austl.	K6	76
Tallapoosa, Ga., U.S.	D13	122
Tallapoosa, stm., U.S.	E12	122
Tallard, Fr.	E11	18
Tallassee, Al., U.S.	E12	122
Tall as-Sulṭān, hist., Gaza	G6	58
Tall Bīsah, Syria	D7	58
Tallinn, Est.	G11	8
Tallmadge, Oh., U.S.	C4	114
Tall Rif'at, Syria	B8	58
Tallulah, La., U.S.	E7	122
Talmage, Ca., U.S.	D2	134
Talmage, Ne., U.S.	K2	118
Tal'menka, Russia	D14	32
Talnah, Russia	C6	34
Taloda, India	H5	54
Taloga, Ok., U.S.	E10	128
Talok, Indon.	C11	50
Tāloqān, Afg.	B10	56
Talovka, Russia	F7	32
Taloyoak, Nu., Can.	B12	106
Talquin, Lake, res., Fl., U.S.	G14	122
Talsi, Lat.	C5	10
Taltal, Chile	B2	92
Taltson, stm., N.T., Can.	C8	106
Talu, Indon.	C1	50
Taluk, Indon.	D2	50
Talumphuk, Laem, c., Thai.	H5	48
Talvikjulja, Russia	B13	8
Talwood, Austl.	G7	76
Tama, Arg.	E4	92
Tama, Ia., U.S.	C5	120
Tamalameque, Col.	C5	86
Tamale, Ghana	H4	64
Tamalea, Indon.	E11	50
Tamalpais, Mount, mtn., Ca., U.S.	F3	134
Tamana, Japan	G3	40
Tamana, Mount, hill, Trin.	s12	105f
Tamanaco, stm., Ven.	C9	86
Tamaniquá, Braz.	I9	86
Taman Negara, p.o.i., Malay.	J6	48
Tamano, Japan	E6	40
Tamanquaré, Ilha, i., Braz.	H9	86
Tamapatz, Mex.	E9	100
Tamar, stm., Austl.	n13	77a
Tamarac, stm., Mn., U.S.	C2	118
Tamaroa, Il., U.S.	F8	120
Tamási, Hung.	C5	26
Tamaulipas, state, Mex.	C9	100
Tamazulapan del Progreso, Mex.	G9	100
Tamazunchale, Mex.	E9	100
Tambacounda, Sen.	G2	64
Tambakboyo, Indon.	G7	50
Tamba-kōchi, plat., Japan	D8	40
Tambangsawah, Indon.	E3	50
Tambara, Moz.	D5	68
Tāmbaram, India	E5	53
Tambej, Russia	B3	34
Tambelan, Kepulauan, is., Indon.	C5	50
Tamberías, Arg.	E3	92
Tambo, stm., Austl.	K6	76
Tambohorano, Madag.	D7	68
Tambolongang, Pulau, i., Indon.	G12	50
Tambora, Gunung, vol., Indon.	H10	50
Tamboril, Braz.	C5	88
Tamboryacu, stm., Peru	H4	86
Tambov, Russia	D6	32
Tambre, stm., Spain	B2	20
Tambu, Teluk, b., Indon.	C11	50
Tambunan, Malay.	H1	52
Tambura, Sudan	F5	62
Tâmchekkeṭ, Maur.	F2	64
Tame, Col.	D6	86
Tameapa, Mex.	C5	100
Tâmega, stm., Port.	C3	20
Tamel Aike, Arg.	I2	90
Tamenghest, Alg.	E6	64
Tamenghest, Oued, stm., Alg.	E5	64
Tamga, Russia	B10	38
Tamgak, Adrar, mtn., Niger	F6	64
Tamiahua, Mex.	E10	100
Tamiahua, Laguna de, l., Mex.	E10	100
Tamiami Canal, can., Fl., U.S.	K4	116
Tamil Nādu, state, India	F4	53
Tamiš (Timiș), stm., Eur.	D7	26
Tâmîya, Egypt	I1	58
Tamkūhi, India	E10	54
Tam Ky, Viet.	E9	48
Tammerfors see Tampere, Fin.	F10	8
Tammisaari, Fin.	G10	8
Tamms, Il., U.S.	G8	120
Tampa, Fl., U.S.	I3	116
Tampa Bay, b., Fl., U.S.	I3	116
Tampang, Indon.	F4	50
Tampaon, stm., Mex.	E9	100
Tampere (Tammerfors), Fin.	F10	8
Tampico, Mex.	D10	100
Tampico, Il., U.S.	C8	120
Tampin, Malay.	K6	48
Tamsagbulag, Mong.	B8	36
Tamshiyacu, Peru	D3	84
Tamsweg, Aus.	C10	22
Tamu, Mya.	D7	46
Tamuning, Guam	i10	78c
Tamworth, Austl.	H8	76
Tamworth, Eng., U.K.	I11	12
Tana (Teno), stm., Eur.	B12	8
Tana, stm., Kenya	D8	66
Tana, Lake see T'ana Hāyk', l., Eth.	E7	62
Tanabe, Japan	F8	40
Tanabi, Braz.	K1	88
Tana bru, Nor.	A12	8
Tanacross, Ak., U.S.	D11	140
Tanafjorden, b., Nor.	A13	8
Tanaga Island, i., Ak., U.S.	g23	140a
T'ana Hāyk', l., Eth.	E7	62
Tanahbala, Pulau, i., Indon.	F2	44
Tanahgrogot, Indon.	D10	50
Tanahjampea, Pulau, i., Indon.	G12	50
Tanahmasa, Pulau, i., Indon.	F2	44
Tanahmerah, Indon.	G10	44
Tanah Merah, Malay.	J6	48
Tanahputih, Indon.	C2	50
Tanakeke, Pulau, i., Indon.	F11	50
Tanakpur, India	D7	54
Tanami Desert, des., Austl.	C5	74
Tan An, Viet.	G8	48
Tanana, Ak., U.S.	C9	140
Tanana, stm., Ak., U.S.	D10	140
Tananarive see Antananarivo, Madag.	D8	68
Tanbar, Austl.	E3	76
Tan Chau, Viet.	G7	48
Tanch'ŏn-ŭp, Kor., N.	D8	38
Tancítaro, Pico de, mtn., Mex.	F7	100
Tanda, Egypt	K1	58
Tānda, India	E9	54
Tānda, India	C5	54
Tandag, Phil.	F6	52
Tandaltī, Sudan	E6	62
Țăndărei, Rom.	E14	26
Tandil, Arg.	H8	92
Tando Ādam, Pak.	F2	54
Tando Allāhyār, Pak.	F2	54
Tandou Lake, l., Austl.	I3	76
Tandula Tank, res., India	H8	54
Tandun, Indon.	C2	50
Tāndūr, India	C3	53
Tanega-shima, i., Japan	I9	38
Tanezrouft, des., Afr.	E4	64
Tang, stm., China	E7	42
Tang, stm., China	E5	42
Tang, stm., China	B6	42
Tanga, Russia	F11	34
Tanga, Tan.	F7	66
Tangail, Bngl.	F12	54
Tanga Islands, is., Pap. N. Gui.	a5	79a
Tanga Langua, c., Gren.	q10	105e
Tanganyika see Tanzania, ctry., Afr.	F6	66
Tanganyika, Lake, l., Afr.	F6	66
Tangarana, stm., Peru	I4	86
Tangarare, Sol. Is.	e8	79b
Tanger (Tangier), Mor.	B3	64
Tangerang, Indon.	G5	50
Tangerhütte, Ger.	D7	16
Tangermünde, Ger.	D7	16
Tanggu, China	B7	42
Tanggulashan, China	A14	54
Tanggula Shan, mts., China	E3	36
Tanggula Shankou, p., China	B13	54
Tanghe, China	E5	42
Tangi, Pak.	A3	54
Tangier, N.S., Can.	F14	110
Tangier see Tanger, Mor.	B3	64
Tangier, Va., U.S.	G10	114
Tangipahoa, stm., U.S.	G8	122
Tangjiagou, China	F7	42
Tangkou, China	F8	42
Tangmai, China	E4	36
Tango-hantō, pen., Japan	D8	40
Tangra Yumco, l., China	C11	54
Tangshan, China	B8	42
Tangtou, China	D8	42
Tangyan, Mya.	A4	48
Tangyin, China	D6	42
Tangyuan, China	B10	36
Tanhoj, Russia	F10	34
Taniantaweng Shan, mts., China	F4	36
Tanigawa-dake, mtn., Japan	C11	40
Tanimbar, Kepulauan, is., Indon.	G9	44
Tanintharyi, state, Mya.	F3	48
Tanis, hist., Egypt	H2	58
Tanjay, Phil.	F4	52
Tanjung, Indon.	H10	50
Tanjung, Indon.	E9	50
Tanjungbalai, Indon.	B1	50
Tanjungbatu, Indon.	C3	50
Tanjungbatu, Indon.	B11	50
Tanjungkarang-Telukbetung, Indon.	F4	50
Tanjunglabu, Indon.	E5	50
Tanjungpandan, Indon.	E5	50
Tanjungpinang, Indon.	C4	50
Tanjungpura, Indon.	K4	48
Tanjungraja, Indon.	E4	50
Tanjungredep, Indon.	B10	50
Tanjungselor, Indon.	B10	50
Tanjunguban, Indon.	C4	50
Tānk, Pak.	B3	54
Tankwa, stm., S. Afr.	H5	70
Tanna, i., Vanuatu	I17	79d
Tannenberg see Stębark, Pol.	C16	16
Tanner, Mount, mtn., B.C., Can.	G12	138
Tannu-Ola, hrebet, mts., Asia	D16	32
Tannūrah, Ra's, c., Sau. Ar.	D7	56
Tanon Strait, strt., Phil.	E4	52
Tanout, Niger	F6	64
Tanquinho, Braz.	G6	88
Tanshui, Tai.	I9	42
Tanta, Egypt	H2	58
Tan-Tan, Mor.	D2	64
Tantoyuca, Mex.	E9	100
Tanuku, India	C5	53
Tanvald, Czech Rep.	F11	16
Tanyang, Kor., S.	C1	40
Tanzania, ctry., Afr.	F6	66
Tao'er, stm., China	B5	38
Taohuazhen, China	A6	42
Taole, China	B2	42
Taonan, China	B5	38
Taongi, at., Marsh. Is.	B7	72
Taormina, Italy	G9	24
Taos, Mo., U.S.	F5	120
Taos, N.M., U.S.	E3	128
Taos Pueblo, N.M., U.S.	E3	128
Taoudenni, Mali	E4	64
Taounate, Mor.	C4	64
Taourirt, Mor.	C4	64
Taoyuan, China	G4	42
Taoyüan, Tai.	I9	42
Tapa, Est.	G11	8
Tapachula, Mex.	H12	100
Tapaga, Cape, c., Samoa	h12	79c
Tapah, Malay.	J5	48
Tapajós, stm., Braz.	D6	84
Tapaktuan, Indon.	K3	48
Tapalqué, Arg.	H7	92
Tapauá, stm., Braz.	E4	84
Tapejara, Braz.	D12	92
Taperoá, Braz.	D7	88
Tapes, Braz.	E12	92
Tapeta, Lib.	H3	64
Taphan Hin, Thai.	D5	48
Taphoen, stm., Thai.	E4	48
Tāpi, stm., India	H4	54
Ta Pi, stm., Thai.	H4	48
Tapiche, stm., Peru	E3	84
Tapini, Pap. N. Gui.	b4	79a
Taplan National Park, p.o.i., Thai.	E6	48
Tāplejungg, Nepal	E11	54
Tappen, N.D., U.S.	H14	124
Tapuae-o-Uenuku, mtn., N.Z.	E5	80
Tapuio, stm., Braz.	C3	88
Tapul Group, is., Phil.	H3	52
Tapun, Mya.	C2	48
Tapuruquara, Braz.	H9	86
Taqāṭu' Hayyā, Sudan	D7	62
Taquara, Braz.	D12	92
Taquaras, Ponta das, c., Braz.	C13	92
Taquari, stm., Braz.	D12	92
Taquari Novo, stm., Braz.	C5	90
Taquaritinga, Braz.	K1	88
Tar, stm., N.C., U.S.	I8	114
Tara, Austl.	F8	76
Tara, Russia	C12	32
Tara, stm., Eur.	G16	22
Tara, stm., Russia	C13	32
Taraba, stm., Nig.	H7	64
Tarabuco, Bol.	C3	90
Ṭarābulus (Tripoli), Leb.	D6	58
Ṭarābulus (Tripoli), Libya	A2	62
Ṭarābulus (Tripolitania), hist. reg., Libya	A2	62
Taraclia, Mol.	D15	26
Tarago, Austl.	J7	76
Taraira (Traíra), stm., S.A.	H7	86
Taraju, Indon.	G6	50
Tarakan, Indon.	B10	50
Tarakan, Pulau, i., Indon.	B10	50
Taralga, Austl.	J7	76
Tara Nacionalni Park, p.o.i., Yugo.	F6	26
Tārānagar, India	D5	54
Taranaki, Mount (Egmont, Mount), vol., N.Z.	D6	80
Tarancón, Spain	D8	20
Taranto, Italy	D11	24
Taranto, Golfo di, b., Italy	E10	24
Tarapoto, Peru	E2	84
Taraquá, Braz.	G7	86
Tarare, Fr.	D10	18
Tarariras, Ur.	G9	92
Tarāsa Dwīp, i., India	G7	46
Tarascon, Fr.	F10	18
Tarascon-sur-Ariège, Fr.	G7	18
Tarasovo, Russia	C19	32
Tarat, Alg.	D6	64
Tarata, Bol.	C3	90
Taratakbuluh, Indon.	C2	50
Tarauacá, stm., Braz.	E3	84
Taravao, Isthme de, isth., Fr. Poly.	v22	78h
Tarawa, at., Kir.	C8	72
Tarawera, N.Z.	D7	80
Tarazona, Spain	C9	20
Tarbagataj, hrebet, mts., Asia	E14	32
Tarbagatay Shan see Tarbagataj, hrebet, mts., Asia	E14	32
Tarbela Reservoir, res., Pak.	A4	54
Tarbert, Scot., U.K.	D6	12
Tarbes, Fr.	F6	18
Tarboro, N.C., U.S.	I8	114
Tarbū, Libya	B3	62
Tarcoola, Austl.	F6	74
Tardoki-Jani, gora, mtn., Russia	G16	34
Taree, Austl.	H9	76
Tareja, Russia	B7	34
Tärendö, Swe.	C10	8
Tarentum, Pa., U.S.	D6	114
Tarfa, Wadi el-, stm., Egypt	J2	58
Tarfaya, Mor.	D2	64
Targhee Pass, p., U.S.	F15	136
Tărgovište, Blg.	F13	26
Târgoviște, Rom.	E12	26
Târgu Bujor, Rom.	D14	26
Târgu Frumos, Rom.	B14	26
Târgu Jiu, Rom.	D10	26
Târgu Mureș, Rom.	C11	26
Târgu-Neamț, Rom.	B13	26
Târgu Ocna, Rom.	C13	26
Târgu Secuiesc, Rom.	D12	26
Tarifa, Spain	H5	20
Tarifa, Punta de, c., Spain	H5	20
Tarija, Bol.	D4	90
Tarikere, India	E2	53
Tarim, stm., China	F14	32
Tarim Pendi, bas., China	F12	30
Taritatu, stm., Indon.	F10	44
Tarkastad, S. Afr.	G8	70
Tarkio, Mo., U.S.	D2	120
Tarkio, stm., U.S.	D2	120
Tarko-Sale, Russia	B13	32
Tarkwa, Ghana	H4	64
Tarlac, Phil.	C3	52
Tarm, Den.	I3	8
Tarma, Peru	F2	84
Tarn, state, Fr.	F8	18
Tarn, stm., Fr.	F7	18
Tärnaby, Swe.	D6	8
Tarnak, stm., Afg.	B1	54
Târnava Mare, stm., Rom.	C11	26
Târnăveni, Rom.	C11	26
Tarn-et-Garonne, state, Fr.	F7	18
Tarnobrzeg, Pol.	F17	16
Tarnobrzeg, state, Pol.	F17	16
Tarnogród, Pol.	F18	16
Târnova, Mol.	A14	26
Tarnów, Pol.	G16	16
Tarnów, state, Pol.	G16	16
Tarnowskie Góry, Pol.	F14	16
Taro, Sol. Is.	d7	79b
Taro, stm., Italy	F7	22
Taron, Pap. N. Gui.	a5	79a
Tarong, Austl.	F8	76
Taroom, Austl.	E7	76
Taroudannt, Mor.	C3	64
Ta Roun, Co, mtn., Viet.	D8	48
Tarpon Springs, Fl., U.S.	H3	116
Tarquinia, Italy	H8	22
Tarra, stm., S.A.	C5	86
Tarrafal, C.V.	k10	65a
Tarragona, Spain	C12	20
Tarragona, co., Spain	D11	20
Tarraleah, Austl.	o13	77a
Tarrasa see Terrassa, Spain	C13	20
Tàrrega, Spain	C12	20
Tárrega see Tàrrega, Spain	C12	20
Tarsus, Tur.	B5	58
Tartagal, Arg.	D4	90
Tartu, Est.	G12	8
Ṭarṭūs, Syria	D6	58
Ṭarṭūs, state, Syria	D7	58
Tarum, stm., Indon.	G5	50
Tarumirim, Braz.	J5	88
Tarumizu, Japan	H3	40
Tarutao, Ko, i., Thai.	I4	48
Tarutao National Park, p.o.i., Thai.	I4	48
Tarutino, Russia	E19	10
Tarutung, Indon.	B1	50
Tarvisio, Italy	D10	22
Tarzan, Tx., U.S.	B6	130
Taşağıl, Tur.	B2	58
Tasāwah, Libya	B2	62
Tasbuget, Kaz.	F11	32
Taseeva, stm., Russia	C16	32
Taseevo, Russia	C17	32
Taseko Lakes, l., B.C., Can.	E7	138
Taseko Mountain, mtn., B.C., Can.	E7	138
Tāsgaon, India	C2	53
Tashi Gang Dzong, Bhu.	E13	54
Ṭashk, Daryācheh-ye, l., Iran	D7	56
Tasikmalaya, Indon.	G5	50
Tåsinge, i., Den.	B6	16
Taškent, Uzb.	F11	32
Taškepri, Turkmen.	B9	56
Taš-Kumyr, Kyrg.	F12	32
Tasman Basin, unds.	N18	142
Tasman Bay, b., N.Z.	E5	80
Tasmania, state, Austl.	n13	77a
Tasmania, i., Austl.	o13	77a
Tasman Peninsula, pen., Austl.	o13	77a
Tasman Sea, Oc.	G7	72
Tășnad, Rom.	B9	26
Tassialouc, Lac, l., Qc., Can.	D16	106
Taštagol, Russia	D15	32
Tastiota, Mex.	A3	100
Tata, Hung.	B5	26
Tata, Mor.	D3	64
Tatabánya, Hung.	B5	26
Tatarbunary, Ukr.	D16	26
Tatarija, state, Russia	C8	32
Tatarinka, Russia	E16	10
Tatarsk, Russia	C13	32
Tatarskij proliv, strt., Russia	G17	34
Tatarskoe-Maklakovo, Russia	I21	8
Tatarstan see Tatarija, state, Russia	C8	32
Tatar Strait see Tatarskij proliv, strt., Russia	G17	34
Tate, Ga., U.S.	B1	116
Tate, stm., Austl.	A4	76
Tateyama, Japan	E12	40
Tate-yama, vol., Japan	C10	40
Tathlina Lake, l., N.T., Can.	C7	106
Tatlayoko Lake, B.C., Can.	E6	138
Tatlayoko Lake, l., B.C., Can.	E6	138
Tatlow, Mount, mtn., B.C., Can.	E7	138
Tatnam, Cape, c., Mb., Can.	D12	106
Tatranský Narodny Park, p.o.i., Slov.	G15	16
Tatrzański Park Narodowy, p.o.i., Pol.	G15	16
Tatsuno, Japan	E7	40
Tatsuno, Japan	D10	40
Tatuí, Braz.	L1	88
Tatum, N.M., U.S.	H5	128
Tatum, Tx., U.S.	E4	122
Tat'ung see Datong, China	A5	42
Tatvan, Tur.	B5	56
Tau, Am. Sam.	h13	79c
Tau, Nor.	G1	8
Tau, i., Am. Sam.	h13	79c
Tauá, Braz.	C5	88
Taubaté, Braz.	L3	88
Tauberbischofsheim, Ger.	G5	16
Taučik, Kaz.	F8	32
Taujskaja guba, b., Russia	E18	34
Taumarunui, N.Z.	D6	80
Taumaturgo, Braz.	E3	84
Taum Sauk Mountain, mtn., Mo., U.S.	G7	120
Taungbon, Mya.	E3	48
Taungdwingyi, Mya.	B2	48
Taunggyi, Mya.	B3	48
Taungnyo Range, mts., Mya.	E3	48
Taungup, Mya.	C2	48
Taungup Pass, p., Mya.	C2	48
Taunsa, Pak.	C3	54
Taunton, Eng., U.K.	J9	12
Taunton, Ma., U.S.	C14	114
Taupo, N.Z.	D6	80
Taupo, Lake, l., N.Z.	D7	80
Tauragė, Lith.	E5	10
Tauranga, N.Z.	C7	80
Taurianova, Italy	F9	24
Taurisano, Italy	E12	24
Tauroa Point, c., N.Z.	B5	80
Taurus Mountains see Toros Dağları, mts., Tur.	A3	58
Tautira, Fr. Poly.	v23	78h
Tavan-Bogdo-Ula, gora, mtn., Asia	E15	32
Tavares, Braz.	D7	88
Tavas, Tur.	F12	28
Tavastehus see Hämeenlinna, Fin.	F10	8
Tavda, Russia	C11	32
Tavda, stm., Russia	C11	32
Tavernes de la Valldigna, Spain	E10	20
Tavernier, Fl., U.S.	K5	116
Taveuni, i., Fiji	p20	79e
Taviano, Italy	E11	24
Tavira, Port.	G3	20
Tavistock, On., Can.	E9	112
Tavistock, Eng., U.K.	K8	12
Tavolara, Isola, i., Italy	D3	24
Tavoliere, reg., Italy	C9	24
Tavolžan, Kaz.	D13	32
Tavor, Har, mtn., Isr.	F6	58
Tavoy Point, c., Mya.	F3	48
Tavşanlı, Tur.	D12	28
Tavua, Fiji	p18	79e
Tawaeli, Indon.	D11	50
Tawakoni, Lake, res., Tx., U.S.	E2	122
Tawas City, Mi., U.S.	D6	112
Tawau, Malay.	A10	50
Tawîla, Gezira, is., Egypt	K4	58
Tawitawi Group, is., Phil.	H3	52
Tawitawi Island, i., Phil.	H2	52
Ṭawkar, Sudan	D7	62
Taxco de Alarcón, Mex.	F8	100
Taxkorgan Tajik Zizhixian, China	B12	56
Tay, stm., Scot., U.K.	E9	12
Tay, Firth of, b., Scot., U.K.	E9	12
Tay, Loch, l., Scot., U.K.	E8	12
Tayabamba, Peru	E2	84
Tayabas Bay, b., Phil.	D3	52
Tayan, Indon.	C7	50
Taylor, Az., U.S.	I6	132
Taylor, Ne., U.S.	F13	126
Taylor, Tx., U.S.	D10	130
Taylor, Mount, mtn., N.M., U.S.	H9	132
Taylors, S.C., U.S.	B3	116
Taylorsville, Ky., U.S.	F12	120
Taylorsville, Ms., U.S.	F9	122
Taylorsville, N.C., U.S.	I4	114
Taylorville, Il., U.S.	E8	120
Taymā', Sau. Ar.	K9	58
Taymouth, N.B., Can.	D10	110
Taymyr Peninsula see Tajmyr, poluostrov, pen., Russia	B7	34
Tay Ninh, Viet.	G8	48
Taytay, Phil.	E2	52
Tayu, Indon.	G7	50
Taz, stm., Russia	A14	32
Taza, Mor.	C4	64
Tazewell, Tn., U.S.	H2	114
Tazewell, Va., U.S.	G4	114
Tazin, stm., Can.	C8	106
Tazin Lake, l., Sk., Can.	D9	106
Tazovskaja guba, b., Russia	A13	32
Tazovskij, Russia	A13	32
Tazovskij poluostrov, pen., Russia	C4	34
Tbessa, Alg.	B6	64
Tbilisi, Geor.	F6	32
Tchaourou, Benin	H5	64
Tchentlo Lake, l., B.C., Can.	A5	138
Tchesinkut Lake, l., B.C., Can.	B5	138
Tchibanga, Gabon	E2	66
Tcho-kiang see Zhejiang, state, China	G8	42
Tchollíré, Cam.	C2	66
Tchula, Ms., U.S.	D8	122
Tczew, Pol.	B14	16
Té, stm., Camb.	F8	48
Teá, stm., Braz.	H9	86
Teaca, Rom.	C11	26
Teaehoa, c., Fr. Poly.	s18	78g
Teague, Tx., U.S.	F2	122
Teahupoo, Fr. Poly.	w22	78h
Te Anau, Lake, l., N.Z.	G2	80
Teapa, Mex.	G12	100
Te Awamutu, N.Z.	C6	80
Teba, Spain	H5	20
Tebakang, Malay.	C7	50
Tebicuary, stm., Para.	C9	92
Tebicuary-mí, stm., Para.	C9	92
Tebingtinggi, Indon.	B1	50
Tebingtinggi, Indon.	E3	50
Tebingtinggi, Pulau, i., Indon.	C3	50
Tébourba, Tun.	H3	24
Téboursouk, Tun.	H3	24
Tecalitlán, Mex.	F7	100
Tecate, Mex.	K9	134
Techirghiol, Rom.	E15	26
Techlé, W. Sah.	E2	64
Techou see Dezhou, China	C7	42
Tecka, Arg.	H2	90
Tecka, stm., Arg.	H2	90
Tecomán, Mex.	F7	100
Tecopa, Ca., U.S.	H9	134
Tecpan de Galeana, Mex.	G8	100
Tecuala, Mex.	D6	100
Tecuci, Rom.	D14	26
Tecumseh, Ok., U.S.	B2	122
Tedžen, Turkmen.	B9	56
Tedžen (Harīrūd), stm., Asia	B9	56
Teec Nos Pos, Az., U.S.	G7	132
Teeli, Russia	D16	32
Tees, stm., Eng., U.K.	G11	12
Teeswater, On., Can.	D8	112
Tefé, Braz.	D5	84
Tefé, stm., Braz.	D4	84
Tefenni, Tur.	F12	28
Tegal, Indon.	G6	50
Tégama, reg., Niger	F6	64
Tegéa, hist., Grc.	F5	28
Tegineneng, Indon.	F4	50
Tegucigalpa, Hond.	E4	102
Tegul'det, Russia	C15	32
Tehachapi, Ca., U.S.	H7	134
Tehachapi Pass, p., Ca., U.S.	H7	134
Tehek Lake, l., Nu., Can.	C12	106
Tehrān (Teheran), Iran	B7	56
Tehrathum, Nepal	E11	54
Tehuacán, Mex.	F10	100
Tehuantepec, Golfo de, b., Mex.	H11	100
Tehuantepec, Gulf of see Tehuantepec, Golfo de, b., Mex.	H11	100
Tehuantepec, Isthmus of see Tehuantepec, Istmo de, isth., Mex.	G11	100
Tehuantepec, Istmo de, isth., Mex.	G11	100
Teignmouth, Eng., U.K.	K9	12
Teixeira, Braz.	D7	88
Teixeira Pinto, Gui.-B.	G1	64
Tejakula, Indon.	H9	50
Tejkovo, Russia	H19	8
Tejon Pass, p., Ca., U.S.	I7	134
Tejupilco de Hidalgo, Mex.	F8	100
Tekamah, Ne., U.S.	C1	120
Tekapo, Lake, l., N.Z.	F4	80
Tekax, Mex.	B3	102
Teke, Tur.	B12	28
Teke Burnu, c., Tur.	E9	28
Tekeli, Kaz.	F13	32
Tekezē (Satīt), stm., Afr.	E7	62
Tekirdağ, Tur.	C10	28
Tekirdağ, state, Tur.	B10	28
Tekkali, India	B7	53
Tekoa, Wa., U.S.	C9	136
Tekonsha, Mi., U.S.	B1	114
Te Kuiti, N.Z.	D6	80
Tel, stm., India	A6	53
Tela, Hond.	E4	102
Telaopengsha Shan, mtn., China	C11	54
Telavi, Geor.	F7	32
Tel Aviv-Jaffa see Tel Aviv-Yafo, Isr.	F5	58
Tel Aviv-Yafo, Isr.	F5	58
Telč, Czech Rep.	G11	16
Teleckoe, ozero, l., Russia	D15	32
Telefomin, Pap. N. Gui.	b3	79a
Telegraph Creek, B.C., Can.	D4	106
Telêmaco Borba, Braz.	B12	92
Telemark, state, Nor.	G3	8
Telembí, stm., Col.	G2	86
Telén, Arg.	H5	92
Telen, stm., Indon.	C10	50
Teleneşti, Mol.	B15	26
Teleno, mtn., Spain	B4	20
Teleorman, state, Rom.	E12	26
Teleorman, stm., Rom.	E12	26
Telescope Point, c., Gren.	q10	105e
Telese, Italy	C8	24
Telford, Eng., U.K.	I10	12
Télimélé, Gui.	G2	64
Telire, stm., C.R.	H6	102
Teljo, Jabal, mtn., Sudan	E5	62
Telkwa, B.C., Can.	B3	138
Tell Basta, hist., Egypt	H2	58
Tell City, In., U.S.	G11	120
Tell El-Amarna, hist., Egypt	K1	58
Tellel Rub, hist., Egypt	H2	58
Teller, Ak., U.S.	C6	140

Name	Map Ref.	Page
Tellicherry, India	F2	53
Tellier, Arg.	I3	90
Tello, Col.	F4	86
Telluride, Co., U.S.	F9	132
Tel Megiddo, hist., Isr.	F6	58
Telmen nuur, l., Mong.	B4	36
Teloloapan, Mex.	F8	100
Telos see Tílos, i., Grc.	G10	28
Telsen, Arg.	H3	90
Telšiai, Lith.	E5	10
Teltow, Ger.	D9	16
Telukbayur, Indon.	D2	50
Telukbayur, Indon.	B10	50
Telukdalem, Indon.	L3	48
Teluk Intan, Malay.	K5	48
Tema, Ghana	H5	64
Temagami, Lake, l., On., Can.	A9	112
Temaju, Pulau, i., Indon.	C6	50
Te Manga, mtn., Cook Is.	a26	78j
Temangga, Indon.	C7	50
Tematangi, at., Fr. Poly.	F12	72
Temax, Mex.	B3	102
Tembeling, stm., Malay.	J6	48
Tembenči, stm., Russia	A17	32
Tembesi, stm., Indon.	D3	50
Tembilahan, Indon.	D3	50
Temblador, Ven.	C10	86
Temblor Range, mts., Ca., U.S.	H6	134
Teme, stm., Eng., U.K.	I10	12
Temecula, Ca., U.S.	J8	134
Temelli, Tur.	D15	28
Temengor, Tasik, res., Malay.	J5	48
Temetiu, mtn., Fr. Poly.	s18	78g
Temir, Kaz.	E9	32
Temirtau, Kaz.	D12	32
Témiscaming, Qc., Can.	B10	112
Témiscamingue, Lac (Timiskaming, Lake), res., Can.	B10	112
Témiscouata, Lac, l., Qc., Can.	C7	110
Tëmkino, Russia	E17	10
Temora, Austl.	J6	76
Temosachic, Mex.	A5	100
Tempe, Az., U.S.	J5	132
Tempe, Danau, l., Indon.	F12	50
Tempino, Indon.	D3	50
Tempio Pausania, Italy	D2	24
Temple, Tx., U.S.	C10	130
Templi, Valle dei, hist., Italy	G7	24
Templin, Ger.	C9	16
Tempoal, stm., Mex.	E9	100
Tempoal de Sánchez, Mex.	E9	100
Tempy, Russia	D20	10
Temuco, Chile	G2	90
Temwen, i., Micron.	m12	78d
Tena, Ec.	H3	86
Tenabo, Mex.	B2	102
Tenaha, Tx., U.S.	F4	122
Tena Kourou, mtn., Burkina	G4	64
Tenāli, India	C5	53
Tenasserim, Mya.	F4	48
Tendaho, Eth.	E8	62
Tende, Col de, p., Eur.	E13	18
Ten Degree Channel, strt., India	G7	46
Tendō, Japan	A13	40
Ténenkou, Mali	G3	64
Ténéré, des., Niger	F7	64
Ténès, Alg.	H12	20
Ténès, Cap, c., Alg.	H12	20
Teng, stm., Mya.	B3	48
Tengah, Kepulauan, is., Indon.	G10	50
Tengchong, China	G4	36
Tenggara, Nusa (Lesser Sunda Islands), is., Indon.	G6	44
Tenggara Celebes see Sulawesi Tenggara, state, Indon.	E12	50
Tenggarong, Indon.	D10	50
Tengger Shamo, des., China	D5	36
Tenghilan, Malay.	G1	52
Tengiz, ozero, l., Kaz.	D11	32
Tengréla, C. Iv.	G3	64
Tengtiao (Na), stm., Asia	A6	48
Tengxian, China	J4	42
Tengxian, China	D7	42
Tenkāsi, India	G3	53
Tenke, D.R.C.	G5	66
Tenkeli, Russia	B17	34
Tenkiller Ferry Lake, res., Ok., U.S.	B4	122
Tenkodogo, Burkina	G4	64
Tennant Creek, Austl.	C6	74
Tennessee, state, U.S.	D10	108
Tennessee, stm., U.S.	A11	122
Tennille, Ga., U.S.	D3	116
Teno, Chile	G2	92
Teno (Tana), stm., Eur.	B12	8
Tenom, Malay.	A9	50
Tenos see Tínos, Grc.	F8	28
Tenos see Tínos, i., Grc.	F8	28
Tenosique, Mex.	D2	102
Tenryū, Japan	E10	40
Tenryū, stm., Japan	E10	40
Tensas, stm., La., U.S.	F7	122
Tensed, Id., U.S.	C10	136
Ten Sleep, Wy., U.S.	C5	126
Tenterfield, Austl.	G8	76
Ten Thousand Islands, is., Fl., U.S.	K4	116
Tentolomatinan, Gunung, mtn., Indon.	E7	44
Teocaltiche, Mex.	E7	100
Teodelina, Arg.	G7	92
Teófilo Otoni, Braz.	I5	88
Teo Lakes, l., Sk., Can.	C4	124
Teotihuacán, hist., Mex.	F9	100
Tepa, Indon.	G8	44
Tepalcatepec, Mex.	F7	100
Tepebaşı, Tur.	B3	58
Tepehuanes, Mex.	C6	100
Tepehuanes, stm., Mex.	C6	100
Tepeji de Ocampo, Mex.	F9	100
Tepelenë, Alb.	D13	24
Tepic, Mex.	E6	100
Teplice, Czech Rep.	F9	16
Tepoca, Bahía de, b., Mex.	F6	98
Tepoca, Punta, c., Mex.	G6	98
Ter, stm., Spain	B14	20
Téra, Niger	G5	64
Tera, stm., Spain	C4	20
Teradomari, Japan	B11	40
Teraina, i., Kir.	C11	72
Teramo, Italy	H10	22
Terbuny, Russia	H21	10
Terceira, i., Port.	C3	60
Tercero, stm., Arg.	F6	92
Terdal, India	C2	53
Terek, stm., Russia	G18	6
Terempa, Indon.	B5	50
Terengganu, state, Malay.	J6	48
Terengganu, stm., Malay.	J6	48
Terenos, Braz.	D6	90
Teresina, Braz.	C4	88
Teresópolis, Braz.	L4	88
Terespol, Pol.	D19	16
Terevaka, Cerro, mtn., Chile	e29	78l
Tergüün Bogd uul, mtn., Mong.	C5	36
Teriang, stm., Malay.	K6	48
Teriberka, Russia	B16	8
Terihi, i., Fr. Poly.	t19	78g
Terlingua, Tx., U.S.	E4	130
Terlingua Creek, stm., Tx., U.S.	E4	130
Termas del Arapey, Ur.	E9	92
Termas de Río Hondo, Arg.	C5	92
Termez, Uzb.	B10	56
Termini Imerese, Italy	G7	24
Termini Imerese, Golfo di, b., Italy	F7	24
Terminillo, Monte, mtn., Italy	H9	22
Términos, Laguna de, b., Mex.	C2	102
Termoli, Italy	H11	22
Termonde see Dendermonde, Bel.	C12	14
Ternej, Russia	B12	38
Terneuzen, Neth.	C12	14
Terni, Italy	H9	22
Ternitz, Aus.	C12	22
Ternopil', Ukr.	F14	6
Terpenija, mys, c., Russia	G17	34
Terpenija, zaliv, b., Russia	G17	34
Terra Alta, W.V., U.S.	E6	114
Terra Bella, Ca., U.S.	H6	134
Terrace, B.C., Can.	B2	138
Terracina, Italy	C7	24
Terra Cotta Army (Qinshihuang Mausoleum), hist., China	D3	42
Terral, Ok., U.S.	H11	128
Terralba, Italy	E2	24
Terra Santa, Braz.	D6	84
Terrassa, Spain	C13	20
Terrebonne Bay, b., La., U.S.	H8	122
Terre-de-Bas, Guad.	i5	105c
Terre-de-Haut, Guad.	i5	105c
Terre-de-Haut, i., Guad.	i5	105c
Terre Haute, In., U.S.	E10	120
Terrell, Tx., U.S.	E2	122
Terre-Neuve see Newfoundland, state, Can.	B17	110
Territoire du Yukon see Yukon, state, Can.	B3	106
Territoires du Nord-Ouest see Northwest Territories, state, Can.	B10	106
Terry, Ms., U.S.	E8	122
Terry, Mt., U.S.	A7	126
Terschelling, i., Neth.	A14	14
Terskej-Alatau, hrebet, mts., Kyrg.	F13	32
Teruel, Col.	F4	86
Teruel, Spain	D9	20
Teruel, co., Spain	D10	20
Terujak, Indon.	J3	48
Tervola, Fin.	C11	8
Terzaghi Dam, dam, B.C., Can.	F8	138
Tes, stm., Asia	D16	32
Tescott, Ks., U.S.	B11	128
Teseney, Erit.	D7	62
Teshekpuk Lake, l., Ak., U.S.	B9	140
Teshio, Japan	B14	38
Teshio, stm., Japan	B15	38
Teslin, Yk., Can.	C4	106
Teslin, stm., Can.	C4	106
Teslin Lake, l., Can.	C4	106
Tësovo, Russia	E17	10
Tësovo-Netyl'skij, Russia	B13	10
Tësovskij, Russia	B13	10
Tessalit, Mali	E5	64
Tessaoua, Niger	G6	64
Testa, Capo, c., Italy	C3	24
Testour, Tun.	H3	24
Tetachuck Lake, res., B.C., Can.	C4	138
Tete, Moz.	D5	68
Tête Jaune Cache, B.C., Can.	D11	138
Tetepare Island, i., Sol. Is.	e7	79b
Teterow, Ger.	C8	16
Tetica, mtn., Spain	G8	20
Teton, Id., U.S.	G15	136
Teton, stm., Id., U.S.	G15	136
Teton, stm., Mt., U.S.	C15	136
Tetonia, Id., U.S.	G15	136
Teton Range, mts., Wy., U.S.	G16	136
Tetouan, Mor.	B4	64
Tetovo, Mac.	A4	28
Tetufera, Mont, mtn., Fr. Poly.	v22	78h
Teuco, stm., Arg.	D4	90
Teulada, Italy	F2	24
Teulada, Capo, c., Italy	F2	24
Teulon, Mb., Can.	D16	124
Teutoburger Wald, hills, Ger.	D4	16
Teuva, Fin.	E9	8
Tevere (Tiber), stm., Italy	H9	22
Teverya, Isr.	F6	58
Te Waewae Bay, b., N.Z.	H2	80
Tewah, Indon.	D8	50
Tewantin-Noosa, Austl.	F9	76
Tewkesbury, Eng., U.K.	I11	12
Texada Island, i., B.C., Can.	G6	138
Texana, Lake, res., Tx., U.S.	F11	130
Texarkana, Ar., U.S.	D4	122
Texarkana, Tx., U.S.	D4	122
Texas, Austl.	G8	76
Texas, state, U.S.	E8	108
Texas City, Tx., U.S.	H4	122
Texel, i., Neth.	A13	14
Texhoma, Ok., U.S.	E7	128
Texico, N.M., U.S.	G5	128
Texoma, Lake, res., U.S.	H11	128
Teyateyaneng, Leso.	F8	70
Teywarah, Afg.	C9	56
Teziutlán, Mex.	F10	100
Tezpur, India	E14	54
Tezzeron Lake, l., B.C., Can.	B6	138
Tha, stm., Laos	B5	48
Tha-anne, stm., Nu., Can.	C11	106
Thabana-Ntlenyana, mtn., Leso.	F9	70
Thabaung, Mya.	D2	48
Thabazimbi, S. Afr.	D8	70
Thabyu, Mya.	E4	48
Thagyettaw, Mya.	F3	48
Thai Binh, Viet.	B8	48
Thailand, ctry., Asia	E5	48
Thailand, Gulf of, b., Asia	G5	48
Thai Nguyen, Viet.	B7	48
Thak, Pak.	C3	54
Thal, Pak.	B3	54
Thala, Tun.	I2	24
Thal Desert, des., Pak.	C3	54
Thalfang, Ger.	G2	16
Tha Li, Thai.	D5	48
Thalia, Tx., U.S.	H9	128
Thālith, Ash-Shallāl ath- (Third Cataract), wtfl, Sudan	D6	62
Thalwil, Switz.	C5	22
Thames, N.Z.	C6	80
Thames, stm., On., Can.	F8	112
Thames, stm., Eng., U.K.	J13	12
Thames, Firth of, b., N.Z.	C6	80
Thamesford, On., Can.	E8	112
Thamesville, On., Can.	F7	112
Thāna, India	B1	53
Thandaung, Mya.	C3	48
Thangoo, Austl.	C4	74
Thangool, Austl.	E8	76
Thanh Hoa, Viet.	C7	48
Thanh Pho Ho Chi Minh (Saigon), Viet.	G8	48
Thanjāvūr, India	F4	53
Thann, Fr.	B12	18
Thap Than, stm., Thai.	E6	48
Tharabwin West, Mya.	F4	48
Tharād, India	F3	54
Thar Desert (Great Indian Desert), des., Asia	D3	54
Thargomindah, Austl.	F5	76
Tharrawaddy, Mya.	D2	48
Tha Sala, Thai.	H4	48
Thásos, Grc.	C7	28
Thásos, i., Grc.	C7	28
Thásos, hist., Grc.	C7	28
Thaton, Mya.	D3	48
Tha Tum, Thai.	E6	48
Thau, Bassin de, l., Fr.	F9	18
Thaungyin (Moei), stm., Asia	D3	48
Thaya (Dyje), stm., Eur.	H12	16
Thayawthadangyi Kyun, i., Mya.	F3	48
Thayer, Ks., U.S.	G2	120
Thayer, Mo., U.S.	H6	120
Thayetchaung, Mya.	F4	48
Thayetmyo, Mya.	C2	48
Thazi, Mya.	B3	48
Thebes see Thíva, Grc.	E6	28
The Bottom, Neth. Ant.	B1	105a
The Cheviot, mtn., Eng., U.K.	F10	12
The Dalles, Or., U.S.	E5	136
Thedford, Ne., U.S.	E12	126
The Father see Ulawun, Mount, vol., Pap. N. Gui.	b5	79a
The Fens, reg., Eng., U.K.	I12	12
The Fishing Lakes, l., Sk., Can.	D10	124
The Granites, hill, Austl.	D6	74
The Hague see 's-Gravenhage, Neth.	B12	14
The Heads, c., Or., U.S.	H2	136
Theinkun, Mya.	G4	48
The Lakes National Park, p.o.i., Austl.	L6	76
The Little Minch, strt., Scot., U.K.	D6	12
Thelon, stm., Can.	C11	106
The Lynd, Austl.	B5	76
The Minch, strt., Scot., U.K.	D6	12
Thenia, Alg.	H14	20
Theodore, Austl.	E8	76
Theodore, Sk., Can.	C10	124
Theodore, Al., U.S.	G10	122
Theodore Roosevelt National Park North Unit, p.o.i., N.D., U.S.	G10	124
Theodore Roosevelt National Park South Unit, p.o.i., N.D., U.S.	G10	124
The Pas, Mb., Can.	E10	106
Thepha, Thai.	I5	48
The Pinnacle, hill, Mo., U.S.	E6	120
The Rand see Witwatersrand, mts., S. Afr.	D8	70
Theresa Creek, stm., Austl.	D6	76
The Rhins, pen., Scot., U.K.	G7	12
Thermaikós Kólpos (Salonika, Gulf of), b., Grc.	C6	28
Thermopolis, Wy., U.S.	D4	126
Thermopylae see Thermopýles, hist., Grc.	E5	28
Thermopýles (Thermopylae), hist., Grc.	E5	28
The Rock, Austl.	J6	76
The Rockies, mtn., Wa., U.S.	D4	136
The Rope, clf, Pit.	c28	78k
Thesiger Bay, b., N.T., Can.	B15	140
The Slot see New Georgia Sound, strt., Sol. Is.	e8	79b
Thessalía, state, Grc.	D5	28
Thessalía, hist. reg., Grc.	D5	28
Thessalon, On., Can.	B6	112
Thessaloníki (Salonika), Grc.	C6	28
Thessaly see Thessalía, hist. reg., Grc.	D5	28
Thetford, Eng., U.K.	I13	12
Thetford Mines, Qc., Can.	D5	110
Theunissen, S. Afr.	F8	70
The Valley, Anguilla	A1	105a
The Village, Ok., U.S.	F11	128
The Wash, b., Eng., U.K.	I13	12
The Weald, reg., Eng., U.K.	J13	12
Thibodaux, La., U.S.	H8	122
Thief Lake, l., Mn., U.S.	C3	118
Thief River Falls, Mn., U.S.	C2	118
Thiene, Italy	E8	22
Thiers, Fr.	D9	18
Thiès, Sen.	G1	64
Thika, Kenya	E7	66
Thimphu, Bhu.	E12	54
Thingvallavatn, l., Ice.	k29	8a
Thingvellir, Ice.	k29	8a
Thingvellir Nasjonalpark, p.o.i., Ice.	k29	8a
Thio, N. Cal.	m16	79d
Thionville, Fr.	E15	14
Thíra, Grc.	G8	28
Thíra (Santorini), i., Grc.	G8	28
Third Cataract see Thālith, Ash-Shallāl ath-, wtfl, Sudan	D6	62
Thiruvananthapuram see Trivandrum, India	G3	53
Thiruvārūr, India	F4	53
Thistilfjörður, b., Ice.	j32	8a
Thíva, Grc.	E6	28
Thiviers, Fr.	D6	18
Thjórsá, stm., Ice.	k30	8a
Thohoyandou, S. Afr.	C10	70
Thoi Binh, Viet.	H7	48
Thomas, Ok., U.S.	F10	128
Thomas, W.V., U.S.	E6	114
Thomaston, Al., U.S.	E11	122
Thomaston, Ga., U.S.	D1	116
Thomaston, Me., U.S.	F7	110
Thomasville, Ga., U.S.	F2	116
Thomasville, N.C., U.S.	I5	114
Thompson, Mb., Can.	D11	106
Thompson, Ia., U.S.	H5	118
Thompson, N.D., U.S.	D1	118
Thompson, stm., B.C., Can.	F9	138
Thompson, stm., U.S.	E4	120
Thompson Falls, Mt., U.S.	C11	136
Thompson Peak, mtn., Ca., U.S.	B3	134
Thomsen, stm., N.T., Can.	B16	140
Thomson, Ga., U.S.	C3	116
Thomson, Il., U.S.	C7	120
Thomson, stm., Austl.	E4	76
Thongwa, Mya.	D3	48
Thonon-les-Bains, Fr.	C12	18
Thonotosassa, Fl., U.S.	H3	116
Thonze, Mya.	D2	48
Thorhild, Ab., Can.	B17	138
Thórisvatn, l., Ice.	k30	8a
Thorlákshöfn, Ice.	I29	8a
Thornaby-on-Tees, Eng., U.K.	G11	12
Thornbury, On., Can.	D9	112
Thorndale, Tx., U.S.	D10	130
Thornton, Co., U.S.	B4	128
Thornton, Tx., U.S.	F2	122
Thorntonville, Tx., U.S.	C4	130
Thorp, Wi., U.S.	G8	118
Thorsby, Ab., Can.	C16	138
Thorshavn see Tórshavn, Far. Is.	n34	8b
Thórshöfn, Ice.	j32	8a
Thouars, Fr.	H8	14
Thoune see Thun, Switz.	D4	22
Thousand Lake Mountain, mtn., Ut., U.S.	E5	132
Thousand Oaks, Ca., U.S.	I7	134
Thousand Ships Bay, b., Sol. Is.	e8	79b
Thousand Springs Creek, stm., U.S.	B2	132
Thrace, hist. reg., Eur.	H13	26
Thrakikó Pélagos, Grc.	C8	28
Three Forks, Mt., U.S.	E15	136
Three Gorges Dam, dam, China	F4	42
Three Hills, Ab., Can.	E17	138
Three Hummock Island, i., Austl.	n12	77a
Three Kings Islands, is., N.Z.	B5	80
Three Mile Plains, N.S., Can.	F12	110
Three Points, Cape, c., Ghana	I4	64
Three Rivers, Mi., U.S.	G4	112
Three Rivers, Tx., U.S.	F9	130
Three Sisters, mtn., Or., U.S.	F5	136
Three Sisters Islands, is., Sol. Is.	f10	79b
Three Springs, Austl.	E3	74
Thrissur see Trichūr, India	F3	53
Throssel, Lake, l., Austl.	E4	74
Thu, Cu Lao, i., Viet.	G9	48
Thuan Chau, Viet.	B6	48
Thu Dau Mot, Viet.	G8	48
Thuin, Bel.	D13	14
Thule (Qaanaaq), Grnld.	B12	141
Thun, Switz.	D4	22
Thun Chang, Thai.	C5	48
Thunder Bay, On., Can.	C9	118
Thunder Bay, b., On., Can.	C9	118
Thunderbird, Lake, res., Ok., U.S.	F11	128
Thunderbolt, Ga., U.S.	D4	116
Thunder Butte Creek, stm., S.D., U.S.	B10	126
Thunder Creek, stm., Sk., Can.	D7	124
Thuner See, l., Switz.	D4	22
Thung Salaeng Luang National Park, p.o.i., Thai.	D5	48
Thung Wa, Thai.	I4	48
Thüringen, state, Ger.	F7	16
Thüringer Wald, mts., Ger.	F6	16
Thuringia see Thüringen, state, Ger.	F7	16
Thurles, Ire.	I5	12
Thurmont, Md., U.S.	E8	114
Thursday Island, Austl.	B8	74
Thurso, Scot., U.K.	C9	12
Thurston Island, i., Ant.	C31	81
Thusis, Switz.	D6	22
Thylungra, Austl.	F4	76
Thyolo, Mwi.	D5	68
Thysville see Mbanza-Ngungu, D.R.C.	F3	66
Tiachiv, Ukr.	A10	26
Tianchang, China	E8	42
Tiandeng, China	J2	42
Tiandong, China	J2	42
Tian'e, China	I2	42
Tiangang, China	C7	38
Tianguá, Braz.	B5	88
Tianjin (Tientsin), China	B7	42
Tianjin, state, China	B7	42
Tianjun, China	D4	36
Tianlin, China	I2	42
Tian Ling, mtn., China	B8	38
Tianmen, China	F5	42
Tianqiaoling, China	C8	38
Tianshifu, China	D6	38
Tianshui, China	D1	42
Tiantai, China	G9	42
Tiantang, China	J4	42
Tianwangsi, China	F8	42
Tianyang, China	J2	42
Tianzhen, China	A6	42
Tianzhu, China	D5	36
Tianzhu, China	H3	42
Tiarei, Fr. Poly.	v22	78h
Tiaro, Austl.	E9	76
Tiassalé, C. Iv.	H4	64
Ti'avea, Samoa	g12	79c
Tibaji, stm., Braz.	A12	92
Tibal-og, Phil.	G5	52
Tibasti, Sarīr, des., Libya	C3	62
Tibati, Cam.	C2	66
Tibbie, Al., U.S.	F10	122
Tiber see Tevere, stm., Italy	H9	22
Tiberias, Lake see Kinneret, Yam, l., Isr.	F6	58
Tibesti, mts., Afr.	C3	62
Tibet see Xizang, state, China	B5	46
Tibet, Plateau of see Qing Zang Gaoyuan, plat., China	B6	46
Tiblawan, Phil.	G6	52
Tibnīn, Leb.	E6	58
Tibooburra, Austl.	G4	76
Tiburón, Cabo, c.	C3	86
Tiburón, Isla, i., Mex.	G6	98
Tiča, Jazovir, res., Blg.	F13	26
Ticao Island, i., Phil.	D4	52
Tîchît, Maur.	F3	64
Ticino, stm., Eur.	D14	18
Tickfaw, stm., U.S.	G8	122
Ticonderoga, N.Y., U.S.	G3	110
Ticul, Mex.	B3	102
Tidioute, Pa., U.S.	C6	114
Tidiquin, Jbel, mtn., Mor.	C4	64
Tidjikja, Maur.	F2	64
Tiébissou, C. Iv.	H3	64
T'iehling see Tieling, China	C5	38
Tiel, Neth.	C14	14
Tieli, China	B10	36
Tieling, China	C5	38
Tielt, Bel.	C12	14
Tiémé, C. Iv.	H3	64
T'ienching see Tianjin, China	B7	42
Tien Giang see Mekong, stm., Asia	F9	46
Tien Shan, mts., Asia	F13	32
T'ienshui see Tianshui, China	D1	42
Tientsin see Tianjin, China	B7	42
Tientsin see Tianjin, state, China	B7	42
Tien Yen, Viet.	B8	48
Tie Plant, Ms., U.S.	D9	122
Tierp, Swe.	F7	8
Tierra Amarilla, Chile	C2	92
Tierra Blanca, Mex.	F10	100
Tierra Blanca, Mex.	G3	130
Tierra Blanca Creek, stm., U.S.	G6	128
Tierra de Campos, reg., Spain	C5	20
Tierra del Fuego, Arg.	J3	90
Tierra del Fuego, i., S.A.	J3	90
Tiétar, stm., Spain	E5	20
Tietê, Braz.	L2	88
Tietê, stm., Braz.	D6	90
Tiéti, N. Cal.	m15	79d
Tiffany Mountain, mtn., Wa., U.S.	B7	136
Tiffin, Oh., U.S.	C2	114
Tifton, Ga., U.S.	E2	116
Tiga, Île, i., N. Cal.	m16	79d
Tigalda Island, i., Ak., U.S.	F7	140
Tigapuluh, Pegunungan, mts., Indon.	D3	50
Tighina, Mol.	C16	26
Tigil', Russia	E20	34
Tignall, Ga., U.S.	C3	116
Tignish, P.E., Can.	D12	110
Tigoda, stm., Russia	A14	10
Tigre, Col.	F7	86
Tigre, stm., Peru	D2	84
Tigre, stm., Ven.	C10	86
Tigris (Dicle) (Dijlah), stm., Asia	C5	56
Tiguentourine, Alg.	D6	64
Tihany, hist., Hung.	C4	26
Tihert, Alg.	B5	64
Tihon, Russia	G22	8
Tihookeanskij, Russia	C10	38
Tihoreck, Russia	E6	32
Tihua see Ürümqi, China	C2	36
Tihuatlán, Mex.	E10	100
Tihvin, Russia	A16	10
Tijuana, Mex.	K8	134
Tijuana, stm., N.A.	K9	134
Tijucas, Braz.	C13	92
Tijucas do Sul, Braz.	B13	92
Tijuco, stm., Braz.	J1	88
Tikal, hist., Guat.	D3	102
Tikal, Parque Nacional, p.o.i., Guat.	D3	102
Tikrīt, Iraq	C5	56
Tikša, Russia	D15	8
Tikšeozero, ozero, l., Russia	C14	8
Tiksi, Russia	B14	34
Tiladummati Atoll, at., Mald.	h12	46a
Tilburg, Neth.	C14	14
Tilbury, On., Can.	F7	112
Tilcha, Austl.	G3	76
Tilden, Il., U.S.	F8	120
Tilden, Ne., U.S.	E15	126
Tilden, Tx., U.S.	F9	130
Tilhar, India	D7	54
Tilimsen, Alg.	C4	64
Tilin, Mya.	B2	48
Tillabéri, Niger	G5	64
Tilley, Ab., Can.	F19	138
Tillia, Niger	F5	64
Tillmans Corner, Al., U.S.	G10	122
Tillson, N.Y., U.S.	C11	114
Tillsonburg, On., Can.	F9	112
Tílos, i., Grc.	G10	28
Tilpa, Austl.	H5	76
Tilton, N.H., U.S.	G5	110
Tiltonsville, Oh., U.S.	D5	114
Tima, Egypt	L2	58
Timaná, Col.	G3	86
Timanskij krjaž, hills, Russia	B8	32
Timaru, N.Z.	G4	80
Timbalier Bay, b., La., U.S.	H8	122
Timbaúba, Braz.	D8	88
Timbavati Game Reserve, S. Afr.	D10	70
Timbedgha, Maur.	F3	64
Timber Lake, S.D., U.S.	B11	126
Timbiras, Braz.	C4	88
Timbó, Braz.	C13	92
Timbo, Lib.	H3	64
Timbuktu see Tombouctou, Mali	F4	64
Timétrine, Mali	F4	64
Timétrine, mts., Mali	F4	64
Timimoun, Alg.	D5	64
Timirist, Râs, c., Maur.	F1	64
Timirjazevo, Russia	E4	10
Timiș, state, Rom.	D8	26
Timiș (Tamiš), stm., Eur.	D7	26
Timiskaming, Lake (Témiscamingue, Lac), res., Can.	B10	112
Timișoara, Rom.	D8	26
Timmendorfer Strand, Ger.	B7	16
Timmins, On., Can.	F14	106
Timmonsville, S.C., U.S.	B6	116
Timms Hill, mtn., Wi., U.S.	F8	118
Timna' see Mikhrot Timna', hist., Isr.	I5	58
Timok, stm., Eur.	E9	26
Timon, Braz.	C4	88
Timor, i., Indon.	G8	44
Timor Sea	K15	142
Timošino, Russia	H21	8
Timotes, Ven.	C6	86
Timpanogos Cave National Monument, p.o.i., Ut., U.S.	C5	132
Timpton, stm., Russia	E14	34
Timšer, Russia	B9	32
Tims Ford Lake, res., Tn., U.S.	B12	122
Tina, stm., S. Afr.	G9	70
Tîna, Khalîg el- (Pelusium Bay), b., Egypt	G3	58
Tinaca Point, c., Phil.	H5	52
Tinambung, Indon.	E11	50
Tinapagee, Austl.	G5	76
Tinaquillo, Ven.	C7	86
Tindivanam, India	E4	53
Tindouf, Alg.	D3	64
Tineba, Pegunungan, mts., Indon.	D12	50
Tineg, stm., Phil.	B3	52
Ting, stm., China	I7	42
Tinggi, Pulau, i., Malay.	K7	48
Tingha, Austl.	G8	76
Tinghert, Ḥamādat (Tinghert, Plateau du), plat., Afr.	D7	64
Tinghert, Plateau du (Tinghert, Ḥamādat), plat., Afr.	D6	64
Tinghsien see Dingxian, China	B6	42
Tinglev, Den.	B5	16
Tingo María, Peru	E2	84
Tingri, China	D11	54
Tingri see Dinggyê, China	D11	54
Tinguiririca, Volcán, vol., Chile	G2	92
Tinharé, Ilha de, i., Braz.	G6	88
Tinh Bien, Viet.	G7	48
Tinian, i., N. Mar. Is.	B5	72
Tinjar, stm., Malay.	B9	50
Tínos, Grc.	F8	28
Tínos, i., Grc.	F8	28
Tinsley, Ms., U.S.	E8	122
Tinsukia, India	C8	46
Tintagel, B.C., Can.	B5	138
Tintina, Arg.	C6	92
Tintinara, Austl.	J3	76
Tio, Erit.	E8	62
Tiobrad Árann see Tipperary, Ire.	I4	12
Tioga, N.D., U.S.	F11	124
Tiojala, Fin.	F10	8
Tioman, Pulau, i., Malay.	K7	48
Tionesta, Pa., U.S.	C6	114
Tipasa, Alg.	H13	20
Tipitapa, Nic.	F4	102
Tippecanoe, stm., In., U.S.	H3	112
Tipperary, Ire.	I4	12
Tipperary, state, Ire.	I5	12
Tipton, Ca., U.S.	G6	134
Tipton, Ia., U.S.	C6	120
Tipton, Mo., U.S.	F5	120
Tipton, Ok., U.S.	G9	128
Tipton, Mount, mtn., Az., U.S.	H2	132
Tiptonville, Tn., U.S.	H8	120
Tip Top Mountain, mtn., On., Can.	F13	106
Tiptūr, India	E3	53
Tiputini, stm., Ec.	H4	86
Tīra, Isr.	F5	58
Tīrān, i., Sau. Ar.	K5	58
Tiran, Strait of, strt.	K5	58
Tirana see Tiranë, Alb.	C13	24
Tiranë, Alb.	C13	24
Tirano, Italy	D7	22
Tiraspol, Mol.	C16	26
Tire, Tur.	E10	28
Tiree, i., Scot., U.K.	E6	12
Tirich Mīr, mtn., Pak.	B11	56
Tirna, stm., India	B3	53
Tírnavos, Grc.	D5	28
Tirodi, India	H7	54
Tirol, state, Aus.	C8	22
Tiros, Braz.	J3	88
Tirso, stm., Italy	E2	24
Tīrthahalli, India	E2	53
Tiruchchirāppalli, India	F4	53
Tiruchengodu, India	F3	53
Tirukkalukkunram, India	E5	53
Tirukkovilūr, India	F4	53
Tiruliai, Lith.	E6	10
Tirunelveli, India	G3	53
Tirupati, India	E4	53
Tiruppattūr, India	E4	53
Tiruppur, India	F3	53
Tirūr, India	F2	53
Tirutturaippūndi, India	F4	53
Tiruvalla, India	G3	53
Tiruvannāmalai, India	E4	53
Tirūvottiyūr, India	E5	53
Tiruvur, India	C5	53
Tisa (Tisza) (Tysa), stm., Eur.	D7	26
Tisaiyanvilai, India	G3	53
Tisdale, Sk., Can.	B9	124
Tishomingo, Ok., U.S.	C2	122
Tisīyah, Syria	F7	58
Tiskilwa, Il., U.S.	C8	120
Tisovec, Slov.	H15	16
Tīsta, stm., Asia	F12	54
Tisza (Tisa) (Tysa), stm., Eur.	C7	26
Tiszaföldvár, Hung.	C7	26
Tiszaújváros, Hung.	B7	26
Tiszavasvári, Hung.	A8	26
Titaf, Alg.	D4	64
Tit-Ary, Russia	B14	34
Titicaca, Lake, l., S.A.	G4	84
Titilāgarh, India	H9	54
Titonka, Ia., U.S.	H4	118
Titov Veles, Mac.	B4	28
Titran, Nor.	E2	8
Tittabawassee, stm., Mi., U.S.	E5	112
Tittmoning, Ger.	H8	16
Titule, D.R.C.	D5	66
Titusville, Fl., U.S.	H5	116
Titusville, Pa., U.S.	C6	114
Tiuni, India	C6	54
Tivaouane, Sen.	F1	64
Tiverton, Eng., U.K.	K9	12
Tivoli, Italy	I9	22
Tivoli, Tx., U.S.	F11	130
Tiyās, Syria	D8	58
Tizimín, Mex.	B3	102
Tizi-Ouzou, Alg.	B5	64
Tizmant el-Zawâya, Egypt	I1	58
Tiznados, stm., Ven.	C8	86
Tiznit, Mor.	D3	64
Tjörn, i., Swe.	G4	8
Tjukalinsk, Russia	C12	32
Tjul'gan, Russia	D9	32
Tjumen', Russia	C10	32
Tjung, stm., Russia	D13	34
Tjuva-Guba, Russia	B15	8
Tlacotalpan, Mex.	F11	100
Tlacotepec, Mex.	G9	100
Tlahualilo de Zaragoza, Mex.	B7	100
Tlalnepantla, Mex.	F9	100
Tlaltenango de Sánchez Román, Mex.	E7	100
Tlapaneco, stm., Mex.	G9	100
Tlaquepaque, Mex.	E7	100
Tlaxcala, state, Mex.	F9	100
Tlaxcala de Xicohténcatl, Mex.	F9	100
Tłuszcz, Pol.	D17	16
Tmassah, Libya	B3	62
Tnâot, stm., Camb.	G7	48
Toa Alta, P.R.	B3	104a
Toa Baja, P.R.	B3	104a
Toachi, stm., Ec.	H2	86
Toahayana, Mex.	B5	100
Toamasina, Madag.	D8	68
Toba, Japan	E9	40
Toba, Danau, l., Indon.	K4	48
Tobago, i., Trin.	r13	105f
Toba Inlet, b., B.C., Can.	F6	138
Toba Kākar Range, mts., Pak.	C10	56
Tobarra, Spain	F9	20
Tobas, Arg.	D6	92
Toba Tek Singh, Pak.	C4	54
Tobejuba, Isla, i., Ven.	C11	86
Tobermorey, Austl.	D7	74
Tobermory, On., Can.	C8	112
Tobermory, Scot., U.K.	E6	12
Tobias, Ne., U.S.	G15	126
Tobias Barreto, Braz.	F6	88
Tobin, Mount, mtn., Nv., U.S.	C8	134
Tobique, stm., N.B., Can.	C9	110
Toboali, Indon.	E5	50
Tobol, Kaz.	D10	32
Tobol, stm., Asia	C11	32
Toboli, Indon.	D12	50
Tobol'sk, Russia	C11	32
Toboso, Phil.	E4	52
Tobruk see Ṭubruq, Libya	A4	62
Tobseda, Russia	B25	8
Tobyhanna, Pa., U.S.	C10	114
Tobyš, stm., Russia	C24	8
Tocantínia, Braz.	E1	88
Tocantinópolis, Braz.	D2	88
Tocantins, state, Braz.	F8	84
Tocantins, stm., Braz.	D8	84
Tocantins, stm., Braz.	F1	88
Tocantinzinho, stm., Braz.	H1	88
Tochcha Lake, l., B.C., Can.	B5	138
Tochigi, Japan	C12	40
Tochigi, state, Japan	C12	40
Tochio, Japan	B12	40
Toco, Trin.	s13	105f
Tocoa, Hond.	E5	102
Toconao, Chile	D3	90
Tocopilla, Chile	D2	90
Tocuco, stm., Ven.	C5	86
Tocumwal, Austl.	J5	76
Tocuyo, stm., Ven.	B7	86
Tocuyo de la Costa, Ven.	B7	86
Toda Rāisingh, India	E5	54
Todi, Italy	H9	22
Todos os Santos, Baia de, b., Braz.	G6	88
Todos Santos, Bol.	C3	90
Todos Santos, Mex.	D3	100
Todos Santos, Bahía de, b., Mex.	L8	134
Tofino, B.C., Can.	G5	138
Toga, i., Vanuatu	i16	79d
Togi, Japan	B9	40
Togiak, Ak., U.S.	E7	140
Togian, Kepulauan, is., Indon.	F7	44
Togo, ctry., Afr.	H5	64
Togtoh, China	A4	42
Togučin, Russia	C14	32
Togur, Russia	C14	32
Togwotee Pass, p., Wy., U.S.	G15	136
Tōhaku, Japan	D6	40
Tohiea, Mont, mtn., Fr. Poly.	v20	78h
Tohopekaliga, Lake, l., Fl., U.S.	H4	116
Tohtamyš, Taj.	B11	56
Toi-misaki, c., Japan	H4	40
Toiyabe Range, mts., Nv., U.S.	D8	134
Tōjō, Japan	E6	40
Tojtepa, Uzb.	F11	32
Tok, Ak., U.S.	D11	140
Tokachi, stm., Japan	C15	38
Tokachi-dake, vol., Japan	C15	38
Tokaj, Hung.	A8	26
Tōkamachi, Japan	B11	40
Tokara-kaikyō, strt., Japan	j19	39a
Tokara-rettō, is., Japan	k19	39a
Tokat, Tur.	A4	56
Tŏkchŏk-kundo, is., Kor., S.	F6	38
Tokelau, dep., Oc.	D9	72

Name | Map Ref. | Page

Tokko, Russia D12 34
Tokma, Russia C19 32
Tokmak, Kyrg. F13 32
Tokoro, stm., Japan C15 38
Tokoroa, N.Z. D6 80
Tok-to, is., Asia B4 40
Toktogul, Kyrg. F12 32
Tokuno-shima, i., Japan I19 39a
Tokur, Russia F15 34
Tokushima, Japan E7 40
Tokushima, state, Japan F7 40
Tokuyama, Japan E4 40
Tokwe, stm., Zimb. B10 70
Tōkyō, Japan D12 40
Tōkyō, state, Japan D12 40
Tokyo Bay see Tōkyō-wan, b., Japan D12 40
Tōkyō-daigaku-uchūkūkan-kenkyūsho, sci., Japan H4 40
Tōkyō-wan, b., Japan D12 40
Tôlañaro, Madag. F8 68
Tolbo, Mong. B3 36
Toledo, Braz. B11 92
Toledo, Col. D5 86
Toledo, Phil. E4 52
Toledo, Spain E6 20
Toledo, Il., U.S. E9 120
Toledo, Oh., U.S. C2 114
Toledo, Or., U.S. F3 136
Toledo, co., Spain E6 20
Toledo, Montes de, mts., Spain E6 20
Toledo Bend Reservoir, res., U.S. F4 122
Tolentino, Italy G10 22
Toli, China B1 36
Toliara, Madag. E7 68
Tolima, state, Col. E4 86
Tolima, Nevado del, vol., Col. E4 86
Tolitoli, Indon. C12 50
Toljatti, Russia D7 32
Tol'ka, Russia B14 32
Tolleson, Az., U.S. J4 132
Tolloche, Arg. B6 92
Tolmači, Russia C18 10
Tolmezzo, Italy D10 22
Tolmin, Slvn. D10 22
Tolna, state, Hung. C5 26
Tolo, Teluk, b., Indon. F7 44
Tolosa, Spain A8 20
Tolstoj, mys, c., Russia E20 34
Tolti, Pak. A6 54
Tolú, Col. C4 86
Toluca, Il., U.S. D8 120
Toluca, Nevado de, vol., Mex. F9 100
Toluca de Lerdo, Mex. F9 100
Tolybaj, Kaz. D10 32
Tom', stm., Russia C14 32
Tomah, Wi., U.S. H8 118
Tomahawk, Wi., U.S. F9 118
Tomakomai, Japan C14 38
Tomanivi, mtn., Fiji p19 79e
Tomar, Port. E2 20
Tomari, Russia G17 34
Tomás Gomensoro, Ur. E9 92
Tomasine, stm., Qc., Can. B13 112
Tomaszów Lubelski, Pol. F19 16
Tomaszów Mazowiecki, Pol. E15 16
Tombador, Serra do, plat., Braz. F6 84
Tomball, Tx., U.S. G3 122
Tombigbee, stm., U.S. F10 122
Tombos, Braz. K5 88
Tombouctou (Timbuktu), Mali F4 64
Tombstone, Az., U.S. L6 132
Tombstone Mountain, mtn., Yk., Can. C3 106
Tombua, Ang. D1 68
Tom Burke, S. Afr. C9 70
Tomé, Chile H1 92
Tomé-Açu, Braz. B1 88
Tomelilla, Swe. I5 8
Tomelloso, Spain E8 20
Tomichi Creek, stm., Co., U.S. C2 128
Tomini, Indon. C12 50
Tomini, Teluk, b., Indon. F7 44
Tomioka, Japan C11 40
Tommot, Russia E14 34
Tomo, stm., Col. E7 86
Tompkins, Sk., Can. D5 124
Tompkinsville, Ky., U.S. H12 120
Tompo, Indon. C12 50
Tom Price, Austl. D3 74
Tomptokan, Russia E15 34
Tomsk, Russia C15 32
Toms River, N.J., U.S. E11 114
Tonalá, Mex. G12 100
Tonami, Japan C9 40
Tonantins, Braz. I7 86
Tonantins, stm., Braz. I7 86
Tonasket, Wa., U.S. B7 136
Tonawanda, N.Y., U.S. B6 114
Tonbo, Mya. C2 48
Tonbridge, Eng., U.K. J13 12
Tondano, Indon. E8 44
Tønder, Den. B4 16
Tondi, India G4 53
Tone, stm., Japan D13 40
Tonekābon, Iran B7 56
Tonga, ctry., Oc. E9 72
Tongaat, S. Afr. F10 70
Tong'an, China I7 42
Tonganoxie, Ks., U.S. E2 120
Tonga Ridge, unds. K21 142
Tongariro National Park, p.o.i., N.Z. D6 80
Tongatapu, state, Tonga o14 78e
Tongatapu, i., Tonga n13 78e
Tonga Trench, unds. L21 142
Tongbai, China E5 42
Tongbai Shan, mts., China E5 42
Tongbei, China B10 36
Tongcheng, China F7 42
Tongchuan, China D3 42
Tongde, China D5 36
Tongeren, Bel. D14 14
Tongguan, China G5 42
Tongguan, China D3 42
Tonghai, China G5 36
Tonghe, China B10 36
Tonghua, China D6 38
Tongjiang, China B11 36
Tongjiang, China F2 42
Tongjosŏn-man, b., Kor., N. E7 38
Tongliang, China G1 42
Tongliao, China C4 38
Tongling, China F7 42
Tongling, China J3 42
Tonglu, China G8 42
Tongnae, Kor., S. D2 40
Tongnan, China F1 42
Tongo, Austl. H4 76
Tongoa, i., Vanuatu k17 79d
Tongoy, Chile E2 92
Tongren, China D5 36
Tongren, China H3 42
Tongres see Tongeren, Bel. D14 14
Tongsa Dzong, Bhu. E13 54
Tongtian, stm., China E4 36
Tongue, Scot., U.K. C8 12
Tongue, stm., U.S. A7 126
Tongue of the Ocean, unds. C9 96
Tongwei, China D1 42
Tongxian, China B7 42
Tongxin, China C1 42
Tongxu, China D6 42
Tongyu, China B5 38
Tongzi, China G2 42
Tonj, Sudan F5 62
Tonk, India E5 54
Tonkawa, Ok., U.S. E11 128
Tonkin see Bac Phan, hist. reg., Viet. A7 48
Tonkin, Gulf of, b., Asia C8 64
Tônlé Sab, Bœng, l., Camb. F6 48
Tonle Sap see Tônlé Sab, Bœng, l., Camb. F6 48
Tonneins, Fr. E6 18
Tonopah, Nv., U.S. E8 134
Tonoshō, Japan E7 40
Tonosí, Pan. D1 86
Tonotha, Bots. B8 70
Tons, stm., India F8 54
Tønsberg, Nor. G4 8
Tonstad, Nor. G2 8
Tonto Creek, stm., Az., U.S. I5 132
Tonto National Monument, p.o.i., Az., U.S. J5 132
Toodyay, Austl. F3 74
Tooele, Ut., U.S. C4 132
Toogoolawah, Austl. F9 76
Toomsboro, Ga., U.S. D2 116
Toora-Hem, Russia D17 32
Toowoomba, Austl. F8 76
Topeka, Ks., U.S. E2 120
Top Hill, hill, Gren. q11 105e
Topia, Mex. C5 100
Topki, Russia C15 32
Topko, gora, mtn., Russia E16 34
Topley, B.C., Can. B4 138
Toplița, Rom. C12 26
Topocalma, Punta, c., Chile G1 92
Topoľčany, Slov. H14 16
Topolobampo, Mex. C4 100
Topolovățu Mare, Rom. D8 26
Toporok, Russia B16 10
Topozero, ozero, l., Russia D14 8
Toppenish, Wa., U.S. D6 136
Topsa, Russia E20 8
Top Springs, Austl. C6 74
Tor, Eth. F6 62
Torbalı, Tur. E10 28
Torbat-e Heydarīyeh, Iran B8 56
Torbat-e Jām, Iran B9 56
Torbrook, N.S., Can. F12 110
Torch Lake, l., Mi., U.S. C4 112
Tordesillas, Spain C5 20
Töre, Swe. C10 8
Torgau, Ger. E8 16
Torhout, Bel. C12 14
Toribulu, Indon. D11 50
Torino (Turin), Italy E4 22
Torit, Sudan G6 62
Tormes, stm., Spain C5 20
Torna, Russia B20 8
Torna, mtn., India B1 53
Torneälven (Tornionjoki), stm., Eur. C10 8
Torneträsk, l., Swe. B8 8
Torngat Mountains, mts., Can. F13 141
Tornillo, Tx., U.S. C1 130
Tornionjoki (Torneälven), stm., Eur. C10 8
Tornquist, Arg. I6 92
Toro, Spain C5 20
Toro, mtn., Mex. F6 100
Toro, Lago del, l., Chile J2 90
Toro, Punta, c., Chile F1 92
Törökszentmiklós, Hung. B7 26
Torom, Russia F16 34
Toronto, On., Can. E10 112
Toronto, Ks., U.S. G1 120
Toronto, S.D., U.S. G2 118
Toropec, Russia D14 10
Tororo, Ug. D6 66
Toros Dağları (Taurus Mountains), mts., Tur. A3 58
Torosozero, Russia E18 8
Toroume, hill, Cook Is. b26 78j
Torquay, Sk., Can. E10 124
Torquay (Torbay), Eng., U.K. K9 12
Torrance, Ca., U.S. J7 134
Torrão, Port. F2 20
Torreblanca, Spain D11 20
Torre del Greco, Italy D8 24
Torredonjimeno, Spain G6 20
Torrejoncillo, Spain E4 20
Torrejón de Ardoz, Spain D7 20
Torrejón-Tiétar, Embalse de, res., Spain E5 20
Torrelavega, Spain A6 20
Torremolinos, Spain H6 20
Torrens, Lake, l., Austl. F7 74
Torrens Creek, Austl. C5 76
Torrens Creek, stm., Austl. C5 76
Torrent, Arg. D9 92
Torrent, Spain E10 20
Torrente see Torrent, Spain E10 20
Torrenueva, Spain F7 20
Torreón, Mex. C7 100
Torre Pellice, Italy F4 22
Torreperogil, Spain F7 20
Torres, Braz. D13 92
Torres, Îles, is., Vanuatu I16 79d
Torres Islands see Torres, Îles, is., Vanuatu I16 79d
Torres Strait, strt., Oc. b3 79a
Torres Vedras, Port. E1 20
Torrevella, Spain G10 20
Torrevieja see Torrevella, Spain G10 20
Torridon, Scot., U.K. D7 12
Torrijos, Spain D6 20
Torrington, Ct., U.S. C12 114
Torrington, Wy., U.S. E8 126
Torröjen, l., Swe. E5 8
Torsa (Amo), stm., Asia E12 54
Torsby, Swe. F5 8
Tórshavn (Thorshavn), Far. Is. n34 8b
Tortola, i., Br. Vir. Is. e8 104b
Tórtolas, Cerro de las (Tórtolas, Cerro), mtn., S.A. D2 92
Tortona, Italy F5 22
Tortorici, Italy F8 24
Tortosa, Spain D11 20
Tortosa, Cap de, c., Spain D11 20
Tortue, Île de la, i., Haiti B11 102
Tortuga Island see Tortue, Île de la, i., Haiti B11 102
Tortuguero, Laguna, b., P.R. B2 104a
Toruń, Pol. C14 16
Toruń, state, Pol. C15 16
Torup, Swe. H5 8
Toržok, Russia C17 10
Torzym, Pol. D11 16
Tosa, Japan F6 40
Tosa-shimizu, Japan G5 40
Tosa-wan, b., Japan F6 40
Tosca, S. Afr. D6 70
Toscana, state, Italy G8 22
Toses, Collada de, p., Spain B12 20
Tosno, Russia A13 10
Toson Hu, l., China D4 36
Tosontsengel, Mong. B4 36
Tostado, Arg. D7 92
Tõstamaa, Est. B6 10
Tosu, Japan F3 40
Totana, Spain G9 20
Toteng, Bots. B6 70
Totiyas, Som. D8 66
Tot'ma, Russia F20 8
Totness, Sur. B6 84
Totoya, i., Fiji q20 79e
Tottenham, Austl. I6 76
Tottenham, On., Can. D10 112
Tottori, Japan D7 40
Tottori, state, Japan D6 40
Touba, C. Iv. H3 64
Toubkal, Jebel, mtn., Mor. C3 64
Touchet, stm., Wa., U.S. D8 136
Touchwood Lake, l., Ab., Can. B19 138
Toudao, stm., China C7 38
Touggourt, Alg. C6 64
Touho, N. Cal. m15 79d
Toul, Fr. F14 14
Touliu, Tai. J9 42
Toulon, Fr. F11 18
Toulon-sur-Arroux, Fr. H13 14
Toulouse, Fr. F7 18
Toumodi, C. Iv. H3 64
Tounassine, Hamada, des., Alg. D3 64
Toungo, Nig. H7 64
Toungoo, Mya. C3 48
Touraine, hist. reg., Fr. G9 14
Tourcoing, Fr. D11 14
Touriñan, Cabo, c., Spain A1 20
Tournai, Bel. D12 14
Tournon, Fr. D10 18
Tournus, Fr. H13 14
Touros, Braz. C8 88
Tours, Fr. G9 14
Toussidé, Pic, vol., Chad C3 62
Touws, stm., S. Afr. H5 70
Toužim, Czech Rep. F9 16
Tovar, Ven. C6 86
Tovarkovskij, Russia G21 10
Tovuz, Azer. A6 56
Tow, Tx., U.S. D9 130
Towada, Japan D14 38
Towanda, Ks., U.S. D12 128
Towanda, Pa., U.S. C9 114
Tower, Mn., U.S. D6 118
Tower City, Pa., U.S. D9 114
Tower Hill, Austl. D5 76
Tower Hill, Il., U.S. E9 120
Towerhill Creek, stm., Austl. C5 76
Towla, Mount, mtn., Zimb. B9 70
Town and Country, Wa., U.S. C9 136
Town Hill, hill, Ber. k16 104e
Townsend, Mt., U.S. D15 136
Townshend Island, i., Austl. D8 76
Townsville, Austl. B6 76
Towson, Md., U.S. E9 114
Towuti, Danau, l., Indon. F7 44
Toyah, Tx., U.S. C4 130
Toyah Creek, stm., Tx., U.S. D4 130
Toyama, Japan C10 40
Toyama, state, Japan C10 40
Toyama-wan, b., Japan C10 40
Tōyo, Japan F6 40
Tōyō, Japan F7 40
Toyohashi, Japan E10 40
Toyokawa, Japan E10 40
Toyonaka, Japan E8 40
Toyooka, Japan D7 40
Toyosaka, Japan B12 40
Toyota, Japan D10 40
Toyoura, Japan E3 40
Tozeur, Tun. C6 64
Trabzon, Tur. A4 56
Tracadie, N.B., Can. C12 110
Tracy, Qc., Can. E3 110
Tracy, Ca., U.S. F4 134
Tracy City, Tn., U.S. B13 122
Tradewater, stm., Ky., U.S. G10 120
Traer, Ia., U.S. B5 120
Trafalgar, Cabo, c., Spain H4 20
Traíd, Spain D9 20
Tráighlí see Tralee, Ire. I3 12
Traiguén, Chile I1 92
Trail, B.C., Can. G13 138
Traill Ø, i., Grnld. C21 141
Traipu, Braz. E7 88
Traíra (Taraira), stm., S.A. H7 86
Trairi, Braz. B6 88
Trakai, Lith. F7 10
Tralee, Ire. I3 12
Trá Lí see Tralee, Ire. I3 12
Trammel, Va., U.S. G3 114
Tramperos Creek (Punta de Agua Creek), stm., U.S. E5 128
Tramping Lake, l., Sk., Can. B5 124
Tra My, Viet. E9 48
Trăn, Blg. G9 26
Tranås, Swe. G6 8
Trancas, Arg. C5 92
Tranco de Beas, Embalse de, res., Spain F8 20
Trang, Thai. I4 48
Trangan, Pulau, i., Indon. G9 44
Trang Dinh, Viet. A8 48
Trani, Italy C10 24
Tran Ninh see Xiangkhoang, Plateau de, plat., Laos C6 48
Tranqueras, Ur. E9 92
Transantarctic Mountains, mts., Ant. D30 81
Transkei, hist. reg., S. Afr. G8 70
Transylvania, hist. reg., Rom. C10 26
Transylvanian Alps see Carpații Meridionali, mts., Rom. D11 26
Trapani, Italy F6 24
Trapper Peak, mtn., Mt., U.S. E12 136
Traralgon, Austl. L6 76
Trârza, reg., Maur. F1 64
Trasimeno, Lago, l., Italy G9 22
Trás-os-Montes, hist. reg., Port. C3 20
Trat, Thai. F6 48
Traun, Aus. B11 22
Traun, stm., Aus. B11 22
Traunstein, Ger. I8 16
Travellers Lake, l., Austl. I4 76
Traverse, Lake, res., U.S. F2 118
Traverse City, Mi., U.S. D4 112
Tra Vinh, Viet. H8 48
Travis, Lake, l., Tx., U.S. D10 130
Travnik, Bos. E4 26
Trayning, Austl. F3 74
Trbovlje, Slvn. D12 22
Třebíč, Czech Rep. G11 16
Trebinje, Bos. G5 26
Trebišov, Slov. H17 16
Treblinka, Pol. D18 16
Trece Martires, Phil. C3 52
Tregoose Islets, is., Austl. A8 76
Treguboyo, Russia B14 10
Treinta y Tres, Ur. F10 92
Trélazé, Fr. G8 14
Trelew, Arg. H3 90
Trelleborg, Swe. I5 8
Tremadog Bay, b., Wales, U.K. I8 12
Tremblant, Mont, mtn., Qc., Can. D2 110
Trembleur Lake, l., B.C., Can. B5 138
Tremiti, Isole, is., Italy H12 22
Tremont, Il., U.S. K9 118
Tremonton, Ut., U.S. B4 132
Tremp, Spain B11 20
Trempealeau, Wi., U.S. G7 118
Trenche, stm., Qc., Can. B4 110
Trenčín, Slov. H14 16
Trenel, Arg. G5 92
Trêng, Camb. F6 48
Trenggalek, Indon. H7 50
Trenque Lauquen, Arg. G6 92
Trent, stm., On., Can. D12 112
Trent, stm., Eng., U.K. H12 12
Trente et Un Milles, Lac des, l., Qc., Can. B13 112
Trentino-Alto Adige, state, Italy D8 22
Trento (Trent), Italy D7 22
Trenton, N.S., Can. E14 110
Trenton, On., Can. D12 112
Trenton, Fl., U.S. G3 116
Trenton, Ga., U.S. C13 122
Trenton, Mo., U.S. D4 120
Trenton, Ne., U.S. A8 128
Trenton, N.J., U.S. D11 114
Trenton, N.C., U.S. A8 116
Trenton, Tn., U.S. I8 120
Trentwood, Wa., U.S. C9 136
Trepassey, Nf., Can. j23 107a
Tres Algarrobos, Arg. G6 92
Tres Arroyos, Arg. I7 92
Três Corações, Braz. K3 88
Tres Coroas, Braz. D12 92
Três de Maio, Braz. C10 92
Tres Esquinas, Col. G4 86
Tres Lagoas, Braz. D6 90
Tres Lagos, Arg. I2 90
Tres Lomas, Arg. H6 92
Três Marias, Braz. J3 88
Tres Marías, Islas, is., Mex. E5 100
Três Marias, Represa de, res., Braz. J3 88
Tres Montes, Península, pen., Chile I1 90
Tres Montosas, mtn., N.M., U.S. I9 132
Tres Palos, Laguna, l., Mex. G9 100
Três Passos, Braz. C11 92
Tres Picos, Cerro, mtn., Arg. I6 92
Três Pontas, Braz. K3 88
Tres Puntas, Cabo, c., Arg. I3 90
Três Rios, Braz. L4 88
Tres Vírgenes, Volcán de las, vol., Mex. B2 100
Tres Zapotes, hist., Mex. F11 100
Tretten, Nor. F4 8
Treuchtlingen, Ger. H6 16
Treuenbrietzen, Ger. D8 16
Treviglio, Italy E6 22
Treviso, Italy E9 22
Trevorton, Pa., U.S. D9 114
Trgovište, Yugo. G9 26
Triabunna, Austl. o13 77a
Triberg, Ger. H4 16
Tribugá, Ensenada de, b., Col. E3 86
Tribune, Sk., Can. E10 124
Tribune, Ks., U.S. C7 128
Tricarico, Italy D10 24
Tricase, Italy E12 24
Trichonída, Límni, l., Grc. E4 28
Trichūr, India F3 53
Tri County Supply Canal, can., Ne., U.S. G12 126
Trida, Austl. I5 76
Trident Peak, mtn., Nv., U.S. B7 134
Trier, Ger. G2 16
Trieste (Trst), Italy E10 22
Trieste, Gulf of, b., Eur. E10 22
Triglav, mtn., Slvn. D10 22
Triglavski narodni park, p.o.i., Slvn. D10 22
Trigueros, Spain G4 20
Tríkala, Grc. D4 28
Trikora, Puncak, mtn., Indon. F10 44
Trilby, Fl., U.S. H3 116
Triman, Pak. D2 54
Trincheras, Mex. F7 98
Trincomalee, Sri L. G5 53
Trindade, Braz. I1 88
Trindade, i., Braz. H12 82
Třinec, Czech Rep. G14 16
Trinidad, Bol. B3 90
Trinidad, Col. E6 86
Trinidad, Cuba B8 102
Trinidad, Co., U.S. D4 128
Trinidad, Tx., U.S. E2 122
Trinidad, Ur. F9 92
Trinidad, i., Trin. s13 105f
Trinidad, Isla, i., Arg. I7 92
Trinidad and Tobago, ctry., N.A. s13 105f
Trinity, Tx., U.S. G3 122
Trinity, stm., Ca., U.S. C2 134
Trinity, stm., Tx., U.S. D13 130
Trinity, Elm Fork, stm., Tx., U.S. H11 128
Trinity, South Fork, stm., Ca., U.S. C2 134
Trinity, West Fork, stm., Tx., U.S. H11 128
Trinity Bay, b., Nf., Can. j23 107a
Trinity Bay, b., Tx., U.S. H4 122
Trinity Islands, is., Ak., U.S. E9 140
Trinity Peak, mtn., Nv., U.S. C7 134
Trinity Site, hist., N.M., U.S. H2 128
Trino, Italy E5 22
Tripa, stm., Indon. J3 48
Tripoli, Grc. F5 28
Tripoli see Tarābulus, Leb. D6 58
Tripoli see Tarābulus, Libya A2 62
Tripoli, Ia., U.S. I6 118
Tripolis, hist., Tur. F12 28
Tripp, S.D., U.S. D15 126
Tripura, state, India G13 54
Tristan da Cunha Group, is., St. Hel. J4 60
Tristao, Îles, is., Gui. G2 64
Triste, Spain B10 20
Triste, Golfo, b., Ven. B7 86
Tri Ton, Viet. G7 48
Triumph, La., U.S. H9 122
Trivandrum, India G3 53
Trnava, Slov. H13 16
Trobriand Islands, is., Pap. N. Gui. b5 79a
Trogir, Cro. G13 22
Troia, Italy C9 24
Troick, Russia D10 32
Troickoe, Russia D15 32
Troickoe, Russia G16 34
Troicko-Pečorsk, Russia B9 32
Troina, Italy G8 24
Trois-Pistoles, Qc., Can. B7 110
Trois Pitons, Morne, vol., Dom. j6 105c
Trois-Rivières, Qc., Can. D4 110
Trois-Rivières, Guad. i5 105c
Trojan, Blg. G11 26
Trojanova Tabla, hist., Yugo. E9 26
Trollhättan, Swe. G5 8
Trombetas, stm., Braz. C6 84
Troms, state, Nor. B8 8
Tromsø, Nor. B8 8
Trona, Ca., U.S. H8 134
Tronador, Cerro, mtn., S.A. H2 90
Trondheim, Nor. E4 8
Trondheimsfjorden, b., Nor. E4 8
Troōdos, Cyp. D3 58
Troodos Mountains, mts., Cyp. D3 58
Troon, Scot., U.K. F8 12
Trophy Mountain, vol., B.C., Can. E11 138
Tropic, Ut., U.S. F4 132
Tropojë, Alb. B14 24
Troškūnai, Lith. E7 10
Trosna, Russia H18 10
Trotuș, stm., Rom. C13 26
Troup, Tx., U.S. E3 122
Trout, La., U.S. F6 122
Trout, stm., N.T., Can. C6 106
Trout Creek, Mi., U.S. E9 118
Trout Creek Pass, p., Co., U.S. C3 128
Trout Lake, l., N.T., Can. C6 106
Trout Lake, l., On., Can. E12 106
Troutville, Va., U.S. G6 114
Trouville-sur-Mer, Fr. E9 14
Trowbridge, Eng., U.K. J10 12
Troy, Al., U.S. F13 122
Troy, Id., U.S. D10 136
Troy, Mo., U.S. F7 120
Troy, N.H., U.S. B13 114
Troy, N.Y., U.S. B12 114
Troy, N.C., U.S. A6 116
Troy, Oh., U.S. D1 114
Troy, Pa., U.S. C9 114
Troy, Tn., U.S. H8 120
Troy, Tx., U.S. C10 130
Troy see Truva, hist., Tur. D9 28
Troyes, Fr. F13 14
Troy Peak, mtn., Nv., U.S. E1 132
Trst see Trieste, Italy E10 22
Trstená, Slov. G15 16
Trubč'evsk, Russia H16 10
Truchas, N.M., U.S. E3 128
Truchas Peak, mtn., N.M., U.S. E3 128
Trucial States see United Arab Emirates, ctry., Asia E7 56
Truckee, Ca., U.S. D5 134
Truckee, stm., U.S. D6 134
Trud, Russia C16 10
Trujillo, Col. E3 86
Trujillo, Hond. E4 102
Trujillo, Peru E2 84
Trujillo, Spain E5 20
Trujillo, Ven. C6 86
Trujillo, state, Ven. C6 86
Trujillo Alto, P.R. B4 104a
Truk Islands see Chuuk, is., Micron. C6 72
Truman, Mn., U.S. H4 118
Trumann, Ar., U.S. B8 122
Trumansburg, N.Y., U.S. B9 114
Trumbull, Ct., U.S. C12 114
Trumbull, Mount, mtn., Az., U.S. G3 132
Trundle, Austl. I6 76
Trung Phan (Annam), hist. reg., Viet. D8 48
Truro, N.S., Can. E13 110
Truro, Eng., U.K. K7 12
Trusan, stm., Malay. A9 50
Truscott, Tx., U.S. H9 128
Trusěni, Mol. B15 26
Truth or Consequences, N.M., U.S. J9 132
Trutnov, Czech Rep. F11 16
Truva (Troy), hist., Tur. D9 28
Truxton Wash, stm., Az., U.S. H3 132
Truyère, stm., Fr. E8 18
Tryduby, Ukr. A17 26
Tryon, Ne., U.S. F12 126
Tryon, N.C., U.S. A3 116
Trzcianka, Pol. C12 16
Trzciel, Pol. D11 16
Trzebiatów, Pol. B11 16
Trzebinia, Pol. F15 16
Trzebnica, Pol. E13 16
Tsagaannuur, Mong. E15 32
Tsaidam Basin see Qaidam Pendi, bas., China D3 36
Tsala Apopka Lake, l., Fl., U.S. H3 116
Tsamkong see Zhanjiang, China K4 42
Ts'anghsien see Cangzhou, China B7 42
T'sangwu see Wuzhou, China J4 42
Tsaratanana, Madag. D8 68
Tsaratanana, mts., Madag. C8 68
Tsau, Bots. E3 68
Tsavo, Kenya E7 66
Tsaydaychuz Peak, mtn., B.C., Can. C4 138
Tsebrykove, Ukr. B17 26
Tses, Nmb. D4 70
Tsetserleg, Mong. B5 36
Tsévié, Togo H5 64
Tshabong, Bots. D6 70
Tshane, Bots. D5 70
Tshela, D.R.C. E2 66
Tshidilamolomo, S. Afr. D7 70
Tshikapa, D.R.C. F4 66
Tshofa, D.R.C. F5 66
Tshuapa, stm., D.R.C. E4 66
Tshumbe (Chiumbe), stm., Afr. B3 68
Tsiafajavona, vol., Madag. D8 68
Tsiigehtchic, N.T., Can. B4 106
Tsimlyansk Reservoir see Cimljanskoe vodohranilišče, res., Russia E6 32
Tsinan see Jinan, China C7 42
Tsineng, S. Afr. E6 70
Tsinghai see Qinghai, state, China D4 36
Tsingkiang see Qingjiang, China E8 42
Tsingtao see Qingdao, China C9 42
Tsingyuan see Baoding, China B6 42
Ts'in-hai see Qinghai, state, China D4 36
Tsining see Jining, China D7 42
Tsinling Shan see Qin Ling, mts., China E3 42
Tsintsabis, Nmb. D2 68
Tsiombe, Madag. F8 68
Tsipa see Cipa, stm., Russia F11 34
Tsiribihina, stm., Madag. D7 68
Tsiroanomandidy, Madag. D8 68
Tsitsihar see Qiqihar, China B9 36
Tsna see Cna, stm., Russia D6 32
Tsomo, stm., S. Afr. H8 70
Tsomog, Mong. B6 36
Tsu, Japan E9 40
Tsubame, Japan B11 40
Tsuchiura, Japan C13 40
Tsugaru-kaikyō, strt., Japan D14 38
Tsukumi, Japan F4 40
Tsukushi-sanchi, mts., Japan F3 40
Tsumeb, Nmb. D2 68
Tsumkwe, Nmb. D3 68
Tsuni see Zunyi, China H2 42
Tsuruga, Japan D9 40
Tsurugi-san, mtn., Japan F7 40
Tsuruoka, Japan A12 40
Tsushima, is., Japan E2 40
Tsushima-kaikyō (Eastern Channel), strt., Japan F2 40
Tsuyama, Japan D7 40
Tswaane, Bots. C6 70
Ttruchchendūr, India G4 53
Tua, D.R.C. E3 66
Tua, stm., Port. C3 20
Tua, Tanjung, c., Indon. F4 50
Tua Chua, Viet. B6 48
Tual, Indon. G9 44
Tuam, Ire. H4 12
Tuamotu, Îles, is., Fr. Poly. E12 72
Tuamotu Archipelago see Tuamotu, Îles, is., Fr. Poly. E12 72
Tuamotu Ridge, unds. K24 142
Tuanan, Indon. E9 50
Tuangku, Pulau, i., Indon. K3 48
Tuapse, Russia F5 32
Tuasivi, Cape, c., Samoa g11 79c
Tuba, Russia C18 32
Tuba, stm., Russia D16 32
Tubac, Az., U.S. L5 132
Tuban, Indon. G8 50
Tubarão, Braz. D13 92
Tūbās, W.B. F6 58
Tübingen, Ger. H4 16
Tubruq, Libya A4 62
Tubuai, i., Fr. Poly. F12 72
Tucacas, Ven. B7 86
Tucano, Braz. F6 88
Tucheng, China G2 42
Tuchów, Pol. G17 16
Tuckerman, Ar., U.S. B7 122
Tuckerton, N.J., U.S. E11 114
Tučkovo, Russia E19 10
Tucson, Az., U.S. K5 132
Tucumán, state, Arg. C5 92
Tucumcari, N.M., U.S. F5 128
Tucunuco, Arg. E3 92
Tucupido, Ven. C9 86
Tucupita, Ven. C11 86
Tucuruí, Braz. D8 84
Tucuruí, Represa de, res., Braz. D8 84
Tudela, Phil. F4 52
Tudela, Spain B9 20
Tudmur (Palmyra), Syria D9 58
Tufānganj, India E12 54
Tufi, Pap. N. Gui. b4 79a
Tugela, stm., S. Afr. F10 70
Tug Fork, stm., U.S. G3 114
Tuggerah Lake, b., Austl. I8 76
Tuguegarao City, Phil. B3 52
Tugur, Russia F16 34
Tuhai, stm., China C7 42
Tuhuangba, China F3 42
Tui, Spain B2 20
Tuibo, China C7 38
Tuira, stm., Pan. D3 86
Tujmazy, Russia D8 32
Tukangbesi, Kepulauan, is., Indon. G7 44
Tukituki, stm., N.Z. D7 80
Tukosméra, Mont, mtn., Vanuatu l17 79d
Tūkrah, Libya A4 62
Tuktoyaktuk, N.T., Can. B4 106
Tukums, Lat. D6 10
Tukuringra, hrebet, mts., Russia F14 34
Tukuyu, Tan. F6 66
Tula, Mex. D9 100
Tula, Russia F20 10
Tulach Mhór see Tullamore, Ire. H5 12
Tulaghi, Sol. Is. e8 79b
Tulancingo, Mex. E9 100
Tulangbawang, stm., Indon. F4 50
Tulare, Ca., U.S. G6 134
Tulare, S.D., U.S. C14 126
Tulare Lake Bed, reg., Ca., U.S. G6 134
Tulare Lake Canal, can., Ca., U.S. G6 134
Tularosa, N.M., U.S. H2 128
Tularosa Valley, bas., N.M., U.S. E9 98
Tulbagh, S. Afr. H4 70
Tulcán, Ec. G3 86
Tulcea, Rom. D15 26
Tulcea, state, Rom. D15 26
Tulelake, Ca., U.S. B4 134
Tule Lake, l., Ca., U.S. B4 134
Tulemalu Lake, l., Nu., Can. C11 106
Tule Valley, val., Ut., U.S. D3 132
Tuli, Zimb. B9 70
Tuliszków, Pol. D14 16
Tulita, N.T., Can. C5 106
Tūlkarm, W.B. F6 58
Tullahoma, Tn., U.S. B12 122
Tullamore, Ire. H5 12
Tulle, Fr. D7 18
Tullibigeal, Austl. I6 76
Tulln, Aus. B13 22
Tullos, La., U.S. F6 122
Tullus, Sudan E4 62
Tully, Austl. A5 76
Tulsa, Ok., U.S. H2 120
Tulsequah, B.C., Can. D4 106
Tul'skaja oblast', co., Russia G20 10
Tuluá, Col. E3 86
Tulum, Mex. B4 102
Tulum, hist., Mex. B4 102
Tulun, Russia D18 32
Tulungagung, Indon. H7 50
Tulungselapan, Indon. E4 50
Tuma, stm., Nic. F5 102
Tumacacori National Historical Park, p.o.i., Az., U.S. L5 132
Tumaco, Col. G2 86
Tumaco, Rada de, b., Col. G2 86
Tuman-gang (Tumen), stm., Asia C8 38
Tumanskij, Russia D24 34
Tumany, Russia D20 34
Tumbarumba, Austl. J6 76
Tumbes, Peru D1 84
Tumbes, Punta, c., Chile H1 92
Tumbler Ridge, B.C., Can. A10 138
Tumen, China C8 38
Tumen (Tuman-gang), stm., Asia C8 38
Tumeremo, Ven. D11 86
Tumiritinga, Braz. J5 88
Tumkūr, India E3 53
Tumoteqi, China A4 42
Tumpat, Malay. I6 48
Tumsar, India H7 54
Tumtum, Wa., U.S. C9 136
Tumu, Ghana G4 64
Tumuc-Humac Mountains, mts., S.A. C6 84
Tumut, Austl. J7 76
Tun, stm., Thai. D4 48
Tunapuna, Trin. s12 105f
Tunari, Cerro, mtn., Bol. C3 90
Tunas de Zaza, Cuba B8 102
Tunchang, China L3 42
T'unch'i see Huangshan, China G8 42
Tunduru, Tan. G7 66
Tundža, stm., Eur. G13 26
Tungabhadra, stm., India D3 53
Tungabhadra Reservoir, res., India D2 53
Tungaru, Sudan E6 62
T'ungchou see Tongxian, China B7 42
T'ungch'uan see Tongchuan, China D3 42
Tung Hai see East China Sea, Asia F9 36
T'unghsien see Tongxian, China B7 42
T'unghua see Tonghua, China D6 38
Tunghwa see Tonghua, China D6 38
Tungkal, stm., Indon. D3 50
Tungku, Malay. A11 50
Tungla, Nic. F5 102
T'ungliao see Tongliao, China C4 38
Tungsha Tao (Pratas Island), i., Tai. K7 42
Tungshih, Tai. I9 42
Tungsten, N.T., Can. C5 106
Tungurahua, state, Ec. H2 86
Tungurahua, vol., Ec. H2 86
Tuni, India C6 53
Tunis, stm., Col. G5 86
Tunis, Tun. H4 24
Tunis, Golfe de, b., Tun. G4 24
Tunis, Gulf of see Tunis, Golfe de, b., Tun. G4 24
Tunisia, ctry., Afr. C6 64
Tunisie see Tunisia, ctry., Afr. C6 64

Name | Map Ref. | Page

Tunja, Col. E5 86
Tunkhannock, Pa., U.S. C9 114
Tunliu, China C5 42
Tunnel Hill, Ga., U.S. C13 122
Tunnelton, W.V., U.S. E6 114
Tunnsjøen, l., Nor. D5 8
Tuntum, Braz. C3 88
Tunu see Østgrønland, state, Grnld. C18 141
Tununak, Ak., U.S. D6 140
Tunuyán, Arg. F3 92
Tunuyán, stm., Arg. F4 92
Tunxi, China G8 42
Tuo, stm., China G1 42
Tuo, stm., China E7 42
Tuobalage, China C12 54
Tuobuja, Russia D13 34
Tuoj-Haja, Russia B20 32
Tuokusidawan Ling, mtn., China A6 46
Tuolumne, can., Ca., U.S. F5 134
Tuong Duong, Viet. C7 48
Tuotuo, stm., China A13 54
Tupã, Braz. D6 90
Tupaciguara, Braz. J1 88
Tupanciretã, Braz. D10 92
Tuparro, stm., Col. E7 86
Tupelo, Ms., U.S. C10 122
Tupelo, Ok., U.S. C2 122
Tupik, Russia F13 34
Tupinambarana, Ilha, i., Braz. D6 84
Tupiraçaba, Braz. H1 88
Tupiza, Bol. D3 90
Tupper Lake, N.Y., U.S. F2 110
Tupungato, Cerro, mtn., S.A. F2 92
Tuquan, China B9 36
Túquerres, Col. G3 86
Tura, India F13 54
Tura, Russia B18 32
Tura, stm., Russia C11 32
Turabah, Sau. Ar. E5 56
Turaiyūr, India F4 53
Turan, Russia D16 32
Turāq al-'Ilab, hills, Syria E9 58
Turau, Bela. H10 10
Turbaco, Col. B4 86
Turbat, Pak. D9 56
Turbo, Col. C3 86
Turčasovo, Russia E18 8
Turda, Rom. C10 26
Turek, Pol. D14 16
Turfan see Turpan, China C2 36
Turfan Depression see Turpan Pendi, depr., China C2 36
Turgaj, Kaz. E10 32
Turgaj, stm., Kaz. E10 32
Turgajskaja ložbina, reg., Kaz. D10 32
Turgajskoe plato, plat., Kaz. D10 32
Turgay see Turgaj, stm., Kaz. E10 32
Turginovo, Russia D18 10
Turgoš, Russia A18 10
Turgutlu, Tur. E10 28
Türi, Est. B8 10
Túria (Turia), stm., Spain D9 20
Túria (Turia), stm., Spain D9 20
Turiaçu, Braz. A3 88
Turiaçu, stm., Braz. B3 88
Turimiquire, Cerro, mtn., Ven. B10 86
Turin, Ab., Can. F18 138
Turin see Torino, Italy E4 22
Turinsk, Russia C10 32
Turka, Ukr. G19 16
Turkana, Lake see Rudolf, Lake, l., Afr. D7 66
Turkestan, Kaz. F11 32
Turkestanskij hrebet, mts., Asia B10 56
Túrkeve, Hung. B7 26
Turkey, ctry., Asia B3 56
Turkey, stm., Ia., U.S. I7 118
Turkey Creek, stm., Ne., U.S. K2 118
Turkish Republic of Northern Cyprus see Cyprus, North, ctry., Asia C4 58
Turkmenbaši, Turkmen. B7 56
Turkmenia see Turkmenistan, ctry., Asia B8 56
Turkmenistan, ctry., Asia B8 56
Türkoğlu, Tur. A7 58
Turks and Caicos Islands, dep., N.A. A12 102
Turks Island Passage, strt., T./C. Is. B12 102
Turks Islands, is., T./C. Is. B12 102
Turku (Åbo), Fin. F9 8
Turku ja Pori, state, Fin. F10 8
Turkwel, stm., Kenya D7 66
Turley, Ok., U.S. H2 120
Turlock, Ca., U.S. F5 134
Turmalina, Braz. I4 88
Turmantas, Lith. E9 10
Turnagain, stm., B.C., Can. D5 106
Turneffe Islands, is., Belize D4 102
Turner, Mt., U.S. F5 124
Turner, Or., U.S. F4 136
Turners Falls, Ma., U.S. B13 114
Turnhout, Bel. C13 14
Turnov, Czech Rep. F11 16
Turnu Măgurele, Rom. F11 26
Turnu Roșu, Pasul, p., Rom. D11 26
Ťuročak, Russia D15 32
Turon, Ks., U.S. D10 128
Turpan, China C2 36
Turpan Pendi (Turfan Depression), depr., China C2 36
Turquino, Pico, mtn., Cuba C9 102
Turrell, Ar., U.S. B8 122
Turret Peak, mtn., Az., U.S. I5 132
Turtle, stm., Mb., Can. D14 124
Turtle-Flambeau Flowage, res., Wi., U.S. E8 118
Turtle Islands, is., S.L. H2 64
Turtle Lake, N.D., U.S. G13 124
Turtle Lake, Wi., U.S. F6 118
Turu, stm., Russia B18 32
Turuhan, stm., Russia A14 32
Turuhansk, Russia C6 34
Turvo, Braz. D13 92
Turvo, stm., Braz. K1 88
Turwi, stm., Zimb. B10 70
Turzovka, Slov. G14 16
Tuscaloosa, Al., U.S. D11 122
Tuscaloosa, Lake, res., Al., U.S. D11 122
Tuscany see Toscana, state, Italy G8 22
Tuscarora Mountain, mts., Pa., U.S. D8 114
Tuscola, Tx., U.S. B8 130
Tuscumbia, Al., U.S. C11 122
Tuscumbia, Mo., U.S. F5 120
Tuskegee, Al., U.S. E13 122
Tustumena Lake, l., Ak., U.S. D9 140
Tutaev, Russia C22 10
Tuticorin, India G4 53
Tutin, Yugo. F8 26
Tutóia, Braz. B4 88
Tutoko, Mount, mtn., N.Z. G3 80
Tutrakan, Blg. E13 26
Tuttle, N.D., U.S. G14 124
Tuttle Creek Lake, res., Ks., U.S. B12 128
Tutuala, Indon. G8 44
Tutuila, i., Am. Sam. h12 79c
Tutupaca, Volcán, vol., Peru G3 84
Tutwiler, Ms., U.S. C8 122
Tutzing, Ger. I7 16
Tuul, stm., Mong. B6 36
Tuva, state, Russia D16 32
Tuvalu, ctry., Oc. D8 72
Tuvuca, i., Fiji p20 79e
Tuwayq, Jabal, mts., Sau. Ar. E6 56
Tuxford, Sk., Can. D8 124
Tuxpan, Mex. E6 100
Tuxpan de Rodríguez Cano, Mex. E10 100
Tuxtepec, Mex. F10 100
Tuxtla Gutiérrez, Mex. G12 100
Túy see Tui, Spain B2 20
Tuy, stm., Ven. B8 86
Tuyen Hoa, Viet. D8 48
Tuyen Quang, Viet. B7 48
Tuy Hoa, Viet. F9 48
Tuyün see Duyun, China H2 42
Tuyūr, Burj at-, hill, Sudan C5 62
Tuz, Iraq C5 56
Tuz Gölü, l., Tur. B3 56
Tuzigoot National Monument, p.o.i., Az., U.S. I4 132
Tuzla, Bos. E5 26
Tuzly, Ukr. D17 26
Tvardita, Mol. C15 26
Tver' (Kalinin), Russia D18 10
Tverca, stm., Russia D18 10
Tverskaja oblast', co., Russia D16 10
Tweed, On., Can. D12 112
Tweed, stm., U.K. F10 12
Tweed Heads, Austl. G9 76
Twee Rivieren, S. Afr. E5 70
Twelve Mile Lake, l., Sk., Can. E7 124
Twenthekanaal, can., Neth. B15 14
Twentynine Palms, Ca., U.S. I9 134
Twin Buttes, mtn., Or., U.S. F4 136
Twin Buttes Reservoir, res., Tx., U.S. C7 130
Twin City, Ga., U.S. D3 116
Twin Falls, Id., U.S. H12 136
Twin Lakes, Ga., U.S. F2 116
Twin Lakes, Wi., U.S. B9 120
Twinsburg, Oh., U.S. C4 114
Twisp, Wa., U.S. B6 136
Twitchell Reservoir, res., Ca., U.S. H5 134
Twitya, stm., N.T., Can. C5 106
Two Butte Creek, stm., Co., U.S. D6 128
Twofold Bay, b., Austl. K7 76
Two Harbors, Mn., U.S. D7 118
Two Medicine, stm., Mt., U.S. B14 136
Two Rivers, Wi., U.S. D2 112
Tybee Island, Ga., U.S. D5 116
Tychy, Pol. F14 16
Tyczyn, Pol. G18 16
Tye, Tx., U.S. B8 130
Tygda, Russia F14 34
Tyler, Mn., U.S. G2 118
Tyler, Tx., U.S. E3 122
Tylertown, Ms., U.S. F8 122
Tylihul, stm., Ukr. B17 26
Tylihul's'kyi lyman, l., Ukr. B17 26
Tym, stm., Russia C14 32
Tymovskoe, Russia F17 34
Tynda, Russia E13 34
Tyndall, S.D., U.S. D15 126
Tyndaris, hist., Italy F8 24
Tynemouth, Eng., U.K. F11 12
Tynset, Nor. E4 8
Tyre see Ṣūr, Leb. E6 58
Tyrifjorden, l., Nor. F3 8
Tyrma, Russia F15 34
Tyrma, stm., Russia F15 34
Tyrone, Ok., U.S. E7 128
Tyrrell, Lake, l., Austl. J4 76
Tyrrhenian Sea, Eur. G11 6
Tysa (Tisa) (Tisza), stm., Eur. A10 26
Tysnesøya, i., Nor. F1 8
Tysse, Nor. F1 8
Tytuvėnai, Lith. E6 10
Ty Ty, Ga., U.S. E2 116
Tyva see Tuva, state, Russia D16 32
Tzaneen, S. Afr. C9 70
Tzekung see Zigong, China F5 36
Tzeliutsing see Zigong, China F5 36
Tzucacab, Mex. B3 102
Tzukung see Zigong, China F5 36
Tzupo see Boshan, China C7 42
Tzupo see Zibo, China C8 42

U

Uatumã, stm., Braz. D6 84
Uauá, Braz. E6 88
Uaupés, Braz. H8 86
Uaupés (Vaupés), stm., S.A. G7 86
Uaxactún, hist., Guat. D3 102
Ubá, Braz. K4 88
Ubagan, stm., Kaz. D10 32
Ubaidullaganj, India G6 54
Ubaitaba, Braz. H6 88
Ubajara, Parque Nacional de, p.o.i., Braz. B5 88
Ubangi (Oubangui), stm., Afr. E3 66
Ubatã, Braz. H6 88
Ubaté, Col. E5 86
Ubatuba, Braz. L3 88
Ube, Japan F4 40
Úbeda, Spain F7 20
Uberaba, Braz. J2 88
Uberlândia, Braz. J1 88
Überlingen, Ger. I5 16
Ubiña, Peña, mtn., Spain B4 20
Ubl'a, Slov. H18 16
Ubly, Mi., U.S. E7 112
Ubombo, S. Afr. E11 70
Ubon Ratchathani, Thai. E7 48
Ubrique, Spain H5 20
Ubundu, D.R.C. E5 66
Učaly, Russia D9 32
Učami, Russia B17 32
Učaral, Kaz. E14 32
Ucayali, stm., Peru D3 84
Uchinoura, Japan H4 40
Uchiura-wan, b., Japan C14 38
Uchiza, Peru E2 84
Uchoa, Braz. K1 88
Uckermark, reg., Ger. C9 16
Ucon, Id., U.S. G15 136
Učur, stm., Russia E15 34
Uda, stm., Russia C17 32
Uda, stm., Russia F15 34
Udagamandalam, India F3 53
Udaipur, India F4 54
Udalguri, India E13 54
Udall, Ks., U.S. D11 128
Udamalpet, India F3 53
Udankudi, India G4 53
Udaquiola, Arg. H8 92
Udaypur, Nepal E11 54
Uddevalla, Swe. G4 8
Uddjaur, l., Swe. D8 8
Udgīr, India B3 53
Udhampur, India B5 54
Udimskij, Russia F21 8
Udine, Italy D10 22
Udmurtia see Udmurtija, state, Russia C8 32
Udmurtija, state, Russia C8 32
Udokan, hrebet, mts., Russia E12 34
Udomlja, Russia C17 10
Udon Thani, Thai. D6 48
Udskaja guba, b., Russia F16 34
Udskoe, Russia F15 34
Udupi, India E2 53
Udža, Russia B12 34
Ueckermünde, Ger. C10 16
Ueda, Japan C11 40
Uele, stm., D.R.C. D4 66
Uelen, Russia C26 34
Uel'kal', Russia C25 34
Uelzen, Ger. C6 16
Ueno, Japan E9 40
Uere, stm., D.R.C. D5 66
Uetersen, Ger. C5 16
Ufa, Russia D9 32
Ufa, stm., Russia C9 32
Uffenheim, Ger. G6 16
Ugab, stm., Nmb. E2 68
Uganda, ctry., Afr. D6 66
Ugărčin, Blg. F11 26
Ugarit, hist., Syria C6 58
Ugashik, Ak., U.S. E8 140
Uglegorsk, Russia G17 34
Uglekamensk, Russia C10 38
Uglič, Russia C21 10
Ugljan, Otok, i., Cro. F12 22
Ugodiči, Russia C22 10
Ugodskij Zavod, Russia E19 10
Ugra, stm., Russia F18 10
Uherské Hradiště, Czech Rep. G13 16
Uherský Brod, Czech Rep. H13 16
Uhlenhorst, Nmb. C3 70
Uhra, stm., Russia B22 10
Uhta, Russia F18 8
Uhta, Russia B8 32
Uíge, Ang. B1 68
Uil, Kaz. E8 32
Uinebona, stm., Ven. E10 86
Uinta Mountains, mts., Ut., U.S. C6 132
Uiraúna, Braz. D6 88
Uisŏng, Kor., S. C1 40
Uitenhage, S. Afr. H7 70
Uithuizermeeden, Neth. A15 14
Uj, stm., Asia D10 32
Ujandina, stm., Russia C17 34
Ujar, Russia C16 32
Ujelang, at., Marsh. Is. C7 72
Újfehértó, Hung. B8 26
Ujhāni, India D7 54
Uji, Japan E8 40
Uji-guntō, is., Japan H2 40
Ujiji, Tan. E5 66
Ujjain, India G5 54
Ujung, Indon. G12 50
Ujunggenteng, Indon. G5 50
Ujungkulon National Park, p.o.i., Indon. G4 50
Ujungpandang (Makasar), Indon. F11 50
Uk, Russia C17 32
Uka, Russia E21 34
Ukara Island, i., Tan. E6 66
Ukerewe Island, i., Tan. E6 66
Ukiah, Ca., U.S. D2 134
Uki Ni Masi Island, i., Sol. Is. f9 79b
Ukmergė, Lith. E7 10
Ukraine, ctry., Eur. F15 6
Ukui, Indon. D3 50
Ukyr, Russia G10 34
Ula, Bela. E12 10
Ulaanbaatar, Mong. B6 36
Ulaangom, Mong. G7 34
Ulan, Austl. I7 76
Ulan Bator see Ulaanbaatar, Mong. B6 36
Ulan Buh Shamo, des., China A2 42
Ulan-Burgasy, hrebet, mts., Russia F10 34
Ulanów, Pol. F18 16
Ulansuhai Nur, l., China A3 42
Ulan-Ude, Russia F10 34
Ulawa Island, i., Sol. Is. e9 79b
Ulawun, Mount (The Father), vol., Pap. N. Gui. b5 79a
Ulchin, Kor., S. B2 40
Ulcinj, Yugo. H6 26
Ulco, S. Afr. F7 70
Uldz, stm., Asia B8 36
Uleåborg see Oulu, Fin. D11 8
Ulen, Mn., U.S. D2 118
Ulety, Russia F11 34
Ulëz, Alb. C13 24
Ulhāsnagar, India B1 53
Uliastaj, Mong. B4 36
Ulindi, stm., D.R.C. E5 66
Ulja, Russia E17 34
Uljanovo, Russia G18 10
Uljanovsk, Russia D7 32
Ul'kan, Russia C19 32
Ulla, stm., Spain B2 20
Ulladulla, Austl. J8 76
Ullin, Il., U.S. G8 120
Ullŭng-do, i., Kor., S. B3 40
Ulm, Ger. H5 16
Ulm, Mt., U.S. C15 136
Ulmarra, Austl. G9 76
Ulmeni, Rom. D13 26
Ulóngüè, Moz. C5 68
Ulsan, Kor., S. D2 40
Ulster, hist. reg., Eur. G5 12
Ulster Canal, can., Eur. G5 12
Ulu, Indon. E8 44
Ulu, Russia D14 34
Ulúa, stm., Hond. E3 102
Ulubat Gölü, l., Tur. C11 28
Uluborlu, Tur. E13 28
Uluçınar, Tur. B6 58
Uludağ, mtn., Tur. C12 28
Uludağ Yarımdası Millî Parkı, p.o.i., Tur. C12 28
Ulukışla, Tur. A5 58
Ulul, i., Micron. C5 72
Ulungur, stm., China B2 36
Ulungur Hu, l., China B2 36
Ulunhan, Russia F11 34
Uluru (Ayers Rock), mtn., Austl. E6 74
Ulutau, gory, mts., Kaz. E11 32
Ulverston, Eng., U.K. G9 12
Ulverstone, Austl. n12 77a
Ulysses, Ks., U.S. D7 128
Uma, China F13 34
Umán, Mex. B3 102
Umanak, Grnld. C15 141
Umanak Fjord, b., Grnld. C15 141
Umargāon, India H4 54
Umaria, India G8 54
Umarizal, Braz. C7 88
Umarkot, Pak. F2 54
Umatac, Guam j9 78c
Umatilla, Fl., U.S. H4 116
Umatilla, Or., U.S. E7 136
Umatilla, stm., Or., U.S. E7 136
Umatilla, Lake, res., U.S. E6 136
Umba, Russia C16 8
Umbertide, Italy G9 22
Umboi Island, i., Pap. N. Gui. b4 79a
Umbria, state, Italy G9 22
Umbukul, Pap. N. Gui. a4 79a
Umbuzero, ozero, l., Russia C16 8
Umeå, Swe. E9 8
Umeälven, stm., Swe. D8 8
Umfolozi Game Reserve, S. Afr. F10 70
Umfors, Swe. D6 8
Umfreville Lake, res., On., Can. A3 118
Umkomaas, S. Afr. G10 70
Umm al-Arānib, Libya B2 62
Umm al-Jimāl, Khirbat, hist., Jord. F7 58
Umm al-Qaywayn, U.A.E. D8 56
Umm as-Sa'd, hist., Syria E7 58
Umm Bel, Sudan E5 62
Umm Durmān (Omdurman), Sudan D6 62
Umm el Fahm, Isr. F6 58
Umm Lajj, Sau. Ar. D4 56
Umm Mitmam, sand, Egypt H3 58
Umm Omeiyid, Râs, mtn., Egypt K3 58
Umm Ruwābah, Sudan E6 62
Umm Sayyālah, Sudan E6 62
Umnak Island, i., Ak., U.S. g25 140a
Umpqua, stm., Or., U.S. G3 136
Umpulo, Ang. C2 68
Umrān, Yemen F5 56
Umraniye, Tur. D14 28
Umred, India H7 54
Umreth, India G4 54
Umtata, S. Afr. G9 70
Umuarama, Braz. A11 92
Umzingwani, stm., Zimb. B9 70
Umzinto, S. Afr. G10 70
Una, Braz. H6 88
Una, India H3 54
Una, stm., Eur. E13 22
Unac, stm., Bos. E3 26
Unadilla, Ga., U.S. D2 116
Unadilla, N.Y., U.S. B10 114
Unaí, Braz. I2 88
Unalakleet, Ak., U.S. D7 140
Unalaska, Ak., U.S. F6 140
Unalaska Island, i., Ak., U.S. F6 140
Unare, stm., Ven. C9 86
'Unayzah, Sau. Ar. D5 56
Uncía, Bol. C3 90
Uncompahgre Peak, mtn., Co., U.S. E9 132
Uncompahgre Plateau, plat., Co., U.S. E8 132
Unden, l., Swe. G5 8
Underberg, S. Afr. F9 70
Undva nina, c., Est. B4 10
Uneča, Russia H15 10
Uneiuxi, stm., Braz. H9 86
Unga Island, i., Ak., U.S. E7 140
Ungava, Péninsule d', pen., Qc., Can. D16 106
Ungava Bay, b., Can. D17 106
Ungava Peninsula see Ungava, Péninsule d', pen., Qc., Can. D16 106
Ungch'ŏn, Kor., S. D1 40
Unggi-ŭp, Kor., N. C9 38
Ungheni, Mol. B14 26
União, Braz. C4 88
União dos Palmares, Braz. E7 88
Unicoi, Tn., U.S. H3 114
Uniejów, Pol. D14 16
Unimak Island, i., Ak., U.S. F7 140
Unimak Pass, strt., Ak., U.S. F6 140
Unini, stm., Braz. H11 86
Unión, Arg. G5 92
Unión, Para. B9 92
Union, Ia., U.S. B4 120
Union, La., U.S. G8 122
Union, N.J., U.S. D11 114
Union, Or., U.S. E9 136
Union, S.C., U.S. B4 116
Union, Wa., U.S. C3 136
Union, W.V., U.S. G5 114
Union Bay, B.C., Can. G6 138
Union City, Ga., U.S. D14 122
Union City, Mi., U.S. F4 112
Union City, Oh., U.S. D1 114
Union City, Pa., U.S. C6 114
Union City, Tn., U.S. H8 120
Unión de Reyes, Cuba A7 102
Unión de Tula, Mex. E7 100
Union Flat Creek, stm., U.S. D9 136
Union Grove, Wi., U.S. F1 112
Union Island, i., St. Vin. p10 105e
Union Point, Ga., U.S. C2 116
Union Springs, Al., U.S. E13 122
Uniontown, Al., U.S. E11 122
Uniontown, Ky., U.S. G10 120
Uniontown, Pa., U.S. E6 114
Unionville, Mi., U.S. E6 112
United, Pa., U.S. D6 114
United Arab Emirates, ctry., Asia E7 56
United Arab Republic see Egypt, ctry., Afr. B5 62
United Kingdom, ctry., Eur. D6 6
United States, ctry., N.A. C10 102
Unity, Sk., Can. B4 124
Universal City, Tx., U.S. E9 130
University, Ms., U.S. C9 122
University City, Mo., U.S. F7 120
University Park, N.M., U.S. K10 132
University Park, Tx., U.S. E2 122
Unjha, India G4 54
Unnāo, India E8 54
Uno, Canal Numero, can., Arg. H9 92
Unquillo, Arg. E5 92
Unst, i., Scot., U.K. n19 12a
Unstrut, stm., Ger. E7 16
Unža, stm., Russia G21 8
Unzen-dake, vol., Japan G3 40
Uong Bi, Viet. B8 48
Uozu, Japan C10 40
Upa, stm., Russia G20 10
Upanema, Braz. C7 88
Upata, Ven. C10 86
Upemba, Lac, l., D.R.C. F5 66
Upernavik, Grnld. C14 141
Upía, stm., Col. E5 86
Upington, S. Afr. F5 70
Upland, Ne., U.S. A10 128
Upleta, India H3 54
Upolu, i., Samoa h11 79c
Upolu Point, c., Hi., U.S. C6 78a
Upper Arlington, Oh., U.S. D2 114
Upper Arrow Lake, l., B.C., Can. F13 138
Upper Austria see Oberösterreich, state, Aus. B10 22
Upper Blackville, N.B., Can. D10 110
Upper Darby, Pa., U.S. E10 114
Upper Egypt see El-Sa'īd, hist. reg., Egypt J2 58
Upper Fraser, B.C., Can. B8 138
Upper Ganga Canal (Upper Ganges Canal), can., India D6 54
Upper Iowa, stm., U.S. H7 118
Upper Kapuas Mountains, mts., Asia C8 50
Upper Klamath Lake, l., Or., U.S. H5 136
Upper Lake, Ca., U.S. D3 134
Upper Lake, l., Ca., U.S. B5 134
Upper Manitou Lake, l., On., Can. B5 118
Upper Musquodoboit, N.S., Can. E14 110
Upper Red Lake, l., Mn., U.S. C4 118
Upper Sandusky, Oh., U.S. D2 114
Upper Takutu-Upper Essequibo, state, Guy. F12 86
Upper Trajan's Wall, misc. cult., Mol. C15 26
Upper Volta see Burkina Faso, ctry., Afr. G4 64
Uppsala, Swe. G7 8
Uppsala, state, Swe. F7 8
Upshi, India B6 54
Upton, Ky., U.S. G12 120
Urabá, Golfo de, b., Col. C3 86
Uracoa, Ven. C10 86
Uraj, Russia B10 32
Urakawa, Japan C15 38
Ural, stm. E8 32
Ural Mountains see Ural'skie gory, mts., Russia C9 32
Ural'sk, Kaz. D8 32
Ural'skie gory (Ural Mountains), mts., Russia C9 32
Urana, Austl. J6 76
Urandangi, Austl. D7 74
Urangan, Austl. E9 76
Urania, La., U.S. F6 122
Uranium City, Sk., Can. D9 106
Uraricaá, stm., Braz. F10 86
Uraricoera, Braz. F11 86
Uraricoera, stm., Braz. F11 86
Ura-Tjube, Taj. B10 56
Uravakonda, India D3 53
Uravan, Co., U.S. E8 132
Urawa, Japan D12 40
Urbana, Ar., U.S. D6 122
Urbana, Il., U.S. D9 120
Urbana, Oh., U.S. D2 114
Urbandale, Ia., U.S. C4 120
Urbania, Italy G9 22
Urbino, Italy G9 22
Urcos, Peru F3 84
Urdinarrain, Arg. F8 92
Urdžar, Kaz. E14 32
Ure, stm., Eng., U.K. G11 12
Urėčča, Bela. H10 10
Uren', Russia H21 8
Ureña, Ven. D5 86
Ures, Mex. G7 98
Ureshino, Japan F2 40
Urewera National Park, p.o.i., N.Z. D7 80
Urgenč, Uzb. F10 32
Urho Kekkosen kansallispuisto, p.o.i., Fin. B12 8
Uriah, Al., U.S. F11 122
Uriah, Mount, mtn., N.Z. E4 80
Uribante, stm., Ven. D6 86
Uribe, Col. F4 86
Uribia, Col. B5 86
Urich, Mo., U.S. F4 120
Urickij, Kaz. D11 32
Urique, stm., Mex. B5 100
Urjung-Haja, Russia B11 34
Urjupinsk, Russia D6 32
Urla, Tur. E9 28
Urlați, Rom. D13 26
Urlings, Antig. f4 105b
Urmia see Orūmīyeh, Iran B6 56
Urmia, Lake see Orūmīyeh, Daryācheh-ye, l., Iran B6 56
Uromi, Nig. H6 64
Uroševac, Yugo. G8 26
Urrao, Col. D3 86
Ursa, Il., U.S. D6 120
Uruaçu, Braz. H1 88
Uruapan, Mex. L9 134
Uruapan del Progreso, Mex. F7 100
Urubamba, Peru F3 84
Urubamba, stm., Peru F3 84
Urubaxi, stm., Braz. H9 86
Urubu, stm., Braz. D6 84
Urubu, stm., Braz. F1 88
Uruburetama, Braz. B6 88
Urucará, Braz. D6 84
Urucu, stm., Braz. D5 84
Uruçuca, Braz. H6 88
Uruçuí, Serra da, hills, Braz. E3 88
Urucuia, stm., Braz. I3 88
Uruçuí-preto, stm., Braz. E3 88
Uruguai (Uruguay), stm., S.A. F8 92
Uruguaiana, Braz. D9 92
Uruguay, ctry., S.A. F10 92
Uruguay (Uruguai), stm., S.A. F8 92
Urumchi see Ürümqi, China C2 36
Ürümqi, China C2 36
Urup, ostrov, i., Russia G19 34
Urupês, Braz. K1 88
Urutaí, Braz. I1 88
Uruwira, Tan. F6 66
Urziceni, Rom. E13 26
Uržum, Russia C7 32
Usa, Japan F4 40
Usa, stm., Russia A9 32
Uşak, Tur. E12 28
Uşak, state, Tur. E12 28
Ušaki, Russia A13 10
Usakos, Nmb. B2 70
Usborne, Mount, mtn., Falk. Is. J5 90
Uščerpe, Russia H14 10
U.S. Department of Energy Hanford Site, sci., Wa., U.S. D7 136
Usedom, i., Eur. B10 16
Ushant see Ouessant, Île d', i., Fr. F3 14
Ushashi, Tan. E6 66
Ushtobe see Uštobe, Kaz. E13 32
Ushuaia, Arg. J3 90
Usingen, Ger. F4 16
Usinsk, Russia A9 32
Usk, Wa., U.S. B9 136
Usk, stm., Wales, U.K. J9 12
Uslar, Ger. E5 16
Usmas ezers, l., Lat. C4 10
Usole, Russia C9 32
Usole-Sibirskoe, Russia D18 32
Uspallata, Arg. F3 92
Uspanapa, stm., Mex. G11 100
Ussuri (Wusuli), stm., Asia C11 36
Ussurijsk, Russia C10 38
Ust'-Barguzin, Russia F11 34
Ust'-Belaja, Russia C23 34
Ust'-Bol'šereck, Russia F20 34
Ust'-Čaun, Russia C23 34
Ust'-Chorna, Ukr. A11 26
Ust'-Cil'ma, Russia D25 8
Uste, Russia B13 32
Uster, Switz. C5 22
Ustica, Isola di, i., Italy F7 24
Ust'-Ilimsk, Russia C18 32
Ust'-Ilimskoe vodohranilišče, res., Russia C18 32
Ústí nad Labem, Czech Rep. F10 16
Ústí nad Orlicí, Czech Rep. G12 16
Ust'-Išim, Russia C12 32
Ustja, stm., Russia F21 8
Ust'-Javron'ga, Russia E21 8
Ustjuckoe, Russia B18 10
Ustjužna, Russia B19 10
Ustka, Pol. B12 16
Ust'-Kamčatsk, Russia E21 34
Ust'-Kamenogorsk, Kaz. E14 32
Ust'-Koksa, Russia D15 32
Ust'-Kujda, Russia B16 34
Ust'-Kulom, Russia B8 32
Ust'-Kut, Russia C19 32
Ust'-Lyža, Russia A9 32
Ust'-Maja, Russia D15 34
Ust'-Man'ja, Russia B10 32
Ust'-Nera, Russia D17 34
Ust'-Njukža, Russia E13 34
Uštobe, Kaz. E13 32
Ust'-Omčug, Russia D18 34
Ust'-Ordynskij, Russia D18 32
Ust'-Ozërnoe, Russia C15 32
Ust'-Pinega, Russia D19 8
Ust'-Reki, Russia E23 8
Ustroń, Pol. G14 16
Ust'-Sumy, Russia D14 32
Ust'-Tym, Russia D24 6
Ust'-Ulagan, Russia D15 32
Ust'-Urgal, Russia F15 34
Ust-Urt Plateau, plat., Asia F9 32
Ust-Vyjskaja, Russia E22 8
Usu, China C1 36
Usuki, Japan F4 40
Usulután, El Sal. F3 102
Usumacinta, stm., N.A. D2 102
Usumbura see Bujumbura, Bdi. E5 66
Ušumun, Russia F14 34
Usvjaty, Russia E13 10
Utah, state, U.S. D5 132
Utah Lake, l., Ut., U.S. C5 132
Utata, Russia D18 32
Ute, Ia., U.S. B2 120
Ute Creek, stm., N.M., U.S. F5 128
Utegi, Tan. E6 66
Utena, Lith. E8 10
Utete, Tan. F7 66
Uthai Thani, Thai. E4 48
Uthal, Pak. D10 56
U Thong, Thai. E4 48
Utiariti, Braz. F6 84
Utica, Ks., U.S. C8 128
Utica, Mi., U.S. F6 112
Utica, Ms., U.S. E8 122
Utica, N.Y., U.S. E14 112
Utica, Oh., U.S. D3 114
Utica see Utique, hist., Tun. G3 24
Utiel, Spain E9 20
Utila, Isla de, i., Hond. D4 102
Utinga, stm., Braz. G5 88
Utique (Utica), hist., Tun. G3 24
Uto, Japan G3 40
Utopia, Tx., U.S. E8 130
Utorgoš, Russia B13 10
Utraula, India E9 54
Utrecht, Neth. B14 14
Utrecht, S. Afr. E10 70
Utrera, Spain G5 20
Utrik, at., Marsh. Is. B7 72
Utroja, stm., Eur. D10 10
Utsunomiya, Japan C12 40
Uttamapālaiyam, India G3 53
Uttaradit, Thai. D4 48
Uttarkāshi, India C7 54
Uttar Pradesh, state, India E7 54
Utuado, P.R. B2 104a
Utukok, stm., Ak., U.S. C7 140
Utupua, i., Sol. Is. E7 72
Uulu, Est. B7 10
Uusimaa, state, Fin. F11 8
Uvá, stm., Col. F7 86
Uvalda, Ga., U.S. D3 116
Uvalde, Tx., U.S. E8 130
Uvaravičy, Bela. H13 10
Uvarovo, Russia D6 32
Uvdal, Nor. F3 8
Uvinza, Tan. F6 66
Uvira, D.R.C. E5 66
Uvs Lake see Uvsu-Nur, ozero, l., Asia F7 34
Uvsu-Nur, ozero, l., Asia F7 34
Uvworé, c., Vanuatu l17 79d
Uwa, Japan F5 40
Uwajima, Japan F5 40
Uwayl, Sudan F5 62
Uxbridge, On., Can. D10 112
Uxmal, hist., Mex. B3 102
Uyo, Nig. H6 64
Uyuni, Bol. D3 90
Uyuni, Salar de, pl., Bol. D3 90
Uzbekistan, ctry., Asia E10 30
Uzda, Bela. G10 10
Uzerche, Fr. D7 18
Uzgen, Kyrg. F12 32
Uzhhorod, Ukr. A9 26
Užice, Yugo. F6 26
Uzlovaja, Russia F20 10
Üzümlü, Tur. G12 28
Uzun Ada, i., Tur. E9 28
Uzunköprü, Tur. B9 28
Uzunkuduk, Uzb. F11 32
Užur, Russia C16 32
Užventis, Lith. E5 10

V

Vaal, stm., S. Afr. F7 70
Vaaldam, res., S. Afr. E8 70
Vaalwater, S. Afr. D8 70
Vaasa (Vasa), Fin. E9 8
Vaasa, state, Fin. E10 8
Vabalninkas, Lith. D7 10
Vác, Hung. B6 26
Vacacaí, stm., Braz. E11 92
Vacaria, Braz. D12 92
Vacaria, stm., Braz. I4 88
Vacaville, Ca., U.S. E4 134
Vaccarès, Étang de, l., Fr. F10 18
Vache, Île à, i., Haiti C11 102
Vad, Russia I21 8
Vadakara see Badagara, India F2 53
Vădeni, Rom. D14 26
Vadnagar, India G4 54
Vado, N.M., U.S. K10 132
Vadodara (Baroda), India G4 54
Vado Ligure, Italy F5 22
Vadsø, Nor. A13 8
Vaduz, Liech. C6 22
Vaga, stm., Russia F20 8
Vågåmo, Nor. F3 8
Vágar, i., Far. Is. m34 8b
Vaghena Island, i., Sol. Is. d7 79b
Vah, stm., Russia B13 32
Váh, stm., Slov. H13 16
Vahsel, Cape, c., S. Geor. J9 90
Vaiden, Ms., U.S. D9 122
Vaigai, stm., India G4 53
Vaigat, strt., Grnld. C15 141
Vaijāpur, India B2 53
Vaikam, India G3 53
Väike-Maarja, Est. A9 10
Vail, Co., U.S. D10 132
Vail, Ia., U.S. B2 120
Vaimali, Vanuatu k17 79d
Vaippār, stm., India G4 53
Vaison-la-Romaine, Fr. E11 18
Vaitahu, Fr. Poly. s18 78g
Vākhān, hist. reg., Afg. B11 56
Valaam, Russia F14 8
Valadeces, Mex. H9 130
Valandovo, Mac. B5 28
Valašské Meziříčí, Czech Rep. G13 16
Valatie, N.Y., U.S. B12 114
Vâlcea, state, Rom. E11 26
Vălčedrăm, Blg. F10 26
Valcheta, Arg. H3 90
Valdagno, Italy E8 22
Valdai Hills see Valdajskaja vozvyšennost', hills, Russia C15 10
Valdaj, Russia E16 8
Valdaj, Russia B16 10
Valdajskaja vozvyšennost' (Valdai Hills), hills, Russia C15 10
Valdarno, val., Italy G8 22
Val-de-Cães, Braz. A1 88
Valdecañas, Embalse de, res., Spain E5 20
Valdemarsvik, Swe. G7 8
Valdepeñas, Spain F7 20
Valderaduey, stm., Spain C5 20
Valdés, Península, pen., Arg. H4 90
Val-des-Bois, Qc., Can. C14 112
Valdez, Ak., U.S. D10 140
Valdivia, Chile G2 90

Name	Map Ref.	Page
Valdivia, Col.	D4	86
Valdobbiadene, Italy	E8	22
Val-d'Oise, state, Fr.	E10	14
Val-d'Or, Qc., Can.	F15	106
Valdosta, Ga., U.S.	F2	116
Valdoviño see Aviño, Spain	A2	20
Vale, Or., U.S.	G9	136
Valemount, B.C., Can.	D11	138
Valença, Braz.	L4	88
Valença, Braz.	G6	88
Valença, Port.	B2	20
Valença do Piauí, Braz.	D4	88
Valence, Fr.	E10	18
Valencia, Phil.	F5	52
València, Spain	E10	20
Valencia, Ven.	B7	86
València, state, Spain	E10	20
València, co., Spain	E10	20
València, Golf de, b., Spain	E10	20
Valencia, Golfo de see València, Golf de, b., Spain	E10	20
Valencia, Gulf of see València, Golf de, b., Spain	E10	20
Valencia, Lago de, l., Ven.	B8	86
Valencia de Alcántara, Spain	E3	20
Valencia de Don Juan, Spain	B5	20
Valencia Island, i., Ire.	J2	12
Valenciennes, Fr.	D12	14
Valente, Braz.	F6	88
Valentin, Russia	C11	38
Valentine, Ne., U.S.	E12	126
Valentine, Tx., U.S.	D3	130
Valenza, Italy	F5	22
Valera, Ven.	C6	86
Valga, Est.	H12	8
Valiente, Península, pen., Pan.	H7	102
Valili, mtn., Fiji	p19	79e
Valjevo, Yugo.	E6	26
Valkeakoski, Fin.	F11	8
Valkenswaard, Neth.	C14	14
Valkininkas, Lith.	F7	10
Valladares, Mex.	H7	130
Valladolid, Mex.	B3	102
Valladolid, Spain	C6	20
Valladolid, co., Spain	C6	20
Vall de Uxó see La Vall d'Uixó, Spain	E10	20
Valle, Lat.	D7	10
Vallecillo, Mex.	H7	130
Valle d'Aosta, state, Italy	E4	22
Valle de Allende, Mex.	H2	130
Valle de la Pascua, Ven.	C8	86
Valle del Cauca, state, Col.	F3	86
Valle del Rosario, Mex.	G1	130
Valle de Olivos, Mex.	B5	100
Valle de Santiago, Mex.	E8	100
Valledupar, Col.	B5	86
Vallée d'Aoste see Valle d'Aosta, state, Italy	E4	22
Valle Edén, Ur.	E9	92
Vallegrande, Bol.	C4	90
Valle Hermoso, Mex.	C10	100
Vallejo, Ca., U.S.	E3	134
Vallenar, Chile	D2	92
Valle Redondo, Mex.	K9	134
Valletta, Malta	I8	24
Valley, Al., U.S.	E13	122
Valley, Ne., U.S.	C1	120
Valley, Wa., U.S.	B9	136
Valley, stm., Mb., Can.	C13	124
Valley Bend, W.V., U.S.	F6	114
Valley City, N.D., U.S.	H16	124
Valley East, On., Can.	B8	112
Valley Falls, Ks., U.S.	E2	120
Valley Farms, Az., U.S.	K5	132
Valley Head, Al., U.S.	C13	122
Valley Mills, Tx., U.S.	C10	130
Valley of the Kings, hist., Egypt	B6	62
Valley Springs, S.D., U.S.	H2	118
Valley Station, Ky., U.S.	F12	120
Valleyview, Ab., Can.	A13	138
Valley View, Tx., U.S.	H11	128
Vallimanca, Arroyo, stm., Arg.	H7	92
Valiorbe, Switz.	D3	22
Valls, Spain	C12	20
Valmeyer, Il., U.S.	F7	120
Valmiera, Lat.	C8	10
Valoria la Buena, Spain	C6	20
Valožyn, Bela.	F9	10
Vālpārai, India	F3	53
Valparaíso, Chile	F2	92
Valparaíso, Mex.	D7	100
Valparaiso, Fl., U.S.	G12	122
Valparaiso, In., U.S.	G2	112
Valparaiso, Ne., U.S.	F16	126
Valparaíso, state, Chile	F2	92
Valréas, Fr.	E10	18
Vals, stm., S. Afr.	E8	70
Vals, Tanjung, c., Indon.	G10	44
Valsbaai see False Bay, b., S. Afr.	I4	70
Valtimo, Fin.	E13	8
Valujki, Russia	D5	32
Valverde del Camino, Spain	G4	20
Valyncy, Bela.	E11	10
Vamori Wash, stm., Az., U.S.	L5	132
Van, Tur.	B5	56
Van, Lake see Van Gölü, l., Tur.	B5	56
Vanadzor, Arm.	A5	56
Vanajavesi, l., Fin.	F10	8
Van Alstyne, Tx., U.S.	D2	122
Vananda, B.C., Can.	G6	138
Vanavara, Russia	B18	32
Van Bruyssel, Qc., Can.	C4	110
Van Buren, Ar., U.S.	B4	122
Van Buren, Me., U.S.	C8	110
Vanceboro, Me., U.S.	E9	110
Vanceburg, Ky., U.S.	F2	114
Vancouver, B.C., Can.	G7	138
Vancouver, Wa., U.S.	E4	136
Vancouver Island, i., B.C., Can.	G4	138
Vancouver Island Ranges, mts., B.C., Can.	G5	138
Vandalia, Il., U.S.	F8	120
Vandalia, Mo., U.S.	E6	120
Vandalia, Oh., U.S.	E1	114
Vandavāsi, India	E4	53
Vanderbijlpark, S. Afr.	E8	70
Vanderbilt, Tx., U.S.	F11	130
Vanderhoof, B.C., Can.	B6	138
Vanderkloof Dam, res., S. Afr.	F7	70
Vanderlin Island, i., Austl.	C7	74
Vandervoort, Ar., U.S.	C4	122
Van Diemen Gulf, b., Austl.	B6	74
Vandry, Qc., Can.	C3	110
Vandžiogala, Lith.	E6	10
Vanegas, Mex.	D8	100
Vänern, l., Swe.	G5	8
Vänersborg, Swe.	G5	8
Vangaindrano, Madag.	E8	68
Van Gölü, l., Tur.	B5	56
Vangunu Island, i., Sol. Is.	e8	79b
Van Horn, Tx., U.S.	C3	130
Van Horne, Ia., U.S.	B5	120
Vanier, On., Can.	C14	112
Vanikolo, i., Sol. Is.	E7	72
Vanimo, Pap. N. Gui.	a3	79a
Vanino, Russia	G17	34
Vānīvilāsa Sāgara, res., India	E3	53
Vāniyambādi, India	E4	53
Vankarem, Russia	C25	34
Vankleek Hill, On., Can.	E2	110
Van Lear, Ky., U.S.	G3	114
Vanna, i., Nor.	A8	8
Vännäs, Swe.	E8	8
Vanndale, Ar., U.S.	B8	122
Vannes, Fr.	G6	14
Van Ninh, Viet.	F9	48
Van Phong, Vung, b., Viet.	F9	48
Van Phong Bay see Van Phong, Vung, b., Viet.	F9	48
Van Reenen, S. Afr.	F9	70
Van Rees, Pegunungan, mts., Indon.	F10	44
Vanrhynsdorp, S. Afr.	G4	70
Vansant, Va., U.S.	G3	114
Vansittart Island, i., Nu., Can.	B14	106
Vanskoe, Russia	B19	10
Vanthali, India	H3	54
Vanua Balavu, i., Fiji	p20	79e
Vanua Lava, i., Vanuatu	i16	79d
Vanua Levu, i., Fiji	p19	79e
Vanuatu (New Hebrides), ctry., Oc.	k16	79d
Van Wert, Oh., U.S.	D1	114
Van Wyksdorp, S. Afr.	H5	70
Van Zylsrus, S. Afr.	E6	70
Vao, N. Cal.	n16	79d
Var, state, Fr.	F12	18
Var, stm., Fr.	F13	18
Varada, stm., India	D2	53
Varallo, Italy	E5	22
Vārānasi (Benares), India	F9	54
Varandej, Russia	A9	32
Varangerfjorden, b., Nor.	A14	8
Varangerhalvøya, pen., Nor.	A13	8
Varano, Lago di, l., Italy	I12	22
Varaždin, Cro.	D13	22
Varazze, Italy	F5	22
Varberg, Swe.	H5	8
Vardak, state, Afg.	A2	54
Vardar (Axiós), stm., Eur.	B5	28
Varde, Den.	I3	8
Vardø, Nor.	A14	8
Varel, Ger.	C4	16
Varela, Arg.	G4	92
Varėna, Lith.	F7	10
Varennes-sur-Allier, Fr.	C9	18
Varese, Italy	E5	22
Vârfurile, Rom.	C9	26
Vargem, Riacho da, stm., Braz.	E6	88
Vargem Grande, Braz.	B3	88
Varginha, Braz.	K3	88
Varkallai, India	G3	53
Varkaus, Fin.	E12	8
Värmeln, l., Swe.	G5	8
Värmland, state, Swe.	G5	8
Varna, Blg.	F14	26
Varna, Russia	D10	32
Varna, state, Blg.	F14	26
Värnamo, Swe.	H6	8
Varniai, Lith.	E5	10
Varnjany, Bela.	F9	10
Varnsdorf, Czech Rep.	F10	16
Varnville, S.C., U.S.	D4	116
Várpalota, Hung.	B5	26
Värska, Est.	C10	10
Varvarin, Yugo.	F8	26
Várzea, stm., Braz.	C11	92
Várzea Alegre, Braz.	D6	88
Várzea da Palma, Braz.	I3	88
Várzea Grande, Braz.	G6	84
Varzino, Russia	B17	8
Vas, state, Hung.	B3	26
Vasa see Vaasa, Fin.	E9	8
Vasa see Vaasa, state, Fin.	E10	8
Vasai, India	E3	46
Vasalemma, Est.	A7	10
Vasco, País see Euskal Herriko, state, Spain	A8	20
Vashkivtsi, Ukr.	A12	26
Vashkivtsi, Ukr.	A14	26
Vashon Island, i., Wa., U.S.	C4	136
Vasilevičy, Bela.	H12	10
Vasilevskij Moh, Russia	C18	10
Vasiliká, Grc.	C6	28
Vasjugan, stm., Russia	C13	32
Vaška, stm., Russia	D21	8
Vaskelovo, Russia	F14	8
Vaslui, Rom.	C14	26
Vaslui, state, Rom.	C14	26
Vass, N.C., U.S.	A6	116
Vassar, Mi., U.S.	E6	112
Västerås, Swe.	G7	8
Västerbotten, state, Swe.	D8	8
Västernorrland, state, Swe.	E7	8
Västervik, Swe.	H7	8
Västmanland, state, Swe.	G7	8
Vasto, Italy	H11	22
Västra Götaland, state, Swe.	G4	8
Vasvár, Hung.	B3	26
Vatan, Fr.	G10	14
Vatican see Vatican City, ctry., Eur.	I9	22
Vatican City, ctry., Eur.	I9	22
Vaticano, Capo, c., Italy	F9	24
Vatnajökull, ice, Ice.	k31	8a
Vatomandry, Madag.	D8	68
Vatra Dornei, Rom.	B12	26
Vättern, l., Swe.	G6	8
Vatu-i-ra Channel, strt., Fiji	p19	79e
Vatukoula, Fiji	p18	79e
Vauclin, Montagne du, mtn., Mart.	k7	105c
Vaucluse, state, Fr.	F11	18
Vaucouleurs, Fr.	F14	14
Vaughan, On., Can.	E10	112
Vaughn, N.M., U.S.	G3	128
Vaukavysk, Bela.	G7	10
Vaupés, state, Col.	G6	86
Vaupés (Uaupés), stm., S.A.	G7	86
Vava'u, i., Tonga	E9	72
Vavoua, C. Iv.	H3	64
Vavuniya, Sri L.	G5	53
Växjö, Swe.	H6	8
Vaza-barris, stm., Braz.	E6	88
Vazante, Braz.	J2	88
Vazuza, stm., Russia	E17	10
Vazuzskoe vodohranilišče, res., Russia	E16	10
Veazie, Me., U.S.	F8	110
Veblen, S.D., U.S.	B15	126
Vecht (Vechte), stm., Eur.	B15	14
Vechta, Ger.	D4	16
Vechte (Vecht), stm., Eur.	B15	14
Vecpiebalga, Lat.	C8	10
Vecsés, Hung.	B6	26
Veddige, Swe.	H4	8
Vedea, stm., Rom.	F12	26
Vedia, Arg.	G7	92
Vednoe, Russia	C19	10
Veedersburg, In., U.S.	H2	112
Veendam, Neth.	A15	14
Veenendaal, Neth.	C14	14
Vega, i., Nor.	D4	8
Vega Alta, P.R.	B3	104a
Vega Baja, P.R.	B3	104a
Vegreville, Ab., Can.	C18	138
Veguita, N.M., U.S.	I10	132
Veinticinco de Mayo, Arg.	G7	92
Veiros, Braz.	D7	84
Veisiejai, Lith.	F6	10
Vejle, Den.	I3	8
Vejle, state, Den.	I3	8
Vela Luka, Cro.	H13	22
Velas, Cabo, c., C.R.	G4	102
Velázquez, Ur.	G10	92
Velden, Ger.	H8	16
Veleka, stm.	G14	26
Veleuščina, Bela.	F11	10
Vélez, Col.	D5	86
Vélez-Málaga, Spain	H6	20
Vel'gija, Russia	B17	10
Velhas, stm., Braz.	I3	88
Velikaja, stm., Russia	C11	10
Velikaja, stm., Russia	D23	34
Velikaja Kema, Russia	B12	38
Velika Morava, stm., Yugo.	E8	26
Velikie Luki, Russia	D13	10
Velikij Ustjug, Russia	F21	8
Veliki Vitorog, mtn., Bos.	E4	26
Velikoe, Russia	G17	8
Velikoe, ozero, l., Russia	C19	10
Velikonda Hills, hills, India	D4	53
Veliko Tărnovo, Blg.	F12	26
Velikovisočnoe, Russia	C25	8
Veli Lošinj, Cro.	F11	22
Vélingara, Sen.	G2	64
Veliž, Russia	E14	10
Vel'ké Kapušany, Slov.	H18	16
Velké Meziříčí, Czech Rep.	G12	16
Vella Gulf, strt., Sol. Is.	d7	79b
Vella Lavella, i., Sol. Is.	d7	79b
Vellār, stm., India	F4	53
Velletri, Italy	I9	22
Vellore, India	E4	53
Velma, Ok., U.S.	G11	128
Vel'sk, Russia	F20	8
Velten, Ger.	D9	16
Velva, N.D., U.S.	F13	124
Velyka Mykhailivka, Ukr.	B16	26
Velykodolyns'ke, Ukr.	C17	26
Velykoplos'ke, Ukr.	C16	26
Velykyi Bychkiv, Ukr.	B11	26
Velykyj Kuialnyk, stm., Ukr.	B17	26
Venadillo, Col.	E4	86
Venado Tuerto, Arg.	F6	92
Venafro, Italy	C8	24
Venâncio Aires, Braz.	D11	92
Vence, Fr.	F13	18
Venda, hist. reg., S. Afr.	C10	70
Vendas Novas, Port.	F2	20
Vendée, state, Fr.	C4	18
Vendéen, Bocage, reg., Fr.	C4	18
Vendôme, Fr.	G10	14
Vendrell see El Vendrell, Spain	C12	20
Veneta, Laguna, b., Italy	E9	22
Venetie, Ak., U.S.	C10	140
Veneto, state, Italy	E8	22
Venev, Russia	F21	10
Venézia (Venice), Italy	E9	22
Venezuela, ctry., S.A.	B4	84
Venezuela, Golfo de, b., S.A.	A3	84
Venezuela, Gulf of see Venezuela, Golfo de, b., S.A.	A3	84
Venezuelan Basin, unds.	G7	144
Vengerovo, Russia	C13	32
Vengurla, India	D1	53
Veniaminof, Mount, vol., Ak., U.S.	E8	140
Venice see Venézia, Italy	E9	22
Venice, Fl., U.S.	I3	116
Venice, La., U.S.	H9	122
Venice, Gulf of, b., Eur.	E9	22
Vénissieux, Fr.	D10	18
Venkatagiri, India	E4	53
Venlo, Neth.	C15	14
Venosa, Italy	D9	24
Venoste, Alpi (Ötztaler Alpen), mts., Eur.	D7	22
Venray, Neth.	C15	14
Venta, stm., Eur.	C4	10
Ventanas, Ec.	H2	86
Ventersdorp, S. Afr.	E8	70
Venterstad, S. Afr.	G7	70
Ventimiglia, Italy	G4	22
Ventotene, Isola, i., Italy	D7	24
Ventspils, Lat.	C4	10
Ventuari, stm., Ven.	E8	86
Ventura, Ca., U.S.	I6	134
Venturia, N.D., U.S.	B13	126
Venustiano Carranza, Mex.	G12	100
Venustiano Carranza, Presa, res., Mex.	B8	100
Vera, Arg.	D7	92
Vera, Spain	G9	20
Vera, Cape, c., Nu., Can.	B8	141
Veracruz, Mex.	F10	100
Veracruz, state, Mex.	F10	100
Veranópolis, Braz.	D12	92
Verāval, India	H3	54
Verbania, Italy	E5	22
Verbano see Maggiore, Lago, l., Eur.	C14	18
Verbeek, Pegunungan, mts., Indon.	E12	50
Verbilki, Russia	D20	10
Vercelli, Italy	E5	22
Vercors, reg., Fr.	E11	18
Verde, stm., Braz.	F6	84
Verde, stm., Braz.	F4	88
Verde, stm., Braz.	J1	88
Verde, stm., Braz.	H1	88
Verde, stm., Braz.	D4	90
Verde, stm., Mex.	E7	100
Verde, stm., Az., U.S.	J5	132
Verde, Cape, c., Bah.	A10	102
Verde Grande, stm., Braz.	H4	88
Verden, Ger.	D5	16
Verden, Ok., U.S.	F10	128
Verde Pequeno, stm., Braz.	H4	88
Verdi, Nv., U.S.	D5	134
Verdigre, Ne., U.S.	E14	126
Verdigris, stm., U.S.	E13	128
Verdon, stm., Fr.	F12	18
Verdun, Qc., Can.	E3	110
Verdun-sur-Garonne, Fr.	F7	18
Verdun-sur-Meuse, Fr.	E14	14
Vereeniging, S. Afr.	E9	70
Veregin, Sk., Can.	C11	124
Vereja, Russia	E19	10
Vereščagino, Russia	B15	32
Vergemont Creek, stm., Austl.	D4	76
Vergennes, Vt., U.S.	F3	110
Verhnedneprovskij, Russia	E16	10
Verhneimbatsk, Russia	B15	32
Verhnemulomskoe vodohranilišče, res., Russia	B14	8
Verhneural'sk, Russia	D9	32
Verhneviljujsk, Russia	D13	34
Verhnij Baskunčak, Russia	E7	32
Verhnij Most, Russia	C11	10
Verhnij Ufalej, Russia	C10	32
Verhnjaja Amga, Russia	E14	34
Verhnjaja Angara, stm., Russia	E11	34
Verhnjaja Inta, Russia	A10	32
Verhnjaja Salda, Russia	C10	32
Verhnjaja Tajmyra, stm., Russia	B8	34
Verhnjaja Tojma, Russia	E21	8
Verhojansk, Russia	C15	34
Verhojanskij hrebet (Verkhoyansk Mountains), mts., Russia	C14	34
Verhopuja, Russia	F19	8
Verhove, Russia	H20	10
Verigin see Veregin, Sk., Can.	C11	124
Verín, Spain	C3	20
Veríssimo, Braz.	J1	88
Verkhovyna, Ukr.	A11	26
Verkhoyansk Mountains see Verhojanskij hrebet, mts., Russia	C14	34
Vermelho, stm., Braz.	E2	88
Vermilion, Oh., U.S.	C3	114
Vermilion, stm., Ab., Can.	C19	138
Vermilion, stm., On., Can.	B8	112
Vermilion, stm., Mn., U.S.	C6	118
Vermilion Bay, b., La., U.S.	H6	122
Vermilion Lake, l., On., Can.	A6	118
Vermilion Lake, l., Mn., U.S.	D5	118
Vermilion Pass, p., Can.	E14	138
Vermillion, S.D., U.S.	E16	126
Vermillion, stm., S.D., U.S.	E15	126
Vermillion, East Fork, stm., S.D., U.S.	D15	126
Vermillon, stm., Qc., Can.	C3	110
Vermont, Il., U.S.	D7	120
Vermont, state, U.S.	F4	110
Vernal, Ut., U.S.	C7	132
Verndale, Mn., U.S.	E3	118
Verneuil, Fr.	F9	14
Vernon, B.C., Can.	F11	138
Vernon, Fr.	E10	14
Vernon, Al., U.S.	D10	122
Vernon, Ct., U.S.	C13	114
Vernon, In., U.S.	F12	120
Vernon, Tx., U.S.	G9	128
Vernon, Ut., U.S.	C4	132
Vernonia, Or., U.S.	E3	136
Vernon Lake, res., La., U.S.	F5	122
Vernon River, P.E., Can.	D13	110
Vero Beach, Fl., U.S.	I5	116
Véroia, Grc.	C5	28
Verona, On., Can.	D13	112
Verona, Italy	E8	22
Verona, Ms., U.S.	C10	122
Verónica, Arg.	G9	92
Versailles, Fr.	F11	14
Versailles, Il., U.S.	E7	120
Versailles, Ky., U.S.	F13	120
Versailles, Mo., U.S.	F5	120
Versailles, Oh., U.S.	D1	114
Veršino-Darasunskij, Russia	F12	34
Veršino-Šahtaminskij, Russia	F12	34
Vertedero, P.R.	B3	104a
Vertientes, Cuba	B8	102
Verulam, S. Afr.	F10	70
Verviers, Bel.	D14	14
Verwoerd Reservoir see Gariep Dam, res., S. Afr.	G7	70
Vescovato, Fr.	G15	18
Veselí nad Lužnicí, Czech Rep.	G10	16
Vesëlyj Jar, Russia	C11	38
Vesole, Monte, mtn., Italy	D9	24
Vesoul, Fr.	G15	14
Vespasiano, Braz.	J4	88
Vesta, C.R.	H6	102
Vest-Agder, state, Nor.	G2	8
Vestavia Hills, Al., U.S.	D12	122
Vesterålen, is., Nor.	B6	8
Vestfjorden, b., Nor.	C5	8
Vestfold, state, Nor.	G4	8
Vestgrønland (Kitaa), state, Grnld.	D16	141
Vestmannaeyjar, Ice.	I29	8a
Vestsjælland, state, Den.	I4	8
Vestvågøya, i., Nor.	B5	8
Vesuvio (Vesuvius), vol., Italy	D8	24
Vesuvius see Vesuvio, vol., Italy	D8	24
Veszprém, Hung.	B4	26
Veszprém, state, Hung.	B4	26
Vésztő, Hung.	C8	26
Vet, stm., S. Afr.	F8	70
Vetapālem, India	D5	53
Vetju, Russia	E24	8
Vetlanda, Swe.	H6	8
Vetluga, Russia	H21	8
Vetluga, stm., Russia	C7	32
Vetlužskij, Russia	G21	8
Vetlužskij, Russia	H21	8
Vetrișoaia, Rom.	C15	26
Vetschau, Ger.	E9	16
Veurne, Bel.	C11	14
Vevey, Switz.	D3	22
Veynes, Fr.	E11	18
Vézère, stm., Fr.	D7	18
Viacha, Bol.	C3	90
Viadana, Italy	F7	22
Viale, Arg.	E8	92
Viamão, Braz.	E12	92
Viamonte, Arg.	F6	92
Vian, Ok., U.S.	B4	122
Viana, Braz.	B3	88
Viana do Bolo, Spain	B3	20
Viana do Castelo, Port.	C1	20
Viana do Castelo, state, Port.	C2	20
Viangchan (Vientiane), Laos	D6	48
Viareggio, Italy	G7	22
Vibank, Sk., Can.	D10	124
Viborg, Den.	H3	8
Viborg, S.D., U.S.	D15	126
Viborg, state, Den.	H3	8
Vibo Valentia, Italy	F10	24
Vic, Spain	C13	20
Vícam, Mex.	B3	100
Vicebsk, Bela.	E13	10
Vicebsk, state, Bela.	E11	10
Vicente Guerrero, Mex.	D6	100
Vicente Guerrero, Presa, res., Mex.	D9	100
Vicenza, Italy	E8	22
Viceroy, Sk., Can.	E8	124
Vich see Vic, Spain	C13	20
Vichada, state, Col.	E7	86
Vichada, stm., Col.	E7	86
Vichadero, Ur.	E10	92
Vichra, stm., Eur.	F14	10
Vichuquén, Chile	G1	92
Vichy, Fr.	C9	18
Vici, Ok., U.S.	E9	128
Vicksburg, Ms., U.S.	E8	122
Viçosa, Braz.	K4	88
Viçosa do Ceará, Braz.	B5	88
Vic-sur-Cère, Fr.	E8	18
Victor, Id., U.S.	G15	136
Victor, Ia., U.S.	C5	120
Victor, Mt., U.S.	D12	136
Victor Harbor, Austl.	J2	76
Victoria, Arg.	F7	92
Victoria, B.C., Can.	H7	138
Victoria, P.E., Can.	D13	110
Victoria, Chile	I1	92
Victoria see Labuan, Malay.	A9	50
Victoria see Rabat, Malta	H8	24
Victoria, Sey.	j13	69b
Victoria, Ks., U.S.	C9	128
Victoria, Tx., U.S.	F11	130
Victoria, Va., U.S.	G7	114
Victoria, state, Austl.	K4	76
Victoria, stm., Austl.	C6	74
Victoria, Chutes see Victoria Falls, wtfl, Afr.	D4	68
Victoria, Lake, l., Afr.	E6	66
Victoria, Lake, l., Austl.	I3	76
Victoria, Mount, mtn., Mya.	B1	48
Victoria, Mount, mtn., Pap. N. Gui.	b4	79a
Victoria Falls, wtfl, Afr.	D4	68
Victoria Fjord, b., Grnld.	A16	141
Victoria Harbour, On., Can.	D10	112
Victoria Island, i., Can.	A8	106
Victoria Land, reg., Ant.	C20	81
Victoria Nile, stm., Afr.	D6	66
Victoria Peak, mtn., Belize	D3	102
Victoria Peak, mtn., B.C., Can.	F4	138
Victoria River Downs, Austl.	C6	74
Victorias, Phil.	E4	52
Victoria Strait, strt., Nu., Can.	B10	106
Victoriaville, Qc., Can.	D4	110
Victoria West, S. Afr.	G6	70
Victorica, Arg.	H5	92
Victorino, Ven.	F8	86
Victorville, Ca., U.S.	I8	134
Vičuga, Russia	H19	8
Vicuña, Chile	E2	92
Vicuña Mackenna, Arg.	F5	92
Vidalia, Ga., U.S.	D3	116
Vidalia, La., U.S.	F7	122
Vidal Ramos, Braz.	C13	92
Videira, Braz.	C12	92
Vidigueira, Port.	F3	20
Vidin, Blg.	E9	26
Vidisha, India	G6	54
Vidor, Tx., U.S.	G4	122
Viđoy, i., Far. Is.	m34	8b
Vidra, Rom.	E13	26
Vidsel, Swe.	D9	8
Vidzeme, hist. reg., Lat.	C8	10
Viechtach, Ger.	G8	16
Viedma, Arg.	H4	90
Viedma, Lago, l., Arg.	I2	90
Vieille Case, Dom.	i6	105c
Viejo, Cerro, mtn., Peru	D2	84
Viella, Spain	B11	20
Vienna see Wien, Aus.	B13	22
Vienna, Ga., U.S.	D2	116
Vienna, Il., U.S.	G9	120
Vienna, Mo., U.S.	F5	120
Vienna, W.V., U.S.	E4	114
Vienna see Wien, state, Aus.	B13	22
Vienna Woods see Wienerwald, mts., Aus.	B13	22
Vienne, Fr.	D10	18
Vienne, state, Fr.	C6	18
Vienne, stm., Fr.	C6	18
Vientiane see Viangchan, Laos	D6	48
Vieques, P.R.	B5	104a
Vieques, Aeropuerto, P.R.	B5	104a
Vieques, Isla de, i., P.R.	B5	104a
Vieremä, Fin.	E12	8
Vierwaldstätter See (Lucerne, Lake of), l., Switz.	D5	22
Vierzon, Fr.	G11	14
Viesca, Mex.	C7	100
Vieste, Italy	I13	22
Vietnam, ctry., Asia	E9	48
Viet Tri, Viet.	B7	48
Vieux-Fort, Qc., Can.	i22	107a
Vieux Fort, St. Luc.	m7	105c
Vieux-Fort, Pointe du, c., Guad.	i5	105c
Vieux-Habitants, Guad.	h5	105c
Vievis, Lith.	F7	10
Vigala, Est.	B7	10
Vigan, Phil.	B3	52
Vigevano, Italy	E5	22
Vigie Airport, St. Luc.	I6	105c
Vignola, Italy	F7	22
Vigo, Spain	B2	20
Vigo, Ría de, est., Spain	B1	20
Vihāri, Pak.	D4	54
Vihorevka, Russia	C18	32
Vihowa, Pak.	C3	54
Vihren, mtn., Blg.	H10	26
Viinijärvi, Fin.	E13	8
Viivikonna, Est.	A10	10
Vijāpur, India	G4	54
Vijayawāda, India	C5	53
Vikārābād, India	C3	53
Viking, Ab., Can.	C19	138
Vikna, Nor.	D4	8
Vikna, i., Nor.	D4	8
Vikramasingapuram, India	G3	53
Vikulovo, Russia	C12	32
Vila da Ribeira Brava, C.V.	k10	65a
Vila de Sena, Moz.	D5	68
Vila do Bispo, Port.	G1	20
Vila do Conde, Port.	C2	20
Vila Fontes, Moz.	D6	68
Vilafranca del Panadés see Vilafranca del Penedès, Spain	C12	20
Vilafranca del Penedès, Spain	C12	20
Vila Franca de Xira, Port.	F2	20
Vila Gamito, Moz.	C5	68
Vilagarcía de Arousa, Spain	B1	20
Vilaine, stm., Fr.	G7	14
Viļaka, Lat.	C10	10
Vilalba, Spain	A3	20
Vilanandro, Tanjona, c., Madag.	D7	68
Viļāni, Lat.	D9	10
Vilankulo, Moz.	B12	70
Vila Nova de Famalicão, Port.	C2	20
Vila Nova de Gaia, Port.	C2	20
Vilanova i la Geltrú, Spain	C12	20
Vila Real, Port.	C3	20
Vila-Real, Spain	E10	20
Vila Real, state, Port.	C3	20
Vila Velha, Braz.	K5	88
Vila Verde, Port.	C2	20
Vilcabamba, Cordillera de, mts., Peru	F3	84
Vilejka, Bela.	F9	10
Vilelas, Arg.	C6	92
Vilhelmina, Swe.	D7	8
Vilhena, Braz.	F5	84
Vilija (Neris), stm., Eur.	F6	10
Viljandi, Est.	G11	8
Viljuj, stm., Russia	D13	34
Viljujsk, Russia	D13	34
Viljujskoe vodohranilišče, res., Russia	B20	32
Vilkaviškis, Lith.	F6	10
Vil'kickogo, ostrov, i., Russia	A19	34
Vil'kickogo, proliv, strt., Russia	A9	34
Vilkija, Lith.	E6	10
Villa Abecia, Bol.	D3	90
Villa Ana, Arg.	D8	92
Villa Ángela, Arg.	C7	92
Villa Atamisqui, Arg.	D6	92
Villa Bella, Bol.	B3	90
Villa Berthet, Arg.	C7	92
Villablino, Spain	B4	20
Villa Bruzual, Ven.	C7	86
Villa Cañás, Arg.	G7	92
Villacañas, Spain	E7	20
Villa Carlos Paz, Arg.	E5	92
Villacarrillo, Spain	F7	20
Villacastín, Spain	D6	20
Villach, Aus.	D10	22
Villacidro, Italy	E2	24
Villa Clara, Arg.	E8	92
Villa Concepción del Tío, Arg.	E6	92
Villa Constitución, Arg.	F7	92
Villa de Arista, Mex.	D8	100
Villa de Cos, Mex.	D7	100
Villa de Cura, Ven.	B8	86
Villa del Carmen, Arg.	F5	92
Villa del Río, Spain	G6	20
Villa del Rosario, Arg.	E8	92
Villa del Rosario, Arg.	E6	92
Villa del Rosario, Ven.	B5	86
Villa de Soto, Arg.	E5	92
Villadiego, Spain	B7	20
Villa Dolores, Arg.	E5	92
Villa Flores, Mex.	G12	100
Villa Florida, Para.	C9	92
Villafranca de los Barros, Spain	F4	20
Villafranca di Verona, Italy	E7	22
Villagarcía de Arosa see Vilagarcía de Arousa, Spain	B1	20
Village see The Village, Ok., U.S.	F11	128
Villa General Roca, Arg.	F4	92
Villa Gesell, Arg.	H9	92
Villagrán, Mex.	C9	100
Villa Grove, Il., U.S.	E9	120
Villaguay, Arg.	E8	92
Villa Guerrero, Mex.	F9	100
Villa Hayes, Para.	B9	92
Villahermosa, Mex.	G12	100
Villa Hidalgo, Mex.	H3	130
Villa Huidobro, Arg.	G5	92
Villa Insurgentes, Mex.	C3	100
Villa Iris, Arg.	I6	92
Villajoyosa see La Vila Joiosa, Spain	F10	20
Villa Juárez, Mex.	B3	100
Villa Krause, Arg.	E3	92
Villalba, P.R.	B3	104a
Villalba see Vilalba, Spain	A3	20
Villaldama, Mex.	B8	100
Villalon, Phil.	E5	52
Villalonga, Arg.	G4	90
Villalpando, Spain	C5	20
Villa Mainero, Mex.	C9	100
Villa María, Arg.	F6	92
Villamartín, Spain	H5	20
Villa Mazán, Arg.	D4	92
Villa Media Agua, Arg.	E3	92
Villa Mercedes, Arg.	F5	92
Villa Montes, Bol.	D4	90
Villa Nueva, Arg.	F6	92
Villanueva, Col.	B5	86
Villanueva, N.M., U.S.	F3	128
Villanueva de Córdoba, Spain	F6	20
Villanueva de la Serena, Spain	F5	20
Villanueva de la Sierra, Spain	D4	20
Villanueva de los Infantes, Spain	F8	20
Villanueva del Río y Minas, Spain	G4	20
Villanueva y Geltrú see Vilanova i la Geltrú, Spain	C12	20
Villa Ocampo, Arg.	D8	92
Villa Ocampo, Mex.	H2	130
Villa Oliva, Para.	B8	92
Villa Pérez, P.R.	B2	104a
Villapinzón, Col.	E5	86
Villarcayo, Spain	B7	20
Villa Regina, Arg.	G3	90
Villa Reynolds, Arg.	F5	92
Villa Rica, Ga., U.S.	D14	122
Villarreal see Vila-Real, Spain	E10	20
Villarrica, Para.	B9	92
Villarrobledo, Spain	E8	20
Villarrubia de los Ojos, Spain	E7	20
Villas, N.J., U.S.	E10	114
Villa San Giovanni, Italy	F9	24
Villa Santa Rita de Catuna, Arg.	E4	92
Villasayas, Spain	C8	20
Villa Serrano, Bol.	C4	90
Villasis, Phil.	C3	52
Villa Unión, Arg.	D3	92
Villa Unión, Arg.	D6	92
Villa Unión, Mex.	D5	100
Villa Valeria, Arg.	G5	92
Villavicencio, Col.	E5	86
Villaviciosa de Córdoba, Spain	F5	20
Villazón, Bol.	D3	90
Villefranche-de-Rouergue, Fr.	E8	18
Villefranche-sur-Saône, Fr.	C10	18
Villena, Spain	F10	20
Villeneuve-sur-Lot, Fr.	E6	18
Villeneuve-sur-Yonne, Fr.	F12	14
Ville Platte, La., U.S.	G6	122
Villers-Cotterêts, Fr.	E12	14
Villerupt, Fr.	E14	14
Villeta, Col.	E4	86
Villeurbanne, Fr.	D10	18
Villiers, S. Afr.	E9	70
Villingen-Schwenningen, Ger.	H4	16
Villisca, Ia., U.S.	D3	120
Villmanstrand see Lappeenranta, Fin.	F12	8
Vilnius, Lith.	F8	10
Vilsbiburg, Ger.	H8	16
Vil'shanka, Ukr.	A17	26
Vilshofen, Ger.	H9	16
Viluppuram, India	E4	53
Vilvoorde, Bel.	D13	14
Vilvorde see Vilvoorde, Bel.	D13	14
Vimmerby, Swe.	H6	8
Vimperk, Czech Rep.	G9	16
Vina, Ca., U.S.	D3	134
Vina, stm., Cam.	C2	66
Viña del Mar, Chile	F2	92
Vinalhaven, Me., U.S.	F8	110
Vinalhaven Island, i., Me., U.S.	F8	110
Vinaròs, Spain	D11	20
Vinaroz see Vinaròs, Spain	D11	20
Vincennes, In., U.S.	F10	120
Vincennes Bay, b., Ant.	B15	81
Vincent, Al., U.S.	D12	122
Vinces, Ec.	H2	86
Vindelälven, stm., Swe.	D8	8
Vindhya Range, mts., India	G6	54
Vinegar Hill, mtn., Or., U.S.	F8	136
Vineland, N.J., U.S.	E10	114
Vinemont, Al., U.S.	C12	122
Vineyard Haven, Ma., U.S.	C15	114
Vineyard Sound, strt., Ma., U.S.	C15	114
Ving Ngün, Mya.	A4	48
Vinh, Viet.	C7	48
Vinhais, Port.	C4	20
Vinh Long, Viet.	G8	48
Vinh Yen, Viet.	B7	48
Vinita, Ok., U.S.	H2	120
Vinkovci, Cro.	E15	22
Vinnytsia, Ukr.	F14	6
Vinnytsia, co., Ukr.	A16	26
Vinson Massif, mtn., Ant.	C32	81
Vintilă Vodă, Rom.	D13	26
Vinton, La., U.S.	G5	122
Vinton, Va., U.S.	G6	114
Viola, Il., U.S.	C7	120
Vioolsdrif, S. Afr.	F3	70
Vipiteno, Italy	D8	22
Vir, Otok, i., Cro.	F11	22
Virac, Phil.	D5	52
Viramgām, India	G3	54
Vīrarājendrapet, India	E2	53
Virbalis, Lith.	F5	10
Virden, Mb., Can.	E13	124
Virden, Il., U.S.	E8	120
Virden, N.M., U.S.	K8	132
Vire, Fr.	F8	14
Virgem da Lapa, Braz.	I4	88
Vírgenes, Cabo, c., S.A.	J3	90
Virgil, Ks., U.S.	C13	128
Virgin, stm., U.S.	G2	132
Virgin Gorda, i., Br. Vir. Is.	e9	104b
Virginia, S. Afr.	F8	70
Virginia, Il., U.S.	E7	120
Virginia, Mn., U.S.	D6	118
Virginia, state, U.S.	G7	114
Virginia Beach, Va., U.S.	H10	114
Virginia City, Mt., U.S.	E14	136
Virginia City, Nv., U.S.	D6	134
Virginia Falls, wtfl, N.T., Can.	C5	106
Virginia Peak, mtn., Nv., U.S.	D6	134
Virgin Islands, dep., N.A.	h14	96a
Virgin Islands, is., N.A.	e7	104b
Virgin Islands National Park, p.o.i., V.I.U.S.	e7	104b
Virgin Passage, strt., N.A.	B5	104a
Virihaure, l., Swe.	C7	8
Virje, Cro.	D13	22
Virojoki, Fin.	F12	8
Viroqua, Wi., U.S.	H7	118
Virovitica, Cro.	E14	22

Name	Map Ref.	Page
Virrat, Fin.	E10	8
Virtaniemi, Fin.	B13	8
Virtsu, Est.	G10	8
Virú, Peru	E2	84
Virudunagar, India	G3	53
Virunga, Parc National de, p.o.i., D.R.C.	D5	66
Viru-Nigula, Est.	A9	10
Virvytė, stm., Lith.	D5	10
Vis see Visrivier, stm., Nmb.	E3	70
Vis, stm., S. Afr.	G5	70
Vis, Otok, i., Cro.	G13	22
Visale, Sol. Is.	e8	79b
Visalia, Ca., U.S.	G6	134
Visayan Islands, is., Phil.	E4	52
Visayan Sea, Phil.	E4	52
Visby, Swe.	H8	8
Viscount, Sk., Can.	C8	124
Viscount Melville Sound, strt., Can.	B11	94
Višegrad, Bos.	F6	26
Viseu, Port.	D3	20
Viseu, state, Port.	D3	20
Vishākhapatnam, India	C6	53
Visnagar, India	G4	54
Višneva, Bela.	F9	10
Visoko, Bos.	E5	26
Visokoi Island, i., S. Geor.	K12	82
Visp, Switz.	D4	22
Visrivier, stm., Nmb.	E3	70
Vista, Ca., U.S.	J8	134
Vistina, Russia	A11	10
Vistula see Wisła, stm., Pol.	B14	16
Vistula Lagoon, b., Eur.	B16	16
Vita, Mb., Can.	E17	124
Vita, stm., Col.	E7	86
Vitarte, Peru	F2	84
Vite, India	C2	53
Viterbo, Italy	H8	22
Viti see Fiji, ctry., Oc.	E8	72
Vitiaz Strait, strt., Pap. N. Gui.	b4	79a
Vitigudino, Spain	C4	20
Viti Levu, i., Fiji	p19	79e
Vitim, Russia	E11	34
Vitim, stm., Russia	E12	34
Vitimskoe ploskogor'e, plat., Russia	F11	34
Vitinja, p., Blg.	G10	26
Vítkov, Czech Rep.	G13	16
Vitória, Braz.	D7	84
Vitória, Braz.	K5	88
Vitoria see Gasteiz, Spain	B8	20
Vitória da Conquista, Braz.	H5	88
Vitória de Santo Antão, Braz.	E8	88
Vitória do Mearim, Braz.	B3	88
Vitorino Freire, Braz.	C3	88
Vitré, Fr.	F7	14
Vitry-le-François, Fr.	F13	14
Vitteaux, Fr.	G13	14
Vittoria, Italy	H8	24
Vittorio Veneto, Italy	D9	22
Viveiro, Spain	A3	20
Viver, Spain	E10	20
Vivero see Viveiro, Spain	A3	20
Vivi, stm., Russia	D8	34
Vivian, La., U.S.	E4	122
Vizcaíno, Desierto de, des., Mex.	B2	100
Vizcaya see Bizkaiko, co., Spain	A8	20
Vize, Tur.	B10	28
Vizianagaram, India	B6	53
Vizille, Fr.	D11	18
Vizinga, Russia	B7	32
Vjalikaja Maščanica, Bela.	G12	10
Vjalikija Radvaničy, Bela.	H7	10
Vjaseja, Bela.	G10	10
Vjatka, stm., Russia	C8	32
Vjatskie Poljany, Russia	C8	32
Vjazemskij, Russia	G15	34
Vjaz'ma, Russia	E17	10
Vjazniki, Russia	H20	8
Vjazyn', Bela.	F10	10
Vjosës (Aóös), stm., Eur.	D13	24
Vlaardingen, Neth.	C13	14
Vlădeasa, Vârful, mtn., Rom.	C9	26
Vladičin Han, Yugo.	G8	26
Vladikavkaz, Russia	F6	32
Vladimir, Russia	H18	8
Vladimirskaja oblast', co., Russia	I19	8
Vladimirskij Tupik, Russia	E16	10
Vladivostok, Russia	C9	38
Vlasenica, Bos.	E5	26
Vlasotince, Yugo.	G9	26
Vlasovo, Russia	B16	34
Vlieland, i., Neth.	A13	14
Vlissingen, Neth.	C12	14
Vlora see Vlorë, Alb.	D13	24
Vlorë, Alb.	D13	24
Vltava (Moldau), stm., Czech Rep.	F10	16
Vnukovo, Russia	E20	10
Vöcklabruck, Aus.	C10	22
Vo Dat, Viet.	G8	48
Vodla, stm., Russia	F17	8
Vodlozero, ozero, l., Russia	E16	8
Vodosalma, Russia	D14	8
Voël, stm., S. Afr.	H7	70
Voghera, Italy	F6	22
Voh, N. Cal.	m15	79d
Vohimena, Tanjona, c., Madag.	F8	68
Vohipeno, Madag.	E8	68
Võhma, Est.	G11	8
Voi, Kenya	E7	66
Voinești, Rom.	B14	26
Voinjama, Lib.	H3	64
Voiron, Fr.	D11	18
Voitsberg, Aus.	C12	22
Vojmsjön, l., Swe.	D6	8
Vojnica, Russia	D14	8
Vojvodina, co., Yugo.	D7	26
Volcán, Pan.	H6	102
Volcano, Hi., U.S.	D6	78a
Volcano Islands see Kazan-rettō, is., Japan	G18	30
Volčiha, Russia	D14	32
Volda, Nor.	E2	8
Volga, S.D., U.S.	G2	118
Volga, stm., Russia	E7	32
Volga-Baltic Canal see Volgo-Baltijskij kanal, can., Russia	G17	8
Volgo, Russia	B16	10
Volgo, ozero, l., Russia	C16	10
Volgo-Baltijskij kanal, can., Russia	G17	8
Volgodonsk, Russia	E6	32
Volgograd, Russia	E6	32
Volgograd Reservoir see Volgogradskoe vodohranilišče, res., Russia	E7	32
Volgogradskoe vodohranilišče, res., Russia	D7	32
Volhov, Russia	A15	10
Volhov, stm., Russia	G14	8
Volissós, Grc.	E8	28
Völkermarkt, Aus.	D11	22
Völklingen, Ger.	G2	16
Volksrust, S. Afr.	E9	70
Voločanka, Russia	B7	34
Volodarskoe, Kaz.	D11	32
Voloe, Russia	F17	10
Vologda, Russia	A22	10
Vologda, stm., Russia	A22	10
Vologodskaja oblast', co., Russia	G19	8
Volokolamsk, Russia	D18	10
Volonga, Russia	C22	8
Vólos, Grc.	D5	28
Volos, Gulf of see Pagasitikós Kólpos, b., Grc.	D5	28
Vološka, Russia	F19	8
Volosovo, Russia	A12	10
Volot, Russia	C13	10
Volovo, Russia	G21	10
Vol'sk, Russia	D7	32
Volta, stm., Ghana	H5	64
Volta Blanche (White Volta), stm., Afr.	G4	64
Volta Lake, res., Ghana	H4	64
Volta Noire (Black Volta) (Mouhoun), stm., Afr.	G4	64
Volta Redonda, Braz.	L3	88
Volterra, Italy	G7	22
Vol'teva, Russia	D21	8
Voltri, ngh., Italy	F5	22
Volturno, stm., Italy	C8	24
Vólvi, Límni, l., Grc.	C6	28
Volyn', co., Ukr.	E20	16
Volžsk, Russia	C7	32
Volžskij, Russia	E6	32
Vonavona Island, i., Sol. Is.	e7	79b
Vonda, Sk., Can.	B7	124
Vondanka, Russia	G22	8
Vondrozo, Madag.	E8	68
Von Frank Mountain, mtn., Ak., U.S.	D8	140
Vopnafjörður, Ice.	k32	8a
Vopnafjörður, b., Ice.	k32	8a
Vorarlberg, state, Aus.	C6	22
Vorau, Aus.	C12	22
Vorderrhein see Rein Anteriur, stm., Switz.	D6	22
Vordingborg, Den.	I4	8
Vóreio Aigaío, state, Grc.	D8	28
Vórioi Sporádhes, is., Grc.	D6	28
Vórios Evvoïkós Kólpos, b., Grc.	E5	28
Vorkuta, Russia	A10	32
Vormsi, i., Est.	G10	8
Vorobevo, Russia	C13	32
Vorobcov, Mol.	B16	26
Voroncovo, Russia	C11	10
Voronež, Russia	D5	32
Voronežskaja oblast', co., Russia	H21	10
Voronja, stm., Russia	B16	8
Voronok, Russia	H15	10
Voronovo, Russia	E5	34
Vorpommern, hist. reg., Ger.	C9	16
Vorsma, Russia	H20	8
Vørterkaka Nunatak, mtn., Ant.	C8	81
Võrtsjärv, l., Est.	G12	8
Võru, Est.	H12	8
Vosburg, S. Afr.	G6	70
Vosges, state, Fr.	F15	14
Vosges, mts., Fr.	F15	14
Voskresensk, Russia	E21	10
Voskresenskoe, Russia	C20	10
Voskresenskoe, Russia	B21	10
Voss, Nor.	F2	8
Vostočno-Kounradskij, Kaz.	E13	32
Vostočno-Sibirskoe more, Russia	B20	34
Vostočnyj Sajan, mts., Russia	D17	32
Vostok, i., Kir.	E11	72
Vostok, sci., Ant.	C15	81
Votice, Czech Rep.	G10	16
Votkinsk, Russia	C8	32
Votuporanga, Braz.	D7	90
Vouga, stm., Port.	D2	20
Vouziers, Fr.	E13	14
Voyageurs National Park, p.o.i., Mn., U.S.	C6	118
Voyeykov Ice Shelf, ice, Ant.	B17	81
Vože, ozero, l., Russia	F18	8
Vožega, Russia	F19	8
Voznesene, Russia	F16	8
Voznoždenija, ostrov, i., Asia	E9	32
Vraca, Blg.	F10	26
Vradyivka, Ukr.	B17	26
Vrancea, state, Rom.	D13	26
Vrangelja, ostrov (Wrangel Island), i., Russia	B24	34
Vranje, Yugo.	G8	26
Vratsa see Vraca, Blg.	F10	26
Vrbas, Yugo.	D6	26
Vrbas, stm., Bos.	E4	26
Vrbovec, Cro.	E13	22
Vrchlabí, Czech Rep.	F11	16
Vrede, S. Afr.	E9	70
Vredenburg, S. Afr.	H3	70
Vredenburgh, Al., U.S.	F11	122
Vredenburg-Saldanha see Vredenburg, S. Afr.	H3	70
Vredendal, S. Afr.	G4	70
Vriddhāchalam, India	F4	53
Vrindāvan, India	E6	54
Vršac, Yugo.	D8	26
Vrútky, Slov.	G14	16
Vryburg, S. Afr.	E7	70
Vryheid, S. Afr.	E10	70
Vselug, ozero, l., Russia	C14	10
Vsetín, Czech Rep.	G13	16
Vsevidof, Mount, mtn., Ak., U.S.	F6	140
Vučitrn, Yugo.	G7	26
Vukovar, Cro.	E16	22
Vulcan, Ab., Can.	F17	138
Vulcan, Rom.	D10	26
Vulcănești, Mol.	D15	26
Vulcano, Isola, i., Italy	F8	24
Vulsino see Bolsena, Lago di, l., Italy	H9	22
Vung Tau, Viet.	G8	48
Vunidawa, Fiji	p19	79e
Vunisea, Fiji	q18	79e
Vuohijärvi, l., Fin.	F11	8
Vuyyūru, India	C5	53
Vyāra, India	H4	54
Vyborg (Viipuri), Russia	F13	8
Vyčegda, stm., Russia	B7	32
Vyčegodskij, Russia	F22	8
Východočeský, state, Czech Rep.	F11	16
Východoslovenský Kraj, state, Slov.	H17	16
Vygoniči, Russia	G16	10
Vygozero, ozero, l., Russia	E16	8
Vyksa, Russia	I20	8
Vylkove, Ukr.	D16	26
Vynohradiv, Ukr.	A10	26
Vypolzovo, Russia	C16	10
Vyrica, Russia	A13	10
Vyšgorodok, Russia	C11	10
Vyškov, Russia	C13	10
Vyškov, Czech Rep.	G12	16
Vyšneol'šanoe, Russia	H20	10
Vyšnevolockoe vodohranilišče, res., Russia	C16	10
Vyšnij Voločok, Russia	C17	10
Vysoké Mýto, Czech Rep.	G12	16
Vysokiniči, Russia	F19	10
Vysokoe, Russia	D17	10
Vysokogornyj, Russia	G16	34
Vysokovsk, Russia	D19	10
Vytebet', stm., Russia	G18	10
Vytegra, Russia	F17	8
Vyzhnytsia, Ukr.	A12	26
W		
Wa, Ghana	G4	64
Waal, stm., Neth.	C14	14
Waalwijk, Neth.	C14	14
Wabag, Pap. N. Gui.	b3	79a
Wabakimi Lake, l., On., Can.	A8	118
Wabamun, Ab., Can.	C16	138
Wabamun Lake, l., Ab., Can.	C15	138
Wabana, Nf., Can.	j23	107a
Wabasca, stm., Ab., Can.	D7	106
Wabasca-Desmarais, Ab., Can.	D8	106
Wabash, In., U.S.	H4	112
Wabash, stm., U.S.	F9	120
Wabasha, Mn., U.S.	G6	118
Wabasso, Mn., U.S.	G3	118
Wabeno, Wi., U.S.	F10	118
Wabera, Eth.	F8	62
Wabowden, Mb., Can.	E11	106
Wąbrzeźno, Pol.	C14	16
Wabu Hu, l., China	E7	42
Waccamaw, stm., U.S.	C7	116
Waccamaw, Lake, l., N.C., U.S.	B7	116
Wachapreague, Va., U.S.	G10	114
Wachau, reg., Aus.	B12	22
Wacissa, Fl., U.S.	F2	116
Waco, Tx., U.S.	C10	130
Waco Lake, res., Tx., U.S.	C10	130
Waconda Lake, res., Ks., U.S.	B10	128
Wadayama, Japan	D7	40
Wad Bandah, Sudan	E5	62
Wadbilliga National Park, p.o.i., Austl.	K7	76
Waddenzee, strt., Neth.	A14	14
Waddington, N.Y., U.S.	D14	112
Waddington, Mount, mtn., B.C., Can.	E5	138
Wadena, Sk., Can.	C10	124
Wadena, Mn., U.S.	E3	118
Wadesboro, N.C., U.S.	B5	116
Wādī as-Sīr, Jord.	G6	58
Wādī Halfā', Sudan	C6	62
Wadley, Al., U.S.	D13	122
Wadley, Ga., U.S.	D3	116
Wad Madanī, Sudan	E6	62
Wadowice, Pol.	G15	16
Wadsworth, Nv., U.S.	D6	134
Wadsworth, Oh., U.S.	C4	114
Wafangdian, China	B9	42
Wageningen, Neth.	C14	14
Wager Bay, b., Nu., Can.	B13	106
Wagga Wagga, Austl.	J6	76
Wagin, Austl.	F3	74
Waging am See, Ger.	I8	16
Wagner, S.D., U.S.	D14	126
Wagoner, Ok., U.S.	I2	120
Wagon Mound, N.M., U.S.	F4	128
Wagontire Mountain, mtn., Or., U.S.	G7	136
Wagrien, reg., Ger.	B6	16
Wągrowiec, Pol.	D13	16
Waha, Libya	B4	62
Wahai, Indon.	F8	44
Wāh Cantonment, Pak.	B4	54
Wahiawa, Hi., U.S.	B3	78a
Wahpeton, N.D., U.S.	E2	118
Wahran (Oran), Alg.	B4	64
Wai, India	B1	53
Waialua, Hi., U.S.	B3	78a
Waianae, Hi., U.S.	B3	78a
Waiau, N.Z.	F5	80
Waiau, stm., N.Z.	G2	80
Waiau, stm., N.Z.	F5	80
Waiblingen, Ger.	H5	16
Waidhofen an der Thaya, Aus.	B12	22
Waidhofen an der Ybbs, Aus.	C11	22
Waigeo, Pulau, i., Indon.	E9	44
Waihi, N.Z.	C6	80
Waikabubak, Indon.	H11	50
Waikato, stm., N.Z.	C6	80
Waikelo, Indon.	H11	50
Waikerie, Austl.	J2	76
Wailuku, Hi., U.S.	C5	78a
Waimate, N.Z.	G4	80
Waimea, Hi., U.S.	A2	78a
Wainganga, stm., India	H7	54
Waingapu, Indon.	H12	50
Waini, stm., Guy.	D12	86
Wainunu Bay, b., Fiji	p19	79e
Wainwright, Ab., Can.	B3	124
Wainwright, Ak., U.S.	B7	140
Waipukurau, N.Z.	E7	80
Wairarapa, Lake, l., N.Z.	E6	80
Wairau, stm., N.Z.	E5	80
Wairoa, N.Z.	D7	80
Wairoa, stm., N.Z.	B6	80
Waïsisi, Vanuatu	l17	79d
Waitaki, stm., N.Z.	G4	80
Waitara, N.Z.	D6	80
Waitemata, N.Z.	C6	80
Waite Park, Mn., U.S.	F4	118
Waitotara, N.Z.	D6	80
Waitsburg, Wa., U.S.	D8	136
Waiwo, Indon.	F9	44
Wajima, Japan	B9	40
Wajir, Kenya	D8	66
Waka, D.R.C.	D4	66
Waka, Eth.	F7	62
Wakarusa, In., U.S.	G3	112
Wakasa-wan, b., Japan	D8	40
Wakatipu, Lake, l., N.Z.	G3	80
Wakaw, Sk., Can.	B8	124
Wakayama, Japan	E8	40
Wakayama, state, Japan	F8	40
WaKeeney, Ks., U.S.	B9	128
Wakefield, Eng., U.K.	H11	12
Wakefield, Ks., U.S.	B11	128
Wakefield, Ne., U.S.	E15	126
Wakefield, Va., U.S.	H8	114
Wake Forest, N.C., U.S.	I7	114
Wake Island, dep., Oc.	B7	72
Wake Island, at., Wake I.	H19	142
Wakema, Mya.	D2	48
Waki, Japan	E7	40
Wakis, Pap. N. Gui.	b5	79a
Wakita, Ok., U.S.	E10	128
Wakkanai, Japan	B14	38
Wakomata Lake, l., On., Can.	B6	112
Wakonda, S.D., U.S.	E15	126
Waku Kungo, Ang.	C2	68
Walachia, hist. reg., Rom.	E11	26
Walanae, stm., Indon.	F12	50
Walawe, stm., Sri L.	H5	53
Wałbrzych, Pol.	F12	16
Wałbrzych, state, Pol.	F12	16
Walcha, Austl.	H8	76
Walcott, Ia., U.S.	C7	120
Walcott, N.D., U.S.	E1	118
Walcott, Lake, res., Id., U.S.	H13	136
Wałcz, Pol.	C12	16
Waldbröl, Ger.	F3	16
Walden, Co., U.S.	C10	132
Waldheim, Sk., Can.	B7	124
Waldkirchen, Ger.	H9	16
Waldmünchen, Ger.	G8	16
Waldo, B.C., Can.	G15	138
Waldoboro, Me., U.S.	F7	110
Waldorf, Md., U.S.	F9	114
Waldport, Or., U.S.	F2	136
Waldron, Sk., Can.	D11	124
Waldron, Ar., U.S.	C4	122
Waldron, In., U.S.	E12	120
Waldshut-Tiengen, Ger.	I4	16
Waldviertel, reg., Aus.	B12	22
Wales, state, U.K.	I9	12
Wales Island, i., Nu., Can.	B13	106
Walewale, Ghana	G4	64
Walgett, Austl.	G6	76
Walgreen Coast, cst., Ant.	C30	81
Walhachin, B.C., Can.	F10	138
Walhalla, N.D., U.S.	F15	124
Walhalla, S.C., U.S.	B2	116
Walhalla, hist., Ger.	G8	16
Walker, Ia., U.S.	B6	120
Walker, stm., Nv., U.S.	D7	134
Walker Bay, b., S. Afr.	I4	70
Walker Lake, l., Nv., U.S.	E7	134
Walkerton, On., Can.	D8	112
Walkerton, In., U.S.	G3	112
Walkertown, N.C., U.S.	H5	114
Walkerville, Mt., U.S.	D14	136
Wall, S.D., U.S.	D10	126
Wallace, Id., U.S.	C11	136
Wallace, Ne., U.S.	G11	126
Wallace, N.C., U.S.	B7	116
Wallaceburg, On., Can.	F7	112
Wallal Downs, Austl.	C4	74
Wallam Creek, stm., Austl.	G6	76
Wallangarra, Austl.	G8	76
Wallaroo, Austl.	F7	74
Wallasey, Eng., U.K.	H9	12
Walla Walla, Wa., U.S.	D8	136
Wallingford, Ct., U.S.	C13	114
Wallingford, Vt., U.S.	G4	110
Wallis, Tx., U.S.	H2	122
Wallis, Îles, is., Wal./F.	E9	72
Wallis and Futuna, dep., Oc.	E9	72
Wallisville Lake, res., Tx., U.S.	H4	122
Wall Lake, Ia., U.S.	I3	118
Wallowa, Or., U.S.	E9	136
Wallowa, stm., Or., U.S.	E9	136
Walls of Jericho National Park, p.o.i., Austl.	n13	77a
Walnut, Il., U.S.	C8	120
Walnut, Ia., U.S.	C2	120
Walnut, Ms., U.S.	C10	122
Walnut, N.C., U.S.	I3	114
Walnut, stm., Ks., U.S.	D11	128
Walnut Canyon National Monument, p.o.i., Az., U.S.	H5	132
Walnut Cove, N.C., U.S.	H5	114
Walnut Creek, stm., Ks., U.S.	C9	128
Walnut Grove, Mn., U.S.	G3	118
Walnut Grove, Ms., U.S.	E9	122
Walnut Ridge, Ar., U.S.	H6	120
Walnut Springs, Tx., U.S.	B10	130
Walpole, Austl.	G3	74
Walpole, N.H., U.S.	G4	110
Walsall, Eng., U.K.	I11	12
Walsenburg, Co., U.S.	D4	128
Walsh, Austl.	C8	74
Walsh, Ab., Can.	E3	124
Walsh, stm., Austl.	A5	76
Walsrode, Ger.	D5	16
Walterboro, S.C., U.S.	D5	116
Walters, Ok., U.S.	G10	128
Waltershausen, Ger.	F6	16
Walthall, Ms., U.S.	D9	122
Walthill, Ne., U.S.	B1	120
Walton, N.S., Can.	E13	110
Walton, In., U.S.	H3	112
Walton, N.Y., U.S.	B10	114
Walvisbaai see Walvis Bay, Nmb.	C2	70
Walvis Bay (Walvisbaai), Nmb.	C2	70
Walvis Bay, b., Nmb.	C2	70
Walvis Ridge, unds.	K14	144
Walworth, Wi., U.S.	B9	120
Wamba, D.R.C.	D5	66
Wamba, Nig.	H6	64
Wamba (Uamba), stm., Afr.	B2	68
Wamego, Ks., U.S.	A10	114
Wampú, Hond.	E5	102
Wampú, stm., Hond.	E5	102
Wampum, Pa., U.S.	D5	114
Wamsutter, Wy., U.S.	B9	132
Wanaka, N.Z.	G3	80
Wanaka, Lake, l., N.Z.	G3	80
Wan'an, China	H6	42
Wanapa, Neth. Ant.	p23	104g
Wanapitei, stm., On., Can.	B8	112
Wanapitei Lake, l., On., Can.	B8	112
Wanbaoshan, China	B6	38
Wanbi, Austl.	J3	76
Wanblee, S.D., U.S.	D11	126
Wanchese, N.C., U.S.	I10	114
Wandel Hav, Grnld.	A22	141
Wandering, stm., Ab., Can.	A18	138
Wanfoxia, China	C4	36
Wang, stm., Thai.	D4	48
Wanganui, N.Z.	D6	80
Wanganui, stm., N.Z.	D6	80
Wangaratta, Austl.	K6	76
Wangcun, China	C7	42
Wangdu Phodrang, Bhu.	E12	54
Wangiwangi, Pulau, i., Indon.	G7	44
Wang Noi, Thai.	E5	48
Wangpan Yang, b., China	F9	42
Wangqing, China	C8	38
Wangtai, China	H7	42
Wangyehmiao see Horqin Youyi Qianqi, China	B9	36
Wanhedian, China	E5	42
Wanhsien see Wanxian, China	F3	42
Wani, India	A4	53
Wanie-Rukula, D.R.C.	D5	66
Wanigela, Pap. N. Gui.	b4	79a
Wanipigow, stm., Can.	C18	124
Wānkāner, India	G3	54
Wanneroo, Austl.	F3	74
Wanning, China	L4	42
Wanning, China	L4	42
Wānparti, India	C4	53
Wantan, China	F3	42
Wanxian, China	F3	42
Wanyuan, China	E3	42
Wanzai, China	G6	42
Wanzleben, Ger.	D7	16
Wapakoneta, Oh., U.S.	H5	112
Wapanucka, Ok., U.S.	C2	122
Wapato, Wa., U.S.	D6	136
Wapello, Ia., U.S.	C6	120
Wāpi, India	H4	54
Wapiti, stm., Can.	A12	138
Wappingers Falls, N.Y., U.S.	C12	114
Wapsipinicon, stm., U.S.	J8	118
War, W.V., U.S.	G4	114
Warangal, India	C4	53
Wārāseoni, India	H7	54
Waratah, Austl.	n12	77a
Waratah Bay, b., Austl.	L5	76
Warburg, Ger.	E4	16
Warburton, Austl.	E5	74
Warburton Bay, b., N.T., Can.	C8	106
Ward, stm., Austl.	E6	76
Warden, S. Afr.	E9	70
Wardha, India	H7	54
Wardha, stm., India	H7	54
Ward Hill, hill, Scot., U.K.	C9	12
Wardlow, Ab., Can.	F19	138
Wardner, B.C., Can.	G15	138
Wardswell Draw, stm., U.S.	B5	130
Waremme, Bel.	D14	14
Waren, Ger.	C8	16
Warenai, stm., Indon.	F10	44
Warenda, Austl.	D3	76
Warendorf, Ger.	E3	16
Ware Shoals, S.C., U.S.	B3	116
Wargla, Alg.	C6	64
Warialda, Austl.	G8	76
Warin Chamrap, Thai.	E7	48
Warminster, Wi., U.S.	D11	112
Warman, Sk., Can.	B7	124
Warmandi, Indon.	F9	44
Warmbad, Nmb.	F4	70
Warmbad, S. Afr.	D9	70
Warm Baths see Warmbad, S. Afr.	D9	70
Warminster, Eng., U.K.	J10	12
Warminster, Pa., U.S.	D10	114
Warm Springs, Ga., U.S.	E14	122
Warm Springs, Mt., U.S.	D14	136
Warm Springs, Or., U.S.	F5	136
Warnemünde, ngh., Ger.	B7	16
Warner, Ab., Can.	G18	138
Warner, N.H., U.S.	G5	110
Warner Lakes, l., Or., U.S.	H6	136
Warner Mountains, mts., U.S.	B5	134
Warner Peak, mtn., Or., U.S.	A6	134
Warner Robins, Ga., U.S.	D2	116
Warnow, stm., Ger.	B8	16
Warra, Austl.	F8	76
Warracknabeal, Austl.	K4	76
Warragul, Austl.	L5	76
Warrawagine, Austl.	D4	74
Warrego, stm., Austl.	G5	76
Warren, Ar., U.S.	D6	122
Warren, In., U.S.	H4	112
Warren, Mi., U.S.	B2	114
Warren, Mn., U.S.	C2	118
Warren, Oh., U.S.	C5	114
Warren, Pa., U.S.	C6	114
Warrens, Wi., U.S.	G8	118
Warrensburg, Mo., U.S.	F4	120
Warrensburg, N.Y., U.S.	G3	110
Warrenton, S. Afr.	F7	70
Warrenton, Mo., U.S.	F6	120
Warrenton, N.C., U.S.	H7	114
Warrenton, Or., U.S.	D2	136
Warri, Nig.	H6	64
Warrington, Eng., U.K.	H10	12
Warrington, Fl., U.S.	G11	122
Warrior, Al., U.S.	D12	122
Warrnambool, Austl.	L4	76
Warroad, Mn., U.S.	C3	118
Warrumbungle National Park, p.o.i., Austl.	H7	76
Warsaw see Warszawa, Pol.	D16	16
Warsaw, Il., U.S.	D6	120
Warsaw, In., U.S.	G4	112
Warsaw, Ky., U.S.	F13	120
Warsaw, Mo., U.S.	F4	120
Warsaw, N.Y., U.S.	B7	114
Warsaw, N.C., U.S.	A7	116
Warspite, Ab., Can.	B18	138
Warszawa (Warsaw), Pol.	D16	16
Warszawa, state, Pol.	D16	16
Warta, Pol.	E14	16
Warta, stm., Pol.	D11	16
Wartburg, Tn., U.S.	H13	120
Wartrace, Tn., U.S.	B12	122
Warud, India	H7	54
Warwick, Austl.	G9	76
Warwick, Eng., U.K.	I11	12
Warwick, R.I., U.S.	C14	114
Warwick Channel, strt., Austl.	B7	74
Wasaga Beach, On., Can.	D10	112
Wasagu, Nig.	G6	64
Wasatch Range, mts., Ut., U.S.	C5	132
Wasbank, S. Afr.	F10	70
Wascana Creek, stm., Sk., Can.	D9	124
Wasco, Ca., U.S.	H6	134
Wasco, Or., U.S.	E6	136
Waseca, Mn., U.S.	G5	118
Wasgomuwa National Park, p.o.i., Sri L.	H5	53
Washademoak Lake, l., N.B., Can.	E11	110
Washburn, Il., U.S.	D8	120
Washburn, N.D., U.S.	G12	124
Washburn, Wi., U.S.	E7	118
Washburn, Mount, mtn., Wy., U.S.	F16	136
Washburn Lake, l., Nu., Can.	A9	106
Wāshīm, India	H6	54
Washington, D.C., U.S.	F8	114
Washington, Ga., U.S.	C3	116
Washington, Il., U.S.	D8	120
Washington, In., U.S.	F10	120
Washington, Ia., U.S.	C6	120
Washington, La., U.S.	G6	122
Washington, Mo., U.S.	F6	120
Washington, N.C., U.S.	A8	116
Washington, Pa., U.S.	D5	114
Washington, Tx., U.S.	G2	122
Washington, Ut., U.S.	F3	132
Washington, Va., U.S.	F7	114
Washington, state, U.S.	C6	136
Washington, Mount, mtn., N.H., U.S.	F5	110
Washington Court House, Oh., U.S.	E2	114
Washington Island, i., Wi., U.S.	C3	112
Washington Land, reg., Grnld.	A12	141
Washington Terrace, Ut., U.S.	B5	132
Washita, stm., U.S.	G12	128
Washow Bay, b., Mb., Can.	C17	124
Washpool National Park, p.o.i., Austl.	G9	76
Washtucna, Wa., U.S.	D8	136
Wasian, Indon.	F9	44
Wasilków, Pol.	C19	16
Wasior, Indon.	F9	44
Waskada, Mb., Can.	E13	124
Waskaganish, Qc., Can.	E15	106
Waskahigan, stm., Ab., Can.	B13	138
Waskom, Tx., U.S.	E4	122
Waspam, Nic.	E5	102
Wassenaar, Neth.	B13	14
Wasseralfingen, Ger.	H6	16
Wassy, Fr.	F13	14
Watampone, Indon.	F12	50
Watansopeng, Indon.	F11	50
Watatic, Mount, mtn., Ma., U.S.	B14	114
Waterberge, mts., S. Afr.	D8	70
Waterbury, Ct., U.S.	C12	114
Wateree Lake, res., S.C., U.S.	B5	116
Waterford (Port Lairge), Ire.	I5	12
Waterford, Ca., U.S.	F5	134
Waterford, Pa., U.S.	C5	114
Waterford, Wi., U.S.	B9	120
Waterford, state, Ire.	I5	12
Waterhen Lake, l., Mb., Can.	B14	124
Water Island, i., V.I.U.S.	e7	104b
Waterloo, Austl.	C5	74
Waterloo, Bel.	D13	14
Waterloo, On., Can.	E9	112
Waterloo, Qc., Can.	E4	110
Waterloo, Al., U.S.	C10	122
Waterloo, Il., U.S.	F7	120
Waterloo, Ia., U.S.	B5	120
Waterloo, N.Y., U.S.	B8	114
Waterloo, Wi., U.S.	A9	120
Waterman, Il., U.S.	C9	120
Waterproof, La., U.S.	F7	122
Watersmeet, Mi., U.S.	E9	118
Waterton-Glacier International Peace Park, p.o.i., N.A.	B13	136
Waterton Lakes National Park, p.o.i., Ab., Can.	G16	138
Watertown, N.Y., U.S.	E14	112
Watertown, S.D., U.S.	C15	126
Watertown, Wi., U.S.	A9	120
Waterval Boven, S. Afr.	D10	70
Water Valley, Ms., U.S.	C9	122
Waterville, N.S., Can.	E12	110
Waterville, Ks., U.S.	B12	128
Waterville, Me., U.S.	F7	110
Waterville, Oh., U.S.	C2	114
Waterville, Wa., U.S.	C6	136
Watervliet, N.Y., U.S.	B12	114
Watford, Eng., U.K.	J12	12
Watford City, N.D., U.S.	G10	124
Wathena, Ks., U.S.	E2	120
Watkins Glen, N.Y., U.S.	B9	114
Watkinsville, Ga., U.S.	C2	116
Watling Island see San Salvador, i., Bah.	C10	96
Watonga, Ok., U.S.	F10	128
Watrous, Sk., Can.	C8	124
Watsa, D.R.C.	D5	66
Watseka, Il., U.S.	H2	112
Watsikengo, D.R.C.	E4	66
Watson, Sk., Can.	B9	124
Watson Lake, Yk., Can.	C5	106
Watsonville, Ca., U.S.	G4	134
Watt Mountain, vol., Dom.	j6	105c
Watts Bar Lake, res., Tn., U.S.	B14	122
Watts Mills, S.C., U.S.	B4	116
Wattwil, Switz.	C5	22
Watubela, Kepulauan, is., Indon.	F9	44
Watzmann, mtn., Ger.	I8	16
Waubay Lake, l., S.D., U.S.	B15	126
Wauchope, Austl.	D6	74
Wauchula, Fl., U.S.	I4	116
Wauconda, Wa., U.S.	B7	136
Waugh, Mb., Can.	E3	118
Waukara, Bukit, mtn., Indon.	D11	50
Waukaringa, Austl.	I2	76
Waukarlycarly, Lake, l., Austl.	D4	74
Waukegan, Il., U.S.	F2	112
Waukesha, Wi., U.S.	A9	120
Waukon, Ia., U.S.	H7	118
Waunakee, Wi., U.S.	A8	120
Wauneta, Ne., U.S.	G11	126
Waupun, Wi., U.S.	H10	118
Waupaca, Wi., U.S.	G11	128
Waurika Lake, res., Ok., U.S.	G10	128
Wausa, Ne., U.S.	E15	126
Wausau, Wi., U.S.	G9	118
Wauseon, Oh., U.S.	C1	114
Wautoma, Wi., U.S.	G9	118
Wauwatosa, Wi., U.S.	E1	112
Wauzeka, Wi., U.S.	A7	120
Wave Hill, Austl.	C6	74
Waverly, Ia., U.S.	B5	120
Waverly, Mo., U.S.	E4	120
Waverly, Ne., U.S.	D1	120
Waverly, N.Y., U.S.	B9	114
Waverly, Oh., U.S.	E2	114
Waverly, Tn., U.S.	H10	120
Waverly, Va., U.S.	G8	114
Waverly Hall, Ga., U.S.	E14	122
Wāw, Sudan	F5	62
Wawa, On., Can.	F14	106
Wawa, Nig.	H5	64
Wawa, stm., Nic.	E5	102
Wāw al-Kabīr, Libya	B3	62
Wawanesa, Mb., Can.	E14	124
Waxahachie, Tx., U.S.	B11	130
Waxhaw, N.C., U.S.	B5	116
Way, Lake, l., Austl.	E4	74
Waya, i., Fiji	p18	79e
Waycross, Ga., U.S.	E3	116
Wayland, Ia., U.S.	C6	120
Wayland, Ky., U.S.	G3	114
Wayland, Mi., U.S.	F4	112
Waylyn, S.C., U.S.	D6	116
Wayne, Ab., Can.	E18	138
Wayne, Mi., U.S.	B2	114
Wayne, Ne., U.S.	E15	126
Wayne, N.J., U.S.	D11	114
Wayne, W.V., U.S.	F3	114
Wayne City, Il., U.S.	F9	120
Waynesboro, Ms., U.S.	F10	122
Waynesboro, Tn., U.S.	B11	122
Waynesboro, Va., U.S.	F6	114
Waynesville, Il., U.S.	D8	120
Waynesville, N.C., U.S.	A3	116
Waynoka, Ok., U.S.	E10	128
Wāzah Khwāh, Afg.	B2	54
Wazīrābād, Pak.	B5	54
Wda, stm., Pol.	C14	16
Wé, N. Cal.	m16	79d
We, Pulau, i., Indon.	J2	48
Weatherford, Ok., U.S.	F10	128
Weatherford, Tx., U.S.	B10	130
Weatherly, Pa., U.S.	D10	114
Weaubleau, Mo., U.S.	G4	120
Weaver Lake, l., Mb., Can.	B17	124
Weaverville, Ca., U.S.	C3	134
Weaverville, N.C., U.S.	I3	114
Webb, Sk., Can.	D5	124
Webb, Ms., U.S.	D8	122
Webbwood, On., Can.	B7	112
Weber, stm., Ut., U.S.	B5	132
Weber City, Va., U.S.	H3	114
Webster, Ab., Can.	A12	138
Webster, Fl., U.S.	H3	116
Webster, Ma., U.S.	B14	114
Webster, Wi., U.S.	F6	118
Webster City, Ia., U.S.	B4	120
Weda, Indon.	E8	44
Weddell Island, i., Falk. Is.	J4	90
Weddell Sea, Ant.	B36	81
Wedderburn, Austl.	K4	76
Wedgeport, N.S., Can.	G11	110
Wedowee, Al., U.S.	D13	122
Weed, Ca., U.S.	B3	134
Weems, Va., U.S.	G9	114
Weenen, S. Afr.	F10	70
Weeping Water, Ne., U.S.	D1	120
Weert, Neth.	C14	14
Wee Waa, Austl.	H7	76
Węgorzewo, Pol.	B17	16
Węgrów, Pol.	D17	16
Wei, stm., China	C8	42
Wei, stm., China	D3	42
Wei, stm., China	C6	42
Weichang, China	C2	38
Weichuan, China	D6	42
Weida, Ger.	F8	16
Weiden in der Oberpfalz, Ger.	G7	16
Weifang, China	C8	42
Weihai, China	C10	42
Weihaiwei see Weihai, China	C10	42
Weihe, China	B8	38
Weilburg, Ger.	F4	16
Weilheim, Ger.	I7	16
Weilmoringle, Austl.	G6	76
Weimar, Ger.	E7	16
Weimar, Tx., U.S.	E11	130
Weinan, China	D3	42
Weinheim, Ger.	G4	16
Weipa, Austl.	B8	74
Weippe, Id., U.S.	D11	136
Weir, Ks., U.S.	D14	128
Weir, Ms., U.S.	D9	122
Weir, stm., Austl.	G8	76
Weirton, W.V., U.S.	D5	114
Weisburd, Arg.	C6	92
Weiser, Id., U.S.	F10	136
Weiser, stm., Id., U.S.	F10	136
Weishan Hu, l., China	D7	42
Weishi, China	D6	42
Weisner Mountain, mtn., Al., U.S.	C13	122
Weissenburg in Bayern, Ger.	G7	16
Weissenfels, Ger.	E7	16
Weiss Lake, res., U.S.	C13	122
Weisswasser, Ger.	E10	16
Weitra, Aus.	B11	22
Weixi, China	F4	36

Name — Map Ref. — Page

Weixian, China C6 42
Weiyuan, stm., China A5 48
Weiz, Aus. C12 22
Wejherowo, Pol. B14 16
Wekoewa Punt, c., Neth. Ant. p23 104g
Welaka, Fl., U.S. G4 116
Welch, Ok., U.S. H2 120
Welch, Tx., U.S. B5 130
Welcome, Mn., U.S. H4 118
Weldiya, Eth. E7 62
Weldon, Sk., Can. A8 124
Weldon, Il., U.S. D9 120
Weldon, stm., U.S. D4 120
Weleetka, Ok., U.S. B2 122
Welk'īṫē, Eth. F7 62
Welkom, S. Afr. E8 70
Welland, On., Can. F10 112
Welland, stm., Eng., U.K. I12 12
Wellborn, Fl., U.S. F3 116
Wellborn, Tx., U.S. G2 122
Wellesley Islands, is., Austl. C8 74
Wellingborough, Eng., U.K. I12 12
Wellington, Austl. I7 76
Wellington, On., Can. E12 112
Wellington, N.Z. E6 80
Wellington, S. Afr. H4 70
Wellington, Eng., U.K. K9 12
Wellington, Co., U.S. G7 126
Wellington, Mo., U.S. E4 120
Wellington, Oh., U.S. C3 114
Wellington, Tx., U.S. G8 128
Wellington, Ut., U.S. D6 132
Wellington, Isla, i., Chile I2 90
Wellington Bay, b., Nu., Can. B9 106
Wellington Channel, strt., Nu., Can. B7 141
Wellman, Ia., U.S. C6 120
Wellman, Tx., U.S. A5 130
Wells, Eng., U.K. J10 12
Wells, Mi., U.S. C2 112
Wells, Mn., U.S. H5 118
Wells, N.Y., U.S. G2 110
Wells, Tx., U.S. F3 122
Wells, Lake, l., Austl. E4 74
Wells, Mount, hill, Austl. C5 74
Wellsboro, Pa., U.S. C8 114
Wellsburg, Ia., U.S. B4 120
Wellsburg, W.V., U.S. D5 114
Wellsford, N.Z. C6 80
Wells-next-the-Sea, Eng., U.K. I13 12
Wellston, Oh., U.S. E3 114
Wellsville, Ks., U.S. C13 128
Wellsville, Mo., U.S. E6 120
Wellsville, N.Y., U.S. B8 114
Wellsville, Oh., U.S. D5 114
Wellton, Az., U.S. K2 132
Wels, Aus. B10 22
Welsford, N.B., Can. E10 110
Welshpool, Wales, U.K. I9 12
Welwyn Garden City, Eng., U.K. J12 12
Wembley, Ab., Can. A11 138
Wena, D.R.C. E4 66
Wenatchee, Wa., U.S. C6 136
Wenatchee Mountains, mts., Wa., U.S. C6 136
Wenceslau Braz, Braz. L1 88
Wenchang, China L4 42
Wencheng, China H8 42
Wenchi, Ghana H4 64
Wenchou see Wenzhou, China F9 36
Wenchow see Wenzhou, China F9 36
Wendell, Id., U.S. H12 136
Wenden, Az., U.S. J3 132
Wendeng, China C10 42
Wendover, Ut., U.S. C2 132
Weng, stm., China I6 42
Weng'an, China H2 42
Wenling, China G9 42
Wenlock, stm., Austl. B8 74
Wenquan, China E14 32
Wenshan, China A7 48
Wenshang, China D7 42
Wenshui, China C4 42
Wenshui, China G2 42
Wensleydale, val., Eng., U.K. G11 12
Wentworth, Austl. J3 76
Wentworth, S.D., U.S. G2 118
Wenxi, China D4 42
Wenxian, China D5 42
Wenzhou, China F9 36
Wepener, S. Afr. F8 70
Werda, Bots. D6 70
Werdau, Ger. F8 16
Werder, Ger. D8 16
Wernadinga, Austl. B2 76
Wernigerode, Ger. E6 16
Werra, stm., Ger. E5 16
Werribee, Austl. K5 76
Werrikimbe National Park, p.o.i., Austl. H9 76
Werris Creek, Austl. H8 76
Wertheim, Ger. G5 16
Wesel, Ger. E2 16
Weser, stm., Ger. C4 16
Weskan, Ks., U.S. C7 128
Weslaco, Tx., U.S. H10 130
Weslemkoon Lake, l., On., Can. C12 112
Wesley, Dom. i6 105c
Wesleyville, Pa., U.S. B5 114
Wessel, Cape, c., Austl. B7 74
Wessel Islands, is., Austl. B7 74
Wessington, S.D., U.S. C14 126
Wessington Springs, S.D., U.S. C14 126
West, Ms., U.S. D9 122
West, Tx., U.S. C10 130
West Allis, Wi., U.S. B9 120
West Antarctica, reg., Ant. D30 81
Westbank, B.C., Can. G11 138
West Bank, dep., Asia F6 58
West Bay, N.S., Can. E15 110
West Bay, b., Tx., U.S. E12 130
West Bend, Ia., U.S. B3 120
West Bend, Wi., U.S. E1 112
West Bengal, state, India G11 54
West Blocton, Al., U.S. D11 122
West Bohemia see Západočeský kraj, state, Czech Rep. G9 16
West Borneo see Kalimantan Barat, state, Indon. D7 50
West Branch, Ia., U.S. C6 120
Westbridge, B.C., Can. G11 138
West Bromwich, Eng., U.K. I11 12
Westbrook, Me., U.S. G6 110
Westbrook, Mn., U.S. G3 118
Westbrook, Tx., U.S. B6 130
West Burlington, Ia., U.S. D6 120
West Burra, i., Scot., U.K. n18 12a
Westby, Austl. J6 76
Westby, Wi., U.S. H8 118
West Cache Creek, stm., Ok., U.S. G10 128
West Caicos, i., T./C. Is. B11 102
West Cape, c., N.Z. G2 80
West Cape Howe, c., Austl. G3 74
West Carlisle, Tx., U.S. H6 128
West Caroline Basin, unds. I16 142
West Chester, Pa., U.S. E10 114
Westchester Station, N.S., Can. E13 110
Westcliffe, Co., U.S. C3 128
West Columbia, S.C., U.S. B4 116
West Columbia, Tx., U.S. H3 122
West Cote Blanche Bay, b., La., U.S. H7 122
West Des Moines, Ia., U.S. C4 120
West Dolores, stm., Co., U.S. F8 132
West Elk Peak, mtn., Co., U.S. E9 132
West End, Ar., U.S. C6 122
West End, N.C., U.S. A6 116
Westerland, Ger. B4 16
Westerly, R.I., U.S. C14 114
Western, state, Sol. Is. e7 79b
Western, stm., Austl. D4 76
Western Australia, state, Austl. D4 74
Western Cape, state, S. Afr. H5 70
Western Channel, strt., Asia E2 40
Western Desert, des., Egypt B5 62
Western Division, state, Fiji p18 79e
Western Dvina (Daugava) (Zahodnjaja Dzvina) (Zapadnaja Dvina), stm., Eur. D7 10
Western Ghāts, mts., India E3 46
Westernport, Md., U.S. E6 114
Western Sahara, dep., Afr. E2 64
Western Samoa see Samoa, ctry., Oc. g12 79c
Western Sayans see Zapadnyj Sajan, mts., Russia D16 32
Western Shore, N.S., Can. F12 110
Westerschelde, est., Neth. C12 14
Westerstede, Ger. C3 16
Westerville, Oh., U.S. D3 114
Westerwald, mts., Ger. F3 16
West European Basin, unds. D12 144
West Falkland, i., Falk. Is. J4 90
West Fargo, N.D., U.S. E1 118
Westfield, Il., U.S. E9 120
Westfield, In., U.S. H3 112
Westfield, Ma., U.S. H4 110
Westfield, N.J., U.S. D11 114
Westfield, Pa., U.S. C8 114
Westfield, Wi., U.S. H9 118
West Fork, Ar., U.S. I3 120
West Frankfort, Il., U.S. G9 120
West Friese Eilanden, is., Neth. A14 14
West Frisian Islands see West Friese Eilanden, is., Neth. A14 14
Westgate, Austl. F6 76
West Grand Lake, res., Me., U.S. E8 110
West Hamlin, W.V., U.S. F3 114
West Hartford, Ct., U.S. C13 114
West Haven, Ct., U.S. C13 114
West Helena, Ar., U.S. C8 122
Westhoff, Tx., U.S. E10 130
Westhope, N.D., U.S. F12 124
West Ice Shelf, ice, Ant. B13 81
West Indies, is. C7 82
West Java see Jawa Barat, state, Indon. G5 50
West Jefferson, N.C., U.S. H4 114
West Jordan, Ut., U.S. C4 132
West Kettle, stm., B.C., Can. G11 138
West Kingston, R.I., U.S. C14 114
West Lafayette, In., U.S. H2 112
Westlake, La., U.S. G5 122
Westland National Park, p.o.i., N.Z. F3 80
West Laramie, Wy., U.S. F7 126
West Lebanon, In., U.S. H2 112
West Liberty, Ky., U.S. G2 114
West Liberty, Oh., U.S. D2 114
Westlock, Ab., Can. B16 138
West Lorne, On., Can. F8 112
Westmeath, state, Ire. H5 12
West Memphis, Ar., U.S. B8 122
Westminster, Co., U.S. B3 128
Westminster, Md., U.S. E9 114
West Monroe, La., U.S. E6 122
Westmoreland, Ks., U.S. B12 128
Westmoreland, Tn., U.S. H11 120
Westmorland, Ca., U.S. J10 134
West Nicholson, Zimb. B9 70
West Nishnabotna, stm., Ia., U.S. C2 120
West Nueces, stm., Tx., U.S. E7 130
West Nusa Tenggara see Nusa Tenggara Barat, state, Indon. G10 50
Weston, Id., U.S. A4 132
Weston, Mo., U.S. E3 120
Weston, Oh., U.S. C2 114
Weston, Or., U.S. E8 136
Weston, W.V., U.S. E5 114
Weston-super-Mare, Eng., U.K. J9 12
West Orange, Tx., U.S. G5 122
Westover, Tn., U.S. B10 122
West Palm Beach, Fl., U.S. J5 116
West Palm Beach Canal, can., Fl., U.S. J5 116
West Pensacola, Fl., U.S. G11 122
Westphalia, Ks., U.S. F2 120
West Plains, Mo., U.S. H6 120
West Point, Ga., U.S. E13 122
West Point, Ia., U.S. D6 120
West Point, Ky., U.S. F11 120
West Point, Ms., U.S. D10 122
West Point, Ne., U.S. J2 118
West Point, N.Y., U.S. C11 114
West Point, Va., U.S. G9 114
West Point Lake, res., U.S. D13 122
West Poplar (Poplar, West Fork), stm., N.A. F8 124
Westport, N.S., Can. F10 110
Westport, On., Can. D13 112
Westport, Ire. H3 12
Westport, Ct., U.S. C12 114
Westport, In., U.S. E12 120
Westport, Or., U.S. D3 136
Westpunt, c., Aruba o19 104g
West Quoddy Head, c., Me., U.S. F10 110
Westray, i., Scot., U.K. B9 12
West Richland, Wa., U.S. D7 136
West Road, stm., B.C., Can. C7 138
West Rutland, Vt., U.S. G3 110
West Salem, Il., U.S. F9 120
West Salem, Oh., U.S. D3 114
West Shoal Lake, l., Mb., Can. D16 124
West Siberian Plain see Zapadno-Sibirskaja ravnina, pl., Russia B12 32
West Slovakia see Západoslovenský Kraj, state, Slov. H14 16
West Spanish Peak, mtn., Co., U.S. D4 128
West Sumatra see Sumatera Barat, state, Indon. D2 50
West Terre Haute, In., U.S. E10 120
West Union, Ia., U.S. B6 120
West Union, Oh., U.S. F2 114
West Unity, Oh., U.S. C1 114
West Valley City, Ut., U.S. C4 132
West Vancouver, B.C., Can. G7 138
Westville, N.S., Can. E14 110
Westville, In., U.S. G3 112
West Virginia, state, U.S. F5 114
West Walker, stm., U.S. E6 134
West Warwick, R.I., U.S. C14 114
West Webster, N.Y., U.S. E12 112
Westwold, B.C., Can. F11 138
Westwood, Ca., U.S. C5 134
Westwood Lakes, Fl., U.S. K5 116
West Wyalong, Austl. I6 76
West Yellowstone, Mt., U.S. F15 136
Wetar, Pulau, i., Indon. G8 44
Wetar, Selat, strt., Indon. G8 44
Wetaskiwin, Ab., Can. C17 138
Wete, Tan. E7 66
Wethersfield, Ct., U.S. C13 114
Wetmore, Ks., U.S. E2 120
Wetumpka, Al., U.S. E12 122
Wetzlar, Ger. F4 16
Wewahitchka, Fl., U.S. G13 122
Wewak, Pap. N. Gui. a3 79a
Wewoka, Ok., U.S. B2 122
Wexford, Ire. I6 12
Wexford, state, Ire. I6 12
Weyburn, Sk., Can. E10 124
Weymontachie, Qc., Can. C3 110
Weymouth, N.S., Can. F10 110
Weymouth, Eng., U.K. K10 12
Weymouth, Ma., U.S. B15 114
Whakatane, N.Z. C7 80
Whangarei, N.Z. B6 80
Whapmagoostui, Qc., Can. D15 106
Wharfe, stm., Eng., U.K. H11 12
Wharton, W.V., U.S. G4 114
Wharton Basin, unds. K12 142
Wharton Lake, l., Nu., Can. C10 106
Whataroa, N.Z. F4 80
What Cheer, Ia., U.S. C5 120
Whatley, Al., U.S. F11 122
Wheatland, Ca., U.S. D4 134
Wheatland, Ia., U.S. C7 120
Wheatley, On., Can. F7 112
Wheatley, Ar., U.S. C7 122
Wheaton, Il., U.S. C9 120
Wheaton, Md., U.S. E8 114
Wheat Ridge, Co., U.S. B3 128
Wheeler, Ms., U.S. C10 122
Wheeler, Tx., U.S. F8 128
Wheeler, stm., Qc., Can. D17 106
Wheeler Lake, res., Al., U.S. C11 122
Wheeler Peak, mtn., Nv., U.S. D2 132
Wheeler Peak, mtn., N.M., U.S. E3 128
Wheeling, W.V., U.S. D5 114
Wheelwright, Arg. F7 92
Wheelwright, Ky., U.S. G3 114
Whidbey Island, i., Wa., U.S. B4 136
Whiskey Peak, mtn., Wy., U.S. E5 126
Whistler, B.C., Can. F8 138
Whitakers, N.C., U.S. H8 114
Whitby, On., Can. E11 112
Whitby, Eng., U.K. G12 12
Whitchurch, Eng., U.K. H10 12
Whitchurch-Stouffville, On., Can. E10 112
White, Ga., U.S. C14 122
White, stm., N.A. C2 106
White, stm., U.S. C7 122
White, stm., U.S. D13 126
White, stm., U.S. C7 132
White, stm., Az., U.S. J6 132
White, stm., In., U.S. F10 120
White, stm., Nv., U.S. F1 132
White, stm., Tx., U.S. H7 128
White, stm., Wa., U.S. C5 136
White, East Fork, stm., In., U.S. F10 120
White, Lake, l., Austl. D5 74
White Bay, b., Nf., Can. i22 107a
White Bear Lake, Mn., U.S. F6 118
White Bluff, Tn., U.S. H10 120
White Butte, mtn., N.D., U.S. A9 126
White Castle, La., U.S. G7 122
White City, Ks., U.S. C12 128
White Cliffs, Austl. H4 76
Whitecourt, Ab., Can. B15 138
White Deer, Tx., U.S. F7 128
Whiteface, stm., Mn., U.S. D6 118
Whiteface Mountain, mtn., N.Y., U.S. F3 110
Whitefield, N.H., U.S. F5 110
Whitefish, Mt., U.S. B12 136
Whitefish Bay, Wi., U.S. A10 120
Whitefish Bay, b., On., Can. B4 118
Whitefish Bay, b., N.A. B5 112
Whitefish Lake, l., Ab., Can. B18 138
Whitefish Lake, l., N.T., Can. C9 106
Whitefish Point, Mi., U.S. B4 112
Whitefish Point, c., Mi., U.S. B4 112
White Hall, Ar., U.S. C6 122
White Hall, Il., U.S. E7 120
Whitehall, Mi., U.S. E3 112
Whitehall, N.Y., U.S. G3 110
Whitehall, Wi., U.S. G7 118
Whitehaven, Eng., U.K. G9 12
Whitehorse, Yk., Can. C4 106
White House, Tn., U.S. H11 120
Whitehouse, Tx., U.S. E3 122
White Island, i., Nu., Can. B13 106
White Island, i., N.Z. C7 80
White Lake, S.D., U.S. D14 126
White Lake, Wi., U.S. F10 118
White Lake, l., On., Can. C13 112
White Lake, l., La., U.S. H6 122
Whitemark, Austl. n13 77a
White Mountain Peak, mtn., Ca., U.S. F7 134
White Mountains, mts., N.H., U.S. F5 110
Whitemouth, stm., Mb., Can. E18 124
Whitemouth Lake, l., Mb., Can. E18 124
Whitemud, stm., Mb., Can. D15 124
White Nile (Abyaḍ, Al-Baḥr al-), stm., Afr. E6 62
White Oak, Tx., U.S. E4 122
White Oak Creek, stm., Tx., U.S. D3 122
White Otter Lake, l., On., Can. B6 118
White Pigeon, Mi., U.S. G4 112
Whitepine, Mt., U.S. C11 136
White Pine, Tn., U.S. H2 114
White Plains, N.Y., U.S. C12 114
White Plains, N.C., U.S. H5 114
Whiteriver, Az., U.S. J6 132
White River, S.D., U.S. D12 126
White River Junction, Vt., U.S. G4 110
White Rock, B.C., Can. G8 138
White Russia see Belarus, ctry., Eur. E14 6
Whitesail Lake, res., B.C., Can. C3 138
Whitesand, stm., Sk., Can. C11 124
White Sands National Monument, p.o.i., N.M., U.S. B1 130
Whitesboro, Tx., U.S. D2 122
White Sea see Beloe more, Russia D18 8
White Settlement, Tx., U.S. B10 130
White Springs, Fl., U.S. F3 116
White Sulphur Springs, Mt., U.S. D16 136
White Sulphur Springs, W.V., U.S. G5 114
Whitesville, Ky., U.S. G11 120
Whiteville, N.C., U.S. B7 116
Whiteville, Tn., U.S. B9 122
White Volta (Volta Blanche), stm., Afr. G4 64
Whitewater, Mt., U.S. F6 124
Whitewater, Wi., U.S. B9 120
Whitewater, stm., U.S. E13 120
Whitewater Baldy, mtn., N.M., U.S. J8 132
Whitewater Creek, stm., N.A. F6 124
Whitewater Lake, l., Mb., Can. E13 124
White Woman Creek, stm., U.S. C7 128
Whitewood, Austl. C4 76
Whitewood, Sk., Can. D11 124
Whitewood, S.D., U.S. C9 126
Whithorn, Jam. i12 104d
Whithorn, Scot., U.K. G8 12
Whiting, Ia., U.S. B1 120
Whiting, Ks., U.S. E2 120
Whitley City, Ky., U.S. H13 120
Whitman, Ma., U.S. B15 114
Whitmire, S.C., U.S. B4 116
Whitmore Mountains, mts., Ant. D31 81
Whitney, On., Can. C11 112
Whitney, Lake, res., Tx., U.S. C10 130
Whitney, Mount, mtn., Ca., U.S. G7 134
Whitney Point, N.Y., U.S. B9 114
Whitsunday Island, i., Austl. C7 76
Whittemore, Ia., U.S. A3 120
Whittemore, Mi., U.S. D6 112
Whittle, Cap, c., Qc., Can. i22 107a
Whittlesea, Austl. K5 76
Whittlesey, Mount, hill, Wi., U.S. E8 118
Whitwell, Tn., U.S. B13 122
Wholdaia Lake, l., N.T., Can. C9 106
Whyalla, Austl. F7 74
Whycocomagh, N.S., Can. E15 110
Wiang Phan, Thai. B4 48
Wiarton, On., Can. D8 112
Wichian Buri, Thai. E5 48
Wichita, Ks., U.S. D11 128
Wichita, stm., Tx., U.S. G10 128
Wichita Falls, Tx., U.S. H10 128
Wick, Scot., U.K. C9 12
Wickenburg, Az., U.S. J4 132
Wickepin, Austl. F3 74
Wickett, Tx., U.S. C5 130
Wickham, Austl. D3 74
Wickiup Reservoir, res., Or., U.S. G5 136
Wickliffe, Ky., U.S. H8 120
Wicklow, Ire. H6 12
Wicklow, state, Ire. H7 12
Wicklow Head, c., Ire. I7 12
Wicklow Mountains, mts., Ire. H6 12
Widgeegoara Creek, stm., Austl. F6 76
Więcbork, Pol. C13 16
Wieleń, Pol. D12 16
Wieliczka, Pol. F16 16
Wielkopolska, reg., Pol. E13 16
Wielkopolski Park Narodowy, p.o.i., Pol. D12 16
Wieluń, Pol. E14 16
Wien (Vienna), Aus. B13 22
Wien, state, Aus. B13 22
Wiener Neustadt, Aus. C13 22
Wienerwald, mts., Aus. B13 22
Wieprz, stm., Pol. E18 16
Wieprza, stm., Pol. B12 16
Wieprz-Krzna, Kanał, can., Pol. E19 16
Wierden, Neth. D2 16
Wiergate, Tx., U.S. F5 122
Wieruszów, Pol. E14 16
Wierzyca, stm., Pol. B14 16
Wiesbaden, Ger. F4 16
Wiesloch, Ger. G4 16
Wigan, Eng., U.K. H10 12
Wiggins, Co., U.S. A4 128
Wiggins, Ms., U.S. G9 122
Wight, Isle of, i., Eng., U.K. K11 12
Wigtown, Scot., U.K. G8 12
Wilbur, Wa., U.S. C8 136
Wilburton, Ok., U.S. C3 122
Wilcannia, Austl. H4 76
Wilcox, Sk., Can. D9 124
Wilcox, Ne., U.S. A9 128
Wildcat Creek, stm., In., U.S. H3 112
Wildcat Hill, mtn., Sk., Can. A11 124
Wild Coast, cst., S. Afr. H9 70
Wilder, Id., U.S. G9 136
Wilderness of Judaea (Midbar Yehuda), des., Asia G6 58
Wildhay, stm., Ab., Can. C13 138
Wildhorse Creek, stm., U.S. G10 126
Wild Horse Lake, l., Mt., U.S. B17 136
Wild Rice, stm., Mn., U.S. D2 118
Wild Rice, stm., N.D., U.S. H17 124
Wildrose, N.D., U.S. F10 124
Wild Rose, Wi., U.S. G9 118
Wildwood, Ab., Can. C15 138
Wildwood, N.J., U.S. F11 114
Wilge, stm., S. Afr. E9 70
Wilhelm, Mount, mtn., Pap. N. Gui. b3 79a
Wilhelmina Gebergte, mts., Sur. C6 84
Wilhelmshaven, Ger. C4 16
Wilhelmstal, Nmb. B3 70
Wilkerson Pass, p., Co., U.S. B3 128
Wilkes-Barre, Pa., U.S. C10 114
Wilkesboro, N.C., U.S. H4 114
Wilkes Land, reg., Ant. C16 81
Wilkie, Sk., Can. B5 124
Willacoochee, Ga., U.S. E2 116
Willamette, stm., Or., U.S. E4 136
Willamette, Middle Fork, stm., Or., U.S. G4 136
Willamina, Or., U.S. E3 136
Willandra Billabong Creek, stm., Austl. I5 76
Willandra National Park, p.o.i., Austl. I5 76
Willapa Bay, b., Wa., U.S. D2 136
Willard, Mo., U.S. G4 120
Willard, Oh., U.S. C3 114
Willard, Ut., U.S. B4 132
Willard, Punta, c., Mex. A2 100
Willcox, Az., U.S. K7 132
Willcox Playa, l., Az., U.S. K7 132
Willemstad, Neth. Ant. p22 104g
Willeroo, Austl. C6 74
William, Mount, mtn., Austl. K4 76
William Bill Dannelly Reservoir, res., Al., U.S. E11 122
Williams, Ca., U.S. D3 134
Williams, Ia., U.S. I5 118
Williams, Mn., U.S. C3 118
Williams, stm., Austl. C3 76
Williamsburg, Ia., U.S. C5 120
Williamsburg, Ky., U.S. H1 114
Williamsburg, Va., U.S. G9 114
Williams Lake, B.C., Can. D8 138
Williamson, N.Y., U.S. E12 112
Williamson, W.V., U.S. G3 114
Williamson, stm., Or., U.S. H5 136
Williamson, Mount, mtn., Ca., U.S. G7 134
Williamsport, Pa., U.S. C8 114
Williamston, Mi., U.S. F5 112
Williamston, S.C., U.S. B3 116
Williamstown, Ky., U.S. F1 114
Williamstown, N.J., U.S. E11 114
Williamstown, W.V., U.S. E4 114
Williamsville, Il., U.S. L9 118
Willikies, Antig. f4 105b
Willimantic, Ct., U.S. C13 114
Willingboro, N.J., U.S. D10 114
Willis, Tx., U.S. G3 122
Willis Group, is., Austl. C10 74
Williston, Fl., U.S. G3 116
Williston, N.D., U.S. F10 124
Williston, S.C., U.S. C4 116
Williston Lake, res., B.C., Can. D6 106
Willits, Ca., U.S. D2 134
Willmar, Mn., U.S. F3 118
Willoughby, Oh., U.S. C4 114
Willoughby Bay, b., Antig. f4 105b
Willow, Ak., U.S. D10 140
Willow, stm., B.C., Can. C8 138
Willowbrook, Sk., Can. C10 124
Willow Bunch, Sk., Can. E8 124
Willow Bunch Lake, l., Sk., Can. E8 124
Willow Creek, Ca., U.S. C2 134
Willow Creek, Mt., U.S. E15 136
Willow Creek, stm., Ab., Can. F17 138
Willow Creek, stm., Or., U.S. F9 136
Willow Creek, stm., Or., U.S. E7 136
Willow Lake, S.D., U.S. C15 126
Willow Lake, l., N.T., Can. C7 106
Willowmore, S. Afr. H6 70
Willowra, Austl. D6 74
Willow Reservoir, res., Wi., U.S. F9 118
Willows, Ca., U.S. D3 134
Willow Springs, Mo., U.S. H6 120
Willowvale, S. Afr. H9 70
Wills Creek, stm., Austl. D2 76
Wills Point, Tx., U.S. E2 122
Wilmar, Ar., U.S. D6 122
Wilmer, Al., U.S. G10 122
Wilmer, Tx., U.S. E2 122
Wilmette, Il., U.S. F2 112
Wilmington, De., U.S. E10 114
Wilmington, N.C., U.S. B7 116
Wilmington, Oh., U.S. E2 114
Wilmington, Vt., U.S. H4 110
Wilmore, Ky., U.S. G13 120
Wilmot, S.D., U.S. F2 118
Wilpattu National Park, p.o.i., Sri L. G4 53
Wilsall, Mt., U.S. D16 136
Wilson, Austl. H2 76
Wilson, Ar., U.S. B8 122
Wilson, La., U.S. G7 122
Wilson, N.Y., U.S. E11 112
Wilson, N.C., U.S. I8 114
Wilson, Ok., U.S. G11 128
Wilson, Tx., U.S. H7 128
Wilson, stm., Austl. F4 76
Wilson, Cape, c., Nu., Can. B14 106
Wilson, Mount, mtn., Az., U.S. H2 132
Wilson, Mount, mtn., Ca., U.S. I7 134
Wilson, Mount, mtn., Co., U.S. F8 132
Wilson Lake, res., Al., U.S. C11 122
Wilson Lake, res., Ks., U.S. C10 128
Wilsons Promontory, pen., Austl. L6 76
Wilsons Promontory National Park, p.o.i., Austl. L6 76
Wilsonville, Ne., U.S. A8 128
Wilton, Eng., U.K. J11 12
Wilton, Me., U.S. F6 110
Wilton, N.H., U.S. B14 114
Wilton, Wi., U.S. H8 118
Wilton, stm., Austl. B6 74
Wiluna, Austl. E4 74
Wimauma, Fl., U.S. I3 116
Wimberley, Tx., U.S. D9 130
Winamac, In., U.S. G3 112
Winburg, S. Afr. F8 70
Winchendon, Ma., U.S. B13 114
Winchester, On., Can. C14 112
Winchester, Eng., U.K. J11 12
Winchester, Il., U.S. E7 120
Winchester, In., U.S. H5 112
Winchester, Ky., U.S. G1 114
Winchester, Tn., U.S. B12 122
Winchester, Va., U.S. E7 114
Wind, stm., Yk., Can. B3 106
Wind, stm., Wy., U.S. D4 126
Wind Cave National Park, p.o.i., S.D., U.S. D9 126
Winder, Ga., U.S. B2 116
Windermere, B.C., Can. F15 138
Windermere, Eng., U.K. G10 12
Windfall, Ab., Can. B14 138
Windhoek, Nmb. C3 70
Windigo, stm., Qc., Can. C3 110
Windom, Mn., U.S. H3 118
Windorah, Austl. E4 76
Window Rock, Az., U.S. H7 132
Wind River Peak, mtn., Wy., U.S. E3 126
Wind River Range, mts., Wy., U.S. D3 126
Windsor, Austl. I8 76
Windsor, N.S., Can. E12 110
Windsor, On., Can. F6 112
Windsor, Qc., Can. E5 110
Windsor, Eng., U.K. J12 12
Windsor, Ca., U.S. E3 134
Windsor, Ct., U.S. C13 114
Windsor, Il., U.S. E9 120
Windsor, Mo., U.S. F4 120
Windsor, N.C., U.S. I9 114
Windsor, Va., U.S. H9 114
Windsor Forest, Ga., U.S. E4 116
Windsor Locks, Ct., U.S. C13 114
Windthorst, Tx., U.S. H10 128
Windward, Gren. p11 105e
Windward Islands, is., N.A. k6 105c
Windward Passage, strt., N.A. C11 102
Windy Peak, mtn., Co., U.S. C2 128
Winfield, Al., U.S. D11 122
Winfield, Ks., U.S. D12 128
Winfield, Mo., U.S. E7 120
Winfield, W.V., U.S. F4 114
Wing, N.D., U.S. G13 124
Wingate, N.C., U.S. B5 116
Wingham, Austl. H9 76
Wingham, On., Can. E8 112
Wingo, Ky., U.S. H9 120
Winisk, On., Can. D13 106
Winisk, stm., On., Can. E13 106
Winisk Lake, l., On., Can. E13 106
Wink, Tx., U.S. C4 130
Winkana, Mya. E4 48
Winkelman, Az., U.S. K6 132
Winkler, Mb., Can. E16 124
Winlock, Wa., U.S. D3 136
Winneba, Ghana H4 64
Winnebago, Mn., U.S. H4 118
Winnebago, Ne., U.S. B1 120
Winnebago, stm., Ia., U.S. H5 118
Winnebago, Lake, l., Wi., U.S. G10 118
Winneconne, Wi., U.S. G10 118
Winnemucca, Nv., U.S. B8 134
Winnemucca Lake, l., Nv., U.S. C6 134
Winner, S.D., U.S. D13 126
Winnetka, Il., U.S. F2 112
Winnett, Mt., U.S. H5 124
Winnibigoshish, Lake, res., Mn., U.S. D4 118
Winnie, Tx., U.S. H4 122
Winning, Austl. D2 74
Winnipeg, Mb., Can. E16 124
Winnipeg, stm., Can. E11 106
Winnipeg, Lake, l., Mb., Can. E11 106
Winnipeg Beach, Mb., Can. D17 124
Winnipegosis, Mb., Can. C13 124
Winnipegosis, Lake, l., Mb., Can. B13 124
Winnipesaukee, Lake, l., N.H., U.S. G5 110
Winnsboro, S.C., U.S. B4 116
Winnsboro, Tx., U.S. E3 122
Winnsboro Mills, S.C., U.S. B4 116
Winona, Ks., U.S. B7 128
Winona, Mn., U.S. G7 118
Winona, Ms., U.S. D9 122
Winona, Mo., U.S. G6 120
Winooski, stm., Vt., U.S. F4 110
Winschoten, Neth. A15 14
Winschoterdiep, can., Neth. A15 14
Winsen, Ger. C6 16
Winslow, Az., U.S. H6 132
Winslow, In., U.S. F10 120
Winslow, Me., U.S. F7 110
Winsted, Mn., U.S. G4 118
Winston, Fl., U.S. H3 116
Winston, Or., U.S. G3 136
Winston-Salem, N.C., U.S. H5 114
Winter, Wi., U.S. F8 118
Winter Garden, Fl., U.S. H4 116
Winter Harbor, Me., U.S. F8 110
Winter Harbour, B.C., Can. F2 138
Winterhaven, Ca., U.S. K2 132
Winter Haven, Fl., U.S. I4 116
Winter Island, i., Nu., Can. B14 106
Winter Park, Fl., U.S. H4 116
Winters, Ca., U.S. E3 134
Winters, Tx., U.S. C8 130
Winterset, Ia., U.S. C4 120
Winterswijk, Neth. B15 14
Winterthur, Switz. C5 22
Winterville, Ga., U.S. C2 116
Winterville, Ms., U.S. D7 122
Winthrop, Me., U.S. F7 110
Winthrop, Wa., U.S. B6 136
Winthrop Harbor, Il., U.S. F2 112
Wintinna, Austl. E6 74
Winton, Austl. D4 76
Winton, N.Z. H3 80
Winton, N.C., U.S. H8 114
Wirāṭnagar, Nepal E11 54
Wīrgañj, Nepal E10 54
Wisbech, Eng., U.K. I12 12
Wiscasset, Me., U.S. G7 110
Wisconsin, state, U.S. G9 118
Wisconsin, stm., Wi., U.S. I8 118
Wisconsin Dells, Wi., U.S. H9 118
Wisconsin Dells, misc. cult., Wi., U.S. H9 118
Wisconsin Rapids, Wi., U.S. G8 118
Wisdom, Mt., U.S. E13 136
Wise, Va., U.S. G3 114
Wiseman, Ak., U.S. C9 140
Wishek, N.D., U.S. A13 126
Wishram, Wa., U.S. E5 136
Wisła, Pol. G14 16
Wisła (Vistula), stm., Pol. B14 16
Wiślany, Mierzeja, spit, Eur. B15 16
Wisłok, stm., Pol. F18 16
Wisłoka, stm., Pol. F17 16
Wismar, Ger. C7 16
Wisner, La., U.S. F7 122
Wister, Ok., U.S. C4 122
Wisznice, Pol. E19 16
Witbank, S. Afr. D9 70
Witham, stm., Eng., U.K. H12 12
Withlacoochee, stm., U.S. F2 116
Witkowo, Pol. D13 16
Wit-Mfolozi, stm., S. Afr. F10 70
Witney, Eng., U.K. J11 12
Wit Nossob, stm., Nmb. C4 70
Witsand, S. Afr. I5 70
Witt, Il., U.S. E8 120
Wittenberg, Wi., U.S. G9 118
Wittenberge, Ger. C7 16
Wittenburg, Ger. C6 16
Wittenoom, Austl. D3 74
Wittingen, Ger. D6 16
Wittlich, Ger. G2 16
Wittmund, Ger. C3 16
Wittstock, Ger. C8 16
Witu Islands, is., Pap. N. Gui. a5 79a
Witvlei, Nmb. C4 70
Witwatersrand, mts., S. Afr. D8 70
Witzenhausen, Ger. E5 16
Wiżajny, Pol. B18 16
Wkra, stm., Pol. C15 16
Wleń, Pol. E11 16
Włocławek, Pol. D15 16
Włocławek, state, Pol. D14 16
Włoszczowa, Pol. F15 16
Woburn, Ma., U.S. B14 114
Wodonga, Austl. K6 76
Wodzisław Śląski, Pol. F14 16
Wokam, Pulau, i., Indon. G10 44
Woking, Eng., U.K. J12 12
Wokingham Creek, stm., Austl. C4 76
Wolbrom, Pol. F15 16
Wolcott, In., U.S. D10 120
Wolcott, N.Y., U.S. E13 112
Wolcottville, In., U.S. G4 112
Woleai, at., Micron. C5 72
Wolf, stm., U.S. B9 122
Wolf, stm., Ms., U.S. G9 122
Wolf, stm., Wi., U.S. G10 118
Wolf, Volcán, vol., Ec. h11 84a
Wolfach, Ger. H4 16
Wolf Creek, Or., U.S. H3 136
Wolf Creek, stm., U.S. E9 128
Wolf Creek, stm., Mt., U.S. C17 136
Wolf Creek Pass, p., Co., U.S. F10 132
Wolf Creek Reservoir, res., Ks., U.S. F2 120
Wolfeboro, N.H., U.S. G5 110
Wolfe Island, i., On., Can. D13 112
Wolfen, Ger. E8 16
Wolfenbüttel, Ger. D6 16
Wolfenden, Mount, mtn., B.C., Can. F3 138
Wolfforth, Tx., U.S. H6 128
Wolfhagen, Ger. E4 16
Wolf Lake, Mi., U.S. E3 112
Wolf Lake, l., Ab., Can. B20 138
Wolf Point, Mt., U.S. F8 124
Wolfratshausen, Ger. I7 16
Wolf Rock, r., Eng., U.K. L7 12
Wolfsberg, Aus. D11 22
Wolfsburg, Ger. D6 16
Wolfville, N.S., Can. E12 110
Wolgast, Ger. B9 16
Woliński Park Narodowy, p.o.i., Pol. C10 16
Wollaston Lake, l., Sk., Can. D10 106
Wollaston Peninsula, pen., Can. B7 106
Wollemi National Park, p.o.i., Austl. I7 76
Wollongong, Austl. J8 76
Wołomin, Pol. D17 16
Wołów, Pol. E12 16
Wolseley, Sk., Can. D10 124
Wolsey, S.D., U.S. C14 126
Wolverhampton, Eng., U.K. I10 12
Wolverton, Eng., U.K. I11 12
Wonarah, Austl. C7 74
Wondai, Austl. F8 76
Wonderland, Ca., U.S. C4 134
Wondinong, Austl. E3 74
Wonewoc, Wi., U.S. H8 118
Wŏnju, Kor., S. F7 38
Wonogiri, Indon. G7 50
Wonosari, Indon. H7 50
Wonosobo, Indon. G6 50
Wŏnsan, Kor., N. E7 38
Wonthaggi, Austl. L5 76
Wood, S.D., U.S. D12 126

Name | Map Ref. | Page

Wood, stm., Ne., U.S. G13 126
Wood, Mount, mtn., Mt., U.S. E17 136
Woodall Mountain, hill, Ms., U.S. C10 122
Woodbine, Ga., U.S. F4 116
Woodbine, Ia., U.S. C2 120
Woodbridge, Eng., U.K. I14 12
Woodbridge, Va., U.S. F8 114
Woodburn, Or., U.S. E4 136
Woodbury, Ga., U.S. E14 122
Woodbury, N.J., U.S. E10 114
Woodbury, Tn., U.S. I11 120
Woodhull, Il., U.S. C7 120
Woodlake, Ca., U.S. G6 134
Wood Lake, Ne., U.S. E12 126
Woodland, Ca., U.S. E4 134
Woodland, Me., U.S. E9 110
Woodland, N.C., U.S. H8 114
Woodland Park, Co., U.S. C3 128
Woodridge, Mb., Can. E17 124
Wood River, Il., U.S. F7 120
Wood River, Ne., U.S. G14 126
Woodroffe, Mount, mtn., Austl. E6 74
Woodruff, Az., U.S. I6 132
Woodruff, S.C., U.S. B3 116
Woodruff, Wi., U.S. F9 118
Woods, Lake, l., Austl. C6 74
Woods, Lake of the, l., N.A. B3 118
Woodsboro, Tx., U.S. F10 130
Woodsfield, Oh., U.S. E4 114
Woods Hole, Ma., U.S. C15 114
Woodside, Austl. L6 76
Woodson, Tx., U.S. A8 130
Woodstock, Austl. D3 76
Woodstock, N.B., Can. D9 110
Woodstock, On., Can. E9 112
Woodstock, Eng., U.K. J11 12
Woodstock, Il., U.S. B9 120
Woodstock, N.Y., U.S. B11 114
Woodstock, Vt., U.S. G4 110
Woodsville, N.H., U.S. F4 110
Woodville, N.Z. E6 80
Woodville, Al., U.S. C12 122
Woodville, Ga., U.S. C2 116
Woodville, Ms., U.S. F7 122
Woodville, Oh., U.S. G6 112
Woodville, Tx., U.S. G4 122
Woodward, Ok., U.S. E9 128
Woody, stm., Can. B12 124
Woody Head, c., Austl. G9 76
Woolmarket, Ms., U.S. G9 122
Woomera, Austl. F7 74
Woonsocket, R.I., U.S. B14 114
Woonsocket, S.D., U.S. C14 126
Woorabinda, Austl. E7 76
Wooramel, Austl. E2 74
Wooramel, stm., Austl. E2 74
Wooster, Oh., U.S. D3 114
Worcester, S. Afr. H4 70
Worcester, Eng., U.K. I10 12
Worcester, Ma., U.S. B14 114
Worden, Mt., U.S. A4 126
Wörgl, Aus. C9 22
Workington, Eng., U.K. G9 12
Worksop, Eng., U.K. H11 12
Worland, Wy., U.S. C5 126
Worms, Ger. G4 16
Worthing, Eng., U.K. K12 12
Worthington, In., U.S. E11 120
Worthington, Mn., U.S. H3 118
Worthington, Oh., U.S. D3 114
Worthington Peak, mtn., Nv., U.S. E1 132
Wotho, at., Marsh. Is. B7 72
Wotu, Indon. E12 50
Wouhnta, Nic. F6 102
Wounded Knee, S.D., U.S. D10 126
Wounded Knee Creek, stm., S.D., U.S. D10 126
Wowan, Austl. D8 76
Wowoni, Pulau, i., Indon. F7 44
Woy Woy, Austl. I8 76
Wrangel Island see Vrangelja, ostrov, i., Russia B24 34
Wrangell, Ak., U.S. E13 140
Wrangell, Cape, c., Ak., U.S. g21 140a
Wrangell Mountains, mts., Ak., U.S. D11 140
Wrath, Cape, c., Scot., U.K. C8 12
Wrens, Ga., U.S. C3 116
Wrentham, Ab., Can. G18 138
Wrexham, Wales, U.K. H10 12
Wright, Mount, mtn., Mt., U.S. B14 136
Wright City, Mo., U.S. F6 120
Wright Patman Lake, res., Tx., U.S. D4 122
Wrightson, Mount, mtn., Az., U.S. L6 132
Wrightstown, Wi., U.S. D1 112
Wrightsville, Ga., U.S. D3 116
Wrightsville Beach, N.C., U.S. B8 116
Wrigley, N.T., Can. C6 106
Wrigley, Tn., U.S. I10 120
Wrocław (Breslau), Pol. E13 16
Wrocław, state, Pol. E13 16
Wrong Lake, l., Mb., Can. B17 124
Wrottesley, Cape, c., N.T., Can. B15 140
Wroxton, Sk., Can. C12 124
Września, Pol. D13 16
Wschowa, Pol. E12 16
Wu, stm., China H3 42
Wu, stm., China G2 42
Wu, stm., China H4 42
Wu, stm., China G7 42
Wu, stm., China I5 42
Wubu, China C4 42
Wuchang, China B7 38
Wuchang Hu, l., China F7 42
Wuchin see Changzhou, China F8 42
Wuchou see Wuzhou, China J4 42
Wuchow see Wuzhou, China J4 42
Wuchuan, China K4 42
Wuchuan, China A4 42
Wuchung see Wuzhong, China C2 42
Wuda, China B2 42
Wudaoliang, China D3 36
Wudi, China C7 42
Wuding, China F5 36
Wuding, stm., China C4 42
Wudu, China E5 36
Wufeng, China F4 42
Wugang, China H4 42
Wugong, China D2 42
Wugong Shan, mts., China H5 42
Wuhai, China B2 42
Wuhan (Hankow), China E6 42
Wuhsi see Wuxi, China F9 42
Wuhsing see Huzhou, China F9 42
Wuhu, China F8 42
Wuhua, China J6 42
Wuhuanchi, China C4 38
Wüjang, China B7 54
Wujia, stm., China A3 42
Wujiangdu, China H2 42
Wukang, China F8 42
Wukari, Nig. H6 64
Wukeshu, China B7 38
Wulateqianqi, China A3 42
Wuliang Shan, mts., China G5 36
Wulong, China G2 42
Wuluhan, Indon. H8 50
Wulumuch'i see Ürümqi, China C2 36
Wuluo, China H3 42
Wuming, China J3 42
Wundwin, Mya. B2 48
Wunnummin Lake, l., On., Can. E13 106
Wunstorf, Ger. D5 16
Wupatki National Monument, p.o.i., Az., U.S. H5 132
Wuppertal, Ger. E3 16
Wuppertal, S. Afr. H4 70
Wuqi, China C3 42
Wuqia, China B12 56
Wuqiang, China B6 42
Wurno, Nig. G6 64
Würzburg, Ger. G5 16
Wurzen, Ger. E8 16
Wushan, China F3 42
Wusheng, China F2 42
Wushenqi, China B3 42
Wushi, China J4 42
Wusih see Wuxi, China F9 42
Wusuli (Ussuri), stm., Asia B11 36
Wutai, China B5 42
Wutai Shan, mtn., China B5 42
Wutong, China I3 42
Wutongqiao, China F5 36
Wutsin see Changzhou, China F8 42
Wut'ungch'iao see Wutongqiao, China F5 36
Wutungkiao see Wutongqiao, China F5 36
Wuvulu Island, i., Pap. N. Gui. a3 79a
Wuwei, China D5 36
Wuwei, China F7 42
Wuxi, China F9 42
Wuxi, China F3 42
Wuxiang, China C5 42
Wuyang, China H4 42
Wuyi, China G8 42
Wuyi Shan, mts., China H7 42
Wuyuan, China A3 42
Wuyuan, China G7 42
Wuzhai, China B4 42
Wuzhi Shan (Wuzhi Peak), mtn., China L3 42
Wuzhong, China C2 42
Wuzhou, China J4 42
Wyaconda, Mo., U.S. D6 120
Wyandotte, Mi., U.S. B2 114
Wyandra, Austl. F5 76
Wyangala, Lake, res., Austl. J7 76
Wyatt, Mo., U.S. H8 120
Wycheproof, Austl. K4 76
Wye, stm., U.K. J10 12
Wyeville, Wi., U.S. G8 118
Wyk, Ger. B4 16
Wykoff, Mn., U.S. H6 118
Wylie, Lake, res., U.S. A4 116
Wymark, Sk., Can. D6 124
Wymondham, Eng., U.K. I13 12
Wymore, Ne., U.S. K2 118
Wyndham, Austl. C5 74
Wyndmere, N.D., U.S. E1 118
Wynne, Ar., U.S. B8 122
Wynnewood, Ok., U.S. G11 128
Wynniatt Bay, b., Can. A8 106
Wynona, Ok., U.S. E12 128
Wynot, Ne., U.S. E15 126
Wynyard, Austl. n12 77a
Wynyard, Sk., Can. C9 124
Wyodak, Wy., U.S. C7 126
Wyoming, On., Can. F7 112
Wyoming, Ia., U.S. B6 120
Wyoming, Mi., U.S. F4 112
Wyoming, state, U.S. E5 126
Wyoming Peak, mtn., Wy., U.S. H16 136
Wyong, Austl. I8 76
Wyperfield National Park, p.o.i., Austl. J3 76
Wyśmierzyce, Pol. E16 16
Wysokie Mazowieckie, Pol. D18 16
Wyszków, Pol. D17 16
Wytheville, Va., U.S. H4 114

X

Xaafuun, Raas, c., Som. B10 66
Xàbia, Spain F11 20
Xaidulla, China A4 46
Xainza, China C12 54
Xai-Xai, Moz. D11 70
Xalapa (Jalapa), Mex. F10 100
Xalin, Som. C9 66
Xam (Chu), stm., Asia B7 48
Xambioá, Braz. D1 88
Xambrê, stm., Braz. A11 92
Xam Nua, Laos B7 48
Xá-Muteba, Ang. B2 68
Xan (San), stm., Asia E8 48
Xangongo, Ang. D2 68
Xankändi, Azer. B6 56
Xánthi, Grc. B7 28
Xanxerê, Braz. C11 92
Xapecó, stm., Braz. C11 92
Xapuri, Braz. F4 84
Xar Moron, stm., China C3 38
Xàtiva, Spain F10 20
Xau, Lake, pl., Bots. B7 70
Xavantina, Braz. D6 90
Xaxim, Braz. C11 92
Xcalak, Mex. C4 102
X-Can, Mex. B4 102
Xelva, Spain E9 20
Xenia, Oh., U.S. E2 114
Xepenehe, N. Cal. m16 79d
Xhumo, Bots. B7 70
Xi, stm., China J5 42
Xiachuan Dao, i., China K5 42
Xiagaixin, China A5 48
Xiamen (Amoy), China I7 42
Xi'an (Sian), China D3 42
Xianfeng, China G3 42
Xiang, stm., China H5 42
Xiangcheng, China E5 42
Xiangfan, China F4 42
Xianggang (Hong Kong), China J6 42
Xiangkhoang, Laos C6 48
Xiangkhoang, Plateau de (Tran Ninh), plat., Laos C6 48
Xiangning, China D4 42
Xiangride, China D4 36
Xiangshan, China G9 42
Xiangtan, China H5 42
Xiangxiang, China H5 42
Xiangyin, China G5 42
Xiangyuan, China C5 42
Xiangzhou, China J3 42
Xianju, China G9 42
Xianshui, stm., China E5 36
Xiantao, China F5 42
Xianyang, China D3 42
Xianyang, China G8 42
Xianyou, China I8 42
Xiao, stm., China I6 42
Xiaochengzi, China C5 38
Xiaogan, China F5 42
Xiaoguai, China B1 36
Xiao Hinggan Ling (Lesser Khingan Range), mts., China B10 36
Xiaojin, China E5 36
Xiaojiu, China B7 38
Xiaoluan, stm., China D2 38
Xiaopingyang, China J3 42
Xiaoshan, China F9 42
Xiaoxian, China D7 42
Xiaoyi, China C4 42
Xiapu, China H9 42
Xiawa, China C4 38
Xiaxian, China D4 42
Xibo, stm., China D3 38
Xichang, China F5 36
Xichong, China F1 42
Xicoténcatl, Mex. D9 100
Xié, stm., Braz. G8 86
Xifei, stm., China E7 42
Xifeng, China C6 38
Xifeng, China H2 42
Xigazê, China D12 54
Xihan, stm., China D1 42
Xihe, China F5 42
Xiheying, China B6 42
Xihua, China E6 42
Xiji, China D1 42
Xiliao, stm., China C5 38
Xilin, China D11 54
Xilinhot, China C2 38
Ximakou, China F5 42
Ximalin, China A6 42
Ximiao, China C5 36
Xin, stm., China G7 42
Xin'an, China C6 38
Xin'anjiang Shuiku, res., China G8 42
Xinavane, Moz. D11 70
Xin Barag Youqi, China B8 36
Xin Barag Zuoqi, China B8 36
Xinbin, China D6 38
Xincai, China E6 42
Xinchang, China G9 42
Xincheng, China G6 36
Xincheng, China B6 42
Xindu, China I4 42
Xinfeng, China I6 42
Xinfeng Shuiku, res., China J6 42
Xing'an, China I4 42
Xingcheng, China A9 42
Xingguo, China H6 42
Xinghai, China D4 36
Xinghe, China A5 42
Xinghua, China E8 42
Xinglong, China D1 42
Xingren, China F6 36
Xingrenbu, China C1 42
Xingtai, China C6 42
Xingtang, China B6 42
Xingu, stm., Braz. D7 84
Xingxian, China B4 42
Xingyi, China F5 36
Xinhe, China C6 42
Xinhua, China H4 42
Xinhui, China J5 42
Xining, China D5 36
Xinji, China C6 42
Xinjiang, China D4 42
Xinjiang, state, China A5 46
Xinjin, China E5 36
Xinjin, China B9 42
Xinjiulong (New Kowloon), China J6 42
Xinkai, stm., China C5 38
Xinli, China B7 38
Xinlitun, China D5 38
Xinmin, China C5 38
Xinning, China H4 42
Xinshao, China H4 42
Xintian, China I5 42
Xinwen, China D7 42
Xinxian, China B5 42
Xinxian, China F6 42
Xinxiang, China D5 42
Xinxing, China C8 38
Xinyang, China E6 42
Xinye, China E5 42
Xinyi, China D8 42
Xinyu, China H6 42
Xinzhou, China L3 42
Xiongyuecheng, China A9 42
Xiping, China E6 42
Xiping, China G8 42
Xiqing Shan, mts., China E5 36
Xique-Xique, Braz. F4 88
Xirdalan, Azer. A6 56
Xishanqiao, China F8 42
Xisha Qundao (Paracel Islands), is., China B5 50
Xishui, China F6 42
Xiti, China B9 54
Xiu, stm., China G6 42
Xi Ujimqin Qi, China B2 38
Xiushui, China G6 42
Xiuyan, China A10 42
Xiva, Spain E10 20
Xixabangma Feng, mtn., China D10 54
Xixi, China H8 42
Xixian, China E6 42
Xixiang, China E2 42
Xixona, Spain F10 20
Xiyang, China C5 42
Xizang (Tibet), state, China B5 46
Xizi, China D3 38
Xochicalco, hist., Mex. F9 100
Xochistlahuaca, Mex. G9 100
Xu, stm., China H7 42
Xuancheng, China F8 42
Xuan'en, China F3 42
Xuang, stm., Laos B6 48
Xuanhan, China F2 42
Xuanhua, China A6 42
Xuanwei, China F5 36
Xuchang, China D5 42
Xun, stm., China J4 42
Xungru, China D10 54
Xunwu, China I6 42
Xupu, China H4 42
Xúquer see Júcar, stm., Spain E10 20
Xuwen, China K4 42
Xuyi, China E8 42
Xuyong, China G1 42
Xuzhou, China D7 42
Xylókastro, Grc. E5 28

Y

Yaak, Mt., U.S. B11 136
Yaan, China E5 36
Yaapeet, Austl. J3 76
Yablonovy Range see Jablonovyj hrebet, mts., Russia F11 34
Yabluniv, Ukr. A12 26
Yabrīn, Sau. Ar. E6 56
Yabucoa, P.R. B4 104a
Yabuli, China B8 38
Yacambu, Parque Nacional, p.o.i., Ven. C7 86
Yacata, i., Fiji p20 79e
Yacheng, China L3 42
Yachi, stm., China H2 42
Yaco see Iaco, stm., S.A. F4 84
Yacuiba, Bol. D4 90
Yacyretá, Isla, i., Para. C9 92
Yādgīr, India C3 53
Yadkin, stm., N.C., U.S. H4 114
Yadkinville, N.C., U.S. H5 114
Yadong, China E12 54
Yafran, Libya A2 62
Yagasa Cluster, i., Fiji q20 79e
Yagoua, Cam. B3 66
Yagradagzê Shan, mtn., China D4 36
Yaguajay, Cuba A8 102
Yaguarón (Jaguarão), stm., S.A. F11 92
Yaguas, stm., S.A. I6 86
Yahe, China B9 38
Yahk, B.C., Can. G14 138
Yahualica, Mex. E7 100
Yai, Khao, mtn., Thai. E4 48
Yainax Butte, mtn., Or., U.S. A4 134
Yaita, Japan C12 40
Yaitopya see Ethiopia, ctry., Afr. F7 62
Yaizu, Japan E11 40
Yajiang, China E5 36
Yakacık, Tur. B7 58
Yakeshi, China B9 36
Yakima, Wa., U.S. D6 136
Yakima, stm., Wa., U.S. D7 136
Yakmach, Pak. D9 56
Yako, Burkina G4 64
Yakoma, D.R.C. D4 66
Yakumo, Japan C14 38
Yaku-shima, i., Japan I9 38
Yakutat Bay, b., Ak., U.S. E11 140
Yakutia see Jakutija, state, Russia D14 34
Yala, Thai. I5 48
Yalahau, Laguna de, b., Mex. B4 102
Yale, B.C., Can. G9 138
Yale, Mi., U.S. E7 112
Yale, Ok., U.S. A2 122
Yale, Mount, mtn., Co., U.S. C2 128
Yalgoo, Austl. E3 74
Yalinga, C.A.R. C4 66
Yalobusha, stm., Ms., U.S. D9 122
Yalong, stm., China E5 36
Yalova, Tur. C12 28
Yalpuh, ozero, l., Ukr. D15 26
Yalu (Amnok-kang), stm., Asia D7 38
Yalu, stm., China D6 38
Yalvaç, Tur. E14 28
Yamaga, Japan F3 40
Yamagata, Japan A13 40
Yamagata, state, Japan A13 40
Yamaguchi, Japan E4 40
Yamaguchi, state, Japan E4 40
Yamal Peninsula see Jamal, poluostrov, pen., Russia B2 34
Yamanaka, Japan C9 40
Yamanashi, state, Japan D11 40
Yamasaki, Japan D7 40
Yamaska, stm., Qc., Can. E4 110
Yamatengwumulu, China D4 36
Yamba, Austl. G9 76
Yambio, Sudan G5 62
Yamdena, Pulau, i., Indon. G9 44
Yame, Japan F3 40
Ya Men, b., China J5 42
Yamethin, Mya. B3 48
Yamma Yamma, Lake, l., Austl. F3 76
Yamoussoukro, C. Iv. H4 64
Yampa, stm., Co., U.S. C8 132
Yampil', Ukr. A15 26
Yamsay Mountain, mtn., Or., U.S. H5 136
Yamuna, stm., India F8 54
Yamzho Yumco, l., China D13 54
Yan, stm., China C4 42
Yan, stm., Sri L. G5 53
Yanac, Austl. K3 76
Yanagawa, Japan F3 40
Yanai, Japan F5 40
Yanam, India C6 53
Yan'an, China C3 42
Yanbu' al-Bahr, Sau. Ar. E4 56
Yanceyville, N.C., U.S. H6 114
Yanchang, China C3 42
Yancheng, China E9 42
Yanchi, China C2 42
Yanco Creek, stm., Austl. J5 76
Yanda Creek, stm., Austl. H5 76
Yandama Creek, stm., Austl. G3 76
Yandé, Île, i., N. Cal. m14 79d
Yandina, Sol. Is. e8 79b
Yandoon, Mya. D2 48
Yanfolila, Mali G3 64
Yang, stm., Thai. D7 48
Yangambi, D.R.C. D4 66
Yang'ang, China I7 42
Yangbajain, China C13 54
Yangcheng, China D5 42
Yangchiang see Yangjiang, China K4 42
Yangchou see Yangzhou, China E8 42
Yangchow see Yangzhou, China E8 42
Yangch'üan see Yangquan, China C5 42
Yangchun, China J4 42
Yangdachengzi, China B6 38
Yanggao, China A5 42
Yanghexi, China G3 42
Yangjiang, China K4 42
Yangku see Taiyuan, China C5 42
Yangliuqing, China B7 42
Yangon (Rangoon), Mya. D2 48
Yangon, state, Mya. D3 48
Yangpingguan, China E1 42
Yangquan, China C5 42
Yangriwan, China F4 42
Yangsan, Kor., S. D2 40
Yangshan, China I5 42
Yangshuo, China I4 42
Yangtze see Chang, stm., China F8 36
Yangtze see Jinsha, stm., China F5 36
Yangxian, China E2 42
Yangxin, China G6 42
Yangyang, Kor., S. A1 40
Yangyuan, China A5 42
Yangzhou, China E8 42
Yanhe, China G3 42
Yanji, China C8 38
Yanji, China C8 38
Yanjiadian, China B9 42
Yankeetown, Fl., U.S. G3 116
Yankton, S.D., U.S. E15 126
Yanqi, China C2 36
Yanqing, China A6 42
Yanshou, China B8 38
Yantabulla, Austl. G5 76
Yantai, China C9 42
Yantan, China G9 42
Yanting, China F1 42
Yantongshan, China C6 38
Yanyuan, China F5 36
Yanzhou, China D7 42
Yao, Chad E3 62
Yaoundé, Cam. D2 66
Yaoxian, China D3 42
Yao Yai, Ko, i., Thai. I4 48
Yap, i., Micron. C4 72
Yapacana, Parque Nacional, p.o.i., Ven. F8 86
Yapacaní, Bol. C4 90
Yapen, Pulau, i., Indon. F10 44
Yapen, Selat, strt., Indon. F10 44
Yappar, stm., Austl. B4 76
Yaque del Norte, stm., Dom. Rep. C12 102
Yaqui, stm., Mex. G8 98
Yaquina, stm., Or., U.S. F3 136
Yaracuy, state, Ven. B7 86
Yaraka, Austl. E5 76
Yardımcı, Tur. A10 58
Yardımcı Burnu, c., Tur. G13 28
Yarí, stm., Col. H5 86
Yariga-take, mtn., Japan C10 40
Yarīm, Yemen G5 56
Yaring, Thai. I5 48
Yaritagua, Ven. B7 86
Yarkand see Shache, China B12 56
Yarkand see Yarkant, stm., China G13 32
Yarkant see Shache, China B12 56
Yarkant, stm., China G13 32
Yarloop, Austl. F3 74
Yarmouth, N.S., Can. G10 110
Yarmouth, Me., U.S. G6 110
Yarmu, Pap. N. Gui. a3 79a
Yarram, Austl. L6 76
Yarraman, Austl. F9 76
Yarrawonga, Austl. K5 76
Yarumal, Col. D4 86
Yasawa Group, is., Fiji p18 79e
Yashiro-jima, i., Japan F5 40
Yasinia, Ukr. A11 26
Yasothon, Thai. E6 48
Yass, Austl. J7 76
Yasugi, Japan D6 40
Yasuní, stm., Ec. H3 86
Yasuni, Parque Nacional, p.o.i., Ec. H4 86
Yata, stm., Bol. B3 90
Yatağan, Tur. F11 28
Yaté, N. Cal. n16 79d
Yates City, Il., U.S. D7 120
Yathkyed Lake, l., Nu., Can. C11 106
Yating, China I2 42
Yatsuga-take, mtn., Japan D11 40
Yatsuo, Japan C10 40
Yatsushiro, Japan G3 40
Yatsushiro-kai, b., Japan G3 40
Yatuá, stm., Ven. G8 86
Yauca, Peru G3 84
Yauco, P.R. B2 104a
Yautepec, Mex. F9 100
Yavarí (Javari), stm., S.A. D3 84
Yavaros, Mex. B4 100
Yavatmāl, India H7 54
Yaví, Cerro, mtn., Ven. E9 86
Yavita, Ven. F8 86
Yaviza, Pan. H9 102
Yavoriv, Ukr. G19 16
Yavuzeli, Tur. A8 58
Yaw, stm., Mya. B2 48
Yawatahama, Japan F5 40
Yaxchilán, hist., Mex. D2 102
Yayladağı, Tur. C7 58
Yayuan, China D7 38
Yazd, Iran C7 56
Yazoo, stm., Ms., U.S. E8 122
Yazoo City, Ms., U.S. E8 122
Ybbs an der Donau, Aus. B12 22
Yding Skovhøj, hill, Den. I3 8
Ýdra (Hydra), i., Grc. F6 28
Ye, Mya. E3 48
Yebyu, Mya. E4 48
Yecheng, China B12 56
Yech'ŏn, Kor., S. C1 40
Yecla, Spain F9 20
Yedashe, Mya. C3 48
Yedi Göller Milli Parkı, p.o.i., Tur. B14 28
Yedseram, stm., Nig. G7 64
Yeeda, Austl. C4 74
Yeghegnador, Arm. B6 56
Yei, Sudan G6 62
Yeji, China F6 42
Yela Island, i., Pap. N. Gui. B10 74
Yelarbon, Austl. G8 76
Yell, i., Scot., U.K. n18 12a
Yellandu, India C5 53
Yellow see Huang, stm., China D8 36
Yellow, stm., Wi., U.S. G8 118
Yellow, stm., Wi., U.S. F7 118
Yellow Grass, Sk., Can. E9 124
Yellowhead Pass, p., Can. D12 138
Yellow House Draw, stm., Tx., U.S. H3 122
Yellowknife, N.T., Can. C8 106
Yellowknife, stm., N.T., Can. C8 106
Yellow Sea, Asia G5 38
Yellowstone, stm., U.S. B7 108
Yellowstone, Clarks Fork, stm., U.S. B3 126
Yellowstone Falls, wtfl, Wy., U.S. F16 136
Yellowstone Lake, l., Wy., U.S. F16 136
Yellowstone National Park, Wy., U.S. F16 136
Yellowstone National Park, p.o.i., U.S. F16 136
Yellowtail Dam, dam, Mt., U.S. B4 126
Yellville, Ar., U.S. H5 120
Yelverton Bay, b., Nu., Can. A9 141
Yemen, ctry., Asia F6 56
Yenagoa, Nig. H6 64
Yenangyaung, Mya. B2 48
Yenanma, Mya. C2 48
Yen Bai, Viet. B7 48
Yench'eng see Yancheng, China E9 42
Yenchi see Yanji, China C8 38
Yenda, Austl. J6 76
Yendéré, Burkina G4 64
Yendi, Ghana H4 64
Ye-ngan, Mya. B3 48
Yengisar, China B12 56
Yengo National Park, p.o.i., Austl. I8 76
Yenice, Tur. A6 58
Yenice, stm., Tur. B15 28
Yenicekale, Tur. A7 58
Yenierenköy, N. Cyp. C5 58
Yenimehmetli, Tur. D15 28
Yenipazar, Tur. C13 28
Yenişehir, Tur. C12 28
Yenisey see Enisej, stm., Russia C6 34
Yenshuichen, Tai. J9 42
Yentai see Yantai, China C9 42
Yeola, India H5 54
Yeo Lake, l., Austl. E4 74
Yeovil, Eng., U.K. K10 12
Yepachic, Mex. A4 100
Yeppoon, Austl. D8 76
Yerevan (Erivan), Arm. A5 56
Yerington, Nv., U.S. E6 134
Yerköy, Tur. B3 56
Yerlisu, Tur. C9 28
Yermo, Ca., U.S. I9 134
Yerupaja, Nevado, mtn., Peru F2 84
Yerushalayim (Jerusalem), Isr. G6 58
Yesa, Embalse de, res., Spain B9 20
Yeşildere, Tur. A4 58
Yeşilköy, Tur. C11 28
Yeşiltepe, Tur. A3 58
Yeso, N.M., U.S. G4 128
Yetman, Austl. G8 76
Yetti, reg., Afr. D3 64
Ye-u, Mya. A2 48
Yeu, Île d', i., Fr. H6 14
Yevlax, Azer. A6 56
Yexian, China E5 42
Yexian, China C8 42
Yeywa, Mya. B3 48
Ygatimí, Para. B10 92
Yguazú, stm., Para. B10 92
Yhú, Para. B10 92
Yi, stm., China B6 42
Yi, stm., China D8 42
Yi, stm., China D5 42
Yi, stm., Ur. F10 92
Yi'allaq, Gebel, mtn., Egypt H4 58
Yi'an, China B10 36
Yibin, China F5 36
Yibug Caka, l., China B11 54
Yichang, China F4 42
Yicheng, China F5 42
Yichuan, China D5 42
Yichuan, China C3 42
Yichuan see Yinchuan, China B2 42
Yichun, China B10 36
Yichun, China H6 42
Yidie, China C4 42
Yidu, China C8 42
Yidu, China F4 42
Yifeng, China G6 42
Yığılca, Tur. C14 28
Yilan, China B10 36
Yilaxi, China C7 38
Yiliang, China F5 36
Yilong, China F2 42
Yin, stm., Mya. B2 48
Yinbaing, Mya. D3 48
Yinchuan, China B2 42
Ying, stm., China E6 42
Yingcheng see Yingchengzi, China B6 38
Yingcheng, China F5 42
Yingchengzi, China B6 38
Yingde, China I5 42
Yingjin, stm., China C3 38
Yingkou, China A10 42
Yingkou, China A9 42
Yingpan, China I2 42
Yingshang, China E6 42
Yingshouyingzi, China A7 42
Yingtan, China G7 42
Yining, China F14 32
Yinjiang, China G3 42
Yinkeng, China H6 42
Yinmatu, stm., China D2 38
Yinnyein, Mya. D3 48
Yin Shan, mts., China C6 36
Yi'ong, stm., China E3 36
Yirga'Alem, Eth. F7 62
Yirol, Sudan F6 62
Yishan, China I3 42
Yishui, China D8 42
Yisuhe, China H5 42
Yitong, stm., China C6 38
Yitulihe, China A9 36
Yiwu, China G8 42
Yiwu, China A5 48
Yixian, China D4 38
Yixing, China F8 42
Yixun, stm., China D2 38
Yiyang, China G5 42
Yiyang, China D4 42
Yiyang, China G7 42
Yiyuan, China C8 42
Yizhang, China I5 42
Yli-Kitka, l., Fin. C13 8
Ylivieska, Fin. D11 8
Ymer Ø, i., Grnld. C21 141
Ynykčanskij, Russia D16 34
Yoakum, Tx., U.S. E10 130
Yocona, stm., Ms., U.S. C9 122
Yog Point, c., Phil. C5 52
Yogyakarta, Indon. G7 50
Yogyakarta, state, Indon. H7 50
Yoho National Park, p.o.i., B.C., Can. E14 138
Yōka, Japan D7 40
Yokadouma, Cam. D2 66
Yōkaichi, Japan D9 40
Yokkaichi, Japan D9 40
Yoko, Cam. C2 66
Yokoate-jima, i., Japan k19 39a
Yokohama, Japan D12 40
Yokosuka, Japan D12 40
Yokote, Japan E14 38
Yola, Nig. H7 64
Yolombo, D.R.C. E4 66
Yom, stm., Thai. D5 48
Yonago, Japan D6 40
Yoncalla, Or., U.S. G3 136
Yonezawa, Japan B12 40
Yong'an, China I7 42
Yongchang, China D5 36
Yongcheng, China D7 42
Yŏngch'ŏn, Kor., S. D1 40
Yongchuan, China G1 42
Yongding, China I7 42
Yongding, stm., China A6 42
Yŏngdŏk, Kor., S. C2 40
Yŏngdong, Kor., S. F7 38
Yongfeng, China H6 42
Yonggi, Kor., S. C1 40
Yongi, China C7 38
Yŏngil-man, b., Kor., S. C2 40
Yŏngju, Kor., S. C1 40
Yongkang, China G9 42
Yongle, stm., China H5 42
Yongnian, China C6 42
Yongning, China J3 42
Yongning, China B1 42
Yongping, China F4 36
Yongren, China F5 36
Yongshan, China F5 36
Yongshou, China D2 42
Yongtai, China I8 42
Yŏngwŏl, Kor., S. B1 40
Yongxing, China B4 42
Yongxing, China H5 42
Yongxiu, China G6 42
Yŏngyang, Kor., S. C2 40
Yongzhou, China H4 42
Yonibana, S.L. H2 64
Yonkers, N.Y., U.S. D12 114
Yonne, state, Fr. G12 14
Yonne, stm., Fr. F12 14
Yopal, Col. E5 86
Yopurga, China B12 56
York, Austl. F3 74
York, Eng., U.K. H11 12
York, Al., U.S. E10 122
York, N.D., U.S. F14 124
York, Pa., U.S. E9 114
York, S.C., U.S. A4 116
York, Cape, c., Austl. B8 74
York, Kap, c., Grnld. B12 141
Yorke Peninsula, pen., Austl. F7 74
Yorketown, Austl. G7 74
York Factory, Mb., Can. D12 106
Yorkshire Dales National Park, p.o.i., Eng., U.K. G10 12
York Sound, strt., Austl. B4 74
Yorkton, Sk., Can. C11 124
Yorktown, Tx., U.S. E10 130
Yorktown, Va., U.S. G9 114
Yorkville, Il., U.S. J10 118
Yorkville, N.Y., U.S. E14 112
Yoro, Hond. E4 102
Yoron-jima, i., Japan I19 39a
Yosemite National Park, p.o.i., Ca., U.S. F6 134
Yosemite Village, Ca., U.S. F6 134
Yoshii, stm., Japan E7 40
Yösöbulag see Altay, Mong. B4 36
Yos Sudarso, Pulau, i., Indon. G10 44
Yŏsu, Kor., S. G7 38
You, stm., China G6 36
You, stm., China G4 42
Youanmi, Austl. E3 74
Youghal, Ire. J5 12
Young, Austl. J7 76
Young, Sk., Can. C8 124
Young, Az., U.S. I5 132
Young, Ur. F9 92
Younghusband Peninsula, pen., Austl. K2 76
Young Island, i., Ant. B21 81
Youngs Rock, r., Pit. c28 78k
Youngstown, Ab., Can. C2 124
Youngstown, N.Y., U.S. E10 112
Youngstown, Oh., U.S. C5 114
Youngsville, La., U.S. G6 122
Youngsville, N.C., U.S. H7 114
Yountville, Ca., U.S. E3 134

Name Map Ref. Page

Youssoufia, Mor. C3 64
Youxian, China H5 42
Youyang, China G3 42
Yŏyang-ni, Kor., S. B1 40
Yozgat, Tur. B3 56
Ypres see Ieper, Bel. D11 14
Ypsilanti, Mi., U.S. B2 114
Yreka, Ca., U.S. B3 134
Ysabel Channel, strt., Pap. N. Gui. a4 79a
Ystad, Swe. I5 8
Ytterhogdal, Swe. E6 8
Yu, stm., China J3 42
Yuam, stm., Thai. C3 48
Yuan see Red, stm., Asia D9 46
Yuan, stm., China H6 42
Yuan, stm., China G4 42
Yuanling, China G4 42
Yuanmou, China F5 36
Yuantan, China J5 42
Yuanyang, China D5 42
Yuasa, Japan E8 40
Yuba City, Ca., U.S. D4 134
Yūbari, Japan C15 38
Yucaipa, Ca., U.S. I8 134
Yucatán, state, Mex. B3 102
Yucatán, Península de (Yucatan Peninsula), pen., N.A. C3 102
Yucatan Channel, strt., N.A. B4 102
Yucatan Peninsula see Yucatán, Península de, pen., N.A. C3 102
Yucca, Az., U.S. I2 132
Yucca Mountain, mtn., Nv., U.S. G9 134
Yucca Valley, Ca., U.S. I9 134
Yucheng, China C7 42
Yuci, China C5 42
Yudu, China I6 42
Yuechi, China F2 42
Yueqing, China G9 42
Yuexi, China F5 36
Yueyang, China G5 42
Yufa, China B7 42
Yugan, China G7 42
Yugoslavia, ctry., Eur. F7 26
Yuhebu, China C3 42
Yuhuan Dao, i., China G9 42
Yuhuang Ding, mtn., China C9 42
Yukon, Ok., U.S. F11 128
Yukon, state, Can. B3 106
Yukon, stm., N.A. D7 140
Yukon Flats, sw., Ak., U.S. C11 140
Yukuhashi, Japan F3 40
Yuli, China F15 32
Yüli, Tai. J9 42
Yulin, China B3 42
Yulin, China J3 42
Yulin, China L3 42
Yuma, Az., U.S. K2 132
Yuma, Co., U.S. A6 128
Yuma, Bahía de, b., Dom. Rep. C13 102
Yumare, Ven. B7 86
Yumbel, Chile H1 92
Yumbo, Col. F3 86
Yumen, China D4 36
Yumt uul, mtn., Mong. C4 36
Yun, stm., China F5 42
Yuna, stm., Dom. Rep. C13 102
Yunak, Tur. E14 28
Yunan, China J4 42
Yuncheng, China D4 42
Yuncheng, China D6 42
Yungay, Chile H2 92
Yungchi see Jilin, China C7 38
Yungchia see Wenzhou, China F9 36
Yungning see Nanning, China J3 42
Yunkai Dashan, mts., China J4 42
Yun Ling, mts., China F4 36
Yunnan, state, China G5 36
Yunnanfu see Kunming, China F5 36
Yunta, Austl. I2 76
Yunwu Shan, mtn., China A7 42
Yunxi, China E4 42
Yunxian, China E4 42
Yunxiao, China I7 42
Yunyang, China F3 42
Yunyang see Yunxian, China E4 42
Yunzalin, stm., Mya. D3 48
Yuping, China H3 42
Yuqing, China H2 42
Yurimaguas, Peru E2 84
Yuriria, Laguna de, l., Mex. E8 100
Yuruá see Juruá, stm., S.A. D4 84
Yuruarí, stm., Ven. D11 86
Yurubí, Parque Nacional, p.o.i., Ven. B7 86
Yurungkax, stm., China A5 46
Yuscarán, Hond. F4 102
Yūsef, Bahr (Yūsuf, Bahr), can., Egypt K1 58
Yushan, China G8 42
Yü Shan, mtn., Tai. J9 42
Yushanzhen, China G3 42
Yushu, China E4 36
Yushu, China B7 38
Yutian, China B7 42
Yutian, China A5 46
Yuty, Para. C9 92
Yütz'u see Yuci, China C5 42
Yuxian, China B6 42
Yuxian, China B5 42
Yuxian, China D5 42
Yuyao, China F9 42
Yuzawa, Japan E14 38
Yvelines, state, Fr. F10 14
Yverdon-les-Bains, Switz. D3 22
Ywathagyi, Mya. A2 48

Z

Zaandam see Zaanstad, Neth. B13 14
Zaanstad, Neth. B13 14
Zabalac', Bela. G7 10
Zābalt, Rom. C8 26
Zabīd, Yemen G5 56
Žabinka, Bela. H6 10
Ząbkowice Śląskie, Pol. F12 16
Žabljak, Yugo. F6 26
Žabno, Pol. F16 16
Zābol, Iran C9 56
Zābol, state, Afg. C1 54
Zabolotiv, Ukr. A12 26
Zabor''e, Bela. E12 10
Zabore, Russia F15 10
Zabory, Russia E15 10
Zabrze, Pol. F14 16
Zabyčanne, Bela. G14 10
Zacapa, Guat. E3 102
Zacapu, Mex. F8 100
Zacatecas, Mex. D7 100
Zacatecas, state, Mex. D7 100
Zacatlán, Mex. F10 100
Zacoalco de Torres, Mex. E7 100
Zacualtipan, Mex. E9 100
Zadar (Zara), Cro. F12 22
Zadetkale Kyun, i., Mya. G3 48
Zadetkyi Kyun, i., Mya. H3 48
Zadoi, China B8 46
Za'farâna, well, Egypt I3 58
Zafer Burnu, c., N. Cyp. C5 58
Zafirovo, Blg. F13 26
Zafra, Spain F4 20
Žagań, Pol. E11 16
Žagare, Lith. D6 10
Zagazig, Egypt H2 58
Zaghouan, Tun. H4 24
Zaghouan, Jebel, mtn., Tun. H4 24
Zagora, Mor. C3 64
Zagórz, Pol. G18 16
Zagreb, Cro. E12 22
Zāgros, Kūhhā-ye, mts., Iran C7 56
Zagros Mountains see Zāgros, Kūhhā-ye, mts., Iran C7 56
Za'gya, stm., China B13 54
Zāhedān, Iran D9 56
Zahirābād, India C3 53
Zahlah, Leb. E6 58
Zahnitkiv, Ukr. A15 26
Zahrebetnoe, Russia B17 8
Zailma, Kaz. D10 32
Zaire see Congo, Democratic Republic of the, ctry., Afr. E4 66
Zaïre see Congo, stm., Afr. F2 66
Zaječar, Yugo. F9 26
Zajsan, Kaz. E14 32
Zajsan, ozero, l., Kaz. E14 32
Zaka, Zimb. B10 70
Zakamensk, Russia F9 34
Zakarpattia, co., Ukr. A10 26
Zakhidnyy Buh (Bug) (Buh), stm., Eur. D17 16
Zakliczyn, Pol. G16 16
Zakopane, Pol. G16 16
Zakouma, Chad E3 62
Zakroczym, Pol. D16 16
Zākynthos, Grc. F3 28
Zákynthos, i., Grc. F3 28
Zala, state, Hung. C3 26
Zala, stm., Hung. C4 26
Zalaegerszeg, Hung. C3 26
Zalamea de la Serena, Spain F5 20
Zalantun, China B9 36
Zalari, Russia D18 32
Zalaszentgrót, Hung. C4 26
Zalău, Rom. B10 26
Zalese, Russia F4 10
Zalim, Sau. Ar. E5 56
Zalingei, Sudan E4 62
Žaltyr, Kaz. D12 32
Žaludok, Bela. G7 10
Zama, Ms., U.S. E9 122
Zamakh, Yemen F6 56
Zamantı, stm., Tur. A6 58
Zambeze, stm., Afr. C3 68
Zambezi, Zam. C3 68
Zambezi, stm., Afr. D5 68
Zambezi Escarpment, clf, Zimb. D4 68
Zambia, ctry., Afr. C4 68
Zamboanga, Phil. G3 52
Zamboanga Peninsula, pen., Phil. G3 52
Zambrów, Pol. C18 16
Žambyl, Kaz. F12 32
Žambyl, Kaz. E12 32
Zameżnaja, Russia D24 8
Zami, stm., Mya. D4 48
Zamora, Ec. D2 84
Zamora, Spain C5 20
Zamora, co., Spain C5 20
Zamora de Hidalgo, Mex. F7 100
Zamość, Pol. F19 16
Zamość, state, Pol. F19 16
Zanaga, Congo E2 66
Žanatas, Kaz. F11 32
Záncara, stm., Spain E8 20
Zanda, China C7 54
Zanesville, Oh., U.S. E3 114
Zanjān, Iran B6 56
Zanjón, Arg. C5 92
Žannetty, ostrov, i., Russia A20 34
Zante see Zákynthos, i., Grc. F3 28
Zanthus, Austl. F4 74
Zanzibar, Tan. F7 66
Zanzibar, i., Tan. F7 66
Zanzibar Channel, strt., Tan. F7 66
Zaostrove, Russia F14 8
Zaō-zan, vol., Japan A13 40
Zaozërnyj, Russia C16 32
Zaozhuang, China D7 42
Zap, N.D., U.S. G12 124
Zapadnaja Dvina, Russia D15 10
Zapadna Morava, stm., Yugo. F8 26
Zapadno-Sibirskaja ravnina (West Siberian Plain), pl., Russia B12 32
Zapadnyj hrebet, mts., Russia F17 34
Zapadnyj Sajan, mts., Russia D16 32
Západočeský kraj, state, Czech Rep. G9 16
Západoslovenský Kraj, state, Slov. H14 16
Zapala, Arg. G2 90
Zapata, Tx., U.S. H8 130
Zapata, Península de, pen., Cuba A7 102
Zapatoca, Col. D5 86
Zapatosa, Ciénaga de, l., Col. C5 86
Zapljuse, Russia B12 10
Zapole, Russia B12 10
Zapoljarnyj, Russia B14 8
Zapopan, Mex. E7 100
Zaporizhzhia, Ukr. E5 32
Zapovednyj, Russia C10 38
Zaprudnja, Russia D20 10
Zaqatala, Azer. A6 56
Zaragoza, Mex. A8 100
Zaragoza, Mex. C1 130
Zaragoza (Saragossa), Spain C10 20
Zaragoza, co., Spain C9 20
Zarajsk, Russia F21 10
Zaranj, Afg. C9 56
Zarasai, Lith. E9 10
Zárate, Arg. G8 92
Zarautz, Spain A8 20
Zarauz see Zarautz, Spain A8 20
Zaraza, Ven. C9 86
Zareče, Russia E21 8
Zarečensk, Russia C14 8
Zarghūn Shahr, Afg. C10 56
Zaria, Nig. G6 64
Žarki, Pol. F15 16
Žarma, Kaz. E13 32
Zărneşti, Rom. D12 26
Zarsuat, Kaz. E12 32
Zarubino, Russia C9 38
Zarumilla, Peru D1 84
Żary, Pol. E11 16
Zarzaïtine, Alg. D6 64
Zarzal, Col. E4 86
Zasa, Lat. D8 10
Zāskār, stm., India B6 54
Zāskār Mountains, mts., Asia B7 54
Zaslaŭe, Bela. F10 10
Zastava, Russia G22 8
Zasulle, Russia D22 8
Žatec, Czech Rep. F9 16
Zatyshshya, Ukr. B16 26
Zavalla, Tx., U.S. F4 122
Zave, Zimb. D5 68
Zavet, Blg. F13 26
Zavodoukovsk, Russia C11 32
Zavodovski Island, i., S. Geor. K12 82
Zavolžsk, Russia H20 8
Zawadzkie, Pol. F14 16
Zawiercie, Pol. F15 16
Zāwiyat al-Mukhaylā, Libya A4 62
Zaydābād, Afg. A2 54
Zaysan see Zajsan, Kaz. E14 32
Zaysan, Lake see Zajsan, ozero, l., Kaz. E14 32
Zayü, stm., China C8 46
Zayzan see Zajsan, Kaz. E14 32
Zaza, stm., Cuba B8 102
Zaza, Presa, res., Cuba B8 102
Zbąszynek, Pol. D11 16
Zbraslav, Czech Rep. G10 16
Žd'ár nad Sazavou, Czech Rep. G11 16
Ždiar, Slov. G16 16
Zduńska Wola, Pol. E14 16
Zearing, Ia., U.S. B4 120
Zeballos, B.C., Can. G4 138
Zebedelia, S. Afr. D9 70
Zebulon, Ga., U.S. C1 116
Zedang, China D13 54
Zeebrugge, Bel. C11 14
Zeehan, Austl. n12 77a
Zeeland, Mi., U.S. F4 112
Zeeland, N.D., U.S. B13 126
Zeerust, S. Afr. D7 70
Zefat, Isr. F6 58
Zehdenick, Ger. D9 16
Zeil, Mount, mtn., Austl. D6 74
Zeist, Neth. B14 14
Zeitz, Ger. E8 16
Zeja, Russia F14 34
Zeja, stm., Russia F14 34
Zejskoe vodohranilišče, res., Russia F14 34
Zelee, Cape, c., Sol. Is. e9 79b
Zelenoborskij, Russia C14 8
Zelenogorsk, Russia F13 8
Zelenograd, Russia D20 10
Zelenogradsk, Russia F3 10
Zelenokumsk, Russia F6 32
Železinka, Kaz. D13 32
Železnodorožnyj, Russia F4 10
Železnodorožnyj, Russia B8 32
Železnogorsk, Russia H18 10
Železnogorsk-Ilimskij, Russia C18 32
Zelienople, Pa., U.S. D5 114
Zella-Mehlis, Ger. F6 16
Zell am See, Aus. C9 22
Zell am Ziller, Aus. C8 22
Zel'va, Bela. G7 10
Želva, Lith. E8 10
Zemaitijos nacionalnis parkas, p.o.i., Lith. D4 10
Zembin, Bela. F11 10
Zembra, Île, i., Tun. G4 24
Zémio, C.A.R. C4 66
Zempoala, hist., Mex. F10 100
Zemun, Yugo. E7 26
Zeng, stm., China J5 42
Zenica, Bos. E4 26
Zenon Park, Sk., Can. A10 124
Zentsūji, Japan E6 40
Zenza do Itombe, Ang. B1 68
Zephyr, Tx., U.S. C9 130
Zephyrhills, Fl., U.S. H3 116
Zepu, China B12 56
Zeravšan, stm., Asia B10 56
Zeravšanskij hrebet, mts., Asia B10 56
Zerbst, Ger. D8 16
Żerków, Pol. D13 16
Zerqan, Alb. C14 24
Žešart, Russia E23 8
Zeulenroda, Ger. F7 16
Zeven, Ger. C5 16
Zevenaar, Neth. E2 16
Zeytinbağı, Tur. C11 28
Zězdy, Kaz. E11 32
Zêzere, stm., Port. E2 20
Žezkazgan, Kaz. E11 32
Zgierz, Pol. E15 16
Zgorzelec, Pol. E11 16
Zhabuchaka Hu, l., China C9 54
Zhakou, China F5 42
Zhambyl see Žambyl, Kaz. F12 32
Zhang, stm., China I6 42
Zhang, stm., China C5 42
Zhangaözen see Novyj Uzen', Kaz. F8 32
Zhangaqazaly see Novokazalinsk, Kaz. F10 32
Zhangbei, China A6 42
Zhangguangcai Ling, mts., China B8 38
Zhanghuang, China K3 42
Zhangjiakou, China A6 42
Zhangping, China I7 42
Zhangpu, China I7 42
Zhangqiu, China C7 42
Zhangshuping, China F4 42
Zhangwu, China C5 38
Zhangye, China D5 36
Zhangzhou, China I7 42
Zhanjiang, China K4 42
Zhanyu, China B5 38
Zhao'an, China J7 42
Zhaodong, China A7 38
Zhaojue, China C9 46
Zhaoping, China I4 42
Zhaoqing, China J5 42
Zhaotong, China F5 36
Zhaoxing, China B11 36
Zhaoyuan, China B10 36
Zhari Namco, l., China C10 54
Zharma see Žarma, Kaz. E14 32
Zhaxi Co, l., China B10 54
Zhaxigang, China B7 54
Zhayyq see Ural, stm. E8 32
Zhecheng, China D6 42
Zhegu, China D13 54
Zhejiang, state, China G8 42
Zhelin, China F9 42
Zhem see Emba, stm., Kaz. E9 32
Zhenbeikou, China B2 42
Zheng'an, China G2 42
Zhengding, China B6 42
Zhenghe, China H8 42
Zhenglan Qi, China C8 36
Zhengning, China D3 42
Zhengyang, China E6 42
Zhengzhou, China D5 42
Zhenhai, China G9 42
Zhenjiang, China E8 42
Zhenlai, China B9 36
Zhenning, China H1 42
Zhenping, China E5 42
Zhentou, stm., China E6 42
Zhenxiong, China F5 36
Zhenyu, China H9 42
Zhenyuan, China H3 42
Zhenyuan, China D2 42
Zherong, China H8 42
Zhetiqara see Džetygara, Kaz. D10 32
Zhijiang, China H3 42
Zhixia, China G8 42
Zhob, Pak. C2 54
Zhob, stm., Pak. C10 56
Zhongba, China C5 46
Zhongdian, China F4 36
Zhongning, China C1 42
Zhongpingchang, China F3 42
Zhongshan, China J5 42
Zhongshan, China I4 42
Zhongshan, sci., Ant. B12 81
Zhongtiao Shan, mts., China D4 42
Zhongwei, China C1 42
Zhongxian, China F3 42
Zhongxiang, China F5 42
Zhongyaozhan, China F14 34
Zhoucun, China C7 42
Zhouning, China H8 42
Zhoushan Dao, i., China F9 42
Zhoushan Qundao, is., China F10 42
Zhouzhi, China D3 42
Zhuanghe, China B10 42
Zhuanglang, China D1 42
Zhucang, China H2 42
Zhucheng, China D8 42
Zhuhe, China G5 42
Zhuji, China G9 42
Zhujia Jian, i., China G10 42
Zhujiang Kou, est., Asia J5 42
Zhumadian, China E5 42
Zhuolu, China A6 42
Zhuozhou, China B6 42
Zhuozi, China A5 42
Zhushan, China E4 42
Zhuxi, China E3 42
Zhuzhou, China H5 42
Zhytomyr, Ukr. E14 6
Zi, stm., China C8 42
Zi, stm., China G4 42
Ziārat, Pak. C10 56
Žiar nad Hronom, Slov. H14 16
Zibo, China C8 42
Zichang, China C3 42
Ziębice, Pol. F13 16
Zielona Góra, Pol. E11 16
Zielona Góra, state, Pol. D11 16
Zierikzee, Neth. C12 14
Ziesar, Ger. D8 16
Zifta, Egypt H2 58
Žigalovo, Russia D19 32
Žigansk, Russia C13 34
Zigong, China F5 36
Zigui, China F4 42
Ziguinchor, Sen. G1 64
Zihuatanejo, Mex. G8 100
Ziyang, China E3 42
Zijin, China J6 42
Zikhron Ya'aqov, Isr. F5 58
Zilaja Tambica, Russia E17 8
Žilina, Slov. G14 16
Žilino, Russia F4 10
Zillah, Libya B3 62
Zillertaler Alpen (Aurine, Alpi), mts., Eur. C8 22
Zilupe, Lat. D11 10
Zilwaukee, Mi., U.S. E6 112
Zima, Russia D18 32
Zimapán, Mex. E9 100
Zimbabwe, ctry., Afr. D4 68
Zimbabwe Ruins, hist., Zimb. B10 70
Zimi, S.L. H2 64
Zimnicea, Rom. F12 26
Zimonino, Russia G14 10
Zinder, Niger G6 64
Zinga Mulike, Tan. F7 66
Zinnik see Soignies, Bel. D12 14
Zion, Il., U.S. F2 112
Zion National Park, p.o.i., Ut., U.S. F4 132
Zionsville, In., U.S. I3 112
Zipaquirá, Col. E5 86
Zirbitzkogel, mtn., Aus. C11 22
Žirjatino, Russia G16 10
Žirovnice, Czech Rep. G11 16
Zitong, China F1 42
Zittau, Ger. F10 16
Ziway, Lake see Ziway Hāyk', l., Eth. F7 62
Ziway Hāyk', l., Eth. F7 62
Zixi, China G7 42
Ziya, stm., China B7 42
Ziyuan, China I4 42
Žizdra, stm., Russia F19 10
Zizhong, China G1 42
Zizhou, China C3 42
Žižica, Russia D14 10
Žižickoe, ozero, l., Russia D14 10
Zlaté Moravce, Slov. H14 16
Zlatoust, Russia C9 32
Zlatoustovsk, Russia F15 34
Zlín, Czech Rep. G13 16
Zlītan, Libya A2 62
Žlobin, Bela. H13 10
Złoczew, Pol. E14 16
Złotoryja, Pol. E11 16
Złotów, Pol. C13 16
Zlynka, Russia H14 10
Zmeinogorsk, Russia D14 32
Żmigród, Pol. E12 16
Zmiinyi, ostriv, i., Ukr. D17 26
Znamenka, Russia F17 10
Znamensk, Russia F4 10
Znamenskoe, Russia C12 32
Żnin, Pol. D13 16
Znojmo, Czech Rep. H12 16
Zoar, S. Afr. H5 70
Zodzina, Bela. F11 10
Zoétélé, Cam. D2 66
Zogang, China F4 36
Zohova, ostrov, i., Russia A19 34
Zohreh, stm., Iran C7 56
Zolotaja Gora, Russia F14 34
Zolymbet, Kaz. D12 32
Zomba, Mwi. D6 68
Zonguldak, Tur. B14 28
Zonguldak, state, Tur. B15 28
Zonza, Fr. H15 18
Zorita, Spain E5 20
Zorra, Arroyo de la, stm., Mex. E6 130
Zouar, Chad C3 62
Zouérat, Maur. E2 64
Zoug see Zug, Switz. C5 22
Zouxian, China D7 42
Zovka, Russia B11 10
Zrenjanin, Yugo. D7 26
Žuantobe, Kaz. F11 32
Zuata, stm., Ven. C9 86
Zubaydīyah, Jabal az-, mtn., Syria E8 58
Zubovo, Russia F17 8
Zudáñez, Bol. C4 90
Zuera, Spain C10 20
Zufar (Dhofar), reg., Oman F7 56
Zug, Switz. C5 22
Zugdidi, Geor. F6 32
Zuger See, l., Switz. C5 22
Zugspitze, mtn., Eur. I6 16
Zújar, stm., Spain F5 20
Žukopa, Russia D15 10
Žukovka, Russia G16 10
Žukovskij, Russia E21 10
Zuli, stm., China D1 42
Zulia, state, Ven. C5 86
Zulia, stm., S.A. C5 86
Zululand, hist. reg., S. Afr. F10 70
Zumbo, Moz. D5 68
Zumbrota, Mn., U.S. G6 118
Zungeru, Nig. H6 64
Zunhua, China A7 42
Zuni, stm., U.S. I7 132
Zuni Pueblo, N.M., U.S. H8 132
Zunyi, China H2 42
Zuo, stm., China J2 42
Zuodeng, China J2 42
Zuomuchedong Hu, l., China D12 54
Zuoyun, China A5 42
Žuraviči, Bela. G13 10
Zurich, On., Can. E8 112
Zürich (Zurigo), Switz. C5 22
Zurich, Lake see Zürichsee, l., Switz. C5 22
Zürichsee, l., Switz. C5 22
Zurigo see Zürich, Switz. C5 22
Zurmi, Nig. G6 64
Žuša, stm., Russia G19 10
Žut, Otok, i., Cro. G12 22
Zutphen, Neth. B15 14
Zuwārah, Libya A2 62
Zuwayzā, Jord. G6 58
Zvenigorod, Russia E19 10
Zvezdec, Blg. G14 26
Zvezdnyj, Russia C19 32
Zvishavane, Zimb. B9 70
Zvolen, Slov. H15 16
Zwedru, Lib. H3 64
Zweibrücken, Ger. G3 16
Zweisimmen, Switz. D4 22
Zwickau, Ger. F8 16
Zwierzyniec, Pol. F18 16
Zwoleń, Pol. E17 16
Zwolle, Neth. B14 14
Zwolle, La., U.S. F5 122
Żyrardów, Pol. D16 16
Zyrjanka, Russia C19 34
Zyrjanovsk, Kaz. E14 32
Zyrjanskoe, Russia C15 32
Zyryan see Zyrjanovsk, Kaz. E14 32
Žytkavičy, Bela. H10 10
Żywiec, Pol. G15 16